CW00662081

牛津簡明英漢醫學辭典

牛津簡明英漢醫學辭典

OXFORD
CONCISE ENGLISH-CHINESE
MEDICAL DICTIONARY

主　編　伊麗莎白·A·馬丁(Elizabeth A. Martin MA)

主　譯　白永權

翻　譯　胡　建　聶文信　張京魚　李　瑩
　　　　司選海　胡海濤　李雲梅　李　明

OXFORD
UNIVERSITY PRESS

OXFORD
UNIVERSITY PRESS

Oxford University Press is a department of the University of Oxford.
It furthers the University's objective of excellence in research, scholarship,
and education by publishing worldwide in

Oxford New York

Auckland Bangkok Buenos Aires Cape Town Chennai
Dar es Salaam Delhi Hong Kong Istanbul Karachi Kolkata
Kuala Lumpur Madrid Melbourne Mexico City Mumbai Nairobi
São Paulo Shanghai Taipei Tokyo Toronto

Oxford is a registered trade mark of Oxford University Press

English text originally published as the fourth edition of the
Concise Medical Dictionary by Oxford University Press 1994
© Market House Ltd, 1980, 1985, 1990, 1994

© Oxford University Press 2000

First published 1999
Second edition 2000
This impression (lowest digit)
7 9 10 8 6

牛津簡明英漢醫學辭典

伊麗莎白 · 馬丁(Elizabeth A. Martin)主編

白永權主譯

ISBN 978-0-19-593237-9 (flexi-cover)
ISBN 978-0-19-591920-2 (paperback)

Printed in Hong Kong
Published by Oxford University Press (China) Ltd
18th Floor, Warwick House East, Taikoo Place, 979 King's Road, Quarry Bay,
Hong Kong

主编

Elizabeth A. Martin MA

参加编寫者及顧問

W. Leslie Alexander FRCS, FRCOphth

J. A. D. Anderson MA, MD, FRCP, FFPHM, FFOM, FRCGP

John Andrewartha BSc, MSc, PhD

J. H. Angel MD, FRCP

John R. Bennett MD, FRCP

Stuart Anthony Bentley MB, BS

Dr Peter Bradbury FRCP

Bruce M. Bryant MB, ChB, MRCP

Robert E. Coleman

Patrick Collins MD, MRCP

J. A. Cullen BSc, MSc

H. L. Dalrymple BSc, MSc

W. J. Dinning FRCS, MRCP

Ivan T. Draper MB, ChB, FRCPEd

J. C. Gingell MB, BCh, FRCSEd, FRCS

John M. Goldman DM, FRCP, FRCPath

W. J. Gordon MD, FRCS(G), FRCOG

Michael Klaber MA, MB, FRCP

H. J. Liebeschuetz MA, FRCP, DCH

Anne Lockhart MIBiol, MIHE, Cert. Ed.

D. J. McFerran MA, FRCS

Gordon Macpherson MB, BS

Charles V. Mann MA, MCh, FRCS

M. A. Openshaw BSc, DPhil

T. R. Pitt Ford PhD, BDS, FDS

D. L. Phillips FRCR, MRCOG

Helen Phillips MBBS, DCH, DROG

Dr John R. Sewell MA, MB, MRCP

Dr Tony Smith MA, BM, BCh

Eric Taylor MA, MB, MRCP, MRCPsych

John Timson BSc, PhD, FLS, MIBiol

H. R. H. Tripp MA, MSc, PhD

Sandra V. Vellucci BSc, PhD, MIBiol

William F. Whimster MRCP, MRCPath

Robert M. Youngson MB, ChB, DTM&H, DO, FRCOpthal

序　言

　　《牛津簡明英漢醫學辭典》（第二版）全面收錄了當今醫學中的所有重要術語和概念。它是由一批傑出的醫學專家和醫學作家編寫而成的，其主要讀者對象是醫學領域中的所有人員：醫生、醫學研究人員、醫學生、護士、藥劑師、理療師、語言治療師、社會工作者、醫院文秘人員、行政管理人員和技師等等。每個詞條都包含一個基本定義，其後是更為詳細的解釋和描述。本辭典的特點是文字簡明準確。因此，對於需要一本家用醫學辭典的讀者，本辭典是非常有價值的。

　　本辭典解釋了解剖學、生理學、生物化學、藥理學以及臨床各學科的主要術語。其中收錄的心理學、精神病學、公共健康學和口腔學詞滙也極為廣泛。另外，此版還編入了許多關於影像、外科技術、不孕症治療、基因篩選實驗和最近研製的藥物的新詞條。同時，此版也刪去了現代醫學中不經常使用的藥物詞條和許多概念模糊而且過時的醫學術語詞條。掌握醫學術語的前綴和後綴的意思是擴大醫學詞滙量的一個途徑，本辭典中收錄了許多常用的醫學術語的前綴和後綴。為了避免出現過多的派生詞詞條，如名詞的形容詞形式等，這些派生詞被列編在派生出它們的詞的定義之後。對有些詞條，除了文字定義解釋外，還配有插圖和圖表。在定義中，有些詞前上方帶一星號（只限於英文），這表明該術語在本辭典中也是一個獨立的詞條，在那裏可找到更多的解釋。有些詞條的解釋是請讀者參閱另一詞條，這說明他們是同義詞；有些詞條的解釋在括號內註出參閱某一詞條，這說明這個詞條有關於它們的較長和有參考價值的解釋。

　　除以上特點之外，《牛津簡明英漢醫學辭典》還為廣大醫務人員學習醫學英語、提高閱讀和翻譯英語醫學資料的能力提供了方便。這一點在該書的翻譯和編排過程中，給予了充分體現。

譯文,在忠實原文和使用規範的中文術語的基礎上,盡可能地保持了原文的篇章結構;英文、中文分按詞條雙欄排版,為讀者將英文與中文對照閱讀提供了方便。

在翻譯的過程中,西安醫科大學的李洞、孔紅梅、董志宏、馬東亮和許崇明對部分譯稿進行了審閱,孫波玲、楊衛寧、李建紅為譯稿錄入計算機及校對稿件做了大量工作,在此表示感謝。

白永權
西安醫科大學外語系主任、教授

A

a- (an-) *prefix denoting* absence of; lacking; not. Examples: *amastia* (absence of breasts); *amorphic* (lacking definite form); *atoxic* (not poisonous).

〔前綴〕**無，缺，不** 例如：無乳房，無定形，無毒的。

ab- *prefix denoting* away from. Example: *abembryonic* (away from or opposite the embryo).

〔前綴〕**（與某部位）分開** 例如：胚外的。

abarticulation *n.* **1.** the dislocation of a joint. **2.** a synovial joint (*see* diarthrosis).

(1) 關節脱位　(2) 滑囊關節（參閲 diarthrosis）。

abasia *n.* an inability to walk for which no physical cause can be identified. *See also* astasia.

步行不能 查找不出軀體性病因的無行走能力。參閲astasia。

abdomen *n.* the part of the body cavity below the chest (*see* thorax), from which it is separated by the *diaphragm. The abdomen contains the organs of digestion – stomach, liver, intestines, etc. – and excretion – kidneys, bladder, etc.; in women it also contains the ovaries and uterus. The regions of the abdomen are shown in the illustration. **–abdominal** *adj.*

腹（部） 由膈肌將其分開的胸部下方的體腔（參閲thorax）。腹內有胃、肝、腸等消化器官與腎、膀胱等排泄器官；女性則還包括卵巢和子宮。腹部各區見圖。

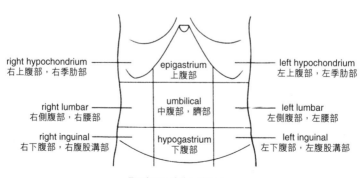

right hypochondrium
右上腹部，右季肋部

epigastrium
上腹部

left hypochondrium
左上腹部，左季肋部

right lumbar
右側腹部，右腰部

umbilical
中腹部，臍部

left lumbar
左側腹部，左腰部

right inguinal
右下腹部，右腹股溝部

hypogastrium
下腹部

left inguinal
左下腹部，左腹股溝部

Regions of the abdomen
腹部分區圖

abdomin- (abdomino-) *combining form denoting* the abdomen. Examples: *abdominalgia* (pain in the abdomen); *abdominothoracic* (relating to the abdomen and thorax).

〔詞幹〕**腹** 例如：腹痛，腹胸的。

abdominoscopy *n. see* laparoscopy.

腹腔鏡檢法 參閱 laparoscopy。

abducens nerve the sixth *cranial nerve (VI), which supplies the lateral rectus muscle of each eyeball, responsible for turning the eye outwards.

展神經 支配雙眼外直肌的第六對腦神經，司眼球外展。

abduct *vb.* to move a limb or any other part away from the midline of the body. **–abduction** *n.*

外展 自身體中線移離一肢或任何其他部位。

abductor *n.* any muscle that moves one part of the body away from another or from the midline of the body.

展肌 使身體的一部分移離另一部分或移離身體中線的肌肉。

aberrant *adj.* abnormal: usually applied to a blood vessel or nerve that does not follow its normal course.

迷行的，異常的 通常用於描述走行異常的血管或神經。

abiotrophy *n.* degeneration or loss of function without apparent cause; for example, *retinal abiotrophy* is progressive degeneration of the retina leading to impaired vision, occurring in genetic disorders such as *retinitis pigmentosa.

生活力缺失 無明顯原因的退化或功能喪失；例如：視網膜生活力缺失是視網膜的進行性變性，可導致視力損害，見於色素性視網膜炎等遺傳性疾病。

ablatio *n.* separation; abruptio. *See* detached retina (ablatio retinae).

脫離 分離，分開。參閱 detached retina (ablatio retinae)。

ablation *n.* the removal of tissue, a part of the body, or an abnormal growth, usually by cutting. *See also* endometrial ablation.

部分切除（術） 去除組織、身體之一部分，或異常生長物，通常用切除術。參閱 endometrial ablation。

ablepharia *n.* absence of or reduction in the size of the eyelids.

無瞼 眼瞼缺失或縮小。

ablepsia *n.* an obsolete term for *blindness.

視覺缺失　盲的廢用詞。

abortifacient *n.* a drug that induces abortion or miscarriage. *See* mifepristone, prostaglandin.

墮胎藥　誘導流產的藥物。參閱 mifepristone，prostaglandin。

abortion *n.* the expulsion or removal of an embryo or fetus from the uterus at a stage of pregnancy when it is incapable of independent survival (i.e. at any time between conception and the 24th week of pregnancy). In *threatened abortion* there may be abdominal pain and bleeding from the uterus but the fetus is still alive; once the fetus is dead abortion becomes *inevitable*. Abortion is *incomplete* so long as the uterus still contains some of the fetus or its membranes. Abortion may be *spontaneous* or it may be *induced* for medical or social reasons (*termination of pregnancy*). *Habitual* (or *recurrent*) *abortion* is the occurrence of three consecutive pregnancy losses before 20 weeks' gestation, with fetuses weighing under 500 grams. The presence of a uterine abnormality, such as *bicornuate uterus or *cervical incompetence, may account for 10–15% of recurrent abortions.

Procuring or attempting to procure abortion are both criminal offences in the UK unless carried out within the terms of the Abortion Act 1967 and the subsequent Abortion Regulations 1991. Two doctors must agree that termination of pregnancy is necessary for one of the reasons specified in the Regulations, and the procedure must be carried out in an approved hospital or clinic. Methods in current use include the administration of drugs, e.g. *mifepristone with or without the addition of prostaglandins (e.g. *gemeprost). The surgical methods of termination of pregnancy include

流產　胚胎或胎兒在尚不能獨立生存時（即介於受孕與妊娠24 周之間）自子宮排出或去除。先兆流產時可有腹痛和子宮出血，但胎兒仍存活；胎兒一旦死亡，流產則不可避免；子宮內存留有部分胎兒或胎膜時是不全流產。流產或為自然流產，亦可為因醫學或社會原因而致的人工流產（終止妊娠）。習慣性流產指連續三次在妊娠 20 周內，胎兒體重不足 500 克時妊娠失敗，其中 10%~15% 因子宮異常所致，如雙角子宮或宮頸閉鎖不全。

在英國，除非符合 1967 年的流產法令和 1991 年的流產法規之條款，流產或企圖流產均屬違法。必須有兩位醫生同意終止妊娠是基於法規中所列原因之一，並須在指定醫院或診所進行。當前使用的方法包括服用藥物，例如：米非司酮單用或與前列腺素合用（如吉美前列素）。終止妊娠的手術方法有經子宮內套管真空吸出胚胎，擴張子宮頸和刮子宮及用卵圓鉗刮取。早期終止妊娠危險性很小，而在妊娠 13 周後有可能出現併發症。

非醫學界人士將流產與小產加以區別，前者是蓄意進行的操作以終止妊娠，後者為一意外事件。醫學界正逐漸認識到這種區別的用處。

vacuum aspiration of the products of conception through an intrauterine cannula, *dilatation and curettage, and uterine evacuation by ovum forceps. Termination carries little risk early in pregnancy, but complications are more likely to occur after the 13th week of pregnancy.

Nonmedical people make a distinction between abortion and *miscarriage*, the former being a procedure deliberately carried out to end the pregnancy, the latter being an accidental occurrence. The medical profession increasingly recognizes this useful distinction.

abortus *n.* a fetus, weighing less than 500 g, that is expelled from the uterus either dead or incapable of surviving.

流產胎　從子宮排出的體重輕於 500 g 的死胎或不能存活的胎兒。

ABO system *see* blood group.

ABO 系統　參閱 blood group。

abrasion *n.* **1.** a graze: a minor wound in which the surface of the skin or a mucous membrane is worn away by rubbing or scraping. **2.** the wearing of the teeth, particularly at the necks by overvigorous brushing. It is frequently enhanced by *erosion. **3.** any rubbing or scraping action that produces surface wear.

(1) 擦傷　因擦或刮而致皮膚或黏膜表面破損的輕傷。**(2) 磨損**　尤指牙齒頸部因過度刷牙的損傷，並常因牙侵蝕而加重。**(3) 擦，刮**　導致表面損傷的任何擦或刮的動作。

abreaction *n.* the release of strong emotion associated with a buried memory. While this can happen spontaneously, it is usually deliberately produced by a therapist using psychotherapy, hypnosis, or drugs such as *thiopentone. The technique is used as a treatment for conversion disorder, anxiety state, and other neurotic conditions, especially when they are thought to be caused by *repression of memories or emotions.

精神發泄　與深藏的記憶有關的強烈情感宣泄。雖可自發產生，但通常由醫生使用心理療法、催眠術或硫噴妥鈉類藥物有意引發，用於治療轉換障礙、焦慮狀態及其他神經性疾患，尤其是被認為因記憶或情感壓抑所致的病症。

abruptio (ablatio) *n.* separation.

分離　分開。

abruptio placentae bleeding from a normally situated placenta causing its complete or partial detachment from the uterine wall after the 24th week of gestation. There may be varying degrees of shock; *hypofibrinogenaemia (a blood coagulation defect) is a further complication. Abruptio placentae ·is often associated with hypertension and pre-eclampsia.

胎盤早期脱離 妊娠 24 周後位置正常的胎盤出血並導致胎盤從子宮壁完全或部分剝離。可有程度不一的休克；進而可出現血纖維蛋白原過少（一種凝血缺陷）的併發症。胎盤早期脱離常與高血壓和先兆子癇有關。

abscess n. a localized collection of pus anywhere in the body, surrounded and walled off by damaged and inflamed tissues. A *boil is an example of an abscess within the skin. The usual cause is local bacterial infection, often by staphylococci, that the body's defences have failed to overcome. In a *cold abscess*, due to tubercle organisms, there is swelling, but little pain or inflammation (as in acute abscesses). Antibiotics, aided by surgical incision to release pus where necessary, are the usual forms of treatment.

The brain and its meninges have a low resistance to infection and a *cerebral abscess* is liable to follow any penetration of these by microorganisms. The condition is fatal unless relieved by aspiration or surgical drainage.

膿腫 身體任何部位的局部膿液聚集，四周被受損和發炎組織包圍隔離。癤即為一種常由局部細菌感染引起的皮膚膿腫，多因身體防禦機制未能抵抗葡萄球菌入侵。寒性膿腫由結核菌所致，有腫脹而幾乎無痛或炎症（不同於急性膿腫）。通常用抗生素治療，輔以在適當部位手術切開排膿。

腦與腦膜的抗感染力低下，而且被任何微生物侵入後均易產生腦膿腫。除非用抽吸法或外科引流法加以緩解，本症可致命。

abscission n. removal of tissue by cutting.

切除 以切除方法去除組織。

absence n. (in neurology) see epilepsy.

失神（神經病學）參閱 epilepsy。

Absidia n. a genus of fungi that sometimes cause disease in man (*see* phycomycosis).

犁頭黴屬 有時可使人致病的真菌一屬（參閱 phycomycosis）。

absorption n. (in physiology) the uptake of fluids or other substances by the tissues of the body. Digested food is absorbed into the blood and lymph from the

吸收（作用）（生理學）人體組織對液體或其他物質的攝取。已消化的食物從消化道吸收進入血液和淋巴。食物吸收

alimentary canal. Most absorption of food occurs in the small intestine – in the jejunum and ileum – although alcohol is readily absorbed from the stomach. The small intestine is lined with minute finger-like processes (*see* villus), which greatly increase its surface area and therefore the speed at which absorption can take place. *See also* assimilation, digestion.

主要在小腸（空腸和迴腸中），而酒精被胃迅速吸收。小腸內襯有微小指狀突起（參閱 villus），可大為增加其表面面積而加快吸收速度。參閱 assimilation，digestion。

abulia *n.* absence or impairment of will power. The individual still has desires but they are not put into action; initiative and energy are lacking. It is commonly a symptom of *schizophrenia.

意志缺失 意志缺乏或薄弱。患者雖有種種願望卻不付諸行動；缺乏主動性與活力。常為精神分裂症的一種症狀。

abutment *n.* (in dentistry) *see* bridge.

橋基 （牙科學）參閱 bridge。

acalculia *n.* an acquired inability to make simple mathematical calculations. It is a symptom of disease in the *parietal lobe of the brain. *See* Gerstmann's syndrome.

計算不能 後天性無簡單數學計算的能力，此為大腦頂葉疾病的一種症狀。參閱 Gerstmann's syndrome。

acantha *n.* **1.** a spine projecting from a *vertebra. **2.** the *backbone.

(1) 棘（突） 脊椎骨的棘突。**(2) 脊柱**。

Acanthamoeba *n.* a genus of widely distributed amoebae some species of which occasionally cause painful corneal ulcers in man.

棘阿米巴屬 分布廣泛的阿米巴一屬，其中一些種類偶爾可對人類引起疼痛的角膜潰瘍。

acanthion *n.* the tip of the spine formed where projecting processes of the upper jaw bones (maxillae) meet at the front of the face.

鼻前棘點 兩側上頜骨突起在臉的前部匯合而形成的棘尖。

acanthosis *n.* an increase in the number of *prickle cells in the innermost layer of the epidermis, leading to thickening of the epidermis. *Acanthosis nigricans* is believed to be associated with insulin resistance; it is characterized by papillomatous growths, mainly in the armpits, giving the skin a pigmented appearance

棘皮症 表皮最深層棘細胞數量增加導致表皮增厚。黑棘皮症據認為與胰島素耐藥性有關，其特徵為主要位於腋下的乳頭狀瘤生長，使皮膚有色素沉着且柔軟光滑，可為良性或惡性。假性黑棘皮症更為常見，且與肥胖症有關。

and a velvety texture. It may be benign or malignant. *Pseudoacanthosis nigricans* is more common and is associated with obesity.

acapnia (hypocapnia) *n.* a condition in which there is an abnormally low concentration of carbon dioxide in the blood. This may be caused by breathing that is exceptionally deep in relation to the physical activity of the individual.

低碳酸血症　血液中二氧化碳濃度過低的狀態，可因與體力活動相關的呼吸過度所致。

acardia *n.* congenital absence of the heart. The condition may occur in conjoined twins; the twin with the heart controls the circulation for both.

無心（畸形）　先天性無心臟。可見於聯胎中；其中有心臟者控制雙胎的循環系統。

acariasis *n.* an infestation of mites and ticks and the symptoms, for example allergy and dermatitis, that their presence may provoke.

蟎病，蜱病　蟎和蜱的侵染及可能誘發的症狀，如變態反應和皮炎。

acaricide *n.* any chemical agent used for destroying mites and ticks.

殺蟎劑　任何用於殺滅蟎和蜱的化學製劑。

acarid *n.* a *mite or *tick.

蟎　蟎或蜱。

Acarina *n.* the group of arthropods that includes the *mites and *ticks.

蟎目　包括蟎和蜱的一類節肢動物。

Acarus (Tyroglyphus) *n.* a genus of mites. The flour mite, *A. siro* (*T. farinae*), is nonparasitic, but its presence in flour can cause a severe allergic dermatitis in flour-mill workers.

蟎屬　蟎之一屬。粉蟎為非寄生蟎，但在麵粉中可引起麵粉廠工人嚴重的變應性皮炎。

acatalasia *n.* an inborn lack of the enzyme *catalase, leading to recurrent infections of the gums (gingivitis) and mouth. It is most common in the Japanese.

過氧化氫酶缺乏（症）　先天性缺乏過氧化氫酶，導致牙齦和口腔的反覆感染（齦炎）。日本人中最多見。

acceptor *n.* (in biochemistry) a substance that helps to bring about oxidation of a reduced *substrate by accepting hydrogen ions.

受體　（生物化學）通過接受氫離子來促使還原底物氧化的物質。

accessory nerve (spinal accessory nerve) the eleventh *cranial nerve (XI), which arises from two roots, cranial and spinal. Fibres from the cranial root travel with the nerve for only a short distance before branching to join the vagus and then forming the recurrent laryngeal nerve, which supplies the internal laryngeal muscles. Fibres from the spinal root supply the sternomastoid and trapezius muscles, in the neck region (front and back).

副神經（脊髓副神經） 發自顱神經根和脊神經根的第十一對腦神經。顱根纖維在與神經短距離並行後分支與迷走神經匯合，形成支配內部喉肌的喉返神經。脊根纖維在頸區（前部和後部）支配胸鎖乳突肌和斜方肌。

accident *n.* a traumatic incident involving any part of the body. *Accident and emergency medicine* (*A and E*) is evolving as a specialized area of patient care.

事故，意外 可涉及身體任何部位的創傷性事件。事故與急症（A 與 E）正在發展成醫護中的一門專門學科。

accommodation *n.* adjustment of the shape of the lens to change the focus of the eye. When the ciliary muscle (*see* ciliary body) is relaxed, suspensory ligaments attached to the ciliary body and holding the lens in position are stretched, which causes the lens to be flattened. The eye is then able to focus on distant objects. To focus the eye on near objects the ciliary muscles contract and the tension in the ligaments is thus lowered, allowing the lens to become rounder.

眼調節 調節晶狀體的形狀以改變眼的焦距。當睫狀肌（參閱 ciliary body）放鬆時，附着於睫狀體之上並保持晶狀體位置的懸韌帶拉緊而使晶狀體變扁，眼睛便能對遠處物體聚焦。若眼睛對近物聚焦，睫狀體則收縮，懸韌帶鬆弛而使晶狀體變圓。

accommodation reaction (convergence reaction) the constriction of the pupil that occurs when an individual focuses on a near object.

調節反應（會聚反應） 個體對近物聚焦時瞳孔的縮小。

accouchement *n.* delivery of a baby. *See also* hydrostatic accouchement.

分娩 產出嬰兒。參閱 hydrostatic accouchement。

acebutolol *n.* a *beta blocker drug commonly used to treat high blood pressure, angina pectoris, and irregular heart rhythms. It is administered by mouth. Possible side-effects include breathing difficulty, especially in asthmatics, and cold hands and feet. Trade name: **Sectral**.

醋丁洛爾 一種β-受體阻滯劑，常用於治療高血壓、心絞痛和心律不齊，供口服。可能產生的副作用有呼吸困難，尤其是哮喘病患者，以及手足發冷。商品名：Sectral。

ACE inhibitor angiotensin-converting enzyme inhibitor: any one of a group of drugs used in the treatment of raised blood pressure and heart failure. ACE inhibitors act by interfering with the action of the enzyme that converts the inactive *angiotensin I to the powerful artery constrictor angiotensin II. The absence of this substance allows arteries to widen and the blood pressure to drop. ACE inhibitors are administered by mouth; they include *captopril and *enalapril. Possible side-effects include weakness, dizziness, loss of appetite, and skin rashes.

血管緊張素轉化酶抑制劑 任何一種治療血壓升高和心力衰竭的藥物，其作用機制為干擾將無活性的血管緊張素 I 轉化成活性強的收縮動脈的血管緊張素 II 的酶的作用。此酶缺乏可使動脈擴張，血壓降低。ACE 抑制劑以口服給藥，包括卡托普利和依那普利。可能產生的副作用有乏力、頭暈、食慾不振及皮疹。

acentric *n.* (in genetics) a chromosome or fragment of a chromosome that has no *centromere. Since acentrics cannot attach to the *spindle they are usually lost during cell division. They are often found in cells damaged by radiation. **–acentric** *adj.*

無着絲粒染色體 （遺傳學）無着絲粒的染色體或染色體片斷。因不能附着於紡錘體而常在細胞分裂中失去。通常見於受放射線損害的細胞。

acephalus *n.* a fetus without a head.

無頭畸胎 無頭胎兒。

acervulus cerebri a collection of granules of calcium-containing material that is sometimes found within the *pineal gland as its calcification proceeds (normally after the 17th year): 'brain sand'.

松果體石 隨其鈣化（通常在 17 歲後）有時可見於松果體內的含鈣顆粒聚集，即腦沙。

acetabulum (cotyloid cavity) *n.* either of the two deep sockets, one on each side of the *hip bone, into which the head of the thigh bone (femur) fits at the *hip joint.

髖臼 髖骨兩側各一的深窩，股骨頭在髖關節處固定於其中。

acetaminophen *n. see* paracetamol.

對乙酰氨基酚 參閱 paracetamol。

acetazolamide *n.* a *diuretic used in the treatment of glaucoma to reduce the pressure inside the eyeball and also as a preventative for altitude sickness. Side-effects include drowsiness and numbness

乙酰唑胺 一種利尿劑，用於在青光眼治療中降低眼球內壓，亦可用於預防高空病。副作用有嗜睡、手足麻木與針刺感。商品名：Diamox。

and tingling of the hands and feet. Trade name: **Diamox**.

acetoacetic acid an organic acid produced in large amounts by the liver under metabolic conditions associated with a high rate of fatty acid oxidation (for example, in starvation). The acetoacetic acid thus formed is subsequently converted to acetone and excreted. *See also* ketone.

乙酰乙酸　一種有機酸，在與脂肪酸高速氧化有關的代謝狀態下（如飢餓時）由肝臟大量產生，隨後轉化為丙酮並排出體外。參閱 ketone。

acetohexamide *n.* a *sulphonylurea oral hypoglycaemic drug used in the treatment of noninsulin-dependent *diabetes mellitus. It is administered by mouth; side-effects include headache, dizziness, and nervousness.

醋磺己脲　一種磺胺醯脲類口服降血糖藥，用於治療非胰島素依賴型糖尿病，口服。副作用有頭痛、頭暈、神經過敏。

acetone *n.* an organic compound that is an intermediate in many bacterial fermentations and is produced by fatty acid oxidation. In certain abnormal conditions (for example, starvation) acetone and other *ketones may accumulate in the blood (*see* ketosis). Acetone is a volatile liquid that is miscible with both fats and water and therefore of great value as a solvent. It is used in chromatography and in the preparation of tissues for enzyme extraction.

丙酮　脂肪酸氧化所產生的一種有機化合物，為多種細菌性發酵的中間產物。丙酮和其他酮類在某些異常狀態下（如飢餓）可蓄積於血液中（參閱 ketosis）。丙酮為揮發性液體，與油脂和水均可混合，因而是一種重要溶媒，用於色譜法和提取酶時的組織標本中。

acetone body (ketone body) *see* ketone.

丙酮體　參閱 ketone。

acetonuria *n. see* ketonuria.

丙酮尿　參閱 ketonuria。

acetylcholine *n.* the acetic acid ester of the organic base choline: the *neurotransmitter released at the synapses of parasympathetic nerves and at *neuromuscular junctions. After relaying a nerve impulse, acetylcholine is rapidly broken down by the enzyme *cholinesterase. *Atropine and curare cause muscular paralysis by blocking the action of acetylcholine at muscle membranes;

乙酰膽鹼　有機膽鹼的醋酸酯；為在副交感神經突觸和神經肌肉接頭所釋放的神經遞質，傳遞神經衝動後迅速被膽鹼酯酶分解。阿托品與箭毒通過阻斷乙酰膽鹼在肌細胞膜的作用而使肌肉麻痺；毒扁豆鹼與其他抗膽鹼酯酶通過阻斷膽鹼酯酶而延長乙酰膽鹼的作用。

physostigmine and other *anticholines-terases prolong the activity of acetyl-choline by blocking cholinesterase.

acetylcysteine *n.* a drug used to break down thick mucous secretions. It is administered as an aerosol, primarily for the treatment of respiratory diseases, such as bronchitis and cystic fibrosis; it is also used to prevent liver damage in paracetamol overdosage. Side-effects may include spasm of the bronchial muscles, nausea, vomiting, and fever. Trade names: **Fabrol**, **Parvolex**.

乙醯半胱氨酸　一種用於稀釋黏稠分泌物的藥物，以氣霧劑投藥，主要用於治療呼吸道疾病，如支氣管炎和囊性纖維變性；亦用於防止對乙醯氨基酚過量時肝臟受損。副作用有支氣管肌肉痙攣、惡心、嘔吐及發熱。商品名：Fabrol，Parvolex。

acetylsalicylic acid *see* aspirin.

乙醯水楊酸　參閱 aspirin。

achalasia (cardiospasm) *n.* a condition in which the normal muscular activity of the oesophagus (gullet) is disturbed, especially failure of an abnormally strong sphincter at the lower end, which delays the passage of swallowed material. It may occur at any age: symptoms include difficulty in swallowing liquids and solids, slowly increasing over years; sometimes regurgitation of undigested food; and occasionally severe chest pain caused by spasm of the oesophagus. Diagnosis is by a barium X-ray examination and sometimes manometric studies (*see* manometry). Treatment is by force-ful stretching of the tight lower end of the oesophagus (cardia) or by surgical splitting of the muscular ring in that area (*cardiomyotomy* or *Heller's operation*).

弛緩不能（賁門痙攣）　食管肌正常活動紊亂，尤其是下端括約肌異常緊張失調引起吞咽困難的狀態。可發生於任何年齡；症狀有逐年緩慢加重的液體和固體吞咽困難；有時出現未消化食物回流；以及偶爾因食管痙攣引起劇烈胸痛。可借鋇餐 X 綫檢查作出診斷，有時採用測壓檢查（參閱 manometry）。治療為擴張食管狹窄的下端（賁門），或手術切開此處的肌肉環（賁門肌切開術或赫勒手術）。

Achilles tendon the tendon of the muscles of the calf of the leg (the *gas-trocnemius and soleus muscles), situated at the back of the ankle and attached to the calcaneus (heel bone).

跟腱　小腿腓腸肌（腓腸肌與比目魚肌）肌腱，位於踝後，附着於跟骨上。

achlorhydria *n.* absence of hydrochloric acid in the stomach. Achlorhydria that

胃酸缺乏　胃內缺乏鹽酸。經給予大劑量組胺後仍存在的胃

persists despite large doses of histamine is associated with atrophy of the lining (mucosa) of the stomach. In this condition there is usually an absence of secretion of *intrinsic factor, which will lead to *pernicious anaemia. In some people, however, achlorhydria is not associated with any disease, produces no ill-effects, and needs no treatment.

酸缺乏與胃黏膜萎縮有關；此時往往無內因子分泌，從而導致惡性貧血。然而有些人胃酸缺乏與任何疾病無關，亦無不適，並不需治療。

acholia *n.* absence or deficiency of bile secretion or failure of the bile to enter the alimentary canal (for example, because of an obstructed bile duct).

無膽汁（症） 無膽汁分泌或分泌不足，或膽汁不能進入消化道（如因膽管阻塞）。

acholuria *n.* absence of the *bile pigments from the urine, which occurs in some forms of jaundice (*acholuric jaundice*). **–acholuric** *adj.*

無膽色素尿 尿中無膽色素，發生於某些類型的黃疸中（無膽色素尿性黃疸）。

achondroplasia *n.* a disorder inherited as a *dominant characteristic, in which the bones of the arms and legs fail to grow to normal size due to a defect in both cartilage and bone. It results in a type of *dwarfism characterized by short limbs, a normal-sized head and body, and normal intelligence. **–achondroplastic** *adj.*

軟骨發育不全 一種顯性遺傳病，患者四肢骨骼因軟骨和骨的缺損而未能發育至正常大小，以致形成以四肢短小而頭顱、軀體和智力正常為特點的一型侏儒。

achromatic *adj.* without colour.

無色的 沒有顏色。

achromatic lenses lenses that are specially designed for use in the eyepieces of microscopes and other scientific instruments. They give clear images, unblurred by the coloured fringes that are produced with ordinary lenses (caused by splitting of the light into different wavelengths).

消色差透鏡 專門設計用於顯微鏡和其他科學儀器目鏡的鏡片。所顯示圖像清晰，而無普通鏡片產生的模糊彩色邊緣（係光綫分解為不同波長所致）。

achromatopsia *n.* the inability to perceive colour. Such complete *colour blindness is very rare and is usually

全色盲 無感色能力。此種全色盲十分罕見，常與視敏度弱有關並由遺傳因素決定。

associated with poor *visual acuity; it is usually determined by hereditary factors.

achylia *n.* absence of secretion. The term is usually applied to a nonsecreting stomach (*achylia gastrica*) whose lining (mucosa) is atrophied (*see* achlorhydria).

胃液缺乏　無分泌。此詞常用來描述胃黏膜萎縮（參閱 achlorhydria）而不分泌（胃液缺乏）。

acidaemia *n.* abnormally high blood acidity. This condition may result from an increase in the concentration of acidic substances and/or a decrease in the level of alkaline substances in the blood. *See also* acidosis. *Compare* alkalaemia.

酸血（症）　血液酸度異常增高，可因血液中酸性物質濃度升高和／或鹼性物質水平降低而致。參閱 acidosis。與 alkalaemia 對比。

acid-base balance the balance between the amount of carbonic acid and bicarbonate in the blood, which must be maintained at a constant ratio of 1:20 in order to keep the hydrogen ion concentration of the plasma at a constant value (pH 7.4). Any alteration in this ratio will disturb the acid-base balance of the blood and tissues and cause either *acidosis or *alkalosis. The lungs and the kidneys play an important role in the regulation of the acid-base balance.

酸鹼平衡　血液中碳酸和碳酸氫鹽之間數量的平衡，二者須保持 1:20 的恆定比率以使血漿中氫離子濃度維持在一恆定值 (pH 7.4)。該比例的任何變動將破壞血液和組織中的酸鹼平衡而引起酸中毒或鹼中毒。肺和腎在調節酸鹼平衡中起着重要作用。

acid-etch technique a technique for bonding resin-based materials to the enamel of teeth; it is used to retain and seal the margins of *fillings, to retain brackets of fixed *orthodontic appliances, and to retain resin-based *fissure sealants and adhesive bridges. A porous surface is created by applying phosphoric acid for approximately one minute.

酸蝕法　使樹脂基質物與牙釉質黏合的技術；用於固定和封閉充填物邊緣，固定固位正牙器托架，以及固定樹脂基質牙裂隙密封劑和黏着橋。用磷酸處理約一分鐘可產生多孔表面。

acid-fast *adj.* **1.** describing bacteria that have been stained and continue to hold the stain after treatment with an acidic solution. For example, tuberculosis bacteria are acid-fast when stained with a *carbol fuchsin preparation. **2.** describing a stain that is not removed from

耐酸的　**(1)** 形容染色後經酸性溶液處理仍保持其着色的細菌。如結核菌用石炭酸品紅液製劑染色時呈耐酸性。**(2)** 形容用酸性溶液沖洗標本仍不褪色的染劑。

a specimen by washing with an acidic solution.

acidophil (acidophilic) *adj.* **1.** (in histology) describing tissues, cells, or parts of cells that stain with acid dyes (such as eosin). **2.** (in bacteriology) describing bacteria that grow well in acid media.

acidosis *n.* a condition in which the acidity of body fluids and tissues is abnormally high. This arises because of a failure of the mechanisms responsible for maintaining a balance between acids and alkalis in the blood (*see* acid-base balance). In *gaseous acidosis* more than the normal amount of carbon dioxide is retained in the body, as in drowning. In *renal acidosis*, kidney failure results in excessive loss of bicarbonate or retention of phosphoric and sulphuric acids. Patients with diabetes mellitus suffer from a form of acidosis in which sodium, potassium, and *ketone bodies are lost in the urine.

acinus *n.* (*pl.* acini) **1.** a small sac or cavity surrounded by the secretory cells of a gland. Some authorities regard the term as synonymous with *alveolus, but others distinguish an acinus by the possession of a narrow passage (lumen) leading from the sac. **2.** (in the lung) the tissue supplied with air by one terminal *bronchiole. *Emphysema is classified by the part of the acinus involved (i.e. *centriacinar*, *panacinar*, or *periacinar*). –**acinous** *adj.*

aclarubicin *n.* an *antimitotic drug administered by injection in the treatment of leukaemia and other cancers. It is an *anthracycline antibiotic; possible side-effects include nausea and vomiting, loss of hair, and damage to bone marrow. Trade name: **Aclacin**.

嗜酸的　**(1)**（組織學）形容能被酸性染料（如曙紅）染色的組織、細胞或細胞的某些部分。**(2)**（細菌學）形容在酸性培養基中生長良好的細菌。

酸中毒　體液與組織的酸度異常高的狀態。因維持血液酸鹼平衡的機制障礙所致（參閱acid-base balance）。二氧化碳性酸中毒時，超過正常量的二氧化碳滯留於體內，如淹溺者。腎性酸中毒時，腎衰竭可導致碳酸氫鹽喪失過多或磷酸和硫酸滯留。糖尿病患者之酸中毒有鈉、鉀和酮體隨尿液排出。

腺泡　**(1)**　由腺體分泌細胞所包圍的小囊或腔。有些專家認為本詞與 alveolus（肺泡）同義，亦有人認為它特指帶有腺腔的腺泡。**(2)**（肺部）由一終末細支氣管供氧的組織。肺氣腫即以所累及的腺泡部位分類（即中心肺泡性肺氣腫，全肺泡性肺氣腫，或周圍肺泡性肺氣腫）。

阿柔比星　注射用治療白血病和其他癌症的抗有絲分裂藥。為蒽環類抗生素；可產生的副作用有惡心、嘔吐、脫髮、以及骨髓損害。商品名：Aclacin。

aclasis *n. see* diaphysial aclasis.

續連症　參閱　diaphysial aclasis。

acne (acne vulgaris) *n.* a common inflammatory disorder of the sebaceous glands. These grease-producing glands are under androgen control, but the cause of acne is unknown. It involves the face, back, and chest and is characterized by the presence of blackheads with papules pustules, and – in more severe cases – cysts and scars. Acne is readily treatable. Mild cases respond to topical therapy with *benzoyl peroxide, while more refractory conditions require treatment with long-term antibiotics or (for treating women only) *anti-androgens, such as Dianette (cyproterone and ethinyloestradiol); severe or cystic acne can be treated with *isotretinoin.

痤瘡　一種常見的皮脂腺發炎的疾病。這些產生油脂的腺體受雄激素控制，但痤瘡的病因仍不明。此病累及面、背和胸部，特徵為伴有丘疹和膿疱的黑頭粉刺，並在病症加重時出現囊腫和瘢痕。痤瘡易於治療。輕症時用過氧苯甲酰局部治療效果良好，較頑固的病程需長期用抗生素治療或（僅對婦女）抗雄激素藥物，如迪安尼特（環丙孕酮和炔雌醇）；重症或囊性痤瘡可用異維甲酸治療。

aconite *n.* the dried roots of the herbaceous plant *Aconitum napellus* (monkshood or wolfbane), containing three *analgesic substances: *aconine, aconitine,* and *picraconitine.* Aconite was formerly used to prepare liniments for muscular pains and a tincture for toothache, but is regarded as too toxic for use today.

烏頭　草本植物歐烏頭的乾燥根莖，含三種止痛物質；烏頭原鹼、烏頭鹼和苦烏頭鹼。過去用於製備肌肉止痛搽劑與牙痛酊劑，現在認為因毒性過大而不宜使用。

acoustic *adj.* of or relating to sound or the sense of hearing.

聽的，聲學的　與聲或聽覺有關的。

acoustic holography a technique of building up a three-dimensional picture of structures within the body using *ultrasound waves. Two separate sound sources cause ultrasound waves to be transmitted through and reflected from the organs being examined. The interference patterns produced on a liquid surface are illuminated by laser light and photographed to form a *hologram.*

傳聲全息照相術　利用超聲波形成體內結構的三維圖像之技術。兩個分離聲源使超聲波穿透被檢器官並自其反射回來，由此在液面產生的干擾圖形經激光照射攝影而形成全息照片。

acoustic nerve *see* vestibulocochlear nerve.

聽神經　參閱　vestibulocochlear nerve。

acquired *adj.* describing a condition or disorder contracted after birth and not attributable to hereditary causes. *Compare* congenital.

獲得的，後天的　描述出生後獲得而非遺傳因素所致的某種狀態或疾病。與 congenital 對比。

acquired immune deficiency syndrome *see* AIDS.

獲得性免疫缺陷綜合徵　參閱 AIDS。

acrania *n.* congenital absence of the skull, either partial or complete, due to a developmental defect.

無顱（畸形）　因發育缺損所致的部分或完全的先天性頭顱缺乏。

acriflavine *n.* a dye used in antiseptic skin preparations and to disinfect contaminated wounds. It may cause sensitivity of the skin to sunlight.

吖啶黄　一種用於皮膚製備中抗菌和受污染傷口消毒的染劑，可導致皮膚對日光過敏。

acrivastine *n.* an *antihistamine drug used to treat hay fever and urticaria (nettle rash). It is administered by mouth. Possible side-effects include drowsiness. Trade name: **Semprex**.

阿伐斯汀　用於治療枯草熱與蕁麻疹的製組胺藥，口服。可致副作用，如嗜睡。商品名：Semprex。

acro- *prefix denoting* **1.** extremity; tip. Example: *acrohypothermy* (abnormal coldness of the extremities (hands and feet)). **2.** height; promontory. Example: *acrophobia* (morbid dread of heights). **3.** extreme; intense. Example: *acromania* (an extreme degree of mania).

〔前綴〕**(1)** 肢端，尖端　例如：手足溫度過低（四肢肢端異常寒冷）。**(2)** 高，岬　例如：高處恐怖（病態恐高）。**(3)** 極端，重度的　例如：重躁狂（極度躁狂）。

acrocentric *n.* a chromosome in which the *centromere is situated at or very near one end. **–acrocentric** *adj.*

近端着絲粒的　着絲粒位於或靠近一端的染色體。

acrocyanosis *n.* bluish-purple discoloration of the hands and feet due to slow circulation of the blood through the small vessels in the skin.

手足發紺　手足因皮膚小血管血液循環緩慢而呈青紫色。

acrodermatitis *n.* inflammation of the skin of the feet or hands. A diffuse chronic variety produces swelling and reddening of the affected areas, followed by atrophy. The cause is unknown and there is no treatment.

肢皮炎　手或足的皮膚炎症。慢性瀰散型肢皮炎患部紅腫，繼而萎縮，其病因不明，亦無有效療法。

acrodynia *n. see* pink disease.

肢痛症　參閱 pink disease。

acromegaly *n.* increase in size of the hands, feet, and the face due to excessive production of *growth hormone (somatotrophin) by a tumour of the anterior pituitary gland. The tumour can be treated with X-rays or surgically removed. *See also* gigantism.

肢端肥大症　垂體前部腫瘤導致生長激素（促生長素）產生過多而致手、足、面部增大。此腫瘤可用 X 綫治療或手術切除。參閱 gigantism。

acromion *n.* an oblong process at the top of the spine of the *scapula, part of which articulates with the clavicle (collar bone) to form the *acromioclavicular joint.* **–acromial** *adj.*

肩峰　肩胛棘頂端的卵圓形突起，其中部分與鎖骨聯接形成肩鎖關節。

acroparaesthesiae *pl. n.* tingling sensations in the hands and feet. *See* paraesthesiae.

肢端感覺異常　手與足的針刺感。參閱 paraesthesiae。

acrosclerosis *n.* a skin disease thought to be a type of generalized *scleroderma. It also has features of *Raynaud's disease with the hands, face, and feet being mainly affected.

肢端硬化病　被認為是一種全身硬皮病的皮膚病。亦具有雷諾病的特點，主要發生於手、面和足。

acrosome *n.* the caplike structure on the front end of a spermatozoon. It breaks down just before fertilization (the *acrosome reaction*), releasing a number of enzymes that assist penetration between the follicle cells that still surround the ovum. Failure of the acrosome reaction is a cause of male infertility (*see also* andrology).

頂體　精子前端的帽狀結構，在即將受精前脫落（頂體反應），並釋放出若干協助精子在仍包圍卵子的卵泡細胞間穿越的酶。頂體反應障礙為男性不育症的病因之一。（參閱 andrology）。

acrylic resin one of a group of polymeric materials used for making denture teeth, denture bases, and formerly as a dental filling material.

丙烯酸樹脂　一種聚合體材料，用於製造托牙、牙列基托，過去也作牙科充填物。

ACTH (adrenocorticotrophic hormone, adrenocorticotrophin, corticotrophin) a hormone synthesized and stored in the anterior pituitary gland,

促腎上腺皮質激素　垂體前葉合成並貯存的激素，在各種應激狀態時大量釋放。此激素控制腎上腺皮質類固醇激素的分

large amounts of which are released in response to any form of stress. ACTH controls the secretion of *corticosteroid hormones from the adrenal gland. It is administered by injection to test adrenal function and to treat conditions such as rheumatic diseases (especially in children) and asthma.

泌。注射用可測腎上腺功能，並可治療風濕病（尤指兒童）和哮喘。

actin *n*. a protein found in muscle, that plays an important role in the process of contraction. *See* striated muscle.

肌纖蛋白 肌肉中的一種蛋白，肌收縮時起重要作用。參閱 striated muscle。

Actinobacillus *n*. a genus of Gram-negative nonmotile aerobic bacteria that are characteristically spherical or rodlike in shape but occasionally grow into branching filaments. Actinobacilli cause disease in animals that can be transmitted to man.

放綫杆菌屬 革蘭氏陰性不運動需氧菌一屬，呈典型的球形或杆狀，偶爾長成分支菌絲。該菌類在動物中致病，並可傳給人類。

Actinomyces *n*. a genus of Gram-positive nonmotile fungus-like bacteria that cause disease in animals and man. The species *A. israelii* is the causative organism of human *actinomycosis.

放綫菌屬 革蘭氏陽性不運動真菌樣細菌一屬，可使人畜致病。伊氏放綫菌為人類放綫菌病的病原體。

actinomycin *n*. a *cytotoxic drug, produced by *Streptomyces* bacteria, that inhibits the growth of cancer cells. There are two forms, both of which are administered by injection. Actinomycin C may damage bone marrow. Actinomycin D (*Cosmegen, Lyovac*) may cause nausea, vomiting, diarrhoea, blood disorders, and bone-marrow damage.

放綫菌素 一種由鏈黴菌產生可抑制癌細胞生長的細胞毒素藥物。有兩型，均為注射給藥。放綫菌素 C 可損害骨髓，放綫菌素 D (Cosmegen，Lyovac) 可引起惡心、嘔吐、腹瀉、血液病及骨髓損害。

actinomycosis *n*. a noncontagious disease caused by the bacterium *Actinomyces israelii*, which most commonly affects the jaw but may also affect the lungs, brain, or intestines. The bacterium is normally present in the mouth but it may become pathogenic following an *apical abscess or extraction of a tooth.

放綫菌病 由伊氏放綫菌所致的一種非接觸傳染性疾病，最常發於頜，亦可侵犯肺、腦或小腸。此菌可正常存在於口腔，但患根尖膿腫或拔牙後則可致病，特徵為有多個開口於皮膚表面的竇道。治療採用引流排膿與長期使用抗生素。

It is characterized by multiple sinuses that open onto the skin. Treatment is by drainage of pus and a prolonged course of antibiotics.

actinotherapy *n.* the treatment of disorders with *infrared or *ultraviolet radiation.

射綫療法　用紅外綫或紫外綫照射治病的方法。

action potential the change in voltage that occurs across the membrane of a nerve or muscle cell when a *nerve impulse is triggered. It is due to the passage of charged particles across the membrane (*see* depolarization) and is an observable manifestation of the passage of an impulse.

動作電位　神經衝動被激發時所發生的穿越神經細胞膜或肌細胞膜的電位變化。由帶電粒子越膜而產生（參閱 depolarization），並為衝動通過的一種可見表現。

active transport (in biochemistry) an energy-dependent process in which certain substances (including ions, some drugs, and amino acids) are able to cross cell membranes against a concentration gradient. The process is inhibited by substances that interfere with cellular metabolism (e.g. high doses of digitalis).

主動轉運　（生物化學）某些物質（包括離子、一些藥物及氨基酸）能夠逆濃度梯度通過細胞膜的需要能量消耗的過程。此過程可被干擾細胞代謝的物質（如大劑量的洋地黃）抑制。

actomyosin *n.* a protein complex formed in muscle between actin and myosin during the process of contraction. *See* striated muscle.

肌纖凝蛋白　肌肉收縮時在肌纖蛋白和肌凝蛋白之間形成的複合體。參閱 striated muscle。

acupuncture *n.* a traditional Chinese system of healing in which symptoms are relieved by thin metal meedles inserted into selected points beneath the skin. The needles are stimulated either by rotation or, more recently, by an electric current. Hypotheses suggest that the needling activates dcep sensory nerves which cause the pituitary and midbrain to release *endorphins – the brain's natural pain-killers. Acupuncture is widely used in the Far East for the relief of pain and in China itself it has become

針灸　一種中國傳統的治療方法，通過將金屬細針刺入皮膚下的特定穴位緩解症狀。可用捻轉法或較新的電流法使針產生刺激。有關理論認為，針刺作用於深部感覺神經，使垂體和中腦釋放腦的天然止痛劑內啡肽。針灸在遠東廣泛應用於解痛，在中國則已成為某些大手術中另一種麻醉的方法。針灸醫師在西方有些具備行醫資格，而多數並無此資格。

an alternative to anaesthesia for some major operations. Acupuncturists in the West may be medically qualified but many are not.

acute *adj.* **1.** describing a disease of rapid onset, severe symptoms, and brief duration. *Compare* chronic. **2.** describing any intense symptom, such as severe pain.

急性的 **(1)** 描述發病急、症狀重而病程短的疾病。與 chronic 對比。**(2)** 描述任何嚴重的症狀,如劇痛。

acute abdomen an emergency surgical condition caused by damage to one or more abdominal organs following injury or disease. The patient is in severe pain and often in shock. Perforation of a peptic ulcer or a severely infected appendix, or rupture of the liver or spleen following a crushing injury, all produce an acute abdomen requiring urgent treatment.

急腹症 外傷或患病後一個或多個腹部器官受損而致的一種外科急症。患者疼痛劇烈並常常休克。消化性潰瘍穿孔,嚴重的闌尾感染,或肝、脾在擠壓傷後穿孔,均導致需緊急處理的急腹症。

acute rheumatism *see* rheumatic fever.

急性風濕病 參閱 rheumatic fever。

acyclovir *n.* an antiviral drug that inhibits DNA synthesis in cells infected by *herpesviruses. Administered topically, by mouth, or intravenously, it is useful in patients whose immune systems are disturbed and also in the treatment of herpes zoster, genital herpes, and herpes encephalitis. Trade name: **Zovirax**.

阿昔洛韋 抑制感染疱疹病毒的細胞內 DNA 合成的抗病毒藥。可局部用藥、口服或靜注,對免疫系統障礙的患者有效,亦用於治療帶狀疱疹、生殖器疱疹及疱疹性腦炎。商品名:Zovirax。

ad- *prefix denoting* towards or near. Examples: *adaxial* (towards the main axis); *adoral* (towards or near the mouth).

〔前綴〕向,近 例如:向軸的;向口的。

ADA deficiency *see* adenosine deaminase deficiency.

腺苷脫氧酶缺乏 參閱 adenosine deaminase deficiency。

Adam's apple (laryngeal prominence) a projection, lying just under the skin, of the thyroid cartilage of the *larynx.

喉結 喉皮膚下甲狀軟骨的突起。

Adams-Stokes syndrome *see* Stokes-Adams syndrome.

亞-斯氏綜合徵　參閱　Stokes-Adams syndrome。

adaptation *n.* the phenomenon in which a sense organ shows a gradually diminishing response to continuous or repetitive stimulation. The nose, for example, may become adapted to the stimulus of an odour that is continuously present so that in time it ceases to report its presence. Similarly, the adaptation of touch receptors in the skin means that the presence of clothes can be forgotten a few minutes after they have been put on.

適應（作用）　感覺器官對持續或重複刺激反應逐漸降低的現象。例如，鼻可適應持續的臭味刺激而最終不再感覺其存在。同樣地，皮膚觸覺感受器的適應意味著穿衣幾分鐘後即不覺其存在。

addiction *n.* a state of *dependence produced by the habitual taking of drugs. Strictly speaking, the term implies the state of physical dependence induced by such drugs as morphine, heroin, and alcohol, but it is also used for the state of psychological dependence, produced by drugs such as barbiturates. Treatment is aimed at gradual withdrawal of the drug and eventually total abstention. *See also* alcoholism, tolerance.

癮，癖　習慣性服藥而產生的一種依賴狀態。嚴格地說，此詞意指嗎啡、海洛因和酒精之類麻醉品所致的軀體依賴狀態，但也用於巴比妥酸鹽類等藥物所致的心理依賴狀態。治療以逐漸脫癮並最終完全戒除為目標。參閱　alcoholism，tolerance。

Addison's disease a syndrome due to inadequate secretion of corticosteroid hormones by the *adrenal glands, sometimes as a result of tuberculous infection. Symptoms include weakness, loss of energy, low blood pressure, and dark pigmentation of the skin. Formerly fatal, the disease is now treatable by replacement hormone therapy.

阿狄森病　一種腎上腺皮質類固醇激素分泌不足而致的綜合徵，有時為結核性感染的結果。症狀有虛弱、無力、低血壓及皮膚的黑色素沉著。過去此病可致死，現可用激素替代療法治療。

adduct *vb.* to move a limb or any other part towards the midline of the body. **–adduction** *n.*

收，內收　肢體或任何其他部分向人體中綫運動。

adductor *n.* any muscle that moves one part of the body towards another or towards the midline of the body.

收肌，內收肌　把身體的一部分拉向另一部分或人體中綫的肌肉。

aden- (adeno-) *prefix denoting* a gland or glands. Examples: *adenalgia* (pain in); *adenogenesis* (development of); *adenopathy* (disease of).

〔前綴〕**腺** 例如：腺痛；腺發生，腺病。

adenine *n.* one of the nitrogen-containing bases (*see* purine) that occurs in the nucleic acids DNA and RNA. *See also* ATP.

腺嘌呤 存在於核酸 DNA 與 RNA 中的含氮鹼類之一。參閱 ATP。

adenitis *n.* inflammation of a gland or group of glands (or glandlike structures). For example, *mesenteric adenitis* affects the lymph nodes (formerly called lymph glands) in the membranous support of the intestines (the mesentery); *cervical adenitis* affects the lymph nodes in the neck.

腺炎 一個或一羣腺體（或腺體樣組織）的炎症。例如，腸繫膜腺炎發生於支持小腸的膜（腸繫膜）中的淋巴結（過去稱淋巴腺），頸淋巴結炎發生於頸部淋巴結。

adenocarcinoma *n.* a malignant epithelial tumour arising from glandular structures, which are constitutent parts of most organs of the body. The term is also applied to tumours showing a glandular growth pattern. These tumours may be subclassified according to the substances that they produce, for example *mucus-secreting* and *serous adenocarcinomas*, or to the microscopic arrangement of their cells into patterns, for example *papillary* and *follicular adenocarcinomas*. They may be solid or cystic (*cystadenocarcinomas*). Each organ may produce tumours showing a variety of histological types; for example, the ovary may produce both mucinous and serous cystadenocarcinomas.

腺癌 源自腺體組織的一種惡性上皮腫瘤，腺體組織為身體多數器官的構成部分。此詞也指呈腺體樣增生型的腫瘤。這些腫瘤可根據所產生物質進一步分類，如黏液分泌性腺癌和漿液性腺癌，或依顯微鏡細胞排列形狀分類，如乳頭狀腺癌和濾泡狀腺癌。腺癌可為實質性或囊性的（囊腺癌）。各個器官可產生呈不同組織型的腫瘤；例如，卵巢既可產生黏液性囊腺癌，也可產生漿液性囊腺癌。

adenohypophysis *n.* the anterior lobe of the *pituitary gland.

腺（性）垂體 垂體前葉。

adenoidectomy *n.* surgical removal of the *adenoids in patients who suffer from either *glue ear or difficulty in breathing through the nose.

增殖腺切除術 對患黏液性耳炎或鼻呼吸困難的病人施行切除腺樣增殖體的手術。

adenoids (nasopharyngeal tonsil) *n.* the collection of lymphatic tissue at the rear of the nose. Enlargement of the adenoids can cause obstruction to breathing through the nose and can block the Eustachian tubes, causing *glus ear.

adenolymphoma *n.* *see* Warthin's tumour.

adenoma *n.* a benign tumour of epithelial origin that is derived from glandular tissue or exhibits clearly defined glandular structures. Adenomas may become malignant (*see* adenocarcinoma). Some show recognizable tissue elements, such as fibrous tissue (*fibroadenomas*), while others, such as bronchial adenomas, produce active compounds giving rise to clinical syndromes (*see* argentaffinoma). Tumours in certain organs, including the pituitary gland, are often classified by their histological staining affinities, for example *eosinophil*, *basophil*, and *chromophobe adenomas*.

adenomyosis *n.* *see* endometriosis.

adenosine *n.* a compound containing adenine and the sugar ribose: it occurs in ATP. *See also* nucleoside.

adenosine deaminase deficiency (ADA deficiency) a genetic disorder affecting about one bady in 25,000 and characterized by a defect in *adenosine deaminase* (*ADA*), an enzyme that is involved in purine metabolism. Deficiency of this enzyme results in selective damage to the antibody-producing lymphocytes; this in turn leads to a condition known as *severe combined immune deficiency* (*SCID*), similar in its effects to AIDS, in which the affected baby has no

腺樣增殖體（鼻咽扁桃體）鼻後部淋巴組織的聚集。它的增大可阻塞鼻呼吸並阻塞咽鼓管而致黏液性耳炎。

腺淋巴瘤　參閱 Warthin's tumour。

腺瘤　源自腺體組織或呈明顯腺狀結構的一種良性上皮腫瘤。可轉為惡性（參閱 adenocarcinoma）。有些腺瘤具有可辨認的組織成分，如纖維組織（纖維腺瘤），有些如支氣管腺瘤產生引起臨床綜合徵的活性化合物（參閱 argentaffinoma）。包括垂體在內的某些部位常根據其組織染色的親和力分類，如嗜酸性、嗜鹼性和拒染性腺瘤。

子宮內膜異位　參閱 endometriosis。

腺苷　一種含腺嘌呤和核糖的化合物，存在於 ATP 中。參閱 nucleoside。

腺苷脱氨酶缺乏　一種以腺苷脱氨酶缺陷為特徵的遺傳病，約 1/25 000 的嬰兒患有此病。腺苷脱氨酶參與嘌呤代謝，此酶缺乏可引起對產生抗體的淋巴細胞的選擇性損害，進而導致稱為嚴重聯合免疫缺陷(SCID) 的狀況，其作用類似於艾滋病，即患兒對感染全無抵抗力，必須自出生便完全置於有保護作用的塑料罩內。這類兒童的半年存活率僅為約

resistance to infection and must be entirely enclosed in a protective plastic bubble from birth. Such children have only about a 50% chance of surviving for six months and are considered to be among the most urgent indications for *gene therapy; the first clinical trials have already begun.

50%，被視為最需基因療法的適應症之一；初步的臨床試驗已經開始。

adenosine diphosphate *see* ADP.

二磷酸腺苷　參閱 ADP。

adenosine monophosphate *see* AMP.

一磷酸腺苷　參閱 AMP。

adenosine triphosphate *see* ATP.

三磷酸腺苷　參閱 ATP。

adenosis *n.* (*pl.* **adenoses**) **1.** excessive growth of development of glands. **2.** any disease of a gland or glandlike structure, especially of a lymph node.

腺病　**(1)** 腺體增長或發育過度。**(2)** 腺體或腺樣結構的任何疾病，尤指淋巴結。

adenovirus *n.* one of a group of DNA-containing viruses causing infections of the upper respiratory tract that produce symptoms resembling those of the common cold.

腺病毒　含 DNA 的一組病毒之一，可致上呼吸道感染，產生類似感冒的症狀。

Adept *n.* antibody-directed enzyme pro-drug therapy: a method under development for the treatment of cancer. It involves the patient being injected first with an antibody-enzyme complex that binds specifically to tumour cells, and later with a *pro-drug*, which is inactive until it comes into contact with the antibody-enzyme complex. The enzyme converts the pro-drug into a *cytotoxic form, which is concentrated around the tumour and can therefore destroy the cancer cells without damaging normal tissue.

抗體引導的酶前（體）藥（物）療法　一種發展中的癌症治療方法。首先給患者注射專與腫瘤細胞結合的抗體-酶複合體，然後再注射接觸抗體-酶複合體之前無活性的前體藥物。此酶將前體藥物轉化成細胞毒素形式，集中在腫瘤周圍，由此可殺滅癌細胞而無損於正常組織。

adhesion *n.* **1.** the union of two normally separate surfaces, such as the moving surfaces of joints, by fibrous connective tissue developing in an inflamed or damaged region. (The fibrous tissue

(1) 黏連　正常狀態下兩個分隔的表面，如關節的活動面，由炎症或受損部位增生的纖維結締組織結合起來（纖維組織本身亦稱黏連）。腸袢間黏連

itself is also called an adhesion.) Adhesions between loops of intestine often occur following abdominal surgery but only rarely cause symptoms, such as intestinal obstruction. If the pericardial sac is affected by adhesion, the movements of the heart may be restricted. **2.** a healing process in which the edges of a wound fit together. In *primary adhesion* there is very little *granulation tissue; in *secondary adhesion* the two edges are joined together by granulation tissue.

常發生在腹部手術後，但僅偶爾產生腸梗阻等症狀。若心包發生黏連則可能限制心臟活動。**(2) 愈合** 傷口邊緣連接起來的愈合過程。一期愈合中幾乎無肉芽組織，二期愈合中則由肉芽組織連接兩邊緣。

adiadochokinesis *n. see* dysdiadochokinesis.

輪替運動不能 參閱 dysdiadochokinesis。

Adie's syndrome (Holmes-Adie syndrome) an abnormality of the pupils of the eyes, often affecting only one eye. The affected pupil reacts slowly to light and the response on convergence of the eyes is also slow. One or more tendon reflexes may be absent. The condition is almost entirely restricted to women.

艾迪綜合徵 一種通常僅影響單眼的瞳孔異常。受累瞳孔對光反應遲緩，會聚反應亦變遲緩，一種或多種腱反射可消失。此症幾乎完全限於女性。

adipocere *n.* a waxlike substance, consisting mainly of fatty acids, into which the soft tissues of the body can be converted after death. This usually occurs when the body is buried in damp earth or is submerged in water. Adipocere delays postmortem decomposition and is a spontaneous form of preservation without mummification.

屍蠟 主要由脂肪酸組成的一種蠟樣物質，死後屍體軟組織可轉變成此種物質，通常發生於屍體葬於濕地或浸入水中時。屍蠟延遲屍體腐敗，是一種無需乾屍化的屍體保存之天然形式。

adipose tissue fibrous *connective tissue packed with masses of fat cells. It forms a thick layer under the skin and occurs around the kidneys and in the buttocks. It serves both as an insulating layer and an energy store; food in excess of requirements is converted into fats and stored within these cells.

脂肪組織 充滿脂肪細胞羣的纖維結締組織。在皮下形成厚層，存在於腎臟和臀部周圍。它兼有隔熱層與能量貯存的功能；過多攝入的食物被轉化為脂肪而貯存於這些細胞內。

adiposis (liposis) *n*. the presence of abnormally large accumulations of fat in the body. The condition may arise from overeating, hormone irregularities, or a metabolic disorder. In *adiposis dolorosa*, a condition affecting women more commonly than men, painful fatty swellings are associated with defects in the nervous system. *See also* obesity.

肥胖症（脂肪過多症） 人體中有異常大量的脂肪蓄積，可因攝食過度，激素分泌紊亂或代謝障礙所致。痛性肥胖症中女性多於男性，引起疼痛的脂肪腫塊與神經系統疾患有關。參閱 obesity。

aditus *n*. an anatomical opening or passage; for example, the opening of the tympanic cavity (middle ear) to the air spaces of the mastoid process.

入口，口 解剖學上的開口或通道。例如，鼓室（中耳）通向乳突氣腔的開口。

adjuvant *n*. any substance used in conjunction with another to enhance its activity. Aluminium salts are used as adjuvants in the preparation of vaccines from the toxins of diphtheria and tetanus: by keeping the toxins in precipitated form, the salts increase the efficacy of the toxins as antigens.

輔藥 任何與另一藥物合用以加強其活性的物質。鋁鹽用作從白喉與破傷風毒素中製備疫苗的輔藥：它通過使毒素保持沉澱狀而增強了毒素的抗原作用。

adjuvant therapy *cytotoxic drug treatment given to patients after surgical removal of, or radiotherapy to, their primary tumour when there is known to be a high risk of future tumour recurrence arising from *micrometastases. Adjuvant therapy is aimed at destroying these secondary tumours and is recommended for some patients with breast cancer. *Compare* neoadjuvant chemotherapy.

輔助療法 在手術切除或放射治療原發性腫瘤後，對微小癌轉移引起腫瘤復發高度危險的患者所給予的細胞毒素藥物治療。輔助療法旨在摧毀這些繼發性腫瘤。現建議某些乳腺癌患者採用輔助療法。與 neoadjuvant chemotherapy 對比。

adnexa *pl. n*, adjoining parts. For example, the *uterine adnexa* are the Fallopian tubes and ovaries (which adjoin the uterus).

附件 毗鄰部分。例如，子宮附件是輸卵管和卵巢（毗鄰子宮）。

ADP (adenosine diphosphate) a compound containing adenine, ribose, and two phosphate groups. ADP occurs in cells and is involved in processes requiring the transfer of energy (*see* ATP).

二磷酸腺苷 一種含腺嘌呤、核糖和兩個磷酸基的化合物。存在於細胞中並參與需要能量轉移的過程（參閱 ATP）。

adrenal glands (suprarenal glands) two triangular *endocrine glands, each of which covers the superior surface of a kidney. Each gland has two parts, the *medulla* and *cortex*. The medulla forms the grey core of the gland; it consists mainly of *chromaffin tissue and is stimulated by the sympathetic nervous system to produce *adrenaline and *noradrenaline. The cortex is a yellowish tissue surrounding the medulla. It is derived embryologically from mesoderm and is stimulated by pituitary hormones (principally *ACTH) to produce three kinds of *corticosteroid hormones, which affect carbohydrate metabolism (e.g. *cortisol), electrolyte metabolism (e.g. *aldosterone), and the sex glands (oestrogens and androgens).

腎上腺 兩個三角形的內分泌腺，均覆蓋在腎的上部。每個腎有髓質與皮質兩部分，主要由嗜鉻組織構成的髓質形成腺的灰色核心，受交感神經刺激而產生腎上腺素和去甲腎上腺素。皮質為包圍髓質的淺黃色組織，在胚胎期由中胚層衍化而來。它受垂體（主要是ACTH）刺激產生三種皮質類固醇激素、可影響碳水化合物代謝（如皮質醇）、電解質代謝（如醛甾酮）及性腺（雌激素和雄激素）。

adrenaline (epinephrine) *n.* an important hormone secreted by the medulla of the adrenal gland. It has the function of preparing the body for 'fright, flight, or fight' and has widespread effects on circulation, the muscles, and sugar metabolism. The action of the heart is increased, the rate and depth of breathing are increased, and the metabolic rate is raised; the force of muscular contraction improves and the onset of muscular fatigue is delayed. At the same time the blood supply to the bladder and intestines is reduced, their muscular walls relax, and the sphincters contract. *Sympathetic nerves were originally thought to act by releasing adrenaline at their endings, and were therefore called *adrenergic* nerves. In fact the main substance released is the related substance *noradrenaline, which also forms a portion of the adrenal secretion.

Adrenaline given by injection is valuable for the relief of bronchial asthma, because it relaxes constricted airways. It

腎上腺素 腎上腺髓質所分泌的一種重要激素，其作用是在面臨恐懼、追逐或戰鬥時使身體作好準備。它對循環、肌肉和糖代謝均也有廣泛影響：使心搏加快、呼吸率與深度增加、代謝率升高、肌肉收縮力增強、疲勞延緩、同時膀胱和腸道供血減少，其肌層鬆弛，括約肌收縮。過去交感神經被認為通過末端釋放腎上腺素而產生作用，因而被稱為腎上腺素能神經。事實上，它所釋放的主要物質是相關的去甲腎上腺素。這種物質也是腎上腺分泌的一部分。

注射腎上腺素可鬆弛氣管的收縮而緩解支氣管性哮喘。腎上腺素亦用於外科手術中或內窺鏡注射時，通過收縮皮膚或黏膜血管而減少出血。一些局麻液中也含有腎上腺素，特別是牙科所用，以延長麻醉作用。

is also used during surgery or by injection through an endoscope to reduce blood loss by constricting vessels in the skin or mucous membranes. It is included in some local anaesthetic solutions, particularly those used in dentistry, to prolong anaesthesia.

adrenergic *adj.* describing nerve fibres that release *noradrenaline as a neurotransmitter. *Compare* cholinergic.

腎上腺素能的　描述釋放神經介質去甲腎上腺素的神經纖維。與 cholinergic 對比。

adrenocorticotrophic hormone (adrenocorticotrophin) *see* ACTH.

促腎上腺皮質激素　參閱 ACTH。

adrenogenital syndrome a hormonal disorder resulting from abnormal steroid production by the adrenal cortex, due to a genetic fault. It may cause masculinization in girls, precocious puberty in boys, and adrenocortical failure (*see* Addison's disease) in both sexes. Treatment is by lifelong steroid replacement.

腎上腺（性）性徵綜合徵　因遺傳缺陷所致腎上腺皮質類固醇產生異常引起的一種激素疾病，可致女孩男性化，男孩青春期早熟，和兩性中均可發生的腎上腺皮質障礙（參閱 Addison's disease）。治療為終身用類固醇替代。

adrenoleukodystrophy *n.* a genetically determined condition of neurological degeneration with childhood and adult forms. It is characterized by progressive *spastic paralysis of the legs and sensory loss, associated with adrenal gland insufficiency and small gonads. The demonstration of abnormal fatty-acid metabolism has implications for future possible drug therapies. *Prenatal diagnosis is possible.

腎上腺白質營養不良　一種遺傳決定的神經病學性變性狀態，分兒童型和成人型。特點為進行性的下肢痙攣麻痺和感覺喪失，伴有腎上腺不足與小性腺。已證實該病有脂肪酸代謝異常，因而顯示出未來可用藥物治療的可能性。可作產前診斷。

adrenolytic *adj.* inhibiting the activity of *adrenergic nerves. Adrenolytic activity is opposite to that of *adrenaline.

抗腎上腺素（作用）的　抑制腎上腺素能神經作用的。抗腎上腺素與腎上腺素其作用相反。

advancement *n.* the detachment by surgery of a muscle, musculocutaneous flap, or tendon from its normal attachment site and its reattachment at a more

徙前術　通過手術使肌肉、肌皮瓣或腱脫離其正常附着部位，使其附着於更前的位置。例如，用於治療斜視，並廣泛

advanced (anterior) point. The technique is used, for example, in the treatment of squint and extensively in plastic surgery to cover large defects (*see also* pedicle)

用於整形外科以遮蓋大片缺陷（參閱 pedicle）。

adventitia (tunica adventitia) *n.* **1.** the outer coat of the wall of a *vein or *artery. It consists of loose connective tissue and networks of small blood vessels, which nourish the walls. **2.** the outer covering of various other organs or parts.

外膜 **(1)** 靜脈或動脈壁的外層，由疏鬆結締組織和小血管網組成並滋養血管壁。**(2)** 其他多種器官或結構的外被。

adventitious *adj.* **1.** occurring in a place other than the usual one. **2.** relating to the adventitia.

偶生的 **(1)** 發生於非正常部位的。**(2)** 與外膜有關的。

Aëdes *n.* a genus of widely distributed mosquitoes occurring throughout the tropics and subtropics. Most species are black with distinct white or silvery-yellow markings on the legs and thorax. *Aëdes* species are not only important as vectors of *dengue, *yellow fever, *filariasis, and Group B viruses causing encephalitis but also constitute a serious biting nuisance. *A. aegypti* is the principal vector of dengue and yellow fever.

伊蚊屬 在熱帶與亞熱帶廣泛分布的蚊屬。多數蚊種呈黑色，在腿部和胸部有明顯的白色或銀黃色斑紋。伊蚊屬蚊不僅是登革熱、黃熱病、絲蟲病及乙型腦炎病毒的重要媒介，還因其叮咬而十分令人討厭。埃及伊蚊是登革熱和黃熱病的主要媒介。

aegophony *n. see* vocal resonance.

羊音 參閱 vocal resonance。

-aemia *suffix denoting* a specified biochemical condition of the blood. Example: *hyperglycaemia* (excess sugar in the blood).

〔後綴〕血症 血液的一種特定生化狀態。如血糖過多（血液中糖分過多）。

aer- (aero-) *prefix denoting* air or gas. Examples: *aerogastria* (gas in the stomach); *aerogenesis* (production of gas).

〔前綴〕氣 空氣或氣體。例如，胃積氣（胃內有氣體）；產氣（產生氣體）。

aerobe *n.* any organism, especially a microbe, that requires the presence of free oxygen for life and growth. *See also* anaerobe, microaerophilic.

需氧菌 任何需有游離氧供其生活與生長的生物體，尤指微生物。參閱 anacrobe，microaerophilic。

aerobic *adj.* **1.** of or relating to aerobes: requiring free oxygen for life and growth. **2.** describing a type of cellular *respiration in which foodstuffs (carbohydrates) are completely oxidized by atmospheric oxygen, with the production of maximum chemical energy from the foodstuffs.

需氧的　**(1)** 需氧菌的或有關需氧菌的：生活生長需要游離氧。**(2)** 描述食物（碳水化合物）被大氣氧完全氧化的一種細胞呼吸，使食物中的化學能量完全釋放出來。

aerobic exercises *see* exercise.

需氧運動　參閱 exercise。

aerodontalgia *n.* pain in the teeth due to change in atmospheric pressure during air travel or the ascent of a mountain.

航空牙痛　航空旅行或登山時因大氣壓改變而致的牙痛。

aeroneurosis *n.* a syndrome of anxiety, agitation, and insomnia found in pilots flying unpressurized aircraft and attributed to *anoxia.

飛行員神經官能症　一種因缺氧導致的有焦慮、激動不安和失眠症狀的綜合徵，見於駕駛無密封艙飛機的飛行員中。

aerophagy *n.* the swallowing of air. This may be done voluntarily to stimulate belching, accidentally during rapid eating or drinking, or unconsciously as a habit. Voluntary aerophagy is used to permit oesophageal speech after surgical removal of the larynx (usually for cancer).

吞氣症　吞入空氣。可隨意吞氣以刺激噯氣，快速吃喝時可偶然吞氣，或可習慣性地無意識吞氣。隨意吞氣被用於喉管切除術後（常因癌症）的食管發音。

aerosol *n.* a suspension of extremely small liquid or solid particles (about 0.001 mm diameter) in the air. Drugs in aerosol form may be administered by inhalation.

氣霧劑　空氣中極其微小的液體或固體粒子（直徑約為 0.001 mm）懸浮。氣霧劑型藥物可以吸入方式給藥。

aetiology (etiology) *n.* **1.** the study or science of the causes of disease. **2.** the cause of a specific disease.

(1) 病因學　疾病原因的研究或科學。**(2)** 病因　特定疾病的原因。

afebrile *adj.* without, or not showing any signs of, a fever.

無熱的　不發熱或不表現任何發熱體徵的。

affect *n.* (in psychiatry) **1.** the predominant emotion in a person's mental state. **2.** the emotion associated with a particular idea. **–affective** *adj.*

情感　（精神病學）**(1)** 個人精神狀態中的主要感情。**(2)** 伴隨某種特定觀念產生的感情。

affective disorder any psychiatric disorder featuring abnormalities of mood or emotion (*affect). The most serious of these are *depression and *mania. Other affective disorders include *SADS (seasonal affective disorder syndrome).

情感性精神病　任何有情緒或感情（情感）異常特點的精神病。其中最為嚴重的是抑鬱和躁狂。其他的情感性精神病包括 SADS（季節性情感紊亂綜合徵）。

afferent *adj.* **1.** designating nerves or neurones that convey impulses from sense organs and other receptors to the brain or spinal cord, i.e. any sensory nerve or neurone. **2.** designating blood vessels that feed a capillary network in an organ or part. **3.** designating lymphatic vessels that enter a lymph node. *Compare* efferent.

傳入的，輸入的 **(1)** 指從感覺器官或其他感受器傳衝動至大腦或脊髓的神經或神經元。即任何感覺神經或感覺神經元。**(2)** 指供給器官或部位毛細管網的血管。**(3)** 指進入淋巴結的淋巴管。與 efferent 對比。

afibrinogenaemia *n.* complete absence of the coagulation factor *fibrinogen in the blood. *Compare* hypofibrinogenaemia.

無纖維蛋白原血症　血液中完全缺乏凝血因子纖維蛋白原。與 hypofibrinogenaemia 對比。

aflatoxin *n.* a poisonous substance produced in the spores of the fungus *Aspergillus flavus*, which infects peanuts. The toxin is known to produce cancer in certain animals and is suspected of being the cause of liver cancers in human beings living in warm and humid regions of the world, where stored nuts and cereals are contaminated by the fungus.

黃曲黴毒素　產生於真菌黃曲黴孢子的一種污染花生的毒物。已知該毒素在某些動物中致癌，並疑為世界溫濕地區人類肝癌的病因，在這些地區貯存的堅果與穀物受到此種真菌的污染。

afterbirth *n.* the placenta, umbilical cord, and ruptured membranes associated with the fetus, which normally become detached from the uterus and expelled within a few hours of birth.

胞衣，胎盤胎膜　與胎兒相連的胎盤、臍帶和破裂的羊膜，正常情況下於產後數小時內自子宮脫落並排出。

aftercare long-term surveillance as an adjunct or supplement to formal medical treatment of those who are chronically sick or *handicapped, including those with mental illness or handicap. Aftercare includes the provision of special aids and the adaptation of homes to improve daily living.

病後調養　對慢性病人或殘疾人，包括精神疾病或障礙患者實行長期監護，為正規醫療的輔助或補充措施。包括提供各類專門援助及幫助適應家庭環境以改善日常生活。

after-image *n.* an impression of an image that is registered by the brain for a brief moment after an object is removed from in front of the eye, or after the eye is closed.

後像　物體從眼前移去或閉目後圖像短暫地保留在腦中的印象。

afterpains *pl. n.* pains caused by uterine contractions after childbirth, especially during breast feeding, due to release of the hormone *oxytocin. The contractions help restore the uterus to its nonpregnant size and are more common in women who have given birth twice or more.

產後痛　產後子宮收縮引起的疼痛，尤在母乳餵養期間，為激素縮宮素釋放所致。子宮收縮有助於子宮復舊，在兩次或多次生育的婦女中更多見。

agammaglobulinaemia *n.* a total deficiency of the plasma protein *gamma globulin. *Compare* hypogammaglobulinaemia

血 γ - 球蛋白缺乏　血漿蛋白 γ - 球蛋白完全缺乏。與 hypogammaglobulinaemia 對比。

agar *n.* an extract of certain seaweeds that forms a gel suitable for the solidification of liquid bacteriological *culture media. *Blood agar* is nutrient agar containing 5–10% horse blood, used for the cultivation of certain bacteria or for detecting haemolytic (blood-destroying) activity.

瓊脂　呈凝膠狀態的某些海草的提取物，適用於液體細菌培養基的固化。血瓊脂為含有 5%~10% 馬血的營養瓊脂，用於培養某些細菌或測定溶血（破壞血液）作用。

Age Concern (in Britain) a voluntary agency with particular interest in the problems of the aged.

老年康采恩　（英國）一個關心老齡問題的志願組織。

agenesis *n.* absence of an organ, usually due to total failure of its development in the embryo.

發育不全　缺乏某一器官，常因胚胎期發育障礙所致。

agglutination (clumping) *n.* the sticking together, by serum antibodies called *agglutinins*, of such microscopic antigenic particles as red blood cells or bacteria so that they form visible clumps. Any substance that stimulates the body to produce an agglutinin is called an

凝集　由稱為凝集素的血清抗體將顯微鏡下才能看見的抗原顆粒如紅細胞或細菌黏結形成明顯的團塊。任何刺激身體產生凝集素的物質稱為凝集原。凝集為一種特異性反應，含不同已知凝集素的各種血清為實

agglutinogen. Agglutination is a specific reaction; in the laboratory, sera containing different known agglutinins provide an invaluable means of identifying unknown bacteria. When blood of different groups is mixed, agglutination occurs because serum contains natural antibodies (*isoagglutinins*) that attack red cells of a foreign group, whether previously encountered or not. This is not the same process as occurs in *blood coagulation.

驗室鑒定不明細菌的一項重要方法。不同血型的血液混合時發生凝集反應，此因血清含有天然抗體（同種凝集素）而對異型紅細胞不論是否曾經接觸過均加以破壞。這不同於凝血過程。

agglutinin *n.* an antibody that brings about the *agglutination of bacteria, blood cells, or other antigenic particles.

凝集素　一種可使細菌、血細胞或其他抗原顆粒凝集的抗體。

agglutinogen *n.* any antigen that provokes formation of an agglutinin in the serum and is therefore likely to be involved in *agglutination.

凝集原　任何促使血清中凝集素形成，並可能參與凝集反應的抗原。

aglossia *n.* congenital absence of the tongue.

無舌（畸形）　先天性缺舌。

agnathia *n.* congenital absence of the lower jaw, either partial or complete.

無（下）頜（畸形）　先天性部分或全部下頜缺失。

agnosia *n.* a disorder of the brain whereby the patient cannot interpret sensations correctly although the sense organs and nerves conducting sensation to the brain are functioning normally. It is due to a disorder of the *association areas in the parietal lobes. In *auditory agnosia* the patient can hear but cannot interpret sounds (including speech). A patient with *tactile agnosia* (*astereognosis*) retains normal sensation in his hands but cannot recognize three-dimensional objects by touch alone. In *visual agnosia* the patient can see but cannot interpret symbols, including letters (*see* alexia).

認識不能　一種腦機能障礙，患者傳導感覺至大腦的感覺器官與神經雖然功能正常，卻不能正確理解各種感覺。為頂葉聯合區病變所致。聽覺性認識不能患者可聽到而不理解聲音（包括語言）。觸覺性認識不能（實體覺缺失）患者有正常手感，但不能僅靠觸摸識別三維物體。視覺性認識不能患者可看到而不能理解符號（包括字母）的含義（參閱 alexia）。

agonal *adj.* describing or relating to the phenomena, such as cessation of breathing or change in the ECG or EEG, that are associated with the moment of death.

瀕死苦悶的 描述瀕死或與瀕死有關的現象，如呼吸停止、心電圖或腦電圖變化。

agonist *n.* **1. (prime mover)** a muscle whose active contraction causes movement of a part of the body. Contraction of an agonist is associated with relaxation of its *antagonist. **2.** a drug or other substance that acts at a cell-receptor site to produce an effect that is the same as, or similar to, that of the body's normal chemical messenger. Cholinergic drugs (*see* parasympathomimetic) are examples.

(1) 主動肌 一種有效活動時引起身體某一部分活動的肌肉。主動肌收縮時伴有其拮抗肌鬆弛。**(2)** 興奮劑、激動劑 作用於細胞受體部位的藥物或其他物質，以產生與體內正常化學信使相同或相似的效力，如膽鹼能藥物（參閱 parasympathomimetic）。

agoraphobia *n.* a morbid fear of public places and/or of open spaces. *See also* phobia.

廣場恐怖，曠野恐怖 對公共場所和/或開闊場地的病態恐懼。參閱 phobia。

agranulocytosis *n.* a disorder in which there is a severe acute deficiency of certain blood cells (*neutrophils) as a result of damage to the bone marrow by toxic drugs or chemicals. It is characterized by fever, with ulceration of the mouth and throat, and may lead rapidly to prostration and death. Treatment is by the administration of antibiotics in large quantities. When feasible, transfusion of white blood cells may be life-saving.

粒細胞缺乏症 因毒性藥或化學品損害骨髓而致的某種血細胞（中性粒細胞）嚴重急性缺乏的疾病。特徵為發熱、口咽潰瘍、可迅速導致衰竭和死亡。可用大劑量抗生素治療，若有條件可輸入白細胞搶救。

agraphia (dysgraphia) *n.* an acquired inability to write, although the strength and coordination of the hand remain normal. It is related to the disorders of language and it is caused by disease in the *parietal lobe of the brain. *see* Gerstmann's syndrome.

書寫不能 後天性無書寫能力，雖然手的力度與協調依然正常。此症與語言障礙有關，為大腦頂葉疾病所致。參閱 Gerstmann's syndrome。

agromania *n.* a pathologically strong impulse to live alone in open country.

隱居癖，野居癖 一種單獨在曠野生活的強烈的病態衝動。

ague *n.* *see* malaria.

瘧（疾） 參閱 malaria。

AIDS (acquired immune deficiency syndrome) a syndrome first identified in Los Angeles in 1981; a description of the causative virus – the human immunodeficiency virus (HIV) – was available in 1983. The virus destroys a subgroup of lymphocytes, resulting in suppression of the body's immune response (*see* immunity). AIDS is essentially a sexually transmitted disease, either homosexually or heterosexually. The two other main routes of spread are via infected blood or blood products (current processing of blood for transfusion and for haemophiliacs has virtually eliminated this danger) and by the maternofetal route. The virus may be transmitted from an infected mother to the child in the uterus or it may be acquired from maternal blood during parturition; it may also be transmitted in breast milk.

Acute infection following exposure to the virus results in the production of antibodies (seroconversion), their presence indicating that infection has taken place. However, not all those who seroconvert progress to chronic infection. For those who do enter a chronic stage there may be illness of varying severity, including persistent generalized involvement of the lymph nodes; what is termed *AIDS-related complex* (*ARC*), including intermittent fever, weight loss, diarrhoea, fatigue, and night sweats; and AIDS itself, presenting as opportunistic infections (especially pneumonia caused by the protozoan *Pneumocystis carinii*) and/or tumours, such as *Kaposi's sarcoma.

HIV has been isolated from semen, cervical secretions, plasma, cerebrospinal fluid, tears, saliva, urine, and breast milk but the concentration shows wide variations. Moreover HIV is a fragile virus and does not survive well outside the body. It is therefore

艾滋病（獲得性免疫缺陷綜合徵） 一種 1981 年首次在洛杉磯確認的綜合徵，1983 年對其致病病毒（人類免疫缺陷病毒，HIV）作出了描述。該病毒破壞多種淋巴細胞，導致身體免疫應答抑制（參閱 immunity）。艾滋病基本上是一種同性或異性間的性傳播疾病。其他兩條主要傳播途徑為污染的血液或血液製品（現在對供輸血及供血友病者的血液處理實際上已消除了這一危險）與母嬰傳播。該病毒可由受感染母親在子宮內傳給胎兒，或在分娩時從母血中感染，亦可經母乳傳播。

接觸艾滋病病毒後的急性感染可致抗體產生（血清轉化），其存在表明已發生感染。然而，並非所有的血清轉化者均發展至慢性感染。慢性患者可有嚴重程度不等的病症，包括持續性全身淋巴結受累；稱為有間歇熱、體重減輕、腹瀉、疲勞和盜汗症狀的艾滋病有關症候羣 (ARC)；以及表現為機會性感染（尤指原生動物卡氏肺囊蟲引起的肺炎）和/或肺瘤（如卡波濟肉瘤）的艾滋病本身。

已從精液、宮頸分泌物、血漿、腦脊液、淚液、唾液、尿液及母乳中分離出艾滋病病毒，但各部位中數量差別很大。此病毒十分脆弱，在體外不易存活，因而一般認為與 HIV 陽性患者的普通社交接觸無感染危險。但對所有衛生工作者在臨床工作中有嚴格的要求，以避免因疏忽而經 HIV 陽性人員的血液、血液製品或體液受到感染。HIV 呈陽性的醫護人員應宣布其狀況並將被予以咨詢。目前認為艾滋病可

considered that ordinary social contact with HIV-positive subjects involves no risk of infection. However, high standards of clinical practice are required by all health workers in order to avoid inadvertent infection via blood, blood products, or body fluids from HIV-positive people. Staff who become HIV-positive are expected to declare their status and will be counselled. Currently AIDS is considered to be fatal, although the type and length of illness preceding death varies considerably. AIDS is pandemic and as yet there is no known cure, although antiviral drugs (such as *zidovudine) are used to prolong the lives of AIDS patients.

致命，雖然其類型與存活時間均有很大差異。艾滋病是一種世界流行病，雖有抗病毒藥物（如齊多夫定）用以延長艾滋病患者生命，迄今仍無已知療法。

AIH *see* artificial insemination.

人工授精 參閱 artificial insemination。

ainhum *n.* loss of one or more toes due to slow growth of a fibrous band around the toe that eventually causes a spontaneous amputation. The condition is found in Black Africans and is associated with going barefoot.

阿洪病 一趾或多趾喪失，因趾周緩慢長出最終引起自發性斷趾的纖維索而致。本病見於非洲黑人，與赤腳行走有關。

air bed a bed with a mattress whose upper surface is perforated with thousands of holes, through which air is forced under pressure. The patient is thus supported, like a hovercraft, on a cushion of air. This type of bed is invaluable for the treatment of patients with large areas of burns.

氣褥 墊褥上有數千氣孔的床，空氣在高壓下穿透氣孔，患者因而如同在氣墊船上一樣，由一層氣墊支撐。這種床對大面積燒傷病人的治療極其重要。

air embolism an air lock that obstructs the outflow of blood from the right ventricle of the heart. Air may gain access to the circulation as a result of surgery, injury, or intravenous infusions. The patient experiences breathlessness and chest discomfort and develops acute heart failure. Tipping the patient head

空氣栓塞 阻塞右心室血流的空氣栓塞。空氣可因手術、受傷或靜注而進入循環系統。病人感覺呼吸困難和胸部不適，進而發展到急性心力衰竭。使病人頭部向下傾斜並取左側臥位可移氣栓。

down, lying on the left side, may move
the air lock.

air sickness *see* travel sickness.

航 空 病　　參 閱　　travel
sickness。

akathisia *n.* a pattern of involuntary
movements induced by antipsychotic
drugs, such as *phenothiazines. An
affected person is driven to restless overactivity, which can be confused with the
agitation for which the drug was originally prescribed.

靜坐不能　精神抑制藥物如吩
噻嗪類所誘發的一種不隨意運
動，迫使患者不停地過度活
動，這一點可與此類藥物本欲
治療的焦慮不安狀態相混淆。

akinesia *n.* a loss of normal muscular
tonicity or responsiveness. In *akinetic
epilepsy* there is a sudden loss of muscular tonicity, making the patient fall
with momentary loss of consciousness.
Akinetic mutism is a state of complete
physical unresponsiveness although the
patient's eyes remain open and appear
to follow movements. It is a consequence
of damage to the base of the brain.
–akinetic *adj.*

運動不能　肌肉喪失正常的緊
張或反應。運動不能性癲癇
時，肌緊張突然喪失而使患者
跌倒，伴意識暫時喪失。運動
不能性緘默症指患者身體完全
無反應能力的狀態，雖然眼仍
睜開並隨物活動，此為腦底受
損之結果。

ala *n.* (*pl.* **alae**) (in anatomy) a winglike
structure; for example, either of the two
lateral flared portions of the external
nose or the winglike expansion of the
ilium.

翼　（解剖學）翼狀結構。例如
外鼻兩側張開的部分或髂骨的
翼狀擴張。

alactasia *n.* absence or deficiency of the
enzyme lactase, which is essential for
the digestion of milk sugar (lactose). All
babies have lactase in their intestines, but
the enzyme disappears during childhood
in about 10% of northern Europeans,
40% of Greeks and Italians, and 80% of
Africans and Asians. Alactasia causes
symptoms only if the diet regularly
includes raw milk, when the undigested
lactose causes diarrhoea and abdominal
pain.

乳糖酶缺乏　乳糖消化所必需
的乳糖酶缺乏或不足。所有嬰
兒的腸道均有乳糖酶，但約有
10% 的北歐兒童、40% 的希
臘和意大利兒童與 80% 的非
洲和亞洲兒童缺乏此酶。僅
在經常飲用生乳時才出現症
狀，未消化的乳糖可致腹瀉或
腹痛。

alanine *n. see* amino acid.

alastrim *n.* a mild form of smallpox, causing only a sparse rash and lowgrade fever. Medical name: **variola minor**.

albendazole *n.* an *anthelmintic drug used to get rid of roundworms, hookworms, and other worm parasites. It is administered by mouth. Possible side-effects include headache, dizziness, fever, skin rashes, and loss of hair. Trade name: **Eskazole**.

Albers-Schönberg disease *see* osteopetrosis.

albinism *n.* the inherited absence of pigmentation in the skin, hair, and eyes (*see* albino).

albino *n.* an individual lacking the normal body pigment (melanin). Albinos have white hair and pink skin and eyes. The pink colour is produced by blood in underlying blood vessels, which are normally masked by pigment.

albumin *n.* a protein that is soluble in water and coagulated by heat. An example is *serum albumin*, which is found in blood plasma and is important for the maintenance of plasma volume. Albumin is synthesized in the liver; the inability to synthesize it is a prominent feature of chronic liver disease (*cirrhosis).

albuminuria (proteinuria) *n.* the presence of serum albumin, serum globulin, or other serum proteins in the urine. This may be associated with kidney or heart disease. Albuminuria is not always associated with disease: it may occur after strenuous exercise or after a long period of standing (*orthostatic albuminuria*).

丙氨酸 參閱 amino acid。

乳白痘，類天花 一種輕型天花，僅引起稀少的疹子和低燒。醫學用語：輕型天花。

阿苯達唑 一種抗蠕蟲藥，用於驅除蛔蟲、鈎蟲及其他蠕蟲寄生物。口服。可致副作用有頭痛、頭暈、發熱、皮疹和脫髮。商品名：Eskazole。

阿爾貝斯-舍恩貝格病，骨硬化病 參閱 osteopetrosis。

白化病 皮膚、頭髮和眼睛的遺傳性色素缺乏（參閱 albino）。

白化病患者 缺乏體內正常色素（黑色素）的人。患者出現白髮，皮膚和眼睛因皮下血管中血液所致為粉紅色，而在正常情況下血液的顏色被色素遮蓋。

白蛋白，清蛋白 一種溶於水並在加熱後凝固的蛋白，如血漿中的血清白蛋白；對維持血漿容量十分重要。白蛋白在肝內合成；失去其合成能力是慢性肝病（肝硬化）的一個顯著特點。

蛋白尿 尿中出現血清白蛋白、血清球蛋白或其他血清蛋白，可伴發於腎病或心臟病。蛋白尿有時與疾病無關，可發生於緊張的鍛煉或長時間站立之後（直立性蛋白尿）。

albumose *n.* a substance, intermediate between albumin and peptones, produced during the digestion of proteins by pepsin and other endopeptidases (*see* peptidase).

alcaptonuria (alkaptonuria) *n.* the congenital absence of an enzyme, homogentisic acid oxidase, that is essential for the normal breakdown of the amino acids tyrosine and phenylalanine. Accumulation of *homogentisic acid casues dark brown discoloration of the skin and eyes (*ochronosis*) and progressive damage to the joints, especially of the spine. The gene responsible for the condition is recessive, so that a child is affected only if both parents are carriers of the defective gene.

alclometazone *n.* a *corticosteroid drug administered externally as a cream or ointment to treat inflammatory skin disorders. Possible side-effects include skin thinning and allergic reactions. Trade name: **Modrasone**.

alcohol *n.* any of a class of organic compounds formed when a hydroxyl group (–OH) is substituted for a hydrogen atom in a hydrocarbon. The alcohol in alcoholic drinks is *ethyl alcohol* (*ethanol*), which has the formula C_2H_5OH. It is produced by the fermentation of sugar by yeast. 'Pure' alcohol contains not less than 94.9% by volume of ethyl alcohol. It is obtained by distillation. A solution of 70% alcohol can be used as a preservative or antiseptic. When taken into the body ethyl alcohol depresses activity of the central nervous system (*see also* alcoholism). *Methyl alcohol (methanol) is extremely poisonous.

Alcoholics Anonymous a voluntary agency of sclf-help that is organized and

（蛋白）腖　介於白蛋白與蛋白腖之間的一種中間產物，產生於蛋白質被胃蛋白酶或其他肽鏈內切酶消化過程中（參閱 peptidase）。

尿黑酸尿　先天性缺乏正常分解酪氨酸與苯丙氨酸兩類氨基酸所必需的尿黑酸氧化酶。尿黑酸蓄積可致皮膚與眼成深棕色（褐黃病），並進行性地損害關節，尤其是脊椎關節。此病致病基因為隱性，故兒童僅在父母均為該缺陷基因携帶者時才患病。

阿氯米松　一種以乳膏或軟膏外用治療炎性皮膚疾患的皮質類固醇藥物。可致副作用有皮膚變薄和變態反應。商品名：Modrasone。

乙醇，酒精　碳氫化合物中的一個氫原子被羥基（–OH）置換時形成的一類有機化合物。酒精性飲料中的酒精是乙醇，分子式為C_2H_5OH，由糖類酵母發酵產生。「純」酒精係蒸餾提取，其中的乙醇含量不少於其容積的 94.9%。70% 的酒精溶液可用作防腐劑或消毒劑。乙醇攝入體內可抑制中樞神經系統的活動（參閱 alcoholism）。甲醇則有劇毒。

嗜酒者互誠協會　由嗜酒者組織並管理的一種地方性自助志

operated locally among those with alcoholic dependency and has national and international support. Members are expected to admit to their drink problems, discuss these openly and frankly at the regular meetings of the group, and also to take part in efficient family support schemes to help those members who have lapses.

alcoholism *n.* the syndrome due to physical *dependence on alcohol, such that sudden deprivation may cause withdrawal symptoms – tremor, anxiety, hallucinations, and delusions (*see* delirium tremens). The risk of alcoholism for an individual and its incidence in a society depend on the amount drunk. Countries such as France, where heavy drinking is socially acceptable, have the highest incidence. Usually several years' heavy drinking is needed for addiction to develop, but the range is from one to 40 years. Alcoholism impairs intellectual function, physical skills, memory, and judgment: social skills, such as conversation, are preserved until a late stage. Heavy consumption of alcohol also causes *cardiomyopathy, peripheral *neuritis, *cirrhosis of the liver, and enteritis. Treatment is usually given in a psychiatric hospital, where the alcoholic is first 'dried out' and then helped to understand the psychological pressures that led to his heavy drinking. Drugs such as *disulfiram (Antabuse), which cause vomiting if alcohol is taken, may help in treatment.

alcuronium *n.* a drug causing profound relaxation of voluntary muscles (*see* muscle relaxant). Used during anaesthesia, it is administered by injection and may delay the resumption of spontaneous breathing, so that

願機構,並得到國家和國際支持。其成員被要求承認自己的酗酒問題,並在定期的小組會上公開坦率地進行討論,同時還要求他們參加行之有效的家庭支持計劃,以幫助有所反覆的成員。

乙醇中毒,酒精中毒 身體對酒精依賴而致的綜合徵,突然禁飲時可產生如震顫、焦慮、幻覺和妄想等戒斷症狀(參閱delirium tremens)。酒精中毒對個人的危害及在社會的發生率取決於飲用量,在酗酒為社會所接受的國家,如法國,發生率最高。通常需有幾年的酗酒才會成癮,但亦可短至 1 年或長達 40 年。酒精中毒損害智能、身體技能、記憶力及判斷力,社交技能,如交談,則可保留至後期。酗酒還可引起心肌病、周圍神經炎、肝硬化與腸炎。通常在精神病醫院治療,嗜酒者在此首先徹底戒酒,繼而接受幫助以理解導致酗酒的心理壓力。飲酒會引起嘔吐的雙硫侖(戒酒硫)一類藥物有助於治療。

雙烯丙毒馬錢鹼 一種引起隨意肌極度鬆弛的麻醉用藥(參閱 muscle relaxant),注射給藥。可延遲自主性呼吸,因而需要人工換氣。商品名:Alloferin。

artificial ventilation is needed. Trade name: **Alloferin**.

aldesleukin *n.* *interleukin 2 produced by recombinant DNA technology (genetic engineering). It enhances the function of the immune system by prompting T-lymphocytes to become *natural killer cells, active against cancer cells. It is administered by injection. The results against certain cancers, including melanomas and kidney-cell cancer, have been encouraging. Trade name: **Proleukin**.

阿地斯白素 由 DNA 重組技術（遺傳工程學）產生的白細胞介素 2。它通過激發 T 淋巴細胞成為對癌細胞有作用的自然殺傷細胞而增強免疫系統功能。注射給藥。對包括黑色素瘤和腎細胞癌在內的一些癌症具有良好效果。商品名：Proleukin。

Aldomet *n. see* methyldopa.

甲基多巴 參閱 methyldopa。

aldosterone *n.* a steroid hormone (*see* corticosteroid) that is synthesized and released by the adrenal cortex and acts on the kidney to regulate salt (potassium and sodium) and water balance. It may be given by injection as replacement therapy when the adrenal cortex secretes insufficient amounts of the hormone and also to treat shock.

醛甾酮 由腎上腺皮質合成並分泌的一種甾類激素（參閱 corticosteroid）。作用於腎臟，調節鹽（鉀和鈉）與水的平衡。腎上腺皮質激素分泌不足時可注射醛甾酮作為替代療法，也可用於治療休克。

aldosteronism *n.* overproduction of aldosterone, one of the hormones secreted by the adrenal cortex, leading to abnormalities in the amounts of sodium, potassium, and water in the body. It is one cause of raised blood pressure (hypertension). *See also* Conn's syndrome.

醛甾酮增多症 腎上腺皮質分泌的激素之一醛甾酮產生過多，引起體內鈉、鉀、水含量異常。為血壓升高（高血壓）的一個因素。參閱 Conn's syndrome。

Aleppo boil *see* oriental sore.

東方癤 皮膚利什曼病 參閱 oriental sore。

aleukaemic *adj.* describing a stage of *leukaemia in which there is no absolute increase in the number of white cells in the blood. The stage is usually followed by one in which excessive numbers of white cells are produced, as typical in leukaemia.

白細胞缺乏的 描述白血病的一期，此時血液白細胞數量無絕對增加。該期之後通常發生為白血病典型表現的白細胞大量增多。

alexia *n.* an acquired inability to read. It is due to disease in the left hemisphere of the brain in a right-handed person. In *agnosic alexia* (*word blindness*) the patient cannot read because he is unable to identify the letters and words, but he retains the ability to write and his speech is normal. This is a form of *agnosia. A patient with *aphasic alexia* (*visual asymblia*) can neither read nor write and often has an accompanying disorder of speech. This is a form of *aphasia. *See also* dyslexia.

讀字不能，失讀（症） 後天性喪失閱讀能力。在善用右手者中是因在腦疾患而致。認識不能性失讀症（詞盲）患者因不能識別字母和單詞而不能閱讀，但仍保持有書寫能力且言語正常。此為認識不能的一種形式。失語性失讀症（視覺性說示不能）患者讀寫均不能，並常伴有語言障礙。此為失語症的一種形式。參閱 dyslexia。

alexin *n.* a former name for the serum component now called *complement.

補體，防禦素 血清成分的舊名，現稱補體（complement）。

alexithymia *n.* a lack of psychological understanding of one's own emotions and moods. It is considered by some psychiatrists to be a way in which people develop *psychosomatic symptoms.

表達心境不能 對自身的感情和心境缺乏心理學的理解。一些精神病學家將其視為產生身心症狀的一種形式。

alfacalcidol *n.* a synthetic form of vitamin D that is used to raise blood calcium levels in *osteomalacia and bone disorders caused by kidney disease. It is administered by mouth or by injection. Trade name: **One-Alpha**.

阿法骨化醇 維生素 D 的一種合成形式，用於在腎病引起的骨軟化和骨骼病時提高血鈣水平。口服或注射給藥。商品名：One-Alpha。

alfentanil hydrochloride a narcotic *analgesic drug used to relieve severe pain. It is administered by injection. Trade name: **Rapifen**.

鹽酸阿芬他尼 用於緩解劇痛的一種麻醉止痛藥。注射給藥。商品名：Rapifen。

ALG antilymphocyte globulin *See* antilymphocyte serum.

抗淋巴細胞球蛋白 參閱 antilymphocyte serum。

algesimeter *n.* a piece of equipment for determining the sensitivity of the skin to various touch stimuli, especially those causing pain.

痛覺計 測定皮膚對各種觸覺刺激，尤其是痛覺刺激敏感性的儀器。

-algia *suffix denoting* pain. Example: *neuralgia* (pain in a nerve).

〔後綴〕痛 例如神經痛。

algid *adj.* cold: usually describing the cold clammy skin associated with certain forms of malaria.

寒冷的 常描述患某型瘧疾時的濕冷皮膚。

alginic acid an *antacid drug used to treat heartburn caused by acid reflux into the gullet and hiatus hernia. It is administered by mouth. Trade names: **Gastrocote**, **Gastron**.

海藻酸 一種解酸劑，用於治療酸回流入食管和食管裂孔疝引起的胃灼熱，口服。商品名：Gastrocote，Gastron。

alienation *n.* (in psychiatry) **1.** the experience that one's thoughts are under the control of somebody else, or that other people participate in one's thinking. It is a symptom of *schizophrenia. **2.** insanity.

(精神病學) **(1) 精神錯亂** 感到自己的思維活動受他人控制，或別人參與到自己的思維活動中之體驗，為精神分裂症的一種症狀。**(2) 精神病**。

alimentary canal the long passage through which food passes to be digested

消化道 食物被消化與吸收所經過的長通道（見圖），從口

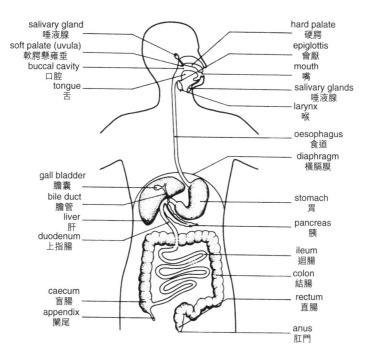

salivary gland 唾液腺	hard palate 硬腭
soft palate (uvula) 軟腭懸雍垂	epiglottis 會厭
buccal cavity 口腔	mouth 嘴
tongue 舌	salivary glands 唾液腺
	larynx 喉
	oesophagus 食道
	diaphragm 橫膈膜
gall bladder 膽囊	
bile duct 膽管	stomach 胃
liver 肝	pancreas 胰
duodenum 上指腸	ileum 迴腸
	colon 結腸
caecum 盲腸	rectum 直腸
appendix 闌尾	anus 肛門

The alimentary canal
消化道

and absorbed (see illustration). It extends from the mouth to the anus and each region is specialized for a different stage in the processing of food, from mechanical breakdown in the mouth to chemical *digestion and *absorption in the stomach and small intestine and finally to faeces formation and water absorption in the colon and rectum.

腔延伸至肛門,每一部位負責食物消化的一個階段。首先在口內機械性粉碎,然後在胃和小腸化學性消化並吸收,最後在結腸與直腸形成糞便,吸收水分。

alizarin (alizarin carmine) *n.* an orange-red dye derived from coal tar and originally isolated from the plant madder (*Rubia tinctorum*). Alizarin is insoluble in water but dissolves in alkalis, alcohol, and ether. It is used as a pH indicator and as a histochemical reagent for calcium, thallium, titanium, and zirconium.

茜素 從煤焦油提取的一種橘紅色染料,最初從歐茜草中分離出來。茜素不溶於水,但溶於鹼、醇和乙醚,用作 pH 指示劑和鈣、鉈、鈦、鋯的組(織)化(學)試劑。

alkalaemia *n.* abnormally high blood alkalinity. This may be caused by an increase in the concentration of alkaline substances and/or a decrease in that of acidic substances in the blood. *See also* alkalosis. *Compare* acidaemia.

鹼血(症) 血液鹼度常升高,可因血內鹼性物質濃度增加和/或酸性物質濃度降低所致。參閱 alkalosis。與 acidaemia 對比。

alkaloid *n.* one of a diverse group of nitrogen-containing substances that are produced by plants and have potent effects on body function. Many alkaloids are important drugs, including *morphine, *quinine, *atropine, and *codeine.

生物鹼 植物所產生的一組不同的含氮物質,對人體功能具有很強作用。許多生物鹼為重要的藥物,包括嗎啡、奎寧、阿托品和可待因。

alkalosis *n.* a condition in which the alkalinity of body fluids and tissues is abnormally high. This arises because of a failure of the mechanisms that usually maintain a balance between alkalis and acids in the arterial blood (*see* acid-base balance). Alkalosis may be associated with loss of acid through vomiting or with excessive sodium bicarbonate intake. Breathing that is abnormally deep in relation to the amount of physical exercise may lead to *respiratory*

鹼中毒 體液和組織內鹼度異常升高的狀態,由於通常維持動脈血中酸鹼平衡的機能障礙而致(參閱 acid-base balance),也可伴發於嘔吐失酸或碳酸氫鈉攝入過多。與體育鍛煉有關的異常深呼吸可致呼吸性鹼中毒。鹼中毒可產生肌無力或痙攣的症狀。

alkalosis. Alkalosis may produce symptoms of muscular weakness or cramp.

alkaptonuria *n. see* alcaptonuria.

尿黑酸尿　參閱 alcaptonuria。

alkylating agents a class of drugs used in chemotherapy that includes *cyclophosphamide and *melphalan. These drugs bind to DNA and prevent complete separation of the two DNA chains during cell division.

烷化劑　包括環磷酰胺和美法侖的一類化療用藥。它們與 DNA 結合，防止細胞分裂時兩個 DNA 鏈的完全分離。

allantois *n.* the membranous sac that develops as an outgrowth of the embryonic hindgut. Its outer (mesodermal) layer carries blood vessels to the *placenta and so forms part of the *umbilical cord. Its cavity is small and becomes reduced further in size during fetal development (*see* urachus). **–allantoic** *adj.*

尿囊　胚胎後腸向外生長發育的膜性囊，其外層（中胚層）有血管通向胎盤並形成臍帶的一部分。尿囊囊腔細小，在胚胎發育過程中進一步縮小（參閱 urachus）。

allele (allelomorph) *n.* one of two or more alternative forms of a *gene, only one of which can be present in a chromosome. Two alleles of a particular gene occupy the same relative positions on a pair of *homologous chromosomes. If the two alleles are the same, the individual is *homozygous for the gene; if they are different he is *heterozygous. *See also* dominant, recessive. **–allelic** *adj.*

等位基因　基因的兩種或多種形式中的一個，在一個染色體中僅能出現一種。一個基因中的兩個等位基因位於同源染色體的同一位點上。若兩個等位基因相同，其個體的基因為純合體，若不同則為雜合體。參閱 dominant，recessive。

allelomorph *n. see* allele.

等位基因　參閱 allele。

allergen *n.* any *antigen that causes *allergy in a hypersensitive person. Allergens are diverse and affect different tissues and organs. Pollens, fur, feathers, mould, and dust may cause hay fever; house mites have been implicated in some forms of asthma; drugs, dyes, cosmetics, and a host of other chemicals can cause rashes and dermatitis; some food allergies may cause diarrhoea or

變應原　任何引起過敏者變態反應的抗原，有多種種類，影響不同的組織和器官。花粉、皮毛、羽毛、戰菌和塵土可引起枯草熱；室內蟎類與某些類型的哮喘有關；藥物、染料、化妝品及多種化學品可致皮疹與皮炎；有些食品變應原可引起腹瀉、便秘，或產生急性細菌性食物中毒。當患者的變應

constipation or simulate acute bacterial food poisoning. When a patient's allergen has been identified (*see* patch test), it may be possible to attempt *desensitization to alleviate or prevent allergic attacks. **–allergenic** *adj*.

allergy *n*. a disorder in which the body becomes hypersensitive to particular antigens (called *allergens), which provoke characteristic symptoms whenever they are subsequently inhaled, ingested, injected, or otherwise contacted. Normally antibodies in the bloodstream and tissues react with and destroy specific antigens without further trouble. In an allergic person, however, the reaction of allergen with tissue-bound antibody (*reagin) also leads, as a side-effect, to cell damage, release of *histamine and *serotonin (5-hydroxytryptamine), inflammation, and all the symptoms of the particular allergy. Different allergies afflict different tissues and may have either local or general effects, varying from asthma and hay fever to severe dermatitis or gastroenteritis or extremely serious shock (*see* anaphylaxis). **–allergic** *adj*.

allogeneic *adj*. describing grafted tissue derived from a donor of the same species as the recipient but with different *histocompatibility.

allograft *n*. *see* homograft.

alloisoleucine *n*. one of the isomers of the amino acid isoleucine.

allopathy *n*. (in homeopathic medicine) the orthodox system of medicine, in which the use of drugs is directed to

原被確定時（參閱 patch test），則可能通過脫敏來減輕或預防變態反應發作。

變態反應　身體對特異抗原（稱為變應原）過敏的疾病，不論在吸入、攝入、注入或經其他方式接觸到這些抗原時則激發產生典型症狀。正常情況下，血流或組織中的抗體與之發生反應並加以破壞而不致發病。但變應性體質者在變應原與組織中抗體（反應素）發生反應時還會產生細胞損害、組胺和 5-羥色胺釋放、炎症以及此種變態反應的特有症狀等副作用。不同變應原損害不同組織，可產生程度不等的局部或全身作用，從哮喘、枯草熱至嚴重皮炎、胃腸炎或重度休克（參閱 anaphylaxis）。

同種（異）的　描述取自與受者種類相同但組織相容性不同的供者的移植組織。

同種（異體）移植物　參閱 homograft。

別異亮氨酸　氨基酸異亮氨酸的異構體之一。

對抗療法（順勢療法）一種傳統的醫療體系，藥物使用的目的為在體內直接對疾病症狀產

producing effects in the body that will directly oppose and so alleviate the symptoms of a disease. *Compare* homeopathy.

生作用而加以緩解。與 homeopathy 對比。

allopurinol *n.* a drug used in the treatment of chronic gout. It acts by reducing the level of uric acid in tissues and blood. It is administered by mouth; side-effects include nausea, vomiting, diarrhoea, headache, fever, stomach pains, and skin rashes. Occasionally, nerve damage and enlargement of the liver may occur. Trade names: **Hamarin, Zyloric**.

別嘌醇　一種用於治療慢性痛風的藥物，作用為降低組織和血液內的尿酸水平，口服。副作用有惡心、嘔吐、腹瀉、頭痛、發熱、胃痛及皮疹。偶爾可發生神經損害和肝腫大。商品名：Hamarin，Zyloric。

allylestrenol (allyloestrenol) *n.* a synthetic female sex hormone (*see* progestogen) that is used in the treatment of abnormal bleeding from the uterus. It is administered by mouth. Trade name: **Gestanin**.

烯丙雌醇　用於治療子宮異常出血的一種合成女性性激素（參閱 progestogen）。口服。商品名：Gestanin。

almoner *n.* a former name for a *medical social worker.

救濟員　醫學社會工作者的舊稱。

alopecia (baldness) *n.* absence of hair from areas where it normally grows. *Non-scarring alopecias* include common baldness in men, which is familial, and *androgenetic alopecia* in women, in which the hair loss is associated with increasing age. Acute hair fall (*telogen effluvium*), in which much or all of the hair is shed but starts to regrow at once, may occur after pregnancy or a serious illness. *Alopecia areata* consists of bald patches that may regrow; it is an example of an organ-specific *autoimmune disease. In *scarring* (or *cicatricial*) *alopecias* the hair does not regrow; examples include *lichen planus and discoid *lupus erythematosus.

脫髮　正常生髮區無髮。非瘢痕性脫髮包括家族性的男性普通脫髮及與年齡增高伴發的女性雄激素性脫髮。急性脫髮（毛髮生長終期脫髮）可發生於妊娠或重病後，此時大量或全部頭髮掉落，但即刻開始重長。斑禿呈若干脫髮小片，可重新長出頭髮，為器官特異性自體免疫疾病之一例。瘢痕性脫髮時掉髮不再重長，如扁平苔癬和盤狀紅斑狼瘡。

aloxiprin *n.* a compound made from aluminium oxide and *aspirin. Its actions

阿洛普令　由氧化鋁和阿司匹林產生的化合物。其作用與用

and uses are similar to those of aspirin, but it is said to be more stable and less liable to cause irritation and bleeding of the stomach. Trade name: **Palaprin forte**.

途類似於阿司匹林，但據說較之更穩定，且更不易引起胃刺激和出血。商品名：Palaprin forte。

alpha blocker (alpha-adrenergic blocker) a drug that prevents the stimulation of alpha-adrenergic receptors at the nerve endings of the sympathetic nervous system by adrenaline-like hormones; it therefore causes widening of arteries (vasodilatation) and a drop in blood pressure. Alpha blockers include *doxazosin, *phentolamine, *phenoxybenzamine, *thymoxamine, *indoramin, and *prazosin. Overdosage causes a severe drop in blood pressure, a rapid pulse, nausea and vomiting, diarrhoea, a dry mouth, flushed skin, convulsions, drowsiness, and coma.

α-受體阻滯劑 通過類似腎上腺素的激素防止交感神經系統神經末梢處的α-腎上腺素能受體興奮的藥物，從而引起動脈擴張（血管舒張）並降低血壓。α-受體阻滯劑包括多沙唑嗪，酚妥拉明、酚苄明、莫西賽利、吲哚拉明和哌唑嗪。劑量過量可引起血壓急劇下降，脈搏急促、惡心嘔吐、腹瀉、口乾、皮膚潮紅、驚厥、嗜睡以及昏迷。

alpha-fetoprotein (afp) *n.* a protein that is formed in the liver and yolk sac of the fetus and is present in the *amniotic fluid and secondarily in maternal blood. The level of afp can be detected by a maternal blood test performed between the 16th and 18th weeks of pregnancy to aid *prenatal diagnosis of certain fetal conditions. Levels are elevated in open *neural tube defects (e.g. spina bifida), twins and triplets, open abdominal wall defects (e.g. *gastroschisis), and fetal death. Levels of afp are decreased in *Down's syndrome. However, afp levels are affected by the length of gestation and the mother's weight, and these factors must be considered when interpreting the results. When levels are unexpectedly high or low, further investigations (for example *ultrasound scanning) are indicated. Alpha-fetoprotein is also produced by certain tumours (*see* tumour marker).

甲胎蛋白 在胎兒肝臟和卵黃囊形成的蛋白，主要在羊水中，其次在母血內。甲胎蛋白水平可於妊娠 16 至 18 周之間通過母體血液試驗測定，以幫助產前診斷胎兒的某些疾病。開放性神經管缺損（如脊柱裂）、雙胞胎和三胞胎、開放性腹壁缺損（如腹裂）及死胎時，甲胎蛋白水平升高。患有唐氏綜合徵時其水平降低。甲胎蛋白水平受妊娠時間和母親體重的影響，因此在看待檢測結果時須對此加以考慮。甲胎蛋白水平異常升高或降低時，應作進一步的檢查（如超聲波掃描）。某些腫瘤亦產生甲胎蛋白（參閱 tumour marker）。

Alport's syndrome a hereditary disease that causes *nephritis accompanied by deafness. Affected males usually die of renal failure before the age of· 40, but females appear to have a better prognosis.

耳-眼-腎綜合徵　導致腎炎並伴有聾症的一種遺傳病。男性患者常在 40 歲之前死於腎衰竭，而女性患者似乎預後較好。

alprazolam n. a *tranquilizer of the benzodiazepine class used to relieve anxiety and as a sedative. It is administered by mouth; side-effects include drowsiness and lightheadedness. Trade name: **Xanax**.

阿普唑侖　苯二氮䓬類安定藥，用於減輕焦慮及用作鎮靜劑，口服。副作用有嗜睡和頭暈目眩。商品名：Xanax。

alprostadil n. a *prostaglandin drug administered by injection to improve lung blood flow in newborn babies with congenital heart defects who are awaiting surgery; it acts by preventing the closure of the blood vessel connecting the aorta to the pulmonary artery (see ductus arteriosus). Possible side-effects include diminished respiratory efforts. Trade name: **Prostin VR**.

前列地爾，前列腺素E₁　一種注射用前列腺素藥物，用於改善正等待手術治療的先天性心臟缺損新生兒的肺部血流。其作用為防止連接主動脈與肺動脈的血管閉合（參閱 ductus arteriosus）。可致副作用有呼吸減弱。商品名：Prostin VR。

AIS 1. see antilymphocyte serum. **2.** amyotrophic lateral sclerosis. See motor neurone disease.

(1) 抗淋巴細胞血清　參閱 antilymphocyte serum。(2) 肌萎縮性（脊髓）側索硬化　參閱 motor neurone disease。

alteplase n. a *tissue plasminogen activator made by recombinant DNA technology (genetic engineering). Alteplase is used to dissolve blood clots (see fibrinolytic), especially in the coronary arteries of the heart. It is administered by injection. Possible side-effects include local bleeding, cerebral haemorrhage, nausea, and vomiting. Trade name: **Actilyse**.

奧特普酶　一種經 DNA 重組技術（遺傳工程學）製成的組織纖維蛋白溶酶原活化劑。用於溶解血塊（參閱 fibrinolytic），尤其在心臟冠狀動脈中。注射給藥。可致副作用有局部出血、腦出血、惡心、嘔吐。商品名：Actilyse。

alternative medicine (complementary medicine, fringe medicine) the various systems of healing, including *homeopathy, herbal remedies, *hypnosis, and faith

補救醫學　包括順勢療法、草藥、催眠和信仰療法在內的各種治療體系，被醫學界排除於傳統療法之外，尤其在由未經

healing, that are not regarded as part of orthodox treatment by the medical profession, especially when offered by unregistered practitioners. Most of the treatments are of unproven benefit but are tried by sufferers of chronic or incurable conditions when orthodox treatment has failed. Many alternative therapies are ridiculed by the medical profession, but *acupuncture and *osteopathy are now generally accepted to be of value in some circumstances. The extent to which individual registered practitioners indulge in or spurn these therapies varies enormously but is governed by the overriding principle (laid down by the General Medical Council) that shared care is only permitted if the registered practitioner remains in overall control; this is often unacceptable to those practising alternative medicine. *See also* chiropractic, holistic, naturopathy.

altitude sickness (mountain sickness) the condition that results from unaccustomed exposure to a high altitude (4500 m or more above sea level). Reduced atmospheric pressure and shortage of oxygen cause deep rapid breathing (*hyperventilation), which lowers the concentration of carbon dioxide in the blood (*see* alkalosis). Symptoms include nausea, exhaustion, and anxiety. In severe cases there may be acute shortness of breath due to fluid collecting in the lungs (pulmonary *oedema), which requires treatment by diuretics and return to a lower altitude.

aluminium hydroxide a safe slow-acting antacid and *laxative. It is administered by mouth as a gel in the treatment of indigestion, gastric and duodenal ulcers, and reflux *oesophagitis. Trade name: **Aludrox**.

註冊的開業者進行時。補救醫學療效多數未經證實,但當傳統療法無效時,慢性病或不治之症患者仍加以試用。雖然醫學界認為許多補救療法荒謬可笑,現已普遍承認針灸和整骨療法在某些情形中有用。是否沉迷於或摒棄這些療法,註冊開業醫師之間行為相差甚多,但均恪守一條至高原則(由醫師總會制定),即只有在註冊醫師的完全控制下方可進行注冊醫師和補救醫學行醫者雙方參與的治療,而奉行補救醫學人士對此常不能接受。參閱 chiropractic,holistic,naturopathy。

高空病(高山病) 對高海拔(海拔 4500 米或以上)不適應引起的一種狀態。低氣壓和缺氧可致深而快速的呼吸(換氣過度)從而降低血液二氧化碳濃度(參閱 alkalosis)。症狀包括惡心、衰竭和焦慮。嚴重時可因肺內液體蓄積(肺水腫)而致急性呼吸短促,需用利尿劑治療,並返回海拔較低地區。

氫氧化鋁 一種安全且作用緩慢的抗酸劑和輕瀉藥。以凝膠劑口服。治療消化不良、胃和十二指腸潰瘍,以及返流性食管炎。商品名:Aludrox。

alveolitis *n*. inflammation of an *alveolus or alveoli. Chronic inflammation of the walls of the alveoli of the lungs is usually caused by inhaled organic dusts (*external allergic alveolitis*; *see* bird-fancier's lung, farmer's lung) but may occur spontaneously (*cryptogenic fibrosing alveolitis*). The latter may be associated with connective tissue diseases, such as rheumatoid arthritis or systemic sclerosis. Both types of alveolitis may progress slowly to a state of fibrosis, and both types usually respond to corticosteroid therapy.

肺泡炎　肺泡的炎症。肺泡壁慢性炎症通常因吸入有機性粉塵所致（外源性變應性肺泡炎，參閱 bird-fancier's lung，farmer's lung），亦可自發產生（隱原性纖維化肺泡炎），後者可與結締組織疾病相關，如類風濕性關節炎或全身性硬化病。兩類肺泡炎均可緩慢發展至纖維變性狀態，亦均可用皮質類固醇治療。

alveolus *n*. (*pl*. **alveoli**) **1.** (in the *lung) a blind-ended air sac of microscopic size. About 30 alveoli open out of each *alveolar duct*, which leads from a respiratory *bronchiole. The *alveolar walls*, which separate alveoli, contain capillaries. The alveoli are lined by a single layer of *pneumocytes, which thus form a very thin layer between air and blood so that exchange of oxygen and carbon dioxide is normally rapid and complete. Children are born with about 20 million alveoli. The adult number of about 300 million is reached around the age of eight. **2.** the part of the upper or lower jawbone that supports the roots of the teeth (*see also* mandible, maxilla). After tooth extraction it is largely absorbed. **3.** the sac of a *racemose gland (*see also* acinus). **4.** any other small cavity, depression, or sac. **–alveolar** *adj*.

(1) 肺泡　（肺內）一個微小的盲端氣囊，約有 30 個肺泡開口於一個由呼吸細支氣管延伸出來的肺泡小管導管。將肺泡分隔開的肺泡壁含有毛細血管。肺泡僅襯有一層肺細胞，因此在空氣與血液之間只有極薄的一層，故正常情況下氧氣與二氧化碳的交換迅速而完全。兒童出生時約有 2000 萬個肺泡，至 8 歲左右達到成人的 3 億個左右。**(2) 牙槽**　上頜骨或下頜骨支持牙根的部分（參閱 mandible，maxilla）。拔牙後被大量吸收。**(3)** 葡萄狀腺的囊（參閱 acinus）。**(4)** 小泡，小窩　任何其他的小腔、陷窩或囊腔。

alverine citrate a bulking agent and *antispasmodic drug used to treat the *irritable bowel syndrome and other colonic disorders. It is administered by mouth. Possible side-effects include occasional mild distension of the bowel. Trade names: **Alvercol**, **Spasmonal**.

枸櫞酸阿爾維林　一種膨脹劑和鎮痙藥，用於治療應激性結腸綜合徵及其他結腸疾病。口服。可致副作用有腸道偶爾輕微膨脹。商品名：Alvercol，Spasmonal。

alveus *n.* a cavity, groove, or canal. The *alveus hippocampi* is the bundle of nerve fibres in the brain forming a depression in which the hippocampus lies.

槽　一個腔、溝或管。海馬槽指大腦神經纖維束形成的一處凹陷，海馬便位於其中。

Alzheimer's disease a progressive form of *dementia occurring in middle age or later, characterized by loss of short-term memory, deterioration in behaviour and intellectual performance, and slowness of thought. The condition may be mimicked by severe depression. The demonstration of damage to the cholinergic pathways in the brain has led to great interest in drug treatments (e.g. *anticholinesterases and vasodilators) but to date none have proved successful. Pathological studies have revealed excess *amyloid protein in the brains of Alzheimer's patients. A genetic locus on chromosome 21 has been found for some inherited forms of Alzheimer's disease.

阿爾茨海默病，早老性痴呆一種發生在中年或中年後的進行性痴呆，特徵為短期記憶喪失，行為與智力表現退化及思維遲鈍。此病可能與嚴重的抑鬱症相仿。已證實本病患者有大腦膽鹼能路徑受損，由此引起了對藥物治療的極大興趣（如抗膽鹼酯酶和血管舒張藥），但迄今仍無一種藥物證明有效。病理學研究揭示本病患者腦內澱粉樣蛋白過多。現已發現某些遺傳型阿爾茨海默病由第 21 對染色體上的一個基因位點所致。

amalgam *n.* any of a group of alloys containing mercury. In dentistry amalgam fillings are made by mixing a silver-tin alloy with mercury in a machine known as an *amalgamator*.

汞合金　任何一種含汞合金。牙科在稱為混汞器的機器中將銀錫合金與汞混合製成汞合金填料。

Amanita *n.* a genus of fungi that contains several species of poisonous toadstools, including *A. phalloides* (death cap), *A. pantherina* (panther cap), and *A. muscaria* (fly agaric). They produce toxins that cause abdominal pain, violent vomiting, and continuous diarrhoea. In the absence of treatment death occurs in approximately 50% of cases, due to severe liver damage.

捕蠅蕈屬　真菌之一屬，其中幾種傘菌有毒，包括條蕈、瓢蕈和捕蠅蕈。它們產生可引起腹痛、劇吐和持續腹瀉的毒素。若不治療，約 50% 的病人因嚴重肝損害死亡。

amantadine *n.* an antiviral drug that probably acts by preventing the penetration of the virus into the host cell and is used in the treatment of influenza infections. Because it stimulates an increase in

金剛烷胺　一種抗病毒藥，其作用可能為防止病毒進入宿主細胞，用於治療流感感染。它可刺激腦內多巴胺濃度升高，而亦用於治療帕金森綜合徵。

the concentration of *dopamine in the brain, it is also used to treat parkinsonism. Common side-effects include nervousness, loss of muscular coordination, and insomnia. Trade name: **Symmetrel**.

常見副作用有神經質、肌肉共濟失調與失眠。商品名：Symmetrel。

amaurosis *n.* partial or complete blindness. For example, *amaurosis fugax* is a condition in which loss of vision is transient. **–amaurotic** *adj.*

黑蒙 部分盲或全盲。例如，一時性黑蒙指短暫的失明狀態。

amaurotic familial idiocy *see* Tay-Sachs disease.

家族性黑蒙性白痴 參閱 Tay-Sachs disease。

ambivalence *n.* (in psychology) the condition of holding opposite feelings (such as love and hate) for the same person or object. Excessive and prevalent ambivalence was thought by Bleuler to be a feature of schizophrenia.

矛盾情緒 （心理學）對同一人或物持有相反感情（如愛與恨）的狀態。布洛伊勒認為極度和經常的矛盾情緒是精神分裂症的一個特點。

Amblyomma *n.* a genus of hard *ticks, several species of which are responsible for transmitting tick *typhus. The bite of this tick can also give rise to a serious and sometimes fatal paralysis.

鈍眼蜱屬 硬蜱的一屬，其中幾種傳播斑疹傷寒。被該類蜱叮咬亦可引起嚴重甚至致命的麻痺。

amblyopia *n.* poor sight, not due to any detectable disease of the eyeball or visual system. In practice this strict definition is not always obeyed. For example, in *toxic amblyopia*, caused by tobacco, alcohol, certain other drugs, and vitamin deficiency, there is a disorder of the *optic nerve. The commonest type is *amblyopia ex anopsia*, in which factors such as squint (*see* strabismus), cataract, and other abnormalities of the optics of the eye (*see* refraction) impair its normal use in early childhood by preventing the formation of a clear image on the retina.

弱視 視力低下，非因眼球或視力系統可查出的疾病所致。實踐中並不始終遵循這一嚴格定義。例如，因煙草、酒精、某些其他藥物及維生素缺乏引起中毒性弱視時，即有視神經障礙。廢用性弱視最為常見，此型弱視在兒童早期即損害視力，如斜視（參閱 strabismus）、白內障及其他眼光學異常（參閱 refraction）之類因素阻礙視網膜清晰成像所致。

amblyoscope (orthoptoscope, synoptophore) *n.* an instrument for measuring the angle of a squint and assessing

弱視鏡 （視軸較正器，同視鏡）測量斜視角度和評定個體使用雙眼程度的儀器，由兩

the degree to which a person uses both eyes together. It consists of two L-shaped tubes, the short arms of which are joined by a hinge so that the long arms point away from each other. The subject looks into the short end and each eye sees, via a system of mirrors and lenses, a different picture, which is placed at the other end of each tube. If a squint is present, the tubes may be adjusted so that the short arms line up with the direction of each eye.

個 L 形管構成。其短柄用鉸鏈連接，長柄則可分開。受試者自短端觀看，各眼可借一組反光鏡和透鏡看見置於各管另一端的不同圖像。若有斜視，則可調節兩管，使短柄與各眼的視綫方向一致。

amelia *n.* congenital total absence of the arms or legs due to a developmental defect. It is one of the fetal abnormalities induced by the drug *thalidomide taken early in pregnancy. *See also* phocomelia.

無肢(畸形) 因發育缺損導致先天性臂或腿全無。為妊娠早期服用沙利度胺造成的一種畸胎。參閱 phocomelia。

ameloblast *n.* a cell that forms the enamel of a tooth and disappears before tooth eruption.

成釉細胞 一種形成牙釉質並在萌牙前消失的細胞。

ameloblastoma *n.* a locally malignant tumour in the jaw. It is considered to develop from ameloblasts although it does not contain enamel. The term *adamantinoma*, formerly used for this tumour, is now no longer in use as it suggests (incorrectly) a growth that is as hard as enamel.

成釉細胞瘤 一種頜局部的惡性腫瘤，雖不含釉質，卻被認為是由成釉細胞發展而來。釉質上皮瘤一詞過去用於指此種瘤，因其（錯誤地）提示生長物硬如釉質而已停用。

amelogenesis *n.* the formation of enamel by *ameloblasts, a process that is completed before tooth eruption. *Amelogenesis imperfecta* is a hereditary condition in which enamel formation is disturbed. The teeth have an unusual surface but are not more prone to decay.

釉質發生 成釉細胞形成釉質的過程，在萌牙前即完成。釉質生長不全為釉質形成受阻的一種遺傳性疾病，此時牙齒表面異常，但並不因而更易腐蝕。

amenorrhoea *n.* the absence or stopping of the menstrual periods. It is normal for the periods to be absent before puberty, during pregnancy and milk secretion, and after the end of the reproductive period

閉經 無月經或停經。青春期前、妊娠期、泌乳期和生育期結束後（參閱 menopause）無經屬正常。原發性閉經為青春期時無經，可因無子宮或卵

(see menopause). In *primary amenor-rhoea* the menstrual periods fail to appear at puberty. This may be due to absence of the uterus or ovaries, a genetic disorder (e.g. *Turner's syndrome), or hormonal imbalance. In *secondary amen-orrhoea* the menstrual periods stop after establishment at puberty. Causes include disorders of the hypothalamus (a part of the brain), deficiency of ovarian, pituitary, or thyroid hormones, mental disturbance, depression, anorexia nervosa, or a major change of surroundings or circumstances.

巢、遺傳性疾病（如特納綜合徵），或激素失衡所致。繼發性閉經指在青春期已有排經後的經期停止，病因有丘腦下部（腦之一部分）疾病、卵巢、垂體或甲狀腺激素缺乏、精神障礙、抑鬱、神經性厭食、以及環境或境遇的重大改變。

amentia *n.* failure of development of the intellectual faculties. *See* mental retardation.

智力缺陷 智力發育不全。參閱 mental retardation。

amethocaine *n.* a potent local anaesthetic. It is applied to skin or mucous membranes for eye, ear, nose and throat surgery, but it has also been employed for *spinal anaesthesia.

丁卡因 一種強效局麻劑。眼、耳、鼻、喉手術時用在皮膚或黏膜上，亦用於脊髓麻醉。

ametropia *n.* any abnormality of *refraction of the eye, resulting in blurring of the image formed on the retina. *See* astigmatism, hypermetropia, myopia. *Compare* emmetropia.

屈光不正 眼的任何折射異常，導致視網膜成像模糊。參閱 astigmatism，hypermetropia，myopia。與 emmetropia 對比。

amiloride *n.* a *diuretic that causes the increased excretion of sodium and chloride; it is often combined with a thiazide diuretic (e.g. hydrochlorothiazide in *Moduretic*) to reduce the potassium loss that occurs with these drugs. Amiloride may produce dizziness and weakness and its continued use may lead to an excessive concentration of potassium in the blood. Trade name: **Midamor**.

阿米洛利 導致鈉和氯排出增加的一種利尿劑，常與一種噻嗪類利尿劑合用（如鹽酸氨氯吡脒中的氫氯噻嗪）以減少此類藥物帶來的鉀喪失。阿米洛利可致頭昏和虛弱，長期服用可引起血鉀濃度過高。商品名：Midamor。

amino acid an organic compound containing an amino group (–NH$_2$) and a carboxyl group (–COOH). Amino acids

氨基酸 一種含有一個氨基（–NH$_2$）和一個羧基（–COOH）的有機化合物，為

are fundamental constituents of all *proteins. Breakdown of proteins found in the body yields the following amino acids: alanine, arginine, asparagine, aspartic acid, cysteine, cystine, glutamic acid, glutamine, glycine, histidine, isoleucine, leucine, lysine, methionine, phenylalanine, proline, serine, threonine, tryptophan, tyrosine, and valine. Some of these amino acids can be synthesized by the body; others, the *essential amino acids, must be obtained from protein in the diet. Certain amino acids present in the body are not found in proteins; these include *citrulline, *ornithine, *taurine, and *gamma-aminobutyric acid.

aminobenzoic acid *see* para-aminobenzoic acid.

aminoglutethimide *n.* a drug used in the treatment of advanced breast cancer. It inhibits synthesis of adrenal steroids (medical adrenalectomy) and the peripheral conversion of androgens to oestrogens. It is administered by mouth, usually with corticosteroid replacement therapy. Side-effects, which are largely dose-related, may include drowsiness, dizziness, and a transient skin rash. Trade name: **Orimeten**.

aminoglycosides *pl. n.* a group of antibiotics active against a wide range of bacteria. Included in the group are *gentamicin, *kanamycin, *neomycin, and *streptomycin. Because of their toxicity (side-effects include ear and kidney damage), they are used only when less toxic antibacterials are ineffective or contraindicated. They are usually administered by injection.

aminopeptidase *n.* any one of several enzymes in the intestine that cause the

所有蛋白質的基本成分。體內蛋白質的分解可產生下述各種氨基酸：丙氨酸、精氨酸、天門冬酰胺、天門冬氨酸、半胱氨酸、胱氨酸、穀氨酸、穀酰胺、甘氨酸、組氨酸、異亮氨酸、亮氨酸、賴氨酸、蛋氨酸、苯基丙氨酸、脯氨酸、絲氨酸、蘇氨酸、色氨酸、酪氨酸、纈氨酸。其中有些可在體內合成，而其他的必需氨基酸則需獲自食物中的蛋白質。體內存在的某些氨基酸不見於蛋白質中，包括瓜氨酸、鳥氨酸、牛磺酸和γ-氨基丁酸。

對氨苯甲酸 參閱 para-aminobenzoic acid。

氨魯米特 用於治療晚期乳腺癌的藥物。抑制腎上腺類固醇的合成（藥物性腎上腺切除術）及外周的雄激素轉化為雌激素，口服。通常用於皮質類固醇替補療法中。副作用主要與劑量有關，可有嗜睡、頭昏和短暫的皮疹。商品名：Orimeten。

氨基糖苷類 一組對多種細菌有效的抗生素，包括慶大黴素、卡那黴素、新黴素和鏈黴素。因具毒性（副作用有耳、腎損害），僅在毒性較小的抗生素無效或有禁忌時使用。一般注射給藥。

氨基肽酶 腸道內分解肽並去除氨基酸的幾種酶之一。

breakdown of a *peptide, removing an amino acid.

aminophylline *n.* a drug that relaxes smooth muscle and stimulates respiration. It is widely used to dilate the air passages in the treatment of asthma and emphysema, to dilate the coronary arteries in angina pectoris, and as a *diuretic, particularly in cases of *oedema. Administered by injection or in suppositories, it may cause nausea, vomiting, dizziness, and fast heart rate. *See also* theophylline. Trade name: **Pecram**.

氨茶鹼　一種鬆弛平滑肌並刺激呼吸的藥物，廣泛用於治療哮喘和肺氣腫時擴張氣管，心絞痛時擴張冠狀動脈，亦為利尿劑，尤其在水腫時。注射或以栓劑給藥，可致惡心、嘔吐、頭昏及心率加快。參閱 theophylline。商品名：Pecram。

amiodarone *n.* an *anti-arrhythmic drug used to control a variety of abnormal heart rhythms, including atrial *fibrillation and abnormally rapid heartbeat. It is administered by mouth or by injection. Side-effects are uncommon. Trade name: **Cordarone X**.

胺碘酮　一種抗心律失常藥物，用於控制多種心律失常，包括心房纖維性顫動與心動異常快速 。口服或注射給藥。副作用罕見 。商品名：Cordarone X。

amitosis *n.* division of the nucleus of a cell by a process, not involving *mitosis, in which the nucleus is constricted into two.

無絲分裂　細胞核通過壓縮分裂為二，不包含有絲分裂。

amitriptyline *n.* a tricyclic *antidepressant drug that has a mild tranquillizing action. Common side-effects include drowsiness, dizziness, numbness, and tingling of limbs. Trade names: **Elatrol**, **Tryptizol**.

阿米替林　一種具有輕微安定作用的三環結構的抗抑鬱藥。常見副作用有嗜睡、頭昏、麻木、和四肢的麻刺感。商品名：Elatrol，Tryptizol。

amlodipine *n.* a *calcium antagonist used to treat angina pectoris. It is administered by mouth. Possible side-effects include headache, dizziness, fatigue, nausea, and fluid retention. Trade name: **Istin**.

氨氯地平　一種用於治療心絞痛的鈣拮抗藥。口服，可致副作用有頭痛、頭昏、疲勞、惡心與液體瀦留。商品名：Istin。

amnesia *n.* total or partial loss of memory following physical injury,

記憶缺失，遺忘（症）　身體受傷、患病、服藥或心理創傷

disease, drugs, or psychological trauma (*see* confabulation, fugue, repression). *Anterograde amnesia* is loss of memory for the events following some trauma; *retrograde amnesia* is loss of memory for events preceding the trauma. Some patients experience both types.

後出現的全部或部分記憶喪失（參閱 confabulation，fugue，repression）。順行性遺忘為失去對受傷後事情的記憶；逆行性遺忘為失去對受傷前事情的記憶。有些患者兼有兩型。

amnihook *n.* a small plastic hooked instrument for performing *amniotomy. The hook is introduced through the cervix.

羊膜鈎 施行羊膜穿破術所用的一種小塑料鈎狀器械，此鈎經子宮頸插入。

amniocentesis *n.* withdrawal of a sample of the fluid (amniotic fluid) surrounding an embryo in the uterus by piercing the amniotic sac through the abdominal wall. As the amniotic fluid contains cells from the embryo (mostly shed from the skin), cell cultures enable chromosome patterns to be studied so that *prenatal diagnosis of chromosomal abnormalities (such as *Down's syndrome) can be made. Metabolic errors and other diseases, such as *spina bifida, can also be diagnosed prenatally from the biochemistry of the cells or that of the fluid (*see* alpha-fetoprotein). Although the risks of amniocentesis, in skilled hands, are extremely low, there is no point in undertaking it unless the parents agree to a termination of the pregnancy if a serious abnormality is discovered.

羊膜穿刺術 經腹壁刺入羊膜囊抽取子宮內胚胎周圍液體（羊水）標本。因羊水含胚胎細胞（大多自皮膚脫落）；其細胞培養可識別染色體模式，從而可對染色體異常（如唐氏綜合徵）作出產前診斷。亦可經細胞或液體的生化檢查產前診斷出代謝障礙與脊柱裂等其他疾病（參閱 alpha-fetoprotein）。雖然由技術熟練人員施行羊膜穿刺術危險極小，只有夫妻雙方均同意若發現嚴重異常即終止妊娠，才有必要施行此術。

amnion *n.* the membrane that forms initially over the dorsal part of the embryo but soon expands to enclose it completely within the *amniotic cavity; it is connected to the embryo at the umbilical cord. It expands outwards and fuses with the chorion, obliterating virtually all the intervening cavity. The double membrane (*amniochorion*) normally ruptures at birth. **–amniotic** *adj.*

羊膜 首先形成於胚胎背部，不久擴展為包圍整個胚胎的膜，與胎兒在臍帶處相連。羊膜外伸與絨毛膜融合，兩者之間腔隙不再存在。此雙層膜（羊膜絨毛膜）正常時在分娩時破裂。

amnioscopy *n.* examination of the inside of the amniotic sac by means of an instrument (*amnioscope*) that is passed through the abdominal wall. This allows the developing fetus within the cavity to be viewed directly. *Cervical amnioscopy*, performed late in pregnancy, enables the amniotic sac to be inspected through the cervix (neck) of the uterus, using a different instrument (a fetoscope). When transilluminated, its fluid volume can be appraised without puncture of the amnion and any meconium observed.

羊膜鏡檢查　用一穿過腹壁的器械（羊膜鏡）檢查羊膜腔內部，可直接觀察腔內胎兒的發育狀況。子宮頸羊膜鏡檢查於妊娠晚期進行，使用另一種器械（胎兒鏡），可經子宮頸檢查羊膜腔。使用透照法時則無需穿刺羊膜和觀察胎糞便可估測羊水量。

amniotic cavity the fluid-filled cavity between the embryo and the *amnion. It forms initially within the inner cell mass of the *blastocyst and later expands over the back of the embryo, eventually enclosing it completely. *See also* amniotic fluid.

羊膜腔　胎兒與羊膜之間充滿液體的腔隙。最初形成於胚泡內層細胞團，爾後擴展至胎兒背部，最後包圍整個胎兒。參閱 amniotic fluid。

amniotic fluid the fluid contained within the *amniotic cavity. It surrounds the growing fetus, protecting it from external pressure. The fluid is initially secreted from the *amnion and is later supplemented by urine from the fetal kidneys. Some of the fluid is swallowed by the fetus and absorbed through its intestine. *See also* amniocentesis.

羊水　羊膜腔內的液體，包圍生長中的胎兒使其免遭外部壓力。最初由羊膜分泌，以後由胎兒腎臟排出的尿液補充。一些羊水被胎兒吞咽並經其腸道吸收。參閱 amniocentesis。

amniotomy (artificial rupture of membranes, ARM) *n.* a method of surgically inducing labour by puncturing the *amnion surrounding the baby in the uterus using an *amnihook or similar instrument.

羊膜穿破術　一種手術引產法，通過使用羊膜鈎或類似器械穿破子宮內包圍胎兒的羊膜進行。

amodiaquine *n.* an antimalarial drug with effects and uses similar to those of *chloroquine. It has also been used for the treatment of lupus erythematosus, leprosy, and rheumatoid arthritis. Doses used to treat malaria have almost no

阿莫地喹　一種作用與用途類似於氯喹的抗瘧藥。也用於治療紅斑狼瘡、麻風病和類風濕性關節炎。治療瘧疾所用劑量幾乎無副作用，但長期使用可致眼角膜、指甲及硬腭上藍灰

side-effects, but prolonged use may cause blue-grey deposits on the cornea of the eye, fingernails, and hard palate. Trade name: **Cordarone X**.

色沉澱。商品名：Cordarone X。

amoeba n. (pl. **amoebae**) any single-celled microscopic animal of jelly-like consistency and irregular and constantly changing shape. Found in water, soil and other damp environments, they move and feed by means of flowing extensions of the body (see pseudopodium). Some amoebae cause disease in man (see Entamoeba). See also Protozoa. **–amoebic** adj.

阿米巴屬，變形蟲屬　任何具膠凍樣稠度和不規則並不斷改變形狀的微小單細胞動物。見於水、土壤及其他潮濕環境中。牠們通過身體的流動和延伸而運動和進食（參閱 pseudopodium）。有些阿米巴屬使人類致病（參閱 Entamoeba）。參閱 Protozoa。

amoebiasis n. see dysentery.

阿米巴病　參閱 dysentery。

amoebocyte n. a cell that moves by sending out processes of its protoplasm in the same way as an amoeba.

變形細胞　以與阿米巴相同的方式依靠伸出原生質突起來活動的細胞。

amoeboma n. a tumour that occurs in the rectum or caecum of the large intestine and is caused by the parasite *Entamoeba histolytica*, a protozoan that invades and destroys the walls of the gut. Tumours may ulcerate and become infected with pus-forming (pyogenic) bacteria, causing severe inflammation of the bowel wall. The tumours usually harden and may even obstruct the bowel.

阿米巴瘤　發生於大腸中直腸或盲腸的一種腫瘤，由侵入並破壞腸壁的原蟲即溶組織內阿米巴寄生所致。腫瘤可發生潰瘍及被化膿菌感染，引起腸壁的嚴重炎症。腫瘤常變硬，甚至可阻塞腸道。

amok n. a sudden outburst of furious and murderous aggression, directed indiscriminately at everybody in the vicinity. It is encountered particularly in certain cultures, such as that of the Malays.

殺人狂　無選擇地針對附近任何人突然暴發的狂怒與謀殺。尤其發生於某些文化背景中，如馬來文化。

amorolfine n. an antifungal drug used to treat ringworm, candidosis, and other fungal infections of the skin and nails. It is applied externally as a cream or nail

阿莫羅芬　用於治療癬、念珠菌病及其他皮膚和指甲真菌感染的抗真菌藥。以乳膏或指甲膠外用。可致副作用有瘙癢與

lacquer; possible side-effects include itching and a transient burning sensation. Trade name: **Loceryl**.

amoxapine *n.* a tricyclic antidepressant drug similar to *imipramine. It is administered by mouth. Overdosage may cause acute kidney failure, convulsions, and coma. Trade name: **Asendis**.

amoxicillin *n.* an antibiotic used to treat infections caused by a wide range of bacteria and other microorganisms. It is administered by mouth. Side-effects include nausea, vomiting, diarrhoea, rashes, and anaemia. Sensitivity to penicillin prohibits its use. Trade name: **Amoxil**.

AMP (adenosine monophosphate) a compound containing adenine, ribose, and one phosphate group. AMP occurs in cells and is involved in processes requiring the transfer of energy (*see* ATP).

ampere *n.* the basic *SI unit of electric current. It is equal to the current flowing through a conductor of resistance 1 ohm when a potential difference of 1 volt is applied between its ends. The formal definition of the ampere is the current that when passed through two parallel conductors of infinite length and negligible cross section, placed 1 metre apart in a vacuum, produces a force of 2×10^{-7} newton per metre between them. Symbol: **A**.

amphetamine *n.* a *sympathomimetic drug that has a marked stimulant action on the central nervous system. It alleviates fatigue and produces a feeling of mental alertness and well-being. The drug has been used in the treatment of

短暫的灼感。商品名：Loceryl。

阿莫沙平 一種與丙咪嗪相似的三環結構抗抑鬱藥，口服。過量可引起腎衰竭、驚厥和昏迷。商品名：Asendis。

阿莫西林 一種用於治療多種細菌及其他微生物感染的抗生素，口服。副作用有惡心、嘔吐、腹瀉、皮疹與貧血。對青黴素過敏者禁用。商品名：Amoxil。

一磷酸腺苷 含腺嘌呤、核糖和一個磷酸基的化合物，產生於細胞內並參與需要能量的轉換過程（參閱 ATP）。

安培 電流的基本國際單位，即導體兩端所加位差為 1 伏特時通過導體電阻為 1 歐姆的電流。正式定義是：通過置於真空中相距 1 米的兩條無限長的平行導綫時，其橫截面小得可忽略不計，所產生的其間每平方米為 2×10^{-7} 牛頓力的電流。符號：A。

苯丙胺 一種對中樞神經系統有顯著興奮作用的擬交感神經藥。可減輕疲勞，使思維敏銳，產生欣快感。此藥用於治療發作性睡眠病，輕度性抑鬱神機能病和肥胖，但主要適用

*narcolepsy, mild depressive neuroses, and obesity, but the chief indication is for the treatment of hyperkinetic syndrome in children. It is administered by mouth; side-effects include insomnia and restlessness. *Tolerance to amphetamine develops rapidly, and prolonged use may lead to *dependence.

於治療兒童的多動綜合徵。口服。副作用有失眠和煩躁。該藥耐藥性發展迅速，長期服用可產生依賴性。

amphiarthrosis *n.* a slightly movable joint in which the bony surfaces are separated by fibrocartilage (*see* symphysis) or hyaline cartilage (*see* synchondrosis).

微動關節 只能稍微活動的關節，骨面由纖維軟骨（參閱 symphysis）或透明軟骨（參閱 synchondrosis）分隔開。

amphoric breath sounds *see* breath sounds.

空甕性呼吸音 參閱 breath sounds。

amphotericin *n.* an *antibiotic, derived from the bacterium *Streptomyces nodosus*, that is used to treat deep-seated fungal infections; it is inactive against bacteria and viruses. It can be administered by mouth, but is usually given by intravenous injection. Common side-effects include headache, fever, muscle pains, and diarrhoea. In some cases kidney damage may occur. Trade names: **Fungilin**, **Fungizone**.

兩性黴素 從結節鏈黴菌提取的一種抗生素。用於治療深部真菌感染，對細菌和病毒無效。可口服，但通常注射給藥。常見副作用有頭痛、發熱、肌肉痛及腹瀉。在一些病例中可發生腎損害。商品名：Fungilin，Fungizone。

ampicillin *n.* an *antibiotic used to treat a variety of infections, including those of the urinary, respiratory, biliary, and intestinal tracts. It is inactivated by *penicillinase and therefore cannot be used against organisms producing this enzyme. It is given by mouth or injection; side-effects include nausea, vomiting, and diarrhoea, and some allergic reactions may occur. Trade names: **Amfipen**, **Penbritin**.

氨苄西林 一種用於治療多種感染的抗生素，包括泌尿道、呼吸道、膽道和腸道感染。可被青黴素酶滅活，因而不能用於殺滅產生此酶的微生物。口服或注射。副作用有惡心、嘔吐、腹瀉、亦可產生一些變態反應。商品名：Amfipen，Penbritin。

ampoule (ampule) *n.* a sealed glass or plastic capsule containing one dose of a drug in the form of a sterile solution for injection.

安瓿 密封的玻璃或塑料小容器，內裝供一次注射用的溶於無菌液體的藥物。

ampulla *n.* (*pl.* **ampullae**) an enlarged or dilated ending of a tube or canal. The semicircular canals of the inner ear are expanded into ampullac at the point where they join the vestibule. The *ampulla of Vater* is the dilated part of the common bile duct where it is joined by the pancreatic duct.

壺腹　管道膨大或擴張的一端。內耳半規管在與前庭相匯處擴展為壺腹，法特壺腹為膽總管與胰管匯合的膨大部分。

amputation *n.* the removal of a limb, part of a limb, or any other portion of the body (such as a breast). The term is customarily modified by an adjective showing the particular type of amputation. Once a common operation in surgery, it is now usually performed only in cases of severe injury to limbs or, particularly in elderly people, when circulation to a limb is inadequate and gangrene develops. In planning an amputation the surgeon takes account of the patient's work and the type of artificial part (prosthesis) that will be fitted.

切斷術　去除一肢，部分肢體，或身體任何其他部位（如一側乳房）。習慣上本詞前用形容詞表明切斷術的特定類型。切斷術為過去常用的外科手術，現只在肢體嚴重受傷或肢體血流不暢而發生壞疽時才施行，尤其是對老年人。外科醫師在制定切斷術方案時，應考慮到患者的工作與將裝配的假肢類型。

amsacrine *n.* a *cytotoxic drug administered by injection to treat various forms of cancer. Possible side-effects include nausea, vomiting, hair loss, and interference with bone marrow blood cell production. Trade name: **Amsidine**.

安吖啶　一種通過注射用於治療多種癌症的細胞毒素藥物。可致副作用有惡心、嘔吐、脫髮、以及干擾骨髓血細胞生成。商品名：Amsidine。

amygdala (amygdaloid nucleus) *n.* one of the *basal ganglia: a roughly almond-shaped mass of grey matter deep inside each cerebral hemisphere. It has extensive connections with the olfactory system and sends nerve fibres to the hypothalamus; its functions are apparently concerned with mood, feeling, instinct, and possibly memory for recent events.

杏仁核　一種基底神經節，為大腦半球各一的深部杏仁形灰質團塊，與嗅覺系統有廣泛聯繫，並發出神經纖維至丘腦下部，其功能與情緒、感覺和本能明顯相關，亦可能與近期記憶有關。

amylase *n.* an enzyme that occurs in saliva and pancreatic juice and aids the digestion of starch, which it breaks down

澱粉酶　一種存在於唾液和胰液中的酶，幫助消化澱粉，使其分解為葡萄糖、麥芽糖和糊

into glucose, maltose, and dextrins. Amylase will also hydrolyse *glycogen to yield glucose, maltose, and dextrins.

amyl nitrite a drug that relaxes smooth muscle, especially that of blood vessels. Given by inhalation, amyl nitrite is used mainly in the treatment of angina pectoris. It is rapidly absorbed and acts quickly, producing a fall in arterial blood pressure. Side-effects include flushing, faintness, and headache. High doses may cause restlessness, vomiting, and blue coloration of the skin.

amylobarbitone *n.* an intermediate-acting *barbiturate. Prolonged use may lead to *dependence and overdosage has serious toxic effects (*see* barbiturism). Trade name: **Amytal**.

amyloid *n.* a *glycoprotein, resembling starch, that is deposited in the internal organs in amyloidosis. β-amyloid protein has been found in the brains of Alzheimer's patients but the significance of this is unclear.

amyloidosis *n.* infiltration of the liver, kidneys, spleen, and other tissues with amyloid, a starchlike substance. In *primary amyloidosis* the disorder arises without any apparent cause; *secondary amyloidosis* occurs as a late complication of such chronic infections as tuberculosis or leprosy and also in *Hodgkin's disease. Amyloidosis is also very common in the genetic disease familial Mediterranean fever (*see* polyserositis).

amylopectin *n.* see starch.

amylose *n.* see starch.

amyotonia congenita (floppy baby syndrome) a former diagnosis for

精。此酶亦水解糖原，產生葡萄糖、麥芽糖和糊精。

亞硝酸（異）戊酯 一種平滑肌鬆弛藥，特別是血管平滑肌鬆弛。吸入投藥。主要用於治療心絞痛。吸收和作用迅速，可降低動脈壓。副作用有顏面潮紅、暈厥和頭痛，大劑量可致煩躁不安，嘔吐及皮膚藍染。

異戊巴比妥 一種中效巴比妥酸鹽，長期使用可產生依賴性，過量則有嚴重毒性（參閱 barbiturism）商品名：Amytal。

澱粉樣蛋白 一種類似澱粉的糖蛋白，在澱粉樣變性時沉積於患者的內部器官，β-澱粉樣蛋白見於阿爾茨海默病患者腦內，但其意義仍未明。

澱粉樣變性 肝、腎、脾及其他組織的澱粉樣蛋白（一種澱粉樣物質）浸潤。原發性澱粉樣變性無明顯發病原因；繼發性澱粉樣變性為某些慢性感染後期的併發症，如結核、麻風病及霍奇金病。在為遺傳性疾病的家族性地中海熱中亦很常見（參閱 polyserositis）。

支鏈澱粉 參閱 starch。

直鏈澱粉 參閱 starch。

先天性肌弛緩（嬰兒鬆弛綜合徵） 過去對多種出生時即存

various conditions, present at birth, in which the baby's muscles are weak and floppy (i.e. hypotonic). The term is becoming obsolete as more specific diagnoses are discovered to explain the cause of floppiness in babies.

在的嬰兒肌肉鬆弛無力（即張力低下）症候羣的診斷，現有更加明確的診斷解釋嬰兒肌肉鬆弛的病因，因而該詞正逐漸廢棄。

amyotrophy *n*. a progressive loss of muscle bulk associated with weakness of these muscles. It is caused by disease of the nerve that activates the affected muscle. Amyotrophy is a feature of any chronic *neuropathy and it may be the most prominent neurological symptom of diabetes mellitus and meningovascular syphilis. A combination of amyotrophy and spasticity may be found in the different forms of *motor neurone disease.

肌萎縮　伴有肌無力的肌肉進行性萎縮，由於支配受累肌肉神經的疾患所致。肌萎縮為任何慢性神經病的特徵，並可能是糖尿病和腦膜血管梅毒最主要的神經病學症狀。肌萎縮伴發肌痙攣可見於各種運動神經元疾病中。

an- *prefix. see* a-.

〔前綴〕　**無**，**缺**，**不**　參閱 a-。

anabolic *adj*. promoting tissue growth by increasing the metabolic processes involved in protein synthesis. Anabolic agents are usually synthetic male sex hormones (*see* androgen); they include *ethyloestrenol, *nandrolone, *oxymetholone, and *stanozolol. They have been used to help weight gain in underweight patients, such as the elderly and those with serious illnesses, and to stimulate the production of blood cells by the bone marrow. Some anabolic steroids cause virilization in women and liver damage.

合成代謝的，**同化的**　增加蛋白質合成的代謝過程以促進組織生長。同化劑通常為人工合成的男性激素（參閱 androgen），包括乙基雌烯醇、南諾龍、羥甲烯龍和司坦唑。它們用於幫助年老或重病患者等體重不足者增加體重，亦用於刺激骨髓產生血細胞。某些同化類固醇可致女性男性化和肝損害。

anabolism *n*. the synthesis of complex molecules, such as proteins and fats, from simpler ones by living things. *See also* anabolic, metabolism.

組成代謝　生物將較簡單分子合成為複雜分子，如蛋白質和脂肪。參閱 anabolic，metabolism。

anacidity *n*. a deficiency or abnormal absence of acid in the body fluids.

酸缺乏　體液內酸不足或異常缺乏。

anacrotism *n.* the condition in which there is an abnormal curve in the ascending line of a pulse tracing. It may be seen in cases of aortic stenosis. **–anacrotic** *adj.*

升綫一波脈（現象） 脈搏描記圖升支中有一異常曲綫的狀態，可見於主動脈瓣狹窄病例中。

anaemia *n.* a reduction in the quantity of the oxygen-carrying pigment *haemoglobin in the blood. The main symptoms are excessive tiredness and fatigability, breathlessness on exertion, pallor, and poor resistance to infection. There are many causes of anaemia. It may be due to loss of blood (*haemorrhagic anaemia*), resulting from an accident, operation, etc., or from chronic bleeding, as from an ulcer or haemorrhoids. *Iron-deficiency anaemia* results from lack of iron, which is necessary for the production of haemoglobin (*see* sideropenia). *Haemolytic anaemias* result from the increased destruction of red blood cells (which contain the pigment). This can be caused by toxic chemicals; *autoimmunity; the action of parasites, especially in *malaria; or conditions such as *thalassaemia and *sickle cell disease, associated with abnormal forms of haemoglobin, or *spherocytosis, which is associated with abnormal red blood cells. (*See also* haemolytic disease of the newborn.) Anaemia can also be caused by the impaired production of red blood cells, as in *leukaemia (when red-cell production in the bone marrow is suppressed) or *pernicious anaemia.

Anaemias can be classified on the basis of the size of the red cells, which may be large (*macrocytic anaemias*), small (*microcytic anaemias*), or normal-sized (*normocytic anaemias*). (*See also* macrocytosis, microcytosis.) The treatment of anaemia depends on the cause. **–anaemic** *adj.*

貧血 血中載氧色素血紅蛋白數量減少。其主要症狀有：極度疲憊和易疲性、用力時氣喘、臉色蒼白及抗感染力低下。貧血有多種原因，可因意外傷害、手術等失血或因潰瘍、痔瘡慢性出血而致（出血性貧血）。缺鐵性貧血因血紅蛋白生成所必需的鐵缺乏所致（參閱 sideropenia）。溶血性貧血則由於紅細胞（含血色素）被大量破壞，原因可為化學毒品、自體免疫、寄生物作用（尤指瘧疾），與血紅蛋白形狀異常有關的情況如地中海貧血和鐮狀細胞病，或與紅細胞有關的球形紅細胞症（參閱 haemolytic disease of the newborn）。貧血還可因紅細胞生成受損而致，如白血病（此時骨髓中紅細胞生成受到抑制）或惡性貧血。

貧血可根據紅細胞大小分類，有大紅細胞性貧血，小紅細胞性貧血，或正常紅細胞性貧血（參閱 macrocytosis，microcytosis）。治療須視其病因而定。

anaerobe *n.* any organism, especially a microbe, that is able to live and grow in the absence of free oxygen. A *facultative anaerobe* is a microorganism that grows best in the presence of oxygen but is capable of some growth in its absence. An *obligate anaerobe* can grow only in the absence of free oxygen. *Compare* aerobe, microaerophilic.

厭氧菌　任何在缺乏游離氧的情況下能存活並生長的生物，特別是微生物。兼性厭氧菌最適於有氧環境，但缺氧時也能生長。專性厭氧菌僅在無游離氧的狀態下生長。與 aerobe，microaerophilic 對比。

anaerobic *adj.* **1.** of or relating to anaerobes. **2.** describing a type of a cellular respiration in which foodstuffs (usually carbohydrates) are never completely oxidized because molecular oxygen is not used. *Fermentation is an example of anaerobic respiration.

(1) 厭氧的　屬於或與厭氧菌有關的。(2) 乏氧的　描述細胞呼吸的一種類型，此時食物（常為碳水化合物）因分子氧未被利用而不能完全氧化，如發酵。

anaesthesia *n.* loss of feeling or sensation in a part or all of the body. Anaesthesia of a part of the body may occur as a result of injury to or disease of a nerve; for example in leprosy. The term is usually applied, however, to the technique of reducing or abolishing an individual's sensation of pain to enable surgery to be performed. This is effected by administering drugs (*see* anaesthetic) or by the use of other methods, such as *acupuncture or hypnosis.

General anaesthesia is total unconsciousness, usually achieved by administering a combination of injections and gases (the latter are inhaled through a mask). *Local anaesthesia* abolishes pain in a limited area of the body and is used for minor operations, particularly many dental procedures. It may be achieved by injections of substances such as lignocaine (commonly used in dentistry) close to a local nerve, which deadens the tissues supplied by that nerve. Local anaesthesia may be combined with intravenous sedation. An appropriate injection into the spinal column produces

感覺缺失，麻醉（法）　身體一部分或全部感覺或知覺喪失。部分感覺缺失可因一條神經受傷或病變而致，如麻風病。但該詞通常指減輕或消除患者痛覺以施行外科手術的技術，以給藥（參閱 anaesthetic）或針灸、催眠等其他方式進行麻醉。

全身麻醉指神志完全喪失，通常經注射與氣體聯合給藥（後者通過面罩吸入）。局部麻醉消除身體某一部分的疼痛而用於小手術，尤其是多種牙科手術。局部麻醉可通過在局部神經附近注射利多卡因類藥物（牙科常用），使該神經支配的組織麻木，並可與靜脈注射鎮靜劑合用。在脊髓適當部位注射麻醉藥可產生下肢或腹部的感覺缺失。區域麻醉通常是肢體的麻醉，用於不適合全身麻醉的情況下，將局部麻醉液注射於手術周圍部位。

*spinal anaesthesia in the lower limbs or abdomen. *Regional anaesthesia*, usually of a limb, is achieved by encircling local anaesthetic solutions and is used in situations where general anaesthesia is not appropriate.

anaesthetic 1. *n.* an agent that reduces or abolishes sensation, affecting either the whole body (*general anaesthetic*) or a particular area or region (*local anaesthetic*). General anaesthetics, used for surgical procedures, depress activity of the central nervous system, producing loss of consciousness. *Anaesthesia is induced by short-acting *barbiturates (such as thiopentone) and maintained by inhalation anaesthetics (such as *halothane). Local anaesthetics inhibit conduction of impulses in sensory nerves in the region where they are injected or applied; they include *amethocaine, *bupivacaine, and *lignocaine. **2.** *adj.* reducing or abolishing sensation.

(1) 麻醉劑 降低或消除全身（全身麻醉）或特定部位（局部麻醉）感覺的藥物。外科手術用的全身麻醉劑抑制中樞神經系統活動而致神志喪失。麻醉可由速效巴比妥酸鹽（如硫噴妥鈉）引起並由吸入麻醉劑（如氟烷）維持。局部麻醉劑抑制其注射或應用部位感覺神經衝動的傳導，包括丁卡因，布比卡因和利多卡因。**(2) 麻醉的** 降低或消除感覺的。

anaesthetist *n.* a medically qualified doctor who administers an anaesthetic to induce unconsciousness in a patient before a surgical operation.

麻醉師 手術前使用麻醉劑使患者喪失意識的有行醫資格的醫師。

anagen *n.* the growth phase of a hair follicle, lasting two to three years. It is followed by a transitional stage, called *catagen*, and then a resting phase, *telogen*, each of which lasts for about two weeks. On average about 85% of hairs are in anagen and hence growing actively. There are abut 100,000 hairs on the human scalp and up to 100 may be shed each day.

毛髮生長初期 持續兩至三年的毛囊生長期，隨之是稱為毛髮生長中期的過渡階段，其後是休養階段的毛髮生長終期。後兩期各持續約兩周。平均有 85% 的毛髮處於生長初期，因此毛髮生長活躍。人類頭皮上大約有 10 萬根頭髮，每天掉髮可達 100 根。

anákhré *n. see* goundou.

根度病（鼻骨增殖性骨膜炎） 參閱 goundou。

anal *adj.* of, relating to, or affecting the anus; for example an anal *fissure or an anal *fistula.

肛門的 屬於、有關或影響肛門的；例如肛門裂或肛門瘻。

anal canal the terminal portion of the large intestine, which is surrounded by the muscles of defecation (*anal sphincters*). The canal ends on the surface at the anal orifice (*see* anus).

肛管　大腸的末端部分，由協助排便的肌肉包圍（肛門括約肌）。肛管終端為肛門口表面（參閱 anus）。

analeptic *n*. a drug that restores consciousness to a patient in a coma or faint; for example, *doxapram, *nikethamide, or *naloxone. Analeptics stimulate the central nervous system to counteract the effects of large doses of narcotic drugs, which depress the central nervous system.

復蘇劑，興奮劑　使昏迷或暈厥患者恢復意識的藥物，如多沙普侖，尼可剎米或納洛酮。復蘇劑刺激中樞神經系統而解除大劑量麻醉劑對中樞神經系統的抑制作用。

anal fissure a break in the skin lining the anal canal, usually causing pain during bowel movements and sometimes bleeding. Anal fissures occur as a consequence of constipation or sometimes of diarrhoea. Treatment is by soothing ointments, but if the condition is severe the operation of *lateral sphincterotomy* (cutting the muscle of the anal sphincter) is required.

肛門裂　肛管內襯的皮膚破裂，常引起排便疼痛，有時出血。肛門裂為便秘的結果，有時因腹瀉所致。治療用軟膏緩解，若病情嚴重則需行外括約肌切開術（切開肛門括約肌）。

analgesia *n*. reduced sensibility to pain without loss of consciousness and without the sense of touch necessarily being affected. The condition may arise accidentally, if nerves are diseased or damaged, or be induced deliberately by the use of pain-killing drugs (*see* analgesic). Strictly speaking, local *anaesthesia should be called *local analgesia*. *See also* relative analgesia.

痛覺缺失，止痛　痛覺降低而無意識喪失，觸覺或亦可不受影響。若神經出現病變或受損可偶然產生痛覺缺失，也可用止痛藥有意引導（參閱 analgesic）。嚴格地説，局部麻醉應稱為局部止痛。參閱 relative analgesia。

analgesic 1. *n*. a drug that relieves pain. Mild analgesics, such as *aspirin and *paracetamol, are used for the relief of headache, toothache, and mild rheumatic pain. More potent *narcotic analgesics*, such as *morphine and *pethidine, are used only to relieve severe pain since these drugs may produce *dependence

(1) 止痛劑　解除疼痛的藥物。輕止痛劑如阿司匹林和對乙酰氨基酚用於緩解頭痛、牙痛和輕度風濕痛，較強的麻醉性止痛劑，如嗎啡和哌替啶，因可產生依賴性和耐藥性（參閱 narcotic，opiate）僅用於緩解劇痛。包括阿司匹林，吲

and *tolerance (*see also* narcotic, opiate). Some analgesics including aspirin, *indomethacin, and *phenylbutazone, also reduce fever and inflammation and are used in rheumatic conditions (*see also* NSAID). **2.** *adj.* relieving pain.

哚美辛和保泰松等的某些止痛劑亦可解熱消炎,而用於風濕性病症(參閱 NSAID)。**(2)** 止痛的

analogous *adj.* describing organs or parts that have similar functions in different organisms although they do not have the same evolutionary origin or development. *Compare* homologous.

同功器官 描述進化的起源與發展均不相同的生物體中具有相似功能的器官或部位。與homologous比較。

analogue *n.* a drug that differs in minor ways in molecular structure from its parent compound. Examples are *calcipotriol (an analogue of vitamin D) and the *LHPH analogues. Useful analogues of existing drugs are either more potent or cause fewer side-effects. *Carboplatin, for example, is a less toxic analogue of *cisplatin.

同型物,類似物 分子結構與其母體化合物略有不同的藥物。如鈣泊三醇(維生素D的一種同型物)和LHRH同型物。現有藥物的各種同型物或療效更強,或產生副作用較少。例如,卡鉑是順鉑的毒性更小的同型物。

analysand *n.* a person undergoing *psychoanalysis.

受精神分析者 接受精神分析的人。

analysis *n.* (in psychology) any means of understanding complex mental processes or experiences. There are several systems of analysis used by different schools of psychology; for example, *psychoanalysis; *transactional analysis*, in which people's relationships are explained in psychoanalytic terms; and *functional analysis*, in which a particular kind of behaviour is thoroughly described with reference to its frequency, its antecedents, and its consequences.

分析 (心理學)了解複雜的心理過程或體驗的任何手段。不同心理學派所採用的分析體系有幾種。如精神分析:用精神分析術語解釋人際關係的相互作用分析;及功能分析,此為參照其頻率、前因與後果對某種類型行為進行詳盡描述。

anamnesis *n.* memory, particularly the recollection by a patient of the symptoms that he noticed at the time when his disease was first contracted.

既往症 記憶,尤指患者對患病初始所注意到的症狀的回憶。

anankastic *adj.* describing a collection of longstanding personality traits, including stubbornness, meanness, an overmeticulous concern to be accurate in small details, a disposition to check things unnecessarily, severe feelings of insecurity about personal worth, and an excessive tendency to doubt evident facts. *See* personality disorder, obsession.

強迫性人格的　描述一系列長期存在的性格特點，包括頑固、自私、過於關注細節、不必要地檢查物品、對個人價值的強烈不安感、以及對明顯事實的過分疑慮。參閱 personality disorder，obsession。

anaphase *n.* the third stage of *mitosis and of each division of *meiosis. In mitosis and anaphase II of meiosis the chromatids separate, becoming daughter chromosomes, and move apart along the spindle fibres towards opposite ends of the cell. In anaphase I of meiosis the pairs of homologous chromosomes separate from each other. *See* disjunction.

後期　有絲分裂和各次減數分裂的第三階段。在有絲分裂和減數分裂後期 II 中，染色單體分開成為子染色體，並沿紡錘絲分別移向細胞兩端。在減數分裂後期 I 中，成對的同源染色體互相分開。參閱 disjunction。

anaphylaxis *n.* an abnormal reaction to a particular *antigen, in which histamine is released from tissues and causes either local or widespread symptoms. An allergic attack (*see* allergy) is an example of localized anaphylaxis. Rarer, but much more serious, is *anaphylactic shock*: an extreme and generalized allergic reaction in which widespread release of histamine causes swelling (*oedema), constriction of the bronchioles, heart failure, circulatory collapse, and sometimes death. **–anaphylactic** *adj.*

過敏症，過敏反應　對某種抗原產生異常反應，組織內釋放出組胺而引起局部或全身症狀。變態反應（參閱 allergy）即為局部過敏症之一種。較罕見但更嚴重的是過敏性休克，為一種極重和全身性的變態反應，此時組胺的釋放引起腫脹（水腫）、細支氣管狹窄、心力衰竭、循環性虛脫，有時導致死亡。

anaplasia *n.* a loss of normal cell characteristics or differentiation, which may be to such a degree that it is impossible to define the origin of the cells. Anaplasia is typical of rapidly growing malignant tumours.

退行發育，間變　細胞的正常特徵或分化喪失，可達到不能識別其來源的程度。此為發展迅速的惡性腫瘤之特點。

anasarca *n.* massive swelling of the legs, trunk, and genitalia due to retention of fluid (*oedema): found in congestive heart failure and some forms of renal failure.

全身水腫　因液體瀦留（水腫）而致的下肢、軀幹和生殖器的大面積腫脹，見於充血性心力衰竭和某些形式的腎衰竭。

anastomosis *n.* **1.** (in anatomy) a communication between two blood vessels without any intervening capillary network. *See* arteriovenous anastomosis. **2.** (in surgery) an artificial connection between tow tubular organs or parts, especially between two normally separate parts of the intestine. *See also* shunt.

(1) 吻合 （解剖學）其間無任何毛細管的兩血管相通。參閱 arteriovenous anastomosis。
(2) 吻合術 （外科學）兩個管狀器官或部位之間，尤指腸的兩段正常分離部分之間的人工連接。參閱 shunt。

anatomy *n.* the study of the structure of living organisms. In medicine it refers to the study of the form and gross structure of the various parts of the human body. The term *morphology* is sometimes used synonymously with anatomy but it is usually used for *comparative anatomy*: the study of differences in form between species. *See also* cytology, histology, physiology. **–anatomical** *adj.* **–anatomist** *n.*

解剖學 對生物體結構的研究，在醫學上指對人體各部分的形狀和肉眼可見結構的研究。形態學一詞有時用作解剖學的同義詞，但通常是指比較解剖學，即對不同種類的形態差異進行研究。參閱 cytology，histology，physiology。

anatoxin *n.* a former name for *toxoid.

類毒素 toxoid的舊稱。

anconeus *n.* a muscle behind the elbow that assists in extending the forearm.

肘（後）肌 位於肘之後協助伸展前臂的肌肉。

Ancylostoma (Ankylostoma) *n.* a genus of small parasitic nematodes (*see* hookworm) that inhabit the small intestine and are widely distributed in Europe, America, Asia, and Africa. The worms suck blood from the gut wall, to which they are attached by means of cutting teeth. Man is the principal and optimum host for *A. duodenale.*

鈎（口綫）蟲屬 寄居小腸的一屬寄生性小綫蟲（參閱 hookworm），廣泛分布於歐洲、美洲、亞洲和非洲。以其切齒附着於腸道吸血。人類是十二指腸鈎蟲的主要與最適宿主。

ancylostomiasis *n.* an infestation of the small intestine by the parasitic hookworm Ancylostoma duodenale. *See* hookworm disease.

鈎（口綫）蟲病 小腸受寄生性鈎蟲十二指腸鈎蟲的侵襲。參閱 hookworm disease。

ANDI an acronym for *ab*normal *d*evelopment and *i*nvolution, used to tabulate benign disorders of the breast.

異常發育和退化 為 abnormal development and involution的首字母縮略詞，用於乳房良性疾患的製表顯示。

andr- (andro-) *prefix denoting* man of the male sex. Example: *androphobia* (morbid fear of).

〔前綴〕**男，雄** 男子或雄性。如，男性恐怖。

androblastoma (arrhenoblastoma) *n.* a tumour of the ovary, composed of Sertoli cells, Leydig cells, or both. It can produce male or female hormones and may give rise to *masculinization; in children it may cause precocious puberty. Up to 30% of these tumours are malignant, but probably as many as 85% of all cases are cured by surgery alone.

男性細胞瘤 由塞爾托利細胞或/和萊迪希細胞組成的一種卵巢瘤，可產生雄激素或雌激素，導致女性男性化和兒童性早熟。其中 30% 為惡性，但大約 85% 的病例僅用手術便可治愈。

androgen *n.* one of a group of steroid hormones, including *testosterone* and *androsterone*, that stimulate the development of male sex organs and male secondary sexual characteristics (e.g. beard growth, deepening of the voice, and muscle development). The principal source of these hormones is the testis (production being stimulated by *luteinizing hormone) but they are also secreted by the adrenal cortex and ovaries in small amounts. In women excessive production of androgens gives rise to *masculinization.

Naturally occurring and synthetic androgens are used in replacement therapy (to treat such conditions as delayed puberty in adolescent boys. *hypogondism, and impotence due to testicular insufficiency); as *anabolic agents; and in the treatment of breast cancer. Side-effects include salt and water retention, increased bone growth, and masculinization in women. Androgens should not be used in patients with cancer of the prostate gland or in pregnant women. **–androgenic** *adj.*

雄激素 包括睾酮和雄甾酮的類固醇激素之一，刺激男性性器官和第二性徵（如胡鬚生長、嗓音變粗及肌肉發育）的發育。主要來自睾丸（由促黃體生成激素刺激其生成），腎上腺皮質和卵巢也有少量分泌。雄激素分泌過多可引起女性的男性化。

天然產生或人工合成的雄激素可用於替代療法（治療男性青少年青春期延遲，性腺機能減退和睾丸機能減退所致陽痿等症），亦用作同化劑或用於治療乳腺癌。副作用有水鹽瀦留、骨質增生及女性男性化。前列腺癌患者或孕婦應禁用。

andrology *n.* **1.** the study of male infertility and impotence. *Seminal analysis reveals the presence of gross

男性學 **(1)** 對男性不育症和陽痿的研究。精液分析可顯示精液濃度及精子形狀與能動性

abnormalities in the shape and motility of spermatozoa, as well as their concentration in the semen, but further procedures are required to diagnose the underlying causes of the sperm dysfunction. These include the diagnosis of abnormalities in the genital tract (e.g. varicocele, obstruction of the vas deferens), which may be corrected surgically, and testing for the presence of antisperm antibodies in the semen and for the ability of the sperm to penetrate the cervical mucus, as well as for the presence of hormonal disorders. More sophisticated techniques include computer-assisted quantitative motility measurements, which monitor the precise speed and motility patterns of individual sperm; biochemical tests for the production of free oxygen radicals, which cause damage to developing sperm; and *acrosome-reaction assays, which reveal the ability of the sperm to penetrate the barriers surrounding the ovum. The development of all these techniques has enabled the identification of several previously undiagnosed causes of infertility and the selection of treatments most likely to succeed in remedying them. **2.** the study of androgen production and the relationship of plasma androgen to androgen action. This study is necessary to understand *hirsutism and other conditions caused by abnormal androgen production.

肉眼可見的異常，但診斷精子機能障礙的潛在原因需作進一步的檢查，包括診斷可用手術矯正的生殖道異常（如精索靜脈曲張和輸精管阻塞），檢測是否存在激素紊亂，精液中是否有精子抗體，以及精子穿過子宮頸黏液的能力。更先進的技術包括計算機輔助能動力定量測定，可監測單個精子的精確速度和運動模式；生化試驗檢測損害發育中精子的氧自由基的產生；以及顯示精子穿透卵巢周圍屏障能力的頂體反應測定。由於這些技術的發展，幾種過去診斷不明的不育症病因現已可鑒別，從而選擇最有效的治療方案。**(2)** 對雄激素產生和血漿雄激素與雄激素作用關係的研究。這種研究對了解多毛症和其他由雄激素生成異常導致的病症很有必要。

androsterone *n.* a steroid hormone (*see* androgen) that is synthesized and released by the testes and is responsible for controlling male sexual development.

雄甾酮　由睾丸合成並釋放的一種類固醇激素（參閱 androgen），具有調節男性性發育的作用。

anencephaly *n.* partial or complete absence of the bones of the rear of the skull and of the cerebral hemispheres of the brain. It occurs as a developmental defect and is not compatible with life for

無腦（畸形）　顱骨後部和大腦半球的部分或完全缺失，為一種發育缺陷，僅能生存數小時。常伴有神經系統的其他缺陷如脊柱裂。有無腦畸形家族

more than a few hours. It is often associated with other defects of the nervous system, such as *spina bifida. Tests for anencephaly can be made early in pregnancy in women with a family history of the condition (*see* amniocentesis, alpha-fetoprotein).

anergy *n.* **1.** lack of response to a specific antigen or allergen. **2.** lack of energy. **–anergic** *adj.*

aneuploidy *n.* the condition in which the chromosome number of a cell is not an exact multiple of the normal basic (haploid) number. *See* monosomy, trisomy; *compare* euploidy. **–aneuploid** *adj., n.*

aneurine *n. see* vitamin B$_1$.

aneurysm *n.* a balloon-like swelling in the wall of an artery. This may be due to degenerative disease or syphilitic infection, which damages the muscular coats of the vessel, or it may be the result of congenital deficiency in the muscular wall. An *aortic aneurysm* may develop anywhere in the aorta. A *dissecting aneurysm* usually affects the first part of the aorta and results from a degenerative condition of its muscular coat. This weakness predisposes to a tear in the lining of the aorta, which allows blood to enter the wall and track along (dissect) the muscular coat. A dissecting aneurysm may rupture or it may compress the blood vessels arising from the aorta and produce infarction (localized necrosis) in the organs they supply. The patient complains of severe chest pain that has a tearing quality and often spreads to the back or abdomen. Surgical repair may help in some cases. A *ventricular aneurysm* may develop in the

史的孕婦，可在妊娠早期對此病進行檢查（參閱 amniocentesis，alpha-fetoprotein）。

(1) 無變應性 對某種抗原或變應原缺乏反應。**(2) 無力**

非整倍性 細胞中染色體數目非正常基數（單倍數）的整倍數的狀態。參閱 monosomy，trisomy。與 euploidy 對比。

硫胺 參閱 vitamin B$_1$。

動脈瘤 動脈壁的氣球樣膨脹。可因損害血管肌層的變性疾病或梅毒感染所致，或為肌壁先天性缺陷的結果。主動脈瘤可發生於主動脈的任何部位。夾層動脈瘤常發生在升主動脈，因其肌層變性而致。肌層受損導致主動脈內膜破裂，使血液進入動脈壁並流過（割裂）肌層。壁間動脈瘤可能破裂或壓迫從主動脈分支的血管，並成所供血器官的梗塞（局部壞死）。患者訴說撕裂樣胸部劇痛，並常放射至背部或腹部。手術修補可用於某些病例。心室動脈瘤可在心肌梗死後發生於左心室壁，部分心肌被瘢痕組織所代替，由此擴張形成動脈瘤囊，可導致心力衰竭，或因動脈瘤內血栓形成引起栓塞。

大多數腦內動脈瘤具先天性，並有破裂而引起蛛網膜下腔出血的危險。顱內小動脈瘤

wall of the left ventricle after myocardial infarction. A segment of myocardium becomes replaced by scar tissue, which expands to form an aneurysmal sac. Heart failure may result or thrombosis within the aneurysm may act as a source of embolism.

Most aneurysms within the brain are congenital: there is a risk that they may burst, causing a *subarachnoid haemorrhage. *Berry aneurysms* are small saccular aneurysms most commonly occurring in the branches of the *circle of Willis. Usually associated with congenital weakness of the vessels, these aneurysms are a cause of fatal intracranial haemorrhage in young adults. *Charcot-Bouchard aneurysms* are small aneurysms found on tiny arteries within the brain of elderly and hypertensive subjects. These aneurysms may rupture, causing cerebral haemorrhage. *See also* arteriovenous aneurysm. **–aneurysmal** *adj.*

angi- (angio-) *prefix denoting* blood or lymph vessels. Examples: *angiectasis* (abnormal dilation of); *angiopathy* (disease of); *angiotomy* (cutting of).

angiitis (vasculitis) *n.* a patchy inflammation of the walls of small blood vessels. It may result from a variety of conditions, including *polyarteritis nodosa, acute nephritis, and serum sickness. Symptoms include skin rashes, arthritis, purpura, and kidney failure. In some cases treatment with cortisone derivatives may be beneficial.

angina *n.* a sense of suffocation of suffocating pain. *See* angina pectoris, Ludwig's angina.

angina pectoris pain in the centre of the chest, which is induced by exercise

為囊狀小動脈瘤,最常發生於韋利斯環,它們常與血管的先天性脆弱有關,是青年人發生致命的顱內出血的一種原因。夏-布氏動脈瘤為見於老年人和高血壓患者腦內小動脈上的小動脈瘤,有可能破裂引起腦出血。參閱 arteriovenous aneurysm。

〔前綴〕**血管** 血管或淋巴管,如血管擴張、血管病、血管切開。

脈管炎 小血管壁的斑塊狀炎症,可因多種病症而致,包括結詳性多動脈炎、急性腎炎和血清病。症狀有皮診、關節炎、紫癜和腎衰竭。可的松類藥物對某些病例有療效。

絞痛 窒息感或窒息痛。參閱 angina pectoris,Ludwig's angina。

心絞痛 由運動誘發並可放射至頷與手臂的胸部正中疼痛,

and relieved by rest and may spread to the jaws and arms. Angina pectoris occurs when the demand for blood by the heart exceeds the supply of the coronary arteries and it usually results from coronary artery *atheroma. It may be prevented or relieved by such drugs as *glyceryl trinitrate and *propranolol. If drug treatment proves ineffective, *coronary angioplasty or *coronary bypass grafts may be required, the former being less invasive than the latter.

休息可緩解。當心臟所需血流超過冠狀動脈供血量時即發生此病，常因冠狀動脈粥樣化所致。某些藥物，如硝酸甘油和普萘洛爾，可預防或緩解本病。若藥物治療無效，則需作冠狀血管成形術或冠狀動脈分流移植，前者比後者損害較輕。

angiocardiography n. X-ray examination of the chambers of the heart after introducing a *radiopaque contrast medium into the blood in the heart. The contrast medium (e.g. Cardioconray) is injected directly into the atria, ventricles, or great vessels of the heart by means of a slim sterile flexible tube (*cardiac catheter*), which is manipulated into position from an accessible point, such as a vein or artery in a limb (*see* (cardiac) catheterization). Its progress through the heart is followed by a rapid series of X-ray films or by the use of cine film (*cineangiocardiography). The X-ray is called an *angiocardiogram*. Angiocardiography is an important aid in diagnosing and planning the surgical repair of heart defects.

心血管造影術　將不透 X 綫的造影劑注入心臟血液後對心臟房室的 X 綫檢查。將無菌柔韌的細管（心導管）從肢體靜脈或動脈等易入部位送達心房、心室或心臟大血管，（參閱（cardiac）catheterization），造影劑（如心康瑞）經此導管直接注入上述部位，其通過心臟的過程用快速系列 X 綫照片或電影軟片（心血管電影造影術）進行跟蹤拍攝，此 X 綫照片稱為心血管照片。心血管造影術是心臟缺損診斷與擬定手術修補方案中一項重要的輔助手段。

angiodysplasia n. an abnormal collection of small blood vessels in the wall of the bowel, which may bleed. It is diagnosed by *colonoscopy or *angiography and may be treated by *diathermy coagulation or by surgical removal.

血管發育不良　腸壁中有出血可能的異常小血管叢，通過結腸鏡檢查或血管造影術做出診斷，可用透熱電凝法或手術切除治療。

angiogenesis n. the formation of new blood vessels. This process is essential for the development of a tumour and is promoted by *growth factors.

血管生成　新血管的形成。此過程為腫瘤發展的必要條件，並受到生長因子的促動。

angiography *n.* X-ray examination of blood vessels. A dye that is opaque to X-rays is injected into the artery and a rapid series of X-ray films is taken (*see* arteriography). *Fluorescein angiography* is a common method of investigation in ophthalmology. *Fluorescein sodium is injected into a vein in the arm, from which it circulates throughout the body. Light of an appropriate wavelength is shone into the eye, causing the dye in the retinal blood vessels to fluoresce. This allows the circulation through the retinal blood vessels to be observed and photographed.

血管造影術　血管的X綫檢查，即將不透X綫的染料注入動脈血管中並拍攝快速系列的X綫照片（參閱 arteriography）。熒光血管造影術是眼科學檢查中的一項常用方法。將熒光素鈉經臂靜脈注入流至全身，用適當波長的光射入眼球，致使視網膜血管中的染料發射熒光，由此可觀察並拍攝到視網膜血管的血流情況。

angiokeratoma *n.* a localized collection of thin-walled blood vessels covered by a cap of warty material. It is most often seen as an isolated malformation in the genital skin of the elderly or on the hands and feet of children. It is not malignant and its cause is unknown. Angiokeratomas may be removed surgically. Multiple angiokeratomas affecting the viscera and skin are seen as a rare inherited and fatal disease (*Fabry's disease*).

血管角質瘤　頂端為疣樣物質的局限性薄壁血管羣，係一種局部畸形。最常見於老年人的生殖器皮膚和兒童的手足部位。此瘤非惡性，其原因不明，可用手術切除。累及內臟與皮膚的血管角質瘤則被視為一種罕見的致死遺傳病（法布里病）。

angioma *n.* a benign tumour composed of blood vessels or lymph vessels. *Cherry angiomas* (or *Campbell de Morgan spots*) are small red spots on the trunk in middle-aged or elderly people. They are completely harmless and consist of a minor vascular malformation. An *arteriovenous angioma* (or *malformation*) is a knot of distended blood vessels overlying and compressing the surface of the brain. It may cause epilepsy, or one of the vessels may burst, causing a *subarachnoid haemorrhage. This type of angioma may be suitable for surgical removal or stereotactic radiotherapy. It may be associated with a purple birthmark on the face: this is called the *Sturge-Weber*

血管瘤　一種由血管或淋巴管構成的良性瘤。櫻桃狀血管瘤（或稱坎貝爾德摩根斑）是中老年人軀幹上的小紅斑，為一種完全無害的輕微血管畸形。動靜脈血管瘤（或畸形）是覆蓋並壓迫腦部表層的擴張的血管羣，可致癲癇，亦可發生血管破裂引起蛛網膜下腔出血。此類血管瘤適於手術切除或立體定位放射療法。可伴發面部紫色胎痣，稱為斯-韋氏綜合徵。參閱 haemangioma，lymphangioma。

syndrome. See also haemangioma, lymphangioma.

angio-oedema (angioneurotic oedema) *n. see* urticaria.

angioplasty *n.* surgical repair or reconstruction of narrowed or completely obstructed arteries (or rarely veins). In *percutaneous transluminal angioplasty* (*PTA*; *balloon angioplasty*) an inflatable balloon, mounted on the tip of a flexible catheter, is placed within the lumen of the affected artery, at the site of the disease, under X-ray screening control (*see* catheterization). On inflation of the balloon the lumen is enlarged, disrupting the *intima (which reduces the chance of stenosis recurring). Common sites for PTA are the coronary, iliac, femoral, and popliteal arteries. *See also* coronary angioplasty.

angiospasm *n. see* Raynaud's disease.

angiotensin *n.* either of two peptides: *angiotensin I* or *angiotensin II.* Angiotensin I is derived, by the action of the enzyme *renin, from a protein (alpha globulin) secreted by the liver into the bloodstream. As blood passes through the lungs, another enzyme acts on angiotensin I to form angiotensin II. This peptide causes constriction of blood vessels and stimulates the release of the hormones *vasopressin and *aldosterone, which increase blood pressure. *See also* ACE inhibitor.

angle *n.* **1.** (in anatomy) a corner. For example, the *angle of the eye* is the outer or inner corner of the eye; the *angle of the mouth* is the site where the upper and lower lips join on either side. **2.** the

血管神經性水腫　參閱 urticaria。

血管成形術　手術修復或重建狹窄或完全阻塞的動脈（偶爾為靜脈）。行經皮腔內血管成形術時（PTA，氣囊血管成形術），將安於柔韌導管頂端的充氣氣囊經 X 綫熒光導引（參閱 catheterization），置於病變部位的受累動脈腔內。此氣囊一經充氣，動脈腔即被擴張使內膜破裂（可減少再次狹窄的機會）。PTA的常行部位為冠狀動脈，髂動脈和膕動脈。參閱 coronary angioplasty。

血管痙攣　參閱 Raynaud's disease。

血管緊張素　兩類肽之一：血管緊張素 I 或血管緊張素 II。通過腎素這種酶的作用，血管緊張素 I 由肝釋放至血流的一種蛋白（α-球蛋白）所衍生。當血液流經肺時，另一種酶作用於血管緊張素 I 而形成血管緊張素 II。這種肽可致血管收縮，並刺激釋放升壓的加壓素和醛甾酮。參閱 ACE inhibitor。

角　(1)（解剖學）解剖學中的角。例如，眼角指眼睛的外角或內角；嘴角指上下唇在兩側的匯合部位。(2) 兩條相交直綫或兩個相交平面所形成的角

degree of divergence of two lines or planes that meet each other; the space between two such lines. The *carrying angle* is the obtuse angle formed between the forearm and the upper arm when the forearm is fully extended and the hand is supinated.

度。臂外偏角為前臂伸直，手後旋時上臂與前臂之間形成的鈍角。

angstrom *n*. a unit of length equal to one ten millionth of a millimetre (10^{-10}m). It is not a recommended *SI unit but is sometimes used to express wavelengths and interatomic distances: the *nanometre (1 nm = 10 Å) is now the preferred unit. Symbol Å.

埃 表示千萬分之一毫米（10^{-10}米）的長度單位，並非公認的一種國際單位，但有時用於表示波長與原子間的距離。現一般使用的單位為毫微米（1 毫微米＝10 埃）。符號：Å。

anhidrosis *n*. the absence of sweating in the presence of an appropriate stimulus for sweating, which may accompany disease or occur as a congenital defect.

無汗（症） 在有適當的刺激出汗條件下無汗，可伴發於疾病或為先天性缺陷。

anhidrotic 1. *n*. any drug that inhibits sweating, such as *parasympatholytic drugs. **2.** *adj.* inhibiting sweating.

(1) 止汗藥 任何抑制出汗的藥物，如抗副交感神經藥。**(2) 止汗的**

anhydraemia *n*. a decrease in the proportion of water, and therefore plasma, in the blood.

缺水血（症） 血液中水分減少，血漿比例隨之降低的狀況。

anhydrase *n*. an enzyme that catalyses the removal of water from a compound.

脫水酶 催化從化合物中去除水分的一種酶。

anima *n*. (in Jungian psychology) an *archetype that is the feminine component of a male's personality.

女性意象（榮格心理學）中的一種原始型，即男子性格中的女性成分。

animus *n*. the *archetype that is the masculine component of a female's personality.

男性意象 女子性格中男性成分的原始型。

anion *n*. an ion of negative charge, such as a bicarbonate ion (HCO_3^-) or a chloride ion (Cl^-) (*see also* electrolyte). The *anion gap* is the difference between the concentrations of cations (positively

陰離子 帶負電荷的離子，如碳酸氫鹽離子（HCO_3^-）或氯化物離子（Cl^-）（參閱electrolyte）。陰離子間隙指陽離子（帶正電荷的離子）與陰

charged ions) and anions, calculated from the formula:

$$(Na^+ + K^+) - (HCO_3^- + Cl^-)$$

It is used to estimate the unaccounted for anions in the blood in cases of metabolic disturbance. The normal anion gap is 10–16 mmol/l.

aniridia *n.* congenital absence of the iris (of the eye). It may be caused by a *deletion on the short arm of chromosome no. 11 and it may be associated with a predisposition to develop nephroblastoma.

aniseikonia *n.* a condition in which the image of an object differs markedly in size or shape in each eye.

anisocytosis *n.* an excessive variation in size between individual red blood cells. Anisocytosis may be noted on microscopical examination of a blood film; from this a graph of the numbers of cells of different sizes may be drawn. Anisocytosis may be a feature of almost any disease affecting the blood.

anisomelia *n.* a difference in size or shape between the arms or the legs.

anisometropia *n.* the condition in which the power of *refraction in one eye differs from that in the other.

anistreplase *n.* a *fibrinolytic drug consisting of a complex of *streptokinase and *plasminogen. It is administered by injection in the treatment of coronary thrombosis. Possible side-effects include local bleeding, slowing of the heart, flushing, low blood pressure, fever, nausea, vomiting, and allergic reactions. Trade name: **Eminase**.

離子的濃度差，根據下述公式進行計算：

$$(Na^+ + K^+) - (HCO_3^- + Cl^-)$$

用於代謝紊亂時估算血液中來源不明的陰離子，其正常值為10~16 mmol/l。

無虹膜　先天性虹膜（眼球）缺失，可因第 11 對染色體短臂上的缺失所致，並可能與產生腎胚細胞瘤的因素有關。

物像不等　物體影像在兩眼中的大小或形狀明顯不同的狀態。

紅細胞（大小）不均　各個紅細胞大小相差極大。可在血膜的顯微鏡檢查中見到此現象，並由此可將不同大小的紅細胞數目繪製成圖。紅細胞不均可為任何影響血液的疾病的特點。

對稱肢體大小不等　兩上肢或兩下肢的大小或形狀不同。

屈光參差　一側眼球的屈光能力與另一側不同的狀態。

鏈道酶　一種由鏈激酶與纖維蛋白溶酶原的絡合酶組成的溶解纖維蛋白藥。注射給藥。治療冠狀動脈血栓形成，可致副作用有局部出血、心率減慢、顏面潮紅、低血壓、發熱、惡心、嘔吐及變態反應。商品名：Eminase。

ankle *n.* **1.** the hinge joint between the leg and the foot. It consists of the *talus (ankle bone), which projects into a socket formed by the lower ends of the *tibia and *fibula. **2.** the whole region of the ankle joint, including the *tarsus and the ends of the tibia and fibula.

踝（關節）（1）腿與足之間由距骨構成的屈戍關節，距骨伸入脛骨和腓骨下端所形成的窩。（2）包括跗骨和脛骨與腓骨下端的整個踝關節。

ankylosing spondylitis *see* spondylitis.

關節強硬性脊椎炎 參閱 spondylitis.。

ankylosis *n.* fusion of the bones across a joint space, either by bony tissue (*bony ankylosis*) or by shortening of connecting fibrous tissue (*fibrous ankylosis*). Ankylosis is a complication of prolonged joint inflammation, as may occur in chronic infection (e.g. tuberculosis) or rheumatic disease (e.g. ankylosing *spondylitis).

關節強硬 關節腔的骨融合，由骨組織融合（骨性關節強硬）或結締纖維組織短縮（纖維性關節強硬）所致。關節強硬是慢性炎症的併發症，如在慢性感染（例如結核病）和風濕病（例如關節強硬性脊椎炎）中所發生的。

Ankylostoma *n. see* Ancylostoma.

鉤（口綫）蟲屬 參閱 Ancylostoma。

annulus *n.* (in anatomy) a circular opening or ring-shaped structure. **–annular** *adj.*

環 （解剖學）環狀孔或環狀結構。

anodontia *n.* absence of the teeth because they have failed to develop. It is more common for only a few teeth to fail to develop (*see* hypodontia).

無牙 因未發育而致的牙齒缺失。通常僅數個牙齒未能發育（參閱 hypodontia）。

anodyne *n.* any treatment or drug that soothes and eases pain.

止痛（劑） 任何緩解或減輕疼痛的治療或藥物。

anomaloscope *n.* an instrument for testing colour discrimination. By adjusting the controls, the subject has to produce a mixture of red and green light to match a yellow light. The matching is done on a brightly illuminated disc viewed down a telescope.

色盲檢查鏡 一種檢測辨色力的儀器。受試者從望遠鏡注視下面一個照亮的圓盤，通過調節控制器在圓盤上展現與黃色相配的紅綠混合色。

anomalous pulmonary venous drainage a congenital abnormality in

肺靜脈血流彷 肺靜脈進入右心房或腔靜脈而非流入左心房

which the pulmonary veins enter the right atrium or vena cava instead of draining into the left atrium. The features are those of an atrial *septal defect.

的一種先天性異常，為房間隔缺損之特點。

anomaly *n.* any deviation from the normal, especially a congenital or developmental defect.

異常　任何偏離正常的情況，尤指先天性或發育上的缺陷。

anomia *n.* **1.** a form of *aphasia in which the patient is unable to give the names of objects, although retaining an understanding of their use and the ability to put words together into speech. **2.** absence of respect for laws and established customs, which is a feature of *psychopathy and *dyssocial personality disorder.

(1) 稱名不能　一種失語症，患者雖仍然理解物品的用途並具組織語言能力，卻不能説出物品的名稱。**(2)** 先天性道德感缺損　無視法律和社會習俗，為一種精神變態及孤僻的人格障礙。

anonychia *n.* congenital absence of one or more nails.

無甲（畸形）　先天性一指或多指指甲缺失。

Anopheles *n.* a genus of widely distributed mosquitoes, occurring in tropical and temperate regions, with some 350 species. The malarial parasite (*see* Plasmodium) is transmitted to man solely through the bite of female *Anopheles* mosquitoes. Some species of *Anopheles* may transmit the parasites of bancroftian *filariasis.

按蚊屬　一個在熱帶與温帶分布廣泛的蚊屬，約有350種。雌性按蚊的叮咬是瘧原蟲傳播給人的唯一途徑（參閲 Plasmodium）。某些按蚊蚊屬可傳播班氏絲蟲病。

anorchism *n.* congenital absence of one or both testes.

無睪（畸形）　先天性單側或雙側無睪丸。

anorexia *n.* loss of appetite.

食慾缺乏　無食慾。

anorexia nervosa a psychological illness, most common in female adolescents, in which the patients starve themselves or use other techniques, such as vomiting or taking laxatives, to induce weight loss. They are motivated by a false perception of their bodies as fat and/or a *phobia of becoming fat. The result is

神經性厭食　多見於青春期女性的一種心理性疾病。患者忍受飢餓或用嘔吐，服輕瀉藥等方法以減輕體重，其動機為一種自感體胖的錯覺和／或肥胖恐怖症，造成體重嚴重下降，常伴有閉經，有時甚至因飢餓而死亡。此病病因複雜，常涉

severe loss of weight, often with *amen-orrhoea, and sometimes even death from starvation. The cause of the illness is complicated – problems within the family and rejection of adult sexuality are often factors involved. Patients must be persuaded to eat enough to maintain a normal body weight and their emotional disturbance is usually treated with *psychotherapy. *See also* bulimia.

及家庭問題，拒絕性行為等因素。必須說服患者進食足夠食物來維持身體正常體重，其情感障礙通常用心理療法進行治療。參閱 bulimia。

anosmia *n.* a loss of the sense of smell. This is most often due to a head cold but it may be caused by a fracture through the anterior fossa of the skull or a frontal brain tumour.

嗅覺缺失 嗅覺喪失。常因鼻傷風引起，亦可因顱骨前窩骨折或大腦額部腫瘤而致。

anovular (anovulatory) *adj.* not associated with the development and release of a female germ cell (ovum) in the ovary, as in *anovular menstruation*.

不排卵的 卵巢中無女性生殖細胞（卵子）發育和排出。如不排卵性月經。

anoxaemia *n.* a condition in which there is less than the normal concentration of oxygen in the blood. *See also* anoxia, hypoxaemia.

缺氧血（症） 血液中氧氣濃度低於正常的狀態。參閱 anoxia，hypoxaemia。

anoxia *n.* a condition in which the tissues of the body receive inadequate amounts of oxygen. This may result from low atmospheric pressure at high altitudes; a shortage of circulating blood, red blood cells, or haemoglobin; or disordered blood flow, such as occurs in heart failure. It can also result from insufficient oxygen reaching the blood in the lungs due to poor breathing movements or because disease, such as pneumonia, is reducing the effective surface area of lung tissue. *See also* hypoxia. –**anoxic** *adj.*

缺氧（症） 身體組織中氧供應不足的狀況，原因可為高原低氣壓；循環血量不足，紅細胞或血紅蛋白減少；或發生於心力衰竭等情況中的循環障礙。呼吸運動減弱或肺組織有效表面積因肺炎等疾病減少時，亦可導致肺部血液含氧不足產生的缺氧。參閱 hypoxia。

ansa *n.* (in anatomy) a loop; for example, the *ansa hypoglossi* is the loop formed by the descending branch of the hypoglossal nerve.

袢 （解剖學）環。例如，舌下神經袢為舌下神經降支所形成的環。

ansiform *adj.* (in anatomy) shaped like a loop. The term is applied to certain lobules of the cerebellum.

祥狀的 （解剖學）形狀如環的，用於小腦的某些小葉。

ant- (anti-) *prefix denoting* opposed to; counteracting; relieving. Examples: *antarthritic* (relieving arthritis); *antibacterial* (destroying or stopping the growth of bacteria.)

〔前綴〕**對抗、抑制、緩解** 例如，抗關節炎的（緩解關節炎）；抗細菌的（殺死或抑制細菌生長）。

Antabuse *n. see* disulfiram.

戒酒硫 參閱 disulfiram。

antacid *n.* a drug that neutralizes the hydrochloric acid secreted in the digestive juices of the stomach. Antacids, which include aluminium hydroxide, calcium carbonate, magnesium hydroxide, and sodium bicarbonate, are used to relieve pain and discomfort in disorders or the digestive system, including peptic ulcer.

解酸劑 中和胃消化液中鹽酸的藥物，其中包括氫氧化鋁、碳酸鈣、氫氧化鎂和碳酸氫鈉，用於緩解消化系統疾病如消化性潰瘍的疼痛與不適。

antagonist *n.* **1.** a muscle whose action (contraction) opposes that of another muscle (called the *agonist* or *prime mover*). Antagonists relax to allow the agonists to effect movement. **2.** a drug or other substance with opposite action to that of another drug or natural body chemical, which it inhibits. Examples are the *antimetabolites. **–antagonism** *n.*

(1) 拮抗肌 其作用（收縮）與另一肌肉（稱為主縮肌或原動肌）相反的肌羣。拮抗肌鬆弛可使主縮肌運動。**(2) 拮抗劑** 與另一藥物作用相反的藥物，或與體內天然的化學物質起相反作用（抑制）的其他物質，例如抗代謝（產）物。

antazoline *n.* a short-acting *antihistamine drug, given by mouth to relieve the symptoms of allergic reactions. It is less irritating than the other antihistamines, but it produces their characteristic side-effects, such as drowsiness, dizziness, and incoordination. Trade name: **Otrivine-Antistin**.

安他唑啉 一種短效抗組胺藥。口服，可減輕變態反應症狀，其刺激性小於其他抗組胺藥，但亦產生典型副作用，如嗜睡、頭昏與共濟失調。商品名：Otrivine-Antistin。

ante- *prefix denoting* before. Examples: *antenatal* (before birth); *anteprandial* (before meals).

〔前綴〕**（在）前** 如出生前的，餐前的。

anteflexion *n.* the bending forward of an organ. A mild degree of anteflexion of the uterus is considered to be normal.

前屈 某一器官的前屈,子宮的輕微前屈視為正常。

ante mortem before death. *Compare* post mortem.

死前 死亡之前。與 post mortem 對比。

antenatal diagnosis *see* prenatal diagnosis.

產前診斷 參閱 prenatal diagnosis。

antepartum *adj.* occurring before the onset of labour.

分娩前的 發生於分娩發作前的。

antepartum haemorrhage bleeding from the genital tract after the 24th week of pregnancy until the birth of the bady.

產前出血 24 孕周至嬰兒出生前的生殖道出血。

anterior *adj.* **1.** describing or relating to the front (ventral) portion of the body or limbs. **2.** describing the front part of any organ.

前的 **(1)** 描述或指身體或四肢的前部。**(2)** 描述任何器官的前部分。

anteversion *n.* the forward inclination of an organ, especially the normal forward inclination of the uterus.

前傾 某一器官向前傾斜,尤指子宮的正常前傾。

anthelmintic 1. *n.* any drug or chemical agent used to destroy parasitic worms (helminths), e.g. tapeworms, round-worms, and flukes, and/or remove them from the body. Anthelmintics include *albendazole, *bephenium hydroxy-naphthoate, *mebendazole, *niclosa-mide, *piperazine, and *praziquantel. **2.** *adj.* having the power to destroy or elimi-nate helminths.

(1)(治)**蠕蟲劑,驅腸蟲劑** 任何殺滅和/或驅除人體寄生性蠕蟲(如絛蟲、蛔蟲與吸蟲)的藥物或化學製劑,包括阿苯達唑、苄酚寧羥萘酸鹽、甲苯達唑、氯硝柳胺、哌嗪、吡喹酮。**(2) 抗蠕蟲的,驅腸蟲的** 具殺滅或除蠕蟲能力的。

anthracosis *n.* *see* coal-worker's pneumoconiosis.

炭末沉着病,炭肺 參閱 coal-worker's pneumoconiosis。

anthracycline *n.* any of 500 or so anti-biotics synthesized or isolated from species of *Streptomyces*. *Doxorubicin is the most important member of this

蒽環類抗生素 由鏈黴菌屬合成或分離出的約 500 種抗生素,其中最重要的一種是阿黴素,具有廣泛的抗腫瘤作用。

group of compounds, which have wide activity against tumours.

anthrax *n.* an acute infectious disease of farm animals caused by the bactcrium *Bacillus anthracis*, which can be transmitted to man by contact with animal hair, hides, or excrement. In man the disease attacks either the lungs, causing pneumonia, or the skin, producing severe ulceration (known as *malignant pustule*). *Woolsorter's disease* is a serious infection of the skin or lungs by *B. anthracis*, affecting those handling wool or pelts (*see* occupational disease). Untreated anthrax can be fatal but administration of large doses of penicillin or tetracycline is usually effective.

炭疽　由炭疽杆菌引起的家畜急性傳染病，可經動物的毛、皮或排泄物傳給人類。此病可侵犯肺部引起肺炎，或侵犯皮膚發生嚴重潰瘍（稱為皮膚炭疽）。揀毛工病是由炭疽杆菌所致的一種嚴重皮膚感染，患者為羊毛或生皮處理工（參閱occupational disease）。炭疽若不治療可致死，但使用大劑量青黴素或四環素通常有效。

anthrop- (anthropo-) *prefix denoting* the human race. Examples: *anthropogenesis* or *anthropogeny* (origin and development of); *anthropoid* (resembling); *anthropology* (science of).

〔前綴〕**人類**　例如，人類發生或人類起源、類人的、人類學。

anthropometry *n.* the taking of measurements of the human body or its parts. Comparisons can then be made between individuals of different sexes, ages, and races to determine the difference between normal and abnormal development. **–anthropometric** *adj.*

人體測量（術）　對人體或人體某一部分的測量，從而可對不同性別、年齡與種族的個體進行比較，以確定正常與異常發育的差值。

anthropozoonosis *n.* a disease that is transmissible from an animal to man, or vice versa, under natural conditions. Diseases that are found primarily in animals and sometimes affect man include *leptospirosis, *anthrax, and *rabies.

人獸病　在自然條件下可從動物傳染到人或從人傳給動物的疾病。主要見於動物但有時感染給人的疾病包括鈎端螺旋體病，炭疽和狂犬病。

anti-androgen *n.* any one of a group of drugs that block the cellular uptake of testosterone by the prostate gland and are therefore used in the treatment of prostate cancer, which is an

抗雄激素　任何阻滯睾酮被前列腺細胞吸收的藥物，用於治療雄激素依賴型腫瘤的前列腺癌以及各種男性性障礙。此類藥包括環丙孕酮。

androgen-dependent tumour, and various sexual disorders in men. Anti-androgens include *cyproterone.

anti-arrhythmic *n.* any of a group of drugs used to correct irregularities in the heart-beat (*see* arrhythmia). They include *atropine, *amiodarone, *verapamil, *quinidine, *disopyramide, and *lignocaine.

antibacterial *adj.* describing an antibiotic that is active against bacteria.

antibiotic *n.* a substance, produced by or derived from a microorganism, that destroys or inhibits the growth of other microorganisms. Antibiotics are used to treat infections caused by organisms that are sensitive to them, usually bacteria or fungi. They may alter the normal microbial content of the body (e.g. in the intestine, lungs, bladder) by destroying one or more groups of harmless organisms, which may result in infections due to overgrowth of resistant organisms. These side-effects are most likely to occur with *broad-spectrum antibiotics* (those active against a wide variety of organisms). Resistance may also develop in the microorganisms being treated (for example, through incorrect dosage), and some antibiotics may cause allergic reactions. *See also* aminoglycosides, antifungal, antiviral drug, cephalosporin, chloramphenicol, penicillin, quinolone, streptomycin, tetracycline.

antibody *n.* a special kind of blood protein that is synthesized in lymphoid tissue in response to the presence of a particular *antigen and circulates in the plasma to attack the antigen and render it harmless. The production of specific antibodies against antigens as diverse as

抗心律失常藥 任何一種用於治療心律不齊的藥物（參閱 arrhythmia），包括阿托品、胺碘酮、維拉帕米、奎尼丁、丙吡胺，及利多卡因。

抗細菌的 描述對細菌有作用的抗生素。

抗生素 由微生物產生或衍生的破壞或抑制其他微生物生長的物質，用於治療對其敏感的微生物（常為細菌或真菌）導致的感染。抗生素可殺死體內一羣或多羣無害微生物而改變正常的菌羣數量（如在腸、肺、膀胱內），引起有耐藥性微生物過度繁殖而致的感染。這些副作用多產生於使用廣譜抗生素時（對多種細菌有效）。抗生素也可使細菌產生耐藥性（如因劑量不當）。一些抗生素並可引起變態反應。參閱 aminoglycosides、antifungal、antiviral drug、cephalosporin、chloramphenicol、penicillin、quinolone、streptomycin、tetracycline。

抗體 因某種抗原出現而在淋巴組織中合成並循環於血漿中的一種特殊血液蛋白，攻擊該抗原使之無害。針對不同抗原，如入侵細菌、吸入花粉和異體紅細胞等所產生的特異性抗體，成為免疫反應和變態反

invading bacteria, inhaled pollen grains, and foreign red blood cells is the basis of both *immunity and *allergy. Antibody formation is also responsible for tissue or organ rejection following transplantation. Chemically, antibodies are proteins of the globulin type; they are classified according to their structure and function (see immunoglobulin).

anticholinergic adj. inhibiting the action of *acetylcholine. *Parasympatholytic drugs are anticholinergic.

anticholinesterase n. any substance that inhibits the action of *cholinesterase, the enzyme that is responsible for the breakdown of the neurotransmitter acetylcholine, and therefore allows acetylcholine to continue transmitting nerve impulses. Drugs with anticholinesterase activity include *distigmine, *neostigmine, *pyridostigmine, and *physostigmine; their uses include the diagnosis and treatment of *myasthenia gravis. See also parasympathomimetic.

anticoagulant n. an agent that prevents the clotting of blood. The natural anticoagulant *heparin directly interferes with blood clotting and is active both within the body and against a sample of blood in a test tube. Synthetic drugs, such as *phenindione and *warfarin, are effective only within the body, since they act by affecting blood *coagulation factors. They take longer to act than heparin. Anticoagulants are used to prevent the formation of blood clots or to break up clots in blood vessels in such conditions as thrombosis and embolism. Incorrect dosage may result in haemorrhage. See also fibrinolytic.

anticonvulsant n. a drug that prevents or reduces the severity and frequency of

應的共同基礎。抗體形成還是組織或器官移植後出現排斥反應的原因。抗體的化學結構為球蛋白型，可按其結構與功能分類（參閱 immunoglobulin）。

抗膽鹼能的 抑制乙醯膽鹼作用的。抗副交感神經藥即屬此類。

抗膽鹼酯酶 任何抑制膽鹼酯酶作用的物質。此酶破壞神經介質乙醯膽鹼，抑制其作用即可使乙醯膽鹼繼續傳遞神經衝動。具抗膽鹼酯酶活性的藥物有地斯的明，新斯的明，吡斯的明及毒扁豆鹼等，用於診斷與治療重症肌無力。參閱 parasympathomimetic。

抗凝（血）劑 防止血液凝固的藥劑。天然抗凝劑肝素直接阻礙血凝固，在體內和對試管內血液標本均有效。合成藥物如苯茚二酮和華法林，因通過影響凝血因子而產生作用，故僅在體內有效，發生作用遲於肝素。抗凝劑用於在血栓形成和栓塞等疾病中防止血管中血塊形成或使其破裂，若劑量使用不當可致出血。參閱 fibrinolytic。

抗驚厥藥 在各型癲癇中預防其發作或減輕發作程度及減少

seizures in various types of epilepsy; the term *antiepileptic drug* is now preferred since not all seizures involve convulsions. The choice of drug is dictated by the type of seizure and the patient's response, and the dosage must be adjusted carefully as individuals vary in their response to these drugs and side-effects may be troublesome. Antiepileptic drugs include *carbamazepine, *lamotrigine, *phenytoin, and *sodium valproate.

發作次數的藥物。並非所有的癲癇發作均出現驚厥，故現多使用抗（癲）癇劑一詞。抗驚厥藥的選擇取決於癲癇發作的類型和病人的反應。對藥物的反應存在個體差異，因此須謹慎調整劑量。副作用可令人煩惱。此類藥包括卡馬西平、拉莫三嗪、苯妥英和丙戊酸鈉。

antidepressant *n.* a drug that alleviates the symptoms of depression. The most widely prescribed antidepressants are a group of drugs with a basic chemical structure of three benzene rings, called *tricyclic antidepressants*, which include *amitriptyline and *imipramine. These drugs are useful in treating a variety of different depressive symptoms. Side-effects commonly include dry mouth, blurred vision, constipation, drowsiness, and difficulty in urination. Other antidepressants include the *MAO inhibitors which have more severe side-effects, and the serotonin (5-HT) reuptake inhibitors (e.g. *fluoxetine. *fluvoxamine).

抗抑鬱藥　緩解抑鬱症狀的藥物。最常用的是一組包括阿米替林和米帕明的基本化學結構式有三個苯環的藥物，稱為三環類抗抑鬱藥，對治療多種不同的抑鬱症狀有效。常見副作用有口乾、視力模糊、便秘、嗜睡及排尿困難。其他抗抑鬱藥有副作用較重的單胺氧化酶抑制劑，以及5-羥色胺再吸收抑制劑（如氟西汀、氟伏沙明）。

antidiuretic hormone (ADH) *see* vasopressin.

抗利尿激素　參閱 vasopressin。

antidote *n.* a drug that counteracts the effects of a poison or of overdosage by another drug. For example, *dimercaprol is an antidote to arsenic, mercury, and other heavy metals.

解毒劑　對抗毒物作用或某種藥物過量產生的作用的藥物。例如，二巰丙醇為砷、汞和其他重金屬的解毒劑。

antidromic *adj.* describing impulses travelling 'the wrong way' in a nerve fibre. This is rare but may happen in shingles, when the irritation caused by the virus in the spinal canal initiates impulses that travel outwards in normally afferent nerves. The area of skin that the sensory

逆向的　描述神經纖維衝動沿錯誤方向傳遞。為一種罕見情況，但可發生於患帶狀疱疹時。病毒所致的椎管刺激使衝動經正常情況下的傳入神經向外傳遞，而使感覺神經分布的皮區（通常為軀幹上一帶狀）

nerves supply (usually a strip on the truck) becomes painfully blistered. Antidromic impulses cannot pass *synapses, which work in one direction only.

出現疼痛水疱。逆行衝動不能通過僅單向傳遞的突觸。

antiemetic *n.* a drug that prevents vomiting. Various drugs have this effect, including some *antihistamines (e.g. cyclizine, promethazine) and *anticholinergic drugs. They are used for such conditions as motion sickness and vertigo; drugs used to counteract nausea and vomiting caused by other drugs include *domperidone, *metoclopramide, and *ondansetron.

止吐劑　預防嘔吐的藥物。多種藥物具此功效,包括某些抗組胺劑(如賽克利嗪和異丙嗪)和抗膽鹼能藥,用於暈動病和眩暈等病症。多潘立酮、甲氧氯普胺及奧丹亞龍等用於消除其他藥物引起的惡心嘔吐。

antiepileptic drug *see* anticonvulsant.

抗(癲)癇劑　參閱 anticonvulsant。

antifibrinolytic *adj.* describing an agent that inhibits the dissolution of blood clots (*see* fibrinolysis). Antifibrinolytic drugs include *aprotinin and *tranexamic acid.

抗纖維蛋白溶解的　描述抑制血凝塊溶解的藥劑(參閱 fibrinolysis),此類藥物包括柳酞酶和氨甲環酸。

antifungal (antimycotic) *adj.* describing a drug that kills or inactivates fungi and is used to treat fungal (including yeast) infections. Antifungal drugs include *amphotericin, *griseofulvin, the *imidazoles, *nystatin, *terbinafine, and *tolnaftate.

抗真菌的(抗黴菌的)　描述殺死或滅活真菌和用於治療真菌(包括酵母菌)感染的藥物。抗真菌藥有兩性黴素、灰黃黴素、咪唑類、制黴菌素、特必萘、及托萘酯。

antigen *n.* any substance that the body regards as foreign or potentially dangerous and against which it produces an *antibody. Antigens are usually proteins, but simple substances, even metals, may become antigenic by combining with and modifying the body's own proteins. These are called *haptens*. **–antigenic** *adj.*

抗原　任何被人體視為異物或有潛在危險並對此產生抗體的物質。抗原通常為蛋白質,但甚至金屬等單純物質,通過與體內蛋白結合並加以改變也可產生抗原性,稱為半抗原。

antihelix (anthelix) *n.* the curved inner ridge of the *pinna of the ear.

對耳輪　耳廓的曲綫形內嵴。

antihistamine n. a drug that inhibits the action of *histamine in the body by blocking the receptors for histamine, of which there are two types: H_1 and H_2. When stimulated by histamine, H_1 receptors may produce such allergic reactions as hay fever, pruritus (itching), and urticaria (nettle rash). Antihistamines that block H_1 receptors (H_1-receptor antagonists), for example *acrivastine, *astemizole, *azatadine, and *chlorpheniramine, are used to relieve these conditions. Many H_1-receptor antagonists, e.g. *cyclizine and *promethazine, also have strong *antiemetic activity and are used to prevent motion sickness. The most common side-effect of these drugs is drowsiness and because of this they are sometimes used to promote sleep. Other side-effects include dizziness, blurred vision, tremors, digestive upsets, and lack of muscular coordination.

H_2 receptors are found mainly in the stomach, where stimulation by histamine causes secretion of acid gastric juice. H_2 antagonists (e.g. *cimetidine, *ranitidine) block these receptors and so reduce gastric acid secretion; they are used in the treatment of *peptic ulcers.

anti-inflammatory 1. adj. describing a drug that reduces *inflammation. The various groups of anti-inflammatory drugs act against one or more of the mediators that initiate or maintain inflammation. Some groups suppress only certain aspects of the inflammatory response. The main groups of anti-inflammatory drugs are the *antihistamines, the glucocorticoids (see corticosteroid), and the nonsteroidal anti-inflammatory drugs (see NSAID). **2.** n. an anti-inflammatory drug.

antiketogenic n. an agent that prevents formation of *ketones in the body.

抗組胺劑 通過阻滯 H_1 和 H_2 兩類組胺受體而抑制體內組胺作用的藥物。H_1 受體在受到組胺刺激時，可產生變態反應如枯草熱、瘙癢與蕁麻疹。阻斷 H_1 受體的抗組胺劑（H_1 受體拮抗劑），如阿伐斯汀，阿司咪唑、阿扎他定和氯苯那敏，可用於減輕這些病症。許多 H_1 受體拮抗劑，如賽克利嗪與異丙嗪，亦有很強的止吐作用而用於預防暈動病。這類藥最常見副作用是嗜睡，因而有時被用來催眠。其他副作用有頭昏、視力模糊、震顫、腸胃不適及肌共濟失調。

H_2 受體主要在胃內，組胺刺激可引起酸性胃液分泌，H_2 受體拮抗劑（如西咪替丁和雷尼替丁）可阻斷 H_2 受體而減少胃酸分泌。用於治療消化性潰瘍。

(1) 抗炎的 描述減輕炎症的藥物。各種抗炎藥對引起或持續炎症的一種或多種介質起作用。有些抗炎藥僅遏制炎性反應的某些方面。主要的抗炎藥有抗組胺劑、糖皮質激素（參閱 corticosteroid）與非甾類抗炎藥（參閱 NSAID）。**(2)** 抗炎藥。

抗生酮藥 防止體內酮體生成的藥物。

antilymphocyte serum (antilymphocyte globulin, ALS, ALG) an *antiserum, containing antibodies that suppress lymphocytic activity, prepared by injecting an animal with lymphocytes. ALS may be given to a patient to prevent the immune reaction that causes tissue rejection following transplantation of such organs as kidneys. Administration naturaly also impairs other immunity mechanisms, making infection a serious hazard.

抗淋巴細胞血清　一種含有抑制淋巴細胞活性的抗血清，通過將淋巴細胞注射到動物體內製備。此種血清可用於器官移植患者，如腎移植，以防止產生導致組織排斥的免疫反應，但其應用亦將損害其他免疫機制，造成嚴重的感染危害。

antimetabolite *n.* a drug that interferes with the normal metabolic processes within cells by combining with the enzymes responsible for them. Some drugs used in the treatment of cancer, e.g. *fluorouracil, *methotrexate, and *mercaptopurine, are antimetabolites that prevent cell growth by interfering with enzyme reactions essential for nucleic acid synthesis. Side-effects of antimetabolites can be severe, involving blood cell disorders and digestive disturbances. *See also* cytotoxic drug.

抗代謝（產）物　通過與催化細胞內代謝過程的酶結合而干擾其正常代謝過程的藥物。一些用於治療腫瘤的藥物，如氟尿嘧啶，甲氨蝶呤和巰嘌呤，是通過干擾核酸合成所必需的酶反應來抑制細胞生長的抗代謝物。此類藥可有嚴重副作用，如血細胞疾病和胃腸功能紊亂。參閱 cytotoxic drug。

antimitotic *n.* a drug that inhibits cell division and growth, e.g. *doxorubicin, *aclarubicin. The drugs used to treat cancer are mainly antimitotics. *See also* antimetabolite, cytotoxic drug.

抗有絲分裂藥　抑制細胞分裂與生長的藥物，如阿黴素和阿柔比星。抗癌藥多為抗有絲分裂藥。參閱 antimetabolite，cytotoxic drug。

antimutagen *n.* a substance that can either reduce the spontaneous production of mutations or prevent or reverse the action of a *mutagen.

抗誘變劑　可減少突變自發產生或防止或逆轉誘變劑作用的物質。

antimycotic *adj. see* antifungal.

抗真菌藥，抗黴菌藥　參閱 antifungal。

anti-oestrogen *n.* one of a group of drugs that oppose the action of *oestrogen. The most important of these drugs is currently *tamoxifen, which

抗雌激素藥　一組對抗雌激素作用的藥物。目前最重要的一種是他莫昔芬，可在組織受體產生抗雌激素的作用，用於治

antagonizes the action of oestrogens at the tissue receptors and is used in the treatment of breast cancers dependent on oestrogen. Because they stimulate the production of pituitary *gonadotrophins, some anti-oestrogens (e.g. *clomiphene) are used to induce or stimulate ovulation in infertility treatment. Side-effects of anti-oestrogens include hot flushes, itching of the vulva, nausea, vomiting, fluid retention, and sometimes vaginal bleeding.

療雌激素依賴型乳腺癌。此類藥可刺激產生垂體促性腺激素，因此某些抗雌激素藥（如氯米芬）用於不孕症治療中誘導或刺激排卵。副作用有熱潮紅、外陰瘙癢、惡心、嘔吐、液體瀦留及有時陰道出血。

antioxidant *n.* a substance capable of neutralizing oxygen free radicals, the highly active and damaging atoms and chemical groups produced by various disease processes and by poisons, radiation, smoking, and other agencies. The body contains its own natural antioxidants but there is growing medical interest in the possibility of controlling cell and tissue damage by means of supplementary antioxidants. Those most commonly used are *vitamin C (ascorbic acid), *vitamin E (tocopherols), and beta *carotene. Evidence is accumulating that these substances can reduce the incidence of a number of serious diseases.

抗氧化劑　可中和氧自由基的物質。氧自由基是多種疾病、毒物、放射、吸煙和其他媒介產生的具很強活性與破壞力的原子和化學團。體內有天然抗氧化劑，但醫學界對通過補充抗氧化劑以控制細胞和組織損害的可能性興趣漸濃。最常用的抗氧化劑為維生素 C（抗壞血酸）、維生素 E（生育酚）和 β-胡蘿蔔素。許多事實表明，此類物質可降低若干嚴重疾病的發生率。

antiperistalsis *n.* a wave of contraction in the alimentary canal that passes in an oral (i.e. upward or backwards) direction (*compare* peristalsis). It was formerly thought to occur in vomiting but modern studies indicate that it never takes place in man.

逆蠕動　消化道向口腔（即向上或往回）方向（與 peristalsis 對比）行進的收縮波。過去認為發生於嘔吐時，但現代研究表明逆蠕動從未發生於人類。

antipruritic *n.* an agent that relieves itching (*pruritus). Examples are *calamine and *crotamiton, applied in creams or lotions, and some *antihistamine drugs (e.g. *trimeprazine), used if the itching is due to an allergy.

止癢劑　減輕瘙癢的藥物。如以乳膏或洗劑使用的爐甘石和克羅米能。一些抗組胺藥（如阿利馬嗪）用於變態反應所致的瘙癢。

antipsychotic *adj.* describing a group of drugs that are used to treat severe mental disorders (psychoses), including schizophrenia and mania; some are administered in small doses to relieve anxiety. Formerly known as *major tranquillizers*, antipsychotic drugs include the *phenothiazines (e.g. *chlorpromazine), *butyrophenones (e.g. *haloperidol), *thioxanthenes* (e.g. *flupenthixol), and *clozapine. Side-effects of many antipsychotics at high doses include abnormal involunatary movements.

抗精神病的　描述一組用於治療精神分裂症和躁狂等嚴重精神障礙的藥物。某些抗精神病藥以小劑量可緩解焦慮症狀。抗精神病藥過去稱為強安定藥，包括吩噻嗪（如氯丙嗪）、丁醯苯（如氟哌啶醇）、噻噸（如三氟噻噸）和氯氮平。許多大劑量精神抑制藥的副作用有異常不隨意運動。

antipyretic *n.* a drug that reduces fever by lowering the body temperature. Several analgesic drugs have antipyretic activity, including *aspirin, *paracetamol, *phenylbutazone, and *mefenamic acid.

退熱劑　一種降低體溫而減輕發熱的藥物，阿司匹林、對乙醯氨基酚、保泰松、甲芬那酸等幾種止痛劑均有解熱作用。

antisecretory drug any drug that reduces the normal rate of secretion of a body fluid, usually one that reduces acid secretion into the stomach. Such drugs include anticholinergic drugs (*see* parasympatholytic), H₂ antagonists (*see* antihistamine), and *proton-pump inhibitors.

抑制分泌藥　任何減少體液正常分泌的藥物。常指減少胃酸分泌的藥物。此類藥包括抗膽鹼能藥（參閱 parasympatholytic），H$_2$ 拮抗藥（參閱 antihistamine）與質子泵抑制劑。

antisepsis *n.* the elimination of bacteria, fungi, viruses, and other microorganisms that cause disease by the use of chemical or physical methods.

抗菌（法）　使用化學或物理方法消滅細菌、真菌、病毒和其他致病微生物。

antiseptic *n.* a chemical that destroys or inhibits the growth of disease-causing bacteria and other microorganisms and is sufficiently nontoxic to be applied to the skin or mucous membranes to cleanse wounds and prevent infections or to be used internally to treat infections of the intestine and bladder. Examples are *cetrimide, *chlorhexidine, *dequalinium, and *hexamine.

防腐劑，抗菌劑　殺死或抑制致病細菌或其他微生物生長的化學藥品，毒性甚微，可用於皮膚或黏膜清潔傷口及預防感染，或內服治療腸道和膀胱感染。例如西曲溴銨、氯己定、克菌定和烏洛托品。

antiserum *n.* (*pl.* **antisera**) a serum that contains antibodies against antigens of a particular kind; it may be injected to treat, or give temporary protection (passive *immunity) against, specific diseases. Antisera are prepared in large quantities in such animals as horses. In the laboratory, they are used to identify unknown organisms responsible for infection (*see* agglutination).

抗血清　含有針對特定抗原之抗體的血清。可經注射治療或短期預防（被動免疫）某種疾病。抗血清用馬等動物大量製取。在實驗室中用於鑒別引起感染的不明微生物（參閱 agglutination）。

antispasmodic *n.* a drug that relieves spasm of smooth muscle. *See* spasmolytic. *Compare* antispastic.

鎮痙劑　緩解平滑肌痙攣的藥物。參閱 spasmolytic。與 antispastic 對比。

antispastic *n.* a drug that relieves spasm of skeletal muscle. *See also* muscle relaxant. *Compare* antispasmodic.

鎮痙劑　緩解骨骼肌痙攣的藥物。參閱 muscle relaxant。與 antispasmodic 對比。

antitoxin *n.* an antibody produced by the body to counteract a toxin formed by invading bacteria or from any other source.

抗毒素　人體所產生的對抗入侵細菌或其他來源之毒素的抗體。

antitragus *n.* a small projection of cartilage above the lobe of the ear, opposite the tragus. *See* pinna.

對耳屏　耳垂上方與耳屏相對的軟骨小突起。參閱 pinna。

antitussive *n.* a drug, such as *dextromethorphan or *pholcodine, that suppresses coughing, possibly by reducing the activity of the cough centre in the brain and by depressing respiration. Some analgesic drugs also have antitussive activity, e.g. *codeine, diamorphine (*see* heroin), and *methadone.

鎮咳劑　通過減少大腦咳嗽中樞活動及抑制呼吸而止咳的藥物，如布美沙芬或福爾可定。一些止痛劑亦有鎮咳作用，如可待因、二醋嗎啡（參閱 heroin）和美沙酮。

antivenene (antivenin) *n.* an *antiserum containing antibodies against specific poisons in the venom of such an animal as a snake, spider, or scorpion.

抗蛇毒素　含有對抗蛇、蜘蛛或蝎等毒液中特種毒素之抗體的抗血清。

antiviral drug a drug effective against viruses that cause disease. Antiviral drugs include *acyclovir, *ganciclovir,

抗病毒藥　對致病病毒有效的藥物，包括阿昔洛韋、更昔洛韋、阿糖腺苷、碘苷、曲氟

*vidarabine, *idoxuridine, *trifluridine* (*Viroptic*), *foscarnet, *zidovudine, *amantadine, and *ribavirin.

antrectomy *n*. **1.** surgical removal of the bony walls of an *antrum. *See* antrostomy. **2.** a surgical operation in which a part of the stomach (the antrum) is removed. Most secretions of acid, pepsin, and the hormone gastrin occur in the antrum and the operation is used (usually combined with *vagotomy) in the treatment of peptic ulcers that have recurred after vagotomy and are resistant to H_2-blocking drugs (*see* antihistamine).

antroscopy *n*. inspection of the inside of the maxillary sinus (*see* paranasal sinuses) using an *endoscope (called an *antroscope*).

antrostomy *n*. a surgical operation to produce a permanent or semipermanent artificial opening to an *antrum in a bone, so providing drainage for any fluid. The operation is sometimes carried out to treat infection of the *paranasal sinuses.

antrum *n*. **1.** a cavity, especially a cavity in a bone. The *mastoid* (or *tympanic*) *antrum* is the space connecting the air cells of the *mastoid process with the chamber of the inner ear. **2.** the part of the *stomach adjoining the pylorus (*pyloric* or *gastric antrum*).

anuria *n*. failure of the kidneys to produce urine. This can occur in a variety of conditions that produce a sustained drop in blood pressure. Urgent assessment is required to differentiate lack of production of urine from an obstruction

尿苷（三氟胸苷）、膦甲酸、齊多夫定、金剛烷胺及利巴韋林。

竇切除術 **(1)** 切除骨質竇壁的手術。參閱 antrostomy。**(2)** 切除胃之一部分（竇部）的手術。大部分胃酸、胃蛋白酶和促胃液素在胃竇分泌，此手術用於（通常同時行迷走神經切斷術）治療迷走神經切斷術後復發並對 H_2 受體阻滯藥有耐藥性的消化性潰瘍（參閱 antihistamine）。

竇透照術，上頜竇鏡檢查 使用內窺鏡（稱為竇透照器）對上頜竇（參閱 paranasal sinuses）內部進行檢查。

竇造口術 在骨竇處作永久性或半永久性人工開口以行引流的外科手術。此手術有時用於治療鼻旁竇感染。

竇 **(1) 腔**。尤指骨腔。鼓竇為連接乳突氣腔與內耳的空間。**(2) 胃鄰近** 幽門的部分（幽門竇）。

無尿（症） 腎臟不能產生尿液。可發生於多種引起血壓持續下降的情況，對此須立即作出判斷，以與因腎臟尿液排出受阻導致的無尿相區別，後者可輕易消除。無尿症伴發於不

to the flow of urine from the kidneys, which can readily be relieved. Anuria is associated with increasing *uraemia and may require *haemodialysis.

斷加重的尿毒症，可能需作血液透析。

anus *n.* the opening at the lower end of the alimentary canal, through which the faeces are discharged. It opens out from the *anal canal and is guarded by two sphincters. The anus is closed except during defecation. **–anal** *adj.*

肛門　消化道下端的開口。糞便經此排出，開口於肛管，由兩括約肌保護。肛門除排便外一般關閉。

anvil *n.* (in anatomy) *see* incus.

砧骨　（解剖學）參閱 incus。

anxiety *n.* generalized pervasive *fear. *Anxiety state* is a condition in which anxiety dominates the patient's life; neuroses are now usually called *anxiety disorders* (*see* neurosis, panic disorder, post-traumatic stress disorder). *See also* generalized anxiety disorder.

焦慮　深層的綜合恐懼，焦慮狀態為患者生活處於焦慮控制下的狀態；神經官能症現通常稱作焦慮症（參閱 neurosis，panic disorder post-traumatic stress disorder）。參閱 generalized anxiety disorder。

aorta *n.* (*pl.* **aortae** or **aortas**) the main artery of the body, from which all others derive. It arises from the left ventricle (*ascending aorta*), arches over the top of the heart (*see* aortic arch) and descends in front of the backbone (*descending aorta*), giving off large and small branches and finally dividing to form the right and left *iliac arteries. The part of the descending aorta from the aortic arch to the diaphragm is called the *thoracic aorta*; the part below the diaphragm is the *abdominal aorta*. **–aortic** *adj.*

主動脈　身體的主要動脈，所有其他動脈均由此發出。主動脈從左心室上升（升主動脈），於心臟上部呈弓狀越過（參閱 aortic arch），在脊柱前下降（降主動脈），分出大小分支，最後形成髂右動脈和髂左動脈。降主動脈從主動脈弓至橫膈的部分稱為胸主動脈。膈下部分稱為腹主動脈。

aortic aneurysm *see* aneurysm.

主動脈（動脈）瘤　參閱 aneurysm。

aortic arch that part of the aorta that extends from the ascending aorta, upward over the heart and then backward and down as far as the fourth

主動脈弓　自升主動脈向上延伸經過心臟，向後向下降至第四胸椎的主動脈段。其外壁中的牽張感受器可監測血壓，係

thoracic vertebra. *Stretch receptors in its outer wall monitor blood pressure and form part of the system maintaining this at a constant level.

aortic regurgitation reflux of blood from the aorta into the left ventricle during diastole. Aortic regurgitation most commonly follows scarring of the aortic valve as a result of previous acute rheumatic fever, but it may also result from other conditions, such as syphilis or dissecting aneurysm. Mild cases are symptom-free, but patients more severely affected develop breathlessness, angina pectoris, and enlargement of the heart; all have a diastolic murmur. A badly affected valve may be replaced surgically with a prosthesis.

aortic replacement a surgical technique used to replace a diseased length of aorta, most often the abdominal aorta. It usually involves inserting into the aorta a flexible tube of artificial material, which functions as a substitute for the diseased section.

aortic stenosis narrowing of the opening of the aortic valve due to fusion of the cusps that comprise the valve. It may result from previous rheumatic fever, or from calcification and scarring in a valve that has two cusps instead of the normal three, or it may be congenital. Aortic stenosis obstructs the flow of blood from the left ventricle to the aorta during systole. Breathlessness on effort, angina pectoris, and fainting may follow. The patient has a systolic murmur. When symptoms develop the valve should be replaced surgically with a mechanical prosthesis (such as a Starr-Edwards ball-cage valve) or with an aortic valve graft.

使血壓保持恆定水平的系統之一部分。

主動脈回流　血液在舒張期從主動脈返流入左心室。最常發生於急性風濕熱所致的主動脈瓣瘢痕形成之後，亦可由梅毒或夾層動脈瘤等疾病引起。輕度返流無症狀，重症者出現氣促、心絞痛和心臟肥大。嚴重受損的瓣膜可手術置換。

主動脈置換　置換主動脈中病段的外科技術，多為腹主動脈的置換。通常為將一人造材料的柔韌管插入主動脈，以替代病段的功能。

主動脈瓣狹窄　因構成瓣膜的瓣葉融合而致的主動脈瓣口狹窄。可由風濕熱引起，或因有兩個瓣葉而非正常情況下三個瓣葉的瓣膜鈣化和瘢痕形成所致，亦可為先天性。主動脈瓣狹窄使心臟收縮期時從左心室流向主動脈的血液受阻，從而發生勞力性氣短、心絞痛及暈厥。患者有收縮期雜音。症狀加重時應以機械瓣膜（如斯塔爾-愛德華籠罩球瓣）或主動脈瓣移植片進行置換。

aortic valve a valve in the heart, lying between the left ventricle and the aorta. It consists of three pockets, shaped like half-moons, that prevent blood returning to the ventricle from the aorta. *See also* semilunar valve.

主動脈瓣　位於左心室與主動脈之間的一種心臟瓣膜，由三個半月狀瓣葉構成；可阻止血液從主動脈返流入左心室。參閱 semilunar valve。

aortitis *n*. inflammation of the aorta, which most commonly occurs as a late complication of syphilis. Aortitis principally affects the ascending thoracic aorta and may result in the formation of an aneurysm and obstruction to the coronary blood flow. Chest pain may occur from pressure on surrounding structures or from the reduced blood supply to the heart. *Aortic regurgitation may be found. The syphilitic infection is treated with penicillin but surgical repair to the aortic aneurysm or valve may be needed.

主動脈炎　主動脈的炎症，最常見為梅毒後期併發症，主要侵犯升主動脈，可致主動脈瘤形成和冠狀動脈血流受阻。可因主動脈周圍組織受壓或心臟供血不足而發生胸痛，亦可出現主動脈回流。梅毒感染用青黴素治療，但主動脈瘤或主動脈瓣損害可能需用外科手術修復。

aortography *n*. X-ray examination of the aorta, which involves the injection into it of a *radiopaque contrast medium, after which a series of X-rays is taken (*see* angiocardiography). Aortography is undertaken to reveal the extent and site of diseases such as atheromatous obstruction or aneurysm; it is an essential aid to the planning of surgical treatment.

主動脈造影術　主動脈的 X 綫檢查，方法是將不透 X 綫的造影劑注入主動脈，然后拍攝一系列 X 綫片（參閱 angiocardiography）。主動脈造影術用於顯示動脈粥樣化梗阻或動脈瘤等病的程度與部位，為外科治療措施中的重要輔助手段。

APC antigen-presenting cell; a macrophage that processes antigen for presentation to T-lymphocytes.

抗原遞呈細胞　處理抗原以遞呈給 T 淋巴細胞的一種巨噬細胞。

aperient *n*. a mild *laxative.

輕瀉劑　輕型瀉藥。

apex *n*. the tip or summit of an organ; for example the heart or lung. The apex of a *tooth is the tip of the root, where there is a small hole (the *apical foramen*) through which vessels and nerves pass from the pulp to the periapical tissues, **–apical** *adj*.

尖　器官的尖端或頂點，如心尖或肺尖。牙尖為牙根的尖，該部位有一小孔（根尖孔），牙髓中的血管和神經經此到達尖周組織。

apex beat the impact of the heart against the chest wall during *systole. It can be felt or heard to the left of the breastbone, in the space between the fifth and sixth ribs.

心尖搏動　心臟收縮時對胸壁的衝擊，在胸骨左側第五與第六肋骨間隙可觸及或聽到。

Apgar score a method of rapidly assessing the general state of a baby immediately after birth. A maximum of 2 points is given for each of the following signs, usually measured at one minute and five minutes after delivery: type of breathing, heart rate, colour, muscle tone, and response to stimuli. Thus an infant scoring 10 points at five minutes after delivery would be in optimum condition. When the score is low, the test is repeated at intervals as a guide to progress.

阿普伽新生兒評分法　嬰兒出生後立即對其一般狀態進行快速評定的方法。通常在產後 1 分鐘與 5 分鐘時測定下列體徵，每項最高值為 2 分：呼吸、心率、顏色、肌張力和對刺激的反應。出生 5 分鐘後因此獲得 10 分的嬰兒處於最佳狀態。對低分者不時重新測定以觀察其進展。

aphakia *n*. absence of the lens of the eye: the state of the eye after a cataract has been removed.

無晶狀體（畸形）　眼晶狀體缺失，為眼摘除白內障後的狀態。

aphasia (dysphasia) *n*. a disorder of language affecting the generation and content of speech and its understanding (it is not a disorder of articulation; *see* dyslalia). It is caused by disease in the left half of the brain (the dominant hemisphere) in a right-handed person. It is commonly accompanied by difficulties in reading and writing. **–aphasic** *adj*.

失語（症）　一種影響言語生成及內容和言語理解的語言障礙（非發育障礙，參閱 dyslalia）。在慣用右手者中為左半腦（優勢半腦）病變所致，常伴有閱讀與書寫困難。

aphonia *n*. absence or loss of the voice caused by disease of the larynx or mouth or by disease of the nerves and muscles involved in the generation and articulation of speech. If loss of speech is due to a defect in the cerebral hemispheres, the disorder is *aphasia.

失音（症）　由喉或口腔疾病導致的發音能力缺失或喪失。亦可因與語言生成與發音有關的神經和肌肉之病變所致。若為大腦半球缺陷引起則為失語症。

aphrenia *n*. failure of development of the intellectual faculties. *See* mental retardation.

痴呆　智能發育缺陷。參閱 mental retardation。

aphrodisiac *n.* an agent that stimulates sexual excitement.

aphtha *n.* (*pl.* **aphthae**) a small ulcer, occurring singly or in groups in the mouth as white or red spots. Their cause is unknown and only palliative treatment is available. **–aphthous** *adj.*

apical abscess an abscess in the bone around the apex of a tooth. An acute abscess is extremely painful, causing swelling of the jaw and sometimes also the face. It invariably results from death and infection of the pulp of the tooth. Treatment is drainage and *root canal treatment or extraction of the tooth.

apicectomy *n.* (in dentistry) surgical removal of the apex of the root of a tooth. It is usually accompanied by placement of a filling in the root end and is carried out when *root canal treatment has failed and cannot be redone.

aplasia *n.* total or partial failure of development of an organ or tissue. *See also* agenesis. **–aplastic** *adj.*

apneusis *n.* a state in which prolonged inhalation occurs. It occurs when the appropriate inhibitory influences are prevented from reaching the inspiratory centre of the brain.

apnoea *n.* temporary cessation of breathing from any cause. Attacks of apnoea are common in newborn babies and should be taken seriously although they do not necessarily indicate serious illness. *See also* sleep apnoea. **–apnoeic** *adj.*

apnoea monitor an electronic alarm that is activated by a sensor that

催慾藥　刺激性興奮的藥物。

口瘡　呈白色或紅色斑點的單個或多個口腔小潰瘍。病因不明，僅可採用姑息療法。

根尖膿腫　牙根尖周圍骨內膿腫。急性根尖膿腫可致劇痛，引起頜部並有時包括面部的腫脹，均由牙髓壞死與感染引起。治療採用引流和根管療法或拔牙。

根尖切除術　（牙科學）牙根尖部的手術切除。常與根端充填同時進行。用於根管療法無效且不能重行時。

發育不全　器官或組織的全部或部分發育不足。參閱 agenesis。

長吸呼吸　吸氣延長的狀態。發生於適當的抑制衝動不能到達大腦吸氣中樞時。

呼吸暫停　任何原因所致的呼吸暫時停止。常見於新生兒。雖不一定表示有嚴重疾病，但應慎重對待。參閱 sleep apnoea。

呼吸暫停監測儀　一種由反應嬰兒呼吸運動的傳感器啟動的

responds to a baby's respiratory movements. It can be used at home to monitor babies thought to be at risk of *cot death.

電子警報器。可用於家庭監護有嬰兒猝死症危險的嬰兒。

apocrine *adj.* **1.** describing sweat glands that occur only in hairy parts of the body, especially the armpit and groin. These glands develop in the hair follicles and appear after puberty has been reached. The strong odours associated with sweating result from the action of bacteria on the sweat produced by apocrine glands. *Compare* eccrine. **2.** describing a type of gland that loses part of its protoplasm when secreting. *See* secretion.

頂分泌 **(1)** 描述身體多毛部位的汗腺，尤其是腋窩和腹股溝的汗腺。這些腺體在毛囊中發育，出現於青春期。出汗時的惡臭來源於細菌對頂泌腺所分泌汗液的作用。與 eccrine 對比。**(2)** 描述分泌時失去部分原漿的一型腺體。參閱 secretion。

apomorphine *n.* an *emetic that produces its effect by direct action on the vomiting centre in the brain. It is given by subcutaneous injection and acts within a few minutes. It is employed in the treatment of poisoning by noncorrosive substances that have been taken by mouth. In nonemetic (lower) dosage, apomorphine has sedative, hypnotic, and expectorant actions.

阿樸嗎啡 一種直接作用於大腦嘔吐中樞的催吐藥。皮下注射幾分鐘後即生效。用於治療經口的非腐蝕性毒物中毒。以不致嘔吐的（低）劑量使用時，具鎮靜、催眠和祛痰作用。

aponeurosis *n.* a thin but strong fibrous sheet of tissue that replaces a *tendon in muscles that are flat and sheetlike and have a wide area of attachment (e.g. to bones). **–aponeurotic** *adj.*

腱膜 取代扁平片狀肌腱的堅實纖維組織薄片，有廣泛的附着面（如與骨）。

apophysis *n.* **1.** a projection from a bone. **2.** a projection of any other part, e.g. of the brain (*apophysis cerebri*: the *pineal gland).

骨突 **(1)** 骨的突出部分。**(2)** 任何其他部位的突出部分，如腦的突出部（松果體）。

apophysitis *n.* inflammation of one or more of the synovial joints between the posterior arches of the vertebrae (*apophyseal joints*). This may occur in rheumatoid arthritis or ankylosing *spondylitis and causes pain. It

骨突炎 椎骨後弓間一個或多個滑膜關節（骨突關節）的炎症。可發生於類風濕性關節炎或關節強硬性脊椎炎中並引起疼痛，致使患關節炎時脊椎不全脫位（半脫位），及關節強

contributes to partial dislocation (sub-luxation) of the vertebrae in arthritis and to rigidity of the spine (due to fusion of the joints) in ankylosing spondylitis.

硬性脊椎炎時脊柱強直（由於關節融合）。

apoplexy *n. see* stroke.

中風，卒中 參閱 stroke。

apotreptic *adj.* describing *response prevention therapy for obsessional neurosis.

預防的 描述治療強迫性神經官能症的應答預防療法。

appendectomy *n.* the usual US term for *appendicectomy.

闌尾切除術 appendicectomy 的美式用語。

appendicectomy *n.* surgical removal of the vermiform appendix. *See also* appendicitis.

闌尾切除術 闌尾的手術切除。參閱 appendicitis。

appendicitis *n.* inflammation of the ver-miform *appendix. *Acute appendicitis*, which has become common this century, usually affects young people. The chief symptom is abdominal pain, first central and later (with tenderness) in the right lower abdomen, over the appendix. Unusual positions of the appendix may cause pain in different sites, leading to difficulty in diagnosis. Vomiting and diarrhoea sometimes occur, but fever is slight. If not treated by surgical removal (appendicectomy) the condition usually progresses to cause an abscess or gener-alized *peritonitis. Conditions that mimic appendicitis include mesenteric *lymphadenitis, acute ileitis (*see* Crohn's disease), *pyelonephritis, and pneumo-nia. *Chronic appendicitis* was a popular diagnosis 20–50 years ago to explain recurrent pains in the lower abdomen. It is rare, and appendicectomy will not usually cure such pains.

闌尾炎 闌尾的炎症。本世紀常見的急性闌尾炎患者通常為年輕人，主要症狀是腹痛，首先在中部，以後（伴有觸痛）在闌尾上方的右下腹。異常位置的闌尾可在不同部位引起疼痛，可使診斷困難。有時發生嘔吐與腹瀉，但熱度不高。若不經手術切除治療（闌尾切除術），病情一般發展引起膿腫或彌漫性腹膜炎。與闌尾炎相似的疾病有腸系膜淋巴結炎、急性迴腸炎（參閱 Crohn's disease）、腎盂腎炎及肺炎。慢性闌尾炎是 20~50 年前常見的解釋下腹反覆疼痛的診斷，現已罕見。闌尾切除術通常不能解除此種疼痛。

appendicostomy *n.* an operation in which the vermiform appendix is brought through the abdominal wall and

闌尾造口術 經腹壁取出闌尾並切開以行腸道引流或減壓的手術。現已極少採用而多選

opened in order to drain or decompress the intestine. It is now rarely performed, *ileostomy, *caecostomy, or *colostomy being preferred.

擇迴腸造口術、盲腸造口術或結腸造口術。

appendicular *adj.* **1.** relating to or affecting the vermiform appendix. **2.** relating to the limbs: the *appendicular skeleton* comprises the bones of the limbs.

(1) 闌尾的　與闌尾相關或影響闌尾的。**(2) 附肢的**　包含肢體所有骨骼的四肢骨骼。

appendix (vermiform appendix) *n.* the short thin blind-ended tube, 7–10 cm long, that is attached to the end of the caecum (a pouch at the start of the large intestine). It has no known function in man and is liable to become infected and inflamed, especially in young adults (*see* appendicitis).

闌尾　附著於盲腸末端（大腸始端的盲囊）的短而細的盲管，長為7~10 cm。在人體的功能尚不明，易感染發炎，尤其在青年人中（參閱 appendicitis）。

apperception *n.* (in psychology) the process by which the qualities of an object, situation, ect., perceived by an individual are correlated with his/her preexisting knowledge.

統覺　（心理學）將所感知的物體、情況等的特性與個人現有知識相互關聯的過程。

appestat *n.* a region in the brain that controls the amount of food intake. Appetite suppressants probably decrease hunger by changing the chemical characteristics of this centre.

食慾中樞　在腦中控制食物攝入量的部位。食慾遏制劑可能通過改變此中樞的化學特性而降低飢餓感。

applicator *n.* any device used to apply medication or treatment to a particular part of the body.

敷料器　對身體某一部位敷藥或治療所用的器械。

apposition *n.* the state of two structures, such as parts of the body, being in close contact. For example, the fingers are brought into apposition when the fist is clenched, and the eyelids when the eyes are closed.

對合　兩種結構，如身體的某些部分，處於密切接觸的狀態。例如，握拳時即使手指處於對合狀態，閉目可使眼瞼處於對合狀態。

apraxia (dyspraxia) *n.* an inability to make skilled movements with accuracy.

（精神性）運用不能　無能力精確地作出技能動作，此係

This is a disorder of the *cerebral cortex resulting in the patient's inability to organize the movements rather than clumsiness due to weakness, sensory loss, or disease of the *cerebellum. It is most often caused by disease of the *parietal lobes of the brain and sometimes by disease of the frontal lobes.

大腦皮質性疾病所致的組織動作能力喪失，而非無力、感覺喪失或小腦病變所致的笨拙。通常有大腦頂葉疾病，有時為額葉疾病引起。

aproctia *n.* congenital absence of the anus or its opening. *See* imperforate anus.

鎖肛，無肛 先天性肛門或肛門孔缺失。參閱 imperforate anus。

aprosexia *n.* inability to fix the attention on any subject, due to poor eyesight, defective hearing, or mental weakness.

注意力減退 因弱視、聽力缺陷或精神衰弱而對任何事物均不能集中注意力。

aprotinin *n.* a drug that prevents the breakdown of blood clots (*see* fibrinolysis) by blocking the action of the enzyme plasmin, i.e. it is an *antifibrinolytic* drug. It is administered by injection to control the severe bleeding that may occur in certain cancers and with *fibrinolytic treatments. Trade name: **Trasylol**.

抑酞酶 一種通過阻滯纖維蛋白溶解酶作用而阻止血凝塊破裂的藥物（參閱 fibrinolysis），即抗纖（維蛋白）溶劑。注射給藥。用於控制某些癌症和溶解纖維蛋白治療中可能發生的嚴重出血。商品名：Trasylol。

APUD cells cells that share the metabolic property of *a*mine-*p*recursor *u*ptake and *d*ecarboxylation. They have a wide distribution, especially in the mucosa of the gastrointestinal tract and pancreas, and are able to form a large variety of peptide hormonal substances; they are often known as the *diffuse endocrine system*.

APUD細胞，胺前體攝取和脫羧細胞 一組均具有攝取胺前體進行脫羧代謝特性的細胞。其分布廣泛，尤其在胃腸道黏膜與胰腺中。可形成種類繁多的肽激素物質。常被稱為擴散性內分泌系統。

APUDoma *n.* a tumour that contains *APUD cells and may give rise to symptoms caused by excessive production of the hormones and other peptides that these cells produce. *Argentaffinomas are a good example of this group of tumours, but there are many others (e.g. *gastrinomas and *vipomas).

APUD瘤 一種含有 APUD 細胞的腫瘤，可引起這些細胞產生的激素和其他肽類過多所致症狀。嗜銀細胞瘤即為一例，但還有多種其他 APUD 瘤（如胃泌素瘤和舒血管腸肽瘤）。

apyrexia *n.* the absence of fever.

無熱期

aqueduct *n.* (in anatomy) a canal containing fluid. For example, the *aqueduct of the midbrain* (*cerebral aqueduct, aqueduct of Sylvius*) connects the third and fourth *ventricles.

導水管　（解剖學）含有液體的管道。例如，連接第三腦室與第四腦室的中腦導水管（西耳維厄斯導水管）。

aqueous humour the watery fluid that fills the chamber of the *eye immediately behind the cornea and in front of the lens. It is continually being formed – chiefly by capillaries of the ciliary processes – and it drains away into Schlemm's canal, at the junction of the cornea and sclera.

水狀液（眼房水）　充滿緊接角膜後晶狀體前的眼房之水狀液體。主要由睫狀突的毛細管不斷產生，並排入到角膜與鞏膜接界的施勤姆管。

arachidonic acid *see* essential fatty acid.

花生烯酸　參閱 essential fatty acid。

arachnidism *n.* poisoning from the bite of a spider. Toxins from the less venomous species of spider cause only local pain, redness, and swelling. Toxins from more venomous species, such as the black widow (*Lactrodectus mactans*), cause muscular pains, convulsions, nausea, and paralysis.

蛛毒中毒　被蜘蛛螫後的中毒。弱毒類蜘蛛的毒素僅引起局部疼痛與紅腫。像黑寡婦強毒類蜘蛛的毒素可引起肌肉疼痛、驚厥、惡心和麻痺。

arachnodactyly *n.* abnormally long and slender fingers: usually associated with excessive height and congenital defects of the heart and eyes in *Marfan's syndrome.

細長指（趾），**蜘蛛腳樣指（趾）**　手指異常纖細修長。常伴發身材過高和心臟與眼的先天性缺陷，見於馬方綜合徵。

arachnoid (arachnoid mater) *n.* the middle of the three membranes covering the brain and spinal cord (*see* meninges), which has a fine, almost cobweb-like, texture. Between it and the pia mater within lies the subarachnoid space, containing cerebrospinal fluid and large blood vessels; the membrane itself has no blood supply.

蛛網膜　覆蓋大腦和脊髓的三層膜之中層（參閱 meninges），其構造纖細近似蛛網。蛛網膜與其內的軟腦（脊）膜之間為內含腦脊液之大血管的蛛網膜下腔，蛛網膜自身無血液供應。

arachnoiditis *n.* an inflammatory process causing thickening and scarring (fibrosis) of the membranous linings (*meninges) of the spinal canal. The resulting entrapment of nerve roots may result in weakness, pain, and numbness in the affected area. The condition may result from infection of the meninges, surgery, or as a response to the oil-based dyes previously used in *myelography. The reaction to myelography is prevented by the current use of water-soluble dyes.

蛛網膜炎 引起脊椎管內（腦脊膜）增厚和瘢痕形成（纖維變性）的炎性過程，神經根受壓可導致受累部位無力、疼痛和麻木。蛛網膜炎可源自腦脊膜感染、外科手術，或是對過去脊髓（X 綫）造影術使用的油類染劑的反應。現已通過使用水溶性染劑防止此種反應。

arachnoid villus one of the thin-walled projections outwards of the arachnoid membrane into the blood-filled sinuses of the dura, acting as a one-way valve for the flow of cerebrospinal fluid from the subarachnoid space into the bloodstream. Large villi, known as *arachnoid granulations* (or *Pacchionian bodies*), are found in the region of the superior sagittal sinus. They may be so distended as to cause pitting of the adjacent bone.

蛛網膜絨毛 從蛛網膜向外伸入硬腦膜血竇內的薄壁突出之一。起着使腦脊液從蛛網膜下腔進入血流的單向閥門作用。稱為蛛網膜粒（或帕基奧尼體）的大絨毛見於上矢狀竇區，此類絨毛的膨脹可致毗鄰骨胳的凹陷。

arbor *n.* (in anatomy) a treelike structure. *Arbor vitae* is the treelike outline of white matter seen in sections of the cerebellum; it also refers to the treelike appearance of the inner folds of the cervix (neck) of the uterus.

樹 （解剖學）樹狀結構。（小腦）活樹是小腦切片所見的樹狀形態，亦指子宮頸內褶的樹狀外觀。

arbovirus *n.* one of a group of RNA-containing viruses that are transmitted from animals to man by insects (i.e. arthropods; hence *ar*thropod-*bo*rne viruses) and cause diseases resulting in encephalitis or serious fever, such as dengue and yellow fever.

蟲媒病毒 一組由昆蟲從動物傳染給人的含核糖核酸病毒。可致腦炎或重症熱病，如登革熱和黃熱病。

ARC AIDS-related complex: *see* AIDS.

艾滋病有關症候群 參閱AIDS。

arc-eye *n.* a painful condition of the eyes caused by damage to the surface of the

弧光眼，電弧眼 因電弧焊紫外綫損傷角膜表面造成的眼部

cornea by ultraviolet light from arc welding. It usually resolves if the eyes are padded for 24 hours. It is similar to *snow blindness and the condition caused by overexposure of the eye to sun-tanning lamps.

疼痛狀態，疼痛常在遮蓋眼部 24 小時後消除。弧光眼與雪盲 和眼受太陽燈照射過度所致狀 態相似。

arch- (arche-, archi-, archo-) *prefix denoting* first; primitive; ancestral. Example: *archinephron* (first-formed embryonic kidney).

〔前綴〕第一，初，原始　如 原腎（最初形成的胚胎腎）。

archenteron *n.* a cavity that forms in the very early embryo as the result of gastrulation (*see* gastrula). In man it forms a tubular cavity, the *archenteric canal*, which connects the amniotic cavity with the yolk sac. **–archenteric** *adj.*

原腸　在最早期胚胎中因原腸 胚形成產生的腔（參閱 gastrula）。在人體形成連接羊膜 腔與卵黃囊的一管狀腔，即神 經腸管。

archetype *n.* (in Jungian psychology) an inherited idea or mode of thought supposed to be present in the *unconscious mind and to derive from the experience of the whole human race, not from the life experience of the individual.

原（始）型　（榮格心理學）被 認為存在於潛意識中的來自全 人類而非個人生活經歷並由遺 傳所得的觀念或思維模式。

archipallium *n.* the *hippocampal formation of the cerebrum. The term is seldom used.

原始外表　大腦的海馬結構。 此詞現已少用。

arcus *n.* (in anatomy) an arch; for example the *arcus aortae* (*aortic arch).

弓　（解剖學）例如主動脈弓。

arcus senilis a greyish line in the periphery of the cornea, concentric with the edge but separated from it by a clear zone. It begins above and below but may become a continuous ring. It consists of an infiltration of fatty material and is common in the elderly. When it occurs in younger people it may indicate abnormal fat metabolism, but there is great racial variation in its incidence. It never affects vision.

老人弓，角膜弓　角膜周圍的 一條淺灰色綫，緊貼角膜邊緣 但由一明亮帶與其分開。此弓 從上下兩方開始，可連接成 環，係脂肪性物質浸潤組成， 常見於老年人。年輕人出現老 人弓可表明脂肪代謝異常，但 其發生率有很大的種族差異。 對視力從無影響。

areola *n*. **1.** the brownish or pink ring of tissue surrounding the nipple of the breast. **2.** the part of the iris that surrounds the pupil of the eye. **3.** a small space in a tissue. **–areolar** *adj*.

areolar tissue loose *connective tissue consisting of a meshwork of collagen, elastic issue, and reticular fibres interspersed with numerous connective tissue cells. It binds the skin to underlying muscles and forms a link between organs while allowing a high degree of relative movement.

Argasidae *n. see* tick.

argentaffin cells cells that stain readily with silver salts. Such cells occur, for example, in the crypts of Lieberkühn in the intestine.

argentaffinoma (carcinoid) *n.* a tumour of the *argentaffin cells in the glands of the intestine (*see* APUDoma). Argentaffinomas typically occur in the tip of the appendix and are among the commonest tumours of the small intestine. They may also occur in the rectum and other parts of the digestive tract and in the bronchial tree (*bronchial carcinoid adenoma*). Argentaffinomas sometimes produce 5-hydroxytryptamine (serotonin), prostaglandins, and other physiologically active substances, which are inactivated in the liver. If the tumour has spread to the liver excess amounts of these substances are released into the systemic circulation and the *carcinoid syndrome* results – flushing, headache, diarrhoea, asthma-like attacks, and in some cases damage to the right side of the heart.

arginine *n.* an *amino acid that plays an important role in the formation of *urea by the liver.

(1) 乳暈 乳頭周圍的淺灰色或粉紅色環形組織。**(2) 暈** 圍繞瞳孔的部分虹膜。**(3) 細隙，小區** 組織內的細隙。

蜂窩組織 由膠原網絡、彈性組織和與無數結締組織細胞交織的網狀纖維構成的疏鬆結締組織。它使皮膚附着於下層的肌肉，並在連接器官的同時使其具有高度的活動自由。

隱喙蜱科 參閱 tick。

嗜銀細胞 易被銀鹽染色的細胞。例如腸利貝屈恩腺中的細胞。

嗜銀細胞瘤 一種腸腺嗜銀細胞的腫瘤（參閱 APUDoma）。多發生於闌尾頂端，為最常見的小腸腫瘤之一，亦可發生於直腸和消化道其他部位及支氣管樹內（支氣管類癌腺瘤）。嗜銀細胞瘤有時產生 S-羥色胺、前列腺素以及其他在肝內被滅活的生理活性物質。若腫瘤擴散至肝，釋放大量此類物質進入體循環，可導致類癌（瘤）綜合徵，出現顏面潮紅、頭痛、腹瀉、哮喘樣發作，以及在一些情況下右心受損。

精氨酸 在肝臟合成尿素中起重要作用的一種氨基酸。

argon laser a type of *laser that produces a beam of intense light, used especially in eye surgery to treat disease of the retina (e.g. diabetic retinopathy). *See also* photocoagulation.

氫激光　一種產生一束強光的激光。尤其用於治療視網膜疾病（如糖尿病性視網膜病）的眼外科手術。參閱 photocoagulation。

Argyll Robertson pupil a disorder of the eyes, common to several diseases of the central nervous system, in which the *pupillary (light) reflex is absent. Although the pupils contract normally for near vision, they fail to contract in bright light.

阿蓋爾羅伯遜瞳孔（徵）　幾種中樞神經系統疾病所共有的一種眼疾患，患者瞳孔（光）反射缺失。瞳孔雖在視近物時正常收縮，卻不能在亮光下收縮。

argyria *n.* the deposition of silver in the skin, either resulting from industrial exposure or following ingestion of silver salts. A slate-grey pigmentation develops slowly; this is accentuated in areas exposed to light.

銀質沉着病　因工業接觸或攝入銀鹽後皮膚中銀質沉積。緩慢發展為藍灰色色素沉着，暴露的部分更為嚴重。

ariboflavinosis *n.* the group of symptoms caused by deficiency of riboflavin (vitamin B_2). These symptoms include inflammation of the tongue and lips and sores in the corners of the mouth.

核黃素缺乏病　核黃素（維生素 B_2）缺乏所致的症候羣，包括舌和唇發炎以及口角潰瘍。

Arnold-Chiari malformation a congenital disorder in which there is distortion of the base of the skull with protrusion of the lower brainstem and parts of the cerebellum through the opening for the spinal cord at the base of the skull. It is commonly associated with *neural tube defects and *hydrocephalus.

阿-希氏畸形　一種顱骨底變形的先天性疾病。伴有腦幹下部與部分小腦從顱骨底的脊髓孔突出，常伴發於神經管缺陷和腦積水。

arousal *n.* **1.** a state of alertness and of high responsiveness to stimuli. It is produced by strong motivation, by anxiety, and by a stimulating environment. **2.** physiological activation of the *cerebral cortex by centres lower in the brain, such as the *reticular activating system, resulting in wakefulness and alertness. It

(1) 警覺　一種戒備並對刺激有強烈反應的狀態。因強烈的動機、焦慮和充滿刺激的環境而產生。(2) 覺醒　大腦中網狀激活系統等低級中樞引起的大腦皮質的生理性激活，可致清醒與警覺。有的假說認為，覺醒程度過高或過低導致神經

is hypothesized that unduly high or low degrees of arousal lead to neuropsychiatric problems, such as *narcolepsy and *mania.

精神性疾病，如發作性睡眠病和躁狂。

arrhenoblastoma *n. see* androblastoma.

男性細胞瘤（卵巢）　參閱 androblastoma。

arrhythmia *n.* any deviation from the normal rhythm (sinus rhythm) of the heart. The natural pacemaker of the heart (the sinoatrial node), which lies in the wall of the right atrium, controls the rate and rhythm of the whole heart under the influence of the autonomic nervous system. It generates electrical impulses that spread to the atria and ventricles, via specialized conducting tissues, and cause them to contract normally. Arrhythmias result from a disturbance of the generation or the conduction of these impulses and may be intermittent or continuous. They include *ectopic beats (extrasystoles), ectopic *tachycardias, *fibrillation, and *heart block (which is often associated with slow heart rates). Symptoms include palpitations, breathlessness, and chest pain. In more serious arrhythmias the *Stokes-Adams syndrome or *cardiac arrest may occur. Arrhythmias may result from most heart diseases but they also occur without apparent cause.

心律失常，心律不齊　心臟正常節律（竇性節律）的任何異常。在自主神經系統影響下，位於右心房壁的天然心臟起搏點（竇房結）控制整個心臟的速度和節律，所發出的電衝動通過特殊的傳導組織傳至心房和心室，使其產生正常收縮。心律失常即因這些衝動的產生或傳導紊亂所致。可為間歇性或持續性的。心律失常包括異位搏動（期外收縮）、異位心動過速、纖維性顫動和心傳導阻滯（常有心率遲緩）。症狀有心悸、氣短和胸痛。嚴重時可出現阿-斯氏綜合徵或心動停止。心律失常可由多種心臟病引起，但亦可無明顯原因。

arsenic *n.* a poisonous greyish metallic element producing the symptoms of nausea, vomiting, diarrhoea, cramps, convulsions, and coma when ingested in large doses. Drugs used as antidotes to arsenic poisoning include *dimercaprol. Arsenic was formerly readily available in the form of rat poison and in fly-papers and was the poisoner's first choice during the 19th century, its presence in a body being then difficult to detect. Today detection is relatively simple. Arsenic was

砷　一種淺灰色有毒金屬元素。大量攝入時可產生惡心、嘔吐、腹瀉、痛性痙攣、驚厥和昏迷等症狀。用作砷中毒解毒劑的有二巰丙醇。過去滅鼠藥和毒蠅紙中多含有砷，並在19世紀為投毒者的首選毒藥，因其在體內的存在那時難以檢測。現在檢測相當簡單。在過去砷曾被用於醫藥，最重要的含砷藥物是治療梅毒和危險的寄生蟲病所用的胂凡納明（灑

formerly used in medicine, the most important arsenical drugs being *arsphenamine* (*Salvarsan*) and *neoarsphenamine*, used in the treatment of syphilis and dangerous parasitic diseases. Symbol: As.

爾佛散）和新肿凡納明。符號：As。

artefact *n. see* artifact.

人為現象　參閱 artifact。

arter- (arteri-, arterio-) *prefix denoting* an artery. Examples: *arteriopathy* (disease of); *arteriorrhaphy* (suture of); *arteriovenous* (relating to arteries and veins).

〔前綴〕**動脈**　例如：動脈病、動脈縫合術、動靜脈的。

arteriectomy *n.* surgical excision of an artery or part of an artery. This may be performed as a diagnostic procedure (for example, to take an arterial biopsy in the diagnosis of arteritis) or during reconstruction of a blocked artery when the blocked segment is replaced by a synthetic graft.

動脈切除術　一條或一段動脈的手術切除。可用作為診斷措施（如動脈炎診斷時取動脈作活檢）或在人造移植物置換阻塞段時用於阻塞動脈之重建。

arteriogram *n.* a tracing of the wave form of an arterial pulse. This can be made directly, by means of an arterial needle puncture and pressure recording, or indirectly, by a recorder placed on the skin over an artery. The tracing may be recorded on a paper strip or on a screen (oscilloscope). Some heart defects produce characteristic pulse wave forms.

動脈搏描記圖　動脈搏動的波形圖。可通過動脈穿刺針和壓力記錄器直接描記，亦可將記錄器置於動脈皮膚上而間接描記。此圖可記錄在紙帶或熒光屏上（示波器）。有些心臟缺損產生具有特徵性的搏動波形圖。

arteriography *n.* X-ray examination of an artery that has been outlined by the injection of a *radiopaque contrast medium. The major uses of arteriography are to demonstrate the site and extent of atheroma, especially in the coronary arteries (*coronary angiography*) and leg arteries (*femoral angiography*), and to reveal the site of aneurysms within the skull or cerebral tumours

動脈造影術　對注入不透 X 綫造影劑顯示其輪廓的動脈進行 X 綫檢查。主要用途為顯示動脈粥樣化的部位與程度。尤其在冠狀動脈（冠狀血管造影術）和下肢動脈（股血管造影術）中，及顯示顱內動脈瘤或大腦腫瘤所在部位（頸動脈和椎動脈血管造影術）。參閱 MUGA scan。

(*carotid* and *vertebral artery angiography*). *See also* MUGA scan.

.

arteriole *n.* a small branch of an *artery, leading into many smaller vessels – the *capillaries. By their constriction and dilation, under the regulation of the sympathetic nervous system, arterioles are the principal controllers of blood flow and pressure.

小動脈　進入許多微小血管即毛細管的動脈小分支。小動脈在交感神經系統調節下，通過其收縮和擴張，對血流和血壓起着主要的控制作用。

arteriolitis *n.* inflammation of the arterioles (the smallest arteries), which may complicate severe hypertension. This produces *necrotizing arteriolitis*, which may result in kidney failure. A similar condition may affect the lung in pulmonary hypertension.

小動脈炎　小動脈（最小動脈）的炎症。可併發於重度高血壓，引起導致腎衰竭的壞死性小動脈炎。肺動脈高血壓小動脈炎可累及肺。

arterioplasty *n.* surgical reconstruction of an artery; for example, in the treatment of *aneurysms.

動脈成形術　動脈的重建手術。如在動脈瘤治療中。

arteriosclerosis *n.* an imprecise term used for any of several conditions affecting the arteries. The term is often used as a synonym for atherosclerosis (*see* atheroma). It may also be used for *Mönckeberg's degeneration*, in which calcium is deposited in the arteries as part of the ageing process, and *arteriolosclerosis*, in which the walls of small arteries become thickened due to ageing or hypertension.

動脈硬化　用於表示幾種累及動脈的狀態之含糊術語。常用作動脈粥樣硬化的同義詞（參閱 atheroma），亦可指隨老化過程產生的動脈內鈣沉積的門克伯格變性，以及小動脈硬化，即小動脈壁由於老化或高血壓而增厚。

arteriotomy *n.* an incision into, or a needle puncture of, the wall of an artery. This is most often performed as a diagnostic procedure in the course of *arteriography or cardiac *catheterization. It may also be required to remove an embolus (*see* embolectomy).

動脈切開術　切開或穿刺動脈壁。最常作為動脈造影術或心導管插入術的一種診斷手段。亦可用於排除栓子（參閱 embolectomy）。

arteriovenous anastomosis a thick-walled blood vessel that connects an

動靜脈吻合　不經毛細管直接連接小動脈和小靜脈的厚壁血

arteriole directly with a venule, thus bypassing the capillaries. Arteriovenous anastomoses are commonly found in the skin of the lips, nose, ears, hands and feet; their muscular walls can constrict to reduce blood flow or dilate to allow blood through to these areas.

管。常見於唇、鼻、耳、手與足的皮膚內。其肌壁可收縮或擴張以減少或增加經過這些區域的血流。

arteriovenous aneurysm a direct communication between an artery and vein, without an intervening capillary bed. It can occur as a congenital abnormality or it may be acquired following injury or surgery. It may affect the limbs, lungs, or viscera and may be single or multiple. If the connection is large, the short-circuiting of blood may produce heart failure. Large isolated arteriovenous aneurysms may be closed surgically.

動靜脈瘤 無毛細管床介入的動脈與靜脈直接相通。可為先天性畸形或發生於受傷或手術後。可發生於四肢、肺部或內臟，單發或多發。若動靜脈瘤很大，血流短路可引起心力衰竭。大而單獨的動靜脈瘤可用手術閉合。

arteriovenous malformation *see* angioma.

動靜脈畸形 參閱 angioma。

arteritis *n.* an inflammatory disease that affects the muscular walls of the arteries. It may be part of a *connective-tissue disease or it may be due to an infection, such as syphilis. The affected vessels are swollen and tender and may become blocked. *Temporal* or *giant-cell arteritis* occurs in the elderly and most commonly affects the arteries of the scalp. The patient complains of severe headache, and blindness may result from thrombosis of the arteries to the eyes. Treatment with cortisone derivatives is rapidly effective.

動脈炎 動脈肌壁的炎性疾病。可為結締組織病之一部分，或因梅毒等感染所致。病變血管腫脹、觸痛，並可能發生阻塞。顳動脈炎，或稱巨細胞動脈炎發生於老年人，多侵犯頭皮的動脈。患者主訴劇烈頭痛，並可因通往眼部動脈的血栓形成造成失明。用可的松衍化物治療可迅速見效。

artery *n.* a blood vessel carrying blood away from the heart. All arteries except the *pulmonary artery carry oxygenated blood. The walls of arteries contain smooth muscle fibres (see illustration),

動脈 從心臟往外運送血液的血管。除肺動脈外的所有動脈均運送含氧血。動脈壁有受交感神經系統控制其收縮或鬆弛的平滑肌纖維（見圖，第 116

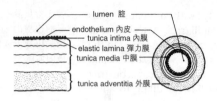

Transverse section through an artery
血管橫切面

which contract or relax under the control of the sympathetic nervous system. *See also* aorta, arteriole.

arthr- (arthro-) *prefix denoting* a joint. Examples: *arthrology* (science of); *arthrosclerosis* (stiffening or hardening of).

arthralgia *n.* pain in a joint, without swelling or other signs of arthritis. *Compare* arthritis.

arthrectomy *n.* surgical excision of a joint. It is usually performed on a painful joint that has ceased to function, as may result from intractable infection.

arthritis *n.* inflammation of one or more joints, characterized by swelling, warmth, redness of the overlying skin, pain, and restriction of motion. Over 200 diseases may cause arthritis, including *rheumatoid arthritis, *osteoarthritis, *gout, *tuberculosis, and other infections. Diagnosis is assisted by examination of the pattern of distribution of affected joints, X-rays, blood tests, and examination of synovial fluid obtained by *aspiration of a swollen joint. *Mono-* or *oligoarthritis* is inflammation of one joint, *pauciarthritis* of a few (four or less), and *polyarthritis* of many joints, either simultaneously or in sequence. Any disease involving the synovial membranes or causing

頁、117 頁）。參閱 aorta，arteriole。

〔前綴〕**關節** 如關節學，關節硬化。

關節痛 無腫脹或其他關節炎體徵的關節痛。與 arthritis 對比。

關節切除術 手術切除某一關節，通常施行於已喪失其功能的疼痛關節，如因難以治愈的感染所致。

關節炎 一個或數個關節的炎症。特徵為表面皮膚腫脹、熱、紅、痛及行動受限。可引起關節炎的疾病超過 200 種，包括類風濕性關節炎、骨關節炎、痛風、結核病以及其他感染。患病關節分布類型檢查、X 綫檢查、血試驗法、抽吸腫脹關節中滑液化驗可輔助診斷。單關節炎指一個關節發炎，少關節炎指幾個（不超過 4 個）關節發炎，多關節炎指多個關節同時或先後發炎。任何累及滑膜或造成軟骨變性的疾病均可引起關節炎。治療取決於其病因，但阿司匹林和類似的止痛劑常用來遏

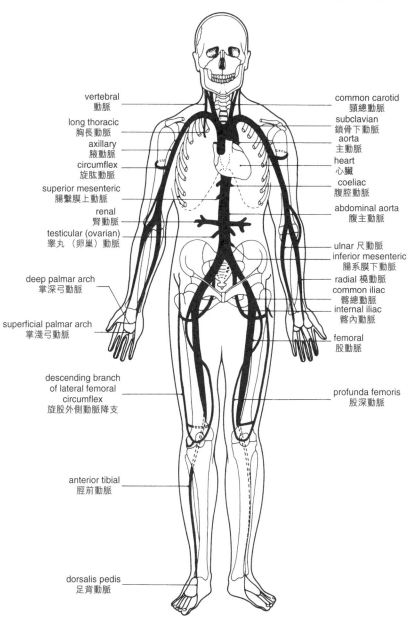

The principal arteries of the body
人體主要動脈

degeneration of cartilage may cause arthritis. Treatment of arthritis depends on the cause, but aspirin and similar analgesics are often used to suppress inflammation, and hence reduce pain and swelling. *See also* psoriatic arthritis, haemarthrosis, pyarthrosis, hydrarthrosis. **–arthritic** *adj.*

arthrodesis *n.* fusion of bones across a joint space by surgical means, which eliminates movement. This operation is performed when a joint is very painful, highly unstable, grossly deformed or chronically infected, or when an *arthroplasty would be inadvisable or impossible.

arthrodic joint (gliding joint) a form of *diarthrosis (freely movable joint) in which the bony surfaces slide over each other without angular or rotational movement. Examples are the joints of the carpus and tarsus.

arthrography *n.* an X-ray technique for examining joints. A *contrast medium (either air or a liquid opaque to X-rays) is injected into the joint space, allowing its outline and contents to be traced accurately.

arthropathy *n.* any disease or disorder involving a joint.

arthroplasty *n.* surgical remodelling of a diseased joint. To prevent the ends of the bones fusing after the operation, a large gap may be created between them (*gap arthroplasty*), a barrier of artificial material may be inserted (*interposition arthroplasty*), or one or both bone ends may be replaced by a *prosthesis of metal or plastic (*replacement arthroplasty*).

arthropod *n.* any member of a large group of animals that possess a hard

制炎症，從而減輕疼痛與腫脹。參閱 psoriatic arthritis，haemarthrosis，pyarthrosis，hydrarthrosis。

關節固定術　用外科方法穿過關節間隙使骨融合而制止關節活動。此項手術用於關節劇痛、過於活動、嚴重畸形或長期感染等情況，或不宜或不能作關節成形術時。

摩動關節　一種動關節（可自由活動的關節）。骨表面無角動或旋動而可互相滑動。如腕關節和跗關節。

關節照相術　檢查關節的 X 綫照相術。將造影劑（不透 X 綫的氣體或液體）注入關節間隙，以準確顯示其輪廓與內容物。

關節病　任何累及關節的疾病或障礙。

關節成形術　病變關節的手術重建。為避免手術後關節骨端融合，可在其間形成較大間隙（間隙關節成形術），亦可插入人造材料為障壁（嵌入關節成形術），或用金屬或塑料假體置換一骨或兩骨骨端（置換關節成形術）。

節肢動物　一大族有堅硬外骨骼和節足及其他附器動物的任

external skeleton and jointed legs and other appendages. Many arthropods are of medical importance, including the *mites, *ticks, and *insects.

arthroscope *n.* an instrument for insertion into the cavity of a joint in order to inspect the contents, before *biopsy or operation on the joint.

arthrotomy *n.* surgical incision of a joint capsule in order to inspect the contents and drain pus (if it is present).

articulation *n.* (in anatomy) the point or type of contact between two bones. *See* joint.

articulator *n.* (in dentistry) an apparatus for relating the upper and lower models of a patient's dentition in a fixed position, usually with maximum tooth contact. Some articulators can reproduce jaw movements. They are used in the construction of crowns, bridges, and dentures.

artifact (artefact) *n.* (in microscopy) a structure seen in a tissue under a microscope that is not present in the living tissue. Artifacts, which are produced by faulty *fixation or staining of the tissue, may give a false impression that disease or abnormality is present in the tissue when it is not.

artificial insemination instrumental introduction of semen into the vagina in order that a woman may conceive. Insemination is timed to coincide with the day on which the woman is expected to ovulate (*see* menstrual cycle). The semen specimen may be provided by the husband (*AIH – artificial insemination husband*), for example in cases of

何成員。其中許多在醫學上有重要意義。包括蟎類、蜱類和昆蟲。

關節（內窺）鏡　關節活組織檢查或手術前，插入關節腔以查看其內容物的器械。

關節切開術　手術切開關節囊以查看其內容物並排膿（若有膿）。

關節　（解剖學）兩骨間的接觸部位或方式。參閱 joint。

殆架，咬合架　（牙科學）將患者上下牙的牙列模型處於某種固定位置並通常使上下牙盡量接觸的器械。有些殆架可模擬頜運動而用於製作牙冠、牙橋和托牙。

人為現象　（顯微鏡檢查）在顯微鏡下組織中所見而並不存在於活組織內的結構。因組織固定或染色錯誤而造成。人為現象可引起一種錯覺，認為某組織內有病變或異常存在，但實際上不存在。

人工授精　用器械將精液導入陰道以使婦女受孕。授精時間安排與婦女預期排卵日相符（參閱 menstrual cycle）。可由其丈夫提供精液（丈夫人工授精），如在陽痿等情況下；或由匿名獻精者提供（供體授精），通常因丈夫患不育症。

*impotence, or by an anonymous donor (*DI – donor insemination*), usually in cases where the husband is sterile.

artificial kidney (dialyser) *see* haemodialysis.

人工腎（透析器）　參閱 haemodialysis。

artificial lung *see* respirator.

人工肺　參閱 respirator。

artificial respiration an emergency procedure for maintaining a flow of air into and out of a patient's lungs when the natural breathing reflexes are absent or insufficient. This may occur after drowning, poisoning, etc., or during a surgical operation on the thorax or abdomen when muscle-relaxing drugs are administered. The simplest and most efficient method is *mouth-to-mouth respiration (the '*kiss of life*'). In hospital the breathing cycle is maintained by means of a *respirator.

人工呼吸　自然呼吸反射消失或減弱時維持患者肺部空氣流通的一項急救措施。這種情況可發生在溺水、中毒等意外事故之後，或在使用肌肉鬆弛藥的胸或腹部外科手術中。最簡單且最有效的方法是口對口呼吸法。在醫院則用呼吸機維持患者的呼吸周期。

artificial rupture of membranes (ARM) *see* amniotomy.

人工破膜　參閱 amniotomy。

arytenoid cartilage either of the two pyramid-shaped cartilages that lie at the back of the *larynx next to the upper edges of the cricoid cartilage.

杓狀軟骨　位於喉部後方鄰近環狀軟骨上緣的兩塊錐形軟骨之一。

arytenoidectomy *n.* surgical excision of the arytenoid cartilage of the larynx in the treatment of paralysis of the vocal cords.

杓狀軟骨切除術　聲帶麻痺治療中喉杓狀軟骨的手術切除。

asbestosis *n.* a lung disease – a form of *pneumoconiosis – caused by fibres of asbestos inhaled by those who are exposed to the mineral. The incidence of lung cancer is high in such patients, particularly if they smoke cigarettes. *See also* mesothelioma.

石棉沉着病　接觸石棉人員因吸入石棉纖維引起的肺部疾病。為肺塵埃沉着病的一種。患者中有很高的肺癌發病率，吸煙者尤甚。參閱 mesothelioma。

asbestos-related pleural disease any one of a variety of conditions involving

石棉相關胸膜病　接觸石棉的患者中累及胸膜而不損害肺部

the *pleura, but not the lungs (*see* asbestosis), in subjects exposed to asbestos. These include the formation of pleural plaques, diffuse pleural thickening, and pleural effusions (*see* oedema).

ascariasis *n.* a disease caused by an infestation with the parasitic worm *Ascaris lumbricoides*. Adult worms in the intestine can cause abdominal pain, vomiting, constipation, diarrhoea, appendicitis, and peritonitis; in large numbers they may cause obstruction of the intestine. The presence of the migrating larvae in the lungs can provoke pneumonia. Ascariasis occurs principally in areas of poor sanitation; it is treated with *piperazine.

Ascaris *n.* a genus of parasitic nematode worms. *A. lumbricoides*, widely distributed throughout the world, is the largest of the human intestinal nematodes – an adult female measures up to 35 cm in length. Eggs, passed out in the stools, may be transmitted to a new host in contaminated food or drink. Larvae hatch out in the intestine and then undergo a complicated migration, via the hepatic portal vein, liver, heart, lungs, windpipe, and pharynx, before returning to the intestine where they later develop into adult worms (*see also* ascariasis).

ascites (hydroperitoneum) *n.* the accumulation of fluid in the peritoneal cavity, causing abdominal swelling. Causes include infections (such as tuberculosis), heart failure, *portal hypertension, *cirrhosis, and various cancers (particularly of the ovary and liver). *See also* oedema.

ascorbic acid *see* vitamin C.

-ase *suffix denoting* an enzyme. Examples: *lactase; dehydrogenase*.

的多種狀況之一（參閱 asbestosis），包括胸膜斑形成、播散性胸膜增厚及胸腔積液（參閱 oedema）。

蛔蟲病 因感染人蛔蟲這一寄生蟲而致的疾病。腸內成蟲可引起腹痛、嘔吐、便秘、腹瀉、闌尾炎和腹膜炎；大量蛔蟲可造成腸梗阻。移動性幼蟲在肺內出現可致肺炎。蛔蟲病主要發生在衛生不良地區，治療用哌嗪。

蛔蟲屬 寄生性綫蟲一屬。廣泛分布於世界各地的人蛔蟲是最長的人類腸綫蟲，雌成蟲可長達 35 cm。隨糞便排出的蟲卵可由受污染的食物或飲料傳播給新宿主。幼蟲在腸內孵化，然後經過肝門靜脈、肝、心臟、肺、氣管和喉的複雜移行過程，回到腸發育為成蟲（參閱 ascariasis）。

腹水 腹腔液體蓄積導致腹部膨脹。病因包括感染（如結核病）、心力衰竭、門靜脈高壓、肝硬化及各種癌症（尤其是卵巢和肝）。參閱 oedema。

抗壞血酸 參閱 vitamin C。

〔後綴〕**酶** 如乳糖酶，脫氫酶。

asepsis *n.* the complete absence of bacteria, fungi, viruses, or other microorganisms that could cause disease. Asepsis is the ideal state for the performance of surgical operations and is achieved by using *sterilization techniques. **–aseptic** *adj.*

無菌 完全沒有細菌、真菌、病毒或其他的致病微生物存在。是施行外科手術的理想狀態。用消毒技術取得。

Asherman syndrome a condition in which *amenorrhoea and infertility follow a major haemorrhage in pregnancy. It may result from overvigorous curettage of the uterus in an attempt to control the bleeding. This removes the lining, the walls adhere, and the cavity is obliterated to a greater or lesser degree. Some 50% of such patients are subsequently infertile, and of those who become pregnant, only a minority achieve an uncomplicated delivery. *Compare* Sheehan's syndrome.

阿謝曼綜合徵 妊娠大出血後閉經和不育的狀況。可因控制出血而刮宮用力過度所致，造成子宮內膜脫落，子宮壁黏連，使子宮腔有程度不等的閉合。這些患者中約 50% 繼而成為不育者，而再次妊娠者中亦僅有少數無併發症。與 Sheehan's syndrome 對比。

asparaginase *n.* an enzyme that inhibits the growth of certain tumours and is used almost exclusively in the treatment of acute lymphoblastic leukaemia. It may cause allergic reactions and *anaphylaxis. Trade name: **Erwinase**.

天門冬酰胺酶 一種抑制某些腫瘤生長的酶。幾乎專用於治療急性淋巴性白血病，可引起變態反應和過敏反應。商品名：Erwinase。

asparagine *n. see* amino acid.

天門冬酰胺 參閱 amino acid。

aspartic acid (aspartate) *see* amino acid.

天門冬氨酸 參閱 amino acid。

Asperger's syndrome a form of abnormal personality characterized by social aloofness, lack of interest in other people, stilted and pedantic styles of speech, and an excessive preoccupation with a very specialized interest (such as timetables). It is often considered to be a mild form of *autism.

阿斯普格爾綜合徵 異常人格的一種形式，特徵為疏遠社會，對他人缺乏興趣，語言呆板迂腐，對某種特別愛好（如時刻表）過於着迷。常被認為是一種輕度的孤獨癖。

aspergillosis *n.* a group of conditions caused by fungi of the genus *Aspergillus*,

曲黴病，曲菌病 由曲黴菌屬黴菌，通常為煙曲黴所引起

usually *Aspergillus fumigatus*. These conditions nearly always arise in patients with pre-existing lung disease and fall into three categories. The allergic form most commonly affects asthmatic patients and may cause collapse of segments or lobes of a lung. The colonizing form leads to formation of a fungus ball (*aspergilloma*), usually within a pre-existing cavity in the lung (such as an emphysematous *bulla or a healed tuberculous cavity). Similar fungus balls may be found in other cavities, such as the eye or the sinuses around the nose. The third form of aspergillosis, in which the fungus spreads throughout the lungs and may even disseminate throughout the body, is rare but potentially fatal. It is usually associated with deficiency in the patient's immunity.

Aspergillus *n.* a genus of fungi, including many common moulds, some of which cause infections of the respiratory system in man. The species *A. fumigatus* causes *aspergillosis. *A. niger* is commonly found in the external ear and can become pathogenic.

aspermia *n.* strictly, a lack or failure of formation of semen. More usually, however, the term is used to mean the total absence of sperm from the semen (*see* azoospermia).

asphyxia *n.* suffocation: a life-threatening condition in which oxygen is prevented from reaching the tissues by obstruction of or damage to any part of the respiratory system. Drowning, choking, and breathing poisonous gas all lead to asphyxia. Unless the condition is remedied by removing the obstruction (when present) and by artificial respiration if necessary, there is progressive

的一組疾病。幾乎總是發生於肺部已有病變的患者中，有三種類型。變態反應型多發於哮喘病人，可致肺段或肺葉萎陷。菌落集成型引起黴菌團（曲黴腫）的形成，通常在肺部原有洞腔內（例如氣腫泡或愈合的結核性腔）。類似的黴菌團亦可見於其他腔內，如眼或鼻旁竇。第三種類型的曲黴病罕見卻具有潛在致命性，霉菌擴散至全肺甚至可播散於全身，通常與患者免疫力缺乏有關。

曲黴屬   包括許多普通黴菌的真菌屬，其中一些可致人呼吸系統感染。煙曲黴可引起曲黴病，常見於外耳的黑曲黴亦可致病。

無精，精液缺乏   嚴格意義上為精液形成不足或不能，然而更通常地指精液中毫無精子（參閱 azoospermia）。

窒息   呼吸系統任何部位阻塞或受損而使氧氣不能到達組織的一種有生命危險的狀況。溺水、氣哽、吸入毒氣均可致窒息。除非排除梗阻（若有）並於必要時作人工呼吸加以搶救，將出現進行性紫紺而造成死亡。腦細胞在無氧狀態下存活不超過大約 4 分鐘。

*cyanosis leading to death. Brain cells cannot live for more than about four minutes without oxygen.

aspiration *n.* the withdrawal of fluid from the body by means of suction using an instrument called an *aspirator*. There are various types of aspirator: some employ hollow needles for removing fluid from cysts, inflamed joint cavities, etc.; another kind is used to suck debris and water from the patient's mouth during dental treatment.

抽吸術　用稱為抽吸器的器械從體內吸出液體。抽吸器有多種類型，有些用空心針管從囊腫、發炎關節腔等處抽液，另一種用於牙科治療中從患者口腔吸出殘渣和水。

aspiration cytology the *aspiration of specimens of cells from tumours or cysts through a hollow needle, using a syringe, and their subsequent examination under the microscope after suitable preparation (by staining, etc.). The technique is now used widely, especially for superficial cysts or tumours, and has become a specialized branch of diagnostic pathology. *See also* fine-needle aspiration cytology.

針吸細胞學　用空心針管從腫瘤或囊腫抽出細胞標本並經適當製備後（如染色等）作顯微鏡檢查。此技術現在應用廣泛，尤其用於淺表囊腫或腫瘤，現已成為診斷病理學的一門專門學科。參閱 fine-needle aspiration cytology。

aspirin (acetylsalicylic acid) *n.* a widely used drug that relieves pain and also reduces inflammation and fever. It is taken by mouth – alone or in combination with other analgesics – for the relief of the less severe types of pain, such as headache, toothache, neuralgias, and the pain of rheumatoid arthritis. It is also taken to reduce fever in influenza and the common cold, and daily doses are used in the prevention of coronary thrombosis and strokes. Aspirin works by inhibiting the production of *prostaglandins; it may irritate the lining of the stomach, causing nausea, vomiting, pain, and bleeding. Tablets should not be held on the gum adjacent to a painful tooth as ulceration may occur. High doses cause dizziness, disturbed

阿司匹林（乙醯水楊酸）　一種廣泛使用的止痛、消炎和解熱藥物。用於解除非劇烈疼痛，如頭痛、牙痛、神經痛及類風濕性關節炎疼痛時，可單獨口服或與其他止痛劑合用。還用於患流行性感冒和普通感冒時解熱。其日常劑量也可用於預防冠狀動脈血栓形成與中風。阿司匹林通過抑制前列腺素生成而生效；但因刺激胃黏膜可引起惡心、嘔吐、疼痛及出血。藥片因可引起潰瘍而不應置於貼近痛牙的牙齦上。大劑量可致頭昏、聽力障礙、精神混亂與呼吸過度（參閱 salicylism）。據認為阿司匹林與雷耶綜合徵病因有關，因此若無專門醫囑，不應

hearing, mental confusion, and over-breathing (*see* salicylism). Aspirin has been implicated as a cause of *Reye's syndrome and should therefore not be given to children below the age of 12 unless specifically indicated. *See also* analgesic.

在 12 歲以下兒童中使用。參閱 analgesic。

assay *n.* a test or trial to determine the strength of a solution, the proportion of a compound in a mixture, the potency of a drug, or the purity of a preparation. *See also* bioassay.

測定，鑒定　為確定溶液濃度、合劑中某種化合物之比例、藥效、或製劑純度而作的檢查或試驗。參閱 bioassay。

assimilation *n.* the process by which food substances are taken into the cells of the body after they have been digested and absorbed.

同化（作用）　食物經消化和吸收後被攝入體內細胞的過程。

association area an area of *cerebral cortex that lies away from the main areas that are concerned with the reception of sensory impulses and the start of motor impulses but is linked to them by many neurones known as *association fibres*. The areas of association are thought to be responsible for the elaboration of the information received by the primary sensory areas and its correlation with the information fed in from memory and from other brain areas. They are thus responsible for the maintenance of many higher mental activities. *See also* body image.

聯合區　位於接受感覺衝動與發出運動衝動的主區之外，而經許多稱為聯想纖維的神經元與之相連的大腦皮質區。此區被認為負責加工初級感覺區所接收信息並使其與來自記憶和其他腦區的信息相聯繫，因此起着維持多種高等精神活動的作用。參閱 body image。

association of ideas (in psychology) linkage of one idea to another in a regular way according to their meaning. In *free association* the linkage of ideas arising in dreams or fantasy may be used to discover the underlying motives of the individual. In *word association tests* stimulus words are produced to which the subject has to respond as quickly as possible.

聯想　（心理學）將一種概念與另一種概念按其含義進行有規律的聯繫。在自由聯想中，產生於睡夢或幻想的概念聯繫可用於揭示某人的潛在動機。在詞聯想試驗中，受試者須對提問詞盡快作答。

astasia *n.* an inability to stand for which no physical cause can be found. *Astasia-abasia* is an inability to stand or walk in the absence of any recognizable physical illness. The patient's attempts are bizarre and careful examination reveals contradictory features. It is most commonly an expression of *conversion disorder.

起立不能 不能查出軀體病因的無站立能力。立行不能指無任何明顯身體疾病時所不能站立或行走。患者意圖站立或行走時動作古怪，仔細檢查可發現相互矛盾的特徵。多為轉換性障礙的一種表現。

astemizole *n.* an *antihistamine drug used to treat hay fever and allergic skin conditions. It is administered by mouth. Possible side-effects include weight gain and, on very high dosage, disordered heart rhythm. Trade name: **Hismanal**.

阿司咪唑 一種用於治療枯草熱和變應性皮膚病的口服抗組胺藥。副作用可有體重增加，大劑量服用並可造成心律紊亂。商品名：Hismanal。

aster *n.* a star-shaped object in a cell that surrounds the *centrosome during mitosis and meiosis and is concerned with the formation of the *spindle.

星體 有絲分裂和減數分裂時細胞內圍繞中心體的星狀體，與紡錘體的形成有關。

astereognosis *n. see* agnosia.

實體覺缺失 參閱 agnosia。

asteroid hyalosis *see* hyalitis.

星形玻璃體炎 參閱 hyalitis。

asthenia *n.* weakness or loss of strength.

無力，衰弱，虛弱

asthenic *adj.* describing a personality disorder characterized by low energy, susceptibility to physical and emotional stress, and a diminished capacity for pleasure.

無力的，虛弱的 描述以精力不濟，容易感受身心壓力以及享樂能力減弱為特點的一種性格障礙。

asthenopia *n. see* eyestrain.

眼疲勞 參閱 eyestrain。

asthenospermia *n. see* oligospermia.

精子活力不足 參閱 oligospermia。

asthma *n.* the condition of subjects with widespread narrowing of the bronchial airways, which changes in severity over short periods of time (either spontaneously or under treatment) and leads to cough, wheezing, and difficulty in breathing. *Bronchial asthma* may be

哮喘 患者支氣管氣道廣泛狹窄，引起咳嗽、喘鳴、呼吸困難的狀態。其嚴重程度可在短時間內發生變化（自發地或經治療後）。支氣管哮喘可因接觸到為數眾多的刺激物之一種或數種而加重，包括變應原、

precipitated by exposure to one or more of a wide range of stimuli, including *allergens, drugs (such as aspirin and other NSAIDs and beta blockers), exertion, emotion, infections, and air pollution. The onset of asthma is usually early in life and in atopic subjects (*see* atopy) may be accompanied by other manifestations of hypersensitivity, such as hay fever and dermatitis; however, the onset may be delayed into adulthood or even middle or old age. Treatment is with *bronchodilators, with or without corticosteroids, usually administered via aerosol or dry-powder inhalers, or – if the condition is more severe – via a nebulizer. Oral corticosteroids are reserved for those patients who fail to respond adequately to these measures. Severe asthmatic attacks may need large doses of oral corticosteroids (*see* status asthmaticus). Avoidance of known allergens, especially the house dust mite, allergens arising from domestic pets, and food additives, will help to reduce the frequency of attacks, as will the discouragement of smoking.

Cardiac asthma occurs in left ventricular heart failure and must be distinguished from bronchial asthma, as the treatment is quite different. **–asthmatic** *adj.*

astigmatism *n.* a defect of vision in which the image of an object is distorted, usually in either the vertical or the horizontal axis, because not all the light rays come to a focus on the retina. Some parts of the object may be in focus but light from other parts may be focused in front of or behind the retina. This is usually due to abnormal curvature of the cornea and/or lens (*see* refraction), whose surface resembles part of the surface of an egg (rather than a sphere). The defect

藥物（例如阿司匹林及其他非類固醇類藥物與β-受體阻滯劑）、勞累、情緒、感染和空氣污染。常在幼年發病，特應性患者可伴有枯草熱和皮炎等其他過敏表現（參閱 atopy）。但哮喘發作亦可延遲到成年後，甚至到中老年時。治療用支氣管擴張藥，可單一給藥或與皮質類固醇聯用，通常以氣霧或乾粉吸入器投藥，若病情較重則用噴霧器投藥。口服皮質類固醇僅用於對此療效不良的患者。嚴重的哮喘發作可需大劑量的口服皮質類固醇（參閱 status asthmaticus）。避免已知變應原，特別是室內塵蟎，來自家庭寵物的變應原和食物添加劑及減少吸烟，將有助於減少發作。

　　心源性哮喘發生於左心室心力衰竭時，因其治療不同而須與支氣管哮喘相區別。

散光　因光綫未均聚焦在視網膜上而產生物體影像變形的一種視力缺陷，通常發生在垂直軸或水平軸。物體某些部分可在視網膜前或後聚焦。通常是因角膜和/或晶狀體曲度異常所致（參閱 refraction），其表面類似蛋形面（而非球面）。此種缺陷可用配戴變形度數恰好相反的圓柱透鏡糾正，從而抵消眼睛自身造成的變形。

can be corrected by wearing *cylindrical lenses*, which produce exactly the opposite degree of distortion and thus cancel out the distortion caused by the eye itself. **–astigmatic** *adj.*

astragalus *n. see* talus.

距骨　參閱 talus。

astringent *n.* a drug that causes cells to shrink by precipitating proteins from their surfaces. Astringents are used in lotions to harden and protect the skin and to reduce bleeding from minor abrasions. They are also used in mouth washes, throat lozenges, eye drops, etc., and in antiperspirants.

收斂劑　使細胞表面蛋白質沉澱而導致細胞皺縮的藥物。用在溶劑中以強化和保護皮膚以及輕微擦傷時止血。亦用於漱口液、喉糖啶、滴眼劑等中，以及用於止汗藥中。

astrocyte (astroglial cell) *n.* a type of cell with numerous sheet-like processes extending from its cell body, found throughout the central nervous system. It is one of the several different types of cell that make up the *glia. The cells have been ascribed the function of providing nutrients for neurones and possibly of taking part in information storage processes.

星形細胞（星形膠質細胞）　一種有許多從細胞體伸出的片狀突起的細胞。見於中樞神經系統各處，是神經膠質的幾種組成細胞之一。據認為有營養神經元的功能並可能參與信息存貯過程。

astrocytoma *n.* a brain tumour derived from non-nervous cells (*glia), which – unlike the neurones – retain the ability to reproduce themselves by mitosis. All grades of malignancy occur, from slow-growing tumours whose histological structure resembles normal glial cells, to rapidly growing highly invasive tumours whose cell structure is poorly differentiated (*see* glioblastoma). In adults astrocytomas are usually found in the cerebral hemispheres but in children they also occur in the cerebellum.

星形細胞瘤　由不同於神經元而仍保留經有絲分裂進行繁殖能力的非神經細胞（神經膠質）所產生的一種腦瘤。其惡性程度各不相同，有組織結構類似正常神經膠質細胞且生長緩慢的腫瘤，亦有細胞分化不良的生長迅速侵犯性強的腫瘤（參閱 glioblastoma）。成人中此瘤通常見於大腦半球，兒童亦可發生在小腦。

asymbolia *n. see* alexia.

説示不能　參閱 alexia。

asymptomatic *adj.* not showing any symptoms of disease, whether disease is present or not.

無症狀的　沒表現出任何疾病症狀，無論疾病是否存在。

asynclitism *n.* tilting of the fetal skull towards one or other shoulder causing the top of the skull to be either nearer to the sacrum (*anterior asynclitism* or *Naegele's obliquity*) or nearer to the pubis (*posterior asynclitism* or *Litzmann's obliquity*). These mechanisms enable the fetal head to pass more easily through the maternal pelvis.

頭盆傾勢不均　胎兒頭顱向一肩傾斜而使頭頂靠近骶骨（前頭盆傾勢不均或稱內格勒傾斜），或靠近恥骨（後頭盆傾勢不均或稱利茨曼傾斜）。這些機製使得胎頭較易通過母體骨盆。

asyndesis *n.* a disorder of thought, in which the normal *association of ideas is disrupted so that thought and speech become fragmentary. It is a symptom of schizophrenia, dementia, or confusion.

思想連貫不能　一種正常聯想被中斷而使思維和語言支離破碎的思維障礙，係精神分裂症、痴呆或精神混亂的一種症狀。

asynergia *n. see* dyssynergia.

協同不能　參閱 dyssynergia。

asystole *n.* a condition in which the heart no longer beats, accompanied by the absence of complexes in the electrocardiogram. The clinical features, causes, and treatment are those of *cardiac arrest.

心搏停止　伴有心電圖復合波消失的心臟停止搏動狀態。其臨床特徵、病因及療法與心動停止相同。

atacurium besylate a *muscle relaxant administered by injection during anaesthesia. Trade name: **Tracrium**.

阿曲庫銨苯碘酸鹽　一種麻醉時注射給藥的肌肉鬆弛劑。商品名：Tracrium。

ataraxia *n.* a state of calmness and freedom from anxiety, especially the state produced by tranquillizing drugs.

心氣和平，心神安定　一種平靜，無憂無慮的狀態，尤指因安定劑所致。

atavism *n.* the phenomenon in which an individual has a character or disease known to have occurred in a remote ancestor but not in his parents.

返祖（現象），隔代遺傳　個體帶有其先祖而非父母的特徵或疾病的現象。

ataxia *n.* the shaky movements and unsteady gait that result from the brain's failure to regulate the body's posture and the strength and direction of limb movements. It may be due to disease of the sensory nerves of the *cerebellum. In *cerebellar ataxia* there is clumsiness of

共濟失調　因腦不能調整身體姿勢和四肢活動的力量與方向造成的步態不穩、行動搖晃。可能由感覺神經或小腦病變所致。小腦性共濟失調時隨意運動笨拙，患者步履蹣跚，吐字不清，並可伴眼球震顫。小腦

willed movements. The patient staggers when walking; he cannot pronounce words properly and may have *nystagmus. *Cerebellar* (or *Nonne's*) *syndrome* is a form of cerebellar ataxia. *Friedreich's ataxia* is an inherited disorder appearing first in adolescence. It has the features of cerebellar ataxia, together with spasticity of the limbs. The unsteady movements of *sensory ataxia* are exaggerated when the patient closes his eyes (*see* Romberg's sign). *See also* tabes dorsalis (*or* locomotor ataxia). **–ataxic** *adj*.

atel- (atelo-) *prefix denoting* imperfect or incomplete development. Examples: *atelencephaly* (of the brain); *atelocardia* (of the heart).

atelectasis *n.* failure of part of the lung to expand. This occurs when the cells lining the air sacs (alveoli) are too immature, as in premature babies, and unable to produce the wetting agent (surfactant) with which the surface tension between the alveolar walls is overcome. It also occurs when the larger bronchial tubes are blocked from within by retained secretions, inhaled foreign bodies, or bronchial cancers, or from without by enlarged lymph nodes, such as are found in patients with tuberculosis and lung cancers. The lung can usually be helped to expand by physiotherapy and removal of the internal block (if present) via a *bronchoscope, but prolonged atelectasis becomes irreversible.

ateleiosis *n.* failure of sexual development owing to lack of *pituitary hormones. *See* infantilism, dwarfism.

atenolol *n.* a drug (*see* beta blocker) used to treat angina and high blood pressure. It is taken by mouth and the

（或農內）綜合徵是小腦性共濟失調的一種類型。弗里德賴希共濟失調是一種首先發生於青春期的遺傳病，具有小腦性共濟失調特徵並伴有四肢痙攣。感覺性共濟失調患者在閉目時，其行動不穩程度有所加重（參閱 Romberg's sign）。參閱 tabes dorsalis（或 locomotor ataxia）。

〔前綴〕**發育不全** 發育不完善或不完全。如腦發育不全，心發育不全。

（肺）**膨脹不全** 部分肺未能擴張。當肺泡壁的細胞過於不成熟，如在早產兒中，而不能產生克服肺泡壁間表面張力的濕潤劑（表面活性劑）時，即發生此種情況。亦發生於較大支氣管因分泌物瀦留，異物吸入或支氣管癌造成內部阻塞，或因淋巴結腫大引起外部阻塞時，如在結核病和肺癌患者中。通常可通過物理療法和用支氣管鏡清除內部阻塞（若有）使肺擴張，但長期的肺膨脹不全則不能治癒。

發育不全，幼稚型 垂體激素缺乏而致的性發育障礙。參閱 infantilism，dwarfism。

阿替洛爾 一種用於治療心絞痛和高血壓的口服藥物（參閱 beta blocker）。最常見副作用

commonest side-effects are fatigue, depression, and digestive upsets. Trade name: **Tenormin**.

atheroma *n.* degeneration of the walls of the arteries due to the formation in them of fatty plaques and scar tissue. This limits blood circulation and predisposes to thrombosis. It is common in adults in Western countries. A diet rich in animal fats (*see* cholesterol) and refined sugar, cigarette smoking, obesity, and inactivity are the principal causes. It may be symptomless but often causes complications from arterial obstruction in middle and late life (such as angina pectoris, heart attack, stroke, and gangrene). Treatment is by prevention, but some symptoms may be ameliorated by drug therapy (e.g. angina by glyceryl trinitrate) or by surgical bypass of the arterial obstruction.

atherosclerosis *n.* a disease of the arteries in which fatty plaques develop on their inner walls, with eventual obstruction of blood flow. *See* atheroma.

athetosis *n.* a writhing involuntary movement especially affecting the hands, face, and tongue. It is usually a form of *cerebral palsy. It impairs the child's ability to speak or use his hands; intelligence is often unaffected. Such movements may also be caused by drugs used to treat *parkinsonism or by the withdrawal of phenothiazines (*see also* dyskinesia). **–athetotic** *adj.*

athlete's foot a fungus infection of the skin between the toes: a type of *ringworm. Medical name: **tinea pedis**.

athyreosis *n.* absence of or lack of function of the thyroid gland, causing *cretinism in infancy and *myxoedema in adult life.

是疲勞、抑鬱和胃腸不適。商品名：Tenormin。

動脈粥樣化　動脈壁內脂肪斑和瘢痕組織形成而致的動脈變性。動脈粥樣化限制血液循環並易於造成血栓形成，常見於西方國家成年人中。主要病因有富於動物脂肪（參閱 cholesterol）和精製食糖的飲食、吸煙、肥胖以及缺乏活動。此病可無症狀，但常在中老年時因動脈阻塞引起併發症（例如心絞痛、心臟病、中風和壞疽）。治療有賴於預防，但有些症狀可用藥物（如心絞痛用硝酸甘油）或做動脈阻塞的旁路手術加以改善。

（動脈）粥樣硬化　脂肪斑在動脈內壁上發展並最終產生血流受阻的一種動脈疾病。參閱 atheroma。

手足徐動症，指痙病　主要發生在手、臉和舌的不隨意的扭曲運動，通常為大腦性麻痺的一型。可損害兒童的說話或用手能力，但智力一般不受影響。治療帕金森綜合徵的藥物或吩噻嗪戒斷（參閱 dyskinesia）亦可引起此類運動。

腳癬　趾間皮膚的真菌感染，為癬的一種。醫學用語：腳癬。

甲狀腺功能缺失　甲狀腺功能缺乏而在嬰兒期造成克汀病和成人期的黏液（性）水腫。

atlas *n.* the first *cervical vertebra, by means of which the skull is articulated to the backbone.

寰椎　構成顱骨和脊柱關節的第一頸椎。

ATLS advanced trauma life support, which comprises the treatment programmes for patients who have been subjected to major trauma (e.g. serious road traffic accidents, missile injuries). Doctors, nurses, and paramedical personnel involved in ATLS receive special training for dealing with such emergencies.

現代創傷救護　包含對經受了重大創傷（如嚴重的道路交通事故、導彈損傷）病人的治療方案。參與 ATLS 的醫生、護士和醫輔人員接受處理此類急症的專門訓練。

atony *n.* a state in which muscles are floppy, lacking their normal elasticity. –**atonic** *adj.*

張力缺乏，弛緩　肌肉鬆弛缺乏正常彈性的狀態。

atopen *n.* any substance responsible for *atopy.

特（異反）應原　任何引起特異反應性的物質。

atopy *n.* a form or *allergy in which there is a hereditary or constitutional tendency to develop hypersensitivity reactions (e.g. hay fever, allergic asthma, atopic *eczema) in response to allergens (*atopens*). –**atopic** *adj.*

特（異反）應性　對變應原（特應原）有產生過敏反應（如枯草熱、變應性哮喘、特異性濕疹）的遺傳或體質趨勢的一種變態反應。

ATP (adenosine triphosphate) a compound that contains adenine, ribose, and three phosphate groups and occurs in cells. The chemical bonds of the phosphate groups store energy needed by the cell, for muscle contraction; this energy is released when ATP is split into ADP or AMP. ATP is formed from ADP or AMP using energy produced by the breakdown of carbohydrates or other food substances. *See also* mitochondrion.

三磷酸腺苷　存在於細胞內的含有腺嘌呤、核糖和三個磷酸基的化合物。磷酸基的化學鍵貯存細胞所需能量供肌肉收縮之用，當三磷酸腺苷分解為二磷酸腺苷或一磷酸腺苷時，能量即被釋放。三磷酸腺苷則利用碳水化合物或其他食物分解所產生的能量由二磷酸腺苷或一磷酸腺苷合成。參閱 mitochondrion。

atresia *n.* **1.** congenital absence or abnormal narrowing of a body opening. *Biliary atresia* (affecting the bile duct) causes obstructive jaundice in infancy and is lethal unless corrected surgically;

閉鎖（畸形）　(1) 身體開口的先天性缺失或異常狹窄。膽道閉鎖（發生於膽管）引起嬰兒期阻塞性黃疸，若不經手術矯正可致死。三尖瓣閉鎖阻礙

tricuspid atresia obstructs the blood flow within the heart from the right atrium to the right ventricle. **2.** the degenerative process that affects the majority of ovarian follicles. Usually only one Graafian follicle will ovulate in each menstrual cycle. **–atretic** *adj.*

atri- (atrio-) *prefix denoting* an atrium, especially the atrium of the heart. Example: *atrioventricular* (relating to the atria and ventricles of the heart).

atrial septal defect (ASD) *see* septal defect.

atrioventricular bundle (AV bundle, bundle of His) a bundle of modified heart muscle fibres (*Purkinje fibres*) passing from the *atrioventricular (AV) node forward to the septum between the ventricles, where it divides into right and left bundles, one for each ventricle. The fibres transmit contraction waves from the atria, via the AV node, to the ventricles.

atrioventricular node a mass of modified heart muscle situated in the lower middle part of the right atrium. It receives the impulse to contract from the *sinoatrial node, via the atria, and transmits it through the *atrioventricular bundle to the ventricles.

atrium *n. (pl.* **atria**) **1.** either of the two upper chambers of the *heart. Their muscular walls are thinner than those of the ventricles; the left atrium receives oxygenated blood from the lungs via the pulmonary vein; the right atrium receives deoxygenated blood from the venae cavae. *See also* auricle. **2.** any of various anatomical chambers into which one or more cavities open. **–atrial** *adj.*

從右心房到右心室的血流。**(2)** 大部分卵泡所發生的退化過程。通常每次月經周期僅有一個格雷夫卵泡排卵。

〔前綴〕（心）**房** 專指心房。例如，房室的（與心房、心室有關的）。

房中隔缺損 參閱 septal defect。

房室束 從房室結向前通向室中隔的一束變異的心肌纖維（浦肯野纖維），由此再向左、右心室分為左束和右束。房室束纖維將來自心房的收縮波經房室結傳遞到心室。

房室結 位於右心房下中部的一團變異的心肌。房室結接受經心房從竇房結傳來的收縮衝動，並通過房室束將其傳遞到心室。

(1) 心房 心臟上部兩腔之一。其肌壁薄於心室肌壁；左心房接受經靜脈來自肺部的含氧血，右心房接受來自腔靜脈的脫氧血。參閱 auricle。**(2)** **房** 泛指解剖學上有一個或數個開口的各種腔室。

Atromid-S *n. see* clofibrate.

atrophy *n.* the wasting away of a normally developed organ or tissue due to degeneration of cells. This may occur through undernourishment, disuse, or ageing. Forms of atrophy peculiar to women include the shrinking of the ovary at the menopause and of the *corpus luteum during the menstrual cycle. *Muscular atrophy* is associated with various diseases, such as poliomyelitis.

atropine *n.* a drug extracted from deadly nightshade (*see* belladonna) that inhibits the action of certain nerves of the autonomic nervous system (*see* parasympatholytic). Atropine relaxes smooth muscle and is used to treat biliary colic and renal colic. It also reduces secretions of the bronchial tubes, salivary glands, stomach, and intestines and is used before general *anaesthesia and to relieve peptic ulcers. It is also used to dilate the pupil of the eye. Atropine is administered by mouth, injection, or as eyedrops; common side-effects include dryness of the throat, thirst, and impaired vision. Trade name: **Minims atropine**.

attachment *n.* **1.** (in psychology) the process of developing the first close selective relationship of a child's life, most commonly with the mother. The relationship acts to reduce anxiety in strange settings and forms a base from which children develop further relationships. **2.** (in the National Health Service) working arrangements by which workers employed by public bodies (such as *community nurses and *social workers) are engaged in association with specific general practitioners, caring for their registered patients rather than working solely on a geographical or district basis.

祛脂乙酯　參閱 clofibrate。

萎縮　因細胞變性所致正常發育的器官或組織體積縮小。可發生於營養不良、廢用或老化。女性特有的萎縮現象包括絕經期卵巢萎縮和月經周期中的黃體萎縮。肌萎縮與脊髓灰質炎等多種疾病有關。

阿托品　從顛茄中（參閱 belladonna）提取的抑制自主神經系統中某些神經作用的藥物（參閱 parasympatholytic）。阿托品鬆弛平滑肌，可用於治療膽石絞痛和腎絞痛，還可減少支氣管、唾液腺、胃及腸的分泌，並用於全身麻醉前給藥及緩解消化性潰瘍，亦用於散瞳。可口服，注射或用作滴眼劑。常見副作用有咽喉乾燥、口渴和視力損害。商品名：Minims atropine。

(1) 依戀　（心理學）培養兒童期最初有選擇的親密關係的過程。多為與其母親。這種關係可減輕兒童在陌生環境中的焦慮不安，並形成兒童發展其他關係的基礎。**(2) 隸屬**　（國民保健服務制）公共機構所僱傭人員（如社區保健護士或社會福利工作者）的工作與專職全科醫師相聯繫的工作安排。使其照顧此醫師的登記患者，而非僅依地理或地區劃區進行工作。

attachment disorder a psychiatric disorder in infants and young children resulting from *institutionalization, emotional neglect, or *child abuse. Affected children are either withdrawn, aggressive, and fearful or attention-seeking and indiscriminately friendly. Treatment requires the provision of stable caring adults as parents over a long period of time.

依附障礙　嬰幼兒因進入收容所，遭受情感忽視或虐待兒童而產生的一種精神障礙。患兒或孤僻、好鬥、膽怯，或尋求他人注意，對人一概友好。治療需要有成年人長期給予父母般的愛護。

attention deficit disorder *see* hyperkinetic syndrome.

注意力短缺障礙　參閱 hyperkinetic syndrome。

attenuation *n.* reduction of the disease-producing ability (virulence) of a bacterium or virus by chemical treatment, heating, drying, by growing under adverse conditions, or by passing through another organism. Treated (*attenuated*) bacteria or viruses are used for many *immunizations.

減毒　通過化學處理、加熱、乾燥、逆境培養，或經其他生物傳代培養而降低細菌或病毒的致病力（毒力）。經過處理（減毒）的細菌或病毒用於多種免疫法中。

atticotomy *n.* a surgical operation to remove *cholesteatoma from the ear. It is a form of limited *mastoidectomy.

鼓室上隱窩切開術　切除耳部膽脂瘤的外科手術，為一種局限的乳突切除術。

attrition *n.* (in dentistry) the wearing of tooth surfaces by the action of opposing teeth. A small amount of attrition occurs with age but accelerated wear may occur in *bruxism and with certain diets.

磨耗　（牙科學）相對牙齒的作用造成的牙表面磨損。輕微磨耗隨年齡增長而發生，但嚴重磨耗可因磨牙症或某些飲食所致。

atypical mole syndrome (dysplastic naevus syndrome) a condition in which affected patients have numerous moles, some of which are relatively large and irregular in shape or pigmentation. There may be a family history of this syndrome or of malignant *melanoma.

非典型痣綜合徵（發育異常痣綜合徵）　患者有無數痣的狀況。其中一些痣較大，形狀和著色不規則，可能有此種綜合徵或惡性黑素瘤的家族史。

atypical pneumonia any one of a group of community-acquired *pneumonias that do not respond to penicillin but do respond to such antibiotics as

非典型性肺炎　任何一種用青黴素無效而四環素和紅黴素類抗生素有效的社區性肺炎，包括肺炎支原體感染、鸚鵡熱衣

tetracycline and erythromycin. They include infection with *Mycoplasma pneumoniae*, *Chlamydia psittaci* (*see* psittacosis), and *Coxiella burnetii* (*see* Q fever).

原體感染（參閱 psittacosis）和伯納特立克次體感染（參閱 Q fever）。

audi- (audio-) *prefix denoting* hearing or sound.

〔前綴〕**聽** 聽力或聲音的。

audiogram *n.* the graphic record of a test of hearing carried out on an audiometer.

聽力圖 用聽力計進行聽力測驗的圖形記錄。

audiology *n.* the study of disorders of hearing.

聽力學 對聽力障礙的研究。

audiometer *n.* an apparatus for measuring hearing at different sound frequencies, so helping in the diagnosis of deafness. **–audiometry** *n.*

聽力計 測驗對不同音頻的聽力的儀器，以此幫助診斷耳聾。

audit *n. see* health service planning.

審計 參閱 health service planning。

auditory *adj.* relating to the ear or to the sense of hearing.

聽覺的 與耳或聽覺有關的。

auditory nerve *see* vestibulocochlear nerve.

聽神經 參閱 vestibulocochlear nerve。

Auerbach's plexus (myenteric plexus) a collection of nerve fibres – fine branches of the *vagus nerve – within the walls of the intestine. It supplies the muscle layers and controls the movements of *peristalsis.

奧厄巴赫神經叢 腸壁內的一簇神經纖維——迷走神經的細支，分布於肌層並控制蠕動運動。

aura *n.* the forewarning of an epileptic or migrainous attack. An *epileptic aura* may take many forms. The *migrainous aura* may affect the patient's eyesight with brilliant flickering lights or blurring of vision, but it may also result in numbness or weakness of the limbs.

先兆 癲癇或偏頭痛發作的預告。癲癇先兆可有多種形式，偏頭痛先兆可影響視力，患者眼前金光閃爍或視覺模糊，但亦可引起肢體麻木或無力。

aural *adj.* relating to the ear.

耳的 與耳有關的。

auranofin *n.* a *gold preparation administered by mouth to treat rheumatoid arthritis. Side-effects include nausea, abdominal pain, diarrhoea, and mouth ulcers. Trade name: **Ridaura**.

金諾芬　一種治療類風濕性關節炎的口服含金製劑。副作用有惡心、腹痛、腹瀉及口腔潰瘍。商品名：Ridaura。

Aureomycin *n.* *see* chlortetracycline.

金黴素　參閱　chlortetracycline。

auricle *n.* **1.** a small pouch in the wall of each *atrium of the heart: the term is also used incorrectly as a synonym for *atrium*. **2.** *see* pinna.

(1) 心耳　兩心房壁內各有的小囊。此詞也被誤用作心房的同義詞。**(2) 耳廓**　參閱pinna。

auriscope (otoscope) *n.* an apparatus for examining the eardrum and the passage leading to it from the ear (external meatus). It consists of a funnel (speculum), a light, and lenses (see illustration).

耳鏡　檢查鼓室及由耳至鼓室通道（外耳道）的器械。由漏斗（窺器）、照明燈和透鏡組成（見圖）。

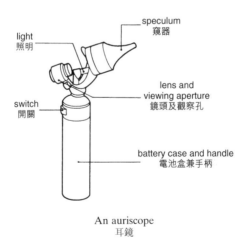

An auriscope
耳鏡

auscultation *n.* the process of listening, usually with the aid of a *stethoscope, to sounds produced by movement of gas or liquid within the body. Auscultation is an aid to diagnosis of abnormalities of the heart, lungs, intestines, and other organs

聽診（法）　通常藉助聽診器聽取體內氣體或液體產生的聲音之過程。聽診是根據不同疾病所引起的特殊聲音變化，而對心、肺、腸和其他器官進行診斷的輔助手段。

according to the characteristic changes in sound pattern caused by different disease processes. **–auscultatory** *adj*.

auscultatory gap a silent period in the knocking sounds heard with a stethoscope over an artery, between the systolic and diastolic blood pressures, when the blood pressure is measured with a *sphygmomanometer.

聽診無音間隙 用血壓計測量血壓時，用聽診器在動脈上聽到的在收縮壓和舒張壓之間的一段無音間歇。

Australia antigen another name for the *hepatitis B antigen, which was first discovered in the blood of an Australian aborigine. This disease is caused by a virus of which the Australia antigen forms part.

澳大利亞抗原 乙型肝炎抗原的另一名稱。最早發現於一位澳大利亞土著人血液內。乙型肝炎由帶有澳大利亞抗原的一種病毒所致。

aut- (auto-) *prefix denoting* self. Example: *autokinesis* (voluntary movement).

〔前綴〕**自己，自體，自動，自發** 如自體運動（隨意運動）。

autism *n*. **1. (Kanner's syndrome, infantile autism)** a rare and severe psychiatric disorder of childhood, with an onset before the age of $2\frac{1}{2}$ years. It is marked by severe difficulties in communicating and forming relationships with other people, in developing language, and in using abstract concepts; repetitive and limited patterns of behaviour (*see* stereotypy); and obsessive resistance to tiny changes in familiar surroundings. Autistic children find it hard to understand how other people feel, and so tend to remain isolated even into adult life. Many are intellectually subnormal, but some are very intelligent and may even be gifted in specific areas (*see* idiot savant). Genetic factors and brain damage are probably important causes. Treatment is not specific, but lengthy specialized education is usually necessary. Behaviour problems and anxiety can be controlled with behaviour therapy

(1) 孤獨癖 一種罕見而嚴重的兒童精神障礙。在兩歲半之前發病。特徵為在與他人交流及建立關係方面，在語言發展方面，及使用抽象概念方面均有嚴重困難，行為方式重複且單調（參閱 stereotypy），以及固執地抗拒熟悉環境中的微小變化。孤獨癖患兒難以理解他人的感覺；因而甚至於成年後依然孤獨。許多患兒智力低下，但有些智力超常，甚至具有特殊方面的天賦（參閱 idiot savant）。遺傳因素和腦損傷可能為其主要病因。無特殊療法，但通常需要長期的特殊教育。行為問題和焦慮不安可用行為療法和藥物加以控制（如吩噻嗪）。**(2) 自我中心主義** 逃避現實的思想轉向以自我為中心的幻想思維狀態，為人格障礙和精神分裂症的一種症狀。

and drugs (such as *phenothiazines). **2.** the condition of retreating from realistic thinking to self-centred fantasy thinking: a symptom of personality disorder and schizophrenia. **–autistic** *adj.*

autoagglutination *n.* the clumping together of the body's own red blood cells by antibodies produced against them, which occurs in acquired haemolytic anaemia (an *autoimmune disease).

自體凝集（作用）　紅細胞受到自體產生的抗體作用而凝集成塊。此種現象發生於獲得性溶血性貧血中（一種自體免疫性疾病）。

autoantibody *n.* an antibody formed against one of the body's own components in an *autoimmune disease.

自體抗體　自體免疫性疾病中產生的作用於身體自身某種組成成分的抗體。

autochthonous *adj.* **1.** remaining at the site of formation. A blood clot that has not been carried in the bloodstream from its point of origin is described as autochthonous. **2.** originating in an organ without external stimulus, like the beating of the heart.

本處發生的　**(1)** 仍在其形成的部位上。如未被從原始部位帶入血流的血塊被描述為本處發生的。**(2)** 無外部刺激而自發於器官內的。如心搏。

autoclave 1. *n.* a piece of equipment for sterilizing surgical instruments, dressings, etc. It consists of a chamber, similar to a domestic pressure cooker, in which the articles are placed and treated with steam at high pressure. **2.** *vb.* to sterilize in an autoclave.

(1) 高壓滅菌器　對外科器械、敷料等進行滅菌的一種裝置。由一個類似家用高壓鍋的容器構成，物品置於其中並用高壓蒸汽處理。**(2) 高壓滅菌**　在高壓滅菌器內消毒。

autocrine *adj.* describing the production by a cell of substances, such as hormones or *growth factors, that can influence the growth of the cell that produces them.

自體分泌　描述激素或生長因子等物質的產生，這些物質可影響其分泌細胞的生長。

autogenous vaccine *see* autovaccine.

自體菌苗　參閱　autovaccine。

autograft *n.* a tissue graft taken from one part of the body and transferred to another part of the same individual. The repair of burns is often done by grafting on strips of skin taken from

自體移植物　取自身體某一部位而移植到同一個體另一部位的組織移植物。燒傷的修復常常是通過從身體其他部位，往往是上臂或股部，移植皮條來

elsewhere on the body, usually the upper arm or thigh. Unlike *homografts, autografts are not rejected by the body's immunity defences. *See also* skin graft, transplantation.

完成。與同種移植物不同，自體移植物不受身體免疫反應排斥。參閱 skin graft，transplantation。

autoimmune disease one of the growing number of otherwise unrelated disorders now suspected of being caused by the inflammation and destruction of tissues by the body's own antibodies (*autoantibodies*). These disorders include acquired haemolytic anaemia, pernicious anaemia, rheumatic fever, rheumatoid arthritis, glomerulonephritis, systemic lupus erythematosus, and several forms of thyroid dysfunction, including Hashimoto's disease. It is not known why the body should lose the ability to distinguish between substances that are 'self' and those that are 'non-self'.

自體免疫性疾病 一組日益增多的疾病。除現在均被懷疑為由身體自身抗體造成的炎症和組織破壞所致而外，彼此別無關聯。此類疾病包括後天性溶血性貧血、惡性貧血、風濕熱、類風濕性關節炎、腎小球性腎炎、系統性紅斑狼瘡，以及包括橋本病的幾種甲狀腺功能障礙。身體失去識別「自身」與「非自身」物質的能力的原因仍未弄明。

autoimmunity *n.* a disorder of the body's defence mechanisms in which antibodies (*autoantibodies*) are produced against certain components or products of its own tissues, treating them as foreign material and attacking them. *See* autoimmune disease, immunity.

自體免疫 一種身體防禦機制的紊亂，此時機體針對自體某組成部分或其組織產物產生抗體，將其視為異物加以攻擊。參閱 autoimmune disease，immunity。

autoinoculation *n.* the accidental transfer of inoculated material from one site in the body to another. Following vaccination against smallpox, for example, satellite lesions may occur around the site of inoculation. Sometimes the conjunctiva is affected.

自體接種 接種物從身體一處意外轉移至另一處。例如接種天花後，接種部位周圍可發生衛星樣損害，有時累及結膜。

autointoxication *n.* poisoning by a toxin formed within the body.

自體中毒 體內形成的毒素引起的中毒。

autologous *adj.* denoting a graft that is derived from the recipient of the graft.

自體固有的 指取自移植接受者自身的移植物。

autolysis *n.* the destruction of tissues or cells brought about by the actions of their own enzymes. *See* lysosome.

自體溶解，自溶　組織或細胞因其酶的作用造成的破壞。參閱 lysosome。

automatism *n.* behaviour that may be associated with *epilepsy, in which the patient performs well-organized movements or tasks. The movements may be simple and repetitive, such as hand clapping, or they may be so complex as to mimic a person's normal conscious activities.

自動症　可能與癲癇有關的行為。患者作出組織有序的動作或工作，可為簡單和重複性的，如拍掌，也可為模仿人們平時有意識活動的複雜動作。

autonomic nervous system the part of the *nervous system responsible for the control of bodily functions that are not consciously directed, including regular beating of the heart, intestinal movements, sweating, salivation, etc. The autonomic system is subdivided into *sympathetic* and *parasympathetic nervous systems*. Sympathetic nerves lead from the middle section of the spinal cord and parasympathetic nerves from the brain and lower spinal cord. The heart, smooth muscles, and most glands receive fibres of both kinds: the interplay of sympathetic and parasympathetic reflex activity (the actions are often antagonistic) governs their working. Sympathetic nerve endings liberate *noradrenaline as a neurotransmitter; parasympathetic nerve endings release *acetylcholine.

自主神經系統　神經系統中負責控制不受意識支配的正常心搏、腸運動、出汗、流涎等身體功能之部分。此系統分為交感神經系統與副交感神經系統。交感神經始於脊髓中段，副交感神經始於腦和脊髓下段。心臟、平滑肌和大部分腺體均接受二者的纖維，交感和副交感神經反射活動的相互作用（常為拮抗作用）則控制其功能。交感神經末梢釋放充當神經介質的去甲腎上腺素，副交感神經末梢釋放乙酰膽鹼。

autoploidy *n.* the normal condition in cells or individuals, in which each cell has a chromosome set consisting of *homologous pairs, enabling cells to divide normally. **–autoploid** *adj., n.*

同源性　細胞或個體的正常狀態。每個細胞均有一套同源偶對組成的染色體，使細胞可以正常分裂。

autopsy (necropsy, post mortem) *n.* dissection and examination of a body after death in order to determine the

屍體解剖　為確定死亡原因或存在某種疾病而在死後進行的屍體解剖和檢查。

cause of death or the presence of disease processes.

autoradiography (radioautography) *n.* a technique for examining the distribution of a radioactive *tracer in the tissues of an experimental animal. The tracer is injected into the animal, which is killed after a certain period. Thin sections of its organs are placed in close contact with a radiation-sensitive material, such as a photographic emulsion, and observed under a microscope. Blackening of the film indicates a high concentration of radioactive material.

自體放射照相術 一種檢查放射性示踪劑在實驗動物組織內分布情況的技術。把示踪劑注入動物，在一段時間後將其殺死，使其器官薄片與放射綫敏感物質，如照相乳膠密切接觸，然後於顯微鏡下進行觀察，底片陰影處表明有高濃度的放射性物質。

autorefractor *n.* a machine that automatically determines the required correction for a spectacle lens. *See also* optometer.

自動式屈光檢查儀 一種自動確定眼鏡鏡片所需的矯正度數的儀器。參閱 optometer。

autoscopy *n.* the experience of seeing one's whole body as though from a vantage point some distance away. It can be a symptom in *epilepsy. *See also* out-of-the-body experience.

自窺幻覺 仿佛從遠方的高處看見自己全身的體驗。可為癲癇的一種症狀。參閱 out-of-the-body experience。

autosome *n.* any chromosome that is not a *sex chromosome and occurs in pairs in diploid cells. **–autosomal** *adj.*

常染色體 任何在二倍體細胞內成對出現的非性染色體。

autosuggestion *n.* self-suggestion or self-conditioning that involves repeating ideas to oneself in order to change psychological or physiological states. Autosuggestion is used primarily in *autogenic training*, a technique used to help patients control their anxiety or their habits. *See* suggestion.

自我暗示 對自己重複某種觀念的自我提示或自我調整，以改變心理或生理狀態。主要用於自律訓練法，即幫助患者控制其焦慮或習慣的一項技術。參閱 suggestion。

autotransfusion *n.* reintroduction into a patient of blood that has been lost from the patient's circulation during surgical operation. The blood is collected by suction during the operation, filtered to

自體輸血 將病人手術時從循環中失去的血液重新輸入體內。這些血液手術時通過抽吸收集，過濾除去氣泡與小血塊後經滴注輸回病人靜脈。

remove bubbles and small blood clots, and returned into one of the patient's veins through a drip.

autotrophic (lithotrophic) *adj.* describing organisms (known as *autotrophs*) that synthesize their organic materials from carbon dioxide and nitrates or ammonium compounds, using an external source of energy. *Photoautotrophic* organisms, including green plants and some bacteria, derive their energy from sunlight; *chemoautotrophic* (or *chemosynthetic*) organisms obtain energy from inorganic chemical reactions. All autotrophic bacteria are nonparasitic. *Compare* heterotrophic.

自營的（無機營養的） 描述利用外界能源從二氧化碳、氮或銨類化合物中合成其有機物質的生物體（稱為自營生物）。包括綠色植物和某些細菌的光自營生物從陽光取得能量；化學自營（或化學合成）生物從無機化學反應中獲得能量。所有自營細菌均為非寄生性菌。與 heterotrophic 對比。

autovaccination *n.* the use of an *autovaccine.

自體菌苗接種 使用自體菌苗進行接種。

autovaccine (autogenous vaccine) *n.* a *vaccine prepared by isolating specimens of bacteria from an infected patient, culturing them, and killing them. By injecting this vaccine back into the patient, it was hoped that the body's resistance to the infection would be stimulated. Although such vaccines were once much favoured for the treatment of boils, there is no good evidence that the dead bacteria are any more likely to stimulate immunity than the living and dead bacteria already present in the body.

自體菌苗 將受感染者體內分離出的細菌標本進行培養和滅活後製成的菌苗。過去曾希望通過將此種菌苗注射給患者而產生抗感染力。雖然這類菌苗曾廣泛用於癤的治療，但並無確證表明這種死菌比體內原有活菌和死菌更易產生免疫力。

aux- (auxo-) *prefix denoting* increase; growth. Example: *auxocardia* (enlargement of the heart).

增加，發育 例如心擴大（心臟的增大）。

auxotroph *n.* a strain of a microorganism, derived by mutation, that requires one or more specific factors for growth not needed by the parent organism.

營養缺陷型 一株由突變產生的微生物，其生長需要一種或數種其母體所不需要的特殊因子。

avascular *adj.* lacking blood vessels or having a poor blood supply. The term is usually used with reference to cartilage.

無血管的　缺乏血管或供血不良的。此詞常用於軟骨。

aversion therapy a form of *behaviour therapy that is used to reduce the occurrence of undesirable behaviour, such as sexual deviations or drug addiction. *Conditioning is used, with repeated pairing of some unpleasant stimulus with a stimulus related to the undesirable behaviour. An example is pairing the taste of beer with electric shock in the treatment of alcoholism. *See also* sensitization.

厭惡療法　一種行為療法。用於減少性慾錯亂或藥癮等不良行為的發生，將令人厭惡的刺激和與惡習有關的刺激反覆配對進行條件反射化。如在酒精中毒治療中將啤酒味道與電休克配對。參閱 sensitization。

avitaminosis *n.* the condition caused by lack of a vitamin. *See also* deficiency disease.

維生素缺乏（病）　維生素缺乏所致的疾病。參閱 deficiency disease。

avoidant *adj.* describing a personality type characterized by self-consciousness, hypersensitivity to rejection and criticism from others, avoidance of normal situations because of their potential risk, high levels of tension and anxiety, and consequently a restricted life.

迴避的　描述一種性格，特徵為害羞，對他人的拒絕和批評過於敏感，迴避有潛在危險的正常情形，高度緊張和焦慮，因此導致生活局限。

avulsion *n.* **1.** (also **evulsion**) the tearing or forcible separation of part of a structure. For example, a tendon may be torn from the bone to which it attaches or the skin of the scalp may be torn from the underlying tissue and bone. **2.** (in dentistry) the knocking out of a tooth by trauma. The tooth may be replanted (*see* replantation).

(1) 撕脱　撕開或強行分開結構的一部分。例如，可將腱從其附着的骨上撕開，或將頭皮從下層組織和骨撕開。**(2) 牙脱落**　（牙科學）外傷所致的牙齒脱落。脱落之牙可重新植入（參閱 replantation）。

axilla *n.* (*pl.* **axillae**) the armpit. –**axillary** *adj.*

腋，腋窩

axis *n.* **1.** a real or imaginary line through the centre of the body or one of its parts or a line about which the body

(1) 軸　通過人體或人體某部分中央的一條真實或想象的直綫，或身體或身體某部分繞其

or a part rotates. **2.** the second *cervical vertebra, which articulates with the atlas vertebra above and allows rotational movement of the head.

旋轉的直綫。**(2) 樞椎** 第二頸椎。上與寰椎聯成關節，使頭可以轉動。

axolemma *n.* the fine cell membrane, visible only under the electron microscope, that encloses the protoplasm of an *axon.

軸膜 僅在電子顯微鏡下可見的包圍軸索原生質的細胞薄膜。

axon *n.* a nerve fibre: a single process extending from the cell body of a *neurone and carrying nerve impulses away from it. An axon may be over a metre in length in certain neurones. In large nerves the axon has a sheath (*neurilemma*) made of *myelin; this is interrupted at intervals by gaps called *nodes of Ranvier*, at which branches of the axon leave. An axon ends by dividing into several branches called *telodendria*, which make contact with other nerves or with muscle or gland membranes.

軸突 一根神經纖維，從神經元細胞體伸出並向外輸送衝動的單個突起。某些神經元的軸突長度超過 1 米。大神經中軸突有髓磷脂形成的鞘（神經鞘），此鞘前稱為郎維埃結的缺口多處隔斷，由斷處發出軸突分支。軸突末端是稱為終樹突的幾根分支，與其他神經、肌肉、或腺體膜相接觸。

axonotmesis *n.* rupture of nerve fibres (axons) within an intact nerve sheath. This may result from prolonged pressure or crushing and it is followed by degeneration of the nerve beyond the point of rupture. The prognosis for *nerve regeneration is good. *Compare* neurapraxia, neurotmesis.

軸索斷傷 完整神經鞘內的神經纖維（軸索）斷裂，可因長期擠壓所致。其遠段隨之發生變性。神經再生的預後良好。與 neurapraxia，neurotmesis 對比。

axoplasm *n.* the semifluid material of which the *axon of a nerve cell is composed. It flows slowly outwards from the cell body.

軸漿，軸質 組成神經細胞軸突的半液體物質，從細胞體緩慢流出。

azapropazone *n.* an anti-inflammatory drug (*see* NSAID) used to treat rheumatoid arthritis, osteoarthritis, ankylosing spondylitis, and gout. It is administered by mouth. Possible side-effects include

阿扎丙宗 用於治療類風濕性關節炎、骨關節炎、關節強硬性脊椎炎和痛風的抗炎藥（參閱 NSAID）。口服。可致副作用有皮膚對光敏感、體液瀦留

sensitivity of skin to light, fluid retention, and bleeding from the bowel. Trade name: **Rheumox**.

和腸道出血。商品名：Rheumox。

azatadine *n.* an *antihistamine drug used to treat hay fever, urticaria, itching, and stings. It is administered by mouth. Possible side-effects include drowsiness, headache, nausea, and loss of appetite. Trade name: **Optimine**.

阿扎他定 用於治療枯草熱、蕁麻疹、瘙癢和螫傷的口服抗組胺藥。可致副作用有嗜睡、頭痛、惡心和食慾不振。商品名：Optimine。

azathioprine *n.* an *immunosuppressive drug, used mainly to aid the survival of organ or tissue transplants. It has also been used in the treatment of acute and chronic leukaemias and inflammatory bowel disease (e.g. ulcerative colitis). Azathioprine may damage bone marrow, causing blood disorders. It may also cause muscle wasting and skin rashes. Trade name: **Imuran**.

硫唑嘌呤 一種免疫抑制劑，主要用於幫助移植器官或組織存活，亦用於治療急性和慢性白血病，以及炎性腸病（如潰瘍性結腸炎）。此藥可損害骨髓引起血液病，亦可引起肌肉萎縮及皮疹。商品名：Imuran。

azelaic acid an antibacterial drug applied externally as a cream in the treatment of acne. Possible side-effects include local irritation and light sensitivity. Trade name: **Skinoren**.

壬二酸 一種以乳膏外用治療痤瘡的抗菌藥。可致副作用有局部刺激和輕微過敏。商品名：Skinoren。

azelastine *n.* an *antihistamine drug administered as a metered-dose nasal spray for the treatment of hay fever. Possible side-effects include nasal irritation and disturbances of taste sensation. Trade name: **Rhinolast**.

氮䓬斯汀 一種按規定劑量用於治療枯草熱的抗組胺鼻噴霧劑。可致副作用有鼻腔刺激與味覺紊亂。商品名：Rhinolast。

azithromycin *n.* an *antibiotic used to treat respiratory, skin, soft-tissue, and other infections, especially those caused by the organism *Chlamydia trachomatis*. It is administered by mouth. Possible side-effects include allergic reactions, nausea, and vomiting. Trade name: **Zithromax**.

阿齊紅黴素 一種用於治療呼吸道、皮膚、軟組織感染和其他尤其是沙眼衣原體所致感染的抗生素。口服。可致副作用有變態反應、惡心和嘔吐。商品名：Zithromax。

azlocillin *n.* a penicillin-type antibiotic used especially to treat infections caused

阿洛西林 一種青黴素類抗生素。特別用於治療綠膿假單胞

by *Pseudomonas aeruginosa*. It is administered by intravenous infusion; possible side-effects include allergic reactions, nausea, and vomiting. Trade name: **Securopen**.

菌引起的感染。靜脈輸注。可致副作用有變態反應、惡心和嘔吐。商品名：Securopen。

azo- (azoto-) *prefix denoting* a nitrogenous compound, such as urea. Example: *azothermia* (raised temperature due to nitrogenous substances in the blood).

〔前綴〕**偶氮基**　指尿素等含氮化合物。如氮血熱（血中含氮物質引起的體溫升高）。

azoospermia (aspermia) *n.* the complete absence of sperm from the seminal fluid. This is due either to failure of formation of sperm by the seminiferous tubules within the testes or to a blockage in the ducts that conduct sperm from the testes. A biopsy of the testis is necessary in order to differentiate these two causes of azoospermia; if a blockage is present it may be possible to relieve it surgically (*see* epididymovasostomy).

精子缺乏（無精）　精液中完全無精子。原因可為睾丸內細精管未能形成精子。或將精子輸出睾丸的導管阻塞，需作睾丸活組織檢查以辨別精子缺乏的這兩種原因。若有阻塞，可用手術排除（參閱 epididymovasostomy）。

azotaemia *n.* a former name for *uraemia.

氮血（症）　尿毒症之舊名。

azoturia *n.* the presence in the urine of an abnormally high concentration of nitrogen-containing compounds, especially urea.

氮尿　尿中含氮化合物尤指尿素濃度過高。

aztreonam *n.* an antibiotic administered by injection used to treat infections of the lungs, bones, skin, and soft tissues caused by Gram-negative organisms (*see* Gram's stain). It is especially useful for treating lung infections in children with cystic fibrosis. Possible side-effects include skin rashes, diarrhoea, and vomiting. Trade name: **Azactam**.

氨曲南　一種用於治療革蘭氏陰性菌引起的肺、骨、皮膚和軟組織感染的注射用抗生素（參閱 Gram's stain）。對治療患囊性纖維變性肺部感染的兒童尤其有效。可致副作用有皮疹、腹瀉及嘔吐。商品名：Azactam。

azygos vein an unpaired vein that arises from the inferior vena cava and drains into the superior vena cava, returning blood from the thorax and abdominal cavities.

奇靜脈　由下腔靜脈發出進入上腔靜脈的一條不成對的靜脈，回流胸腔與腹腔的血液。

B

Babinski reflex *see* plantar reflex.

baby blues a colloquial name for the fleeting misery and tearfulness that affects about half of all pregnant women, especially those having their first baby. The state should not be confused with the condition of *puerperal depression.

bacillaemia *n.* the presence of bacilli in the blood, resulting from infection.

bacille Calmette-Guérin *see* BCG.

bacilluria *n.* the presence of bacilli in the urine, resulting from a bladder or kidney infection. *See* cystitis.

bacillus *n.* (*pl.* **bacilli**) any rod-shaped bacterium. *See also* Bacillus, Lactobacillus, Streptobacillus.

Bacillus *n.* a large genus of Gram-positive spore-bearing rodlike bacteria. They are widely distributed in soil and air (usually as spores). Most feed on dead organic material and are responsible for food spoilage. The species *B. anthracis*, which is nonmotile, causes *anthrax, a disease of farm animals transmissible to man. *B. polymyxa*, commonly found in soil, is the source of the *polymyxin group of antibiotics. *B. subtilis* may cause conjunctivitis in man; it also produces the antibiotic *bacitracin.

bacitracin *n.* an antibiotic produced by certain strains of bacteria and effective against a number of microorganisms. It is usually applied externally, to treat

巴賓斯基反射　參閱 plantar reflex。

嬰兒憂鬱症　約半數孕婦，尤其是初孕者，所感受的短時痛苦和悲哀之通俗名稱。此種狀態須與產褥抑鬱症相區別。

桿菌血症　因感染而引起血液中存在桿菌。

卡介苗　參閱 BCG。

桿菌尿　因膀胱或腎臟感染而導致的尿液中含有桿菌。參閱 cystitis。

桿菌　任何桿狀細菌。參閱 Bacillus，Lactobacillus，Streptobacillus。

芽胞桿菌屬　產生芽胞的革蘭氏陽性桿狀細菌一大屬。廣泛分布在土壤和空氣中（常以芽胞形式）。大多數以死亡的有機物為能量並引起食物腐敗。不運動的炭疽桿菌引起牲畜炭疽病，並可傳染給人。土壤中常有的多黏芽胞桿菌是多黏菌素類抗生素的來源。枯草桿菌可在人類引起結膜炎，也產生抗生素桿菌肽。

桿菌肽　一種由某些菌株所產生並對多種微生物有效的抗生素。通常外用以治療皮膚、眼或鼻的感染，亦可用作腸道抗

infections of the skin, eyes, or nose, but can be given by mouth as an intestinal antiseptic or by injection. The principal toxic effect is on the kidneys. Trade names: **Cicatrin**, **Polybactrin**.

backbone (spinal column, spine, vertebral column) *n.* a flexible bony column extending from the base of the skull to the small of the back. It encloses and protects the spinal cord, articulates with the skull, ribs, and hip girdle, and provides attachment for the muscles of the back. It is made up of individual bones (*see* vertebra) connected by discs of fibrocartilage (*see* intervertebral disc) and bound together by ligaments. The backbone of a newborn baby contains 33 vertebrae: seven cervical (neck), 12

菌劑口服或注射。主要的毒性反應為腎損害。商品名：Cicatrin，Polybactrin。

脊柱 從顱骨底部延伸至骶尾部的可彎曲骨性柱。它包繞並保護脊髓，與顱骨、肋骨和髖帶形成關節，為背肌之附着點。脊柱由經纖維軟骨盤連接（參閱 intervertebral disc）和韌帶結合在一起的單塊椎骨組成（參閱 vertebra）。新生兒脊柱有 33 塊椎骨：7 塊頸椎、12 塊胸椎、5 塊腰椎、5 塊骶椎和 4 塊尾椎。成人的骶椎和尾椎融合而成兩塊獨立的骨頭（分別為骶骨和尾骨）；因此成

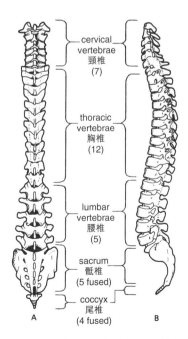

cervical vertebrae 頸椎 (7)

thoracic vertebrae 胸椎 (12)

lumbar vertebrae 腰椎 (5)

sacrum 骶椎 (5 fused)

coccyx 尾椎 (4 fused)

A   B

The backbone, seen from the back (A) and left side (B)
脊椎背面觀 (A) 和左側面觀 (B)

thoracic (chest), five lumbar (lower back), five sacral (hip), and four coccygeal. In the adult the sacral and coccygeal vertebrae become fused into two single bones (sacrum and coccyx, respectively); the adult vertebral column therefore contains 26 bones (see illustration). Anatomical name: **rachis**.

人脊柱只有26塊椎骨（見圖）。解剖學用語：脊柱。

bacteraemia *n.* the presence of bacteria in the blood: a sign of infection.

菌血症 血液中存在細菌。為感染的一種體徵。

bacteri- (bacterio-) *prefix denoting* bacteria. Example: *bacteriolysis* (dissolution of).

〔前綴〕**細菌，菌** 例如溶菌（作用）。

bacteria *pl. n.* (*sing.* **bacterium**) a group of microorganisms all of which lack a distinct nuclear membrane (and hence are considered more primitive than animal and plant cells) and have a cell wall of unique composition (many antibiotics act by destroying the bacterial cell wall). Most bacteria are unicellular; the cells may be spherical (*coccus), rod-shaped (*bacillus), spiral (*Spirillum), comma-shaped (*Vibrio) or corkscrew-shaped (*spirochaete). Generally, they range in size between 0.5 and 5µm. Motile species bear one or more fine hairs (flagella) arising from their surface. Many possess an outer slimy *capsule, and some have the ability to produce an encysted or resting form (*endospore). Bacteria reproduce asexually by simple division of cells; incomplete separation of daughter cells leads to the formation of *colonies consisting of different numbers and arrangements of cells. Some colonies are filamentous in shape, resembling those of fungi. Some bacteria may reproduce sexually by *conjugation.

Bacteria are very widely distributed. Some live in soil, water, or air; others are parasites of man, animals, and plants.

細菌 一類均無明顯核膜（因而被認為較動物和植物細胞原始），只有由獨特成分組成細胞壁的微生物（許多抗生素通過破壞細菌的細胞壁而起作用）。細菌多為單細胞，細胞可為球狀（球菌）、桿狀（桿菌）、螺旋形（螺旋菌）、弧形（弧菌）或螺旋狀（螺旋體）。大小一般在 0.5~5µm 之間。可動的細菌帶有一根或多根源於體表的細毛（鞭毛），許多細菌外層有一黏性莢膜，有些具有形成包囊或靜止狀態（內孢子）的能力。細菌經細胞簡單分裂無性繁殖，子細胞的不完全分裂導致細胞數量和排列各異的菌落形成。有些菌落為與真菌形狀相似的絲狀。有些細菌可經接合而有性繁殖。

細菌分布廣泛，一些存在於土壤、水或空氣中，其他的則寄生於人、動物或植物。許多寄生菌對宿主無害，有些則產生毒素而致病（參閱 endotoxin，exotoxin）。

Many parasitic bacteria do not harm their hosts; some cause diseases by producing poisons (*see* endotoxin, exotoxin).

bactericidal *adj.* being capable of killing bacteria. Substances with this property include antibiotics, antiseptics, and disinfectants; they are known as *bactericides*. *Compare* bacteriostatic.

殺菌的 能殺滅細菌的，具此特性的物質包括抗生素、防腐劑和消毒劑，統稱為殺菌劑。與 bacteriostatic 對比。

bacteriology *n.* the science concerned with the study of bacteria. It is a branch of microbiology. **-bacteriological** *adj.* **-bacteriologist** *n.*

細菌學 研究細菌的科學，為微生物學的一門分支學科。

bacteriolysin *n. see* lysin.

溶菌素 參閱 lysin。

bacteriophage (phage) *n.* a virus that attacks bacteria. In general, a phage consists of a head, tail, and tail fibres, all composed of protein molecules, and a core of DNA. The tail and tail fibres are responsible for attachment to the bacterial surface and for injection of the DNA core into the host cell. The phage grows and replicates in the bacterial cell, which is eventually destroyed with the release of new phages. Each phage acts specifically against a particular species of bacterium. This is utilized in *phage typing*, a technique of identifying bacteria by the action of known phages on them. *See also* lysogeny.

噬菌體 一種侵襲細菌的病毒。一般包括頭、尾和尾部纖維，均由蛋白質分子和一個 DNA 核心組成。其尾和尾部纖維使噬菌體附着於細菌表面，並將 DNA 核心注入宿主細胞。它在細菌細胞內生長並複製，最終隨新噬菌的釋放而破壞細菌細胞。每一種噬菌體專門作用於一種細菌，這一特點被用於噬菌體分型，即一種通過已知噬菌體對細菌的作用來鑒別細菌的技術。參閱 lysogeny。

bacteriostatic *adj.* capable of inhibiting or retarding the growth and multiplication of bacteria. Erythromycin is bacteriostatic. *Compare* bactericidal.

抑菌的 能抑制或延緩細菌生長和繁殖的。紅黴素為一種抑菌劑。與 bactericidal 對比。

bacterium *n. see* bacteria.

細菌 參閱 bacteria。

Bacteroides *n.* a genus of Gram-negative, mostly nonmotile, anaerobic rodlike bacteria. They are normally

擬桿菌屬 革蘭氏陰性厭氧桿狀細菌一屬，多數不運動。正常存在於哺乳動物消化道和泌

present in the alimentary and urinogenital tracts of mammals and are found in the mouth, particularly in dental plaque associated with periodontal disease. Some species have now been classified into new genera, *Porphyromonas* and *Prevotella*.

尿生殖道中，亦見於口腔，尤其在與牙周病有關的牙斑中。其中一些菌株現已歸入擬桿菌屬。

Bactrim *n. see* co-trimoxazole.

複方新諾明　參閱 co-trimoxazole。

bagassosis *n.* a form of external allergic *alveolitis caused by exposure to the dust of mouldy bagasse, the residue of sugar cane after the sugar has been extracted, which is used in the production of hardboard and other thermal boards. Symptoms usually appear in the evening after exposure during the day and include fever, malaise, irritant cough, and respiratory distress.

蔗塵沉着病，蔗塵肺　因接觸發霉的蔗塵所致的一種外源性變應性肺泡炎。蔗渣是榨糖後的甘蔗殘渣，用於生產硬質纖維板和耐熱板。通常為白天接觸蔗塵後於傍晚出現發熱、不適、刺激性咳嗽和呼吸窘迫等症狀。

Baghdad boil *see* oriental sore.

巴格達癤　參閱 oriental sore。

Baker's cyst a cyst that occurs behind the knee, either originating from a naturally occurring bursa or resulting from the protrusion of synovial membrane through a weakness in the knee-joint capsule.

貝克囊腫　膝後部囊腫，可源於自然形成的囊或因膝關節滑膜向後膨出所致。

BAL 1. *see* bronchoalveolar lavage. **2.** British Anti-Lewisite (*see* dimercaprol).

(1) 支氣管肺泡灌洗　參閱 bronchoalveolar lavage。
(2) 二巰丙醇　參閱 dimercaprol。

balanitis *n.* inflammation of the glans penis, usually associated with tightness of the foreskin (*phimosis). It is more common in childhood than in adult life. An acute attack is associated with redness and swelling of the glans. Treatment is by antibiotics, and further attacks are prevented by *circumcision. In *Zoon's plasma cell balanitis* persistent

龜頭炎　陰莖龜頭的炎症。常與包皮過緊（包莖）有關，兒童較成人多見。急性期龜頭紅腫用抗生素治療，並行包皮環切術以防復發。佐恩漿細胞龜頭炎患者龜頭上持續出現發亮紅斑，其病因不明。乾燥性龜頭炎是一種以龜頭上乳白斑為特徵的自體免疫疾病。

shiny red patches develop on the glans; the cause is unknown. *Balanitis xerotica obliterans* is an autoimmune condition characterized by ivory-white patches on the glans.

balanoposthitis *n.* inflammation of the foreskin and the surface of the underlying glans penis. It usually occurs as a consequence of *phimosis and represents a more extensive local reaction than simple *balanitis. The affected areas become red and swollen, which further narrows the opening of the foreskin and makes passing urine difficult and painful. Treatment of an acute attack is by administration of antibiotics, and further attacks are prevented by *circumcision.

龜頭包皮炎 包皮和陰莖龜頭表面的炎症，常由包莖所致。較單純性龜頭炎局部反應更為廣泛。炎症區域紅腫，使得包皮開口處進一步狹窄，引起排尿困難和疼痛。急性炎症用抗生素治療，並行包皮環切術預防復發。

balantidiasis *n.* an infestation of the large intestine of man with the parasitic protozoan *Balantidium coli*. Man usually becomes infected by ingesting food or drink contaminated with cysts from the faeces of a pig. The parasite invades and destroys the intestinal wall, causing ulceration and *necrosis, and the patient may experience diarrhoea and dysentery. Balantidiasis is a rare cause of dysentery, mainly affecting farm workers; it is treated with various antibiotics, carbarsone, and *diiodohydroxyquinoline.

小袋纖毛蟲病 寄生性原生動物結腸小袋纖毛蟲所致的人體大腸感染。通常因攝入豬糞中包囊污染的食物或飲料而致。結腸小袋纖毛蟲入侵並破壞腸壁，引起潰瘍與壞死，病人可出現腹瀉和痢疾。小袋纖毛蟲病罕見引起痢疾，患者主要為農場工人。治療可用多種抗生素、卡巴肿和雙碘喹啉。

Balantidium *n.* a genus of one of the largest parasitic *protozoans affecting man (70μm or more in length). The oval body is covered with threadlike cilia (for locomotion). *B. coli*, normally living in the gut of pigs as a harmless *commensal, occasionally infects man (*see* balantidiasis).

小袋纖毛蟲屬 感染人類的最大寄生性原生動物屬之一（70 μm 或更長）。卵圓形軀體由綫狀纖毛覆蓋（利於運動）。結腸小袋纖毛蟲正常情況下作為無害共生體寄居於豬腸，偶爾感染人（參閱 balantidiasis）。

baldness *n. see* alopecia.

禿（髮），脫髮 參閱 alopecia。

Balkan nephropathy a type of kidney failure that is prevalent in the former Yugoslavia. The cause is unknown. It is associated with a high incidence of carcinoma of the epithelium of the proximal renal tubules.

巴爾幹腎病　流行於前南斯拉夫的腎衰竭之一型，其病因不明，與近曲腎小管上皮癌的高發生率有關。

ball-and-socket joint *see* enarthrosis.

球窩關節，杵臼關節　參閱 enarthrosis。

ballistocardiograph *n.* an instrument for recording the displacement of the whole body produced by the ejection of blood with each heartbeat. The normal record produced by such an instrument (*ballistocardiogram*) may be altered by disease of the heart or aortic valve (*see* aortic regurgitation, aortic stenosis).

心衝擊描記器　記錄每次心搏射出血液引起全身移位的儀器。據此產生的正常記錄（心衝擊描記圖）可因心臟或主動脈瓣病變而改變（參閱 aortic regurgitation，aortic stenosis）。

balloon *n.* an inflatable plastic cylinder of variable size that is mounted on a thin tube and used for dilating narrow areas in blood vessels (*see* coronary angioplasty) or in the alimentary tract (*strictures). It is also used to prevent the reflux of solutions being injected, e.g. into a vessel during *angiography.

氣囊　裝在細管上大小各異的可膨脹塑料筒。用於擴張血管內狹窄部分（參閱 coronary angioplasty）或消化道狹窄部分。亦用於防止注入溶液的回流，如血管造影術時注入靜脈的溶液回流。

ballottement *n.* the technique of examining a fluid-filled part of the body to detect a floating object. During pregnancy, a sharp tap with the fingers, applied to the uterus through the abdominal wall or the vagina, causes the fetus to move away and then return to impart an answering tap to the examiner's hand as it floats back to its original position. This confirms that swelling of the uterus is due to a fetus rather than a tumour or other abnormality.

衝擊觸診（法）　檢查體內某一充滿液體部分以探測某個浮動物體的手法。孕期中用手指經腹壁或陰道衝擊子宮，可使胎兒移開，當胎兒浮回原位時產生對檢查者手的振盪。由此證實子宮腫大是因胎兒而非腫瘤或其他異常所致。

balneotherapy *n.* the treatment of disease by bathing, usually in the

浴療法　通常在溫泉的礦泉水中以洗浴治療疾病。曾一度流

mineral-containing waters of hot springs. The once fashionable 'water cures', taken at spas, certainly had a more psychological than physical effect. Today, specialized remedial treatment in baths, under the supervision of physiotherapists, is used to alleviate pain and improve blood circulation and limb mobility in arthritis and in nerve and muscle disorders.

行的溫泉「水療」，其心理作用大於生理作用。如今在理療醫師的監督管理下，專業化浴療用於減輕疼痛，加速血液循環及增強關節炎和神經與肌肉疾患病人肢體的靈活性。

bandage *n.* a piece of material, in the form of a pad or strip, applied to a wound or used to bind around an injured or diseased part of the body.

綳帶 塊狀或帶狀材料，用於敷蓋傷口或包繞身體受傷或患病部位。

Bandl's ring *see* retraction ring.

班德爾環 參閱 retraction ring。

Banti's syndrome a disorder in which enlargement and overactivity of the spleen occurs as a result of increased pressure within the splenic vein. The commonest cause is *cirrhosis of the liver.

班蒂綜合徵 脾靜脈壓力升高導致脾腫大和功能亢進的疾病。最常見病因為肝硬化。

barbiturate *n.* any of a group of drugs, derived from barbituric acid, that depress activity of the central nervous system and were formerly used as sedatives and hypnotics. They are classified into three groups according to their duration of action – short, medium, and long. Because they produce *tolerance and psychological and physical *dependence, have serious toxic side-effects (*see* barbiturism), and can be fatal following large overdosage, barbiturates have been largely replaced in clinical use by safer drugs. The main exceptions are the very short-acting drug *thiopentone, which is still used to induce anaesthesia, and the long-acting *phenobarbitone, used to control some forms of epilepsy.

巴比妥酸鹽 一組抑制中樞神經系統的巴比妥酸衍化藥物。過去用作鎮靜劑和催眠藥。根據其作用持續時間分為三類：短效、中效和長效。此類藥產生耐藥性和心理與生理依賴性，有嚴重毒副作用（參閱 barbiturism），大劑量可致死，因此在臨床上基本已被其他較為安全的藥物替代。主要的例外有超短效的硫噴妥鈉，仍用於誘導麻醉；和長效的苯巴比妥，用於控制某些類型的癲癇。

barbiturism *n.* addiction to drugs of the barbiturate group. Signs of intoxication include confusion, slurring of speech, yawning, sleepiness, loss of memory, loss of balance, and reduction in muscular reflexes. Withdrawal of the drugs must be undertaken slowly, over 1–3 weeks, to avoid the withdrawal symptoms of tremors and convulsions, which can prove fatal.

巴比妥中毒 對巴比妥類藥物成癮。中毒體徵包括精神混亂、語言含糊、打呵欠、嗜睡、健忘、平衡喪失和肌反射減弱。停藥必須緩慢，需 1~3 周，以避免震顫和驚厥等可致死的停藥症狀。

barefoot doctor *see* medical assistant.

赤腳醫生 參閱 medical assistant。

baritosis *n.* a lung disease – a form of *pneumoconiosis – caused by inhaling barium dust. It gives dramatic shadows on chest X-rays but no respiratory disability.

鋇塵沉着病，鋇塵肺 吸入鋇塵引起的肺部疾病，為塵肺的一種。X 綫胸片有明顯陰影，但無呼吸障礙。

barium sulphate a barium salt, insoluble in water, that is opaque to X-rays and is used as a contrast medium in radiography of the stomach and intestines. *See also* enema.

硫酸鋇 一種不溶於水並不透 X 綫的鋇鹽。用作胃腸放射照相術的造影劑。參閱 enema。

Barlow's sign *see* congenital dislocation of the hip.

巴洛徵 參閱 congenital dislocation of the hip。

baroreceptor (baroceptor) *n.* a collection of sensory nerve endings specialized to monitor changes in blood pressure. The main receptors lie in the *carotid sinuses and the *aortic arch; others are found in the walls of other large arteries and veins and some within the walls of the heart. Impulses from the receptors reach centres in the medulla; from here autonomic activity is directed so that the heart rate and resistance of the peripheral blood vessels can be adjusted appropriately.

壓力感受器 一羣專門監測血壓變化的感覺神經末梢。主要感受器位於頸動脈竇和主動脈弓，另外一些位於其他大動脈壁與大靜脈壁，還有一些位於心壁內。來自感受器的衝動傳至延髓中樞，由此調整自主神經活動，使心率和外周血管阻力可作適當調節。

barotitis *n.* disease of the ear caused by changing air pressure, as experienced during air travel.

氣壓耳炎 氣壓變化引起的耳病。如在空中旅行時。

barotrauma *n.* damage to the ear, *Eustachian tube, or paranasal sinuses caused by changes in ambient pressure, as experienced during air flight or deep-sea diving.

氣壓傷　空中旅行或深海潛水時周圍氣壓改變所致的耳、咽鼓管或鼻旁竇損傷。

Barr body *see* sex chromatin.

巴爾小體　參閱 sex chromatin。

Barrett's oesophagus a condition in which the normal squamous *epithelium lining the oesophagus is replaced by columnar epithelium because of damage caused by *gastro-oesophageal reflux. The condition may be associated with an ulcer (*Barrett's ulcer*), and the epithelium has an abnormally high likelihood of undergoing malignant change.

巴雷特食管　由胃食管返流所致的損傷使食管內壁正常的鱗狀上皮被柱狀上皮取代的狀況。可伴有潰瘍（巴雷特潰瘍），此種上皮發生惡變的可能性極高。

barrier cream a preparation used to protect the skin against water-soluble irritants (e.g. detergents, breakdown products of urine). Usually applied in the form of a cream or ointment and often containing a silicone (such as *dimethicone), barrier creams are useful in the alleviation of various skin disorders, including napkin rash and bedsores.

護膚脂　保護皮膚不受水溶性刺激物（如去污劑、尿液分解物）損害的製劑。往往為乳膏或軟膏，常含有硅酮（如二甲硅油），對減輕尿布疹和褥瘡等多種皮膚病有效。

bartholinitis *n.* inflammation of *Bartholin's glands. In *chronic bartholinitis* cysts may form in the glands as a result of blockage of their ducts. In *acute bartholinitis* abscess formation may occur (*Bartholin's abscess*).

前庭大腺炎　巴托林腺的炎症。患慢性前庭大腺炎時，可因腺管阻塞而形成管內囊腫，急性前庭大腺炎患者可有膿腫形成（巴托林膿腫）。

Bartholin's glands (greater vestibular glands) a pair of glands that open at the junction of the vagina and the external genitalia (vulva). Their secretions lubricate the vulva and so assist penetration by the penis during coitus. The *lesser vestibular glands*, around the vaginal opening, perform the same function.

巴托林腺　開口於陰道和外生殖器（外陰）接合處的一對腺體。其分泌物潤滑外陰而利於性交時陰莖的插入。位於陰道口周圍的前庭小腺功能與此相同。

Bartonella (Haemobartonella) *n*. a genus of parasitic rod-shaped or rounded microorganisms, usually regarded as rickettsiae. They occur in the red blood cells and cells of the lymphatic system, spleen, liver, and kidneys. *B. bacilliformis* causes *bartonellosis in man.

巴爾通體屬　通常被視為立克次體的寄生性桿狀或球形微生物一屬。存在於紅細胞和淋巴系統、脾、肝及腎細胞中。桿菌狀巴爾通體引起人類巴爾通體病。

bartonellosis *n*. an infectious disease, confined to high river valleys in Peru, Ecuador, and Colombia, caused by the rickettsia *Bartonella bacilliformis*. The parasite, present in red blood cells and cells of the lymphatic system, is transmitted to man by sandflies. There are two clinical types of the disease: *Oroya fever* (*Carrion's disease*), whose symptoms include fever, anaemia, and enlargement of the liver, spleen, and lymph nodes; and *verruga peruana*, characterized by wart-like eruptions on the skin that can bleed easily and ulcerate. Oroya fever accounts for nearly all fatalities. Bartonellosis can be treated successfully with penicillin and other antibiotics and blood transfusions may be given to relieve the anaemia.

巴爾通體病　由立克次體桿菌狀巴爾通體引起的一種傳染病，限發於秘魯、厄瓜多爾和哥倫比亞的高原河谷。存在於紅細胞和淋巴系統細胞中的這種寄生蟲由白蛉傳播給人。該病有兩種臨床類型；奧羅亞熱（卡里翁病），症狀有發熱、貧血和肝、脾、淋巴結腫大；秘魯疣，特徵為易出血和形成潰瘍的皮膚疣狀疹。該病中死亡幾乎均由奧羅亞熱所致。青黴素或其他抗生素治療巴爾通體病療效很好，可輸血以減輕貧血。

basal cell carcinoma (BCC) the commonest form of skin cancer. Although classified as a malignant tumour, it grows very slowly. BCC usually occurs on the central area of the face, especially in fair-skinned people; the prevalence increases greatly with exposure to sunlight. The initial sign is a spot or lump that fails to heal, enlarging to a diameter of 1 cm over five years or so. Treatment is straightforward, using *curettage and cautery, surgical excision, *cryotherapy, or *radiotherapy. Only if neglected for decades does a BCC eventually become a so-called *rodent ulcer* and destroy the surrounding tissue. However, the term

基底細胞癌　最常見的皮膚癌。雖被列為惡性腫瘤但生長緩慢。通常出現於面部正中，尤在淺膚色人種中；日光照射可大為增加其發生率。最初體徵是不能愈合的一個斑點或腫塊，約經 5 年時間擴大至 1 cm。須用刮除術和烙術、手術切除術、冷凍療法或放射療法治療，僅在數十年不經治療的情況下，基底細胞癌才會最終發展為所謂的侵蝕性潰瘍而破壞周圍組織。而「侵蝕性潰瘍」一詞有時仍用於任何基底細胞癌。

'rodent ulcer' is still sometimes used to mean any basal cell carcinoma.

basal ganglia several large masses of grey matter embedded deep within the white matter of the *cerebrum (see illustration). They include the *caudate* and *lenticular nuclei* (together known as the *corpus striatum*) and the *amygdaloid nucleus*. The lenticular nucleus consists of the *putamen* and *globus pallidus*. The basal ganglia have complex neural connections with both the cerebral cortex and thalamus: they are involved with the regulation of voluntary movements at a subconscious level.

基底神經節　深藏於大腦白質中的幾個大灰質團塊（見圖），包括尾狀核與豆狀核（合稱紋狀體）及杏仁核。豆狀核由殼和蒼白球組成。基底神經節與大腦皮質和丘腦均有複雜的神經聯繫，參與下意識層次的隨意運動調節。

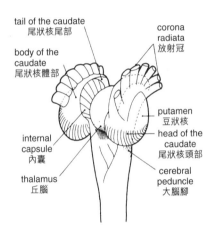

tail of the caudate
尾狀核尾部

body of the caudate
尾狀核體部

corona radiata
放射冠

internal capsule
內囊

putamen
豆狀核

head of the caudate
尾狀核頭部

thalamus
丘腦

cerebral peduncle
大腦腳

The basal ganglia and neighbouring parts
(seen from the front)
基底神經節及附近結構
（前面觀）

basal metabolism the minimum amount of energy expended by the body to maintain vital processes, e.g. respiration, circulation, and digestion. It is expressed in terms of heat production per unit of body surface area per day (*basal metabolic rate – BMR*), and for an

基礎代謝　身體維持呼吸、循環和消化等生命過程的最低耗能量，用每天每單位體表面積產熱量來表示（基礎代謝率）。男性基礎代謝平均每天為 1.7 千卡（7.115 千焦耳）。基礎代謝率可用直接測

average man the BMR is 1.7 Calories (7.115 kilojoules) per day. BMR may be determined by the direct method, in which the subject is placed in a respiratory chamber and the amount of heat evolved is measured, or (more normally) by the indirect method, based on the *respiratory quotient. Measurements are best taken during a period of least activity, i.e. during sleep and 12–18 hours after a meal, under controlled temperature conditions. Various factors, such as age, sex, and particularly thyroid activity, influence the value of the BMR.

定法測量；即受試者位於呼吸室內測量所放出的熱量，或（更常見）採用基於呼吸商的間接測定法。活動最少時測量最佳，即在控制溫度條件下於進食後 12~18 小時的睡眠中進行。許多因素影響基礎代謝率的值，如年齡、性別、尤其是甲狀腺功能。

basement membrane the thin delicate membrane that lies at the base of an *epithelium. It is composed of mucopolysaccharide and fibres of protein.

基膜 位於上皮基底的脆弱薄膜。由黏多糖和蛋白纖維構成。

base pairing the linking of the two strands of a DNA molecule by means of hydrogen bonds between the bases of the nucleotides. Adenine always pairs with thymine and cytosine with guanine. *See* DNA.

鹼基配對 一個 DNA 分子中的雙鏈在核苷酸內鹼基之間由氫鍵的連接。腺嘌呤始終與胸腺嘧啶配對，胞嘧啶則與鳥嘌呤配對。參閱 DNA。

basilar artery an artery in the base of the brain, formed by the union of the two vertebral arteries. It extends from the lower to the upper border of the pons Varolii and then divides to form the two posterior cerebral arteries.

基底動脈 由兩側椎動脈匯合而成的位於大腦基底部的一根動脈。從腦橋下部伸向上部邊緣，然後分支形成兩支大腦後動脈。

basilar membrane a membrane in the *cochlea of the ear that separates two of the three channels (scalae) that run the length of the spiral cochlea. The organ of Corti is situated on the basilar membrane, inside the scala media.

基（底）層 耳蝸內將貫穿整個螺旋耳蝸的三個腔管（階）中的二個分開的一層膜。柯蒂器位於蝸管內基底層上。

basilic vein a large vein in the arm, extending from the hand along the back of the forearm, then passing

貴要靜脈 上臂的一條大靜脈；從手部沿前臂上行，於肘部向前轉入上臂內側。

forward to the inner side of the arm at the elbow.

basion *n.* the midpoint of the anterior border of the large hole (foramen magnum) at the base of the *skull.

顱底點　顱骨底部大孔（枕骨大孔）前緣中點。

basophil *n.* a variety of white blood cell distinguished by the presence in its cytoplasm of coarse granules that stain purple-black with *Romanowsky stains. The function of basophils is poorly understood, but they are capable of ingesting foreign particles and contain *histamine and *heparin. There are normally $30–150 \times 10^6$ basophils per litre of blood.

嗜鹼細胞　胞漿中用羅曼諾夫斯基染劑染色時為紫黑色粗顆粒的多種白細胞，對其功能了解甚少，但具有攝取外來微粒的能力，並含有組胺與肝素。正常狀態下每升血液中有 $30~150 \times 10^6$ 個嗜鹼細胞。

basophilia *n.* **1.** a property of a microscopic structure whereby it shows an affinity for basic dyes. **2.** an increase in the number of certain white blood cells (*basophils) in the blood, which may occur in a variety of blood diseases.

(1) 嗜鹼性　對鹼性染劑顯示親和力的顯微結構特性。**(2)** 嗜鹼細胞增多（症）　血液某些白細胞（嗜鹼細胞）數量增加，可發生在多種血液病中。

basophilic *adj.* readily stainable by basic dyes: showing *basophilia.

嗜鹼（染色）的　易為鹼性染劑着色的，顯示嗜鹼性的。

bathyaesthesia *n.* sensation experienced in the deeper parts of the body, such as the joints and muscles.

深部感覺　軀體較深部位如關節和肌肉的感覺。

Batten's disease one of a group of rare hereditary disorders (known as the *neuronal ceroid lipofuscinoses*) that also includes *Tay-Sachs disease. Fatty substances accumulate in the cells of the nervous system, causing progressive dementia, epilepsy, spasticity, and visual failure. The condition starts in late infancy or childhood. There is no treatment.

巴滕病，少年型神經元蠟樣脂褐質症　一類罕見的遺傳性疾病（稱為神經元蠟樣脂褐質沉積症），其中亦包括泰薩氏病。脂肪物質在神經系統細胞中蓄積，引起進行性痴呆、癲癇、痙攣狀態和視力障礙。此病始於嬰兒後期或兒童期，且不能治療。

battered baby syndrome *see* nonaccidental injury.

虐兒綜合徵，受虐嬰兒綜合徵　參閱 nonaccidental injury。

Bazin's disease a rare disease of young women in which tender nodules develop under the skin in the calves. The nodules may break down and ulcerate, though they may clear up spontaneously. The cause is unknown. Medical name: **erythema induratum**.

巴贊病，硬結性皮結核 一種小腿皮下出現觸痛性結節的罕見疾病，發生於年輕女性。結節可破裂形成潰瘍，雖然亦可自然愈合。病因不明。醫學用語：硬結性紅斑。

BCC *see* basal cell carcinoma.

基底細胞癌 參閱 basal cell carcinoma。

BCG (bacille Calmette-Guérin) a strain of tubercle bacillus that has lost the power to cause tuberculosis but retains its antigenic activity; it is therefore used to prepare a vaccine against the disease.

卡介苗 喪失致病力而保留抗原性的結核桿菌菌株；用於製備抗結核病疫苗。

Beau's lines transverse depressions on the nails appearing some weeks after a severe illness, such as pneumonia or a heart attack.

博氏綫 患肺炎或心臟病發作等重病數周後，指甲上所出現的橫凹綫。

beclomethasone *n.* a *corticosteroid drug that is administered by inhaler to treat hay fever and asthma and is applied externally in the treatment of inflammatory skin disorders. Possible side-effects include nasal irritation and hoarseness. Trade names: **Beconase**, **Becotide**, **Propaderm**.

倍氯米松 一種治療枯草熱和哮喘的皮質類固醇藥物，亦外用於治療炎性皮膚病。可致副作用有鼻腔刺激和聲音嘶啞。商品名：Beconase，Becotide，Propaderm。

becquerel *n.* the *SI unit of activity of a radioactive source, being the activity of a radionuclide decaying at a rate of one spontaneous nuclear transition per second. It has replaced the curie. Symbol: Bq.

貝可（勒爾） 放射源強度的國際單位。即放射性核素以每秒發生一次自發原子核躍遷的速度蛻變時的強度。已取代居里。符號：Bq。

bed bug a bloodsucking insect of the genus *Cimex*. *C. hemipterus* of the tropics and *C. lectularius* of temperate regions have reddish flattened bodies and vestigial wings. They live and lay their eggs in the crevices of walls and furniture and emerge at night to suck blood; although

臭蟲 臭蟲屬的一種吸血昆蟲。熱帶的熱帶臭蟲和溫帶的溫帶臭蟲有淺紅色扁平軀體和發育不全的翅膀，在牆壁和家具縫隙中棲息及產卵，夜間出來吸血。雖然臭蟲非已知的疾病傳播媒介，但被其叮咬處易

bed bugs are not known vectors of disease, their bites leave a route for bacterial infection. Premises can be disinfested with appropriate insecticides.

受細菌感染。臭蟲活動之處可用合適的殺蟲劑消滅。

bed occupancy the number of hospital beds occupied by patients expressed as a percentage of the total beds available in the ward, specialty, hospital, area, or region. It may be recorded in relation to a defined point in time or more usefully for a period, when the calculation is based on bed-days. It is used with other indices (such as *discharge rate) to assess the demands for hospital beds in relation to diseases, specialties, or populations and hence to gauge an appropriate balance between health needs and residential (hospital) resources.

床位占有率 某病房、專科、醫院、地區或行政區總床位中病床所占百分率。按床位占有日統計時，可根據時點或更有用的時期進行記錄。床位占有率與其他指標（如出院率）共同用於評估疾病、專科或人羣的醫院床位需要量，以求達到醫療需求之間的平衡。

bedsore (decubitus ulcer, pressure sore) *n.* an ulcerated area of skin caused by irritation and continuous pressure on part of the body: a hazard to be guarded against in all bedridden (especially unconscious) patients. Healing is hindered by the reduced blood supply to the area, and careful nursing is necessary to prevent local gangrene. The patient's position should be changed frequently, and the buttocks, heels, elbows, and other regions at risk kept dry and clean.

褥瘡 因刺激和長期壓迫身體某部分引起的皮膚潰瘍。所有臥床病人（尤其昏迷病人）都需預防。褥瘡的愈合因該部位血流減少而受到妨礙，須細緻護理以防止局部壞疽。病人體位應經常變換，並保持臀部、足跟、肘及其他易患部位乾燥清潔。

bedwetting *n. see* enuresis.

遺尿 參閱 enuresis。

behaviourism *n.* an approach to psychology postulating that only observable behaviour need be studied, thus denying any importance to unconscious processes. Behaviourists are concerned with the laws regulating the occurrence of behaviour (*see* conditioning).
–behaviourist *n.*

行為主義 主張只需研究可觀察到的行為而否認潛意識過程具有重要性的心理學派。行為主義者注重研究控制行為發生的規律（參閱 conditioning）。

behaviour modification the use of the methods of behaviourist psychology (*see* behaviourism) – especially operant *conditioning – to alter people's behaviour. Behaviour modification has wider applications than *behaviour therapy, since it is also used in situations in which the client is not ill; for example, in education. *See also* chaining, prompting.

行為矯正法　行為心理學方法的運用（參閱 behaviourism），尤其是操作性條件反射化，以改變人的行為。行為矯正法亦用於當事人無病的情形中，如教育中，故較行為療法運用更廣。參閱 chaining, prompting。

behaviour therapy treatment based on the belief that psychological problems are the products of faulty learning and not the symptoms of an underlying disease. Treatment is directed at the problem or target behaviour and is designed for the particular patient, not for the particular diagnostic label that has been attached to him. *See also* aversion therapy, conditioning, desensitization, response prevention.

行為療法　基於心理問題是由錯誤感知所致，而非某一潛在疾病之症狀這種信念而採取的治療。針對患者的心理問題或目標行為進行，根據患者的特定情況而非所診斷的疾病設計治療方案。參閱 aversion therapy, conditioning, desensitization, response prevention。

bejel (endemic syphilis) *n.* a long-lasting nonvenereal form of *syphilis that occurs in the Balkans, Turkey, eastern Mediterranean countries, and the dry savannah regions of North Africa; it is particularly prevalent where standards of personal hygiene are low. The disease is spread among children and adults by direct body contact. Early skin lesions are obvious in the moist areas of the body (mouth, armpits, and groin) and later there may be considerable destruction of the tissues of the skin, nasopharynx, and long bones. Wartlike eruptions in the anal and genital regions are common. Bejel, which is rarely fatal, is treated with penicillin.

非性病性梅毒（地方性梅毒）　一種持久的非性病性梅毒，發生於巴爾幹半島各國、土耳其、東地中海各國和北非的熱帶大草原地區。在個人衛生水平低下的地區尤其流行。此病由身體直接接觸在兒童與成人中傳播。早期時身體潮濕部位（口腔、腋窩和腹股溝）的皮膚損害明顯，後期時可有皮膚、鼻咽與長骨組織很大的破壞。肛門及生殖器部位常有疣狀疹。此病致死罕見，治療用青黴素。

bel *n. see* decibel.

貝（耳）　參閱 decibel。

belladonna *n.* **1.** deadly nightshade (*Atropa belladonna*): the plant from which the drug atropine is obtained.

顛茄 (1) 從中可提取阿托品的植物。(2) 從顛茄獲得並從中提取阿托品的毒性生物鹼。顛

2. the poisonous alkaloid derived from deadly nightshade, from which atropine is extracted. Preparations of belladonna are used as an anticholinergic drug (*see* parasympatholytic). Trade names: **Alophen**, **Bellocarb**.

bell and pad a psychological method of treating bed-wetting in children and adults. When the subject starts to pass urine it is detected by a pad (or by sheets of metallic mesh) and this sets off a bell (or loud buzzer). The modern form of the apparatus has a small electronic sensor worn under the underclothes and produces a loud bleep. The purpose of the alarm is to waken the subject, who then empties the bladder fully. A process of conditioning leads to the subject learning to be dry. It is effective in about 80% of cases.

belle indifference a symptom of *conversion disorder in which an apparently grave physical affliction (which has no physical cause) is accepted in a smiling and calm fashion.

Bell's palsy paralysis of the *facial nerve causing weakness of the muscles of one side of the face and an inability to close the eye. In some patients hearing may be affected so that sounds seem abnormally loud, and a loss of taste sensation may occur. The cause of this condition is unknown and recovery normally occurs spontaneously.

belly *n.* **1.** the *abdomen or abdominal cavity. **2.** the central fleshy portion of a muscle.

Bence-Jones protein (Bence-Jones albumose) a protein of low molecular

茄製劑用作抗膽鹼能藥（參閱 parasympatholytic）。商品名：Alophen，Bellocarb。

鈴墊療法 一種治療兒童與成人遺尿的心理學方法。受試者開始排尿時由一墊子（或金屬網片）測知並觸響鈴（或蜂鳴器），新式裝置中有一個佩在內衣下的小型電子傳感器可發出嘟嘟之聲。響鈴是為了喚醒受試者，然後排空膀胱。建立條件反射過程可使受試者學會控制排尿，約80%的病例有效。

快意淡漠 一種轉換性障礙症狀。表現為微笑鎮定地接受明顯的嚴重軀體痛苦（無生理性病因）。

貝爾麻痺 面神經麻痺導致一側面部肌無力和閉眼不能。有些患者聽力可受影響而感覺聲音過高，並可出現味覺喪失。其病因不明，常自發痊愈。

腹 （**1**） 腹部或腹腔。（**2**）肌肉的中央多質部分。

本斯-瓊斯蛋白 一種見於多發性骨髓瘤、淋巴瘤、白血病和

weight found in the urine of patients with multiple *myeloma, *lymphoma, *leukaemia, and *Hodgkin's disease.

霍奇金病患者尿中的低分子量蛋白。

bendrofluazide (bendroflumethazide) *n.* a potent diuretic used in the treatment of conditions involving retention of fluid, such as congestive heart failure, hypertension, and *oedema. Its actions and side-effects are similar to those of *chlorothiazide. Trade names: **Aprinox**, **Contyl**.

苄氟噻嗪 一種強效利尿劑。用於治療充血性心力衰竭、高血壓和水腫之類液體瀦留狀況；其作用與副作用與氯噻嗪相似。商品名：Aprinox，Contyl。

bends *n. see* compressed air illness.

減壓病 參閱 compressed air illness。

Benedict's test a test for the presence of sugar in urine or other liquids. A few drops of the test solution are added to *Benedict's solution*, prepared from sodium or potassium citrate, sodium carbonate, and copper sulphate. The mixture is boiled and shaken for about two minutes, then left to cool. The presence of up to 2% glucose is indicated by the formation of a reddish, yellowish, or greenish precipitate, the highest levels corresponding to the red coloration, the lowest (about 0.05%) to the green.

本尼迪克特試驗 檢測尿液或其他液體中是否存在糖的試驗。將幾滴被測溶液加入用枸橼酸鈉或枸橼酸鉀，碳酸鈉及硫酸銅配製的本尼迪克特溶液中，煮沸並搖晃約 2 分鐘後待其冷卻；達 2% 的葡萄糖含量可由淺紅、淺黃或淺綠色沉澱顯示，含糖量最高呈紅色，最低（約 0.05%）則呈綠色。

benethamine penicillin an antibiotic effective against most Gram-positive bacteria (streptococci, staphylococci, and pneumococci). A derivative of *penicillin G, it can be administered by mouth but is usually given as an intramuscular injection, from which it liberates penicillin G slowly. Patients hypersensitive to penicillins may suffer allergic reactions.

苄胺青黴素 一種對多數革蘭氏陽性菌（鏈球菌、葡萄球菌和肺炎球菌）有效的抗生素，為青黴素 G 的衍化物。可口服，但通常肌內注射緩慢釋放青黴素 G。青黴素過敏者可產生變態反應。

benign *adj.* **1.** describing a tumour that does not invade and destroy the tissue in which it originates or spread to distant sites in the body, i.e. a tumour that is not

良性的 (1) 描述不侵犯或破壞其發源組織或不播散至體內較遠部位的腫瘤，即非癌性腫瘤。(2) 描述任何不產生有害

cancerous. **2.** describing any disorder or condition that does not produce harmful effects. *Compare* malignant.

後果的疾病或狀態。與 malignant 對比。

benign intracranial hypertension (pseudotumour cerebri) a syndrome of raised pressure within the skull caused by impaired reabsorption of cerebrospinal fluid. The symptoms include headache, vomiting, double vision, and *papilloedema. It normally subsides spontaneously but treatment may be required to protect the patient's vision.

良性顱內高壓 一種因腦脊液重吸收障礙所致顱內壓升高的綜合徵。症狀有頭痛、嘔吐、複視和視神經乳頭水腫。一般自行緩解，但可因保護患者視力而需治療。

benign prostatic hypertrophy (BPH) *see* prostate gland.

良性前列腺肥大 參閱 prostate gland。

benorylate *n.* a compound of *aspirin and *paracetamol that relieves pain, inflammation, and fever. It is an alternative to aspirin, particularly in the treatment of rheumatoid arthritis. Side-effects may include drowsiness, noises in the ears, and skin rashes. Trade name: **Benoral**.

貝諾酯 一種阿司匹林和對乙酰氨基酚的化合物。具解熱止痛抗炎作用，為阿司匹林的一種替代藥，尤其在治療類風濕性關節炎時。副作用可有嗜睡、耳鳴和皮疹。商品名：Benoral。

benperidol *n.* a *butyrophenone antipsychotic drug used mainly to treat deviant and antisocial sexual behaviour. It is administered by mouth. Trade name: **Anquil**.

苯哌利多 一種主要用於治療不軌和性行為反常的丁酰苯抗精神病藥。口服。商品名：Anquil。

benserazide *n.* a drug that prevents the breakdown of *levodopa to dopamine outside the brain by inhibiting the enzyme dopa decarboxylase. Administered by mouth in combination with levodopa (as *Madopar*), it is used to treat parkinsonism following encephalitis (post-encephalitic parkinsonism). Possible side-effects include nausea, vomiting, loss of appetite, involuntary movements, and faintness on standing up.

苄絲肼 一種抑制多巴脫羧酶而防止左旋多巴在腦外分解為多巴胺的藥物。口服並與左旋多巴類藥（如經苄絲肼）合用，治療腦炎後帕金森綜合徵。可致副作用有惡心、嘔吐、食慾不振、不隨意運動與起立暈厥。

benzalkonium *n.* a detergent disinfectant with the same uses and effects as *cetrimide.

苯甲烴銨　用途和效果與西曲溴銨相同的一種去污消毒劑。

benzathine penicillin a long-acting antibiotic, given by mouth or intramuscular injection, that is slowly absorbed and effective against most Gram-positive bacteria (streptococci, staphylococci, and pneumococci). Patients hypersensitive to the penicillins suffer allergic reactions. Trade name: **Penidural**. *See also* penicillin.

苄星青黴素　一種長效抗生素。口服或肌注，吸收緩慢，對多數革蘭氏陽性菌（鏈球菌、葡萄球菌和肺炎球菌）有效。青黴素過敏者有變態反應。商品名：Penidural。參閱penicillin。

benzhexol *n.* a drug that has actions and side-effects similar to those of *atropine. Taken by mouth, it is used mainly to reduce muscle spasm in parkinsonism. Trade names: **Artane**, **Broflex**.

苯海索　一種作用和副作用類似於阿托品的藥物。口服。主要用於減輕帕金森綜合徵的肌痙攣。商品名：Artane，Broflex。

benzocaine *n.* a local anaesthetic used in the form of an ointment, suppository, or aerosol to relieve painful conditions of the skin and mucous membranes. Virtually non-toxic, it can also be taken by mouth in the form of lozenges to treat such conditions as lacerations of the mouth or tongue and gastric ulcers.

苯佐卡因　一種以軟膏、栓劑或氣霧劑等形式用於緩解皮膚和黏膜疼痛的局麻藥。幾乎無毒，亦可以錠劑口服治療口腔裂傷或舌、胃潰瘍之類疾病。

benzodiazepines *n.* a group of pharmacologically active compounds used as minor *tranquillizers and hypnotics. The group includes *bromazepam, *chlordiazepoxide, *diazepam, and *oxazepam.

苯二氮䓬類　一組用作為弱安定藥和催眠藥的活性化合物。包括嗅西泮、氯氮䓬、地西泮和奧沙西泮。

benzoic acid an antiseptic, active against fungi and bacteria, used as a preservative in foods and pharmaceutical preparations, as well as for the treatment of fungal infections of the skin.

苯甲酸　一種對真菌和細菌有效的抗菌劑。用於治療皮膚真菌感染，亦用作食物和藥學製劑防腐劑。

benzoyl peroxide a preparation used in the treatment of acne and other skin conditions. It acts by removing the surface

過氧苯甲酰　一種用於治療痤瘡和其他皮膚病的製劑。其作用為除去表皮上層與疏通

layers of the epidermis and unblocking skin pores and has an antiseptic effect on skin bacteria. It is administered as a cream, lotion, or gel. Side-effects include skin irritation, excessive peeling, and (occasionally) blistering. Trade names: **Acetoxyl**, **Acnegel**, **Benoxyl**.

皮膚毛孔，並對皮膚細菌有抗菌作用。以乳膏、洗劑或凝膠給藥。副作用有皮膚刺激、大量脫屑及（偶爾）起疱。商品名：Acetoxyl，Acnegel，Benoxyl。

benzthiazide *n.* a *diuretic used in the treatment of conditions involving fluid retention, such as congestive heart failure, *oedema, and hypertension. Trade name: **Dytide**.

苄噻嗪 一種用於治療充血性心力衰竭、水腫和高血壓等液體瀦留狀態的利尿劑。商品名：Dytide。

benztropine *n.* a drug that is similar to *atropine but also acts as an antihistamine, local anaesthetic, and sedative. Given by mouth, it is used mainly in the treatment of parkinsonism to reduce rigidity and muscle cramps. It is well tolerated, but produces drowsiness and confusion.

苄扎托品 一種與阿托品類似，但亦具抗組胺、局部麻醉與鎮靜作用的藥物。口服。主要用於帕金森綜合徵中減輕強直和肌痙攣。其耐藥性良好，但可致嗜睡與精神混亂。

benzydamine hydrochloride an anti-inflammatory drug (*see* NSAID) used to treat muscle pain. It is administered as a cream for external use. Trade name: **Difflam**.

鹽酸苄達明 一種用於治療肌肉痛的抗炎藥（參閱NSAID）。以乳膏外用。商品名：Difflam。

benzyl benzoate an oily aromatic liquid that is applied to the body – in the form of a lotion – for the treatment of scabies. It is also useful in treating pediculosis. Trade name: **Ascabiol**.

苯甲酸苄酯 一種以洗劑用於治療疥瘡的油性芳香液體。治療虱病亦有效。商品名：Ascabiol。

benzylpenicillin *n. see* penicillin.

苄青黴素，青黴素 G 參閱penicillin。

bephenium hydroxynaphthoate an *anthelmintic drug used to get rid of hookworms and other nematodes. It is administered by mouth. Possible side-effects include stomach irritation. Trade name: **Alcopar**.

苄芬寧羥萘酸鹽 一種用於驅除鉤蟲和其他綫蟲的治蠕蟲劑。口服，可致副作用有胃刺激。商品名：Alcopar。

beriberi *n.* a nutritional disorder due to deficiency of vitamin B₁ (thiamin). It is widespread in rice-eating communities in which the diet is based on polished rice, from which the seed coat (which is rich in thiamin) has been removed. Beriberi takes two forms: *wet beriberi*, in which there is an accumulation of tissue fluid (*oedema), and *dry beriberi*, in which there is extreme emaciation. There is nervous degeneration in both forms of the disease and death from heart failure is often the outcome.

berry aneurysm *see* aneurysm.

berylliosis *n.* poisoning by beryllium or its compounds, either by inhalation or by skin contamination. Inhalation of fumes from molten beryllium causes an acute *alveolitis and is usually fatal. Subacute and chronic forms can result from extremely low levels of exposure to the powder and can produce granulomata in the skin or lungs very similar to those seen in *sarcoidosis. In the lungs, these lead to fibrosis, which can, however, be prevented by prompt use of oral corticosteroids. Although the incidence of berylliosis has been greatly reduced since the use of beryllium compounds in the manufacture of fluorescent light tubes was discontinued in Britain in 1948, new cases are still occurring.

beta blocker a drug that prevents stimulation of the beta-adrenergic receptors at the nerve endings of the sympathetic nervous system and therefore decreases the activity of the heart. Beta blockers include *acebutolol, *betaxolol, *bisoprolol, *oxprenolol, *propranolol, and *sotalol; they are used to control abnormal heart rhythms, to treat angina, and

腳氣（病） 一種維生素 B₁（硫胺）缺乏所致的營養性疾病。流行於以去除了富含硫胺的種衣而精製的大米為主食的社區。腳氣病分兩型：有組織液蓄積（水腫）的濕性腳氣病和有嚴重消瘦的乾性腳氣病。兩種類型均有神經變性，後果常為死於心力衰竭。

顱內小動脈瘤 參閱 aneurysm。

鈹中毒 吸入或皮膚接觸鈹或其化合物所致的中毒。吸入熔鈹煙霧引起急性肺泡炎，常可致死。接觸極其少量的鈹粉可引起亞急性或慢性肺泡炎。並可產生極似肉樣瘤病中所見的皮膚或肺肉芽腫。它們在肺部引起纖維變性，但可立即口服皮質類固醇藥物予以防止。在英國，自 1948 年停止熒光管製造中使用鈹化合物以來鈹中毒發生率已大為減少，但仍有新病例出現。

β-受體阻滯劑 一類阻止交感神經系統神經末梢處的 β-腎上腺素能受體興奮，從而減弱心臟活動的藥物。包括醋丁洛爾、倍他洛爾、比索洛爾、氧烯洛爾、普萘洛爾和索他洛爾。用於控制心律不齊、治療心絞痛與降低血壓。阻斷 β-受體可引起肺內氣道縮窄，故任

to reduce high blood pressure. Blockade of beta receptors may cause constriction of air passages in the lungs and care has to be taken with the use of beta blockers in patients with any bronchial conditions. *See also* sympatholytic.

betahistine *n*. a drug that has properties similar to those of *histamine and is administered by mouth to treat *Ménière's disease. A common side-effect is nausea. Trade name: **Serc**.

beta-lactam antibiotic one of a group of drugs that includes the *penicillins and the *cephalosporins. All have a four-membered *beta-lactam* ring as part of their molecular structure. Beta-lactam antibiotics function by interfering with the growth of the cell walls of multiplying bacteria. Bacteria become resistant to these antibiotics by producing *beta-lactamases*, enzymes (such as *penicillinase) that disrupt the beta-lactam ring.

betamethasone *n*. a synthetic corticosteroid drug with effects and uses similar to those of *prednisolone. The side-effects are those of *cortisone. Trade names: **Betnelan**, **Betnesol**, **Betnovate**.

betatron *n*. a device used to accelerate a stream of electrons (*beta particles*) into a beam of radiation that can be used in *radiotherapy.

betaxolol *n*. a *beta blocker drug used to treat high blood pressure and chronic simple *glaucoma. It is administered by mouth and as eye drops. Possible side-effects include breathing difficulty, fatigue, cold extremities, and sleep disturbances. Trade names: **Kerlone**, **Betoptic**.

何支氣管疾病患者須謹慎使用此類藥物。參閱 sympatholytic。

倍他司汀 一種其特性類似於組胺的藥物。口服治療梅尼埃病。常見副作用有惡心。商品名：Serc。

β-內醯胺抗生素 一組包括青黴素類和頭孢菌素類的藥物。其分子結構均有一個 4 位的 β-內醯胺環，通過干擾繁殖細菌的細胞壁生長而起作用。細菌通過產生 β-內醯胺酶，即使 β-內醯胺環破裂的酶（如青黴素酶），而對此類抗生素產生耐藥性。

倍他米松 一種作用與用途類似於潑尼松龍的合成皮質類固醇藥物。副作用同可的松。商品名：Betnelan，Betnesol，Betnovate。

電子迴旋加速器 一種將電子流（β-粒子）加速成為可用於放射治療的放射束的裝置。

倍他洛爾 一種用於治療高血壓和慢性單純性青光眼的 β-受體阻滯劑，口服或用作滴眼劑。可致副作用有呼吸困難、疲乏、四肢發冷及睡眠障礙。商品名：Kerlone，Betoptic。

bethanechol *n.* a cholinergic drug (*see* parasympathomimetic) that acts mainly on the bowel and bladder, stimulating these organs to empty. It is administered by mouth. Possible side-effects include nausea, vomiting, and abdominal cramps. Trade name: **Myotonine**.

烏拉膽鹼　一種主要作用於腸與膀胱，刺激它們排空的膽鹼能藥（參閱 parasympathomimetic）。口服，可致副作用有惡心、嘔吐和腹部痙攣。商品名：Myotonine。

bethanidine *n.* a drug that lowers blood pressure. It is given by mouth and acts by blocking the sympathetic nerves that supply the blood vessels. Common side-effects include dizziness, fainting, oedema, and breathlessness.

倍他尼定　一種口服降壓藥，通過阻滯支配血管的交感神經而起作用。常見副作用包括頭昏、暈厥、水腫及呼吸困難。

bezafibrate *n.* a drug that reduces blood *cholesterol levels and is used to treat hypercholesterolaemia that fails to respond to diet. It is administered by mouth. Possible side-effects include skin rashes, nausea and vomiting, and muscle pain. Trade name: **Bezalip**.

苯扎貝特　一種降低血膽固醇水平的藥物。用於治療改變飲食無效的血膽固醇過高。口服。可致副作用有皮疹、惡心嘔吐及肌痛。商品名：Bezalip。

bezoar *n.* a mass of swallowed foreign material within the stomach. The material, which is usually swallowed by psychiatrically disturbed patients, accumulates and ultimately causes gastric obstruction. Its removal often requires a surgical operation. *See also* trichobezoar.

糞石　吞咽的異物在胃內積聚，常係精神病者所為，異物在胃內聚積，最終導致胃梗阻，常需手術取出。參閱 trichobezoar。

bi- *prefix denoting* two; double. Examples: *biciliate* (having two cilia); *binucleate* (having two nuclei).

〔前綴〕二，雙　例如：雙纖毛的，雙核的。

biceps *n.* a muscle with two heads. The *biceps brachii* extends from the shoulder joint to the elbow (see illustration). It flexes the arm and forearm and supinates the forearm and hand. The *biceps femoris* is situated at the back of the thigh and is responsible for flexing the knee, extending the thigh, and rotating the leg outwards.

二頭肌　具有雙頭的肌肉。肱二頭肌從肩關節延伸至肘部（見圖），使上臂和前臂屈曲並使前臂和手旋後。股二頭肌位於大腿後部，使膝部屈曲，大腿伸展和小腿外旋。

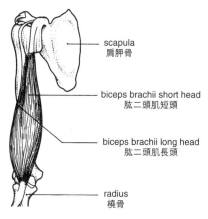

The biceps muscle of the arm
肱二頭肌

biconcave *adj.* having a hollowed surface on both sides. Biconcave lenses are used to correct short-sightedness. *Compare* biconvex.

雙凹（形）的　兩面均為凹面的。雙凹透鏡用於矯正近視。與 biconvex 對比。

biconvex *adj.* having a surface on each side that curves outwards. Biconvex lenses are used to correct long-sightedness. *Compare* biconcave.

雙凸（形）的　兩面均為凸面的。雙凸透鏡用於矯正遠視。與 biconcave 對比。

bicornuate *adj.* having two hornlike processes or projections. The term is applied to an abnormal uterus that is divided into two separate halves at the upper end.

雙角的　有兩個角狀突起的。用於描述在上端分為兩個獨立部分的異常子宮。

bicuspid 1. *adj.* having two *cusps, as in the premolar teeth and the mitral valve of the heart. **2.** *n.* (in the USA) a premolar tooth.

(1) 二尖的　有兩個尖的。如前磨牙和心臟二尖瓣。**(2)**（美國）**雙尖牙**

bicuspid valve *see* mitral valve.

二尖瓣　參閱 mitral valve。

bifid *adj.* split or cleft into two parts.

兩叉的，對裂的　裂為兩部分。

bifocal lenses glasses in which the upper part of the lens gives a sharp image of distant objects and the lower part is for near vision, such as reading. *See also* trifocal lenses, multifocal lenses.

雙焦點透鏡　一種上部對遠物成像清晰而下部適合於近處視物如閱讀的眼鏡。參閱 trifocal lenses，multifocal lenses。

bifurcation *n*. (in anatomy) the point at which division into two branches occurs; for example in blood vessels or in the trachea.

杈　（解剖學）分支開始之點，如在血管或氣管中。

bigeminal body one of the two swellings that develop in the roof of the midbrain during its development in the embryo.

二疊體　胚胎發育期間中腦頂部形成的兩個隆突之一。

bigeminy *n*. the condition in which alternate *ectopic beats of the heart are transmitted to the pulse and felt as a double pulse beat (*pulsus bigeminus*). It is a common manifestation of digitalis poisoning.

二聯律　心臟交替出現的異位搏動傳遞至脈搏而呈二聯脈搏動（二聯脈）的狀態。是洋地黃中毒的一種常見表現。

biguanide *n*. one of the group of drugs including *metformin, which is used to treat noninsulin-dependent (Type II) diabetes mellitus. Biguanides are *oral hypoglycaemic drugs: they act by reducing the release of glucose from the liver and increasing glucose uptake by muscles.

雙胍，縮二胍　一組包括二甲雙胍的用於治療非胰島素依賴型（II 型）糖尿病的藥物。為口服降血糖藥，通過減少肝臟釋放葡萄糖和增加肌肉吸收葡萄糖而發揮作用。

bilateral *adj*. (in anatomy) relating to or affecting both sides of the body or of a tissue or organ or both of a pair of organs (e.g. the eyes, breasts, or ovaries).

兩側的　（解剖學）涉及或影響軀體、某組織或器官兩側的，或某成對器官的（如眼、乳房或卵巢）。

bile *n*. a thick alkaline fluid that is secreted by the *liver and stored in the *gall bladder, from which it is ejected intermittently into the duodenum via the common *bile duct. Bile may be yellow, green, or brown, according to the proportions of the *bile pigments (excretory products) present; other constituents are lecithin, cholesterol, and *bile salts. The

膽汁　一種由肝臟分泌、貯存於膽囊並經膽總管間斷排入十二指腸的鹼性黏稠液體。根據其中膽色素（排泄產物）所占比例，膽汁可為黃色、綠色或棕色，其他成分有卵磷脂、膽固醇和膽鹽。膽鹽有助於在十二指腸內乳化脂肪，使之更易被胰脂酶分解為脂肪酸和甘

bile salts help to emulsify fats in the duodenum so that they can be more easily digested by pancreatic *lipase into fatty acids and glycerol. Bile salts also form compounds with fatty acids, which can then be transported into the *lacteals. Bile also helps to stimulate *peristalsis in the duodenum.

bile acids the organic acids in bile; mostly occurring as bile salts (sodium glycocholate and sodium taurocholate). They are cholic acid, deoxycholic acid, glycocholic acid, and taurocholic acid.

bile duct any of the ducts that convey bile from the liver. Bile is drained from the liver cells by many small ducts that unite to form the main bile duct of the liver, the *hepatic duct*. This joins the *cystic duct*, which leads from the *gall bladder, to from the *common bile duct*, which drains into the duodenum.

bile pigments coloured compounds – breakdown products of the blood pigment *haemoglobin – that are excreted in *bile. The two most important bile pigments are *bilirubin*, which is orange or yellow, and its oxidized form *biliverdin*, which is green. Mixed with the intestinal contents, they give the brown colour to the faeces (*see* urobilinogen).

bile salts sodium glycocholate and sodium taurocholate – the alkaline salts of *bile – necessary for the emulsification of fats. After they have been absorbed from the intestine they are transported to the liver for reuse.

Bilharzia *n. see* Schistosoma.

bilharziasis *n. see* schistosomiasis.

油。膽鹽亦與脂肪酸形成化合物，然後可被轉運到乳糜管。膽汁還有助於刺激十二指腸的蠕動。

膽汁酸 膽汁中的有機酸。大多數以膽鹽存在（甘氨膽酸鈉和牛磺膽酸鈉），包括膽酸、去氧膽酸、甘氨膽酸和牛磺膽酸。

膽管 任何從肝臟運送膽汁的管道。膽汁經許多小管從肝細胞排出，這些小管集合成肝臟的主要膽管即肝管，再與由膽囊發出的膽囊管匯合形成膽總管進入十二指腸。

膽色素 隨膽汁排泄的有色化合物。為血液色素血紅蛋白的分解產物。最重要的兩種膽色素是呈橙色或黃色的膽紅素，和其氧化形式呈綠色的膽綠素。它們與腸道內容物混合後使糞便呈棕色（參閱 urobilinogen）。

膽鹽 膽汁的鹼性鹽類，即乳化脂肪酸必需的甘氨膽酸鈉和牛磺膽酸鈉。經腸道吸收後被送至肝臟以供重新使用。

裂體吸蟲屬 參閱 Schistosoma。

裂體吸蟲病 參閱 schistosomiasis。

bili- *prefix denoting* bile.

〔前綴〕**膽汁**

biliary *adj.* relating to or affecting the bile duct or bile. *See also* fistula.

膽汁的，膽的 涉及或影響膽管或膽汁的。參閱 fistula。

biliary colic pain resulting from obstruction of the gall bladder or common bile duct, usually by a stone. The pain, which is very severe, is usually felt in the upper abdomen (in the mid-line or to the right). It often occurs about an hour after a meal (particularly if fatty), may last several hours, and is usually steady in severity (unlike other forms of *colic). Vomiting often occurs simultaneously.

膽絞痛 膽囊或膽總管梗阻引起的疼痛，常為結石所致。疼痛極其劇烈，一般出現在上腹部（位於中綫或偏右），通常發生在餐後一小時左右（若為脂肪性飲食尤其如此）。可持續數小時，疼痛程度穩定（不同於其他類型絞痛），常伴有嘔吐。

bilious *adj.* **1.** containing bile; for example *bilious vomiting* is the vomiting of bile-containing fluid. **2.** a lay term used to describe attacks of nausea or vomiting.

膽汁（質）的 **(1)** 含膽汁的，如膽汁性嘔吐為嘔吐含膽汁的液體。**(2)** 用於描述惡心或嘔吐發作的非專業詞。

bilirubin *n. see* bile pigments.

膽紅素 參閱 bile pigments。

bilirubinaemia *n.* an excess of the *bile pigment bilirubin in the blood. Normally there is under 0.8 mg bilirubin per 100 ml blood (17 μmol/l); when the concentration of bilirubin is above 1–1.5 mg per 100 ml (20–30 μmol/l), visible *jaundice occurs.

膽紅素血症 血液中膽色素（膽紅素）過多。正常情況下每 100 ml 血液中膽紅素少於 0.8 mg（17 μmol/l）；當其濃度超過 1~1.5 mg/100 ml（20–30 μmol/l）時，即發生黃疸。

biliuria (choluria) *n.* the presence of bile in the urine: a feature of certain forms of jaundice.

膽汁尿 尿液中含有膽汁，為某類型黃疸的一種特徵。

biliverdin *n. see* bile pigments.

膽綠素 參閱 bile pigments。

Billings method a method of planning pregnancy, now rarely used, involving the daily examination of cervical mucus in the vagina, which varies in consistency and colour throughout the menstrual cycle. Use of a *Billings mucus observation chart* to help identify the type of

比林思法 現已罕用的一種計劃法。每日檢查陰道子宮頸黏液，其稠度和顏色在月經周期均有所變化。運用比林思黏液觀察圖來幫助鑒別黏液類型，可使婦女（在大約50％的情形中）提前六天獲知即將排

mucus enables the woman (in about 50% of cases) to have six days' warning of impending ovulation. It is a rather unreliable method of contraception.

卵。此為一種相當不可靠的避孕法。

bimanual *adj.* using two hands to perform an activity, such as a gynaecological examination.

雙手的 用雙手進行某種活動,如作婦科檢查。

binaural *adj.* relating to or involving the use of both ears.

兩耳的 有關或涉及使用雙耳的。

binder *n.* a bandage that is wound around a part of the body, usually the abdomen, to apply pressure or to give support or protection.

腹帶 包繞身體某一部分,通常是腹部,以加壓來提供支持或保護的繃帶。

binge–purge syndrome *see* bulimia.

食-瀉綜合徵 參閱 bulimia。

binocular *adj.* relating to or involving the use of both eyes.

雙眼的 有關或涉及使用雙眼的。

binocular vision the ability to focus both eyes on an object at the same time, so that a person sees one image of the object he is looking at. It is not inborn, but acquired during the first few months of life. Binocular vision enables judgment of distance and perception of depth. *See also* stereoscopic vision.

雙眼視覺 同時將雙眼聚焦於一物體而使所視物體成為一個影像的能力。此種能力非先天所有,而在出生後頭幾個月中獲得。雙眼視覺使人能夠判斷距離和知覺深度。參閱 stereoscopic vision。

bio- *prefix denoting* life or living organisms. Example: *biosynthesis* (formation of a compound within a living organism).

〔前綴〕**生命,生物** 如生物合成(生物體內化合物的形成)。

bioassay *n.* estimation of the activity or potency of a drug or other substance by comparing its effects on living organisms with effects of a preparation of known strength. Bioassay is used to determine the strength of preparations of hormones or other material of biological origin when other physical or chemical methods are not available.

生物鑒定 通過將某藥物或其他物質對生物體的效力與已知效力的標本相比較,對其活動性或效力做出鑒定。用於當其他物理或化學方法不能使用時測定激素或其他生物源性物質標本的效力。

bioavailability *n.* the proportion of a drug that is delivered to its site of action in the body. This is usually the amount entering the circulation and may be low when the drugs are given by mouth.

生物有效率　某藥物抵達體內作用部位的比率。通常為進入體內循環的量，口服時含量可能較低。

biochemistry *n.* the study of the chemical processes and substances occurring in living things. **–biochemical** *adj.* **–biochemist** *n.*

生物化學　對生物的化學反應過程和物質的研究。

biofeedback *n.* the giving of immediate information to a subject about his bodily processes (such as heart rate), which are usually unconscious. These processes can then be subject to operant *conditioning. This is an experimental treatment for disturbances of bodily regulation, such as hypertension.

生物反饋　將有關通常無意識的身體變化過程（如心率）信息立即告知患者。然後可使這些過程形成操作性條件反射化。為對身體調節功能紊亂如高血壓的一種試驗治療。

biological response modifier a therapeutic agent, such as *interferon or *interleukin, that influences the body's defence mechanisms to act against a cancer cell. These substances are normally produced in small amounts by the body; relatively large doses are being studied for cancer treatment.

生物應答調節劑　一種影響機體防禦機制而對某種癌細胞產生作用的治療劑，如干擾素或白細胞介素。機體正常產生少量這些物質；現在研究將較大劑量用於癌症治療。

biology *n.* the study of living organisms – plants, animals, and microorganisms – including their structure and function and their relationships with one another and with the inanimate world. **–biological** *adj.*

生物學　對生物即植物、動物和微生物的結構、活動、相互關係以及與非生物界關係的研究。

biometry *n.* the measurement of living things and the processes associated with life, including the application of mathematics, particularly statistics, to problems in biology.

生物統計學　對生物及有關生命過程的測量。包括將數學尤其是統計學用於生物學問題。

bionics *n.* the science of mechanical or electronic systems that function in the same way as, or have characteristics of,

仿生學　功能或特徵與生物系統相同的機械或電子系統的科學。與 cybernetics 對比。

living systems. *Compare* cybernetics.
–bionic *adj.*

bionomics *n. see* ecology.

biopsy *n.* the removal of a small piece of living tissue from an organ or part of the body for microscopic examination. Biopsy is an important means of diagnosing cancer from examination of a fragment of tumour. It is often carried out with a special hollow needle, inserted into the liver, kidney, or other organ, with relatively little discomfort to the patient.

biostatistics *n.* statistical information and techniques used with special reference to studies of health and social problems. It embraces, overlaps, and is to some extent synonymous with the fields of *vital statistics* (e.g. *fertility and *mortality rates) and *demography.

biotechnology *n.* the development of techniques for the application of biological processes to the production of materials of use in medicine and industry. For example, the production of many antibiotics relies on the activity of various fungi and bacteria. Recent techniques of *genetic engineering, in which human genes are cloned in bacterial cells, have enabled the large-scale production of hormones (notably insulin), vaccines, interferon, and other useful products.

biotin *n.* a vitamin of the B complex that is essential for the metabolism of fat, being involved in fatty acid synthesis and *gluconeogenesis. A biotin deficiency is extremely rare in man; it can be induced by eating large quantities of raw egg white, which contains a

個體生態學　參閱 ecology。

活組織檢查　從某器官或身體某部分獲取一小片活組織進行顯微鏡檢查。是一種根據檢查腫瘤碎片診斷癌症的重要方法。通常用一專用空針插入肝、腎或其他器官，患者微感不適。

生命統計　專門用於有關健康和社會問題研究的統計學資料與技術。與生命統計學（如生育率和死亡率）和人口學有所重疊交叉，並在一定程度上含義相同。

生物技術　發展運用生物過程生產有醫學和工業用途材料的技術。例如，許多抗生素的生產依賴於多種真菌和細菌活性。最近將人體基因在細菌細胞內克隆（無性繁殖）的遺傳工程學技術，使得可以大量生產激素（如胰島素）、疫苗、干擾素和其他有用產品。

生物素，維生素 H　一種脂肪代謝必需的 B 族複合維生素，參與脂肪酸合成和糖原異生。生物素缺乏在人類極為罕見，可因食入大量生蛋清所致。生蛋清含有一種與生物素結合的抗生物素蛋白而使其不為身體

protein – avidin – that combines with biotin, making it unavailable to the body. Rich sources of the vitamin are egg yolk and liver.

所用。生物素在蛋黃和肝臟中含量豐富。

biperiden *n.* a drug with effects similar to those of atropine, used in the treatment of parkinsonism, certain forms of spasticity, and to control the muscular incoordination that may result from the use of some tranquillizers. It is given by mouth; side-effects are those of *atropine. Trade name: **Akineton**.

比哌立登 一種作用與阿托品相似的藥物。用於治療帕金森綜合徵、某些類型的強直以及控制某些鎮靜劑所致的肌共濟失調。口服。副作用與阿托品相同。商品名：Akineton。

bipolar *adj.* (in neurology) describing a neurone (nerve cell) that has two processes extending in different directions from its cell body.

雙極的 （神經病學）描述有兩個從細胞體向不同方向伸展的突起的神經元（神經細胞）。

bipolar disorder *see* manic-depressive psychosis.

雙相（情感性）障礙 參閱 manic-depressive psychosis。

bird-fancier's lung a form of external allergic *alveolitis caused by the inhalation of avian proteins present in the droppings and feathers of certain birds, especially pigeons and caged birds (such as budgerigars). As in *farmer's lung, there is an acute and a chronic form.

養鳥者肺 一種外源性變應性肺泡炎。因吸入某些鳥類的糞和羽毛中的鳥蛋白所致，特別是鴿子和籠中鳥（如澳洲長尾小鸚鵡）。與農夫肺一樣有急性和慢性兩型。

birefringence *n.* the property possessed by some naturally occurring substances (such as cell membranes) of doubly refracting a beam of light, i.e. of bending it in two different directions. **–birefringent** *adj.*

雙折射 某些自然存在物質（如細胞膜）所具有的雙重折射一束光的特性，即使其向兩個不同方向折射。

birth *n.* (in obstetrics) *see* labour.

生產 （產科學）參閱 labour。

birth control the use of *contraception or *sterilization (male or female) to prevent unwanted pregnancies.

節（制生）育 利用避孕或絕育（男性或女性）方法預防意外妊娠。

birthing chair a chair specially adapted to allow childbirth to take place in a sitting position. Its recent introduction in the Western world followed the increasing demand by women for greater mobility during labour. The chair is electronically powered and can be tilted back quickly and easily should the need arise.

產椅　一種專門適用於坐位分娩的椅子。在西方國家因婦女要求分娩中有更多的活動自由而新近採用。產椅為電動，若有需要可迅速輕易地向後傾斜。

birthmark *n.* a skin blemish or mark present at birth. The cause is unknown but most birthmarks grow before the baby is born. *See* naevus.

胎記，胎痣　出生時就有的皮膚斑記。其原因不明，但大多數在嬰兒出生前即已長出。參閱 naevus。

birth rate *see* fertility rate.

出生率　參閱 fertility rate。

bisacodyl *n.* a *laxative that acts on the large intestine to cause reflex movement and bowel evacuation. Bisacodyl is administered by mouth or in a suppository. The commonest side-effect is the development of abdominal cramps. Trade name: **Dulco-lax**.

比沙可啶，雙醋苯啶　一種作用於大腸引起反射運動和排便的輕瀉劑。口服或栓劑給藥。最常見副作用為腸痙攣。商品名：Dulco-lax。

bisexual *adj.* **1.** describing an individual who is sexually attracted to both men and women. **2.** describing an individual who possesses the qualities of both sexes.

兩性的　**(1)** 描述對男性或女性均可產生性戀的個人。**(2)** 描述具有兩性特徵的個人。

Bismarck brown a basic aniline dye used for staining and counterstaining histological and bacterial specimens.

苯胺棕　一種用於對組織和細菌標本染色與復染色的鹼性苯胺染劑。

bismuth carbonate a drug used to treat peptic ulcer, especially cases in which the organism *Helicobacter pylori* is a causal agent. It is administered by mouth. Trade name: **APP**.

碳酸鉍　一種用於治療消化性潰瘍的藥物。尤其是病原體為幽門螺桿菌的病例中。口服。商品名：APP。

bisoprolol *n.* a *beta blocker drug used to treat angina pectoris. It is administered by mouth. Possible side-effects include breathing difficulty, fatigue, cold extremities, and sleep disturbances. Trade names: **Emcor**, **Monocor**.

比索洛爾　一種用於治療心絞痛的 β-受體阻滯劑，口服。可致副作用有呼吸困難、疲勞、四肢發冷和睡眠障礙。商品名：Emcor，Monocor。

bistoury *n.* a narrow surgical knife, with a straight or curved blade (see illustration).

細長刀　一種刀刃為直形或彎形的狹長外科手術刀（見圖）。

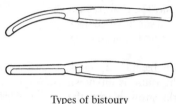

Types of bistoury
細長刀類型

bite-raiser *n.* an appliance to prevent normal closure of the teeth in orthodontic treatment and in the treatment of the *temporomandibular joint syndrome.

增高𬌗　在正牙療法和顳下頜關節綜合徵治療中阻止牙齒正常閉合的器械。

bite-wing *n.* a dental X-ray film that provides a view of the crowns of the teeth in part of both upper and lower jaws. This view is used in the diagnosis of caries and periodontal disease.

𬌗翼片　一種顯示部分上下牙冠的牙冠科 X 綫片。用於診斷齲齒和牙周病。

bivalent *n.* (in genetics) a structure consisting of homologous chromosomes attached to each other by *chiasmata during the first division of *meiosis. **–bivalent** *adj.*

二價（染色）體　（遺傳學）在第一次減數分裂中經交叉而相互依附的同源染色體所構成的一種結構。

blackdamp (chokedamp) *n.* (in mining) the poisonous gas containing carbon dioxide, carbon monoxide, or other suffocating material, sometimes found in pockets in underground workings. *Compare* firedamp.

烏煙，窒息性毒氣　（礦業）含有二氧化碳、一氧化碳或其他窒息性物質的毒氣。有時見於地下巷道空穴中。與 firedamp 對比。

Black Death *see* plague.

黑死病，鼠疫　參閱 plague。

black eye bruising of the eyelids.

黑眼　眼瞼的挫傷瘀血。

black fly a small widely distributed blood-sucking insect of the genus

黑蠅　一種分布廣泛的蚋屬吸血小昆蟲。因其弓背形狀亦稱

Simulium. Black flies are also known as buffalo gnats from their humpbacked appearance. Female flies can inflict painful bites and constitute a serious pest to man at certain times of the year. *S. damnosum* in Africa and *S. ochraceum* in Central America and Venezuela transmit the parasites causing *onchocerciasis.

blackhead *n.* a plug formed of fatty material (sebum and keratin) in the outlet of a *sebaceous gland in the skin. *See also* acne. Medical name: **comedo**.

black heel a black area, usually over the Achilles tendon, resulting from the rupture of capillaries in the skin in those who play basketball, squash, etc. It may be mistaken for malignant melanoma.

blackwater fever a rare and serious complication of malignant tertian (falciparum) *malaria in which there is massive destruction of the red blood cells, leading to the presence of the blood pigment haemoglobin in the urine. The condition is probably brought on by inadequate treatment with *quinine; it is marked by fever, bloody urine, jaundice, vomiting, enlarged liver and spleen, anaemia, exhaustion, and – in fatal cases – a reduced flow of urine resulting from a blockage of the kidney tubules. Treatment involves rest, administration of alkaline fluids and intravenous glucose, and blood transfusions.

bladder *n.* **1. (urinary bladder)** a sac-shaped organ that has a wall of smooth muscle and stores the urine produced by the kidneys. Urine passes into the bladder through the *ureters; the release of urine from the bladder is controlled by a sphincter at its junction with the *urethra. The *bladder neck* is the outlet

為蚋。雌性黑蠅叮咬疼痛，在一年中某些時候對人構成危害。非洲的憎蚋和中美洲與委內瑞拉的淡黃蚋傳播盤尾絲蟲病。

黑頭粉刺　皮膚皮脂腺開口處脂肪物質（皮脂和角蛋白）形成的栓。參閱　acne。醫學用語：黑頭粉刺。

黑踵　在打籃球、軟式網球等的人中，皮膚毛細血管破裂產生的一黑區，常在跟腱上方，可被誤認為惡性黑瘤。

黑水熱　惡性間日瘧（惡性瘧疾）的一種罕見而嚴重的併發症。因紅細胞大量破壞而導致尿中出現血色素即血紅蛋白，可能因奎寧治療不充分而引起。特徵為發熱、血尿、黃疸、嘔吐、肝脾腫大、貧血、衰竭，以及在危及生命的病例中因腎小管阻塞導致尿量減少。治療包括休息、注射鹼性液體和靜脈注射葡萄糖及輸血。

(1) 膀胱　其壁為平滑肌並貯存腎臟產生的尿液的囊狀器官。尿液經輸尿管進入膀胱，膀胱排尿則由膀胱與尿道交界處的括約肌控制。膀胱頸為膀胱出口並在此與尿道會合。在男性與前列腺相接，受骨盆的植物神經控制。膀胱頸是尿豬

of the bladder where it joins the urethra and in males it is in contact with the *prostate gland; it is under the control of the autonomic nerves of the pelvis. The neck of the bladder is the commonest site for *retention of urine, usually by an enlarged prostate or a urethral *stricture. **2.** any of several other hollow organs containing fluid, such as the *gall bladder.

留最常見的部位，通常因前列腺肥大或尿道狹窄所致。**(2)** 囊　其他的幾個內含液體的中空器官，如膽囊。

bladder augmentation (bladder enhancement) a surgical method of increasing the capacity of the bladder. This is usually achieved by ileocaecocystoplasty (*see* cystoplasty).

膀胱擴大術　一種增加膀胱容量的外科方法。通常為施行迴腸結腸膀胱成形術（參閱 cystoplasty）。

bladder replacement *see* cystectomy.

膀胱置換　參閱 cystectomy。

bladderworm *n.* *see* cysticercus.

囊蟲　參閱 cysticercus。

blast *n.* an important cause of serious soft-tissue injury that is associated with explosions or high-velocity missiles. The eardrums, lungs, and gastrointestinal tract are especially vulnerable to the indirect effects of the blast wave.

衝擊波　與爆炸或高速導彈有關的嚴重軟組織損傷的一個重要原因。耳室、肺和胃腸道尤其易受到衝擊波的間接作用。

-blast *suffix denoting* a formative cell. Example: *osteoblast* (formative bone cell).

〔後綴〕成……細胞　指胚性細胞，如成骨細胞。

blastema *n.* any zone of embryonic tissue that is still differentiating and growing into a particular organ. The term is usually applied to the tissue that develops into the kidneys and gonads.

胚基，芽基　任何仍在分化和生長為某一特定器官的胚胎組織區。一般用於指將發育為腎和性腺的組織。

blasto- *prefix denoting* a germ cell or embryo. Example: *blastogenesis* (early development of an embryo).

〔前綴〕胚，芽　指生殖細胞或胚胎。如芽生（胚胎的早期發育）。

blastocoele *n.* the fluid-filled cavity that develops within the *blastocyst. The

囊胚腔，分裂腔　胚泡內充滿液體的腔隙。此腔增加了胚胎

cavity increases the surface area of the embryo and thus improves its ability to absorb nutrients and oxygen.

blastocyst *n.* an early stage of embryonic development that consists of a hollow ball of cells with a localized thickening (the *inner cell mass*) that will develop into the actual embryo; the remainder of the blastocyst is composed of *trophoblast (see illustration). At first the blastocyst is unattached, but it soon implants in the wall of the uterus. *See also* implantation.

胚泡 胚胎發育的早期階段，由具有將發育成胚胎的局部增厚區（泡內細胞羣）的細胞中空球構成；胚泡的其餘部分由滋養層組成（見圖）。胚泡最初呈游離狀，但很快便植入子宮壁。參閱 implantation。

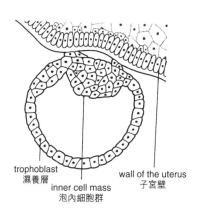

trophoblast
濕養層
inner cell mass
泡內細胞群
wall of the uterus
子宮壁

Section through a blastocyst
胚泡斷面觀

blastomere *n.* any of the cells produced by *cleavage of the zygote, comprising the earliest stages of embryonic development until the formation of the *blastocyst. Blastomeres divide repeatedly without growth and so decrease in size.

（分）裂球 任何由合子卵裂產生的細胞。為胚胎發育至卵泡形成的最早階段。分裂球反覆分裂而不生長，因此體積縮小。

blastomycosis *n.* any disease caused by parasitic fungi of the genus *Blastomyces*, which may affect the skin (forming wart-like ulcers and tumours on the face, neck, hands, arms, feet, and legs) or involve

芽生菌病 任何由芽生菌屬寄生性真菌引起的疾病。可侵犯皮膚（在面、頸、手、臂、腳和腿部形成疣狀潰瘍和腫塊）；或累及肺、骨、肝、脾

various internal tissues, such as the lungs, bones, liver, spleen, and lymphatics. There are two principal forms of the disease: *North American blastomycosis* (*Gilchrist's disease*), caused by *B. dermatitidis*; and *South American blastomycosis*, caused by *B. brasiliensis*. Both diseases are treated with antifungal drugs (such as amphotericin).

和淋巴管等多種內部組織。有兩種主要類型,即皮炎芽生菌導致的北美芽生菌病(吉爾克里斯特病)和巴西芽生菌導致的南美芽生菌病。兩型均用抗真菌藥治療(如兩性黴素)。

blastopore *n.* the opening that forms as a result of invagination of the surface layer of the early embryo (*gastrula). It is very much reduced in man, in which it gives rise to the archenteric canal (*see* archenteron).

胚孔 早期胚胎(原腸胚)表層內陷形成的開口。在人類已大為縮小,神經腸管在其內形成(參閱 archenteron)。

blastula *n.* an early stage of the embryonic development of many animals. The equivalent stage in mammals (including man) is the *blastocyst.

囊胚,囊胚泡 許多動物胚胎發育的一個早期階段。哺乳動物(包括人類)的相應階段為胚泡。

bleeding *n. see* haemorrhage.

出血 參閱 haemorrhage。

blenn- (blenno-) *prefix denoting* mucus. Example: *blennorrhagia* (excessive production of).

〔前綴〕黏液 如黏液溢出。

blennophthalmia *n. Obsolete.* *conjunctivitis in which there is a sticky yellow discharge from the eye.

眼膿溢 廢用詞。有黏性黃色分泌物的眼結膜炎。

blennorrhagia *n.* a copious discharge of mucus, particularly from the urethra. This usually accompanies *urethritis and sometimes occurs with acute *prostatitis. Treatment is directed to clearing the underlying causative organism by antibiotic administration.

淋病 大量的黏液排出,尤其從尿道。常伴有尿道炎,有時伴有急性前列腺炎。治療為用抗生素消滅病原體。

blennorrhoea *n.* a profuse watery discharge from the urethra. This, like *blenorrhagia, is associated with either prostatitis or urethritis, and is cleared by

黏液溢出 從尿道排出大量水樣物。與淋病一樣和前列腺炎或尿道炎有關。治療同此類疾病的常規療法。

the usual measures undertaken in the treatment of these conditions.

bleomycin *n.* an antibiotic with action against cancer cells, used in the treatment of Hodgkin's disease and other lymphomas and in squamous cell carcinoma. It is administered by injection and can cause toxic side-effects in the skin and lungs; it should not be used in patients with impaired kidney function or lung disease.

博萊黴素，爭光黴素　一種有抗癌細胞作用的抗生素。用於治療霍奇金病和其他淋巴瘤及鱗狀上皮細胞癌。注射給藥，對皮膚和肺有毒副作用，腎功能損害或肺病患者禁用。

blephar- (blepharo-) *prefix denoting* the eyelid. Example: *blepharotomy* (incision into).

〔前綴〕**眼瞼，瞼**　如瞼切開術。

blepharitis *n.* inflammation of the eyelids. In *squamous blepharitis*, often associated with dandruff of the scalp, white scales accumulate among the lashes. *Chronic ulcerative blepharitis* is characterized by yellow crusts overlying ulcers of the lid margins. The lashes become matted together and tend to fall out or become distorted. *Allergic blepharitis* may occur in response to drugs or cosmetics put in the eye or on the eyelids.

瞼炎　眼瞼的炎症。鱗屑性瞼炎常伴有頭皮脫屑，白色鱗屑在睫毛中堆積。慢性潰瘍性瞼炎特徵為瞼緣潰瘍處覆有黃痂，睫毛纏結，往往倒伏或扭曲。變應性瞼炎可因在眼部或眼瞼使用藥物或化妝品所致。

blepharon *n. see* eyelid.

眼瞼　參閱 eyelid。

blepharophimosis *n.* a small aperture between the eyelids. It is usually congenital.

瞼裂狹小　眼瞼之間距離短小，常為先天性。

blepharoplasty (tarsoplasty) *n.* any operation to repair or reconstruct the eyelid. It involves either rearrangement of the tissues of the lid or the use of tissue from other sites (e.g. skin or mucous membrane).

瞼成形術　任何修復或重建眼瞼的手術，包括重新調整眼瞼組織或使用其他部位的細胞組織（如皮膚或黏膜）。

blepharospasm *n.* involuntary tight contraction of the eyelids, either in response to painful conditions of the eye or as a form of *dystonia.

瞼痙攣　眼瞼非隨意性緊張收縮。為對眼部疼痛的反應或張力障礙的一種形式。

blind loop syndrome (stagnant loop syndrome) a condition of stasis of the small intestine allowing the overgrowth of bacteria, which causes *malabsorption and the passage of fatty stools (*see* steatorrhoea). It is usually the result of chronic obstruction (resulting, for example, from *Crohn's disease, a *stricture, or intestinal tuberculosis), or surgical bypass operations producing a stagnant length of bowel, or conditions (e.g. a jejunal *diverticulum) in which a segment of intestine is out of continuity with the rest.

blindness *n.* the inability to see. Lack of all light perception constitutes total blindness but there are degrees of visual impairment far less severe than this that may be classed as blindness for administrative or statutory purposes. For example, marked reduction in the *visual field is classified as blindness, even if objects are still seen sharply. The commonest causes of blindness worldwide are *trachoma, *onchocerciasis, and vitamin A deficiency (*see* night blindness) but there is wide geographic variation. In Great Britain the commonest causes are age-related degeneration of the *macula, *glaucoma, *cataract, myopic retinal degeneration, and diabetes mellitus.

blind register (in Britain) a list of persons who are technically blind due to reduced visual acuity (inability to read a car number plate from a distance of three metres) or who have severely restricted fields of vision (*see* blindness). Such people are entitled to special education and to financial and other social benefits. *See also* partially sighted register.

盲袢綜合徵 一種小腸停滯而使細菌生長過多，導致吸收障礙和脂肪糞的狀態（參閱 steatorrhoea）。通常源自慢性梗阻（如克羅恩病、狹窄、或腸結核所致），或引起某段腸腔停滯的外科旁路手術，或某一腸腔與其餘部分分離的狀態（如空腸憩室）。

盲，視覺缺失 無視覺能力。喪失所有光感為全盲，但還有依行政管理法或法令可列為盲人的遠輕於此程度的視力損害。例如，即使可清楚視物，但視野明顯縮小則列為視覺缺失。全球性最常見病因有沙眼、盤尾絲蟲病和維生素 A 缺乏症（參閱 night blindness），但病因有很大的地區差異。在英國，最常見病因為與年齡有關的黃斑變性、青光眼、白內障、近視性視網膜變性以及糖尿病。

視力缺失登記簿 （英國）因視敏度降低而為法定盲人（在三米外不能看清汽車牌號）或視野嚴重縮小者（參閱 blindness）之名冊。此類人享有特殊教育、經濟補助及其他社會福利的權利。參閱 partially sighted register。

blind spot the small area of the *retina of the eye where the nerve fibres from the light-sensitive cells (*see* cone, rod) lead into the optic nerve. There are no rods or cones in this area and hence it does not register light. Anatomical name: **punctum caecum**.

盲點　眼球視網膜小區，光感細胞（參閱 cone，rod）發出的神經纖維在此進入視神經。此區既無視桿細胞亦無視錐細胞，因而不能感光。醫學用語：盲點。

blind trial *see* intervention study.

盲法試驗　參閱 intervention study。

blinking *n.* the action of closing and opening the eyelids, which wipes the front of the eyeball and helps to spread the *tears. Reflex blinking may be caused by suddenly bringing an object near to the eye: the eyelids close involuntarily in order to protect the eye.

瞬目　閉合眼瞼的活動，可擦洗眼球前部並有助於淚液擴散。反射性瞬目可由某物突然靠近眼引起眼瞼自行關閉以保護眼睛。

blister *n.* a swelling containing watery fluid (serum) and sometimes also blood (*blood blister*) or pus, within or just beneath the skin. Blisters commonly develop as a result of unaccustomed friction on the hands or feet or at the site of a burn. Blisters may be treated with antiseptics and dressings. An unduly painful blister may be punctured with a sterile needle so that the fluid is released.

疱　皮內或皮下含有水樣液體（血清），有時亦有血（血疱）或膿的腫塊。常因手、足或燒傷部位不習慣摩擦而發生。可用抗菌劑和敷料加以治療。劇烈疼痛的水疱可用無菌針穿刺排除液體。

block *n.* any interruption of physiological or mental function, brought about intentionally (as part of a therapeutic procedure) or by disease. *See also* heart block, nerve block.

阻滯　人為的（作為治療措施的一部分）或由疾病所致的生理或精神功能阻斷。參閱 heart block，nerve block。

blocking *n.* (in psychiatry) **1.** a sudden halting of the flow of thought or speech. Blocking of thought, accompanied by the sensation of thoughts being removed from the mind, is a symptom of *schizophrenia. Blocking of speech may be a consequence of thought block or a result of a mechanical impediment in speech, such as *stammering. **2.** the failure to

中斷　（精神病學）**(1)** 思維或語言的突然停止。伴有腦中思想喪失感覺的思維中斷為精神分裂症的一種症狀。語言中斷可為思維中斷或機械性語言障礙如口吃的結果。**(2)** 因其不愉快的聯想而不能回憶某一特定事件，或就某一特定思潮進行思考。

recall a specific event, or to explore a specific train of thought, because of its unpleasant associations.

blood *n.* a fluid tissue that circulates throughout the body, via the arteries and veins, providing a vehicle by which an immense variety of different substances are transported between the various organs and tissues. It is composed of *blood cells, which are suspended in a liquid medium, the *plasma. An average individual has approximately 70 ml of blood per kilogram body weight (about 5 litres in an average adult male).

血　一種經動脈或靜脈循環於全身的液體組織。為在不同器官和組織間運送大量不同物質的媒介物，由懸浮於血漿這種液體介質中的血細胞組成。人體平均含量約為 70 ml/kg（成年男性平均約為 5 升）。

blood bank a department within a hospital or blood transfusion centre in which blood collected from donors is stored prior to transfusion. Blood must be kept at a temperature of 4°C and may be used up to four weeks after collection.

血庫　醫院或輸血中心內貯存供血者血液以備輸血用的部門。血液必須保持在 4°C，可在採集後 4 周內使用。

blood-brain barrier the mechanism whereby the circulating blood is kept separate from the tissue fluids surrounding the brain cells. It is a semipermeable membrane allowing solutions to pass through it but excluding solid particles and large molecules.

血腦屏障　使循環血液與圍繞腦細胞的組織液分隔開的機制。為一層可使溶液通過但將固體顆粒和大分子排斥在外的半透膜。

blood cell (blood corpuscle) any of the cells that are present in the blood in health or disease. The cells may be subclassified into two major categories, namely red cells (*erythrocytes), and white cells (*leucocytes), which include granulocytes, lymphocytes, and monocytes (see illustration). The blood cells (including *platelets) account for approximately 40% of the total volume of the blood in health; red cells comprise the vast majority.

血細胞　健康或患病時血液中存在的所有細胞。可分為兩大類；即紅細胞與包括粒細胞、淋巴細胞和單核細胞的白細胞（見圖）。血細胞（包括血小板）大約占正常血液總量的 40%，絕大多數為紅細胞。

blood clot a solid mass formed as the result of *blood coagulation, either

血塊　因血液凝固在血管和心臟內或其他部位形成的固體塊

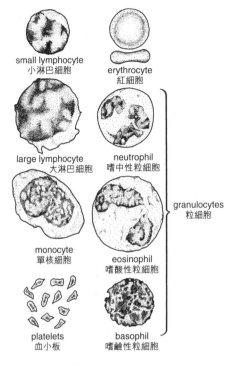

Types of blood cells
血細胞類型

within the blood vessels and heart or elsewhere (*compare* thrombus). A blood clot consists of a meshwork of the protein *fibrin in which various blood cells are trapped.

blood clotting *see* blood coagulation.

blood coagulation (blood clotting) the process whereby blood is converted from a liquid to a solid state. The process may be initiated by contact of blood with a foreign surface (*intrinsic system*) or with damaged tissue (*extrinsic system*). These systems involve the interaction of a variety of substances (*coagulation

（與 thrombus 對比）。由包含各種血細胞的纖維蛋白網組成。

凝血　參閱 blood coagulation。

凝血　血液由液體轉變為固體的過程。此過程可始於血液接觸異物表面（內源性系統）或接觸損傷組織（外源性系統）。這些系統參與多種物質（凝血因子）的相互作用並導致凝血酶的生成，凝血酶將可溶性纖維蛋白原轉變為不溶性

factors) and lead to the production of the enzyme thrombin, which converts the soluble blood protein *fibrinogen to the insoluble protein *fibrin. Blood coagulation is an essential mechanism for the arrest of bleeding (*haemostasis).

纖維蛋白。血凝固為止血的基本機制。

blood corpuscle *see* blood cell.

血細胞　參閱 blood cell。

blood count the numbers of different blood cells in a known volume of blood, usually expressed as the number of cells per litre. A sample of blood at known dilution is examined in a special counting chamber. Blood-count investigations are important in the diagnosis of blood diseases. *See also* differential leucocyte count.

血細胞計數　已知血容量內不同血細胞的數量，一般用每升血液中的細胞數表示。已知其稀釋度的血液標本在專用計數室內進行檢查。血細胞計數在血液病診斷中有重要意義。參閱 differential leucocyte count。

blood donor a person who gives blood for storage in a *blood bank. The blood can then be used for *transfusion into another patient. In Britain collection is organized by the National Blood Transfusion Services, but the armed forces have their own services. *See also* blood group.

供血者　獻血以供血庫貯存備用者。血液可輸給另一患者。在英國，採血由國家輸血服務中心組織實施，但軍隊有其獨立機構。參閱 blood group。

blood group any one of the many types into which a person's blood may be classified. Based on the presence or absence of certain inherited antigens on the surface of the red blood cells. Blood of one group contains antibodies in the serum that react against the cells of other groups.

There are more than 30 blood group systems, one of the most important of which is the *ABO system*. This system is based on the presence or absence of antigens A and B: blood of groups A and B contains antigens A and B, respectively; group AB contains both antigens and group O neither. Blood of group A

血型　根據紅細胞表面是否存在某種遺傳性抗原，人體血液可以分為多種類型。一種血型血清中的抗體與其他型的細胞發生反應。血型系統有三十多種，最重要的一種為 ABO 系統。這一系統的基礎為是否存在 A 抗原和 B 抗原。A 型血和 B 型血分別含有 A 抗原和 B 抗原；AB 型血中 A、B 兩種抗原均有，O 型血中均無。A 型血含抗 B 抗原的抗體，B 型血含抗 A 抗原的抗體。AB 型血兩種抗原均無，O 型血均有。血液中含有某類抗體的人不能接受含有相應抗原血液的

contains antibodies to antigen B; group B blood contains anti-A antibodies; group AB has neither antibody and group O has both. A person whose blood contains either (or both) of these antibodies cannot receive a transfusion of blood containing the corresponding antigens. The table illustrates which blood groups can be used in transfusion for each of the four groups.

輸血。下表列出了輸血中四種血型的使用方法。

Donor's blood group 供血者血型	Blood group of people donor can receive blood from 供血者可接受其 血液的人的血型	Blood group of people donor can give blood to 供血者可供血給 他的人的血型
A	A, O	A, AB
B	B, O	B, AB
AB	A, B, AB, O	AB
O	O	A, B, AB, O

blood plasma *see* plasma.

血漿　參閱 plasma。

blood poisoning the presence of either bacterial toxins or large numbers of bacteria in the bloodstream causing serious illness. *See* pyaemia, septicaemia, toxaemia.

敗血症　血流中存在細菌毒素或大量細菌，引起嚴重疾病。參閱 pyaemia，septicaemia，toxaemia。

blood pressure the pressure of blood against the walls of the main arteries. Pressure is highest during *systole, when the ventricles are contracting (*systolic pressure*), and lowest during *diastole, when the ventricles are relaxing and refilling (*diastolic pressure*). Blood pressure is measured – in millimetres of mercury – by means of a *sphygmomanometer at the brachial artery of the arm, where the pressure is most similar to that of blood leaving the heart. The

血壓　血液對大動脈壁的壓力。血壓在心室收縮的收縮期最高（收縮壓），在心室舒張和再充盈的舒張期最低（舒張壓）。血壓用 mmHg 表示，通過置於上臂肱動脈部位的血壓計測量，此處壓力與血液離開心臟時的壓力最為近似。血壓的正常範圍隨年齡而變化，年輕人的收縮壓預期值大約為 120mm，舒張壓約為 80mm。簡寫為 120/80。

normal range varies with age, but a young adult would be expected to have a systolic pressure of around 120 mm and a diastolic pressure of 80 mm. These are recorded as 120/80.

Individual variations are common. Muscular exertion and emotional factors, such as fear, stress, and excitement, all raise systolic blood pressure (*see* hypertension). Systolic blood pressure is normally at its lowest during sleep. Severe shock may lead to an abnormally low blood pressure and possible circulatory failure (*see* hypotension). Blood pressure is adjusted to its normal level by the *sympathetic nervous system and hormonal controls.

blood serum *see* serum.

blood sugar the concentration of glucose in the blood, normally expressed in millimoles per litre. The normal range is 3.5–5.5 mmol/l. Blood-sugar estimation is an important investigation in a variety of diseases, most notably in diabetes mellitus. *See also* hyperglycaemia, hypoglycaemia.

blood test any test designed to discover abnormalities in a sample of a person's blood, such as the presence of alcohol, drugs, or bacteria, or to determine the *blood group.

blood transfusion *see* transfusion.

blood vessel a tube carrying blood away from or towards the heart. Blood vessels are the means by which blood circulates throughout the body. *See* artery, arteriole, vein, venule, capillary.

blue baby an infant suffering from congenital cyanotic heart disease, the

個體差異常見。肌肉勞累和恐懼、緊張、興奮等感情因素均使收縮壓升高（參閱 hypertension）。通常睡眠時收縮壓最低。嚴重休克可導致異常低血壓並可發生循環衰竭（參閱 hypotension）。血壓由交感神經系統和激素控制調節在正常水平。

血清 參閱 serum。

血糖 血液中葡萄糖的濃度，常以 mmol/l 表示。正常值為 3.5~5.5 µmol/l。血糖測定是多種疾病的一項重要檢查內容，尤其是糖尿病。參閱 hyperglycaemia，hypoglycaemia。

血液檢驗 用於發現人體血液標本中異常狀況的檢驗，如檢測酒精、藥物或細菌，或確定血型。

輸血 參閱 transfusion。

血管 運送血液離開或流向心臟的管道。血管為血液在全身循環之工具。參閱 artery，arteriole，vein，venule，capillary。

青紫嬰兒 患有先天性青紫性心臟病的嬰兒。最常見類型為

commonest forms of which are *tetralogy of Fallot and *transposition of the great vessels, in which the circulation is misdirected. Both of these conditions result in the presence of partially deoxygenated blood (which is blue in colour) in the peripheral circulation, which gives the skin and lips a characteristic purple colour. Surgical correction is often possible at an early stage. If untreated, infants may survive months or years with persistent *cyanosis.

Boari flap an operation in which a tube of bladder tissue is constructed to replace the lower third of the ureter when this has been destroyed or damaged or has to be removed because of the presence of a tumour. *See also* ureteroplasty.

body *n.* **1.** an entire animal organism. **2.** the trunk of an individual, excluding the limbs. **3.** the main or largest part of an organ (such as the stomach or uterus). **4.** a solid discrete mass of tissue; e.g. the carotid body. *See also* corpus.

body image (body schema) the individual's concept of the disposition of his limbs and the identity of the different parts of his body. It is a function of the *association areas of the brain. *See also* Gerstmann's syndrome.

body temperature the intensity of heat of the body, as measured by a thermometer. Body temperature is accurately controlled by a small area at the base of the brain (the *hypothalamus); in normal individuals it is maintained at about 37°C (98.4°F). Heat production by the body arises as the result of vital activities (e.g. respiration, heartbeat, circulation, secretion) and from the muscular effort of exercise and shivering.

法樂四聯症和引起逆向循環的大血管錯位。兩種狀況均導致外周循環中有部分未氧合血（呈藍色），使皮膚和口唇呈現典型的紫色。常可在早期進行手術矯正。若不治療，這類嬰兒可存活數月或數年，紫紺則長期存在。

博厄里瓣　輸尿管的下三分之一段被破壞或損傷時，或因腫瘤而切除時，用膀胱組織建造一管道來替代的手術。參閱 ureteroplasty。

體　**(1)** 完整的動物機體。**(2)** 除肢體外的軀幹。**(3)** 器官主要或最大的部分（如胃或子宮）。**(4)** 獨立的實質性組織塊，如頸動脈球。參閱 corpus。

體像　個體對四肢位置和身體各部分特徵的概念，為大腦聯合區的一種功能。參閱 Gerstmann's syndrome。

體溫　用溫度計所測的體熱強度。體溫受腦底部一小區（丘腦下部）的精確控制；正常維持在 37°C (98.4°F) 左右。身體因生命活動（如呼吸、心搏、循環、分泌），肌肉運動和戰栗而產熱，發熱時體溫升高。

A rise in body temperature occurs in fever.

body type (somatotype) the characteristic anatomical appearance of an individual, based on the predominance of the structures derived from the three germ layers (ectoderm, mesoderm, endoderm). The three types are described as *ectomorphic, *mesomorphic, and *endomorphic.

體型　個體的特徵性解剖學表現。取決於來自三個胚層（外胚層、中胚層、內胚層）的結構優勢。三種類型分別稱為外胚層體型、中胚層體型和內胚層體型。

boil *n.* a tender inflamed area of the skin containing pus. The infection is usually caused by the bacterium *Staphylococcus aureus* entering through a hair follicle or a break in the skin, and local injury or lowered constitutional resistance may encourage the development of boils. Boils usually heal when the pus is released or with antibiotic treatment, though occasionally they may cause more widespread infection. Medical name: **furuncle**.

癤　皮膚含膿的觸痛性炎區。感染常由經毛囊或皮膚破損侵入的金黃色葡萄球菌所致，局部損傷或機體抵抗力降低可促使癤的發展。一般在排膿或用抗生素治療後愈合。偶爾可致感染擴散。醫學用語：癤。

bolus *n.* a soft mass of chewed food or a pharmaceutical preparation that is ready to be swallowed.

大丸劑，團　適於吞咽的咀嚼後的食物軟團或藥學製劑。

bonding *n.* **1.** (in psychology) the development of a close and selective relationship, such as that of *attachment. *Mother-child bonding* is the supposed process in which physical contact between mother and child in the child's first hours of life promotes the mother's loving and caring for her baby. **2.** (in dentistry) the attachment of dental restorations, sealants, and appliances to teeth. Bonding may be mechanical (*see* acid-etch technique) or chemical, by the use of adhesive *cements.

(1) 依附　（心理學）選擇性親密關係的產生，如依戀。母子依附指想象中嬰兒出生後即有的母子身體接觸促使母親對嬰兒愛戀與關懷的過程。**(2) 黏合**　（牙科學）將牙修復體、密封劑和其他材料黏固於牙。黏合可為機械性的（參閱 acid-etch technique）或使用黏固粉的化學性的。

bone *n.* the hard extremely dense connective tissue that forms the skeleton of

骨　構成人體骨骼的堅硬而致密的結締組織。由充滿骨鹽

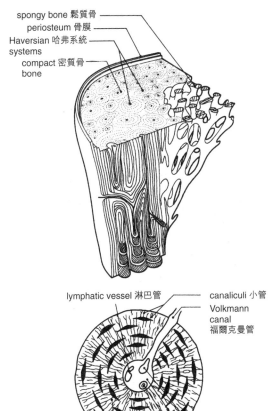

spongy bone 鬆質骨
periosteum 骨膜
Haversian 哈弗系統 systems
compact 密質骨 bone

lymphatic vessel 淋巴管
canaliculi 小管
Volkmann canal 福爾克曼管

two lamellae of matrix 兩個基質板
lacunae containing bone cells 骨陷窩內含骨細胞

vein 靜脈
Haversian canal 哈弗管
artery 動脈

Section of the shaft of a long bone (above)
with detail of a single Haversian system (below)
長骨幹（上）和一個哈弗
系統（下）的微細構造圖

the body. It is composed of a matrix of collagen fibres impregnated with bone salts (chiefly calcium carbonate and calcium phosphate). *Compact* (or *cortical*) *bone* forms the outer shell of bones; it consists of a hard virtually solid mass made up of bony tissue arranged in concentric layers (*Haversian systems*). *Spongy* (or *cancellous*) *bone*, found beneath compact bone, consists of a meshwork of bony bars (*trabeculae*) with many interconnecting spaces containing marrow. (See illustration.) Individual bones may be classed as long, short, flat, or irregular. The outer layer of a bone is called the *periosteum. The *medullary cavity* is lined with *endosteum and contains the marrow. Bones not only form the skeleton but also act as stores for mineral salts and play an important part in the formation of blood cells.

（主要是碳酸鈣和磷酸鈣）的膠原纖維基質組成。密質骨（骨皮質）形成骨的外殼，由以同心層排列的骨性組織（哈弗系統）組成的堅硬物質構成。鬆質骨位於密質骨之下，由骨小梁網絡及許多相互貫通的含有骨髓的腔隙構成（見圖）。單塊骨可分為長骨、短骨、扁骨或異形骨。骨的外層稱為骨膜，骨髓腔有骨內膜覆蓋並含有骨髓。骨不僅形成骨骼，而且是無機鹽貯存所，並在血細胞形成中起重要作用。

bone marrow (marrow) the tissue contained within the internal cavities of the bones. At birth, these cavities are filled entirely with blood-forming *myeloid tissue* (*red marrow*) but in later life the marrow in the limb bones is replaced by fat (*yellow marrow*). Samples of bone marrow may be obtained for examination by *aspiration through a stout needle or by *trephine biopsy. *See also* haemopoiesis.

骨髓　骨內腔隙中所含組織。出生時這些腔隙全部充滿骨髓組織（紅骨髓），四肢骨的骨髓以後被脂肪所取代（黃骨髓）。可用粗針抽吸或環鑽活檢取得骨髓標本進行檢查。參閱 haemopoiesis。

bony labyrinth *see* labyrinth.

骨迷路　參閱 labyrinth。

borax *n.* a mild astringent with a weak antiseptic action, applied externally to skin and mucous membranes. Borax and boric acid are used in mouth and nasal washes, gargles, eye lotions and contact-lens solutions, and in dusting powder. Side-effects from external application are rare; most reported cases of poisoning are in infants.

硼砂　一種具有弱抗菌作用的温和收斂劑，外用於皮膚和黏膜。硼砂和硼酸用於口腔和鼻腔沖洗、含漱液、洗眼液、接觸鏡片溶液和撒粉中。外用副作用罕見，報道的中毒病例多為嬰兒。

borborygmus *n.* (*pl.* **borborygmi**) an abdominal gurgle due to movement of fluid and gas in the intestine. Excessive borborygmi occur when intestinal movement is increased, for example in the *irritable bowel syndrome and in intestinal obstruction, or when there is more intestinal gas than normal.

腹鳴　腸內液體和氣體運動引起的腹部咕嚕聲。腸道運動增強時腹鳴音亢進，如在應激性結腸綜合徵、腸梗阻或腸積氣時。

borderline *adj.* **1.** describing a personality disorder characterized by unstable and intense relationships, exploiting and manipulating other people, rapidly changing moods, recurrent suicidal or self-injuring acts, and a pervasive inner feeling of emptiness and boredom. **2.** *see* schizotypal.

邊緣型的　**(1)** 描述一種性格障礙，特點為人際關係不穩定、緊張、利用和操縱他人、情緒多變、經常性的自殺或自傷行為，以及充滿空虛和厭煩的內在感覺。**(2)** 參閱 schizotypal。

Bordetella *n.* a genus of tiny Gram-negative aerobic bacteria. *B. pertussis* causes *whooping cough, and all the other species are able to break down red blood cells and cause diseases resembling whooping cough.

博戴桿菌屬　一屬微小的革蘭氏陰性需氧菌。百日咳博戴桿菌引起百日咳，其他菌種均能破壞紅細胞，導致百日咳樣疾病。

boric acid *see* borax.

硼酸　參閱 borax。

borneol *n.* an essential oil used, in preparations with other essential oils, such as menthol, menthone, and camphene, to disperse gallstones and kidney stones. It is administered by mouth. Trade names: **Rowachol**, **Rowatinex**.

龍腦（冰片）　與薄荷腦、薄荷酮和樟腦萜等揮發油合用於製劑中以排出膽石和腎結石的一種揮發油，口服。商品名：Rowachol，Rowatinex。

Bornholm disease (devil's grip, epidemic myalgia, epidemic pleurodynia) a disease caused by *Coxsackie viruses. It is spread by contact and epidemics usually occur during warm weather in temperate regions and at any time in the tropics. Symptoms include fever, headache, and attacks of severe pain in the lower chest. The illness lasts about a week and is rarely fatal. There is no specific treatment.

流行性胸肌痛　一種由柯薩奇病毒所致的疾病。通過接觸傳播，流行通常發生在溫帶的暖季和熱帶的任何季節。症狀有發熱、頭痛、下胸部陣發性劇痛。病程約為一周，極少致死，無特效治療。

Borrelia *n.* a genus of large parasitic *spirochaete bacteria. The species *B. duttonii*, *B. persica*, and *B. recurrentis* cause *relapsing fever in Africa, Asia, North America, and Europe. The species *B. burghdorferi* causes *Lyme disease.

包柔螺旋體屬，疏螺旋體屬 大型寄生性螺旋體屬細菌。達氏疏螺旋體、波斯疏螺旋體和回歸熱疏螺旋體引起非洲、亞洲、北美洲和歐洲各地的回歸熱。博氏疏螺旋體可致萊姆病。

botulinum toxin a powerful nerve toxin, produced by the bacterium *Clostridium botulinum*, that has proved effective, in minute dosage, for the treatment of various conditions of muscle overaction, such as strabismus (squint) and various dystonic conditions (*see* dystonia), including spasm of the orbicularis muscle in patients with *blepharospasm. It is administered by injection. Possible side-effects include prolonged local muscle paralysis. Trade name: **Dysport**.

肉毒桿菌毒素 肉毒桿菌所產生的一種強效神經毒素。微劑量可用於治療多種肌運動過度狀態如斜視，和各種肌張力障礙疾病（參閱 dystonia），包括瞼痙攣患者的輪匝肌痙攣。注射給藥。可致副作用為長期局部肌麻痺。商品名：Dysport。

botulism *n.* a serious form of *food poisoning from foods containing the toxin produced by the bacterium *Clostridium botulinum*. The toxin selectively affects the central nervous system; in fatal cases, death is often caused by heart and lung failure resulting from a malfunction of the cardiac and respiratory centres of the brain. The bacterium thrives in improperly preserved foods, typically canned raw meats. The toxin, being rather unstable to heat, is invariably destroyed in cooking.

肉毒中毒 含有肉毒桿菌毒素的食物引起的嚴重食物中毒。毒素選擇性作用於中樞神經系統，危重病例常因心臟和腦呼吸中樞功能障礙導致心肺衰竭而死亡。肉毒桿菌在保存不當的食物如罐裝生肉中大量繁殖。肉毒桿菌毒素非常不耐熱，總在烹飪中被破壞。

Bouchard's node a lump of cartilage-covered bone arising at the proximal interphalangeal joint of a finger in osteoarthritis. It is often found together with *Heberden's nodes.

布夏爾結 骨關節炎患者近端指骨間關節出現的軟骨覆蓋的骨塊。常同見於希伯登結。

bougie *n.* a hollow or solid cylindrical instrument, usually flexible, that is inserted into tubular passages, such as the

探條 插入食管、直腸或尿道等管狀通道的中空或實心圓柱形器械，常可彎曲。用於診斷

oesophagus (gullet), rectum, or urethra. Bougies are used in diagnosis and treatment, particularly by enlarging *strictures (for example, in the urethra).

和治療，尤其是擴張狹窄（如擴張尿道狹窄）。

bovine spongiform encephalopathy (BSE) *see* spongiform encephalopathy.

牛海綿狀腦病 參閱 spongiform encephalopathy。

bowel *n. see* intestine.

腸 參閱 intestine。

Bowen's disease a type of carcinoma of the squamous epidermal cells of the skin that does not spread to the basal layers.

鮑恩病 未擴散至基底層的皮膚鱗狀上皮細胞癌。

bow-legs *pl. n.* abnormal out-curving of the legs, resulting in a gap between the knees on standing. A certain degree of bowing is normal in small children, but persistence into adult life or later development of this deformity, results from abnormal growth of the *epiphysis (as in *Still's disease) or arthritis. The condition can be corrected by *osteotomy or interposition *arthroplasty. Medical name: **genu varum**.

弓形腿，膝外翻 雙腿異常外曲，以至站立時雙膝不能並攏。幼兒可有一定程度的正常彎曲，但持續至成年或畸形有所發展時，則為骺發育異常（如斯蒂爾病）或關節炎所致。可用骨切開術或嵌入關節成形術矯正。醫學用語：膝外翻。

Bowman's capsule the cup-shaped end of a *nephron, which encloses a knot of blood capillaries (*glomerulus*). It is the site of primary filtration of the blood into the kidney tubule.

鮑曼囊 腎單位的杯狀末端，包繞毛細血管結（腎小球）。為血液進入腎小管的初級過濾部位。

BPH benign prostatic hypertrophy. *See* prostate gland.

良性前列腺肥大 參閱 prostate gland。

brachi- (brachio-) *prefix denoting* the arm. Example: *brachialgia* (pain in).

〔前綴〕**臂** 如臂痛。

brachial *adj.* relating to or affecting the arm.

臂的，肱的

brachial artery an artery that extends from the axillary artery, at the armpit, down the side and inner surface of the

肱動脈 於腋窩處從腋動脈沿上臂內側下行至肘部的動脈，在此分為橈動脈和尺動脈。

upper arm to the elbow, where it divides into the radial and ulnar arteries.

brachialis *n.* a muscle that is situated at the front of the upper arm and contracts to flex the forearm (see illustration). It works against the triceps brachii.

肱肌　位於上臂前面的肌肉，其收縮屈曲前臂（見圖），與肱三頭肌拮抗。

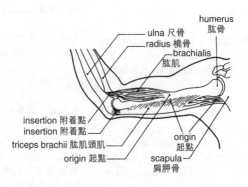

Brachialis and triceps muscles
肱肌和三頭肌

brachial plexus a network of nerves, arising from the spine at the base of the neck, from which arise the nerves supplying the arm, forearm and hand, and parts of the shoulder girdle (see illustration). *See also* radial nerve.

臂叢　源於頸部脊髓的神經網，由此產生支配上臂、前臂和手，以及部分肩胛帶的神經（見圖）。參閱 radial nerve。

brachiocephalic artery *see* innominate artery.

頭臂動脈　參閱 innominate artery。

brachium *n.* (*pl.* **brachia**) the arm, especially the part of the arm between the shoulder and the elbow.

臂　尤指肩與肘之間的臂部。

brachy- *prefix denoting* shortness. Example: *brachydactylia* (shortness of the fingers or toes).

〔前綴〕短　如短指（趾）畸形（手指或腳趾短小）。

brachycephaly *n.* shortness of the skull, with a *cephalic index of about 80. **–brachycephalic** *adj.*

短頭（畸形）　顱骨短小，顱指數約為 80。

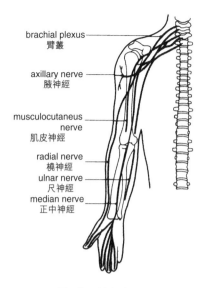

brachial plexus
臂叢

axillary nerve
腋神經

musculocutaneus
nerve
肌皮神經

radial nerve
橈神經
ulnar nerve
尺神經
median nerve
正中神經

The brachial plexus
臂叢

brachytherapy *n.* radiotherapy adminis-tered by implanting radioactive wires or grains into or close to a tumour. This technique is used in the treatment of many accessible tumours (e.g. breast cancer).

近距（放射）療法　將放射性導綫或微粒植入或靠近腫瘤的放射療法。用於治療多種易受影響的腫瘤（如乳腺癌）。

brady- *prefix denoting* slowness. Example: *bradylalia* (abnormally slow speech).

〔前綴〕**徐緩**　緩慢或遲鈍。如言語徐緩（言語異常緩慢）。

bradycardia *n.* slowing of the heart rate to less than 50 beats per minute. *Sinus bradycardia* is often found in healthy individuals, especially athletes, but it is also seen in some patients with reduced thyroid activity, jaundice, hypothermia, or *vasovagal attacks. Bradycardia may also result from *arrhythmias, especially complete *heart block, when the slowing is often extreme and often causes loss of consciousness.

心搏過緩　心率低於 50 次／分。竇性心搏過緩常見於正常人尤其是運動員中，但亦見於一些甲狀腺功能減弱、黃疸、低溫或血管迷走神經性發作患者中。心搏過緩也可因心律失常所致，尤其是完全性心傳導阻滯，此時心搏極其緩慢並常引起意識喪失。

bradykinesia *n.* a symptom of *parkinsonism comprising a difficulty in initiating movements and slowness in executing movements and in maintaining body posture.

運動徐緩　帕金森綜合徵的一種症狀，包括起始運動困難，完成運動緩慢和保持體姿笨拙。

bradykinin *n.* a naturally occurring polypeptide consisting of nine amino acids. Bradykinin is a very powerful vasodilator and causes contraction of smooth muscle; it is formed in the blood under certain conditions and is thought to play an important role as a mediator of inflammation. *See* kinin.

緩激肽　9 個氨基酸組成的天然多肽。為一種強效血管舒張藥並可致平滑肌收縮。在一定條件下形成於血液中，被認為是一種炎症介質而發揮重要作用。參閱 kinin。

braille *n.* an alphabet, developed by Louis Braille (1809–1852) in 1837, in which each letter is represented by a pattern of raised dots, which are read by feeling with the finger tips. It is the main method of reading used by the blind today.

點字法（盲人用）　1837 年由路易・布萊葉 (1809~1852) 發明的一種字母表。每個字母用凸起的點狀模型表示，通過指尖感覺閱讀。為現代盲人閱讀的主要方法。

brain *n.* the enlarged and highly developed mass of nervous tissue that forms the upper end of the *central nervous system (see illustration). The average adult human brain weighs about 1400 g (approximately 2% of total body weight) and is continuous below with the spinal cord. It is invested by three connective tissue membranes, the *meninges, and floats in *cerebrospinal fluid within the rigid casing formed by the bones of the skull. The brain is divided into the hindbrain (rhombencephalon), consisting of the *medulla oblongata, *pons Varolii, and *cerebellum; the *midbrain (mesencephalon); and the forebrain (prosencephalon), subdivided into the *cerebrum and the *diencephalon (including the *thalamus and *hypothalamus). Anatomical name: **encephalon**.

腦　形成中樞神經系統上端的膨大和高度發育的神經組織團（見圖）。成人平均腦重約為 1400 克（約佔體重的 2%），向下移行為脊髓。腦由三層結締組織膜即腦脊膜覆蓋，浮於被堅硬顱骨所包圍的腦脊液中。腦分為由延髓、腦橋和小腦組成的菱腦，中腦，和由大腦與間腦（包括丘腦和丘腦下部）組成的前腦。醫學用語：腦。

brain death *see* death.

腦死亡　參閱 death。

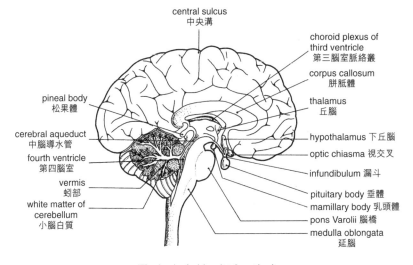

The brain (midsagittal section)
腦（矢狀面）

brainstem *n.* the enlarged extension upwards within the skull of the spinal cord, consisting of the medulla oblongata, the pons, and the midbrain. The pons and medulla are together known as the *bulb*, or *bulbar area*. Attached to the midbrain are the two cerebral hemispheres. *See* brain.

腦幹　顱內脊髓向上延伸的膨大部分，由延髓、腦橋和中腦組成。腦橋和延髓統稱為球部。大腦半球附着於中腦。參閱 brain。

brain tumour *see* cerebral tumour.

腦腫瘤　參閱　cerebral tumour。

branchial arch *see* pharyngeal arch.

鰓弓　參閱 pharyngeal arch。

branchial cleft *see* pharyngeal cleft.

鰓裂　參閱 pharyngeal cleft。

branchial cyst a cyst that arises at the site of one of the embryonic *pharyngeal pouches due to a developmental anomaly.

鰓裂囊腫　發育異常所致胚胎咽囊處產生的囊腫。

branchial pouch *see* pharyngeal pouch.

鰓囊　參閱　pharyngeal pouch。

Brandt Andrews method a technique for expelling the placenta from the uterus. Upward pressure is applied to the uterus through the abdominal wall while holding the umbilical cord taut. When the uterus is elevated in this way, the placenta will be in the cervix or upper vagina and is then expelled by applying pressure below the base of the uterus.

breakbone fever *see* dengue.

breast *n*. **1.** the mammary gland of a woman: one of two compound glands that produce milk. Each breast consists of glandular lobules – the milk-secreting areas – embedded in fatty tissue (see illustration). The milk passes from the lobules into ducts, which join up to form 15–20 *lactiferous ducts*. Near the front of the breast the lactiferous ducts are dilated into *ampullae*, which act as

布-安氏法　從子宮出胎盤術。拉緊臍帶同時經腹壁將子宮向上推壓，子宮因此升高時，胎盤即處於子宮頸或陰道上方，再經子宮底向下施壓排出。

登革熱　參閱 dengue。

(1) 乳房　女性的乳腺。泌乳的兩複腺之一，由包埋於脂肪組織中的乳腺小葉（乳汁分泌區）組成（見圖）。乳汁經乳腺小葉進入乳腺導管，爾後匯合形成 15~20 個輸乳管。輸乳管在近乳房前部處擴大為壺腹以貯存乳汁。每一輸乳管在乳頭各有一個開口。乳頭周圍的較暗部分稱為乳暈。參閱

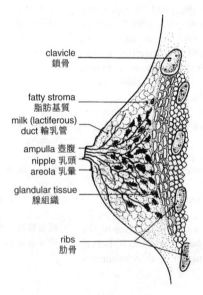

clavicle
鎖骨

fatty stroma
脂肪基質

milk (lactiferous)
duct 輸乳管

ampulla 壺腹
nipple 乳頭
areola 乳暈

glandular tissue
腺組織

ribs
肋骨

Longitudinal section through a breast
乳房縱切面觀

reservoirs for the milk. Each lactiferous duct discharges through a separate orifice in the nipple. The dark area around the nipple is called the *areola. See also* lactation. Anatomical name: **mamma. 2.** the front part of the chest (thorax).

breastbone *n. see* sternum.

breast cancer a malignant tumour of the breast, usually a *carcinoma, rarely a *sarcoma. It is unusual in men but is the commonest form of cancer in women, in some cases involving both breasts. Despite extensive research the cause is not known, but it would appear to have a familial link.

The classic sign is a lump in the breast, which is often noticed after minor local injury; bleeding or discharge from the nipple may occur infrequently. Sometimes the first thing to be noticed is a lump in the armpit, which is due to spread of the cancer to the drainage lymph nodes. The tumour may also spread to the bones, lungs, and liver. Current treatment of a localized tumour is usually by surgery (*see* lumpectomy, mastectomy), with or without radiotherapy; cytotoxic drugs and hormone therapy may be used as *adjuvant therapy and for widespread (metastatic) disease. *Tamoxifen is the hormonal treatment of choice for breast cancer in postmenopausal women with metastatic disease; it is also increasingly used as a first-line treatment for premenopausal women.

breast implant a prosthesis to replace breast tissue that has been removed surgically during a simple *mastectomy in the treatment of breast cancer. The type of implant in current use is a silicone sac filled with silicone gel; it has recently

lactation。醫學用語：乳房。
(2) 胸　胸廓前部。

胸骨　參閱 sternum。

乳腺癌　乳房的惡性腫瘤。一般為癌，偶爾為肉瘤，男性罕見，卻是女性最常見癌症。一些病例累及雙側乳房。雖有廣泛研究仍病因不明。但似有家族性。

　　典型體徵是乳房腫塊，常在局部輕傷後被發現，很少發生乳頭出血或溢乳。有時因癌症擴散至引流淋巴結而首先注意到腋窩腫塊。乳腺癌亦可擴散至骨、肺與肝。目前對局限性腫瘤通常用手術治療（參閱 lumpectomy，mastectomy），或兼用放射療法。細胞毒素藥物和激素療法可用作輔助療法及用於發生廣泛轉移的病例。他莫昔芬是已發生轉移的經絕期乳腺癌患者的最佳激素治療，也愈來愈多地用作經絕期前婦女的重要治療激素。

乳房植入物　取代乳腺癌治療時單純性乳房切除術中所切除的乳房組織的假體。現代使用的植入物為填充硅酮凝膠的硅酮囊狀物；最近發現，用聚氨酯材料塗在硅酮囊外層使其表

been found that coating the sac with polyurethane to give a textured surface reduces the incidence of fibrosis around the implant and consequent hardening of breast tissue. The implant is inserted subcutaneously at the time of operation (the skin and nipple are retained), and follow-up radiotherapy is not normally required. Implants are also used to augment existing breast tissue.

面具有一定結構，可減少植入物周圍發生纖維變性而使乳房組織硬化。植入物在行乳房切除術時經皮下植入（保留皮膚和乳頭），之後一般不需要放射治療。植入物亦用於增大現有乳房組織。

breath-holding attacks episodes in which a child cries, holds its breath, and goes blue. They are common in toddlers and are usually precipitated by not getting their own way. The attacks may cause loss of consciousness. Drug treatment is not necessary and the attacks cease spontaneously.

屏氣發作 小孩哭泣、屏氣並發紺。幼兒中常見，一般因未能隨心所欲所致。發作可引起意識喪失。無需藥物治療而自行停止。

breathing *n.* the alternation of active *inhalation* (or *inspiration*) of air into the lungs through the mouth or nose with the passive *exhalation* (or *expiration*) of the air. During inhalation the *diaphragm and *intercostal muscles con-

呼吸 經口或鼻將空氣主動吸入肺內（吸氣）和被動呼出空氣（呼氣）的更迭。吸氣時膈肌和肋間肌收縮，使胸腔擴大吸入空氣。呼氣時這些肌肉鬆弛將空氣從肺中迫出（見

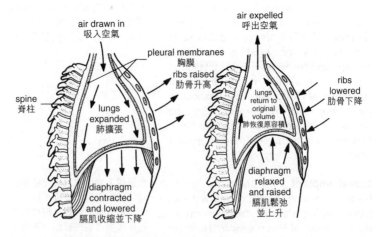

Position of the diaphragm (from the side) during breathing
呼吸時膈的位置（側面觀）

tract, which enlarges the chest cavity and draws air into the lungs. Relaxation of these muscles forces air out of the lungs at exhalation. (See illustration.) Breathing is part of *respiration and is sometimes called external respiration. There are many types of breathing in which the rhythm, rate, or character is abnormal. *See also* apnoea, bronchospasm, Cheyne-Stokes respiration, dyspnoea, stridor.

breathlessness *n. see* dyspnoea.

breath sounds the sounds heard through a stethoscope placed over the lungs during breathing. Normal breath sounds are soft and called *vesicular* – they may be increased or decreased in disease states. The sounds heard over the larger bronchi are louder and harsher. Breath sounds transmitted through consolidated lungs in pneumonia are louder and harsher; they are similar to the sounds heard normally over the larger bronchi and are termed *bronchial breath sounds*. *Crepitations and *rhonchi are sounds added to the breath sounds in abnormal states of the lung. *Amphoric* or *cavernous* sounds have a hollow quality and are heard over cavities in the lung; the amphoric quality may also be heard in voice sounds and on percussion.

breech presentation the position of a baby in the uterus such that it will be delivered buttocks first (instead of the normal head-first position). This type of delivery increases the risk of damage to the baby. *See also* cephalic version, Lovset's manoeuvre.

bregma *n.* the point on the top of the skull at which the coronal and sagittal *sutures meet. In a young infant this is an opening, the anterior *fontanelle.

圖）。此為呼吸作用的一部分，有時稱為外呼吸。有多種類型的呼吸節律、呼吸率和呼吸性質異常。參閱 apnoea，bronchospasm，Cheyne-Stokes respiration，dyspnoea，stridor。

氣促 參閱 dyspnoea。

呼吸音 經置於肺部的聽診器於呼吸時聽到的聲音。正常呼吸音柔和，稱為肺泡呼吸音，患病時可增強或減弱。大支氣管部位呼吸音較響而粗，肺炎時經實變肺臟傳遞的呼吸音較響而粗，類似於正常在大支氣管部位聽到的聲音，稱為支氣管呼吸音。捻發音和乾囉音是肺部異常狀態下的呼吸附加音。空甕性質亦可在語音和叩診中聽到。

臀先露 胎兒在子宮內的位置，分娩時臀部首先娩出（而非正常的頭先露胎位），此種分娩增加了胎兒受損傷的危險。參閱 cephalic version，Lovset's manoeuvre。

前囟 顱骨頂部冠狀縫與矢狀縫連接之處。嬰兒此處為未閉間隙，即前囟。

bretylium tosylate a drug used in patients with cardiac arrest to reverse ventricular *fibrillation that has failed to respond to electrical *defibrillation. It is administered by intravenous injection. Trade name: **Bretylate**.

溴苄銨托西酸鹽　一種用於電除纖顫無效的使心搏停止患者逆轉心室纖維性顫動的藥物。靜脈注射給藥。商品名：Bretylate。

bridge *n.* (in dentistry) a fixed replacement for missing teeth. The artificial tooth is attached to one or more natural teeth, usually by a crown. Bridges may also be fitted on dental *implants. The supporting teeth (or implants) are referred to as *abutments*, and the artificial teeth that fit over them are referred to as *retainers*. The replacements of missing teeth are known as *pontics. Adhesive bridges* are attached to one or more adjacent teeth by a metal plate that adheres to the enamel on the tooth surface prepared by the *acid-etch technique; these bridges require minimal tooth preparation compared with conventional types of bridges.

牙橋　（牙科學）缺牙的固定替代物。假牙通常靠牙冠相連在一個或多個真牙上。牙橋亦可裝在牙植入物上，支持牙（或植入物）稱為基牙，裝在基牙上的假牙稱為固位體。缺牙替代物稱為橋體。黏結橋通過用酸蝕法黏連在牙面釉質上的金屬托基而附着於一個或數個毗鄰牙上。與常規型齒橋相比，此種齒橋所需的牙製備最少。

Bright's disease *see* nephritis.

布賴特病，腎炎　參閱 nephritis。

Briquet's syndrome *see* somatization disorder.

布里奎特綜合徵　參閱 somatization disorder。

British Anti-Lewisite (BAL) *see* dimercaprol.

抗路易士藥劑，二巰丙醇　參閱 dimercaprol。

British thermal unit a unit of heat equal to the quantity of heat required to raise the temperature of 1 pound of water by 1° Fahrenheit. 1 British thermal unit = 1055 joules. Abbrev.: Btu.

英制熱量單位　相當於使 1 磅水溫度升高華氏 1 度的熱量單位。1 英制熱量單位等於 1055 焦耳。縮寫為 Btu。

Broca's area the area of cerebral motor cortex responsible for the initiation of speech. It is situated in the left frontal

布羅卡區，旁嗅區　支配言語運動的大腦皮質區。在大多數（但非全部）右利者中位於左

lobe in most (but not all) right-handed people, in the region of *Brodmann areas 44 and 45.

額葉的布羅德曼皮質區 44 和 45 區。

Brodie's abscess an abscess of bone: a form of chronic bacterial *osteomyelitis, not due to tuberculosis or syphilis. Treatment is by surgical drainage and antibiotics.

布羅迪膿腫（幹骺端膿腫） 骨膿腫；一種非結核病或梅毒所致的慢性細菌性骨髓炎。用外科引流和抗生素治療。

Brodmann areas the numbered areas (1–47) into which a map of the *cerebral cortex may conveniently be divided for descriptive purposes, based upon the arrangement of neurones seen in stained sections under the microscope. On the map area 4, for example, corresponds to primary motor cortex, while the primary visual cortex comes into area 17.

布羅德曼皮質區 根據顯微鏡下染色切片中神經元的排列情況，便於劃分大腦皮質進行描述的編號區域 (1–47)。例如，4 區相當於第 1 運動皮質區，而第 1 視覺皮質區在 17 區。

bromazepam *n.* a long-acting *benzodiazepine drug used in the short-term treatment of disabling anxiety. It is administered by mouth. Trade name: **Loxetan**.

溴西泮 一種用於傷殘性焦慮的短期治療的長效苯二氮草。口服。商品名：Loxetan。

bromism *n.* a group of symptoms caused by excessive intake of bromides, formerly widely used as sedatives. Overuse for long periods leads to mental dullness, weakness, drowsiness, loss of sensation, slurred speech, and sometimes coma. A form of acne may also develop.

溴中毒 溴化物攝入過多產生的一種症狀。溴化物曾廣泛用作鎮靜劑。長期過量使用可致精神遲鈍、虛弱、嗜睡、感覺喪失、語言模糊、有時昏迷。亦可出現痤瘡。

bromocriptine *n.* a drug, derived from ergot, that has effects similar to those of *dopamine. It is used in the treatment of *parkinsonism and to prevent lactation by inhibiting the secretion of the hormone *prolactin by the pituitary gland. The drug is administered by mouth. Fairly common side-effects are dizziness and confusion. Trade name: **Parlodel**.

溴隱亭 一種源於麥角而作用類似於多巴胺的藥物。用於治療帕金森綜合徵及抑制垂體腺分泌催乳素而抑制泌乳，口服。常見副作用為頭昏和精神混亂。商品名：Parlodel。

brompheniramine *n.* an *antihistamine given by mouth to relieve the symptoms of allergic reactions, especially hay fever and rhinitis. Common side-effects include drowsiness, dizziness, dryness of the throat, and digestive upsets. Trade name: **Dimotane**.

溴苯那敏　一種減輕變態反應症狀，尤其是枯草熱和鼻炎的口服抗組胺藥，常見副作用有嗜睡、頭昏、口乾和胃腸不適。商品名：Dimotane。

Brompton cocktail a mixture of alcohol, morphine, and cocaine sometimes given to control severe pain in terminally ill people, especially those dying of cancer. The mixture was first tried at the Brompton Hospital, London, and has given relief to thousands.

布朗普頓雞尾酒　一種由酒精、嗎啡和可卡因配製的合劑。有時用於晚期患者尤其是癌症患者控制劇痛。此合劑首先在倫敦的布朗普頓醫院試用並使數以千計的患者減輕病痛。

bromsulphthalein *n.* a blue dye used in tests of liver function. A small quantity of the dye is injected into the bloodstream, and its concentration in the blood is measured after 5 and then 45 minutes. The presence of more than 10% of the dose in the circulation after 45 minutes indicates that the liver is not functioning normally.

磺溴酞鈉　檢測肝功的藍色染劑。小劑量染劑 5 分鐘和 45 分鐘注入血液後分別測定血液中其濃度。45 分鐘後血流中染劑超過注入量的10%則提示肝功能異常。

bronch- (broncho-) *prefix denoting* the bronchial tree. Examples: *bronchoalveolar* (relating to the bronchi and alveoli); *bronchopulmonary* (relating to the bronchi and lungs).

〔前綴〕支氣管　指支氣管樹。例如，支氣管肺泡的（有關支氣管和肺泡的），支氣管肺的（有關支氣管和肺的）。

bronchial carcinoma cancer of the bronchus, one the commonest causes of death in smokers. *See also* lung cancer, oat cell.

支氣管癌　吸煙者死亡的最常見原因之一。參閱 lung cancer，oat cell。

bronchial tree a branching system of tubes conducting air from the trachea (windpipe) to the lungs: includes the bronchi (*see* bronchus) and their subdivisions and the *bronchioles.

支氣管樹　從氣管運送空氣至肺部的管道分支系統，包括支氣管（參閱 bronchus）及其分支和細支氣管。

bronchiectasis *n.* widening of the bronchi or their branches. It may be

支氣管擴張　支氣管或其分支擴大。可為先天性的，或由感

congenital or it may result from infection (especially whooping cough or measles in childhood) or from obstruction, either by an inhaled foreign body or by a growth (including cancer). Pus may form in the widened bronchus so that the patient coughs up purulent sputum, which may contain blood. Diagnosis is on the clinical symptoms and by X-ray and CT scan. Treatment consists of antibiotic drugs to control the infection and physiotherapy to drain the sputum. Surgery may be used if only a few segments of the bronchi are affected.

bronchiole *n.* a subdivision of the bronchial tree that does not contain cartilage or mucous glands in its wall. Bronchioles open from the fifth or sixth generation of bronchi and extend for up to 20 more generations before reaching the *terminal bronchioles*. Each terminal bronchiole divides into a number of *respiratory bronchioles*, from which the *alveoli open. Each terminal bronchiole conducts air to an acinus in the *lung. **–bronchiolar** *adj.*

bronchiolitis *n.* inflammation of the small airways in the lungs (*see* bronchiole) due to viral infection, usually the *respiratory syncytial virus. Bronchiolitis occurs in epidemics and is commonest in infants of less than one year. The bronchioles become swollen, the lining cells die, and the tubes become blocked with debris and mucopus. This prevents air reaching the alveoli and the child becomes short of oxygen (hypoxic), breathless, and possibly cyanosed; the breathlessness may prevent feeding. Bronchiolitis is treated with oxygen and supportive measures, e.g., feeding via a nasogastric tube. Antibiotics are indicated only if there is evidence of a

染所致（兒童尤其因百日咳或麻疹），亦可因異物吸入或有腫物（包括癌）造成支氣管阻塞而致。擴大的支氣管中可有膿形成，故患者咳出可能帶血的膿性痰。依據臨床症狀和 X 綫檢查與 CT 掃描作診斷，治療包括用抗生素控制感染和理療排痰。若病變僅限於幾段支氣管時可行手術治療。

細支氣管　管壁中無軟骨或黏液腺的支氣管樹分支。從第 5 或第 6 級支氣管分出，並不斷分支達 20 級而變為終末細支氣管。每一終末細支氣管分為若干呼吸細支氣管，下為肺泡。每一終末細支氣管輸送空氣至一組肺泡。

細支氣管炎　通常為呼吸道合胞病毒感染所致的肺內小導管炎症（參閱 bronchiole）。係流行性疾病，在不滿 1 歲的幼兒中最常見。患病時細支氣管腫脹，內襯細胞死亡，氣管被碎屑和黏液性膿阻塞，從而阻礙空氣到達肺泡，造成患兒缺氧（氧過少）、氣促並可能發紺；氣促還可妨礙餵養。治療採用給氧和支持措施，如用鼻胃管餵養，抗生素僅適用於有繼發感染的情況。若患兒特別虛弱，用利巴韋林特效治療可能有益。細支氣管炎反覆發作可能預示發生哮喘。

secondary infection. If the child is particularly vulnerable, specific treatment with *ribavirin may be beneficial. Recurrent attacks of bronchiolitis may herald the onset of *asthma.

bronchitis *n.* inflammation of the bronchi (*see* bronchus). *Acute bronchitis* is caused by viruses or bacteria and is characterized by coughing, the production of mucopurulent sputum, and narrowing of the bronchi due to spasmodic contraction (*see* bronchospasm). In *chronic bronchitis* the patient coughs up excessive mucus secreted by enlarged bronchial mucous glands; the bronchospasm cannot always be relieved by bronchodilator drugs. It is not primarily an inflammatory condition, although it is frequently complicated by acute infections. The disease is particularly prevalent in Britain in association with cigarette smoking, air pollution, and *emphysema.

支氣管炎　支氣管的炎症（參閱 bronchus）。急性支氣管炎由病毒或細菌所致，特徵為咳嗽、有黏液膿性痰及痙攣性收縮引起的支氣管狹窄（參閱 bronchospasm）。慢性支氣管炎患者因支氣管黏液腺增殖而咳出大量黏液。支氣管擴張劑不能緩解所有的支氣管痙攣。本病雖常併發於急性感染，卻非一種炎性為主的疾病。在英國尤其流行，與吸煙、空氣污染和肺氣腫有關。

bronchoalveolar lavage (BAL) a method of obtaining cellular material from the lungs that is used particularly in the investigation and monitoring of interstitial lung disease and in the investigation of pulmonary infiltrates in immunosuppressed patients. Examination of the cells in the lavage fluid may help to identify the cause of interstitial lung disease. The combination of cytological and microbiological examination can lead to a very high rate of diagnostic accuracy in such conditions as *Pneumocystis carinii* pneumonia.

支氣管肺泡灌洗　一種從肺部獲取細胞物質的方法。特別用於檢查和探測間質性肺病和檢查免疫抑制患者的肺浸潤。檢查灌洗液中的細胞有助於鑒定間質性肺病的病因。細胞學和微生物學的聯合檢查可在卡氏肺囊蟲性肺炎之類疾病中作出高度準確的診斷。

bronchoconstrictor *n.* a drug that causes narrowing of the air passages by producing spasm of bronchial smooth muscle.

支氣管收縮藥　使支氣管平滑肌收縮導致氣道變窄的藥物。

bronchodilator *n.* an agent that causes widening of the air passages by relaxing bronchial smooth muscle. *Sympathomimetic drugs that stimulate beta-receptors, such as *ephedrine, *isoprenaline, *salbutamol, and *terbutaline, are potent bronchodilators and are used for relief of bronchial asthma and chronic bronchitis. These drugs are often administered as aerosols, giving rapid relief, but at high doses they may stimulate the heart.

支氣管擴張藥　使支氣管平滑肌鬆弛導致氣道擴張的藥物。刺激 β-受體的擬交感神經藥為強效支氣管擴張藥，如麻黃鹼、異丙腎上腺素、沙丁胺醇和特布他林，用於緩解支氣管哮喘和慢性支氣管炎。常以氣霧劑使用，生效迅速，但大劑量可刺激心臟。

bronchography *n.* X-ray examination of the bronchial tree after it has been made visible by the injection of *radiopaque dye or contrast medium. It was used particularly in the diagnosis of *bronchiectasis, but has now been largely superseded by CT scanning.

支氣管造影術　注入不透 X 綫的染劑或造影劑使其顯影後對支氣管樹的 X 綫檢查。尤其用於診斷支氣管擴張，現已基本被 CT 掃描取代。

bronchophony *n. see* vocal resonance.

支氣管（語）音　參閱 vocal resonance。

bronchopneumonia *n. see* pneumonia.

支氣管肺炎　參閱 pneumonia。

bronchoscope *n.* an instrument used to look into the trachea and bronchi. In addition to the rigid tubular metal type, used for many years, there is now a narrower flexible *fibreoptic instrument with which previously inaccessible bronchi can be inspected. With either instrument the bronchial tree can be washed out (*see* bronchoalveolar lavage) and samples of tissue and foreign bodies can be removed with long forceps. **–bronchoscopy** *n.*

支氣管鏡　一種用於窺視氣管和支氣管的器械。除沿用多年的金屬硬管型外，現有一種可檢查過去不能抵達的支氣管的較細而易彎的纖維光學鏡。兩型均可沖洗支氣管樹（參閱 bronchoalveolar lavage），並均可用長鉗取出組織標本和異物。

bronchospasm *n.* narrowing of bronchi by muscular contraction in response to some stimulus, as in *asthma and *bronchitis. The patient can usually inhale air into the lungs, but exhalation may

支氣管痙攣　因某種刺激如哮喘和支氣管炎引起肌肉收縮而致支氣管狹窄。患者通常能吸氣，而呼氣則需明顯的肌肉運動，伴有聽診器可清晰聽見或

require visible muscular effort and is accompanied by expiratory noises that are clearly audible (*see* wheeze) or detectable with a stethoscope. The condition in which bronchospasm can usually be relieved by bronchodilator drugs is known as *reversible obstructive airways disease* and includes asthma; that in which bronchodilator drugs usually have no effect is *irreversible obstructive airways disease* and includes chronic bronchitis.

bronchus *n.* (*pl.* **bronchi**) any of the air passages beyond the *trachea (windpipe) that has cartilage and mucous glands in its wall (see illustration). The trachea divides into two main bronchi, which divide successively into five *lobar bronchi*, 20 *segmental bronchi*, and two or three more divisions. *See also* bronchiole. **–bronchial** *adj.*

發現的呼氣音（參閱 wheeze）。可被支氣管擴張藥緩解的病症稱為可逆性氣道阻塞性疾病，包括哮喘；支氣管擴張藥無效的病症為不可逆性氣道阻塞性疾病，包括慢性支氣管炎。

支氣管 氣管以下管壁有軟骨和黏液腺的氣道（見圖）。氣管分為兩個主支氣管，進而相繼分成 5 個葉支氣管，20 個段支氣管以及 2 至 3 個更多分支。參閱 bronchiole。

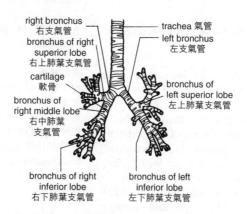

The bronchi and their principal (lobar) branches
支氣管及其主要（葉）分支

brown fat a form of fat in adipose tissue that is a rich source of energy and can be converted rapidly to heat. There is speculation that a rapid turnover of brown fat

褐色脂肪 脂肪組織中貯存豐富能量並可迅速轉化為熱量的一種脂肪。據推測褐色脂肪迅速轉化，以平衡食物攝入過多

occurs to balance excessive intake of food and unnecessary production of white fat (making up the bulk of adipose tissue). Some forms of obesity may be linked to lack of – or inability to synthesize – brown fat.

與白色脂肪（組成脂肪組織的大部分）不必要的生成。某些肥胖症可能與缺少或不能合成褐色脂肪有關。

Brown-Séquard syndrome the neurological condition resulting when the spinal cord has been partly cut through. In those parts of the body supplied by the damaged segment there is a flaccid weakness and loss of feeling in the skin. Below the lesion there is a spastic paralysis on the same side and a loss of pain and temperature sensation on the opposite side.

布朗-塞卡爾綜合徵 脊髓被部分截斷時產生的神經病學症狀。損傷節段所支配的身體部位肌弛緩無力和皮膚感覺喪失。損傷節段以下有同側痙攣性麻痺和對側痛覺和溫度覺喪失。

Brucella *n.* a genus of Gram-negative aerobic spherical or rodlike parasitic bacteria responsible for *brucellosis (undulant fever) in man and contagious abortion in cattle, pigs, sheep, and goats. The principal species are *B. abortus* and *B. melitensis. Brucella ring test* is a diagnostic test for brucellosis involving the clumping together of a standard *Brucella* strain by antibodies in an infected person's serum.

布氏桿菌屬 一屬在人類引起布氏桿菌病（波狀熱）與牛、豬、綿羊和山羊傳染性流產的革蘭氏陰性球狀或桿狀需氧寄生性細菌。主要菌種為流產布氏桿菌和馬爾他布氏桿菌。布氏桿菌環狀試驗用於診斷布氏桿菌病，方法為使感染者血清中的抗體與標準布氏桿菌菌株發生凝集反應。

brucellosis (Malta fever, Mediterranean fever, undulant fever) *n.* a chronic disease of farm animals caused by bacteria of the genus *Brucella*, which can be transmitted to man either by contact with an infected animal or by drinking nonpasteurized contaminated milk. Symptoms include headache, fever, aches and pains, sickness, loss of appetite, and weakness; occasionally a chronic form develops, with recurrent symptoms. Untreated the disease may last for years but prolonged administration of tetracycline antibiotics or streptomycin is effective.

布氏桿菌病 由布氏桿菌屬細菌引起的家畜的慢性疾病，可經接觸受感染動物或飲用未經消毒的污染牛乳而傳染於人。症狀有頭痛、發熱、疼痛、惡心、食慾喪失及乏力。偶爾發展為慢性，伴復發症狀。若不治療此病可持續數年，但長期使用四環素類抗生素或鏈黴素對此病有效。

Brufen *n. see* ibuprofen.

布洛芬 參閱 ibuprofen。

Brugia *n.* a genus of threadlike parasitic worms (*see* filaria). *B. malayi* infects man throughout southeast Asia, causing *filariasis and *elephantiasis (especially of the feet and legs). *B. pahangi*, a parasite of wild cats and domestic animals, produces an allergic condition in man, with coughing, breathing difficulty, and an increase in the number of *eosinophils in the blood. *Brugia* undergoes part of its development in mosquitoes of the genera *Anopheles* and *Mansonia*, which transmit the parasite from host to host.

馬來絲蟲屬 一屬綫狀蠕蟲（參閱 filaria）。在全東南亞，馬來絲蟲感染人類引起絲蟲病和象皮病（尤其在腳和腿）。寄生於野貓和家畜的彭亨絲蟲在人類引起變應症狀，伴咳嗽、呼吸困難和血液嗜酸性細胞增多。馬來絲蟲屬在按蚊屬和曼蚊屬蚊體內度過部分發育階段，絲蟲經此蚊媒從宿主傳給另一宿主。

bruise (contusion) *n.* an area of skin discoloration caused by the escape of blood from ruptured underlying vessels following injury. Initially red or pink, a bruise gradually becomes bluish, and then greenish yellow, as the haemoglobin in the tissues breaks down chemically and is absorbed. It may be necessary to draw off blood from very severe bruises through a needle, to aid healing.

挫傷 受傷後血液逸出破裂血管而致的局部皮膚變色。最初為紅色或桃紅色，隨組織中血紅蛋白化學分解與吸收而逐漸變藍，然後變成綠黃色。嚴重挫傷時可需用針吸出淤血以利愈合。

bruit *n. see* murmur.

（雜）音 參閱 murmur。

Brunner's glands compound glands of the small intestine, found in the *duodenum and the upper part of the jejunum. They are embedded in the submucosa and secrete mucus.

布倫內腺 見於十二指腸和空腸上段的小腸複腺，包埋於黏膜下層並分泌黏液。

brush border *see* microvillus.

刷狀緣 參閱 microvillus。

bruxism *n.* a habit in which an individual grinds his teeth, which leads to excessive wear. This usually occurs during sleep.

磨牙症 一種磨牙的習慣，致使牙過多磨損，一般發生於睡眠中。

BSE bovine *spongiform encephalopathy.

牛海綿狀腦病

bubo *n.* a swollen inflamed lymph node in the armpit or groin, commonly developing in some sexually transmitted diseases (e.g. soft sore), bubonic plague, and leishmaniasis.

腹股溝淋巴結炎　腋窩或腹股溝淋巴結腫脹發炎。通常發生於某些性傳播疾病（如軟下疳）、腺鼠疫和利什曼病中。

bubonic plague *see* plague.

腺鼠疫，腹股溝淋巴結鼠疫　參閱 plague。

buccal *adj.* **1.** relating to the mouth or the hollow part of the cheek. **2.** describing the surface of a tooth adjacent to the cheek.

頰的　**(1)** 與口腔或頰中空部位有關的。**(2)** 描述與面頰毗鄰的牙表面。

buccal cavity the cavity of the mouth, which contains the tongue and teeth and leads to the pharynx. Here food is tasted, chewed, and mixed with saliva, which begins the process of digestion.

口腔前庭　包含舌與牙的口腔部，通向咽部。食物在此品嘗、咀嚼並與唾液混合開始消化過程。

buccal glands small glands in the mucous membrane lining the mouth. They secrete material that mixes with saliva.

頰腺　口腔黏膜內的小腺體，其分泌物與唾液混合。

buccinator *n.* a muscle of the cheek that has its origin in the maxilla and mandible (jaw bones). It is responsible for compressing the cheek and is important in mastication.

頰肌　源於上頜骨和下頜骨的頰部肌肉。起收縮頰部之作用，有重要的咀嚼功能。

buclizine *n.* an *antihistamine with marked sedative properties. Given by mouth, it is used (combined with codeine and paracetamol in *Migraleve*) to treat migraine and is also used to relieve mild anxiety states and tension. Side-effects include drowsiness, dizziness, dryness of the throat, and gastrointestinal upsets. Occasionally it may cause teratogenic effects.

布克利嗪，安其敏　一種鎮靜作用顯著的口服抗組胺藥。（與可待因和對乙酰氨基酚結合）用於治療偏頭痛及緩解輕度焦慮狀態和緊張。副作用有嗜睡、頭昏、咽喉乾燥和胃腸不適，偶爾致畸。

Budd-Chiari syndrome a rare condition that follows obstruction of the hepatic vein by a blood clot or tumour.

巴-希氏綜合徵　血塊或腫瘤阻塞肝靜脈引起的一種罕見疾病，特徵為腹水和肝硬化。

It is characterized by ascites and cirrhosis of the liver.

budesonide *n.* a *corticosteroid drug used in a nasal spray to treat hay fever or as an inhalant for asthma. It is also administered as a cream or ointment for the treatment of eczema, psoriasis, and similar conditions. Trade names: **Pulmicort, Preferid**.

布地奈德 一種以鼻腔噴霧治療枯草熱或作為吸入劑用於哮喘的皮質類固醇藥物。亦用作乳膏或軟膏治療濕疹、銀屑病和類似疾病。商品名：Pulmincort，Preferid。

Buerger's disease an inflammatory condition of the arteries, especially in the legs, that predominantly affects young male cigarette smokers. Intermittent *claudication (pain due to reduced blood supply) and gangrene of the limbs may develop. Coronary thrombosis may occur and venous thrombosis is common. The treatment is similar to that of *atheroma but cessation of smoking is essential to prevent progression of the disease. Medical name: **thromboangiitis obliterans**.

伯格病，血栓閉塞性脈管炎 一種主要發生於年輕男性吸煙者的動脈炎性疾患，尤其在下肢。可發生間歇性跛行（血液供應不足引起疼痛）和肢體壞疽，亦可發生冠狀動脈血栓形成，靜脈血栓形成常見。治療與動脈粥樣化的治療相似，但必須戒煙以防止病情發展。醫學用語：血栓閉塞性脈管炎。

bufexamac *n.* an anti-inflammatory drug (*see* NSAID) administered externally in the form of a cream for the treatment of skin inflammation and to relieve itching.

丁苯羥酸 一種以乳膏，外用治療皮膚炎症及減輕瘙癢的抗炎藥（參閱 NSAID）。

buffer *n.* a solution whose hydrogen ion concentration (pH) remains virtually unchanged by dilution or by the addition of acid or alkali. The chief buffer of the blood and extracellular body fluids is the bicarbonate (H_2CO_3/HCO_3^-) system. *See also* acid-base balance.

緩衝劑 稀釋、加酸或加鹼後氫離子濃度 (pH) 保持不變的溶液。血液和細胞外液的主要緩衝劑是碳酸氫鹽系統 (H_2CO_3/HCO_3^-)。參閱 acid-base balance。

bulb *n.* (in anatomy) any rounded structure or a rounded expansion at the end of an organ or part.

球 （解剖學）器官或部分末端的圓形結構或圓形擴張。

bulbar *adj.* **1.** relating to or affecting the medulla oblongata. **2.** relating to a bulb. **3.** relating to the eyeball.

(1) 延髓的 有關或影響延髓的。(2) 球的 (3) 眼球的

bulbourethral glands *see* Cowper's glands.

尿道球腺　參閱 Cowper's glands。

bulimia *n.* insatiable overeating. This symptom may be psychogenic, occurring, for example, as a phase of *anorexia nervosa (*bulimia nervosa* or the *binge–purge syndrome*); or it may be due to neurological causes, such as a lesion of the *hypothalamus.

食慾過盛　不能滿足的進食過多。此症狀可為精神性的，如為神經性厭食的一個階段（神經性食慾過盛），或由神經性病因所致，如下丘腦損傷。

bulla *n.* (*pl.* **bullae**) **1.** a large blister, containing serous fluid. **2.** (in anatomy) a rounded bony prominence. **3.** a thin-walled air-filled space within the lung, arising congenitally or in *emphysema. It may cause trouble by rupturing into the pleural space (*see* pneumothorax), by adding to the air that does not contribute to gas exchange, and/or by compressing the surrounding lung and making it inefficient. **–bullous** *adj.*

大疱，大泡　**(1)** 含有漿液的大水疱。**(2)**（解剖學）圓形骨性隆凸。**(3)** 先天性的或見於肺氣腫中肺內充滿空氣的薄壁空隙。可由於破裂進入胸腔（參閱 pneumothorax），增加不參與交換的氣體量和／或壓迫肺部影響通氣效率而致病。

bumetanide *n.* a quick-acting *diuretic used to relieve the fluid retention (oedema) occurring in heart failure, kidney disease, and cirrhosis of the liver. It is administered by mouth or by injection. A possible side-effect is dizziness. Trade name: **Burinex**.

布美他尼　一種用於減輕心力衰竭、腎病和肝硬化中液體瀦留（水腫）的速效利尿劑。口服或注射給藥。可致副作用為頭昏。商品名：Burinex。

bundle *n.* a group of muscle or nerve fibres situated close together and running in the same direction; e.g. the *atrioventricular bundle.

束　一組緊密排列並走向一致的肌或神經纖維，如房室束。

bundle branch block a defect in the specialized conducting tissue of the heart (*see* arrhythmia) that is recognized as an electrocardiographic abnormality. Left or right bundle branch blocks, affecting the respective ventricles, may be seen. Occasionally both left and right bundle branch blocks occur simultaneously and the patient develops complete *heart

束支性傳導阻滯　一種心臟特殊傳導組織病變（參閱 arrhythmia），有心電圖異常的表現。左或右束支性傳導阻滯分別影響左心室或右心室。左右束支偶爾同時發生傳導阻滯，患者出現完全性心傳導阻滯，病因類似於完全性心傳導阻滯。

block. The causes are similar to those of complete heart block.

bundle of His *see* atrioventricular bundle.

希斯束 參閱 atrioventricular bundle。

bunion *n*. a swelling of the joint between the great toe and the first metatarsal bone. A *bursa often develops over the site and the great toe becomes displaced towards the others. Bunions are usually caused by ill-fitting shoes and may require surgical treatment.

拇囊炎 拇趾與第一跖骨間關節的腫脹，常在此形成黏液囊並使拇趾移位。一般因穿鞋不適引起，可能需要外科治療。

buphthalmos (hydrophthalmos) *n*. infantile or congenital glaucoma: increased pressure within the eye due to a defect in the development of the tissues through which fluid drains from the eye. Since the outer coat (sclera) of the eyeball of children is distensible, the eye enlarges as the inflow of fluid continues. It affects both eyes and may accompany congenital malformations in other parts of the body. Treatment is by surgical operation, e.g. *goniotomy, to improve drainage of fluid from the eye. Spontaneous arrest of buphthalmos may occur before vision is completely lost.

牛眼 嬰兒青光眼或先天性青光眼；因引流房水的組織發育缺陷引起眼內壓升高，由於兒童眼球外膜（鞏膜）可膨脹，眼球隨房水不斷進入而擴大。此病累及雙眼，可伴有身體其他部位的先天性畸形。治療採用外科手術，如前房角切開術，以增加房水引流。可在完全失明前自然停止。

bupivacaine *n*. a potent local anaesthetic, used mainly for regional *nerve block. It is significantly longer acting than many other local anaesthetics. It has been used in childbirth, but may cause slowing of the baby's heart, with a risk of death. Trade name: **Marcain**.

布比卡因 主要用於區域神經阻滯的強效局部麻醉劑。其作用時間明顯長於許多其他局部麻醉藥。已用於分娩中，但可引起嬰兒心搏減慢甚至死亡。商品名：Marcain。

buprenorphine *n*. a powerful synthetic *opiate painkilling drug; it acts for 6–8 hours and is administered by mouth. Side-effects include drowsiness, nausea, dizziness, and sweating. Trade name: **Temgesic**.

丁丙諾啡 一種合成的強效阿片製劑止痛藥；作用時間為 6~8 小時，口服。副作用有嗜睡、惡心、頭昏和出汗。商品名：Temgesic。

bur (burr) *n.* **1.** a cutting drill that fits in a dentist's handpiece. Burs are mainly used for cutting cavities in teeth. **2.** a surgical drill for cutting through bone.

bur hole a circular hole drilled through the skull to release intracranial tension (due to blood, pus, or cerebrospinal fluid) or to facilitate such procedures as needle aspiration or biopsy.

Burkitt's lymphoma (Burkitt's tumour) a malignant tumour of the lymphatic system, most commonly affecting children and largely confined to tropical Africa in a zone 15° north and south of the equator. It is the most rapidly growing malignancy, with a tumour doubling time of about five days. It can arise at various sites, most commonly the facial structures, such as the jaw, and in the abdomen. The *Epstein-Barr virus plays a role in the origin and growth of the tumour. Complications affecting the nervous system occur in up to 50% of cases. Non-African Burkitt's lymphoma is increasingly being recognized. All forms are very sensitive to cytotoxic drug therapy but cure is uncommon.

burn *n.* tissue damage caused by such agents as heat, chemicals, electricity, sunlight, or nuclear radiation. A *first-degree burn* affects only the outer layer (epidermis) of the skin. In a *second-degree burn* both the epidermis and the underlying dermis are damaged. A *third-degree burn* involves damage or destruction of the skin to its full depth and damage to the tissues beneath. Burns cause swelling and blistering, due to loss of plasma from damaged blood vessels. In serious burns, affecting 15% or more

（牙）鑽 **(1)** 牙醫手機上的切削鑽頭，主要用於牙齒鑽洞。**(2)** 鑿穿骨骼的外科錐。

鑽孔 鑽穿顱骨的圓孔。以減小顱內壓（血液、膿液或腦脊液所致）或利於作針吸法或活組織檢查。

伯基特淋巴瘤 一種淋巴系統的惡性腫瘤，最常發生於兒童及熱帶非洲赤道南北各 15 度區域內。其惡性程度發展極快，大約 5 天腫瘤即增長一倍。可發生在不同部位，最常見於面部如頜以及腹部。EB 病毒為腫瘤發生和生長的因素之一，達 50% 的病例有神經系統的併發症，非非洲型伯基特淋巴瘤正日益增多。各型均對細胞毒素藥物治療敏感，但治愈少見。

灼傷、燒傷 由熱、化學品、電、日光或核放射等造成的組織損傷。I度燒傷僅累及皮膚外層（表層），II度燒傷時表皮層與其下的真皮層均受損傷，III度燒傷時皮膚全層及皮下組織均受損。因受損血管中的血漿喪失而產生腫脹與水疱。在成人燒傷面積達 15%（兒童 10% 或更多）的嚴重燒傷中，這種血漿喪失導致嚴重休克，需立即輸血或輸注鹽溶液。燒傷還可引起細菌感染，

of the body surface in adults (10% or more in children), this loss of plasma results in severe *shock and requires immediate transfusion of blood or saline solution. Burns may also lead to bacterial infection, which can be prevented by administration of antibiotics. Third-degree burns may require skin grafting.

可用抗生素預防。III 度燒傷需皮膚移植。

burr *n.* *see* bur.

（牙）鑽　參閱 bur。

bursa *n.* (*pl.* **bursae**) a small sac of fibrous tissue that is lined with *synovial membrane and filled with fluid (synovia). Bursae occur where parts move over one another; they help to reduce friction. They are normally formed round joints and in places where ligaments and tendons pass over bones. However, they may be formed in other places in response to unusual pressure or friction.

黏液囊　一種內襯滑膜並充滿液體（滑液）的纖維組織小囊。見於相互在其面上運動的部位處，有助於減少摩擦。正常形成於關節周圍和韌帶與肌腱通過骨的地方。亦可在異常壓力或摩擦的其他地方形成。

bursitis *n.* inflammation of a *bursa, resulting from injury, infection, or rheumatoid *synovitis. It produces pain and tenderness and sometimes restricts movement at a nearby joint; for example, at the shoulder. Treatment of bursitis not due to infection is by rest and corticosteroid injection. *See also* housemaid's knee.

黏液囊炎　受傷、感染或類風濕性滑膜炎所致的黏液囊的炎症。使附近關節如肩疼痛和觸痛，有時運動受限。非感染所致黏液囊炎的治療為休息和注射皮質類固醇藥物。參閱 housemaid's knee。

buserelin *n.* an *LHRH analogue that is administered as a nasal spray for the treatment of endometriosis and to help in the management of advanced cancer of the prostate gland. Possible side-effects include hot flushes, headache, emotional upset, and loss of libido. Trade names: **Suprecur, Suprefact**.

布舍瑞林　一種以鼻腔噴霧劑治療子宮內膜異位和幫助控制晚期前列腺癌的 LHRH 類似物。可致副作用有熱潮紅、頭痛、情感紊亂、性慾喪失。商品名：Suprecur，Suprefact。

buspirone *n.* a *tranquillizer used to relieve the symptoms of anxiety. It

丁螺環酮　一種用於減輕焦慮症狀的安定藥，口服。常見副

is administered by mouth; common side-effects are headache, nausea, dizziness, and nervousness. Trade name: **Buspar**.

busulphan *n.* a drug that destroys cancer cells by acting on the bone marrow. It is administered by mouth, mainly in the treatment of chronic myeloid leukaemia. It may cause blood disorders producing bleeding. Trade name: **Myleran**.

butobarbitone (butobarbital) *n.* an intermediate-acting *barbiturate, used for the treatment of insomnia and for sedation. It produces sleep within 30 minutes when given by mouth and its sedative effect lasts for about six hours. Prolonged administration may lead to *dependence and its use with alcohol should be avoided; overdosage has serious effects (*see* barbiturism). Trade name: **Soneryl**.

butriptyline *n.* a tricyclic *antidepressant drug administered by mouth. Possible side-effects include difficulty in urination.

butyrophenone *n.* one of a group of chemically related *antipsychotic drugs that includes *haloperidol, *droperidol, and *benperidol. Butyrophenones inhibit the effects of *dopamine by occupying dopamine receptor sites in the body.

byssinosis *n.* an industrial disease of the lungs caused by inhalation of dusts of cotton, flax, hemp, or sisal. The patient characteristically has chest tightness and *wheeze after the weekend break, which wears off during the working week. The causal agent has not been identified.

作用為頭痛、惡心、頭昏及神經過敏。商品名：Buspar。

白消安 一種作用於骨髓來破壞癌細胞的口服藥物。主要用於治療慢性骨髓樣白血病，可引起出血。商品名：Myleran。

丁巴比妥 一種用於治療失眠和鎮靜的中效巴比妥酸鹽。口服後 30 分鐘內入眠，其鎮靜作用持續約 6 小時，長期服用可產生依賴性，應避免與乙醇合用。過量有嚴重後果（參閱 barbiturism）。商品名：Soneryl。

布替林 一種口服三環類抗抑鬱藥。可致副作用為排尿困難。

丁酰苯 一組化學結構相關的抗精神病藥物，包括氟哌啶醇、氟哌利多、苯哌利多。通過占據體內多巴胺受體位置而抑制其作用。

棉屑病，棉屑沉着病 一種吸入棉花、亞麻、大麻或西沙爾麻塵而引起的職業性肺病。患者在周末休息後出現典型的胸悶和喘鳴，而在工作日中逐漸減弱。致病因子尚未確定。

C

cac- (caco-) *prefix denoting* disease or deformity. Example: *cacosmia* (unpleasant odour).

〔前綴〕**惡，有病** 指病態或畸形。如惡臭。

cachet *n.* a flat capsule containing a drug that has an unpleasant taste. The cachet is swallowed intact by the patient.

扁囊劑 內裝不良味道藥物的扁形膠囊。患者將其完整吞下。

cachexia *n.* a condition of abnormally low weight, weakness, and general bodily decline associated with chronic disease. It occurs in such conditions as cancer, pulmonary tuberculosis, and malaria.

惡液質 慢性病時出現的體重異常減輕、虛弱和全身衰竭的狀態。見於癌症、肺結核與瘧疾等。

cacosmia *n.* a disorder of the sense of smell in which scents that are inoffensive to most people are objectionable to the sufferer or in which a bad smell seems to be perpetually present. The disorder is usually due to damage to pathways within the brain rather than in the nose or olfactory nerve.

惡臭幻覺 一種嗅覺障礙。患者難以忍受對多數人無礙的氣味，或似乎有臭味持續存在，通常因腦內神經而非嗅神經路徑損傷而致。

cadmium *n.* a silvery metallic element that can cause serious lung irritation if the fumes of the molten metal are inhaled. Long-term exposure may also cause kidney damage. Symbol: Cd.

鎘 一種似銀的金屬元素。大量吸入其蒸氣時可對肺產生嚴重刺激，長期接觸還可致腎損害。符號：Cd。

caecostomy *n.* an operation in which the caecum is brought through the abdominal wall and opened in order to drain or decompress the intestine, usually when the colon is obstructed or injured.

盲腸造口術 經腹壁取出盲腸作一開口的手術。用於腸道引流與減壓，通常在結腸梗阻或損傷時。

caecum *n.* a blind-ended pouch at the junction of the small and large intestines, situated below the *ileocaecal valve. The upper end is continuous with the colon and the lower end bears the vermiform appendix. *See* alimentary canal.

盲腸 位於迴盲瓣下方的小腸與大腸接合處的盲端囊。其上端與結腸相延續，下端附有闌尾。參閱 alimentary canal。

caeruloplasmin *n.* a copper-containing protein present in blood plasma. Congenital deficiency of caeruloplasmin leads to abnormalities of the brain and liver (*see* Wilson's disease).

血漿銅藍蛋白　一種存在於血漿的含銅蛋白。先天性缺乏此種蛋白可致腦和肝異常（參閱 Wilson's disease）。

Caesarean section a surgical operation for delivering a baby through the abdominal wall. The operation most commonly performed is *lower uterine segment Caesarean section* (*LUSCS*), carried out through an incision (usually transverse) in the lower segment of the uterus. *Classical Caesarean section*, in which the upper segment of the uterus is incised vertically, is now rarely performed. In addition to its use in cases of obstructed labour, *malpresentation (breech, brow, and shoulder), and in severe *antepartum haemorrhage, Caesarean section is being performed increasingly when the baby is at risk and is exhibiting signs of distress. Because of improved techniques in perinatal care, particularly of the preterm baby, the operation may be performed, if necessary, as soon as the child is viable.

剖宮產術　經腹壁使嬰兒娩出的手術。最常施行的為子宮下段剖宮產術 (LUSCS)，即在子宮下段作一切口（常為橫切）。垂直切開子宮上段的古典式剖宮產術現已少用。剖宮產術用於有產道阻礙的分娩、先露異常（臀先露，額先露和肩先露）和嚴重的產前出血，亦越來越多地用於胎兒有危險並顯示窘迫徵象時。由於圍產期保健技術的提高，尤其是對早產兒，若有必要，一旦胎兒具備了存活能力即可行此手術。

caesium-137 *n.* an artificial radioactive isotope of the metallic element caesium. The radiation given off by caesium-137 is employed in the technique of *radiotherapy. Symbol: ^{137}Cs. *See also* telecurietherapy.

^{137}銫　金屬元素銫的人工放射性同位素。其射綫用於放射治療。符號：^{137}Cs。參閱 telecurietherapy。

café au lait spots well-defined pale-brown patches on the skin. They are present in up to 20% of the normal population, but the presence of six or more in an individual is strongly suggestive of *neurofibromatosis.

咖啡牛乳色斑　皮膚上邊界明確的淡棕色斑，出現在達 20% 的正常人羣中。但個體有 6 個或更多色斑則極有可能為神經纖維瘤病。

caffeine *n.* an alkaloid drug, obtained from coffee and tea, that has a stimulant action, particularly on the central

咖啡因　從咖啡和茶葉中提取的生物鹼藥。對中樞神經系統有興奮作用，用於促進清醒狀

nervous system. It is used to promote wakefulness and increase mental activity; it also possesses diuretic properties and will help relieve certain forms of headache. It is often administered with aspirin or codeine in analgesic preparations.

態和增強腦力活動；亦具利尿特性，有助於緩解某些類型的頭痛。常與阿司匹林或可待因合用於止痛藥中。

caisson disease *see* compressed air illness.

潛水員病　參閱 compressed air illness。

calamine *n.* a preparation of zinc carbonate used as a mild astringent on the skin in the form of a lotion, cream, or ointment.

鑪甘石　以洗劑、乳膏或軟膏用作温和的皮膚收斂劑的碳酸鋅製劑。

calc- (calci-, calco-) *prefix denoting* calcium or calcium salts.

〔前綴〕**鈣**　指鈣元素或鈣鹽。

calcaneus (heel bone) *n.* the large bone in the *tarsus of the foot that forms the projection of the heel behind the foot. It articulates with the cuboid bone in front and with the talus above.

跟骨　於足後形成跟部突起的足跗骨中的一塊大骨，與在前的骰骨和在上的距骨形成關節。

calcar *n.* a spurlike projection. The *calcar avis* is the projection in the medial wall of the lateral ventricle of the brain.

距　刺狀突起。禽距指側腦室內壁的突起。

calcicosis *n.* *pneumoconiosis in marble cutters. The term is not in current use.

灰石肺，灰石沉着病　採石工人的肺塵埃沉着病。此詞現已棄用。

calciferol *n. see* vitamin D.

維生素D₂，骨化醇　參閱 vitamin D。

calcification *n.* the deposition of calcium salts in tissue. This occurs as part of the normal process of bone formation (*see* ossification).

鈣化　組織中鈣鹽沉積，為骨生成正常過程的一部分（參閱 ossification）。

calcinosis *n.* the abnormal deposition of calcium salts in the tissues. This may occur only in the fat layer beneath the skin or it may be more widespread.

鈣質沉着　鈣鹽在組織中異常沉澱。可僅限於皮下脂肪層，亦可更為廣泛。

calcipotriol *n.* a vitamin D analogue administered as an ointment for the treatment of psoriasis. Possible side-effects include skin irritation and facial dermatitis. Trade name: **Dovonex**.

鈣泊三醇　以軟膏用於治療銀屑病的維生素 D 同型物。可致副作用有皮膚刺激和面部皮炎。商品名：Dovonex。

calcitonin *n. see* thyrocalcitonin.

降鈣素　參閱　thyrocalci-tonin。

calcium *n.* a metallic element essential for the normal development and functioning of the body. Calcium is an important constituent of bones and teeth: the matrix of *bone, consisting principally of calcium phosphate, accounts for about 99% of the body's calcium. It is present in the blood at a concentration of about 10mg/100ml, being maintained at this level by hormones (*see* thyrocalcitonin, parathyroid hormone). It is essential for many metabolic processes, including nerve function, muscle contraction, and blood clotting.

The normal dietary requirement of calcium is about 1 g per day: dairy products (milk and cheese) are the principal sources. Its uptake by the body is facilitated by *vitamin D; a deficiency of this vitamin may therefore result in such conditions as *rickets, *osteoporosis, and *osteomalacia. A deficiency of calcium in the blood may lead to *tetany. Excess calcium may be deposited in the body as *calculi (stones), especially in the gall bladder and kidney. Symbol: Ca.

鈣　一種人體正常發育和功能所必需的金屬元素。為骨骼與牙的重要成分，主要由磷酸鈣構成的骨基質大約占體內鈣量的 99%，以 10 mg/100 ml 左右的濃度存在於血液中，並由激素維持此水平（參閱　thyrocalcitonin，parathyroid hormone）。鈣對許多代謝過程必不可少，包括神經功能、肌肉收縮和血凝固。

對鈣的正常飲食需求約為每日 1 克；乳製品（奶和奶酪）為其主要來源。維生素 D 促進身體對鈣的吸收，缺乏此種維生素則可導致佝僂病、骨質疏鬆症和骨軟化疾病。血鈣缺乏可引起手足搐搦。鈣量過高可以結石沉積於體內，尤其在膽囊和腎內。符號：Ca。

calcium antagonist a drug that inhibits the influx of calciumions into cardiac and smooth-muscle cells; it therefore reduces the strength of heart-muscle contraction, reduces conduction of impulses in the heart, and causes vasodilatation. Calcium antagonists include *amlodipine, *diltiazem, *nicardepine, *nifedipine, and

鈣拮抗劑　抑制鈣離子進入心肌細胞和平滑肌細胞的藥物。從而降低心肌收縮力，降低心衝動的傳導而使血管舒張。用於治療心絞痛和高血壓，包括氨氯地平、地爾硫䓬、尼卡地平、硝苯地平和維拉帕米。

*verapamil, which are used to treat angina and high blood pressure.

calculosis *n*. the presence of multiple calculi (stones) in the body. *See* calculus.

calculus *n*. (*pl.* **calculi**) **1.** a stone: a hard pebble-like mass formed within the body, particularly in the gall bladder (*see* gallstone) or anywhere in the urinary tract (*see* cystolithiasis, nephrolithiasis, staghorn calculus). Calculi in the urinary tract are commonly composed of calcium oxalate and are usually visible on X-ray examination. Most of these stones cause pain, whether sited in the kidney, ureter, or bladder; stones passing down a duct (such as the ureter) cause severe colicky pain. Such stones are usually removed surgically, either by crushing (*see* litholopaxy), or by *lithotripsy to prevent or cure urinary obstruction and infection. Calculi may also occur in the ducts of the salivary glands. **2.** a calcified deposit that forms on the surfaces of teeth. *Supragingival calculus* forms above the *gingivae (gums), principally in relation to the openings of the salivary gland ducts. *Subgingival calculus* forms beneath the crest of the gingivae. Calculus hinders the cleaning of teeth and its presence contributes to *gingivitis.

calibrator *n*. **1.** an instrument used for measuring the size of a tube or opening. **2.** an instrument used for dilating a tubular part, such as the gullet.

caliectasis (hydrocalycosis) *n*. dilatation or distension of the calyces of the kidney, which is mainly associated with *hydronephrosis and usually demonstrated by ultrasound or IVP (*see* intravenous pyelogram).

結石病　體內有多個結石。參閱 calculus。

結石　**(1)**　石：體內形成的堅硬卵石樣團塊，尤其在膽囊（參閱 gallstone）或泌尿道的任何部位（參閱 cystolithiasis，nephrolithiasis，staghorn calculus）。泌尿道結石通常為草酸鈣，X 綫檢查一般可見到。此類結石不論位於腎臟、輸尿管或膀胱多引起疼痛；沿管道（如輸尿管）移動則造成劇烈絞痛。常用粉碎（參閱 litholopaxy）或碎石術排除這類結石，以防止或治愈尿道梗阻和感染，結石還可產生在唾液腺管內。**(2)**　形成於牙表面的鈣質沉積物。齦上積石主要在唾液腺管開口附近的牙齦上方形成，齦下積石形成於齦崤下方。牙積石妨礙清潔牙齒，並促使齦炎發生。

管徑測量器　**(1)**　用於測量管道或開口大小的儀器。**(2)**　用於擴張管狀部位如食管的器械。

腎盞擴張　腎盞的擴張或膨脹，主要發生於腎盂積水，常可由超聲波或靜脈腎盞 X 綫片顯示（參閱 intravenous pyelogram）。

calliper (caliper) *n*. **1.** an instrument with two prongs or jaws, used for measuring diameters: used particularly in obstetrics for measuring the diameter of the pelvis. **2.** (also called **calliper splint**) a leg splint that consists of metal rods attached to a padded ring at the top of the leg, taking the weight of the body at the pelvis. Calliper splints can be used to exert *traction on a deformed or paralysed leg as part of orthopaedic treatment.

(1) 測徑器 用於測量直徑的有兩叉或夾片的器械，尤其用於產科測量骨盆徑。**(2) 雙腳規** 在下肢頂端與一墊圈連接的金屬桿下肢夾，於骨盆處支撐體重。可在矯形療法中用於畸形或麻痺下肢的牽引。

callosity (callus) *n*. a hard thick area of skin occurring in parts of the body subject to pressure or friction. The soles of the feet and palms of the hands are common sites, and if much hard dead skin develops a callosity can become painful. A *corn is a type of callosity.

胼胝 身體某些部位因受壓或摩擦產生的皮膚變硬增厚。足底和手掌多見。若產生大量死硬皮可引起疼痛。雞眼即為一種胼胝。

callus *n*. **1.** a mass of blood and *granulation tissue, containing bone-forming cells, that forms around the bone ends following a fracture. Callus formation is an essential part of the process of healthy union in a fractured bone. The callus, which is visible on X-ray as a slightly opaque area, eventually becomes calcified and modelled. **2.** *see* callosity.

(1) 骨痂 骨折後斷端周圍形成的內含成骨細胞的血液和肉芽組織塊。骨痂形成為骨折康復愈合過程所必需。骨痂在 X 線片中為一高度透明區，最終鈣化成型。**(2) 胼胝** 參閱 callosity。

calor *n*. heat: one of the classical signs of inflammation in a tissue, the other three being *rubor (redness), *dolor (pain), and *tumor (swelling). An inflamed region has a higher temperature than normal because of the distended blood vessels, which allow an increased flow of blood.

灼熱 組織炎症的典型體徵之一。其他三者為紅、痛、腫脹。炎症區因血管擴張使血流增加造成溫度高於正常。

calorie *n*. a unit of heat equal to the amount of heat required to raise the temperature of 1 gram of water from 14.5°C to 15.5°C (the 15° calorie). One Calorie (also known as the *kilocalorie* or *kilogram*

卡（路里） 熱量單位，相當於使 1 克水的溫度從 14.5°C 升至 15.5°C（15° 卡）所需熱量。1 大卡（也稱千卡或千克卡）等於 1000 卡，此單位用於表示

calorie) is equal to 1000 calories; this unit is used to indicate the energy value of foods. Except in this context, the calorie has largely been replaced by the *joule (1 calorie = 4.1855 joules).

食物能量值。其他情況下已多為焦耳所取代（1卡 = 4.1855焦耳）。

calorimeter *n.* any apparatus used to measure the heat lost or gained during various chemical and physical changes. For example, calorimeters may be used to determine the total energy values of different foods in terms of calories. **–calorimetry** *n.*

測熱計　任何用於測量各種化學和物理變化中熱量增減的器械。例如，測熱計可用於測定不同食物的總能量卡值。

calvaria *n.* the vault of the *skull.

顱蓋　顱頂。

calyx *n.* (*pl.* **calyces**) a cup-shaped part, especially any of the divisions of the pelvis of the *kidney. Each calyx receives urine from the urine-collecting tubes in one sector of the kidney.

盞　杯狀部分，尤指腎盞的任何分支。每支腎盞接受來自一個部分腎集合管的尿液。

Campbell de Morgan spots *see* angioma.

德摩根斑　參閱 angioma。

camphor *n.* a crystalline substance obtained from the tree *Cinnamomum camphora* that has been used to treat flatulence. It is used in the form of *camphorated oil* (camphor in cottonseed oil) in liniments as a counterirritant.

樟腦　一種取自樟樹的用於治療（腸胃）氣脹的晶狀物質。以樟腦油（樟腦溶於棉籽油）形式用於搽劑中，作為抗刺激劑。

campimetry *n.* a method of assessing the central part of the *visual field. The patient fixes his gaze with one eye at a target in the centre of a black screen two metres away. A small object on the end of a black rod is moved onto the screen and the patient tells the examiner when he sees it. This is repeated many times from different directions until a map is built up of the area in front of the eye in which such an object can be seen. Campimetry allows examination only of

平面視野計　一種評估中央視野的方法。患者一目凝視兩米外黑色屏幕中心的目標，將一黑色桿端上的小物體移上屏幕，患者見後即告之檢查者。從不同方向多次重複進行，直至將患者眼前所能視此物的區域繪製成圖。此法只能檢查視野中心 30° 以內範圍。

that part of the field of vision within 30°
in all directions from the centre.

camptodactylia *n*. congenital inward
bending of a finger, most commonly the
little finger.

屈曲指　先天性指內屈，多為
小指。

Campylobacter *n*. a genus of spiral
motile Gram-negative bacteria. Species
of *Campylobacter* are a common cause
of food poisoning, producing headache,
nausea, diarrhoea, and vomiting lasting
for 3–5 days. *See also* Helicobacter.

彎曲桿菌屬　一屬可活動的革
蘭氏陰性螺旋狀細菌。為食物
中毒的一個常見原因，引起頭
痛、惡心、腹瀉、嘔吐，持續
3~5 日。參閱 Helicobacter。

canal *n*. a tubular channel or passage;
e.g. the *alimentary canal and the auditory canal of the ear.

管，道　管狀通道。如消化道
和耳道。

canaliculus *n*. (*pl*. **canaliculi**) a small
channel or canal. Canaliculi occur, for
example, in compact bone, linking
lacunae containing bone cells. *Bile
canaliculi* are minute channels within the
liver that transport bile to the bile duct.

小管　小管道。例如，密質骨
中有小管連接含有骨細胞的腔
隙。膽小管是肝內輸送膽汁至
膽管的微小通道。

cancellous *adj*. lattice-like: applied to
the bony tissue laid down by *osteoblasts
during development of bone and in the
*consolidation stage of fracture repair.

網狀骨質的　網絡狀的：指成
骨細胞在骨發育期間和骨折愈
合的骨化期所形成的骨組織。

cancer *n*. any *malignant tumour,
including *carcinoma and *sarcoma. It
arises from the abnormal and uncontrolled division of cells that then invade
and destroy the surrounding tissues.
Spread of cancer cells (*metastasis) may
occur via the bloodstream or the lymphatic channels or across body cavities
such as the pleural and peritoneal spaces,
thus setting up secondary tumours at
sites distant from the original tumour.
Each individual primary tumour has its
own pattern of local behaviour and
metastasis; for example, bone metastasis
is very common in breast cancer but very

癌症　包括癌和肉瘤的任何惡
性腫瘤。產生於不正常細胞的
失控分裂，之後侵入並破壞周
圍組織。癌細胞可經血流、淋
巴管或通過胸腔和腹腔等體腔
播散（轉移），因而在遠離原
發瘤的部位產生繼發性瘤。每
種原發瘤均有其局部行為特徵
和轉移途徑，例如、乳腺癌中
骨轉移多見而卵巢癌中則少
見。可能有多種致病因子，有
些已為人所知。如吸煙與肺癌
有關，放射則和某些骨肉瘤及
白血病有關。亦已知有幾類病
毒可致癌（參閱 oncogenic）。

rare in cancer of the ovary. There are probably many causative factors, some of which are known; for example, cigarette smoking is associated with lung cancer, radiation with some bone sarcomas and leukaemia, and several viruses are known to cause tumours (*see* oncogenic). A genetic element is implicated in the development of some cancers. Treatment of cancer depends on the type of tumour, the site of the primary tumour, and the extent of spread.

某些癌的發生涉及遺傳因素。治療需視腫瘤類型，原發瘤位置及擴散程度而定。

cancer phobia a personality disorder of the phobic type leading to compulsively performed rituals, especially repeated hand-washing, changing of clothes that have been touched by others, avoidance of air breathed by others, and even avoidance of any contact with other persons. Minor symptoms are interpreted as signs of cancer and panic attacks may occur. As with any other phobic disorder, cancer phobia cannot be treated by appeals to reason. Some success has been achieved by various forms of *behaviour therapy.

癌症恐怖 一種恐怖型人格障礙，導致強迫性作出某些動作，尤其是反覆洗手，更換他人觸碰過的衣物，避開他人呼出的空氣，甚至避免與他人的任何接觸。略有疾病症狀即視為患癌的表現並可能產生恐慌。與其他類型的恐怖症相同，癌症恐怖不能靠理智加以治療。運用各種行為療法已取得一些效果。

cancrum oris ulceration of the lips and mouth. *See also* noma.

壞疽性口炎 唇與口部的潰瘍。參閱 noma。

candela *n.* the *SI unit of luminous intensity, equal to the intensity in a given direction of a source that emits monochromatic radiation of frequency 540×10^{12} Hz and has a radiant intensity in that direction of 1/683 watt per steradian. Symbol: cd.

堪（德拉） 發光強度的國際單位，相當於在某方向頻率為 540×10^{12} 赫茲的單色發射的光源強度，在此方向的放射強度為每球面度 1/683 瓦特。符號：cd。

Candida *n.* a genus of *yeasts (formerly called *Monilia*) that inhabit the vagina and alimentary tract and can – under certain conditions – cause *candidosis. The species *C. albicans*, a small oval budding fungus, is primarily responsible for candidosis.

念珠菌屬 一屬寄居於陰道和消化道的酵母（舊稱叢梗孢屬）。在一定條件下可引起念珠菌病。白色念珠菌為一種小的卵圓形芽生菌，是念珠菌病的主要致病菌。

candidosis (candidiasis) n. a common *yeast infection of moist areas of the body, usually caused by *Candida albicans*. It is espccially common in the vagina, where it is known as *thrush*, but is also found in the mouth and skin folds. On the skin the lesions are bright red with small satellite pustules, while in the mouth candidosis appears as white patches on the tongue or inside the cheeks. In the vagina it produces itching and sometimes a thick white discharge. Candidosis may develop in patients receiving broad-spectrum antibiotics as well as in those who are *immunocompromised. Topical, intravaginal, or oral therapy with *imidazoles is effective; oral *nystatin helps to reduce candidal infection of the bowel.

念珠菌病　身體潮濕部位常見的酵母感染。一般為白色念珠菌所致，尤多見於陰道，稱為鵝口瘡，亦見於口腔和皮膚皺褶。損傷在皮膚上呈鮮紅色並伴有小衛星狀膿疱，在口腔內則為舌部或頰內白斑。念珠菌病引起陰道瘙癢，有時伴有黏稠白色分泌物。此病可發生於免疫缺乏者及接受廣譜抗生素治療的患者。用咪唑類局部、陰道內給藥或口服治療有效；口服製黴菌素有助於減少腸念珠菌感染。

canine n. the third tooth from the midline of each jaw. There are thus four canines, two in each jaw, in both the permanent and deciduous (milk) *dentitions. It is known colloquially as the *eye tooth*.

犬牙　每側頜骨中綫的第三枚牙。每側各有兩枚，故在恆牙列和乳牙列中共有四枚。俗稱眼牙。

canities n. loss of pigment in the hair, which causes greying or whitening. It is usually part of the ageing process, when it starts at the temples. White patches may occur as a result of *alopecia areata or *vitiligo.

灰髮（症）　頭髮色素喪失造成頭髮變灰或變白。始於顳部時，常為衰老過程的一部分。白色斑塊則可因斑禿或白斑所致。

cannabis n. a drug prepared from the Indian hemp plant (*Cannabis sativa*), also known as *pot*, *marijuana*, *hashish*, and *bhang*. Smoked or swallowed, it produces euphoria and hallucinations and affects perception and awareness, particularly of time. Cannabis has little therapeutic value and its nonmedical use is illegal: there is evidence that prolonged use may cause brain damage and lead the

大麻　一種以印度大麻植物（印度大麻）製取的藥物。吸入或吞下後可產生欣快感或幻覺並影響知覺和意識，尤其對時間。大麻的醫療價值甚微，其非醫學使用則違法：有證據說明長期使用大麻可致腦損害，並進而使用海洛因等麻醉品。參閱 dependence。

user onto 'hard' drugs, such as heroin. *See also* dependence.

cannula *n.* a hollow tube designed for insertion into a body cavity, such as the bladder, or a blood vessel. The tube contains a sharp pointed solid core (*trocar*), which facilitates its insertion and is withdrawn when the cannula is in place.

套管，插管 設計用於插入膀胱或血管等體腔的中空管。內有一尖銳實芯（套針）便於插入，套管抵位後即取出。

cantharidin *n.* the active principle of *cantharides*, or *Spanish fly* (the dried bodies of a blister beetle, *Lytta vesicatoria*). A toxic and irritant chemical, cantharidin causes blistering of the skin and was formerly used in veterinary medicine as a counterirritant and vesicant. If swallowed it causes nausea, vomiting, and inflammation of the urinary tract, the latter giving rise to its reputation as an aphrodisiac. It is very dangerous and may cause death.

斑蝥素 斑蝥或稱歐蕪菁（一種稱為西班牙蠅的斑蝥之乾屍）中的成分。為一種具毒性和刺激性的化學物質，可使皮膚起疱，獸醫曾用作抗刺激劑和起疱劑。若吞入可引起惡心、嘔吐及泌尿道炎症，後者使其得到催慾藥之名。本品危險性大，可致死。

canthus *n.* either corner of the eye; the angle at which the upper and lower eyelids meet. **–canthal** *adj.*

眥 兩眼角之一，上下眼瞼會合於此。

cap *n.* a covering or a cover-like part. The *duodenal cap* is the superior part of the duodenum as seen on X-ray after a barium meal.

蓋，帽 覆蓋物或蓋狀部分。十二指腸冠是鋇餐後X綫所顯示的十二指腸的上部。

Capgras' syndrome (illusion of doubles) the delusion that a person closely involved with the patient has been replaced by an identical-looking impostor. It is often, but not necessarily, a form of paranoid *schizophrenia.

卡普格拉斯綜合徵 患者熟悉之人被相貌相同的外來者替代的幻想。通常但不一定為一種妄想狂型精神分裂症。

capillary *n.* an extremely narrow blood vessel, approximately 5–20 μm in diameter. Capillaries form networks in most tissues; they are supplied with blood by arterioles and drained by venules. The

毛細血管 直徑約為 5~20μm 的極細的血管。在大多數組織內形成毛細血管網，由小動脈供血，小靜脈排血。管壁僅一層細胞，可使氧、二氧化碳、

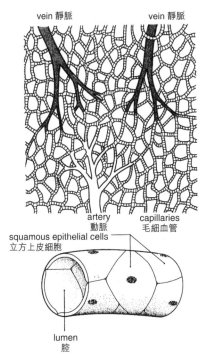

A network of capillaries (above); a single capillary (below)
毛細血管網（上）與單一毛細血管（下）

vessel wall is only one cell thick, which enables exchange of oxygen, carbon dioxide, water, salts, etc., between the blood and the tissues (see illustrations).

水、鹽等在血液和組織間進行交換（見圖）。

capitate *adj.* head-shaped; having a rounded extremity.

頭狀的 具有圓形末端的。

capitate bone the largest bone of the wrist (*see* carpus). It articulates with the scaphoid and lunate bones behind, with the second, third, and fourth metacarpal bones in front, and with the trapezoid and hamate laterally.

頭狀骨 最大的腕骨（參閱 carpus）。與在後的舟骨和月骨，在前的第二、三、四掌骨和側面的小多角骨和鈎骨形成關節。

capitellum *n.* see capitulum.

肱骨小頭 參閱 capitulum。

capitulum *n.* the small rounded end of a bone that articulates with another bone. For example, the *capitulum humeri* (or *capitellum*) is the round prominence at the elbow end of the humerus that articulates with the radius.

小頭　骨與另一骨形成關節的小而圓的末端。如肱骨小頭是肱骨肘端與橈骨構成關節的圓形隆凸。

capping *n.* (in dentistry) **1.** crowning: the technique of fitting a tooth with an artificial *crown. **2.** *see* pulp capping.

（牙科學）**(1) 造冠術**　在牙上裝配人工牙冠的技術。**(2) 蓋髓術**　參閱 pulp capping。

capreomycin *n.* an antibiotic, derived from the bacterium *Streptomyces capreolus*, that is used in the treatment of tuberculosis. It is given with other anti-tuberculosis drugs to reduce the development of resistance by the infective bacteria. Capreomycin is poorly absorbed from the gastrointestinal tract and therefore must be administered by intramuscular injection. The more serious side-effects include ear and kidney damage. Trade name: **Capastat**.

卷曲黴素　一種獲自卷曲鏈黴菌的用於治療結核病的抗生素。與其他抗結核藥合用以減少其傳染菌產生耐藥性。卷曲黴素胃腸道吸收不良，故須肌注給藥。較嚴重的副作用有耳和腎損害。商品名：Capastat。

capsule *n.* **1.** a membrane, sheath, or other structure that encloses a tissue or organ. For example, the kidney, adrenal gland, and lens of the eye are enclosed within capsules. A *joint capsule* is the fibrous tissue, including the synovial membrane, that surrounds a freely movable joint. **2.** a soluble case, usually made of gelatin, in which certain drugs are administered. **3.** the slimy substance that forms a protective layer around certain bacteria. It is usually made of *polysaccharide.

(1) 囊，被膜　包繞組織或器官的膜、鞘或其他結構，如腎、腎上腺和晶狀體均為囊所包繞。關節囊是包繞可動關節的纖維組織，包括滑膜。**(2) 膠囊**　常用明膠製作的可溶性囊，包裹某些藥物。**(3) 莢膜**　形成某些細菌周圍保護層的黏性物質，通常為多糖構成。

capsulitis *n.* inflammation of the capsule surrounding a joint.

囊炎　關節囊的炎症。

capsulotomy *n.* an incision into the capsule of the lens. In modern operations for cataract the lens capsule is not removed and tends, after months or

晶狀體囊切開術　切開晶狀體囊。在現代白內障手術中保留的晶狀體囊往往在數年後變混濁。採用激光手術之前，用一

years, to become opaque. Before the advent of laser surgery a tiny knife (*cystitome*) was inserted into the eye and a hole cut in the centre of the capsule, thus providing a clear path for light rays to reach the retina. Currently this procedure is routinely performed with a *YAG laser at an out-patient clinic.

小刀（晶狀體囊刀）在晶狀體囊中央切開一孔，使光綫可抵視網膜。現在可在門診部用釔鋁石榴石激光常規施行此手術。

captopril *n.* a drug used in the treatment of heart failure and hypertension; it acts by inhibiting the action of angiotensin (*see* ACE inhibitor). Side-effects include rash, *neutropenia or *agranulocytosis, hypotension, and loss of taste. Trade names: **Acepril**, **Capoten**.

卡托普利　一種用於治療心力衰竭和高血壓的藥物。通過抑制血管緊張素的作用而生效（參閱 ACE inhibitor）。副作用有皮疹、中性白細胞減少或粒細胞缺乏、低血壓，以及味覺喪失。商品名：Acepril，Capoten。

caput succedaneum a temporary swelling of the soft parts of the head of a newly born infant that occurs during birth, due to compression by the muscles of the cervix (neck) of the uterus.

胎頭腫塊　新生兒在娩出時頭軟組織的暫時性腫脹。因受子宮頸肌肉壓迫所致。

carbachol *n.* a *parasympathomimetic drug that is used after surgical operations to restore the function of inactive bowels or bladder. It is also (but now infrequently) used as a treatment for glaucoma. Side-effects may include sweating, nausea, and faintness.

卡巴膽鹼　擬副交感神經藥。用於手術後恢復腸或膀胱功能，亦用於（現已不多）治療青光眼。副作用可有出汗、惡心、暈厥。

carbamazepine *n.* an *anticonvulsant drug used in the treatment of epilepsy and to relieve the pain of trigeminal neuralgia. Common side-effects include drowsiness, dizziness, and muscular incoordination; abnormalities of liver and bone marrow may occur with long-term treatment. Trade name: **Tegretol**.

卡馬西平　抗驚厥藥，用於治療癲癇和緩解三叉神經痛。常見副作用有嗜睡、頭昏和肌共濟失調；長期使用可致肝與骨髓損害。商品名：Tegretol。

carbaryl *n.* a drug administered in the form of a lotion or shampoo to kill head and pubic lice. Trade names: **Carylderm**, **Clinicide**.

卡巴立　一種以洗劑或洗髮液殺頭虱和陰虱的藥物。商品名：Carylderm，Clinicide。

carbenicillin *n.* a synthetic penicillin: an antibiotic that is effective against a wide range of bacterial infections. It is poorly absorbed from the gastrointestinal tract and must be given by intramuscular injection. Allergic reactions are common side-effects. Trade name: **Pyopen**.

羧苄西林 一種合成青黴素：對多種細菌感染有效的一種抗生素。胃腸道吸收不佳，必須肌注。變態反應為常見副作用。商品名：Pyopen。

carbenoxolone *n.* a drug that reduces inflammation, used mainly to promote healing in the treatment of gastric ulcers or ulcers of the mouth. It is given by mouth; side-effects include the retention of salt and water (*see* oedema), weight gain, and raised blood pressure. Trade names: **Bioplex, Bioral**.

甘珀酸，生胃酮 一種減輕炎症的藥物。主要用於胃潰瘍或口腔潰瘍治療中促進愈合，口服，副作用有水鹽瀦留（參閱 oedema）、體重增加和血壓升高。商品名：Bioplex，Bioral。

carbimazole *n.* a drug used to reduce the production of thyroid hormone in cases of overactivity of the gland (thyrotoxicosis). It is administered by mouth; some allergic reactions may occur and high dosage may cause enlargement of the thyroid gland, which may obstruct the windpipe. Trade name: **Neo-Mercazole**.

卡比馬唑 一種在甲狀腺功能亢進時（甲狀腺毒症）用於減少甲狀腺激素產生的藥物。口服，可產生一些變態反應，大劑量可致甲狀腺腫大而阻塞氣管。商品名：Neo-Mercazole。

carbohydrate *n.* any one of a large group of compounds, including the *sugars and *starch, that contain carbon, hydrogen, and oxygen and have the general formula $C_x(H_2O)_y$. Carbohydrates are important as a source of energy: they are manufactured by plants and obtained by animals and man from the diet, being one of the three main constituents of food (*see also* fat, protein). All carbohydrates are eventually broken down in the body to the simple sugar *glucose, which can then take part in energy-producing metabolic processes. Excess carbohydrate, not immediately required by the body, is stored in the liver and muscles in the form of *glycogen. In plants carbohydrates are

碳水化合物 包括糖和澱粉的一大組化合物，含碳、氫、氧，均有 $C_x(H_2O)_y$ 分子式。是重要的能量來源：由植物製造，動物或人類從飲食中獲取。為食物的三大主要成分之一（參閱 fat，protein）。所有的碳水化合物最終在體內分解為單糖即葡萄糖，爾後參與產能的代謝過程，不為身體急需的多餘碳水化合物則以糖原形式貯存於肝臟和肌肉。碳水化合物在植物中是重要的結構物質（如纖維素）和貯存產品（常以澱粉形式）。參閱 disaccharide，monosaccharide，polysaccharide。

important structural materials (e.g. cellulose) and storage products (commonly in the form of starch). *See also* disaccharide, monosaccharide, polysaccharide.

carbol fuchsin a red stain for bacteria and fungi, consisting of carbolic acid and *fuchsin dissolved in alcohol and water.

石炭酸品紅液　用於細菌和真菌染色的紅色染劑。為石炭酸和品紅在酒精與水中的溶液。

carbolic acid *see* phenol.

石炭酸　參閱 phenol。

carbon dioxide a colourless gas formed in the tissues during metabolism and carried in the blood to the lungs, where it is exhaled (an increase in the concentration of this gas in the blood stimulates respiration). Carbon dioxide occurs in small amounts in the atmosphere; it is used by plants in the process of *photosynthesis. It forms a solid (dry ice) at −75°C (at atmospheric pressure) and in this form is used as a refrigerant. Formula: CO_2.

二氧化碳　組織代謝時產生的無色氣體，經血液運至肺呼出（血中二氧化碳濃度升高刺激呼吸）。大氣中有少量二氧化碳；植物在光合作用過程中加以利用。二氧化碳在 −75°C（大氣壓下）形成固體（乾冰），並以此作冷凍劑使用。分子式：CO_2。

carbon monoxide a colourless almost odourless gas that is very poisonous. When breathed in it combines with haemoglobin in the red blood cells to form *carboxyhaemoglobin, which is bright red in colour. This compound is chemically stable and thus the haemoglobin can no longer combine with oxygen. Carbon monoxide is present in coal gas and motor exhaust fumes. Formula: CO.

一氧化碳　一種無色並幾乎無味的劇毒氣體。吸入後與紅細胞中的血紅蛋白結合形成鮮紅色的碳氧血紅蛋白。該化合物化學性質穩定，因此血紅蛋白不再能與氧結合。一氧化碳存在於煤氣和汽車廢氣中。分子式：CO。

carbon tetrachloride a pungent volatile fluid used as a dry-cleaner. When inhaled or swallowed it may severely damage the heart, liver, and kidneys, causing cirrhosis and nephrosis, and it can also affect the optic nerve and other nerves. Treatment is by administration of oxygen. Formula: CCl_4.

四氯化碳　一種用作乾洗劑的刺激性揮發液體。吸入或吞咽後可嚴重損害心、肝、腎，導致肝硬化和腎病，還可累及視神經與其他神經。用輸氧治療。分子式：CCl_4。

carboplatin *n.* a derivative of platinum that is used in the treatment of certain types of cancer. It is similar to *cisplatin but has fewer side-effects.

卡鉑 一種鉑的衍生物。用於治療某些類型的癌症，與順鉑相似，但副作用較少。

carboxyhaemoglobin *n.* a substance formed when carbon monoxide combines with the pigment *haemoglobin in the blood. Carboxyhaemoglobin is incapable of transporting oxygen to the tissues and this is the cause of death in carbon monoxide poisoning. Large quantities of carboxyhaemoglobin are formed in carbon monoxide poisoning, and low levels are always present in the blood of smokers and city dwellers.

碳氧血紅蛋白 一氧化碳與血液色素血紅蛋白結合時形成的物質。碳氧血紅蛋白不能運送氧至組織，此乃一氧化碳中毒死亡的原因。一氧化碳中毒時有大量碳氧血紅蛋白形成，吸煙者和城市居民的血液中常有少量存在。

carboxylase *n.* an enzyme that catalyses the addition of carbon dioxide to a substance.

羧化酶 將二氧化碳引入某物質的催化酶。

carbuncle *n.* a collection of *boils with multiple drainage channels. The infection is usually caused by *Staphylococcus aureus* and may result in an extensive slough of skin. Treatment is with antibiotics and sometimes also by surgery.

癰 一叢有多個引流道的癤。感染常因金黃色葡萄球菌所致，可引起皮膚大面積脫落。用抗生素有時亦用手術治療。

carcin- (carcino-) *prefix denoting* cancer or carcinoma. Example: *carcinogenesis* (development of).

〔前綴〕癌 如致癌作用。

carcino-embryonic antigen (CEA) a protein produced in the fetus but not in normal adult life. It may be produced by carcinomas, particularly of the colon, and is a rather insensitive marker of malignancy. It is an example of an *oncofetal antigen that is used as a *tumour marker.

癌胚抗原 胎兒體內產生但正常成人中不產生的一種蛋白。可能由癌所產生，尤其是結腸癌，是一種低敏感度的惡性標記物。例如，癌胚抗原被用作為腫瘤標記。

carcinogen *n.* any substance that, when exposed to living tissue, may cause the production of cancer. Known carcinogens include ionizing radiation and many chemicals, e.g. those found in cigarette

致癌物（質） 任何接觸到活組織時可致癌的物質。已知致癌物有離子射綫和多種化學物質，如在香煙中發現的與某些工業所產生的化學物質。致癌

smoke and those produced in certain industries. They cause damage to the DNA of cells that may persist if the cell divides before the damage is repaired. Damaged cells may subsequently develop into a cancer (*see* carcinogenesis). An inherent susceptibility to cancer is probably necessary for a carcinogen to promote the development of cancer. *See also* oncogenic. **–carcinogenic** *adj.*

carcinogenesis *n.* the evolution of an invasive cancer cell from a normal cell. Intermediate stages, sometimes called *premalignant*, *preinvasive*, or *noninvasive* may be recognizable.

carcinoid *n. see* argentaffinoma.

carcinoma *n.* *cancer that arises in epithelium, the tissue that lines the skin and internal organs of the body. It may occur in any tissue containing epithelial cells. In many cases the site of origin of the tumour may be identified by the nature of the cells it contains. Organs may exhibit more than one type of carcinoma; for example, an adenocarcinoma and a squamous carcinoma may be found in the cervix (but not usually concurrently). Treatment depends on the nature of the primary tumour, different types responding to different drug combinations. **–carcinomatous** *adj.*

carcinomatosis *n.* carcinoma that has spread widely throughout the body. Spread of the cancer cells occurs via the lymphatic channels and bloodstream and across body cavities, for example the peritoneal cavity.

carcinosarcoma *n.* a malignant tumour of the cervix, uterus, or vagina containing

物導致對細胞DNA的破壞，若細胞在這種損害得到修復前分裂，損害則持續進行。受損細胞可隨之發展成癌（參閱 carcinogenesis）。致癌物可能需要癌症的先天易感性來促使癌症發生。參閱 oncogenic。

癌發生 由一正常細胞到侵襲性癌細胞的發展過程。其中間階段，有時稱為惡性前的、侵襲前的、或非侵襲性的，可以予以識別。

類癌（瘤） 參閱 argentaffinoma。

癌 發生於上皮組織的癌症。該組織覆蓋機體皮膚和內臟器官。癌可出現在任何含有上皮細胞的組織。在許多情況下，癌瘤的原發部位可由其所含細胞的性質來確定。同一器官可能會出現幾種癌，如腺癌和鱗狀癌均可見於子宮頸（但通常不是同時發生）。治療取決於原發癌的性質，不同類型的癌對不同的藥物配伍產生反應。

癌病 癌廣泛擴散到全身。癌細胞的擴散通過淋巴管道和血流並穿越體腔而發生，如腹膜腔。

癌肉瘤 宮頸、子宮體或陰道的一種惡性腫瘤。內含腺癌、

a mixture of *adenocarcinoma, sarcoma cells, and stroma. It may be bulky and polypoid, with grapelike fronds (*sarcoma botryoides*). Tissues of mesodermal origin, such as bone, cartilage, or striated muscle, may also be present.

肉瘤細胞和基質混合物。它可能巨大且呈息肉狀，並具有葡萄樣分葉。存在源自中胚層的組織，如骨、軟骨或橫紋肌等。

cardi- (cardio-) *prefix denoting* the heart. *Examples: cardiomegaly* (enlargement of); *cardiopathy* (disease of).

〔前綴〕心　指心臟，如心臟肥大（擴大），心臟病。

cardia *n.* **1.** the opening at the upper end of the *stomach that connects with the oesophagus (gullet). **2.** the heart.

(1) 賁門　開口於胃的上端，聯接食管。**(2) 心臟**

cardiac *adj.* **1.** of, relating to, or affecting the heart. **2.** of or relating to the upper part of the stomach (*see* cardia).

(1) 心臟的　與心臟有關係的，患及心臟的。**(2) 賁門的**　與胃的上部有關的（參閱cardia）。

cardiac arrest the cessation of effective pumping action of the heart, which most commonly occurs when the muscle fibres of the ventricles start to beat rapidly without pumping any blood (ventricular *fibrillation) or when the heart stops beating completely (*asystole). There is abrupt loss of consciousness, absence of the pulse, and breathing stops. The most common cause is *myocardial infarction. Unless treated promptly, irreversible brain damage and death follow within minutes. Some patients may be resuscitated by massage of the heart, artificial respiration, and *defibrillation.

心動停止　心臟的有效泵血行為的停止。最常見的多發生於當心室肌肉纖維開始快速搏動而沒有血液泵出（心室纖維性顫動）時，或當心臟完全停止搏動（心搏停止）。出現突然喪失意識，脈搏消失，呼吸停止。最常見的原因是心肌梗死。除非立刻予以治療，不可逆的大腦損害以及死亡就會在隨後幾分鐘內發生。一些病人通過心臟按摩、人工呼吸和除纖顫法可得以復蘇。

cardiac cycle the sequence of events between one heartbeat and the next, normally occupying less than a second. The atria contract simultaneously and force blood into the relaxed ventricles. The ventricles then contract very strongly and pump blood out through the aorta and pulmonary artery. During ventricular contraction, the atria relax and fill up again with blood. *See* diastole, systole.

心動周期　在兩次心跳之間心臟的一連串活動，通常歷時不到一秒鐘。左右心房同時收縮，將血液驅入舒張的心室。然後，心室非常強烈地收縮，通過主動脈和肺動脈將血液泵出。在心室收縮期間，心房舒張，再次充滿血液。參閱 diastole，systole。

cardiac muscle the specialized muscle of which the walls of the *heart are composed. It is composed of a network of branching elongated cells (fibres) whose junctions with neighbouring cells are marked by irregular transverse bands known as *intercalated discs*.

心肌 組成心臟壁的特殊肌肉。它由分支伸長的細胞（肌纖維）所組成的網絡構成。通過稱為閏板的不規則橫帶與相鄰的細胞聯結。

cardiac reflex reflex control of the heart rate. Sensory fibres in the walls of the heart are stimulated when the heart rate increases above normal. Impulses are sent to the cardiac centre in the brain, stimulating the vagus nerve and leading to slowing of the heart rate.

心臟反射 控制心率的反射。當心率增加到超過正常時，心臟壁內的感覺纖維就受到刺激。衝動就被傳送至大腦內的心跳中樞，從而刺激迷走神經，導致心率減慢。

cardinal veins two pairs of veins in the embryo that carry blood from the head (*anterior cardinal veins*) and trunk (*posterior cardinal veins*); they unite to form the *common cardinal vein*, which drains into the sinus venosus of the heart.

主靜脈 胚胎的兩對靜脈，引導血液從頭部（前主靜脈）和軀幹部（後主靜脈）返回心臟。它們匯合形成總主靜脈，注入心臟靜脈竇。

cardiology *n.* the science concerned with the study of the structure, function, and diseases of the heart. *See also* nuclear cardiology. **–cardiologist** *n.*

心臟病學 與研究心臟結構、功能和疾病有關的科學。參閱 nuclear cardiology。

cardiomyopathy *n.* any chronic disorder affecting the muscle of the heart. It may be inherited but can be caused by various conditions, including virus infections, alcoholism, beriberi (vitamin B_1 deficiency), and amyloidosis. The cause is often unknown. It may result in enlargement of the heart, *heart failure, *arrhythmias, and embolism. There is often no specific treatment but patients improve following the control of heart failure and arrhythmias.

心肌病 任何損害心肌的慢性疾病。心肌病可遺傳而得，也可由不同疾病引起，包括病毒感染、酒精中毒、腳氣病（維生素B_1缺乏）以及澱粉樣變性。病因常不清楚。可能導致心臟膨大、心力衰竭、心律不齊與栓塞。通常沒有特效治療方法，但經過控制心力衰竭和心律不齊，病人的病情可以好轉。

cardiomyoplasty *n.* a recent surgical technique to replace or reinforce damaged cardiac muscle with skeletal muscle.

心肌成形術 一種新的外科技術，用骨骼肌代替或加強已經受損的心肌。

cardiomyotomy *n. see* achalasia.

心麻痺術　使心臟停跳的技術，可通過給心臟注射一種鹽液，或降溫，或電擊。這一技術使得複雜心臟外科手術和移植能夠安全進行。

cardioplegia *n.* a technique in which the heart is stopped by injecting it with a solution of salts, by hypothermia, or by an electrical stimulus. This has enabled complex cardiac surgery and transplants to be performed safely.

心肺分流術　該方法使體循環被維持而心臟搏動被故意停止，用於心臟外科手術時心臟和肺的功能由氧泵（參閱 heart-lung machine）來維持，直到自然循環恢復。

cardiopulmonary bypass a method by which the circulation to the body is maintained while the heart is deliberately stopped during heart surgery. The function of the heart and lungs is carried out by a pump-oxygenator (*see* heart-lung machine) until the natural circulation is restored.

賁門痙攣　參閱 achalasia。

cardiospasm *n. see* achalasia.

胎心與分娩力描記儀　該儀器用於胎心與分娩力描記法中，以產生胎心與分娩力描記圖，從而獲得測量圖形打印結果。

cardiotocograph *n.* the instrument used in *cardiotocography to produce a *cardiotocogram*, the graphic printout of the measurements obtained.

胎心與分娩力描記法　電子監測胎心率及節律，可通過體外麥克風或換能器、或通過給胎兒頭皮處使用電極，來記錄胎兒心電圖和心率。這一過程還包括測量子宮收縮力和收縮頻率，可採用外加換能器或宮內導管。

cardiotocography *n.* the electronic monitoring of the fetal heart rate and rhythm, either by an external microphone or transducer or by applying an electrode to the fetal scalp, recording the fetal ECG and hence the heart rate. The procedure also includes a measurement of the strength and frequency of uterine contractions by means of an external transducer or an intrauterine catheter.

心切開綜合徵（心切開後綜合徵）　該徵可發生於心臟或包裹着它的膜（心包）手術後數周或數月，其特徵為發熱和心包炎。肺炎和胸膜炎可能構成綜合徵的一部分。這被認為是一種自體免疫性疾患，而且可能會反覆發作。一種類似的綜合徵（德雷斯勒綜合徵）可見於

cardiotomy syndrome (postcardiotomy syndrome) a condition that may develop weeks or months after surgery to the heart and the membrane surrounding it (pericardium) and is characterized by fever and also *pericarditis. Pneumonia and pleurisy may form part of the syndrome. It is thought to be an *autoimmune condition and may be recurrent. A similar syndrome (*Dressler's syndrome*) may follow myocardial infarction. It may respond to anti-inflammatory drugs.

cardiovascular system (circulatory system) the heart together with two networks of blood vessels – the *systemic circulation and the *pulmonary circulation (see illustration). The cardiovascular system effects the circulation of blood around the body, which brings about transport of nutrients and oxygen to the tissues and the removal of waste products.

心肌梗死後。消炎藥物可能
有效。

心血管系統（循環系統） 心臟
和兩種血管網絡——體循環和
肺循環（見圖）。心血管系統
作用於全身的血液循環，傳輸
營養和氧氣到組織，並把廢物
運走。

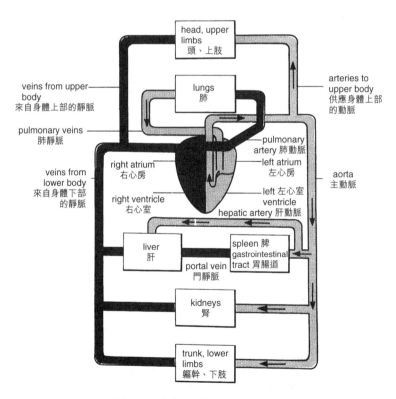

Diagram of the cardiovascular system
心血管系統

cardioversion (countershock) *n.* a method of restoring the normal rhythm of the heart in patients with increased heart rate due to arrhythmia. A controlled direct-current shock, synchronized with the R wave of the electrocardiograph, is given through electrodes placed on the chest wall of the anaesthetized patient. The apparatus is called a *cardiovertor* and is a modified defibrillator (*see* defibrillation).

心臟復律法（反休克法） 該方法恢復心臟正常節律，用於因心律不齊而心動過速的病人。受控直流電休克，與心電圖上 R 波同步。該電擊經處於麻醉狀態患者胸壁上的電極施行。這一裝置被稱為心臟復律器，是一改良的除顫器（參閱 defibrillation）。

caries *n.* decay and crumbling of the substance of a tooth (*see* dental caries) or a bone. **–carious** *adj.*

(1) 齲 (2) 骨疽 牙（參閱 dental caries）或骨質的變質和破碎。

carina *n.* a keel-like structure, such as the keel-shaped cartilage at the bifurcation of the trachea into the two main bronchi.

隆凸 龍骨狀結構，例如位於氣管分成兩支主支氣管的分叉處的龍骨狀軟骨。

cariogenic *adj.* causing caries, particularly dental caries.

生齲的 能引起齲的，特別是引起齲齒的。

carminative *n.* a drug that relieves flatulence, used to treat gastric discomfort and colic.

驅風劑 該藥物減輕脹氣，用於治療胃不適和急腹痛。

carmustine (BCNU) *n.* a drug (an *alkylating agent) used in the treatment of certain cancers, including lymphomas and brain tumours.

卡莫司汀（卡氮芥） 用於治療某些癌症，包括淋巴瘤和腦瘤的藥（一種烷化劑）。

carneous mole a fleshy mass in the uterus consisting of pieces of placenta and products of conception that have not been expelled after abortion.

肉樣胎塊 子宮內的肉狀塊，由胎盤碎片和妊娠產物組成，在流產後尚未被排除掉。

carotenaemia *n. see* xanthaemia.

胡蘿蔔素血症 參閱 xanthaemia。

carotene *n.* a yellow or orange plant pigment – one of the carothenoids – that occurs in four forms: alpha (α), beta (β), gamma (γ), and delta (δ). The most

胡蘿蔔素 一種黃色或橘紅色的植物色素，是胡蘿蔔素類中的一種，以四種形式出現：α、β、γ 和 δ。最重要的是 β

important form is β-carotene, which is an *antioxidant and can be converted in the body to retinol (vitamin A). Foods containing β-carotene (milk and some vegetables) are therefore a source of the vitamin.

胡蘿蔔素，是一種抗氧化劑，在體內被轉化為視黃醇（維生素 A）。含有 β 胡蘿蔔素的食物（牛奶和一些蔬菜）因此就是該維生素的來源。

carotenoid *n.* any one of a group of about 100 naturally occurring yellow to red pigments found mostly in plants. The group includes the *carotenes.

類胡蘿蔔素   一組大約一百種天然存在的、黃色至紅色的色素，多見於植物。其中包括胡蘿蔔素。

carotid artery either of the two main arteries in the neck whose branches supply the head and neck. The *common carotid artery* arises on the left side directly from the aortic arch and on the right from the innominate artery. They ascend the neck on either side as far as the thyroid cartilage (Adam's apple), where they each divide into two branches, the *internal carotid*, supplying the cerebrum, forehead, nose, eye, and middle ear, and the *external carotid*, sending branches to the face, scalp, and neck.

頸動脈   頸部兩個大動脈的任何一個。其分支供應頭頸部。左頸總動脈直接源於主動脈弓，而右頸總動脈則源於無名動脈。它們各自上行至頸部兩側，直至甲狀軟骨（喉結），由此各自分為兩支：頸內動脈供應腦部、前額、鼻、眼睛和中耳；頸外動脈供應面部、頭皮和頸部。

carotid-artery stenosis (carotid stenosis) narrowing of the carotid artery, which reduces the supply of blood to the brain and is a cause of strokes. Sometimes the condition is due to a tumour of the *carotid body. Many cases can be treated by surgical excision or bypass of the narrowed segment (*see also* endarterectomy).

頸動脈狹窄   頸動脈變得狹窄，減少向大腦的血液供應，是中風的一個病因。有時是由頸動脈體瘤引起的。許多病例可予以外科切除或狹窄段旁路來治療。參閱 endarterectomy。

carotid body a small mass of tissue in the carotid sinus containing *chemoreceptors that monitor levels of oxygen, carbon dioxide, and hydrogen ions in the blood. If the oxygen level falls, the chemoreceptors send impulses to the cardiac and respiratory centres in the brain, which promote increases in heart and respiration rates.

頸動脈體   該小塊組織位於頸動脈竇中，含有化學感受器，監控血液中氧氣、二氧化碳和氫離子含量。如果氧含量減少，化學感受器發放衝動到腦內的心跳中樞和呼吸中樞，促之增加心率和呼吸節律。

carotid sinus a pocket in the wall of the carotid artery, at its division in the neck, containing receptors that monitor blood pressure (*see* baroreceptor). When blood pressure is raised, impulses travel from the receptors to the vasomotor centre in the brain, which initiates a reflex *vasodilatation and slowing of heart rate to lower the blood pressure to normal.

頸動脈竇　該袋狀結構位於頸動脈壁，在頸部分叉處，內含感受器監控血壓（參閱 baroreceptor）。當血壓上升時，脈衝由感受器傳向大腦的血管運動中樞，引起反射性血管舒張，減慢心率，將血壓降至正常。

carp- (carpo-) *prefix denoting* the wrist (carpus).

〔前綴〕腕

carpal 1. *adj.* relating to the wrist. **2.** *n.* any of the bones forming the carpus.

(1) 腕的　與腕有關的。**(2)** 腕骨　構成腕的任何骨頭。

carpal tunnel the space between the carpal bones of the wrist and the connective tissue (retinaculum) over the flexor tendons. It contains the flexor tendons and the median nerve.

腕管　該空隙位於腕部的腕骨與屈肌腱上的結締組織（支持帶）之間。它包含屈肌腱和正中神經。

carpal tunnel syndrome compression of the median nerve as it passes through the wrist (*see* carpal tunnel). This causes pain and numbness in the index and middle fingers and weakness of the thumb.

腕管綜合徵　正中神經穿過腕時受壓，使得食指和中指感到疼痛和麻木，並使拇指無力。

carphology (floccillation) *n.* plucking at the bedclothes by a delirious patient. This is often a sign of extreme exhaustion and may be the prelude to death.

捉空摸床　譫妄患者抓拽被褥的行為。常常為極度虛弱的表現，或死亡前的徵兆。

carpopedal spasm *see* spasm.

腕足痙攣　參閱 spasm。

carpus *n.* the eight bones of the wrist (see illustration). The carpus articulates with the metacarpals distally and with the ulna and radius proximally.

腕骨　腕部的八塊骨頭（見圖）。腕骨遠端與掌骨、近端與尺骨和橈骨構成關節。

carrier *n.* **1.** a person who harbours the microorganisms causing a particular disease without experiencing signs or symptoms of infection and who can

(1) 病原攜帶者　一個帶有引起某種疾病的微生物而沒有傳染病體徵和症狀，但能把這一疾病傳播給他人的人。**(2)** 基

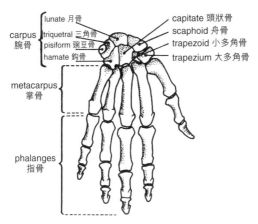

Bones of the left wrist and hand (from the front)
左腕、掌骨前面觀

transmit the disease to others. **2.** (in genetics) a person who bears a gene for an abnormal trait without showing any signs of the disorder; the carrier is usually *heterozygous for the gene concerned, which is *recessive. **3.** an animal, usually an insect, that passively transmits infectious organisms from one animal to another or from an animal to man. *See also* vector.

cartilage *n.* a dense connective tissue composed of a matrix produced by cells called *chondroblasts*, which become embedded in the matrix as *chondrocytes*. It is a semiopaque grey or white substance, consisting chiefly of *chondroitin sulphate, that is capable of withstanding considerable pressure. There are three types: *hyaline cartilage*, *elastic cartilage*, and *fibrocartilage* (see illustration). In the fetus and infant cartilage occurs in many parts of the body, but most of this cartilage disappears during development. In the adult, hyaline cartilage is found in the

因攜帶者 （遺傳學）帶有一種異常特性基因而沒有疾病體徵的人。通常為該隱性基因的雜合體。**(3) 媒介動物** 一種動物，能被動地將傳染性生物從一動物傳給另一動物或從一動物傳給人。參閱 vector。

軟骨 一種致密結締組織，由成軟骨細胞產生的基質構成。而成軟骨細胞變成軟骨細胞，被包埋在基質裏。軟骨是一種半透明的灰色或白色的物質，主要由硫酸軟骨素組成，它能承受相當的壓力。可分為三種：透明軟骨、彈力軟骨和纖維軟骨（見圖）。在胎兒和嬰兒中，軟骨見於身體的許多部位。其大多數在成長過程中消失。在成人，透明軟骨可見於肋骨、喉、氣管、支氣管、鼻和可動骨的關節部位。彈性軟

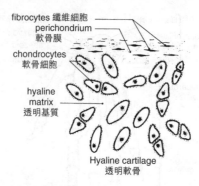

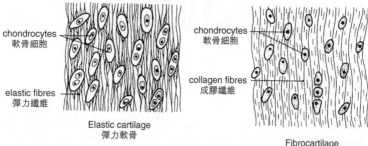

Types of cartilage
軟骨的種類

costal cartilages, larynx, trachea, bronchi, nose, and at the joints of movable bones. Elastic cartilage occurs in the external ear, and fibrocartilage in the intervertebral discs and tendons.

骨出現於外耳，而纖維軟骨則位於椎間盤和肌腱。

caruncle *n.* a small red fleshy swelling. The *lacrimal caruncle* is the red prominence at the inner angle of the eye. *Hymenal caruncles* occur around the mucous membrane lining the vaginal opening.

肉阜 微小的紅色肉樣隆突。淚阜是眼內角處紅色突起。處女膜痕是圍繞陰道口的黏膜突起。

caseation *n.* the breakdown of diseased tissue into a dry cheeselike mass: a type of degeneration associated with tubercular lesions.

乾酪化 病變組織崩解成乾酪樣物質的過程，是一種與結核損害有關的變性。

case control study comparison of a group of people who have a disease with another group free from that disease, in term of *variables in their backgrounds (e.g. cigarette smoking in those who have died from lung cancer and in those dying from other causes). In the more precise *matched pair study* every individual with the disease is paired with a control matched on the basis of (say) age, sex, and/or occupation in order to place greater emphasis on a factor for which the pairs have not been matched. *Compare* cohort study, cross-sectional study.

病例對照研究　將一組患有某種疾病的病人與另一組未患該種疾病的病人根據其背景變量進行比較（例如，死於肺癌的吸煙者與死於其他因素的吸煙者）。在更精確的配對比較研究中，每一位患有該種疾病的人根據其年齡、性別或者職業與另一位對照者配對，以強調其在配對中沒有構成對應關係的某一因素。與 cohort study，cross-sectional study 對比。

case fatality ratio the number of fatalities from a specified disease in a given period per 100 episodes of the disease arising in the same period. Unless all such deaths occur rapidly after the onset of the disease (e.g. cholera) they are likely to be the outcome of episodes that started in an earlier period (hence the term *ratio* rather than *rate*). Comparison of the annual number of admissions and fatalities in a given hospital in respect of a specific disease is known as the *hospital fatality ratio*.

病死比率　某一時期某一特定疾病在每一百例中的死亡數字。除非所有那樣的死亡在該疾病發生後迅速出現（如霍亂），否則這些死亡很可能是在特定時間以前已經開始發病的結果。因此，用「比」(ratio) 而不用「率」(rate)。比較每年某醫院患某病而入院的病人數量與死亡數之間的比率稱為住院死亡比率。

casein *n*. a milk protein. Casein is precipitated out of milk in acid conditions or by the action of rennin: it is the principal protein of cheese. Casein is very easily prepared and is useful as a protein supplement, particularly in the treatment of malnutrition.

酪蛋白　一種乳蛋白。酪蛋白沉澱見於酸化的乳汁，或由凝乳酶作用引起，是奶酪的主要蛋白質。酪蛋白製取容易，可用做蛋白補充品，特別是用於營養不良的治療。

case work *see* social services.

病案調查　參閱 social services。

cassette *n*. (in radiography) a thin light-proof box in which a piece of X-ray film is placed during the taking of an X-ray. It usually contains special screens that

貯片盒　（放射照相術）一薄壁暗盒，放置一張 X 綫片，用於 X 綫攝影。通常包括特殊的屏幕，在 X 綫照射下可發出熒

fluoresce under the influence of X-rays and so intensify the image that is formed on the film.

光，從而增強在膠片上形成的影像。

cast *n.* **1.** a rigid casing for a limb or other part of the body, made of plastic or with open-woven bandage impregnated with plaster of Paris and applied while wet. A plaster cast is designed to protect a broken bone and prevent movement of the aligned bone ends until healing has progressed sufficiently. **2.** a mass of dead cellular, fatty, and other material that forms within a body cavity and takes its shape. It may then be released and appear elsewhere. For example, *granular casts appearing in the urine indicate kidney disease.

(1) 模型 一個硬的模型，用於肢體或身體其他部位，由塑料或由石膏繃帶趁濕製成。石膏托用以保護斷骨，且防止對正的骨折斷端的活動，直至愈合充分。**(2) 管型** 一堆死亡細胞、脂肪和其他物質，在一體腔內形成，並與其形狀一樣。隨後，該物體可被排出，出現於其他部位。如，顆粒管型見於尿中，提示有腎臟疾病。

castor oil *see* laxative.

蓖麻油 參閱 laxative。

castration *n.* removal of the sex glands (the testes or the ovaries). Castration in childhood causes failure of sexual development but when done in adult life (usually as part of hormonal treatment for cancer) it produces less marked physical changes in both sexes. Castration inevitably causes sterility but it need not cause impotence or loss of sexual desire.

閹割 除去性腺（睾丸或卵巢）。兒童時期閹割引起性發育障礙，但成年期閹割（通常是癌症的激素療法的一部分），很少產生明顯的器質改變，無論雌雄。閹割不可避免地引起生育能力的喪失，但它不一定會引起陽痿或性慾喪失。

CAT computerized axial tomography, now usually referred to as *computerized tomography (CT).

計算機軸向斷層照相術 現在通常被稱為電子計算機斷層照相術 (CT)。

cata- *prefix denoting* downward or against.

〔前綴〕**(1)** 向下　**(2)** 對抗

catabolism *n.* the chemical decomposition of complex substances by the body to form simpler ones, accompanied by the release of energy. The substances broken down include nutrients in food (carbohydrates, proteins, etc.) as well as the body's storage products (such as glycogen). *See also* metabolism. **–catabolic** *adj.*

分解代謝 體內化學分解複雜物質以形成簡單物質，並伴隨有能量的釋放。分解的物質包括食物中的營養素（碳水化合物、蛋白質等）以及身體的貯存物質（如糖原）。參閱 metabolism。

catagen *n. see* anagen.

catalase *n.* an enzyme, present in many cells (including red blood cells and liver cells), that catalyses the breakdown of hydrogen peroxide.

catalepsy *n.* the abnormal maintenance of postures or physical attitudes, occurring in *catatonia. These may have arisen spontaneously or they may be induced by the examiner.

catalyst *n.* a substance that alters the rate of a chemical reaction but is itself unchanged at the end of the reaction. The catalysts of biochemical reactions are the *enzymes.

cataphoresis *n.* the introduction into the tissues of positively charged ionized substances (cations) by the use of a direct electric current. *See* iontophoresis.

cataplasia *n.* degeneration of tissues to an earlier developmental form.

cataplexy *n.* a recurrent condition in which the patient suddenly collapses to the ground without loss of consciousness. Laughter or any strong emotion can provoke an attack. It is usually associated with *narcolepsy.

cataract *n.* any opacity in the lens of the eye, resulting in blurred vision. The commonest type is *senile cataract*, seen frequently in the elderly, but some cataracts are congenital, while others are due to metabolic disease, such as *diabetes. Cataracts may also result from direct or indirect injury to the lens and prolonged exposure of the eye to infrared rays (e.g. *glass-blowers' cataract*) or ionizing radiation. Minor degrees of cataract do not necessarily impair vision seriously.

毛髮生長中期 參閱 anagen。

過氧化氫酶 一種酶，見於許多細胞（包括紅細胞和肝細胞），催化過氧化氫分解。

木僵 異常保持的姿勢或體位，見於緊張症。可自發出現或由檢查者誘發。

觸媒 一種物質，能改變一個化學反應的速度而本身在反應結束後不發生變化。生化反應的觸媒被稱為酶。

陽離子電泳 通過直流電把陽離子化的物質引入組織。參閱 iontophoresis。

組織退化 組織退化到一種較早期的發育形式。

猝倒 一種反覆發作的狀態，患者突然倒地，並伴隨意識喪失。大笑或任何強烈的情緒都可激起發作。它常併發有發作性睡眠。

白內障 眼球晶狀體的混濁，導致視力模糊。最常見的種類是老年性白內障，常見於老年人，但一些白內障是先天性的，而其他則由代謝性疾病引起，如糖尿病。白內障也可由於晶狀體的直接或間接的受損，以及眼睛長期受到紅外綫的照射（如吹玻璃工白內障）或電離輻射所致。輕度白內障不一定會嚴重損傷視力。

白內障可通過外科摘除病

Cataract is treated by surgical removal of the affected lens (*cataract extraction*; *see also* phacoemulsification); patients may wear a contact lens or appropriate spectacles to compensate for the missing lens but in modern practice an intraocular lens is routinely inserted (*lens implantation*).

變晶狀體而得以治療（白內障摘除術。參閱 phacoemulsification）。病人可配戴隱形眼鏡或合適的普通眼鏡以代償晶狀體的損傷。但在現代實踐中，眼睛內晶狀體植入是常規措施（晶狀體植入法）。

catarrh *n.* the excessive secretion of thick phlegm or mucus by the mucous membrane of the nose, nasal sinuses, nasopharynx, or air passages. The term is not used in any precise or scientific sense.

卡他 過多分泌的濃稠痰液或黏液，來自鼻、鼻竇、鼻咽或空氣通道。此術語不用於精確和科學的表達。

catatonia *n.* a state in which a person becomes mute or stuporous or adopts bizarre postures. The features include *flexibilitas cerea*, in which the limbs may be moved passively by another person into positions that are then retained for hours on end. Catatonia was once a noted feature of *schizophrenia but is now hardly ever seen in developed countries. It remains common in Third World countries. **–catatonic** *adj.*

緊張症 該狀態指一個人變得一言不發或恍惚或採取怪異的姿勢。其特點包括蠟樣屈曲。在此種情況下，其四肢被另一個人被動地置於某種位置後，可保持數小時不變。緊張症曾經是精神分裂症的一個明顯特徵，但目前在發達國家少見。此種病症仍多見於第三世界國家。

catchment area the geographic area from which a hospital can expect to receive patients and on which in Britain the designated population of the hospital is based. There is no statutory requirement forcing patients to use the hospital(s) of their area, but a code of zoning practice exists for some specialties (e.g. geriatrics, mental illness). A hospital may have a smaller catchment area (e.g. a National Health Service District) for common specialties than for rarer ones, which may be shared between several districts (*regional specialty*) or regions (*supraregional specialty*). *See also* independent contact.

保健地段 一個醫院預期接診病人的地理區域。在英國，醫院接診的病人根據此區域來劃分。不存在法律依據強制病人使用他們居住區域的醫院，但對某些專科疾病（如老年病、精神病）要求分區就診。如果一個醫院承擔的常見病應診保健地段（如國民保健服務制所屬地段）比罕見病應診範圍小，則後者可由幾個地段（地區專科）或地區（跨地區專科）共同分擔。參閱 independent contact。

catecholamines *pl. n.* a group of physiologically important substances, including

兒茶酚胺 一組具有生理重要性的物質，包括腎上腺素、去

*adrenaline, *noradrenaline, and *dopamine, having various different roles (mainly as *neurotransmitters) in the functioning of the sympathetic and central nervous systems. Chemically, all contain a benzene ring with adjacent hydroxyl groups (catechol) and an amine group on a side chain.

甲腎上腺素和多巴胺。各自施加不同作用（主要為神經遞質）於交感神經和中樞神經系統。化學結構上，都含有一個苯環，及鄰位羥基（兒茶酚）和一個氨基於支鏈上。

catgut *n.* a natural fibrous material prepared from the tissues of animals, usually from the walls of sheep intestines, twisted into strands of different thicknesses and used to sew up wounds (*see* suture) and tie off blood vessels during surgery. The catgut gradually dissolves and is absorbed by the tissues, so that the stitches do not have to be removed later. This also minimizes the possibility of long-term irritation at the site of operation. Some catgut is treated with chromic acid for different periods during manufacture (*chromic catgut*). This gives catguts that last for longer lengths of time before absorption is complete.

腸綫 一種天然纖維物質，由動物組織，通常為羊的小腸壁，紡成不同粗細的綫。在外科手術當中，用於縫合傷口（參閱 suture）和結紮血管。腸綫逐漸溶解，並被組織吸收，因此，縫綫不必後期拆除。從而將對手術部位的長期刺激減少至最小程度。在製備過程中，一些腸綫經鉻酸處理的時間不同（鉻腸綫）。這使得腸綫在完全吸收之前保持較長時間。

catharsis *n.* purging or cleansing out of the bowels by giving the patient a *laxative (cathartic) to stimulate intestinal activity.

導瀉 通過給病人用輕瀉藥（導瀉藥）刺激腸管運動來排泄或清理腸管。

cathartic *n. see* laxative.

導瀉藥 參閱 laxative。

cathepsin *n.* one of a group of enzymes found in animal tissues, particularly the spleen, that digest proteins.

組織蛋白酶 一種酶，見於動物組織，特別是脾臟，能消化蛋白。

catheter *n.* a flexible tube for insertion into a narrow opening so that fluids may be introduced or removed. *Urinary catheters* are passed into the bladder through the urethra to allow drainage of urine in certain disorders and to empty the bladder before abdominal operations.

導管 一種軟管，能插入狹窄開口，從而將液體注入或排出。在某些疾病中，導尿管通過尿道穿入膀胱以排出尿液，在腹部手術前排空膀胱。

catheterization *n.* the introduction of a *catheter into a hollow organ. This is most often performed as *urethral catheterization*, when a catheter is introduced into the bladder to relieve obstruction to the outflow of urine (*see also* intermittent self-cathetization). *Cardiac catheterization* entails the introduction of special catheters into the arteries and veins of the arms or legs through which their tips are manipulated into the various chambers of the heart. Cardiac catheterization provides data on pressures and blood flow within the various chambers of the heart. It permits *angiocardiography. *Arterial catheterization* enables the introduction into the arteries of dyes for radiographic purposes, of drugs to constrict or expand the vessels for treatment purposes, and of insoluble microspheres to block the vessel and arrest haemorrhage or necrose tumours.

導管插入術 將導管插入中空器官。最常見的是導尿管插入術。導管被插入膀胱，解除梗塞而排出尿液（參閱 intermittent self-catheterization）。心導管插入術是指將特殊的導管插入上肢或下肢的動脈和靜脈，由此使其尖端抵達心臟各房室。心導管插入術提供心臟各房室內的血壓和血流信息。此法也可用來進行心血管造影。動脈導管插入法是指將導管插入動脈，為放射照相目的而將染料注入、為治療目的而注入藥物以收縮或擴張血管，以及導入不溶性微球以堵塞血管，停止出血或使腫塊壞死。

cation *n.* an ion of positive charge, such as a sodium ion (Na^+). *Compare* anion. *See* electrolyte.

陽離子 帶正電荷的離子，如鈉離子（Na^+）。與 anion 對比。參閱 electrolyte。

cation-exchange resins complex insoluble chemical compounds that may be administered with the diet to alter the *electrolyte balance of the body in the treatment of heart, kidney, and metabolic disorders. For example, in patients on a strict low-sodium diet such resins combine with sodium in the food so that it cannot be absorbed and passes out in the faeces.

陽離子交換樹脂 能夠同飲食一同服用的複雜的不溶性化合物，用於治療心臟、腎臟和代謝疾患中改變體內電解質平衡。例如，嚴格進低鹽飲食的病人，食用鈉鹽時並用此類樹脂，可防止鈉鹽吸收，從而在糞便中排泄掉。

cat-scratch fever an infectious disease, possibly viral in origin, transmitted to man following injury to the skin by a cat scratch, splinter, or thorn. The injury becomes inflamed and mild fever and swelling of the lymph nodes (usually

貓抓熱 病原體可能是病毒的一種傳染病。由於貓抓、鋒利碎片或棘刺造成皮膚損傷而傳播給人。損傷處發炎，有輕度發熱，感染後大約一周，淋巴結腫大（通常是那些接近傷口

those closest to the wound) develop about a week after infection. In some cases serious abscess formation occurs, but generally recovery is complete.

處的淋巴結）。一些病人出現嚴重膿腫，但通常能完全恢復。

cauda *n.* a tail-like structure. The *cauda equina* is a bundle of nerve roots from the lumbar, sacral, and coccygeal spinal nerves that descend nearly vertically from the spinal cord until they reach their respective openings in the vertebral column.

尾　尾樣結構。馬尾指的是一束來自腰、骶和尾骨部脊神經根。它們從脊髓開始垂直下行，到脊柱上各自的出口為止。

caudal *adj.* relating to the lower part or tail end of the body.

(1) 尾的　(2) 身體下部的　涉及身體下部的或尾端的。

caul *n.* **1.** (in obstetrics) a membrane that may surround an infant at birth. It consists of an intact *amnion. **2.** (in anatomy) *see* omentum.

(1) 胎頭羊膜　（產科學）分娩時可包繞胎兒的一層膜。它由一完整的羊膜組成。**(2) 大網膜**（解剖學）參閱 omentum。

causal agent a factor associated with the definitive onset of an illness (or other response, including an accident). Examples of causal agents are bacteria, trauma, and noxious agents. The relationship is more direct than in the case of a *risk factor, and in general the specific ill health will only occur if the agent is a precursor.

致病因子　與一種疾病的發生確實有關的因素（或其他情況，包括事故）。如細菌、外傷、有毒或有害物質。與危險因素比較，致病因子與疾病的關係更為直接，而且，通常情況下，只有致病因子出現後，某一特定的病態才會發生。

causalgia *n.* an intensely unpleasant burning pain felt in a limb where there has been partial damage to the sympathetic and somatic sensory nerves.

灼痛　當肢體交感神經和軀體感覺神經受到部分損傷時，肢體所感受到的一種強烈的灼傷痛。

caustic *n.* an agent, such as silver nitrate, that causes irritation and burning and destroys tissue. Caustic agents may be used to remove dead skin, warts, etc., but care must be taken not to damage the surrounding area.

腐蝕劑　一種如硝酸銀那樣能引起刺激、灼燒且破壞組織的物質。腐蝕劑可以被用來除去死皮和疣等，但使用時，須注意不要損傷周圍的部位。

caustic soda *see* sodium hydroxide.

苛性鈉　參閱 sodium hydroxide。

cauterize *vb.* to destroy tissues by direct application of a heated instrument (known as a *cautery*): used for the removal of small warts or other growths (*see also* curettage) and also to stop bleeding from small vessels. –**cautery** *n.*

烙 通過直接使用一加熱的器械破壞組織（稱為烙器）。這一器械被用來除去小疣或其他增生物（參閱 curettage），也用來止住小血管出血。

cavernitis *n.* inflammation of the corpora cavernosa of the *penis or the corpus cavernosum of the clitoris.

海綿體炎 陰莖海綿體或陰蒂海綿體的炎症。

cavernosography *n.* a radiological examination of the penis that entails the infusion of a radiopaque contrast material into the corpora cavernosa of the penis via a small butterfly needle. X-rays taken during the infusion give information regarding the veins draining the penis.

海綿體造影術 陰莖部的放射性檢查。需要通過一小的蝶形針將一種不透 X 綫的造影劑注入陰莖海綿體。在注入過程中所攝的 X 綫照相提供關於陰莖靜脈引流的信息。

cavernosometry *n.* the measurement of pressure within the corpora cavernosa of the penis during infusion. The flow rate required to produce an erection is recorded and also the flow necessary to maintain the induced erection. The examination is important in the investigation of failure of erection and impotence.

海綿體壓力測量 在灌注期間對陰莖海綿體內壓力的測量。產生勃起所需要的流速被記錄下來。還要記錄保持已誘發的勃起所需要的流速。這一檢查對於研究勃起不能和陽痿很重要。

cavernous breathing *see* breath sounds.

空洞性呼吸 參閱 breath sounds。

cavernous sinus one of the paired cavities within the *sphenoid bone, at the base of the skull behind the eye sockets, into which blood drains from the brain, eye, nose, and upper cheek before leaving the skull through connections with the internal jugular and facial veins. Through the sinus, in its walls, pass the internal carotid artery and the abducens, oculomotor, trochlear, ophthalmic, and maxillary nerves.

海綿竇 位於顱骨底部眼眶後方蝶骨內的一對腔隙之一。接納來自腦、眼、鼻和面頰上部的血液，使之離開顱部與頸內靜脈和面靜脈匯合。通過竇壁，穿行的有頸內動脈以及展神經、動眼神經、滑車神經、眼神經和上頜神經。

cavity *n.* **1.** (in anatomy) a hollow enclosed area; for example, the abdominal cavity or the buccal cavity (mouth). **2.** (in dentistry) **a.** the hole in a tooth caused by *caries or abrasion. **b.** the hole shaped in a tooth by a dentist to retain a filling.

(1) 腔 （解剖學）中空封閉的區域，如腹腔或口腔前庭。**(2)** 洞 （牙科學）**a.** 由齲變或磨損而形成的牙孔。**b.** 牙科醫生為進行補牙而修製的備填洞。

cavity varnish (in dentistry) a solution of natural or synthetic resin in an organic solvent. It is used as a sealer for amalgam fillings or as a coating over newly inserted cement fillings.

洞襯劑 （牙科學）溶於有機溶劑的一種天然的或合成樹脂溶液，用以封閉汞合金填料或覆蓋新充填的黏固粉。

CBW (chemical and biological warfare) the use of poisonous gases and other chemicals, bacteria, viruses, and toxins during war.

化學和生物戰 戰爭期間對有毒氣體和其他化學品、細菌、病毒和毒素的使用。

CCDC *see* public health physician.

傳染病控制高級醫師 參閱 public health physician。

CD cluster of differentiation: a numerical system for classifying antigens expressed on the surface of leucocytes.

分化群集性 一種數字系統，用於分類在白細胞表面表達的抗原。

CDH *see* congenital dislocation of the hip.

先天髖部脫位 參閱 congenital dislocation of the hip。

cefaclor *n.* a *cephalosporin antibiotic used in the treatment of otitis media, upper and lower respiratory-tract infections, urinary-tract infections, and skin infections. It is administered by mouth; side-effects include diarrhoea and skin eruptions. Trade name: **Distaclor.**

頭孢克洛 一種頭孢菌素類抗生素，用於治療中耳炎、上下呼吸道感染、尿道感染和皮膚感染。口服。副作用包括腹瀉和皮膚斑疹。商品名：Distaclor。

cefadroxil *n.* a *cephalosporin antibiotic used in the treatment of urinary-tract infections, skin infections, pharyngitis, and tonsillitis. It is administered by mouth; side-effects include skin rash and generalized itching. Trade name: **Baxan.**

頭孢羥氨苄 一種頭孢菌素類抗生素，用於治療尿道感染、皮膚感染、咽炎以及扁桃體炎。副作用包括皮疹和全身搔癢。商品名：Baxan。

-CELE   262

-cele (-coele) *suffix denoting* swelling, hernia, or tumour. Example: *gastrocele* (hernia of the stomach).

cell *n.* the basic unit of all living organisms, which can reproduce itself exactly (*see* mitosis). Each cell is bounded by a *cell membrane* of lipids and protein, which controls the passage of substances into and out of the cell. Cells contain *cytoplasm, in which are suspended a *nucleus and other structures (*organelles) specialized to carry out particular activities in the cell (see illustration).

Complex organisms such as man are built up of millions of cells that are specially adapted to carry out particular functions. The process of cell differentiation begins early on in the development of the embryo and cells of a particular type (e.g. blood cells, liver cells) always give rise to cells of the same type. Each cell has a particular number of *chromosomes

〔後綴〕**膨脹，疝，腫物** 表示膨腫、疝或腫物。如胃疝。

細胞 所有生物的基本單位，它能進行嚴格的自我複製（參閱 mitosis）。每個細胞都有一個脂質和蛋白構成的細胞膜。該膜控制物質進出細胞。細胞中的細胞漿包繞着細胞核和其他結構（細胞器），它們在細胞內完成特定的活動。（見圖）。

像人這樣複雜的生物由數百萬具有特定功能的細胞組成。細胞的分化在胚胎發展的早期就開始了。某一具體類型的細胞（如血細胞、肝細胞）總會產生同一種細胞。每一細胞在其核中都有一定數量的染色體。性細胞（精子和卵子）總是只有身體所有其他細胞的染色體數量的一半（參閱

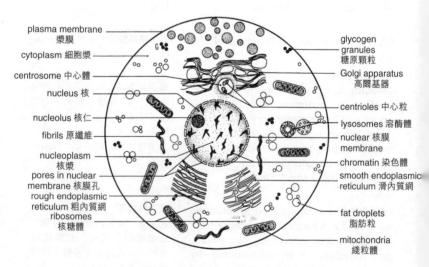

An animal cell (microscopical structure)
動物細胞（顯微鏡下結構）

in its nucleus. The sex cells (sperm and ova) always contain half the number of chromosomes of all the other cells of the body (*see* meiosis); at fertilization a sperm and ovum combine to form a cell with a complete set of chromosomes that will develop into the embryo.

cell body (perikaryon) the enlarged portion of a *neurone (nerve cell), containing the nucleus. It is concerned more with the nutrition of the cell than with propagation of nerve impulses.

cell division reproduction of cells by division first of the chromosomes (karyokinesis) and then of the cytoplasm (cytokinesis). Cell division to produce more body (somatic) cells is by *mitosis; cell division during the formation of gametes is by *meiosis.

cellulitis *n.* inflammation of the connective tissue between adjacent tissues and organs. This is commonly due to bacterial infection by streptococci (occasionally by staphylococci) and usually requires antibiotic treatment to prevent its spread to the bloodstream.

cellulose *n.* a carbohydrate consisting of linked glucose units. It is an important constituent of plant cell walls. Cellulose cannot be digested by man and is a component of *dietary fibre (roughage).

Celsius temperature (centigrade temperature) temperature expressed on a scale in which the melting point of ice is assigned a temperature of 0° and the boiling point of water a temperature of 100°. For many medical purposes this scale has superseded the Fahrenheit scale (*see* Fahrenheit temperature). The

meiosis）。受精時，精子和卵子結合生成具有完整的一套染色體的細胞，從而發育成胚胎。

胞體（核周體） 神經元（神經細胞）的膨大部分，內含有核。它主要與細胞的營養有關，而與神經衝動的傳導關係不大。

細胞分裂 細胞通過分裂方式繁殖時，先是染色體的分裂（核分裂），然後才是細胞漿的分裂（胞質分裂）。細胞通過有絲分裂以產生更多體細胞。配子形成時的細胞分裂是通過減數分裂而進行的。

蜂窩織炎 相鄰的組織和器官之間的結締組織的炎症。通常是由於鏈球菌引起的細菌感染（偶爾由葡萄球菌引起），而且通常需要使用抗生素治療以防止其沿血流傳播。

纖維素 以連結起來的葡萄糖單位構成的碳水化合物。它是植物細胞壁的重要組成成分。纖維素不能被人類消化，是食物纖維的一個組成成分（粗食）。

攝氏溫度 刻度上冰的融點被定為 0 度，而水的沸點被定為 100 度的溫度單位。因許多醫學目的，這一溫度取代了華氏溫度（參閱 Fahrenheit temperature）。從攝氏 (C) 到華氏 (F) 溫度的轉換公式為：$F = {}^9/_5C + 32$。

formula for converting from Celsius (C) to Fahrenheit (F) is: $F = \frac{9}{5}C + 32$.

cement *n.* **1.** any of a group of materials used in dentistry either as fillings or as *lutes for crowns. Glass ionomer cements are used for filling, and zinc phosphate, zinc polycarboxylate, and glass ionomer cements are used for luting. Zinc oxide–eugenol cements are widely used as temporary fillings. **2.** *see* cementum.

(1) 黏固粉 一組牙科中用做牙冠填料或密封粉的物質。玻璃離聚物黏固粉被用做填料，磷酸鋅、聚羧酸鋅和玻璃離聚物被用作密封粉。氧化鋅丁香酚黏固粉被廣泛地用做暫時的填料。**(2) 牙骨質** 參閱 cementum。

cementocyte *n.* a cell found in cementum.

牙骨質細胞 牙骨質中存在的一種細胞。

cementoma *n.* a benign overgrowth of cementum.

牙骨質瘤 牙骨質的良性增生。

cementum (cement) *n.* a thin layer of hard tissue on the surface of the root of a *tooth. It attaches the fibres of the periodontal membrane to the tooth.

牙骨質 牙根表面的一薄層硬組織。這層組織使牙周膜纖維固定在牙齒上。

censor *n.* (in psychology) the mechanism, postulated by Freud, that suppresses or modifies desires that are inappropriate or feared. The censor is usually regarded as being located in the *superego but was also described by Freud as being in the *ego itself.

潛意識抑制 （心理學）弗洛伊德提出的一種心理機制，即壓抑或修正令人害怕的慾望。通常認為這種抑制存在於超我，但也被弗洛伊德描述為存在於自我本身。

-centesis *suffix denoting* puncture or perforation. Example: *amniocentesis* (surgical puncture of the amnion).

〔後綴〕**穿刺術** 表示穿刺術或穿孔術，如羊膜穿刺術（羊膜的外科穿刺）。

centi- *prefix denoting* one hundredth or a hundred.

〔前綴〕**百分的，一百的** 百分之一或表示一百。

centigrade temperature *see* Celsius temperature.

百度溫標 參閱 Celsius temperature。

centile chart a graph with lines showing average measurements of height and weight compared to age and sex, against which a child's progress can be assessed.

百分曲線圖 一種線性圖，含有與年齡和性別相對應的平均高度和體重的測量值。對照該圖可以評價一個兒童的發育。

The number of a centile predicts the percentage of children who are below a particular measurement at a given age; for example, the 10th centile means 10% of the population will be smaller and 90% bigger at that age. A child will normally follow a particular centile line. Children who are above the 97th or below the 3rd centile, or whose growth rapidly changes centiles, should be investigated.

百分曲綫圖上的一個數字可以預測在某一年齡低於某一具體測量值的兒童的百分比。例如，第十個百分比表示在那個年齡的總人口中，百分之十的人會小於該值，而百分之九十要大於該值。一個兒童通常隨着某一具體的百分綫而成長。高於第百分之九十七或者低於第三個百分綫的兒童，或者那些發育過程迅速變換百分曲綫的兒童要予以檢查。

centoxin *n.* a *monoclonal antibody that neutralizes the effects of bacterial *endotoxins. It is administered by injection in cases of dangerous bacterial infection with overwhelming toxicity.

消內毒素 一種單克隆抗體，能中和細菌性內毒素的作用。注射用於治療巨毒性危險細菌感染。

Central Manpower Committee *see* manpower committee.

中央衛生人力委員會 參閱 manpower committee。

central nervous system (CNS) the *brain and the *spinal cord, as opposed to the cranial and spinal nerves and the *autonomic nervous system, which together form the *peripheral nervous system*. The CNS is responsible for the *integration of all nervous activities.

中樞神經系統 腦和脊髓，與組成外周神經系統的腦神經、脊神經和自主神經相對應，中樞神經系統負責所有神經活動的整合。

central venous pressure (CVP) the pressure of blood within the right atrium. Measurement of CVP is obtained by *catheterization of the right side of the heart; the catheter is attached to a manometer. CVP measurements are used to estimate circulatory function and blood volume in cases of shock or severe haemorrhage and to monitor blood replacement. In a recumbent patient, with the zero point of the manometer level with the mid-axilla (centre of the armpit), CVP should measure between 5 and 8 cm saline under normal conditions.

中心靜脈壓 右心房內的血壓。對心臟右側實施導管插入可獲得中心靜脈壓值。將導管與一測壓計聯結。中心靜脈壓測量用於在休克或嚴重出血情況下估計循環功能和血量，也用於監控換血過程。當病人平臥時，將腋窩中部與壓力計的零點水平對齊。正常情況下，中心靜脈壓力為 5~8 cm 鹽水柱。

centre *n.* (in neurology) a collection of neurones (nerve cells) whose activities control a particular function. The *respiratory* and *cardiovascular centres*, for example, are regions in the lower brainstem that control the movements of respiration and the functioning of the circulatory system, respectively.

中樞 （神經病學）一神經元（神經細胞）集羣，它們的活動控制一特定的功能。例如，呼吸中樞和心血管中樞位於腦幹下部，它們分別控制呼吸運動和循環系統的功能。

centrencephalic *adj.* (in electroencephalography) describing discharges that can be recorded synchronously from all parts of the brain. The source of this activity is in the *reticular formation of the midbrain. *Centrencephalic epilepsy* is associated with a congenital predisposition to seizures.

中腦型的 （腦電描記術）描述可以從腦的各個部分同時記錄到的放電現象。這一活動來源於中腦網狀結構。中腦型癲癇與先天素質有關。

centri- *prefix denoting* centre. Example: *centrilobular* (in the centre of a lobule (especially of the liver)).

〔前綴〕中心的，中央的 指中心，如小葉中心的（尤指肝臟內）。

centrifugal *adj.* moving away from a centre, as from the brain to the peripheral tissues.

離心的 離開中心的，如從腦到外周組織。

centrifuge *n.* a device for separating components of different densities in a liquid, using centrifugal force. The liquid is placed in special containers that are spun at high speed around a central axis.

離心機 利用離心力將液體中不同密度的成分進行分離的器械。將液體置於特製容器內，繞中心軸高速旋轉。

centriole *n.* a small particle found in the cytoplasm of cells, near the nucleus. Centrioles are involved in the formation of the *spindle and aster during cell division. During interphase there are usually two centrioles in the *centrosome; when cell division occurs these separate and move to opposite sides of the nucleus, and the spindle is formed between them.

中心粒 一種靠近細胞核、存在於細胞漿中的小粒。在細胞分裂過程中，中心粒參與紡錘體和星體的形成。在分裂間期，通常在中心體裏有兩個中心粒。當細胞分裂開始時，它們就分開，移到核的對應兩側，它們中間形成紡錘體。

centripetal *adj.* moving towards a centre, as from the peripheral tissues to the brain.

向心的 向中心移動，例如由外周組織向腦的移動。

centromere (kinetochore) *n.* the part of a chromosome that joins the two *chromatids to each other and becomes attached to the spindle during *mitosis and *meiosis. When chromosome division takes place the centromeres split longitudinally.

着絲粒（動原體）　染色體中將兩個染色單體相互聯結起來的部分，並在有絲分裂和減數分裂時附着於紡錘體。當染色體分裂發生時，着絲粒沿縱向分裂。

centrosome (centrosphere) *n.* an area of clear cytoplasm, found next to the nucleus in nondividing cells, that contains the *centrioles.

中心體（中心球）　在非分裂細胞的核附近存在的澄清的細胞漿區，它含有中心粒。

centrosphere *n.* **1.** an area of clear cytoplasm seen in dividing cells around the poles of the spindle. **2.** *see* centrosome.

(1) 中心球　細胞分裂時紡錘體兩極周圍澄清的細胞漿區域。**(2)** 中心體　參閱 centrosome。

centrum *n.* (*pl.* **centra**) the solid rod-shaped central portion of a *vertebra.

椎體　椎骨中央實心的棒狀部分。

cephal- (cephalo-) *prefix denoting* the head. Example: *cephalalgia* (pain in).

〔前綴〕頭部　表示頭，如頭痛。

cephalad *adj.* towards the head.

向頭方向的

cephalexin *n.* a *cephalosporin antibiotic used in the treatment of respiratory-tract and genitourinary-tract infections, bone and skin infections, and otitis media. It is administered by mouth; diarrhoea is the most common side-effect. Trade names: **Ceporex**, **Keflex**.

頭孢氨苄　一種頭孢菌素類抗生素，用於治療呼吸道和泌尿生殖道的感染、骨和皮膚感染以及中耳炎。用於口服。腹瀉是最常見的副作用。商品名：Ceporex，Keflex。

cephalhaematoma *n.* an egg-sized swelling on the head caused by a collection of bloody fluid between one or more of the skull bones (usually the *parietal bone) and its covering membrane (periosteum). It is most commonly seen in newborn infants delivered with the aid of forceps or subjected to pressures during passage through the birth canal. No treatment is necessary and the swelling disappears in a few months. If it is

頭皮血腫　頭部雞蛋大小的腫脹，位於一個或多個顱骨（通常是頂骨）與覆蓋膜（骨膜）之間，由血性液體的聚積而成。此種疾患常見於新生兒中，由於出生過程借助於產鉗的幫助，或者是在通過產道時受到了擠壓。不需要進行治療，血腫在數月內消失。如果面積較大，液體裏面的血液就會分解，將膽紅素釋放進入血

extensive, the blood within the fluid may break down, releasing bilirubin into the bloodstream and causing *jaundice. A cephalhaematoma in an older baby or child is evidence of some recent injury to the head; occasionally an unsuspected fracture is revealed on X-ray.

液，引起黃疸。較大的嬰兒或兒童頭部出現血腫證明其頭部近期受到損傷。偶爾，X 綫檢查揭示意外的骨折。

cephalic *adj.* of or relating to the head.

頭的　涉及頭部的。

cephalic index a measure of the shape of a skull, commonly used in *craniometry: the ratio of the greatest breadth, multiplied by 100, to the greatest length of the skull. *See also* brachycephaly, dolichocephaly.

顱骨指數　常用於顱測量法中。顱骨形狀的測量即最大顱寬乘以 100，再與最大顱長的比值。參閱 brachycephaly，dolichocephaly。

cephalic version a procedure for turning a fetus that is lying in a breech or transverse position so that its head will enter the birth canal first. It may give rise to complications and is therefore only carried out in selected cases.

胎頭倒轉術　一種使臀位或橫位的胎兒旋轉，使其頭首先進入產道的方法。它可能會引起併發症，因此只能施予有選擇的病例。

cephalin *n.* one of a group of *phospholipids that are constituents of cell membranes and are particularly abundant in the brain.

腦磷脂　一組磷脂，是細胞的構成成分，且在腦中含量豐富。

cephalocele *n. see* neural tube defects.

腦膨出　參閱 neural tube defects。

cephalogram *n.* a special standardized X-ray picture that can be used to measure alterations in the growth of skull bones.

測顱 X 綫照片　一種特殊的標準 X 綫照片，用於測量顱骨生長的改變。

cephalometry *n.* the study of facial growth by examination of standardized lateral radiographs of the head. It is used mainly for diagnosis in *orthodontics.

顱測量術　採用頭部標準側位 X 綫攝影檢查面部發育情況的方法。主要用於口腔正畸科的診斷。

cephalosporin *n.* any one of a group of semisynthetic *beta-lactam antibiotics, derived from the mould

頭孢菌素類　一組半合成 β-內酰胺抗生素，提取於頭孢子菌屬，能有效作用於廣譜微生

Cephalosporium, which are effective against a wide range of microorganisms and are therefore used in a variety of infections (*see* cefaclor, cefadroxil, cephalexin, cephazolin). Cross-sensitivity with penicillin may occur and the principal side-effects are allergic reactions and irritation of the digestive tract.

cephazolin *n.* a semisynthetic antibiotic, given by intramuscular or intravenous injection in the treatment of a number of infections. *See* cephalosporin. Trade name: **Kefzol**.

cercaria *n.* (*pl.* **cercariae**) the final larval stage of any parasitic trematode (*see* fluke). The cercariae, which have tails but otherwise resemble the adults, are released into water from the snail host in which the parasite undergoes part of its development. Several thousand cercariae may emerge from a single snail in a day.

cerebellar syndrome (Nonne's syndrome) *see* (cerebellar) ataxia.

cerebellum *n.* the largest part of the hind-brain, bulging back behind the pons and the medulla oblongata and overhung by the occipital lobes of the cerebrum. Like the cerebrum, it has an outer grey cortex and a core of white matter. Three broad bands of nerve fibres – the inferior, middle, and superior cerebellar peduncles – connect it to the medulla, the pons, and the midbrain respectively. It has two hemispheres, one on each side of the central region (the *vermis*), and its surface is thrown into thin folds called *folia* (see illustration). Within lie four pairs of nuclei.

The cerebellum is essential for the maintenance of muscle tone, balance,

物，因此用於治療多種感染（參閱 cefaclor，cefadroxil，cephalexin，cephazolin）。與青黴素具有交叉敏感性。主要副作用為過敏反應和消化道刺激。

頭孢唑啉 一種半合成抗生素，肌肉或靜脈注射，用於治療某些感染。參閱 cephalosporin。商品名：Kefzol。

尾蚴 任何寄生吸蟲的最後幼蟲期（參閱 fluke）。尾蚴有尾，除此之外就與成蟲相似。它先在螺體宿主經歷部分發展，隨後被釋放入水裏。一個螺體宿主一天可產出數千尾蚴。

小腦綜合徵（農內綜合徵） 參閱 (cerebellar) ataxia。

小腦 後腦最大的部分，從橋腦和延腦向後膨出，懸於大腦枕葉之下。像大腦一樣，其外層為灰質，內核為白質。三束粗大的神經纖維（包括上、中、下小腦腳）將其分別與延腦、橋腦和中腦相連。它有兩個半球，分別位於中央部（蚓部）兩側，其表面形成微細的皺褶，稱為葉（見圖），內部含有四對神經核。

小腦在維持肌肉緊持性、平衡和隨意控制肌肉羣的活動的協調方面是重要的，從而將肌肉收縮運動轉換成平穩的協調運動。但它不能引起運動，在有意識的知覺和智力方面不起作用。

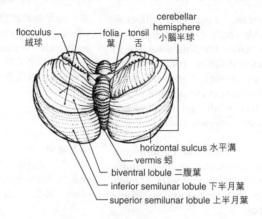

The cerebellum (anterior view)
小腦（前觀）

and the synchronization of activity in groups of muscles under voluntary control, converting muscular contractions into smooth coordinated movement. It does not, however, initiate movement and plays no part in the perception of conscious sensations or in intelligence. **–cerebellar** *adj.*

cerebr- (cerebri-, cerebro-) *prefix denoting* the cerebrum or brain.

〔前綴〕**大腦，腦** 表示大腦或腦。

cerebral abscess *see* abscess.

大腦膿腫 參閱 abscess。

cerebral aqueduct (aqueduct of Sylvius) the narrow channel, containing cerebrospinal fluid, that connects the third and fourth *ventricles of the brain.

大腦導水管 溝通大腦第三和第四腦室的狹窄管道，內含腦脊液。

cerebral cortex the intricately folded outer layer of the *cerebrum, making up some 40% of the brain by weight and composed of an estimated 15 thousand million neurones (*see* grey matter). This is the part of the brain most directly responsible for consciousness, with essential roles in perception, memory, thought, mental ability, and intellect, and

大腦皮質 大腦裏呈密集皺褶的外層，構成腦重量的 40%，估計由 150 億個神經元組成（參閱 grey matter）。這部分是腦中最直接負責意識的部分。其基本的作用在於感覺、記憶、思維和智力活動，它還負責產生隨意運動。它與全身的所有部位都直接或間接的聯繫

it is responsible for initiating, voluntary activity. It has connections, direct or indirect, with all parts of the body. The folding of the cortex provides a large surface area, the greater part lying in the clefts (*sulci*), which divide the upraised convolutions (*gyri*). On the basis of its microscopic appearance in section, the cortex is mapped into *Brodmann's areas; it is also divided into functional regions; including *motor cortex, *sensory cortex, and *association areas. Within, and continuous with it, lies the *white matter, through which connection is made with the rest of the nervous system.

cerebral haemorrhage bleeding from a cerebral artery into the tissue of the brain. It is commonly caused by degenerative disease of the blood vessels and high blood pressure but it may result from bleeding from congenital abnormalities of blood vessels. The extent and severity of the symptoms depend upon the site and volume of the haemorrhage; they vary from a transient weakness or numbness to profound coma and death. *See also* atheroma, hypertension, stroke.

cerebral hemisphere one of the two paired halves of the *cerebrum.

cerebral palsy a nonprogressive disorder of movement resulting from damage to the brain before, during, or immediately after birth. It is often complicated by other neurological and mental problems. The underlying brain damage is permanent. There are many causes, including birth injury, *hypoxia, *hypoglycaemia, jaundice, and infection. The most common disability is a *spastic paralysis. Sensation is often affected, leading to a lack of balance, and intelligence, posture,

着。皮質的皺褶提供了一個大的表面積，最大的部分位於將隆起的腦回隔開的溝裏。根據顯微鏡切片觀察所見，皮質按布羅德曼皮質區被化分成若干區域。它也被劃分成若干功能區域，包括運動皮質區、感覺皮質區和聯想區。白質位於其內，且與其相伴延續，從而與神經系統的其餘部分相聯繫。

腦出血 腦動脈出血，流入腦組織。它通常是由血管變性病和高血壓引起，也可由血管先天畸形引起。症狀的多少和嚴重程度取決於出血的部位和出血量的多少。其症狀表現為短暫性無力或麻痺到深度昏迷和死亡。參閱 atheroma，hypertension，stroke。

大腦半球 大腦的兩個對應的半球。

大腦性麻痺 一種由於產前、產中、或剛出生後大腦的損害而引起的非漸進性運動疾病。它常併發其他神經和智力疾患。潛在的腦損傷是永久性的。原因有多種，包括產傷、缺氧、血糖過少、黃疸和感染。最常見的缺陷為痙攣性麻痺。感覺常常受累，導致缺乏平衡感。智力、姿態和語言常常受損。四肢的攣縮可引起固定的畸形。其他相關的特徵包

and speech are frequently impaired. Contractures of the limbs may cause fixed abnormalities. Other associated features include epilepsy, visual impairment, squint, reduced hearing, and behavioural problems.

Management of cerebral palsy requires a multidisciplinary approach, the mainstays of which are physiotherapy, speech therapy, and appropriate appliances. Surgery may be necessary to relieve the contractures.

cerebral tumour an abnormal multiplication of brain cells. This forms a swelling that compresses or destroys the healthy brain cells and – because of the rigid nature of the skull – increases the pressure on the brain tissue. Malignant tumours grow rapidly, spreading through the otherwise normal brain tissue and causing progressive neurological disability. Benign tumours grow slowly and compress the brain tissue. Both benign and malignant tumours commonly cause fits.

cerebration *n.* **1.** the functioning of the brain as a whole. **2.** the unconscious activities of the brain.

cerebroside *n.* one of a group of compounds occurring in the *myelin sheaths of nerve fibres. They are *glycolipids, containing *sphingosine, a fatty acid, and a sugar, usually galactose (in *galactocerebrosides*) or glucose (in *glucocerebrosides*).

cerebrospinal fever (spotted fever) *see* meningitis.

cerebrospinal fluid (CSF) the clear watery fluid that surrounds the brain and

括癲癇、視力損傷、斜視、聽力減退和行為障礙。

大腦性麻痹的治療需要多學科介入,主要是生理療法、語言療法和適當的器械。可能也需要用外科手術以消除攣縮。

腦腫瘤 腦細胞的一種異常增殖。由此所形成的腫物則壓迫或破壞健康的腦細胞。而且,由於顱骨質地堅硬,因此,增加了對腦組織的壓力。惡性腫瘤生長迅速,向本來是正常的腦組織擴散,引起進行性神經功能缺陷。良性腫瘤生長緩慢,壓迫腦組織。良性和惡性腫瘤通常都可引起癲癇。

精神活動 **(1)** 腦的整體功能活動。**(2)** 腦的潛意識活動。

腦苷 一組存在於神經纖維髓鞘中的化合物之一。是糖脂類,含有鞘氨醇、脂肪酸和糖。通常為半乳糖(在半乳糖腦苷裏)或者葡萄糖(在葡萄糖腦苷裏)。

流行性腦膜炎(斑疹熱) 參閱 meningitis。

腦脊液 在腦和脊髓周圍的澄清水樣液體。它含於蛛網膜下

spinal cord. It is contained in the *subarachnoid space and circulates in the *ventricles of the brain and in the central canal of the spinal cord. The brain floats in the fluid (its weight so being reduced from about 1400 g to less than 100 g) and is cushioned by it from contact with the skull when the head is moved vigorously. The CSF is secreted by the *choroid plexuses in the ventricles, circulates through them to reach the subarachnoid space, and is eventually absorbed into the bloodstream through the *arachnoid villi, Its normal contents are glucose, salts, enzymes, and a few white cells, but no red blood cells.

cerebrovascular disease any disorder of the blood vessels of the brain and its covering membranes (meninges). Most cases are due to atheroma and/or hypertension, clinical effects being caused by rupture of diseased blood vessels (*cerebral or *subarachnoid haemorrhage) or inadequacy of the blood supply to the brain (ischaemia), due to cerebral thrombosis or embolism. The term *cerebrovascular accident* is given to the clinical syndrome accompanying a sudden and sometimes severe attack, which leads to a *stroke.

cerebrum (telencephalon) *n.* the largest and most highly developed part of the brain, composed of the two *cerebral hemispheres*, separated from each other by the *longitudinal fissure* in the midline (see illustration). Each hemisphere has an outer layer of grey matter, the *cerebral cortex, below which lies white matter containing the *basal ganglia. Connecting the two hemispheres at the bottom of the longitudinal fissure is the *corpus callosum*, a massive bundle of nerve fibres. Within each hemisphere

腔，在腦室和脊髓中央管內循環。腦懸浮於該液體中（因此腦的重量由 1400 g 逐漸減少至不到 100 g）。當頭部激烈運動時，腦脊液可緩衝腦，以防與顱骨相接觸。腦脊液由腦室內的脈絡叢分泌，循環通過腦室而到達蛛網膜下腔，最後通過蛛網膜絨毛吸收而進入血液。正常情況下內含葡萄糖、鹽、酶、少量白細胞，但無紅細胞。

腦血管疾病 腦血管和其覆膜（腦膜）的任何疾病。大多數腦血管疾病源於動脈粥樣化和／或高血壓，受累血管的破裂（腦出血或蛛網膜下出血）或因為腦血栓或腦栓塞而引起的腦部血液供應不足（局部缺血）都可以引起臨床表現。腦血管意外一詞指伴有突然和有時嚴重發作的臨床綜合徵。它常導致中風。

大腦（終腦） 腦的最大、最發達部分，含有兩個腦半球。兩個半球由位於中綫的縱裂隔開（見圖）。每一腦半球都有灰質外層，即大腦皮質，其下為含有基底神經結的白質。在縱裂底部的胼胝體將兩半球聯結起來。胼胝體是粗大的神經纖維束。每一半球內都有新月形、充滿液體的腔（側腦室），該腔與間腦中的中心第三腦室相通。大腦負責身體所有隨意活動的產生和協調，並且控制低

is a crescent-shaped fluid-filled cavity (lateral *ventricle), connected to the central third ventricle in the *diencephalon. The cerebrum is responsible for the initiation and coordination of all voluntary activity in the body and for governing the functioning of lower parts of the nervous system. The cortex is the seat of all intelligent behaviour. —**cerebral** *adj.*

級神經系統的功能活動。大腦皮質是所有智力行為的中樞。

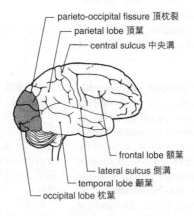

parieto-occipital fissure 頂枕裂
parietal lobe 頂葉
central sulcus 中央溝
frontal lobe 額葉
lateral sulcus 側溝
temporal lobe 顳葉
occipital lobe 枕葉

Lobes of the cerebrum (from the right side)
大腦葉（右面觀）

cerumen (earwax) *n.* the waxy material that is secreted by the sebaceous glands in the external auditory meatus of the outer ear. Its function is to protect the delicate skin that lines the inside of the meatus.

耵聹　外耳道皮脂腺所分泌的蠟樣物質。其作用是保護附着於外耳道內表面的脆嫩的皮膚。

cervic- (cervico-) *prefix denoting* **1.** the neck. Example: *cervicodynia* (pain in). **2.** the cervix, especially of the uterus. Example: *cervicectomy* (surgical removal of).

〔前綴〕頸　**(1)** 頭頸，如頸痛。**(2)** 頸部，尤指子宮頸部，如子宮切除術。

cervical *adj.* **1.** of or relating to the neck. **2.** of, relating to, or affecting the cervix

(1) 頸的　與頸有關聯的。**(2)** 頸部的　與某器官的頸部有

(neck region) of an organ, especially the cervix of the uterus.

cervical cancer (cervical carcinoma) cancer of the neck (cervix) of the uterus. The tumour may develop from the surface epithelium of the cervix (squamous carcinoma) or from the epithelial lining of the cervical canal (adenocarcinoma). In both cases the tumour is invasive, spreading to involve surrounding tissue and subsequently to neighbouring lymph nodes and adjacent organs, such as the bladder and rectum. In carcinoma in situ (*see* cervical intraepithelial neoplasia) the tumour is confined to the epithelium: there is no invasion of surrounding tissue but, if untreated, it can become malignant. Cancer of the cervix can be detected in an early stage of development (*see* cervical smear). Features of cervical cancer include vaginal discharge, often foul-smelling and usually blood-stained. Treatment is by irradiation or surgery, or a combination of both, and cytotoxic drugs may also be used. *See also* human papillomavirus.

cervical cerclage a procedure to help prevent *preterm delivery. It involves placing a stitch around the cervix of the uterus to keep it closed and reduce the possibility of preterm cervical dilatation and rupture of membranes.

cervical fracture *see* whiplash injury.

cervical incompetence unnatural spontaneous dilatation of the cervix of the uterus during the second trimester of pregnancy. The membranes bulge and subsequently rupture, and the fetus is expelled prematurely. It may be caused by forcible dilatation of the cervix during

關聯或有影響的，特別是子宮頸。

宮頸癌 子宮頸部的癌。瘤可能從子宮頸的表皮發生（鱗狀癌）或者在宮頸管上皮發生（腺癌）。在兩種情形中，瘤是侵入性的，向外擴散，累及周圍組織，並隨後擴散到鄰近淋巴結和器官，如膀胱和直腸。在原位癌中（參閱 cervical intraepithelial neoplasia）癌局限於上皮，不侵害周圍組織，但如果不治療的話，它會變成惡性。宮頸癌可早期被檢查出來（參閱 cervical smear）。宮頸癌的特徵包括陰道惡臭的血性分泌物增加。治療方法為放射療法或外科手術，或者二者結合，也可使用細胞毒素藥物。參閱 human papillomavirus。

宮頸環紮法 一種防止早產的方法。即將子宮頸紮住，使其閉合以減少早產宮頸擴張和膜破裂的可能性。

宮頸擦傷 參閱 whiplash injury。

宮頸閉鎖不全 妊娠的第二個三月期子宮頸的異常的自主擴張。膜向前突出，隨後破裂，胎兒被提前娩出。這可能是由於刮宮和擴張術中宮頸的強迫擴張所致，或者與以前的分娩中宮頸損傷有關。

the operation of *dilatation and curettage or it may be related to laceration of the cervix during a previous confinement.

cervical intraepithelial neoplasia (CIN) cellular changes in the cervix of the uterus preceding the invasive stages of *cervical cancer. The CIN grading system distinguishes three stages: *CIN 1* (mild dysplasia); *CIN 2* (moderate dysplasia); and *CIN 3* (severe dysplasia, carcinoma in situ). CIN is uncommon after the menopause. Treatment may be by *laser beam, which destroys the tissue, or by large loop excision of the *transformation zone of the cervix, a procedure performed through a colposcope, under local anaesthetic, using diathermy.

宮頸上皮內瘤生成 宮頸癌侵襲期子宮頸的細胞變化。宮頸上皮內瘤分類系統有三期：CIN 一期（輕度增生），CIN 二期（中度增生），CIN 三期（嚴重增生，原位癌）。絕經後該病少見。可通過激光治療，這一療法可破壞組織。或者將宮頸上皮移形區大環切除來進行治療，這是在陰道鏡下，經局部麻醉，採用透熱法而進行的一種技術。

cervical smear (Papanicolaou (Pap) test) a specimen of cellular material scraped from the neck (cervix) of the uterus that is stained and examined under a microscope in order to detect cell changes indicating the presence of cancer. The *transformation zone of the cervix is most likely to produce evidence of *cervical intraepithelial neoplasia if present. Routine cervical smears are taken to detect precancerous and early cancerous changes.

宮頸塗片法（帕帕尼科拉烏試驗） 將子宮頸擦拭下來的細胞標本塗色，在顯微鏡下進行觀察以發現提示癌存在的細胞變化。如宮頸上皮內瘤生成出現，宮頸上皮移形區很可能提示病變證據。常規宮頸塗片檢查可檢測出癌症前期或早期癌症變化。

cervical vertebrae the seven bones making up the neck region of the *backbone. The first cervical vertebra – the *atlas* – consists basically of a ring of bone that supports the skull by articulating with the occipital condyles (*see* occipital bone). The second vertebra – the *axis* – has an upward-pointing process (the *odontoid process* or *dens*) that forms a pivot on which the atlas can rotate, enabling the head to be turned. *See also* vertebra.

頸椎 組成脊柱頸部的 7 塊骨。第一塊頸椎是寰椎，基本由一環狀骨組成，與枕髁相關節以支撐顱骨（參閱 occipital bone）。第二塊頸椎是樞椎，它有一向上的尖突（牙樣突或齒突）形成支軸。寰椎可在此軸上旋轉，頭部因之可以轉動。參閱 vertebra。

cervicitis *n.* inflammation of the neck (cervix) of the uterus.

宮頸炎 子宮頸的炎症。

cervix *n.* a necklike part, especially the *cervix uteri* (neck of the uterus), which projects into the vagina. The cervical canal passes through it, linking the cavity of the uterus with the vagina; the canal normally contains mucus, the viscosity of which changes throughout the menstrual cycle. The cervix is capable of wide dilation during childbirth.

cestode *n.* *see* tapeworm.

cetrimide *n.* a detergent disinfectant, used for cleansing skin surfaces and wounds, sterilizing surgical instruments and babies' napkins, and in shampoos. There are few adverse reactions from external application; most toxic effects are due to poisoning from ingestion. Trade name: **Cetavlon**.

cetylpyridinium *n.* a detergent disinfectant, used for the disinfection of skin, wounds, and burns, as a mouthwash, and in the form of throat lozenges. Trade name: **Merocet**.

Chagas' disease a disease caused by the protozoan parasite *Trypanosoma cruzi*. It is transmitted to man when the trypanosomes, present in the faeces of nocturnal bloodsucking *reduviid bugs, come into contact with wounds and scratches on the skin or the delicate internal tissues of the nose and mouth. The presence of the parasite in the heart muscles and central nervous system results in serious inflammation and lesions, which can prove fatal. The disease, limited to poor rural areas of South and Central America, is especially prevalent in children and young adults. It may be treated with nifurtimox. *See also* trypanosomiasis.

頸部　頸樣部分，尤指突入陰道的子宮頸。宮頸管穿過頸部，將宮腔和陰道聯結起來。宮頸管道通常含黏膜，其黏度在整個月經周期都在變化。分娩時，宮頸能擴張很大。

縧蟲　參閱 tapeworm。

西曲溴銨　一種防腐除污劑，用於清洗皮膚表面和傷口，對外科器械和嬰兒尿布進行消毒，亦用於洗髮劑中。外用。副作用極少。多數毒性作用來自誤服中毒。商品名：Cetavlon。

十六烷基吡啶　一種防腐除污劑，用於皮膚、傷口和燒傷消毒，也可用於含漱劑以及咽喉含片。商品名：Merocet。

恰加斯病　一種由寄生性原蟲克氏錐蟲引起的疾病。錐蟲存在於夜間出沒的吸血豬蝽的糞便內，通過皮膚傷口、搔抓處或口鼻等脆弱的內部組織而傳入人體。在心臟和中樞神經系統出現該寄生蟲可引起致命的嚴重炎症與損害。該病局限在中美和南美洲的貧困區，主要發生於兒童和青年。它可用硝呋莫司治療。參閱 trypanosomiasis。

chaining *n.* a technique of *behaviour modification in which a complex skill is taught by being broken down into its separate components, which are gradually built up into the full sequence. Usually the last component in the sequence is taught first, because it is this component that is followed by *reinforcement: this is termed *backwards chaining*.

連鎖法 一種行為矯正方法。將一個複雜的技能分解成獨立的部分，再將其漸漸地構成一完整的程序。通常先講授程序的最後一部分，因為緊跟着這一部分之後就可進行強化。這種方法被稱為逆向連鎖法。

chalazion (meibomian cyst) *n.* a swollen sebaceous gland in the eyelid, caused by chronic inflammation following blockage of the gland's duct. The gland becomes converted into a jelly-like mass, producing disfigurement of the lid. It may become secondarily infected, when it will be painful and may discharge. Treatment is by application of antibiotic ointments or surgical incision and curettage of the gland.

霰粒腫（瞼板腺囊腫）一種眼瞼皮脂腺的腫脹，在腺管阻塞之後由慢性炎症引起。腺體變成了膠凍樣物質，引起眼瞼變形。當感到疼痛，且有分泌物時，它可能受到繼發感染。治療採用抗生素類油膏外用，或外科切除，以及腺體刮治。

chancre *n.* a painless ulcer that develops at the site where infection enters the body, e.g. on the lips, penis, urethra, or eyelid. It is the primary symptom of such infections as sleeping sickness and syphilis.

下疳，初瘡 發生於身體感染侵入部位的一種無痛潰瘍，如在唇、陰莖、尿道、或眼瞼處。它是昏睡病和梅毒感染的初期症狀。

chancroid *n. see* soft sore.

軟下疳 參閱 soft sore。

Charcot-Leyden crystals fine colourless sharp-pointed crystals seen in the sputum of asthmatics.

夏-萊氏晶體 哮喘病人痰液中出現的細小、無色、尖形的晶體。

Charcot-Marie-Tooth disease (peroneal muscular atrophy) an inherited disease of the peripheral nerves, also known as *hereditary sensorimotor neuropathy*, causing a gradually progressive weakness and wasting of the muscles of the legs and the lower part of the thighs. The hands and arms are eventually affected.

夏-瑪-圖氏病（腓骨肌萎縮）一種遺傳性的周圍神經疾病，也叫遺傳性感覺運動神經病。它引起小腿肌肉和大腿下端緩慢而具漸進性的無力與萎縮。最後手部和上肢被感染。

Charcot's joint a damaged, swollen, and deformed joint, often the knee, resulting from repeated minor injuries of which the patient is unaware because the nerves that normally register pain are not functioning. The condition may occur in syphilis, diabetes mellitus, and syringomyelia.

夏爾科關節 由於反覆輕度外傷而引起的關節損傷、腫脹和變形，常常是膝關節。因為通常接受痛感的神經失去功能，病人受傷時並未察覺。該病可見於梅毒、糖尿病和脊髓空洞症。

Charcot's triad the combination of fever, figors, and jaundice that indicates acute *cholangitis.

夏爾科三聯徵 提示急性膽管炎的發燒、寒戰和黃疸的聯合徵狀。

Charnley clamps parallel metal rods driven through the ends of two bones that are to be joined to form an *arthrodesis. The rods are connected on each side of the joint by bolts bearing wing nuts; tightening of the screw arrangements forces the surfaces of the bones together. When the two bones have joined, by growth and reshaping, the clamps can be removed.

查利夾 一種關節固定術。將需要融合的骨的兩端分別釘入相互平行的金屬桿，關節兩側的金屬桿由帶有翼狀螺絲釘的螺桿相連接。擰緊螺絲可使兩側骨面靠攏。當兩骨通過生長和成形而融合時，即可拆除該夾。

Chart *n.* continuous hyperfractionated accelerated radiotherapy: a recently developed radiotherapeutic technique aimed at the rapid destruction of tumour cells when they are actively proliferating and therefore most sensitive to radiation. The technique is still at a very experimental stage and is currently being evaluated at research level.

查特放射綫療法 連續、超量、加速放射綫療法。這是一個近期發展的放射綫治療技術，目的在於迅速地破壞瘤細胞。用於當瘤細胞增殖旺盛，從而也對放射治療極為敏感時。這一技術仍然處於初級實驗階段，目前正在研究評價。

cheil- (cheilo-) *prefix denoting* the lip(s). Example: *cheiloplasty* (plastic surgery of).

〔前綴〕**唇** 如唇成形術。

cheilitis *n.* inflammation of the lips. *Angular cheilitis* affects the angles of the lips and is associated with candidosis in denture wearers.

唇炎 唇部的炎症。傳染性口角炎累及口唇的角部，與戴托牙者中的白色念珠菌病有關。

cheiloplasty *n. see* labioplasty.

唇成形術 參閱 labioplasty。

cheiloschisis *n. see* harelip.

唇裂　參閱 harelip。

cheilosis *n.* swollen cracked bright-red lips. This is a common symptom of many nutritional disorders, including ariboflavinosis (vitamin B$_2$ deficiency).

唇乾裂　唇腫脹、裂開、鮮紅。這是許多營養不良症的常見症狀，包括核黃素缺乏（維生素 B$_2$ 缺乏）。

cheir- (cheiro-) *prefix denoting* the hand(s). Examples: *cheiralgia* (pain in); *cheiroplasty* (plastic surgery of).

〔前綴〕手　如手痛、手成形術。

cheiropompholyx *n.* a type of *eczema affecting the palms and fingers. The thickness of the skin in these areas prevents the pinhead vesicles from breaking and eventually the skin peels after a period of intense itching. *See* pompholyx.

掌蹠汗疱　一種影響手掌和指頭的濕疹。這些部位的皮膚厚，阻止針頭樣水泡的破裂，所以，在經過一段強烈的搔癢之後，最終，皮膚脫皮。參閱 pompholyx。

chelating agent a chemical compound that forms complexes by binding metal ions. Some chelating agents, including *desferrioxamine and *penicillamine, are drugs used to treat metal poisoning: the metal is bound to the drug and excreted safely. Chelating agents often form the active centres of enzymes.

螯合劑　一種通過與金屬離子結合形成螯合物的化合物。有些螯合劑，如去鐵胺、青黴胺等，是用於治療金屬中毒的藥物：金屬與之結合，然後安全地排出體外。螯合劑常形成酶的活性中心。

chem- (chemo-) *prefix denoting* chemical or chemistry.

〔前綴〕化學的，化學

chemoreceptor *n.* a cell or group of cells that responds to the presence of specific chemical compounds by initiating an impulse in a sensory nerve. Chemoreceptors are found in the taste buds and in the mucous membranes of the nose. *See also* receptor.

化學感受器　對特定的化學物質的存在產生反應的一個或一組細胞，其反應方式是在感覺神經內產生一次衝動。化學感受器存在於味蕾和鼻黏膜內。參閱 receptor。

chemosis *n.* swelling (oedema) of the *conjunctiva. It is usually due to inflammation but may occur if the drainage of blood and lymph from around the eye is obstructed.

球結膜水腫　結膜的腫脹（水腫）。通常該病由炎症引起。但是，如果眼周圍的血液和淋巴循環阻塞時也可發生該病。

chemotaxis *n.* movement of a cell or organism in response to the stimulus of a gradient of chemical concentration.

趨化性，趨藥性　一細胞或微生物對各種濃度化學物質的刺激做出反應而產生的運動。

chemotherapy *n.* the prevention or treatment of disease by the use of chemical substances. The term is sometimes restricted to the treatment of infectious diseases with antibiotics and other drugs or to the control of cancer with antimetabolites and similar drugs (in contrast to *radiotherapy).

chenodeoxycholic acid a drug used in the treatment of cholesterol gallstones, which it gradually dissolves over a period of up to 18 months. It is administered by mouth. A common side-effect is diarrhoea. Trade names: **Chendol**, **Chenofalk**, **Chenocedon**.

cherry angioma *see* angioma.

chest *n. see* thorax.

Cheyne-Stokes respiration a striking form of breathing in which there is a cyclical variation in the rate, which becomes slower until breathing stops for several seconds before speeding up to a peak and then slowing again. It occurs when the sensitivity of the respiratory centres in the brain is impaired, particularly in states of coma.

chiasma *n.* (*pl.* **chiasmata**) **1.** (in genetics) the point at which homologous chromosomes remain in contact after they have started to separate in the first division of *meiosis. Chiasmata occur from the end of prophase to anaphase and represent the point at which mutual exchange of genetic material takes place (*see* crossing over). **2.** *see* optic chiasma.

chickenpox *n.* a mild highly infectious disease caused by a *herpesvirus that is transmitted by airborne droplets. After

化學療法　通過使用化學物質來預防或治療疾病。這一術語有時僅限於用抗生素和其他藥物治療傳染性疾病，或用抗代謝藥和類似的藥品控制癌症（相對於放射療法而言）。

鵝去氧膽酸　一種用於治療膽固醇膽結石的藥物。結石在最多 18 個月內溶解。用於口服。常見的副作用為腹瀉。商品名：Chendol，Chenofalk，Chenocedon。

櫻桃樣血管瘤　參閱 angioma。

胸　參閱 thorax。

陳-施呼吸　一種呼吸率有周期變化的呼吸類型。呼吸變慢，直至停止。數秒鐘後，呼吸加快至一頂峯，然後又再次減慢。該病見於腦內呼吸中樞受損時，特別是在昏迷狀態。

（1）交叉　（遺傳學）同源染色體在減數分裂第一期中已分離但保持接觸的時刻。交叉持續於第一期末至第三期。此時，遺傳物質相互進行交換（參閱 crossing over）。（2）視交叉　參閱 optic chiasma。

水痘　一種通過空氣飛沫傳播的，由疱疹病毒引起的症狀輕微的高度傳染性疾病。在

an incubation period of 11–18 days a mild fever develops, followed within 24 hours by an itchy rash of dark red pimples. The pimples spread from the trunk to the face, scalp, and limbs; they develop into blisters and then scabs, which drop off after about 12 days. The only treatment is bed rest and the application of calamine lotion to the spots to discourage scratching; scarring is unusual. Complications are rare but include secondary infection and occasionally *encephalitis. The patient is infectious from the onset of symptoms until all the spots have gone. Since an attack in childhood generally confers life-long immunity, chickenpox is rare among adults, although the virus may reactivate to cause shingles (*see* herpes). In adult patients who are particularly vulnerable, e.g. those with AIDS or who are otherwise immunosuppressed, chickenpox can be a serious disease, which may be treated with *acyclovir. Medical name: **varicella**.

11~18 天的潛伏期之後，開始有輕度發燒，24 小時內出現暗紅色瘙癢性丘疹。丘疹從軀幹部向頭部、頭皮及四肢擴散。隨後發展成水痘，最後結痂。大約 12 天後全部脫落。唯一的治療就是臥床休息和用爐甘石洗劑塗抹患處來止癢。很少形成瘢痕。併發症很少見，但包括繼發感染，偶爾有腦炎。病人從有症狀開始就具傳染性，直到所有的皮疹消失。兒童期患此病一般可產生終生免疫力，因此，成人很少有患此病的，儘管病毒可能重新產生活性而引起帶狀疱疹（參閱 herpes）。在特別易於被感染的成年病人中，例如那些患有艾滋病的，或者那些由於其他原因免疫被抑制的人，水痘可能成為一個嚴重的疾病。這可用阿昔洛韋治療。醫學用語：水痘。

chiclero's ulcer a form of *leishmaniasis of the skin caused by the parasite *Leishmania tropica mexicana*. The disease, occurring in Panama, Honduras, and the Amazon, primarily affects men who visit the forests to collect chicle (gum) and takes the form of an ulcerating lesion on the ear lobe. The sore usually heals spontaneously within six months.

糖膠樹膠工人潰瘍 一種由墨西哥熱帶利什曼原蟲引起的皮膚利什曼病。本病見於巴拿馬、洪都拉斯和亞馬遜河流域，主要侵襲進森林採集糖膠樹膠（製口香糖原料）的成年男人，表現為耳廓處的潰瘍性病變。潰瘍常在 6 個月內自然愈合。

Chief Administrative Medical Officer a public health physician at area level under the NHS (Scotland) Act and the terms of the NHS Act applicable to Wales. *See* National Health Service.

行政區主管醫師 據蘇格蘭國家保健計劃，在蘇格蘭和威爾士，負責地段公共衛生的醫生，參閱 National Health Service。

chigger *n. see* Trombicula.

恙蟎 參閱 Trombicula。

chigoe *n. see* Tunga.

Chikungunya fever a disease, occurring in Africa and Asia, caused by an *arbovirus and transmitted to man by mosquitoes of the genus *Aëdes*. The disease is similar to *dengue and symptoms include fever, headache, generalized body pain, and an irritating rash. The patient is given drugs to relieve the pain and reduce the fever.

chilblains (perniosis) *pl. n.* dusky red itchy swellings that develop on the extremities in cold weather. They usually settle in two weeks but treatment with *nifedipine is helpful in severe cases. There may be a genetic predisposition to chilblains.

child abuse the maltreatment of children. It may take the form of *sexual abuse*, when a child is involved in sexual activity by an adult; *physical abuse*, when physical injury is caused by cruelty or undue punishment (*see* nonaccidental injury); *neglect*, when basic physical provision for needs is lacking; and *emotional abuse*, when lack of affection and/or hostility from caregivers damage a child's emotional development (*see* attachment disorder).

childbirth *n. see* labour.

child health clinic (CHC) (in Britain) a special clinic for the routine care of infants and preschool children, formerly known as a *child welfare centre*. Sometimes these chinics are staffed by doctors, *health visitors, and clinic nurses employed by District Health Authorities; the children attending them are drawn from the neighbourhood around the clinic. Alternatively general practitioners

沙蚤　參閱 Tunga。

奇孔岡亞熱　一種由蟲媒病毒引起的、通過伊蚊傳播給人類的疾病。發生於非洲和亞洲。該病類似登革熱。症狀包括發熱、頭痛、全身疼痛與刺激性皮疹。給予藥物以止痛和退熱。

凍瘡（凍瘡病）　寒冷季節發生於肢端的暗紅色瘙癢性腫脹。它們通常在兩周內消失，但對嚴重病例，用硝苯地平治療有效。凍瘡可能與遺傳易感性體質有關。

虐待兒童　對兒童的虐待。當兒童涉及成人的性活動時，虐待兒童的方式即為性虐待。當殘酷的行為或過度的體罰引起身體傷害時，就是身體虐待（參閱 non-accidental injury）。當所需要的最基本的物質供給缺乏時，就是失職虐待。當缺乏來自撫養者的愛和／或受到敵視，而損傷兒童的情感發育時，就是情感虐待。參閱 attachment disorder。

分娩　參閱 labour。

兒童保健站　（英國）一種對幼兒與學齡前兒童提供常規保健服務的機構，以前叫兒童福利中心。其工作人員由地段衛生當局僱傭的醫生、保健員以及門診護士組成。在這些保健站接受保健服務的兒童來自保健站周圍的地區。另一種形式的兒童保健站是全科醫生自己辦的，每周一次，出診醫生和其

may run their own CHC, say once a week, with health visitors and other staff in attendance; it is unusual for children not registered with the practice to attend such clinics. The service provides screening tests for such conditions as congenital dislocation of hips, suppressed squint (*see* cover test), thyroid insufficiency, and impaired speech and/or hearing. The *Guthrie test may also be performed if this has not been done before the baby leaves hospital. The staff of CHCs also educate mothers (especially those having their first child) in feeding techniques and hygiene and see that children receive the recommended immunizations against infectious diseases. They also ensure that the families of handicapped children receive maximum support from health and social services and that such children achieve their maximum potential in the preschool period. *See also* community paediatrician.

他職員都參加。不參與此類保健門診的兒童比較少見。該保健站進行普查活動：先天性髖關節脫位、隱斜視（參閱 cover test）、甲狀腺功能不全以及言語和／或聽力損傷。如果幼兒在出院前未做格思里試驗，還可在這裏補做。兒童保健站的工作人員還針對幼兒餵養方法和衛生對母親（特別是那些初產婦）進行教育。且監督兒童接受對抗各種傳染病的推薦的免疫（注射）。他們也保證殘疾兒童的家庭獲得最大可能的保健和社會福利。支持且保證那些兒童在學前期獲得充分和最大程度的發展。參閱 community paediatrician。

chir- (chiro-) *prefix denoting* the hand (s). *See also* cheir-.

〔前綴〕手　表示「手」。參閱 cheir-。

chiropody (podiatry) *n.* the study and care of the foot, including its normal structure, its diseases, and their treatment. **–chiropodist** *n.*

足病治療　研究和照料足的正常結構、足病及其治療。

chiropractic *n.* a system of treating diseases by manipulation, mainly of the vertebrae of the backbone. It is based on the theory that nearly all disorders can be traced to the incorrect alignment of bones, with consequent malfunctioning of nerves and muscle throughout the body.

捏脊療法　一種利用按摩而治療疾病的方法，主要是按摩脊椎骨。該方法的理論基礎為：幾乎所有的疾病都可以追溯到骨的聯結不當，因而產生全身神經和肌肉功能障礙。

Chlamydia *n.* a genus of virus-like bacteria that cause disease in man and birds. *Chlamydia psittaci* causes *psittacosis, and *C. trachomatis* is the causative agent

衣原體　能引起人和鳥類疾病的一種像病毒的細菌，鸚鵡熱衣原體引起鸚鵡熱。沙眼衣原體是沙眼這一眼疾的致病因

of the eye disease *trachoma. Some strains of *Chlamydia*, especially *C. trachomatis*, are a common cause of sexually transmitted infections. The organisms are usually regarded as Gram-negative bacteria but are of similar size to viruses and all are obligate parasites. **–chlamydial** *adj.*

子。一些衣原體株，特別是沙眼衣原體，是通過性傳播感染的一個常見原因。這些生物通常被認為是革蘭氏陰性細菌，而與病毒大小相似，且所有都是專性寄生物。

chloasma (melasma) *n.* ill-defined symmetrical brown patches on the cheeks or elsewhere on the face. Chloasma is a *photosensitivity reaction in women on combined oral contraceptive pills or who are pregnant; very rarely it occurs in men. It can usually be prevented by the use of sunscreens.   .

褐黃斑（黑斑病） 頰或面部其他部位出現的邊緣不規則的對稱性的褐黃色斑。褐黃斑是口服複合性避孕藥或者妊娠婦女的光敏反應。男性很少發生。常通過遮陽而得以防止。

chlor- (chloro-) *prefix denoting* **1.** chlorine or chlorides. **2.** green.

〔前綴〕**(1)** 氯，氯化物 **(2)** 綠色

chloracne *n.* an occupational acne-like skin disorder that occurs after regular contact with chlorinated hydrocarbons. These chemicals are derived from oil and tar products; 'cutting oils' used in engineering also cause the disease. The skin develops blackheads, papules, and pustules, mainly on hairy parts (such as the forearm). Warts and skin cancer may develop after many years of exposure to these chemicals.

氯痤瘡 一種因經常接觸氯化烴類而引起的痤瘡樣職業性皮膚病。這些化學物質來源於石油和瀝青產物。工業用切削油也可引起這一疾病。皮膚出現黑頭粉刺、丘疹和膿疱，多見於有毛髮的部位（如前臂）。長年與這些化學品相接觸，可產生疣和皮膚癌。

chloral hydrate a sedative and hypnotic drug used, mainly in children and the elderly, to induce sleep or as a daytime sedative. It is rapidly absorbed from the alimentary canal and is usually given by mouth as a syrup, although it can be administered rectally. Toxic effects are usually only seen with overdosage. Prolonged use may lead to *dependence. Trade names: **Noctec**, **Welldorm elixir**. *Chloral betaine*, in the form of tablets

水合氯醛 一種鎮靜催眠藥，主要用於兒童和老人催眠或作為白天用鎮靜劑。它迅速地從消化道吸收。雖然可以直接直腸給藥的方式使用，但通常作為一種糖漿劑而用於口服。通常超量服用才出現毒性影響。長期服用可導致藥物依賴。商品名：Noctec，Welldorm elixir。氯醛甜菜鹼（片劑形式）在體內被分解成水合氯醛。

(*Welldorm tablets*), is broken down in the body to chloral hydrate.

chlorambucil *n.* a drug that destroys cancer cells. It is given by mouth and used mainly in the treatment of chronic leukaemias. Prolonged large doses may cause damage to the bone marrow. Trade name: **Leukeran**.

苯丁酸氮芥 一種能破壞癌細胞的藥物。口服且主要用於治療慢性白血病。長期的大量服用可以引起對骨髓的損害。商品名：Leukeran。

chloramphenicol *n.* an antibiotic, derived from the bacterium *Streptomyces venezuelae* and also produced synthetically, that is effective against a wide variety of microorganisms. However, due to its serious side-effects, especially damage to the bone marrow, it is usually reserved for serious infections (such as typhoid fever) when less toxic drugs are ineffective. It is also used, in the form of eye drops or ointment, to treat bacterial conjunctivitis. Trade names: **Chloromycetin**, **Kemicetine**.

氯黴素 由委內瑞拉鏈黴菌中提取的一種抗生素，也可人工合成生產。它能有效地消滅許多種微生物。但是，由於其嚴重的副作用，特別是對骨髓的損害，通常僅用於毒性較小的藥物不起作用時的嚴重感染（如傷寒）。也以眼藥水或者軟膏劑的形式，用於治療細菌性結膜炎。商品名：Chloromycetin，Kemicetine。

chlorbutol *n.* an antibacterial and anti-fungal agent used as a preservative in injection solutions, in eye and nose drops, in powder form for topical use in irritational skin conditions, and as a gargle or mouthwash (combined with chlorhexidine in *Eludril*).

三氯叔丁醇 一種抗細菌和抗真菌劑。在注射液、眼藥和滴鼻劑中用做防腐劑。以粉劑形式局部外用，治療刺激性皮膚疾病。偶爾可用作嗽口劑（與氯己啶合用）。

chlordiazepoxide *n.* a sedative and tranquillizing drug with *muscle relaxant properties, used to relieve tension, fears and anxiety and in the treatment of alcoholism. It is administered by mouth or injection. Common side-effects are nausea, skin reactions, and muscular incoordination. Trade names: **Librium**, **Diapox**, **Elenium**. *See also* tranquillizer.

氯氮䓬 一種具有肌肉鬆弛作用的鎮靜和安定藥物。用於治療乙醇中毒以及消除緊張、恐懼和憂慮。可口服和注射。常見的副作用有惡心、皮膚反應和肌肉運動失調。商品名：Librium，Diapox，Elenium。參閱 tranquillizer。

chlorhexidine *n.* an antiseptic used as a general disinfectant for skin and mucous membranes or as a preservative (for

氯己啶（洗必太） 一種用於皮膚和黏膜的普通消毒劑，或做為一種防腐劑（如用做眼藥

example, in eye drops). Chlorhexidine is used in solution, creams, gels, and lozenges and in some preparations is combined with *cetrimide. In very dilute solutions it can be used as an effective mouthwash for the control of infections of the mouth. Skin sensitivity to chlorhexidine occurs rarely. Trade name: **Hibitane**.

chlorination *n.* the addition of noninjurious traces of chlorine (often one part per million) to water supplies before human consumption to ensure that disease-causing organisms are destroyed. *See also* fluoridation.

chlorine *n.* an extremely pungent gaseous element with antiseptic and bleaching properties. It is widely used to sterilize drinking water and purify swimming pools. In high concentrations it is toxic; it was used in World War I as a poison gas in the trenches. Symbol: Cl.

chlormethiazole *n.* a *sedative and hypnotic drug used to treat insomnia in the elderly (when associated with confusion, agitation, and restlessness) and drug withdrawal symptoms (especially in alcoholism). It is administered by mouth or injection and the most common side-effects are tingling sensations in the nose and sneezing. Trade name: **Heminevrin**.

chlormezanone *n.* a tranquillizing drug used in the treatment of mild anxiety and tension, including premenstrual tension. It is also used to relieve pain and muscle spasm. Chlormezanone is administered by mouth; the most common side-effects are drowsiness and dizziness. Trade name: **Trancopal**.

chlorocresol *n.* an antiseptic derived from phenol, used as a general

水）。氯己啶用於溶液、乳膏、凝膠和含片中。在一些製劑中，它與西曲溴銨合用。濃度很低的氯己啶溶液，可用作有效的漱口劑，控制口腔感染。皮膚很少對氯己啶過敏。商品名：Hibitane。

加氯消毒法 加入非傷害性痕量（百萬分之一）的氯於水中，確保在人們使用前殺滅所有致病菌。參閱 fluoridation。

氯 一種具有抗菌和漂白特性的強烈刺激性氣體元素。廣泛用於消毒飲用水和淨化游泳池水。高濃度時有毒性。第一次世界大戰時，在戰壕裏，它曾被當做毒氣使用。符號：Cl。

氯美噻唑 一種鎮定催眠藥物，用於治療老年人失眠症（當與精神錯亂、激動和不安有關時）和藥物戒斷症狀（特別在乙醇中毒時）。可口服和注射。最常見的副作用是鼻子的麻刺感和打噴嚏。商品名：Heminevrin。

氯美扎酮 一種安定藥，用於治療輕度焦慮和緊張，包括經前緊張。它也可以用於消除疼痛和肌肉痙攣。該藥為口服，最常見的副作用是倦睡和頭暈。商品名：Trancopal。

氯甲酚 一種來自苯酚的殺菌藥，用於一般消毒劑。低濃度

disinfectant and, at low concentrations, as a preservative in injections, creams, and lotions. Strong solutions applied to the skin may cause sensitivity reactions.

chloroform *n.* a volatile liquid formerly widely used as a general anaesthetic. Because its use as such causes liver damage and affects heart rhythm, chloroform is now used only in low concentrations as a flavouring agent and preservative, in the treatment of flatulence, and in liniments as a *rubefacient.

chloroma *n.* a tumour that arises in association with *myeloid leukaemia and consists essentially of a mass of leukaemic cells. A freshly cut specimen of the tumour appears green, but the colour rapidly disappears on exposure to air. It shows red fluorescence with ultraviolet light and responds to specific antileukaemic treatment.

chlorophenothane *n. see* DDT.

chlorophyll *n.* one of a group of green pigments, found in all green plants and some bacteria, that absorb light to provide energy for the synthesis of carbohydrates from carbon dioxide and water (photosynthesis). The two major chlorophylls, a and b, consist of a porphyrin/magnesium complex.

chloropsia *n.* green vision: a rare symptom of digitalis poisoning.

chloroquine *n.* a drug used principally in the treatment and prevention of malaria but also used in rheumatoid arthritis, certain liver infections and skin conditions, and lupus erythematosus. It is administered by mouth or injection;

時，作為防腐劑用於注射劑、乳膏劑和洗劑。作用於皮膚的高濃度氯甲酚可引起過敏反應。

氯仿 一種過去曾被廣泛用做全身麻醉劑的揮發性液體。因為如此使用可引起肝臟損害和影響心臟節律，現在僅以其低濃度用做調味劑和防腐劑，用於治療脹氣和發紅藥擦劑。

綠色（肉瘤） 一種與髓樣白血病伴隨發生的腫瘤，主要由白血病細胞團組成。新鮮切片標本呈綠色，但暴露於空氣後顏色迅速消失。用紫外綫照射時，可發紅色熒光。治療特異性抗白血病有效。

滴滴涕 參閱 DDT。

葉綠素 存在於所有綠色植物和一些細菌中的一組綠色色素中的一種，能吸收光綫能量將二氧化碳和水合成為碳水化合物（光合作用）。a 和 b 兩種主要葉綠素，由卟啉／鎂絡合物組成。

綠視症 視物呈綠色，少見的洋地黃中毒症狀。

氯喹 一種藥物，主要用於治療和預防瘧疾，但也用於類風濕性關節炎，某些肝臟傳染病和皮膚疾患與紅斑性狼瘡。用於口服或注射。大劑量長期使用的一個副作用就是眼損

a side-effect of prolonged use in large doses is eye damage. Trade names: **Avloclor**, **Nivaquine**.

chlorothiazide *n.* a *diuretic used to treat fluid retention (oedema) and high blood pressure (hypertension). It is administered by mouth and may cause skin sensitivity reactions, stomach pains, nausea, and reduced blood potassium levels. Trade name: **Saluric**.

chloroxylenol *n.* an *antiseptic, derived from *phenol but less toxic and more selective in bactericidal activity, used mainly in solution as a skin disinfectant. Trade name: **Dettol**.

chlorphenesin *n.* a compound, active against bacteria and fungi, that is applied to the skin as a cream or dusting powder to treat fungal infections, such as athlete's foot. Trade name: **Mycil**.

chlorpheniramine *n.* a potent *antihistamine used to treat such allergies as hay fever, rhinitis, and urticaria. It is administered by mouth or, to relieve severe conditions, by injection. Trade name: **Piriton**.

chlorpromazine *n.* a phenothiazine *antipsychotic drug used in the treatment of *schizophrenia and *mania; it is also used to treat severe anxiety and agitation and to control nausea and vomiting. It also enhances the effects of *analgesics and is used in terminal illness and preparation for anaesthesia. Chlorpromazine is administered by mouth or injection or as a rectal suppository; common side-effects are drowsiness and dry mouth. It also causes abnormalities of movement, especially *dystonias, *dyskinesia, and *parkinsonism. Trade name: **Largactil**.

害。商品名：Avloclor，Nivaquine。

氯噻嗪 一種治療水瀦留（水腫）和高血壓的利尿藥。口服，可引起皮膚過敏性反應、胃痛、惡心和血鉀降低。商品名：Saluric。

氯二甲酚 一種由苯酚衍生的抗菌劑，但毒性小，而在殺菌活動中更具選擇性。主要用於作為皮膚消毒劑的溶液中。商品名：Dettol。

氯苯甘醚 一種抗細菌和真菌的化合物。作為乳膏劑或粉劑，用於皮膚以治療真菌感染，如足癬。商品名：Mycil。

氯苯那敏 一種高效抗組胺藥，用於治療諸如枯草熱、鼻炎和蕁麻疹等過敏性疾病。口服或注射，以消除嚴重病症。商品名：Piriton。

氯丙嗪 一種吩噻嗪抗精神病藥，用於治療精神分裂症和躁狂症。它也用於治療嚴重焦慮和激動，控制惡心和嘔吐。它可加強止痛藥的效果，用於晚期疾病止痛和基礎麻醉。該藥可口服或注射或作為直腸栓劑。常見的副作用為嗜睡和口乾。它還引起運動異常，特別是肌張力減小、運動障礙和帕金森綜合徵。商品名：Largactil。

chlorpropamide *n.* a drug that reduces blood sugar levels and is used to treat noninsulin-dependent diabetes in adults. It is administered by mouth and can cause such side-effects as skin sensitivity reactions and digestive upsets. Trade name: **Diabinese**. *See also* sulphonylurea.

氯磺丙脲　一種降低血糖量的藥物，用於治療成人非胰島素依賴性糖尿病。口服。可引起皮膚過敏性反應和消化不良。商品名：Diabinese。參閱 sulphonylurea。

chlortetracycline *n.* an *antibiotic active against many bacteria and fungi. It is administered by mouth or injection or as ointment or cream (for skin and eye infections); side-effects are those of the other *tetracyclines. Trade names: **Aureomycin, Deteclo**.

金黴素　一種可消滅多種細菌和真菌的抗生素。口服或注射，或作為軟膏劑或乳膏劑（用於皮膚和眼感染）。副作用與其他四環素相同。商品名：Aureomycin，Deteclo。

chlorthalidone *n.* a *diuretic used to treat fluid retention (oedema) and high blood pressure (hypertension). It is administered by mouth and may cause skin sensitivity reactions, stomach pains, nausea, and reduced blood potassium levels. Trade name: **Hygroton**.

氯噻酮　一種利尿藥，用於治療水滯留（水腫）和高血壓病。口服，可引起皮膚過敏反應、胃痛、惡心以及血鉀量減少。商品名：Hygroton。

choana *n.* (*pl.* **choanae**) a funnel-shaped opening, particularly either of the two openings between the nasal cavity and the pharynx.

漏斗　漏斗狀開口，尤指鼻腔和咽喉之間的兩個開口。

chokedamp *n. see* blackdamp.

窒息性毒氣　參閱 blackdamp。

chol- (chole-, cholo-) *prefix denoting* bile. Example: *cholemesis* (vomiting of).

〔前綴〕膽汁　如嘔膽。

cholagogue *n.* a drug that stimulates the flow of bile from the gall bladder and bile ducts into the duodenum.

利膽藥　一種能刺激膽汁從膽囊和膽管流向十二指腸的藥物。

cholangiocarcinoma *n.* a malignant tumour of the bile ducts. It is particularly likely to occur at the junction of the two main bile ducts within the liver, causing obstructive jaundice.

膽管癌　膽管的惡性腫瘤。尤可出現在肝臟內兩條主要膽管匯合處，引起梗阻性黃疸。

cholangiography *n.* X-ray examination of the bile ducts, used to demonstrate the site and nature of any obstruction to the ducts or to show the presence of stones within them. A medium that is opaque to X-rays is introduced into the ducts either by injection into the bloodstream (*intravenous cholangiography*); direct injection into the liver (*percutaneous transhepatic cholangiography*); direct injection into the bile ducts at operation (*operative cholangiography*); or by injection into the duodenal opening of the bile ducts through a *duodenoscope (*endoscopic retrograde cholangiopancreatography*; *see* ERCP). *See also* percutaneous transhepatic cholangiopancreatography.

膽管造影術 膽管的 X 綫檢查，用於顯示膽管的任何梗阻的部位和性質，或證明膽管內有膽石存在。一種不透 X 綫的造影劑通過以下任何一種方法注入膽管：注入血流（靜脈膽管造影術）、直接注入肝臟（經皮肝膽管造影術）、術中直接注入膽管（術中膽管造影術）、或通過十二指腸鏡注入膽管的十二指腸開口（內窺鏡逆行性胰膽管造影術，參閱 ERCP）。參閱 percutaneous transhepatic cholangiopancreatography。

cholangiolitis *n.* inflammation of the smallest bile ducts (*cholangioles*). *See* cholangitis.

膽小管炎 最小的膽管（毛細膽管）的炎症。

cholangioma *n.* a rare tumour originating from the bile duct.

膽管瘤 一種源自膽管的少見腫瘤。

cholangitis *n.* inflammation of the bile ducts. It usually occurs when the ducts are obstructed, especially by stones, or after operations on the bile ducts. Symptoms include intermittent fever, usually with *rigors, and intermittent jaundice (a combination known as *Charcot's triad*). Initial treatment is by antibiotics, but removal of the obstruction is essential for permanent cure. Liver abscess is a possible complication, and recurrent episodes of cholangitis lead to secondary biliary *cirrhosis. *Sclerosing cholangitis* is a characteristic but rare complication of ulcerative colitis in which all the bile ducts develop irregularities and narrowing.

膽管炎 膽管的炎症。通常發生在膽管梗阻時，特別是被結石梗阻，或在膽管手術之後。症狀包括間歇性發熱，通常伴有寒戰。另一症狀為周期性黃疸（稱為夏爾科三聯症）。初期治療用抗生素，但根治需要消除梗阻。肝膿腫可能是一併發症。反覆發作的膽管炎可導致繼發性肝硬化。硬化性膽管炎是潰瘍性結腸炎的特有的但很少見的併發症，此時，所有膽管發育不規則，而且變窄。

cholecalciferol *n. see* vitamin D.

膽骨化醇 參閱 vitamin D。

cholecyst- *prefix denoting* the gall bladder. Example: *cholecystotomy* (incision of).

〔前綴〕**膽囊**　如膽囊切開術。

cholecystectomy *n.* surgical removal of the gall bladder, usually for *cholecystitis or gallstones. Formerly always performed by *laparotomy, the operation is now often done by *laparoscopy (*percutaneous laparoscopic cholecystectomy*). *See also* minimally invasive surgery.

膽囊切除術　通常為治療膽囊炎或膽結石而將膽囊切除的外科手術。以前總是通過剖腹術進行切除，現在則常通過腹腔鏡檢查來進行這一手術（經皮腹腔鏡膽囊切除術）。參閱 minimally invasive surgery。

cholecystenterostomy *n.* a surgical procedure in which the gall bladder is joined to the small intestine. It is performed in order to allow bile to pass from the liver to the intestine when the common bile duct is obstructed by an irremovable cause.

膽囊小腸吻合術　一種外科手術方法，將膽囊與小腸吻合起來。當膽總管被一無法解除的因素梗阻時，則行此手術，目的在於讓膽汁從肝臟流入小腸。

cholecystitis *n.* inflammation of the gall bladder. *Acute cholecystitis* is due to bacterial infection, causing fever and acute pain over the gall bladder. It is usually treated by rest and antibiotics. *Chronic cholecystitis* is often associated with *gallstones and causes recurrent episodes of upper abdominal pain. (*See also* Murphy's sign.) Recurrent bacterial infection may be the cause, but the physical processes leading to gallstone formation may also be important. It may require treatment by *cholecystectomy. *See also* cholesterosis.

膽囊炎　膽囊的炎症。急性膽囊炎由細菌感染引起，有發熱和膽囊區的劇烈疼痛。通常通過休息和抗生素治療而得以治愈。慢性膽囊炎則常常與膽結石相關，引起反覆發作的上腹部疼痛（參閱 Murphy's sign）。反覆的細菌感染可能是病因，但是導致膽結石形成的體質因素可能也很重要。可能需要膽囊切除術進行治療。參閱 cholesterosis。

cholecystoduodenostomy *n.* a form of *cholecystenterostomy in which the gall bladder is joined to the duodenum.

膽囊十二指腸吻合術　膽囊小腸吻合術的一種。該術將膽囊與十二指腸相吻合。

cholecystogastrostomy *n.* a form of *cholecystenterostomy in which the gall bladder is joined to the stomach. It is rarely performed.

膽囊胃吻合術　膽囊小腸吻合術的一種，把膽囊與胃相吻合。現在很少做此手術。

cholecystography *n.* X-ray examination of the gall bladder. A compound

膽囊造影術　膽囊的 X 綫檢查。口服一種不透 X 綫的化合

that is opaque to X-rays is taken by mouth, absorbed by the intestine, and excreted by the liver into the bile, which is concentrated in the gall bladder. An X-ray photograph (*cholecystogram*) of the gall bladder indicates whether or not it is functioning, and gallstones may be seen as contrasting (non-opaque) areas within it. A fatty meal is usually also given, to demonstrate the ability of the gall bladder to contract.

物，經小腸吸收，並由肝臟排泄進入膽汁。膽汁在膽囊內濃縮。膽囊的 X 綫照片（膽囊照片）提示是否功能正常，通過與造影劑區域（不透 X 綫的）對比可以看見結石。為顯示膽囊收縮功能，通常給予病人脂肪多的食物。

cholecystokinin *n.* a hormone secreted by the cells of the duodenum in response to the presence of partly digested food in the duodenum. It causes contraction of the gall bladder and expulsion of bile into the intestine and stimulates the production of digestive enzymes by the pancreas. *See also* pancreatic juice.

縮膽囊素　因十二指腸內出現未完全消化的食物而使得十二指腸細胞分泌的一種激素。它引起膽囊的收縮，將膽汁排出而進入小腸，刺激胰腺消化酶的產生。參閱 pancreatic juice。

cholecystotomy *n.* a surgical operation in which the gall bladder is opened, usually to remove gallstones. It is performed only when *cholecystectomy would be impracticable or dangerous.

膽囊切開術　一種外科手術。膽囊被切開，通常是為了摘取膽石。只有在膽囊切除術不能進行或者危險時才行此手術。

choledoch- (choledocho-) *prefix denoting* the common bile duct. Example: *choledochoplasty* (plastic surgery of).

〔前綴〕**膽總管**　如膽總管成形術。

choledocholithiasis *n.* stones within the common bile duct. The stones usually form in the gall bladder and pass into the bile duct, but they may develop within the duct after *cholecystectotomy.

膽總管結石　膽總管內的結石。通常結石在膽囊形成，然後進入膽道，但它們在膽囊切除後可在膽道內形成。

choledochotomy *n.* a surgical operation in which the common bile duct is opened, to search for or to remove stones within it. It may be performed at the same time as *cholecystectomy or if stones occur in the bile duct after cholecystectomy.

膽總管切開術　一種外科手術。切開膽總管以搜尋或摘取裏面的結石。可在膽囊切除術進行的同時行此手術。或者當結石位於膽道時，此術可在膽囊切除術後進行。

cholelithiasis n. the formation of stones in the gall bladder (*see* gallstone).

膽石病　膽囊內膽石生成（參閱 gallstone）。

cholelithotomy n. removal of gallstones by *cholecystomy.

膽石取出術　通過膽囊切開術而摘取結石的手術。

cholera n. an acute infection of the small intestine by the bacterium *Vibrio cholerae*, which causes severe vomiting and diarrhoea (known as *ricewater stools*) leading to dehydration. The disease is contracted from food or drinking water contaminated by faeces from a patient. Cholera often occurs in epidemics; outbreaks are rare in good sanitary conditions. After an incubation period of 1–5 days symptoms commence suddenly; the resulting dehydration and the imbalance in the concentration of body fluids can cause death within 24 hours. Initial treatment involves replacing the fluid loss by *oral rehydration therapy; tetracycline eradicates the bacteria and hastens recovery. The mortality rate in untreated cases is over 50%. Vaccination against cholera is effective for only 6–9 months.

霍亂　由霍亂弧菌引起的小腸急性感染。引起嚴重的嘔吐和腹瀉（稱為米泔樣便）而導致脫水。通過食用被病人糞便污染的水或食物而感染。霍亂常呈暴發流行，在衞生條件好的地方很少發生。在經過 1~5 天的潛伏期之後，症狀突然開始出現。脫水和體液的濃度失去平衡可在 24 小時內引起死亡。初期治療包括口服補液來補充體液的丟失。四環素可殺滅霍亂弧菌，並加速恢復。未治療病例的病死率為 50%。抗霍亂的疫苗接種有效期僅 6~9 個月。

choleresis n. the production of bile by the liver.

膽汁分泌　肝臟的膽汁生產。

choleretic n. an agent that stimulates the secretion of bile by the liver thereby increasing the flow of bile.

利膽劑　一種刺激肝臟膽汁分泌從而增加膽汁流出的藥物。

cholestasis n. failure of normal amounts of bile to reach the intestine, resulting in obstructive *jaundice. The cause may be a mechanical block in the bile ducts, such as a stone (*extrahepatic biliary obstruction*), or liver disease, such as that caused by the drug *chlorpromazine in some hypersensitive individuals (*intrahepatic cholestasis*). The symptoms are jaundice with dark urine, pale faeces, and usually itching (pruritus).

膽汁阻塞　膽汁不能正常到達小腸，從而引起阻塞性黃疸。其原因可能是膽管的機械梗塞，如結石（肝外性膽汁阻塞）或肝臟疾病，如在一些過敏性極強的個體病人中由藥物氯丙嗪引起的肝臟疾病（肝內性膽汁阻塞）。症狀為黃疸、黑色尿、糞便灰白色、且通常發癢（瘙癢）。

cholesteatoma *n.* a skin-lined sac containing debris from dead skin cells that grows from the eardrum into the *mastoid bone, eroding normal structures in its path. Left untreated, it can carry infection to the brain, causing meningitis or a cerebral *abscess. Treatment is by means of *mastoidectomy. Rarely, cholesteatoma can arise congenitally in the *temporal bone or central nervous system.

膽脂瘤　一個皮膚包裹的囊，內含死亡的皮膚細胞的碎屑。該囊從鼓室開始生長，伸入乳突骨，並在其經路上侵蝕正常的結構。若不治療，可感染腦，引起腦膜炎或腦膿腫。用乳突切除術治療。膽脂瘤可先天出現於顳骨或中樞神經系統，但很少見。

cholesterol *n.* a fatlike material (a *sterol) present in the blood and most tissues, especially nervous tissue. Cholesterol and its esters are important constituents of cell membranes and are precursors of many steroid hormones and bile salts. Western dietary intake is approximately 500–1000 mg/day. Cholesterol is synthesized in the body from acetate, mainly in the liver, and blood concentration is normally 140–300 mg/100 ml (3.6–7.8 mmol/l). An elevated concentration of cholesterol in the blood (*hypercholesterolaemia*) is often associated with *atheroma, of which cholesterol is a major component. People with *primary* (or *familial*) *hypercholesterolaemia* have a genetic defect causing a lack of low-density *lipoprotein (LDL) receptors, which remove cholesterol from the bloodstream. Drugs are available that lower serum cholesterol and LDL levels. Cholesterol is also a constituent of *gallstones.

膽固醇　存在於血液和大多數組織，特別是神經組織內的一種脂肪樣物質（一種甾醇）。膽固醇和其酯類是細胞膜的重要成分，也是許多固醇類激素與膽鹽的前體。西方的膳食攝入量大約為每天500~1000mg。膽固醇在體內由乙酸鹽合成，主要合成於肝臟，血液中的濃度通常為140~300mg/100ml (3.6~7.8mmol/l)。血液中膽固醇含量升高（高膽固醇血症）常提示動脈粥樣化。膽固醇是該疾病的主要構成成分。原發性（或家族性）高膽固醇血症的病人有遺傳缺陷。這一缺陷引起將膽固醇從血流中消除掉的低密度脂蛋白（LDL）受體缺乏。藥物能夠降低血清膽固醇和 LDL 含量。膽固醇也是膽結石的一個構成成分。

cholesterosis *n.* a form of chronic *cholecystitis in which small crystals of cholesterol are deposited on the internal wall of the gall bladder, like the pips of a strawberry; hence its descriptive term *strawberry gall bladder*. The crystals may enlarge to become *gallstones.

膽固醇沉着病　慢性膽囊炎的一種。膽固醇的微小顆粒沉着在膽囊的內壁，似草莓種子，因此用以描述其形狀的詞語為草莓樣膽囊。這些顆粒可變大，發展成膽結石。

cholestyramine *n.* a drug that binds with bile salts so that they are excreted. It is administered by mouth to relieve conditions due to irritant effects of bile salts – such as the itching that occurs in obstructive jaundice – and also to lower the blood levels of cholesterol and other fats. Common side-effects include constipation, diarrhoea, heartburn, and nausea. Trade name: **Questran**.

考來烯胺 一種與膽鹽結合而被排出的藥物。用於口服以解除因膽鹽刺激作用而產生的症狀，如阻塞性黃疸中所出現的瘙癢。還可用以降低血中膽固醇和其他脂肪的含量。常見的副作用包括便秘、腹瀉、燒心和惡心。商品名：Questran。

cholic acid (cholalic acid) *see* bile acids.

膽酸 參閱 bile acids。

choline *n.* a basic compound important in the synthesis of phosphatidylcholine (lecithin) and other *phospholipids and of *acetylcholine. It is also involved in the transport of fat in the body. Choline is sometimes classed as a vitamin but, although it is essential for life, it can be synthesized in the body.

膽鹼 在合成磷脂酰膽鹼（卵磷脂）和其他磷脂類以及乙酰膽鹼過程中的一種重要鹼性化合物。它還參與體內脂肪的運輸。膽鹼有時被歸類為維生素，然而，儘管它對生命活動至關重要，但它可在體內合成。

cholinergic *adj.* **1.** describing nerve fibres that release *acetylcholine as a neurotransmitter. **2.** describing drugs that mimic the actions of acetylcholine (*see* parasympathomimetic). *Compare* adrenergic.

(1) 膽鹼能的 能釋放神經遞質乙酰膽鹼的神經纖維。**(2) 膽鹼能藥** 模仿乙酰膽鹼作用的藥物（參閱 parasympathomimetic）。與 adrenergic 對比。

cholinesterase *n.* an enzyme that breaks down a choline ester into its choline and acid components. The term usually refers to *acetylcholinesterase,* which breaks down the neurotransmitter *acetylcholine into choline and acetic acid. It is found in all *cholinergic nerve junctions, Where it rapidly destroys the acetylcholine released during the transmission of a nerve impulse so that subsequent impulses may pass. Other cholinesterases are found in the blood and other tissues.

膽鹼酯酶 一種將膽鹼酯分解成膽鹼和酸性部分的酶。這一術語常指乙酰膽鹼酯酶。它將神經遞質分解成膽鹼和乙酸。乙酰膽鹼酯酶存在於所有膽鹼能神經接頭處。在這裏，它將在一神經衝動的傳遞中釋放的乙酰膽鹼迅速破壞，以使隨後的衝動通過。其他膽鹼酯酶存在於血液和其他組織中。

choline theophyllinate a drug used to dilate the air passages in asthma and

膽茶鹼 一種用於治療哮喘和慢性支氣管炎的氣管擴張藥

chronic bronchitis. It is administered by mouth and can cause digestive upsets and nausea. Trade name: **Choledyl**.

物。口服。能引起消化不良和惡心。商品名：Choledyl。

choluria *n.* bile in the urine, which occurs when the level of bile in the blood is raised, especially in obstructive *jaundice. The urine becomes dark brown or orange, and bile pigments and bile salts may be detected in it.

膽汁尿　尿中出現膽汁。當血液中膽汁含量升高時會產生這種現象，特別是在阻塞性黃疸中。尿會變成暗褐色。可在其中檢測出膽色素和膽鹽。

chondr- (chondro-) *prefix denoting* cartilage. Example: *chondrogenesis* (formation of).

〔前綴〕**軟骨**　如軟骨形成。

chondrin *n.* a material that resembles gelatin, produced when cartilage is boiled.

軟骨膠（素）　一種當軟骨被煮沸時產生的類膠狀物質。

chondriosome *n. see* mitochondrion.

綫粒體　參閱 mitochondrion。

chondroblast *n.* a cell that produces the matrix of *cartilage.

成軟骨細胞　一種產生軟骨基質的細胞。

chondroblastoma *n.* a tumour derived from *chondroblasts, having the appearance of a mass of well-differentiated cartilage.

成軟骨細胞瘤　由成軟骨細胞產生的腫瘤，其外觀呈良好分化的軟骨腫塊。

chondrocalcinosis *n.* the presence of calcium pyrophosphate crystals in joint cartilage, as seen in *pseudogout by means of X-ray.

軟骨鈣質沉着病　在關節軟骨中出現焦磷酸鈣結晶的現象，就如在假痛風中 X 綫檢查所見。

chondroclast *n.* a cell that is concerned with the absorption of cartilage.

破軟骨細胞　一種與軟骨吸收有關的細胞。

chondrocranium *n.* the embryonic skull, which is composed entirely of cartilage and is later replaced by bone. *See also* meninx.

軟骨頂　胚胎期的顱骨，全部由軟骨構成，隨後被骨所取代。參閱 meninx。

chondrocyte *n.* a *cartilage cell, found embedded in the matrix.

軟骨細胞　埋植於基質中的一種軟骨細胞。

chondrodermatitis nodulans helicis a fairly common painful nodule on the upper part of the ear. It occurs mainly in middle-aged or elderly men and characteristically prevents the sufferer from sleeping on the affected side; it is readily treated by being cut out.

耳輪結節性軟骨皮炎 耳的上部非常常見的痛性結節。主要發生於中年或老年人。其特徵為患者不能側向患側入睡。治療採用切除。

chondrodysplasia (chondro-osteo-dystrophy, chondrodystrophy) *n.* a hereditary disorder of cartilage formation, also known as *Morquio-Brailsford disease*, that results from a defect in mucopolysaccharide metabolism. It results in deformities in the weight-bearing bones, which leads to dwarfism. *Osteoporosis is marked, and the cornea and heart may also develop abnormally. The condition is diagnosed by X-rays, which show characteristic malformation of the growing ends (epiphyses) of the bones, and by examination of the urine.

軟骨發育不良（骨軟骨營養障礙，軟骨營養障礙） 一種遺傳性軟骨形成不良症，又叫莫-布氏病。該病源於黏多糖代謝缺陷。它引起承重骨畸形可導致侏儒症。骨質疏鬆顯著，且角膜和心臟也可發生病變。通過X綫和尿檢可以診斷該病。X綫可見骨的生長端（骨骺）有特徵性畸形。

chondrodystrophy *n. see* chondrodysplasia.

軟骨營養障礙 參閱 chondrodysplasia。

chondroitin sulphate a mucopolysaccharide that forms an important constituent of cartilage, bone, and other connective tissues. It is composed of glucuronic acid and N-acetyl-D-galactosamine units.

硫酸軟骨素 構成軟骨、骨和其他結締組織的重要組成成分的一種黏多糖。它由葡萄糖醛酸與N-乙酰半乳糖胺單位組成。

chondroma *n.* a benign tumour of cartilage-forming cells, which may occur at the growing end of any bone but is found most commonly in the bones of the feet and hands. *See also* dyschondroplasia, enchondroma, ecchondroma.

軟骨瘤 軟骨生成細胞的一種良性腫瘤，可發生於任何骨的生長端，但最常見於腳和手的骨頭。參閱 dyschondroplasia，enchondroma，ecchondroma。

chondromalacia *n.* degeneration of cartilage at a joint. *Chondromalacia patellae* is a roughening of the inner surface of the kneecap, resulting in a pain, a grating

軟骨軟化 關節軟骨變性。髕骨軟骨軟化指的是髕骨內表面粗糙不平，引起疼痛、摩擦感和運動不穩感。

sensation, and a feeling of instability on movement.

chondro-osteodystrophy *n. see* chondrodysplasia.

骨軟骨營養障礙　參閱 chondrodysplasia。

chondrosarcoma *n.* a malignant tumour of cartilage cells, occurring in a bone. Treatment is by surgical removal and radiotherapy.

軟骨肉瘤　骨組織中軟骨細胞的惡性腫瘤。治療用外科切除和放射治療。

chord- (chordo-) *prefix denoting* **1.** a cord. **2.** the notochord.

〔前綴〕**(1)** 索狀物，帶狀物 **(2)** 脊索

chorda *n.* (*pl.* **chordae**) a cord, tendon, or nerve fibre. The *chordae tendineae* are stringlike processes in the heart that attach the margins of the mitral and tricuspid valve leaflets to projections of the wall of the ventricle (*papillary muscles*). Rupture of the chordae, through injury, endocarditis, or degenerative changes, results in *mitral incompetence.

索　索、腱索或神經纖維。腱索指心臟內繩索樣的突起，它將二尖瓣的瓣葉與心室壁的乳頭肌連接起來。外傷，心內膜炎或變性改變可引起腱索斷裂，而發生二尖瓣閉鎖不全。

chordee *n.* acute angulation of the penis. In *Peyronie's disease, this is due to a localized fibrous plaque in the penis, which fails to engorge on erection. As a result, the penis angulates at this point making intercourse impossible. In a child, downward chordee is an associated deformity in *hypospadias and the more severe forms are corrected surgically.

塑形陰莖　陰莖勃起時呈現銳角彎曲。在佩羅尼病中，陰莖有局限性纖維瘢痕，在勃起時，不能很好充血。結果，陰莖在這一位置變曲而使性交無法進行。在兒童，塑形陰莖與尿道下裂畸形有關。嚴重者需用手術予以矯正。

chordoma *n.* a rare tumour arising from remnants of the embryologic *notochord. The classical sites are the base of skull and the region of the sacrum.

脊索瘤　由胚胎期脊索的殘餘物產生的罕見腫瘤。最常見的部位在顱骨底部和骶部。

chorea *n.* a jerky involuntary movement particularly affecting the head, face, or limbs. Each movement is sudden but the resulting posture may be prolonged for a few seconds. The symptoms are usually due to disease of the *basal ganglia but

舞蹈病　一種抽搐樣不自主運動，影響頭、臉、或四肢。每一運動都是突然發生，但所形成的姿勢可延續數秒。症狀通常由於基底神經節疾病而產生，也可由於治療帕金森綜合

may result from drug therapy for *parkinsonism or on the withdrawal of phenothiazines. Such movements are characteristic of *Huntington's disease, in which they are associated with progressive dementia. *Senile chorea* occurs sporadically in elderly people and there is no dementia. *Sydenham's chorea* affects children and is associated with rheumatic fever. It responds to mild sedatives.

徵的藥物引起，或者吩噻嗪戒斷引起。這種運動是亨廷頓病的特點，並與進行性癡呆有關。老年性舞蹈病散見於老人，但無癡呆。西德納姆舞蹈病影響兒童，與風濕熱有關，可用輕鎮靜藥治療。

chorion *n.* the embryonic membrane that totally surrounds the embryo from the time of implantation. It is formed from *trophoblast lined with mesoderm and becomes closely associated with the *allantois. The blood vessels (supplied by the allantois) are concentrated in the region of the chorion that is attached to the wall of the uterus and forms the *placenta. *See also* villus. **–chorionic** *adj.*

絨毛膜　自胚泡植入宮內之時起包裹整個胚胎的胚膜。它由中胚層的滋養層形成，且與尿囊緊密相連。血管（來自尿囊）集中在絨毛膜區。這一區與子宮壁相連，形成胎盤。參閱villus。

chorionepithelioma (choriocarcinoma) *n.* a rare form of cancer originating in the outermost of the membranes (chorion) surrounding the fetus. It is a highly malignant tumour usually following a *hydatidiform mole, although it may follow abortion or even a normal pregnancy. The tumour rapidly spreads to the lungs, but is relatively sensitive to treatment with *cytotoxic drugs.

絨毛膜上皮癌　一種少見的癌。起源於包圍胎兒的最外層的膜（絨毛膜）。是一種極為惡性的腫瘤，常發生在葡萄胎之後，但也可能在流產甚至正常妊娠之後發生。腫瘤迅速擴散到肺。但對細胞毒素藥物治療相對敏感。

chorionic villus sampling (CVS) a fetal monitoring technique in which a sample of chorionic *villus is taken between the eighth and eleventh weeks of pregnancy. Sampling is carried out through the cervix or abdomen under ultrasound visualization. The cells so obtained are subjected to chromosomal and biochemical studies to determine if any abnormalities are present in the

絨膜絨毛取樣　一種胎兒監護技術，在妊娠 8~11 周期間採集絨膜絨毛的樣品。取樣在超聲顯影下通過宮頸或腹部進行。以此法獲得的細胞要進行染色體和生化研究以確定胎兒是否出現任何異常。這一技術能夠進行產前診斷諸如唐氏綜合徵和地中海貧血等先天性疾病。

fetus. This enables the *prenatal diagnosis of such congenital disorders as Down's syndrome and thalassaemia.

choroid *n.* the layer of the eyeball between the retina and the sclera. It contains blood vessels and a pigment that absorbs excess light and so prevents blurring of vision. *See* eye.

脈絡膜　眼球視網膜和鞏膜之間的一層膜。它含有血管和能吸收過強光綫的色素，以防止視力模糊。參閱 eye。

choroiditis *n.* inflammation of the choroid layer of the eye. It may be inflamed together with the iris and ciliary body, but often is involved alone and in patches (*focal* or *multifocal choroiditis*). Vision becomes blurred but the eye is usually painless. *See* uveitis.

脈絡膜炎　眼的脈絡膜炎症。可與虹膜和睫狀體炎症同時發生，但常單獨發生，且呈斑狀（病竈性或多病竈性脈絡膜炎）。視力變得模糊，但眼部通常無痛感。參閱 uveitis。

choroid plexus a rich network of blood vessels, derived from those of the pia-mater, in each of the brain's ventricles. It is responsible for the production of *cerebrospinal fluid.

脈絡叢　在各腦室內的軟腦膜發出的密集血管網絡。它負責產生腦脊液。

Christmas disease a disorder that is identical in its effects to *haemophilia, but is due to a deficiency of a different blood coagulation factor, the *Christmas factor* (Factor IX).

克里斯馬斯病　一種臨床表現與血友病類似的疾病，但本病是由於另一不同的凝血因子——克里斯馬斯因子而引起的（第 IX 因子）。

chrom- (chromo-) *prefix denoting* colour or pigment.

〔前綴〕顏色，色素

chromaffin *n.* tissue in the medulla of the *adrenal gland consisting of modified neural cells containing granules that are stained brown by chromates. Adrenaline and noradrenaline are released from the granules when the adrenal gland is stimulated by its sympathetic nerve supply. *See also* neurohormone.

嗜鉻組織　在腎上腺髓質中由變異的神經細胞構成的組織。這種細胞內含有可被鉻染成褐色的顆粒。當腎上腺受到交感神經的刺激時，這些顆粒就釋放出腎上腺素和去甲腎上腺素。參閱 neurohormone。

-chromasia *suffix denoting* staining or pigmentation.

〔後綴〕染色，色素沉着

chromat- (chromato-) *prefix denoting* colour or pigmentation.

〔前綴〕**顏色，色素沉着**

chromatid *n.* one of the two threadlike strands formed by longitudinal division of a chromosome during *mitosis and *meiosis. They remain attached at the *centromere. Chromatids can be seen between early prophase and metaphase in mitosis and between diplotene and the second metaphase of meiosis, after which they divide at the centromere to form daughter chromosomes.

染色單體 染色體在有絲分裂和減數分裂期間沿縱向分裂而形成的兩條綫樣絲條的一條。它們仍與着絲粒相連。在有絲分裂的前期與中期之間，減數分裂的兩綫相和第二中期之間可以看到。在此之後，它們在着絲粒處分裂，形成子染色體。

chromatin *n.* the material of a cell nucleus that stains with basic dyes and consists of DNA and protein: the substance of which the chromosomes are made. *See* euchromatin, heterochromatin.

染色質 細胞核內由脫氧核糖核酸和蛋白質組成的並能被鹼性染料着色的物質。染色體即由此物質組成。參閱 euchromatin，heterochromatin。

chromatography *n.* any of several techniques for separating the components of a mixture by selective absorption. Two such techniques are quite widely used in medicine, for example to separate mixtures of amino acids. In one of these, *paper chromatography*, a sample of the mixture is placed at the edge of a sheet of filter paper. As the solvent soaks along the paper, the components are absorbed to different extents and thus move along the paper at different rates. In *column chromatography* the components separate out along a column of a powdered absorbent, such as silica or aluminum oxide.

色譜法 任何通過選擇性吸收將一混合物的成分予以分離的技術。有兩個這樣的技術廣泛應用於醫學來分離氨基酸混合物。其中之一是紙層析法。將混合物的標本放在濾紙的邊緣。隨着溶劑浸漬濾紙，因各成分被吸收的程度不同，它們在紙上運動的速度也不同。在柱層析法中，成分通過裝有粉狀吸收劑的柱進行分離，如二氧化硅或氧化鋁。

chromatolysis *n.* the dispersal or disintegration of the microscopic structures within the nerve cells that normally produce proteins. It is part of the cell's response to injury.

染色質溶解 通常產生蛋白的神經細胞內的顯微結構的分散或崩解。它是細胞對損傷反應的一部分。

chromatophore *n.* a cell containing pigment. In man chromatophores

色素細胞 一種含有色素的細胞。人類的色素細胞含有

containing *melanin are found in the skin, hair, and eyes.

黑素，存在於皮膚、頭髮和眼睛。

chromatopsia *n.* abnormal coloured vision: a rare symptom of various conditions. Sometimes everything looks reddish to patients after removal of their cataracts; patients suffering from digitalis poisoning may see things in green or yellow. Similar disturbances of colour may be experienced by people recovering from inflammation of the optic nerve.

色視症 色視覺異常，多種不同疾病表現出的一種少見症狀。有時，當病人內障摘除術後，所有東西看起來呈紅色。洋地黃中毒患者視物呈綠色或黃色。患視神經炎症的病人恢復後也可出現類似的視色紊亂。

chromoblastomycosis (chromomycosis) *n.* a chronic fungal infection of the skin usually occurring at the site of an injury; for example, a wound from a wood splinter. It produces pigmented wartlike lumps – mainly on the feet and legs – that sometimes ulcerate. The disease is often found in adult male agricultural workers.

着色真菌病 皮膚的一種慢性真菌感染。通常發生於受傷部位，如由木頭碎片造成的創傷。出現有色素沉着的疣狀腫塊，主要在腳和腿，有時可見潰瘍。該病常見於成年男性農業工人中。

chromosome *n.* one of the threadlike structures in a cell nucleus that carry the genetic information in the form of *genes. It is composed of a long double filament of *DNA coiled into a helix together with associated proteins, with the genes arranged in a linear manner along its length. It stains deeply with basic dyes during cell division (*see* meiosis, mitosis). The nucleus of each human somatic cell contains 46 chromosomes, 23 of which are of maternal and 23 of paternal origin (see illustration). Each chromosome can duplicate an exact copy of itself between each cell division (*see* interphase) so that each new cell formed receives a full set of chromosomes. *See also* chromatid, centromere, sex chromosome. **–chromosomal** *adj.*

染色體 細胞核中一種細綫形結構。它們以基因的形式攜帶遺傳信息。由一對長的脫氧核糖核酸細絲與相關的蛋白質盤繞而形成螺旋狀，基因即按其長軸呈綫性排列。在細胞分裂期間，它能被鹼性染料着色（參閱 meiosis，mitosis）。每個人類體細胞核內包括 46 個染色體，其中 23 個來自母體，23 個來自父體（見圖）。在每次細胞分裂期間，每一個染色體都能把自己進行準確的複製（參閱 interphase）。因此，每一新形成的細胞都接受到完整的一套染色體。參閱 chromatid，centromere，sex chromosome。

chron- (chrono-) *prefix denoting* time. Example: *chronophobia* (abnormal fear of).

〔前綴〕**時 間** 如時間恐怖症。

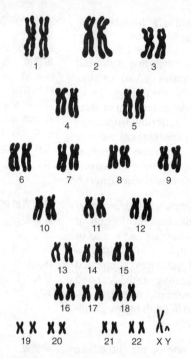

Human male chromosomes, arranged in numbered pairs according to a standard classification. The female set differs only in the sex chromosomes (XX instead of XY).

男性染色體，按標準分類法編號成對排列。女性染色體僅用 XX 取代 XY 即可。

chronic *adj.* describing a disease of long duration involving very slow changes. Such disease is often of gradual onset. The term does not imply anything about the severity of a disease. *Compare* acute.

慢性的 描述一持續時間長、變化緩慢的疾病。這種疾病的發生是漸進性的。該術語不暗示疾病的任何嚴重程度。與 acute 對比。

chronic fatigue syndrome *see* myalgic encephalomyelitis.

慢性疲勞綜合徵 參閱 myalgic encephalomyelitis。

Chronic Sick and Disabled Persons Act 1970 (in Britain) an Act providing for the identification and care of those suffering from a chronic or degenerative disease for which there is no cure and which can be only partially alleviated by

慢性病和殘疾人法 1970 （英國）一個旨在對那些患有慢性病或變性疾病，而該病又無法治療或治療僅能獲得部分好轉的病人提供鑒定和照顧的法案。這樣的病人要與那些可能

treatment. Such patients are usually distinguished from the elderly who may also suffer from chronic diseases. It is the responsibility of local authorities to identify those with such problems and to ensure that services are available to meet their needs and that the people concerned are aware of the available services. Identification can be difficult because of the lack of clear and agreed definition of what constitutes a disability of such severity as to warrant inclusion in such a register. As there is no compulsion, many general practitioners and community nurses fail to notify the appropriate *social service department for reasons of confidentiality and also because many patients fear the stigma of being included on such a register. *See* handicap.

也會患有慢性疾病的老人區分開來。地方當局的責任在於發現那些有此類問題的人，並確保所提供的服務可以滿足其需要和使這些人知道可獲得的服務。此類人員的識別可能會困難一些，因為缺乏明確和統一的定義，甚麼樣的嚴重性才能構成殘疾以保證被列入登記名單。因為沒有硬性規定，許多全科醫生和地區護士不給相應社會福利部門通知這些病人的名字，其原因在於個人保密，也因為許多病人害怕被列入登記單上這一恥辱。參閱 handicap。

chrys- (chryso-) *prefix denoting* gold or gold salts.

〔前綴〕金，金鹽

Chrysops *n.* a genus of bloodsucking flies, commonly called deer flies. Female flies, found in shady wooded areas, bite man during the day. Certain species in Africa may transmit the tropical disease *loiasis to man. In the USA *C. discalis* is a vector of *tularaemia.

斑虻屬　一種吸血的蠅屬，通常稱為鹿虻。雌蠅見於蔭密林區，白天叮咬人類。非洲的某些種類可將熱帶羅阿絲蟲病傳播給人類。在美國，中室斑虻是傳播兔熱病的媒介昆蟲。

chrysotherapy *n.* the treatment of disease by the administration of gold or its compounds. The injection or oral administration of *gold salts is extremely effective in the treatment of arthritis in some patients. However, some patients develop potentially severe side-effects, including blood disorders, dermatitis, and impairment of kidney function.

金療法　使用金或其化合物治療疾病的方法。一些關節炎病人注射或口服金鹽對治療其病特別有效。但是，一些病人卻發生潛在的嚴重副作用，包括血液病、皮炎和腎功能損傷。

Chvosteck's sign twitching of the facial muscles elicited by stimulation of the facial nerve by tapping. This indicates

沃斯特克徵　輕扣後，由於面部神經的刺激而引發面部肌肉抽搐。這提示肌肉過敏性，通

muscular irritability, usually due to calcium depletion (*see* tetany).

常是由於鈣缺乏引起（參閱 tetany）。

chyle *n.* an alkaline milky liquid found within the *lacteals after a period of absorption. It consists of lymph with a suspension of minute droplets of digested fats, which have been absorbed from the small intestine. It is transported in the lymphatic system to the thoracic duct, which drains into the subclavian vein.

乳糜 食物被吸收一段時間後在乳糜管內出現的一種鹼性乳白色液體。它由淋巴液和懸浮於其中的被小腸吸收消化了的脂肪微粒組成。乳糜液從淋巴系統被運輸到胸導管，隨後進入鎖骨下靜脈。

chylomicron *n.* a microscopic particle of fat present in the blood after fat has been digested and absorbed from the small intestine.

乳糜微粒 脂肪在小腸被吸收和消化後出現在血液中的一種微小的脂肪顆粒。

chyluria *n.* the presence of *chyle in the urine.

乳糜尿 尿中出現乳糜。

chyme *n.* the semiliquid acid mass that is the form in which food passes from the stomach to the small intestine. It is produced by the action of *gastric juice and the churning movements of the stomach.

食糜 食物從胃進入小腸時形成的半液體酸性團塊。是由胃液和胃攪拌運動的作用而形成的。

chymotrypsin *n.* a protein-digesting enzyme (*see* peptidase). It is secreted by the pancreas in an inactive form, *chymotrypsinogen*, that is converted into chymotrypsin in the duodenum by the action of *trypsin.

胰凝乳蛋白 一種蛋白消化酶（參閱 peptidase）。是由胰腺分泌的一種無活性胰凝乳蛋白酶原，在十二指腸內通過胰蛋白酶的作用，轉化成胰凝乳蛋白。

chymotrypsinogen *n.* *see* chymotrypsin.

胰凝乳蛋白酶原 參閱 chymotrypsin。

cicatricial *adj.* associated with scarring. For example, *cicatricial alopecia* is a type of baldness associated with scarring, as opposed to non-scarring alopecia (*see* alopecia).

瘢痕的 與瘢痕有關的。如瘢痕狀脫髮是一種與結疤有關的禿頂。與之相對的是非瘢痕性脫髮（參閱 alopecia）。

-cide *suffix denoting* killer or killing. Examples: *bactericide* (of bacteria); *infanticide* (of children).

〔後綴〕**殺手，殺死** 如殺菌劑，殺嬰。

ciliary body the part of the *eye that connects the choroid with the iris. It consists of three zones: the *ciliary ring*, which adjoins the choroid; the *ciliary processes*, a series of about 70 radial ridges behind the iris to which the suspensory ligament of the lens is attached; and the *ciliary muscle*, contraction of which alters the curvature of the lens (*see* accommodation).

睫狀體 眼內將脈絡膜和虹膜連接起來的部分。共分三帶：與脈絡膜相連的睫狀環；與晶狀體懸韌帶相連的虹膜後呈放射狀排列的約 70 根突起（睫狀突）；通過收縮改變晶狀體曲度的睫狀肌（參閱 accommodation）。

cilium *n.* (*pl.* **cilia**) **1.** a hairlike process, large numbers of which are found on certain epithelial cells and on certain (ciliate) protozoa. Cilia are particularly characteristic of the epithelium that lines the upper respiratory tract, where their beating serves to remove particles of dust and other foreign material. **2.** an eyelash or eyelid. **–ciliary** *adj.*

(1) 纖毛 在某種上皮細胞和某些（纖毛蟲）原蟲上存在的大量毛髮樣突起。上呼吸道上皮細胞的一個特徵就是有纖毛。它們的抖動可排掉灰塵顆粒和其他異物。**(2) 睫（毛），瞼**

cimetidine *n.* an *antihistamine drug that reduces secretion of acid in the stomach and is used to treat stomach and duodenal ulcers, inflammation of the oesophagus, and other digestive disorders. It is administered by mouth or injection and the most common side-effects are dizziness, diarrhoea, muscular pains, and rash. Trade names: **Dyspamet**, **Galenamet**, **Tagamet**.

西咪替丁（甲氰咪胍） 一種減少胃酸分泌的抗組胺藥，用於治療胃和十二指腸潰瘍、食管炎及其他消化道疾病。口服或注射。最常見的副作用是頭昏、腹瀉、肌肉痛和皮疹。商品名：Dyspamet，Galenamet，Tagamet。

Cimex *n. see* bed bug.

臭蟲屬 參閱 bed bug。

CIN *see* cervical intraepithelial neoplasia.

宮頸上皮內瘤生成 參閱 cervical intraepithelial neoplasia。

cinchocaine *n.* a local anaesthetic used in dental and other operations and to relieve pain. It is applied directly to the skin or mucous membranes or injected at the site where anaesthesia is required or into the spine. Side-effects

辛可卡因 一種用於牙和其他手術的局部麻醉劑。可直接用於皮膚或黏膜或直接注射到需要麻醉的部位，或注射入脊髓腔。副作用為打呵欠、坐立不安、激動、惡心、嘔吐，有時

such as yawning, restlessness, excitement, nausea, vomiting, and allergic reactions can sometimes occur. Trade name: **Nupercainal**.

可出現過敏反應。商品名：Nupercainal。

cinchona n. the dried bark of *Cinchona* trees, formerly used in medicine to stimulate the appetite and to prevent haemorrhage and diarrhoea. Taken over prolonged periods, it may cause *cinchonism. Cinchona is the source of *quinine.

金雞納樹皮 金雞納樹的乾燥樹皮。過去用來入藥以開胃、止血和止腹瀉。長期服用引起金雞納中毒。奎寧取自金雞納樹皮。

cinchonism n. poisoning caused by an overdose of cinchona or the alkaloids quinine, quinidine, or cinchonine derived from it. The symptoms are commonly ringing noises in the ears, dizziness, blurring of vision (and sometimes complete blindness), rashes, fever, and low blood pressure. Treatment with *diuretics increases the rate of excretion of the toxic compounds from the body.

金雞納中毒 由過量服用金雞納或生物鹼奎寧、奎尼丁或金雞寧等引起的中毒。通常症狀有耳鳴、頭暈、視力模糊（有時全盲）、皮疹、發熱和低血壓。採用利尿劑將毒性化合物加速排出體外。

cineangiocardiography n. a form of *angiocardiography in which the X-ray pictures are recorded on cine film. This allows the dynamic movements of the heart to be studied when the film is projected.

心血管電影造影術 一種心血管造影術。將X綫照片記錄在電影膠片上。當電影被放映時，就可對心臟的動態運動進行研究。

cinefluorography n. the technique of taking a rapid succession of photographs of the fluorescent screen of a *fluoroscope, so that the recorded events may be later analysed.

熒光電影照相術 將熒光鏡的熒光屏上一系列迅速變化的圖像拍攝下來的技術。因此，所記錄下來的活動可供以後進行研究。

cineradiography n. the technique of taking a rapid succession of X-ray photographs, to capture on film events that occur rapidly during a particular radiographic investigation.

電影放射照相術 一種迅速拍攝的一系列X綫照片的技術。在進行一項特殊的X綫研究時可將迅速發生的活動拍攝在膠片上。

cingulectomy n. surgical excision of the *cingulum, the part of the brain

扣帶回切除術 切除扣帶的外科手術。扣帶是腦中與憤怒和

concerned with anger and depression. The procedure has occasionally been carried out as *psychosurgery for intractable mental illness.

沮喪情感有關的部位。這一手術偶爾用作精神外科療法治療難治的精神病。

cingulum *n.* (*pl.* **cingula**) **1.** a curved bundle of nerve fibres in each cerebral hemisphere, nearly encircling its connection with the corpus callosum. *See* cerebrum. **2.** a small protuberance on the lingual surface of the crowns of incisor and canine teeth.

(1) **扣帶** 在每一大腦半球中的彎形神經纖維束，幾乎全部包圍其與胼胝體的連接部分。
(2) **頰帶** 切牙和尖牙冠舌面上的一種小突起。

ciprofloxacin *n.* a broad-spectrum antibiotic that can be given orally and is particularly useful against Gram-negative bacteria, such as *Pseudomonas*, that are resistant to all other oral antibiotics. Side-effects can include nausea, diarrhoea, abdominal pain, and headache. Trade name: **Ciproxin**.

環丙氟哌酸 一種廣譜抗生素，口服，特別用於對所有其他口服抗生素都有耐藥性的革蘭氏陰性細菌，如假單胞菌屬。副作用包括惡心、腹瀉、腹痛和頭痛。商品名：Ciproxin。

circle of Willis a circle on the undersurface of the brain formed by linked branches of the arteries that supply the brain (see illustration). This helps to maintain the blood supply in the event of a feeding vessel being blocked. Most cerebral *aneurysms occur on or near the circle of Willis.

威利斯環 顱底表面由向腦部供血的動脈分支形成的環（見圖）。這使得在一個供血支管發生阻塞時，仍能保持血流供應。大多數顱內動脈瘤發生於此環或在此環附近。

circulatory system see cardiovascular system.

循環系統 參閱 cardiovascular system。

circum- *prefix denoting* around: surrounding. Example: *circumanal* (surrounding the anus).

〔前綴〕**環繞，周圍** 如肛周。

circumcision *n.* surgical removal of the foreskin of the penis. This operation is usually performed for religious and ethnic reasons but is sometimes required for medical conditions, mainly *phimosis and *paraphimosis. *Female circumcision* involves removal of the clitoris, *labia

包皮環切術 陰莖包皮的外科切除手術。此手術的施行是因宗教和種族原因，但有時是由於治療疾病的需要，主要是包莖和嵌頓包莖。女性陰蒂切開術涉及陰蒂、小陰唇及大陰唇的切除。切除的程度不同部

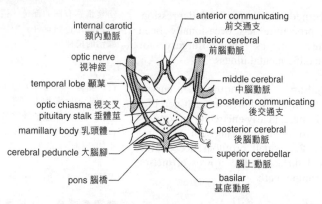

internal carotid
頸內動脈

optic nerve
視神經

temporal lobe 顳葉

optic chiasma 視交叉
pituitary stalk 垂體莖
mamillary body 乳頭體

cerebral peduncle 大腦腳

pons 腦橋

anterior communicating
前交通支

anterior cerebral
前腦動脈

middle cerebral
中腦動脈

posterior communicating
後交通支

posterior cerebral
後腦動脈

superior cerebellar
腦上動脈

basilar
基底動脈

Arterial branches forming the circle of Willis
(from below)
動脈交通支形成韋利斯環（下面觀）

minora, and labia majora. The extent of excision varies from tribe to tribe and from country to country. The simplest and least damaging form is *clitoridectomy* (removal of the clitoris); the next form entails excision of the prepuce, clitoris, and all or part of the labia minora. The most extensive form, *infibulation*, involves excision of clitoris, labia minora, and labia majora. The vulval lips are sutured together and a piece of wood or reed is inserted to preserve a small passage for urine and menstrual fluid. In the majority of women who are circumcised, *episiotomy, often extensive, is required to allow delivery of a child.

circumduction *n*. a circular movement, such as that made by a limb.

circumflex nerve a mixed sensory and motor nerve of the upper arm. It arises from the fifth and sixth cervical segments of the spinal cord and is distributed to the deltoid muscle of the shoulder and the overlying skin.

落、不同國家都不同。最簡單的和損害性最小的一種形式是陰蒂切除術（切除陰蒂）。另一種形式涉及陰蒂、包皮、全部或部分小陰唇的切除。切除範圍最大的形式是鎖陰術。它涉及切除陰蒂、小陰唇和大陰唇。外陰唇被縫在一起，並置一木條或蘆葦棍以保留一狹窄通道以供尿液和月經排出。大多數被施行陰蒂切開術的婦女需行外陰切開術以便分娩，這一手術常涉及範圍較大。

環形運動 一種環形運動，如肢體所做的環形運動。

腋神經 手臂上部的一支感覺和運動的混合神經。它從脊髓的第五和第六頸段發出，並分布於肩三角肌及表皮中。

circumoral *adj.* situated around the mouth.

circumstantiality *n.* a disorder of thought in which thinking and speech proceed slowly and with many unnecessary trivial details. It is sometimes seen in organic *psychosis, in *schizophrenia, and in people of pedantic and obsessional personality.

cirrhosis *n.* a condition in which the liver responds to injury or death of some of its cells by producing interlacing strands of fibrous tissue between which are nodules of regenerating cells. The liver becomes tawny and characteristically knobbly (due to the nodules). Causes include *alcoholism (*alcoholic cirrhosis*), viral *hepatitis (*postnecrotic cirrhosis*), chronic obstruction of the common bile duct (*secondary biliary cirrhosis*), autoimmune diseases (*chronic aggressive hepatitis, primary biliary cirrhosis*), and chronic heart failure (*cardiac cirrhosis*). In at least half the cases of cirrhosis no cause is found (*cryptogenic cirrhosis*). Complications include *portal hypertension, *ascites, *hepatic encephalopathy, and *hepatoma. Cirrhosis cannot be cured but its progress may be stopped if the cause can be removed. This particularly applies in alcoholism (when all alcohol must be prohibited); in chronic hepatitis (in which corticosteroid treatment may reduce inflammation); in secondary biliary cirrhosis (in which surgery may relieve obstruction); and in cardiac failure that can be treated. **–cirrhotic** *adj.*

cirs- (cirso-) *prefix denoting* a varicose vein. Example: *cirsectomy* (excision of).

cirsoid *adj.* describing the distended knotted appearance of a varicose vein.

口周　位於口的周圍。

瑣談症　一種思維障礙病。患者思維和言語進行緩慢，且有許多不必要的不重要的細節。有時見於器質性精神病、精神分裂症以及古板型人格和強迫型人格。

肝硬化　肝臟通過產生交錯的纖維組織索來應答肝損傷或一些肝細胞的死亡。在纖維組織索之間是再生細胞結。肝臟變成黃褐色，並出現富有特點的結節狀（由於結節引起）。原因包括酒精中毒（酒精性肝硬化）、病毒性肝炎（壞死性肝硬化）、慢性膽總管梗塞（繼發性膽汁性肝硬化）、自體免疫性疾病（慢性侵襲性肝炎、原發性膽汁性肝硬化）和慢性心力衰竭（心臟性肝硬化）。在至少一半的肝硬化病例中，病發原因不明（病因不明性肝硬化）。併發症包括門靜脈高壓、腹水、肝性腦病以及肝癌。肝硬化尚不能治愈，但如果消除病因，則可扼制其病情發展。這特別適用於乙醇中毒（必須禁止一切酒類）、慢性肝炎（皮質類固醇治療可減輕炎症）、繼發性膽汁性肝硬化（外科手術可減輕梗阻）和可予以治療的心力衰竭。

〔前綴〕**靜脈曲張**　表示曲張的靜脈，如靜脈曲張切除術。

曲張的　描述一曲張靜脈擴張而致的結節狀外觀。本術語用

The term is used for a type of tumour of the scalp (*cirsoid aneurysm*), which is an arteriovenous aneurysm.

於指頭皮的一種動靜脈瘤（曲張性動脈瘤）。

cisplatin *n.* a heavy-metal compound: a *cytotoxic drug that impedes cell division by damaging DNA. Administered intravenously, it is important in the treatment of testicular and ovarian tumours. It is highly toxic; side-effects include nausea, vomiting, kidney damage, peripheral neuropathy, and hearing loss. Less toxic *analogues of cisplatin are now available (*see* carboplatin). Trade name: **Neoplatin.**

順鉑　一種重金屬化合物，是一種細胞毒素藥物，它通過破壞脫氧核糖核酸而制止細胞分裂。該藥通過靜脈注射使用。在治療睪丸與卵巢腫瘤時很重要。該藥有高度毒性。副作用包括惡心、嘔吐、腎損壞、末梢神經病以及失聽。現在已有毒性較輕的順鉑的同類藥物（參閱 carboplatin）。商品名：Neoplatin。

cisterna *n.* (*pl.* **cisternae**) **1.** one of the enlarged spaces beneath the *arachnoid that act as reservoirs for cerebrospinal fluid. The largest (*cisterna magna*) lies beneath the cerebellum and behind the medulla oblongata. **2.** a dilatation at the lower end of the thoracic duct, into which the great lymph ducts of the lower limbs drain.

池　(1) 蛛網膜下腔充當腦脊液貯積處的擴大間隙。最大的池（小腦延髓池）位於小腦之下，延髓之後。(2) 胸導管下端的擴大部分。下肢的大淋巴管注入該部分。

cistron *n.* the section of a DNA or RNA chain that controls the amino-acid sequence of a single polypeptide chain in protein synthesis. A cistron can be regarded as the functional equivalent of a *gene.

順反子　在蛋白合成中，控制某一多肽鏈的氨基酸排列順序的脫氧核糖核酸或其鏈的一部分。順反子被認為其功能與基因相同。

citric acid an organic acid found naturally in citrus fruits. Citric acid is formed in the first stage of the *Krebs cycle, the important energy-producing cycle in the body.

枸櫞酸　柑橘類果實中自然存在的一種有機酸。枸櫞酸是在三羧酸循環的第一階段形成的。這一循環是體內重要的產能循環。

citric acid cycle *see* Krebs cycle.

枸櫞酸循環　參閱 Krebs cycle。

Citrobacter *n.* a genus of Gram-negative anaerobic rod-shaped bacteria widely distributed in nature. The organisms cause infections of the intestinal and

枸櫞酸菌屬　自然界中廣為分布的一種革蘭氏陰性厭氧桿狀細菌。這些生物引起小腸和尿道、膽囊和腦膜等的感染。這

urinary tracts, gall bladder, and the meninges that are usually secondary, occurring in the elderly, newborn, debilitated, and immunocompromised.

些感染通常是繼發的，見於老年人、新生兒、體弱者和免疫受損的人中。

citrullinaemia *n.* an inborn lack of one of the enzymes concerned with the chemical breakdown of proteins to urea: in consequence both the amino acid citrulline and ammonia accumulate in the blood. Affected children fail to thrive, and show signs of mental retardation.

瓜氨酸血症 先天性缺乏把蛋白化學分解成尿素的酶。結果是血中氨基酸瓜氨酸和氨同時增加。患兒不能茁壯成長，且表現出智力障礙的體徵。

citrulline *n.* an *amino acid produced by the liver as a by-product during the conversion of ammonia to *urea.

瓜氨酸 肝臟生成的一種氨基酸，是氨轉化為尿素時的一種副產物。

clamp *n.* a surgical instrument designed to compress a structure, such as a blood vessel or a cut end of the intestine (see illustration). A variety of clamps have been designed for specific surgical procedures. Blood-vessel clamps are used to stop bleeding from the cut vessels. Intestinal clamps prevent the intestinal contents from leaking into the abdominal cavity during operations on the intestines and are designed either not to damage the intestinal wall (noncrushing clamps) or to close the open end (crushing clamps) prior to suturing.

鉗 用以壓迫一結構的外科器械，如一根血管或小腸的斷端（見圖）。為了具體的外科手術，設計有不同的鉗。血管鉗被用來止住血管斷端的流血。在對小腸進行手術期間，小腸鉗防止小腸內容物漏到腹腔。小腸鉗設計成能不損傷小腸壁（非粉碎性鉗）或者在縫合前關閉切開的端口（粉碎性鉗）。

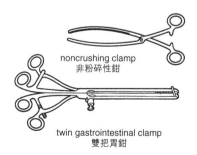

noncrushing clamp
非粉碎性鉗

twin gastrointestinal clamp
雙把胃鉗

Intestinal clamps
腸鉗

clasmocyte *n. see* macrophage.

大吞噬細胞　參閱 macrophage。

clasp *n.* (in dentistry) the part of a *denture that keeps it in place. It is made of flexible metal.

卡環　（牙科學）使托牙固定位置的部分。它由可塑性金屬製成。

claudication *n.* limping. *Intermittent claudication* is a cramping pain, induced by exercise and relieved by rest, that is caused by an inadequate supply of blood to the affected muscles. It is most often seen in the calf and leg muscles as a result of *atheroma of the leg arteries. The leg pulses are often absent and the feet may be cold. The treatment is that of atheroma.

跛行　間歇性跛行是一種痙攣性疼痛，運動誘發，休息可緩解，因患病肌肉的血液供應不足引起。多見於小腿或腿部，是由下肢動脈粥樣化所致。下肢脈搏常消失，足發冷。治療方法與治療動脈粥樣化相同。

claustrophobia *n.* a morbid fear of enclosed places. *See also* phobia.

幽閉恐怖　對密閉場所的一種病態恐懼。參閱 phobia。

claustrum *n.* a thin vertical layer of grey matter in each cerebral hemisphere, between the surface of the *insula and the lenticular nucleus (*see* basal ganglia).

屏狀核　位於腦島表面和豆狀核之間的每一大腦半球內的一薄層灰質。參閱 basal ganglia。

clavicle *n.* the collar bone: a long slender curved bone, a pair of which form the front part of the shoulder girdle. Each clavicle articulates laterally with the *scapula and medially with the manubrium of the sternum (breastbone). Fracture of the clavicle is a common *sports injury: the majority of cases require no treatment other than supporting the weight of the arm in a sling. **–clavicular** *adj.*

鎖骨　一根細長彎曲的骨頭，一對該骨構成肩胛帶的前部。每一鎖骨外側與肩胛骨，內側與胸骨柄聯成關節（胸骨）。鎖骨骨折是一常見的體育運動損傷：絕大多數此類損傷除了用一懸帶支持手臂重量外無需治療。

clavulanic acid a drug that interferes with the *penicillinases that inactivate many penicillin-type antibiotics, such as *amoxycillin. Combined with the antibiotic (in *Augmentin* or *Timentin*), clavulanic acid can overcome drug resistance.

克拉維酸（棒酸）　一種使青黴素類抗生素（如阿莫西林）失去活性的青黴素酶藥物。與抗生素合用（奧格門汀或泰門丁）能消除藥物的耐藥性。

clavus *n*. **1.** *see* corn. **2.** a sharp pain in the head, as if a nail were being driven in.

(1) 雞眼 (2) 釘腦感　腦內一種銳痛，就像釘進一根釘子一樣。

claw-foot *n*. an excessively arched foot, giving an unnaturally high instep. In most cases the cause is unknown, but the deformity may sometimes be due to an imbalance between the muscles flexing the toes and the shorter muscles that extend them; this type is found in some neuromuscular diseases, such as Friedreich's *ataxia. Surgical treatment is effective in childhood but less so in adult life. Medical name: **pes cavus**.

爪形足　一種極度弓形足，表現出一種不自然的高隆起。大多數病例原因不明，但有時可能因為屈趾的肌肉與伸趾的短肌不平衡所致。這類疾患常見於一些神經肌肉疾病，如弗里德賴希共濟失調。兒童期外科手術治療有效。但對成年人則不太有效。醫學用語：弓形足。

claw-hand *n*. flexion and contraction of the fingers with extension at the joints between the fingers and the hand, giving a claw-like appearance. Any kind of damage to the nerves or muscles may lead to claw-hand; causes include injuries, *syringomyelia, and leprosy. *See also* Dupuytren's contracture.

爪形手　掌指關節伸開手指的屈曲和攣縮而形成的爪樣外觀。任何形式的神經或肌肉損傷都可導致爪形手。原因包括外傷、脊髓空洞症和麻風病。參閱 Dupuytren's contracture。

clearance (renal clearance) *n*. a quantitative measure of the rate at which waste products are removed from the blood by the kidneys. It is expressed in terms of the volume of blood that could be completely cleared of a particular substance in one minute.

清除率（腎清除率）　血液中廢物被腎臟排出速度的數量測量。清除率的表示是根據一分鐘之內血液中某種物質被全部排出的量。

clearing *n*. (in microscopy) the process of removing the cloudiness from microscopical specimens after *dehydration by means of a *clearing agent*. This increases the transparency of the specimens. Xylene, cedar oil, methyl benzoate plus benzol, and methyl salicylate plus benzol are commonly used as clearing agents.

透明法　（顯微鏡檢查法）脫水後借助於透明劑除掉顯微標本的模糊現象的過程。這一過程能增加標本的透明度。二甲苯、香柏油、苯甲酸甲酯加苯、水楊酸甲酯加苯是常用的透明劑。

cleavage *n*. (in embryology) the process of repeated cell division of the fertilized

卵裂　（胚胎學）受精卵的不斷的細胞分裂過程，結果形成細

egg to form a ball of cells that becomes the *blastocyst. The cells (*blastomeres*) do not grow between divisions and so they decrease in size.

胞球，細胞球變成胚泡。這些細胞（分裂球）在分裂期間不再生長。因此，在體積上減小。

cleft palate a fissure in the midline of the palate due to failure of the two sides to fuse in embryonic development. Only part of the palate may be affected, or the cleft may extend the full length with bilateral clefts at the front of the maxilla; it may be accompanied by a *harelip and disturbance of tooth formation. Cleft palates can be corrected by surgery.

腭裂 由於在胚胎發育期腭的兩側未能融合而在腭的中綫處形成的裂。它可僅是部分性的，也可延伸至全長，在上頜骨前方的兩側出現腭裂。腭裂可伴有兔唇與牙齒形成障礙。腭裂可借助外科手術予以矯正。

cleid- (cleido-, clid-, clido-) *prefix denoting* the clavicle (collar bone). Example: *cleidocranial* (of the clavicle and cranium).

〔前綴〕鎖骨 如鎖骨顱骨的。

cleidocranial dysostosis a congenital defect of bone formation in which the skull bones ossify inperfectly and the collar bones (clavicles) are absent.

鎖骨顱骨發育不全 一種先天性骨形成缺陷。顱骨骨化不全，鎖骨缺乏。

clemastine *n.* an antihistamine used for the treatment of symptoms of hay fever, urticaria, and angioneurotic oedema because of its drying effects. It is administered by mouth; commonest side-effects are dizziness, sleepiness, and stomach upset. Trade names: **Allereze**, **Tavegil**.

氯馬斯汀 一種抗組胺藥，因其乾燥作用而用於治療枯草熱、蕁麻疹和血管神經病性水腫。口服。最常見的副作用是頭暈、嗜睡和胃部不適。商品名：Allereze，Tavegil。

clenbuterol *n.* a beta-adrenergic drug (*see* sympathomimetic) useful in the treatment of asthma. It is capable of causing a considerable increase in the bulk of voluntary muscle (hypertrophy) with an increase in force and a reduction in relaxation time. It also prevents the atrophy of muscle that has been deprived of its nerve supply during the long period of nerve regeneration.

克侖特羅 一種 β-腎上腺素能藥物（參閱 sympathomimetic），用於治療哮喘。它能引起隨意肌塊的增加（肥大），使肌力增加，舒張時間縮短。它還防止由於長期的神經變性造成失去神經支配而引起的肌肉萎縮。

client-centred therapy (Rogerian therapy) a method of psychotherapy in which the therapist refrains from directing his client in what he should do and instead concentrates on communicating understanding and acceptance. Frequently he reflects the client's own words or feelings back to him. The aim is to enable the client to solve his own problems.

climacteric *n.* **1.** *see* menopause. **2. (male climacteric)** declining sexual drive and fertility in men, usually occurring around or after middle age.

clindamycin *n.* an *antibiotic used to treat serious bacterial infections. It is administered by mouth; possible side-effects are nausea, vomiting, diarrhoea, and occasional hypersensitivity reactions. Trade name: **Dalacin C**.

clinic *n.* **1.** an establishment or department of a hospital devoted to the treatment of particular diseases or the medical care of out-patients. **2.** a gathering of instructors, students, and patients, usually in a hospital ward, for the examination and treatment of the patients.

clinical medical officer *see* community health.

clinical medicine the branch of medicine dealing with the study of actual patients and the diagnosis and treatment of disease at the bedside, as opposed to the study of disease by *pathology or other laboratory work.

clitoridectomy *n.* the surgical removal of the clitoris (*see* (female) circumcision).

clitoris *n.* the female counterpart of the penis, which contains erectile tissue (*see*

患者中心療法（羅傑蘭療法）一種心理治療方法。治療者避開指導患者應該做什麼，而將精力放在交流、理解和接受上。通常他將患者自己的語言或情感反射給患者本身，目的在於讓患者能夠解決自己的問題。

(1) 絕經期　參閱 menopause。
(2) 更年期　（男性更年期）男性性慾和生育能力的下降，通常發生於中年前後或以後。

克林黴素　一種用於治療嚴重細菌感染的抗生素。口服。可能具有的副作用為惡心、嘔吐、腹瀉和偶爾有過敏反應。商品名：Dalacin C。

(1) 臨床科室　醫院中從事治療某些專門病症的機構或科室或者醫療保健門診。**(2)** 大查房　在醫院病房裏教師、學生和病人會集在一起旨在對病人進行檢查和治療。

臨床醫師　參閱 community health。

臨床醫學　醫學的一個分支，它涉及對實際病人進行研究，並進行臨床疾病的診斷和治療，這與通過病理學或其他實驗室工作對疾病進行研究相反。

陰蒂切除術　陰蒂的外科切除。參閱 (female) circumcision。

陰蒂　女性的相當於男性陰莖的部分，內含勃起組織（參閱

corpus cavernosum) but is unconnected with the urethra. Like the penis it becomes erect under conditions of sexual stimulation, to which it is very sensitive.

clivus *n*. (in anatomy) a surface that slopes, such as occurs in part of the sphenoid bone.

cloaca *n*. the most posterior part of the embryonic *hindgut. It becomes divided into the rectum and the urinogenital sinus, which receives the bladder together with the urinary and genital ducts.

clofibrate *n*. a drug that reduces the levels of blood lipids, including cholesterol, and is used to treat atherosclerosis and angina. It is administered by mouth; side-effects can include stomach discomfort, nausea, and diarrhoea. Trade name: **Atromid-S**.

Clomid *n*. *see* clomiphene.

clomiphene *n*. a synthetic nonsteroidal compound (*see* anti-oestrogen) that induces ovulation and subsequent menstruation in women who fail to ovulate and is used in the treatment of infertility. It is also used to stimulate ovulation (*see* superovulation) for some procedures of assisted conception (e.g. IVF) and to treat some cases of male infertility. Trade name: **Clomid**.

clomipramine *n*. a drug used to treat various depressive states (*see* antidepressant). It is administered by mouth or injection; common side-effects are dry mouth and blurred vision. Trade name: **Anafranil**.

clonazepam *n*. a drug with *anticonvulsant properties, used to treat epilepsy

corpus cavernosum)，但不與尿道連通。像陰莖一樣，性興奮時勃起。此部位對性刺激非常敏感。

斜坡 （解剖學）一個傾斜的表面，如在蝶骨的一部分中所出現的。

泄殖腔 胚胎期後腸的最後的部分。隨後分成直腸和尿生殖竇。尿生殖竇與膀胱及尿道和生殖管相聯接。

氯貝特 一種減少血脂（包括膽固醇在內）含量的藥物。該藥用於動脈粥樣硬化和心絞痛。口服。副作用包括胃部不適、惡心和腹瀉。商品名：Atromid-S。

氯蔗酚（舒經酚）參閱 clomiphene。

氯米芬 一種合成的非甾類化合物（參閱 anti-oestrogen）。能對不排卵的婦女誘發排卵和隨後的行經。該藥用於治療不孕症。它也用於人工授孕手術中（如 IVF）刺激排卵（參閱 superovulation），以及用於治療一些男性不育症。商品名：Clomid。

氯米帕明（氯丙咪嗪）一種用於治療不同抑鬱狀態的藥物（參閱 antidepressant）。口服或注射。常見副作用包括口乾和視力模糊。商品名：Anafranil。

氯硝西泮 一種具有抗驚厥特性的藥物，用於治療癲癇和其

and other conditions involving seizures. It is administered by mouth or injection; drowsiness is a common sideeffect. Trade name: **Rivotril**.

clone 1. *n.* a group of cells (usually bacteria) descended from a single cell by asexual reproduction and therefore genetically identical to each other and to the parent cell. **2.** *n.* (**gene clone**) a group of identical genes produced by techniques of *genetic engineering. The parent gene is isolated using *restriction enzymes and inserted, via a *cloning vector* (e.g. a bacteriophage), into a bacterium, in which it is replicated. *See also* vector. **3.** *vb.* to form a clone.

clonic *adj.* of, relating to, or resembling clonus. The term is most commonly used to describe the rhythmical limb movements in convulsive *epilepsy.

clonidine *n.* a drug used to treat high blood pressure (hypertension) and migraine. It is administered by mouth or injection and commonly causes drowsiness and dry mouth. Trade names: **Catapres**, **Dixarit**.

clonogenic *adj.* describing a cell capable of producing a colony of cells of a predetermined minimum size. Such a cell is known as a *colony forming unit* (*CFU*).

clonorchiasis *n.* a condition caused by the presence of the fluke *Clonorchis sinensis* in the bile ducts. The infection, common in the Far East, is acquired through eating undercooked, salted, or pickled freshwater fish harbouring the larval stage of the parasite. Symptoms include fever, abdominal pain, diarrhoea, liver enlargement, loss of

他伴有驚厥的疾病。口服或注射。嗜睡是常見的副作用。商品名：Rivotril。

(1) 克隆 通過無性繁殖而由一單一細胞生成的一組細胞羣（通常是細菌）。因此，這些細胞相互之間及與母細胞在遺傳學上相同。**(2) 克隆基因** （基因克隆）通過遺傳工程技術產生的一組相同基因。通過限制酶將親代基因分離，並通過克隆載體（如噬菌體）導入一個細菌裏進行複製（參閱vector）。**(3) 形成克隆**

陣攣性的 與陣攣有關的或類似陣攣的。本術語最常用於描述驚厥性癲癇時肢體有節律的運動。

可樂定 一種治療高血壓和偏頭痛的藥物。口服或注射。常引起嗜睡和口乾。商品名：Catapres，Dixarit。

克隆形成的 描述一種能夠產生預定大小的細胞集羣的細胞。這樣一個細胞被稱為集落形成單位 (CFU)。

支睾吸蟲病 華支睾吸蟲在膽道出現引起的疾病。該病常見於遠東，通過食用帶有寄生蟲幼蟲的未煮熟的、鹹的、或者醃製的淡水魚而引起。症狀包括發熱、腹痛、腹瀉、肝增大、食慾減退、消瘦，而且，在此類病症晚期中，有肝硬化和黃疸。儘管吡喹酮在一些病

appetite, emaciation and – in advanced cases – cirrhosis and jaundice. Treatment is unsatisfactory although *praziquantel has proved beneficial in some cases.

Clonorchis *n.* a genus of liver flukes, common parasites of man and other fish-eating mammals in the Far East. The adults of *C. sinensis* cause clonorchiasis. Eggs are passed out in the stools and the larvae undergo their development in two other hosts, a snail and a fish.

clonus *n.* rhythmical contraction of a muscle in response to a suddenly applied and then sustained stretch stimulus. It is most readily obtained at the ankle when the examiner bends the foot sharply upwards and then maintains an upward pressure on the sole. It is caused by an exaggeration of the stretch reflexes and is usually a sign of disease in the brain or spinal cord.

clopamide *n.* a *diuretic used to treat fluid retention (oedema) and high blood pressure (hypertension). It is administered by mouth and side-effects are uncommon. Trade name: **Viskaldix**.

clorazepate potassium a tranquillizing drug used to relieve anxiety, tension, and agitation. It is administered by mouth; side-effects can include dizziness, digestive upsets, blurred vision, and, occasionally, drowsiness. Trade name: **Tranxene**.

Clostridium *n.* a genus of mostly Gram-positive anaerobic spore-forming rodlike bacteria commonly found in soil and in the intestinal tract of man and animals. Many species cause disease in man and animals and produce extremely potent *exotoxins. *C. botulinum* grows freely in badly preserved canned foods, producing

例中已經證明有效，但治療不滿意。

支睪吸蟲屬 一種肝吸蟲屬，是遠東人類和其他食魚哺乳動物中常見的寄生蟲。華支睪吸蟲的成蟲引起支睪吸蟲病。蟲卵隨糞便排出。幼蟲在其他兩種宿主螺和魚體內經歷其發育過程。

陣攣 肌肉對一突然施加的且然後維持緊張狀態的刺激做出反應的節律收縮。當檢查者將足突然向上扳，並在足底持續加壓時，就可出現這一現象。這是牽張反射過強引起的，而且通常是腦或脊髓疾病的體徵。

氯帕胺 一種利尿藥，用於治療液體瀦留（水腫）和高血壓病。口服。副作用不常見。商品名：Viskaldix。

氯氮草二鉀 一種安定類藥物，用於治療焦慮、緊張和激動。口服。副作用包括頭暈、消化道不適、視力模糊以及偶爾發生嗜睡。商品名：Tranxene。

梭狀芽胞桿菌屬 多數為革蘭氏陽性、厭氧，形成芽胞的桿狀細菌屬，常見於土壤以及人類和動物腸道中。此屬中多種細菌為人類和動物致病菌，且產生極為強烈的外毒素。肉毒梭狀芽胞桿菌在保存不好的罐裝食器裏迅速生長，產生引起

a toxin causing serious food poisoning (*botulism); an extremely dilute form of this toxin is now used to treat muscle spasm (*see* botulinum toxin). *C. histolyticum*, *C. oedematiens*, and *C. septicum* all cause *gas gangrene when they infect wounds. *C. tetani* lives as a harmless *commensal in the intestine of animals and man but causes *tetanus on contamination of wounds (with manured soil). The species *C. perfringens* – Welch's bacillus – causes blood poisoning, *food poisoning, and gas gangrene. Overgrowth of *C. difficile*, a normal inhabitant of the human large intestine, is not uncommon as a complication of some antibiotic therapy and produces a specific condition – *pseudomembranous colitis* – which is life-threatening unless treated promptly.

clotrimazole *n.* an antifungal drug used to treat all types of fungal skin infections (including ringworm) and vaginal infections. It is applied to the infected part as a cream or solution or as vaginal pessaries and occasionally causes mild burning or irritation. Trade name: **Canesten**.

clotting factors *see* coagulation factors.

clotting time *see* coagulation time.

cloxacillin sodium an antibiotic, derived from penicillin, used to treat many bacterial infections. It is administered by mouth or injection; possible side-effects include diarrhoea and hypersensitivity reactions occur in penicillin-sensitive patients. Trade name: **Orbenin**.

clozapine *n.* an *antipsychotic drug used in the treatment of schizophrenia

嚴重食物中毒（肉毒桿菌中毒）的毒素。這種毒素的極大稀釋製劑現已用於治療肌肉痙攣（參閱 botulinum toxin）。當溶組織梭狀芽胞桿菌、水腫梭狀芽胞桿菌及敗血梭狀芽胞桿菌感染傷口時，都能引起氣性壞疽。破傷風梭狀芽胞桿菌作為一種無害的共生菌生存於動物和人類的腸道中，但傷口污染時可引起破傷風（通過澆灌過人糞尿的土壤）。產氣莢膜梭狀芽胞桿菌引起毒血症、食物中毒和氣性壞疽。難辨梭狀芽胞桿菌是人類大腸的普通寄生菌。它的生長過剩是一些抗生素治療的常見結果，且產生一種特有的疾病——假膜性結腸炎，如不立刻予以治療，將危及生命。

克黴唑　一種抗真菌藥，用於治療各種各樣真菌皮膚感染（包括癬）和陰道感染。可製成乳膏劑或溶液或陰道栓劑用於患處。使用該藥偶爾引起輕微灼燒或刺激感。商品名：Canesten。

凝血因子　參閱 coagulation factors。

凝血時間　參閱 coagulation time。

鄰氯青黴素鈉　一種青黴素衍生的抗生素。用於治療許多細菌感染。口服或注射。可能有的副作用包括腹瀉以及對青黴素過敏的病人發生強烈過敏反應。商品名：Orbenin。

氯氮平　一種抗精神病藥物，用於對其他藥物有耐藥性的精

resistant to other drugs. Administered by mouth, it is notable for the absence of tremors and repetitive movements that are associated with other antipsychotic drugs. However, it may seriously affect white blood cell production by the bone marrow and it may cause drowsiness, salivation, fatigue, dizziness, headache, and urinary retention. Trade name: **Clozaril**.

clubbing *n.* thickening of the tissues at the bases of the finger and toe nails so that the normal angle between the nail and the digit is filled in. The nail becomes convex in all directions and in extreme cases the digit end becomes bulbous like a club or drumstick. Clubbing is seen in pulmonary tuberculosis, bronchiectasis, empyema, infective endocarditis, cyanotic congenital heart disease, and lung cancer and as a harmless congenital abnormality.

club-foot (talipes) *n.* a deformity of one or both feet in which the patient cannot stand with the sole of the foot flat on the ground. In the most common variety (*talipes equinovarus*) the foot is twisted downwards and inwards so that the patient walks on the outer edge of the upper surface of his foot. Other varieties are *talipes varus*, in which the sole of the foot is turned inwards, and *talipes valgus*, in which it is twisted outwards. The defect is present at birth and can be corrected by orthopaedic splinting in the early months of infancy. It is more common in male children. It may also occur as a complication of muscular paralysis due to poliomyelitis.

clumping *n. see* agglutination.

cluttering *n.* an erratic unrhythmical way of speaking in rapid jerky bursts. It

神分裂症。口服。明顯的功效在於消除其他抗精神病藥物引起的震顫和重複性動作。然而，它可能通過骨髓嚴重影響白細胞的產生，且可引起嗜睡、流涎、疲勞、頭暈、頭痛和尿液瀦留。商品名：Clozaril。

杵狀變 指或趾基底部組織增厚，以致指（趾）甲與指（趾）之間的正常角度消失。指（趾）甲四面隆起，且在極嚴重病例中，指（趾）端呈球形，像球棒或鼓槌。杵狀變發生於肺結核、支氣管擴張、肺氣腫、感染性心內膜炎、青紫型先天性心臟病和肺癌，也可能是一種無害的先天性畸形。

畸形足 單足或雙足畸形，患者因之不能足底放平站立。在常見的一種形式中（馬蹄內翻足），足向下向內扭轉，因此患者用足背外側邊緣行走。其他類型有內翻足（足底向內翻轉）和外翻足（足底向外翻轉）。這一缺陷是先天的，且可於嬰兒早期用矯形夾板予以糾正。它也可為脊髓灰質炎所致肌肉麻痺的合併症。

凝集 參閱 agglutination。

語言急促 一陣急促的斷續無定沒有節律的講話。它可使語

can make speech hard to understand, and speech therapy is usually helpful. Unlike *stammering, there are no repetitions or prolonged hesitations of speech.

言難以理解。語言療法通常有助於該問題的解決。不像口吃，這一語言障礙沒有語言的重複或者延長的口吃。

Clutton's joint a swollen joint, usually the knee, caused by inflammation of the synovial membranes due to congenital syphilis.

克拉頓關節　一種因先天性梅毒引起的滑膜炎症造成的關節腫脹（通常為膝關節）。

clyster *n.* an old-fashioned term for an *enema.

灌腸法　enema 的舊稱。

CMV *see* cytomegalovirus.

巨細胞病毒　參閱 cytomegalovirus。

CNS *see* central nervous system.

中樞神經系統　參閱 central nervous system。

coagulant *n.* any substance capable of converting blood from a liquid to a solid state. *See* blood coagulation.

促凝劑　任何能將血液從液態轉變為固態的物質。參閱 blood coagulation。

coagulase *n.* an enzyme, formed by disease-producing varieties of certain bacteria of the genus *Staphylococcus*, that causes blood plasma to coagulate. Staphylococci that are positive when tested for coagulase production are classified as belonging to the species *Staphylococcus aureus*.

凝固酶　由一些致病葡萄球菌屬的細菌產生的，能使血漿凝固的酶。凝固酶實驗呈陽性的葡萄球菌被分類為屬於金黃色葡萄球菌。

coagulation *n.* the process by which a colloidal liquid changes to a jelly-like mass. *See* blood coagulation.

凝固　膠態液體轉變成膠凍樣固體的過程。

coagulation factors (clotting factors) a group of substances present in blood plasma that, under certain circumstances, undergo a series of chemical reactions leading to the conversion of blood from a liquid to a solid state (*see* blood coagulation). Although they have specific names, most coagulation factors are

凝血因子　在一定條件下，經歷一系列化學變化，導致血液由液態向固態轉變的一組存在於血漿中的物質（參閱 blood coagulation）。雖然它們有具體的名字，絕大多數凝血因子用一組統一的羅馬數字來表示（如第 VIII 因子，第 IX 因

referred to by an agreed set of Roman numerals (e.g. Factor VIII, Factor IX). Lack of any of these factors in the blood results in the inability of the blood to clot. *See also* haemophilia.

子）。缺乏這些因子的任何一個都會導致凝血障礙。參閱 haemophilia。

coagulation time (clotting time) the time taken for blood or blood plasma to coagulate (*see* blood coagulation). When measured under controlled conditions and using appropriate techniques, coagulation times may be used to test the function of the various stages of the blood coagulation process.

凝血時間 血液或血漿凝固所需要的時間（參閱 blood coagulation）。用適當的技術在控制的條件下進行測量時，凝血時間可用來測試血液凝固過程中不同階段的功能。

coagulum *n.* a mass of coagulated matter, such as that formed when blood clots.

凝塊 凝固的物質團塊，如血液凝固時所形成的團塊。

coalesce *vb.* to grow together or unite. **—coalescence** *n.*

併合 融合或連合。

coal-worker's pneumoconiosis a lung disease caused by coal dust. It affects mainly coal miners but also other exposed workers, such as lightermen, if the lungs' capacity to accommodate and remove the particles is exceeded. *See* pneumoconiosis.

煤礦工人塵肺 由煤塵埃引起的一種疾病。它主要累及煤礦工人，但也累及其他暴露於煤塵的工人，如駁船工人。這種情況是肺臟容納和排除塵埃顆粒的功能超負荷所致。參閱 pneumoconiosis。

coarctation *n.* (of the aorta) a congenital narrowing of a short segment of the aorta. The most common site of coarctation is just beyond the origin of the left subclavian artery from the aorta. This results in high blood pressure (*hypertension) in the upper part of the body and arms and low blood pressure in the legs. The defect is corrected surgically.

縮窄 （主動脈的）縮窄是主動脈一小段的先天性狹窄。最常見的縮窄部位是在左鎖骨下動脈的遠端。結果在軀體上部和上肢引起高血壓，在下肢引起低血壓。這一疾患用手術予以糾正。

cobalamin *n. see* vitamin B₁₂.

鈷胺（素） 參閱 vitamin B₁₂。

cobalt *n.* a metallic element. The artificial radioisotope *cobalt-60*, or *radiocobalt*, is a powerful emitter of gamma radiation

鈷 一種金屬元素。人工放射性同位素 ⁶⁰鈷（或放射性鈷）是一種 γ 放射綫的強大放射

and is used in the radiation treatment of cancer (*see* radiotherapy, telecurietherapy). Cobalt itself forms part of the *vitamin B_{12} molecule. Symbol: Co.

源。用於治療癌症（參閱 radiotherapy，telecurietherapy）。鈷本身構成維生素 B_{12} 分子的一部分。符號：Co。

cobalt-chromium *n.* a silver-coloured nonprecious alloy of cobalt and chromium used for the metal frame of partial *dentures.

鈷鉻合金 一種銀色的非貴重的鈷和鉻的金屬。用於製作部分托牙牷架。

cocaine *n.* an alkaloid that is derived from the leaves of the coca plant (*Erythroxylon coca*) or prepared synthetically and is sometimes used as a local anaesthetic in eye, ear, nose, and throat surgery. It constricts the small blood vessels at the site of application and therefore need not be given with *adrenaline. Since it causes efflings of exhilaration and may lead to psychological *dependence, cocaine has largely been replaced by safer anaesthetics.

可卡因 一種從古柯植物（古柯樹）的葉子中提取的或人工合成的生物鹼。有時用做眼、耳、鼻和喉外科手術的局部麻醉劑。能收縮用藥部位的小血管，因此，不必再給予腎上腺素。因為它可引起欣快感，且可導致心理依賴感，可卡因多被較為安全的麻醉藥所代替。

cocainism *n.* **1.** the habitual use of, or addiction to, *cocaine in order to experience its intoxicating effects. **2.** the mental and physical deterioration resulting from addiction to cocaine.

(1) 可卡因癮 為享受可卡因令人欣快的效果而養成可卡因使用習慣或對之成癮。**(2) 可卡因中毒** 由於對可卡因成癮而導致心理和體質狀態的惡化。

cocarcinogen *n.* a substance that enhances the effect of a *carcinogen.

輔致癌物質 強化致癌物作用的物質。

coccidioidomycosis *n.* an infection caused by inhaling the spores of the fungus *Coccidioides immitis*. In 60% of patients infection produces no symptoms at all. In the primary form there is an influenza-like illness that usually resolves within about eight weeks. In a few patients the disease becomes progressive and resembles tuberculosis. Severe or progressive infections are treated with intravenous injections of amphotericin B. The disease is endemic in the desert areas of the Americas, especially the

球孢子菌病 一種因吸入粗球孢子菌的真菌孢子所致的感染。60% 的病人的感染不產生任何症狀。最初感染時，疾病類似流感，通常大約 8 周之內就可痊愈。在少數病人中疾病變得漸進性，且類似結核病。嚴重或漸進性感染用兩性黴素 B 靜脈注射治療。該疾病在美洲沙漠地帶，特別是在美國西南部、墨西哥北部和阿根廷北部流行。

southwestern United States, northern Mexico, and northern Argentina.

coccobacillus *n.* a rod-shaped bacterium (bacillus) that is so small that it resembles a spherical bacterium (coccus). Examples of such bacteria are *Bacteroides* and *Brucella*.

球桿菌　一種非常小，類似一球形細菌（球菌）的桿狀細菌（桿菌）。如擬桿菌屬和布氏桿菌屬。

coccus *n.* (*pl.* **cocci**) any spherical bacterium. *See also* gonococcus, meningococcus, Micrococcus, pneumococcus, Staphylococcus, Streptococcus.

球菌　任何球形細菌。參閱 gonococcus，meningococcus，Micrococcus，pneumococcus，Staphylococcus，Streptococcus。

coccy- (coccyg-, coccygo-) *prefix denoting* the coccyx. Example: *coccygectomy* (excision of).

〔前綴〕尾　如尾骨切除術。

coccygodynia (coccydynia) *n.* pain in the lowermost segment of the spine (coccyx) and the neighbouring area.

尾骨痛　脊柱最下段（尾骨）和鄰近區域的疼痛。

coccyx *n.* (*pl.* **coccyges** or **coccyxes**) the lowermost element of the *backbone: the vestigial human tail. It consists of four rudimentary *coccygeal vertebrae* fused to form a triangular bone that articulates with the sacrum. *See also* vertebra. **–coccygeal** *adj.*

尾骨　脊椎骨的最下部分：殘留的人尾。它包括融合在一起形成一塊三角形骨的四塊退化的骨。這一三角形骨與骶骨關節連接。參閱 vertebra。

cochlea *n.* the spiral organ of the *labyrinth of the ear, which is concerned with the reception and analysis of sound. As vibrations pass from the middle ear through the cochlea, different frequencies cause particular regions of the basilar membrane to vibrate: high notes cause vibration in the region nearest the middle ear; low notes cause vibration in the region nearest the tip of the spiral. The *organ of Corti*, which lies within a central triangular membrane-bound canal (*scala media* or *cochlear duct*), contains sensory hair cells attached to an overlying *tectorial membrane* (see

耳蝸　耳迷路中的螺旋形器官，它負責聲音的接收和分析。當震動由中耳傳播穿過耳蝸時，不同的頻率使得基膜的不同部位震動。高音引起距中耳最近的區域震動，而低音引起耳蝸頂部最近區域的震動。位於中心呈三角形膜性管道（中階或蝸管）中的柯蒂器含有附着於上方蓋膜（見圖）的感覺性毛細胞。當基膜震動時，感覺細胞就變形，並將神經衝動通過耳蝸神經傳向大腦。

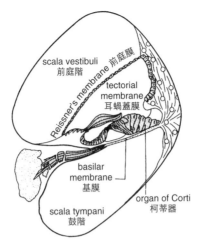

scala vestibuli
前庭階

Reissners membrane 前庭膜

tectorial
membrane
耳蝸蓋膜

basilar
membrane
基膜

organ of Corti
柯蒂器

scala tympani
鼓階

Section through a turn of the cochlea
耳蝸經螺旋切面

illustration). When the basilar membrane vibrates the sensory cells become distorted and send nerve impulses to the brain via the *cochlear nerve. **–cochlear** *adj.*

cochlear duct (scala media) *see* cochlea.

蝸管（中階）　參閱 cochlea。

cochlear implant a device to improve the hearing of profoundly deaf people who derive no benefit from conventional *hearing aids. It consists of an electrode that is permanently implanted into the inner ear (*cochlea). An external device with a microphone and an electronic processing unit passes information to the electrode using radio-frequency waves. The implant is powered by batteries in the external part of the device.

人工耳蝸　一種改善重度耳聾人聽力的裝置。這些人使用傳統的助聽器無效。這種耳蝸由一永久植入內耳（耳蝸）的一根電極組成。一個帶有麥克風和電子傳送元件的外部裝置用無綫頻率波將信息傳向電極。通過外部裝置的電池供給電源。

cochlear nerve the nerve connecting the cochlea to the brain and therefore responsible for the nerve impulses

耳蝸神經　將耳蝸與大腦連接起來，並因而負責傳導與聽覺有關的神經衝動的神經。它構

relating to hearing. It forms part of the *vestibulocochlear nerve (cranial nerve VIII).

成前庭耳蝸神經（第 VIII 對腦神經）的一部分。

codeine *n.* an *analgesic derived from morphine but less potent as a pain-killer and sedative and less toxic. It is administered by mouth or injection to relieve pain and also to suppress coughs. Common side-effects include constipation, nausea, vomiting, dizziness, and drowsiness, but *dependence is uncommon.

可待因　一種從嗎啡提取的止痛藥，但作為鎮痛和鎮靜藥作用較小，毒性較輕。口服或注射以止痛，也用以鎮咳。常見副作用包括便秘、惡心、嘔吐、頭暈和嗜睡，但依賴性較少見。

Codman's triangle the characteristic X-ray appearance of *Ewing's sarcoma: a triangular area on the surface of the bone resulting from elevation of the *periosteum by malignant tissue, the extremes forming an angle with the normal bony cortex.

科德曼三角　尤因瘤的典型 X 綫表像：骨表面的一個三角形區域。這是由於惡性組織引起的骨膜升高，其遠端與正常骨皮質構成三角而引起的。

codon *n.* the unit of the *genetic code that determines the synthesis of one particular amino acid. Each codon consists of a section of the DNA molecule, and the order of the codons along the molecule determines the order of amino acids in each protein made in the cell.

密碼子　決定一個特定氨基酸合成的遺傳密碼單位。每個密碼子由 DNA 分子的片斷組成。而且，分子中密碼子的排列順序決定了細胞中合成的每個蛋白中氨基酸的排列順序。

-coele *suffix denoting* **1.** a body cavity. Example: *blastocoele* (cavity of blastocyst). **2.** *see* -cele.

〔後綴〕**(1)** 體腔　如囊腔。**(2)** 疝，膨出瘤　腫大（參閱 -cele）。

coeli- (coelio-) *prefix denoting* the abdomen or belly. Example: *coeliectasia* (abnormal distension of).

〔前綴〕腹，腹腔　如腹脹（腹部異常脹大）。

coeliac *adj.* of or relating to the abdominal region. The *coeliac trunk* is a branch of the abdominal *aorta supplying the stomach, spleen, liver, and gall bladder.

腹部的　屬於或與腹部有關的。腹腔幹是向胃、脾、肝臟和膽囊供血的腹主動脈的分支。

coeliac disease a condition in which the small intestine fails to digest and

麥膠過敏性腸病　一種小腸不能消化和吸收食物的疾病。

absorb food. Affecting 0.1–0.2% of the population (but much more common is SW Ireland), it is due to a permanent sensitivity of the intestinal lining to the protein gliadin, which is contained in *gluten in the germ of wheat and rye and causes atrophy of the digestive and absorptive cells of the intestine. Symptoms include stunted growth, distended abdomen, and pale frothy foul-smelling stools; the disease can be diagnosed by *biopsy of the jejunum and is treated successfully by a strict and lifelong gluten-free diet. Medical name: **gluten enteropathy**.

該病波及 0.1%~0.2% 的人口（但在愛爾蘭西南部更為常見）。它是由小腸黏膜對含於小麥和黑麥胚芽穀蛋白內的麥膠蛋白的永久性過敏引起的，且引起腸的消化和吸收細胞萎縮。症狀包括生長發育障礙、腹脹、蒼白色多泡沫惡臭的大便。此病可通過空腸組織活檢予以診斷，嚴格的終身不含穀蛋白的膳食可成功地治療此症。醫學用語：非熱帶性口炎性腹瀉。

coelioscopy n. the technique of introducing an *endoscope through an incision in the abdominal wall to examine the intestines and other organs within the abdominal cavity.

體腔鏡檢查 一種將內窺鏡通過腹壁切口插入以檢查腹腔內腸和其他器官的技術。

coelom n. the cavity in an embryo between the two layers of mesoderm. It develops into the body cavity.

原始體腔 胚胎期兩層中胚層之間的腔隙。以後發展成為體腔。

coenzyme n. a nonprotein organic compound that, in the presence of an *enzyme, plays an essential role in the reaction that is catalysed by the enzyme. Coenzymes, which frequently contain the B vitamins in their molecular structure, include *coenzyme A, *FAD, and *NAD.

輔酶 一種非蛋白有機化合物。在有酶存在的情況下，它對該酶所催化的反應起着重要的作用。輔酶常常在其分子結構中含有維生素 B 族。輔酶包括輔酶 A、黃素腺嘌呤二核苷酸和烟酰胺腺嘌呤二核苷酸。

coenzyme A a *nucleotide containing pantothenic acid, which is an important coenzyme in the Krebs cycle and in the metabolism of fatty acids.

輔酶 A 一種含有泛酸的核苷是三羧酸椒環和脂肪代謝中的一種重要的輔酶。

cofactor n. a nonprotein substance that must be present in suitable amounts before certain *enzymes can act. Cofactors include *coenzymes and metal ions (e.g. sodium and potassium ions).

輔因子 某些酶發生作用前必須從適量存在的一種非蛋白質物質。輔因子包括輔酶和金屬離子（如鈉和鉀離子）。

cognition *n.* the mental processes by which knowledge is acquired. These include perception, reasoning, acts of creativity, problem-solving, and possibly intuition. *Compare* conation.

cognitive psychology the branch of psychology concerned with all human activities relating to knowledge. More specifically, cognitive psychology is concerned with how knowledge is acquired, stored, correlated, and retrieved, by studying the mental processes underlying attention, concept formation, information processing, memory, and speech (*psycholinguistics*). Cognitive psychology views the brain as an information-processing system operating on, and storing, the data acquired by the senses. It investigates this function by experiments designed to measure and analyse human performance in carrying out a wide range of mental tasks. The data obtained allows possible models of the underlying mental processes to be constructed. These models do not purport to represent the actual physiological activity of the brain. Nevertheless, as they are refined by testing and criticism, it is hoped that they may approach close to reality and gradually lead to a clearer understanding of how the brain operates.

cognitive therapy a form of *psychotherapy based on the belief that psychological problems are the products of faulty ways of thinking about the world. For example, a depressed patient may have come to see him- or herself as powerless to change in any way. The therapist assists the patient to identify these false ways of thinking and to avoid them.

cohort study (longitudinal study, prospective study) a systematic follow-up

認識　知識被獲得的精神過程。包括知覺、推理、創造活動、解決問題和可能具有的直覺。與 conation 對比。

認識心理學　心理學涉及與知識有關的一切人類活動的一個分支學科。更具體地講，認識心理學涉及知識是如何獲得、貯存、相互關聯和恢復的。這一切需通過研究注意、概念的形成、信息處理、記憶和語言（心理語言學）這些活動的基本意識過程來了解。認識心理學將大腦看成是運轉的並進行貯存的信息處理系統，信息是通過感覺獲得的。通過測定和分析人類在執行廣泛意識活動任務的表現而設計的實驗來研究這一功能。所獲得的信息使得構築基本的意識過程的模型成為可能。這些模型並不意味着要表現大腦的實際的生理活動。不管怎麼樣，隨着這些模型通過實驗和校正而改進，人們希望這些模型可能接近現實，且漸漸引向更清楚地了解大腦是如何運轉的。

認知療法　一種心理療法，建立在心理障礙是思維方法錯誤這一基礎上。例如，一個抑鬱型的病人可能發展到把自己看成無論從那方面都沒有能力進行改變。治療者幫助患者認識到這些錯誤的思維方法並且避免它們。

隊列性研究（縱向研究，前瞻性研究）　對一組病人在一定時

of a group of people for a defined period of time or until the occurrence of a specified event (e.g. onset of illness, retirement, or death) in order to observe their pattern of disease and/or cause of death. On the basis of factors prevailing at the outset of the study or arising during the period of follow-up, two or more separate cohorts may be identified and compared in relation to outcome.

期內或直到一具體事件的發生為止而進行的系統性的隨訪研究，以觀察其疾病譜和／或死亡的原因。根據研究開始時表現的或者在隨訪期間出現的因素，可識別兩個或更多隊列，對結果進行比較。

coitus (sexual intercourse, copulation) *n.* sexual contact between a man and a woman during which the erect penis enters the vagina and is moved within it by pelvic thrusts until *ejaculation occurs. *See also* orgasm. **–coital** *adj.*

性交 男女之間發生的性行為。在此期間，勃起的陰莖插入陰道，並通過骨盆的推進在其內運動，直至射精發生。參閱 orgasm。

coitus interruptus a contraceptive method in which the penis is removed from the vagina before ejaculation of semen (orgasm). The method is unreliable (10–20 pregnancies per 100 woman-years) and it may lead to sexual disharmony and anxiety in one or both partners.

中斷性交 一種避孕方法。在精液射出之前將陰莖拔出陰道。這一方法不可靠（每年每一百名婦女中有 10~20 次懷孕發生），而且可導致性生活不協調和單方或雙方出現焦慮。

col- (coli-, colo-) *prefix denoting* the colon. Example: *coloptosis* (prolapse of).

〔前綴〕**結腸** 如腸下垂。

colchicine *n.* a drug obtained from the meadow saffron (*Colchicum autumnale*), used to relieve pain in attacks of gout and in the prevention of attacks of polyserositis. It is administered by mouth; common side-effects are nausea, vomiting, diarrhoea, and stomach pains.

秋水仙鹼 一種從秋水仙屬提取的藥物，用於痛風發作時止痛，以及預防多漿膜炎的發作。口服。常見副作用為惡心、嘔吐、腹瀉和胃痛。

cold (common cold) *n.* a widespread infectious virus disease causing inflammation of the mucous membranes of the nose, throat, and bronchial tubes. The disease is transmitted by coughing and sneezing. Symptoms commence 1–2 days after infection and include a sore throat,

感冒 一種廣泛存在的傳染性病毒病。它引起鼻、喉和支氣管的黏膜發炎。該疾病通過咳嗽和打噴嚏傳播。症狀在感染 1~2 天之後開始出現，包括咽痛、鼻塞或流鼻涕、頭痛、咳嗽和全身不適。該病較輕，持

stuffy or runny nose, headache, cough, and general malaise. The disease is mild and lasts only about a week but it can prove serious to young babies and to patients with a pre-existing respiratory complaint.

續僅約一周，但對嬰兒和有呼吸道疾患的病人可能是非常嚴重的。

cold sore *see* herpes.

唇疱疹 參閱 herpes。

colectomy *n.* surgical removal of the colon. *Total colectomy* is removal of the whole colon, usually for extensive *colitis; partial colectomy* is removal of a segment of the colon. *See also* hemicolectomy, proctocolectomy.

結腸切除術 結腸的外科切除。全結腸切除術是將結腸全部切除，通常是為治療彌漫性結腸炎而採取此法。部分結腸切除是切除結腸的一段。參閱 hemicolectomy，proto-colectomy。

colestipol *n.* a drug used, in conjunction with dietary reduction of cholesterol, to lower *cholesterol levels in the blood in patients with primary hypercholesterolaemia. It binds bile acids, forming a complex that is excreted in the faeces. The reduction in bile acids causes cholesterol to be oxidized to bile acids, decreases low-density *lipoprotein serum levels, and decreases serum cholesterol levels. It is administered by mouth; side-effects include headache, constipation, and abdominal discomfort. Trade name: **Colestid**.

考來替泊 與減少飲食中膽固醇聯用以降低原發性高膽固醇血症病人血中膽固醇含量的一種藥物。它與膽酸結合，形成一種複合物，從糞便裏排泄掉。膽酸的降低引起膽固醇氧化成為膽酸，降低了低密度脂蛋白血清的含量。口服。副作用包括頭疼、便秘和腹部不適。商品名：Colestid。

colic *n.* severe abdominal pain, usually of fluctuating severity, with waves of pain seconds or a few minutes apart. *Infantile colic* is common among babies, due to wind in the intestine associated with feeding difficulties. *Intestinal colic* is due to partial or complete obstruction of the intestine or to constipation. Colic arising from the small intestine is felt in the upper abdomen; colic from the colon is felt in the lower abdomen. Medical names: **enteralgia**, **tormina**. *See also* biliary colic.

絞痛 嚴重的腹痛，通常疼痛嚴重程度呈現波動性變化、每隔幾秒鐘或幾分鐘疼痛就一陣陣發作。嬰兒腹絞痛在嬰兒中常見，這是由於與餵飼困難有關的腸內脹氣引起的。腸絞痛是由於腸的部分或完全阻塞所致或由於便秘所致。來源於小腸的絞痛出現於上腹部；來自於結腸的絞痛出現於下腹部。醫學用語：腸痛、絞痛。參閱 biliary colic。

coliform bacteria a group of Gram-negative rodlike bacteria that are normally found in the gastrointestinal tract and have the ability to ferment the sugar lactose. The group includes the genera *Enterobacter*, **Escherichia*, and **Klebsiella*.

大腸桿菌群　一組革蘭氏陰性桿狀細菌。正常情況下存在於胃腸道，並具有使乳糖發酵的能力。這一組細菌包括腸桿菌屬、埃希桿菌屬和克雷白菌屬。

colistin *n*. an **antibiotic administered by mouth to treat gastroenteritis and other bacterial infections. Colistin is a mixture of antimicrobial substances produced by a strain of the bacterium *Bacillus polymyxa*. Trade name: **Colomycin**.

多黏菌素 E　一種口服抗生素，用於治療胃腸炎和其他細菌感染。多黏菌素 E 是多黏芽胞桿菌菌株產生的抗菌物質的混合物。商品名：Colomycin。

colitis *n*. inflammation of the colon. The usual symptoms are diarrhoea, sometimes with blood and mucus, and lower abdominal pain. It is diagnosed by demonstrating inflammation of the colon's lining (mucosa) by **sigmoidoscopy or barium **enema X-ray. Colitis may be due to infection by **Entamoeba histolytica* (*amoebic colitis*) or by bacteria (*infective colitis*); it may also occur in **Crohn's disease (*Crohn's colitis*). Partial or temporary cessation of blood supply to the colon may cause *ischaemic colitis*. *Ulcerative colitis* (*idiopathic proctocolitis*) almost always involves the rectum (*see* proctitis) as well as a varying amount of the colon, which become inflamed and ulcerated. Its cause is unknown. It varies in severity from month to month, relapses being treated by drugs, including corticosteroids and drugs containing 5-aminosalicylic acid (sulphasalazine, mesalazine, and olsalazine, as tablets or enemas), and bed rest. Severe, continuous, or extensive colitis may be treated by surgery (*see* colectomy, proctocolectomy). Diarrhoea or pain where inflammation is absent is often due to *mucous colitis* (*see* irritable bowel syndrome).

結腸炎　結腸的炎症。通常症狀為腹瀉，有時伴有血和黏液以及下腹部疼痛。本病可通過乙狀結腸鏡或鋇劑灌腸 X 綫檢查結腸黏膜的炎症來得以診斷。結腸炎可能由於溶組織內阿米巴（阿米巴性結腸炎）或細菌（傳染性結腸炎）的感染引起，該病也可發生於克羅恩病（克羅恩結腸炎）。結腸的血液供應部分或暫時的停止可引起缺血性結腸炎。潰瘍性結腸炎（特發性直腸炎）幾乎總是侵犯直腸與不同長度的結腸，使之發炎和形成潰瘍。原因不明，嚴重程度逐月變化，復發時可用藥物治療，包括皮質類固醇和含有 5-氨基水楊酸的藥物（柳氮磺胺吡啶、美沙拉嗪、奧沙拉嗪等用作片劑或灌腸劑）以及卧床休息。嚴重、持續或彌漫性結腸炎可用外科手術予以治療（參閱 colectomy，proctocolectomy）。出現腹瀉或疼痛但無炎症存在時，常為黏液性結腸炎（參閱 irritable bowel syndrome）。

collagen *n.* a protein that is the principal constituent of white fibrous connective tissue (as occurs in tendons). Collagen is also found in skin, bone, cartilage, and ligaments. It is relatively inelastic but has a high tensile strength.

膠原　一種蛋白，是白色纖維性結締組織的主要成分（如腱中），膠原還存在於皮膚、骨、軟骨和韌帶中。其彈性較小，但具有極強的可伸力。

collagen disease an obsolete term for *connective-tissue disease.

膠原病　結締組織病的舊名。

collar bone *see* clavicle.

鎖骨　參閱 clavicle。

collateral 1. *adj.* accessory or secondary. **2.** *n.* a branch (e.g. of a nerve fibre) that is at right angles to the mainpart.

(1) 副的，次要的　(2) 側方橫向分支　如某一神經纖維的分支。

collateral circulation 1. an alternative route provided for the blood by secondary vessels when a primary vessel becomes blocked. **2.** the channels of communication between the blood vessels supplying the heart. At the apex of the heart, where the coronary arteries form *anastomoses, these are very complex.

(1) 側支循環　當某一主要血管被阻塞後由次要的血管構成血液供應的替代路綫。**(2) 心臟血管間交通支**　向心臟供血的血管間交通系統。在冠狀動脈吻合的心尖部，這些系統非常複雜。

Colles' fracture a fracture just above the wrist, across the lower end of the *radius, usually caused by a fall on the outstretched hand. The hand and wrist below the fracture are displaced backwards. The bone is restored to its normal position under anaesthesia, and a plaster slab is applied. The fracture usually unites within six weeks. *Malunion is a common complication, resulting in deformity.

科利斯骨折　手腕上部、越過橈骨下端的骨折。通常是由於手外伸時跌倒而引起。骨折下方的手和腕部向後移位。在麻醉下使骨恢復到其正常位置，並使用石膏夾板。骨折通常在6周內愈合。骨接合不正是一常見併發症。產生畸形。

colliculus *n.* (*pl.* **colliculi**) a small protuberance or swelling. Two pairs of colliculi, the *superior* and *inferior colliculi*, protrude from the roof of the midbrain (*see* tectum).

丘，小阜　一個微小的隆凸。中腦的兩對小丘：上丘和下丘從腦室頂部向前凸出（參閱 tectum）。

collimation *n.* the production of a thin parallel-sided beam of radiation by

準直　通過調節光綫路徑上不同點的縫隙以產生細而平行的

means of adjustable slits placed at strategic points along the beam. A collimated beam of radiation is necessary in the technique of scintigraphy (when an organ is scanned for radioactivity; *see* scintigram) and also in radiotherapy.

放射光束。準直光束在閃爍法技術（當一器官被掃描檢查放射性時；參閱 scintigram）和放射療法中是必需的。

collodion *n.* a syrupy solution of nitrocellulose in a mixture of alcohol and ether. When applied to the surface of the body it evaporates to leave a thin clear transparent skin, useful for the protection of minor wounds. Flexible collodion also contains camphor and castor oil, which allow the skin to stretch a little more.

火棉膠 溶於酒精和乙醚混合物中的硝基纖維素糖漿樣溶液。當本品被塗抹於體表面時，揮發後留下一層透明的薄膜。這層薄膜有益於保護小傷口。彈性火棉膠含有樟腦和蓖麻油，這可使皮膚伸展稍大點。

collyrium *n.* a medicated solution used to bathe the eyes.

洗眼劑 一種用於清洗眼的藥液。

coloboma *n.* a defect in the development of the eye causing abnormalities ranging in severity from a notch in the lower part of the iris, making the pupil pear-shaped, to defects behind the iris in the *fundus. The enlarged pupil causes dazzle symptoms. A coloboma of the eyelid is a congenital notch in the lid margin.

缺損 一種引起畸形的眼生長發育缺陷。嚴重程度不等，從虹膜下部出現切迹使瞳孔呈梨形，到眼底虹膜後部的缺陷。擴大的瞳孔可引起眩目症狀。眼瞼缺損是瞼緣的一種先天性切迹。

colon *n.* the main part of the large intestine, which consists of four sections – the *ascending*, *transverse*, *descending*, and *sigmoid colons* (see illustration). The colon has no digestive function but it absorbs large amounts of water and electrolytes from the undigested food passed on from the small intestine. At intervals strong peristaltic movements move the dehydrated contents (faeces) towards the rectum. **–colonic** *adj.*

結腸 大腸的主要部分，包括四個部分——升結腸、橫結腸、降結腸和乙狀結腸（見圖）。結腸沒有消化功能，但能吸收來自小腸的未消化的食物中的大量水分。強有力的間斷蠕動性運動把已失水的腸內容物（糞便）推向直腸。

colonic irrigation washing out the contents of the large bowel by means of

結腸灌洗術 使用大量灌腸劑把大腸內容物洗出，可用水

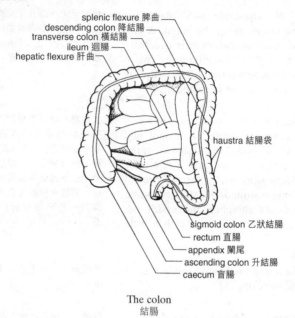

splenic flexure 脾曲
descending colon 降結腸
transverse colon 橫結腸
ileum 迴腸
hepatic flexure 肝曲

haustra 結腸袋

sigmoid colon 乙狀結腸
rectum 直腸
appendix 闌尾
ascending colon 升結腸
caecum 盲腸

The colon
結腸

copious enemas, using either water, with or without soap, or other medication.

（加或不加肥皂）或用其他藥物。

colonoscopy *n.* a procedure for examining the interior of the entire colon and rectum using a flexible illuminated *fibreoptic or video-camera instrument (*colonoscope*) introduced through the anus and guided up the colon by a combination of visual and X-ray control. It is possible to obtain specimens for microscopic examination using flexible forceps passed through the colonoscope and to remove polyps using a *diathermy snare.

結腸鏡檢查 檢查全部結腸和直腸內壁的一種技術，用可彎曲並帶有光源的光學纖維或可視照相器械（結腸鏡），通過肛門，靠目視結合 X 綫控制導向結腸。使用可彎曲的鉗子，通過結腸鏡能獲得顯微鏡檢標本，也可用燒灼圈套器切除息肉。

colony *n.* a discrete population or mass of microorganisms, usually bacteria, all of which are considered to have developed from a single parent cell. Bacterial colonies that grow on agar plates differ in shape, size, colour, elevation,

菌落 一稀疏的微生物（通常指細菌）羣體或羣落，其中所有細菌都來自一個親代細胞。由於菌種的原因，生長在瓊脂平板上的細菌菌落在形狀、大小、顏色、厚度、透明度和表

translucency, and surface texture, depending on the species. This is used as a means of identification. *See also* culture.

面結構不盡相同。這些均可作為鑒定之用。參閱 culture。

colony-stimulating factor (CSF) one of a group of substances (haemopoietic growth factors or hormones) that are produced in the bone marrow and stimulate the production of specific blood cells. Genetically engineered granulocyte colony-stimulating factor (G-CSF) stimulates neutrophil production and also limits bone marrow toxicity from chemotherapy.

細胞集落刺激因子 骨髓內產生的並能刺激產生某種血細胞的一組物質（血細胞生長因子或激素）。基因工程粒細胞集落刺激因子 (G-CSF) 刺激中性粒細胞的產生，並減少來自化療對骨髓的毒性。

colorimeter *n.* an instrument for determining the concentration of a particular compound in a preparation by comparing the intensity of colour in it with that in a standard preparation of known concentration. The instrument is used particularly for measuring the amount of haemoglobin in the blood.

比色計 一種測定某一製劑中某一化合物濃度的儀器。其方法為將該製劑的色度與已知濃度的標準製劑的色度進行比較。這一儀器特別用於測定血中血紅蛋白的含量。

colostomy *n.* a surgical operation in which a part of the colon is brought through the abdominal wall and opened in order to drain or decompress the intestine. The part of the colon chosen depends on the site of obstruction. An *iliac colostomy* opens onto the left lower abdomen; a *transverse colostomy* on the upper abdomen. The colostomy may be temporary, eventually being closed after weeks or months to restore continuity; or permanent, usually when the rectum or lower colon has been removed. An appliance is usually worn over the colostomy opening (*stoma) to prevent soiling the clothes.

結腸造口術 將部分結腸通過腹壁拉出進行造口以對腸進行引流或減壓的外科手術。所選的結腸部分取決於梗阻部位。迴腸造口術開口於左下腹。橫結腸造口術開口於上腹部。結腸造口可以是暫時的，在數周或數月後縫合以恢復腸管通路。也可是永久性的，通常是當直腸或下段結腸被切除後。通常將一裝置覆蓋於結腸開口處（口）以防糞便污染衣物。

colostrum *n.* the first secretion from the breast, occurring shortly after, or sometimes before, birth prior to the secretion

初乳 分娩後或有時在分娩前在真正乳液分泌之前的乳房最初的分泌物。它是一種比較清

of true milk. It is a relatively clear fluid containing serum, white blood cells, and protective antibodies.

colour blindness any of various conditions in which certain colours are confused with one another. True lack of colour appreciation is extremely rare (*see* monochromat), but some defect of colour discrimination is present in about 8% of Caucasian males, and 0.4% of Caucasian females. The most common type of colour blindness is *Daltonism* (*protanopia*) – red-blindness – in which the person cannot distinguish between reds and greens. Occasional cases are due to acquired disease of the retina but in the vast majority it is inherited. The defect is thought to be in the functioning of the light-sensitive cells in the retina responsible for colour perception (*see* cone). *See also* deuteranopia, trichromatic.

colp- (colpo-) *prefix denoting* the vagina. Example: *colpoplasty* (plastic surgery of).

colpoperineorrhaphy *n.* an operation to repair tears in the vagina and the muscles surrounding its opening, particularly posteriorly.

colporrhaphy *n.* an operation designed to remove lax and redundant vaginal tissue and so reduce the diameter of the vagina in cases of prolapse of the anterior vaginal wall (*anterior colporrhaphy*) or posterior vaginal wall (*see* proctocele) (*posterior colporrhaphy*).

colposcope (vaginoscope) *n.* an instrument that is inserted into the vagina and permits visual examination of the cervix and the upper part of the vagina (vaginal vault). It is used in the

亮的液體，含有血清、白細胞和保護性抗體。

色盲 把某一顏色與另一顏色相互混淆的任一疾病。完全缺乏識別顏色能力是極為少見的（參閱 monochromat），但部分缺乏顏色識別能力在男性白種人中約占 8%。在女性白種人中約占 0.4%。最常見的色盲類型為紅綠色盲（紅色盲）。患者不能分辨紅色和綠色。偶然有些色盲病例是由於視網膜疾患，但大多數色盲是遺傳的。負責感知顏色的視網膜的感光細胞功能缺陷被認為是該疾病的原因（參閱 cone）。參閱 deuteranopia，trichromatic。

〔前綴〕**陰道** 如陰道成形術。

陰道會陰縫合術 一種修補陰道和陰道口周圍，特別是其後部肌肉裂傷的手術。

陰道縫合術 一種切除鬆弛多餘陰道組織的手術，在陰道前壁脫垂（前陰道縫合術）或者陰道後壁脫垂（參閱 proctocele）（後陰道縫合術）的情形下，其結果減小了陰道的直徑。

陰道鏡 一種插入陰道的器械，使其能在直視下檢查宮頸和陰道上部（陰道穹窿）。它用於診斷宮頸惡性變前或早期惡性（非侵襲性）變。

diagnosis of premalignant and early malignant (noninvasive) changes in the cervix. –**colposcopy** *n*.

colposuspension *n*. a surgical operation in which the upper part of the vaginal wall is fixed to the anterior abdominal wall by unabsorbable suture material. Performed through an abdominal incision, this sling operation is used in the surgical treatment of prolapse of the vaginal wall, particularly when stress incontinence exists. *See also* Stamey procedure.

陰道懸吊術　用不能吸收的縫綫把陰道壁的上部固定於腹壁前部的一種外科手術。手術通過腹部切口進行。這一懸吊性手術用於治療陰道壁脱垂的外科治療，特別是當壓迫性尿失禁存在時。參閱 Stamey procedure。

colpotomy *n*. an incision made into the wall of the vagina, usually the posterior vaginal wall, close to the cervix (*posterior colpotomy*). This was formerly used to confirm the diagnosis of ectopic pregnancy, but has now been largely superseded by *laparoscopy. Colpotomy is sometimes referred to as *culdocentesis*.

陰道切開術　將陰道壁切開的手術，通常切開靠近宮頸的陰道壁後部（後穹窿切開術）。這一手術過去被用來證實異位妊娠。但現在卻已被腹腔鏡檢查所代替。陰道切開術有時稱作後穹窿穿刺術。

columella *n*. (in anatomy) a part resembling a small column. For example, the *columella cochleae* (*modiolus*) is the central pillar of the cochlea, around which the spiral cochlear canal winds. The *columella nasi* is the anterior part of the nasal septum.

小柱，軸　（解剖學）類似一個小柱狀的部分。如耳蝸軸（蝸軸）就是耳蝸的中央柱，螺旋狀的耳蝸管沿其盤繞。鼻柱是鼻中隔的前部。

column *n*. (in anatomy) any pillar-shaped structure, especially any of the tracts of grey matter found in the spinal cord.

柱　（解剖學）任何柱狀結構，尤指脊髓中的灰質束。

coma *n*. a state of unrousable unconsciousness. *See also* Glasgow scoring system.

昏迷　不能喚醒的意識喪失狀態。參閱 Glasgow scoring system。

comedo *n*. (*pl.* **comedones**) *see* blackhead.

粉刺　參閱 blackhead。

commando operation a major operation performed to remove a malignant tumour from the head and neck. Extensive dissection, often involving the face,

頭頸部清除術　切除頭頸部惡性腫瘤的大手術。廣泛性切除（常累及面部）後要隨之進行整形以恢復功能和面容。

is followed by reconstruction to restore function and cosmetic acceptability.

commensal *n.* an organism that lives in close association with another of a different species without either harming or benefiting it. For example, some microorganisms living in the gut obtain both food and a suitable habitat but neither harm nor benefit man. *Compare* symbiosis. **–commensalism** *n.*

共生體　與另一不同種的生物共同生活，並對之不產生任何利害影響的生物體。例如，一些生活於腸道的微生物獲得食物和一合適的生活環境，但對人既無益處又無害處。與symbiosis 對比。

comminuted fracture a fracture in which the bone is broken into more than two pieces. A crushing force is usually responsible and there is often extensive injury to surrounding soft tissues.

粉碎性骨折　一種骨被折成兩塊以上的骨折。通常由擠壓性壓力所致，而且經常對周圍軟組織有廣泛損傷。

commissure *n.* **1.** a bundle of nerve fibres that crosses the midline of the central nervous system, often connecting similar structures on each side. **2.** any other tissue connecting two similar structures.

連合　**(1)** 穿越中樞神經系統中綫，且常連接兩側同樣結構的神經纖維索。**(2)** 任何其他連接兩個同樣結構的組織。

communicable disease (contagious disease, infectious disease) any disease that can be transmitted from one person to another. This may occur by direct physical contact, by common handling of an object that has picked up infective microorganisms (*see* fomes), through a disease *carrier, or by spread of infected droplets coughed or exhaled into the air. The most dangerous communicable disease are on the list of *notifiable diseases.

傳染病　任何能從一人傳播給另一個人的疾病。可通過以下方法發生：直接身體接觸，共同使用某一已染傳染微生物的物體（參閱 fomes），疾病攜帶者咳出或呼出的傳染性飛沫均可傳染。最危險的傳染病被列在法定傳染病名單上。

communicable disease control *see* public health physician.

傳染病控制　參閱 public health physician。

communicans *adj.* communicating or connecting. The term is applied particularly to blood vessels or nerve fibres connecting two similar structures.

交通的　聯繫或連接。本術語特別用於指連接兩個類似結構的血管或神經纖維。

community dentistry the branch of NHS dentistry under the control of the health authorities. It has been principally concerned with the treatment of children, but now also treats priority groups. Its staff, who may be part-time, are generally salaried for this aspect of their work.

community health preventive services, mainly outside the hospital, involving the surveillance of special groups of the population, such as preschool and school children, women, and the elderly, by means of routine clinical assessment and *screening tests. Routine preventive measures, such as immunization, birth control, and dietary advice, are offered in special clinics staffed by *community nurses and subconsultant grades of doctors (*clinical medical officers* and *senior clinical medical officers*) and sometimes by *community paediatricians employed by Health Authorities. When somebody is identified as having an illness, he (or she) is referred for treatment to a *general practitioner or hospital as appropriate. *See also* child health clinic, community dentistry, school health service.

Community Health Council (CHC) (in Britain) a group of local residents (usually one per district) appointed to voice the views of patients in relation to the *National Health Service. Serviced by a salaried secretary, these Councils have no executive power but their views must be sought by District Health Authorities (DHA) on all matters that affect the provision of health services in the district. The DHA must also receive and consider the annual report of each CHC within its district. Members of a CHC may pay site visits to hospitals or

社區牙醫公會 衛生當局領導下的國民保健服務制牙醫界的一個分支組織。它過去主要關注兒童牙科疾病的治療，但現在也優先治療羣體病人。其工作人員可能是兼職的，通常對其這方面的工作給予工資。

社區衛生保健 主要為醫院外預防服務。涉及通過常規臨床檢查和篩查來對人羣中的特殊羣體進行監查，如學前和學齡兒童、婦女和老人。常規的預防措施，如免疫接種、計劃生育、飲食咨詢等，都由專科門診機構提供。其工作人員由社區保健護士和主治醫師（臨床醫師和高級臨床醫師）組成，有時由衛生當局僱傭的社區兒科醫師組成。當查出某人有病時，則將他（或她）轉診給一個全科醫師或相應的醫院。參閱 child health clinic，community dentistry，school health service。

社區衛生委員會 （英國）由當地提名的居民（通常為一個地段一個代表）組成的一個羣體。其職能是傳達患者對國民保健服務制的意見。在該組織任職的幹部享受月工資待遇，但這些機構沒有行政權力，但地段衛生當局在所有涉及提供該地段保健服務方面必須徵求他們的意見。地段衛生當局也必須聽取和考慮本區內每一社區衛生委員會的年度報告。社區衛生委員會的成員可實際考察醫院或者其他衛生機構，但

other health service property but not to the private premises of general practitioners or private nursing homes. Patients who are dissatisfied with treatment may be advised by the CHC as to how to submit complaints to the DHA; indeed a letter from the secretary of the CHC showing an interest in such a complaint will usually ensure serious consideration even though the CHC lacks the authority of the *health service commissioner to investigate complaints.

不能去視察私人全科醫師診所或私人護理院。對治療不滿意的病人在如何向地段衛生當局提出陳訴方面可接受社區衛生委員會的咨詢。確實，一封來自社區衛生委員會幹事的關於對這一陳訴表示關注的信，通常會保證對此事的嚴肅對待，儘管社區衛生委員會沒有衛生事業專員那樣調查投訴的權力。

community hospital *see* hospital.

社區醫院　參閱 hospital。

community medicine 1. *see* public health medicine. **2.** (loosely) public health medicine combined with general practice, especially in areas where medical manpower is scarce and one doctor may be filling both roles for a large population.

社區醫學　**(1)** 參閱 public health medicine。**(2)**（不確切）與綜合醫療相結合的公共衛生醫學，特別是在醫療人力缺乏、一個醫生對一很大的人羣身兼二職的地區。

community midwife *see* domiciliary midwife.

社區助產士　參閱 domiciliary midwife。

community nurses (in Britain) a generic term for *health visitors, *domiciliary midwives, and *home nurses. *See also* domiciliary services.

社區保健護士　（英國）對保健員、家庭助產士和家庭護士的統稱。參閱 domiciliary services。

community paediatrician a consultant in child health with special responsibility outside the hospital. *See also* community health.

社區兒科醫師　一個在醫院外負有特殊責任的兒童保健的咨詢員。參閱 community health。

community physician *see* public health physician.

社區醫師　參閱 public health physician。

community services *see* domiciliary services.

社區保健服務　參閱 domiciliary services。

comparative mortality figure *see* occupational mortality.

相對死亡率數字　參閱 occupational mortality。

compartment syndrome any of the neural or muscular disabilities of the limbs that can be produced by tight bandages or plasters in the treatment of fractures. The tissues of the limbs are divided up by thick sheets of fascia into separate compartments. If tension arises in these compartments due to internal bleeding, the blood supply may be cut off and both neural and muscular *ischaemia may ensue, with serious resulting disabilities (*acute compartment syndromes*). *See also* Volkmann's contracture.

腔隙綜合徵　在治療骨折中，繃帶或石膏夾板太緊而產生肢體的任何神經或肌肉功能的喪失。肢體的組織被厚厚的繃帶層分成了相互獨立的腔隙。如果因為內出血而在這些腔隙出現壓力的話，血供可能被切斷，神經和肌肉局部缺血會接着發生，結果導致嚴重的功能喪失（急性腔隙綜合徵）。參閱 Volkmann's contracture。

compatibility *n.* the degree to which the body's defence systems will tolerate the presence of intruding foreign material, such as blood when transfused or a kidney when transplanted. Complete compatibility exists between identical twins: a blood transfusion between identical twins will evoke no *antibody formation in the recipient. In severe *incompatibility*, for example between completely unrelated people, there are likely to be swift immune reactions as antibodies attack and destroy any offending antigenic material. *See also* histocompatibility, immunity. **–compatible** *adj.*

相容性　機體免疫防禦系統對外來異物的耐受程度，如血液（當被輸入時）和腎（當被移植時）。同卵雙胎之間存在有完全相容性：同卵雙胎之間的輸血在受血者體內不引起抗體形成。在嚴重不相容時，如在血型完全不相容的人們之間，很可能有立刻免疫反應，因為抗體襲擊和破壞任何外來抗原物質。參閱 histocompatibility，immunity。

compensation *n.* the act of making up for a functional or structural deficiency. For example, compensation for the loss of a diseased kidney is brought about by an increase in size of the remaining kidney, so restoring the urine-producing capacity.

代償　對功能或結構缺陷進行彌補的行為。例如，摘除的病腎因餘留腎臟的體積增大得以補償，因而恢復尿液生成能力。

compensation neurosis a fixed preoccupation with real or imaginary disability following an industrial or civil injury, when there is a possibility of financial compensation. The condition tends to deprive the affected person of the motive to overcome the alleged disability and

賠償性神經官能症　由於工業或民用損傷而產生的一種真正或假想病殘的固定觀念。此時常有一種經濟上補償的可能性。這種疾病趨於使患者失去克服所疑病傷的信心，也使之失去承認自然的恢復過程的能

to acknowledge the natural processes of recovery. Uncompensated disability often persists for many years, but the disorder often clears up soon after a satisfactory settlement.

complement *n*. a substance in the blood, consisting of a group of nine different fractions, that aids the body's defences when antibodies combine with invading antigens. Complement is involved with the breaking up (*lysis), *agglutination, and *opsonization of foreign cells. Following antibody-antigen reaction it may also attract scavenging cells (*phagocytes) to the area of conflict. *See also* immunity.

complementary medicine *see* alternative medicine.

complement fixation the binding of *complement to the complex that is formed when an antibody reacts with a specific antigen. Because complement is taken up from the serum only when such a reaction has occurred, testing for the presence of complement after mixing a suspension of a known organism with a patient's serum can give confirmation of infection with a suspected organism. The *Wassermann reaction for diagnosing syphilis is a complement-fixation test.

complex *n*. (in psychoanalysis) an emotionally charged and repressed group of ideas and beliefs that is capable of influencing an individual's behaviour. The term in this sense was originally used by Jung, but it is now widely used in a looser sense to denote an unconscious motive.

complication *n*. a disease or condition arising during the course of or as a consequence of another disease.

補體 血液中的一種物質，包括一組 9 種不同的成分。當抗體與外來抗原結合時，它能幫助機體的防禦。補體參與外來細胞的分解（溶解）、凝集和調理作用。在抗體-抗原反應之後，它也可將具有清除功能的細胞（吞噬細胞）吸引到反應部位來。參閱 immunity。

補救醫學 參閱 alternative medicine。

補體結合反應 抗體和特異抗原反應時產生的複合物與補體結合的現象。因為僅僅在此反應發生時，補體才從血清中被吸引，因此，將一已知生物體的懸液和患者的血清相混合之後測定補體的出現，可證實是否感染某種被懷疑的生物體。用於診斷梅毒的瓦塞爾曼反應就是一種補體結合試驗。

情結，情綜 （精神分析）一些充滿感情但又被壓抑的，且能影響個體行為的思想和信念。該術語的這一意義最初是由榮格使用的，但現在它以不太嚴格的含義廣泛用於指某種潛意識的動機。

併發症 在某一疾病過程中或由於某一疾病而發生的其他疾病。

composite resin a tooth-coloured filling material for teeth. It is composed of two different materials: an inorganic filler chemically held in an organic resin. Composite resins are usually hardened by polymerization initiated by intense light.

compress *n.* a pad of material soaked in hot or cold water and applied to an injured part of the body to relieve the pain of inflammation.

compressed air illness (caisson disease) a syndrome occurring in people working under high pressure in diving bells or at great depths with breathing apparatus. On return to normal atmospheric pressure nitrogen dissolved in the bloodstream expands to form bubbles, causing pain (the *bends*) and blocking the circulation in small blood vessels in the brain and elsewhere (*decompression sickness*). Pain, paralysis, and other features may be eliminated by returning the victim to a higher atmospheric pressure and reducing this gradually, so causing the bubbles to redissolve. Chronic compressed air illness may cause damage to the bones (*avascular necrosis*), heart, and lungs.

compulsion *n.* an *obsession that takes the form of a motor act, such as repetitive washing based on a fear of contamination.

compulsory admission (in Britain) the entry and detention of a person within an institution (hospital or *Part III accommodation) without his consent, either because of mental illness (*see* Mental Health Act) or severe social deprivation. Application by a *mental welfare officer or *social worker supported by a general practitioner and/or a suitably qualified

複合樹脂 填牙用的與牙同色的填料。它由兩種不同的材料組成：一種無機填料和使之含於其中的有機樹脂。複合樹脂通常因強光照射而發生的聚合作用而硬化。

敷布 在熱水或冷水中浸泡過的纖物墊。用於機體損傷部位以緩解炎症所引起的疼痛。

壓縮空氣病（潛水員病） 在高壓潛水艙中或配戴呼吸裝置在深水進行作業的人所出現的一種綜合徵。當他們一回到正常大氣壓環境時，溶解於血流中的氮膨脹而形成氣泡，引起疼痛（沉箱病），堵塞腦和其他部位小血管的血液循環（減壓病）。疼痛、麻痺和其他症狀可通過將患者送回更高氣壓環境，並逐漸減壓，使氣泡重新溶解的方法予以消除。慢性壓縮空氣病可引起骨（缺血性壞死）、心臟和肺的損害。

強迫症 以一種運動行為為形式而出現的強迫意念，如基於一種怕髒而反覆的盥洗行為。

強迫收容（英國）對某一個人在未經本人同意的情況下強制將其收留在某一機構內（醫院或第三部分收容所）。其原因為精神病（參閱 Mental Health Act）或因為嚴重的社會生活能力喪失。由精神病福利官員或者社會福利工作者會同一全科醫師和/或具有一定

specialist must be approved by a court of law except in emergencies relating to mental illness, in which the patient must either agree to stay as a voluntary admission or the emergency order is ratified by a court within seven days. Detained patients who consider themselves wrongly held have a right of appeal to a *Mental Health Review Tribunal. When a patient has committed a dangerous act the court may order compulsory admission to a hospital with special security arrangements (e.g. Broadmoor). *Compare* voluntary admission.

資格的專家提出的強迫收容申請必須經法院批准，但與精神病有關的緊急情況例外。在此種情況下，患者須同意自願進入或在七天之內由法院批准緊急決議。那些認為自己被錯誤監禁的患者有向精神保健審查法庭申訴的權利。當一患者做了危險行為時，法院可下達將其強迫收容於有特殊安全措施的醫院的決議（如布羅德莫爾醫院）。與 voluntary admission 對比。

computerized tomography (CT) a development of diagnostic radiology for the examination of the soft tissues of the body. For example, within the skull it can be used to diagnose pathological conditions of the brain, such as tumours, abscesses, and haematomas. The technique involves the recording of 'slices' of the body with an X-ray scanner (*CT scanner*); these records are then integrated by computer to give a cross-sectional image. This investigation is without risk to the patient. *See also* tomography. *Compare* positron emission tomography (PET).

電子計算機斷層照相術 檢查體內軟組織的一種放射診斷學新技術。例如，在顱內，這一技術可用於診斷腦的病理性疾病，如腫瘤、膿腫和血腫。這一技術涉及運用X綫掃描儀（CT掃描儀）記錄身體多層次狀況。這些記錄被計算機綜合在一起而產生斷面圖像。這一檢查對病人沒有危險。參閱 tomography。與 positron emission tomography (PET) 對比。

conation *n.* the group of mental activities (including drives, will, and *instincts) that leads to purposeful action. *Compare* cognition.

意動 導致有目的的動作的心理活動（包括慾望、意念和本能）。與 cognition 對比。

conception *n.* **1.** (in gynaecology) the start of pregnancy, when a male germ cell (sperm) fertilizes a female germ cell (ovum) in the *Fallopian tube. **2.** (in psychology) an idea or mental impression.

(1) 受孕 （產科學）妊娠的開始，此時，在輸卵管中，一個雄性生殖細胞（精子）使一雌性生殖細胞（卵子）受精。**(2) 概念** （心理學）某種觀念或心理印象。

conceptus *n.* the products of conception: the developing fetus and its enclosing membrane at all stages in the uterus.

孕體 妊娠的產物：子宮內各階段發育的胎兒和包膜。

concha *n*. (*pl.* **conchae**) (in anatomy) any part resembling a shell. For example, the *concha auriculae* is a depression on the outer surface of the pinna (auricle), which leads to the external auditory meatus of the outer ear. *See also* nasal concha.

甲　(解剖學) 任何類似介殼的部分。如耳甲是耳廓外表面凹陷部分，它通向外耳的外耳道。參閱 nasal concha。

concordance *n*. similarity of any physical characteristic that is found in both of a pair of twins.

一致性　在一對雙胞胎身上存在的任何外部特點的相似性。

concretion *n*. a stony mass formed within such an organ as the kidney, especially the coating of an internal organ (or a foreign body, such as a urinary catheter) with calcium salts. *See also* calculus.

結石　在如腎臟那樣的器官內形成的石質塊狀物，特別是體內臟器（或者異物，如導尿管）由鈣鹽構成的包被。參閱 calculus。

concussion *n*. a limited period of unconsciousness caused by injury to the head. It may last for a few seconds or a few hours. There may be no recognizable structural damage to the brain, but scans may reveal evidence of contusion (bruising) within the brain. Repeated concussion eventually causes symptoms suggesting brain damage. *See also* punch drunk syndrome.

腦震盪　由頭部外傷引起的短期意識喪失。它可持續數秒鐘或數小時。或許沒有可識別的對腦的器質性損害，但掃描可顯示腦內挫傷的迹象。反覆發生的腦震盪最終引起提示腦損害的症狀。參閱 punch drunk syndrome。

condenser *n*. (in microscopy) an arrangement of lenses beneath the stage of a microscope. It can be adjusted to provide correct focusing of light on the microscope slide.

聚光器　(顯微鏡檢查) 顯微鏡臺架下方的透鏡裝置，可對其調節以在顯微鏡載物片上產生正確的光線聚點。

conditioned reflex a reflex in which the response occurs not to the sensory stimulus that normally causes it but to a separate stimulus, which has been learnt to be associated with it. In Pavlov's classic experiments, dogs learned to associate the sound of a bell with feeding, time and would salivate at the bell's sound whether food was then presented to them or not.

條件反射　一種對正常情況下引起反應的感覺刺激不發生反應，而是對一經過訓練才與之聯繫的不相關刺激的反射。在巴甫洛夫的經典實驗中，狗學會把鈴聲與進食的時間聯繫起來，無論是否給予食物，一聽見鈴聲，狗都會分泌唾液。

conditioning *n.* the establishment of new behaviour by modifying the stimulus/response associations. In *classical conditioning* a stimulus not normally associated with a particular response is presented together with the stimulus that evokes the response automatically. This is repeated until the first stimulus evokes the response by itself (*see* conditioned reflex). In *operant conditioning* a response is rewarded (or punished) each time it occurs, so that in time it comes to occur more (or less) frequently (*see* reinforcement).

condom *n.* a sheath made of latex rubber, plastic, or silk that is fitted over the penis during sexual intercourse. Use of a condom protects both partners against sexually transmitted disease (including AIDS) and, carefully used, it is reasonably reliable contraceptive (between 2 and 10 pregnancies per 100 woman-years). A more recent development is the *female condom* (e.g. *Femidom*), which is fitted into the vagina. Manufactured from similar materials as male condoms, they too act as both contraceptives and as barriers to sexually transmitted diseases.

conduct disorder a repetitive and persistent pattern of aggressive or otherwise antisocial behaviour. It is usually recognized in childhood or adolescence and can lead to a *dyssocial or impulsive personality disorder. Treatment is usually with *behaviour therapy or *family therapy.

condylarthrosis (condyloid joint) *n.* a form of *diarthrosis (freely movable joint) in which an ovoid head fits into an elliptical cavity. Examples are the knee joint and the joint between the mandible

條件反射化 通過改變刺激與反應之間的聯繫以建立新的行為方式。在經典的條件反射化中,一種正常情況下不與一特定反應相聯繫的刺激與自動引起該種反應的刺激同時給予。這一過程不斷重複,直到第一個刺激本身引起該種反應(參閱 conditioned reflex)。在操作性條件反射化中,一種反應在每次產生時被給予獎勵(或懲罰)。因此,在經過一段時間後,該反應能經常(或不常)出現(參閱 reinforcement)。

陰莖套 一種由膠乳橡膠、塑料或絲製成的護套,在性交時套在陰莖上。使用陰莖套可使雙方免受性傳播疾病(包括艾滋病)感染。如小心使用可成為一種可靠的避孕器具(每年每百名婦女中妊娠數為 2~10 次)。最近新研製了一種女性陰道套(如女用陰道套),可置入陰道內。女性陰道套製造的材料與男性陰莖套一樣。它也起着避孕和防止性傳播疾病的作用。

行為障礙 一種反覆的、頑固的進攻性或者反社會的行為方式。通常發生於童年或青春期,能導致孤僻或衝動性人格障礙。治療通常用行為療法或家庭療法。

髁狀關節 一種動關節(能自由活動的關節),卵圓形關節頭嵌入一橢圓形關節腔,如膝關節以及下頜骨和顱部的顳骨之間的關節。

(lower jaw) and the temporal bone of the skull.

condyle *n.* a rounded protuberance that occurs at the ends of some bones, e.g. the *occipital bone, and forms an articulation with another bone.

condyloma *n.* a raised wartlike growth. The commonest type, *condyloma acuminatum*, is found on the vulva, under the foreskin, or on the skin of the anal region. Condylomas are infectious and are probably transmitted during sexual contact. *Condyloma latum* is an infectious warty lesion of the secondary stage of syphilis, occurring around the vulva or anus.

cone *n.* one of the two types of light-sensitive cells in the *retina of the eye (*compare* rod). The human retina contains 6–7 million cones; they function best in bright light and are essential for acute vision (receiving a sharp accurate image). The area of the retina called the *fovea contains the greatest concentration of cones. Cones can also distinguish colours. It is thought that there are three types of cone, each sensitive to the wavelength of a different primary colour – red, green, or blue. Other colours are seen as combinations of these three primary colours.

cone biopsy surgical removal, via a colposcope, of a cone-shaped segment of tissue from the cervix of the uterus. It may be performed if a cervical smear reveals evidence of *cervical intraepithelial neoplasia (CIN): the affected tissue is removed and examined microscopically for confirmation of the diagnosis.

confabulation *n.* the invention of circumstantial but fictitious detail about

髁　一些骨（如枕骨）的末端出現的圓形突起，它與另一骨構成關節。

濕疣　疣狀突起生長物。最常見的一種類型為尖銳濕疣，見於外陰部、包皮下或肛門區的皮膚。濕疣有傳染性，可能在性接觸期間傳播。扁平濕疣是二期梅毒有傳染性的疣狀病變，出現於外陰或肛門周圍。

視錐細胞　眼的視網膜中兩種感光細胞之一（與 rod 對比）。人類視網膜含有 600 萬~700 萬個視錐細胞。在光亮下，它們功能最佳，對精密視覺（接受精細準確的形象）至關重要。視網膜中被稱為中央凹的區域所含的視錐細胞密度最高。視錐細胞也能分辨顏色。一般認為有三種視錐細胞，每一種能感受不同原色波長——紅、綠或藍色。其他顏色被看成是此三種原色的不同結合。

錐形活檢　通過陰道鏡將子宮頸組織的一段椎形部分外科切除。如果宮頸塗片檢查顯示宮頸內皮瘤形成迹象時，則施行該活檢：切除病變組織，然後在顯微鏡下進行檢查以證實診斷。

虛談症　對假想中的過去已經發生的事件細節進行詳細地但

events supposed to have occurred in the past. Usually this is to disguise an inability to remember past events. It may be a symptom of any form of loss of memory, but typically occurs in *Korsakoff's syndrome.

又是想像的虛構。通常是對不能回憶過去事件的一種掩飾。它可能是任何形式記憶力喪失的一種症狀，但典型地發生於科爾薩科夫綜合徵。

confection *n.* (in pharmacy) a sweet substance that is combined with a medicinal preparation to make it suitable for administration.

糖膏劑 （藥劑學）與藥物混合使之適合於服用的有甜味的物質。

conflict *n.* (in psychology) the state produced when a stimulus produces two opposing reactions. The basic types of conflict situation are *approach–approach*, in which the individual is drawn towards two attractive – but mutually incompatible – goals; *approach–avoidance*, where the stimulus evokes reactions both to approach and to avoid; and *avoidance–avoidance*, in which the avoidance reaction to one stimulus would bring the individual closer to an equally unpleasant stimulus. Conflict has been used to explain the development of neurotic disorders, and the resolution of conflict remains an important part of psychoanalysis. *See also* conversion.

衝突 （心理學）當一種刺激產生兩種相反的反應時所產生的狀態。衝突狀態的基本類型有以下幾種。接近-接近衝突：患者被吸引向兩個有吸引力的但又相互不相容的目標。接近-迴避衝突：刺激引起接近和迴避兩種反應的衝突。迴避-迴避衝突：對於一種刺激的迴避反應使得一個人接近另一同樣不愉快的刺激。衝突被用來解釋神經障礙疾病的發展。衝突的解決仍然是精神分析的重要部分。參閱 conversion。

confluence *n.* a point of coalescence. The *confluence of the sinuses* is the meeting point of the superior sagittal, transverse, straight, and occipital venous sinuses in the dura mater in the occipital region of the skull.

匯合 連合的點。竇滙是上矢狀竇、橫竇、直竇和顳骨枕骨區硬膜內枕靜脈竇的匯合點。

congenital *adj.* describing a condition that is recognized at birth or that is believed to have been present since birth. Congenital malformations include all disorders present at birth whether they are inherited or caused by an environmental factor.

先天的 描述一種出生時就被發現的或認為從出生時就一直存在的疾病。先天畸形包括所有出生時就出現的障礙，無論是遺傳性的還是因環境因素引起的。

congenital dislocation of the hip (CDH) one of the commonest abnormalities present at birth, in which the head of the femur is displaced from the acetabulum (socket) of the ilium, which is poorly developed; it frequently affects both hip joints. CDH can be detected by *Barlow's* (or *Von Rosen's*) *sign*, a click elicited in newborn babies when the hip is gently dislocated by manual flexion and abduction of the joint.

先天性髖關節脫位　出生時出現的最常見的畸形之一。股骨頭與發育不良的髂骨的髖臼移位。它常常影響髖關節。先天性髖關節脫位可以借助巴洛體徵（或馮‧羅森體徵）發現，當使新生兒髖部關節屈曲和外展時其輕微移位而發出咔塔聲。

congestion *n.* an accumulation of blood within an organ, which is the result of back pressure within its veins (for example congestion of the lungs and of the liver occurs in heart failure). Congestion may be associated with *oedema (accumulation of fluid in the tissues). It is relieved by treatment of the cause.

充血　靜脈回流壓力而引起的某器官內血液的集聚（如心力衰竭時所發生的肺部鬱血和肝鬱血），充血可能與水腫有關（組織內液體集聚）。可通過病因治療獲得緩解。

Congo red a dark-red or reddish-brown pigment that becomes blue in acidic conditions. It is used as a histological *stain. *Amyloidosis is indicated if over 60% of the dye disappears from the blood within one hour of injection.

剛果紅　在酸性情況下變成藍色的一種暗紅色或紅棕色色素。它用做組織染色的染色劑。如注射後一小時 60% 以上的剛果紅自血液中消失，則提示有澱粉樣變。

coniine *n.* an extremely poisonous alkaloid, found in hemlock (*Conium maculatum*), that paralyses the nerves, mainly the motor nerves. Coniine has been included in drug preparations for the treatment of asthma and whooping cough.

歐毒芹鹼　存在於毒茴類毒草中的一種劇毒生物鹼。它麻痺神經（主要是運動神經）。歐毒芹鹼用於一些藥物製劑當中治療哮喘和百日咳。

coning *n.* prolapse of the brainstem through the *foramen magnum as a result of raised intracranial pressure: it is usually immediately fatal. A similar emergency can occur through the hiatus of the *tentorium.

錐形（疝）　因顱內壓的上升而使腦幹從枕骨大孔脫出。通常它會立刻致命。類似的急症可通過幕孔發生。

conization *n.* surgical removal of a cone of tissue. The technique is commonly

錐形切除術　對組織行錐形切除的外科手術。這一技術通常

used in excising a portion of the cervix (neck) of the uterus (*see* cone biopsy).

conjoined twins *see* Siamese twins.

conjugate (conjugate diameter, true conjugate) *n.* the distance between the front and rear of the pelvis measured from the most prominent part of the sacrum to the back of the pubic symphysis. Since the true conjugate cannot normally be measured during life it is estimated by subtracting 1.3–1.9 cm from the *diagonal conjugate*, the distance between the lower edge of the symphysis and the sacrum (usually about 12.7 cm). If the true conjugate is less than about 10.2 cm, delivery of an infant through the natural passages may be difficult or impossible, and *Caesarean section may have to be performed.

conjugation *n.* the union of two microorganisms in which genetic material (DNA) passes from one organism to the other. In some bacteria a minute projection on the donor 'male' cell (a *pilus*) forms a bridge with the recipient 'female' cell through which the DNA is transferred. Conjugation is comparable to sexual reproduction in higher organisms.

conjunctiva *n.* the delicate mucous membrane that covers that front of the eye and lines the inside of the eyelids. The conjunctiva lining the eyelids contains many blood vessels but that over the eyeball contains few and is transparent. **–conjunctival** *adj.*

conjunctivitis (pink eye) *n.* inflammation of the conjunctiva, which becomes red and swollen and produces a watery or pus containing discharge. It causes discomfort rather than pain and does not

用於切除子宮頸的一部分（參閱 cone biopsy）。

聯胎　參閱 Siamese twins。

骨盆直徑　從骶骨最突出部分至恥骨聯合後部測得的骨盆前後的距離。因骨盆直徑通常在生前無法測出，因此，通過從對角徑（恥骨聯合下緣至骶骨，通常大約為 12.7 cm）減去 1.3~1.9 cm 而估計得出骨盆直徑。如果骨盆直徑小於 10.2 cm，從自然產道分娩嬰兒可能會有困難或者不可能，因此，可能需施行剖宮產。

接合　兩個微生物的連合。在此過程中，遺傳物質（脫氧核糖核酸）從一生物傳遞給另一生物。在一些細菌中，在供體「雄性」細胞（菌毛）上的微小突起與受體「雌性」細胞形成一橋。脫氧核糖核酸就從此橋得以傳遞。接合與高等生物的有性生殖類似。

結膜　覆蓋於眼球前部和眼瞼內部的一層脆弱的黏膜。覆蓋於眼瞼的結膜含有許多血管，但是覆蓋於眼球的結膜含有少數血管，且是透明的。

結膜炎（紅眼）　結膜的炎症。結膜變紅變腫脹，產生水樣或膿性分泌物。引起不適，而非疼痛，且通常不影響視力。結膜炎由細菌或病毒感染（在

usually affect vision. Conjunctivitis is caused by infection by bacteria or viruses (in which case it usually spreads rapidly to the other eye), allergy, or physical or chemical irritation. The patient usually recovers with no after-effects in one to three weeks; bacterial infections respond to antibiotic eye drops. *See also* trachoma, ophthalmia neonatorum.

此情況下，感染通常迅速傳給另一隻眼）、過敏反應或物理或化學刺激引起。患者通常在 1~3 周內痊愈，無後遺症。細菌感染使用抗生素眼藥水有效。參閱 trachoma，ophthalmia neonatorum。

connective tissue the tissue that supports, binds, or separates more specialized tissues and organs or functions as a packing tissue of the body. It consists of an amorphous *ground substance* of mucopolysaccharides in which may be embedded white (collagenous), yellow (elastic), and reticular fibres, fat cells, *fibroblasts, *mast cells, and *macrophages (see illustration). Variations in chemical composition of the ground substance and in the proportions and quantities of cells and fibres give rise to tissues of widely differing characteristics, including bone, cartilage, tendons, and ligaments as well as *adipose, *areolar, and *elastic tissues.

結締組織 支持、聯結或分隔更為專門化的組織和器官或起着身體充填組織功能的組織。它由一種黏多糖類無定形基質與嵌於黏多糖類的白色（膠原）纖維、黃色（彈力）纖維和網狀纖維、脂肪細胞、成纖維細胞、肥大細胞和巨噬細胞組成（見圖）。基質中化學成分的不同和各種細胞與纖維的比例和數量的不同產生廣為不同特點的組織，包括骨、軟骨、肌腱、韌帶和脂肪組織、疏鬆結締組織與彈力組織等。

connective-tissue disease any one of a group of diseases that are characterized by inflammatory changes in connective tissue and can affect virtually any body system. Formerly known as *collagen diseases* (connective-tissue disease has been the preferred term since 1978), they include *dermatomyositis, systemic and discoid *lupus erythematosus, *morphoea, *polyarteritis nodosa, and *rheumatoid arthritis.

結締組織病 一組以結締組織發生炎性變化為特點的任何疾病，且可影響幾乎任何身體系統。以前該種疾病被稱為膠原疾病（從 1978 年起，結締組織病一直是人們習慣使用的名稱）。此種疾病包括皮肌炎、系統性和盤狀紅斑狼瘡、硬皮病、多關節炎和類風濕性關節炎。

Conn's syndrome the combination of muscular weakness, abnormally intense thirst (polydipsia), the production of large volumes of urine (polyuria), and hypertension, resulting from excessive

康恩綜合徵，原發性醛固酮增多症 由於腎上腺皮質所分泌的激素醛甾酮過多而產生的肌無力、異常強烈的口渴（煩渴）、尿量產出較大（多尿）

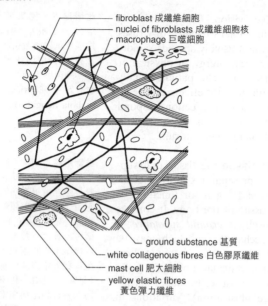

fibroblast 成纖維細胞
nuclei of fibroblasts 成纖維細胞核
macrophage 巨噬細胞

ground substance 基質
white collagenous fibres 白色膠原纖維
mast cell 肥大細胞
yellow elastic fibres
黃色彈力纖維

Loose (areolar) connective tissue
疏鬆結締組織

production of the hormone aldosterone by the adrenal cortex. Two percent of cases of hypertension are due to it.

consanguinity *n.* relationship by blood; the sharing of a common ancestor within a few generations.

conservative treatment treatment aimed at preventing a condition from becoming worse, in the expectation that either natural healing will occur or progress of the disease will be so slow that no drastic treatment will be justified. *Compare* radical treatment.

consolidation *n.* **1.** the state of the lung in which the alveoli (air sacs) are filled with fluid produced by inflamed tissue, as in *pneumonia. It is diagnosed from its dullness to *percussion, bronchial

和高血壓等綜合症狀。2% 的高血壓病都是由此引起的。

血親 血緣關係。在近幾代內有共同的祖先。

保守療法 旨在防止疾病惡化，希望自然痊愈出現或病程減慢，以致不需使用烈性藥物治療的一種療法。與 radical treatment 對比。

(1) 實變 肺泡被炎性組織產生的液體充滿（如肺炎）時肺的狀態。其診斷可由病人叩診出現濁音、支氣管性呼吸音（參閱 breath sounds）和胸部

breathing (*see* breath sounds) in the patient, and from the distribution of shadows on the chest X-ray. **2.** the stage of repair of a broken bone following *callus formation, during which the callus is transformed by *osteoblasts into mature bone.

X 綫陰影分布等做出。**(2) 骨化** 在骨痂形成後折骨修復的階段。在此期間，成骨細胞將骨痂轉變成發育成熟骨。

constipation *n.* a condition in which bowel evacuations occur infrequently, or in which the faeces are hard and small, or where passage of faeces causes difficulty or pain. The frequency of bowel evacuation varies considerably from person to person and the normal cannot be precisely defined. Constipation developing in a person of previously regular bowel habit may be a symptom of intestinal disease. Recurrent or longstanding constipation is treated by increasing *dietary fibre (roughage), *laxatives, or *enemas. *Faecal impaction*, the endresult of chronic constipation common in senile patients, often requires manual removal of the faecal bolus under an anaesthetic.

便秘 排便次數減少，或糞質變硬，糞量少，或者排便產生困難或疼痛的一種疾病。排便次數每人差異很大，正常排便次數很難進行準確定義。一個以前有規律排便習慣的人出現便秘可能是腸道疾患的一個症狀。反覆發作的或長期的便秘可以通過增加食物纖維（粗糙食物）、緩瀉劑、或灌腸等方法加以治療。糞便嵌塞是老年慢性便秘患者中常見的最終結果，它常需在麻醉情況下用手將糞塊排除。

constrictor *n.* any muscle that compresses an organ or causes a hollow organ or part to contract.

縮肌 任何能壓迫某一器官或使某一空腔器官或該器官的一部分收縮的肌肉。

consultant *n.* a fully trained specialist in a branch of medicine who accepts total responsibility for patient care. In Britain consultants are usually responsible for the care of patients in hospital wards but they are allowed to opt for some sessions in private practice in addition to any National Health Service commitments. After registration, doctors continuing in hospital service are appointed successively *senior house officer*, *registrar*, and *senior registrar* (all full-time training grades with increasing responsibilities).

高級醫師 在醫學的某一分支具有完備知識和技能並對患者醫療護理承擔全部責任的專家。在英國，高級醫師通常負責醫院病房患者的治療。除了完成任何國民服務制的職責外，他們被允許選擇一些時間進行私人營業。在取得註冊資格後，繼續在醫院工作的醫生可逐級連續被晉升為住院醫師、專科主治醫師和主任醫師（所有職業受訓等級上升伴隨着責任的遞增）。在受訓等級

While in the training grades specialist examinations are taken and consultant appointment is based on a combination of qualifications by examination and practical experience in post. Doctors who do not complete full specialist training, including *general practitioners with an interest in a particular specialty, may work in hospitals in subconsultant grades with a variety of titles carrying increasing responsibility, such as *clinical assistant, hospital practitioner grade, associate specialist,* and *staff grade. See also* Doctor.

晉升時，要參加專家資格考試。高級醫師的晉升建立在考試和崗位實踐經驗資格的綜合考慮基礎之上。那些沒有完成完全的專門醫師訓練的醫生，包括對某一具體專業感興趣的全科醫師，可在醫院的副專科高級醫師級別工作，此種級別有許多責任遞增的不同工作，如臨床助理醫師、醫院醫師助理、副專科大夫和職員助理。參閱 Doctor。

consumption *n.* any disease causing wasting of tissues, especially (formerly) pulmonary tuberculosis. **−consumptive** *adj.*

癆病 任何引起組織消耗的疾病，特別是（過去）肺結核。

contact *n.* transmission of an infectious disease by touching or handling an infected person or animal (*direct contact*) or by *indirect contact* with airborne droplets, faeces, etc., containing the infective microorganism.

接觸傳染 傳染病的一種傳播方式。通過接觸或處理受感染的病人或動物（直接接觸）或通過與帶有傳染性微生物的飛沫、糞便等的間接接觸而感染。

contact lenses lenses worn directly against the eye, separated from it only by a film of tear fluid. *Corneal microlenses* cover only the cornea, while *haptic lenses* cover some of the surrounding sclera as well. Contact lenses are used mainly in place of glasses to correct long- and short-sightedness and other errors of refraction, but they may be used in a protective capacity in some types of corneal disease. Contact lenses may be made of hard or soft materials, which have very different properties. Hard Perspex lenses have been partly replaced by newer gas-permeable lenses, which allow oxygen to pass from the atmosphere to the cornea.

隱形眼鏡 直接戴在眼睛上、與眼睛僅有一層淚液相隔的透鏡。角膜微型鏡片僅覆蓋角膜，而眼白鏡片還覆蓋周圍的鞏膜。主要用於代替普通眼鏡以糾正近視和遠視和其他屈光不正，但它們可在一些角膜疾病中用於保護功能。可由硬的或軟的材料製成，它們的特性也大大不同。硬的丙烯酸樹脂鏡片已大多用更新的、透氣的鏡片所代替。這種鏡片可使氧氣從大氣裏進入角膜。

contact therapy a form of *radiotherapy in which a radioactive substance is

接觸放射療法 一種將放射性物質置於身體需要治療部位的

brought into close contact with the part of the body being treated. Needles or capsules of the isotope may be implanted in or around a tumour so that the radiation they emit will destroy it. *Compare* telecurietherapy.

放射療法。將製成針狀或膠囊狀的同位素植入腫瘤內部或其周圍，因此，它們所發射的放射綫會破壞腫瘤。與 telecurietherapy 對比。

contagious disease originally, a disease transmitted only by direct physical contact: now usually taken to mean any *communicable disease.

接觸性疾病 原來指僅通過直接的身體接觸而傳播的疾病。現在，它通常用來指任何傳染性疾病。

continent diversion *see* urinary diversion.

節制性改道 參閱 urinary diversion。

contra- *prefix denoting* against or opposite. Example: *contraversion* (turning away from).

〔前綴〕反，抗，逆，對 如反轉。

contraception *n.* the prevention of unwanted pregnancy, which can be achieved by various means. Hormonal contraceptives (oestrogen and progestogen or progestogen only) act by preventing ovulation. They are usually taken in regular doses in the form of the Pill (*see* oral contraceptive), but may also be administered through the skin, by means of an adhesive patch impregnated with the hormones, or by three- or two-monthly injections of a long-acting progestogen. Recently developed methods for continuous administration of the hormones are subcutaneous implants of progestogen (e.g. *Norplant*) and vaginal rings containing progestogen, which is released over a period of three months. Methods that aim to prevent fertilization of the ovum include *coitus interruptus, the *condom, the *diaphragm, and surgical intervention (tubal occlusion and vasectomy: *see* sterilization). Methods that aim to prevent implantation of a fertilized ovum in the uterus include the intrauterine contraceptive device

避孕 不願懷孕的預防措施。可通過各種辦法來實現。激素避孕藥（雌激素和孕激素類或單用孕激素類）通過防止排卵而發揮作用。通常以片劑的形式定期口服（參閱 oral contraceptive），但也可借助於浸滲有激素的黏貼性膏藥敷在皮膚上用藥，或通過每三個月或兩個月注射一種長效的孕激素。新近發展的持續使用激素的方法是皮下植入孕激素（如左18-乙基炔諾酮）和含有孕激素的陰道環。三個月後取出。旨在防止卵子受精的方法包括終止性交、陰莖套、子宮帽和外科手術（輸卵管閉合術和輸精管切除術，參閱 sterilization）。旨在防止子宮內已受精卵子植入的方法包括宮內避孕器（參閱 IUCD）；這些方法可用於性交後，但必須在植入前（參閱 postcoital contraception）。其宗教信仰阻止使用機械或激素避孕方法的夫婦可使用安全期避孕方法。在此種方

(*see* IUCD); these methods can be used after intercourse but before implantation (*see* postcoital contraception). Couples whose religious beliefs forbid the use of mechanical or hormonal contraceptives may use the *rhythm method, in which intercourse is limited to those days in the menstrual cycle when conception is least likely.

法下，性交僅限於月經周期中最不可能懷孕的那幾天。

contraction *n.* the shortening of a muscle in response to a motor nerve impulse. This generates tension in the muscle, usually causing movement.

收縮 對運動神經衝動反應的肌肉短縮。這激發肌肉緊張，通常會引起運動。

contracture *n.* *fibrosis of muscle or connective tissue producing shrinkage and shortening without generating any strength. It is usually a consequence of pain in or disuse of a muscle or limb. *See also* Dupuytren's contracture, Volkmann's contracture.

攣縮 產生肌肉短縮而不產生任何力量的肌肉組織的纖維性變。通常由於肌肉疼痛或肢體或肌肉廢用性萎縮的結果。參閱 Dupuytren's contracture，Volkmann's contracture。

contraindication *n.* any factor in a patient's condition that makes it unwise to pursue a certain line of treatment. For example, an attack of pneumonia in a patient would be a strong contraindication against the use of a general anaesthetic.

禁忌症 疾病狀態下使用任何不利於疾病治療的方法及因素。例如，肺炎是使用全身麻醉劑的最大禁忌症。

contralateral *adj.* on or affecting the opposite side of the body: applied particularly to paralysis (or other symptoms) occurring on the opposite side of the body from the brain lesion that caused them.

對側的 位於或影響身體的相反一側的，特別用於因腦損傷而引起的身體的相反一側發生麻痺（或其他症狀）。

contrast medium any substance that is used to improve the visibility of structures during radiography. Barium, given orally or as an enema to show up the alimentary tract on X-ray, is an example of a contrast medium. Air is occasionally

造影劑 在放射照相中用以提高結構可見度的任何物質。口服鋇或灌腸鋇在 X 綫下更清楚顯示消化道就是造影劑的範例。空氣偶爾也用作造影劑。它可在 X 綫檢查腦室時用以

useful as a contrast medium; it may be used to displace the cerebrospinal fluid during X-ray examination of the ventricles of the brain. *See also* radiopaque.

取代腦脊液的位置。參閱 radiopaque。

contrecoup *n.* injury of a part resulting from a blow on its opposite side. This may happen, for example, if a blow on the back of the head causes the front of the brain to be pushed against the inner surface of the skull.

對衝傷 一側受到打擊時引起的另一側的損傷。例如,當腦後部受到的打擊引起腦前部與顱內表面相碰撞,這種損傷就可發生。

contusion *n. see* bruise.

挫傷 參閱 bruise。

conus arteriosus the front upper portion of the right ventricle adjoining the pulmonary arteries.

動脈圓錐 與肺動脈相連的右心室的前上部分。

conus medullaris the conical end of the spinal cord, at the level of the lower end of the first lumbar vertebra.

脊髓圓錐 脊髓的圓錐形末端,位於第一腰椎下端水平位置。

convergence *n.* **1.** (in neurology) the formation of nerve tracts by fibres coming together into one pathway from different regions of the brain. **2.** (in ophthalmology) the ability of the eyes to turn inwards and focus on a near point so that a single image is formed on both retinas. The closer the object, the greater the degree of convergence.

(1) 集合束 (神經病學) 來自腦的不同部位的神經纖維形成的神經束。**(2) 會聚** (眼科學) 眼睛向內轉,集中於一近點,因而在兩個視網膜上形成同一影像的能力。物體愈近,會聚的程度愈高。

conversion *n.* (in psychiatry) the expression of *conflict as physical symptoms. Psychoanalysts believe that the repressed instinctual drive is manifested as motor or sensory loss, such as paralysis, rather than as speech or action. This is thought to be one of the ways in which *conversion disorder is produced.

轉換 (心理學) 內心衝突以軀體症狀形式表示出來的現象。精神分析學家認為,被壓抑的本能性衝動表現為運動或感覺喪失,如麻痺,而不是表現為語言或行動。這被認為是轉換性障礙產生的原因之一。

conversion disorder a psychological conflict or need that manifests itself as an organic dysfunction or physical symptom. The sufferer may display symptoms of

轉換性障礙 一種心理衝突或需求,表現為一種器質性功能障礙或身體症狀。患者可能顯示以下症狀:失明、耳聾、感

blindness, deafness, loss of sensation, gait abnormalities, or paralysis of various parts of the body. None of these can be accounted for by organic disease. Conversion disorder was formerly known as *hysteria.

覺缺失、步態異常或者身體不同部位出現麻痺。這些症狀都不是由器質性疾病引起的。轉換性障礙過去叫作癔病。

convolution *n.* a folding or twisting, such as one of the many that cause the fissures, sulci, and gyri of the surface of the *cerebrum.

迴 一種褶疊或卷曲的結構，如在大腦表面引起的許多裂、溝和迴等結構。

convulsion *n.* an involuntary contraction of the muscles producing contortion of the body and limbs. Rhythmic convulsions of the limbs are a feature of major *epilepsy. *Febrile convulsions* are provoked by fever in otherwise healthy infants and young children. An afebrile *infantile convulsion* is likely to be due to birth injury or a developmental defect of the brain.

抽搐 引起軀幹和肢體扭曲的非自主性肌肉收縮。節律性肢體抽搐是癲癇大發作的一個特徵。熱性抽搐是由本來健康的嬰兒和幼兒的發燒引起。非熱性嬰兒抽搐很可能是由於產傷或大腦發育缺陷引起。

Cooley's anaemia *see* thalassaemia.

庫利貧血 參閱 thalassaemia。

Coombs' test a means of detecting rhesus antibodies on the surface of red blood cells that precipitate proteins (globulins) in the blood serum. The test is used in the diagnosis of haemolytic *anaemia in babies with rhesus incompatibility in whom there is destruction of red blood cells.

庫姆斯試驗 一種檢測紅細胞表面 Rh 抗體的方法。此時，血清中的蛋白（球蛋白）沉澱在紅細胞上。本試驗用於診斷在體內有紅細胞破壞的 Rh 不相容的幼兒是否患有溶血性貧血。

copr- (copro-) *prefix denoting* faeces. Example: *coprophobia* (abnormal fear of).

〔前綴〕糞 如糞便恐怖（對糞便的異常畏懼）。

coprolalia *n.* the repetitive speaking of obscene words. It can be involuntary, as part of the *Gilles de la Tourette syndrome.

穢褻語言 反覆使用穢褻字眼說話。它可以是不自主的，是圖雷特綜合徵的一部分。

coprolith *n.* a mass of hard faeces within the colon or rectum, due to chronic constipation. It may become calcified.

糞石 因慢性便秘而引起的結腸或直腸中出現堅硬的糞塊。它可發生鈣化。

coproporphyrin *n.* a *porphyrin compound formed during the synthesis of protoporphyrin IX, a precursor of *haem. Copoporphyrin is excreted in the faeces in *hereditary coproporphyria*.

co-proxamol *n.* an *analgesic drug consisting of a combination of the drug *paracetamol and the weakly narcotic drug *dextropropoxyphene. It is administered by mouth. Possible side-effects include dizziness, drowsiness, nausea, and vomiting. Trade names: **Distalgesic**, **Paxalgesic**.

copulation *n. see* coitus.

cor *n.* the heart.

coracoid process a beaklike process that curves upwards and forwards from the top of the *scapula, over the shoulder joint.

cord *n.* any long flexible structure, which may be solid or tubular. Examples include the spermatic cord, spinal cord, umbilical cord, and vocal cord.

cordectomy *n.* surgical removal of a vocal cord or, more usually, a piece of the vocal cord (*partial cordectomy*).

cordocentesis *n.* the removal of a sample of fetal blood by inserting a hollow needle through the abdominal wall of a pregnant woman, under ultrasound guidance, into the umbilical vein. The blood is subjected to chromosome analysis and biochemical and other tests to determine the presence of abnormalities. *See also* prenatal diagnosis.

cordotomy *n.* a surgical procedure for the relief of severe and persistent pain in

糞卟啉 在原卟啉 IX 合成期間形成的卟啉化合物。是血紅素的前體。在遺傳性糞卟啉症中，糞卟啉從糞便中排出。

右丙氧芬醋氨酚合劑 一種鎮痛藥物，是由醋氨酚和具有微弱麻醉作用的右丙氧芬結合而成。用於口服。可能具有的副作用包括頭暈、嗜睡、惡心和嘔吐。商品名：Distalgesic，Paxalgesic。

交媾 參閱 coitus。

心臟

喙突 由肩胛骨上部向前上方彎曲的鳥嘴樣突起。位於肩關節上方。

索，帶 任何實心或空心的長而柔軟的結構。例如精索、脊索、臍帶和聲帶。

聲帶切除術 用外科手術切除全部聲帶。更常用的作法為切除一部分聲帶（部分聲帶切除術）。

臍帶穿刺術 在超聲引導下，將一空心針從妊娠婦女的腹壁刺入到胎兒臍帶靜脈採集胎兒血樣的技術。對血液進行染色體分析及生化和其他試驗以確定是否出現畸形。參閱 prenatal diagnosis。

脊髓前側柱切斷術 一種為解除盆腔或下肢嚴重而持久的疼

the pelvis or lower limbs. The nerve fibres that transmit the sensation of pain to consciousness pass up the spinal cord in special tracts (the *spinothalamic tracts*). In cordotomy the spinothalamic tracts are severed in the cervical (neck) region.

痛所施行的外科手術。將痛覺傳導到感覺區的神經纖維在特殊的傳導束內（脊髓丘腦束）經過脊髓上行。在脊髓前側柱切斷術中，脊髓丘腦束在頸部被切斷。

Cordylobia *n. see* tumbu fly.

瘤蠅屬　參閱 tumbu fly。

core-and-cluster *n.* a form of housing for handicapped or subnormal people. Institutional organizations are replaced by small self-contained living units associated with a central facility providing more intensive resources.

分居式收養院　殘疾人或亞正常人的一種居住方式。大型的有組織集中居住被小型而獨立的生活小區所代替。這些小區由一中心設施提供更為完全的服務。

corectopia *n.* displacement of the pupil towards one side from its normal position in the centre of the iris. When present from birth, the displacement is usually inwards towards the nose. Scarring of the iris from inflammation may also draw the pupil out of position.

瞳孔異位　瞳孔從虹膜中央的正常位置向一側移位。先天性瞳孔異位通常是向鼻部內向移位。虹膜炎症後的瘢痕亦可引起瞳孔位置不正。

corium *n. see* dermis.

真皮　參閱 dermis。

corn *n.* an area of hard thickened skin on or between the toes: a type of *callosity produced by ill-fitting shoes. The horny skin layers form an inverted pyramid that presses down into the deeper skin layers, causing pain. A corn may be treated by applying salicylic acid or by chiropody. Medical name: **clavus**.

雞眼　足趾間或底部的皮膚變硬增厚的部分。是由穿不合適的鞋引起的一種胼胝。皮膚角質層形成一種逆向生長的錐體，壓迫皮膚深層，引起疼痛。雞眼可通過使用水楊酸或足病治療術得以治療。醫學用語：雞眼。

cornea *n.* the transparent circular part of the front of the eyeball. It refracts the light entering the eye onto the lens, which then focuses it onto the retina. The cornea contains no blood vessels and it is extremely sensitive to pain. **–corneal** *adj.*

角膜　眼球前部的圓形透明部分。把進入眼內的光綫折射到晶體上，然後晶體聚焦到視網膜上。角膜不含有任何血管，對疼痛極為敏感。

corneal graft *see* keratoplasty.

角膜移植　參閱 keratoplasty。

corneal ring a ring designed to be inserted into the peripheral tissue of the cornea in order to alter the curvature of the corneal surface. It is undergoing trials to assess its ability to correct errors of refraction. In myopia (short-sightedness), for example, the ring would be required to stretch the corneal tissue peripherally and thus flatten the central corneal curvature in order to correct the myopia.

cornification *n. see* keratinization.

cornu *n.* (*pl.* **cornua**) (in anatomy) a horn-shaped structure, such as the horn-shaped processes of the hyoid bone and thyroid cartilage. *See also* horn.

corona *n.* a crown or crownlike structure. The *corona capitis* is the crown of the head.

coronal *adj.* relating to the crown of the head or of a tooth. The *coronal plane* divides the body into dorsal and ventral parts (see illustration).

coronal suture *see* suture (def. 1).

corona radiata 1. a series of radiating fibres between the cerebral cortex and the internal capsule of the brain. **2.** a layer of follicle cells that surrounds a freshly ovulated ovum. The cells are elongated radially to the ovum when seen in section.

coronary angioplasty a procedure, not requiring *thoracotomy, in which a segment of coronary, artery narrowed by atheroma is stretched by the inflation of a balloon introduced into it by means of cardiac *catheterization under X-ray screening (*see* angioplasty). The site of the obstruction is identified by prior

角膜環 為了改變角膜表面的凸度而設計的一種嵌入角膜周圍組織的環。經過試驗可以評估其矯正反射誤差的能力。例如，在近視的情況下，需要此環以將角膜組織向外圍擴展，從而使中央角膜凸度變小以糾正近視。

角化 參閱 keratinization。

角 （解剖學）一種角狀結構，如舌骨和甲狀軟骨的角狀突起。參閱 horn。

冠 一種冠或冠狀結構。頭頂即頭的冠部。

冠的 與頭頂部或牙冠相關的。冠狀面將身體分成前後兩部分（見圖）。

冠狀縫 參閱 suture（釋義1）。

放射冠 **(1)** 大腦皮質和內囊之間一系列呈放射狀排列的神經纖維。**(2)** 環繞着一個新排出的卵子的一層卵泡細胞。在剖面下進行觀察，可見細胞呈放射狀向卵子延伸。

冠狀血管成形術 一種不需要胸廓切開術的一種技術。在 X 綫掃描下利用心臟導管插入術導入一充氣氣囊使因動脈粥樣硬化而變得狹窄的冠狀動脈段擴張（參閱 angioplasty）。被阻塞的部位首先通過心血管造影術確認。不是所有變得狹窄

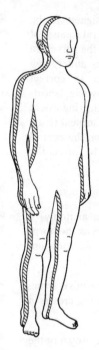

Coronal plane of section through the body
身體的冠狀切面

*angiocardiography. Not all narrowed segments can be improved by angioplasty. *See also* coronary bypass graft.

coronary arteries the arteries supplying blood to the heart. The *right* and *left coronary arteries* arise from the aorta, just above the aortic valve, and form branches encircling the heart. *See* coronary angioplasty, coronary bypass graft.

coronary bypass graft *coronary revascularization in which a segment of a coronary artery narrowed by atheroma is bypassed by an autologous section of healthy saphenous vein or internal mammary artery at *thoracotomy. The

的血管部分都可通過血管成形術得以改善。參閱 coronary bypass graft。

冠狀動脈 向心臟供應血液的動脈。左右冠狀動脈起自主動脈，正好在主動脈瓣的上方，形成包繞整個心臟的分支。參閱 coronary angioplasty，coronary bypass graft。

冠狀動脈分流移植 冠狀動脈血管再通術。因動脈粥樣硬化而造成的冠狀動脈狹窄的部分通過胸廓切開術用其自體健康隱靜脈或乳房動脈段搭橋分流。由於一個或多個移植血管

improved blood flow resulting from one or more such grafts relieves *angina pectoris and reduces the risk of *myocardial infarction.

使得血流改善緩解了心絞痛，減少了心肌梗死的危險性。

coronary revascularization a surgical method of improving the blood flow through coronary arteries narrowed by atheroma. *See* coronary bypass graft.

冠狀動脈血管再通術 一種改善因動脈粥樣硬化產生的冠狀動脈狹窄處血流的外科方法。參閱 coronary bypass graft。

coronary thrombosis the formation of a blood clot (thrombus) in the coronary artery, which obstructs the flow of blood to the heart. This is usually due to *atheroma and results in the death (infarction) of part of the heart muscle. For symptoms and treatment *see* myocardial infarction.

冠狀動脈血栓形成 冠狀動脈內血凝塊（血栓）形成的過程。它阻塞血液流向心臟。該疾病通常由於動脈粥樣硬化而引起，且導致心肌的部分死亡（梗死）。症狀和治療，參閱 myocardial infarction。

coroner *n.* the official who presides at an *inquest. He must be either a medical practitioner or a lawyer of at least five years' standing.

驗屍官 主持驗屍的官員。他必須是一位至少有五年工作經驗的醫師或律師。

coronoid process 1. a process on the upper end of the *ulna. It forms part of the notch that articulates with the humerus. **2.** the process on the ramus of the *mandible to which the temporalis muscle is attached.

(1) 尺骨喙突 尺骨上端的突起。它形成與肱骨相關節的切迹部分。**(2) 下頜骨冠突** 下頜支上的突起。顳肌即附着於該處。

cor pulmonale enlargement of the right ventricle of the heart that results from diseases of the lungs or the pulmonary arteries. Such diseases include those affecting the structure of the lungs (e.g. emphysema) or their function (e.g. obesity) except when these changes result from congenital heart disease or diseases primarily affecting the left side of the heart.

肺心病 因肺臟或肺動脈疾病引起的右心室擴大。這些疾病包括導致肺結構異常（如肺氣腫）或肺功能障礙（如肥胖）的疾病，但導致這些變化的先天性心臟病或主要累及左側心臟的疾病除外。

corpus *n.* (*pl.* **corpora**) any mass of tissue that can be distinguished from its surroundings.

主體 任何有別於外圍組織的結構。

corpus albicans the residual body of scar tissue that remains in the ovary at the point where a *corpus luteum has regressed after its secretory activity has ceased.

白體　卵巢中的黃體分泌活動停止後退化形成的殘餘瘢痕組織。

corpus callosum the broad band of nervous tissue that connects the two cerebral hemispheres, containing an estimated 300 million fibres. *See* cerebrum.

胼胝體　連接兩側大腦半球的闊帶狀神經組織。其中含有約 3 億條神經纖維。參閱 cerebrum。

corpus cavernosum either of a pair of cylindrical blood sinuses that form the erectile tissue of the *penis and clitoris. In the penis a third sinus, the corpus spongiosum, encloses the urethra and extends into the glans. All these sinuses have a spongelike structure that allows them to expand when filled with blood.

海綿體　構成陰莖和陰蒂中的勃起組織的一對圓柱形血竇。在陰莖中，還有第三個竇，即尿道海綿體。它包繞尿道，並直達龜頭。所有這些血竇都有海綿狀結構。當充血時，該結構使血竇膨脹。

corpuscle *n*. any small particle, cell, or mass of tissue.

小體　任何微小的顆粒、細胞或組織團塊。

corpus luteum the glandular tissue in the ovary that forms at the site of a ruptured *Graafian follicle after ovulation. It secretes the hormone *progesterone, which prepares the uterus for implantation. If implantation fails the corpus luteum becomes inactive and degenerates. If an embryo becomes implanted the corpus luteum continues to secrete progesterone until the fourth month of pregnancy, by which time the placenta has taken over this function.

黃體　排卵後在卵巢破裂的格雷夫卵泡處形成的腺體組織。它分泌激素孕酮以準備子宮內受精着床。如卵泡植入失敗，黃體則變得失去活性，然後變性。如果胚胎植入的話，黃體就繼續分泌孕酮，直至妊娠第四個月。此時，胎盤已代替其功能。

corpus spongiosum the blood sinus that surrounds the urethra of the male. Together with the corpora cavernosa, it forms the erectile tissue of the *penis. It is expanded at the base of the penis to form the urethral bulb and at the tip to form the glans penis.

尿道海綿體　包繞男性尿道的血竇。它與陰莖海綿體共同形成陰莖的勃起組織。在陰莖底部，它變得膨大而形成尿道球，其頂部也變得膨大，形成陰莖頭。

corpus striatum the part of the *basal ganglia in the cerebral hemispheres of the brain consisting of the caudate nucleus and the lentiform nucleus.

correlation *n.* (in statistics) the extent to which one of a pair of characteristics affects the other in a series of individuals. Such pairs of observations can be plotted as a series of points on a graph. If all the points on the resulting *scatter diagram* are in a straight line (which is neither horizontal nor vertical), the *correlation coefficient* may vary within the range of +1, where an increase of one variable is always associated with the corresponding increase in the other, to –1, where an increase of one variable is associated with a constant decrease of the other; a coefficient of 0 indicates no dependence of the one characteristic on the other of a straight line type. The *regression coefficient* is the average extent to which a unit increase of one characteristic influences the increase/decrease of the other. Where several factors appear to correlate with the onset of disease the relative importance of each may be calculated by the statistical technique known as *multivariate analysis.*

cortex *n.* (*pl.* **cortices**) the outer part of an organ, situated immediately beneath its capsule or outer membrane; for example, the *adrenal cortex* (*see* adrenal glands), *renal cortex* (*see* kidney), or *cerebral cortex. **–cortical** adj.*

corticosteroid (corticoid) *n.* any steroid hormone synthesized by the adrenal cortex. There are two main groups of corticosteroids. The *glucocorticoids* (e.g. *hydrocortisone (cortisol), *cortisone, and corticosterone) are essential for the utilization of carbohydrate, fat, and

紋狀體　大腦半球基底神經節的一部分。含有尾狀核和豆狀核。

相關　（統計學）在一組個體中，一對特徵因素的某一個對另一個的影響程度。這種成對的觀測值可以繪製成圖。如果所構成的散點圖上的所有的點構成一條直綫（非水平綫，也非垂直綫）時，則相關係數可在 +1 到 –1 的範圍內變動。在 +1 時，一個變量的增加總與另一變量的增加相關；在 –1 時，一個變量的增加與另一變量的不斷減少相關。相關係數為 0 表示兩個特徵因素相互之間無綫性依賴關係。迴歸係數表示某一特徵因素的值增加一個單位時影響另一特徵因素的增加／減少的平均程度。當幾種因素看來都與某種疾病的發生有關時，通過被稱為多變量分析的統計技術即可算出各種因素的重要程度。

皮質　直接位於包膜下或外膜下的某器官的外表部分。如腎上腺皮質（參閱 adrenal glands），腎皮質（參閱 kidney）或大腦皮質。

皮質類固醇　由腎上腺皮質合成的任何固醇類激素。主要有兩大類皮質類固醇。糖皮質激素（如氫化可的松、可的松和皮質酮）對身體利用糖、脂肪、蛋白和正常應激作用至關重要。天然的和人工的糖皮質

protein by the body and for a normal response to stress. Naturally occurring and synthetic glucocorticoids have very powerful anti-inflammatory effects and are used to treat conditions that involve inflammation. The *mineralocorticoids* (e.g. *aldosterone) are necessary for the regulation of salt and water balance.

激素具有極強的抗炎作用，因此用於治療炎症疾病。鹽皮質激素（如醛甾酮）對於鹽和水平衡的調節很有必要。

corticosterone *n.* a steroid hormone (*see* corticosteroid) synthesized and released in small amounts by the adrenal cortex.

皮質酮 由腎上腺皮質合成並分泌的少量固醇類激素（參閱 corticosteroid）。

corticotrophin *n.* see ACTH.

促腎上腺皮質激素 參閱 ACTH。

cortisol *n.* see hydrocortisone.

皮質醇 參閱 hydrocortisone。

cortisone *n.* a naturally occurring *corticosteroid that is used mainly to treat deficiency of corticosteroid hormones in *Addison's disease and following surgical removal of the adrenal glands. It is administered by mouth or injection and may cause serious side-effects such as stomach ulcers and bleeding, nervous and hormone disturbances, muscle and bone damage, and eye changes.

可的松 一種天然存在的皮質類固醇。主要用於阿狄森病的皮質類固醇缺乏和腎上腺摘除後。口服或注射。可引起嚴重副作用，如胃潰瘍和出血、神經與內分泌紊亂、肌肉和骨骼的損傷和眼的病變。

cor triloculare a rare congenital condition in which there are three instead of four chambers of the heart due to the presence of a single common ventricle. *Cyanosis (blueness) is common. Most patients die in infancy.

三腔心 一種少見的先天性心臟病。因為只有一個共同的心室，因此，心臟有三個腔，而不是四個。常有紫紺（青藍）。大多數病人在嬰兒期就會死亡。

Corynebacterium *n.* a genus of Gram-positive, mostly aerobic, nonmotile, rodlike bacteria that frequently bear club-shaped swellings. Many species cause disease in man, domestic animals, birds, and plants; some are found in dairy products. The species *C. diphtheriae*

棒狀桿菌屬 一種革蘭氏陽性、多數為需氧性、無活動能力的、有杵狀隆起的桿狀細菌。許多此類細菌在人類、家畜、鳥類與植物中引起疾病。一些細菌見於奶製品。白喉桿菌（克-勒氏桿菌）是白喉的致

(*Klebs-Loeffler bacillus*) is the causative organism of *diphtheria, producing a powerful *exotoxin that is harmful to heart and nerve tissue. It occurs in one of three forms: *gravis*, *intermedius*, and *mitis*.

病菌，能產生一種對心臟和神經組織有害的強烈的外毒素。它以三種形式出現：重型、中型和輕型。

coryza (**cold in the head**) *n*. a catarrhal inflammation of the mucous membrane in the nose due to either a *cold or *hay fever. *See also* catarrh.

鼻卡他 由感冒或枯草熱所引起的鼻黏膜的卡他性炎症。參閱 catarrh。

COSHH (control of substances hazardous to health) (in occupational health) legislation and resulting regulations concerning the duties and responsibilities of employers and employees to ensure that *hazardous substances* used in a workplace (e.g. toxic chemicals in factories, anaesthetic gases in operating theatres, carbonaceous dust arising from photocopying machines in offices) do not affect adversely the operatives themselves or their colleagues.

健康有害物質的控制 （職業衛生）立法以及由此而產生的規定。這些規定涉及僱主和僱員的義務和責任，以確保在一工作場所所使用的有害物質（如工廠裏的有害化學物質、手術室裏的麻醉氣體、辦公室裏複印機產生的含碳粉塵）不對操作者自己或其同事產生不利影響。

cost- (costo-) *prefix denoting* the ribs. Example: *costectomy* (excision of).

〔前綴〕**肋** 例如肋骨切除術。

costal *adj*. of or relating to the ribs.

肋的 肋的或與肋有關的。

costal cartilage a cartilage that connects a *rib to the breastbone (*sternum). The first seven ribs (true ribs) are directly connected to the sternum by individual costal cartilages. The next three ribs are indirectly connected to the sternum by three costal cartilages, each of which is connected to the one immediately above it.

肋軟骨 將肋骨和胸骨連接起來的軟骨。前七根肋骨（真肋）通過各自肋軟骨與胸骨直接相連。其餘三根肋軟骨通過與其上一根肋軟骨的連接與胸骨間接相連。

costalgia *n*. pain localized to the ribs. This term is now rarely used.

肋痛 局限於肋骨區的疼痛。該詞現在罕用。

costive *adj*. constipated.

便秘的

costochondritis *n.* *see* Tietze's syndrome.

肋骨軟骨炎 痛性非化膿性肋軟骨腫大症。參閱 Tietze's syndrome。

cot death (sudden infant death syndrome, SIDS) the sudden unexpected death of an infant less than two years old (peak occurrence between two and six months) from an unidentifiable cause. There appear to be many factors involved, the most important of which is the position in which the baby is laid to sleep: babies who sleep on their fronts (the prone position) have an increased risk. Other factors increasing the risk include parental smoking, overheating with bedding, prematurity, and a history of cot death within the family. About half the affected infants will have had a viral upper respiratory tract infection within the 48 hours preceding their death, many of these being due to the *respiratory syncytial virus. *See also* apnoea monitor.

嬰兒猝死症 因不明原因而致不到兩歲嬰兒突然不可預料的死亡（高峯發病在兩個月至六個月之間）。似有許多因素，其中最重要的因素是嬰兒被放置睡覺的位置。爬位（前位）睡覺的幼兒發病危險性較高。其他增加這一猝死症危險性的因素包括父母親吸煙、寢具過熱、早產和其家族中有嬰兒猝死的家庭史。大約一半患此症的嬰兒在其死亡前 48 小時內會有上呼吸道病毒感染。其中多為呼吸道合胞病毒感染。參閱 apnoea monitor。

co-trimoxazole *n.* an antibacterial drug consisting of *sulphamethoxazole and *trimethoprim. Since both these drugs are well absorbed and rapidly excreted – and each potentiates the action of the other – co-trimoxazole is taken by mouth and is particularly useful for treating urinary-tract infections (such as cystitis). Side-effects are those of the *sulphonamides. Trade names: **Bactrim**, **Septrin**.

增效磺胺甲基異噁唑 一種由磺胺甲基異噁唑和甲氧苄啶組成的抗菌藥。這兩種藥物吸收良好，排泄迅速，且相互之間能增強效果，因此，增效磺胺甲基異噁唑用於口服，特別對泌尿道感染有效（如膀胱炎）。副作用同磺胺類藥物。商品名：Bactrim，Septrin。

cotton-wool spots accumulations of *axoplasm in the nerve-fibre layer of the retina, which indicate disease (e.g. hypertension, connective-tissue disease, or AIDS).

棉絮狀滲出點 視網膜神經纖維層軸漿的積聚。它提示疾患（如高血壓、結締組織病或艾滋病）。

cotyledon *n.* any of the major convex subdivisions of the mature *placenta. Each cotyledon contains a major branch

胎盤葉 成熟胎盤的任何主要凸面分區。每個胎盤葉都有臍血管的一個大分支。這一分支

of the umbilical blood vessels, which branch further into the numerous villi that make up the surface of the cotyledon.

再繼續分成胎盤葉表面的大量絨毛。

cotyloid cavity *see* acetabulum.

髖臼　參閱 acetabulum。

couching *n*. an operation for cataract in which the lens is pushed out of the pupil downwards and backwards into the jelly-like vitreous humour by a small knife inserted through the edge of the cornea. It was widely employed in ancient Hindu civilizations and has been practised ever since. Its sole advantage is speed of performance, but modern developments in surgery and anaesthesia leave little place for it today. The complication rate is very high.

針撥術　一種摘除白內障的手術。用一小刀沿角膜邊緣插入，將晶狀體自瞳孔向下或向後撥入膠凍樣玻璃體液中。此術在古印度文明中被廣泛使用，並沿用至今。其唯一優點是手術迅速，但是，外科和麻醉的現代發展已使此術失去實用價值。此術合併症發生率很高。

coughing *n*. a form of violent exhalation by which irritant particles in the airways can be expelled. Stimulation of the cough reflexes results in the glottis being kept closed until a high expiratory pressure has built up, which is then suddenly released. Medical name: **tussis**.

咳嗽　一種猛烈的呼吸，借此排出呼吸道中的刺激物。咳嗽反射的刺激引起聲門關閉，直至強大的呼氣壓形成它又突然開放。醫學用語：咳。

coulomb *n*. the *SI unit of electric charge, equal to the quantity of electricity transferred by 1 ampere in 1 second. Symbol: C.

庫倫　電荷的國際單位，等於一秒鐘內通過一安培電流的電量。符號：C。

coumarin *n*. a drug used to prevent coagulation in the treatment of thrombophlebitis and pulmonary embolism. The main side-effect is haemorrhage.

香豆素　一種在治療血栓性靜脈炎和肺栓塞中用於預防凝血的藥物。主要的副作用是出血。

counselling *n*. **1.** a method of approaching psychological difficulties in adjustment that aims to help the client work out his own problems. The counsellor listens sympathetically, attempting to identify with the client, tries to clarify current problems, and sometimes gives advice. It involves less emphasis on

(1) 咨詢　一種解決適應性心理障礙的方法。其方法旨在幫助患者弄清自己的問題。咨詢員滿懷同情地聽取患者的陳述，並試圖和患者打成一片。努力澄清現存的問題，有時也給予建議。本法比心理療法或心理分析療法較少地涉及強調

insight and interpretation than does psychotherapy or psychoanalytic therapy. See also client-centred therapy. **2.** *see* genetic counselling.

對內心世界的洞察和解釋。參閱 client-centred therapy。**(2)** **遺傳咨詢** 參閱 genetic counselling。

counterextension *n.* an orthopaedic procedure consisting of *traction on one part of a limb, while the remainder of the limb is held steady: used particularly in the treatment of a fractured femur (thigh bone).

對抗牽引術 一種矯形外科方法，包括對肢體某一部分進行牽引，在該肢體其餘部分固定的情況下。特別用於治療股骨骨折。

counterirritant *n.* an agent, such as methyl salicylate, that causes irritation when applied to the skin and is used in order to relieve more deep-seated pain or discomfort. **–counterirritation** *n.*

抗刺激劑 一種用於塗搽在皮膚上能引起刺激的物質，如水楊酸甲酯。用以減輕深部的疼痛與不適。

countertraction *n.* the use of a balancing opposing force during *traction, when a strong continuous pull is applied to a limb so that broken bones can be kept in alignment during healing. To ensure that traction on a limb by weights and pulleys does not pull the patient out of bed, countertraction is often produced by applying tension to metal pins temporarily inserted into the opposite end of the bone.

對抗牽引 在牽引中，當一肢體被給予強力持續牽拉時，對肢體施加能保持平衡的相反作用力，以便在愈合期間斷骨能保持對位。為確保通過重物和滑輪對肢體進行牽引時患者不致被拉出床外，通常對臨時骨折對端的金屬釘加拉力以產生對抗牽引。

couvade *n.* **1.** a custom in some tribes whereby a father takes to his bed during or after the birth of his child. **2.** a symptom of abdominal pain experienced by a man in relation to his wife's giving birth. It may be due to *conversion disorder, anxiety, or sympathy.

(1) 父代母育 一些部落的一種風俗。在其孩子生育時或生育後，父親臥床的作法。**(2)** **夫代妻痛** 男子在其妻分娩時感到的腹部疼痛症狀。它可能由於轉換性障礙、焦慮、或同情而致。

cover-slip *n.* an extremely thin square or circle of glass used to protect the upper surface of a preparation on a microscope slide.

蓋玻片 用於保護顯微鏡載物片上的標本的方形或圓形薄玻璃片。

cover test a text used to detect a suppressed *strabismus (squint) in children.

覆蓋試驗 一種檢查兒童隱性斜視的試驗。讓兒童用一目注

The child is asked to look fixedly at an object with one eye while the other is kept open but covered by the hand of the observer. The hand is then withdrawn: if the eye that had been covered is seen to move towards the nose to adjust to the focus of the uncovered eye the child is assumed to have a divergent squint; movement of the eye away from the nose implies a convergent squint.

視某物，而另一目卻保持睜開，但被檢查者用手蓋住。然後取開此手。如果看到曾被遮蓋的眼睛向鼻側移動以調節未被遮蓋的眼睛的焦距，則認為該兒童可能有外隱斜視。如果向離開鼻側方向移動，則提示內隱斜視。

Cowper's glands (bulbourethral glands) a pair of small glands that open into the urethra at the base of the penis. Their secretion contributes to the seminal fluid, but less than that of the prostate gland or seminal vesicles.

考珀腺（尿道球腺） 一對在陰莖底部開口於尿道的小腺體。它們的分泌物構成精液的一部分，但比前列腺和精囊的分泌物少。

cowpox *n.* a virus infection of cows' udders, transmitted to man by direct contact, causing very mild symptoms similar to *smallpox. An attack confers immunity to smallpox. Medical name: **vaccinia**.

牛痘 牛乳腺的一種病毒感染。通過直接接觸而傳播給人，引起與天花類似的輕度症狀。患病後對天花有免疫力。醫學用語：牛痘。

cox- (coxo-) *prefix denoting* the hip. Example: *coxalgia* (pain in).

〔前綴〕**髖** 如髖關節痛。

coxa *n.* (*pl.* **coxae**) **1.** the hip bone. **2.** the hip joint.

(1) 髖骨 (2) 髖關節

Coxiella *n.* a genus of rickettsiae that cause disease in animals and man. They are transmitted to man by inhalation and produce disease characterized by inflammation of the lungs, without a rash (*compare* typhus). The single species, *C. burnetii*, causes *Q fever.

柯克斯體屬 一種能引起動物和人患病的立克次體。通過呼吸傳播給人，引起肺部炎症，但無皮疹（與 typhus 對比）為特點的疾病。伯納特柯克斯體單獨可引起 Q 熱。

Coxsackie virus (echovirus) one of a group of RNA-containing viruses that are able to multiply in the gastrointestinal tract (*see* enterovirus). About 30 different types exist. *Type A Coxsackie viruses* generally cause less severe and

柯薩奇病毒屬（埃可病毒） 一組在胃腸道中繁殖的含有 RNA 的病毒羣（參閱 enterovirus）。存在有大約 30 種不同類型。甲型柯薩奇病毒通常引起不太嚴重、界綫不太清楚的

less well-defined diseases, although some cause meningitis and severe throat infections (*see* herpangina). *Type B Coxsackie viruses* cause inflammation or degeneration of brain, skeletal muscle, or heart tissue (*see* Bornholm disease).

疾病，儘管一些引起腦膜炎和嚴重喉部感染（參閱 herpangina）。乙型柯薩奇病毒引起腦、骨骼肌或心肌組織的炎症或者變性（參閱 Bornholm disease）。

CPA *see* cyproterone.

醋酸環丙孕酮 參閱 cyproterone。

crab louse *see* Phthirus.

陰虱 參閱 Phthirus。

cradle *n*. a framework of metal strips or other material that forms a cage over an injured part of the body of a patient lying in bed, to protect it from the pressure of the bedclothes.

支架 由金屬條或其他材料做成的支架，它在臥床病人的身體損傷部位上方構成籠架，以保護其不受被褥的壓蓋。

cradle cap a common condition in young babies in which crusty white or yellow scales form a 'cap' on the scalp. It is treated by applying oil or using a special shampoo and usually resolves in the first year of life, although it may represent the start of seborrhoeic *eczema.

乳痂 幼兒中一種常見疾患。結痂性白色或黃色鱗屑在頭皮上形成一種「罩」。它通過搽塗油或運用特殊的洗髮劑而得以治療，且通常在第一年就消失，儘管它可能發展成脂溢性濕疹。

cramp *n*. prolonged painful contraction of a muscle. It is sometimes caused by an imbalance of the salts in the body, but is more often a result of fatigue, imperfect posture, or stress. Spasm in the muscles making it impossible to perform a specific task but allowing the use of these muscles for any other movement is called *occupational cramp*. It most often affects the hand muscles for writing (*writer's cramp*).

痛性痙攣 肌肉持續的痛性收縮。有時它是由體內鹽類失去平衡引起，但更經常是由疲勞、姿勢不當或壓力引起。如果肌肉無法完成某一特殊任務但可進行其他任何活動，這種痙攣稱為職業性痙攣。它最常累及寫字的手部肌肉（書寫痙攣）。

crani- (cranio-) *prefix denoting* the skull. Example: *cranioplasty* (plastic surgery of).

〔前綴〕**顱** 如顱成形術（整形外科的）。

cranial nerves the 12 pairs of nerves that arise directly from the brain and leave the skull through separate

腦神經 由腦直接發出，並通過不同孔裂而離開顱骨的12對神經。習慣上用羅馬數字

apertures; they are conventionally given Roman numbers, as follows: I *olfactory; II *optic; III *oculomotor; IV *trochlear; V *trigeminal; VI *abducens; VII *facial; VIII *vestibulocochlear; IX *glossopharyngeal; X *vagus; XI *accessory; XII *hypoglossal. *Compare* spinal nerves.

craniometry *n.* the science of measuring the differences in size and shape of skulls.

craniopharyngioma *n.* a brain tumour derived from remnants of *Rathke's pouch*, an embryologic structure from which the pituitary gland is partly formed. The patient may show raised intracranial pressure and *diabetes insipidus due to reduced secretion of the hormone *vasopressin. An X-ray of the skull typically shows calcification within the tumour and loss of the normal skull structure around the pituitary gland.

craniostenosis *n.* premature closing of the *sutures between the cranial bones during development, resulting in the skull remaining abnormally small. *Compare* craniosynostosis.

craniosynostosis *n.* premature fusion of some of the cranial bones, usually before birth, so that the skull is unable to expand in certain directions to assume its normal shape under the influence of the growing brain. Depending on which cranial *sutures fuse early, the skull may become elongated from front to back, broad and short, peaked (*oxycephaly or turricephaly*), or asymmetrical. *Compare* craniostenosis.

craniotomy *n.* **1.** surgical removal of a portion of the skull, to expose the brain and *meninges for inspection or biopsy

表示：I 嗅、II 視、III 動眼、IV 滑車、V 三叉、VI 展、VII 面、VIII 前庭耳蝸、IX 舌咽、X 迷走、XI 副、XII 舌下。與 spinal nerves 對比。

顱測量法　測量顱的大小和形狀差異的科學。

顱咽管瘤　由拉特克囊的殘餘部分形成的腦腫瘤，這是一種胚胎結構，由此形成腦垂體。患者可表現出顱內壓升高，並由於加壓素分泌減少而出現尿崩症。顱骨 X 綫典型表現為瘤體內鈣化、垂體周圍正常顱骨結構受到破壞。

顱狹小　在發育期顱骨間骨縫的過早閉合，導致顱異常小。與 craniosynostosis 對比。

顱縫早閉　一些顱骨的過早融合，通常在出生前就發生，從而，顱骨不能在大腦生長的影響下向某些方向膨大以實現其正常形狀。顱可能會從前到後拉長，變得寬而短、峯狀（尖頭或塔頭），或不對稱。這取決於那一顱縫融合過早。與 craniostenosis 對比。

(1) 顱骨切開術　外科切除部分顱骨以暴露腦和軟腦膜以便進行觀察病變或活檢，或減小

or to relieve excessive intracranial pressure (as in a subdural *haematoma). **2.** surgical perforation of the skull of a dead fetus during difficult labour, so that delivery may continue. For both operations the instrument used is called a *craniotome*.

過高的顱內壓（如在硬膜下血腫時）。**(2) 穿顱術** 難產時將死胎頭顱穿破的手術，以使分娩繼續。以上兩種手術所用的器械稱為開顱器。

cranium *n.* the part of the skeleton that encloses the brain. It consists of eight bones connected together by immovable joints (*see* skull). **–cranial** *adj.*

顱 包容腦的那部分骨骼。它由相互之間以不動關節連接的八塊骨組成（參閱 skull）。

creatinase (creatine kinase) *n.* an enzyme involved in the metabolic breakdown of creatine to creatinine.

肌酸酶 一種將肌酸分解代謝成肌酐的酶。

creatine *n.* a product of protein metabolism found in muscle. Its phosphate, *creatine phosphate* (*phosphocreatine*, *phosphagen*), acts as a store of highenergy phosphate in muscle and serves to maintain adequate amounts of *ATP (the source of energy for muscular contraction).

肌酸 肌肉中蛋白質代謝的一種產物。其磷酸鹽——磷酸肌酸在肌肉中起着高能磷酸鹽的貯存作用，以便保持足夠量的三磷酸腺苷（三磷酸腺苷為肌肉收縮的能量來源）。

creatinine *n.* a substance derived from creatine and creatine phosphate in muscle. Creatinine is excreted in the urine.

肌酸酐 肌肉中肌酸與磷酸肌酸的代謝產物。肌酸酐在尿中被排出。

creatinuria *n.* an excess of the nitrogenous compound creatine in the urine.

肌酸尿 尿中出現過量的含氮化合物——肌酸。

creatorrhoea *n.* the passage of excessive nitrogen in the faeces due to failure of digestion or absorption in the small intestine. It is found particularly in pancreatic failure. *See* cystic fibrosis, pancreatitis.

肉質泄瀉 由於小腸消化或吸收障礙而在糞便中排出過量氮質。特別在胰腺功能障礙時易見。參閱 cystic fibrosis，pancreatitis。

Credé's method a technique for expelling the placenta from the uterus. With the uterus contracted, downward pressure is applied to it through the abdominal wall in the direction of the birth canal.

克雷德法 將胎盤從子宮排出的技術。隨着子宮的收縮，經腹壁朝產道方向推壓。這一方法現已大多被布-安氏法所代替。

This method has now been largely replaced by the *Brandt Andrews method.

creeping eruption (larva migrans) a skin disease caused either by larvae of certain nematode worms (e.g. *Ancylostoma braziliense*) normally parasitic in dogs and cats or by the maggots of certain flies (*see* Hypoderma, Gasterophilus). The larvae burrow within the skin tissues, their movements marked by long thin red lines that cause the patient intense irritation. The nematode infections are treated with diethylcarbamazine or thiabendazole; maggots can be surgically removed.

匐行疹（幼蟲遊走症） 由通常寄生於狗和貓的某些綫蟲（如巴西鈎口綫蟲）的幼蟲或某些蠅類（參閱 Hypoderma Gasterophilus）的蛆引起的皮膚病。幼蟲在皮膚組織內掘溝移動並引起病人強烈刺癢，外表以細長的紅綫為特徵。綫蟲感染用乙胺嗪或噻苯達唑治療；蛆則可用外科方法切除。

crenation *n.* an abnormal appearance of red blood cells seen under a microscope, in which the normally smooth cell margins appear crinkly or irregular. Crenation may be a feature of certain blood disorders, but most commonly occurs as a result of prolonged storage of a blood specimen prior to preparation of a blood film.

皺縮紅細胞 顯微鏡下觀察到的一種紅細胞的異常外觀。此時，正常平滑的邊緣表現出皺縮狀或不規則。皺縮紅細胞可能是某些血液病的一個特徵，但大多數由於血標本製作血片前保存過久所致。

crepitation (rale) *n.* a soft fine crackling sound heard in the lungs through the stethoscope. Crepitations are made either by air passages and alveoli (air sacs) opening up during inspiration or by air bubbling through fluid. They are not normally heard in healthy lungs.

捻發音（囉音） 通過聽診器在肺部所聽到的一種輕微細小的破裂音。捻發音是由於吸氣時氣管和肺泡開放所致，或者氣泡通過液體產生的。通常，在健康肺臟，這些音聽不到。

crepitus *n.* **1.** a crackling sound or grating feeling produced by bone rubbing on bone or roughened cartilage, detected on movement of an arthritic joint. Crepitus in the knee joint is a common sign of *chondromalacia patellae in the young and *osteoarthritis in the elderly. **2.** a similar sound heard with a stethoscope over an inflamed lung when the patient breathes in.

(1) 骨摩擦音 骨與骨摩擦或與粗糙的軟骨摩擦產生的破裂音或摩擦感，出現於發炎的關節活動時。膝關節的骨摩擦音是年輕人髕骨軟骨軟化和老年人骨關節炎的常見體徵。**(2) 捻發音** 用聽診器在發炎肺部吸氣時所聽到的一種類似的音。

cresol *n.* a strong antiseptic effective against many microorganisms and used mostly in soap solutions as a general disinfectant. It is sometimes used in low concentrations as a preservative in injections. Cresol solutions irritate the skin and if taken by mouth are corrosive and cause pain, nausea, and vomiting.

crest *n.* a ridge or linear protuberance, particularly on a bone. Examples include the crest of fibula and the iliac crest (of the ilium).

cretinism *n.* a syndrome of *dwarfism, mental retardation, and coarseness of the skin and facial features due to lack of thyroid hormone from birth (congenital *hypothyroidism).

Creutzfeldt-Jakob disease *see* spongiform encephalopathy.

cribriform plate *see* ethmoid bone.

cricoid cartilage the cartilage, shaped like a signet ring, that forms part of the anterior and lateral walls and most of the posterior wall of the *larynx.

cri-du-chat syndrome a congenital condition of mental retardation associated with multiple physical abnormalities and an abnormal catlike cry in infancy. It results from a chromosomal abnormality in which one of the arms of chromosome no. 5 is missing.

crisis *n.* **1.** the turning point of a disease, after which the patient either improves or deteriorates. Since the advent of antibiotics, infections seldom reach the point of crisis. **2.** the occurrence of sudden severe pain in certain diseases. *See also* Dietl's crisis.

甲酚 一種對許多微生物都有很好效果的殺菌劑，常以肥皂溶液的形式作為一般消毒劑。有時用其低濃度做為注射液的防腐劑。甲酚溶液刺激皮膚，若吞服，則具腐蝕作用，引起疼痛、惡心和嘔吐。

嵴 脊狀或綫性隆凸，特別指骨上的這種結構。如腓骨嵴和髂嵴。

克汀病 因先天缺乏甲狀腺激素（先天甲狀腺機能減退）而導致的以侏儒症、智力低下、皮膚和面部粗糙為特徵的一種綜合徵。

克-雅氏病 參閱 spongiform encephalopathy。

篩板 參閱 ethmoid bone。

環狀軟骨 形狀類似圖章戒指的軟骨，形成喉的前壁和側壁的一部分，後壁的大部分。

貓叫綜合徵 嬰兒期有多種身體畸形，並伴有像貓叫樣的一種先天性智力障礙疾患。它是由染色體異常引起的，第五號染色體的一臂丟失。

(1) 極期 病人疾病好轉或惡化的轉折點。由於抗生素的出現，感染很少有達到極期的。
(2) 危象 某些疾病突然出現嚴重的疼痛。參閱 Dietl's crisis。

crista *n.* (*pl.* **cristae**) **1.** the sensory structure within the ampulla of a *semicircular canal within the inner ear (see illustration). The cristae respond to changes in the rate of movement of the head, being activated by pressure from the fluid in the semicircular canals. **2.** one of the infoldings of the inner membrane of a *mitochondrion. **3.** any anatomical structure resembling a crest.

(1) 壺腹嵴 內耳半規管壺腹內的感覺末梢器（見圖）。壺腹嵴通過接受半規管內液體壓力的刺激而對頭部運動速度的變化發生反應。**(2) 綫粒體嵴** 綫粒體內膜向內褶疊的部分。**(3) 嵴狀結構** 任何類似嵴狀的解剖結構。

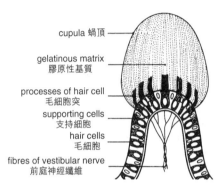

cupula 蝸頂

gelatinous matrix 膠原性基質

processes of hair cell 毛細胞突

supporting cells 支持細胞

hair cells 毛細胞

fibres of vestibular nerve 前庭神經纖維

A crista in the ampulla of a semicircular canal
內耳半規管的壺腹嵴

Crohn's disease a condition in which segments of the alimentary tract become inflamed, thickened, and ulcerated. It usually affects the terminal part of the ileum; its acute form (*acute ileitis*) may mimic *appendicitis. Chronic disease often causes partial obstruction of the intestine, leading to pain, diarrhoea, and *malabsorption. *Fistulae around the anus, between adjacent loops of intestine, or from intestine to skin, bladder, etc. are characteristic complications. The cause is unknown. Treatment includes rest, corticosteroids, immunosuppressive drugs, antibiotics, dietary modification, or (in some cases) surgical removal of the affected part of the intestine. Alternative

克羅恩病 消化道的某些節段出現炎症、增厚和潰瘍的一種疾病。它多累及迴腸末段。其急性型（急性迴腸炎）可能與闌尾炎相似。慢性病常引起部分迴腸梗阻，導致疼痛、腹瀉和吸收不良。肛周、相鄰腸袢之間，或由腸管到皮膚、膀胱等部位形成的瘻管是本病的典型併發症。病因不明。治療包括休息，使用皮質醇類、免疫抑制劑、抗生素、改變飲食或者（在一些病例中）對患病腸段進行外科切除。其他可代替名稱有：局部性腸炎、節段性迴腸炎。

names: **regional enteritis**, **regional ileitis**.

cromolyn sodium a drug used to prevent and treat asthma and allergic bronchitis. It is administered by inhalation and may cause throat irritation. Trade name: **Intal**.

色甘酸鈉 一種用於預防和治療哮喘和變應性支氣管炎的藥物。通過吸入使用，可引起喉頭刺激。商品名：Intal。

crossbite *n.* a condition in which some or all of the lower teeth close outside the upper teeth when the mandible is as far back as it will go.

反殆 下頜骨盡力回縮時下牙仍部分或全部關閉在上牙之外的情況。

cross-dressing *n. see* transvestism.

易裝癖 參閱 transvestism。

crossing over (in genetics) the exchange of sections of chromatids that occurs between pairs of homologous chromosomes, which results in the recombination of genetic material. It occurs during *meiosis at a *chiasma.

交換 （遺傳學）在成對的同源染色體之間發生的染色單體的部分交換。它導致遺傳物質的重組。它發生於交叉時的減數分裂期間。

cross-over trial *see* intervention study.

交叉實驗 參閱 intervention study。

cross-sectional study the collection and analysis of information relating to persons in a population or group at a defined point in time (or within a defined period), with particular reference to their individual characteristics and exposure to factors thought likely to predispose to disease. *See also* prevalence rate.

橫面調查 在一特定的時間（或在一特定時期）對一人羣或羣體進行的資料收集和分析。着重了解其個體特徵和接觸可疑病因的情況。參閱 prevalence rate。

crotamiton *n.* a drug that destroys mites and is used to treat scabies and similar skin infections and also to relieve itching. It is applied to the skin as a lotion or ointment and sometimes causes reddening and hypersensitivity reactions. Trade name: **Eurax**.

克羅米能 一種殺蟎藥。用於治療疥瘡和類似的皮膚感染，也用於止癢。以洗劑或軟膏外用於皮膚，有時引起皮膚發紅或過敏。商品名：Eurax。

croup *n.* acute inflammation and obstruction of the respiratory tract, involving the

哮吼 累及幼兒（通常 6 個月至 3 歲之間）喉部和主要呼吸

larynx and the main air passages (trachea and bronchi), in young children (usually aged between six months and three years). The usual cause is a virus infection but bacterial secondary infection can occur. The symptoms are those of *laryngitis, accompanied by signs of obstruction – harsh difficult breathing (*see* stridor), a rising pulse rate, restlessness, and *cyanosis. Treatment by reassurance and humidification of the inspired air usually reverses the alarming symptoms. In severe cases the obstruction may require treatment by *intubation or *tracheostomy. *See also* epiglottitis.

管道（氣管和支氣管）的呼吸道急性炎症和梗阻。通常病因是病毒感染，但細菌繼發性感染亦可發生。症狀與喉炎症狀相同，伴隨梗塞體徵：喘鳴性呼吸困難（參閱 stridor）、脈率加快、坐卧不安和紫紺。通過安慰和增加吸入空氣的濕度治療通常可緩解症狀。在嚴重病例中，可能需要插管或行氣管切開術。參閱 epiglottitis。

crown *n.* **1.** the part of a tooth normally visible in the mouth and usually covered by enamel. **2.** a dental *restoration that covers most or all of the natural crown. It may be made of porcelain, gold, a combination of these, or less commonly other materials. Most crowns are like thimbles and are custom made to fit over a trimmed-down tooth. A *post crown* is used to restore a tooth when insufficient of the natural crown remains. A post is inserted into the root and the missing centre of the tooth is built up; over it is fitted a thimble-like crown to restore the natural shape of the tooth. *Root canal treatment is required before a post crown can be made.

(1) 牙冠 通常指口腔內牙齒的可見和被釉質覆蓋部分。**(2) 人工牙冠** 覆蓋大部分或所有自然牙冠的牙科修復體。它可由瓷、金或瓷金結合製作而成，偶爾也用其他材料製作。多數牙冠像罩冠，要根據修整了的牙齒預先定製，以便嵌戴。當自然牙冠所留部分不足時則用樁冠修復該牙。冠樁插入牙根，從而使該牙齒所失中心得以建立；外面再套一個套筒樣罩冠以恢復牙齒的自然外形。樁冠施行前要進行根管治療。

crowning *n.* **1.** the stage of labour when the upper part of the infant's head is encircled by, and just passing through, the vaginal opening. **2.** (in dentistry) the technique of treating and fitting a tooth with an artificial *crown.

(1) 着冠 分娩的一個階段。此時嬰兒頭的上部被陰道口包圍或剛穿過陰道口。**(2) 造冠術** （牙科學）用一人造牙冠修復並安裝牙齒的技術。

cruciate ligaments a pair (anterior and posterior) of ligaments inside each knee joint, which help to prevent excessive

膝十字韌帶 每一膝關節內的一對（前和後）韌帶。它防止過度地前後滑動。膝十字韌帶

anteroposterior glide. Damage to the cruciate ligaments is a common *sports injury, especially in football players.

損傷是常見的一種運動損傷，特別在足球運動員中。

crude rate the total number of events (e.g. cases of lung cancer) expressed as a percentage (or rate per 1000, etc.) of the whole population. When factors such as age structure or sex of populations may seriously affect their rates (as in *mortality or *morbidity rates) it is more meaningful to compare age/sex specific rates using one or more age groups of a designated sex (e.g. lung cancer in males aged 55–64 years). More complex calculations, which take account of the age bias of a population as a whole, can produce *standardized rates* or – as has been used for deciding resource allocation in the British National Health Service – *standardized mortality ratios* (SMR). In these the ratios of subgroups are expressed as percentages of that for a designated or standard population (e.g. England and Wales), particularly applied to the age bracket 15–64 years.

總發生率 按百分率（或千分率）表示的全體人口中某一疾病（如肺癌）發生的總數。當總人口中諸如年齡結構或性別嚴重影響這些比率時（如在死亡率和發病率中），採用一個或多個指定性別年齡組來比較具體的年齡和性別的某一疾病發生的比率，則更有意義（如 55~64 歲的男性中肺癌死亡率和發病率）。通過總人口中年齡結構差異的更為複雜的計算法可算出標準化率或者就像英國國民保健服務制在決定財政撥款時一直使用的標準化死亡率（SMR）。在這些情況下，各分組的比率是用指定的或標準的人口中的百分比來表示（如英格蘭和威爾士）。這種方法特別適用於 15~64 歲年齡組。

crural *adj.* **1.** relating to the thigh or leg. **2.** relating to the crura cerebri (*see* crus).

(1) 腳的 與大腿或腿相關的。**(2) 大腦腳的** 與大腦腳有關的（參閱 crus）。

crus *n.* (*pl.* **crura**) an elongated process or part of a structure. The *crus cerebri* is one of two symmetrical nerve tracts situated between the medulla oblongata and the cerebral hemispheres.

腳 一長條形突起或一結構的長條形部分。大腦腳是位於延腦和大腦半球之間的一對相互對稱的神經束。

crush syndrome kidney failure following massive trauma to, and necrosis of, muscle. It results from acute necrosis of the renal tubules associated with the presence in the blood of *myohaemoglobin, released from the damaged muscle.

擠壓綜合徵 大面積肌肉損傷和壞死後出現的腎功能衰竭。其原因是由於血中出現由損壞的肌肉所釋放的肌紅蛋白而產生的腎小管壞死引起的。

cry- (cryo-) *prefix denoting* cold.

〔前綴〕冷 表示冷。

cryaesthesia *n*. **1.** exceptional sensitivity to low temperature. **2.** a sensation of coldness.

冷凝球蛋白 在某些病中有可能在血液中出現的一種異常蛋白——免疫球蛋白（參閱para-protein）。在低溫時，冷凝球蛋白變得不能溶解。在寒冷天氣裏導致手指和腳趾頭的小血管阻塞，並產生典型的皮疹。冷凝蛋白的出現（冷凝蛋白血症）可能是多種疾病的一個特徵，包括巨球蛋白血症、系統性紅斑狼瘡和某些感染。

(1) 冷覺過敏 對低溫的異常過敏。(2) 冷覺 對寒冷的感覺。

cryoglobulin *n*. an abnormal protein – an *immunoglobulin (see paraprotein) – that may be present in the blood in certain diseases. Cryoglobulins become insoluble at low temperatures, leading to obstruction of small blood vessels in the fingers and toes in cold weather and producing a characteristic rash. The presence of cryoglobulins (*cryoglobulinaemia*) may be a feature of a variety of diseases, including *macroglobulinaemia, systemic *lupus erythematosus, and certain infections.

冷沉澱物 在人工控制的條件下通過冷凍和解凍而產生的沉澱物質。冷沉澱物的一個例子是在 4°C 時解凍被冷凍的新鮮血液所得到的沉澱物。這種沉澱物富含凝血因子Ⅷ（抗血友病因子），用於控制血友病出血。

cryoprecipitate *n*. a precipitate produced by freezing and thawing under controlled conditions. An example of a cryoprecipitate is the residue obtained from fresh frozen blood plasma that has been thawed at 4°C. This residue is extremely rich in a clotting factor, Factor VIII (antihaemophilic factor), and is used in the control of bleeding in *haemophilia.

冷藏 通過冷凍來保存組織。胚胎的冷藏被作為體外受精技術的一部分，例如因醫療原因而推遲妊娠時。

cryopreservation *n*. preservation of tissues by freezing. Cryopreservation of embryos may be employed as part of *in vitro fertilization procedures, for example if there are medical reasons for delaying the pregnancy.

冷刀 參閱 cryosurgery。

cryoprobe *n*. *see* cryosurgery.

(1) 冷凍切片機 一種裝有切片機來切割冷凍組織的小盒。(2) 低溫控制器 一種用於保持一特定低溫的裝置。

cryostat *n*.**1.** a chamber in which frozen tissue is sectioned with a *microtome. **2.** a device for maintaining a specific low temperature.

冷凍手術 在身體的局部採用高度冷卻以冷凍和破壞不想要的組織。冷凍手術通常借用一

cryosurgery *n*. the use of extreme cold in a localized part of the body to freeze and destroy unwanted tissues.

Cryosurgery is usually undertaken with an instrument called a *cryoprobe*, which has a fine tip cooled by allowing carbon dioxide or nitrous oxide gas to expand within it. Cryosurgery is commonly used for the treatment of detached retina, the destruction of certain bone tumours, and the obliteration of skin blemishes.

種稱做冷刀的儀器進行。這一冷刀有一尖端，通過使其內部的二氧化碳或氧化亞氮氣體膨脹而致冷。冷凍手術通常用於治療視網膜剝脫、破壞某些骨腫瘤和去除皮膚贅生物。

cryotherapy *n.* the use of cold in the treatment of disorders. *See* cryosurgery, hypothermia (def. 2). *Compare* thermotherapy.

冷凍療法 在治療疾病中使用冷卻的方法。參閱 cryosurgery，hypothermia（第二個釋義）。與 thermotherapy 對比。

crypt *n.* a small sac, follicle, or cavity; for example, the crypts of Lieberkühn (*see* Lieberkühn's glands), which are intestinal glands.

小囊，小泡，小腔 如利貝屈恩腺（參閱 Lieberkühn's glands），為腸腺。

crypt- (crypto-) *prefix denoting* concealed. Example: *cryptogenic* (of unknown origin).

〔前綴〕隱 表示隱蔽的。如隱原性的（不明原因的）。

cryptococcosis (torulosis) *n.* a disease of worldwide distribution, but recognized mainly in the USA, caused by the fungus *Cryptococcus neoformans*. The fungus attacks the lung, resulting in a tumour-like solid mass (*toruloma*), but produces few or no symptoms referable to the lungs. It may spread to the brain, leading to meningitis. The condition responds well to treatment with *amphotericin B.

隱球菌病 在世界範圍內都有，但主要在美國發現，由叫做新型隱球菌的真菌引起的一種疾病。該真菌侵襲肺，導致瘤樣實塊（隱球菌結節），但很少產生或不產生有關肺部病變的症狀。它可能擴散至腦，導致腦膜炎。本病用兩性黴素 B 治療效果好。

Cryptococcus *n.* a genus of unicellular yeastlike fungi that cause disease in man. They are found in soil (particularly when enriched with pigeon droppings), and they are common in pigeon roosts and nests. The species *C. neoformans* causes *cryptococcosis.

隱球菌屬 一種引起人類疾病的單細胞酵母樣真菌。它們見於土壤裏（特別是被施以鴿糞而肥沃的土壤）。而且，它們在鴿棚和鴿巢內常見。新型隱球菌可引起隱球菌病。

cryptomenorrhoea *n.* absence of blood flow when the internal symptoms of

隱發月經 有月經的體內症狀但無月經流出的現象。這一疾

menstruation are present. The condition may arise because the hymen at the entrance to the vagina lacks an opening (*imperforate hymen) or because of some other obstruction.

病的發生是由於陰道口處女膜沒有開口（處女膜閉鎖）或因其他阻塞而引起。

cryptophthalmos *n.* apparent absence of the eyes due to failure of normal eyelid formation during embryonic development, resulting in absence of the opening between the upper and lower eyelids.

隱眼畸形 在胚胎發育期間由於正常眼瞼形成障礙而出現明顯的無眼，從而導致上眼瞼和下眼瞼間沒有開口。

cryptorchidism (cryptorchism) *n.* the condition in which the testes fail to descend into the scrotum and are retained within the abdomen or inguinal canal. The operation of *orchidopexy is necessary to bring the testes into the scrotum before puberty in order to allow subsequent normal development; it is thought that the higher temperature in the abdomen interferes with sperm production. **–cryptorchid** *adj., n.*

隱睾症 睾丸未能降入陰囊而停留於腹腔或腹股溝管內的疾病。睾丸固定手術有必要在青春期前施行以便使睾丸能降入陰囊，從而保證隨後的正常發育。一般認為腹腔內的高溫影響精子的產生。

CSF 1. *see* cerebrospinal fluid. **2.** *see* colony-stimulating factor.

(1) 腦脊液 參閱 cerebrospinal fluid。**(2) 細胞集落刺激因子** 參閱 colony-stimulating factor。

CS gas a powerful incapacitating gas used in warfare and riot control. The sufferer experiences a burning sensation in the eyes, difficulty in breathing, tightness of the chest, nausea, vomiting, and streaming from the eyes and nose. In confined spaces the gas can prove fatal.

CS 毒氣 用於戰爭和暴力控制的一種烈性使人失去能力的氣體。受害者眼內感受到一種灼燒感，呼吸困難、胸悶、惡心、嘔吐、大量流眼淚和鼻涕。在通氣不良環境裏，該氣體被證明是致命的。

CT *see* computerized tomography.

電子計算機斷層照相術 參閱 computerized tomography。

cubital *adj.* relating to the elbow or forearm; for example the *cubital fossa* is the depression at the front of the elbow.

肘的 與肘或前臂相聯繫的。如肘窩是肘前部的凹陷處。

cuboid bone the outer bone of the *tarsus, which articulates with the fourth and fifth metatarsal bones in front and with the calcaneus (heel bone) behind.

骰骨　跗骨中的外側骨，前與第四、第五蹠骨構成關節，後與跟骨構成關節。

cuirass *n. see* respirator.

護胸甲　參閱 respirator。

culdocentesis *n. see* colpotomy.

後穹窿穿刺術　參閱 colpotomy。

culdoscope *n.* a tubular instrument with lenses and a light source, used for direct observation of the uterus, ovaries, and Fallopian tubes (*culdoscopy*). The instrument is passed through the wall of the vagina behind to the neck of the uterus. The culdoscope has now been largely replaced by the *laparoscope.

後穹窿鏡　一種管狀器械，帶有透鏡和光源，用於直接觀察子宮、卵巢和輸卵管（後穹窿檢查術）。該器械通過子宮頸後部穿過陰道壁。現在，後穹窿鏡已大多被腹腔鏡所取代。

Culex *n.* a genus of mosquitoes, world-wide in distribution, of which there are some 600 species. Certain species are important as vectors of filariasis (*see also* Wuchereria) and viral encephalitis.

庫蚊屬　分布於全球的一屬蚊子，大約有 600 種。某些種類具有臨床重要性，因其是絲蟲病（參閱 Wuchereria）和病毒性腦炎的傳播媒介。

culicide *n.* an agent that destroys mosquitoes or gnats.

殺蚊劑　一種殺死蚊和蚋的藥劑。

culmen *n.* an area of the upper surface of the *cerebellum, anterior to the declive and posterior to the central lobule and separated from them by deep fissures.

山頂　小腦上部表面的一個區域，位於小腦山坡前，中央小葉後，並通過深溝與它們隔開。

culture 1. *n.* a population of microorganisms, usually bacteria, grown in a solid or liquid laboratory medium (*culture medium*), which is usually *agar, broth, or *gelatin. A *pure culture* consists of a single bacterial species. A *stab culture* is a bacterial culture growing in a plug of solid medium within a bottle (or tube); the medium is inoculated by 'stabbing' it with a bacteria-coated

(1) 培養物　在固體或液體實驗室培養基中生長的微生物種羣（通常為細菌）。培養基通常是瓊脂、肉湯或明膠。純培養物由單一菌種構成。穿刺培養物是用染菌的直金屬絲刺入瓶（或試管）內的固體培養基中進行接種生長。存貯培養物是一種恆久細菌培養物，可進行傳代培養（參閱 tissue

straight wire. A *stock culture* is a permanent bacterial culture, from which subcultures are made. *See also* tissue culture.
2. *vb.* to grow bacteria or other microorganisms in cultures.

culture）。**(2) 培養**　在培養基內培養細菌或其他微生物。

cumulative action the toxic effects of a drug produced by repeated administration of small doses at intervals that are not long enough for it to be either broken down or excreted by the body.

蓄積作用　重複小劑量用藥而產生的毒性作用。用藥的間隔不長，藥物未被身體分解或排出體外。

cumulus oophoricus a cluster of follicle cells that surround a freshly ovulated ovum. By increasing the effective size of the ovum they may assist its entrance into the end of the Fallopian tube. They are dispersed at fertilization by the contents of the *acrosome.

卵丘　在剛排出的卵子周圍的一羣卵泡細胞。通過增加卵子的有效體積，這些卵泡細胞可幫助其進入輸卵管末端。在受精時，它們被精子頂體的內容物所溶解。

cuneiform bones three bones in the *tarsus – the *lateral* (external), *intermediate* (middle), and *medial* (internal) cuneiform bones – that articulate respectively with the first, second, and third metatarsal bones in front. All three bones articulate with the navicular bone behind.

楔骨　跗骨中的三塊骨頭：外側楔骨、中間楔骨和內側楔骨。前與第一、第二和第三蹠骨構成關節。所有三塊骨頭後與舟狀骨構成關節。

cuneus *n.* a wedge-shaped area of *cerebral cortex that forms the inner surface of the occipital lobe.

楔葉　大腦皮層中形成枕葉內側面的楔形部分。

Cuniculus *n.* a genus of large forest-dwelling rodents, the pacas or spotted cavies, found in South and Central America. In Brazil these animals are a natural reservoir of the parasite *Leishmania braziliensis*, which causes espundia (*see* leishmaniasis).

隧鼠屬　生活在森林裏的一類大型嚙齒動物。如天竺鼠（又稱花斑豚鼠）。見於南美和中美洲。在巴西，這些動物是巴西利什曼原蟲的自然貯主，它能引起鼻咽黏膜利什曼病（參閱 leishmaniasis）。

cupola *n.* **1.** the small dome at the end of the cochlea. **2.** any of several dome-shaped anatomical structures.

頂　**(1)** 耳蝸末端的小圓頂。
(2) 任一圓頂狀解剖學結構。

cupping *n.* the former practice of applying a heated cup to the skin and allowing it to cool, which causes swelling of the tissues beneath and an increase in the flow of blood in the area. This was thought to draw out harmful excess blood from diseased organs nearby and so promote healing. In *wet cupping* the skin was previously cut, so that blood would actually flow into the cup and could be removed.

杯吸術　過去使用的一種治療方法。把一加熱的杯子置於皮膚上，並待其冷卻，這引起皮下組織腫脹，並增加該區域的血流。一般認為此方法能吸出鄰近病變器官中過多的有害血液，並因而促進痊愈。在濕杯吸術中，皮膚事先切開，因此，血液實際上流入杯內，並被清除。

cupula *n.* a small dome-shaped structure consisting of sensory hairs embedded in gelatinous material, forming part of a *crista in the ampullae of the semicircular canals of the ear.

蝸頂　一種小的圓頂狀結構，由浸埋於膠樣物質中的感覺性毛細胞構成。它構成耳的半規管壺腹嵴的一部分。

curare *n.* an extract from the bark of South American trees (*Strychnos* and *Chondodendron* species) that relaxes and paralyses voluntary muscle. Used for centuries as an arrow poison by South American Indians, curare was formerly employed to control the muscle spasms of tetanus and, more recently, as a muscle relaxant in surgical operations. It has now been replaced in surgery by *tubocurarine.

箭毒　從南美一種樹（馬錢屬和剛多防己屬）的皮中提取的物質。這種物質鬆弛和麻痺隨意肌。數世紀來，南美印第安人將其用做箭毒，以前也用它控制破傷風時的肌肉痙攣。後來，在外科手術中用做肌肉鬆弛劑。現在，已被筒箭毒鹼所代替。

curettage *n.* the scraping of the skin or the internal surface of an organ or body cavity by means of a spoon-shaped instrument (*curette*), usually to remove diseased tissue or to obtain a specimen for diagnostic purposes (*see also* dilatation and curettage). Curettage of the skin is combined with cauterization; it may be used for the removal of *basal cell carcinoma, seborrhoeic *keratoses, etc., and usually causes little scarring.

刮除術　用一勺形器械（刮匙）刮擦皮膚或者一器官或體腔內表面的手術，通常是為了刮除病變組織或者是為了診斷目的而獲取標本（參閱 dilatation and curettage）。皮膚刮除術要與燒灼術相結合。它可用於摘除基底細胞瘤、脂溢性角化病等。通常遺留小瘢痕。

curette *n.* a spoon-shaped instrument for scraping tissue from a cavity (*see* curettage, dilatation and curettage).

刮匙　從體腔上刮擦組織的一種勺狀器械（參閱 curettage，dilatation and curettage）。

curie *n*. a former unit for expressing the activity of a radioactive substance. It has been replaced by the *becquerel. Symbol: Ci.

居里 過去使用的一種表示放射性物質的放射性的單位。它已被「貝可」取代。符號：Ci。

Curling's ulcers gastric or duodenal ulcers associated with stress from severe injury of major burns.

柯林潰瘍 因嚴重外傷或大面積燒傷而致的應激性胃潰瘍或十二指腸潰瘍。

Curschmann's spirals elongated *casts of the smaller bronchi, which are coughed up in bronchial asthma. They unroll to a length of 2 cm or more and have a central core ensheathed in mucus and cell debris.

庫施曼螺旋 支氣管哮喘咳出的細支氣管管型。它們伸開可達 2 cm 長或者更長些，且在黏膜和細胞碎片裏包繞有一中心核。

Cushing's syndrome the condition resulting from excess amounts of *corti-costeroid hormones in the body. Symptoms include weight gain, reddening of the face and neck, excess growth of body and facial hair, raised blood pressure, loss of mineral from the bones (osteo-porosis), raised blood glucose levels, and sometimes mental disturbances. The syndrome may be due to overstimulation of the adrenal glands by excessive amounts of the hormone ACTH, secreted either by a tumour of the pituitary gland (*Cushing's disease*) or by a malignant tumour in the lung or elsewhere. Other causes include a benign or malignant tumour of the adrenal gland(s) resulting in excess activity of the gland and pro-longed therapy with high doses of corti-costeroid drugs (such as prednisone).

庫欣綜合徵 因體內皮質類固醇類激素過多而引起的疾病。症狀包括體重增加、面部和頸部潮紅、體毛和面部毛髮過多生長、血壓升高、骨內礦物質脫失（骨質疏鬆病）、血糖升高，且有時有精神障礙。該疾病可能是由於過量的促腎上腺皮質激素過強刺激腎上腺所致。垂體腫瘤（庫欣病）或肺部或其他部位的惡性腫瘤都會分泌大量促腎上腺皮質激素。其他病因包括腎上腺本身引起腺體過多活動的良性或惡性腫瘤。使用大劑量的皮質類固醇藥物（如潑尼松）進行長期治療。

cusp *n*. **1.** any of the cone-shaped promi-nences on teeth, especially the molars and premolars. **2.** a pocket or fold of the mem-brane (endocardium) lining the heart or of the layer of the wall of a vein, several of which form a *valve. When the blood flows backwards the cusps fill up and become distended, so closing the valve.

(1) 牙尖 牙齒上的任一圓錐形突起，尤指磨牙和前磨牙上的突起。**(2)** 瓣尖 附於心臟內膜（心內膜）或血管內壁上的褶疊物或袋狀物。幾個此種結構構成瓣。當血液逆流時，瓣尖充盈，變得擴張，因此該瓣就關閉。

cutaneous *adj.* relating to the skin.

皮膚的 與皮膚相關的。

cuticle *n.* **1.** the *epidermis of the skin. **2.** a layer of solid or semisolid material that is secreted by and covers an *epithelium. **3.** a layer of cells, such as the outer layer of cells in a hair.

(1) 表皮 皮膚外表層。**(2) 護膜** 由某種上皮細胞分泌並覆蓋於該上皮細胞的固體層或半固體物質層。**(3) 角質層** 一層細胞，如毛髮細胞的外層。

cutis *n. see* skin.

皮膚 參閱 skin。

CVP *see* central venous pressure.

中心靜脈壓 參閱 central venous pressure。

CVS *see* chorionic villus sampling.

絨膜絨毛取樣 參閱 chorionic villus sampling。

cyan- (cyano-) *prefix denoting* blue.

〔前綴〕青紫色，藍色

cyanide *n.* any of the notoriously poisonous salts of hydrocyanic acid. Cyanides combine with and render inactive the enzymes of the tissues responsible for cellular respiration, and therefore they kill extremely quickly; unconsciousness is followed by convulsions and death. Hydrogen cyanide vapour is fatal in less than a minute when inhaled. Sodium or potassium cyanide taken by mouth may also kill within minutes. Prompt treatment with amyl nitrite and sodium thiosulphate or dicobalt *edetate may save life. Cyanides give off a smell of bitter almonds.

氰化物 眾所周知的氫氰酸的有毒鹽類。氰化物與組織內負責細胞呼吸的酶相結合，使之失去活性，因此，它們引起死亡極快。患者意識喪失，隨之為驚厥和死亡。吸入氫氰酸蒸氣後不到一分鐘就可致命。口服氰化鉀或氰化鈉也可以幾分鐘內致死。用亞硝酸異戊酯和硫代硫酸鈉或依地酸二鈷進行立刻治療可挽救生命。氰化物釋放一種苦杏仁味。

cyanocobalamin *n. see* vitamin B_{12}.

氰鈷胺 參閱 vitamin B_{12}。

cyanopsia *n.* a condition in which everything looks bluish.

藍視症 一切視物皆呈藍色的疾病。

cyanosis *n.* a bluish discoloration of the skin and mucous membranes resulting from an inadequate amount of oxygen in the blood. Cyanosis is associated with heart failure, lung diseases, the breathing of oxygen-deficient atmospheres, and

紫紺 由於血液中氧量不足而導致的皮膚和黏膜變藍的病症。紫紺發生於心力衰竭、肺病、呼吸含氧量不足的大氣以及窒息時，也見於患先天性心臟病的青紫嬰兒。

asphyxia. Cyanosis is also seen in *blue babies, because of congenital heart defects. **–cyanotic** *adj.*

cybernetics *n.* the science of communication processes and automatic control systems in both machines and living things: a study linking the working of the brain and nervous system with the functioning of computers and automated feedback devices. *See also* bionics.

控制論　研究機器和生物中信息傳遞過程和自動控制系統的科學。這是一門把腦和神經系統的運作和計算機和自動反饋裝置的功能聯繫起來研究的科學。參閱 bionics。

cycl- (cyclo-) *prefix denoting* **1.** cycle or cyclic. **2.** the ciliary body. Example: *cyclectomy* (excision of).

〔前綴〕**(1)** 環　環或環的。**(2)** 睫狀體　如睫狀體切除術。

cyclamate *n.* either of two compounds, sodium or calcium cyclamate, that are thirty times as sweet as sugar and, unlike saccharin, stable to heat. Cyclamates were used as sweetening agents in the food industry until 1969, when their use was banned because they were suspected of causing cancer.

環己氨磺酸鹽　比糖甜 30 倍的兩種化合物：環己氨磺酸鈉和環己氨磺酸鈣。與糖精不同的是它們耐熱。在 1969 年以前，環己氨磺酸鹽在食品工業中用做甜味劑。此後因懷疑它引起癌症而被禁止使用。

cyclitis *n.* inflammation of the *ciliary body of the eye (*see* uveitis).

睫狀體炎　眼的睫狀體的炎症（參閱 uveitis）。

cyclizine *n.* a drug with *antihistamine properties, used to prevent and relieve nausea and vomiting in travel sickness, vertigo, disorders of the inner ear, and postoperative sickness. It is administered by mouth; common side-effects are drowsiness and dizziness. Trade name: **Valoid**.

賽克利嗪　一種具有抗組胺特性的藥物，用於預防和緩解旅行病、暈眩、內耳疾患和術後病。口服。常見的副作用為嗜睡和頭暈。商品名：Valoid。

cyclodialysis *n.* an operation for *glaucoma in which part of the *ciliary body is separated from its attachment to the sclera, producing a cleft between the two. The aqueous humour comes into contact with the exposed surface of the ciliary body and some of it is absorbed from this

睫狀體分離術　一種治療青光眼的手術。將部分睫狀體與其鞏膜的附着分離，在它們二者之間留一裂隙。房水得以與暴露出來的睫狀體表面相接觸，部分房水則從其表面被吸收，如果這一吸收對眼睛液體的

surface. The pressure within the eye will be reduced if this absorption adds significantly to the drainage of fluid from the eye.

引流增加顯著，則眼內壓可減低。

cyclopenthiazide *n.* a *diuretic used to treat fluid retention (oedema), high blood pressure (hypertension), and heart failure. It is administered by mouth and may cause skin sensitivity reactions, nausea, constipation, diarrhoea, and reduced blood potassium levels. Trade name: **Navidrex**.

環戊噻嗪 一種利尿劑，用以治療液體瀦留（水腫）、高血壓和心力衰竭。口服。可引起皮膚過敏反應、惡心、便秘、腹瀉和血鉀含量降低。商品名：Navidrex。

cyclopentolate *n.* a drug, similar to *atropine, that is used in eye drops to paralyse the ciliary muscles and dilate the pupil for eye examinations and to treat some types of eye inflammation. Trade names: **Minims cyclopentolate**, **Mydrilate**.

環噴托酯 一種類似阿托品的藥物。以眼藥水的形式用以麻痺睫狀肌，擴張瞳孔以進行眼部檢查和治療某些眼部炎症。商品名：Minims cyclopentolate，Mydrilate。

cyclophoria *n.* a type of squint (*see* strabismus) in which the eye, when tested, tends to rotate slightly clockwise or anticlockwise.

旋轉隱斜視 一種斜視（參閱 strabismus）。當檢查時，眼球傾向於輕度順時針或逆時針方向轉動。

cyclophosphamide *n.* a drug used to treat some cancers, often in combination with other *cytotoxic drugs. It also has *immunosuppressive properties and is used in prolonging the survival of tissue transplants and in other conditions requiring a reduced immune response. Cyclophosphamide is administered by mouth or by injection; common side-effects are nausea, vomiting, and – particularly at high doses – hair loss. Trade name: **Endoxana**.

環磷酰胺 一種用於治療腫瘤的藥物，通常與其他細胞毒類藥物並用。它還具有免疫抑制特性，用於延長組織移植物的生存以及其他需要減輕免疫反應的疾病。環磷酰胺用於口服或注射。常見的副作用是惡心、嘔吐。特別在大劑量時，可發生脫髮。商品名：Endoxana。

cycloplegia *n.* paralysis of the ciliary muscle of the eye (*see* ciliary body). This causes inability to alter the focus of the eye and is usually accompanied by paralysis of the muscles of the pupil,

睫狀肌麻痺 眼的睫狀肌麻痺（參閱 ciliary body）。它使眼睛不能改變焦距，並通常伴隨有瞳孔肌肉麻痺，導致瞳孔的固定擴張（瞳孔擴大）。其病因

resulting in fixed dilation of the pupil (*mydriasis*). It is induced by the use of atropine or similar drugs in order to inactivate the muscle in cases of inflammation of the iris and ciliary body. It may also occur after injuries to the eye.

是在患虹膜炎或睫狀體炎時，為了使肌肉處於失活狀態而使用阿托品或類似藥品而誘發的。它也可在眼外傷之後發生。

cyclopropane *n.* a general *anaesthetic, administered by inhalation for all types of surgical operation. It can cause postoperative nausea, vomiting, and headache.

環丙烷　一種全身麻醉藥，各種外科手術都吸入使用。它引起術後惡心、嘔吐和頭痛。

cycloserine *n.* an *antibiotic, active against a wide range of bacteria, that may be used as supporting treatment in tuberculosis. It is administered by mouth; side-effects, which can be severe, include dizziness, drowsiness, convulsions, and mental confusion.

環絲氨酸　一種有效的廣譜抗生素。在肺結核中用做輔助治療，也用於治療某些尿道感染。口服。副作用可能會很嚴重，包括頭暈、嗜睡、驚厥和精神錯亂。

cyclosporin A a drug that suppresses the immune system and is administered to prevent and treat rejection of a transplanted organ or bone marrow. Trade name: **Sandimmun**.

環孢菌素A　一種抑制免疫系統的藥物，用於防治器官或骨髓移植的排異反應。商品名：Sandimmun。

cyclothymia *n.* the occurrence of marked swings of mood from cheerfulness to misery. These fluctuations are not as great as those of *manic-depressive psychosis. They usually represent a personality disorder, for which *psychotherapy is sometimes helpful.

循環情感性氣質　從高興到悲哀的情緒明顯交替變化。這種波動不像躁狂抑鬱性精神病那樣大。它們通常表示一種人格障礙。對此，有時心理療法會奏效。

cyclotron *n.* a machine in which charged particles following a spiral path within a magnetic field are accelerated by an alternating electric field. It produces very high-energy electromagnetic radiation, which has been used in the treatment of certain cancers, particularly of the eye. It is now little used on account of severe adverse effects on the tissues following treatment.

迴旋加速器　一種通過交替改變電場使帶電粒子在磁場中沿螺旋路綫加速前進的機器。它產生非常高的高能電磁輻射，一直用於治療某些癌症，特別是眼的癌症。現在，它很少用，原因是治療之後對組織有極嚴重的副作用。

cyesis *n. see* pregnancy.

妊娠　參閱 pregnancy。

cyn- (cyno-) *prefix denoting* a dog or dogs. Example: *cynophobia* (morbid fear of).

〔前綴〕犬　表示一條狗或數條狗。如犬恐怖病（對狗的不正常恐懼）。

cyproheptadine *n.* a potent *antihistamine administered by mouth to treat allergies and itching skin conditions; it is also used to stimulate the appetite. Drowsiness is a common side-effect. Trade name: **Periactin**.

賽庚啶　一種強力抗組胺藥，口服。治療變態反應和皮膚瘙癢性疾患。它也用於刺激食慾。嗜睡是一常見的副作用。商品名：Periactin。

cyproterone (cyproterone acetate, CPA) *n.* a steroid drug that inhibits the effects of male sex hormones (*see* antiandrogen) and is used to treat various sexual disorders and advanced prostate cancer in men. It is administered by mouth and common side-effects include tiredness, loss of strength, inhibition of sperm formation, infertility, and breast enlargement (gynaecomastia). Trade names: **Androcur**, **Cyprostat**.

環丙孕酮（醋酸環丙孕酮）　一種抑制雄激素作用的藥物，用於治療各種男子性功能障礙和晚期前列腺癌。口服。常見的副作用包括倦怠、無力、精子形成抑制、不育和乳房增大（男子女性型乳房）。商品名：Androcur，Cyprostat。

cyrtometer *n.* a device for measuring the shape of the chest and its movements during breathing.

胸圍計　一種測量胸圍形狀及其呼吸時運動的器械。

cyst *n.* **1.** an abnormal sac or closed cavity lined with *epithelium and filled with liquid or semisolid matter. There are many varieties of cysts occurring in different parts of the body. *Retention cysts* arise when the outlet of a glandular duct is blocked, as in *sebaceous cysts. Some cysts are congenital, due to abnormal embryonic development; for example, *dermoid cysts. Others are tumours containing cells that secrete mucus or other substances, and another type of cyst is formed by parasites in the body (*see* hydatid cyst). Cysts may occur in the jaws: a *dental cyst* occurs at the apex of a tooth,

(1) 囊腫　襯有上皮並充滿液體或半液體物質的一種異常囊袋或封閉的腔隙。在身體的不同部位有許多不同種類的囊腫。當腺管出口被阻塞時會發生瀦留囊腫，如皮脂腺囊腫。有些囊腫是先天性的，其原因是胚胎期發育異常，如皮樣囊腫。其他囊腫為腫瘤，內含分泌黏液或其他物質的細胞。另一種囊腫是由體內寄生蟲形成的（參閱 hydatid cyst）。囊腫可出現於頜部。牙囊腫出現於牙尖，含牙囊腫發生於未萌出牙的牙冠周圍，萌牙囊腫在一

a *dentigerous cyst* occurs around the crown of an unerupted tooth, and an *eruption cyst* forms over an erupting tooth. *See also* fimbrial cyst, ovarian cyst. **2.** a dormant stage produced during the life cycle of certain protozoan parasites of the alimentary canal, including *Giardia* and *Entamoeba*. Cysts, passed out in the faeces, have tough outer coats that protect the parasites from unfavourable conditions. The parasites emerge from their cysts when they are eaten by a new host. **3.** a structure formed by and surrounding the larvae of certain parasitic worms.

萌牙上方出現。參閱 fimbrial cyst，ovarian cyst。**(2) 包囊期** 消化道內某些寄生蟲（包括賈第蟲屬與內阿米巴屬）生活周期中的休眠階段。由糞便排出的包囊帶有硬的外層包殼。這一外層包殼保護原蟲免受不利環境的影響。當包囊被一新的宿主食入後，寄生蟲則從包囊中出來。**(3) 包囊** 由某些寄生蟲幼蟲形成並包圍着它們的結構。

cyst- (cysto-) *prefix denoting* **1.** a bladder, especially the urinary bladder. Example: *cystoplasty* (plastic surgery of). **2.** a cyst.

〔前綴〕**(1) 膀胱** 表示囊形物，尤指膀胱，如膀胱成形術。**(2) 囊**

cystadenoma *n.* an *adenoma showing a cystic structure.

囊腺瘤 一種腺瘤，呈囊狀結構。

cystalgia *n.* pain in the urinary bladder. This is common in *cystitis and when there are stones in the bladder and is occasionally present in bladder cancer. Treatment is directed to the underlying cause.

膀胱痛 膀胱部位的疼痛。這種情況在膀胱炎和膀胱內有結石時較為普遍，偶爾見於膀胱癌，治療針對病因。

cystectomy *n.* surgical removal of the urinary bladder. This is necessary in the treatment of certain bladder conditions, notably cancer, and necessitates subsequent *urinary diversion. The ureters draining the urine from the kidneys are reimplanted into the colon (*see* ureterosigmoidostomy) or into an isolated segment of intestine (usually the ileum), which is brought to the skin surface as a spout (*see* ileal conduit). Alternatively, in *bladder replacement*, a segment of ileum or colon is reconstructed to form a pouch, which is

膀胱切除術 膀胱的外科切除。在治療某些膀胱疾患時，特別是膀胱癌時，該手術是必要的，並隨後需要進行泌尿改道。由腎引流尿液的輸尿管被植入結腸上（參閱 ureterosigmoidostomy）或者植入分離的一段小腸上（通常是迴腸），再被引至皮膚表面以作為尿液導出口（參閱 ileal conduit）。作為一種替代方法，膀胱替代術指的是將迴腸或結腸的一段被重新構建而成一個囊，與尿道吻合，起着尿液貯存器的作

anastomosed to the urethra and acts as a reservoir for the urine. Emptying may be achieved by abdominal straining or *intermittent self-catheterization.

用。通過腹部滲出或間歇性自我導管插入可以排空該囊。

cysteine *n.* a sulphur-containing *amino acid that is an important constituent of many enzymes. The disulphide (S–S) links between adjacent cysteine molecules in polypeptide chains contribute to the three-dimensional molecular structure of proteins.

半胱胺酸 一種含硫的氨基酸，是許多種酶的重要組成分。多肽鏈中兩個相鄰半胱氨酸分子間的二硫 (S–S) 鍵構成了蛋白質的主體分子結構。

cystic *adj.* **1.** of, relating to, or characterized by cysts. **2.** of or relating to the gall bladder or urinary bladder.

(1) 囊的，包囊的 與囊有關的，或者具有囊的特點的。**(2)** 膽囊的，膀胱的 膽囊的或與膽囊有關的；膀胱的或與膀胱有關的。

cystic duct *see* bile duct.

膽囊管 參閱 bile duct。

cysticercosis *n.* a disease caused by the presence of tapeworm larvae (*see* cysticercus) of the species *Taenia solium* in any of the body tissues. Man becomes infected on ingesting tapeworm eggs in contaminated food or drink. The presence of cysticerci in the muscles causes pain and weakness; in the brain the symptoms are more serious, including mental deterioration, paralysis, giddiness, epileptic attacks, and convulsions, which may be fatal. There is no specific treatment for this cosmopolitan disease although surgical removal of cysticerci may be necessary to relieve pressure on the brain.

囊尾蚴病 任何人體組織中由有鉤縧蟲幼蟲（參閱 cysticercus）所引起的疾病。人類在食入被縧蟲卵污染的食物後而感染此病。肌肉內的囊尾蚴的存在會引起疼痛和無力。腦內的囊尾蚴引起的症狀則較嚴重，包括智力減退、麻痺、眩暈、癲癇和驚厥，可致死。儘管為了減低顱內壓力可能需外科切除囊尾蚴，但對此全球性疾病尚無特效療法。

cysticercus (bladderworm) *n.* a larval stage of some *tapeworms in which the scolex and neck are invaginated into a large fluid-filled cyst. The cysts develop in the muscles or brain of the host following ingestion of tapeworm eggs. *See* cysticercosis.

囊尾蚴 某些縧蟲的幼蟲期。幼蟲的頭節和頸節包在一個大的充滿液體的包囊內。在縧蟲卵被食入後，包囊就在宿主的肌肉或腦中生長。參閱 cysticercosis。

cystic fibrosis (fibrocystic disease of the pancreas, mucoviscidosis) a hereditary disease affecting cells of the exocrine glands (including mucus-secreting glands, sweat glands, and others). The faulty gene responsible has been identified as lying on chromosome no. 7 and is recessive, i.e. both parents of the patient can be *carriers without being affected by the disease. Affected individuals lack a protein, *cystic fibrosis transmembrane regulator* (*CFTR*), that enables the transport of chloride ions across cell membranes: this results in the production of thick mucus, which obstructs the intestinal glands (causing meconium *ileus in newborn babies), pancreas (causing deficiency of pancreatic enzymes resulting in *malabsorption and *failure to thrive), and bronchi (causing *bronchiectasis). Respiratory infections, which may be severe, are a common complication. The sweat contains excessive amounts of sodium and chloride, which is an aid to diagnosis.

Treatment consists of minimizing the effects of the disease by administration of pancreatic enzymes and physiotherapy for the lungs and by preventing and combating secondary infection. *Genetic counselling is essential, as each subsequent child of carrier parents has a one in four chance of being affected (*See also* mouthwash test). Some patients are benefiting from revolutionary new treatments, including transplantation of heart and lungs and treatment aimed at altering the genetic content of the faulty cells (*see* gene therapy).

cystine *n. see* amino acid.

cystinosis *n.* an inborn defect in the metabolism of amino acids, leading to

囊腫性纖維變性（胰纖維性囊腫病，胰管黏稠物阻塞症）一種遺傳性疾病，影響外分泌腺體細胞（包括黏液分泌腺、汗腺和其他腺體）。引起病變的錯誤基因被發現位於第七染色體內，且是隱性的。也就是說病人的父母親可能同是攜帶該種基因而不患此疾病。患此病者缺少一種蛋白：囊腫性纖維變性跨膜調節器（CFTR）。該蛋白使得氯化物離子被運輸而穿過細胞膜，這導致黏稠的液體的產生，阻塞腸腺（引起新生兒胎糞性腸梗阻），阻塞胰腺（引起胰腺酶缺乏症，導致吸收不良和發育障礙），阻塞支氣管（引起支氣管擴張）。呼吸道感染是常見的併發症，可能十分嚴重。汗裏含有過量的鈉和氯化物，此點有助於診斷。

治療包括通過服用胰酶、肺部理療和防治繼發感染來最大限度減小疾病的影響。遺傳咨詢是基本需要的，因為攜帶該種基因的父母親隨後的每一個孩子都有四分之一的可能性患此病（參閱 mouthwash test）。一些病人從革新的治療方法中獲得效果，包括心和肺的移植、以及旨在改變缺陷細胞的基因表達（參閱 gene therapy）。

胱氨酸 參閱 amino acid。

胱氨酸病 先天性氨基酸代謝障礙，導致氨基酸胱氨酸在

abnormal accumulation of the amino acid cystine in the blood, kidneys, and lymphatic system. *See also* Fanconi syndrome.

血、腎和淋巴系統的異常積聚。參閱 Fanconi syndrome。

cystinuria *n.* excessive excretion of the amino acid cystine in the urine due to an inborn defect of reabsorption by the kidney tubules. It leads to the formation of cystine stones in the kidney.

胱氨酸尿 由於先天性腎小管重吸收障礙而引起的氨基酸胱氨酸在尿中的過量排出。它導致腎胱氨酸結石形成。

cystitis *n.* inflammation of the urinary bladder, often caused by infection (most commonly by the bacterium *Escherichia coli*). It is usually accompanied by the desire to pass urine frequently, with a degree of burning. More severe attacks are often associated with the painful passage of blood in the urine, which is accompanied by a cramplike pain in the lower abdomen persisting after the bladder has been emptied. An acute attack is treated by antibiotic administration and a copious fluid intake. *See also* interstitial cystitis.

膀胱炎 膀胱的炎症，常由感染引起（最常見的是由大腸桿菌引起的）。通常伴有頻繁排尿感，帶有燒灼感。嚴重者有痛性血尿，伴隨有膀胱排空後的下腹部持續性絞痛。急性膀胱炎用抗生素治療，並大量飲水。參閱 interstitial cystitis。

cystitome *n.* a small knife with a tiny curved or hooked blade, used to cut the lens capsule in the type of operation for cataract in which the capsule is left behind (*extracapsular cataract extraction*). *See also* capsulotomy.

晶狀體囊刀 一種帶有微小彎曲或鈎形刀口的微型手術刀，用於白內障手術中切開晶狀體囊而將晶狀體囊保留下來（晶狀體囊內障摘除術）。參閱 capsulotomy。

cystocele *n.* prolapse of the base of the bladder in women. It is usually due to weakness of the pelvic floor after childbirth and causes bulging of the anterior wall of the vagina on straining. When accompanied by stress incontinence of urine, surgical repair (anterior *colporrhaphy) is indicated.

膀胱突出 女子膀胱基底部脫垂。通常是由於骨盆底鬆弛引起，導致陰道前壁用力時膨出。當伴有應激性尿失禁時，它提示應進行手術修復（前陰道縫合術）。

cystography *n.* X-ray examination of the urinary bladder after the injection of a contrast medium. The X-ray

膀胱造影術 在注入一種造影劑後對膀胱進行 X 綫檢查。以此所獲的 X 綫照片或膠片被稱

photographs or films thus obtained are known as *cystograms*. Cystography is most commonly performed to detect reflux of urine from the bladder to the ureters, usually in children (*see* vesicoureteric reflux). If films are taken during voiding then the urethra can also be observed (*see* urethrography).

cystolithiasis *n.* the presence of stones (calculi) in the urinary bladder. The stones are either formed in the bladder, due to obstruction, urinary retention, and infection (*primary calculi*), or pass to the bladder after being formed in the kidneys (*secondary calculi*). They cause pain, the passage of bloody urine, and interruption of the urinary stream and should be removed surgically. *See* calculus.

cystometer *n.* an apparatus for measuring the pressure within the bladder. Modern investigations also include measurement of urine flow, and the resultant bladder pressure/flow study (*urodynamic investigation*) provides useful information regarding bladder function.

cystopexy (vesicofixation) *n.* a surgical operation to fix the urinary bladder (or a portion of it) in a different position. It may be performed as part of the repair or correction of a prolapsed bladder.

cystoplasty *n.* the operation of enlarging the capacity of the bladder by incorporating a segment of bowel. In a *clam cystoplasty*, the bladder is cut across longitudinally from one side of the neck to the other side through the dome (fundus) of the bladder and a length of the ileum or colon is inserted as a patch. In the operation of *ileocaecocystoplasty*, the dome is removed by cutting across

為膀胱 X 綫照片。施行膀胱造影術最常見的是為了檢查從膀胱到輸尿管的尿液的返流（參閱 vesicoureteric reflux）。如在膀胱排空時拍照片，那麼，對尿道也可進行觀察（urethrography）。

膀胱結石病 膀胱中出現結石。結石可形成於膀胱內，其原因為梗阻、尿瀦留和感染（原發性結石），也可在腎裏形成後排入膀胱（繼發性結石）。它們引起疼痛、血尿及間歇性排尿，應通過外科手術取出。參閱 calculus。

膀胱內壓測量器 一種測量膀胱內壓力的器械。現代檢查包括尿流量的測定。膀胱內壓力／流量研究（尿流動力學檢查）提供有關膀胱功能的有益信息。

膀胱固定術 一種將膀胱（或其一部分）固定於另一不同部位的外科手術。該手術也可是修復或糾正膀胱脫垂術的一部分。

膀胱成形術 通過一段結腸來擴大膀胱容量的手術。在蛤形膀胱成形術中，將膀胱從其頸部沿縱向並通過膀胱穹窿部（基底）切開，插入作為補片的一段迴腸或結腸。在行迴腸盲腸膀胱成形術時，通過在輸尿管的開口上方橫向切開膀胱，切除膀胱基底。並用一節切除的盲腸和末端迴腸取而代

the bladder transversely above the openings of the ureters; it is replaced by an isolated segment of caecum and terminal ileum. In *ileocystoplasty* the bladder is enlarged by an opened-out portion of small intestine. The bladder may be totally replaced by a reservoir constructed from either small or large intestine (*see* cystectomy).

之。在行迴腸膀胱成形術時，通過一部分切開的小腸使膀胱得以擴大。也可用小腸或大腸構建一貯器而完全代替膀胱（參閱 cystectomy）。

cystosarcoma phylloides a malignant tumour of the connective tissue of the breast: it accounts for approximately 1% of all breast cancers. Such tumours may show a wide variation in cell structure. The best treatment for a localized tumour is simple *mastectomy.

葉狀囊性內瘤 乳房的結締組織惡性腫瘤，約占所有乳腺癌的 1%。該腫瘤表現出許多不同的細胞結構。對局限性腫瘤的最好治療方法是做簡單的乳房切除術。

cystoscopy *n.* examination of the bladder by means of an instrument (*cystoscope*) inserted via the urethra. The cystoscope consists of a metal sheath surrounding a telescope and light-conducting bundles. Irrigating fluid is conducted via the sheath into the bladder and additional channels are available for the catheters to be inserted into the ureters, diathermy electrodes for removing polyps, etc. or biopsy forceps for taking specimens of tumours or other growths.

膀胱鏡檢查 通過使用經輸尿管插入的一器械對膀胱的檢查。膀胱鏡由一個環繞望遠鏡的金屬護套和光導纖維束組成。灌洗液通過金屬套管注入膀胱。其他通道用以把導管插入尿道，用透熱電極去除息肉，或者用組織鉗採集瘤樣或其他新生物的活體。

cystostomy *n.* The operation of creating an artificial opening between the bladder and the anterior abdominal wall. This provides a temporary or permanent drainage route for urine.

膀胱造口術 在膀胱和前腹壁之間開一人工造口的手術。這一手術為尿液提供了暫時或永久性的引流。

cystotomy *n.* surgical incision into the urinary bladder, usually by cutting through the abdominal wall above the pubic symphysis (*suprapubic cystotomy*). This is necessary for such operations as removing stones or tumours from the bladder and for gaining access

膀胱切開術 切開膀胱的外科手術，通常在恥骨聯合上方的腹壁切開（恥骨弓上膀胱切開術）。對於從膀胱切除結石或腫瘤以及在膀胱前列腺切除術中為了到達前列腺，都需施行此手術。

to the prostate gland in the operation of transvesical *prostatectomy.

cyt- (cyto-) *prefix denoting* **1.** cell(s). **2.** cytoplasm.

〔前綴〕**(1)** 細胞 **(2)** 細胞質

cytarabine *n.* a *cytotoxic drug used to suppress the symptoms of some types of leukaemia. It is administered by injection and can damage the bone marrow, leading to various blood cell disorders. Other side-effects are nausea, vomiting, mouth ulcers, and diarrhoea. Trade names: **Alexan**, **Cytosar**.

阿糖胞苷　一種用於抑制某些類型的白血病症狀的細胞毒素藥物。注射。可損害骨髓，導致各種血細胞疾病。其他副作用為惡心、嘔吐、口腔潰瘍和腹瀉。商品名：Alexan，Cytosar。

-cyte *suffix denoting* a cell. Examples: *chondrocyte* (cartilage cell); *osteocyte* (bone cell).

〔後綴〕**細胞**　如軟骨細胞，骨細胞。

cytidine *n.* a compound containing cytosine and the sugar ribose. *See also* nucleoside.

胞（嘧啶核）苷　一種含有胞嘧啶和核糖的化合物。參閱 nucleoside。

cytochemistry *n.* the study of chemical compounds and their activities in living cells.

細胞化學　研究活細胞的化學成分及其活動的學科。

cytochrome *n.* a compound consisting of a protein linked to *haem. Cytochromes act as electron transfer agents in biological oxidation-reduction reactions, particularly those associated with the mitochondria in cellular respiration. *See* electron transport chain.

細胞色素　一種由血紅素及與其相連的蛋白質組成的化合物。在生物氧化還原反應中，細胞色素起着電子傳遞體的作用，特別是細胞呼吸中的綫粒體的傳遞介質。參閱 electron transport chain。

cytogenetics *n.* a science that links the study of inheritance (genetics) with that of cells (cytology); it is concerned mainly with the study of the *chromosomes, especially their origin, structure, and functions.

細胞遺傳學　一門把遺傳研究（遺傳學）和細胞研究（細胞學）連結起來的科學。主要涉及染色體，尤其是它們的起源、結構和功能。

cytokinesis *n.* division of the cytoplasm of a cell, which occurs at the end of cell

胞質分裂　細胞質的分離，發生於細胞分裂末期，細胞核分裂之

division, after division of the nucleus, to form two daughter cells. *Compare* karyokinesis.

後，從而形成兩個子細胞。與 karyokinesis 對比。

cytology *n.* the study of the structure and function of cells. The examination of cells under a microscope is used in the diagnosis of various diseases. These cells are obtained by scraping an organ, as in *cervical cytology* (*see* cervical smear), by aspiration (*see* aspiration cytology), or they are collected from cells already shed (*exfoliative cytology*). *See also* biopsy. –**cytological** *adj.*

細胞學　研究細胞結構和功能的學科。在顯微鏡下觀察細胞可用來診斷各種各樣的疾病。這些細胞可通過刮擦某一器官而獲得，如宮頸細胞學檢查（參閱 cervical smear）。也可通過抽吸（參閱 aspiration cytology）或者通過收集已經脫落的細胞獲得（表皮脫落細胞學檢查）。參閱 biopsy。

cytolysis *n.* the breakdown of cells, particularly by destruction of their outer membranes.

細胞溶解　細胞的分解，特別是由於細胞外膜被破壞而引起的分解。

cytomegalovirus (CMV) *n.* a member of the herpes group of viruses (*see* herpesvirus). It commonly occurs in man and normally produces symptoms milder than the common cold. However, in individuals whose immune systems are compromised (e.g. by cancer or AIDS) it can cause more severe effects, and it has been found to be the cause of congenital handicap in infants born to women who have contracted the virus during pregnancy.

巨細胞病毒　疱疹病毒屬中的一個種（參閱 herpesvirus）。常見於人類，且通常產生比感冒較輕的症狀。但是，在免疫系統功能低下的患者中（如癌症或艾滋病），它可引起更嚴重的感染，已發現在妊娠期間感染這一病毒的婦女，會分娩出先天性畸形的胎兒。

cytometer *n.* an instrument for determining the number of cells in a given quantity of fluid, such as blood, cerebrospinal fluid, or urine. *See* haemocytometer.

血細胞計數器　在一特定量的液體中，如血液、腦脊液，或尿液中，測定細胞數量的器械。參閱 haemocytometer。

cytomorphosis *n.* the changes undergone by a cell in the course of its life cycle.

細胞變形　細胞生命周期中所發生的形態變化。

cytopenia *n.* a deficiency of one or more of the various types of blood cells. *See* eosinopenia, erythropenia,

血細胞減少症　一種或多種血細胞的缺乏。參閱 eosinopenia，erythropenia，lympho-

lymphopenia, neutropenia, pancytopenia, thrombocytopenia.

penia，neutropenia，pancyto-
penia，thrombocytopenia。

cytophotometry *n.* the study of chemical compounds in living cells by means of a *cytophotometer*, an instrument that measures light intensity through stained areas of cytoplasm.

細胞光度測定法　通過細胞光度測定儀研究活細胞裏的化學成分。這是一種測量細胞質染色區域光點強度的儀器。

cytoplasm *n.* the jelly-like substance that surrounds the nucleus of a cell. *See also* ectoplasm, endoplasm, protoplasm. **–cytoplasmic** *adj.*

細胞質，細胞漿　包圍一細胞核的膠凍樣物質。參閱ectoplasm，endoplasm，protoplasm。

cytoplasmic inheritance the inheritance of characters controlled by factors present in the cell cytoplasm rather than by genes on the chromosomes in the cell nucleus. Cytoplasmic inheritance is known to occur in lower animals and in plants but has not so far been found in man.

細胞質遺傳　由出現於細胞的細胞質裏的因子而不是由細胞核裏的染色體上的基因所控制的特徵的遺傳。細胞質遺傳見於低等動物與植物中，至今尚未在人類身上發現。

cytosine *n.* one of the nitrogen-containing bases (*see* pyrimidine) that occurs in the nucleic acid DNA.

胞嘧啶　存在於脱氧核糖核酸中的一種含氮鹼基（參閱pyrimidine）。

cytosome *n.* the part of a cell that is outside the nucleus.

細胞質體　細胞核外的細胞的部分。

cytotoxic drug a drug that damages or destroys cells and is used to treat various types of cancer either with or without the use of *radiotherapy. Examples are *amsacrine, *cisplatin, *cyclophosphamide, *cytarabine, *mustine, and *anthracycline antibiotics; they offer successful treatment in some conditions and help reduce symptoms and prolong life in others. Cytotoxic drugs destroy cancer cells by inhibiting cell division (i.e. they are *antimitotic*) but they also affect normal cells, particularly in bone marrow, skin, stomach lining, and fetal tissue, and dosage must be carefully controlled. *See also* antimetabolite.

細胞毒素藥物　一種破壞細胞的藥物，用於治療各種各樣的癌症，可同時使用放射療法，也可不用。例如安吖啶、順鉑、環磷酰胺、阿糖胞苷、氮芥和蒽環類抗生素。在一些疾病中，它們的療效很好，在另外一些疾病中，它們幫助減少症狀，延長生命。細胞毒素藥物通過抑制細胞分裂破壞癌細胞（也就是説它們是抗有絲分裂的），但是，它們也破壞正常細胞，尤其是骨髓、皮膚、胃黏膜和胎兒組織，因此劑量應謹慎控制。參閱　antimetabolite。

cytotrophoblast *n.* the part of a *trophoblast that retains its cellular structure and does not invade the maternal tissues. It forms the outer surface of the *chorion.

細胞滋養層　滋養層中保持其細胞結構，但不侵犯母體組織的部分。它構成絨毛膜的外表面。

D

dacarbazine (DTIC) *n.* a drug used in the treatment of certain cancers, including *Hodgkin's disease and malignant melanoma. Side-effects include severe vomiting.

達卡巴嗪　一種用於治療某些癌症的藥物，包括霍奇金病和惡性黑素瘤。副作用包括嚴重的嘔吐。

dacry- (dacryo-) *prefix denoting* 1. tears. 2. the lacrimal apparatus.

〔前綴〕(1) 淚液 (2) 淚器

dacryoadenitis *n.* inflammation of the tear-producing gland (*see* lacrimal apparatus).

淚腺炎　產生淚液的腺體的炎症（參閱 lacrimal apparatus）。

dacryocystitis *n.* inflammation of the lacrimal sac (in which tears collect), usually occurring when the duct draining the tears into the nose is blocked (*see* lacrimal apparatus).

淚囊炎　淚囊（收集淚液的囊）的炎症，通常發生在將淚液引流入鼻腔的導管被阻塞時（參閱 lacrimal apparatus）。

dacryocystorhinostomy *n.* an operation to relieve blockage of the nasolacrimal duct (which drains tears into the nose), in which a communication is made between the lacrimal sac and the nose by removing the intervening bone. *See* dacryocystitis, lacrimal apparatus.

淚囊鼻腔造口術　解除鼻淚管（引流淚液入鼻腔的導管）阻塞的手術。該手術通過摘除中間的骨而使淚囊和鼻腔溝通。參閱 dacryocystitis，lacrimal apparatus。

dacryops *n. Obsolete.* a watering eye.

淚眼　廢用詞：充滿淚水的眼睛。

dactyl- *prefix denoting* the digits (fingers or toes). Examples: *dactylomegaly*

〔前綴〕指，趾　表示指或趾（即手指或腳趾）。如指、趾巨

(abnormally large size of); *dactylospasm* (painful contraction of).

大（手指頭或腳趾頭異常的大）和指、趾痙攣（指趾疼痛性收縮）。

dactylitis *n.* inflammation of a finger or toe caused by bone infection (as in tuberculous *osteomyelitis) or rheumatic disease.

指（趾）炎　因骨感染（如結核性骨髓炎）或風濕性疾病而引起的手指或腳趾發炎。

dactylology *n.* the representation of speech by finger movements: sign language.

手語　借助手指的動作表達語言；聾啞人語言。

Daltonism (protanopia) *n.* red-blindness: a defect in colour vision in which a person cannot distinguish between reds and greens. The term has been used to refer to *colour blindness in general.

色盲　紅色盲，一種色覺缺陷。患者不能區分紅色和綠色。本詞泛指色盲。

damp *n.* (in mining) any gas encountered underground other than air. *See* blackdamp, firedamp.

礦內毒氣　（採礦）在地下遇到的除了空氣外的任何氣體。參閱 blackdamp，firedamp。

danazol *n.* a synthetic *progestogen that inhibits the secretion by the pituitary gland of gonadotrophins. It is used to treat precocious puberty, breast enlargement in males (gynaecomastia), excessively heavy menstrual periods, and *endometriosis. It is administered by mouth. Possible side-effects include nausea, swelling of the feet and ankles, weight gain, oiliness of the skin, and, in women, excessive growth of facial and body hair. Trade name: **Danol**.

達那唑　一種人工合成的孕激素，能抑制垂體的促性腺激素的分泌。它用於治療性早熟、男子乳房增大（男子女性型乳房）、白帶過多和子宮內膜異位。口服。可能具有的副作用包括惡心、腳和踝的腫脹、體重增加和油性皮膚。女性的副作用還有面部和體毛的過分生長，商品名：Danol。

D and C *see* dilatation and curettage.

擴張術和刮除術　參閱 dilatation and curettage。

dandruff *n.* visible scaling from the surface of the scalp. It is extremely common, occurring in about 50% of the population, and is associated with the presence of the yeast *Pityrosporum*

頭皮屑　頭皮表面可見的脫落。此種情況極為常見，發生於大約 50% 的人羣，與瓶形酵母有關，是頭皮脂溢性濕疹的前體。患頭皮脂溢性濕疹

ovale. It is the precursor of seborrhoeic *eczema of the scalp, in which there is a degree of inflammation in addition to the greasy scaling. Dandruff can be controlled by shampoos containing tar, selenium sulphide, or zinc pyrithione. Medical name: **pityriasis capitis**.

時，除了油性膜脱落外還有一定程度的炎症。頭皮屑可用含有焦油、二硫化硒或巰氧吡啶鋅的洗髮香精治療。醫學用語：頭皮糠疹。

Dandy-Walker syndrome a form of *cerebral palsy in which the *cerebellum is usually the part of the brain affected. It leads to unsteadiness of balance and an abnormal gait and may be associated with *hydrocephalus.

丹-沃氏綜合徵 一種腦麻痺，通常侵害的部位是小腦。該病導致平衡不穩和步態異常，伴有腦積水。

dangerous drugs *see* Misuse of Drugs Act 1971.

危險藥物 參閱 Misuse of Drugs Act 1971。

danthron *n.* a *laxative administered by mouth; it sometimes colours the urine pink or red. It is usually combined with a faecal softener (e.g. in *Codalax*, *Normax*).

丹蒽醌 一種口服的緩瀉劑，有時可將尿液染成粉紅色，通常與糞便軟化劑（如 Codalax，Normax）合用。

dantrolene *n.* a *muscle relaxant drug used to relieve muscle spasm in such conditions as cerebral palsy, multiple sclerosis, or spinal cord injury. It is administered by mouth or by injection. Possible side-effects include weakness, dizziness, drowsiness, and vertigo; liver damage sometimes occurs. Trade name: **Dantrium**.

硝苯呋海因 用以緩除肌肉痙攣的肌肉鬆弛藥，用於治療諸如腦麻痺、多發性硬化或者脊髓的外傷等病症。可能有的副作用有虛弱、頭暈、嗜睡、眩暈，有時還發生肝損傷。商品名：Dantrium。

dapsone *n.* a drug (*see* sulphone) used to treat *leprosy and dermatitis herpetiformis. It is administered by mouth or injection; the most common side-effects are allergic skin reactions.

氨苯碸 一種用於治療麻風病和疱疹樣皮炎的藥。口服或注射給藥。常見的副作用包括過敏性皮膚反應。

dark adaptation the changes that take place in the retina and pupil of the eye enabling vision in very dim light. Dark adaptation involves activation of the *rods – the cells of the retina that

暗適應 眼睛的視網膜和瞳孔為能在極弱的光下視物而生的變化。暗適應涉及激活桿細胞（在弱光下發揮着最佳作用的視網膜細胞）和瞳孔的

function best in dim light – and the reflex enlargement of the pupil (*see* pupillary reflex). *Compare* light adaptation.

反射性開關（參閱 pupillary reflex）。與 light adaptation 對比。

Data Protection Act 1984 (in the UK) legislation by which anyone storing personal information relating to an individual on a computer is responsible for the accuracy of that information and may neither use the information nor pass it on to others without the knowledge and consent of that individual. Users of the information are required to be registered. Individuals about whom information is held can require to see a printout of the information relevant to them and demand to have inaccurate or misleading information amended. Specific exceptions include police, state security, and medical research, but not medical information that may affect employment or promotion.

個人信息保護法 **(1984)** （英國）一項立法。任何在電腦上存貯有關某一個人信息的人要對信息的準確性負責任，且在不經告知該個人，並取得其同意的情況下，不能使用該個人的信息，也不能將信息傳給其他人。信息的使用者須進行登記。其信息被存貯的個人可要求一份有關他們的信息的打印件並要求將不準確的或引起誤解的信息予以修正。特殊的例外包括警察、國家安全、醫學研究，但並不包括影響僱傭或提升的醫療信息。

daunorubicin *n.* an antibiotic that interferes with DNA synthesis and is used in the treatment of acute leukaemia. It is administered by injection. Possible side-effects include loss of hair and damage to bone marrow and heart muscle.

柔紅黴素 一種抑制脱氧核糖核酸的合成的抗生素，用於治療急性白血病。注射使用。可能具有的副作用包括脱髮、對骨髓和心肌的損害。

day blindness comparatively good vision in poor light but poor vision in good illumination. The condition is usually congenital and associated with poor *visual acuity and defective colour vision. Acquired cases occur when the *cones (light-sensitive cells) at the back of the retina are selectively destroyed by disease. Medical name: **hemeralopia**. *Compare* night blindness.

晝盲 在弱光下相對視力尚好，但在良好照明下視力反而差的現象。該疾病通常是先天性的且伴有視敏度差和色覺缺陷。當視網膜後部的錐細胞（感光細胞）被選擇性地破壞時，獲得性晝盲就可發生。醫學用語：晝盲症。與 night blindness 對比。

day-case surgery surgical procedures that can be performed in a single day, without the need to admit the patient for an overnight stay in hospital. Modern

一日外科手術 一天可以做完而不需讓病人住院呆一晚上的外科手術。現代外科手術和麻醉技術能使許多輕、中度外科

techniques of surgery and anaesthesia now enable many surgical cases of minor and intermediate degrees of severity to be treated in this way: examples include many breast lesions, dilatation and curettage, and operations for hernia and varicose veins. Special units are established in many hospitals.

病例以此種方式治療。例子包括乳房損傷、擴張術和刮除術、疝和靜脈曲張手術。在許多醫院都設立了專科。

day hospital a hospital in which patients spend a substantial part of the day under medical supervision but do not stay overnight. Day hospitals are mainly used for the treatment of elderly patients and those with mental disorders.

晝間醫院 病人在醫療護理下度過一天的大部分時間，但卻不在醫院過夜的醫院。晝間醫院主要是為治療老年病人和那些有精神疾病的人。

DDAVP *see* desmopressin.

去氨加壓素 參閱 desmopressin。

DDT (chlorophenothane, dicophane) *n.* a powerful insecticide that was formerly widely used against lice, fleas, flies, bed bugs, cockroaches, and other disease-carrying and destructive insects. It is a relatively stable compound that is stored in animal fats, and the quantities now present in the environment – in the form of stores accumulated in animal tissues – have led to its use being restricted. Acute poisoning, from swallowing more than 20g, produces nervous irritability, muscle twitching, convulsions, and coma, but only a few fatalities have been reported.

滴滴涕（二氯二苯基三氯乙烷，氯苯乙烷） 一種強力殺蟲劑，曾被廣泛用於殺滅虱、跳蚤、蠅、臭蟲、蟑螂和其他攜帶疾病和具有破壞作用的昆蟲。是一種蓄積於動物脂肪中的相對穩定的化合物，現在由於在環境中（以在動物組織中蓄積的形式）大量存在而導致了限制該藥物的使用。因吞服20克以上的滴滴涕而導致的急性中毒產生神經過敏、肌肉抽搐、驚厥和昏迷，但死亡報道僅為少數。

de- *prefix denoting* **1.** removal or loss. Examples: *demineralization* (of minerals from bones or teeth); *devascularization* (of blood supply). **2.** reversal.

〔前綴〕**(1)** 脫，去 除去或丟失。如脫礦質作用（從骨或牙中脫去礦物質），血供阻斷（失去血液供應）。**(2)** 逆轉，反向

deafness *n.* partial or total loss of hearing in one or both ears. *Conductive deafness* is due to a defect in the conduction of sound from the external ear to

聾 一耳或雙耳的部分或完全性聽力喪失。傳導性聾是由於聲音從外耳到內耳的傳導缺陷所致。這可能是由於耳鼓穿

the inner ear. This may be due to perforations of the eardrum, fluid or infection in the middle ear (*see* glue ear, otitis media), or disorders of the small bones in the middle ear (*ossicles). *Sensorineural* (or *perceptive*) *deafness* may be due to a lesion of the *cochlea in the inner ear, the auditory nerve, or the auditory centres in the brain. It may be present from birth (for example if the mother was affected with German measles during pregnancy). In adults it may be brought on by injury, disease (e.g. *Ménière's disease), or prolonged exposure to loud noise; progressive sensorineural deafness (*presbyacusis*) is common with advancing age.

The type of deafness can be diagnosed by various hearing tests (*see* Rinne's test, Weber's test), and the treatment depends on the cause. *See also* cochlear implant, hearing aid.

deamination *n*. a process, occurring in the liver, that occurs during the metabolism of amino acids. The amino group ($-NH_2$) is removed from an amino acid and converted to ammonia, which is ultimately converted to *urea and excreted.

death *n*. absence of vital functions. Death is diagnosed by permanent cessation of the heartbeat. *Brain death* is defined as permanent functional death of the centres in the brainstem that control the breathing, pupillary, and other vital reflexes. Usually two independent medical opinions are required before brain death is agreed, but organs such as kidneys may then legally be removed for transplantation surgery before the heart has stopped.

death certificate a medical certificate stating the cause of a person's death,

孔、中耳積液或感染（參閱 glue ear，otitis media），或由中耳小骨疾患所引起的。感音神經（感覺性）性聾可能是由於內耳的耳蝸、聽神經或者大腦的聽覺中樞的損傷引起的。此種耳聾可出生就有（如母親在妊娠期間感染上風疹時）。在成人，該疾患可能由於外傷、疾病（如梅尼埃病）或者長期暴露於高音而引起的。漸進性感音神經性聾隨着年齡的增長而較為普遍（老年聾）。

通過各種聽力測試（參閱 Rinne's test，Weber's test）可以診斷出耳聾類型。治療取決於病因。參閱 cochlear implant，hearing aid。

脱氨基作用 在肝內氨基酸代謝中發生的一個過程。氨基（$-NH_2$）從氨基酸中脱掉，轉化成氨，氨最終轉化成尿素而被排出。

死亡 生命機能的喪失。通過心跳的永久停止可以判斷死亡。腦死亡被定義為腦幹中控制呼吸、瞳孔和其他生命反射的中樞永久性的功能喪失。通常腦死亡被確定之前須有兩份獨立的醫學鑒定，但是，像腎等器官在心臟停止跳動之前可以合法地予以切除以進行外科移植手術。

死亡證明書 一份説明一個人死亡原因的證書，通常也説明

usually also stating the deceased's marital status, occupation, and age. A doctor's diagnosis of the main cause of death, and any contributory causes of death, and his signature are registered in Great Britain at St Catherine's House, London. Death certificates are required by law in the majority of countries throughout the world.

死者的婚姻狀況、職業和年齡。在英國，醫生對死亡的主要原因以及與死亡有關的任何原因所作的診斷及其簽名，須在倫敦卡塞琳院登記備案。世界上多數國家的法律都要求死亡證明書。

debridement *n.* the process of cleaning an open wound by removal of foreign material and dead tissue, so that healing may occur without hindrance.

清創術 通過去除異物和壞死組織而對開放性創傷進行清除的過程，以使愈合能毫無障礙地進行。

debrisoquine *n.* a potent drug used to treat high blood pressure (hypertension). It is administered by mouth; common side-effects are nausea, headache, sweating, and general malaise. Trade name: **Declinax**.

異喹胍 一種用於治療高血壓的強效藥物。口服。常見副作用有惡心、頭疼、出汗和全身不適。商品名：Declinax。

dec- (deca-) *prefix denoting* ten.

〔前綴〕十，癸

Decadron *n. see* dexamethasone.

地塞米松 參閱 dexamethasone。

decalcification *n.* loss or removal of calcium salts from a bone or tooth.

脫鈣 鈣鹽從骨或牙齒丟失或去除。

decapitation *n.* removal of the head, usually the head of a dead fetus to enable delivery to take place. This procedure is very rare nowadays, being undertaken only in dire circumstances when the fetal head is too large to pass through the birth canal, the mother's life is endangered, and Caesarean section impossible.

斷頭術 將頭截除。通常是截除死胎的頭以使分娩得以進行。此術現今罕見，僅在胎頭過大，難以通過產道，危及產婦生命，但剖宮產又不可能的情況下才使用斷頭術。

decapsulation (decortication) *n.* the surgical removal of a *capsule from an organ; for example, the stripping of the membrane that envelops the kidney or of

被膜切除術（皮質剝除術） 外科去除一器官的被膜，如剝除包裹腎的膜或者剝除包裹慢性膿腫的發炎被膜。

the inflammatory capsule that encloses a chronic abscess.

decay *n*. (in bacteriology) the decomposition of organic matter due to microbial action.

腐敗 （細菌學）因細菌作用而發生的有機物的分解。

decerebration *n*. the removal of the higher centres of the brain or cutting across the brain below the cerebrum so that cerebral functions are eliminated. This procedure is carried out on experimental animals, but certain injuries to the brain in man may cause the same severe neurological signs as occur in an animal that has been decerebrated.

去大腦 切除大腦高級中樞或在大腦以下將腦橫切，從而大腦機能被消除。此手術施行於實驗動物，但在人類，有些大腦損傷時也會發生類似去大腦動物的嚴重神經學體徵。

deci- *prefix denoting* a tenth.

〔前綴〕**十分之一**

decibel (dB) *n*. one tenth of a bel: a unit for comparing levels of power (especially sound) on a logarithmic scale. A power source of intensity P has a power level of $10 \log_{10} P/P_0$ decibels, where P_0 is the intensity of a reference source. The decibel is much more widely used than the bel. Silence is 0 dB; a whisper has an intensity of 20 dB, normal speech 50 dB, heavy traffic 80 dB, and a jet aircraft 120 dB.

分貝 十分之一貝爾：用對數值表示功率（尤其是聲音功率）的單位。強度的功率源 P 等於 $10 \log_{10} P/P_0$ 分貝的功率水平，P_0 為參照率的強度。分貝較貝爾使用廣泛得多。寂靜為 0 分貝，耳語的強度為 20 分貝，正常說話為 50 分貝，繁忙的交通強度為 80 分貝，噴氣式飛機的強度則是 120 分貝。

decidua *n*. the modified mucous membrane that lines the wall of the uterus during pregnancy and is shed with the afterbirth at parturition (*see* endometrium). There are three regions: the *decidua capsularis*, a thin layer that covers the embryo; the *decidua basalis*, where the embryo is attached; and the *decidua parietalis*, which is not in contact with the embryo. **–decidual** *adj*.

蛻膜 妊娠期鋪襯在子宮壁上的改變了的黏膜。此膜在分娩時隨胎盤胎膜一塊脫落（參閱 endometrium）。分三個部分：包蛻膜（覆蓋胚胎的一薄層）、基蛻膜（胚胎附着的地方）、壁蛻膜（與胚胎不相接觸的膜）。

deciduoma *n*. a mass of tissue within the uterus derived from remnants of

蛻膜瘤 子宮內由蛻膜的殘留物生成的組織塊。參閱

*decidua. *See also* chorionepithelioma (malignant deciduoma).

chorionepithelioma（惡性蛻膜瘤）。

deciduous teeth the primary teeth, which are shed just before eruption of their permanent successors. In the absence of permanent successors they can remain functional for many years. *See* dentition.

乳牙　初生牙，在恆牙臨萌出前脫落。在恆牙缺失情況下，它們可維持發揮功能多年。參閱 dentition。

declive *n.* an area of the upper surface of the *cerebellum, posterior to the culmen and anterior to the folium of the middle lobe.

小腦山坡　小腦的上部表面、山頂之後中央小葉之前的區域。

decomposition *n.* the gradual disintegration of dead organic matter, usually foodstuffs or tissues, by the chemical action of bacteria and/or fungi.

腐敗分解　死亡的有機物（通常為食物或組織）通過細菌和／或真菌的化學作用而發生的逐漸分解過程。

decompression *n.* **1.** the reduction of pressure on an organ or part of the body by surgical intervention. Surgical decompression can be effected at many sites: the pressure of tissues on a nerve may be relieved by incision; raised pressure in the fluid of the brain can be lowered by cutting into the *dura mater; and cardiac compression – the abnormal presence of blood or fluid round the heart – can be cured by cutting the sac (pericardium) enclosing the heart. **2.** the gradual reduction of atmospheric pressure for deepsea divers, who work at artificially high pressures. *See* compressed air illness.

減壓　(1) 用外科手術減輕對器官或身體局部的壓力。外科減壓可在許多部位進行：通過切開手術可以使組織對某一神經的壓力得以緩解；通過切開硬腦脊膜可以降低升高的腦脊液壓力；通過切開包裹心臟的囊（心包）可以治愈心臟壓迫（心臟周圍血液或液體積存的異常狀態）。(2) 對在人工高壓下工作的深海潛水員進行逐漸減低大氣壓力的過程。參閱 compressed air illness。

decompression sickness *see* compressed air illness.

減壓病　參閱 compressed air illness。

decongestant *n.* an agent that reduces or relieves nasal congestion. Most nasal decongestants are *sympathomimetic drugs, applied either locally, in the form of nasal sprays or drops, or taken by mouth.

減充血劑　一種減輕或消除鼻充血的藥物。大多數減充血劑都是擬交感藥物，局部以噴霧或滴入形式使用或口服使用。

decortication *n.* **1.** the removal of the outside layer (cortex) from an organ or structure, such as the kidney. **2.** an operation for removing the blood clot and scar tissue that forms after bleeding into the chest cavity (haemothorax). **3.** *see* decapsulation.

(1) 皮質剝除術　去除器官或結構的外層（皮層），如腎臟的外層。**(2) 胸膜外纖維層剝離術**　將胸腔出血（血胸）後形成的血塊和瘢痕組織剝除的手術。**(3) 被膜剝離術**　參閱 decapsulation。

decubitus *n.* the recumbent position.

臥位　躺臥的體位。

decubitus ulcer *see* bedsore.

褥瘡性潰瘍　參閱 bedsore。

decussation *n.* a point at which two or more structures of the body cross to the opposite side. The term is used particularly for the point at which nerve fibres cross over in the central nervous system.

交叉　身體兩種或多種結構向對側交叉的部位。該術語主要指中樞神經系統中神經纖維向對側跨越交叉的部位。

deer fly *see* Chrysops.

鹿虻　參閱 Chrysops。

defecation *n.* a bowel movement in which faeces are evacuated through the rectum and anus. The amount and composition of the food eaten determine to a large degree the bulk of the faeces, and the transit time through the intestinal tract determines the water content. *See* constipation, diarrhoea.

排糞　糞便由直腸和肛門排出的腸運動。所吃食物的量和成分在很大程度上決定糞便的量，通過腸道的時間決定水分含量。參閱 constipation，diarrhoea。

defence mechanism the means whereby an undesirable impulse can be avoided or controlled. Many defence mechanisms have been described, including *repression, *projection, *reaction formation, *sublimation, and *splitting. They may be partly responsible for such problems as tics, stammering, and phobias.

心理防禦機制　避免或控制不需要的衝動的心理手段。已有許多防禦機制被描述清楚，包括壓抑機制、投射（推諉）機制、反應形成機制、昇華作用機制和分裂機制。它們可能是產生抽搐、口吃和恐怖等問題的部分原因。

deferent *adj.* **1.** carrying away from or down from. **2.** relating to the vas deferens.

(1) 輸出的　載離或向下載運。**(2) 輸精管的**　與輸精管相關的。

defervescence *n*. the disappearance of a fever, a process that may occur rapidly or take several days, depending upon the cause and treatment given.

退熱　發熱的消退。這一過程可迅速發生或幾天內完成。這取決於病因和採用的治療。

defibrillation *n*. administration of a controlled electric shock to restore normal heart rhythm in cases of cardiac arrest due to ventricular *fibrillation. The apparatus (*defibrillator*) administers the shock either through electrodes placed on the chest wall over the heart or directly to the heart after the chest has been opened surgically.

除纖顫　對因心室纖維性顫動而導致的心臟停搏給予一控制電擊以恢復正常心臟節律。該儀器（除纖顫器）通過置於胸壁上心臟部位的電極給予電擊，或在外科開胸情況下直接給予心臟電擊。

defibrination *n*. the removal of *fibrin, one of the plasma proteins that causes coagulation, from a sample of blood. It is normally done by whisking the blood with a bundle of fine wires, to which the strands of fibrin that form in the blood adhere.

去纖維蛋白法　從血樣中除去纖維蛋白（一種能引起凝血的血漿蛋白）。一般是用一束細金屬絲在血中攪動，使在血中形成的纖維蛋白絲附着於金屬絲上。

deficiency *n*. (in genetics) *see* deletion.

缺乏，不足　（遺傳學）參閱 deletion。

deficiency disease any disease caused by the lack of an essential nutrient in the diet. Such nutrients include *vitamins, *essential amino acids, and *essential fatty acids.

營養缺乏病　由於膳食中缺乏某種基本營養素而引起的任何疾病。這種營養素包括維生素、必需氨基酸和脂肪酸。

degeneration *n*. the deterioration and loss of specialized function of the cells of a tissue or organ. The changes may be caused by a defective blood supply or by disease. Degeneration may involve the deposition of calcium salts, fat (*see* fatty degeneration), or fibrous tissue in the affected organ or tissue. *See also* infiltration.

變性　一組織或器官中細胞特殊功能的衰退與喪失。這些變化可能是由於血供障礙或者是由於疾病引起的。變性可能包含受累器官或組織內的鈣鹽、脂肪（參閱 fatty degeneration）或纖維組織沉積。參閱 infiltration。

deglutition *n*. *see* swallowing.

吞咽　參閱 swallowing。

dehiscence *n*. a splitting open, as of a surgical wound.

裂開　如外科傷口裂開。

dehydration *n*. **1.** loss or deficiency of water in body tissues. The condition may result from inadequate water intake and/or from excessive removal of water from the body; for example, by sweating, vomiting, or diarrhoea. Symptoms include great thirst, nausea, and exhaustion. The condition is treated by drinking plenty of water, severe cases require *oral rehydration therapy or intravenous administration of water and salts (which have been lost with the water). **2.** the removal of water from tissue during its preparation for microscopical study, by placing it successively in stronger solutions of ethyl alcohol. Dehydration follows *fixation and precedes *clearing.

dehydrogenase *n. see* oxidoreductase.

déjà vu a vivid psychic experience in which immediately contemporary events seem to be a repetition of previous happenings. It is a symptom of some forms of *epilepsy. *See also* jamais vu.

delayed suture a technique used in the closure of contaminated wounds and wounds associated with tissue necrosis, such as are produced by missile injuries. The superficial layers of the wound are left open, to be closed later when the tissues have been cleaned.

deletion (deficiency) *n*. (in genetics) a type of mutation involving the loss of DNA. The deletion may be small, affecting only a portion of a single gene, or large, resulting in loss of a part of a chromosome and affecting many genes.

Delhi boil *see* oriental sore.

delirium *n*. an acute disorder of the mental processes accompanying organic

失水，脫水 **(1)** 身體組織的水分喪失或不足。這一疾患的原因在於水攝入量不足以及/或者從身體排出水量過多所致（如通過出汗、嘔吐、或者腹瀉）。症狀包括煩渴、惡心、衰竭。這一疾患的治療可通過大量飲水，嚴重者須口服補液療法或靜脈給水和鹽（隨水分丟失而丟失）。**(2)** 製備顯微鏡研究用標本時，將組織塊依次浸入濃度遞增的乙醇溶液中，以除去組織中水分。脫水前，需做固定；脫水後，要使用透明法。

脫氫酶 參閱 oxidoreductase。

似曾相識症 一種生動的心理體驗：把當前事件看成似乎是以前發生過的事件的重複。是某些形式的癲癇症的一個症狀。參閱 jamais vu。

延遲縫合 一種縫合技術，用於感染傷口或與組織壞死有關傷口的縫合，如彈道傷。傷口的表層不予縫合，當組織被清洗乾淨後再進行縫合。

缺失（缺乏） （遺傳學）一種涉及脫氧核糖核酸丟失的突變。缺失可小，僅涉及單個基因的一部分；缺失也可大，導致染色體部分丟失，累及許多基因。

德里癤 參閱 oriental sore。

譫妄，妄想 伴有大腦皮質性疾病的一種急性精神活動障

brain disease. It may be manifested by illusions, disorientation, hallucinations, or extreme excitement and occurs in metabolic disorders, intoxication, deficiency diseases, and infections.

delirium tremens a psychosis caused by *alcoholism, usually seen as a withdrawal syndrome in chronic alcoholics. Typically it is precipitated by a head injury or an acute infection causing abstinence from alcohol. Features include anxiety, tremor, sweating, and vivid and terrifying visual and sensory hallucinations, often of animals and insects. Severe cases may end fatally.

delivery *n. see* labour.

deltoid *n.* a thick triangular muscle that covers the shoulder joint (see illustration). It is responsible for raising the arm away from the side of the body.

礙。該病症表現為錯覺、定向障礙、幻覺或極度興奮，發生於代謝性疾病、中毒、營養缺乏病和傳染病。

震顫性譫妄 由乙醇中毒引起的精神疾病，常被看作是慢性酒精中毒患者的戒斷綜合徵。典型情況是該患者先有因頭部損傷或急性感染而戒酒的病史。症狀包括焦慮、震顫、出汗和逼真而嚇人的視覺和感覺幻覺，常常是動物和昆蟲。嚴重者可致死。

分娩 參閱 labour。

三角肌 覆蓋肩關節（見圖）的一厚三角形肌肉。它支配手臂從身體的側部上舉。

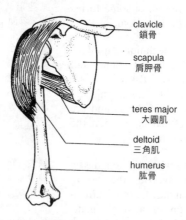

clavicle
鎖骨

scapula
肩胛骨

teres major
大圓肌

deltoid
三角肌

humerus
肱骨

The deltoid muscle
三角肌

delusion *n.* an irrationally held belief that cannot be altered by rational argument. In mental illness it is often a false

妄想 一種用理性論證無法改變的不合理固執信念。在精神病中，它常是一種錯誤的信

belief that the individual is persecuted by others, is very powerful, is controlled by others, or is a victim of physical disease (*see* paranoia). Delusions may be a symptom of *schizophrenia, *manic-depressive psychosis, or an organic psychosis.

念，認為自己受到他人迫害、自己很強大、自己被人控制或者自己是身體疾病的受害者（參閱 paranoia）。妄想可以是精神分裂症、躁狂抑鬱性精神病或器質性精神病的一種症狀。

demeclocycline *n.* an antibiotic that is active against a wide range of bacteria and is used to treat various infections. It is administered by mouth; common side-effects are nausea, diarrhoea, and symptoms resulting from the growth of organisms not sensitive to the drug. Trade name: **Ledermycin**.

地美環素 一種抗菌範圍廣的抗生素，用於治療各種感染。口服。常見副作用為惡心、腹瀉以及對藥物不敏感細菌的生長所導致的症狀。商品名：Ledermycin。

dementia *n.* a chronic or persistent disorder of the mental processes due to organic brain disease. It is marked by memory disorders, changes in personality, deterioration in personal care, impaired reasoning ability, and disorientation. *Presenile dementia* occurs in young or middle-aged people. The term is sometimes reserved for *Alzheimer's disease and *Pick's disease, but it is important to distinguish these conditions from those brain diseases for which curative treatment may be available.

痴呆 由於大腦器質性疾病而引起的慢性頑固性精神活動障礙。其特點為記憶障礙、個性改變、自理能力衰退、推理能力障礙和定向障礙。早老性痴呆發生於年輕人或中年人。該術語有時用於阿爾茨海默病和皮克病，但重要的是要把這些疾患與可以治好的大腦疾病區分開來。

demi- *prefix denoting* half.

〔前綴〕半

Demodex *n.* a genus of harmless parasitic mites, the follicle mites, found in the hair follicles and associated sebaceous glands of the face. They resemble tiny worms, about 0.4 mm in length, and their presence may give rise to dermatitis.

脂蟎屬 一種無害的寄生蟎，即毛囊脂蟎。見於面部毛囊和相關的面部皮脂腺內。牠們類似細小蠕蟲，長約 0.4 mm，其出現可引起皮炎。

demography *n.* the study of populations on a national, regional, or local basis in terms of age, sex, and other *variables, including patterns of migration and survival. It is used in *public health

人口學 研究一個國家、地區和局部地段人口的年齡、性別和其他變量（包括人口遷移和生存方式）的科學。用於公共衛生醫學以幫助確定衛生需

medicine to help identify health needs and *risk factors. *See also* biostatistics.

求和危險因素。參閱 biostatistics。

demulcent *n.* a soothing agent that protects the mucous membranes and relieves irritation. Demulcents form a protective film and are used in mouth washes, gargles, etc., to soothe irritation or inflammation in the mouth.

緩和藥 一種保護黏膜、緩和刺激的緩解劑。緩和藥形成一層保護膜，用作漱口劑，含漱液以緩解口腔刺激或炎症。

demyelination *n.* a disease process selectively damaging the *myelin sheaths surrounding the nerve fibres in the central or peripheral nervous system. This in turn affects the function of the nerve fibres, which the myelin normally supports. Demyelination may be the primary disorder, as in *multiple sclerosis, or it may occur after head injury or strokes.

脫髓鞘 選擇性損害包圍中樞和周圍神經系統的神經纖維的髓鞘的病變過程。這反過來影響通常由髓鞘支持的神經纖維的功能。脫髓鞘可為原發性疾病（如多發性硬化症），也可在頭部損傷或中風後發生。

denaturation *n.* the changes in the physical and physiological properties of a protein that are brought about by heat, X-rays, or chemicals. These changes include loss of activity (in the case of enzymes) and loss (or alteration) of antigenicity (in the case of *antigens).

變性作用 由熱、X 綫或化學物質引起的蛋白物理和生理特性的變化。這些變化包括活性（酶）和抗原性（抗原）的喪失。

dendrite *n.* one of the shorter branching processes of the cell body of a *neurone, which makes contact with other neurones at synapses and carries nerve impulses from them into the cell body.

樹突 神經元的細胞體的較短分支狀突起，與其他神經元在突觸部位發生接觸，並從突觸處將神經衝動傳入細胞體內。

dendritic ulcer a branching ulcer of the surface of the cornea caused by *herpes simplex virus. A similar appearance may be produced by a healing corneal abrasion. Dendritic ulcers tend to recur because the virus lies dormant in the tissues; years may elapse between attacks.

樹枝狀潰瘍 由單純性疱疹病毒引起的角膜表面分支狀潰瘍。相似的潰瘍現象也可由角膜擦傷的愈合產生。樹枝狀潰瘍有復發傾向，因為病毒潛伏於組織內。兩次發作之間可相隔數年。

denervation *n.* interruption of the nerve supply to the muscles and skin. The

去神經支配 中斷神經對肌肉和皮膚的支配。肌肉癱瘓，其

muscle is paralysed and its normal tone (elasticity) is lost. The muscle fibres shrink and are replaced by fat. A denervated area of skin loses all forms of sensation and its subsequent ability to heal and renew its tissues may be impaired.

dengue (breakbone fever) *n.* a disease caused by arboviruses and transmitted to man principally by the mosquito *Aëdes aegypti*. Symptoms, which last for a few days, include severe pains in the joints and muscles, headache, sore throat, fever, running of the eyes, and an irritating rash. These symptoms recur in a usually milder form after an interval of two or three days. Death rarely occurs, but the patient is left debilitated and requires considerable convalescence. A more severe form, *dengue haemorrhagic fever*, characterized by a breakdown of the blood-clotting mechanism with internal bleeding, can affect children. Dengue occurs throughout the tropics and subtropics. Patients are given aspirin and codeine to relieve the pain and calamine lotion is helpful in easing the irritating rash.

dens *n.* a tooth or tooth-shaped structure.

dens invaginatus literally, an infolded tooth: a specific type of tooth malformation that mainly affects upper lateral incisors to varying degrees.

dent- (denti-, dento-) *prefix denoting* the teeth. Example: *dentoalveolar* (relating to the teeth and associated jaw).

dental auxiliary any of several assistants to a dentist. A *dental hygienist* performs scaling and instruction in oral hygiene under the prescription of the dentist. A *dental surgery assistant* helps the dentist

登革熱（斷骨熱） 一種由蟲媒病毒引起的疾病，主要由埃及伊蚊傳播給人。症狀持續數天，包括關節和肌肉劇烈疼痛、頭痛、咽喉炎、發熱、流淚、瘙癢性皮疹。這些症狀經過 2~3 天的間隔後會重複出現，表現較輕。死亡很少發生，但患者卻變得虛弱，需要好好恢復。登革出血熱是一種較嚴重的登革熱，其特點是凝血機制發生障礙，並伴有內出血，該病可感染兒童。登革熱發生於熱帶和亞熱帶地區。病人可給予阿司匹林和可待因以緩解疼痛，爐甘石洗劑有助於減輕瘙癢性皮疹。

牙，齒 牙齒或齒狀結構。

牙內陷 按字面意義，即可知其意義為陷入的牙，是一種特殊類型的牙畸形，不同程度地影響着上側切牙。

〔前綴〕牙 如牙槽的（與牙和與之相連的頜骨有關的）。

牙科輔助人員 牙科醫生數名助手中的任何一個。一個牙科衛生員根據牙科醫生的處方施行牙齒潔治術和口腔衛生指導。牙外科助手則在牙科椅旁

at the chairside by preparing materials, passing instruments, and aspirating fluids from the patient's mouth. A *dental technician* constructs dentures, crowns, and orthodontic appliances in the laboratory for the dentist. A *dental therapist* performs treatment on children under the direction of a dentist in the community dental services and in hospitals.

dental caries decay and crumbling of the substance of a tooth. Dental caries is caused by the metabolism of the bacteria in *plaque attached to the surface of the tooth. Acid formed by bacterial breakdown of sugar in the diet causes demineralization of the enamel of the tooth. If no preventive measure or treatment is carried out it spreads into the dentine and progressively destroys the tooth. It is the most common cause of toothache, and once infection has spread to the pulp it may extend through the root canal into the periapical tissues to cause an *apical abscess. Frequent intake of sugar is a major cause, and the disease is more common in young people and has a predilection for specific sites. Dental caries can be most effectively prevented by restricting the frequency of sugar intake and avoiding sweet food and drinks at bedtime. The resistance of enamel to dental caries can be increased by the application of *fluoride salts to the tooth surface from toothpastes or mouth rinses. *Fluoridation of water also makes teeth resistant to caries during the period of tooth development. Once caries has spread into the dentine, treatment usually consists of removing the decayed part of the tooth using a *drill and replacing it with a *filling.

dental chair the chair on which a patient lies for dental treatment. Electric

邊幫助牙科醫生，如準備材料、傳遞器械和從患者口腔中抽吸液體。牙科技師在牙醫實驗室製備托牙、牙冠和矯正器。在社區牙科防治站和醫院裏在牙科醫生的指導下牙科治療師對兒童施行治療。

齲　牙質的腐朽和破碎。齲是由附着於牙表面牙斑中的細菌代謝所致。膳食中的糖經細菌分解而形成的酸引起牙釉質的脫礦作用。如果不採取預防性措施或者治療，它會殃及牙本質並漸進性破壞該牙。它是牙疼的最常見的原因。一旦感染擴散至牙髓，它可以延伸至整個牙根管以達根尖周組織，引起根尖膿腫。經常吃糖是一主要原因，該病在年輕人中多見，且特別易發生於一定的部位。齲可通過嚴格地限制糖的攝入和睡覺前避免甜食和甜味飲料而得以有效預防。使用含氟鹽的牙膏或漱口液，可增強牙釉質的抗齲能力。水的氟化作用可使處於發育期的牙具有抗齲能力。一旦齲擴展至牙本質，治療則通常包括用牙鑽除掉牙的腐朽部分，並用填料代替它。

牙椅　患者能躺着進行牙科治療的椅子。電動開關改變病人

switches change the position of the patient, and the chair is frequently attached to the *dental unit.

dental floss fine thread, usually of nylon, used to clean some surfaces of teeth.

dental nerve either of two nerves that supply the teeth; they are branches of the trigeminal nerve. The *inferior dental nerve* supplies the lower teeth and for most of its length exists as a single large bundle; thus anaesthesia of it has a widespread effect (*see* inferior dental block). The *superior dental nerve*, which supplies the upper teeth, breaks into separate branches at some distance from the teeth and it is possible to anaesthetize these individually with less widespread effect for the patient.

dental pantomogram (DPT) a special form of tomogram (*see* tomography) that provides a picture of all the teeth of both jaws on one film.

dental unit a major fixed piece of dental equipment to which are attached the dental drills, aspirator, compressed air syringe, and ultrasonic scaler.

dentate *adj.* **1.** having teeth. **2.** serrated; having toothlike projections.

dentifrice *n.* a paste or powder for cleaning the teeth. Toothpastes contain a fine abrasive; an essential ingredient is suitable flavouring to make their use pleasant. Most toothpastes contain *fluoride salts, which help to prevent dental caries.

dentine *n.* a hard tissue that forms the bulk of a tooth. The dentine of the crown

牙線　用以清潔部分牙面的細線，通常由尼龍製成。

牙神經　支配牙的兩條神經。它們是三叉神經的分支。下牙神經支配下列牙，其全長的大部分是一粗大的神經束，因此，對其進行麻醉可獲得較大範圍的麻醉效果（參閱 inferior dental block）。上牙神經支配上列牙，在距離牙不遠處分為獨立的分支，因此可對這些神經進行單個麻醉而獲得範圍不太大的麻醉效果。

牙全體 X 線斷層照片　一種特殊的 X 線體層照片（參閱 tomography）：在一張膠片上提供一幅上下頜所有牙齒的照片。

牙科綜合治療裝置　一件主要的固定性牙科設備，連帶器械包括牙鑽、吸引器、壓縮空氣槍和超聲刮牙器。

(1) 有牙的　(2) 鋸齒狀的　有齒狀突起的。

牙粉（膏）　清潔牙齒的膏或粉。牙膏中含有一種很細的磨料。基本成分中有一種合適的香料使應用者樂於接受。大多數牙膏含有氟鹽，它們有助於預防齲。

牙本質　構成牙主體的一種堅硬組織。牙冠的牙本質由牙釉

is covered by enamel and that of the root by cementum. The dentine is permeated by fine tubules, which near the centre of the tooth contain cellular processes from the pulp. Exposed dentine is sensitive to touch, heat, and cold.

所覆蓋，牙根的牙本質由牙骨質所覆蓋。牙本質有微細小管穿透，小管在近牙中心的部位含有來自牙髓的細胞突起。暴露的牙本質對觸摸、熱和寒冷敏感。

dentinogenesis *n.* the formation of *dentine by *odontoblasts. Although dentinogenesis continues throughout life, very little dentine is formed later than a few years after tooth eruption. *Dentinogenesis imperfecta* is a hereditary condition in which dentine formation is disturbed, resulting in loss of overlying enamel.

牙本質生成 由成牙質細胞形成牙本質。儘管牙本質在一生中斷續生成，但是，與牙萌出後數年間牙本質形成相比，以後的生成很慢。不完全性牙本質生成是一種遺傳性病變，表現為牙本質形成被干擾，導致覆蓋在上面的牙釉缺失。

dentist *n.* a member of the dental profession, who in the UK must be registered with the General Dental Council unless he holds a medical qualification.

牙科醫生 牙科職業的一名從業人員，在英國，除非他有行醫資格證書，否則他必須在牙醫公會註冊。

dentistry *n.* the study, management, and treatment of diseases and conditions affecting the mouth, jaws, teeth, and their supporting tissues. Sub-disciplines are: dental public health, *endodontics, oral medicine, oral surgery, *orthodontics, *paedodontics, *periodontics, preventive dentistry, *prosthetic dentistry, and restorative dentistry.

牙科學 對患及口、頜、牙和它們的支持組織的疾病和情況的研究、處理和治療的科學。分支學科有牙科公共衛生學、牙髓病學、口腔醫學、口腔外科學、正牙學、兒童牙科學、牙周病學、預防牙科學、假牙修復學和恢復牙科學。

dentition *n.* the arrangement of teeth in the mouth. The *deciduous dentition* comprises the teeth of young children. It consists of 20 teeth, made up of incisors, canines, and molars only. The lower incisor erupts first at about 6 months of age, and all the deciduous teeth have usually erupted by the age of $2^1/_2$ years. The lower incisors are shed first at about 6 years of age, and from this time until about 12 years old both deciduous and permanent teeth are present; i.e. there is a *mixed dentition*.

牙列 在口腔內牙的排列。乳牙列是由幼兒的牙構成的。它由 20 個牙組成，僅包括切牙、尖牙和磨牙。在大約 6 個月時，下切牙首先萌出，所有的乳牙到 2 歲半時通常都已萌出。下切牙在大約 6 歲時首先脫落，並且，從此時直到大約 12 歲，乳牙和恆牙同時存在，也就是說，有一混合牙列。恆牙多達 32 顆，由切牙、尖牙和磨牙組成。第一個萌出的牙就是第一個磨牙（在大約 6 歲

The *permanent dentition* consists of up to 32 teeth, made up of incisors, canines, premolars, and molars. The first tooth to erupt is the first molar (at the age of 6) and most have appeared by the age of 14 years, although the third molars may not erupt until the age of 18–21 years. See illustrations.

時），而大多數則要到 14 歲時才出現，儘管第三個磨牙可能一直要到 18~21 歲時才萌出，見圖。

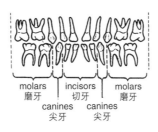

molars　incisors　molars
磨牙　　切牙　　磨牙
canines　　canines
尖牙　　　尖牙

Deciduous dentition
乳牙列

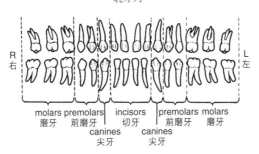

R　　　　　　　　　　　　　　　　L
右　　　　　　　　　　　　　　　　左

molars premolars　incisors　premolars molars
磨牙　前磨牙　　切牙　　前磨牙　磨牙
　　　canines　　　canines
　　　尖牙　　　　尖牙

Permanent dentition
恆牙列

denture *n.* a removable replacement for one or more teeth carried on some type of plate or frame. A *complete denture* replaces all the teeth in one jaw. It is usually made entirely of acrylic resin. A *partial denture* replaces some teeth because others still remain. It is designed to restore function with the least potential damage to the remaining teeth. The framework of the denture base is often made of metal (*cobalt-chromium) because of its strength. (*See*

托牙　裝在某種托板或支架上，可以取下來的一個或多個牙齒的替代物。全口托牙取代單頜的所有牙齒。通常完全用丙烯酸樹脂製成。部分托牙只取代一些牙齒，因為其他的牙仍然存留着。此種設計旨在恢復功能而對存留牙的潛在損害卻最小。托牙基的支架常由金屬（鈷-鉻）製成，其原因是其強度（參閱 prosthesis）。托牙口瘡是一種與托牙基托清潔不

also prosthesis.) *Denture sore mouth* is a form of candidosis related to inadequately cleaned denture bases. *Denture hyperplasia* is an overgrowth of fibrous tissue covered by mucous membrane, resulting from chronic irritation by a denture.

足有關的念珠菌病所致。托牙性增生是由黏膜覆蓋的纖維組織過度增生，其原因是由於托牙的慢性刺激引起的。

deodorant *n.* an agent that reduces or removes unpleasant body odours by destroying bacteria that live on the skin and break down sweat. Deodorant preparations often contain an antiseptic.

除臭劑 一種通過殺滅生存於皮膚並能分解汗液的細菌以減輕或消除體臭的藥物。除臭劑中常含有一種防腐劑。

deontology *n.* the study of ethics and correct behaviour or duty. In medicine this includes consideration of the proper behaviour of a doctor towards his patient, whether a patient should be told if his condition is fatal or not, and similar problems for which there may be no written guidelines. The best-known code of conduct is the *Hippocratic oath.

道義學 研究倫理、正確行為或職責的學科。在醫學中，道義學包括醫生面對其病人的正確行為，即病人是否應被告知其病情致命與否以及類似無章可循的問題。最知名的行為準則是希波克拉底誓言。

deoxycholic acid *see* bile acids.

去氧膽酸 參閱 bile acids。

deoxycorticosterone *n.* a hormone, synthesized and released by the adrenal cortex, that regulates salt and water balance. *See also* corticosteroid.

脫氧皮質酮 由腎上腺皮質合成和分泌的一種激素，調節鹽和水的平衡。參閱 corticosteroid。

deoxyribonuclease *n.* an enzyme, located in the *lysosomes of cells, that splits DNA at specific places in the molecule.

脫氧核糖核酸酶 一種存在於細胞溶酶體內的酶，能在分子的特定部位降解 DNA。

deoxyribonucleic acid *see* DNA.

脫氧核糖核酸 參閱 DNA。

Department of Health a department of central government that supports the Secretary of State for Health in meeting his obligations, which include the *National Health Service and the prevention and control of infectious diseases. Information is collated, priorities

衛生部 中央政府的一個部。其職能是支持國家衛生大臣履行其職能，如：負責國家保健服務制的工作和傳染病的預防和控制，收集資料，評估優先考慮的事務，並向地區和地段級衛生局撥款。該部的人員配

assessed, and resources allocated to Regional and District Health Authorities. The department is staffed by civil servants, including medical and nursing personnel and those from other health professions. Equivalent departments support the ministers responsible for health services in Scotland, Wales, and Northern Ireland. Formerly, the department was joined with the *Department of Social Security.

置是由公務人員組成，包括醫療和護理人員和其他衛生專業人員。在蘇格蘭、威爾士和北愛爾蘭，則有級別等同的部分協助主管衛生事務的大臣工作。過去，該部是和社會福利部合在一起的。

Department of Social Security a department of central government that supports the Secretary of State for Social Security in meeting his obligations, which include the *social services, *National Insurance, and income support and other benefits for those with welfare needs.

社會福利部 由社會福利大臣所主持的中央政府的一個部，該部門完成的工作職責包括社會福利項目、國民保險業務和那些對社會福利需要的人的收入補貼和其他福利。

dependence (drug dependence) *n.* the physical and/or psychological effects produced by the habitual taking of certain drugs, characterized by a compulsion to continue taking the drug. In *physical dependence* withdrawal of the drug causes specific symptoms (*withdrawal symptoms*), such as sweating, vomiting, or tremors, that are reversed by further doses. Substances that may induce physical dependence include alcohol and the 'hard' drugs morphine, heroin, and cocaine. Dependence on 'hard' drugs carries a high mortality, partly because overdosage may be fatal and partly because their casual injection intravenously may lead to infections such as *hepatitis and *AIDS. Treatment is difficult and requires specialist skills. Much more common is *psychological dependence*, in which repeated use of a drug induces reliance on it for a state of well-being and contentment, but there are no physical withdrawal symptoms if

依賴（藥物依賴） 由習慣性服用某些藥物所產生的身體和／或心理效應。其特點是迫使繼續服用該藥品。身體性依賴表現為停止服藥會引起具體的症狀（脫癮症狀），如出汗、嘔吐或者震顫等。這些症狀通過進一步服藥後可消除。可誘發身體依賴的物質包括酒精和麻醉品嗎啡、海洛因和可卡因。對麻醉品的依賴有很高的死亡率，部分原因是因為消毒不嚴格的靜脈注射可導致傳染病，如肝炎和艾滋病。治療起來較難，且需要專門技術。而更為普遍的是心理依賴：一種藥物的重複服用誘發對該藥物的依賴，以求得一種良好狀態和滿足感。但是當該藥的服用被停止時，並無身體脫癮症狀。可誘發心理依賴的物質包括煙草裏的尼古丁、大麻和許多「軟性」毒品，如巴比妥類和苯丙胺類。

use of the drug is stopped. Substances that may induce psychological dependence include nicotine in tobacco, cannabis, and many 'soft' drugs, such as barbiturates and amphetamines.

depersonalization *n.* a state in which a person feels himself becoming unreal or strangely altered, or feels that his mind is becoming separated from his body. Minor degrees of this feeling are common in normal people under stress. Severe feelings of depersonalization occur in anxiety neurosis, in states of *dissociation, in depression and schizophrenia, and in epilepsy (particularly temporal-lobe epilepsy). *See also* derealization, out-of-the-body experience.

人格解體 一個人感覺自己變得不真實或發生了奇怪變化、或感覺自己的思維和軀體相分離的一種狀態。在有壓力的情況下，正常人可常有這種輕度的感覺。嚴重的人格解體感覺發生於焦慮性神經症、分裂狀態、抑鬱症和精神分裂症以及癲癇（特別是顳葉癲癇）。參閱 derealization，out-of-the-body experience。

depilatory *n.* an agent applied to the skin to remove hair.

脫毛劑 一種塗於皮膚以脫毛的藥物。

depolarization *n.* the sudden surge of charged particles across the membrane of a nerve cell or a muscle cell that accompanies a physicochemical change in the membrane and cancels out, or reverses, its resting potential to produce an *action potential. The passage of a *nerve impulse is a rapid wave of depolarization along the membrane of a nerve fibre.

去極化 帶電粒子突然大量透過神經細胞或肌肉細胞的膜，伴隨着膜的物理化學變化，使靜息電位消除或逆轉，從而產生動作電位的過程。一個神經衝動的傳遞是一個沿着一條神經纖維膜行進的快速去極波。

depressant *n.* an agent that reduces the normal activity of any body system or function. Drugs such as general *anaesthetics, *barbiturates, and opiates are depressants of the central nervous system and respiration. *Cytotoxic drugs, such as azathioprine, are depressants of the levels of white blood cells.

抑制劑 一種降低身體任何系統或功能的正常活動的藥物。諸如全身麻醉劑、巴比妥類和阿片類藥物是中樞神經系統和呼吸系統的抑制劑。細胞毒素藥物（如硫唑嘌呤）是白細胞數量的抑制劑。

depression *n.* a mental state characterized by excessive sadness. Activity can be agitated and restless or slow and

抑鬱症 以過分悲哀為特徵的精神狀態。活動可以是焦慮和不安，或者緩慢和遲鈍。行為

retarded. Behaviour is governed by pessimistic or despairing beliefs, and sleep, appetite, and concentration are disturbed. There are several causes. *Manic-depressive psychosis causes severe depression, a. major *affective disorder, in which there may be delusions of being worthless, ill, wicked, or impoverished and hallucinations of accusing voices. Loss and frustration also cause depression, which may be prolonged and disproportionate in *dysthymic disorder* (formerly known as depressive *neurosis). (*See also* puerperal depression.) Treatment is with *antidepressant drugs, *cognitive therapy, and/or *psychotherapy. Severe cases may need *electroconvulsive therapy.

受悲觀或絕望的信念所支配，睡眠、食慾和注意力均受到擾亂。此症有幾個原因。躁狂抑鬱性精神病引起嚴重抑鬱，這是一種主要的情感性精神病。此時，會有無生存價值、生病、邪惡、虛弱無力等妄想和譴責聲音幻覺。失敗和挫折也引起抑鬱。這種抑鬱症可以持久不愈，精神抑鬱性障礙可以表現為不均衡型（以前稱為抑鬱性神經症）。治療使用抗抑鬱藥物、內心療法和／或心理療法。嚴重者可能需要電休克療法。

depressor *n*. **1.** a muscle that causes lowering of part of the body. The *depressor labii inferioris* is a muscle that draws down and everts the lower lip. **2.** a nerve that lowers blood pressure.

(1) 降肌 一種使身體的一部分下降的肌肉。下唇方肌是一種將唇下拉並外翻的肌肉。**(2) 減壓神經** 一條降低血壓的神經。

dequalinium *n*. an antiseptic, active against some bacteria and fungi, used as lozenges or paint to treat mouth and throat infections. Trade name: **Labosept**.

克菌定 一種治療某些細菌和真菌的有效抗菌劑。以錠劑或搽劑方式用於治療口腔和咽喉感染。商品名：Labosept。

derealization *n*. a feeling of unreality in which the environment is experienced as unreal and as flat, dull, or strange. The experience is unwelcome and often frightening. It occurs in association with *depersonalization or with the conditions that cause depersonalization.

現實感喪失 一種不真實的感覺，此時，環境被體驗為不切實存在的、單調、乏味或者奇怪的。此種經歷令人不快，且常為之恐懼。它常與人格解體或者與引起人格解體的疾患有關。

dereism *n*. undirected fantasy thinking that fails to respect the realities of life. When this becomes markedly dominant it may be a feature of *schizoid personality or of *schizophrenia.

空想癖 不尊重現實生活的無定向的幻想思維。當這種情況變得極為明顯時，它可能會是精神分裂樣人格或精神分裂症的一個特徵。

derm- (derma-, dermo-, dermat(o)-) *prefix denoting* the skin.

〔前綴〕**皮膚** 表示皮膚。

-derm *suffix denoting* **1.** the skin. **2.** a germ layer.

〔後綴〕**(1) 皮膚 (2) 胚層**

Dermacentor *n.* a genus of hard *ticks, worldwide in distribution, the adults of which are parasites of man and other mammals. The wood tick, *D. andersoni*, transmits Rocky Mountain spotted fever to man in the western USA and the dog tick, *D. variabilis*, is the vector of the milder form of this disease in the east.

革蜱屬 一類全球分布的硬蜱。成蟲是人類和其他哺乳動物的寄生蟲。在美國西部，安革蜱將落基山斑疹熱傳播給人類，而犬血蜱（變異革蜱）是東部該病輕型的媒介。

dermal *adj.* relating to or affecting the skin, especially the *dermis.

皮的 與皮膚（特別是真皮）相關的或使其受到影響的。

Dermanyssus *n.* a genus of widespread parasitic mites. The red poultry mite, *D. gallinae*, is a common parasite of wild birds in temperate regions but can also infest poultry. It occasionally attacks and takes a blood meal from man, causing itching and mild dermatitis.

皮刺蜱屬 一廣泛分布的寄生蟎。紅色家禽蟎（雞皮刺蟎）是温帶地區野生鳥類中常見寄生蟲，但也可侵襲家禽。它偶爾從人身上吸血，引起瘙癢和輕度皮炎。

dermatitis *n.* an inflammatory condition of the skin caused by outside agents (*compare* eczema, an endogenous disease in which such agents do not play a primary role). *Primary irritant dermatitis* may occur in anyone who has sufficient contact with such irritants as acids, alkalis, solvents, and (especially) detergents. It is the commonest cause of *occupational dermatitis* in hairdressers, nurses, cooks, etc.) (*See also* napkin rash.) In *allergic contact dermatitis* skin changes resembling those of eczema develop as a delayed reaction to contact with a particular allergen, which may be present at low concentrations. The commonest example in women is *nickel dermatitis* from jewellery, jeans studs, etc., in men *chromium dermatitis* is relatively

皮炎 一種由外界因子（與這種因子不起作用的內源疾病 eczeme 對比）引起的皮膚炎症。原發刺激性皮炎可在任何與諸如酸、鹼、溶劑和（尤其是）去污劑等刺激物有足夠接觸時間的人身上發生。在美髮師、護士、廚師等人，它是職業性皮炎的最常見的原因（參閱 napkin rash）。在過敏性接觸性皮炎中，類似於濕疹皮膚改變的產生是由於對接觸某一特定變應原的一種延遲反應。低濃度的變應原也可使此種現象出現。在婦女中，最常見的例子則是由於珠寶、牛仔服的飾釘等引起的鎳皮炎。在男人中，鉻皮炎較為常見。皮炎的治療取決於病因。

common. Treatment of dermatitis depends upon the cause.

Dermatitis herpetiformis is an uncommon, very itchy rash with symmetrical blistering, especially on the knees, elbows, buttocks, and shoulders. It is associated with *gluten sensitivity and responds well to treatment with dapsone.

疱疹樣皮炎是一種不常見的、非常瘙癢的皮疹，並伴有對稱的水疱（尤其在膝、肘、臀部和肩部）。與穀蛋白過敏有關，用氨苯碸治療有效。

Dermatobia *n.* a genus of nonbloodsucking flies inhabiting lowland woods and forests of South and Central America. The parasitic maggots of *D. hominis* can cause a serious disease of the skin in man (*see* myiasis). The maggots burrow into the skin, after emerging from eggs transported by bloodsucking insects (e.g. mosquitoes), and produce painful boil-like swellings. Treatment involves surgical removal of the maggots.

皮蠅屬 一類棲息於中美洲和南美洲低地樹林和森林中的非吸血蠅。人皮蠅的寄生蛆在人類可引起一種嚴重的皮膚病（參閱 myiasis）。吸血昆蟲（如蚊）將蠅卵傳給人。在寄生蛆從卵中孵出之後，牠們則鑽入皮膚內，從而產生疼痛性的癤腫樣的腫脹。治療涉及外科切除蠅蛆。

dermatofibrosarcoma protuberans a tumour probably derived from *histiocytes that may occur in any part of the body. It is locally invasive but does not *metastasize. It often recurs locally despite excision.

隆凸性皮膚纖維肉瘤 一種可出現在身體任何部位、可能起源於組織細胞的腫瘤。具有局部侵襲性，但不轉移。即使切除之後，它常會局部復發。

dermatoglyphics *n.* the study of the patterns of finger, palm, toe, and sole prints. These patterns are formed by skin ridges, the distribution of which is unique to each individual. Abnormalities are found in those with chromosomal aberrations, such as *Down's syndrome. Dermatoglyphics is of value in criminology and is also of interest to anthropologists. *See also* fingerprint.

膚紋學 研究手指、手掌、腳趾和腳跟皮紋型的學科。這些皮紋型是由皮嵴形成的。皮嵴的分布每一個人都是獨特的。在那些有染色體畸變（如唐氏綜合徵）的人中可見皮紋畸形。在犯罪學中膚紋學有價值，人類學家也對之感興趣。參閱 fingerprint。

dermatology *n.* the medical specialty concerned with the diagnosis and treatment of skin disorders. **–dermatological** *adj.* **–dermatologist** *n.*

皮膚病學 有關皮膚疾病的診斷和治療的醫學專業。

dermatome *n.* **1.** a surgical instrument used for cutting thin slices of skin in

(1) 植皮刀 在一些皮膚移植手術中用以將皮膚切割成薄片

some skin grafting operations. **2.** that part of the segmented mesoderm in the early embryo that forms the deeper layers of the skin (dermis) and associated tissues. *See* somite.

的外科器械。**(2) 生皮節** 在早期胚胎內形成皮膚深層（真皮）和附屬組織的胚層體節部分。參閱 somite。

dermatomyositis *n.* an inflammatory disorder of the skin and underlying tissues, including the muscles. The condition is one of the *connective-tissue diseases. A bluish-red skin eruption occurs on the face, scalp, neck, shoulders, and knuckles and is later accompanied by severe swelling. Dermatomyositis is often associated with internal cancer in adults, though not in children.

皮肌炎 皮膚和皮下組織（包括肌肉）的一種炎症。這種疾患是結締組織病的一種。表現為面部、頭皮、頸、肩和手部出現紫紅色皮膚疱疹，隨後伴有嚴重的腫脹。皮肌炎在成人中常與內臟癌症有關，在兒童並無此伴隨關係。

Dermatophagoides *n.* a genus of *mites that have been detected in samples of dust taken from houses in various parts of Europe. The mites may occasionally infest the skin of the scalp and cause dermatitis.

塵蟎屬 從歐洲不同地區所採集的室塵樣品中檢測出來的一類蟎。這類蟎可偶爾侵襲頭皮，引起皮炎。

dermatophyte *n.* a fungus belonging to any one of the three genera (*Microsporum*, *Trichophyton*, and *Epidermophyton*) that can feed on *keratin and cause *ringworm (tinea).

皮真菌 一種以角蛋白為食並引起癬菌病（癬）的真菌。有三類：小孢子菌屬、發癬菌屬和表皮癬菌屬。

dermatosis *n.* any disease of skin, particularly one without inflammation. In *juvenile plantar dermatosis*, which affects children up to the age of 14, the skin on the front of the sole becomes red, glazed, and symmetrically cracked. This condition, which settles spontaneously after a number of years, is believed to be related to the wearing of trainers.

皮膚病 皮膚的任何疾病，特別是沒有炎症的疾病。侵襲 14 歲以下兒童和青少年，足底皮膚病表現為足底前部變紅、發亮和對稱裂開。這一疾患在數年之後自然痊愈。一般認為是與穿着訓練鞋有關。

dermis (corium) *n.* the true *skin: the thick layer of living tissue that lies beneath the epidermis. It consists mainly of loose connective tissue within which

真皮 真正的皮膚即位於表皮下方的厚層活組織。主要由疏鬆結締組織組成。在其內是血管、淋巴管、感覺神經末梢、

are blood capillaries, lymph vessels, sensory nerve endings, sweat glands and their ducts, hair follicles, sebaceous glands, and smooth muscle fibres. **–dermal** *adj*.

汗腺及其導管、毛囊、皮脂腺和平滑肌纖維。

dermographism *n*. a local reaction caused by pressure on the skin. People with such highly sensitive skin can 'write' on it with a finger or blunt instrument, the pressure producing weals.

皮膚劃痕現象　一種按壓皮膚所引起的局部反應。具有這種高度過敏性皮膚的人可以用手指或鈍器在皮膚上「寫字」。其壓力可產生持續一段時間的劃痕。

dermoid cyst (dermoid) a cyst containing hair, hair follicles, and *sebaceous glands, usually found at sites marking the fusion of developing sections of the body in the embryo. Sometimes a dermoid cyst may develop after an injury. Treatment is by surgical removal.

皮樣囊腫　含有毛髮、毛囊和皮脂腺的囊腫，通常見於胚胎發育體節的融合部位。有時在一次外傷後可產生皮樣囊腫。治療方法是通過外科摘除。

Descemet's membrane the membrane that forms the deepest layer of the *stroma of the cornea of the eye. The endothelium lies between it and the aqueous humour.

後彈性層　形成眼角膜基質最深層的膜。內皮位於它和房水之間。

desensitization *n*. **1.** (*or* **hyposensitization**) a method for reducing the effects of a known allergen by injecting, over a period, gradually increasing doses of the allergen, until resistance is built up. *See* allergy. **2.** a technique used in the *behaviour therapy of phobic states. The thing that is feared is very gradually introduced to the patient, first in imagination and then in reality. At the same time the patient is taught relaxation to inhibit the development of anxiety (*see* relaxation therapy). In this way he is able to cope with progressively closer approximations to the feared object or situation.

脫敏　(1)　一種通過在一段時間內，逐漸增加已知變應原的注射劑量，直至對變應原的耐受性建立，從而減弱該變應原作用的方法（參閱 allergy）。(2)　一種用於恐怖症的行為療法技術。先對患者將其所害怕的事物逐漸向其介紹，開始為想像，然後再為實物。同時，教會患者放鬆以防止焦慮的產生（參閱 relaxation therapy）。採用此種方法，患者能夠對付逐漸接近的所懼怕的事物或情形。

desferrioxamine *n*. a drug that combines with iron in body tissues and fluids

去鐵胺　一種能與身體組織和體液內的鐵相結合的藥物，用

and is used to treat iron poisoning (including that resulting from prolonged or constant blood transfusion, as for thalassaemia), diseases involving iron storage in parts of the body (*see* haemochromatosis), and for the diagnosis of such diseases. It is administered by mouth, injection, or as eye drops; reactions and pain sometimes occur on injection. Trade name: **Desferal**.

於治療鐵中毒（包括由於長期的或者經常性的輸血所致鐵中毒，如治療地中海貧血），和涉及身體某些部位鐵蓄積的疾病（參閱 haemochromatosis）以及此疾病的診斷。口服、注射或作為滴眼劑。有時注射發生反應並引起疼痛。商品名：Desferal。

desipramine *n.* a tricyclic *antidepressant drug administered by mouth or injection; common side-effects are dry mouth, blurred vision, insomnia, and unsteadiness in walking. Trade name: **Pertofran**.

地昔帕明 一種三環結構的抗抑鬱藥。口服或注射。常見副作用為口乾、視物模糊、失眠和步態不穩。商品名：Pertofran。

desmopressin *n.* a synthetic derivative of *vasopressin that causes a decrease in urine output and is used to treat diabetes insipidus. It is also effective in mild haemophilia and von Willebrand's disease. Side-effects include stomach cramps, headache, and flushing of the skin. It is taken intranasally to treat diabetes insipidus and intravenously to treat haemophilia and von Willebrand's disease. Trade name: **DDAVP**.

去氨加壓素 一種人工合成能減少排尿量的加壓素的衍生物。用於治療尿崩症。對輕度血友病和遺傳性假血友病也有效。副作用包括胃絞痛、頭痛和皮膚潮紅。鼻內使用可治尿崩症，靜脈注射可治療血友病和遺傳性假血友病。商品名：DDAVP。

desmosome *n.* an area of contact between two adjacent cells, occurring particularly in epithelia. The cell membranes at a desmosome are thickened and fine fibres (*tonofibrils*) extend from the desmosome into the cytoplasm.

橋粒 兩個相鄰細胞之間（主要出現於上皮）的接觸區。橋粒處的細胞膜變厚，並有細纖維（張力原纖維）自橋粒延伸至細胞漿內。

desogestrel *n.* a *progestogen used in various *oral contraceptives, usually in combination with an oestrogen. Trade names: **Marvelon**, **Mercilon**.

去氧孕烯 一種孕激素，用於各種口服避孕藥中，通常與雌激素合用。商品名：Marvelon，Mercilon。

desoximethasone *n.* a corticosteroid applied to the skin as a cream or

去羥米松 一種皮質類固醇。用做霜劑或軟膏塗抹於皮膚以

ointment to reduce inflammation and pruritus. Side-effects include burning, itching, and local skin irritation. Trade name: **Stiedex**.

減輕炎症和瘙癢。副作用包括灼燒感、瘙癢和局部皮膚刺激。商品名：Stiedex。

desquamation *n.* the process in which the outer layer of the *epidermis of the skin is removed by scaling.

脱皮　通過脱落而使皮膚的表皮外層去除的過程。

detached retina separation of the inner nervous layer of the *retina from the outer pigmented layer (retinal pigment epithelium) to which it is attached. It commonly occurs when one or more holes in the retina allow fluid from the vitreous cavity of the eyeball to accumulate under the retina. Vision is lost in the affected part of the retina. The condition can be treated surgically by creating patches of scar tissue between the retina and the choroid by application of extreme cold (*see* cryosurgery) or heat (*see* photocoagulation); this, combined with *plombage, allows reattachment of the retina.

視網膜剝離　視網膜內神經層從所附着的外色素沉着層（視網膜色素上皮）分離。它通常發生於當視網膜上的一個或幾個洞使得來自眼球玻璃體腔的液體在視網膜下蓄積時。在視網膜病變的部分，視力喪失。此種疾患可在極冷（參閱cryosurgery）或者極熱（參閱photocoagulation）下通過在視網膜和脈絡膜之間形成瘢痕組織黏連而得以外科治療。在配合使用異物填充後，可使之重新附着於視網膜上。

detergent *n.* a synthetic cleansing agent that removes all impurities from a surface by reacting with grease and suspended particles, including bacteria and other microorganisms. Some detergents, e.g. *cetrimide, are used solely for cleansing; others may be used as *antiseptics and *disinfectants.

去污劑　一種合成的清潔劑，能通過與油脂和懸浮粒子（包括細菌和其他微生物）發生反應而將物體表面的雜質清除掉。一些去污劑（如西曲溴銨）只用於清除污垢，而其他方面則用作抗菌劑和消毒劑。

detoxication (detoxification) *n.* **1.** the process whereby toxic substances are removed or toxic effects neutralized. It is one of the functions of the liver. **2.** the 'drying-out' of a patient suffering from *alcoholism.

解毒（解毒療法）　**(1)** 有毒物質被清除或毒性作用被中和的過程。這是肝臟的功能之一。**(2)** 乙醇中毒患者的戒酒。

detrition *n.* the process of wearing away solid bodies (e.g. bones) by friction or use.

磨耗　由於磨擦或使用而磨損固體物質（如骨）的過程。

detrusor *n.* the muscle of the urinary bladder wall. The functioning of the detrusor and urethral sphincter is assessed by a urodynamic investigation (*see* urodynamics). This is used to diagnose dysfunction, absent and exaggerated reflexes, and instability in the muscle and lack of coordination between the muscle and the sphincter (bladder/sphincter dyssynergia).

逼尿肌 膀胱壁的肌肉。逼尿肌和尿道括約肌功能的執行通過尿動力學研究加以測定（參閱 urodynamics）。這被用來診斷功能障礙、反射缺失和亢進、肌無力以及逼尿肌和括約肌之間失調（膀胱／括約肌協同失調症）等症。

Dettol *n. see* chloroxylenol.

對氯間二甲酚 參閱 chloroxylenol。

detumescence *n.* **1.** the reverse of erection, whereby the erect penis or clitoris becomes flaccid after orgasm. **2.** subsidence of a swelling.

(1) 勃起消退 勃起的反向過程，即性慾高潮之後勃起的陰莖或陰蒂變軟。**(2)** 消腫 腫脹的消退。

deut- (deuto-, deuter(o)-) *prefix denoting* two, second, or secondary.

〔前綴〕二，第二，繼發

deuteranopia *n.* a defect in colour vision in which reds, yellows, and greens are confused. It is thought that the mechanisms for perceiving red light and green light are in some way combined in people with this defect. *Compare* protanopia, tritanopia. *See also* colour blindness.

綠色盲 紅、黃和綠色相混淆的一種色覺缺陷。一般認為，有此種缺陷的患者，其分辨紅色光的機制和分辨綠色光的機制以某種方式結合在一起。與 protanopia，tritanopia 對比。參閱 colour blindness。

deutoplasm *n. see* yolk.

副漿 參閱 yolk。

developmental disorder any one of a group of conditions, arising in infancy or childhood, that are characterized by delays in biologically determined psychological functions, such as language. They are more common in males than females and tend to follow a course of handicap with gradual improvement. They are classified into *pervasive* conditions, in which many types of development are involved (e.g. *autism), and *specific* disorders, in which the

發育障礙 在幼兒期或兒童期出現的，以生物性心理功能（如語言）延緩為特徵的任何一種疾病。此種情況男性多於女性，並傾向於有一種障礙，並逐漸改善。它們被分為兩種：綜合性發育障礙，即涉及許多類型發育障礙（如孤獨症）；特異性發育障礙，即障礙是一種孤立的問題（如誦讀困難）。

handicap is an isolated problem (such as *dyslexia).

deviance *n.* variation from normal behaviour beyond the limits acceptable to the majority of the conforming peer group; particularly (though not exclusively) applied to sexual habits (*see also* sexual deviation).

deviation *n.* **1.** (in ophthalmology) any abnormal position of one or both eyes. For example, if the eyes are both looking to one side when the head is facing forwards, they are said to be *deviated* to that side. Such deviations of both eyes may occur in brain disease. Deviations of one eye come into the category of squint (*see* strabismus). **2.** *see* sexual deviation.

Devic's disease *see* neuromyelitis optica.

devitalization *n.* (in dentistry) removal of the pulp of a tooth. *See* root canal treatment.

dew-point hygrometer *see* hygrometer.

dexamethasone *n.* a *corticosteroid drug used principally to treat severe allergies, skin and eye diseases, rheumatic and other inflammatory conditions, and hormone and blood disorders. It is administered by mouth or injection; side-effects include sodium and fluid retention, muscle weakness, convulsions, vertigo, headache, and hormonal disturbances (including menstrual irregularities). Trade names: **Decadron**, **Maxidex**.

dexamphetamine *n.* a drug with actions and effects similar to those of *amphetamine. Trade name: **Dexedrine**.

乖僻 偏離正常行為的程度超出了相互一致的大多數同等羣體可以接受的範圍。本術語特別用於（儘管不是完全地）指性習慣（參閱 sexual deviation）。

(1) 偏斜 （眼科學）一眼或雙眼的任何畸形位置。如當頭面向前方時，假如雙眼都向一邊看，它們被稱為向某一側偏斜。此類雙眼偏斜可發生於腦病。一眼偏斜屬於斜視這一類（參閱 strabismus）。(2) 性變異 參閱 sexual deviation。

德維克病，視神經腦脊髓炎 參閱 neuromyelitis optica。

殺髓 （牙科學）牙髓的去除。參閱 root canal treatment。

露點溫度計 參閱 hygrometer。

地塞米松 一種皮質類固醇藥物，主要用於治療嚴重過敏、皮膚和眼病、風濕性和其他炎症性疾患以及激素和血液病。口服或注射。副作用包括鈉和液體的瀦留、肌無力、抽搐、眩暈、頭痛和激素分泌紊亂（包括月經不調）。商品名：Decadron，Maxidex。

右旋苯丙胺 一種作用和效果與苯丙胺相類似的藥物。商品名：Dexedrine。

dextr- (dextro-) *prefix denoting* **1.** the right side. Example: *dextroposition* (displacement to the right). **2.** (in chemistry) dextrorotation.

〔前綴〕**(1)** 右邊　如右移位（向右偏移）。**(2)** 右旋（化學）。

dextran *n.* a carbohydrate, consisting of branched chains of glucose units, that is a storage product of bacteria and yeasts. Preparations of dextran solution are used in transfusions, to increase the volume of plasma.

右旋糖酐，葡聚糖　一種碳水化合物，由支鏈葡萄糖組成，為細菌和酵母的貯藏產物。右旋糖酐溶液製劑用於輸液以增加血漿量。

dextrin *n.* a carbohydrate formed as an intermediate product in the digestion of starch by the enzyme amylase. Dextrin is used in the preparation of pharmaceutical products (as an *excipient) and surgical dressings.

糊精　在澱粉酶的作用下，澱粉的消化過程中作為中間產物而形成的一種碳水化合物。糊精用於藥劑產品（作為賦形劑）和外科敷料的製備。

dextrocardia *n.* a congenital defect in which the position of the heart is a mirror image of its normal position, with the apex of the ventricles pointing to the right. It may be associated with other congenital defects and is often combined with *situs invertus*, in which the appendix and liver lie on the left side of the abdomen and the stomach lies on the right side. Isolated dextrocardia produces no adverse effects.

右位心　一種先天性缺陷：心臟的位置與其正常位置正好相反，心室尖部指向右側，該疾病可能與其他先天性缺陷有關，並常與心臟轉位共存。此時，闌尾和肝臟位於腹部左側，而胃則位於右側。單純右位心不產生有害影響。

dextromethorphan *n.* a drug used in lozenges, syrups, and linctuses to suppress coughs (*see* antitussive). It sometimes causes drowsiness, dizziness, and digestive upsets. *See also* triprolidine.

右美沙芬　一種用於糖錠、糖漿和舐膏劑中的鎮咳藥物（參閱 antitussive）。它有時引起嗜眠、頭暈和消化紊亂。參閱 triprolidine。

dextromoramide *n.* an *analgesic used to relieve moderate or severe pain. It is given by mouth, injection, or as suppositories and sometimes causes dizziness, reduced blood pressure, nausea,

右嗎拉胺　一種用於解除中度或重度疼痛的鎮痛劑。口服、注射、或製成栓劑。有時引起頭暈、血壓下降、惡心、嘔吐和嗜睡。右嗎拉胺與嗎啡相

vomiting, and sleepiness. Dextromoramide is similar to *morphine and can cause morphine-type dependence. Trade name: **Palfium**.

dextropropoxyphene *n.* an *analgesic used to relieve mild or moderate pain. It is administered by mouth, often in combination with other analgesics (*see* co-proxamol), and sometimes causes dizziness, drowsiness, nausea, and vomiting. Trade name: **Doxolene**.

dextrose *n. see* glucose.

dhobie itch a fungal infection of the skin that chiefly affects the groin but may spread to the thighs and buttocks. It is caused by *dermatophyte fungi, usually *Trichophyton rubrum*, *T. interdigitale*, and *Epidermophyton floccosum*. Medical name: **tinea cruris**. *See also* ringworm.

DI *see* artificial insemination.

di- *prefix denoting* two or double.

dia- *prefix denoting* **1.** through. **2.** completely or throughout. **3.** apart.

diabetes *n.* any disorder of metabolism causing excessive thirst and the production of large volumes of urine. Used alone, the term most commonly refers to *diabetes mellitus. *See also* diabetes insipidus, haemochromatosis (bronze diabetes). **–diabetic** *adj., n.*

diabetes insipidus a rare metabolic disorder in which the patient produces large quantities of dilute urine and is constantly thirsty. It is due to deficiency of the pituitary hormone *vasopressin, which regulates reabsorption of water in

似，可引起嗎啡型賴藥性。商品名：Palfium。

右丙氧芬 一種用於解除輕度或中度疼痛的鎮痛劑。用於口服，常與其他止痛藥共用（參閱 co-proxamol）。有時可引起頭暈、嗜眠、惡心和嘔吐。商品名：Doxolene。

右旋糖 參閱 glucose。

朵比癬 一種主要侵襲腹股溝，但可擴散至大腿和髖部的真菌感染，由皮膚真菌（通常為深紅色發癬菌屬，指（趾）間發癬菌和絮狀表皮癬菌）引起。醫學用語：股癬。參閱 ringworm。

供體人工授精 參閱 artificial insemination。

〔前綴〕二，雙

〔前綴〕(1) 通過 (2) 完全，貫穿 (3) 分開

多尿症 引起過度口渴和大量尿液產生的任何代謝疾病。該術語單獨使用時通常指糖尿病。參閱 diabetes insipidus，haemochromatosis (bronze diabetes)。

尿崩症 一種少見的代謝病，患者排出大量稀淡的尿液，且一直口渴。此症緣於垂體激素加壓素缺乏所致。加壓素調節腎臟內水的重吸收，通過給予激素而得以治療。

the kidneys, and is treated by administration of the hormone.

diabetes mellitus a disorder of carbohydrate metabolism in which sugars in the body are not oxidized to produce energy due to lack of the pancreatic hormone *insulin. The accumulation of sugar leads to its appearance in the blood (*hyperglycaemia*), then in the urine; symptoms include thirst, loss of weight, and the excessive production of urine. The use of fats as an alternative source of energy leads to disturbances of the *acid-base balance, the accumulation of ketones in the bloodstream (*ketosis), and eventually to convulsions preceding *diabetic coma*. There appears to be an inherited tendency to diabetes; the disorder may be triggered by various factors, including physical stress.

Diabetes that starts in childhood or adolescence is usually more severe than that beginning in middle or old age. It is known as *Type I* (or *insulin-dependent*) *diabetes mellitus* as patients have little or no ability to produce the hormone and are entirely dependent on insulin injections for survival. In *Type II* (or *noninsulin-dependent*) *diabetes mellitus*, usually occurring after the age of 40, the pancreas retains some ability to produce insulin but this is inadequate for the body's needs; patients may require treatment with *oral hypoglycaemic drugs. In both types of diabetes the diet must be carefully controlled, with adequate carbohydrate for the body's needs. Lack of balance in the diet or in the amount of insulin taken leads to *hypoglycaemia. Long-term complications of diabetes include thickening of the arteries, which can affect the eyes (diabetic *retinopathy).

糖尿病 一種碳水化合物代謝疾病。因缺乏胰腺激素胰島素而使得體內糖不能氧化以產生能量。糖的蓄積導致血中出現糖（血糖過多），隨後在尿中出現。症狀包括口渴、體重減輕和尿液過量產出。作為能量的替代來源而使用脂肪導致酸鹼平衡紊亂，血流中酮體蓄積（酮症），並最終發生糖尿病性昏迷以至抽搐。糖尿病似有遺傳傾向。該症可由多種因素誘發，包括身體應激反應。

始於兒童期或青少年時期的糖尿病通常比始於中年或老年的糖尿病更嚴重。糖尿病I型（或胰島素依賴性糖尿病）是患者幾乎沒有或者完全沒有生成激素的能力而完全依賴胰島素注射而得以生存。而糖尿病II型（或非胰島素依賴性糖尿病）通常發生於 40 歲以後。胰腺保持了一些生成胰島素的能力，但這不足以滿足身體之需。患者可能必須使用口服低血糖藥物進行治療。在兩種糖尿病類型中，飲食都要進行控制，供以充足的碳水化合物以供身體之需。膳食缺乏平衡或所攝入的胰島素的量失去平衡會導致血糖減少。糖尿病的遠期併發症包括動脈壁變厚。它可影響眼睛（糖尿病性視網膜病）。

diaclasia *n.* a fracture made deliberately by a surgeon to correct a deformity in a bone, which has usually resulted from a badly set or untreated fracture.

折骨術　外科大夫有意進行的骨折以矯正通常因接骨不良或未治骨折所致的骨畸形。

diaclast *n.* a surgical instrument used for the destruction of the skull of a fetus. This rare procedure enables a dead fetus to be delivered through the birth canal.

穿顱器　用以破碎胎兒顱骨的一種外科器械。這種不常用的技術可使死胎從產道得以分娩。

diagnosis *n.* the process of determining the nature of a disorder by considering the patient's *signs and *symptoms, medical background, and – when necessary – results of laboratory tests and X-ray examinations. *See also* differential diagnosis, prenatal diagnosis. *Compare* prognosis. **–diagnostic** *adj.*

診斷　通過對患者的體徵和症狀、治療背景以及（如必要的話）實驗室檢查和 X 綫檢查結果的分析而對疾病的本質進行確定的過程。參閱 differential diagnosis，prenatal diagnosis。與 prognosis 對比。

diakinesis *n.* the final stage in the first prophase of *meiosis, in which homologous chromosomes, between which crossing over has occurred, are ready to separate.

終變期　減數分裂前期第一時期的最後階段。此時，已經發生了交換的兩條同源染色體正準備分開。

dialyser *n.* a piece of apparatus for separating components of a liquid mixture by *dialysis, especially an artificial kidney (*see* haemodialysis).

透析器　通過透析作用而將一液態混合物的組成成分分離的一種裝置，尤指人工腎（參閱 haemodialysis）。

dialysis *n.* a method of separating particles of different dimensions in a liquid mixture, using a thin semipermeable membrane whose pores are too small to allow the passage of large particles, such as proteins, but large enough to permit the passage of dissolved crystalline material. A solution of the mixture is separated from distilled water by the membrane; the solutes pass through the membrane into the water while the proteins, etc., are retained. The principle of dialysis is used in the artificial kidney (*see* haemodialysis). The peritoneum is used as an autogenous semipermeable

透析　運用薄半透膜將液體混合物中不同大小的粒子進行分離的一種方法。半透膜上的小孔很小，大的粒子（如蛋白）不能通過，但小孔的大小卻足以讓溶解的晶體物質通過。用半透膜把混合物溶液與蒸餾水隔開，溶質通過膜進入水中，而蛋白等則被留下，透析原理被用於人工腎（參閱 haemodialysis）。在腹膜透析技術中，腹膜被用做自體半透膜。腹膜透析用於不宜使用血液透析時的情況。

membrane in the technique of *peritoneal dialysis*, which is employed when haemodialysis is not appropriate.

diamorphine *n. see* heroin.

二醋嗎啡 （海洛因） 參閱 heroin。

diapedesis *n.* migration of cells through the walls of blood capillaries into the tissue spaces. Diapedesis is an important part of the reaction of tissues to injury (*see* inflammation).

血細胞滲出 細胞穿過毛細血管而遷移至組織間隙。血細胞滲出是組織對損傷反應的重要的組成部分（參閱 inflammation）。

diaphoresis *n.* the process of sweating, especially excessive sweating. *See* sweat.

出汗 出汗的過程，尤指過量出汗。參閱 sweat。

diaphoretic (sudorific) *n.* a drug that causes an increase in sweating, such as *pilocarpine, which stimulates the sweat glands directly. *Antipyretic drugs also have diaphoretic activity, which helps reduce the body temperature in fevers.

發汗劑 一種引起出汗增加的藥物，如直接刺激汗腺的毛果蕓香鹼。退熱藥物也有發汗效能，這有助於在發熱時降低體溫。

diaphragm *n.* **1.** (in anatomy) a thin musculomembranous dome-shaped muscle that separates the thoracic and abdominal cavities. The diaphragm is attached to the lower ribs at each side and to the breastbone and the backbone at the front and back. It bulges upwards against the heart and the lungs, arching over the stomach, liver, and spleen. There are openings in the diaphragm through which the oesophagus, blood vessels, and nerves pass. The diaphragm plays an important role in *breathing. It contracts with each inspiration, becoming flattened downwards and increasing the volume of the thoracic cavity. With each expiration it relaxes and is restored to its dome shape. **2.** a hemispherical rubber cap fitted inside the vagina over the neck (cervix) of the uterus as a contraceptive. When combined with the use of a chemical spermicide the diaphragm

(1) 膈肌 （解剖學）是分隔胸腔和腹腔的肌膜型圓穹狀薄肌。膈肌兩側附着於下位肋骨，前方和後方附着於胸骨和脊椎。它向上方膨隆，抵着心臟和兩肺，並在胃、肝臟和脾上方構成拱形。在膈肌上有開口，有食管、血管和神經穿過。膈肌在呼吸中起着重要的作用。吸氣時，膈肌緊張，下降變為扁平形，從而增加胸腔容量。每呼一次氣，膈肌鬆弛，恢復成圓穹狀態。**(2)** 子宮帽 一種半球形橡膠帽，用做避孕器具，放置於陰道內覆蓋子宮頸部。子宮帽與化學性殺精子劑合用時，可提供可靠的避孕效果，避孕失敗率低達每100名婦女中，一年僅為2~10次妊娠。

provides reliable contraception with a failure rate as low as 2–10 pregnancies per 100 woman-years.

diaphysial aclasis a hereditary abnormality of cartilage and bone growth, resulting in many cartilaginous outgrowths (exostoses) from the long bones. Bone growth may also be retarded, causing stunting and deformity.

骨幹性續連症　一種遺傳性軟骨和骨生長異常，導致從長骨長出許多軟骨贅（外生軟骨疣）。骨生長也可停滯，引起發育不良和畸形。

diaphysis *n*. the shaft (central part) of a long bone. *Compare* epiphysis.

骨幹　長骨的幹部（中段部分）。與 epiphysis 對比。

diaphysitis *n*. inflammation of the diaphysis (shaft) of a bone, through infection or rheumatic disease. It may result in impaired growth of the bone and consequent deformity.

骨幹炎　骨幹的炎症，由感染或風濕性疾病所致，可導致骨生長損傷和隨之而產生畸形。

diarrhoea *n*. frequent bowel evacuation or the passage of abnormally soft or liquid faeces. It may be caused by intestinal infections, other forms of intestinal inflammation (such as *colitis or *Crohn's disease), *malabsorption, anxiety, and *irritable bowel syndrome. Severe or prolonged diarrhoea may lead to excess losses of fluid, salts, and nutrients in the faeces.

腹瀉　頻繁的糞便排出或排出異常軟便或水樣便。其原因可能是腸道感染，其他形式的腸道炎症（如結腸炎或克羅恩病）、吸收障礙、焦慮和應激性腸綜合徵。嚴重或長期腹瀉可導致糞便中液體、鹽和營養的過度喪失。

diarthrosis (synovial joint) *n*. a freely movable joint. The ends of the adjoining bones are covered with a thin cartilaginous sheet, and the bones are linked by a ligament (*capsule*) lined with *synovial membrane, which secretes synovial fluid (see illustration). Such joints are classified according to the type of connection between the bones and the type of movement allowed. *See* arthrodic joint, condylarthrosis, enarthrosis, ginglymus, saddle joint, trochoid joint.

動關節（滑膜關節）　一種可自由活動的關節。毗連骨的末端被一薄的軟骨層所覆蓋，骨通過韌帶（關節囊）而連接。韌帶和分泌滑液的滑膜相連（見圖）。這類關節的分類是根據骨間連接的類型和所能進行的運動類型進行的。參閱 arthrodic joint，condylarthrosis，enarthrosis，ginglymus，saddle joint，trochoid joint。

diaschisis *n*. a temporary loss of reflex activity in the brainstem or spinal cord

神經機能聯繫不能　大腦皮質破壞後發生的腦幹或脊髓反射

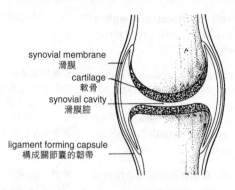

synovial membrane
滑膜

cartilage
軟骨

synovial cavity
滑膜腔

ligament forming capsule
構成關節囊的韌帶

A synovial joint
滑膜關節

following destruction of the cerebral cortex. As time passes this state of suppressed reflex activity is replaced by one of unduly exaggerated reflexes and spasticity of the limbs.

活動的暫時喪失。隨着時間的流逝，這種反射活動的抑制狀態被反射異常亢奮和肢體強直狀態所取代。

diastase *n.* an enzyme that hydrolyses starch in barley grain to produce maltose during the malting process. It has been used to aid the digestion of starch in some digestive disorders.

澱粉酶 一種在製麥芽過程中將大麥芽中的澱粉水解為麥芽糖的酶。在一些消化道紊亂中，澱粉酶一直被用於幫助澱粉的消化。

diastole *n.* the period between two contractions of the heart, when the muscle of the heart relaxes and allows the chambers to fill with blood. The term usually refers to *ventricular diastole*, which lasts about 0.5 seconds in a normal heart rate of about 70/minute. During exertion this period shortens, so allowing the heart rate to increase. *See also* blood pressure, systole. **–diastolic** *adj.*

舒張期 心臟兩次收縮之間的時期，此時，心肌鬆弛，使心腔為血液所充盈。這一術語通常指心室舒張。在每分鐘 70 次的正常心律下，心室舒張持續約 0.5 秒。用力時，這一期間縮短，以使心率增加。參閱 blood pressure，systole。

diastolic pressure *see* blood pressure.

舒張壓 參閱 blood pressure。

diathermy *n.* the production of heat in a part of the body by means of a high-frequency electric current passed

透熱療法 通過流經置於患者皮膚上的兩個電極之間的高壓電流而在身體的局部產熱的療

between two electrodes placed on the patient's skin. The heat generated increases blood flow and can be used in the treatment of deep-seated pain in rheumatic and arthritic conditions. *See also* microwave therapy.

The principle of diathermy is also utilized in various surgical instruments: a *diathermy knife*, for example, is used to coagulate tissues. The knife is itself one electrode, the other being a large moistened pad applied to another part of the patient's body. Because blood is coagulated as the knife is used, and small vessels sealed off, virtually bloodless incisions may be made. *Diathermy snares* and *needles* can be used to destroy unwanted tissue and to remove small superficial neoplasms. *See also* electrosurgery.

diathesis *n.* a higher than average tendency to acquire certain diseases, such as allergies, rheumatic diseases, or gout. Such diseases may run in families, but they are not inherited.

diazepam *n.* a long-acting *benzodiazepine used to treat acute anxiety, delirium tremens, epilepsy, and muscle spasms; it is also used as a *premedication. Diazepam is administered by mouth or injection and can cause addiction; side-effects include drowsiness and lethargy, vertigo, low blood pressure, and skin rashes. Trade names: **Diazemuls**, **Valium**.

diazoxide *n.* a drug used to lower blood pressure in patients with hypertension and also used to treat conditions in which the levels of blood sugar are low (including *insulinoma). It is usually administered (by mouth or (for hypertension) injection) with a diuretic as it causes salt and water retention. Trade name: **Eudemine**.

法。所產之熱增加了血流，可用以治療風濕性和關節性疾患的深部疼痛。參閱 microwave therapy。

透熱療法的原理也用於各種外科器械中。例如，用透熱刀來凝固組織。刀本身是一根電極，而另一根則是置於患者身上的一個大而濕潤的墊子。當使用刀子時，血液凝固，小血管被封閉，所以，可以進行完全的無血切開術。透熱勒除器和透熱烙針可用來破壞不想要的組織，摘除小的表皮贅生物。參閱 electrosurgery。

素質 比一般人更易患某些疾病（如變態反應性疾病、風濕性疾病或者痛風）的傾向。這些疾病可累及一些家庭成員，但不遺傳。

地西泮（安定） 一種長效苯二氮䓬，用於治療急性焦慮症、震顫性譫妄、癲癇和肌肉攣縮。它也用作麻醉前用藥。地西泮可口服或注射，且可引起藥癮。副作用包括嗜眠和困倦、眩暈、低血壓和皮疹。商品名：Diazemuls，Valium。

二氮嗪 一種用於降低高血壓病人的血壓和用於治療血糖量低的疾病的藥物（包括胰島素瘤）。因其引起鹽和水滯留，所以通常和利尿劑合用。口服或（為高血壓）注射。商品名：Eudemine。

DIC *see* disseminated intravascular coagulation.

彌散性血管內凝血 參閱 disseminated intravascular coagulation。

dicephalus *n. see* craniopagus.

雙頭畸胎 參閱 craniopagus。

dichlorphenamide *n.* a *diuretic used to reduce pressure within the eye in the treatment of glaucoma. It is administered by mouth; side-effects include drowsiness, dizziness, digestive upsets, and skin rashes. Trade name: **Daranide**.

二氯磺酰胺 一種利尿劑，在治療青光眼時，用以降低眼內壓。口服。副作用包括嗜眠、頭暈、消化紊亂和皮疹。商品名：Daranide。

dichromatic *adj.* describing the state of colour vision of those who can appreciate only two of the three primary colours. People with such vision match any given colour by a mixture of the two they can distinguish. *Compare* trichromatic.

二色視的 描述那些能看清三原色中兩種原色的色覺狀態。有此色覺異常者只能用他們能夠分辨的二原色來混合配色。與 trichromatic 對比。

DICI *see* direct intracytoplasmic injection.

直接細胞質內注射 參閱 direct intracytoplasmic injection。

Dick test a test for susceptibility to *scarlet fever. If a small quantity of toxin from the bacteria responsible (haemolytic streptococci) is injected under the skin of a person not immune to the disease, a positive reaction results, causing local reddening of the skin.

迪克試驗 一種檢查猩紅熱易感性的試驗。如果來自相關細菌（溶血性鏈球菌）的少量毒素皮下注入對猩紅熱無免疫力的人時，會產生陽性反應，引起皮膚局部發紅。

diclofenac *n.* an anti-inflammatory drug (*see* NSAID) used to relieve joint pain in osteoarthritis, rheumatoid arthritis, and ankylosing spondylitis. It is administered by mouth; possible side-effects include abdominal pain, nausea, and diarrhoea. Trade names: **Volraman**, **Voltarol**.

雙氯芬酸 一種抗炎藥物（參閱 NSAID），用於解除骨關節病、類風濕性關節炎和關節強硬性脊椎炎等的關節痛。口服。可能有的副作用包括腹痛、惡心和腹瀉。商品名：Volraman，Voltarol。

dicophane *n. see* DDT.

滴滴涕 參閱 DDT。

dicrotism *n*. a condition in which the pulse is felt as a double beat for each contraction of the heart. It may be seen in typhoid fever. **–dicrotic** *adj*.

dictyoma *n*. a tumour of the epithelium lining the *ciliary body of the eye. It may be benign or malignant.

dicyclomine *n*. a drug that reduces spasms of smooth muscle and is used to relieve peptic ulcer, infantile colic, colitis, and related conditions. It is administered by mouth; side-effects include dry mouth, thirst, and dizziness. Trade name: **Merbentyl**.

didanosine *n*. an antiviral drug that interferes with the action of the enzyme *reverse transcriptase, by means of which HIV, the cause of AIDS, is able to incorporate itself into the human host cell. The drug is administered by mouth in attempts to prolong the lives of sufferers from AIDS. Possible side-effects include damage to nerves, severe pancreatitis, nausea, vomiting, and headache.

didronel *n*. a drug used to improve mineralization of bone in women suffering from postmenopausal osteoporosis (PMO), especially those who have already suffered fractures. It is administered by mouth. Possible side-effects include nausea, diarrhoea, and a metallic taste in the mouth. Trade name: **Didronel PMO**.

didym- (didymo-) *prefix denoting* the testis.

dieldrin *n*. an insecticide that attacks the central nervous system of insects and has proved useful in the control of various beetles, flies, and larvae that attack crops.

二波脈 在每次心臟收縮中能感到兩次脈搏的情況。可見於傷寒。

視網膜胚瘤 襯於眼睫狀體的上皮瘤。可以是良性的或惡性的。

雙環維林 一種減輕平滑肌攣縮的藥物，用於治療消化性潰瘍、嬰兒腹絞痛、結腸炎和相關疾病。口服。副作用包括口乾、口渴和頭暈。商品名：Merbentyl。

二脫氧肌苷（地丹諾辛） 一種抗病毒藥物，能干擾逆轉錄酶的作用。通過逆轉錄酶，人體免疫缺陷病毒（艾滋病的病因）能夠將自己移植入人體宿主細胞。該藥口服，以期延長艾滋病患者的生命。可能具有的副作用包括神經損傷、嚴重胰腺炎、惡心、嘔吐和頭痛。

羥乙二磷酸鈉 一種用以改進絕經後患骨質疏鬆症婦女的骨礦化作用的藥物，特別用於那些已患骨折的患者。口服。可能有的副作用包括惡心、腹瀉和口中金屬味覺。商品名：Didronel PMO。

〔前綴〕睾丸

狄氏劑 一種殺蟲劑，能襲擊昆蟲的中樞神經系統，在控制各種甲蟲、蠅和襲擊莊稼的昆蟲幼蟲時證明有效。因其殘留

Because of its persistence in and contamination of the environment, its use in the UK is now severely restricted.

於環境中，並對環境產生污染，該藥物在英國被嚴格限制使用。

diencephalon *n.* an anatomical division of the forebrain, consisting of the epithalamus, thalamus (dorsal thalamus), hypothalamus, and ventral thalamus (subthalamus). *See* brain.

間腦 前腦的解剖小區，由上丘腦、丘腦（背側丘腦）、下丘腦和丘腦底部（腹側丘腦）組成。參閱 brain。

dienoestrol *n.* a synthetic female sex hormone (*see* oestrogen) administered by mouth to treat symptoms of the menopause, to suppress lactation, and to relieve symptoms in cancer of the breast or prostate. It is also applied as a cream to relieve itching or inflammation of the vagina and in acne. Trade name: **Ortho Dienoestrol**.

己二烯雌酚 一種用於口服的合成雌性激素（參閱 oestrogen）以治療絕經症狀，抑制泌乳、緩解乳腺或前列腺癌症的症狀，它還用做乳膏劑以消除陰道和痤瘡的瘙癢或炎症。商品名：Ortho Dienoestrol。

diet *n.* the mixture of foods that a person eats. A *balanced diet* contains adequate quantities of all the *nutrients.

膳食 一個人所吃食物的混合。平衡膳食含有足夠的所有營養素。

dietary fibre (roughage) the part of food that cannot be digested and absorbed to produce energy. Dietary fibre falls into four groups: *cellulose, hemicelluloses, lignins*, and *pectins*. Highly refined foods, such as sucrose, contain no dietary fibre. Foods with a high fibre content include wholemeal cereals and flour, root vegetables, nuts, and fruit. Dietary fibre is considered by some to be helpful in the prevention of many of the diseases of Western civilization, such as *diverticulosis, constipation, appendicitis, obesity, and diabetes mellitus. Communities consuming high-fibre diets very rarely have any of these diseases.

食物纖維（粗糙食物） 食物中不能被消化和吸收以產生能量的部分。食物纖維分為四類：纖維素、半纖維素、木質素和果膠。高度精製的食物（如蔗糖）不含食物纖維。纖維含量高的食物包括粗穀類食物和粗麵粉、根類蔬菜、果仁和水果。一些人認為食物纖維有助於預防許多西方文明的疾病，如憩室病、便秘、闌尾炎、肥胖症和糖尿病。消耗高纖維膳食的人羣很少患這些疾病。

dietetics *n.* the application of the principles of *nutrition to the selection of food and the feeding of individuals and groups.

營養學，膳食學 運用營養原理選擇食物和為個體和羣體配食的科學。

diethylcarbamazine *n.* an anthelmintic drug that destroys filariae and is therefore used in the treatment of filariasis, loiasis, and onchocerciasis. It is administered as tablets. Side-effects may include headache, malaise, joint pains, nausea, and vomiting.

乙胺嗪 一種驅腸蟲藥，能殺死絲蟲屬，因之用於治療絲蟲病、羅阿絲蟲病和盤尾絲蟲病。製成片劑服用。副作用可包括頭痛、不適、關節痛、惡心和嘔吐。

diethylpropion *n.* a drug, similar to *amphetamine, that suppresses the appetite and is used in the treatment of obesity. It is administered by mouth and may cause dry mouth, insomnia, depression, headache, constipation, and allergic rashes. Dependence of the amphetamine type can occur. Trade names: **Apesate**, **Tenuate Dospan**.

安非拉酮 一種類似苯丙胺的藥物，能抑制食慾，用於治療肥胖症。該藥口服。可引起口乾、失眠、抑鬱、頭痛、便秘和變態反應性皮疹。可發生苯丙胺型依賴。商品名：Apesate，Tenuate Dospan。

Dietl's crisis acute obstruction of a kidney causing severe pain in the loins. The obstruction usually occurs at the junction of the renal pelvis and the ureter, causing the kidney to become distended with accumulated urine (*see* hydronephrosis). Sometimes the pelvis drains spontaneously, with relief of pain, but acute decompression of the kidney may be required with surgical relief of the obstruction (*pyeloplasty).

迪特爾危象 引起腰部劇痛的急性腎梗阻。梗阻通常發生於腎盂和輸尿管的接合部，由於尿潴留而使腎擴張（腎積水）。有時，腎盂自行分流，疼痛可消失。但腎臟迅速減壓可能需要外科解除梗阻來實現（腎盂成形術）。

differential diagnosis *diagnosis of a condition whose signs and/or symptoms are shared by various other conditions. For example, abdominal pain may be due to any of a large number of different disorders, which must be ruled out in arriving at a correct diagnosis.

鑒別診斷 對具有與其他疾病相同的體徵和／或症狀的疾病的診斷。如，腹部疼痛可能由於許多不同疾病所致。在作出正確診斷時，要對它們進行排除。

differential leucocyte count (differential blood count) a determination of the proportions of the different kinds of white cells (leucocytes) present in a sample of blood. Usually 100 white cells are counted and classified under the microscope or by electronic apparatus,

白細胞分類計數（血細胞分類計數） 測定在一血樣中出現的不同種類的白細胞的比例。通常，在顯微鏡下或借助電子器械計數100個白細胞，並進行分類。其結果以在白細胞總數所占的百分比和在每升血液中

so that the results can readily be expressed as percentages of the total number of leucocytes and the absolute numbers per litre of blood. The information often aids diagnosis of disease.

differentiation *n.* **1.** (in embryology) the process in embryonic development during which unspecialized cells or tissues become specialized for particular functions. **2.** (in oncology) the degree of similarity of tumour cells to the structure of the organ from which the tumour arose. Tumours are classified as well, moderately, or poorly differentiated.

diflunisal *n.* an anti-inflammatory drug (*see* NSAID) derived from salicylic acid and used to control symptoms in osteoarthritis and other painful conditions. It is administered by mouth. Possible side-effects include dyspepsia, diarrhoea, headache, dizziness, tinnitus, and skin rashes. Trade name: **Dolobid**.

di George syndrome a hereditary condition resulting in an inability to fight infections (immunodeficiency) associated with absence of the parathyroid and thymus glands, abnormalities of the heart, and low calcium levels. Affected children are prone to *Candida infections and often present with *failure to thrive.

digestion *n.* the process in which ingested food is broken down in the alimentary canal into a form that can be absorbed and assimilated by the tissues of the body. Digestion includes mechanical processes, such as chewing, churning, and grinding food, as well as the chemical action of digestive enzymes and other substances (bile, acid, etc.) Chemical digestion begins in the mouth with the

的絕對數來表示。該資料常有助於對疾病的診斷。

分化 **(1)**（胚胎學）胚胎發育中無特定功能的細胞或組織變得專門適於特定功能的過程。**(2)**（腫瘤學）腫瘤細胞和腫瘤生成器官的結構的相似程度。腫瘤被分類為分化良好、分化中等和分化不良型。

二氟尼柳 一種由水楊酸衍生的抗炎藥物（參閱 NSAID），用於控制骨關節炎和其他痛性疾病的症狀。口服。可能有的副作用包括消化不良、腹瀉、頭疼、頭暈、耳鳴和皮疹。商品名：Dolobid。

迪喬治綜合徵，胸腺甲狀旁腺發育不全 一種遺傳性疾患（免疫缺乏），不能抵抗感染，與甲狀旁腺和胸腺缺失、心臟畸形和鈣量低有關。患此疾病的兒童易受念珠菌感染，且常發育停滯。

消化 攝入的食物在消化道內分解為可被身體組織吸收和同化的物質的過程。消化包括一些機械過程，如咀嚼、攪拌、磨碎食物以及消化酶和其他物質（膽汁、酸等）的化學作用。化學消化開始於口腔（唾液對食物的作用），但其主要過程發生於胃和小腸。在那裏，食物受到胃液、胰液和腸液的作用。

action of *saliva on food, but most of it takes place in the stomach and small intestine, where the food is subjected to *gastric juice, *pancreatic juice, and *succus entericus.

digitalis *n.* an extract from the dried leaves of foxgloves (*Digitalis* species), which contains various substances, including *digitoxin and *digoxin, that stimulate heart muscle. Used to treat heart failure, it is administered by mouth or, in emergency, by injection. High doses can cause nausea, vomiting, loss of appetite, diarrhoea, abdominal pain, and abnormal heart activity. *See also* digitalization.

洋地黃 乾洋地黃葉（洋地黃屬）的提取物，內含多種物質，包括洋地黃毒甙和地高辛。它們能刺激心肌。用於治療心力衰竭。口服。在緊急情況下，則進行注射。高劑量能引起惡心、嘔吐、食慾減退、腹瀉、腹痛和心臟活動異常。參閱 digitalizaion。

digitalization *n.* the administration of the drug digitalis or one of its purified derivatives to a patient with heart failure until the optimum level has been reached in the heart tissues. At this stage the control of heart failure should be adequate and there should be few side-effects. The process of digitalization may take several days.

洋地黃化 給心力衰竭患者服用洋地黃或其純化的衍生物，直至心肌組織內的藥物達到最適濃度。在此階段，應足以控制心力衰竭，而副作用應最少。洋地黃化過程可需幾天。

digitoxin *n.* a drug that increases heart muscle contraction and is used in heart failure. It is slow-acting but the effects are prolonged. Digitoxin is administered by mouth or injection; possible side-effects are those of *digitalis.

洋地黃毒甙 一種增強心肌收縮，治療心力衰竭的藥物。該藥物起效慢，但作用卻能延長較長時間。洋地黃毒甙用於口服或注射。可能有的副作用與洋地黃相同。

digoxin *n.* a drug that increases heart muscle contraction and is used in heart failure. It is rapidly effective and the effects are short-lived. Digoxin is administered by mouth or injection; side-effects are those of *digitalis. Trade name: **Lanoxin**.

地高辛 一種用於增強心肌收縮，治療心力衰竭的藥物。該藥起效快，持續時間短。地高辛用於口服或注射。副作用與洋地黃相同。商品名：Lanoxin。

dihydrocodeine *n.* a drug used to relieve pain and suppress coughs (*see*

雙氫可待因 一種用於緩解疼痛和鎮咳（參閱 analgesic，

analgesic, antitussive). It is administered by mouth or injection and sometimes causes nausea, dizziness, and constipation. Dependence of the *morphine type can also occur, but this is rare. Trade name: **DHC Continus**.

antitussive）的藥物。該藥用於口服或注射。有時引起惡心、頭暈和便秘。嗎啡型依賴也可發生，但這種情況少見。商品名：DHC Continus。

dihydroergotamine n. a derivative of *ergotamine used to prevent and relieve migraine attacks. It is administered by mouth or injection; side-effects are rare but nausea sometimes occurs. Trade name: **Dihydergot**.

雙氫麥角胺 一種麥角胺的衍生物，用於預防和解除偏頭痛發作。用於口服或注射。副作用少見，但有時發生惡心。商品名：Dihydergot。

dihydrofolate reductase inhibitor any of various drugs that interfere with the conversion of folic acid to its active form in the body. They include *pyrimethamine, *trimethoprim, *triamterene, and *methotrexate. When such drugs are necessary, folate deficiency is treated with *folinic acid rather than folic acid.

二氫葉酸還原酶抑制劑 干擾葉酸在體內轉化為活性狀態的多種藥物。這些藥物包括乙氨嘧啶，甲氧苄啶、氨苯蝶啶、甲氨蝶呤。當需要此類藥物時，葉酸缺乏時使用亞葉酸治療，而不用葉酸治療。

diiodohydroxyquinoline n. an antiseptic used to treat bowel infections and dysentery caused by amoebae. It is administered by mouth or as pessaries and occasionally causes irritation of the digestive system, headache, itching, and boils.

雙碘喹啉 一種抗菌劑，用於治療因阿米巴屬引起的腸道感染和痢疾。用作口服或栓劑。偶爾引起消化系統刺激、頭痛、瘙癢和癤腫。

diiodotyrosine n. an iodine-containing substance produced in the thyroid gland from which the *thyroid hormones are derived.

二碘酪氨酸 一種由甲狀腺產生的含碘物質，由之生成甲狀腺激素。

dilaceration n. a condition affecting some teeth after traumatic injury, in which the root and crown are at an abnormal angle to each other. It usually necessitates removal of the tooth.

彎曲牙 創傷之後侵害一些牙齒的疾患。在此種情況下，牙根和牙冠之間呈現異常的角度。此疾患通常需要拔除患牙。

dilatation n. the enlargement or expansion of a hollow organ (such as a blood vessel) or cavity.

擴張 中空器官（如血管）或腔室的增大或擴張。

dilatation and curettage (D and C)
an operation in which the cervix (neck) of the uterus is dilated, using an instrument called a *dilator, and the lining (endometrium) of the uterus is lightly scraped off with a curette (*see* curettage). It is performed for a variety of reasons, including the removal of any material remaining after abortion, removal of small tumours, and obtaining a sample of endometrium for histological examination in the diagnosis of gynaecological disorders. Special types of curette to which suction is applied (vabra or suction curettes) may be used to obtain a specimen of endometrium (*vabra curettage*) or to remove the products of conception in abortion (*suction curettage*).

擴張子宮頸和刮子宮（擴刮）
一種手術。採用一種被稱為擴張器的器械使子宮的頸部擴張，用刮器將子宮的襯裏（子宮內膜）輕輕刮掉（參閱curettage）。此手術的施行基於多種原因，包括流產後除去任何殘留物質，小腫瘤的摘除以及在診斷婦科疾病中由子宮內膜取樣以進行組織學檢查。能進行吸取的特殊擴刮器（吸空器或吸刮器）可用來採集子宮內膜樣品（吸空器刮除術）或用來除掉流產後妊娠產物（吸刮子宮術）。

dilator *n.* **1.** an instrument used to enlarge a body opening or cavity. For example, the male urethra may become narrowed by disease and it can sometimes be restored to its original size by inserting a dilator. Dilators (such as Hegar's dilator) are also used to enlarge the canal in the cervix of the uterus in the procedure of *dilatation and curettage. **2.** a drug, applied either locally or systemically, that causes expansion of a structure, such as the pupil of the eye or a blood vessel. *See also* vasodilator. **3.** a muscle that, by its action, opens an aperture or orifice in the body.

(1) 擴張器 一種用於擴張身體小孔或體腔的器械。例如男性輸尿管因疾病可能變窄，它有時可通過插入一擴張器而使之恢復到原來的大小。擴張器（如黑加擴張器）在子宮頸擴張和刮子宮技術中用以擴張子宮頸管。**(2) 擴張藥** 局部或全身使用的可使某一結構擴大的藥物，如眼睛瞳孔或血管。參閱 vasodilator。**(3) 開大肌** 通過自體活動使身體開口或孔開大的肌肉。

diltiazem *n.* a *calcium antagonist used in the treatment of effort-associated angina and high blood pressure (hypertension). It acts as a vasodilator and is administered by mouth; side-effects include oedema, headache, nausea, dizziness, and skin rash. Trade names: **Britiazem**, **Tildiem**.

地爾硫䓬 一種鈣拮抗劑，用於治療與勞累相關的心絞痛和高血壓。它起着血管擴張劑的作用，口服。副作用包括水腫、頭痛、惡心、頭暈和皮疹。商品名：Britiazem，Tildiem。

dimenhydrinate *n.* an *antihistamine used to prevent and treat travel sickness, nausea and vomiting due to other causes, vertigo, and inner ear disturbances. It is administered by mouth or injection and commonly causes drowsiness, dizziness, digestive upsets, dry mouth, and headache. Trade name: **Dramamine**.

茶苯海明　一種抗組胺藥物，用於預防和治療暈車、其他原因所致的惡心和嘔吐、眩暈和內耳疾病。口服或注射。通常引起嗜眠、頭暈、消化不良、口乾和頭痛。商品名：Dramamine。

dimercaprol *n.* a drug that combines with metals in the body and is used to treat poisoning by antimony, arsenic, bismuth, gold, mercury, and thallium and in Wilson's disease. It is administered by injection and commonly causes nausea, vomiting, and watering of the eyes. Trade name: **British Anti-Lewisite (BAL)**.

二巰丙醇　一種能在體內與金屬結合的藥物。用於治療銻、砷、鉍、金、汞和鉈中毒以及威爾遜病。注射用藥。通常引起惡心、嘔吐和流淚。商品名：British Anti-Lewisite (BAL)。

dimethicone *n.* a silicone preparation used externally to prevent undue drying of the skin and to protect it against irritating external agents. It is commonly used to prevent napkin rash in babies. Trade names: **Conotrane**, **Siopel**.

二甲硅油　一種硅酮製劑，外用以預防皮膚過度乾燥，防止皮膚受外界刺激性因子的影響。通常用於預防幼兒尿布疹。商品名：Conotrane，Siopel。

dimethindine maleate an *antihistamine drug used to treat hay fever, urticaria, and other allergic conditions. It is administered by mouth. Possible side-effects include drowsiness and slowed reactions. Trade names: **Fenostil Retard**, **Vibrocil**.

馬來酸二甲茚定　一種抗組胺藥，用於治療枯草熱、蕁麻疹和其他變態反應性疾病。口服用藥。可能有的副作用包括嗜眠和反應遲緩。商品名：Fenostil Retard，Vibrocil。

dimethyl sulphoxide (DMSO) a chemical used in an ointment to treat skin inflammations or in combination with other topically applied drugs to improve their absorption. It may cause skin irritation.

二甲亞碸　一種用做軟膏的化學物質。用以治療皮膚炎症，或與其他外用藥物合用，以促進吸收，它可引起皮膚刺激。

dinoprost *n.* a *prostaglandin drug used to terminate pregnancy or to expel a fetus that has died. It is administered by mouth or as a vaginal tablet or gel. Trade name: **Prostin F2 alpha**.

地諾前列素（前列腺素 F2a）一種前列腺素藥，用以終止妊娠或排出已死的胎兒。口服，或用作陰道片劑或凝膠。商品名：Prostin F2 alpha。

dioctyl sodium sulphosuccinate a softening agent that is given by mouth or in suppositories, often together with a laxative, to relieve constipation. It is also used in solution to soften ear wax.

多庫酚鈉　一種軟化劑，口服或栓劑用藥。常與緩瀉藥合用以解除便秘。主要製成溶液，用以軟化耳垢。

diode laser a portable laser used for treating diseases of the retina of the eye by producing small burns in the retina (*see* photocoagulation).

二極管激光器　一種便攜式激光器，通過在視網膜上進行小面積灼燒以治療眼睛視網膜疾病（參閱 photocoagulation）。

diodone *n.* an iodine-containing compound that is *radiopaque and therefore useful in radiographic examination of parts of the body. Injected into the bloodstream, it is concentrated by the kidneys as it is excreted and forms a useful medium for showing up the urinary tract and any abnormalities that may be present (*see* pyelography).

碘奧酮（碘吡拉哈）　一種含碘化合物，不透 X 綫，因之有助於局部放射照相檢查。該化合物被注入血液後，在腎內集中，在排出時，可顯示尿道和可能存在的任何疾病。參閱 pyelography。

dioptre *n.* the unit of measurement of the power of *refraction of a lens. One dioptre is the power of a lens that brings parallel light rays to a focus at a point one metre from the lens, after passing through it. A stronger lens brings light rays to a focus at a point closer to it than a weaker lens and has a higher dioptric power.

屈光度　測量透鏡屈光能力的量度單位。一個屈光度是指透鏡使通過它的平行光綫在透鏡後 1 米處聚焦的能力。功率強的透鏡把光綫聚焦在距離自己較近的一點上，而功率弱的透鏡不能，且屈光度數也較大。

dipeptidase *n.* an enzyme, found in digestive juices, that splits certain products of protein digestion (dipeptides) into their constituent amino acids. The latter are then absorbed by the body.

二肽酶　消化液內的一種酶，能使蛋白質消化產物（二肽）分解為其組成的氨基酸。後者隨後被身體所吸收。

dipeptide *n.* a compound consisting of two amino acids joined together by a peptide bond (e.g. glycylalanine, a combination of the amino acids glycine and alanine). *See* dipeptidase.

二肽　由肽鍵將兩種氨基酸結合在一起而組成的化合物（甘氨酰丙氨酸由甘氨酸和丙氨酸兩種氨基酸結合而成）。參閱 dipeptidase。

diphenhydramine *n.* an *antihistamine with sedative properties used to treat

苯海拉明　一種具有鎮靜特性的抗組胺藥，用於治療變應性

allergic conditions, such as hay fever and rhinitis, and – in combination with other drugs – in cough mixtures (e.g. *Benylin*). It is administered by mouth or injection; side-effects include drowsiness, dry mouth, dizziness, and nausea.

diphenoxylate *n*. a drug used, often in combination with *atropine (in *Lomotil*), to treat diarrhoea. It is also used after *colostomy or ileostomy to reduce the frequency and fluidity of the stools. It is administered by mouth; side-effects can include nausea, drowsiness, dizziness, skin reactions, and restlessness.

diphosphonate *n*. any of a class of compounds that bind strongly to bone. This property makes them useful in imaging the skeleton and treating certain bone disorders, such as *Paget's disease of bone.

diphtheria *n*. an acute highly contagious infection, caused by the bacterium *Corynebacterium diphtheriae*, generally affecting the throat but occasionally other mucous membranes and the skin. The disease is spread by direct contact with a patient or carrier or by contaminated milk. After an incubation period of 2–6 days a sore throat, weakness, and mild fever develop. Later, a soft grey membrane forms across the throat, constricting the air passages and causing difficulty in breathing and swallowing; a *tracheostomy may be necessary. Bacteria multiply at the site of infection and release a toxin into the bloodstream, which damages heart and nerves. Death from heart failure or general collapse can follow within four days but prompt administration of antitoxin and penicillin arrests the disease; complete recovery requires prolonged bed rest. An effective

疾病（如枯草熱和鼻炎）。與其他藥物合用，用做止咳合劑（如苯海拉明）。口服或注射。副作用包括嗜眠、口乾、頭暈和惡心。

地芬諾酯 一種常與阿托品（在鹽酸苯乙呱啶中）合用以治療腹瀉的藥物。該藥物也用於結腸造口術或迴腸造口術後以減少排便次數和減少稀便。口服用藥。副作用包括惡心、嗜眠、頭暈、皮膚反應和焦躁不安。

二碳膦酸酯 一類強力與骨骼結合的化合物。這一特性使得這一類化合物有助於骨骼顯像和治療某些骨病，如骨的變形性骨炎。

白喉 一種因白喉棒狀桿菌引起的急性接觸性傳染病。通常累及咽喉，偶爾也侵犯其他黏膜和皮膚。該病通過與一患者或致病菌攜帶者的直接接觸而得以傳播或通過污染的乳汁傳播，通過2~6天的潛伏期後，出現咽喉痛、虛弱和輕度發熱。隨後，在喉部形成一軟性灰色膜，阻礙氣管，引起呼吸和吞咽困難。需要施行氣管造口術。細菌在感染部位繁殖，並向血流釋放一種毒素。該毒素損害心臟和神經。可在四天內因心力衰竭或全身虛脫而死亡。但及時應用抗毒素和青黴素可控制本病。完全恢復需要長時間臥床休息。一種有效的免疫計劃使得在大多數西方國家裏白喉已屬罕見。參閱 Schick test。

immunization programme has now made diphtheria rare in most Western countries (*see also* Schick test).

diphtheroid *adj.* resembling diphtheria (especially the membrane formed in diphtheria) or the bacteria that cause it.

類白喉　與白喉（尤指白喉中所形成的膜）或引起白喉的細菌類似的。

diphyllobothriasis *n.* an infestation of the intestine with the broad tapeworm, *Diphyllobothrium latum*, which sometimes causes nausea, malnutrition, diarrhoea, and anaemia resulting from impaired absorption of vitamin B_{12} through the gut. The infestation, common in Baltic countries, is contracted following ingestion of uncooked fish infected with the larval stage of the tapeworm. The tapeworm can be expelled from the gut with the anthelmintic *mepacrine.

裂頭絛蟲病　由闊節裂頭絛蟲引起的腸道感染。有時引起惡心、營養不良、腹瀉和貧血。其原因為腸內維生素 B_{12} 吸收障礙。該病在波羅的海國家常見，是因食用被裂頭絛蟲幼蟲感染的生魚而感染的，裂頭絛蟲可通過驅腸蟲藥米帕林從腸中排除。

Diphyllobothrium *n.* a genus of large tapeworms that can grow to a length of 3–10 m. The adult of *D. latum*, the broad (or fish) tapeworm, infects fish-eating mammals including man, in whom it may cause serious anaemia (*see* diphyllobothriasis). The parasite has two intermediate hosts: a freshwater crustacean and a fish (*see also* plerocercoid).

裂頭絛蟲屬　一類可長達 3~10 m 的巨大絛蟲。闊節裂頭絛蟲的成蟲感染食魚的哺乳動物，包括人類，引起嚴重貧血（參閱 diphyllobothriasis）。這一寄生蟲有兩個中間宿主：淡水甲殼類和魚類。參閱 plerocercoid。

dipipanone *n.* a potent *analgesic drug used to relieve severe pain. It is administered by mouth or injection and may cause nausea, vomiting, dizziness, and drowsiness. Trade name: **Diconal**.

地匹呱酮　一種強效鎮痛藥物，用於解除劇痛。口服或注射。可引起惡心、嘔吐、頭暈和嗜眠。商品名：Diconal。

dipl- (diplo-) *prefix denoting* double.

〔前綴〕雙倍

diplacusis *n.* perception of a single sound as double owing to a defect of the *cochlea in the inner ear.

複聽　因內耳耳蝸缺陷所致將單聲感知為雙聲的現象。

diplegia *n.* paralysis involving both sides of the body and affecting the legs more

兩側癱　身體兩側癱瘓，腿的損害比臂嚴重。大腦性兩側癱

severely than the arms. *Cerebral diplegia* is a form of *cerebral palsy in which there is widespread damage, in both cerebral hemispheres, of the brain cells that control the movements of the limbs. **–diplegic** *adj.*

是一種大腦性麻痺，大腦兩半球控制肢體運動的腦細胞遭受廣泛損害。

diplococcus *n.* any of a group of non-motile parasitic spherical bacteria that occur in pairs. The group includes the *pneumococcus.

雙球菌 一類成對存在沒有運動能力的寄生性球形細菌。這一類細菌包括肺炎雙球菌。

diploë *n.* the lattice-like tissue that lies between the inner and outer layers of the *skull.

板障 顱骨內板和外板之間的網格狀組織。

diploid *adj.* describing cells, nuclei, or organisms in which each chromosome except the Y sex chromosome is represented twice. *Compare* haploid, triploid. **–diploid** *n.*

二倍體的 描述除 Y 性染色體外每條染色體均成雙存在的細胞，細胞核或機體。與 haploid，triploid 對比。

diplopia *n.* double vision: the simultaneous awareness of two images of the one object. It is usually due to limitation of movement of one eye so that the two eyes cannot simultaneously look at the same object. This may be caused by a defect of the nerves or muscles controlling eye movement or a mechanical restriction of eyeball movement in the orbit. Double vision that does not disappear on covering one eye can be caused by early cataract (*see also* polyopia).

複視 雙視覺：對一個物體同時產生兩個物像的現象。通常由於一隻眼的運動受到限制，兩隻眼睛同時看到同一物體。這可能因控制眼睛運動的神經或肌肉損傷所致，或者眼球在眼眶內運動機械障礙所致。覆蓋一隻眼雙視覺也不消失可能是由於早期白內障所致。（參閱 polyopia）。

diplotene *n.* the fourth stage in the first prophase of *meiosis, in which *crossing over occurs between the paired chromatids of homologous chromosomes, which then begin to separate.

雙綫期 減數分裂前期中的第四階段，同源染色體的配對染色單體之間發生交換，然後開始分離。

diprosopus *n.* a fetal monster with a single trunk and normal limbs but with some degree of duplication of the face.

雙面畸胎 一種不能存活的畸胎。有一軀幹和正常的四肢，但有不同程度的雙面部畸形。

dipsomania *n*. morbid and insatiable craving for alcohol, occurring in paroxysms. Only a small proportion of alcoholics show this symptom. *See* alcoholism.

間發性酒狂 以陣發形式發生的對酒精的病態和不可控制的渴求。只有少數嗜酒者表現出這一症狀。參閱 alcoholism。

Diptera *n*. a large group of insects, including *mosquitoes, gnats, midges, house flies, and *tsetse flies, that possess a single pair of wings. The mouthparts of many species, e.g. mosquitoes and tsetse flies, are specialized for sucking blood; these forms are important in the transmission of disease (*see* vector). *See also* fly.

雙翅目 一大目昆蟲，包括有一對翅膀的蚊、蚋、蠓、家蠅和采采蠅。許多種類（如蚊和采采蠅）的口器特化而能吸血。這些類型在傳播疾病方面起着重要作用（參閱 vector）。參閱 fly。

Dipylidium *n*. a genus of tapeworms. *D. caninum*, a common parasite of the small intestine of dogs and cats, which occasionally infects man but usually produces no obvious symptoms. Fleas are the intermediate hosts, and children in close contact with pets become infected on ingesting fleas harbouring the parasite.

複孔縧蟲屬 縧蟲的一個屬。犬複孔縧蟲是狗和貓的小腸常見寄生蟲，偶爾侵襲人，但通常不產生明顯症狀。蚤為中間宿主。當兒童與狗、貓密切接觸時，因吞入帶寄生蟲的蚤而被感染。

dipyridamole *n*. a drug that dilates the blood vessels of the heart and reduces platelet aggregation. It is given by mouth or injection to prevent thrombosis around prosthetic heart valves. It may cause headache, stomach upsets, and dizziness. Trade name: **Persantin**.

雙嘧達莫 一種擴張心臟血管和減少血小板聚集的藥物。口服或注射以預防在修復性心臟瓣膜周圍發生血栓。它可引起頭痛、胃部不適和頭暈。商品名：Persantin。

direct intracytoplasmic injection (DICI) a technique for assisting conception in cases of male infertility caused by inability of the spermatozoa to penetrate the barriers surrounding the ovum, in which a single spermatozoon is injected into the cytoplasm of an ovum.

直接細胞質內注射 在男性不育病例中幫助受孕的技術。男性不育是由精子沒有能力穿透在卵子周圍的屏障所致。在此種技術中，一個精子被注射入一個卵子的細胞質內。

director *n*. an instrument used to guide the extent and direction of a surgical incision.

探針 一種在外科切開術中用於探測深度和指導方向的器械。

Director of Public Health (DPH) *see* public health physician.

公共衛生主任　參閱 public health physician。

dis- *prefix denoting* separation.

〔前綴〕**分離**

disability *n. see* handicap.

殘疾　參閱 handicap。

Disabled Living Foundation (in Britain) a voluntary agency interested in all aspects of the care of those with *handicaps and in improving their quality of life. It is particularly concerned with aids to daily living, some of which can be inspected by clients, doctors, and others at a permanent exhibition at the headquarters of the Foundation.

殘疾人生活基金會　（英國）對殘疾人的所有方面進行照顧，並改善他們的生活質量的一個志願機構。它特別注重日常生活的幫助，其中一些可在委托人和醫生監督下進行，而其他則由基金會總部的常設機構監督。

disabled person *see* Employment Service, handicap.

殘疾人　參閱 Employment Service，handicap。

disablement *n. see* handicap.

缺陷，殘疾　參閱 handicap。

Disablement Resettlement Service *see* Employment Service.

殘疾人再就業服務機構　參閱 Employment Service。

disaccharide *n.* a carbohydrate consisting of two linked *monosaccharide units. The most common disaccharides are *maltose, *lactose, and *sucrose.

二糖　一種由兩個單糖單位連結而成的碳水化合物。最常見的二糖是麥芽糖、乳糖和蔗糖。

disarticulation *n.* separation of two bones at a joint. This may be the result of an injury or it may be done by the surgeon at operation in the course of amputation; for example of a limb, finger, or toe.

關節離斷　關節部位兩骨的分離。這可能是外傷的結果，也可是截斷術中由外科醫師施行，如一肢體、手指或趾的截斷手術。

disc *n.* (in anatomy) a rounded flattened structure, such as an *intervertebral disc or the *optic disc.

盤　（解剖學）一圓形扁平結構，如椎間盤或視盤。

discharge rate the number of cases of a specified disease discharged from hospitals related to the population of the *catchment area: usually expressed regionally per 10,000.

出院率　某種疾病出院的數字和該保健地段人口之比，通常以該地區每一萬人中出院的人數表示。

discission *n.* an obsolete operation for cataract in which the lens capsule was ruptured by a fine knife or needle to allow the substance of the lens to be absorbed naturally into the surrounding fluid of the eye.

內障刺開術　一種白內障的過時的手術方法。用一小刀或細針將晶狀體囊刺破以使晶體物質被眼的周圍液體所自然吸收。

discoid lupus erythematosus (DLE) *see* lupus erythematosus.

盤狀紅斑狼瘡　參閱 lupus erythematosus。

disease *n.* a disorder with a specific cause and recognizable signs and symptoms; any bodily abnormality or failure to function properly, except that resulting directly from physical injury (the latter, however, may open the way for disease).

疾病　有一特定原因，並有可以識別的體徵和症狀的病症，包括任何軀體畸形或者功能不能正常發揮，但不包括由直接物理損傷所致的障礙（但後者卻可導致疾病）。

disimpaction *n.* the process of separating the broken ends of a bone when they have been forcibly driven together during a fracture. *Traction may be required to keep the bone ends separate but in good alignment.

嵌插分離　將骨折時被強力嵌插在一起的骨的斷端分離的過程。需要用牽引方法使骨端保持分離，但應在正確的對位綫上。

disinfectant *n.* an agent that destroys or removes bacteria and other microorganisms and is used to cleanse surgical instruments and other objects. Examples are *cresol, *hexachlorophane, and *phenol. Dilute solutions of some disinfectants may be used as *antiseptics or as preservatives in solutions of eye drops or injections.

消毒劑　一種破壞或去除細菌和其他微生物的藥劑，用於清潔手術器械和其他物品。如甲酚、六氯酚和苯酚。一些消毒劑的稀釋液可作為抗菌劑，但在眼藥水或注射液中可用作防腐劑。

disinfection *n.* the process of eliminating infective microorganisms from contaminated instruments, clothing, or surroundings by using physical means or chemicals (*disinfectants).

消毒　通過物理方法或化學物質（消毒劑）從污染的器械、衣物和被褥或環境中殺滅病源性微生物的過程。

disinfestation *n.* the destruction of insect pests and other animal parasites. This generally involves the use of

殺滅病媒法　殺滅有害昆蟲和其他動物寄生蟲。這通常包括局部運用殺蟲劑（如滅虱），

insecticides applied either topically, as in delousing, or as a spray for eliminating an infestation of fleas or bed bugs in the home.

或用作噴灑劑以消除室內跳蚤和臭蟲的感染。

disintegrative psychosis 1. *see* Heller's syndrome. **2.** a pervasive *developmental disorder, often with features of *autism, occurring as a result of a brain disease, such as encephalitis, in childhood.

(1) 分裂性精神病 參閱 Heller's syndrome。**(2) 精神發育障礙** 一種綜合性發育障礙，常因腦病而出現孤獨症的特徵，如兒童期腦炎。

disjunction *n.* the separation of pairs of homologous chromosomes during meiosis or of the chromatids of a chromosome during *anaphase of mitosis or meiosis. *Compare* nondisjunction.

分離 減數分裂期間成對的同源染色體的分離，或在有絲分裂或減數分裂後期一染色體的染色單體的分離。與 nondisjunction 對比。

dislocation (luxation) *n.* displacement from their normal position of bones meeting at a joint. Dislocation of the shoulder is common in sports injuries, and congenital abnormalities may lead to repeated dislocations of the hip. The bones are restored to their normal positions by manipulation, which may require local or general anaesthesia (*see* reduction). *Compare* subluxation.

脫位 相會於關節部位的骨從正常位置脫離。在運動損傷中，肩的脫位較為普遍，而先天性畸形可導致髖骨反覆脫位。通過推拿可使骨恢復到其正常位置，這可能需要局部或全身麻醉（參閱 reduction）。與 subluxation 對比。

dismemberment *n.* the amputation of a leg, arm, or part of a limb.

截斷術 一隻腿、臂或肢體的部分的截斷。

disoma *n.* a double-bodied fetal monster with a single head.

雙軀幹畸胎 有一個頭，但有雙身的畸胎。

disopyramide *n.* a *parasympatholytic drug used to treat various heart conditions involving abnormal heart rates. It is administered by mouth; side-effects such as dry mouth, blurred vision, difficulty in urination, and digestive upsets may occur. Trade names: **Dirythmin SA**, **Rythmodan**.

丙吡胺 一種擬副交感神經藥。用於治療涉及異常心律的各種心臟疾患。口服。可能發生的副作用包括口乾、視力模糊、排尿困難和消化道不適。商品名：Dirythmin SA，Rythmodan。

disorientation *n.* the state produced by loss of awareness of space, time, or

定向力障礙 對空間、時間或人物的感知能力的喪失所產生

personality. It can be the result of drugs, anxiety, or organic disease (such as dementia or *Korsakoff's syndrome).

的狀態。它可能是藥物、焦慮，或器質性疾病（如痴呆或柯爾薩科夫綜合徵）的結果所致。

dispensary *n.* a place where medicines are made up by a pharmacist according to the doctor's prescription and dispensed to patients. A dispensary is often part of an out-patient department in a hospital.

藥房 藥劑師按醫生的處方配製藥品並分發給患者的地方。藥房常為醫院門診部的一部分。

dispensing practice (in Britain) a general practice (usually in remote areas) in which doctors receive special allowances under the terms of the *National Health Service for dispensing the medications they prescribe for their patients. *See also* general practitioner.

藥品配發業務 （英國）一種綜合性業務（通常在邊遠地區）。根據國民保健服務制的規定，醫生給其患者配發他們自己所開的藥物可獲得特殊的補貼。參閱 general practitioner。

displacement *n.* (in psychology) the substitution of one type of behaviour for another, usually the substitution of a relatively harmless activity for a harmful one; for example, kicking the cat instead of one's boss.

替代 （心理學）用一種行為代替另一種行為的現象，通常是用相對無害的活動代替一種有害的活動。例如，用腳踢貓來代替踢老板。

dissection *n.* the cutting apart and separation of the body tissues along the natural divisions of the organs and different tissues in the course of an operation. Dissection of corpses is carried out for the study of anatomy.

解剖 在手術過程中，沿着器官和不同組織的自然分界予以切開和分離身體組織。屍體解剖是為解剖學研究而進行的。

disseminated *adj.* widely distributed in an organ (or organs) or in the whole body. The term may refer to disease organisms or to pathological changes.

播散的 在一器官（或多個器官內）或全身廣泛分布的。這一術語可指患病的機體或指病理變化。

disseminated intravascular coagulation (DIC) a condition resulting from overstimulation of the blood-clotting mechanisms in response to disease or injury, such as severe infection, asphyxia, hypothermia, abruptio placentae, or

彌散性血管內凝血 對於疾病和外傷應答時凝血機制的過度應激狀態，如嚴重感染、窒息、低溫、胎盤分離或宮內胎兒死亡。過度應激導致全身血液凝固和凝血因子的過分消

intrauterine fetal death. The overstimulation results in generalized blood coagulation and excessive consumption of coagulation factors. The resulting deficiency of these may lead to spontaneous bleeding. Transfusions of plasma are given to replace the depleted clotting factors, and treatment of the underlying cause is essential.

耗。由此所引起的凝血因子的缺乏可導致自動出血。給患者輸入血漿以替代所消耗掉的凝血因子。治療病因是最重要的。

disseminated sclerosis *see* multiple sclerosis.

播散性硬化　參閱　multiple sclerosis。

dissociation *n.* (in psychiatry) the process whereby thoughts and ideas can be split off from consciousness and may function independently, thus (for example) allowing conflicting opinions to be held at the same time about the same object. Dissociation may be the main factor in cases of dissociative *fugue and multiple personalities.

分裂　(精神病學) 思想和觀念與意識相分離而能獨立活動的過程，因此 (例如)，對同一主題可保持有相互矛盾的觀點。分裂在散漫性癔症和多重人格病例中可能是主要因素。

dissociative disorder any one of a group of extreme *defence mechanisms that include loss of memory for important personal details (*see* amnesia); wandering away from home and the assumption of a new identity (*see* fugue); splitting of the personality into two or more distinct personalities (*see* multiple personality disorder); and trancelike states with severely reduced response to external stimuli.

聯想散漫性障礙　任一極端個人的保護機制。包括忘卻重要的個人情況 (參閱 amnesia)，離家漫游，假裝一種新身份 (參閱 fugue)，分裂出兩種以上相互不同的人格 (參閱 multiple personality disorder) 和對外界刺激的反應嚴重減小的恍惚狀態。

distal *adj.* **1.** (in anatomy) situated away from the origin or point of attachment or from the median line of the body. For example, the term is applied to a part of a limb that is furthest from the body; to a blood vessel that is far from the heart; and to a nerve fibre that is far from the central nervous system. *Compare* proximal. **2.** (in dentistry) describing the surface of a tooth away from the midline of the jaw.

(1) 遠側的　(解剖學) 指位於起端或附着點的遠側，或身體中綫遠側的。例如，該術語用於指距軀幹較遠的肢體部分，遠離心臟的血管，遠離中樞神經系統的一根神經纖維。與 proximal 對比。**(2) 遠中的** (牙科學) 描述頜中綫遠側的牙齒表面。

Distalgesic *n. see* co-proxamol.

右 丙 氧 芬　參 閱　co-proxamol。

distichiasis *n.* a very rare condition in which there is an extra row of eyelashes behind the normal row. They may rub on the cornea.

雙行睫　在正常眼睫毛後面又長出一排睫毛的一種罕見疾患。它們可擦傷角膜。

distigmine *n.* an *anticholinesterase drug used to treat myasthenia gravis. It is administered by mouth. Possible side-effects include nausea, vomiting, diarrhoea, and excessive salivation. Trade name: **Ubretid**.

地斯的明　一種用於治療重症肌無力的抗膽鹼酯酶。口服。可能具有的副作用包括惡心、嘔吐、腹瀉和過度唾液分泌。商品名：Ubretid。

District Health Authority *see* National Health Service.

地段衛生局　參閱　National Health Service。

District Medical Committee *see* medical committee.

地段醫療委員會　參閱 medical committee。

District Medical Officer (DMD) *see* public health physician.

地段醫官　參閱 public health physician。

district nurse *see* home nurse.

地段護士　參閱 home nurse。

District Planning Team a multidisciplinary group of doctors, nurses, and others established in a health district to identify gaps in the services and to suggest how they can be improved. Outside agencies (e.g. *social services) are included when appropriate. Some terms are permanent (e.g. those dealing with the elderly and mentally sick); others are established on and *ad hoc* basis.

地段計劃小組　在一衛生地段內設立的由醫生、護士和其他人構成的一個多學科小組，以鑒定服務的差距，並建議它們如何得以改進。如合適的話，外部機構（如社會福利機構）也被包括在內。有些小組是常設的（如負責老年人和精神病患者的小組），而其他的小組則是基於特定要求設立的。

disulfiram *n.* a drug used in the treatment of chronic alcoholism. It acts as a deterrent by producing unpleasant effects when taken with alcohol, including flushing, breathing difficulties, headache, palpitations, nausea, and vomiting. It is administered by mouth; common side-effects are fatigue, nausea, and constipation. Trade name: **Antabuse**.

雙硫侖　一種用於治療慢性乙醇中毒的藥物。當與酒精合用時，它可做為抑制藥物產生不適的反應，包括顏面潮紅、呼吸困難、頭痛、心悸、惡心和嘔吐。口服。常見的副作用是疲乏、惡心和便秘。商品名：Antabuse。

dithranol *n.* a drug applied to the skin as an ointment or paste to treat *psoriasis. It may irritate the skin on application. Trade names: **Alphodith, Dithrolan.**

地蔥酚　一種皮膚外用藥。用做軟膏或糊劑以治療銀屑病。在使用時，可刺激皮膚。商品名：Alphodith，Dithrolan。

diuresis *n.* increased secretion of urine by the kidneys. This normally follows the drinking of more fluid than the body requires, but it can be stimulated by the administration of a *diuretic.

尿液增多　腎臟尿液分泌的增加。通常飲水量超過身體需要時則尿液增多，但是，也可通過服用利尿劑刺激尿液增多。

diuretic *n.* a drug that increases the volume of urine produced by promoting the excretion of salts and water from the kidney. Examples are the *thiazide diuretics* (e.g. *chlorothiazide and *chlorthalidone), *frusemide, *spironolactone, and *triamterene. Diuretics are used to reduce the oedema due to salt and water retention in disorders of the heart, kidneys, liver, or lungs. Some mild diuretics, including *acetazolamide, are used to reduce the pressure within the eyeball in glaucoma. Diuretics are also used – in conjunction with other drugs – in the treatment of high blood pressure. Treatment with thiazide diuretics often results in potassium deficiency; this is corrected by simultaneous administration of potassium salts.

利尿劑　通過促進腎臟排出鹽和水使尿液量增加的藥物。如噻嗪類利尿劑（如氫氯噻嗪和氯噻酮）、呋噻米、螺內酯和氨苯蝶啶。利尿劑用於減少心臟、腎臟、肝臟或肺部疾病中因鹽和水的瀦留所致水腫。一些輕度利尿劑（包括乙醯唑胺）被用來減輕青光眼的眼球內的壓力。利尿劑在與其他藥物聯用時，也用於治療高血壓。用噻嗪類利尿劑進行治療常導致鉀缺乏。鉀缺乏可通過同時服用鉀鹽得以糾正。

divagation *n.* rambling discursive thought and speech. It is not specific to any one psychiatric condition.

語無倫次　零亂而不着邊際的思維和言語。這種現象並非是任何一種精神疾病所特有的。

divarication *n.* the separation or stretching of bodily structures. *Rectus divarication* is stretching of the *rectus abdominis muscle, a common condition associated with pregnancy or obesity.

分離　軀體結構的分離或拉長。直肌分離指的是腹直肌肌肉的拉長。這是與妊娠或肥胖有關的常見情況。

divaricator *n.* a scissor-like surgical instrument used to divide portions of tissue into two separate parts during an operation.

分離器　一種在手術過程中將組織分離成各不相連的兩個部分的剪刀樣外科器械。

diverticular disease a condition in which there are diverticula (*see* diverticulum) in the colon associated with lower abdominal pain and disturbed bowel habit. The pain is due to spasm of the muscles of the intestine and not to inflammation of the diverticula (*compare* diverticulitis).

diverticulitis *n.* inflammation of a *diverticulum, most commonly of one or more colonic diverticula. This type of diverticulitis is caused by infection and causes lower abdominal pain with diarrhoea or constipation; it may lead to abscess formation, which often requires surgical drainage. A Meckel's diverticulum sometimes becomes inflamed due to infection, causing symptoms similar to *appendicitis. Diverticula elsewhere in the alimentary tract are not subject to diverticulitis. *Compare* diverticular disease.

diverticulosis *n.* a condition in which diverticula exist in a segment of the intestine without evidence of inflammation (*compare* diverticulitis).

diverticulum *n.* (*pl.* **diverticula**) a sac or pouch formed at weak points in the walls of the alimentary tract. They may be caused by increased pressure from within (*pulsion diverticula*) or by pulling from without (*traction diverticula*). A *pharyngeal diverticulum* occurs in the pharynx and may cause difficulty in swallowing. *Oesophageal diverticula* occur in the middle or lower oesophagus (gullet); they may be associated with muscular disorders of the oesophagus but rarely cause symptoms. *Gastric diverticula* affect the stomach (usually the upper part) and cause no symptoms. *Duodenal diverticula* occur on the

憩室病　併發有下腹痛和大腸功能紊亂的結腸憩室病（參閱diverticulum）。疼痛是由於腸肌肉攣縮，而不是由於憩室的炎症所致（與 diverticulitis 對比）。

憩室炎　結腸憩室（最常見的為一個或多個）的炎症。這類憩室炎是由感染引起的，並引起下腹疼痛，伴有腹瀉或便秘。它可導致膿腫形成。此時，常需外科引流。梅克爾憩室有時因感染而發炎，引起與闌尾炎類似的症狀。消化道其他部位的憩室不發生憩室炎。（與 diverticular disease 對比）。

腸憩室病　腸的某節段存在多個憩室而無炎症證據的疾患（與 diverticulitis 對比）。

憩室　在消化道壁的薄弱處形成的囊或袋。它們可由於內壓增加（推壓性憩室）或外部牽拉（牽引性憩室）而發生。咽憩室發生於咽部，可引起吞嚥困難。食管憩室發生於食管中部或下部。它們可與食管肌肉的疾病有關，但很少引起症狀。胃憩室發生在胃（通常在上部），不引起任何症狀。十二指腸憩室發生於十二指腸曲的凹面，它們可合併消化不良，並增加膽總管結石病的危險性，但通常很少引起症狀。空腸憩室發生在小腸，常為多發性，並且因細菌在內繁殖而

concave surface of the duodenal loop; they may be associated with *dyspepsia and an increased risk of choledocholithiasis, but usually cause few symptoms. *Jejunal diverticula* affect the small intestine, are often multiple, and may give rise to abdominal discomfort and *malabsorption due to growth of bacteria within them. *Meckel's diverticulum* occurs in the ileum, about 35 cm from its termination, as a congenital abnormality. It may become inflamed, mimicking *appendicitis; if it contains embryonic remnants of stomach mucosa it may form a *peptic ulcer, causing pain, bleeding, or perforation. *Colonic diverticula*, affecting the colon (particularly the lowest portion), become commoner with increasing age and often cause no symptoms. However they are sometimes associated with abdominal pain or altered bowel habit (*see* diverticular disease) or they may become inflamed (*see* diverticulitis).

引起腹部不適和吸收障礙。梅克爾憩室發生於迴腸，距其末端約35cm，是先天性異常。可發生炎症，類似闌尾炎。假如它含有胃黏膜胚胎殘留物，它會形成消化性潰瘍，引起疼痛、出血或穿孔。隨着年齡增長，發生在結腸（尤其是其下部）的憩室變得較為常見，且常不引起任何症狀。然而，它們可伴發腹部疼痛或大便習慣改變（參閱 diverticular disease），或可發生炎症（參閱 diverticulitis）。

division *n.* the separation of an organ or tissue into parts by surgery.

分離　手術中將器官或組織分成幾個部分。

divulsor *n.* a surgical instrument used to dilate forcibly any canal or cavity, usually the urethra.

擴張器　一種施加力量擴張任何管道或腔室（通常為尿道）的外科器械。

dizygotic twins *see* twins.

雙卵雙胎兒　參閱 twins。

DLE discoid lupus erythematosus. *See* lupus erythematosus.

盤形紅斑狼瘡　參閱 lupus erythematosus。

DMD (Duchenne muscular dystrophy) *see* muscular dystrophy.

迪歇納肌營養不良　參閱 muscular dystrophy。

DMSA dimercaptosuccinic acid labelled with *technetium-99, used as a tracer to obtain *scintigrams of the kidney, particularly to show scarring resulting from infection.

二巰基丁二酸　由^{99}鎝所標記的二巰基丁二酸，用作示踪物以獲得腎臟的閃爍圖，尤以顯示因感染所致瘢痕。

DNA (deoxyribonucleic acid) the genetic material of nearly all living organisms, which controls heredity and is located in the cell nucleus (*see* chromosome, gene). DNA is a *nucleic acid composed of two strands made up of units called *nucleotides (see illustration). The two strands are wound around each other into a d'ouble helix and linked together by hydrogen bonds between the bases of the nucleotides (*see* base pairing). The genetic information of the DNA is contained in the sequence of bases along the molecule (*see* genetic code); changes in the DNA cause *mutations. The DNA molecule can make exact copies of itself by the process of *replication, thereby passing on the genetic information to the daughter cells when the cell divides.

脫氧核糖核酸 幾乎所有活的生物體的遺傳物質。它控制遺傳，位於細胞核裏（參閱 chromosome，gene）。DNA 為一種由兩條被稱為核苷酸鏈構成的核酸（見圖）。兩條鏈相互纏繞形成一雙螺旋結構，通過核苷酸的鹼基之間的氫鏈結合在一起（參閱 base pairing）。DNA 的遺傳信息被包含在沿着分子的鹼基順序中（參閱 genetic code）。DNA 內的變化引起突變。DNA 分子通過複製過程對其進行準確無誤的複製。當細胞分裂時，將遺傳信息傳遞給子代細胞。

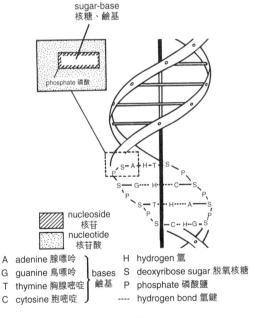

Structure of part of a DNA molecule
DNA分子的部分結構

dobutamine *n.* a *sympathomimetic drug used to assist in the management of heart failure. It increases the force of contraction of the ventricles and improves the heart output and it may be given by continuous intravenous drip.

多巴酚丁胺 一種擬交感神經藥，用於幫助治療心力衰竭。它增加心室的收縮力，並改進心臟搏出量，可通過持續靜脈滴注給予患者。

Doctor *n.* **1.** the title given to a recipient of a higher university degree than a Master's degree. The degree *Medicinae Doctor* (MD) is awarded by some British universities as a research degree. In the US the degree is awarded on qualification. **2.** a courtesy title given to a qualified medical practitioner, i.e. one who has been registered by the General Medical Council (GMC). Most doctors in the UK obtain bachelors' degrees in medicine and surgery (MB, BS) or the diplomas of the conjoint boards of the Royal Colleges of Physicians and Surgeons of England and Scotland or the Society of Apothecaries (e.g. LRCP, MRCS, LMSSA): these degrees or diplomas and one year's hospital experience are required by the GMC before they will register a person as a doctor. Normally it is compulsory to hold two full-time *preregistration appointments* in general subjects at hospitals recognized for this purpose. The doctor has the title *house physician* (or *surgeon*), *resident*, or *intern* and is debarred from independent practice. Surgeons in the UK do not use the title Doctor and are referred to, as a mark of distinction, as Mr. In the US qualified dentists and pharmacists also use the courtesy title Doctor. *See also* consultant.

(1) 博士 授予接受者比碩士更高的大學學位的稱號。在英國，醫學博士 (MD) 是作為一科研學位授予的。在美國，此項學位則是按照所具資格授予的。**(2)** 醫生 對一獲得行醫資格的醫療從業人員的尊稱，也就是在醫師總會註冊的人。在英國，多數醫生獲得內科和外科學士學位 (MB, BS)，或者持有英格蘭和蘇格蘭的皇家內科醫師和外科醫師學會證書，或者藥劑師學會等的證書（如皇家內科醫師學會資格認定證書、皇家外科醫師學會成員證書、藥劑師學會內科和外科資格認定證書）。這些學位或證書和一年的醫院工作經歷是醫師總會將一個人註冊為醫生前所要求具備的。通常，註冊人員必須在指定醫院的綜合科裏擔任兩份全日制見習期醫生職務。醫生具有住院內科總醫師（或住院外科總醫師）、住院醫師或見習醫師職稱，並不許獨立行醫。在英國，外科醫師不用醫生稱呼。作為一種區別的標誌，他們被稱呼為先生。在美國，符合資格的牙醫和藥劑師也用醫生這一尊稱。參閱consultant。

dolich- (dolicho-) *prefix denoting* long. Example: *dolichocolon* (abnormally long colon).

〔前綴〕長的 如長結腸（異常長的結腸）。

dolichocephaly *n.* the condition of having a relatively long skull, with

長頭 頭圍指數為 75 或者更小的顱骨相對較長的狀態。

a *cephalic index of 75 or less.
–dolichocephalic *adj.*

dolor *n.* pain: one of the classical signs of inflammation in a tissue, the other three being *calor (heat), *rubor (redness), and *tumor (swelling). The pain in inflammation is thought to be due to the release of chemicals from damaged cells.

痛　疼痛：組織炎症的傳統的體徵之一。其他三個體徵為灼熱、發紅和腫脹。炎症疼痛被認為是受損細胞釋放化學物質所致。

dolorimetry *n.* the measurement of pain. *See* algesimeter.

測痛法　測量疼痛。參閱 algesimeter。

domiciliary consultation 1. a house call by a *general practitioner made at the request of a patient. **2.** (in Britain) an arrangement in the *National Health Service whereby a hospital specialist sees a patient at home, often to assess the need to admit elderly patients for hospital care. The specialist receives special remuneration for this service.

(1) 出診　根據病人要求，一全科醫師去病人家裏進行診治的做法。**(2) 家訪**　（英國）國民保健服務制的一種安排，醫院的專科醫師在病人家裏對病人進行診視，常常是為了評估有無必要讓老年病人住院治療。專科醫師因此服務而獲得特殊的酬金。

domiciliary midwife (community midwife) (in Britain) a registered general *nurse with special training in midwifery (both hospital and domiciliary practice). She must be registered with the UKCC in order to practise; this requires regular refresher courses to supplement the basic qualification of *Registered Midwife* (*RM*). Planned *home deliveries* are comparatively rare; the work of domiciliary midwives is mainly concerned with antenatal, intranatal, and postnatal care, especially in those discharged 48 hours or less after delivery, and in some cases conducting deliveries in community hospitals.

家庭助產士（社區助產士）（英國）受過助產特殊教育（醫院和家庭接生）的註冊護士。他們必須在 UKCC 註冊方可開業。這要求定期進修課程以提高註冊助產士 (RM) 的基本資格。有計劃的家庭接生比較少見。家庭助產士的工作主要涉及產前、產間和產後護理，特別對那些產後出院後 48 小時或者更短時間內的產婦的護理。在一些情況下，在社區醫院進行接生。

domiciliary services (in Britain) health and social services that are available in the home and are distinguished from hospital-based services. They include the services of such personnel as

家庭保健服務　（英國）在家裏能夠獲得的保健和社會福利服務。這種服務有別於醫院裏的服務。它們包括由以下人員提供的服務：由地段衛生局僱傭

community nurses employed by District Health Authorities (*see* home nurse, domiciliary midwife, health visitor) and social workers, home helps, and bath attendants employed by social service departments of local authorities. Also included are services such as meals on wheels, loan equipment for home care, and ambulatory aids. The term *community services* is also applied to these services, but strictly speaking, hospitals and other residential institutes should be included under the latter heading.

dominant *adj.* (in genetics) describing a gene (or its corresponding characteristic) whose effect is shown in the individual whether its *allele is the same or different. If the allele is different it is described as *recessive and its effect is masked. **–dominant** *n.*

domiphen *n.* an *antiseptic administered in the form of lozenges to treat bacterial and fungal infections of the mouth and throat. It is also used in solution for cleansing wounds and burns, for treating fungal infections of the skin, and for general disinfection of skin and mucous membranes. Trade name: **Bradosol**.

domperidone *n.* an antiemetic drug used especially to reduce the nausea and vomiting caused by other drugs (e.g. anticancer drugs). It inhibits the effects of *dopamine, acting to close the sphincter muscle at the upper opening of the stomach (the cardia) and to relax the sphincter at the lower opening (the pylorus). It is administered by mouth or suppository; possible side-effects include breast enlargement and milk secretion. Trade names: **Evoxin**, **Motilium**.

的社區護士（參閱 home nurse，domiciliary midwife，health visitor）和由地方當局的社會福利部門所僱傭的社會福利工作者、家務服務和浴室服務員。還包括諸如流動送餐、租賃家庭護理用具和流動服務等服務項目。社區服務這一術語也適用於這些服務項目，但嚴格地來說，醫院和其他收容患者的機構應包括在後一類。

顯性的 （遺傳學）描述一作用能在個體身上顯示的基因，無論其等位基因是一樣的還是不同的。如果等位基因不同，它被描述為隱性的，其影響被遮蔽。

度米芬 一種抗菌劑，做成糖錠劑服用，以治療口腔和咽喉的細菌和真菌感染。它也用於溶液以清潔傷口和燒傷、治療皮膚真菌感染和用於一般皮膚及黏膜消毒。商品名：Bradosol。

多潘立酮 一種止吐藥，特別用於減輕由其他藥物（如抗癌藥物）所引起的惡心和嘔吐。它抑制多巴胺的作用，從而關閉胃的上部開口（賁門）的括約肌，並鬆弛其下部開口的括約肌（幽門）。用於口服或栓劑。可能有的副作用包括乳腺增大和泌乳。商品名：Evoxin，Motilium。

Donald-Fothergill operation (Manchester operation) a surgical operation consisting of anterior *colporrhaphy, amputation of the cervix, and *colpoperineorrhaphy. It is performed for genital prolapse.

donor *n.* a person who makes his own tissues or organs available for use by someone else. For example, a donor may provide blood for transfusion (*see* blood donor), a kidney for transplantation, or sex cells for *artificial insemination or *oocyte donation.

donor insemination *see* artificial insemination.

dopa *n.* dihydroxyphenylalanine: a physiologically important compound that forms an intermediate stage in the synthesis of catecholamines (dopamine, adrenaline, and noradrenaline) from the essential amino acid tyrosine. It also plays a role itself in the functioning of certain parts of the brain. The laevorotatory form, *levodopa, is administered for the treatment of *parkinsonism, in which there is a deficiency of dopamine in the brain.

dopamine *n.* a *catecholamine derived from dopa that functions as a *neurotransmitter acting on specific dopamine receptors and also on adrenergic receptors throughout the body, especially in the *limbic system and *extrapyramidal system of the brain and in the arteries and the heart. It also stimulates the release of noradrenaline from nerve endings. The effects vary with the concentration. Dopamine is used as a drug to increase the strength of contraction of the heart in heart failure, shock, severe trauma, and septicaemia. It is

多納德-福瑟吉爾手術（曼徹斯特手術） 一種外科手術，包括陰道前壁縫合術、宮頸截斷術和陰道會陰成形術。該手術的施行是為了治療生殖器脫垂。

供者 提供自己的組織或器官以供他人使用的人。例如，一供者可為輸血提供血液（參閱 blood donor），為移植提供腎臟，或者為人工授精提供性細胞，或卵母細胞捐獻。

供體授精 參閱 artificial insemination。

多巴 是一種具有重要生理作用的化合物，是由基本氨基酸酪氨酸合成兒茶酚胺（多巴胺、腎上腺素和去甲腎上腺素）過程中的中間產物。它自身在大腦的某些部分的機能發揮中起作用。左旋型多巴藥左旋多巴用以治療帕金森綜合徵。患此病的病人腦中缺乏多巴胺。

多巴胺 由多巴衍生的一種兒茶酚胺，具有神經遞質的功能。作用於全身（尤其是四肢系統和大腦錐體外系統以及動脈和心臟的多巴胺受體和腎上腺素能受體）。它也刺激來自神經末梢的去甲腎上腺素的釋放。其作用濃度不同而異。多巴胺可用來作為一種在心力衰竭、休克、嚴重創傷和敗血症等症中增強心臟收縮力的藥物。以嚴格控制的劑量用於注射。可能具有的副作用包括心跳異常加快或心律不齊、惡

administered by injection in carefully controlled dosage. Possible side-effects include unduly rapid or irregular heartbeat, nausea, vomiting, breathlessness, angina pectoris, and kidney damage.

Certain drugs (*dopamine receptor agonists*) have an effect on the body similar to that of dopamine. They include *amantadine and *bromocriptine and are used to treat *parkinsonism, *acromegaly (as they suppress the release of growth hormone), and to suppress or prevent milk secretion (through their action in blocking the release of prolactin). Drugs that compete with dopamine to occupy and block the dopamine receptor sites in the body are known as *dopamine receptor antagonists*. They include some *antipsychotic drugs (e.g. the phenothiazines and *butyrophenones) and certain drugs (e.g. *domperidone and *metoclopramide) used to treat nausea and vomiting.

dopamine hypothesis the theory that schizophrenia is caused in part by abnormalities in the metabolism of *dopamine and can be treated in part by drugs (such as *chlorpromazine) that antagonize its action as a neurotransmitter.

Doppler technique a diagnostic technique that utilizes changes in frequency when *ultrasound waves are bounced back from tissues of various densities to demonstrate their consistency and structure. It is used extensively in the diagnosis of tumours and other lesions of soft tissues and also for investigating cardiac function (*see* echocardiography) and the blood flow in peripheral arteries, as the relative speed of the blood flow alters the frequency of the sound beam. The latter property is also utilized for examining uterine and placental circulation

心、嘔吐、呼吸困難、心絞痛和腎損傷。

某些藥物（多巴胺受體藥）對身體具有與多巴胺相似的作用。它們包括金剛烷胺和溴隱亭。用於治療帕金森綜合徵、肢端肥大症（因其抑制生長激素的分泌）和抑制或預防泌乳（通過其阻斷催乳素的分泌作用）。與多巴相對抗的以占據和阻斷身體多巴胺受體部位的藥物被稱為多巴胺受體拮抗劑。它們包括一些抗精神病藥（如吩噻嗪類和丁酰苯類）和某些用於治療惡心和嘔吐的藥物（如多潘立酮和甲氧氯普胺）。

多巴胺假說 一種理論。認為精神分裂症部分原因是由多巴胺的代謝異常引起的，因之可用神經遞質的藥物（如氯丙嗪）通過其對抗多巴胺的作用而進行部分治療。

多普勒技術 一種診斷技術。方法是利用超聲波被不同密度的組織反射後的頻率的變化來顯示它們的堅固性和結構。它廣泛用於診斷腫瘤和軟組織損傷，也用於檢查心肌功能和周圍動脈的血流，因為血流的相對速度可改變聲波的頻率。後面這一特性在妊娠期間被用來檢查子宮和胎盤循環以對胎兒健康狀況和胎兒異常做出產前預測和診斷。結果可提示有無必要實施進一步的（侵入性）診斷技術（如臍帶穿刺術）。

during pregnancy to enable prenatal prediction and diagnosis of fetal well-being and of fetal anomalies. The results may indicate the necessity for further (invasive) diagnostic procedures, such as *cordocentesis.

dors- (dorsi-, dorso-) *prefix denoting* **1.** the back. Example: *dorsalgia* (pain in). **2.** dorsal.

〔前綴〕**(1)** 背　　如背痛。**(2)** 背側的

dorsal *adj.* relating to or situated at or close to the back of the body or to the posterior part of an organ.

背側的　與身體背部或一器官的後部相關的，或位於或接近身體背部或一器官的後部。

dorsiflexion *n.* backward flexion of the foot or hand or their digits; i.e. bending towards the upper surface.

背屈　腳或手、指或趾的向後屈曲，即向着上表面彎曲。

dorsoventral *adj.* (in anatomy) extending from the back (dorsal) surface to the front (ventral) surface.

背腹側的　（解剖學）從後（背）側表面向前（腹）側表面的延伸。

dorsum *n.* **1.** the back. **2.** the upper or posterior surface of a part of the body; for example, of the hand. *See also* dorsal.

(1) 背　**(2)** 背面　身體的某部分的上表面或後表面。例如手背。參閱 dorsal。

dose *n.* a carefully measured quantity of a drug that is prescribed by a doctor to be given to a patient at any one time. The *median effective dose* (ED_{50}) is the dose of a drug that produces desired effects in 50% of individuals tested. *See also* LD_{50}.

劑量　醫生給患者開出處方中仔細稱量的一次藥物量。半數有效量（ED_{50}）是指 50% 的受試個體產生預期效果的藥物劑量。參閱 LD_{50}。

dosimeter *n.* a device to record the amount of radiation received by workers with X-rays or other radiation, usually consisting of a small piece of photographic film in a holder attached to the clothing. At regular intervals the film is examined to discover the amount of radiation it (and therefore the wearer) has received.

放射量計　一種記錄接觸 X 綫或其他輻射的工人所接受的輻射量的儀器，通常由內裝感光膠片的可掛在衣物上的小盒組成。膠片被定期檢查以確定它及佩戴者所接受的輻射量。

dosimetry *n.* the calculation of appropriate doses for given conditions, usually the calculation of correct amounts of radiation for the treatment of cancer in different parts of the body. *See* radiotherapy.

劑量測定 對某一確定疾病計算出合適的劑量的過程。通常是指計算出治療身體不同部位的腫瘤的正確的輻射量。參閱 radiotherapy。

double-bind *n.* a disordered pattern of family relationships in which one family member gives contradictory instructions to another (as when a mother asks her child verbally for affection but simultaneously, by her gestures, indicates that the child should remain distant). The result is that any action the child makes will be wrong, and furthermore he cannot escape from the situation. This has been supposed, but not proved, to be a factor in causing schizophrenia.

矛盾性牽制 一種異常型的家庭關係。一個家庭成員給另一家庭發出相互矛盾的指示（如當一母親口頭表達讓孩子表示親近，但同時卻用其體態暗示孩子應保持距離）。結果是孩子所做的任何行為都是錯的，而且，他不能逃避這一狀況。這一直被認為（但未被證明）是引起精神分裂症的一個因素。

double-blind trial *see* intervention study.

雙盲試驗 參閱 intervention study。

double J stents *see* stent.

雙重斯坦特固定膜 參閱 stent。

double uterus *see* uterus didelphys.

雙子宮 參閱 uterus didelphys。

double vision *see* diplopia.

複視 參閱 diplopia。

douche *n.* a forceful jet of water used for cleaning any part of the body, most commonly the vagina. A vaginal douche is extremely unreliable as a method of contraception.

沖洗 以加壓噴頭噴水以清潔身體的任何部位（最常見為陰道）。作為一種避孕方法，陰道沖洗是極不可靠的。

Down's syndrome a condition resulting from a genetic abnormality in which an extra chromosome is present (three are three no. 21 chromosomes instead of the usual two), giving a total of 47 chromosomes rather than the normal 46. The chances of having a Down's child are higher with increasing maternal age.

唐氏綜合徵 一種因遺傳異常而致的疾患。出現了一條多餘的染色體（有三條 21 號染色體，而不像通常那樣有兩條）。因之，染色體總數達 47 條，而並非通常情況的 46 條。隨着母親的年齡增大，生育患有唐氏綜合徵的孩

Affected individuals share certain clinical features, including a characteristic flat facial appearance with slanting eyes (as in Mongolian races, which gave the former name, *mongolism*, to the condition), broad hands with short fingers and a single crease across the palm, malformed ears, eyes with a speckled iris (*Brushfield's spots*), short stature, and *hypotonia. Many individuals also have a degree of mental handicap, although the range of ability is wide and some individuals are of normal intelligence. Associated abnormalities, including heart defects (which affect about 40% of Down's children), intestinal malformation, deafness, and squints, may also be present.

*Prenatal diagnosis of Down's syndrome can be obtained by *amniocentesis. *chorionic villus sampling, and the *triple marker test: the condition can be confirmed by chromosomal analysis. Down's syndrome can also occur as a result of chromosomal rearrangement (*translocation) and as part of a *mosaicism. Medical name: **trisomy 21**.

doxapram *n*. a drug that stimulates breathing and has similar effects and uses to those of *nikethamide. Trade name: **Dopram**.

doxazosin *n*. an *alpha blocker drug used to treat high blood pressure. It is administered by mouth. Possible side-effects include faintness on standing up, weakness, dizziness, and headache. Trade name: **Cardura**.

doxepin *n*. a drug used to relieve depression, especially when associated with anxiety (*see* antidepressant, tranquilizer). It is administered by mouth;

子的可能性就增高。患病的個人有某些臨床特徵，包括有面部扁平、雙眼斜視如蒙古族的面貌特徵，手掌寬闊、指頭短、有一皺褶穿過手掌、耳朵畸形、帶有斑點虹膜的眼睛（布拉什菲爾德斑）、身材矮小和張力減退。許多患者有某種程度的智力障礙，儘管能力範圍很寬，且有些患者智力正常。相關異常也可出現，包括心臟缺陷（波及 40% 的唐氏綜合徵的兒童）、腸道畸形、耳聾和斜眼。

通過羊膜穿刺術、絨膜絨毛取樣術和三聯標記測試對唐氏綜合徵進行產前診斷。這一疾病可通過染色體分析來加以證實。唐氏綜合徵也可因基因重組（易位）而發生，是染色體鑲嵌現象的一部分。醫學用語：21 號三倍體病。

多沙普侖　一種能促進呼吸的藥物。該藥和尼可剎米具有類似的作用和用途。商品名：Dopram。

多沙唑嗪　一種 α-受體阻滯劑藥物，用於治療高血壓。口服。副作用包括站起暈厥、虛弱、頭暈和頭痛。商品名：Cardura。

多塞平　一種用於消除抑鬱（特別是合併焦慮時）的藥物（參照 antidepressant，tranquillizer）。口服。副作用包括

side-effects can include drowsiness, dry mouth, blurred vision, and digestive upsets. Trade name: **Sinequan**.

嗜眠、口乾、視力模糊和消化道不適。商品名：Sinequan。

doxorubicin *n.* an *anthracycline antibiotic isolated from *Streptomyces peucetius caesius* and used mainly in the treatment of leukaemia and various other forms of cancer. Doxorubicin acts by interfering with the production of DNA and RNA (*see also* cytotoxic drug). It is administered by injection or infusion; side-effects include bone marrow depression, baldness, gastrointestinal disturbances, and heart damage. Trade name: **Adriamycin**.

阿黴素 一種從由波賽青灰鏈黴菌中分離出來的蒽環類抗生素，主要用於治療白血病和各類其他癌症。阿黴素通過干擾 DNA 和 RNA（參閱 cytotoxic drug）的生成而發揮作用。注射或滴注。副作用包括骨髓抑制、脫髮、胃腸道紊亂和心臟損害。商品名：Adriamycin。

doxycycline *n.* an *antibiotic used to treat infections caused by a wide range of bacteria and other microorganisms. It is administered by mouth and side-effects are those of the other *tetracyclines. Trade names: **Nordox, Vibramycin**.

多西環素 一種用於治療由許多種細菌和其他微生物引起的感染的抗生素。口服。副作用和其他四環素類的副作用相同。商品名：Nordox，Vibramycin。

DPT *see* dental pantomogram.

牙全體 X 綫斷層照片 參閱 dental pantomogram。

DPT vaccine a combined *vaccine against diphtheria, whooping cough, and tetanus organisms, prepared from their *toxoids and other antigens.

白百破疫苗 抗白喉、百日咳和破傷風病原體的一種聯合疫苗。是用上述生物的類毒素和其他抗原製備的。

drachm *n.* **1.** a unit of weight used in pharmacy. 1 drachm = 3.883 g (60 grains). **2.** a unit of volume used in pharmacy. 1 fluid drachm = 3.696 ml (1/8 fluid ounce).

打蘭 (1) 用於藥學中的一種重量單位。1 打蘭等於 3.883 克（60 格令）。(2) 藥學中使用的一種容量單位。1 液量打蘭等於 3.696 毫升（1/8 液量盎斯）。

dracontiasis *n.* a tropical disease caused by the parasitic nematode *Dracunculus medinensis* (*see* guinea worm) in the tissues beneath the skin. The disease is transmitted to man via contaminated drinking water. The initial symptoms, which appear a year after infection,

麥地那龍綫蟲病 一種熱帶疾病，是由皮下組織裏寄生綫蟲麥地那龍綫蟲所致。這一疾病是通過被污染的飲用水而傳播給人類。最初症狀出現於感染一年後，是由綫蟲向皮膚表面遷移而引起的，這些症狀包括

result from the migration of the worm to the skin surface and include itching, giddiness, difficulty in breathing, vomiting, and diarrhoea. Later a large blister forms on the skin, usually on the legs or arms, which eventually bursts and may ulcerate and become infected. Dracontiasis is common in India and West Africa but also occurs in Arabia, Iran East Africa, and Afghanistan. Treatment involves extracting the worm or administering *thiabendazole, *metronidazole, or *niridazole.

Dracunculus *n. see* guinea worm.

dragee *n.* a *pill that has been coated with sugar.

drain 1. *n.* a device, usually a tube or wick, used to draw fluid from an internal body cavity to the surface. A drain is sometimes inserted during an operation to ensure that any fluid formed immediately passes to the surface, so preventing an accumulation that may become infected or cause pressure in the operation site. Negative pressure (suction) can be applied through a tube drain to increase its effectiveness. **2.** *vb. see* drainage.

drainage *n.* the drawing off of fluid from a cavity in the body, usually fluid that has accumulated abnormally. For example, serous fluid may be drained from a swollen joint, pus removed from an internal abscess, or urine from an over-distended bladder. *See also* drain.

drastic *n.* any agent causing a major change in a body system or function, e.g. strong laxatives.

瘙癢、頭暈、呼吸困難、嘔吐和腹瀉。隨後，在皮膚上形成一大疱，通常是在腿或臂部，最後破裂，並且可能發生潰瘍和感染。麥地那龍綫蟲病在印度和西非普遍，但也見於阿拉伯半島、伊朗、東非和阿富汗。治療包括取出綫蟲或使用噻苯達唑、甲硝唑或尼立達唑。

龍綫蟲屬　參閱　guinea worm。

糖衣丸　一種包裹了一層糖的藥丸。

(1) 引流器　用以將體內腔隙的液體吸至體表的器械（通常為一吸管或紗布條）。在手術中，有時放置一引流器以確保所形成的任何液體能立刻流向體表，以預防液體蓄積，避免感染發生，或引起手術部位的壓迫。負壓（吸力）能通過管子提高引流效果。**(2) 引流**　參閱　drainage。

引流　從體內腔隙內引出液體（通常為異常蓄積的液體）。例如，從腫脹關節將漿液性液體引流出來，從一體內膿腫處將膿液排出，從脹滿異常的膀胱內引流尿液。參閱　drain。

峻烈藥　引起機體系統或功能的巨大改變的任何藥物，如峻瀉劑。

draw-sheet *n.* a sheet placed beneath a patient in bed that, when one portion has been soiled or becomes uncomfortably wrinkled, may be pulled under the patient so that another portion may be used. The bed does not have to be remade, and the patient does not have to leave bed.

墊單　置於臥床患者身下的單子。當其一部分被弄髒或起皺而使患者感到不適時，可將其從患者身下抽出，而另一部分則仍可使用。不需重新鋪床，而患者也不需離床。

drepanocyte (sickle cell) *n. see* sickle-cell disease.

鐮狀細胞　參閱　sickle-cell disease。

drepanocytosis *n. see* sickle-cell disease.

鐮狀細胞增多症　參閱　sickle-cell disease。

dressing *n.* material applied to a wound or diseased part of the body, with or without medication, to give protection and assist healing.

敷料　貼敷於傷口或身體患病部位的材料。含或不含藥物，起着保護和促進痊愈的作用。

drill *n.* (in dentistry) a rotary instrument used to remove tooth substance, particularly in the treatment of caries. It consists of a handpiece that takes variously shaped *burs. Most drilling is done with an air-driven turbine handpiece, but some is performed with a much slower mechanically driven handpiece. Drills usually have a waterspray coolant.

牙鑽　（牙科學）一種轉動的器械，用以除去牙質。特別用於治療齲病。由可裝多種形狀鑽頭的握柄構成。多數鑽牙都是用氣動渦輪牙鑽來進行的，但一些鑽牙卻是以轉速很低的機械驅動的牙鑽進行的。牙鑽通常有一噴水冷卻裝置。

drip (intravenous drip) *n.* apparatus for the continuous injection (*transfusion) of blood, plasma, saline, glucose solution, or other fluid into a vein. The fluid flows under gravity from a suspended bottle through a tube ending in a hollow needle inserted into the patient's vein. The rate of flow can be adjusted according to the rate of drips seen in a transparent section of the tube, which also serves as a trap for bubbles.

輸注器　（靜脈輸注器）　供靜脈內連續輸注血液、血漿、鹽水、葡萄糖溶液或其他液體的裝置。在重力作用下，液體通過一條管子，並經過末端插進病人靜脈內的中空針頭流入患者靜脈內。液流速度可根據管子的一段透明部分所觀察到的液滴速度而加以調節。透明部分還可用以排除氣泡。

drom- (dromo-) *prefix denoting* movement or speed.

〔前綴〕運動，速度

dromomania *n.* a pathologically strong impulse to travel, which is said to be present in some vagabonds.

droperidol *n.* a *butyrophenone anti-psychotic drug that produces a state of emotional quietness and mental detachment. It is sometimes used as a pre-medication before surgery. Trade name: **Droleptan**.

dropsy *n. see* oedema.

Drosophila *n.* a genus of very small flies, commonly called fruit flies, that breed in decaying fruit and vegetables. *D. melanogaster* has been extensively used in genetic research as it has only four pairs of chromosomes and those in its salivary glands are easily recognizable. Adult *D. repleta* sometimes feed on faecal matter and may transmit disease organisms.

drug *n.* any substance that affects the structure of functioning of a living organism. Drugs are widely used for the prevention, diagnosis, and treatment of disease and for the relief of symptoms. The term *medicine* is sometimes preferred for therapeutic drugs in order to distinguish them from narcotics and other addictive drugs that are used illegally.

drug dependence *see* dependence.

dry mouth a condition that occurs as a result of reduced salivary flow because of *Sjögren's syndrome, excision of a major salivary gland, or radiotherapy to the head that destroys the salivary glands. It causes an increased incidence of dental caries and loss of denture stability in

漂泊癖 一種病態的想要旅行的強烈衝動。據說見於一些流浪者中。

氟呱科多 一種丁酰苯抗精神病藥，能產生一種情緒平靜和精神寄托的狀態。有時用作術前用藥。商品名：Droleptan。

水腫 參閱 oedema。

果蠅屬 一類很小的蠅，通常稱為果蠅。能在腐爛水果和蔬菜中繁殖。黑腹果蠅被廣泛用於遺傳學研究，因其只有四對染色體和其唾液腺裏的染色體很容易辨認。果蠅成蟲有時食取糞便物質，因而可傳播病原體。

藥物 任何能影響一個生物的結構或功能的物質。藥物被廣泛用於疾病的預防、診斷和治療以及解除症狀。medicine 一詞有時被用來指治療用藥物，以區別麻醉藥和其他非法使用的或成癮性藥物。

藥物依賴 參閱 dependence。

口乾 一種因唾液分泌減少而發生的情況。唾液分泌減少是由乾燥綜合徵、主要唾液腺被切除，或頭部放射治療破壞唾液腺所致。口乾引起齲齒發病率上升，並使缺齒人的托牙穩定性喪失。有牙齒的患者應被

people who have lost their teeth. Patients with their own teeth should be given nonacidic saliva substitutes, strict dietary advice, and chlorhexidine mouthwashes; they require special monitoring by their dentist. Medical name: **xerostomia**.

給予非酸性唾液替代物、嚴格的膳食建議和氯己定漱口液；他們需要牙醫的特殊監理。醫學用語：口腔乾燥。

dry socket a painful condition in which the normal healing of a tooth socket has been disturbed. Instead of being filled with a blood clot the socket is empty as a result of a nonspecific infection; treatment is palliative and the condition resolves in 10–14 days.

乾槽症　一種牙槽的正常修復過程受到破壞的疼痛性疾患。牙槽除由血凝塊充填外沒有其他物質，此乃非特異性感染而致。採取姑息治療，疾患在10~14天可解除。

DSM Diagnostic and Statistical Manual: an influential publication of the American Psychiatric Association in which psychiatric disorders are classified and defined. *DSM-III-R* is the current (1989) version, the revision of the third edition (1980).

診斷和統計手冊　美國精神學協會的一種極有影響力的出版物。該書對精神病進行了分類和定義。*DSM-III-R* 是最新版本 (1989)，是第三版 (1980) 的修訂本。

DTIC *n. see* dacarbazine.

達卡巴嗪　參閱 dacarbazine。

DTPA diethylenetriaminepentaacetic acid labelled with *technetium-99, used as a tracer to obtain *scintigrams of the kidney to show function and reflux.

二乙烯三胺五乙酸　以 ^{99} 鎝進行標記的二乙烯三胺五乙酸，用作示蹤劑以獲得腎臟閃爍圖以顯示其功能和回流。

Duchenne dystrophy *see* muscular dystrophy.

迪歇納肌營養不良　參閱 muscular dystrophy。

duct *n.* a tubelike structure or channel, especially one for carrying glandular secretions.

管，導管　管樣結構或管道，尤指輸送腺體分泌物的管道。

ductless gland *see* endocrine gland.

無管腺　參閱 endocrine gland。

ductule *n.* a small duct or channel.

小管　一種小導管或管道。

ductus *n.* a duct. The *ductus deferens* is the *vas deferens.

管，導管　如輸精管。

ductus arteriosus a blood vessel in the fetus connecting the pulmonary artery directly to the ascending aorta, so bypassing the pulmonary circulation. It normally closes after birth. Failure of the ductus to close (*patent ductus arteriosus*) produces a continuous *murmur, and the consequences are similar to those of a *septal defect. It may close spontaneously in childhood but often requires surgical closure.

動脈導管　胎兒期把肺動脈和升主動脈直接連通，因而使血液繞過肺循環的血管。通常，出生後即關閉。動脈導管未閉（動脈導管開放）產生持續性的雜音。其後果和房室間隔缺損的後果相同。它可在兒童期自行關閉，但常需做外科閉合手術。

Dukes staging a system devised by Sir Cuthbert Dukes that compares the extent of tumours of the colon and rectum with their cure rates. It formed the basis for many later systems of cancer staging and is still used.

杜克斯結腸和直腸腫瘤病期分類法　由庫斯伯特·杜克斯設計的一種將迴腸和直腸腫瘤的程度和其治愈率進行比較的方法。它是後來構成許多癌症分期系統的基礎，並繼續被使用。

dumbness *n. see* mutism.

啞　參閱 mutism。

Dumdum fever *see* kala-azar.

黑熱病　參閱 kala-azar。

dumping syndrome a group of symptoms that sometimes occur after operations on the stomach, particularly *gastrectomy. After a meal, especially one rich in carbohydrate, the patient feels faint and weak and may sweat and become pale. The attack lasts 30 minutes to two hours and is caused by rapid stomach emptying, leading to falls in blood sugar and the drawing of flunom the blood into the intestine. Avoidance of carbohydrate meals may relieve the syndrome but further surgery is sometimes required.

傾倒綜合徵　胃手術（特別胃切除）後有時發生的一些症狀。飯後（特別是富含碳水化合物的飲食），患者感覺虛弱無力，可出汗，臉色蒼白。發作持續 30 分鐘至 2 小時。該病是由胃內容物被迅速排空，導致血糖降低，並使血中的水分被吸入腸內。避免含碳水化合物的飲食可緩解此綜合徵，但有時需要更進一步手術治療。

duo- *prefix denoting* two.

〔前綴〕**兩，二**

duoden- (duodeno-) *prefix denoting* the duodenum, Example: *duodenectomy* (excision of).

〔前綴〕**十二指腸**　如十二指腸切除術。

duodenal ulcer an ulcer in the duodenum, caused by the action of acid and pepsin on the duodenal lining (mucosa) of a susceptible individual. It is usually associated with an increased output of stomach acid and affects people with blood group O more commonly than others. Infection of the *antrum of the stomach with *Helicobacter pylori* is always present. Symptoms include pain in the upper abdomen, especially when the stomach is empty, which often disappears completely for weeks or months; vomiting may occur. Complications include bleeding (see haematemesis), *perforation, and obstruction due to scarring (see pyloric stenosis). Symptoms are relieved by antacid medicines; most ulcers heal if treated by an *antisecretory drug, or if *H. pylori* is eradicated by a combination of a bismuth compound and antibiotics. Surgery (see gastrectomy, vagotomy) is now rarely required.

十二指腸潰瘍 十二指腸的潰瘍，是由胃酸和胃蛋白酶作用於易感者的十二指腸襯裏（黏膜）而致。通常與胃酸分泌量升高有關，侵犯 O 型血者比其他血型的人較普遍。胃竇部總是存在幽門螺桿菌的感染。症狀包括上腹疼痛，尤其是當胃排空時。疼痛常可完全消失數周或數月。可發生嘔吐。併發症包括出血（參閱 haematemesis）、穿孔和因瘢痕而發生梗阻（參閱 pyloric stenosis）。症狀通過制酸藥物而得以緩解。如果採用抗分泌藥物進行治療，或通過合用鉍化合物和抗生素消除幽門螺桿菌，多數潰瘍可痊愈。現在，很少採用外科方法（參閱 gastrectomy，vagotomy）。

duodenoscope n. a fibreoptic or video instrument for examining the interior of the duodenum. An end-viewing instrument is used for most examinations, but a side-viewing instrument is used for *ERCP. The end-viewing instrument is also used for examination of the stomach (it is also known as a *gastroduodenoscope*) and it is usual to combine the two examinations (*gastroduodenoscopy*).

十二指腸鏡 一種檢查十二指腸內部的光纖或圖像儀器。多數檢查使用前視式十二指腸鏡，但對於內窺鏡逆行至胰膽管造影術則要用側視式內窺鏡。前視式儀器也用於胃的檢查（也稱為胃十二指腸鏡）。通常要結合這兩種檢查（胃十二指腸鏡檢查）。

duodenostomy n. an operation in which the duodenum is brough through the abdominal wall and opened, usually in order to introduce food. See also gastroduodenostomy.

十二指腸造口術 十二指腸被引導穿過腹壁，並進行開口以便灌注食物的手術。參閱 gastroduodenostomy。

duodenum n. the first of the three parts of the small *intestine. It extends from the pylorus of the stomach to the jejunum. The duodenum receives bile from

十二指腸 小腸三部分的第一部分。它從胃幽門向下延伸至空腸。十二指腸接受來自膽囊的膽汁（通過膽總管）和來自

the gall bladder (via the common bile duct) and pancreatic juice from the pancreas. Its wall contains various glands (including *Brunner's glands*) that secrete an alkaline juice, rich in mucus, that protects the duodenum from the effects of the acidic *chyme passing from the stomach. **–duodenal** *adj.*

胰腺的胰液。腸壁含有各種腺體（包括布倫納腺）。這些腺體分泌一種富含黏液的鹼液，保護十二指腸不受通過胃的酸性食糜的作用。

duplex imaging a method for measuring blood flow using an ultrasound source and coupled Doppler probe (*see* Doppler technique). It is especially useful for estimating venous blood flow.

複式顯像法 採用超聲裝置和一連接的多普勒探針測量血流的方法（參閱 Doppler technique）。它尤其有助於估計靜脈血流。

Dupuytren's contracture forward curvature of one or more fingers (usually the third and/or fourth) due to fixation of the flexor tendon of the affected finger to the skin of the palm. The condition is treated by surgical *division of the fibrous bands joining tendon and skin.

迪皮特倫攣縮 一指或多指（通常為第三和/或第四指）由於其屈肌腱黏連在手掌肌肉而發生向前彎曲。這一疾病通過外科分離聯結屈肌腱和肌肉的纖維素而得以治療。

dura (dura mater, pachymeninx) *n.* the thickest and outermost of the three *meninges surrounding the brain and spinal cord. It consists of two closely adherent layers, the outer of which is identical with the periosteum of the skull. The inner dura extends downwards between the cerebral hemispheres to form the *falx cerebri* and forwards between the cerebrum and cerebellum to form the *tentorium*. A thin film of fluid (not cerebrospinal fluid) separates the inner dura from the arachnoid.

硬（腦脊）膜 包繞腦和脊髓的三層腦脊膜中最厚和最外面的一層。它由兩層相互緊密黏連組成，外層就是顱骨的骨膜。內層在兩大腦半球之間下延形成大腦鐮，在大腦和小腦之間向前延伸形成小腦幕。一薄層液體（不是腦脊液）將硬膜內層和蛛網膜分隔開來。

dural *adj.* of, relating to, or affecting the *dura.

硬（腦脊）膜的 與硬膜相關的或影響硬膜的。

dwarfism *n.* abnormally short stature from any cause. The most common type of dwarf is the *achondroplastic dwarf* (*see* achondroplasia). *Pituitary dwarfs* have a deficiency of *growth hormone

侏儒症 因任何原因所致異常矮小身材的現象，最常見的類型是軟骨發育不全性侏儒（參閱 achondroplasia）。垂體性侏儒係垂體缺陷而致生長激素缺

due to a defect in the pituitary gland; they are well proportioned and show no mental retardation, but may be sexually underdeveloped. *Primordial dwarfs* have a genetic defect in their response to growth hormone. Dwarfism is also associated with thyroid deficiency (*see* cretinism), in which both physical and mental development is retarded; chronic diseases such as rickets; renal failure; and intestinal malabsorption.

乏所致。這種侏儒身材各部勻稱，無智力發育停滯，但可有性發育不良。先天性侏儒症是與生長激素有關的基因缺陷所致。侏儒症也與甲狀腺功能低下並存（參閱 cretinism）。此時體格和智力發育均停滯。還和諸如佝僂症、腎功能衰竭和腸吸收障礙等慢性疾病共存。

dydrogesterone *n.* a synthetic female sex hormone (*see* progestogen) used to treat menstrual abnormalities (such as dysmenorrhoea) and infertility and to prevent miscarriage. It is administered by mouth and may cause mild nausea and break through bleeding. Trade name: **Duphaston**.

地屈孕酮　一種合成的雌性激素（參閱 progestogen），用於治療月經失調（如痛經）和不孕，預防流產。口服，可引起輕度惡心和突發性出血。商品名：Duphaston。

dynamometer *n.* a device for recording the force of a muscular contraction. A small hand-held dynamometer may be used to record the strength of a patient's grip. A special optical dynamometer measures the action of the muscles controlling the shape of the lens of the eye.

肌力計　記錄肌肉收縮力量的裝置。一種小型手握式肌力計可測定患者的握力。一種特殊的光學肌力計可測量控制眼晶狀體形狀的肌肉活動。

dyne *n.* a unit of force equal to the force required to impart to a mass of 1 gram an acceleration of 1 centimetre per second per second. 1 dyne = 10^{-5} newton.

達因　力的單位，等於 1 克質量獲得1厘米／秒^{2}的加速度所需的力。1 達因等於 10^{-5} 牛頓。

-dynia *suffix denoting* pain. Example: *proctodynia* (in the rectum).

〔後綴〕痛　如（直腸內）肛部痛。

dys- *prefix denoting* difficult, abnormal, or impaired. Examples: *dysbasia* (difficulty in walking); *dysgeusia* (impairment of taste).

〔前綴〕困難，異常，障礙　如步行困難，味覺障礙。

dysaesthesiae *pl. n.* the abnormal and sometimes unpleasant sensations felt by

感覺異常　感覺神經纖維部分受損的患者在其皮膚被觸及時

a patient with partial damage to sensory nerve fibres when his skin is touched. *Compare* paraesthesiae.

感受到的異常和不舒服的感覺，與 paraesthesiae 對比。

dysarthria *n.* a speech disorder in which the pronunciation is unclear although the linguistic content and meaning are normal.

發音障礙 一種語言障礙。發音不清，但語言內容和意義卻是正常的。

dysbarism *n.* any clinical syndrome due to a difference between the atmospheric pressure outside the body and the pressure of air or gas within a body cavity (such as the paranasal sinuses or the middle ear). *See* compressed air illness.

氣壓病 任何由於體外的大氣壓和體腔內（如鼻旁竇或中耳）氣體壓力的差異而產生的臨床綜合徵。參閱 compressed air illness。

dysbulia *n.* any disturbance of the will or of the mental processes that lead to purposeful action.

意志障礙 一切意志或導致有目的行動的心理過程的障礙。

dyschezia *n.* a form of constipation resulting from a long period of voluntary suppression of the urge to defecate. The rectum becomes distended with faeces and bowel movements are difficult or painful.

大便困難 因長期有意識壓抑便意而造成的便秘類型。直腸因糞便而變得膨脹，排便困難或有疼痛。

dyschondroplasia *n.* a condition due to faulty ossification of cartilage, resulting in development of many benign cartilaginous tumours (*see* chondroma). The bones involved may become stunted and deformed.

軟骨發育不良 由於軟骨鈣化異常導致產生許多良性軟骨腫瘤（參閱 chondroma）的疾病。受累骨可發生生長受阻，並變形。

dyscrasia *n.* an abnormal state of the body or part of the body, especially one due to abnormal development or metabolism. In classical medicine the term was used for the imbalance of the four *humours, which was believed to be the basic cause of all diseases.

體液失調 因異常發育或代謝所致身體或部分身體的異常狀態。在古典醫學中，這一術語用於指四種體液失去平衡。當時認為這是所有疾病的最根本原因。

dysdiadochokinesis (**adiadochokinesis**) *n.* clumsiness in performing

輪替運動障礙 快速變換動作不靈活。常通過讓患者用手指

rapidly alternating movements. It is often recognized by asking the patient to tap with his fingers on the back of his other hand. It is a sign of disease of the cerebellum.

dysentery *n.* an infection of the intestinal tract causing severe diarrhoea with blood and mucus. *Amoebic dysentery* (*amoebiasis*) is caused by the protozoan *Entamoeba histolytica* and results in ulceration of the intestines and occasionally in the formation of abscesses in the liver (*see* hepatitis), lungs, testes, or brain. The parasite is spread by food or water contaminated by infected faeces. Symptoms appear days or even years after infection and include diarrhoea, indigestion, loss of weight, and anaemia. Prolonged treatment with drugs, including metronidazole and tetracyclines, is usually effective in treating the condition. Amoebic dysentery is mainly confined to tropical and subtropical countries.

Bacillary dysentery is caused by bacteria of the genus *Shigella* and is spread by contact with a patient or carrier or through food or water contaminated by their faeces. Epidemics are common in overcrowded insanitary conditions. Symptoms, which develop 1–6 days after infection, include diarrhoea, nausea, cramp, and fever and they persist for about a week. An attack may vary from mild diarrhoea to an acute infection causing serious dehydration and bleeding from the gut. In most cases, provided fluid losses are replaced, recovery occurs within 7–10 days; antibiotics may be given to eliminate the bacteria. *Compare* cholera.

dysgenesis *n.* faulty development; *gonadal dysgenesis* is failure of the

輕叩另一手背來判斷。它是小腦疾病的一個症狀。

痢疾　引起嚴重腹瀉（便中帶有血和黏液）的腸道感染。阿米巴痢疾（阿米巴病）是由溶組織內阿米巴引起並導致腸潰瘍形成和偶爾在肝臟（參閱hepatitis）、肺臟、睾丸或腦內有膿腫的形成。寄生蟲通過被感染的糞便污染食物或水進行傳播。在感染後，症狀可於數天或數年後出現，包括腹瀉、消化不良、體重減輕和貧血。長期使用藥物治療（包括甲硝達唑和四環素）通常能有效地治療該症。阿米巴痢疾主要局限於熱帶和亞熱帶國家。

　　細菌性痢疾是由志賀桿菌屬細菌引起的，可通過患者或細菌攜帶者或通過被其糞便污染的食物或水進行傳播。在居民密集不衛生的環境裏，痢疾流行較為常見。症狀在感染 1~6 天後出現，包括腹瀉、惡心、腹絞痛和發熱，並持續一周。發作可表現出多種形式：從輕度腹瀉到引起嚴重脫水和腸出血的急性感染。在多數情況下，如果液體丟失被補充的話，可在 7~10 天恢復。可給予抗生素以殺滅細菌。與 cholera 對比。

發育不全　發育缺陷。生殖發育障礙是卵巢或睾丸發

ovaries or testes to develop (*see* Turner's syndrome).

dysgerminoma (germinoma, gonocytoma) *n.* a malignant tumour of the ovary, thought to arise from primitive germ cells; it is homologous to the *seminoma of the testis. About 15% of such tumours affect both ovaries; outside the ovary they have been recorded in the anterior mediastinum and in the pineal gland. Dysgerminomas may occur from infancy to old age, but the average age of patients is about 20 years. They are very sensitive to *radiotherapy. Dysgerminomas are also known as *large cell carcinomas* or *alveolar sarcomas of the ovary*.

dysgraphia *n. see* agraphia.

dyskariosis *n.* the abnormal condition of a cell that has a nucleus showing the features characteristic of the earliest stage of malignancy, while retaining relatively normal cytoplasm. It may be seen, for example, in the squamous and columnar epithelial cells of a *cervical smear.

dyskinesia *n.* a group of involuntary movements that appear to be a fragmentation of the normal smoothly controlled limb and facial movements. They include *chorea, *dystonia, and those involuntary movements occurring as side-effects to the use of levodopa and the phenothiazines.

dyslalia *n.* a speech disorder in which the patient uses a vocabulary or range of sounds that is peculiar to him. It is a feature of the defective speech acquired by children who have been aphasic from birth (*see* aphasia).

dyslexia *n.* a developmental disorder selectively affecting a child's ability to

育不全（參閱 Turner's syndrome）。

無性細胞瘤（生殖母細胞瘤） 卵巢的一種惡性腫瘤，被認為源自原始生殖細胞。該瘤和睾丸的精原細胞瘤同源。15% 的此種腫瘤侵襲兩側卵巢。在卵巢之外，有在前縱隔和松果體附近發生該腫瘤的病例報告。無性細胞瘤可發生於從嬰兒到老年所有人羣。但患者的平均年齡為 20 歲。它們對放射治療很敏感。無性細胞瘤也被稱為卵巢大細胞癌或卵巢蜂窩狀肉瘤。

書寫困難 參閱 agraphia。

核異常 細胞的異常狀態，細胞核表現出典型的惡性早期特徵但同時保持相對正常的細胞質。例如，它可見於宮頸塗片的鱗狀和柱狀上皮細胞裏。

運動障礙 一組不隨意運動，表現為正常平穩控制的肢體和面部運動變得支離散亂。此類障礙包括舞蹈症、張力障礙以及使用左旋多巴和吩噻嗪而出現的不隨意運動副作用。

出語障礙 一種言語障礙，患者運用其特有的詞匯或音域說話。這是患先天性失語症的兒童所具有的言語缺陷的一個特徵。參閱 aphasia。

誦讀困難 一種選擇性地影響兒童學習閱讀和書寫能力的發

learn to read and write. It is an uncommon condition, affecting boys more often than girls, and can create serious educational problems. Always apparent by the age of seven (or, in severe cases, earlier), it is sometimes called *specific dyslexia*, *developmental reading disorder*, or *developmental word blindness* to distinguish it from acquired difficulties with reading and writing. *Compare* alexia. **–dyslexic** *adj.*

育障礙。這是一種不常見疾患，患兒中男孩多於女孩，可造成嚴重教育問題。一般在 7 歲時就表現出來（嚴重病例更早些）。有時稱為特異性誦讀困難、發育性誦讀障礙或發育性詞盲，以與後天讀寫困難相區別。與 alexia 對比。

dyslogia *n.* disturbed and incoherent speech. This may be due to *dementia, *aphasia, *mental retardation, or mental illness.

難語症 言語支離破碎，不連貫。這可能由於癡呆、失語症、智力低下或精神疾病所致。

dysmenorrhoea *n.* painful menstruation, of which there are two main forms. *Primary* (*spasmodic*) *dysmenorrhoea* usually begins with the first period and is heralded by cramping lower abdominal pains starting just before or with the menstrual flow and continuing during menstruation. Is it often associated with nausea, vomiting, headache, faintness, and symptoms of peripheral vasodilatation. The cause is thought to be related to excessive *prostaglandin production. *Secondary* (*congestive*) *dysmenorrhoea* usually affects older women who complain of a congested ache with lower abdominal cramps, which usually start from a few days to two weeks before menstruation. Causes include *pelvic inflammatory disease, *endometriosis, fibroids, and the presence of an IUCD.

痛經 月經疼痛。主要有兩種類型。原發性（痙攣性）痛經始於月經初潮，出現下腹部痙攣性疼痛。該疼痛始於月經前或月經期間，並且持續整個月經期間。常伴發惡心、嘔吐、頭痛、暈厥和周圍血管舒張症狀。一般認為病因與過多的前列腺素分泌有關。繼發性（充血性）痛經通常發生於年齡較大的婦女，她們主訴充血性疼痛，伴有下腹部絞痛。通常始於月經前數天到兩周。病因包括骨盆炎性疾病、子宮內膜異位，纖維瘤和宮內避孕器等。

dysmnesic syndrome a disorder of memory in which new information is not learned but old material is well remembered. *See* Korsakoff's syndrome.

記憶綜合徵 對新鮮信息記不住而對往事卻記憶清楚的記憶障礙。參閱 Korsakoff's syndrome。

dysmorphophobia *n.* a fixed distressing belief that one's body is deformed and

畸形恐懼 一種頑固的令其不安的信念，認為其軀體是畸形

repulsive, or an excessive fear that it might become so.

dysostosis *n.* the abnormal formation of bone or the formation of bone in abnormal places, such as a replacement of cartilage by bone.

dyspareunia *n.* painful or difficult sexual intercourse experienced by a woman. Psychological or physical factors may be responsible (*see* vaginismus).

dyspepsia (indigestion) *n.* disordered digestion: usually applied to pain or discomfort in the lower chest or abdomen after eating and sometimes accompanied by nausea or vomiting. **–dyspeptic** *adj.*

dysphagia *n.* a condition in which the action of swallowing is either difficult to perform, painful (*see* odynophagia), or in which swallowed material seems to be held up in its passage to the stomach. It is caused by painful conditions of the mouth and throat, obstruction of the pharynx or oesophagus by diseases of the wall or pressure from outside, or by abnormalities of muscular activity of the pharynx or oesophagus.

dysphasia *n. see* aphasia.

dysphemia *n. see* stammering.

dysphonia *n.* difficulty in voice production. This may be due to a disorder of the larynx, pharynx, tongue, or mouth, or it may be *psychogenic. *Compare* dysarthria, aphasia.

dysplasia (alloplasia, heteroplasia) *n.* abnormal development of skin, bone, or other tissues. *See also* fibrous dysplasia. **–dysplastic** *adj.*

和令人厭惡的，或者是一種認為其軀體會變成這種情況的極度恐懼。

骨發育不全　骨形成異常，或在異位形成的骨，如骨代替軟骨。

性交困難　婦女體驗的痛性性交或性交困難。精神或軀體因素可能是此種情況的原因（參閱 vaginismus）。

消化不良　障礙性消化：通常指飯後下胸部或腹部疼痛或不適，有時可伴有惡心或嘔吐。

吞咽困難　吞咽動作難以進行或引起疼痛（參閱 odynophagia），或感覺被吞咽的東西似乎停滯在通向胃的中途的一種疾患。是因口腔和喉部疼痛性病症、咽或食管阻塞（管壁病變或外來壓迫所致，或由於咽或食管肌活動異常所致）等原因所致。

言語困難　參閱 aphasia。

口吃　參閱 stammering。

發音困難　發音困難。這可能是由於喉、咽、舌或口腔疾病所致，或者是精神性原因所致。與 dysarthria，aphasia 對比。

發育不良（發育異常，再生異常）　皮膚、骨或其他組織的異常發育。參閱 fibrous dysplasia。

dyspnoea *n.* laboured or difficult breathing. (The term is often used for a sign of laboured breathing apparent to the doctor, *breathlessness* being used for the subjective feeling of laboured breathing). Dyspnoea can be due to obstruction to the flow of air into and out of the lungs (as in bronchitis and asthma), various diseases affecting the tissue of the lung (including pneumoconiosis, emphysema, tuberculosis, and cancer), and heart disease.

呼吸困難　費力的或困難的呼吸（本詞常用以指醫生所能觀察到的費力呼吸體徵，而氣短則被用以指費力呼吸的主觀感覺）。呼吸困難可因以下原因所致：進出肺的氣流受阻（如支氣管炎和哮喘），肺臟組織的各種疾病（包括塵肺、肺氣腫、肺結核和癌症）和心臟疾病。

dyspraxia *n. see* apraxia.

運用障礙　參閱 apraxia。

dyssocial *adj.* describing a personality disorder characterized by callous unconcern for others, irresponsibility, violence, disregard for social rules, and an incapacity to maintain enduring relationships.

孤僻的　描述一種人格障礙，特別為對他人無感情、不關心、不負責任、粗暴、不遵守社會法則，且沒有能力保持持久關係。

dyssynergia (asynergia) *n.* lack of co-ordination, especially clumsily uncoordinated movements found in patients with disease of the cerebellum. They include *dysmetria* (the application of inappropriate force for a movement), intention *tremor, *dysdiadochokinesis, and a staggering wide-based gait.

共濟失調（協同不能）　缺乏協調，尤指見於患小腦疾病患者的笨拙的不協調的運動。它們包括辨距障礙（做一動作時用力不當）、意向震顫、輪替運動障礙和兩腿分開的蹣跚步態。

dysthymic disorder *see* depression, neurosis.

精神抑鬱性障礙　參閱 depression，neurosis。

dystocia *n.* difficult birth, caused by abnormalities in the fetus or the mother. The most common causes of *fetal dystocia* are excessive size or *malpresentation of the baby. *Maternal dystocia* may result if the pelvis is abnormally small, the uterine muscles fail to contract, or the neck of the uterus fails to expand. If the cause of dystocia cannot be eliminated, it may be necessary to deliver the

難產　因胎兒或母親異常所致分娩困難。最常見的胎兒性難產的原因是胎兒過大或胎先露異常。母親性難產可發生於骨盆異常的小，子宮肌肉不收縮，或子宮頸不擴張。如果難產原因不能被消除，可能需做剖宮產術，或採用對母親危險性最小的手術來分娩胎兒。

baby by Caesarean section or to operate in such a way that it can be removed with the minimum possible risk to the mother.

dystonia *n.* a postural disorder caused by disease of the *basal ganglia in the brain. There may be spasm in the muscles of the shoulders, neck, trunk, and limbs. The arm is often held in a rotated position and the head is drawn back and to one side. Dystonic conditions, including *blepharospasm, may be helped by the injection of *botulinum toxin. **–dystonic** *adj.*

張力障礙　一種因大腦基底神經節病變引起的姿態障礙。可表現為肩、頸、軀幹和四肢的肌肉痙攣。上臂常保持一種轉動姿勢，頭被拉向一側，並向後。張力性疾病（包括眼瞼痙攣）可通過注射肉桿菌毒素得以治療。

dystrophia myotonica (myotonic dystrophy) a type of *muscular dystrophy in which the muscle weakness and wasting is accompanied by an unnatural prolongation of the muscular contraction after any voluntary effort (*see* myotonia). The muscles of the face, temples, and neck are especially wasted. Baldness, endocrine malfunction, and cataracts also occur. The disease can affect both sexes (it is inherited as an autosomal *dominant character).

肌強直性營養不良　一種肌營養不良，肌肉無力和消瘦，並在有意識用力之後，則伴有肌肉收縮非自然性時間延長（參閱 myotonia）。面部、兩顳和頸部肌肉尤其消瘦。脫髮、內分泌功能失調和內障也可發生。該病男女都可罹患（作為常染色體顯性特點而遺傳）。

dystrophy (dystrophia) *n.* a disorder of an organ or tissue, usually muscle, due to impaired nourishment of the affected part. The term is applied to several unrelated conditions; for example, *muscular dystrophy and *dystrophia adiposogenitalis* (*see* Fröhlich's syndrome).

營養不良症　因患病部位營養障礙而致的一器官或組織（通常為肌肉）的病變。本術語適用於幾種互不相關的疾病，如肌肉營養不良症和肥胖性生殖營養不良（參閱 Fröhlich's syndrome）。

dysuria *n.* difficult or painful urination. This is usually associated with urgency and frequency of urination if due to *cystitis or *urethritis. The pain is burning in nature and is relieved by curing the underlying cause. A high fluid intake usually helps.

排尿困難　排尿困難或痛性排尿。在膀胱炎或尿道炎時常與尿急和尿頻同時存在。疼痛為灼燒性質，通過治療根本原因而得以解除。大量進水通常奏效。

E

ear *n.* the sense organ concerned with hearing and balance (see illustration). Sound waves, transmitted from the outside into the external auditory meatus, cause the eardrum (tympanic membrane) to vibrate. The small bones (ossicles) of the middle ear – the malleus, incus, and stapes – transmit the sound vibrations to the fenestra ovalis, which leads to the inner ear (*see* labyrinth). Inside the *cochlea the sound vibrations are converted into nerve impulses. Vibrations emerging from the cochlea could cause pressure to build up inside the ear, but this is released through the *Eustachian tube. The *semicircular canals, *saccule, and *utricle – also in the inner ear – are all concerned with balance.

earache *n. see* otitis, otalgia.

耳 主司聽力和平衡的感覺器官（見圖）。從外界傳入外耳道的聲波引起鼓膜振動。中耳小骨（聽骨）——錘骨、砧骨和鐙骨——將聲波振動傳入前庭窗，再由此傳入內耳（參閱 labyrinth）。在耳蝸內，聲波振動轉化成神經衝動。來自耳蝸的振動可引起壓力在耳內逐漸增大，但可通過咽內管被解除。內耳中的半規管、球囊和橢圓囊都涉及平衡。

耳痛 參閱 otitis，otalgia。

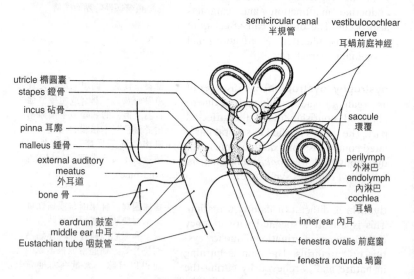

Structure of the ear
耳的結構

eardrum *n. see* tympanic membrane.

鼓膜　參閱　tympanic membrane。

earwax *n. see* cerumen.

耳垢　參閱　cerumen。

eburnation *n.* the wearing down of the cartilage at the articulating surface of a bone, exposing the underlying bone. This is an end result of *osteoarthritis.

骨質致密化　骨關節面的軟骨磨損，使位於下面的骨暴露。這是骨關節炎的最終結果。

ec- *prefix denoting* out of or outside.

〔前綴〕外，在外

ecbolic *n.* an agent, such as *oxytocin, that induces childbirth by stimulating contractions of the uterus.

催產劑　一種藥，如縮宮素。能通過刺激子宮收縮來誘使胎兒娩出。

ecchondroma *n.* (*pl.* **ecchondromata**) a benign cartilaginous tumour (*see* chondroma) that protrudes beyond the margins of a bone. *Compare* enchondroma.

外生軟骨瘤　一種突出骨緣的良性軟骨腫瘤（參閱 chondroma）。與 enchondroma 對比。

ecchymosis *n.* a bruise: an initially bluish-black mark on the skin, resulting from the release of blood into the tissues either through injury or through the spontaneous leaking of blood from the vessels (as in some blood diseases).

瘀斑　一種挫傷。皮膚上最初出現的藍黑色斑迹，因外傷而使血液進入組織所致，或因血液從血管自然滲出而使血液進入組織所致（如在一些血液病中）。

eccrine *adj.* **1.** describing sweat glands that are distributed all over the body. Their ducts open directly onto the surface of the skin and they are densest on the soles of the feet and the palms of the hands. *Compare* apocrine. **2.** *see* merocrine.

(1) 外分泌的　描述遍布全身的汗腺。它們的導管直接開口於皮膚表面，且在足底和手掌最為密集。與 apocrine 對比。(2) 部分分泌的　參閱 merocrine。

ecdemic *adj.* not occurring normally in the population of a country: applied sometimes to unusual diseases brought in from abroad by immigrants or travellers. *Compare* endemic.

外來的　不常見的發生於某一國家人口之中的。有時用以指由移民或旅遊者由海外帶進的不常見疾病。與 endemic 對比。

ecdysis *n.* the act of shedding skin; *desquamation.

蛻皮　皮膚蛻落的表現；脫皮。

ECG *n. see* electrocardiogram.

echinococciasis (echinococcosis) *n. see* hydatid disease.

棘球蚴病　參閱　hydatid disease。

Echinococcus *n.* a genus of small parasitic tapeworms that reach a maximum length of only 8mm. Adults are found in the intestines of dogs, wolves, or jackals. If the eggs are swallowed by man, who can act as a secondary host, the resulting larvae penetrate the intestine and settle in the lungs, liver, or brain to form large cysts, usually 5–10cm in diameter (*see* hydatid disease). Two species causing this condition are *E. granulosus* and *E. multilocularis.*

棘球屬　一類最長可達8mm 的小型寄生縧蟲。成蟲可見 於狗、狼、豺的腸道。如其 卵被人吞入，則人就成為第 二宿主，長成的幼蟲則可穿 腸壁而在肺、肝臟或腦定居， 從而形成大的囊腫，直徑通 常為5~10cm（參閱 hydatid disease）。引起這一病症的兩 類是細粒棘球縧蟲和多房棘球 縧蟲。

echoacousia *n.* a false sensation of echoing after normally heard sound owing to a defect of the cochlea in the inner ear.

回聲感覺　在聽到正常聲音後 又聽到一種回聲的錯覺，其原 因為內耳耳蝸的缺陷。

echocardiography *n.* the use of *ultrasound waves to investigate and display the action of the heart as it beats. Used in the diagnosis and assessment of congenital and acquired heart diseases, it is safe, painless, and reliable and reduces the need for cardiac *catheterization. *M-mode echocardiography* uses a single beam of ultrasound. The image produced is not anatomical but permits precise measurement of cardiac dimensions and the diagnosis of valvular, myocardial, and pericardial disease, *Cross-section echocardiography* (*two-dimensional* or *real-time echocardiography*) uses multiple ultrasound beams to produce tomographic images (*see* tomography) that are clearly recognizable as cardiac structure. In *Doppler echocardiography* ultrasound reflected from moving red blood cells is subject to the Doppler effect

超聲心動描記法　在心臟跳動 時，用超聲波來研究並展示心 臟活動的方法。該方法用於先 天性和後天性心臟疾病的診斷 和評估。這一方法安全、無 痛、可靠、並且減少了向心臟 插入導管的必要性。M-型超聲 心動描記法採用單一超聲波。 所產生之圖像不具備解剖特 點，但能進行心臟周邊的準確 測量，以及診斷瓣膜、心肌和 心包疾病。橫斷面超聲心動描 記法（平面或實時超聲心動描 記法）採用多種超聲波，可產 生心臟結構容易辨認的X綫體 層圖像（參閱 tomography）。 在多普勒超聲心動描記法中， 從流動的紅細胞反射來的超聲 波受多普勒效應的支配（即隨 着觀察者的快慢程度，音頻也 隨着變化）。這可以用來計算

(change of pitch with velocity relative to the observer), which can be used to calculate blood flow and pressure within the heart and great vessels. It is useful in the diagnosis and assessment of valve disease and intracardial shunts.

心臟和大血管內的血流和壓力。它有助於診斷和評估瓣膜疾病和心內分流術。

echoencephalography *n*. investigation of structures within the skull by detecting the echoes of ultrasonic pulses. The chief value of the method was in detecting those disorders causing a displacement of the midline structures of the brain. The technique has largely been superseded by *computerized tomography (CT) and *magnetic resonance imaging (MRI).

腦超聲波檢查法　通過檢測超聲脈衝的回波來檢查顱內結構的方法。此方法的主要價值在於檢測那些引起大腦中綫結構移位的疾病。這一技術在很大程度上已被電子計算機斷層照相術和磁共振成像術所代替。

echography *n*. the technique of using *ultrasound waves to map out and study the internal structure of the body. Ultrasound waves are reflected to different degrees by different structures within the body. The visual recording of these reflected waves is called an *echogram*. *See also* echocardiography, echoencephalography, ultrasonography.

超聲波描記術　採用超聲波來給出和檢查身體的內部結構的技術。身體內不同結構對超聲波的反射程度各不相同。這些反射的超聲波的圖像描記被稱為回波圖。參閱 echocardiography，echoencephalography，ultrasonography。

echokinesis *n*. *see* echopraxia.

模仿運動　參閱 echopraxia。

echolalia *n*. pathological repetition of the words spoken by another person. It may be a symptom of language disorders, *autism, *catatonia, or *Gilles de la Tourette syndrome.

模仿語言　病理性地重複他人所説的話，它可能是語言障礙、孤獨僻、緊張症或圖雷特底綜合徵的一種症狀。

echo planar imaging (EPI) an imaging technique, based on *nuclear magnetic resonance (NMR), that provides a real-time snapshot with, apparently, the same image quality as NMR. This method, which is still in the early stages of development, may provide new insights into fetal pathology.

回波平面成像技術　採用核磁共振 (NMR)，能夠產生表面上與核磁共振一樣成像質量的實時快照的成像技術。這一技術仍處於發展階段，可為胎兒病理學提供新的突破。

echopraxia (echokinesis) *n.* pathological imitation of the actions of another person. It may be a symptom of *catatonia or of *latah.

模仿行動　病理性的模仿他人行動的現象。它可能是緊張症或拉塔病的一個症狀。

echotomography *n. see* ultrasonotomography.

超聲波斷層描記法　參閱 ultrasonotomography。

echovirus *n.* one of a group of about 30 RNA-containing viruses, originally isolated from the human intestinal tract, that were found to produce pathological changes in cells grown in culture, although they were not clearly associated with any specific disease. These viruses – which were accordingly termed *e*nteric *c*ytopathic *h*uman *o*rphan viruses – are now more commonly known as *Coxsackie viruses. *Compare* reovirus.

埃可病毒　一組約 30 種含有 RNA 的病毒，最早從人體腸道中分離出來，能使培養基中的細胞產生病理變化，但它們是否與任何特異性疾病有關，還不清楚。這些病毒原來被相應地稱作「腸道細胞病變人類孤兒病毒」，現在則更多稱為柯薩奇病毒。與 reovirus 對比。

eclabium *n.* the turning outward of a lip.

唇外翻　唇向外翻。

eclampsia *n.* the occurrence of one or more convulsions not caused by other conditions, such as epilepsy or cerebral haemorrhage, in a woman with *pre-eclampsia. The onset of convulsions may be preceded by a sudden rise in blood pressure and/or a sudden increase in *oedema and development of *oliguria. The convulsions are usually followed by coma. Eclampsis is a threat to both mother and baby and must be treated immediately.

子癇　在先兆子癇婦女中發生的一次或多次驚厥狀態。這些驚厥並非因其他疾病所致，如癲癇或腦出血。驚厥發作前可有血壓突然上升和／或水腫增多，產生少尿症狀。驚厥之後即發生昏迷。子癇對母親和胎兒都有威脅，應予以及時治療。

ecology (bionomics) *n.* the study of the relationships between man, plants and animals, and the environment, including the way in which human activities may affect other animal populations and alter natural surroundings. **–ecological** *adj.* **–ecologist** *n.*

生態學　研究人、植物和動物以及環境關係的科學，也包括人類活動可能影響其他動物羣體並改變自然環境的方法。

econazole *n.* an antifungal drug used to treat ringworm and candidosis. It is

益康唑　一種抗真菌藥物，用於治療癬菌病和念珠病。用

administered as a cream, lotion, spray powder, or vaginal pessary. Possible side-effects may include local irritation and burning. Trade names: **Ecostatin**, **Pevaryl**.

做膏劑、塗搽劑、噴粉劑或陰道栓劑。商品名：Ecostatin，Pevaryl。

ecraseur *n.* a surgical device, resembling a *snare, that is used to sever the base of a tumour during its surgical removal.

絞勒器 一種類似勒除器的外科器械。用於外科切除術時除去腫瘤根底。

ecstasy *n.* a sense of extreme wellbeing and bliss. The word applies particularly to *trance states dominated by religious thinking. While not necessarily pathological, it can be caused by epilepsy (especially of the temporal lobe) or by schizophrenia.

入迷 一種極度幸福和喜悅的感覺。該術語尤指因被宗教思想所支配的迷惘狀態。它不一定是病理性的，但是，它可由癲癇（尤其是顳葉病變引起的）或精神分裂症所引起。

ECT *see* electroconvulsive therapy.

電驚厥療法 參閱 electroconvulsive therapy。

ect- (ecto-) *prefix denoting* outer or external.

〔前綴〕外，外部，外面

ectasia (ectasis) *n.* the dilatation of a tube, duct, or hollow organ.

擴張 管、道或中空臟器的膨脹。

ecthyma *n.* an infection of the skin, usually caused by *Staphylococcus aureus*, in which the full thickness of the epidermis is involved (*compare* impetigo, which is a superficial infection). Ecthyma heals more slowly than impetigo and causes scarring.

深膿疱 通常由金黃色葡萄球菌引起的一種皮膚感染。表皮完全變厚（參閱 impetigo：一種表面感染）。深膿腫比膿疱病痊愈更為緩慢，且致瘢痕。

ectoderm *n.* the outer of the three *germ layers of the early embryo. It gives rise to the nervous system and sense organs, the teeth and lining of the mouth, and to the *epidermis and its associated structures (hair, nails, etc.). **—ectodermal** *adj.*

外胚層 早期胚胎三胚層的外層，由此產生神經系統和感覺器官、牙齒和口腔黏膜、表皮層及其相關結構（頭髮、指甲等）。

ectomorphic *adj.* describing a *body type that is relatively thin, with a large skin surface in comparison to weight. **—ectomorph** *n.* **—ectomorphy** *n.*

外胚層體型的 描述一種身材類型。比較瘦，與體重相比有一大的皮膚表面。

-ectomy *suffix denoting* surgical removal of a segment or all of an organ or part. Examples: *appendicectomy* (of the appendix); *prostatectomy* (of the prostate gland).

〔後綴〕**切除術**　外科切除一器官或部位的一段或全部。如闌尾切除術，前列腺切除術。

ectoparasite *n.* a parasite that lives on the outer surface of its host. Some ectoparasites, such as bed bugs, maintain only periodic contact with their hosts, whereas others, such as the crab louse, have a permanent association. *Compare* endoparasite.

外寄生物　一種寄生於其宿主外表層的寄生蟲。一些外寄生物（如臭蟲）僅與宿主保持一段時期的接觸，但是，其他外寄生物（如陰虱）卻與宿主有一永久接觸的關係。與 endoparasite 對比。

ectopia *n.* **1.** the misplacement, due either to a congenital defect or injury, of a bodily part. **2.** the occurrence of something in an unnatural location (*see also* ectopic beat, ectopic pregnancy). **–ectopic** *adj.*

異位　**(1)** 身體某部位因先天性缺陷或損傷而產生的錯位。**(2)** 某事物發生於不正常的部位（參閱 ectopic beat，ectopic pregnancy）。

ectopic beat (extrasystole) a heartbeat due to an impulse generated somewhere in the heart outside the sinoatrial node. Ectopic beats are generally premature in timing; they are classified as *supraventricular* if they originate in the atria and *ventricular* if they arise from a focus in the ventricles. They may be produced by any heart disease, by nicotine from smoking, or by caffeine from excessive tea or coffee consumption; they are common in normal individuals. The patient may be unaware of their presence or may feel that his heart has 'missed a beat'. Ectopic beats may be suppressed by drugs such as quinidine, propranolol, and lignocaine; avoidance of smoking and reduction in excessive tea or coffee intake may help. *See* arrhythmia.

異位搏動（期外收縮）　因心臟竇房結以外的部位發出的衝動所致的心臟跳動。異位搏動通常是期前收縮。它們分為兩種：室上性異位搏動（如果衝動來自心房）和室性異位搏動（如果衝動源自心室）。它們可能由任何心臟疾病、吸煙中的尼古丁或由過量飲用茶或咖啡中的咖啡因等原因所致，在正常個體，此種情況也可見到。患者可能意識不到異位搏動的出現，或感覺到他的心臟有「漏搏」，異位搏動可用諸如奎尼丁、普萘洛爾和利多卡因等藥物抑制。避免吸煙和減少過量飲茶和咖啡有助於緩解。參閱 arrhythmia。

ectopic hormone a hormone produced by cells that do not usually produce it. Some tumour cells secrete hormones; for example, lung cancer cells secrete vasopressin.

異位激素　通常不產生該激素的細胞所產生的一種激素。一些癌細胞分泌激素。如肺癌細胞分泌加壓素。

ectopic pregnancy (extrauterine pregnancy) the development of a fetus at a site other than in the uterus. This may happen if the fertilized egg cell remains in the ovary or in the tube lending from near the ovary to the uterus (the Fallopian tube) or if it lodges in the free abdominal cavity. The most common type of ectopic pregnancy is *atubal* (or *oviducal*) *pregnancy*, which occurs in Fallopian tubes that become blocked or inflamed. The growth of the fetus may cause the tube to rupture and bleed. In many cases the fetus dies within three months of conception and the products are absorbed into the maternal circulation. Rarely, the pregnancy may continue until a live baby can be delivered by Caesarean section. The condition may be diagnosed by ultrasound and the products of conception may be removed by laparoscopy before damage is done to the Fallopian tube.

異位妊娠（宮外孕）胎兒的發育不在子宮內。如果受精卵細胞滯留在卵巢，或從卵巢附近通向子宮的管內（輸卵管），或停留於腹腔，異位妊娠就可發生。最常見的異位妊娠為輸卵管妊娠，即妊娠發生於輸卵管，輸卵管發生堵塞或炎症。胎兒的生長可引起輸卵管破裂和出血。在許多情況下，胎兒在妊娠三個月之內就死亡，死亡殘留物被吸收至母體循環內。但有時妊娠繼續，直至通過剖宮產取出活嬰。此種疾病可通過超聲診斷，且受孕產物可在輸卵管損害前通過腹腔鏡取出。

ectoplasm *n.* the outer layer of cytoplasm in cells, which is denser than the inner cytoplasm (*endoplasm) and concerned with activities such as cell movement. **–ectoplasmic** *adj.*

外（胞）質（漿）細胞質的外層，比內細胞質（細胞內質）要稠密，並與活動（如細胞運動）有關。

ectro- *prefix denoting* congenital absence.

〔前綴〕先天性缺失

ectrodactyly *n.* congenital absence of all or part of one or more fingers.

缺指　一個或多個手指的全部或部分先天性缺失。

ectromelia *n.* congenital absence or gross shortening (aplasia) of the long bones of one or more limbs. *See also* amelia, hemimelia, phocomelia.

缺肢　單肢或多肢的長骨先天性缺失或整體變短（發育不全）的情況。參閱 amelia hemimelia，phocomelia。

ectropion *n.* turning out of the eyelid, away from the eyeball. The commonest type is *senile ectropion*, in which the lower eyelid droops because of laxity of

瞼外翻　眼瞼離開眼球，向外翻轉的現象。最常見的是老年性瞼外翻。因老年時眼瞼鬆弛，使得下眼瞼下垂。如果閉

the eyelid in old age. If the muscle that closes the eye (orbicularis oculi) is paralysed the lower lid also droops. Ectropion may also occur if scarring causes contraction of the surrounding facial skin.

眼的肌肉（眼輪匝肌）麻痺，下眼瞼也下垂。如果瘢痕引起周圍面部肌肉的收縮，瞼外翻也可發生。

eczema *n.* a common itchy skin disease characterized by reddening (*erythema) and vesicle formation, which may lead to weeping and crusting. It is endogenous, or constitutional, i.e. outside agents do not play a primary role (*compare* dermatitis), but in some contexts the terms 'dermatitis' and 'eczema' are used interchangeably. There are five main types: (1) *atopic eczema*, which affects up to 20% of the population and is associated with asthma and hay fever; (2) *seborrhoeic eczema* (or *dermatitis*), which involves the scalp, eyelids, nose, and lips and is associated with the presence of *Pityrosporum* yeasts; (3) *discoid* (or *nummular*) *eczema*, which is characterized by coin-shaped lesions and occurs only in adults; (4) *pompholyx, affecting the hands and feet; (5) *gravitational* (or *stasis*) *eczema*, associated with poor venous circulation and incorrectly known as *varicose eczema*.

Treatment of eczema is with topical or systemic corticosteroids but emollients are very important, especially in treating mild cases. **–eczematous** *adj.*

濕疹 一種常見瘙癢性皮膚病，特點為皮膚變紅（紅斑）和疱疹形成，並導致液體流出和結痂。本病為內源性或體質性，即外界因子不產生主要作用（與 dermatitis 對比），但在一些情況下，皮炎和濕疹兩術語可相互換用。有五種主要類型：(1) 變態反應性濕疹，有20% 的人患病，與哮喘和枯草熱有關；(2) 脂溢性濕疹（或皮炎）侵害頭皮、眼瞼、鼻和嘴唇，與瓶形酵母的出現有關；(3) 盤形（或錢幣形）濕疹的特點是錢幣形損傷，並僅發生於成人；(4) 汗疱發生於手和腳；(5) 重力型（停滯型）濕疹與靜脈循環不良有關，並被誤認為是靜脈曲張型濕疹。

濕疹的治療是採用外用或全身性使用皮質類固醇，但潤膚劑的使用很重要，尤其是在治療輕度濕疹時。

edentulous *adj.* lacking teeth: usually applied to people who have lost some or all of their teeth.

無牙的 缺牙，常用於指失去部分或全部牙齒的人。

edetate *n.* a salt of *ethylenediaminetetraacetic acid* (*EDTA*), which is used as a *chelating agent in the treatment of poisoning. *Dicobalt edetate* is an antidote to cyanide, administered by intravenous injection as soon as possible after poisoning. *Calcium disodium edetate* is used

依地酸鹽 乙二胺四乙酸的一種鹽，在治療中毒症時，用作螯合劑。依地酸二鈷是氰化物的一種解毒藥。在中毒後立刻靜脈注射。依地酸鈣鈉用於治療重金屬中毒，如鉛和鍶。

to treat poisoning by heavy metals, such as lead and strontium.

edrophonium *n.* a drug that stimulates skeletal muscles (*see* parasympathomimetic). It is administered by injection in a test for diagnosis of *myasthenia gravis. Side-effects can include nausea and vomiting, increased saliva flow, diarrhoea, and stomach pains. Trade name: **Tensilon**.

依酚氯銨（騰喜龍）　一種刺激骨骼肌的藥物（參閱 parasympathomimetic）。檢查中，用於注射以診斷重症肌無力。副作用包括惡心、嘔吐、流涎增多、腹瀉和胃痛。商品名：Tensilon。

EDTA (ethylenediaminetetraacetic acid) *see* edetate.

乙二胺四乙酸　參閱 edetate。

Edwards' syndrome the condition of a baby born with multiple congenital abnormalities, including mental retardation, due to *trisomy of chromosome no. 18.

愛德華綜合徵　因 18 號染色體的三倍體而致新生兒患有多發性先天畸形的病症。

EEG (electroencephalogram) *see* electroencephalography.

腦電圖　參閱 electroencephalography。

effector *n.* any structure or agent that brings about activity in a muscle or gland, such as a motor nerve that causes muscular contraction or glandular secretion. The term is also used for the muscle or gland itself.

效應器　引起肌肉或腺體活動的任何結構或物質。如運動神經，它能引起肌肉收縮或腺體分泌。此術語也可用於肌肉或腺體本身。

efferent *adj.* **1.** designating nerves or neurones that convey impulses from the brain or spinal cord to muscles, glands, and other effectors; i.e. any motor nerve or neurone. **2.** designating vessels or ducts that drain fluid (such as lymph) from an organ or part. *Compare* afferent.

輸出的，傳出的　**(1)** 指能將大腦或脊髓發出的衝動傳送到肌肉、腺體或其他效應器上的神經或神經元，如任何運動神經或神經元。**(2)** 指能引流某一器官或部位液體（如淋巴液）的脈管或管道。與 afferent 對比。

effleurage *n.* a form of *massage in which the hands are passed continuously and rhythmically over a patient's skin in one direction only, with the aim of

輕撫法　一種按摩的方式。按摩時用雙手在患者的皮膚表面僅向一個方面連續有規律地按壓，以增加此方向的血流量，

increasing blood flow in that direction and aiding the dispersal of any swelling due to *oedema.

並促進由水腫引起的各種腫脹的消散。

effort syndrome a condition of marked anxiety about the condition of one's heart and circulatory system. This is accompanied by a heightened consciousness of heartbeat and respiration, which in turn is worsened by the anxiety it induces. Treatment is commonly with reassurance and *tranquillizers; the use of psychotherapy is only occasionally necessary.

奮力綜合徵 一種對自己心臟及循環系統狀況過分擔憂的病症。它伴有對心跳和呼吸的高度知覺，此知覺依次會因其引起的擔憂而加重。治療方法通常是消除疑慮及服用鎮靜藥；心理療法只是偶爾需要。

effusion *n.* **1.** the escape of pus, serum, blood, lymph, or other fluid into a body cavity as a result of inflammation or the presence of excess blood or tissue fluid in an organ or tissue. **2.** fluid that has escaped into a body cavity.

滲漏 **(1)** 某器官或組織因炎症或血液、組織液過多而引起膿、血清、血液、淋巴液及其他液體向體腔的滲入。**(2)** 滲入體腔的液體。

eflornithine *n.* a drug recently approved by the World Health Organization for the treatment of *sleeping sickness. It is administered by mouth and intravenous injection. Possible side-effects include diarrhoea, hair loss, convulsions, and damage to bone marrow. Trade name: **DMFO**.

依氟鳥氨酸 世界衛生組織最近批准的治療昏睡病的一種藥物。口服和靜脈注射。可能的副作用包括腹瀉、脫髮、痙攣和骨髓損害。商品名：DMFO。

egg cell *see* ovum.

卵細胞 參閱 ovum。

ego *n.* (in psychoanalysis) the part of the mind that develops from a person's experience of the outside world and is most in touch with external realities. In Freudian terms the ego is said to reconcile the demands of the *id (the instinctive unconscious mind), the *superego (moral conscience), and reality.

自我 （精神分析）來自人對外界的體驗且與外部現實密切相關的那部分意識。弗洛伊德學說認為，自我能協調伊德（本能的潛意識），超我（道德良心）和現實之間的需要。

eidetic *adj. see* imagery.

遺覺的 參閱 imagery。

eikonometer *n.* an instrument for measuring the size of images on the retina of the eye.

影像計　一種測量眼視網膜成像大小的儀器。

Eisenmenger reaction a condition in which *pulmonary hypertension is associated with a *septal defect, so that blood flows from the right to the left side of the heart or from the pulmonary artery to the aorta. This allows blue blood, poor in oxygen, to bypass the lungs and enter the general circulation. This reduces the oxygen content of the arterial blood in the aorta and its branches, resulting in a patient with a dusky blue appearance (*cyanosis) and an increased number of red blood cells (*polycythaemia). There is no curative treatment at this stage, but the patient may be helped by the control of heart failure and polycythaemia. The condition may be prevented by appropriate treatment of the septal defect before irreversible pulmonary hypertension develops.

艾森門格爾反應　一種因心室間隔缺損而產生的肺動脈高壓，使血液從心臟右側流向左側或從肺動脈流向主動脈的病症。這使低氧血不通過肺部就直接進入體循環，降低進入主動脈及其分支裏動脈血氧含量，使患者出現紫紺面容和紅細胞數增加。目前尚無治療方法，但可通過控制心力衰竭及紅細胞增多來緩解患者病痛。在不可逆性肺動脈高壓發生之前，此病可通過治療室間隔缺損來預防。

ejaculation *n.* the discharge of semen from the erect penis at the moment of sexual climax (orgasm) in the male. The constituents of semen are not released simultaneously, but in the following sequence: the secretion of *Cowper's glands followed by that of the *prostate gland and the spermatozoa and finally the secretion of the *seminal vesicles. *See also* premature ejaculation.

射精　男性在性高潮時精液從勃起的陰莖射出的過程。精液的成分不是同時而是按下列順序釋放出來的：考珀腺分泌液，接着是前列腺液和精子，最後是精囊分泌液。參閱 premature ejaculation。

elastic cartilage a type of *cartilage in which elastic fibres are distributed in the matrix. It is yellowish in colour and is found in the external ear.

彈性軟骨　一種軟骨，其彈性纖維分布於基質。呈淡黃色，見於外耳。

elastic tissue strong extensible flexible *connective tissue rich in yellow *elastic fibres*. These fibres are long, thin, and branching and are composed primarily of

彈性組織　彈性極強的結締組織，富於黃色彈性纖維。細長且有分支，主要由類似白蛋白的蛋白質——彈性硬蛋白構

an albumin-like protein, *elastic*. Elastic tissue is found in the dermis of the skin, in arterial walls, and in the walls of the alveoli of the lungs.

成。它見於皮膚真皮、動脈壁及肺泡壁。

elastin *n*. protein forming the major constituent of *elastic tissue fibres.

彈性硬蛋白 組成彈性組織纖維主要成分的蛋白質。

elastosis *n*. degeneration of the yellow fibres in connective tissues and skin (*see* elastic tissue).

彈性組織變性 結締組織和皮膚的黃色纖維變性。（參閱 elastic tissue）。

elation (exaltation) *n*. a state of cheerful excitement and enthusiasm. Marked elation of mood is a characteristic of *mania or *hypomania.

得意 興高采烈且熱情洋溢的狀態，明顯得意的情緒是躁狂或輕躁狂症的一種特徵。

elbow *n*. the hinge joint (*see* ginglymus) between the bones of the upper arm (humerus) and the forearm (radius and ulna). It is a common site of fractures and dislocation.

肘 上臂和前臂骨頭之間的屈戌關節（參閱 ginglymus）。常發生骨折和脫位。

electrocardiogram (ECG) *n*. a recording of the electrical activity of the heart on a moving paper strip (see illustration). The ECG tracing is recorded by means of an apparatus called an *electrocardiograph* (*see* electrocardiography). It aids in the diagnosis of heart disease, which may produce characteristic changes in the ECG.

心電圖 心臟電活動在移動的紙條上記錄下來的曲綫（見圖）。心電圖的描繪是由心電描記器進行的。它有助於診斷心臟病，該病可能使心電圖產生有特徵的變化。

electrocardiography *n*. a technique for recording the electrical activity of the heart. Electrodes connected to the recording apparatus (*electrocardiograph*) are placed on the skin of the four limbs and chest wall; the record itself is called an *electrocardiogram (ECG). In conventional *scalar electrocardiography* 12 leads (*see* lead[2]) are recorded, but more may be employed in special circumstances (for example, an oesophageal

心電描記術 記錄心臟電活動的一種技術。將連接記錄儀（心電描記器）的電極與四肢和胸壁皮膚相接觸，所作出的記錄本身稱作心電圖。在常規的標量法中，可記錄12個導聯。在特殊情況下，會使用更多的導聯（如從插入食管內的電極引出的食管導聯可用於分析心律不齊）。

　　心向量描記術在英國較少

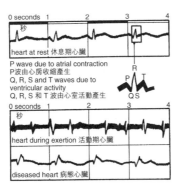

Typical electrocardiograms
典型的心電圖

lead, from an electrode within the gullet, may be used in the analysis of arrhythmias).

Vectorcardiography is less commonly used in Britain, but may be employed to obtain a three-dimensional impression of electrical activity of the heart.

使用，但可用來獲得心臟電活動的三維印象。

electrocardiophonography *n.* a technique for recording heart sounds and murmurs simultaneously with the ECG, which is used as a reference tracing. The sound is picked up by a microphone placed over the heart. The tracing is a *phonocardiogram*. It provides a permanent record of heart sounds and murmurs and is useful in their analysis.

心音電描記術 與作為參考標誌的心電圖同時進行記錄心音及其雜音的技術。心音由放在心臟上方的擴音器所接收。所記錄下的曲綫即心音圖。它提供了心音及其雜音的永久性記錄，在其分析中很有用。

electrocautery *n.* the destruction of diseased or unwanted tissue by means of a needle or snare that is electrically heated. Warts, polyps, and other growths can be burned away by this method.

電烙術 用電熱針或電熱勒除器將病變組織或不需要組織毀壞掉。疣、息肉和其他生長物可用此方法灼除。

electrocoagulation *n.* the coagulation of body tissues by means of a high-frequency electric current concentrated at one point as it passes through them.

電凝法 當高頻電流經過組織時通過聚集在某一點而使該組織凝固。電凝法在手術中用透熱刀做無血切口。

Electrocoagulation, using a *diathermy knife, permits bloodless incisions to be made during operation.

electroconvulsive therapy (ECT) a treatment for severe depression and occasionally for schizophrenia and mania. A convulsion is produced by passing an electric current through the brain. The convulsion is modified by giving a *muscle relaxant drug and an *anaesthetic, so that in fact only a few muscle twitches are produced. The means by which ECT acts is not yet known. The procedure can also produce confusion, loss of memory, and headache, which almost always pass off within a few hours. These side-effects are reduced by unilateral treatment, in which the current is passed only through the nondominant hemisphere of the brain.

電驚厥療法 對嚴重抑鬱症，偶爾也對精神分裂症及躁狂症的一種治療方法。使電流通過大腦會引起驚厥。驚厥可用肌肉鬆弛劑和麻醉劑予以控制，實際上只有少數肌肉發生抽搐。電驚厥療法的原理還不為人們所知。驚厥過程也會導致精神錯亂、記憶喪失及頭痛等副作用，但它們幾小時後幾乎總是全部消失。這些副作用也可通過單側治療而減輕。單側治療即電流只通過大腦的非優勢半球。

electrodesiccation n. see fulguration.

電乾燥法 參閱 fulguration。

electroencephalogram (EEG) n. see electroencephalography.

腦電圖 參閱 electroencephalography。

electroencephalography n. the technique for recording the electrical activity from different parts of the brain and converting it into a tracing called an _electroencephalogram_ (_EEG_). The machine that records this activity is known as an _encephalograph_. The pattern of the EEG reflects the state of the patient's brain and his level of consciousness in a characteristic manner. Electroencephalography is mostly used in the diagnosis and management of epilepsy.

腦電描記術 從大腦不同部位記錄腦電活動並將其轉換成稱作腦電圖的描繪技術。記錄這種活動的機器叫腦造影儀。腦電圖的模式能有特徵地反映患者的大腦狀態及其清醒程度。此技術用來探查和確定器質性疾病，如腦內腫瘤，亦可用於診斷和監控癲癇。

electrokymography n. the technique of recording the movements of an organ, especially the heart, by means of a *fluoroscope and a photoelectric recording system.

電記波照相術 通過熒光鏡及光電記錄系統記錄器官，特別是心臟活動的技術。

electrolyte *n.* a solution that produces ions (an ion is an atom or group of atoms that conduct electricity); for example, sodium chloride solution consists of free sodium and free chloride ions. In medical usage electrolyte usually means the ion itself; thus the term *serum electrolyte level* means the concentration of separate ions (sodium, potassium, chloride, bicarbonate, etc.) in the circulating blood. Concentrations of various electrolyte levels can be altered by many diseases, in which electrolytes are lost from the body (as in vomiting or diarrhoea) or are not excreted and accumulate (as in renal failure). When electrolyte concentrations are severely diminished they can be corrected by administering the appropriate substance by mouth or by intravenous drip. When excess of an electrolyte exists it may be removed by *dialysis or by special resins in the intestine, taken by mouth or by enema. *See also* anion.

electromyography *n.* continuous recording of the electrical activity of a muscle by means of electrodes inserted into the muscle fibres. The tracing is displayed on an oscilloscope. The technique is used for diagnosing various nerve and muscle disorders and assessing progress in recovery from some forms of paralysis.

electronarcosis *n.* the induction of sleep by passing weak electrical currents through the brain. It is seldom used in Western psychiatry.

electron microscope a microscope that uses a beam of electrons as a radiation source for viewing the specimen. The resolving power (ability to register fine detail) is a thousand times greater than

電解質 產生離子的溶液（離子是一種能導電的原子或原子團）；如氯化鈉溶液是由游離鈉離子和游離氯離子組成的。在醫學上，電解質通常指離子本身；因此，血清電解質濃度術語指在循環血液中各種離子（鈉、鉀、氯、碳酸氫鹽等）的濃度。各種電解質濃度可因很多疾病而改變，使電解質從體內消失（如嘔吐和腹瀉時）或不能排泄而聚積在體內（如腎衰竭時）。當電解質濃度嚴重下降時，可通過口服或靜脈點滴適當的物質得到糾正。當電解質過多時，可通過透析或腸內通過口服或灌腸的特殊樹脂而排除。參閱 anion。

肌電描記術 將電極放入肌肉纖維內，連續記錄肌肉電活動的技術。描記圖可顯示在示波器上。此技術用於各種神經及肌肉疾病的診斷及估計某些麻痺症的恢復進程。

電麻醉 微弱電流通過大腦所誘發的睡眠。在西方精神病學中很少使用。

電子顯微鏡 用電子束做放射源來觀察標本的顯微鏡。其分辨率比一般光學顯微鏡大一千倍。標本須在特殊技術製成的真空器裏檢查，電子通常聚集

that of an ordinary light microscope. The specimen must be examined in a vacuum, which necessitates special techniques for preparing it, and the electrons are usually focused onto a fluorescent screen (for direct viewing) or onto a photographic plate (for a photograph, or *electron micrograph*). A *transmission electron microscope* is used to examine thin sections at high magnification. A *scanning electron microscope* reveals the surfaces of objects at various magnifications; its great depth of focus is advantageous.

到熒光屏上（為直接觀察）或照像底板上（為拍照片或電子顯微照像）。透射電子顯微鏡用於放大檢查超薄切片。掃描電子顯微鏡可顯示不同放大倍數的物體表面，焦距深是其優點。

electron transport chain a series of enzymes and proteins in living cells through which electrons are transferred, via a series of oxidation-reduction reactions. This ultimately leads to the conversion of chemical energy into a readily usable and storable form. The most important electron transport chain is the *respiratory chain*, present in mitochondria and functioning in cellular respiration.

電子轉移鏈 活細胞內能通過一系列氧化還原反應轉移電子的一組酶和蛋白質。這最終是將化學能量轉化成易使用和貯存的能量形式。最重要的電子轉移鏈是呼吸鏈，它存在於綫粒體內，在細胞呼吸中發揮作用。

electrooculography *n.* an electrical method of recording eye movements. Tiny electrodes are attached to the skin at the inner and outer corners of the eye, and as the eye moves an alteration in the potential between these electrodes is recorded. The size of this potential at rest also gives an indication of the health of the retina.

眼電描記法 記錄眼運動的一種電學方法。將微小電極與眼內外角處的皮膚相接觸，當眼動時，電極之間的電勢變化就被記錄下來。眼休息時的電勢大小也能表明視網膜的健康狀況。

electrophoresis *n.* the technique of separating electrically charged particles, particularly proteins, in a solution by passing an electric current through the solution. The rate of movement of the different components depends upon their charge, so that they gradually separate into bands. Electrophoresis is widely

電泳 電流經過溶液來分離其中帶電離子，特別是蛋白質的技術。不同成分的移動速度依其電荷大小而異，因此，它們會逐漸分離成不同的帶。電泳廣泛用於體內化學成分的研究，如血清中不同蛋白質的分析。

used in the investigation of body chemicals, such as the analysis of the different proteins in blood serum.

electroretinography *n.* a method of recording changes in the electrical potential of the retina when it is stimulated by light. One electrode is placed on the eye in a contact lens and the other is usually attached to the back of the head. In retinal disease the pattern of electrical change is altered. The technique is useful in diagnosing retinal diseases when opacities, such as cataract, make it difficult to view the retina or when the disease produces little visible change in the retina.

視網膜電描記法　記錄光綫刺激視網膜時其電熱變化的方法。一電極置於眼睛上的隱形眼鏡裏，另一電極通常接於頭後。視網膜有病時，電勢記錄圖發生改變。此技術在診斷視網膜疾病時很有用。如在白內障之類疾病使視網膜不易看清時，或在視網膜發生難以看到的病變時。

electrosurgery *n.* the use of a high-frequency electric current from a fine wire electrode (a *diathermy knife) to cut tissue. The ground electrode is a large metal plate. When used correctly, little heat spreads to the surrounding tissues, in contrast to *electrocautery.

電外科　使用從纖細的金屬綫電極發出的高頻電流（透熱刀）來切割組織。接地電極為一大金屬板。當使用得當時，與電烙術相比幾乎沒有熱量擴散到周圍組織。

electrotherapy *n.* the passage of electric currents through the body's tissues to stimulate the functioning of nerves and the muscles that they supply. The technique is used to bring about improvement in the muscles of patients with various forms of paralysis due to nerve disease or muscle disorder. *See also* faradism, galvanism.

電療法　使電流通過體內各組織以刺激神經和肌肉發揮其應有的功能。此技術用於由神經或肌肉疾病所導致的各種麻痺患者肌肉功能的改善。參閱 faradism，galvanism。

electuary *n.* a pharmaceutical preparation in which the drug is made up into a paste with syrup or honey.

藥糖劑　一種藥物製劑。在其製作中，將藥物與糖漿或蜂蜜混製成膏劑。

elephantiasis *n.* gross enlargement of the skin and underlying connective tissues caused by obstruction of the lymph vessels, which prevents drainage of lymph from the surrounding tissues.

象皮病　因淋巴管堵塞而阻礙淋巴液從其周圍組織引流所引起的皮膚及皮下結締組織的明顯腫脹。淋巴管壁炎症，增厚及最終的淋巴管堵塞通常是由

Inflammation and thickening of the walls of the vessels and their eventual blocking is commonly caused by the parasitic filarial worms *Wuchereria bancrofti* and *Brugia malayi*. The parts most commonly affected are the legs but the scrotum, breasts, and vulva may also be involved. Elastic bandaging is applied to the affected parts and the limbs are elevated and rested. Larval forms in the blood are killed with diethylcarbamazine. *See also* filariasis.

寄生絲蟲：班氏吳策綫蟲和馬來絲蟲引起的。最常見的發病部位在腿部，但陰囊、乳房及女性外陰也可染上。患部纏上彈性繃帶，抬高並休息肢體。血液中的幼蟲用乙胺嗪殺死。參閱 filariasis。

elevator *n.* **1.** an instrument that is used to raise a depressed broken bone, for example in the skull or cheek. A specialized *periosteal elevator* is used in orthopaedics to strip the fibrous tissue (periosteum) covering bone. **2.** a lever-like instrument used to ease a tooth out of its socket during extraction.

(1) 起子　用來托起凹陷性斷骨（如顱骨、顴骨骨折）的工具。特製的骨膜起子在骨科用來剝下包繞骨的纖維組織。**(2) 牙挺**　拔牙時用來將牙挺出齒槽的桿狀工具。

elimination *n.* (in physiology) the entire process of excretion of metabolic waste products from the blood by the kidneys and urinary tract.

排泄　（生理學）將血液中代謝廢物通過腎臟及尿道排出的整個過程。

ELISA *see* enzyme-linked immunosorbent assay.

酶聯免疫吸附試驗　參閱 enzyme-linked immunosorbent assay。

elixir *n.* a preparation containing alcohol (ethanol) or glycerine, which is used as the vehicle for bitter or nauseous drugs.

酏劑　含有酒精（乙醇）或甘油的製劑。用作苦味的或令人惡心的藥物的賦形劑。

elliptocytosis *n.* the presence of significant numbers of abnormal elliptical red cells (*elliptocytes*) in the blood. Elliptocytosis may occur as a hereditary disorder or be a feature of certain blood diseases, such as *myelofibrosis or iron-deficiency *anaemia.

橢圓形紅細胞症　血液中存在着相當數量的非正常橢圓形紅細胞。它能在遺傳病中發現，也可能是某些血液病的特徵，如骨髓纖維變性或缺鐵性貧血。

elutriation *n.* the separation of a fine powder from a coarser powder by mixing

淘析法　從粗粉末中分離出細粉末。通過將它們與水混合，

them with water and decanting the upper layer while it still contains the finer particles. The heavier coarse particles sink to the bottom more rapidly.

當表面層含有細顆粒時，將其傾析。較重的粗顆粒沉入底部較快。

em- *prefix. see* en-.

〔前綴〕**在裏面，包住** 參閱 en-。

emaciation *n.* wasting of the body, caused by such conditions as malnutrition, tuberculosis, cancer, or parasitic worms.

消瘦 由諸如營養不良、結核病、癌或寄生蟲引起的身體耗損。

emasculation *n.* strictly, surgical removal of the penis. The term is often used to mean loss of male physical and emotional characteristics, either as a result of removal of the testes (castration) or of emotional stress.

閹割，去勢，去雄 嚴格地講指切除陰莖的手術。但本詞常用來指由於切除睾丸或因情緒緊張而引起的男性生理和情緒特徵的喪失。

embalming *n.* the preservation of a dead body by the introduction of chemical compounds that delay putrefaction. Embalming is employed mainly so that a body can be transported long distances and funeral rites can be conducted without undue haste. In the USA it is a routine hygienic measure.

屍體防腐 用延緩腐爛的化學物質保存屍體。古埃及人在製作木乃伊方面將這一技術提到了很高水平。今天使用屍體防腐主要使屍體能長距離運送，葬禮不至於匆忙進行。在美國，屍體防腐是常規衛生措施。

embedding *n.* (in microscopy) the fixing of a specimen within a mass of firm material in order to facilitate the cutting of thin sections for microscopical study. The embedding medium, e.g. paraffin wax for light microscopy or Araldite for electron microscopy, helps to keep the specimen intact.

包埋 （顯微鏡檢查）將標本固定在一塊堅固的物質裏，以利於做成用於顯微鏡研究的切片。包埋介質，如用於光學顯微鏡的石蠟，或用於電子顯微鏡的環氧樹脂，有助於保護標本完整無損。

embolectomy *n.* surgical removal of an *embolus in order to relieve arterial obstruction. The embolus may be removed by cutting directly into the affected artery (*arteriotomy*). In some instances it is removed by a balloon *catheter, which is manipulated beyond

栓子切除術 手術切除栓子以去除動脈阻塞。栓子可通過直接切開受阻動脈（動脈切開術）而去除。在某些情況下，栓子還可以用氣囊導管去除。該導管是從易到達栓子部位的動脈小切口插入，越過栓子後進行

the embolus from a small arteriotomy in an accessible artery. The catheter is then withdrawn carrying the embolus with it. In some cases of pulmonary embolism, embolectomy may be life-saving. It may also prevent gangrene in cases of a limb artery embolus.

操作的,然後將帶有栓子的導管抽出。在一些肺動脈栓塞的病例中,栓子切除術能挽救生命。在肢體動脈栓塞的病例中,它也可預防能導致截肢的壞死。

embolism *n.* the condition in which an embolus becomes lodged in an artery and obstructs its blood flow. The most common form of embolism is *pulmonary embolism, in which a blood clot is carried in the circulation to lodge in the pulmonary artery. An embolus in any other artery constitutes a *systemic embolism*. In this case a common source of the embolus is a blood clot within the heart in mitral valve disease or following *myocardial infarction. The clinical features depend upon the site at which an embolus lodges (for example, a stroke may result from a cerebral embolism and gangrene caused by a limb embolism). Treatment is by *anticoagulant therapy with heparin and warfarin. Major embolism is treated by *embolectomy or *streptokinase to remove or dissolve the embolus. *See also* air embolism.

栓塞 栓子停留在動脈裏,阻礙血液循環。最常見的栓塞形式為肺動脈栓塞,即循環中的血塊被攜帶並停留在肺動脈裏。任何其他動脈裏的栓子都能構成體循環栓塞。在這種情況下,常見的栓子來源是二尖瓣疾病時或心肌梗死後心臟裏的血塊。臨床特點取決於栓子停留的部位(如中風會由腦栓塞引起,壞疽由肢體動脈栓塞導致)。治療可用肝素及華法林抗凝療法。較大的栓塞則用栓子切除術治療,或用鏈激酶去溶解栓子。參閱 air embolism。

embolization (therapeutic embolization) *n.* the introduction of embolic material to reduce or conpletely obstruct bloodflow in such conditions as congenital arteriovenous malformations (*see* angioma), angiodysplasia, malignant tumours, or arterial rupture. Under X-ray screening control, a cannula is inserted into the artery supplying the affected area and occluding material, such as microspheres, metallic coils, or PVA (polyvinyl alcohol) foam, is injected, The procedure simplifies subsequent surgery or replaces it.

栓塞形成 注入栓塞物質以減少或完全堵塞血流的方法,常用於諸如先天動靜脈畸形、血管發育不良症(參閱 angioma)、惡性腫瘤、或者動脈破裂等疾病。在 X 線熒光屏監控下,將一套管插入動脈患部並注射閉塞物質如微球體、金屬綫圈或 PVA(聚乙烯醇)泡沫。此方法簡化了隨後的手術或取而代之。

embolus *n.* (*pl.* **emboli**) material, such as a blood clot, fat, air, or a foreign body, that is carried by the blood from one point in the circulation to lodge at another point (*see* embolism).

embrasure *n.* the space formed between adjacent teeth.

embrocation *n.* a lotion rubbed onto the body to treat sprains and strains.

embryo *n.* an animal at an early stage of development, before birth. In man the term refers to the products of conception within the uterus up to the eighth week of development, during which time all the main organs are formed (see illustration). *Compare* fetus. –**embryonic** *adj.*

栓子　血液在循環中從一點攜帶至另一點的物質，如血塊、脂肪、空氣或異物（參閱embolism）。

楔狀隙　相鄰牙齒之間所形成的縫隙。

擦劑　為治療扭傷和勞損而塗擦在身體上的洗劑。

胚胎　出生之前發育早期的動物。在人類，指在子宮內發育的前八周懷孕產物。在此期間，所有的主要器官均已形成（見圖）。與 fetus 對比。

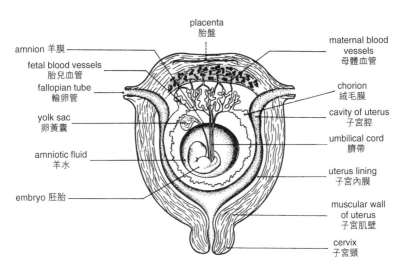

A developing embryo
胚胎的發育

embryology *n.* the study of growth and development of the embryo and fetus from fertilization of the ovum until birth. –**embryological** *adj.*

胚胎學　研究從卵子受精到胎兒出生這一時期胚胎及胎兒生長發育的科學。

embryonic disc the early embryo before the formation of *somites. It is a flat disc of tissue bounded dorsally by the amniotic cavity and ventrally by the yolk sac. The formation of the *primitive streak and *archenteron in the embryonic disc determines the orientation of the embryo, which then becomes progressively elongated.

胚盤 體節形成之前的早期胚胎。扁平盤狀組織，背側與羊膜腔相鄰，腹側與卵黃囊相接。胚盤中的原條和原腸的形成決定了胚胎的定向，然後，使其逐漸延長。

embryoscopy *n.* examination of an embryo or fetus during the first 12 weeks of pregnancy by means of a fibreoptic *endoscope inserted through the cervix; it can be performed as early as five weeks' gestation. Access to the fetal circulation may be obtained through the instrument and direct visualization of the embryo permits the diagnosis of malformations.

胚胎鏡檢查 通過子宮頸插入纖維內鏡檢查在孕期頭12周的胚胎和胎兒；此檢查可早到妊娠5周時進行。通過該器械能得到胎兒循環資料，對胎兒的直接觀察能夠診斷畸形。

embryo transfer the transfer of an embryo from an in vitro culture into the uterus. *See also* in vitro fertilization.

胚胎移植 把一個體外培養的胚胎轉移到子宮中去。參閱 in vitro fertilization。

emesis *n. see* vomiting.

嘔吐 參閱 vomiting。

emetic *n.* an agent that causes vomiting. Strong emetics, such as *apomorphine, are used to induce vomiting following drug overdose. Substances such as common salt, which irritate the stomach nerves if taken in sufficient quantities, also cause vomiting. Some emetics, e.g. ipecacuanha, are *expectorants at low doses.

催吐藥 引起嘔吐的一種藥物。強催吐藥，如阿樸嗎啡，在服藥過量時用來誘發嘔吐。某些物質，如食鹽，若食用過多，會刺激胃神經，也能引起嘔吐。一些催吐藥，如吐根，劑量小時，也是祛痰劑。

eminence *n.* a projection, often rounded, on an organ or tissue, particularly on a bone. An example is the *iliopubic eminence* on the hip bone.

突起 在器官或組織上，特別是在骨上的一種隆起，常常為圓形。髖骨上的髖恥隆起為一例。

Emiscan *n.* trade name for *computerized tomography.

艾梅斯康 電子計算機斷層照相術的商品名。

emissary veins a group of veins within the skull that drain blood from the venous sinuses of the dura mater to veins outside the skull.

導血管靜脈　一組顱內靜脈，它們將硬腦膜靜脈竇的血液引流到顱外靜脈。

emission *n.* the flow of semen from the erect penis, usually occurring while the subject is asleep (*nocturnal emission*).

遺精　精液從勃起的陰莖中的流出，通常發生在睡眠期間（夢遺）。

EMLA cream a cream containing a *e*utectic *m*ixture of *l*ocal *a*naesthetics (hence the name). Applied to the skin as a thick coating, it gives a helpful degree of local anaesthesia, allowing blood samples to be taken and facilitating biopsy procedures in young children.

低共熔混合局麻膏　一種含有局部麻醉劑的低共熔混合物膏。厚厚地塗於皮膚，它能起局部麻醉的作用，使幼兒血樣易被採集並有助於活組織檢查的操作。

emmetropia *n.* the state of refraction of the normal eye, in which parallel light rays are brought to a focus on the retina with the accommodation relaxed. Distant objects are seen clearly without any effort to focus. *Compare* ametropia, hypermetropia, myopia.

正視眼　具有正常屈光能力的眼。即平行光線在視網膜上不用調節即可聚焦。距眼 6 米以外的物體，不用調整焦距，就可清楚看到。與 ametropia，hypermetropia，myopia 對比。

emollient *n.* an agent that soothes and softens the skin. Emollients are fats and oils, such as lanolin and liquid paraffin; they are used alone as moisturizers to lessen the need for active drug therapy (such as corticosteroids for eczema) and in skin preparations as a base for a more active drug, such as an antibiotic.

潤滑劑　使皮膚光滑和柔軟的製劑。係脂肪和油脂類物質，如羊毛脂和液體石蠟。它們單獨作為增濕劑來減輕對特效藥治療的需要（如皮質類固醇治療濕疹）利用在皮膚製劑中作為速效的藥物，如抗生素的基質。

emotion *n.* a state of arousal that can be experienced as pleasant or unpleasant. Emotions can have three components: *subjective*, *physiological*, and *behavioural*. For example, fear can involve an unpleasant subjective experience, an increase in physiological measures such as heart rate, sweating, etc, and a tendency to flee from the fear-provoking situation.

情緒　能夠引起快樂或痛苦的心理狀態。情緒有三個組成部分：主觀上的、生理上的和行為上的。如恐懼包括不愉快的主觀感受；生理上的反應加速，如心動過速、出汗等；及逃離引起恐懼的環境的傾向。

empathy *n.* the ability to understand the thoughts and emotions of another person. In a psychotherapist empathy is often considered to be one of the necessary qualities enabling successful treatment. *See* alexithymia.

神入　理解他人想法和感情的能力。對心理治療的醫生來説，神入常被認為是能進行成功治療的必備特點之一。參閲 alexithymia。

emphysema *n.* air in the tissues. In *pulmonary emphysema* the air sacs (*alveoli) of the lungs are enlarged and damaged, which reduces the surface area for the exchange of oxygen and carbon dioxide. Severe emphysema causes breathlessness, which is made worse by infections. There is no specific treatment, and the patient may become dependent on oxygen. The mechanism by which emphysema develops is not understood, although it is known to be particularly common in men in Britain and is associated with chronic bronchitis, smoking, and advancing age.

In surgical *emphysema* air may escape into the tissues of the chest and neck from leaks in the lungs or oesophagus; occasionally air escapes into other tissues during surgery, and bacteria may form gas in soft tissues. The presence of gas or air gives the affected tissues a characteristic crackling feeling to the touch, and it may be visible on X-rays. It is easily absorbed once the leak or production is stopped.

氣腫　存在於組織中的氣體。在肺氣腫病中，肺泡腫大並受損，減少了氧氣和二氧化碳交換的面積。嚴重的肺氣腫可引起呼吸困難，並可因感染而加重。此病無特殊療法，患者要依靠吸氧生活。儘管肺氣腫在英國是人人皆知和極為常見的疾病，並與慢性氣管炎、吸煙、年齡的增長有關，但其發病機制尚未搞清。

在外科性氣腫中，氣體可能從肺和食管的裂縫中漏到胸部和頸部組織中去。在外科手術中，氣體有時也會漏到其他組織中去，而且細菌也會在軟組織中產生氣體。因為存在氣體，在觸摸患部組織時，有捻發感。X 綫透視可見到氣體。當漏氣被阻止，或產氣停止時，氣體易被吸收。

empirical *adj.* describing a system of treatment based on experience or observation, rather than of logic or reason.

經驗主義的　指根據經驗或觀察而不是邏輯或推理的治療體系。

Employment Service (in Britain) an executive agency within the Department of Employment for running public employment services. It has special responsibility to find employment for and if necessary train (or retrain) those who are handicapped from any cause. Its

就業服務機構　（英國）就業部內管理公眾就業的執行機構。它有特殊的責任來為因任何原因而致殘的人找到職業，必要時培訓或再培訓他們。其「殘疾人一再就業服務機構」依靠職業中心受過專門訓練的

Disablement Resettlement Service relies on specially trained Officers (*DROs*), based in jobcentres, who see that those with handicaps find satisfactory employment. Recommendations made by DROs include that of registration as *disabled people*, which helps in obtaining and retaining employment. Other ways of assisting include referral to an *Employment Rehabilitation Centre* for assessment of potential and/or reacclimatization to a working environment for those who have been absent from work through ill health over a long period. Special training course may be arranged for handicapped people. These courses, covering a wide range of skilled and semiskilled occupations and lasting about six months, may be held at colleges, *special skill centres*, or at the premises of potential employers. For those with severe disabilities there is also a *sheltered placement scheme*, while for the blind there are special *Blind Persons Resettlement Officers* (*BPRO*), though *total* blindness is not a prerequisite for registration.

官員，負責為殘疾人找到滿意的工作。由殘疾人再就業服務機構官員提供的推薦包括殘疾人登記證，它有助於殘疾人得到並保留工作。其他的幫助包括將因病長期脫離工作的人分配到「就業康復中心」以評估其重新工作的能力和/或對工作環境的適應能力。特殊訓練班是為殘疾人安排的。這些培訓班培訓的職業項目很廣，有純技術性的和半技術性的，為期六個月，可在學院、專業技術中心或在僱主的單位裏舉辦。對那些具有嚴重傷殘的殘疾人還有「保護性分配方案」；對盲人來説有專門的盲人再就業官員為其服務，儘管全盲並不是註冊登記的先決條件。

empyema (pyothorax) *n.* pus in the *pleural cavity, usually secondary to infection in the lung or in the space below the diaphragm. Empyema is a life-threatening condition, which can usually only be relieved by surgical drainage of the pus.

膿胸 胸腔積膿，通常繼發於肺或膈下腔隙的感染。這是一種有生命危險的疾病。通常只有通過外科引流膿汁而緩解。

emulsion *n.* a preparation in which fine droplets of one liquid (such as oil) are dispersed in another liquid (such as water). In pharmacy medicines are prepared in the form of emulsions to disguise the taste of an oil, which is dispersed in a flavoured liquid.

乳劑 一種液體的微小顆粒（如油）分散在另一液體（如水）之中的製劑。在製藥業中，藥物被製成乳劑形式以除去油味。油液被分散到有香味的液體之中。

en- (em-) *prefix* denoting in; inside.

〔前綴〕在……之內

enalapril *n.* a drug used in the treatment of high blood pressure (hypertension) and heart failure. It inhibits the action of angiotensin (*see* ACE inhibitor), which results in decreased vasopressor (blood-vessel constricting) activity and decreased aldosterone secretion. It is administered by mouth; side-effects include headache, dizziness, fatigue, and diarrhoea. Trade name: **Innovace**.

依那普利　一種用以治療高血壓和心力衰竭的藥物。它可阻滯血管緊張肽的作用（參閱 ACE inhibitor），從而導致血管收縮力降低及醛甾酮分泌的降低。口服；副作用包括頭痛、頭暈、疲勞及腹瀉。商品名：Innovace。

enamel *n.* the extremely hard outer covering of the crown of a *tooth. It is formed before tooth eruption by *ameloblasts.

釉質　牙冠的外層，極硬。在牙齒生長之前由成釉細胞形成。

enarthrosis *n.* a ball-and-socket joint: a type of *diarthrosis (freely movable joint), e.g. the shoulder joint and the hip joint. Such a joint always involves a long bone, which is thus allowed to move in all planes.

杵臼關節　一種球囊關節。動關節（可自由移動的關節）的一種，例如肩關節和髖關節。這種關節總是與長骨有關聯，使長骨在各個平面都能活動。

encapsulated *adj.* (of an organ, tumour, etc.) enclosed in a capsule.

包囊內的　被包囊包裹的（器官、腫瘤等）。

encephal- (encephalo-) *prefix denoting* the brain.

〔前綴〕腦

encephalin (enkephalin) *n.* a peptide occurring naturally in the brain and having effects resembling those of morphine or other opiates. *See also* endorphin.

腦啡肽　自然產生於腦內的任何一種肽，有類似嗎啡或其他阿片製劑的作用。參閱 endorphin。

encephalitis *n.* inflammation of the brain. It may be caused by a viral or bacterial infection or it may be part of an allergic response to a systemic viral illness or vaccination (*see* encephalomyelitis). *Viral encephalitis* is endemic in some parts of the world; it may also occur epidemically or sporadically. One form – *encephalitis lethargica* – reached epidemic proportions shortly after World

腦炎　大腦炎症。可由病毒或細菌感染引起，也可是對全身病毒疾病或疫苗接種過敏反應的一部分（參閱 encephalomyelitis）。病毒性腦炎是世界某些地區的地方病，也可呈流行性或散發性發病。腦炎的一種——昏睡性腦炎在第一次世界大戰後很快成為流行病，以頭痛、嗜眠及迅速進入昏迷狀態

War I and was marked by headache and drowsiness, progressing to coma (hence its popular name – *sleepy sickness*). Occasional cases still occur as a complication of mumps. It can cause postencephalitic *parkinsonism. Another type of encephalitis that occurs sporadically is due to herpes simplex.

為特點（因此，其俗名又叫昏睡病）。偶發的病例仍見於流行性腮腺炎的併發症。它還可引起腦炎後帕金森綜合徵。另一種散發性腦炎由單純疱疹引起。

encephalocele *n. see* neural tube defects.

腦突出　參閱 neural tube defects。

encephalography *n.* any of various techniques for recording the structure of the brain or the activity of the brain cells. Examples are *echoencephalography, *electroencephalography, and *pneumoencephalography.

腦描記術　能記錄腦結構或腦細胞活動的各種技術。例如，腦超聲檢查術、腦電描記術和氣腦造影術。

encephaloid *adj.* having the appearance of brain tissue: applied to certain tumours for example *encephaloid carcinoma of the breast*.

髓樣的　具有腦髓組織外觀的。用於描述某些腫瘤，例如，乳房髓樣癌。

encephalomyelitis *n.* an acute inflammatory disease affecting the brain and spinal cord. It is sometimes part of an overwhelming virus infection but *acute disseminated encephalomyelitis* is a form of delayed tissue hypersensitivity provoked by a mild infection or vaccination 7–10 days earlier. Survival through the acute phase of the illness is often followed by a remarkably complete recovery.

腦脊髓炎　侵害到腦和脊髓的急性炎症。有時是全身嚴重病毒感染的一部分。但急性播散性腦脊髓炎是一種遲發的組織過敏反應，由輕度感染或疫苗接種後7~10天內發生。能夠渡過此急性期的患者會很快康復。

encephalomyelopathy *n.* any condition in which there is widespread disease of the brain and spinal cord. *Necrotizing encephalomyelopathy of childhood* is a progressive illness with extensive destruction of nerve cells throughout the central nervous system. It is thought to be caused by a disorder of metabolism.

腦脊髓病　廣泛分布於腦和脊髓的疾病總稱。兒童壞死性腦脊髓病是一種進行性疾病，中樞神經系統的神經細胞遭到廣泛破壞。此病被認為是代謝障礙引起的。

encephalon *n. see* brain

腦　參閱 brain。

encephalopathy *n.* any of various diseases that affect the functioning of the brain. *See* hepatic encephalopathy, spongiform encephalopathy, Wernicke's encephalopathy.

腦病　任何損傷腦功能的疾病。參閱 hepatic encephalopathy，spongiform encephalopathy，Wernicke's encephalopathy。

enchondroma *n.* (*pl.* **enchondromata**) a benign cartilaginous tumour (*see* chondroma) occurring in the growing zone (metaphysis) of a bone and not protruding beyond its margins. Such tumours are often solitary; when multiple tumours occur the condition is known as *enchondromatosis*. *Compare* ecchondroma.

內生軟骨瘤　一種良性軟骨瘤（參閱 chondroma），生長於骨生長帶（幹骺端），但不超出其邊緣。這種瘤通常是單發的。當有多個這種瘤發生時，就叫作多發性內生軟骨瘤病。與 ecchondroma 對比。

encopresis *n.* incontinence of faeces. The term is used for faecal soiling associated with psychiatric disturbance.

大便失禁　排便失控。此術語用於指與精神紊亂有關的排便失禁。

encounter group a form of group psychotherapy. The emphasis is on encouraging close relationships between group members and on the expression of feelings. To this end, physical contact and confrontations between group members are arranged by the group leader. The stress of the experience can be damaging to maladjusted people.

談心治療小組　心理療法的一種小組形式。重點在於促進小組成員密切相處，交流感情。為達到這個目的，小組負責人安排成員接觸和交流。參加小組帶來的緊張不安會對適應不良的成員造成傷害。

encysted *adj.* enclosed in a cyst.

包囊內的　被囊包裹着的。

end- (endo-) *prefix denoting* within or inner. Example: *endonasal* (within the nose).

〔前綴〕在……之內，內部　例如：鼻內的。

endarterectomy *n.* a surgical 're-bore' of an artery that has become obstructed by *atheroma with or without a blood clot (thrombus); the former operation is known as *thromboendarterectomy*. The inner part of the wall is removed together with any clot that is present. This restores patency and arterial blood

動脈內膜切除術　一種外科手術。將帶有或不帶有血塊（栓子）的被粥樣斑塊堵塞的動脈打通。前一種手術稱做血栓動脈內膜切除術，是將動脈壁內膜與存在的血塊一起除去。這可使動脈恢復通暢，使動脈血液流到曾發生動脈阻塞的組織

flow to the tissues beyond the obstruction. The technique is most often applied to obstruction of the carotid arteries or of the arteries that supply the legs.

中去。這種手術常用於頸動脈阻塞或供應腿部血液的動脈堵塞。

endarteritis *n.* chronic inflammation of the inner (intimal) portion of the wall of an artery, which most often results from late syphilis. Thickening of the wall produces progressive arterial obstruction and symptoms from inadequate blood supply to the affected part (*ischaemia). The arteries to the brain are often involved, giving rise to meningovascular syphilis. Endarteritis of the aorta may obstruct the mouths of the coronary arteries, supplying the heart. Endarteritis of the arteries to the wall of the aorta (the vasa vasorum) contributes to *aneurysm formation. The syphilitic infection may be eradicated with penicillin.

動脈內膜炎 動脈壁內膜的慢性炎症，常因晚期梅毒引起。動脈壁的增厚逐漸形成動脈堵塞，引起受損部位供血不足（缺血）而出現症狀。腦動脈經常受損，引起腦膜血管梅毒。主動脈內膜炎可堵塞營養心臟的冠狀動脈口。營養主動脈壁的動脈（血管滋養管）內膜炎可形成動脈瘤。青黴素可治愈梅毒性感染。

end artery the terminal branch of an artery, which does not communicate with other branches. The tissue it supplies is therefore probably completely dependent on it for its blood supply.

終末動脈 動脈的最終分支。不與其他動脈分支相交通。因此，它供給的組織要完全依靠它的血運。

endemic *adj.* occurring frequently in a particular region or population: applied to diseases that are generally or constantly found among people in a particular area. *Compare* ecdemic, epidemic, pandemic.

地方性的 在特定的區域或人羣中頻繁發生的。指在特定地區經常或不斷在人羣中發生的疾病。與 ecdemic，epidemic，pandemic 對比。

endemic syphilis *see* bejel.

非性病性梅毒 參閱 bejel。

endocarditis *n.* inflammation of the lining of the heart cavity (endocardium) and valves. It is most often due to rheumatic fever or results from bacterial infection (*bacterial endocarditis*). Temporary or permanent damage to the heart valves may result. The main

心內膜炎 心腔內膜（心內膜）和瓣膜的炎症。主要因風濕熱或細菌性感染（細菌性心內膜炎）引起。可造成心瓣膜暫時或永久性的破壞。主要特點是發熱、多變的心臟雜音，心力衰竭及栓塞。治療包括休息，

features are fever, changing heart murmurs, heart failure, and embolism. Treatment consists of rest and antibiotics; surgery may be required to repair damaged heart valves.

用抗生素；外科可修復損害的心瓣膜。

endocardium *n.* a delicate membrane, formed of flat endothelial cells, that lines the heart and is continuous with the lining of arteries and veins. At the openings of the heart cavities it is folded back on itself to form the cusps of the valves. It presents a smooth slippery surface, which does not impede blood flow. **–endocardial** *adj.*

心內膜 由扁平細胞組成的，內襯心臟的薄膜，並與動、靜脈內膜相連。在心臟開口處，心內膜反褶形成了心瓣膜尖部。其表面光滑，因而不妨礙血流。

endocervicitis *n.* inflammation of the membrane lining the cervix (neck) of the uterus, usually caused by infection. Surface cells (epithelium) may die, resulting in a new growth of healthy epithelium over the affected area. The condition is accompanied by a thick mucoid discharge.

子宮頸內膜炎 子宮頸內膜炎症，通常由感染引起。表皮細胞（上皮細胞）可能死亡，受損傷部位有新的健康上皮生長，此病伴有濃稠黏液分泌物。

endocervix *n.* the mucous membrane (*endometrium) that lines the cervix (neck) of the uterus.

子宮頸內膜 子宮頸的黏膜（子宮內膜）。

endochondral *adj.* within the material of a cartilage.

軟骨內的 在軟骨質內部的。

endocrine gland (ductless gland) a gland that manufactures one or more *hormones and secretes them directly into the bloodstream (and not through a duct to the exterior). Endocrine glands include the pituitary, thyroid, parathyroid, and adrenal glands, the ovary and testis, the placenta, and part of the pancreas.

內分泌腺 一種腺體，分泌一種或多種激素並直接將其分泌入血流（而不是通過導管分泌到外界）。內分泌腺包括腦垂體、甲狀腺、甲狀旁腺及腎上腺、卵巢、睪丸、胎盤和部分胰腺。

endocrinology *n.* the study of the *endocrine glands and the substances

內分泌學 研究內分泌腺及其分泌物（激素）的學科。

they secrete (*hormones). **–endocrinol-ogist** *n.*

endoderm *n.* the inner of the three *germ layers of the early embryo, which gives rise to the lining of most of the alimentary canal and its associated glands, the liver, gall bladder, and pancreas. It also forms the lining of the bronchi and alveoli of the lung and most of the urinary tract. **–endodermal** *adj.*

內胚層　早期胚胎三胚層的內層。負責絕大部分消化道內膜及其附屬腺體、肝臟、膽囊及胰腺的生長。也負責形成支氣管、肺泡及大部分泌尿道的內膜。

endodermal sinus tumour a rare tumour of fetal remnants of the ovaries or testes.

內胚層竇腫瘤　一種罕見的腫瘤，由胎兒卵巢或睾丸的殘留物形成。

endodontics *n.* the study, treatment, and prevention of diseases of the pulp of teeth and their sequelae. A major part of treatment is *root canal treatment.

牙髓病學　研究和治療牙髓病變及其後遺症的科學。主要的治療手段是根管治療。

endogenous *adj.* arising within or derived from the body. *Compare* exogenous.

內生的　由體內因素產生或衍生的。與 exogenous 對比。

endolymph *n.* the fluid that fills the membranous *labyrinth of the ear.

內淋巴液　流入耳膜迷路的液體。

endolymphatic duct a blind-ended duct that leads from the sacculus and joins a duct from the utriculus of the membranous *labyrinth of the ear.

內淋巴管　一側為盲端的管道。從球囊發出，又與耳膜迷路橢圓囊發出的管道匯合。

endolymphatic sac a dilatation at the end of the *endolymphatic duct that removes waste products from the inner ear.

內淋巴囊　內淋巴管一端的膨隆，排除內耳內的廢物。

endometrial ablation the removal of the entire endometrium by means of a technique (*laser ablation*) in which a special type of laser, known as a *Nd: YAG laser* (neodymium: yttrium–aluminium–garnet laser), is used to destroy the endometrium in situ. The

子宮內膜摘除　使用激光技術，將全部子宮內膜摘除。這種特殊類型的激光Nd：YAG 激光（釹：釔－鋁－石榴石激光）被用以在原位摧毀子宮內膜。手術通常在局部麻醉後使用宮腔鏡實施，使用電凝法

operation is usually performed under local anaesthetic by using a *hysteroscope. The same effect may be achieved by *electrocoagulation (see also transcervical resection of the endometrium). Ablation may be used as an alternative to hysterectomy or hormone therapy in the treatment of abnormally heavy menstrual bleeding (see menorrhagia).

endometriosis *n.* the presence of tissue similar to the lining of the uterus (see endometrium) at other sites in the pelvis; it is thought to be caused by retrograde *menstruation. When the tissue has infiltrated the wall of the uterus (myometrium) the condition is known as *adenomyosis*. The tissue may also be found in the ovary, Fallopian tubes, pelvic ligaments, on the pelvic peritoneum, and even in the cervix and the vagina. This tissue undergoes the periodic changes similar to those of the endometrium and causes pelvic pain and severe *dysmenorrhoea. The pain continues throughout and after menstruation. Symptoms disappear if pregnancy occurs and after the menopause. Treatment during the reproductive years is largely confined to the use of drugs (e.g. *danazol), although restricted surgical treatment may also be necessary. The formation of pelvic *adhesions is a common sequel to endometriosis. In such circumstances the uterus, Fallopian tubes, and ovaries may need to be surgically removed in order to alleviate the symptoms.

endometritis *n.* inflammation of the *endometrium due to acute or chronic infection. It may be caused by foreign bodies, bacteria, viruses, or parasites. In the acute phase it may occur in the period immediately after childbirth

也可達到相同效果（參閱 transcervical resection of the endometrium）。子宮內膜摘除可能作為子宮切除術或者激素療法的替代方法，也可用於治療異常經血過多（參閱 menorrhagia）。

子宮內膜異位 子宮內膜樣物質存在於盆腔內其他部位（參閱 endometrium）。一般認為這是由逆行月經引起的。當異位組織侵入到子宮壁時，此狀態稱為子宮內膜異位。子宮內膜也可在卵巢、輸卵管、盆腔韌帶、盆腔腹膜上甚至在子宮頸和陰道發現。這些異位組織同子宮內膜一樣有周期性變化，引起盆腔疼和痛經。疼痛持續到月經之後。症狀可在懷孕和絕經期消失。在生育年齡治療局限於使用藥物（如達那唑），有條件的手術治療也是需要的。產生盆腔黏連是子宮內膜異位常見的後遺症。在此情況下，子宮、輸卵管和卵巢可能需要手術摘除，以使症狀緩解。

子宮內膜炎 由急性和慢性感染引起的子宮內膜炎症。可由異物、細菌、病毒或寄生蟲引起。急性發病可在產後（產褥期）即刻發生，而慢性可不伴有妊娠（如結核性子宮內膜

(puerperium) but the chronic phase may not be associated with pregnancy (as in tuberculous endometritis). Chronic endometritis in women with IUDs may be responsible for the contraceptive action.

炎）。放置宮內避孕器婦女的慢性子宮內膜炎可能起避孕作用。

endometrium *n.* the mucous membrane lining the uterus, which becomes progressively thicker and more glandular and has an increased blood supply in the latter part of the menstrual cycle. This prepares the endometrium for implantation of the embryo, but if this does not occur much of the endometrium breaks down and is lost in menstruation. If pregnancy is established the endometrium becomes the *decidua, which is shed after birth. **–endometrial** *adj.*

子宮內膜 附着於子宮內壁的黏膜。在月經周期的後期逐漸增厚，腺體增多，血供更多，這就為胚胎的種植做好了準備。如果沒有妊娠，大部分子宮內膜將脫落並在月經時排出體外，一旦妊娠，內膜將變成蛻膜，並在胎兒娩出後脫落。

endomorphic *adj.* describing a *body type that is relatively fat, with highly developed viscera and weak muscular and skeletal development. **–endomorph** *n.* **–endomorphy** *n.*

內胚層體形的 形容體態比較臃腫，內臟高度發達，而肌肉、骨骼發育較差的體型。

endomyocarditis *n.* an acute or chronic inflammatory disorder of the muscle and lining membrane of the heart. When the membrane surrounding the heart (pericardium) is also involved the condition is termed *pancarditis*. The principal causes are rheumatic fever and virus infections. There is enlargement of the heart, murmurs, embolism, and frequently arrhythmias. The treatment is that of the cause and complications. *See also* endocarditis.

A chronic condition, *endomyocardial fibrosis*, is seen in Black Africans: the cause is unknown.

心肌內膜炎 心肌和心內膜的急性或慢性炎症。炎症見於心外膜（心包）時，叫做全心炎。主要病因是風濕熱和病毒感染，症狀表現為心臟擴大、心臟雜音、栓塞及頻發的心律不齊。治療以病因和併發症的治療為主。參閱endocarditis。

一種慢性病症——心內膜肌纖維變性見於非洲黑人，其病因不明。

endomysium *n.* the fine connective tissue sheath that surrounds a single *muscle fibre.

肌內膜 包繞單個肌纖維，極薄的結締組織鞘。

endoneurium *n.* the layer of fibrous tissue that separates individual fibres within a *nerve.

神經內膜　一根神經內，分隔單個纖維的纖維組織層。

endoparasite *n.* a parasite that lives inside its host, for example in the liver, lungs, gut, or other tissues of the body. *Compare* ectoparasite.

內寄生物　寄生在宿主體內，例如在肝臟、肺、腸道或其他組織內生存的寄生物。與 ectoparasite 對比。

endopeptidase *n.* a digestive enzyme (e.g. *pepsin) that splits a whole protein into small peptide fractions by splitting the linkages between peptides in the interior of the molecule. *Compare* exopeptidase. *See also* peptidase.

肽鍵內切酶　一種消化酶（如胃蛋白酶）。可分解分子內兩肽之間的鍵，將整個蛋白質分解成若干個肽。與 exopeptidase 對比。參閱 peptidase。

endophthalmitis *n.* inflammation, usually due to imfection, within the eye.

眼內炎　眼內炎症，通常由感染引起。

endoplasm *n.* the inner cytoplasm of cells, which is less dense that the *ectoplasm and contains most of the cell's structures. **–endoplasmic** *adj.*

內質　細胞內胞質，不如細胞外質稠密，具有細胞內絕大部分結構。

endoplasmic reticulum (ER) a system of membranes present in the cytoplasm of cells. ER is described as *rough* when it has *ribosomes attached to its surface and *smooth* when ribosomes are absent. It is the site of manufacture of proteins and lipids and is concerned with the transport of these products within the cell (*see also* Golgi apparatus).

內質網　存在於細胞內胞質裏的膜系統。當其表面附有核糖體時，稱粗面內質網；沒有核糖體附着時為滑面內質網。內質網是產生蛋白質和脂類的部位，並參與它們在細胞內的轉移（參閱 Golgi apparatus）。

end organ a specialized structure at the end of a peripheral nerve, acting as a receptor for a particular sensation. Taste buds, in the tongue, are end organs subserving the sense of taste.

末梢裝置　周圍神經末梢處的一種特殊結構。有感受器作用，接受特殊感覺。舌上的味蕾就是感受味覺的末梢裝置。

endorphin *n.* one of a group of chemical compounds, similar to the *encephalins, that occur naturally in the brain and have pain-relieving properties similar

內啡肽　與腦啡肽類似的一組化合物。產生於腦內，有類似麻醉劑的鎮痛特性。內啡肽來自腦垂體中一種叫做 β-趨脂素

to those of the opiates. The endorphins are derived from a substance found in the pituitary gland known as *beta-lipotrophin*; they are thought to be concerned with controlling the activity of the endocrine glands.

endoscope *n.* any instrument used to obtain a view of the interior of the body. Examples of endoscopes include the *auriscope, used for examining the ear canal and eardrum, and the *gastroscope, for examining the inside of the stomach. Essentially, most endoscopes consist of a tube with a light at the end and an optical system or a miniature video camera for transmitting an image to the examiner's eye. *See also* fibrescope. **–endoscopic** *adj.* **–endoscopy** *n.*

endoscopic retrograde cholangiopancreatography *see* ERCP.

endospore *n.* the resting stage of certain bacteria, particularly species of the genera *Bacillus* and *Clostridium*. In adverse conditions the nucleus and cytoplasm within the normal vegetative stage of the bacterium can become enclosed within a tough protective coat, allowing the cell to survive. On return of favourable conditions the spore changes back to the vegetative form.

endosteum *n.* the membrane that lines the marrow cavity of a bone.

endothelioma *n.* any tumour arising from or resembling endothelium. It may arise from the linings of blood or lymph vessels (*haemangioendothelioma* and *lymphangioendothelioma* respectively); from the linings of the pleural cavity or the peritoneal cavity (*see* mesothelioma); or from the meninges (*see* meningioma).

的物質，並被認為與控制內分泌腺活動有關。

內窺鏡 用於觀察體內結構的任何儀器。例如，耳鏡，檢查耳道和耳鼓；胃鏡，檢查胃內結構。大多內窺鏡的基本結構是由尾部帶光源的管子和將映像轉送到檢驗者眼內的光學系統組成。參閱 fibrescope。

內窺鏡逆行性胰膽管造影術 參閱 ERCP。

內芽胞 某種細菌，特別是桿菌和梭狀芽胞菌屬的靜止期。在不利情況下，細菌內正常生長期的胞核和胞質可被堅硬的保護層包裹起來，使細胞免遭損害。回到有利時機時，芽胞又恢復到生長期的形態。

骨內膜 覆蓋骨髓腔的膜。

內皮瘤 源於內皮或類似內皮的任何腫瘤。也可起源於血管或淋巴管內皮（血管內皮瘤及淋巴管內皮瘤）、胸膜、腹膜（參閱 mesothelioma）或腦膜（參閱 meningioma）。

endothelium *n.* the single layer of cells that lines the heart, blood vessels, and lymphatic vessels. It is derived from embryonic mesoderm. *Compare* epithelium.

內皮　內襯心臟、血管及淋巴管的單層細胞層。來源於胚胎的中胚層。與 epithelium 對比。

endothermic *adj.* describing a chemical reaction associated with the absorption of heat. *Compare* exothermic.

吸熱的　用於描述吸收熱量的化學反應。與 exothermic 對比。

endotoxin *n.* a poison generally harmful to all body tissues, contained within certain Gram-negative bacteria and released only when the bacterial cell is broken down or dies and disintegrates. *Compare* exotoxin.

內毒素　通常對人體所有組織都有害的毒物。存在於特定的革蘭氏陰性細菌體內，只有在細菌細胞被破壞、死亡及分解時才釋放出來。與 exotoxin 對比。

end-plate *n.* the area of muscle cell membrane immediately beneath the motor nerve ending at a *neuromuscular junction. Special receptors in this area trigger muscular contraction when the nerve ending releases its *neurotransmitter.

終板　在神經肌肉結合處，直接位於運動神經末梢下的肌細胞膜的區域。當神經末梢釋放神經遞質時，該區域的特殊受體就促使肌肉收縮。

enema *n.* (*pl.* **enemata** or **enemas**) a quantity of fluid infused into the rectum through a tube passed into the anus. An *evacuant enema* (soap or olive oil) is used to remove faeces. A *barium enema* using barium sulphate, which is opaque to X-rays, is given to demonstrate the colon by X-ray. A *therapeutic enema* is used to insert drugs into the rectum, usually corticosteroids in the treatment of *proctocolitis.

灌腸法　將一定量的液體通過從肛門插管注入直腸。清洗灌腸（用肥皂或橄欖油）用於排出糞便。硫酸鋇能對X綫顯影，所以鋇灌腸用於使結腸在X綫下顯影。治療性灌腸用於把藥灌入直腸，皮質類固醇灌腸常用來治療直腸結腸炎。

enervation *n.* **1.** weakness; loss of strength. **2.** the surgical removal of a nerve.

(1) 虛弱無力；喪失力量　(2) 神經切除

enflurane *n.* a volatile drug used to induce and maintain general anaesthesia. It is administered by inhalation. Possible side-effects include seizures, hepatitis, and kidney damage.

恩氟烷　用於引起和保持全身麻醉的揮發性藥物。吸入麻醉劑，可能的副作用包括癲癇發作、肝炎和腎臟受損。

engagement *n.* (in obstetrics) the stage of pregnancy that occurs when the presenting part of the fetus has descended into the mother's pelvis. Engagement of the fetal head occurs when the widest part has passed through the pelvic inlet.

engram *n.* the supposed physical basis of an individual memory.

enkephalin *n. see* encephalin.

enophthalmos *n.* a condition in which the eye is abnormally sunken into the socket. It may follow fractures of the floor of the orbit that allow the eye to sink downwards and backwards.

enoxacin *n. see* quinolone.

enoxaparin *n. see* low-molecular-weight heparin.

enoximone *n.* an *inotropic drug used in heart failure to increase the force and output of the heart. It is administered by injection. Trade name: **Perfan**.

ensiform cartilage *see* xiphoid process.

ENT *see* otorhinolaryngology.

Entamoeba *n.* a genus of widely distributed amoebae, of which some species are parasites of the digestive tract of man. *E. histolytica* invades and destroys the tissues of the intestinal wall, causing amoebic *dysentery and ulceration of the gut wall (*see also* amoeboma); infection of the liver with this species (amoebic hepatitis) is common in

銜接 （產科學）產程的一部分，指胎兒先露部降至母親骨盆。胎頭部銜接發生指胎頭最寬大部分已通過骨盆入口。

興奮痕迹 個體記憶的假設生理基礎。

腦啡肽 參閱 encephalin。

眼球陷沒 眼睛失常陷入眼眶中，眶底骨折時，眼睛可向後下方凹陷。

依諾沙星 參閱 quinolone。

依諾肝素 參閱 low-molecular-weight heparin。

依諾昔酮 一種可影響收縮力的藥物，用於心臟衰竭的治療，它可增強心收縮力，增大心輸出量。注射劑。商品名：Perfan。

劍突軟骨 參閱 xiphoid process。

耳鼻喉科 參閱 otorhinolaryngology。

內阿米巴屬 廣泛分布的阿米巴原蟲屬，其中一些種類是人類消化道的寄生蟲。溶組織內阿米巴侵入並破壞腸壁組織，引起痢疾和腸壁潰瘍（參閱 amoeboma）。這種阿米巴感染肝臟（阿米巴肝炎）在熱帶國家很普遍。結腸內阿米巴是無害的腸內寄生物。釀內阿米巴

tropical countries. *E. coli* is a harmless intestinal parasite; E. *gingivalis*, found within the spaces between the teeth, is associated with periodontal disease and gingivitis.

見於兩齒之間的縫隙，與牙周病及齒齦炎有關。

enter- (entero-) *prefix denoting* the intestine   Example: *enterolith* (calculus in).

〔前綴〕**腸**　如腸結石。

enteral *adj.* of or relating to the intestinal tract.

腸的　與腸道有關的。

enteral feeding *see* nutrition.

腸營養法　參閱 nutrition。

enteralgia *n. see* colic.

腸痛　參閱 colic。

enterectomy *n.* surgical removal of part of the intestine.

腸切除術　部分腸切除手術。

enteric *adj.* relating to or affecting the intestine.

腸的　指腸或侵犯腸的。

enteric-coated *adj.* describing tablets that are coated with a substance that enables them to pass through the stomach and into the intestine unchanged. Enteric-coated tablets contain drugs that are destroyed by the acid contents of the stomach.

包有腸衣的　指被一層物質包裹的藥片。使此藥片通過胃進入腸道而不發生變化。包有腸衣的藥片含有能被胃酸破壞的藥物。

enteric fever *see* paratyphoid fever, typhoid fever.

腸熱病　參閱 paratyphoid fever，typhoid fever。

enteritis *n.* inflammation of the small intestine, usually causing diarrhoea. *Infective enteritis* is caused by viruses or bacteria; *radiation enteritis* is caused by X-rays or radioactive isotopes. *See also* Crohn's disease (regional enteritis), gastroenteritis.

腸炎　小腸炎症，通常引起腹瀉。感染性腸炎由病毒和細菌引起；放射性腸炎由 X 綫或放射性同位素引起。參閱 Crohn's disease，gastroenteritis。

enterobiasis (oxyuriasis) *n.* a disease, common in children throughout the world, caused by the parasitic nematode

蟯蟲病　世界常見的一種兒童疾病。由寄生在大腸裏的蟯蟲引起。儘管此寄生蟲不會給腸

Enterobius vermicularis (*see* pinworm) in the large intestine. The worms do not cause any serious lesions of the gut wall although, rarely, they may provoke appendicitis. The emergence of the female from the anus at night irritates and inflames the surrounding skin, causing the patient to scratch and thereby contaminate fingers and nails with infective eggs. The eggs may reinfect the same child or be spread to other children. Worms may occasionally enter the vulva and cause a discharge from the vagina. Enterobiasis responds well to treatment with *piperazine compounds.

壁造成嚴重病變，但偶爾也引起闌尾炎。夜間，雌蟯蟲從肛門爬出，刺激周圍皮膚並引起炎症，促使患者去搔抓，因此，患者手指及指甲被傳染性蟲卵污染。蟲卵又可重新感染同一兒童或傳播給另一兒童。蟯蟲偶可進入陰道刺激陰道分泌。哌嗪治療蟯蟲病效果良好。

Enterobius (Oxyuris) *n. see* pinworm.

蟯蟲屬 參閱 pinworm。

enterocele *n.* a hernia of the *pouch of Douglas (between the rectum and uterus) into the upper part of the posterior vaginal wall. It may contain loops of small bowel.

後陰道疝 道格拉斯腔疝（直腸和子宮之間），在陰道後壁上部。可含有小腸祥。

enterocentesis *n.* a surgical procedure in which a hollow needle is pushed through the wall of the stomach or intestines to release an abnormal accumulation of gas or fluid or to introduce a catheter for feeding (*see* gastrostomy, enterostomy).

腸穿刺 一種外科手術。將空心針通過胃壁或腸壁刺入其內來釋放不正常的積氣或積液，或者插入飼管（參閱 gastrostomy enterostomy）。

enterocolitis *n.* inflammation of the colon and small intestine. *See also* colitis, enteritis, necrotizing enterocolitis.

小腸結腸炎 結腸和小腸炎症。參閱 colitis，enteritis，necrotizing enterocolitis。

enterogastrone *n.* a hormone from the small intestine (duodenum) that inhibits the secretion of gastric juice by the stomach. It is released when the stomach contents pass into the small intestine.

腸抑胃素 小腸（十二指腸）分泌的激素，抑制胃液的分泌。胃內容物進入小腸時，此激素才被分泌出來。

enterogenous *adj.* borne by or carried in the intestine.

腸源的 由腸道產生的或被腸道輸送的。

enterokinase *n.* the former name for
*enteropeptidase.

腸激酶　腸肽酶的舊稱。

enterolith *n.* a stone within the intestine.
It usually builds up around a gallstone or
a swallowed fruit stone.

腸石　腸道內的石頭。是圍繞
着膽石或被吞入的果核產生
的。

enteromegaly *n.* *Rare.* enlargement
(usually increased diameter) of the
intestine.

巨腸　罕見的腸增大（通常為
直徑增大）。

enteropathy *n.* disease of the small
intestine. *See also* coeliac disease
(gluten-induced enteropathy).

腸病　小腸疾病，參閱 coeliac
disease (gluten-induced enteropathy)。

enteropeptidase *n.* an enzyme secreted
by the glands of the small intestine that
acts on trypsinogen to produce *trypsin.

腸肽酶　小腸腺分泌的一種
酶，作用於胰蛋白酶原，產生
胰蛋白酶。

enteropexy *n.* a surgical operation in
which part of the intestine is fixed to
the abdominal wall. This was formerly
performed for visceroptosis (a condition
in which the abdominal organs were
thought to have descended to a lower
than normal position), but it is no longer
carried out.

腸固定術　將部分腸管固定在
腹壁上的一種外科手術。以
前，此手術用以治療內臟下垂
（腹腔臟器離開正常位置而下
傾）。現已不實施此手術。

enteroptosis *n.* a condition in which
loops of intestine (especially transverse
*colon) are in a low anatomical position.
At one time this was thought to cause
various abdominal symptoms, and operations were devised to correct it. It is now
known that no symptoms result from
simple anatomical variations of this sort.

腸下垂　腸袢（特別是橫結腸）
低於其固有解剖位置。曾有一
時期，此類情況被認為是腹部
各種症狀的原因，並設計手術
予以糾正。現在已知這種單純
的解剖位置變化是不會引起任
何症狀的。

enterorrhaphy *n.* the surgical procedure
of stitching an intestine that has either
perforated or been divided during an
operation.

腸縫合術　因腸穿孔或手術時
腸斷離而將其縫合的一種外科
手術。

enterostomy *n.* an operation in which
the small intestine is brought through
the abdominal wall and opened (*see*

腸造口術　將小腸經腹壁拉
出並造口（參閱 duodeno-
stomy，jejunostomy，ileo-

duodenostomy, jejunostomy, ileostomy) or is joined to the stomach (*gastroenterostomy*) or to another loop of small intestine (*enteroenterostomy.*)

stomy）或將其與胃或其他腸祥相連接的手術。

enterotomy *n.* surgical incision into the intestine.

腸切開術　切開腸道的手術。

enterotoxin *n.* a poisonous substance that has a particularly marked effect upon the gastrointestinal tract, causing vomiting, diarrhoea, and abdominal pain.

腸毒素　一種有毒物質，對胃腸道有明顯作用，可引起嘔吐、腹瀉和腹痛。

enterovirus *n.* any virus that enters the body through the gastrointestinal tract, multiplies there and then (generally) invades the central nervous system. Enteroviruses include *Coxsackie viruses and *polioviruses.

腸道病毒　通過胃腸道進入體內，並在腸內繁殖，然後侵犯中樞神經系統的任何病毒，包括柯薩奇病毒和脊髓灰質炎病毒。

enterozoon *n.* any animal species inhabiting or infecting the gut of another. *See also* endoparasite.

腸寄生物　任何寄生於他種動物腸道中的動物種類。參閱 endoparasite。

enthesis *n.* the junction of tendon and bone.

填補法　肌腱與骨的連接方法。

enthesopathy *n.* any rheumatic disease resulting in inflammation of *entheses. Ankylosing *spondylitis, *psoriatic arthritis, and *Reiter's disease are examples.

腱端病　任何能導致肌肉與腱在骨起止點處炎症的風濕病。例如關節強硬性脊椎炎、銀屑病關節炎及賴特爾病。

entoptic phenomena visual sensations caused by changes within the eye itself, rather than by the normal light stimulation process. The commonest are tiny-floating spots (*floaters*) that most people can see occasionally, especially when gazing at a brightly illuminated background (such as a blue sky).

內視現象　因眼內本身變化，而非正常光綫的刺激所引起的視覺。最常見的眼內變化是大多數人都能偶爾見到的小懸浮點（懸浮物），特別是在凝視光芒耀眼的背景（如藍天）時。

entropion *n.* inturning of the eyelid towards the eyeball. The lashes may rub

瞼內翻　眼瞼向內翻向眼球，睫毛可因此摩擦眼睛，引起炎

against the eye and cause irritation (*see* trichiasis). The commonest type is *spastic entropion of the lower eyelid*, due to spasm of the muscles that closes the eye (orbicularis oculi). Entropion may also be caused by scarring of the lining membrane (conjunctiva) of the lid.

症。最常見的炎症類型是下眼瞼痙攣性內翻，因眼輪匝肌痙攣引起。內翻也可因結膜瘢痕引起。

enucleation *n.* a surgical operation in which an organ, tumour, or cyst is completely removed. In ophthalmology it is an operation in which the eyeball is removed but the other structures in the socket (e.g. eye muscles) are left in place. Commonly a plastic ball is temporarily buried in the socket to give a better cosmetic result.

剜出術 將器官、腫瘤或囊腫全部除去的手術。在眼科學中，指將眼球除去，保留眼眶內其他結構（如眼肌）的手術。通常是將一個塑料球植入眼眶獲得較好的整容效果。

enuresis *n.* the involuntary passing of urine, especially bedwetting by children at night (*nocturnal enuresis*). (The majority of children are dry during daytime by the age of three years and at night by four.) Nocturnal enuresis can be caused by underlying disorders of the urinary tract, particularly infection, but is usually functional in nature. The condition settles spontaneously as the child grows older, but it may persist into teenage – and rarely adult – life. It can be treated by the use of a nocturnal alarm (*see* bell and pad), by *reinforcement of periods of continence with a reward system, or by drug treatment. *See also* incontinence. **–enuretic** *adj.*

遺尿 無意識地排尿，尤其是兒童在夜間的尿床（夜尿症）。夜尿症可由潛在的尿道疾病引起，特別是感染。但通常為功能性遺尿。隨兒童年齡的增長，發病可逐漸停止，但也可持續到青少年，個別人還可持續到成年，直到終生。治療可在夜間使用鬧鐘（參閱 bell and pad），通過獎勵辦法強化其克制時間，或者用藥物治療。參閱 incontinence。

environment *n.* any or all aspects of the surroundings of an organism, both internal and external, which influence its growth, development, and behaviour.

環境 生物體周圍的各個方面，包括內外環境，能影響生物體的生長、發育及其行為。

Environmental Health Officer (EHO) a person, employed by a local authority with special training in such aspects of

環境衛生官員 當地政府僱傭的人員，他們在環境衛生和人群的居住衛生、衛生設施、飲

environmental health and pollution as housing, sanitation, food, clean air, and water supplies (formerly known as a *Public Health Inspector*). Though not a registered medical practitioner, the EHO is responsible for the organization of the environmental health department. If medical (epidemiological) advice is required, the appropriate *public health physician (proper officer) acts in an advisory or consultant capacity.

食衛生、空氣淨化和供水衛生等方面受過專門訓練（舊稱公共衛生督察）。他們雖然不是註冊醫生，但他們負責環境衛生部門的組織工作。如果需要醫學（流行病學）咨詢，相應的公共衛生醫師（專職官員）將擔負顧問或高級醫師職務。

enzyme *n.* a protein that, in small amounts, speeds up the rate of a biological reaction without itself being used up in the reaction (i.e. it acts as a catalyst). An enzyme acts by binding with the substance involved in the reaction (the *substrate*) and converting it into another substance (the *product* of the reaction). An enzyme is relatively specific in the type of reaction it catalyses; hence there are many different enzymes for the various biochemical reactions. Each enzyme requires certain conditions for optimum activity, particularly correct temperature and pH, the presence of *coenzymes, and the absence of specific inhibitors. Enzymes are unstable and are easily inactivated by heat or certain chemicals. They are produced within living cells and may act either within the cell (as in cellular respiration) or outside it (as in digestion). The names of enzymes usually end in -*ase*; enzymes are named according to the substrate upon which they act (as in *lactase*), or the type of reaction they catalyse (as in *hydrolase*).

Enzymes are essential for the normal functioning and development of the body. Failure in the production or activity of a single enzyme may result in metabolic disorders; such disorders are often inherited and some have serious effects. **–enzymatic** *adj.*

酶 一種蛋白質，只需少量就可加速生化反應，而其自身並不參加反應（即起催化劑作用）。酶是通過與反應中的物質（底物）結合，又將該物質轉變成另一物質（反應的產物）而發揮作用的。酶對其催化反應的種類是有特異性的。因此，有很多不同的酶參與各種生化反應。為達到其最佳活性，每種酶都需一定條件，特別是適宜的溫度和 pH 值及輔酶的存在和無特異性抑制劑參與。酶是不穩定的，很易受熱及某些化學物質影響而失活。它們在活細胞內產生，並可在細胞內和細胞外起作用（前者如細胞呼吸，後者如消化）。酶的名稱通常以 -ase 結尾，並根據其作用的物質或催化反應而命名（前者如乳糖酶，後者如水解酶）。

酶對身體的正常功能和發育是必要的。一種酶的產生或活性受阻可引起代謝性疾病。這種病通常是遺傳的，有些病還可導致嚴重的後果。

enzyme-linked immunosorbent assay (ELISA) a sensitive technique for measuring the amount of a substance. An antibody that will bind to the substance is produced; the amount of an easily measured enzyme that then binds to the antibody complex enables accurate measurement.

酶聯免疫吸附試驗 測定物質含量的一種靈敏技術。一種抗體附着於待測物質上；已知含量的酶再附着於抗體化合物上，這樣來測定一種物質的準確含量。

eonism *n.* the adoption of female manners and dress by a man. *See* transsexualism, transvestitism.

易裝癖 男性採用女性的舉止和裝束。參閱 transsexualism，transvestitism。

eosin *n.* a red acidic dye, produced by the reaction of bromine and fluorescein, used to stain biological specimens for microscopical examination. Eosin may be used in conjunction with a contrasting blue alkaline dye taken up by different parts of the same specimen.

伊紅 紅色酸性染料。為溴和熒光素反應的產物，用以對生物標本進行染色來進行顯微鏡下檢查。作為對照，伊紅可與能被同一標本不同部位所吸收的鹼性藍染料聯合使用。

eosinopenia *n.* a decrease in the number of eosinophils in the blood.

嗜酸性細胞減少 血液中嗜酸性細胞數量下降。

eosinophil *n.* a variety of white blood cell distinguished by the presence in its cytoplasm of coarse granules that stain orange-red with *Romanowsky stains. The function of the eosinophil is poorly understood, but it is capable of ingesting foreign particles, is present in large numbers in lining or covering surfaces within the body, and is involved in allergic responses. There are normally 40–400 $\times 10^6$ eosinophils per litre of blood.

嗜酸性細胞 血液中能用羅曼諾夫斯基染色法將胞質內粗顆粒染成橘紅色的各種白細胞。此細胞的功能不清楚，但能消化外來顆粒，並大量存在於體內臟器的內層或外表，還與過敏反應有關。正常情況下，每升血液中有 40~400 $\times 10^6$ 個嗜酸性細胞。

eosinophilia *n.* an increase in the number of eosinophils in the blood. Eosinophilia occurs in response to certain drugs and in a variety of diseases, including allergies, parasitic infestations, and certain forms of leukaemia.

嗜酸性細胞增多 血液中嗜酸性細胞數量增多。可發生於各種疾病，包括變態反應、寄生蟲感染及某些類型的白血病。

eparterial *adj.* situated on or above an artery.

動脈上的 位於動脈上或動脈以上的。

ependyma *n.* the extremely thin membrane, composed of cells of the *glia (*ependymal cells*), that lines the ventricles of the brain and the choroid plexuses. It is responsible for helping to form cerebrospinal fluid. **–ependymal** *adj.*

室管膜　由神經膠質經胞（室管膜細胞）組成的薄膜。內襯腦室和脈絡叢，由此產生腦脊液。

ependymoma *n.* a cerebral tumour derived from the glial (non-nervous) cells lining the cavities of the ventricles of the brain (*see* ependyma). It may obstruct the flow of cerebrospinal fluid, causing a *hydrocephalus.

室管膜瘤　生長於腦室腔內膜膠質細胞的（非神經細胞的）腦腫瘤。可堵塞腦脊液的流動，引起腦積水。

ephebiatrics *n.* the branch of medicine concerned with the common disorders of children and adolescents. *Compare* paediatrics.

青年病學　研究兒童和青少年常見病的醫學分支。與 paediatrics 對比。

ephedrine *n.* a drug that causes constriction of blood vessels and widening of the bronchial passages (*see* sympathomimetic). It is used mainly in the treatment of asthma and other allergic conditions and chronic bronchitis. It is administered by mouth or by inhalation and may cause nausea, vomiting, insomnia, headache, and nervousness.

麻黃鹼　能使血管收縮、支氣管擴張的藥物（參閱 sympathomimetic）。主要治療哮喘、某些過敏性疾病及慢性支氣管炎。口服或吸入藥。可引起惡心、嘔吐、失眠、頭痛及神經過敏。

EPI *see* echo planar imaging.

回波平面成像技術　參閱 echo planar imaging。

epi- *prefix denoting* above or upon.

〔前綴〕上，在……之上

epiblepharon *n.* an abnormal fold of skin, present from birth, stretching across the eye just above the lashes of the upper eyelid or in front of them in the lower lid. It may cause the lower lashes to turn upwards or inwards against the eye. It usually disappears within the first year of life.

瞼贅皮　出生時就存在的不正常的皮膚皺褶。占據上眼瞼睫毛上部的整個眼部或下眼瞼睫毛的前部。可使下睫毛上翻或內翻而摩擦眼睛。一般一歲時消退。

epicanthus (epicanthic fold) *n.* a vertical fold of skin from the upper eyelid

內眥贅皮　從上眼瞼下垂，覆蓋內眼角的垂直皮膚皺褶。在

that covers the inner corner of the eye. It is normal in Mongolian races and occurs abnormally in certain congenital conditions, e.g. *Down's syndrome. **–epicanthal**, **epicanthic** *adj*.

蒙古人種是正常現象，也可發生於某種先天性疾患，如唐氏綜合徵。

epicardia *n*. the part of the *oesophagus, about 2 cm long, that extends from the level of the diaphragm to the stomach.

食管腹部 從橫膈到胃的那部分食管，約2cm長。

epicardium *n*. the outermost layer of the heart wall, enveloping the myocardium. It is a serous membrane that forms the inner layer of the serous *pericardium. **–epicardial** *adj*.

心外膜 包裹心肌的心壁最外層。是一層漿膜，構成了心包漿膜層的內層。

epicondyle *n*. the protuberance above a *condyle at the end of an articulating bone.

上髁 骨關節端髁上部的突起。

epicranium *n*. the structures that cover the cranium, i.e. all layers of the scalp.

頭被 覆蓋頭顱的結構，例如頭皮各層。

epicranius *n*. the muscle of the scalp. The *frontal* portion, at the forehead, is responsible for raising the eyebrows and wrinkling the forehead; the *occipital* portion, at the base of the skull, draws the scalp backwards.

顱頂肌 頭皮中的肌肉。額部的額肌負責提眉和皺額。顱底枕部肌肉能向後牽拉頭皮。

epicritic *adj*. describing or relating to sensory nerve fibres responsible for the fine degrees of sensation, as of temperature and touch. *Compare* protopathic.

細覺的 用於描述細微感覺，或與負責接收細微感覺，如溫度、觸覺的神經纖維有關的。與 protopathic 對比。

epidemic *n*. a sudden outbreak of infectious disease that spreads rapidly through the population, affecting a large proportion of people. The commonest epidemics today are of influenza. *Compare* endemic, pandemic. **–epidemic** *adj*.

流行病 突然爆發，迅速在人羣中傳播，危害大批人的傳染病。當今，最常見的流行病是流行性感冒。與 endemic，pandemic 對比。

epidemiology *n*. the study of epidemic disease, with a view to finding means of control and future prevention. This

流行病學 研究控制和預防流行病措施的科學。不僅只研究典型的流行病，如鼠疫、天

not only applies to the study of such classical epidemics as plague, smallpox, and cholera but also includes all forms of disease that relate to the environment and ways of life. It thus includes the study of the links between smoking and cancer, and diet and coronary disease, as well as *communicable diseases.

花、霍亂，也研究與環境和生活方式有關的所有類型的疾病。因此，流行病學也包括研究吸烟與癌症、膳食與冠心病以及傳染性疾病的關係。

epidermis *n.* the outer layer of the *skin, which is divided into four layers (see illustration). The innermost *Malpighian or germinative layer* (*stratum germinativum*) consists of continuously dividing cells. The other three layers are continually renewed as cells from the germinative layer are gradually pushed outwards and become progressively impregnated with keratin (*see* keratinization). The outermost layer (stratum corneum) consists of dead cells whose cytoplasm has been entirely replaced by keratin. It is thickest on the soles of the feet and palms of the hands. **–epidermal** *adj.*

表皮 皮膚的最外層。可分為四層（見圖）。最內層是馬爾皮基層或稱生發層（表皮生發層），由不斷分裂的細胞組成。其他三層隨生發層細胞的逐漸上擠而不斷更新，並不斷產生角蛋白（參閱 keratinization）。最外層（角質層）由死亡細胞組成，其胞質已完全被角蛋白取代。在腳跟和手掌部位，它是最厚的。

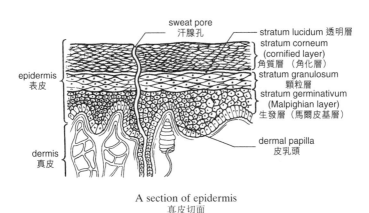

sweat pore
汗腺孔

stratum lucidum 透明層
stratum corneum
(cornified layer)
角質層 （角化層）
stratum granulosum
顆粒層
stratum germinativum
(Malpighian layer)
生發層（馬爾皮基層）

epidermis
表皮

dermal papilla
皮乳頭

dermis
真皮

A section of epidermis
真皮切面

epidermoid *adj.* having the appearance of epidermis (the outer layer of the skin): used to describe certain tumours of tissues other than the skin.

表皮樣的 具有表皮外觀的。用以形容某些腫瘤組織，不是形容皮膚。

epidermoid cyst *see* sebaceous cyst.

表皮樣囊腫 參閱 sebaceous cyst。

epidermolysis bullosa any one of a group of genetically determined disorders characterized by blistering of skin and mucous membranes. In the simple forms the blistering is induced by injury. In the more serious (dystrophic) forms the blistering may occur spontaneously; some of the dystrophic forms of the disease are fatal.

大疱性表皮鬆解 先天性疾病之一。表現為皮膚和黏膜起疱，單純症狀是由創傷引起，嚴重時（營養不良性的），可自發性地起疱；一些營養不良性的起疱是致命的。

Epidermophyton *n.* a genus of fungi that grow on the skin, causing *ringworm. *See also* dermatophyte.

表皮癬菌屬 生長在皮膚上的真菌屬。可引起皮膚感染性腳癬及朵比癬。參閱 dermatophyte。

epidiascope *n.* an apparatus for projecting a greatly magnified image of an object, such as a specimen on a microscope slide, on to a screen.

實物幻燈機 能將物體（如顯微鏡載物片上的標本）高倍放大到屏幕上的投影裝置。

epididymectomy *n.* the surgical removal or excision of the epididymis.

附睾切除術 摘除或完整切除附睾的手術。

epididymis *n.* (*pl.* **epididymides**) a highly convoluted tube, about seven metres long, that connects the *testis to the vas deferens. The spermatozoa are moved passively along the tube over a period of several days, during which time they mature and become capable of fertilization. They are concentrated and stored in the lower part of the epididymis until ejaculation. **–epididymal** *adj.*

附睾 高度卷曲的管道，連接睾丸和輸精管，約7米長。精子沿管道被動移動需幾天時間，在此期間，精子成熟並有能力授精。精子在附睾下部濃縮並貯存，直到射精。

epididymitis *n.* inflammation of the epididymis. The usual cause is infection spreading down the vas deferens from the bladder or urethra, resulting in pain, swelling, and redness of the affected half of the scrotum. The inflammation may spread to the testicle (*epididymo-*

附睾炎 附睾炎症。常見病因是源於膀胱或尿道經輸精管蔓延的感染。患側陰囊疼痛、紅腫。炎症還可擴散到睾丸。可用抗生素及鎮痛藥物治療。

orchitis). Treatment is by administration of antibiotics and analgesics.

epididymovasostomy *n.* the operation of connecting the vas deferens to the epididymis to bypass obstruction of the latter. It is performed in an attempt to cure *azoospermia caused by this blockage.

輸精管附睾吻合術　連接輸精管與附睾的手術，以繞過附睾阻塞，此手術用於治療由於附睾阻塞而導致的精子缺乏。

epidural (extradural) *adj.* on or over the dura mater (the outermost of the three membranes covering the brain and spinal cord). The *epidural space* is the space between the dura mater of the spinal cord and the vertebral canal. The spinal epidural space is used for anaesthetizing spinal nerve roots, especially to provide pain relief during childbirth. *See also* spinal anaesthesia.

硬膜外的　在硬腦脊膜（覆蓋腦及脊髓的三層膜中的最外層）以外的。硬膜外腔是硬脊膜和椎管之間的間隙。硬脊膜外腔被用於脊神經根麻醉，特別適於緩解分娩時疼痛。參閱 spinal anaesthesia。

epigastrium *n.* the upper central region of the *abdomen. **–epigastric** *adj.*

上腹部的　腹部的中上部位。

epigastrocele *n.* a *hernia through the upper central abdominal wall.

上腹疝　中上腹壁疝。

epiglottis *n.* a thin leaf-shaped flap of cartilage, covered with mucous membrane, situated immediately behind the root of the tongue. It covers the entrance to the *larynx during swallowing.

會厭　由黏膜覆蓋的葉狀軟骨薄瓣。直接位於舌根後部。在吞咽時，蓋住喉頭入口處。

epiglottitis *n.* swelling and inflammation of the epiglottis and other parts of the *supraglottis, obstructing air flow to the lungs. It is usually caused by the bacterium *Haemophilus influenzae*. Treatment is by administration of antibiotics, careful observation, and possible *intubation or *tracheostomy.

會厭炎　會厭炎和聲門其他部分炎症的水腫及發炎堵塞了通入肺部的氣流，通常由流感嗜血桿菌引起。治療上可採用抗生素，仔細觀察，必要時用插管法或者氣管切開術。

epilation *n.* the removal of a hair by its roots. This can be done mechanically

脫毛法　從根部除去毛髮。可機械性拔除（一根根地拔掉或

(by pulling the hairs individually or using wax to strip an area of hair) or by electrolysis.

用蠟除去某一部位的毛髮），或通過電解法除去。

epilepsy *n.* a disorder of brain function characterized by recurrent seizures that have a sudden onset. *Idiopathic epilepsy* is not associated with structural damage to the brain and includes *generalized epilepsy*. This may take the form of *major*, or *tonic-clonic*, seizures (formerly called *grand mal*). At the onset the patient falls to the ground unconscious with his muscles in a state of spasm. The lack of any respiratory movement may result in a bluish discoloration of the skin and lips (cyanosis). This – the tonic phase – is replaced by convulsive movements, when the tongue may be bitten and urinary incontinence may occur (the clonic phase). Movements gradually cease and the patient may rouse in a state of confusion, complaining of headache, or he may fall asleep.

In another type of idiopathic epilepsy, mainly affecting children, the seizures take the form of *absences* (formerly called *petit mal*): brief spells of unconsciousness, lasting for a few seconds, during which posture and balance are maintained. The eyes stare blankly and there may be fluttering movements of the lids and momentary twitching of the fingers and mouth. The electroencephalogram characteristically shows bisynchronous wave and spike discharges (3 per second) during the seizures and at other times. Attacks are sometimes provoked by over-breathing or intermittent photic stimulation. As the stream of thought is completely interrupted, children with frequent seizures may have learning difficulties. This form of epilepsy seldom appears before the age of three or after adoles-

癲癇 以反覆突然發作為特徵的腦功能失常疾病。特發性癲癇不伴有大腦的結構損傷，包括廣義上的癲癇。特發性癲癇形式是較大的，或者陣發性強直痙攣發作（正式稱為癲癇大發作）。病人發作時倒地，神志不清伴有抽搐。呼吸運動的缺乏導致皮膚、口唇變藍色（紫紺）。強直期後是抽搐，此時可能發生舌咬傷和尿失禁（痙攣期）。抽搐可逐漸停止，病人神志混亂，主訴頭疼或者入睡。

特發性癲癇的另一類型主要發生於兒童，表現為失神（以前稱為小發作）：短暫數秒鐘的神志不清，此時能保持身體姿勢和平衡。雙眼毫無表情地發呆，眼瞼不停地閉合及手指和唇部的瞬間抽動。在發作和平時腦電圖能特徵性地顯示雙同時性波，波峯形狀改變（每秒3次）。有時深呼吸和間斷的光刺激可誘發癲癇。由於完全打斷了思維過程，經常發作的兒童學習會有困難。此種形式的癲癇很少在3歲以前和青春期之後出現，到成年可自發消失，但也可能在大發作和不完全癲癇之後發作。

不全性（病竈性或症狀性）癲癇是腦結構有損傷的表現症狀。發作特點取決於腦部受損的部位。在傑克遜運動性發作中，抽搐從拇指傳到手、肩、臉（這種傳播方式稱為進行型）。顳葉癲癇（精神運動型癲癇）是由大腦顳葉或鄰近頂葉皮質層疾病引起。其症狀包括嗅幻覺、味幻覺、視幻覺及

cence. It often subsides spontaneously in adult life, but it may be followed by the onset of major or partial epilepsy.

Partial (or *focal* or *symptomatic*) *epilepsy* is a symptom of structural damage to the brain, and the nature of the seizure depends upon the location of the damage in the brain. In a *Jacksonian* motor seizure the convulsive movements might spread from the thumb to the hand, arm, and face (this spread of symptoms is called the *march*). *Temporal lobe* (or *psychomotor*) *epilepsy* is caused by disease in the cortex of the temporal lobe or the adjacent paritetal lobe of the brain. Its symptoms may include *hallucinations of smell, taste, sight, and hearing, paroxysmal disorders of memory, and *automatism. Throughout an attack the patient is in a state of clouded awareness and afterwards he may have no recollection of the event (*see also* déjà vu, jamais vu).

The different forms of epilepsy can be controlled by the use of *antiepileptic drugs. **–epileptic** *adj*., *n*.

聽幻覺，還時常出現記憶障礙和自動症。在整個發作期間，患者始終意識不清。發作後，患者回憶不起這一過程（參閱déjà vu，jamais vu）。

用抗癲癇藥物能夠控制不同類型的癲癇。

epileptogenic *adj*. having the capacity to provoke epileptic seizures.

引起癲癇的 具有引起癲癇發作能力的。

epiloia *n*. *see* tuberous sclerosis.

結節性腦硬化 參閱 tuberous sclerosis。

epimenorrhagia *n*. *see* menorrhagia.

月經過多 參閱 menorrhagia。

epimenorrhoea *n*. menstruation at shorter intervals than is normal.

月經過頻 月經間期縮短。

epimysium *n*. the fibrous elastic tissue that surrounds a *muscle.

肌外膜 包繞肌肉的彈性纖維組織。

epinephrine *n*. *see* adrenaline.

腎上腺素 參閱 adrenaline。

epineural *adj*. derived from or situated on the neural arch of a vertebra.

神經弓上的 源於或位於椎骨神經弓上的。

epineurium *n.* the outer sheath of connective tissue that encloses the bundles (fascicles) of fibres that make up a *nerve.

神經外膜　包繞組成神經纖維束的結締組織外鞘。

epiphenomenon *n.* an unusual symptom or event that may occur simultaneously with a disease but is not necessarily directly related to it. *Compare* complication.

副現象　不正常的症狀或事態。可與疾病同時發生，但不一定與其有直接的關係。與 complication 對比。

epiphora *n.* watering of the eye, in which tears flow onto the cheek. It is due to some abnormality of the tear drainage system (*see* lacrimal apparatus).

淚溢　眼睛流淚，且流到頰部。因淚液引流系統不正常引起。

epiphysis *n.* **1.** the end of a long bone, which is initially separated by cartilage from the shaft (diaphysis) of the bone and develops separately. It eventually fuses with the diaphysis to form a complete bone. Injuries of the epiphysis are defined in the *Salter and Harris classification*. **2.** *see* pineal gland. **–epiphyseal** *adj.*

(1) 骺　長骨末端。最初由軟骨將其與骨幹分開，獨自生長發育。最後與骨幹融合，形成一整骨。在沙特爾和哈利斯分類中為骺損傷下了定義。**(2)** 參閱 pineal gland。

epiphysitis *n.* inflammation of the end (epiphysis) of a long bone. It may result in retardation of growth and deformity of the affected bone.

骺炎　長骨末端（骺）炎症。可使受損骨生長遲緩及變形。

epiplo- *prefix denoting* the omentum. Example: *epiplocele* (hernia containing omentum).

〔前綴〕網膜　如，網膜疝。

epiploon *n. see* omentum.

網膜　參閱 omentum。

episio- *prefix denoting* the vulva. Example: *episioplasty* (plastic surgery of).

〔前綴〕外陰　如外陰成形術。

episiotomy *n.* an incision into the tissues surrounding the opening of the vagina (perineum) during a difficult birth, at the stage when the infant's head has partly

外陰切開術　將陰道口周圍組織切開。用於在胎頭部分露出產道的難產時。目的在於有限度地擴大產道口，使胎兒易於

emerged through the opening of the birth passage. The aim is to enlarge the opening in a controlled manner so as to make delivery easier and to avoid extensive tearing of adjacent tissues.

婉出及避免陰道附近組織進一步撕裂。

epispadias *n.* a congenital abnormality in which the opening of the *urethra is on the dorsal (upper) surface of the penis. Surgical correction is carried out in infancy.

尿道上裂 尿道口開在陰莖背表面（上部）的一種先天性異常。可在嬰兒時進行外科矯正。

epistasis *n.* **1.** the stopping of a flow or discharge, as of blood. **2.** a type of gene action in which one gene can suppress the action of another (nonallelic) gene. The term is sometimes used for any interaction between nonallelic genes. **–epistatic** *adj.*

(1) 流體抑制 流體或排出液的停止，如血液。**(2) 上位性** 基因功能的一個類型，即一種基因抑制另外一個基因（非等位基因）的作用。有時該術語也用於兩個非等位基因之間的相互作用。

epistaxis *n. see* nosebleed.

鼻出血 參閱 nosebleed。

epithalamus *n.* part of the forebrain, consisting of a narrow band of nerve tissue in the roof of the third ventricle (including the region where the choroid plexus is attached) and the *pineal gland. *See also* brain.

丘腦上部 前腦的一部分。由第三腦室頂部（包括有脈絡叢的部位）中的神經組織窄索及松果體組成。參閱 brain。

epithalaxia *n.* loss of layers of epithelial cells from the lining of the intestine.

上皮脫屑 皮膚或腸內膜上皮細胞層脫落。

epithelioma *n.* a tumour of *epithelium, the covering of internal and external surfaces of the body: a former term for *carcinoma.

上皮瘤 身體內、外表面的上皮腫瘤。上皮瘤過去指上皮癌。

epithelium *n.* the tissue that covers the external surface of the body and lines hollow structures (except blood and lymphatic vessels). It is derived from embryonic ectoderm and endoderm. Epithelial cells may be flat and scalelike (*squamous*), *cuboidal*, or *columnar*. The latter may bear cilia or brush borders or

上皮 覆蓋身體外表及內襯空腔結構（除血管和淋巴管）的組織。來自胚胎的內、外胚層。上皮細胞可呈扁平、鱗狀、立方或柱狀。後者還長有纖毛，或呈刷狀緣，或分泌黏液或其他物質。細胞下面是一層基底膜，將上皮細胞與其下

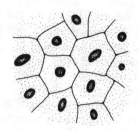

Stratified squamous epithelium, surface view above and sectional view below
複層鱗狀上皮，上圖是表面觀，下圖是切面觀

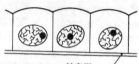

basement membrane 基底膜
Simple cuboidal epithelium
單層立方上皮

goblet cell 杯狀細胞

Ciliated columnar epithelium
纖毛柱狀上皮

basement membrane 基底膜
Pseudostratified ciliated epithelium
假複層纖毛上皮

Types of epithelium
上皮的種類

secrete mucus or other substances (*see* goblet cell). The cells rest on a common *basement membrane*, which separates epithelium from underlying *connective tissue. Epithelium may be either *simple*,

的結締組織分開。上皮細胞可以是單層，即由一層細胞組成；也可是複層，含有幾層細胞；或是假複層，從細胞的排列上看像多層，但事實上，

consisting of a single layer of cells; *stratified*, consisting of several layers; or *pseudostratified*, in which the cells appear to be arranged in layers but in fact share a common basement membrane (see illustration). *See also* endothelium, mesothelium. **–epithelial** *adj.*

這些細胞共有同一層基底膜（見圖）。參閱 endothelium，mesothelium。

epitrichium (periderm) *n.* the most superficial layer of the skin, one cell in thickness, that is only present early in embryonic development. It protects the underlying *epidermis until it is fully formed.

皮上層 皮膚的最表層，單細胞表面，只存在於胚胎發育期，保護下面的表皮直至表皮完全形成。

eponychium *n. see* nail.

甲上皮 參閱 nail。

eponym *n.* a disease, structure or species named after a particular person, usually the person who first discovered or described it. Eponyms are widespread in medicine, but they are being replaced as more descriptive terms become necessary. Thus the eponyms islets of Langerhans, aqueduct of Sylvius, and Hashimoto's disease are more likely to be designated in text books as pancreatic islands, cerebral aqueduct, and autoimmune thyroiditis, respectively. **–eponymous** *adj.*

冠名名詞 用某人名字命名的一種疾病、結構或物種。通常此人是第一個發現或描述該疾病、結構或物種的人。冠名名詞廣泛見於醫學，但現正被取代，因為更多的描述性術語是必要的。因此，屬冠名名詞的朗格罕斯島、西爾維厄斯導水管、橋本病很可能在教科書中被分別命名為胰島、大腦導水管、自體免疫性甲狀腺炎。

epoophoron *n. see* paroophoron.

卵巢冠 參閱 paroophoron。

epoprostenol *n.* a *prostaglandin drug used immediately before and during renal dialysis to prevent clotting of blood in the shunt. It is administered by intravenous injection.

依前列醇 一種前列腺素藥物，在腎透析術之前或術中即刻使用以防止旁路中血栓形成，此為靜脈注射藥物。

Epstein-Barr virus the virus, belonging to the *herpesvirus group, that is the causative agent of *glandular fever. It is also implicated in hepatitis and in certain cancers (e.g. *Burkitt's lymphoma and *Hodgkin's disease).

愛-巴氏病毒，EB 病毒 屬皰疹病毒科病毒，可引起腺熱。與肝炎和某些癌症發生有關（如伯基特淋巴瘤和霍奇金病）。

epulis *n.* a swelling on the gum. Most such swellings are due to fibrous hyperplasia, but an epulis may be the opening of a *sinus tract.

齦瘤　齒齦腫大。大多數的這種腫大是由纖維增生引起，但它也可能是竇道的開口。

equi- *prefix denoting* equality.

〔前綴〕相等

equinia *n. see* glanders.

馬鼻疽　參閱 glanders。

Erb's palsy a partial paralysis of the arm caused by injury to a baby's *brachial plexus during birth. This may happen if-during a difficult delivery – excess traction applied to the head damages the fifth cervical root of the spinal cord. The muscles of the shoulder and the flexors of the elbow are paralysed and the arm hangs at the side internally rotated at the shoulder.

埃爾布麻痺　在嬰兒出生時，損傷其臂叢引起的上肢部分麻痺。過度牽拉頭部（如在難產時）時損傷脊髓第五頸神經根可導致此病。肩部肌肉及肘部屈肌麻痺，而且上肢在肩部內旋。

ERCP (endoscopic retrograde cholangiopancreatography) the technique in which a catheter is passed through a *duodenoscope into the *ampulla of Vater of the common bile duct and injected with a radiopaque medium to outline the pancreatic duct and bile ducts radiologically. It is now widely used in the diagnosis of obstructive jaundice and pancreatic disease. *See also* papillotomy.

內窺鏡逆行性胰膽管造影術　將導管通過十二指腸鏡進入總膽管的法特壺腹部，注入造影劑，使胰導管、膽管顯影。現已廣泛用於診斷阻塞性黃疸和胰腺病。參閱 papillotomy。

erectile *adj.* capable of causing erection or becoming erect. The penis is composed largely of erectile tissue.

能勃起的　有勃起能力的。陰莖主要是由能勃起的組織組成。

erection *n.* the sexually active state of the penis, which becomes enlarged and rigid (due to the erectile tissue being swollen with blood) and capable of penetrating the vagina. The term is also applied to the clitoris in a state of sexual arousal.

勃起　陰莖的性興奮狀態。陰莖變得粗大，堅硬（因勃起組織充血腫大），有能力插入陰道。此術語也用以指性興奮期的陰蒂。

erepsin *n.* a nixture of protein-digesting enzymes (*see* peptidase) secreted by the intestinal glands. It is part of the *succus entericus.

腸肽酶　腸腺分泌的蛋白消化酶的混合物（參閱 peptidase）。是腸液的一部分。

erethism *n.* **1.** a state of abnormal mental excitement or irritability. **2.** rapid response to a stimulus.

(1) 病態興奮　不正常的精神興奮和煩躁狀態。(2) 興奮增強　對刺激的迅速反應。

erg *n.* a unit of work or energy equal to the work done when the point of application of a force of 1 dyne is displaced through a distance of 1 cm in the direction of the force. 1 erg = 10^{-7} joule.

爾格　功或能量的單位。即用 1 達因的力使某物沿力的方向移動 1 厘米所做的功。1 爾格 = 10^{-7} 焦耳。

erg- (ergo-) *prefix denoting* work or activity.

〔前綴〕功能，活動能力

ergocalciferol *n. see* vitamin D.

麥角骨化醇　參閱 vitamin D。

ergograph *n.* an apparatus for recording the work performed by the muscles of the body when undergoing activity. Ergographs are useful for assessment of the capabilities of athletes undergoing training.

測力器　在身體活動時，測量肌肉活動的儀器。對估價進行訓練的運動員的能力很有用。

ergometrine *n.* a drug that stimulates contractions of the uterus. It is administered by injection to assist labour and to control bleeding following delivery. Trade name: **Syntometrine**.

麥角新鹼　刺激子宮收縮的藥物。注射用藥，助產及控制產後出血。商品名：Syntometrine。

ergonomics *n.* the study of man in relation to his work and working surroundings. This broad science involves the application of psychological as well as physiological principles to the design of buildings, machinery, vehicles, packaging, implements, and anything else with which man comes into contact.

人體功率學　研究人與其工作及其工作環境的科學。這一內容廣泛的科學包括運用心理學及生理學原理對建築物、機器、車輛、包裝、日用工具及其他人類所接觸的東西進行設計。

ergosterol *n.* a plant sterol that, when irradiated with ultraviolet light, is

麥角固醇　一種植物固醇。當受到紫外綫照射時，可轉化成

converted to ergocalciferol (vitamin D$_2$). *See* vitamin D.

麥角骨化醇（維生素 D$_2$）。參閱 vitamin D。

ergot *n.* a fungus (*Claviceps purpurea*) that grows on rye. It produces several important alkaloids, chemically related to LSD, including *ergotamine and *ergometrine, which are used in medicine in the treatment of migraine and in childbirth. Eating bread made with rye infected with the fungus has led to sporadic outbreaks of *ergotism over the centuries.

麥角 生長在黑麥上的一種真菌。能產生出一些重要的在化學結構上與麥角二乙酰胺有關的生物鹼，包括麥角胺和麥角新鹼。在醫學上，它們用在偏頭痛及分娩時。過去好幾個世紀，食用有真菌感染的黑麥麵包曾引起散發性麥角中毒。

ergotamine *n.* a drug that causes constriction of blood vessels and is used to relieve migraine. It is administered by mouth, injection, inhalation, or in suppositories. Common side-effects are nausea and vomiting, and ergotism may develop as a result of high doses. Trade names: **Lingraine**, **Migril**.

麥角胺 引起血管收縮，用於治療偏頭痛的藥物。可口服、注射、吸入或以栓劑形式給藥。常見的副作用有惡心、嘔吐、大劑量使用時，可引起麥角中毒。商品名：Lingraine，Migril。

ergotism *n.* poisoning caused by eating rye infected with the fungus *ergot. The chief symptom is gangrene of the fingers and toes, with diarrhoea and vomiting, nausea, and headache. In the Middle Ages the disease was known as *St Anthony's fire*, because of the inflamed appearance of the tissues afflicted with gangrene and the belief that a pilgrimage to St Anthony's tomb would result in cure.

麥角中毒 食入麥角真菌感染的黑麥麵包而引起的中毒。主要症狀是手指、腳趾壞死，伴有腹瀉、嘔吐、惡心及頭痛。在中世紀時，此病叫做聖安東尼熱。這是因為壞死組織呈火焰樣外觀，而且人們還認為朝拜聖安東尼墓可治愈此病。

erogenous *adj.* describing certain parts of the body, the physical stimulation of which leads to sexual arousal.

性慾發生的 指身體某些部位因生理性刺激而引起性興奮。

erosion *n.* **1.** an eating away of surface tissue by physical or chemical processes, including those associated with inflammation. A *cervical erosion* is an abnormal area of epithelium that may develop at the neck of the uterus due to tissue

(1) 糜爛 因物理和化學過程，包括炎症引起的組織表面缺損。宮頸糜爛就是在分娩或人工流產時組織操作而引起的宮頸上皮異常。在皮膚，糜爛可呈表面潰瘍型因而容易治

damage caused at childbirth or by attempts at abortion. In the skin an erosion represents a superficial type of ulceration and therefore heals quite readily. **2.** (in dentistry) loss of surface tooth substance, usually caused by repeated application of acid, as may occur with excessive intake of citrus fruits or regurgitation of acid from the stomach in bulimia nervosa.

愈。**(2)** **侵蝕** （牙科學）牙表面物質缺損。通常因反覆的酸刺激引起。如大量食入柑橘類水果或食慾亢進胃酸返流時。

erot- (eroto-) *prefix denoting* sexual desire or love. Example: *erotophobia* (morbid dread of).

〔前綴〕 **性慾，性愛** 如，性慾恐懼。

eroticism *n.* **1.** those elements in thought, imagination, pictorial imagery, literature, or the arts that tend to arouse sexual excitement or desire. **2.** actual sexual arousal. **3.** a greater than average disposition for sex and all its manifestations. **4.** sexual interest or excitement prompted by contemplation or stimulation of areas of the body not normally associated with sexuality. The terms *anal eroticism* and *oral eroticism* are used both in a theoretical Freudian sense and in reference to adult physical sexual activity.

(1) **色情** 思想、想象、繪畫中的形象、文字或藝術中，趨於引起性興奮或性慾的因素。**(2)** **性衝動** 實際的性慾望。**(3)** **好色** 偏好於性及其表現。**(4)** **性愛** 由思想或刺激與通常性行為無關的身體部位所引起的性興趣或性興奮。肛交和口交術語，既用來指理論上的弗洛伊德學說，也指成人身體性活動。

erotomania *n.* a delusion that the individual is loved by some person, often a person of importance. Sometimes, but not always, this progresses to schizophrenia.

色情狂 某人幻想被另一人，通常是重要人物所愛。有時，這種情況可逐漸發展成精神分裂症。

eructation *n.* belching: the sudden raising of gas from the stomach.

噯氣 氣體突然從胃裏竄出。

eruption *n.* **1.** the outbreak of a rash. A *bullous eruption* is an outbreak of blisters. **2.** (in dentistry) the emergence of a growing tooth from the gum into the mouth.

(1) **發疹** 疹的突然出現。大疱性發疹是一種水疱疹的出現。**(2)** **萌出** （牙科學）正在生長的牙從牙齦長到口腔的短時狀態。

erysipelas *n.* an infection of the skin and underlying tissues with the bacterium *Streptococcus pyogenes*. The affected areas, usually the face and scalp, become inflamed and swollen, with the development of raised patches that may be several inches across. The patient is ill, with a high temperature. Attacks may recur in certain individuals, possibly because of a defect in their lymphatic systems. Treatment is with penicillin.

丹毒 由化膿鏈球菌感染的皮膚及皮下組織感染。感染部位通常是臉及頭皮。表現為炎性水腫，伴有直徑幾英寸長的斑片狀隆起。患者發病時有高燒，個別患者其病情可反覆發作。可能是因淋巴組織有缺陷所致。可使用青黴素治療。

erysipeloid *n.* an infection of the skin and underlying tissues with *Erysipelothrix insidiosa*, developing usually in people handling fish, poultry, or meat. Infection enters through scratches or cuts on the hands, and is normally confined to a finger or hand, which becomes reddened; sometimes systemic illness develops. Treatment is with penicillin.

類丹毒 詭譎丹毒絲菌引起的皮膚及皮下組織感染。當手被刮破或有切口時，就可因此發生感染並出現紅腫。正常情況下，感染只限於手指或手；有時，可引起全身疾病。治療使用青黴素。

Erysipelothrix *n.* a genus of Gram-positive nonmotile rod-shaped bacteria with a tendency to form filaments. They are parasites of mammals, birds, and fish. *E. insidiosa* (formerly *E. rhusiopathiae*) is a widely distributed species causing the disease *erysipeloid*.

丹毒絲菌屬 一種革蘭氏染色陽性、非活動性能形成絲的桿菌屬。寄生在哺乳動物、鳥類及魚類身上。詭譎丹毒絲菌（以前稱紅斑丹毒絲菌）是廣泛分布的菌種，能引起丹毒。

erythema *n.* flushing of the skin due to dilatation of the blood capillaries in the dermis. It may be physiological or a sign of inflammation or infection. *Erythema nodosum* is characterized by tender bruiselike swellings on the shins and is often associated with streptococcal infection. In *erythema multiforme* the eruption, which can take various forms, is characterized by so-called target lesions that may be recurrent and follow herpes simplex infection. *Erythema ab igne* is a reticular pigmented rash on the lower

紅斑 因毛細血管擴張而引起的皮膚不正常的發紅。可能是生理性的或者是炎症和感染的特徵。結節性紅斑的特徵是小腿脛部具有壓疼的挫傷樣水腫，常伴有鏈球菌感染。多形性紅斑（紅斑形狀多種多樣）是反覆發作的固定皮損，隨後有單純疱疹感染。火激紅斑則是持續暴露於輻射熱源引起的小腿上呈網狀的着色皮疹。

legs caused by persistent exposure to radiant heat.

erythr- (erythro-) *prefix denoting* **1.** redness. Example: *erythuria* (excretion of red urine). **2.** erythrocytes.

〔前綴〕。**(1) 紅色** 如紅尿症（排紅色尿）。**(2) 紅細胞**

erythraemia *n. see* polycythaemia vera.

紅細胞增多症 參閱 polycythaemia vera。

erythrasma *n.* a chronic skin infection due to the bacterium *Corynebacterium minutissimum*, occurring in such areas as the armpits, groin, and toes, where skin surfaces are in contact.

紅癬 微小棒狀桿菌引起的慢性皮膚感染。發生在皮膚表面相互密切接觸的部位，如腋窩、腹股溝及腳趾間。

erythroblast *n.* any of a series of nucleated cells (*see* normoblast, proerythroblast) that pass through a succession of stages of maturation to form red blood cells (*erythrocytes). Erythroblasts are normally present in the blood-forming tissue of the bone marrow, but they may appear in the circulation in a variety of diseases (*see* erythroblastosis). *See also* erythropoiesis.

成紅細胞 經過成熟期各階段而最終形成紅細胞的一系列有核細胞中的任何一種。在正常情況下，成紅細胞存在於骨髓造血組織中。但在某些疾病中可出現於血循環中。參閱 erythropoiesis。

erythroblastosis *n.* the presence in the blood of the nucleated precursors of the red blood cells (*erythroblasts). This may occur when there is an increase in the rate of red cell production, as in haemorrhagic or haemolytic *anaemia, or in infiltrations of the bone marrow by tumours, etc.

成紅細胞增多症 血中存在着紅細胞的前身細胞，可發生於紅細胞生成速度過快時。如出血性和溶血性貧血時，或骨髓受到腫瘤侵襲時。

erythroblastosis foetalis a severe but rare haemolytic *anaemia affecting newborn infants due to destruction of the infant's red blood cells by factors present in the mother's serum. It is usually caused by incompatibility of the rhesus blood groups between mother and infant (*see* rhesus factor).

新生兒成紅細胞增多症 因母體血清中因子作用於新生胎兒使胎兒紅細胞受破壞而引起的嚴重而又十分罕見一種溶血性貧血。通常因母體與胎兒的血液中 Rh 因子不一致而引起（參閱 rhesus factor）。

erythrocyanosis *n.* mottled purplish discoloration on the legs and thighs, usually of adolescent girls or fat boys before puberty. The disorder sometimes occurs in older women. The condition is worse in cold weather and there is no satisfactory treatment apart from weight loss.

紺紅皮病　在小腿和大腿上出現紫色斑紋。通常見於青春期前的少女、肥胖男孩。有時，也見於老年婦女。寒冷氣候時病情加重，除了減輕體重外尚無滿意療法。

erythrocyte (red blood cell) *n.* a *blood cell containing the red pigment *haemoglobin, the principal function of which is the transport of oxygen. A mature erythrocyte has no nucleus and its shape is that of a biconcave disc, approximately $7\mu m$ in diameter. There are normally about 5×10^{12} erythrocytes per litre of blood. *See also* erythropoiesis.

紅細胞　一種含有血紅蛋白的血細胞。主要功能是輸送氧。成熟紅細胞無核，呈雙凹形，直徑約$7\mu m$。正常情況下，每升血液中約有5×10^{12}個紅細胞。參閱 erythropoiesis。

erythrocyte sedimentation rate *see* ESR.

紅細胞沉降率　參閱 ESR。

erythrocytic *adj.* describing those stages in the life cycle of the malarial parasite (*see* Plasmodium) that develop inside the red blood cells (*see* trophozoite). *Compare* exoerythrocytic.

紅細胞內的　指瘧原蟲（參閱 Plasmodium）在紅細胞（參閱 trophozoite）內生長發育的生活周期的各個階段。與 exo-erythrocytic 對比。

erythroderma (exfoliative dermatitis) *n.* abnormal reddening, flaking, and thickening of the skin affecting a wide area of the body. Commoner after the age of 50, erythroderma affects men three times as often as women; it may result from pre-existing skin disease, such as eczema or psoriasis, or be caused by drugs or lymphoma.

紅皮病　皮膚不正常的紅腫、片狀脫屑及增厚。此病能侵犯身體的大面積。常見於50歲以上患者。男性發病率是女性的三倍。多繼發於原有的皮膚病，如濕疹、銀屑病或者由藥物和淋巴瘤引起。

erythroedema *n. see* pink disease.

紅皮水腫病　參閱 pink disease。

erythrogenesis *n. see* erythropoiesis.

紅細胞發生　參閱 erythro-poiesis。

erythromelalgia *n.* painful paroxysmal dilation of the blood vessels of the skin, usually affecting the feet and extremities.

紅斑性肢痛　皮膚血管陣發性擴張、疼痛。常侵犯腳及肢體。

erythromycin *n*. an *antibiotic used to treat infections caused by a wide range of bacteria and other microorganisms. It is administered by mouth or injection. Side-effects are rare and mild, though nausea, vomiting, and diarrhoea occur occasionally. Trade names: **Erymax**, **Erythrocin**.

紅黴素　治療多種細菌及其他微生物感染的一種抗生素。可口服也可注射。副作用少且輕。偶見惡心、嘔吐及腹瀉。商品名：　Erymax，Erythrocin。

erythron *n*. that part of the blood-forming system of the body that is directed towards the production of red blood cells. The erythron is not a single organ but is dispersed throughout the blood-forming tissue of the *bone marrow. *See also* erythropoiesis.

紅細胞系　身體造血系統中，可直接產生紅細胞的那一部分。它不是單獨的器官，而是遍布於骨髓的造血組織之中。參閱 erythropoiesis。

erythropenia *n*. a reduction in the number of red blood cells (*erythrocytes) in the blood. This usually, but not invariably, occurs in *anaemia.

紅細胞減少　血液中紅細胞數量下降。常見於貧血，但也有例外。

erythroplasia *n*. an abnormal red patch of skin that occurs in the mouth or on the genitalia and is precancerous.

增殖性紅斑　一種異常的紅色皮膚塊，發生於口內或生殖器上，為癌前期病變。

erythropoiesis (erythrogenesis) *n*. the process of red blood cell (*erythrocyte) production, which normally occurs in the blood-forming tissue of the *bone marrow. The ultimate precursor of the red cell is the *haemopoietic stem cell, but the earliest precursor that can be identified microscopically is the *proerythroblast. This divides and passes through a series of stages of maturation termed respectively early, intermediate, and late *normoblasts, the latter finally losing its nucleus to become a mature red cell. *See also* haemopoiesis.

紅細胞生成　紅細胞產生的過程。正常情況下，產生於骨髓的造血組織中。最早的紅細胞的前身是造血幹細胞。但在顯微鏡下可識別的最早前身是原成紅細胞。它不斷分裂，並分別經過早幼、中幼、晚幼紅細胞這一系列的成熟期，最後脫核成為成熟紅細胞。參閱 haemopoiesis。

erythropoietin *n*. a hormone secreted by certain cells in the kidney in response

紅細胞生成素　腎臟中某些細胞因組織內氧含量下降而分泌

to a reduction in the amount of oxygen reaching the tissues. Erythropoietin increases the rate of red cell production (*erythropoiesis) and is the mechanism by which the rate of erythropoiesis is controlled.

出來的一種激素。它能加快並控制紅細胞的生成速度。

erythropsia *n.* red vision: a symptom sometimes experienced after removal of a cataract and also in snow blindness.

紅視症　紅視覺，一種少見的症狀。有時出現在白內障手術之後，也出現在雪盲時。

eschar *n.* a scab or slough, as produced by the action of heat or a corrosive substance on living tissue.

焦痂　因熱或腐蝕作用於活組織而產生的痂和腐肉。

Escherichia *n.* a genus of Gram-negative, generally motile, rodlike bacteria that have the ability to ferment carbohydrates, usually with production of gas, and are found in the intestines of man and many animals. *E. coli* – a lactose-fermenting species – is usually not harmful but some strains cause gastrointestinal infections. It is also widely used in laboratory experiments for bacteriological and genetic studies.

埃希桿菌屬　一種革蘭氏陰性，通常有活動性的桿狀菌屬。能使碳水化合物發酵，並產生氣體，見於人類及多種動物的腸道。大腸桿菌是能發酵乳糖的菌種，通常無害。但在某些情況下可引起泌尿道感染及小兒腹瀉。大腸桿菌還被廣泛用於實驗室內細菌學及遺傳學研究。

eserine *n. see* physostigmine.

毒扁豆鹼　參閱 physostigmine。

esophoria *n.* a tendency to squint in which the eye, when covered, tends to turn inwards towards the nose. *See also* heterophoria.

內隱斜視　當閉眼時，眼睛向鼻側內移的一種斜視現象。參閱 heterophoria。

esotropia *n.* convergent *strabismus: a type of squint.

內斜視　會聚性斜視。斜視的一種。

espundia (mucocutaneous leishmaniasis) *n.* a disease of the skin and mucous membranes caused by the parasitic protozoan *Leishmania braziliensis* (*see* leishmaniasis). Occurring in South and Central America, espundia takes the form of ulcerating lesions on the arms

皮膚黏膜利什曼病　由寄生原蟲巴西利什曼原蟲引起的一種皮膚和黏膜疾病。發生於南美和中美。此病可使上肢和下肢發生潰瘍性病變。病變還可波及到鼻、口腔黏膜，使組織受到嚴重破壞。

and legs; the infection may also spread to the mucous membranes of the nose and mouth, causing serious destruction of the tissues.

ESR (erythrocyte sedimentation rate) the rate at which red blood cells (erythrocytes) settle out of suspension in blood plasma, measured under standardized conditions. The ESR increases if the level of certain proteins in the plasma rises, as in rheumatic diseases, chronic infections, and malignant disease, and thus provides a simple but valuable screening test for these conditions.

essence *n.* a solution consisting of an essential oil dissolved in alcohol.

essential *adj.* describing a disorder that is not apparently attributable to an outside cause; for example, essential *hypertension.

essential amino acid an *amino acid that is essential for normal growth and development but cannot be synthesized by the body. Essential amino acids are normally obtained from protein-rich foods in the diet, such as liver, eggs, and dairy products. There are nine essential amino acids: tryptophan, lysine, phenylalanine, histidine, threonine, valine, methionine, leucine, and isoleucine.

essential fatty acid one of a group of unsaturated fatty acids that are essential for growth but cannot be synthesized by the body. The three essential fatty acids are *linoleic, linolenic*, and *arachidonic acids*; of these, only linoleic acid need be included in the diet as the other two can be synthesized from it in the body. Large amounts of linoleic acid occur in maize

紅細胞沉降率 在標準條件下測得紅細胞在血漿懸液中沉降的速度。如果血漿中某些蛋白質增加，則沉降率增快，如在風濕病、慢性感染及惡性病時。因此檢查惡性病時，它可做為簡單而又有價值的篩查試驗。

香精劑 溶解在乙醇內的揮發性油溶液。

原發的 指沒有明顯外因的疾病。如原發性高血壓。

必需氨基酸 正常生長發育所必需，而體內又不能合成的氨基酸。正常情況下，可從含蛋白質豐富的食物中攝取。如肝、蛋及乳製品。有九種必需氨基酸：色氨酸、賴氨酸、苯丙氨酸、組氨酸、蘇氨酸、纈氨酸、蛋氨酸、亮氨酸及異亮氨酸。

必需脂肪酸 體內不能合成而又是生長所必需的一組非飽和脂肪酸。它們是：亞油酸、亞麻酸和花生四烯酸。其中，只有亞油酸需從食物中攝取。其他兩種可從進入體內的亞油酸合成。大量的亞油酸來自玉米油和豆油，少量來自豬肉脂肪。

(corn) oil and soya bean oil; smaller amounts in pork fat.

essential oil a volatile oil derived from an aromatic plant. Essential oils are used in various pharmaceutical preparations.

揮發油　來自芳香植物的易揮發的油。用於各種藥物製劑。

esterase *n.* an enzyme that catalyses the hydrolysis of esters into their constituent acids and alcohols. For example, fatty-acid esters are broken down to form fatty acids plus alcohol.

酯酶　一種催化脂類水解，使其生成相應的酸和乙醇的酶。如脂肪酸脂可被分解成脂肪酸和乙醇。

ethacrynic acid a *diuretic used to treat fluid retention (oedema), such as that associated with heart failure and kidney and liver disorders. It is administered by mouth or injection. Common side-effects are loss of appetite, difficulty in swallowing, nausea, vomiting, and diarrhoea. Trade name: **Edecrin**.

利尿酸　利尿藥。用於治療液體瀦留（水腫），如因心力衰竭及腎、肝疾病引起的水腫。口服或注射用藥，常見的副作用有食慾不振、吞咽困難、惡心、嘔吐及腹瀉。商品名：Edecrin。

ethambutol *n.* a drug used in the treatment of tuberculosis, in conjunction with other drugs. It is administered by mouth and occasionally causes visual disturbances, which cease when the drug is withdrawn. Allergic rashes and digestive upsets may also occur. Trade name: **Myambutol**.

乙胺丁醇　與其他藥物聯用的治療結核病藥。口服。偶可引起視力障礙，但停藥後消失。也可引起過敏疹及消化不良。商品名：Myambutol。

ethanol (ethyl alcohol) *n. see* alcohol.

乙醇　參閱 alcohol。

ether *n.* a volatile liquid formerly used as an anaesthetic administered by inhalation, though now largely replaced by safer and more efficient drugs. It also has laxative action when administered by mouth. Ether irritates the respiratory tract and affects the circulation.

乙醚，醚　一種揮發性液體。以前用作吸入麻醉劑，現大部分已被更安全有效的藥物所替代。口服時，也有輕瀉作用。醚能刺激消化道並損害循環系統。

ethical committee (in Britain) a group of consultants and other experts set up (especially in a hospital) to monitor investigations concerned with teaching

醫德委員會　（英國）由高級醫師和其他專家組成的團體（特別是在醫院裏），以監督把人用於教學和科研的情況。該委

or research, that involve the use of human subjects. It is responsible for ensuring that patients are adequately informed of the procedures involved in a research project (including the use of dummy or placebo treatments as controls), that the tests and/or therapies are safe, and that no-one is pressurized into participating.

員會負責讓患者充分了解科研項目的所有過程（包括使用對照治療用的安慰劑），保證實驗和治療是安全的，而且保證沒有人是被迫參加上述活動的。

ethinyloestradiol *n.* a synthetic female sex hormone (*see* oestrogen) administered by mouth to treat symptoms of the menopause and menstrual disorders and to suppress lactation in mothers not breast-feeding. It is mainly used, however, in combination with a progestogen, in *oral contraceptives (e.g. *Conova 30, Femodene*).

炔雌醇 一種合成的雌性激素（參閱 oestrogen）。口服，治療閉經和月經失調，抑制停止哺乳母親泌乳，還治療前列腺癌。但主要與孕酮合用，作為口服避孕藥。

ethionamide *n.* a drug used to treat tuberculosis, usually in conjunction with other drugs. It is administered by mouth or in suppositories. Loss of appetite, nausea, and vomiting are common side-effects. Trade name: **Trescatyl.**

乙硫異烟胺 治療結核病藥。常與其他藥合用。口服或以栓劑形式給藥。常見的副作用是食慾不振、惡心及嘔吐。商品名：Trescatyl。

ethisterone *n.* a synthetic female sex-hormone (*see* progestogen) used, often in combination with an *oestrogen, to treat menstrual disorders, particularly amenorrhoea. It was formerly used in hormone pregnancy tests. It is administered by mouth.

炔孕酮 一種合成的女性激素（參閱 progestogen）。常與雌激素聯合使用，治療月經不調，特別是閉經。以前用於孕激素檢驗。口服。

ethmoid bone a bone in the floor of the cranium that contributes to the nasal cavity and orbits. The part of the ethmoid forming the roof of the nasal cavity – the *cribriform plate* – is pierced with many small holes through which the olfactory nerves pass. *See also* nasal concha, skull.

篩骨 一塊構成鼻腔和眼眶顱顳底的一部分的骨頭。在形成鼻腔頂部——篩板的部分有很多小孔，嗅神經就從中穿過。參閱 nasal concha, skull。

ethnology *n.* the study of the different races of mankind and their variations: a

人種學 研究人類不同種族及他們不同之處的科學。是人類

branch of anthropology that deals mainly with cultural and social differences between groups and the problems, medical and otherwise, that arise from their particular ways of life. **–ethnic** *adj.*

ethosuximide *n.* an *anticonvulsant drug used to control epileptic seizures. It is administered by mouth; side-effects such as drowsiness, depression, and digestive disturbances may occur but are usually temporary. Trade names: **Emeside, Zarontin**.

ethylene *n.* an inflammable gas sometimes used as an anaesthetic administered by inhalation. There are usually no toxic effects, but nausea and vomiting commonly occur after its use.

ethyloestrenol *n.* a steroid drug with *anabolic properties, used to treat conditions involving wasting of protein and bone, such as osteoporosis. It is administered by mouth and sometimes causes nausea, water retention, and menstrual disturbances at high doses. Trade name: **Orabolin**.

ethynodiol *n.* a synthetic female sex hormone (*see* progestogen) that is used to treat menstrual disorders and in *oral contraceptives. It is administered by mouth, usually in combination with an *oestrogen. Side-effects can include nausea, vomiting, headache, breast swelling, weight gain, fluid retention, and breakthrough bleeding. Trade name: **Femulen**.

etiology *n. see* aetiology.

etoposide (VP16-213) *n.* a *cytotoxic drug derived from an extract of the mandrake plant. It is administered

學的分支。人種學主要研究不同種族之間文化及社會的區別，及因他們的特殊生活方式而出現的醫療和其他方面的問題。

乙琥胺 一種抗驚厥藥。用於治療癲癇發作。口服。副作用有嗜睡、抑鬱及消化道紊亂，但通常只是暫時性的。商品名：Emeside，Zarontin。

乙烯 一種易燃性氣體。有時用作吸入性麻醉劑。通常無毒性作用。使用後常發生惡心、嘔吐。

乙雌烯醇 一種具有同化作用的類固醇藥物。用於治療與蛋白質和骨質消耗有關的疾病，如骨質疏鬆症。口服。有時引起惡心、水瀦留。大劑量時可引起月經失調。商品名：Orabolin。

炔諾醇 一種合成的雌性激素（參閱 progestogen）。用於治療月經失調及用作口服避孕藥。口服。常與雌激素合用。副作用有惡心、嘔吐、頭痛、乳房腫脹、體重增加、液體瀦留及突發性出血。商品名：Femulen。

病因學 參閱 aetiology。

依托泊甙 從毒參茄植物中提取的一種細胞毒素藥物。靜脈注射或口服。主要治療支氣管

intravenously or by mouth, primarily in the treatment of bronchial carcinoma, lymphomas, and testicular tumours. Side-effects include alopecia, nausea, and marrow suppression. Trade name: **Vepesid**.

癌、淋巴瘤和睪丸腫瘤。副作用有脫髮、惡心及骨髓抑制。商品名：Vepesid。

eu- *prefix denoting* **1.** good, well, or easy. **2.** normal.

〔前綴〕**(1)** 好，優，容易 **(2)** 正常

eubacteria *pl. n.* a very large group of bacteria with rigid cell walls and – typically – flagella for movement. The group comprises the so-called 'true' bacteria, excluding those, such as spirochaetes and mycoplasmas, with flexible cell walls.

真細菌 有堅硬的細胞壁，並有典型鞭毛運動的一大類細菌。這類細菌就是所謂的「真」細菌。但不包括有柔韌細胞壁的如螺旋體和支原體之類。

eucalyptol *n.* a volatile oil that has a mild irritant effect on the mucous membranes of the mouth and digestive system. It is taken as pastilles or inhaled as vapour to relieve catarrh. Large doses may cause nausea, vomiting, and diarrhoea.

桉油精 一種揮發性油，對口腔及消化道黏膜有輕微刺激作用，可製成錠劑服用或吸入其蒸氣，以消除卡他。大劑量時，可引起惡心、嘔吐及腹瀉。

euchromatin *n.* chromosome material (*see* chromatin) that stains most deeply during mitosis and represents the major genes. *Compare* heterochromatin.

常染色質 絲分裂時，染色最深並代表主要基因的染色質（參閱 chromatin）。與 heterochromatin 對比。

eugenics *n.* the science that is concerned with the improvement of the human race by means of the principles of genetics. It is mainly concerned with the detection and, where possible, the elimination of genetic disease in man.

優生學 用遺傳學原理改良人種的科學。主要是檢查人類遺傳病，並在可能的情況下，消除它們。

eumenorrhoea *n.* regular menstruation. This does not necessarily indicate regular ovulation.

月經正常 月經周期正常。這並不代表排卵周期正常。

eupepsia *n.* the state of normal or good digestion: freedom from digestive symptoms.

消化正常 正常或良好的消化狀態，沒有消化道症狀。

euphoria *n.* a state of optimism, cheerfulness, and well-being. A morbid degree of euphoria is characteristic of *mania and *hypomania. *See also* ecstasy, elation.

欣快 得意、歡樂和幸福的表現。病態的歡快是躁狂症及輕躁狂症的特點。參閱 ecstasy，elation。

euplastic *adj.* describing a tissue that heals quickly after injury.

易於機化的 指組織損傷後很快愈合。

euploidy *n.* the condition of cells, tissues, or organisms in which there is one complete set of chromosomes or a whole multiple of this set in each cell. *Compare* aneupolidy. **–euploid** *adj., n.*

整倍體 細胞、組織或生物的一種狀態。即在其每一細胞內有一整套的染色體或有整數的多套染色體。與 aneuploidy 對比。

Eustachian tube the tube that connects the middle *ear to the pharynx. It allows the pressure on the inner side of the eardrum to remain equal to the external pressure.

咽鼓管 連接口耳和咽部的管道。它使作用在鼓膜內側的壓力與外部的相等。

euthanasia *n.* the act of taking life to relieve suffering. In *voluntary euthanasia* the sufferer asks for measures to be taken to end his life. This may be accomplished by active steps, usually the administration of a drug, or by *passive euthanasia* – the deliberate withholding of treatment. In *compulsory euthanasia* society or a person acting on authority gives instructions to terminate the life of a person, such as an infant, who cannot express his wishes. In no country is compulsory euthanasia legal, but many societies exist to promote the cause of voluntary euthanasia.

安樂死術 為除去身體的痛苦而結束生命的一種方法。自願安樂死術是指患者本人要求採取措施結束其生命。可採取主動方式，通常是用藥，或採用被動安樂死術——停止治療。強制安樂死術是指權威性團體或個人下令來結束某人的生命，如對不能表達其願望的嬰兒。儘管在很多社會裏都存在鼓勵採用安樂死術現象，但還沒有一個國家制定出強制性安樂死術的法律。

euthyroid *adj.* having a thyroid gland that functions normally. *Compare* hyperthyroidism, hypothyroidism. **–euthyroidism** *n.*

甲狀腺機能正常的 指有正常功能的甲狀腺。與 hyperthyroidism，hypothyroidism 對比。

evacuator *n.* a device for sucking fluid out of a cavity. In its simplest form it consists of a hollow rubber bulb that

排出器 從腔中吸出液體的工具。它最簡單的形式是由一個空心膠皮球和一個插入腔內的

is attached, via a valve system, to a tube inserted into the cavity. Another valve leads to discharge tube. Evacuators may be used to empty the bladder of unwanted material during such operations as the removal of a calculus or transurethral *prostatectomy.

管子通過閥門系統相連而組成，另一閥門在管道的排出端。排出器在手術時用於吸除囊中的廢物，如在結石切除時和經尿道前列腺摘除術。

evagination *n.* the protrusion of a part or organ from a sheathlike covering or by eversion of its inner surface.

外突 某部位或器官自鞘樣結構中伸出的突起，或因內表面外翻而出現的突起。

eventration *n.* **1.** protrusion of the intestines through the abdominal wall. **2.** (of the diaghragm) abnormal elevation of part of the diaphragm due to a congenital weakness (but without true herniation), as observed by X-ray.

(1) 腸突出 腸經腹壁突出。
(2) 膈突出 橫膈因先天性薄弱而部分不正常地上升（但不是真疝），X 綫可查出。

event sampling (in psychology) a way of recording behaviour in which the presence of a particular kind of behaviour is noted whenever it occurs. It is used for precise descriptions of behaviour and for following the course of *behaviour modification. *See also* time sampling.

事件採樣 （心理學）一種記錄行為的方法。只要某種特殊行為發生時，就立即把它記錄下來。此法用於準確描述行為及跟蹤行為改變的過程。參閱 time sampling。

eversion *n.* a turning outward; in *eversion of the cervix* the edges of the cervix (neck) of the uterus turn outward after having been torn during childbirth.

外翻 向外翻轉。在宮頸外翻中，宮頸緣在分娩時被撕裂後向外翻轉。

evisceration *n.* **1.** (in surgery) the protrusion of an organ through a surgical incision. **2.** (in ophthalmology) an operation in which the contents of the eyeball are removed, the empty outer envelope (sclera) being left behind. *Compare* enucleation.

(1) 外置術 （外科學）經外科切開術使一器官突出。**(2) 眼內容剜出術** （眼科學）除去眼球內容物，只留下空外殼（鞏膜）的手術。與 enucleation 對比。

evulsion *n. see* avulsion.

撕脫 參閱 avulsion。

Ewing's sarcoma a malignant tumour of bone occurring in children and young adults (*see* Codman's triangle).

尤因瘤 發生於兒童和青年的惡性骨腫瘤（參閱 Codman's triangle）。1921年吉·尤因將

Distinguished from *osteosarcoma by J. Ewing in 1921, it commonly arises in the femur but is liable to spread to other bones and to the lung. It usually presents with pain, often associated with fever and *leucocytosis. The tumour is sensitive to radiotherapy, and systemic therapy with *cytotoxic drugs has improved its prognosis.

此瘤與骨肉瘤區分開。此腫瘤常發生在股骨，容易轉移到其他骨和肺部，通常表現為疼痛，常伴發燒和白細胞增多。該腫瘤對放療敏感。系統地進行細胞毒素藥物治療也可改善其預後。

ex- (exo-) *prefix denoting* outside or outer.

〔前綴〕在……之外，外

exaltation *n. see* elation.

異常興奮　參閱 elation。

exanthem *n.* a rash or eruption, such as that occurring in measles. **–exanthematous** *adj.*

疹病　皮疹或發疹疾病，如麻疹時發生的皮疹。

excavator *n.* **1.** a spoon-shaped surgical instrument that is used to scrape out diseased tissue, usually for laboratory examination. **2.** a type of hand instrument with spoon ends used for removing decayed dentine from teeth. It may also be used as a *curette.

剜器　(1) 通常為實驗室檢查而用於剜出病變組織的匙樣外科器械。(2) 一種手用器械，尾端帶匙，用於從牙齒中除去腐爛牙質，也可做刮匙用。

exchange transfusion a technique for treating *haemolytic disease in newborn infants. Using a syringe with a three-way tap, blood is withdrawn from the baby (via the umbilical vein), ejected, and replaced by an equal amount of donor blood compatible with the mother's blood, without detaching the syringe. By many repetitions of this exchange, red blood cells liable to be destroyed and bilirubin released from those already destroyed are removed, while keeping the baby's blood volume and number of red cells constant. Exchange transfusion can also be used in *sickle-cell disease, as a temporary treatment during a crisis.

交換輸血法　治療新生兒溶血性疾病的一種技術。用一隻帶三通接頭的 20 ml 注射器通過臍靜脈從嬰兒體內抽出 Rh 陽性血液，不用更換注射器，再注入與母親血液相容的等體積供體血液。反覆重複這種交換，容易破壞的紅細胞及從已被破壞的紅細胞中釋放出來的膽紅素就可被除去。同時，又保持了嬰兒血容量及紅細胞數穩定不變。交換輸血法也用於鐮狀細胞病危象時的臨時治療手段。

excimer laser a laser that can remove very thin sheets of tissue from the

激態原子激光　一種激光，可除去眼角膜表面薄的組織，用

surface of the cornea of the eye. This can be done to alter the curvature of the corneal surface, for example to treat myopia (*photorefractive keratectomy*), or to remove diseased (e.g. calcified) tissue from the corneal surface (*photothera-peutic keratectomy*).

於改變角膜弧度。例如，用於治療近視或從角膜表面去除病變組織。

excipient *n.* a substance that is combined with a drug in order to render it suitable for administration; for example, in the form of pills. Excipients should have no pharmacological action themselves.

賦形劑 為使藥物易於服用（如丸劑形式）而與其結合的物質。但其本身不應有藥理作用。

excise *vb.* to cut out tissue, an organ, or a tumour from the body. **–excision** *n.*

切除 將組織、器官或腫瘤從體內切除。

excitation *n.* (in neurophysiology) the triggering of a conducted impulse in the membrane of a muscle cell or nerve fibre. During excitation a polarized membrane becomes momentarily depolarized and an *action potential is set up.

興奮 （神經生理學）激發肌細胞膜或神經纖維產生傳導性衝動的動因。興奮時，極化膜暫時去極化，並形成動作電位。

excoriation *n.* the destruction and removal of the surface of the skin or the covering of an organ by scraping, the application of a chemical, or other means.

表皮脫落 因搔抓、使用化學物質或其他方法使皮膚表面或器官外膜遭到破壞並脫落。

excrescence *n.* an abnormal outgrowth on the surface of the body, such as a wart.

贅生物 體表面不正常的生長物，如疣。

excreta *n.* any waste material discharged from the body, especially faeces.

排泄物 從體內排出的任何廢物，特別是糞便。

excretion *n.* the removal of the waste products of metabolism from the body, mainly through the action of the *kidneys. Excretion also includes the loss of water, salts, and some urea through the sweat glands and carbon dioxide and water vapour from the lungs, and the term is also used to include the egestion of faeces.

排泄 體內的代謝廢物通過腎臟的作用排出體外。但也包括水、鹽及一些尿素從汗腺排出及二氧化碳和水蒸氣從肺臟排出的過程。此術語也用以指排便。

exenteration *n.* (in ophthalmology) an operation in which all the contents of the eye socket (orbit) are removed, leaving only the bony walls intact. The bone is covered by a skin graft. This operation is sometimes necessary when there is a malignant tumour in the orbit.

眼眶內容物剜出術　（眼科學）除去眼眶內所有內容物，只留下完整骨壁的手術。用移植的皮膚覆蓋骨壁。在眼眶內有惡性腫瘤時，有時必需施行這種手術。

exercise *n.* any activity resulting in physical exertion that is intended to maintain physical fitness, to condition the body, or to correct a physical deformity. Exercises may be done actively by the person or passively by a therapist. *Aerobic exercises* are intended to increase oxygen consumption (as in running) and to benefit the lungs and cardiovascular system, in contrast to *isometric exercises. In *isotonic exercises*, the muscles contract and there is movement, but the force remains the same; this improves joint mobility and muscle strength.

運動　能導致身體用力的任何活動，可保持身體適應性，改善身體條件，或矯正身體畸形。運動可由某人主動去做或由治療師來被動完成。需氧運動可提高氧氣消耗，有益於肺和心血管系統，與無氧運動相反。等張運動中，肌肉收縮、運動，但力保持不變；這樣可提高關節活動能力和肌肉的力量。

exflagellation *n.* the formation and release of mature flagellated male sex cells (*see* plasmodium) by the *microgametocytes of the malarial parasite (*see* microgamete). The process, which is completed in 10–15 minutes, occurs after the microgametocytes have been transferred from man to the stomach of a mosquito.

小配子形成　由瘧原蟲小配子母細胞形成並釋放有鞭毛的成熟雄性細胞的過程。整個過程在10~15分鐘之內完成，發生在小配子母細胞從人體轉移到蚊胃之後。

exfoliation *n.* **1.** flaking off of the upper layers of the skin. **2.** separation of a surface epithelium from the underlying tissue. **3.** the natural shedding of deciduous teeth. **–exfoliative** *adj.*

脫落　**(1)** 皮膚外層剝落。**(2)** 表面上皮與皮下組織分離。**(3)** 乳齒自然掉落。

exhalation (expiration) *n.* the act of breathing air from the lungs out through the mouth and nose. *See* breathing.

呼出　肺部的氣體從口及鼻排出的動作。參閱 breathing。

exhibitionism *n.* exposure of the genitals to another person, as a sexually

裸露癖，露陰癖　向他人暴露自己的生殖器。一種不正常的

deviant act. The word is often broadened to mean public flaunting of any quality of the individual.

性變態行為。該詞的意思還被擴大為公開誇耀自己的長處。

exo- *prefix. see* ex-.

〔前綴〕**外** 參閱 ex-。

exocoelom *n. see* extraembryonic coelom.

外體腔 參閱 extraembryonic coelom。

exocrine gland a gland that discharges its secretion by means of a duct, which opens onto an epithelial surface. An exocrine gland may be *simple*, with a single unbranched duct, or *compound*, with branched ducts and multiple secretory sacs. The illustration shows some different types of these glands. Examples of exocrine glands are the sebaceous and sweat glands. *See also* secretion.

外分泌腺 通過導管排出其分泌液的腺體。導管口開向上皮表面。可分為單管外分泌腺：只有一個不分支的導管；複管外分泌腺：有多個分支的導管和分泌囊。下圖是這些腺體的不同類型。外分泌腺包括皮脂腺和汗腺等。參閱 secretion。

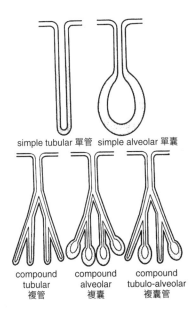

simple tubular 單管   simple alveolar 單囊

compound
tubular
複管

compound
alveolar
複囊

compound
tubulo-alveolar
複囊管

Types of exocrine gland
外分泌腺種類

exoenzyme *n.* an *enzyme that acts outside the cell that produced it. Examples of exoenzymes are the digestive enzymes.

胞外酶　在分泌細胞外發揮作用的酶。如消化酶等。

exoerythrocytic *adj.* describing those stages in the life cycle of the malarial parasite (*see* Plasmodium) that develop in the cells of the liver. Each parasite (*sporozoite) divides repeatedly to produce a *schizont containing many merozoites.

紅細胞外的　指在肝細胞內生長發育的瘧原蟲（參閱 Plasmodium）生活周期中的各個階段。每一瘧原蟲又反覆分裂，可產生出含有裂殖子的裂殖體。

exogenous *adj.* originating outside the body or part of the body: applied particularly to substances in the body that are derived from the diet rather than built up by the body's own processes of metabolism. *Compare* endogenous.

外原的　源於身體外或身體某部位外的。專指從膳食中得來，而不是因身體本身的代謝過程所產生的體內物質。與 endogenous 對比。

exomphalos *n.* an umbilical *hernia.

臍疝　一種臍部的疝。

exopeptidase *n.* an enzyme (e.g. *trypsin) that takes part in the digestion of proteins by splitting off the terminal amino acids of a polypeptide chain. *Compare* endopeptidase. *See also* peptidase.

肽鏈外切酶　通過分解多肽鏈末端氨基酸而參與蛋白質消化的酶（如胰蛋白酶）。與 endopeptidase 對比。參閱 peptidase。

exophoria *n.* a tendency to squint in which the eye, when covered, tends to turn outwards. *See also* heterophoria.

外隱斜視　當閉眼時，眼睛向外移的斜視現象。參閱 heterophoria。

exophthalmic goitre (Graves's disease) *see* thyrotoxicosis.

突眼性甲狀腺腫　參閱 thyrotoxicosis。

exophthalmometer (proptometer) *n.* an instrument for measuring the degree of protrusion of the eyeball. The distance measured is that from the rim of bone at the outer edge of the eye, forwards to the surface of the front of the cornea.

突眼計　測量眼球突出程度的儀器，測量的距離是從眼外緣的骨緣向前到角膜的前表面。

exophthalmos *n.* protrusion of the eyeballs in their sockets. This can result from

突眼，眼球突出　眼球在其眼眶內突出。可因眼球及眼眶損

injury or disease of the eyeball or socket but is most commonly associated with overactivity of the thyroid gland (*see* thyrotoxicosis).

傷或疾病引起，但主要與甲狀腺功能亢進有關（參閱 thyrotoxicosis）。

exosmosis *n.* outward osmotic flow. *See also* osmosis.

外滲 體液向外滲出。參閱 osmosis。

exostosis *n.* a benign cartilaginous outgrowth from a bone. *See* osteoma.

外生骨疣 生長於骨上的良性軟骨新生物。參閱 osteoma。

exothermic *adj.* describing a chemical reaction in which energy is released in the form of heat. *Compare* endothermic.

放熱的 指以熱的形式釋放能量的化學反應。與 endothermic 對比。

exotic *adj.* describing a disease occurring in a region of the world far from where it might be expected. Thus malaria and leishmaniasis are regarded as exotic when they are diagnosed in patients in Britain.

外來的 指某地區發生了原本只發生在遠離該地區的世界其他地區的疾病。因此，當在英國的患者被診斷為患瘧疾和利什曼病時，這些病就被認為是外來的。

exotoxin *n.* a highly potent poison, often harmful to only a limited range of tissues, that is produced by a bacterial cell and secreted into its surrounding medium. It is generally unstable, being rendered inactive by heat, light, and chemicals. Exotoxins are produced by such bacteria as those causing *botulism, *diphtheria, and *tetanus. *Compare* endotoxin.

外毒素 由細菌產生，並釋放到其周圍環境的劇毒物質。通常只對組織的有限範圍有害。一般不穩定，可被熱、光、化學物質滅活。外毒素由能引起肉毒中毒、白喉及破傷風一類的細菌產生。與 endotoxin 對比。

exotropia *n.* divergent *strabismus: a type of squint.

外斜視 散開性斜視，斜視的一種。

expectorant *n.* a drug that enhances the secretion of sputum by the air passages so that it is easier to cough up. Expectorants are used in cough mixtures; they act by increasing the bronchial secretion or make it less viscous (*see* mucolytic). Drugs such as *ipecacuanha are *stimulant expectorants* in small quantities: they irritate the lining of the stomach, which provides a stimulus for the reflex

祛痰劑 促進氣道分泌痰液，使其易於咳出的藥物。用於止咳合劑中。是通過增加支氣管的分泌或使痰液稀薄而發揮作用的（參閱 mucolytic）。小劑量的藥物如吐根屬刺激性祛痰劑：它們通過激惹胃黏膜反射地刺激支氣管黏膜內的腺體產生痰液。大劑量的吐根可導致嘔吐。

production of sputum by the glands in the bronchial mucous membrane. At higher doses they produce vomiting.

expectoration *n*. the act of spitting out material brought into the mouth by coughing.

排痰　吐出因咳嗽帶到嘴裏的東西。

expiration *n*. **1.** the act of breathing out air from the lungs: exhalation. **2.** dying.

(1) 呼出　排出肺部氣體的動作。**(2) 臨終**

explant 1. *n*. live tissue transferred from the body (or any organism) to a suitable artificial medium for culture. The tissue grows in the artificial medium and can be studied for diagnostic or experimental purposes. Tumour growths are sometimes examined in this way. **2.** silicone rubber material sutured to the outside of the eyeball over a retinal tear or hole (*see* detached retina, plombage). The resulting indent allows the retina to reattach. **3.** *vb.* to transfer live tissue for culture outside the body. **–explantation** *n*.

(1) 移出物　從體內（或任何生物體內）移到適宜的人工培養基上進行培養的活組織。此組織在人工培養基上生長，並為診斷或實驗的目的而對其進行研究。腫瘤生長物有時就是用這種方法進行檢查的。**(2) 充填術**　硅膠物質縫在眼球外覆蓋視網膜破損或裂孔。產生的壓力使得視網膜恢復原位。**(3) 移出**　將活組織移到體外進行培養。

exploration *n*. (in surgery) an investigative operation to determine the cause of symptoms. **–exploratory** *adj*.

探查術　（外科學）為確定症狀的原因而進行的探查性手術。

exposure *n*. (in behaviour therapy) a method of treating fears and phobias that involves confronting the individual with the situation he has been avoiding, so allowing the fears to wane by *extinction. It can be achieved gradually by *desensitization or suddenly by *flooding.

暴露療法　（行為療法）治療害怕或恐懼的方法。讓患者親臨其曾避免遇到的現場，使懼怕心理因消退作用而消失。這種療法可通過脫敏作用而逐漸達到目的，或通過暴露於恐怖環境之中而迅速達到目的。

expressed emotion a measure of the degree of warmth or hostility in a relationship between two people, assessed when one person is talking about the other. High levels of criticism and hostility from family members can worsen the prognosis of mentally ill patients.

情感表示　兩個人間關係熱烈程度的衡量方法，在一個人談論另一個時可獲得。家庭成員的過度批評和熱情可使精神病患者的治療變得更加困難。

exsanguinate *vb.* to deprive the body of blood; for example, as a result of an accident causing severe bleeding or – very rarely – through uncontrollable bleeding during a surgical operation. **–exsanguination** *n.*

失血 體內血液的流失。如因意外事故而嚴重出血，或外科手術時不能控制的出血。後者很少見。

exsiccation *n.* drying up, as may occur in tissues deprived of an adequate supply of water during dehydration or starvation.

乾燥 缺水。常發生於脫水或饑餓時沒有充分供水的組織。

exstrophy *n.* a severe congenital abnormality in which the bladder fails to close during development: the baby is born with an absent lower abdominal wall and the internal surface of the posterior bladder wall is exposed. It is associated with *epispadias, total urinary incontinence, and undescended testes.

外翻 一種嚴重的先天性疾病，膀胱在發育過程中不能關閉。胎兒出生時下腹壁缺損，膀胱後壁內表面外露。此病伴有尿道上裂，完全性尿失禁和睾丸下降不全。

exsufflation *n.* the forcible removal of secretions from the air passages by some form of suction apparatus.

抽吸 用某種形式的抽吸器強力抽出氣道中的分泌物。

extension *n.* **1.** the act of extending or stretching, especially the muscular movement by which a limb is straightened. **2.** the application of *traction to a fractured or dislocated limb in order to restore it to its normal position.

(1) 伸展 伸直或展開的動作。特別是肌肉運動，這樣可使肢體伸直。**(2) 牽引** 用牽引的方法使骨折或錯位的肢體恢復其正常位置。

extensor *n.* any muscle that causes the straightening of a limb or other part.

伸肌 使肢體或其他部位伸直的所有肌肉。

exteriorization *n.* a surgical procedure in which an organ is brought from its normal site to the surface of the body. This may be done as a temporary or permanent measure; for example, the intestine may be brought to the surface of the abdomen (*see* colostomy). The process is also sometimes used in physiological experiments on animals.

外置術 將某器官從其正常位置移到身體表面的外科手術。可作為暫時或永久性措施。如將腸道拉出腹壁表面。這一手術有時也用於動物的生理實驗。

exteroceptor *n.* a sensory nerve, ending in the skin or a mucous membrane, that is responsive to stimuli from outside the body. *See also* chemoreceptor, receptor.

外感受器　在皮膚或黏膜內的感覺神經末梢，傳導體外的刺激。參閱 chemoreceptor，receptor。

extinction *n.* (in psychology) the weakening of a conditioned reflex that takes place if it is not maintained by *reinforcement. This is used as a method of treatment when undesirable behaviour (e.g. destructiveness) is reduced simply by withdrawing whatever rewards it (e.g. the fuss made by other people).

消失作用　（心理學）如果不持續強化條件，則這種條件反射會逐漸減弱，此作用可作為一種治療方法。當發生令人不快的行為時（如破壞行為），只要不去理睬（如其他人大驚小怪），這種行為是會減少的。

extirpation *n.* the complete surgical removal of tissue, an organ, or a growth.

摘除　將組織、器官或生長物完全外科切除。

extra- *prefix denoting* outside or beyond.

〔前綴〕外，在……之外

extracellular *adj.* situated or occurring outside cells; for example, *extracellular fluid* is the fluid surrounding cells.

細胞外的　位於或發生於細胞之外的。例如細胞外液是細胞周圍的液體。

extracorporeal *adj.* situated or occurring outside the body. *Extracorporeal circulation* is the circulation of the blood outside the body, as through a *heart-lung machine or an artificial kidney (*see* haemodialysis).

體外的　位於或發生於體外的。體外循環是身體之外的血液循環，例如通過心肺機或人工腎臟的血液循環（參閱 haemodialysis）。

extract *n.* a preparation containing the pharmacologically active principles of a drug, made by evaporating a solution of the drug in water, alcohol, or ether.

浸膏　具有藥物有效成分的製劑。經蒸發藥的水溶液、酒精溶液及乙醚溶液而製成。

extraction *n.* **1.** the surgical removal of a part of the body. Extraction of teeth is usually achieved by applying extraction *forceps to the crown or root of the tooth to dislocate it from its socket. When this is not possible, for example because the tooth or root is deeply buried within the bone, extraction is performed surgically by removing bone and, where necessary, dividing the tooth. **2.** the act of pulling

(1) 摘除術　外科切除身體某部位。牙齒摘除術是用拔牙鉗夾住牙冠或牙根部使其脫離牙槽而完成的。如使用這一方法不能成功，譬如牙齒或牙根部深深埋入骨內，就要切除牙槽骨，再分離出牙齒來完成摘除術。**(2) 取出**　在分娩時，從母體中拉出嬰兒的動作。

out a baby from the body of its mother during childbirth.

extractor *n.* an instrument used to pull out a natural part of the body, to remove a foreign object, or to assist delivery of a baby (*see* vacuum extractor).

取出器　摘出體內某自然部分，除去異物或幫助嬰兒娩出的器械（參閱 vacuum extractor）。

extradural *adj. see* epidural.

硬膜外的　參閱 epidural。

extraembryonic coelom (exocoelom) the cavity, lined with mesoderm, that surrounds the embryo from the earliest stages of development. It communicates temporarily with the coelomic cavity within the embryo (peritoneal cavity). Late in pregnancy it becomes almost entirely obliterated by the growth of the *amnion, which fuses with the *chorion.

胚外體腔　最早發育期的胚胎周圍的腔。內襯以中胚層。與胚胎內體腔（腹腔）暫時相交通。妊娠後期，該腔幾乎完全被生長的與絨毛膜融合的羊膜所閉合。

extraembryonic membranes the membranous structures that surround the embryo and contribute to the placenta and umbilical cord. They include the *amnion, *chorion, *allantois, and *yolk sac. In man the allantois is always very small and by the end of pregnancy the amnion and chorion have fused into a single membrane and the yolk sac has disappeared.

胚外膜　包繞胚胎並構成胎盤和臍帶的膜樣結構。包括羊膜、絨毛膜、尿囊和卵黃囊。在人類，尿囊總是很小；而且在妊娠末期時，羊膜和絨毛膜融合在一起，形成單層膜；卵黃囊也已消失。

extrapleural *adj.* relating to the tissues of the chest wall outside the parietal *pleura.

胸膜外的　指胸膜壁層外的胸壁組織。

extrapyramidal system the system of nerve tracts and pathways connecting the cerebral cortex, basal ganglia, thalamus, cerebellum, reticular formation, and spinal neurones in complex circuits not included in the *pyramidal system. The extrapyramidal system is mainly concerned with the regulation of stereotyped reflex muscular movements.

錐體外系統　在錐體系以外的連接大腦皮層、基底神經節、丘腦、小腦網狀結構及脊神經元的神經束和傳導系統。是一套複雜的神經環路。錐體外系統主要是調節固有的肌肉運動反射。

extrasensory perception (ESP) a supposed way of perceiving that involves none of the known senses. *Clairvoyance* is the extrasensory perception of current events; *precognition* is extrasensory perception of future events; *telepathy* is the extrasensory perception of the thoughts of others.

超感知覺 假設的不包括已知感覺的察覺方式。洞察力就是對現實事物的超感知覺，預感就是對將來事件的超感知覺，心靈感應就是對他人想法的超感知覺。

extrasystole *n. see* ectopic beat.

期外收縮 參閱 ectopic beat。

extrauterine *adj.* outside the uterus.

子宮外的 子宮以外的。

extravasation *n.* the leakage and spread of blood or fluid from vessels into the surrounding tissues, which follows, injury, burns, inflammation, and allergy.

外滲 血液或液體從血管內滲出並擴散到周圍組織。通常發生在損傷、燒傷、炎症及變態反應以後。

extraversion *n. see* extroversion.

外向性格 參閱 extroversion。

extrinsic muscle a muscle, such as any of those controlling movements of the eyeball, that has its origin some distance from the part it acts on. *See also* eye.

外附肌 其起源與其作用部位有一定距離的肌肉。如控制眼球運動的所有肌肉。參閱 eye。

extroversion *n.* **1.** (or **extraversion**) an enduring personality trait characterized by interest in the outside world rather than the self. People high in extroversion (*extroverts*), as measured by questionnaires and tests, are gregarious and outgoing, prefer to change activities frequently, and are not susceptible to permanent *conditioning. Extroversion was first described by Carl Jung as a tendency to action rather than thought, to scientific rather than philosophical interests, and to emotional rather than intellectual reactions. *Compare* introversion. **2.** a turning inside out of a hollow organ, such as the uterus (which sometimes occurs after childbirth).

(1) 外向性格 以對外界而不是對自己感興趣為特點的個性。以外向性格為主的人，經詢問和考查證明，是愛交際而且開朗的，寧願頻繁更換活動種類，也不願持續在一種恆定的環境之中生活。卡爾·榮格是第一位描述外向性格的人。他認為：外向性格表現為願意活動而不願意思考；喜歡科學而不喜歡哲學；善於感情用事而不是理智地處事。與 introversion 對比。**(2) 外翻** 某空腔臟器由內翻向外。如子宮外翻（有時分娩後發生）。

extrovert *n. see* extroversion.

extrusion *n.* (in dentistry) the forced eruption of a tooth by means of an orthodontic appliance; for example, to realign a tooth that has been accidentally forced into the jaw.

exudation *n.* the slow escape of liquid (called the *exudate*) containing proteins and white cells through the walls of intact blood vessels, usually as a result of inflammation. Exudation is a normal part of the body's defence mechanisms.

eye *n.* the organ of sight: a three-layered roughly spherical structure specialized for receiving and responding to light. The outer fibrous coat consists of the sclera and the transparent cornea; the middle vascular layer comprises the choroid, ciliary body, and iris; and the inner sensory layer is the retina (see illustration).

　　Light enters the eye through the cornea, which refracts the light through

外向性格者　參閱　extroversion。

擠壓成形　（牙科學）使用牙科矯正器械迫使牙齒生長成形；如將偶爾發生倒向頜骨的牙齒進行重新復位。

滲出　含蛋白質和白細胞的液體（滲出液）從完整的血管緩慢溢出。通常是炎症的結果。滲出是身體防禦機制的一正常部分。

眼　視覺器官。大體分三層專門接收並轉送光綫的球狀結構。外部纖維層由鞏膜和角膜組成；中間脈管層由脈絡膜、睫狀體和虹膜組成；內部的感覺層即視網膜（見圖）。

　　光通過角膜進入眼內，角膜又將光通過房水折射到晶狀體上。經晶狀體的調節（參閱accommodation），光通過玻璃體集中到視網膜上。在視網

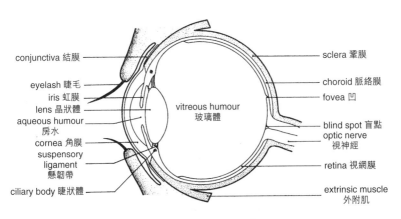

The eye (sagittal section)
眼 （矢狀面）

the aqueous humour onto the lens. By adjustment of the shape of the lens (*see* accommodation) light is focused through the vitreous humour onto the retina. In the retina light-sensitive cells (*see* cone, rod) send nerve impulses to the brain via the optic nerve. The arrangement of the two eyes at the front of the head provides *binocular vision. Each eye is contained in an *orbit, and movement of the eye within the orbit is controlled by extrinsic eye muscles (see illustration).

膜裏，光感細胞（參閱 cone，rod）通過視神經將神經衝動送入大腦。腦前的兩眼提供了雙眼視覺。每一眼眶裏有一隻眼，眼眶內眼的移動由眼外附肌控制（見圖）。

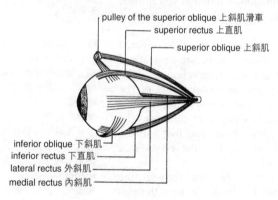

pulley of the superior oblique 上斜肌滑車
superior rectus 上直肌
superior oblique 上斜肌
inferior oblique 下斜肌
inferior rectus 下直肌
lateral rectus 外斜肌
medial rectus 內斜肌

Extrinsic muscles of the eye
眼外附肌

eyeball *n.* the body of the *eye, which is roughly spherical, is bounded by the *sclera, and lies in the *orbit. It is closely associated with accessory structures – the eyelids, conjunctiva, and lacrimal (tear-producing) apparatus – and its movements are controlled by three pairs of extrinsic eye muscles (see illustration).

眼球 眼的主體，它近似球形，被鞏膜包繞，處於眼眶內。它與其附屬結構——眼瞼、結膜和淚器密切相關；其運動由三對眼外附肌控制（見圖）。

eyebrow *n.* the small fringe of hair on the bony ridge just above the eye. It helps to prevent moisture from running into the eye. Anatomical name: **supercilium**.

眼眉 眼上方骨嵴部位上的小毛緣。它可防止液體流入眼內。解剖學用語：眉。

eyeground *n.* the inside of the eye as seen through an ophthalmoscope; the ocular fundus.

眼底　通過眼底鏡所見到的眼內結構；眼底。

eyelash *n.* one of the long stiff hairs that form a row projecting outwards from the front edge of the upper and lower eyelids. The eyelashes help keep dust away from the eye. Anatomical name: **cilium**.

睫毛　從上下眼瞼前緣向外長出的一排較長較硬的毛。它有助於避免灰塵進入眼內。解剖學用語：睫。

eyelid *n.* the protective covering of the eye. Each eye has two eyelids consisting of skin, muscle, connective tissue (*tarsus*), and sebaceous glands (*meibomian* or *tarsal glands*). Each eyelid is lined with membrane (*conjunctiva) and fringed with eyelashes. Stimulation of the pain receptors in the cornea causes the eyelids to close in a reflex action. Inflammation of a meibomian gland can result in a *chalazion. Anatomical names: **blepharon**, **palpebra**.

眼瞼　遮蓋眼的保護性皺襞。每隻眼睛有兩個眼瞼，由皮膚、肌肉、結締組織和皮脂腺體組成。每一眼瞼由黏膜（結膜）內襯，由睫毛落緣。刺激角膜的疼痛感受器可引起眼瞼反射性關閉。瞼板腺炎症可引起瞼板腺囊腫。解剖學用語：瞼。

eyepiece *n.* the lens or system of lenses of an optical instrument, such as a microscope, that is nearest to the eye of the examiner. It usually produces a magnified image of the previous image formed by the instrument. *Compare* objective.

目鏡　光學儀器如顯微鏡中距離檢查者眼睛最近的部件。一般把由儀器形成圖像再進行放大。與 objective 對比。

eyespot *n.* a small light-sensitive area of pigment found in some protozoans and other lower organisms.

眼點　一些原生動物和其他低級生物中具有顏色的小光敏感區。

eyestrain *n.* a sense of fatigue brought on by use of the eyes for prolonged close work or in persons who have an uncorrected error of *refraction or an imbalance of the muscles that move the eyes. Symptoms are usually aching or burning of the eyes, accompanied by headache and even general fatigue if the eyes are not rested. Medical name: **asthenopia**.

眼疲勞　因長期用眼進行工作或者某些人因屈光不正或動眼肌不協調而引起的一種疲勞感覺。症狀通常為眼疼或燒灼感，如眼睛不休息，會伴有頭痛，甚至全身疲勞。醫學用語：視力疲勞。

F

Fabry's disease *see* angiokeratoma.

法布里病　參閱　angiokera-toma。

face-bow *n*. (in dentistry) an instrument for transferring the jaw relationship of a patient to an *articulator to allow reproduction of the lateral and protrusive movements of the lower jaw.

面弓　（牙科學）將患者頜關係轉移到𬌗架上的一種器械。它用以複製出能夠向外或向前移動的下頜。

face-lift *n*. plastic surgery designed to correct the sagging facial tissues of the elderly. Eyelid drooping can be corrected at the same procedure.

面皺伸平　用以矯正老年人鬆弛下垂的面部組織的整容手術。眼瞼下垂也可以同樣方法矯正。

facet *n*. a small flat surface on a bone or tooth, especially a surface of articulation.

小平面　骨或牙齒上的小平面，特別是關節面。

facial nerve the seventh *cranial nerve (VII): a mixed sensory and motor nerve that supplies the muscles of facial expression, the taste buds of the front part of the tongue, the sublingual salivary glands, and the lacrimal glands. A small branch to the middle ear regulates the tension on the ear ossicles.

面神經　第七對腦神經(VII)：感覺和運動的混合神經，它分布於面部表情肌、舌前的味蕾、舌下唾液腺及淚腺。其一小分支分布到中耳以調節聽小骨的張力。

facial paralysis paralysis of the facial nerve, causing weakness and loss of function of the muscles it serves. It occurs in *Bell's palsy.

面神經麻痺　面部神經麻痺引起它所控制的肌肉功能的減弱或喪失。它常發生於貝爾麻痺。

-facient *suffix denoting* causing or making. Example: *abortifacient* (causing abortion).

〔後綴〕引起，使產生　如，墮胎藥（引起流產）。

facies *n*. **1.** facial expression, often a guide to a patient's state of health as well as his emotions. The typical facies seen in adenoids is the vacant look, with the mouth drooping open. A *Hippocratic facies* is the sallow face, sagging and with

(1) 面容　面部表情，通常是患者健康狀況及情緒的表現。增殖腺患者的典型面容是無表情及張着下垂的嘴。希波克拉底面容是面色灰黃、精神萎靡、無神而凝視的目光，此面

listless staring eyes, that some read as the expression of approaching death. **2.** (in anatomy) a specified surface of a bone or other body part.

容有人稱之為死相。**(2)** 表面 （解剖學）骨或身體其他部分 的表面。

facilitation *n.* (in neurology) the phenomenon that occurs when a neurone receives, through a number of different synapses, impulses that are not powerful enough individually to start an *action potential but whose combined activity brings about some *depolarization of the membrane. In this facilitated state any small additional depolarization will suffice to trigger off an impulse in the cell.

接通作用 （神經學）此現象發 生於當神經元通過多種不同的 突觸接受衝動時，單個的衝動 如不足以引起動作電位，所有 的衝動合在一起，就能引起膜 的去極化。在接通期間，小量 附加的去極化作用就能激發細 胞內的衝動。

facio- *prefix denoting* the face. Examples: *faciobrachial* (relating to the face and arm); *faciolingual* (relating to the face and tongue); *facioplegia* (paralysis of).

〔前綴〕面　如面臂的（有關 面和臂的），面舌的（有關面 和舌的），面癱（面神經麻 痺）。

factitious *adj.* produced artificially, either deliberately or by accident, and therefore not to be taken into account when the results of an experiment are considered or a diagnosis is being made.

人為的　有意或無意地人為產 生的。因此，在分析實驗結果 或做出診斷時，應不予考慮。

factor *n.* (in biochemistry) a substance that is essential to a physiological process, often a substance the nature of which is unknown. *See also* coagulation factors, growth factor.

因子 （生物化學）生理活動過 程中的基礎物質，此物質的本 質常不明。參閱 coagulation factor，growth factor。

Factor VIII (antihaemophilic factor) a *coagulation factor normally present in blood. Deficiency of the factor, which is inherited by males from their mothers, results in classic *haemophilia.

（凝血）因子 VIII（抗血友病 因子）　正常存在於血液的凝血 因子。此因子的缺乏（多為男 性從其母親那裏遺傳下來）會 導致典型的血友病。

Factor IX (Christmas factor) a *coagulation factor normally present in blood. Deficiency of the factor results in *haemophilia.

（凝血）因子 IX（克里斯馬斯 因子）　正常存在於血液中的凝 血因子。此因子缺乏會引起血 友病。

Factory Inspectorate the largest and oldest of the statutory bodies responsible for monitoring the health and safety of factory workers. It is administered by the Department of Employment through the Health and Safety Executive under the terms of the Health and Safety at Work Act. Requirements include a routine examination of young persons and those exposed to toxic hazards (e.g. lead) and the adequate guarding of machinery. Ensuring that the atmosphere inside the factory is free from poisonous fumes and chemicals may cause some conflict with local authorities, whose *Environmental Health Officers have responsibility to prevent atmospheric pollution.

工廠視察團 （英國）負責管理工廠裏工人健康和安全的最大最早的法定團體。按勞動法中健康和安全的條例要求，該視察團由就業部的健康與安全局管理。要求包括：對青年人及暴露於有害毒物（如鉛）之中的人們進行常規檢查，保證不受機器的損傷。確保廠內空氣中無毒氣及無有害化學物質。但這可能與當地政府相矛盾，因他們的環境衞生官員也負責預防大氣污染的工作。

facultative *adj.* describing an organism that is not restricted to one way of life. A *facultative parasite* can live either as a parasite or, in different conditions, as a nonparasite able to survive without a host. *Compare* obligate.

兼性的 指不局限於一種生活方式的生物。兼性寄生物既可作為寄生物生存，也可在不同的環境中不需宿主而作為非寄生物生存。與 obligate 對比。

FAD (flavin adenine dinucleotide) a *coenzyme, derived from riboflavin, that takes part in many important oxidation-reduction reactions. It consists of two phosphate groups, adenine, and ribose.

黃素腺嘌呤二核苷酸 能參與很多重要的氧化還原反應的輔酶，來源於核黃素。由二個磷酸基團、腺嘌呤和核糖組成。

fading *n.* (in behaviour modification) *see* prompting.

消退 行為矯正法用語。參閱 prompting。

faecal impaction *see* constipation, impacted.

糞便阻塞 參閱 constipation，impacted。

faecalith *n.* a small hard mass of faeces, found particularly in the vermiform appendix: a cause of inflammation.

糞石 小的硬糞便團塊，主要見於闌尾，可引起炎症。

faeces *n.* the waste material that is eliminated through the anus. It is formed in the *colon and consists of a solid or

糞便 從肛門排出的廢物。形成於結腸，由未被消化的食物殘渣（主要是纖維素）與膽色

semisolid mass of undigested food remains (chiefly cellulose) mixed with *bile pigments (which are responsible for the colour), bacteria, various secretions (e.g. mucus), and some water. **–faecal** *adj*.

素（着色物質）、細菌、各種分泌物（如黏液）及水混合而成的固體和半固體物質組成。

Fahrenheit temperature temperature expressed on a scale in which the melting point of ice is assigned a temperature of 32° and the boiling point of water a temperature of 212°. For most medical purposes the Celsius (centigrade) scale has replaced the Fahrenheit scale. The formula for converting from Fahrenheit (F) to Celsius (C) is: $C = (5/9)(F - 32)$. *See also* Celsius temperature.

華氏溫度 在溫標上以冰的融點為32°，水的沸點為212°表現出來的溫度。在醫學上，華氏溫標多數已被攝氏溫標所取代。華氏溫度換算成攝氏溫度的公式為：$C = (5/9)(F - 32)$。參閱 Celsius temperature。

failure to thrive (FTT) failure of an infant to grow satisfactorily compared with the average for that community. It is detected by regular measurements and plotting on *centile charts. It can be the first indication of a serious underlying condition, such as kidney or heart disease or malabsorption, or it may result from problems at home, particularly *nonaccidental injury.

發育不足 指一嬰兒與其社區的嬰兒平均標準相比未能令人滿意地發育成長。它是通過經常的測量和在百分位點圖表上繪圖而檢查出來。它可能是諸如腎、心臟或者吸收障礙等嚴重的潛在疾病的最早迹像，或者是由家庭問題所致，特別指非事故性損傷。

fainting *n. see* syncope.

昏厥 參閱 syncope。

falciform ligament a fold of peritoneum separating the right and left lobes of the liver and attaching it to the diaphragm and the anterior abdominal wall as far as the umbilicus.

鐮狀韌帶 分隔肝臟左右葉的腹膜皺襞。通過它，上與橫膈相連，下與前腹壁以及臍相連。

Fallopian tube (oviduct, uterine tube) either of a pair of tubes that conduct ova (egg cells) from the ovary to the uterus (*see* reproductive system). The ovarian end opens into the abdominal cavity via a funnel-shaped structure with finger-like projections (*fimbriae*) surrounding the opening. Movements of the fimbriae at ovulation assist in directing the ovum to

輸卵管 將卵細胞從卵巢運送到子宮（參閱 reproductive system）的一對管道之一。卵巢端通過漏斗狀結構開口於腹腔。圍繞開口處，漏斗狀結構上帶有很多指樣突起（傘）。在排卵期，傘的運動有助於卵子直接進入輸卵管。卵子在輸卵管的卵巢端附近受精。

the Fallopian tube. The ovum is fertilized near the ovarian end of the tube.

falloposcope *n.* a narrow flexible fibreoptic *endoscope used to view the inner lining of the Fallopian tubes (*see* falloposcopy).

輸卵管鏡 用來觀察輸卵管內部結構的細小柔韌的纖維內窺鏡（參閱 falloposcopy）。

falloposcopy *n.* observation of the interior of a Fallopian tube using a *falloposcope introduced via a *hysteroscope.

輸卵管鏡檢查 使用通過宮腔鏡插入的輸卵管鏡對輸卵管內部的觀察檢查。

Fallot's tetralogy *see* tetralogy of Fallot.

法樂四聯症 參閱 tetralogy of Fallot。

false pregnancy *see* pseudocyesis.

假妊娠 參閱 pseudocyesis。

false rib *see* rib.

假肋 參閱 rib。

falx (falx cerebri) *n.* (*pl.* **falces**) a sickle-shaped fold of the *dura mater that dips inwards from the skull in the midline, between the cerebral hemispheres.

大腦鐮 從顱骨突入大腦半球之間的鐮刀狀硬腦膜皺襞。

familial *adj.* describing a condition or character that is found in some families but not in others. It is often inherited.

家族的 指在同一家庭而不是其他家庭裏發現的疾病或特徵。通常是遺傳的。

family doctor *see* general practitioner.

家庭醫生 參閱 general practitioner。

Family Health Services Authority (FHSA) (in Britain) an authority responsible for running general medical services (general practitioners and also dentists, pharmacists, and opticians working outside hospitals) for the population served by one or more District Health Authorities. FHSAs include representatives of the local *medical committee, the local dental committee, the local pharmaceutical committee, and the local optical committee. Recent legislation established FHSAs to replace

家庭保健服務管理局 （英國）負責管理由一個或多個地段衛生局管轄的所有綜合醫療服務部門（包括全科醫師、也包括在醫院外工作的牙科醫師、藥劑師、眼科醫生）的管理機構。家庭保健服務管理局包括當地醫學委員會、當地牙科委員會、當地藥學委員會及當地眼科委員會的代表。最近的立法確定家庭保健服務管理局取代開業醫師管理委員會。後者像前者一樣負責對全科醫師的

Family Practitioner Committees (FPCs), which – like FHSAs – were responsible for the supervision of *general practitioners (including adjudicating on misdemeanors). However, FHSAs have additional managerial duties, including responsibility for remuneration from a predetermined budget. The general practitioners have *independent contracts (as distinct from salaries) with the FHSA, which must approve all names included on the *medical list* (a special list of general practitioners working in the National Health Service). Such inclusion is subject to overall monitoring of the *Medical Practices Committee*, which advises the Department of Health; Similar arrangements exist for the other three services (*see* general dental services). Refusal to include a registered practitioner, who has successfully undertaken an approved postgraduate training programme, is usually the result of there being a surplus for the population being served. However, the FHSA must also approve the premises and the hours of service. The committee meets regularly (e.g. every two months) and has separate subcommittees concerned with vacancies, hours of availability, and allocation of patients who are refused acceptance by all general practitioners in the vicinity. It also receives the views of the professional groups for which it is responsible.

family planning 1. the use of *contraception to limit or space out the numbers of children born to a couple. **2.** provision of contraceptive methods within a community or nation. *See also* genetic counselling.

family practitioner *see* general practitioner.

管理（包括對不端行為的裁決）。但是家庭保健服務管理局有附加的管理職責，包括負責從預先確定的預算中支付酬勞。全科醫師與家庭保健服務管理局簽有獨立的合同（與拿工資的醫生不同）。醫生名單（在國民保健服務制中工作的全科醫師的特殊名單）必須由管理局批准，再由醫學實踐委員會全面監督。該委員會還向衛生部提供咨詢。其他三個醫療服務部門（參閱 general dental services）也有類似的規定。如果不給一醫師註冊登記，而此醫師已成功地進行了經批准的畢業後培訓，通常是因為在這一地區人口服務的醫生已滿額。但家庭保健服務管理局必須規定行醫的地點及時間。委員會定期開會（如每兩月一次），並召開分會處理醫生空缺、工作時間及分配被該地區全科醫師拒絕接受病人的去向。它還接受其負責的專業團體的意見。

計劃生育 (1) 使用避孕措施來限制一對夫妻所生孩子的人數或者孩子之間的時距。**(2)** 在社區或者全國範圍內規定的避孕措施。參閱 genetic counselling。

家 庭 醫 生 參 閱 general practitioner。

family therapy a form of *psychotherapy based on the belief that psychological problems are the products of abnormalities in communication between family members. All family members are therefore seen together, when possible, in order to clarify and modify the ways they relate together (*see* genogram, paradox, sculpting).

家庭療法　一種心理療法形式，它是基於心理問題是家庭成員之間交流異常的結果的觀念。因此，所有家庭成員，可能時，都出席治療能澄清和改善他們之間的關係。（參閱 genogram，paradox，sculpting）。

famotidine *n.* a drug used for the treatment of duodenal ulcers and conditions of excessive gastric acid secretion, such as the Zollinger-Ellison syndrome. It is administered by mouth and intravenously; side-effects are headache, diarrhoea, and dizziness. Trade name: **Pepcid**.

法莫替丁　一種用以治療十二指腸潰瘍和過量胃酸分泌症（如佐-埃氏綜合徵）的藥物。口服和靜脈注射；副作用有頭痛、腹瀉及頭暈。商品名：Pepcid。

Fanconi syndrome a disorder of the proximal kidney tubules, which may be inherited or acquired and is most common in children. It is characterized by the urinary excretion of large amounts of amino acids, glucose, and phosphates (though blood levels of these substances are normal). Symptoms may include osteomalacia, rickets, muscle weakness, and *cystinosis. Treatment is directed to the cause.

范康尼綜合徵　腎臟近曲小管的疾病，可遺傳或後天獲得，最常見於兒童。特點為從尿液中排洩出大量的氨基酸、葡萄糖及磷酸鹽（儘管這些物質在血液裏的量是正常的）。症狀包括骨軟化、佝僂病、肌無力及胱氨酸病。治療應針對病因。

fantasy *n.* a complex sequence of imagination in which several imaginary elements are woven together into a story. An excessive preoccupation with one's own imaginings may be symptomatic of a difficulty in coping with reality. In psychoanalytic psychology, *unconscious fantasies* are supposed to control behaviour, so that psychological symptoms can be symbols of or defences against such fantasies (*see* symbolism).

幻想　把幾種想象的情節編織成一個完整故事的複雜的幻想序列。過分沉醉於這種幻想可能是難於與現實相適應的症狀。在精神分析心理學中，潛意識的幻想被認為能控制人的行為，因而，心理上的症狀可能是這些幻想的象徵，或者是對這些幻想的抵制。（參閱 symbolism）。

farad *n.* the *SI unit of capacitance, equal to the capacitance of a capacitor

法拉　電容的國際單位，等於當通入1庫侖電流時，兩個電

between the plates of which a potential difference of 1 volt appears when it is charged with 1 coulomb of electricity. Symbol: F.

壓差為1伏特的電容器之間的電容量。符號：F。

faradism *n.* the use of induced rapidly alternating electric currents to stimulate nerve and muscle activity. *See also* electrotherapy.

感應電療法 使用快速感應交流電激發神經和肌肉的活動。參閱 electrotherapy。

farcy *n. see* glanders.

馬鼻疽 參閱 glanders。

farmer's lung an occupational lung disease caused by allergy to fungal spores that grow in inadequately dried stored hay, straw, or grain, which then becomes mouldy. It is an allergic *alveolitis, such as also results from sensitivity to many other allergens. An acute reversible form can develop a few hours after exposure; a chronic form, with the gradual development of irreversible breathlessness, occurs with or without preceding acute attacks. Avoidance of the allergen is the main principle of treatment, but most farmers are able to continue to farm by taking appropriate precautions.

農夫肺 一種職業性肺病，因對貯存不當而發霉的乾草、稻桿及穀物堆裏生長的真菌孢子過敏而致。此病是一種變態反應性肺泡炎，與其他變應原在肺部引起的結果相似。急性可逆型在接觸變態原數小時後發病；慢性型可在急性發作後逐漸發展成不可逆性呼吸困難，也可直接發病。避免接觸變應原是主要治療原則。

fascia *n.* (*pl.* **fasciae**) connective tissue forming membranous layers of variable thickness in all regions of the body. Fascia surrounds the softer or more delicate organs and is divided into *superficial fascia* (found immediately beneath the skin) and *deep fascia* (which forms sheaths for muscles).

筋膜 在身體所有部位形成各種厚度膜樣層的結締組織。筋膜包繞着較柔軟或較嬌嫩的器官。分為淺筋膜（直接位於皮膚之下）和深筋膜（形成肌鞘）。

fasciculation *n.* brief spontaneous contraction of a few muscle fibres, which is seen as a flicker of movement under the skin. It is most often associated with disease of the motor neurones in the spinal cord or of the nerve fibres.

自發性收縮 少量肌纖維短暫地、自動地收縮。表現為皮下抽動。常與脊髓中運動神經元疾病或神經纖維疾病有關。自發性收縮也可在正常人腓腸肌處看到。

Fasciculation may be seen in the calf muscles of normal individuals.

fasciculus (fascicle) *n.* a bundle, e.g. of nerve or muscle fibres.

束　束狀物，如神經束或肌纖維束。

fasciitis *n.* inflammation of *fascia. It may result from bacterial infection or from a rheumatic disease, such as *Reiter's syndrome or ankylosing spondylitis.

筋膜炎　筋膜發炎。它可因細菌感染或風濕性疾病，如賴特爾綜合徵或強直性脊椎炎引起。

Fasciola *n.* a genus of *flukes. *F. hepatica*, the liver fluke, normally lives as a parasite of sheep and other herbivorous animals but sometimes infects man (*see* fascioliasis).

片吸蟲屬　吸蟲的一屬。肝吸蟲在正常情況下寄生在羊及其他食草動物身上，但有時也侵犯人類（參閱 fascioliasis）。

fascioliasis *n.* an infestation of the bile ducts and liver with the liver fluke, *Fasciola hepatica*. Man acquires the infection through eating wild watercress on which the larval stages of the parasite are present. The symptoms include fever, dyspepsia, vomiting, loss of appetite, abdominal pain, and coughing; the liver may also be extensively damaged (causing *liver rot*). Anthelmintics are used in the treatment of fascioliasis.

片吸蟲病　肝吸蟲侵犯膽囊和肝引起的疾病。人類是通過食入附有寄生蟲幼蟲的野生水芹而感染。症狀有發熱、消化不良、嘔吐、食慾減退、腹痛及咳嗽。肝臟可有廣泛損害（肝吸蟲病）。抗蠕蟲藥物可用來治療片吸蟲病。

fasciolopsiasis *n.* a disease, common in the Far East, caused by the fluke *Fasciolopsis buski* in the small intestine. At the site of attachment of the adult flukes in the intestine there may be inflammation with some ulceration and bleeding. Symptoms include diarrhoea, and in heavy infections the patient may experience loss of appetite, vomiting, and (later) swelling of the face, abdomen, and legs. Death may follow in cases of severe ill health and malnutrition. The flukes can be removed with an anthelmintic (such as praziquantel).

薑片蟲病　一種疾病，常見於遠東，由小腸內布氏薑片蟲引起。被吸蟲成蟲侵犯的小腸部位有炎症，伴有潰瘍及出血。症狀包括腹瀉。嚴重感染的患者還有食慾不振，嘔吐，面部、腹部及腿部水腫（晚期）。健康狀態極差及營養不良的患者可能死亡。吸蟲可由驅腸蟲藥驅除（如吡喹酮）。

Fasciolopsis *n.* a genus of large parasitic flukes widely distributed throughout eastern Asia and especially common in China. The adults of *F. buski*, the giant intestinal fluke, live in the human small intestine. Man becomes infected with the fluck on eating uncooked water chestnuts contaminated with fluke larvae and the resulting symptoms can be serious (*see* fasciolopsiasis).

薑片蟲屬 大型寄生吸蟲屬，廣泛分布於東亞，尤其是中國。布氏薑片蟲的成蟲是一種大型腸道吸蟲，寄生於小腸。人類在食入含有幼蟲的荸薺後感染，並引起嚴重症狀（參閱 fasciolopsiasis）。

fastigium *n.* the highest point of a fever.

極變 發燒的最高度。

fat *n.* a substance that contains one or more fatty acids (in the form of *triglycerides) and is the principal form in which energy is stored by the body (in *adipose tissue). It also serves as an insulating material beneath the skin (in the subcutaneous tissue) and around certain organs (including the kidneys). Fat is one of the three main constituents of food (*see also* carbohydrate, protein); it is necessary in the diet to provide an adequate supply of *essential fatty acids and for the efficient absorption of fat-soluble vitamins from the intestine. Excessive deposition of fat in the body leads to *obesity. *See also* brown fat, lipid.

脂肪 含有一種或多種脂肪酸（以甘油三酯的形式）的物質，並且是身體（在脂肪組織）貯存能量的主要形式，也可做為皮下的絕熱物（在皮下組織），包繞某些器官（包括腎臟）。食物中大部分的碳水化合物在作為能量被消耗之前要轉化成脂肪。為獲得充分必需脂肪酸及吸收腸道內脂溶性維生素，膳食中必備一定量的脂肪。體內脂肪過分積存可導致肥胖症。參閱 brown fat，lipid。

fatigue *n.* **1.** mental or physical tiredness, following prolonged or intense activity. Muscle fatigue may be due to the waste products of metabolism accumulating in the muscles faster than they can be removed by the venous blood. Incorrect or inadequate food intake or disease may predispose a person to fatigue. **2.** the inability of an organism, an organ, or a tissue to give a normal response to a stimulus until a certain recovery period has elapsed.

疲勞 **(1)** 在過長或緊張的活動之後，精神和體力上的疲乏。肌疲勞可能是由於肌肉中代謝廢物的積累比靜脈血液清除它們的速度快而引起。飲食不當或不足或生病容易使人感到疲勞。**(2)** 某生物體、器官或組織在恢復期到來以前對刺激不能產生正常反應的狀態。

fatty acid an organic acid with a long straight hydrocarbon chain and an even

脂肪酸 帶有碳氫直長鏈和偶數碳原子的有機酸。脂肪酸是

number of carbon atoms. Fatty acids are the fundamental constituents of many important lipids, including *triglycerides. Some fatty acids can be synthesized by the body; others, the *essential fatty acids, must be obtained from the diet. Examples of fatty acids are *palmitic acid*, *oleic acid*, and *stearic acid*. See also fat.

很多重要脂類，包括甘油三酯的基本成分。有些脂肪酸可在體內合成，另一些必需脂肪酸則必須從食物中獲取。脂肪酸有棕櫚酸、油酸、硬脂酸等。參閱 fat。

fatty degeneration deterioration in the health of a tissue due to the deposition of abnormally large amounts of fat in its cells. The accumulation of fat in the liver and heart may seriously impair their functioning. The deposition of fat may be linked with incorrect diet, excessive alcohol consumption, or a shortage of oxygen in the tissues caused by poor circulation or a deficiency of haemoglobin.

脂肪變性 某組織因其細胞內不正常地蓄積大量的脂肪而變質。肝臟和心臟脂肪蓄積能嚴重地影響其功能。脂肪的沉積可與飲食不當、酗酒、或因血液循環不良或血紅蛋白不足引起的組織缺氧有關。

fauces *n.* the opening leading from the mouth into the pharynx. It is surrounded by the *glossopalatine arch* (which forms the anterior pillars of the fauces) and the *pharyngopalatine arch* (the posterior pillars).

咽門 從口腔通向咽部的開口。它由舌腭弓（構成前咽弓）和咽腭弓（構成後弓）所環繞。

favism *n.* an inherited defect in the enzyme glucose-6-phosphate dehydrogenase causing the red blood cells to become sensitive to a chemical in broad beans. It results in destruction of red blood cells (haemolysis), which may lead to severe anaemia, requiring blood transfusion. Favism occurs in parts of the Mediterranean and Iran. See also glucose-6-phosphate dehydrogenase deficiency.

蠶豆病 一種遺傳缺陷，缺乏葡萄糖 6 磷酸脫氫酶而引起紅細胞對蠶豆中的化學物質敏感。紅細胞受到破壞可導致嚴重貧血，需輸血治療。蠶豆病發生於地中海和伊朗的一些地區。參閱 glucose-6-phosphate dehydrogenase deficiency。

favus *n.* a type of *ringworm of the scalp that is caused by the fungus *Trichophyton schoenleini*. Favus, which is rare in Europe, is typified by yellow crusts made up of the threads of fungus and skin debris, which form honeycomb-like masses.

黃癬 頭皮發癬的一種，由舍氏發癬菌引起。黃癬，在歐州罕見，以菌絲和皮屑組成的黃痂為特點，黃痂又形成蜂窩狀斑塊。

fear *n.* an emotional state evoked by the threat of danger and usually characterized by unpleasant subjective experiences as well as physiological and behavioural changes. Fear is often distinguished from *anxiety in having a specific object. Associated physiological changes can include increases in heart rate, blood pressure, sweating, etc. Behavioural changes can include an avoidance of fear-producing objects or situations and may be extremely disabling; for example, fear of open spaces. These specific disabling fears are known as *phobias. *Beta blockers relieve the physiological manifestations of fear and are useful in the treatment of short-term fears, such as the fear of hearing the results of an examination. Tranquillizers, such as diazepam, carry a risk of developing dependence, and *behaviour therapy or *cognitive therapy are preferred for disabling and persistent fears.

febricula *n.* a fever of low intensity or short duration.

febrifuge *n.* a treatment or drug that reduces or prevents fever. *See* antipyretic.

febrile *adj.* relating to or affected with fever.

feedback *n.* the coupling of the output of a process to the input. Feedback mechanisms are important in regulating many physiological processes; for example, hormone output and enzyme-mediated reactions. In *negative feedback*, a rise in the output of a substance (e.g. a hormone) will inhibit a further increase in its production, either directly or indirectly. In *positive feedback*, a rise in the output of a substance is associated with

恐懼 因受到危險威脅而引起的一種情緒狀態，通常以不愉快的主觀體驗和生理、行為上的變化為特點。恐懼與焦慮的區別在於它是針對某一具體對象產生的。生理上的變化包括心動過速、血壓上升、出汗增加。行為上的變化包括離開引起恐懼的對象或環境，甚至使人喪失正常生活能力，如曠野恐懼。這些具體的使人喪失能力的恐懼稱做恐懼症。β-受體阻滯劑能減輕恐懼的生理反應，對治療短期恐懼，如害怕聽到考試結果非常有用。安定藥如地西泮有產生對藥物依賴的危險；相比起來，行為療法或者認知療法更適合於治療使人喪失能力的和持續性恐懼。

微熱 低度或短期發熱。

解熱藥 退熱或預防發熱的藥。參閱 antipyretic。

發熱的 發熱的或者熱病的。

反饋 聯於輸出反應的輸入信息過程。反饋機制在調節生理過程中是很重要的，如激素的釋放和酶促反應。在負反饋中，某物質釋放增加（如激素）將直接和間接地抑制其進一步增加。在正反饋中，某物質釋放增加將直接或間接地促進另一物質數量的增加。

an increase in the output of another substance, either directly or indirectly.

Fehling's test a test for detecting the presence of sugar in urine; it has now been replaced by better and easier methods. It uses *Fehling's solution*, of which there are two components: Fehling's I (a copper sulphate solution) and Fehling's II (a solution of potassium sodium tartrate and sodium hydroxide). Boiling Fegling's solution is added to an equal volume of boiling urine; a yellowish or brownish coloration indicates the presence of sugar.

費林試驗 檢測尿糖的一種試驗，現已被更好、更容易的試驗所替代。使用兩種費林溶液：費林 I 液（硫酸銅溶液）和費林 II 液（枸櫞酸鈉鉀和氫氧化鈉溶液）。把等體積尿和費林溶液煮沸，黃色或棕色表示糖的存在。

Feingold diet a diet that purports to treat many illnesses by the elimination of artificial food colourings, preservatives, and salicylates from the diet. It has been recommended for the treatment of *hyperkinetic syndrome, but is of unproved value.

芬哥德膳食 用以治療多種疾病的一種膳食，不含有人造食物色素、防腐劑和水楊酸。被特別推薦用來治療運動過度綜合徵，但其效果未得到證實。

feminization *n.* the development of female secondary sexual characteristics (enlargement of the breasts, loss of facial hair, and fat beneath the skin) in the male, either as a result of an endocrine disorder or of hormone therapy.

男子女性化 男子表現出女性的第二性徵（乳房增大、無鬍鬚、皮下脂肪增厚）。因內分泌紊亂或激素療法引起。

femoral *adj.* of or relating to the thigh or to the femur.

股的 指大腿或股骨的或與之有關的。

femoral artery an artery arising from the external iliac artery at the inguinal ligament. It is situated superficially, running down the front medial aspect of the thigh. Two-thirds of the way down it passes into the back of the thigh, continuing downward behind the knee as the *popliteal artery*.

股動脈 在腹股溝韌帶附近從髂外動脈發出的一支動脈。位置表淺，向下走行到大腿的前內側。在下行的三分之二處，該動脈穿入大腿的後側，改名為膕動脈，繼續在膝後向下走行。

femoral epiphysis *see* femur.

股骺 參閱 femur。

femoral nerve the nerve that supplies the quadriceps muscle at the front of the thigh and receives sensation from the front and inner sides of the thigh. It arises from the second, third, and fourth lumbar nerves.

股神經 支配大腿前方股四頭肌，並接收大腿前內側感覺的神經。它是從第二、第三、第四腰神經發出的。

femoral triangle (Scarpa's triangle) a triangular depression on the inner side of the thigh bounded by the sartorius and adductor longus muscles and the inguinal ligament. The pulse can be felt here as the femoral artery lies over the depression.

股三角（斯卡帕三角） 大腿內側面的三角形凹陷，其邊界為縫匠肌、內收肌和腹股溝韌帶。脈搏在此可觸摸到，因股動脈通過此凹陷。

femur (thigh bone) *n.* a long bone between the hip and the knee (see illustration). The head of the femur articulates with the acetabulum of the *hip

股骨 位於髖骨和膝之間的長骨（見圖）。股骨頭與髖骨的髖臼相關節。大轉子和小轉子為股骨上的隆凸，臀肌和腰大

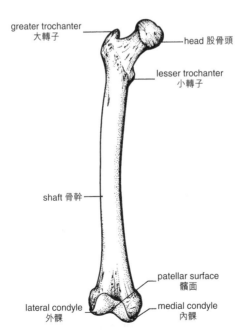

greater trochanter 大轉子
head 股骨頭
lesser trochanter 小轉子
shaft 骨幹
patellar surface 髕面
lateral condyle 外髁
medial condyle 內髁

The femur (front view)
股骨（前面觀）

bone. The *greater* and *lesser trochanters* are protuberances on which the gluteus and psoas major muscles, respectively, are inserted. The *lateral* and *medial condyles* articulate with the *tibia and the concave grooved *patellar surface* accommodates the kneecap (patella). The narrowed end of the femur (femoral neck), which carries the head, is the commonest site of fracture of the leg in elderly women. Partial dislocation of the *femoral epiphysis*, the growth area of the upper end of the bone, leads to deformity of the head of the femur and premature degeneration of the hip joint.

肌分別附着於其上。外髁和內髁與脛骨相關節，凹陷的髕面與髕骨相接。股骨的縮窄端（股骨頸），支撐股骨頭，是老年婦女大腿骨折最常見處。股骺的部分錯位（股骨上端的生長區）導致股骨頭的畸形和髖關節的過早退化。

fenbufen *n*. an anti-inflammatory drug (*see* NSAID) used to relieve inflammation and the resulting pain and stiffness. It is administered by mouth. Possible side-effects include nausea, vomiting, and skin rashes. Trade name: **Lederfen**.

芬布芬　一種用來減輕發炎和發炎引起疼痛和強直的抗炎藥。口服。可能的副作用包括惡心、嘔吐及皮疹。商品名：Lederfen。

fenestra *n*. (in anatomy) an opening resembling a window. The *fenestra ovalis* (*fenestra vestibuli*) – the oval window – is the opening between the middle *ear and the vestibule of the inner ear. It is closed by a membrane to which the stapes is attached. The *fenestra rotunda* (*fenestra cochleae*) – the round window – is the opening between the scala tympani of the cochlea and the middle ear. Sound vibrations leave the cochlea through the fenestra rotunda which, like the fenestra ovalis, is closed by a membrane.

窗　（解剖學）一種類似窗戶的開口。前庭窗即卵圓窗，是中耳和內耳前庭之間的開口。該口被一層膜覆蓋，鐙骨就附着在該膜上。蝸窗為圓形窗，是耳蝸鼓階和中耳之間的開口。振動聲波從蝸窗離開耳蝸。同前庭窗一樣，蝸窗也被一層膜覆蓋。

fenestration *n*. a surgical operation in which a new opening is formed in the bony *labyrinth of the inner ear as part of the treatment of deafness due to *otosclerosis. It is rarely performed today, having been superseded by *stapedectomy.

開窗術　一種外科手術，即在內耳骨迷路造一新口，是因耳硬化症而致聾的治療方法的一部分。現在很少使用，已被鐙骨切除術所取代。

fenfluramine *n.* a drug, similar to *amphetamine, that reduces the appetite and is used in the treatment of obesity. It is administered by mouth; common side-effects are drowsiness and diarrhoea. Trade name: **Ponderax**.

fenoprofen *n.* an *analgesic drug that also reduces inflammation (*see* NSAID) and is used to treat arthritic conditions. It is administered by mouth and may cause digestive upsets, drowsiness, dizziness, sweating, and headache. Trade name: **Fenopron**, **Progesic**.

fermentation *n.* the biochemical process by which organic substances, particularly carbohydrate compounds, are decomposed by the action of enzymes to provide chemical energy. An example is *alcoholic fermentation*, in which enzymes in yeast decompose sugar to form ethyl alcohol and carbon dioxide.

ferri- (ferro-) *prefix denoting* iron.

ferritin *n.* an iron-protein complex that is one of the forms in which iron is stored in the tissues.

ferrous sulphate an *iron salt administered by mouth to treat or prevent iron-deficiency anaemia. There are few serious side-effects; stomach upsets and diarrhoea may be prevented by taking the drug with meals. Similar preparations used to treat anaemia include ferrous fumarate and ferrous succinate.

fertility rate the number of live births occurring in a year per 1000 women of child-bearing age (usually 15 to 44 years). A less reliable measure of fertility can be obtained from the *live birth*

芬氟拉明　類似苯丙胺的一種藥物，能抑制食慾，用於治療肥胖症。口服。常見的副作用有嗜眠和腹瀉。商品名：Ponderax。

非諾洛芬　有消炎作用的鎮痛藥，用於治療關節病。口服。可引起消化道不適、嗜眠、眩暈、出汗及頭痛。商品名：Fenopron，Progesic。

發酵　有機物，特別是碳水化合物，在酶的作用下分解以提供能量的生化過程。例如：乙醇發酵是用酵母中的酶將糖分解成乙醇和二氧化碳。

〔前綴〕鐵

鐵蛋白　一種鐵蛋白質化合物。它是鐵貯存在組織中的一種形式。

硫酸亞鐵　口服的一種鐵鹽。用來治療或預防缺鐵性貧血。幾乎無嚴重的副作用。若出現胃不適或腹瀉，則可在吃飯時服入藥物。治療貧血的類似製劑還有富馬酸亞鐵、琥珀酸亞鐵。

生育率　每千名育齡婦女（一般在15~44歲之間）每年生產活嬰的數量。從活嬰出產率（每千人中活嬰出生數量）或自然增長率（超死亡數的活嬰

rate (the number of live births per 1000 of the population) or the *natural increase* (the excess of live births over deaths). More rarely quoted are the *gross reproduction rate* (the rate at which the child-bearing female population is reproducing itself) and the *net reproduction rate*, which takes into account female mortality before the age of reproduction. Other measures of fertility include the *legitimate birth rate* (the number of live births per 1000 women married once and aged 16 to 44) and the *illegitimate birth rate* (the number of illegitimate births per 1000 unmarried women and widows aged 15 to 44).

數）中得出的生育率是不十分可靠的。粗再生率（有生育能力的婦女的繁殖率）及考慮到育齡前女性死亡率的純再生率更少使用。其他生育率的統計有婚生率（每千名16~44歲的已婚婦女中活嬰出生數）及非婚生率（每千名15~44歲的未婚婦女和寡婦中非婚生活嬰出生數）等。

fertilization *n.* the fusion of a spermatozoon and an ovum. Rapid changes in the membrane of the ovum prevent other spermatozoa from penetrating. Penetration stimulates the completion of meiosis and the formation of the second polar body. Once the male and female pronuclei have fused the zygote starts to divide by cleavage.

受精 精子和卵子融合成一體。卵細胞膜的快速變化能防止其他精子穿入。精子進入卵子能刺激減數分裂的完成和第二極體的形成。一旦雌、雄原核融合為一體，合子便開始卵裂。

festination *n.* the short tottering steps that characterize the gait of a patient with *parkinsonism.

慌張步態 短促跟蹌的步態，是帕金森綜合徵患者步態的特點。

fetal blood sampling a technique, usually carried out during labour, in which a sample of blood is withdrawn from a vein in the scalp of the fetus. From this is determined the degree of fetal *acidosis. The normal pH of fetal blood is 7.35 (range 7.45–7.25). The lower the level, the more likely is the fetus to be suffering from *hypoxia, indicating an urgent need to terminate the labour; if the pH is allowed to fall below a level of 7.10, the life of the fetus is endangered.

胎血取樣 分娩期間所採用的一種技術，即從胎兒的頭皮靜脈抽出血樣。以此確定胎兒酸中毒的程度。胎血正常的pH值是7.35（範圍7.45~7.25）。水平越低，胎兒越可能患供氧不足，表明急需終止分娩；如果pH值降到7.10水平以下，胎兒的生命會有危險。

fetal implant (fetal graft) the introduction of an ovum, fertilized in vitro and developed to the *blastocyst stage, into the uterus of a postmenopausal woman in order that she may become pregnant. Before this procedure, the woman's uterus must be prepared, by hormone therapy, to receive and nurture the blastocyst. Hormone treatment is continued throughout the pregnancy.

胎植入（胎兒移植） 將在體外受精並發育到胚細胞階段的卵植入一絕經期後的婦女的子宮裏以使她能懷孕。在植入之前，此婦女的子宮須用激素療法特別處理過來接收並滋養胚細胞。激素治療持續懷孕全過程。

fetal transplant specific cells taken from a healthy newly aborted fetus and transplanted into a person suffering from a specific disease. These fetal cells take over the function of the specific diseased or damaged cells of the host. Examples are fetal brain cells transplanted into the affected part of the brain in a patient suffering from Parkinson's disease, and fetal pancreatic cells transplanted into the pancreas of a juvenile diabetic. Other diseases are being investigated experimentally with a view to using fetal transplants. Potentially, such procedures involve ethical considerations.

胎移植 將從剛墮胎的健康胎兒體內所取的特殊細胞移植進患某種特異病的患者體內。這些胎細胞接替患者不健全或者受損細胞的功能。例如胎腦細胞移植進患帕金森病患者的大腦患部，胎胰細胞移植進少年糖尿病患者的胰腺。其他疾病也在進行以使用胎移植為目的實驗性調查研究。這些手術潛在地牽涉倫理問題。

fetishism *n.* sexual attraction to an inappropriate object (known as a *fetish*). This may be a part of the body (e.g. the foot or the hair), clothing (e.g. underwear or shoes), or other objects (e.g. leather handbags or rubber sheets). In all these cases the fetish has replaced the normal object of sexual love, in some cases to the point at which sexual relationships with another person are impossible or are possible only if the fetish is either present or fantasized. Treatment can involve *psychotherapy or behaviour therapy using *aversion therapy and masturbatory conditioning of desirable sexual behaviour. *See also* sexual deviation.

戀物癖 對非性感的物體發生的性戀。戀物對象可能是身體的某些部位（如腳和體毛）或衣物（褲衩和鞋）或其他物品（如皮革手提包、橡膠薄片）。在所有這些病例中，正常的性愛對象被取代，在有些病例中，患者甚至不能與他人有性關係，或者只有在戀物對象存在或幻想到才有可能。治療牽涉心理和行為療法使用厭惡療法和手淫法來塑造患者的性行為。參閱 sexual deviation。

feto- *prefix denoting* a fetus.

〔前綴〕胎兒

fetor (foetor) *n.* an unpleasant smell. *Fetor oris* is bad breath (*halitosis).

臭味　令人厭惡的氣味。口臭是從口裏呼出的難聞的氣味。

fetoscopy *n.* the inspection of a fetus before birth by passing special fibreoptic instrument known as a *fetoscope* through the abdomen of a pregnant woman into her uterus. Fetoscopy, usually performed in the 18th–20th week of gestation, allows the inspection of the fetus for visible abnormalities and blood sampling by inserting a hollow needle under direct vision into a placental blood vessel. The blood can then be examined for abnormalities and hence the *prenatal diagnosis of blood disorders (such as thalassaemia, haemophilia, and sickle-cell disease) and Duchenne muscular dystrophy.

胎兒鏡觀察術　對出生前胎兒的觀察，是通過孕婦腹壁刺入其子宮內的一種叫做胎兒鏡的特殊纖維儀進行的。此方法通常在妊娠的第18~20周使用以檢查胎兒是否有看得見的異常和在直接觀察下通過空心針刺入胎盤血管中採集血樣。然後檢查血液是否存在異常及對血液病（如地中海貧血、血友病及鐮狀細胞病）及迪歇納肌肉萎縮做出產前診斷。

fetus (foetus) *n.* a mammalian *embryo during the later stages of development within the uterus. In human reproduction it refers to an unborn child from its eighth week of development. **–fetal** *adj.*

胎兒　在子宮內發育後期的哺乳類動物的胚胎。在人類，它是指從妊娠第八周到出生這一時期的懷孕產物。

fetus papyraceous a twin fetus that has died in the uterus and become flattened and mummified.

薄紙樣胎　死於子宮內的雙胎，變平成木乃伊狀。

Feulgen reaction a method of demonstrating the presence of DNA in cell nuclei. The tissue section under investigation is first hydrolysed with dilute hydrochloric acid and then treated with *Schiff's reagent. A purple coloration develops in the presence of DNA.

福伊爾根反應　檢查細胞核內DNA的方法。將被檢查的組織切片，用稀鹽酸處理後，再用席夫試劑進行染色。有DNA的部位將呈現紫色。

fever (pyrexia) *n.* a rise in body temperature above the normal, i.e. above an oral temperature of 98.6°F (37°C) or a rectal temperature of 99°F (37.2°C).

發熱　身體的溫度超過正常度數，即口溫超過37°C (98.6°F)或肛溫超過37.2°C (99°F)。發熱常伴有寒顫、頭痛、惡心、

Fever is generally accompanied by shivering, headache, nausea, constipation, or diarrhoea. A rise in temperature above 105°F (40.5°C) may cause delirium and, in young children, *convulsions too. Fevers are usually caused by bacterial or viral infections and can accompany any infectious illness, from the common cold to *malaria. An *intermittent fever* is a periodic rise and fall in body temperature, often returning to normal during the day and reaching its peak at night, as in malaria. A *remittent fever* is one in which body temperature fluctuates but does not return to normal. *See also* relapsing fever.

便秘或腹瀉。超過 40.5°C (105°F) 的高燒可引起譫妄，嬰幼兒患者還可出現驚厥。發熱通常由細菌和病毒感染引起，並伴隨感冒、瘧疾等傳染病出現。間歇熱為身體周期性發熱，通常在白天體溫恢復到正常，在夜間體溫又升到其最高度數，如在患瘧疾時。弛張熱是一種溫度有波動但不恢復正常的發熱。參閱 relapsing fever。

FHSA *see* Family Health Services Authority.

家庭保健服務管理局　參閱 Family Health Services Authority。

fibr- (fibro-) *prefix denoting* fibres or fibrous tissue.

〔前綴〕纖維或纖維組織

fibre *n.* **1.** (in anatomy) a threadlike structure, such as a muscle cell, a nerve fibre, or a collagen fibre. **2.** (in dietetics) *see* dietary fibre. **–fibrous** *adj.*

纖維　(1)（解剖學）一種綫狀結構，如肌細胞、神經纖維、或膠原纖維。(2)（營養學）參閱 dietary fibre。

fibre optics the use of fibres for the transmission of light images. Synthetic fibres with special optical properties can be used in instruments to relay pictures of the inside of the body for direct observation or photography. *See* fibrescope. **–fibreoptic** *adj.*

纖維光學　用纖維傳導光學形象的方法。合成的光導纖維可用在能分程傳遞體內情況的器械上，以進行直接觀察或拍照。參閱 fibrescope。

fibrescope *n.* an *endoscope that uses *fibre optics for the transmission of images from the interior of the body. Fibrescopes have a great advantage over the older endoscopes as they are flexible and can be introduced into relatively inaccessible cavities of the body.

纖維鏡　用纖維光學傳遞體內情況形象的內窺鏡。纖維鏡與老式內窺鏡比較有明顯的優點，它們能彎曲，而且能插入很難進入的體內腔道。

fibril *n.* a very small fibre or a constituent thread of a fibre (for example, a *myofibril of a muscle fibre). **–fibrillar**, **fibrillary** *adj.*

原纖維　纖細纖維或者組成纖維的纖維絲（如肌纖維中的肌原纖維）。

fibrillation *n.* a rapid and chaotic beating of the many individual muscle fibres of the heart, which is consequently unable to maintain effective synchronous contraction. The affected part of the heart then ceases to pump blood. Fibrillation may affect the atria or ventricles independently. *Atrial fibrillation*, a common type of *arrhythmia, results in rapid and irregular heart and pulse rates. The main causes are atherosclerosis, chronic rheumatic heart disease, and hypertensive heart disease. It may also complicate various other conditions, including chest infections and thyroid overactivity. The heart rate is controlled by the administration of *digoxin; in some cases the heart rhythm can be restored to normal by *cardioversion.

When *ventricular fibrillation* occurs the heart stops beating (*see* cardiac arrest). It is most commonly the result of *myocardial infarction.

纖維性顫動　許多心肌纖維快速、雜亂無章的跳動，導致心臟不能保持有效、同步的收縮。心臟受損部位停止泵血。纖維性顫動可單獨發生在心房或心室。心房纖維性顫動是心律不齊的常見類型，可導致快速和不規則心率及脈率。主要原因為動脈粥樣硬化、慢性風濕性心臟病及高血壓性心臟病。此顫動還可發生於其他各種疾病，包括肺部感染及甲亢。服用地高辛可控制心率；在有些病例，心律還可通過心臟復律術恢復正常。

當發生心室纖維顫動時，心臟停止跳動，是心肌梗死最常見的結果。

fibrin *n.* the final product of the process of *blood coagulation, produced by the action of the enzyme thrombin on a soluble precursor fibrinogen. The product thus formed (*fibrin monomer*) links up (polymerizes) with similar molecules to give a fibrous meshwork that forms the basis of a blood clot, which seals off the damaged blood vessel.

纖維蛋白　凝血過程中的最後產物，由凝血酶作用於可溶性纖維蛋白原而產生。所形成的物質（纖維蛋白質單體）與相似的分子結合（聚合）形成纖維蛋白網，該網是形成血塊的基礎，血塊能封住損傷的血管。

fibrinogen *n.* a substance (*coagulation factor), present in blood plasma, that is acted upon by the enzyme thrombin to produce the insoluble protein fibrin in the final stage of *blood coagulation. The

纖維蛋白原　存在於血漿中的一種物質（凝血因子），經凝血酶作用後，在凝血的最後階段產生不溶性纖維蛋白。血漿中纖維蛋白原的

normal level of fibrinogen in plasma is 2–4 g/l (4–6 g/l during pregnancy).

正 常 值 是 2~4 g/1 （孕 期 4~6 g/l）。

fibrinogenopenia *n. see* hypofibrinogenaemia.

纖維蛋白原減少　　參閱 hypofibrinogenaemia。

fibrinoid *adj.* resembling the protein fibrin.

纖維蛋白樣的　類似纖維蛋白的。

fibrinokinase *n.* one of a group of substances (activators) that convert the in active substance plasminogen to the active enzyme *plasmin, which digests blood clots (*see* fibrinolysis). Fibrinokinase is insoluble in water and can be extracted from animal tissue.

纖維蛋白激酶　將無活性的纖維蛋白溶酶原轉化成能溶解血塊的活性纖維蛋白溶酶的一組物質（激活因子）中之一種。不溶於水，可從動物組織中提取。

fibrinolysin *n. see* plasmin.

纖 維 蛋 白 溶 酶　　參 閱 plasmin。

fibrinolysis *n.* the process by which blood clots are removed from the circulation, involving digestion of the insoluble protein *fibrin by the enzyme *plasmin. The latter exists in the plasma as an inactive precursor (plasminogen), which is activated in parallel with the *blood coagulation process. Normally a balance is maintained between the processes of coagulation and fibrinolysis in the body; an abnormal increase in fibrinolysis leads to excessive bleeding.

纖維蛋白溶解　消除循環中的血塊，包括由纖維蛋白溶酶溶解非溶解狀態的纖維蛋白的過程。纖維蛋白溶酶以無活性纖維蛋白溶酶原存在於血漿中，在凝血過程中同時被激活。正常情況下，體內的凝血過程和纖維蛋白溶解過程處於平衡狀態。不正常的纖維蛋白溶解過程增強可導致大量出血。

fibrinolytic *adj.* describing a group of drugs that are capable of breaking down the protein fibrin, which is the main constituent of blood clots, and are therefore used to disperse blood clots (thrombi) that have formed within the circulation. They include *streptokinase, *alteplase, *anistreplase, and *urokinase. Possible side-effects include bleeding at needle puncture sites, headache, backache, blood spots in the skin, and allergic reactions.

溶解纖維蛋白的　指一組能分解纖維蛋白（血塊的主要組成成分）的藥物，因此被用來分解循環中所形成的血塊。它們包括鏈激酶、奧特普酶、鏈道酶及尿激酶。可能的副作用包括針刺點出血、頭痛、皮膚出血斑及過敏反應。

fibroadenoma *n. see* adenoma.

纖維腺瘤 參閱 adenoma。

fibroblast *n.* a widely distributed cell in *connective tissue that is responsible for the production of both the ground substance and of the precursors of collagen, elastic fibres, and reticular fibres.

成纖維細胞 廣泛分布於結締組織中的細胞，是產生基質、膠原、彈力纖維及網狀纖維的前體。

fibrocartilage *n.* a tough kind of *cartilage in which there are dense bundles of fibres in the matrix. It is found in the intervertebral discs and pubic symphysis.

纖維軟骨 一種在其基質內存在着稠密纖維束的韌性軟骨。見於椎間盤和恥骨聯合。

fibrocyst *n.* a benign tumour of fibrous connective tissue containing cystic spaces-. –**fibrocystic** *adj.*

囊變性纖維瘤 含有囊間隙的良性纖維組織瘤。

fibrocystic disease of the pancreas *see* cystic fibrosis.

胰腺纖維囊性病 參閱 cystic fibrosis。

fibrocyte *n.* an inactive cell present in fully differentiated *connective tissue. It is derived form a *fibroblast.

纖維細胞 存在於完全分化的結締組織中的無活性細胞。由成纖維細胞演變而來。

fibrodysplasia *n.* abnormal development affecting connective tissue.

纖維發育不良 結締組織發育異常。

fibroelastosis *n.* overgrowth or disturbed growth of the yellow (elastic) fibres in *connective tissue, especially *endocardial fibroelastosis*, overgrowth and thickening of the wall of the heart's left ventricle.

彈力纖維組織增生 結締組織中的黃色纖維（彈力纖維）生長過度或生長紊亂，特別是心內膜彈力纖維組織增生，即左心室壁增生並增厚。

fibroepithelial polyp a fibrous overgrowth covered by epithelium, often occurring inside the mouth in response to chronic irritation. It is sometimes called an *epulis.

纖維上皮息肉 纖維組織增生並由上皮覆蓋，經常發生於口腔，由慢性刺激引起。有時叫作齦瘤。

fibroid 1. *n.* (**fibromyoma, uterine fibroid**) a benign tumour of fibrous and muscular tissue, one or more of which may develop in the muscular wall of the uterus. Fibroids often cause pain and

(1) 纖維性瘤（纖維肌瘤，子宮平滑肌瘤） 纖維和肌組織的良性腫瘤，單發或多發生長在子宮壁上。常引起疼痛和月經過多，並可長得極大。纖維瘤

excessive menstrual bleeding and they may become extremely large. They do not threaten life, but render pregnancy unlikely. It is usually women over 30 years of age who are affected. Some fibroids can be removed surgically; in other cases removal of the uterus (hysterectomy) may be necessary. If, as frequently happens, discomfort and other symptoms are absent, surgery is not required. **2.** *adj.* resembling or containing fibres.

fibroma *n*. (*pl.* **fibromas** or **fibromata**) a nonmalignant tumour of connective tissue.

fibromyoma *n*. a tumour of muscular and fibrous material, usually occurring in the uterus (*see* fibroid).

fibronectin *n*. a large glycoprotein that acts as a host defence mechanism. In the plasma it induces phagocytosis and on the cell surface it induces protein linkage. It is also involved in platelet aggregation. It is concentrated in connective tissue and the endothelium of the capillaries.

fibroplasia *n*. the production of fibrous tissue, occurring normally during the healing of wounds. *Retrolental fibroplasia* is the abnormal proliferation of fibrous tissue immediately behind the lens of the eye, leading to blindness. It is most commonly seen in newborn preterm infants, in whom it is associated with high concentrations of inhaled oxygen.

fibrosarcoma *n*. a malignant tumour of connective tissue, derived from *fibroblasts. Fibrosarcomas may arise in soft tissue or bone: they can effect any organ but are most common in the limbs,

雖沒有生命危險，但卻影響懷孕。患此病婦女通常大於30歲。可做外科切除；有些病例則需子宮切除（子宮切除術）。多數情況下，若無不適感和其他症狀，無需外科手術。**(2) 類纖維的，含纖維的**

纖維瘤　結締組織的一種非惡性腫瘤。

纖維肌瘤　由肌肉和纖維物質構成的腫瘤，通常發生於子宮（參閱 fibroid）。

纖維糖蛋白　擔當宿主防禦機制的大糖蛋白。在血漿中它誘導吞噬作用；在細胞表層，它誘導蛋白結合。它還會引起血小板集合。它集中於結締組織和毛細管的內皮。

纖維組織增生　纖維組織的生成，通常發生於傷口愈合過程中。晶狀體後纖維組織增生是指直接位於眼晶狀體後的纖維組織不正常的增生，可導致失明。以前見於早產兒，由吸氧過度而產生。

纖維肉瘤　結締組織的一種惡性腫瘤，超源於成纖維細胞。可生長在軟組織和骨上；能侵犯任何器官，但常發生在肢體上，特別是腿。此病可見於任

particularly the leg. They occur in people of all ages and may be congenital. The cells of these tumours show varying degrees of differentiation; the less well differentiated tumours containing elements of histiocytes have been recently reclassified as *malignant fibrous histiocytomas*.

何年齡的患者，可能是先天性疾病。這些腫瘤細胞表現出不同的分化程度。分化較低的含有組織細胞成分的腫瘤，最近被重新分類為惡性纖維組織細胞瘤。

fibrosis *n.* thickening and scarring of connective tissue, most often a consequence of inflammation or injury. *Pulmonary interstitial fibrosis* is thickening and stiffening of the lining of the air sacs (alveoli) of the lungs, causing progressive breathlessness. *See also* cystic fibrosis, retroperitoneal fibrosis.

纖維化 結締組織增厚並有瘢痕形成，通常是炎症或者損傷的結果。肺間質纖維化是肺泡膜增厚、僵硬，可引起進行性呼吸困難。參閱 cystic fibrosis，retroperitoneal fibrosis。

fibrositis *n.* inflammation of fibrous connective tissue, especially an acute inflammation of back muscles and their sheaths, causing pain and stiffness. *See also* muscular rheumatism.

纖維織炎 纖維結締組織炎症，特別是腰背肌肉及其肌鞘的急性炎症，可引起疼痛和強直。參閱 muscular rheumatism。

fibrous dysplasia a developmental abnormality in which changes occur in bony tissue, resulting in aching and a tendency to pathological fracture. In *monostotic fibrous dysplasia* one bone is affected; *polyostotic fibrous dysplasia* involves many bones.

纖維性發育不良 骨組織發育不正常，其病變可引起疼痛與病理性骨折，單骨性纖維性發育不良是一個骨受損。多骨性纖維性發育不良是多個骨受損。

fibula *n.* the long thin outer bone of the lower leg. The head of the fibula articulates with the *tibia just below the knee; the lower end projects laterally as the *lateral malleolus*, which articulates with one side of the *talus.

腓骨 小腿外側的細長骨。在膝下，腓骨頭與脛骨聯成關節；腓骨下端外側的突起為外踝，與距骨的一側聯成關節。

field *n.* (in radiotherapy) an area of the body selected for treatment with radiotherapy. For example, a *mantle field* comprises the neck, armpits, and central chest, for the radiotherapy of Hodgkin's disease. Radiation is administered to the

區 （放療學）選擇用放療法治療的身體區域。例如斗蓬式放射野由頸部、腋窩和胸腔中心部位組成對霍奇金病進行放療。通過聚集從放療機中發射出來的微粒束到限定部位進

defined area by focusing the beam of particles emitted by the radiotherapy machine and shielding the surrounding area of the body.

行放療，同時保護身體的周圍區域。

field of vision *see* visual field.

視野　參閱 visual field。

figlu test a test for folic acid or vitamin B_{12} deficiency . A dose of the amino acid histidine, which requires the presence of folic acid or vitamin B_{12} for its complete breakdown. is given by mouth. In the absence of these vitamins, *formiminoglutamic* acid (figlu) – an intermediate product in histidine metabolism – accumulates and can be detected in the urine.

亞胺甲基榖氨酸試驗　檢驗葉酸或維生素 B_{12} 是否缺乏的一種試驗。口服一定量的氨基酸（組氨酸），該酸只有在葉酸或維生素 B_{12} 存在時可完全分解。如缺乏這些維生素，組氨酸代謝的中間產物亞胺甲基榖氨酸增加，並可在尿中查出。

FIGO staging a classification drawn up by the International Federation of Gynaecology and Obstetrics to define the extent of the spread of cancers of the ovary, uterus, and cervix.

國際婦產科（聯合會）腫瘤分類　由國際婦產科（聯合會）制定的卵巢癌、子宮癌和子宮頸癌的大小及侵襲程度分類。

filament *n.* a very fine threadlike structure, such as a chain of bacterial cells. **–filamentous** *adj.*

絲　非常纖細的綫狀結構，如菌絲。

filaria *n.* (*pl.* **filariae**) any of the long threadlike nematode worms that, as adults, are parasites of the connective and lymphatic tissues of man capable of causing disease. They include the genera *Brugia, *Loa, *Onchocerca*, and *Wuchereria*. Filariae differ from the intestinal nematodes (*see* hookworm) in that they undergo part of their development in the body of a bloodsucking insect, e.g. a mosquito, on which they subsequently depend for their transmission to another human host. *See also* microfilaria. **–filarial** *adj.*

絲蟲　長絲狀綫蟲，其成蟲寄生於人類結締組織內，能夠致病。包括有馬來絲蟲、羅阿絲蟲、盤尾絲蟲及吳策綫蟲。絲蟲與腸道綫蟲（參閱 hookworm）不同，因為絲蟲要在吸血性昆蟲（如蚊子）體內經歷一段發育期，並依靠這類昆蟲傳播給他人。參閱 microfilaria。

filariasis *n.* a disease, common in the tropics and subtropics, caused by

絲蟲病　常見於熱帶和亞熱帶地區的一種疾病，由存在於淋

the presence in the lymph vessels of the parasitic nematode worms *Wuchereria bancrofti* and *Brugia malayi* (*see* filaria). The worms, which are transmitted to man by various mosquitoes (including *Aëdes*, *Culex*, *Anopheles*, and *Mansonia*), bring about inflammation and eventual blocking of lymph vessels, which causes the surrounding tissues to swell (*see* elephantiasis). The rupture of urinary lymphatics may lead to the presence of *chyle in the urine. Filariasis is treated with the drug *diethylcarbamazine.

巴管內的班氏吳策綫蟲和馬來絲蟲（參閱 filaria）引起。這些絲蟲通過各種蚊子（包括伊蚊、庫蚊、按蚊和曼蚊）轉移到人體，引起淋巴管炎，並最終導致淋巴管阻塞，使其周圍組織水腫（參閱 elephantiasis）。尿道淋巴管破裂可使尿液中出現乳糜液。絲蟲病可用乙胺嗪治療。

filiform *adj.* shaped like a thread; for example, the threadlike *filiform papillae* of the *tongue.

絲狀的 形狀像綫的，如舌絲狀乳頭。

filling *n.* (in dentistry) the operation of inserting a specially prepared substance into a cavity drilled in a tooth, often in the treatment of dental caries. The filling may be *temporary* or *permanent*, and various materials may be used (*see* amalgam, cement, composite resin, gold).

充填 （牙科學）將特殊製備的物質填入齲齒上鑽開的腔內的手術，常用於齲牙的治療。充填可以是暫時的也可是永久的，而且很多物質都可用做填充物（參閱 amalgam，cement，composite resin，gold）。

filum *n.* a threadlike structure. The *filum terminale* is the slender tapering terminal section of the spinal cord.

絲 綫狀結構。終絲是脊髓圓椎下端的細長絲。

fimbria *n.* (*pl.* **fimbriae**) a fringe or fringelike process, such as any of the finger-like projections that surround the opening of the ovarian end of the *Fallopian tube. **–fimbrial** *adj.*

傘 穗或穗樣突，如圍繞輸卵管卵巢端開口的指樣突起。

fimbrial cyst a simple cyst of the *fimbria of the Fallopian tube.

傘囊腫 輸卵管傘的單純囊腫。

finasteride *n.* a drug that causes shrinkage of the prostate gland and is administered by mouth for relieving the symptoms caused by an enlarged

非那甾胺 一種能引起前列腺縮小的藥物，口服以減輕由腺體增大阻塞尿從膀胱流出的症狀。此藥通過減少前列腺產生

gland obstructing the outflow of urine from the bladder. The drug acts by reducing androgenic stimulation of the prostate, inhibiting the enzyme responsible for converting testosterone to its more active metabolite, 5-dehydroxytestosterone (5-DHT), within the gland. Trade name: **Proscar**.

fine-needle aspiration cytology (FNAC) a technique that uses samples obtained by fine-needle aspiration to provide information on the cells of tumours or cysts. It is useful for excluding the presence of malignant cells in cysts of the breast and thyroid. *See also* aspiration cytology.

fingerprint *n.* the distinctive pattern of minute ridges in the outer horny layer of the skin. Every individual has his or her own unique pattern of loops (70%), whorls (25%), or arches (5%) (see illustration). Fingerprint patterns can show the presence of inherited disorders. *See also* dermatoglyphics.

firedamp *n.* (in mining) an explosive mixture of gases, usually containing a high proportion of methane, occasionally encountered in pockets underground. It can be distinguished from *blackdamp (chokedamp), which does not ignite.

first aid procedures used in an emergency to help a wounded or ill patient before the arrival of a doctor or admission to hospital.

first intention *see* intention.

fission *n.* a method of asexual reproduction in which the body of a protozoan or bacterium splits into two equal parts (*binary fission*), as in the *amoebae, or

男性徵的刺激作用，抑制能引起腺體內睪酮轉化為其更活躍代謝物——5-脱氫二甲睪酮。商品名：Proscar。

細針吸引細胞學 使用通過細針吸引所得的樣本來提供腫瘤或者囊腫細胞情況的技術。此技術在排除乳腺和甲狀腺囊腫惡性細胞的存在很有用。參閱 aspiration cytology。

指紋 皮膚角化層上的微小皮嵴的特殊圖型。每個人都有他（她）自己獨特圈狀紋型（70%），輪狀紋（25%），或者弓狀紋（5%）（見圖）。指紋圖型能表明是否患有遺傳病。參閱 dermatoglyphics。

沼氣 （採礦業）一種爆炸性混合氣體，通常含較高比例的甲烷，偶可見於地下坑道。沼氣與礦內窒息性氣體不同，後者不能點燃。

急救 在醫生到來之前或入院前，搶救傷員或患者所採取的緊急措施。

第一期愈合 參閱 intention。

分裂 無性繁殖的方法。原生動物體或細菌分裂成兩個相等的部分（二分裂），如阿米巴；或分裂成兩個以上的相等

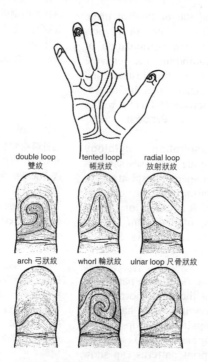

double loop 雙紋　　tented loop 帳狀紋　　radial loop 放射狀紋

arch 弓狀紋　　whorl 輪狀紋　　ulnar loop 尺骨狀紋

Ridges on the hand, with details of the most common fingerprints
手指皮嵴的最常見指紋圖型

more than two equal parts (*multiple fission*), for example, sporozoite formation in the malarial parasite (*see* Plasmodium). The resulting products of fission eventually grow into complete organisms.

fissure *n.* **1.** (in anatomy) a groove or cleft; e.g. the *fissure of Sylvius* is the groove that separates the temporal lobe of the brain from the frontal and parietal lobes. **2.** (in pathology) a cleftlike defect in the skin or mucous membrane caused by some disease process. *See* anal fissure. **3.** (in dentistry) a naturally occurring groove in the enamel on the surface of a tooth, especially a molar.

部分（多分裂），如在瘧原蟲體內的子孢子。分裂出的產物最終長成完整的生物。

裂 **(1)**（解剖學）溝或縫，如大腦側裂就是分隔大腦顳葉和額葉及頂葉的溝。**(2)**（病理學）在疾病過程中產生的皮膚和黏膜裂縫樣缺損，例如肛裂就是肛門皮膚的撕裂。**(3)**（牙科學）自然出現在牙釉質表面上的溝，特別是磨牙。

fissure sealant (in dentistry) a material that is bonded to the enamel surface of teeth to seal the fissures, in order to prevent dental caries. Composite resins, unfilled resins, and glass ionomer cements have been used as fissure sealants.

fistula *n.* (*pl.* **fistulae**) an abnormal communication between two hollow organs or between a hollow organ and the exterior. Many fistulae are caused by infection or injury. For example an *anal fistula* may develop after an abscess in the rectum has burst (*see* ischiorectal abscess), creating an opening between the anal canal and the surface of the skin. (*See also* vesicovaginal fistula.) Some fistulae result from malignant growths or ulceration: a carcinoma of the colon may invade and ulcerate the adjacent wall of the stomach, causing a *gastrocolic fistula*. Other fistulae develop as complications of surgery: after gall-bladder surgery, for example, bile may continually escape to the surface through the wound producing a *biliary fistula*. Fistulae may also be a form of congenital abnormality; examples include a *tracheo-oesophageal fistula* (between the windpipe and gullet) and a *rectovaginal fistula* (between the rectum and vagina).

fit *n.* a sudden attack. The term is commonly used specifically for the seizures of *epilepsy but it is also used more generally, e.g. a fit of coughing.

fixation *n.* **1.** (in psychoanalysis) a failure of psychological development, in which traumatic events prevent a child from progressing to the next developmental stage. This is said to be a cause of mental illness and of personality disorder. *See also* psychosexual development.

牙裂隙充填劑 （牙科學）用來附着在牙釉質表面上的物質，以封閉（牙）裂隙，防止出現齲齒。複合樹脂、直接填充樹脂和玻璃離聚物黏固劑都已被用作牙裂隙充填劑。

瘻 指兩個空心器官或一個空心器官與體外異常通道。很多瘻是由感染和損傷引起的。如肛瘻可發生在直腸膿腫破裂之後（參閱 ischiorectal abscess），使肛管和皮膚之間出現通道（參閱 vesicovaginal fistula）。有一些瘻是由惡性腫瘤和潰瘍引起：結腸癌可侵犯或腐蝕鄰近的胃壁，導致胃結腸瘻；其他一些瘻可由手術的併發症引起，如膽囊手術後，膽汁可不斷地從刀口流出體外，形成膽瘻。瘻也可能是一種先天性異常，如食管支氣管瘻和陰道直腸瘻。

發作 突然發病。此術語通常用來指癲癇的發病，但也普遍地用於其他疾病的發作，如咳嗽發作。

(1) 固結 （精神分析）心理發展受阻，即創傷性事件妨礙了兒童心理繼續向下一個階段發展。這被認為是精神上的疾病及病態人格的原因（參閱 psychosexual development）。**(2) 固定** 為進行顯微鏡下檢查而

2. a procedure for the hardening and preservation of tissues of microorganisms to be examined under a microscope. Fixation kills the tissues and ensures that their original shape and structure are retained as closely as possible. It also prepares them for sectioning and staining. The specimens can be immersed in a chemical *fixative or subjected to *freeze-drying.

使組織或微生物變硬並將其保存起來的方法。固定雖使組織失活，但盡可能使組織的形狀、結構與其固定前基本相同。固定也是組織切片與染色前的準備。可將標本浸入化學固定液中或用冷凍法進行固定。

fixative (fixing agent) *n.* a chemical agent, e.g. alcohol or osmium tetroxide, used for the preservation and hardening of tissues for microscopical study. *See* fixation (def. 2).

固定液 一種化學試劑，如乙醇或四氧化鋨，用於保護組織並使其變硬以進行顯微鏡檢查。參閱 fixation（釋義 2）。

FK506 a powerful *immunosuppressive drug used to prevent rejection of transplanted organs. FK506 has also been used to treat allergic skin conditions and psoriasis. Side-effects include damage to the kidneys, and there is an increased risk of developing certain cancers.

FK506 一種高效抑制免疫反應的藥物，用來防止移植器官的排異作用。此藥也已被用來治療過敏性皮膚病和銀屑病。副作用包括腎損害並有引起某些癌症的危險。

flaccid *adj.* **1.** flabby and lacking in firmness. **2.** characterized by a decrease in muscle tone (e.g. flaccid *paralysis). **–flaccidity** *n.*

弛緩的 **(1)** 不結實的、不堅硬的。**(2)** 肌張力下降的（如弛緩性麻痺）。

flagellate *n.* a type of *protozoan with one or more fine whiplike threads (*see* flagellum) projecting from its body surface, by means of which it is able to swim. Some flagellates are parasites of humans and are therefore of medical importance. *See* Trypanosoma, Leishmania, Giardia, Trichomonas.

鞭毛蟲 原生動物的一種，其身體表面有一個或多個鞭狀綫突起（參閱 flagellum），通過這種突起的作用，該蟲可以移動。有些鞭毛蟲是人類的寄生蟲，因此在醫學上很重要。參閱 Trypanosoma，Leishmania，Giardia，Trichomonas。

flagellation *n.* the act of whipping oneself or others as a means of obtaining sexual pleasure (*see* masochism, sadism). A person displaying this sexual deviation is called a *flagellant* or *flagellomane.*

鞭笞狂 用鞭抽打自己或他人而獲得性滿足的一種性心理變態（參閱 masochism，sadism）。表現此種性變態的人稱做鞭笞狂者。

flagellum *n.* (*pl.* **flagella**) a fine long whiplike thread attached to certain types of cell (e.g. spermatozoa and some unicellular organisms). Flagella are responsible for the movement of the organisms to which they are attached.

鞭毛　附着在某些種類細胞上的細長鞭樣細絲（如精子及一些單細胞生物）。鞭毛能使其所附着的生物體移動。

flail chest a condition of the chest associated with an unstable ribcage following multiple fractures of the ribs and sternum. It leads to asphyxia unless corrected promptly.

連枷狀胸　在肋骨和胸骨多發骨折後所形成的不穩定的與肋骨支架有關的一種狀態。如不及時糾正，可導致窒息。

flap *n.* **1.** (in surgery) a strip of tissue dissected away from the underlying structures but left attached at one end so that it retains its blood and nerve supply in a *pedicle. The flap is then used to repair a defect in another part of the body. The free end of the flap is sewn into the area to be repaired and after about three weeks, when the flap has 'healed into' its new site, the other end is detached and the remainder of the flap is sewn in. Flaps are commonly used by plastic surgeons in treating patients who have suffered severe skin and tissue loss after mutilating operations (e.g. *mastectomy) or after burns or injuries not amenable to repair by split skin grafting (*see* skin graft). Skin flaps may also be used to cover the end of a bone in an amputated limb. **2.** (in dentistry) a piece of mucous membrane and periosteum attached by a broad base. It is lifted back to expose the underlying bone and enable a procedure such as surgical *extraction to be performed. It is subsequently replaced.

瓣　**(1)**（外科學）從某部分離出的一種條形組織，但一端與下面的組織相連以保持血運及神經支配。瓣被用來修復身體其他部位的缺損。將瓣的游離端縫到要修復的部位上，約三周後，當瓣與新組織「愈合」時，再將另一端（蒂）分離，瓣的其他部分即縫到新的部位上。瓣通常用於整形外科，以治療燒傷或損傷後皮膚或組織嚴重缺損而已不可能進行植皮修復的患者（參閱 skin graft）。皮瓣也用來覆蓋斷肢的骨端。**(2)**（牙科學）留有較寬蒂的一片黏膜和骨膜。將其揭開，可暴露出其下的骨，使手術如拔牙能夠進行，然後再將其復位。

flare *n.* **1.** reddening of the skin that spreads outwards from a focus of infection or irritation in the skin. **2.** the red area surrounding an urticarial weal.

潮紅　**(1)** 感染竈或受刺激部位周圍的皮膚發紅。**(2)** 蕁麻疹周圍的發紅部位。

flashback *n.* vivid involuntary reliving of the perceptual abnormalities experienced during a previous episode of drug intoxication, including *hallucinations and *derealization.

閃回 清楚地不自覺地（憑想象）重新體驗在以前麻醉品中毒事件中所經歷的知覺上的異常，包括幻覺和現實感喪失。

flat-foot *n.* absence of the arching of the foot, so that the sole lies flat upon the ground. It may be present in infancy or be acquired in adult life, usually either from prolonged standing or from excessive weight. Flat feet need treatment (exercises) only if they cause pain. Medical name: **pes planus**.

扁平足 足弓缺乏，腳底着地處呈扁平形。可在嬰兒時就存在，也可在成年時出現，通常因長期站立或身體超重所引起。扁平足只有在出現疼痛時才需要治療（鍛煉）。醫學用語：扁平足。

flatulence *n.* **1.** the expulsion of gas or air from the stomach through the mouth; belching. **2.** a sensation of abdominal distension. **–flatulent** *adj.*

(1) 噯氣 胃內氣體通過口腔竄出；**(2)** 腹脹 腹部脹氣的感覺。

flatus *n.* intestinal gas, composed partly of swallowed air and partly of gas produced by bacterial fermentation of intestinal contents. It consists mainly of hydrogen, carbon dioxide, and methane in varying proportions. Indigestible nonabsorbable carbohydrates in some foods (e.g. beans) cause increased volumes of flatus.

腸氣 腸道內氣體，由吞咽的氣體和腸內容物裏的細菌發酵所產生的氣體組成。含有不同比例的氫氣、二氧化碳和甲烷。有些食物（如豆類）裏未被消化的非吸收性碳水化合物能引起大量腸氣。

flatworm (platyhelminth) *n.* any of the flat-bodied worms, including the *flukes and *tapeworms. Both these groups contain many parasites of medical importance.

扁蟲 身體呈扁平形的蠕蟲，包括吸蟲和縧蟲。這兩組蟲中有很多在醫學上有其重要性的寄生蟲。

flav- (flavo-) *prefix denoting* yellow.

〔前綴〕黃色

flavin adenine dinucleotide *see* FAD.

黃素腺嘌呤二核苷酸 參閱 FAD。

flavin mononucleotide *see* FMN.

黃素單核苷酸 參閱 FMN。

flavoprotein *n.* a compound consisting of a protein bound to either *FAD or

黃素蛋白 蛋白質與黃素腺嘌呤二核苷酸或者黃素單核苷酸

*FMN (called *flavins*). Flavoproteins are constituents of several enzyme systems involved in intermediary metabolism.

（黃素）相結合的化合物。黃素蛋白是一些酶系統的成分，這些酶與調節代謝有關。

flea *n.* a small wingless bloodsucking insect with a laterally compressed body and long legs adapted for jumping. Adult fleas are temporary parasites on birds and mammals and those species that attack man (*Pulex*, *Xenopsylla*, and *Nosopsyllus*) may be important in the transmission of various diseases. Their bites are not only a nuisance but may become a focus of infection. Appropriate insecticide powders are used to destroy fleas in the home.

蚤 無翅吸血性小昆蟲，其身體側向扁平，腿長以適應跳躍。蚤的成蟲可暫時寄生在鳥及哺乳類動物身上，侵襲人類的蚤（蚤屬、客蚤屬、病蚤屬）在傳播疾病方面有重要作用。蚤的刺吸不僅令人厭惡，而刺吸部位還會成為感染病竈。適當的殺蟲劑粉可消除家裏的蚤。

flecainide *n.* a drug used to control irregular heart rhythms. It is administered by mouth. Possible side-effects include nausea, vomiting, dizziness, vertigo, jaundice, visual disturbances, and some nerve damage. Trade name: **Tambocor**.

氟卡尼 用來控制不規則心臟節律的一種藥物。口服。可能的副作用包括噁心、嘔吐、頭暈、眩暈、黃疸、視覺障礙及某些神經損害。商品名：Tambocor。

flexibilitas cerea *see* catatonia.

蠟樣屈曲 參閱 catatonia。

flexion *n.* the bending of a joint so that the bones forming it are brought towards each other. *Plantar flexion* is the bending of the toes (or fingers) downwards, towards the sole (or palm). *See also* dorsiflexion.

屈曲 關節彎曲，使形成此關節的骨互相靠攏。跖屈是足趾（或手指）向下朝腳（或手）掌方向彎曲。參閱 dorsiflexion。

flexor *n.* any muscle that causes bending of a limb or other part.

屈肌 能引起肢體和其他部位彎曲的任何肌肉。

flexure *n.* a bend in an organ or part, such as the *hepatic* and *splenic flexures* of the *colon.

曲 某器官或部位的彎曲，如結腸的肝曲和脾曲。

floaters *pl. n.* opacities in the vitreous humour of the eye, which cast a shadow on the retina and are therefore seen as

懸浮物 眼玻璃體裏的濁斑，在視網膜上產生投射陰影，因此在強照明下相對於明亮背景

dark shapes against a bright background in good illumination. They are a form of *entopic phenomenon.

floccillation *n. see* carphology.

摸空　參閱 carphology。

flocculation *n.* a reaction in which normally invisible material leaves solution to form a coarse suspension or precipitate as a result of a change in physical or chemical conditions. Flocculation tests using serum and special reagents are useful in diagnosing liver abnormalities. *See also* agglutination.

絮凝作用　因物理或化學變化而使溶液中正常時見不到的物質形成粗大懸浮物或沉澱物的一種反應。用血清和特殊試劑做的絮凝試驗在診斷肝臟是否異常方面很有用。參閱agglutination。

flocculus *n.* a small ovoid lobe of the *cerebellum, overhung by the posterior lobe and connected centrally with the nodulus in the midline.

絨球　位於小腦的卵圓形小葉，懸於後葉之下，其中央部與中綫小結相連。

flooding *n.* **1.** excessive bleeding from the uterus, as in *menorrhagia or miscarriage. **2.** (in psychology) (also called **implosion**) a method of treating *phobias in which the patient is exposed intensively and at length to the feared object, either in reality or fantasy. Although it is distressing and needs good motivation if treatment is to be completed, it is an effective and rapid form of therapy.

(1) 血崩　子宮大出血，如在月經過多或流產時。**(2)** 以恐治恐法（心理學）治療恐怖症的一種方法。有意讓這類患者接觸或接近可怕的事物，無論該事物是真實的或者想象中的。儘管這種療法令患者痛苦，而且需要很好地動員患者接受此療法，但如果要進行徹底治療的話，此療法有效且見效快。

floppy baby syndrome *see* amyotonia congenita.

嬰兒鬆弛綜合徵　參閱 amyotonia congenita。

flosequinan *n.* a drug that acts on the smooth muscle of arteries and veins to cause these to relax and widen. This greatly reduces the load on the heart in patients with heart failure without affecting the blood supply to the various parts of the body. The drug is still being evaluated; side-effects include headache, dizziness, and palpitations.

氟司喹南　作用於動、靜脈平滑肌而使其鬆弛和增寬的一種藥物，能大大減輕患心臟衰竭病人的心臟負擔而不影響向身體各部位供血。此藥仍在評估階段；副作用包括頭痛、頭暈及心悸。

flow cytometry a technique in which cells are tagged with a fluorescent dye and then directed single file through a laser beam. The intensity of *fluorescence induced by the laser beam is proportional to the amount of DNA in the cells.

流式細胞計數術　用熒光染料標記細胞並通過激光束將其確定為單個細胞的技術。激光束誘導的熒光強度與細胞內脫氧核糖核酸數量相稱。

flowmeter *n.* an instrument for measuring the flow of a liquid or gas. Anaesthetic equipment has to be fitted with flowmeters so that the administration of anaesthetic gases in different proportions can be controlled. Flowmeters are widely used by asthma sufferers to measure their ability to expire air.

流量計　測量液體或氣體流量的儀器。麻醉設備須裝備流量計以便控制不同比例的麻醉氣體用量。流量計廣泛使用於哮喘患者以測量他們呼氣的能力。

flucloxacillin *n.* a semisynthetic *penicillin. readily absorbed when taken by mouth and effective against bacteria that produce *penicillinase. A possible side-effect is an allergic reaction to penicillin. Trade names: **Floxapen**, **Magnapen**.

氟氯西林　半合成的青黴素，口服極易吸收，對殺死產生青黴素酶的細菌很有效。可能的副作用為對青黴素的過敏反應。商品名：Floxapen，Magnapen。

fluconazole *n.* an antifungal drug used to treat candidosis in any part of the body, externally or internally. It is administered by mouth. Possible side-effects include nausea and vomiting. Trade name: **Diflucan**.

氟康唑　一種抗真菌藥，用來治療身體任何部位，內部或外部的念珠菌病。可能的副作用包括惡心及嘔吐。商品名：Diflucan。

fluctuation *n.* the characteristic feeling of a wave motion produced in a fluid-filled part of the body by an examiner's fingers. If fluctuation is present when a swelling is examined, this is an indication that there is fluid within it and that the swelling is not due to a solid growth.

波動　檢查者的手在身體某充滿液體的部位感覺到的一種特殊的波動震動感。當檢查腫脹部位時出現這種感覺，則表明內有液體而非固體生長。

flucytosine *n.* an antifungal drug that is effective against systemic infections, including cryptococcosis and candidosis. It can be administered by mouth; side-effects may include nausea and vomiting, diarrhoea, rashes, and blood disorders.

氟胞嘧啶　一種抗真菌藥，對全身感染，包括隱球菌病和念珠菌病很有效。可口服；副作用可能包括惡心及嘔吐、腹瀉、皮疹及血液病。

fludrocortisone *n.* a synthetic *corticosteroid used to treat disorders of the adrenal glands. It is administered by mouth and side-effects include muscle weakness, bone disorders, digestive and skin disorders, and fluid retention. Trade name: **Florinef**.

氟氫可的松　合成的皮質類固醇，用於治療腎上腺疾病。口服；副作用包括肌無力、骨疾病、消化道及皮膚出現異常及液體瀦留。商品名：Florinef。

fluke *n.* any of the parasitic flatworms belonging to the group Trematoda. Adult flukes, which have suckers for attachment to their host, are parasites of man, occurring in the liver (*liver flukes*; *see* Fasciola), lungs (*see* Paragonimus), gut (*see* Heterophyes), and blood vessels (*blood flukes*; *see* Schistosoma) and often cause serious disease. Eggs, passed out with the stools, hatch into larvae called *miracidia, which penetrate an intermediate snail host. Miracidia give rise asexually to *redia larvae and finally *cercariae in the snail's tissues. The released cercariae may enter a second intermediate host (such as a fish or crustacean); form a cyst (*metacercaria) on vegetation; or directly penetrate the human skin.

吸蟲　任何屬於吸蟲綱類的寄生扁蟲。吸蟲成蟲與其宿主有連接吸盤，是人類的寄生蟲，發生於肝（肝吸蟲，參閱 Fasciola）、肺（參閱 Paragonimus）、腸（參閱 Heterophyes）及血管（血吸蟲；參閱 Schistosoma），經常引起嚴重疾病。其卵通過糞便排出，孵化成叫作毛蚴的幼蟲，該幼蟲能滲進中間宿主螺類體內，並在此無性繁殖出雷蚴並最後在螺類體中發展成尾蚴。釋放出來的尾蚴可能進入第二中間宿主（如魚或甲殼綱類動物）；在增殖體上形成囊腫（後囊蚴）；或者直接穿透人類皮膚進入體內。

flumazenil *n.* a *benzodiazepine antagonist drug, used in anaesthesia to reverse the effects of benzodiazepines on the nervous system. It is administered by injection. Trade name: **Anexate**.

氟馬西尼　苯二氮䓬類拮抗藥，用於麻醉中逆轉苯二氮䓬類藥對神經系統的效應。注射用。商品名：Anexate。

flunisolide *n.* an anti-inflammatory corticosteroid drug used in the long-term treatment of bronchial asthma and rhinitis. It is administered as an inhalation or a spray; the most common side-effects are nausea and vomiting, headache, upper respiratory-tract infections, and local irritation. Trade name: **Syntaris**.

氟尼縮松　一種抗炎症皮質類固醇藥物，用於支氣管哮喘和鼻炎的長期治療。用藥法為吸入劑或者噴霧劑；最常見的副作用有惡心和嘔吐、頭痛、上呼吸道感染及局部刺激。商品名：Syntaris。

flunitrazepam *n.* a *benzodiazepine drug used for the short-term treatment of insomnia. It is administered by mouth. Trade name: **Rohypnol**.

氟硝西泮　苯二氮泮類藥，用於失眠症的短期治療。口服。商品名：Rohypnol。

fluocinonide *n.* a synthetic corticosteroid used topically to reduce inflammation. It is applied to the skin as a cream, gel, ointment, or solution. Side-effects include burning, itching, and local eruptions. Trade name: **Metosyn**.

fluorescein sodium a water-soluble orange dye that glows with a brilliant green colour when blue light is shone on it. A dilute solution is used to detect defects in the surface of the cornea, since it stains areas where the *epithelium is not intact. In retinal *angiography it is injected into a vein and its circulation through the blood vessels of the retina is viewed and photographed by a special camera.

fluorescence *n.* the emission of light by a material as it absorbs radiation from outside. The radiation absorbed may be visible or invisible (e.g. ultraviolet rays or X-rays). *See* fluoroscope. **–fluorescent** *adj.*

fluoridation *n.* the addition of *fluoride to drinking water in order to reduce *dental caries. Drinking water with a fluoride ion content of one part per million is effective in reducing caries throughout life when given during the years of tooth development. *See also* fluorosis.

fluoride *n.* a compound of fluorine. The incorporation of fluoride ions in the enamel of teeth makes them more resistant to *dental caries. The ions enter enamel during its formation, and after tooth eruption by surface absorption. The addition of fluoride to public water supplies is called *fluoridation. Fluoride may also be applied topically in toothpaste or by a dentist. If the water supply contains too little fluoride, fluoride salts

氟輕松 一合成皮質類固醇，局部使用來減輕炎症。常以霜、膠、膏或者溶液塗於皮膚表面。副作用包括灼熱、瘙癢和局部發疹。商品名：Metosyn。

熒光素鈉 一種水溶性染料，用光照射時能放出光芒燦爛的綠色。其稀釋液用於探查角膜表面是否有缺損，因為它能使上皮細胞受損部位着色。在視網膜血管造影時，將該染料注射到靜脈內，就可見到視網膜的血管，並用特殊鏡頭進行拍照。

熒光 某物質在吸收外界的光綫後所發射出來的光。所吸收的外界的光綫可以是可見光或不可見光（如紫外綫和X綫）。參閱 fluoroscope。

氟化 為減少齲牙的發生而向飲用水中加入適量的氟。在牙齒發育的年齡，飲用氟離子含量為百萬分之一的飲用水能有效地減少人們一生的齲齒發病率。參閱 fluorosis。

氟化物 氟的化合物。將氟離子加進牙釉質內，能使牙釉質有較強的抗齲能力。氟離子是在釉質形成時由其表面吸收到釉質內的。將適量的氟投放到公用飲水中叫做氟化。氟化物還可加在牙膏內或由牙醫使用。如果公用飲水含氟量太少，可給兒童以漱口藥、滴劑或片劑的形式添加氟鹽。

may be given to children in the from of mouthwashes, drops, or tablets.

fluoroscope *n.* an instrument on which X-ray images may be viewed directly without taking and developing X-ray photographs. It consists basically of a *fluorescent screen*, which is coated with chemicals that exhibit the property of *fluorescence when exposed to X-rays. Fluoroscopes are used for mass chest X-ray examinations.

熒光鏡 不用拍照和沖洗X綫照片就可直接顯示出X綫物像的儀器。基本上由熒光屏組成,熒光屏表面有一層化學物質覆蓋。當被X綫照射時,這層物質能顯示出特徵性的熒光。熒光鏡用於胸部X綫普查。

fluorosis *n.* the effects of high *fluoride intake. Dental fluorosis is characterized by mottled enamel, which is opaque and may be stained. Its incidence increases when the level of fluoride in the water supply is above 2 parts per million. The mottled enamel is resistant to dental caries. When the level is over 8 parts per million systemic fluorosis may occur, with calcification of ligaments.

氟中毒 服入大量氟化物的結果。牙齒氟中毒的特點是:出現斑釉色,即釉質無光澤並着色。當公用飲水裏的氟化物超過百萬分之二時,氟中毒的發病率就會增加。斑釉有抗齲能力。當水中氟化物超過百萬分之八時,可能發生機體氟中毒,同時伴有韌帶鈣化。

fluorouracil *n.* a drug that prevents cell growth (*see* antimetabolite) and is used in the treatment of cancers of the digestive system and breast. It can be administered by mouth or by injection. Side-effects, which may be severe, include digestive and skin disorders, mouth ulcers, hair loss, nail changes, and blood disorders. Fluorouracil is also applied as a cream to treat certain skin conditions, including skin cancer.

氟尿嘧啶 能抑止細胞生長(參閱 antimetabolite),用來治療消化系統和乳腺癌的一種藥物。口服或注射給藥。副作用可能很嚴重,包括消化道和皮膚異常、口腔潰瘍、脫髮、指甲發生變化及血液病。該藥物可以霜劑的形式治療某些皮膚病,包括皮膚癌。

fluoxetine *n.* an *antidepressant drug that acts by prolonging the action of the neurotransmitter *serotonin (5-hydroxytryptamine) in the brain. It is administered by mouth. Possible side-effects include nausea, vomiting, diarrhoea, insomnia, anxiety, fever, skin rash, and convulsions. Trade name: **Prozac**.

氟西汀 一種抗抑鬱藥,通過延長腦神經介質 5-羥色胺的作用而發揮作用。口服。可能的副作用包括惡心、嘔吐、腹瀉、失眠、焦慮、發熱、皮疹及驚厥等。商品名:Prozac。

flupenthixol *n.* a thioxanthene *antipsychotic drug used to treat schizophrenia and other psychoses. It is administered by mouth and by injection. Possible side-effects include sedation and involuntary movements. Trade names: **Depixol**, **Fluanxol**.

三氟噻噸　一種噻噸抗精神病藥物，用來治療精神分裂症及其他精神病。口服和注射給藥。可能的副作用包括鎮靜及不隨意運動。商品名：Depixol，Fluanxol。

fluphenazine *n.* a phenothiazine *antipsychotic drug used for the treatment of schizophrenia and other psychotic disorders. It is administered by mouth or injection. Side-effects include abnormal muscular movements. Trade names: **Modecate**, **Moditen**.

氟奮乃靜　一種吩噻嗪抗精神病藥物，用於精神分裂症和其他精神病的治療。口服或注射給藥。副作用包括不正常肌肉運動。商品名：Modecate，Moditen。

flurazepam *n.* a benzodiazepine drug used to treat insomnia and sleep disturbances (*see* hypnotic). It is administered by mouth and sometimes causes morning drowsiness, dizziness, and muscle incoordination. Trade name: **Dalmane**.

氟西泮　一種苯二氮䓬類藥，用來治療失眠和睡眠障礙（參閱 hypnotic）。口服。有時引起清晨嗜眠、眩暈及肌肉不協調。商品名：Dalmane。

flurbiprofen *n.* an analgesic that relieves inflammation (*see* NSAID), used in the treatment of rheumatoid arthritis and osteoarthritis and to prevent contraction of the pupil during eye surgery. Side-effects may include gastrointestinal upset, diarrhoea, and nausea. Trade names: **Froben**, **Ocufen**.

氟比洛芬　減輕炎症的止痛藥（參閱 NSAID），用於類風濕性關節炎和骨關節炎的治療及用來防止眼手術期間瞳孔收縮。副作用可能包括胃腸不適、腹瀉及惡心。商品名：Froben，Ocufen。

flush *n.* reddening of the face and/or neck. *Hectic flush* occurs in such wasting diseases as pulmonary tuberculosis. A *hot flush*, accompanied by a feeling of heat, occurs in some emotional disorders and during the menopause.

潮紅　臉和（或）脖子發紅。癆病性潮紅見於消耗性疾病，如肺結核。熱性潮紅伴有發熱感，發生於感情失常及絕經期。

fluspirilene *n.* an *antipsychotic drug used to treat schizophrenia. It is administered by injection; side-effects can include fatigue, digestive upsets, and drowsiness. Trade name: **Redeptin**.

氟司必林　治療精神分裂症的一種抗精神病藥。注射給藥。副作用有疲乏、消化道不適和嗜眠。商品名：Redeptin。

flutter *n.* a disturbance of normal heart rhythm that – like *fibrillation – may affect the atria or ventricles. However, the arrhythmia is less rapid and less chaotic. The causes and treatment are similar to those of fibrillation. *See also* cardiac arrest, defibrillation.

撲動　心律紊亂的一種，類似纖維性顫動，可發生在心房或心室，但這種心律紊亂速度較慢且表現較不雜亂。病因及治療與纖維性顫動類似。參閱 cardiac arrest，defibrillation。

fluvoxamine *n.* an *antidepressant drug that acts by prolonging the action of the neurotransmitter *serotonin (5-hydroxy-tryptamine) in the brain. It is taken by mouth; side-effects may include sleepi-ness, agitation, tremor, vomiting, and diarrhoea. Trade name: **Faverin**.

氟伏沙明　一種抗抑鬱藥，通過延長腦神經介質 5-羥色胺的作用而起作用。口服。副作用可能包括嗜睡、焦慮、發抖、嘔吐及腹瀉。商品名：Faverin。

flux *n.* an abnormally copious flow from an organ or cavity. *Alvine flux* is *diarrhoea.

流出　器官或體腔內的大量液體不正常地溢出。Alvine flux 即腹瀉。

fly *n.* a two-winged insect belonging to a large group called the Diptera. The mouthparts of flies are adapted for sucking and sometimes also for piercing and biting. Fly larvae (maggots) may infest human tissues and cause disease (*see* myiasis).

蠅　雙翅目中的一種雙翅昆蟲。其口器適於吸吮，有時也用來刺入及叮咬。蠅蛆可感染人體組織並致病（參閱 myiasis）。

FMN (flavin mononucleotide) a deriva-tive of riboflavin (vitamin B_2) that is the immediate precursor of *FAD and functions as a *coenzyme in various oxidation-reduction reactions.

黃素單核苷酸　核黃素（維生素B_2）的衍生物，是黃素腺嘌呤二核苷酸的前體。在各種氧化還原反應中起輔酶作用。

focal distance (of the eye) the distance between the lens and the point behind the lens at which light from a distant object is focused. In a normally sighted person the point of focus is on the retina, but in *myopia (short-sightedness) the focus is in front of the retina and in *hypermetropia (long-sightedness) the point of focus is beyond the retina.

（眼的）焦點距離　晶狀體和晶狀體後的某一點（遠處物體的光綫所聚焦的那一點）之間的距離。正常視力的人，這一聚焦點在視網膜上，但近視眼的人，這一聚焦點在視網膜之前，遠視眼在視網膜之後。

focus *n.* **1.** the point at which rays of light converge after passing through a

(1) 焦點　光綫經過晶狀體集中的點。(2) 病竈　感染或其

lens. **2.** *n.* the principal site of an infection or other disease. **3.** *vb.* (in ophthalmology) to accommodate (*see also* accommodation).

foetus *n. see* fetus.

fold *n.* (in anatomy and embryology) the infolding of two surfaces or membranes.

folic acid (pteroylglutamic acid) a B vitamin that is important in the synthesis of nucleic acids. The metabolic role of folic acid is interdependent with that of *vitamin B$_{12}$ (both are required by rapidly dividing cells) and a deficiency of one may lead to deficiency of the other. A deficiency of folic acid results in the condition of megaloblastic anaemia. Good sources of folic acid are liver, yeast extract, and green leafy vegetables. The actual daily requirement of folate is not known but the suggested daily intake is 200μg/day for an adult, which should be doubled during pregnancy to prevent neural tube defects (e.g. spina bifida) in the fetus.

folie à deux (communicated insanity) a condition in which two people who are closely involved with each other share a system of *delusions. Sometimes one member of the pair has developed a *psychosis and has imposed it on the other by a process of suggestion; sometimes both members are schizophrenic and elaborate their delusions or hallucinations together. More than two people may be involved (*folie à trois*, *folie à quatre*, etc.). Treatment usually involves separation of the affected people and management according to their individual requirements.

folinic acid a derivative of folic acid involved in purine synthesis. Administered

他疾病的主要部位。**(3)** 調節眼科學術語（參閱 accommodation）。

胎兒　參閱 fetus。

皺襞　（解剖學和胚胎學）膜表面褶疊所形成的結構。

葉酸　一種維生素B，對核酸的合成很重要。葉酸的代謝與維生素 B$_{12}$ 的代謝互相依賴（兩者都被快速分裂的細胞所需要）。兩者缺一都可導致另一物質的缺乏。葉酸不足可引起巨成紅細胞性貧血。葉酸的主要來源是肝臟、酵母浸出物和綠葉。每日葉酸鹽的實際需要量是多少還不清楚，但建議的每日攝入量是成人每天200μg，孕婦應加倍以防止胎兒神經管缺損（如脊柱裂）。

二聯性精神病　兩個有血緣關係的人患有同樣妄想症狀的一種疾病。有時，其中一人發展成精神病，可通過暗示的方式使另一人發病。有時兩人同是精神分裂症患者。可同時具有同樣的妄想或幻想。此病還可牽涉兩人以上（三聯性精神病、四聯性精神病）。通常的治療方法是將患者分開，並根據個體的需要進行治療。

亞葉酸　與嘌呤合成有關的葉酸的衍生物。口服或注射給

by mouth or by injection, it is used to reverse the biological effects of methotrexate and other *dihydrofolate reductase inhibitors and so to prevent excessive toxicity. This action is termed *folinic acid rescue*. Trade name: **Leucovorin**.

藥，用於逆轉甲氨蝶呤和其他二氫葉酸還原酶抑制劑的生化效應，以防止毒性過大。這個作用叫作亞葉酸解毒。商品名：Leucovorin。

folium *n.* (*pl.* **folia**) a thin leaflike structure, such as any of the folds on the surface of the cerebellum.

葉 薄片葉狀結構，如小腦表面上的皺襞。

follicle *n.* a small secretory cavity, sac, or gland, such as any of the cavities in the *ovary in which the ova are formed. *See also* Graafian follicle, hair follicle. **–follicular** *adj.*

濾泡 小分泌腔、囊或腺體，如卵巢裏任何腔，卵子就是在這些腔內形成的。參閱 Graafian follicle，hair follicle。

follicle-stimulating hormone (FSH) a hormone (*see* gonadotrophin) synthesized and released by the anterior pituitary gland. FSH stimulates ripening of the follicles in the ovary and formation of sperm in the testes. It is administered by injection to treat sterility due to lack of ovulation, amenorrhoea, and decreased sperm production. Stimulation of ovulation by FSH may, in some cases, lead to multiple pregnancy.

卵泡刺激素 由垂體前葉合成並釋放出的一種激素（參閱 gonadotrophin）。該激素能刺激卵巢內卵泡成熟及睪丸內精子的形成。注射給藥來治療因不排卵、閉經及精子生成過少而引起的不孕症。在某些病例中，用該激素刺激排卵可導致多胎妊娠。

folliculitis *n.* inflammation of hair follicles in the skin, commonly caused by infection. Folliculitis caused by *Pityrosporum* yeasts may be a marker for the diagnosis of AIDS.

毛囊炎 皮膚毛囊發炎，通常由感染引起。由瓶形酵母引起的毛囊炎是艾滋病診斷的一個標誌。

fomentation *n.* *see* poultice.

罨劑 參閱 poultice。

fomes *n.* (*pl.* **fomites**) any object that is used or handled by a person with a *communicable disease and may therefore become contaminated with the infective organisms and transmit the disease to a subsequent user. Common fomites are towels, bed-clothes, cups, and money.

污染物 任何被傳染病患者使用或接觸過的、並因此被感染物污染而且將疾病傳染給下一個使用者的物品。常見的污染物為毛巾、床單、杯及貨幣。

fontanelle *n.* an opening in the skull of a fetus or young infant due to incomplete *ossification of the cranial bones and the resulting incomplete closure of the *sutures. The *anterior fontanelle* occurs where the coronal, frontal, and sagittal sutures meet; the *posterior fontanelle* occurs where the sagittal and lambdoidal sutures meet (see illustration).

囟　胎兒或嬰兒的顱骨因未完全骨化而出現的開口及由此而形成的未完全閉合的骨縫。前囟是由冠狀縫、額縫、矢狀縫相匯合而形成的。後囟見於矢狀縫和人字縫匯合處（見圖）。

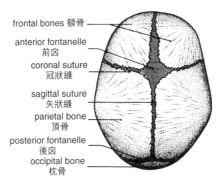

frontal bones 額骨
anterior fontanelle 前囟
coronal suture 冠狀縫
sagittal suture 矢狀縫
parietal bone 頂骨
posterior fontanelle 後囟
occipital bone 枕骨

Fontanelles in the skull of a newborn infant (from above)
新生兒顱骨囟（上面觀）

food handler a person engaged in the preparation, storage, cooking, and serving of food. Such people should be free from infectious conditions, either in the form of overt disease or as carriers. They may be subject to inspection to prove freedom from infection, particularly those who handle food that is either to be eaten raw or has previously been subjected to cooking (e.g. meat pies, paté).

飲食服務人員　從事食物製備、貯存、烹調及餐廳服務人員的總稱。此類人應避免接觸傳染病，既不能是患者也不應是**攜帶者**。他們應接受檢查以證明他們未受到過傳染，特別是那些親手接觸食物（無論是生吃食物還是熟食品如肉餅、餡餅）的人。

food poisoning an illness affecting the digestive system that results from eating food that is contaminated either by bacteria or bacterial toxins or, less commonly, by residues of insecticides

食物中毒　因食入污染的食物而引起消化系統症狀的疾病。這些食物可被細菌、細菌毒素污染，偶可被殘留的殺蟲劑（如在水果和蔬菜上）或有毒

(on fruit and vegetables) or poisonous chemicals such as lead or mercury. It can also be caused by eating poisonous fungi, berries, etc. Symptoms commence 1–24 hours after ingestion and include vomiting, diarrhoea, abdominal pain, and nausea. Food-borne infections are caused by bacteria of the genera *Salmonella*, *Campylobacter*, and *Listeria* in foods of animal origin. The disease is transmitted by human carriers who handle the food, by shellfish growing in sewage-polluted waters, or by vegetables fertilized by manure. Toxin-producing bacteria causing food poisoning include those of the genus *Staphylococcus*, which rapidly multiply in warm foods, and the species *Clostridium perfringens*, which multiplies in reheated cooked meals. A rare form of food poisoning – *botulism – is caused by toxins produced by the bacterium *Clostridium botulinum*, which may contaminate badly preserved canned foods. *See also* gastroenteritis.

的化學物質如鉛或汞污染。還可因食入有毒的蘑菇或漿果引起。食入污染物後1~24小時開始出現症狀。症狀包括嘔吐、腹瀉、腹痛及惡心。來於食物的感染是由動物臟器中的沙門菌屬、彎曲菌屬和李斯特菌屬引起。疾病能由處理食物的帶菌者、污水裏生長的貝殼動物或施過糞肥的蔬菜而傳染。引起食物中毒的產毒細菌包括能在熱食中快速繁殖的葡萄球菌屬及在熟肉食中繁殖的產氣莢膜梭狀芽胞桿菌。不常見的一種食物中毒——肉毒中毒——是由肉毒桿菌產生的毒素引起的,這種菌能污染保存不良的罐頭食物。參閱 gastroenteritis。

foot *n.* the terminal organ of the lower-limb. From a surgical point of view, the human foot comprises the seven bones of the *tarsus, the five metatarsal bones, and the phalangeal bones plus the surrounding tissues; anatomically, the bones and tissues of the ankle are excluded.

足　下肢的終末器官。從外科觀點看,人腳是由七塊跗骨、五塊跖骨和趾骨及其周圍的組織組成。解剖學上,踝部的骨和組織被排除在外。

foramen *n.* (*pl.* **foramina**) an opening or hole, particularly in a bone. The *apical foramen* is the small opening at the apex of a tooth. The *foramen magnum* is a large hole in the occipital bone through which the spinal cord passes. The *foramen ovale* is the opening between the two atria of the fetal heart, which allows blood to flow from the right to the left side of the heart by displacing a membranous valve.

孔　口或洞,尤指骨頭上的孔或洞。根尖孔是牙尖上的小孔。枕骨大孔是枕骨上的一個大孔,脊髓由此孔通過。卵圓孔是胎兒心臟兩心房之間的開口,使右心房的血液沖開膜瓣後流入左心房。

forceps *n.* a pincer-like instrument designed to grasp an object so that it can be held firm or pulled. Specially designed forceps – of which there are many varieties – are used by surgeons and dentists in operations (see illustration). The forceps used in childbirth are so designed as to fit firmly round the baby's head without damaging it. Dental

鉗　能牢牢夾住或拉出物體的鉗形器械。特殊設計的鉗種類很多，用於外科和牙科手術（見圖）。用於分娩的鉗是為能恰好夾住胎兒頭又不引起損傷而設計的。拔牙鉗是為能適合各種牙齒形狀而特殊設計的。以其柄長、嘴短的形狀，這些鉗能起到相當大的槓桿作用。

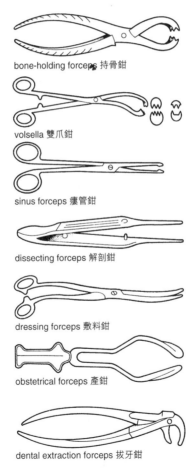

bone-holding forceps 持骨鉗

volsella 雙爪鉗

sinus forceps 瘻管鉗

dissecting forceps 解剖鉗

dressing forceps 敷料鉗

obstetrical forceps 產鉗

dental extraction forceps 拔牙鉗

Types of forceps
鉗的種類

extraction forceps are specially designed to fit the various shapes of teeth. By having long handles and short beaks they provide considerable leverage.

forebrain *n.* the furthest forward division of the *brain, consisting of the *diencephalon and the two cerebral hemispheres.

前腦　腦的最前部分，由間腦和兩側大腦半球組成。

foregut *n.* the front part of the embryonic gut, which gives rise to the oesophagus (gullet), stomach, and part of the small intestine (from which the liver and pancreas develop).

前腸　胚腸的前部分，將生長出食道、胃和部分小腸（肝和胰就從此部分小腸中發育而成）。

forensic medicine the branch of medicine concerned with the scientific investigation of the causes of injury and death in unexplained circumstances, particularly when criminal activity is suspected. Such investigations are carried out chiefly by pathologists at the request of a *coroner, in conjunction with other experts and police investigators.

法醫學　一醫學分支，用科學的方法調查無法解釋的，特別是懷疑與犯罪有關的損傷和死亡原因。此種調查主要是在驗屍官的邀請下由病理學家進行，並與其他方面的專家和警方調查人員相配合。

forequarter amputation an operation involving removal of an entire arm, including the scapula and clavicle. It is usually performed for soft tissue or bone sarcomas arising from the upper arm or shoulder. *Compare* hindquarter amputation.

上肢切斷術　切除全部上肢，包括肩胛和鎖骨的手術。通常因上肢或肩部軟組織肉瘤或骨肉瘤而施行。與 hindquarter amputation 對比。

foreskin *n. see* prepuce.

包皮　參閱 prepuce。

forewaters *n.* the *amniotic fluid that escapes from the uterus through the vagina when that part of the amnion lying in front of the presenting part of the fetus ruptures, either spontaneously or by *amniotomy. Spontaneous rupture is usual in labour but rupture may occur before labour starts (premature rupture of membranes).

前羊水　指胎兒先露部分之前的那部分羊膜破裂後，從子宮通過陰道流出的羊膜液體，破裂可是自發地也可通過羊膜穿破術。自發破裂通常在分娩時發生，但破裂也可發生在分娩之前（羊膜的過早破裂）。

formaldehyde *n.* the aldehyde derivative of formic acid, formerly used as a vapour to sterilize and disinfect rooms and such items as mattresses and blankets. The toxic vapour is produced by boiling *formalin in an open container or using it in a sealed autoclave.

甲醛　甲酸的醛衍生物，做為蒸氣用於房間及床墊和毯子等物件的滅菌和消毒。在敞口容器內煮沸福爾馬林溶液或使用密封的高壓滅菌鍋均可產生這種毒氣。

formalin *n.* a solution containing 40% formaldehyde in water, used as a sterilizing agent and, in pathology, as a fixative. It is lethal to bacteria, viruses, fungi, and spores and is used to treat wools and hides to kill anthrax spores. Heating the solution produces the irritating vapour of *formaldehyde, which is also used for disinfection.

福爾馬林　含40%甲醛的水溶液，用作消毒劑，在病理學中作為一種固定劑使用。該溶液可殺死細菌、病毒、真菌和芽胞。用來處理羊毛和獸皮，以殺死炭疽芽胞。加熱此溶液能產生出有刺激性氣體甲醛，該氣體也可用作消毒劑。

forme fruste an atypical form of a disease in which the usual symptoms fail to appear and its progress is stopped at an earlier stage than would ordinarily be expected.

頓挫型　疾病的非典型形式。通常症狀不表現出來，病情在早期階段即停止發展。

formication *n.* a prickling sensation said to resemble the feeling of ants crawling over the skin. It is a form of *paraesthesiae and it is sometimes a symptom of drug intoxication.

蟻走感　常被形容成類似螞蟻在皮膚上爬行感覺的一種刺激感。是感覺異常的一種形式，有時是藥物中毒的症狀。

formulary *n.* a compendium of formulae used in the preparation of medicinal drugs.

處方集　用於配製醫藥的處方冊。

fornix *n.* (*pl.* **fornices**) an arched or vault-like structure, especially the *fornix cerebri*, a triangular structure of white matter in the brain, situated between the hippocampus and hypothalamus. The *fornix of the vagina* is any of three vaulted spaces at the top of the vagina, around the cervix of the uterus.

穹窿　弓狀或拱頂狀結構，尤指大腦穹窿，是大腦白質的三角形結構，位於海馬和丘腦下部之間。陰道穹窿是子宮頸周圍的陰道頂部的三個拱形空間。

foscarnet *n.* an antiviral drug used in the treatment of infections caused by

膦甲酸　一種抗病毒藥，用於治療對阿昔洛韋耐藥的疱疹病

herpesviruses, including *cytomegaloviruses, that are resistant to *acyclovir, especially in patients with AIDS. It is administered by intravenous injection. Possible side-effects include thirt and increased urine output, nausea and vomiting, fatigue, headache, and kidney, damage. Trade name: **Foscavir**.

毒感染，包括巨細胞病毒，特別是在艾滋病患者身上所引起的感染。靜脈注射給藥。可能的副作用包括口渴及尿量增多、惡心及嘔吐、疲勞、頭痛和腎損害。商品名：Foscavir。

fossa n. (pl. **fossae**) a depression or hollow. The *cubital fossa* is the triangular hollow at the front of the elbow joint; the *iliac fossa* is the depression in the inner surface of the ilium; the *pituitary fossa* is the hollow in the sphenoid bone in which the pituitary gland is situated; a *tooth fossa* is a pit in the enamel on the surface of a tooth.

窩 一種凹陷或穴。肘窩是肘關節前面的三角形凹陷；髂窩是髂骨內表面的凹陷；垂體窩是蝶骨上的穴，垂體腺就位於此穴內；齒窩是牙齒表面釉質上的小坑。

fovea n. (in anatomy) a small depression, especially the shallow pit in the retina at the back of the eye. It contains a large number of *cones and is therefore the area of greatest acuity of vision: when the eye is directed at an object, the part of the image that is focused on the fovea is the part that is most accurately registered by the brain. *See also* macula (lutea).

凹 （解剖學）小凹陷，尤指眼後視網膜上的淺窩。在此窩內，含有大量視錐細胞，因此是視覺最敏感的區域：當眼睛直視物體時，聚焦在小凹上的物像部分是被大腦最精確感知到的部分。參閱 macula (lutea)。

foveola n. (in anatomy) a small depression.

小凹 （解剖學）小凹陷。

fracture n. breakage of a bone, either complete or incomplete. A *simple fracture* involves a clean break with little damage to surrounding tissues and no break in the overlying skin. If a bone end pierces the overlying skin the fracture is *compound*, and there is a risk of infection (*see* osteomyelitis). Fracture of an already diseased bone is termed a *pathological fracture* and may occur after minor injuries. Treatment of a simple

骨折 骨頭完全或不完全折斷。單純性骨折指有整齊骨裂，周圍組織損傷很小，而骨折部位的皮膚無破裂的骨折。如骨折端刺破骨折部位的皮膚則為複合骨折，有感染的危險（參閱 osteomyelitis）。病骨骨折叫做病理性骨折，可發生在很輕微損傷之後。單純骨折的治療包括重新將錯位的骨折端對位，進行夾板固定或內固

fracture includes realignment of the bone ends where there is displacement, immobilization by external splints or internal fixation, followed by *rehabilitation. *See also* comminuted fracture, greenstick fracture.

fraenectomy *n.* an operation to remove the fraenum, including the underlying fibrous tissue.

fraenum (frenum, frenulum) *n.* **1.** any of the folds of mucous membrane under the tongue or between the gums and the upper or lower lips. **2.** any of several other structures of similar appearance.

fragile-X syndrome a major genetic dirorder caused by a constriction near the end of the long arm of an *X chromosome. The fragile-X syndrome is second only to *Down's sydrome as a cause of mental retardation. Affected males have unusually high foreheads, unbalanced faces, large jaws, long protruding ears, and large testicles. They have an IQ below 50 and are prone to violent outbursts. Folic acid helps to control their behaviour. About one-third of the females with this mutation on one of their two X chromosomes are also mentally retarded. Screening for the characteristic chromosome can be done by *amniocentesis or *chorionic villus sampling.

fragilitas *n.* abnormal brittleness or fragility, for example of the hair (*fragilitas crinium*) or the bones (*fragilitas ossium*; *see* osteogenesis imperfecta).

framboesia *n. see* yaws.

framycetin *n.* an *antibiotic used mainly in the form of an ointment, cream, or

定，直至康復。參閱 comminuted fracture，greenstick fracture。

繫帶切除術　去除繫帶，包括其下方纖維組織的手術。

繫帶　**(1)** 舌下或齦唇之間的黏膜皺襞。**(2)** 任何類似皺襞的其他結構。

X 染色體脆弱綜合徵　由 X 染色體長臂端附近的狹窄而引起的一主要遺傳疾病。是僅次於唐氏綜合徵引起智力低下的原因。患此病的男性前額非常高，臉發育不平衡，有大頜骨、前突的大耳朵及大睪丸。他們的智商在 50 以下，易於狂暴發作。葉酸有助於控制他們的行為。女性約三分之一在兩個 X 染色體之一上有這種突變，也會智力低下。對特異染色體的檢查可通過羊膜穿刺術或絨膜絨毛取樣的方法進行。

脆弱　不正常的易碎、易斷現象，如脆髮症或脆骨症。

雅司病　參閱 yaws。

新黴素 B　以軟膏、乳膏劑或溶液的形式治療皮膚、眼睛、

eye or ear drops to treat skin, eye, and ear infections. Skin sensitivity sometimes occurs. Trade names: **Sofradex**, **Soframycin**.

耳朵感染的抗生素。亦可口服治療胃腸炎和食物中毒，有時可出現皮膚過敏。商品名：Sofradex，Soframycin。

fraternal twins *see* twins.

雙卵性雙胎　參閱 twins。

freckle *n.* a brown spot on the skin commonly found on the arms and face of red-haired or blond people. Freckles, which are harmless, appear where there is excessive production of the pigment melanin without any increase in numbers of melanoyctes after exposure to sunlight. *Compare* lentigo.

雀斑　皮膚上的小黃斑點，通常見於皮膚白皙的青年人上肢及臉部。雀斑對人體無害，是由於陽光照射後，黑色素在皮膚個別部位過量產生的結果。與 lentigo 對比。

free association (in *psychoanalysis) a technique in which the patient is encouraged to pursue a particular train of ideas as they enter consciousness. *See also* association of ideas.

自由聯想　（精神分析）鼓勵病人繼續追尋其進入意識領域裏的思想序列的方法。參閱 association of ideas。

free-floating anxiety an all-pervasive unfocused fear that is not produced by any appropriate cause or attached to any particular idea. Such anxiety is a feature of the *generalized anxiety disorder.

游離性焦慮　廣泛而無中心的恐懼，不是由任何適當的原因或因任何特殊的思想而引起。此類焦慮是泛發性焦慮症的特點。

freeze drying a method for the *fixation of histological specimens, involving a minimum of chemical and physical change. Specimens are immersed in isopentane cooled to $-190°C$ in liquid air. This fixes the tissue instantly, without the formation of large ice crystals (which would cause structural changes). The tissue is then dehydrated in a vacuum for about 72 hours at $-32.5°C$.

冷凍乾燥　固定組織標本的一種方法，能使標本只發生微小的化學和物理變化。將標本浸入異戊烷內，放在 $-190°C$ 的液化氣內冷凍。這種方法可使組織長期固定而沒有大結晶冰形成（因結晶冰可引起結構變化）。然後再將該組織在 $-32.5°C$ 的真空容器內脫水 72 小時。

freeze etching a technique for preparing specimens for electron microscopy. The unfixed tissue is frozen and then split with a knife and a layer of ice is sublimed from the exposed surface. The resultant

冷凍蝕刻法　製備電子顯微鏡標本的技術。將未固定的組織冷凍，再用刀將其切成片，這樣，冰層就會從組織的切面上昇華出來。因此，用這種方法

image is thus not distorted by chemical fixatives.

Frei test a rarely used diagnostic test for the sexually transmitted disease *lymphogranuloma venereum. A small quantity of the virus, inactivated by heat, is injected into the patient's skin. If the disease is present a small red swelling appears at the site of injection within 48 hours.

fremitus *n.* vibrations or tremors in a part of the body, detected by feeling with the fingers of hand (*palpation) or by listening (*auscultation). The term is most commonly applied to vibrations perceived through the chest when a patient breathes, speaks (*vocal fremitus*), or coughs. The nature of the fremitus gives an indication as to whether the chest is affected by disease. For example, loss of vocal fremitus suggests the presence of fluid in the pleural cavity; its increase suggests consolidation of the underlying lung.

frenulum *n. see* fraenum.

frenum *n. see* fraenum.

frequency *n.* (of urine) the frequent passage of urine, which usually indicates genitourinary disorders and diseases but also accompanies *polyuria.

frequency distribution (in statistics) presentation of the characteristics (*variables) of a series of individuals (e.g. their heights, weights, or blood pressures) in tabular form or as a histogram (bar chart) so as to indicate the proportion of the series that have different measurements. In a *normal* or *Gaussian distribution* the number of readings and their

製成的標本不會被化學固定劑所破壞。

弗賴試驗 較少使用的一種性病性淋巴肉芽腫的診斷試驗。將被熱滅活的小量病毒注射到患者皮內,如患者患有此病,48小時內,注射部位有小紅腫出現。

震顫 身體某部位的震動或顫動,可用手指或手的感覺(觸診)感到,或被聽到(聽診)。此術語最常用於描述在患者呼吸、説話(語音震顫)或咳嗽時通過胸部所察覺到的震顫。震顫的特點是提示胸部是否有病。例如,語音震顫消失表明胸腔內存在積液,語顫音增強説明肺部有實質病變。

繫帶 參閲 fraenum。

繫帶 參閲 fraenum。

尿頻 頻繁的排尿,通常表明泌尿生殖器障礙和疾病,但它也伴隨多尿症。

頻數分布 (統計學)以表格和直方圖的形式表現一系列個體的特點(如身高、體重或血壓),並能表示出用不同測定方法所得此系列差異的比例。在正態分布和高斯分布中,資料上的數字和其在平均值兩側的分布是對稱的。在偏態分布中(如泊松分布),測得的數

range on either side of the *mean value is symmetrical; in a *skewed distribution* (e.g. *Poisson*) the measurements are bunched on one side of the mean and spread out over a wider range on the other.

字集中在平均值的一側，而另一側呈分散分布。

Freudian *adj.* relating to or describing the work and ideas of Sigmund Freud (1856–1939): applied particularly to the school of psychiatry based on his teachings (*see* psychoanalysis).

弗洛伊德學派的 指與西格蒙·弗洛伊德 (1856~1939) 工作和觀點有關的：尤指基於他的學說而發展起來的精神病學派。參閱 psychoanalysis。

friction murmur (friction rub) a scratching sound, heard over the heart with the aid of the stethoscope, in patients who have *pericarditis. It results from the two inflamed layers of the pericardium rubbing together during activity of the heart.

摩擦音 用聽診器在心包炎患者心臟部位的胸壁上聽到的一種搔抓音。這是在心臟活動時，心包的兩層發炎的膜互相摩擦的結果。

Friedman's test an obsolete pregnancy test based on the ability of urine of pregnant women (containing human chorionic gonadotrophin) to induce the development of corpora lutea in a female rabbit.

弗里德曼試驗 一種過時的妊娠試驗，是根據孕婦尿（含有人絨毛膜促性腺激素）促使雌兔體內黃體發育能力而定。

Friedreich's ataxia *see* ataxia.

弗里德賴希共濟失調 參閱 ataxia。

frigidity *n.* lack of sexual desire or inability to achieve orgasm. The phenomenon may affect either sex, but the term is almost always applied to women only. In some cases the woman feels revulsion towards sexual activity.

性冷淡 缺乏性慾，或無能力達到性高潮。男性或女性都可患性冷淡，但該術語幾乎總是只用於女性，在某些病例中，女性對性行為感到厭惡。

fringe medicine *see* alternative medicine.

非正統醫學 參閱 alternative medicine。

Fröhlich's syndrome a disorder of the *hypothalamus (part of the brain) affecting males: the boy is overweight with

弗勒利希綜合徵 男性丘腦下部（腦的一部分）疾病：男孩過度肥胖、性器官不發育及睡

sexual development absent and disturbances of sleep and appetite. Medical name: **dystrophia adiposogenitalis**.

眠和食慾紊亂。醫學用語：肥胖性生殖器退化。

frontal *adj*. **1.** of or relating to the forehead (*see* frontal bone). **2.** denoting the *anterior part of a body or organ.

(1) 額的　**(2)** 前面的　指身體和器官前面的。

frontal bone the bone forming the forehead and the upper parts of the orbits; it contains several air spaces (*frontal sinuses*: *see* paranasal sinuses). At birth it consists of right and left halves, joined by a suture that usually closes during infancy. *See* skull.

額骨　形成前額及眶上部的骨，含有很多氣竇（參閱 paranasal sinuses）。出生時由左右兩半組成，中間為骨縫，該縫在嬰兒時閉合。參閱 skull。

frontal lobe the anterior part of each cerebral hemisphere (*see* cerebrum), extending as far back as the deep central sulcus (cleft) of its upper and outer surface. Immediately anterior to the central sulcus lies the motor cortex, responsible for the control of voluntary movement; the area further forward – the *prefrontal lobe – is concerned with behaviour, learning, judgment, and personality.

額葉　大腦半球的前部分（參閱 cerebrum），向後延伸到大腦外上表面的中央溝。緊靠中央溝以前的部分是皮質運動區，負責控制自主運動。再前面的部位——前額葉——與行為、學習、判斷及個性有關。

frontal sinus *see* paranasal sinuses.

額竇　參閱 paranasal sinuses。

frostbite *n*. damage to the tissues caused by freezing. The affected parts, usually the nose, fingers, or toes, become pale and numb. Ice forms in the tissues, which may thus be destroyed, and amputation may become necessary. Frostbitten parts should not be rubbed, since there is no blood circulation in the tissues, but they may be gently warmed in tepid water. Precautions must be taken against bacterial infection, to which frostbitten skin is highly susceptible.

凍瘡　因受凍而引起的組織損傷。受損部位通常為鼻、手指或腳趾，表現為蒼白與麻木。如組織內有冰形成，可使組織受到破壞，必要時需截肢。凍瘡部位不應揉擦，因該部位內無血液循環，但可用溫水逐漸加溫。須預防細菌感染，凍瘡皮膚對細菌有極高的易感性。

frottage *n*. rubbing up against somebody (usually in a crowd) as a means of

摩擦淫　以摩擦他人身體（通常是在人羣中）作為獲得性滿

obtaining sexual pleasure. A person displaying this sexual deviation is called a *frotteur*; frotteurs are almost exclusively males.

足的手段。表現出這種性變態的人叫做摩擦淫者；他們幾乎全是男性。

frozen shoulder chronic painful stiffness of the shoulder joint. This may follow injury a stroke, or *myocardial infarction or may gradually develop for no apparent reason. Treatment is by gentle stretching and exercises, sometimes combined with *corticosteroid injection into the joint. *See also* capsulitis.

凍肩 肩關節慢性疼痛性强直。這可出現在外傷、中風或心肌梗死之後，或無明顯原因而逐漸發展成病。治療是通過輕輕牽拉，做運動，有時可在肩關節內注射皮質類固醇。參閱 capsulitis。

fructose *n.* a simple sugar found in honey and in such fruit as figs. Fructose is one of the two sugars in *sucrose. Fructose from the diet can be used to produce energy by the process known as *glycolysis, which takes place in the liver. Fructose is important in the diet of diabetics since, unlike glucose, fructose metabolism is not dependent on insulin.

果糖 存在於蜂蜜和水果（如無花果）中的一種單糖。它是蔗糖中兩種單糖之一。食物中的果糖可通過肝臟進行糖酵解產生能量。果糖是糖尿病患者膳食中的重要成分，因它與葡萄糖不同，是不依靠胰島素代謝的。

fructosuria (levulosuria) *n.* the presence of fructose (levulose) in the urine.

果糖尿 尿裏存在有果糖。

frusemide *n.* a *diuretic used to treat fluid retention (oedema) associated with heart, liver, or kidney disease and also high blood pressure. It is administered by mouth or injection; common side-effects are nausea and vomiting. Trade name: **Lasix**.

呋噻米 一種利尿藥，用於治療因心臟病、肝病或腎病及高血壓病引起的液體瀦留（水腫）。口服或注射給藥；常見的副作用是惡心和嘔吐。商品名：Lasix。

FSH *see* follicle-stimulating hormone.

卵泡刺激素 參閱 follicle-stimulating hormone。

FTT *see* failure to thrive.

發育不足 參閱 failure to thrive。

fuchsin (magenta) *n.* any one of a group of reddish to purplish dyes used in staining bacteria for microscopic observation and capable of killing various disease-causing microorganisms. *Acid*

品紅 一組顏色從紅到紫的染料中的任何一種，用於對細菌染色，以進行顯微鏡下觀察且能殺死各種致病性微生物。酸性品紅是硫化品紅的混合物。

fuchsin (*acid magenta*) is a mixture of sulphonated fuchsins; *basic fuchsin* (*basic magenta*) and *new* (*trimethyl*) *fuchsin* are basic histological dyes (basic fuchsin is also an antifungal agent).

鹼性品紅和新品紅（三甲基）是最基本的組織學染料（鹼性品紅還是一種抗真菌劑）。

-fuge *suffix denoting* an agent that drives away, repels, or eliminates. Example: *febrifuge* (a drug that reduces fever).

〔後綴〕指有驅除、抵制或消減作用的藥。如退熱藥（退燒藥）。

fugue *n.* a period of memory loss during which the patient leaves his usual surroundings and wanders aimlessly or starts a new life elsewhere. It is often preceded by psychological conflict and depression (*see* dissociative disorder) or it may be associated with organic mental disease.

神游症　患者離開他常住的環境，無目的地漫游，或在其他地方開始新生活。患者事後對這段時期失去記憶。患病前患者通常有心理衝突和壓抑感（參閱 dissociative disorder）或者和器質性精神病有關。

fulguration (electrodesiccation) *n.* the destruction with a *diathermy instrument of warts, growths, or unwanted areas of tissue, particularly inside the bladder. This latter operation is performed via the urethra and viewed through a cystoscope.

電灼療法（電乾燥法）用透熱器械破壞疣、新生物或病變組織，特別是膀胱內的病變組織。後一種手術要通過膀胱鏡在尿道內施行。

fulminating (fulminant, fulgurant) *adj.* describing a condition or symptom that is of very sudden onset, severe, and of short duration.

暴發的　指突然發作、病情嚴重、且持續期短的疾病或症狀。

fumigation *n.* the use of gases or vapours to bring about *disinfestation of clothing, buildings, etc. Sulphur dioxide, formaldehyde, and chlorine are common fumigating agents.

薰蒸消毒法　一種用氣體或蒸氣消毒衣服、房屋等的方法。二氧化硫、甲醛及氯氣是常見的薰蒸劑。

functional disorder a condition in which a patient complains of symptoms for which no physical cause can be found. Such a condition is frequently an indication of a psychiatric disorder. *Compare* organic disorder.

功能性疾病　從患者主訴症狀中不能找出軀體性原因的一種疾病。此種疾病經常是精神病的一種表現。與 organic disorder 對比。

fundholder *n.* (in the NHS) *see* general practitioner.

公債持有人（國民保健服務制）參閱 general practitioner。

fundoplication *n.* a surgical operation for *gastro-oesophageal reflux disease in which the upper part of the stomach is wrapped around the lower oesophagus. The commonest technique is named after Rudolf Nissen, a Swiss surgeon.

胃底摺術　治療胃食管返流病的一種外科手術。在此病中，胃的上部被包繞在下食管的周圍。這一常用技術被命名為魯道夫·尼森（一瑞士外科醫生）手術。

fundus *n.* **1.** the base of a hollow organ: the part farthest from the opening; e.g. the fundus of the stomach, bladder, or uterus. **2.** the interior concavity forming the back of the eyeball, opposite the pupil.

(1) 底　空心器官的底部，距開口部最遠的部分。如胃底、膀胱底或子宮底。**(2) 眼底**　眼睛內部與瞳孔位置相對的部位。

fungicide *n.* an agent that kills fungi. *See also* antifungal.

殺真菌劑　殺死真菌的藥物。參閱 antifungal。

fungoid **1.** *adj.* resembling a fungus. **2.** *n.* a fungus-like growth.

(1) 蕈狀的　**(2) 蕈樣新生物**

fungus *n.* (*pl.* **fungi**) a simple organism (formerly regarded as a plant) that lacks the green pigment chlorophyll. Fungi include the *yeasts, rusts, moulds, and mushrooms. They live either as *saprophytes or as *parasites of plants and animals; some species infect and cause disease in man. Some yeasts are a good source of vitamin B and many antibiotics are obtained from the moulds (*see* penicillin). **–fungal** *adj.*

真菌　一種無葉綠素的簡單生物（以前認為是植物）。真菌包括酵母菌、銹菌、黴及蕈。它們既可作為植物和動物的腐生物生存，也可作為寄生物生存。有些菌種還可以使人類感染致病。有些酵母菌是維生素 B 的重要來源而且許多抗生素也是從黴菌中獲得的（參閱 penicillin）。

funiculitis *n.* inflammation of the spermatic cord. This usually arises in association with *epididymitis and causes pain and swelling of the involved cord. Treatment is by administration of antibiotics and analgesics.

精索炎　精索炎症。通常因附睾炎而發病引起受損的精索疼痛和腫脹。治療為服用抗生素和鎮痛藥。

funiculus *n.* **1.** any of the three main columns of white matter found in each lateral half of the spinal cord. **2.** a bundle

(1) 脊索　脊髓兩側所見到的白質中三個主要柱狀結構。**(2) 神經索**　被鞘膜包繞着的一束

of nerve fibres enclosed in a sheath; a fasciculus. **3.** (formerly) the spermatic cord or umbilical cord.

神經纖維。**(3)精索或臍帶**（舊稱）。

funis *n.* (in anatomy) any cordlike structure, especially the umbilical cord.

索條 （解剖學）任何繩索狀結構，尤指臍帶。

funnel chest depression of the breastbone and inward curving of the costal cartilages articulating with it, resulting in deformity of the chest. Medical name: **pectus excavatum**.

漏斗胸 胸骨的下凹及與之關節連接的肋軟骨向裏彎曲，引起胸部畸形。醫學用語：漏斗胸。

furcation *n.* the place where the roots fork on a multirooted tooth.

分叉 多根牙上的牙根分支處。

furor *n.* indiscriminate violence and destructiveness, occurring especially during a period of mental confusion due to *epilepsy.

狂暴 隨意的暴力和破壞行為，特別是發生在因癲癇而失去理智的時期。

furuncle *n. see* boil.

癤 參閱 boil。

furunculosis *n.* the occurrence of several *boils (furuncles) at the same time, usually caused by *Staphylococcus aureus* infection. Treatment includes thorough daily disinfection of the skin as well as antibiotic therapy.

癤病 同一時間出現多個癤腫，通常是由葡萄球菌感染引起的。治療包括每天做身體皮膚消毒及抗生素療法。

fusidic acid a steroid antibiotic used in the form of its salt, sodium fusidate, against penicillin-resistant staphylococci. It has no value against streptococci and is usually prescribed in conjunction with another antibiotic, such as *flucloxacillin. It is administered by mouth. Possible side-effects include nausea, vomiting, and skin rashes. Trade name: **Fucidin**.

夫西地酸 一種甾族抗生素，用其鹽的形式——夫西地酸鈉來殺死抗青黴素葡萄球菌。它本身沒有抗葡萄球菌價值，通常與另一抗生素如氟氯西林一起連用。口服。可能的副作用包括惡心、嘔吐和皮疹。商品名：Fucidin。

fusiform *adj.* spindle-shaped; tapering as both ends.

梭形的 紡錘形的；兩端呈圓錐形的。

fusion *n.* (in surgery) the joining together of two structures. For example,

融合 （外科學）兩結構結合在一起。例如將兩個或更多的脊

fusion of two or more vertebra is performed to stabilize an unstable spine.

椎融合在一起，就形成一個穩固的脊柱。

Fusobacterium *n.* a genus of Gram-negative rodlike bacteria with tapering ends. Most species are normal inhabitants of the mouth of animals and man and produce no harmful effects, but anaerobic *Fusobacterium* species are associated with *ulcerative gingivitis.

梭形桿菌屬 革蘭氏陰性兩端呈圓錐形的桿狀菌屬。大多數菌種正常生活在動物和人類的口腔裏，而且不產生危害，但一種厭氧梭形桿菌可與潰瘍性齦炎有關。

G

GABA *see* gamma-aminobutyric acid.

γ-氨基丁酸 參閱 gamma-aminobutyric acid。

Gaffkya *n.* a genus of bacteria now classified as *Micrococcus*.

加夫基球菌屬 微球菌屬的舊稱。

gag *n.* (in medicine) an instrument that is placed between a patient's teeth to keep his mouth open.

張𧮼器 （醫學）放在患者牙齒之間使口保持張開的一種器械。

galact- (galacto-) *prefix denoting* **1.** milk. Example: *galactosis* (formation of). **2.** galactose.

〔前綴〕**(1)** 乳 例如乳汁生成。**(2)** 半乳糖

galactagogue *n.* an agent that stimulates the secretion of milk or increases milk flow.

催乳藥 刺激乳汁分泌或增加乳汁流量的藥物。

galactocele *n.* **1.** a breast cyst containing milk, caused by closure of a milk duct. **2.** an accumulation of milky liquid in the sac surrounding the testis (*see* hydrocele).

(1) 乳腺囊腫 含有乳汁的乳腺腫瘤，由輸乳管閉合所致。**(2) 乳性鞘膜積液** 陰囊內積聚乳狀液體（參閱 hydrocele）。

galactorrhoea *n.* **1.** abnormally copious milk secretion. **2.** secretion of milk after breast feeding has been stopped.

溢乳 **(1)** 乳汁分泌異常豐富。**(2)** 母乳餵養停止後的乳汁分泌。

galactosaemia *n.* an inborn inability to utilize the sugar galactose, which in consequence accumulates in the blood. Untreated, affected infants fail to thrive and become mentally retarded, but if galactose is eliminated from the diet growth and development may be normal.

galactose *n.* a simple sugar and a constituent of the milk sugar *lactose. Galactose is converted to glucose in the liver. The enzyme necessary for this conversion is missing in infants with a rare inherited metabolic disease called *galactosaemia.

galea *n.* **1.** a helmet-shaped part, especially the *galea aponeurotica*, a flat sheet of fibrous tissue (*see* aponeurosis) that caps the skull and links the two parts of the *epicranius muscle. **2.** a type of head bandage.

galenical *n.* a pharmaceutical preparation of a drug of animal or plant origin.

gallamine *n.* a drug administered by injection to produce muscle relaxation during anaesthesia (*see* muscle relaxant). It is also used in a diagnostic test for *myasthenia gravis. Trade name: **Flaxedil**.

gall bladder a pear-shaped sac (7–10 cm long), lying underneath the right lobe of the liver, in which *bile is stored (see illustration). Bile passes (via the hepatic duct) to the gall bladder from the liver, where it is formed, and is released into the duodenum (through the common bile duct) under the influence of the hormone *cholecystokinin, which is secreted when food is present in the duodenum. The gall bladder is a common site of stone formation (*see* gallstone).

半乳糖血症 一種不能利用半乳糖的先天性疾病，其結果使半乳糖蓄積於血內。如不治療，患兒不能茁壯成長，智力發育遲緩；但如飲食中消除了半乳糖，生長發育可以恢復正常。

半乳糖 一種單糖和乳糖的一種成分。半乳糖在肝內轉變為葡萄糖。半乳糖血症是嬰兒的一種罕見的遺傳性代謝病，是由於體內缺少半乳糖轉變為葡萄糖所必需的酶所致。

(1) 帽狀腱膜 顱頂肌的頭盔狀腱膜。大片腱膜（參閱 aponeurosis）覆蓋於顱頂上，前後各與顱頂肌的額腹和枕腹相連。(2) 帽狀繃帶 頭部繃帶的一類型。

蓋倫製劑 一種以動物或植物為原料的藥物製劑。

加拉碘銨 麻醉時使用的一種注射用的肌肉鬆弛藥（參閱 muscle relaxant）。亦用於對重症肌無力的診斷試驗。商品名：Flaxedil。

膽囊 一個貯存膽汁的梨形囊（長7~10 cm），位於肝右葉下面（見圖）。在肝內生成的膽汁（經肝管）進入膽囊貯存。當食物進入十二指腸，分泌縮膽囊素激素，此激素使膽汁（經膽總管）進入十二指腸。膽囊是結石形成的常見處（參閱 gallstone）。

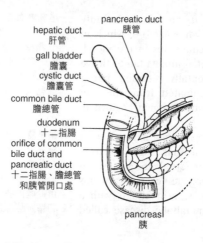

pancreatic duct
胰管

hepatic duct
肝管

gall bladder
膽囊

cystic duct
膽囊管

common bile duct
膽總管

duodenum
十二指腸

orifice of common
bile duct and
pancreatic duct
十二指腸、膽總管
和胰管開口處

pancreas
胰

The gall bladder and pancreas and their associated ducts
膽囊和胰及其導管

gallium *n.* a silvery metallic element. A radioisotope of gallium is used for the detection of lymphomas and areas of infection (such as an abscess).

鎵 一銀白金屬元素。鎵的放射性同位素被用來探側淋巴瘤和感染區域（如膿腫）。

gallstone *n.* a hard mass composed of bile pigments, cholesterol, and calcium salts, in varying proportions, that can form in the gall bladder. The formation of gallstones (*cholelithiasis*) occurs when the physical characteristics of bile alter so that cholesterol is less soluble, though chronic inflammation of the gall bladder (*see* cholecystitis) may also be a contributory factor. Gallstones may exist for many years without causing symptoms. However, they may cause severe pain (*see* biliary colic) or they may pass into the common bile duct and cause obstructive *jaundice or *cholangitis. Gallstones containing calcium may be seen on a plain X-ray (opaque stones), but if their calcium content is low they can be seen only by *cholecystography. Cholelithiasis is usually treated by surgical removal of

膽結石 一種由不同比例的膽色素、膽固醇和鈣鹽組成的硬的凝結物，可在膽囊內形成。當膽汁發生物理特性改變時，膽固醇的溶解度減低，導致膽結石形成（膽石病）。慢性膽囊炎（參閱 cholecystitis）也是引起膽結石形成的一個因素。膽結石可存在許多年而不出現症狀。膽結石可引起劇烈疼痛（參閱 biliary colic），或進入膽總管而導致阻塞性黃疸或膽囊炎。含鈣質的膽結石可於 X 綫平片下顯影（不透明膽石），但如其所含鈣的量少，則只能見於膽囊造影。膽石病常通過手術摘除膽囊（參閱 cholecystectomy）或從膽囊中取出膽石來治療。膽石既可通過口服的膽酸鹽溶解也可通

the gall bladder (*see* cholecystectomy) or by removing the stones themselves, which can be either dissolved using bile salts given by mouth or shattered by ultrasound waves. There is no need for treatment if the stones are causing no symptoms.

過超聲波擊碎。如膽石不引起任何症狀則無需治療。

galvanism *n.* (formerly) any form of medical treatment using electricity. *Interrupted galvanism* is a form of *electrotherapy in which direct current, in impulses lasting for 30 to 100 milliseconds, is used to stimulate the activity of nerves or the muscles they supply. *See also* faradism.

電療法 （舊稱）採用任何形式的電流進行治療的醫療方法。斷續電療是電療法的一種形式。這種電療採用持續 30 至 100 毫秒的直流電脈衝，以刺激神經及其所支配的肌肉的活動。參閱 faradism。

Gam-Anon *n.* *see* Gamblers Anonymous.

賭博者互誠協會 參閱 Gamblers Anonymous。

Gamblers Anonymous (GA) an organization, founded in the US in 1957 and established in the UK in 1964, that seeks to assist compulsive gamblers. The despair, humiliation, and loneliness of compulsive gamblers is neither widely known nor understood. Invariably their addiction leads to bankruptcy, loss of jobs, rejection by family and friends, and ultimately to criminal means of obtaining money with which to gamble. GA offers a form of group therapy similar to that provided by *Alcoholics Anonymous. Senior members help the new members to face their creditors and to work out repayment budgets that will eventually free them from their obligations. The sister organization, *Gam-Anon*, provides advice and encouragement for the families of compulsive gamblers.

賭博者互誠協會 一個設法幫助不能自拔的賭博者的組織。此組織 1957 年創建於美國，1964 年設立於英國。不能自拔的賭博者的失望、羞辱、孤立情緒，是既不為人所知，也不為人理解的。他們的癖嗜肯定會導致破產、失業、被家庭和朋友拋棄，最終用犯罪的手段去獲得金錢，再去賭博。此協會和嗜酒者互誠協會一樣，採用一種集體治療的方式，以老會員幫助新會員，制定向債權人償還債務的計劃，最終使他們從債務中擺脫出來。與此協會配合的婦女組織對不能自拔的賭博者的家屬進行勸告和鼓勵。

gamete *n.* a mature sex cell: the *ovum of the female or the *spermatozoon of the male. Gametes are haploid, containing half the normal number of chromosomes.

配子 一種成熟的性細胞，如女性的卵子或男性的精子。配子是單倍體的，含有正常染色體數量的一半。

gamete intrafallopian transfer (GIFT) a procedure for assisting conception, suitable only for women with healthy Fallopian tubes. In over 50% of women in whom infertility is diagnosed, the tubes are normal but some other factor, such as endometriosis, prevents conception. Using needle *aspiration, under laparoscopic or ultrasonic guidance, ova are removed from the ovary. After being mixed with the partner's spermatozoa, they are introduced into a Fallopian tube, where fertilization takes place. The fertilized ovum can subsequently become implanted in the uterus.

配子輸卵管內轉移　一幫助妊娠的技術，只適合於具有健全輸卵管的婦女。在 50% 以上診斷出有不孕症的婦女，輸卵管是正常的，但某些其他因素如子宮內膜異位阻止懷孕，使用針吸引術，在腹腔鏡或超聲指導下，將卵子從卵巢裏取出。在與其配偶的精子混合後，再導入輸卵管進行受精。受精的卵隨後可移植在子宮內。

gametocide *n.* a drug that kills *gametocytes. Drugs such as *primaquine destroy gametocytes of the malaria parasite (*see* Plasmodium), so interrupting the life cycle and preventing infection of the mosquito.

殺配子（體）劑　一種殺滅配子體的藥物。例如破壞瘧原蟲（參閱 Plasmodium）配子體的藥物伯氨喹啉，能中斷瘧原蟲的生活周期，防止蚊蟲感染。

gametocyte *n.* any of the cells that are in the process of developing into gametes by undergoing *gametogenesis. *See also* oocyte, spermatocyte.

配子體　在配子形成過程中發育成為配子的任何細胞，參閱 oocyte，spermatocyte。

gametogenesis *n.* the process by which spermatozoa and ova are formed. In both sexes the precursor cells undergo *meiosis, which halves the number of chromosomes. However, the timing of events and the size and number of gametes produced are very different in the male and female. *See* oogenesis, spermatogenesis.

配子形成　精子和卵子形成的過程。精子和卵子的母細胞進行減數分裂，使其染色體數目減少一半。然而，雄性和雌性配子形成時間的長短、大小和數目是極不相同的。參閱 oogenesis，spermatogenesis。

gamma aminobutyric acid (GABA) an amino acid found in the central nervous system, predominantly in the brain, where it acts as an inhibitory *neurotransmitter.

γ-氨基丁酸　一種氨基酸，存在於中樞神經系統，主要在腦內。起抑制神經遞質的作用。

gamma benzene hexachloride an insecticide used in creams, lotions,

丙體六六六　一種殺蟲劑，用作乳劑、洗劑、溶液劑或洗髮

solutions, or shampoos to treat infestations caused by scabies, mites, and lice (including head lice). Mild skin reactions occasionally occur.

gamma camera a piece of apparatus for taking photographs of parts of the body into which radioactive isotopes that give off *gamma rays have been introduced as *tracers.

gamma globulin any of a class of proteins, present in the blood *plasma, identified by their characteristic rate of movement in an electric field (*see* electrophoresis). Almost all gamma globulins are *immunoglobulins. Injection of gamma globulin provides temporary protection against *hepatitis A and has recently been shown to reduce the incidence of coronary artery involvement in *Kawasaki disease. *See also* globulin.

gamma rays electromagnetic radiation of wavelengths shorter than X-rays, given off by certain radioactive substances. Gamma rays have greater penetration than X-rays; they are harmful to living tissues and can be used to sterilize certain materials. Controlled doses are used in *radiotherapy.

gamo- *prefix denoting* marriage.

ganciclovir *n.* an antiviral drug used to treat severe *cytomegalovirus infections, mainly in patients with AIDS. It is administered by injection. Possible side-effects include nausea, vomiting, diarrhoea, infertility, confusion, seizures, and disturbance of bone marrow blood-cell production. Trade name: **Cymevene**.

gangli- (ganglio-) *prefix denoting* a ganglion.

劑，以治療由疥蟎和虱（包括頭虱）引起的感染。偶有輕微的皮膚反應。

γ 照相機　一種拍攝 γ 射綫的照相機。所拍攝的 γ 射綫是由置入體內作為示蹤物的放射性核素釋放出的。

γ 球蛋白（丙種球蛋白）　存在於血漿中的一類蛋白質。此類蛋白質根據其在電場（參閱 electrophoresis）內特定的移動速度來測定。幾乎所有的 γ 球蛋白都是免疫球蛋白。注射 γ 球蛋白能起暫時的抗甲肝作用，最近顯示能降低川崎病中冠狀動脈受損的發病率。參閱 globulin。

γ 射綫　一種電磁輻射，波長短於 X 綫，由某些放射性物質所釋放。γ 射綫有較 X 綫更強的穿透力，對活組織有危害，可用於消毒某些用具。嚴格控制劑量的 γ 射綫可用於放射治療。

〔前綴〕婚配

更昔洛韋　一種抗病毒藥，用於治療嚴重巨細胞病毒感染，主要是艾滋病患者身上。注射給藥。可能的副作用包括惡心、嘔吐、腹瀉、不育（孕）症、精神錯亂、癲癇發作及骨髓血細胞生成障礙。商品名：Cymevene。

〔前綴〕神經節

ganglion n. (pl. **ganglia**) **1.** (in neurology) any structure containing a collection of nerve cell bodies and often also numbers of synapses. In the *sympathetic nervous system chains of ganglia are found on each side of the spinal cord, while in the *parasympathetic system ganglia are situated in or nearer to the organs innervated. Swellings in the posterior sensory *roots of the spinal nerves are termed ganglia; these contain cell bodies but no synapses. Within the central nervous system certain well-defined masses of nerve cells are called ganglia (or *nuclei*); for example, the *basal ganglia. **2.** an abnormal but harmless swelling (cyst) that sometimes forms in tendon sheaths, especially at the wrist.

(1) 神經節 （神經病學）含有神經細胞集合體，並常有許多突觸的結構。在交感神經系統，神經節鏈排於脊柱兩側；而在副交感系統，神經節位於所支配的器官內或其附近。含有感覺纖維的脊神經後根的膨大部也稱為神經節。這些神經節有細胞體而無突觸。在中樞神經系統內某些清晰的神經團也稱為神經節（或核），如基底神經節。**(2) 腱鞘囊腫** 一種異常但無危害的腫塊（囊腫），有時見於腱鞘內，尤其在腕部。

ganglioside n. one of a group of *glycolipids found in the brain, liver, spleen, and red blood cells (they are particularly abundant in nerve cell membranes). Gangliosides are chemically similar to *cerebrosides but contain additional carbohydrate groups.

神經節苷脂 為糖脂類的一種，見於腦、肝、脾和紅細胞（在神經細胞中尤其豐富）。神經節苷脂和腦苷脂在化學結構上近似，但前者具有一個額外的糖基。

gangosa n. a lesion that occasionally appears in the final stage of *yaws, involving considerable destruction of the tissues of both the hard palate and the nose.

毀形性鼻咽類 在雅司病末期偶爾出現的一種損害，硬腭和鼻的組織都遭到相當的破壞。

gangrene n. death and decay of part of the body due to deficiency or cessation of blood supply. The causes include disease, injury, or *atheroma in major blood vessels, frostbite or severe burns, and diseases such as *diabetes mellitus and *Raynaud's disease. *Dry gangrene* is death and withering of tissues caused simply by a cessation of local blood circulation. *Moist gangrene* is death and putrefactive decay of tissue caused by bacterial infection. *See also* gas gangrene.

壞疽 由於血液供應缺乏或停止而使身體的一部分壞死和腐爛。其病因包括疾病、損傷、大血管粥樣化、凍瘡或嚴重燒傷，以及糖尿病、雷諾病等。乾性壞疽係單純由於局部血管的循環停止所致，組織壞死和乾枯。濕性壞疽係由於細菌感染所致的組織壞死並腐爛。參閱 gas gangrene。

Ganser state (pseudodementia) a syndrome characterized by *approximate answers*, i.e. the patient gives grossly and absurdly false replies to questions, but the reply shows that the question has been understood. For example, the question "What colour is snow?" may elicit the reply "Green". This can be accompanied by odd behaviour or episodes of *stupor. The condition is due to *conversion disorder or to conscious malingering.

gargoylism *n. see* Hunter's syndrome, Hurler's syndrome.

gas gangrene death and decay of wound tissue infected by the soil bacterium *Clostridium perfringens*. Toxins produced by the bacterium cause putrefactive decay of connective tissue with the generation of gas. Treatment is usually by surgery.

Gasterophilus *n.* a genus of widely distributed non-bloodsucking beelike flies. The parasitic maggots normally live in the alimentary canal of horses but, rarely, can also infect man and cause an inflamed itching eruption of the skin (*see* creeping eruption).

gastr- (gastro-) *prefix denoting* the stomach. Examples: *gastralgia* (pain in); *gastrocolic* (relating to the stomach and colon).

gastrectasia *n.* dilatation of the stomach. This may be caused by *pyloric stenosis or it may occur as a complication of some abdominal operations or trauma.

gastrectomy *n.* a surgical operation in which the whole or a part of the

甘塞症（假性痴呆） 一種以似是而非的回答為特徵的綜合徵。病人對問題做出荒謬頂透的錯誤回答，但從回答中可以看出他對所提的問題是理解的。例如，問「雪是甚麼顏色？」回答「綠色的。」答話時伴有古怪的舉止或木僵發作。這種病態是由於（心理）轉換障礙，或者是由於詐病所致。

脂肪軟骨營養不良 參閱 Hunter's syndrome，Hurler's syndrome。

氣性壞疽 由土壤中產氣莢膜桿菌感染傷口組織所致的壞死和腐爛。桿菌毒素引起結締組織腐爛，產生氣體。常用外科治療。

胃蠅屬 一種廣泛分布的蜜蜂狀非吸血蠅屬。其蛆正常寄生於馬的消化道中，但偶爾也能感染人，引起瘙癢的炎性皮疹（參閱 creeping eruption）。

〔前綴〕胃 例如：胃痛，胃結腸的。

胃擴張 胃的膨脹。可由幽門狹窄引起或作為腸道的手術或損傷的併發症。

胃切除術 把全胃或一部分胃切除的外科手術。全胃切除術

stomach is removed. *Total gastrectomy*, in which the oesophagus is joined to the duodenum, is usually performed for stomach cancer but occasionally for the *Zollinger-Ellison syndrome. In *partial* (or *subtotal*) *gastrectomy* the upper third or half of the stomach is joined to the duodenum or small intestine (*gastroenterostomy*): an operation usually carried out in severe cases of *peptic ulcers. After gastrectomy capacity for food is reduced, sometimes leading to weight loss. Other complications of gastrectomy include *dumping syndrome, anaemia, and *malabsorption.

gastric *adj.* relating to or affecting the stomach.

gastric glands tubular glands that lie in the mucous membrane of the stomach wall. There are three varieties: the *cardiac*, *fundic* (*oxyntic*), and *pyloric glands*, and they secrete *gastric juice.

gastric juice the liquid secreted by the *gastric glands of the stomach. Its main digestive constituents are hydrochloric acid, mucin, *rennin, and pepsinogen. The acid acts on pepsinogen to produce *pepsin, which functions best in an acid medium. The acidity of the stomach contents also kills unwanted bacteria and other organisms that have been ingested with the food. Gastric juice also contains *intrinsic factor, which is necessary for the absorption of vitamin B_{12}.

gastric ulcer an ulcer in the stomach, caused by the action of acid, pepsin, and bile on the stomach lining (mucosa). The output of stomach acid is not usually increased. Symptoms include vomiting and pain in the upper abdomen soon after eating, and such complications as

是將食道與十二指腸吻合，用於胃癌，偶爾用於佐-埃氏綜合徵的治療。部分胃切除術是將上 1/3 或 1/2 的胃與十二指腸或小腸吻合，用於治療嚴重的消化道潰瘍。胃切除術後，食物容量將減少，有時會導致體重減輕。其他胃切除術後的併發症包括傾倒綜合徵、貧血及吸收障礙。

胃的 與胃有關或影響胃的。

胃腺 胃黏膜上的管狀腺。胃腺分三種：賁門腺、胃底腺（胃酸腺）和幽門腺，它們分泌胃液。

胃液 胃腺分泌的液體。其主要的具有消化功能的成分有鹽酸、黏蛋白、凝乳酶和胃蛋白酶原。鹽酸作用於胃蛋白酶原使之轉化成胃蛋白酶，這種酶在酸性環境中功能最強。胃內的酸性物質也能殺死隨食物攝入的有害細菌或其他微生物。胃液還含有為吸收維生素 B_{12} 所必需的內因子。

胃潰瘍 胃部的潰瘍。由於胃酸、胃蛋白酶和膽汁作用於胃黏膜所致。胃酸的分泌量不一定增加。胃潰瘍的症狀包括進食後不久即發生嘔吐和上腹部疼痛。可發生出血、穿孔或由於瘢痕形成所致的梗阻等併發

bleeding (see also haematemesis), *perforation, and obstruction due to scarring may occur. Symptoms are relieved by antacid medicines, but most ulcers heal if treated by an *antisecretory drug. Surgery may be required if the ulcer fails to heal. Since stomach cancer may mimic a gastric ulcer, all gastric ulcers should be examined by a *gastroscope to aid in their differentiation.

症。服用抗酸藥物可使症狀緩解，但如用抑制分泌藥物治療，多數潰瘍能愈合。如潰瘍不愈，則需手術治療。由於胃癌的症狀與胃潰瘍極相似，因此所有胃潰瘍患者都應做胃鏡檢查，以資鑒別。

gastrin n. a hormone produced in the mucous membrane of the pyloric region of the stomach (see G-cell). Its secretion is stimulated by the presence of food. It is circulated in the blood to the rest of the stomach, where it stimulates the production of *gastric juice.

胃泌素，促胃液素 胃幽門區黏膜產生的一種激素（參閱 G-cell）。此激素受食物的刺激而分泌，通過血液循環至胃的其餘部分，刺激胃液的產生。

gastrinoma n. a rare tumour that secretes excess amounts of the hormone gastrin, causing the *Zollinger-Ellison syndrome. Such tumours most frequently occur in the pancreas; about half of them are malignant.

胃泌素瘤 一種罕見腫瘤，分泌過量胃泌素，引起佐-埃氏綜合徵。此類腫瘤最常發生於胰腺，大約一半是惡性的。

gastritis n. inflammation of the lining (mucosa) of the stomach. Acute gastritis is caused by ingesting excess alcohol or other irritating or corrosive substances, resulting in vomiting. Chronic gastritis is associated with smoking and chronic alcoholism and may be caused by bile entering the stomach from the duodenum. Many cases are caused by the baterium *Helicobacter pylori. It has no definite symptoms, but the patient is liable to develop gastric ulcers. Atrophic gastritis, in which the stomach lining is atrophied, may succeed chronic gastritis but may occur spontaneously as an *autoimmune disease.

胃炎 胃黏膜的炎症。急性胃炎是由於飲酒過多或攝入其他刺激性或腐蝕性物質所致，可引起嘔吐。慢性胃炎與吸烟和慢性酒精中毒有關，可能由膽汁從十二指腸返流於胃內引起。許多病例由幽門螺桿菌所致。慢性胃炎缺乏特異性症狀，但易發展為胃潰瘍。萎縮性胃炎的胃黏膜的萎縮性改變，可能是慢性胃炎繼發的，但可能是一種特發的自體免疫性疾病。

gastrocele n. a *hernia of the stomach.

胃膨出 胃疝。

gastrocnemius *n.* a muscle that forms the greater part of the calf of the leg (see illustration). It flexes the knee and foot (so that the toes point downwards).

腓腸肌　一塊佔有大部分小腿肚子的肌肉（見圖）腓腸肌使膝和足彎曲（致使腳趾向下）。

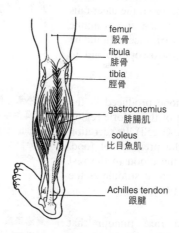

femur
股骨

fibula
腓骨

tibia
脛骨

gastrocnemius
腓腸肌

soleus
比目魚肌

Achilles tendon
跟腱

Gastrocnemius and soleus muscles
腓腸肌和比目魚肌

gastrocolic reflex a wave of peristalsis produced in the colon by introducing food into a fasting stomach.

胃結腸反射　空腹進食時引起的結腸蠕動波。

gastroduodenoscope *n. see* duodeno-scope, gastroscope.

胃十二指腸鏡　參閱 duodeno-scope，gastroscope。

gastroduodenoscopy *n.* the technique of viewing the inside of the stomach and duodenum with an endoscope. *See also* duodenoscope.

胃十二指腸鏡檢查　用內窺鏡窺探胃和十二指腸內部的技術。參閱 duodenoscope。

gastroduodenostomy *n.* a surgical operation in which the *duodenum (usually the third or fourth part) is joined to an opening made in the stomach in order to bypass an obstruction (such as *pyloric stenosis) or to facilitate the exit of food from the stomach after vago-tomy. *See also* duodenostomy.

胃十二指腸吻合術　在十二指腸（通常在 1/3 或 1/4 處）與胃之間造一通道的手術。此手術使胃梗阻（如幽門梗阻）有旁道相通，或者便於施行迷走神經切斷術後胃內食物的排空。參閱 duodenostomy。

gastroenteritis *n.* inflammation of the stomach and intestine. It is usually due to acute infection by viruses or bacteria or to food-poisoning toxins and causes vomiting and diarrhoea. The illness usually lasts 3–5 days. Fluid loss is sometimes severe, especially in infants, and intravenous fluid replacement may be necessary.

胃腸炎　胃和腸的炎症。常由於細菌或病毒的急性感染或食物中毒所致，引起嘔吐和腹瀉。病程通常為 3~5 天。有時體液喪失嚴重，尤其在嬰兒，可能需要靜脈補液。

gastroenterology *n.* the study of gastrointestinal disease, which includes disease of any part of the digestive tract and also of the liver, biliary tract, and pancreas.

胃腸病學　研究胃腸疾病的學科，包括消化道任何部位的疾病，也包括肝、膽道和胰的疾病。

gastroenterostomy *n.* a surgical operation in which the small intestine is joined to an opening made in the stomach. The usual technique is *gastroduodenostomy.

胃腸吻合術　在小腸與胃之間造一通道的手術。通常做的是胃十二指腸吻合術。

gastroileac reflex the relaxation of the *ileocaecal valve caused by the presence of food in the stomach.

胃迴腸反射　由胃中存在的食物引起的迴盲瓣開放。

gastrojejunostomy *n.* a surgical operation in which the *jejunum is joined to an opening made in the stomach. This is done in preference to *gastroduodenostomy if the latter operation is technically difficult or in special operations to avoid a backflow of bile into the stomach.

胃空腸吻合術　在空腸與胃之間造一通道的手術。如果施行胃十二指腸手術在技術上有困難，或者要避免手術後膽汁返流，則以施行胃空腸吻合術為好。

gastrolith *n.* a stone in the stomach, which usually builds up around a *bezoar.

胃結石　胃內的石塊，通常圍繞果核等異物形成胃腸結石。

gastro-oesophageal reflux a condition in which the stomach contents reflux into the oesophagus because of permanent or intermittent impairment of the usual mechanisms preventing this. It may give rise to *oesophagitis.

胃-食管返流　一種胃內食物返流進食管的疾病，由於阻止此病發生的生理機制永久性或間隙性損傷所致，可導致食管炎。

gastro-oesophageal reflux disease (GORD) the syndrome caused by abnormal gastro-oesophageal reflux, which includes symptoms of *heartburn, regurgitation, and *odynophagia, in which *oesophagitis may be present.

胃-食管返流病　由異常的胃-食管返流引起的綜合徵，包括胃灼熱，反胃和食管炎可能存在的吞咽痛等症狀。

gastro-oesophagostomy *n.* a surgical operation in which the *oesophagus (gullet) is joined to the stomach, bypassing the natural junction when this is obstructed by *achalasia, *stricture (narrowing) of the oesophagus, or cancer. This operation is rarely performed, because gastric juices entering the oesophagus through the artificial junction cause inflammation and stricture.

胃食管吻合術　食管和胃管之間繞過自然連接處相連接的手術。施行於當食管由於賁門失弛緩症、食管狹窄或食管癌而阻塞時，此手術已較少施行，因為胃液會通過人工連接處進入食管，引起炎症和狹窄。

gastropexy *n.* surgical attachment of the stomach to the abdominal wall.

胃固定術　將胃附着於腹壁的手術。

gastroplasty *n.* surgical alteration of the shape of the stomach without removal of any part. The term was originally used for correction of an acquired deformity, e.g. narrowing due to a peptic ulcer, but has more recently been applied to techniques for reducing the size of the stomach in the treatment of morbid obesity, e.g. vertical banded gastroplasty.

胃成形術　不切除任何胃部而改變胃形狀的手術。此術語起先用來指後天畸形，如由於消化性潰瘍引起的狹窄。但最近被用來指在治療病態肥胖症所用的減小胃體積的手術（如垂直綁紮胃成形術）。

gastroptosis *n.* a condition in which the stomach hangs low in the abdomen. Although the diagnosis was once used to explain various abdominal complaints, it is now known that the stomach may assume various anatomical positions without causing any symptoms.

胃下垂　胃向下腹移位。儘管胃下垂的診斷曾用於解釋種種腹部病痛，但現在認為胃可以有不同的解剖位置，而不引起任何症狀。

gastroschisis *n.* a congenital defect in the abdominal wall, which fails to close to the right of a normal umbilical cord. Gut prolapses through the defect and has no covering. Treatment is surgical.

腹裂（畸形）　腹壁的先天性缺損，在正常臍帶的右側不能閉合。內臟經過缺損處脫垂，無覆蓋。治療需外科手術。

gastroscope *n.* an illuminated optical instrument used to inspect the interior of the stomach. For many years these were rigid or semirigid instruments affording only limited views, but modern fully flexible instruments, which transmit the image through a fibreoptic bundle or by a tiny video camera, allow all areas of the stomach to be seen and photographed and specimens taken for microscopic examination. Therapeutic procedures (e.g. to arrest haemorrhage, remove a polyp, or produce a *gastrostomy) may be performed. As the same instruments can usually be introduced into the duodenum they are also known as *gastroduodenoscopes* or *oesophagogastroduodenoscopes*. **–gastroscopy** *n.*

胃鏡 一種用於檢查胃內部的光學照明器械。多年來採用的胃鏡管是硬質的或半硬質的，只能用以看到有限的胃區，而現代使用十分柔軟的光學纖維管，可以看到胃的各個部分，並可攝影和採取標本做顯微鏡檢查。可施行治療方法（如阻止出血、切除息肉或者進行胃造口術）。因此鏡亦可用以檢查十二指腸，故也稱為胃十二指腸鏡或食管胃十二指腸鏡。

gastrostaxis *n.* an obsolete term for *haematemesis (bleeding from the stomach).

胃滲血 嘔血的廢用詞（胃出血）。

gastrostomy *n.* a surgical procedure in which an opening is made into the stomach from the outside. It is usually performed to allow food and fluid to be poured directly into the stomach when swallowing is impossible because of disease or obstruction of the oesophagus. Sometimes it is used temporarily after operations on the oesophagus, until healing has occurred. Formerly a gastrostomy was always performed surgically, but it can now be done using an *endoscope (*percutaneous endoscopic gastrostomy*).

胃造口術 在胃與腹壁間造一瘻管至體外的手術。當因食管疾患或阻塞而不能吞咽時，常施行此手術以便把食物直接送入胃中。有時在施行食管手術後暫時用此方法，直至食管愈合為止。以前，胃造口術總是施行外科手術，但現在可通過內窺鏡進行（經皮內窺鏡胃造口術）。

gastrotomy *n.* a procedure during abdominal surgery in which the stomach is opened, usually to allow inspection of the interior (e.g. to find a point of bleeding), to remove a foreign body, or to allow the oesophagus to be approached

胃切口術 切開胃壁的手術，常用於檢查胃內部（尋找出血點），或去除胃內異物，或從下端接近食管（例如，穿過腫瘤狹窄處將導管拉下來）。

from below (e.g. to pull down a tube through a constricting growth).

gastrula *n.* an early stage in the development of many animal embryos. It consists of a double-layered ball of cells formed by invagination and movement of cells in the preceding single-layered stage (blastula) in the process of *gastrulation*. It contains a central cavity, the *archenteron, which opens through the *blastopore* to the outside. True gastrulation only occurs in the embryos of amphibians and certain fish, but a similar process occurs in the embryonic disc in other vertebrates, including man.

原腸胚 為許多動物胚胎發育中的早期階段。在原腸胚胎形成的過程中，由單層的囊胚泡內陷和移動而形成兩層的細胞球。原腸胚含有一個中心腔，即原腸，開口於胚孔。真性原腸胚形成僅發生於兩棲類和某些魚類的胚胎，但其他脊椎動物（包括人類）的胚盤形成，也有類似的過程。

Gaucher's disease a genetically determined (autosomal *recessive) disease resulting from the deposition of glucocerebrosides (*see* cerebroside) in the brain and other tissues (especially bone). It causes mental retardation, abnormal limb posture and spasticity, and difficulty with swallowing. Carrier detection and *prenatal diagnosis are possible; enzyme replacement therapy is used in treatment.

戈歇病 一遺傳確定（常染色體缺陷性）疾病，由腦內和其他組織（尤指骨）內葡萄糖腦苷脂（參閱 cerebroside）分解所致。可引起智力發育遲緩、異常肢體姿勢和痙攣狀態及吞咽困難。可作負荷試驗和產前診斷。治療用酶替代療法。

gauss *n.* a unit of magnetic flux density equal to 1 maxwell per square centimetre. 1 gauss = 10^{-4} tesla.

高斯 磁場強度單位。每個單位等於每平方厘米 1 麥克斯威。1 高斯 = 10^{-4} 特斯拉。

Gaussian distribution *see* frequency distribution, significance.

高斯分布 參閱 frequency distribution，significance。

gauze *n.* thin open-woven material used in several layers for the preparation of dressings and swabs.

紗布 細薄的稀疏織品，用幾層紗布可製成敷料或拭子。

gavage *n.* forced feeding: any means used to get an unwilling or incapacitated patient to take in food by mouth, especially via a stomach tube.

管飼法 強制餵養的方法：使不願意或無能力進食的病人從口進食，尤指用胃管餵飼。

G-cell *n.* any of the cells of the mucous membrane of the stomach that are responsible for the production of *gastrin. They occur mainly in the gastric *antrum. Increased production of G-cells is associated with duodenal ulcer and the *Zollinger-Ellison syndrome: gastrin acts to increase the production of acid by the oxyntic (parietal) cells of the gastric glands.

G細胞 能產生胃泌素的任何胃黏膜細胞。主要分布於幽門竇。G 細胞生成增加與十二指腸潰瘍和佐-埃氏綜合徵有關：胃泌激素作用通過胃腺泌酸細胞增加酸的生成。

gel *n.* a colloidal suspension that has set to form a jelly. Some insoluble drugs are administered in the form of gels.

凝膠 一種混懸膠體，放置後形成膠凍。有些不溶解的藥物常採用凝膠劑型。

gelatin *n.* a jelly-like substance formed when tendons, ligaments, etc. containing *collagen (a protein) are boiled in water. Gelatin has been used in medicine as a source of protein in the treatment of malnutrition, in pharmacy for the manufacture of capsules and suppositories, and in bacteriology for preparing culture media.

明膠 一種膠凍狀物質，是當肌腱、韌帶等含有膠原（一種蛋白質）的物質在水中煮沸後形成的。明膠在醫學中作為蛋白質的一種來源，一直用以治療營養不良；在製藥中用以製造膠囊和栓劑；在細菌學中用以配製培養基。

gemeprost *n.* a *prostaglandin drug, administered as a vaginal pessary to terminate pregnancy. It causes powerful contractions of the uterus at any stage of pregnancy. Trade name: **Cervagem**.

吉美前列素 一種前列腺素藥，用作陰道栓劑終止妊娠。可在懷孕的任何時期引起強有力的宮縮。商品名：Cervagem。

gemfibrozil *n.* a drug used to lower very low-density *lipoproteins in patients with high *triglyceride serum levels who have not responded to diet, weight reduction, or exercise. It is administered by mouth; side-effects include diarrhoea, abdominal pain, and nausea and vomiting. Trade name: **Lopid**.

吉非貝齊 用以降低高脂血症患者的極低密度脂蛋白水平的藥物。這些患者血中的高水平甘油三酯用節食、減輕體重及鍛煉的方法難以下降。用以口服，產生的副作用包括腹瀉、腹痛、惡心和嘔吐。商品名：Lopid。

gemmule *n.* one of the minute spines or surface extensions of a *dendrite, through which contact is made with another neurone at a *synapse.

樹突棘 神經細胞樹突表面的一種細刺狀突起或棘，通過樹突棘與另一個神經元的突觸相接觸。

gene *n.* the basic unit of genetic material, which is carried at a particular place on a *chromosome. Originally it was regarded as the unit of inheritance and mutation but is now usually defined as a sequence of *DNA or *RNA that acts as the unit controlling the formation of a single polypeptide chain (*see* cistron). In diploid organisms, including man, genes occur as pairs of *alleles. Various kinds of gene have been discovered: *structural genes* determine the biochemical makeup of the proteins; *regulator genes* control the rate of protein production (*see* operon). *Architectural genes* are responsible for the integration of the protein into the structure of the cell, and *temporal genes* control the time and place of action of the other genes and largely control the *differentiation of the cells and tissues of the body.

gene clone *see* clone.

general dental services a part of the NHS dental service. Dentists are included on the dental list of the appropriate *Family Health Services Authority and are independent contractors. They are paid partly by capitation (per head) and partly by item of service. They are entirely responsible for the financial management of their own practices.

generalized anxiety disorder a state of inappropriate and sometimes severe anxiety, without adequate cause, that lasts for at least six months. It affects about 2% of the population, women twice as often as men, and often develops in early adult life. It can, however, start at any age. There is a hereditary tendency to develop the disorder and about 25% of immediate relatives of sufferers are also affected. The disorder is thought

基因 遺傳物質的基本單位，位於染色體的特定位置上。最初基因被認為是遺傳和突變的生物單位，而現在基因常被看作是一種脫氧核糖核酸或核糖核酸的順序，是控制一條多肽單鏈形成的功能單位（參閱 cistron）。在二倍體的生物，包括人類，基因是以成對的等位基因出現的。發現有很多種的基因：結構基因，決定蛋白質的生物化學組成；調節基因，控制蛋白質生成的速度（參閱 operon）。構建基因，負責把蛋白質結合於細胞結構中去；時間基因，控制其他基因作用的時間和地點，在很大程度上控制身體的細胞和組織的分化。

基因克隆 參閱 clone。

普通牙醫服務所 國民保健服務制牙醫服務部的一部分。牙醫在所屬的家庭保健服務管理局牙醫花名冊上登記，是單獨與患者簽訂合同的。他們按所服務的項目支酬，與病人簽訂的合同僅是一個療程。他們完全自負盈虧。

泛發性焦慮症 不正常狀態，有時嚴重焦慮，無確定原因，至少持續六個月。2% 的患病率，女性為男性的 2 倍。並通常發生在成人早期階段。但是，這種紊亂可發生在任何年齡段，有遺傳趨向，患者直系親屬中大約有 25% 也受影響。此病被認為是由神經介質，如大腦前葉或邊緣系統的腎上腺素或 γ-氨基丁酸，功能

to be caused by a disturbance of the functions of neurotransmitters, such as adrenaline or GABA, in the frontal lobes or the *limbic system of the brain. Symptoms include shakiness, *bruxism, restlessness, fatigability, breathlessness, palpitations, sweating, clammy hands, dry mouth, lightheadedness, diarrhoea, flushing, and *globus hystericus. Treatment is with beta blockers, antihistamines, tricyclic antidepressants, and MAO inhibitors.

General Manager *see* National Health Service.

general paralysis of the insane (GPI) a late consequence of syphilitic infection. The symptoms are those of a *dementia and spastic weakness of the limbs. Deafness, epilepsy, and *dysarthria (defective pronunciation) may occur. The infecting organism can be detected in the brain cells and tests for syphilis in blood and cerebrospinal fluid are usually positive. When the symptoms are combined with those of *tabes dorsalis, the resulting condition is called *tabo-paresis*. Vigorous treatment with procaine penicillin is required, but recovery is likely to be limited.

general practitioner (GP) a doctor (also known as a *family doctor* or *family practitioner*) who is the main agent of *primary health care, through whom patients make first contact with health services for a new episode of illness or fresh developments of chronic diseases. Advice and treatment are provided for those who do not require the expertise of a *consultant or other specialist services of hospitals (*see* secondary health care). In the British *National Health Service patients on the practice list of a GP

障礙所致。症狀包括發抖、磨牙症、不寧、易疲勞、氣喘、心悸、出汗、手冷濕、口乾、頭暈、腹瀉、臉紅和癔病球。治療用 β-受體阻滯劑、抗組胺劑、三環抗抑制藥和單胺氧化酶抑制劑。

總幹事 參閱 National Health Sevice。

麻痺性痴呆 梅毒感染的晚期結果。具有痴呆病人症狀並且肢體強直性無力。可能出現耳聾、癲癇、發音困難。腦細胞中能檢出梅毒螺旋體，血液和腦脊液中梅毒試驗常呈陽性。當症狀伴有脊髓癆症時，稱為脊髓癆性麻痺性痴呆。需用大劑量的普魯卡因青黴素治療，但治療效果欠佳。

全科醫師 承擔初級衛生保健工作的主要醫師，若病人初患新病或其慢性病有新的變化，病人首先通過他們與衛生保健機構接觸。病人若不需要高級醫師會診或轉送其他醫院專科治療（參閱 secondary health care），則由全科醫師為病人提供建議和治療。在英國參加國民保健服務制的病人，接受全科醫師的保健服務不需支付費用。全科醫師除了為參加國民保健服務制的病人服務外，可

receive care without payment on an open-access basis. A practitioner may have private patients in addition to NHS patients; a few have exclusively private practices. No NHS patient may be charged for an NHS prescription by the GP (except in a *dispensing practice, where a statutory charge is made for the medication); similarly a medical certificate on which to base a claim for *social security payment must be given without charge. Conversely, no private patient may receive an NHS prescription. Two or more practitioners may form a partnership sharing fees and work loads, including cross-cover for each other's NHS patients. When they share premises, secretarial help, and other resources this constitutes a *group practice*; the premises from which they operate may be privately owned or may be a publicly owned *health centre. Remuneration of GPs is based on a quarterly capitation fee for each registered patient (higher for those over 65 years of age) regardless of the number of consultations; however, additional claims can be made for a few services (e.g. antenatal care and household calls during sleeping hours). A practice with at least 7000 patients may apply to become a *fundholder*, with responsibility for managing its own NHS budget, including the power to purchase the services it requires for its own patients from whichever hospital or other health-care provider gives the best service. *See also* independent contract.

以有自己的病人，少數全科醫師只私人開業。參加國民保健服務制的病人不需要負擔國民保健服務制處方或醫療證明的費用；相反，沒有參加國民保健服務制的病人則不能獲取國民保健服務制的處方。兩個或兩個以上的全科醫師可結成同伴共同做事、分享收入，並可交換診治各自的國民保健服務制的病人。與他們有共同的房產、辦事人員和其他資源時，即組成一個聯合診所，其辦公的房產可以是私人擁有的，也可以是公有的一衛生保健中心。全科醫師的報酬來自每個登記參加國民保健服務制的病人每季度交付的保健稅（65歲以上的病人交付較多），而與病人求治的次數無關。然而，有些服務需收額外的費用（如產前衛生保健服務和夜間出診）。擁有至少7000病人的行醫者可申請成為公債持有人，具有負責管理自己的國民保健服務制預算，包括有權利從任何能提供最好服務的醫院或其他衛生保健提供者那裏獲得其病人所需要的服務。參閱independent contract。

generic *adj.* **1.** denoting a drug name that is not protected by a trademark. **2.** of or relating to a *genus.

屬的 **(1)** 指不受商標所保護的藥品名。**(2)** 屬的或有關屬的。

-genesis *suffix denoting* origin or development. Example: *spermatogenesis* (development of spermatozoa).

〔後綴〕起源，發生 例如：精子發生。

gene therapy treatment directed to curing genetic disease by introducing normal genes into patients to overcome the effects of defective genes, using techniques of *genetic engineering. The most radical approach would be to do this at a very early stage in the embryo, so that the new gene would be incorporated into the germ cells (ova and sperm) and would therefore be inheritable. However, this approach is not considered to be either safe or ethical, because the consequences would affect all descendants of the patient, and it is not being pursued. In *somatic cell gene therapy* the healthy gene is inserted into *somatic cells (such as the *stem cells of the bone marrow) that give rise to other cells. All the surviving descendants of these modified cells will then be normal and, if present in sufficient numbers, the condition will be cured (the defective gene will, however, still be present in the germ cells).

At present, gene therapy is most feasible for treating disorders caused by a defect in a single recessive gene, so that the deficiency can be overcome by the introduction of a normal allele (therapy for disorders caused by dominant genes (e.g. Huntington's disease) would require the modification or replacement of the defective allele as its effect is expressed in the presence of a normal allele). Examples of such recessive disorders include *adenosine deaminase (ADA) deficiency and *cystic fibrosis. Gene therapy trials for the former condition have already begun: lymphocyte stem cells are isolated from the patient, using *monoclonal antibodies, and incubated with *retroviruses that have been genetically engineered to contain the normal ADA gene (*see* vector). This gene thus becomes integrated into the

基因治療 利用基因工程的方法，將正常基因導入因基因異常而發病的病人體內，以補償異常基因的功能。最根本的方法是在胚胎很早期實行，這樣，新的基因可與生殖細胞（卵和精子）融合而能被遺傳。然而，這種方法並不被認為是安全的或人道的，因為這將導致病人的後代全患病，故而不被採用。在體細胞基因治療中，健康基因被插入到體細胞中（如骨髓中的幹細胞）。這些被改造的細胞的所有存活的子代細胞將全部正常，如果其數量足夠，病態將得到治療（但異常基因仍存在於胚細胞中）。

目前，在原基因隱性疾病中的治療中，這種方法最可行。因為導入的正常等位基因可以補償基因引起的缺陷。（顯性基因起作用，如亨廷頓病）正常等位基因將修改或替代有缺陷的等位基因。例如隱性遺傳疾病包括腺苷脫氨酶（ADA）、缺乏和囊性纖維變性。基因治療在這些疾病中的嘗試已經進行：從病人體內分離出淋巴幹細胞，用單克隆抗體和被基因工程改造的含有正常 ADA 基因（參閱 vector）的逆轉錄病毒共同孵育，這樣，正常 ADA 基因將插入到幹細胞中去，然後再把這種幹細胞重新導入病人骨髓中，病人將產生正常的淋巴細胞。臨床上囊性纖維變性的基因治療的嘗試是利用脂質體通過一個吸管導入患者的肺部。也嘗試對有些腫瘤的基因治療（如黑素瘤和乳腺瘤），目的是導入腫瘤組織一些基因，這些基因可指導生成能特定殺滅腫瘤細胞的物質。

stem cells, which – when returned to the patient's bone marrow – can then produce normal lymphocytes. Clinical trials for the gene therapy of cystic fibrosis involve using *liposomes to introduce the normal gene into the lungs of sufferers via an inhaler. Gene therapy for certain types of cancer (e.g. melanoma and breast cancer) is also being tested. Here the approach is aimed at introducing into the cancerous tissue genes that direct the production of substances that specifically destroy the tumour cells.

genetic code the information carried by *DNA and *messenger RNA that determines the sequence of amino acids in every protein and thereby controls the nature of all proteins made by the cell. The genetic code is expressed by the sequence of *nucleotide bases in the nucleic acid molecule, a unit of three consecutive bases (a *codon*) coding for each amino acid. The code is translated into protein at the ribosomes (*see* transcription, translation). Any changes in the genetic code result in the insertion of incorrect amino acids in a protein chain, giving a *mutation.

遺傳密碼　由脫氧核糖核酸和信使核糖核酸傳遞的遺傳信息，決定每個蛋白質中氨基酸順序，控制細胞所有蛋白質的性能。遺傳密碼是由核酸分子中的核苷酸鹼基的順序來表示的，每個氨基酸的密碼都是連續的三個核苷酸（密碼子）的組合。在核糖體上密碼被翻譯到蛋白質（參閱 transcription，translation）。遺傳密碼的改變導致蛋白質鏈內插入錯誤的氨基酸，從而引起突變。

genetic counselling the procedure by which patients and their families are given advice about the nature and consequences of inherited disorders, the possibility of becoming affected or having affected children, and the various options that are available to them for the prevention, diagnosis, and management of such conditions. Genetic counselling should be available at prenatal and postnatal clinics, and also through family planning clinics.

遺傳咨詢　給病人及其家屬提供遺傳病的本質和後果及本人患病或孩子患病的可能性，提供預防、診斷和控制這種疾病的各種選擇。產前、產後及計劃生育都需遺傳咨詢。

genetic drift the tendency for variations to occur in the genetic composition of

遺傳漂變　遺傳成分的隨機變異，這種變異傾向出現在與外

small isolated inbreeding populations by chance. Such populations become genetically rather different from the original population from which they were derived.

界隔離的近親婚配的小羣體中，這種羣體在遺傳學上與他們原先的羣體變得頗為不同。

genetic engineering (recombinant DNA technology) the techniques involved in altering the characteristics of an organism by inserting genes from another organism into its DNA. This altered DNA (known as *recombinant DNA*) is usually produced by isolating foreign genes, often by the use of *restriction enzymes, and inserting them into bacterial DNA, often using viruses as *vectors. Once inserted, the foreign gene may use the cell machinery of its host to synthesize the protein that it originally coded for in the organism it was derived from. For example, the human genes for *insulin, *interferon, and *growth hormone production have been incorporated into bacterial DNA and such genetically engineered bacteria are used in the commercial production of these substances. Some other applications of genetic engineering include DNA analysis, the production of *monoclonal antibodies, and – more recently – *gene therapy.

基因工程（重組 DNA 技術） 改變一生物特徵的技術，是通過將另一生物的基因插入其 DNA 中進行的。已經改變的 DNA（稱做重組 DNA）通常是通過分離外源基因產生的；分離外源基因經常通過使用限制性內切酶，並將其插入細菌 DNA 中，常常使用病毒作為載體。一旦插入，外源基因可能使用宿主的細胞機制合成其自身編碼的蛋白質。例如，負責生產胰島素、干擾素和生長激素的人體基因已被納入到細菌 DNA 中，這類以遺傳工程改造的菌已用於商品化生產。基因工程的其他應用包括 DNA 分析、單克隆抗體的生產以及最近的基因療法。

genetics *n.* the science of inheritance. It attempts to explain the differences and similarities between related organisms and the ways in which characters are passed from parents to their offspring. *Human* and *medical genetics* are concerned with the study of inherited diseases. *See also* cytogenetics, Mendel's laws.

遺傳學 遺傳的科學。它致力於闡明有關的生物之間的不同點和相似點，以及雙親的特徵傳給後代的各種方式，人類遺傳學和醫學遺傳學主要研究遺傳性疾病。參閱 cytogenetics，Mendel's laws。

genetic screening *screening tests to discover individuals whose *genotypes are associated with specific diseases (*see*

基因篩查 發現基因型與特定疾病有關的人的篩查（參閱 mouthwash test）。這類人以後

also mouthwash test). Such individuals may later develop the disease itself or pass it on to their children (*see* carrier). The recent use of genetic screening to diagnose the sex of the fetus so that the parents may 'choose' the sex of their children has caused considerable controversy.

可能自己患此病或將其遺傳給他們的子女（參閱 carrier）。最近使用基因篩查來診斷胎兒的性別以便父母能選擇他們的子女的性別，這種方法已引起了相當大的爭議。

geni- (genio-) *prefix denoting* the chin.

〔前綴〕頦

-genic *suffix denoting* **1.** producing. **2.** produced by.

〔後綴〕(1) 產生的 (2) 被產生的

genicular *adj.* relating to the knee joint: applied to arteries that supply the knee.

膝的　有關膝關節的。以動脈為例：供應膝的動脈。

geniculum *n.* a sharp bend in an anatomical structure, such as the bend in the facial nerve in the medial wall of the middle ear.

膝　明顯彎曲的解剖學結構，比如中耳內側壁的面神經的膝狀神經節。

genion *n.* (in *craniometry) the tip of the protuberance of the chin.

頦尖　（顱測量法）頦的隆凸尖端。

genioplasty *n.* an operation performed in plastic surgery to alter the size and shape of the chin. This can be built up with grafted bone, cartilage, or artificial material.

頦成形術　一種整形外科手術，是用移植的骨、軟骨或人工材料重建面頰骨的。

genital *adj.* relating to the reproductive organs or to reproduction.

生殖的　有關生殖器的或有關生殖的。

genital herpes *see* herpes.

生殖器疱疹　參閱 herpes。

genitalia *pl. n.* the reproductive organs of either the male or the female. However, the term is usually used in reference to the external parts of the reproductive system. *See also* vulva.

生殖器　男性或女性的生殖器官，但是此術語常指外生殖器系統。參閱 vulva。

genito- *prefix denoting* the reproductive organs. Examples: *genitoplasty* (plastic surgery of); *genitourinary* (relating

〔前綴〕生殖器　例如：生殖器成形術，泌尿生殖的。

to the reproductive and excretory systems).

genitourinary medicine the medical specialty concerned with the study and treatment of *sexually transmitted diseases.

泌尿生殖學　專門從事有關性傳播疾病的研究及治療的醫學。

genogram *n*. a technique of family *psychotherapy, in which a family tree and a family history of a particular psychological disorder are constructed in view of the whole family to help them understand each other better.

遺傳圖　一種家庭心理治療採用的方法，把家譜和家庭史編出來，以便幫助所有家庭成員更好地相互了解。

genome *n*. the total genetic material of an organism, comprising the genes contained in its chromosomes; sometimes the term is used for the basic *haploid set of chromosomes of an organism. The human genome comprises 23 pairs of chromosomes (*see* Human Genome Project).

基因組　一個生物體所有的遺傳物質，位於染色體上。有時指單倍體的染色體，人類共有 23 對染色體（參閱 Human Genome Project）。

genotype *n*. **1.** the genetic constitution of an individual or group, as determined by the particular set of genes it possesses. **2.** the genetic information carried by a pair of alleles, which determines a particular characteristic. **3.** a gene or pattern of genes the precise details of which are defined. *Compare* phenotype.

(1) 遺傳型　個體或羣體的遺傳組成，是由其攜帶的基因組決定。(2) 基因型　一對等位基因傳遞的遺傳信息，決定一種獨特的特徵。(3) 基因類型　指其精確的細節已被定義的基因或基因類型。與 phenotype 對比。

gentamicin *n*. an *aminoglycoside antibiotic used to treat infections caused by a wide range of bacteria. It can be administered by injection or applied in a cream to the skin or in drops to the ears and eyes. Kidney and ear damage may occur at high doses. Trade names: **Cidomycin**, **Garamycin**, **Genticin**.

慶大黴素　一種治療感染的廣譜氨基糖苷類抗生素。可注射，或以乳膏用於皮膚，或製成滴耳劑，滴眼劑。大劑量用時，可能出現腎毒性和耳毒性。商品名：Cidomycin，Garamycin，Genticin。

gentian violet 1. a dye used for staining tissues and microorganisms for microscopical study. **2.** *see* methyl violet.

(1) 龍膽紫　一種染料，可染色組織和微生物用以顯微鏡觀察。(2) 甲紫　參閱 methyl violet。

genu *n.* **1.** the knee. **2.** any bent anatomical structure resembling the knee. **–genual** *adj.*

膝 **(1)** 膝蓋。**(2)** 任何類似膝狀彎曲的解剖學結構。

genus *n.* (*pl.* **genera**) a category used in the classification of animals and plants. A genus consists of several closely related and similar species; for example, the genus *Canis* includes the dog, wolf, and jackal.

屬 動、植物分類所用的類目。一個屬由一些密切相關和近似的物種組成；例如：犬屬包括狗、狼和豺。

genu valgum abnormal in-curving of the legs, resulting in excessive separation of the feet when the knees are in contact. *See* knock-knee.

膝外翻 大腿異常內曲，導致兩膝靠攏時兩腳過度分開。參閱 knock-knee。

genu varum abnormal outward curving of the legs, resulting in separation of the knees. *See* bow-legs.

膝內翻 大腿異常外曲，導致兩膝分開。參閱 bow-legs。

geo- *prefix denoting* the earth or soil.

〔前綴〕土、地

geophagia *n.* the eating of dirt. *See* pica.

食土癖 吃髒物。參閱 pica。

ger- (gero-, geront(o)-) *prefix denoting* old age.

〔前綴〕老年

geriatrics *n.* the branch of medicine concerned with the diagnosis and treatment of disorders that occur in old age and with the care of the aged. *See also* gerontology.

老年病學 醫學的一個分支。研究對老年期發生疾病的診斷和治療，以及老年人的衛生保健。參閱 gerontology。

germ *n.* any microorganism, especially one that causes disease. *See also* infection.

微生物 任何微小的生物，尤指致病的微生物。參閱 infection。

German measles a mild highly contagious virus infection, mainly of childhood, causing enlargement of lymph nodes in the neck and a widespread pink rash. The disease is spread by close contact with a patient. After an incubation period of 2–3 weeks a headache, sore throat, and slight fever develop,

風疹 一種症狀較輕但有高度傳染性的病毒性傳染病。主要見於兒童，引起頸部淋巴結腫大和廣泛的淺紅色皮疹。此病通過與患者密切接觸而傳播。經 2~3 周的潛伏期後出現頭痛、喉痛和輕微發熱，繼而出現頸部腫脹、疼痛以及淺紅色

followed by swelling and soreness of the neck and the eruption of a rash of minute pink spots, spreading from the face and neck to the rest of the body. The spots disappear within seven days but the patient remains infectious for a further 3–4 days. An infection usually confers immunity. As German measles can cause fetal malformations during early pregnancy, girls should be immunized against the disease before puberty. Most children now receive immunization via the *MMR vaccine in their second year. Medical name: **rubella**. *Compare* scarlet fever.

的細小斑點狀皮疹，從面頸部擴散至全身。皮疹在 7 天內消失，但患者在其後的 3~4 天內仍具傳染性。通常一次感染就可獲得免疫。由於在妊娠早期感染風疹可導致胎兒畸形，因而女孩在青春期前就應接受免疫以預防此病。現在大多數兒童在兩歲時通過 MMR 疫苗注射獲得免疫。醫學用語：風疹。與 scarlet fever 對比。

germ cell (gonocyte) any of the embryonic cells that have the potential to develop into spermatozoa or ova. The term is also applied to any of the cells undergoing gametogenesis and to the gametes themselves.

生殖細胞　任何能夠發育成為精子或卵子的胚胎細胞。此詞亦指任何經歷配子而形成的細胞或配子本身。

germicide *n.* an agent that destroys microorganisms, particularly those causing disease. *See* antibiotic, antifungal, antiseptic, disinfectant.

殺菌劑　一種消滅微生物的製劑，尤指消滅致病微生物的製劑。參閱 antibiotic，antifungal，antiseptic，disinfectant。

germinal *adj.* **1.** relating to the early developmental stages of an embryo or tissue. **2.** relating to a germ.

(1) 生發的　有關胚胎或組織早期發育的。**(2) 病菌的**　有關致病菌的。

germinal epithelium the epithelial covering of the ovary, which was formerly thought to be the site of formation of *oogonia. It is now thought that the oogonia persist in a dormant state from the prenatal period until required in reproductive life.

生殖上皮　覆蓋於卵巢的上皮。先前認為是卵原細胞生成的場所。現在認為卵原細胞自出生前直到育齡時長期處於休眠狀態。

germinal vesicle the nucleus of a mature *oocyte, prior to fertilization. It is considerably larger than the nucleus of other cells.

生發泡　成熟的卵母細胞受精前的細胞核。此核要比其他細胞的胞核大得多。

germ layer any of the three distinct types of tissue found in the very early stages of embryonic development (*see* ectoderm, endoderm, mesoderm). The germ layers can be traced throughout embryonic development as they differentiate to form the entire range of body tissues.

胚層　在胚胎發育最早期見到的三層分界清晰的組織中的任何一層（參閱 ectoderm，endoderm，mesoderm）。在整個胚胎發育期間能見到三個胚層分化形成機體各組織的全部過程。

germ plasm the substance postulated by 19th-century biologists (notably Weismann) to be transmitted via the gametes from one generation to the next and to give rise to the body cells.

胚質，種質　19世紀生物學家（尤其是魏斯曼）的假説認為，有一種通過生殖細胞代代相傳的種質。種質產生體細胞。

gerontology *n.* the study of the changes in the mind and body that accompany ageing and the problems associated with them.

老年學　研究老年人心理和身體改變及其相關問題的學科。

Gerstmann's syndrome a group of symptoms that represent a partial disintegration of the patient's recognition of his *body image. It consists of an inability to name the individual fingers, misidentification of the right and left sides of the body, and inability to write or make mathematical calculations (*see* acalculia, agraphia). It is caused by disease in the association area of the left parietal lobe of the brain.

格斯特曼綜合徵　病人對其身體某部分形象不能分辨的一組症狀。包括手指認識不能、左右失認、失寫、計算不能（參閱 acalculia，agraphia）。此綜合徵由大腦左側頂葉聯合區的病竈引起。

gestaltism *n.* a school of psychology that regards mental processes as wholes (*gestalts*) that cannot be broken down into constituent parts. From this was developed *gestalt therapy*, which aims at achieving a suitable gestalt within the patient that includes all facets of functioning.

完形心理學　一種心理學學説。認為整體（完形）的心理過程不能被細分為各個組成部分。由此學説而發展為完形心理療法，旨在使病人獲得一個適宜的、包括各方面功能活動的完形心態。

gestation *n.* the period during which a fertilized egg cell develops into a baby that is ready to be delivered. Gestation

妊娠　受精卵細胞發育成為即將出生的嬰兒的過程。人的妊娠期平均為266天（或者自末

averages 266 days in humans (or 280 days from the first day of the last menstrual period). *See also* pregnancy.

次月經的第一天算起為 280 天)。參閱 pregnancy。

gestodene *n.* a *progestogen used in oral contraceptives in combination with an oestrogen. Trade names: **Femodene**, **Minulet**.

孕二烯酮　一種孕激素藥，可與雌激素合用的口服避孕藥。商品名：Femodene，Minulet。

GFR *see* glomerular filtration rate.

腎小球濾過率　參閱 glomerular filtration rate。

Ghon's focus the lesion produced in the lung of a previously uninfected person by tubercle bacilli. It is a small focus of granulomatous inflammation, which may become visible on a chest X-ray if it grows large enough or if it calcifies. A Ghon's focus usually heals without further trouble, but in some patients tuberculosis spreads from it via the lymphatics, the air spaces, or the bloodstream.

岡氏病竈　一個先前未曾受過結核桿菌感染的人所受的肺部結核性損害。它是一個小的肉芽腫性炎症病竈。當其長得足夠大或者鈣化時，可在胸部 X 綫透視中見到。一個岡氏病竈通常愈合而無進一步病變，但在某些病人結核由此病竈經淋巴管、氣管或血流擴散開。

giant cell any large cell, such as a *megakaryocyte. Giant cells may have one or many nuclei.

巨細胞　任何巨大的細胞，如巨核細胞。巨細胞可有一個或多個細胞核。

giant-cell arteritis *see* arteritis.

巨細胞性動脈炎　參閱動脈炎。

Giardia *n.* a genus of parasitic pear-shaped protozoa inhabiting the small intestine of man. They have four pairs of *flagella, two nuclei, and two sucking discs used for attachment to the intestinal wall. *Giardia* is usually harmless but may occasionally cause diarrhoea (*see* giardiasis).

賈第蟲屬　寄生於人體小腸內的一種梨形原蟲屬。它們有四對鞭毛、兩個細胞核以及兩個用於吸附於腸壁的吸盤。賈第蟲屬通常不致病，但偶可引起腹瀉（參閱 giardiasis）。

giardiasis (lambliasis) *n.* a disease caused by the parasitic protozoan *Giardia lamblia* in the small intestine. Man becomes infected by eating food contaminated with cysts containing the

賈第蟲病　由寄生於小腸內的原蟲蘭伯賈第蟲所引起的一種疾病。人吃了染有此寄生蟲包囊的食物而感染。症狀包括腹瀉、惡心、腹痛、腹脹、並排

parasite. Symptoms include diarrhoea, nausea, bellyache, and flatulence, as well as the passage of pale fatty stools (steatorrhoea). Large numbers of the parasite may interfere with the absorption of food through the gut wall. The disease occurs throughout the world and is particularly common in children; it responds well to oral doses of quinacrine and *metronidazole.

出帶有脂肪的灰白色糞便（脂肪瀉）。大數量的寄生蟲可阻礙腸壁對食物的吸收。此病發生於世界各地，兒童中尤為常見；口服米帕林（阿的平）和甲硝唑（滅滴靈）治療有效。

gibbus (gibbosity) n. a sharply angled curvature of the backbone, resulting from collapse of a vertebra. Infection with tuberculosis was a common cause.

駝背 脊柱呈銳角形彎曲，由脊椎萎陷所致。結核感染為其常見病因。

Giemsa's stain a mixture of *methylene blue and *eosin, used for distinguishing different types of white blood cell and for detecting parasitic microorganisms in blood smears. It is one of the *Romanowsky stains.

吉姆薩染劑 一種亞甲藍和曙紅的混合液，用以區分白細胞的不同類型，以及檢驗血塗片中的寄生微生物。它是羅曼諾夫斯基染劑的一種。

GIFT see gamete intrafallopian transfer.

配子輸卵管內轉移 參閱 gamete intrafallopian transfer。

gigantism n. abnormal growth causing excessive height, most commonly due to oversecretion during childhood of *growth hormone (somatotrophin) by the pituitary gland. In eunuchoid gigantism the tall stature is due to delayed puberty, which results in continued growth of the long bones before their growing ends (epiphyses) fuse. See also acromegaly.

巨人症 身體異常生長而導致的過分高大，大多由於兒童期垂體分泌生長激素過多所致。在無睾性巨人症中，其高大體型是由於青春期延遲，導致長骨在其生長端（骺）融合前繼續生長。參閱 acromegaly。

Gilbert's syndrome familial unconjugated hyperbilirubinaemia: a condition due to an inherited congenital deficiency of the enzyme UDP glucuronyl transferase in the liver cells. Patients become mildly jaundiced, especially if they fast or have some minor infection. Occasionally

吉爾貝綜合徵 家庭性非結合型高膽紅素血症：是肝細胞中缺乏尿苷二磷酸葡萄糖醛酰轉移酶的一種先天性遺傳性疾患。病人有輕度黃疸，尤其在他們空腹或有輕度感染時。偶爾可出現輕微胃腸不適。小劑

they have mild abdominal discomfort. The jaundice can be diminished by small doses of phenobarbitone, which stimulates enzyme activity. The condition is harmless.

量苯巴比妥剌激酶的活力而使黃疸消失。本病預後良好。

Gilles de la Tourette syndrome (Tourette's syndrome) a condition of severe and multiple *tics, including vocal tics, grunts, and involuntary obscene speech (*coprolalia). The patient may also involuntarily repeat the words or imitate the actions of others (*see* palilalia). The condition usually starts in childhood and becomes chronic; the causes are unknown. Drug treatment (for example, with *pimozide) is sometimes successful.

圖雷特綜合徵 一種嚴重的多發性抽搐疾患，包括爆發性發聲、喉鳴和不隨意的猥褻言語（穢褻言語）。病人也可不隨意地重複他人的言語或模仿他人動作（參閱 palilalia）。此病常始於兒童期並轉為慢性；病因未明。藥物治療（如用匹莫齊特）有時見效。

gingiv- (gingivo-) *prefix denoting* the gums. Example: *gingivoplasty* (plastic surgery of).

〔前綴〕齦 指齒齦 例如：齦成形術。

gingiva *n.* (*pl.* **gingivae**) the gum: the layer of dense connective tissue and overlying mucous membrane that covers the alveolar bone and necks of the teeth. **–gingival** *adj.*

齦 齒齦：包裹牙槽骨和牙頸的一層結締組織，外有黏膜覆蓋。

gingivectomy *n.* the surgical removal of excess gum tissue. It is a specific procedure of periodontal surgery.

齦切除術 手術除去多餘的齦組織。它是牙周外科的一個特定程序。

gingivitis *n.* inflammation of the gums (*see* gingiva) caused by *plaque on the surfaces of the teeth at their necks. The gums are swollen and bleed easily. *Chronic gingivitis* is an early stage of *periodontal disease but is reversible with good oral hygiene. *Ulcerative gingivitis is painful and destructive.

齦炎 由牙頸表面的菌斑引起的齒齦炎症（參閱 gingiva）。齒齦腫脹並易出血。慢性齦炎是牙周病的早期階段，但良好的口腔衛生可使其復原。潰瘍性齦炎疼痛並具破壞性。

ginglymus (hinge joint) *n.* a form of *diarthrosis (freely movable joint) that allows angular movement in one plane

屈戌關節 動關節（可自由活動的關節）中的一種類型。這種關節只能在一個平面上成角

only, increasing or decreasing the angle between the bones. Examples are the knee joint and the elbow joint.

girdle *n.* (in anatomy) an encircling or arching arrangement of bones. *See also* pelvic girdle, shoulder girdle.

帶 （解剖學）環形或半圓形的骨性支架。參閱 pelvic girdle，shoulder girdle。

glabella *n.* the smooth rounded surface of the *frontal bone in the middle of the forehead, between the two eyebrows.

眉間 額中圓而光滑的額骨面，兩眉之間。

gladiolus *n.* the middle and largest segment of the *sternum.

胸骨體 胸骨中間的最大節塊。

gland *n.* an organ or group of cells that is specialized for synthesizing and secreting certain fluids, either for use in the body or for excretion. There are two main groups of glands: the *exocrine glands, which discharge their secretions by means of ducts, and the *endocrine glands, which secrete their products – hormones – directly into the bloodstream. *See also* secretion.

腺 專門合成和分泌某種體液的一個器官或細胞羣，這種體液或在體內利用，或排出。腺體有兩大類：外分泌腺，通過導管排出其分泌物；內分泌腺，其分泌物——激素——直接進入血流。參閱 secretion。

glanders (equinia) *n.* an infectious disease of horses, donkeys, and mules that is caused by the bacterium *Pseudomonas mallei* and can be transmitted to man. Symptoms include fever and inflammation (with possible ulceration) of the lymph nodes (a form of the disease known as *farcy*), skin, and nasal mucous membranes. In the untreated acute form death may follow in 2–20 days. In the more common chronic form, many patients survive without treatment. Administration of sulphonamides or streptomycin is usually effective.

鼻疽（馬鼻疽） 馬、猴和騾的一種傳染病，由鼻疽假單胞菌引起，能傳播於人。症狀有發燒、淋巴結炎症（一種稱為馬皮疽的疾病），皮膚和鼻黏膜炎症（可伴有潰瘍）。未經治療的急性病人可於 2~20 天內死亡。較為常見的慢性病人大多不經治療也可存活。用磺胺類藥物或鏈黴素治療常有效。

glandular fever an infectious disease, caused by the Epstein-Barr virus, that affects the lymph nodes in the neck, armpits, and groin; it mainly affects

腺熱 認為係由 EB 病毒所致的一種傳染病。病變累及頸部、腋窩和腹股溝淋巴結；主要感染青少年。經過 5~7 天的

adolescents and young adults. After an incubation period of 5–7 days, symptoms commence with swelling and tenderness of the lymph nodes, fever, headache, a sore throat, and loss of appetite. In some cases the liver is affected, causing *hepatitis, or the spleen is enlarged. Glandular fever is diagnosed by the presence of large numbers of *monocytes in the blood. Complications are rare but symptoms may persist for weeks before recovery. Medical name: **infectious mononucleosis**.

glans (glans penis) n. the acorn-shaped end part of the *penis, formed by the expanded end of the corpus spongiosum (erectile tissue). It is normally covered by the prepuce (foreskin), unless this has been removed by circumcision. The term glans is also applied to the end of the *clitoris.

Glasgow scoring system (Glasgow coma scale) a numerical system used to estimate a patient's level of consciousness after head injury. Each of the following are numerically graded: eye opening (4), motor response (6), and verbal response (5). The higher the score, the greater the level of consciousness: a score of 7 indicates a coma.

glaucoma n. a condition in which loss of vision occurs because of an abnormally high pressure in the eye. In most cases there is no other ocular disease. This is known as *primary glaucoma* and there are two pathologically distinct types: *acute glaucoma*, in which a sudden rise in pressure is accompanied by pain and marked blurring of vision; and the more common *chronic simple glaucoma*, in which the pressure increases gradually, usually without producing pain, and the

潛伏期後，開始出現淋巴結腫大及觸痛、發燒、頭痛、咽喉痛和食慾不振等症狀。有的病例累及肝臟，引起肝炎，或有脾臟腫大。腺熱可根據血液中存在的大量單核細胞來診斷。併發症少見，但在痊癒前症狀可持續數周。醫學用語：傳染性單核細胞增多症。

陰莖頭 陰莖的橡實形末端。由尿道海棉體（勃起組織）末端的膨大部分組成。正常有包皮覆蓋，除非實行包皮環切術將其切除。此術語亦用於陰蒂的末端。

格拉斯哥計分系統 用來衡量病人腦傷後意識水平的一個數字系統。下列每項都經數量分度。眼開度（4），運動反應（6），及言語反應（5）。分值越高，意識水平越高：分值 7 分表明昏迷。

青光眼 眼內壓異常升高引起的視力喪失病變。大多數病例中無其他眼疾存在，稱為原發性青光眼。原發性青光眼在病理學上有兩種不同類型：急性充血性青光眼，眼壓突然升高，伴有疼痛和明顯的視力模糊；慢性單純性青光眼，眼壓逐漸升高，常無疼痛，隱襲性視力喪失。同樣的視力喪失可發生於眼壓正常的眼睛，稱為低眼壓性青光眼。原發性青光

visual loss is insidious. The same type of visual loss may rarely occur in eyes with a normal pressure: this is called *low-tension glaucoma*. Primary glaucoma occurs increasingly with age and is an important cause of blindness. *Secondary glaucoma* may occur when other ocular disease impairs the normal circulation of the aqueous humour and causes the intraocular pressure to rise.

In all types of glaucoma the eventual problem is to reduce the intraocular pressure. Drops are inserted into the eye at regular intervals to improve the outflow of aqueous humour from the eye, and drops and tablets (such as *acetazolamide) are used to reduce the production of aqueous humour. If this treatment is ineffective, surgery may be performed to make a new channel through which the aqueous humour may drain from the eye in sufficient quantities to allow the pressure to return to normal. Such operations are known as *drainage* or *filtering operations*.

眼的發生隨年齡增大而增多，是失明的一個重要原因。繼發性青光眼可由其他眼疾引起，眼疾破壞房水的正常循環而導致眼內壓升高。

所有類型的青光眼其根本的問題是降低眼內壓。使用眼藥水按規定間隔滴入眼內以增加房水引流，以及使用眼藥水和內服片劑（如乙醯唑胺）以減少房水的產生。如治療無效，可施行手術，選一輔助的通道使有足夠量的房水流出，以恢復正常眼內壓。這種手術稱為引流手術或過濾手術。

gleet *n.* a discharge of purulent mucus from the penis or vagina resulting from chronic *gonorrhoea.

後淋　自陰莖或陰道排出的膿性黏液，係由慢性淋病引起。

glenohumeral *adj.* relating to the glenoid cavity and the humerus: the region of the shoulder joint.

盂肱的　與關節盂和肱骨有關的，肩關節部位。

glenoid cavity (glenoid fossa) the socket of the shoulder joint: the pear-shaped cavity at the top of the *scapula into which the head of the humerus fits.

關節盂　肩關節臼：肩胛骨頂端的梨形腔，適合肱骨頭置於其中。

gli- (glio-) *prefix denoting* **1.** glia. **2.** a glutionous substance.

〔前綴〕**膠質**　**(1)** 神經膠質。**(2)** 膠狀物質。

glia (neuroglia) *n.* the special connective tissue of the central nervous system, composed of different cells, including the

神經膠質　中樞神經系統的特殊結締組織，由不同細胞組成，包括少突膠質細胞、星形

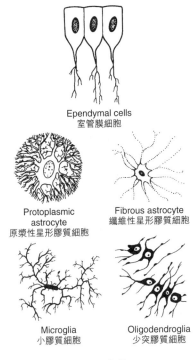

Ependymal cells
室管膜細胞

Protoplasmic
astrocyte
原漿性星形膠質細胞

Fibrous astrocyte
纖維性星形膠質細胞

Microglia
小膠質細胞

Oligodendroglia
少突膠質細胞

Types of glia
神經膠質細胞的類型

*oligodendrocytes, *astrocytes, ependymal cells (*see* ependyma), and *microglia, with various supportive and nutritive functions (see illustration). Glial cells outnumber the neurones by between five and ten to one, and make up some 40% of the total volume of the brain and spinal cord. **–glial** *adj.*

膠質細胞、室管膜細胞（參閱 ependyma）和小膠質細胞。這些細胞具有各種支持和營養功能（見圖）。神經膠質細胞的數量為神經元的 5~10 倍，約占腦和脊髓全部體積的 40%。

gliadin *n.* a protein, soluble in alcohol, that is obtained from wheat. It is one of the constituents of *gluten.

麥膠蛋白　一種從小麥中獲取的蛋白質，溶於酒精。是麩質的一個組成部分。

glibenclamide *n.* a drug that reduces the level of sugar in the blood and is used to treat noninsulin-dependent diabetes (*see* sulphonylurea). It is administered by

格列本脲　降低血糖水平的藥物。用於治療非胰島素依賴性糖尿病（參閱 sulphonylurea）。口服。副作用包括輕

mouth. Side-effects include mild digestive upsets and skin reactions. Trade name: **Daonil**, **Euglucon**.

度胃腸不適和皮膚過敏。商品名：Daonil，Euglucon。

gliclazide *n.* a *sulphonylurea oral hypoglycaemic drug used in the treatment of noninsulin-dependent (Type II) *diabetes. Trade name: **Diamicron**.

格列齊特 一種磺酰脲口服低血糖藥，用於治療非胰島素依賴性（II 型）糖尿病。商品名：Diamicron。

gliding joint *see* arthrodic joint.

滑膜關節 參閱 arthrodic joint。

glioblastoma (spongioblastoma) *n.* the most aggressive type of brain tumour derived from non-nervous (glial) tissue (*see* astrocytoma). Its rapid enlargement destroys normal brain cells, with a progressive loss of function, and raises the intracranial pressure, causing headache, vomiting, and drowsiness. Treatment is rarely curative and the prognosis is poor.

成膠質細胞瘤 最具侵襲性的一種腦瘤，起源於非神經的（神經膠質的）組織（參閱 astrocytoma）。腦瘤迅速擴大，破壞正常腦細胞，使腦功能逐漸喪失，腦壓升高，引起頭痛，嘔吐和嗜睡。療效不明，預後差。

glioma *n.* any tumour of non-nervous cells (*glia) in the nervous system. The term is sometimes also used for all tumours that arise in the central nervous system, including *astrocytomas, *oligodendrogliomas, medulloblastomas, and ependymomas. Tumours of low-grade malignancy produce symptoms by pressure on surrounding structures; those of high-grade malignancy may be invasive.

神經膠質瘤 神經系統中的任何非神經細胞性（神經膠質性）腫瘤。此詞有時用於中樞神經系統發生的所有腫瘤，包括星形細胞瘤、少突膠質細胞瘤、成神經管細胞瘤和室管膜細胞瘤。惡性度低的腫瘤產生周圍結構受壓的症狀；惡性度高的腫瘤可有侵犯性。

gliosome *n.* a *lysosome in an *astrocyte.

膠質粒 星形細胞內的一種溶酶體。

glipizide *n.* a drug used to control high blood-glucose levels (hyperglycaemia) in patients with noninsulin-dependent diabetes after diet control has failed (*see* sulphonylurea). It is administered by mouth; side-effects are hypoglycaemia, nausea and vomiting, and skin rash. Trade names: **Glibenese**, **Minodiab**.

格列吡嗪 一種用於控制高血糖（血糖過多）的藥物，適於經飲食控制無效的非胰島素依賴性糖尿病患者（參閱 sulphonylurea）。口服，副作用有低血糖、惡心、嘔吐及皮疹。商品名：Glibenese，Minodiab。

globin *n*. a protein, found in the body, that can combine with iron-containing groups to form *haemoglobin (which is found in red blood cells) and *myohaemoglobin (found in muscle).

globulin *n*. one of a group of simple proteins that are soluble in dilute salt solutions and can be coagulated by heat. A range of different globulins is present in the blood (the *serum globulins*, including alpha (α), beta (β), and *gamma (γ) globulins) Some globulins have important functions as antibodies (*see* immunoglobulin); others are responsible for the transport of lipids, iron, or copper in the blood.

globulinuria *n*. the presence in the urine of globulins.

globus *n*. a spherical or globe-shaped structure; for example, the *globus pallidus*, part of the lenticular nucleus in the brain (*see* basal ganglia).

globus hystericus the sense of having a 'lump in the throat' that can neither be swallowed nor brought up. This feeling often accompanies acute anxiety, sadness, or mental conflict and is due to a constriction of the circularly placed muscles around the lower part of the pharynx.

glomangioma (glomus tumour) *n. see* glomus.

glomerular filtration rate (GFR) the rate at which substances are filtered from the blood of the glomeruli into the Bowman's capsules of the *nephrons. It is calculated by measuring the *clearance of specific substances (e.g. creatinine) and is an index of renal function.

珠蛋白　見於人體內的一種蛋白質。能與含鐵的基團結合形成血紅蛋白（見於紅細胞）和肌紅蛋白（見於肌肉）。

球蛋白　一類單純蛋白質中的一種，可溶於稀鹽溶液，加熱後凝結。血液中有一系列不同的球蛋白（血清蛋白、包括α、β和γ球蛋白）。有些球蛋白具有抗體的重要功能（參閱immunoglobulin）；另外一些球蛋白具有運載血中脂類、鐵或銅的作用。

球蛋白尿　尿中存在球蛋白。

球　一種球形結構；例如蒼白球，是大腦豆狀核的一部分（參閱 basal ganglia）。

癔病球　喉內有塊狀物的感覺，不能吞下也不能吐出。這種感覺常伴有急性焦慮、憂鬱或心理矛盾，是咽喉下部周圍的肌肉收縮所致。

血管球瘤　參閱 glomus。

腎小球濾過率　由腎小球從血液中濾入到腎單位鮑曼囊中物質的比率。他由測量某特定物質的清除率來計算（如肌酸酐），是腎功能的指標。

glomerulitis *n.* any one of a variety of lesions of the glomeruli (*see* glomerulus) associated with acute or chronic kidney disease. Such lesions are recognized by electron microscopic examination, using immunofluorescent staining techniques, of kidney biopsy specimens taken during the course of the disease.

腎小球炎　與急性或慢性腎病有關的任何腎小球損害。這種損害可經電子顯微鏡檢查進行識別，在發病過程中取腎的活組織標本，運用熒光免疫染色技術。

glomerulonephritis (glomerular nephritis) *n.* any of a group of kidney diseases involving the glomeruli (*see* glomerulus), usually thought to be the result of antibody-antigen reactions that localize in the kidneys because of their filtering function. *Acute nephritis* is marked by blood in the urine and fluid and urea retention. It may be related to a recent streptococcal throat infection and usually settles completely, with rapid return of normal kidney function. Other forms of nephritis present with chronic *haematuria or with the *nephrotic syndrome; children often eventually recover completely, but adults are more likely to progress to *chronic nephritis* and eventual kidney failure.

腎小球腎炎　累及腎小球的一組腎疾病（參閱 glomerulus）。通常認為此病是腎中抗體－抗原反應的結果，由於腎的濾過作用。急性腎炎的標誌為血尿，液體瀦留及尿素瀦留。可與近期咽喉部鏈球菌感染有關，通常痊愈，腎功能迅速恢復。其他類型的腎炎出現慢性血尿或腎病綜合徵；兒童最終常可痊愈，而成人更可能發展為慢性腎炎以至最終腎功衰竭。

glomerulus *n.* (*pl.* **glomeruli**) **1.** the network of blood capillaries contained within the cuplike end (*Bowman's capsule*) of a *nephron. It is the site of primary filtration of waste products from the blood into the kidney tubule. **2.** any other small rounded mass.

(1) 腎小球　包含在某腎單位的杯狀囊（鮑曼囊）內的毛細血管網。是血液中的廢物以原尿形式濾入腎小管的場所。**(2)** 小球　任何其他小圓球狀物。

glomus *n.* (*pl.* **glomera**) a small communication between a tiny artery and vein in the skin of the limbs. It is concerned with the regulation of temperature. Occasionally its malformation and overgrowth produces a harmless but often painful tumour (*glomus tumour* or *glomangioma*), usually occurring in the skin at the ends of the fingers or

血管球　肢體皮膚內細小動脈與靜脈間的一個小的脈絡球。與溫度調節有關。偶爾其畸變與生長過度造成一無害但經常疼痛的腫瘤（血管球瘤），常發生在指端或趾端的皮膚。可通過手術烙除或切除。

toes. It may be cauterized or removed surgically.

gloss- (glosso-) *prefix denoting* the tongue. Examples: *glossopharyngeal* (relating to the tongue and pharynx); *glossoplasty* (plastic surgery of).

〔前綴〕舌　例如：舌咽的，舌成形術。

glossa *n. see* tongue.

舌　參閱 tongue。

glossectomy *n.* surgical removal of the tongue, an operation usually carried out for cancer in this structure.

舌切除術　舌的手術切除，一種常用於治療舌癌的手術。

Glossina *n. see* tsetse.

舌蠅屬　參閱 tsetse。

glossitis *n.* inflammation of the tongue. Causes include anaemia, candidosis, and vitamin deficiency.

舌炎　舌的炎症。病因包括貧血、念珠菌病及維生素缺乏。

glossolalia *n.* nonsense speech that mimics normal speech in that it is appropriately formed into an imitation of syllables, words, and sentences. It can be uttered in *trance states and during sleep.

癲語　毫無意義的言語。患者模仿正常的言語，幾乎形成仿造的音節、單詞和句子。這些言語可在恍惚狀態和睡眠時說出來。

glossopharyngeal nerve the ninth *cranial nerve (IX), which supplies motor fibres to part of the pharynx and to the parotid salivary glands and sensory fibres to the posterior third of the tongue and the soft palate.

舌咽神經　第九腦神經(IX)，它為部分咽部和腮腺提供運動纖維，為舌的後三分之一部分和軟腭提供感覺纖維。

glossoplegia *n.* paralysis of the tongue.

舌癱瘓　舌麻痺。

glottis *n.* the space between the two *vocal cords. The term is often applied to the vocal cords themselves or to that part of the larynx associated with the production of sound.

聲門　兩條聲帶之間的空隙。此詞亦常用於聲帶本身或指喉的發聲部分。

gluc- (gluco-) *prefix denoting* glucose. Example: *glucosuria* (urinary excretion of).

〔前綴〕糖　葡萄糖。例如：糖尿。

glucagon *n.* a hormone, produced by the pancreas, that causes an increase in the blood sugar level and thus has an effect opposite to that of *insulin. Glucagon is administered by injection to counteract diabetic *hypoglycaemia.

高血糖素 由胰臟產生的一種激素，可導致血糖水平升高，因而具有與胰島素相反的作用。高血糖素用於對抗糖尿病性血糖過少，注射用。

glucagonoma *n.* a pancreatic tumour that secretes glucagon and produces attacks of *hypoglycaemia.

高血糖瘤 一種胰腺瘤，它分泌高血糖素並引起血糖過少的發作。

glucocorticoid *n. see* corticosteroid.

糖皮質激素 參閱 corticosteroid。

glucokinase *n.* an enzyme (a *hexokinase), found in the liver, that catalyses the conversion of glucose to glucose-6-phosphate. This is the first stage of *glycolysis.

葡萄糖激酶 見於肝內的一種酶（己糖激酶），它可催化葡萄糖轉變為 6-磷酸葡萄糖。這是糖酵解的第一個步驟。

gluconeogenesis *n.* the biochemical process in which glucose, an important source of energy, is synthesized from non-carbohydrate sources, such as amino acids. Gluconeogenesis occurs mainly in the liver and kidney and meets the needs of the body for glucose when carbohydrate is not available in sufficient amounts in the diet.

糖原異生 由非糖物質（如氨基酸）合成葡萄糖（能量的一個重要來源）的生化過程。糖原異生主要在肝和腎內發生，當飲食中缺少足夠糖類時，它可滿足機體對葡萄糖的需要。

glucosamine *n.* the amino sugar of glucose, i.e. glucose in which the hydroxyl group is replaced by an amino group. Glucosamine is a component of *mucopolysaccharides and *glycoproteins: for example, hyaluronic acid, a mucopolysaccharide found in synovial fluid, and *heparin.

葡糖氨 氨基葡萄糖係葡萄糖的羥基被氨基所替代。葡糖氨是黏多糖和糖蛋白的一種成分：如透明質酸（在滑液中見到的一種黏多糖）和肝素。

glucose (dextrose) *n.* a simple sugar containing six carbon atoms (a hexose). Glucose is an important source of energy in the body and the sole source of energy for the brain. Free glucose is not found in many foods (grapes are an exception);

葡萄糖 一種含有六個碳原子的單糖（己糖）。葡萄糖是身體能量的一個重要來源，並是腦能量的唯一來源。在許多食物中並無游離的葡萄糖（葡萄除外），然而，葡萄糖是蔗糖

however, glucose is one of the constituents of both sucrose and starch, both of which yield glucose after digestion. Glucose is stored in the body in the form of *glycogen. The concentration of glucose in the blood is maintained at around 5mmol/l by a variety of hormones, principally *insulin and *glucagon. If the blood-glucose concentration falls below this level neurological and other symptoms may result (*see* hypoglycaemia). Conversely, if the blood-glucose level is raised above its normal level, to 10mmol/l, the condition of *hyperglycaemia develops. This is a symptom of *diabetes mellitus.

和澱粉的一個成分，二者被消化後都可產生葡萄糖。葡萄糖以糖原的形式貯存於體內。血液中葡萄糖的濃度維持在5mmol/l 左右，受幾種激素主要是胰島素和高血糖素調節。血糖濃度低於此水平會出現神經方面的或其他的症狀（參閱 hypoglycaemia）。相反，若血糖濃度高於其正常水平，達10mmol/l，則將出現高血糖症。這是糖尿病的一個症狀。

glucose-6-phosphate dehydrogenase deficiency a hereditary condition in which the enzyme glucose-6-phosphate dehydrogenase (G6PD), which functions in carbohydrate metabolism, is absent. It becomes apparent in infancy, causing enlargement of the liver and low blood sugars. Treatment is by frequent glucose feeds and restriction of dietary galactose and fructose. *Compare* favism.

葡萄糖-6-磷酸鹽脫氫酶缺乏症 一種葡萄糖-6-磷酸鹽脫氫酶 (G6PD) 缺失的遺傳病，這種酶作用於碳水化合物代謝。此病在嬰兒期明顯，引起肝腫大及低血糖。治療是經常服葡萄糖及限食含半乳糖、左旋糖食物。與 favism 對比。

glucose tolerance test a test used in the diagnosis of *diabetes mellitus. A quantity of glucose is given to the patient by mouth, after 10–16 hours of fasting, and the concentration of sugar in the blood and urine is determined at 30-minute intervals during the next two hours. These readings indicate the ability of the patient's body to utilize glucose.

葡萄糖耐量試驗 一種用於診斷葡萄糖的試驗。在病人禁食一段時間後給其口服一定量的葡萄糖，其後的10~16小時禁食，每隔 30 分鐘測定血中和尿中糖的濃度。所得曲綫代表病人體內利用葡萄糖的能力。

glucoside *n. see* glycoside.

葡萄糖苷 參閱 glycoside。

glucuronic acid a sugar acid derived from glucose. Glucuronic acid is an important constituent of *chondroitin

葡萄糖醛酸 由葡萄糖衍生的一種糖酸。葡萄糖醛酸是硫酸軟骨素（見於軟骨中）和透明

sulphate (found in cartilage) and *hyaluronic acid (found in synovial fluid).

glue ear a common condition in which viscous fluid accumulates in the middle ear, causing *deafness. It is most frequently seen in children and is due to malfunction of the *Eustachian tube. Many cases resolve spontaneously; treatment, if required, consists of surgical incision of the eardrum (*myringotomy), drainage of the fluid, and the insertion of a *grommet. Medical name: **secretory otitis media**.

glutamate dehydrogenase (glutamic acid dehydrogenase) an important enzyme involved in the *deamination of amino acids.

glutamic acid (glutamate) *see* amino acid.

glutamic oxaloacetic transaminase (GOT) an enzyme involved in the *transamination of amino acids. This enzyme is present in blood serum (*serum GOT, SGOT*); measurement of SGOT may be used in the diagnosis of acute *myocardial infarction and acute liver disease. This enzyme has been renamed *aspartate aminotransferase* (*AST*), but the old abbreviation is still widely used.

glutamic pyruvic transaminase (GPT) an enzyme involved in the *transamination of amino acids. High levels of this enzyme are found in the liver, and measurement of GPT in the serum (*serum GPT, SGPT*) is of use in the diagnosis and study of acute liver disease. This enzyme has been renamed *alanine aminotransferase* (*ALT*), but the old abbreviation is still widely used.

質酸（見於滑膜液）的重要成分。

膠耳 黏液積聚於中耳的一種常見病，能引起耳聾。此病兒童最常見，病因為咽鼓管機能失常。許多病例可自動消退；必要時治療可包括鼓膜切除術，液體引流及植入墊圈。醫學用語：分泌性中耳炎。

穀氨酸脫氫酶 涉及氨基酸脫氨基作用的一種重要的酶。

穀氨酸 參閱 amino acid。

穀氨酸草酰乙酸轉氨酶 涉及氨基酸氨基轉移的一種酶，這種酶存在於血漿中（血漿穀草轉氨酶）；測量其濃度可用於診斷急性心肌梗死和急性肝病。此酶已被重新命名為天門冬氨酸轉氨酶(AST)，但其舊的縮寫名仍廣泛使用。

穀氨酸丙酮酸轉氨酶 涉及氨基酸氨基轉移的一種酶。這種酶在肝內的濃度高，測量血漿中穀丙轉氨酶的濃度可用於診斷和研究急性肝病。此酶已被重新命名為丙氨酸轉氨酶(ALT)，但其舊的縮寫仍廣泛使用。

glutaminase *n.* an enzyme, found in the kidney, that catalyses the breakdown of the amino acid glutamine to ammonia and glutamic acid: a stage in the production of urea.

穀氨醯胺酶　見於腎中的一種酶。此酶催化穀氨醯胺分解為氨和穀氨酸：這是產生尿素的一個步驟。

glutamine *n. see* amino acid.

穀氨醯胺　參閱 amino acid。

glutathione *n.* a peptide containing the amino acids glutamic acid, cysteine, and glycine. It functions as a *coenzyme in several oxidation-reduction reactions.

穀胱甘肽　包含穀氨酸、半胱氨酸和甘氨酸的一種肽。在幾種氧化-還原反應中起輔酶作用。

glutelin *n.* one of a group of simple proteins found in plants and soluble only in dilute acids and bases. An example is *glutenin*, found in wheat (*see* gluten).

穀蛋白　見於植物中的一組單純蛋白質中的一種。僅溶於稀酸和稀鹼中。例如：小麥中的麥穀蛋白（參閱 gluten）。

gluten *n.* a mixture of the two proteins *gliadin* and *glutenin*. Gluten is present in wheat and rye and is important for its baking properties: when mixed with water it becomes sticky and enables air to be trapped and dough to be formed, sensitivity to gluten leads to *coeliac disease in children.

穀蛋白麩質　兩種蛋白質麥膠蛋白和麥穀蛋白的混合物。麩質存在於小麥和黑麥中，它有一種重要的特性適於烘烤：與水混合後即成為黏性的，含有空氣的麵團。兒童對麩質的敏感可導致腹部疾患。

gluteus *n.* one of three paired muscles of the buttocks (*gluteus maximus*, *gluteus medius* and *gluteus minimus*). They are responsible for movements of the thigh. **–gluteal** *adj.*

臀肌　臀部的三對肌肉之一（臀大肌、臀中肌、臀小肌）。臀肌司大腿的運動。

glyc- (glyco-) *prefix denoting* sugar.

〔前綴〕　糖

glyceride *n.* a *lipid consisting of glycerol (an alcohol) combined with one or more fatty acids. *See also* triglyceride.

甘油酯　由甘油（一種醇）與一個或多個脂肪酸結合成的一種脂。參閱 triglyceride。

glycerin (glycerol) *n.* a clear viscous liquid obtained by hydrolysis of fats and mixed oils and produced as a by-product in the manufacture of soap. It is used as an *emollient in many skin preparations,

甘油　由脂肪及混合的油水解而獲得的一種清澈的黏性液體。是肥皂生產中的副產品。在許多皮膚製劑中用作潤滑劑，或用作輕瀉劑（特別是製

as a laxative (particularly in the form of *suppositories), and as a sweetening agent in the pharmaceutical industry.

glyceryl trinitrate (nitroglycerin) a drug that dilates blood vessels and is used to prevent and treat angina (*see* vasodilator). It is administered by mouth and by skin patches; large doses may cause flushing, headache, and fainting. Trade names: **Nitrocontin, Sustac**.

glycine *n. see* amino acid.

glycobiology *n.* the study of the chemistry, biochemistry, and other aspects of carbohydrates and carbohydrate complexes, especially *glycoproteins. Elucidation of the structure and role of the sugar molecules of glycoproteins has important medical implications and has led to the development of new drugs, such as *tissue plasminogen activators, drugs that affect the immune system, antiviral drugs, and drugs used to treat *rheumatoid arthritis.

glycocholic acid *see* bile acids.

glycogen *n.* a carbohydrate consisting of branched chains of glucose units. Glycogen is the principal form in which carbohydrate is stored in the body: it is the counterpart of starch in plants. Glycogen is stored in the liver and muscles and may be readily broken down to glucose.

glycogenesis *n.* the biochemical process, occurring chiefly in the liver and in muscle, by which glucose is converted into glycogen.

glycogenolysis *n.* a biochemical process, occurring chiefly in the liver and in muscle, by which glycogen is broken down into glucose.

成栓劑），在製藥業中用作甜味劑。

硝酸甘油 一種擴張血管的藥物，用於預防和治療心絞痛（參閱 vasodilator）。口服及皮膚貼片；大劑量可引起面部潮紅、頭痛及昏厥。商品名：Nitrocontin，Sustac。

甘氨酸 參閱 amino acid。

葡萄糖生物學 研究糖類和糖類複合物，尤其是糖蛋白化學、生物化學及其他方面的學科。闡明糖蛋白中糖分子的結構及功能有重要的醫學意義，已導致發展新藥，如組織纖維蛋白溶酶原激活劑、影響免疫系統藥物、抗病毒藥、以及用以治療類風濕關節炎的藥物。

甘氨膽酸 參閱 bile acids。

糖原 由許多葡萄糖單位的支鏈組成的碳水化合物。糖原是機體貯存糖的主要形式：它與植物中的澱粉類似。糖原貯存於肝和肌肉中，可隨時分解為葡萄糖。

糖原生成 葡萄糖轉化為糖原的生化過程。主要發生於肝和肌肉內。

糖原分解 糖原分解為葡萄糖的生化過程。主要發生於肝和肌肉內。

glycolipid *n*. a *lipid containing a sugar molecule (usually galactose or glucose). The *cerebrosides are examples of glycolipids.

糖脂　一種含糖分子（通常是半乳糖或葡萄糖）的脂類。如腦苷脂。

glycolysis *n*. the conversion of glucose, by a series of ten enzyme-catalysed reactions, to lactic acid. Glycolysis takes place in the cytoplasm of cells and the first nine reactions (converting glucose to pyruvate) form the first stage of cellular *respiration. The process involves the production of a small amount of energy (in the form of ATP), which is used for biochemical work. The final reaction of glycolysis (converting pyruvate to lactic acid) provides energy for short periods of time when oxygen consumption exceeds demand; for example, during bursts of intense muscular activity. *See also* lactic acid.

糖酵解　葡萄糖轉變為乳糖的過程，經十種酶促反應。糖酵解發生的細胞的胞漿中，其前九種反應（葡萄糖轉變為丙酮酸）構成細胞呼吸的第一階段。此過程中產生的少量能量（以三磷酸腺苷的形式）用於生化反應。糖酵解的最後一種反應（丙酮酸轉變為乳酸），是為在短時間內耗氧超過正常需要時提供能量；例如：在肌肉劇烈活動時。參閱　lactic acid。

glycoprotein *n*. one of a group of compounds consisting of a protein combined with a carbohydrate (such as galactose or mannose). Examples of glycoproteins are certain enzymes, hormones, and antigens.

糖蛋白　由蛋白質和糖（如半乳糖或甘露糖）結合組成的一類化合物。例如某些酶、激素和抗原都是糖蛋白。

glycoside *n*. a compound formed by replacing the hydroxyl (–OH) group of a sugar by another group. (If the sugar is glucose the compound is known as a *glucoside*.) Glycosides found in plants include some pharmacologically important products (such as *digitalis). Other plant glycosides are natural food toxins, present in cassava, almonds, and other plant products, and may yield hydrogen cyanide if the plant is not prepared properly before eating.

糖苷　糖的羥基（–OH）被其他基團替代而形成的一種化合物。（如果此糖是葡萄糖，其形成的化合物稱為葡萄糖苷。）植物中發現的糖苷包括某些有重要藥理作用的製品（如洋地黃）。其他植物糖苷是天然的食物毒素，存在於木薯、杏仁或其他植物產品中，如在食用前未適當處理，可產生氰化氫。

glycosuria *n*. the presence of glucose in the urine in abnormally large amounts. Only very minute quantities of this sugar

糖尿　尿內出現異常大量的葡萄糖。正常情況下尿內只能見到極微量的葡萄糖。糖尿濃度

may be found normally in the urine. Higher levels may be associated with diabetes mellitus, kidney disease, and some other conditions.

高可能與糖尿病、腎病或某些其他疾病有關。

gnath- (gnatho-) *prefix denoting* the jaw. Example: *gnathoplasty* (plastic surgery of).

〔前綴〕頷 如：頷成形術。

gnathion *n.* the lowest point of the midline of the lower jaw (mandible).

頷下點 下頷骨中綫的最下點。

Gnathostoma *n.* a genus of parasitic nematodes. Adult worms are commonly found in the intestines of tigers, leopards, and dogs. The presence of the larval stage of *G. spinigerum* in man, who is not the normal host, causes a skin condition called *creeping eruption.

腭口（綫）蟲屬 一屬寄生性綫蟲。其成蟲常見於虎、豹和狗的腸內。棘腭口綫蟲的正常宿主不是人類，其幼蟲侵入人體，引起一種叫匐行疹的皮膚病。

gnotobiotic *adj.* describing germ-free conditions or a germ-free animal that has been inoculated with known microorganisms.

無菌生物的 描述處於無菌狀態的生物，或者接種了已知微生物的無菌動物。

GnRH *see* gonadotrophin-releasing hormone.

促性腺激素釋放激素 參閱 gonadotrophin-releasing hormone。

goblet cell a column-shaped secretory cell found in the *epithelium of the respiratory and intestinal tracts. Goblet cells secrete the principal constituents of mucus.

杯狀細胞 一種柱形的分泌細胞，見於呼吸道和腸道的上皮內。杯狀細胞分泌黏液的主要成分。

goitre *n.* a swelling of the neck due to enlargement of the thyroid gland. This may be due to lack of dietary iodine, which is necessary for the production of thyroid hormone: the gland enlarges in an attempt to increase the output of hormone. This was the cause of *endemic goitre*, formerly common in regions where the diet lacked iodine. *Sporadic goitre* may be due to simple overgrowth

甲狀腺腫 由於甲狀腺腫大引起的頸部腫塊。可因膳食中缺乏碘引起，碘是產生甲狀腺激素所必需的：甲狀腺增大是為了增加激素排出量。這就是地方性甲狀腺腫的發生原因，此病以往常發生於膳食中缺碘的地區。散發性甲狀腺腫可由於腺體單純肥大（增生）或腫瘤所致。突眼性甲狀腺腫（格雷

(hyperplasia) of the gland or to a tumour. In *exophthalmic goitre* (*Graves's disease*) the swelling is associated with overactivity of the gland and is accompanied by other symptoms (*see* thyrotoxicosis). Autoimmune thyroiditis can be associated with goitre (*see* Hashimoto's disease).

gold *n.* **1.** a bright yellow metal that is very malleable. In dentistry pure gold is occasionally used as a filling. Alloys are used extensively for *crowns, *inlays, and *bridges, either alone or veneered with a tooth-coloured material. Gold alloys are now only rarely used as the metal framework for partial dentures, *cobalt-chromium alloys being used instead. **2.** (in pharmacology) any of several compounds of the metal gold, used in the treatment of rheumatoid arthritis. *Sodium aurothiomalate* (*Myocrisin*) is administered by intramuscular injection. Common side-effects include mouth ulcers, itching, blood disorders, skin reactions, and inflammation of the colon and kidneys. *Auranofin is a gold compound administered orally.

Golgi apparatus a collection of vesicles and folded membranes in a cell, usually connected to the *endoplasmic reticulum. It stores and later transports the proteins manufactured in the endoplasmic reticulum. The Golgi apparatus is well developed in cells that produce secretions, e.g. pancreatic cells producing digestive enzymes.

Golgi cells types of *neurones (nerve cells) within the central nervous system. *Golgi type* I *neurones* have very long axons that connect different parts of the system; *Golgi type* II *neurones*, also

夫斯病）與腺體過度活動有關，並伴有其他症狀（參閱 thyrotoxicosis）。自體免疫甲狀腺炎可與甲狀腺腫有關（參閱 Hashimoto's disease）。

金 **(1)** 一種極具延展性的發亮黃色金屬。在牙科學中純金偶爾用作填料。其合金被廣泛用作套冠、嵌體和橋體，可單獨使用，或覆蓋一層牙色的材料。金合金已很少用作部分托牙的金屬構架，現已用鈷鉻合金替代。**(2)**（藥理學）用於治療類風濕關節炎的幾種金的化合物。肌肉內注射硫代蘋果酸金鈉。常見的副作用包括口腔潰瘍、瘙癢、血液病、皮膚反應及結腸和腎的炎症。金諾芬是口服的金化合物。

高爾基體　細胞內一羣囊泡和褶膜的複合體，常與內質網相連接。高爾基體貯存並接着轉運內質網內生產的蛋白質。高爾基體在產生分泌物的細胞（例如產生消化酶的胰細胞）內發育良好。

高爾基細胞　中樞神經系統內的各型神經元（神經細胞）。高爾基 I 型神經元具有很長的軸突，與神經系統各部分相連接；高爾基 II 型神經元又稱作

known as *microneurones*, have only short axons or sometimes none.

小神經元，僅有短的軸突，或有的沒有軸突。

Golgi tendon organ *see* tendon organ.

高爾基腱器　參閱　tendon organ。

Gomori's method a method of staining for the demonstration of enzymes, especially phosphatases and lipases, in histological specimens.

戈莫里法　一種顯示組織學標本中的酶的染色法，尤其用於顯示磷酸酶和脂酶。

gomphosis *n.* a form of *synarthrosis (immovable joint) in which a conical process fits into a socket. An example is the joint between the root of a tooth and the socket in the jawbone.

釘狀嵌合　不動關節的一種形式。這種關節由一個圓錐形突起插在臼窩內組成。例如牙根與下頜骨牙槽之間的關節。

gonad *n.* a male or female reproductive organ that produces the gametes. *See* ovary, testis.

性腺　產生配子的雄性或雌性生殖器官。參閱　ovary，testis。

gonadorelin *n.* a synthetic analogue of gonadotrophin-releasing hormone (*see* LHRH analogue), administered by intravenous injection to stimulate the production of pituitary gonadotrophins. It is used in the treatment of *amenorrhoea and certain types of infertility.

戈那瑞林　促性腺激素釋放激素的合成類似物（參閱 LHRH analogue），靜脈內注射給藥以刺激垂體促性腺激素的生成。用於閉經和某些類型的不孕症的治療。

gonadotrophin (gonadotrophic hormone) *n.* any of several hormones synthesized and released by the pituitary gland that act on the testes or ovaries (gonads) to promote production of sex hormones and either sperm or ova. Their production is controlled by *gonadotrophin-releasing hormone. The main gonadotrophins are *follicle-stimulating hormone and *luteinizing hormone. They may be given by injection to treat infertility. *See also* human chorionic gonadotrophin.

促性腺激素　作用於睾丸或卵巢（性腺）促使其產生性激素和精子或卵子的幾種激素。這些激素由垂體合成並釋放。他們的生成是由促性腺激素釋放激素控制的。主要的促性腺激素是卵泡刺激素和黃體生成素，可用來注射，治療不育（孕）症。參閱 human chorionic gonadotrophin。

gonadotrophin-releasing hormone (GnRH) a peptide hormone produced in

促性腺激素釋放激素　產生於下丘腦的肽激素，通過血流運

the hypothalamus and transported via the bloodstream to the pituitary gland, where it controls the synthesis and release of pituitary *gonadotrophins. GnRH and its analogues (*see* LHRH analogue) are used to treat hormonal sexual disorders and some types of infertility.

送到垂體。在垂體，它控制垂體促性腺激素的合成與釋放。促性腺激素釋放激素及其類似物（參閱 LHRH analogue）被用來治療激素性疾病和有些類型的不育（孕）症。

gonagra *n.* gout in the knee.

膝痛風　膝關節痛風。

goni- (gonio-) *prefix denoting* an anatomical angle or corner.

〔前綴〕**角**　指解剖學的角或角度。

goniometer *n.* an instrument for measuring angles, such as those made in joint movements.

測角計　一種測量角度的儀器，如測量關節移動的測角計。

gonion *n.* the point of the angle of the lower jawbone (mandible).

下頜骨點　下頜骨角的尖端。

goniopuncture *n.* a rarely performed operation for congenital glaucoma (*see* buphthalmos) to enable fluid to be drawn from the eye. Using a fine knife, an incision is made from within the eye into Schlemm's canal, at the junction of the cornea and sclera, and continued outwards until the knife appears beneath the conjunctiva. This creates a pathway for fluid to drain from the anterior chamber of the eye to the subconjunctival tissue. The tip of the knife within the eye is observed through a special contact lens.

前房角穿刺術　一種較少使用治療先天性青光眼的手術（參閱 buphthalmos），使房水得以從眼內流出。在角膜和鞏膜結合處用鋒利小刀在眼內做一切口，進入施勒姆管，繼而向外直至刀口出現於結膜下面。這樣就建造了一個通道，使房水得以從眼的前房流入結膜下組織。手術時用一種特殊的接觸鏡來觀察眼內的刀尖。

gonioscope *n.* a special lens used for viewing the structures around the edge of the anterior chamber of the eye (in front of the iris). These structures are hidden behind the sclera at the periphery of the cornea and are not accessible to direct viewing.

前房角鏡　一種用以觀察眼前房角周圍結構（在晶體前面）的特殊鏡片。這些結構隱藏於鞏膜後面，恰好在角膜緣之外，不易直接觀察到。

goniotomy (trabeculotomy) *n.* an operation for congenital glaucoma (*see*

前房角切開術　一種用於治療先天性青光眼的手術，用一把

buphthalmos). A fine knife is used to make an incision into Schlemm's canal from within the eye. It is the first stage of *goniopuncture.

鋒利小刀向眼內作一切口進入施勒姆管，這是前房角穿刺術的第一步驟。

gonococcus n. (pl. **gonococci**) the causative agent of gonorrhoea: the bacterium *Neisseria gonorrhoeae*. –**gonococcal** adj.

淋球菌　淋病的致病菌：即淋病奈瑟菌。

gonocyte n. see germ cell.

生殖母細胞　參閱 germ cell。

gonorrhoea n. a sexually transmitted disease, caused by the bacterium *Neisseria gonorrhoeae*, that affects the genital mucous membranes of either sex. Symptoms develop about a week after infection and include pain on passing urine and discharge of pus (known as *gleet*) from the penis (in men) or vagina (in women); some infected women, however, experience no symptoms. If a pregnant woman has gonorrhoea, her baby's eyes may become infected during passage through the birth canal (see ophthalmia neonatorum). In untreated cases, the infection may spread throughout the reproductive system, causing sterility; severe inflammation of the urethra in men can prevent passage of urine (a condition known as *stricture). Later complications include arthritis, inflammation of the heart valves (*endocarditis), and infection of the eyes, causing conjunctivitis. Treatment with sulphonamides, penicillin, or tetracycline in the early stages of the disease is usually effective.

淋病　由淋病奈瑟菌引起的一種性傳播疾病，累及兩性的生殖器黏膜。感染後約一周出現症狀，包括排尿時疼痛並從陰莖（男性）或從陰道（女性）排膿（稱為後淋），但也有些被感染的婦女未感到有症狀。如孕婦患有淋病，其嬰兒的眼睛可在出生時通過產道而受感染（參閱 ophthalium neonatorum）。在未經治療的病例，感染可遍及整個生殖系統而導致不孕。男子的尿道有嚴重炎症時可使排尿困難（尿道狹窄）。晚期合併症包括關節炎、心臟瓣膜炎（心內膜炎）以及眼受感染引起的結膜炎。在患病早期用磺胺類藥物、青黴素或四環素治療往往奏效。

good neighbour scheme (in Britain) a voluntary experimental scheme organized by social service departments of local authorities to bridge the gap in the care of the elderly between total

睦鄰組合　（在英國）由地方當局社會福利部門組織的一種志願的試驗性組合。這種組合為解決老年人的保健問題，在完全自理和提供家務服務之間

independence and the provision of a home help. *See also* social services.

goose flesh the reaction of the skin to cold or fear. The blood vessels contract and the small muscle attached to the base of each hair follicle also contracts, causing the hairs to stand up: this gives the skin an appearance of plucked goose skin.

GORD *see* gastro-oesophageal reflux disease.

gorget *n.* an instrument used in the operation for removal of stones from the bladder. It is a *director or guide with a wide groove.

goserelin *n. see* LHRH analogue.

gouge *n.* a curved chisel used in orthopaedic operations to cut and remove bone (see illustration).

A gouge
圓鑿

goundou (anákhré) *n.* a condition following an infection with *yaws in which the nasal processes of the upper jaw bone thicken (*see* hyperostosis) to form two large bony swellings, about 7 cm in diameter, on either side of the nose. The swellings not only obstruct the nostrils but also interfere with the field of vision. Initial symptoms include persistent headache and a bloody purulent discharge from the nose. Early cases can be treated with injections of penicillin; otherwise surgical removal of the

搭起橋樑。參閱 social services。

雞皮疙瘩 對冷或驚恐的皮膚反應。血管收縮，附於每個毛囊底部的細小肌肉也收縮，導致毛髮豎立；這使皮膚的外貌如同拔了毛的雞（鵝）皮。

胃食管返流病 參閱 gastro-oesophageal reflux disease。

有槽導引器 用於膽結石摘除手術的一種器械。它是一種具有寬闊槽溝的探針或探條。

戈舍瑞林 參閱 LHRH analogue。

圓鑿 一種彎曲形鑿子，骨科手術中用以切割和去除骨頭（見圖）。

根度病 （鼻骨增生性骨膜炎）感染雅司病後的一種疾病。上頜骨的鼻突增厚（參閱 hyperostosis），形成鼻兩側骨性腫大，直徑約 7 cm。腫塊不僅堵塞鼻孔，而且干擾視野。最初的症狀包括持續頭痛和流出膿血性鼻涕。早期病例可注射青黴素治療，否則需要外科切除腫塊。根度病發生於中非洲和南美洲。

growths is necessary. Goundou occurs in central Africa and South America.

gout *n.* a disease in which a defect in uric acid metabolism causes an excess of the acid and its salts (urates) to accumulate in the bloodstream and the joints respectively. It results in attacks of acute gouty arthritis and chronic destruction of the joints and deposits of urates (*tophi*) in the skin and cartilage, especially of the ears. The excess of urates also damages the kidneys, in which stones may form. Treatment with drugs that increase the excretion of urates (*uricosuric drugs) or with *allopurinol, which slows their formation, can control the disease. *See also* podagra.

痛風　一種尿酸代謝紊亂的疾病，使過多尿酸和尿酸鹽蓄積在血流和關節內，導致急性痛風性關節炎發作和慢性關節組織破壞，以及皮膚、軟骨、特別是耳的軟骨內尿酸鹽（痛風石）沉積。過多的尿鹽亦使腎臟受損，形成腎結石。治療用加快尿酸鹽排泄的藥物（促尿酸尿藥物）或減慢尿酸鹽形成的藥物——別嘌醇能有效地控制本病。參閱 podagra。

Graafian follicle a mature follicle in the ovary prior to ovulation, containing a large fluid-filled cavity that distends the surface of the ovary. The *oocyte develops inside the follicle, attached to one side.

格雷夫卵泡　在排卵前卵巢內的一種成熟卵泡，含有一個充滿液體的大囊腔，使卵巢表面膨脹。卵母細胞在卵泡內發育，附着於卵泡的一側。

graft **1.** *n.* any organ, tissue, or object used for *transplantation to replace a faulty part of the body. A *skin graft is a piece of skin cut from a healthy part of the body and used to heal a damaged area of skin. A healthy kidney removed from one person and transplanted to another individual is described as a *kidney* (or *renal*) *graft*. Corneal grafts are taken from a recently dead individual to repair corneal opacity (*see* keratoplasty). Artificial tubes and valves are used to replace diseased peripheral arteries and heart valves, respectively. **2.** *vb.* to transplant an organ or tissue.

(1) 移植物　任何用來移植以替代身體受損部分的器官、組織或物體。皮膚移植是切取身體健康部分的一片皮膚用來愈合受損傷部位的皮膚，腎移植是切除一人的健康腎臟用來移植於另一人。角膜移植是從新近死亡的人身上取下的眼角膜用來醫治角膜混濁（參閱 keratoplasty）。人工瓣膜移植物用來替換受損的心臟瓣膜。
(2) 移植　移植一個器官或組織。

graft-versus-host disease (GVHD) a condition that occurs following bone marrow transplantation and sometimes

移植物抗宿主病　骨髓移植術後發生的一種疾病。由於供者骨髓的淋巴細胞排斥宿主的組

blood transfusion, in which lymphocytes from the graft attack specific tissues in the host. The skin, gut, and liver are the most severely affected. Drugs that suppress the immune reaction, such as steroids and *cyclosporin A, reduce the severity of the rejection.

織所致。皮膚、腸和肝受影響最為嚴重。抑制免疫反應的藥物，如類固醇和環孢菌素 A 可減輕排斥的嚴重程度。

grain *n.* a unit of mass equal to 1/7000 of a pound (avoirdupois). 1 grain = 0.0648 gram.

厘　質量的一種單位，等於 1/7000 磅（英衡制）。1 厘 = 0.0648 克。

gram *n.* a unit of mass equal to one thousandth of a kilogram. Symbol: g.

克　質量的一種單位，等於一公斤的千分之一。符號：g。

-gram *suffix denoting* a record; tracing. Example; *electrocardiogram* (record of an electrocardiograph).

〔後綴〕圖，像　指一種記錄或描寫。例如心電圖（心電描記器的記錄）。

gramicidin *n.* an *antibiotic that acts against a wide range of bacteria. It is used alone or in combination with other antibiotics or antiseptics in ointments, solutions, or sprays for the treatment of infected ulcers, wounds, and burns.

短桿菌肽　一種具有廣譜抗菌作用的抗生素。單獨使用，或與其他抗生素或防腐劑聯合使用，用作軟膏、液劑或氣霧劑，以治療受感染的潰瘍、創傷和燒傷。

Gram's stain a method of staining bacterial cells, used as a primary means of identification. A film of bacteria spread onto a glass slide is dried and heat-fixed, stained with a violet dye, treated with decolourizer (e.g. alcohol), and then counterstained with red dye. *Gram-negative* bacteria lose the initial stain but take up the counterstain, so that they appear red microscopically. *Gram-positive* bacteria retain the initial stain, appearing violet microscopically. These staining differences are based on variations in the structure of the cell wall in the two groups.

革蘭氏染色法　細菌細胞染色的一種方法，係用於鑒別細菌的一種主要手段。將細菌標本置於載玻片上塗成薄膜，晾乾並加熱固定，用紫色染料染色，經脫色劑（如酒精）處理後再用紅色染料復染。革蘭氏陰性細菌失去最初的染劑而攝取復染劑，故在顯微鏡下呈現紅色。革蘭氏陽性細菌保留最初的染劑而在顯微鏡下呈現紫色。這兩種染色差別是根據兩類不同的細胞壁結構決定的。

grand mal (major epilepsy) *see* epilepsy.

癲癇大發作　參閱 epilepsy。

grand multiparity the condition of a woman who has had six or more previous pregnancies. Such women are more prone to the accidents of labour and to some of the diseases of pregnancy.

多經產 指以前已懷孕六次以上婦女的身體狀況。此類婦女更易發生分娩事故和一些妊娠疾病。

granular cast a cellular *cast derived from a kidney tubule. In certain kidney diseases, notably acute *glomerulonephritis, abnormal collections of renal tubular cells are shed from the kidney, often as a cast of the tubule. The casts can be observed on microscopic examination of the centrifuged deposit of a specimen of urine. Their presence in the urine indicates continued activity of the disease.

顆粒管型 自腎小管衍生的一種細胞管型。在某些腎臟疾病，特別是急性腎小球腎炎，從腎小管脫落的異常積聚物常像一種小管的模型。可用尿標本離心後取渣作顯微鏡檢查，以觀察管型。尿內出現管型表示疾病在繼續活動。

granulation n. the growth of small rounded outgrowths, made up of small blood vessels and connective tissue, on the healing surface of a wound (when the edges do not fit closely together) or an ulcer. Granulation is a normal stage in the healing process.

肉芽 由許多小血管和結締組織長出的小圓肉團，生長於傷口愈合面（當其邊緣不能合攏時）或潰瘍上。肉芽發生是愈合的一個正常步驟。

granulocyte n. any of a group of white blood cells that, when stained with *Romanowsky stains, are seen to contain granules in their cytoplasm. They can be subclassified on the basis of the colour of the stained granules into *neutrophils, *eosinophils, and *basophils.

粒細胞 用羅曼諾夫斯基染劑染色時可見到細胞質內含有顆粒的任何一類白細胞。粒細胞按其所染顆粒的顏色可分為中性、嗜酸性和嗜鹼性三類。

granulocytopenia n. a reduction in the number of *granulocytes (a type of white cell) in the blood. See neutropenia.

粒細胞減少 血液中粒細胞（白細胞的一種類型）的數目減少。參閱 neutropenia。

granuloma n. (pl. **granulomata** or **granulomas**) a mass of *granulation tissue produced in response to chronic infection, inflammation, a foreign body, or to unknown causes. Infections giving rise to granulomata include tuberculosis, syphilis, *granuloma inguinale, leprosy,

肉芽腫 由肉芽組織形成的腫塊。係由慢性感染、炎症、異物或不明病因引起。由感染引起的肉芽腫包括結核病、梅毒、腹股溝肉芽腫、麻風病和某些真菌病，如球孢子菌病。肉芽腫可由於澱粉或外科治療

and some fungal diseases, such as coccidioidomycosis. Granulomata may occur as reactions to such foreign bodies as starch and talc following surgical procedures or to some metals, such as beryllium and zirconium. Sarcoidosis and Crohn's disease are granulomatous diseases of which the causes are not known. A granuloma may also occur around the apex of a tooth root as a result of inflammation or infection of its pulp. **–granulomatous** *adj.*

後的滑石粉等異物，或由於諸如鈹、鋯等金屬所引起的反應所致。肉樣瘤病和克羅恩病是病因未明的肉芽腫性疾病。肉芽腫也可發生於牙根尖端的周圍，係牙髓的炎症或感染的結果。

granuloma annulare a chronic skin condition of unknown cause. In the common localized type there is a ring or rings of closely set papules, 1–5 cm in diameter, found principally on the hands and arms.

環形肉芽腫　一種慢性皮膚病，病因不明。在其常局限的類型有一個或多個密布的丘疹環，直徑為 1~5 cm，主要見於手和臂上。

granuloma inguinale an infectious disease caused by *Calymmatobacterium granulomatis*, which is known to be transmitted during sexual intercourse. It is marked by a pimply rash on and around the genital organs, which develops into a granulomatous ulcer. The disease responds to treatment with tetracyclines and streptomycin.

腹股溝肉芽腫　由肉芽腫鞘桿菌引起的一種傳染性疾病，通常經性交傳染。在外生殖器周圍皮膚上出現膿疱性丘疹，並形成肉芽性潰瘍。本病用四環素族抗生素和鏈黴素治療有效。

granulomatosis *n.* any condition marked by multiple widespread *granulomata. *See also* Wegener's granulomatosis.

肉芽腫病　以蔓延的多發性肉芽腫為特徵的任何一種疾病。參閱　Wegener's granulomatosis。

granulopoiesis *n.* the process of production of *granulocytes, which normally occurs in the blood-forming tissue of the *bone marrow. Granulocytes are ultimately derived from a *haemopoietic stem cell, but the earliest precursor that can be identified microscopically is the *myeloblast. This divides and passes through a series of stages of maturation termed respectively *promyelocyte,

粒細胞生成　粒細胞產生的過程，通常發生於骨髓的造血組織。粒細胞淵源於造血幹細胞，但在顯微鏡下可辨認的最早的前體是原粒細胞，由原粒細胞經過一系列的成熟期，分別稱為早幼粒細胞、中幼粒細胞和晚幼粒細胞，而分化演變為成熟的粒細胞。參閱 haemopoiesis。

GRAPH- 690

*myelocyte, and *metamyelocyte, before becoming a mature granulocyte. *See also* haemopoiesis.

graph- (grapho-) *prefix denoting* handwriting.

〔前綴〕**書寫的** 指與書寫有關的。

-graph *suffix denoting* an instrument that records. Example: *electrocardiograph* (instrument recording heart activity).

〔後綴〕**描記器** 指一種記錄儀器。例如：心電描記器（記錄心臟活動的儀器）。

graphology *n.* the study of the characteristics of handwriting to obtain indications about a person's psychological make-up or state of health. It is possible to detect certain signs of physical disease, such as fine nervous tremors or irregularity of the pulse.

筆體學 研究書寫特徵以獲得人的心理氣質或健康狀態特徵的科學。根據筆體來察知軀體疾病的某些體徵是可能的，例如細微的神經性震顫或不整脈。

grattage *n.* the process of brushing or scraping the surface of a slowly healing ulcer or wound to remove *granulation tissue, which – though a stage in the healing process – sometimes overgrows or becomes infected and therefore delays healing. Grattage is used in the treatment of *trachoma.

刷除術 用刷除或刮除緩慢愈合的潰瘍或傷口的表面以去除肉芽組織，肉芽組織的發生雖然是愈合過程的一個步驟，但其有時過度生長或受感染時，可延遲愈合。刷除術用於沙眼的治療。

gravel *n.* small stones formed in the urinary tract. The stones usually consist of calcareous debris or aggregations of other crystalline material. The passage of gravel from the kidneys is usually associated with severe pain (*ureteric colic*) and may cause blood in the urine. *See also* calculus.

尿結石 在泌尿道內形成的小石子。這些石子常由石灰質的碎屑或其他晶體物質的聚集體組成。尿結石從腎內排出時常伴有劇痛（輸尿管絞痛）並可導致血尿。參閱 calculus。

Graves's disease (exophthalmic goitre) *see* thyrotoxicosis.

格雷夫斯病（突眼性甲狀腺腫） 參閱 thyrotoxicosis。

gravid *adj.* pregnant.

妊娠的 懷孕的。

Grawitz tumour *see* hypernephroma.

格拉維茨瘤 參閱 hypernephroma。

gray *n.* the *SI unit of absorbed dose of ionizing radiation, being the absorbed dose when the energy per unit mass imparted to matter by ionizing radiation is 1 joule per kilogram. It has replaced the rad. Symbol: Gy.

戈瑞　電離輻射吸收劑量國際單位。電離輻射給予物體的能量為每千克 1 焦耳的吸收劑量時，即為 1 戈瑞。它已替代拉德單位。符號：Gy。

green monkey disease *see* Marburg disease.

綠猴病　參閱　Marburg disease。

greenstick fracture an incomplete break in a long bone occurring in children, whose bones have greater flexibility. *See also* fracture.

青枝骨折　一種不完全骨折，發生於兒童的長骨。因兒童長骨有較大的韌性。參閱　fracture。

grey matter the darker coloured tissues of the central nervous system, composed mainly of the cell bodies of neurones, branching dendrites, and glial cells (*compare* white matter). In the brain grey matter forms the *cerebral cortex and the outer layer of the cerebellum; in the spinal cord the grey matter lies centrally and is surrounded by white matter.

灰質　中樞神經系統的顏色較深的組織（與 white matter 對比），主要由神經元的細胞體、分支的樹突和神經膠質細胞組成。在腦內的灰質形成大腦皮質和小腦外層；在脊髓內灰質居於中央，四周被白質包圍。

gripe *n.* severe abdominal pain (*see* colic).

腸絞痛　嚴重的腹痛。參閱 colic。

griseofulvin *n.* an *antibiotic administered by mouth to treat fungal infections of the hair, skin, and nails, such as ringworm. Mild and temporary side-effects such as headache, skin rashes, and digestive upsets may occur. Trade names: **Fulcin**, **Grisovin**.

灰黃黴素　一種口服抗生素，用於治療頭髮、皮膚和指甲的真菌感染，如癬菌病。可有暫時的輕微副作用，如頭痛、皮疹和胃腸道不適。商品名：Fulcin，Grisovin。

groin *n.* the external depression on the front of the body that marks the junction of the abdomen with either of the thighs. *See also* inguinal.

腹股溝　在身體前面腹部與兩側大腿相接處呈現的外表凹陷。參閱 inguinal。

grommet *n.* a flanged metal or plastic tube that is inserted in the eardrum in cases of *glue ear. It allows air to enter the middle ear, bypassing the

通氣管　一種翼緣的金屬或塑料管子。用以插入膠耳病人鼓膜內使空氣進入中耳，繞過患者自己喪失功能的咽鼓管。

patient's own nonfunctioning *Eustachian tube.

ground substance the matrix of *connective tissue, in which various cells and fibres are embedded.

基質　結締組織的細胞間質，其中包埋着各種細胞和纖維。

group practice *see* general practitioner.

聯合診所　參閱 general practitioner。

group therapy 1. (group psychotherapy) *psychotherapy involving at least two patients and a therapist. The patients are encouraged to understand and to analyse their own and one another's problems. *See also* encounter group, psychodrama. **2.** therapy in which people with the same problem, such as *alcoholism, meet and discuss together their difficulties and possible ways of overcoming them.

集體治療　**(1)**（集體心理治療）至少有兩個病人和一個治療師在一起進行的心理治療。鼓勵病人互相了解和分析自己的和他人的問題。參閱 encounter group，psychodrama。**(2)** 對病情相同，如酒精中毒的病人在一起進行的治療。病人聚在一起討論他們的困難和克服困難的可能途徑。

growth factor a *polypeptide that is produced by cells and stimulates them to proliferate. Some may be involved in the abnormal regulation of growth seen in cancer when produced in excessive amounts. An example is *platelet-derived growth factor* (*PDGF*).

生長因子　由細胞產生並刺激其增殖的多肽。有些生長因子與當產生過量時見於癌症的生長異常調節有關。例如血小板衍生生長因子。

growth hormone (GH, somatotrophin) a hormone, synthesized and stored in the anterior pituitary gland, that promotes growth of the long bones in the limbs and increases protein synthesis (via *somatomedin). Its release is controlled by the opposing actions of *growth-hormone releasing hormone* and *somatostatin. Excessive production of growth hormone results in *gigantism before puberty and *acromegaly in adults. Lack of growth hormone in children causes *dwarfism.

生長激素　在垂體前葉內合成並貯藏的一種激素，促進四肢長骨的生長和增加蛋白質的合成（通過促生長因子）。它的釋放是通過生長激素釋放激素和生長激素釋放抑制因子的反作用而控制的。生長激素產生過多導致青春期前的巨人症和成人的肢端肥大症。在兒童時缺少生長激素會引起侏儒症。

grumous *adj.* coarse; lumpy; clotted; often used to describe the appearance of

凝塊的　粗糙的、結塊的、凝結的，常用於描述創傷或患病

the centre of wounds or diseased cells or the surface of a bacterial culture.

細胞中央部分，或細菌培養基表面的外貌。

guaiphenesin *n.* an *expectorant used in cough mixtures and tablets.

愈創甘油醚　一種祛痰劑，用作止咳合劑或片劑。

guanethidine *n.* a drug that is used to reduce high blood pressure (*see* sympatholytic). It is administered by mouth; common side-effects are diarrhoea, faintness, and dizziness. Trade name: **Ismelin**.

胍乙啶　一種降血壓藥物（參閱 sympatholytic）。口服。常見副作用有腹瀉、乏力和眩暈。商品名：Ismelin。

guanine *n.* one of the nitrogen-containing bases (*see* purine) that occurs in the nucleic acids DNA and RNA.

鳥嘌呤　含氮鹼基中的一種（參閱 purine），存在於脫氧核糖核酸和核糖核酸的核酸中。

guanosine *n.* a compound containing guanine and the sugar ribose. *See also* nucleotide.

鳥苷　一種含有鳥嘌呤和核糖的化合物。參閱 nucleotide。

gubernaculum *n.* (*pl.* **gubernacula**) either of a pair of fibrous strands of tissue that connect the gonads to the inguinal region in the fetus. In the male they guide and possibly move the testes into the scrotum before birth. In the female the ovaries descend only slightly within the abdominal cavity and the gubernacula persist as the round ligaments connecting the ovaries and uterus to the abdominal wall.

引帶　在胚胎期連接生殖腺於腹股溝區的一對索狀纖維組織的任何一個。在男性出生前引帶引導睾丸並可能牽拉睾丸進入陰囊中。在女性卵巢於腹腔內僅稍微下降，其引帶成為連接卵巢和子宮於腹壁的圓韌帶。

Guillain-Barré syndrome (postinfective polyneuropathy) a disease of the peripheral nerves in which there is numbness and weakness in the limbs. It usually develops 10–12 days after a respiratory infection that provokes an allergic response in the peripheral nerves; recovery is usually excellent although often prolonged. A rapidly progressive form of the disease is called *Landry's paralysis*. *See* polyradiculitis.

吉-巴氏綜合徵　周圍神經的一種疾病。具有四肢麻木無力的症狀。常在一次呼吸系統感染後 10~20 天發生，係感染引起周圍神經的一種變態反應；恢復通常很好，儘管經常拖長。此病的一種急進型稱為朗德里麻痺。參閱 polyradiculitis。

guillotine *n.* **1.** a surgical instrument used for removing the tonsils. It is loop-shaped and contains a sliding knife blade (see illustration). **2.** an encircling suture to control the escape of fluid or blood from an orifice or to close a gap.

(1) 鍘除刀 用於切除扁桃體的一種外科器械，環狀，並裝有滑動的刀片（見圖）。**(2) 環繞縫合** 用於控制液體或血液從一開口流失或關閉裂隙。

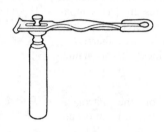

A tonsil guillotine
扁桃體鍘除刀

guinea worm a nematode worm, *Dracunculus medinensis*, that is a parasite of man. The white threadlike adult female, 60–120 cm long, lives in the connective tissues beneath the skin. It releases its larvae into a large blister on the legs or arms; when the limbs are immersed in water the larvae escape and are subsequently eaten by tiny water fleas (*Cyclops*), inside which their development continues. The disease *dracontiasis results from drinking water contaminated with *Cyclops*.

麥地那龍綫蟲 是人類的一種寄生綫蟲。白色綫狀雌性成蟲體長 60~120cm，寄生於皮下結締組織內。其幼蟲在小腿或手臂上形成一個大疱；當人的肢體浸入水中時，幼蟲即逸出，繼而被小水蚤（劍水蚤）吞食，並在其體內繼續發育。麥地那龍綫蟲病係飲了受劍水蚤污染的水所致。

gullet *n. see* oesophagus.

食管 參閱 oesophagus。

gum *n.* (in anatomy) *see* gingiva.

齦 （解剖學）參閱 gingiva。

gumboil *n.* the opening on the surface of the gum of a *sinus tract from a chronic abscess associated with the roots of a tooth. It may be accompanied by varying degrees of swelling, pain, and discharge and is more often related to deciduous than to permanent teeth.

齦膿腫 開口於牙齦表面與牙根相通的慢性膿腫的竇道。有不同程度的腫脹、疼痛和膿溢，在乳牙較在恆牙更為常見。

gumma *n.* a small soft tumour, characteristic of the tertiary stage of *syphilis, that occurs in connective tissue, the liver, brain, testes, heart, or bone.

gumshield *n.* a soft flexible cover that fits over the teeth for protection in contact sports. The best type is specially made to fit the individual.

gunshot wound a common cause of both military and civil injuries. Gunshot wounds are usually produced by high-velocity missiles: deep-seated tissue destruction of thermal origin is a major complication.

gustation *n.* the sense of taste or the act of tasting.

gustatory *adj.* relating to the sense of taste or to the organs of taste.

gut *n.* **1.** *see* intestine. **2.** *see* catgut.

Guthrie test examination of a drop of blood to exclude the presence of *phenylketonuria. This rare metabolic disorder (with an estimated incidence of 1/20,000) has severe consequences in terms of mental handicap unless the child receives a special diet from an early age. It is performed once milk feeding has been established, on the sixth or seventh day of life.

gutta *n.* (*pl.* **guttae**) (in pharmacy) a drop. Drops are the form in which medicines are applied to the eyes and ears.

gutta-percha *n.* the juice of an evergreen Malaysian tree, which is hard at room temperature but becomes soft and elastic when heated in hot water. On cooling, gutta-percha will retain any

梅毒瘤，樹膠腫　一種小的軟瘤，為第三期梅毒的特徵。發生於結締組織、肝、腦、睾丸、心和骨內。

護齒　一種柔軟的套在牙齒上的保護罩，在交手運動項目中作保護用。最好的護齒是專門為個人而特製的。

彈傷　軍事和民事損傷的常見原因。通常由高速導彈所致。熱源破壞深位組織是主要的併發症。

味覺　味道的感覺或嘗味。

味覺的　有關味覺或味覺器官的。

(1) 腸　參閱 intestine。(2) 腸綫　參閱 catgut。

格思里試驗　檢查一滴血以排除苯丙酮酸尿的試驗。這種罕見的代謝缺陷（估計發生率為1/20 000）能產生嚴重的精神障礙後遺症。除非在幼年時給兒童一種特殊的膳食才可避免。一旦乳餵養建立起來，即出生後第六、七天施行此檢查。

滴　（藥劑學）一種滴劑。滴劑是用於眼和耳的醫藥的一種劑型。

馬來乳膠　馬來西亞的一種常綠樹的膠汁。這種乳膠在室溫時是堅硬的，而在沸水中加熱則變得柔軟而有彈性。冷卻後乳膠保持其加熱時所具有的形

deformity imparted to it when hot; thus it was used in dentistry as an impression material and as a temporary filling material. It has been superseded by better materials but is still used in the form of gutta-percha points as the core of *root fillings.

態。因此曾用於牙科學作為印模材料和暫時充填的材料。這種乳膠現已被更好的材料所替代，但仍用於作為根管充填的填料。

guttate *adj.* describing lesions in the skin that are shaped like drops.

滴狀的 描述形如滴狀的皮膚損害。

GVHD *see* graft-versus-host disease.

移植物抗宿主病 參閱 graft-versus-host disease。

gyn- (gyno-, gynaec(o)-) *prefix denoting* women or the female reproductive organs.

〔前綴〕**女性** 指女子或女性生殖器官。

gynaecology *n.* the study of diseases of women and girls, particularly those affecting the female reproductive system. *Compare* obstetrics. **–gynaecological** *adj.* **–gynaecologist** *n.*

婦科學 研究婦女和少女的疾病，特別是累及女性生殖系統疾病的學科。與 obstetrics 對比。

gynaecomastia *n.* enlargement of the breasts in the male, due either to hormone imbalance or to hormone therapy.

男子女性型乳房 男子乳腺增大，或由於激素失衡或由於激素治療所致。

gypsum *n. see* plaster of Paris.

石膏 參閱 plaster of Paris。

gyr- (gyro-) *prefix denoting* **1.** a gyrus. **2.** a ring or circle.

〔前綴〕**(1)** 回 腦回。**(2)** 環 圓環或圈。

gyrus *n.* (*pl.* **gyri**) a raised convolution of the *cerebral cortex, between two sulci (clefts).

腦回 大腦皮層兩條裂溝（裂口）之間高起的回旋。

H

habit *n.* a sequence of learned behaviour occurring in a particular context or as a

習慣 產生於特殊場合或者作為對特別事件的反應的一些獲

response to particular events. Habits organize life, often in minute detail. They are often the result of *conditioning, are performed automatically and unconsciously, and reduce decision-making. Habits, once established, often persist after the original causal factors no longer operate. Behavioural psychology is based on the premise that one form of conditioning can be replaced by another.

得性行為。習慣常以細微的細節組織生活。它們常常是條件作用的結果，自動和無意識地進行並且減少做決定。習慣一旦建立起來，在起先促使的因素不再起作用之後常常會持續不變。行為心理學是基於一種形式的條件作用會被另一種所取代為前提。

habitual abortion *see* abortion.

習慣性流產 參閱 abortion。

habituation *n.* (in pharmacology) the condition of being psychologically dependent on a drug, following repeated consumption, marked by reduced sensitivity to its effects and a craving for the drug if it is withdrawn. *See also* dependence.

習慣化 （藥理學）指反覆使用某種藥物後，在生理上產生依賴性的狀態，其特徵為對藥物作用的敏感度降低和一旦停藥後就渴望得到該藥。參閱 dependence。

habitus *n.* an individual's general physical appearance, especially when this is associated with a constitutional tendency to a particular disease.

體型 一個人身體的一般外貌，尤指與患某種病的體質有聯繫時。

haem *n.* an iron-containing compound (a *porphyrin) that combines with the protein globin to form *haemoglobin, found in the red blood cells.

血紅素 一種含鐵化合物，與珠蛋白結合形成血紅蛋白，見於紅細胞中。

haem- (haema-, haemo-, haemat(o)-) *prefix denoting* blood. Examples: *haematogenesis* (formation of); *haemophobia* (fear of).

〔前綴〕血 如造血（血的形成），血恐怖（對血的恐懼）。

haemagglutination *n.* the clumping of red blood cells (*see* agglutination). It is caused by an antibody-antigen reaction or some viruses and other substances.

血細胞凝集 紅細胞的凝集（參閱 agglutination）。它是由一種抗體-抗原反應或者某些病毒和其他物質引起的。

haemangioblastoma (Lindau's tumour) *n.* a tumour of the brain or spinal cord arising in the blood vessels

成血管細胞瘤 （林道瘤）產生於腦膜或腦血管的腦脊髓腫瘤。它常伴有嗜鉻細胞瘤

of the meninges or brain. It is often associated with *phaeochromocytoma and *syringomyelia. *See also* von Hippel-Lindau disease.

haemangioma *n.* a benign tumour of blood vessels. It often appears on the skin as a type of birthmark; the strawberry *naevus is an example. *See also* angioma.

Haemaphysalis *n.* a genus of hard *ticks. Certain species transmit tick *typhus in the Old World; *H. spinigera* transmits the virus causing *Kyasanur Forest disease in India.

haemarthrosis *n.* joint pain and swelling caused by bleeding into a joint. This may follow injury or may occur spontaneously in a disease of the blood, such as *haemophilia. Treatment is by immobilization, cold compresses, and correction of the blood disorder (if present). Removal of blood from the joint may relieve the pain.

haematemesis *n.* the act of vomiting blood. The blood may have been swallowed (e.g. following nosebleed or tonsillectomy) but more often arises from bleeding in the oesophagus, stomach, or duodenum. Common causes are gastric and duodenal ulcers, gastritis brought on by irritating food or drink, and varicose veins in the oesophagus. If much blood is lost, it is usually replaced by blood transfusion. If bleeding does not stop spontaneously it may be arrested by coagulation of the bleeding point using either a *laser or a *heater-probe, or by the injection of *adrenaline or a sclerosing material: all these techniques are applied through an *endoscope. *See also* melaena.

和脊髓空洞症。參閱 von Hippel-Lindau disease。

血管瘤 一種血管的良性腫瘤。它常以一種胎痣出現於皮膚上，例如莓樣痣。參閱 angioma。

血蜱屬 硬蜱的一屬。在歐洲，某些種（類）可傳播蜱傳斑疹傷寒。在印度，距刺血蜱可傳播病毒，引起基亞薩努爾森林病。

關節積血 因出血進入關節內所致的關節疼痛和腫脹。此病可發生於損傷後，在血液病中也可自發產生，如血友病時。治療包括固定關節、冷敷，有血液病者治療該病。排除關節中積血可減輕疼痛。

嘔血 嘔吐血液的動作。血液可被吞咽（如鼻出血或扁桃體切除後），而更多見於食管、胃或十二指腸出血時發生嘔血。常見的原因有胃和十二指腸潰瘍、飲食刺激引起的胃炎以及食管靜脈曲張。如失血過多，往往需要輸血。如果流血不能自發停止，可通過使用激光、加熱探針或者注射腎上腺素或者硬化物質使出血點凝結的方法抑制。以上所有方法都是通過內窺鏡操作的。參閱 melaena。

haemathidrosis (haematidrosis) *n. see* haematohidrosis.

血汗症　參閱　haematohidrosis。

haematin *n.* a chemical derivative of *haemoglobin formed by removal of the protein part of the molecule and oxidation of the iron atom from the ferrous to the ferric form.

高鐵血紅素　血紅蛋白的化學衍生物。通過去掉血紅蛋白分子中的蛋白部分，以及將鐵原子由亞鐵氧化成高鐵所形成。

haematinic *n.* a drug that increases the amount of *haemoglobin in the blood, e.g. *ferrous sulphate and other iron-containing compounds. Haematinics are used, often in combination with vitamins and *folic acid, to prevent and treat anaemia due to iron deficiency. They are used particularly to prevent anaemia during pregnancy. Digestive disturbances sometimes occur with haematinics.

補血藥　增加血液中血紅蛋白含量的藥物，如硫酸亞鐵以及其他含鐵化合物。補血藥通常與維生素類及葉酸聯合使用，用於預防和治療缺鐵性貧血。此藥尤多用於預防妊娠期貧血。服用補血藥有時可發生消化功能紊亂。

haematocoele *n.* a swelling caused by leakage of blood into a cavity, especially that of the membrane overlying the front and sides of the testis. A *parametric* (*pelvic*) *haematocoele* is a swelling near the uterus formed by the escape of blood, usually from a Fallopian tube in ectopic pregnancy.

體腔積血　血液漏入腔內引起的一種腫脹，尤其指睾丸鞘膜的積血。子宮旁（盆腔）積血，通常是由於輸卵管異位妊娠，血液漏出，在子宮附近形成的一種腫脹。

haematocolpos *n.* the accumulation of menstrual blood in the vagina because the hymen at the entrance to the vagina lacks an opening. *See* cryptomenorrhoea.

陰道積血　由於陰道入口處的處女膜閉鎖，月經血集積於陰道內所致。參閱 cryptomenorrhoea。

haematocrit *n. see* packed cell volume.

紅細胞壓積　參閱 packed cell volume。

haematocyst *n.* a cyst that contains blood.

血囊腫　內含血液的囊腫。

haematogenous (haematogenic) *adj.* **1.** relating to the production of blood or its constituents; haematopoietic. **2.** produced by, originating in, or carried by the blood.

(1) 生血的　與血或血液成分的產生有關的。**(2) 血源性的**　由血產生的，起源於血的或由血攜帶的。

haematohidrosis (haemathidrosis, haematidrosis) *n.* the secretion of sweat containing blood.

血汗症　排出含血的汗液。

haematology *n.* the study of blood and blood-forming tissues and the disorders associated with them. **–haematological** *adj.* **–haematologist** *n.*

血液學　研究血液和造血組織及其疾病的學科。

haematoma *n.* an accumulation of blood within the tissues that clots to form a solid swelling. Injury, disease of the blood vessels, or a clotting disorder of the blood are the usual causative factors. An *intracranial haematoma* causes symptoms by compressing the brain and by raising the pressure within the skull. A blunt injury to the head, especially the temple, may tear the middle meningeal artery, giving rise to a rapidly accumulating *extradural haematoma* requiring urgent surgical treatment. In elderly people a relatively slight head injury may tear the veins where they cross the space beneath the dura, giving rise to a *subdural haematoma*. Excellent results are obtained by surgical treatment. An *intracerebral haematoma* may be a consequence of severe head injury but is more often due to *atherosclerosis of the cerebral arteries and high blood pressure resulting in bleeding into the brain. *See also* perianal haematoma.

血腫　血液在組織內蓄積，凝結成一固性腫塊。血管病、凝血障礙是引起本病的常見因素。顱內血腫能引起腦受壓和顱內壓升高的症狀。頭部損傷可戳破腦膜中的動脈，迅速引起血液集積而形成硬膜外血腫。此病需要緊急外科治療。對老年人，較輕的頭部損傷可戳破穿過硬腦膜下部的靜脈，引起硬腦膜下血腫。外科治療可獲顯效。顱內血腫可能是嚴重的頭部外傷的結果。但較常見的是由於腦動脈硬化和高血壓導致血液進入大腦。參閱 perianal haematoma。

haematometra *n.* **1.** accumulation of menstrual blood in the uterus. **2.** any abnormally copious bleeding in the uterus.

子宮積血　**(1)** 月經血蓄積於子宮內。**(2)** 子宮內異常的大量出血。

haematomyelia *n.* bleeding into the tissue of the spinal cord. This has been thought to be the cause of acutely developing symptoms that mimic *syringomyelia.

骨髓出血　出血時血液進入脊髓組織內。本病被認為是假性脊髓空洞症症狀急性發展的原因。

haematopoiesis *n. see* haemopoiesis.

血細胞生成　參閱 haemopoiesis。

haematoporphyrin *n.* a type of **por-phyrin produced during the metabolism of haemoglobin.

血卟啉　卟啉的一種類型，產生於血紅蛋白代謝過程中。

haematosalpinx (haemosalpinx) *n.* the accumulation of menstrual blood in the Fallopian tubes.

輸卵管積血　經血蓄積於輸卵管內。

haematoxylin *n.* a colourless crystalline compound extracted from logwood (*Haematoxylon campechianum*) and used in various histological stains. When oxidized haematoxylin is converted to *haematein*, which imparts a blue colour to certain parts of cells, especially cell nuclei. *Heidenhain's iron haematoxylin* is used to stain sections that are to be photographed, since it gives great clarity at high magnification.

蘇木精　一種無色的晶狀化合物，由洋蘇木提取，用於各種組織學染色。蘇木精可氧化成氧化蘇木精，它可使細胞的某些部分染成藍色，尤其是細胞核部分。由於海登海因鐵蘇木精在高倍放大下呈現高的清晰度，故常用於染拍照用的切片。

haematuria *n.* the presence of blood in the urine. The blood may come from the kidneys, one or both ureters, the bladder, or the urethra, as a result of injury or disease.

血尿　尿中有血液存在，血液可來自腎、一側或兩側輸尿管、膀胱或尿道、因損傷或疾病所致。

haemin *n.* a chemical derivative of haemoglobin formed by removal of the protein part of the molecule, oxidation of the iron atom, and combination with an acid to form a salt (*compare* haematin). *Chlorohaemin* forms characteristic crystals, the identification of which provides the basis of a chemical test for blood stains.

氯化血紅素　血紅蛋白的化學衍生物，通過去掉血紅蛋白分子中的蛋白部分，使鐵原子氧化，以及與酸結合成鹽形成的（與 haematin 對比）。氯化血紅素形成有特徵性的晶體，其晶體特徵之辨認為血痕（法醫）化驗的基礎。

haemo- *prefix. see* haem-.

〔前綴〕血

Haemobartonella *n. see* Bartonella.

血巴爾通體屬　參閱 Bartonella。

haemochromatosis (bronze diabetes, iron-storage disease) *n.* a hereditary

血色素沉着症（青銅色糖尿病，鐵貯積病）　鐵貯積過多的

disorder in which there is excessive absorption and storage of iron. This leads to damage and functional impairment of many organs, including the liver, pancreas, and endocrine glands. The main features are a bronze colour of the skin, diabetes, and liver failure. Iron may be removed from the body by blood letting or an iron *chelating agent may be administered. *Compare* haemosiderosis.

一種遺傳性疾病。它可導致許多器官包括肝、胰和內分泌腺損傷和功能降低。其主要特徵是：青銅色皮膚、糖尿病和肝功能衰竭。可通過放血或鐵螯合劑使鐵從體內排出。與 haemosiderosis 對比。

haemoconcentration *n.* an increase in the proportion of red blood cells relative to the plasma, brought about by a decrease in the volume of plasma. Haemoconcentration may occur in any condition in which there is a severe loss of water from the body. *Compare* haemodilution.

血濃縮 由於血漿容量下降，造成紅細胞與血漿之比相對增加。血濃縮可發生於任何身體失水的情況。與 haemodilution 對比。

haemocytometer *n.* a special glass chamber of known volume into which diluted blood is introduced. The numbers of the various blood cells present are then counted visually, through a microscope. Haemocytometers have been largely replaced by electronic cell counters.

血細胞計數器 已知容積的特製玻璃池。將稀釋的血液滴入池內，爾後通過顯微鏡，以目視計算存在的各種血細胞的數目。血細胞計數器已基本被電子計數器所取代。

haemodialysis *n.* a technique of removing waste materials or poisons from the blood using the principle of *dialysis. Haemodialysis is performed on patients whose kidneys have ceased to function; the process takes place in an *artificial kidney*, or *dialyser*. The stream of blood taken from an artery is circulated through the dialyser on one side of a semipermeable membrane, while a solution of similar electrolytic composition to the patient's blood circulates on the other side. Water and waste products from the patient's blood filter through the membrane, whose pores are too small to allow passage of blood cells and

血液透析 運用透析的原理排除血中廢物和毒物的一種技術。血液透析施行於兩側腎已喪失功能的病人，透析通過人工腎或透析器進行。方法是引出一動脈血流，使在透析器中半透膜的一側循環，在半透膜的另一側循環著與病人的血液電解質成分類似的溶液，病人血中的水分和廢物通過此膜濾過。由於膜孔很小，血細胞和蛋白質不能通過，然後純淨的血經靜脈回流至病人體內。

proteins. The purified blood is then returned to the patient's body through a vein.

haemodilution *n.* a decrease in the proportion of red blood cells relative to the plasma, brought about by an increase in the total volume of plasma. This may occur in a variety of conditions, including pregnancy and enlargement of the spleen (*see* hypersplenism). *Compare* haemoconcentration.

血液稀釋　由於血漿總容量的增加，血細胞與血漿之比相對下降。血液稀釋可發生於各種情況，包括妊娠和脾腫大（參閱 hypersplenism）。與 haemoconcentration 對比。

haemoglobin *n.* a substance contained within the red blood cells (*erythrocytes) and responsible for their colour, composed of the pigment *haem* (an iron-containing *porphyrin) linked to the protein *globin*. Haemoglobin has the unique property of combining reversibly with oxygen and is the medium by which oxygen is transported within the body. It takes up oxygen as blood passes through the lungs and releases it as blood passes through the tissues. Blood normally contains 12–18 g/dl of haemoglobin. *See also* myohaemoglobin, oxyhaemoglobin.

血紅蛋白　存在於紅細胞內，決定紅細胞顏色的一種物質，由血色素（一種含鐵卟啉）與珠蛋白連接組成。血紅蛋白具有獨特的性質，即與氧呈可逆性結合，在體內作為輸送氧的媒介。當血流通過肺部時血紅蛋白即吸取氧，而當通過組織時則將氧釋放出來。正常血紅蛋白含量為 12~18 g/dl。參閱 myohaemoglobin，oxyhaemoglobin。

haemoglobinometer *n.* an instrument for determining the concentration of *haemoglobin in a sample of blood, which is a measure of its ability to carry oxygen.

血紅蛋白計　一種測定血標本中血紅蛋白濃度的儀器，也是測定血紅蛋白攜氧能力的儀器。

haemoglobinopathy *n.* any of a group of inherited diseases, such as *thalassaemia and *sickle-cell disease, in which there is an abnormality in the production of haemoglobin.

血紅蛋白病　血紅蛋白生成異常的遺傳性疾病中任何一種，包括地中海貧血、鐮狀細胞病等。

haemoglobinuria *n.* the presence in the urine of free haemoglobin. The condition occurs if haemoglobin, released from disintegrating red blood cells, cannot be taken up rapidly enough by blood

血紅蛋白尿　指尿中出現游離的血紅蛋白。當血紅蛋白從破壞的紅細胞中大量釋放出來，而且不能快速地與足夠的血漿蛋白結合時，即可發生血紅

proteins. The condition sometimes follows strenuous exercise. It is also associated with certain infectious diseases (such as blackwater fever), ingestion of certain chemicals (such as arsenic), and injury.

蛋白尿。此病有時發生於劇烈的鍛煉以後，也可能與某些傳染病（如黑尿熱）、攝入某些化學制品（如砷）和損傷等有關。

haemogram *n.* the results of a routine blood test, including an estimate of the blood haemoglobin level, the *packed cell volume, and the numbers of red and white blood cells (*see* blood count). Any abnormalities seen in microscopic examination of the blood are also noted.

血像 血常規檢驗的結果，包括血紅蛋白水平、血細胞壓積量以及紅、白細胞計數（參閱 blood count）。並記錄血液顯微鏡檢查中發現的任何異常情況。

haemolysin *n.* a substance capable of bringing about destruction of red blood cells (*haemolysis). It may be an antibody or a bacterial toxin.

溶血素 能引起紅細胞破壞的一種物質。它可能是一種抗體或一種細菌毒素。

haemolysis *n.* the destruction of red blood cells (*erythrocytes). Within the body, haemolysis may result from defects within the red cells or from poisoning, infection, or the action of antibodies; it may occur in mismatched blood transfusions. It usually leads to anaemia. Haemolysis of blood specimens may result from unsatisfactory collection or storage or be brought about intentionally as part of an analytical procedure (*see* laking).

溶血 紅細胞的破壞。在體內，溶血可由於紅細胞本身的缺陷，或因中毒、感染，或因輸血配血不當時抗體的作用引起，它可導致貧血。血標本溶血可由採集或貯存不當造成，或為了做化驗分析而有意造成的（參閱 laking）。

haemolytic *adj.* causing, associated with, or resulting from destruction of red blood cells (*erythrocytes). For example, a *haemolytic antibody* is one that causes destruction of red cells; a *haemolytic anaemia* is due to red-cell destruction (*see* anaemia).

溶血的 引起、伴有或由紅細胞的破壞導致的，例如溶血性抗體是引起紅細胞溶血的一種物質，溶血性貧血是由紅細胞的破壞引起的（參閱 anaemia）。

haemolytic disease of the newborn the condition resulting from destruction (haemolysis) of the red blood cells of the fetus by antibodies in the mother's blood passing through the placenta. This most

新生兒溶血性疾病 胎兒紅細胞破壞（溶血）引起的疾病，由母血中的抗體通過胎盤進入胎兒血循環所致。當胎兒紅細胞是 Rh 陽性（即紅細胞具有

commonly happens when the red blood cells of the fetus are Rh positive (i.e. they have the *rhesus factor) but the mother's red cells are Rh negative. The fetal cells are therefore incompatible in her circulation and evoke the production of antibodies. This may result in very severe anaemia of the fetus, leading to heart failure with oedema (*hydrops fetalis) or stillbirth. When the anaemia is less severe the fetus may reach term in good condition, but the accumulation of the bile pigment bilirubin from the destroyed cells causes severe jaundice after birth, which may require *exchange transfusion. If untreated it may cause serious brain damage (*see* kernicterus).

A blood test early in pregnancy enables the detection of antibodies in the mother's blood and the adoption of various precautions for the infant's safety. Some cases of predictably very severe haemolytic disease have been successfully treated by intrauterine transfusion. The incidence of the disease has been greatly reduced by preventing the formation of antibodies in a Rh negative mother. If at birth or after an abortion the baby's blood is found to be incompatible with the mother's (i.e. Rh positive) she is given an injection of Rh antibody (anti-D immunoglobulin). This rapidly destroys any Rh positive fetal cells so that they do not remain long enough to stimulate antibody production in her blood (which could affect her next pregnancy).

haemolytic uraemic syndrome a condition in which sudden rapid destruction of red blood cells (*see* haemolysis) causes acute renal failure due partly to obstruction of small arteries in the kidneys. The haemolysis also causes a reduction in the number of platelets, which can lead to

Rh 因子），而母親紅細胞是 Rh 陰性極易發生本病。胎兒的血細胞在母親的血循環中不相適應而引起抗體的產生。本病可造成胎兒嚴重貧血，進而導致心力衰竭與水腫（胎兒水腫）或死胎。當貧血不太嚴重時，胎兒可足月順產，但當紅細胞破壞引起的膽汁色素（膽紅素）積集時，胎兒出生後可發生嚴重黃疸，可能需予換血。如未予治療，可引起嚴重的腦損傷（參閱 kernicterus）。

妊娠早期做血液檢查能檢測母血中的抗體，進而採取各種預防措施，以保證嬰兒的安全。某些預示嚴重的溶血性疾病的病例，通過子宮內輸血已治療成功。通過預防 Rh 陰性母體內抗體的形成，本病的發病率已大為減少。如一個婦女在分娩後或流產後發現胎兒血與母血不相容（即 Rh 陽性），則這位婦女應予注射 Rh 抗體（抗-D 免疫球蛋白）。此抗體能迅速地破壞 Rh 陽性胎兒細胞，以使 Rh 陽性胎兒細胞不能長時間存在，不能在該婦女血中刺激抗體的產生（此種抗體可影響母親下次妊娠）。

溶血性尿毒症綜合徵　紅細胞突然迅速地破壞（參閱 haemolysis），引起急性腎動能衰竭，部分由於腎內小動脈梗阻的一種病症。這種溶血也引起血小板計數減少，導致嚴重出血。此綜合徵可因敗血症、

severe haemorrhage. The syndrome may occur as a result of septicaemia, eclamptic fits in pregnancy (*see* eclampsia), or as a reaction to certain drugs. There may also be small sporadic outbreaks of the condition without any obvious cause.

haemopericardium *n.* the presence of blood within the membranous sac (pericardium) surrounding the heart, which may result from injury, tumours, rupture of the heart (e.g. following myocardial infarction), or a leaking aneurysm. The heart is compressed (*cardiac tamponade*) and the circulation impaired; a large fall in blood pressure and cardiac arrest may result. Surgical drainage of the blood may be life saving.

haemoperitoneum *n.* the presence of blood in the peritoneal cavity, between the lining of the abdomen or pelvis and the membrane covering the organs within.

haemophilia *n.* a hereditary disorder in which the blood clots very slowly, due to a deficiency of either of two *coagulation factors: Factor VIII (antihaemophilic factor) or Factor IX (Christmas factor). The patient may experience prolonged bleeding following any injury or wound, and in severe cases there is spontaneous bleeding into muscles and joints. Bleeding in haemophilia may be treated by transfusions of plasma (which contains the missing factor). Alternatively concentrated preparations of Factor VIII or Factor IX, obtained by freezing fresh plasma, may be administered (*see* cryoprecipitate). Haemophilia is controlled by a *sex-linked gene, which means that it is almost exclusively restricted to males: women can carry the disease – and pass it on to their sons – without being affected themselves. **–haemophiliac** *n.*

妊娠子癇（參閱 eclampsia）發作或某些藥物反應而發生。有些輕度散發病例沒有明顯的原因。

心包積血 指包繞心臟的膜性囊（心包）內積有血液。可由損傷、腫瘤、心臟破裂（例如心肌梗死後）或漏血性動脈瘤引起。心臟受壓（心包填塞）和循環受阻，可引起血壓下降和心搏停止。血液外科引流可挽救患者生命。

腹腔積血 腹腔內存有血液。血液積於腹部或骨盆內面的腹膜與臟器表面的腹膜之間。

血友病 一種遺傳性疾病。本病因缺乏兩種凝血因子的任何一種：凝血因子 VIII（抗血友病因子 A）或者凝血因子 IX（抗血友病因子 B），血液凝固極為緩慢。病人可能有操作或創傷後出血延長的病史。嚴重病例可有自發性出血、血液進入肌肉和關節中。血友病出血可用輸血漿（其中含所缺因子）來治療。亦可給予由冷凍新鮮血漿（參閱 cryoprecipitate）獲得的凝血因子 VIII 或 IX 濃縮製劑。血友病是由性連鎖基因控制。發病者幾乎全部只限於男性，而女性可攜帶本病基因，並將本病基因傳給她們的兒子，而她們自己並不發病。

Haemophilus *n.* a genus of Gram-negative aerobic nonmotile parasitic rodlike bacteria frequently found in the respiratory tract. They can grow only in the presence of certain factors in the blood and/or certain coenzymes: they are cultured on fresh blood *agar. Most species are pathogenic: *H. aegyptius* causes conjunctivitis, and *H. ducreyi* soft sore (chancroid). *H. influenzae* is associated with acute and chronic respiratory infections (*see also* epiglottitis) and is a common secondary cause of *influenza infections; *H. influenzae* type B is an important cause of bacterial *meningitis in young children (*see* Hib vaccine).

嗜血桿菌屬　革蘭氏陰性需氧型桿菌的一屬。無活動能力，屬寄生菌，常見於呼吸道。它只能生長於具有一定因子的血液和／或某些輔酶中。可培養於新鮮血液瓊脂。其多數菌種是致病性的：結膜炎嗜血桿菌引起結膜炎；杜克雷嗜血桿菌引起軟下疳；流感嗜血桿菌引起急性和慢性呼吸道感染（參閱 epiglottitis），而且是流感繼發感染的常見原因。B 型流感嗜血桿菌是少兒細菌性腦膜炎的重要原因（參閱 Hib vaccine）。

haemophthalmia *n.* bleeding into the *vitreous humour of the eye: vitreous haemorrhage.

眼球積血　血液進入眼的玻璃體中：玻璃體出血。

haemopneumothorax *n.* the presence of both blood and air in the pleural cavity, usually as a result of injury. Both must be drained out to allow the lung to expand normally. *See also* haemothorax.

血氣胸　胸膜腔中存有血液及氣體，通常係外傷的結果。必須將血液及氣體自胸膜腔引流出，使肺能正常地擴張。參閱 haemothorax。

haemopoiesis *n.* the process of production of blood cells and platelets which continues throughout life, replacing aged cells (which are removed from the circulation). In healthy adults, haemopoiesis is confined to the *bone marrow, but in embryonic life and in early infancy, as well as in certain diseases, it may occur in other sites (*extramedullary haemopoiesis*). *See also* erythropoiesis, leucopoiesis, thrombopoiesis. **–haemopoietic** *adj.*

血生成　血細胞和血小板的產生過程。此過程持續終身，以取代老的細胞（從血液循環中排除）。在健康的成人中，血生成限於骨髓中，而在胚胎期，幼小嬰兒以及某些疾病中，血生成則可發生於其他部位（骨髓外造血）。參閱 erythropoiesis，leucopoiesis，thrombopoiesis。

haemopoietic stem cell the cell from which all classes of blood cells are derived. It cannot be identified microscopically, although some workers believe that it is identical in appearance

造血幹細胞　衍生所有各級血細胞的原始造血細胞。儘管有些人認為，其外觀與淋巴細胞完全相同，在顯微鏡下無法辨別，它通過骨髓以及某些其他

with a *lymphocyte. It can be demonstrated by *tissue culture of the blood-forming tissue of the bone marrow, as well as in certain other sites. *See also* haemopoiesis.

部位造血組織的組織培養可得到證明。參閱 haemopoiesis。

haemoptysis *n.* the coughing up of blood. This symptom should always be taken seriously, however small the amount. In some patients the cause is not serious; in others it is never found. But it should always be reported to a doctor.

咯血 咳出血液，無論出血量多少，對這種症狀應採取認真的態度。儘管有些病人出血的原因是不嚴重的，甚至有些病人未找到原因，但都應該向醫生報告。

haemorrhage (bleeding) *n.* the escape of blood from a ruptured blood vessel, externally or internally. Arterial blood is bright red and emerges in spurts, venous blood is dark red and flows steadily, while damage to minor vessels may produce only an oozing. Rupture of a major blood vessel such as the femoral artery can lead to the loss of several litres of blood in a few minutes, resulting in *shock, collapse, and death, if untreated. *See also* haematemesis, haematuria, haemoptysis.

出血 血液從破裂的血管向體外或體內漏出。動脈血鮮紅，是湧出的；靜脈血暗紅，是緩緩流出的。當傷及小血管時，可引起滲血。大血管破裂，如股動脈出血，可在幾分鐘內丟失幾升血液。如未經治療可造成休克、虛脫及死亡。參閱 haematemesis，haematuria，haemoptysis。

haemorrhagic *adj.* associated with or resulting from blood loss (*see* haemorrhage). For example, *haemorrhagic anaemia* is due to blood loss (*see* anaemia).

出血的 與失血有關的或失血引起的（參閱 haemorrhage）。例如，出血性貧血是失血所致（參閱 anaemia）。

haemorrhagic disease of the newborn a temporary disturbance in blood clotting caused by *vitamin K deficiency and affecting infants on the second to fourth day of life. It causes gastrointestinal bleeding and is more common in breast-fed and *preterm infants. The condition can be prevented by giving all babies vitamin K, either by injection or orally, shortly after birth. Medical name: **melaena neonatorum**.

新生兒出血病 一種由維生素 K 缺乏引起的暫時性凝血障礙，影響第二天至第四天的新生嬰兒。它引起胃腸出血，在母乳餵養和早產兒更常見。此病可通過給出產後所有嬰兒注射或口服維生素 K 得到預防。醫學用語：新生兒黑糞症。

haemorrhoidectomy *n.* the surgical operation for removing *haemorrhoids, which are tied and then excised. Possible complications are bleeding or, later, anal stricture (narrowing). The operation is usually performed only for second- or third-degree haemorrhoids that have not responded to simple measures.

痔切除術 切除痔的外科手術。手術時先將痔核結紮，然後再予切除。可能的併發症是出血，或晚期的肛門狹窄。這種手術通常只用於簡單治療無效的第二或第三度痔。

haemorrhoids (piles) *pl. n.* enlargement of the normal spongy blood-filled cushions, in the wall of the anus (*internal haemorrhoids*), usually a consequence of prolonged constipation or, occasionally, diarrhoea. They most commonly occur at three main points equidistant around the circumference of the anus. Uncomplicated haemorrhoids are seldom painful; any pain is usually caused by a *fissure. The main symptom is bleeding, and in *first-degree haemorrhoids*, which never appear at the anus, bleeding at the end of defecation is the only symptom. *Second-degree haemorrhoids* protrude beyond the anus as an uncomfortable swelling but return spontaneously; *third-degree haemorrhoids* remain outside the anus and need to be returned by pressure.

First- and second-degree haemorrhoids may respond to bowel regulation using a high-fibre diet with faecal softening agents. If bleeding persists, an irritant fluid (a sclerosing agent) may be injected around the swollen cushions to make them shrivel up. Other effective treatments are infrared coagulation and the application of elastic bands. Third-degree haemorrhoids often require surgery (*see* haemorrhoidectomy), especially if they become *strangulated (producing severe pain and further enlargement).

External haemorrhoids are either prolapsed internal haemorrhoids or – more often – *perianal haematomas or

痔 肛門壁中海綿狀血管墊部位的擴張（內痔）。通常繼發於長期便秘，或偶爾繼發於腹瀉。內痔最常發生於圍繞肛周等距離的三個主要點。沒有併發症的痔少有疼痛；任何疼痛通常是肛裂所致。其主要症狀為出血。第一度痔肛門內還未出現痔核時，排便後出血是唯一的症狀；第二度痔是肛一側凸出，並有不舒適的腫脹感，但能自行回復；第三度痔脫出於肛門外，並需用壓力托回。

第一和第二度痔，用高纖維軟食及潤滑劑，以使有規律地排便，可能是有效的。如持續出血，可圍繞腫脹的靜脈注入一種刺激性液體（一種硬化劑），使痔萎縮。其他有效的治療為紅外綫凝結和敷用彈性繃帶。第三度痔，經常需行外科手術治療（參閱 haemorrhoidectomy），尤其如痔形成絞窄時（造成劇烈疼痛並進一步增大）。

外痔或是脫出的內痔，或（較常見的）是肛周血腫愈合後餘留的殘餘皮贅。

the residual skin tags remaining after a perianal haematoma has healed.

haemosalpinx *n. see* haematosalpinx.

輸卵管積血 參閱 haemato-salpinx。

haemosiderin *n.* a substance composed of a protein shell containing iron salts which may be present inside certain cells, being one of the forms in which iron is stored within the body. It is insoluble and may be demonstrated microscopically in suitably stained tissue preparations.

含鐵血黃素 由含鐵鹽蛋白殼組成的物質。它可存於某些細胞內，是鐵貯存於人體內的一種形式。它是不可溶的，在經過適當染色的組織製劑中，可在顯微鏡下顯示出。

haemosiderosis *n.* a disorder caused by excessive deposition of iron, which in turn results from excessive intake or administration of iron, usually in the form of blood transfusions. It results in damage to various organs, including the heart and liver. *Compare* haemo-chromatosis.

含鐵血黃素沉積症 鐵沉積過多引起的疾患。本病是由於攝取或投予鐵過多引起，且通常是以輸血的形式輸入。本症可導致各種器官——包括心和肝的損傷。與 haemochromato-sis 比較。

haemostasis *n.* the arrest of bleeding, involving the physiological processes of *blood coagulations and the contraction of damaged blood vessels. The term is also applied to various surgical procedures (for example the application of *ligatures or *diathermy to cut vessels) used to stop bleeding.

止血 阻止出血，包括凝血和損傷血管收縮的生理過程。此術語也適用於用來止血的各種手術操作（例如結紮或燒灼血管）。

haemostatic (styptic) *n.* an agent that stops or prevents haemorrhage: for example, *phytomenadione and *thromboplastin. Haemostatics are used to control bleeding due to various causes and may be used in treating bleeding disorders, such as haemophilia.

止血劑 止住或預防出血的製劑，例如維生素 K_1 及凝血激酶。止血劑用於控制各種原因引起的出血，還可用於治療各種出血性疾病，如血友病。

haemothorax *n.* blood in the pleural cavity, usually due to injury. If the blood is not drained dense fibrous *adhesions occur between the pleural surfaces,

血胸 血液存在於胸膜腔中，通常由損傷引起。如血液不引流出來，胸膜表面之間就會發生致密的纖維黏連。可損害肺

which can impair the normal movement of the lung. The blood may also become infected (*see* empyema).

haemozoin *n.* an iron-containing pigment present in the organisms that cause malaria (*Plasmodium* species).

hair *n.* a threadlike keratinized outgrowth of the epidermis of the *skin. It develops inside a tubular *hair follicle*. The part above the skin consists of three layers: an outer *cuticle*; a *cortex*, forming the bulk of the hair and containing the pigment that gives the hair its colour; and a central core (*medulla*), which may be hollow. The *root* of the hair, beneath the surface of the skin, is expanded at its base to form the *bulb*, which contains a matrix of dividing cells. As new cells are formed the older ones are pushed upwards and become keratinized to form the root and shaft. A hair may be raised by a small erector muscle in the dermis, attached to the hair follicle.

hairball *n. see* trichobezoar.

hair follicle a sheath of epidermal cells and connective tissue that surrounds the root of a *hair.

hair papilla a projection of the dermis that is surrounded by the base of the hair bulb. It contains the capillaries that supply blood to the growing *hair.

hairy cell an abnormal white blood cell that has the appearance of an immature lymphocyte with fine hairlike cytoplasmic projections around the perimeter of the cell. It is found in a rare form of leukaemia (*hairy-cell leukaemia*) most commonly occurring in young men.

的正常運動。積血也可被感染（參閱 empyema）。

瘧原蟲色素 存在於瘧疾病原體（症原蟲）內的含鐵色素。

毛髮 皮膚表皮上絨樣的角質化生出物。它在管狀的毛囊內發育。皮膚上面的部分由三層組成：外面有一層小皮；中層是皮質，構成毛髮的主體，並含有色素，使毛髮呈特有的顏色，核心（髓質）可以是中空的；毛根位於皮膚表面下，在其基部膨大形成毛球，球內含有分裂細胞的母質。當新的細胞形成時，老的細胞則被上推，然後角質化，形成毛根和毛幹。一根毛髮可通過真皮內的、附着於毛囊上的、小的立毛肌將其豎起。

毛團 參閱 trichobezoar。

毛囊 圍繞毛根的表皮細胞和結締組織鞘。

毛乳頭 被毛球基底面圍繞着的真皮突起。它含有許多毛細血管，對毛髮的生長提供血液。

毛狀細胞 一種不正常的白細胞。它具有不成熟淋巴細胞的外形以及圍繞細胞周邊的細毛髮樣的胞漿突起，這種細胞主要見於年輕人的罕見型的白血病（毛狀細胞白血病）。

halfway house a residential home for a group of people where some professional supervision is available. It is used as a stage in the rehabilitation of the mentally ill, usually when they have just been discharged from hospital and are able to work but are not yet ready for independent life.

重返社會訓練所　為一羣人而設的，可獲得某些專業性管理的住所。它用於精神病人的康復階段，通常是在病人剛出院，雖能工作但尚不能獨立生活時。

halitosis *n.* bad breath. Causes of temporary halitosis include recently eaten strongly flavoured food, such as garlic or onions, and drugs such as paraldehyde. Other causes include mouth breathing, *periodontal disease, and infective conditions of the nose, throat, and lungs (especially *bronchiectasis). Constipation, indigestion, and some liver diseases may also cause the condition.

口臭　呼出難聞的氣味。暫時性口臭的原因包括新近食入濃味食物，如蒜頭或洋葱，以及藥物如副醛。其他原因包括口呼吸、牙周病以及鼻、咽和肺（特別是支氣管擴張）的感染性疾病。便秘、消化不良以及某些肝病也可引起此症。

hallucination *n.* a false perception of something that is not really there. Hallucinations may be visual, auditory, tactile, gustatory (of taste), or olfactory (of smell). They may be provoked by psychological illness (such as *schizophrenia) or physical disorders in the brain (such as temporal lobe *epilepsy or stroke) or they may be caused by drugs or sensory deprivation. Hallucinations should be distinguished from dreams and from *illusions (since they occur at the same time as real perceptions and are not based upon real stimuli).

幻覺　一種並非真實存在的事物的虛假知覺。幻覺可以是視覺的、聽覺的、觸覺的、味覺的或者是嗅覺的。這些幻覺可由精神病（如精神分裂症）或腦的器質性疾患（如顳葉癲癇）或者由藥物或感覺喪失引起。幻覺應與夢和錯覺相區別（因這些錯覺與真實知覺同時發生而非基於真正刺激所產生）。

hallucinogen *n.* a drug that produces hallucinations, e.g. *cannabis and *lysergic acid diethylamide. Hallucinogens were formerly used to treat certain types of mental illness. **–hallucinogenic** *adj.*

致幻劑　引起幻覺的一種藥劑，如大麻、麥角酰二乙胺等。致幻劑過去用於治療某些類型的精神病。

hallux *n.* (*pl.* **halluces**) the big toe.

拇　大趾。

hallux rigidus painful stiffness of the joint between the big toe and the first

拇強直　與第一跖骨之間關節的疼痛強直。是對簡單（保守）

metatarsal bone. It is a common cause of painful disability that responds to simple (conservative) management.

治療有反應的引起疼痛性功能喪失的常見原因。

hallux valgus displacement of the big toe towards the others. It is often associated with a *bunion.

拇外翻 向其他趾的移位。常與拇囊炎有關。

hallux varus displacement of the big toe away from the others.

拇內翻 離開其他趾的移位。

haloperidol *n.* a *butyrophenone antipsychotic drug used to relieve anxiety and tension in the treatment of schizophrenia and other psychiatric disorders. It is administered by mouth or injection; muscular incoordination and restlessness are common side-effects. Trade names: **Haldol, Serenace**.

氟哌啶醇 一種丁酰苯抗精神病藥物,用於精神分裂症和其他精神病中以減輕焦慮和緊張。口服或注射給藥。肌共濟失調和不安是其常見的副作用。商品名:Haldol, Serenace。

halophilic *adj.* requiring solutions of high salt concentration for healthy growth. Certain bacteria are halophilic. **–halophile** *n.*

嗜鹽的 需要有高濃度鹽溶液才能健康生長的,某些細菌是嗜鹽的。

halos *pl. n.* coloured rings seen around lights by people with acute congestive glaucoma and sometimes by people with cataract.

暈 急性充血性青光眼患者所見的圍繞燈光的彩色環。白內障患者有時亦有此症狀。

halothane *n.* a potent general *anaesthetic administered by inhalation, used for inducing and maintaining anaesthesia in all types of surgical operations. Reduced blood pressure and irregular heartbeat may occur during halothane anaesthesia. Trade name: **Fluothane**.

氟烷 有效的吸入性全身麻醉藥,用於在所有類型外科手術中誘導和維持麻醉。氟烷麻醉過程中可發生血壓下降與心律不齊。商品名:Fluothane。

hamartoma *n.* an overgrowth of mature tissue in which the elements show disordered arrangement and proportion in comparison to normal. The overgrowth is benign but malignancy may occur in any of the constituent tissue elements.

錯構瘤 一種過度生長的成熟組織。與正常組織相比,其成分在排列及比例上顯得混亂。這種過度的生長物是良性的。但其中任何一種組織成分均可發生惡性變。

hamate bone (unciform bone) a hook-shaped bone of the wrist (*see* carpus). It articulates with the capitate and triquetral bones at the sides, with the lunate bone behind, and with the fourth and fifth metacarpal bones in front.

hammer *n.* (in anatomy) *see* malleus.

hammer toe a deformity of a toe, most often the second, caused by fixed flexion of the first joint. A corn often forms over the deformity, which may be painful. If severe pain does not respond to strapping or corrective footwear, it may be necessary to perform *arthrodesis at the affected joint.

hamstring *n.* any of the tendons at the back of the knee. They attach the *hamstring muscles* (the biceps femoris, semitendinosus, and semimembranosus) to their insertions in the tibia and fibula.

hamulus *n.* (*pl.* **hamuli**) any hooklike process, such as occurs on the hamate, lacrimal, and sphenoid bones and on the cochlea.

hand *n.* the terminal organ of the upper limb. From a surgical point of view, the human hand comprises the eight bones of the *carpus (wrist), the five metacarpal bones, and the phalangeal bones plus the surrounding tissues; anatomically, the bones and tissues of the wrist are excluded. The hand is a common site of infections and injuries, many of which are of industrial origin for which compensation may be claimed.

handedness *n.* the preferential use of one hand, rather than the other, in

鈎骨　腕的鈎狀骨（參閱 carpus）。與一側的頭狀骨和三角骨，與其後的月骨，與前方的第四及第五掌骨分別組成關節。

錘骨　（解剖學）參閱 malleus。

錘狀趾　足趾的一種畸形，最常見於第二趾骨，因第一趾關節固定於屈曲位所致。在畸形處常形成雞眼而致疼痛。如貼絆創膏或穿矯正鞋無效的話，則有必要做受影響關節的關節固定術。

膕繩肌腱　膝後的任何肌腱。它們連接膕繩肌羣（股二頭肌、半腱肌及半膜肌）至其在脛骨與腓骨的附着處。

鈎　任何鈎形的突起，例如發生於鈎骨的、淚骨的、蝶骨的以及耳蝸的。

手　上肢的終端器官。從外科的觀點，人手是由八隻腕骨、五隻掌骨和指骨及其周圍組織組成；解剖學上，腕骨和組織被排除在外。手是感染和損傷的常見處。許多損傷是工業起因，可索賠。

手偏利（用手習慣）　在隨意活動中，偏於用一側手，而非另

voluntary actions. Ambidexterity – the ability to use either hand with equal skill – is very rare. About 90% of people are right-handed and this correlates with the half of the brain that is dominant for speech: some 97% of right-handed people have left-hemisphere dominance for speech, whereas only 60% of left-handed people are right-hemisphere dominant for speech.

一側手。雙手同利（以同樣技能使用雙手的能力）很少見。大約 90% 的人是右偏利；這與大腦的言語優勢半球有關：大約 97% 的右偏利人有左半球言語優勢，而只有 60% 的左偏利人是右半腦言語優勢。

hand, foot, and mouth disease a self-limiting disease, mainly affecting young children, caused by *Coxsackie viruses. A feeling of mild illness is accompanied by mouth ulcers and painful blisters on the hands and feet.

手 - 足 - 口病　一種自限性疾病，主要影響少兒，由柯薩奇病毒引起。輕度的患病感伴隨口腔潰瘍和手足疼痛性水疱。

handicap *n.* **1.** partial or total inability to perform a social, occupational, or other activity that the affected person wants to do. It reflects the extent to which an individual is disadvantaged by some partial or total *disability* when compared with those in a peer group who have no such disability. A handicap is usually related to an identifiable struc-tural *impairment*, often based on a range of two standard deviations from the *mean observation obtained from study-ing a large number of apparently healthy subjects. It may also reflect functional impairment, which may be unsuspected by the individual and discovered by clinical observation or testing. The alternative terms *abnormality*, *defect*, or *malformation* (for impairment) and *mal-function* (for disability) are used by many authorities, which may sometimes cause confusion; in an attempt to resolve this, a working group of the *World Health Organization has suggested using the generic term *disablement*, but this has gained only limited acceptance. *See also* Employment Service, International

缺陷　**(1)** 部分或完全不能履行患者想要做的社會、職務或者其他方面的活動。它反映某個人當與那些沒有同樣缺陷的同等人羣比較時，由於某些方面的部分或完全缺陷而不能利用其有利條件的程度。缺陷通常是涉及某一明顯的結構上的損害，也可是在大量調查明顯健康人羣獲得的平均數（觀測值）兩個標準差範圍基礎上確定。缺陷也可反映功能性的損傷，本人可能沒有覺察到，而是通過臨床觀察和測試才發現的。其他作者有用異常、缺損、畸形（對損傷）及功能障礙（對喪失勞動力）等替換的術語，但有時可引起混亂。在解決此問題的嘗試中，世界衛生組織的一個工作組建議使用普通術語殘疾，但這只獲得有限的接受。（參閱 Employment Service，International Classification of Diseases）**(2)** 參閱 mental handicap。

Classification of Diseases. **2.** *see* mental handicap.

Hand-Schüller-Christian disease *see* reticuloendotheliosis.

漢-許-克氏病　參閱 reticuloendotheliosis。

Hansen's bacillus *see* Mycobacterium.

漢森桿菌　參閱 Mycobacterium。

hantavirus *n.* one of a genus of viruses that infect rats, mice, and voles and cause disease in humans when the secretions or excreta of these rodents are inhaled or ingested. The disease was first reported from the area of the Hantaan river, which separates North from South Korea, but hantavirus infections also occur in Japan, China, Russia, Europe, and the USA: in Britain it can affect farm, nature conservancy, and sewage workers and those engaged in water sports. The symptoms vary according to the strain of the infecting virus. Many patients have a mild influenza-like illness, but severe cases are characterized by high fever, headache, shock, nausea and vomiting, and *petechiae in the skin; there may be kidney pain and rapidly progressive kidney damage leading to kidney failure. A particularly virulent strain in the USA attacks the lungs, leading to rapid respiratory failure. The mortality rate in these severe cases is high.

漢坦病毒　一個病毒屬，可感染大鼠、小鼠及田鼠，當這些鼠類分泌物及排泄物被吸入或食入可引起人類疾病。本病首次報道自漢坦河域（分隔南、北朝鮮的界河），但漢坦病毒感染在日本、中國、俄羅斯、歐洲及美國也有出現。在英國，它可感染農場、自然保護區、污水工作者、水上運動員。由於感染病毒株不同，症狀不盡相同。許多病人僅呈輕流感樣表現，但有些嚴重病人則以高熱、頭疼、休克、惡心、嘔吐和皮膚瘀斑為特徵，可發生腎區疼痛及快速發展的進行性腎損害，導致腎功能衰竭。在美國，一種毒力特別強的毒株可感染肺臟，引起急性呼吸功能衰竭。這些重症病例，病死率很高。

haploid (monoploid) *adj.* describing cells, nuclei, or organisms that have a single set of unpaired chromosomes. In man the gametes are haploid following *meiosis. *Compare* diploid, triploid. **—haploid** *n.*

單倍的　描述細胞、核或生物體具有單套不成對的染色體。在人類生殖細胞減數分裂後的精子和卵子是單倍的。與 diploid，triploid 對比。

haplotype *n.* a complete set of *HLA antigens inherited from either parent.

單倍型　親代任何一方所遺傳的一整套人白細胞抗原。

hapt- (hapto-) *prefix denoting* touch.

〔前綴〕**接觸**

hapten *n. see* antigen.

半抗原 參閱 antigen。

haptoglobin *n.* a protein present in blood plasma that binds with free haemoglobin to form a complex that is rapidly removed from the circulation by the liver. Depletion of plasma haptoglobin is a feature of anaemias in which red blood cells are destroyed inside the circulation with the release of haemoglobin into the plasma and its loss in the urine.

結合珠蛋白 血漿中存在的一種蛋白。與游離的血紅蛋白結合，形成一種複合物，由肝臟很快從血循環中消除。血漿該蛋白的缺失是多種貧血的特徵，此類貧血時，血循環中紅細胞破壞，血紅蛋白釋放到血漿中，結合珠蛋白從尿中丟失。

harara *n.* a severe and itchy inflammation of the skin occurring in people continuously subjected to the bites of the *sandfly *Phlebotomus papatasii*. The incidence of this allergic skin reaction, prevalent in the Middle East, may be checked by controlling the numbers of sandflies.

白蛉皮炎 一種嚴重且發癢的皮膚炎症，發生於持續遭受巴浦白蛉叮咬的人。這種在中東流行的過敏性皮膚反應，可通過控制白蛉的數量來阻止。

harelip *n.* the congenital deformity of a cleft in the upper lip, on one or both sides of the midline. It occurs when the three blocks of embryonic tissue that go to form the upper lip fail to fuse and it is often associated with a *cleft palate. Medical name: **cheiloschisis**.

唇裂 上唇中線一側或兩側發生裂口的先天性畸形。在胚胎時期形成上唇的三塊組織不能融合時可發生此病症。醫學用語：唇裂（畸形）。

Harrison's sulcus a depression on both sides of the chest wall of a child between the pectoral muscles and the lower margin of the ribcage. It is caused by exaggerated suction of the diaphragm when breathing in and develops in conditions in which the airways are partially obstructed or when the lungs are abnormally congested due to some congenital abnormality of the heart.

哈里森溝 小兒兩側胸壁上，在胸肌與肋骨下緣之間的一種凹陷。當吸氣時以及發生呼吸道部分受阻的情況時，或由於某些心臟先天性異常所致的肺異常充血時，因膈肌過度牽引胸壁所致。

Hartnup disease a rare hereditary defect in the absorption of the amino acid tryptophan, leading to mental

哈特納普病 一種罕見的遺傳性色氨酸吸收缺陷、可導致智力低下，皮膚增厚、粗糙，以

retardation, thickening and roughening of the skin on exposure to light, and lack of muscular coordination. The condition is similar to *pellagra. Treatment with nicotinamide is usually effective.

harvest mite *see* Trombicula.

Hashimoto's disease chronic inflammation of the thyroid gland (*thyroiditis*) due to the formation of antibodies against normal thyroid tissue (autoantibodies). Its features include a firm swelling of the thyroid and partial or total failure of secretion of thyroid hormones; often there are auto-antibodies to other organs, such as the stomach. Women are more often affected than men and the condition often occurs in families.

hashish *n. see* cannabis.

haustrum *n.* one of the pouches on the external surface of the *colon.

Haversian canal one of the small canals (diameter about 50 μm) that ramify throughout compact *bone. *See also* Haversian system.

Haversian system one of the cylindrical units of which compact *bone is made. A *Haversian canal* forms a central tube, around which are alternate layers of bone matrix (*lamellae*) and *lacunae* containing bone cells. The lacunae are linked by minute channels (*canaliculi*).

hay fever a form of *allergy due to the pollen of grasses, trees, and other plants, characterized by inflammation of the membrane lining the nose and sometimes of the conjunctiva (*vernal*

及肌共濟失調。此病與糙皮病相似。用煙醯胺治療通常有效。

沙蟎（秋蚲） 參閱 Trombicula。

橋本病 甲狀腺的慢性炎症（甲狀腺炎）。由於形成抗正常甲狀腺組織的抗體（自身抗體）引起。其特徵包括甲狀腺硬性腫大，甲狀腺激素的分泌部分或完全停止，往往對其他器官如胃也有自身抗體。女子比男子更常累及且此病經常發生於家庭內。

大麻 參閱 cannabis。

袋 結腸外表面上的囊之一。

哈弗管 貫穿密質骨並成網狀的一種小管（直徑約50μm）。參閱 Haversian system。

哈弗系統 組成密質骨的圓柱形骨單位。即以哈弗管為中心，繞以一層一層的骨基質（板）以及含骨細胞的腔隙。這些腔隙由許多小管連接起來。

枯草熱 由草、樹木以及其他植物引起的變態反應的一種類型。其特徵為鼻粘膜發炎，有時為結膜炎（春季結膜炎）。打噴嚏、流鼻涕或鼻塞以及流

conjunctivitis). The symptoms of sneezing, running or blocked nose, and watering eyes are due to histamine release and often respond to treatment with *antihistamines. If the allergen is identified, it may be possible to undertake *desensitization. Medical name: **allergic rhinitis**.

hazardous substance (in occupational health) *see* COSHH.

HCG *see* human chorionic gonadotrophin.

head *n.* **1.** the part of the body that contains the brain and the organs of sight, hearing, smell, and taste. **2.** the rounded portion of a bone, which fits into a groove of another to form a joint; for example, the head of the humerus or femur.

headache *n.* pain felt deep within the skull. Most headaches are caused by emotional stress or fatigue but some are symptoms of serious intracranial disease. *See also* migraine.

headgear *n.* (in dentistry) a strap that is fixed round the back of the head and attached to an *orthodontic appliance to aid tooth movement. It is normally worn at night and for part of the day.

head injury an injury usually resulting from a blow to the head and often associated with brain injury. It may result in *concussion or – if the blood vessels in the head are torn – to a *haematoma. The level of consciousness of a patient following a head injury can be assessed using the *Glasgow scoring system. Head injuries are an important cause

淚等症狀是由於組胺釋放之故。用抗組胺類藥物治療往往有效。如能鑒定其變應原，就有可能做脫敏治療。醫學用語：變態反應性鼻炎。

有害物質　（職業衛生）參閱 COSHH。

人絨毛膜促性腺激素　參閱 human chorionic gonadotrophin。

頭　**(1)** 包含腦以及視、聽、味與嗅覺等器官的那部分人體。**(2)** 骨的圓形部。它的形狀適宜於進入另一相應的窩，以形成關節；例如肱骨或股骨的頭。

頭痛　顱內疼痛。多數由情緒緊張或疲乏引起，但有些是顱內嚴重疾患的症狀。參閱 migraine。

頭帽　（牙科學）繞頭後部固定並與牙正常器具相縛以幫助牙運動的帶子。它正常在夜晚和部分白天戴。

頭部損傷　通常由頭部的打擊所致的損傷，經常與腦損傷有關。它可能導致腦震盪或者——如果頭部血管撕裂——導致血腫。病人的清醒度，在頭部損傷後，可用格拉斯哥計分系統得到評估。頭部損傷是由事故致死的主要原因；立法強制在工業場所和建築工地戴保

of death due to accidents: legislation to impose protective headgear at industrial sites and on construction workers and motorcyclists has reduced their incidence.

護性安全帽，已使工人和騎摩托車的人事故降低。

Heaf test a skin test to determine whether or not an individual is immune to tuberculosis. A spring-loaded gun mounted with very short needles produces a circle of six punctures in the forearm through which *tuberculin is introduced. If the test is positive a reaction causes the skin to become red and raised, indicating that the individual is immune. If the test is negative a vaccine (*BCG) can be given.

希夫試驗 一種確定人是否對結核有免疫力的皮膚試驗。裝有極為短小針頭的彈簧槍在前臂擊出一圈六個穿刺點。經過這些穿刺注入結核菌素。如果試驗是陽性的，反應會引起皮膚變紅並凸起，表明此人是有免疫力的。如果試驗呈陰性，可注射疫苗（卡介苗）。

Health and Safety Executive (HSE) (in Britain) a statutory body responsible for the health and safety of workers (including factory, office, and agricultural workers). *See also* COSHH.

健康與安全局 （英國）一法定機構，負責工人健康與安全（包括工廠、辦公室和農業工人）。參閱 COSHH。

Health Board (in Scotland and Northern Ireland) another name for Health Authority. *See* National Health Service.

衛生委員會 （蘇格蘭和北愛爾蘭）衛生局的另一名稱。參閱 National Health Service。

health care *see* primary health care, secondary health care, tertiary health care.

衛生保健 參閱 primary health care，secondary health care，tertiary health care。

health centre (in Britain) a building, owned or leased by a District Health Authority, that houses personnel and/or services from one or several sections of the National Health Service (e.g. *general practitioners, *community nurses, dentists, *child health clinics, facilities for X-rays, laboratory tests, and electrocardiography). Services provided by local authorities, such as social services, chiropody, and child psychology, may also operate from such a centre.

衛生中心 （在英國）指地段衛生局自己所擁有或由該局租賃的一建築物，容納來自國民保健服務制的一個或幾個部門的工作人員及/或服務設施（例如全科醫師、社區保健護士、牙科醫師、兒童保健站、以及 X 綫、實驗室檢查、心電描記技術等設備）。衛生中心也可承擔由地方當局提供的服務項目，如社會福利、足病治療以及兒童心理咨詢等。

health education persuasive methods used to encourage people (either individually or collectively) to adopt life styles that the educators believe will improve health and to reject habits regarded as harmful to health or likely to shorten life expectancy. The term is also used in a broader sense to include instruction about bodily function, etc., so that the public is better informed about health issues. *See also* health promotion.

health promotion a programme of surveillance planned on a community basis to maintain the best possible health and quality of life of the members of that community, both collectively and individually. Programmes include a blend of such personal services as *health education, immunization, and *screening tests, with environmental monitoring of the atmosphere, housing, and water and food supplies, as well as occupational hazards (*see* occupational health service).

health service commissioner (ombudsman) an official responsible to Parliament and appointed to protect the interests of patients in relation to administration of the *National Health Service. He can investigate complaints and allegations of maladministration but not of professional negligence.

health service manager an administrator with special training and skills in management who is concerned with running hospitals and other health services. Generally, the basic training for managers is in disciplines other than health; however, doctors, nurses, and others may fill such posts, sometimes combining them with professional appointments, such as Regional (or District) Medical Officer (or Nursing

健康教育 說服教育的方法，用來鼓勵人們（單個的或集體的）採納教育家認為會增進健康的生活方式，並拋棄那些有害健康或很可能縮短預期壽命的習慣。此術語廣義上也包括講授有關人體的功能等，以便使民眾了解有關的健康常識。參閱 health promotion。

健康促進 以社區為基礎而計劃的監督項目，以維持社區成員，個人和集體兩方面的可能的最高健康和生活質量。項目包括將諸如健康教育、免疫、篩查等個人服務與大氣的環境監測、住房、水和食物的供給以及職業危害融合為一體（參閱 occupational health service）。

衛生事業專員（巡視員） 一對（英國）議會負責的官員，被委任來維護病人在國民保健服務制中應享受的權益。他可調查有關行政管理不當方面的投訴和陳述，但不過問技術事故。

衛生事業管理人員 在管理方面受過訓練有技能的管理人員，負責管理醫院和其他服務機構。一般來講，管理人員的基本培訓是在規章制度方面，而不是衛生方面；然而，醫生、護士和其他人員也可擔任這樣的職位，有時與他們的職業委任相結合，如地區（或地段）醫官（或護師）。參閱 National Health Service，

Officer). *See also* National Health Service, nursing officer, public health physician.

health service planning balancing the needs of a community, assessed by such indices as mortality, morbidity, and disability, with the resources available to meet these needs in terms of medical manpower (ensuring the numbers in training grades meet but do not exceed future requirements for career grades) and technical resources, such as hospitals (capital planning), equipment, and medicines. Success is measured by a process of *medical audit* in which the use of resources is weighed against the efficiency of their use (e.g. treatments undertaken, bed occupancy) and effectiveness in terms of outcome (e.g. deaths, complications, quality of life, return to work).

health visitor (public health nurse) a trained nurse with experience in midwifery and with special training in preventive medicine (including health education). The training usually takes place at a university or technical college over three academic terms, the course being approved by the United Kingdom Central Council for Nursing, Midwifery, and Health Visiting (UKCC), with which body the practising health visitor is required to be registered. All births are notified to the appropriate health visitor, most of whose work is concerned with routine visiting of selected preschool children (through the elderly and chronic sick may also receive routine visits). Health visitors do not carry out practical nursing care but seek to educate parents or relatives how best to care for their charges, in particular by drawing attention to unmet needs in terms of health

nursing officer，public health physician。

衛生事業規劃 以現有可應用的資源平衡社會的需求，這需要通過評估諸如死亡率、發病率和傷殘率指數而得到。根據醫學人力（保證培訓數量滿足並不超過未來職業等級的需要）和技術資源，如醫院（資金規劃）、設備和醫藥等，來滿足這些需要。其成功率由醫學審計的方法來衡量：審計時，將資源的使用與他們的使用效率（如所做的治療、床位占有率）及依照結果的有效性（如死亡、併發症、生活質量和重返工作）進行衡量。

保健員（公共衛生護士） （英國）一種受過預防醫學（包括健康教育）特別訓練，對助產有經驗的護士。通常大學或技校培訓三個學期。課程由英國護士、助產士和保健員委員會(UKCC) 提供，此機構要求實習保健員註冊。所有出生的嬰兒向相應的保健員報告。多數保健員的工作是定期訪問經選擇的學齡前兒童（儘管是年齡較大的以及慢性疾患的兒童也可受到定期訪問）。保健員不做實際的護理工作，而是力求做好對雙親或家庭成員的宣傳教育，指導他們如何很好地負起責任，特別要注意，在衛生保健方面，以及增進健康的社會福利方面，哪些需要沒有得到滿足。少數保健員具有專業任務（例如對老年人、殘疾兒童的照顧）。許多保健員屬於

care and those of the social services likely to improve health. A few health visitors have specialist roles (e.g. handi-capped children or the elderly). Many belong to a professional body known as the *Health Visitors Association* but mem-bership is not obligatory.

專業團體保健員協會的成員，但入會不是強制性的。

hearing aid an electronic device to enable a deaf person to hear, consisting of a miniature sound receiver, an ampli-fier, and either an earpiece or a vibrator to transfer the amplified sound to the ear. The earpiece fits into the ear; the vibra-tor (used in cases of conductive *deaf-ness) fits behind the ear and transmits through the bone directly to the inner ear. The aid is powered by a battery, and the whole unit is usually small enough to fit behind or within the ear inconspicuously.

助聽器 一種能使聾人聽到聲音的電子設備，由小型的聲音接受器、放大器和耳機（或振動器）組成。耳機將放大的聲音傳入耳內。耳機置於耳內，振動器（用於傳導性耳聾的病例）置於耳後，使聲音通過骨直接傳入內耳。助聽器由電池啟動，其總的體積往往很小，可裝在耳後或耳內而不致顯眼。

heart *n.* a hollow muscular cone-shaped organ, lying between the lungs, with the pointed end (*apex*) directed downwards, forwards, and to the left. The heart is about the size of a closed fist. Its wall consists largely of *cardiac muscle (myocardium), lined and surrounded by membranes (*see* endocardium, peri-cardium). It is divided by a *septum* into separate right and left halves, each of which is divided into an upper *atrium and a lower *ventricle (see illustration). Deoxygenated blood from the *venae cavae passes through the right atrium to the right ventricle. This contracts and pumps blood to the lungs via the *pul-monary artery. The newly oxygenated blood returns to the left atrium via the pulmonary veins and passes through to the left ventricle. This forcefully con-tracts, pumping blood out to the body via the *aorta. The direction of blood flow within the heart is controlled by *valves.

心臟 中空的圓錐形肌性器官，位於兩肺之間，尖端向左前下方。心臟約有握拳大小。心壁大體上由心肌、心內膜以及心臟外面的心包組成（參閱 endocardium，peri-cardium）。它由一間隔分成左右兩個部分。每一半側心又分成上面的心房和下面的心室（見圖）。脫氧血由腔靜脈經右心房到右心室。右心室收縮將血經肺動脈泵入肺內。攜氧血經肺靜脈重新回到左心房，然後到左心室，左心室有力地收縮，將血泵出，通過主動脈輸送到全身。心臟內血流的方向是由瓣膜來控制的。

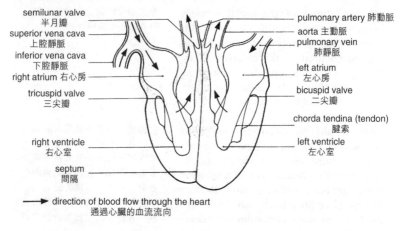

semilunar valve 半月瓣
superior vena cava 上腔靜脈
inferior vena cava 下腔靜脈
right atrium 右心房
tricuspid valve 三尖瓣
right ventricle 右心室
septum 間隔

pulmonary artery 肺動脈
aorta 主動脈
pulmonary vein 肺靜脈
left atrium 左心房
bicuspid valve 二尖瓣
chorda tendina (tendon) 腱索
left ventricle 左心室

→ direction of blood flow through the heart
通過心臟的血流流向

Vertical section through the heart
心臟的垂直切面

heart attack *see* myocardial infarction.

心臟驟停 參閱 myocardial infarction。

heart block a condition in which conduction of the electrical impulses generated by the natural pacemaker of the heart (the *sinoatrial node) is impaired, so that the pumping action of the heart is slowed down. In *partial* or *incomplete heart block* conduction between atria and ventricles is delayed (*first degree heart block*) or not all the impulses are conducted from the atria to the ventricles (*second degree heart block*). In *third degree* or *complete heart block* no impulses are conducted and the ventricles beat at their own slow intrinsic rate (20–40 per minute).

Heart block may be congenital or it may be due to heart disease, including myocardial infarction, myocarditis, cardiomyopathy, and disease of the valves. It is most frequently seen in the elderly as the result of chronic degenerative scarring around the conducting tissue. There may be no symptoms, but when

心傳導阻滯 一種由於心臟自然起搏點發出的電衝動的傳導受到損害，以致其泵血作用減緩的心臟疾患。部分或不完全傳導阻滯是心房和心室之間的傳導延遲（I 度心傳導阻滯）或不能傳導所有心房到心室的衝動（II 度心傳導阻滯）。III 度或完全心傳導阻滯是不能傳導衝動，心室以其自身緩慢的固有心率（20~40 次/分）搏動。

心傳導阻滯可以是先天性的，也可能是由於心臟病（包括心肌梗死、心肌炎、心肌病以及瓣膜病）引起。心傳導阻滯最常見於較年長者，這是由於傳導組織周圍慢性退化的瘢痕形成的結果，本病可無症狀，但當心率和脈搏非常緩慢時可出現症狀，病人可發生心力衰竭或阿-斯氏綜合徵。可使用人工起搏器消除症狀。

very slow heart and pulse rates occur the patient may develop heart failure or *Stokes-Adams syndrome. Symptoms may be abolished by the use of an artificial *pacemaker.

heartburn (pyrosis) *n.* discomfort or pain, usually burning in character, that is felt behind the breastbone and often appears to rise from the abdomen towards or into the throat. It may be accompanied by the appearance of acid or bitter fluid in the mouth and is usually caused by regurgitation of stomach contents into the gullet or by *oesophagitis.

胃灼熱 以燒灼感為特徵的胃部不適或疼痛。燒灼感位於胸骨後，經常從腹部上升到咽喉部。可伴有吐酸水或苦水，這通常是由於胃內容物返流到食管或由食管炎引起。

heart failure a condition in which the pumping action of the ventricle of the heart is inadequate. This results in back pressure of blood, with congestion of the lungs and liver. The veins in the neck becomed engorged and fluid accumulates in the tissues (*see* oedema). There is a reduced flow of arterial blood from the heart, which in extreme cases results in perpheral circulatory failure (cardiogenic shock). Heart failure may result from any condition that overloads, damages, or reduces the efficiency of the heart muscle. Common causes are coronary thrombosis, hypertension, chronic disease of the valves, and arrhythmias. The patient experiences breathlessness, even when lying flat, and oedema of the legs.

Treatment consists of rest, a low salt diet, diuretic drugs (e.g. frusemide), and digitalis derivatives (e.g. digoxin). Structural abnormalities, such as defective valves, may be corrected surgically.

心力衰竭 心室的泵血作用不足的一種疾病，可導致血壓下降、肺和肝充血。頸靜脈充盈，液體蓄積於組織內（參閱 oedema）。來自心臟的動脈血流量減少，在嚴重病例中導致周圍循環衰竭（心源性休克），心力衰竭可由任何情況如負荷過重、損傷、心肌效力下降等引起。常見的原因是冠狀動脈血栓形成、高血壓、慢性瓣膜疾患以及心律不齊。病人呼吸急促（甚至在平臥時）以及腿腫。

治療包括休息、低鹽飲食、服利尿藥（例如呋噻米）以及洋地黃類（如地高辛）。結構上的異常，如瓣膜疾患，可用外科方法糾正。

heart-lung machine an apparatus for taking over temporarily the functions of both the heart and the lungs during heart surgery. It incorporates a pump, to

心肺機 心肺手術時用於暫時替代心肺功能的一種器械。它將用於維持循環的泵和用於充氧的器械結合起來。血液是通

maintain the circulation, and equipment to oxygenate the blood. Blood is taken from the body by tubes inserted into the superior and inferior venae cavae, and the oxygenated blood is returned under pressure into a large artery, such as the femoral artery. The surgeon is therefore able to undertake the repair or replacement of heart valves or perform other surgical operations involving the heart and great blood vessels.

過插進上下腔靜脈的小管引出身體，而含氧血在壓力下返回大動脈，例如股動脈。因此，外科醫師就可着手作心瓣膜的修復或更換手術，或者做其他外科手術，包括心臟或大血管的手術。

heater-probe *n.* a device that can be passed through an endoscope to apply controlled heat in order to coagulate a bleeding peptic ulcer.

加熱探針 一種穿過內窺鏡並能控制產熱的器械，用來凝結正在出血的消化性潰瘍。

heat exhaustion fatigue and collapse due to the low blood pressure and blood volume that result from loss of body fluids and salts after prolonged or unaccustomed exposure to heat. It is most common in new arrivals in a hot climate and is treated by giving drinks or intravenous injections of salted water.

中暑虛脫 由血壓低和血容量下降引起的疲勞和虛脫。是長期或不習慣暴露於熱環境後體液和鹽分丟失造成的。本病最常見於初到熱帶的人。可予飲水或靜脈注射鹽水治療。

heatstroke (sunstroke) *n.* raised body temperatrue (pyrexia), absence of sweating, and eventual loss of consciousness due to failure or exhaustion of the temperature-regulating mechanism of the body. It is potentially fatal unless treated immediately: the body should be cooled by applying damp cloths and body fluids restored by giving drinks or intravenous injections of salted water.

中暑（日射病） 由體溫調節機制衰竭引起的體溫升高（發熱）、不出汗以及最終意識喪失。如不立即治療，可能致死。治療：披蓋濕布使身體涼下來，並通過飲水或靜脈注射鹽水使體液恢復。

hebephrenia *n.* a form of *schizophrenia. It is typically a chronic condition, and the most prominent features are disordered thinking; inappropriate emotions with thoughtless cheerfulness, apathy, or querulousness; and silly behaviour. It typically starts in adolescence or young adulthood. Social

青春期痴呆 精神分裂症的一個類型。它是一種典型的慢性疾患。其突出的特徵是思維紊亂、不適當的感情以及無思想內容的高興、冷淡、發牢騷和愚蠢行為。此病典型的發病始於青春期或年輕的成年人。對多數患者來講，恢復正常的社

and occupational rehabilitation are the most important therapies for most patients; drugs such as the *phenothiazines or butyrophenones can also help. **–hebephrenic** adj.

Heberden's node a lump of cartilage-covered bone arising at the terminal joint of a finger in *osteoarthritis. It is often inherited.

hebetude n. apathy and emotional dullness. This is not a symptom specific to any one condition; extreme degrees are found in *schizophrenia and *dementia.

hectic adj. occurring regularly. A hectic fever is a fever that typically develops in the afternoons, in cases of pulmonary tuberculosis.

hecto- prefix denoting a hundred.

heel n. the part of the foot that extends behind the ankle joint, formed by the heel bone (see calcaneus).

Hegar's sign an indication of pregnancy detectable between the 6th and 12th weeks: used before modern urine tests for pregnancy were available. If the fingers of one hand are inserted into the vagina and those of the other are placed over the pelvic cavity, the lower part of the uterus feels very soft compared with the body of the uterus above and the cervix below.

helc- (helco-) prefix denoting an ulcer.

Helicobacter n. a genus of spiral flagellated Gram-negative bacteria. The species H. pylori (formerly classified as Campylobacter pylori) is found in the stomach within the mucous layer. It

會生活和職業是最重要的治療方法，藥物如吩噻嗪類或丁醯苯類可能也是有幫助的。

希伯登結 覆蓋軟骨的一種腫塊，骨關節炎時發生於指關節末端。往往是遺傳性的。

精神遲鈍 冷淡和感情遲鈍。它不是某一疾病特有的症狀。極重度精神遲鈍見於精神分裂症和痴呆。

潮式的 有規律發生的。潮熱，在肺結核病中，典型的發生於下午。

〔前綴〕百

(足) 跟 足的一部分，延伸到踝關節後，由跟骨形成（參閱 calcaneus）。

黑加徵 妊娠的一種指徵。妊娠第六至第十二周之間查出：用於現代妊娠尿試驗使用之前。將一隻手的手指插入陰道內，另一隻手的手指置於盆腔上面，子宮的下部與它上方子宮體及子宮頸下部相比感覺很鬆軟。

〔前綴〕潰瘍

螺桿菌 螺旋、鞭毛狀革蘭氏陰性細菌的一屬。幽門螺桿菌種（過去分類為幽門彎曲菌）見於胃黏膜層內。發生於大部分中年人，但總是存在於十二

occurs in the majority of middle-aged people, but is invariably present in duodenal ulceration. Eradication of the organism (using various combinations of bismuth, antibiotics, and antisecretory drugs) leads to healing of the ulcer.

指腸潰瘍中。消除此微生物（使用各種鉍、抗生素及抑制分泌藥物的複合劑）可使潰瘍愈合。

helicotrema *n.* the narrow opening between the scala vestibuli and the scala tympani at the tip of the *cochlea in the ear.

蝸孔 耳蝸尖端前庭階和鼓階之間的狹窄開口。

helio- *prefix denoting* the sun.

〔前綴〕日（光）

heliotherapy *n.* the use of sunlight to promote healing; sunbathing.

日光療法 利用陽光促進治愈；日光浴。

helix *n.* the outer curved fleshy ridge of the *pinna of the outer ear.

耳輪 外耳耳廓外部的曲綫形肉質緣。

Heller's operation *see* achalasia.

赫勒手術 參閱 achalasia。

Heller's syndrome (disintegrative psychosis) a rare mental illness of childhood. Abnormalities of behaviour may be the only sign at first but the condition progresses to psychotic manifestations, such as *stereotypies and hallucinations, and ultimately to dementia. Nearly always a physical cause can be found. The illness progresses to severe incapacity or death.

赫勒綜合徵 少兒的一種罕見的精神病。初起時，行為異常可能是唯一的體徵，爾後發展為精神病的表現，如有刻板動作及幻覺，終至痴呆。幾乎總能找到軀體性病因。此病可發展到嚴重的能力喪失或死亡。

Heller's test a test for the presence of protein (albumin) in the urine. A quantity of urine is carefully poured onto the same quantity of pure nitric acid in a test tube. A white ring forms at the junction of the liquids if albumin is present. However, a similar result may be obtained if the urine contains certain drugs or is very concentrated. A dark brown ring indicates the presence of an abnormally high level of potassium

赫勒試驗 檢查尿中蛋白（白蛋白）的一種試驗。將一定的尿量倒入同量純硝酸的試管中，如尿中含有白蛋白，在兩種液體接觸面形成一白色環。但是如尿中含有某些藥物或尿液是很濃縮的，也可獲得同樣結果。深棕色環表明尿中有異常高濃度的吲哚酚硫酸鉀（參閱 indicanuria）。

indoxyl sulphate in the urine (*see* indicanuria).

HELLP syndrome a form of severe *pre-eclampsia affecting many body systems and characterized by *h*aemolysis, *e*levated *l*iver enzymes, and a *l*ow *p*latelet count (hence the name). It constitutes an emergency requiring prompt termination of the pregnancy.

Helly's fluid a mixture of potassium dichromate, sodium sulphate, mercuric chloride, formaldehyde, and distilled water, used in the preservation of bone marrow.

helminth *n.* any of the various parasitic worms, including the *flukes, *tapeworms, and *nematodes.

helminthiasis *n.* the diseased condition resulting from an infestation with parasitic worms (helminths).

helminthology *n.* the study of parasitic worms.

hemeralopia *n. see* day blindness.

hemi- *prefix denoting* (in medicine) the right or left half of the body. Example: *hemianaesthesia* (anaesthesia of one side of the body).

hemiachromatopsia *n.* loss of colour appreciation in one half of the visual field.

hemianopia *n.* absence of half of the normal field of vision. The commonest type is *homonymous hemianopia*, in which the same half (right or left) is lost in both eyes. Sometimes the inner halves of the visual field are lost in both eyes,

溶血、高肝酶及低血小板綜合徵　嚴重子癇前期的一種形式，影響許多人體系統，其特點是溶血，肝臟酶量升高及血小板數目減少（因此而得名）。它構成急症，需及時終止妊娠。

赫利液　重鉻酸鉀、硫酸鈉、氯化汞、甲醛和蒸餾水的混合物，用於骨髓的保存。

蠕蟲　各種寄生蠕蟲的任意一種。包括吸蟲類、縧蟲類和綫蟲類。

蠕蟲病　感染寄生性蠕蟲引起的疾病。

蠕蟲學　研究寄生性蠕蟲的學科。

夜盲症　參閱 day blindness。

〔前綴〕偏（單）側　（醫學）指人體的右或左半側。例如：偏側感覺缺失（人體的一側感覺缺失）。

偏（側）色盲　一半視野不能認別顏色。

偏盲　正常視野的一半缺失。最常見的類型是同側偏盲，即兩眼的同一半側（右或左）偏盲。有時是兩眼視野的內半部缺失，引起兩鼻側偏盲；而其他外半部視野缺失則產生顳側

producing a *binasal hemianopia*, while in others the outer halves are lost, producing a *bitemporal hemianopia*. Very rarely both upper halves or both lower halves are lost, producing an *altitudinal hemianopia*.

偏盲。罕見的兩眼上半或下半視野缺失,產生上下側偏盲。

hemiballismus *n.* a violent involuntary movement usually restricted to one arm and primarily involving the proximal muscles. It is a symptom of disease of the *basal ganglia.

偏身顫搐 一種強烈的不隨意的運動,通常限於某一手臂,而且首先侵犯附近的肌肉。此症是基底神經節疾患的一種症狀。

hemicolectomy *n.* surgical removal of about half the *colon (large intestine), usually the right section (*right hemicolectomy*) with subsequent joining of the *ileum to the transverse colon. This is performed for disease of the terminal part of the ileum (such as *Crohn's disease) or of the caecum or ascending colon (such as cancer or Crohn's disease).

結腸部分切除術 外科切除約1/2 的結腸(大腸),通常是結腸右部(右半結腸切除術),其後使迴腸與橫結腸相連。這種手術可用於迴腸末端疾患(例如克羅恩病),或盲腸端及升結腸疾患(例如癌或克羅恩病)。

hemicrania *n.* **1.** a headache affecting only one side of the head, usually *migraine. **2.** absence of half of the skull in a developing fetus.

(1) 偏側頭痛 只侵犯一側頭部的一種頭痛。通常是指偏頭痛。**(2) 半無腦** 在胎兒發育中,頭顱的一半缺失。

hemimelia *n.* congenital absence or gross shortening (aplasia) of the distal portion of the arms or legs. Sometimes only one of the two bones of the distal arm (radius and ulna) or leg (tibia and fibula) may be affected. *See also* ectromelia.

半肢畸形 手臂或腿的遠側部先天性缺失或短(發育不全)。有時只是遠側臂骨(橈骨與尺骨)或小腿骨(脛骨與腓骨)二個中的一個受累。參閱 ectromelia。

hemiparesis *n. see* hemiplegia.

輕偏癱 參閱 hemiplegia。

hemiplegia (hemiparesis) *n.* paralysis of one side of the body. Movements of the face and arm are often more severely affected than those of the leg. It is caused by disease affecting the opposite (contralateral) hemisphere of the brain.

偏癱 身體一側癱瘓。面部與手臂的運動通常比腿部受累較為嚴重。此病由對側大腦半球疾病引起。

hemisacralization *n.* fusion of the fifth lumbar vertebra to one side only of the sacrum. *See* sacralization.

半骶化　第五腰椎與只一側骶骨融合。參閱 sacralization。

hemisphere *n.* one of the two halves of the *cerebrum, not in fact hemispherical but more nearly quarter-spherical.

半球　大腦的兩半球之一，事實上並非半球狀的，而是呈 1/4 球面狀。

hemizygous *adj.* describing genes that are carried on an unpaired chromosome, for example the genes on the X chromosome in man. **–hemizygote** *n.*

半合子的　描述具有不成對染色體的基因，男性 X 染色體上的基因。

hemlock *n.* the plant *Conium maculatum*, found in Britain and central Europe. It is a source of the poisonous alkaloid *coniine.

毒芹，鐵杉　毒茴類植物歐毒芹，見於英國及中歐。它是有毒生物鹼歐毒芹鹼的來源。

hemp *n. see* cannabis.

大麻　參閱 cannabis。

Henle's loop the part of a kidney tubule that forms a loop extending towards the centre of the kidney. It is surrounded by blood capillaries, which absorb water and selected soluble substances back into the bloodstream.

亨利袢（細尿管袢）　腎小管的一部分。它形成一袢狀，伸向腎中心。袢周圍有毛細血管圍繞，其功能是將水分、選擇的可溶性物質重吸收回血流中。

Henoch-Schönlein purpura (Schönlein-Henoch purpura, anaphylactoid purpura) a common, and frequently recurrent, form of *purpura found especially (but not exclusively) in young children. It is characterized by red weals and a purple rash on the buttocks and lower legs due to bleeding into the skin from inflamed capillaries, together with arthritis, gastrointestinal symptoms, and (in some cases) nephritis. There is no specific treatment.

亨-舍氏紫癜（過敏樣紫癜）　一種常見的，經常復發的紫癜類型，尤見於（但不僅僅指）少兒。其特徵為臀部和下腿部紅斑、紫疹（由於發炎的毛細血管出血至皮膚所致）和關節炎、胃腸道症狀及（在某些病例中）腎病。無具體的治療方法。

henry *n.* the *SI unit of inductance, equal to the inductance of a closed circuit with a magnetic flux of 1 weber per ampere of current. Symbol: H.

亨（利）　電感的國際單位。等於在閉合電路中每安（培）電流產生 1 韋（伯）磁通量的電感。符號：H。

Hensen's node (primitive knot) the rounded front end of the embryonic *primitive streak.

亨森結（原結） 胚胎原條前端的圓形結節。

heparin *n.* an *anticoagulant produced in liver cells, some white blood cells, and certain other sites, which acts by inhibiting the action of the enzyme *thrombin in the final stage of *blood coagulation. An extracted purified form of heparin is widely used for the prevention of blood coagulation both in patients with thrombosis and similar conditions and in blood collected for examination. The drug is usually administered by injection and the most important side-effect is bleeding. *See also* low-molecular-weight heparin.

肝素 在肝細胞、有些白細胞以及某些其他部位產生的抗凝血物質。其作用是抑制血液凝固最後階段的酶（凝血酶）的活動。提純的肝素廣泛用於治療血栓形成和類似的疾患，以及採血檢查時用作抗凝劑。治療用時通常是注射給藥，其最主要的副作用是出血。參閱 low-molecular-weight heparin。

hepat- (hepato-) *prefix denoting* the liver. Examples: *hepatopexy* (surgical fixation of); *hepatorenal* (relating to the liver and kidney).

〔前綴〕肝 例如：肝固定術（外科固定肝的手術），肝腎的（與肝及腎有關的）。

hepatalgia *n.* pain in or over the liver. It is caused by liver inflammation (especially an abscess) or swelling (as in cardiac failure or *steatosis).

肝痛 肝內或肝區疼痛。可由肝臟的炎症（尤其是膿腫）或腫大（如心力衰竭或脂肪變性時）引起。

hepatectomy *n.* the operation of removing the liver. *Partial hepatectomy* is the removal of one or more lobes of the liver; it may be carried out after severe injury or to remove a tumour localized in one part of the liver.

肝切除術 切除肝的手術。部分肝切除術是切除一葉或一葉以上肝臟；肝損傷後可行這種手術，局限於肝臟某一部位的腫瘤可用這種手術切除。

hepatic *adj.* relating to the liver.

肝的 與肝有關的。

hepatic duct *see* bile duct.

肝管 參閱 bile duct。

hepatic encephalopathy (portosystemic encephalopathy) a condition in which brain function is impaired by the presence of toxic substances, absorbed from the colon, which are normally removed or detoxified by the liver. It occurs when the liver is severely

肝性腦病（門體靜脈性腦病） 由於毒性物質的存在使大腦功能損害的一種疾病。這些毒性物質從結腸中吸收，在正常情況下是由肝排除或解毒的。它發生於當肝嚴重損傷（如肝硬化）或側支循環形成時。症狀

damaged (as in cirrhosis) or bypassed. Symptoms include drowsiness, confusion, difficulty in performing tasks (e.g. writing), and coma. Treatment consists of stopping protein intake and administering antibiotics (to prevent bacterial production of toxins) and enemas and cathartics (to remove colonic toxins).

hepatic flexure the bend in the *colon, just underneath the liver, where the ascending colon joins the transverse colon.

hepaticostomy *n.* a surgical operation in which a temporary or permanent opening is made into the main duct carrying bile from the liver.

hepatic vein one of several short veins originating within the lobes of the liver as small branches, which unite to form the hepatic veins. These lead directly to the inferior vena cava, draining blood from the liver.

hepatitis *n.* inflammation of the liver caused by viruses, toxic substances, or immunological abnormalities. *Infectious hepatitis* is caused by viruses, four main types of which have been isolated as specific causes of the disease and can be detected by blood tests: hepatitis A, hepatitis B, hepatitis C, and hepatitis D; other viral causes of hepatitis include the *Epstein-Barr virus. *See also* Entamoeba.

Hepatitis A (*epidemic ·hepatitis*) is transmitted by food or drink contaminated by a carrier or patient and commonly occurs where sanitation is poor. After an incubation period of 15–40 days, the patient develops fever and sickness. Yellow discoloration of the skin (*see* jaundice) appears about a week later

包括倦睡、精神錯亂、難於完成某些任務（如寫字）以及昏迷。治療：限制蛋白質攝入，給予抗生素（預防細菌性毒素產物），灌腸以及瀉藥（排除結腸毒素）。

結腸右曲 結腸的彎曲，正好在肝的下面，在升結腸連接橫結腸處。

肝管造口術 在膽總管處做一暫時性的或持久性開口的外科療法，以從肝臟運送膽汁。

肝靜脈 幾條短靜脈中的一條，其小分支起於肝葉內，爾後合併成肝靜脈。這些肝靜脈直接通入下腔靜脈，從肝臟引流血液。

肝炎 由病毒、有毒物質或免疫異常所致的肝臟炎症。傳染性肝炎是由病毒引起的。以疾病的特殊病因並結合血液檢驗測定結果，可分為四個主要類型：甲型肝炎、乙型肝炎、丙型肝炎和丁型肝炎；肝炎的其他病毒原因包括 E-B 病毒。參閱 Entamoeba。

甲型肝炎（流行性肝炎）是通過病毒攜帶者或病人污染的食物或飲水傳播的。常見於衛生條件差的地區。潛伏期 15~40 天，然後病人出現發熱和惡心、嘔吐。一週後，皮膚發黃（參閱 jaundice），可持續到三周。在這期間，病人可能有傳染性。嚴重的併發症是不常見的，一旦發病後常產

and persists for up to three weeks. The patient may be infectious throughout this period. Serious complications are unusual and an attack often confers immunity. Injection of *gamma globulin provides temporary protection, but active immunization is preferable.

Hepatitis B (formerly known as *serum hepatitis*) is transmitted by infected blood or blood products contaminating hypodermic needles, blood transfusions, or tattooing needles or by sexual contact: is often occurs in drug addicts. Symptoms, which develop suddenly after an incubation period of 1–6 months, include headache, fever, chills, general weakness, and jaundice. Most patients make a gradual recovery but the mortality rate is 5–20%.

Hepatitis C has only recently been isolated (it was formerly known as non-A, non-B hepatitis); its mode of transmission is similar to that of hepatitis B. *Hepatitis D* occurs only with or after infection with hepatitis B.

Chronic hepatitis continues for months or years, eventually leading to *cirrhosis (*see also* hepatoma). It may be caused by persistent infection with a hepatitis virus (usually hepatitis B or C), which may respond to treatment with *interferon, or by *autoimmune disease, treated by *corticosteroids or *immunosuppressive therapy.

hepatization *n.* the conversion of lung tissue, which normally holds air, into a solid liver-like mass during the course of acute lobar *pneumonia.

hepato- *prefix. see* hepat-.

hepatoblastoma *n.* a malignant tumour of the liver occurring in children, made

生免疫力。注射丙種球蛋白可提供暫時性預防，但自動免疫更可取。

乙型肝炎（過去稱作血清型肝炎）可通過感染的血或血製品污染皮下注射針頭、輸血、或皮膚刺紋針傳染，或經性接觸傳染：它常發生於吸毒者。在潛伏期1~6個月後，症狀突然發生，包括頭痛、發熱、寒戰、虛弱和黃疸。多數病人可逐漸恢復，病死率是5%~20%。

丙型肝炎是最近才被分離出來的（過去叫做非甲、非乙型肝炎）；它的傳染方式與乙型肝炎的傳染方式相似。丁型肝炎只與乙型肝炎一起或在乙型肝炎感染後發生。

慢性肝炎持續數月或幾年，最終導致肝硬化（參閱 hepatoma）。它可能是由持續的肝炎病毒（通常是乙型和丙型肝炎）感染所致，此病毒對干擾素治療有反應；或者是由自體免疫疾病所引起，此病用皮質類固醇或免疫抑制療法治療。

肝樣變 肺組織轉變成肝樣。在正常情況下肺組織含有空氣，在急性大葉性肺炎的過程中，則變為實質性的肝樣團塊。

〔前綴〕**肝** 參閱 hepat-。

肝胚細胞瘤 一種肝的惡性腫瘤，發生於兒童，由胚胎的肝

up of embryonic liver cells. It is often confined to one lobe of the liver; such cases may be treated by a partial *hepatectomy.

細胞組成。它通常局限於肝的一個葉，這樣的病例可通過部分肝切除術治療。

hepatocellular *adj.* relating to or affecting the cells of the liver.

肝細胞的　與肝細胞有關的或影響肝細胞的。

hepatocyte *n.* the principal cell type in the *liver: a large cell with many metabolic functions, including synthesis, storage, detoxification, and bile production.

肝細胞　肝的主要細胞類型：具有許多代謝功能（包括合成、貯存、解毒和產生膽汁）的大細胞。

hepatoma *n.* a malignant tumour of the liver, originating in mature liver cells. In Western countries it is rare in normal livers, but often develops in patients with cirrhosis, particularly after hepatitis B infection. In Africa and other tropical countries it is frequent, possible causes including fungi (*see* aflatoxin) and other ingested toxins. Hepatomas often synthesize *alphafetoprotein, which circulates in the blood and is a useful indicator of these tumours.

The term hepatoma is often, though incorrectly, used to include malignant tumours arising in the bile duct (*see* cholangiocarcinoma).

肝細胞癌　一種肝的惡性腫瘤，起源於成熟的肝細胞。在西方國家裏，此病在正常肝中是很少見的，但經常發生於肝硬化患者。此病在非洲和其他熱帶國家很常見，其可能原因包括真菌（參見 aflatoxin）和其他攝入的毒素。這些肝細胞癌往往合成甲胎蛋白，在血中循環，因而它是診斷這種腫瘤有用的標誌。

　　肝細胞癌這術語常常（不正確地）包括發生於膽管的惡性腫瘤（參閱 cholangiocarcinoma）。

hepatomegaly *n.* enlargement of the liver to such an extent that it can be felt below the rib margin. This may be due to congestion (as in heart failure), inflammation, infiltration (e.g. by fat), or tumour.

肝大　肝臟增大到可在肋緣下觸及的程度。此症可由充血（如心力衰竭時）、炎症、浸潤（如脂肪）或腫瘤引起。

hepatotoxic *adj.* damaging or destroying liver cells. Certain drugs, such as *paracetamol, can cause liver damage at high doses or with prolonged use.

肝細胞毒的　損傷或破壞肝細胞的。一些藥物如對乙酰氨基酚在高劑量和長期使用的情況下，可引起肝損害。

hept- (hepta-) *prefix denoting* seven.

〔前綴〕七

hereditary *adj.* transmitted from parents to their offspring; inherited.

遺傳的　由父母傳給他們的子女的。

heredity *n.* the process that causes the biological similarity between parents and their offspring. *Genetics is the study of heredity.

遺傳　引起父母與子女之間生物學相似性的過程。遺傳學是研究遺傳的學科。

heredo- *prefix denoting* heredity.

〔前綴〕遺傳

hermaphrodite *n.* an individual in which both male and female sex organs are present or in which the sex organs contain both ovarian and testicular cells. Human hermaphrodites are very rare. **–hermaphroditism** *n.*

兩性體　出現男性和女性兩性器官，或性器官含有卵巢細胞和睾丸細胞的人。人類兩性體是很罕見的。

hernia *n.* the protrusion of an organ or tissue out of the body cavity in which it normally lies. An *inguinal hernia* (or *rupture*) occurs in the lower abdomen; a sac of peritoneum, containing fat or part of the bowel, bulges through a weak part (*inguinal canal*) of the abdominal wall. It may result from physical straining or coughing. A *scrotal hernia* is an inguinal hernia so large that it passes into the scrotum; a *femoral hernia* is similar to an inguinal hernia but protrudes at the top of the thigh, through the point at which the femoral artery passes from the abdomen to the thigh. A *diaphragmatic hernia* is the protrusion of an abdominal organ through the diaphragm into the chest cavity; the most common type is the *hiatus hernia*, in which the stomach passes partly or completely into the chest cavity through the hole (*hiatus*) for the oesophagus (gullet). This may be associated with *gastro-oesophageal reflux. An *umbilical hernia* (or *exomphalos*) is the protrusion of abdominal organs into the umbilical cord, due to a fault in embryonic development. It is present at birth and can be treated surgically.

疝　某一器官或組織從體腔的正常位置向外突出。腹股溝疝發生於下腹部：為一腹膜囊，內含脂肪或一部分腸，經腹壁的薄弱部（腹股溝管）膨出。它可因全身用力或咳嗽引起。陰囊疝是由於腹股溝疝過大，以致通入陰囊內；股疝與腹股溝疝類似，不同的是經過股動脈從腹部到大腿通過的點突出至大腿上部。膈疝是某一腹部器官經膈肌突入胸腔內；最常見的類型是裂孔疝，它是胃的一部分或全部經食管裂孔突入胸腔。這可能與胃食管返流病有關。臍疝（或臍凸出）是腹部器官向臍帶膨出，由於胚胎發育缺陷所致。出生時發生可用手術治療。

這些疝有時因不能回復到它們正常的位置（不能還原的）而變得複雜化，增大，且固定於其囊內（嵌頓性的），或失去血液供應，出現疼痛，終至壞死（絞窄性）。這種疝最好的治療方法——尤其如有疼痛時——是外科修補術（參閱hernioplasty）。

Hernias may be complicated by becoming impossible to return to their normal site (*irreducible*); swollen and fixed within their sac (*incarcerated*); or cut off from their blood supply, becoming painful and eventually gangrenous (*strangulated*). The best treatment for hernias, especially if they are painful, is surgical repair (*see* hernioplasty).

hernio- *prefix denoting* a hernia.

hernioplasty *n.* the surgical operation to repair a hernia, in which the abnormal opening is sewn up and/or the weakness strengthened with suture material. The recommended techniques for repair include a layered suture repair (*Shouldice operation*) or the insertion of a mesh of polypropylene (*Lichtenstein operation*).

herniorrhaphy *n.* surgical repair of a hernia.

heroin (diamorphine) *n.* a white crystalline powder derived from *morphine but with a shorter duration of action. Like morphine it is a powerful narcotic analgesic whose continued use leads to *dependence.

herpangina *n.* a viral infectious disease of sudden onset that causes fever, blisters, and ulceration of the soft palate and tonsillar area. It usually lasts 2–5 days.

herpes *n.* inflammation of the skin or mucous membranes that is caused by *herpesviruses and characterized by collections of small blisters. There are two types of *herpes simplex virus* (*HSV*): type I causes the common *cold sore*, usually present on or around the lips; type II is mainly associated with *genital

〔前綴〕疝

疝根治術 修補疝的外科手術。即縫合疝的異常開口，及/或用縫綫加強薄弱部位。建議的修復手術包括分層縫合修復術（舒德戴斯手術）和聚丙烯網孔填補術（林克斯頓手術）。

疝縫合術 疝的外科修補術。

海洛因（二醋嗎啡） 由嗎啡衍生的白色結晶形粉劑，但作用時間比嗎啡短。和嗎啡一樣，它是強麻醉鎮痛劑，長期應用可導致藥物依賴性。

疱疹性咽峽炎 突然發作的病毒感染性疾病。它引起發熱、水疱和軟腭與扁桃體區的潰瘍。通常持續2~5天。

疱疹 由疱疹病毒引起的皮膚或黏膜炎症，其特徵為成堆的小水疱。有兩種類型的單純疱疹病毒（HSV）：I型引起普通感冒疱疹，通常存在於唇上或周圍；II型主要與生殖器疱疹有關，是性交傳播的。但是，I型和II型都能引起生殖器疱

herpes and is sexually transmitted. However, types I and II can both cause either genital herpes or cold sores, depending on the site of initial infection. HSV blisters are contagious through skin-to-skin contact and are recurrent in some people. HSV can also affect the conjunctiva (*see also* dendritic ulcer).

Herpes zoster (*shingles*) is caused by the varicella-zoster virus, which also causes chickenpox. Following an attack of chickenpox, the virus lays dormant in the dorsal root ganglia of the spinal cord. Later, under one of a number of influences, the virus migrates down the sensory nerve to affect one or more *dermatomes on the skin in a band. One side of the face or an eye (*ophthalmic zoster*) may be involved. Shingles may be chronically painful, especially in the elderly. *See also* Ramsay Hunt syndrome.

Treatment of all forms of herpes is with an appropriate preparation of *acyclovir; analgesics may be required for shingles.

herpesvirus *n.* one of a group of DNA-containing viruses causing latent infections in both man and animals. The herpesviruses are the causative agents of *herpes and chickenpox. The group also includes the *cytomegalovirus and *Epstein-Barr virus. *Herpesvirus simiae* (*virus B*) causes and infection in monkeys similar to herpes simplex, but when transmitted to man it can produce fatal encephalitis.

hertz *n.* the *SI unit of frequency, equal to one cycle per second. Symbol: Hz.

Herxheimer reaction *see* Jarisch-Herxheimer reaction.

heter- (hetero-) *prefix denoting* difference; dissimilarity.

疹和感冒疱疹，根據最初感染點而定。單純疱疹水疱通過皮膚與皮膚接觸傳染，有些人復發。單純疱疹還可感染結膜（參閱 dendritic ulcer）。

帶狀疱疹是由水痘疱疹病毒引起；此病毒還引起水痘。繼水痘發作後，此病毒在脊髓的背側根神經節處處於潛伏狀態。之後，在某一影響因素作用下，此病毒沿感覺神經遷移累及皮膚的一個或多個皮區，呈帶狀。面部一側或一隻眼（眼疱疹）可能累及。帶狀疱疹可能長期疼痛，特別是老年人。參閱 Ramsay Hunt syndrome。

所有形式疱疹的治療均可用無阿昔洛韋這一有效製劑；帶狀疱疹可能需要止痛藥。

疱疹病毒 含 DNA 病毒羣的一種，在人類和動物中引起潛伏性感染。疱疹病毒是疱疹和水痘的病因。此病毒羣也包括巨細胞病毒和 EB 病毒。猿猴疱疹病毒（B 病毒）在猿猴中引起與單純疱疹相似的一種感染，但傳染到人類時則發生致死性的腦炎。

赫（茲） 頻率的國際單位，等於每秒一周。符號：Hz。

赫克斯海默反應 參閱 Jarisch-Herxheimer reaction。

〔前綴〕異

heterochromatin *n.* chromosome material (*see* chromatin) that stains most deeply when the cell is not dividing. It is thought not to represent major genes but may be involved in controlling these genes, and also in controlling mitosis and development. *Compare* euchromatin.

異染色質　細胞不分裂時染色體中染色最深的物質（參閱 chromatin）。它被認為不代表多數基因，但它可參與控制這些基因，而且也控制有絲分裂和發育。與 euchromatin 對比。

heterochromia *n.* colour difference in the iris of the eye, which is usually congenital but is occasionally secondary to inflammation of the iris. In *heterochromia iridis* one iris differs in colour from the other; in *heterochromia iridum* one part of the iris differs in colour from the rest.

異色性　指眼虹膜的顏色的差異。它通常是先天性的，但偶爾是虹膜炎症的繼發感染。一眼虹膜異色是一眼虹膜的顏色與另一眼不同；兩眼虹膜異色是兩眼虹膜某一部分的顏色與其餘部分不同。

heterogametic *adj.* describing the sex that produces two different kinds of gamete, which carry different *sex chromosomes, and that therefore determines the sex of the offspring. In humans men are the heterogametic sex: the sperm cells carry either an X or a Y chromosome. *Compare* homogametic.

異型配子的　描述產生兩種不同類型配子的性別。此配子帶有不同的性染色體，因而可確定子女的性別。在人類男性是異型配子性別：其精子細胞帶一個 X 或一個 Y 染色體。與 homogametic 對比。

heterogeneity *n.* (in oncology) variability or differences in the properties of cells within a tumour.

異種性　（腫瘤學）腫瘤內細胞特性的變異性或差異。

heterograft (xenograft) *n.* a living tissue graft that is made from an animal of one species to another of a different species. For example, attempts have been made to graft animal organs into humans. *See also* transplantation.

異種移植物　從一種動物種移到另一種不同動物種的活組織移植物。例如將動物器官移植到人類。參閱 transplantation。

heterophoria *n.* a tendency to squint. Under normal circumstances both the eyes work together and look at the same point simultaneously, but if one eye is covered it will move out of alignment with the object the other eye is sill viewing. When the cover is removed the eye immediately returns to its normal

隱斜視　一種斜眼的傾向。在正常情況下，兩眼一起動作，同時看到物體的同一點上，但如遮住一隻眼，此眼的視綫就離開物體，而另一眼則仍注視着物體。當遮蔽物被移去時，該眼立即回到正常的位置。多數人都有點外隱斜視（隱斜視

position. Most people have some small degree of the type of heterophoria known as *exophoria*, in which the covered eye turns outwards, away from the nose (*compare* esophoria). Heterophoria often produces eyestrain because of the unconscious effort required to keep the two eyes aligned. *See also* strabismus.

的一型），此型隱斜視，被遮住的眼球離鼻側向外轉動（與esophoria 對比）。隱斜視時，由於需要無意識的用力，以使兩眼協調，因此常引起眼疲勞。參閱 strabismus。

Heterophyes *n.* a genus of small parasitic *flukes occurring in Egypt and the Far East. Adult flukes of the species *H. heterophyes* live in the small intestine of man and other fish-eating animals; in man the flukes can produce serious symptoms (*see* heterophyiasis). The fluke has two intermediate hosts, a snail and a mullet fish.

異形吸蟲屬 發生於埃及和遠東的小型寄生性吸蟲，其成蟲寄生於人和其他食魚類動物的小腸中；在人體此吸蟲可引起嚴重症狀（參閱 heterophyiasis）。這種吸蟲有兩個中間宿主，即蝸牛和鯔魚。

heterophyiasis *n.* an infestation of the small intestine with the parasitic fluke *Heterophyes heterophyes*. Man becomes infected on eating raw or salted fish that contains the larval stage of the fluke. The presence of adult flukes may provoke symptoms of abdominal pain and diarrhoea; if the eggs reach the brain, spinal cord, and heart (via the bloodstream) they produce serious lesions. Tetrachloroethylene may be used in treatment of the infection.

異形吸蟲病 由寄生性吸蟲異形吸蟲引起的小腸感染。人因食進含有吸蟲幼蟲的生魚或醃魚而感染。吸蟲成蟲的存在可引起腹痛和腹瀉症狀；其蟲卵移行至大腦、脊髓和心臟（經血流）時可引起該部位的嚴重損害。可用四氯乙烯治療。

heteroplasty *n.* the grafting of tissue from an animal of one species to another of a different species.

異種移植術 把某一個種的動物組織移植到另一個種。

heteropsia *n.* different vision in each eye.

雙眼不等視 每隻眼的視力不相同。

heterosexuality *n.* the pattern of sexuality in which sexual behaviour and thinking are directed towards people of the opposite sex. It includes both normal

異性性慾 性慾的類型，其性行為和思維針對着相反性別的人。它包括正常和變態型性活動。

and deviant forms of sexual activity. **–heterosexual** *adj. n.*

heterosis *n.* hybrid vigour: the increased sturdiness, resistance to disease, etc., of individuals whose parents are of different races or species compared both with their parents and with the offspring of genetically similar parents.

雜種優勢 雜種生物的活力增強：父母是不同族或不同種，其子女的個體與他們的父母比，或者與遺傳學上相似的父母所生子女比較時更加健壯，抗病力強。

heterotopia (heterotopy) *n.* the displacement of an organ or part of the body from its normal position.

異位 人體某一器官或身體某一部位離開其正常位置。

heterotrophic (organotrophic) *adj.* describing organisms (known as heterotrophs) that use complex organic compounds to synthesize their own organic materials. Most heterotrophs are *chemoheterotrophic*, i.e. they use the organic compounds as an energy source. This group includes the majority of bacteria and all animals and fungi. *Compare* autotrophic.

異養的（有機營養的） 指用複雜的有機化合物合成自然有機物的生物體（通稱異養生物）。多數是化學異養的，即它們用有機化合物作為能量的來源。這羣生物包括多數細菌、所有動物和真菌。與 autotrophic 對比。

heterotropia *n. see* strabismus.

斜視 參閱 strabismus。

heterozygous *adj.* describing an individual in whom the members of a pair of genes determining a particular characteristic are dissimilar. *See* allele. *Compare* homozygous. **–heterozygote** *n.*

雜合的 描述決定某一個人某一性狀的一對基因互不相同。參閱 allele。與 homozygous 對比。

hex- (hexa-) *prefix denoting* six.

〔前綴〕六

hexacanth *n. see* oncosphere.

六鈎蚴 參閱 oncosphere。

hexachlorophane *n.* a disinfectant similar to *phenol, formerly used in soaps and creams to treat skin disorders. Its use in medicinal products was limited by law in 1973 because of the toxic effects it might produce when absorbed into the body. Trade names: **Dermalex**, **Ster-Zac D. C.**

六氯酚 與苯酚相同的一種消毒劑，過去用其肥皂類和乳劑類以治療皮膚疾患。由於當此藥吸收進入人體時可能產生毒性作用，因此其醫藥產品的應用，（在英國）已被 1973 年的法令限制。商品名：Dermalex，Ster-Zac D. C.。

hexachromia *n.* the ability to distinguish only six of the seven colours of the spectrum, the exception being indigo. Most people cannot distinguish indigo from blue or violet.

六色症 只能分辨七色光譜中六色的能力，靛藍除外。多數人不能分辨藍色和紫色。

hexamine (methenamine) *n.* an *antiseptic with a wide range of antibacterial activity, used to treat infections and inflammation of the urinary tract, such as cystitis. High doses may cause irritation of the stomach or bladder. Trade name: **Hiprex**.

烏洛托品 抗菌效力廣泛的一種抗菌劑，用於治療泌尿道感染和炎症，如膀胱炎。大劑量可引起胃和膀胱的刺激反應。商品名：Hiprex。

hexokinase *n.* an enzyme that catalyses the conversion of glucose to glucose-6-phosphate. This is the first stage of *glycolysis.

己糖激酶 催化葡萄糖轉化為6-磷酸葡萄糖的一種酶。此乃糖酵解的第一階段。

hexosamine *n.* the amino derivative of a *hexose sugar. The two most important hexosamines are *glucosamine and galactosamine.

己糖胺 己糖的氨基衍生物。兩種最重要的己糖胺類是氨基葡萄糖和氨基半乳糖。

hexose *n.* a simple sugar with six carbon atoms. Hexose sugars are the sugars most frequently found in food. The most important hexose is *glucose.

己糖 含六個碳原子的單糖。是食物中最多見的糖類。最重要的己糖是葡萄糖。

hiatus *n.* an opening or aperture. For example, the diaphragm contains hiatuses for the oesophagus and aorta.

裂孔 一種開口或孔。如膈肌含有食管裂孔和主動脈裂孔。

hiatus hernia *see* hernia.

裂孔疝 參閱 hernia。

Hib vaccine a vaccine that gives protection against the bacterium *Haemophilus influenzae* type B, which causes *meningitis, *epiglottitis, and joint infections. The vaccine is given with the triple DPT vaccine during the first year of life.

流感嗜血桿菌 B 型疫苗 能預防流感嗜血桿菌 B 型感染的疫苗。流感嗜血桿菌 B 型能引起腦膜炎、會厭炎和關節感染。此疫苗與白喉百日咳破傷風三聯菌苗在一歲時一起使用。

hiccup *n.* abrupt involuntary lowering of the diaphragm and closure of the sound-producing folds at the upper end of the

呃逆 膈肌突然不自主地下降和氣管上端的聲帶皺襞突然關閉，當空氣吸入時產生一種獨

trachea, producing a characteristic sound as the breath is draw in. Hiccups, which usually occur repeatedly, may be caused by indigestion or more serious disorders, such as alcoholism. Medical name: **singultus**.

特的聲音。呃逆往往反覆發生，可因消化不良或更嚴重的疾病（如乙醇中毒）引起。醫學用語：呃逆。

Hickman catheter a fine plastic cannula inserted into a vein in the neck to allow administration of drugs and repeated blood samples. The catheter is tunnelled for several centimetres beneath the skin to prevent infection entering the bloodstream. It is used most frequently in patients receiving long-term chemotherapy.

希克曼導管　一纖細塑料導管，插進頸部靜脈給藥和重複採血樣。此導管在皮膚下插入幾厘米，以防止感染進入血流。最常使用於接受長期化療的病人。

hidr- (hidro-) *prefix denoting* sweat. Example: *hidropoiesis* (formation of).

〔前綴〕汗　例如：汗生成。

hidradenitis suppurativa an inflammatory condition of the *apocrine sweat glands, which first become active at adolescence; it occurs in the armpits and groin. In women the condition responds to *anti-androgen therapy.

化膿性汗腺炎　頂（漿分）泌汗腺的炎症，在青春期時首先顯現。發生於腋窩和腹股溝。在女子，此症對抗雄激素療法有反應。

hidrosis *n.* **1.** the excretion of sweat. **2.** excessive sweating.

(1) 出汗　**(2)** 多汗

hidrotic *n.* an agent that causes sweating. *Parasympathomimetic drugs are hidrotics.

發汗藥　引起發汗的一種藥。擬副交感神經藥為發汗藥。

hilum *n.* (*pl.* **hila**) a hollow situated on the surface of an organ, such as the kidney or spleen, at which structures such as blood vessels, nerve fibres, and ducts enter or leave it.

門　位於某一器官如腎或脾表面的凹洞。該器官的血管、神經以及管道等結構由此進出。

hindbrain *n.* the part of the *brain comprising the cerebellum, pons, and medulla oblongata. The pons and medulla contain the nuclei of many of

菱腦　由小腦、腦橋以及延髓組成的腦的一部分。腦橋和腦髓內有許多腦神經核（腦神經由其外部發出）和網狀結構。

the cranial nerves, which issue from their surfaces, and the reticular formation. The fluid-filled cavity in the midline is the fourth *ventricle.

其中綫上充滿液體的腔隙是第四腦室。

hindgut *n.* the back part of the embryonic gut, which gives rise to part of the large intestine, the rectum, bladder, and urinary ducts. *See also* cloaca.

後腸 胚胎腸的後部，由此發生大腸的一部分、直腸、膀胱和尿道。參閱 cloaca。

hindquarter amputation an operation involving removal of an entire leg and part or all of the pelvis associated with it. It is usually performed for soft tissue or bone sarcomas arising from the upper thigh, hip, or buttock. *Compare* forequarter amputation.

髂腹間切斷術 包括切除整個腿以及部分或全部骨盆在內的一種手術。在股、髂或臀上部產生軟組織或骨肉瘤時通常施行此手術。與 forequarter amputation 對比。

hinge joint *see* ginglymus.

屈戌關節 參閱 ginglymus。

hip *n.* the region of the body where the thigh bone (femur) articulates with the *pelvis: the region on each side of the pelvis.

髖部 股骨與骨盆形成關節連接的人體的部位：此部位在骨盆兩側。

hip bone (innominate bone) a bone formed by the fusion of the ilium, ischium, and pubis. It articulates with the femur by the *acetabulum* of the ilium, a deep socket into which the head of the femur fits (*see* hip joint). Between the pubis and ischium, below and slightly in front of the acetabulum, is a large opening – the *obturator foramen*. The right and left hip bones form part of the *pelvis.

髖骨 由髂骨、坐骨和恥骨融合形成的骨。通過髖臼與股骨形成關節連接，即股骨頭進入髖臼窩（參閱 hip joint）。恥骨與坐骨間、髖臼下稍前方是一大的開口——閉孔。左、右側髖骨形成骨盆的一部分。

hip girdle *see* pelvic girdle.

髖帶 參閱 pelvic girdle。

hip joint the ball-and-socket joint (*see* enarthrosis) between the head of the femur and the acetabulum (socket) of the ilium (*see* hip bone). It is a common site of osteoarthritis and rheumatoid

髖關節 股骨頭和髂骨（參閱 enarthrosis）髖臼之間的球與臼關節，是骨關節炎和風濕性關節炎的常見處，經常用外科治療（通過髖置換）。參閱

arthritis, which is often treated surgically (by *hip replacement). *See also* congenital dislocation of the hip.

Hippelates *n.* a genus of small flies. The adults of *H. pallipes* are suspected of transmitting *yaws in the West Indies. Other species of *Hippelates* may be involved in the transmission of conjunctivitis.

hippocampal formation a curved band of cortex lying within each cerebral hemisphere: in evolutionary terms one of the brain's most primitive parts. It forms a portion of the *limbic system and is involved in the complex physical aspects of behaviour governed by emotion and instinct.

hippocampus *n.* a swelling in the floor of the lateral *ventricle of the brain. It contains complex foldings of cortical tissue and is involved, with other connections of the *hippocampal formation, in the workings of the *limbic system. **–hippocampal** *adj.*

Hippocratic oath the oath taken by a doctor that binds him to observe the code of behaviour and practice followed by the Greek physician Hippocrates (460–370 BC), called the 'Father of Medicine', and the students of the medical school in Cos where he taught.

hippus *n.* abnormal rhythmical variations in the size of the pupils, independent of the intensity of the light falling on the eyes. It is occasionally seen in various diseases of the nervous system.

hip replacement a surgical procedure developed for replacing a diseased hip joint with a prosthesis: many types of prosthesis are available. *See also* arthroplasty.

congenital dislocation of the hip。

潛蠅屬 小蠅的一屬。在西印度羣島，懷疑淡色潛蠅成蟲傳播雅司病。潛蠅屬的其他蟲種參與傳播結膜炎。

海馬結構 位於每側大腦半球內的皮質的彎曲帶：從進化的觀點來看，是腦最古老的部分之一。它形成邊緣系統的一部分，由情緒和本能所控制的複雜行為的生理活動與此結構有關。

海馬 大腦的側腦室底的一隆突。內含有皮質組織的複雜皺褶，與海馬有關的其他結構聯繫在一起，參與邊緣系統的種種活動。

希波克拉底誓言 醫生立的誓言，用以約束自己要按照醫學之父——希臘醫生希波克拉底（公元前 460~370）及他任教的科斯島醫學院的學生們的行醫準則行事。

虹膜震顫 瞳孔大小發生異常的節律性的變化，與進入眼中的光的強度無關。偶爾見於各種神經系統疾病。

髖置換 用假體替代患病髖關節的外科手術：許多類型的假體均可應用。參閱 arthroplasty。

Hirschsprung's disease a congenital condition in which the rectum and sometimes part of the lower colon have work. The affected portion does not expand or conduct the contents of the bowel, which accumulate in and distend the upper colon. Symptoms, which are usually apparent in the first weeks of life, are abdominal pain and swelling and severe or complete constipation. Diagnosis is by X-ray and by microscopic examination of samples of the bowel wall, which shows the absence of nerve cells. Treatment is by surgery to remove the affected segment and join the remaining (normal) colon to the anus. *See also* megacolon.

赫希施普龍病 一種先天性疾病：在胚胎發育中直腸和部分下段結腸未形成正常的神經網。受累部位不能擴張或輸送腸內容物，以致腸內容物在腸內聚積，而其上段結腸擴張。其症狀往往在出生後幾周內出現，有腹痛、腹脹以及嚴重便秘或完全不能排便。通過X綫以及腸壁標本的顯微鏡檢查來診斷，顯微鏡檢查顯示神經細胞缺失。治療是通過外科手術切除受累腸段，將剩餘的結腸（正常的）接到肛門上。參閱 megacolon。

hirsutism *n.* the presence of coarse pigmented hair on the face, chest, upper back, or abdomen in a female as a result of *hyperandrogenism (excessive production of androgen). *See also* virilization.

多毛症 存在於女性面部、胸、上脊部或腹部粗着色的毛髮，係雄激素過多症（雄激素產生過量）的結果。參閱 virilization。

hirudin *n.* an *anticoagulant present in the salivary glands of leeches and in certain snake venoms, that prevents *blood coagulation by inhibiting the action of the enzyme *thrombin.

水蛭素 存在於水蛭腮腺和某些蛇毒液中的抗凝血劑。它通過抑制凝血酶的作用以阻止血液凝固。

hist- (histio-, histo-) *prefix denoting* tissue.

〔前綴〕**組織**

histaminase *n.* an enzyme, widely distributed in the body, that is responsible for the inactivation of histamine.

組胺酶 廣泛分布於體內的一種酶，能滅活組胺。

histamine *n.* a compound derived from the amino acid histidine. It is found in nearly all tissues of the body, associated mainly with the *mast cells. Histamine has pronounced pharmacological activity, causing dilation of blood vessels and contraction of smooth muscle (for example, in the lungs). It is an important

組胺 由氨基酸組氨酸衍生的一種化合物。它幾乎見於人體的所有組織，主要與肥大細胞有關。組胺有顯著的藥理學作用，引起血管擴張和平滑肌（如肺中）收縮。組胺是炎症的一種重要介質，皮膚損傷後（例如由於動物毒液和毒素）

mediator of inflammation and is released in large amounts after skin damage (such as that due to animal venoms and toxins), producing a characteristic skin reaction (consisting of flushing, a flare, and a weal). Histamine is also released in anaphylactic reactions and allergic conditions, including asthma, and gives rise to some of the symptoms of these conditions. *See also* anaphylaxis, antihistamine.

大量釋放，產生獨特的皮膚反應（由潮紅、風疹塊組成）。在過敏反應和變態反應病中，包括哮喘，也釋放出組胺，引發此類疾病的某些症狀。參閱anaphylaxis，antihistamine。

histamine acid phosphate a derivative of *histamine used to test for acid secretion in the stomach in conditions involving abnormal gastric secretion, such as *Zollinger-Ellison syndrome. It is administered by injection and can cause headache, wheezing, rapid heartbeat, disturbed vision, and digestive upsets.

磷酸組胺　組胺的一種衍生物，用於包括胃分泌異常（如佐-埃氏綜合徵）的胃酸分泌試驗。注射給藥。可引起頭痛、哮鳴、心跳加快、視力模糊以及消化紊亂。

histidine *n.* an *amino acid from which *histamine is derived.

組氨酸　一種氨基酸，組胺由其衍生。

histiocyte *n.* a fixed *macrophage, i.e. one that is stationary within connective tissue.

組織細胞　一靜止的巨噬細胞，即在結締組織內靜止不動的巨噬細胞。

histiocytoma *n.* a tumour that contains *macrophages or *histiocytes, large cells with the ability to engulf foreign matter and bacteria. *See also* fibrosarcoma (malignant fibrous histiocytoma).

組織細胞瘤　一種含有巨噬細胞或組織細胞的腫瘤，即具有吞噬異物和細菌能力的大細胞。參閱 fibrosarcoma (malignant fibrous histiocytoma)。

histiocytosis *n.* any of a group of diseases in which there are abnormalities in certain large phagocytic cells (*histiocytes), leading to biochemical defects, such as abnormal storage of fats (as in *Gaucher's disease), and other poorly understood conditions, such as Hand-Schüller-Christian disease (*see* reticuloendotheliosis) and Letterer-Siwe disease.

組織細胞增生症　某種大吞噬細胞（組織細胞）發生異常的一組疾病。可導致生化方面的缺陷，例如脂肪異常貯積（戈歇病），以及其他病因不明的疾病，例如漢-許-克氏病（參閱 reticuloendotheliosis）和萊-賽氏病。

histochemistry *n.* the study of the identification and distribution of chemical compounds within and between cells, by means of stains, indicators, and light and electron microscopy. **–histochemical** *adj.*

組織化學 以染劑、指示劑以及光學顯微鏡和電子顯微鏡檢查，研究細胞內或細胞間化合物的成分和分布的學科。

histocompatibility *n.* the form of *compatibility that depends upon tissue components, mainly specific glycoprotein antigens in cell membranes. A high degree of histocompatibility is necessary for a tissue graft or organ transplant to be successful. **–histocompatible** *adj.*

組織相容性 與組織成分，主要是細胞膜內特異性糖蛋白相容的形式。為使組織移植或器官移植成功，需要高度的組織相容性。

histogenesis *n.* the formation of tissues.

組織生成 組織的形成。

histogram *n.* a form of statistical graph in which values are plotted in the form of rectangles on a chart; a bar-chart.

直方圖 統計圖的一種類型。其值以長方形繪製於圖表上；直條圖。

histoid *adj.* **1.** resembling normal tissue. **2.** composed of one type of tissue.

(1)組織樣的 類似正常組織的。(2) 單一組織的 由一種類型的組織構成的。

histological grade the degree of *differentiation of a tumour, typically a breast tumour.

組織學等級 腫瘤的鑑別程度，乳腺瘤有典型性。

histology *n.* the study of the structure of tissues by means of special staining techniques combined with light and electron microscopy. **–histological** *adj.*

組織學 以特殊的染色技術以及光學顯微鏡和電子顯微鏡檢查研究組織結構的學科。

histone *n.* a simple protein that combines with a nucleic acid to form a *nucleoprotein.

組蛋白 一種單純蛋白，能與核酸結合，形成一種核蛋白。

Histoplasma *n.* a genus of parasitic yeast-like fungi. The species *H. capsulatum* causes the respiratory infection *histoplasmosis.

組織胞漿菌屬 寄生性類酵母真菌的一屬。該菌屬的莢膜組織胞漿菌能引起呼吸道感染——組織胞漿菌病。

histoplasmin *n.* a preparation of antigenic material from a culture of

莢膜組織胞漿菌素 由真菌——莢膜組織胞漿菌培養出的

the fungus *Histoplasma capsulatum*, used to test for the presence of the disease *histoplasmosis by subcutaneous injection.

抗原性物質的一種製劑。通過皮下注射，用來檢驗組織胞漿菌病的存在。

histoplasmosis *n.* an infection caused by inhaling spores of the fungus *Histoplasma capsulatum*. The primary pulmonary form usually produces no symptoms or harmful effects and is recognized retrospectively by X-rays and positive *histoplasmin skin testing. Occasionally, progressive histoplasmosis, which resembles tuberculosis, develops. Symptomatic disease is treated with intravenous amphotericin-B. The spores are found in soil contaminated by faeces, especially from chickens and bats. The disease is endemic in the northern and central USA, Argentina, Brazil, Venezuela, and parts of Africa.

組織胞漿菌病 通過吸入真菌——莢膜組織胞漿菌的孢子引起的一種感染。初期的肺型通常不引起症狀或有害作用，通過 X 綫和陽性莢膜組織胞漿菌素皮膚試驗確認。偶爾發生進行性的組織細胞漿菌病。該病發展類似肺結核。有症狀的組織胞漿菌病可用靜脈注射兩性黴素 B 治療。孢子見於被糞便（尤其是鳥類和蝙蝠類）污染的土壤。此病流行於美國北部和中部、阿根廷、巴西、委內瑞拉以及非洲部分地區。

histotoxic *adj.* poisonous to tissues: applied to certain substances and conditions.

組織毒的 對組織有毒的：描述某些物質和疾患。

HIV (human immunodeficiency virus) a *retrovirus responsible for *AIDS. *See also* HTLV.

人類免疫缺陷病毒 引起艾滋病的逆轉錄病毒。參閱 HTLV。

hives *n. see* urticaria.

蕁麻疹 參閱 urticaria。

HLA system human leucocyte antigen system: a series of four gene families (termed A, B, C, and D) that code for polymorphic proteins expressed on the surface of most nucleated cells. Individuals inherit from each parent one gene (or set of genes) for each subdivision of the HLA system. If two individuals have identical HLA types, they are said to be histocompatible. Successful tissue transplantation requires a minimum number of HLA differences between donor and recipient tissues.

人白細胞抗原系統 人白細胞抗原系統：包括四個基因系（稱做 A、B、C、D）。它們編碼多數有核細胞表面的多形蛋白。由個體所遺傳來自每一親代的某一基因（或一套基因）導致 HLA 系統的各個亞型。如果兩個人有相同的人白細胞抗原類型，他們被認為是組織相容的。成功的組織移植要求供體和受體組織之間人白細胞抗原具有最小差異。

hobnail liver the liver of a patient with cirrhosis, which has a knobbly appearance caused by regenerating nodules separated by bands of fibrous tissue.

結節樣肝臟　肝硬化病人的肝臟，具有結節樣外觀，由於纖維組織索將再生的小結分隔開所致。

Hodgkin's disease a malignant disease of lymphatic tissues – a form of *lymphoma – usually characterized by painless enlargement of one or more groups of lymph nodes in the neck, armpits, groin, chest, or abdomen; the spleen, liver, bone marrow, and bones may also be involved. Apart from the enlarging nodes, there may also be weight loss, fever, profuse sweating at night, and itching (known as *B symptoms*). Hodgkin's disease is distinguished from other forms of lymphoma by the presence of large binucleate cells (*Sternberg-Reed cells*) in the cancerous lymph nodes. Treatment depends on the extent of disease and may include surgery, radiotherapy, drug therapy, or a combination of these. Drugs used in the treatment of the disease include nitrogen mustard, vincristine, procarbazine, prednisone, chlorambucil, and vinblastine. Many patients can be cured; in the early stages of the disease this may be in the order of 85% or more.

霍奇金病　淋巴組織的一種惡性疾病——淋巴組織瘤的一種類型——通常以頸、腋、腹股溝、胸或腹部的單個或多羣淋巴結的無痛性腫大為特徵，脾、骨髓和骨也受累。除腺體腫大外，也可有體重下降、發熱、夜間大量出汗以及瘙癢（稱為 B 綜合徵）。從霍奇金病者癌性淋巴結中存在大雙核細胞（斯-里氏細胞）而區別於淋巴瘤的其他類型。依病者程度治療包括外科手術、放射治療、藥物治療或者它們的綜合療法。治療此病的藥物有氮芥、長春新鹼、丙卡巴肼、強的松、苯丁酸氮芥和長春花鹼。多數病人可以治療，在疾病早期階段有效治療可達 85% 或以上。

holistic *adj.* describing an approach to patient care in which the physical, mental, and social factors in the patient's condition are taken into account, rather than just the diagnosed disease. The term is applied to a range of orthodox and unorthodox methods of treatment. *See also* alternative medicine.

機能整體性的　描述照料病人的一種思路：應考慮病人的身體、精神以及社會等各方面因素，而不是僅僅考慮經診斷的疾病。此術語適用於一系列正統的和非正統的治療方法。參閱 alternative medicine。

Holmes-Adie syndrome *see* Adie's syndrome.

霍-艾氏綜合徵　參閱 Adie's syndrome。

holo- *prefix denoting* complete or entire.

〔前綴〕完全、全部

holocrine *adj.* describing a gland or type of secretion in which the entire cell disintegrates when the product is released.

全漿分泌　描述腺體或分泌的類型。當釋放其產物時，整個細胞發生解體。

home delivery *see* domiciliary midwife.

家庭分娩　參閱 domiciliary midwife。

home help *see* social services.

家務服務　參閱 social services。

home nurse (district nurse) (in Britain) a trained nurse with special training in *domiciliary services. Formerly all home nurses had to be registered, but increasing numbers of enrolled nurses are now working in this field. Prior to 1974 they were employed either by voluntary agencies on repayment from local health authorities or by these authorities directly. The home nursing service is now the responsibility of District Health Authorities; normally day care only is provided but under special circumstances out of hours nursing can be arranged. Formerly each nurse was allocated to a geographical district and doctors requiring the services for their patients had to contact the local headquarters. However, it is now common for nurses to be allocated to a designated general practice, an arrangement known as *attachment.

家庭護士（地段護士）　（在英國）在家庭保健服務部門受過專門訓練的護士。過去所有的家庭護士都必須是國家註冊護士，但近幾年來在此領域工作的僱傭護士逐步增加。1974 年以前他們或是由地方衛生當局付報酬的志願機構來僱傭，或是由這些衛生局直接僱傭。家庭護理工作目前是地段衛生局負責；正常情況下只提供日間護理，在特殊情況下可安排超時護理。過去，每一護士被分配到一定的地段，當醫生要求為他們的病人提供服務時，必須與地方總部聯繫。但現在通常是分配護士從事指定的一般護理工作，這種安排稱之為附加護理。

homeo- (homoeo-) *prefix denoting* similar; like.

〔前綴〕相同，類似

homeopathic (homoeopathic) *adj.* **1.** of or relating to *homeopathy. **2.** infinitesimally small, as applied to the dose of a drug.

(1) 順勢療法的　與順勢療法有關的。(2) 極小的　指一藥物的劑量。

homeopathy (homoeopathy) *n.* a system of medicine based on the theory that 'like cures like'. The patient is treated with extremely small quantities

順勢療法　以「以毒攻毒」理論為基礎的醫學體系。用極小量的藥物治療病人，而該藥本身就能產生病人所患疾病的症

of drugs that are themselves capable of producing symptoms of his particular disease. The system was founded by Samuel Hahnemann (1755–1843) at the end of the 18th century and is followed by a minority of doctors in the UK. There is a Royal London Homeopathic Hospital. *See also* alternative medicine. **–homeopathist** *n.*

狀。該體系由塞繆爾·哈曼 (1755~1843) 創立於 18 世紀末，目前在英國仍被少數醫生沿用。並有一所倫敦皇家順勢療法醫院。參閱 alternative medicine。

homeostasis *n.* the physiological process by which the internal systems of the body (e.g. blood pressure, body temperature, *acid-base balance) are maintained at equilibrium, despite variations in the external conditions. **–homeostatic** *adj.*

體內平衡，自身穩定 儘管身體外部條件有種種變化，但是內部系統（如血壓、體溫、酸鹼平衡）被這種生理學過程維持在平衡狀態。

homo- *prefix denoting* the same or common.

〔前綴〕**相同，共同**

homocystinuria *n.* an inherited disease caused by an enzyme deficiency resulting in an excess of homocysteine (an intermediate in the synthesis of the amino acid *cysteine) in the blood and the presence of homocystine (an oxidized form of cysteine) in the urine. Clinically affected individuals are mentally retarded, excessively tall with long fingers (due to overgrowth of bones), and have a tendency to form blood clots in the veins and arteries. Treatment is by diet.

高胱氨酸尿 一種遺傳性疾病，病因是酶的缺乏導致血液中高胱氨酸（氨基酸半胱氨酸合成的中間物）過量和尿中出現高胱氨酸（半胱氨酸的氧化形式）。臨床患者智力低下，身長過高，手指過長（骨頭過度生長所致），並且動脈和靜脈血管中易形成血塊。飲食治療。

homoeopathy *n. see* homeopathy.

順勢療法 參閱 homeopathy。

homogametic *adj.* describing the sex that produces only one kind of gamete, which carries the same *sex chromosome, and that therefore does not determine the sex of the offspring. In humans women are the homogametic sex: each egg cell carries an X chromosome. *Compare* heterogametic.

同型配子的 描述只能產生一種配子的性別。其配子的性染色體相同，因而不決定後代的性別。在人類，婦女為同型配子性別：每個卵細胞攜帶一個 X 染色體。與 heterogametic 對比。

homogenize *vb.* to reduce material to a uniform consistency, e.g. by crushing and mixing. Organs and tissues are homogenized to determine their overall content of a particular enzyme or other substance. **–homogenization** *n.*

使均匀、匀化 使物質濃度均衡，例如通過壓碎和混合。均化器官和組織，以測定其中某種酶或其他物質的總含量。

homogentisic acid a product formed during the metabolism of the amino acids phenylalanine and tyrosine. In normal individuals homogentisic acid is oxidized by the enzyme *homogentisic acid oxidase*. In rare cases this enzyme is lacking and a condition known as *alcaptonuria, in which large amounts of homogentisic acid are excreted in the urine, results.

尿黑酸 氨基酸（苯丙氨酸和酪氨酸）代謝過程中的產物。在正常個體中，尿黑酸由尿黑酸氧化酶氧化。在極少數病人中，該酶缺乏，導致大量尿黑酸由尿液排出，這種疾病被稱為尿黑酸尿。

homograft (allograft) *n.* a living tissue or organ graft between two members of the same species; for example, a heart transplant from one person to another. Such grafts will not survive unless the recipient is treated to suppress his body's automatic rejection of the foreign tissue. *See also* transplantation.

同種移植物（同種移植） 供同一物種的兩個個體間使用的活組織或器官移植物；如兩個人間的心臟移植。這種移植物不會存活，除非受體接受抑制其機體對異物的自動排斥反應的治療。參閱 transplantation。

homoiothermic *adj.* warm-blooded: able to maintain a constant body temperature independently of, and despite variations in, the temperature of the surroundings. Mammals (including humans) and birds are homoiothermic. *Compare* poikilothermic. **–homoiothermy** *n.*

恆溫的 溫血的；能夠不受環境溫度控制或不受環境溫度變化的影響，保持某一恆定體溫的。哺乳動物（包括人）和鳥類都是恆溫的。與 poikilothermic 對比。

homolateral *adj. see* ipsilateral.

同側的 參閱 ipsilateral。

homologous *adj.* **1.** (in anatomy) describing organs or parts that have the same basic structure and evolutionary origin, but not necessarily the same function or superficial structure. *Compare* analogous. **2.** (in genetics) describing a pair of chromosomes of similar shape and size and having identical gene loci.

(1) 同種的 （解剖學）指器官或部位基本結構和進化起源相同，但功能或表面結構不一定相同。與 analogous 對比。**(2)** 同源的 （遺傳學）用以描述形狀和大小相似，基因位點相同的一對染色體。其中一條來於母親，另一條來於父親。

One member of the pair is derived from the mother, the other from the father.

homonymous *adj.* describing a visual defect in which the visual field to one side of the body is restricted in both eyes (*see* hemianopia).

同側的，同一關係的　描述雙目對身體一側的視野同時受限的視力缺陷（參閱 hemianopia）。

homoplasty *n.* surgical repair of defective or damaged tissues or organs with a *homograft.

同種移植術　以同種移植物對有缺陷或損傷的組織或器官的手術修復。

homosexuality *n.* the condition of being sexually attracted, covertly or overtly, by members of one's own sex: it can affect either sex (*see also* lesbianism). The cause of homosexuality remains unclear, although there is some evidence of a genetic basis. Homosexuality is no longer regarded as a psychological disorder, but help is sometimes offered to individuals wishing to change their sexual orientation. There are no drugs available for changing sexual orientation, although it is possible to depress the sexual drive. Persons seeking help for their homosexuality are more likely to benefit from *counselling to reduce any anxiety and guilt that may be associated with the condition, rather than trying to change their sexual behaviour. **–homosexual** *adj., n.*

同性戀慾，同性戀　公開或隱密地被與自己同性的個體發生性吸引的狀況。兩性均可發生（參閱 lesbianism）。同性戀的原因尚不清楚，但有一些證據表明與遺傳基礎有關。同性戀不再被認為是一種心理異常，但對希望改變其性指向的人，常可給予幫助。儘管可以壓抑性衝動，但對改變性指向沒有有效的藥物。尋求幫助的人常常得益於心理咨詢，以減輕同性戀帶來的焦慮和犯罪感，而不是試圖改變他們的性行為。

homozygous *adj.* describing an individual in whom the members of a pair of genes determining a particular characteristic are identical. *See* allele. *Compare* heterozygous. **–homozygote** *n.*

純合的　描述決定個體某個特徵的一對基因是相同的。參閱 allele。與 heterozygous 對比。

homunculus *n.* **1.** (manikin) a dwarf with no deformity or abnormality other than small size. **2.** (manikin) a small jointed anatomical model of a man. **3.** (in early biological theory) a miniature human being thought to be contained within each of the reproductive cells.

(1)（人體模型）矮人　沒有畸形或發育異常，只是身材矮小的人。(2)（人體模型）人體模型　小型的有活動關節的人體解剖模型。(3) 小人（早期生物學理論）被認為存在於每個生殖細胞內的微型小人。

hook *n.* a surgical instrument with a bent or curved tip, used to hold, lift, or retract tissue at operation.

鈎　一種尖端彎曲的外科器械，手術中用於拉住、提起或牽開組織。

hookworm *n.* either of two nematode worms, *Necator americanus* or *Ancylostoma duodenale*, which live as parasites in the intestine of man. Both species, also known as the New and Old World hookworms respectively, are of great medical importance (*see* hookworm disease).

鈎蟲　美洲板口綫蟲或十二指腸鈎蟲，為人體腸道內寄生綫蟲。這兩種蟲分別又被稱為新大陸鈎蟲和舊大陸鈎蟲，是醫學上兩種重要綫蟲（參閱 hookworm disease）。

hookworm disease a condition resulting from an infestation of the small intestine by hookworms. Hookworm larvae live in the soil and infect man by penetrating the skin. The worms travel to the lungs in the bloodstream and from there pass via the windpipe and gullet to the small intestine. Heavy hookworm infections may cause considerable damage to the wall of the intestine, leading to a serious loss of blood; this, in conjunction with malnutrition, can provoke severe anaemia. Symptoms include abdominal pain, diarrhoea, debility, and mental inertia. The disease occurs throughout the tropics and subtropics and is prevalent in areas of poor personal hygiene and sanitation. *Bephenium hydroxynaphthoate, reliable and easy to administer, is used in treatment.

鈎蟲病　小腸受鈎蟲感染引起的一種疾病。鈎蟲幼蟲生活在土壤中並通過穿透皮膚感染人體。鈎蟲隨血流移動到肺，然後經氣管及食管到達小腸。大量的鈎蟲感染可引起腸壁嚴重損傷，導致嚴重失血。失血和營養不良共同引起嚴重貧血。症狀包括腹痛、腹瀉、虛弱及精神不振。該病發生在熱帶及亞熱帶所有地區並流行於個人衛生和環境衛生條件差的地區。苄芬寧羥萘酸鹽常用於治療，療效可靠，用藥方便。

hordeolum *n. see* stye.

瞼腺炎　參閱 stye。

hormone *n.* a substance that is produced in one part of the body (by an *endocrine gland, such as the thyroid, adrenal, or pituitary), passes into the bloodstream and is carried to other (distant) organs or tissues, where it acts to modify their structure or function. Examples of hormones are corticosteroids (from the adrenal cortex), growth hormone (from

激素　身體某一部位（內分泌腺如甲狀腺、腎上腺或垂體）產生的一種物質。它進入血流後被帶到其他（遠離的）器官或組織，從而改變該器官或組織的結構或功能。例如皮質類固醇（由腎上腺皮質產生）、生長素（由垂體產生）和雄激素（由睾丸產生）。

the pituitary gland), and androgens (from the testes).

hormone replacement therapy (HRT)

the use of female hormones for the relief of symptoms resulting from cessation of ovarian function, either at the time of the natural *menopause or following surgical removal of the ovaries. Oestrogenic hormones may be prescribed orally, transdermally, or by subcutaneous implant. The combination of progestogen with oestrogen is preferred if the woman has retained her uterus, since administration of oestrogen alone might cause overstimulation of the endometrium or even cancer; over-stimulation may result in uterine bleeding. HRT is effective against vasomotor upsets (e.g. hot flushes), genitourinary atrophy (causing vaginal dryness), and in preventing *osteoporosis; there is usually also an improvement in psychological wellbeing, and HRT is claimed to prevent coronary heart disease. It is most efficacious in preventing the above conditions if prescribed as soon as the earliest symptoms of the menopause are detected.

horn *n.* (in anatomy) a process, outgrowth, or extension of an organ or other structure. It is often paired. In the spinal cord crescent-shaped areas of grey matter (seen in cross section) are known as the dorsal and ventral horns.

Horner's syndrome a group of symptoms that are due to a disorder of the sympathetic nerves in the brainstem or cervical (neck) region. The syndrome consists of a constricted pupil, drooping of the upper eyelid (*ptosis), and an absence of sweating over the affected side of the face.

激素替代療法 使用雌性激素，以緩解自然絕經或手術摘除卵巢後卵巢功能停止引起的症狀。雌激素可以口服或經皮給藥，也可皮下植入。如果患者仍有子宮，則優先選用雌激素和孕酮聯合用藥。因為單獨使用雌激素，可能引起子宮內膜過分刺激徵，甚至癌症。前者可以引起子宮出血。激素替代療法對於血管舒縮紊亂（熱潮紅）、生殖泌尿系統萎縮（導致陰道乾燥），以及預防骨質疏鬆症都有效果，還常出現心理健康水平的改善。據稱，激素替代療法還能預防冠心病。絕經的最早期症狀一旦發現便立即給予激素替代療法，療效最佳。

角 （解剖學）指器官或其他結構的一個突起，向外生長物或延伸部分。通常是成對的。在脊髓灰質中月牙形區域（見於橫斷面）稱為後角和前角。

霍納綜合徵 腦幹頸部交感神經失常引起的一組症狀，包括瞳孔收縮，上瞼下垂及患側臉部無汗。

horseshoe kidney an anatomical variation in kidney development whereby the lower poles of both kidneys are joined together. This usually causes no trouble but it may be associated with impaired drainage of urine from the kidney by the ureters, which cross in front of the united lower segment.

蹄鐵形腎 腎臟發育過程中的解剖變異，指兩腎的下極結合在一起。這種變異通常不引起不適，但可伴有從腎到輸尿管的排尿障礙，輸尿管從前方橫跨兩腎連結下段。

hospice *n.* an institution that specializes in the care of terminally ill patients with special concern for death with dignity: narcotic drugs are used in carefully controlled doses for the relief of pain.

臨終病室 專門看護臨終病人的一種機構，特別注意死亡的尊嚴：以謹慎控制的劑量使用鎮痛藥來緩解疼痛。

hospital *n.* an institution offering residential, investigatory, and/or therapeutic care regarded as too complex or specialized for provision as a *domiciliary service. Such care may be residential (in-patient), including the care of patients for a whole day and their return home at night (*day hospital*). Out-patient services include consultation with designated specialists by prior appointment, X-rays, laboratory tests, physiotherapy, and accident and emergency services for those requiring urgent care. Most Health Districts have a *general hospital* (*DGH*), which provides sufficient basic services for the population of the District. Some larger hospitals have resources that are more highly specialized, to meet the needs of a wider population, providing so-called *regional* or *supraregional* (*national*) services. Such hospitals often provide training for medical students (*teaching* or *university hospitals*) and for postgraduate education. Some smaller hospitals – known as *community hospitals* – are staffed mainly or exclusively by general practitioners and are intended for people for whom home care is not practicable on social grounds. Hospitals

醫院 一種提供住宿、觀察和/或治療的機構。它所提供的服務像家庭服務，但複雜和專業化得多。這種護理可分為住院性的（住院病人），包括全日看護，和夜晚病人回家的（晝間醫院）。門診病人的服務項目包括預約指定專家的診治、X線檢查、實驗室檢查、理療和對需要緊急處理的病人提供的事故和急診服務。多數衛生保健地段都擁有一家綜合醫院，為該地段人口提供充足的基本醫療服務項目。一些較大的醫院擁有更為專業化的醫療資源，提供所謂的地區性或跨地區性（全國性）服務，以滿足較廣大人口的需求。這類醫院通常為醫學生（教學醫院或大學醫院）和研究生提供培訓。一些較小的醫院稱為社區醫院，其主要或全部工作人員為全科醫師，它們專門為由於社會原因不能進行家庭護理的病人服務。醫院可以申請成為自治的國民保健服務制中的托管機構，不受衛生當局的管轄，其收入主要來源於與衛生當局簽訂的提供服務的合同和

may apply to become self-governing *NHS trusts*, independent of health authority control, their income deriving chiefly from contracts to provide services to health authorities and fundholding general practitioners. *See also* independent contract.

掌握資金的全科醫師。參閱 independent contract。

Hospital Activity Analysis *see* Hospital In-patient Enquiry.

醫院活動分析　參閱 Hospital In-patient Enquiry。

hospital fatality ratio *see* case fatality ratio.

住院死亡率　參閱 case fatality ratio。

hospital infection *see* nosocomial infection.

醫院傳染　參閱 nosocomial infection。

Hospital In-patient Enquiry (in Britain) a statistical review, organized jointly by the *Department of Health and the *Office of Population Censuses and Surveys, providing information about in-patients treated in National Health Service hospitals. The data, based on a sample of episodes of illness (as distinct from individual patients), include diagnosis on discharge or death, duration on the waiting list, and length of stay. More detailed information, including aspects of therapy while in the hospital, are included in *Hospital Activity Analysis. Compare* record linkage.

住院病人調查　（英國）由衛生部和人口普查辦公室聯合組織的統計學調查，提供在國民保健服務制醫院中住院治療的病人信息。資料以疾病抽樣為基礎（不同於個體病人），內容包括出院診斷、死亡診斷、等候入院及住院的時間長短。更為具體的信息，包括入院後治療方面的情況，則被收入醫院活動分析中。與 record linkage 對比。

host *n*. an animal or plant in or upon which a *parasite lives. An *intermediate host* is one in which the parasite passes its larval or asexual stages; a *definitive* host is one in which the parasite develops to its sexual stage.

宿主　寄生物寄生於其內或其表面的動物或植物。中間宿主是寄生物過其幼蟲或無性期的場所；終宿主則為寄生物發育至其性生殖階段的場所。

housemaid's knee (prepatellar bursitis) a fluid-filled swelling of the bursa in front of the kneecap, often resulting from frequent kneeling. Treatment – and prevention – is by avoidance of kneeling. *See also* bursitis.

髕前囊炎　髕骨前部囊的充液性腫脹，常由頻繁下跪所致。防治方法是避免下跪動作。參閱 bursitis。

house physician/surgeon *see* Doctor.

住院內科醫師／外科醫師　參閱 Doctor。

HPV *see* human papillomavirus.

人類乳頭瘤病毒　參閱 human papillomavirus。

H₂-receptor antagonist *see* antihistamine.

H_2 受體拮抗劑　參閱 antihistamine。

H₂ receptors *see* antihistamine.

H_2 受體　參閱 antihistamine。

HRT *see* hormone replacement therapy.

激素替代療法　參閱 hormone replacement therapy。

HSE *see* Health and Safety Executive.

健康與安全局　參閱 Health and Safety Executive。

5-HT 5-hydroxytryptamine (*see* serotonin).

5-羥色氨　參閱 serotonin。

HTLV (human T-cell lymphocytotrophic virus) a family of viruses that includes the *AIDS virus, HTLV III (or HIV). Other HTLV viruses may cause lymphomas and leukaemias.

人類 T 細胞淋巴細胞滋養病毒　病毒的一種，包括艾滋病病毒，即人類 T 細胞淋巴細胞滋養病毒 III（或人類免疫缺陷病毒）。其他的人類 T 細胞淋巴細胞滋養病毒可引起淋巴瘤和白血病。

human chorionic gonadotrophin (HCG) a hormone, similar to the pituitary *gonadotrophins that is produced by the placenta during pregnancy. Large amounts are excreted in the urine, and this is used as the basis for most *pregnancy tests. The level of HCG in the serum is one of the indicators used in the *triple marker test for Down's syndrome. HCG maintains the secretion of *progesterone by the corpus luteum of the ovary, the secretion of pituitary gonadotrophins being blocked during pregnancy. HCG is given by injection to treat delayed puberty, undescended testes, premenstrual tension, and (with

人絨毛膜促性腺激素　一種激素，與垂體促性腺激素相似。在妊娠期由胎盤產生。該激素由尿液中大量排出，作為多種妊娠測試的基礎。血清中人絨毛膜促性腺激素水平是唐氏綜合徵三重標記試驗的指徵之一。妊娠期垂體促性腺激素的分泌被阻斷，因此，絨毛膜促性腺激素維持卵巢黃體分泌黃體酮。注射該種激素可治療青春期遲緩、隱睾、經前緊張；與卵泡刺激素聯用，還可治療不排卵引起的不孕症。

*follicle-stimulating hormone) sterility due to lack of ovulation.

Human Fertilization and Embryology Act 1990 an Act of Parliament that makes provisions for human embryos and children produced as a result of artificial insemination, in vitro fertilization, or any other method of assisted conception. The increasing use of such methods means that it is no longer possible to define legal parentage solely on a genetic basis. Under the Act, the legal mother is defined as the woman who has given birth to the child, regardless of genetic parentage, unless the child is subsequently adopted or (in the case of children born to *surrogate mothers) a *section 30 order is made. The legal father is generally the genetic father except when the latter is a licensed sperm donor or when the donor's sperm is used after his death. When a wife conceives as a result of assisted conception, her spouse may be regarded as the child's legal father, even if he is not the genetic father, as long as he consented to her treatment. The Act also established a *Human Fertilization and Embryology Authority*, which controls and reviews research involving the use of embryos and issues licences for this research and for treatment in assisted conception. It also maintains a register of persons whose gametes are used for assisted conception and of children born as a result. Children over the age of 18 can apply to the Authority for information concerning their ethnic and genetic background.

Human Genome Project a massive international research project to elucidate the entire sequence of genes on all the human chromosomes. The human

人類授精和胚胎學法案 1990 英國一項議會法案、對人工授精、試管授精和其他人工授精方法產生的人類胚胎和兒童作出規定。這些方法不斷增多的使用意味着不能再僅僅以基因基礎定義法律上的父母親關係。根據這項法案,法定母親的定義是娩出孩子的婦女,而與基因母親身分無關,除非孩子生後接着被領養或者(在代用母親產出孩子的情況下)法院根據 30 款做出判決。法定的父親通常是遺傳學意義上的父親,除非這位遺傳學意義上的父親是一位持有許可證的精子供體或者供體的精子在他去世後才被使用。當一位妻子通過人工授精而懷孕,只要她的丈夫同意過她接受人工授精,他就可以被認為是這個孩子的法定父親,即使他不是遺傳學意義上的父親。

該項法案還建立了一個人類授精和胚胎學管理委員會,控制和審查涉及胚胎使用的研究和頒發從事這項研究和接受人工授精的許可證。它還對其配子用於人工授精的人和人工授精出生的孩子進行登記。18 歲以上的孩子可以向該管理委員會申請獲取有關他們的種族和遺傳背景方面的信息。

Human Genome Project 人類基因組項目 一項大型國際研究項目,目的是闡明所有人類染色體上的整個基因排列順序。人類基因組包含約 30

genome comprises some 3000 million nucleotide base pairs (*see* DNA) forming about 100,000 genes, distributed between 23 pairs of chromosomes. The sequence of these bases, along the length of each chromosome, is currently being determined in several centres in different parts of the world. The Human Genome Project is by far the most ambitious biological research programme of all time. Beginning in 1988, it was scheduled to last for 15 years, but recent advances in methods of automating gene sequencing, made in a French laboratory, suggest that the project will be completed sooner than this. Knowledge of the entire human genome will be of incalculable value to medicine and human biology. It has already resulted in the identification of the genes associated with many hereditary disorders and revealed the existence of a genetic basis or component for many other diseases not previously known to have one. Theoretically, this would enable the development of drugs to alleviate conditions caused by deficiency of specific proteins and the large-scale genetic screening of populations known to be susceptible to particular disorders.

human immunodeficiency virus *see* HIV.

human leucocyte antigen system *see* HLA system.

human papillomavirus (HPV) a virus – a member of the *papovavirus group – that causes warts, including genital warts. There are over 50 strains of HPV: certain strains are considered to be causative factors in the development of anal and genital cancers, especially cervical cancer, but additional factors are necessary

億個核苷酸基對（參閱 DNA），它們組成大約 10 萬個基因，分布在 23 對染色體間。目前，世界各地的幾個中心正在測定這些基因在每條染色體上的排列順序。人類基因組項目顯然是人類歷史上最雄心勃勃的生物學研究項目。這個項目始於 1988 年，按計劃要持續 15 年，但是，最近一個法國實驗室在基因自動排序方法上的進展預示這個項目將提前完成。全部人類基因組的知識對於醫學和人類生物學都有不可估量的價值。它已經使人們識別了與許多遺傳性疾病有關的基因，並且揭示了許多其他疾病以前不為人知的遺傳學基礎或成分。理論上，這將使人們能夠研製緩解特異性蛋白不足引起的疾病的藥物，並且形成對某一疾病敏感人羣的大範圍基因篩查。

人類免疫缺陷病毒　參閱 HIV。

人白細胞抗原系統　參閱 HLA system。

人類乳頭瘤病毒　乳多泡病毒羣的一員，引起疣，包括生殖器疣的一種病毒。它有 50 多個亞種，其中有些被認為是引起肛門癌和生殖器癌，尤其是子宮頸癌的致病因子，但是細胞惡變必須還有其他因素。這種病毒是最常見的性傳染病之

before the cells become malignant. HPV is one of the most common sexually transmitted infections. In women the presence of HPV may be detected on colposcopic examination, although techniques using DNA amplification (*see* polymerase chain reaction) give more accurate results and suggest that up to 40% of a normal, apparently healthy, female population may harbour these viruses. In women with an abnormal cervical smear, the DNA test is found to be positive in a much higher percentage and is therefore a useful indicator of a high risk of developing cancer of the cervix.

一。在女性，陰道鏡檢可以發現這種病毒的存在。但是，DNA 放大技術（參閱 polymerase chain reaction）的結果更為精確，並且表明高達 40% 的正常健康女性可能攜帶這種病毒。宮頸塗片異常的女性，DNA 檢驗的陽性率更高，因此，DNA 檢驗是查出患宮頸癌高風險的一項有用指標。

humectant 1. *n.* a substance that is used for moistening. **2.** *adj.* causing moistening.

(1) 致濕劑 用於引起潮濕的物質。**(2) 致濕的** 引起潮濕的。

humerus *n.* the bone of the upper arm. The *head* of the humerus articulates with the *scapula at the shoulder joint. At the lower end of the shaft the *trochlea* articulates with the *ulna and part of the radius. The radius also articulates with a rounded protuberance (the *capitulum*) close to the trochlea. Depressions (*fossae*) at the front and back of the humerus accommodate the ulna and radius, respectively, when the arm is flexed or straightened.

肱骨 上臂骨。肱骨頭在肩關節處與肩胛骨連接。在肱骨體下端，滑車與尺骨和部分橈骨連接形成關節。橈骨還和一個圓形隆凸（肱骨小頭）在滑車附近形成關節。在屈曲或伸直上肢時，肱骨前、後的兩個凹陷（窩）分別與尺骨和橈骨吻合。

humoral *adj.* circulating in the bloodstream; humoral *immunity requires circulating antibodies.

體液的 在血流中循環的；體液免疫需要循環抗體。

humour *n.* a body fluid. *See* aqueous humour, vitreous humour.

體液 身體的一種液體。參閱 aqueous humour，vitreous humour。

Hünner's ulcer *see* interstitial cystitis.

亨納潰瘍，全（膀胱）壁纖維變性 參閱 interstitial cystitis。

Hunter's syndrome a hereditary disorder caused by deficiency of an enzyme that results in the accumulation of protein-carbohydrate complexes and fats in the cells of the body. This leads to mental retardation, enlargement of the liver and spleen, and prominent coarse facial features (*gargoylism*). The disease is *sex-linked, being restricted to males, although females can be *carriers. Medical name: **mucopolysaccharidosis type II**.

亨特綜合徵　一種酶的缺乏引起身體細胞內蛋白質-碳水化合物複合體和脂肪蓄積所致的一種遺傳性疾病。導致精神發育遲緩，肝脾增大和面部特徵突起粗糙（脂肪軟骨營養不良）。該病為性連鎖疾病，僅限於男性，女性可成為攜帶者。醫學用語：黏多糖貯積病 II 型。

Huntington's disease (Huntington's chorea) a hereditary disease caused by a defect in a single gene that is inherited as a *dominant characteristic, tending to appear in half of the children of the parents with this condition. Symptoms, which begin to appear in early middle age, include jerky involuntary movements (*see* chorea) accompanied by behavioural changes and progressive dementia. The defective gene, which is located on chromosome no. 4, has now been identified, which will have important implications for the *genetic screening of those at risk.

亨廷頓舞蹈病　由單個基因缺陷引起的一種遺傳病，為顯性特徵遺傳，患此病的父母親所生的子女中，有一半可能發病。症狀開始出現於中年早期，包括不自主地抽動（參閱 chorea）並伴有行為改變和進行性精神衰退。有缺陷的基因位於 4 號染色體上，目前已被識別。這對危險人羣的基因篩查有重要意義。

Hurler's syndrome a hereditary disorder caused by deficiency of an enzyme that results in the accumulation of protein-carbohydrate complexes and fats in the cells of the body. This leads to severe mental retardation, enlargement of the liver and spleen, heart defects, deformities of the bones, and coarsening and thickening of facial features (*gargoylism*). Medical name: **mucopolysaccharidosis type I**.

胡爾勒綜合徵　一種酶的缺乏引起身體細胞內蛋白質、碳水化合物複合體和脂肪蓄積所致的遺傳性疾病。引起嚴重的智力低下，肝脾增大，心臟缺損，骨骼畸形，顏面變粗增厚（脂肪軟骨營養不良）。醫學用語：黏多糖貯積病 I 型。

Hutchinson's teeth narrowed and notched permanent incisor teeth; a sign of congenital *syphilis.

哈欽森牙、鋸齒形牙　狹小而有切口的恆切牙，為先天性梅毒的體徵。

hyal- (hyalo-) *prefix denoting* **1.** glassy; transparent. **2.** hyalin. **3.** the vitreous humour of the eye.

〔前綴〕**(1)** 玻璃的，透明的 **(2)** 透明蛋白 **(3)** 眼睛的房水

hyalin *n.* a clear glassy material produced as the result of degeneration in certain tissues, particularly connective tissue and epithelial cells.

透明蛋白 一種透明的玻璃樣物質，由某些組織變性所致，尤其是結締組織和上皮細胞。

hyaline cartilage the most common type of *cartilage: a bluish-white elastic material with a matrix of chondroitin sulphate in which fine collagen fibrils are embedded.

透明軟骨 最常見的軟骨類型：一種藍白色彈性物質，以硫酸軟骨素為基質，其中嵌有纖細的膠原纖維。

hyaline membrane disease *see* respiratory distress syndrome.

透明膜病 參閱 respiratory distress syndrome。

hyalitis *n.* inflammation of the *vitreous body of the eye. *Asteroid hyalosis* (formerly known as *asteroid hyalitis*) is a degenerative condition (rather than an inflammation), in which the vitreous contains many small white opacities.

玻璃體炎 眼睛玻璃體的炎症。星形玻璃體病（曾被稱作星形玻璃體炎）是一種變性疾病（而不是炎症），玻璃體內含有許多小的白色濁斑。

hyaloid artery a fetal artery lying in the *hyaloid canal of the eye and supplying the lens.

玻璃體動脈 一條胎兒動脈，位於眼睛玻璃體管內，給晶狀體提供血液。

hyaloid canal a channel within the vitreous humour of the *eye. It extends from the centre of the optic disc, where it communicates with the lymph spaces of the optic nerve, to the posterior wall of the lens.

玻璃體管 位於眼睛玻璃體內的一條管道，從視盤中央延伸至晶狀體後壁，並在視盤中央與視神經淋巴間隙相通。

hyaloid membrane the transparent membrane that surrounds the *vitreous humour of the eye, separating it from the retina.

玻璃體膜 包繞眼睛玻璃體的透明膜，將玻璃體與視網膜分開。

hyaluronic acid an acid *mucopolysaccharide that acts as the binding and protective agent of the ground substance of connective tissue. It is also present in

透明質酸 一種酸性黏多糖，為結締組織基質的黏合劑和保護劑。也存在於關節周圍滑液中以及眼的玻璃體和房水中。

the synovial fluid around joints and in the vitreous and aqueous humours of the eye.

hyaluronidase *n.* an enzyme that depolymerizes *hyaluronic acid and therefore increases the permeability of connective tissue. Hyaluronidase is found in the testes, in semen, and in other tissues.

透明質酸酶　一種分解透明質酸，增加結締組織通透性的酶。見於睾丸、精子和其他組織。

hybrid *n.* the offspring of a cross between two genetically unlike individuals. A hybrid, whose parents are usually of different species or varieties, is often sterile.

雜種　兩個基因不同的個體雜交的後代。雜種的雙親往往屬於不同的種或變種。雜種常常是不育的。

hydatid *n.* a bladder-like cyst formed in various human tissues following the growth of the larval stage of an *Echinococcus tapeworm. E. granulosus produces a single large fluid-filled cyst, called *unilocular hydatid*, which gives rise internally to smaller daughter cysts. The entire hydatid is bound by a fibrous capsule. E. multilocularis forms aggregates of many smaller cysts with a jelly-like matrix, called an *alveolar hydatid*, and enlarges by budding off external daughter cysts. Alveolar hydatids are not delimited by fibrous capsules and produce malignant tumours, which invade and destroy human tissues. *See also* hydatid disease.

棘球蚴囊　棘球屬絛蟲經過幼蟲階段生長後在人體各種組織中形成的球狀囊。細粒棘球絛蟲產生一個單一的、大的、充滿液體的囊，叫單房性棘球蚴囊，囊內又形成小的子囊。整個棘球蚴囊由一層纖維被膜包繞。多房型棘球絛蟲形成內含膠狀基質的許多較小蚴囊的聚集體，叫泡狀棘球蚴囊。多房型棘球絛蟲通過向外萌發子囊而增大。泡狀棘球蚴囊不受纖維被膜限制，而且產生惡性腫瘤。此瘤侵入和破壞人體組織。參閱 hydatid disease。

hydatid disease (hydatidosis, echinococciasis, echinococcosis) a condition resulting from the presence in the liver, lungs, or brain of *hydatid cysts. The cysts of *Echinococcus multilocularis* form malignant tumours; those of *E. granulosus* exert pressure as they grow and thereby damage surrounding tissues. The presence of hydatids in the brain may result in blindness and epilepsy, and

棘球蚴病　由於棘球蚴囊存在於肝、肺和腦中而引起的一種疾病。多房型棘球絛蟲的棘球蚴囊形成惡性腫瘤；細粒棘球絛蟲的棘球蚴囊生長時產生壓力而破壞周圍組織。棘球蚴囊存在於腦中可引起失明和癲癇；任何蚴囊的破裂均可引起嚴重變態反應，包括發熱和蕁麻疹。治療必須行手術摘除蚴

the rupture of any cyst can cause severe allergic reactions including fever and *urticaria. Treatment may necessitate surgical removal of the cysts. Spread of hydatid disease, particularly common in sheep-raising countries, can be prevented by the deworming of dogs.

囊。棘球蚴病的傳播在養羊的國家尤為常見，可通過給狗驅蟲來預防。

hydatidiform mole (hydatid mole, vesicular mole) a collection of fluid-filled sacs that develop when the membrane (chorion) surrounding the embryo degenerates in early pregnancy. These sacs give the placenta the appearance of a bunch of grapes. The embryo dies, the uterus enlarges, and there is a discharge of pinkish liquid and cysts from the vagina. A malignant condition may subsequently develop (*see* chorionepithelioma).

水泡狀胎塊（葡萄胎） 妊娠早期，包繞胚胎的膜（絨毛膜）變性產生的一團充滿液體的囊。這些囊使胎盤外觀尤如一串葡萄。胚胎死亡，子宮擴大，陰道內排出粉紅色液體和囊。可繼發惡性疾病（參閱 chorionepithelioma）。

hydatidosis *n. see* hydatid disease.

棘球蚴病 參閱 hydatid disease。

hydr- (hydro-) *prefix denoting* water or a watery fluid.

〔前綴〕水，水狀液

hydraemia *n.* the presence in the blood of more than the normal proportion of water.

稀血症 水在血中的比例高於正常值。

hydralazine *n.* a drug that lowers blood pressure and is used, usually in conjunction with *diuretics, to treat hypertension. It is given by mouth or by injection; side-effects, including rapid heart rate, headache, faintness, and digestive upsets, can occur, especially at high doses. Trade name: **Apresoline**.

肼屈嗪 一種降壓藥，通常和利尿劑合用治療高血壓。口服或注射給藥；會發生心率加快、頭痛、暈厥和消化不適等副作用，尤其當大劑量使用時。商品名：Apresoline。

hydramnios (hydramnion) *n.* the presence of an abnormally large amount of *amniotic fluid surrounding the fetus from about the 20th week of pregnancy. The uterus becomes swollen, which

羊水過多 妊娠約 20 周起，在胎兒周圍存在着異常大量羊水。子宮脹大，可引起呼吸困難；身體內液體過多，可能會發生難產。羊水過多常和雙胎

causes breathlessness, there is excess fluid in the body tissues, and there may be a difficult birth. Hydramnios is often associated with twin pregnancies or with fetal abnormalities, e.g. *anencephaly. The diagnosis is confirmed by ultrasound scan.

妊娠或胎兒畸形，尤其是無腦畸形有關。通過超聲掃描可確診。

hydrargyria *n. see* mercurialism.

汞中毒　參閱 mercurialism。

hydrarthrosis *n.* swelling at a joint caused by excessive synovial fluid. The condition usually involves the knees and may be recurrent. Often no cause is apparent; in some cases rheumatoid arthritis develops later.

關節積水　滑膜液過多引起的關節腫脹。此病常累及膝部，並可復發。常常無明顯病因，有些病例以後發生類風濕性關節炎。

hydrocalycosis *n. see* caliectasis.

腎盞積水　參閱 caliectasis。

hydrocele *n.* the accumulation of watery liquid in a sac, usually the sac surrounding the testes. This condition is characterized by painless enlargement of the scrotum; it is treated surgically, by drainage of the fluid or removal of the sac.

鞘膜積液　水樣液在囊內，通常是在包繞睾丸的囊內聚積。此病以陰囊無痛性增大為特徵，可通過外科排液或囊腫摘除來治療。

hydrocephalus *n.* an abnormal increase in the amount of cerebrospinal fluid within the ventricles of the brain. In childhood, before the sutures of the skull have fused, hydrocephalus makes the head enlarge. In adults, because of the unyielding nature of the skull, hydrocephalus raises the intracranial pressure with consequent drowsiness and vomiting. Hydrocephalus may be caused by obstruction to the outflow of cerebrospinal fluid from the ventricles or a failure of its reabsorption into the cerebral sinuses. *Spina bifida is commonly associated with hydrocephalus. Treatment is to divert the excess cerebrospinal fluid into the abdominal cavity, where it is absorbed. This is achieved by

腦積水　腦室內的腦脊液量異常增大。在兒童期，顱縫閉合以前，腦積水使頭部增大。在成人，由於顱骨形狀不易改變，腦積水使顱內壓增高，隨之引起倦睡和嘔吐。腦積水可因腦脊液由腦室流出受阻或再吸收回大腦靜脈竇障礙引起。常伴有脊柱裂。治療時可將過量的腦脊液分流引入腹腔內重吸收。在腦室至腹部間造一細管可完成此分流（腦室-腹膜分流）。

tunnelling a thin tube from the ventricles to the abdomen (a *ventriculo-peritoneal shunt*).

hydrochloric acid a strong acid present, in a very dilute form, in gastric juice. The secretion of excess hydrochloric acid by the stomach results in the condition *hyperchlorhydria.

鹽酸　一種強酸，以極為稀釋的形式存在於胃液中。胃內分泌鹽酸過多引起胃酸過多症。

hydrochlorothiazide *n.* a *diuretic used to treat fluid retention (oedema) and high blood pressure. It is administered by mouth, and side-effects can include digestive upsets, skin reactions, and dizziness. Trade names: **Esidrex**, **Hydrosaluric**.

氫氯噻嗪　用以治療體液瀦留（水腫）和高血壓的利尿劑。口服給藥，副作用包括消化系統不適，皮膚反應和頭暈。商品名：Esidrex，Hydrosaluric。

hydrocortisone (cortisol) *n.* a steroid hormone: the major glucocorticoid synthesized and released by the human adrenal cortex (*see* corticosteroid). It is important for normal carbohydrate metabolism and for the normal response to any stress. Hydrocortisone is used in the treatment of adrenal failure (*Addison's disease) and inflammatory, allergic, and rheumatic conditions (including rheumatoid arthritis, colitis, and eczema). It may be given by mouth, by injection, or in the form of a cream or ointment. Possible side-effects of hydrocortisone therapy include peptic ulcers, bone and muscle damage, suppression of growth in children, and the signs of *Cushing's syndrome.

氫化可的鬆　類固醇激素：人腎上腺皮質合成和分泌的重要糖皮質激素（參閱 corticosteroid）。它對正常的碳水化合物代謝和對來自任何刺激的正常應答都是重要的。氫化可的鬆用以治療腎上腺衰竭（阿狄森病）和炎性，變態反應性和風濕性疾病（包括風濕性關節炎，結腸炎和濕疹）。可口服，注射或以乳劑或軟膏劑的形式給藥。氫化可的鬆治療可能產生的副作用包括消化性潰瘍，骨和肌肉損害，兒童生長抑制以及庫欣綜合徵的體徵。

hydrocyanic acid (prussic acid) an intensely poisonous volatile acid that can cause death within a minute if inhaled. It has a smell of bitter almonds. *See* cyanide.

氫氰酸　一種劇毒性，揮發性酸；一旦吸入，可在1分鐘內致死。有苦杏仁味。參閱 cyanide。

hydrogenase *n.* an enzyme that catalyses the addition of hydrogen to a compound in reduction reactions.

氫化酶　在還原反應中，催化某化合物加氫作用的酶。

hydrogen bond a weak electrostatic bond formed by linking a hydrogen atom between two electronegative atoms (e.g. nitrogen or oxygen). The large number of hydrogen bonds in proteins and nucleic acids are responsible for maintaining the stable molecular structure of these compounds.

hydrogen peroxide a colourless liquid used as a disinfectant for cleansing wounds and, diluted, as a deodorant mouthwash or as ear drops for removing wax. Strong solutions irritate the skin.

hydrolase *n.* an enzyme that catalyses the hydrolysis of compounds. Examples are the *peptidases.

hydroma *n. see* hygroma.

hydronephrosis *n.* distension and dilatation of the pelvis of the kidney. This is due to an obstruction to the free flow of urine from the kidney. An obstruction at or below the neck of the bladder will result in hydronephrosis of both kidneys. The term *primary pelvic hydronephrosis* is used when the obstruction, usually functional, is at the junction of the renal pelvis and ureter. Surgical relief by *pyeloplasty is advisable to avoid the back pressure atrophy of the kidney and the complications of infection and stone formation. **–hydronephrotic** *adj.*

hydropericarditis *n. see* hydropericardium.

hydropericardium *n.* accumulation of a clear serous fluid within the membranous sac surrounding the heart. It occurs in many cases of *pericarditis (*hydropericarditis*). If the heart is compressed the fluid is withdrawn (aspirated) via a

氫鍵 兩個負電荷原子（如氮原子和氧原子）通過一個氫原子連接起來而形成的一種弱的靜電結合鍵。蛋白質或核酸中大量的氫鍵維持着這些化合物穩定的分子結構。

過氧化氫 一種無色液體。用作清洗傷口的消毒劑；稀釋後，用作除臭性漱口藥或清除耵聹的滴耳劑。其濃溶液刺激皮膚。

水解酶 催化化合物水解的酶。例如肽酶。

水囊瘤 參閱 hygroma。

腎盂積水 腎盂擴張膨大。這是由於尿液從腎臟的自由流出發生阻塞所致。發生於膀胱頸處或以下的阻塞導致雙腎腎盂積水。當阻塞（通常是功能性阻塞）發生在腎盂和輸尿管的連接處時，可用原發性腎盂積水這一術語。可行腎盂成形術來緩解腎盂積水，從而避免腎返壓性萎縮以及感染、結石形成等合併症。

積水性心包炎 參閱 hydropericardium。

心包積液 一種清澈的漿液在包圍心臟的膜性囊內積聚。心包積液發生於許多心包炎（積水性心包炎）病例中。如果心臟因此受到擠壓可通過胸壁將一根針插入心包囊抽吸液

needle inserted into the pericardial sac through the chest wall (*pericardiocentesis*). See also hydropneumopericardium.

hydroperitoneum *n. see* ascites.

hydrophobia *n. see* rabies.

hydrophthalmos *n. see* buphthalmos.

hydropneumopericardium *n.* the presence of air and clear fluid within the pericardial sac around the heart, which is most commonly due to entry of air during pericardiocentesis (*see* hydropericardium). The presence of air does not affect the management of the patient.

hydropneumoperitoneum *n.* the presence of fluid and gas in the peritoneal cavity. This may be due either to the introduction of air through an instrument being used to remove the fluid; because a perforation in the digestive tract has allowed the escape of fluid and gas; or because gas-forming bacteria are growing in the peritoneal fluid.

hydropneumothorax *n.* the presence of air and fluid in the pleural cavity. If the patient is shaken the fluid makes a splashing sound (called a *succussion splash*). An *effusion of serous fluid commonly complicates a *pneumothorax, and must be drained.

hydrops fetalis the state of a baby born with severe *oedema: fluid accumulates in the body cavities, especially in the peritoneal and pleural cavities (*see* ascites). It is associated with a high mortality. There are many causes for this condition but commonest is severe anaemia associated with *haemolytic disease. Congential heart abnormalities

體（心包穿刺術）。參閱 hydropneumopericardium。

腹水 參閱 ascites。

狂犬病 參閱 rabies。

水眼 參閱 buphthalmos。

液氣心包 空氣和清澈的液體存在於包繞心臟的心包囊內。最常見的病因是心包穿刺術（參閱 hydropericardium）過程中，空氣進入。對病人的治療處理不因空氣的存在而受影響。

液氣腹 空氣和液體存在於腹膜腔內。這可能是由於空氣通過抽取液體的器械進入；也可能由於消化道穿孔使液體和氣體漏入；也可能由於產氣細菌在腹水中生長。

液氣胸 空氣和液體存在於胸膜腔內。搖動病人時，液體發出擊水聲（稱作振蕩音）。漿液性滲漏常常合併氣胸，必須予以引流。

胎兒水腫 嬰兒生來伴有嚴重水腫的狀態：液體積聚在體腔，尤其是腹腔和胸腔內（參閱 ascites）。此病死亡率高。病因有許多種，其中最常見的是與溶血性疾病有關的嚴重貧血。先天性心臟畸形和腎、肺疾病也是偶見的病因。妊娠期反覆向母體子宮內行胎兒腹膜

and kidney and lung disease are occasional causes. Repeated intrauterine transfusions into the fetal peritoneum during pregnancy have saved infants in whom haemolytic disease severe enough to cause hydrops fetalis was predicted.

腔輸血術曾挽救過一些據預測將患嚴重溶血性疾病，足以發生胎兒水腫的嬰兒。

hydrosalpinx *n.* the accumulation of watery fluid in one of the *Fallopian tubes, which becomes swollen.

輸卵管積水　水樣液在一個輸卵管內積聚，使之發生腫脹。

hydrostatic accouchement the management of normal labour with the mother partially immersed in a water bath.

水下分娩法　母親局部浸入水中的一種正常分娩處理方法。

hydrotherapy *n.* the use of water in the treatment of disorders: today restricted in orthodox medicine to exercises done in remedial swimming pools for the *rehabilitation of arthritic or partially paralysed patients.

水療法　在治療疾病時使用水。現在，在正統醫學中，該詞只限指關節炎或部分癱瘓病人為康復而在治療性游泳池內進行的各種鍛煉。

hydrothorax *n.* fluid in the pleural cavity. *See also* hydropneumothorax.

胸腔積液　液體存在於胸腔內。參閱　hydropneumothorax。

hydrotubation *n.* the introduction of a fluid (usually a dye) through the cervix (neck) of the uterus under pressure to allow visualization, by *laparoscopy, of the passage of the dye through the Fallopian tubes. It is used to test whether or not the tubes are blocked in the investigation of infertility.

輸卵管通水　在壓力下將液體（通常為染料）通過子宮頸注入，從而能夠用輸卵管鏡觀察到染料經過輸卵管的路徑。在研究不孕症原因時，可用來檢查輸卵管是否阻塞。

hydroureter *n.* an accumulation of urine in one of the tubes (ureters) leading from the kidneys to the bladder. The ureter becomes swollen and the condition usually results from obstruction of the ureter by a stone or a misplaced artery.

輸尿管積水　尿液積聚在連接腎和膀胱的一個管道（輸尿管）內。輸尿管腫脹，此病通常由結石或異位動脈引起的尿道阻塞所致。

hydroxocobalamin *n.* a cobalt-containing drug administered by

羥鈷胺　一種含鈷藥物，注射給藥，用以治療累及維生素

injection to treat conditions involving vitamin B_{12} deficiency, such as pernicious anaemia. Trade names: **Cobalin-H, Neo-Cytamen**.

hydroxychloroquine *n.* a drug similar to *chloroquine, used mainly to treat lupus erythematosus and rheumatoid arthritis. Side-effects such as skin reactions, hair loss, and digestive upsets may occur and prolonged use can lead to eye damage. Trade name: **Plaquenil**.

hydroxyprogesterone *n.* a synthetic female sex hormone (*see* progestogen) administered by injection to prevent miscarriage and to treat menstrual disorders. There may be pain at the injection site, and progestogens taken by mouth are often preferred. Trade name: **Porluton**.

hydroxyproline *n.* a compound, similar in structure to the *amino acids, found only in *collagen.

5-hydroxytryptamine *n. see* serotonin.

hydroxyurea *n.* a drug that prevents cell growth and is used to treat some types of leukaemia. It is administered by mouth. Hydroxyurea may lower the white cell content of the blood due to its effects on the bone marrow. Trade name: **Hydrea**.

hydroxyzine *n.* an *antihistamine drug with sedative properties, used to relieve anxiety, tension, and agitation and to treat nausea and vomiting. It is administered by mouth and may cause drowsiness, headache, dry mouth, and itching. Trade name: **Atarax**.

hygiene *n.* the science of health and the study of ways of preserving it, particularly by promoting cleanliness.

B_{12} 缺乏的疾病，如惡性貧血。商品名：Cobalin-H，Neo-Cytamen。

羥氯喹 和氯喹相似的一種藥物，主要用於治療紅斑狼瘡和類風濕性關節炎。可能發生副作用，例如皮膚反應、脫髮以及消化系統不適；長期使用可損害眼睛。商品名：Plaquenil。

羥孕酮 一種合成的女性激素。（參閱 progestogen）。注射給藥，用於預防流產和治療月經疾病。注射部位可能有疼痛，因而常常先用口服孕激素類藥物。商品名：Proluton。

羥脯氨酸 一種結構與氨基酸相似的化合物，僅見於膠原組織中。

5-羥色胺 參閱 serotonin。

羥基脲 一種阻止細胞生長的藥物，用於治療某些類型的白血病。口服給藥。羥基脲由於其對骨髓的作用，可降低血中白細胞含量。商品名：Hydrea。

羥嗪 一種具有鎮靜性質的抗組胺藥物，用於緩解焦慮、緊張和煩躁以及治療惡心和嘔吐。口服給藥，可能引起倦睡、頭痛、口乾和瘙癢。商品名：Atarax。

衛生學 研究健康和保健，尤其通過促進清潔衛生保護健康的途徑的科學。

hygr- (hygro-) *prefix denoting* moisture.

〔前綴〕潮濕

hygroma (hydroma) *n.* a type of cyst. It may develop from a *lymphangioma (*cystic hygroma*) or from the liquified remains of a subdural *haematoma (*subdural hygroma*).

水囊瘤 一種囊腫，可能由淋巴管瘤（水囊狀淋巴管瘤）或硬膜下血腫的液化殘留物（硬膜下水囊瘤）而發生。

hygrometer *n.* an instrument for measuring the relative humidity of the atmosphere, i.e. the ratio of the moisture in the air to the moisture it would contain if it were saturated at the same temperature and pressure. In the *dew-point hygrometer* a polished surface is reduced in temperature until the water vapour from the atmosphere forms on it. The temperature of this dew point enables the relative humidity of the atmosphere to be calculated. In the *wet-and-dry bulb hygrometer*, there are two thermometers mounted side by side, the bulb of one being surrounded by moistened muslin. The thermometer with the wet bulb will register a lower temperature than that with the dry bulb owing to the cooling effect of the evaporating water. The temperature difference enables the relative humidity to be calculated.

濕度計 一種測量大氣相對濕度的儀器，例如，空氣含水量和在同樣溫度、壓力下空氣達到飽和態時的含水量的比率。用露點濕度計，降低一個光滑平面的溫度，直到大氣中的水蒸氣形成於其上。通過露點溫度，可以計算出大氣相對濕度。用濕乾球濕度計，有兩個溫度計並排豎立，其中一個的球部被濕潤的紗布包裹。由於水分蒸發時的冷卻作用，球部濕潤的溫度計比球部乾燥的溫度計記錄的溫度低。通過這個溫度差可算出相對濕度。

hymen *n.* the membrane that covers the opening of the vagina at birth but usually perforates spontaneously before puberty. If the initial opening is small it may tear, with slight loss of blood, at the first occasion of sexual intercourse.

處女膜 出生時覆蓋陰道開口的膜，但在成熟前往往自然穿孔。如果原來的口小，在第一次性交時可撕裂，並伴有少量出血。

Hymenolepis *n.* a genus of small widely distributed parasitic tapeworms. The dwarf tapeworm, *H. nana*, only 40 mm in length, lives in the human intestine. Fleas can be important vectors of this species, and children in close contact with flea-infested dogs are particularly prone to infection. *H. diminuta* is a common

膜殼絛蟲屬 分布廣泛的小型寄生性絛蟲的一屬。其中短小的絛蟲，短膜殼絛蟲，長僅40 mm，寄居在人類腸內。蚤可以成為這種絛蟲的重要媒介，所以，與被蚤類侵擾的狗密切接觸的兒童易被感染。長膜殼絛蟲是嚙齒動物的常見寄

parasite of rodents; man occasionally becomes infected on swallowing stored cereals contaminated with insect pests – the intermediate hosts for this parasite. Symptoms of abdominal pain, diarrhoea, loss of appetite, and headache are obvious only in heavy infections of either species. Treatment involves a course of *anthelmintics.

生蟲，人類若吞食了被害蟲污染的儲存穀物（這種寄生蟲的中間宿主），偶爾可被感染。只有在這兩種縧蟲感染嚴重時，才表現出明顯的腹痛、腹瀉、食慾減退和頭痛症狀。治療包括一個療程的治蠕蟲劑。

hymenotomy *n.* incision of the hymen at the entrance to the vagina. This operation may be performed on a young girl if the membrane completely closes the vagina and thus impedes the flow of menstrual blood. It is also carried out to alleviate dyspareunia (painful intercourse).

處女膜切除術 在陰道入口處切開處女膜。如果年輕姑娘處女膜完全封閉陰道，以致阻礙經血流出時，可行此手術。還可行此手術緩解痛性交媾困難。

hyo- *prefix denoting* the hyoid bone. Example: *hyoglossal* (relating to the hyoid bone and tongue).

〔前綴〕**舌骨** 例如舌骨舌的（與舌骨和舌有關的）。

hyoglossus *n.* a muscle that serves to depress the tongue. It has its origin in the hyoid bone.

舌骨舌肌 使舌下降的肌肉，起點在舌骨上。

hyoid bone a small isolated U-shaped bone in the neck, below and supporting the tongue. It is held in position by muscles and ligaments between it and the styloid process of the temporal bone.

舌骨 頸部一塊小型孤立的 U 型骨，位於舌下支撐着舌。舌骨通過它和顳骨莖突之間的肌肉和韌帶保持其位置。

hyoscine (scopolamine) *n.* a drug that prevents muscle spasm (*see* parasympatholytic). It is used in the treatment of gastric or duodenal ulcers, spasm in the digestive system, and difficult or painful menstruation and also to relax the uterus in labour. It can also be used to calm excitement in some psychiatric conditions, for preoperative medication, for travel sickness, and to dilate the pupil and paralyse the muscles of the eye for examination. It is administered by mouth

東莨菪鹼 一種預防肌肉痙攣的藥物（參閱 parasympatholytic）。用於治療胃或十二指腸潰瘍，消化系統痙攣，月經困難或痛經，以及分娩時用於鬆弛子宮。還可用於某些精神病，起鎮靜作用，用於術前給藥、治療旅行病、眼檢查時擴張瞳孔和麻痹肌肉。口服或注射給藥。副作用罕見，但可能包括口乾、視力模糊、排尿困難和心跳加

or injection. Side-effects are rare but can include dry mouth, blurred vision, difficulty in urination, and increased heart rate. Trade names: **Buscopan**, **Scopoderm**.

hyp- (hypo-) *prefix denoting* **1.** deficiency, lack, or small size. Example: *hypognathous* (having a small lower jaw). **2.** (in anatomy) below; beneath. Example: *hypoglossal* (under the tongue).

hypalgesia *n.* an abnormally low sensitivity to pain.

hyper- *prefix denoting* **1.** excessive; abnormally increased. **2.** (in anatomy) above.

hyperacusis *n.* abnormally acute hearing or painful sensitivity to sounds.

hyperadrenalism *n.* overactivity of the adrenal glands. *See* Cushing's syndrome.

hyperaemia *n.* the presence of excess blood in the vessels supplying a part of the body. In *active hyperaemia* (*arterial hyperaemia*) the arterioles are relaxed and there is an increased blood flow. In *passive hyperaemia* the blood flow from the affected part is obstructed.

hyperaesthesia *n.* excessive sensibility, especially of the skin.

hyperalgesia *n.* an abnormal state of increased sensitivity to painful stimuli.

hyperandrogenism *n.* excessive secretion of androgen in women. It is associated with *hirsutism, acne, sparse or infrequent menstruation (oligomenor-

快。商品名：Buscopan Scopoderm。

〔前綴〕**(1)** 不足、缺乏、體積小　例如，下頜突出的（下頜骨過小的）。**(2)** 在……下面，低於……（解剖學）例如，舌下的（在舌的下面）。

痛覺減退　對疼痛敏感性異常低。

〔前綴〕**(1)** 過度的，異常增大的　**(2)**（解剖學）在……上，高於

聽覺過敏　聽覺異常靈敏或對聲音令人痛苦的敏感性。

腎上腺機能亢進　腎上腺過分活躍。參閱 Cushing's syndrome。

充血　供應身體某一部位的血管中血液量過多。在主動性充血（動脈性充血）中，小動脈擴張，所以血液流量增大。在被動性充血（靜脈充血）中，來自受累部位的血流受阻。

感覺過敏　過分的敏感性，尤指皮膚。

痛覺過敏　對疼痛刺激的敏感性增加的異常狀態。

雄激素過多症　婦女的雄激素分泌過度。伴有多毛症、痤瘡、經量或經次稀少（月經過少）、子宮出血、無排卵或少

rhoea), *metrorrhagia, absent or infrequent ovulation, infertility, endometrial *hyperplasia, *hyperlipidaemia, *hyperglycaemia, and hypertension; all these conditions may be the result of mutations in specific genes. *See also* virilization.

排卵、不孕症、子宮內膜增生、高脂血症、血糖過多和高血壓。所有這些病症可能均由特異基因突變所致。參閱virilization。

hyperbaric *adj.* at a pressure greater than atmospheric pressure.

高壓的 壓力高於大氣壓的。

hyperbaric oxygenation a technique for exposing a patient to oxygen at high pressure. It is used to treat carbon monoxide poisoning, gas gangrene, compressed air illness, and acute breathing difficulties. It is also used in some cases during heart surgery.

高壓氧療法 一種使病人暴露於高壓氧的技術。用於治療二氧化碳中毒，氣性壞疽，壓縮空氣病和急性呼吸困難。還用於一些心臟手術病人。

hypercalcaemia *n.* the presence in the blood of an abnormally high concentration of calcium. *Idiopathic hypercalcaemia* is a congenital condition associated with mental retardation and heart defects. Hypercalcaemia can also be caused by excessive ingestion of vitamin D. *Compare* hypocalcaemia.

高鈣血症 血液中鈣的濃度異常高。原發性高鈣血症是先天性疾病，並伴有智力發育遲緩和心臟缺損。高鈣血症還可由維生素 D 過分攝入引起。與 hypocalcaemia 對比。

hypercalcinuria (hypercalcuria) *n.* the presence in the urine of an abnormally high concentration of calcium.

高鈣尿症 尿液中存在濃度異常高的鈣。

hypercapnia (hypercarbia) *n.* the presence in the blood of an abnormally high concentration of carbon dioxide.

高碳酸血症 血液中存在濃度異常高的二氧化碳。

hyperchloraemia *n.* the presence in the blood of an abnormally high concentration of chloride.

高氯血症 血液中氯化物濃度異常高。

hyperchlorhydria *n.* a greater than normal secretion of hydrochloric acid by the stomach, usually associated with a *duodenal ulcer. Extremely high levels

胃酸過多症 胃中鹽酸的分泌量高於正常，常常伴有胃潰瘍。胃酸分泌量極度高者見於佐-埃氏綜合徵。

of acid secretion are found in the *Zollinger-Ellison syndrome.

hypercholesterolaemia *n. see* cholesterol.

高膽固醇血症　參閱 cholesterol。

hyperchromatism *n.* the property of the nuclei of certain cells (for example, those of tumours) to stain more deeply than normal. **–hyperchromatic** *adj.*

着色過度　某些細胞（如腫瘤細胞）核的染色比正常深的特性。

hyperdactylism (polydactylism) *n.* the condition of having more than the normal number of fingers or toes. The extra digits are commonly undersized (rudimentary) and are usually removed surgically shortly after birth.

多指（趾）　手指或腳趾數目多於正常。多出的指（趾）常比正常的小（發育不完全），並且常在出生後不久被手術切除。

hyperdynamia *n.* excessive activity of muscles.

肌力過度　肌肉活動過度。

hyperemesis gravidarum severe vomiting during pregnancy. It starts in early pregnancy and may continue to produce marked dehydration and subsequent liver damage. Rarely, the condition worsens in spite of active treatment; under such circumstances it may be necessary to terminate the pregnancy.

妊娠嘔吐　妊娠期嚴重嘔吐。開始於妊娠早期，可能持續，以致引起明顯的脫水和繼發的肝臟損傷。如果給予積極治療，妊娠嘔吐很少惡化；但如果惡化，可能有必要終止妊娠。

hyperextension *n.* excessive and forceful extension of a limb beyond the normal limits, usually as part of an orthopaedic procedure to correct deformity.

伸展過度　肢體超過正常限度的過度和用力伸展。通常作為矯形方法的一部分，以矯正畸形。

hyperglycaemia *n.* an excess of glucose in the bloodstream. It may occur in a variety of diseases, most notably in *diabetes mellitus, due to insufficient insulin in the blood and excessive intake of carbohydrates. Untreated it may progress to diabetic coma.

血糖過多　血流中的葡萄糖過多。可能發生在多種疾病中，尤其值得注意的是糖尿病。由血中胰島素不足和碳水化合物過分攝入所致。如果不予治療，可發展成糖尿病性昏迷。

hypergraphia *n.* a style of writing characterized by excessive verbosity,

多寫症　以過分冗長，拘泥於不重要的細節及喜歡涵蓋一切

pedantic insistence on much nonessential detail, and obsessive inclusiveness that is a feature of the type of personality disturbance frequently associated with severe epilepsy. People manifesting hypergraphia will seldom accept that they have a communication problem.

為特點的一種寫作風格。這是常與嚴重癲癇有關的一種人格障礙類型。表現出此症狀的人一般不承認他們存在交往問題。

hyperidrosis (hyperhidrosis) *n.* excessive sweating, which may occur in certain diseases, such as thyrotoxicosis of fevers, or following the use of certain drugs.

多汗症 過度出汗，可以發生於某些疾病中，如甲狀腺毒症或發熱性疾病，或使用某些藥物之後。

hyperinsulinism *n.* **1.** excessive secretion of the hormone insulin by the islet cells of the pancreas. **2.** metabolic disturbance due to administration of too much insulin.

(1) 胰島素分泌過多 胰腺的胰島素細胞分泌過多的胰島激素。**(2) 胰島素過多症** 由於使用過多的胰島素而引起的代謝紊亂。

hyperkalaemia *n.* the presence in the blood of an abnormally high concentration of *potassium, usually due to failure of the kidneys to excrete it. *See also* electrolyte.

高鉀血症 血液中存在的鉀的濃度異常高，常常由於腎臟衰竭，使鉀不能排出所致。參閱 electrolyte。

hyperkeratosis *n.* thickening of the outer horny layer of the skin. It may occur as an inherited disorder, affecting the palms and soles.

角化過度（症） 皮膚外角質層變厚。可能是一種遺傳病，侵犯手掌和蹠部。

hyperkinesia *n.* a state of overactive restlessness in children. *See* hyperkinetic syndrome. **–hyperkinetic** *adj.*

多動症 兒童過分活動不安定的狀態。參閱 hyperkinetic syndrome。

hyperkinetic syndrome (attention deficit disorder) a mental disorder, usually of children, characterized by a grossly excessive level of activity and a marked impairment of the ability to attend. Learning is impaired as a result, and behaviour is disruptive and may be defiant or aggressive. The syndrome is more common in the intellectually subnormal, the epileptic, and the brain-damaged. Treatment usually involves

多動綜合徵（注意力短缺障礙） 常見於兒童的一種精神病，特徵為顯著的過分活動和明顯的注意力不能集中。結果是學習受到影響，而且行為異常，可能是挑釁性或進攻性的。該病多發於智力低下、癲癇及腦部損傷的兒童。治療包括藥物（例如苯丙胺類）和行為療法；家屬需要咨詢和實際幫助。

drugs (such as amphetamines) and behaviour therapy; the family needs advice and practical help.

hyperlipidaemia (hyperlipaemia) *n.* the presence in the blood of an abnormally high concentration of fats.

高脂血症 血液中脂肪濃度異常高。

hyperlipoproteinaemia *n.* the presence in the blood of abnormally high concentrations of *lipoproteins.

高脂蛋白血症 血液中脂蛋白濃度異常高。

hypermetropia (long-sightedness) *n.* the condition in which parallel light rays are brought to a focus behind the retina when the *accommodation is relaxed (see illustration). Moderate degrees of hypermetropia may not cause blurred vision in children and young adults because of their ability to accommodate, but for older people and those with greater degrees of hypermetropia near vision is more blurred than distance

遠視 當眼調節鬆弛時，平行光綫聚焦於視網膜後（見圖）。在兒童和青年人中，輕度遠視可能不會引起視力模糊，因為他們有能力調節；但對於年齡較大者及遠視度數較深者，近景比遠景更模糊。通過戴凸面鏡可恢復到正常視力。與 emmetropia，myopia 對比。

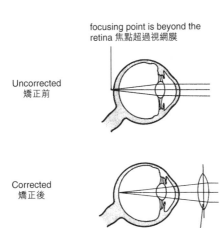

focusing point is beyond the retina 焦點超過視網膜

Uncorrected 矯正前

Corrected 矯正後

convex lens converges light rays falling on the eye 凸透鏡集中光綫至眼內

Hypermetropia (long-sightedness)
遠視

vision. Normal vision can be restored by wearing spectacles with convex lenses. *Compare* emmetropia, myopia.

hypermotility *n.* excessive movement or activity, especially of the stomach or intestine.

運動過強　過度運動或活動，尤指胃和腸。

hypernatraemia *n.* the presence in the blood of an abnormally high concentration of *sodium. *See also* electrolyte.

高鈉血症　血液中鈉濃度異常高。參閱 electrolyte。

hypernephroma (Grawitz tumour, renal cell carcinoma) *n.* a malignant tumour of kidney cells, so called because it is said to resemble part of the adrenal gland and at one time was thought to originate from this site. It may be present for some years before giving rise to symptoms, which include fever, loin pain, and blood in the urine. Treatment is by surgery but tumours are apt to recur locally. The tumour spreads via the bloodstream and can often be seen growing along the renal vein. Secondary growths from a renal cell carcinoma in the lung have a characteristic 'cannon-ball' appearance. These tumours are relatively insensitive to radiotherapy and cytotoxic drugs but some respond to such hormones as progestogens and testosterone.

腎上腺樣瘤（格拉維茨瘤，腎細胞瘤）　一種腎細胞的惡性腫瘤，因為據說與腎上腺的一部分相似，並且曾被認為起源於這個部位，所以得此名。可能存在多年後才產生症狀，包括發熱、腰痛和血尿。採用手術治療，但腫瘤易於局部復發。腫瘤通過血流傳播，而且常常可見沿着腎靜脈生長。腎細胞瘤在肺中的繼發瘤呈典型的「炮彈」外觀。這些腫瘤對放療治療和細胞毒性藥物相對來說較不敏感，但有些對黃體酮和睾酮等激素有反應。

hyperopia *n.* the usual US term for *hypermetropia.

遠視　美國常用的術語。

hyperosmia *n.* an abnormally acute sense of smell.

嗅覺過敏　嗅覺異常靈敏。

hyperostosis *n.* excessive enlargement of the outer layer of a bone. The condition is harmless and is usually recognized as an incidental finding on X-ray. It commonly affects the frontal bone of the skull (*hyperostosis frontalis*).

骨肥厚　骨外層過度膨大，這種情況無害，並且常常在 X 綫檢查時偶然發現。它通常侵犯顱骨前方（額骨肥厚）。

hyperparathyroidism *n.* overactivity of the parathyroid glands. *See also* von Recklinghausen's disease.

甲狀旁腺功能亢進　甲狀旁腺活動過度，參閱 von Recklinghausen's disease。

hyperpiesia *n. see* hypertension.

高血壓　參閱 hypertension。

hyperplasia *n.* the increased production and growth of normal cells in a tissue or organ. The affected part becomes larger but retains its normal form. During pregnancy the breasts grow in this manner. *Compare* hypertrophy, neoplasm.

增生　組織或器官中正常細胞的繁殖和生長加快。受累部位變大，但仍保持其正常類型。妊娠期，乳房以這種方式生長。與 hypertrophy，neoplasm 對比。

hyperpnoea *n.* an increase in the rate of breathing that is proportional to an increase in metabolism; for example, on exercise. *Compare* hyperventilation.

呼吸過度　與代謝的增加成正比的呼吸率增加，如鍛煉時。與 hyperventilation 對比。

hyperpraxia *n.* excessive motor activity, such as is seen in *mania and the *hyperkinetic syndrome.

活動過度　運動活動過度，如見於躁狂和多動綜合徵。

hyperpyrexia *n.* a rise in body temperature above 106°F (41.1°C). *See* fever.

高熱　體溫升高到 41.1°C 以上。參閱 fever。

hypersensitive *adj.* prone to respond abnormally to the presence of a particular antigen, which may cause a variety of tissue reactions ranging from *serum sickness to an allergy (such as hay fever) or, at the severest, to anaphylactic shock (*see* anaphylaxis). It is thought that when the normal antigen-antibody defence reaction is followed by tissue damage this may be due to an abnormality in the working of the *complement system. *See also* allergy, immunity, **–hypersensitivity** *n.*

過敏的　易於對某種特定抗原的存在作出異常反應的。它可引起各種組織反應，從血清病到變態反應（例如枯草熱），最嚴重的可引起過敏性休克（參閱 anaphylaxis）。人們認為，如果正常的抗原——抗體防禦反應之後發生組織損傷，這可能是由於補體系統功能的異常。參閱 allergy，immunity。

hypersomnia *n.* sleep lasting for exceptionally long periods, as occurs in some cases of brain inflammation.

睡眠過度　睡眠持續時間異常長，如發生於一些腦炎病例中。

hypersplenism *n.* a decrease in the numbers of red cells, white cells, and

脾機能亢進　血液中紅細胞、白細胞和血小板數量增加，這

platelets in the blood resulting from destruction or pooling of these cells by an enlarged spleen. Hypersplenism may occur in any condition in which there is enlargement of the spleen (*see* splenomegaly).

hypersthenia *n.* an abnormally high degree of strength or physical tension in all or part of the body.

hypertension *n.* high *blood pressure, i.e. elevation of the arterial blood pressure above the normal range expected in a particular age group. Hypertension may be of unknown cause (*essential hypertension* or *hyperpiesia*). It may also result from kidney disease, including narrowing (stenosis) of the renal artery (*renal hypertension*), endocrine diseases (such as Cushing's disease or phaeochromocytoma) or disease of the arteries (such as coarctation of the aorta), when it is known as *secondary* or *symptomatic hypertension*. Complications that may arise from hypertension include atherosclerosis, heart failure, cerebral haemorrhage, and kidney failure, but treatment may prevent their development. Hypertension is symptomless until the symptoms of its complications develop. Some cases of hypertension may be cured by eradicating the cause. Most cases, however, depend upon long-term drug therapy to lower the blood pressure and maintain it within the normal range. The drugs used include thiazide *diuretics, *beta blockers, *methyldopa, *guanethidine, and many others. Combinations of drugs may be needed to obtain optimum control. *See also* portal hypertension, pulmonary hypertension.

hyperthermia (hyperthermy) *n.* **1.** exceptionally high body temperature

是由於脾增大而使這些細胞被破壞和淤積所致。脾機能亢進可發生於任何有脾增大的疾病（參閱 splenomegaly）。

體力過盛 身體全部或部分的力量或肌張力異常大。

高血壓 血壓增高，即動脈血壓增高超出某一特定年齡組所預期的正常範圍。高血壓可以是不明原因的（特發性高血壓或高壓病），也可能是由腎臟疾病，包括腎動脈狹窄（腎性高血壓），內分泌疾病（如庫欣病或嗜鉻細胞瘤）或動脈疾病（如主動脈狹窄）所致，這時稱之為繼發性或症狀性高血壓。

由高血壓引起的併發症包括動脈粥樣硬化、心臟衰竭、腦出血和腎衰竭，治療可預防這些併發症的發生。在其併發症症狀發生之前，高血壓不表現出症狀。一些高血壓可以通過消除病因而治愈。然而，多數病例依賴長期藥物療法降低血壓並維持其在正常範圍內。使用的藥物包括噻嗪類，利尿藥類、β-受體阻滯劑，甲基多巴、胍乙啶以及許多其他藥。為了獲得最佳控制，可能需要聯合用藥。參閱 portal hypertension，pulmonary hypertension。

(1) 高溫 身體溫度異常高（大約 41°C 或以上）。參閱

(about 41°C or above). *See* fever. **2.** treatment of disease by inducing fever. *Compare* hypothermia.

fever。**(2) 高溫治療** 通過促使發熱來治療疾病。與 hypothermia 對比。

hyperthyroidism *n.* overactivity of the thyroid gland, either due to a tumour, overgrowth of the gland, or Graves's disease. *See* thyrotoxicosis.

甲狀腺功能亢進 甲狀腺過度活躍，由腫瘤、甲狀腺過度生長、或格雷夫斯病所致。參閱 thyrotoxicosis。

hypertonia (hypertonicity) *n.* exceptionally high tension in muscles.

張力過高 肌張力異常高。

hypertonic *adj.* **1.** describing a solution that has a greater osmotic pressure than another solution. *See* osmosis. **2.** describing muscles that demonstrate an abnormal increase in *tonicity.

(1) 高滲的 描述一種溶液的滲透壓高於其他溶液的。參閱 osmosis。**(2) 高張的** 描述肌肉的緊張性異常增高。

hypertrichosis *n.* excessive growth of hair (*see* hirsutism).

多毛症 毛髮過度生長（參閱 hirsutism）。

hypertrophy (hypertrophia) *n.* increase in the size of a tissue or organ brought about by the enlargement of its cells rather than by cell multiplication (as during normal growth and tumour formation). Muscles undergo this change in response to increased work. *Compare* hyperplasia.

肥大 由細胞的增大而不是細胞的增殖引起的組織或器官體積的增大（在正常生長或腫瘤形成期間）。肌肉負荷增加時，會發生這種變化。與 hyperplasia 對比。

hypertropia *n. see* strabismus.

上斜肌 參閱 strabismus。

hyperuricaemia (lithaemia) *n.* the presence in the blood of an abnormally high concentration of uric acid. *See* gout.

高尿酸血症 血液中尿酸的濃度異常高。參閱 gout。

hyperuricuria (lithuria) *n.* the presence in the urine of an abnormally high concentration of uric acid.

高尿酸尿症 尿液中尿酸的濃度異常高。

hyperventilation *n.* breathing at an abnormally rapid rate at rest. This causes a reduction of the carbon dioxide concentration of arterial blood, leading to dizziness, tingling (paraesthesiae) in the

換氣過度 靜止時，呼吸速率異常快。這導致血液中二氧化碳濃度降低，引起頭暈，唇和四肢麻刺感（異常感覺），手部強直性痙攣和胸部發緊。若

lips and limbs, tetanic cramps in the hands, and tightness across the chest. If continued, hyperventilation may cause loss of consciousness. This sequence of events occurs in the *hyperventilation syndrome (HVS)*, which has been estimated to contribute to 10% of out-patient referrals to hospital.

持續則可導致神志喪失。這一系列病症常見於過度換氣綜合徵。據估計，過度換氣綜合徵占醫院門診病人的 10%。

hypervitaminosis *n.* the condition resulting from excessive consumption of vitamins. This is not serious in the case of water-soluble vitamins, when any intake in excess of requirements is easily excreted in the urine. However, the fat-soluble vitamins A and D are toxic if taken in excessive amounts.

維生素過多症　攝入維生素過多造成的疾病。水溶性維生素過多症的病例並不嚴重，因為超過需要的攝入量易從尿中排出。然而，如果攝入過量脂溶性維生素 A 和 D 是有毒的。

hypervolaemia *n.* an increase in the volume of circulating blood.

血量增多　循環血液容量的增加。

hyphaema *n.* a collection of blood in the chamber of the eye that lies in front of the iris.

眼前房積血　血液積聚在虹膜前方的眼房內。

hyphedonia *n.* a lower than normal capacity for achieving enjoyment.

快感減少　獲得快感的能力低於正常人。

hypn- (hypno-) *prefix denoting* 1. sleep. 2. hypnosis.

〔前綴〕(1) 睡眠　(2) 催眠

hypnagogic *adj. see* imagery.

入睡前的　參閱 imagery。

hypnopompic *adj. see* imagery.

半醒的　參閱 imagery。

hypnosis *n.* a sleeplike state, artificially induced in a person by a *hypnotist*, in which the mind is more than usually receptive to suggestion and memories of past events – apparently forgotten – may be elicited by questioning. Hypnotic suggestion has been used for a variety of purposes in medicine, for example as a cure for addiction and in other forms of *psychotherapy.

催眠狀態　由催眠師對某人人工誘發產生的類似睡眠的狀態。處於這種狀態的人比通常更易接受暗示，而且有關過去的記憶——明顯被遺忘的——可以通過提問引發。催眠暗示在醫學上有多種用途，例如用來治療吸毒成癮和用於其他形式的心理療法中。

hypnotic (soporific) *n.* a drug that produces sleep by depressing brain function. Hypnotics include benzodiazepines (such as *nitrazepam and *temazepam), *chloral hydrate, and some sedative *antihistamines (e.g. *promethazine). Hypnotics are used for insomnia and sleep disturbances, especially in mental illnesses and in the elderly. They often cause hangover effects in the morning.

催眠藥　通過抑制大腦功能引發睡眠的一種藥物。催眠類藥包括苯二氮䓬類（例如硝西泮和替馬西泮），水合氯醛和一些鎮靜性抗組胺藥物（如異丙嗪）。催眠藥用於治療失眠和睡眠障礙，尤其用於精神疾病及老年病人。常在早晨造成延續效應。

hypnotism *n.* the induction of *hypnosis.

催眠術　催眠狀態的誘發。

hypo- *prefix. see* hyp-.

〔前綴〕**(1)** 不足、缺乏、體積小　**(2)** 下、低於……。參閱 hyp-。

hypoaesthesia *n.* a condition in which the sense of touch is diminished; uncommonly this may be extended to include other forms of sensation.

感覺減退　觸覺減低的一種疾病。不常累及其他感覺形式。

hypobaric *adj.* at a pressure lower than that of the atmosphere.

低壓的　壓力低於大氣壓的。

hypobulia *n.* mild deficiency of will power. *See* abulia.

意志薄弱　意志力輕度缺乏。參閱 abulia。

hypocalcaemia *n.* the presence in the blood of an abnormally low concentration of calcium. *See* tetany. *Compare* hypercalcaemia.

低鈣血症　血液中鈣濃度異常低。參閱 tetany。與 hypercalcaemia 對比。

hypocapnia *n. see* acapnia.

低碳酸血症　參閱 acapnia。

hypochloraemia *n.* the presence in the blood of an abnormally low concentration of chloride.

低氯血症　血液中氯濃度異常低。

hypochlorhydria *n.* reduced secretion of hydrochloric acid by the stomach. *See* achlorhydria.

胃酸過少症　胃分泌的鹽酸量減少。參閱 achlorhydria。

hypochondria *n.* preoccupation with the physical functioning of the body and

疑病症　過分關注身體的生理功能和幻想的病體。可能導致

with fancied ill health. It may amount to a handicapping neurosis and dominate a person's life. In the most severe form there are delusions of ill health, usually due to underlying *depression. Treatment with reassurance, *antidepressant drugs, and/or psychotherapy is usual, but the condition is often chronic. **–hypochondriac** adj., n.

神經機能障礙並影響一個人的一生。最嚴重時幻想身體有病，這常由潛在的抑鬱所致。常見的治療有安慰，抗抑鬱藥和/或心理療法，但此病常為慢性。

hypochondrium n. the upper lateral portion of the *abdomen, situated beneath the lower ribs. **–hypochondriac** adj.

季肋部 腹部的上外側區，位於肋弓的下面。

Hypoderma n. a genus of non-bloodsucking beelike insects – the warble flies – widely distributed in Europe, North America, and Asia. Cattle are the usual hosts for the parasitic maggots, but rare and accidental infections of man have occurred (see myiasis), especially in farm workers. The maggots migrate beneath the skin surface, producing an inflamed linear lesion similar to that of *creeping eruption.

皮下蠅屬 非吸血性蜜蜂樣昆蟲的一屬——牛皮下蠅，廣泛分布在歐洲、北美洲和亞洲。牛羣是其寄生蛆常見的宿主，但也發生過偶然的人的感染（參閱 myiasis），尤其是農夫中。其蛆在皮表下面游走，產生與匐行疹相似的綫形炎性感染。

hypodermic adj. beneath the skin: usually applied to subcutaneous *injections. The term is also applied to the syringe used for such injections, and sometimes – loosely – to any injection.

皮下的 皮膚下面的：常用於皮下注射。此術語還用於進行皮下注射的注射器，有時廣義地用於任何注射。

hypodontia n. a reduction in the normal number of teeth through congenital absence.

牙發育不全 先天性缺失導致牙的數目減少。

hypofibrinogenaemia (fibrinogenopenia) n. a deficiency of the clotting factor *fibrinogen in the blood, which results in an increased tendency to bleed. It may occur as an inherited disorder in which either production of fibrinogen is impaired or the fibrinogen produced does not function in the normal way

血纖維蛋白原過少（纖維蛋白原減少） 血液中凝血因子——纖維蛋白原缺乏，導致出血傾向增加。它可能是遺傳性疾病，由於纖維蛋白原的產生發生障礙，或者生產的纖維蛋白原不能正常作用（血纖維蛋白原異常）。血纖維蛋白原過少

(*dysfibrinogenaemia*). Alternatively, it may be acquired. For example, it is the commonest cause of blood coagulation failure during pregnancy, when the blood fibrinogen level falls below the normal pregnancy level of 4–6g/l. This usually occurs as a complication of severe *abruptio placentae, prolonged retention of a dead fetus, or amniotic fluid embolism.

也可以是後天的。例如，當血纖維蛋白原水平降低至正常妊娠水平 (4~6g/l) 以下時，它是妊娠期血液不能凝集的最常見原因。這通常表現為嚴重的胎盤早期脫離、死胎長期滯留或羊水栓塞的併發症。

hypogammaglobulinaemia *n.* a deficiency of the protein *gamma globulin in the blood. It may occur in a variety of inherited disorders or as an acquired defect, as in certain *lymphomas. Since gamma globulin consists mainly of antibodies (*immunoglobulins), hypogammaglobulinaemia results in an increased susceptibility to infections.

血丙種球蛋白減少 血液中丙種球蛋白缺乏。它可以發生於多種遺傳性疾病，也可以是後天性缺陷，如在某些淋巴瘤中。由於丙種球蛋白主要由抗體（免疫球蛋白）組成，所以，血丙種球蛋白減少會導致對各種感染的易感性增加。

hypogastrium *n.* that part of the central *abdomen situated below the region of the stomach. **–hypogastric** *adj.*

下腹 中腹的一部分，位於胃區下方。

hypogeusia *n.* a condition in which the sense of taste is abnormally weak. *See also* hypoaesthesia.

味覺減退 味覺異常差的一種疾病。參閱 hypoaesthesia。

hypoglossal nerve the twelfth *cranial nerve (XII), which supplies the muscles of the tongue and is therefore responsible for the movements of talking and swallowing.

舌下神經 第十二對 (XII) 腦神經，分布於舌部肌肉，因而支配說話和吞咽的動作。

hypoglycaemia *n.* a deficiency of glucose in the bloodstream, causing muscular weakness and incoordination, mental confusion, and sweating. If severe it may lead to *hypoglycaemic coma*. Hypoglycaemia most commonly occurs in *diabetes mellitus, as a result of insulin overdosage and insufficient intake of carbohydrates. It is treated by administration of glucose: by injection if the patient

血糖過少 血流中葡萄糖缺乏可造成肌肉無力和肌運動失調、精神混亂以及出汗。嚴重時，可造成低血糖性昏迷。血糖過少最常發生於糖尿病，由胰島素使用過量和碳水化合物攝入不足所致。給予葡萄糖治療：昏迷病人注射給藥，其他病人口服給藥。

is in a coma, by mouth otherwise.
–hypoglycaemic *adj.*

hypogonadism *n.* impaired function of the testes or ovaries, causing absence or impairment of the *secondary sexual characteristics.

性腺機能減退　睾丸或卵巢功能障礙，導致第二性徵缺失或不明顯。

hypoidrosis (hypohidrosis) *n.* the production of an abnormally small amount of sweat relative to the environmental temperature, bodily activity, or other relevant circumstances.

少汗　相對於環境溫度，身體活動量或其他相關情況而言，汗量的產生異常少。

hypoinsulinism *n.* a deficiency of insulin due either to inadequate secretion of the hormone by the pancreas or to inadequate treatment of diabetes mellitus.

胰島素分泌過少　胰腺激素分泌不足或糖尿病治療不當引起的腺島素缺乏。

hypokalaemia *n.* the presence of abnormally low levels of potassium in the blood: occurs in dehydration. *See* electrolyte.

低鉀血症　血液中鉀的含量異常低：發生於脫水。參閱 electrolyte。

hypomania *n.* a mild degree of *mania. Elated mood leads to faulty judgment; behaviour lacks the usual social restraints and the sexual drive is increased; speech is rapid and animated; the individual is energetic but not persistent and tends to be irritable. The abnormality is not so great as in mania and the patient may appear normal and 'a bit of a character' to those who do not know him (*see* elation, euphoria). Treatment follows the same principles as for mania, and it may be difficult to prevent an individual from damaging his own interests with extravagant behaviour. **–hypomanic** *adj., n.*

輕躁狂症　一種輕度躁狂症。高漲的情緒導致判斷失誤；行為失去通常的社會約束；性慾增強；說話快而且興奮；患者精力充沛，但不持久，而且易生氣。所有這些異常表現沒有躁狂病患者嚴重；因此，病人可以貌似正常，而對於不認識他的人來說，他還「略有個性」（參閱 elation，euphoria）。治療原則和躁狂症相同，但是，可能難以防止患者因過度行為損害他自己的利益。

hypomenorrhoea *n.* the release of an abnormally small quantity of blood at menstruation. The duration of bleeding may be normal or less than normal.

月經過少　行經時排出的血量異常少。出血時間正常或短於正常。

hyponatraemia *n.* the presence in the blood of an abnormally low concentration of *sodium: occurs in dehydration. *See* electrolyte.

低 鈉 血 症　　血液中鈉濃度異常低：發生於脱水。參閱 electrolyte。

hypoparathyroidism *n.* subnormal activity of the parathyroid glands, causing a fall in the blood concentration of calcium and muscular spasms (*see* tetany).

甲狀旁腺機能減退　甲狀旁腺活動低於正常，導致血液鈣濃度降低和肌痙攣（參閱 tetany）。

hypopharynx *n. see* laryngopharynx.

喉 咽 部　　參閱 laryngo-pharynx。

hypophysectomy *n.* the surgical removal or destruction of the pituitary gland (hypophysis) in the brain. The operation may be conducted by opening the skull or by the insertion of special needles that produce a very low temperature (*see* cryosurgery).

垂體切除術　手術切除或破壞大腦垂體。此手術可開顱進行，也可用特製的超低温穿刺針進行（參閱 cryosurgery）。

hypophysis *n. see* pituitary gland.

垂 體　　參閱 pituitary gland。

hypopiesis *n.* abnormally reduced blood pressure in the absence of organic disease (*see* hypotension).

低 血 壓　　在不存在器質性疾病的情況下，血壓異常降低（參閱 hypotension）。

hypopituitarism *n.* subnormal activity of the pituitary gland, causing *dwarfism in childhood and a syndrome of impaired sexual function, pallor and premature ageing in adult life (*see* Simmond's disease).

垂體機能減退　垂體活動低於正常。在兒童時期引起侏儒症，在成人期引起性功能障礙、面色蒼白及早老的綜合徵（參閱 Simmond's disease）。

hypoplasia *n.* underdevelopment of an organ or tissue. *Dental hypoplasia* is the defective formation of parts of a tooth due to illnesses such as measles or starvation while the tooth is being formed. It is marked by transverse lines of brown defective enamel, which define the date of the illness.

發育不全　器官或組織發育低下。牙齒發育不全是由於牙形成期內患病，如麻疹或飢餓造成牙齒某些部分的缺陷性形成。其特徵為棕色缺陷性牙釉質上的橫綫，這表明患病時間。

hypopraxia *n.* **1.** a condition of diminished and enfeebled activity. **2.** a lack of interest in, or a disinclination for, activity; listlessness.

活動減退 **(1)** 活動減少且虛弱的情況。**(2)** 對於活動不感興趣或不願參加；倦怠。

hypoproteinaemia *n.* a decrease in the quantity of protein in the blood. It may result from malnutrition, impaired protein production (as in liver disease), or increased loss of protein from the body (as in the *nephrotic syndrome). It results in swelling (*oedema), because of the accumulation of fluid in the tissues, and increased susceptibility to infections. *See also* hypogammaglobulinaemia.

低蛋白血症 血液中蛋白量減少，可由營養不良，蛋白生成障礙（如患肝病時），或蛋白從體內丟失增加（如患腎病綜合徵時）所致。液體在組織內積聚，可導致水腫。而且對各種感染的異感性增加。參閱 hypogammaglobulinaemia。

hypoprothrombinaemia *n.* a deficiency of the clotting factor prothrombin in the blood, which results in an increased tendency to bleed. It may occur as an inherited defect, as the result of liver disease, vitamin K deficiency, or anticoagulant treatment.

低凝血酶原血症 血液中凝血因子——凝血酶原缺乏，導致出血傾向增加。它可以是遺傳性的，也可由肝病、維生素 K 缺乏或抗凝血治療引起。

hypopyon *n.* pus in the chamber of the eye that lies in front of the iris.

眼前房積膿 膿液積於虹膜前方的眼房內。

hyposensitive *adj.* less than normally responsive to the presence of antigenic material. *Compare* hypersensitive. **–hyposensitivity** *n.*

低敏感的 對抗原性物質存在的反應性低於正常。與 hypersensitive 對比。

hyposensitization *n. see* desensitization.

脫敏作用 參閱 desensitization。

hyposmia *n.* a condition in which the sense of smell is exceptionally weak. *See also* hypoaesthesia.

嗅覺減退 對氣味的感覺異常差的疾病。參閱 hypoaesthesia。

hypospadias *n.* a congenital abnormality in which the opening of the *urethra is on the underside of the penis: either on the glans penis (*glandular hypospadias*), at the junction of the glans with the shaft (*coronal hypospadias*), or on the shaft

尿道下裂 一種先天異常，尿道開口位於陰莖下側，或者在陰莖頭上（龜頭尿道下裂），或者在陰莖頭和陰莖體的連接處（冠狀尿道下裂），或者在陰莖體本身（陰莖尿道

itself (*penile hypospadias*). All varieties of hypospadias can be treated surgically, and neither micturition nor sexual function need be impaired. *See* MAGPI operation.

下裂)。各種尿道下裂均可手術治療，排尿和性功能都不一定受影響。參閱 MAGPI operation。

hypostasis *n.* accumulation of fluid or blood in a dependent part of the body, under the influence of gravity in cases of poor circulation. Hypostatic congestion of the lung bases may be seen in debilitated patients who are confined to bed. It predisposes to pneumonia (hypostatic pneumonia) but it may be prevented by careful nursing and physiotherapy. A similar condition affects the dependent parts of the body after death. **–hypostatic** *adj.*

墜積 在循環不良的病例中，由於重力的影響，液體或血液積聚在身體一個下垂部位。肺底的墜積性充血可見於臥床虛弱病人。這情況易導致肺炎（墜積性肺炎），但也可通過精心護理和理療預防。同樣的情況發生於死後人體的下垂部分。

hyposthenia *n.* a state of physical weakness or abnormally low muscular tension.

衰弱 身體虛弱或肌張力異常低的狀態。

hyposthenuria *n.* the secretion of urine of low specific gravity. The inability to concentrate the urine occurs in patients at the final stage of chronic renal failure.

低滲尿 排出低比重的尿。慢性腎功能衰竭晚期，病人喪失濃縮尿的能力。

hypotension *n.* a condition in which the arterial *blood pressure is abnormally low. It occurs after excessive fluid loss (e.g. through diarrhoea, burns, or vomiting) or following severe blood loss (haemorrhage) from any cause. Other causes include myocardial infarction, pulmonary embolism, severe infections, allergic reactions arrhythmias, acute abdominal conditions (e.g. pancreatitis), Addison's disease, and drugs (e.g. an overdose of the drugs used to treat hypertension).

Some people experience a temporary fall in blood pressure when rising from a horizontal position (*orthostatic hypotension*). Temporary hypotension may result

低血壓 動脈血壓異常低的狀況。它發生於任何原因引起的液體過分喪失（例如，由於腹瀉、燒傷或嘔吐）或嚴重失血（出血）之後。其他原因包括心肌梗死、肺栓塞、各種嚴重感染、變態反應、心律失常、急腹症（如胰腺炎），阿狄森病以及藥物（例如過量使用某些藥物治療高血壓）。

一些人從水平位起立時會發生暫時性血壓降低（直立性低血壓）。暫時性低血壓可以導致單純性暈厥。病人出現頭暈、出汗、並且可能發生意識障礙。嚴重時，發生周圍循環衰竭（心源性休克），並伴有

in a simple faint (syncope). The patient becomes light-headed, sweats, and may develop impaired consciousness. In severe cases peripheral circulatory failure (cardiogenic shock) develops, with unrecordable blood pressure, weak pulses, and suppression of urine production. The patient is placed flat, with legs elevated, and given oxygen. Fluid and blood are replaced by an intravenous infusion as required. Specific treatment of the cause is provided (e.g. corticosteroids in Addison's disease).

血壓不能測出，脈搏微弱以及尿量減少。使病人平臥，抬高雙腿，並且給予氧氣。根據需要，靜脈輸注液體和血液。同時，針對起因，給予特殊治療（例如阿狄森病時用皮質類固醇）。

hypothalamus *n.* the region of the forebrain in the floor of the third ventricle, linked with the thalamus above and the *pituitary gland below (*see* brain). It contains several important centres controlling body temperature, thirst, hunger, and eating, water balance, and sexual function. It is also closely connected with emotional activity and sleep and functions as a centre for the integration of hormonal and autonomic nervous activity though its control of the pituitary secretions (*see* neuroendocrine system, pituitary gland). **–hypothalamic** *adj.*

下丘腦　位於第三腦室底部的前腦區，上與丘腦相接，下與垂體相接（參閱 brain）。它包含幾個重要中樞，控制體溫、渴、飢餓、吃飯、水平衡以及性功能。它還與情緒活動和睡眠密切相關，而且它通過控制垂體的分泌，發揮着激素和自主神經活動結合的中樞功能（參閱 neuroendocrine system，pituitary gland）。

hypothenar *adj.* describing or relating to the fleshy prominent part of the palm of the hand below the little finger. *Compare* thenar.

小魚際的　描述手掌小指下部的肉質隆起部，或與此部位有關。與 thenar 對比。

hypothermia *n.* **1.** accidental reduction of body temperature below the normal range in the absence of protective reflex actions, such as shivering. Often insidious in onset, it is particularly liable to occur in babies and the elderly if they are living in poorly heated homes and have inadequate clothing. **2.** deliberate lowering of body temperature for therapeutic purposes. This may be done during

(1) 低溫　在無保護性反射作用下（如發抖），體溫意外降至正常範圍以下。常常隱伏發生，尤其易發生於嬰兒和老年人，如果他們的居室供暖不足和穿衣不夠時。**(2) 降溫**　為了治療，有意降低體溫。此法常用於手術過程中，以減少病人的需氧量。

surgery, in order to reduce the patient's requirement for oxygen.

hypothymia *n.* a diminished intensity of emotional response. It is a feature of *asthenic personalities, and of some chronic schizophrenics and some depressives.

情感減退 情緒反應強度減弱，它是虛弱人格、一些慢性精神分裂症以及一些抑鬱症的特徵。

hypothyroidism *n.* subnormal activity of the thyroid gland. If present at birth and untreated it leads to *cretinism. In adult life it causes mental and physical slowing, undue sensitivity to cold, slowing of the pulse, weight gain, and coarsening of the skin (*myxoedema*). The condition can be treated by administration of thyroxine.

甲狀腺功能減退 甲狀腺活性低於正常。如果出生時就存在，並且不予治療，可導致克汀病。在成人，它可以引起精神和身體活動遲緩，對寒冷過分敏感，脈搏緩慢，體重增加以及皮膚粗糙（黏液性水腫）。此病可通過使用甲狀腺素治療。

hypotonia *n.* a state of reduced tension in muscle.

張力減退 肌肉張力降低的狀態。

hypotonic *adj.* **1.** describing a solution that has a lower osmotic pressure than another solution. *See* osmosis. **2.** describing muscles that demonstrate diminished *tonicity.

(1) 低滲的 描述滲透壓低於其他溶液的。參閱 osmosis。
(2) 低張力的 描述肌緊張性降低的。

hypotrichosis *n.* a condition in which less hair develops than normal.

毛髮稀少 毛髮生長較正常少。

hypotropia *n. see* strabismus.

下斜視 參閱 strabismus。

hypoventilation *n.* breathing at an abnormally shallow and slow rate, which results in an increased concentration of carbon dioxide in the blood. *Alveolar hypoventilation* may be primary, which is very rare, or secondary, which can be due to destructive lesions of the brain or to an acquired blunting of respiratory drive arising from failure of the respiratory pump.

肺換氣不足 以異常表淺和緩慢的速率呼吸，造成血中二氧化碳濃度增加。肺泡性換氣不足可以是原發性的，但非常罕見；也可以是繼發性的，由大腦破壞性損傷所致，或由呼吸泵衰竭造成的後天性呼吸動力減弱所致。

hypovitaminosis *n.* a deficiency of a vitamin caused either through lack of the vitamin in the diet or from an inability to absorb or utilize it.

維生素缺少症　某種維生素缺乏，由食物中缺少維生素或不能吸收或利用維生素所致。

hypovolaemia (oligaemia) *n.* a decrease in the volume of circulating blood. *See* shock.

血容量減少　循環血容量的減少。參閱 shock。

hypoxaemia *n.* reduction of the oxygen concentration in the arterial blood, recognized clinically by the presence of central and peripheral *cyanosis. When the partial pressure of oxygen (PO$_2$) falls below 8.0 kPa (60 mmHg), the condition is defined as respiratory failure.

低氧血症　動脈血中氧濃度降低。臨床上可由中央或外周紫紺的存在來識別此病。當氧分壓 (PO$_2$) 降至 8.0 kPa (60 mmHg) 以下時，被定義為呼吸衰竭。

hypoxia *n.* a deficiency of oxygen in the tissues. *See also* anoxia, hypoxaemia.

缺氧　組織中氧氣缺乏。參閱 anoxia，hypoxaemia。

hypsarrhythmia *n.* an abnormal and chaotic pattern of brain activity, demonstrated by *encephalography, that is usually associated with *infantile spasms.

嚴重腦電節律失常　腦照相術顯示的異常的，混亂的腦活動波型，常伴有嬰兒痙攣。

hyster- (hystero-) *prefix denoting* **1.** the uterus. **2.** hysteria.

〔前綴〕(1) 子宮　(2) 癔病

hysterectomy *n.* the surgical removal of the uterus, either through an incision in the abdominal wall (*abdominal hysterectomy*) or through the vagina (*vaginal hysterctomy*). *Subtotal hysterectomy* (rarely performed now) involves removing the body of the uterus but leaving the neck (cervix); in *total hysterectomy* the entire uterus is removed. The operation is performed for cancerous conditions affecting the uterus and for nonmalignant conditions (e.g. fibroids) in which there is excessive menstrual bleeding. Although pregnancy is no longer possible, hysterectomy does not affect sexual desire or activity.

子宮切除術　經腹壁切口（腹部子宮切除術）或經陰道（陰道子宮切除術）手術切除子宮。次全子宮切除術（現在很少進行）是切除子宮體，但保留子宮頸；全子宮切除術時，切除整個子宮。此手術用於累及子宮的癌性疾病以及經血量過多的非惡性疾病（如子宮肌瘤）。儘管術後不再有妊娠的可能性，但是子宮切除術不影響性慾和性活動。

hysteria *n.* **1.** formerly, a neurosis characterized by emotional instability, repression, dissociation, some physical symptoms (*see* hysterical), and vulnerability to suggestion. Two types were recognized: *conversion hysteria*, now known as *conversion disorder; and *dissociative hysteria*, comprising a group of conditions now generally regarded as *dissociative disorders. *See also* neurosis. **2.** a state of great emotional excitement.

(1) 癔病 從前指一種神經官能症，其特徵為情緒不穩定、壓抑、分裂，一些身體症狀及對暗示的敏感性（參閱 hysterical）。曾識別為兩種類型：轉換性癔病，現在稱為轉換性障礙；分裂性癔病，由現在一般被認為是聯想散漫性障礙的一組病態組成。參閱 neurosis。**(2) 歇斯底里** 情緒非常激動的狀態。

hysterical *adj.* **1.** formerly, describing a symptom that is not due to organic disease, is produced unconsciously, and from which the individual derives some gain. What were known as hysterical symptoms are characteristic of *conversion disorder. **2.** describing a kind of *personality disorder characterized by instability and shallowness of feelings and by superficiality and a tendency to manipulate in personal relationships.

(1) 癔病的 描述由非器質性疾病引起的某種症狀，無意識產生但患者從中獲得滿足。過去所認為的癔病症狀是轉換性障礙的特徵。**(2) 歇斯底里的** 描述一種人格障礙，其特徵是情緒不穩定，易動感情以及人際關係中的淺薄和喜歡控制人。

hysterosalpingography *n. see* uterosalpingography.

子宮輸卵管造影術 參閱 uterosalpingography。

hysterosalpingosonography *n.* visualization of the Fallopian tubes by means of an ultrasound beam, usually directed via a vaginal probe, after a contrast medium has been passed through them via the cervix. *See also* transvaginal ultrasonography.

子宮輸卵管超聲造影術 將造影劑經宮頸注入兩個輸卵管，然後通過一超聲光束對輸卵管造影，此超聲光束通常經陰道探針導入。參閱 transvaginal ultrasonography。

hysteroscope (uteroscope) *n.* a tubular instrument with a light source for observing the interior of the uterus. *See also* endoscope.

宮腔鏡 帶一光源的管形器械，用於觀察子宮內部。參閱 endoscope。

hysterotomy *n.* an operation for removal of the fetus by incision of the uterus through the abdomen before the 24th week of gestation; after this

子宮切開術 妊娠第 24 周以前，經由腹腔切開子宮，取出胎兒的一種手術，24 周後，此手術被稱為剖宮產術。現在，

time the operation is called *Caesarean section. Hysterotomy is now rarely performed owing to improvements in the efficiency of drugs now available for induction abortion, e.g. *mifepristone.

由於用於引產的藥物（如米非司酮）效力的提高，子宮切開術很少做。

I

-iasis *suffix denoting* a diseased condition. Example: *leishmaniasis* (disease caused by *Leishmania* species).

〔後綴〕病　例如：利什曼病（利什曼原蟲屬引起的疾病）。

iatro- *prefix denoting* **1.** medicine. **2.** doctors.

〔前綴〕**(1)** 醫學　**(2)** 醫生

iatrogenic *adj.* describing a condition that has resulted from treatment, as either an unforeseen or inevitable side-effect.

醫源性的　描述由治療引起的疾病，是治療不可預見或難以避免的副作用。

ibuprofen *n.* an anti-inflammatory drug (*see* NSAID), used in the treatment of arthritic conditions. It is administered by mouth and sometimes causes skin rashes and digestive upsets. Trade names: **Brufen, Junifen**.

布洛芬　一種抗炎藥物（參閱 NSAID），用於治療關節疾病。口服用藥，有時引起皮疹和消化系統不適。商品名：Brufen，Junifen。

ICD *see* International Classification of Diseases.

國際疾病分類　參閱 International Classification of Diseases。

ichor *n.* a watery material oozing from wounds or ulcers.

敗液　由傷口或潰瘍滲出的水樣物質。

ichthyosis *n.* any one of a group of disorders, usually hereditary, in which there is persistent noninflammatory scaling of the skin. *Autosomal dominant ichthyosis*, in which the affected gene is *dominant, affects 1 in 300 people and first appears in infancy; mild cases show only trivial

魚鱗癬　指一組疾病中的任何一種，常常是遺傳性的，表現為皮膚持續的非炎性鱗屑脱落。常染色體顯性魚鱗癬的患病基因是顯性的；每 300 人中有 1 人發病，而且在嬰兒期即開始。輕度病例僅表現出輕微

scaling. *Xeroderma is a very mild form of the disorder. Treatment of ichthyosis is mainly by the regular use of emollients.

鱗屑脱落。乾皮病是本病的一種極輕形式。治療主要通過長期使用潤膚劑。

ICIDH *see* International Classification of Diseases.

國際損傷、傷殘和殘疾分類 參閱 International Classification of Diseases。

ICSH (interstitial-cell-stimulating hormone) *see* luteinizing hormone.

間質細胞刺激素 參閱 luteinizing hormone。

icterus *n. see* jaundice.

黃疸 參閱 jaundice。

ictus *n.* a stroke or any sudden attack. The term is often used for an epileptic seizure, stressing the suddenness of its onset.

突發 中風或任何突然的疾病發作。本術語常用於癲癇發作，強調其發病的突然性。

id *n.* (in psychoanalysis) a part of the unconscious mind governed by the instinctive forces of *libido and the death wish. These violent forces seek immediate release in action or in symbolic form. The id is therefore said to be governed by the pleasure principle and not by the demands of reality or of logic. In the course of individual development some of the functions of the id are taken over by the *ego.

伊德 （精神分析）潛意識心理的一部分，由性慾和死的願望的本能力量支配。這些強大的力量在行動或象徵性的形式中尋求突然的釋放。所以，據說伊德是由求樂原則，而不是現實或邏輯要求控制。在個體發育過程中，伊德的一些功能由自我代替。

-id *suffix denoting* relationship or resemblance to. Example: *spermatid* (a stage of sperm formation).

〔後綴〕與……有關或相似 例如：精子細胞（精子形成的一個階段）。

ideation *n.* the process of thinking or of having *imagery or ideas.

思想作用 思維或者產生意象或想法的過程。

identical twins *see* twins.

單卵性雙胎 參閱 twins。

identification *n.* (in psychological development) the process of adopting other people's characteristics more or less permanently. Identification with a parent is important in personality formation, and has been especially implicated in the

認同 （心理發展）或多或少持久地接納他人特點的過程。與父母親相認同對個性形成有重要意義，特別與道德感及適當性角色的發展有關。

development of a moral sense and of an appropriate sex role.

ideo- *prefix denoting* **1.** the mind or mental activity. **2.** ideas.

〔前綴〕**(1) 心理或心理活動 (2) 觀念**

ideomotor *adj.* describing or relating to a motor action that is evoked by an idea. *Ideomotor apraxia* is the inability to translate the idea of a complex behaviour into action.

意念動作的 描述由某一觀念引發的動作或與此動作有關的。意念動作性運用不能是不能把一個複雜活動的觀念轉變為動作。

idio- *prefix denoting* peculiarity to the individual.

〔前綴〕**自體、自發、特異** 某個個體的特性。

idiopathic *adj.* denoting a disease or condition the cause of which is not known or that arises spontaneously. **–idiopathy** *n.*

自發的 指原因不明或自然發生的某種疾病或狀態。

idiopathic facial pain a *neuralgia that has no known cause and is typified by pain in the face that does not fit the distribution of nerves. It is often stress-related, and in many cases appears to be associated with defective metabolism of *tyramine.

自發性顏面痛 一種原因不明的神經痛,特點是與神經分布不符合的臉部疼痛。它常常與緊張有關,在許多病例中,似乎和酪胺代謝缺陷相關。

idiosyncrasy *n.* an unusual and unexpected sensitivity exhibited by an individual to a particular drug or food. **–idiosyncratic** *adj.*

特異反應性 個體對某種特殊藥物或食品所表現出的罕見和意外的敏感性。

idiot savant an individual whose overall functioning is at the level of mental retardation but who has one or more special intellectual abilities that are advanced to a high level. Musical ability, calculating ability, and rote memory are examples of abilities that may be highly developed. Many such individuals suffer from *autism.

低能特才者 這種個體的綜合機能處於精神發育遲緩水平,但有一項或多項智力能力發展到高水平。可能高度發展的能力的例子包括音樂能力、計算能力和死記硬背能力。許多此類個體患有孤獨癖。

idioventricular *adj.* affecting or peculiar to the ventricles of the heart. The term is

心室自身的 影響心室的或心室特有的。此術語最常用於描

most often used to describe the very slow beat of the heart's ventricles under the influence of their own natural subsidiary pacemaker (*idioventricular rhythm*).

述心室在其自身自然輔助起搏點（心室自身節律）作用下的非常緩慢的搏動。

idoxuridine *n.* an iodine-containing antiviral drug that inhibits the growth of viruses and is used to treat herpes infections of the eye. It is administered in eye drops or ointment and may cause irritation and stinging on application. Trade names: **Herpid**, **Idoxene**.

碘苷　一種含碘的抗病毒藥物，可抑制病毒生長，用於治療眼疱疹感染，以滴眼劑或軟膏形式給藥，使用時可引起刺激和刺痛。商品名：Herpid，Idoxene。

ifosfamide *n.* a *cytotoxic drug used in the treatment of malignant disease, particularly sarcomas, testicular tumours, and lymphomas. It is administered intravenously by injection or infusion. Side-effects include nausea, vomiting, alopecia, and haemorrhagic cystitis; concomitant administration of *mesna is recommended to prevent cystitis. Trade name: **Mitoxana**.

異環磷酰胺　一種細胞毒素藥物，用於治療癌症，特別是肉瘤、睾丸腫瘤及淋巴瘤。靜脈注射或滴注給藥。副作用包括惡心、嘔吐、脫髮及出血性膀胱炎。建議同時使用美司鈉以預防膀胱炎。商品名：Mitoxana。

IL-2 *n. see* interleukin.

白細胞介素-2　參閱　interleukin。

ile- (ileo-) *prefix denoting* the ileum. Examples: *ileocaecal* (relating to the ileum and caecum); *ileocolic* (relating to the ileum and colon).

〔前綴〕**迴腸**　例如迴盲腸的（與迴腸和盲腸有關的），迴結腸的（與迴腸和結腸有關的）。

ileal conduit a segment of small intestine (ileum) used to convey urine from the ureters to the exterior into an appliance (*see also* urinary diversion). The ureters are implanted into an isolated segment of bowel, usually ileum but sometimes sigmoid colon, one end of which is brought through the abdominal wall to the skin surface. This end forms a spout, or *stoma*, which projects into a suitable urinary appliance. The ureters themselves cannot be used for this purpose as they tend to narrow and retract

迴腸導水管　將尿液從輸尿管運送至體外一容器內的一段小腸（迴腸）。（參閱 urinary diversion）。將輸尿管植入一節游離的腸段，常為迴腸，但有時為乙狀結腸。將該腸段的一端經腹壁拉出到皮膚表面。此端形成一出水口或孔，突入一合適的尿容器。輸尿管本身不能作此用途，因為一旦拉出皮膚，它會變窄和迴縮。只有在膀胱必須被切除或改道時，如因為癌，才做這種手術。

if brought through the skin. The operation is performed if the bladder has to be removed or bypassed; for example, because of cancer.

ileal pouch (perineal pouch) a reservoir made from loops of ileum to replace a surgically removed rectum, avoiding the need for a permanent *ileostomy.

迴腸囊 由迴腸袢造成的一貯器，以代替手術摘除的直腸，而不必行永久性的迴腸造口術。

ileectomy *n*. surgical removal of the ileum (small intestine) or part of the ileum.

迴腸切除術 手術切除迴腸（小腸）或部分迴腸。

ileitis *n*. inflammation of the ileum (small intestine). It may be caused by *Crohn's disease, tuberculosis, the bacterium *Yersinia enterocolitica*, or typhoid or it may occur in association with ulcerative *colitis (when it is known as *backwash ileitis*).

迴腸炎 迴腸（小腸）的炎症。它可以由克羅恩病、結核病、耶爾森菌小腸結腸炎或傷寒引起，也可與潰瘍性結腸炎同時發生（稱為返流性迴腸炎）。

ileocaecal valve a valve at the junction of the small and large intestines consisting of two membranous folds that close to prevent the backflow of food from the colon and caecum to the ileum.

迴盲瓣 大小腸連接處的一個瓣膜，由兩片膜性皺襞組成，關閉時可防止食物由結腸和盲腸返流到迴腸。

ileocolitis *n*. inflammation of the ileum and the colon (small and large intestines). The commonest causes are *Crohn's disease and tuberculosis.

迴腸結腸炎 迴腸和結腸（小腸和大腸）的炎症，最常見的病因是克羅恩病和結核病。

ileocolostomy *n*. a surgical operation in which the ileum is joined to some part of the colon. It is usually performed when the right side of the colon has been removed or if it is desired to bypass either the terminal part of the ileum or right side of the colon.

迴腸結腸吻合術 一種把迴腸連接到結腸某部位的外科手術。該手術常在結腸右側已被切除或需做迴腸末端或結腸右側改道時施行。

ileocystoplasty *n*. *see* cystoplasty.

迴腸膀胱成形術 參閱 cystoplasty。

ileoproctostomy (ileorectal anastomosis) *n*. a surgical operation in which

迴腸直腸吻合術 一種把迴腸連接到直腸上的外科手術，通

the ileum is joined to the rectum, usually after surgical removal of the colon (*see* colectomy).

ileostomy *n.* a surgical operation in which the ileum is brought through the abdominal wall to create an artificial opening (*stoma*) through which the intestinal contents can discharge, thus bypassing the colon. Various types of bag may be worn to collect the effluent. The operation is usually performed in association with *colectomy; or to allow the colon to rest and heal in cases of colitis; or following injury or surgery to the colon. It can be used as an alternative to a *colostomy.

ileum *n.* the lowest of the three portions of the small *intestine. It runs from the jejunum to the *ileocaecal valve. **–ileal**, **ileac** *adj.*

ileus *n.* intestinal obstruction, usually obstruction of the small intestine (ileum). *Paralytic* or *adynamic ileus* is functional obstruction of the ileum due to loss of intestinal movement (peristalsis), which may be caused by abdominal surgery (*see* laparotomy), spinal injuries, deficiency of potassium in the blood (hypokalaemia), or peritonitis. Treatment consists of intravenous administration of fluid and nutrients and removal of excess stomach secretions by tube until peristalsis returns. If possible, the underlying condition is treated. Mechanical obstruction of the ileum may be caused by a gallstone entering the bowel through a fistula or widened bile duct (*gallstone ileus*); thickened *meconium in newborn babies with *cystic fibrosis (*meconium ileus*); or intestinal worms, usually the threadworm *Enterobius vermicularis* (*verminous ileus*).

常在手術切除結腸後施行（參閱 colectomy）。

迴腸造口術　將迴腸經腹壁拉出，造成一個人工開口的外科手術。腸道內容物可經由開口排出，從而繞過結腸。可佩戴多種類型的袋子來收集流出物。該手術常與結腸切除術同時進行；或用於結腸炎病例中，使結腸得到休息和痊愈；或在結腸損傷或手術後用作結腸造口術的替代療法。

迴腸　小腸三部分中最下方的一段，這由空腸延伸至盲瓣。

腸梗阻　腸道梗阻。通常為小腸（迴腸）梗阻。麻痺性或無力性腸梗阻是由小腸運動（蠕動）喪失引起的功能性梗阻；可由腹部手術（參閱 laparotomy）、脊髓損傷、血中缺鉀（低鉀血症）或腹膜炎所致。治療包括靜脈輸入液體和營養物質，以及用吸管排出過多的胃分泌物，直至蠕動恢復。如可能，治療原發疾病。機械性腸梗阻可由膽石通過瘻管或擴大的膽道進入腸內（膽石性腸梗阻）；或由囊性纖維化新生兒黏稠的胎糞（胎糞性腸梗阻）；或腸道蠕蟲——通常是綫蠕蟲引起（蠕蟲性腸梗阻）。

ili- (ilio-) *prefix denoting* the ilium.

iliac arteries the arteries that supply most of the blood to the lower limbs and pelvic region. The right and left *common iliac arteries* form the terminal branches of the abdominal aorta. Each branches into the *external iliac artery* and the smaller *internal iliac artery*.

iliacus *n.* a flat triangular muscle situated in the area of the groin. This muscle acts in conjunction with the *psoas muscle to flex the thigh.

iliac veins the veins draining most of the blood from the lower limbs and pelvic region. The right and left *common iliac veins* unite to form the inferior vena cava. They are each formed by the union of the *internal* and *external iliac veins*.

iliopsoas *n.* a composite muscle made up of the *iliacus and *psoas muscles, which have a common tendon.

ilium *n.* the haunch bone: a wide bone forming the upper part of each side of the *hip bone (*see also* pelvis). There is a concave depression (*iliac fossa*) on the inside of the pelvis; the right iliac fossa provides space for the vermiform appendix. **–iliac** *adj.*

illusion *n.* a false perception due to misinterpretation of the stimuli arising from an object. For example, a patient may misinterpret the conversation of others as the voices of enemies conspiring to destroy him. Illusions can occur in quite normal people, when they are usually spontaneously corrected. They may also occur in almost any psychiatric syndrome, especially *depression. *Compare* hallucination.

〔前綴〕**髂** 髂骨。

髂動脈 供給骨盆區和下肢大部分血液的動脈。左、右髂總動脈形成腹主動脈的終末支。每支又分支為髂外動脈和較小的髂內動脈。

髂肌 位於腹股溝區的扁平三角形肌肉。此肌肉與腰大肌聯合作用，以屈曲大腿。

髂靜脈 從下肢和盆骨區引流大部分血液的靜脈。左、右髂總靜脈聯合形成下腔靜脈。每條髂總靜脈又由髂內和髂外靜脈聯合形成。

髂腰肌 由髂肌和腰肌組成的複合肌肉，它們有一共同的肌腱。

髂骨 髂骨：形成每側髂骨上部的寬大骨頭（參閱 pelvis）。在骨盆內側面有一凹窩（髂窩），右髂窩為闌尾提供空間。

錯覺 由於對某一物體引起的刺激的曲解所形成的一種錯誤的知覺。例如，患者可能把他人的談話誤認為是陰謀陷害他的敵人的說話聲音。錯覺可以發生於十分正常的人，這時，它可自然得到糾正。錯覺也可發生於幾乎各種精神病綜合徵，尤其是抑鬱症中。與 hallucination 對比。

視覺錯覺是不符合外部世

Optical illusions are perceptions that do not agree with the actual object in the external world. They are produced by deceptive qualities of the stimulus and are in no way pathological.

界中的實際物體的知覺。它是由刺激的假象所致，而絲毫不是病理性的。

imagery *n.* the production of vivid mental representations by the normal processes of thought. *Hypnagogic imagery* occurs just before falling asleep, and the images are often very distinct. *Hypnopompic imagery* occurs in the state between sleep and full wakefulness. Like hypnagogic imagery, the experiences may be very vivid. *Eidetic imagery*, commoner in children than adults, is the production of images of exceptional clarity, which may be recalled long after being first experienced.

意象活動 正常的思維過程產生逼真的心理表象。催眠意象發生於臨入睡前，意象經常非常清晰。覺醒意象發生於睡眠和充分覺醒之間的狀態。與催眠意象一樣，這種體驗可以是十分逼真的。遺覺意象活動，兒童較成人常見，是指產生了異常清晰的意象，以致於在首次體驗相當長時間後仍然能被回憶起來。

imaging *n.* the production of images of organs or tissues using radiological procedures, particularly by using scanning techniques. *See also* computerized tomography, magnetic resonance imaging, ultrasonography.

影像術 利用放射學方法，特別是利用掃描技術使器官或組織成像。參閱 computerized tomography，magnetic resonance imaging，ultrasonography。

imago *n.* (in psychoanalysis) the internal unconscious representation of an important person in the individual's life, particularly a parent.

意象 （心理分析）對在某人生命中一位重要人物，尤其是父親或母親的內在的、潛意識的再現。

imidazole *n.* one of a group of chemically related antifungal drugs that are also effective against a wide range of bacteria; some (e.g. *thiabendazole and *mebendazole) are also used as anthelmintics. The group includes *econazole, *clotrimazole, *ketoconazole, and *miconazole. They are administered by mouth or externally as creams.

咪唑 化學組成相關的一組抗真菌藥。此類藥對多種細菌也有療效；其中一些（如噻苯達唑和甲苯達唑）還被用作抗蠕蟲藥。這組藥包括：益康唑、克黴唑、酮康唑，以及咪康唑。口服或用作外用乳膏。

imipramine *n.* a drug administered by mouth or injection to treat depression (*see* antidepressant). Its effects may be

米帕明（丙咪嗪） 口服或注射給藥治療抑鬱症的一種藥物（參閱 antidepressant）。藥效

slow to develop; common side-effects include dry mouth, blurred vision, constipation, sweating, and rapid heartbeat. Trade name: **Tofranil**.

發生緩慢，常見的副作用包括口乾、視力模糊、便秘、出汗和心跳過速。商品名：Tofranil。

imitation *n*. acting in the same way as another person, either temporarily or permanently. This is one of the mechanisms of *identification. It can be used in therapy (*see* modelling).

模仿 暫時或永久地與他人相同的行為。這是認同機制的一種，可用於治療（參閱 modelling）。

immersion foot *see* trench foot.

浸泡足 參閱 trench foot。

immobilization *n*. the procedure of making a normally movable part of the body, such as a joint, immovable. This helps an infected, diseased, or injured tissue (bone, joint, or muscle) to heal. Immobilization may be temporary (for example, by means of a plaster of Paris cast on a limb) or it may be permanent. Permanent immobilization of a joint is achieved by means of the operation of *arthrodesis.

固定術 使身體正常活動部位，如關節，不能活動的措施。這可以幫助一個感染和生病或受傷的組織（骨，關節或肌肉）瘂愈。固定術可是暫時性的（如用煆石膏貼於肢體上），也可是永久性的。關節的永久固定可通過關節固定術完成。

immune *adj*. protected against a particular infection by the presence of specific antibodies against the organisms concerned. *See* immunity.

免疫的 由於存在對抗相關微生物的特異性抗體，而不受某種感染。參閱 immunity。

immune response the response of the *immune system to antigens. There are two types of immune response produced by two populations of *lymphocytes. B-lymphocytes are responsible for *humoral immunity*, producing free antibodies that circulate in the bloodstream; and T-lymphocytes are responsible for *cell-mediated immunity*.

免疫應答 免疫系統對抗原作出的應答反應。免疫應答有兩種類型，分別由兩種淋巴細胞作出。B-淋巴細胞負責體液免疫，產生循環在血流中的自由抗體；T-淋巴細胞負責細胞免疫。

immune system the organs responsible for *immunity. The primary *lymphoid organs are the thymus and the bone marrow; the secondary lymphoid organs

免疫系統 負責免疫的器官。初級淋巴器官包括甲狀腺和骨髓；次級淋巴器官是淋巴結和淋巴樣組織聚合體（脾臟、扁

are the lymph nodes and lymphoid aggregates (spleen, tonsils, gastrointestinal lymph tissue, and Peyer's patches).

immunity *n.* the body's ability to resist infection, afforded by the presence of circulating *antibodies and white blood cells. Antibodies are manufactured specifically to deal with the antigens associated with different diseases as they are encountered. *Active immunity* arises when the body's own cells produce, and remain able to produce, appropriate antibodies following an attack of a disease or deliberate stimulation (*see* immunization). *Passive immunity*, which is only short-lived, is provided by injecting ready-made antibodies in *antiserum taken from another person or an animal already immune. Babies have passive immunity, conferred by antibodies from the maternal blood and *colostrum, to common diseases for several weeks after birth. *See also* immune response.

immunization *n.* the production of *immunity by artificial means. Passive immunity, which is temporary, may be conferred by the injection of an *antiserum, but the production of active immunity calls for the use of treated antigens, to stimulate the body to produce its own antibodies: this is the procedure of *vaccination (also called *inoculation*). The material used for immunization (the *vaccine) may consist of live bacteria or viruses so treated that they are harmless while remaining antigenic or completely dead organisms or their products (e.g. toxins) chemically or physically altered to produce the same effect.

immuno- *prefix denoting* immunity or immunological response.

桃體、胃腸道淋巴組織和派伊爾結）。

免疫性 由於循環抗體和白細胞的存在而使機體具有的抵抗感染的能力。機體遭遇不同疾病時，產生出特異的抗體，以對付與某種疾病相關的抗原。機體受到疾病侵襲或有意刺激後，其自身細胞產生並且能夠持續產生相應的抗體，這便產生了自動免疫（參閱 immunization）。被動免疫維持時間短，是通過注射由其他人或動物已具免疫力的抗血清製備所得的抗體獲得的。嬰兒在生後幾周內具有對常見疾病的被動免疫力，這是從母血和初乳中獲得的抗體產生的。參閱 immune response。

免疫 用人工的方法產生免疫力。被動免疫是暫時性的，可由注射一種抗血清獲得，而自動免疫的產生則需要用處理過的抗原，刺激機體產生自身的抗體，這個過程稱為預防接種（也稱為預防注射）。用於免疫的材料（疫苗）可以是經過處理的活細菌或病毒，它們無害而保留抗原性；也可以是完全滅活的生物體或其產物（如毒素），在經過化學或物理學改變後產生同樣效果。

〔前綴〕**免疫** 指免疫性或免疫應答。

immunoassay *n.* any of various techniques for determining the levels of antigen and antibody in a tissue. *See* immunoelectrophoresis, immunofluorescence, radioimmunoassay.

免疫測定法 用於測定某一組織中抗原和抗體水平的任何一種技術。參閱 immunoelectrophoresis，immunofluorescence，radioimmunoassay。

immunocompromised *adj.* describing patients in whom the immune response is reduced or defective due to *immunosuppression. Such patients are vulnerable to opportunistic infections.

免疫缺乏的 由於免疫抑制而使免疫應答減弱或者有缺陷的患者。這些患者易受機會性致病菌感染。

immunoelectrophoresis *n.* a technique for identifying antigenic fractions in a serum. The components of the serum are separated by *electrophoresis and allowed to diffuse through agar gel towards a particular antiserum. Where the antibody meets its antigen, a band of precipitation occurs. *See also* precipitin.

免疫電泳 用於鑒定血清中抗原部分的一種技術。通過電泳使血清中的成分被分開，並通過瓊脂凝膠向特異的抗血清擴散，當抗體遇到它的抗原時，即產生一沉澱區。參閱 precipitin。

immunofluorescence *n.* a technique for observing the amount and/or distribution of antibody or antigen in a tissue section. The antibodies are labelled (directly or indirectly) with a fluorescent dye (e.g. fluorescein) and applied to the tissue, which is observed through an ultraviolet microscope. In *direct immunofluorescence* the antibody is labelled before being applied to the tissue. In *indirect immunofluorescence* the antibody is labelled after it has bound to the antigen, by means of fluorescein-labelled anti-immunoglobulin serum. **–immunofluorescent** *adj.*

免疫熒光法 用於觀察組織切片中抗體或抗原的數量和／或分布的一種技術。用熒光染劑（如熒光素）標記（直接或間接）抗體，然後將其用於組織，通過紫外綫顯微鏡觀察。直接免疫熒光法是先標記抗體，然後把它用於組織。間接免疫熒光法是抗體與抗原結合後，再用熒光素標記過的抗免疫球蛋白血清來標記抗體。

immunoglobulin (Ig) *n.* one of a group of structurally related proteins (gamma *globulins) that act as antibodies. Several classes of Ig with different functions are distinguished – IgA, IgD, IgE, IgG, and IgM. They can be separated by *immunoelectrophoresis. *See* antibody.

免疫球蛋白 在結構上相關的一組蛋白質中的一種（丙種球蛋白），起抗體作用。依不同的功能區分為幾種——免疫球蛋白 A、免疫球蛋白 D、免疫球蛋白 E、免疫球蛋白 G 和免疫球蛋白 M。可通過電泳把它們分開。參閱 antibody。

immunological tolerance a failure of the body to distinguish between materials that are 'self', and therefore to be tolerated, and those that are 'not self', against which antibodies are produced. For example, the body fails to produce antibodies against foreign materials if an antigen has previously been introduced into the body before the antibody-producing system is mature; apparently the presence of antigen within the growing cells inhibits antibody formation.

immunology *n.* the study of *immunity and all of the phenomena connected with the defence mechanisms of the body. –**immunological** *adj.*

immunophoresis *n.* a technique, relying upon the *precipitin reaction, for identifying an unknown antigen or testing for an antibody in a serum. Antibody and antigen are allowed to diffuse towards each other in agar gel.

immunosuppression *n.* suppression of the *immune response, usually by disease (e.g. AIDS) or by drugs (e.g. steroids, azathioprine, cyclosporin A).

immunosuppressive *n.* a drug, such as *azathioprine or *cyclophosphamide, that reduces the body's resistance to infection and other foreign bodies by suppressing the immune system. Immunosuppressives are used to maintain the survival of organ and tissue transplants and to treat various *autoimmune diseases, including rheumatoid arthritis. *Cyclosporin A is the immunosuppressive usually used in organ transplant recipients. Because immunity is lowered during treatment with immunosuppressives, there is an increased susceptibility to infection and certain types of cancer.

免疫耐受性　機體缺乏鑒別自身物質（可耐受的）和非自身物質（機體對其產生抗體）的能力。例如，如果在產生抗體的系統成熟之前，抗原就先進入體內，機體就不能產生抗體以抵禦異物；生長細胞內抗原的存在似乎抑制抗體的形成。

免疫學　研究免疫力及所有與機體防禦機制有關現象的學科。

免疫滲透　一種以沉澱素反應為基礎的技術，用於鑒定某一未知抗原或檢驗血清中某一抗體。抗原和抗體可以在瓊脂凝膠中彼此互相擴散。

免疫抑制　免疫應答受到抑制，常由疾病（如艾滋病）或藥物（如類固醇、硫唑嘌呤、環孢菌素 A）所致。

免疫抑制劑　通過抑制免疫系統減少機體對感染和其他異物的抵抗力的一類藥物，如硫唑嘌呤或環磷酰胺。免疫抑制劑用於維持器官和組織移植物的存活，以及治療各種自身免疫性疾病，包括類風濕性關節炎。環孢菌素 A 是經常用於器官移植受體的免疫抑制劑。由於在用免疫抑制劑治療期間免疫力下降，所以對感染和某些癌症的易感性增加。

immunotherapy *n.* the prevention or treatment of disease using agents that may modify the immune response. It is a largely experimental approach, studied most widely in the treatment of cancer. *See* biological response modifier.

免疫療法　使用能改變免疫應答的制劑預防和治療疾病。目前，它主要是一種實驗性治療方法，較廣泛地試用於癌症的治療。參閱　biological response modifier。

immunotoxin *n.* one of a new class of drugs undergoing clinical trials for the treatment of leukaemia. Immunotoxins combine *monoclonal antibodies, which can specifically target cancerous cells, with a highly toxic compound (such as *ricin) that inactivates the cells' *ribosomes and thus inhibits protein synthesis. Because the toxin does not attack the whole cell only tiny amounts are required.

免疫毒素　臨床上正在試用於白血病治療的一種新型藥物。免疫毒素使單克隆抗體和毒性極強的化合物（如蓖麻毒蛋白）結合起來，前者能夠特異性地瞄準癌症細胞，後者滅活細胞核糖體，從而抑制蛋白質合成。由於免疫毒素並不攻擊整個細胞，所以僅需微量。

immunotransfusion *n.* the transfusion of an *antiserum to treat or give temporary protection against a disease.

免疫製劑輸入法　輸入一種抗血清以治療或暫時預防某種疾病。

impacted *adj.* firmly wedged. An *impacted tooth* (usually a wisdom tooth) is one that cannot erupt into a normal position because it is obstructed by other tissues. *Impacted faeces* are so hard and dry that they cannot pass through the anus without special measures being taken (*see* constipation). An *impacted fracture* is one in which the bone ends are driven into each other. **–impaction** *n.*

嵌入的，阻生的，嵌塞的　牢固地楔入的。阻生牙（通常是智齒）是由於其他組織的阻塞而不能在正常位置萌出的牙。嵌塞糞便非常硬而且乾燥，因此，不採取特殊措施，不能通過肛門（參閱　constipation）。嵌塞性骨折是指骨端互相嵌入的骨折。

impairment *n. see* handicap.

損害　參閱　handicap。

impalpable *adj.* describing a structure within the body that cannot be detected (or that can be detected only with difficulty) by feeling with the hand.

不可觸知的　描述體內某個憑手感不能（或者難於）檢清的結構。

imperforate *adj.* lacking an opening. Occasionally girls at puberty are found to have an *imperforate hymen* (a fold of membrane close to the vaginal orifice),

閉鎖的　缺少某種開口的。偶爾可見一些青春期女孩的處女膜閉鎖（膜的皺襞接近陰道口），因而阻礙經血的流出。

which impedes the flow of menstrual blood.

imperforate anus (proctatresia) partial or complete obstruction of the anus: a condition, discovered at birth, due to failure of the anus to develop normally in the embryo. There are several different types of imperforate anus; these include *developmental anal stenosis*, *persistent anal membrane*, and *covered anus* (due to fused genital folds). If the anal canal fails to develop, the rectum ends blindly above the muscles of the perineum. Most mild cases of imperforate anus can be treated by a simple operation. If the defect is extensive a temporary opening is made in the colon (*see* colostomy), with later surgical reconstruction of the rectum and anus.

impetigo *n*. a superficial bacterial infection of the skin. *Nonbullous impetigo* is caused by *Staphylococcus aureus*, *Streptococcus* species, or both organisms; it mainly affects young children and is highly contagious, with yellowish-brown crusting. *Bullous impetigo* is caused by *Staph. aureus*; it is characterized by blisters, is less contagious than the nonbullous form, and occurs at any age. Treatment of impetigo is with topical antibiotics; systemic antibiotics may occasionally be needed.

implant *n*. **1.** a drug (such as a subcutaneous hormone implant), a prosthesis (such as an artificial hip, a *breast implant, or a *cochlear implant), or a radioactive source (such as radium needles) that is put into the body. **2.** (in dentistry) a rigid structure that is embedded in bone or under its periosteum to provide support for replacement teeth on a *denture or a *bridge. Recent types

肛門閉鎖 肛門的部分或完全阻塞。這種病在出生時被發現，是由於胚胎期肛門未能正常發育所致。肛門閉鎖有幾種類型，包括肛門發育不全，肛膜未破和隱蔽肛門（由生殖皺襞融合所致）。如果肛管停止發育，直腸就會在會陰肌上形成一個盲端。多數輕度肛門閉鎖可以通過一個簡單手術得到治療。如果缺陷是廣泛的，則在結腸上作一臨時開口（參閱colostomy），以後再行直腸和肛門的重建手術。

膿疱症 皮膚表面的細菌感染。非大疱性膿疱症由金黃色葡萄球菌、鏈球菌或兩者共同引起，主要發生於幼兒，接觸傳染性高，有黃褐色痂。大疱性膿疱症由金黃色葡萄球菌引起，特點為水疱，接觸傳染性較非大疱性膿疱症弱，任何年齡均可發病。治療：膿疱局部用抗生素；偶爾需要全身使用抗生素。

植入物 **(1)** 植入體內的藥物（如皮下激素植入），假體（如人造髖骨，乳房植入或耳蝸植入）或者放射源（如鐳針）。**(2)**（牙科學）埋入骨內或骨膜下的堅硬的結構，用於支撐托牙或齒橋上的義齒。新型的骨結合性植入物具有許多特殊的金屬插入物（通常是鈦）；將這些金屬插入物置於頜骨內，

(*osseo-integrated implants*) consist of a number of special metal inserts (often titanium), placed in the jawbone, onto which an artificial tooth superstructure is subsequently bolted. Osseo-integrated implants are also used to retain facial *prostheses.

義齒的上層結構插在其上。骨結合植入物也用於保持顏面假體。

implantation *n.* **1.** (or **nidation**) the attachment of the early embryo to the lining of the uterus, which occurs at the *blastocyst stage of development, six to eight days after ovulation, of implantation determines the position of the placenta. **2.** the placing of a substance (e.g. a drug) or an object (e.g. an artificial pacemaker) within a tissue. **3.** the surgical replacement of damaged tissue with healthy tissue (*see* transplantation).

(1) **着床** 早期胚胎附着於子宮內膜上。它發生於排卵後 6 天至 8 天的胚泡發育階段。着床位置決定胎盤的位置。 **(2)** **植入** 將某一物質（如藥物）或物體（如人工起搏器）埋於組織內。 **(3) 移植** 用健康組織替代損傷組織的置換手術（參閱 transplantation）。

implosion *n. see* flooding.

血崩 參閱 flooding。

impotence *n.* inability in a man to have sexual intercourse. Impotence may be *erectile*, in which the penis does not become firm enough to enter the vagina, or *ejaculatory*, in which penetration occurs but there is no ejaculation of semen (orgasm). Either of these kinds of impotence may be due to a physical disease, such as diabetes (*organic*), or to a psychological or emotional problem (*psychogenic*).

陽痿 指男性不能性交。陽痿可以是勃起性的，即陰莖勃起不夠堅硬，以致不能進入陰道內，也可以是射精性的，即陰莖雖能插入，但沒有精液射出（性慾高潮）。這兩種陽痿都可能由身體疾病，如糖尿病所致（器質性的），或由心理和情感問題所致（精神性的）。

impression *n.* (in dentistry) an elastic mould made of the teeth and surrounding soft tissues or of a toothless jaw. A soft impression material (e.g. silicone or alginate) is placed over the teeth or jaw and sets within several minutes. After removal from the mouth a plaster model is made; on this are constructed *restorations of teeth, *dentures, or *orthodontic appliances.

印模 （牙科學）指牙齒和周圍軟組織或無牙頜的一個彈性模子。將一種軟的印模材料（如矽酮或藻酸鹽）置於牙齒或頜骨上數分鐘。從口腔中取出後即成一石膏模子。在此模子上製造牙的修復體、托牙和口腔正畸矯正器。

imprinting *n.* (in animal behaviour) a rapid and irreversible form of learning that takes place in some animals during the first hours of life. Animals attach themselves in this way to members of their own species, but if they are exposed to creatures of a different species during this short period, they become attached to this species instead.

印刻 （動物行為）指一些動物生後最初數小時所發生的迅速而不可逆的學習形式。通過這種學習方式，動物把自己與同種的其他成員關聯起來；如果在這段短時間內，牠們接觸過不同種的動物，牠們則把自己與那種動物關聯起來。

impulse *n.* (in neurology) *see* nerve impulse.

衝動 （神經病學）參閱 nerve impulse。

in- (im-) *prefix denoting* **1.** not. **2.** in; within; into.

〔前綴〕**(1)** 不 (2) 在……裏，在……內，進入到……

inanition *n.* a condition of exhaustion caused by lack of nutrients in the blood. This may arise through starvation, malnutrition, or intestinal disease.

營養不足 血中養分缺乏引起的消耗性疾病。這可以由於飢餓、營養不良或腸道疾病而引起。

inappetence *n.* lack of desire, usually for food.

食慾不振 通常指對食物缺乏慾望。

in articulo mortis Latin: at the moment of death.

臨終時 拉丁語：死亡的時刻。

inbreeding *n.* the production of offspring by parents who are closely related; for example, who are first cousins or siblings. The amount of inbreeding in a population is largely controlled by culture and tradition. *Compare* outbreeding.

近親交配 血緣關係很近的父母親生育後代。如堂（表）兄妹之間或親兄妹之間。人口中近親交配的數量主要由文化和傳統影響。與 outbreeding 對比。

incarcerated *adj.* confined or constricted so as to be immovable: applied particularly to a type of *hernia.

箝閉的 受限制或被縮窄以至不能活動，特別用於一種疝。

incidence rate (inception rate) a measure of morbidity based on the number of new episodes of illness arising in a population over an estimated period. It can be expressed in terms of sick persons or episodes per 1000 individuals at risk. *Compare* prevalence rate.

發病率 根據一定時期內某一人羣中新發某病的例數，來衡量疾病情況的指標。它可用每1000 風險人口中的病人數或發病數來表示。與 prevalence rate 對比。

incision *n.* **1.** the surgical cutting of soft tissues, such as skin or muscle, with a knife or scalpel. **2.** the cut so made.

(1) **切開** 用刀或解剖刀手術切開軟組織，如皮膚或肌肉。
(2) **切口**

incisor *n.* any of the four front teeth in each jaw, two on each side of the midline. *See also* dentition.

切牙 每個頜骨上四個前牙中的任何一個，中綫每側各兩個。參閱 dentition。

incisure *n.* (in anatomy) a notch, small hollow, or depression.

切跡 （解剖學）指切跡、小洞或凹陷。

inclusion bodies particles occurring in the nucleus and cytoplasm of cells usually as a result of virus infection. Their presence can sometimes be used to diagnose such an infection.

包涵體 發生於細胞核和細胞漿中的顆粒，通常是病毒感染的結果。它們的存在有時可用於診斷此類感染。

income support an income-related benefit payable to those whose income does not exceed a specified minimum. It replaced supplementary benefit in 1988.

收入津貼 （英國）一項與收入有關的津貼，給予收入未超過某一規定的最低值的人；1988年取代了額外津貼。

incompatibility *n. see* compatibility.

不相容性 參閱 compatibility。

incompetence *n.* impaired function of the valves of the heart or veins, which allows backward leakage of blood. *See* aortic regurgitation, mitral incompetence, varicose veins.

關閉不全 心臟或靜脈瓣膜的功能損傷，致使血液可以返流。參閱 aortic regurgitation，mitral incompetence，varicose veins。

incontinence *n.* **1.** the inappropriate involuntary passage of urine, resulting in wetting. *Stress incontinence* is the leak of urine on coughing and straining. It is common in women in whom the muscles of the pelvic floor are weakened after childbirth. *Overflow incontinence* is leakage from a full bladder, which occurs most commonly in elderly men with bladder outflow obstruction or in patients with neurological conditions affecting bladder control. *Urge incontinence* is leakage of urine that

(1) **尿失禁** 不適宜的不隨意排尿，造成尿漏。壓迫性尿失禁是指咳嗽或用力時尿液漏出。常見於產後骨盆底肌無力的婦女。溢流性尿失禁是指尿液由充溢的膀胱內漏出，最常見於膀胱排尿梗阻的老年男性或者神經性疾病累及膀胱神經控制的患者。尿意性尿失禁是指有強烈排尿慾望而又不能控制的尿液漏出。參閱 enuresis。 (2) **大便失禁** 不能控制排便。

accompanies an intense desire to pass water with failure of restraint. *See also* enuresis. **2.** inability to control bowel movements (*faecal incontinence*).

incoordination *n.* (in neurology) an impairment in the performance of precise movements. These are dependent upon the normal function of the whole nervous system, and incoordination may result from a disorder in any part of it. *See* apraxia, ataxia, dyssynergia.

共濟失調 （神經病學）指完成精確運動的能力障礙。這些精確運動依賴於整個神經系統的正常功能，而共濟失調可能由神經系統任何部位的疾病所致。參閱 apraxia，ataxia，dyssynergia。

incubation *n.* **1.** the process of development of an egg or a culture of bacteria. **2.** the care of a premature baby in an *incubator.

(1) 孵育 卵或細菌培養物的發育過程。 **(2) 保溫** 將早產兒放在恆溫箱內護理。

incubation period (latent period) 1. the interval between exposure to an infection and the appearance of the first symptoms. **2.** (in bacteriology) the period of development of a bacterial culture.

潛伏期 (1) 暴露於某種感染和首發症狀之間的時期。 **(2)** （細菌學）指細菌培養基的發育時期。

incubator *n.* a transparent container for keeping premature babies in controlled conditions and protecting them from infection. Other forms of incubator are used for cultivating bacteria in Petri dishes and for hatching eggs.

恆溫箱 用於控制早產兒的生活條件和保護他們免受感染的透明容器。其他形式的恆溫箱用於佩特里培養皿中的細菌培養和孵卵。

incus *n.* a small anvil-shaped bone in the middle *ear that articulates with the malleus and the stapes. *See* ossicle.

砧骨 中耳內的一塊小鐵砧樣骨頭，與錘骨和鐙骨以關節連接。參閱 ossicle。

independent contract (in Britain) a special arrangement whereby *hospitals or *general practitioners working in the *National Health Service receive budgeted funds to provide services of their own selection, without direction from health authorities. However, basic services must be provided for the population of the District Health Authority in

獨立合同 （英國）一種特殊方式，規定在國民保健服務制內工作的醫院或全科醫師獲得預算基金，以便提供他們自己選擇的醫療服務，而不受衛生機構的指導。但是，他們必須向地段衛生局負責的人羣提供基本服務，而這種服務是按協議比例計劃的。

which the service is located at an agreed rate.

Inderal *n. see* propranolol.

心得安　參閱 propranolol。

indican *n.* a compound excreted in the urine as a detoxification product of *indoxyl. Indican is formed by the conjugation of indoxyl with sulphuric acid and potassium on the decomposition of tryptophan.

尿藍母　隨尿排出的一種化合物，是吲哚酚的一種解毒產物。色氨酸分解時，吲哚酚與硫酸和鉀結合形成尿藍母。

indicanuria *n.* the presence in the urine of an abnormally high concentration of *indican. This may be a sign that the intestine is obstructed.

尿藍母尿　尿液中尿藍母濃度異常高，這是腸道梗阻的可能體徵。

indication *n.* (in medicine) a strong reason for believing that a particular course of action is desirable. In a wounded patient, the loss of blood, which would lead to circulatory collapse, is an indication for blood transfusion. *Compare* contraindication.

適應症　（醫學）指使人相信某種做法是符合需要的一個有力的理由。對某位外傷病人，失血會導致循環衰竭，因而是輸血的適應症。與 contraindication 對比。

indigestion *n. see* dyspepsia.

消化不良　參閱 dyspepsia。

indole *n.* a derivative of the amino acid tryptophan, excreted in the urine and faeces. Abnormal patterns of urinary indole excretion are found in some mentally retarded patients.

吲哚　由尿和糞中排出的一種氨基酸（色氨酸）的衍生物。尿中吲哚排泄的異常情況可見於精神發育遲緩的病人。

indolent *adj.* describing a disease process that is failing to heal or has persisted. The term is applied particularly to ulcers of skin or mucous membrane.

難愈合的　描述一種未能痊愈或者持續未愈的病程。此術語特指皮膚或黏膜潰瘍。

indomethacin *n.* an anti-inflammatory drug (*see* NSAID), used in the treatment of arthritic conditions. It is administered either by mouth or in suppositories; common side-effects are headache, dizziness, and digestive upsets. Trade names: **Indocid, Indomod**.

吲哚美辛　一種抗炎藥物（參閱 NSAID），用於治療關節炎性疾病。口服或栓劑給藥。常見的副作用包括頭痛、頭暈以及消化系統不適。商品名：Indocid，Indomod。

indoramin *n.* an *alpha blocker drug used to treat high blood pressure. It is administered by mouth. Possible side-effects can include drowsiness, nasal congestion, dry mouth, and failure of ejaculation. Trade names: **Baratol, Doralese**.

吲哚拉明　一種用於治療高血壓的α-受體阻滯劑。口服給藥，可能的副作用包括倦睡、鼻腔阻塞、口乾和射精障礙。商品名：Baratol，Doralese。

indoxyl *n.* an alcohol derived from *indole by bacterial action. It is excreted in the urine as *indican.

吲哚酚　通過細菌的作用，由吲哚衍生的一種醇。它以尿藍母的形式從尿中排出。

induction *n.* **1.** (in obstetrics) the starting of labour by artificial means. *Medical induction* is carried out using such drugs as *prostaglandins or *oxytocin, which stimulate uterine contractions. *Surgical induction* is performed by *amniotomy (artificial rupture of membranes), usually supplemented by oxytocic drugs. Induction of labour is carried out if the wellbeing or life of mother or child is threatened by continuance of the pregnancy **2.** (in anaesthesia) initiation of *anaesthesia. General anaesthesia is usually induced by the intravenous injection of rapid short-acting narcotic drugs, e.g. thiopentone.

(1) 引產　（產科學）指用人工方法引起分娩。藥物引產通過使用前列腺素或縮宮素等藥物進行，這些藥物刺激子宮收縮。手術引產通過羊膜穿破術（人工穿破膜）進行，並常輔以催產藥。如果妊娠的繼續威脅母親或胎兒的生命和健康，則行引產術。**(2) 誘導麻醉**（麻醉學）指開始麻醉。全身麻醉往往通過靜脈注射快速、短效的麻醉藥誘導，如硫噴妥鈉。

induration *n.* abnormal hardening of a tissue or organ. *See also* sclerosis.

硬結　組織或器官不正常地變硬。參閱 sclerosis。

indusium *n.* a thin layer of grey matter covering the upper surface of the *corpus callosum between the two cerebral hemispheres.

被蓋　覆蓋兩個大腦半球間的胼胝體表面的一薄層灰質。

industrial disease *see* occupational disease.

工業病　參閱 occupational disease。

inertia *n.* (in physiology) sluggishness or absence of activity in certain smooth muscles. In *uterine inertia* the muscular wall of the uterus fails to contract adequately during labour, making the

無力　（生理學）指某些平滑肌的活動遲緩或消失。在子宮無力的病例中，因分娩時子宮肌層不能充分收縮，致使分娩時間過長。這種無力分娩開始就

process excessively long. This inertia may be present from the start of labour or it may develop because of exhaustion following strong contractions.

可出現，或因強烈收縮後肌力衰竭而發生。

in extremis Latin: at the point of death.

瀕死　　拉丁語：在死亡之時。

infant *n.* a child incapable of any form of independence from its mother: a child under one year of age, especially a premature or newborn child. In legal use the term denotes a child up to the age of seven years.

嬰兒　　各方面均需依賴母親的小兒：一歲以下的小兒，尤指早產兒或新生兒。在法律上，此術語指七歲以下的小孩。

infanticide *n.* (in Britain) under the terms of the Infanticide Act 1938, the felony of child destruction by the natural mother within 12 months of birth when the balance of her mind is disturbed because she has not fully recovered from childbirth and/or lactation. Under such circumstances a charge that would have been one of murder is reduced to manslaughter.

殺嬰罪　　（英國）指根據 1938 年殺嬰罪法的條款，在孩子出生後 12 個月內，母親尚未完全從分娩及/或哺乳中恢復而出現精神混亂，殺死嬰兒的犯罪行為。在這種情況下，本應為謀殺罪的指控減輕為過失殺人。

infantile *adj.* **1.** denoting conditions occurring in adults that are recognizable in childhood, e.g. poliomylitis (*infantile paralysis*) and *infantile scurvy*. **2.** of, relating to, or affecting infants.

嬰兒的　　**(1)** 指成人發生的某些常見於兒童期的疾病，如脊髓灰質炎（嬰兒癱）以及嬰兒壞血病。 **(2)** 嬰兒的，與嬰兒有關的，發於嬰兒的。

infantile spasms (salaam attacks) a form of epilepsy caused by serious congenital or acquired brain disease, usually beginning under the age of six months. The spasms are involuntary flexing movements of the arms, legs, neck, and trunk; each spasm lasts 1–3 seconds and is associated with flushing of the face, and runs of spasms occur over a period of several minutes. They may occur many times in one day. The baby fails to respond to human contact and development is profoundly slowed. An EEG pattern of *hypsarrhythmia

嬰兒痙攣　　由嚴重先天或後天性腦部疾病引起的一種癲癇，常首次發病於 6 個月以內。這種痙攣是臂、腿、頸和軀幹的不隨意屈曲運動，每次痙攣持續 1~3 秒鐘，並伴有面部潮紅，幾分鐘連續發生數次痙攣。

這種痙攣一天內可多次發生。嬰兒對人們的接觸無反應，而且發育嚴重延遲。有時可見高度腦節律失常的腦電圖型。將痙攣誤診為小兒驚風，往往延誤了診斷。及早發現，

is sometimes seen. Interpretation of the spasms as wind has often delayed diagnosis. Immediate recognition and treatment with corticosteroids or ACTH offers a chance of arresting the disease, but outcome depends primarily on the nature of the underlying brain abnormality.

並用皮質類固醇和促腎上腺皮質激素治療，有終止發作的可能性，但預後主要取決於潛在的腦部異常的性質。

infantilism *n.* persistence of childlike physical or psychological characteristics into adult life.

幼稚型　類似兒童的身體和心理特點持續至成人期。

infant mortality rate (IMR) the number of deaths of infants under one year of age per 1000 live births in a given year. Included in the IMR are the *neonatal death rate* (calculated from deaths occurring in the first four weeks of life) and *postneonatal death rate* (from deaths in the remainder of the first year). Neonatal deaths are further subdivided into *early* (first week) and *late* (second, third, and fourth weeks). In prosperous countries neonatal deaths account for about two-thirds of infant mortalities, the majority being in the first week. The IMR is usually regarded more as a measure of social affluence than a measure of the quality of antenatal and/or obstetric care; the latter is more truly reflected in the *perinatal mortality rate* (the sum of stillbirths and first-week or early neonatal deaths per 1000 total births). *See also* stillbirth rate.

嬰兒死亡率　在特定的一年中，每1000個活產中1歲以內嬰兒的死亡數目。嬰兒死亡率包括新生兒死亡率（出生後頭四周內發生的死亡數目）和新生兒期後死亡率（第一年剩餘時間內的死亡數目）。新生兒死亡又進一步被分為早期（第一周）和後期（第二、三和四周）。在發達國家，新生兒死亡率占嬰兒死亡率的2/3，而其中多數發生於第一周。通常，與其把嬰兒死亡率看作為出生前及／或生產時護理質量的指標，不如把它看作為社會富裕程度的指標。而生前及產時護理質量更真實地反映在圍產期死亡率中（每1000次分娩中的死產數和產後第一周或早期新生兒期死亡數）。

infarct *n. see* infarction.

梗塞　參閱 infarction。

infarction *n.* the death of part or the whole of an organ that occurs when the artery carrying its blood supply is obstructed by a blood clot (thrombus) or an *embolus. For example, *myocardial infarction, affecting the muscle of the heart, follows coronary thrombosis. A small localized area of dead tissue

梗死　器官的部分或全部死亡，發生於當為它提供血液的動脈被血凝塊（血栓）或栓子阻塞時。例如，累及心臟肌肉的心肌梗死隨冠狀動脈血栓形成而發生。由於供血不足造成小的、局部壞死組織區被稱為梗塞。

produced as a result of an inadequate blood supply is known as an *infarct*.

infection *n.* invasion of the body by harmful organisms (pathogens), such as bacteria, fungi, protozoa, rickettsiae, or viruses. The infective agent may be transmitted by a patient or *carrier in airborne droplets expelled during coughing and sneezing or by direct contact, such as kissing or sexual intercourse (*see* sexually transmitted disease); by animal or insect *vectors; by ingestion of contaminated food or drink; or from an infected mother to the fetus during pregnancy or birth. Pathogenic organisms present in soil, organisms from animal intermediate hosts, or those living as *commensals on the body can also cause infections. Organisms may invade via a wound or bite or through mucous membranes. After an *incubation period symptoms appear, usually consisting of either localized inflammation and pain or more remote effects. Treatment with drugs is usually effective against most infections, but there is no specific treatment for many of the common viral infections, including the common cold and influenza.

傳染 致病微生物（病原體）侵入人體，如細菌、真菌、原蟲、立克次體或病毒。傳染性病原體的傳播可通過病人或攜帶者咳嗽或打噴嚏排出的飛沫；或通過直接接觸，如接吻或性交（參閱 sexually transmitted disease）；或通過動物或昆蟲媒介物，或由於食入被污染的食物或飲料；或在妊娠或分娩時，由被感染的母親傳給胎兒。傳染還可以由土壤中的病原性微生物，來自動物中間宿主的微生物或者人體上生活的共生體微生物引起。微生物可通過傷口、咬傷或黏膜侵入。潛伏期後出現症狀，通常包括局部炎症和疼痛或者遠離部位的反應。對大多數感染，藥物治療通常是有效的，但對許多常見的病毒性感染，包括普通感冒和流行性感冒，尚無特殊治療方法。

infectious disease *see* communicable disease.

傳染性疾病 參閱 communicable disease。

infectious mononucleosis *see* glandular fever.

傳染性單核細胞增多症 參閱 glandular fever。

inferior *adj.* (in anatomy) lower in the body in relation to another structure or surface.

下面的 （解剖學）指人體內相對另一結構或表面位置靠下的。

inferior dental block a type of injection to anaesthetize the inferior *dental nerve. Inferior dental block is routinely performed to allow dental procedures to

下牙阻滯 用於麻醉下牙神經的一種注射方法。臨床上常行下牙阻滯，從而使口腔一側的下牙手術得以進行。

be carried out on the lower teeth on one side of the mouth.

inferior dental canal a bony canal in the *mandible on each side. It carries the inferrior *dental nerve and vessels and for part of its length its outline is visible on a radiograph.　·

下牙管　位於每側下顎內的一個骨性管道，內有下牙神經和血管通過，X 綫片上可見一段下牙管的外形。

inferiority complex 1. an unconscious and extreme exaggeration of feelings of insignificance or inferiority, which is shown by behaviour that is defensive or compensatory (such as aggression). **2.** (in psychoanalysis) a *complex said to result from the conflict between Oedipal wishes (*see* Oedipus complex) and the reality of the child's lack of power. This gives rise to repressed feelings of personal inferiority.

(1)　自卑情緒　一種微不足道或卑微低下的感覺被下意識地極端誇大的情形，通過防衛性或補償性（如攻擊）行為表現出來。**(2)　自卑情綜**（精神分析）指戀母情結的願望（參閱 Oedipus complex）與孩子缺乏力量的現實間的衝突所產生的綜合徵。它造成自我卑下的壓抑情感。

infertility *n.* inability in a woman to conceive or in a man to induce conception. Female infertility may be due to failure to ovulate, to obstruction of the *Fallopian tubes, or to disease of the lining of the uterus (endometrium). Possible treatments (depending on the cause) include administration of drugs (such as *clomiphene or *LHRH analogues), surgery (*see* salpingostomy, salpingolysis) to restore patency of the Fallopian tubes, *gamete intrafallopian transfer (GIFT), and *in vitro fertilization. Causes of male infertility include decreased numbers of motility of spermatozoa (*see* oligospermia) and total absence of sperm (*see* azoospermia). *See also* andrology, sterility.

不孕症　婦女不能懷孕或者男性不能使之懷孕。女性不孕症可能由於不排卵、輸卵管阻塞或者子宮內膜的疾患所致。可行的治療（取決於病因），包括使用藥物（如克羅米芬或促黃體激素釋放激素類似物），手術（參閱 salpingostomy, salpingolysis）疏通輸卵管，配子輸卵管內轉移，以及試管授精。男性不孕症的原因包括精子活性降低或數目減少（參閱 oligospermia）和完全無精子（參閱 azoospermia）。參閱 andrology，sterility。

infestation *n.* the presence of animal parasites either on the skin (for example, ticks) or inside the body (for example, tapeworms).　.

寄生　動物寄生物存在於皮膚上（如：蜱）或體內（如：絛蟲）。

infibulation *n. see* (female) circumcision.

infiltration *n.* **1.** the abnormal entry of a substance (*infiltrate*) into a cell, tissue, or organ. Examples of infiltrates are blood cells, cancer cells, fat, starch, or calcium and magnesium salts. **2.** the injection of a local anaesthetic solution into the tissues to cause local *anaesthesia. Infiltration anaesthesia is routinely used to anaesthetize upper teeth to allow dental procedures to be carried out.

inflammation *n.* the body's response to injury, which may be acute or chronic. *Acute inflammation* is the immediate defensive reaction of tissue to any injury, which may be caused by infection, chemicals, or physical agents. It involves pain, heat, redness, swelling, and loss of function of the affected part. Blood vessels near the site of injury are dilated, so that blood flow is locally increased. White blood cells enter the tissue and begin to engulf bacteria and other foreign particles. Similar cells from the tissues remove and consume the dead cells, sometimes with the production of pus, enabling the process of healing to commence. In certain circumstances healing does not occur and *chronic inflammation* ensues.

influenza *n.* a highly contagious virus infection that affects the respiratory system. The viruses are transmitted by coughing and sneezing. Symptoms commence after an incubation period of 1–4 days and include headache, fever, loss of appetite, weakness, and general aches and pains. They may continue for about a week. With bed rest and aspirin most patients recover, but a few may go on to develop pneumonia, either a primary influenzal viral pneumonia or a

鎖陰術 參閱 (female) circumcision。

浸潤 **(1)** 某種物質（浸潤物）非正常地進入細胞、組織或器官中。浸潤物的例子有血細胞、癌細胞、脂肪、澱粉、或鈣及鎂鹽。**(2)** 把局部麻醉劑注射入組織內，以造成局部麻醉。通常慣用浸潤性麻醉來麻醉上牙以使牙手術操作得以完成。

炎症 人體對損傷的反應，可以是急性的或慢性的。急性炎症是組織對任何損傷的迅速防禦性反應，它可由傳染、化學藥品或物理因素引起。有累及部位的痛、熱、紅、腫和功能喪失。損傷部位附近的血管擴張，以致局部血流增加。白細胞進入組織，並且開始吞噬細菌和其他外來的微粒。組織中與白細胞相似的細胞清除吞入所有的死細胞，有時產生膿液，使癒合過程開始。在某些情況下，癒合不發生，而慢性炎症接着發生。

流行性感冒 一種具有高度傳染性的病毒感染，累及呼吸系統。病毒通過咳嗽或噴嚏傳播。1~4 天潛伏期後，症狀開始，包括頭痛、發熱、無食慾、虛弱、以及全身疼痛。症狀可持續約一周。通過臥床休息和服用阿司匹林，多數病人可康復，但一些病人可能繼續發展為肺炎，為原發性流感病毒肺炎或繼發性流感病毒肺炎。這兩種肺炎都可因肺內出

secondary bacterial pneumonia. Either of these may lead to death from haemorrhage within the lungs. The main bacterial organisms responsible for secondary infection are *Streptococcus pneumoniae*, *Haemophilus influenzae*, and *Staphylococcus aureus*, against which appropriate antibiotic therapy must be given. An influenzal infection provides later protection only against the specific strain of virus concerned; the same holds true for immunization.

血而導致死亡。造成繼發性感染的主要細菌是肺炎鏈球菌、流感嗜血桿菌和金黃色葡萄球菌。對於這些細菌，必須使用適當的抗生素治療。一種流感感染僅能對特異株的病毒提供後來的預防；免疫也是如此。

infra- *prefix denoting* below.

〔前綴〕下

infrared radiation the band of electromagnetic radiation that is longer in wavelength than the red of the visible spectrum. Infrared radiation is responsible for the transmission of radiant heat. It may be used in physiotherapy to warm tissues, reduce pain, and improve circulation, but is not as effective as *diathermy for deep structures. Special photographic film, which is sensitive to infrared radiation, is used in *thermography.

紅外綫照射 波長比可見光譜的紅光長的電磁射綫帶。紅外綫照射造成輻射熱的傳導。它可用於理療中，溫暖組織，減少疼痛，以及促進循環，但對深層結構不如透熱療法有效。對紅外綫照射敏感的特殊攝影膠片被用於溫度記錄法中。

infundibulum *n.* any funnel-shaped channel or passage, particularly the hollow conical stalk that extends downwards from the hypothalamus and is continuous with the posterior lobe of the pituitary gland.

漏斗 任何漏斗狀的管道或通道，特指從丘腦下部向下延伸並與垂體後葉相連的圓錐形空心柄。

infusion *n.* **1.** the slow injection of a substance, usually into a vein (*intravenous infusion*). This is a common method for replacing water, electrolytes, and blood products and is also used for the continuous administration of drugs (e.g. antibiotics, painkillers) or *nutrition. *See also* drip. **2.** the process whereby the active principles are extracted from plant

(1) 輸注 緩慢地注射某種物質，通常注入靜脈（靜脈輸注）。這是一種補充水、電解質以及血製品的常用方法，也用於連續地給予藥物（如抗生素、止疼藥）或營養。參閱 drip。**(2) 浸出** 通過把植物材料浸入已加熱至沸點的水中以提取出其中有效成分的過程

material by steeping it in water that has been heated to boiling point (as in the making of tea). **3.** the solution produced by this process.

（如沏茶）。**(3) 浸劑** 通過浸出過程產生的溶液。

ingesta *pl. n.* food and drink that is introduced into the alimentary canal through the mouth.

飲食物 通過口腔插管注入消化道的食物和飲料。

ingestion *n.* **1.** the process by which food is taken into the alimentary canal. It involves chewing and swallowing. **2.** the process by which a phagocytic cell takes in solid material, such as bacteria.

(1) 攝食 食物被攝入消化道的過程，包括咀嚼和吞咽。**(2) 吞噬** 吞噬細胞攝入固體物質，如細菌的過程。

ingravescent *adj.* gradually increasing in severity.

漸重的 嚴重程度逐漸增大的。

ingrowing toenail downward curving of the sides of the big toenail, which causes chafing of the skin alongside the nail resulting in inflammation around the base of the nail.

嵌甲生趾 大腳趾甲兩側向下彎曲，引起趾甲沿綫的皮膚受到摩擦傷，造成甲基周圍炎症。

inguinal *adj.* relating to or affecting the region of the groin (inguen).

腹股溝的 與腹股溝有關的，影響腹股溝區的。

inguinal canal either of a pair of openings that connect the abdominal cavity with the scrotum in the male fetus. The inguinal canals provide a route for the descent of the testes into the scrotum, after which they normally become obliterated.

腹股溝管 在男性胎兒中，連接腹腔和陰囊的一對開口。腹股溝管為睾丸降入陰囊提供了路徑。此後，在正常情況下，此開口閉合。

inguinal hernia *see* hernia.

腹股溝疝 參閱 hernia。

inguinal ligament (Poupart's ligament) a ligament in the groin that extends from the anterior superior iliac spine to the pubic tubercle. It is part of the *aponeurosis of the external oblique muscle of the abdomen.

腹股溝韌帶 腹股溝內，由髂前上棘延伸至恥骨結節的一條韌帶。它是腹外斜肌腱膜的一部分。

INH *see* isoniazid.

異煙肼 參閱 isoniazid。

inhalation *n.* **1.** (*or* **inspiration**) the act of breathing air into the lungs through the mouth and nose. *See* breathing. **2.** a gas, vapour, or aerosol breathed in for the treatment of conditions of the respiratory tract. **–inhaler** *n.*

inhibition *n.* **1.** (in physiology) the prevention or reduction of the functioning of an organ, muscle, etc., by the action of certain nerve impulses. **2.** (in psychoanalysis) an inner command that prevents one from doing something forbidden. Some inhibitions are essential for social adjustment, but excessive inhibitions can severely restrict one's life. **3.** (in psychology) a tendency not to carry out a specific action, produced each time the action is carried out.

inhibitor *n.* a substance that prevents the occurrence of a given process or reaction. *See also* MAO inhibitor.

inion *n.* the projection of the occipital bone that can be felt at the base of the skull.

initiation *n.* (in oncology) the first step in the development of cancer (*see* carcinogenesis).

injection *n.* introduction into the body of drugs or other fluids by means of a syringe, usually drugs that would be destroyed by the digestive processes if taken by mouth. Common routes for injection are into the skin (*intracutaneous* or *intradermal*); below the skin (*subcutaneous*), e.g. for insulin; into a muscle (*intramuscular*), for drugs that are slowly absorbed; and into a vein (*intravenous*), for drugs to be rapidly absorbed. *Enemas are also regarded as injections.

(1) 吸入 經口和鼻把空氣吸進肺的動作。參閱 breathing。**(2)** 吸入劑 吸進的氣體、蒸氣或氣霧劑，用於治療呼吸道疾病。

抑制 **(1)** （生理學）指通過某些神經衝動的作用，使器官、肌肉等的功能受阻或減少。**(2)** （精神分析）指阻止某人做某件被禁止的事情的一種內在命令。有些抑制對適應社會非常重要，但過分的抑制可嚴重約束一個人的生活。**(3)** （心理學）指不進行某個特殊行為的一種傾向。每次進行該行為時，便產生這種傾向。

抑制劑 阻止某個特定過程或反應發生的物質。參閱 MAO inhibitor。

枕外隆突 在顱骨底可觸摸到的枕骨突起部分。

發生 （腫瘤學）指癌症發展的第一步（參閱 carcinogenesis）。

注射 用注射器將藥物或者其他液體注入體內，通常是口服時會被消化過程破壞的藥物。常用的注射途徑是：皮內（真皮內的）；皮下（如用於胰島素注射）；肌肉內（用於吸收緩慢的藥物）；以及靜脈內（用於吸收迅速的藥物）。各種灌腸也被看作為注射。

inlay *n.* **1.** a substance or piece of tissue inserted to replace a defect in a tissue. For example, a bone graft may be inlaid into an area of missing or damaged bone. **2.** (in dentistry) a rigid restoration inserted into a tapered cavity in a tooth. It is held in place with a cement *lute. While cast gold has been the most widely used material, porcelain and composite resin are also used.

嵌體　(1) 將一種物質或一片組織嵌入以替代一個組織缺損。例如：可將骨移植物嵌入骨缺失或骨損傷的區域。(2)（牙科學）指插入逐漸變小的牙洞中的一塊堅硬的修復物。用黏固粉將其固定。合金是應用最廣的材料，另外，也使用瓷料和合成樹脂。

inlet *n.* an aperture providing the entrance to a cavity, such as that of the pelvis.

入口　進入某一洞腔的開口，如骨盆的開口。

innate *adj.* describing a condition or characteristic that is present in an individual at birth and is inherited from his parents. *See also* congenital.

先天的　描述生來就有的和由父母親遺傳而來的一種狀況或特徵。參閱 congenital。

inner ear *see* labyrinth.

內耳　參閱 labyrinth。

innervation *n.* the nerve supply to an area or organ of the body, which can carry either motor impulses to the structure or sensory impulses away from it towards the brain.

神經支配　身體某一區域或器官的神經分布，它既可以向該結構傳入運動衝動，也可以把感覺衝動從該結構傳向大腦。

innocent *adj.* (of a tumour) benign; not malignant.

良性的　（腫瘤）非惡性的。

innominate artery (brachiocephalic artery) a short artery originating as the first large branch of the *aortic arch, passing upwards to the right, and ending at the lower neck near the right sternoclavicular joint. Here it divides into the right common carotid and the right subclavian arteries.

無名動脈　起於主動脈弓第一大分支的一條短動脈，向右側上行，止於頸部下方右胸鎖關節附近。在此處分為右頸總動脈和鎖骨下動脈。

innominate bone *see* hip bone.

髂骨　參閱 hip bone。

innominate vein (brachiocephalic vein) either of two veins, one on each side of the neck, formed by the junction of the external jugular and subclavian

無名靜脈　分別位於頸部兩側的兩條靜脈，由頸外靜脈和鎖骨下靜脈匯合而成。這兩條靜脈匯成上腔靜脈。

veins. The two veins join to form the superior vena cava.

ino- *prefix denoting* **1.** fibrous tissue. **2.** muscle.

〔前綴〕**(1)** 纖維組織　**(2)** 肌肉

inoculation *n.* the introduction of a small quantity of material, such as a vaccine, in the process of *immunization: a more general name for *vaccination.

接種　免疫過程中，將少量物質，如疫苗注入體內；是 vaccination 的一個較為通用的名稱。

inoculum *n.* any material that is used for inoculation.

接種物　用於接種的任何物質。

inosine pranobex a drug that increases the efficiency of the immune system by increasing the number of T-lymphocytes and enhancing the activity of natural killer cells. Some early trials in HIV-positive people suggest that the drug could delay progression to AIDS. Trade name: **Imunovir**.

肌苷　通過增加 T-淋巴細胞數目和加強自然殺傷細胞的活性來增強免疫系統效率的一種藥物。在 HIV 陽性病人中進行的早期試驗表明：此藥能延緩艾滋病的進行。商品名：Imunovir

inositol *n.* a compound, similar to a hexose sugar, that is a constituent of some cell phospholipids. Inositol is present in many foods, in particular in the bran of cereal grain. It is sometimes classified as a vitamin but it can be synthesized by most animals and there is no evidence that it is an essential in humans.

肌醇　與己糖類似的一種化合物，是某些細胞磷脂的一種成分。肌醇存在於許多食物中，特別在穀糠中。它有時被分類為一種維生素，但可由多數動物合成，而且無證據表明它是人體的一種要素。

inositol triphosphate a short-lived biochemical *second messenger formed from *phospholipid in the cell membrane when a chemical messenger (e.g. a hormone or serotonin) binds to receptors on the cell surface. Inositol triphosphate triggers the rapid release of calcium into the cell fluid, which initiates various cellular processes, such as smooth muscle contraction and the release of glucose, histamine, etc. Inositol triphosphate exists for only a few

肌醇三磷酸鹽　一種化學信使（如激素或 5-羥色胺）與細胞表面受體結合時，細胞膜內的磷脂形成的一種存在時間短的生化第二信使。肌醇三磷酸鹽激發鈣迅速釋放到細胞液中，這又開始了多種細胞功能，如收縮平滑肌和釋放葡萄糖和組胺等。肌醇三磷酸鹽僅存在幾秒鐘，便通過一序列酶的作用，被轉化為肌醇。

seconds before being converted to inositol by the action of a sequence of enzymes.

inotropic *adj.* affecting the contraction of heart muscle. Drugs such as *digitalis, *dobutamine, and *enoximone have positive inotropic action, stimulating heart muscle contractions and causing the heart rate to increase. *Beta-blocker drugs, such as *propranolol, have negative inotropic action, reducing heart muscle contractions and causing the heart rate to decrease.

變力性的 影響心肌的收縮的。洋地黃，多巴酚丁胺和依諾昔酮等藥物都有正性變力作用，它們刺激心肌收縮，並且導致心率加快。β-受體阻滯劑類藥物，如普萘洛爾，有負性變力作用，它們減少心臟收縮，並且導致心率降低。

in-patient *n.* a patient who is admitted to a bed in a hospital ward and remains there for a period of time for treatment, examination, or observation. *Compare* out-patient.

住院病人 收住醫院病房某一床位，並且留住一段時間進行治療、檢查和觀察的病人。與 out-patient 對比。

inquest *n.* an official judicial enquiry into the cause of a person's death: carried out when the death is sudden or takes place under suspicious circumstances. The results of medical and legal investigations that have been carried out are considered by a *coroner, sitting with or without a jury, and made publicly known. *See also* autopsy.

驗屍 對某人死亡原因的官方司法性調查。當死亡突然或者發生在可疑的情況下時進行。醫學和法律調查的結果由驗屍官在有或沒有陪審團的情況下考慮，並且公布於眾。參閱 autopsy。

insanity *n.* a degree of mental illness such that the affected individual is not responsible for his actions or is not capable of entering into a legal contract. The term is a legal rather than a medical one.

精神病 某種程度的精神疾病，此病患者不對他的行為負責，並且不能訂立法律契約。此術語為法學術語，而非醫學術語。

insect *n.* a member of a large group of mainly land-dwelling *arthropods. The body of the adult is divided into a head, thorax, and abdomen. The head bears a single pair of sensory antennae; the thorax bears three pairs of legs and, in most insects, wings (these are

昆蟲 主要為陸生的一大類節肢動物。成蟲身體分為頭、胸和腹。頭部長有一對觸角；胸部長有三對足，多數昆蟲的胸部還有翅（一些寄生類則沒有，例如虱和蚤）。一些昆蟲在醫學上很重要。各種吸血性

absent in some parasitic groups, such as lice and fleas). Some insects are of medical importance. Various bloodsucking insects transmit tropical diseases, for example the female *Anopheles* mosquito transmits malaria and the tsetse fly transmits sleeping sickness. The bites of lice can cause intense irritation and, secondarily, bacterial infection. The organisms causing diarrhoea and dysentery can be conveyed to food on the bodies of flies. *See also* myiasis.

昆蟲傳播熱帶疾病，例如雌性按蚊傳播瘧疾，采采蠅傳播昏睡病。虱叮咬可引起強烈刺激作用，並且繼發細菌感染。能引起腹瀉和痢疾的微生物可通過蒼蠅身體被傳播到食物中。參閱 myiasis。

insecticide *n*. a preparation used to kill destructive or disease-carrying insects. Ideally, an insecticide should have no toxic effects when ingested by human beings or animals, but modern powerful compounds have inherent dangers and have caused fatalities. Some insect powders contain organic phosphorus compounds and fluorides; when ingested accidentally they may cause damage to the nervous system. The use of such compounds is generally under strict control. *See also* DDT, dieldrin.

殺昆蟲藥　用於殺死有害或帶病昆蟲的一種製劑。理想的殺蟲藥被人類或動物食入時，應該沒有毒作用，但是現代強有力的化合物有其固有的危險，而且曾引起死亡。一些殺昆蟲的藥粉含有有機磷化合物和氟化物類；如被誤食，可以導致神經系統的損傷。此類化合物的使用通常受到嚴格控制。參閱 DDT，dieldrin。

insemination *n*. introduction of semen into the vagina. *See also* artificial insemination, intrauterine insemination.

授精　使精子進入陰道　參閱 artificial insemination，intrauterine insemination。

insertion *n*. (in anatomy) the point of attachment of a muscle (e.g. to a bone) that is relatively movable when the muscle contracts. *Compare* origin.

附着　（解剖學）指肌肉的附着點（如：附着於骨），當肌肉收縮時，此點相對而言可以移動。與 origin 對比。

insight *n*. (in psychology) knowledge of oneself. The term is applied particularly to a patient's recognition that he has psychological problems; in this sense absence of insight is a feature of psychosis. The term is also applied to the patient's accuracy of understanding the development of his personality and

自知力　（心理學）指對自己的認識。此術語尤指患者認識到他自己有心理問題；在這個意義上，沒有自知力是精神病的一個特徵。此術語亦指病人對自己的個性發展和存在的問題的準確認識；在這個意義上，心理療法可以加強自知力。

his problems; in this sense insight is enhanced by psychotherapy.

insolation *n.* exposure to the sun's rays. *See also* heatstroke.

日射　暴露於太陽光綫下。參閱 heatstroke。

insomnia *n.* inability to fall asleep or to remain asleep for an adequate length of time, so that tiredness is virtually permanent. Insomnia may be associated with disease, particularly if there are painful symptoms, but is more often caused by worry.

失眠症　不能入睡或者不能保持足夠時間的睡眠，幾乎導致持久性疲勞。失眠可能與疾病有關，尤其當有疼痛的症狀時，但是，憂慮是失眠更常見的原因。

inspiration *n.* see inhalation.

吸氣　參閱 inhalation。

instillation *n.* **1.** the application of liquid medication drop by drop, as into the eye. **2.** the medication, such as eye drops, applied in this way.

(1) 滴注法　一滴一滴地使用液體藥物，如滴入眼中。**(2)** 滴劑　按此法應用的藥物，如滴眼劑。

instinct *n.* **1.** a complex pattern of behaviour innately determined, which is characteristic of all individuals of the same species. The behaviour is released and modified by environmental stimuli, but its pattern is relatively uniform and predetermined. **2.** an innate drive that urges the individual towards a particular goal (for example, *libido in psychoanalytic psychology).

本能　**(1)** 先天決定的複雜行為方式。它是同種所有個體的特徵。這種行為由環境刺激而表現出來；但它的方式相對而言是無變化的和事先確定的。**(2)** 推動個體達到某一特定目標的先天驅動力（例如，精神分析心理學中的性慾）。

institutionalization *n.* a condition produced by long-term residence in an unstimulating impersonal institution (such as some residential care homes and orphanages). The individual adapts to the behaviour characteristic of the institution to such an extent that he is handicapped in other environments. The features often include apathy, dependence, and a lack of personal responsibility. Some symptoms, such as *stereotypy, are commoner in the institutionalized.

收容所症　由於長期居住在一種沒有刺激，沒有人情味的機構中（例如某些收養所和孤兒院）引起的一種狀態。個體適應這種機構特有的行為，以致在其他環境中，他要發生障礙。其特徵常包括感情淡漠、依賴性，及缺乏自理能力。有些症狀，如刻板症，在收容者中更常見。

insufficiency *n.* inability of an organ or part, such as the heart or kidney, to carry out its normal function.

功能不全　一個器官或者部分，如心臟或者腎臟，不能行使其正常功能。

insufflation *n.* the act of blowing gas or a powder, such as a medication, into a body cavity.

吹入　把氣體或者粉末（例如一種藥物）吹入體腔的動作。

insula *n.* an area of the *cerebral cortex that is overlapped by the sides of the deep lateral sulcus (cleft) in each hemisphere.

腦島　大腦皮質的一個區域。它被兩側大腦半球外側裂的深面邊緣所覆蓋。

insulin *n.* a protein hormone, produced in the pancreas by the beta cells of the *islets of Langerhans, that is important for regulating the amount of sugar (glucose) in the blood. Insulin secretion is stimulated by a high concentration of blood sugar. Lack of this hormone gives rise to *diabetes mellitus, in which large amounts of sugar are present in the blood and urine. This condition may be treated successfully by insulin injections.

胰島素　一種蛋白質激素，它在胰腺內由朗格漢斯島的 β 細胞產生。它對於調節血中糖（葡萄糖）量很重要。血糖的高濃度刺激胰島素的分泌。這種激素的缺乏導致糖尿病：血和尿中出現大量糖。這種疾病可通過注射胰島素而成功治療。

insulinase *n.* an enzyme, found in such tissues as the liver and kidney, that is responsible for the normal breakdown of insulin in the body.

胰島素酶　一種見於肝、腎組織的酶，它負責體內胰島素的正常分解。

insulinoma *n.* an insulin-producing tumour of the beta cells in the *islets of Langerhans of the pancreas. Symptoms can include sweating, faintness, episodic loss of consciousness, and other features of *hypoglycaemia (*see* Whipple's triad). Single tumours can be removed surgically. Multiple very small tumours scattered throughout the pancreas cannot be treated by surgery but do respond to drugs that poison the beta cells, including *diazoxide.

胰島素瘤　一種產生胰島素的胰腺朗格漢斯島內β細胞瘤。症狀可以包括出汗、暈厥、陣發性神志喪失，以及血糖過少的其他症狀（參閱 Whipple's triad）。單個腫瘤可手術摘除；散布於整個胰腺的多個小腫瘤不能用手術治療，而用破壞β細胞的藥物，包括二氮嗪很有效果。

Intal *n. see* cromolyn sodium.

色甘酸鈉　參閱 cromolyn sodium。

integration *n.* the blending together of the *nerve impulses that arrive through the thousands of synapses at a nerve cell body. Impulses from some synapses cause *excitation, and from others *inhibition; the overall pattern decides whether an individual nerve cell is activated to transmit a message or not.

整合作用 把通過上千個突觸到達一個神經細胞體的神經衝動混合在一起。從一些突觸傳來的衝動引起興奮，從另一些突觸傳來的衝動引起抑制。總的方式決定該神經細胞是否被激活而傳遞某個信息。

integument *n.* **1.** the skin. **2.** a membrane or layer of tissue covering any organ of the body.

(1) 皮膚。**(2)** 包膜 覆蓋身體某個器官的一層黏膜或者組織。

intelligence quotient (IQ) an index of intellectual development. In childhood and adult life it represents intellectual ability relative to the rest of the population; in children it can also represent rate of development (*mental age as a percentage of chronological age). Most *intelligence tests are constructed so that the resulting intelligence quotients in the general population have a *mean of about 100 and a *standard deviation of about 15.

智商 一種智力發育情況的指標。在兒童及成人，它表示相對於人羣中其他人的智力能力；在兒童，它還表示發育的速度（智力年齡，為實足年齡的百分數）。多數智力測驗設計時使所得的一般人羣的平均智商數約為 100，標準差約為 15。

intelligence test a standardized assessment procedure for the determination of intellectual ability. The score produced is usually expressed as an *intelligence quotient. Most tests present a series of different kinds of problems to be solved. The best known are the Wechsler Adult Intelligence Scale (WAIS), the Wechsler Intelligence Scale for Children (WISC), and the Stanford Binet Intelligence Scale. Scores on intelligence tests are used for such purposes as the diagnosis of *mental retardation and the assessment of intellectual deterioration.

智力測驗 用於測定智力的一個標準化評估方法。所得的分值通常表示為智商。多數測驗提出一系列不同類型需要解決的問題。最著名的有韋克斯勒成人智力量表，韋克斯勒兒童智力量表以及斯比氏智能測驗表。智力測驗的得分被用於診斷智力發育低下以及評估智力退化。

intensive therapy unit (ITU) a hospital unit designed to give intensive care, provided by specialist multidisciplinary staff,

特療病房 一種專門設計的醫院病房。由多學科專家向所選擇的病情嚴重的病人或者需要

to a selected group of seriously ill patients or to those in need of special postoperative techniques (e.g. heart or chest patients).

特殊術後技術的病人提供精心治療（如心臟或胸部病人）。

intention *n.* a process of healing. Healing by *first intention* is the natural healing of a wound or surgical incision when the edges are brought together under aseptic conditions and *granulation tissue forms. In healing by *second intention* the wound edges are separated and the cavity is filled with granulation tissue over which epithelial tissue grows from the wound edges. In healing by *third intention* the wound ulcerates, granulations are slow to form, and a scar forms at the wound site.

愈合　傷口長好的過程。一期愈合指傷口或者手術切口自然長好，這時，創緣在無菌狀態中合攏在一起，並有肉芽組織形成。二期愈合時，創緣分開，其間腔隙長滿肉芽組織而肉芽組織上方是從創面長出的上皮組織。三期愈合時傷口發生潰瘍，肉芽組織形成緩慢，同時，傷口位置形成瘢痕。

intention tremor *see* tremor.

意向震顫　參閱 tremor。

inter- *prefix denoting* between. Examples: *intercostal* (between the ribs); *intertrochanteric* (between the trochanters).

〔前綴〕在……之間的　例如：肋間的（在肋骨之間的），轉子間的（在轉子之間的）。

intercalated *adj.* describing structures, tissues, etc., that are inserted or situated between other structures.

插入的　描述被插入或者位於其他結構之間的結構和組織等。

intercellular *adj.* situated or occurring between cells.

細胞間的　位於或者發生於細胞之間的。

intercostal muscles muscles that occupy the spaces between the ribs and are responsible for controlling some of the movements of the ribs. The superficial *external intercostals* lift the ribs during inspiration; the deep *internal intercostals* draw the ribs together during expiration.

肋間肌　占據兩肋之間的空間並且負責支配肋骨的一些活動的肌肉。吸氣時，表淺的肋間外肌抬起肋骨；呼氣時，深部的肋間內肌拉攏肋骨。

intercurrent *adj.* going on at the same time: applied to an infection contracted by a patient who is already suffering from an infection or other disease.

間發的　同時進行的：指已感染或者已患某種疾病的病人又傳染上另一種感染。

interferon *n.* a substance that is produced by cells infected with a virus and has the ability to inhibit viral growth. Interferon is active against many different viruses, but particular interferons are effective only in the species that produces them. There are three types of human interferon; *alpha* (from white blood cells), *beta* (from fibroblasts), and *gamma* (from lymphocytes). Human interferon can now be produced in bacterial host cells by *genetic engineering for clinical use in treating hepatitis B and C, and certain forms of cancer, and multiple sclerosis.

干擾素　由被病毒感染的細胞產生的一種物質，它能抑制病毒生長。干擾素對於許多不同的病毒都有效，但是，特殊的干擾素只對產生它們的那種病毒有效。人類干擾素有三種：α（來於白細胞），β（來於成纖維細胞）和 γ（來於淋巴細胞）。現在，人們可通過基因工程，在細菌宿主的細胞中產生人類干擾素，臨床用於治療乙型肝炎、丙型肝炎、某些類型的癌症和多發性硬化症。

interkinesis *n.* **1.** the resting stage between the two divisions of *meiosis. **2.** *see* interphase.

分裂間期　**(1)** 兩期減數分裂之間的靜止期。**(2)** 參閱 interphase。

interleukin *n.* any of a family of proteins that control some aspects of haemopoiesis and the immune response. Twelve interleukins are currently characterized; *interleukin* 2 (IL-2) stimulates T-lymphocytes and is being investigated for the treatment of cancer (*see* aldesleukin).

白細胞介素　控制血細胞生成和免疫應答的某些方面的一組蛋白質。目前已鑒別出 12 種白細胞介素，白細胞介素 2(IL-2) 刺激 T 淋巴細胞，因此，目前正研究它對癌症的治療作用（參閱 aldesleukin）。

intermittent claudication *see* claudication.

間歇性跛行　參閱 claudication。

intermittent fever a fever that rises, subsides, then returns again. *See* malaria.

間歇熱　升高、減退、又回升的一種熱型。參閱 malaria。

intermittent self-catheterization (ISC) a procedure in which the patient periodically passes a disposable catheter through the urethra into the bladder for the purpose of emptying it of urine. It is increasingly used in the management of patients of both sexes (including children) with chronic *retention and large residual urine volumes, often due to *neuropathic bladder. ISC may prevent

間歇性自我導管插入　病人周期性地把一次性導管經尿道插入膀胱排空其中尿液的一種方法。它愈來愈多地用於男女兩性（包括兒童）患有因神經病性膀胱所致慢性尿瀦留和殘餘尿量大的病人的護理。可以預防背部壓力和輸尿管上部擴張，以及隨之發生的感染和尿失禁。

back pressure and dilatation of the upper urinary tract with consequent infection and incontinence.

intern *n. see* Doctor.

實習醫生　參閱 Doctor。

International Classification of Diseases (ICD) a list of all known diseases and syndromes published by the *World Health Organization every ten years (approximately). Diseases are grouped either according to system (e.g. cardiovascular, respiratory) or type (e.g. malignant growths, accidents); each is allocated a three-digit number for computerization and hence comparison of mortality and morbidity rates, both regionally and nationally. Agreed simplified groupings exist, and some rubrics are subdivided by the use of a fourth digit. A parallel list, the *International Classification of Impairments, Disabilities and Handicaps* (*ICIDH*), has also been compiled and is being used experimentally. *See also* handicap.

國際疾病分類　所有已知疾病和綜合症的一個目錄，由世界衛生組織（大約）每 10 年出版一次。疾病根據系統（如心血管和呼吸）或者類型（如惡性腫瘤和事故）分類。每一類給予一個三位數字，用於計算機管理，借此，可以比較地區和全國的死亡率與患病率。公認的簡化分類法在使用，同時，第四位數的使用使某些目錄產生分類。人們還編纂了一個相同的目錄《國際損傷、傷殘和殘疾分類》並正在試用中。參閱 handicap。

interneurone *n.* a neurone in the central nervous system that acts as a link between the different neurones in a *reflex arc. It usually possesses numerous branching processes (dendrites) that make possible extensive and complex circuits and pathways within the brain and spinal cord.

中間神經元　中樞神經系統中，在反射弧上連接不同神經元的神經元。它通常具有許多分支樣突起（樹突），這使得大腦和脊髓內有可能形成廣泛而複雜的環路和通路。

internode *n.* the length of *axon covered with a myelin sheath. Internodes are separated by nodes of Ranvier, where the sheath is absent.

結間隙　被覆髓鞘的一段軸索。結間隙被郎維埃結分隔，而郎維埃結區沒有髓鞘。

interobserver error (in statistical surveys) *see* validity.

觀察者之間誤差　用於統計學調查。參閱 validity。

interoceptor *n.* any *receptor organ composed of sensory nerve cells that

內感受器　由對體內變化（如肌肉的伸展或血的酸度）作出

respond to and monitor changes within the body, such as the stretching of muscles or the acidity of the blood.

反應，並監控此變化的感覺神經細胞組成的任何感受器官。

interparietal bone (inca bone, incarial bone) the bone lying between the *parietal bones, at the back of the skull.

頂間骨　位於顱骨後部，兩頂骨間的骨。

interpeduncular *adj.* situated between the peduncles of the cerebrum or cerebellum.

腦腳間的　位於大腦腳或小腦腳間的。

interphase (interkinesis) *n.* the period when a cell is not undergoing division (mitosis), during which activities such as DNA synthesis occur.

分裂間期　細胞不進行分裂（有絲分裂）的時期，此間，發生 DNA 合成等活動。

intersex *n.* an individual who shows anatomical characteristics of both sexes. *See* hermaphrodite, pseudohermaphroditism. **–intersexuality** *n.*

雌雄間體　表現出兩性解剖特點的個體。參閱 hermaphrodite，pseudohermaphroditism。

interstice *n.* a small space in a tissue or between parts of the body. **–interstitital** *adj.*

小間隙　位於組織內或者身體兩部位間的小間隙。

interstitial cells (Leydig cells) the cells interspersed between the seminiferous tubules of the *testis. They secrete *androgens in response to stimulation by *luteinizing hormone from the anterior pituitary gland.

間質細胞　散在於睪丸內的生精小管間的細胞。它們在垂體前葉分泌的黃體激素刺激下，分泌雄性激素。

interstitial-cell-stimulating hormone *see* luteinizing hormone.

促間質細胞激素　參閱 luteinizing hormone。

interstitial cystitis a chronic non-bacterial inflammation of the bladder accompanied by an urgent desire to pass urine frequently and bladder pain; it is usually associated with an ulcer in the bladder wall (*Hünner's ulcer*). The cause is unknown and *contracture of the bladder eventually occurs. Treatment is by *balloon distension of the bladder

間質性膀胱炎　膀胱的慢性非細菌性炎症，伴隨頻繁的急迫的尿欲和膀胱痛。它通常與膀胱壁上的潰瘍（亨納潰瘍）有關。病因不明，但最終發生膀胱攣縮。治療包括在脊髓或硬膜下麻醉下，氣囊擴張膀胱，膀胱內滴注抗炎溶液，以及給予類固醇和非甾類抗炎藥。對

under spinal or epidural anaesthetic, instillation of anti-inflammatory solutions into the bladder, and administration of steroids or *NSAIDs. Bladder enhancement or augmentation (*see* cystoplasty) may be required for a contracted bladder.

於狹小的膀胱，可能需要做膀胱擴大術（參閱 cystoplasty）。

intertrigo *n.* superficial inflammation of two skin surfaces that are in contact, such as between the thighs or under the breasts, particularly in obese people. It is caused by friction and sweat and is often aggravated by infection, especially with *Candida*.

擦爛 兩個互相接觸的皮膚表面的淺表炎症，如兩個大腿間或者乳房下面，尤其見於肥胖的人。它是由於摩擦和汗液造成的，常因感染而加重，特別是念珠菌屬感染。

interventional radiology an application of radiology whereby therapeutic or diagnostic procedures can be performed under direct radiological vision. It is used in many forms of *minimally invasive surgery, including *coronary angioplasty, visualization of obstructions in the bile ducts (*see* (percutaneous) cholangiography), and the removal of kidney stones (*see* percutaneous nephrolithotomy).

介入性放射學 放射學的一種應用方法；借此，治療和診斷過程都可直接在放射視野中進行。它被用於許多形式的最小侵入性手術中，包括冠狀血管成形術，膽管內阻塞造影術，（參閱 (percutaneous) cholangiography）以及腎結石切除術（參閱 percutaneous nephrolithotomy）。

intervention study a comparison of the outcome between two or more groups of patients that are deliberately subjected to different regimes (usually of treatment but sometimes of a preventive measure, such as vaccination). Wherever possible those entering the trial should be allocated to their respective groups by means of random numbers, and one such group (*controls*) should have no active treatment (*randomized controlled trial*). Ideally neither the patient nor the person assessing the outcome should be aware of which therapy is allocated to which patient (*blind trial*), nor should the doctor responsible for treatment (*double-blind trial*), and the groups

防治實驗研究 有意讓兩組或更多組病人接受不同的方案（通常為治療方案，但有時是預防方案，如接種），然後比較各組的結果。應盡可能通過隨機數字將參與實驗者分配到不同的組中，而且，其中有一組（對照組）不接受有效的治療（隨機對照試驗）。最好是病人及實驗結果評估者都不知道治療給予了哪些病人（單盲試驗），而負責治療的醫生也不知道（雙盲試驗），同時，預定的時間後，各組應交換治療（交叉試驗）。

should exchange treatment after a pre-arranged period (*cross-over trial*).

intervertebral disc the flexible plate of fibrocartilage that connects any two adjacent vertebrae in the backbone. At birth the central part of the disc – the *nucleus pulposus* – consists of a gelatinous substance, which becomes replaced by cartilage with age. The intervertebral discs account for one quarter of the total length of the backbone; they act as shock absorbers, protecting the brain and spinal cord from the impact produced by running and other movements. *See also* prolapsed intervertebral disc.

椎間盤 在脊柱內連接任何兩個相鄰椎骨的柔韌的纖維軟骨盤。出生時，盤的中央部分——髓核——由膠狀物質組成；隨着年齡的增加，它逐漸由軟骨所代替。椎間盤占脊柱總長度的四分之一；它們起緩衝器的作用，保護大腦和脊髓不受跑步和其他活動所引起的衝擊。參閱 prolapsed intervertebral disc。

intestinal flora bacteria normally present in the intestinal tract. Some are responsible for the synthesis of *vitamin K. By producing a highly acidic environment in the intestine they may also prevent infection by pathogenic bacteria that cannot tolerate such conditions.

腸內菌群 腸道內正常存在的細菌。一些能合成維生素 K。同時，它們在腸內產生一個酸性極高的環境，從而可以防止不能耐受這種條件的病原菌的感染。

intestinal juice *see* succus entericus.

腸液 參閱 succus entericus。

intestinal obstruction blockage of the intestines producing symptoms of vomiting, distension, and abdominal pain; failure to pass flatus or faeces (complete constipation) is usual. The causes may be acute (e.g. hernia) or chronic (e.g. tumours, Crohn's disease). Conservative management is by nasogastric suction ('suck') and replacement of water and electrolytes ('drip'), but most cases require surgical cure by removing the underlying cause.

腸梗阻 腸道阻塞，產生嘔吐、腹脹和腹痛症狀。同時，不能排氣或排便（完全性便秘）也很常見。病因可以是急性（如疝氣）或者慢性的（如腫瘤，克羅恩病）。保守處理是採用鼻胃抽吸，同時補充水和電解質（滴注），但是多數病例需要手術治療來排除潛在的病因。

intestine (bowel, gut) *n.* the part of the *alimentary canal that extends from the stomach to the anus. It is divided into two main parts – the small intestine and the large intestine. The *small intestine* is divided into the *duodenum, *jejunum,

腸 從胃延伸至肛門的一部分消化道。它被分為兩個主要部分——小腸和大腸。小腸被分為十二指腸、空腸和迴腸。消化吸收過程大部分發生在小腸。被稱作絨毛（見圖）的指

and *ileum. It is here that most of the processes of digestion and absorption of food taken place. The surface area of the inside of the small intestine is increased by the presence of finger-like projections called *villi* (see illustration). Glands in the mucous layer of the intestine secrete digestive enzymes and mucus. The *large intestine* consists of the *caecum, vermiform *appendix, *colon, and *rectum. It is largely concerned with the absorption of water from the material passed from the small intestine. The contents of the intestines are propelled forwards by means of rhythmic muscular contractions (*see* peristalsis). **–intestinal** *adj.*

狀突起的存在使小腸內表面積增加。位於小腸黏膜層的腺體分泌消化酶和黏液。大腸由盲腸、闌尾、結腸和直腸組成，主要與從來自於小腸的物質中吸收水分有關。腸道內容物通過有節律的肌肉收縮（參閱 peristalsis）被推向前進。

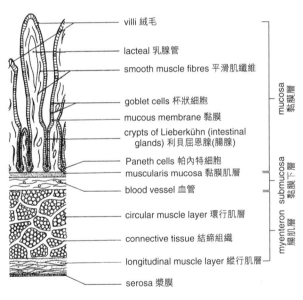

Longitudinal section through the ileum
迴腸縱切面

intima (tunica intima) *n.* **1.** the inner layer of the wall of an *artery or *vein. It is composed of a lining of endothelial cells and an elastic membrane. **2.** the

內膜 （1）動脈或靜脈壁的內層。它由一層內皮細胞和一層彈性膜組成。（2）其他多種器官或部位的內膜。

inner layer of various other organs or parts.

intolerance *n.* the inability of a patient to tolerate a particular drug, manifested by various adverse reaction.

不耐性　病人不能耐受某種藥物，通過多種副反應表現出來。

intoxication *n.* the symptoms of poisoning due to ingestion of any toxic material, including alcohol and heavy metals.

中毒　攝入任何有毒物質，包括酒精和重金屬而引起的中毒症狀。

intra- *prefix denoting* inside; within. Examples: *intralobular* (within a lobule); *intrauterine* (within the uterus).

〔前綴〕**內的、裏的**　例如：小葉內的、子宮內的。

intracellular *adj.* situated or occurring inside a cell or cells.

細胞內的　位於或者發生於一個或多個細胞內的。

intracranial *adj.* within the skull.

顱內的　在頭顱內的。

intradermal *adj.* within the skin. An *intradermal injection* is made into the skin.

皮內的　在皮膚內的。皮內注射即在皮膚內注射。

intramuscular *adj.* within a muscle. An *intramuscular injection* is made into a muscle.

肌內的　在肌肉內的。肌內注射即在肌肉內注射。

intraobserver error (in statistical surveys) *see* validity.

觀察者誤差　用於統計學調查中。參閱 validity。

intraocular *adj.* of or relating to the area within the eyeball.

眼內的　眼球內部的區域的或者與此區域有關的。

intrastromal keratomileusis an operation undergoing trials for its ability to correct severe degrees of myopia (shortsightedness) that cannot normally be treated by other surgical techniques (e.g. *radial keratotomy). A disc of corneal tissue (from the *stroma of the cornea) is removed, frozen, and remodelled on a lathe, then replaced into the cornea to alter its curvature and thus reduce the myopia. *Excimer laser treatment, which

基質內角膜成形術　一種正在嘗試中的手術，用於矯正不能通過其他手術方法（如放射性角膜切開術）正常治療的高度近視。（從角膜基質）取下一個盤狀角膜組織，冷凍並且在車床上使其重新成形，然後將其放回角膜，從而改變角膜的屈度，由此減輕近視。激態原子激光術治療目前也被用於治療高度近視，此法較易操作。

is easier to perform, is also now being used for treating severe myopia.

intrathecal *adj.* **1.** within the *meninges of the spinal cord. An *intrathecal injection* is made into the meninges. **2.** within a sheath, e.g. a nerve sheath.

鞘內的 **(1)** 在脊髓膜內的。鞘內注射即在脊髓膜內的注射。**(2)** 在鞘內的，如在神經鞘內。

intrauterine contraceptive device *see* IUCD.

宮內避孕器 參閱 IUCD。

intrauterine growth retardation (IUGR) the condition resulting in the birth of a baby with a weight on or below the 10th centile (*see* centile chart) predicted for gestational age (i.e. *small for dates*; *SFD*). Causes include maternal disease (e.g. infection, malnutrition, high blood pressure, smoking, and alcoholism), poor socioeconomic conditions, multiple pregnancy (e.g. twins), and fetal disease. It may be associated with *preterm birth.

宮內發育遲緩 嬰兒出生時體重等於或低於按妊娠年齡所預測的第十百分位數（參閱 centile chart）（即低體重嬰兒）。其原因包括母親患病（如感染、營養不良、高血壓、吸煙和酗酒）、社會經濟狀況低下、多胎妊娠（如雙胞胎）以及胎兒患病。它可以與早產有關。

intrauterine insemination (IUI) a procedure for assisting conception in cases of male infertility caused by inability of the spermatozoa to penetrate the cervical mucus or the barriers surrounding the ovum. The spermatozoa, which may be chemically treated in vitro to improve their motility and *acrosome reaction, are injected into the uterus through the vagina.

宮內授精 一種人工授精方法，用於精子不能穿破子宮頸黏膜或者卵巢周圍屏障所造成的男性不孕症。精子可以在試管中處理以增加其活性及頂體反應，然後經陰道被注入子宮。

intravenous *adj.* into or within a vein. *See* infusion, injection.

靜脈內的 進入靜脈的或在靜脈內的。參閱 infusion，injection。

intravenous feeding *see* nutrition.

靜脈飼養 參閱 nutrition。

intravenous pyelogram (IVP) a succession of X-ray films of the urinary tract following the injection into a vein of an iodine-containing substance (which is

靜脈腎盂造影片 靜脈注射一種含碘物質（它不透 X 綫）後所拍攝的泌尿道 X 綫連續片。這種物質由腎濃縮和排泄。靜

opaque to X-rays). This material is concentrated and excreted by the kidneys, and the IVP reveals details of the kidneys, the ureters, and subsequently the bladder. An IVP tests kidney function and reveals the presence of stones in the kidneys or ureters and other abnormalities of the urinary tract. *See also* pyelography.

脈腎盂造影片顯示出腎、輸尿管以及膀胱的詳細情況。它能檢測腎功能，顯示腎或者輸尿管中存在的結石及其他泌尿道異常。參閱 pyelography。

intraversion *n. see* introversion.

內向　參閱 introversion。

intra vitam Latin: during life.

生活期間　拉丁語。

intrinsic factor a glycoprotein secreted in the stomach. The secretion of intrinsic factor is necessary for the absorption of *vitamin B_{12}; a failure of secretion of intrinsic factor leads to a deficiency of the vitamin and the condition of *pernicious anaemia.

內因子　胃分泌的一種糖蛋白。內因子的分泌是吸收維生素 B_{12} 所必需的；因此，內因子分泌缺乏導致維生素 B_{12} 缺乏和惡性貧血。

intrinsic muscle a muscle that is contained entirely within the organ or part it acts on. For example, there are intrinsic muscles of the tongue, whose contractions change the shape of the tongue.

內附肌　完全被包圍在它所作用的器官或部分內的一塊肌肉。例如：舌內附肌的收縮改變舌的形狀。

intro- *prefix denoting* in; into.

〔前綴〕在……內，進到……裏

introitus *n.* (in anatomy) an entrance into a hollow organ or cavity.

入口　（解剖學）指一空腔或空洞器官的開口。

introjection *n.* (in psychoanalysis) the process of adopting, or of believing that one possesses, the qualities of another person. This can be a form of *defence mechanism. *See also* identification.

內向投射　（精神分析）指某人相信自己具有或接納他人品質的過程。這可以是一種形式的防禦機制。參閱 identification。

intromission *n.* the introduction of one organ or part into another, e.g. the penis into the vagina.

插入　某一器官或其一部分進入另一器官或其部分，如陰莖插入陰道。

introversion *n.* **1.** (*or* **intraversion**) an enduring personality trait characterized

(1) 內向　一種持續的個性特徵，其特點是對自我感興趣，

by interest in the self rather than the outside world. People high in introversion (*introverts*), as measured by questionnaires and psychological tests, tend to have a small circle of friends, like to persist in activities once they have started, and are highly susceptible to permanent *conditioning. Introversion was first described by Carl Jung as a tendency to distancing oneself from others, to philosophical interests, and to reserved defensive reactions. *Compare* extroversion. **2.** a turning inwards of a hollow organ (such as the uterus) on itself.

對外部世界無興趣。由問卷和心理測驗檢測出的高度內向性的人（內向者），他們一般朋友少，一旦開始做某事，喜歡持續下去以及高度因循守舊。卡爾·榮格首次把內向描述成一種與他人疏遠、喜歡哲學以及緘默的防禦反應性格傾向。與 extroversion 對比。**(2) 內翻** 空腔器官向內翻轉（如子宮）。

introvert *n. see* introversion.

內向者 參閱 introversion。

intubation *n.* the introduction of a tube into part of the body for the purpose of diagnosis or treatment. Thus *gastric intubation* may be performed to remove a sample of the stomach contents for analysis or to administer drugs directly into the stomach.

插管法 為診斷或者治療而把一個管子導入身體某部分。當需取出胃內容物標本作分析，或者直接向胃內用藥，可行胃插管。

intumescence *n.* a swelling or an increase in the volume of an organ.

腫大 某一器官的體積腫脹變大。

intussusception *n.* the telescoping (*invagination*) of one part of the bowel into another; most common in young children under the age of four. As the contents of the intestine are pushed onwards by muscular contraction more and more intestine is dragged into the invaginating portion, resulting in obstruction. Symptoms include intermittent colic or pain, vomiting, and the passing of red jelly with the stools; if the condition does not receive prompt surgical treatment, shock from gangrene of the bowel may result. A barium or Gastrografin enema may confirm the diagnosis and in many cases may relieve the intussusception.

腸套疊 腸的一部分套入另一部分中：最常發生於四歲以下幼兒。由於肌肉收縮，腸內容物被向前推進，愈來愈多的腸被拉入套疊部分，引起梗阻。症狀包括間歇性絞痛或疼痛，隨糞便排出紅色膠狀物；如果沒有及時給予手術治療，可因腸壞死造成休克。鋇或者泛影葡胺灌腸可明確診斷，同時，對許多病人還可緩解套疊。

inulin *n.* a carbohydrate with a high molecular weight, used in a test of kidney function called *inulin clearance*. Inulin is filtered from the bloodstream by the kidneys. By injecting it into the blood and measuring the amount that appears in the urine over a given period, it is possible to calculate how much filtrate the kidneys are producing in a given time.

菊粉 一種高分子量碳水化合物，用於一種稱作菊粉擴清率的腎功能檢測。菊粉由腎臟從血流中濾出。通過把菊粉注射入血液並且測量一定時間後尿中出現的菊粉量，可計算出在該時間內腎臟產生的濾出液量。

inunction *n.* the rubbing in with the fingers of an ointment or liniment.

塗擦法 用手指塗擦軟膏或擦劑。

invagination *n.* **1.** the infolding of the wall of a solid structure to form a cavity. This occurs in some stages of the development of embryos. **2.** *see* intussusception.

(1) 凹入 實心結構的壁凹入形成一個空腔。這發生於胚胎發育的某些階段。**(2) 腸套疊** 參閱 intussusception。

invalidity benefit *see* sickness benefit.

病廢救濟金 參閱 sickness benefit。

invasion *n.* the spread of *cancer into neighbouring normal structures; it is one of the cardinal features of malignancy.

侵襲，侵入 癌症擴散到其周圍的正常結構中，這是惡性腫瘤的主要症狀之一。

inversion *n.* **1.** the turning inwards or inside-out of a part or organ: commonly applied to the state of the uterus after childbirth when its upper part is pulled through the cervical canal. **2.** a chromosome mutation in which a block of genes within a chromosome are in reverse order, due to that section of the chromosome becoming inverted. The centromere may be included in the inverted segment (*pericentric inversion*) or not (*paracentric inversion*).

(1) 內翻 某器官或者某部分向內翻轉或者由內向外翻出：常指分娩後子宮上部通過宮頸管被拉出的狀態。**(2) 倒位** 一種染色體突變。指一條染色體內的一組基因順序顛倒，這是由於該段染色體倒轉所致。著絲粒可包括在倒轉段內（臂間倒位）或不包括在內（臂內倒位）。

invertebrate 1. *n.* an animal without a backbone. The following are invertebrate groups of medical importance: *insects, *ticks, *nematodes, *flukes, *protozoans, and *tapeworms. **2.** *adj.* not possessing a backbone.

(1) 無脊椎動物 沒有脊柱的動物。下面是幾種醫學上重要的無脊椎動物：昆蟲類、蜱類、綫蟲類、吸蟲類、原蟲類和絛蟲類。**(2) 無脊椎的** 沒有脊柱的。

in vitro Latin: describing biological phenomena that are made to occur outside the living body (traditionally in a test-tube).

in vitro fertilization (IVF) fertilization of an ovum outside the body, the resultant *zygote being incubated to the *blastocyst stage and then implanted in the uterus. The technique, pioneered in Britain, resulted in 1978 in the birth or the first *test-tube baby*. IVF is employed when a woman has blocked Fallopian tubes or some other impediment to the union of sperm and ovum in the reproductive tract. The mother-to-be is given hormone therapy causing a number of ova to mature at the same time (*see* superovulation). Several of them are then removed from the ovary through a laparoscope. The ova are mixed with spermatozoa from her partner and incubated in a culture medium until the blastocyst is formed. The blastocyst is then implanted in the mother's uterus and the pregnancy allowed to continue normally.

in vivo Latin: describing biological phenomena that occur or are observed occurring within the bodies of living organisms.

involucrum *n.* a growth of new bone, formed from the *periosteum, that sometimes surrounds a mass of infected and dead bone in osteomyelitis.

involuntary muscle muscle that is not under conscious control, such as the muscle of the gut, stomach, blood vessels, and heart. *See also* cardiac muscle, smooth muscle.

involution *n.* **1.** the shrinking of the womb to its normal size after childbirth. **2.** atrophy of an organ in old age.

在活體外 拉丁語：描述在活體外促使發生的生物現象（傳統上在試管內）。

試管內授精 卵子體外受精後，將所產生的受精卵孵育至囊胚期，然後將其植入子宮。這項技術在英國首先被利用並且於 1978 年，導致了第一例試管嬰兒的誕生。如果婦女患輸卵管阻塞或者其他疾病妨礙精子和卵子在生殖道內結合時，採用試管內授精。對未來的母親給予激素療法，使多個卵子同時成熟（參閱 super-ovulation）。然後，通過腹腔鏡取出幾個卵子。將卵子與來源於配偶的精子混合，並且在培養基內孵育，直到形成囊胚。然後，將囊胚植入母親的子宮，妊娠得以正常繼續。

在活體內 拉丁語：描述在活的生物體內發生或者被觀察到正在發生的生物現象。

包殼 新骨的生長。由骨膜形成。在骨髓炎中，有時包圍受感染和壞死的骨塊。

不隨意肌 不受意識控制的肌肉，如腸、胃、血管以及心臟的肌肉。參閱 cardiac muscle，smooth muscle。

(1) 復舊 產後子宮收縮到其正常大小。**(2) 退化** 年老時某一器官的萎縮。

involutional melancholia a severe *depression, usually psychotic, appearing for the first time in the involutional period of middle life (approximately 40–55 for women, 50–65 for men). Such an illness classically has characteristic features, including agitation; delusions of ill-health, poverty, sin, and sometimes of the nonexistence of the world; and preoccupations with death and loss. However, the features are not always classical, and many authorities do not regard the condition as a clinical entity separate from depressive psychosis. *See* manic-depressive psychosis.

更年期憂鬱症　一種嚴重的抑鬱症，通常是精神病性的。首發於中年的更年期（女性約為45~55歲，男性約為50~65歲）。典型的更年期憂鬱症的特點包括：焦慮不安；有關不健康、貧窮、犯罪和有時關於虛無世界的幻想；有關死亡和損失的偏執想法。但是，這些特徵往往並不典型，而且許多專家認為這不是一種可從抑鬱型精神病獨立出來的臨床病種。參閱　manic-depressive psychosis。

iodine *n.* an element required in small amounts for healthy growth and development. An adult body contains about 30 mg of iodine, mostly concentrated in the thyroid gland: this gland requires iodine to synthesize *thyroid hormones. A deficiency of iodine leads to *goitre. The daily requirement of iodine in an adult is thought to be about 150 μg per day; dietary sources of iodine are sea food and vegetables grown in soil containing iodide and also iodized table salt. Radioactive isotopes of iodine (usually iodine-131), which are *radiopaque, are used in the diagnosis and treatment of diseases of the thyroid gland. Iodine is also used as an antiseptic. Symbol: I.

碘　健康成長和發育少量需要的一種元素。成人體內含碘約30 mg，大部分集中在甲狀腺內：甲狀腺需要碘以合成甲狀腺激素。碘缺乏導致甲狀腺腫。據認為：成人每日需碘量是150 μg；碘的食物來源是海產品和含碘土壤上生長的蔬菜，以及加碘的食鹽。碘的放射性同位素（通常為[131]碘）是不透 X 綫的，因而用於診斷和治療甲狀腺疾病。碘也用作抗菌劑。化學符號：I。

iodipamide *n.* a *radiopaque iodine-containing compound used as a *contrast medium in radiography.

膽影酸　一種不透 X 綫的含碘化合物，用作放射造影術中的一種造影劑。

iodism *n.* iodine poisoning. The main features are a characteristic staining of the mouth and odour on the breath. Vomited material may be yellowish or bluish. There is pain and burning in the throat, intense thirst, and diarrhoea, with

碘中毒　碘中毒的主要特徵為口腔中典型的着色和呼吸氣味。嘔吐物可能為淺黃或淺藍色。喉部有疼痛燒灼感，有劇渴和腹瀉，並伴有頭暈、虛弱和驚厥。緊急處理包括服用溶

dizziness, weakness, and convulsions. Emergency treatment includes administration of starch or flour in water and lavage with sodium thiosulphate solution.

於水的澱粉或麪粉和用硫代硫酸鈉溶液灌洗。

iontophoresis *n.* the technique of introducing through the skin, by means of an electric current, charged particles of a drug, so that it reaches a deep site. The method has been used to transfer salicylate ions through the skin in the treatment of deep rheumatic pain. *See also* cataphoresis.

離子透入療法 用電流經過皮膚導入帶電荷的藥物離子使之達到深層部位的一種技術。在治療深部風濕痛時，此法已被用於經皮膚透入水楊酸鹽離子。參閱 cataphoresis。

iopanoic acid *n.* a *radiopaque iodine-containing compound used in radiography to outline the gall bladder (*see* cholecystography). Given by intravenous injection, the iopanoic acid is concentrated in the bile by the liver and thus shows up the gall bladder clearly during X-ray examination.

碘番酸 一種不透射綫的含碘化合物。在放射攝影中，用於顯示膽囊的輪廓（參閱 cholecystography）。靜脈注射後，碘番酸由肝濃縮於膽汁中，於是在 X 綫檢查時，清晰地顯示出膽囊。

iophendylate *n.* a *radiopaque iodine-containing compound that is sometimes used in radiography to show up the spinal canal (*see* myelography). It is injected through a *lumbar puncture needle.

碘芬酯 一種不透射綫的含碘化合物。有時用於放射攝影中顯示椎管（參閱 myelography）。用腰穿針注射。

ipecacuanha *n.* a plant extract used in small doses, usually in the form of tinctures and syrups, as an *expectorant to relieve coughing and to induce vomiting. Ipecacuanha irritates the digestive system, and high doses may cause severe digestive upsets.

吐根 通常以酊劑和糖漿的形式小劑量使用的一種植物提取物，用作祛痰劑以減輕咳嗽和誘發嘔吐。吐根刺激消化系統，因此，大劑量可以引起嚴重消化道不適。

ipratropium *n.* a bronchodilator drug used in the treatment of chronic reversible airways obstruction (*see* bronchospasm). Ipratropium is administered by inhalation; side-effects include nausea, palpitations, and headache. Trade name: **Atrovent**.

異丙托銨 一種氣管擴張藥，用於治療慢性可逆性氣道阻塞（參閱 bronchospasm）。吸入給藥；其副作用包括惡心、心悸以及頭痛。商品名：Atrovent。

iprindole *n.* a drug administered by mouth for the treatment of depression (*see* antidepressant). Response may take place gradually, and side-effects, such as dry mouth, blurred vision, constipation, and sweating, may occur. Trade name: **Prondol**.

伊普吲哚　用於治療抑鬱症的一種口服藥（參閱 antidepressant）。藥效可能逐漸發生，而且可能發生口乾、視力模糊、便秘以及出汗等副作用。商品名：Prondol。

ipsilateral (ipselateral, homolateral) *adj.* on or affecting the same side of the body: applied particularly to paralysis (or other symptoms) occurring on the same side of the body as the brain lesion that caused them. *Compare* contralateral.

同側的　位於或者影響機體同側的，尤指大腦損傷引起的並與該損傷同側的癱瘓（或其他症狀）。與 contralateral 對比。

IQ *see* intelligence quotient.

智商　參閱 intelligence quotient。

irid- (irido-) *prefix denoting* the iris.

〔前綴〕虹膜

iridectomy *n.* an operation on the eye in which a part of the iris is removed.

虹膜切除術　切除部分虹膜的眼科手術。

iridencleisis *n.* an operation for *glaucoma in which a small incision is made into the eye, beneath the *conjunctiva and close to the cornea, and part of the iris is drawn into it. The iris acts like a wick and keeps the incision open for the drainage of fluid from the front chamber of the eye to the tissue beneath the conjunctiva.

虹膜嵌頓術　治療青光眼的一種手術。在結膜下靠近角膜處向眼內做一小切口，將一部分虹膜拉入切口內。拉入的虹膜起着類似燈芯的作用和保持切口開放，使液體從眼前房流到結膜下組織。

iridocyclitis *n.* inflammation of the iris and ciliary body of the eye. *See* uveitis.

虹膜睫狀體炎　眼球虹膜和睫狀體的炎症。參閱 uveitis。

iridodialysis *n.* a tear, caused by injury to the eye, in the attachment of the iris to the ciliary body. Usually a dark crescentic gap is seen at the edge of the iris where the tear has occurred, and the pupil pulls away from the site of the tear.

虹膜脫離　眼球損傷造成的虹膜和睫狀體附着部位撕裂。通常在撕裂發生處的虹膜邊緣可見黑色新月型裂隙，瞳孔從撕裂處移開。

iridodonesis *n.* tremulousness of the iris when the eye is moved. It is due to absence of support from the lens, against which the iris normally lies, and occurs when the lens is absent or dislocated from its normal position.

iridoplegia *n.* paralysis of the iris, which is usually associated with *cycloplegia and results from injury, inflammation, or the use of pupil-dilating eye drops. In the case of injury, the pupil is usually larger than normal and moves little, if at all, in response to light and drugs.

iridotomy *n.* an operation on the eye in which an incision is made in the iris using a knife or a *YAG laser.

iris *n.* the part of the eye that regulates the amount of light that enters. It forms a coloured muscular diaphragm across the front of the lens; light enters through a central opening, the *pupil*. A ring of muscle round the margin contracts in bright light, causing the pupil to become smaller (*see* pupillary reflex). In dim light a set of radiating muscles contract and the constricting muscles relax, increasing the size of the pupil. The outer margin of the iris is attached to the *ciliary body.

iris bombé an abnormal condition of the eye in which the iris bulges forward towards the cornea. It is due to pressure from the aqueous humour behind the iris when its passage through the pupil to the anterior chamber of the eye is blocked (*pupil-block glaucoma*).

iritis *n.* inflammation of the iris. *See* uveitis.

iron *n.* an element essential to life. The body of an adult contains on average

虹膜震顫　眼球運動時虹膜顫動。由於失去晶狀體的支持所致（正常情況下，虹膜依賴於晶狀體的支持）。當晶狀體缺乏或者脫離其正常位置時可發生此症。

虹膜麻痺　虹膜的麻痺，通常伴有睫狀肌麻痺，由損傷、炎症、或者使用擴瞳滴眼劑所致。在有損傷的病例中，瞳孔較正常大而且對光綫和藥物即使有反應，也是極小的。

虹膜切開術　用手術刀或者釔-鋁-石榴石激光在虹膜上做一切口的眼科手術。

虹膜　調節進入眼內的光量的眼球部分。它在晶狀體前形成一個着色的肌性隔膜；光綫經過一個中央開口——瞳孔——進入眼內。光綫明亮時，圍繞虹膜邊緣的環形肌收縮，瞳孔變小（參閱 pupillary reflex）。光綫昏暗時，一羣放射狀肌肉收縮，而收縮的肌肉鬆弛，瞳孔增大。虹膜外緣附着於睫狀體上。

虹膜膨起　虹膜朝前向角膜鼓起的一種眼球異常狀態。當房水從瞳孔流到眼前房的通路受阻時（瞳孔阻塞性青光眼），由虹膜後房水壓力所引起。

虹膜炎　虹膜的炎症。參閱 uveitis。

鐵　生命必需的一種元素。成人身體平均含鐵 4 克，其中一

4 g of iron, over half of which is contained in *haemoglobin in the red blood cells, the rest being distributed between *myohaemoglobin in muscles, *cytochromes, and iron stores in the form of *ferritin and *haemosiderin. Iron is an essential component in the transfer of oxygen in the body. The absorption and loss of iron is very finely controlled. A good dietary source is meat, particularly liver. The recommended daily intake of iron is 10 mg per day for men and 12 mg per day for women during their reproductive life. A deficiency of iron may lead to *anaemia. Symbol: Fe.

Many preparations of iron are used to treat iron-deficiency anaemia. These include preparations taken by mouth, such as *ferrous sulphate, and those administered by injection, such as *iron dextran.

iron dextran a drug containing *iron and *dextran, administered by intramuscular or intravenous injection to treat iron-deficiency anaemia. Side-effects can include pain at the site of injection, rapid beating of the heart, and allergic reactions. Trade name: **Imferon**.

iron lung *see* respirator.

iron-storage disease *see* haemochromatosis.

irradiation *n.* the therapeutic application of electromagnetic radiation (usually alpha, beta, gamma, or X-rays) to a particular structure or tissue. *See* radiotherapy.

irreducible *adj.* unable to be replaced in a normal position: applied particularly to a type of *hernia.

半以上存在於紅細胞的血紅蛋白中,其餘部分則分布於肌肉的肌紅蛋白和細胞色素內。鐵以含鐵蛋白和含鐵血黃素的形式貯存。鐵是人體內氧氣運輸必不可少的一個成分。鐵的吸收和丟失受到極為精細的控制。肉類,尤其是肝,是鐵的良好的食物來源。鐵的每日建議攝取量是:男性每天 10 毫克,育齡女性每天 12 毫克。鐵缺乏可導致貧血。化學符號:Fe。

有多種用於治療缺鐵性貧血的鐵製劑,包括口服製劑(如硫酸亞鐵)和注射製劑(如葡聚糖鐵)。

葡聚糖鐵 含鐵和葡聚糖的一種藥物,肌肉或靜脈注射給藥,用於治療缺鐵性貧血。副作用可能包括注射部位疼痛、心跳加快和變態反應。商品名:Imferon。

鐵肺 參閱 respirator。

鐵貯積病 參閱 haemochromatosis。

照射 對某一特殊結構或者組織治療性地應用電磁射綫(通常是 α、β、γ 或者 X 射綫)。參閱 radiotherapy。

不能還原的 不能回復到正常位置的:尤指疝的一種類型。

irrigation *n.* the process of washing out a wound or hollow organ with a continuous flow of water or medicated solution.

沖洗法　用持續水流或藥液沖洗傷口或者空腔器官的過程。

irritability *n.* (in physiology) the property of certain kinds of tissue that enables them to respond in a specific way to outside stimuli. Irritability is shown by nerve cells, which can generate and transmit electrical impulses when stimulated appropriately, and by muscle cells, which contract when stimulated by nerve impulses.

應激性　（生理學）指某種組織的特性。它使這些組織能夠以特殊方式對外界刺激作出反應。神經細胞顯示應激性，在受到適當刺激時，能夠產生並且傳導電衝動；肌細胞也顯示應激性：受到神經衝動刺激時收縮。

irritable bowel syndrome (spastic colon, mucous colitis) a common condition in which recurrent abdominal pain with constipation and/or diarrhoea continues for years without any general deterioration in health. There is no detectable structural disease; the symptoms are caused by abnormal muscular contractions in the intestine. The cause is unknown, but the condition is often associated with stress or anxiety and may follow severe infection of the intestine. Tests may be needed to rule out organic disease. Treatment is based on removing anxiety (psychotherapy), dietary adjustment and faecal softening agents, and antispasmodic drugs.

應激性腸綜合徵（痙攣性結腸，黏液性結腸炎）　一種常見的疾病：復發性腹痛伴有便秘和／或腹瀉，持續數年而全身健康沒有下降。無任何可查出的結構性疾病；症狀由腸內肌肉異常收縮引起。病因不明，但此病常與緊張和焦慮有關，也可發生於嚴重腸道感染之後。需做檢查排除器質性疾病的可能性。治療基於消除焦慮（心理療法）、調節飲食、糞便軟化劑以及抗痙攣藥。

irritant *n.* any material that causes irritation of a tissue, ranging from nettles (causing pain and swelling) to tear gas (causing watering of the eyes). Chronic irritation by various chemicals can give rise to *dermatitis.

刺激物　能刺激組織的任何物質，從蕁麻類（引起疼痛腫脹）到催淚氣體（引起眼睛流淚）。由多種化學物質引起的慢性刺激作用能夠引起皮炎。

isch- (ischo-) *prefix denoting* suppression or deficiency.

〔前綴〕抑制、缺乏

ischaemia *n.* an inadequate flow of blood to a part of the body, caused by constriction or blockage of the blood

局部缺血　身體某一部分血流量不足，由供應該部分的血管收縮或者阻滯所致。心肌局部

vessels suppying it. Ischaemia of heart muscle produces *angina pectoris. Ischaemia of the calf muscles of the legs on exercise (causing intermittent *claudication) or at rest (producing *rest pain) is common in elderly subjects with atherosclerosis of the vessels at or distal to the point where the aorta divides into the iliac arteries.

缺血造成心絞痛；腿部腓腸肌運動時缺血（引起間歇性跛行）或靜止時缺血（引起靜止痛）常見於一些老年人，這些老年人患有動脈粥樣硬化，部位在主動脈與髂動脈分叉處或者在髂動脈遠側。

ischi- (ischio-) *prefix denoting* the ischium.

〔前綴〕坐骨

ischiorectal abscess an abscess in the space between the sheet of muscle that assists in control of the rectum (levator ani) and the pelvic bone. It may occur spontaneously, but is often secondary to an anal fissure, thrombosed *haemorrhoids, or other disease of the anus. Symptoms are severe throbbing pain near the anus with swelling and fever; it may cause an anal *fistula. Pus is drained from the abscess by surgical incision.

坐骨直腸窩膿腫　協助控制直腸的大片肌肉（肛提肌）與骨盆之間的膿腫。可自發產生，但常常繼發於肛裂、血栓性痔或者其他肛門疾病。症狀有肛門附近的跳痛，並伴有腫脹和發熱。本病可引起肛瘻。可通過手術切開將膿液從膿腫處引流。

ischium *n.* a bone forming the lower part of each side of the *hip bone (*see also* pelvis). **–ischiac, ischial** *adj.*

坐骨　形成雙側髖骨下部的骨骼（參閱 pelvis）。

ischuria *n.* retention or suppression of the urine. *See* anuria, retention.

尿閉　尿瀦留或受阻。參閱 anuria，retention。

island *n.* (in anatomy) an area of tissue or group of cells clearly differentiated from surrounding tissues.

島　（解剖學）指與周圍組織有明顯區別的一塊組織或者一羣細胞。

islet *n.* (in anatomy) a small group of cells that is structurally distinct from the cells surrounding it.

小島　（解剖學）結構不同於其周圍細胞的一小羣細胞。

islets of Langerhans small groups of cells, scattered through the material of the *pancreas, that secrete the hormones *insulin and *glucagon. There are three

朗格罕斯島　散在於胰腺組織中的小羣細胞，它們分泌胰島素和胰高血糖素。組織學中，有三組主要的細胞類型：α、β

main histological types of cells: alpha (α), beta (β), and delta cells; these cells produce glucagon, insulin, and *somatostatin, respectively.

和 δ 細胞，分別產生胰高血糖素、胰島素及生長抑制素。

iso- *prefix denoting* equality, uniformity, or similarity.

〔前綴〕**相等、均勻、類同**

isoagglutinin (isohaemagglutinin) *n.* one of the antibodies occurring naturally in the plasma that cause *agglutination of red blood cells of a different group.

同種凝集素　血漿中自然存在的抗體之一。它使不同型的紅細胞凝集。

isoagglutinogen *n.* one of the *antigens naturally occurring on the surface of red blood cells that is attacked by an isoagglutinin in blood plasma of a different group, so causing *agglutination.

同種凝集素原　紅細胞表面自然存在的抗原之一，在不同血型血漿中同種凝集素原的作用下引起凝集。

isoantibody *n.* an *antibody that occurs naturally against the components of foreign tissues from an individual of the same species.

同種抗體　自然存在的一種抗體，對抗來自同種個體的異體組織成分。

isoantigen *n.* an antigen that forms a natural component of an individual's tissues. Thus the antigens of the *HLA system are isoantigens, as are the agglutinogens of the different *blood groups.

同種抗原　形成個體組織天然成分的一種抗原，因此白細胞抗原系統是同種抗原，不同血型的凝集原也是。

isodactylism *n.* a congenital defect in which all the fingers are the same length.

指等長　所有指長度相等的一種先天性缺陷。

isoenzyme (isozyme) *n.* a physically distinct form of a given enzyme. Isoenzymes catalyse the same type of reaction but have slight physical and immunological differences. Isoenzymes of dehydrogenases, oxidases, transaminases, phosphatases, and proteolytic enzymes are known to exist.

同功酶　某種酶的一個物理結構不同的形式。同功酶催化同種類型的反應，但有輕微的物理學和免疫學差異。已知存在的同功酶有：脫氫酶、氧化酶、轉氨酶、磷酸酶、以及蛋白水解酶。

isohaemagglutinin *n. see* isoagglutinin.

同種血凝素　參閱 isoagglutinin。

isoimmunization *n.* the development of antibodies (*isoantibodies*) within an individual against antigens from another individual of the same species.

同種免疫作用　某一個體內所產生的對抗同種另一個體的抗體。

isolation *n.* **1.** the separation of a person with an infectious disease from non-infected people. *See also* quarantine. **2.** (in surgery) the separation of a structure from surrounding structures by the use of instruments.

(1) 隔離　將患有某種傳染病的人與未感染者分開。參閱 quarantine。**(2) 分離**　（外科學）指通過器械的使用，將一個結構與其周圍結構分離。

isoleucine *n.* an *essential amino acid. *See also* amino acid.

異亮氨酸　一種必需氨基酸。參閱 amino acid。

isomerase *n.* any one of a group of enzymes that catalyse the conversion of one isomer of a compound into another.

異構酶　一組酶，催化某種化合物的一種異構體向另一種異構體轉變。

isometheptene *n.* a *sympathomimetic drug used in the treatment of migraine. It is administered by mouth. Possible side-effects include dizziness. Trade name: **Midrid**.

異美汀　用於治療偏頭痛的一種擬交感神經藥。口服給藥。可能的副作用包括頭暈。商品名：Midrid。

isometric exercises (isometrics) a system of exercises based on the principle of *isometric contraction* of muscles. This occurs when the fibres are called upon to contract and do work, but despite an increase in tension do not shorten in length. It can be induced in muscles that are used when a limb is made to pull or push against something that does not move. The exercises increase fitness and build muscle.

等長收縮鍛煉　以肌肉等長收縮原理為基礎的一套鍛煉方法。當肌纖維收縮做功時，若肌張力增加而長度不縮短，即發生肌肉等長收縮。當用某一肢體推拉某一不動的物體時，可在參與動作的肌肉內產生等長收縮。這種鍛煉可以使身體健康，肌肉發達。

isometropia *n.* an equal power of *refraction in both eyes.

屈光相等　兩眼屈光度相等。

isomorphism *n.* the condition of two or more objects being alike in shape or structure. It can exist at any structural level, from molecules to whole organisms. –**isomorphic**, **isomorphous** *adj.*

同形　兩個或者更多的物體在形狀或結構上相同的情況。同形可存在於從分子到整個有機體的任何結構水平。

isoniazid (isonicotinic acid hydrazide, INH) *n.* a drug used in the treatment of *tuberculosis, usually taken by mouth. Because tuberculosis bacteria soon become resistant to isoniazid, it is usually given in conjunction with streptomycin and other antibiotics. Occasional side-effects include digestive disturbances and dry mouth; high doses or prolonged treatment may cause inflammation of the nerves, which can be countered by including pyridoxine (vitamin B₆) in the preparation.

異煙肼　用於治療結核病的一種藥物，通常口服給藥。由於結核菌很快對異煙肼形成抗藥性，所以異煙肼通常與鏈黴素以及其他抗生素聯合使用。偶見的副作用包括消化紊亂和口乾；大劑量或長期用藥可引起神經炎，這種情況可通過在製劑中加入吡多辛（維生素B₆）得到扭轉。

isoprenaline *n.* a *sympathomimetic drug used to dilate the air passages in asthma and other bronchial conditions. It also stimulates the heart and is used to treat some heart conditions involving reduced heart activity. It is administered by inhalation, by mouth, by injection, or in suppositories. Side-effects such as increased heart rate, palpitations, chest pain, dizziness, and fainting may occur. Trade names: **Medihaler-Iso**, **Saventrine**.

異丙腎上腺素　一種擬交感神經藥。哮喘或其他支氣管疾病時，用以擴張氣道。它也興奮心臟，用於治療心臟活動降低的某些心臟病。口服、吸入、注射或栓劑給藥。可能發生的副作用包括：心率加速、心悸、胸痛、頭暈和暈眩。商品名：Medihaler-Iso，Saventrine。

isosorbide dinitrate a drug used for the treatment of angina in patients unable to take glyceryl trinitrate. It acts by relaxing the smooth muscle of both arteries and veins, thus causing dilation. It is administered by mouth; side-effects are rare, but include headache, hypotension, nausea and vomiting, and skin rash. Trade names: **Cedocard**, **Isoket**, **Isordil**, **Sorbitrate**.

硝酸異山梨酯　一種治療心絞痛的藥物，用於不能使用硝酸甘油的患者。它同時鬆弛動脈和靜脈平滑肌，從而引起擴張。口服給藥，副作用很少見，但可包括：頭痛、低血壓、惡心嘔吐以及皮疹。商品名：Cedocard，Isoket，Isordil，Sorbitrate。

isosthenuria *n.* inability of the kidneys to produce either a concentrated or a dilute urine. This occurs in the final stages of renal failure.

等滲尿　兩腎不能產生濃縮尿或稀釋尿，見於腎功能衰竭晚期。

isotonic *adj.* **1.** describing solutions that have the same osmotic pressure. *See*

(1) 等滲的　描述滲透壓相等的溶液。參閱 osmosis。**(2)** 等

osmosis. **2.** describing muscles that have equal *tonicity.

張的　描述具有同樣張性的肌肉。

isotonic exercises *see* exercise.

等張鍛煉　參閱 exercise。

isotope *n.* any one of the different forms of an element, possessing the same number of protons (positively charged particles) in the nucleus, and thus the same atomic number, but different numbers of neutrons. Isotopes therefore have different atomic weights. Radioactive isotopes decay into other isotopes or elements, emitting alpha, beta, or gamma radiation. Some radioactive isotopes may be produced artificially by bombarding elements with neutrons. These are known as *nuclides* and are used extensively in *radiotherapy for the treatment of cancer.

同位素　某種元素的多種不同形式。其原子核中具有相同數量的質子（正電荷粒子），相同的原子序數和不同的中子數。因此，各種同位素具有不同的原子量。放射性同位素衰變成其他同位素或元素，並放射出 α、β 或 γ 射綫。某些放射性同位素可通過中子轟擊元素人工產生。這些放射性同位素被稱為核素，廣泛用於癌症的放射治療。

isotope investigations investigations of the structure and functions of organs and tissues by labelling with radioactive isotopes substances that are concentrated by the body. Once introduced into the body, the radioactive *tracers can be detected on a *scintigram or using a *gamma camera, revealing the outline of the shape, or demonstrating the function, of organs and tissues. It is also possible to follow the formation of abnormal collections of blood or pus.

同位素檢測　通過人體內含有的放射性同位素標記法，來檢測器官和組織的結構和功能。放射性示蹤劑進入體內，便可由閃爍圖測到或用 γ 照相機顯示器官和組織的形狀輪廓，或演示其功能。它還可跟蹤血液或膿液的異常聚集和形成。

isotretinoin *n.* a drug related to vitamin A (*see* retinoid) and used in the treatment of severe acne that has failed to respond to other treatment. It is administered by mouth. Possible side-effects include dry skin, nose bleeds, eyelid and lip inflammation, muscle, joint, and abdominal pains, diarrhoea, and some disturbances of vision. Trade name: **Roaccutane**.

異維甲酸　一種與維生素A（參閱 retinoid）有關的藥物，用於治療其他治療方法無效的嚴重痤瘡。口服給藥，可能的副作用包括皮膚乾燥、鼻血、眼瞼和口唇炎症，肌肉、關節和腹部疼痛，腹瀉以及某些視力障礙。商品名：Roaccutane。

isoxsuprine *n.* a drug that dilates blood vessels and is used to improve blood flow in such conditions as cerebrovascular disease and arteriosclerosis and to inhibit contractions in premature labour. It is administered by mouth or injection and rarely it may cause flushing, increased heart rate, dizziness, and nausea. Trade name: **Duvalidan**.

isozyme *n. see* isoenzyme.

ispaghula husk a bulking agent (*see* laxative) used to treat constipation, *diverticulitis, and *irritable bowel syndrome. It is administered by mouth. Trade names: **Colven**, **Fybogel**.

isthmus *n.* a constricted or narrowed part of an organ or tissue, such as the band of thyroid tissue connecting the two lobes of the thyroid gland.

itch *n.* local discomfort or irritation of the skin, prompting the sufferer to scratch or rub the affected area. It is the main symptom of skin disease. *See* pruritus.

-itis *suffix denoting* inflammation of an organ, tissue, etc. Examples: *arthritis* (or a joint); *peritonitis* (of the peritoneum).

ITU *see* intensive therapy unit.

IUCD (intrauterine contraceptive device) a plastic or metal coil, spiral, or other shape, about 25 mm long, that is inserted into the cavity of the uterus to prevent conception. Its exact mode of action is unknown but it is thought to interfere with implantation of the embryo. Early IUCDs (such as the *Lippes loop*) were made of plastic; later variants (such as the *Gravigard*) are

異克舒令　一種擴血管藥。腦血管病或動脈硬化病時，用於擴張血管；早產時，用於抑制子宮收縮。口服或注射給藥，極少數情況下，它可引起潮紅、心率加速、頭暈以及惡心。商品名：Duvalidan。

同功酶　參閱 isoenzyme。

卵葉車前殼　一種增容劑（參閱 laxative），用於治療便秘、憩室炎以及應激性腸綜合徵。口服給藥。商品名：Colven，Fybogel。

峽　某一器官或組織的縮小或狹窄部分，如連接甲狀腺兩葉的甲狀腺組織帶。

癢　皮膚局部不適或刺激，迫使患者去搔抓該患病部位。癢是皮膚病的主要症狀。參閱 pruritus。

〔後綴〕炎症　器官、組織等的炎症。如關節炎（關節的），骨膜炎（骨膜的）。

特療病房　參閱 intensive therapy unit。

宮內避孕器　一種塑料或金屬環，呈螺旋或其他形狀，長約25 mm，將其置入子宮腔以避免受孕。它確切的作用方式未知，但據認為能阻止胚胎植入。早期的宮內避孕器（如利佩斯環）由塑料製成，後來的改良型（如格利維加德環）包以銅。銅緩慢融解，增加了避孕作用。一些避孕器，如

covered with copper, which slowly dissolves and augments the contraceptive action. Devices such as the *Progestasert* release small amounts of a contraceptive hormone drug. About one-third of women fitted with an IUCD find the side-effects (heavy menstrual bleeding or back pain) unacceptable, but most have no complaints. The unwanted pregnancy rate is about 2 per 100 woman-years. If pregnancy should occur there is normally no need to remove the device (it may, however, be shed spontaneously). *See also* postcoital contraception.

IUGR *see* intrauterine growth retardation.

IUI *see* intrauterine insemination.

ivermectin *n.* a drug used in the treatment of *onchocerciasis. It is administered by mouth and acts by killing the immature forms (*microfilariae) of the parasite. Side-effects, which are mild, include itching and swollen lymph nodes.

IVF *see* in vitro fertilization.

IVP *see* intravenous pyelogram.

Ixodes *n.* a genus of widely distributed parasitic ticks. Several species are responsible for transmitting *Lyme disease, *tularaemia, Queensland tick typhus, and *Russian spring-summer encephalitis. The bite of a few species can give rise to a serious paralysis, caused by a toxin in the tick's saliva.

ixodiasis *n.* any disease caused by the presence of *ticks.

Ixodidae *n.* a family of *ticks.

Progestasert 可釋放少量避孕激素藥物。約三分之一安放宮內避孕器的婦女出現難以忍受的副作用（經血過多或背痛），但多數無任何不適。帶環婦女妊娠率每年約為2%。如發生妊娠，正常情況下不需去掉避孕器（它可自然脫落）。參閱 postcoital contraception。

宮內發育遲緩　參閱 intrauterine growth retardation。

宮內授精　參閱 intrauterine insemination。

伊維菌素　一種用於治療盤尾絲蟲病的藥物。口服可藥，它通過殺死該寄生蟲的未成熟體（微絲蚴）而起作用。輕微的副作用包括癢及淋巴結腫。

試管授精　參閱 in vitro fertilization。

靜脈腎盂造影片　參閱 intravenous pyelogram。

硬蜱屬　一屬分布廣泛的寄生蜱。有幾個種能傳播萊姆病、兔熱病、昆士蘭蜱傳斑疹傷寒和俄羅斯春夏型腦炎。幾種蜱的叮咬可引起嚴重麻痺，由其唾液中所含毒素所致。

蜱病　蜱的存在而引起的任何疾病。

硬蜱科　蜱類的一科。

J

Jacksonian epilepsy *see* epilepsy.

Jacquemier's sIgn a bluish or purplish coloration of the vagina: a possible indication of pregnancy.

jactitation *n.* restless tossing and turning of a person suffering from a severe disease, frequently one with a high fever.

jamais vu one of the manifestations of temporal lobe *epilepsy, in which there is a sudden feeling of unfamiliarity with everyday surroundings.

Jarisch-Herxheimer reaction (Herxheimer reaction) exacerbation of the symptoms of syphilis that may occur on starting antibiotic therapy for the disease. The effect is transient and requires no treatment.

jaundice *n.* a yellowing of the skin or whites of the eyes, indicating excess bilirubin (a bile pigment) in the blood. Jaundice is classified into three types. *Obstructive jaundice* occurs when bile made in the liver fails to reach the intestine due to obstruction of the *bile ducts (e.g. by gallstones) or to *cholestasis. The urine is dark, the faeces pale, and the patient may itch. *Hepatocellular jaundice* is due to disease of the liver cells, such as *hepatitis, when the liver is unable to utilize the bilirubin, which accumulates in the blood. The urine may be dark but the faeces retain their colour. *Haemolytic jaundice* occurs when there is excessive destruction of red cells in the blood (*see* haemloysis). Urine and faeces retain their normal colour. Medical name: **icterus**.

傑克遜癲癇　參閱 epilepsy。

雅克米埃徵　陰道着色變成淺藍或淺紫，為妊娠的一個可能指徵。

輾轉不安　患嚴重疾病的人，通常為高燒患者，不安地翻來覆去。

舊事如新症　顳葉癲癇的表現之一，患者突然對日常環境感到陌生。

賈-赫氏反應（赫克斯海默爾反應）　在梅毒的抗菌治療開始時，梅毒症狀加重。其影響短暫，不需治療。

黃疸　皮膚或眼白發黃，表示血中膽紅素（一種膽色素）過多。黃疸分為三型。肝臟中生成的膽汁，由於膽道梗阻（如結石）或膽汁阻塞，不能到達腸道時，則發生梗阻性黃疸。尿色深，糞便色灰白，患者可覺瘙癢。肝細胞性黃疸是由肝細胞疾病所致，如肝炎。此時，肝臟不能利用膽紅素，膽紅素聚積於血中。尿色可能深，而糞便保留原色。當血中紅細胞破壞過多時（參閱 haemolysis），發生溶血性黃疸。尿及糞便保持其正常顏色。醫學用語：黃疸。

jaw *n.* either the *maxilla (upper jaw) or the *mandible (lower jaw). The jaws form the framework of the mouth and provide attachment for the teeth.

領 上頜骨（上頜）或下頜骨（下頜）。上、下頜形成口的構架，並為牙齒提供附着處。

jejun- (jejuno-) *prefix denoting* the jejunum.

〔前綴〕空腸

jejunal biopsy removal of a piece of the lining (mucosa) of the upper small intestine. This can be done by a surgical operation but is usually performed by a gastroduodenoscope or a special metal capsule, swallowed by the patient. When the capsule is in the *jejunum a small knife within it is triggered by suction on an attached tube, cutting off a small piece of mucosa. The specimen may be examined microscopically to assist in the diagnosis of *coeliac disease, *Whipple's disease, or intestinal infections, or its enzyme content may be measured chemically to detect, for example, *lactase deficiency.

空腸活組織檢查 切取小腸上部的一片腸黏膜。這可通過外科手術進行；但通常是通過胃十二指腸鏡或者由病人吞下特製的金屬囊進行。此囊到達空腸內後，其內的小刀由所連接的管上的抽吸裝置啟動，切取一小片黏膜，標本可在顯微鏡下檢查，以輔助腹腔疾病、惠普爾病或腸道疾病的診斷；或者用化學方法測定標本中的酶含量，以檢測，如乳糖酶缺乏。

jejunal ulcer *see* peptic ulcer, Zollinger-Ellison syndrome.

空腸潰瘍 參閱 peptic ulcer，Zollinger-Ellison syndrome。

jejunectomy *n.* surgical removal of the jejunum or part of the jejunum.

空腸切除術 手術切除空腸或部分空腸。

jejunoileostomy *n.* an operation in which the jejunum is joined to the ileum (small intestine), when either the end of the jejunum or the beginning of the ileum has been removed or is to be bypassed. It is usually performed for intestinal disease (e.g. Crohn's disease). It was formerly used for the treatment of obesity but has been abandoned because of serious side-effects.

空腸迴腸吻合術 把空腸和迴腸（小腸）相連接的一種手術。當空腸末端或者迴腸起始端已被切除或者需被繞過時行此手術。手術常用於治療腸道疾病（如克羅恩病）；此手術曾用於治療肥胖症，但由於嚴重副作用，已棄用。

jejunostomy *n.* a surgical operation in which the jejunum is brought through

空腸造口術 將空腸拉出腹壁並且造口的外科手術。它使導

the abdominal wall and opened. It can enable the insertion of a catheter into the jejunum for short-term infusion of nutrients or other substances.

管能插入空腸，短期輸入營養或其他物質。

jejunotomy *n.* a surgical incision into the jejunum in order to inspect the interior or remove something from within it.

空腸切開術 手術切開空腸，以便檢查其內部，或從中取出某物。

jejunum *n.* part of the small *intestine. It comprises about two-fifths of the whole small intestine and connects the duodenum to the ileum. **–jejunal** *adj.*

空腸 小腸的一部分。它約占整個小腸的 2/5，並且連接十二指腸和迴腸。

jerk *n.* the sudden contraction of a muscle in response to a nerve impulse. The *knee jerk* (*see* patellar reflex) is the reflex kicking movement produced by contraction of the quadriceps muscle of the thigh after it has been stretched by tapping the tendon below the knee. Eliciting this and other jerks, such as the ankle and elbow jerks, is a means of testing the nerve pathways, via the spinal cord, which are involved in *reflexes.

反射 神經衝動引起的肌肉突然收縮。膝反射是踢腿反射，其產生是通過伸直大腿後叩擊膝下肌腱，使股四頭肌收縮。引發膝反射和其他反射，如踝、肘反射是檢查參與反射的脊髓神經通路的方法。

jigger *n. see* Tunga.

沙蚤 參閱 Tunga。

joint *n.* the point at which two or more bones are connected. The opposing surfaces of the two bones are lined with cartilaginous, fibrous, or soft (synovial) tissue. The three main classes of joint are *diarthrosis (freely movable), *amphiarthrosis (slightly movable), and *synarthrosis (immovable).

關節 兩個或者更多骨的連接處。兩骨相對的骨面襯有軟骨、纖維或軟組織（滑膜）。關節的三種主要類型是動關節（可自由活動的），微動關節（可輕微活動的）及不動關節（不能活動的）。

joule *n.* the *SI unit of work or energy, equal to the work done when the point of application of a force of 1 newton is displaced through a distance of 1 metre in the direction of the force. In electrical terms the joule is the work done per second when a current of 1 ampere flows through a resistance of 1 ohm. Symbol: J. *See also* calorie.

焦耳 功或能量的國際單位，等於用一牛頓的力將物體沿力的方向移動一米的距離所做的功。在電學術語中，焦耳指 1 安培的電流通過一歐姆的電阻時每秒鐘所做的功。符號：J。參閱 calorie。

jugular *adj.* relating to or supplying the neck or throat.

頸的 與頸部或喉部有關的，供應頸部或喉部的。

jugular vein any one of several veins in the neck. The *internal jugular* is a very large paired vein running vertically down the side of the neck and draining blood from the brain, face, and neck. It ends behind the sternoclavicular joint, where it joins the subclavian vein. The *external jugular* is a smaller paired vein running superficially down the neck to the subclavian vein and draining blood from the face, scalp, and neck. Its tributary, the *anterior jugular*, runs down the front of the neck.

頸靜脈 頸部幾條靜脈中的任何一條。頸內靜脈是很大的成對靜脈，沿頸側垂直向下，引流來自腦、面部及頸部的血液。它止於胸鎖關節後，在此處連接鎖骨下靜脈。頸外動脈是較小的成對靜脈，在淺表部沿頸向下至鎖骨下靜脈，引流來自面部、頭皮和頸部的血流。其分支頸前靜脈沿頸前向下。

jugum *n.* (in anatomy) a ridge or furrow that connects two parts of a bone.

軛 （解剖學）連接骨的兩個部分的嵴或溝。

junction *n.* (in anatomy) the point at which two different tissues or structures are in contact. *See also* neuromuscular junction.

接點 （解剖學）兩個不同的組織或結構的接觸點。參閱 neuromuscular junction。

juvenile polyp *see* polyp.

幼年息肉 參閱 polyp。

juxta- *prefix denoting* proximity to. Example: *juxta-articular* (near a joint).

〔前綴〕接近於 例如近骨節的（靠近關節）。

K

Kahn reaction a test for syphilis, in which antibodies specific to the disease are detected in a sample of the patient's blood by means of a *precipitin reaction. This test is not as reliable as some.

康氏反應 用於檢查梅毒的一種試驗。通過沉澱反應檢測患者血液樣本的梅毒特異性抗體。此試驗不如其他某些試驗可靠。

kala-azar (visceral leishmaniasis, Dumdum fever) *n.* a tropical diseas, caused by the parasitic protozoan

黑熱病 由寄生性原蟲杜氏利什曼原蟲引起的一種熱帶病。這種寄生蟲通過白蛉傳播給

Leishmania donovani. The parasite, which is transmitted to man by *sandflies, invades the cells of the lymphatic system, spleen, and bone marrow. Symptoms include enlargement and subsequent lesions of the liver and spleen; anaemia; a low *leucocyte count; weight loss; and irregular fevers. The disease occurs in Asia, South America, the Mediterranean area, and Africa. Drugs containing antimony, with supplementary pentamidine, are used in the treatment of this potentially fatal disease.

kallidin *n.* a naturally occurring polypeptide consisting of ten amino acids. Kallidin is a powerful vasodilator and causes contraction of smooth muscle; it is formed in the blood under certain conditions. *See* kinin.

kallikrein *n.* one of a group of enzymes found in the blood and body fluids that act on certain plasma globulins to produce bradykinin and kallidin. *See* kinin.

kanamycin *n.* an *antibiotic used to treat a wide range of bacterial infections. It is administered mainly by injection but is given by mouth for infections of the intestine and by inhalation for respiratory infections. Mild side-effects sometimes occur; these include skin rashes, fever, headache, nausea, vomiting, and tingling sensations. Trade name: **Kannasyn**.

kaolin *n.* a white clay that contains aluminium and silicon and is purified and powdered for use as an adsorbent. It is taken by mouth to treat the diarrhoea and vomiting due to food poisoning and other digestive disorders. Kaolin is also used in dusting powders and poultices.

人，侵犯淋巴系統、脾和骨髓細胞。症狀包括肝臟和脾臟的腫大及繼發性病變、貧血，白細胞計數低，體重減輕和不規則發熱。此病發於亞洲、南美洲、地中海地區，以及非洲。含銻的藥品及補充噴他脒可用於治療這種可能致死的疾病。

卡里定 一種天然存在的多肽，由 10 種氨基酸組成。它是一種強力血管舒張藥，可引起平滑肌收縮。在特定條件下，它在血中形成。參閱 kinin。

激肽釋放酶 見於血液和體液中的一組酶。這些酶作用於某些血漿球蛋白，以產生緩激肽及卡里定。參閱 kinin。

卡那黴素 一種用於治療細菌感染的廣譜抗生素，主要通過注射給藥，但腸道感染時可口服，呼吸系統感染時可吸入。有時可能發生輕微副作用，包括：皮疹、發燒、頭痛、惡心、嘔吐及麻刺感。商品名：Kannasyn。

白陶土 一種含有鋁和硅的白色黏土。將其提純並研成粉末，可用作吸附劑。它口服可治療食物中毒以及其他消化系統疾病引起的腹瀉嘔吐。白陶土也可用於撲粉和泥罨劑。

Kaposi's sarcoma a malignant tumour arising from blood vessels in the skin and appearing as purple to dark brown plaques or nodules. It is common in Africa but rare in the Western world, except in patients with *AIDS. The tumour evolves slowly; radiotherapy is the treatment of choice but chemotherapy may be of value in metastatic disease.

卡波濟肉瘤　發生於皮膚血管的一種惡性腫瘤，呈紫至深褐色斑塊或結節。常見於非洲，而罕見於西方，艾滋病患者除外。本病發展緩慢；放射治療是首選的治療方法，但化學療法對轉移瘤可能有價值。

kary- (karyo-) *prefix denoting* a cell nucleus.

〔前綴〕核　細胞核。

karyokinesis *n.* division of the nucleus of a cell, which occurs during cell division before division of the cytoplasm (*cytokinesis*). *See* mitosis.

核分裂　細胞核的分裂，它發生於細胞分裂期，細胞漿分裂（細胞質變動）之前。參閱 mitosis。

karyolysis *n.* the breakdown of the cell nucleus in mitosis.

核溶解　有絲分裂時細胞核崩潰。

karyoplasm *n. see* nucleoplasm.

核質　參閱 nucleoplasm。

karyosome *n.* the dense mass of *chromatin found in the cell nucleus, which is composed mainly of chromosomes.

核粒　見於細胞核中的致密染色質團，它主要由染色體組成。

karyotype 1. *n.* the *chromosome set of an individual or species described in terms of both the number and structure of the chromosomes. **2.** *n.* the representation of the chromosome set in a diagram. **3.** *vb.* to determine the karyotype of a cell, as by microscopic examination.

核型　**(1)** 以染色體的數目和結構所表述的某個體或某物種的染色體組。**(2)** 染色體組的圖表表示法。**(3)** 測定細胞的核型，如通過顯微鏡檢查。

katathermometer *n.* a thermometer used to measure the cooling power of the air surrounding it, having its bulb covered with water-moistened material. The instrument is brought to a steady temperature of 100°F and then exposed to the air. The time taken for the temperature recorded by the thermometer

乾濕球溫度計　用於測量其周圍空氣冷卻力的一種溫度計。它的球部蓋有用水浸濕的材料。先使該溫度計達到穩定的 100°F（37.8°C），然後暴露於空氣中。溫度計上記錄的溫度降至 95°F 所需的時間，就是該空氣冷卻力的指標。

to fall to 95°F gives an index of the air's cooling power.

Kawasaki disease (mucocutaneous lymph node syndrome) a condition of unknown cause affecting young children, usually less than five years old, and characterized by fever, conjunctivitis, a sore throat, and a generalized rash and reddening of the palms and soles. This is followed by peeling of the fingers and toes. The fever usually persists for 1–2 weeks. In approximately one-fifth of children there is involvement of the coronary arteries and heart muscle (myocardium), resulting in *myocarditis and *aneurysms of the coronary arteries. About 2% of cases are fatal. The aneurysms will usually resolve spontaneously but slowly. Treatment involves aspirin therapy, and *gamma globulin has recently been shown to reduce the risk of coronary artery disease.

川崎病 一種病因不明的疾病，發病於幼兒，通常是 5 歲以下幼兒。其特徵是發熱、結膜炎、咽喉痛和全身性皮疹和手掌、足掌發紅。隨後，手指和腳趾脫皮。發燒通常持續 1~2 周。在約 1/5 兒童中，該病侵犯冠狀動脈和心肌，導致心肌炎和冠狀動脈瘤。約 2% 的病例是致命的。動脈瘤會自發，但緩慢溶解。治療包括阿司匹林療法。最近已證明丙種球蛋白減小冠狀動脈疾病的風險。

Kayser-Fleischer ring a brownish-yellow ring in the outer rim of the cornea of the eye. It is a deposit of copper granules and is diagnostic of *Wilson's disease. When well developed it can be seen by unaided observation, but faint Kayser-Fleischer rings may only be detected by specialized ophthalmological examination.

凱-弗氏環 眼角膜外緣的棕黃色環。它是沉積的銅粒，是威爾遜病的診斷依據。當充分發展時，它可用肉眼觀察到，而輕微的凱-弗氏環只能通過專門的眼科檢查檢定。

Kell antigens a group of antigens that may or may not be present on the surface of red blood cells, forming the basis of a *blood group. This group is important in blood transfusion reactions.

凱爾抗原 紅細胞表面可能存在或不存在的一組抗原，它們形成血型的基礎。這組抗原對輸血反應很重要。

Keller's operation a common operation for *bunions associated with displacement of the big toe towards the others (hallux valgus). It involves remodelling of the joint after excision of the base of the first phalanx of the big toe.

克勒爾手術 治療與大拇趾向其他趾錯位（拇外翻）有關的拇囊炎的一種常見手術。手術包括在切除大拇趾第一趾骨基部後重造關節。

keloid *n.* an overgrowth of fibrous scar tissue following trauma to the skin. It does not resolve spontaneously but may be flattened by applied pressure or with injections of potent corticosteroids. Keloid formation is particularly common at certain sites, such as the breastbone or ear lobe; surgical excision of benign (nonmalignant) lesions from such sites is therefore best avoided. A *hypertrophic scar* is similar, but resolves over a period of months.

瘢痕疙瘩　皮膚創傷後過度生長的纖維瘢痕組織。它不會自發溶解，但若用壓力或者注射有效力的皮質類固醇，可變平。瘢痕疙瘩的形成特別常發於某些部位，如胸骨或耳垂；因此，在這些部位最好避免手術切除良性（非惡性）病變。肥大性瘢痕與此類似，但可在數月內溶解。

kelvin *n.* the *SI unit of temperature, formally defined as the fraction 1/273.16 of the temperature of the triple point of water. A temperature in kelvins is equal to a Celsius temperature plus 273.15°C. Symbol: K.

開（爾文）　溫度的國際單位，正式定義為水三相點溫度的 1/273.16。開爾文溫度等於攝氏溫度加上 273.15°C。符號：K。

kerat- (kerato-) *prefix denoting* **1.** the cornea. Example: *keratopathy* (disease of). **2.** horny tissue, especially of the skin.

〔前綴〕**(1)** 角膜　例如：角膜病（角膜的疾病）。**(2)** 角質組織　尤指皮膚角質組織。

keratalgia *n.* pain arising from the cornea.

角膜痛　發生於角膜的疼痛。

keratectasia *n.* bulging of the cornea at the site of scar tissue (which is thinner than normal corneal tissue).

角膜突出　瘢痕組織處的角膜（較正常角膜薄）膨出。

keratectomy *n.* an operation in which a part of the cornea is removed, usually a superficial layer. This procedure is now frequently done by an *excimer laser.

角膜切除術　手術切除部分角膜，通常為淺表層。現在，此手術常用激態原子激光做。

keratin *n.* one of a family of proteins that are the major constituents of the nails, hair, and the outermost layers of the skin. The cytoplasm of epithelial cells, including *keratinocytes, contains a network of keratin filaments.

角蛋白　一組蛋白。它們是指甲、頭髮及皮膚最外層的主要成分。上皮細胞的細胞漿，包括角化細胞的胞漿，含有一個角蛋白絲網狀物。

keratinization (cornification) *n.* the process by which cells become horny due

角質化　由於角蛋白在細胞內沉積使細胞成角質的過程。它

to the deposition of *keratin within them. It occurs in the *epidermis of the skin and associated structures (hair, nails, etc.), where the cells become flattened, lose their nuclei, and are filled with keratin as they approach the surface.

發生於皮膚表皮層及其附屬結構（頭髮和指甲等）。在此處，細胞在接近表面時變平，失去細胞核，並且充滿角蛋白。

keratinocyte *n.* a type of cell that makes up 95% of the cells of the epidermis. Keratinocytes migrate from the deeper layers of the epidermis and are finally shed from the surface of the skin.

角質化細胞　占表皮層細胞95%的一種細胞類型。角質化細胞從表皮深層向外遷移，最後從皮膚表面脫落。

keratitis *n.* inflammation of the *cornea of the eye. The eye waters and is very painful and vision is blurred. It may be due to physical or chemical agents (abrasions, exposure to dust, chemicals, ultraviolet light, etc.) or result from infection. Keratitis not due to infection usually responds to keeping the eyes covered until the corneal surface has healed; infections often require specific drug treatment, e.g. with antibiotics.

角膜炎　眼球角膜的炎症。眼睛流淚，劇痛，而且視力模糊。它可由物理的或化學的因素（擦傷、接觸塵土、化學物品，紫外綫等）或感染引起。對於非感染性角膜炎，覆蓋眼睛，直至角膜表面愈合往往有效。感染性角膜炎常需特異藥物治療，如用抗生素。

keratoacanthoma *n.* a firm nodule that appears singly on the skin, grows to 1–2 cm across in about six weeks, and usually disappears gradually during the next few months. Men are affected more often than women, commonly between the ages of 50 and 70. Keratoacanthomas occur mainly on the face; the cause is not known. Although they may disappear spontaneously this may leave an unsightly scar; therefore treatment by curettage and cautery, or excision, may be required.

角化棘皮瘤　出現於皮膚上的單個硬結。約六周，直徑可長至 1~2 cm，在以後的幾個月裏，通常逐漸消失。男性患者較女性多，常發於 50~70 歲間。角化棘皮瘤主要發生於面部，其原因不明。儘管它可自發消失，但可留下難看的瘢痕；因此，可能需要通過刮除術和燒灼術或切除術治療。

keratocele (descemetocele) *n.* outward bulging of the base of a deep ulcer of the cornea. The deep layer of the cornea (Descemet's membrane) is elastic

角膜後（彈性）層突出　角膜深部潰瘍的基底部向外膨出。角膜深層（德塞梅膜）有彈性，且相對不易穿孔。因此，

and relatively resistant to perforation; it therefore bulges when the overlying cornea has been destroyed.

當位於其上的角膜被破壞時，角膜深層即膨出。

keratoconjunctivitis *n.* combined inflammation of the cornea and conjunctiva of the eye.

角膜結膜炎　眼球角膜和結膜的合併發炎。

keratoconus *n.* conical cornea: an abnormal condition of the eye in which the cornea, instead of having a regular curvature, comes to a rounded apex towards its centre. The 'cone' tends to become sharper over a period of years.

圓錐形角膜　圓錐形的角膜：眼的異常狀態，角膜沒有規則的曲度，其中心呈圓頂狀態。這種圓錐形數年後變得更明顯。

keratoglobus (megalocornea) *n.* a congenital disorder of the eye in which the whole cornea bulges forward in a regular curve. *Compare* keratoconus.

球型角膜　眼球的一種先天性疾病，整個角膜以規則的屈度向前突出。與 keratoconus 對比。

keratomalacia *n.* a progressive nutritional disease of the eye due to vitamin A deficiency. The cornea softens and may become perforated. This condition is very serious and blindness is usually inevitable. *See also* xerophthalmia.

角膜軟化　因維生素缺乏引起的進行性眼病。眼球變軟，且可能穿孔。此病極為嚴重，失明往往難以避免。參閱 xerophthalmia。

keratome *n.* any instrument designed for cutting the cornea. The simplest type has a flat triangular blade attached at its base to a handle, the other two sides being very sharp and tapering to a point. Power-driven keratomes have oscillating or rotating blades.

角膜刀　切開角膜專用的一種器械。最簡單的類型有一扁三角形刀片，其底連接刀柄，另外兩邊極鋭利，而且逐漸變細變尖。電動角膜刀具有擺動或旋轉刀片。

keratometer (ophthalmometer) *n.* an instrument for measuring the radius of curvature of the cornea. It is used for assessing the degree of abnormal curvature of the cornea in *astigmatism. Usually the vertical and horizontal curvatures are measured. All keratometers work on the principle that the size of the image of an object reflected from a convex mirror (in this case, the cornea)

角膜曲度計　用於測量角膜曲度半徑的一種儀器。它用於判定散光時角膜異常曲度的程度。通常測量水平和垂直曲度。所有角膜曲度計的工作原理是：從一凸鏡（此處是角膜）上反射的某一物像的大小取決於鏡面的曲度。曲度愈大，物像愈小。

depends on the curvature of the mirror. The steeper the curve, the smaller the image. –**keratometry** *n.*

keratoplasty (corneal graft) *n.* an eye operation in which any diseased parts of the cornea are replaced by clear corneal tissue from a donor. All layers of the cornea may be replaced (*penetrating keratoplasty*) or only some of its layers, the deeper layer remaining (*lamellar keratoplasty*). In the latter case the thickness of the replacement cornea is correspondingly reduced.

角膜成形術 用來自供體的透明角膜組織替換任一病變角膜部位的手術。角膜各層均可替換（穿透性角膜替換術），或僅替換角膜的某些層，而保留其深層（板層角膜替換術）。在後一種情況下，替換角膜的厚度也相應減小。

keratoscope (Placido's disc) *n.* an instrument for detecting abnormal curvature of the cornea. It consists of a black disc, about 20 cm in diameter, marked with concentric white rings. The examiner looks through a small lens in the centre at the reflection of the rings in the patient's cornea. A normal cornea will reflect regular concentric images of the rings; a cornea that is abnormally curved (for example in *keratoconus) or scarred reflects distorted rings. Modern keratoscopes can print out a contour map of the corneal surface.

角膜鏡 用於檢測角膜異常曲度的一種儀器。它是一個黑色圓盤，直徑約 20 cm，標有白色同心圓。檢查者通過鏡中心的小凸鏡觀察圓在患者角膜上的成像。正常角膜可反射出圓環的規則同心圓成像，而屈度異常（如圓錐形角膜）或有瘢痕的角膜則反射出扭曲的圓環。現代角膜鏡可打印出一張角膜表面輪廓圖。

keratosis *n.* a horny overgrowth of the skin. *Actinic* (or *solar*) *keratoses* are red spots with a scaly surface, found in older fair-skinned people who have been chronically overexposed to the sun. The spots may become malignant. *Seborrhoeic keratoses* (or *basal-cell papillomas*), less correctly known as *seborrhoeic warts*, never become malignant. They are superficial yellowish spots, occurring especially on the trunk in middle age, that slowly darken and become warty over the years.

角化病 皮膚的角質過度生長。光化性角化病是具有鱗狀表面的紅色斑塊，見於長期暴露於陽光的白皮膚的老年人。斑塊可惡變。脂溢性角化病（基底細胞乳頭狀瘤），不正確地稱為脂溢性疣，不會惡變。它們是淺表的淡黃色斑塊，尤其發生於中年人的軀幹部，數年後，顏色逐漸加深，變成疣狀。

keratotomy *n.* an incision into the cornea. *See also* radial keratotomy.

角膜切開術 將角膜切開。參閱 radial keratotomy。

kerion *n.* an uncommon and severe form of *ringworm of the scalp consisting of a painful inflamed mass. It is caused by a type of ringworm fungus that usually infects animal species.

膿癬　頭皮癬的一種罕見而嚴重的形式，為一疼痛的炎性塊。它由一種通常感染動物的癬菌引起。

kernicterus *n.* staining and subsequent damage of the brain by bile pigment (bilirubin), which may occur in severe cases of *haemolytic disease of the newborn. Immature brain cells in the *basal ganglia are affected, and as brain development proceeds a pattern of *cerebral palsy emerges at about six months, with uncoordinated movements, deafness, disturbed vision, and feeding and speech difficulties.

核黃疸　由膽色素（膽紅素）引起的腦部着色及繼發損傷。本病可發生於嚴重的新生兒溶血病患兒。基底神經節中的未成熟腦細胞受累，且隨着腦的發育，在約 6 個月時，出現某種形式的大腦性麻痺，伴發運動不協調、耳聾、視力障礙和餵養及説話困難。

Kernig's sign a symptom of *meningitis in which the hamstring muscles in the legs are so stiff that the patient is unable to extend his legs at the knee when the thighs are held at a right angle to the body.

克尼格徵　腦膜炎的一種症狀。大腿的膕繩肌極為僵硬，以致當患者大腿與身體成直角時，膝部不能伸直。

ketamine *n.* a drug used to produce anaesthesia, mainly in children. It is administered by injection. Trade name: **Ketalar**.

氯胺酮　用於誘導麻醉的一種藥物，主要用於兒童，注射給藥。商品名：Ketalar。

ketoconazole *n.* an antifungal drug (*see* imidazole) used in the treatment of such fungal diseases as *candidosis, *histoplasmosis, and *blastomycosis. It is taken by mouth; side-effects include dizziness, drowsiness, nausea, and vomiting. Trade name: **Nizoral**.

酮康唑　一種抗真菌藥（參閱 imidazole）。用於治療真菌性疾病，如念珠菌病、組織胞漿菌病及芽生菌病。口服，副作用包括：頭暈、嗜睡、惡心及嘔吐。商品名：Nizoral。

ketogenesis *n.* the production of *ketone bodies. These are normal products of lipid metabolism and can be used to provide energy. The condition of *ketosis can occur when excess ketone bodies are produced.

酮生成　產生酮體。酮體是脂代謝的正常產物，且可用於提供能量。但若產生過多的酮體，可能發生酮病。

ketogenic diet a diet that promotes the formation of *ketone bodies in the tissues. A ketogenic diet is one in which the principal energy source is fat rather than carbohydrate.

生酮膳食　促使組織內酮體形成的膳食。在生酮膳食中，主要的能量來源是脂肪，而不是碳水化合物。

ketonaemia n. the presence in the blood of *ketone bodies.

酮血（症）　血中出現酮體。

ketone n. any member of a group of organic compounds consisting of a carbonyl group (=CO) flanked by two alkyl groups. The ketones acetoacetic acid, acetone, and β-hydroxybutyrate (known as *ketone* (or *acetone*) *bodies*) are produced during the metabolism of fats. *See also* ketosis.

酮　羰基（=CO）兩側各連接着一個烴基構成的一組有機化合物。酮類（乙醯乙酸、丙酮及 β-羥丁酸）（稱為酮或丙酮體）是脂肪代謝過程中產生的。參閱 ketosis。

ketonuria (acetonuria) n. the presence in the urine of *ketone (acetone) bodies. This may occur in diabetes mellitus, starvation, or after persistent vomiting and results from the partial oxidation of fats. Ketone bodies may be detected by adding a few drops of 5% sodium nitroprusside solution and a solution of ammonia to the urine; the gradual development of a purplish-red colour indicates their presence.

酮尿（症）　尿中存在酮（丙酮）體。這可發生於糖尿病、飢餓或持續嘔吐之後；它是由脂肪不完全氧化所致。在尿中加入幾滴 5% 的亞硝基鐵氰化鈉及氨液可檢測出酮體；逐漸變成紫紅色表明酮體的存在。

ketoprofen n. an anti-inflammatory drug (*see* NSAID), administered by mouth to treat various arthritic and rheumatic diseases. Side-effects are rare, but indigestion sometimes occurs. Trade names: **Orudis**, **Oruvail**.

酮洛芬　一種抗炎藥物（參閱 NSAID），口服用藥，用於治療關節疾病和風濕病。副作用罕見，但有時可出現消化不良。商品名：Orudis，Oruvail。

ketose n. a simple sugar that terminates with a keto group (−C=O); for example, *fructose.

酮糖　末端為一個酮基（−C=O）的單糖，例如果糖。

ketosis n. raised levels of *ketone bodies in the body tissues. Ketone bodies are normal products of fat metabolism and can be oxidized to produce energy.

酮病　人體組織中的酮體水平升高。酮體是脂肪代謝的正常產物，且可被氧化產生能量。當發生脂肪代謝不平衡時，酮

Elevated levels arise when there is an imbalance in fat metabolism, such as occurs in diabetes mellitus or starvation. Ketosis may result in severe *acidosis. *See also* ketonuria.

體水平升高，如糖尿病或飢餓時。酮病可導致嚴重的酸中毒。參閱 ketonuria。

keyhole surgery *see* minimally invasive surgery.

鎖眼外科 參閱 minimally invasive surgery。

khat (qat, kat) *n.* the leaves of the shrub *Catha edulis*, which contain a stimulant. In the Yemen these leaves are wrapped around betel nuts and chewed: this habit is associated with the development of oral *leucoplakia.

卡塔葉 灌木衛矛科植物卡塔的葉子，其中含一種興奮劑。在也門，將這種葉子包在檳榔上嚼食。這種習慣與口腔黏膜白斑病的發生有關。

kidney *n.* either of the pair of organs responsible for the excretion of nitrogenous wastes, principally urea, from the blood (see illustration). The kidneys are situated at the back of the abdomen, below the diaphragm, one on each side of the spine; they are supplied with blood by the renal arteries. Each kidney is enclosed in a fibrous capsule and is composed of an outer *cortex* and an inner *medulla*. The active units of the kidney are the *nephrons, within the cortex and medulla, which filter the blood under pressure and then reabsorb water and

腎 負責血液中含氮廢物，主要是排出尿素的一對器官（見圖）。腎位於腹部的後面，膈肌下方，分別位於脊柱兩側；它們由腎動脈供給血液。每個腎由一個纖維囊包繞，並且由外面的皮質和裏面的髓質組成。腎的功能單位是腎單位，位於皮質和髓質內，在壓力下過濾血液，然後重吸收水分及所選擇的物質回到血液中。如此形成的尿從腎單位經腎小管進入腎盂，再由此至輸尿管，導入膀胱。參閱 haemodialy-

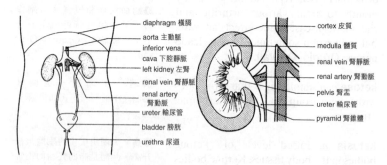

Position of the kidneys
腎的位置

Section through a kidney
腎的切面

selected substances back into the blood. The *urine thus formed is conducted from the nephrons via the renal tubules into the *renal pelvis* and from here to the ureter, which leads to the bladder. *See also* haemodialysis, horseshoe kidney, renal function tests.

Kienböck's disease necrosis of the *lunate bone of the wrist, caused by the cutting off of its blood supply. It most commonly follows injury, often trivial.

killer cell *see* lymphocyte, natural killer cell.

kilo- *prefix denoting* a thousand.

kilocalorie *n.* one thousand calories. *See* calorie.

kilogram *n.* the *SI unit of mass equal to 1000 grams and defined in terms of the international prototype (a cylinder of platinum-iridium alloy) kept at Sèvres, near Paris. Symbol: kg.

kin- (kine-) *prefix denoting* movement.

kinaesthesia *n.* the sense that enables the brain to be constantly aware of the position and movement of muscles in different parts of the body. This is achieved by means of *proprioceptors, which send impulses from muscles, joints, and tendons. Without this sense, coordinated movement would be impossible with the eyes closed.

kinaesthesiometer *n.* an instrument for measuring a patient's awareness of the muscular and joint movements of his own body: used during the investigation of nervous and muscular disorders and certain forms of brain damage.

sis，horseshoe kidney，renal function tests。

金伯克病 腕半月骨的壞死，由其血供被切斷引起，最常發生在損傷，尤其是不嚴重的損傷之後。

殺傷細胞 參閱 lymphocyte，natural killer cell。

〔前綴〕千 一千。

千卡 一千卡。參閱 calorie。

千克 質量的國際單位，等於 1000 克，它是由保存在巴黎附近的塞夫爾國際原器（鉑-銥合金的圓柱）規定的。符號：kg。

〔前綴〕運動

運動覺 使人腦總是能意識到身體各個部位肌肉的位置和運動的感覺。這是通過從肌肉、關節及肌腱發出衝動的本體感覺器獲得的。沒有這種感覺，閉眼時就不可能產生協調運動。

肌動覺測量器 用於測量患者對其本身肌肉和關節運動的知覺的一種儀器。在神經和肌肉疾病及某些類型腦損傷的調查研究中使用。

kinanaesthesia *n*. inability to sense the positions and movements of parts of the body, with consequent disordered physical activity.

運動感覺缺失　不能感覺身體各部分的位置和運動以及隨之發生的身體運動障礙。

kinase *n*. **1.** an agent that can convert the inactive form of an enzyme (*see* proenzyme) to the active form. **2.** an enzyme that catalyses the transfer of phosphate groups. An example is *phosphofructokinase.

激（活）酶　**(1)** 能使某種酶的無活性型（參閱 proenzyme）轉變為活性型的一種因子。**(2)** 催化磷酸基轉移的一種酶，如：磷酸果糖激酶。

kinematics *n*. the study of motion and the forces required to produce it. This includes the different forces at work during the movement of a single part of the body, and more complex movements such as running and climbing.

運動學　有關運動和產生運動所需的力的學科。它包括人體單一部位運動時，及更為複雜的運動時，如跑步及爬山時，做功的各種力。

kineplasty *n*. method of amputation in which the muscles and tendons of the affected limb are arranged so that they can be integrated with a specially made artificial replacement. This enables direct movement of the artificial hand or limb by the muscles.

運動整形截肢術　截肢術的一種方法。術中，整理患肢肌肉和肌腱，以使它能與特製的人工替換物結合為一整體。這樣就可通過肌肉，使人工手或人工肢體直接運動。

-kinesis *suffix denoting* movement.

〔後綴〕運動

kinetochore *n*. *see* centromere.

着絲點　參閱 centromere。

kinin *n*. one of a group of naturally occurring polypeptides that are powerful *vasodilators, which lower blood pressure, and cause contraction of smooth muscle. The kinins *bradykinin* and *kallidin* are formed in the blood by the action of proteolytic enzymes (*kallikreins*) on certain plasma globulins (*kininogens*). Kinins are not normally present in the blood, but are formed under certain conditions; for example when tissue is damaged or when there are changes in the pH and temperature

激肽　天然存在的一組多肽，它們是強有力的血管擴張劑，可降低血壓，引起平滑肌收縮。激肽類緩激肽和卡里定是通過蛋白水解酶（激肽釋放酶）對某些血漿球蛋白（激肽原）的作用在血中形成的（激肽形成）。正常情況下，激肽不存在於血液中，它們在一定條件下形成。例如，當組織受損或血液酸鹼度或溫度變化時。據認為：激肽在炎症反應中起作用。

of the blood. They are thought to play a role in inflammatory response.

kiss of life *see* mouth-to-mouth respiration.

口對口復蘇法　參閱 mouth-to-mouth respiration。

Klebsiella *n.* a genus of Gram-negative rodlike nonmotile bacteria, mostly lactose-fermenting, found in the respiratory, intestinal, and urinogenital tracts of animals and man. The species *K. oxytoca* is associated with human urinary infections; *K. pneumoniae* is associated with pneumonia and other respiratory infections. The species *K. rhinoscleromatis* causes *rhinoscleroma, a chronic infection of the nose and pharynx.

克雷白桿菌屬　一屬革蘭氏陰性不動型桿狀菌，大部分能發酵乳糖，見於動物和人的呼吸道、腸道及泌尿生殖道。泌尿克雷白桿菌與人類泌尿道感染有關；肺炎克雷白桿菌與肺炎及其他呼吸道感染有關；鼻硬結克雷白桿菌引起鼻硬結症——鼻咽的一種慢性感染。

Klebs-Loeffler bacillus *see* Corynebacterium.

克-勒氏桿菌　參閱 Corynebacterium。

Kleine-Levin syndrome a rare episodic disorder characterized by periods (usually of a few days or weeks) in which sufferers eat enormously, sleep for most of the day and night, and may become more dependent or aggressive than normal. Between episodes they are usually quite unaffected. The disorder almost always resolves spontaneously.

克-萊氏綜合徵　具有發作期（常為幾天或幾周）的一種罕見的陣發性疾病。發作期內，病人飯量極大，白天晚上多數時間睡覺，可比正常狀態時更具依賴性或好鬥性。不發作時，病人通常正常。此病常自然痊愈。

klepto- *prefix denoting* stealing.

〔前級〕偷竊

kleptomania *n.* a pathologically strong impulse to steal, often in the absence of any desire for the stolen object(s). It is sometimes associated with *depression.

偷竊狂　一種病態的強烈的偷竊衝動，常常並不是想要所偷的東西。它有時伴有抑鬱症。

Klinefelter's syndrome a genetic disorder in which there are three sex chromosomes, XXY, rather than the normal XX or XY. Affected individuals are apparently male, but are tall and thin, with small testes, failure of normal sperm

克萊因費爾特綜合徵　一種遺傳病。患者有三條性染色體：XXY，而不是正常的 XX 或 XY。患者表面上是男性，但體瘦細高，睾丸小，無正常精子產生（精子缺乏），乳房增

production (azoospermia), enlargement of the breasts (gynaecomastia), and absence of facial and body hair.

大（男子女性型乳房）及面部和身體無毛。

Klumpke's paralysis a partial paralysis of the arm caused by injury to a baby's *brachial plexus during birth. This may result from an obstetric manoeuvre in which the arm is raised at the shoulder to an extreme degree, which damages the lower cervical (neck) and upper thoracic (chest) nerve roots of the spinal cord. It results in weakness and wasting of the muscles of the hand.

克隆普克麻痺 分娩過程中嬰兒臂神經叢損傷引起的臂部部分性麻痺。這可能是由於某種助產措施使肩臂過度抬高，損傷了脊髓的下頸和上胸脊神經根所致。本病導致手部肌肉無力和消瘦。

kneading *n. see* petrissage.

揉捏法 參閱 petrissage。

knee *n.* the hinge joint (*see* ginglymus) between the end of the femur, the top of the tibia, and the back of the *patella (kneecap). It is commonly involved in *sports injuries (such as a torn meniscus or ligament) and is a common site of osteoarthritis and rheumatoid arthritis; it can be replaced by an artificial joint.

膝 股骨端、脛骨頂和髕骨後之間的鉸鏈式關節（參閱 ginglymus）。此關節常在運動損傷（如半月板或韌帶撕傷）中受累，並且是骨關節炎和類風濕性關節炎的常發部位；它可由人工關節替換。

knight's-move thought a form of thought disorder, characteristic of *schizophrenia, in which the *associations of ideas are bizarre and tortuous.

騎士思維 思維紊亂的一種形式，是精神分裂症的特徵。患者的聯想離奇而扭曲。

knock-knee *n.* abnormal in-curving of the legs, resulting in a gap between the feet when the knees are in contact. In severe cases there is stress on the knee, ankle, and foot joints, resulting eventually in degenerative arthritis. The condition may be corrected by *osteotomy. Medical name: **genu valgum**.

膝外翻 兩腿的異常內曲，導致兩膝接觸時，兩足間形成一間隙。嚴重的病例有膝、踝及足關節的壓迫感，最終造成退行性關節炎。本病可通過骨切開術糾正。醫學用語：膝外翻。

Kocher manoeuvre a method for *reduction of a dislocated shoulder by manipulation.

科赫爾手法 一種通過推拿使錯位關節復位的方法。

Koch's bacillus *see* Mycobacterium.

科赫桿菌 參閱 Mycobacterium。

Koebner phenomenon (isomorphic response) a phenomenon that occurs in skin diseases, especially psoriasis and lichen planus, in which the characteristic lesions of the disease appear in linear form in response to such trauma as cuts, burns, or scratches.

科布內現象　皮膚病中見到的一種現象，尤其見於牛皮癬和扁平苔癬。切傷、燒傷或搔刮傷後，典型的疾病損傷呈直綫形。

Köhler's disease inflammation of the *navicular bone of the foot (see osteochondritis). It occurs in children, causing pain and limping, and is treated by strapping the foot.

克勒病　足舟狀骨的炎症（參閱 osteochondritis）。本病發生於兒童，引起疼痛和跛行，可用橡皮膏貼足治療。

koilonychia n. the development of thin (brittle) concave (spoon-shaped) nails, a common disorder that can occur with anaemia due to iron deficiency, though the cause is not known. Any underlying disease should be treated.

反甲　形成薄（脆）、凹陷（匙狀）的指甲。本病是一種常見病，可發生於缺鐵性貧血。病因不明，應治療任何原發病。

Koplik's spots small red spots with bluish-white centres that often appear on the mucous membranes of the mouth in *measles.

科普利克斑　中央是淡藍發白的小紅斑，常出現於麻疹患者的口腔黏膜上。

koro n. a state of acute anxiety, seen especially in certain cultures (such as that of the Chinese of SE Asia), characterized by a sudden belief that the penis is shrinking into the abdomen and will disappear: the sufferer is convinced that disappearance of the penis means death. Occasionally women have a similar belief that their breasts are disappearing into their body. It is usually treated with tranquillizing drugs and reassurance.

陰縮，縮陰　一種極度憂慮的狀態，尤其見於某些特定文化的人羣中（如東南亞華裔），其特徵是突然相信其陰莖縮入腹內，並會消失，患者深信陰莖消失意味着死亡。偶爾，女性也有類似的想法，認為她們的乳房正在向體內消失。本病通常用安定藥和安慰法來治療。

Korsakoff's syndrome (Korsakoff's psychosis) an organic disorder affecting the brain that results in a memory defect in which new information fails to be learnt although events from the past are still recalled; *disorientation for time and place; and a tendency to invent

科爾薩科夫綜合徵　又稱科爾薩科夫精神病，侵犯大腦的一種器質性疾病，導致一種記憶缺陷，不能學到新信息，但能回想起過去的事件；時間及空間定向力障礙；傾向於虛構素材以填充記憶空白（參閱

material to fill memory blanks (*see* confabulation). The commonest cause of the condition is alcoholism, especially when this has led to deficiency of thiamin (vitamin B₁). Large doses of thiamin are given as treatment. The condition often becomes chronic.

confabulation）。本病最常見的病因是酒精中毒，尤其是在酒精中毒導致硫胺（維生素 B₁）缺乏時。治療使用大劑量硫胺。本病常變為慢性。

KPTT kaolin partial thromboplastin time: a method for estimating the degree of anticoagulation induced by heparin therapy for venous thrombosis.

白陶土部分凝血激酶時間　肝素療法治療靜脈血栓形成時用於估計所產生的抗凝程度的一種方法。

kraurosis *n.* shrinking of a body part, usually the vulva in elderly women (*kraurosis vulvae*).

乾皺　身體某一部分皺縮，通常指老年婦女的外陰。

Krebs cycle (citric acid cycle) a complex cycle of enzyme-catalysed reactions, occurring within the cells of all living animals, in which acetate, in the presence of oxygen, is broken down to produce energy in the form of *ATP (via the *electron transport chain) and carbon dioxide. The cycle is the final step in the oxidation of carbohydrates, fats, and proteins; some of the intermediary products of the cycle are used in the synthesis of amino acids.

克雷布斯循環（三羧酸循環）一種酶促反應的複雜循環，發生於所有活動物的細胞內。在此循環中，乙酸化合物在有氧存在的情況下被分解，產生 ATP 形式的能量（通過電子轉移鏈）和二氧化碳。此循環是糖類、脂肪類和蛋白質類氧化作用的最終步驟；有些循環中間產物用於合成氨基酸。

Krukenberg tumour a rapidly developing malignant growth in one or (more often) both ovaries. The tumour is secondary to a primary growth in the stomach or intestine.

克魯肯貝格瘤　在一側或兩側（更常見）卵巢內一種發展迅速的惡性腫瘤，它繼發於胃或腸的原發瘤。

krypton-81m *n.* a radioactive gas that is the shortest-lived isotope in medical use (half-life 13 seconds). It can be used to investigate the function of the lungs. The patient breathes a small quantity of the gas, the arrival of which in different parts of the lungs is recorded by means of a *gamma camera. *See also* rubidium-81.

氪-81 m　一種放射性氣體，是醫學上使用的壽命最短的（半衰期 13 秒）放射性同位素。它可用於研究肺功能。病人吸入少量該種氣體，用 γ 照相機記錄氣體到達肺不同部位的情況。參閱 rubidium-81。

Küntscher nail a metal rod that is inserted down the middle of the femur (thigh bone) to stabilize a transverse fracture of the shaft.

金切爾釘　沿股骨（大腿骨）中部插入的一根金屬釘，用於固定股骨體的橫向骨折。

Kupffer cells phagocytic cells that line the sinusoids of the *liver (see macrophage). They are particularly concerned with the formation of *bile and are often seen to contain fragments of red blood cells and pigment granules that are derived from the breakdown of haemoglobin.

庫普費爾細胞　覆蓋肝竇內面的巨噬細胞（參閱 macrophage）。它們尤其與膽汁的形成有關，常發現此細胞內含有紅細胞碎片以及血紅蛋白分解產生的色素顆粒。

kuru (trembling disease) *n.* a disease that affects only members of the Fore tribe of New Guinea. It involves a progressive degeneration of the nerve cells of the central nervous system, particularly in the region of the brain that controls movement. Muscular control becomes defective and shiver-like tremors occur in the trunk, limbs, and head. Kuru affects mainly women and children and usually proves fatal within 9–12 months. It is thought to be caused by a *prion and transmitted by cannibalism. *See also* spongiform encephalopathy.

庫魯病（震顫病）　僅發生於新幾內亞富爾族居民的一種病。本病引起中樞神經系統神經細胞的進行性變性，尤其在控制運動的大腦區域。由於肌肉控制變得有缺陷，所以軀幹、四肢和頭部發生顫抖樣震顫。庫魯病主要發生於婦女和兒童，通常在 9~12 個月內致死。據認為，本病由蛋白質性感染粒子引起，並通過同類相食作用傳播。參閱 spongiform encephalopathy。

Kussmaul breathing the slow deep respiration associated with acidosis.

庫斯毛爾呼吸　與酸中毒有關的緩慢呼吸。

Kveim test a test used for the diagnosis of *sarcoidosis. Tissue from a lymph node of a person suffering from the disease is injected intradermally; the development of a granuloma at the injection site indicates that the subject has sarcoidosis.

克維姆試驗　用於肉樣瘤病的診斷試驗。將從該病患者淋巴結取下的組織注入皮下，如果在注射部位形成肉芽腫，則表明患者確實患有肉樣瘤病。

kwashiorkor *n.* a form of malnutrition due to a diet deficient in protein and energy-producing foods, common among certain African tribes. Kwashiorkor develops when, after prolonged breast

克瓦希奧科病　由於飲食中蛋白質和產能食物不足引起的一種營養不良，常見於非洲某些部落中。本病發生於長期哺乳後，小兒斷乳並且開始不適宜

feeding, the child is weaned onto an inadequate traditional family diet. The diet is such that it is physically impossible for the child to consume the required quantity in order to obtain sufficient protein and energy. Kwashiorkor is most common in children between the ages of one and three years. The symptoms are *oedema, loss of appetite, diarrhoea, general discomfort, and apathy; the child fails to thrive and there is usually associated gastrointestinal infection.

的傳統家庭飲食時。這種飲食從生理學角度講，小兒不可能攝入所需要的數量，來獲取足夠的蛋白質和能量。本病最常見於1~3歲的小兒。症狀有：水腫、食慾減退、腹瀉、全身不適和冷淡；小兒不能茁壯成長，且伴有胃腸感染。

Kyasanur Forest disease a tropical disease, common in southern India, caused by a virus transmitted to man through the bite of the forest-dwelling tick *Haemaphysalis spinigera*. Symptoms include fever, headache, muscular pains, vomiting, conjunctivitis, exhaustion, bleeding of nose and gums and, subsequently, internal bleeding and the *necrosis of various tissues. General therapy, in the absence of specific treatment, involves relief of dehydration and loss of blood; analgesics are given to alleviate pain.

基亞薩努爾森林病 一種熱帶病，常見於印度南部，由一種病毒引起，通過一種森林蜱距刺血蜱的叮咬傳播給人。症狀包括：發燒、頭痛、肌肉痛、惡心、結膜炎、疲憊、鼻腔及牙齦出血，以及繼發的內出血及各種組織壞死。在沒有特異性療法的情況下，全身療法包括減輕脫水和失血；給予鎮痛藥以緩解疼痛。

kymograph *n.* an instrument for recording the flow and varying pressure of the blood within the blood vessels. **–kymography** *n.*

記波器 用於記錄血管內血液流動和壓力變化的一種儀器。

kypho- *prefix denoting* a hump.

〔前綴〕**駝背**

kyphos *n.* a sharply localized forward angulation of the spine, resulting in the appearance of a lump (the deformity of the traditional hunchback). The deformity is due to collapse of the anterior part of a vertebra, usually caused by osteoporosis, a secondary malignant deposit, or tuberculosis.

脊柱後凸 脊柱局部明顯的向前彎曲，以致出現一隆突（傳統的駝背畸形）。這種畸形是由於椎骨的前部萎陷所致，而椎骨前部萎陷往往由骨質疏鬆症、繼發性惡性沉積物或結核病引起。

kyphoscoliosis *n.* abnormal curvature of the spine both forwards and sideways:

脊柱後側凸 脊柱向前和向側異常彎曲，即脊柱後凸合併脊

*kyphosis combined with *scoliosis. The deformity may occur during growth for no apparent reason (*idiopathic kyphoscoliosis*) or may result from any of several diseases involving the vertebrae and spinal muscles. Special braces can reduce the extent of the deformity; *osteotomy of the backbone may be required to correct severe deformity.

kyphosis *n.* excessive outward curvature of the spine, causing hunching of the back. A *mobile kyphosis* may be caused by bad posture or muscle weakness or may develop to compensate for another condition, such as hip deformity. A *fixed kyphosis may result* from collapse of the vertebrae (as in senile *osteoporosis), from *osteochondritis in the young, or from ankylosing *spondylitis. Lesser degrees of fixed kyphosis may be balanced by *lordosis (inward curvature) in another part of the spine. Treatment depends on the cause, and may include physiotherapy, bracing, and spinal *osteotomy in severe cases. *See also* kyphos, kyphoscoliosis.

柱側凸。這種畸形可發生於成長期間而無明顯原因（自發性脊柱後側凸），也可由某些疾病累及脊椎和棘肌引起。特製的支撐物可減少畸形的程度；糾正嚴重畸形需行脊柱骨切開術。

脊柱後凸　脊柱過度向外彎曲，引起駝背。可動性脊柱後凸可由不良的姿勢或肌肉衰弱引起，或者為代償其他疾病，如髖畸形而產生。不動性脊柱後凸可由椎骨萎陷（如老年性骨質疏鬆時）、年輕人骨軟骨炎或強直性脊椎炎引起。較輕的不動性脊柱後凸可通過脊柱其他部分的脊柱前凸（向內彎曲）得到平衡。治療取決於病因，包括理療、支撐，嚴重病例可行脊椎骨切開術。參閱 kyphos，kyphoscoliosis。

L

labelling index the proportion of cells in a sample of tissue that are producing DNA. Cells that are synthesizing DNA take up tritiated thymidine, which shows up on an autoradiograph (*see* autoradiography) of the sample.

标记指数　某個組織樣品中，正在生產 DNA 的細胞的比例。合成 DNA 的細胞吸收氚標誌的胸苷，而這種胸苷在該樣品的自體放射照片上顯示出來（參閱 autoradiography）。

labetalol *n.* a combined alpha- and beta-blocking drug (*see* sympatholytic), sometimes found to be more effective in the treatment of high blood pressure than

拉貝洛爾　一種 α-β-受體聯合阻滯藥，（參閱 sympatholytic），治療高血壓時，有時比 β-受體阻滯劑更有效。

beta blockers. It is administered by mouth or intravenous infusion. Possible side-effects include faintness on standing up, scalp tingling, and difficulty with urination and ejaculation. Trade names: **Labrocol**, **Trandate**.

口服或靜脈輸注給藥。可能的副作用包括：起立時暈厥、頭皮麻刺感，以及排尿和射精困難。商品名：Labrocol，Trandate。

labial *adj*. **1.** relating to the lips or to a labium. **2.** designating the surface of a tooth adjacent to the lips.

唇的　**(1)** 與雙唇或某一唇樣結構有關的。**(2)** 指與唇相鄰的牙齒表面。

labio- *prefix denoting* the lip(s).

〔前綴〕嘴唇

labiomancy *n*. lip-reading.

唇讀

labioplasty (cheiloplasty) *n*. surgical repair of injury or deformity of the lips.

唇成形術　手術修復唇損傷或畸形。

labium *n* (*pl*. **labia**) a lip-shaped structure, especially either of the two pairs of skin folds that enclose the *vulva. The larger outer pair are known as the *labia majora* and the smaller inner pair the *labia minora*.

唇　唇形結構，尤指封閉外陰的兩對皮膚皺褶，外面稍大的一對稱為大陰唇，裏面稍小的一對稱為小陰唇。

labour *n*. the sequence of actions by which a baby and the afterbirth (placenta) are expelled from the uterus at childbirth. The process usually starts spontaneously about 280 days after conception, but it may be started by artificial means (*see* induction). In the first stage the muscular wall of the uterus begins contracting while the muscle fibres of the cervix relax so that the cervix expands. A portion of the membranous sac (amnion) surrounding the baby is pushed into the opening and ruptures under the pressure, releasing *amniotic fluid to the exterior. In the second stage the baby's head appears at the cervix and the contractions of the uterus strengthen. The passage of the infant through the vagina is assisted by contractions of the abdominal muscles and conscious pushing by

分娩　出生時嬰兒和胎盤從子宮排出的一系列動作。通常在受孕後約 280 天，此過程自動開始，但也可人工手段啟動（參閱 induction）。第一產程時，子宮壁的肌肉開始收縮而子宮頸肌纖維鬆弛，於是宮頸擴張。包繞胎兒的膜性囊（羊膜）的一部分被推入子宮頸口，並在壓力下破裂，釋放出羊水，流向體外。第二產程時，胎兒頭部出現在子宮頸，子宮收縮加強。在母親腹肌收縮和有意識的推動下，嬰兒得以通過陰道。當胎兒頭頂部出現在陰道口時，整個胎兒便可順利娩出陰道，然後剪斷臍帶。如果胎頭娩出受阻，則可在周圍組織上作一切口（參閱 episiotomy）。最後產程時，由

the mother. When the top of the baby's head appears at the vaginal opening the whole infant is eased clear of the vagina, and the umbilical cord is cut. If the emergence of the head is impeded an incision may be made in the surrounding tissue (*see* episiotomy). In the final stage the placenta and membranes are pushed out by the continuing contraction of the uterus, which eventually returns to its unexpanded state. The average duration of labour is about 12 hours in first pregnancies and about 8 hours in subsequent pregnancies. The pain of labour may be reduced if the mother trains her abdominal muscles during the prenatal period and by the use of drugs (*accelerated labour*). *See also* Caesarean section.

labrum *n.* (*pl.* **labra**) a lip or liplike structure; occurring, for example, around the margins of the articulating socket (acetabulum) of the hip bone.

labyrinth (inner ear) *n. a* convoluted system of cavities and ducts comprising the organs of hearing and balance. The *membranous labyrinth* is a series of interconnected membranous canals and chambers consisting of the *semicircular canals, *utricle, and *saccule (concerned

於子宮的持續收縮，胎盤和胎膜被推出，而子宮最終恢復到其不擴張狀態。初產婦平均分娩時間約為 12 小時，經產婦約為 8 小時。母親在產前鍛煉腹肌並且使用藥物，分娩的疼痛可以減輕（加速性分娩）。參閱 Caesarean section。

唇 唇或唇樣結構，如位於髖臼的關節盂邊緣周圍。

迷路 由組成聽覺和平衡器官的腔室和管道形成的螺旋形系統。膜迷路是一系列相連的膜性管道和腔室，包括半規管、橢圓囊、球囊（與平衡有關）和蝸管的中央腔（與聽覺有關）（見圖）。膜迷路內充滿液體

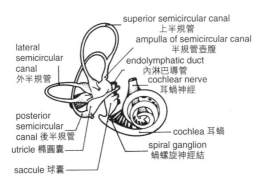

Membranous labyrinth of the right ear
右耳膜迷路

with balance) and the central cavity of the *cochlea (concerned with hearing). (See illustration.) It is filled with a fluid, *endolymph*. The *bony labyrinth* is the system of the bony canals and chambers that surround the membranous labyrinth. It is embedded in the petrous part of the *temporal bone and is filled with fluid (*perilymph*).

——內淋巴。骨迷路是圍繞在膜迷路外面的骨質管道和腔室系統。它嵌在顳骨岩部,充滿液體(外淋巴)。

labyrinthitis (otitis interna) *n.* inflammation of the inner ear (labyrinth). *See* otitis.

迷路炎 內耳(迷路)發炎。參閱 otitis。

laceration *n.* a tear in the flesh producing a wound with irregular edges.

撕裂 造成傷口邊緣不規則的軟組織撕裂。

lacertus *n.* a band of fibres or a tendon-like structure.

纖維束 一束纖維或腱樣結構。

lacrimal apparatus the structures that produce and drain away fluid from the eye (see illustration). The *lacrimal gland* secretes *tears, which drain away through small openings (*puncta*) at the inner corner of the eye into two *lacrimal canaliculi*. From there the tears pass into the nasal cavity via the *lacrimal sac* and the *nasolacrimal duct.

淚器 產生並從眼內排出液體的結構(見圖)。淚腺分泌淚液,淚液經眼內眥的兩個小開口(淚點)流入淚小管。由此,眼淚經淚囊和鼻淚管流入鼻腔。

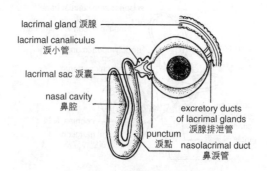

lacrimal gland 淚腺
lacrimal canaliculus 淚小管
lacrimal sac 淚囊
nasal cavity 鼻腔
excretory ducts of lacrimal glands 淚腺排泄管
punctum 淚點
nasolacrimal duct 鼻淚管

The lacrimal apparatus
淚器

lacrimal bone the smallest bone of the face: either of a pair of rectangular bones that contribute to the orbits. *See* skull.

涙骨　面部最小的骨頭；參與構成眼眶的一對長方形骨。參閱 skull。

lacrimal nerve a branch of the *ophthalmic nerve that supplies the lacrimal gland (*see* lacrimal apparatus) and conjunctiva.

涙神經　視神經的一支，支配涙腺（參閱 lacrimal apparatus）和結膜。

lacrimation *n.* the production of excess tears; crying. *See also* lacrimal apparatus.

流涙　生成大量涙液；哭泣。參閱 lacrimal apparatus。

lacrimator *n.* an agent that irritates the eyes, causing excessive secretion of tears.

催涙劑　刺激眼引起大量涙液分泌的製劑。

lact- (lacti-, lacto-) *prefix denoting* **1.** milk. **2.** lactic acid.

〔前綴〕**(1)** 乳　**(2)** 乳酸

lactalbumin *n.* a milk protein present in milk at a lower concentration than *casein. Unlike casein, it is not precipitated from milk under acid conditions; it is therefore a constituent of cheese made from whey rather than curd.

乳白蛋白　乳汁中存在的一種乳蛋白，其濃度低於酪蛋白。乳白蛋白不同於酪蛋白，它不是乳汁在酸性環境中沉澱下來的；所以，它是用乳清，而非凝乳製成的乳酪的成分。

lactase *n.* an enzyme, secreted by the glands of the small intestine, that converts lactose (milk sugar) into glucose and galactose during digestion.

乳糖酶　指腸腺分泌的一種酶。在消化過程中，將乳糖轉化為葡萄糖和半乳糖。

lactation *n.* the secretion of milk by the *mammary glands of the breasts, which usually begins at the end of pregnancy. A fluid called *colostrum is secreted before the milk is produced; both secretions are released in response to the sucking action of the infant on the nipple. Lactation is controlled by hormones (*see* prolactin, oxytocin); it stops when the baby is no longer fed at the breast.

泌乳　乳房的乳腺分泌乳汁，它通常在妊娠末期開始。在乳汁生成前分泌所謂的初乳；嬰兒吸吮乳頭反射地引起初乳和乳汁分泌。泌乳過程由激素（參閱 prolactin，oxytocin）控制；嬰兒斷奶後，泌乳停止。

lacteal *n.* a blind-ended lymphatic vessel that extends into a villus of the small *intestine. Digested fats are absorbed into the lacteals.

乳糜管　伸入小腸絨毛中的盲端淋巴管；消化了的脂肪被吸收進入乳糜管。

lactic acid a compound that forms in the cells as the end-product of glucose metabolism in the absence of oxygen (*see* glycolysis). During strenuous exercise pyruvic acid is reduced to lactic acid, which may accumulate in the muscles and cause cramp. Lactic acid (owing to its low pH) is an important food preservative. The lactic acid produced by the fermentation of milk is responsible for the preservation and flavour of cheese, yoghurt, and other fermented milk products.

乳酸　作為無氧葡萄糖代謝的終產物在細胞內形成的一種化合物（參閱 glycolysis）。在大強度的鍛煉過程中，丙酮酸被分解為乳酸，乳酸在肌肉內蓄積並引起肌肉痙攣。乳酸（由於其 pH 值低）是一種重要的食物防腐劑。牛乳發酵生成的乳酸可防止乳酪、酸乳及其他發酵奶製品腐敗，並賦予其美好味道。

lactiferous *adj*. transporting or secreting milk, as the *lactiferous ducts* of the breast.

輸乳的　輸送或分泌乳汁的，例如乳腺的輸乳管。

lactifuge *n*. a drug that reduces the secretion of milk. Some oestrogenic drugs have this effect and are used to suppress milk production in mothers not breast-feeding.

回乳劑　減少乳汁分泌的一種藥物。雌激素類藥物有此作用，所以可用於抑制不哺乳母親的乳汁產生。

Lactobacillus *n*. a genus of Gram-positive nonmotile rodlike bacteria capable of growth in acid media and of producing lactic acid from the fermentation of carbohydrates. They are found in fermenting animal and plant products, especially dairy products, and in the alimentary tract and vagina. They are responsible for the souring of milk. The species *L. acidophilus* is found in milk and is associated with dental caries. It occurs in very high numbers in the faeces of breast- or bottle-fed infants.

乳桿菌屬　無活動能力的革蘭氏陽性桿菌的一屬，能在酸性培養基中生活，且能使碳水化合物發酵生成乳酸。該屬細菌可見於發酵的動植物產品，尤其是奶製品中，以及消化道和陰道中。它們可以使牛乳變酸。嗜酸乳桿菌見於奶中，且與齲齒有關。母乳餵養和人工餵養的嬰兒糞便中有大量嗜酸乳桿菌存在。

lactogenic hormone *see* prolactin.

催乳激素　參閱 prolactin。

lactose *n*. a sugar, consisting of one molecule of glucose and one of galactose, found only in milk. Lactose is split into its constituent sugars by the enzyme *lactase, which is secreted in the small intestine. This enzyme is missing or is of

乳糖　一種糖，由一分子葡萄糖和一分子半乳糖組成，僅見於乳中。在小腸中分泌的乳糖酶的作用下，乳糖分解成其組成成分單糖。而在一些東方或非洲種族的某些人羣中，乳糖

low activity in certain people of some Eastern and African races. This leads to the inability to absorb lactose, known as *lactose intolerance*.

酶缺失，或其活性低下，導致
不能吸收乳糖，稱為乳糖耐受
不良。

lactosuria *n.* the presence of milk sugar (*lactose) in the urine. This often occurs during pregnancy and breastfeeding or if the milk flow is suppressed.

乳糖尿　尿中存在乳糖。常發
生於妊娠期和哺乳期或者乳汁
流動受阻時。

lactulose *n.* a disaccharide sugar that acts as a gentle but effective *laxative. It is administered by mouth but is not absorbed or broken down, remaining intact until it reaches the colon. There it is split by bacteria into simpler sugars that help to retain water, thereby softening the stools. Trade names: **Duphalac**, **Lactulose**.

乳果糖　一種雙糖，用作温和
而有效的輕瀉藥。口服給藥，
但在到達結腸之前不被吸收，
也不被分解。在結腸內，由細
菌分解為較簡單的糖類；這些
糖類有助於保留水分，從而軟
化糞便。商品名：Duphalac，
Lactulose。

lacuna *n.* (*pl.* **lacunae**) (in anatomy) a small cavity or depression; for example, one of the spaces in compact bone in which a bone cell lies.

腔隙、陷窩　（解剖學）小的
腔室或凹陷。例如密質骨內一
個骨細胞所在的腔隙。

laetrile *n.* a cyanide-containing compound extracted from peach stones. It has been used in *alternative medicine in the treatment of various forms of cancer.

扁桃甙製劑　一種從桃仁中提
取的含氰化物的化合物，在補
救醫學中用於治療多種類型癌
症。

laevo- *prefix. see* levo-.

〔前綴〕左　參閱 levo-。

laevocardia *n.* the normal position of the heart, in which its apex is directed towards the left. *Compare* dextrocardia.

左位心　心臟的正常位置，心
尖指向左方。與 dextrocardia
對比。

lagaena (lagena) *n.* the closed end of the spiral *cochlea. This term is more commonly used to describe the structure homologous to the cochlea in primitive vertebrates.

壺　螺旋形蝸管的盲端，此術
語更常用於指初級脊椎動物的
與耳蝸類似的結構。

lagophthalmos *n.* any condition in which the eye does not close completely. It may lead to corneal damage from undue exposure.

兔眼　眼不能完全閉合的任何
疾病。由於過度暴露，可導致
角膜損傷。

laking *n.* the physical or chemical treatment of blood to abolish the structure of the red cells and thus form a homogeneous solution. Laking is an important preliminary step in the analysis of haemoglobin or enzymes present in red cells.

紅細胞溶解 用化學或物理方法處理紅細胞，從而破壞紅細胞結構，形成同質溶液。紅細胞溶解是分析紅細胞內血紅蛋白和酶的首要步驟。

-lalia *suffix denoting* a condition involving speech.

〔後綴〕**言語** 和言語有關的疾病。

lallation (lalling) *n.* **1.** unintelligible speech-like babbling, as heard from infants. **2.** the immature substitution of one consonant for another (e.g. *l* for *r*).

(1) 嬰兒樣語 像嬰兒一樣的含糊、難懂地說話。**(2) 輔音混淆** 一個輔音對另一個輔音的不完全地替代（如 l 替代 r）。

lambda *n.* the point on the skull at which the lambdoidal and sagittal *sutures meet.

人字縫尖 顱骨上人字縫和矢狀縫的匯合點。

lambdoidal suture *see* suture (def. 1).

人字縫 參閱 suture（釋義1）。

lambliasis *n. see* giardiasis.

賈第蟲病 參閱 giardiasis。

lamella *n.* (*pl.* **lamellae**) **1.** a thin layer, membrane, scale, or plate-like tissue of part. In *bone tissue, lamellae are thin bands of calcified matrix arranged concentrically around a Haversian canal. **2.** a thin gelatinous medicated disc used to apply drugs to the eye. The disc is placed on the eyeball; the gelatinous material dissolves and the drug is absorbed.

(1) 板 一薄層膜，鱗片或者板狀組織或結構。在骨組織中，骨板是圍繞一個哈弗管向心排列的鈣化基質薄板。**(2) 眼片** 眼部用藥時使用的一種凝膠藥物薄片。將眼片貼在眼球上，凝膠物質溶解，藥物被吸收。

lamina *n.* (*pl.* **laminae**) a thin membrane or layer of tissue.

板 薄膜或組織層。

laminectomy (rachiotomy) *n.* surgical cutting into the backbone to obtain access to the spinal cord. The surgeon excises the rear part (the posterior arch) of one or more vertebrae. The operation is performed to remove tumours, to treat injuries to the spine, such as prolapsed

椎板切除術 手術切開椎骨以接近骨髓。外科醫生切開一個或多個椎骨的後部（後弓），行此手術以切除腫瘤，治療脊柱損傷，如椎間盤脫出（術中，將受累的椎間盤切除）或解除脊神經的壓迫。

intervertebral (slipped) disc (in which the affected disc is removed), or to relieve pressure on a spinal nerve.

lamotrigine *n.* an anticonvulsant drug used in the control of epilepsy. It is administered by mouth. Possible side-effects include nausea, headache, double vision, dizziness, *ataxia, and skin rashes. Trade name: **Lamictal**.

拉莫三嗪　用於控制癲癇的抗痙攣藥。口服給藥。可能的副作用包括惡心、頭痛、複視、頭暈、共濟失調和皮疹。商品名：Lamictal。

lanatoside *n.* a drug similar to *digitalis, used in the treatment of heart failure. It is administered by mouth or injection. High doses may cause loss of appetite, nausea, vomiting, headache, disturbed vision, and abnormal heart activity. Trade name: **Cedilanid**.

毛花苷　類似洋地黃的藥物，用於治療心力衰竭。口服或注射給藥。大劑量可引起食慾喪失、惡心、嘔吐、頭痛、視力障礙和心臟活動異常。商品名：Cedilanid。

Lancefield classification a classification of the *Streptococcus* bacteria based on the presence or absence of antigenic carbohydrate on the cell surface. Species are classified into the groups A–S. Most species causing disease in man belong to groups A, B, and D.

蘭斯菲爾德分類法　一種以細胞表面是否存在抗原性糖類為基礎的鏈球菌分類法。鏈球菌分為 A~S 組。多數人類致病菌屬 A、B 和 D 組。

lancet *n.* a broad two-edged surgical knife with a sharp point.

柳葉刀　一種尖頭面寬的雙刃手術刀。

lancinating *adj.* describing a sharp stabbing or cutting pain.

刺割樣的　描述一種尖銳的戳刺或刀割樣疼痛。

Landry's paralysis a rapidly progressive form of the *Guillain-Barré syndrome.

朗德里麻痺　吉-巴氏綜合徵的快速進展型。

Lange curve an obsolescent method of detecting excess globulins in the protein of the cerebrospinal fluid. It was useful in the diagnosis of neurosyphilis and multiple sclerosis but has been superseded by more specific tests.

朗格曲綫　檢測腦脊髓液蛋白質內球蛋白過量的一種已廢用的方法。它曾用於診斷神經梅毒和多發性硬化症，但已被更特異性的試驗取代。

lanugo *n.* fine hair covering the body and limbs of the human fetus. It is most

胎毛　覆蓋人胎軀體和四肢的細微毛髮。大約在妊娠 28 周

profuse at about the 28th week of gestation and is shed around 40 weeks.

時最多，在 40 周左右時脫落。

laparo- *prefix denoting* the loins or abdomen.

〔前綴〕**腰，腹**

laparoscope (peritoneoscope) *n.* a surgical instrument (a type of *endoscope) comprising an illuminated viewing tube that is inserted through the abdominal wall to enable the surgeon to view the abdominal organs (*see* laparoscopy).

腹腔鏡 一種外科器械（一種內窺鏡），由一根帶照明的窺管組成。將此窺管經腹壁插入，外科醫生便可以觀察腹腔器官（參閱 laparoscopy）。

laparoscopy (abdominoscopy, peritoneoscopy) *n.* examination of the abdominal structures (which are contained within the peritoneum) by means of an illuminated tubular instrument (*laparoscope). This is passed through a small incision in the wall of the abdomen after injecting carbon dioxide into the abdominal cavity (pneumoperitoneum). In addition to being a diagnostic aid, it is used when taking a biopsy, aspirating cysts, and dividing adhesions. Surgery, including *cholecystectomy, *fundoplication, *colectomy, *hemicolectomy, and the occlusion of Fallopian tubes for sterilization, can also be performed through a laparoscope, using either a laser or diathermy to control bleeding (*see also* minimally invasive surgery). The laparoscope is also used for collecting ova for *in vitro fertilization and in performing certain gynaecological operations using a laser (*laser laparoscopy*). **–laparoscopic** *adj.*

腹腔鏡檢查 利用一個帶照明的管狀器械（腹腔鏡）檢察腹腔結構（包容在腹膜以內）。將二氧化碳注入腹腔（氣腹）後，經腹壁上一小切口插入腹腔鏡。除用作一種輔助診斷手段，此檢查還用於做活檢，抽吸囊內容物，及分開黏連物。若用激光器或透熱法控制出血（參閱 minimally invasive surgery），通過腹腔鏡還可進行膽囊切除術、胃底摺術結腸切除術，結腸部分切除術，以及絕育術時閉塞輸卵管等等。腹腔鏡還用於試管授精時收集卵子及使用激光器的某些婦科手術（激光腹腔鏡）。

laparotomy *n.* a surgical incision into the abdominal cavity. The operation is done to examine the abdominal organs as a help to diagnosis; for example, to establish the spread of a growth (*exploratory laparotomy*) or as a prelude to major surgery.

剖腹術 手術切開腹腔。行此手術是為了檢查腹腔器官以輔助診斷，例如確定腫物的擴散（剖腹探查）或作為大手術的先期手術。

lardaceous *adj.* resembling lard: often applied to tissue infiltrated with the starch-like substance amyloid (*see* amyloidosis).

豚脂性的　豬油樣的，常用於指澱粉樣物質（澱粉樣蛋白）浸潤的組織（參閱 amyloidosis）。

larva *n.* (*pl.* **larvae**) the preadult or immature stage hatching from the egg of some animal groups, e.g. insects and nematodes, which may be markedly different from the sexually mature adult and have a totally different way of life. For example, the larvae of some flies are parasites of animals and cause disease whereas the adults are free-living. –**larval** *adj.*

幼蟲　某些動物，如昆蟲和綫蟲由卵孵出成蟲前的未成熟階段。幼蟲可明顯不同於性成熟的成蟲，且有完全不同的生活方式。如某些蠅的幼蟲是動物的寄生蟲並能引起疾病，而成蟲則是非寄生性的。

larva migrans *see* creeping eruption.

幼蟲游走症　參閱 creeping eruption。

laryng- (laryngo-) *prefix denoting* the larynx.

〔前綴〕喉

laryngeal reflex a cough produced by irritating the larynx.

喉反射　刺激喉引起的反射。

laryngectomy *n.* surgical removal of the whole or a part of the larynx, as in the treatment of laryngeal carcinoma. Speech can be partially restored in many patients using special appliances.

喉切除術　手術切除整個或部分喉，如治療喉癌時。通過使用特殊矯正器，許多病人可重新獲得部分說話能力。

laryngismus *n.* closure of the vocal cords by sudden contraction of the laryngeal muscles, followed by a noisy indrawing of breath. It occurs in young children and was in the past associated with low-calcium rickets. Now it occurs when the larynx has been irritated following administration of anaesthetic, when a foreign body has lodged in the larynx, or in *croup.

喉痙攣　喉肌突然收縮引起的聲帶關閉，接着是一個聲音很大的吸氣。喉痙攣發生於幼兒，以前與低鈣性佝僂病有關；現在，喉痙攣發生於給予麻醉藥後刺激喉時，或異物堵在喉內時，或患白喉時。

laryngitis *n.* inflammation of the larynx and vocal cords, due to infection by bacteria or viruses or irritation by gases,

喉炎　細菌或病毒感染或氣體、化學物質等刺激引起的喉和聲帶發炎。聲帶不能振動

chemicals, etc. The cords lose their vibrance (owing to swelling) and the voice becomes husky or is lost completely; breathing is harsh and difficult (*see* stridor); and the cough is painful and honking. Obstruction of the airways may occasionally be serious, especially in children (*see* croup). The patient should rest his voice and remain in a warm moisture-laden atmosphere; steam inhalations for 15–20 minutes every 2–3 hours are traditionally beneficial. The patient should avoid cold air or fog and smoking.

（由於腫脹）且聲音變得粗啞或完全喪失，呼吸粗糙困難（參閱 stridor）；咳嗽時疼痛且有雁鳴聲。氣管阻塞有時很嚴重，尤其見於兒童（參閱 croup）。患者應讓聲帶休息並且保持在溫暖濕潤的環境中，每 2~3 小時作 15~20 分鐘蒸汽吸入一般是有益的。避免接觸冷空氣、霧和烟。

laryngocele *n.* a developmental defect in which an air sac communicates with the larynx. The sac forms a swelling in the neck that dilates on coughing or straining.

喉囊腫　有氣囊與喉通連的一種發育缺陷。該囊在頸部形成一腫脹，咳嗽或用力時擴張。

laryngofissure *n.* a surgical operation to open the larynx, enabling access for further procedures.

喉切開術　切開喉的一種外科手術，以便進行進一步的手術操作。

laryngology *n.* the study of diseases of the larynx and vocal cords.

喉科學　關於喉和聲帶疾病的學科。

laryngomalacia *n.* a condition characterized by paroxysmal attacks of breathing difficulty and *stridor. It occurs in small children and is caused by flaccidity of the structure of the larynx. It usually resolves spontaneously by the age of two years.

喉軟化　一種以陣發性呼吸困難和喘鳴為特點的疾病。它發病於幼兒，由喉部結構鬆弛引起。通常在 2 歲前自行痊愈。

laryngopharynx (hypopharynx) *n.* the part of the pharynx that lies below the hyoid bone.

喉咽　位於舌骨下的咽的一部分。

laryngoscope *n.* an instrument (a type of *endoscope) for examining the larynx. *See* laryngoscopy.

喉鏡　用於檢查喉的一種器械（一種內窺鏡）。參閱 laryngoscopy。

laryngoscopy *n.* examination of the larynx. This may be done indirectly using a small mirror or directly using a laryngoscope.

喉鏡檢查　檢查喉部，可用一小鏡子間接檢查，或用喉鏡直接檢查。

laryngospasm *n.* involuntary closure of the larynx, obstructing the flow of air to the lungs.

喉痙攣 喉不隨意的關閉，阻塞了流向肺的氣流。

laryngotomy *n.* surgical incision of the larynx. *Inferior laryngotomy*, in which an incision is made in the cricothyroid membrane beneath the larynx, is a life-saving operation for patients in whom there is obstruction to breathing at or above the larynx. *See* tracheostomy.

喉切開術 手術切開喉。喉下部切開術是在喉下部環甲膜處切開，它是喉或喉以上呼吸阻塞時的急救手術。參閱 tracheostomy。

laryngotracheobronchitis *n.* a severe and almost exclusively viral infection of the respiratory tract, especially of young children, in whom there may be a dangerous degree of obstruction either at the larynx (*see* croup) or main air passages (bronchi) due to the thickness and stickiness of the fluid (exudate) produced by the inflamed tissues. Symptoms normally start at night. Treatment: as for *laryngitis, with endotracheal *intubation or *tracheostomy if necessary and bronchoscopy in addition, during which it may be possible to clear the obstructing exudate by bronchial lavage and suction. The condition may recur.

喉氣管支氣管炎 一種嚴重的呼吸道感染，幾乎全是病毒性的，尤發於小兒。由於炎症組織分泌的液體（滲出液）濃度稠和黏性大，患兒可有喉部（參閱 croup）或主氣道（支氣管）阻塞的危險。症狀通常開始於夜間。治療與喉炎的治療相同，必要時做氣管插管或氣管造口術，還可做支氣管鏡檢查，以便通過支氣管灌洗和抽吸清除阻塞的滲出液。本病可復發。

larynx *n.* the organ responsible for the production of vocal sounds, also serving as an air passage conveying air from the pharynx to the lungs. It is situated in the front of the neck, above the trachea. It is made up of a framework of nine cartilages (see illustration) – the epiglottis, thyroid, cricoid, arytenoid (two), corniculate (two), and cuneiform (two) – bound together by ligaments and muscles and lined with mucous membrane. Within are a pair of *vocal cords, which function in the production of voice. **–laryngeal** *adj.*

喉 產生聲音的器官，也是空氣由咽輸送至肺的通道。位於頸前部氣管上方。它由一個 9 塊軟骨的支架構成（見圖）——會厭軟骨、甲狀軟骨、環狀軟骨、杓狀軟骨（2 塊）、角狀軟骨（2 塊）和楔狀軟骨（2 塊）。這些軟骨由韌帶和肌肉連在一起，內面襯有黏膜。喉內有一對聲帶，在發聲時起作用。

laser *n.* a device that produces a very thin beam of light in which high energies

激光器 產生集中高能量的極細光束的一種裝置（此詞是受

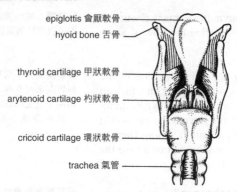

epiglottis 會厭軟骨

hyoid bone 舌骨

thyroid cartilage 甲狀軟骨

arytenoid cartilage 杓狀軟骨

cricoid cartilage 環狀軟骨

trachea 氣管

Cartilages of the larynx
喉的軟骨

are concentrated (the word derives from *l*ight *a*mplification by *s*timulated *e*mission of *r*adiation). In surgery, lasers can be used to operate on small areas of abnormality without damaging delicate surrounding tissue. For example, lasers are used to unblock coronary arteries narrowed by atheroma and to remove certain types of birthmark (*see* naevus). Different types of laser are used in eye surgery for operations on the cornea, lens capsule, and retina (*see* argon laser, diode laser, excimer laser, YAG laser). Lasers are also used in the treatment of *cervical intraepithelial neoplasia and in a specialized form (the *Nd: YAG laser*) for *endometrial ablation.

激輻射光放大的縮寫）。在外科，激光器可用於小病變的手術，而不損傷周圍精細的組織。例如：激光器可用於通暢由動脈粥樣腫而變狹的冠狀動脈，及摘除某些胎記（參閱naevus）。在眼外科，不同類型的激光器用於角膜、晶狀體囊和視網膜手術（參閱 argon laser，diode laser，excimer laser，YAG laser）。激光器還用於治療宮頸上皮內瘤；一種特殊形式的激光器（Nd：YAG激光），還可用於切除子宮內膜。

laser Doppler flowmeter an instrument for measuring blood flow through tissue (e.g. skin) utilizing a laser beam.

激光多普勒流速計　利用激光光束測量通過組織（如皮膚）的血流的一種儀器。

laser laparoscopy *see* laparoscopy.

激光腹腔鏡檢查　參閱 laparoscopy。

Lasix *n. see* frusemide.

速尿　參閱 frusemide。

Lassa fever a serious virus disease confined to Central West Africa. After

拉沙熱　一種嚴重的病毒性疾病，局限於中西非。經 3~21

an incubation period of 3–21 days, headache, high fever, and severe muscular pains develop; difficulty in swallowing often arises. Death from kidney or heart failure occurs in over 50% of cases. Treatment with plasma from recovered patients is the best therapy, and the causative virus is susceptible to ribavirin.

latah *n.* a pattern of behaviour seen especially in certain cultures, such as that of Malaysia. After a psychological shock the affected individual becomes very anxious and very suggestible and shows excessive obedience and pathological imitation of the actions of another person (echopraxia).

latamoxef *n.* a type of *cephalosporin antibiotic active against many Gram-negative bacilli (*see* Gram's stain). Trade name: **Moxalactam**.

latent period (in neurology) the pause of a few milliseconds between the time that a nerve impulse reaches a muscle fibre and the time that the fibre starts to contract.

lateral *adj.* **1.** situated at or relating to the side of an organ or organism. **2.** (in anatomy) relating to the region or parts of the body that are furthest from the *median plane. **3.** (in radiology) in the *sagittal plane.

lathyrism *n.* a disease, characterized by muscular weakness and paralysis, found among people whose staple diet consists mostly of large quantites of *Lathyrus sativus*, a kind of chick pea, and/or vetches and pulses related to it. Except in mild cases complete recovery does not occur, despite administration of an adequate diet and physiotherapy.

天的潛伏期後，發生頭痛、高燒和劇烈的肌肉痛，常常還有吞咽困難。50% 以上的病人因腎臟或心臟功能衰竭死亡。用康復病人的血漿治療是最佳治療方法，致病病毒對利巴韋林敏感。

拉塔病 一種行為方式，尤見於某些文化中，如馬來西亞文化。在一次精神衝擊後，患者變得非常憂慮，易為暗示影響，表現出過分順從，以及病態地模仿他人的動作（模仿行動）。

拉氧頭孢 一種頭孢菌屬抗生素，對治療許多革蘭氏陰性桿菌（參閱 Gram's stain）有效。商品名：Moxalactam。

潛伏期 （神經病學）神經衝動到達肌纖維和肌纖維開始收縮之間的幾個毫秒的時間間歇。

(1) 側的 位於器官或機體側方的或與此有關的。**(2) 外側的** （解剖學）與離身體正中斷面最遠的身體區域或部分有關的。**(3) 矢狀面** （放射學）在矢狀面上。

山黧豆中毒 一種以肌肉無力和麻痺為特點的疾病。見於以大量草香豌豆（鷹嘴豆的一種）和／或野豌豆及有關豆類為主食的人羣。儘管可給予適當的飲食及理療，除輕病例外，不可能完全恢復。

laudanum *n.* a hydroalcoholic solution containing 1% morphine, prepared from macerated raw opium. It was formerly widely used as a narcotic analgesic, taken by mouth.

阿片酊　含 1% 嗎啡的酊劑，用浸製的生阿片製成。曾廣泛用作口服麻醉止痛藥。

laughing gas *see* nitrous oxide.

笑氣　參閱 nitrous oxide。

lavage *n.* washing out a body cavity, such as the colon or stomach, with water or a medicated solution.

灌洗　用水或藥液沖洗體腔，如結腸和胃。

laxative *n.* a drug used to stimulate or increase the frequency of bowel evacuation (also called a *cathartic* or *purgative*), or to encourage the passage of a softer or bulkier stool. The common laxatives are the stimulants castor oil, bisacodyl, and senna and its derivatives; magnesium sulphate and other mineral salts; and methylcellulose, ispaghula husk, and other bulking agents.

輕瀉藥　用於刺激或增加排便次數，或促使糞便軟化或使大量糞便排出的藥物（也稱作導瀉藥或催瀉藥）。常用的輕瀉藥有蓖麻油，比沙可啶和番瀉葉及其衍生物；硫酸鎂和其他礦物鹽；甲基纖維素，卵葉車前殼以及其他膨脹劑。

LD₅₀ the dose of a toxic compound that causes death in 50% of a group of experimental animals to which it is administered: used as a measure of the toxicity of drugs.

半數致死量　一種毒性化合物可使 50% 的實驗動物死亡的劑量。用於衡量藥物毒性。

LDL low-density lipoprotein. *See* lipoprotein.

低密度脂蛋白　參閱 lipoprotein。

L-dopa *n. see* levodopa.

左旋多巴　參閱 levodopa。

lead[1] *n.* a soft bluish-grey metallic element that forms several poisonous compounds. Acute lead poisoning, which may follow inhalation of lead fumes or dust, causes abdominal pains, vomiting, and diarrhoea, with paralysis and convulsions and sometimes *encephalitis. In chronic poisoning a characteristic bluish marking of the gums ('lead line') is seen and the peripheral nerves are affected; there is also anaemia. Treatment is with

鉛　一種柔軟的藍灰色金屬元素，形成幾種有毒化合物。急性鉛中毒可發生於吸入鉛蒸氣或鉛塵後，引起腹痛、惡心、腹瀉、並伴有麻痺和抽搐，有時發生腦炎。慢性鉛中毒時牙齦可見典型的藍色標誌（鉛綫），周圍神經受累，並有貧血。治療用依地酸鹽。現在已嚴格控制在顏料中用鉛。符號：Pb。

*edetate. The use of lead in paints is now strictly controlled. Symbol: Pb.

lead[2] *n.* a portion of an electrocardiographic record that is obtained from a single electrode or a combination of electrodes placed on a particular part of the body (*see* electrocardiogram, electrocardiography). In the conventional ECG, 12 leads are recorded. Each lead represents the electrical activity of the heart as 'viewed' from a different position on the body surface and may help to localize myocardial damage.

導程　將單個電極或一組電極置於身體特定部位以獲得的心電描記記錄的一部分（參閱 electrocardiogram，electrocardiography）。常規心電描記法中，記錄 12 個導程。每個導程代表從體表一個不同部位觀察到的心臟電活動，有助於確定心肌損傷的部位。

learning difficulty *see* mental handicap.

學習困難　參閱 mental handicap。

leather-bottle stomach *see* linitis plastica.

皮革狀胃　參閱 linitis plastica。

lecithin *n.* one of a group of *phospholipids that are important constituents of cell membranes and are involved in the metabolism of fat by the liver. An example is *phosphatidylcholine*. Lecithins are present in the *surfactant that occurs in fetal lung tissue. The *lecithin-sphingomyeli ratio* (*LS ratio*) is used as a measure of fetal lung maturity; an LS ratio below 2 indicates a higher risk of *respiratory distress syndrome (RDS). In such cases cortisone may be given to stimulate fetal lung maturity and hence reduce the risk of RDS in the newborn.

卵磷脂　磷脂族中的一種，是細胞膜的重要組成成分，參與肝的脂肪代謝。磷脂酰膽鹼就是個例子。在胎兒肺組織上發生的表面活性物質上存在有卵磷脂，因此，卵磷脂與鞘磷脂的比率（LS 比率）用於衡量胎兒肺成熟性；LS 比率低於 2 表明發生呼吸窘迫綜合徵的風險較高。對這種病人，可給予可的松，以促進胎兒肺成熟，從而減小新生兒患呼吸窘迫綜合徵的風險。

lecithinase *n.* an enzyme from the small intestine that breaks *lecithin down into glycerol, fatty acids, phosphoric acid, and choline.

卵磷脂酶　小腸分泌的一種酶，能將卵磷脂分解為甘油、脂肪酸、磷酸和膽鹼。

leech *n.* a type of worm that possesses suckers at both ends of its body. Leeches occur in tropical forests and grasslands

水蛭　一種身體兩端有吸盤的蠕蟲。見於熱帶森林、草地或水中。某些寄生種吸吮動物和

and in water. Certain parasitic species suck blood from animals and humans, and their bites cause irritation and, in some cases, infection. Rarely, leeches are taken in with foul drinking water and pass from the mouth to the nose, where they provoke headache and nose bleeds. A leech can be detached from its host by applying salt; calamine lotion eases the irritation of the bites. Formerly widely used for letting blood, the medicinal leech (*Hirudo medicinalis*) is now used in some surgical operations to remove excess blood. The anticoagulants in its salivary glands are being investigated for the treatment of some types of heart disease.

人血，其叮咬可引起刺激，有時會導致感染。偶見用污水時誤食水蛭，水蛭經口入鼻，在鼻內引起頭痛和鼻衄。用鹽可使水蛭與其宿主分離。爐甘石洗劑可減輕水蛭叮咬的刺激。藥用水蛭從前曾廣泛用於放血，現在在一些外科手術中，仍用於清除過多血液。人們正在研究水蛭唾液腺中抗凝劑對治療某些類型的心臟病的效果。

Le Fort classification a classification of fractures involving the *maxilla (upper jaw) and *orbit. Type I involves the maxilla only, type II the anterior orbit, and type III the posterior orbit.

勒福特分類法 累及上頜骨及眼窩的骨折的一種分類法。I 型僅累及上頜骨，II 型累及前眶，III 型累及後眶。

Legg-Calvé-Perthes disease (Perthes disease, pseudocoxalgia) inflammation of the heads of the femurs (thighbones), resulting in loss of the blood supply and death of the outer layer of bone (avascular necrosis) (*see* osteochondritis). It occurs most commonly in boys between the ages of 5 and 10, and causes aching and a limp. Deformity, shortening, and secondary osteoarthritis of the bones result.

萊-卡-佩氏病 股骨（大腿骨）頭的炎症，導致血供障礙和骨外層壞死（無血管性壞死）。（參閱 osteochondritis）。最常發於 5~10 歲男孩，引起疼痛和跛行。會發生該骨變形、變短和繼發性骨關節炎。

legionnaires' disease an infection of the lungs caused by the bacterium *Legionella pneumophila*, named after an outbreak at the American Legion convention in Pennsylvania in 1976. *Legionella* organisms are widely found in water; outbreaks of the disease have been associated with defective central heating, air conditioning, and

軍團病 肺炎軍團菌引起的肺感染，以在 1976 年美國賓夕法尼亞州的美國軍團代表大會上的爆發而命名。軍團屬微生物廣泛見於水中，此病的爆發一直與不良的中央供暖、空調、及其他通氣系統有關。2~10 天潛伏期後，表現出症狀：不適及肌肉疼痛，接着有

other ventilating systems. Symptoms appear after an incubation period of 2–10 days; malaise and muscle pain are succeeded by a fever, dry cough, chest pain, and breathlessness. X-ray of the lungs shows patchy consolidation. Erythromycin provides the most effective therapy.

發燒、乾咳、胸痛和呼吸困難。肺 X 綫檢查見斑塊樣實變。紅黴素療效最佳。

leio- *prefix denoting* smoothness. Example: *leiodermia* (abnormal smoothness of the skin).

〔前綴〕**平滑** 如滑澤皮（皮膚異常光滑）。

leiomyoma *n.* a benign tumour of smooth muscle. Such tumours occur most commonly in the uterus (*see* fibroid) but can also arise in the digestive tract, walls of blood vessels, etc. They may undergo malignant change (*see* leiomyosarcoma).

平滑肌瘤 平滑肌的良性腫瘤。此類瘤最常發生於子宮（參閱 fibroid），但亦可發生於消化道、血管壁等等。它們可惡變（參閱 leiomyosarcoma）。

leiomyosarcoma *n.* a malignant tumour of smooth muscle, most commonly found in the uterus, stomach, small bowel, and at the base of the bladder. It is the second most common *sarcoma of soft tissues. This tumour is rare in children, occurring most commonly in the bladder, prostate, and stomach.

平滑肌肉瘤 平滑肌的惡性腫瘤，最常見於子宮、胃、小腸及膀胱底部。是第二位最常見的軟組織肉瘤。少見於兒童，最常發生於膀胱、前列腺和胃。

Leishman-Donovan body *see* Leishmania.

利-杜氏小體 參閱 Leishmania。

Leishmania *n.* a genus of parasitic flagellate protozoans, several species of which cause disease in man (*see* leishmaniasis). The parasite assumes a different form in each of its two hosts. In man, especially in *kala-azar patients, it is a small rounded structure, with no flagellum, called a *Leishman-Donovan body*, which is found within the cells of the lymphatic system, spleen, and bone marrow. In the insect carrier it is long and flagellated.

利什曼原蟲屬 一種有鞭毛的寄生原蟲，其中幾種能引起人類疾病（參閱 leishmaniasis）。該寄生蟲在兩種不同宿主體內採取不同的形式。在人體內，尤其是黑熱病患者體內，它是小的圓形結構，無鞭毛，稱為利-杜氏小體，見於淋巴系統，脾及骨髓的細胞內。在昆蟲攜帶者體內，它呈長形且有鞭毛。

leishmaniasis *n.* a disease, common in the tropics and subtropics, caused by parasitic protozoans of the genus *Leishmania*, which are transmitted by the bite of sandflies. There are two principal forms of the disease: *visceral leishmaniasis*, in which the cells of various internal organs are affected (*see* kala-azar); and *cutaneous leishmaniasis*, which affects the tissues of the skin. Cutaneous leishmaniasis itself has several different forms, depending on the region in which it occurs and the species of *Leishmania* involved. In Asia it is common in the form of *oriental sore. In America there are several forms of leishmaniasis (*see* chiclero's ulcer, espundia). Cutaneous leishmaniasis is treated with drugs containing antimony.

黑熱病，利什曼病　一種常見於熱帶和亞熱帶的疾病，由利什曼原蟲屬的一些寄生原蟲引起，通過白蛉的叮咬傳播。該病有兩種主要類型：內臟利什曼病，即各種內臟器官的細胞均受累（參閱 kala-azar）；和皮膚利什曼病，即皮膚組織受累。皮膚利什曼病本身根據其發病區域及致病種，又可分為幾種類型。在亞洲，常見的是東方癤；在美洲有幾類（參閱 chiclero's ulcer，espundia）。用含銻的藥物治療皮膚利什曼病。

lemniscus *n.* a ribbon-like tract of nerve tissue conveying information from the spinal cord and brainstem up wards through the midbrain to the higher centres. On each side a *medial lemniscus* acts as a pathway from the spinal cord, while an outer *lateral lemniscus* commences higher up and is mainly concerned with hearing.

丘系　一條神經組織的帶狀束，將信息從脊髓和腦幹向上經過中腦傳到更高級中樞。在每一側，內側丘系是傳送來自脊髓的信息路徑，而外側丘系起始於較高部位，主要與聽覺有關。

lens *n.* **1.** (in anatomy) the transparent crystalline structure situated behind the pupil of the eye and enclosed in a thin transparent *capsule*. It helps to refract incoming light and focus it onto the *retina. *See also* accommodation. **2.** (in optics) a piece of glass shaped to refract rays of light in a particular direction. *Convex lenses* converge the light, and *concave lenses* diverge it; they are worn to correct faulty eyesight. *See also* bifocal lenses, contact lenses, trifocal lenses.

(1) 晶狀體　（解剖學）位於眼球瞳孔後方包在一薄層透明囊膜內的透明水晶狀結構。它參與折射進入眼球的光綫，並將其聚焦於視網膜上。參閱 accommodation。**(2) 鏡片**（光學）一層玻璃片，做成能使光綫向特定方向折射的形狀。凸透鏡會聚光綫，凹透鏡分散光綫；戴此類鏡片以矯正視力異常。參閱 bifocal lenses，contact lenses，trifocal lenses。

lens implantation *see* cataract.

晶狀體植入　參閱 cataract。

lenticonus *n.* a condition in which the central part of the front surface of the lens of the eye (or sometimes, the back) has a much steeper curvature than normal and bulges forwards in a blunted cone. It is usually congenital.

錐狀晶狀體　一種疾病，眼晶狀體前表面（有時為後表面）中央部分的曲度較正常大，呈鈍圓錐形向前膨出。通常為先天性。

lenticular nucleus (lentiform nucleus) *see* basal ganglia.

豆狀核　參閱 basal ganglia。

lentigo *n.* a flat dark brown spot found mainly in the elderly on skin exposed to light. Lentigo is characterized by increased numbers of *melanocytes in the basal layer of the epidermis (freckles, by contrast, do not show an increase in these cells). In *lentigo maligna* (or *Hutchinson's lentigo*), which occurs on the cheeks of the elderly, the spot is larger than 2 cm in diameter and has variable pigmentation; it is a malignant *melanoma that has not spread to other sites.

着色斑　主要見於老年人日曬皮膚上的黑褐色扁平斑。其特點是表皮基底層黑色素細胞增加（與之相比，雀斑不表現出此類細胞數目的增加）。着色斑痣（或哈欽森痣）發生於老年人頰部，其斑塊直徑大於2 cm，且色素沉積情況不同，是一種尚未轉移到其他部位的惡性黑素瘤。

leontiasis *n.* overgrowth of the skull bones, said to resemble the appearance of a lion's head: a rare feature of untreated *Paget's disease. Medical name: **leontiasis ossea**.

骨性獅面　顱骨過度生長，據說是如獅頭的外觀，係未治療的佩吉特病的一種少見特徵。醫學用語：骨性獅面。

lepra reaction an aggravation of lumps on the skin caused by *leprosy, accompanied by fever and malaise.

麻風反應　麻風病造成的皮膚結節的惡化現像，伴有發熱和不適。

leproma *n.* a lump on the skin characteristic of *leprosy.

麻風結節　麻風病特有的皮膚結節。

lepromin *n.* a chemical prepared from lumps on the skin caused by lepromatous *leprosy.

麻風菌素　由瘤型麻風病的皮膚結節製備的一種化學製劑。

leprosy (Hansen's disease) *n.* a chronic disease, caused by the bacterium *Mycobacterium leprae*, that affects the skin, mucous membranes, and nerves. It

麻風病　一種慢性疾病，由麻風分枝桿菌引起，侵犯皮膚、黏膜及神經。它主要局限於熱帶，直接接觸傳染。1~30 年潛

is confined mainly to the tropics and is transmitted by direct contact. After an incubation period of 1–30 years, symptoms develop gradually and mainly involve the skin and nerves. *Lepromatous (multibacillary) leprosy* is a contagious steadily progressive form of the disease characterized by the development of widely distributed lumps on the skin, thickening of the skin and nerves, and in serious cases by severe numbness of the skin, muscle weakness, and paralysis, which leads to disfigurement and deformity. Tuberculosis is a common complication. *Tuberculoid leprosy* is a benign, often self-limiting, form of leprosy causing discoloration and disfiguration of patches of skin (sparsely distributed) associated with localized-numbness. *Indeterminate leprosy* is a form of the disease in which skin manifestations represent a combination of the two main types; tuberculoid and indeterminate leprosy are known as *paucibacillary leprosy*.

Like tuberculosis, leprosy should be treated with a combination of antibacterial drugs, to overcome the problem of resistance developing to a single drug; the WHO advocates a combination of rifampicin and dapsone for six months to treat paucibacillary leprosy and these drugs with the addition of clofazimine for multibacillary leprosy, this *multidrug therapy* (*MDT*) to be continued for two years. The WHO is conducting a trial in which ofloxacin is used in combination with other drugs to shorten the treatment time before cure. Reconstructive surgery can repair some of the damage caused by the disease. A vaccine is being developed and tested.

伏期後,逐漸出現症狀且主要累及皮膚和神經。瘤型麻風病是本病一種持續惡化的傳染型,特徵是廣泛發生皮膚結節,皮膚和神經增厚變粗,在重病人中發生嚴重的皮膚麻木、肌肉無力和癱瘓,進而導致毀形和畸形。常見合併症是結核病。結核樣型麻風病是一種良性,且常自限的麻風病類型,引起皮膚斑塊(稀散分布的)褪色和變形,伴有局部麻木感。未定型麻風病是其皮膚表現代表了上述兩型的一種類型;結核樣型和未定型麻風病稱為少菌的麻風病。

與結核病一樣,治療麻風病應聯合使用多種抗菌藥物,以克服對某種單一藥物產生的抗藥性。世界衛生組織提倡:治療少菌的麻風病時,利福平和氨苯碸聯合使用 6 個月;而對多菌的麻風病,除這兩種藥物外,再加用氯法齊明。這種多藥物療法持續 2 年。世界衛生組織正在實驗氧氟沙星和其他藥物合用,從而縮短治愈時間。修復手術可以修復本病造成的一些損傷。另外,人們正在研製疫苗。

lept- (lepto-) *prefix denoting* **1.** slender; thin. **2.** small. **3.** mild; slight.

〔前綴〕**(1)** 細、薄　**(2)** 小　**(3)** 輕度,輕微

leptocyte *n.* a red blood cell (*erythrocyte) that is abnormally narrow. Leptocytes are seen in certain types of anaemia.

薄紅細胞　一種異常薄的紅細胞，見於某些類型的貧血。

leptomeninges *pl. n.* the inner two *meninges: the arachnoid and pia mater.

柔腦（脊）膜　兩層內腦膜，即蛛網膜和軟腦膜。

leptomeningitis *n.* inflammation of the inner membranes (the *pia mater and *arachnoid) of the brain and spinal cord. *See also* meningitis.

柔腦（脊）膜炎　腦和脊髓內層腦膜（軟腦膜和蛛網膜）的炎症。參閱 meningitis。

leptophonia *n.* weakness of the voice.

聲弱　聲音微弱。

Leptospira *n.* a genus of spirochaete bacteria, commonly bearing hooked ends. They are not visible with ordinary light microscopy and are best seen using dark-ground microscopy. The parasitic species *L. icterohaemorrhagiae* is the main causative agent of Weil's disease (*see* leptospirosis), but many closely related species cause similar symptoms.

鈎端螺旋體屬　一種螺旋體菌，通常兩端呈鈎狀。在普通光學顯微鏡下不可見，而在暗視野下看得最清楚。寄生性的出血性黃疸鈎端螺旋體是韋爾病（參閱 leptospirosis）的主要致病菌，但許多近緣種引起類似症狀。

leptospirosis (Weil's disease) *n.* an infectious disease, caused by bacteria of the genus *Leptospira* (especially *L. icterohaemorrhagiae*), that occurs in rodents, dogs, and other mammals and may be transmitted to people whose work brings them into contact with these animals. The disease begins with a fever and may affect the liver (causing jaundice) or meninges (resulting in meningitis); in some cases the kidneys are involved.

鈎端螺旋體病　由鈎端螺旋體屬細菌（尤其是出血性黃疸鈎端螺旋體）引起的傳染病，發生於嚙齒動物、狗及其他哺乳動物，且可傳播給因工作與這些動物接觸的人。本病開始表現為發熱，可累及肝臟（引起黃疸）或腦膜（引起腦膜炎）；有些病人的腎臟受累。

leptotene *n.* the first stage in the first prophase of meiosis, in which the chromosomes become visible as single long threads.

細綫期　減數分裂的第一期的第一階段。這時，染色體變得可見，呈單個長綫形。

leresis *n.* rambling speech, immature both in syntax and pronunciation. It is a feature of dementia.

饒舌　説話雜亂無章，句法和發音都幼稚，是癡呆的一種特性。

Leriche's syndrome a condition in males characterized by absence of penile erection combined with absence of pulses in the femoral arteries and wasting of the buttock muscles. It is caused by occlusion of the abdominal aorta and iliac arteries.

勒靈什綜合徵　一種男性疾病，特徵是陰莖不能勃起，伴有股動脈搏動缺失及臀肌無力。由腹主動脈和髂動脈阻塞所致。

lesbianism *n.* female *homosexuality: the condition in which a woman is sexually attracted to, or engages in sexual behaviour with, another woman. Lesbianism is not an illness. **–lesbian** *adj., n.*

女子同性戀　表現為一女性對另一女性產生性愛，或與其發生性行為的狀況。女子同性戀不是一種疾病。

Lesch-Nyhan disease a *sex-linked hereditary disease caused by an enzyme deficiency resulting in overproduction of uric acid. Affected boys are mentally retarded and suffer from *spasticity and gouty arthritis. They also have a compulsion for self-mutilation.

萊-尼氏病　某種酶缺乏導致尿酸分泌過量引起的一種性連鎖的遺傳病。患病男孩智力發育低下，並患有痙攣和痛風性關節炎。他們還有一種自殘強迫性。

lesion *n.* a zone of tissue with impaired function as a result of damage by disease or wounding. Apart from direct physical injury, examples of primary lesions include abscesses, ulcers, and tumours; secondary lesions (such as crusts and scars) are derived from primary ones.

損害　由疾病或外傷的損傷造成功能障礙的組織部位。原發性損害除直接的物理損傷外，還有膿腫、潰瘍及腫瘤。繼發性損傷，如結痂和瘢痕，來自於原發性損傷。

lethal gene a gene that, under certain conditions, causes the death of the individual carrying it. Lethal genes are usually *recessive: an individual will die only if both his parents carry the gene. If only one parent is affected, the lethal effects of the gene will be masked by the dominant *allele inherited from the normal parent.

致死性基因　在一定條件下能引起其攜帶者死亡的基因。致死性基因通常為隱性：只有父母雙方均攜有此種基因的子代才會死亡。如果父母僅有一方攜帶該基因，則其致死作用將被從正常父母一方遺傳而來的顯性等位基因所掩蓋。

lethargy *n.* mental and physical sluggishness: a degree of inactivity and unresponsiveness approaching or verging on the unconscious. The condition results from disease (such as sleeping sickness) or hypnosis.

昏睡，嗜睡　精神和體力的遲鈍狀態：接近或瀕臨喪失意識前的某種程度的無活動和無反應狀態。這種狀態由疾病（如昏睡病）或催眠造成。

Letterer-Siwe disease *see* reticuloendotheliosis.

萊-賽氏病　參閱　reticuloendotheliosis。

leuc- (leuco-, leuk-, leuko-) *prefix denoting* **1.** lack of colour; white. **2.** leucocytes.

〔前綴〕**(1)** 無色，白　**(2)** 白細胞

leucine *n.* an *essential amino acid. *See also* amino acid.

亮氨酸　一種必需氨基酸。參閱 amino acid。

leucocidin *n.* a bacterial *exotoxin that selectively destroys white blood cells (leucocytes).

殺白細胞素　一種選擇性地破壞白細胞的細菌外毒素。

leucocyte (white blood cell) *n.* any blood cell that contains a nucleus. In health there are three major subdivisions: *granulocytes, *lymphocytes and *monocytes, which are involved in protecting the body against foreign substances and in antibody production. In disease, a variety of other types may appear in the blood, most notably immature forms of the normal red or white blood cells.

白細胞　一切有核的血細胞。健康良好時，白細胞有三種主要亞型：粒細胞，淋巴細胞和單核細胞，它們參與保護機體，對抗異物，及產生抗體。疾病時多種其他類型可出現在血液中，其中最值得注意的是正常紅細胞或白細胞的幼稚型。

leucocytosis *n.* an increase in the number of white blood cells (leucocytes) in the blood. *See* basophilia, eosinophilia, lymphocytosis, monocytosis.

白細胞增多　血中白細胞數目增加。參閱 basophilia，eosinophilia，lymphocytosis，monocytosis。

leucoderma *n.* loss of pigment in areas of the skin, resulting in the appearance of white patches or bands.

白斑病　皮膚某些區域色素缺乏，以致呈現出白斑或白帶。

leucolysin *n. see* lysin.

白細胞溶素　參閱 lysin。

leucoma *n.* a white opacity occurring in the cornea. Most leucomas result from scarring after corneal inflammation or ulceration. Congenital types may be associated with other abnormalities of the eye.

角膜白斑　角膜上的白色混濁物，多數角膜白斑由角膜炎症或潰瘍後瘢痕形成所致。先天型角膜白斑可伴有其他眼異常。

leuconychia *n.* white discoloration of the nails, which may be total or partial. The cause is unknown.

白甲病 全部或部分指甲變為白色，病因未明。

leucopenia *n.* a reduction in the number of white blood cells (leucocytes) in the blood. *See* eosinopenia, lymphopenia, neutropenia.

白細胞減少 血液中白細胞數目減少。參閱 eosinopenia，lymphopenia，neutropenia。

leucoplakia (leukoplakia) *n.* a thickened white patch on a mucous membrane, such as the mouth lining or vulva, that cannot be rubbed off. It is not a specific disease and is present in about 1% of the elderly. Occasionally leucoplakia can become malignant and it may be the first sign of AIDS. *See also* khat.

白斑病 黏膜上不能擦去的厚白色斑塊，如口腔黏膜或陰唇上。這是一種非特異性疾病，可見於 1% 的老年人。黏膜白斑偶爾可惡化，並可以是艾滋病的第一個徵兆。參閱 khat。

leucopoiesis *n.* the process of the production of white blood cells (leucocytes), which normally occurs in the blood-forming tissue of the *bone marrow. *See also* granulopoiesis, haemopoiesis, lymphopoiesis, monoblast.

白細胞生成 白細胞生成的過程。正常情況下，該過程發生於骨髓造血組織內。參閱 granulopoiesis，haemopoiesis，lymphopoiesis，monoblast。

leucorrhoea *n.* a whitish or yellowish discharge of mucus from the vaginal opening. It may occur normally, the quantity usually increasing before and after menstruation. An abnormally large discharge may indicate infection of the lower reproductive tract, e.g. by the protozoan *Trichomonas vaginalis* (*see* vaginitis).

白帶 陰道口流出的蒼白或淺黃色黏液。正常情況下可有白帶，月經前後量通常增多。異常大量白帶可能表明下生殖道感染，如陰道毛滴蟲感染（參閱 vaginitis）。

leucotomy *n.* the surgical operation of interrupting the pathways of white nerve fibres within the brain: it is the most common procedure in *psychosurgery. In the original form, *prefrontal leucotomy* (*lobotomy*), the operation involved cutting through the nerve fibres connecting the *frontal lobe with the *thalamus and the association fibres of the frontal-lobe. This was often successful in

腦白質切斷術 切除腦內白色神經纖維通路的外科手術：是精神外科學中最常用的。其原型為前額葉腦白質切斷術（葉切斷術），即手術切斷額葉和丘腦白神經纖維以及額葉間的聯絡纖維。過去常可成功地減輕情緒緊張。但前額葉腦白質切斷術有嚴重副作用，因此，現在已不再使用。

reducing severe emotional tension. However, prefrontal leucotomy had serious side-effects and the procedure has now been abandoned.

Modern procedures use *stereotaxy and make selective lesions in smaller areas of the brain. Side-effects are uncommon and the operation is occasionally used for intractable pain, severe depression, obsessional neurosis, and chronic anxiety, where very severe emotional tension has not been relieved by other treatments.

現代的做法是採用立體定位法，在腦的較小範圍內造成選擇性損傷。副作用不常見，手術用於頑固性頭痛、嚴重抑鬱症、強迫性神經症和慢性焦慮症，這些病例中，極其嚴重的情緒緊張未能通過其他治療緩解。

leukaemia *n.* any of a group of malignant diseases in which the bone marrow and other blood-forming organs produce increased numbers of certain types of white blood cells (*leucocytes). Overproduction of these white cells, which are immature or abnormal forms, suppresses the production of normal white cells, red cells, and platelets. This leads to increased susceptibility to infection (due to *neutropenia), *anaemia, and bleeding (due to *thrombocytopenia). Other symptoms include enlargement of the spleen, liver, and lymph nodes.

Leukaemias are classified into *acute* or *chronic* varieties depending on the rate of progression of the disease. They are also classified according to the type of white cell that is proliferating abnormally; for example *acute lymphoblastic leukaemia* (*see* lymphoblast) and *acute myeloblastic leukaemia* (*see* myeloblast). (*See also* myeloid leukaemia.) Leukaemias are treated with radiotherapy or *cytotoxic drugs, which are aimed at suppressing the production of the abnormal cells.

白血病　一組惡性疾病，骨髓及其他造血器官生成的某型白細胞數目增加。這些幼稚型或異常型白細胞的過量生成抑制了正常細胞、紅細胞和血小板的生成，導致易感染性（由於中性白細胞減少）、貧血和出血（由於血小板減少）。其他症狀包括脾、肝和淋巴結腫大。

根據其進程，白血病可分為急性或慢性兩種；也可根據異常增殖的白細胞類型分型；如急性淋巴母細胞性白血病（參閱 lymphoblast）和急性原粒細胞白血病（參閱 myeloblast）。（參閱 myeloid leukaemia）治療白血病採用放射治療或細胞毒素藥物，目的是抑制異常細胞生成。

leukoplakia *n. see* leucoplakia.

白斑病　參閱 leucoplakia。

leukotaxine *n.* a chemical, present in inflammatory exudates, that attracts

白細胞趨化素　存在於炎性滲出物中的一種化學物質。它吸

white blood cells (leucocytes) and increases the permeability of blood capillaries. It is probably produced by injured cells.

引白細胞，增加毛細血管通透性。可能由受損傷細胞產生。

leuprorelin *n. see* **LHRH** analogue.

亮丙瑞林 參閱 LHRH analogue。

levallorphan *n.* a drug that counteracts the depression in breathing caused by narcotic analgesics such as morphine without affecting their pain-relieving effects. It is administered by injection, usually before or at the same time as the analgesic. Trade name: **Lorfan**.

左洛啡烷 一種藥物，能對抗麻醉性鎮痛藥（如嗎啡）引起的呼吸抑制，而不影響其鎮痛效果。注射給藥，通常在給鎮痛藥之前或同時給藥。商品名：Lorfan。

levamisole *n.* an *anthelmintic drug used to remove roundworms. It has also been found to have an unexpected effect in stimulating the immune system by increasing T-cell responsiveness and encouraging the activity of *phagocytes. It is effective in rheumatoid arthritis. The drug is administered by mouth; possible side-effects include joint pain and interference with blood-cell production, which limit its use.

左旋咪唑 一種驅除蛔蟲的治蟯蟲劑。另外，人們意外地發現它能增加 T 細胞反應性和增加巨噬細胞活性，從而激發免疫系統。它對於類風濕關節炎有效。口服用藥。可能的副作用包括關節痛和對血細胞生成過程的干擾作用，而後者限制了它的應用。

levator *n.* **1.** a surgical instrument used for levering up displaced bone fragments in a depressed fracture of the skull. **2.** any muscle that lifts the structure into which it is inserted; for example, the *levator scapulis* helps to lift the shoulder blade.

(1) 起子 顱骨凹陷骨折時，用於撬起錯位骨折片的外科器械。(2) 提肌 提升其所附着結構的肌肉。如肩胛提肌協助提升肩胛骨。

levo- (laevo-) *prefix denoting* **1.** the left side. **2.** (in chemistry) levorotation.

〔前綴〕(1) 左側 (2) 左旋（化學）。

levodopa (L-dopa) *n.* a naturally occurring amino acid (*see* dopa) administered by mouth to treat *parkinsonism. Common side-effects are nausea, vomiting, loss of appetite, and involuntary facial movements; high doses may cause

左旋多巴 一種天然存在的氨基酸（參閱 dopa）。口服。治療帕金森綜合徵。常見的副作用有惡心、嘔吐、食慾喪失及不隨意面部運動。大劑量可引起無力、暈厥和頭暈。商品

weakness, faintness, and dizziness. Trade names: **Brocadopa**, **Larodopa**. *See also* benserazide.

levonorgestrel *n.* a synthetic female sex hormone – a *progestogen – used mainly in *oral contraceptives, either in combination with an oestrogen or as a progestogen-only preparation.

levorphanol *n.* a narcotic analgesic, similar to *morphine, that is used to relieve severe pain. It is administered by mouth or injection and may cause nausea, vomiting, loss of appetite, constipation, and confusion. Dependence may develop. Trade name: **Dromoran**.

levulosuria *n. see* fructosuria.

Leydig cells *see* interstitial cells.

Leydig tumour a tumour of the *interstitial (Leydig) cells of the testis. Such tumours often secrete testosterone, which in prepubertal boys causes *virilization.

LH *see* luteinizing hormone.

Lhermitte's sign a tingling shocklike sensation passing down the arms or trunk when the neck is flexed. It is a nonspecific indication of disease in the cervical (neck) region of the spinal cord.

LHRH analogue any one of a group of analogues of *luteinizing hormone releasing hormone*, which stimulates the release of *luteinizing hormone (LH) from the pituitary gland (*see also* gonadotrophin-releasing hormone). LHRH analogues are more powerful

名：Brocadopa，Larodopa。參閱 benserazide。

左旋諾孕酮 一種合成的雌性激素（黃體酮），主要用於口服避孕藥中，或與雌激素合用，或用作單純的黃體酮製劑。

左啡諾 一種類似於嗎啡的麻醉性鎮痛藥，用於解除劇烈疼痛。口服或注射用藥，可引起惡心、嘔吐、食慾喪失、便秘和神經錯亂。可產生藥物依賴。商品名：Dromoran。

果糖尿 參閱 fructosuria。

萊迪希細胞 參閱 interstitial cells。

萊迪希腫瘤 睪丸間質細胞（萊迪希細胞）的一種腫瘤。這種腫瘤常分泌睪酮，使青春期前的男孩男性化。

黃體生成素 參閱 luteinizing hormone。

萊爾米特徵 當屈頸時沿手臂或軀幹傳遞的一種電震樣麻刺的感覺。它是脊髓頸區疾病的一個非特異性指徵。

黃體生成素釋放激素類似物 一組黃體生成素釋放激素的類似物，刺激垂體分泌黃體生成素（參閱gonadotrophin-releasing hormone）。黃體生成素釋放激素類似物較天然存在的激素更有效力，它首先增

than the naturally occurring hormone, initially increasing the secretion of LH by the pituitary: this acts to block the hormone receptors and to inhibit the release of further LH. Two LHRH analogues, *goserelin* (Zoladex) and *leuprorelin* (Prostap), are increasingly being used in the treatment of advanced prostate cancer. Both are given subcutaneously in depot form into the abdominal wall at monthly intervals. After causing an initial rise in plasma testosterone for approximately ten days the level then falls to the same low level as that achieved by castration. *See also* buserelin.

Some LHRH analogues, given in the form of a snuff, are used in the treatment of female infertility.

加垂體對黃體生成素的分泌量：這具有阻滯激素受體和抑制黃體生成素的進一步分泌作用。戈舍瑞林和亮丙瑞林，這兩種黃體生成素釋放激素愈來愈多地用於治療晚期前列腺癌。它們都是每月一次以貯存形式皮下給藥注入腹壁。最初十天左右，血清睾酮水平會升高，然後，該水平降至卵巢切除術後的低水平。參閱 buserelin。

有些黃體生成素釋放激素類似物以鼻吸劑形式用藥，可用於治療女性不孕。

libido *n.* the sexual drive: the term is often used to refer to the intensity of sexual desires. In psychoanalytic theory, the libido (like the death instinct) is said to be one of the fundamental sources of energy for all mental life. The normal course of development (*see* psychosexual development) can be altered by fixation at one level and by regression.

性慾 性衝動：此術語常用於指性衝動的強度。在精神分析理論中，性慾（猶如死亡本能）被說成是所有精神生活的基本能源之一。正常的性慾發展進程（參閱 psychosexual development）可由於在某一水平的停滯或者倒退而改變。

Librium *n. see* chlordiazepoxide.

利眠寧 參閱 chlordiazepoxide。

lice *pl. n. see* louse, pediculosis.

虱 參閱 louse，pediculosis。

lichenification *n.* thickening of the epidermis of the skin with exaggeration of the normal creases. The cause is abnormal scratching or rubbing of the skin.

苔蘚化 皮膚表皮增厚，正常皮膚褶痕增粗。由於搔抓或摩擦皮膚所致。

lichenoid *adj.* describing any skin disease that resembles *lichen planus.

苔蘚樣的 描述類似扁平苔蘚的任何皮膚疾病。

lichen planus an extremely itchy skin disease of unknown cause. Shiny flat-

扁平苔蘚 一種病因不明，極度瘙癢的皮膚疾病。發亮的紫

topped mauve spots may occur anywhere but are characteristically found on the inside of the wrists. It may take the form of a white lacy pattern in the mouth, which usually produces no symptoms. Trauma, such as a scratch, may induce a linear form of the disease (*see* Koebner phenomenon).

紅色扁平斑可發生於各個部位，腕部內側是典型的發病部位。在口腔中，扁平苔蘚呈白色花邊形，且通常不產生症狀。創傷，如搔抓傷可使該病呈綫形（參閱 Koebner phenomenon）。

lichen sclerosus et atrophicus a chronic skin disease affecting the anogenital area, especially in women, and characterized by sheets of thin ivory-white skin. In 20% of patients other skin areas are also affected.

硬化萎縮苔蘚　一種侵犯肛門外生殖器區域（尤其女性）的慢性皮膚病，其特徵為成片的乳白色薄皮膚。在 20% 患者中，其他皮膚區域也會受累。

lichen simplex chronicus *see* neurodermatitis.

單純慢性苔蘚　參閱 neurodermatitis。

Lieberkühn's glands (crypts of Lieberkühn) simple tubular glands in the mucous membrane of the *intestine. In the small intestine they lie between the villi. They are lined with columnar *epithelium in which various types of secretory cells are found. In the large intestine Lieberkühn's glands are longer and contain more mucus-secreting cells.

利貝屈恩腺，腸腺　腸黏膜內的單管腺。在小腸內，腸腺位於絨毛之間。它們的內表面覆蓋着含有各種分泌細胞的柱狀上皮。在大腸內腸腺較長，且含有更多的黏液分泌細胞。

lien *n. see* spleen.

脾　參閱 spleen。

lien- (lieno-) *prefix denoting* the spleen. Example: *lienopathy* (disease of).

〔前綴〕脾　如脾病。

life table an actuarial presentation of the ages at which a group of males and/or females will die and from which mean *life expectancy* at any age can be estimated, based on the assumption that mortality patterns current at the time of preparation of the table will continue to apply.

壽命表　對一組男性和／或女性將來死亡年齡精確計算的描述。據此，可估算出任何年齡時的平均預期壽命。它以下述假設為基礎：即制定此表當時的死亡率構成將持續不變。

ligament *n.* **1.** a tough band of white fibrous connective tissue that links two bones together at a joint. Ligaments

韌帶　**(1)** 將兩塊骨連接於關節處的一條堅韌的白色纖維結締組織索帶。韌帶無彈性但可

are inelastic but flexible; they both strengthen the joint and limit its movements to certain directions. **2.** a sheet of peritoneum that supports or links together abdominal organs.

彎曲，它能強固關節並限制其向特定方向活動。**(2)** 支持和連結腹腔器官的片狀腹膜。

ligation *n.* the application of a *ligature.

結紮　結紮綫的應用。

ligature *n.* any material – for example, nylon, silk, catgut, or wire – that is tied firmly round a blood vessel to stop it bleeding or around the base of structure (such as the *pedicle of a growth) to constrict it.

結紮綫　任何緊紮在血管上以止血或者某結構基部（如生長物的蒂）以使之縮小的材料，如尼龍綫、絲綫、腸綫和金屬綫。

light adaptation reflex changes in the eye to enable vision either in normal light after being in darkness or in very bright light after being in normal light. The pupil contracts (*see* pupillary reflex) and the pigment in the *rods is bleached. *Compare* dark adaptation.

光適應　眼的反射變化，在從暗處轉入光綫明亮處或從正常光綫處轉入非常明亮處時，使眼能看見物體。瞳孔收縮（參閱 pupillary reflex）和視桿細胞內色素脫色。與 dark adaptation 對比。

lightening *n.* the sensation experienced, usually after the 36th week of gestation, by many pregnant women, particularly those carrying their first child, as the presenting part of the fetus enters the pelvis. This reduces the pressure on the diaphragm and the woman notices that it is easier to breathe. *Compare* engagement.

（孕腹）輕鬆感　許多孕婦，尤其是初次懷孕的婦女通常在妊娠 36 周後所體驗到的感覺。此時，胎兒先露部進入骨盆，膈肌壓力減小，孕婦感覺到呼吸變得容易了。與 engagement 對比。

light reflex *see* pupillary reflex.

光反射　參閱 pupillary reflex。

lignocaine *n.* a widely used local *anaesthetic administered by injection for minor surgery and dental procedures. It can also be applied directly to the eye, throat, and mouth as it is absorbed through mucous membranes. Lignocaine is also injected to treat conditions involving abnormal heart rhythm, particularly myocardial infarction. When used

利多卡因　一種使用廣泛的局部麻醉藥，注射用藥，用於小手術或口腔科手術。也可直接用於眼、喉和口腔，經黏膜吸收。注射利多卡因還可治療有心率失常的疾病，尤其是心肌梗死。作局麻藥用時，副作用不常見。商品名：Xylocaine，Xylocard。

as a local anaesthetic, side-effects are uncommon. Trade names: **Xylocaine**, **Xylocard**.

limbic system a complex system of nerve pathways and networks in the brain, involving several different nuclei, that is involved in the expression of instinct and mood in activities of the endocrine and motor systems of the body. Among the brain regions involved are the *amygdala, *hippocampal formation, and *hypothalamus. The activities of the body that are governed are those concerned with self-preservation (e.g. searching for food, fighting) and preservation of the species (e.g. reproduction and the care of offspring), the expression of fear, rage, and pleasure, and the establishment of memory patterns. *See also* reticular activating system.

邊緣系統 大腦內神經通路和網絡的複雜系統，包括幾種不同的核團。它參與機體內分泌和運動系統活動中本能和情緒的表達。邊緣系統所包括的腦區有杏仁核、海馬結構和下丘腦。受其控制的機體活動有：保存身體（如覓食、搏鬥）和保存種系（如繁殖和養育後代）的活動，恐懼、憤怒和喜悅的表達，以及記憶模式的建立。參閱 reticular activating system。

limbus *n.* (in anatomy) an edge or border; for example, the *limbus sclerae* is the junction of the cornea and sclera of the eye.

緣 （解剖學）邊緣或邊界。例如，鞏膜緣是眼角膜和鞏膜的接合部。

limen *n.* (in anatomy) a border or boundary. The *limen nasi* is the boundary between the bony and cartilaginous parts of the nasal cavity.

閾 （解剖學）邊界或分界綫。鼻閾是鼻腔骨部與軟骨部的分界處。

liminal *adj.* (in physiology) relating to the threshold of perception.

閾的 （生理學）與知覺閾有關的。

limosis *n.* abnormal hunger or an excessive desire for food.

善饑症 異常的飢餓或過分的進食慾望。

lincomycin *n.* an *antibiotic used to treat infections caused by a narrow range of bacteria, including osteomyelitis. It is administered by mouth or injection and occasionally causes diarrhoea, nausea, and stomach pains. Trade name: **Lincocin**.

林可黴素 一種抗生素，用於治療由少數細菌引起的感染，包括骨髓炎。口服或注射用藥，偶爾引起腹瀉、惡心和胃痛。商品名：Lincocin。

linctus *n.* a syrupy liquid medicine, particularly one used in the treatment of irritating coughs.

舔膏劑 一種糖漿型藥，特別是用於治療刺激性咳嗽的藥。

lindane *n.* an insecticide drug applied as a lotion or cream to kill such parasites as lice and the scabies mite, *Sarcoptes scabei*. Possible side-effects include skin irritation and rashes, but these are rare. Trade names: **Esoderm**, **Lorexane**.

林旦 一種殺昆蟲藥，用作洗液或乳膏，殺死虱、疥蟎等寄生蟲。可能的副作用包括皮膚刺激和皮疹，但罕見。商品名：Esoderm，Lorexane。

Lindau's tumour *see* haemangioblastoma.

林道瘤 參閱 haemangioblastoma。

linea *n.* (*pl.* **lineae**) (in anatomy) a line, narrow streak, or stripe. The *linea alba* is a tendinous line, extending from the xiphoid process to the pubic symphysis, where the flat abdominal muscles are attached.

縫 (解剖學) 一條綫、痕或條紋。白綫是從劍突延伸至恥骨聯合的一條腱，其上有扁平肌附着。

linear accelerator (linac) a machine that accelerates particles to produce high-energy radiation, used in the treatment (radiotherapy) of malignant disease.

直綫加速器 一種加速分子以產生高能輻射的儀器，用於治療 (放射療法) 惡性腫瘤。

lingual *adj.* relating to, situated close to, or resembling the tongue (lingua). The lingual surface of a tooth is the surface adjacent to the tongue.

舌的 與舌有關的，位於舌附近的，像舌的。牙齒的舌面指與舌貼近的牙面。

lingula *n.* **1.** the thin forward-projecting portion of the anterior lobe of the cerebellum, in the midline. **2.** a small section of the upper lobe of the left lung, extending downwards in front of the heart. **3.** a bony spur on the inside of the mandible, above the angle of the jaw. **4.** a small backward-pointing projection on each side of the sphenoid bone.

(1) 小腦舌 小腦前葉正中綫上向前突出的薄的部分。**(2)** 左肺小舌 左肺上葉的一小部分，向下延伸至心臟前方。**(3)** 下頜小舌 下頜內面、下頜角上方的骨突。**(4)** 蝶骨小舌 蝶骨兩側向後的小突起。

liniment *n.* a medicinal preparation that is rubbed onto the skin or applied on a surgical dressing. Liniments often contain camphor.

搽劑 塗搽在皮膚或外科敷料上的藥劑。搽劑常含樟腦。

lining *n.* (in dentistry) a protective layer placed in a prepared tooth cavity before a restoration is inserted.

linitis plastica (leather-bottle stomach) diffuse infiltration of the stomach submucosa with malignant tissue, producing rigidity and narrowing. Diagnosis by endoscopy may be difficult but radiological changes are more marked.

linkage *n.* (in genetics) the situation in which two or more genes lie close to each other on a chromosome and are therefore very likely to be inherited together. The further two genes are apart the more likely they are to be separated by *crossing over during meiosis.

linoleic acid *see* essential fatty acid.

linolenic acid *see* essential fatty acid.

lint *n.* a material used in surgical dressings, made of scraped linen or a cotton substitute. It is usually fluffy on one side and smooth on the other.

liothyronine *n.* a hormone produced by the thyroid gland that is similar to *thyroxine and used to treat conditions of thyroid deficiency. It is administered by mouth or injection and has a rapid but short-lived effect. Trade name: **Tertroxin**.

lip- (lipo-) *prefix denoting* **1.** fat. **2.** lipid.

lipaemia *n.* the presence in the blood of an abnormally large amount of fat.

lipase (steapsin) *n.* an enzyme, produced by the pancreas and the glands of the small intestine, that breaks down

襯料 （牙科學）在處理好的牙洞中，填入修復體前放入的一層保護性物質。

皮革狀胃 癌組織在胃黏膜下層的彌散性浸潤，造成胃僵硬和變窄。難以通過內窺鏡診斷，但放射學改變較顯著。

連鎖 （遺傳學）兩個或兩個以上基因在同一染色體上緊密相鄰的狀態，因此，這些基因很可能一起遺傳。兩個基因相距愈遠，它們就愈容易在減數分裂期間通過交換而分開。

亞油酸 參閱 essential fatty acid。

亞麻酸 參閱 essential fatty acid。

絨布 一種用作外科敷料的材料，用刮擦過的亞麻布或棉質代用品製成。通常一面呈絨毛狀，另一面光滑。

三碘甲狀腺氨酸 甲狀腺產生的一種類似甲狀腺素的激素，用於治療甲狀腺功能不足的疾病。口服或注射給藥。藥效出現快而維持時間短。商品名：Tertroxin。

〔前綴〕**(1)** 脂肪 **(2)** 脂質

脂血症 血液中存在異常大量的脂肪。

脂酶 胰腺和小腸腺產生的一種酶，在消化過程中將脂肪分解為甘油和脂肪酸。

fats into glycerol and fatty acids during digestion.

lipid *n.* one of a group of naturally occurring compounds that are soluble in solvents such as chloroform or alcohol, but insoluble in water. Lipids are important dietary constituents, not only because of their high energy value but also because certain vitamins and essential fatty acids are associated with them. The group includes *fats, the *steroids, *phospholipids, and *glycolipids.

脂質，脂類　天然存在的一組化合物，溶於氯仿或乙醇等溶媒，不溶於水。脂類是重要的膳食成分，這不僅是因為它們重要的能量價值，而且因為某些維生素和必需脂肪酸都與它們有關。這組化合物包括脂肪、類固醇、磷脂和甘油脂。

lipidosis (lipoidosis) *n.* (*pl.* **-ses**) any disorder of lipid metabolism within the cells of the body. The *brain lipidoses* (*see* Gaucher's disease, Hunter's syndrome, Hurler's syndrome, Tay-Sachs disease) are inborn defects causing the accumulation of lipids within the brain.

脂沉積　機體細胞內的任何脂肪代謝障礙。大腦脂肪沉積症（參閱 Gaucher's disease，Hunter's syndrome，Hurler's syndrome，Tay-Sachs disease）是引起脂質在大腦內蓄積的先天性缺陷。

lipochondrodystrophy *n.* multiple congenital defects affecting lipid (fat) metabolism, cartilage and bone, skin, and the major internal organs, leading to mental retardation, dwarfism, and deformities of the bones.

脂肪軟骨營養不良　一種多發性先天性缺陷，累及脂肪代謝、軟骨、骨、皮膚和主要內臟器官，導致智力發育低下、侏儒症和骨變形。

lipochrome *n.* a pigment that is soluble in fat and therefore gives colour to fatty materials. An example is *carotene, the pigment responsible for the colour of egg yolks and butter.

脂色素　一種色素，可溶於脂肪，因而使脂肪物質着色。例如胡蘿蔔素是給予蛋黃和黃油顏色的色素。

lipodystrophy *n.* any disturbance of fat metabolism or of the distribution of fat in the body. In *inferior lipodystrophy* fat is absent from the legs; in *insulin lipodystrophy*, sometimes occurring in diabetics, it disappears from the areas at which insulin is injected.

脂肪營養不良　體內脂肪代謝或分布障礙。下肢脂肪營養不良時腿部沒有脂肪；糖尿病時有時發生胰島素性脂肪營養不良：注射胰島素的部位脂肪消失。

lipofuscin *n.* a brownish pigment staining with certain fat stains. It is most

脂褐質　一種被某些脂肪染劑染成淺褐色的色素，最常見於

common in the cells of heart muscle, nerves, and liver and is normally contained within the *lysosomes.

心肌、神經及肝細胞內，正常情況下存在於溶酶體內。

lipogenesis *n.* the process by which glucose and other substances, derived from carbohydrate in the diet, are converted to *fatty acids in the body.

脂肪生成 從膳食中的碳水化合物衍生來的葡萄糖和其他物質在體內轉變為脂肪酸的過程。

lipogranulomatosis *n.* an abnormality of lipid metabolism causing deposition of yellowish nodules in the skin.

脂肪肉芽腫病 引起皮膚內黃色結節沉積的一種脂肪代謝異常。

lipoic acid a sulphur-containing compound that can be readily interconverted to and from its reduced form, *dihydrolipoic acid*. Lipoic acid functions in carbohydrate metabolism as one of the *coenzymes in the oxidative decarboxylation of pyruvate and other α-keto acids.

硫辛酸 一種含硫化合物，它與其還原形式——二氫硫辛酸——能很容易地相互轉換。在碳水化合物代謝中，硫辛酸在丙酮酸鹽及其他α-酮酸氧化脫羧過程中起着一種輔酶的作用。

lipoid factor one of the substances involved in the clotting of blood, which is important for the activation of plasma *thromboplastin.

脂樣因子 參與血液凝固的一種物質，對血漿凝血激酶的激活很重要。

lipoidosis *n. see* lipidosis.

脂沉積症 參閱 lipidosis。

lipolysis *n.* the process by which lipids, particularly triglycerides in fat, are broken down into their constituent fatty acids in the body by the enzyme *lipase. **–lipolytic** *adj.*

脂肪分解 體內脂類，尤其是脂肪中的三酸甘油酯，在脂酶作用下分解為其組成成分脂肪酸的過程。

lipoma *n.* a common benign tumour composed of well-differentiated fat cells.

脂肪瘤 由分化良好的脂肪細胞構成的一種常見的良性腫瘤。

lipomatosis *n.* **1.** the presence of an abnormally large amount of fat occurring in the tissues. **2.** the presence of multiple *lipomas.

(1) 脂肪過多症 組織內存在異常大量的脂肪。**(2) 脂肪瘤病** 多發性脂肪瘤的存在。

lipopolysaccharide *n.* a complex molecule containing both a lipid component

脂多糖 含一個脂質成分和一個多糖成分的複雜分子。脂多

and a polysaccharide component. Lipopolysaccharides are constituents of the cell walls of Gram-negative bacteria and are important in determining the antigenic properties of these bacteria.

糖是革蘭氏陰性菌細胞壁的組成成分，對於決定這些細菌的抗原性很重要。

lipoprotein *n.* one of a group of proteins, found in blood plasma and lymph, that are combined with fats or other lipids. Lipoproteins are important for the transport of lipids in the blood and lymph. *Cholesterol is transported in the bloodstream in the form of the *low-density lipoproteins* (*LDLs*). Cholesterol is removed from the bloodstream by means of special LDL receptors, which are inserted into the membranes of cells and bind the LDLs, which are then taken into the cells. Other forms of lipoprotein are *high-density lipoprotein* (*HDL*) and *very low-density lipoprotein*.

脂蛋白 見於血漿和淋巴中，與脂肪或其他脂質結合的一組蛋白質。脂蛋白對於脂質在血液和淋巴中的運輸有重要作用。膽固醇以低密度脂蛋白的形式被運輸，並通過特殊的低密度脂蛋白受體排出血流。此受體被插入細胞膜內，並且和低密度脂蛋白結合。然後，低密度脂蛋白被攝入細胞內。脂蛋白的其他形式是高密度脂蛋白和極低密度脂蛋白。

liposarcoma *n.* a rare malignant tumour of fat cells. It is most commonly found in the thigh and is rare under the age of 30 years. There are four main histological types: *well-differentiated, myxoid, pleomorphic, and round-cell liposarcomas*, the first two of which are the most sensitive to treatment, usually by surgery.

脂肉瘤 一種罕見的脂肪細胞惡性腫瘤。最常見於大腿，30歲以前少見。有 4 種主要的組織學類型：分化良好型、黏液樣型、多形型和圓細胞型。前兩種對治療（通常為手術治療）最敏感。

liposome *n.* a microscopic spherical membrane-enclosed vesicle or sac (20–30 nm in diameter) made artificially in the laboratory by the addition of an aqueous solution to a phospholipid gel. The membrane resembles a cell membrane and the whole vesicle is similar to a cell organelle. Liposomes can be incorporated into living cells and may be used to transport relatively toxic drugs into diseased cells, where they can exert their maximum effects. For example, liposomes containing *methotrexate can be injected into the patient's blood. The

脂質體 一種顯微鏡下可見的球形泡或囊（直徑20~30 nm），包裹在膜內，實驗室中將水溶液加入磷脂凝膠中人工可製成。其膜類似於細胞膜，整個囊泡則與細胞器類似。脂質體可進入活細胞內，用於運載有一定毒性的藥物到病變細胞，使藥物在細胞內發揮最大作用。例如可將含甲氨喋呤的脂質體注射入病人血液。癌症器官溫度較正常體溫高，所以，當脂質體通過該器官血管時，囊膜融化，藥物被釋放。人們

cancerous organ is at higher temperature than normal body temperature, so that when the liposome passes through its blood vessels the membrane melts and the drug is released. Liposomes are also being investigated for use as vehicles in *gene therapy.

還在研究脂質體在基因治療中的載體作用。

liposuction *n.* a technique for removing unwanted collections of subcutaneous fat by using a powerful suction tube passed through the skin at different locations.

吸脂術 在不同部位的皮膚插入大功率吸管去除不想要的皮下堆積的脂肪的一種技術。

lipotrophin *n.* a hormone-like substance from the anterior pituitary gland that stimulates the transfer of fat from the body stores to the bloodstream.

促脂激素 垂體前葉分泌的一種激素類物質，刺激脂肪從體內脂庫進入血流。

lipotropic *adj.* describing a substance that promotes the transport of fatty acids from the liver to the tissues or accelerates the utilization of fat in the liver itself. An example of such a substance is the amino acid methionine.

促脂肪的 描述一種能促進脂肪酸從肝臟轉運到組織或加速脂肪在肝臟自身利用的物質。蛋氨酸為此類物質之一例。

lipping *n.* overgrowth of bone as seen in X-rays near a joint margin. This is a characteristic sign of degenerative or inflammatory joint disease and occurs most frequently and prominently in osteoarthrosis. *See also* osteophyte.

唇樣變 X 綫檢查顯示的關節緣附近骨的過度生長。這是變性或炎性關節病的典型體徵，在骨關節病中，最常發生，也最顯著，參閱 osteophyte。

lipuria *n.* the presence of fat or oil droplets in the urine.

脂肪尿 尿中出現脂肪或油滴。

liquor *n.* (in pharmacy) any solution, usually an aqueous solution.

液 （藥劑學）任何溶液，通常指水溶液。

Listeria *n.* a genus of Gram-positive aerobic motile rodlike bacteria that are parasites of warm-blooded animals. The single species. *L. monocytogenes*, infects many domestic and wild animals. If it is transmitted to man, by eating infected animals or animal products, it may cause

李斯忒菌屬 革蘭氏陽性需氧能運動的桿狀菌的一屬，寄生於溫血動物體內。單核細胞增多性李司忒菌單株能感染許多家畜和野生動物。如果通過食入感染動物或動物製品傳播給人時，它可致病（李斯忒菌

disease (*listeriosis*), especially in the frail, ranging from influenza-like symptoms to meningoencephalitis. In pregnant women it may terminate the pregnancy or damage the fetus.

病），尤其在身體虛弱者中，引起從流感樣症狀到腦膜炎一系列病症。在孕婦，它可結束妊娠或損傷胎兒。

lith- (litho-) *prefix denoting* a calculus (stone). Example: *lithogenesis* (formation of).

〔前綴〕**結石** 如：結石形成。

-lith *suffix denoting* a calculus (stone). Example: *faecalith* (a stony mass of faeces).

〔後綴〕**結石** 如：糞石。

lithaemia *n. see* hyperuricaemia.

尿酸鹽血症 參閱 hyperuricaemia。

lithiasis *n.* formation of stones (*see* calculus) in an internal organ, such as the gall bladder (*see* gallstone), urinary system, pancreas, or appendix.

結石病 內臟器官內形成結石（參閱 calculus），如膽囊內（參閱 gallstone）、泌尿系統、胰腺內或闌尾內。

lithium (lithium carbonate) *n.* a drug given by mouth to prevent episodes of manic-depressive psychosis or to treat mania. Side-effects include tremor, weakness, nausea, thirst, and excessive urination. Thyroid function can be interfered with, and changes in the kidney can appear after long-term lithium treatment. Excessive doses can cause an *encephalopathy and even death. The levels of lithium in the blood are therefore usually checked during long-term therapy. Trade names: **Camcolit**, **Litarex**, **Priadel**.

鋰劑（碳酸鋰） 一種預防躁狂抑鬱性精神病發作或治療躁狂症的口服藥物。副作用包括震顫、無力、惡心、口渴和多尿。甲狀腺功能可受干擾，長期鋰劑治療後，可出現腎臟變化。過量可引起腦病甚至死亡。所以，長期治療時，通常須監測血鋰水平。商品名：Camcolit，Litarex，Priadel。

litholapaxy (lithotripsy) *n.* the operation of crushing a stone in the bladder, using an instrument called a *lithotrite*. The small fragments of stone can then be removed by irrigation and suction.

碎石術 用碎石器粉碎膀胱內結石的過程。然後，通過沖洗或抽吸除去小的結石碎片。

lithonephrotomy *n.* surgical removal of a stone from the kidney. *See* nephrolithotomy, pyelolithotomy.

腎石切除術 手術取出腎內結石。參閱 nephrolithotomy，pyelolithotomy。

lithopaedion *n.* a fetus that has died in the uterus or abdominal cavity and has become calcified.

胎兒石化　在子宮或腹腔內死亡並發生鈣化的胎兒。

lithotomy *n.* the surgical removal of a stone (calculus) from the urinary tract. *See* nephrolithotomy, pyelolithotomy, ureterolithotomy.

腎石切除術　手術取出泌尿道內的結石。參閱 nephrolithotomy，pyelolithotomy，ureterolithotomy。

lithotripsy *n.* **1.** the destruction of calculi (stones) by the application of shock waves. In *extracorporeal shockwave lithotripsy* (*ESWL*), used for destroying calculi in the upper urinary tract and gallstones, the shock waves are generated and transmitted by an external power source. The specialized machine (a *lithotripter*) consists of a sophisticated radiological system to localize the stone accurately by biplanar X-ray or ultrasound and a shock head or transducer to produce and focus the energy source. The prototype machines required the patient to be anaesthetized and immersed in a water bath for treatment, but the newer machines require neither water bath nor general anaesthesia. In *electrohydraulic lithotripsy* (*EHL*), used for destroying urinary calculi, an electrically generated shock wave is transmitted to the stone by a contact probe delivered via a *nephroscope. **2.** *see* litholapaxy.

(1) 電震碎石術　利用電震波破壞結石。體外電震波碎石，用於破壞上尿道及膽囊結石，其電震波由一體外電源產生並發射。這種專門機器（碎石器）含有一個通過雙平面 X 綫或超聲準確定位結石的複雜放射學系統和一個震頭或集中能源的換能器。老式的機器要求病人治療時麻醉並浸入水中，而較新式的機器則不需水浴或全麻。電液壓電震碎石法用於破壞尿道結石。電射震動波由一經腎鏡插入的接觸探針傳遞給結石。**(2) 碎石術**　參閱 litholapaxy。

lithotrite *n.* a surgical instrument used for crushing a stone in the bladder. *See* litholapaxy.

碎石器　用於粉碎膀胱內結石的外科器械。參閱 litholapaxy。

lithotrophic *adj. see* autotrophic.

自營的　參閱 autotrophic。

lithuresis *n.* the passage of small stones or *gravel in the urine.

石尿症　尿中排出小石頭或尿結石。

lithuria *n. see* hyperuricuria.

尿酸鹽尿症　參閱 hyperuricuria。

litre *n.* a unit of volume equal to the volume occupied by 1 kilogram of pure water at 4°C and 760 mmHg pressure. In *SI units the litre is treated as a special name for the cubic decimetre, but is not used when a high degree of accuracy is required (1 litre = $1.0000028 \, dm^3$). For approximate purposes 1 litre is assumed to be equal to 1000 cubic centimetres (cm^3), therefore 1 millilitre (ml) is often taken to be equal to $1 \, cm^3$. This practice is now deprecated.

升 體積單位，相當於 1 kg 純水在 4°C 760 mmHg（約 101 kPa）壓力下所占的體積。在國際單位中，升是 $1 \, m^3$ 的專門術語，但當要求高度精確時則不使用（1 升＝1.0000028 立方分米）。為了取近似值，假定 1 升等於 1000 立方厘米，因而 1 毫升通常當作 1 立方厘米。這種作法現已遭到反對。

Little's disease a form of *cerebral palsy involving both sides of the body and affecting the legs more severely than the arms.

利特爾病 一種大腦性麻痺，累及身體兩側，對兩腿的影響較兩臂嚴重。

Litzmann's obliquity *see* asynclitism.

利茨曼傾斜 參閱 asynclitism。

livedo *n.* a discoloured area or spot on the skin, often caused by local congestion of the circulation.

青斑 皮膚上的變色區域或斑點，常由局部血管充血引起。

liver *n.* the largest gland of the body, weighing 1200–1600 g. Situated in the top right portion of the abdominal cavity, the liver is divided by fissures (*fossae*) into four lobes: the *right* (the largest lobe), *left*, *quadrate*, and *caudate lobes*. It is connected to the diaphragm and abdominal walls by five ligaments: the membranous *falciform* (which separates the right and left lobes), *coronary*, and *right* and *left triangular ligaments* and the fibrous *round ligament*, which is derived from the embryonic umbilical vein. Venous blood containing digested food is brought to the liver in the *hepatic portal vein* (*see* portal system). Branches of this vein pass in between the lobules and terminate in the *sinusoids* (see illustration). Oxygenated blood is supplied in the *hepatic artery*. The blood leaves the liver

肝 身體最大的腺體，重 1200~1600 g，位於腹腔右上方。肝由裂隙分為四葉：右葉（最大），左葉，方形葉和尾形葉。它由 5 條韌帶與膈及腹壁相連：膜性的鐮狀韌帶（將肝區分為左右葉），冠狀韌帶，左和右三角韌帶以及纖維性的肝圓韌帶（由胚胎期的臍靜脈演化而成）。含有已消化食物的靜脈血經肝門靜脈進入肝（參閱 portal system）。門靜脈分支在小葉間行進，止於肝竇（見圖）。氧合血由肝動脈供應。血液經每個小葉的中央靜脈離開肝臟，流入肝靜脈內。肝臟由來自迷走神經的副交感神經纖維和來自太陽叢的交感神經纖維支配。肝臟有多種重要功能。它合成膽汁，膽汁流

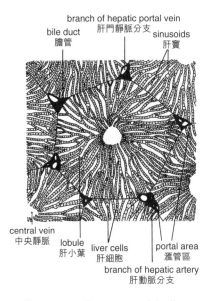

bile duct
膽管

branch of hepatic portal vein
肝門靜脈分支

sinusoids
肝竇

central vein
中央靜脈

lobule
肝小葉

liver cells
肝細胞

portal area
滙管區

branch of hepatic artery
肝動脈分支

The microscopic structure of the liver
肝的顯微結構

via a central vein in each lobule, which drains into the *hepatic vein. The liver is supplied by parasympathetic nerve fibres from the vagus nerve, and by sympathetic fibres from the solar plexus. The liver has a number of important functions. It synthesizes *bile, which drains into the *gall bladder before being released into the duodenum. The liver is an important site of metabolism of carbohydrates, proteins, and fats. It regulates the amount of blood sugar, converting excess glucose to *glycogen; it removes excess amino acids by breaking them down into ammonia and finally *urea; and it stores and metabolizes fats. The liver also synthesizes *fibrinogen and *prothrombin (essential blood-clotting substances) and *heparin, an anticoagulant. It forms red blood cells in the fetus and is the site of production of plasma proteins. It has an important

入膽囊,然後排入十二指腸。肝是碳水化合物、蛋白質和脂肪代謝的重要場所。它調節血糖量,將過剩的葡萄糖轉變為糖原;它把過剩的氨基酸分解為氨和最終產物尿素來排除過剩的氨基酸;它還貯存和代謝脂肪。肝還合成纖維蛋白原、凝血酶原(主要的凝血物質)和肝素(抗凝劑)。胚胎期肝生成紅細胞,並且是製造血漿蛋白的場所。肝在毒性物質的解毒過程中有重要作用;它分解衰老的紅細胞及其他無用物質,如男性體內過多的雌激素(參閱 Kupffer's cells)。肝也是維生素 A 合成的場所,維生素 A 和維生素 B_{12}、D 及 K 共同貯存在肝內。

　　肝臟是多種重要疾病的部位,包括肝炎、肝硬化、阿米巴病、棘球蚴病及肝細胞癌。

role in the detoxification of poisonous substances and it breaks down worn out red cells and other unwanted substances, such as excess oestrogen in the male (*see also* Kupffer's cells). The liver is also the site of *vitamin A synthesis; this vitamin is stored in the liver, together with vitamins B$_{12}$, D, and K.

The liver is the site of many important diseases, including *hepatitis, *cirrhosis, *amoebiasis, *hydatid disease, and *hepatomas.

livid *adj.* denoting a bluish colour of the skin, such as that produced locally by a bruise or of the general complexion in *cyanosis.

青紫的　指皮膚帶藍色的。如挫傷所致的局部青紫或紫紺時全身的皮膚顏色。

Loa *n.* a genus of parasitic nematode worms (*see* filaria). The adult eye worm, *L. loa*, lives within the tissues beneath the skin, where it causes inflammation and swelling (*see* loiasis). The motile embryos, present in the blood during the day, may be taken up by bloodsucking *Chrysops* flies. Here they develop into infective larvae, ready for transmission to a new human host.

羅阿絲蟲屬　一屬寄生性綫蟲（參閱 filaria）。羅阿絲蟲成蟲生活在皮下組織內，並在該處引起炎症和水腫（參閱 loiasis）。晝間存在於血內的能活動的蟲胚可被吸血斑虻所吸取。在虻體內，牠們發育為感染性的幼蟲，傳給新的人宿主。

lobe *n.* a major division of an organ or part of an organ, especially one having a rounded form and often separated from other lobes by fissures or bands of connective tissue. For example, the brain, liver, and lung are divided into lobes. **–lobar** *adj.*

葉　某一器官或部分器官的一個主要部分，尤指圓形且常由裂隙或結締組織帶與其他葉分開的部分。例如：腦、肝和肺都被分為葉。

lobectomy *n.* the surgical removal of a lobe of an organ or gland, such as the lung, thyroid, or brain. Lobectomy of the lung may be performed for cancer or other disease of the lung.

葉切除術　手術切除器官或腺體的某個葉，如肺、甲狀腺或腦的某葉。患肺癌或其他肺部疾病時，可行肺葉切除術。

lobotomy (prefrontal leucotomy) *n.* *see* leucotomy.

葉切斷術　參閱 leucotomy。

lobule *n*. a subdivision of a part or organ that can be distinguished from the whole by boundaries, such as septa, that are visible with or without a microscope. For example, the *lobule of the liver* is a structural and functional unit seen in cross-section under a microscope as a column of cells drained by a central vein and bounded by a branch of the portal vein. The *lung lobule* is a practical subdivision of the lung tissue seen macroscopically in lung slices as outlined by incomplete septa of fibrous tissue. It is made up of three to five lung *acini.

小葉　器官或某個部位的一個分葉，由隔等分界將其與整體區分開來。有時肉眼可見，有時顯微鏡下可見。如：肝小葉是肝的結構和功能單位，在顯微鏡下可見其橫切面為由中央靜脈引流，由一門靜脈分支為界的一個細胞柱。肺小葉實際是肺組織的分葉，在肺切片上肉眼可見由不完全的纖維組織中隔構成的輪廓，3~5 個腺泡組成一個肺小葉。

lochia *n*. the material eliminated from the uterus through the vagina after the completion of labour. The first discharge, *lochia rubra* (*lochia cruenta*), consists largely of blood. This is followed by *lochia serosa*, a brownish mixture of blood and mucus, and finally *lochia alba* (*lochia purulenta*), a yellowish or whitish discharge containing microorganisms and cell fragments. Each stage may last for several days. **–lochial** *adj*.

惡露　分娩後由子宮經陰道排出的物質。最初的排出物——紅色惡露——主要由血液組成；然後是漿液性惡露。為血液和黏液的褐色混合物；最後是白色惡露，一種內含細菌和細胞碎片的白色分泌物。每種惡露持續幾天。

locked-in syndrome *see* persistent vegetative state.

關閉綜合徵　參閱 persistent vegetative state。

lockjaw *n*. *see* tetanus.

破傷風　參閱 tetanus。

locomotor ataxia *see* tabes dorsalis.

運動性共濟失調　參閱 tabes dorsalis。

loculus *n*. (in anatomy) a small space or cavity.

小腔　（解剖學）小的空間或腔室。

locum tenens a doctor who stands in temporarily for a colleague who is absent or ill and looks after the patients in his practice. Often shortened to **locum**.

代理醫師　暫時代替缺席或生病的同事照料其病人的醫生。常簡稱為 locum。

locus *n*. **1.** (in anatomy) a region or site. The *locus caeruleus* is s small pigmented

部位　(1)（解剖學）一個區域或位置。藍斑是第四腦室底的

region in the floor of the fourth ventricle of the brain. **2.** (in genetics) the region of a chromosome occupied by a particular gene.

一個着色區域。**(2)**（遺傳學）特定基因在染色體上所占的位置。

lofepramine *n.* a tricyclic *antidepressant that is administered by mouth or injection. Possible side-effects include flushing, sweating, dry mouth, blurred vision, difficulty in passing urine, and drowsiness. Trade name: **Gamanil**.

洛非帕明 一種三環抗抑鬱藥，口服或注射給藥。可能的副作用包括臉紅、出汗、口乾、視力模糊、排尿困難及嗜睡。商品名：Gamanil。

log- (logo-) *prefix denoting* words; speech.

〔前綴〕言，語言

logopaedics *n.* the scientific study of defects and disabilities of speech and of the methods used to treat them; speech therapy.

言語矯正學 關於語言缺陷和語言能力喪失及其治療方法的科學研究；言語治療。

logorrhoea *n.* a rapid flow of voluble speech, often with incoherence, such as is encountered in *mania.

多言症 口若懸河，但常語無倫次，見於躁狂症。

-logy (-ology) *suffix denoting* field of study. Example: *cytology* (study of cells).

〔後綴〕**學** 指學術領域。如細胞學（關於細胞的學科）。

loiasis *n.* a disease, occurring in West and Central Africa, caused by the eye worm *Loa loa*. The adult worms live and migrate within the skin tissues, causing the appearance of transitory *calabar* swellings. These are probably an allergic reaction to the worms' waste products, and they sometimes lead to fever and itching. Worms often migrate across the eyeball just beneath the conjunctiva, where they cause irritation and congestion. Loiasis is treated with *diethylcarbamazine, which kills both the adults and larval forms.

羅阿絲蟲病 一種發生於西非和中非，由眼絲蟲（羅阿絲蟲）引起的疾病。成蟲在皮膚組織內生活游走，引起短暫的卡拉巴絲蟲腫。這可能是對蟲排泄物的變態反應，有時導致發熱和瘙癢。蟲常在眼結膜下穿越眼球游走，引起該處刺激及充血。羅阿絲蟲病的治療使用乙胺嗪，它可殺死幼蟲和成蟲。

loin *n.* the region of the back and side of the body between the lowest rib and the pelvis.

腰 位於最低位肋骨和骨盆之間的身體後面和側面區域。

Lomotil *n*. *see* diphenoxylate.

止瀉寧　參閱　diphenoxy-late。

long-sightedness *n*. *see* hypermetropia.

遠視　參閱 hypermetropia。

loop *n*. **1.** a bend in a tubular organ, e.g. *Henle's loop in a kidney tubule. **2.** one of the patterns of dermal ridges in *fingerprints.

袢　(1) 管狀器官的彎曲部。如腎小管的亨利袢。(2) 指紋中皮嵴類型的一種。

loperamide *n*. a drug used in the treatment of diarrhoea. It acts by reducing *peristalsis of the digestive tract and is administered by mouth; side-effects are rare, but include abdominal distension, drowsiness, and skin rash. Trade name: **Imodium**.

洛哌丁胺　一種治療腹瀉的藥物，通過減弱消化道蠕動起作用，口服用藥。副作用少見，但包括腹脹、嗜睡和皮疹。商品名：Imodium。

loprazolam *n*. a long-acting *benzodiazepine drug administered by mouth. Possible side-effects include addiction and rebound insomnia. Trade name: **Loprazolam**.

氯普唑侖　一種長效苯二氮䓬類藥物，口服，可能的副作用包括成癮及反跳性失眠。商品名：Loprazolam。

lorazepam *n*. a *benzodiazepine used to relieve moderate or severe anxiety and tension and to treat insomnia. It is administered by mouth and may cause drowsiness, dizziness, blurred vision, and nausea. Trade name: **Ativan**.

勞拉西泮　一種苯二氮䓬類藥物，用於解除中度或嚴重焦慮症和緊張，及治療失眠。口服用藥，可引起嗜睡、頭暈、視力模糊和噁心。商品名：Ativan。

lordosis *n*. inward curvature of the spine. A certain degree of lordosis is normal in the lumbar and cervical regions of the spine: loss of this is a sign of ankylosing *spondylitis. Exaggerated lordosis may occur in adolescence, through faulty posture or as a result of disease affecting the vertebrae and spinal muscles. *Compare* kyphosis.

脊柱前凸　脊柱向內彎曲。脊柱腰區和頸區一定程度的前凸是正常的，失去此前凸則是關節強硬性脊椎炎的體徵。過度的脊柱前凸可發生於青春期，由姿勢不正確或疾病累及脊椎和棘肌所致。與 kyphosis 對比。

lotion *n*. a medicinal solution for washing or bathing the external parts of the body. Lotions usually have a cooling, soothing, or antiseptic action.

洗液　用於洗浴身體外部的藥液。洗液通常有涼爽、舒適和抗菌的作用。

loupe *n.* a small magnifying hand lens used for examining the front part of the eye, usually with a pocket torch to provide illumination. In modern practice a slit-lamp microscope is used.

角膜放大鏡　袖珍放大鏡，用於檢查眼球前部，通常用手電提供照明。現代醫學中，使用裂隙燈顯微鏡。

louse *n.* (*pl.* **lice**) a small wingless insect that is an external parasite of man. Lice attach themselves to hair and clothing using their well-developed legs and claws. Their flattened leathery bodies are resistant to crushing and their mouthparts are adapted for sucking blood. Lice thrive in overcrowded and unhygienic conditions; they can infest humans (*see* pediculosis) and they may transmit disease. *See also* Pediculus, Phthirus.

虱　一種無翅昆蟲，寄生於人體外部。虱用發育良好的腿和爪貼附在頭髮和衣服上。其平坦、堅韌的身體能抗擠壓，其口器適於吸血。虱在人羣密集和不衞生的環境中繁殖旺盛，它們可寄生於人類（參閱pediculosis）且可傳播疾病。參閱 Pediculus，Phthirus。

lovastatin *n.* a drug that interferes with the synthesis of cholesterol in the liver and is used to reduce abnormally high blood cholesterol levels. Possible side-effects include muscle pain and weakness, liver damage, insomnia, headache, nausea, dyspepsia, diarrhoea, and abdominal cramps.

洛伐他汀　一種干擾肝臟合成膽固醇的藥物，用於降低異常高的血液膽固醇水平。可能的副作用包括肌肉疼痛和無力，肝臟損傷、失眠、頭痛、惡心、消化不良、腹瀉和腹部痙攣。

Lovset's manoeuvre rotation and traction of the trunk of the fetus during a breech birth to facilitate delivery of the arms and the shoulders.

羅福斯特手法　臀位分娩後旋轉牽引胎兒軀幹以利臂及肩娩出。

low-density lipoprotein (LDL) *see* lipoprotein.

低密度脂蛋白　參閱 lipoprotein。

low-molecular-weight heparin a type of *heparin that is more readily absorbed and requires less frequent administration than standard heparin preparations used as anticoagulant therapy to prevent deep-vein thrombosis following surgery or during kidney dialysis. It also produces less risk of bleeding. Preparations in use include *enoxaparin*.

低分子量肝素　一種比標準肝素製劑易於吸收，且所需的用藥頻率也低的一種肝素類型。作為一種抗凝治療，預防手術後或腎透析過程中深部靜脈血栓形成。它引起出血的風險也較小。使用的製劑包括依諾肝素。

lozenge *n.* a medicated tablet containing sugar. Lozenges should dissolve slowly in the mouth so that the medication is applied to the mouth and throat.

LSD *see* lysergic acid diethylamide.

lubb-dupp *n.* a representation of the normal heart sounds as heard through the stethoscope. Lubb (the first heart sound) coincides with closure of the mitral and tricuspid valves; dupp (the second heart sound) is due to closure of the aortic and pulmonary valves.

lucid interval temporary recovery of consciousness after a blow to the head, before relapse into coma. It is a sign of intracranial arterial bleeding.

Ludwig's angina severe inflammation caused by infection of both sides of the floor of the mouth, resulting in massive swelling of the neck. If untreated, it may obstruct the airways, necessitating tracheostomy.

lues *n.* a serious infections disease such as syphilis.

lumbago *n.* low backache, of any cause or description. Severe lumbago, of sudden onset while bending or lifting, can be due either to a slipped disc or to a strained muscle or ligament. When associated with *sciatica it is often due to a slipped disc.

lumbar *adj.* relating to the loin.

lumbar puncture a procedure in which cerebrospinal fluid is withdrawn by means of a hollow needle inserted into the *subarachnoid space in the region of

錠劑（糖錠） 含糖的藥片。錠劑應在口內緩慢溶解，以便給腔和咽喉用藥。

麥角二乙胺 參閱 lysergic acid diethylamide。

路布-杜普 比擬用聽診器聽到的正常心音。路布（第一心音）發生於二尖瓣和三尖瓣關閉時，杜普（第二心音）發生於主動脈瓣和肺動脈瓣關閉時。

神志清明期 頭部受擊後暫時的知覺恢復，爾後又陷入昏迷。這是顱內出血的指徵。

路德維希咽峽炎 口底兩側感染引起的嚴重炎症，導致頸部大面積水腫。若不治，它可阻塞氣道而需氣管切開術。

梅毒 一種嚴重的傳染性疾病。

腰痛 各種原因引起的形形色色的下背部痛。彎腰或提物時突然發作的嚴重腰痛可由椎間盤脫出或肌肉或韌帶拉傷所致。若伴有坐骨神經痛，則常由椎間盤脫出所致。

腰的 與腰有關的。

腰椎穿刺 用一根空芯針在腰部（通常是第三與第四腰椎之間）刺入蛛網膜下腔抽出腦脊液的操作。由此得到的體液可

the lower back (usually between the third and fourth lumbar vertebrae). The fluid thus obtained is examined for diagnostic purposes. The procedure is usually without risk to the patient, but in patients with raised intracranial pressure it may be hazardous and the optic fundi must be examined for the presence of *papilloedema. *See also* Queckenstedt test.

用於診斷性檢查。這種操作對病人一般無危險，但對顱壓高的病人會有害，所以必須檢查眼底有無視神經乳頭水腫。參閱 Queckenstedt test。

lumbar vertebrae the five bones of the backbone that are situated between the thoracic vertebrae and the sacrum, in the lower part of the back. They are the largest of the unfused vertebrae and have stout processes for attachment of the strong muscles of the lower back. *See also* vertebra.

腰椎 位於腰部、胸椎和骶椎之間的五塊椎骨。它們是未融合的椎骨中最大的，有粗的突起供腰部強有力的肌肉附着。參閱 vertebra。

lumbo- *prefix denoting* the loin; lumbar region.

〔前綴〕**腰**，腰區

lumbosacral *adj.* relating to part of the spine composed of the lumbar vertebrae and the sacrum.

腰骶的 與腰椎和骶椎組成的脊柱部分有關的。

lumen *n.* **1.** the space within a tubular or sac-like part, such as a blood vessel, the intestine, or the stomach. **2.** the SI unit of luminous flux, equal to the amount of light emitted per second in unit solid angle of 1 steradian by a point source of 1 candela. Symbol: lm.

(1) 腔 管道或囊樣結構內的空間，如血管腔、腸腔或胃腔。**(2) 流明** 國際單位制中的光通量單位，相當於 1 堪德拉的點光源每秒經 1 球面度單位立體角發出的光量。符號：lm。

lumpectomy *n.* an operation for *breast cancer in which the tumour and surrounding breast tissue are removed: muscles, skin, and lymph nodes are left intact (*compare* mastectomy). The procedure, usually followed by radiation, is indicated for patients with a tumour less than 2 cm in diameter and who have no metastases to local lymph nodes or to distant organs.

腫塊切除術 一種治療乳腺癌的手術。手術中，切除腫瘤及其周圍乳腺組織；而保留肌肉、皮膚和淋巴結不動（與 mastectomy 對比）。手術後通常進行放療。這種手術適用於腫瘤直徑小於 2cm 且未發生局部淋巴結或遠端器官轉移的患者。

lunate bone a bone of the wrist (*see* carpus). It articulates with the capitate and hamate bones in front, with the radius behind, and with the triquetral and scaphoid at the sides.

lung *n*. one of the pair of organs of *respiration, situated in the chest cavity on either side of the heart and enclosed by a serous membrane (*see* pleura). The lungs are fibrous elastic sacs that are expanded and compressed by movements of the rib cage and diaphragm during *breathing. They communicate with the atmosphere through the *trachea, which opens into the pharynx. The trachea divides into two bronchi (*see* bronchus), which enter the lungs and branch into *bronchioles. These divide further and terminate in minute air sacs (*see* alveolus), the sites of gaseous exchange. (See illustration.) Atmospheric oxygen is absorbed and

月骨 腕部的一塊骨頭（參閱 carpus）。它在前方與頭狀骨和鈎骨形成關節，後方與橈骨形成關節，側面分別與三角骨和舟骨形成關節。

肺 一對呼吸器官，位於胸腔內心臟兩側，由一層漿膜（參閱 pleura）包裹。肺是纖維性的彈性囊。呼吸時，隨肋骨架和膈的運動而被擴張和壓縮。它通過開口於咽的氣管與大氣相通。氣管分支為兩個支氣管（參閱 bronchus），支氣管進入肺並分支為細支氣管。這些細支氣管進一步分支，終止為小的氣囊（參閱 alveolus）——氣體交換的部位（見圖）。大氣中的氧被吸收入肺，而來自肺毛細血管的二氧化碳被釋放入肺；兩者均按濃度梯度進行（參閱 pulmonary circula-

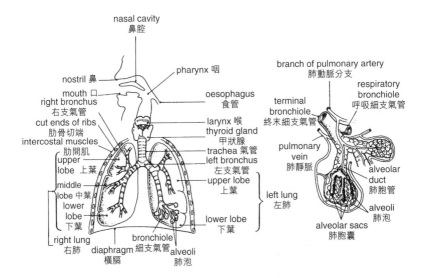

The lungs and main air passages, with details of the alveoli
肺和主要氣管，附肺泡細部

carbon dioxide from the blood of the pulmonary capillaries is released into the lungs; in each case down a concentration gradient (*see* pulmonary circulation). The total capacity of the lungs in an adult male is about 5.5 litres, but during normal breathing only about 500 ml of air is exchanged (*see also* residual volume). Other functions of the lung include water evaporation: an important factor in the fluid balance and heat regulation of the body.

lung cancer cancer arising in the epithelium of the air passages (*bronchial cancer*) or lung. It is a very common form of cancer, particularly in Britain, and is strongly associated with cigarette smoking and exposure to industrial air pollutants (including asbestos). There are often no symptoms in the early stages of the disease, when diagnosis is made on X-ray examination. Treatment includes surgical removal of the affected lobe or lung (20% of cases are suitable for surgery), radiotherapy, and chemotherapy.

lunula *n*. the whitish crescent-shaped area at the base of a *nail.

lupus *n*. any of several chronic skin diseases. *See* lupus erythematosus, lupus verrucosus, lupus vulgaris.

lupus erythematosus (LE) a chronic inflammatory disease of connective tissue, affecting the skin and various internal organs (*systemic LE, SLE*). Typically, there is a red scaly rash on the face, affecting the nose and cheeks; arthritis; and progressive damage to the kidneys. Often the heart, lungs, and brain are also affected by progressive attacks of inflammation followed by the formation of scar tissue (fibrosis). In a

tion)。成年男女的肺總氣量約為 5.5 升，但正常呼吸過程中，僅有約 500 ml 的氣體被交換（參閱 residual volume）。肺的其他功能包括水分蒸發：這是機體液體平衡和體溫調節的一個重要因素。

肺癌 發生於氣道的（支氣管癌）或肺的上皮的癌瘤。它是一種極常見的癌症形式，尤其在英國，且與吸烟和接觸工業大氣污染物（包括石棉）有密切關係。本病早期常無症狀，此時，可據 X 綫檢查做出診斷。治療包括手術切除受累的肺葉或肺（20% 病例適於手術），放射治療和化學治療。

弧形 指甲基部發白的新月形區域。

狼瘡 幾種慢性皮膚病。參閱 lupus erythematosus，lupus verrucosus，lupus vulgaris。

紅斑狼瘡 結締組織的一種慢性炎性疾病，侵犯皮膚和各種內臟器官（系統性紅斑狼瘡）。典型表現有：侵犯鼻和兩頰的面部脫屑性紅色皮疹；關節炎和腎臟的漸進性損傷。心、肺和腦也常反覆遭受炎症侵襲，繼而有瘢痕組織形成（纖維化）。輕型時僅皮膚受累，稱為盤狀紅斑狼瘡。本病被認為是一種自體免疫性疾

milder form, known as *discoid LE* (*DLE*), only the skin is affected. LE is regarded as an *autoimmune disease and can be diagnosed by the presence of abnormal antibodies in the bloodstream. The disease is treated with corticosteroids or immunosuppressive drugs.

病，可根據血流中存在的異常抗體做出診斷。本病用皮質類固醇或免疫抑制劑治療。

lupus verrucosus a rare tuberculous infection of the skin – commonly the arm or hand – typified by warty lesions. It occurs in those who have been reinfected with tuberculosis.

疣狀狼瘡　一種以疣狀損傷為特徵的罕見的皮膚結核性感染，常發於臂或手。該病發生於再次感染結核的病人。

lupus vulgaris tuberculous infection of the skin, usually due to direct inoculation of the tuberculosis bacillus into the skin. This type of lupus often starts in childhood, with dark red patches on the nose or cheek. Unless treated lupus vulgaris spreads, ulcerates, and causes extensive scarring. Treatment is with antituberculous drugs.

尋常狼瘡　皮膚的結核性感染，通常由於直接的皮膚內注射結核桿菌引起。此型狼瘡通常始於兒童期，鼻或頰部有暗紅色斑。若不治療，尋常狼瘡可蔓延，形成潰瘍，導致廣泛的瘢痕形成。治療用抗結核藥。

lute *n.* (in dentistry) a thin layer of cement inserted into the minute space between a prepared tooth and a crown or inlay to hold it permanently in place.

密封粉　（牙科學）一薄層黏固粉，填入已製備好的牙和牙冠或嵌體之間微小腔洞內，使之永遠固定在原位。

lutein *n.* **1.** *see* xanthophyll. **2.** the yellow pigment of the corpus luteum.

(1)　葉黃素　參閱 xanthophyll。**(2)　黃體素**　黃體的黃色色素。

luteinizing hormone (LH) a hormone (*see* gonadotrophin), synthesized and released by the anterior pituitary gland, that stimulates ovulation, *corpus luteum formation, progesterone synthesis by the ovary (*see also* menstrual cycle), and androgen synthesis by the interstitial cells of the testes. Also called: **interstitial cell stimulating hormone (ICSH)**.

黃體生成素　一種激素（參閱 gonadotrophin），由垂體前葉合成和分泌。它刺激排卵、黃體形成、卵巢合成孕酮（參閱 menstrual cycle）和睪丸間質細胞合成睪丸酮。也稱為間質細胞刺激素 (ICSH)。

luteo- *prefix denoting* **1.** yellow. **2.** the corpus luteum.

〔前綴〕**(1)** 黃色　**(2)** 黃體

luteotrophic hormone (luteotrophin) *see* prolactin.

促黃體激素　參閱 prolactin。

lux *n.* the *SI unit of intensity of illumination, equal to 1 lumen per square metre. This unit was formerly called the metre candle. Symbol: lx.

勒　照明強度的國際單位，相當於每平方米 1 流明。此單位過去稱為米燭光。符號：lx。

luxation *n. see* dislocation.

脫位　參閱 dislocation。

lyase *n.* one of a group of enzymes that catalyse the linking of groups by double bonds.

裂解酶　通過雙鍵催化化學基團結合的一種酶。

lycanthropy *n.* a very rare symptom of mental disorder in which an individual believes that he can change into a wolf.

變狼妄想　一種極少見的精神病症狀，病人相信自己能變為一隻狼。

Lyell's disease *see* staphylococcal scalded skin syndrome.

萊爾病　參閱 staphylococcal scalded skin syndrome。

Lyme disease a disease caused by a spirochaete, *Borrelia burghdorferl*, and transmitted by certain ticks of the genus *Ixodes*. Following a 3–32-day incubation period, a slowly extending red rash develops in approximately 75% of cases; intermittent systemic symptoms include fever, malaise, headache and neck stiffness, and muscle and joint pains. Later, 60% of patients suffer intermittent attacks of arthritis, especially of the knees, each attack lasting months and recurring over several years. The spirochaete has been identified in synovium and synovial fluid. Neurological and cardiac involvement occurs in a smaller percentage of cases. Treatment is with tetracycline or penicillin.

萊姆病　一種由螺旋體（博氏疏螺旋體）引起，並由硬蜱屬的某些蜱傳播的疾病。3~32 天的潛伏期後，75% 左右的病人發生一種緩慢蔓延的紅色皮疹；間歇性的全身症狀，包括：發熱、不適、頭痛、頸部僵硬及肌肉關節痛。此後，60% 的病人有間歇性發作的關節炎，尤其在膝部，每次發作持續數月，幾年後復發。在滑膜和滑液中，已發現這種螺旋體。少數病例中，發生神經系統及心臟受累。治療用四環素和青黴素。

lymph *n.* the fluid present within the vessels of the *lymphatic system. It

淋巴　存在於淋巴系統的淋巴管內的液體。淋巴是組織的清

consists of the fluid that bathes the tissues, which is derived from the blood and is drained by the lymphatic vessels. Lymph passes through a series of filters (*lymph nodes) and is ultimately returned to the blood-stream via the *thoracic duct. It is similar in composition to plasma, but contains less protein and some cells, mainly *lymphocytes.

洗液，它來自血液，在淋巴管內流動。淋巴通過一系列濾過器（淋巴結），最終經胸導管返回血液。淋巴的組成與血漿相似，但含較少量蛋白質和一些細胞，主要為淋巴細胞。

lymphaden- (lymphadeno-) *prefix denoting* lymph node(s).

〔前綴〕**淋巴結**

lymphadenectomy *n.* surgical removal of lymph nodes, an operation commonly performed when a cancer has invaded nodes in the drainage area of an organ infiltrated by a malignant growth.

淋巴結切除術 切除淋巴結的手術。當惡性腫瘤浸潤某器官的淋巴引流區的淋巴結時，常行此手術。

lymphadenitis *n.* inflammation of lymph nodes, which become swollen, painful, and tender. Some cases may be chronic (e.g. tuberculous lymphadenitis) but most are acute and localized adjacent to an area of infection. The most commonly affected lymph nodes are those in the neck, in association with tonsillitis. The lymph nodes help to contain and combat the infection. Occasionally generalized lymphadenitis occurs as a result of virus infections. The treatment is that of the cause.

淋巴結炎 淋巴結發炎，變得腫脹和疼痛。有些病例可為慢性（如結核性淋巴結炎），但多數為急性，局限於感染部位附近。最常受累的是頸部淋巴結，並伴有扁桃體炎。淋巴結能抑制和抵抗感染。偶爾會因病毒感染引起全身性淋巴結炎。根據病因來治療。

lymphadenoma *n.* an obsolete term for *lymphoma.

淋巴組織瘤 淋巴瘤的廢用名。

lymphangi- (lymphangio-) *prefix denoting* a lymphatic vessel.

〔前綴〕**淋巴管**

lymphangiectasis *n.* dilatation of the lymphatic vessels, which is usually congenital and produces enlargement of various parts of the body (e.g. the leg in Milroy's disease). It may also be caused by obstruction of the lymphatic vessels. *See* lymphoedema.

淋巴管擴張 淋巴管的擴張。通常為先天性的，導致身體各個部位腫大（如米爾羅伊病的腿腫）。本病也可由淋巴管阻塞引起。參閱 lymphoedema。

lymphangiography *n*. X-ray examination of the lymphatic vessels and lymph nodes after a contrast medium has been injected into them (*see* angiography). Its main uses are in the investigation of the extent and spread of cancer of the lymphatic system and in the investigation of lymphoedema.

淋巴管造影術　將造影劑注入淋巴管和淋巴結後，對兩者進行 X 綫檢查（參閱 angiography）。主要用於檢查淋巴系統癌瘤的範圍及蔓延，以及檢查淋巴水腫。

lymphangioma *n*. a localized collection of distended lymphatic vessels, which may result in a large cyst in the neck or armpit (*cystic hygroma*). This can be removed surgically.

淋巴管瘤　擴張淋巴管的局部聚集，可在頸部或腋窩形成一個大囊腫（囊性水瘤）。可手術摘除。

lymphangiosarcoma *n*. a very rare malignant tumour of the lymphatic vessels. It is most commonly seen in the chronically swollen (oedematous) arms of women who have had a mastectomy for breast cancer.

淋巴管肉瘤　一種罕見的淋巴管惡性腫瘤。最常見於因乳腺癌行乳房切除術的婦女的臂部，該部位長期水腫。

lymphangitis *n*. inflammation of the lymphatic vessels, which can be seen most commonly as red streaks in the skin adjacent to a focus of streptococcal infection. Occasionally a more chronic form results in *lymphoedema. The infected part is rested and the infection can be eliminated by an antibiotic (e.g. penicillin).

淋巴管炎　淋巴管的炎症。最常表現為鏈球菌感染病竈附近皮膚上的一條紅綫。較慢性形式偶爾可導致淋巴水腫。患部休息，並使用抗生素（如青黴素）可消除感染。

lymphatic 1. *n*. a lymphatic vessel. *See* lymphatic system. **2.** *adj*. relating to or transporting lymph.

(1) 淋巴管　參閱 lymphatic system。**(2) 淋巴的**，與淋巴有關的，輸送淋巴的

lymphatic system a network of vessels that conveys electrolytes, water, proteins, etc. – in the form of *lymph – from the tissue fluids to the bloodstream (see illustration). It consists of fine blind-ended lymphatic capillaries, which unite to form lymphatic vessels. At various points along the lymphatic vessels are *lymph nodes. Lymph drains into the capillaries

淋巴（管）系統　以淋巴的形式，將電解質、水、蛋白質等從組織液運輸到血液的一個管道網絡（見圖）。它由盲端的纖細毛細淋巴管構成，而毛細淋巴管匯合形成淋巴管。淋巴結分佈於順淋巴管走行的各個部位。淋巴流入毛細淋巴管，然後進入淋巴管，淋巴管內有

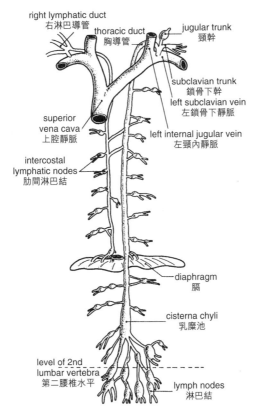

right lymphatic duct
右淋巴導管

thoracic duct
胸導管

jugular trunk
頸幹

subclavian trunk
鎖骨下幹
left subclavian vein
左鎖骨下靜脈

superior
vena cava
上腔靜脈

left internal jugular vein
左頸內靜脈

intercostal
lymphatic nodes
肋間淋巴結

diaphragm
膈

cisterna chyli
乳糜池

level of 2nd
lumbar vertebra
第二腰椎水平

lymph nodes
淋巴結

The lymphatic system
淋巴系統

and passes into the lymphatic vessels, which have valves to prevent backflow of lymph. The lymphatics lead to two large channels – the *thoracic duct* and the *right lymphatic duct* – which return the lymph to the bloodstream via the innominate veins.

lymph node one of a number of small swellings found at intervals along the lymphatic system. Groups of nodes are found in many parts of the body; for example, in the groin and armpit and

瓣膜防止淋巴倒流。淋巴管匯成兩條大的管道——胸導管和右淋巴導管，它們通過無名靜脈使淋巴回流入血流。

淋巴結 淋巴系統內間隔可見的許多小的膨大物。成組的淋巴結可見於身體許多部位，如腹股溝、腋窩及耳後。淋巴結由淋巴組織組成，起淋巴過濾

behind the ear. They are composed of lymphoid tissue and act as filters for the lymph, preventing foreign particles from entering the bloodstream; they also produce lymphocytes.

lympho- *prefix denoting* lymph or the lymphatic system.

lymphoblast *n.* an abnormal cell present in the blood and the blood-forming organs in one type of leukaemia (*lymphoblastic leukaemia*). It has a large nucleus with very scanty cytoplasm and was once thought to be the precursor of the lymphocyte. **–lymphoblastic** *adj.*

lymphocyte *n.* a variety of white blood cell (leucocyte), present also in the lymph nodes, spleen, thymus gland, gut wall, and bone marrow. With *Romanowsky stains, lymphocytes can be seen to have dense nuclei with clear pale-blue cytoplasm. Lymphocytes with scanty cytoplasm are *small lymphocytes*; those with abundant cytoplasm are *large lymphocytes*. There are normally 1.5–4.0 × 10^9 lymphocytes per litre of blood. They are involved in *immunity and can be subdivided into *B-lymphocytes*, which produce circulating antibodies, and *T-lymphocytes*, which are primarily responsible for cell-mediated immunity. T-lymphocytes can differentiate into helper, killer, or suppressor cells. **–lymphocytic** *adj.*

lymphocytopenia *n. see* lymphopenia.

lymphocytosis *n.* an increase in the number of *lymphocytes in the blood. Lymphocytosis may occur in a wide variety of diseases, including chronic lymphocytic *leukaemia and infections due to viruses.

器的作用，防止異物進入血流。淋巴結還生成淋巴細胞。

〔前綴〕淋巴，淋巴系統

淋巴母細胞 某種類型白血病（淋巴母細胞性白血病）時出現於血液和造血器官中的一種異常細胞。它的核大而胞漿極少，一度曾被認為是淋巴細胞的前體細胞。

淋巴細胞 白細胞的一種類型，也存在於淋巴結、脾、胸腺、腸壁和骨髓內。羅曼諾夫斯基染色可見淋巴細胞有致密的胞核和清亮、淺藍色胞漿。胞漿稀少的淋巴細胞是小淋巴細胞，胞漿豐富的是大淋巴細胞。正常情況下，每升血液中有 1.5–4.0 × 10^9 個淋巴細胞。它們參與免疫反應，可進一步分為 B 淋巴細胞和 T 淋巴細胞。前者產生循環抗體，後者主要與細胞免疫有關。T 淋巴細胞可分化為輔助細胞、殺傷細胞及抑制細胞。

淋巴細胞減少 參閱 lymphopenia。

淋巴細胞增多 血液中淋巴細胞數目增加。可發生於多種疾病中，如慢性淋巴細胞性白血病和病毒性感染。

lymphoedema *n.* an accumulation of lymph in the tissues, producing swelling; the legs are most often affected. It may be due to a congenital abnormality of the lymphatic vessels (as in *Milroy's disease*, congenital lymphoedema of the legs) or result from obstruction of the lymphatic vessels by a tumour, parasites, inflammation, or injury. Treatment consists of elastic support, by stockings or bandages, and diuretic drugs. A variety of surgical procedures have been devised but with little success.

淋巴水腫 淋巴在組織內積聚，導致水腫；最常累及雙腿。可由某種淋巴管的先天異常（米爾羅伊病時的先天性腿部淋巴水腫）所致；也可由腫瘤、寄生蟲、炎症或損傷阻塞淋巴管引起。治療包括用彈性支持物，如長統襪和繃帶，以及利尿藥。曾設計了多種外科方法但均療效甚微。

lymphogranuloma venereum a sexually transmitted disease that is caused by *Chlamydia* and is most common in tropical regions. An initial lesion on the genitals is followed by swelling and inflammation of the lymph nodes in the groin; the lymph vessels in the genital region may become blocked, causing thickening of the skin of that area. Early treatment with sulphonamides or tetracyclines is usually effective.

性病性淋巴肉芽腫 一種性傳播病，由衣原體屬引起，最常見於熱帶地區。最先為生殖器的損傷，接着腹股溝淋巴結發炎、腫大。生殖器區的淋巴管可能被堵塞，引起該區皮膚變厚。早期用磺胺類或四環素治療通常有效。

lymphography *n.* the technique of injecting *radiopaque material into the lymphatic system in a particular region of the body so that X-ray photographs may be taken of the lymph vessels and nodes. Lymphography can indicate the presence of tumours in the lymphatic system.

淋巴造影術 將不透 X 綫的物質注射入身體某個區域的淋巴系統以拍攝淋巴結和淋巴管 X 綫照片的技術。此法可查出淋巴系統內存在的腫瘤。

lymphoid tissue a tissue responsible for the production of lymphocytes and antibodies. It occurs as discrete organs, in the form of the lymph nodes, tonsils, thymus, and spleen, and also as diffuse groups of cells not separated from surrounding tissue. *See also* immune system.

淋巴組織 負責產生淋巴細胞和抗體的組織。它以淋巴結、扁桃體、胸腺和脾的形式形成獨立的器官，也可不與周圍組織分開，形成彌散的細胞羣。參閱 immune system。

lymphokine *n.* a substance produced by lymphocytes that has effects on other

淋巴因子 淋巴細胞產生的一種物質，對參與免疫系統的其

cells involved in the immune system. An example is *interleukin 2 (IL-2).

他細胞有影響。例如：白細胞介素 2。

lymphoma *n.* any malignant tumour of lymph nodes, including *Hodgkin's disease. There is a broad spectrum of malignancy, with prognosis ranging from a few months to many years. The patient usually shows evidence of multiple enlarged lymph nodes and may have constitutional symptoms such as weight loss, fever, and sweating. Disease may be widespread, but in some cases is confined to a single area, such as the tonsil. Treatment is with drugs such as chlorambucil or combinations of cyclophosphamide, vincristine, and prednisone, sometimes with the addition of doxorubicin and/or bleomycin; response to these drugs is often dramatic. Localized disease may be treated with radiotherapy followed by drugs. Patients with non-Hodgkin's lymphoma that does not respond to chemotherapy may be considered for a bone-marrow transplant.

淋巴瘤 包括霍奇金病在內的所有淋巴結惡性腫瘤。惡性程度很不一致，預後從數月到數年。病人通常表現出多發性淋巴結腫大迹象，並可有全身性症狀，如體重下降、發熱及出汗。疾病可廣泛蔓延，但某些病例僅局限於某個部位，如扁桃體。治療藥物有苯丁酸氮芥或者環磷酰胺、長春新鹼和強的松聯合使用，有時還可加上阿黴素和／或博來黴素。對這些藥物的反應常非常顯著。局限性的淋巴瘤可先放療，再用藥物治療。對化學治療無反應的非霍奇金淋巴瘤患者可考慮骨髓移植。

lymphopenia (lymphocytopenia) *n.* a decrease in the number of *lymphocytes in the blood, which may occur in a wide variety of disease.

淋巴細胞減少 血液中淋巴細胞數目的減少，可見於多種疾病。

lymphopoiesis *n.* the process of the production of *lymphocytes, which occurs in the *bone marrow as well as in the lymph nodes, spleen, thymus gland, and gut wall. The precursor cell from which lymphocytes are derived has not yet been identified.

淋巴細胞生成 淋巴細胞生成的過程，發生於骨髓、淋巴結、脾、胸腺及腸壁。產生淋巴細胞的前體細胞仍未確定。

lymphorrhagia *n.* the escape of the lymph from lymphatic vessels that have been injured.

淋巴溢 淋巴逸出受損傷的淋巴管。

lymphosarcoma *n.* an old term for non-Hodgkin's *lymphoma.

淋巴肉瘤 非霍奇金淋巴瘤的曾用名。

lymphuria *n.* the presence in the urine of lymph.

淋巴尿　尿中出現淋巴。

lys- (lysi-, lyso-) *prefix denoting* lysis; dissolution.

〔前綴〕**溶解**

lysergic acid diethylamide (LSD) a *psychedelic drug that is also a *hallucinogen. It has been used to aid treatment of psychological disorders. Side-effects include digestive upsets, dizziness, tingling, anxiety, sweating, dilated pupils, muscle incoordination and tremor. Alterations in sight, hearing and other senses occur, psychotic effects, depression, and confusion are common, and tolerance to the drug develops rapidly. Because of these toxic effects, LSD is no longer used clinically.

麥角二乙胺　一種致幻劑。一直用於心理疾病的輔助治療。副作用包括：消化系統不適、頭暈、麻刺感、焦慮、出汗、瞳孔擴張、肌肉共濟失調及震顫。會發生視力、聽力及其他感覺改變，常見精神症狀、抑鬱以及精神錯亂，快速產生耐藥性。由於這些毒作用，此藥不再用於臨床。

lysin *n.* a protein component in the blood that is capable of bringing about the destruction (lysis) of whole cells. Names are given to varieties of lysin with different targets; for example, *haemolysin* attacks red blood cells; *leucolysin* attacks white cells; and a *bacteriolysin* targets bacterial cells.

溶素　血液中一種能導致整個細胞破壞（溶解）的蛋白質成分。靶細胞不同的各種溶素有不同的名稱。如溶血素攻擊紅細胞；白細胞溶素攻擊白細胞；細菌溶素則溶解細菌細胞。

lysine *n.* an *essential amino acid. *See also* amino acid.

賴氨酸　一種必需氨基酸。參閱 amino acid。

lysis *n.* the destruction of cells through damage or rupture of the plasma membrane, allowing escape of the cell contents. *See also* autolysis, lysozyme.

溶解　通過損傷或破裂細胞膜，使細胞內容物逸出而破壞細胞。參閱 autolysis，lysozyme。

-lysis *suffix denoting* **1.** lysis; dissolution. **2.** remission of symptoms.

〔後綴〕**(1) 溶解　(2) 症狀減輕**

lysogenic *adj.* producing *lysis.

致溶的　引起溶解的。

lysogeny *n.* an interaction between a *bacteriophage and its host in which a latent form of the phage (*prophage*)

噬菌體生成　噬菌體與其宿主間的一種相互作用。在這種作用中，噬菌體的一種潛伏形式

exists within the bacterial cell, which is not destroyed. Under certain conditions (e.g. irradiation of the bacterium) the phage can develop into an active form, which reproduces itself and eventually destroys the bacterial cell.

lysosome *n*. a particle in the cytoplasm of cells that contains enzymes responsible for breaking down substances in the cell and is bounded by a single membrane. Lysosomes are especially abundant in liver and kidney cells. Foreign particles (e.g. bacteria) taken into the cell are broken down by the enzymes of the lysosomes. When the cell dies, these enzymes are released to break down the cell's components.

lysozyme *n*. an enzyme found in tears and egg white. It catalyses the destruction of the cell walls of certain bacteria. Bacterial cells that are attacked by lysozyme are said to have been *lysed*.

（前噬菌體）存在於未被破壞的細菌細胞內。在特定條件下（如射綫照射細菌），這種前噬菌體發育為其活躍形式，進行自身繁殖，並最終破壞細菌細胞。

溶酶體 細胞胞漿內的一種顆粒，內含一些專門分解細胞內物質的酶，並由一單層膜包裹。肝和腎細胞內溶酶體尤其多。進入細胞的異物（如細菌）由溶酶體的酶分解。細胞死亡時，這些溶酶體被釋放出來分解細胞成分。

溶菌酶 見於淚液和蛋白中的一種酶。它催化對某些細菌細胞壁的破壞。細菌細胞被溶菌酶攻擊稱為溶菌。

M

maceration *n*. **1.** the softening of a solid by leaving it immersed in a liquid. **2.** (in obsterics) the natural breakdown of a dead fetus within the uterus.

Macleod's syndrome (Swyer-James syndrome) pulmonary *emphysema affecting only one lung and beginning in childhood or in adolescence; it occurs secondarily to necrotising bronchitis, probably caused by a virus.

macr- (macro-) *prefix denoting* large size. Example: *macrencephaly* (abnormally enlarged brain).

浸漬 （1）把固體浸泡在液體中使其變軟。（2）（產科學）死胎在子宮內自然分解。

麥克勞德綜合徵（斯-詹氏綜合徵） 僅累及一側肺的肺氣腫，開始於兒童期或青少年期，它繼發於壞死性支氣管炎，可能由某種病毒引起。

〔前綴〕**大** 如巨腦（腦異常增大）。

macrocephaly (megalocephaly) *n.* abnormal largeness of the head in relation to the rest of the body. *Compare* microcephaly.

巨頭 與身體其他部位相比，頭部異常大。與 microcephaly 對比。

macrocheilia *n.* hypertrophy of the lips: a congenital condition in which the lips are abnormally large. *Compare* microcheilia.

巨唇 唇部肥厚：一種雙唇異常大的先天性疾病。與 microcheilia 對比。

macrocyte (megalocyte) *n.* an abnormally large red blood cell (*erythrocyte), seen in certain anaemias. *See also* macrocytosis. **–macrocytic** *adj.*

巨紅細胞 異常大的紅細胞，見於某些貧血。參閱 macrocytosis。

macrocytosis *n.* the presence of abnormally large red cells (*macrocytes*) in the blood. Macrocytosis is a feature of certain anaemias (*macrocytic anaemias*), including those due to deficiency of vitamin B_{12} or folic acid, and also of anaemias in which there is a increase in the rate of red cell production.

巨紅細胞症 血液中有異常大紅細胞存在。本症是某些貧血（巨紅細胞型貧血）的特點，包括維生素 B_{12} 或葉酸缺乏導致的貧血和紅細胞生成速度增加的貧血。

macrodactyly *n.* abnormally large size of one or more of the fingers or toes.

巨指（趾） 一個或多個指或趾異常大。

macrodontia *n.* a condition in which the teeth are unusually large.

巨牙 牙齒異常大的情形。

macrogamete *n.* the nonmotile female sex cell of the malarial parasite (*Plasmodium*) and other single-celled animals (*see* Protozoa). The macrogamete is similar to the ovum of higher animal groups and larger than the male sex cell (*see* microgamete).

大配子 瘧疾寄生物（瘧原蟲）和其他單細胞動物（參閱 Protozoa）的不運動的雌性性細胞。大配子類似於高等動物的卵，並且較雄性性細胞大（參閱 microgamete）。

macrogametocyte *n.* a cell that undergoes meiosis to form mature female sex cells (macrogametes) of the malarial parasite (*see* Plasmodium). Macrogametocytes are found in the blood of man but must be ingested by a mosquito before developing into macrogametes.

大配子體 經過減數分裂而形成瘧疾寄生物（參閱 Plasmodium）成熟雌性性細胞（大配子）的一種細胞。大配子體可見於人血中，但必須被蚊蟲吞入後才能發育成大配子。

macrogenitosoma n. excessive bodily growth with marked enlargement of the genitalia. *Macrogenitosoma praecox* is a variant occurring in early childhood.

巨生殖器巨體　身體過分生長，伴有生殖器明顯增大。早熟性巨生殖器巨體是發生在幼年的一種變異型。

macroglia n. one of the two basic classes of *glia (the non-nervous cells of the central nervous system), divided into *astrocytes and *oligodendrocytes. *Compare* microglia.

大神經膠質　兩種基本神經膠質（中樞神經系統的非神經細胞）類型的一種，分為星形膠質細胞和少突神經膠質細胞。與 microglia 對比。

macroglobulin n. **1. (immunoglobulin M, IgM)** a protein of the globulin series that is present in the blood and functions as an antibody, forming an effective firstline defence against bacteria in the bloodstream. *See also* immunoglobulin. **2.** an abnormal form of **IgM** (*see* paraprotein).

(1) 巨球蛋白　球蛋白系列中的一種蛋白，存在於血液中，有抗體功能，形成血流中抵禦細菌的第一道防綫（參閱 immunoglobulin）。**(2)** 病變蛋白　免疫球蛋白的一種異常形式（參閱 paraprotein）。

macroglobulinaemia n. the presence in the blood of excessive amounts of macroglobulin, produced by a malignant proliferation of the lymphocytes.

巨球蛋白血症　血中出現過量的巨球蛋白，由淋巴細胞的惡性增殖產生。

macroglossia n. an abnormally large tongue. It may be due to a congenital defect, such as thyroid deficiency (cretinism); to infiltration of the tongue with *amyloid or a tumour; or to obstruction of the lymph vessels.

巨舌　舌異常大。它可由先天性缺陷引起，如甲狀腺功能低下（克汀病），或舌受澱粉樣蛋白或腫瘤浸潤引起；或由淋巴管阻塞引起。

macrognathia n. marked overgrowth of one jaw relative to the growth of the other.

巨頜　與另一頜的生長相比，一頜明顯生長過度。

macromelia n. abnormally large size of the arms or legs. *Compare* micromelia.

巨肢　臂或腿異常大。與 micromelia 對比。

macronormoblast n. an abnormal form of any of the cells (*normoblasts) that form a series of precursors of red blood cells. Macronormoblasts are unusually large but have normal nuclei (*compare* megaloblast); they are seen in certain

巨幼紅細胞　形成一系列紅細胞的前體細胞（幼紅細胞）的異常形式。這種細胞異常大，但核正常（與 megaloblast 對比）。它們可見於紅細胞生成障礙的某些貧血。

anaemias in which red cell production is impaired.

macrophage (clasmocyte) *n.* a large scavenger cell (a *phagocyte) present in connective tissue and many major organs and tissues, including the bone marrow, spleen, *lymph nodes, liver (*see* Kupffer cells), and the central nervous system (*see* microglia). They are closely related to *monocytes. *Fixed macrophages* (*histiocytes*) are stationary within connective tissue; *free macrophages* wander between cells and aggregate at focal sites of infection, where they remove bacteria or other foreign bodies from blood or tissues. *See also* reticuloendothelial system.

巨噬細胞　一種大的清掃細胞（吞噬細胞），存在於結締組織及許多主要的器官和組織中，包括骨髓、脾、淋巴結、肝臟（參閱 Kupffer cells），及中樞神經系統（參閱 microglia）。它們與單核細胞有密切關係。固定的巨噬細胞（組織細胞）靜止地存在於結締組織內；游離的巨噬細胞游走於細胞之間，並聚集於感染竈部位，從血液或組織中清除細菌或其他異物。參閱 reticuloendothelial system。

macropsia *n.* a condition in which objects appear larger than they really are. It is usually due to disease of the retina affecting the *macula but may also occur in spasm of *accommodation.

視物顯大症　視物體顯得比其實際大的一種疾病。常由於累及黃斑的視網膜疾病引起，也可發生於眼調節痙攣時。

macroscopic *adj.* visible to the naked eye. *Compare* microscopic.

目視的　肉眼可看見的。與 microscopic 對比。

macrosomia *n.* abnormally large size. In *fetal macrosomia* a large baby is associated with poorly controlled maternal diabetes. The increased size is due to excessive production of fetal insulin and thence to increased deposition of glycogen in the fetus.

巨體症　身體異常大。在胎兒巨體症中，嬰兒巨體與其母親糖尿病未很好控制有關，胎兒胰島素過度生成和由此引起的胎兒體內糖原的沉積增加，造成胎兒身體增大。

macula *n.* (*pl.* **maculae**) a small anatomical area that is distinguishable from the surrounding tissue. The *macula lutea* is the yellow spot on the retina at the back of the eye, which surrounds the greatest concentration of cones (*see* fovea). Maculae occur in the saccule and utricle of the inner ear (see illustration). Tilting of the head causes the otoliths to

斑　區別於周圍組織的一塊小的解剖學區域。黃斑是位於眼球後面視網膜上的黃點，該區域內視椎細胞最為密集（參閱 fovea）。聽斑位於內耳的小囊和橢圓囊內（見圖）。頭部傾斜使耳石將毛細胞變彎曲。毛細胞將神經衝動經前庭傳向大腦。參閱 labyrinth。

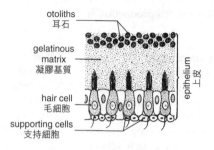

A macula of the inner ear
內耳的斑

bend the hair cells, which send impulses to the brain via the vestibular nerve. *See also* labyrinth.

macule *n.* a flat circumscribed area of skin or an area of altered skin colour (e.g. a freckle). *Compare* papule.

斑（點）　皮膚的一個扁平局限部位或皮膚顏色改變的一個部位（如雀斑）。與 papule 對比。

maculopapular *adj.* describing a rash that consists of both *macules and *papules.

斑丘疹的　描述由斑（點）和丘疹組成的皮疹。

madarosis *n.* **1.** a congenital deficiency of the eyelashes and eyebrows, which are sometimes absent altogether. **2.** a deficiency of the eyelashes alone, caused by chronic *blepharitis.

睫毛脫落　(1) 睫毛和眉毛的先天性缺失，有時兩者可一同發生。(2) 由慢性眼瞼炎引起的單純睫毛缺失。

Madopar *n. see* benserazide.

羥苄綠胼　參閱 benserazide。

Madura foot an infection of the tissues and bones of the foot producing chronic inflammation (mycetoma), occurring in the tropics. It is caused by various filamentous fungi (including *Madurella*) and certain bacteria of the general *Nocardia* and *Streptomyces*. Medical name: **maduromycosis**.

足分支菌病　足組織和足骨的感染造成慢性炎症（足分支菌病），發生於熱帶地區。由多種絲狀真菌（包括馬杜拉分支菌屬）及諾卡菌屬和鏈黴菌屬的某些細菌引起。醫學用語：足分支菌病。

Madurella *n.* a genus of widely distributed fungi. The species *M. grisea* and

馬杜拉分支菌屬　廣泛分布的一屬真菌。灰色馬杜拉菌和足

M. mycetomi cause the tropical infection
*Madura foot.

腫馬杜拉菌造成熱帶感染——
足分支菌病。

maduromycosis *n. see* Madura foot.

足分支菌病　參閱　Madura
foot。

magenta *n. see* fuchsin.

品紅　參閱 fuchsin。

maggot *n.* the wormlike larva of a fly,
which occasionally infests human tissues
(*see* myiasis). Formerly maggots were, in
some cases, allowed to feed on dead and
rotting tissues and so assist in the cleaning and healing of serious wounds.

蛆　蒼蠅的蠕蟲樣幼蟲，偶爾
感染人類（參閱 myiasis）。以
前，在某些病例中，人們讓蛆
吞食死亡和腐爛的組織，以幫
助清潔和愈合嚴重的傷口。

magnesium *n.* a metallic element
essential to life. The body of an average
adult contains about 25 g of magnesium,
concentrated mostly in the bones.
Magnesium is necessary for the proper
functioning of muscle and nervous tissue.
It is required as a *cofactor for approximately 90 enzymes. A good source of
magnesium is green leafy vegetables.
Symbol: Mg.

鎂　生命必需的一種金屬元
素。成年人身體平均含鎂約 25
克，主要集中於骨內。鎂是肌
肉和神經組織發揮正常功能所
必需的。它是約 90 種酶所需
要的輔因子。綠葉蔬菜是良好
的鎂源。符號：Mg。

magnesium carbonate a weak *antacid
used to relieve indigestion and also pain
due to stomach and duodenal ulcers; it is
also used as a mild laxative. It is usually
given with other compounds in mixtures,
powders, and tablets.

碳酸鎂　一種弱的抗酸製劑，
用於緩解消化不良及胃和十二
指腸潰瘍引起的疼痛。還被用
作為溫和的緩瀉劑。它通常以
合劑、粉劑和片劑與其他化合
物一起使用。

magnesium hydroxide a magnesium
salt with effects and uses similar to those
of *magnesium carbonate. Trade name:
Milk of Magnesia.

氫氧化鎂　一種效果和用途類
似於碳酸鎂的鎂鹽。商品名：
Milk of Magnesia。

magnesium sulphate a magnesium salt
given in mixtures or enemas to treat constipation (*see* laxative). It is also administered by injection to treat magnesium
deficiency.

硫酸鎂　一種用以治療便秘
（參閱 laxative）的鎂鹽合劑或
灌腸劑。也可注射治療鎂缺
乏。

magnesium trisilicate a compound of
magnesium with antacid and absorbent

三硅酸鎂　一種具有抗酸和吸
收特性的鎂化合物，用於治療

properties, used in the treatment of peptic ulcers and other digestive disorders.

消化性潰瘍和其他消化性疾病。

magnetic resonance imaging (MRI) a diagnostic technique based on analysis of the absorption and transmission of high-frequency radio waves by the water molecules in tissues placed in a strong magnetic field (*see* nuclear magnetic resonance). Using modern high-speed computers, this analysis can be used to 'map out' the variation in tissue signals in any plane and thus produce images of the tissues. It is particularly useful for examining the central nervous system and musculoskeletal system, and to a lesser extent the chest and abdomen. MRI can be used for the noninvasive diagnosis and treatment planning of a wide range of diseases, including cancer: it has the advantage that it does not use potentially harmful ionizing radiation, such as X-rays.

磁共振成像術　一種以分析置於強磁場中的組織內水分子對高頻放射波的吸收和傳遞為基礎的診斷技術（參閱 nuclear magnetic resonance）。利用現代高速計算機，這種分析可描繪出各個平面組織信號的變化，從而產生組織影像。它對檢查中樞神經系統和肌肉骨骼系統尤其有用，對檢查胸及腹也有一定用處。本技術可用作包括癌症在內的多種疾病的非介入性診斷和治療：其優點是它不用可能有害的電離輻射，如 X 綫。

magnetic resonance spectroscopy (MRS) a diagnostic technique that utilizes the phenomenon of *nuclear magnetic resonance to obtain a biochemical profile of tissues. It is particularly useful for biochemical analysis of tissues, especially muscle, that are otherwise difficult to investigate and would require a biopsy.

磁共振分光術　一種利用核磁共振現象獲得組織的生化輪廓的診斷技術。它對於組織（尤其是肌肉的）生化分析非常有用，否則，這些組織難以檢查且需要活檢。

MAGPI operation meatal advancement and glanuloplasty operation: a simple surgical procedure designed to correct minor to moderate degrees of coronal or subcoronal *hypospadias. This single-stage operation corrects and associated minor degrees of *chordee and transfers the urethral opening to the glans.

尿道徙前及成形手術　用於矯正輕度或中度冠向的或冠向下的尿道下裂的一個簡單手術。這個一步性手術可矯正任何併發的輕度痛性陰莖勃起，並將尿道口移至陰莖頭。

mal *n.* illness or disease.

疾病

mal- *prefix. denoting* disease, disorder, or abnormality.

malabsorption *n.* a state in which absorption of one or more substances by the small intestine is reduced. It most commonly affects fat (causing *steatorrhoea), some vitamins (such as B₁₂, folic acid, vitamin D, and vitamin K), *electrolytes (such as calcium, potassium), iron, and amino acids. Symptoms (depending on the substances involved) include weight loss, diarrhoea, anaemia, swelling (oedema), and vitamin deficiencies. The commonest causes are *coeliac disease, *pancreatitis, *cystic fibrosis, *blind loop syndrome, or surgical removal of a length of small intestine.

malacia *n.* abnormal softening of a part, organ, or tissue, such as bone (*see* osteomalacia).

-malacia *suffix denoting* abnormal softening of a tissue. Example: *keratomalacia* (of the cornea).

malaise *n.* a general feeling of being unwell. The feeling may be accompanied by identifiable physical discomfort and may indicate the presence of disease.

malar bone *see.* zygomatic bone.

malaria (ague, marsh fever, periodic fever, paludism) *n.* an infectious disease due to the presence of parasitic protozoa of the genus *Plasmodium* (*P. falciparum*, *P. malariae*, *P. ovale*, or *P. vivax*) within the red blood cells. The disease is transmitted by the *Anopheles* mosquito and is confined mainly to tropical and subtropical areas.

Parasites in the blood of an infected person are taken into the stomach of the

〔前綴〕疾病，紊亂，障礙，異常

吸收障礙 小腸對一種或多種物質的吸收作用減弱的一種狀態。最常影響脂肪（引起脂肪痢）、某些維生素（如維生素 B₁₂、葉酸、維生素 D 和維生素 K）、電解質（如鈣、鉀）、鐵及氨基酸的吸收。症狀（取決於所涉及的物質）包括體重下降、腹瀉、貧血、水腫及維生素缺乏。最常見的原因是腹腔疾病、胰腺炎、膽囊纖維化、盲袢綜合徵及手術切除部分小腸。

軟化 身體的一部分、一個器官或組織的異常軟化，如骨（參閱 osteomalacia）。

〔後綴〕軟化 組織異常變軟，如角膜軟化。

不適 一種全身的不適感。這種感覺可伴有明確的身體不適，並可表示疾病的存在。

顴骨 參閱 zygomatic bone。

瘧（疾）由瘧原蟲屬（惡性瘧原蟲、三日瘧原蟲、卵形瘧原蟲或間日瘧原蟲）寄生蟲在紅細胞內的存在而引起的傳染性疾病。本病由按蚊傳播，主要局限於熱帶和亞熱帶。

蚊子叮食被感染者時，將其血中的寄生蟲吸入胃中。在這裏牠們繁殖並侵入蚊子的唾液腺。當蚊子叮咬另一人時，寄生蟲被注入血流並遷移到肝

mosquito as it feeds. Here they multiply and then invade the salivary glands. When the mosquito bites and individual, parasites are injected into the bloodstream and migrate to the liver and other organs, where they multiply. After an incubation period varying from 12 days (*P. falciparum*) to 10 months (some varieties of *P. vivax*), parasites return to the bloodstream and invade the red blood cells. Rapid multiplication of the parasites results in destruction of the red cells and the release of more parasites capable of infecting other red cells. This causes a short bout of shivering, fever, and sweating, and the loss of healthy red cells results in anaemia. When the next batch of parasites is released symptoms reappear. The interval between fever attacks varies in different types of malaria: in *quartan malaria* (or *fever*), caused by *P. malariae*, it is three days; in *tertian malaria* (*P. ovale* or *P. vivax*) two days; and in *malignant tertian* (or *quotidian*) *malaria* (*P. falciparum*) – the most severe kind – from a few hours to two days (*see also* backwater fever). Preventive and curative treatment includes such drugs as *chloroquine, *proguanil, *mefloquine, and *pyrimethamine. A vaccine is being tested.

和其他器官，開始繁殖。在 12 天（惡性瘧原蟲）至 10 個月（某些間日瘧原蟲的變種）不等的潛伏期後，寄生蟲返回血流且侵入紅細胞。寄生蟲的快速繁殖導致紅細胞破壞和更多能感染其他紅細胞的寄生蟲被釋放。這引起短暫的寒顫、發熱及出汗；正常紅細胞的減少導致貧血。當下一批寄生蟲被釋放時，這些症狀再次出現。不同類型的瘧疾有不同的發熱間隔：由三日瘧原蟲引起的三日瘧（或熱），間隔是三天；由卵形瘧原蟲或間日瘧原蟲引起的間日瘧，間隔期是二天；由惡生瘧原蟲引起的惡性瘧（或日發瘧）是最嚴重的類型，間隔期從數小時到 2 天（參閱 blackwater fever）。防治藥物包括：氯喹、氯胍、甲氟喹及乙氨嘧啶。其疫苗正在試製中。

malathion *n.* an organophosphorous insecticide used to treat head and pubic lice and scabies. It is applied externally in the form of a lotion; possible side-effects are skin irritation and allergic reactions. Trade names; **Derbac-M**, **Prioderm**, **Soleo-M**.

馬拉硫磷 一種有機磷殺蟲劑，用於治療頭虱、陰虱或蟎。為外用洗劑；可能的副作用有：皮膚刺激和過敏反應。商品名：Derbac-M，Prioderm，Soleo-M。

malformation *n.* any variation from the normal physical structure, due either to congenital or developmental defects or to disease or injury.

畸形 由先天或發育缺陷，或由疾病或損傷造成的正常身體結構的變化。

malignant *adj.* **1.** describing a tumour that invades and destroys the tissue in which it originates and can spread to other sites in the body via the bloodstream and lymphatic system. If untreated such tumours cause progressive deterioration and death. *See* cancer. **2.** describing any disorder that becomes life-threatening if untreated (e.g. *malignant hypertension*). *Compare* benign.

malignant melanoma (MM) *see* melanoma.

malingering *n.* pretending to be ill, usually in order to avoid work or gain attention. It may be a sign of mental disorder (*see also* Munchausen's syndrome).

malleolus *n.* either of the two protuberances on each side of the ankle: the *lateral malleolus* at the lower end of the *fibula or the *medial malleolus* at the lower end of the *tibia.

mallet finger a condition in which the little finger is bent downwards, due to tearing of the attachment of the long extensor tendon.

malleus *n.* a hammer-shaped bone in the middle *ear that articulates with the incus and is attached to the eardrum. *See* ossicle.

Mallory's triple stain a histological stain consisting of water-soluble aniline blue or methyl blue, orange G, and oxalic acid. Before the stain is applied the tissue is mordanted, then treated with acid fuchsin and phosphomolybdic acid. Nuclei stain red, muscle red to orange, nervous tissue lilac, collagen dark blue, and mucus and connective tissue become blue.

惡性的　**(1)** 描述侵入和破壞其原發部位並能隨血流和淋巴系統擴散到身體其他部位的腫瘤。如未經治療，這種腫瘤可引起進行性惡化及死亡。參閱 cancer。**(2)** 描述未經治療則可危及生命的任何疾病（如惡性高血壓）。與 benign 對比。

惡性黑色素瘤　參閱 melanoma。

裝病　通常為了逃避工作或引起注意而假裝生病。它也可以是精神病的一種徵象（參閱 Munchausen's syndrome）。

踝　腳脖子兩側的兩個突起：外踝在腓骨下端，內踝在脛骨下端。

槌狀指　長伸肌肌腱附着處撕裂引起的一種小指彎向下側的異常狀態。

錘骨　位於中耳內的錘形骨，與砧骨連接並附着於鼓膜上。參閱 ossicle。

馬洛里三重染劑　由水溶性苯胺藍或甲基藍、橙黃 G 和草酸組成的一種組織學染劑。使用該染劑前，先將組織用染劑染色，然後用酸品紅和磷鉬酸處理。核染成紅色，肌肉由紅到橙黃色，神經組織淡藍色，膠原組織深藍色，黏液和結締組織則為藍色。

Mallory-Weiss syndrome tearing of the tissues around the junction of the oesophagus (gullet) and stomach as a result of violent vomiting. It is associated with *haematemesis and perforation of the oesophagus.

馬-韋氏綜合徵　劇烈嘔吐引起的食管與胃相交處周圍組織的撕裂，伴有嘔血和食管穿孔。

malnutrition *n.* the condition caused by an improper balance between what an individual eats and what he requires to maintain health. This can result from eating too little (*subnutrition* or *starvation*) but may also imply dietary excess or an incorrect balance of basic foodstuffs such as protein, fat, and carbohydrate. A deficiency (or excess) of one or more minerals, vitamins, or other essential ingredients may arise from *malabsorption of digested food or metabolic malfunction of one or more parts of the body as well as from an unbalanced diet.

營養不良　人體攝入的食物和維持健康所需的營養不平衡所致的疾病。可由飲食過少（營養不足或飢餓）引起，但也包含飲食過度或蛋白質、脂肪和碳水化合物等基本食物攝入不平衡。已消化的食物的吸收障礙，或身體某個或多個部位代謝機能障礙或膳食不平衡可造成一種或多種礦物質、維生素或其他基本成分缺乏（或過多）。

malocclusion *n.* the condition in which the upper and lower teeth are abnormally related.

錯𬌗　上下齒相對關係異常的狀態。

Malpighian body the part of a *nephron comprising the blood capillaries of the glomerulus and its surrounding Bowman's capsule.

馬爾皮基小體　由腎小球的毛細血管及其周圍的鮑曼囊組成的腎單位的一部分。

Malpighian layer the stratum germinativum: one of the layers of the *epidermis.

馬爾皮基層　表皮生發層：表皮的一層。

malposition *n.* (in obstetrics) an abnormal position of the fetal head when this is the presenting part in labour. The head is in such a position that the diameter of the skull in relation to the pelvic opening is greater than normal. This is likely to result in a prolonged and complicated labour.

錯位　（產科學）胎頭的一種異常位置，以致胎頭成為生產中的先露部。胎頭的位置使顱骨，相對於骨盆口而言，較正常大。這可能造成分娩延長和複雜化。

malpractice *n.* professional misconduct: treatment falling short of the standards

醫療差錯　職業過失：治療未達到技術及護理標準，而這一

of skill and care that can reasonably be expected from a qualified medical practitioner.

malpresentation *n.* the condition in which the presenting part of the fetus (*see* presentation) is other than the head. Malpresentation is likely to complicate labour and may necessitate delivery by *Caesarean section.

malt *n.* a mixture of carbohydrates, predominantly maltose, produced by the breakdown of starch contained in barley or wheat grains. The cereal grain is allowed to germinate and the malt is extracted with hot water. Malt is used for brewing and distilling; it has been used as a source of nutrients in wasting diseases.

Malta fever *see* brucellosis.

maltase *n.* an enzyme, present in saliva and pancreatic juice, that converts maltose into glucose during digestion.

maltose *n.* a sugar that consists of two molecules of glucose. Maltose is formed from the digestion of starch and glycogen and is found in germinating cereal seeds.

malunion *n.* deformity of a bone resulting from *union of a fracture in which the bone ends are poorly aligned. Arthritis of adjoining joints may develop as a complication later. *Osteotomy may be needed to correct the deformity and prevent the complication.

mamilla *n. see* nipple.

mamillary bodies two paired rounded swellings in the floor of the *hypothalamus, immediately behind the pituitary gland.

標準是有理由從合格的醫務人員那裏期望達到的。

先露異常 胎兒先露部（參閱 presentation）不是頭部的狀態。先露異常可能使分娩複雜化，而且可能需做剖宮產。

麥芽浸液 由大麥或小麥粒中的澱粉分解產生的以麥芽糖為主的碳水化合物的混合液。使麥粒生芽，再用鹽水浸出麥芽汁。麥芽浸液用於釀造和蒸餾，還用作消耗性疾病中營養物的一種來源。

馬耳他熱 參閱 brucellosis。

麥芽糖酶 唾液和胰液中的一種酶；消化過程中，該酶將麥芽糖轉化為葡萄糖。

麥芽糖 由兩分子葡萄糖組成的一種糖。麥芽糖在澱粉和糖原消化時形成，並見於生芽的穀種中。

（骨）連接不正 骨折愈合時斷端連接不良所致的骨畸形。可繼發鄰近關節的關節炎。可能需行截骨術，以矯正畸形，預防併發症。

乳頭 參閱 nipple。

乳頭體 位於下丘腦底部，垂體緊後方的一對圓形突起。

mamma *n. see* breast.

乳房　參閱 breast。

mammary gland the milk-producing gland of female mammals. *See* breast.

乳腺　雌性哺乳動物的生乳腺。參閱 breast。

mammography *n.* the making of X-ray or infrared ray photographs of the breast. It is used for the early detection of abnormal growths. *See also* radiography, thermography.

乳房 X 綫照相片　對乳房進行 X 綫或紅外綫照相，用於早期探測異常腫物。參閱 radiography，thermography。

mammoplasty *n.* plastic surgery of the breasts, in order to alter their shape or increase or decrease their size. In the case of sagging breasts skin and glandular tissue are removed and the remaining breast tissue is fixed in the normal position. After a mastectomy, or when the breasts are too small, a prosthesis (*see* breast implant) may be inserted to improve the contour.

乳房成形術　改變乳房形狀或增大，減小其體積的乳房整形手術。對乳房下垂的病人，去除皮膚及腺體組織，然後將剩餘的乳房組織固定在正常位置上。乳房切除後，或乳房過小時，可塞入假體（參閱 breast implant）以改善外形。

mammothermography *n.* the technique of examining the breasts for the presence of tumours or other abnormalities by *thermography.

乳房溫度記錄法　用溫度記錄法檢查乳房腫瘤或其他異常的技術。

M-AMSA (amsacrine) *n.* a *cytotoxic drug undergoing evaluation in the treatment of malignant disease. Side-effects include marrow suppression.

安吖啶　一種細胞毒性藥，其治療惡性疾病的效果正在評估中。副作用包括骨髓抑制。

Manchester operation *see* Donald-Fothergill operation.

曼徹斯特手術　參閱 Donald-Fothergill operation。

mancinism *n.* the condition of being left-handed.

左利　善用左手。

mandelic acid a drug that prevents bacterial growth and was formerly used (in the form of the ammonium or calcium salt) to treat infections of the urinary system (it has now largely been replaced by antibiotics). Mandelic acid is administered as a catheter solution.

扁桃酸　預防細菌生長的一種藥物，曾用於治療泌尿系統感染（以銨鹽或鈣鹽的形式，現已基本被抗生素取代）。扁桃酸作為導管溶液使用。

mandible *n.* the lower jawbone. It consists of a horseshoe-shaped *body*, the upper surface of which bears the lower teeth (*see* alveolus (def. 2)), and two vertical parts (*rami*). Each ramus divides into a *condyle* and a *coronoid process. The condyle articulates with the temporal bone of the cranium to form the *temporomandibular joint* (a hinge joint). *See also* maxilla, skull. **–mandibular** *adj.*

下**頜骨** 下部頜骨。由一塊上表面支撐下齒的馬蹄形骨體（參閱 alveolus 釋義 2）和兩個垂直的部分組成。每一個支分為一個髁和一個冠狀突。髁與顳的顳骨連接形成顳下頜關節（屈戌關節）。參閱 maxilla，skull。

manganese *n.* a greyish metallic element, the oxide of which, when in haled by miners in underventilated mines, causes brain damage and symptoms very similar to those of *parkinsonism. Minute quantities of the element are required by the body (*see* trace element). Symbol: Mn.

錳 淺灰色的金屬元素，其氧化物在通風不良的礦井中被礦工吸入後，引起腦損傷及類似於帕金森綜合徵的症狀。微量錳是身體需要的（參閱 trace element）。符號：Mn。

mania *n.* a state of mind characterized by excessive cheerfulness and increased activity. The mood is euphoric and changes rapidly to irritability. Thought and speech are rapid to the point of incoherence and the connections between ideas may be impossible to follow. Behaviour is also overactive, extravagant, overbearing, and sometimes violent. Judgment is impaired, and therefore the sufferer may damage his own interests. There may be grandiose delusions. Treatment is usually with drugs, such as lithium or phenothiazines, and hospital admission is frequently necessary. *See also* affective disorder, manic-depressive psychosis. **–manic** *adj.*

躁狂 以過度歡欣和異常活躍為特徵的一種情緒狀態。病人情緒欣快並且極易激動。思想和語言很快，以至於不連貫。想法之間的聯繫難以把握。行為過度活躍、誇張、專橫、有時狂暴。患者判斷力受損以至損害自身利益。可有誇大妄想。通常用鋰或吩噻嗪類藥物治療，常需入院。參閱 affective disorder，manic-depressive psychosis。

-mania *suffix denoting* obsession, compulsion, or exaggerated feeling for. Example: *pyromania* (for starting fires).

〔後綴〕**狂，癖** 對……的執迷，強迫性或過分的喜愛。例如：縱火癖。

manic-depressive psychosis (bipolar disorder) a severe mental illness causing repeated episodes of *depression,

躁狂抑鬱性精神病 引起抑鬱症、躁狂症或二者反覆發作的嚴重精神病。這種發作可由煩

*mania, or both. These episodes can be precipitated by upsetting events but are out of proportion to these causes. Sometimes chronic depression or chronic mania can result. There is a genetically inherited predisposition to the illness. Treatment is with *phenothiazine drugs for mania, and *antidepressant drugs or, in severe cases, *electroconvulsive therapy for depression. *Lithium and carbamazepine can prevent or reduce the frequency and severity of attacks, and the sufferer is usually well in the intervals between them.

心的事情誘發，但病情和病因不成比例。有時，可造成慢性抑鬱症或慢性躁狂症。本病有基因遺傳傾向。治療：用吩噻嗪類藥物治療躁狂，用抗抑鬱藥治療抑鬱症，或對於嚴重的病例，用電驚厥療法治療抑鬱症。鋰和卡馬西平可預防和降低發作的頻率和嚴重性，發作間隙，患者通常情況良好。

manikin *n. see* homunculus.

人體模型 參閱 homunculus。

manipulation *n.* the use of the hands to produce a desired movement or therapeutic effect in part of the body. Both physiotherapists and osteopaths use manipulation to restore normal working to stiff joints.

推拿術 用手使身體某部位產生理想的動作或治療效果。理療師和整骨師用推拿術恢復僵硬關節的正常功能。

mannitol *n.* a *diuretic administered by injection to supplement other diuretics in the treatment of fluid retention (oedema), to treat some kidney disorders, and to relieve pressure in brain injuries. Headache, chest pain, and dry mouth may occur following injection.

甘露醇 一種利尿劑。注射給藥，治療液體瀦留（水腫）；輔助其他利尿劑治療腎病及緩解腦損傷後的顱內壓。注射後可發生頭痛、胸痛和口乾。

Mann-Whitney U test *see* significance.

曼-惠（特尼）U 檢驗 參閱 significance。

manometer *n.* a device for measuring pressure in a liquid or gas. A manometer often consists of a U-tube containing mercury, water, or other liquid, open at one end and exposed to the fluid under pressure at the other end. The pressure can be read directly from a graduated scale. *See also* sphygmomanometer.

測壓計 測量氣體或液體中壓力的一種儀器。測壓計常由一U 型管組成；該管含有水銀、水或其他液體，一端開放，另一端與受壓液體接觸。該壓力可直接從刻度上讀出。參閱 sphygmomanometer。

manometry *n.* measurement of pressures within organs of the body. The technique is used to record changes within fluid-filled chambers (e.g. cerebral ventricles) or to indicate muscular activity in motile tubes, such as the oesophagus, rectum, or bile duct.

測壓法　測量身體器官內的壓力。該技術可用於記錄充滿液體的腔室（如腦室）內的變化，或指示活動的管道（如食管、直腸、或膽管）中的肌肉活動。

manpower committee (in Britain) a special committee established regionally (*Regional Manpower Committee*) and centrally (*Central Manpower Committee*) by the Department of Health to advise on medical staffing by specialty and to consider the relative numbers of consultants and training grades of doctors in the National Health Service.

人力委員會　（英國）由衛生部建立的地區性（地區人力委員會）和中央性（中央人力委員會）的特殊委員會。它對專業醫務人員提出建議，並考慮國民保健服務制中高級醫師的相對數量和醫生的培訓級別。

mantle *adj. see* field.

斗篷式放射野　參閱 field。

mantoux test *see* tuberculin.

芒圖試驗　參閱 tuberculin。

manubrium *n.* (*pl.* **manubria**) **1.** the upper section of the breastbone (*see* sternum). It articulates with the clavicles and the first costal cartilage; the second costal cartilage articulates at the junction between the manubrium and body of the sternum. **2.** the handle-like part of the *malleus (an ear ossicle), attached to the eardrum. –**manubrial** *adj.*

柄　(1) 胸骨上部（參閱 sternum）。它連接鎖骨和第一肋軟骨，第二肋軟骨連接在胸骨柄和胸骨體的接合處。(2) 附着於鼓膜上的錘骨（一個耳小骨）的柄狀部分。

MAO *see* monoamine oxidase.

單胺氧化酶　參閱 monoamine oxidase。

MAO inhibitor a drug that prevents the activity of the enzyme *monoamine oxidase (MAO) in brain tissue and therefore affects mood. MAO inhibitors include isocarboxazid, *phenelzine, and *tranylcypromin. These drugs are *antidepressants, whose use is now restricted because of the severity of their side-effects. These include interactions with other drugs (e.g. ephedrine,

單胺氧化酶抑制劑　阻止單胺氧化酶在腦組織中的活性並因此影響情緒的一種藥物。該抑制劑包括異卡波肼、苯乙肼和反苯環丙胺。這些都是抗抑鬱藥，其使用現在已經由於其嚴重的副作用而受到限制。副作用包括與其他藥物（如麻黃鹼、苯丙胺）和含酪胺的食物（如乳酪）相互作用而使血

amphetamine) and with foods containing *tyramine (e.g. cheese) to produce a sudden increase in blood pressure. *See also* moclobemide, selegiline.

壓突然增高。參閱 moclobemide，selegiline。

maple syrup urine disease an inborn defect of amino acid metabolism causing an excess of valine, leucine, isoleucine, and alloisoleucine in the urine, which has an odour like maple syrup. Treatment is dietary; if untreated, the condition leads to mental retardation and death in infancy.

楓糖尿症 一種先天性的氨基酸代謝缺陷，造成尿中纈氨酸、亮氨酸、異亮氨酸和別亮氨酸過多，使尿具有楓糖氣味。飲食治療；若不治，可引起智力發育遲緩和嬰兒死亡。

maprotiline *n.* a drug used to treat all types of depression, including that associated with anxiety (*see* antidepressant). It is administered by mouth and may cause drowsiness, dizziness, and tremor. Trade name: **Ludiomil**.

馬普替林 治療與焦慮有關的各型抑鬱症的一種藥物（參閱 antidepressant）。口服給藥，可引起嗜睡、頭暈和震顫。商品名：Ludiomil。

marasmus *n.* severe wasting in infants, when body weight is below 75% of that expected for age. The infant looks 'old', pallid, apathetic, lacks skin fat, and has subnormal temperature. The condition may be due to *malabsorption, wrong feeding, metabolic disorders, repeated vomiting, diarrhoea, severe disease of the heart, lungs, kidneys, or urinary tract, or chronic bacterial or parasitic disease (especially in tropical climates). Maternal rejection of an infant may cause marasmus through undereating. Acute infection may precipitate death. Treatment depends on the underlying cause, but initially very gentle nursing and the provision of nourishment and fluids by gradual steps is appropriate for all.

兒童消瘦 嬰兒嚴重消耗性疾病，患者體重低於其年齡標準體重的 75%。患者顯得「老」，皮膚蒼白，淡漠，缺少皮下脂肪且體溫低於正常。病因可為吸收不良，餵養不當，代謝紊亂，反覆嘔吐，腹瀉，嚴重的心、肺、腎或泌尿道疾病及慢性細菌或寄生蟲病（特別在熱帶）。嬰兒因母親的厭棄而進食不足亦可引起此病。急性感染可突然造成死亡。治療取決於病因，但最初細心的護理和逐步供給營養和液體適用於所有病例。

marble-bone disease *see* osteopetrosis.

骨硬化病 參閱 osteopetrosis。

Marburg disease (green monkey disease) a virus disease of vervet

馬爾堡病 綠猴的一種病毒性疾病，由接觸感染動物的血液

(green) monkeys transmitted to man by contact (usually in laboratories) with blood or tissues from an infected animal. Symptoms include fever, malaise, severe headache, vomiting, diarrhoea and bleeding from mucous membranes in the mouth and elsewhere. Treatment with antiserum and measures to reduce the bleeding are sometimes effective.

或組織（通常在實驗室中）而傳播給人。症狀包括發熱、不適、嚴重頭痛、嘔吐、腹瀉以及口腔及其他部位黏膜出血。有時抗血清療法和減少出血的措施有效。

march fracture a fracture through the neck of the second or third metatarsal bone, associated with excessive walking.

行軍骨折　穿過第二或第三跖骨頸的骨折，與走路過量有關。

Marfan's syndrome an inherited disorder of connective tissue characterized by excessive tallness, abnormally long and slender fingers and toes (*arachnodactyly*), heart defects, and partial dislocation of the lenses of the eyes.

馬方綜合徵　結締組織的一種遺傳病，其特徵是身材過高，指和趾異常長而細，心臟缺陷及眼晶狀體部分脱位。

marijuana *n. see* cannabis.

大麻葉　參閱 cannabis。

Marion's disease obstruction of the outlet of the bladder caused by enlargement of the muscle cells in the neck of the bladder.

馬里恩病　由膀胱頸肌細胞增大導致的膀胱出口阻塞。

Marjolin's ulcer a carcinoma that develops at the edge of a chronic *ulcer of the skin, usually a varicose ulcer in the ankle region.

馬喬林潰瘍　發生於慢性皮膚潰瘍（常為踝區的靜脈屈張性潰瘍）邊緣的癌。

marrow *n. see* bone marrow.

骨髓　參閱 bone marrow。

marsupialization *n.* an operative technique for curing a cyst. The cyst is opened, its contents removed, and the edges then stitched to the skin incision. The wound is kept open until it has healed by *granulation.

造袋術　治療囊腫的手術方法，切開囊腫，清除內容物，然後把囊腫邊緣與皮膚切口縫合。在肉芽組織產生之前，傷口保持開放。

masculinization *n.* development of excess body and facial hair, deepening of the voice, and increase in muscle bulk

男性化　由於激素紊亂或激素療法，使女性體毛和髭鬚過多，嗓音低沉，肌肉發達（男

(secondary male sexual characteristics) in a female due to a hormone disorder or to hormone therapy. *See also* virilism, virilization.

性第二性徵）。參閱 virilism, virilization。

masochism *n*. sexual pleasure derived from the experience of pain. The word is sometimes used loosely for all forms of behaviour that lead to pain or humiliation. *See* sexual deviation. **–masochist** *n*. **–masochistic** *adj*.

受虐狂　因經受痛苦而獲得的性快感。此詞有時可泛指各種引起痛苦或羞辱的行為。參閱 sexual deviation。

massage *n*. manipulation of the soft tissues of the body with the hands. Massage is used to improve circulation, reduce oedema where present, prevent *adhesions in tissues after injury, reduce muscular spasm, and improve the tone of muscles. *See also* effleurage, petrissage, tapotement.

按摩法　用手推拿身體軟組織。推拿術用於改善循環，緩解存在的水腫，預防損傷後組織黏連，減少肌肉痙攣，以及改善肌肉的緊張度。參閱 effleurage, petrissage, tapotement。

masseter *n*. a thick muscle in the cheek extending from the zygomatic arch to the outer corner of the mandible. It is important for mastication and acts by closing the jaws.

咬肌　從顴骨弓延至下頜骨外角的頰部厚肌肉；它通過關閉上下頜而對咀嚼起有重要作用。

mast- (masto-) *prefix denoting* the breast.

〔前綴〕乳房

mastalgia *n*. pain in the breast.

乳腺痛　乳房疼痛。

mast cell a large cell in *connective tissue with many coarse cytoplasmic granules. These granules contain the chemicals *heparin, *histamine, and *serotonin, which are released during inflammation and allergic responses.

肥大細胞　結締組織中帶有許多粗細胞質顆粒的一種大細胞。這些顆粒中含有肝素、組胺及血清素等化學物質；炎症和過敏反應時，釋放這些物質。

mastectomy *n*. surgical removal of a breast. *Simple mastectomy*, performed for extensive but not necessarily invasive tumours, involves simple removal of the breast; the skin and if possible the nipple may be retained and a prosthesis (*see*

乳房切除術　手術切除乳房。若腫瘤面積大，但不一定為侵襲性時，可行單純性乳房切除術，即僅切除乳房，而保留皮膚，並且在可能的情況下，可保留乳頭；同時，可向皮下植

breast implant) may be inserted under the skin to give the appearance of normality. When breast cancer has spread to involve the lymph nodes, *radical mastectomy* may be preformed. This classically involves removal of the breast with the skin and underlying pectoral muscles together with all the lymphatic tissue of the armpit. This treatment may be followed up with radiotherapy and/or chemotherapy. In modern surgical practice a modified radical mastectomy, preserving the pectoral muscles, is more usual than the classical technique. *See also* lumpectomy.

入假體（參閱 breast implant）以恢復其正常外觀。若腫瘤擴散累及淋巴結，則可行乳房根治術。傳統的乳房根治術包括切除乳房及皮膚，其下方的胸肌，連同腋窩的所有淋巴組織。這種治療後可進行放射治療和／或化學治療。現代外科實踐中的乳房切除術有所改變；即保留胸肌，這種做法比傳統乳房根治術常見。參閱 lumpectomy。

mastication *n.* the process of chewing food.

咀嚼 咀嚼食物的過程。

mastitis *n.* inflammation of the breast, usually caused by bacterial infection via damaged nipples. It most often occurs as acute *puerperal mastitis*, which develops during the period of breastfeeding, about a month after childbirth, and sometimes involves the discharge of pus. Chronic *cystic mastitis* has a different cause and does not involve inflammation. The breast feels lumpy due to the presence of cysts, and the condition is thought to be caused by hormone imbalance.

乳腺炎 乳房發炎，常由受損乳頭的細菌感染引起。急性產後乳腺炎最常見，它有時發生於產後約 1 個月的哺乳期，有時流膿。慢性囊性乳腺炎病因不同，並且沒有炎症。因有囊腫，乳房感覺凹凸不平，此病被認為由激素不平衡所致。

mastoid *n.* the *mastoid process of the temporal bone. *See also* mastoiditis.

乳突 顳骨的乳突。參閱 mastoiditis。

mastoidectomy *n.* an operation to remove some or all of the air cells in the bone behind the ear (the *mastoid process of the temporal bone) when they have become infected (*See* mastoiditis) or invaded by *cholesteatoma. *See also* atticotomy.

乳突切除術 手術切除耳後骨內（顳骨的乳狀突）部分或全部受感染（參閱 mastoiditis）或被膽脂瘤侵入的含氣腔。參閱 atticotomy。

mastoiditis *n.* inflammation of the *mastoid process behind the ear and of

乳突炎 耳後乳突以及連接乳突至中耳腔的氣腔（乳突竇）

the air space (*mastoid antrum*) connecting it to the cavity of the middle ear. It is usually caused by bacterial infection that spreads from the middle ear (*see* otitis (media)). Usually the infection responds to antibiotics, but surgery (*see* mastoidectomy) may be required in severe cases.

mastoid process a nipple-shaped process on the *temporal bone that extends downward and forward behind the ear canal and is the point of attachment of several neck muscles. It contains many air spaces (*mastoid cells*), which communicate with the cavity of the middle ear via an air-filled channel, the *mastoid antrum*. This provides a possible route for the spread of infection from the middle ear (*see* mastoiditis).

masturbation *n.* physical self-stimulation of the male or female external genital organs in order to produce sexual pleasure, which may result in orgasm.

matched pair study *see* case control study.

materia medica the study of drugs used in medicine and dentistry, including *pharmacognosy, *pharmacy, *pharmacology, and therapeutics.

maternal mortality rate the number of deaths due to complications of pregnancy, childbirth, and the puerperium expressed as a proportion of all births (i.e. including *stillbirths). Formerly the rate was expressed per 1000 births but with the low levels currently reported it is customary to use a base of a 100,000 births. Concern with maternal mortality resulted in Britain in a special

的炎症。常由來自於中耳的細菌感染引起（參閱 otitis (media)）。該感染通常可用抗生素治愈，但嚴重病人可能需行手術（參閱 mastoidectomy）。

乳突 顳骨上的乳頭狀突，在耳道後向前下方延伸，是幾條頸肌的附着點。它含有許多氣腔（乳突房）；這些氣腔經過一條充滿氣體的管道（乳突竇）與中耳腔相通。這為感染由中耳傳播提供了一條可能的途徑（參閱 mastoiditis）。

手淫 男性或女性為產生性快感而自我物理刺激生殖器官。手淫可產生性高潮。

配對研究 參閱 case control study。

藥學 醫學和牙科學用藥的研究，包括生藥學、藥物學、藥理學以及治療學。

母親死亡率 以占所有出生數目（即包括死產）的比率表示的妊娠、分娩和產褥期的併發症造成的死亡數目。以前是以每 1000 出生次數表示，但由於最近報告的死亡率低，所以習慣上以 10 萬出生次數為基數表示。隨着對母親死亡率的關注，在英國對每一例此類死亡進行了特殊的秘密調查，以

confidential enquiry being held into every such deaty to try and pinpoint the possible shortfall in resources or care.

matrix *n.* the substance of a tissue or organ in which nore specialized structures are embedded; for example, the ground substance of connective tissue.

matrix band a flexible strip that is placed round a tooth to restore a wall, thus simplifying insertion of a dental filling.

maturation *n.* the process of attaining full development. The term is applied particularly to the development of mature germ cells (ova and sperm).

maxilla *n.* (*pl.* **maxillae**) loosely, the upper jaw, which bears the upper teeth. Strictly, the maxilla is one of a pair of bones that partly form the upper jaw, the outer walls of the maxillary sinus, and the floor of the orbit. *See also* mandible, skull. **–maxillary** *adj.*

maxillary sinus (maxillary antrum) *see* paranasal sinuses.

maxillofacial *adj.* describing or relating to the region of the face, jaws, and related structures.

maxwell *n.* a unit of magnetic flux equal to a flux of 1 gauss per square centimetre.

mazindol *n.* a drug that reduces the appetite and is used in the treatment of obesity. It is administered by mouth and may cause constipation, dry mouth, and insomnia. Trade name: **Teronac**.

求指出醫療資源及護理方面可能的不足。

基質　某一組織或器官的物質，其中包埋着較為特異化的結構。例如，結締組織的基質。

基質帶　置於牙周圍形成一個壁的一條柔性帶，以便簡化牙充塞物的插入。

成熟　達到充分發育的過程。特指成熟的胚芽細胞（卵子和精子）的發育。

上頜骨　泛指支撐上齒的整個上頜。嚴格地説，上頜骨是形成上頜的一對骨中的一塊骨，它形成上頜竇外壁和眼眶底的一部分。參閲　mandible，skull。

上頜竇　參閲　paranasal sinuses。

頜面的　描述面部、頜部及其有關結構的；與面部、頜部及其有關結構有關的。

麥克斯韋　相當於每平方厘米1 高斯通量的磁通量單位。

馬吲哚　減少食慾，用於治療肥胖症的一種藥物。口服用藥，可引起便秘、口乾和失眠。商品名：Teronac。

McBurney's point the point on the abdomen that overlies the anatomical position of the appendix and is the site of maximum tenderness in acute appendicitis. It lies one-third of the way along a line drawn from the anterior superior iliac spine (the projecting part of the hipbone) to the umbilicus.

麥克伯尼點 相應於闌尾解剖部位腹壁上的點，它是急性闌尾炎時最大觸痛的位置。它位於髂前上棘（髖骨的突出部分）到臍連綫上髂前上棘側三分之一處。

ME *see* myalgic encephalomyelitis.

肌痛性腦脊髓炎 參閱 myalgic encephalomyelitis。

meals on wheels *see* social services.

上門福利餐 參閱 social services。

mean (arithmetic mean) *n.* the average of a group of observations calculated by adding their values and dividing by the number in the group. When one or more observations are substantially different from the rest, which can influence the arithmetic mean unduly, it is preferable to use the *geometric mean* (a similar calculation based on the logarithmic values of the observations) or – more commonly – the *median* (the middle observation of the series arranged in ascending order). A further method of obtaining an average value of a group is to identify the *mode* – the observation (or group of observations when these occur as a continuous quantitative *variable) that occurs most often in the series.

均值 將觀測組中各觀測值相加，再除以觀測次數，所得到的該組觀測平均數。當一個或更多的觀測值與其他觀測值差異懸殊，以至過度影響算術平均數時，最好使用幾何均數（一種基於觀測對數的類似計算法）或更常用的中位數（按遞增順序排列的數列的中間觀察值）。獲得某組平均值的另一個方法是識別衆數，即在數列中最常出現的一個觀測值（如觀測值為連續的變量，則為一組觀測值）。

measles *n.* a highly infectious virus disease that tends to appear in epidemics every 2–3 years and mainly affects children. After an incubation period of 8–15 days, symptoms resembling those of a cold develop accompanied by a high fever. Small red spots with white centres (*Koplik's spots*) may appear on the inside of the cheeks. On the third to fifth day a blotchy, slightly elevated pink rash develops, first behind the ears then on the face

麻疹 傳染性極強的一種病毒性疾病，常每隔 2~3 年流行一次，主要累及兒童。8~15 天潛伏期後，出現類似感冒的症狀，並伴有高熱。頰內出現中心發白的小紅點（科普利克斑）。在第 3~5 天，首先是耳後，接着在臉和其他部位出現粉紅色扁丘疹，持續 3~5 天。在這期間，病人具有傳染性。在大多數病例中，這些症狀很

and elsewhere; it lasts 3–5 days. The patient is infectious throughout this period. In most cases the symptoms soon subside but patients are susceptible to pneumonia and middle ear infections. Complete recovery may take 2–4 weeks. Severe complications include encephalitis (one in 1000 cases) and *subacute sclerosing panencephalitis. Measles is a common cause of childhood mortality in malnourished children, particularly in the developing world, Vaccination against measles provides effective immunity (*see* MMR vaccine). Medical names: **rubeola, morbilli**.

快消失，但病人易患肺炎和中耳炎。完全恢復可需 2~4 周。嚴重的併發症包括大腦炎（1/1000 例）和亞急性硬化性全腦炎。麻疹是營養不良兒童中，尤其是在發展中國家，兒童死亡的一個常見原因。麻疹疫苗接種產生有效的免疫力（參閱 MMR vaccine）。醫學用語：麻疹。

meat- (meato-) *prefix denoting* a meatus. Example: *meatotomy* incision into the urethral meatus).

〔前綴〕**道或口** 例如尿道口切開術（切開尿道口）。

meatus *n.* (in anatomy) a passage or opening. The *external auditory meatus* is the passage leading from the pinna of the outer *ear to the eardrum. A *nasal meatus* is one of three groovelike parts of the nasal cavity beneath each of the nasal conchae. The *urethral meatus* is the external opening of the urethra.

道 （解剖學）一個通道或者開口。外耳道是從外耳耳廓到鼓室的通道。鼻道是每個下鼻甲下方鼻腔的三個溝樣部分。尿道口是尿道外口。

mebendazole *n.* an *anthelmintic drug used to get rid of roundworms, hookworms, pinworms, and whipworms. Side-effects may include stomach upsets. Trade name: **Vermox**. *See also* imidazole.

甲苯達唑 一種用於驅除蛔蟲、鈎蟲、蟯蟲和鞭蟲的抗蠕蟲藥。副作用可有胃部不適。商品名：Vermox。參閱imidazole。

mebhydrolin *n.* an *antihistamine drug used to treat allergic conditions, such as hay fever and urticaria. Trade name: **Fabahistin**.

美海屈林 用於治療枯草熱和蕁麻疹等過敏性疾病的一種抗組胺劑。商品名：Fabahistin。

mechanoreceptor *n.* a group of cells that respond to mechanical distortion, such as that caused by stretching or compressing a tissue, by generating a nerve impulse in a sensory nerve (*see* receptor).

機械感受器 通過在感覺神經中產生一個神經衝動，對牽拉或壓迫組織等引起的機械變形起反應的一組細胞（參閱receptor）。其中包括觸覺感受

Touch receptors, *proprioceptors, and the receptors for hearing and balance all belong to this class.

器、本體感受器和聽覺及平衡感受器。

mechanotherapy *n.* the use of mechanical equipment during physiotherapy to produce regularly repeated movements in part of the body. This is done to improve the functioning of muscles and joints.

機械療法 在理療中，運用機械器械具身體某部位產生有規律的反覆運動。此法用於改善肌肉和關節的功能。

Meckel's cartilage a cartilaginous bar in the fetus around which the *mandible develops. Part of Meckel's cartilage develops into the malleus (an ear ossicle) in the adult.

梅克爾軟骨 下頜骨在其周圍發育的胎兒棒狀軟骨。成人後，部分梅克爾軟骨發育為錘骨（一個耳骨）。

Meckel's diverticulum *see* diverticulum.

梅克爾憩室 參閱 diverticulum。

meclozine *n.* an *antihistamine drug used mainly to prevent and treat nausea and vomiting, particularly in travel sickness, and also to relieve allergic reactions. It is administered by mouth.

美克洛嗪 一種抗組胺劑，主要用於預防和治療惡心和嘔吐，特別是旅行病，以及用於緩解變態反應。口服用藥。

meconism *n.* poisoning from the effects of eating or smoking *opium or the products derived from it, especially *morphine.

阿片中毒 食入或吸入阿片或其製品，尤其是嗎啡引起的中毒。

meconium *n.* the first stools of a newborn baby, which are sticky and dark green and composed of cellular debris, mucus, and bile pigments. The presence of meconium in the amniotic fluid during labour indicates fetal distress. *See also* (meconium) ileus.

胎糞 由細胞碎屑、黏液和膽汁色素組成的黏稠暗綠色新生兒初便。分娩時羊水中出現胎糞表明胎兒有危險。參閱 (meconium) ileus。

media (tunica media) *n.* **1.** the middle layer of the wall of a *vein or *artery. It is the thickest of the three layers, being composed of elastic fibres and smooth muscle fibres in alternating layers. **2.** the middle layer of various other organs or parts.

(1) 血管中膜 靜脈或動脈壁的中層。由彈性纖維層和平滑肌層交錯組成，是三層中最厚的一層。**(2) 中層** 其他各種器官或部位的中層。

medial *adj.* relating to or situated in the central region of an organ, tissue, or the body.

中部的　位於某個器官、組織或身體中部的或與之有關的。

median *adj.* **1.** (in anatomy) situated in or towards the plane that divides the body into right and left halves. **2.** (in statistics) *see* mean.

(1) 正中的　（解剖學）位於把身體分成左右兩半的平面上或接近該平面的。**(2) 中位數**（統計學）參閱 mean。

mediastinitis *n.* inflammation of the midline partition of the chest cavity (mediastinum), usually complicating a rupture of the oesophagus (gullet). *Sclerosing mediastinitis* often leads to *fibrosis, which may cause compression of other structures in the thorax, such as the superior vena cava, the bronchial tree, or the oesophagus.

縱隔炎　胸腔中綫隔膜（縱隔）的炎症，通常合併食管破裂。硬化性縱隔炎常導致纖維化，而引起胸腔其他結構的壓迫，如上腔靜脈、支氣管樹以及食管。

mediastinum *n.* the space in the thorax (chest cavity) between the two pleural sacs. The mediastinum contains the heart, aorta, trachea, oesophagus, and thymus gland and is divided into anterior, middle, posterior, and superior regions.

縱隔　位於胸腔內兩個胸膜囊之間的間隙。縱隔被分為前、中、後和上部，其中有心臟、主動脈、氣管、食管和胸腺。

medical *adj.* **1.** of or relating to medicine, the diagnosis, treatment and prevention of disease. **2.** of or relating to conditions that require the attention of a physician rather than a surgeon. For example, a *medical ward* of a hospital accommodates patients with such conditions.

(1) 醫學的　醫藥的，即疾病的診斷、治療和預防的或與之有關的。**(2) 內科的**　需要內科醫生，而不是外科醫生照管的疾病的或與之有關的。例如，醫院的內科病房收住患此類疾病的人。

medical assistant a health service worker who is not a registered medical practitioner (often a nurse or an ex-serviceman with experience as a senior medical orderly) working in association with a doctor to undertake minor treatments and preliminary assessments. In poorer countries, particularly in rural areas where qualified resources are short

醫生助理　一種保健服務人員，他（她）不是註冊的行醫者（常為護士或高級醫務兵的退伍軍人），而協助醫生從事小的治療以及前期診斷。在貧窮的國家，特別是在合格的人材短缺的農村（如中國），農民接受有限的衛生保健培訓，就開始「赤腳醫生」的雙

(e.g. China), agricultural workers receive limited training in health care and continue in a dual role as *barefoot doctors*; elsewhere, limited training concentrates more on environmental issues: the workers so trained are known as *sanitarians*.

重角色；在其他地方，有限的培訓更多地集中於環境問題，經過這樣培訓的人稱為衛生員。

medical audit *see* health service planning.

醫療帳目審核 參閱 health service planning。

medical certificate a certificate stating a doctor's diagnosis of a patient's medical condition, disability, or fitness to work.

診斷書 表明醫生對病人病情、傷殘程度或工作能力的診斷證明。

medical committee 1. (in a hospital) a group of doctors of consultant grade (some or all of the consultants on the hospital staff) who give medical viewpoints on affairs concerned with overall policies on patient care, resource allocation, and the running of the hospital. Representatives of other hospital professions (nursing, administration, planning, and junior doctors) are usually in attendance. It is generally divided into those specialist subgroups representing the broad divisions of hospital practice (medical, surgical, paediatric, etc.). However, alternative subdivisions (e.g. acute services, priority services) are the subject of experimentation in some Health Authorities. Usually the chairmen of divisions form an executive committee for day-to-day decisions that are ratified at less frequent meetings of the medical committee. **2. (local medical committee)** (in Britain) a group of representatives of the general practitioners under cntract with a single *Family Health Services Authority. The members act as spokespersons for the local practitioners, by whom they are elected. Similar arrangements and

醫學委員會 **(1)** （醫院裏）對病人護理、資源分配和醫院管理等事項提供醫學觀點的高級醫師組織（醫院的部分或全部高級醫師）。醫院內其他方面的代表（護理、管理、計劃、及低年資醫生）常出席此委員會會議。委員會常分為專家小組，代表醫院內各科室部門（內科、外科、兒科等）。然而，有些衛生局正在試驗可供選擇的專家分組辦法（如：急診服務，優先服務）。通常，各個小組的主席組成執行委員會，負責日常決策，而這些決策在醫學委員會不太經常召開的會議上通過。**(2)** 地方醫學委員會是（英國）與一個家庭保健服務管理局簽有合同的全科醫師的代表。這些人由當地全科醫師選出並作為他們的發言人。國民保健服務制中醫院外服務的牙科醫師、藥劑師和眼科醫師也有類似的組織及責任。**(3)** （英國）由一些專家及全科醫師的代表組成的團體，他們是地區或地段衛生局（地區或地段醫療委員會）的醫學顧問和發言人。

responsibilities apply for the dentists, pharmacists, and opticians practising in the NHS outside hospitals. **3.** (in Britain) a group of representative specialists and general practitioners who serve as medical advisors and spokespersons to a District or Regional Health Authority (*District Medical Committee or Regional Medical Committee*). *See also* National Health Service.

medical jurisprudence the study or practice of the legal aspects of medicine. *See* forensic medicine.

Medical Officer of Health (formerly in Britain) the chief health executive of local government. The title is still used in many countries. *See* Environmental Health Officer, public health physician.

medical social worker a person with some medical training, employed to assist patients with domestic problems that may arise through illness. *See also* social services.

medicated *adj.* containing a medicinal drug: applied to lotions, soaps, sweets, etc.

medication *n.* **1.** a substance administered by mouth, applied to the body, or introduced into the body for the purpose of treatment. Medicated dressings are applied to wounds to prevent infection and allow normal healing. *See also* premedication. **2.** treatment of a patient using drugs.

medicine *n.* **1.** the science or practice of the diagnosis, treatment, and prevention of disease. **2.** the science or practice of nonsurgical methods of treating disease. **3.** any drug or preparation used for the

參閱 National Health Service。

法醫學 醫學法律方面的研究或實踐。參閱 forensic medicine。

衛生醫官 （從前在英國）地方政府的衛生長官。這一頭銜仍用於許多國家。參閱 Environmental Health Officer，public health physician。

醫學社會福利工作者 受過一些醫學培訓，受聘幫助病人處理疾病期間可能出現的家庭問題的人員。參閱 social services。

加藥的 含有起醫療作用的藥物的；用於洗劑、肥皂、甜食等。

(1) 藥物 為了治療而口服、敷於身體或注入體內的一種物質。加熱的敷料用於傷口可預防感染，使其恢復正常。參閱 premedication。**(2) 藥物療法** 使用藥物治療病人。

(1) 醫學 疾病的診斷、治療和預防的科學或實踐。**(2) 內科學** 用非手術方法治療疾病的科學或實踐。**(3) 藥物** 用於治療或預防疾病的任

treatment or prevention of disease, particularly a drug that is taken by mouth.

medicochirurgical *adj.* of or describing matters that are related to both medicine and surgery. A medicochirurgical disorder is one that calls for treatment by both a physician and a surgeon.

Mediterranean fever 1. *see* brucellosis. **2.** *see* polyserositis.

medium *n.* **1.** any substance, usually a broth, agar, or gelatin, used for the *culture of microorganisms or tissue cells. An *assay medium* is used to determine the concentration of a growth factor or chemical by measuring the amount of growth it produces in a particular microorganism; all other nutrients are present in amounts adequate for growth. **2.** *see* contrast medium.

medroxyprogesterone *n.* a synthetic female sex hormone (*see* progestogen) used to treat menstrual disorders, including amenorrhoea, to prevent miscarriage, and (in combination with an oestrogen) in *oral contraceptives. It is administered by mouth or injection. Trade names: **Farlutal**, **Provera**.

medulla *n.* **1.** the inner region of any organ or tissue when it is distinguishable from the outer region (the cortex), particularly the inner part of the kidney, adrenal glands, or lymph nodes. **2.** *see* medulla oblongata. **3.** the *myelin layer of certain nerve fibres. **–medullary** *adj.*

medulla oblongata (myelencephalon) the extension within the skull of the upper end of the spinal cord, forming the lowest part of the *brainstem. Besides

何藥物或製劑，尤指口服藥物。

內外科的 描述與內科和外科都有關的情況。內外科疾病是需要內科和外科醫生共同治療的疾病。

地中海熱 **(1)** 參閱 brucellosis。**(2)** 參閱 polyserositis。

培養基 **(1)** 用於微生物或組織細胞培養的任何物質，通常為肉湯、瓊脂或明膠。鑒定培養基通過測定特殊微生物的生長量，來測定引起這種生長的某種生長因子或化學物質的濃度；培養基中所有其他營養物質的量足夠生長所需。**(2)** 參閱 contrast medium。

甲羥孕酮 一種合成的雌性性激素（參閱 progestogen），用於治療月經不調，包括閉經；預防自然流產以及（與雌激素合用）口服避孕。口服或注射用藥。商品名：Farlutal，Provera。

髓 **(1)** 與其外部結構（皮質）不同的任何器官或組織的內部結構，特別是腎、腎上腺或淋巴結的內部結構。**(2)** 參閱 medulla oblongata。**(3)** 某些神經纖維的髓鞘層。

延髓 形成腦幹最下部的脊髓上端在顱內的延伸部分。除了構成神經衝動進出顱內的主要通路外，延髓內有負責心臟和

forming the major pathway for nerve impulses entering and leaving the skull, the medulla contains centres that are responsible for the regulation of the heart and blood vessels, respiration, salivation, and swallowing. *Cranial nerves VI–XII leave the brain in this region.

血管的調節、呼吸、唾液分泌和吞咽的中樞。第 6~12 腦神經在此離腦。

medullated (myelinated) nerve fibre any nerve fibre that has a sheath of *myelin surrounding and insulating its axon.

脊髓神經纖維 有髓鞘包繞並隔離其軸索的任何神經纖維。

medulloblastoma *n*. a *cerebral tumour that occurs during childhood. It is derived from cells that have the apparent potential to mature into neurones. The medulloblastoma usually develops in the central region (vermis) of the cerebellum adjacent to the fourth ventricle. It causes an unsteady gait and shaky limb movements. Obstruction to the flow of cerebrospinal fluid (CSF) causes *hydrocephalus. Treatment involves surgery to remove most of the tumour and restore CSF flow, followed by radiotherapy. 40% of children affected survive for five years.

成神經管細胞瘤 發生於兒童期的腦瘤。由有明顯潛力發育為神經元的細胞衍變而來。成神經管細胞瘤通常發生於鄰近於第四腦室的小腦中部。它引起不穩定步態和震顫性四肢運動。腦脊液流動受阻可引起腦積水。治療包括手術摘除大部分腫瘤和恢復腦脊液流動，然後放射治療。40% 的患兒存活五年。

mefenamic acid an anti-inflammatory drug (*see* NSAID) used to treat headache, toothache, rheumatic pain, and similar conditions. It is administered by mouth; side-effects include digestive upsets, drowsiness, and skin rashes. Trade name: **Ponstan**.

甲芬那酸 用於治療頭痛、牙痛、風濕痛及類似疾病的一種抗炎藥（參閱 NSAID）。口服用藥，副作用包括消化系統不適，嗜睡和皮疹。商品名：Ponstan。

mefloquine *n*. a drug used in the treatment of malaria that is resistant to other drugs. It is administered by mouth but should not be taken during pregnancy, by psychiatric patients, or with beta blockers. Trade name: **Lariam**.

甲氟噻 用於治療對其他藥物產生耐藥性的瘧疾的一種藥物。口服用藥，妊娠期病人、精神病人及使用 β-受體阻滯劑的病人禁服。商品名：Lariam。

mefruside *n*. a thiazide-like *diuretic used to treat high blood pressure and get

美夫西特 一種噻嗪類利尿劑，用於治療高血壓及排除過

rid of excess body fluid. It is administered by mouth. Possible side-effects include nausea and indigestion. Trade name: **Baycaron**.

量的體液。口服用藥。可能的副作用包括惡心和消化不良。商品名：Baycaron。

mega- *prefix denoting* **1.** large size, or abnormal enlargement or distension. Example: *megacaecum* (of the caecum). **2.** a million. Example: *megavolt* (a million volts).

〔前綴〕**(1)** 巨　體積大或異常增大或膨脹，例如：巨盲腸。**(2)** 一百萬　例如兆伏（一百萬伏）。

megacolon *n.* dilatation, and sometimes lengthening, of the colon. It is caused by obstruction of the colon, *Hirschsprung's disease, or longstanding constipation, or it may occur as a complication of ulcerative *colitis (*toxic megacolon*).

巨結腸　結腸的擴張，並有時拉長。它由結腸阻塞，赫希施普龍病，長期便秘引起，或可以成為潰瘍性結腸炎（中毒性巨結腸）的併發症。

megakaryoblast *n.* a cell that gives rise to the platelet-forming cell *megakaryocyte, found in the blood-forming tissue of the bone marrow. It is derived from a *haemopoietic stem cell and matures via an intermediate stage (*promegakaryocyte*) into a megakaryocyte.

巨核母細胞　見於骨髓造血組織內生成巨核細胞（一種生成血小板的細胞）的一種細胞。它由造血幹細胞衍變而來，並且經過中間階段（幼巨核細胞）發育成熟為巨核細胞。

megakaryocyte *n.* a cell in the bone marrow that produces *platelets. It is large (35–160μm in diameter), with an irregular multilobed mucleus, and with *Romanowsky stains its abundant cytoplasm appears pale blue with fine reddish granules. *See also* thrombopoiesis.

巨核細胞　骨髓內生成血小板的一種細胞。它體積大（直徑為 35–160μm），具有不規則的多葉核。羅曼諾夫斯基染色時，其豐富的胞漿呈淡藍色並帶有細小的淡紅色顆粒。參閱 thrombopoiesis。

megal- (megalo-) *prefix denoting* abnormal enlargement. Example: *megalomelia* (of limbs).

〔前綴〕巨　異常增大。例如：巨肢。

megaloblast *n.* an abnormal form of any of the cells that are precursors of red blood cells (*see* erythroblast). Megaloblasts are unusually large and their nuclei fail to mature in the normal way; they are seen in the bone marrow in certain anaemias (*megaloblastic*

巨紅母細胞　任何一種紅細胞前體細胞的異常形態（參閱 erythroblast）。巨紅母細胞通常異常大，並且胞核不能以正常形式成熟。此細胞常見於因缺乏維生素 B_{12} 或葉酸引起的貧血病人骨髓中。

anaemias) due to dificiency of vitamin B$_{12}$ or folic acid. **–megaloblastic** *adj.*

megalocephaly *n.* **1.** *see* macrocephaly. **2.** overgrowth and distortion of skull bones (*see* leontiasis).

(1) 巨頭　參閱 macrocephaly。**(2)** 顱骨的過度生長和變形（參閱 leontiasis）。

megalocyte *n. see* macrocyte.

巨紅細胞　參閱 macrocyte。

megalomania *n.* delusions of grandeur, such as being God, royalty, etc. It may be a feature of a schizophrenic or manic illness or of cerebral syphilis.

誇大狂　把自己想象為上帝、皇族等偉大人物的一種妄想症。它是精神分裂症或躁狂病或腦梅毒的一個特點。

-megaly *suffix denoting* abnormal enlargement. Example: *splenomegaly* (of spleen).

〔後綴〕大、巨　異常增大。例如：脾大。

megaureter *n.* gross dilatation of the *ureter. This occurs above the site of a long-standing obstruction in the ureter, which blocks the free flow of urine from the kidney. A common cause of megaureter is reflux of urine from the bladder into the ureters (*see* vesicoureteric reflux), but some of the most striking examples are found in so-called *idiopathic megaureter*. In this condition, which may affect one or both ureters, there is a segment of normal ureter of varying length at the extreme lower end of the bladder, above which the ureter is enormously dilated. Both reflux and idiopathic megaureter progress to urinary infection and/or renal impairment. Treatment is by corrective surgery.

巨輸尿管　輸尿管極度擴張。發生於輸尿管長期阻塞部位的上方，堵塞了尿液從腎臟流出。巨輸尿管的一個常見病因是從膀胱到輸尿管的尿返流（參閱 vesicoureteric reflux），但一些最典型的病例見於所謂的原發性巨輸尿管。在這種一條或兩條輸尿管受累的病例中，與膀胱相連的最下端處有一段長度不等的正常輸尿管，而此段之上的輸尿管明顯擴大。返流性和原發性巨輸尿管發展成泌尿系統感染和／或腎臟損傷。施行矯正手術來治療。

megestrol *n.* a synthetic female sex hormone (*see* progestogen) that is used in the treatment of metastatic breast cancer and metastatic endometrial cancer. Trade name: **Megace**.

甲地孕酮　用於治療轉移性乳腺癌和子宮內膜癌的一種合成雌性激素（參閱 progestogen）。商品名：Megace。

meibomian cyst *n. see* chalazion.

瞼板腺囊腫，邁博姆腺囊腫　參閱 chalazion。

meibomian glands (tarsal glands) small sebaceous glands that lie under the conjunctiva of the eyelids.

邁博姆腺（瞼板腺）位於眼瞼結膜下方的小皮脂腺。

meiosis (reduction division) *n.* a type of cell division that produces four daughter cells, each having half the number of chromosomes of the original cell. It occurs before the formation of sperm and ova and the normal (*diploid) number of chromosomes is restored after fertilization. Meiosis also produces genetic variation in the daughter cells, brought about the process of *crossing over. Meiosis consists of two successive divisions, each divided into four stages (*see* prophase, metaphase, anaphase, telophase). (See illustration.) *Compare* mitosis. **–meiotic** *adj.*

減數分裂　細胞分裂的一種類型，由此產生 4 個子細胞，每個子細胞含原始細胞的染色體數目的一半。它發生於精子和卵子形成之前，而授精後染色體數恢復正常（二倍體）。減數分裂也由交換過程導致子細胞的基因變異。減數分裂由兩次連續的分裂組成，每次分為四個階段。（參閱 prophase，metaphase，anaphase，telophase）（見圖）。與 mitosis 對比。

Meissner's plexus (submucous plexus) a fine network of parasympathetic nerve fibres in the wall of the alimentary canal, supplying the muscles and mucous membrane.

邁斯納叢　位於消化道壁內，支配肌肉和黏膜的一個小副交感神經纖維網。

melaena *n.* black tarry faeces due to the presence of partly digested blood from higher up the digestive tract. Melaena is not apparent unless at least 500 ml of blood has entered the gut. It often occurs after vomiting blood (*see* haematemesis), having the same causes, but may be due to disease in the small intestine or upper colon, such as carcinoma or *angiodysplasia. *See also* haemorrhagic disease of the newborn (melaena neonatorum).

黑糞症　黑色柏油樣糞便，由於消化道上部出血，血液經部分消化後所致。至少 500 毫升血進入腸道才出現黑糞症。此病常發生於嘔血（參閱 haematemesis）後，但可由小腸或上結腸疾病，如癌症或血管發育不良引起，病因相同。參閱 haemorrhagic disease of the newborn (melaena neonatorum)。

melan- (melano-) *prefix denoting* **1.** black coloration. **2.** melanin. Example: *melanaemia* (the presence in the blood of melanin).

〔前綴〕**(1)** 黑色　**(2)** 黑素例如：黑血症（血中有黑素）。

melancholia *n. see* depression, involutional melancholia.

憂鬱症　參閱 depression，involutional melancholia。

Prophase I leptotene 前期 I 細綫期

cytoplasm
細胞漿
chromosome
染色體
cell membrane
細胞膜

centriole 中心粒

nuclear membrane
核膜

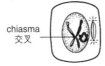

zygotene to pachytene 偶綫期到粗綫期

bivalent of
homologous
chromosomes
同源二價染色體

diplotene to diakinesis 雙綫期到終變期

chiasma
交叉

Metaphase I 中期 I

one chromosome
of each pair goes
to each pole
每對染色體中的
每條分別移向兩極

Anaphase I 後期 I

Telophase I 末期 I

Metaphase II to Anaphase II 中期 II 到後期 II

chromatids
separate
染色單體分離

four haploid nuclei
4 個單倍體核

Telophase II 末期 II

Stages in meiosis
減數分裂各期

melanin *n.* a dark-brown to black pigment occurring in the hair, the skin, and in the iris and choroid layer of the eyes. Melanin is contained within special cells (*chromatophores* or *melanophores*) and is produced by the metabolism of the amino acid tyrosine. Production of melanin by *melanocytes* in the epidermis of the skin is increased by the action of sunlight (producing tanning), which protects the underlying skin layers from the sun's radiation.

melanism (melanosis) *n.* an unusually pronounced darkening of body tissues caused by excessive production of the pigment *melanin. For example, melanism may affect the hair, the skin (after sunburn, during pregnancy, or in *Addison's disease), or the eye.

melanocyte *n.* any one of the cells, concentrated within the epidermis of skin, that produces the dark brown pigment *melanin.

melanocyte-stimulating hormone (MSH) a hormone synthesized and released by the pituitary gland. In amphibians MSH brings about colour changes in the skin but its physiological role in man is uncertain.

melanoma (malignant melanoma, MM) *n.* a highly malignant tumour of melanin-forming cells, the *melanocytes. Such tumours usually occur in the skin (excessive exposure to sunlight is a contributory factor) but are also found in the eye and the mucous membranes. They may contain melanin or be free of pigment (*amelanotic melanomas*). Spread of this cancer to other parts of the body, especially to the lymph nodes and liver, is common. In these cases melanin

黑素 毛髮、皮膚、虹膜及脈絡膜層中深褐到黑色的色素。黑素位於特殊細胞（色素細胞或黑色素細胞）內，並且由酪氨酸（一種氨基酸）代謝生成。日光的作用使表皮內黑素細胞的黑素生成增加（曬黑），由此保護皮膚下層不受日光照射。

黑變病 因黑素生成過多引起的身體組織異常明顯變暗。例如：黑變病可發生於頭髮、皮膚（日曬後，妊娠期間，或患有阿狄森病時）或眼睛。

黑素細胞 集中於皮膚表皮中，產生深褐色黑素的細胞。

促黑素細胞激素 由垂體生成和釋放的一種激素。在兩棲動物中，它可改變皮膚顏色，對人體的生理作用還不確定。

黑素瘤（惡性黑素瘤） 黑素細胞（生成黑素的細胞）的一種高度惡性腫瘤。此瘤常發生於皮膚內（過度暴露於日光是一個致病因素），但也可見於眼睛和黏膜內。瘤內可含或不含黑素（無黑色素性黑素瘤）。這種癌常擴散到身體其他部位，特別是淋巴結和肝臟。在這種病例中，黑素或其前體（黑素原）可從尿中排出，並且整個皮膚可被色素染成深

or its precursors (*melanogens*) may be excreted in the urine and the whole of the skin may be deeply pigmented. The prognosis is inversely related to the thickness of the tumour; almost all patients with tumours less than 0.76 mm survive following surgical excision.

色。其預後和瘤的厚度呈逆相關，手術治療後，黑素瘤小於 0.76 mm 的病人幾乎都可存活。

melanonychia *n.* blackening of the nails with the pigment *melanin.

黑甲 由於黑素而變黑的指甲。

melanophore *n. see* melanin.

黑素細胞 參閱 melanin。

melanoplakia *n.* pigmented areas of *melanin in the mucous membrane lining the inside of the cheeks.

黏膜黑斑 頰內黏膜的黑素沉着區域。

melanosis *n.* **1.** *see* melanism. **2.** a disorder in the body's production of the pigment melanin. **3.** *cachexia associated with the spread of the skin cancer *melanoma. **–melanotic** *adj.*

黑變病 (1) 參閱 melanism。(2) 人體生成黑素時的一種疾病。(3) 與黑素瘤擴散有關的惡病質。

melanuria *n.* the presence of dark pigment in the urine. this may be caused by the presence of melanin or its precursors, in some cases of *melanoma; it may alternatively be caused by metabolic disease, such as *porphyria.

黑尿 尿中存在黑色色素。可由尿中存在黑素或其前體引起，在一些黑素瘤病人中，也可由代謝性疾病引起，如卟啉症。

melasma *n. see* chloasma.

黑斑病 參閱 chloasma。

melatonin *n.* a hormone produced by the *pineal gland in darkness but not in bright light. Melatonin receptors in the brain, in a nucleus immediately above the *optic chiasma, react to this hormone and synchronize the nucleus to the 24-hours day/night rhythm, thus informing the brain when it is day and when it is night. Melatonin is a derivative of *serotonin, with which it works to regulate the sleep cycle, and is being used experimentally to treat jet lag, *SADS, and insomnia in shift workers and the elderly.

褪黑激素 松果體在光綫暗淡時，而不是在光綫明亮時產生的一種激素。神經核內的受體對褪黑激素起反應，並將此核與 24 小時的晝夜節律同步，從而使大腦知道白天與黑夜。褪黑激素是 5-羥色胺的一種衍生物，並與之共同調節睡眠周期，並且正被試用於治療時差症、季節性情感紊亂綜合徵、倒班工人和老年人的失眠症。

melioidosis *n.* a disease of wild rodents caused by the bacterium *Pseudomonas pseudomallei*. It can be transmitted to man, possibly by rat fleas, causing pneumonia, multiple abscesses, and septicaemia. It is often fatal.

類鼻疽 由類鼻疽假單胞菌引起的野生囓齒動物的疾病。它可傳播給人（可能通過鼠蚤），引起肺炎、多發性膿腫和敗血症。它常常是致命的。

melomelus *n.* a fetus with one or more pairs of supernumery limbs.

贅肢畸胎 有一對或多對額外肢體的胎兒。

melphalan *n.* a drug used to treat various types of cancer, including malignant melanoma, tumours of the breast and ovaries, and Hodgkin's disease. It is administered by mouth or injection. Side-effects include digestive upsets, mouth ulcers, and temporary hair loss. Trade name: **Alkeran**.

美法侖 用於治療多種癌症的一種藥物，包括惡性黑色素瘤，乳腺和卵巢癌，以及霍奇金病。口服或注射用藥。副作用包括消化道不適，口腔潰瘍和暫時性脱髮。商品名：Alkeran。

membrane *n.* **1.** a thin layer of tissue surrounding the whole or part of an organ or tissue lining a cavity, or separating adjacent structures or cavities. *See also* basement membrane, mucous membrane, serous membrane. **2.** the lipoprotein envelope surrounding a cell (*plasma* or *cell membrane*). **–membranous** *adj.*

膜 **(1)** 全部或部分包繞某個組織或器官，覆蓋於某個腔室內，或者分隔毗鄰結構或腔室的一薄層組織。**(2)** 包繞某個細胞的脂蛋白被膜（血漿或細胞膜）。

membrane bone a bone that develops in connective tissue by direct *ossification, without cartilage being formed first. The bones of the face and skull are membrane bones.

膜骨 最初沒有軟骨形成，在結締組織中通過直接骨化形成的一種骨。面骨和顱骨均是膜骨。

membranous labyrinth *see* labyrinth.

膜迷路 參閱 labyrinth。

men- (meno-) *prefix denoting* menstruation.

〔前綴〕 **月經**

menarche *n.* the start of the menstrual periods and other physical and mental changes associated with puberty. The menarche occurs when the reproductive organs become functionally active and may take place at any time between 10 and 18 years of age.

月經初潮 月經期和其他青春期有關的生理、心理變化的開始。生殖器官具有功能活性時，月經初潮來臨，這可發生於 10~18 歲期間任何時候。

MENCAP a British voluntary association that promotes the welfare of the mentally handicapped and their families, through education, campaigning, and the provision of resources for projects.

mendelism *n.* the theory of inheritance based on *Mendel's laws.

Mendel's laws rules of inheritance based on the breeding experiments of Gregor Mendel, which showed that the inheritance of characteristics is controlled by particles now known as *genes. In modern terms they are as follows. (1) Each body (somatic) cell of an individual carries two factors (genes) for every characteristic and each gamete carries only one. It is now known that the genes are arranged on chromosomes, which are present in pairs in somatic cells and separate during gamete formation by the process of *meiosis. (2) Each pair of factors segregates independently of all other pairs at meiosis, so that the gametes show all possible combinations of factors. This law applies only to genes on different chromosomes; those on the same chromosome are affected by *linkage. *See also* dominant, recessive.

Mendelson's syndrome inhalation of regurgitated stomach contents by an anaesthetized patient, which may result in death from anoxia or cause extensive lung damage or pulmonary *oedema with severe *bronchospasm. It is a well-recognized hazard of general anaesthesia in obstetrics and may be prevented by giving gastric-acid inhibitors (e.g. *cimetidine or *ranitidine) or sodium citrate before inducing anaesthesia.

Ménétrier's disease a disorder in which gross enlargement (*see* hypertro-

孟坎普　一個英國志願者協會，通過教育、宣傳、活動及提供各種項目資源來改進精神障礙者及其家庭的生活福利。

孟德爾遺傳學説　以孟德爾定律為基礎的遺傳理論。

孟德爾定律　基於喬治‧孟德爾育種實驗的遺傳規律，它表明特性的遺傳受到現稱為基因的顆粒控制。現代術語表述如下：(1) 每個個體的體細胞含有每個特性的兩個基因，而每個配子中僅含有一個。現已知道，基因排列在染色體上，在體細胞中，染色體成對存在，在形成配子時通過減數分裂過程而分開。(2) 在減數分裂時，每對基因不受其他對基因影響而獨立分離，這樣，配子可有所有可能的基因組合方式。此定律僅適用於位於不同染色體上的基因，而同一染色體上的基因受連鎖影響。參閱 dominant，recessive。

門德爾森綜合徵　麻醉病人吸入返流的胃內容物。它可由缺氧而致死，還可造成大面積肺損傷或肺水腫，伴有嚴重的支氣管痙攣。是產科全身麻醉已被公認的風險，可通過麻醉誘導前給予胃酸抑制劑（如西咪替丁或雷尼替丁）或枸櫞酸鈉預防。

巨大肥厚性胃炎　胃內黏膜細胞過度增大（參閱 hypertrophy) of the cells of the mucous membrane lining the stomach is associated with anaemia.

Ménière's disease a disease of the inner ear characterized by episodes of deafness, buzzing in the ears (*tinnitus), and *vertigo. Typically the attacks are preceded by a sensation of fullness in the ear. Symptoms last for several hours and between attacks the affected ear may return to normal. It is caused by the build-up of fluid in the inner ear and is treated by drugs or surgery. Medical name: **endolymphatic hydrops**.

mening- (meningo-) *prefix denoting* the meninges.

meninges *pl. n.* (*sing.* **meninx**) the three connective tissue membranes that line the skull and vertebral canal and enclose the brain and spinal cord (see illustration). The outermost layer – the

phy）並且伴有貧血的一種疾病。

梅尼埃病 以發作性的耳聾、耳鳴和眩暈為特點的一種內耳疾病。典型病例中，疾病發作前耳內有脹滿感。症狀持續數小時，而在發作間期，患耳可恢復正常。它由內耳積液引起，可通過藥物或手術治療。醫學用語：迷路積水。

〔前綴〕腦膜

腦脊膜 覆蓋在顱骨和椎管內並包圍腦和脊髓的三層結締組織膜（見圖）。最外層是硬腦（脊）膜，沒有彈性，堅硬，比中層（蛛網膜）和最內層

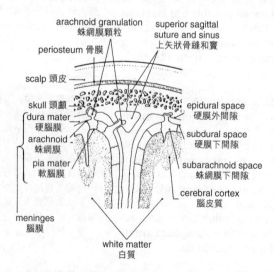

arachnoid granulation 蛛網膜顆粒
superior sagittal suture and sinus 上矢狀骨縫和竇
periosteum 骨膜
scalp 頭皮
skull 頭顱
dura mater 硬腦膜
arachnoid 蛛網膜
pia mater 軟腦膜
epidural space 硬膜外間隙
subdural space 硬膜下間隙
subarachnoid space 蛛網膜下間隙
cerebral cortex 腦皮質
meninges 腦膜
white matter 白質

Section through the skull and brain to show meninges
腦和顱骨切面以示腦脊膜

*dura mater (pachymeninx) – is inelastic, tough, and thicker than the middle layer (the *arachnoid mater) and the innermost layer (the *pia mater). The inner two membranes are together called the *leptomeninges*; between them circulates the *cerebrospinal fluid.

（軟腦膜）厚。裏面的兩層統稱為柔腦（脊）膜,腦脊液在這兩層之間循環。

meningioma *n.* a tumour arising from the fibrous coverings of the brain and spinal cord (*meninges). It is usually slow-growing and produces symptoms by pressure on the underlying nervous tissue. In the brain the tumour is a cause of focal *epilepsy and gradually progressive neurological disability. In the spinal cord it causes paraplegia and the *Brown-Séquard syndrome. Some meningiomas (known as *meningeal sarcomas*) are malignant and can invade neighbouring tissues. Treatment of the majority of cases is by surgical removal if the tumour is accessible. The more malignant varieties may also require additional radiotherapy. Some patients have been known to have symptoms for as long as 30 years before the tumour has been discovered.

腦（脊）膜瘤　發生於腦和脊髓的纖維性覆蓋物上（腦脊膜）的一種腫瘤。通常生長緩慢,並因壓迫下面的神經組織而產生症狀。在腦部,腫瘤是病竈性癲癇和漸進性神經功能喪失的一個病因。在脊髓,它可引起截癱和布朗-塞卡爾綜合徵。一些腦（脊）膜瘤（稱為腦脊膜肉瘤）是惡性的,可侵犯鄰近組織。如果腫瘤可接近,大多數病例通過手術摘除治療。惡性度較高的類型則需輔助放射治療。一些病人在腫瘤發現前,其症狀已存在了 30 年。

meningism *n.* stiffness of the neck mimicking that found in meningitis. It is most common in childhood and is usually a symptom of chest infection or inflammation in the upper respiratory tract. Examination of the *cerebrospinal fluid reveals no abnormalities.

假性腦（脊）膜炎　酷似可見於腦膜炎的那種頸部僵硬。最常發於兒童,它通常是胸腔感染或上呼吸道炎症的症狀。腦脊液檢查未見異常。

meningitis *n.* an inflammation of the *meninges due to infection by viruses or bacteria. Meningitis causes an intense headache, fever, loss of appetite, intolerance to light and sound, rigidity of muscles, especially those in the neck (*see also* Kernig's sign), and in severe cases convulsions, vomiting, and delirium

腦（脊）膜炎　細菌或病毒感染所致的腦（脊）膜炎症。可造成劇烈頭痛,食慾喪失,發燒,不耐受光和聲音,肌肉,特別是頸部肌肉強直（參閱 Kernig's sign）；嚴重的病人由驚厥、嘔吐和譫妄導致死亡。小兒細菌性腦（脊）膜炎

leading to death. The most important causes of bacterial meningitis in young children are *Haemophilus influenzae* and *Neisseria meningitidis* (the meningococcus); immunization against *Haemophilus* meningitis is now possible (*see* Hib vaccine). In *meningococcal meningitis* (also known as *cerebrospinal fever* and *spotted fever*) the symptoms appear suddenly and the bacteria can cause widespread meningococcal infection culminating in *meningococcal septicaemia*, with its characteristic haemorrhagic rash anywhere on the body. Unless rapidly diagnosed and treated, death can occur within a week. Bacterial meningitis is treated with large doses of antibiotics administered as soon as possible after diagnosis. With the exception of herpes simplex *encephalitis (which is treated with acyclovir), viral meningitis does not respond to drugs. *See also* leptomeningitis, pachymeningitis.

最重要的病因是流感嗜血桿菌和腦膜炎奈瑟菌（腦膜炎雙球菌）。現在可針對嗜血桿菌性腦膜炎進行免疫接種（參閱 Hib vaccine）。在腦膜炎雙球菌性腦膜炎（亦稱腦脊熱和斑疹熱）中，症狀突然出現，細菌可引起廣泛的腦膜炎雙球菌感染，並且以腦膜炎雙球菌性敗血症告終，全身出現典型的出血疹。若不迅速診斷治療，一周內可發生死亡。細菌性腦（脊）膜炎在確診後盡快給予大劑量抗生素治療。病毒性腦（脊）膜炎中，除單純疱疹性腦炎（用阿昔洛韋治療）外，其餘都對藥物無反應。參閱 leptomeningitis，pachymeningitis。

meningocele *n.* see neural tube defects.

腦（脊）膜膨出 參閱 neural tube defects。

meningococcaemia *n.* the presence of meningococci (bacteria of the species *Neisseria meningitidis*) in the bloodstream. *See* meningitis.

腦膜炎雙球菌血症 血流中有腦膜炎雙球菌（腦膜炎奈瑟菌菌種的細菌）。參閱 meningitis。

meningococcus *n.* (*pl.* **meningococci**) the bacterium *Neisseria meningitidis*, which can cause a serious form of septicaemia and is a common cause of *meningitis. **–meningococcal** *adj.*

腦膜炎雙球菌 腦膜炎奈瑟菌，能引起嚴重的敗血症，並且是腦膜炎的常見病因。

meningoencephalitis *n.* inflammation of the brain and its membranous coverings (the meninges) caused by bacterial or viral infection. The disease may also involve the spinal cord, producing *myelitis with paralysis of both legs, sometimes called *meningomyelitis*.

腦膜腦炎 細菌或病毒感染引起的腦及其膜性覆蓋物（腦脊膜）的炎症。該病還可累及脊髓，產生伴有雙下肢癱瘓的脊髓炎，有時亦稱作脊髓脊膜炎。

meningoencephalocele *n. see* neural tube defects.

meningomyelitis *n. see* meningoen-cephalitis.

meningomyelocele *n. see* neural tube defects.

meningovascular *adj.* relating to or affecting the meninges covering the brain and spinal cord and the blood vessels that penetrate them to supply the underlying neural tissues. The term is also used to describe secondary syphilitic infection of the nervous system.

meninx *n.* **1.** the thin layer of mesoderm that surrounds the brain of the embryo. It gives rise to most of the skull and the membranes that surround the brain. *See also* chondrocranium. **2.** *see* meninges.

meniscectomy *n.* surgical removal of a cartilage (meniscus) in the knee. This is carried out when the meniscus has been torn or is diseased, to relieve pain and 'locking' of the knee joint. The operation can now be performed through an *arthroscope.

meniscus *n.* (in anatomy) a crescent-shaped structure, such as the fibrocarti-laginous disc that divides the cavity of a synovial joint.

menopause (climacteric) *n.* the time in a woman's life when the ovaries cease to produce an egg cell every four weeks: menstruation ceases and the woman is no longer able to bear children. The menopause can occur at any age between the middle thirties and the middle fifties, most commonly between 45 and 55. Menstruation may decrease gradually

腦腦膜膨出 參閱 neural tube defects。

脊髓脊膜炎 參閱 menin-goencephalitis。

脊髓脊膜膨出 參閱 neural tube defects。

腦脊膜血管的 累及覆蓋腦和脊髓的腦脊膜以及穿過腦脊膜供應下面神經組織的血管的，或與它們有關的。此術語亦用於描述神經系統的繼發性梅毒感染。

(1) 原腦（脊）膜 包圍胚胎的薄的中胚層組織。它形成大部分顱骨以及包圍腦的膜。參閱 chondrocranium。**(2)** 腦（脊）膜 參閱 meninges。

半月板切除術 手術切除膝部一軟骨（半月板）。當半月板撕裂或有病變時，可行此手術緩解疼痛並且「固定」膝關節。現在可通過關節內窺鏡行此手術。

半月板 （解剖學）一半月形結構，如分隔滑膜關節腔的纖維軟骨盤。

絕經 婦女到一定年齡，卵巢停止每四周產生一個卵子，月經停止，婦女不再生育。絕經可發生於 35 歲至 55 歲之間任何年齡，最常發於 45~55 歲之間。在連續的經期內，月經可逐漸減少，或者月經間期延長；月經也可以突然完全停止。絕經時，體內性激素的平

in successive periods or the intervals between the periods may lengthen; alternatively there may be a sudden and complete stoppage of the periods. At the time of the menopause there is a change in the balance of sex hormones in the body, which sometimes leads to hot flushes, palpitations, and dryness of the mucous membrane lining the vagina. Some women may also experience emotional disturbances. Some of these symptoms may be alleviated by *hormone replacement therapy. **–menopausal** *adj.*

衡有所改變，有時引起發熱、潮紅、心悸和陰道內黏膜乾燥。有些婦女還產生情緒紊亂。以上有些症狀可通過激素替代療法緩解。

menorrhagia (epimenorrhagia, dysfunctional bleeding) *n.* abnormally heavy bleeding at menstruation, which may or may not be associated with abnormally long periods. Menorrhagia may be associated with hormonal imbalance, inflammation or tumours (e.g. fibroids) in the pelvic cavity, and anaemia. In some cases no obvious pathology can be demonstrated.

月經過多 經期出血量異常大，可伴有或不伴有經期異常長。月經過多可與激素失衡、盆腔內炎症或腫瘤（如纖維瘤）及貧血有關。有些病例無可見的病理改變。

MENS multiple endocrine neoplasia syndromes: a group of syndromes characterized by combinations of endocrine-based symptoms and signs caused by tumours. The tumours may involve the pituitary, thyroid, parathyroid, and adrenal glands and the pancreas, but some combinations predominate and are designated Types I, IIa, and IIIb. *See also* APUD cells.

多發性內分泌瘤綜合徵 由腫瘤引起的，基於內分泌系統的症狀和體徵的各種組合為特點的一類綜合徵。這些腫瘤可發生於垂體、甲狀腺、甲狀旁腺、腎上腺和胰腺，但有些組合較突出，並命名為 I 型、IIa 型和 IIb 型。參閱 APUD cells。

menses *n.* **1.** the blood and other materials discharged from the uterus at menstruation. **2.** *see* menstruation.

月經 **(1)** 經期時，從子宮排出的血液及其他物質。**(2)** 參閱 menstruation。

menstrual cycle the periodic sequence of events in sexually mature nonpregnant women by which an egg cell (ovum) is released from the ovary at four-weekly intervals until the change of life (*see*

月經周期 在性成熟的非妊娠婦女中出現的周期性連續生理活動，以每四周的間隔從卵巢內釋放一個卵細胞，直到生理機能有所改變（參閱

menopause). The stages of the menstrual cycle are shown in the diagram. An ovum develops within a *Graafian follicle in the ovary. When mature, it bursts from the follicle and travels along the Fallopian tube to the uterus. A temporary endocrine gland – the corpus luteum – develops in the ruptured follicle and secretes the hormone *progesterone, which causes the lining of the uterus (endometrium) to become thicker and richly supplied with blood in preparation for pregnancy. If the ovum is not fertilized the cycle continues: the corpus luteum shrinks and the endometrium is shed at *menstruation. If fertilization does take place the fertilized ovum becomes attached to the endometrium and the corpus luteum continues to secrete progesterone, i.e. pregnancy begins.

menopause）。月經周期的各階段如圖所示。卵子在卵巢的格雷夫卵泡內發育。成熟時，它從破裂的卵泡內出來，並且沿輸卵管行至子宮。暫時的內分泌腺體——黃體在破裂的卵泡內形成，並且分泌黃體酮，引起子宮內膜增厚，並且有豐富的血供，從而為妊娠作好準備。若卵子未受精，則該周期繼續：黃體萎縮，經期內膜脫落。若發生受精，則受精卵附着於內膜，黃體繼續分泌黃體酮，即妊娠開始。

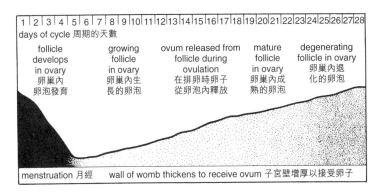

The menstrual cycle
月經周期

menstruation (menses) *n.* the discharge of blood and of fragments of *endometrium from the vagina at intervals of about one month in women of childbearing age (*see* menarche, menopause). Menstruation is that stage

月經　生育年齡的婦女以大約一個月的間隔從陰道內排出血液及子宮內膜碎片（參閱 menarche，menopause）。在月經周期的月經期，由於未發生受精，增厚準備接收受精卵

of the *menstrual cycle during which the endometrium, thickened in readiness to receive a fertilized egg cell (ovum), is shed because fertilization has not occurred. The normal duration of discharge varies from three to seven days. In *anovular menstruation*, discharge takes place without previous release of an egg cell from the ovary. *Vicarious menstruation* is bleeding from a mucous membrane other than the endometrium when normal menstruation is due. *Retrograde menstruation* is the backflow of blood and endometrial cells through the Fallopian tubes (*see* endometriosis). *See also* amenorrhoea, dysmenorrhoea, epimenorrhoea, hypomenorrhoea, menorrhagia, oligomenorrhoea.

的子宮內膜脫落。正常的月經排出期 3~7 天不等。無排卵性月經中，月經排出前卵巢沒有釋放卵子。代償性月經是正常月經來臨時，出血的是其他黏膜，而不是子宮內膜。返流性月經是血液和子宮內膜細胞由輸卵管返流（參閱 endometriosis）。參閱 amenorrhoea，dysmenorrhea，epimenorrhoea，hypomenorrhoea，menorrhagia，oligomenorrhoea。

mental[1] *adj.* relating to or affecting the mind.

精神的　與精神有關的，影響精神的。

mental[2] *adj.* relating to the chin.

頦的　與頦有關的。

mental age a measure of the intellectual level at which an individual functions; for example, someone described as having a mental age of 6 years would be functioning at the level of an average 6-year-old child. This measure has largely been replaced by a comparison of the functioning of persons of the same age group (*see* intelligence quotient, intelligence test).

智力年齡　某個人智能水平的一種測量指標。例如，稱某人具有 6 歲的智力年齡，即指他／她有 6 歲兒童的平均智力水平。同年齡組人的智能比較已基本替代了這種測量。（參閱 intelligence quotient，intelligence test）。

mental deficiency *see* mental retardation.

智力低下　參閱 mental retardation。

mental handicap delayed or incomplete intellectual development combined with some form of social malfunction, such as educational or occupational failure or inability to look after oneself. Good education alters the course of the handicap, for which the term *learning difficulty*

智力障礙　智力發育遲緩或不全，伴有某種形式社會功能障礙，如不能受教育，不能工作或不能照顧自己。良好的教育可改變智力障礙的程度，現在廣泛使用學習困難一詞指此意。參閱 mental retardation。

is now widely used. *See also* mental retardation.

Mental Health Act Commission a regulating body governed by the Mental Health Act 1983. Its members comprise some 90 psychiatrists, nurses, lawyers, members of other clinical professions, and lay people. They have the responsibilities of regularly visiting psychiatric hospitals (yearly for ordinary hospitals; more frequently for *special hospitals), reviewing psychiatric care, giving second opinions on the need for certain psychiatric treatments, and acting as a forum for the discussion of psychiatric issues.

精神保健法委員會　受（英國）1983 年精神保健法支配的一個調節機構。其成員包括 90 多位精神病學家、護士、律師、其他臨床專業人員及非專業人員。他們的職責是周期性地查訪精神病醫院（普通醫院每年一次，專科醫院更頻繁），檢查精神病醫療情況，就某種精神病治療的需要給予參考性意見，並就精神病有關問題進行討論。

Mental Health Acts the Acts of Parliament governing the care of the mentally disordered. The Mental Health Act 1959 provided the framework for England and Wales; similar Acts in 1960 and 1961 provided for Scotland and Northern Ireland. They abolished the old system of certification and established a legal framework for voluntary treatment of the mentally ill on the same basis as other patients. The Act also provides for *compulsory admission when the mentally disordered put themselves or other people into danger. It also enjoined local authorities to provide for the community treatment of mental disorder. The Mental Health (Amendment) Act of 1982 made further provisions for the protection of the civil rights of patients, the restriction of grounds for their detention and compulsory treatment, and for a commission to regulate aspects of the practice of psychiatry (*see* Mental Health Act Commission). The provisions of the 1959 and 1982 Acts are now codified in a single statute, the Mental Health Act 1983.

精神保健法　關於精神病人醫療的（英國）議會法令。1959 年的精神保健法令為英格蘭和威爾士提供了精神保健的基本框架；1960 年和 1961 年類似的法令為蘇格蘭和北愛爾蘭提供了精神保健的基本框架。它們廢除了舊的鑒定制度，建立了精神病病人在與其他病人一樣的基礎上自願進行治療的法律框架。該條例也提供了當精神病人使自己或他人處境危險時的強制收容的框架。它還責成地方當局對精神疾病提供社區治療。1982 年的精神病保健法令（修正案），就保護病人的公民權，限制禁閉病人和強行治療，以及成立一個委員會管理精神病醫療工作作出了進一步的規定（參閱 Mental Health Act Commission）。1959 和 1982 年法令中的規定現被編纂成一份單獨的文件——1983 年精神保健法。

Mental Health Review Tribunal one of a number of tribunals, established under the Mental Health Act 1959 and now operating under the Mental Health Act 1983, to which applications may be made for the discharge from hospital of a person compulsorily detained there under provisions of the Act (*see* compulsory admission). When a patient is subject to a restriction order an application may only be made after his first six months of detention. The powers of the tribunals, which comprise both legally and medically qualified members, include reclassifying unrestricted patients, recommending leave of absence for a patient, delaying discharge, and transferring patients to other hospitals.

精神保健審查法庭 根據（英國）1959 年精神保健條例成立，現在按 1983 年精神保健法運行的許多審查法庭。按 1983 年精神保健法規定：被強迫住院的病人可向此審查法庭申請出院（參閱 compulsory admission）。當病人受某個限制命令的控制時，只有在其入院六個月後才能提出申請。審查法庭由法律和醫療人員組成；其權力包括將未受限制的病人重新分類，建議病人離院，延遲病人出院，及將病人轉院。

mental illness a disorder of one or more of the functions of the mind (such as emotion, perception, memory, or thought), which causes suffering to the patient or others. If the sole problem is that the individual's behaviour as a whole is out of line with society's expectations, then the term 'illness' is not appropriate.

Mental illness should be distinguished from *mental retardation, in which an individual has a general failure of development of the normal intellectual capacities. It is broadly divided into *psychosis, in which the capacity for appreciating reality is lost, and *neurosis, in which insight is retained.

精神病 使病人或他人痛苦的一種或多種腦功能（如情感、知覺、記憶或思維）障礙。如果唯一的問題是個人的整個行為不符合社會的預期標準，那麼「病」這個詞就不恰當了。

精神病應區別於智力低下，後者為個體的總的智能發育未達到正常水平。精神病被廣義地分為喪失了理解現實能力的精神病和保留有自知力的神經官能症。

mental impairment (mostly in legal usage) the condition of significant or severe impairment of intellectual and social functioning associated with abnormally aggressive or seriously irresponsible behaviour.

精神損傷 （主要用於法律）智力及社會功能的顯著而嚴重損傷的疾病，伴有異常攻擊性的或嚴重不負責任的行為。

mental retardation the state of those whose intellectual powers have failed to develop to such an extent that they are in need of care and protection and require special education. It is also known as *mental deficiency* and *mental handicap. The handicap may be classified according to the *intelligence quotient (IQ) as mild (IQ 50–70), moderate to severe (IQ 20–50), and profound (IQ less than 20). Mildly handicapped people often make a good adjustment to life after special help with education. The moderately and severely handicapped usually need much more help and most are permanently dependent on other people, while the profoundly handicapped usually need constant attention. There are very many causes of mental retardation, including *Down's syndrome, inherited metabolic disorders, brain injury, and gross psyshological deprivation; some are preventable or treatable.

智力低下 其智力未充分發育以致需要照顧、保護及特殊教育的人員的狀態。也稱為智力不足或智力障礙。根據智商，這種障礙可分類為：輕度（智商為 50~70），中度至重度（智商為 20~50），以及深度（智商低於 20）。輕度障礙的病人經過特殊教育後可良好地適應生活。中度和重度障礙者常需較多的幫助，並且多數人永遠依賴於他人。重度障礙者常需持續地看護。智力低下的原因很多，包括唐氏綜合徵，遺傳性代謝紊亂，腦損傷和過度心理失落。有些智力低下是可以預防或治愈的。

mental welfare officer (in Britain) formerly, an employee of a local authority with special training in and responsibility for people with mental illness. *See also* social services.

精神病福利官員 （英國）過去指地方當局的受過特殊訓練並負責精神病人的僱員。參閱 social services。

mento- *prefix denoting* the chin.

〔前綴〕**頦** 指頦骨。

mentum *n.* the chin.

頦

mepacrine *n.* a drug used to treat various infestations, particularly giardiasis and taeniasis; it was formerly widely used to treat malaria but has now largely been replaced by safer drugs. It is administered by mouth. Digestive upsets and headache may occur and the skin often turns yellow.

米帕林 用於治療各種傳染病的藥物，特別是梨形鞭毛蟲病和縧蟲病。以前曾廣泛用於瘧疾的治療，但現在已被更安全的藥物所取代。口服用藥。可能發生消化道不適及頭痛，皮膚常變黃。

meperidine *n.* *see* pethidine.

度冷丁 參閱 pethidine。

meprobamate n. a mild *tranquillizer used to relieve anxiety and nervous tension. It is administered by mouth or injection; side-effects include digestive upsets, headache, and drowsiness. Trade name: **Equanil**.

meralgia paraesthetica painful tingling and numbness felt over the outer surface of the thigh when the lateral cutaneous nerve is trapped as it passes through the fibrous and muscular tissues of the thigh.

mercaptopurine n. a drug that prevents the growth of cancer cells and is administered by mouth, chiefly in the treatment of some types of leukaemia (see antimetabolite). It commonly reduces the numbers of white blood cells; mouth ulcers and digestive upsets may also occur. Trade name: **Puri-Nethol**.

mercurialism (hydrargyria) n. mercury poisoning. Metallic mercury is absorbed through the skin and alimentary canal, and its vapour is taken in through the lungs. Acute poisoning causes vomiting, severe abdominal pains, bloody diarrhoea, and kidney damage, with failure to produce urine. Treatment is with *dimercaprol. Chronic poisoning causes mouth ulceration, loose teeth, loss of appetite, and intestinal and renal disturbances, with anaemia and nervous irritability. Treatment is removing the patient from further exposure.

mercury n. a silvery metallic element that is liquid at room temperature. Its toxicity has caused a decline in the use of its compounds in medicine during this century, but mercurial compounds in the form of ointments were formerly used in the treatment of syphilis. The main uses of mercury salts today are in antiseptics,

甲丙氨酯眠爾適 解除焦慮和神經緊張的一種輕型安定藥。口服或注射用藥，副作用包括消化道不適、頭痛和嗜睡。商品名：Equanil。

感覺異常性股痛 當股外側皮神經在通過股纖維和肌組織時受到牽扯，股的外表面可有刺痛感和麻木感。

巰嘌呤 防止癌細胞生長的一種藥物，口服用藥，主要用於治療某些類型的白血病（參閱 antimetabolite）。它常可引起白細胞減少，也可發生口腔潰瘍和消化道不適。商品名：Puri-Nethol。

汞中毒 金屬汞通過皮膚和消化道被吸收，其蒸氣通過肺被吸入。急性中毒引起惡心、嚴重的腹痛、血性腹瀉和腎臟損傷，伴有尿生成障礙。治療用二巰（基）丙醇。慢性中毒引起口腔潰瘍、牙齒鬆動、食慾喪失和腸道及腎功能紊亂，伴有貧血及神經過敏。治療方法是讓病人不再接觸汞。

汞 室溫下呈液態的銀白色金屬元素。本世紀內，其毒性使其化合物在醫藥中的應用有所減少，過去，汞化合物的膏劑用於治療梅毒。現在，汞鹽主要用於防腐劑，殺真菌劑和抗寄生物劑。它還廣泛用於口腔科，作為汞合金填充物的成

fungicides, and antiparasitic agents. It is widely used in dentistry as a component of *amalgam fillings; when the mercury is combined with the filling alloy, it is nontoxic. Symbol: Hg. *See also* mercurialism.

分；當汞與填充合金結合，它沒有毒性。符號：Hg。參閱 mercurialism。

merocrine (eccrine) *adj.* describing a type of *secretion in which the glandular cells remain intact during the process of secretion.

部分分泌 描述分泌過程中，腺細胞保持不變的一種分泌。

merozoite *n.* a stage in the life cycle of the malaria parasite (*Plasmodium*). Many merozoites are formed during the asexual division of the schizont (*see* schizogony). The released merozoites may invade new red blood cells or new liver cells, and continue the asexual phase with the production of yet more merozoites, effectively spreading the infection. Alternatively, merozoites invade red blood cells and begin the sexual cycle with the formation of male and female sex cells (*see* microgametocyte, macrogametocyte).

裂殖子 瘧疾寄生物（瘧原蟲）生活周期的一個階段。許多裂殖子形成於裂殖體（參閱 schizogony）的無性分裂期。釋放的裂殖子可侵入新的紅細胞或肝細胞，並繼續其無性期，產生更多的裂殖子，從而有效傳播感染。或者，裂殖子侵入紅細胞，開始其有性周期，形成雌性、雄性性細胞（參閱 microgametocyte，macrogametocyte）。

mes- (meso-) *prefix denoting* middle or medial.

〔前綴〕**中間的，中層的**

Mesa *see* microsurgical epididymal sperm aspiration.

顯微外科附睪精子吸出術 參閱 microsurgical epididymal sperm aspiration。

mesaortitis *n.* inflammation of the middle layer (media) of the wall of the aorta, generally the result of late syphilis. Aneurysm formation may result. The infection can be eradicated with penicillin.

主動脈中層炎 一般為晚期梅毒所致的主動脈壁中層的炎症。可形成動脈瘤。青黴素可根治此感染。

mesarteritis *n.* inflammation of the middle layer (media) of an artery, which is often combined with inflammation in all layers of the artery wall. It is seen in

動脈中層炎 動脈壁中層的炎症，常合併動脈壁各層的炎症。見於梅毒、多動脈炎、顳動脈炎和伯格病。

syphilis, polyarteritis, temporal arteritis, and Buerger's disease.

mescaline *n.* an alkaloid present in *mescal buttons* (the dried tops of the Mexican cactus *Lophophora williamsii*) that produces inebriation and vivid colourful hallucinations when ingested.

仙人球毒鹼　威廉斯仙人球（墨西哥仙人掌屬威廉斯仙人球的乾燥頂部）中的一種鹼。食入後，能產生酒醉狀和鮮明多彩的幻覺。

mesencephalon *n. see* midbrain.

中腦　參閱 midbrain。

mesenchyme *n.* the undifferentiated tissue of the early embryo that forms almost entirely from *mesoderm. It is loosely organized and the individual cells migrate to different parts of the body where they form most of the skeletal and connective tissue, the blood and blood system, and the visceral (smooth) muscles.

間（充）質　幾乎完全由中胚層形成的早期胚胎的未分化組織。它的結構疏鬆，其單個細胞可移行到身體不同部位，而在各部位形成骨骼和結締組織、血液和血液系統及內臟（平滑）肌的大部分。

mesentery *n.* a double layer of *peritoneum attaching the stomach, small intestine, pancreas, spleen, and other abdominal organs to the posterior wall of the abdomen. It contains blood and lymph vessels and nerves supplying these organs. **–mesenteric** *adj.*

腸繫膜　將胃、小腸、胰、脾和其他腹部器官附着於腹後壁上的雙層腹膜，內含有供應這些器官的血管、淋巴管和神經。

mesial *adj.* **1.** medial. **2.** relating to or situated in the *median line or plane. **3.** designating the surface of a tooth towards the midline of the jaw.

正中的　(1) 中間的。(2) 位於中綫或正中面的，與此有關的。(3) 指朝向頜中綫的牙面的。

mesiodens *n.* an extra tooth that may occur in the midline of the palate, between the central incisors, and may interfere with their eruption.

額外牙　發生於腭中綫上中切牙間的一顆多出的牙齒，可阻礙中切牙的萌生。

mesmerism *n.* *hypnosis based on the ideas of the 18th-century physician Franz Mesmer, sometimes employing magnets and a variety of other equipment.

催眠術　基於 18 世紀弗朗茲·梅斯梅爾醫生的觀點的催眠術，有時使用磁鐵和其他多種設備。

mesna *n.* a drug administered intravenously by injection or infusion to prevent the toxic effect of *ifosfamide and *cyclophosphamide on the bladder. It binds with the toxic metabolite acrolein in the urine.

美司鈉　預防異環磷酰胺和環磷酰胺對膀胱的毒性作用的一種靜脈注射或輸注藥。它與尿中毒性代謝物丙烯醛結合。

mesoappendix *n.* the *mesentery of the appendix.

闌尾繫膜　闌尾的腸繫膜。

mesocolon *n.* the fold of peritoneum by which the colon is fixed to the posterior abdominal wall. Usually only the *transverse* and *sigmoid mesocolons* persist in the adult, attached to the transverse and sigmoid colon, respectively.

結腸繫膜　將結腸固定於腹後壁的腹膜皺襞。成人中通常僅存留有橫結腸和乙狀結腸繫膜，分別附着於橫結腸和乙狀結腸上。

mesoderm *n.* the middle *germ layer of the early embryo. It gives rise to cartilage, muscle, bone, blood, kidneys, gonads and their ducts, and connective tissue. It separates into two layers – an outer *somatic* and an inner *splanchnic mesoderm*, separated by a cavity (*coelom*) that becomes the body cavity. The dorsal somatic mesoderm becomes segmented into a number of *somites. *See also* mesenchyme. **–mesodermal** *adj.*

中胚層　早期胚胎的中胚芽層。形成軟骨、肌肉、骨、血液、腎臟、性腺及其管道，以及結締組織。它分成兩層，即外層的體中胚層和內層的內臟中胚層，其間由腔分隔，此腔變成體腔。背側的體中胚層分成許多個體節。參閱 mesenchyme。

mesometrium *n.* the broad ligament of the uterus: a sheet of connective tissue that carries blood vessels to the uterus and attaches it to the abdominal wall.

子宮繫膜　子宮寬闊的韌帶。它是攜帶血管到子宮並且將子宮附着於腹壁上的一層結締組織。

mesomorphic *adj.* describing a *body type that has a well developed skeletal and muscular structure and a sturdy upright posture. **–mesomorph** *n.* **–mesomorphy** *n.*

中型身材的　描述骨骼及肌肉結構發育良好並具有強健筆直姿態的體型。

mesonephros (Wolffian body) *n.* the second area of kidney tissue to develop in the embryo. Its excretory function only lasts for a very brief period before it degenerates. However, parts of it

中腎　胚胎內第二個腎組織發育區。它的分泌功能僅維持短時間便退化。但是，它的部分組織併入男性生殖結構。它的管道——中腎（或沃爾夫中腎）

become incorporated into the male reproductive structures. Its duct – the *mesonephric* (or *Wolffian*) *duct* – persists in males as the epididymis and vas deferens, which conduct sperm from the testis. **–mesonephric** *adj.*

管在男性體中存留，成為從睾丸中引導精液的附睾和輸精管。

mesophilic *adj.* describing organisms, especially bacteria, that grow best at temperatures of about 25–45°C. *Compare* psychrophilic, thermophilic.

適温的 描述在約 25°C~45°C 間生長最佳的有機物，特別是細菌。與 psychrophilic，thermophilic 對比。

mesosalpinx *n.* a fold of peritoneum that surrounds the Fallopian tubes. It is the upper part of the broad ligament that surrounds the uterus.

輸卵管繫膜 包圍輸卵管的腹膜皺襞。它是包繞子宮的闊韌帶的上部。

mesosome *n.* a structure occurring in some bacterial cells, formed by infolding of the cell membrane. Mesosomes are associated with the DNA and play a part in cell division.

間體 一些細菌細胞中由細胞膜內摺而形成的結構。它與 DNA 有關，而且參與細胞分裂。

mesotendon *n.* the delicate connective tissue membrane that surrounds a tendon.

腱繫膜 圍繞腱的纖細結締組織膜。

mesothelioma *n.* a tumour of the pleura, peritoneum, or pericardium. The occurrence or pleural mesothelioma has a very strong association with exposure to asbestos dust (*see* asbestosis), and workers in the asbestos industry who develop such tumours are entitled to industrial compensation. In other cases there is no history of direct exposure to asbestos at work, but the patients had been exposed to asbestos via the clothes of relatives who had had direct contact with asbestos, or they themselves had lived very close to an asbestos factory. There is no curative treatment for the disease, but good results have occasionally been obtained from radical surgery for limited disease, from radiotherapy, and from chemotherapy.

間皮瘤 胸膜、腹膜或心包膜上的腫瘤。胸膜間皮瘤的發生與接觸石棉粉塵有極大關係（參閱 asbestosis），所以，患此瘤的石棉工人有權享受企業補助。在其他的病例中，病人沒有工作上直接接觸石棉的病史，但可通過直接接觸石棉的其親戚的衣服接觸石棉，或其住處離石棉工廠很近。此病沒有治愈的方法，但極少數病人曾通過根治手術，放射治療或化學治療獲得好的效果。

mesothelium *n.* the single layer of cells that lines *serous membranes. It is derived from embryonic mesoderm. *Compare* epithelium.

間皮　覆在漿膜表面的單層細胞。它由胚胎的中胚層衍變而來。與 epithelium 對比。

mesovarium *n.* the *mesentery of the ovaries.

卵巢繫膜　卵巢的繫膜。

messenger RNA a type of RNA that carries the information of the *genetic code of the DNA from the cell nucleus to the ribosomes, where the code is translated into protein. *See* transcription, translation.

信使 **RNA**　將 DNA 的遺傳密碼信息從細胞核攜帶到核糖體的一種 RNA。在核糖體，遺傳信息被轉譯成蛋白質。參閱 transcription，translation。

mestranol *n.* a synthetic female sex hormone (*see* oestrogen) used in combination with a progestogen to treat menopausal symptoms (*see* hormone replacement therapy) and as a constituent of *oral contraceptive pills. Trade names: **Menophase**, **Norinyl-1**.

美雌醇　一種合成的雌性性激素（參閱 oestrogen），與黃體酮聯合使用治療更年期綜合徵（參閱 hormone replacement therapy），並且是口服避孕藥片的組成成分。商品名：Menophase，Norinyl-1。

met- (meta-) *prefix denothing* **1.** distal to; beyond; behind. **2.** change; transformation.

〔前綴〕**(1)** 遠離的、超出、後面　**(2)** 改變、轉變

metabolism *n.* **1.** the sum of all the chemical and physical changes that take place within the body and enable its continued growth and functioning. Metabolism involves the breakdown of complex organic constituents of the body with the liberation of energy, which is required for other processes (*see* catabolism) and the building up of complex substances, which form the material of the tissues and organs, from simple ones (*see* anabolism). *See also* basal metabolism. **2.** the sum of the biochemical changes undergone by a particular constituent of the body; for example, protein metabolism. **–metabolic** *adj.*

（新陳）代謝　**(1)** 體內發生的能使身體繼續生長和維持功能的所有化學和物理變化的總和。新陳代謝包括複雜的有機成分的分解，伴有其他過程所必需的能量的釋放（參閱 catabolism）和由簡單物質合成複雜物質，以構成組織和器官的成分（參閱 anabolism）。參閱 basal metabolism。**(2)** 身體某個特殊成分所發生的生化變化的總和。例如蛋白代謝。

metabolite *n.* a substance that takes part in the process of *metabolism. Metabolites are either produced during metabolism or are constituents of food taken into the body.

代謝物　參與代謝過程的一種物質。代謝物是新陳代謝過程的產物或攝入體內的食物的組成成分。

metacarpal 1. *adj.* relating to the bones of the hand (*metacarpus). **2.** *n.* any of the bones forming the metacarpus.

(1) 掌的　與手骨（掌）有關的。(2) 掌骨　構成掌的骨頭。

metacarpus *n.* the five bones of the hand that connect the *carpus (wrist) to the *phalanges (digits).

掌　連接腕和指（趾）的 5 個手骨。

metacentric *n.* a chromosome in which the centromere is at or near the centre of the chromosome. **–metacentric** *adj.*

中間着絲粒的　着絲粒位於或接近染色體中心的一種染色體。

metacercaria *n.* (*pl.* **metacercariae**) a mature form of the *cercaria larva of a fluke. Liver fluke metacercariae are enveloped by thin cysts and develop on various kinds of vegetation.

後囊蚴　吸蟲尾蚴的成熟形式。肝吸蟲後囊蚴被一薄囊包繞，並在多種植被上發育。

metachromasia (metachromatism) *n.* **1.** the property of a dye of staining certain tissues or cells a colour that is different from that of the stain itself. **2.** the variation in colour produced in certain tissue elements that are stained with the same dye. **3.** abnormal coloration of a tissue produced by a particular stain. **–metachromatic** *adj.*

異染性　(1) 所染出的組織或細胞的顏色不同於染料本身顏色的染劑特性。(2) 用同種染劑染出的組織成分產生不同顏色。(3) 某種特殊染劑產生的異常的組織染色。

Metagonimus *n.* a genus of small flukes, usually less than 3 mm in length, that are common as parasites of dogs and cats in the Far East, N Siberia, and the Balkan States. Adult flukes of *M. yokogawai* occasionally infect the duodenum of man if undercooked fish (the intermediate host) is eaten. They may cause inflammation and some ulceration of the intestinal lining, which produces a mild

後殖吸蟲屬　一屬小吸蟲，長度通常小於 3 毫米，常為遠東、西伯利亞北部和巴爾幹半島地區狗和貓的寄生物。如果吃了生魚（中間宿主），橫川後殖吸蟲的成蟲偶然會感染人的十二指腸，可引起腸黏膜的炎症和潰瘍，造成輕度腹瀉。四氯乙烯可有效驅除吸蟲。

diarrhoea. Flukes can be easily removed with tetrachlorethylene.

metamorphopsia *n.* a condition in which objects appear distorted. It is usually due to a disorder of the retinal affecting the *macula (the most sensitive part).

metamyelocyte *n.* an immature *granulocyte (a type of white blood cell), having a kidney-shaped nucleus (*compare* myelocyte) and cytoplasm containing neutrophil, eosinophil, or basophil granules. It is normally found in the blood-forming tissue of the bone marrow but may appear in the blood in a wide variety of diseases, including acute infections. *See also* granulopoiesis.

metanephros *n.* the excretory organ of the fetus, which develops into the kidney and is formed from the rear portion of the *nephrogenic cord. It does not become functional until birth, since urea is transferred across the placenta to the mother.

metaphase *n.* the second stage of *mitosis and of each division of *meiosis, in which the chromosomes line up at the centre of the *spindle, with their centromeres attached to the spindle fibres.

metaphysis *n.* the growing portion of a long bone that lies between the *epiphyses (the ends) and the *diaphysis (the shaft).

metaplasia *n.* an abnormal change in the nature of a tissue. For instance, columnar epithelium lining the bronchi may be converted to squamous epithelium (*squamous metaplasia*): this may be an early sign of malignant change.

視物變形症　視物變形的一種疾病。常由累及黃斑（最敏感部位）的視網膜疾病所致。

晚幼粒細胞　一種不成熟的粒細胞（一種白細胞），有腎形核（與 myelocyte 對比）且胞漿內含有嗜中性、嗜酸性或嗜鹼性顆粒。正常情況下，可見於骨髓造血組織內；在患急性感染等多種疾病時，可出現於血液中。參閱 granulopoiesis。

後腎　由生腎索後部形成並發育成腎臟的胎兒排泄器官。出生前，由於尿素經過胎盤被轉移到母體，後腎不發揮功能。

中期　有絲分裂的第二階段和減數分裂每次分裂的第二個階段。在此期間，染色體排列於紡錘體中央，其着絲粒附着於紡錘體纖維上。

幹骺端　位於骨骺（骨端）和骨幹（骨體）之間的長骨的生長部分。

（組織）轉化（化生）　組織特性的異常改變。例如，覆蓋支氣管內的柱狀上皮可轉化為鱗狀上皮（鱗狀組織化生）；這可為惡性變的早期徵象。骨髓組織轉化是正常情況下僅見於

Myeloid metaplasia is the development of bone marrow elements, normally found only within the marrow cavities of the bones, in organs such as the spleen and liver. This may occur after bone marrow failure.

骨髓腔內的骨髓成分在脾、肝等器官中發育。這可發生於骨髓衰竭後。

metaraminol *n.* a *sympathomimetic drug that stimulates alpha receptors and is used to treat severe anaphylactic shock (*see* anaphylaxis). It is administered by injection. Trade name: **Aramine**.

間羥胺　刺激 α 受體，用於治療嚴重的過敏性休克（參閱 anaphylaxis）的一種擬交感神經藥。注射用藥。商品名：Aramine。

metastasis *n.* the distant spread of malignant tumour from its site of origin. This occurs by three main routes: **(1)** through the bloodstream; **(2)** through the lymphatic system; **(3)** across body cavities, e.g. through the peritoneum. Highly malignant tumours have a greater potential for metastasis. Individual tumours may spread by one or all of the above routes, although *carcinoma is said classically to metastasize via the lymphatics and *sarcoma via the bloodstream. **–metastatic** *adj.*

轉移　惡性腫瘤從原發部位向遠處擴散。轉移有三個途徑：**(1)** 通過血流；**(2)** 通過淋巴系統；**(3)** 穿過體腔，如穿過腹膜。高度惡性的腫瘤轉移的可能性較大。雖然一般認為癌症通過淋巴管轉移，肉瘤通過血流轉移，但個別腫瘤可通過上述一種或所有途徑轉移。

metastasize *vb.* (of a malignant tumour) to spread by *metastasis.

轉移　（惡性腫瘤）經轉移擴散。

metatarsal 1. *adj.* relating to the bones of the foot (*metatarsus). **2.** *n.* any of the bones forming the metatarsus.

蹠的　**(1)** 與腳骨（蹠）有關的。**(2)** 形成蹠的任何骨頭。

metatarsalgia *n.* aching pain in the metatarsal bones of the foot. Repeated injury and deformities of the foot are common causes, and corrective footwear may be prescribed.

蹠（骨）痛　腳蹠骨的鈍痛。足部的反覆損傷或畸形是常見的病因，可穿矯正鞋治療。

metatarsus *n.* the five bones of the foot that connect the *tarsus (ankle) to the *phalanges (toes).

蹠　將跗骨（踝）連接於腳骨（趾）的 5 塊骨頭。

metathalamus *n.* a part of the *thalamus consisting of two nuclei through which impulses pass from the eyes and ears to be distributed to the cerebral cortex.

丘腦後部　含有兩個核的那部分丘腦。眼和耳的衝動通過此處分布於腦皮質。

metencephalon *n.* part of the hind-brain, formed by the pons and the cere-bellum and continuous below with the medulla oblongata. *See* brain.

後腦　菱腦的一部分，由腦橋和小腦組成，向下與延腦相連。參閱 brain。

meteorism *n.* *see* tympanites.

鼓脹　參閱 tympanites。

-meter *suffix denoting* an instrument for measuring. Example: *perimeter* instrument for measuring the field of vision).

〔後綴〕**計、表、量器**　用於測量的儀器，例如：視野計（測量視野的儀器）。

metformin *n.* a *biguanide drug that reduces blood sugar levels and is used to treat noninsulin-dependent *diabetes. It is administered by mouth and may cause loss of appetite and minor digestive upsets. Trade name: **Glucophage**. *See also* oral hypoglycaemic drug.

甲福明　降低血糖水平，用於治療非胰島素依賴型糖尿病的一種雙胍藥。口服用藥，副作用包括食慾喪失及輕度消化系統不適。商品名：Glu-cophage。參閱 oral hypogly-caemic drug。

methadone *n.* a potent narcotic *anal-gesic drug administered by mouth or injection to relieve severe pain and as a linctus to suppress coughs. It is also used to treat heroin addiction. Digestive upsets, drowsiness, and dizziness may occur, and prolonged use may lead to dependence. Trade name: **Physeptone**.

美沙酮　一種口服或注射用的強麻醉鎮痛藥，用於解除劇痛或用作止咳舐膏劑。也用於治療海洛因成癮。可有消化系統不適、嗜睡和眩暈；長期使用可導致賴藥性。商品名：Phy-septone。

methaemalbumin *n.* a chemical complex of the pigment portion of haemoglobin (*haem*) with the plasma protein *albumin. It is formed in the blood in those anaemias in which red blood cells are destroyed and free haemoglobin is released into the plasma. In such conditions methaemalbumin can be detected in both the blood and urine.

正鐵白蛋白　血紅蛋白的色素部分（血紅素）與血漿蛋白（白蛋白）的化學複合物。貧血病人的紅細胞被破壞，自由的血紅蛋白被釋放進入血漿，因而在其血中形成正鐵白蛋白。在這種疾病中，血和尿中均可檢出正鐵白蛋白。

methaemoglobin *n.* a substance formed when the iron atoms of the blood

正鐵血紅蛋白　當血色素（血紅蛋白）的鐵原子從亞鐵氧化

pigment *haemoglobin have been oxidized from the ferrous to the ferric form (*compare* oxyhaemoglobin). The methaemoglobin cannot bind molecular oxygen and therefore it cannot transport oxygen round the body. The presence of methaemoglobin in the blood (*methaemoglobinaemia*) may result from the ingestion of oxidizing drugs or from an inherited abnormality of the haemoglobin molecule. Symptoms include fatigue, headache, dizziness and *cyanosis.

成高鐵時形成的一種物質（與 oxyhaemoglobin 對比）。正鐵血紅蛋白不能與氧分子結合，所以，它不能向全身運送氧氣。血中存在正鐵血紅蛋白（正鐵血紅蛋白症）可由攝入氧化藥物或血紅蛋白分子遺傳異常所致。症狀包括疲勞、頭痛、眩暈及紫紺。

methanol *n. see* methyl alcohol.

甲醇　參閱 methyl alcohol。

methenamine *n. see* hexamine.

烏洛托品　參閱 hexamine。

methionine *n.* a sulphur-containing *essential amino acid. *See also* amino acid.

蛋氨酸　一種含硫的必需氨基酸。參閱 amino acid。

methixene *n.* a drug with effects similar to those of *atropine, used to control the tremors and other symptoms in parkinsonism and to relieve spasm of smooth muscle in digestive disorders. It is administered by mouth; side-effects can include dry mouth, disturbed vision, flushing, and dizziness. Trade name: **Tremonil**.

美噻嗪　效果類似於阿托品的一種藥物，用於控制帕金森綜合徵中的震顫及其他徵狀，以及解除消化道疾病中的平滑肌痙攣。副作用包括口乾、視力障礙、潮紅和眩暈。商品名：Tremonil。

methoserpidine *n.* a drug that lowers the blood pressure. It is administered by mouth; common side-effects include lethargy, drowsiness, and digestive upsets. Trade name: **Decaserpyl**.

美索舍平　一種降血壓藥。口服用藥，副作用包括昏睡、嗜睡和消化系統障礙。商品名：Decaserpyl。

methotrexate *n.* a drug that interferes with cell growth and is used to treat various types of cancer, including leukaemia (*see* antimetabolite). It is administered by mouth or injection; common side-effects include mouth sores, digestive upsets, skin rashes, and hair loss. Trade name: **Maxtrex**.

甲氨蝶呤　干擾細胞生長，治療包括白血病的多種癌症的一種藥物（參閱 antimetabolite）。口服或注射用藥，常見的副作用包括口腔潰瘍、皮疹及脫髮。商品名：Maxtrex。

methotrimeprazine *n.* a tranquillizing, sedative, and analgesic drug used to treat anxiety, tension, and agitation and to relieve moderate or severe pain. It is administered by mouth or by injection; common side-effects include drowsiness and weakness. Trade name: **Nozinan**.

左甲硫拉嗪　治療焦慮、緊張、激動及解除中度或重度頭痛的安定、鎮靜和止痛藥。口服或注射用藥，常見的副作用包括嗜睡和虛弱。商品名：Nozinan。

methoxamine *n.* a *sympathomimetic drug that causes blood vessels to constrict and thus raises blood pressure. It is administered by injection to maintain the blood pressure during surgical operations. High doses may cause headache and vomiting. Trade name: **Vasoxine**.

甲氧明　使血管收縮從而升高血壓的一種擬交感神經藥。手術期間，可注射甲氧明以維持血壓。大劑量可引起頭痛和嘔吐。商品名：Vasoxine。

methyclothiazide *n.* a thiazide *diuretic used in the treatment of high blood pressure (*hypertension) and oedema associated with congestive heart failure, cirrhosis, other drug therapy, and kidney dysfunction. It prevents reabsorption of sodium, chloride, and, to a lesser extent, potassium. It is administered by mouth; side-effects include loss of appetite, dizziness, and hypotension. Trade name: **Enduron**.

甲氯噻嗪　一種噻嗪利尿藥。用於治療與充血性心力衰竭、肝硬化，其他藥物治療及腎機能不良有關的高血壓和水腫。它可防止鈉、氯和較小程度的鉀的重吸收。口服用藥，副作用包括食慾喪失、眩暈及低血壓。商品名：Enduron。

methyl alcohol (methanol) wood alcohol: an alcohol that is oxidized in the body much more slowly than ethyl alcohol and forms poisonous products. As little as 10 ml of pure methyl alcohol can produce permanent blindness, and 100 ml is likely to be fatal. The breakdown product formaldehyde is responsible for damage to the eyes; it is itself converted to formic acid, which causes acidosis and death from respiratory failure. *See also* methylated spirits.

甲醇　木醇：在體內比乙醇氧化慢得多並形成有毒產物的一種醇。僅 10 毫升的純甲醇可致永久性失明，而 100 毫升則可能致死。裂解產物甲醛造成眼睛損傷；甲醛又轉變為甲酸，甲酸引起酸中毒和呼吸衰竭而死亡。參閱 methylated spirits。

methylamphetamine *n.* a drug with actions and side-effects similar to those of *amphetamine. It is administered by mouth to treat narcolepsy and

去氧麻黃鹼　作用和副作用類似於苯丙胺的一種藥物。口服使用可治療發作性睡眠、帕金森綜合徵及一些抑鬱狀態，也

parkinsonism and some depressive states, and to reduce appetite. It is also administered by injection in psychiatry, to restore the blood pressure in surgical procedures, and to treat drug overdosage. Its use is restricted to hospitals.

可減小食慾。注射使用可用於精神病人，可在手術操作中恢復血壓，並可治療藥物過量。此藥限於醫院內使用。

methylated spirits a mixture consisting mainly of ethyl alcohol with *methyl alcohol and petroleum hydrocarbons. The addition of pyridine gives it an objectionable smell, and the dye methyl violet is added to make it recognizable as unfit to drink. It is used as a solvent, cleaning fluid, and fuel.

甲基化醑劑 主要由乙醇，甲醇及石油烴組成的混合製劑。添加吡啶使其具有難聞的氣味。另外，加入甲基紫染劑使其易於識別，不能飲用。可用作溶劑、清潔劑和燃料。

methylcellulose *n.* a compound that absorbs water and is used as a bulk *laxative to treat constipation, to control diarrhoea, and in patients with a *colostomy. It is administered by mouth and usually has no side-effects. Trade name: **Celevac**.

甲基纖維素 一種吸水的化合物，用作容積性輕瀉劑治療便秘，控制腹瀉並用於結腸造口術病人。口服用藥，常無副作用。商品名：Celevac。

methyldopa *n.* a drug that reduces blood pressure (*see* sympatholytic). It is administered by mouth or injection, and drowsiness commonly occurs during the first days of treatment. Trade names: **Aldomet**, **Dopamet**, **Hydromet**, **Medomet**.

甲基多巴 一種降血壓的藥物（參閱 sympatholytic）。口服或注射用藥，治療的前幾天常發生嗜睡。商品名：Aldomet，Dopamet，Hydromet，Medomet。

methylene blue a blue dye used to stain bacterial cells for microscopic examination.

亞甲藍 一種用來染細菌細胞以供顯微鏡檢查的藍色染劑。

methyl green a basic dye used for colouring the stainable part of the cell nucleus (chromatin) and – with pyronin – for the differential staining of RNA and DNA, which give a red and a green colour respectively.

甲（基）綠 一種鹼性染劑，用於染細胞核（染色質）中可染部分；與派洛寧合用，可作 RNA 和 DNA 的鑑別染色，分別呈紅色和綠色。

methylphenidate *n.* a *sympathomimetic drug that also stimulates the

哌醋甲酯 一種擬交感神經藥，也可刺激中樞神經系統。

central nervous system. It is used to treat hyperkinetic syndrome in children, to improve mental activity in convalescence and some depressive states, and to overcome lethargy associated with drug treatment. It is administered by mouth or injection; side-effects such as nervousness and insomnia may occur. Trade name: **Ritalin**.

用於治療兒童多動綜合徵，改善病後恢復期及抑鬱狀態病人的精神活動，並克服與藥物治療有關的嗜睡。口服或注射；可發生神經過敏、失眠等副作用。商品名：Ritalin。

methylprednisolone *n*. a glucocorticoid (*see* corticosteroid) used in the treatment of inflammatory conditions, such as rheumatoid arthritis, rheumatic fever, and allergic states, and for adrenocortical insufficiency. It is administered by mouth, intravenously, and intramuscularly; side-effects include *electrolyte imbalance, muscle weakness, and abdominal distension. Trade names: **Depo-Medrone**, **Medrone**, **Solu-Medrone**.

甲潑尼龍 一種糖皮質激素（參閱 corticosteroid），用於治療炎症，如類風濕關節炎、風濕熱、過敏狀態以及腎上腺皮質功能不足。口服，靜脈注射或肌肉注射。副作用包括電解質失衡，肌無力及腹脹。商品名：Depo-Medrone，Medrone，Solu-Medrone。

methyl salicylate oil of wintergreen: a liquid with *counterirritant and *analgesic properties, applied to the skin to relieve pain in lumbago, sciatica, and rheumatic conditions.

水楊酸甲酯 冬青油，具有抗刺激及止痛特性的液體，用於皮膚以解除腰痛、坐骨神經痛和風濕病的疼痛。

methyltestosterone *n*. a synthetic male sex hormone (*see* androgen) administered by mouth to treat sexual underdevelopment in men. It is also used to suppress lactation, to treat menstrual and menopausal disorders, and to treat breast cancer in women. Side-effects are those of *testosterone.

甲睾酮 一種合成的男性性激素（參閱 androgen），口服，可治療男性性發育不全。也可用於女性抑制泌乳，治療月經和絕經時的疾病以及治療乳腺癌。副作用同睾丸酮的副作用。

methylthiouracil *n*. a drug that inhibits thyroid activity, formerly administered by mouth to treat overactivity of the thyroid gland (*see* thyrotoxicosis). Side-effects may include rashes, digestive upsets, and headache, and *carbimazole is now preferred.

甲硫氧嘧啶 一種抑制甲狀腺活動的藥物。過去曾口服治療甲狀腺功能亢進（參閱 thyrotoxicosis）。副作用可包括皮疹、消化道不適及頭痛。現常選用卡比馬唑。

methyl violet (gentian violet) a dye used mainly for staining Protozoa.

甲（基）紫　主要用於原生動物染色的一種染劑。

methysergide *n.* a drug used to prevent severe migraine attacks and to control diarrhoea associated with tumours in the digestive system. It is administered by mouth; common side-effects are digestive upsets, dizziness, and drowsiness. Trade name: **Deseril**.

美西麥角　用於預防嚴重偏頭痛發作，控制與消化系統腫瘤有關的腹瀉的藥物。口服，常見的副作用包括消化系統不適、眩暈及嗜睡。商品名：Deseril。

metoclopramide *n.* a drug that antagonizes the actions of *dopamine; it is used to treat nausea, vomiting, indigestion, heartburn, and flatulence. It is administered by mouth or injection; high doses may cause drowsiness and muscle spasms. Trade names: **Gastromax**, **Maxolon**.

甲氧氯普胺　對抗多巴胺作用的一種藥物。用於治療惡心、嘔吐、消化不良、胃灼熱、以及腸胃脹氣。口服或注射，大劑量可引起嗜睡和肌痙攣。商品名：Gastromax，Maxolon。

metolazone *n.* a *diuretic used to treat fluid retention (oedema) and high blood pressure. It is administered by mouth; side-effects include headache, loss of appetite, and digestive upsets, and blood potassium levels may be reduced. Trade name: **Metenix**, **Xuret**.

美扎拉宗　治療液體瀦留（水腫）及高血壓的一種利尿劑。口服，副作用包括頭痛、食慾喪失、消化系統不適，同時血鉀水平可能降低。商品名：Metenix，Xuret。

metoprolol *n.* a drug that controls the activity of the heart (*see* beta blocker) and is used to treat high blood pressure and angina. It is administered by mouth; the commonest side-effects are tiredness and digestive upsets. Trade names: **Betaloc**, **Lopresor**.

美托洛爾　控制心臟活動的一種藥物（參閱 beta blocker），用於治療高血壓和心絞痛。口服，最常見的副作用有疲倦和消化系統不適。商品名：Betaloc，Lopresor。

metr- (metro-) *prefix denoting* the uterus.

〔前綴〕子宮

metre *n.* the *SI unit of length that is equal to 39.37 inches. It is formally defined as the length of the path travelled by light in vacuum during a time interval of 1/299,792,458 of a second. Symbol: m.

米　相當於 39.37 英寸的國際長度單位。正式規定為在 1/299792458 秒的時間間隔內，光在真空中傳播路綫的長度。符號：m。

metritis *n*. inflammation of the uterus. *See also* endometritis, myometritis.

子宮炎　子宮的炎症。參閱 endometritis，myometritis。

metronidazole *n*. a drug used to treat infections of the urinary, genital, and digestive systems, such as trichomoniasis, amoebiasis, and giardiasis, and acute ulcerative gingivitis. It is administered by mouth or in suppositories; side-effects are rare but may include digestive upsets, drowsiness, and headache. Trade names: **Flagyl, Metrozol**.

甲硝唑　治療泌尿、生殖、消化系統感染，如毛滴蟲病、阿米巴病、梨形鞭毛蟲病、以及急性潰瘍性牙齦炎的藥物。口服或栓劑用藥。副作用少見，但可有消化系統不適、嗜睡和頭痛。商品名：Flagyl，Metrozol。

metropathia haemorrhagica irregular episodes of bleeding from the uterus, without previous ovulation, due to excessive oestrogenic activity. It is associated with endometrial *hyperplasia and usually with follicular cysts of the ovary.

功能性子宮出血　雌激素過分活躍引起的無先期排卵的子宮不規律出血。可併發子宮內膜增生，並且卵巢內常有卵泡囊腫。

metrorrhagia *n*. bleeding from the uterus other than the normal menstrusl periods. It may indicate serious disease and should always be investigated.

子宮出血　非正常月經的子宮出血。可表示有嚴重疾病，應作檢查。

-metry *suffix denoting* measuring or measurement.

〔後綴〕測量

metyrapone *n*. a drug that interferes with the production of the hormone *aldosterone and is used in the treatment of *Cushing's syndrome. It is administered by mouth. Side-effects may include nausea, vomiting, low blood pressure, and allergic reactions. Trade name: **Metopirone**.

美替拉酮　干擾醛甾酮生成，治療庫欣綜合徵的一種藥物。口服，副作用包括惡心、嘔吐、低血壓、及過敏反應。商品名：Metopirone。

mexiletine *n*. an *anti-arrhythmic drug used in the treatment or prevention of severe heart irregularity arising in the lower chambers (ventricles). It is administered by mouth. Possible side-effects include nausea and vomiting, dizziness, and double vision. Trade name: **Mexitil**.

美西律　預防治療心室產生的嚴重心律不齊的一種抗心律不齊藥。口服，可能的副作用包括惡心、嘔吐、眩暈及複視。商品名：Mexitil。

MHC major histocompatibility complex: a series of genes located on chromosome no. 6 that code for antigens, including the *HLA antigens, that are important in the determination of histocompatibility.

主要組織相容性複合體　位於 6 號染色體上的一個染色體序列，它是包括人類白細胞抗原在內的，對決定組織相容性有重要意義的抗原編碼。

mianserin *n.* a drug used to relieve moderate or severe depression and anxiety. It is administered by mouth; side-effects are usually milder than with other potent antidepressants, the commonest being drowsiness. Trade names: **Bolvidon, Norval**.

米安色林　解除中度或重度抑鬱症和焦慮症的一種藥物。口服，副作用較其他強效抗抑鬱藥輕，最常見為嗜睡。商品名：Bolvidon，Norval。

micelle *n.* one of the microscopic particles into which the products of fat digestion (i.e. fatty acids and monoglycerides), present in the gut, are dispersed by the action of *bile salts. Fatty material in this finely dispersed form is more easily absorbed by the small intestine.

微膠粒　顯微鏡下可見的一種微粒。在膽鹽的作用下，腸道內的脂肪消化的產物（即脂肪酸和單酸甘油酯）被分散進入這些微粒中。這種小的分散形式更易被小腸吸收。

miconazole *n.* a drug used to treat fungal infections, such as *ringworm of the scalp, body, and feet, and candidosis. It is administered by intravenous injection, intravaginally, and topically; side-effects include itching, skin rash, and nausea and vomiting. Trade names: **Daktarin, Gynodaktarin**.

咪康唑　治療真菌感染如頭皮、身體和足部癬病，以及念珠菌病的一種藥物。可靜脈注射，陰道內或皮膚表面用藥。副作用包括瘙癢、皮疹、惡心和嘔吐。商品名：Daktarin，Gynodaktarin。

micr- (micro-) *prefix denoting* **1.** small size. **2.** one millionth part.

〔前綴〕(1) 小　(2) 微　百萬分之一。

microaerophilic *adj.* describing microorganisms that grow best at very low oxygen concentrations (i.e. below the atmospheric level).

微需氧的　描述在氧濃度極低時（即：低於大氣壓水平）生長最佳的微生物。

microaneurysm *n.* a minute localized swelling of a capillary wall, which is found in the retina of patients with diabetic *retinopathy. It is recognized as a small red dot when the interior of the eye is examined with an *ophthalmoscope.

微動脈瘤　毛細血管壁的局限性小腫物可見於糖尿病性視網膜病病人視網膜內。眼底鏡檢查眼內時，呈一小紅點。

microangiopathy *n.* damage to the walls of the smallest blood vessels. It may result from a variety of diseases, including diabetes mellitus, connective-tissue diseases, infections, and cancer. Some common manifestations of microangiopathy are kidney failure, haemolysis (damage to red blood cells), and purpura (bleeding into the skin). The treatment is that of the underlying cause.

微血管病　最小血管壁的損傷。它可由多種疾病引起，其中包括糖尿病、結締組織病、感染和癌症。一些常見的微血管病的表現有腎功能衰竭、溶血（紅細胞損傷）和紫癜（皮下出血）。治療針對原發病。

microbe *n. see* microorganism.

微生物　參閱 microorganism。

microbiology *n.* the science of *microorganisms. Microbiology in relation to medicine is concerned mainly with the isolation and identification of the microorganisms that cause disease. **–microbiological** *adj.* **–microbiologist** *n.*

微生物學　關於微生物的科學。與醫學有關的微生物學主要研究致病微生物的分離和鑒定。

microblepharon (microblepharism) *n.* the condition of having abnormally small eyelids.

小（眼）瞼　眼瞼異常小。

microcephaly *n.* abnormal smallness of the head in relation to the size of the rest of the body: a congenital condition in which the brain is not fully developed. *Compare* macrocephaly.

小頭　相對於身體其他部位的大小，頭部異常小。這是一種腦未充分發育的先天性疾病。與 macrocephaly 對比。

microcheilia *n.* abnormally small size of the lips. *Compare* macrocheilia.

小唇　唇異常小。與 macrocheilia 對比。

Micrococcus *n.* a genus of spherical Gram-positive bacteria occurring in colonies. They are saprophytes or parasites. The species *M. tetragenus* (formerly *Gaffkya tetragena*) is normally a harmless parasite in man but it can become pathogenic, causing arthritis, endocarditis, meningitis, or abscesses in tissues. It occurs in groups of four.

微球菌屬　以菌落存在的一屬革蘭氏陰性球形菌。為腐物寄生物或寄生物。其中一種四聯細球菌（以前稱四聯球菌）正常情況下是人體無害寄生物，但可變成致病菌，引起關節炎、心內膜炎、腦（脊）膜炎或組織膿腫。它以四個一組的形式存在。

microcyte *n.* an abnormally small red blood cell (*erythrocyte). *See also* microcytosis. **–microcytic** *adj.*

小紅細胞　異常小的紅細胞。參閱 microcytosis。

microcytosis *n.* the presence of abnormally small red cells (*microcytes*) in the blood. Microcytosis is a feature of certain anaemias (*microcytic anaemias*), including iron-deficiency anaemias, certain *haemoglobinopathies, anaemias associated with chronic infections, etc.

小紅細胞症　血中有異常小的紅細胞。小紅細胞是某些貧血（小紅細胞性貧血）的一個特點，其中有缺鐵性貧血、某種血紅蛋白病、與慢性感染有關的貧血等等。

microdactyly *n.* abnormal smallness or shortness of the fingers.

細指（趾）　指（趾）異常小短。

microdiscectomy *n.* surgical removal of all or part of a *prolapsed intervertebral disc using an *operating microscope, a very short incision, and very fine instruments that can be inserted between the individual vertebrae of the backbone. The procedure is used to relieve pressure on spinal nerve roots or on the spinal cord caused by protrusion of the pulpy matter of the disc (*nucleus pulposus*). This is a form of *minimally invasive surgery.

顯微椎間盤切除術　使用手術顯微鏡，通過一個小切口和可插入脊柱每個椎骨間的細小器械，手術切除部分或全部脱出的椎間盤。此手術可用於解除椎間盤髓質（髓核）突出造成的對脊神經根或脊髓的壓迫。這是最少侵入的外科手術。

microdissection *n.* the process of dissecting minute structures under the microscope. Miniature surgical instruments, such as knives made of glass, are manipulated by means of geared connections that reduce the relatively coarse movements of the operator's fingers into microscopic movements, Using this technique it is possible to dissect the nuclei of cells and even to separate individual chromosomes. *See also* microsurgery.

顯微解剖　通過顯微鏡解剖細微結構的過程。微型外科器械，如玻璃刀是通過把手術者手指相對粗大的動作轉變為細微動作的傳動裝置來操縱的。使用這種技術，可以解剖細胞核，甚至分離單個染色體。參閱 microsurgery。

microdochectomy *n.* an exploratory operation on the mammary ducts, usually to detect (or exclude) the presence of a suspected tumour.

顯微乳管探查術　乳腺管的一種探查手術，常用於檢出（或排出）可疑腫瘤的存在。

microdontia *n.* a condition in which the teeth are unusually small.

小牙　牙齒異常小。

microelectrode *n.* an extremely fine wire used as an electrode to measure the electrical activity in small areas of tissue. Microelectrodes can be used for recording the electrical changes that occur in the membranes of cells, such as those of nerve and muscle.

微電極　一根極其微細的電綫，用作電極來測量小面積組織內電活動。微電極可用於記錄細胞膜內，如神經和肌肉細胞膜內的電變化。

microfilaria *n.* (*pl.* **microfilariae**) the motile embryo of certain nematodes (*see* filaria). The slender microfilariae, 150–300μm in length, are commonly found in the circulating blood or lymph of patients suffering an infection with any of the filarial worms, e.g. *Wuchereria*. They mature into larvae, which are infective, within the body of a bloodsucking insect, such as a mosquito.

微絲蚴　某些綫蟲可活動的胚胎（參閱 filaria）。纖細的微絲蚴，長度為 150~300μm，常見於任何一種絲蟲（如吳策綫蟲屬）感染的病人的循環血液和淋巴中。牠們在吸血昆蟲（如蚊子）體內成熟為有感染性的幼蟲。

microgamete *n.* the motile flagellate male sex cell of the malarial parasite (*Plasmodium*) and other single-celled animals (*see* Protozoa). The microgamete is similar to the sperm cell of higher animal groups and smaller than the female sex cell (*see* macrogamete).

小配子　瘧疾寄生物（瘧原蟲屬）和其他單細胞動物（參閱 Protozoa）能活動的有鞭毛的雄性性細胞。小配子類似於較高級動物的精子細胞，但小於雌性性細胞（參閱 macrogamete）。

microgametocyte *n.* a cell that undergoes meiosis to form 6–8 mature male sex cells (microgametes) of the malarial parasite (*see* Plasmodium). Microgametocytes are found in the blood of man but must be ingested by a mosquito before developing into microgametes.

小配子體　經過減數分裂，形成 6~8 個成熟的雄性性細胞（小配子）的瘧疾寄生物（參閱 Plasmodium）的一種細胞。小配子體見於人血中，但必須被蚊子吞入，然後才能發育為小配子。

microglia *n.* one of the two basic classes of *glia (the non-nervous cells of the central nervous system), having a mainly scavenging function (*see* macrophage). *Compare* macroglia.

小神經膠質（細胞）　兩類基本的神經膠質（中樞神經系統的非神經細胞），具有主要的清除功能（參閱 macrophage）。與 macroglia 對比。

microglossia *n.* abnormally small size of the tongue.

小舌　舌異常小。

micrognathia *n.* a condition in which one or both jaws are unusually small.

小頜　頜異常小。

microgram *n.* one millionth of a gram. Symbol: μg.

微克　一克的百萬分之一。符號：μg。

micrograph (photomicrograph) *n.* a photograph of an object as viewed through a microscope. An *electron micrograph* is photographed through an electron microscope; a *light micrograph* through a light microscope.

顯微照片　通過顯微鏡觀察到的物體的照片。電子顯微照片是通過電子顯微鏡拍攝的，光學顯微照片是通過光學顯微鏡拍攝的。

microgyria *n.* a developmental disorder of the brain in which the folds (convolutions) in its surface are small and its surface layer (cortex) is structurally abnormal. It is associated with mental and physical retardation.

腦迴小　腦表面褶（腦迴）小而且其表面層（皮質）結構異常的一種腦發育疾病。伴有智力和體力低下。

microhaematocrit *n.* a measurement of the proportion of red blood cells in a volume of circulating blood. It is determined by taking a sample of the patient's blood in a fine tube and spinning it in a centrifuge until settling is complete. *See* packed cell volume.

微量紅細胞比容　一定容量的循環血液中紅細胞所占比例的一種測量方法。測量方法是將病人血樣採集在一細管內，將小管在離心機上旋轉直至完全沉澱。參閱　packed cell volume。

micromanipulation *n.* the manipulation of extremely small structures under the microscope, as in *microdissection, or *microsurgery.

顯微操作　通過顯微鏡，在極其小的結構上操作，如顯微解剖，或顯微手術。

micromelia *n.* abnormally small size of the arms or legs. *Compare* macromelia.

四肢短小　手臂或腿的長度小於正常。與　macromelia　對比。

micrometastasis *n.* a secondary tumour that is undetectable by clinical examination or diagnostic tests.

轉移癌　臨床檢查或診斷測試中發現不了的繼發性腫瘤。

micrometer *n.* an instrument for making extremely fine measurements of thickness or length, often relying upon the movement of a screw thread and the principle of the *vernier.

測微計　一種常借助於螺紋的運動和游標尺原理來極其精確地測量厚度或長度的儀器。

micrometre *n.* one millionth of a metre (10^{-6} m). Symbol: μm.

微米　　百萬分之一米（10^{-6} m）。符號：μm。

microorganism (microbe) *n.* any organism too small to be visible to the naked eye. Microorganisms include *bacteria, some *fungi, *mycoplasmas, *protozoa, *rickettsiae, and *viruses.

微生物　由於太小而無法用肉眼看到的任何生物體。微生物包括細菌、某些種類的真菌、支原體、原生動物、立克次體和病毒。

microphotograph *n.* **1.** a photograph reduced to microscopic proportions. **2.** (loosely) a *photomicrograph.

(1) 縮微照片　一種縮小到微觀比例的照片。**(2)**（泛指）顯微照片

micropipette *n.* an extremely fine tube from which minute volumes of liquid can be delivered. It can also be used to draw up minute quantities of liquid for examination. Using a micropipette it is possible to add or take away material from individual cells under the microscope.

微量管　用來輸送微量液體的極細管，也可用來吸取小量液體供檢查用。使用微量管可在顯微鏡下給單個細胞添加物質或從中取走物質。

micropsia *n.* a condition in which objects appear smaller than they really are. It is usually due to disease of the retina affecting the *macula but may occur in paralysis of *accommodation.

視物顯小症　所視物體比其實際尺寸要小的病態。此病通常由影響黃斑的視網膜疾病引起，但也可發生於調節麻痺。

microscope *n.* an instrument for producing a greatly magnified image of an object, which may be so small as to be invisible to the naked eye. *Light or optical microscopes* use light as a radiation source for viewing the specimen and combinations of lenses to magnify the image; these are usually an *objective and an *eyepiece. *See also* electron microscope, operating microscope, ultramicroscope. **–microscopical** *adj.* **–microscopy** *n.*

顯微鏡　一種使物體圖像高度放大的儀器，該物體可能很小，肉眼無法看到。光學顯微鏡用光作為射綫源來觀察標本，用組合在一起的透鏡來放大圖像。這些透鏡通常有一個物鏡和一個目鏡。參閱 electron microscope，operating microscope，ultramicroscope。

microscopic *adj.* **1.** too small to be seen clearly without the use of a microscope. **2.** of, relating to, or using a microscope.

(1) 顯微的　小到不使用顯微鏡就看不清楚的。**(2)** 顯微鏡的，和顯微鏡相關的，使用顯微鏡的

microsome *n.* a small particle consisting of a piece of *endoplasmic reticulum to which ribosomes are attached. Microsomes are formed when homogenized cells are centrifuged. **–microsomal** *adj.*

微粒體 由一小塊附着有核糖體的內質網組織構成的小微粒。勻化細胞被離心時形成微粒體。

microsonation *n.* the use of ultrasound waves generated inside the body from an extremely small source, such as the tip of a needle or a bubble within the tissues. This technique is used to obtain a picture of the fine structure of the neighbouring tissues. It is a specialized form of *ultrasonography.

微超聲檢查法 體內極小聲源（例如針尖或組織內的氣泡等）產生的超聲波的使用。這一技術用於獲取鄰近組織的細微結構圖像。它是超聲描記術的一種特殊形式。

Microsporum *n.* a genus of fungi causing *ringworm. *See also* dermatophyte.

小孢子菌屬 一類引起癬菌病的真菌。參閱 dermatophyte。

microsurgery *n.* the branch of surgery in which extremely intricate operations are performed through highly refined *operating microscopes using miniaturized precision instruments (forceps, scissors, needles, etc.). The technique enables surgery of previously inaccessible parts of the eye, inner ear, spinal cord, and brain (e.g. for the removal of tumours and repair of cerebral aneurysms), as well as the reattachment of amputated fingers (necessitating the suturing of minute nerves and blood vessels) and the reversal of vasectomies.

顯微外科 通過精度極高的手術顯微鏡，使用微型精密儀器（鑷子、剪子、針等）來完成極複雜手術的一個外科分支。這項技術使得外科手術能夠在眼睛、內耳、脊髓和腦的從前不能手術的部分進行（例如切除腫瘤和修復腦動脈瘤），也使斷指再植（縫合小神經和血管時是必需的）和輸精管切斷後的接通成為可能。

microsurgical epididymal sperm aspiration (Mesa) the removal of spermatozoa from the epididymis by needle *aspiration. This procedure, performed under anaesthetic, may be undertaken to assist conception in cases where the normal passage of sperm from the testis is obstructed, for example by blockage (through infection) of the ducts or by vasectomy. The extracted sperm are subjected to special treatment to select the

顯微外科附睾精液吸引術 通過針刺吸引術從附睾中取出精子。此技術在麻醉下進行，用來幫助精子從睾丸的正常排出受阻的病例受孕，如輸精管阻塞（因為感染）或輸精管切除術。抽取出來的精液要進行特殊處理，挑選最強健和活動性最大的精子，然後再進行化學處理來激活和用於試管受精。

strongest and most motile; these are then chemically treated to activate them and used for *in vitro fertilization.

microtome *n.* an instrument for cutting extremely thin slices of material that can be examined under a microscope. The material is usually embedded in a suitable medium, such as paraffin wax. A common type of microtome is a steel knife.

切片機　用於把材料切成能夠在顯微鏡下檢查的超薄片的儀器。所切材料通常包埋在一個合適的培養基中，例如包埋在石蠟中，常見的切片機是不銹鋼刀片。

microvascular *adj.* involving small vessels. The term is often applied to techniques of *microsurgery for reuniting small blood vessels (the same techniques are applied frequently to nerve suture).

微血管的　涉及小血管的。此術語常用於顯微外科技術中小血管的吻合（該技術也頻繁用於神經縫合）。

microvillus *n.* (*pl.* **microvilli**) one of a number of microscopic hairlike structures (about 5μm long) projecting from the surface of epithelial cells (*see* epithelium). They serve to increase the surface area of the cell and are seen on absorptive and secretory cells. In some regions (particularly the intestinal tract) microvilli form a dense covering on the free surface of the cells: this is called a *brush border*.

微絨毛　上皮細胞（參閱 epithelium）表面突出的顯微毛髮樣結構的一種（長約 5μm）。它們有助於增加細胞的表面積，在吸收和分泌細胞上可看到。在有些部位（特別是腸道），微絨毛在細胞的游離面上形成一個致密的覆蓋層，稱為刷狀緣。

microwave therapy a form of *diathermy using electromagnetic waves of extremely short wavelength. In modern apparatus the electric currents induced in the tissues have frequencies of up to 25,000 million cycles per second.

微波療法　一種使用波長極短的電磁波的透熱療法。用現代儀器，組織中產生的感應電頻率可達到每秒 250 億周。

micturition *n. see* urination.

排尿　參閱 urination。

midazolam *n.* a *benzodiazepine drug used as a sedative for minor surgery, as a premedication, and to induce general anaesthesia. It is administered by injection. Possible side-effects include headache, dizziness, and difficulty in breathing. Trade name: **Hypnovel**.

咪達唑侖　一種苯二氮䓬類藥，用作小手術鎮靜劑，術前用藥和誘導全身麻醉。注射給藥。可能產生的副作用有頭痛、頭暈和呼吸困難。商品名：Hypnovel。

midbrain (mesencephalon) *n.* the small portion of the *brainstem, excluding the pons and the medulla, that joins the hindbrain to the forebrain.

中腦　腦幹的一小部分，不包括連接後腦和前腦的腦橋和延髓。

middle ear (tympanic cavity) the part of the *ear that consists of an air-filled space within the petrous part of the temporal bone. It is lined with mucous membrane and is connected to the pharynx by the *Eustachian tube and to the outer ear by the eardrum (*tympanic membrane). Within the middle ear are three bones – the auditory *ossicles – which transmit sound vibrations from the outer ear to the inner ear (*see* labyrinth).

中耳（耳室腔）　顳骨岩部內由含氣腔構成的耳部分。中耳內壁有黏膜覆蓋，借助咽鼓管與咽腔連接，借助鼓膜與外耳連接。中耳內有三塊骨，即聽小骨，它們把聲波由外耳傳向內耳（參閱 labyrinth）。

midgut *n.* the middle portion of the embryonic gut, which gives rise to most of the small intestine and part of the large intestine. Early in development it is connected with the *yolk sac outside the embryo via the *umbilicus.

中腸　產生大部分小腸和部分大腸的胚胎腸的中間部分。在發育早期，它憑借臍與胚胎外面的卵黃囊相連。

midwifery *n.* the profession of providing assistance and medical care to women undergoing labour and childbirth. *See also* domiciliary midwife, obstetrics. **–midwife** *n.*

助產學　給臨床和分娩的婦女提供幫助和醫療的專業。參閱 domiciliary midwife，obstetrics。

mifepristone *n.* a drug used to produce an abortion within the first 63 days of pregnancy: it acts by blocking the action of *progesterone, which is essential for maintaining pregnancy. If a second drug, one of the prostaglandins (e.g. *gemeprost), is taken within 48 hours to complete the expulsion of the fertilized egg cell, the method is said to be 95% effective.

米非司酮　一種用來在懷孕最初 63 天內引產的藥物：此藥通過抑制維持懷孕所必需的孕酮而起作用。如果第二種藥，即前列腺素的一種（吉美前列素），在 48 小時內服用以完成受精卵細胞的排除，據報導該法的成功率為 95%。

migraine *n.* a recurrent throbbing headache that characteristically affects one side of the head. There is sometimes forewarning of an attack (an *aura*)

偏頭痛　一種反覆發作的跳動性頭痛，其特點為影響頭的一側。有時有發作先兆，如視力障礙或麻木及/或肢體無力。

consisting of visual disturbance or numbness and/or weakness of the limbs, which clear up as the headache develops. It is often accompanied by prostration and vomiting. Effective preventive therapies now exist and drugs such as *sumatriptan may be used to treat acute attacks.

頭痛出現後這些先兆會消失。偏頭痛常伴有虛脫或嘔吐。現已有了有效的預防性療法，像舒馬坦這樣的藥物可用來治療急性發作。

Mikulicz's disease damage to the lacrimal and salivary glands resulting in enlargement of these glands, narrowing of the corners of the eyes, conjunctivitis, and dryness of the mouth. The cause may be autoimmune disease or malignancy.

米庫利奇病　淚腺和唾液腺損害，可導致這些腺體增大、眼角狹窄、結膜炎和口乾。病因可能是自體免疫疾病或惡性腫瘤。

miliaria *n. see* prickly heat.

粟疹，痱子　參閱 prickly heat。

miliary *adj.* describing or characterized by very small nodules or lesions, resembling millet seed.

粟粒性的　描述或特徵為非常小的結節或損害，類似小米粒。

miliary tuberculosis acute generalized *tuberculosis characterized by lesions in affected organs, which resemble millet seeds.

粟粒性結核　急性全身性結核，其特點為受累器官內有類似小米粒的損害。

milium *n.* (*pl.* **milia**) a white nodule in the skin, particularly on the face. Up to 4 mm in diameter, milia are tiny *keratin cysts occurring just beneath the outer layer (epidermis) of the skin. Milia are commonly seen in newborn babies around the nose; they disappear without active treatment.

粟粒疹　皮膚，特別是面部皮膚的白色小結。粟粒疹直徑可達 4 mm，是緊靠皮膚外層（表皮）下出現的小的角蛋白囊腫。粟粒疹常見於新生兒鼻部周圍，無需主動治療即可消失。

milk *n.* the liquid food secreted by female mammals from the mammary gland. It is the sole source of food for the young of most mammals at the start of life. Milk is a complete food in that it has most of the nutrients necessary for life: protein, carbohydrate, fat, minerals, and vitamins. The composition of milk varies very much from mammal to mammal.

奶　雌性哺乳動物乳腺中分泌出來的液體食物，是大多數哺乳動物幼崽生命初期時唯一的食物源。奶是一種營養全面的食品，因為其中含有生命必需的大多數營養物質：蛋白質、碳水化合物、脂肪、礦物質和維生素。奶的成分因哺乳動物的種類不同變化很大。牛奶中

Cows' milk contains nearly all the essential nutrients but is comparatively deficient in vitamins C and D. Human milk contains more sugar (lactose) and less protein than cows' milk.

含有幾乎所有的基本營養物質，但是相對缺少維生素 C 和維生素 D。和牛奶相比，人奶中含有較多的糖（乳糖），但是蛋白質含量較少。

milk rash a spotty red facial rash that is common during the first few months of life; it disappears without treatment.

乳疹 出生頭幾個月內常見的點狀、紅色面部皮疹。無需治療即可消失。

milk teeth *Colloquial.* the deciduous teeth of young children. *See* dentition.

乳牙 （口頭語）幼兒的暫牙。參閱 dentition。

milli- *prefix denoting* one thousandth part.

〔前綴〕千分之一

milliampere *n.* one thousandth of an ampere (10^{-3} A). Symbol: mA.

毫安〔培〕 千分之一安培（10^{-3} A）。符號：mA。

milligram *n.* one thousandth of a gram. Symbol: mg.

毫克 千分之一克。符號：mg。

millilitre *n.* one thousandth of a litre. Symbol: ml. *See* litre.

毫升 千分之一升。符號：ml。參閱 litre。

millimetre *n.* one thousandth of a metre (10^{-3} m). Symbol: mm.

毫米 千分之一米（10^{-3} m）。符號：mm。

Milroy's disease *see* lymphoedema.

米爾羅伊病 參閱 lymphoedema。

Minamata disease a form of mercury poisoning (from ingesting methyl mercury in contaminated fish) that caused 43 deaths in the Japanese coastal town of Minamata during 1953–56. The source of mercury was traced to an effluent containing mercuric sulphate from a local PVC factory. Symptoms include numbness, difficulty in controlling the limbs, and impaired speech and hearing.

水俁病 1953 年至 1956 年間發生在日本沿海城鎮水俁鎮，引起 43 人死亡的一種汞中毒（因為食用含有甲基汞的污染魚類引起）。汞的來源是當地一家聚氯乙烯工廠排放的含有硫酸汞的污水。症狀包括麻木、四肢失控、語言和聽覺損傷。

MIND the National Association for Mental Health. It is a voluntary association, registered as a charity, that

國家精神衛生協會 （英國）一志願者協會，註冊為慈善機構，旨在通過建議、教育、運

promotes the welfare of those with *mental illness through advice, education, campaigning, and the provision of resources.

mineralocorticoid *n. see* corticosteroid.

minim *n.* a unit of volume used in pharmacy, equivalent to one sixtieth part of a fluid *drachm.

minimally invasive surgery surgical intervention involving the least possible physical trauma to the patient, particularly surgery performed using an operating laparoscope or other endoscope (*see* laparoscopy) passed through a tiny incision; it is known popularly as *keyhole surgery*. Several types of abdominal surgery, including gall bladder removal (*see* cholecystectomy) and extracorporeal shock-wave *lithotripsy for stones in the urinary or bile drainage system, are commonly performed in this way. Such methods usually allow the patient to resume normal activity much sooner than would be possible after more conventional procedures. *See also* interventional radiology.

minitracheostomy *n.* temporary *tracheostomy using a needle or fine-bore tube inserted through the skin.

minocycline *n.* a tetracycline antibiotic active against a wide range of bacteria and against rickettsial infections, mycoplasmal pneumonia, and relapsing fever. It is administered by mouth and by intravenous injection; side-effects include loss of appetite, skin rash, and dizziness. Trade name: **Minocin**.

minoxidil *n.* a peripheral vasodilator used in the treatment of high blood

動和提供物資來促進精神病患者的福利事業。

鹽（腎上腺）皮質激素 參閱 corticosteroid。

量滴 用於藥學的容量單位，等於一液量打蘭的六十分之一。

最小侵入外科 給病人造成最小身體損傷的外科介入，特別是通過一個小切口使用手術用腹腔鏡或其他內窺鏡（參閱 laparoscopy）進行的外科手術。常被稱作鎖഼外科。若干種腹部手術，包括膽囊切除術（參閱 cholecystectomy）和尿道及膽道系統結石體外衝擊波電震碎石術，常採用此法。和更為常規的方法相比較，此法通常可使病人更早地恢復正常的活動。參閱 interventional radiology。

最小氣管造口術 用針或毛細管通過皮膚插入的臨時氣管造口術。

米諾環素 四環素類抗生素，能有效地抑制廣譜細菌和治療克次體感染、支原體肺炎和回歸熱。口服或靜脈注射。副作用包括無食慾、皮疹及頭暈。商品名：Minocin。

米諾地爾 在其他藥物無效時用於治療高血壓的周圍血管舒

pressure (hypertension) when other drugs are not effective; it is administered by mouth in conjunction with a *diuretic. It is also applied to the scalp, in the form of a lotion, to restore hair growth. Side-effects include ECG changes and transient oedema. Trade names: **Loniten**, **Regaine**.

張藥。此藥和利尿劑一起口服。也可作為洗劑用於頭皮，以恢復頭髮生長。副作用包括心電圖改變和短暫的水腫。商品名：Loniten，Regaine。

mio- *prefix denoting* **1.** reduction or diminution. **2.** rudimentary.

〔前綴〕**(1)** 減少，縮小 **(2)** 原基的，已退化的

miosis (myosis) *n.* constriction of the pupil. This occurs normally in bright light, but persistent miosis is most commonly caused by certain types of eye drops used to treat glaucoma. *See also* miotic. *Compare* mydriasis.

瞳孔縮小 瞳孔的收縮。瞳孔縮小通常在光很亮時出現。但是持續的瞳孔縮小最常由用於治療青光眼的某些滴眼藥引起。參閱 miotic。與 mydriasis 對比。

miotic *n.* a drug that causes the pupil of the eye to contract. Miotics, such as *physostigmine and *pilocarpine, are used to counteract the dilation of the pupil caused by drugs such as ephedrine and phenylephrine and to reduce the pressure in the eye in the treatment of glaucoma.

縮瞳藥 使眼睛瞳孔收縮的藥物。縮瞳藥，如毒扁豆鹼和毛果芸香鹼，用於對抗諸如麻廣鹼和苯福林等藥物造成的瞳孔擴張。在治療青光眼時用於降低眼壓。

miracidium *n.* (*pl.* **miracidia**) the first-stage larva of a parasitic *fluke. Miracidia hatch from eggs released into water with the host's excreta. They have *cilia and swim about until they reach a snail. The miracidia then bore into the snail's soft tissues and there continue their development as *sporocysts.

毛蚴 寄生性吸蟲的第一階段幼蟲。毛蚴從隨着宿主的排泄物一起釋放到水中的卵裏孵出。牠們有纖毛，在水中游動直到接觸螺類。毛蚴接着鑽入螺體的軟組織並在那裏繼續發育成包蚴。

miscarriage *n. see* abortion.

流產 參閱 abortion。

miso- *prefix denoting* hatred. Example: *misopedia* (of children).

〔前綴〕厭惡，憎恨 如：厭子女症。

misoprostol *n.* a *prostaglandin drug used in the prevention and treatment of peptic ulcer caused by nonsteroidal

米索前列醇 一種前列腺素藥，用於預防和治療由非類固醇消炎藥引起的消化性潰瘍

anti-inflammatory drugs (*see* NSAID). It is administered by mouth. Possible side-effects include nausea, vomiting, diar-rhoea, and abdominal pain. Trade names: **Cytotec**, **Napratec**.

（參閱 NSAID）。口服。可能產生的副作用包括惡心、嘔吐、腹瀉和腹痛。商品名：Cytotec，Napratec。

missed case a person suffering from an infection in whom the symptoms and signs are so minimal that either there is no request for medical assistance or the doctor fails to make the diagnosis. The patient usually has partial immunity to the disease, but since the infecting organisms (pathogens) are of normal viru-lence, nonimmune contacts can be affected with the full manifestations of the illness. The period of infectivity is confined to the shortened duration of the illness (in contrast to a *carrier, in whom the pathogen is present without neces-sarily causing any ill effect). Alterna-tively the subject has had the disease but retains some of the pathogens (e.g. in the throat or bowel) and so acts as a contin-uing reservoir of infection.

漏診病例 傳染病患者身上的症狀和體徵如此之輕以致病人沒有求醫或者醫生未能做出診斷。病人對於該病通常有部分免疫力，但是因為致病菌（病原體）具有正常的毒力，沒有免疫力者接觸感染會產生疾病的全部表現。傳染期局限在縮短的病期內（與體內有病原體但不一定產生病症的帶菌者形成對比）。另一種情況是，病人已患過本病，但保留着一些病原體（如在喉或腸內），因此持續充當傳染貯主。

Misuse of Drugs Act 1971 (in the UK) an Act of Parliament restricting the use of dangerous drugs. These controlled drugs include the natural *opiates and their synthetic substitutes, many stimu-lants (including amphetamine, cocaine, and pemoline), and hallucinogens such as LSD and cannabis. The Act specifies certain requirements for writing pre-scriptions for these drugs. The Misuse of Drugs (Notification of and Supply to Addicts) Regulations (1973) and the Misuse of Drugs Regulations, which are updated from time to time, also lay down who may supply controlled drugs. Five categories of persons are defined.

濫用藥物條例 (1971) （英國）限制使用危險藥物的國會法令。被控制的藥物包括天然的阿片製劑以及它們的合成替代物、許多興奮劑（包括苯丙胺、可卡因和匹莫林）、致幻劑類藥如：麥角二乙胺和大麻。法令規定了開這些藥物處方的一些要求。濫用藥物的規定 (1973) 以及不斷增補的濫用藥物條例同樣規定了誰可以供應限制性藥物。五類人被列舉了出來。

mite *n.* a free-living or parasitic arthro-pod belonging to a group (Acarina) that

蟎 一種自由生存或寄生性的節肢動物，屬於亦包括蜱在內

also includes the *ticks. Most mites are small, averaging 1 mm or less in length. A mite has no antennae or wings, and its body is not divided into a distinct head, thorax, and abdomen. Medically important mites include the many species causing dermatitis (e.g. *Dermatophagoides*) and the harvest mite (*see* Trombicula), which transmits scrub typhus.

mithramycin (plicamycin) *n.* an antibiotic that prevents the growth of cancer cells. It was formerly used for treating certain forms of cancer but is now used only to reduce high levels of calcium in the blood. Common side-effects are digestive upsets and mouth ulcers and, more seriously, nosebleeds and vomiting of blood.

mitochondrion (chondriosome) *n.* (*pl.* **mitochondria**) a structure, occurring in varying numbers in the cytoplasm of every cell, that is the site of the cell's energy production. Mitochondria contain *ATP and the enzymes involved in the cell's metabolic activities; each is bounded by a double membrane, the inner being folded inwards to form projections (*cristae*). **–mitochondrial** *adj.*

mitogen *n.* any substance that can cause cells to begin division (*mitosis).

mitomycin C an antibiotic that inhibits the growth of cancer cells. It causes severe marrow suppression but is of use in the treatment of stomach and breast cancers. Trade name: **Mutamycin**.

mitosis *n.* a type of cell division in which a single cell produces two genetically identical daughter cells. It is the way in

的屬（蟎目）。多數蟎不大，平均長 1 mm 或更短。蟎無觸鬚和翼，身體沒有清楚地分成頭、胸和腹。有醫學意義的蟎包括許多可引起皮炎的蟎屬（例如：表皮蟎屬）及傳播恙蟲病的秋蟎（參閱 Trombicula）。

普卡黴素 一種防止癌細胞生長的抗生素。以前用於治療某些種類的癌症，但是現在僅用於降低血液中鈣的高濃度。常見副作用是消化不良和口腔潰瘍，更為嚴重的副作用是鼻出血和吐血。

綫粒體 以不同數目存在於每個細胞胞漿內的一種結構，是細胞能量生成的地方。綫粒體含有三磷酸腺苷和參與細胞代謝活動的酶；每個綫粒體都由一個雙層膜包裹，內膜向裏摺皺，構成突起。

有絲分裂原，促細胞分裂劑 能使細胞開始分裂（有絲分裂）的任何物質。

絲裂黴素 C 抑制癌細胞生長的一種抗生素。可引起嚴重的骨髓抑制，但用於治療胃癌和乳腺癌。商品名：Mutamycin。

有絲分裂 一個單細胞產生兩個基因相同的子細胞的細胞分裂類型。它是為了生長和修

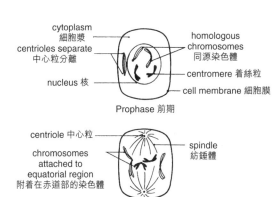

cytoplasm
細胞漿

centrioles separate
中心粒分離

nucleus 核

homologous
chromosomes
同源染色體

centromere 着絲粒

cell membrane 細胞膜

Prophase 前期

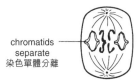

centriole 中心粒

chromosomes
attached to
equatorial region
附着在赤道部的染色體

spindle
紡錘體

Metaphase 中期

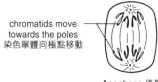

chromatids
separate
染色單體分離

Early anaphase 早後期

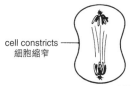

chromatids move
towards the poles
染色單體向極點移動

Anaphase 後期

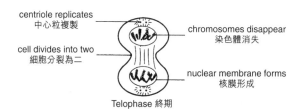

cell constricts
細胞縮窄

Late anaphase 晚後期

centriole replicates
中心粒複製

cell divides into two
細胞分裂為二

chromosomes disappear
染色體消失

nuclear membrane forms
核膜形成

Telophase 終期

Stages in mitosis
有絲分裂各期

which new body cells are produced for both growth and repair. Division of the nucleus (*karyokinesis*) takes place in four stages (*see* prophase, metaphase, anaphase, telophase) and is followed by division of the cytoplasm (*cytokinesis*) to form the two daughter cells (see illustration). *Compare* meiosis. **–mitotic** *adj.*

復而產生新體細胞的途徑。核分裂分為四個階段（參閱 prophase，metaphase，anaphase，telophase），之後是細胞漿的分裂（胞質分裂），形成兩個子細胞（見圖）。與 meiosis 對比。

mitotic index the proportion of cells in a tissue that are dividing at a given time.

有絲分裂指數 在一定時間內組織裏正在分裂的細胞比例。

mitoxantrone *n.* a drug used in the treatment of certain cancers, including breast cancer, leukaemia, and lymphomas. Side-effects are usually mild. Trade name: **Novantrone**.

米托蒽醌 一種藥物，用於治療包括乳腺癌、白血病和淋巴瘤在內的某些癌症。副作用通常很輕微。商品名：Novantrone。

mitral incompetence failure of the *mitral valve to close, allowing a reflux of blood from the left ventricle of the heart to the left atrium. It most often results from scarring of the mitral valve by rheumatic fever, but it can also develop as a complication of myocardial infarction or cardiomyopathies. It may occur as a congenital defect. Its manifestations include breathlessness, atrial *fibrillation, embolism, enlargement of the left ventricle, and a systolic *murmur. Mild cases are symptomless and require no treatment, but in severe cases the affected valve should be replaced with an artificial one (*mitral prosthesis*).

二尖瓣關閉不全 二尖瓣膜不能關閉，使血液從心臟的左心室返流到左心房。其最常見的病因是風濕熱引起的二尖瓣瘢痕形成，但也能發展成心肌梗死或心肌病的併發症。它可作為先天性缺陷。其表現包括氣短、心房纖維性顫動、栓塞、左心室擴大和收縮期雜音。輕者無症狀，無需治療，但是重者應用人工瓣膜更換受累瓣膜。

mitral stenosis narrowing of the opening of the mitral valve: a result of chronic scarring that follows rheumatic fever. It may be seen alone or combined with *mitral incompetence. The symptoms are similar to those of mitral incompetence except that the patient has a diastolic *murmur. Mild cases need no treatment, but severe cases are treated surgically by reopening the stenosis

二尖瓣狹窄 二尖瓣開口變窄，為風濕熱後的慢性瘢痕形成所致。可單獨存在或與二尖瓣關閉不全一起存在。患者除有舒張期雜音外，病症和二尖瓣關閉不全相似。輕者無需治療，但重者則需要手術切開狹窄或裝上人工瓣膜來治療。

(*mitral valvotomy*) or by inserting an artificial valve (*mitral prosthesis*).

mitral valve (bicuspid valve) a valve in the heart consisting of two flaps (cusps) attached to the walls at the opening between the left atrium and left ventricle. It allows blood to pass from the atrium to the ventricle, but prevents any backward flow.

二尖瓣　附着在心臟左心房的左心室之間的開口壁上的、由兩個小片（瓣尖）構成的心臟瓣膜。它可使血液從心房流向心室，但阻止任何回流。

mittelschmerz *n.* pain in the lower abdomen experienced about midway between successive menstrual periods, i.e. when the egg cell is being released from the ovary. *See also* menstrual cycle.

經間痛　在兩次相連的月經的大約中間所感到的下腹痛，例如：當卵細胞從卵巢中排出時。參閱 menstrual cycle。

mixed connective tissue disease a disease with many features in common with systemic *lupus erythematosus, *polymyositis, and *scleroderma. Some authorities dispute its status as a separate entity.

混合性結締組織病　許多特點與系統性紅斑狼瘡、多肌炎和硬皮病相同的一種疾病。有些專家對把它當作單獨的病種持有異議。

ml *abbrev. for* millilitre. See litre.

〔縮寫〕毫升　參閱 litre。

MLC (MLR) mixed lymphocyte culture (or reaction): a test in which lymphocytes from prospective donor and recipient are cultured together in a test tube to assess the suitability of transplanting organs or bone marrow cells.

混合淋巴細胞培養（混合淋巴細胞反應）　把預期的供體和受體的淋巴細胞一起在一個試管內培養，用以評估器官移植或骨髓細胞移植的適應性試驗。

MLD minimal lethal dose: the smallest quantity of a toxic compound that is recorded as having caused death. *See also* LD_{50}.

最小致死量　根據記載能造成死亡的毒性化合物的最小量。參閱 LD_{50}。

MLR *see* MLC.

混合淋巴細胞反應　參閱 MLC。

MM malignant melanoma (*see* melanoma).

惡性黑素瘤　（參閱 melanoma）。

mmHg a unit of pressure equal to 1 millimetre of mercury. 1 mmHg = 133.3224 pascals.

毫米汞柱 等於 1 毫米汞的壓力單位。1 毫米汞柱 = 133.3224 帕斯卡。

MMR vaccine a combined vaccine against measles, mumps, and German measles (rubella). It is now recommended that this vaccine is given to all children between 12 and 15 months old. Specific contraindications include immunosuppression, allergy to neomycin, and anaphylactic reaction to eggs.

麻疹、流行性腮腺炎和風疹疫苗 用於防治麻疹、流行性腮腺炎和風疹的聯合疫苗。這種疫苗現在已經被推薦給 12~15 個月的所有兒童使用。具體的禁忌症包括免疫抑制、新黴素過敏及蛋類過敏反應。

MND *see* motor neurone disease.

運動神經元疾病 參閱 motor neurone disease。

moclobemide *n.* an antidepressant drug that reversibly inhibits the enzyme monoamine oxidase. The adverse effects of existing *MAO inhibitors, which include severe reactions when cheese or other tyramine-containing foods are eaten by patients taking them, are less likely with reversible inhibitors.

摩氯苯胺 可逆性抑制單胺氧化酶的抗抑鬱藥。現有的單胺氧化酶抑制劑的副作用包括服用此類藥物的病人食用奶酪或其他含酪胺的食物後產生生嚴重反應，但這些副作用在服用可逆性抑制劑後不大可能出現。

modality *n.* **1.** a form of sensation, such as smell, hearing, tasting, or detecting temperature. Differences in modality are not due to differences in the structure of the nerves concerned, but to differences in the working of the sensory receptors and the areas of brain that receive the messages. **2.** one form of therapy as opposed to another, such as the modality of physiotherapy contrasted with that of radiotherapy.

(1) 感覺模式 一種感覺方式，例如：嗅、聽、味或溫度感。感覺模式的差異不是因為相關的神經結構的不同，而是因為感覺接受器的功能和接受信息的大腦區域不同。**(2) 治療模式** 與另外一種療法相反的治療模式，例如物理療法模式和放射療法模式完全不同。

mode *n.* *see* mean.

眾數 參閱 mean。

Modecate *n.* *see* fluphenazine.

氟非那嗪，氟奮乃靜 參閱 fluphenazine。

modelling *n.* a technique used in *behaviour modification, whereby an individual learns a behaviour by observing someone

模擬法 一種用於改變行為的技術。通過觀察他人做事的方式來學習一種行為。這種方式

else doing it. Together with *prompting, it is useful for introducing new behaviours to the individual.

加上激勵，對於個人學習新行為是有用的。

modiolus *n.* the conical central pillar of the *cochlea in the inner ear.

蝸軸　內耳蝸的圓錐形中心柱。

Moduretic *n. see* amiloride.

鹽酸氨氯吡咪　參閱 amiloride。

Mogadon *n. see* nitrazepam.

硝基安定　參閱 nitrazepam。

molar *n.* in the permanent *dentition, the sixth, seventh, or eighth tooth from the midline on each side in each jaw (*see also* wisdom tooth). In the deciduous dentition, molars are the fourth and fifth teeth from the midline on each side in each jaw.

磨牙　在恆牙列中從上下頜中綫數起，每邊第六、七或八顆牙（參閱 wisdom tooth）。在暫牙列中，磨牙是從上下頜中綫數起每邊第四和第五顆牙。

molarity *n.* the strength of a solution, expressed as the weight of dissolved substance in grams per litre divided by its molecular weight, i.e. the number of moles per litre. Molarity is indicated as 0.1 M, 1 M, 2 M, etc.

體積克分子濃度　溶液的濃度，以每升中克單位溶質的重量除以其分子量來表示，即每升的克分子數。體積克分子濃度表示為 0.1 M，1 M，2 M 等。

molar solution a solution in which the number of grams of dissolved substance per litre equals its molecular weight, i.e. a solution of molarity 1 M.

容積克分子溶液　一種每升中溶質的克數等於其分子量的溶液，即體積克分子濃度等於 1 M 的溶液。

mole[1] *n.* the *SI unit of amount of substance, equal to the amount of substance that contains as many elementary units as there are atoms in 0.012 kilograms of carbon-12. The elementary units, which must be specified, may be atoms, molecules, ions, electrons, etc, or a specified group of such entities. One mole of a compound has a mass equal to its molecular weight expressed in grams. Symbol: mol.

摩爾　物質量的國際單位，等於含有和 0.012 千克的 ^{12} 碳中原子數一樣多的基本單位的物質量。必須具體説明的是，基本單位可以是原子、分子、離子、電子等，或這類物體的特定組合。1 摩爾的化合物的質量等於以克表示的該化合物的分子量。符號：mol。

mole² *n.* a nonmalignant collection of pigmented cells in the skin. Moles are rare in infancy, increase in numbers during childhood and especially in adolescence, but decline in numbers in old age. They vary widely in appearance, being flat or raised, smooth or hairy. Changes in the shape, colour, etc., of moles in adult life should be investigated as this may be an early sign of malignant *melanoma. Medical name: **melanotic naevus**. *See also* atypical mole syndrome.

痣 皮膚中色素細胞的非惡性集合。痣在嬰兒期少見，兒童期，特別是青春期數目增加，但進入老年期數目減少。痣在外型上區別很大，有扁平的、凸起的、平滑的或長毛的等。在成年人中，痣的形狀、顏色等發生變化應檢查，因為這有可能是惡性黑素瘤的早期體徵。醫學名：黑素痣。參閱 atypical mole syndrome。

molecular biology the study of the molecules that are associated with living organisms, especially proteins and nucleic acids.

分子生物學 與生物，特別是蛋白質和核酸相關的分子的研究。

molluscum contagiosum a common disease of the skin, mainly affecting children. Characterized by papules less than 5 mm in diameter, each with a central depression, the disease is caused by a *poxvirus and is spread by direct contact. Untreated, the papules disappear in 6–9 months.

傳染性軟疣 一種常見皮膚病，主要侵襲兒童。特徵為皮膚出現直徑小於 5mm、中間有凹陷的丘疹。由痘病毒所致，通過直接接觸傳染。丘疹在 6~9 個月內無需治療即可消失。

mon- (mono-) *prefix denoting* one, single, or alone.

〔前綴〕一個，單個或單獨

Mongolian blue spots blue-black pigmented areas seen at the base of the back and on the buttocks of babies. They are more common in Asian babies and usually fade during the first year of life.

蒙古青斑 可見於幼兒背底和臀部的青黑色色素區。常見於亞洲幼兒，通常在出生的第一年內消失。

mongolism *n.* *see* Down's syndrome.

先天愚型 參閱 Down's syndrome。

Monilia *n.* the former name of the genus of yeasts now known as *Candida.

念珠菌屬 念珠菌屬真菌的舊名，現稱為 Candida。

moniliasis *n.* an obsolete name for *candidosis.

念珠菌病 candidosis 的廢用名。

monoamine oxidase (MAO) an enzyme that catalyses the oxidation of a large variety of monoamines, including adrenaline, noradrenaline, and serotonin. Monoamine oxidase is found in most tissues, particularly the liver and nervous system. Drugs that act as inhibitors of this enzyme are widely used in the treatment of depression (*see* MAO inhibitor).

單胺氧化酶 用於催化包括腎上腺素、去甲腎上腺素和血清素等許多種類不同的單胺酶。單胺氧化酶可見於大多數組織中,特別是肝臟及神經系統。這種酶的抑制劑被廣泛用於治療抑鬱症(參閱 MAO inhibitor)。

monoarthritis *n. see* arthritis.

單關節炎 參閱 arthritis。

monoblast *n.* the earliest identifiable cell that gives rise to a *monocyte. It is probably identical with the *myeloblast and matures via an intermediate stage (*promonocyte*). It is normally found in the blood-forming tissue of the *bone marrow but may appear in the blood in certain diseases, most notably in acute monoblastic *leukaemia.

成單核細胞 能生長成單核細胞的最早可識別細胞。它可能和成髓細胞相同,並通過中間階段(前單核細胞)成熟。正常情況下見於骨髓的造血組織,但可出現在某些疾病患者的血液中,在急性成單核細胞性白血病中最典型。

monochromat *n.* a person who is completely colour-blind. There are two types. *The rod monochromat* apprears to have totally defective *cones: he has very poor visual acuity as well as the inability to discriminate colours. The *cone monochromat* has normal visual acuity: his cones appear to respond normally to light but to be completely unable to discriminate colours. It is possible in this case that the defect does not lie in the cones themselves but in the integration of the nerve impulses as they pass from the cones to the brain. Both types of colour blindness are probably inherited.

全色盲者 完全色盲的人。有兩類。視桿細胞性全盲者表示出完全有缺陷的視錐:患者視敏度很差且不能區別顏色。視錐細胞性全色盲者視敏度正常:患者的錐體對光表現出正常反應,但不能區分顏色。在這兩種病例中,缺陷可能不在於錐體本身,而是神經衝動從視錐傳往大腦的整合作用。兩種色盲可能都是遺傳的。

monoclonal antibody an antibody produced artificially from a cell *clone and therefore consisting of a single type of immunoglobulin. Monoclonal antibodies are produced by fusing antibody-forming lymphocytes from mouse spleen with

單克隆抗體 從一個細胞無性繁殖人工生產的並因此由一個類型免疫球蛋白構成的抗體。單克隆抗體通過融合鼠脾中的抗體生成淋巴細胞和鼠骨髓瘤細胞而形成。由此產生的雜交

mouse myeloma cells. The resulting hybrid cells multiply rapidly (like cancer cells) and produce the same antibody as their parent lymphocytes.

細胞繁殖很快（像癌細胞一樣）並產生與母體本淋巴細胞相同的抗體。

monocular adj. relating to or used by one eye only. Compare binocular.

單眼的 僅和一隻眼相關或供一隻眼使用的。與 binocular 對比。

monocyte n. a variety of white blood cell, 16–20μm in diameter, that has a kidney-shaped nucleus and greyish-blue cytoplasm (when treated with *Romanowsky stains). Its function is the ingestion of foreign particles, such as bacteria and tissue debris. There are normally 0.2–0.8 × 10^9 monocytes per litre of blood. **–monocytic** adj.

單核細胞 直徑在 16~20μm，有腎形核和灰藍色胞漿的白細胞（用羅曼諾夫斯基染色法處理時）。其功能為吞噬異物微粒，如細菌和組織細屑。每升血液中正常時有 0.2~0.8 × 10^9 個單核細胞。

monocytosis n. an increase in the number of *monocytes in the blood. It occurs in a variety of diseases, including certain leukaemias (monocytic leukaemias) and infections due to some bacteria and protozoa.

單核細胞增多症 血液中單核細胞數的增加。它可產生於許多疾病之中，包括某些白血病（單核細胞性白血病）及由細菌和原生動物造成的感染。

monodactylism n. the congenital absence of all but one digit on each hand and foot.

單指（趾）（畸形） 每隻手和腳上先天性除了一個指（趾）外其餘缺失。

monoiodotyrosine n. an iodine-containing substance produced in the thyroid gland from which the *thyroid hormones are derived.

一碘酪氨酸 甲狀腺中產生的含碘物質。從中衍生出甲狀腺激素。

monomania n. the state in which a particular delusion or set of delusions is present in an otherwise normally functioning person. See also paranoia.

單狂 其他功能均正常的人所有的一種特殊的或一套幻覺狀態。參閱 paranoia。

mononeuritis n. disease affecting a single peripheral nerve. Entrapment of the nerve or interference with its blood supply are the commonest causes.

單神經炎 影響一根周圍神經的病症。神經的黏連和神經供血障礙是最常見的病因。多數性單神經炎是兩根或更多根神

Mononeuritis multiplex is the separate involvement of two or more nerves. *Compare* polyneuropathy.

經分別受累。與 polyneuro-pathy 對比。

mononucleosis *n*. the condition in which the blood contains an abnormally high number of mononuclear leucocytes (*monocytes). *See* glandular fever (infectious mononucleosis).

單核細胞增多（症） 血液中含有異常增多的單核白細胞（單核細胞）。參閱 glandular fever (infectious mononucleosis)。

monophobia *n*. an extreme fear of being alone.

孤身恐怖（症） 極度害怕孤獨生活。

monophyletic *adj*. describing a number of individuals, species, etc., that have evolved from a single ancestral group. *Compare* polyphyletic.

一元的 形容由一個祖系衍生出來的許多個體和物種等。與 polyphyletic 對比。

monoplegia *n*. paralysis of one limb. **–monoplegic** *adj*.

單癱 單肢癱瘓。

monoploid *adj*. *see* haploid.

單倍的 參閱 haploid。

monorchism *n*. absence of one testis. This is usually due to failure of one testicle to descent into the scrotum before birth. The term is sometimes used for the condition in which on testicle has been removed surgically or destroyed by injury or disease. If the single testis is normal, no adverse effects result from the absence of the other.

單睪丸 缺少一個睪丸。通常是因為出生前一側睪丸沒有下降到陰囊所致。這個術語有時也用於表示一側睪丸被外科切除或被外傷或疾病損壞情況。如果單側睪丸正常，另一側睪丸的缺失不會產生有害的作用。

monosaccharide *n*. a simple sugar having the general formula $(CH_2O)_n$. Monosaccharides may have between three and nine carbon atoms, but the most common number is five or six. Monosaccharides are classified according to the number of carbon atoms they possess. Thus *trioses* have three carbon atoms, *tetroses* four, *pentoses* five, and *hexoses* six. The most abundant monosaccharide is glucose (a hexose).

單糖 通用分子式為 $(CH_2O)_n$ 的一種糖。單糖可有 3~9 個碳原子，但最常見的為 5 個或 6 個。單糖按其所含的碳原子數目分類。因此丙糖有三個碳原子，丁糖有 4 個，戊糖有 5 個，己糖有 6 個。最大量的單糖是葡萄糖（一種己糖）。

monosomy n. a condition in which there is one chromosome missing from the normal (*diploid) set. *Compare* trisomy. **–monosomic** adj.

單體性 一套正常的染色體（二倍體）中缺少一條染色體的狀態。與 trisomy 對比。

monozygotic twins see twins.

單卵雙生子 參閱 twins。

mons n. (in anatomy) a rounded eminence. The *mons pubis* is the mound of fatty tissue lying over the pubic symphysis.

阜 （解剖學）圓形隆起。陰阜是位於恥骨聯合上方的脂肪組織的隆起。

Moraxella n. a genus of short rodlike Gram-negative aerobic bacteria, usually occurring in pairs. They exist as parasites in many warm-blooded animals. The species *M. lacunata* causes conjunctivitis.

莫拉菌屬 通常成對出現、短桿狀革蘭氏陰性需氧菌屬。它們作為寄生菌存在於許多溫血動物體內。結膜炎莫拉菌會導致結膜炎。

morbid adj. diseased or abnormal; pathological.

疾病的 疾病的或不正常的；病理學的。

morbidity n. the state of being diseased. The *morbidity rate* is the number of cases of a disease found to occur in a stated number of the population, usually given as cases per 100,000 or per million (the number may be smaller for common diseases). Annual figures for morbidity rate give the incidence of the disease, which is the number of new cases reported in the year. *See also* incidence rate, prevalence rate.

患病 患病的狀態。患病率是一定數目的人群中所發現的一種疾病的病例數，通常定為每十萬或百萬（普通疾病此數字可小些）人中的病例數。年患病率數字表示該病當年所報告的新病例數。參閱 incidence rate，prevalence rate。

morbilli n. see measles.

麻疹 參閱 measles。

morbilliform adj. describing a skin rash resembling that of measles.

麻疹樣的 描述與麻疹相似的一種皮疹。

morbus n. disease. The term is usually used as part of the medical name of a specific disease.

（疾）病 此術語通常用作一種具體疾病的醫學名稱的一部分。

mordant n. (in microscopy) a substance, such as alum or phenol, used to fix a *stain in a tissue.

媒染劑 （顯微鏡檢查）用於固定組織染色的一種物質，例如：明礬或石炭酸。

moribund *adj.* dying.

瀕死的　臨死的。

moricizine *n.* a drug administered by mouth to treat life-threatening irregularity of the heartbeat (*arrhythmia). Possible side-effects include worsening of the arrhythmia and heart failure, and it is used only in cases in which these risks are thought to be justified.

莫雷西嗪　一種口服藥，用於治療危及生命的心律不齊。可能存在的副作用包括加重心律不齊或心臟衰竭。此藥僅用於這些危險被認為可接受的病例中。

morning sickness nausea and vomiting occurring during early pregnancy. In some women the symptoms disappear if a small amount of food is eaten before rising in the morning. *Compare* hyperemesis gravidarum.

晨吐　妊娠早期出現的惡心和嘔吐。對少數婦女來說，晨起前吃少量食物，症狀即可消失。與 hyperemesis gravidarum 對比。

morphine *n.* a potent analgesic and *narcotic drug used mainly to relieve severe and persistent pain. It is administered by mouth or injection; common side-effects are loss of appetite, nausea, constipation, and confusion. Morphine causes feelings of euphoria; *tolerance develops rapidly and *dependence may occur.

嗎啡　主要用於減輕嚴重且持續疼痛的一種強效止痛及麻醉藥。口服或注射。常見副作用有無食慾、惡心、便秘及精神混亂。嗎啡能產生欣快感，耐受性形成快，可產生藥物依賴。

morpho- *prefix denoting* form or structure.

〔前綴〕形態　形狀或結構。

morphoea *n.* a localized form of *scleroderma characterized by firm ivory-coloured waxy plaques in the skin without any internal sclerosis. The plaques may often disappear spontaneously but resolution is slow.

硬斑病　一種局限型硬皮病，表現為皮膚中有堅硬的乳白色光滑斑塊，內無硬節。斑塊可自行消失但較緩慢。

morphogenesis *n.* the development of form and structure of the body and its parts.

形態形成　身體及其各部的形態和結構的發育。

morphology *n. see* anatomy.

形態學　參閱 anatomy。

-morphous *suffix denoting* form or structure (of a specified kind).

〔後綴〕（一個特定類型的）形態或結構

Morquio-Brailsford disease *see* chondrodysplasia.

莫爾基奧-布雷爾斯福病　參閱 chondrodysplasia。

mortality (mortality rate) *n.* the incidence of death in the population in a given period. The *annual mortality rate* is the number of registered deaths in a year, multiplied by 1000 and divided by the population at the middle of the year. *See also* infant mortality rate, maternal mortality rate.

死亡率　一定時期內人口中的死亡發生率。年度死亡率等於一年中在冊死亡人數乘以 1000，除以年中人口數。參閱 infant mortality rate，maternal mortality rate。

mortification *n. see* necrosis.

壞疽　參閱 necrosis。

morula *n.* an early stage of embryonic development formed by *cleavage of the fertilized ovum. It consists of a solid ball of cells and is an intermediate stage between the zygote and *blastocyst.

桑葚胚　受精卵分裂形成的胚胎發育的早期階段。它由一個堅固的細胞球組成，是介於合子和胚泡之間的中期階段。

mosaicism *n.* a condition in which the cells of an individual do not all contain identical chromosomes; there may be two or more genetically different populations of cells. Often one of the cell populations is normal and the other carries a chromosome defect such as *Down's syndrome or *Turner's syndrome. In affected individuals the chromosome defect is usually not fully expressed. **–mosaic** *adj.*

鑲嵌體　一個人的細胞中並不都包含着相同染色體的情況。可以有兩個或更多基因不同的細胞羣體。通常細胞羣體中的一個是正常的，而其他的攜帶有染色體缺陷，例如唐氏綜合徵或特納綜合徵。在患病人羣中，染色體缺陷通常沒有完全顯現出來。

mosquito *n.* a small winged bloodsucking insect belonging to a large group the *Diptera (two-winged flies). Its mouthparts are formed into a long proboscis for piercing the skin and sucking blood. Female mosquitoes transmit the parasites responsible for several major infectious diseases, such as *malaria. *See* Anopheles, Aëdes, Culex.

蚊　屬於一個大的組別——雙翅目的有翅吸血小昆蟲。它的口部由長喙構成，以刺入皮膚吸血。雌蚊傳播能導致幾種主要傳染病（如瘧疾）的寄生蟲。參閱 Anopheles，Aëdes，Culex。

motile *adj.* being able to move spontaneously, without external aid: usually applied to a *microorganism or a cell (e.g. a sperm cell).

能動的　不用外力幫助可以自行移動的：常用於指微生物或細胞（如精子）。

motion sickness *see* travel sickness

量 動 病　　參 閱　　travel sickness。

motor cortex the region of the *cerebral cortex that is responsible for initiating nerve impulses that bring about voluntary activity in the muscles of the body. It is possible to map out the cortex to show which of its areas is responsible for which particular part of the body. The motor cortex of the left cerebral hemisphere is responsible for muscular activity in the right side of the body.

運動皮層　負責產生支配身體肌肉隨意運動的神經衝動的大腦皮層區域。可以標出皮層以顯示它的某個區域支配身體的某個特殊部位。左側腦運動皮層支配身體右側的肌肉運動。

motor nerve one of the nerves that carry impulses outwards from the central nervous system to bring about activity in a muscle or gland. *Compare* sensory nerve.

運動神經　從中樞神經系統外傳衝動，以使肌肉或腺體活動的一條神經。與 sensory nerve 對比。

motor neurone one of the units (*neurones) that goes to make up the nerve pathway between the brain and an effector organ, such as a skeletal muscle. An *upper motor neurone* has a cell body in the brain and an axon that extends into the spinal cord, where it ends in synapses. It is thus entirely within the central nervous system. A *lower motor neurone*, on the other hand, has a cell body in the spinal cord or brainstem and an axon that extends outwards in a cranial or spinal motor nerve to reach an effector.

運動神經元　構成大腦和效應器（如骨骼肌）之間神經傳導路的一個單位。上行運動神經元在腦中有一個細胞體和一個延伸到骨髓、終止於突觸處的軸索。因此它完全在中樞神經系統內。下行運動神經元在脊髓或腦幹裏有細胞體及從顱和脊髓運動神經中向外延伸到一個效應器的軸索。

motor neurone disease (MND) a progressive degenerative disease of the motor system occurring in middle age and causing muscle weakness and wasting. It primarily affects the cells of the anterior horn of the spinal cord, the motor muclei in the brainstem, and the corticospinal fibres. There are three clinically distinct forms: *amyotrophic lateral sclerosis* (*ALS*), *progressive muscular atrophy*, and *progressive bulbar*

運動神經元病　發生於中年，引起肌肉無力和萎縮的一種運動神經進行性退化病。主要影響脊髓前角細胞、腦幹的運動核和皮質脊髓纖維。臨床上有三種明顯不同的類型：肌萎縮、進行性肌萎縮及進行性延髓麻痺。有些類型的運動神經元病是家族性的。迄今尚無特異療法，但廣泛的支持療法可幫助保持病人的自立和功能。

palsy. Some forms of MND are familial (inherited). No specific treatment is available to date but extensive support-ive therapy may help maintain patients' independence and function. Current research on nerve growth factors may offer future specific therapies.

目前對神經生長因子的研究可能為未來提供特異療法。

mould *n.* any multicellular filamentous fungus that commonly forms a rough furry coating on decaying matter.

黴菌 任何多細胞絲狀真菌，通常形成腐爛物上的粗糙毛皮狀包被。

moulding *n.* the changing of the shape of an infant's head during labour, brought about by the pressures to which it is subjected when passing through the birth canal.

兒頭變形 分娩時胎頭形狀的變化，由通過產道時胎頭受壓產生。

mountain sickness *see* altitude sick-ness.

高山病 參閱 altitude sick-ness。

mouth-to-mouth respiration a form of *artificial respiration, performed mouth-to-mouth, by blowing air into the victim's lungs to inflate them and then allowing exhalation to occur automatically. It is commonly known as the *kiss of life*. The operator should aim to produce roughly 20 cycles of respiration per minute, or more for a younger victim.

口對口呼吸 人工呼吸的一種類型，口對口地將空氣吹入受害者的肺裏使其擴張，然後使空氣自動呼出。它通常被稱為「生命之吻」。操作者目的在於產生每分鐘大約 20 個呼吸周期，對年齡較輕者可多一些。

mouthwash *n.* an aqueous solution with antiseptic, astringent, or deodorizing properties used for daily rinsing of the mouth and teeth. Mouthwashes are used to prevent dental *caries (*see also* chlorhexidine, fluoride) and to treat mild throat infections.

漱口液 具有防腐、收斂或除臭特徵的水性溶液，用於每日漱口和潔牙。漱口液被用來預防齲齒（參閱 chlorhexidine，fluoride）及治療輕度咽喉感染。

mouthwash test a simple noninvasive procedure that enables the detection of *carriers for single gene defects, e.g. *cystic fibrosis. Epithelial cells from the buccal cavity are obtained from a saline mouthwash: from these it is possible to

漱口液檢查 一種簡單的非侵入性手術，它能檢測單基因缺陷，例如囊性纖維變性的基因攜帶者。從鹽漱口液中獲取頰腔中的上皮細胞：從中能分離出 DNA，DNA 通過聚合

isolate DNA, which is amplified by the *polymerase chain reaction to enable gene analysis.

酶鏈反應被放大以供基因分析。

moxibustion *n.* a form of treatment favoured in Japan, in which cones of sunflower pith or down from the leaves of the plant *Artemisia moxa* are stuck to the skin and ignited. The heat produced by the smouldering cones acts as a counterirritant and is reputed to cure a variety of disorders.

灸術　在日本備受喜愛的一種治療形式，灸法是把向日葵莖髓或艾絨灸柱貼近皮膚並點燃。燻燒的灸柱產生的熱量起抗刺激作用並被認為能治愈多種疾病。

MRI *see* magnetic resonance imaging.

磁共振成像術　參閱 magnetic resonance imaging。

MRS *see* magnetic resonance spectroscopy.

磁共振分光術　參閱 magnetic resonance spectroscopy。

MS *see* multiple sclerosis.

多發性硬化　參閱 multiple sclerosis。

MSH *see* melanocyte-stimulating hormone.

促黑素細胞激素　參閱 melanocyte-stimulating hormone。

mucilage *n.* (in pharmacy) a thick aqueous solution of a gum used as a lubricant in skin preparations (*see also* glycerin), for the production of pills, and for the suspension of insoluble substances. The most important mucilages are of acacia, tragacanth, and starch.

膠漿　（藥劑學）濃稠的樹膠水性溶液，可用作皮膚藥劑的潤滑劑（參閱 glycerin），生產藥丸及不溶物質的懸浮液。最重要的膠漿有阿拉伯膠、西黃芪膠和澱粉。

mucin *n.* the principal constituent of *mucus. Mucin is a *glycoprotein.

黏蛋白　黏液的主要成分。黏蛋白是一種糖蛋白。

muco- *prefix denoting* **1.** mucus. **2.** mucous membrane.

〔前綴〕(1) 黏液　(2) 黏膜

mucocoele *n.* a space or organ distended with mucus. For example, it may occur in the gall bladder when the exit duct becomes obstructed so that the mucus secretions are retained and dilate

黏液囊腫　因為黏液而膨脹的腔或器官。例如：當排出管阻塞造成黏液分泌物滯留，膽囊腔擴大時，就會產生膽囊黏液囊腫。管道阻塞或破裂

the cavity of the organ. A mucocoele in the soft tissues arising from a salivary gland occurs when the duct is blocked or ruptured.

時，唾液腺軟組織產生黏液囊腫。

mucolytic *n.* an agent, such as carbocysteine or tyloxapol, that dissolves or breaks down mucus. Mucolytics are used to treat chest conditions involving excessive or thickened mucus secretions.

黏液溶解劑 一種藥劑，例如羧甲半胱氨酸或泰洛沙泊等，能溶解或分解黏液。用於治療胸部疾病時黏液分泌過多或黏稠。

mucopolysaccharide *n.* one of a group of complex carbohydrates functioning mainly as structural components in connective tissue. Mucopolysaccharide molecules are usually built up of two repeating sugar units, one of which is an amino sugar. An example of a mucopolysaccharide is *chondroitin, occurring in cartilage.

黏多糖 主要作為結締組織結構成分的一組複雜的碳水化合物之一。通常由兩個重複的糖單位組成，其中有一個是一種氨基糖，如產生在軟骨中的軟骨素。

mucopolysaccharidosis *n.* *see* Hunter's syndrome, Hurler's syndrome.

黏多糖貯積病 參閱 Hunter's syndrome，Hurler's syndrome。

mucoprotein *n.* one of a group of proteins found in the *globulin fraction of blood plasma. Mucoproteins are globulins combined with a carbohydrate group (an amino sugar). They are similar to *glycoproteins but contain a greater proportion of carbohydrate.

黏蛋白 血漿球蛋白片斷中的一組蛋白之一。是球蛋白與一種糖類（一種氨基糖）結合的產物。它們和糖蛋白相似，但碳水化合物的比例較大。

mucopurulent *adj.* containing mucus and pus. *See* mucopus.

黏液膿性的 含黏液和膿的。參閱 mucopus。

mucopus *n.* a mixture of *mucus and *pus.

黏液性膿 黏液和膿的混合物。

Mucor *n.* a genus of mould fungi commonly seen on dead and decaying organic matter. They can be pathogenic in man.

毛黴菌屬 死亡或腐爛的有機物上常見的真菌屬。在人身上可致病。

mucosa *n.* *See* mucous membrane. —**mucosal** *adj.*

黏膜 參閱 mucous membrane。

mucous membrane (mucosa) the moist membrane lining many tubular structures and cavities, including the nasal sinuses, respiratory tract, gastrointestinal tract, biliary, and pancreatic systems. The surface of the mouth is lined by mucous membrane, the nature of which varies according to its site. The mucous membrane consists of a surface layer of *epithelium, which contains glands secreting *mucus, with underlying layers of connective tissue (lamina propria) and muscularis mucosae, which forms the inner boundary of the mucous membrane.

黏膜　襯於鼻竇、呼吸道、胃腸道、膽和胰腺等許多管腔內壁的濕潤膜。口腔內壁襯有黏膜，並因其位置不同性質各異。黏膜由含有能分泌黏液的腺體的上皮表層、下層的結締組織（黏膜固有層）和形成黏膜內界的肌層組成。

mucoviscidosis *n. see* cystic fibrosis.

（胰管）黏稠物阻塞症　參閱 cystic fibrosis。

mucus *n.* a viscous fluid secreted by *mucous membranes. Mucus acts as a protective barrier over the membranes, a lubricant, and a carrier of enzymes. It consists chiefly of *glycoproteins, particularly *mucin*. **–mucous** *adj.*

黏液　黏膜分泌的一種黏性液體。可作為黏膜表面的保護層、潤滑劑和酶的載體。主要由糖蛋白，特別是黏蛋白組成。

MUGA scan (multiple-gated arteriography) a method of studying the left-ventricular function and wall motion of the heart by injecting the patient's red cells with radioactive technetium-99 to form an image of the blood pool within the heart at specific points in the cardiac cycle, using an ECG, *gamma camera, and computer.

多門動脈造影術　一種研究心臟左心室功能和內壁運動的方法。其作法是向患者的紅細胞中注射放射活性 ^{99} 鎝，使用心電圖、γ 照像機和計算機對心內的特定點於心搏周期中形成圖像。

Müllerian duct *see* paramesonephric duct.

米勒管　參閱 paramesonephric duct。

multifactorial *adj.* describing a condition that is believed to have resulted from the interaction of genetic factors, usually polygenes, with an environmental factor or factors. Many disorders, e.g. spina bifida and anencephaly, are thought to be multifactorial.

多因子的　描述人們認為由於基因，通常是多基因和一種或多種環境因素相互作用而產生的一種狀況。許多疾病，例如脊柱裂和無腦（畸形），被認為是多種因素所致。

multifocal lenses lenses in which the power (*see* dioptre) of the lower part gradually increases towards the lower edge. There is no dividing line on the lens as there is between the upper and lower segments of *bifocal lenses. The wearer can see clearly at any distance by lowering or raising his eyes.

多焦點透鏡　放大率從下部向下邊緣逐漸增加的透鏡（參閱 dioptre）。多焦點透鏡上沒有分界綫，而雙焦點透鏡上下部分之間則有。戴鏡者降低或抬高眼睛就能清楚地看到任何距離。

multigravida *n.* a woman who has been pregnant at least twice.

經產孕婦　至少有兩次妊娠的婦女。

multi-organ failure (MOF) the terminal stage of serious illness.

多器官衰竭　嚴重疾病的最後階段。

multipara *n.* a woman who has given birth to a live child after each of at least two pregnancies. *See also* grand multiparity.

經產婦　至少有兩次妊娠且每次都產下活嬰的婦女。參閱 grand multiparity。

multiple personality disorder a psychiatric disorder in which the affected person has two or more distinct, and often contrasting, personalities. As each personality assumes dominance, it determines attitudes and behaviour and usually appears to be unaware of the other personality (or personalities). Transition is sudden and the mental states of the different personalities are normal. The condition is thought to be a late result of *child abuse. Treatment is by psychotherapy.

多重性格症　一種精神疾病，患者有兩種或更多顯著且通常相反的個性。當一種個性占主導地位時，它會決定患者的態度及行為，使其忘記另一種（或其他的）個性。這種轉換很突然。不同個性的精神狀態均正常。此病被看作是虐待兒童的晚期的結果。用精神療法治療。

multiple sclerosis (MS, disseminated sclerosis) a chronic disease of the nervous system affecting young and middle-aged adults. The *myelin sheaths surrounding nerves in the brain and spinal cord are damaged, which affects the function of the nerves involved. The course of the illness is usually characterized by recurrent relapses followed by remissions, but a proportion of patients

多發性硬化　影響青年和中年神經系統的慢性病。包繞大腦和脊髓內神經的髓鞘質破壞，繼而影響到有關神經的功能。病程特點為復發後又緩解，但部分病人呈慢性進行性病程。此病影響腦和脊髓的不同部位，導致典型的分散症狀。這些症狀包括步態不穩、四肢震顫性運動（共濟失調）、眼球

run a chronic progressive course. The disease affects different parts of the brain and spinal cord, resulting in typically scattered symptoms. These include unsteady gait and shaky movements of the limbs (ataxia), rapid involuntary movements of the eyes (*nystagmus), defects in speech pronunciation (dysarthria), spastic weakness, and *retrobulbar neuritis. The underlying cause of the nerve damage remains unknown. Steroid treatment may be used in an acute relapse, and beta-*interferon therapy may reduce the relapse rate.

快速不隨意運動（眼球震顫）、發音缺陷（構音障礙）、肌力減退和球後視神經炎。神經損壞的基本原因尚不清楚。急性發作可用甾類化合物治療，β 干擾素可減少復發率。

multisystem *adj.* describing a disease that affects many systems of the body.

多系統的 描述影響機體多系統的疾病。

multivariate analysis *see* correlation.

多變量分析 參閱 correlation。

mummification *n.* **1.** the conversion of dead tissue into a hard shrunken mass, chiefly by dehydration. **2.** (in dentistry) the application of a fixative to the dental pulp to prevent decomposition.

(1) 乾屍化 死亡組織轉化成硬縮塊，主要通過脫水。**(2) 乾髓法** （牙科學）把固定液應用於牙髓以防止其腐敗。

mumps *n.* a common virus infection mainly affecting school-age children. Symptoms appear 2–3 weeks after exposure: fever, headache, and vomiting may precede a typical swelling of the *parotid salivary glands. The gland on the side of the face often swells up days before the other but sometimes only one side is affected. The symptoms usually vanish within three days, the patient remaining infectious until the swelling has completely disappeared, but the infection may spread to other salivary glands and to the pancreas, brain (causing an aseptic meningitis), and testicles. In adult men, mumps can cause sterility. Vaccination against mumps provides effective

流行性腮腺炎 主要影響學齡兒童的一種常見病毒感染。接觸病毒後 2~3 周出現症狀：典型的腮腺腫脹出現前會產生發熱、頭痛和嘔吐。面部一側腮腺常比另一側早幾天腫脹，但有時僅一側腮腺受影響。症狀通常在三天內消失，病人在腫脹消失前仍有傳染性，但傳染可以擴散到其他涎腺、胰腺、腦（引起無菌性腦膜炎）和睾丸。在成年男性中，流行性腮腺炎可引起不育。對抗流行性腮腺炎的疫苗能產生有效的免疫力（參閱 MMR vaccine）。醫學用語：傳染性腮腺炎。

immunity (*see* MMR vaccine). Medical name: **infectious parotitis**.

Munchausen's syndrome a mental disorder in which the patient persistently tries to obtain hospital treatment, especially surgery, for an illness that is nonexistent: it is an extreme form of malingering. The disease may be described in vivid detail, and in some cases injury may be deliberately self-inflicted in an attempt to give the appearance of authenticity to the claims being made. In *Munchausen's syndrome by proxy*, the patient inflicts harm on others (often children) in order to attract medical attention.

明肖森綜合徵　一種精神病，病人為不存在的疾病不斷地試圖得到醫治，特別是外科手術：是裝病的一種極端形式。病人可以極其逼真的細節描述病情。在有些病例中，病人為了給所作宣稱以真實感，會故意傷害自己。在代擬明肖森綜合徵中，病人會傷害其他人（通常是兒童）以吸引醫療方面的關注。

murmur (bruit) *n.* a noise, heard with the aid of a stethoscope, that is generated by turbulent blood flow within the heart of blood vessels. Turbulent flow is produced by damaged valves, *septal defects, narrowed arteries, or arteriovenous communications. Heart murmurs can also be heard in normal individuals, especially those who have hyperactive circulation, and frequently in normal children (*innocent murmurs*). Murmurs are classified as *systolic* or *diastolic* (heard in ventricular *systole or *diastole respectively); *continuous murmurs* are heard throughout systole and diastole.

雜音　借助聽診器聽到的心臟和血管內血液渦流產生的聲音。渦流是由瓣膜損傷、間隔缺陷、動脈或動靜脈回流造成的。正常成人可存在心臟雜音，特別是循環旺盛的人中，亦可頻繁見於正常的兒童（良性雜音）。雜音可以分為收縮期或舒張期雜音（分別在心室收縮期或舒張期聽到）；連續性雜音在整個收縮期和舒張期可聽到。

Murphy's sign a sign of inflammation of the gall bladder: continuous pressure over the gall bladder while the patient is taking a deep breath will cause a catch in the breath at the point of maximum inhalation.

墨菲徵　膽囊炎的一種體徵。病人深吸氣時，持續的壓力會在吸氣量達到最大時引起屏息。

muscae volitantes *pl. n.* black spots seen floating before the eyes usually due to the presence of opacities in the

飛蠅幻視　浮在眼前的可見黑點，通常是由於隨着年齡的增加，玻璃體變得更不固

vitreous humour as it becomes more fluid with age.

muscle *n.* a tissue whose cells have the ability to contract, producing movement or force (see illustration). Muscles possess mechanisms for converting energy derived from chemical reactions into mechanical energy. The major functions of muscles are to produce movements of the body, to maintain the position of the body against the force of gravity, to produce movements of structures inside the body, and to alter pressures or tensions of structures in the body. There are three types of muscle: *striated muscle, attached to the skeleton; *smooth muscle, which is found in such tissues as the stomach, gut, and blood vessels; and *cardiac muscle, which forms the walls of the heart.

定而出現的玻璃體不透明所致。

肌肉 其細胞能收縮、產生運動或力量的組織（見圖）。肌肉具有把化學反應的能量轉化成機械能的機制。肌肉的主要功能有：使身體運動，維持身體在重力作用下的位置，使體內諸結構運動，改變體內諸結構的壓力或緊張感等。肌肉分三類：附着於骨骼上的橫紋肌；在胃、腸道和血管等上見到的平滑肌和構成心臟壁的心肌。

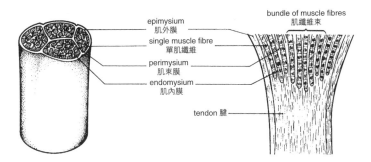

A voluntary muscle in transverse section (left) and in longitudinal section at its junction with a tendon (right)
隨意肌的橫切面（左）及其與腱接合處的縱切面（右）

muscle relaxant an agent that reduces tension in muscles. Drugs such as *dantrolene and *diazepam are used to relieve skeletal muscular spasms in various spastic conditions, parkinsonism, and tetanus. Other drugs, e.g. *alcuronium, *gallamine, *suxamethonium, and

肌肉鬆弛劑 減少肌肉緊張度的藥物。丹曲林和地西泮等藥物被用來緩解各種痙攣性疾病、帕金森綜合徵和破傷風中的骨骼肌痙攣。其他藥物，例如雙烯丙毒馬錢鹼、加拉碘銨、琥珀膽鹼和筒箭毒鹼在神

*tubocurarine, block the transmission of impulses at neuromuscular junctions and are used to relax voluntary muscles during the administration of anaesthetics in surgical operations.

經肌肉的接合處阻斷衝動的傳遞並在外科手術施行麻醉時放鬆隨意肌。

muscle spindle a specialized receptor, sensitive to stretch, that is embedded between and parallel to the fibres of striated muscles. These receptors are important for coordinated muscular movement. *See also* stretch receptor.

肌梭 一種特殊的受體，對牽張敏感，包埋在橫紋肌之間並與橫紋肌纖維平行。這些受體對於協調肌肉運動很重要。參閱 stretch receptor。

muscular dystrophy a group of muscle diseases, marked by weakness and wasting of selected muscles, in which there is a recognizable pattern of inheritance. The affected muscle fibres degenerate and are replaced by fatty tissue. The muscular dystrophies are classified according to the patient's age at onset, distribution of the weakness, the progression of the disease, and the mode of inheritance. Isolated cases may occur as a result of gene mutation. Confirmation of the diagnosis is based upon *electromyography and muscle biopsy.

The most common form is *Duchenne dystrophy*, which is inherited as a sex-linked recessive character and is nearly always restricted to boys. It usually begins before the age of four, with selective weakness and wasting of the muscles of the pelvic girdle and back. The child has a waddling gait and *lordosis of the lumbar spine. The calf muscles – and later the shoulders and upper limbs – often become firm and bulky. Although the disease cannot be cured, physiotherapy and orthopaedic measures can relieve the disability. The identification of the gene abnormality raises the possibility of *gene therapy in the future. *See also* dystrophia myotonica (myotonic dystrophy).

肌營養不良 一組肌肉疾病，其特點是選擇性的肌無力和肌萎縮，有遺傳性。受累的肌纖維退化並被脂肪組織代替。肌營養不良根據病人發病年齡、肌無力的範圍、病程和遺傳模式等分類。孤立的病例可發生於基因變異。確診依靠肌電描記術和肌肉活組織檢查。

最常見的類型是迪歇納肌營養不良，為性連鎖隱性遺傳，幾乎均局限於男孩。此病通常在四歲前開始，表現為骨盆帶和腰部肌肉選擇性肌無力和肌萎縮。兒童有蹣跚步態及腰脊柱前凸。小腿肌肉，隨後是雙肩及上肢肌肉常變硬且膨大。雖然此病不能治愈，但物理療法和矯形措施能減輕殘疾。基因異常的發現為將來使用基因治療增加了可能性。參閱 dystrophia myotonica (myotonic dystrophy)。

muscularis *n.* a muscular layer of the wall of a hollow organ (such as the stomach) or a tubular structure (such as the intestine or the ureter). The *muscularis mucosae* is the muscular layer of a mucous membrane complex, especially that of the stomach or intestine.

肌層　空腔器官（例如胃）或管狀結構（例如腸或輸尿管）的肌層。黏膜肌層是黏膜複合體的肌層，特別是胃或腸的肌層。

muscular rheumatism any aching pain in the muscles and joints. Commonly the symptoms are due to *fibrositis; wear and tear of the joints (*osteoarthritis); or to inflammation of the muscles associated with abnormal immune reactions (*polymyalgia rheumatica).

肌風濕病　肌肉和關節酸痛。通常情況下症狀是由於纖維織炎，關節的磨損及撕裂（骨關節炎）或與異常免疫反應相關的肌肉炎症（風濕性多肌痛）所導致。

musculo- *prefix denoting* muscle.

〔前綴〕肌肉

musculocutaneous nerve a nerve of the *brachial plexus that supplies some muscles of the arm and the skin of the lateral part of the forearm.

肌皮神經　臂叢的一根神經，支配手臂的一些肌肉和前臂側部皮膚。

mushroom *n.* the aerial fruiting (spore-producing) body of various fungi. Edible species include field mushrooms and cultivated mushrooms (*Agaricus campestris* and *A. bisporus*), the chanterelle (*Cantherellus cibarius*), and the parasol (*Lepiota procera*). However, great care must be taken in identifying edible fungi. Many species are poisonous, especially the death cap and panther cap (*see* Amanita).

蕈類（植物）　各種真菌的氣生子實體（孢子生成）。可食蕈包括野生和培育的蕈（食用蘑菇和傘菌屬雙孢子）、雞油菌屬植物（雞油菌）和小傘菌屬。但是在鑒定食用真菌時必須十分謹慎。許多種類的真菌有毒，特別是毒傘和斑毒傘（參閱 Amanita）。

mustine (nitrogen mustard) *n.* a drug used to treat various types of cancer, including Hodgkin's disease and some types of leukaemia. It is administered by injection; common side-effects include nausea and vomiting, and the drug may damage the bone marrow, causing serious blood disorders.

氮芥　治療霍奇金病和某些類型的白血病等各類癌症的藥物。注射給藥。常見的副作用包括惡心和嘔吐，此藥可損害骨髓，造成嚴重的血液病。

mutagen *n.* an external agent that, when applied to cells or organisms, can

誘變劑　一種外用藥劑，用於細胞或機體時能增加突變率。

increase the rate of *mutation. Mutagens usually only increase the number of mutants formed and do not cause mutations not found under natural conditions. Several kinds of radiation, many chemicals, and certain viruses can act as mutagens, *Compare* antimutagen.

mutant *n.* **1.** an individual in which a mutation has occurred, especially when the effect of the mutation is visible. **2.** a characteristic showing the effects of a mutation. **–mutant** *adj.*

mutation *n.* a change in the genetic material (*DNA) of a cell, or the change this causes in a characteristic of the individual, which is not caused by normal genetic processes. In a *point* (or *gene*) *mutation* there is a change in a single gene; in a *chromosome mutation* there is a change in the structure or number of the chromosomes. All mutations are rare events and may occur spontaneously or be caused by external agents (*mutagens). If a mutation occurs in developing sex cells (gametes) it may be inherited. Mutations in any other cells (*somatic mutations*) are not inherited.

mutism *n.* inability or refusal to speak; dumbness. Innate speechlessness most commonly occurs in those who have been totally deaf since birth (*deafmutism*). Inability to speak may result from brain damage (*see* aphasia). It may also be caused by depression or psychological trauma, in which case the patient either does not speak at all or speaks only to particular persons or in particular situations. This latter condition is called elective mutism.

Treatment of mutism due to psychological causes is now increasingly by behavioural means, such as *prompting:

通常只能增加已形成的突變體的數目，但不會引起自然情況下觀察不到的突變。許多種類的射綫、化學物品和某些病毒能起誘變劑的作用。與antimutagen 對比。

(1) 突變體 發生突變的個體，尤指突變作用可見的個體。**(2) 突變性** 表現出突變作用的特性。

突變 正常遺傳過程中不會產生的細胞遺傳物質（脱氧核糖核酸）的變化，或因此而引起的個體特性的變化。在一個點（或基因）突變中，有單個基因的變化，在染色體突變中有結構或染色體數目的變化。所有的突變都是少見的，可自發產生或由外部作用物（誘變劑）引起。如果突變產生在發育中的性細胞（配子）中，則可遺傳。其他任何細胞內的突變（體細胞突變）沒有遺傳性。

啞症 不會講話或拒絕講話；啞（症）。先天性啞最常發生在從出生時起便耳聾的人中（聾啞症）。失語症可因腦損傷造成（參閱 aphasia），也可由抑鬱或心理創傷引起，在此種病例中，患者可根本不講話或只對某些人講話，或僅在某些特定情況下講話。後一種情況被稱為選擇性啞症。

現在越來越多地採用行為療法，例如激勵，來治療因為心理原因造成的啞症：把病人對其不講話的人慢慢地介紹到病人講話的情景中去。此法可

people that the patient does not address are slowly introduced into the situation where the patient does speak. This may be done either alone or in combination with more traditional psychotherapy. **–mute** *adj.*, *n.*

單獨使用或與更為傳統的心理療法混合使用。

mutualism *n.* the intimate but not necessarily obligatory association between two different species of organism in which there is mutual aid and benefit. *Compare* symbiosis.

共生現象 兩種不同種類的生物之間互助互利的、親密的、但不一定是必需的關係。與 symbiosis 對比。

my- (myo-) *prefix denoting* muscle.

〔前綴〕肌肉

myalgia *n.* pain in the muscles. **–myalgic** *adj.*

肌痛 肌肉的疼痛。

myalgic encephalomyelitis (ME) a disease characterized by extreme fatigue (it is also known as *chronic fatigue syndrome*), poor coordination, giddiness, depression, and general malaise, which can last for months or years. The cause has not been, established, but the condition frequently occurs as a sequel to such viral infections as glandular fever and it may be an extreme postviral reaction: it is frequently known as *postviral fatigue syndrome*.

肌痛性腦脊髓炎 一種疾病，特點為持續數月或數年的極度疲勞（亦稱慢性疲勞綜合徵）、協調性差、眩暈、抑鬱和全身不適。病因尚不清楚，但此病常作為腺熱等病毒性感染的後遺症發作，可能是極端的病毒後反應：常稱為病毒後疲勞綜合徵。

myasthenia gravis a chronic disease marked by abnormal fatigability and weakness of selected muscles, which is relieved by rest or *anticholinesterase drugs. The degree of fatigue is so extreme that these muscles are temporarily paralysed. Other symptoms include drooping of the upper eyelid (ptosis), double vision, and *dysarthria. The cause is uncertain, but appears to be associated with impaired ability of the neurotransmitter acetylcholine to induce muscular contraction. It chiefly affects adolescents and young adults (usually

重症肌無力 以選擇性肌肉異常疲勞及無力為特點的一種慢性病，通過休息或抗膽鹼酯酶藥可緩解此病。疲勞的程度極高，以致這些肌肉會出現暫時性癱瘓。其他症狀包括上瞼下垂、複視和構音障礙。病因尚不明確，但似乎與神經遞質乙酰膽鹼誘導肌肉收縮能力受損相關。它主要影響青少年和青春期成人（通常是婦女）及 40 歲以上的成年人。藥物治療和外科手術切除胸腺能減輕症狀。甾類化合物療法或血漿交

women) and adults over 40. Drug treatment and surgical removal of the thymus lessen the severity of the symptoms. Steroid therapy or plasma exchange may be used to treat the more severely affected patients.

換可用於治療更為嚴重的受累患者。

myc- (myco-, mycet(o)-) *prefix denoting* a fungus.

〔前綴〕真菌

mycelium *n.* (*pl.* **mycelia**) the tangled mass of fine branching threads that make up the feeding and growing part of a *fungus.

菌絲體 構成真菌攝取養料及生長部分的細絲狀纏結團。

mycetoma *n.* a chronic inflammation of tissues caused by a fungus. *See* Madura foot.

足分支菌病 真菌引起的組織慢性炎症。參閱 Madura foot。

Mycobacterium *n.* a genus of rodlike Gram-positive aerobic bacteria that can form filamentous branching structures. Some species are pathogenic to animals and man: *M. leprae* (*Hansen's bacillus*) causes *leprosy; *M. tuberculosis* (*Koch's bacillus*) causes *tuberculosis. *M. bovis* causes tuberculosis in cattle but can also infect the lungs, joints, and intestines of man.

分支桿菌屬 能形成絲狀分支結構的桿狀革蘭氏陽性需氧菌屬。有些種類對人和動物有致病性：麻風分支桿菌（漢森桿菌）能引起麻風病；結核分支桿菌（科赫桿菌）能導致結核病。牛（型）結核分支桿菌可使牛患結核病，亦可感染人的肺、關節和腸道。

mycology *n.* the science of fungi. *See also* microbiology. **–mycologist** *n.*

真菌學 研究真菌的科學。參閱 microbiology。

mycoplasma *n.* one of a group of minute nonmotile microorganisms that lack a rigid cell wall and hence display a variety of forms. They are regarded by some authorities as primitive bacteria. The group includes some species that cause severe respiratory disease in cattle, sheep, and goats; one of these, *Mycoplasma pneumoniae*, causes *atypical pneumonia in man. The group also includes the *pleuropneumonia-like organisms* (*PPLO*).

支原體 一組微小，不運動的微生物。這些微生物沒有堅硬的細胞壁，因此顯示出各種形態。有些專家認為它們是原始的細菌，這組中包括一些能引起牛、羊和山羊等嚴重呼吸道疾病的種類；其中，肺炎支原體可引起人類非典型性肺炎。支原體也包括類胸膜肺炎菌（鳥型支原體）。

mycosis *n.* any disease caused by a fungus, including actinomycosis, aspergillosis, cryptococcosis, rhinosporidiosis, ringworm, and sporotrichosis.

mycosis fungoides a disease that is a variety of *reticulosis confined to the skin, with plaques and later nodules infiltrated with T-lymphocytes. It progresses slowly and can be treated initially with topical corticosteroids, later with *PUVA and electron-beam therapy; chemotherapy is not helpful.

Mycota *n. see* undecenoic acid.

mydriasis *n.* widening of the pupil, which occurs normally in dim light. The commonest cause of prolonged mydriasis is drug therapy (*see* mydriatic) or injury to the eye. *See also* cycloplegia. *Compare* miosis.

mydriatic *n.* a drug that causes the pupil of the eye to dilate. Examples are *atropine, *cyclopentolate, and *phenylephrine. Mydriatics are used to aid examination of the eye and to treat some eye inflammations such as iritis and cyclitis.

myectomy *n.* a surgical operation to remove part of a muscle.

myel- (myelo-) *prefix denoting* **1.** the spinal cord. **2.** bone marrow. **3.** myelin.

myelencephalon *n. see* medulla oblongata.

myelin *n.* a complex material formed of protein and *phospholipid that is laid down as a sheath around the *axons of

真菌病　真菌引起的任何疾病，其中包括放綫菌病、曲菌病、隱球菌病、鼻孢子蟲病、癬菌病和孢子絲菌病。

蕈樣真菌病　一種局限於皮膚的網狀細胞增多症，伴有斑片和隨後發生的 T 細胞浸潤性結節。病情發展緩慢，患病初期可用表面的皮質類固醇治療，以後用光化學療法和電子射綫療法，化療無效。

十一碳烯酸　參閱 undecenoic acid。

瞳孔散大　在光綫暗淡時，使正常瞳孔散大。持續性瞳孔散大的最常見原因是藥物治療（參閱 mydriatic）或眼外傷。參閱 cycloplegia。與 miosis 對比。

擴瞳藥　使瞳孔擴張的藥。例如阿托品、環噴托酯和苯福林。擴瞳藥被用於輔助檢查眼睛及治療一些眼炎，如虹膜炎和睫狀體炎。

肌（部分）切除術　切除部分肌肉的外科手術。

〔前綴〕脊髓，髓　**(1)** 脊髓。**(2)** 骨髓。　**(3)** 髓鞘質，髓磷脂。

腦髓末腦　參閱 medulla oblongata。

髓鞘質，髓磷脂　一種由蛋白質和磷脂組成的複合物，圍繞某些神經元的軸突，稱為有髓

certain neurones, known as *myelinated* (or *medullated*) *nerve fibres*. The material is produced and laid down in concentric layers by *Schwann cells at regular intervals along the nerve fibre (see illustrations). Myelinated nerves conduct impulses more rapidly than nonmyelinated nerves.

鞘神經纖維。沿神經纖維的一定間隔，施萬細胞產生這種物質並以同心層鋪設（見圖）。有髓鞘的神經傳遞衝動要比無髓鞘的神經快。

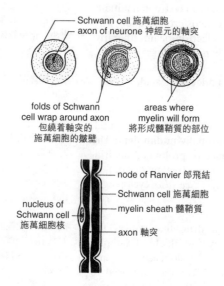

folds of Schwann cell wrap around axon
包繞着軸突的施萬細胞的皺壁

areas where myelin will form
將形成髓鞘質的部位

Schwann cell 施萬細胞
axon of neurone 神經元的軸突

node of Ranvier 郎飛結
Schwann cell 施萬細胞
myelin sheath 髓鞘質
axon 軸突

nucleus of Schwann cell 施萬細胞核

Longitudinal section through a myelinated nerve fibre
有髓鞘神經纖維的縱切面

myelination *n.* the process in which *myelin is laid down as an insulating layer around the axons of certain nerves. Myelination of nerve tracts in the central nervous system is completed by the second year of life.

髓鞘形成 髓鞘質圍繞某些神經元的軸突形成絕緣層的過程。中樞神經系統中神經束的髓鞘形成是兩歲時完成的。

myelitis *n.* **1.** an inflammatory disease of the spinal cord. The most usual kind (*transverse myelitis*) most often occurs during the development of multiple sclerosis, but it is sometimes a manifestation of *encephalomyelities, when it can

(1) 脊髓炎 脊髓的炎症。最常見的類型（橫貫性脊髓炎）最常發生於多發性硬化中，但有時是腦脊髓炎的一種表現，這時它能作為單獨疾病出現。炎症或多或少地擴散到脊髓組

occur as an isolated attack. The inflammation spreads more or less completely across the tissue of the spinal cord, resulting in a loss of its normal function to transmit nerve impulses up and down. It is as though the spinal cord had been severed: paralysis and numbness affects the legs and trunk below the level of the diseased tissue. **2.** inflammation of the bone marrow. *See* osteomyelitis.

myeloblast *n.* the earliest identifiable cell that gives rise to a *granulocyte, having a large mucleus and scanty cytoplasm. It is normally found in the blood-forming tissue of the bone marrow, but may appear in the blood in a variety of diseases, most notably in acute myeloblastic *leukaemia. *See also* granulopoiesis. **–myeloblastic** *adj.*

myelocele *n. see* neural tube defects.

myelocyte *n.* an immature form of *granulocyte having a round nucleus (*compare* metamyelocyte) and neutrophil, eosinophil, or basophil granules within its cytoplasm (*compare* promyelocyte). It is normally found in the blood-forming tissue of the bone marrow, but may appear in the blood in a variety of diseases, including infections, infiltrations of the bone marrow, and certain leukaemias. *See also* granulopoiesis.

myelofibrosis *n.* a chronic but progressive disease characterized by *fibrosis of the bone marrow, which leads to anaemia and the presence of immature red and white blood cells in the circulation. Other features include enlargement of the spleen and the presence of blood-forming (myeloid) tissue in abnormal

織各處，導致神經衝動向上或向下傳導的正常功能喪失。就好似脊髓被切斷：癱瘓和麻木會影響於患病組織下方的下肢和軀體。**(2) 骨髓炎** 骨髓的炎症。參閱 osteomyelitis。

成髓細胞，原（始）粒細胞 生成一個粒細胞、有一個大核及稀疏細胞漿胞的最早期可鑒別的細胞。成髓細胞正常情況下見於骨髓的造血組織中，但在某些種類的疾病中，最明顯的是急性原粒細胞性白血病中，它可出現在血液中。參閱 granulopoiesis。

脊髓突出 參閱 neural tube defects。

髓細胞，中幼粒細胞 粒細胞的一種未成熟形式，其胞漿（與 promyelocyte 對比）內有一圓形核（與 metamyelocyte 對比）和嗜中性、嗜酸性或嗜鹼性（顆）粒。正常情況下見於骨髓的造血組織中，但在感染、骨髓浸潤及某些白血病等疾病時可出現在病人的血液中。參閱 granulopoiesis。

骨髓纖維變性 一種慢性進行性疾病，特點為骨髓纖維變性，可導致貧血及血液循環中出現未成熟的紅細胞和白細胞。其他特徵包括脾腫大和在異常部位，如脾和肝中出現造血（骨髓樣）組織。其病因不明。

sites, such as the spleen and liver. Its cause is unknown.

myelography *n.* a specialized method of X-ray examination to demonstrate the spinal canal that involves injection of a radiopaque contrast medium into the subarachnoid space. The X-rays obtained are called *myelograms*. It is of importance in the recognition of tumours of the spinal cord and other conditions compressing the cord or the nerve roots. The former use of oil-based dyes in myelography was an occasional cause of *arachnoiditis. This complication is now avoided by the use of water-soluble contrast media.

myeloid *adj.* **1.** like, derived from, or relating to bone marrow. **2.** resembling a *myelocyte. **3.** relating to the spinal cord.

myeloid leukaemia a variety of *leukaemia in which the type of blood cell that proliferates abnormally originates in the blood-forming (myeloid) tissue of the bone marrow. Myeloid leukaemias may be acute or chronic and may involve any one of the cells produced by the marrow.

myeloid tissue a tissue in the *bone marrow in which the various classes of blood cells are produced. *See also* haemopoiesis.

myeloma (multiple myeloma, myelomatosis) *n.* a malignant disease of the bone marrow, characterized by two or more of the following criteria: (1) the presence of an excess of abnormal malignant plasma cells in the bone marrow; (2) typical deposits in the bones on X-ray, giving the appearance of holes;

脊髓（X綫）造影術　顯示脊髓的X綫檢查的專業化方法，它涉及蛛網膜下腔注射一種不透X綫的造影劑。得到的X綫照片叫「脊髓X綫（造影）照片」。在識別脊髓腫瘤及脊髓或神經根受壓性疾患中此法具有重大意義。過去在脊髓（X綫）造影術中使用的油質染劑偶然會導致蛛網膜炎。現在使用水溶性造影劑避免了這一併發症。

(1) 骨髓樣的　類似於，衍生於或與骨髓相關的。**(2)** 中幼粒細胞樣的　與中幼粒細胞相似的。**(3)** 脊髓的　與脊髓有關的。

粒細胞性白血病　一種白血病，其異常增加的血細胞來源於骨髓造血（骨髓的）組織。粒細胞性白血病可以是急性或慢性，並可涉及由骨髓生成的任何細胞。

骨髓造血組織　骨髓中生成各類血細胞的一種組織。參閱haemopoiesis。

骨髓瘤（多發性骨髓瘤，骨髓瘤病）　骨髓的一種惡性病，有以下兩種或數種特點：(1) 骨髓中出現過多的異常惡性漿細胞；(2) X綫片上可見骨中有典型沉積物，呈多孔樣外觀；(3) 血清中出現異常的 γ 球蛋白，常為 IgG（一種免疫球蛋

(3) the presence in the serum of an abnormal gamma globulin, usually IgG (an immunoglobulin; *see* paraprotein). *Bence-Jones protein may also be found in the serum or urine. The patient may complain of tiredness due to anaemia and of bone pain and may develop pathological fractures. Treatment is usually with such drugs as melphalan or cyclophosphamide, with local radiotherapy to particular areas of pain. Radiotherapy of the whole body is also used in the primary treatment of myeloma. *See also* plasmacytoma.

白，參閱 paraprotein）。本斯-瓊斯蛋白也可出現在血清或尿中。病人會主訴因貧血出現的疲勞和骨痛，並可發展成病理性骨折。通常用美法侖或環磷酰胺等藥及疼痛的特殊部位局部放射治療。在骨髓瘤的初期治療中，也使用全身放射療法。參閱 plasmacytoma。

myelomalacia *n.* softening of the tissues of the spinal cord, most often caused by an impaired blood supply.

脊髓軟化 脊髓組織的軟化，最常見的病因是血供不足。

myelomatosis *n. see* myeloma.

骨髓瘤病 參閱 myeloma。

myelomeningocele *n. see* neural tube defects.

脊髓脊膜突出 參閱 neural tube defects。

myelosuppression *n.* a reduction in blood-cell production by the bone marrow. It commonly occurs after chemotherapy and may result in anaemia, infection, and abnormal bleeding (*see* thrombocytopenia, neutropenia). **–myelosuppressive** *adj.*

髓抑制 骨髓引起的造血細胞生成減少。一般情況出現在化療之後，可導致貧血、感染及異常出血（參閱 thrombocytopenia，neutropenia）。

myenteric reflex a reflex action of the intestine in which a physical stimulus causes the intestine to contract above and relax below the point of stimulation.

腸（肌）反射 腸道的一種反射活動，在這種反射活動中物理刺激使刺激點以上的腸管收縮，刺激點以下的腸管放鬆。

myenteron *n.* the muscular layer of the *intestine, consisting of a layer of circular muscle inside a layer of longitudinal muscle. These muscles are used in *peristalsis. **–myenteric** *adj.*

腸肌層 腸道的肌層，由縱向肌層內層的環狀肌層構成。用於腸蠕動。

myiasis *n.* an infestation of a living organ or tissue by maggots. The flies

蠅蛆病 蛆對活器官或組織的感染。正常情況下蠅在腐爛的

normally breed in decaying animal and vegetable matter; myiasis therefore generally occurs only in regions of poor hygiene, and in most cases the infestations are accidental. Various genera may infect humans. *Gasterophilus*, *Hypoderma*, *Dermatobia*, and *Cordylobia* affect the skin; *Fannia* invades the alimentary canal and the urinary system; *Phormia* and *Wohlfahrtia* can infest open wounds and ulcers; *Oestrus* attacks the eyes; and *Cochliomyia* invades the nasal passages. Treatment of external myiases involves the destruction and removal of maggots followed by the application of antibiotics to wounds and lesions.

動物或蔬菜中繁殖。因此蠅蛆病一般出現在衛生差的地域，而且在大多數情況下，感染都是偶然的。許多種類的蠅可感染人。胃蠅屬、皮下蠅屬、皮蠅屬和瘤蠅屬侵襲皮膚；廁蠅屬侵襲消化道和泌尿系統；黑花蠅屬和肉蠅屬感染開放性創傷和潰瘍；狂蠅屬侵襲眼睛；而錐蠅屬則侵襲鼻腔。治療外部蠅蛆病包括消滅及去除蛆蟲，然後針對傷口及損害部位使用抗生素。

mylohyoid *n.* a muscle in the floor of the mouth, attached at one end to the mandible and at the other to the hyoid bone.

下頜舌骨肌 口腔底部的一塊肌肉，其一端附着於頜骨，另一端附着於舌骨。

myo- *prefix. see* my-.

〔前綴〕肌 參閱 my-。

myoblast *n.* a cell that develops into a muscle fibre. **–myoblastic** *adj.*

成肌細胞 發展成肌纖維的細胞。

myocardial infarction death of a segment of heart muscle, which follows interruption of its blood supply (*see* coronary thrombosis). Myocardial infarction is usually confined to the left ventricle. The patient experiences a 'heart attack': sudden severe chest pain, which may spread to the arms and throat. The main danger is that of ventricular *fibrillation, which accounts for most of the fatalities. Other *arrhythmias are also frequent; *ectopic beats in the ventricle are especially important as they predispose to ventricular fibrillation. Other complications include heart failure, rupture of the heart, phlebothrombosis, pulmonary embolism, pericarditis, shock, mitral

心肌梗死 部分心肌血供中斷後壞死（參閱 coronary thrombosis）。心肌梗死通常局限於左心室。患者「心臟病發作」時感到胸部突然嚴重疼痛，可擴散到手臂和咽喉。主要的危險在於引起大多數死亡的心室纖顫。其他心率失常也常見，心室的異位搏動預示心室纖顫。其他併發症包括心衰、心臟破裂、靜脈血栓形成、肺栓塞、心包炎、休克、二尖瓣關閉不全和室間隔穿孔。

　　在流動及住院的冠心病護理中，使用早期發現、預防和治療心律失常及心跳停止的設

incompetence, and perforation of the septum between the ventricles.

The best results from the management of patients with myocardial infarction follow mobile and hospital-based coronary care with facilities for the early detection, prevention, and treatment of arrhythmias and *cardiac arrest. Most survivors of myocardial infarction are able to return to a full and active life, including those who have been successfully resuscitated from cardiac arrest.

myocarditis *n.* acute or chronic inflammation of the heart muscle. It may be seen alone or as part of pancarditis (*see* endomyocarditis).

myocardium *n.* the middle of the three layers forming the wall of the heart (*see also* endocardium, epicardium). It is composed of *cardiac muscle and forms the greater part of the heart wall, being thicker in the ventricles than in the atria. **–myocardial** *adj.*

myoclonus *n.* a sudden spasm of the muscles typically lifting and flexing the arms. Occasional *myoclonic jerks* occur between seizures in patients with idiopathic *epilepsy, and myoclonus is a major feature of some progressive neurological illnesses with extensive degeneration of the brain cells (including the *spongiform encephalopathies). Myoclonic jerks on falling asleep (*nocturnal myoclonus*) occur in normal individuals. **–myoclonic** *adj.*

myocyte *n.* a muscle cell.

myodynia *n.* pain in the muscles.

myoepithelium *n.* a tissue consisting of cells of epithelial origin having a contractile cytoplasm. Myoepithelial cells

備，取得了對患心肌梗死病人處理的最好效果。大多數心肌梗死的倖存者，包括那些成功地從心跳停止中復蘇者，都能恢復到完全且活躍的生活。

心肌炎 心肌的急性或慢性炎症。它可單獨或作為全心炎的一部分出現。（參閱 endomyocarditis）。

心肌（層） 構成心臟壁的三層肌肉的中間層（參閱 endocardium，epicardium）。由心肌構成並形成心臟壁的大部分，在心室處比心房處要厚一些。

肌陣攣 以抬起及屈曲手臂為典型特點的突發性肌肉痙攣。偶爾會發生在原發性癲癇病患者的兩次發作之間，肌陣攣是腦細胞廣泛變性的某些進行性疾病的一個主要特徵（包括海綿狀腦）。正常人睡眠時會產生肌陣攣。

肌細胞 肌肉細胞。

肌痛 肌肉的疼痛。

肌上皮 由具有收縮性胞漿的上皮組織細胞構成的一種組織。肌上皮細胞在促進物

play an important role in encouraging the secretion of substances into ducts.

myofibril *n.* one of numerous contractile filaments found within the cytoplasm of *striated muscle cells. When viewed under a microscope myofibrils show alternating bands of high and low refractive index, which give striated muscle its characteristic appearance.

myogenic *adj.* originating in muscle: applied to the inherent rhythmicity of contraction of some muscles (e.g. cardiac muscle), which does not depend on neural influences.

myoglobin *n. see* myohaemoglobin.

myoglobinuria *n. see* myohaemoglobinuria.

myogram *n.* a recording of the activity of a muscle. *See* electromyography.

myography *n.* an instrument for recording the activity of muscular tissues. *See* electromyography.

myohaemoglobin (myoglobin) *n.* an iron-containing protein, resembling *haemoglobin, found in muscle cells. Like haemoglobin it contains a haem group, which binds reversibly with oxygen, and so acts as an oxygen reservoir within the muscle fibres.

myohaemoglobinuria (myoglobinuria) *n.* the presence in the urine of the pigment myohaemoglobin.

myokymia *n.* prominent quivering of a few muscle fibres, not associated with

質分泌物進入導管中起重要作用。

肌原纖維 橫紋肌細胞胞漿內所發現的許多收縮絲的一種。在顯微鏡下觀察時，肌原纖維呈現出高低折射指數的交替帶，這使橫紋肌有具有特性的外觀。

肌（原）性的 起源於肌肉內的：適用於某些肌肉（例如心肌）收縮在內的節律，而不是依靠神經的影響。

肌紅蛋白 參閱 myohaemoglobin。

肌紅蛋白尿 參閱 myohaemoglobinuria。

肌動（描記）圖 肌肉活動的一種記錄。參閱 electromyography。

肌動描記器 一種用於記錄肌肉組織活動的儀器。參閱 electromyography。

肌紅蛋白 一種含鐵蛋白質，類似於肌細胞中的血紅蛋白。像血紅蛋白一樣，它含有能夠可逆地和氧結合的血紅素，因此在肌肉內起到氧氣庫的作用。

肌紅蛋白尿 尿中出現肌紅蛋白這種色素。

肌纖維顫搐 和其他任何異常特徵無關的，少數肌纖維的明

any other abnormal features. It is a benign condition. *See also* fasciculation.

顫顫動。這是一種良性情況。參閱 fasciculation。

myology *n.* the study of the structure, function, and diseases of the muscles.

肌學 研究肌肉的結構、功能和疾病的科學。

myoma *n.* a benign tumour of muscle. It may originate in smooth muscle (*see* leiomyoma) or in striated muscle (*see* rhabdomyoma).

肌瘤 肌肉的一種良性腫瘤。它可能起源於平滑肌（參閱 leiomyoma）或橫紋肌（參閱 rhabdomyoma）中。

myomectomy *n.* an operation in which benign tumours (fibroids) are removed from the muscular wall of the uterus.

肌瘤切除術 從子宮的肌壁切除良性腫瘤（子宮肌瘤）的一種手術。

myometritis *n.* inflammation of the muscular wall (myometrium) of the uterus.

子宮肌（層）炎 子宮肌壁（子宮肌層）的炎症。

myometrium *n.* the muscular tissue of the uterus, which surrounds the *endometrium. It is composed of smooth muscle that undergoes small regular spontaneous contractions. The frequency and amplitude of these contractions alter in response to the hormones *oestrogen, *progesterone, and *oxytocin, which are present at particular stages of the menstrual cycle and pregnancy.

子宮肌層 圍繞子宮內膜的肌肉組織。由平滑肌組成，能夠產生小而有節律的自動收縮。收縮的頻率和幅度隨着月經周期和妊娠期的特殊階段中產生的雌激素、孕酮和縮宮素等的影響而變化。

myoneural junction *see* neuromuscular junction.

肌神經接點 參閱 neuromuscular junction。

myopathy *n.* any disease of the muscles. The myopathies are usually subdivided into those that are inherited (*see* muscular dystrophy) and those that are acquired. The acquired myopathies include *polymyositis and muscular diseases complicating endocrine disorders or carcinoma. All are typified by weakness and wasting of the muscles, which may be associated with pain and tenderness.

肌病 肌肉的任何疾病。通常分為遺傳性的（參閱 muscular dystrophy）和獲得性的。獲得性肌病包括多肌炎及合併有內分泌病或腫瘤的肌病。以伴有疼痛及觸痛的肌無力和肌萎縮為特點。

myopia (short-sightedness) *n.* the condition in which parallel light rays

近視 平行光綫在視網膜前面聚焦的疾病（見圖）。遠處的

are brought to a focus in front of the retina (see illustration). Distant objects are blurred and cannot be made sharp by *accommodation. The condition is corrected by wearing spectacles with concave lenses and can now be treated by surgery (*see* excimer laser, intrastromal keratomileusis, radial keratotomy). *Compare* emmetropia, hypermetropia. **–myopic** *adj.*

物體模糊不清，而且通過調節也不能變清楚。可通過配戴凹透鏡得到糾正，現在可用外科手術治療（參閱 excimer laser，intrastromal keratomileusis，radial keratotomy）。與 emmetropia，hypermetropia 對比。

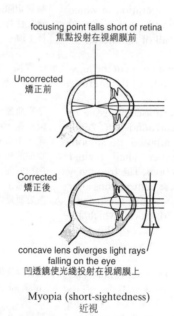

focusing point falls short of retina
焦點投射在視網膜前

Uncorrected
矯正前

Corrected
矯正後

concave lens diverges light rays falling on the eye
凹透鏡使光綫投射在視網膜上

Myopia (short-sightedness)
近視

myoplasm *n. see* sarcoplasm.

肌漿 參閱 sarcoplasm。

myoplasty *n.* the plastic surgery of muscle, in which part of a muscle is partly detached and used to repair tissue defects or deformities in the vicinity of the muscle.

肌整形術 肌肉的整形手術，肌肉被部分分開並被用來修復附近肌肉組織缺陷或畸形。

myosarcoma *n.* malignant tumour of muscle. *See also* leiomyosarcoma, rhabdomyosarcoma.

肌肉瘤 肌肉的惡性腫瘤。參閱 leiomyosarcoma，rhabdomyosarcoma。

myosin *n.* the most abundant protein in muscle fibrils, having the important properties of elasticity and contractility. With actin, it comprises the principal contractile element of muscles. *See* striated muscle.

肌漿球蛋白　肌原纖維中最豐富的蛋白，其重要的特徵是具有彈性和收縮性。它與肌動蛋白一起構成了肌肉的主要收縮元素。參閱 striated muscle。

myosis *n. see* miosis.

瞳孔縮小　參閱 miosis。

myositis *n.* any of a group of muscle diseases in which inflammation and degenerative changes occur. *Polymyositis is the most commonly occurring example, but myositis may be found in relation to systemic *connective-tissue diseases and a minority are caused by bacterial or parasitic infections.

肌炎　任何產生炎症和變性變化的肌肉疾病。多肌炎是最常見的病例，與系統性結締組織病有關，少數由細菌或寄生蟲感染引起。

myositis ossificans the formation of bone in a *haematoma that occurs after fractures, especially around the elbow.

骨折性肌炎　骨折，特別是肘部周圍骨折之後的血腫中骨的形成。

myotactic *adj.* relating to the sense of touch in muscles.

肌（觸）覺的　和肌肉的觸覺相關的。

myotatic reflex *see* stretch reflex.

牽張反射　參閱 stretch reflex。

myotome *n.* that part of the segmented mesoderm in the early embryo that gives rise to all the skeletal muscle of the body. Visceral (smooth) muscles develop from unsegmented mesoderm (*see* mesenchyme). *See also* somite.

肌節　早期胚胎中節段狀的中層胚部分，發育成身體所有的骨骼肌。內臟（平滑）肌由沒有節段的中層胚（參閱 mesenchyme）發展而來。參閱 somite。

myotomy *n.* the dissection or surgical division of a muscle.

肌切開術　肌肉的解剖或外科切開。

myotonia *n.* a disorder of the muscle fibres that results in abnormally prolonged contractions. The patient has difficulty in relaxing a movement (e.g. his grip) after any vigorous effort. It is a feature of a hereditary condition starting in infancy or early childhood (*myotonia*

肌強直　導致肌纖維收縮異常延長的一種疾病。患者在任何強有力的努力之後會產生鬆弛困難（例如握拳）。肌強直是從嬰兒期或幼兒期開始的某種遺傳病（先天性肌強直）的一個特徵，並且是肌肉營養不良

congenita) and of a form of muscular dystrophy (*dystrophia myotonica).

（肌強直性營養不良）的一種形式。

myotonic *adj.* relating to muscle tone.

肌緊張的，肌強直的　和肌肉緊張性相關的。

myotonus *n.* **1.** a tonic muscular spasm. **2.** muscle tone.

(1) 肌強直　強直性肌肉痙攣。　**(2)** 肌緊張

myringa *n.* the eardrum (*see* tympanic membrane).

鼓膜　參閱 tympanic membrane。

myringitis *n.* inflammation of the eardrum. *See* otitis (media).

鼓膜炎　鼓膜的炎症。參閱 otitis (media)。

myringoplasty (tympanoplasty) *n.* surgical repair of a perforated eardrum by grafting.

鼓膜成形術　通過移植術修復穿孔的鼓膜。

myringotomy *n.* incision of the eardrum to create an artificial opening, either to allow infected fluid to drain from the middle ear in acute *otitis media or to remove fluid in *glue ear and permit the insertion of a *grommet.

鼓膜切開術　人工切開鼓膜造口。此開口在急性中耳炎時可引流液體或在膠耳時引流液體及置入通氣管。

myx- (myxo-) *prefix denoting* mucus.

〔前綴〕**黏液**

myxoedema *n.* **1.** a dry firm waxy swelling of the skin and subcutaneous tissues found in patients with underactive thyroid glands (*see* hypothyroidism). **2.** the clinical syndrome due to hypothyroidism in adult life, including coarsening of the skin, intolerance to cold, weight gain, and mental dullness. The symptoms are abolished with thyroxine treatment.

黏液（性）水腫　**(1)** 甲狀腺功能低下患者皮膚和皮下組織的乾燥、堅固的蠟樣腫脹（參閱 hypothyroidism）。　**(2)** 成年人甲狀腺機能減退引起的臨床綜合徵，包括皮膚變粗糙、不耐寒、體重增加及精神遲鈍。用甲狀腺素治療可消除症狀。

myxofibroma *n.* a benign tumour of fibrous tissue that contains myxomatous elements (*see* myxoma) or has undergone mucoid degeneration.

黏液纖維瘤　纖維組織的良性腫瘤，含有黏液瘤成分（參閱 myxoma）或經歷過黏液退化。

myxoid cyst a small cyst containing a thick sticky fluid. It develops over the end

黏液樣囊腫　含有黏稠液體的小囊腫，從手指或腳趾的末端

joint of a finger or toe and should not be cut out, because the cyst is usually in communication with the underlying joint.

myxoma *n.* a benign gelatinous tumour of connective tissue. *Atrial myxoma* is a tumour of the heart, usually of the left side, arising from the septum dividing the two upper chambers. Symptoms may include fever, lassitude, joint pains, and sudden loss of consciousness due to obstruction of the blood-flow. The tumour may be wrongly · diagnosed as stenosis of the mitral valve as it can produce a similar murmur. Treatment requires surgical removal. **–myxomatous** *adj.*

myxosarcoma *n.* a *sarcoma containing mucoid material. It is doubtful whether this represents a true entity and it may be simply a variant of other sarcomas, such as a *liposarcoma or a *fibrosarcoma.

myxovirus *n.* one of a group of RNA-containing viruses that includes those causing influenza in animals and man. The related *paramyxoviruses* include the *respiratory syncytial virus (RSV) and the agents that cause measles, mumps, and parainfluenza.

N

nabilone *n.* a drug related to cannabis, used to control severe nausea and vomiting, especially when caused by anticancer drugs. Administered by mouth, it is thought to act on opiate receptors in the nervous system. Trade name: **Cesamet**.

關節發展而來。不能切除，因為囊腫通常和其下面的關節相關。

黏液瘤 結締組織的良性膠狀瘤。心房黏液瘤是心臟的腫瘤，常在心臟的左側，起源於房間隔，症狀有發熱、倦怠、關節痛及由血流受阻引起的突然意識喪失。因為能產生與二尖瓣狹窄相似的雜音，可產生誤診。需手術治療。

黏液肉瘤 含有黏液樣物質的肉瘤。對此病是否構成一個真正的實體尚有疑問。可能僅是其他肉瘤（如脂肉瘤及纖維肉瘤）的一個變種。

黏液病毒 含有 RNA 的病毒屬中的一種，包括那些使動物和人患流感的病毒。有關的副黏液病毒包括呼吸道合胞病毒 (RSV) 和引起麻疹、流行性腮腺炎和副流感病毒。

大麻隆 和大麻相關的一種藥物，用於控制嚴重的惡心和嘔吐，特別是由抗癌藥物引起的惡心和嘔吐。口服。此藥被認為能作用於神經系統的阿片受體。商品名：Cesamet。

nabothian follicle (nabothian cyst, nabothian gland) one of a number of cysts on the neck (cervix) of the uterus, near its opening to the vagina. The sacs, which contain mucus, form when the ducts of the glands in the cervix are blocked by a new growth of surface cells (epithelium) over an area damaged because of infection.

納博特濾泡（納博特囊腫、納博特腺）子宮頸接近其通向陰道開口部位上的許多囊腫之一。當感染造成局部表層細胞（上皮細胞）新的生長，從而堵塞了子宮頸腺體的導管時，含有黏液的囊腫就形成了。

NAD (nicotinamide adenine dinucleotide) a *coenzyme that acts as a hydrogen acceptor in oxidation-reduction reactions, particularly in the *electron transport chain in cellular respiration. NAD and the closely related coenzyme NADP (nicotinamide adenine dinucleotide phosphate) are derived from nicotinic acid; they are reduced to NADH and NADPH, respectively.

煙酰胺腺嘌呤二核苷酸，輔酶Ⅰ　在氧化還原反應中，特別是在細胞呼吸的電子轉移鏈中作為氫受體的輔酶。煙酰胺腺嘌呤二核苷酸和與其密切相關的煙酰胺腺嘌呤二核苷酸磷酸都由煙酸衍生而來。它們分別被還原為 NADH 和 NADPH。

nadolol n. a *beta blocker used in the treatment of angina pectoris and high blood pressure (hypertension). It is administered by mouth; side-effects include decreased heart *rate, dizziness, and low blood pressure. Trade name: **Corgard**.

納多洛爾　一種β-受體阻滯劑，用於治療心絞痛和高血壓。口服。副作用包括心率減緩、頭暈和低血壓。商品名：Corgard。

NADP (nicotinamide adenine dinucleotide phosphate) see NAD.

煙酰胺腺嘌呤二核苷酸磷酸，輔酶Ⅱ　參閱 NAD。

Naegele rule a method used to estimate the probable date of the onset of labour: nine months and seven days are added to the date of the first day of the last menstrual period. A correction is required if the woman does not have 28-day menstrual cycles.

內格勒規則　估算分娩大致日期的方法。方法是自末次月經的第一天加上九個月零七天。如果婦女的月經期不是 28 天，則要對此規則加以調整。

Naegele's obliquity see asynclitism.

內格勒傾斜　參閱 asynclitism。

Naegleria n. a genus of *amoebae that normally live in damp soil or mud.

耐格里原蟲屬（阿米巴原蟲）正常情況下生長在潮濕土壤或

Naegleria species can, however, live as parasites in man and are believed to have caused some rare, but fatal, infections of the brain.

泥土中的阿米巴蟲屬。但是耐格里原蟲可寄生於人體內，據信曾引起某些罕見但致命的大腦感染。

naevus *n.* (*pl.* **naevi**) a birthmark: a clearly defined malformation of the skin, present at birth. There are may different types of naevi. Some, including the strawberry naevus and port-wine stain, are composed of small blood vessels (*see* haemangioma). The *strawberry naevus* (or *strawberry mark*) is a raised red lump usually appearing on the face and growing rapidly in the first month of life. These birthmarks slowly resolve and spontaneously disappear between the ages of five and ten. The *port-wine stain* (or *capillary naevus*) is a permanent purplish discoloration that may occur anywhere but usually appears on the upper half of the body. Laser treatment can reduce the discoloration. Occasionally a port-wine stain may be associated with a malformation of blood vessels over the brain, for example in the Sturge-Weber syndrome (*see* angioma).

It is not uncommon for a pale or white halo to develop around an ordinary pigmented naevus, especially on the trunk, forming a *halo naevus*. The pigmented naevus disappears over the course of a few months; this is followed by resolution of the pale area. A *blue naevus* is a small blue-grey papule appearing at birth or later in life, mainly on the extremities. Progression to malignant melanoma is very rare. *See also* mole[2].

痣 一種胎記：出生時就有的，邊界明確的皮膚畸形。有許多不同的種類。有些痣，包括草莓狀痣和葡萄酒樣色素斑，由小血管組成（參閱 haemangioma）。草莓狀痣（或草莓斑）通常是皮膚表面上的一個隆起的紅色腫塊，在人出生的一個月內生長迅速。這些胎記在 5~10 個月之間會逐漸溶解並自動消失。葡萄酒樣色素斑（或毛細管痣）是一種永久性的紫色變色，可出現在身體的任何部位，但常出現在身體的上半部分。激光治療可以減少變色。葡萄酒樣色素斑偶爾會和大腦的血管畸形，如斯-韋氏綜合徵（參閱 angioma）相關。

在一個普通的色素痣周圍，特別是軀幹上的色素痣周圍，淡色或白色的暈圈發展成暈圈痣並非少見。色素痣在數月內會消失，這通常出現在淡色區域消退後，藍痣是出生時或生長中出現的一種藍灰色小丘疹。很少發展成惡性腫瘤。參閱 mole[2]。

Naga sore *see* tropical ulcer.

納加潰瘍 參閱 tropical ulcer。

NAI *see* nonaccidental injury.

非事故性外傷 參閱 nonaccidental injury。

nail *n*. a horny structure, composed of keratin, formed from the epidermis on the dorsal surface of each finger and toe (see illustration). The exposed part of the nail is the *body*, behind which is the *root*. The whitish crescent-shaped area at the base of the body is called the *lunula*. Growth of the nail occurs at the end of the nail root by division of the germinative layer of the underlying *epidermis (which forms part of the *matrix*). The growing nail slides forward over the *nail bed*. The fold of skin that lies above the root is the *nail fold*; folds of skin on either side of the nail are the *nail walls*. The epidermis of the nail fold that lies next to the nail root is called the *eponychium* (forming the 'cuticle' at the base of the nail). Anatomical name: **unguis**.

甲　由角蛋白構成的一種角質結構，形成於每個指和趾的背面表皮（見圖）。甲的暴露部分是甲體，其後面是甲根。甲體基底部的白色新月形區域叫弧影。甲的生長通過下面的表皮生長層（它形成甲床的一部分）的分裂產生於甲根的末端。生長中的甲在甲床上向前滑動。甲根上的皮膚皺襞是甲褶，甲兩側的皮膚皺襞叫甲壁，緊挨着甲根的甲褶的表皮叫甲上皮（在甲的基底部形成「護膜」。）解剖學名：指（趾）甲。

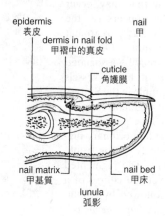

epidermis
表皮
dermis in nail fold
甲褶中的真皮
cuticle
角護膜
nail
甲
nail matrix
甲基質
lunula
弧影
nail bed
甲床

Longitudinal section through the fingertip and nail
指尖和甲的縱切面

nalidixic acid a *quinolone antibiotic active against various bacteria and used to treat infections of the urinary and digestive systems. It is administered by mouth; common side-effects are nausea, vomiting, and skin reactions. Trade names: **Negram**, **Uriben**.

萘啶酸　一種喹啉抗生素，能作用於各種細菌，用於治療泌尿系統和消化系統的感染。口服。常見的副作用有惡心、嘔吐和皮膚反應。商品名：Negram，Uriben。

naloxone *n.* a drug that is a specific antidote to morphine and similar narcotic drugs. It is administered by intravenous or subcutaneous injection. As it is short-acting, repeated doses may be necessary. Trade name: **Narcan**.

納洛酮　嗎啡或與其類似麻醉藥的一種專門解毒藥。靜脈或皮下注射，因為其藥效短，須反覆注射。商品名：Narcan。

naltrexone *n.* a narcotic antagonist drug that is used in the maintenance treatment of heroin- and other opiate-dependent patients. It is administered by mouth. Possible side-effects include abdominal cramps, nausea and vomiting, sleep difficulties, and dizziness. Trade name: **Nalorex**.

納曲酮　用於海洛因及其他阿片依賴患者維持療法的麻醉藥對抗劑。口服。可能產生的副作用有下腹絞痛、惡心、嘔吐、失眠和頭暈。商品名：Nalorex。

nandrolone *n.* a synthetic male sex hormone with *anabolic effects. It is administered by injection and high doses may cause signs of *virilization in women. Trade name: **Deca-Durabolin**.

南諾龍　具有組成代謝作用的人工合成雄性激素。注射給藥，婦女大劑量使用可造成男性化的微兆。商品名：Deca-Durabolin。

nano- *prefix denoting* **1.** extremely small size. **2.** one thousand-millionth part (10^{-9}).

〔前綴〕**(1)** 矮，小　極小。**(2)** 纖，毫微　10 億分之一 (10^{-9})。

nanometre *n.* one thousand-millionth of a metre $(10^{-9}\,\text{m})$. One nanometre is equal to 10 angstrom. Symbol: nm.

毫微米　10 億分之一米 (10^{-9}m)。1 毫微米等於 10 個埃。符號：nm。

naphazoline *n.* a drug that constricts small blood vessels and is used to relieve congestion in rhinitis and sinusitis. It is administered as nasal drops and may cause slight irritation. Trade name: **Vasocon-A**.

荼甲哇啉　收縮小血管的藥物。用於解除鼻炎和鼻竇炎時出現的充血現象。作為滴鼻劑給藥，可造成輕度的刺激。商品名：Vasocon-A。

napkin rash (nappy rash) a red skin rash within the napkin area, usually causes by chemical irritation (ammoniacal *dermatitis) or infection with *Candida*. Ammoniacal dermatitis is caused by skin contact with wet soiled nappies, the stool bacteria reacting with urine to form irritant ammonia.

尿布疹　尿布覆蓋區域內的紅色皮疹，通常由化學刺激（氨性皮炎）或念珠菌感染引起。氨性皮炎由皮膚接觸髒濕的尿布、糞便細菌與尿反應形成的刺激性氨造成。治療包括接觸空氣，使用氨防護霜及勤換尿布。念珠菌性尿布疹用抗真菌

Treatment involves exposure to air, application of barrier creams, and frequent nappy changes. Candidal nappy rash is treated with antifungal creams. Other causes of napkin rash include eczema and psoriasis.

霜治療。尿布疹的其他病因包括濕疹和牛皮癬。

naprapathy *n.* a system of medicine based on the belief that a great many diseases are attributable to displacement of ligaments, tendons, and other connective tissues and that cure can be brought about only by manipulation to correct these displacements.

推拿療法 一種醫療體系,其基礎是認為許多疾病都是韌帶、肌腱以及其他結締組織移位引起,並且只有通過推拿糾正移位才能治愈疾病。

naproxen *n.* an analgesic drug that also reduces inflammation and fever (*see* NSAID). It is used to treat rheumatoid arthritis, ankylosing spondylitis, and gout. It is administered by mouth; side-effects may include digestive upsets and rashes. Trade names: **Naprosyn**, **Nycopren**.

萘普生 一種亦具有消炎和解熱作用的鎮痛藥(參閱NSAID)。用於治療風濕性關節炎。強直性脊椎炎和痛風。口服給藥。副作用有消化不良和皮疹。商品名:Naprosyn,Nycopren。

narcissism *n.* an excessive involvement with oneself and one's self-importance. In Freudian terms it is a state in which the *ego has taken itself as a love object. Some degree of narcissism is present in most individuals, but when it is shown to an extreme degree it may be a symptom of schizophrenia, personality disorder, or other conditions. **–narcissistic** *adj.*

自戀,自戀癖 過度涉及自我及自大。在弗洛伊德學派的術語中,自戀是一種把自我作為戀愛對象的狀態。大多數人都有某種程度的自戀,但是自戀達到極端狀態時,可能是精神分裂症,人格障礙或其他疾病的一種症狀。

narco- *prefix denoting* narcosis; stupor.

〔前綴〕**麻醉,昏糊,木僵**

narcolepsy *n.* an extreme tendency to fall asleep in quiet surroundings or when engaged in monotonous activities. The patient can be woken easily and is immediately alert. It is often associated with *cataplexy, and when falling asleep the patient may experience hallucinations or transient attacks of muscular paralysis. **–narcoleptic** *adj., n.*

發作性睡(眠)病 在安靜環境中或從事單調活動時極度傾向於睡眠。病人很容易被喚醒並馬上活躍。本病通常和猝倒相關,睡著時病人可產生幻覺或短暫發作肌肉麻痺。

narcosis *n.* a state of diminished consciousness or complete unconsciousness caused by the use of *narcotic drugs, which have a depressant action on the nervous system. The body's normal reactions to stimuli are diminished and the body may become sedated or completely anaesthetized.

narcotic *n.* a drug that induces stupor and insensibility and relieves pain. The term is used particularly for *morphine and other derivatives of opium (*see* opiate) but is also applied to other drugs that depress brain function (e.g. general anaesthetics and hypnotics). In legal terms a narcotic is any addictive drug subject to illegal use. Narcotics (i.e. morphine and morphine-like drugs) have been largely replaced as sleeping drugs because of their ability to cause *dependence and tolerance; they are still used for relief of severe pain (*see* analgesic).

nares *pl. n.* (*sing.* **naris**) openings of the nose. The two *external* (or *anterior*) *nares* are the nostrils, leading from the nasal cavity to the outside. The two *internal* (or *posterior*) *nares* (*choanae*) are the openings leading from the nasal cavity into the pharynx.

nasal bone either of a pair of narrow oblong bones that together form the bridge and root of the nose. *See* skull.

nasal cavity the space inside the nose that lies between the floor of the cranium and the roof of the mouth. It is divided into two halves by a septum: each half communicates with the outside via the nostrils and with the nasopharynx through the posterior nares.

nasal concha (turbinate bone) any of three thin scroll-like bones that form the

麻醉　使用對神經系統有抑制作用的麻醉藥後引起的意識減少或完全喪失狀態。身體對刺激的正常反應減小，因此會進入鎮靜狀態或被完全麻醉。

麻醉藥　誘導昏糊和無知覺並緩解疼痛的一種藥物。這個術語特指嗎啡和阿片的其他衍化物（參閱 opiate），但亦可指抑制大腦功能的其他藥物（例如全身麻醉藥和安眠藥）。在法律術語中，麻醉藥泛指非法使用的成癮藥。因為麻醉藥能引起藥物依賴和耐藥性，它們（例如嗎啡和嗎啡類藥）大部分已被安眠藥取代。麻醉藥仍被用於緩解嚴重疼痛（參閱 analgesic）。

鼻孔　鼻子的開口。兩個前鼻孔是鼻腔通向外界的鼻孔，兩個後鼻孔是鼻腔通向咽喉的開口。

鼻骨　一對狹窄的長方形骨中的一個，它們共同組成鼻梁和鼻根。參閱 skull。

鼻腔　鼻內位於顱底和口腔頂之間的空間。鼻腔被中隔分為兩部分。每一半都通過前鼻孔與外界相連，通過後鼻孔與鼻咽相連。

鼻甲　構成鼻腔壁的三塊薄的卷形骨中的任何一個。上鼻甲

sides of the *nasal cavity. The *superior* and *middle nasal conchae* are part of the *ethmoid bone; the *inferior nasal conchae* are a separate pair of bones of the face. *See* skull.

和中鼻甲是篩骨的一部分；下鼻甲是一對獨立的面骨。參閱 skull。

nasion *n.* the point on the bridge of the nose at the centre of the suture between the nasal and frontal bones.

鼻根點 位於鼻骨和額骨的骨縫中央、鼻梁上的點。

naso- *prefix denoting* the nose.

〔前綴〕**鼻**

nasogastric tube a tube passed through the nose into the stomach, used to aspirate fluid from, or introduce material into, the stomach (*see* Ryle's tube).

鼻胃管 一條從鼻進入胃的管，用於從胃中抽吸液體或向胃中輸入物質（參閱 Ryle's tube）。

nasolacrimal *adj.* relating to the nose and the lacrimal (tear-producing) apparatus.

鼻淚的 與鼻和淚（產生淚的）器相關的。

nasolacrimal duct the duct that passes through the hole (*nasolacrimal canal*) in the palatine bone of the skull. It drains the tears away from the *lacrimal apparatus into the inferior meatus of the nose.

鼻淚管 穿過顱的腭骨內孔（鼻淚管）的管道。它把淚從淚器導向下鼻道。

nasopharynx (rhinopharynx) *n.* the part of the *pharynx that lies above the soft palate.

鼻咽 位於軟腭上的咽部分。

nates *pl. n.* the buttocks. **—natal** *adj.*

臀

national census *see* Office of Population Censuses and Surveys.

全國人口普查 參閱 Office of Population Censuses and Surveys。

National Health Service (in Britain) a comprehensive service offering therapeutic and preventive medical and surgical care, including the prescription and dispensing of medicines, spectacles, and medical and dental appliances. Exchequer funds pay for the services of doctors, nurses, and other professionals, as well as residential costs in NHS

國民保健服務制 （英國）一個綜合性服務制度，提供內科和外科治療和預防，包括處方和配藥、配眼鏡以及醫療和牙科器械等。醫生、護士和其他專業人員的服務、在實行國民保健服務制醫院的住院費以及相當部分的醫藥器械費用全由國庫資金支付。1946 年通過的

hospitals, and meet a substantial part of the cost of the medicines and appliances. Legislation enacted in 1946 was implemented in 1948 and the services were subjected to substantial reorganization in 1974 and again in 1982 and 1993. In England overall responsibility is vested in the Secretary of State for Health assisted by a comprehensive department (*see* Department of Health). Administration is based on a system of delegation downwards and accountability upwards through a hierarchy of 14 regions, each subdivided into a number of districts. In general, *Regional Health Authorities (RHAs)*, whose members are all appointed by the Secretary of State, are responsible for overall (strategic) planning and monitoring and for allocating funds to the *District Health Authorities (DHAs)*. DHAs, whose chairmen are appointed by the Secretary of State and the majority of their members by the RHAs, are responsible for local (tactical) planning and for acquiring the services required for their districts. Each tier has a team of officers including a doctor (*see* public health physician), *nursing officer, administrator, and treasurer responsible for the smooth working of their respective aspects of the Service. Formerly the team functioned on the basis of consensus management, which was often unsatisfactory because of failure to reach decisions; now each officer, though self-accountable in professional terms, is answerable managerially to the *Regional* (or *District*) *General Manager*.

Health authorities are expected to provide all the normal health services from their own resources except the salaries and fees for general practitioners, pharmacists, opticians, and dentists, which come from a separate fund through the *Family Health Services

法律於 1948 年執行。這些服務機構在 1974 年、1982 年和 1992 年重新改組。在英格蘭，衛生國務大臣在一個綜合部門（參閱 Department of Health）的協助下全權負責這些服務機構。行政體系建立在向下的委派制和向上的負責制，實行分級管理，把全國分成 14 個區，每個區又細分成若干地段。一般說來，地區衛生局 (RHAs) 的所有成員由國務大臣任命，RHAs 負責全面的（戰略的）規劃和監督，並負責向地段衛生局 (DHAs) 下撥資金。DHAs 的局長由國務大臣任命，大多數成員由 RHAs 任命，DHAs 負責局部（戰術上的）計劃並負責安排他們所在地段需要的服務。每一級都有一個工作組包括一名醫生（參閱 public health physician）、護師、行政人員和財務人員在內，負責所分管的服務工作順利進行。以前這個工作組在意見完全一致時方可發揮作用，但是因為不能作出決定，經常不盡人意。現在每位職員儘管在專業方面各行其職，但在整體管理上對地區（或地段）總幹事負責。

各衛生當局應從它們自己的資金中向所有的正常保健服務項目提供資金，但不支付全科醫生、藥劑師、配鏡師及牙科醫生的薪水及費用，這部分費用的來源是家庭保健服務管理的單獨基金。一些少見病病人的專項費用由地區和跨地區部門分擔。地段的劃分盡量與地方當局管理的範圍相同，這樣便於努力取得並保證與社會福利部門間的聯繫，這些部門提供許多重要的服務項目支持病人和老年人（參閱 social

Authority. Some of the special resources for patients with rarer complaints are shared on a regional or supraregional basis. Wherever possible, districts have common boundaries with local authorities in order to try and ensure liaison with the social service departments, which provide many important services to support the sick and aged (*see* social services). However, many districts include part of more than one local authority since the division tends to be made on the basis of the *catchment area of a district general hospital.

Different arrangements apply in Northern Ireland, Wales, and Scotland (for which there is a separate Act), where the appropriate Secretary of State is responsible and the regional tier is omitted. In Wales and Scotland there is an intermediate tier by which districts are grouped into areas (*see* Chief Administrative Medical Officer).

National Insurance (in Britain) a compulsory scheme of insurance under the terms of which employers and employees make joint contributions so that those who have contributed for a qualifying period may claim benefits in times of sickness, injury, maternity leave, unemployment, and retirement; self-employed persons pay all their own contributions. Those who do not qualify under the terms of this insurance scheme may also receive financial payments in times of need, but only subject to a stringent means test.

natriuresis *n.* the excretion of sodium in the urine, especially in greater than normal amounts.

natriuretic *n.* an agent that promotes the excretion of sodium salts in the urine. Most *diuretics are natriuretics.

services），但是，因為地段的劃分趨於以地段綜合醫院的保健地段為基礎，所以許多地段範圍包括不止一個地方當局的一部分。

北愛爾蘭、威爾士和蘇格蘭應用不同的管理辦法（因為它們有單獨的法令），在這些地方，相應的國務大臣負責這項工作，沒有地區一層。在威爾士和蘇格蘭，有一個中間層，通過中間層把地段劃分為行政區（參閱 Chief Administrative Medical Officer）。

國民保險 （英國）一種強制性保險計劃，按其條款規定，僱主和僱員要共同交保險金以便於那些交足有資格期限保險金者可以在生病、受傷、休產假、失業和退休時可獲取利益。個體戶要付全部的保險金。按保險計劃條款規定沒有資格者在需要時也可獲得經濟賠償，但需要通過嚴格的測試。

尿鈉排泄 尿中鈉的排泄，特別指鈉的排泄比正常量大。

（促）尿鈉排泄藥 促使尿中鈉鹽排泄的藥物。大多數利尿劑是（促）尿鈉排泄藥。

natural killer cell (NK cell) a type of *lymphocyte that is able to kill certain types of cancer cells. Patients with cancer typically have fewer of these cells in the blood.

自然殺傷細胞　一種能夠殺滅某些類型癌細胞的一種淋巴細胞，癌症患者的血液中這些細胞要少一些，這是很典型的。

naturopathy *n.* a system of medicine that relies upon the use of only 'natural' substances for the treatment of disease, rather than drugs. Herbs, food grown without artificial fertilizers and prepared without the use of preservatives or colouring material, pure water, sunlight, and fresh air are all employed in an effort to rid the body of 'unnatural' substances, which are said to be at the root of most illnesses.

自然醫術　僅依靠「自然」物質來治療疾病而不使用藥物的醫療體系。草藥、沒有使用化肥培植的糧食、沒有使用防腐劑或色素加工的食物、純水、陽光和新鮮空氣都被用來去除身體內的非自然物質，據說這些非自然物質是大多數疾病的根源。

nausea *n.* the feeling that one is about to vomit, as experienced in seasickness and in morning sickness of early pregnancy. Actual vomiting often occurs subsequently.

惡心　一種想嘔吐的感覺，如暈船或妊娠早期反應時所感到的那樣。隨後常會產生真正的嘔吐。

navel *n.* see umbilicus.

臍　參閱 umbilicus。

navicular bone a boat-shaped bone of the ankle (*see* tarsus) that articulates with the three cuneiform bones in front and with the talus behind.

舟狀骨　踝部的船形骨（參閱 tarsus），它和前面的三塊楔骨及後面的距骨構成關節。

nearthrosis *n. see* pseudarthrosis.

人造關節　參閱 pseudarthrosis。

nebula *n.* a faint opacity of the cornea that remains after an ulcer has healed.

角膜雲翳　潰瘍痊愈後角膜上存留的輕度混濁。

nebulizer *n.* an instrument used for applying a liquid in the form of a fine spray.

噴霧器　用於把液體變成氣霧的器械。

NEC *see* necrotizing enterocolitis.

壞死性小腸結腸炎　參閱 necrotizing enterocolitis。

Necator *n.* a genus of *hookworms that live in the small intestine. The human

板口綫蟲屬　生活在小腸中的鈎蟲屬。人類鈎蟲，即美洲板

hookworm, *N. americanus*, occurs in tropical Africa, Central and South America, India, and the Pacific Islands. The worm possesses two pairs of sharp cutting plates inside its mouth cavity, which enable it to feed on the blood and tissues of the gut wall. *Compare* Ancylostoma.

口綫蟲屬，出現於熱帶非洲、中美洲、南美洲、印度和太平洋諸島。這種蟲的口腔內有兩對鋒利的切板，用以攝食腸壁的血液和組織。與 Ancylostoma 對比。

necatoriasis *n.* an infestation of the small intestine by the parasitic hookworm *Necator americanus*. *See also* hookworm disease.

板口綫蟲病 寄生鉤蟲美洲板口綫蟲屬對於小腸的感染。參閱 hookworm disease。

neck *n.* **1.** the part of the body that connects the head and the trunk. It is the region supported by the *cervical vertebras. **2.** *see* cervix.

(1) 頸 連接頭和軀幹的身體部分，這一區域由頸椎支持。**(2) 子宮頸** 參閱 cervix。

necro- *prefix denoting* death or dissolution.

〔前綴〕**壞死** 死亡，溶解。

necrobiosis *n.* a gradual process by which cells lose their function and die. *Necrobiosis lipoidica* is a disease in which degeneration of collagen produces sharply demarcated yellowish-brown plaques, especially on the shins of women. It is often, but not exclusively, associated with diabetes mellitus.

漸遺性（細胞）壞死 細胞喪失其功能並死亡的緩慢過程。脂性漸進性壞死是一種病，患病時膠原的變性產生界限明顯的黃褐斑，特別出現於婦女的脛部。本病通常但不完全和糖尿病相關。

necrology *n.* the study of the phenomena of death, involving determination of the moment of death and the different changes that occur in the tissues of the body after death.

死亡學 研究死亡現象的科學，它涉及確定死亡的瞬間和死亡後身體組織內產生的不同變化。

necromania *n.* morbid desire for a dead body or bodies. This may be necrophilism, but the attraction is sometimes not sexual. A bereaved person, for instance, who is not grieving normally, may occasionally treasure the body of a loved one.

戀屍狂 對屍體的病態喜好。它可以表現為戀屍癖，但有時不是性吸引。例如：一個喪偶者因為悲傷，偶爾會珍藏愛人的屍體。

necrophilism (necrophilia) *n*. sexual attraction to corpses. *See also* sexual deviation. **–necrophile** *n*.

戀屍癖　對屍體產生的性吸引。參閱 sexual deviation。

necropsy *n. see* autopsy.

屍體解剖　參閱 autopsy。

necrosis (mortification) *n*. the death of some or all of the cells in an organ or tissue, caused by disease, physical or chemical injury, or interference with the blood supply (*see* gangrene). *Caseous necrosis* occurs in pulmonary tuberculosis, the long tissue becoming soft, dry, and cheese-like.

壞死（壞疽）　由於疾病、物理或化學創傷或血液供應障礙（參閱 gangrene）所致的器官或組織內細胞部分或全部死亡。乾酪樣壞死產生在肺結核中，肺組織變軟、變乾，像奶酪。

necrospermia *n*. the presence of either dead or motionless spermatozoa in the semen. *See* infertility.

死精症　精液中出現死的或無活動能力的精子。參閱 infertility。

necrotizing enterocolitis (NEC) a serious disease affecting the bowel during the first three weeks of life; it is much more common in *preterm babies. The abdomen distends and blood and mucus appear in the stools; the bowel may perforate. Treatment is to rest the bowel and administer antibiotics. If the bowel becomes necrotic, surgery may be necessary.

壞死性小腸結腸炎　在出生後的前三周中影響腸道的嚴重疾病。此病在早產兒中更常見。腹部腫脹，糞便中出現血和黏液。腸道會發生穿孔。治療時要讓腸道休息並使用抗生素。如果出現腸壞死，則需要手術。

nedocromil *n*. an anti-inflammatory drug used to treat bronchitis and bronchial asthma. It is administered by metered-dose aerosol inhaler; possible side-effects include nausea and brief headaches. Trade name: **Tilade**.

奈多羅米　用於治療支氣管炎和支氣管痙攣的一種抗炎藥。通過計量氣霧吸入器給藥。副作用包括惡心和短暫的頭痛。商品名：Tilade。

needle *n*. a slender sharp-pointed instrument used for a variety of purposes. Needles used for sewing up tissue during surgery are of various designs, for specific operations; they are equipped with an eye for threading suture material or they have the suture material fused onto them (so-called *atraumatic needles*).

針　用於各種不同目的的、纖細的、頂端呈尖形的器械。手術中用來縫合組織的針設計各異，以滿足具體的手術。這些針有穿縫合材料的針眼或與縫合材料熔合在一起（所謂的無損傷針）。空心針用於向體內（皮下注射器）注射液體，

Hollow needles are used to inject substances into the body (in hypodermic syringes), to obtain specimens of tissue, or to withdraw fluid from a cavity (*see* aspiration, biopsy). *See also* stop needle.

獲取組織標本或從腔室中抽取液體（參閱 aspiration，biopsy）。參閱 stop needle。

needle-stick injury a common accidental injury to the fingers and hands of nurses and doctors by contaminated injection needles. It can result in transmitted infections (e.g. hepatitis, AIDS).

針刺外傷 被污染的注射針對護士和醫生手指和手造成的常見的意外傷害。會導致感染（例如肝炎、艾滋病）。

needling *n*. a form of *capsulotomy in which a sharp needle is used to make a hole in the capsule surrounding the lens of the eye. This technique has now largely been replaced by use of the *YAG laser.

針刺術 一種晶狀體囊切除術，用一根尖針在眼睛晶狀體周圍的囊上刺一個孔。這一技術大部分已被 YAG 激光取代。

negativism *n*. behaviour that is the opposite of that suggested by others. In *active negativism* the individual does the opposite of what he is asked (for example, he screws his eyes up when asked to open them). This is uncommon in adult life and is usually associated with other features of *catatonia. In *passive negativism* the person fails to cooperate (for example, he does not eat). This occurs in *schizophrenia and *depression.

違拗症 與其他人的建議相反的行為。在主動違拗症中，病人幹與他人要求相反的事（例如：要求他睜開眼睛時，病人會緊閉雙眼）。此病在成人中不常見，通常和緊張症的其他特徵相關。在被動違拗症中，患者不合作（例如：不吃飯）。這發生於精神分裂症和抑鬱症。

Neisseria *n*. a genus of spherical Gram-negative aerobic nonmotile bacteria characteristically grouped in pairs. They are parasites of animals, and some species are normal inhabitants of the respiratory tract of man. The species *N. gonorrhoeae* (the *gonococcus*) causes *gonorrhoea. Gonococci are found within pus cells of urethral and vaginal discharge; they can be cultured only on serum or blood agar. *N. meningitidis* (the *meningococcus*) causes meningococcal *meningitis. Meningococci are found within pus cells of infected cerebrospinal

奈瑟菌屬 特點為成對聚集在一起的球形、革蘭氏陰性、需氧、非運動細菌屬。它們是動物的寄生菌，某些種類寄生於人類呼吸道。淋病拉瑟菌（淋球菌）引起淋病。淋球菌可見於尿道和陰道排出物的膿細胞內。只能在血清或血瓊脂平板上培養。腦膜炎奈瑟菌屬（腦膜炎雙球菌）引起腦（脊）膜炎。腦膜炎雙球菌可見於被感染的腦脊液和血液的膿細胞內或帶菌者的鼻道內。也只能在血清或血瓊脂平板上培養。

fluid and blood or in the nasal passages of carriers. They too can only be cultured on serum or blood agar.

nematode (roundworm) *n.* any one of a large group of worms having an unsegmented cylindrical body, tapering at both ends. This distinguishes nematodes from other *helminths. Nematodes occur either as free-living forms in the sea, fresh water, and soil or as parasites of plants, animals, and man. *Hookworms and *pinworms infest the alimentary canal. *Filariae are found in the lymphatic tissues. The *guinea worm and *Onchocerca affect connective tissue. Some nematodes (e.g. pinworms) are transmitted from host to host by the ingestion of eggs; others (e.g. *Wuchereria) by the bite of a bloodsucking insect.

neo- *prefix denoting* new or newly formed.

neoadjuvant chemotherapy chemotherapy that is given before the treatment of a primary tumour with the aim of improving the results of surgery or radiotherapy and preventing the development of metastases. *Compare* adjuvant therapy.

neocerebellum *n.* the middle lobe of the *cerebellum, excluding the pyramid and uvula. In evolutionary terms it is the newest part, occurring only in mammals.

neologism *n.* (in psychiatry) the invention of words to which meanings are attached. It is common in childhood, but when it occurs in an adult it may be a symptom of a psychotic illness, such as *schizophrenia. It should be distinguished from *paraphasia, in which new

綫蟲 任何無體節、圓柱形、兩端逐漸變細的一大類蠕蟲。這使綫蟲與其他蠕蟲不同。綫蟲既可以離體形式生存在海水、淡水和土壤中，又可作為植物、動物和人的寄生蟲。鈎蟲和蟯蟲寄生於消化道。絲蟲見於淋巴組織中。麥地那龍綫蟲和盤尾絲蟲屬影響結締組織。有些綫蟲（例如蟯蟲）通過卵的攝入從一個宿主傳向另一個宿主。其他綫蟲（例如：吳策綫蟲屬）則通過吸血昆蟲的叮咬傳播。

〔前綴〕**新** 新的或新形成的。

新輔助化學療法 治療原發性腫瘤之前使用的化學療法，其目的在於加強手術或放射療法的結果，並預防轉移的發展。與 adjuvant therapy 對比。

新小腦 不包括蚓錐體和蚓垂在內的小腦的中葉。在進化論的範疇中，新小腦是最新部分，僅產生於哺乳動物。

新語症 （精神病學）發明具有意義的詞語。常見於兒童，但成人產生新語症時，可能是精神病，如精神分裂症的一種症狀。應把新語症和言語錯亂分開。後者指給普通詞匯加上新意義。

meanings are attached to ordinary words.

neomycin *n.* an *aminoglycoside antibiotic used to treat infections caused by a wide range of bacteria, mainly those affecting the skin and eyes. It is usually applied in creams or drops with other antibiotics, but can also be given by mouth.

新黴素　一種氨基糖甙類抗生素，用於治療由許多不同種類的細菌，主要是那些影響皮膚和眼睛的細菌引起的感染。通常與其他抗生素混合製成藥膏或滴劑使用，但也能口服。

neonatal death rate *see* infant mortality rate.

新生兒（期）死亡率　參閱 infant mortality rate。

neonatal screening *screening tests carried out on newborn babies to detect diseases that appear in the neonatal period, such as phenylketonuria (*see* Guthrie test), Duchenne muscular dystrophy, and cystic fibrosis.

新生兒普查　在新生兒中進行的普查，目的是發現新生兒出現的疾病，如苯丙酮酸尿（參閱 Guthrie test）、迪歇納肌營養不良和囊性纖維變性。

neonate *n.* an infant at any time during the first four weeks of life. The word is particularly applied to infants just born or in the first week of life. **–neonatal** *adj.*

新生兒　出生後頭四周內的嬰兒。此詞尤指剛出生或出生第一周的嬰兒。

neopallium *n.* an enlargement of the wall of each cerebral hemisphere. In evolutionary terms it is the newest part of the cerebrum, formed by the development of new pathways for sight and hearing in mammals.

新大腦皮質　每個大腦半球壁的增大。在進化論的範疇中，它是大腦的最新部分。在哺乳動物中，它由視、聽覺新路徑的發展形成。

neoplasm *n.* any new and abnormal growth: any *benign or *malignant tumour.

新生物　任何新且異常的生長物：任何良性或惡性腫瘤。

neostigmine *n.* a *parasympathomimetic drug that functions by inhibiting the enzyme cholinesterase (*see also* anticholinesterase). It is used mainly to diagnose and treat *myasthenia gravis and as an antidote to some *muscle-relaxant drugs, such as tubocurarine. It is also used to treat some intestinal

新斯的明　抑制膽鹼酯酶的擬副交感神經藥（參閱 anticholinesterase）。主要用於診斷和治療重症肌無力，並作為某些肌肉鬆弛劑，如筒箭毒鹼的解毒劑。也用於治療某些腸道疾病和青光眼。口服、注射或用作滴眼藥。副作用包括消

disorders and glaucoma. Neostigmine is administered by mouth, injection, or in eye-drops; side-effects include digestive upsets and increased saliva flow. Trade name: **Prostigmin**.

化不良和唾液增加。商品名：Prostigmin。

nephr- (nephro-) *prexifx denoting* the kidney(s).

〔前綴〕**腎**

nephralgia *n*. pain in the kidney. The pain is felt in the loin and can be caused by a variety of kidney complaints.

腎痛 腎臟的疼痛。患者感到腰痛，可能由多種腎病引起。

nephrectomy *n*. surgical removal of a kidney. When performed for cancer of the kidney, the entire organ is removed together with its surrounding fat and the adjacent adrenal gland (*radical nephrectomy*). Removal of either the upper or lower pole of the kidney is termed *partial nephrectomy*.

腎切除術 腎臟的外科切除。切除腎癌時，整個器官和周圍脂肪和附近的腎上腺都要切除（腎全切除術）。腎臟的上極和下極切除叫腎部分切除術。

nephritis (Bright's disease) *n*. inflammation of the kidney. Nephritis is a non-specific term used to describe a condition resulting from a variety of causes. *See* glomerulonephritis.

腎炎（布賴特病） 腎臟的炎症。腎炎是一個非專門術語，用於描述由各種原因導致的腎病。參閱 glomerulonephritis。

nephroblastoma (Wilms' tumour) *n*. a malignant tumour of the kidney found in children (*see* cancer). It is rare over the age of eight years and the most obvious symptom is an abdominal swelling. Treatment of the tumour is by *nephrectomy followed by radiotherapy and *cytotoxic drugs. Considerable improvement in the results of treatment has occurred in recent years since the use of cytotoxic drugs as a routine.

腎胚細胞瘤（維爾姆斯瘤） 見於兒童的惡性腎臟腫瘤（參閱 cancer）。八歲後罕見，最明顯的症狀是腹部腫脹。用腎切除術治療，然後用放射治療和細胞毒素藥物。從細胞毒素藥物作為常規藥以來，近年治療效果產生了很大的改進。

nephrocalcinosis *n*. the presence of calcium deposits in the kidneys. This can be caused by excess calcium in the blood, as caused by overactivity of the parathyroid glands, or it may result from an

腎鈣質沉着 腎臟中產生鈣沉積物。病因可能是甲狀旁腺機能亢進所致的血鈣過多，或者是腎臟的潛在異常。腎鈣質沉着的原因必須通過全面的生

underlying abnormality of the kidney. The cause of nephrocalcinosis must be detected by full biochemical, radiological, and urological investigation so that appropriate treatment can be undertaken.

化、放射和泌尿檢查弄清楚，以便於進行適當治療。

nephrogenic cord either of the paired ridges of tissue that run along the dorsal surface of the abdominal cavity of the embryo. Parts of it develop into the kidney, ovary, or testis and their associated ducts. Intermediate stages of these developments are the *pronephros, *mesonephros, and *metanephros.

生腎索 成對組織嵴中的一個，在胚胎腹腔背側排列。其中一部分發育成腎臟、卵巢或睾丸及其相關的導管。這些發育的中期叫前腎、中腎和後腎。

nephrolithiasis n. the presence of stones in the kidney (see calculus). Such stones can cause pain and blood in the urine, but they may produce no symptoms. Full investigation is undertaken to determine the underlying cause of stone formation. When stones are associated with urinary obstruction and infection they usually require surgical removal (see nephrolithotomy, psyelolithotomy).

腎石病 腎臟中存在的結石（參閱 calculus）。這類結石能造成疼痛及血尿，可無症狀。需全面檢查以確定結石形成的原因。結石與尿導阻塞和感染相關時，要手術去除結石（參閱 nephrolithotomy, pyelolithotomy）。

nephrolithotomy n. the surgical removal of a stone from the kidney by an incision into the kidney substance. It is normally performed in combination with an incision into the renal pelvis (see pyelolithotomy). See also percutaneous nephrolithotomy.

腎石切除術 經腎實質切口從腎臟中手術切除結石。常和腎盂切開同時進行（參閱 pyelolithotomy）。參閱 percutaneous nephrolithotomy。

nephrology n. the branch of medicine concerned with the study, investigation, and management of diseases of the kidney. See also urology. **–nephrologist** n.

腎病學 和腎病的研究、調查及管理相關的醫學分支。參閱 urology。

nephron n. the active unit of excretion in the kidney (see illustration). Blood, which is supplied by branches of the renal artery, is filtered through a knot of

腎單位 腎臟中排泄活性單位（見圖）。腎動脈分支提供的血液由毛細管結（腎小球）過濾進入杯狀的鮑曼囊，以便於

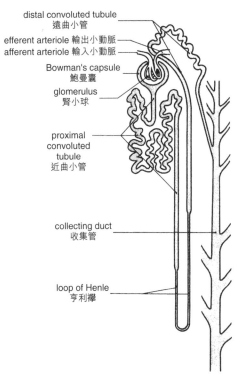

A single nephron
一個腎單位

capillaries (*glomerulus*) into the cup-shaped *Bowman's capsule* so that water, nitrogenous waste, and many other substances (excluding colloids) pass into the *renal tubule*. Here most of the substances are reabsorbed back into the blood, the remaining fluid (*urine) passing into the collecting duct, which drains into the *ureter.

水、含氮的代謝物和許多其他物質（不包括膠體）進入腎小管。大多數物質在此被重新吸收回血液中，剩餘的液體（尿）進入收集管，收集管把尿排入輸尿管。

nephropathy *n*. disease of the kidney. *See also* Balkan nephropathy.

腎病　腎臟的疾病。參閱 Balkan nephropathy。

nephropexy *n*. an operation to fix a mobile kidney. The kidney is fixed to

腎固定術　固定活動性腎的手術。將腎臟固定在第十二肋骨

the twelfth rib and adjacent posterior abdominal wall to prevent descent of the kidney on standing (*see* nephroptosis).

和鄰近的後腹壁上以防止站立時腎臟下垂（參閱 nephroptosis）。

nephroptosis *n*. abnormal descent of a kidney into the pelvis on standing, which may occur if it is excessively mobile (for example, in thin women). If this is accompanied by pain and obstruction to free drainage of urine by the kidney, *nephropexy may be advised.

腎下垂 站立時腎臟進入骨盆的異常下垂，如果腎臟活動性過大時，可出現腎下垂（例如在瘦小的婦女中），如果腎下垂時伴有疼痛和排尿阻塞，可施行腎固定術。

nephrosclerosis *n*. hardening of the arteries and arterioles of the kidneys. *Arteriolar nephrosclerosis* is associated with *hypertension.

腎硬化 腎臟動脈和小動脈變硬。小動脈性腎硬化和高血壓有關。

nephroscope *n*. an instrument (*endoscope) used for examining the interior of the kidney, usually passed into the renal pelvis through a track from the skin surface after needle *nephrostomy and dilatation of the tract over a guide wire. The nephroscope allows the passage of instruments under direct vision to remove calculi (*see* percutaneous nephrolithotomy) or disintegrate them by ultrasound probes or electrohydraulic shock waves (*see* lithotripsy).

腎鏡 用於檢查腎內部的一種儀器（內窺鏡），通常在針腎造口術和用一根引導綫對管道擴張後，從皮膚表面經過一個路徑將其進入腎盂。可在腎鏡直視下將儀器插入取出結石（參閱 percutaneous nephrolithotomy）或用超聲探針或電動液壓衝擊波粉碎結石（參閱 lithotripsy）。

nephroscopy *n*. inspection of the interior of the kidney with a *nephroscope.

腎鏡檢查 使用腎鏡對腎臟內部的檢查。

nephrosis *n*. (in pathology) degenerative changes in the epithelium of the kidney tubules. The term is sometimes used loosely for the *nephrotic syndrome.

腎病 （病理學）腎小管上皮變性。該術語有時泛指腎病綜合徵。

nephrostomy *n*. drainage of urine from the kidney by a tube (catheter) passing through the kidney via the skin surface. This is commonly used as a temporary procedure after operations on the kidney. Long-term urine drainage by nephrostomy may be complicated by the

腎造口術 通過皮膚表面用一根導管從腎臟中引流尿液。腎造口術常被用作為腎臟手術後的暫時措施。經過腎造口術長期導尿伴隨有感染問題及碎屑阻塞導管，因此較複雜。腎造口術也能使腎鏡通過。

attendant problems of infection and obstruction of the catheter by debris. Nephrostomy is also performed to enable the passage of a *nephroscope.)

nephrotic syndrome a condition in which there is great loss of protein in the urine, reduced levels of albumin in the blood, and generalized swelling of the tissues due to *oedema. It can be caused by a variety of disorders, most usually *glomerulonephritis.

nephrotomy n. surgical incision into the substance of the kidney. This is usually undertaken to remove a kidney stone (see nephrolithotomy).

nephroureterectomy (ureterone- phrectomy) n. the surgical removal of a kidney together with its ureter. This operation is performed for cancer of the kidney pelvis or ureter. It is also under- taken when the kidney has been destroyed by *vesicoureteric reflux, to prevent subsequent continuing reflux into the stump of the ureter that would occur if the kidney alone were removed.

nerve n. a bundle of conducting *nerve fibres (see illustration) that transmit impulses from the brain or spinal cord to the muscles and glands (*motor nerves*) or inwards from the sense organs to the brain and spinal cord (*sensory nerves*). Most large nerves and *mixed nerves*, con- taining both motor and sensory nerve fibres running to and from a particular region of the body.

nerve block a method of producing *anaesthesia in part of the body by blocking the passage of pain impulses in the sensory nerves supplying it. A local anaesthetic, such as lignocaine, is

腎病綜合徵　一種病症，本病中大量蛋白喪失在尿中，血液中白蛋白水平降低，水腫導致全身性組織腫脹。可由多種疾病引起，最常見的是腎小球腎炎。

腎切開術　腎實質的手術切開。它通常用於去除腎結石（參閱 nephrolithotomy）。

腎輸尿管切除術（輸尿管腎切除術）　腎和輸尿管的切除手術。腎盂癌或輸尿管癌時做此手術。腎臟被膀胱輸尿管返流破壞時也可做此手術，以防如果單獨切除腎臟以後膀胱輸尿管返流進入輸尿管的殘餘部分。

神經　一束傳導神經纖維（見圖），它們把衝動從大腦或脊髓導向肌肉和腺體（衝動神經）或向內從感覺器官傳向大腦和脊髓（感覺神經）。大多數大神經都是混合神經，它們含有通向身體某一特殊區域和來自此區域的運動和感覺神經纖維。

神經傳導阻滯　在身體的一部分產生麻醉的方法，其作法是阻滯感覺神經中痛覺的傳導。例如將局麻藥利多因注射到神經區域的組織內，麻醉就被

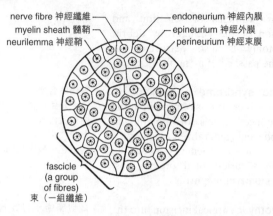

Transverse section through a nerve
神經的橫切面

injected into the tissues in the region of a nerve. In this way anaesthesia can be localized, so that minor operations can be performed without the necessity of giving a general anaesthetic.

限制在一個局部，這樣無須全身性麻醉即可作小手術。

nerve cell *see* neurone.

神經細胞　參閱 neurone。

nerve ending the final part (terminal) of one of the branches of a nerve fibre, where a *neurone makes contact either with another neurone at a synapse or with a muscle or gland cell at a neuro-muscular or neuroglandular junction.

神經末梢　神經纖維分支的最後部分，在此一個神經元和另一個神經元在突觸處接觸或與肌肉或腺體細胞在神經肌肉接頭或神經腺體接頭處接觸。

nerve entrapment syndrome any syndrome resulting from pressure on a nerve from surrounding structures. Examples include the *carpal tunnel syndrome and *meralgia paraesthetica.

神經壓迫綜合徵　神經周圍結構壓迫神經導致的任何綜合徵，例如腕管綜合徵和感覺異常性股痛。

nerve fibre the long fine process that extends from the cell body of a *neurone and carries nerve impulses. Bundles of nerve fibres running together form a *nerve. Each fibre has a sheath, which in medullated nerve fibres is a relatively

神經纖維　從神經元細胞體延伸出來並傳導神經衝動的長細突。並行的纖維束形成神經。每根纖維都有鞘，鞘是有髓神經纖維中的較厚層，含脂肪性絕緣物質，即髓鞘質。

thick layer containing the fatty insulating material *myelin.

nerve gas any gas that disrupts the normal functioning of nerves and thus of the muscles they supply. There are two groups, the *G agents* and the *V agents*. The latter are more than 300 times as deadly as mustard gas: one inhalation can kill by paralysing the respiratory muscles. V agents also act through the skin, therefore gas masks are ineffective protection against them.

神經性毒氣　破壞神經的正常功能，並由此破壞神經所支配的肌肉的毒氣。它們可分為兩類：G 類毒氣和 V 類毒氣。後者的毒性比芥子毒氣大 300 倍：吸入可因呼吸肌麻痹導致死亡。V 類毒氣也通過皮膚發生效力，所以用防毒面具無效。

nerve impulse the electrical activity in the membrane of a *neurone that – by its rapid spread from one region to the next – is the means by which information is transmitted within the nervous system along the axons of the neurones. The membrane of a resting nerve is charged (*polarized*) because of the different concentrations of ions inside and outside the cell. When a nerve impulse is triggered, a wave of *depolarization spreads, and ions flow across the membrane (*see* action potential). Until the nerve has undergone *repolarization no further nerve impulses can pass.

神經衝動　神經元膜裏的電活動，通過從一個區域迅速傳向另一個區域成為沿神經元軸索傳遞信息的媒體。由於細胞內外離子濃度不同，靜止的神經膜被極化。神經衝動產生時，去極化波傳播，離子沿膜流動（參閱 action potential）。神經經歷重新極化以前，後面的神經衝動無法通過。

nerve regeneration the growth of new nerve tissue, which occurs at a very slow rate (1–2 mm per day) after a nerve has been severed and is often partially or totally incomplete. *Microsurgery has improved the results by facilitating primary repair in the immediate aftermath of injury. *See also* axonotmesis, neurotmesis.

神經再生　新神經組織的生長，在神經被切斷後，緩慢生長（每天 1~2 mm）並且通常是部分或完全不完整。通過採用顯微外科對外傷進行及時的基本修復已增加了其再生結果。參閱　axonotmesis，neurotmesis。

nervous breakdown a popular term applied to a range of emotional crises varying from a brief attack of 'hysterical' behaviour to a major psychoneurotic illness with severe long-term effects

神經崩潰　指多種情緒危機的廣泛術語，涉及範圍從短暫發作的「歇斯底里」行為到對患者生活造成長期嚴重影響的主要心理疾病。這個詞有時被用

on the life of the sufferer. The term is also sometimes used as a euphemism for a frank psychiatric illness, such as *schizophrenia.

作症狀明顯的精神性疾病，例如精神分裂症的婉言。

nervous system the vast network of cells specialized to carry information (in the form of *nerve impulses) to and from all parts of the body in order to bring about bodily activity. The brain and spinal cord together form the *central nervous system; the remaining nervous tissue is known as the *peripheral nervous system and includes the *autonomic nervous system, which is itself divided into the sympathetic and parasympathetic nervous systems. The basic functional unit of the nervous system is the *neurone (nerve cell).

神經系統　專門來回傳遞信息（以神經衝動的形式）到身體各個部位，以產生身體活動的巨大細胞網。大腦和脊髓共同形成中樞神經系統，其餘的神經組織叫周圍神經系統並包括自主神經系統，自主神經系統本身被分成交感神經系統和副交感神經系統。神經系統的基本功能單位是神經元（神經細胞）。

Nesbit's operation an operation devised to surgically straighten a congenitally curved penis but now more frequently employed to correct the penile curvature caused by *Peyronie's disease.

內斯比特手術　一種外科手術，旨在通過外科整直先天性彎曲的陰莖，但現在更多地用於糾正佩羅尼病引起的陰莖彎曲。

nettle rash see urticaria.

蕁麻疹　參閱 urticaria。

neur- (neuro-) prefix denoting nerves or the nervous system.

〔前綴〕神經　神經或神經系統。

neural arch see vertebra.

神經弓　參閱 vertebra。

neural crest the two bands of ectodermal tissue that flank the *neural plate of the early embryo. Cells of the neural crest migrate throughout the embryo and develop into sensory nerve cells and peripheral nerve cells of the autonomic nervous system.

神經嵴　位於早期胚胎神經板側面的兩條外胚胎層組織帶。神經嵴細胞在整個胚胎中游動並發育成感覺神經細胞和自主神經系統的周圍神經細胞。

neuralgia n. a severe burning or stabbing pain often following the course of a nerve. Postherpetic neuralgia is an intense debilitating pain felt at the site of

神經痛　通常沿神經通路產生的嚴重灼痛或刺痛。帶狀疱疹（後）神經痛是在以前發生疱疹部位感覺到的強烈的使人衰

a previous attack of shingles. In *trigeminal neuralgia* (*tic douloureux*) there are brief paroxysms of searing pain felt in the distribution of one or more branches of the *trigeminal nerve in the face. The facial pain of *migrainous neuralgia* lasts for 30–60 minutes and occurs at roughly the same time on successive days.

弱的疼痛。在三叉神經痛中，面部三叉神經一個或在三個神經分支的分布區有短暫的、陣發性的灼燒樣疼痛。偏頭痛性神經痛的面部疼痛持續 30~60 分鐘，在以後幾天內的大約同一時間裏產生。

neural plate the strip of ectoderm lying along the central axis of the early embryo that forms the *neural tube and subsequently the central nervous system.

神經板　形成神經管，並在以後形成中樞神經系統的，沿早期胚胎中軸排列的外胚層帶。

neural spine the spinous process situated on the neural arch of a *vertebra.

椎骨棘突　位於椎骨神經弓上的棘突。

neural tube the embryological structure from which the brain and spinal cord develop. It is a hollow tube of ectodermal tissue formed when two edges of a groove in a plate of primitive neural tissue (*neural plate*) come together and fuse. Failure of normal fusion results in a number of congenital defects (*see* neural tube defects).

神經管　發育成大腦和脊髓的胚胎結構。它是一個外胚層組織的空管，是原始神經組織盤（神經板）中一個溝的兩個邊緣結合在一起並融合時形成的。正常融合失敗時會導致諸多先天性缺陷（參閱 neural tube defects）。

neural tube defects a group of congenital abnormalities caused by failure of the *neural tube to form normally. In *spina bifida the bony arches of the spine, which protect the spinal cord and its coverings (the meninges), fail to close. More severe defects of fusion of these bones will result in increasingly serious neurological conditions. A *meningocele* is the protrusion of the meninges through the gap in the spine, the skin covering being vestigial. There is a constant risk of damage to the meninges, with resulting infection. Urgent surgical treatment to protect the meninges is therefore required. In a *meningomyelocele* (*myelomeningocele, myelocele*) the spinal cord and the nerve roots are

神經管缺陷　神經管形成異常導致的一組先天性異常。在脊柱裂中，保護脊髓及其外膜（脊膜）的脊柱骨弓不能閉合。更嚴重的骨融合缺陷會導致嚴重的進行性神經性疾病。脊膜突出是脊膜從脊柱的空隙突出，有皮膚覆蓋殘留。有持久的脊膜受損的危險，並伴有感染。因此需要緊急外科手術以保護脊膜。在脊髓膜突出（脊髓突出）中，脊髓及神經根暴露，常與位於其上面的薄膜黏連。有引起持續感染的危險，而且伴有下肢癱瘓和麻木及尿失禁。常出現腦積水和阿-希氏畸形。神經管顱末端融合不良（顱對裂）會發展成類似

exposed, often adhering to the fine membrane that overlies them. There is a constant risk of infection and this condition is accompanied by paralysis and numbness of the legs and urinary incontinence. *Hydrocephalus and the *Arnold-Chiari malformation are usually present. A failure of fusion at the cranial end of the neural tube (*cranium bifidum*) gives rise to comparable disorders. The bone defect is most often in the occipital region of the skull but it may occur in the frontal or basal regions. A protrusion of the meninges alone is known as a *cranial meningocele*. The terms *meningoencephalocele, encephalocele*, and *cephalocele* are used for the protrusion of brain tissue through the skull defect. This is accompanied by severe mental and physical disorders.

病情。骨缺陷最常出現在顱的枕部，但亦可發生於額部和顱底部。單純的脊膜突出叫顱腦脊膜突出。腦腦膜突出、腦突出和腦膨出等術語用於指腦組織通過顱骨缺陷向外突出。此病伴有嚴重的精神和軀體疾病。

neurapraxia *n.* temporary loss of nerve function resulting in tingling, numbness, and weakness. It is usually caused by compression of the nerve and there is no structural damage involved. Complete recovery occurs. *Compare* axonotmesis, neurotmesis.

神經失用症　導致麻刺感、麻木和無力的神經功能暫時喪失。此症通常由神經壓迫引起，沒有結構損害。可完全恢復。與 axonotmesis，neurotmesis 對比。

neurasthenia *n.* a set of psychological and physical symptoms, including fatigue, irritability, headache, dizziness, anxiety, and intolerance of noise. It can be caused by organic damage, such as a head injury, or it can be due to neurosis. **–neurasthenic** *adj., n.*

神經衰弱　一組心理和軀體症狀，包括困倦、易怒、頭痛、眩暈、焦慮和不能忍受噪音等。此病可由器官損傷引起，如頭部損傷，或由神經官能症引起。

neurectasis *n.* the surgical procedure for stretching a peripheral nerve.

神經牽伸術　用外科手術拉長周圍神經。

neurectomy *n.* the surgical removal of the whole or part of a nerve.

神經切除術　外科全部或部分切除某根神經。

neurilemma (neurolemma) *n.* the sheath of the *axon of a nerve fibre. The neurilemma of a medullated fibre

神經鞘　神經纖維軸索的鞘。有髓（鞘）纖維的神經鞘含有施萬細胞生成的髓鞘質。

contains *myelin laid down by Schwann cells. **–neurilemmal** *adj.*

neurilemmoma *n. see* neurofibroma.

神經鞘瘤　參閱　neurofibroma。

neurinoma *n. see* neurofibroma.

神經鞘瘤　參閱　neurofibroma。

neuritis *n.* a disease of the peripheral nerves showing the pathological changes of inflammation. The term is also used in a less precise sense as an alternative to *neuropathy. *See also* retrobulbar neuritis.

神經炎　呈現炎症病理變化的周圍神經疾病。此術語在不太準確時也用作神經病的代名詞。參閱　retrobulbar neuritis。

neuroanatomy *n.* the study of the structure of the nervous system, from the gross anatomy of the brain down to the microscopic details of neurones.

神經解剖學　研究神經系統結構的科學，範圍覆蓋從大腦的大體解剖學到神經元的顯微細節。

neurobiotaxis *n.* the predisposition of a nerve cell to move towards the source of its stimuli during development.

神經細胞趨生物性　發育期間神經細胞向其刺激源移動的趨向。

neuroblast *n.* any of the nerve cells of the embryo that give rise to functional nerve cells (neurones).

成神經細胞　生成功能性神經細胞（神經元）的胚胎神經細胞。

neuroblastoma *n.* a malignant tumour composed of embryonic nerve cells. It may originate in any part of the sympathetic nervous system, most commonly in the medulla of the adrenal gland, and secondary growths are often widespread in other organs and in bones.

神經母細胞瘤　由胚胎神經細胞構成的惡性腫瘤。發源於交感神經系統的任何部位。最常發生於腎上腺的髓質，繼發性生長常廣泛分布於其他器官和骨中。

neurocranium *n.* the part of the skull that encloses the brain.

腦顱　容納大腦的顱骨部分。

neurodermatitis (lichen simplex chronicus) *n.* thickened eczematous skin that develops at the site of constant rubbing in susceptible individuals. Common sites are the nape of the neck

神經性皮炎（單純慢性苔癬）易受感染的人中經常摩擦部位形成的變厚濕疹性皮膚。常發生部位是女性的頸背及男性的小腿。應激是一個致病因素。

in women and the lower legs in men. Stress is a causative factor.

neuroendocrine system the system of dual control of certain activities of the body by means of both nerves and circulating hormones. The functioning of the autonomic nervous system is particularly closely linked to that of the pituitary and adrenal glands. *See also* neurohormone, neurosecretion.

神經內分泌系統 借助神經和循環中的激素對身體的某些活動進行雙重控制的系統。自主神經系統的功能與垂體和腎上腺的功能之間關係特別密切。參閱 neurohormone，neurosecretion。

neuroepithelioma *n.* a malignant tumour of the retina of the eye. It is a form of *glioma and may spread into the brain if not treated early.

神經上皮瘤 視網膜的惡性腫瘤。是一種神經膠質瘤，如不盡早治療，可擴散到大腦。

neuroepithelium *n.* a type of epithelium associated with organs of special sense. It contains sensory nerve endings and is found in the retina, the membranous labyrinth of the inner ear, the mucous membrane lining the nasal cavity, and the taste buds. **–neuroepithelial** *adj.*

神經上皮 和特殊感覺器官相關的一種上皮。含有感覺神經末梢，並見於視網膜、內耳膜迷路、鼻腔黏膜和味蕾中。

neurofibril *n.* one of the microscopic threads of cytoplasm found in the cell body of a *neurone and also in the *axoplasm of peripheral nerves.

神經原纖維 存在於神經元細胞體內，亦見於周圍神經的軸漿中的細胞質的顯微細絲。

neurofibroma **(neurilemmoma, neurinoma, neuroma, Schwannoma)** *n.* a benign tumour growing from the fibrous coverings of a peripheral nerve: it is usually symptomless. When it develops from the sheath of a nerve root, it causes pain and may compress the spinal cord.

神經纖維瘤（神經鞘瘤，神經瘤） 周圍神經的纖維膜上產生的良性腫瘤：通常無症狀，從神經根的鞘上生長時可引起疼痛並壓迫脊髓。

neurofibromatosis (von Recklinghausen's disease) *n.* a congenital disease that is typified by numerous benign tumours growing from the fibrous coverings of nerves (*see* neurofibroma). Tumours may occur in the spinal canal, where they may press on the spinal cord.

神經纖維瘤病（馮雷克林豪森病） 一種先天性疾病，其特點是神經的纖維膜上產生無數良性腫瘤（參閱 neurofibroma）。腫瘤可產生於脊髓管中，在此壓迫脊髓。沿神經走向可在皮下觸摸到腫瘤。有時

The tumours can be felt beneath the skin along the course of the nerves; they sometimes become malignant, giving rise to *neurofibrosarcomas*. Pigmented patches on the skin (*see* café au lait spots) are commonly found. This condition is occasionally associated with the adrenal tumour *phaeochromocytoma.

惡變成神經纖維肉瘤。皮膚常可出現色素斑（參閱 café au lait spots）。此病偶爾和腎上腺腫瘤——嗜鉻細胞瘤相關。

neurogenesis *n.* the growth and development of nerve cells.

神經發生　神經細胞的生長和發育。

neurogenic *adj.* **1.** caused by disease or dysfunction of the nervous system. **2.** arising in nervous tissue. **3.** caused by nerve stimulation.

神經發生的　**(1)** 神經系統疾病或功能障礙引起的。**(2)** 神經組織中產生的。**(3)** 神經刺激造成的。

neuroglia *n. see* glia.

神經膠質　參閱 glia。

neurohormone *n.* a hormone that is produced within specialized nerve cells and is secreted from the nerve endings into the circulation. Examples are the hormones oxytocin and vasopressin, produced within the nerve cells of the hypothalamus and released into the circulation in the posterior pituitary gland, and noradrenaline, released from *chromaffin tissue in the adrenal medulla.

神經激素　特殊的神經細胞內產生的並從神經末梢分泌出來進入循環中的一種激素。例如縮宮素和加壓素在下丘腦的神經細胞中產生並在後垂體腺被釋放進循環，去甲腎上腺素從腎上腺髓質的嗜鉻組織中釋放。

neurohumour *n.* a *neurohormone or a *neurotransmitter.

神經體液　一種神經激素或神經遞質。

neurohypophysis *n.* the posterior lobe of the *pituitary gland.

垂體神經部　垂體的後葉。

neurolemma *n. see* neurilemma.

神經鞘　參閱 neurilemma。

neurology *n.* the study of the structure, functioning, and diseases of the nervous system (including the brain, spinal cord, and all the peripheral nerves). **–neurological** *adj.* **–neurologist** *n.*

神經病學　研究神經系統（包括大腦、脊髓和所有周圍神經）的結構、功能和疾病的科學。

neuroma *n. see* neurofibroma.

神經瘤　參閱 neurofibroma。

neuromuscular junction (myoneural junction) the meeting point of a nerve fibre and the muscle fibre that it supplies. Between the enlarged end of the nerve fibre (*motor end-plate*) and the membrane of the muscle is a gap across which a *neurotransmitter must diffuse from the nerve to trigger contraction of the muscle.

神經肌肉接頭　神經纖維與其所支配的肌肉纖維的會合點。在神經纖維增大端（運動終板）與肌膜之間是一個間隙，神經遞質必須穿越此間隙彌散以引起肌肉的收縮。

neuromyelitis optica (Devic's disease) a condition that is closely related to multiple sclerosis. Typically there is a transverse *myelitis, producing paralysis and numbness of the legs and trunk below the inflamed spinal cord, and *retrobulbar (optic) neuritis affecting both optic nerves. The attacks of myelitis and optic neuritis may coincide or they may be separated by days or weeks. Recovery from the initial attack is often incomplete, but relapses appear to be less common than in conventional multiple sclerosis.

視神經脊髓炎（德維克病）與多發性硬化密切相關的一種疾病。有典型的橫貫性脊髓炎，產生脊髓發炎部位以下下肢和軀幹的癱瘓和麻木，以及影響兩側視神經的球後（視）神經炎。脊髓炎和視神經炎的發作可以偶合，也可以相隔數日或數週。初次發作後的恢復常不完全，但與常規多發性硬化相比，復發較少。

neurone (nerve cell) *n.* one of the basic functional units of the nervous system: a cell specialized to transmit electrical *nerve impulses and so carry information from one part of the body to another (see illustration). Each neurone has an enlarged portion, the *cell body* (*perikaryon*), containing the nucleus; from the body extend several processes (*dendrites*) through which impulses enter from their branches. A longer process, the nerve fibre (*see* axon), extends outwards and carries impulses away from the cell body. This is normally unbranched except at the *nerve ending. The point of contact of one neurone with another is known as a *synapse.

神經元（神經細胞）　神經系統的基本功能單位之一：專門用於傳遞電神經衝動的細胞，這樣把信息從身體的一個部分傳送到另外一個部分（見圖）。每個神經元都有一個增大的部分，即細胞體（核周體），含有核；從胞體伸出許多突起（樹突），通過這些突起，衝動從分支中傳入細胞體。一個較長的突起，即神經纖維（參閱 axon），向外延伸並傳導衝動離開細胞體。除了在神經末梢部位以外，它通常沒有分支。一個神經元和另一個神經元接觸的點叫突觸。

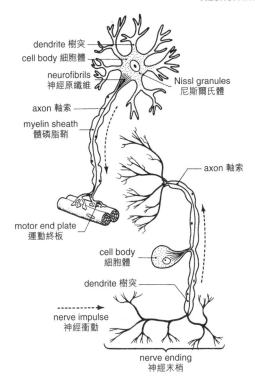

Types of neurone: motor (left) and sensory (right)
神經元的類型：運動（左）和感覺（右）

neuronophagia *n.* the process whereby damaged or degenerating nerve cells finally disintegrate and are removed by scavenger cells (*phagocytes).

噬神經細胞作用　受損或變性的神經細胞最終裂解並被吞噬細胞清除的過程。

neuronoplasty *n.* reconstructive surgery for damaged or severed peripheral nerves.

神經整形術　受損或被切斷的周圍神經的重建手術。

neuropathic bladder a malfunctioning bladder due to partial or complete interruption of its nerve supply. Causes include injury to the spinal cord, spina bifida, multiple sclerosis, and diabetic neuropathy.

神經病理性膀胱　支配膀胱的神經部分或完全中斷所致的膀胱功能失調。病因包括脊髓受傷、脊柱對裂、多發性硬化和糖尿病性神經病。

neuropathy *n.* any disease of the peripheral nerves, usually causing weakness and numbness. In a *mononeuropathy* a single nerve is affected and the extent of the symptoms depends upon the distribution of that nerve. In a *polyneuropathy* many or all of the nerves are involved and the symptoms are most profound at the extremities of the limbs.

神經病　常引起無力和麻木的周圍神經的任何疾病。在單一神經病中，一根單獨的神經受累，症狀的範圍取決於該神經的分布區域。在多神經病中，許多或所有的神經受累，在肢體末端症狀最嚴重。

neurophysiology *n.* the study of the complex chemical and physical changes that are associated with the activity of the nervous system.

神經生理學　研究與神經系統活動相關的複雜的化學和物理變化的科學。

neuropil *n.* nerve tissue that is visible microscopically as a mass of interwoven and interconnected nerve endings, dendrites, and other neurone components, rather than an ordered array of axons.

神經纖維網　顯微鏡下看到的神經組織，它是相互交織和相互聯繫起來的神經末梢、樹突及其他神經元成分，而不是有序排列的軸。

neuropsychiatry *n.* the branch of medicine concerned with the psychiatric effects of disorders of neurological function or structure. Increasingly, the correlation is being drawn between demonstrable brain changes and the resulting effects on the mind. It is the function of the growing speciality of neuropsychiatry to investigate this relationship.

神經精神病學　涉及神經功能或結構紊亂的精神病學作用的醫學分支。可用證據證明的大腦變化及其對精神所產生的影響之間的相關性越來越受重視。調查這種關係是神經精神病學的作用。

neuroretinitis *n.* combined inflammation of the optic nerve and the retina.

視神經（視）網膜炎　視神經和視網膜的共同炎症。

neurosecretion *n.* any substance produced within, and secreted by, a nerve cell. Important examples are the hormone-releasing factors produced by the cells of the *hypothalamus and released into blood vessels of the pituitary gland, on which they act.

神經分泌　神經細胞內產生並分泌的物質。下丘腦細胞產生的激素釋放因子被釋放到它們作用的垂體血管內就是重要的例證。

neurosis *n.* (*pl.* **neuroses**) any long-term mental or behavioural disorder in

神經官能症　任何長期的精神或行為疾病，患者保持與現實

which contact with reality is retained and the condition is recognized by the sufferer as abnormal. A neurosis essentially features anxiety or behaviour exaggeratedly designed to avoid anxiety. Defence mechanisms against anxiety take various forms and may appear as phobias, obsessions, compulsions, or sexual dysfunctions. In recent attempts at classification, the disorders formerly included under the neuroses have been renamed. The general term is now *anxiety disorder*; hysteria has become *conversion disorder; amnesia, fugue, multiple personality, and depersonalization are *dissociative disorders; obsessional neurosis is now known as *obsessive-compulsive disorder* (*see* obsession); and depressive neurosis has become *dysthymic disorder* (*see* depression). Psychoanalysis has proved of little value in curing these conditions and Freud's speculations as to their origins are not now widely accepted outside Freudian schools of thought. Neurotic disorders are probably best regarded as being the result of inappropriate early programming. *Behaviour therapy seems effective in some cases. **–neurotic** *adj.*

neurosurgery *n.* the surgical or operative treatment of diseases of the brain and spinal cord. This includes the management of head injuries, the relief of raised intracranial pressure and compression of the spinal cord, the eradication of infection, the control of intracranial haemorrhage, and the diagnosis and treatment of tumours. The development of neurosurgery has been supported by advances in anaesthetics, radiology, antiseptics, and scanning techniques.

neurosyphilis *n.* *syphilis affecting the nervous system.

接觸，能意識到此病不正常。神經官能症基本特徵是焦慮或誇張性地為了避免焦慮而引起的行為。對抗焦慮的防禦機制形式各異，可表現為恐怖、煩擾、強迫或性功能障礙。在最近的分類嘗試中，神經官能症中以前所包括的疾病已被重新命名。現在使用的通用術語為焦慮性疾病；癔病現稱轉換性障礙；遺忘症、神游症、多重性格和去人格症等改名為聯想散漫性障礙，強迫性神經官能症現稱強迫觀念與強迫症（參閱 obsession），抑鬱性神經官能症已更名為心境惡劣病（參閱 depression）。現已證實用心理分析療法治療這些疾病價值不大。在弗洛伊德學派之外，弗洛伊德對其病因的猜想現在尚未被廣泛接受。最好把神經性疾病看作是早期教育不當的結果。在有些病例中，行為療法似乎有效。

神經外科學 外科或手術治療大腦和脊髓的疾病。包括處理頭痛受傷、降低顱內壓和脊髓的壓力、控制顱內出血及診斷和治療腫瘤。麻醉學、放射學、消毒滅菌法和掃描技術等的發展支持了神經外科學的發展。

神經梅毒 累及神經系統的梅毒。

neuroticism *n.* a dimension of personality derived from questionnaires and psychological tests. People with high scores in neuroticism are anxious and intense and more prone to develop *neurosis.

神經過敏症 從問卷調查和心理測驗得出的人格量度。在神經過敏症測驗中得分高者表現為焦慮和緊張，並容易發展成神經官能症。

neurotmesis *n.* the complete severance of a peripheral nerve, which is associated with degeneration of the nerve fibres distal to the point of severance and slow *nerve regeneration. *Compare* axonotmesis, neurapraxia.

神經斷傷 周圍神經的完全切斷，它和靠近切斷點一側的神經纖維相關並減緩神經的再生。與 axonotmesis，neurapraxia 對比。

neurotomy *n.* the surgical procedure of severing a nerve.

神經切斷術 切斷神經的外科手術。

neurotoxic *adj.* poisonous or harmful to nerve cells.

神經毒性的 對神經細胞有毒或有害的。

neurotransmitter *n.* a chemical substance released from nerve endings to transmit impulses across *synapses to other nerves and across the minute gaps between the nerves and the muscles or glands that they supply. Outside the central nervous system the chief neurotransmitter is *acetylcholine; *noradrenaline is released by nerve endings of the sympathetic system. In the central nervous system, as well as acetylcholine and noradrenaline, *dopamine, *serotonin, *gamma aminobutyric acid and several other substances act as transmitters.

神經遞質 神經末梢釋放的化學物質。能傳導衝動穿越突觸到達其他神經及與其支配的肌肉或腺體之間的小空隙。在中樞神經系統之外，主要的神經遞質是乙醯膽鹼；去甲腎上腺素是由交感神經的神經末梢釋放的。在中樞神經系統中，除了乙醯膽鹼和去甲腎上腺素之外，多巴胺、5-羥色胺、γ-氨基丁酸和許多其他物質起遞質作用。

neurotrophic *adj.* relating to the growth and nutrition of neural tissue in the body.

神經營養的 與體內神經組織的生長和營養相關的。

neurotropic *adj.* growing towards or having an affinity for neural tissue. The term may be applied to viruses, chemicals, or toxins.

親神經的 向神經組織方向生長或與神經組織有親合性的。此術語可用於病毒、化學物質或毒素。

neutropenia *n.* a decrease in the number of *neutrophils in the blood. Neutropenia

中性白細胞減少（症） 血液中中性白細胞數目的降低。中

may occur in a wide variety of diseases, including certain hereditary defects, aplastic *anaemias, tumours of the bone marrow, *agranulocytosis, and acute leukaemias. It results in an increased susceptibility to infections.

性白細胞減少（症）可以發生在包括某些遺傳缺陷、再生障礙性貧血、骨髓腫瘤、粒細胞缺乏症和急性白血病在內的許多種類不同的疾病中，此症導致對感染的易感性增加。

neutrophil (polymorph) *n.* a variety of *granulocyte (a type of white blood cell) distinguished by a lobed nucleus and the presence in its cytoplasm of fine granules that stain purple with *Romanowsky stains. It is capable of ingesting and killing bacteria and provides an important defence against infection. There are normally $2.0–7.5 \times 10^9$ neutrophils per litre of blood.

中性粒細胞（多形核白細胞） 一種粒細胞（白細胞的一種類型），其特點為分葉核和胞漿中出現用羅曼諾夫斯基染劑染成的紫色細小微粒。中性粒細胞能夠消化和殺滅細菌以預防感染。正常情況下每升血液中有 $2.0~7.5 \times 10^9$ 個中性粒細胞。

newton *n.* the *SI unit of force, equal to the force required to impart of 1 kilogram an acceleration of 1 metre per second per second. Symbol: N.

牛頓 力的國際單位。1 牛頓等於使 1000 克的物體產生 1 米／平方秒加速度的力。符號：N。

nexus *n.* (in anatomy) a connection or link.

連結 （解剖學）連結或結合。

niacin *n. see* nicotinic acid.

煙酸 參閱 nicotinic acid。

nicardipine *n.* a *calcium antagonist used to treat long-term angina. It is administered by mouth. Possible side-effects include nausea, chest pain, dizziness, headache, flushing, and palpitations. Trade name: **Cardene**.

尼卡地平 用於治療長期咽峽炎的鈣拮抗藥。口服。可能產生的副作用包括惡心、胸痛、頭暈、頭痛、面紅和心悸。商品名：Cardene。

niche *n.* (in anatomy) a recess or depression in a smooth surface.

龕 （解剖學）平滑表面上的隱窩或凹陷。

niclosamide *n.* an *anthelmintic drug used to remove tapeworms. It is administered by mouth; unlike older treatments, it is free from side-effects. Trade name: **Yomesan**.

氯硝柳胺，滅縧靈 用於清除縧蟲的抗蠕蟲藥。口服。與舊治療藥不同的是此藥無副作用。商品名：Yomesan。

nicotinamide *n.* a B vitamin: the amide of *nicotinic acid.

煙醯胺 一種 B 族維生素：煙酸的醯胺。

nicotinamide adenine dinucleotide *see* NAD.

煙酰胺腺嘌呤二核苷酸　參閱 NAD。

nicotine *n.* a poisonous alkaloid derived from *tobacco, responsible for the dependence of regular smokers on cigarettes. In small doses nicotine has a stimulating effect on the autonomic nervous system, causing in regular smokers such effects as raised blood pressure and pulse rate and impaired appetite. Large doses cause paralysis of the autonomic ganglia.

煙鹼，尼古丁　從煙草中提取的一種有毒生物鹼，可造成經常吸煙者對煙草的依賴。小劑量對自主神經系統有刺激作用，使經常吸煙者血壓升高、脈搏增快和食慾不振。大劑量引起自主神經節麻痺。

nicotinic acid (niacin) a B vitamin. Nicotinic acid is a derivative of pyridine and is interchangeable with its amide, *nicotinamide*. Both forms of the vitamin are equally active. Nicotinamide is a component of the coenzymes *NAD (nicotinamide adenine dinucleotide) and NADP, its phosphate. Nicotinic acid is required in the diet but can also be formed in small amounts in the body from the essential amino acid tryptophan. A deficiency of the vitamin leads to *pellagra. Good sources of nicotinic acid are meat, yeast extracts, and some cereals. Nicotinic acid is present in some cereals (e.g. maize) in a bound unavailable form. The adult recommended intake is 18 mg equivalent per day (1 mg equivalent is equal to 1 mg of available nicotinic acid or 60 mg tryptophan).

煙酸　一種 B 族維生素。煙酸是吡啶的衍生物，它可與其酰胺，即煙酰胺相互轉換。這兩種形式的維生素活性相同。煙酰胺是輔酶 NAD（煙酰胺腺嘌呤二核苷酸）和其磷酸鹽 NADP 的一種成分。飲食中需要煙酸，但它也可以小量地在體內從必需的氨基酸即色氨酸中形成。這種維生素的缺乏會導致糙皮病。煙酸富含於肉、酵母浸出物和一些穀類中。煙酸在有些穀物（例如玉米）中以結合起來的、無法利用的形式存在。成人每日推薦攝入量是 18mg 當量（1mg 當量等於 1mg 可利用的煙酸或 60mg 色氨酸）。

nicotinyl *n.* a drug that dilates blood vessels. It is similar to *nicotinic acid and is used to treat disorders due to poor circulation, such as chilblains and Raynaud's disease. It is administered by mouth; side-effects are rare, but temporary flushing of the face may occur. Trade name: **Ronicol**.

煙醇　擴張血管的藥物。它與煙酸類似，用於治療由於循環不良所致的疾病，如凍瘡和雷諾病。口服，副作用罕見，但會出現短暫的面紅。商品：Ronicol。

nictitation *n.* exaggerated and frequent blinking or winking of the eyes.

瞬眼（眨眼）　誇大和頻繁的瞬眼或眨眼。

nidation *n. see* implantation.

nidus *n.* a place in which bacteria have settled and multiplied because of particularly suitable conditions: a focus of infection.

nifedipine *n.* a *calcium antagonist used in the treatment of angina and high blood pressure (hypertension). It is administered by mouth; side-effects include dizziness, headache, and nausea. Trade names: **Adalat**, **Calcilat**.

night blindness the inability to see in dim light or at night. It is due to a disorder of the cells in the retina that are responsible for vision in dim light (*see* rod), and can result from dietary deficiency of *vitamin A. If the vitamin deficiency is allowed to continue, its manifestations may progress to include *xerophthalmia and *keratomalacia. Night blindness may be caused by other retinal diseases, e.g. *retinitis pigmentosa. Medical name: **nyctalopia**. *Compare* day blindness.

night sweat copious sweating during sleep. Night sweats may be an early indication of tuberculosis, AIDS, or other disease.

night terror the condition in which a child (usually aged 2–4 years), soon after falling asleep, starts screaming and appears terrified. The child cannot be comforted because he remains mentally inaccessible; the attack ceases when he wakes up fully and is never remembered. Attacks sometimes follow a stressful experience.

nikethamide *n.* an *analeptic drug used to raise the level of consciousness in

着床　參閱 implantation。

病竈　因為條件特別適合，細菌居住並繁殖的地方：感染的病竈。

硝苯地平　用於治療咽峽炎和高血壓的一種鈣拮抗藥。口服。副作用包括頭暈、頭痛及惡心。商品名：Adalat，Calcilat。

夜盲（症）　在光綫昏暗處或夜間不能看見東西。病因是視網膜中負責在昏暗光綫下視物的細胞疾病（參閱 rod），也可因膳食中缺乏維生素 A 所致。如果聽任這種維生素缺乏，夜盲（症）的表現可發展到包括乾眼病和角膜軟化在內的多種疾病。夜盲症可能由其他視網膜疾病引起，例如：色素沉着性視網炎。醫學名：夜盲症。與 day blindness 對比。

盗汗　睡眠時大量出汗。盜汗可能是結核病、艾滋病或其他疾病的早期表現。

夜驚　兒童（通常是 2~4 歲）入睡後不久開始尖叫並表現出驚恐的現象。因為兒童在思維上難以捉摸，所以無法安慰。兒童完全清醒後發作停止且永遠回憶不起來。有時在緊張之後會發作。

尼克刹米　一種興奮劑，用於提高昏迷病人的意識水平，以

comatose patients so that they can be encouraged to cough and bring up bronchial secretions. It is administered by mouth or injection. Possible side-effects include nausea, rapid and irregular heartbeat, dizziness, restlessness, and tremor.

刺激咳出氣管分泌物。口服或注射。可能產生的副作用有惡心、心跳加快、心律不齊、頭暈、煩躁和顫抖。

Nile blue an oxazine chloride, used for staining lipids and lipid pigments. *Nile blue A* (*Nile bule sulphate*), which stains fatty acids, changes from blue to purplish at pH 10–11.

尼羅藍　惡嗪氯化物，用於脂類及脂色素的染色。給脂肪酸染色的尼羅藍 A（硫酸尼羅藍）在 pH 10~11 之間由藍變紫。

ninhydrin reaction a histochemical test for proteins, in which ninhydrin (triketo-hydrindene hydrate) is boiled with the test solution and gives a blue colour in the presence of amino acids and proteins.

（水合）茚三酮反應　蛋白質的組織化學試驗，在這種試驗中，（水合）茚三酮和試驗溶液一起被煮沸，有氨基酸和蛋白質存在則呈現出藍色。

nipple (mamilla, papilla) *n.* the protuberance at the centre of the *breast. In females the milk ducts open at the nipple.

乳頭　乳房中央的隆起。在雌性動物中，乳腺管在乳頭上有開口。

niridazole *n.* an anthelmintic drug used particularly in the treatment of schistosomiasis. It is administered by mouth and side-effects may include agitation and confusion, abdominal discomfort, some digestive upset, and headache. Niridazole should not be used in patients with impaired liver function.

尼立達唑　專門用於治療血吸蟲病的一種抗蠕蟲藥。口服。副作用包括煩躁、精神混亂、下腹不適、某些消化不良和頭痛。肝功能受損者不能使用。

Nissl granules collections of darkstaining material, containing RNA, seen in the cell bodies of neurones on microscopic examination.

尼斯爾體　深色染色物質的集合，含 RNA，顯微鏡檢查時見於神經元的細胞體內。

nit *n.* the egg of a *louse. The eggs of head lice are firmly cemented to the hair, usually at the back of the head; those of body lice are fixed to the clothing. Nits, 0.8 × 0.3 mm, are visible as light white specks.

蟣　虱卵。頭虱的卵牢固地黏在頭髮上，通常在頭的後部。體虱的卵依附在衣服上。蟣大小為 0.8 × 0.3 mm。肉眼看到的呈淡白點。

nitrazepam *n.* a *hypnotic drug administered by mouth to treat insomnia and sleep disturbances. It is often preferred to other hypnotics since side-effects are not severe, though morning drowsiness can sometimes occur. Trade name: **Mogadon**.

硝西泮 治療失眠（症）和睡眠障礙的口服安眠藥。儘管有時會造成早晨困倦，但因為副作用不嚴重，常選用此藥，而不是其他安眠藥。商品名：Mogadon。

nitric acid a strong corrosive mineral acid, HNO_3, the concentrated form of which is capable of producing severe burns of the skin. Swallowing the acid leads to intense burning pain and ulceration of the mouth and throat. Treatment is by immediate administration of alkaline solutions, followed by milk or olive oil.

硝酸 一種強腐蝕性無機酸：HNO_3。濃硝酸會造成皮膚的嚴重燒傷。吞服硝酸可導致強烈的灼痛和口腔及咽喉潰瘍。治療採取立即服用鹼性溶液，然後服用牛奶和橄欖油。

nitrofurantoin *n.* a drug used to treat bacterial infections of the urinary system. It is administered by mouth and may cause nausea, vomiting, and skin rashes. Trade names: **Furadantin**, **Macrodantin**.

呋喃妥因 治療泌尿系統細菌感染的一種藥物。口服。可造成惡心、嘔吐和皮疹。商品名：Furadantin，Macrodantin。

nitrogen *n.* a gaseous element and a major constituent of air (79 per cent). Nitrogen is an essential constituent of proteins and nucleic acids and is obtained by man in the form of protein-containing foods (atmospheric nitrogen cannot be utilized directly). Nitrogenous waste is excreted as *urea. Liquid nitrogen is used to freeze some specimens before pathological examination. Symbol: N.

氮 一種氣體元素，大氣的主要成分（79%）。氮是蛋白質和核酸的基本成分，人從蛋白質食物中獲取（空氣中的氮不能被直接利用）。氮的廢料作為尿素被排出。液態氮在病理檢查前用於冷凍某些標本。符號：N。

nitrogen balance the relationship between the nitrogen taken into the body and that excreted, denoting the balance between the manufacture and breakdown of the body mass. A negative nitrogen balance, when excretion exceeds intake, is usual after injury or operations as the energy requirements

氮平衡 身體吸收和排出的氮之間的關係，它表示身體物質的製造和分解之間的平衡。分泌大於吸收時出現負氮平衡，因為外傷或手術後身體對能量的需要沒有從內生源得到均衡的滿足，經常發生負氮平衡。

of the body are met disproportionately from endogenous sources.

nitrogen mustard *see* mustine.

氮芥　參閱 mustine。

nitroglycerin *n. see* glyceryl trinitrate.

硝酸甘油　參閱 glyceryl trinitrate。

nitroprusside *n.* a cyanide-containing drug used in the emergency treatment of high blood pressure. Given by controlled infusion into a vein, it is the most effective known means of reducing dangerously high pressure, but its effects and level in the blood must be closely monitored. Possible side-effects include nausea, vomiting, headache, palpitations, sweating, and chest pain.

硝普鹽　高血壓急診治療時使用的一種含氰化物藥物。以控制劑量輸注靜脈時是已知的最有效的降低危險性高血壓的方法，但必須嚴密監視它在血液中的作用和水平。可能產生的副作用包括噁心、嘔吐、頭痛、心悸、出汗和胸痛。

nitrous oxide a colourless gas used as an *anaesthetic with good *analgesic properties. It is administered by inhalation, in conjunction with oxygen, and is used as a vehicle for potent anaesthetic vapours, such as halothane. A mixture of oxygen and nitrous oxide provides effective analgesia for some dental procedures and in childbirth; such a state is known as *relative analgesia. Nitrous oxide was formerly referred to as *laughing gas* because of its tendency to excite the patient when used alone.

氧化亞氮　一種無色氣體，用作麻醉劑，具有良好的鎮痛作用。通過和氧氣一起吸入給藥，並被用作強麻醉劑蒸氣，如氟烷的載體。氧氣和氧化亞氮的混合物在某些牙科手術和分娩中作為有效的止痛法；這種狀態叫相對止痛藥。氧化亞氮以前被稱作笑氣，因為它單獨使用時趨向於使病人激動。

nm *abbrev. for* nanometre.

〔縮寫〕毫微米

NMR *see* nuclear magnetic resonance.

核磁共振　參閱 nuclear magnetic resonance。

Nocardia *n.* a genus of rodlike or filamentous Gram-positive nonmotile bacteria found in the soil. As cultures age, filaments form branches, but these soon break up into rodlike or spherical cells. Three or more spores may form in each cell; these germinate to form filaments.

諾卡菌屬　見於土壤中的桿狀或絲狀革蘭氏陽性無運動菌屬。培養成熟時，菌絲形成分支，但這些分支很快分裂成桿狀或球形細胞，每個細胞中會形成三個或更多的孢子；這些孢子生長形成菌絲。有些種類

Some species are pathogenic: *N. asteroides* causes *nocardiosis and *N. madurae* is associated with the disease *Madura foot.

有致病性。星形諾卡菌引起諾卡放綫菌病，馬杜拉諾卡菌與足分支菌病有關。

nocardiosis *n.* a disease caused by bacteria of the genus *Nocardia*, primarily affecting the lungs, skin, and brain, resulting in the formation of abscesses. Treatment involves antibiotics and sulphonamides.

諾卡放綫菌病 諾卡菌屬細菌引起的一種疾病。此病主要影響肺、皮膚和大腦，導致膿腫形成。用抗生素和磺胺類藥治療。

noci- *prefix denoting* pain or injury.

〔前綴〕**疼痛，傷害**

nociceptive *adj.* describing nerve fibres, endings, or pathways that are concerned the with condition of pain.

感受傷害的 與疼痛有關的神經纖維、末梢或傳導路的。

noct- (nocti-) *prefix denoting* night.

〔前綴〕**夜晚**

noctambulation *n. see* somnambulism.

夢行（症） 參閱 somnambulism。

nocturia *n.* the passage of urine at night. In the absence of a high fluid intake, sleep is not normally interrupted by the need to pass urine. Nocturia usually occurs in elderly men with enlarged prostate glands, and is a common reason for patients to request *prostatectomy.

夜尿症 夜間排尿。不大量攝入液體時，睡眠不會被需要排尿而打斷。夜尿症常產生於老年男性前列腺增大，是病人需要作前列腺切除術的常見原因。

node *n.* a small swelling or knot of tissue. *See* atrioventricular node, lymph node, sinoatrial node.

結 組織的小腫塊或結節。參閱 atrioventricular node，lymph node，sinoatrial node。

node of Ranvier one of the gaps that occur at regular intervals in the *myelin sheath of medullated nerve fibres, between adjacent *Schwann cells.

郎飛結 有髓鞘神經纖維的髓鞘中每隔一定距離出現的小空隙，位於相鄰的施萬細胞之間。

nodule *n.* a small swelling or aggregation of cells.

小結 細胞的小腫塊或聚集。

noma *n.* a gangrenous infection of the mouth that spreads to involve the face. It

走馬疳 擴散到涉及面部的口腔的壞疽性感染。在文明化的

is rare in civilized communities and is usually found in debilitated or malnourished individuals. Noma is a severe form of *ulcerative gingivitis.

nonaccidental injury (NAI) injury inflicted on babies and young children by parents (usually step-parents) or carers. Most commonly seen in babies aged six months or less, it usually takes the form of bruising, particularly on the face; bite marks; burns or scalds, particularly cigarette burns; and bone injuries, especially spiral fractures of the long bones in the limbs and skull fractures. Internal injuries may be fatal. Careful examination often reveals several injuries of different ages, indicating long-term abuse. NAI usually has serious consequences for the child, including *failure to thrive and behavioural problems.

Known colloquially as the *battered baby* (or *child*) *syndrome*, it may be precipitated by many factors, including relationship difficulties, social problems, and ill health, and is more common if the child is handicapped. It is often found that abusers suffered similar abuse themselves when young. Many abused children suffer further injury if discharged into the same environment with no support (*see also* risk register). A child at considerable risk may need to be removed from the family home.

nondisjunction *n.* a condition in which pairs of homologous chromosomes fail to separate during meiosis or a chromosome fails to divide at *anaphase of mitosis or mitosis. It results in a cell with an abnormal number of chromosomes (*see* monosomy, trisomy).

noninvasive *adj.* **1.** denoting techniques of investigation or treatment that do not

社區中，此病不常見，常見於衰弱或營養不良的人。走馬疳是潰瘍性齦炎的嚴重形式。

非事故性傷害 父母（通常是繼父繼母）或看護者對嬰兒及幼兒的傷害。最常見於六個月或更小一些的嬰兒。常見形式有挫傷，尤其是臉上挫傷、咬痕、燒傷或燙傷、煙頭燒傷、骨外傷和四肢長骨的螺旋形骨折和顱骨骨折。內傷可能致命。詳細的檢查經常會揭示出不同年齡的許多傷害，這說明是長期虐待。非事故性傷害通常對兒童產生嚴重的後果，包括發育停滯和行為異常。

非事故性傷害俗稱受虐嬰兒（或兒童）綜合徵，可能由諸多因素所致，包括關係困難、社會問題和疾病，兒童殘疾時較為常見。亦常見於幼年時經歷過相似虐待的虐待者。許多已受到虐待的兒童在沒有支持時如果被送到相同的環境中，會受到更大的傷害（參閱 risk register）。需要從家中接出處於極大危險中的兒童。

不分開現象 減數分裂期間成對的同源染色體不能分開，或在有絲分裂或減數分裂後期染色體不能分開的情況。會導致細胞帶有染色體的數目異常（參閱 monosomy，trisomy）。

非侵入性 **(1)** 表示不用針或刀穿透皮膚的檢查或治療技

involve penetration of the skin by needles of knives. **2.** denoting tumours that do not spread into surounding tissues (*see* benign).

術。**(2)** 表示不擴散到周圍組織的腫瘤（參閱 benign）。

Nonne's syndrome (cerebellar syndrome) *see* (cerebellar) ataxia.

農內綜合徵（小腦綜合徵）參閱 (cerebellar) ataxia。

nonsecretor *n.* a person in whose body fluids it is not possible to detect soluble forms of the A, B or O agglutinogens that determine blood group. *Compare* secretor.

非分泌者 體液中不能找到可決定血型的可溶性 A、B 或 O 血型凝集原的人。與 secretor 對比。

nonsteroidal anti-inflammatory drug *see* NSAID.

非甾類抗炎藥 參閱 NSAID。

noradrenaline (norepinephrine) *n.* a hormone, closely related to *adrenaline and with similar actions, secreted by the medulla of the *adrenal gland and also released as a *neurotransmitter by sympathetic nerve endings. Among its many actions are constriction of small blood vessels leading to an increase in blood pressure, increased blood flow through the coronary arteries and a slowing of the heart rate, increase in the rate and depth of breathing, and relaxation of the smooth muscle in intestinal walls.

去甲腎上腺素 一種激素，和腎上腺素密切相關，並具有類似的作用。由腎上腺的髓質分泌，也由交感神經末梢釋放，作為神經遞質。具有收縮小血管使血壓升高，增加冠狀動脈血流、降低心率、增加呼吸速度和深度及鬆弛小腸壁的平滑肌的功能。

norepinephrine *n. see* noradrenaline.

去甲腎上腺素 參閱 noradrenaline。

norethisterone *n.* a synthetic female sexhormone (see progestogen) administered by mouth to treat menstrual disorders, including amenorrhoea. Its main use, however, is in oral contraceptives, often in combination with an oestrogen. Trade name: **Primolut.**

炔諾酮 口服，治療包括閉經在內的月經紊亂的合成雌性激素（參閱 progestogen）。但其主要用途是常與雌激素結合用作口服避孕藥。商品名：Primolut。

norma *n.* a view of the skull from one of several positions, from which it can be described or measured. For example the

顱外觀 從不同位置觀察顱骨，借此描述或測量顱骨。例如側面觀是從側面觀察顱骨，

norma lateralis is a side view of the skull; the *norma verticalis* is the view of the top of the skull.

垂直面觀是對顱骨頂部進行觀察。

normalization *n.* (in psychiatry) the process of making the living conditions of people with *mental handicap as similar as possible to those of people who are not handicapped. This includes moves to living outside institutions and encouragement to cope with work, pay, social life, sexuality, and civil rights.

正常化 （精神病學）盡可能地使有智力障礙的人的生活條件和正常人的生活條件相似的過程。包括移居到醫院外生活及鼓勵他們工作、賺錢、參加社交活動、享受性生活和行使公民權。

normo- *prefix denoting* normality.

〔前綴〕正常

normoblast *n.* a nucleated cell that forms part of the series giving rise to the red blood cells and is normally found in the blood-forming tissue of the bone marrow. Normoblasts pass through three stages of maturation: *early* (or *basophilic*), *intermediate* (or *polychromatic*), and *late* (or *orthochromatic*) forms. *See also* erythroblast, erythropoiesis.

幼紅細胞 生成紅細胞過程中某個部分所形成的有核細胞，正常情況下見於骨髓的造血組織中。幼紅細胞經過三個成熟階段：早期（或嗜鹼染色的）、中期（或多色的）及晚期（或正染的）形式。參閱 erythroblast，erythropoiesis。

normocyte *n.* a red blood cell of normal size. A *normocytic anaemia* is one characterized by the presence of such cells. **—normocytic** *adj.*

正常紅細胞 正常大小的紅細胞。正常紅細胞性貧血以出現這種細胞為特徵。

normotensive *adj.* describing the state in which the arterial blood pressure is within the normal range. *Compare* hypertension, hypotension.

血壓正常的 描述動脈血壓處於正常範圍內的狀態。與 hypertension，hypotension 對比。

Northern blot analysis a technique for identifying a specific form of messenger RNA in cells. It uses a gene *probe known to match the RNA being sought. *Compare* Southern blot analysis, Western blot analysis.

RNA 印迹分析 用於鑒別細胞中特異型信使 RNA 的技術。它使用一種已知的基因探針和要尋找的 RNA 相配。與 Southern blot analysis，Western blot analysis 對比。

nortriptyline *n.* a tricyclic *antidepressant drug that is used to relieve all types of depression. It is administered by

去甲替林 用於治療各種類型的抑鬱症的一種三環抗抑鬱藥。口服。副作用有口乾和

mouth; side-effects may include dry mouth and drowsiness. Trade names: **Allegron**, **Aventyl**.

nose *n.* the organ of olfaction, which also acts as an air passage that warms, moistens, and filters the air on its way to the lungs. The *external nose* is a triangular projection in the front of the face that is composed of cartilage and covered with skin. It leads to the *nasal cavity* (*internal nose*), which is lined with mucous membrane containing olfactory cells and is divided into two chambers (*fossae*) by the *nasal septum*. The lateral wall of each chamber is formed by the three scroll-shaped *nasal conchae, below each of which is a groovelike passage (*meatus*). The *paranasal sinuses open into these meatuses.

nosebleed *n.* bleeding from the nose, which may be caused by physical injury or may be associated with fever, high blood pressure, or blood disorders. The blood often comes from a vessel just inside the nostril, in which case the flow may be stopped by applying pressure on the side of the nose. Otherwise gauze packing may be effective in controlling the loss of blood. Medical name: **epistaxis**.

noso- *prefix denoting* disease.

nosocomial infection (hospital infection) an infection whose development is favoured by a hospital environment. It may develop in a hospitalized patient without having been present or incubating at the time of admission, or it may be acquired in hospital but only appears after discharge. Such infections include fungal and opportunist bacterial infections. They are aggravated by factors favouring the spread of organisms (cross-contamination) and by reduced

困倦。商品名：Allegron，Aventyl。

鼻　嗅覺器官，也可作為空氣流向肺時温暖、濕潤和過濾空氣的氣道。外鼻是面部前面的三角形突起，由軟骨構成並覆以皮膚。與鼻腔（內鼻）相通。鼻腔內襯含有嗅覺細胞的黏膜，並被鼻中隔分成兩腔（鼻前庭），每個腔的側壁由三個卷形鼻甲構成，每個鼻甲的下面是溝狀通道（鼻道），鼻旁竇開口於這些鼻道。

鼻出血　鼻中出血，可由物理損傷引起或與發熱、高血壓或血液病有關。血液經常來自鼻孔淺部的血管，可以通過向鼻側加壓阻止出血。另外紗布填塞可以有效地止血。醫學用語：鼻衄。

〔前綴〕**疾病**

醫院內感染　醫院環境對其發生有利的感染。醫院內感染可發生在入院時並沒有出現感染或正處在潛伏期的住院病人，或者是住院以後受感染，但出院以後感染才出現。這類感染包括真菌及條件致病菌感染。在有利於微生物擴散的諸多因素（交叉感染）、病人抵抗力下降及細菌對抗生素產生耐藥性時，感染會加重。此術語也包括醫務人員中產生的感染。

resistance of individual patients, as well as by antibiotic-resistant strains of bacteria. The term also includes infections developing among hospital staff.

nosology *n.* the naming and classification of diseases.

疾病分類學 疾病的命名和分類。

Nosopsyllus *n.* a genus of fleas. The common rat flea of temperate regions, *N. fasciatus*, will, in the absence of rats, bite man and may therefore transmit plague or murine typhus from an infected rat population. The rat flea is also an intermediate host for the larval stage of two tapeworms, *Hymenolepis diminuta* and *H. nana*.

病蚤屬 蚤的一個屬。温帶地區常見的鼠蚤，即具帶病蚤，在沒有老鼠時會叮咬人，因此從被感染的鼠羣中傳播鼠疫或鼠斑疹傷寒。鼠蚤也是兩種縧蟲，即縮小膜殼縧蟲和短膜殼縧蟲幼蟲階段的中間宿主。

nostrils *n. see* nares.

鼻孔 參閱 nares。

notch *n.* (in anatomy) an indentation, especially one in a bone.

切迹 （解剖學）一種缺口，特別是骨中的缺口。

notifiable disease a disease that must be reported to the health authorities in order that speedy control and preventive action may be undertaken if necessary. In Great Britain such diseases must be notified to the proper officer for the control of communicable diseases (formerly to the Medical Officer of Health). They include AIDS (but not HIV positivity), diphtheria, dysentery, food poisoning, infective jaundice, malaria, measles, poliomyelitis, tuberculosis, typhoid, and whooping cough. The list varies for different countries, and some diseases are internationally notifiable through the *World Health Organization; these include cholera, plague, relapsing fever, typhus, and yellow fever.

法定傳染病 一種必須報告衛生當局以便必要時可採取快速控制及預防行動的疾病。在英國，這種疾病必須報告給負責傳染病控制的有關官員（以前報告給衛生醫官）。法定傳染病包括艾滋病（HIV 陽性者除外）、白喉、痢疾、食物中毒、傳染性黃疸、瘧疾、麻疹、脊髓灰質炎、結核病、傷寒及百日咳。此名單因國家而異，有些疾病通過世界衛生組織向國際通報，這些疾病包括霍亂、鼠疫、回歸熱、斑疹傷寒和黃熱病。

notochord *n.* a strip of mesodermal tissue that develops along the dorsal surface of the early embryo, beneath the *neural tube. It becomes almost entirely obliterated by the development of the

脊索 位於神經管下的、沿早期胚胎的側面發育的中胚層組織帶。因為脊椎的發育，脊索會變得幾乎完全閉合，僅留作椎間盤的一部分。

vertebrae, persisting only as part of the intervertebral discs.

NSAID (nonsteroidal anti-inflammatory drug) any one of a large group of drugs used for pain relief, particularly in rheumatic disease. NSAIDs act by inhibiting the enzymes responsible for the formation or *prostaglandins, which are important mediators of inflammation. They include *aspirin, *azapropazone, *diflunisal, *ibuprofen, *ketoprofen, and *naproxen, Adverse effects include gastric bleeding and ulceration.

非甾類抗炎藥 用於解除疼痛，特別是風濕熱的一大類藥物。這類藥物通過抑制負責前列腺素形成的酶而產生作用，前列腺素是炎症的重要調節者。這類藥物包括阿司匹林、二氟尼柳、阿扎丙宗、布洛芬、酮洛芬和萘普生。有害作用有胃出血和胃潰瘍。

nucha *n.* the nape of the neck. –**nuchal** *adj.*

項 頸的後部。

nuclear cardiology the study and diagnosis of heart disease by the intravenous injection of a *radionuclide. The radionuclide emits gamma rays, enabling a gamma camera and computer to form an image of the heart. *See* MUGA scan, thallium scan.

核心臟病學 通過靜脈注射放射性核素研究和診斷心臟病。放射性核素能發出 γ 射綫，使 γ 照相機及計算機能夠形成心臟的圖像。參閱 MUGA scan，thallium scan。

nuclear magnetic resonance (NMR) the absorption and transmission of high-frequency radio waves by the nuclei of molecules when placed in a strong magnetic field. The effect is highly dependent on the concentration of hydrogen nuclei within each molecule, and is therefore particularly useful for analysing biological material. It has important applications in noninvasive diagnostic techniques (*see* magnetic resonance imaging, magnetic resonance spectroscopy).

核磁共振 分子的核置於強磁場中時發出的高頻放射波的吸收和傳導。其作用高度依賴於每個分子中的氫核，因此對於分析生物材料特別有用。核磁共振在非侵入性診斷技術中有重要的應用價值（參閱 magnetic resonance imaging，magnetic resonance spectroscopy）。

nuclear medicine the branch of medicine concerned with the use of *radionuclides in the study and diagnosis of diseases. *See also* nuclear cardiology.

核醫學 涉及使用放射核素研究和診斷疾病的醫學分支。參閱 nuclear cardiology。

nuclease *n.* an enzyme that catalyses the breakdown of nucleic acids by cleaving the bonds between adjacent nucleotides. Examples are *ribonuclease*, which acts on RNA, and *deoxyribonuclease*, which acts on DNA.

nucleic acid either of two organic acids, *DNA or *RNA, present in the nucleus and in some cases the cytoplasm of all living cells. Their main functions are in heredity and protein synthesis.

nucleolus *n.* (*pl.* **nucleoli**) a dense spherical structure within the cell *nucleus that disappears during cell division. The nucleolus contains *RNA for the synthesis of *ribosomes and plays an important part in RNA and protein synthesis.

nucleoplasm (karyoplasm) *n.* the protoplasm making up the nucleus of a cell.

nucleoprotein *n.* a compound that occurs in cells and consists of nucleic acid and protein tightly bound together. *Ribosomes are nucleoproteins containing RNA; *chromosomes are nucleoproteins containing DNA.

nucleoside *n.* a compound consisting of a nitrogen-containing base (a *purine or *pyrimidine) linked to a sugar. Examples are *adenosine, *guanosine, *cytidine, *thymidine, and *uracil.

nucleotide *n.* a compound consisting of a nitrogen-containing base (a *purine or *pyrimidine) linked to a sugar and a phosphate group. Nucleic acids (DNA and RNA) are long chains of linked nucleotides (*polynucleotide* chains), which in DNA contain the purine bases

核酸酶 通過鄰近核苷酸之間的鍵裂解催化核酸分解的一種酶。例如作用於 RNA 的核糖核酸酶和作用於 DNA 的脫氧核糖核酸酶。

核酸 兩種有機酸 DNA 和 RNA 之一，存在於所有活細胞的核中，有些情況下存在於活細胞的胞漿中。主要功能是遺傳和合成蛋白質。

核仁 細胞分裂過程中消失的、細胞核內的稠密的球形結構。核仁中含有核糖體合成用的 RNA 並在 RNA 和蛋白質合成中起重要作用。

核質（核漿）組成細胞核的原生質。

核蛋白 細胞中產生的一種化合物，由核酸和蛋白質緊密結合在一起構成。核糖體是含有 RNA 的核蛋白；染色體是含 DNA 的核蛋白。

核苷 由含氮鹼（嘌呤或嘧啶）連接糖構成的一種化合物。例如腺苷、鳥苷、胞核嘧啶、胸腺核苷和尿嘧啶。

核苷酸 由含氮鹼（嘌呤或嘧啶）連接糖和磷基組成的一種化合物。核酸（DNA 和 RNA）是被連在一起的核苷酸的長鏈（多核苷酸鏈），在 DNA 中，它含有嘌呤鹼，即腺嘌呤和鳥嘌呤，及嘧啶鹼，即胸腺

adenine and guanine and the pyrimidines thymine and cytosine; in RNA, thymine is replaced by uracil.

嘧啶和胞嘧啶；在 RNA 中，胸腺嘧啶被尿嘧啶代替。

nucleus *n.* **1.** the part of a *cell that contains the genetic material, *DNA. The DNA, which is combined with protein, is normally dispersed throughout the nucleus as *chromatin. During cell division the chromatin becomes visible as *chromosomes. The nucleus also contains *RNA, most of which is located in the *nucleolus. The nucleus is separated from the cytoplasm by a double membrane, the *nuclear envelope*. **2.** an anatomically and functionally distinct mass of nerve cells within the brain or spinal cord.

核 **(1)** 含有遺傳物質 DNA 的細胞部分。與蛋白質結合的 DNA 在正常情況下作為染色質彌散到核的各處。在細胞分裂過程中，染色質作為染色體變得可以看到。核中也含 RNA，大多數位於核仁中。核與胞漿被一個雙層膜（核膜）分開。**(2)** 大腦或脊髓中在解剖上和功能上特點明顯的神經細胞團。

nude mouse a mouse born without a thymus and therefore no T-lymphocytes. Human tumours will often grow in these mice. For unknown reasons these mice are hairless, hence the name.

裸鼠 先天無胸腺，因此無 T 型淋巴細胞的老鼠。人類腫瘤常會在這些老鼠體內生長。這種老鼠無毛，故得此名。牠無毛的原因不明。

nuisance *n.* any noxious substance, accumulating in refuse or as dust or effluent, that is deemed by British law to be injurious to health or offensive. It can also include dwellings, work premises, or animals.

有害物 英國法律認定為有損健康或具有侵擾性的、在垃圾中堆積或作為灰塵或廢水的任何有毒物質。有害物也包括住宅、工作場所或動物。

null hypothesis *see* significance.

無效假說 參閱 significance。

nullipara *n.* a woman who has never given birth to an infant capable of survival.

未產婦 從未生過能夠存活的嬰兒的婦女。

nurse *n.* a person trained and experienced in medical matters and entrusted with the care of the sick and the carrying out of medical and surgical routines under the supervision of a doctor. In Britain student nurses must receive a specified period of training in a hospital

護士 在醫療事務方面受過培訓、具有一定經驗的、負責照看病人、並在醫生的指導下執行內外科常規工作的人。在英國，見習護士必須在全國護士理事會認可的醫院裏接受一定時期的培訓並通過考試，才能

approved by the General Nursing Council and pass an examination before qualifying for registration with the UKCC (United Kingdom Central Council for Nursing, Midwifery, and Health Visiting) as a *general nurse* (*RGN*). *See also* domiciliary midwife, health visitor, home nurse, nursing officer, practice nurse, school nurse.

nursing officer a higher grade of nurse concerned with administration and management in either tier of the British *National Health Service (*Regional* or *District Nursing Officer*). There are in addition the grades of *Principal Nursing Officer*, who is responsible for part of the nursing organization within a hospital or in community nursing, and *Senior Nursing Officer*, who is responsible for a group of nurses caring for a designated specialty (e.g. surgical).

nutation *n*. the act of nodding the head.

nutrient *n*. a substance that must be consumed as part of the diet to provide a source of energy, material for growth, or substances that regulate growth or energy production. Nutrients include carbohydrates, fats, proteins, minerals, and vitamins.

nutrition *n*. **1.** the study of food in relation to the physiological processes that depend on its absorption by the body (growth, energy production, repair of body tissues, etc.). The science of nutrition includes the study of diets and of deficiency diseases. **2.** the intake of nutrients and their subsequent absorption and assimilation by the tissues. Patients who cannot be fed in a normal way can be given nutrients by tubes into the intestines (*enteral feeding*) or by infusion into a vein (*intravenous feeding*).

有資格作為全科護士（註冊護士），在英國護士、助產士和保健員委員會 (UKCC) 註冊。參閱 domiciliary midwife，health visitor，home nurse，nursing officer，practice nurse，school nurse。

護師 在英國國民保健服務制（地區或地段護師）兩級中的一個負責行政和管理的高級護士。另外還有主任護師，負責醫院內或社區內的部分護理組織工作；高級護師，負責某一指定專科（例如外科）一組護士的工作。

點頭 點頭的動作。

營養素 作為膳食的一部分必須攝食的物質，目的在於提供生長所需的能量和材料來源，或者是調節生長或能量製造的物質。營養素包括碳水化合物、脂肪、蛋白質、礦物質和維生素。

營養 **(1)** 研究食物與食物被身體吸收的生理過程（生長、能量製造、身體組織的恢復）之間的相互關係。營養科學包括膳食和營養缺乏症的研究。**(2)** 營養素的攝入及其接着被組織吸收和同化。不能以正常方式進食的患者可以用導管向腸道供給營養素（腸道飼養）或靜脈滴注（靜脈飼養）。

nux vomica the seed of the tree *Strychnos nux-vomica*, which contains the poisonous alkaloid *strychnine.

馬錢子　馬錢樹的種子，含毒性生物鹼士的寧。

nyct- (nycto-) *prefix denoting* night or darkness.

〔前綴〕**夜間，黑暗**

nyctalopia *n. see* night blindness.

夜盲症　參閱　night blindness。

nyctophilia *n.* an intense preference for the darkness and an avoidance of activity in daylight hours. This is sometimes a form of social *phobia.

嗜夜癖　極度喜愛黑夜並避免在白天活動。有時是一種形式的社會恐怖症。

nyctophobia *n.* extreme fear of the dark. It is common in children and not unusual in normal adults.

黑夜恐怖　極度害怕黑暗。常見於兒童，正常成人中不多見。

nyctophonia *n.* speaking in the night but not in the daytime: a form of elective *mutism.

白晝失語　夜間講話但白天不講：一種選擇性啞症。

nymph *n.* **1.** an immature stage in the life history of certain insects, such as grasshoppers and *reduviid bugs. On emerging from the eggs, nymphs resemble the adult insects except that they are smaller, do not have fully developed wings, and are not sexually mature. **2.** the late larval stage of a tick.

若蟲　**(1)** 某些昆蟲，例如蚱蜢和獵蝽生活史中的不成熟階段。從卵中孵化出來時，若蟲與成蟲相似，只是牠們較小，沒有完全發育的翼，性不成熟。**(2)** 壁虱的晚期幼蟲。

nympho- *prefix denoting* **1.** the labia minora. **2.** female sexuality.

〔前綴〕**(1) 小陰唇　(2) 女性性慾**

nymphomania *n.* an extreme degree of sexual promiscuity in a woman. *Compare* satyriasis. **–nymphomaniac** *adj., n.*

慕男狂　女性極度的性亂交。與 satyriasis 對比。

nystagmus *n.* rapid involuntary movements of the eyes that may be from side to side, up and down, or rotatory. Nystagmus may be congenital and associated with poor sight; it also occurs in disorders of the part of the brain responsible for

眼球震顫　眼球不隨意地快速運動。運動可呈兩側、上下或旋轉式。可為先天性的並與視力不佳有關。也可產生於負責眼球運動及其協調的大腦部分的疾病、耳內平衡器官或大腦

eye movements and their coordination and in disorders of the organ of balance in the ear or the associated parts of the brain. *Optokinetic nystagmus* occurs in normal people when they try to look at a succession of objects moving quickly across their line of sight. Jerking eye movements may occur in normal people when tired, on concentrating their gaze in any direction. These are called *nystagmoid jerks* and they do not imply disease.

nystatin *n.* an antifungal drug used especially to treat yeast infections, such as candidosis. It is formulated, often in conjunction with other drugs (e.g. tetracycline in *Mysteclin* and *Trimovate*), as a cream for skin infections, as tablets for oral and intestinal infections, as pessaries of suppositories for vaginal or anal infections, or as eye drops for eye infections. Side-effects include mild digestive upsets. Trade name: **Nystan**.

相關部分的疾病中。正常人在盡力看從他眼前掠過的一系列物體時，可產生視動性眼球震顫。正常人困倦、凝視任何方向時可出現震顫性眼球運動。這些叫眼球震顫樣反射，它們不表示有病。

製黴菌素　一種抗真菌藥，特別用於治療酵母菌感染，例如念珠菌病。常和其他藥物（如黴死泰素和去黴特中的四環素）一起配製成治療皮膚感染的霜劑、治療口腔及腸道感染的片劑、治療陰道及肛門感染的子宮托或栓劑或治療眼部感染的滴眼藥。副作用包括輕度消化不良。商品名：Nystan。

O

oat cell a cell type of carcinoma of the bronchus. Oat cells are small round or oval cells with darkly staining nuclei and scanty indistinct cytoplasm. Oat-cell carcinoma is usually related to smoking and accounts for about one-quarter of bronchial carcinomas. Also known as *small-cell lung cancer*, it is very sensitive to chemotherapy and radiotherapy.

obesity *n.* the condition in which excess fat has accumulated in the body, mostly in the subcutaneous tissues. Obesity is usually considered to be present when a person is 20% above the recommended

燕麥細胞　支氣管癌的一種細胞類型。燕麥細胞是具有黑染色細胞核和少量模糊不清的胞漿的小圓形或卵圓形細胞。通常與吸烟相關，並占支氣管癌的大約 1/4。也稱小細胞肺癌，對化療和放療非常敏感。

肥胖　體內，主要是皮下組織，脂肪大量聚積的狀態。一個人的體重比其身高及體形相應的推薦體重高出 20% 時，常被認為肥胖。脂肪的聚集通

weight for his/her height and build. The accumulation of fat is usually caused by the consumption of more food than is required for producing enough energy for daily activities. Obesity is the most common nutritional disorder of recent years in Western societies: some patients may require surgical treatment to attain worthwhile weight reduction. **–obese** *adj.*

常是由於進食量大於日常活動所需要的能量。肥胖是西方社會中近年來最常見的營養性疾病：有些病人可能需要手術治療以使體重降低到理想水平。

obex *n.* the curved lower margin of the fourth *ventricle of the brain, between the medulla oblongata and the cerebellum.

閂　第四腦室的曲綫狀下邊緣，位於延髓和小腦之間。

objective *n.* (in microscopy) the lens or system of lenses in a light microscope that is nearest to the object under examination and furthest from the *eyepiece. In many types of microscope interchangeable objectives with different powers of magnification are provided.

物鏡　（顯微鏡檢查）光學顯微鏡中距受檢物體最近、距目鏡最遠的透鏡或一組透鏡。許多類型的顯微鏡都配備具有不同放大能力的可替換的物鏡。

obligate *adj.* describing an organism that is restricted to one particular way of life; for example, an *obligate parasite* cannot exist without a host. *Compare* facultative.

專性的　描述僅限於一種特殊生活方式的生物體；例如專性寄生蟲離開了宿主就不能生存。與 facultative 對比。

observer error *see* validity.

觀察者誤差　參閱 validity。

obsession *n.* a recurrent thought, feeling, or action that is unpleasant and provokes anxiety but cannot be got rid of. Although an obsession dominates the person, he (or she) realizes its senselessness and struggles to expel it. The obsession may be a vivid image, a thought, a fear (for example, of contamination), or an impulse (for example, to wash the hands repetitively). It is a feature of *obsessive-compulsive disorder* (*see also* neurosis) and sometimes of depression and of organic states, such as

強迫觀念　令人不愉快、引起焦慮且不能擺脱的反覆性想法、感覺或行為。儘管強迫觀念控制着一個人，但他（或她）能認識到強迫觀念沒有意義且盡力去驅除它。強迫觀念可能是一幅栩栩如生的圖像、一種思想、一種恐懼（例如害怕傳染）或一種衝動（例如反覆洗手）。它是強迫觀念與強迫症（參閱 neurosis）的一個特徵，有時是抑鬱症及器質性狀態（例如腦炎）的特徵。可以用

encephalitis. It can be treated with behaviour therapy and also with psychotherapy and tranquillizers. *See also* anankastic. **–obsessional** *adj.*

行為療法治療，也可用心理療法及安定藥治療。參閱 anankastic。

obsessive–compulsive disorder *see* neurosis, obsession.

強迫觀念與強迫症　參閱 neurosis，obsession。

obstetrics *n.* the branch of medical science concerned with the care of women during pregnancy, childbirth, and the period of about six weeks following the birth, when the reproductive organs are recovering. *Compare* gynaecology. **–obstetrical** *adj.* **–obstetrician** *n.*

產科學　醫學科學的一個分支，涉及懷孕期間、生產期間及產後大約六星期，即生殖器處於恢復中的婦女護理。與 gynaecology 對比。

obstipation *n. Chiefly US.* severe of complete constipation.

頑固性便秘（主要是美國用語）嚴重的或完全的便秘。

obstructive airways disease *see* bronchospasm.

阻塞性呼吸道疾病　參閱 bronchospasm。

obstructive sleep apnoea a serious condition in which airflow from the nose and mouth to the lungs is restricted during sleep. It is characteristically associated with loud snoring and a fall in the oxygen concentration in the blood, and it can lead to heart failure. In children the cause is usually enlargement of the tonsils and adenoids and treatment is by removing these structures. In adults the tonsils may be implicated but there are often other abnormalities of the *pharynx and the patients are often obese. Treatment may include weight reduction or nocturnal breathing support using a *ventilator; alternatively *tonsillectomy, *uvulopalatopharyngoplasty, or *tracheostomy may be required.

阻塞性睡眠窒息　睡眠時氣流從鼻及口腔流向肺受阻的一種嚴重疾病，特點是大聲打鼾及血液中氧氣濃度下降，可導致心衰。在兒童，病因通常是扁桃體及增殖腺增大。治療方法是摘除這些結構。在成人，可因扁桃體影響且咽常有其他異常，病人常過度肥胖。治療包括降低體重或用呼吸機進行夜間呼吸支持。作為另一種治療方案，可能需要做扁桃體摘除術、懸雍垂軟腭扁桃體切除術或氣管造口術。

obtund *vb.* to blunt or deaden sensitivity; for example, by the application of a local anaesthetic, which reduces

使遲鈍　使感覺遲鈍或麻木；如使用局部麻醉使附近神經感覺降低或喪失。

or causes complete loss of sensation in nearby nerves.

obturator *n.* **1.** *see* obturator muscle. **2.** a wire or rod within a cannula or hollow needle for piercing tissues or fitting aspirating needles. **3.** a removable form of denture that both closes a defect in the palate and also bears artificial teeth for cosmetic purposes. The defect may be congenital, as in a cleft palate, or result from the removal of a tumour.

obturator foramen a large opening in the *hip bone, below and slightly in front of the acetabulum. *See also* pelvis.

obturator muscle either of two muscles that cover the outer surface of the anterior wall of the pelvis (the *obturator externus* and *obturator internus*) and are responsible for lateral rotation of the thigh and movements of the hip.

obtusion *n.* the weakening or blunting of normal sensations. This may be associated with disease.

occipital bone a saucer-shaped bone of the *skull that forms the back and part of the base of the cranium. At the base of the occipital are two *occipital condyles*: rounded surfaces that articulate with the first (atlas) vertebra of the backbone. Between the condyles is the *foramen magnum*, the cavity through which the spinal cord passes.

occiput *n.* the back of the head. **–occipital** *adj.*

occlusal *adj.* (in dental anatomy) denoting or relating to the biting surface of a premolar or molar tooth.

(1) 閉孔肌　參閱 obturator muscle。**(2)** 填充物　套管中的綫或桿或用於針刺組織或安裝吸液的空心針。**(3)** 腭裂充填體　一種可摘除的托牙，既可閉合腭缺陷，又可安裝具有美容意義的假牙。缺陷可能是先天性的，例如腭裂，或因摘除腫瘤所致。

閉孔　髖骨中的一個大孔，位於髖臼之下並稍靠前處。參閱 pelvis。

閉孔肌　覆蓋骨盆前壁外表面的兩塊肌肉（閉孔內肌和閉孔外肌），它負責股骨的外展和髖骨的運動。

感覺遲鈍　正常感覺的減弱或麻木。可能與疾病有關。

枕骨　構成顱骨底後部的部分碟形顱骨。枕骨的底部是兩個枕骨髁，與第一頸椎（環椎）聯成關節的圓形表面。在兩個枕骨髁之間是枕骨大孔，脊髓由此通過。

枕部　頭顱的後部。

殆面的　（口腔解剖學）指磨牙的咬合面或磨牙；與磨牙的咬合面或磨牙相關的。

occlusal rim the occlusal extension of a denture base to allow analysis of jaw relations and to record jaw relations for the construction of *dentures, bridges, and extensive crowning.

殆堤　製造托牙、齒橋及廣泛造冠術時，用於分析和記錄頜關係的牙托基上的延長部分。

occlusion *n.* **1.** the closing or obstruction of a hollow organ or part. **2.** (in dentistry) the relation of the upper and lower teeth when they are in contact. Maximum contact between the teeth is known as *intercuspal* (or *centric*) *occlusion. See also* malocclusion.

(1) 閉塞　空腔器官或其部分的關閉或阻塞。**(2)** 殆　（口腔學）上下牙接觸時的關係。牙與牙之間最大的接觸叫牙尖間　（或正中殆）。參閱 malocclusion。

occult *adj.* not apparent to the naked eye; not easily determined or detected. For example *occult blood* is blood present in such small quantities, for example in the faeces, that it can only be detected microscopically or by chemical testing.

潛隱性　肉眼觀察不明顯的；不易確定或覺察的。例如隱血是出血（如在糞便中）很少，只有顯微鏡觀察或化學檢查才可測出。

occupational disease any one of various specific diseases to which workers in certain occupations are particularly prone. *Industrial diseases*, associated with a particular industry or group of industries, fall within this category. Examples of such diseases include the various forms of *pneumoconiosis, which affect the lungs of workers continually exposed to dusty atmospheres; cataracts in glassblowers; decompression sickness in divers; poisoning from toxic metals in factory and other workers; and infectious diseases contracted from animals by farm workers, such as woolsorter's disease (*see* anthrax). *See also* COSHH, prescribed disease, sickness benefit.

職業病　從事某些職業的工人特別容易感染的各種特殊疾病。與某一特殊工業或工業集團相關的工業性疾病就屬於這一類。例如長期置身於布滿灰塵的空氣中而致的肺塵埃沉着病，吹玻璃工人患的白內障；潛水員患的減壓症；工廠中有毒金屬引起的中毒及其他工人的中毒；農場工人接觸動物所致的傳染性疾病，例如羊毛分揀工疾病（參閱 anthrax）。參閱 COSHH，prescribed disease，sickness benefit。

occupational health service (OHS) a voluntary scheme by which employers provide a mainly preventive health service for employees during working hours. Specially trained doctors and

職業衛生服務　一種自願的計劃，僱主通過此計劃向在上班的工人主要提供預防性衛生服務。訓練有素的醫生及護士就有害的工作環境，包括飯廳、

nurses advise management on hazardous situations at work, including canteens, washrooms, etc. Advice is also given to management in relation to employees with prolonged or repeated sickness absence and on the potential for rehabilitation programmes for those with *handicap. Instruction is given to the work force on simple first aid procedures and *health promotion programmes in relation to nutrition, exercise, and stress; there is also surveillance of stretchers and other equipment for coping with emergencies. Smaller employing units may band together and obtain such services from a common source or hire them on a sessional basis as required. With the approval of the *Health and Safety Executive, the OHS may conduct routine statutory tests on employees working with potentially hazardous substances, such as lead. *See also* COSHH.

洗手間等向經理提出建議。就僱員延長或反覆請病假及對有缺陷者的療養計劃向經理提供咨詢。指導工人簡單的急救操作和與營養、鍛煉、壓力等相關的健康促進計劃。也有供處理急救的擔架和其他設備管理。較小的傭工單位可以聯合起來從一個共同的來源獲得這些服務，或按需要短期僱傭他們。經健康與安全局的批准，職業衛生服務可以給接觸有害物質（例如鉛）的工人做常規法定檢查。參閱 COSHH。

occupational mortality rates and causes of death in relation to different jobs, occupational and socioeconomic groups, or *social class. Because some occupations have older incumbents than others (e.g. judges) allowance for age bias is made by comparing either *standardized mortality ratios* for those aged 15–64 years or related but less familiar indices, such as *comparative mortality figure* or *proportional mortality ratio*.

職業死亡率　與不同工作、職業和社會經濟團體或社會階層相關的死亡率及死亡原因，因為有些職業比起其他職業（例如法官）有更多年齡較大的從業者，年齡偏差津貼根據比較 15~64 歲間的標準死亡率而制定，或根據相關但不太常用的指標而制定，例如根據比較死亡率或死亡率比制定。

occupational therapy the treatment of physical and psychiatric conditions by encouraging patients to undertake specific selected activities that will help them to reach their maximum level of function and independence in all aspects of daily life. These activities are designed to make the best use of the patient's capabilities and are based on individual requirements. They range from

職業療法　通過鼓勵病人從事專門的、有選擇的、能夠幫助他們在日常生活的各方面達到最佳功能和水平來治療軀體及精神性疾病。這些活動旨在充分利用病人的能力，且以個人需要為基礎，可包括木工、金屬工、製陶和其他藝術性活動、家政管理、社交技巧（針對精神病人）及休閒活動（針

woodwork, metalwork, and printing to pottery and other artistic activities, household management, social skills (for psychiatric patients), and leisure activities (for geriatric patients). Occupational therapy also includes assessment for mechanical aids and adaptations in the home.

對老年病人）。職業療法也包括對機械性輔助設備及對療養所適應過程的評估。

ochronosis *n.* the presence of brown-black pigment in the skin, cartilage, and other tissues due to the abnormal accumulation of homogentisic acid that occurs in the metabolic disease *alcaptonuria.

褐黃症 代謝性疾病尿黑酸尿症中產生的尿黑酸異常所導致的皮膚、軟骨及其他組織中出現褐黑色色素斑。

oct- (octa-, octi-, octo-) *prefix denoting* eight.

〔前綴〕八

ocular *adj.* of or concerned with the eye or vision.

眼的 眼的、視覺的、或與眼、視覺相關的。

oculist *n.* an old term for an *ophthalmologist

眼科醫師 ophthalmologist（眼科醫師）一詞的舊稱。

oculo- *prefix denoting* the eye(s).

〔前綴〕眼

oculogyric *adj.* causing or concerned with movements of the eye.

眼動的 引起眼球運動的或與之相關的。

oculomotor *adj.* concerned with eye movements.

眼球運動的 與眼球運動相關的。

oculomotor nerve the third *cranial nerve (III), which is composed of motor fibres distributed to muscles in and around the eye. Fibres of the parasympathetic system are responsible for altering the size of the pupil and the lens of the eye. Fibres outside the eye run to the upper eyelid and to muscles that turn the eyeball in different directions.

動眼神經 第三對腦神經，由分布在眼睛內部和周圍肌肉的運動性神經纖維組成。副交感神經系統的纖維調節瞳孔的大小及眼睛的晶狀體。眼外的纖維支配上眼瞼及使眼球向不同方向轉動的肌肉。

oculonasal *adj.* concerned with the eye and nose.

眼鼻的 與眼睛和鼻子相關的。

odont- (odonto-) *prefix denoting* a tooth. Example: *odontalgia* (toothache).

〔前綴〕牙 如：牙痛。

odontoblast *n.* a cell that forms dentine. Odontoblasts line the pulp and have small processes that extend into the dentine.

成牙質細胞　形成牙本質的細胞。成牙質細胞覆蓋牙髓並有通向牙本質的小突起。

odontogenic tumour any one of a group of rare tumours composed of dental tissue; the most important example is the *ameloblastoma.

牙原性腫瘤　由牙質組織構成的一類罕見腫瘤；最重要的例子是成釉細胞瘤。

odontoid process a toothlike process from the upper surface of the axis vertebra. *See* cervical vertebrae.

齒突　樞椎表面上的牙齒樣突起。參閱 cervical vertebrae。

odontology *n.* the study of the teeth.

牙科學　研究牙齒的科學。

odontome *n.* an abnormal mass of calcified dental tissue, which usually represents a developmental abnormality. *Compare* hamartoma.

牙瘤　鈣化的牙組織的一種異常團塊，通常代表發育異常。與 hamartoma 對比。

-odynia *suffix denoting* pain in (a specified part).

〔後綴〕痛　（一個特定區域的）疼痛。

odynophagia *n.* a sensation of pain behind the sternum as food or fluid is swallowed; particularly, the burning sensation experienced by patients with *oesophagitis when hot, spicy or alcoholic liquid is swallowed.

吞咽痛　吞咽食物或液體時胸骨後的疼痛感；特別是食管炎患者吞咽熱、辣、酒精飲料時所感到的灼燒感。

oedema *n.* excessive accumulation of fluid in the body tissues: popularly known as *dropsy*. The resultant swelling may be local, as with an injury or inflammation, or more general, as in heart or kidney failure. In generalized oedema there may be collections of fluid within the chest cavity (*pleural effusions*), obdomen (*see* ascites), or within the air spaces of the lung (*pulmonary oedema*). It may result from heart or kidney failure, cirrhosis of the liver, acute nephritis, the nephrotic syndrome, starvation, allergy, or drugs (e.g. phenylbutazone

水腫　人體組織中液體的過多聚積：俗稱浮腫。產生的結果即腫脹可以是局部的，例如外傷或感染，亦可為廣泛的，如心衰或腎衰。全身性水腫時，胸腔（胸腔積液）、腹腔（參閱 ascites）或肺（胸腔積液）氣泡中會有積液（肺水腫）。產生的原因包括心衰竭、腎衰竭、肝硬化、急性腎炎、腎病綜合徵、飢餓、過敏或藥物（如保泰松或可的松類等）。在這些病例中，服用利尿藥可刺激腎臟排出過多的液體。由於

or cortisone derivatives). In such cases the kidneys can usually be stimulated to get rid of the excess fluid by the administration of *diuretic drugs. *Subcutaneous oedema* commonly occurs in the legs and ankles due to the influence of gravity and (in women) before menstruation; the swelling subsides with rest and elevation of the legs. **–oedematous** *adj.*

重力的影響和在（婦女）月經前，腿和踝常會產生皮下水腫。休息及抬高下肢時，腫脹消失。

Oedipus complex repressed sexual feelings of a child for its opposite-sexed parent, combined with rivalry towards the same-sexed parent: said, in Freudian psychoanalytic theory, to be a normal stage of development. The end of the Oedipus complex in children is marked by a loss of sexual feelings towards the opposite-sexed parent and an increase in identification with the same-sexed parent. Arrest of development at the Oedipal stage is said to be responsible for sexual deviations and other neurotic behaviour.

戀母情結（伊迪普斯情結） 孩子對異性父母持有的被抑制的性感情，這種感情和對同性父母的敵意結合在一起。弗洛伊德心理分析理論稱其為成長中的正常階段。伊迪普斯情結結束的特點是對異性父母的性感情消失及與同性父母的認同增加。在伊迪普斯發育階段停止發育據信可導致性慾倒錯及其他神經質的行為。

oesophag- (oesophago-) *prefix* *denoting* the oesophagus. Example: *oesophagectomy* (surgical removal of).

〔前綴〕**食管** 如：食管切除術。

oesophageal ulcer *see* peptic ulcer, oesophagitis.

食管潰瘍 參閱 peptic ulcer，oesophagitis。

oesophageal varices dilated veins in the lower oesophagus due to *portal hypertension. These may rupture and bleed, resulting in *haematemesis; serious bleeding may endanger life. Bleeding may be arrested by a compression balloon, by *sclerotherapy, by applying elastic bands via an endoscope, or by injections of *vasopressin or *somatostatin.

食管靜脈曲張 門靜脈高血壓引起的食管下靜脈擴張。這些擴張的靜脈可破裂並出血，產生嘔血；嚴重的出血會危及生命。用加壓氣球、硬化療法、經內窺鏡應用橡皮帶或注射加壓素或生長激素抑制素等可阻止出血。

oesophagitis *n.* inflammation of the oesophagus (gullet). Frequent

食管炎 食管的炎症。由於胃返酸及消化液返流引起的返流

regurgitation of acid and peptic juices from the stomach causes *reflux oesophagitis*, the commonest form, which may be associated with a hiatus *hernia. The main symptoms are heartburn, regurgitation of bitter fluid, and sometimes difficulty in swallowing; complications include bleeding, narrowing (*stricture) of the oesophageal canal, ulceration, and *Barrett's oesophagus. It is treated by antacid medicines, drugs to reduce acid secretion, weight reduction, and avoidance of bending; in severe cases surgery may be required. *Corrosive oesophagitis* is caused by the ingestion of caustic acid or alkali. It is often severe and may lead to perforation of the oesophagus or to extensive stricture formation. Treatment includes avoidance of food and administration of antibiotics; later dilatation of the stricture may also be needed. *Infective oesophagitis* is most commonly due to a fungus (*Candida*) infection in debilitated patients, especially those being treated with antibiotics, corticosteroids, and immunosuppressive drugs, but is occasionally due to viruses (such as cytomegalovirus or herpes virus).

oesophagocele *n.* protrusion of the lining (mucosa) of the oesophagus (gullet) through a tear in its muscular wall.

oesophagogastroduodenoscopy (OGD) *n.* endoscopic examination of the upper alimentary tract using a fibreoptic or video instrument. *See also* gastroscope.

oesophagoscope *n.* an illuminated optical instrument used to inspect the interior of the oesophagus (gullet), dilate its canal (in cases of stricture), obtain material for biopsy, or remove a foreign

性食管炎是最常見的形式，它可能和食管裂孔疝相關。主要症狀有胃灼熱、苦液的返流，有時出現吞咽困難；併發症包括食管出血、食管狹窄、潰瘍和巴雷特食管。治療可用抗酸藥、抑制酸分泌藥、降低體重、避免彎腰；嚴重病例需手術治療。腐蝕性食管炎由攝食腐蝕酸或鹼引起，經常很嚴重，可導致食管穿孔或廣泛的狹窄形成。治療包括避免進食，服用抗生素，以後還需擴張狹窄部位。感染性食管炎最常見的原因是虛弱患者的真菌（念珠菌屬）感染，特別是使用抗生素、皮質類固醇和免疫抑制藥物治療者的真菌感染，偶爾由病毒（例如巨細胞病毒或疱疹病毒）引起。

食管膨出　經食管肌壁裂口的食管黏膜的突起。

食管胃十二指腸檢查　使用纖維光學或影像儀器對上消化道進行內窺鏡檢查。參閱gastroscope。

食管鏡　一種有照明裝置的光學儀器，用於檢查食管內腔、擴張食管（在狹窄病例中）、獲取用於活檢的材料或去除異物。它可以是硬金屬管或能彎

body. It may be a rigid metal tube or a flexible fibreoptic or video-camera instrument (*see* gastroscope). **–oesophagoscopy** *n.*

曲的纖維光學或影像照像儀器（參閱 gastroscope）。

Oesophagostomum *n.* a genus of parasitic nematodes occurring in Brazil, Africa, and Indonesia. It is a rare intestinal parasite of man, producing symptoms of dysentery in cases of heavy infection. The worms may also invade the tissues of the gut wall, giving rise to abscesses. The worms can be eliminated with anthelmintics.

結節綫蟲屬 巴西、非洲及印度尼西亞出現的寄生性綫蟲屬。是一種罕見的人類腸道寄生蟲，嚴重時產生痢疾症狀。也侵襲腸壁組織，造成膿腫。可以使用治蠕蟲藥驅蟲。

oesophagostomy *n.* a surgical operation in which the oesophagus (gullet) is opened onto the neck. It is usually performed after operations on the throat as a temporary measure to allow feeding.

食管造口術 食管在頸部開口的外科手術。在咽部手術後，常採用此法作為進食的臨時措施。

oesophagotomy *n.* surgical opening of the oesophagus (gullet) in order to inspect its interior or to remove or insert something.

食管切開術 為了檢查食管內腔、去除異物或插入器械，手術切開食管。

oesophagus *n.* the gullet: a muscular tube, about 23 cm long, that extends from the pharynx to the stomach. It is lined with mucous membrane, whose secretions lubricate food as it passes from the mouth to the stomach. Waves of *peristalsis assist the passage of food.

Diseases of the oesophagus include *achalasis, carcinoma, hiatus hernia, *oesophageal varices, *oesophagitis, and *peptic ulcer. **–oesophageal** *adj.*

食管 一個肌性管道，長約 23 cm，從咽喉通向胃。內襯黏膜，其分泌物在食物從口腔向胃運動過程中能潤滑食物。食管蠕動波幫助食物通過。

食管疾病包括食管弛緩不能、腫瘤、食管裂孔疝、食管靜脈曲張、食管炎及消化性潰瘍。

oestradiol *n.* the major female sex hormone produced by the ovary. *See* oestrogen.

雌二醇 卵巢產生的主要雌性激素。參閱 oestrogen。

oestriol *n.* one of the female sex hormones produced by the ovary. *See* oestrogen.

雌三醇 卵巢產生的一種雌性激素。參閱 oestrogen。

oestrogen *n.* one of a group of steroid hormones (including oestriol, oestrone, and oestradiol) that control female sexual development, promoting the growth and function of the female sex organs (*see* menstrual cycle) and female secondary sexual characteristics (such as breast development). Oestrogens are synthesized mainly by the ovary; small amounts are also produced by the adrenal cortex, testes, and placenta. In men excessive production of oestrogen gives rise to *feminization.

Naturally occurring and synthetic oestrogens, given by mouth or injection, are used to treat *amenorrhoea and menopausal symptoms (*see* hormone replacement therapy), as well as androgen-dependent cancers (e.g. cancer of the prostate), and also to inhibit lactation. Synthetic oestrogens are a major constituent of *oral contraceptives. Side-effects of oestrogen therapy may include nausea and vomiting, headache and dizziness, irregular vaginal bleeding, fluid and salt retention, and feminization in men. Oestrogens should not be used in patients with a history of cancer of the breast, uterus, or genital tract. **–oestrogenic** *adj.*

oestrone *n.* one of the female sex hormones produced by the ovary. *See* oestrogen.

Oestrus *n.* genus of widely distributed nonbloodsucking flies, occurring wherever sheep and goats are raised. The parasitic larvae of *O. ovis*, the sheep nostril fly, may occasionally and accidentally infect man. By means of large mouth hooks, it attaches itself to the conjunctiva of the eye, causing a painful *myiasis that may result in loss of sight. This is an occupational disease of shepherds. Larvae

雌激素 類固醇類激素的一種（包括雌三醇、雌酮和雌二醇），控制女性性發育、促進女性性器官的生長和功能（參閱 menstrual cycle）及女性第二性徵（例如乳房發育）。雌激素主要由卵巢合成。腎上腺皮質、睪丸及胎盤也製造少量的雌激素。男性過量產生雌激素會導致女性化。

口服或注射天然及人工合成的雌激素用於治療閉經、女性更年期症狀（參閱 hormone replacement therapy）、雄激素依賴性癌（如前列腺癌）及抑制泌乳。人工合成雌激素是口服避孕藥的主要成分。副作用包括惡心、嘔吐、頭痛、陰道不規則出血、水鹽瀦留和男性女性化。有乳腺癌、子宮癌或生殖道癌等病史者不能使用雌激素。

雌酮 卵巢產生的一種雌性激素。參閱 oestrogen。

狂蠅屬 分布廣泛的不吸血蠅屬，產於飼養綿羊和山羊的地方。羊狂蠅寄生性幼蟲，即綿羊鼻腔飛蠅，會偶然且無意中感染人類。牠借助其巨大的口鈎依附在人眼的結膜，引起疼痛性蠅蛆病，可導致失明。這是牧羊人的職業病。麻醉後用鑷子可取走幼蟲。

can be removed with forceps following anaesthesia.

Office of Population Censuses and Surveys (in Britain) a department of central government responsible for the compilation and publication of statistics relating to national and local populations and the demographic patterns of births, marriages, and deaths (including the medical cause of death). It organizes a *national census* at ten-yearly intervals based on the actual presence of individuals in a house or institution on a designated night (known as a *de facto census*), contrasting with the approach in the US, where enumeration is based on official address (*de jure census*).

人口普查及調查辦公室 （英國）中央政府部門，負責匯編、出版與全國和地方人口相關的統計數字及出生率、成婚率、死亡率（包括死亡的醫學原因）等的統計模式。根據某一指定夜間家庭或機構中的實際人口數（稱作事實普查），每隔十年組織一次全國性人口普查，它與美國採用的方法不同，後者計數以官方地址為基礎（法律意義上的普查）。

ofloxacin *n.* a *quinolone antibiotic used to treat urinary-tract and sexually transmitted infections and undergoing trials for multidrug therapy of leprosy. It is administered by mouth or injection; possible side-effects include nausea, vomiting, and skin rashes. Trade name: **Tarivid**.

氧氟沙星 一種喹啉抗生素，用於治療尿路感染及性傳播性感染，並正在作麻風病多藥治療試驗。可能產生的副作用包括惡心、嘔吐及皮疹。商品名：Tarivid。

OGD *n. see* oesophagogastroduodenoscopy.

食管胃十二指腸檢查 參閱 oesophagogastroduodenoscopy。

ohm *n.* the *SI unit of electrical resistance, equal to the resistance between two points on a conductor when a constant potential difference of 1 volt applied between these points produces a current of 1 ampere. Symbol: Ω.

歐姆 電阻的國際單位。1歐姆等於在某一導體的兩端之間用1伏特電壓產生1安培電流時的電流阻力。符號：Ω。

-oid *suffix denoting* like; resembling. Example: *pemphigoid* (condition resembling pemphigus).

〔前綴〕……樣的，……狀的，如……的 例如：類天疱疹樣的（天疱疹狀的）。

ointment *n.* a greasy material, usually containing a medicament, applied to the skin or mucous membranes.

軟膏 常含有藥物，塗於皮膚或黏膜上的多脂物質。

olecranon process the large process of the *ulna that projects behind the elbow joint.

鷹嘴 肘關節後面突出的尺骨的大的突起。

oleic acid *see* fatty acid.

油酸 參閱 fatty acid。

oleo- *prefix denoting* oil.

〔前綴〕油

oleothorax *n.* the procedure of introducing paraffin wax extrapleurally so that the lung is allowed to collapse. This was sometimes formerly undertaken to allow closure of tuberculous cavities within the lung.

人工油胸療法 胸膜外使用石蠟使肺萎縮的方法。以前此療法有時用於使肺中結核性腔閉合。

oleum *n.* (in pharmacy) an oil.

油 （藥劑學）一種油。

olfaction *n.* **1.** the sense of smell. **2.** the process of smelling. Sensory cells in the mucous membrane that lines the nasal cavity are stimulated by the presence of chemical particles dissolved in the mucus. *See* nose. **—olfactory** *adj.*

(1) 嗅覺 (2) 嗅功能 嗅的過程。襯於鼻腔的黏膜中的感覺細胞受溶解在黏膜中化學微粒刺激。參閱 nose。

olfactory nerve the first *carnial nerve (I): the special sensory nerve of smell. Fibres of the nerve run upwards from smell receptors in the nasal mucosa high in the roof of the nose, through minute holes in the skull, join to form the olfactory tract, and pass back to reach the brain.

嗅神經 第一對腦神經：嗅覺的專門感覺神經。神經纖維從鼻頂部黏膜的嗅覺感受器上行穿過顱骨中的小孔，與嗅束連接，再向後行返回大腦。

olig- (oligo-) *prefix denoting* **1.** few. **2.** a deficiency.

〔前綴〕**(1) 少 (2) 缺少**

oligaemia *n. see* hypovolaemia.

血量減少 參閱 hypovolaemia。

oligoarthritis *n. see* arthritis.

單關節炎 參閱 arthritis。

oligodactylism *n.* the congenital absence of some of the fingers and toes.

少指（趾）畸形 先天性指（趾）的部分缺失。

oligodendrocyte *n.* one of the cells of the *glia, responsible for producing the

少突神經膠質細胞 一種神經膠質細胞，負責產生中樞神經

*myelin sheaths of the neurones of the central nervous system and therefore equivalent to the *Schwann cells of the peripheral nerves.

系統神經元髓鞘，因此相當於周圍神經的施萬細胞。

oligodendroglioma *n.* a tumour of the central nervous system derived from a type of *glia (the supporting tissue) rather than from the nerve cells themselves. *See also* glioma.

少突神經膠質細胞瘤　中樞神經系統的一種腫瘤，由一種神經膠質（支持組織）而不是神經細胞本身衍化而來。參閱 glioma。

oligodipsia *n.* a condition in which thirst is diminished or absent.

渴感過弱　口渴感減弱或缺失。

oligodontia *n.* the congenital absence of some of the teeth.

少牙（畸形）　部分牙齒先天性缺失。

oligohydramnios *n.* a condition in which the amount of amniotic fluid bathing a fetus during pregnancy is abnormally small (0–200 ml in the third trimester). It is usually associated with retarded fetal growth and may indicate serious fetal kidney abnormalities. *See* Potter syndrome.

羊水過少　妊娠期間浸泡胎兒的羊水異常減少的疾病（在第三個三個月期為 0~200 ml）。它常和胎兒生長遲緩相關並可預示嚴重的胎兒腎畸形。參閱 Potter syndrome。

oligomenorrhoea *n.* sparse or infrequent menstruation.

月經過少　月經稀少或很少發生。

oligo-ovulation *n.* infrequent occurrence of ovulation.

排卵過少　排卵很少發生。

oligospermia *n.* the presence of less than the normal amount of spermatozoa in the semen (*see* seminal analysis). In oligospermia there are less than 20 million spermatozoa per ml with poor motility (*asthenospermia*) and often including many bizarre and immature forms (*teratospermia*). Treatment is directed to any underlying cause (such as *varicocele). *See also* andrology, infertility.

精子減少　精液中精子數量小於正常（參閱 seminal analysis）。每毫升精液中精子少於兩千萬，活動性差（精子活力不足），且常包含許多異常和未成熟的形狀（畸形精子症）。治療針對病因（例如精索靜脈曲張）。參閱 andrology，infertility。

oliguria *n.* the production of an abnormally small volume of urine. This may be

少尿　尿量異常少。可能與強體力活動和／或天氣炎熱而產

a result of copious sweating associated with intense physical activity and/or hot weather. It can also be due to kidney disease, retention of water in the tissues (*see* oedema), loss of blood, diarrhoea, or poisoning.

生的大量出汗有關。也可由腎病、組織內水瀦留（參閱 oedema）、失血、腹瀉或中毒引起。

olive *n.* a smooth oval swelling in the upper part of the medulla oblongata on each side. It contains a mass of nerve cells, mainly grey matter (*olivary nucleus*). **—olivary** *adj.*

橄欖體 位於延髓上部各邊的光滑的、卵形隆起。含有神經團塊，主要是灰質（橄欖核）。

-ology *suffix. see* -logy.

〔後綴〕**學** 參閱 -logy。

olsalazine *n.* a salicylate preparation used to treat mild ulcerative colitis. It is administered by mouth. Possible side-effects include nausea, vomiting, headache, joint paint, and skin rashes. Trade name: **Dipentum**.

奧沙拉秦 用於治療輕度潰瘍性結腸炎的一種水楊酸鹽製劑。口服。可能產生的副作用包括惡心、嘔吐、頭痛、關節痛及皮疹。商品名：Dipentum。

om- (omo-) *prefix denoting* the shoulder.

〔前綴〕**肩**

-oma *suffic denoting* a tumour. Examples: *hepatoma* (of the liver); *lymphoma* (of the lymph nodes).

〔後綴〕**瘤** 例如：肝細胞瘤（肝臟的腫瘤），淋巴瘤（淋巴結瘤）。

omentectomy *n.* the removal of all or part of the omentum (the fold of peritoneum between the stomach and other abdominal organs).

網膜切除術 切除所有或部分網膜（胃或其他腹腔器官之間的腹膜皺襞）。

omentopexy *n.* an operation in which the *omentum is attached to some other tissue, usually the abdominal wall (in order to improve blood flow through the liver) or the heart (to increase the blood supply to the heart).

網膜固定術 使網膜附着於其他組織，通常是腹壁（以增加流經肝臟的血流）或心臟（以增加心臟的血液供應）的手術。

omentum (epiploon) *n.* a double layer of *peritoneum attached to the stomach and linking it with other abdominal organs, such as the liver, spleen, and intestine. The *great omentum* is a highly

網膜 附着於胃並把胃與其他腹腔器官，例如肝臟、脾及腸管等，連接起來的一個雙層腹膜。大網膜是一個高度摺疊的網膜的一部分，含豐富的脂肪

folded portion of the omentum, rich in fatty tissue, that covers the intestines in an apron-like fashion. It acts as a heat insulator and prevents friction between abdominal organs. The *lesser omentum* links the stomach with the liver. **–omental** *adj*.

組織，呈裙狀覆蓋於腸。作為熱絕緣層並防止腹腔器官間摩擦。小網膜連接胃和肝臟。

omeprazole *n*. a *proton-pump inhibitor used to treat gastric and duodenal ulcers and the *Zollinger-Ellison syndrome. Omeprazole can be effective in cases that have failed to respond to H$_2$-receptor antagonists, such as *ranitidine. Administered by mouth, it is long-acting and need only be taken once a day. Possible side-effects include nausea, diarrhoea, headache, constipation, and skin rashes. Trade name: **Losec**.

奧美拉唑　用於治療胃和十二指腸潰瘍及佐-埃氏綜合徵的質子泵抑制劑。對氫感受器抑制藥，如雷尼替丁沒有反應時，使用奧美拉唑可能有效。口服。藥效持久，每日只需服用一次。可能產生的副作用包括噁心、腹瀉、頭痛、便秘及皮疹。商品名：Losec。

Ommaya reservoir a device inserted into the ventricles of the brain to enable the repeated injection of drugs into the cerebrospinal fluid. It is used, for example, in the treatment of malignant meningitis, particularly in children with leukaemia.

御廠貯器　為了能反覆向腦脊髓液中注射藥而插入到腦室的一種裝置。如：用它治療惡性腦膜炎，特別用於治療白血病患兒。

omphal- (omphalo-) *prefix denoting* the navel or umbilical cord.

〔前綴〕臍，臍帶

omphalitis *n*. inflammation of the navel, especially in newborn infants.

臍炎　臍部的炎症，特別是新生兒臍部的炎症。

omphalocele *n*. an umbilical *hernia.

臍突出　一種臍疝。

omphalus *n. see* umbilicus.

臍　參閱 umbilicus。

Onchocerca *n*. a genus of parasitic worms (*see* filaria) occurring in central Africa and central America. The adult worms are found in fibrous nodules within the connective tissues beneath the skin and their presence causes disease (*see* onchocerciasis). Various species of

盤尾絲蟲屬　非洲中部及美洲中部出現的一種寄生蟲屬（參閱 filaria）。成蟲見於皮下結締組織內的纖維性結節中，其出現會引起疾病（參閱 onchocerciasis）。盤尾絲蟲在各種黑蠅體內經過其部分發

black fly, in which *Onchocerca* undergoes part of its development, transmit the infective larvae to man.

onchocerciasis *n.* a tropical disease of the skin and underlying connective tissue caused by the parasitic worm *Onchocerca volvulus*. Fibrous nodular tumours grow around the adult worms in the skin; these may take several months to appear, and if secondary bacterial infection occurs they may degenerate into abscesses. The skin also becomes inflamed and itches. The migration of the *microfilariae into the eye can cause total or partial blindness – called *river blindness* in Africa. Onchocerciasis occurs in Africa and Central and South America. The drugs *suramin, *diethylcarbamazine, and – more recently – *ivermectin are used in treatment; if possible, the nodules are removed as and when they appear.

onco- *prefix denoting* **1.** a tumour. **2.** volume.

oncofetal antigen a protein normally produced only by fetal tissue but often produced by certain tumours. An example is *carcino-embryonic antigen (CEA), which has been used as a *tumour marker.

oncogene *n.* a gene in viruses and mammalian cells that can cause cancer. It probably produces proteins (growth factors) regulating cell division that, under certain conditions, become uncontrolled and may transform a normal cell to a malignant state.

oncogenesis *n.* the development of a new abnormal growth (a benign or malignant tumour).

育，這些種類的黑蠅把傳染性幼蟲傳播給人類。

盤尾絲蟲病 由寄生蟲旋盤尾絲蟲引起的熱帶皮膚及皮下結締組織病。皮膚中的成蟲周圍生長堅韌的纖維結節瘤。這些腫瘤數月後才出現，如果繼發細菌性感染，腫瘤會變成膿腫。皮膚亦會發炎、發癢。微絲蚴移行到眼睛會引起完全或部分失明，稱作非洲河盲。盤尾絲蟲病發生於非洲、中美和南美洲。治療用蘇拉明和乙胺嗪，最近使用伊維菌素。如果可能的話，當結節出現時予以切除。

〔前綴〕**(1)** 腫瘤　**(2)** 體積

瘤胎抗原 正常情況下只有胎兒組織產生的，但常由某些腫瘤產生的一種蛋白質。例如：已被當作腫瘤標記的癌胚抗原(CEA)。

致癌基因 病毒及哺乳動物細胞中能引起腫瘤的基因。可產生調節細胞分裂的蛋白質（生長因子），在某種情況下會失控，使正常細胞轉變成癌細胞。

瘤形成 一種異常的新生物的形成（良性或惡性腫瘤）。

oncogenic *adj.* describing a substance, organism, or environment that is known to be a causal factor in the production of a tumour. Some viruses are considered to be oncogenic; these include the *papovaviruses, the *retroviruses, certain *adenoviruses and *herpesviruses, and the *Epstein-Barr virus. *See also* carcinogen.

致腫瘤的　在腫瘤產生過程中作為致病因子的一種物質、生物體或環境。有些病毒被看作是致腫瘤的，其中包括乳多泡病毒、逆轉錄病毒、某些腺病毒和疱疹病毒及 EB 病毒。參閱 carcinogen。

oncology *n.* the study and practice of treating tumours. It is often subdivided into medical, surgical, and radiation oncology. **–oncologist** *n.*

腫瘤學　研究及治療腫瘤的科學，通常再分為內科、外科及放射腫瘤學。

oncolysis *n.* the destruction of tumours and tumour cells. This may occur spontaneously or, more usually, in response to treatment with drugs or by radiotherapy.

癌細胞溶解　腫瘤及腫瘤細胞的破壞。可自發產生，更常見的是對藥療或放療的反應。

oncometer *n.* an instrument for measuring the volume of blood circulating in one of the limbs. *See* plethysmography.

器官體積測量器　測量一個肢體中血液循環量的儀器。參閱 plethysmography。

oncosphere (hexacanth) *n.* the six-hooked larva of a *tapeworm. If ingested by a suitable intermediate host, such as a pig or an ox, the larva will use its hooks to penetrate the wall of the intestine. The larva subsequently migrates to the muscles, where it develops into a *cysticercus.

六鈎蚴　絛蟲的六個口鈎幼蟲。如果被其合適的中間宿主，例如豬或牛，攝入體內，幼蟲會用其口鈎穿透宿主的腸壁，接着移動到肌肉，在此發育成囊尾蚴。

oncotic *adj.* **1.** characterized by a tumour or swelling. **2.** relating to an increase in volume or pressure.

(1) 腫瘤的　以腫瘤或腫脹為特點的。**(2) 膨出的**　與體積或壓力的增加相關的。

oncotic pressure a pressure represented by the pressure difference that exists between the osmotic pressure of blood and that of the lymph or tissue fluid. Oncotic pressure is important for regulating the flow of water between blood and tissue fluid. *See also* osmosis.

膨脹壓，膠體滲透壓　血液和淋巴或組織液滲透壓之間的差別而產生的壓力。膨脹壓在調節血壓和組織液之間的水流動時起重要作用。參閱 osmosis。

ondansetron *n.* a drug used to control severe nausea and vomiting, especially

奧丹亞龍　一種藥物，用於控制嚴重的惡心和嘔吐，特別是

when it results from chemotherapy and radiotherapy. Ondansetron works by opposing the action of the neurotransmitter *serotonin (5-hydroxytryptamine) and is undergoing trials for its ability to improve memory in patients with Alzheimer's disease and to treat anxiety. Trade name: **Zofran**.

由化療及放療而引起的惡心和嘔吐。通過對抗神經遞質 5-羥色胺發揮作用。目前正在進行增進阿爾茨海默病患者記憶能力及治療抑鬱症試驗。商品名：Zofran。

oneir- (oneiro-) *prefix denoting* dreams or dreaming.

〔前綴〕**夢，作夢**

oneirism *n.* day-dreaming. Obviously this is a normal phenomenon, but in excess it may impair the ability to cope with life. This is a feature of *schizoid and *asthenic personalities.

夢樣狀態 白日夢。明顯屬於正常現象，但頻繁出現會影響處理日常生活能力。是精神分裂樣人格和無力型人格的特徵。

onomatomania *n.* the repeated intrusion of a specific word or a name into a person's thoughts: a form of *obsession.

稱名癖，強迫性詞語症 一個特殊的單詞或名字反覆闖進人的思想之中：一種強迫觀念。

onomatopoiesis *n.* inventing words that reflect the sound made by the object or event to be described. It is one of the principles guiding some schizophrenics in the production of *neologisms.

詞語創新 創造詞語以表現要描述的物體或事物發出的聲音。是指導精神分裂症患者產生新語症時的一個原則。

ontogeny *n.* the history of the development of an individual from the fertilized egg to maturity.

個體發生 個體從受精卵到成熟的發育史。

onych- (onycho-) *prefix denoting* the nail(s).

〔前綴〕**甲**

onychogryphosis *n.* thickening and lateral curvature of a nail, usually the big toenail.

甲彎曲 甲，常指大趾甲的變厚及外側彎曲。

onycholysis *n.* separation or loosening of part or all of a nail from its bed. The condition may occur in *psoriasis and in fungal infection of the skin and nail bed. It is commoner in women and may return to normal spontaneously.

甲脫離 指（趾）甲從甲床部分或完全分開。此病可由銀屑病及皮膚和甲床的真菌感染引起。常發生於婦女，可自行恢復正常。

onychomycosis *n.* fungus infection of the nails caused by *dermatophytes or *Candida*. The nails become yellow, opaque, and thickened. *See also* ringworm.

甲癬 由表皮癬菌屬或念珠菌屬引起的指（趾）甲真菌感染。指（趾）甲變黃、無光澤、變硬。參閱 ringworm．

O'nyong nyong fever (joint-breaker fever) a disease of East Africa and Malaysia, caused by an *arbovirus and transmitted to man by mosquitoes of the genus *Anopheles*. The disease is similar to *dengue and symptoms include rigor, severe headache, an irritating rash, fever, and pains in the joints. The patient is given drugs to relieve the pain and fever.

奧絨絨熱（關節裂痛熱） 東非和馬來西亞發現的一種病。由蟲媒病毒引起，由按蚊屬中的蚊蟲傳播給人類。此病與登革熱相似。病狀包括寒顫、劇烈頭痛、搔癢性皮疹、發熱和關節痛。患者用藥可緩解疼痛及發熱。

oo- *prefix denoting* an egg; ovum.

〔前級〕卵，卵巢

oocyst *n.* a spherical structure, 50–60 μm in diameter, that develops from the zygote (*see* ookinete) of the malarial parasite (*Plasmodium*) on the outer wall of the mosquito's stomach. The oocyst steadily grows in size and its contents divide repeatedly to form *sporozoites, which are released into the body cavity of the mosquito when the oocyst bursts.

卵囊 一種球形結構，直徑為50~60μm。由蚊胃外壁上瘧疾寄生蟲（瘧原蟲）的受精卵（參閱 ookinete）發育而來。卵囊不斷增大，其內容反覆分裂形成子孢子，卵囊破裂時，孢子被釋放進蚊的體腔。

oocyte *n.* a cell in the ovary that undergoes *meiosis to form an ovum. *Primary oocytes* develop from *oogonia in the fetal ovary as they enter the early stages of meiosis. Only a fraction of the primary oocytes survive until puberty, and even fewer will be ovulated. At ovulation the first meiotic division is completed and a *secondary oocyte* and a *polar body* are formed. Fertilization stimulates the completion of the second meiotic division, which produces a second polar body and an ovum.

卵母細胞 經過減數分裂形成卵子的卵巢細胞。卵原細胞進入減數分裂的早期階段時，在胚胎期卵巢中形成初級卵母細胞。只有一部分初級卵母細胞能生存到青春期，能被排卵者為數更少。排卵時第一次減數分裂結束，次級卵母細胞和極體形成。受精刺激次級減數分裂的完成，產生次級體和卵子。

oocyte donation the transfer of oocytes from one woman to another. Possible

卵母細胞捐獻 卵母細胞從一位婦女移植到另一位婦女。可

recipients include women with primary or secondary ovarian failure or severe genetic disorders, and women in whom ovulation has been suppressed as an incidental result of drug treatment for another condition (e.g. cancer). Pregnancy rates are higher than with *in vitro fertilization.

能接受的人包括原發或繼發性卵巢衰竭婦女、有嚴重遺傳病的婦女、由於治療其他疾病（例如癌）的藥物副作用、排卵被抑制的婦女。受孕率比試管受精高。

oogenesis *n.* the process by which mature ova (egg cells) are produced in the ovary (see illustration). Primordial germ cells multiply to form *oogonia, which start their first meiotic division to become *oocytes in the fetus. This division is not completed until each oocyte is ovulated. The second division is only completed on fertilization. Each meiotic division is unequal, so that one large ovum is produced with a much smaller polar body.

卵發生 卵巢中產生成熟卵細胞的過程（見圖）。原始胚細胞繁殖形成卵原細胞，卵原細胞在胚胎期開始它們的第一次減數分裂，形成卵母細胞。這種分裂直到每個卵母細胞排卵時才完成。第二次減數分裂僅在受精時才完成。每次減數分裂不相等，以致產生一個大的卵和很小的極體。

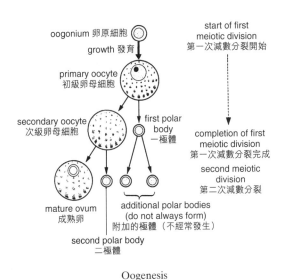

Oogenesis
卵發生

oogonium *n.* (*pl.* **oogonia**) a cell produced at an early stage in the formation

卵原細胞 卵細胞形成的早期階段產生的一種細胞。移行到

of an ovum (egg cell). Primordial germ cells that have migrated to the embryonic ovary multiply to form numerous small oogonia. After the fifth month of pregnancy they enter the early stages of the first meiotic division to form the *oocytes. *See also* oogenesis.

胚胎卵巢的原始胚細胞繁殖形成許多小卵原細胞。妊娠五個月後，進入第一次減數分裂的初級階段，形成卵母細胞。參閱 oogenesis。

ookinete *n.* the motile elongated *zygote of the malarial parasite (*Plamodium*), formed after fertilization of the *macrogamete. The ookinete bores through the lining of the mosquito's stomach and attaches itself to the outer wall, where it later forms an *oocyst.

動合子 巨配子受精後形成的、能活動的細長形瘧原蟲（瘧原蟲屬）合子。動合子穿透蚊的胃黏膜並依附在外壁上，隨後在此形成卵囊。

oophor- (oophoro-) *prefix denoting* the ovary.

〔前綴〕卵巢

oophorectomy (ovariectomy) *n.* surgical removal of an ovary, performed, for example, when the ovary contains tumours or cysts or is otherwise diseased. *See also* ovariotomy.

卵巢切除術 手術切除卵巢，例如卵巢發生腫瘤、囊腫或其他疾病時，做此手術。參閱 ovariotomy。

oophoritis (ovaritis) *n.* inflammation of an ovary, either on the surface of within the organ. Oophoritis may be associated with infection of the Fallopian tubes (*see* salpingitis) or the lower part of the abdominal cavity. *Follicular oophoritis* is inflammation of the ovarian (Graafian) follicles. A bacterial infection usually responds to antibiotics.

卵巢炎 卵巢表面或內部的炎症。卵巢炎可能與輸卵管感染（參閱 salpingitis）或下腹腔炎有關。卵泡卵巢炎是卵泡（囊狀卵泡）的炎症。細菌性炎症通常用抗生素治療，效果顯著。

oophoropexy *n.* the stitching of a displaced ovary to the wall of the pelvic cavity.

卵巢固定術 將移位的卵巢縫合在盆腔壁上的手術。

operant *adj.* describing a unit of behaviour that is defined by its effect on the environment. *See* conditioning.

操作的 根據其對環境產生的影響而定義的一種行為。參閱 conditioning。

operating microscope a binocular microscope commonly in use for micro-

手術顯微鏡 常用於顯微外科的雙筒顯微鏡。顯微鏡內的光

surgery. The field of operation is illuminated through the objective lens by a light source within the microscope (see illustration). Many models incorporate a beam splitter and a second set of eyepieces, to enable the surgeon's assistant to view the operation.

源通過物鏡給手術區域照明（見圖）。許多型號的手術顯微鏡裝配分光鏡和一套附加的目鏡，使外科醫生的助手能夠觀看手術。

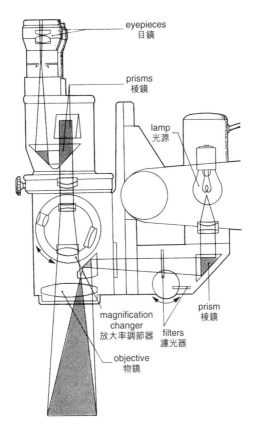

eyepieces
目鏡

prisms
棱鏡

lamp
光源

prism
棱鏡

magnification
changer
放大率調節器

filters
濾光器

objective
物鏡

An operating microscope
手術顯微鏡

operculum *n.* (*pl.* **opercula**) **1.** a plug of mucus that blocks the cervical canal of the uterus in a pregnant woman. When the cervix begins to dilate at the start of

(1) 栓 阻塞妊娠期婦女子宮頸管的黏液栓。分娩開始時子宮頸開始擴張，稍帶有血液的栓作為流出物排出。**(2) 滋養**

labour, the operculum, slightly stained with blood, comes away as a discharge ('show'). **2.** (in embryology) a plug of fibrin and blood cells that develops over the side at which a developing fertilized ovum has become embedded in the wall of the uterus. **3.** (in neurology) one of the folded and overlapping regions of cerebral cortex that conceal the *insula on each side of the brain. **4.** (in dentistry) a flap of gingival tissue that overlies the crown of a partially erupted tooth.

層蓋 （胚胎學）發育中受精卵在子宮腔着床處之上出現的纖維素和血細胞的栓子。**(3) 島蓋** （神經學）大腦兩側掩蓋腦島的大腦皮質摺疊區。**(4) 齦蓋**（口腔學）位於部分冒出的牙冠上的牙齦組織片。

operon *n.* a group of closely linked genes that regulate the production of enzymes. An operon is composed of one or more *structural genes*, which determine the nature of the enzymes made, and an *operator gene*, which controls the working of the structural genes and is itself controlled by a *regulator gene*, which is not part of the operon.

操縱子 調節酶生產的一組緊密相連的基因。一個操縱子由一個或更多的結構基因組成，結構基因決定生產出來酶的性質。操縱基因控制結構基因的功能，本身又受調節基因的控制，調節基因不是操縱子的一部分。

ophthalm- (ophthalmo-) *prefix denoting* the eye or eyeball. Examples: *ophthalmectomy* (surgical removal of); *ophthalmorrhexis* (rupture of); *ophthalmotomy* (incision into).

〔前綴〕眼，眼球 例如：眼球切除術（外科切除），眼滲血（刺破），眼球切開術（切入）。

ophthalmia *n. Obsolete.* inflammation of the eye, particularly the conjunctiva (*see* conjunctivitis).

眼炎 （廢用詞）眼，特別是結膜的炎症（參閱 conjunctivitis）。

ophthalmia neonatorum a form of conjunctivitis occurring in newborn infants, who contract the disease as they pass through an infected birth canal. The most serious condition, gonococcal conjunctivitis, occurs if the mother has a gonorrhoeal infection: blindness will result unless antibiotic treatment or silver nitrate eye drops are given promptly.

新生兒眼炎 一種發生於新生兒的結膜炎，新生兒通過被感染的產道時感染此病。如果新生兒的母親有淋病感染，會出現最嚴重的疾病即淋病性結膜炎。除非迅速用抗生素治療或用硝酸銀滴眼藥，否則會導致新生兒失明。

ophthalmic *adj.* concerned with the eye.

眼的，眼科的 和眼相關的。

ophthalmic nerve the smallest of the three branches of the *trigeminal nerve. It supplies sensory fibres to the eyeball, conjunctiva, and lacrimal gland, to a small region of the nasal mucous membrane, and to the skin of the nose, brows, and scalp.

眼神經　三叉神經三個分支中最小的分支。它給眼球、結膜、淚腺、鼻黏膜的小區域及鼻、額和頭等的皮膚提供感覺神經。

ophthalmitis n. inflammation of the eye. *See* conjunctivitis, uveitis.

眼炎　眼的炎症。參閱 conjunctivitis、uveitis。

ophthalmodynamometry n. measurement of the blood pressure in the vessels of the retina of the eye. A small instrument is pressed against the eye until the vessels are seen (through an *ophthalmoscope) to collapse. The pressure recorded by the instrument reflects the pressure within the vessels of the retina. In certain disorders of the blood circulation to the eye, the pressure in the vessels is reduced and the vessels can be made to collapse by a lower than normal pressure on the eyeball.

視網膜血壓檢查法　眼視網膜的血管中血壓的測量方法。用一個小儀器擠壓眼球直到（用眼底鏡）看到血管萎縮。儀器記錄的壓力即視網膜血管內的血壓。在某些眼部血液循環疾病中，血管的壓力降低，血管會因為對眼球的壓力小於正常而萎縮。

ophthalmologist n. a doctor who specializes in the diagnosis and treatment of eye diseases.

眼科醫師　專門診斷和治療眼科疾病的醫生。

ophthalmology n. the branch of medicine that is devoted to the study and treatment of eye diseases. **—opthalmological** *adj.*

眼科學　醫學的一個分支，專門研究和治療眼科疾病。

ophthalmometer n. *see* keratometer.

檢眼計，眼屈光計　參閱 keratometer。

ophthalmoplegia n. paralysis of the muscles of the eye. *Internal ophthalmoplegia* affects the muscles inside the eye: the iris (which controls the size of the pupil) and also the ciliary muscle (which is responsible for *accommodation). *External ophthalmoplegia* affects the muscles moving the eye. Ophthalmoplegia

眼肌麻痺　眼部肌肉的癱瘓。眼內肌麻痺影響眼內部的肌肉：虹膜肌（控制瞳孔的大小）及睫狀肌（負責調節）。眼外肌麻痺影響運動眼球的肌肉。眼肌麻痺會伴有甲狀腺毒症所致的眼球突出。

may accompany *exophthalmos due to thyrotoxicosis.

ophthalmoscope *n.* an instrument for examining the interior of the eye (see illustration). There are two types. The *direct ophthalmoscope* enables a fine beam of light to be directed into the eye and at the same time allows the examiner to see the spot where the beam falls inside the eye. Examiner and subject are very close together. In the *indirect ophthalmoscope* an image of the inside of the eye is formed between the subject and the examiner; it is this image that the examiner sees. The examiner and subject are almost an arm's length apart. There have been recent attempts to develop a *scanning laser ophthalmoscope*, which uses a scanning camera, rather than a human observer, to view the inside of the eye. **–ophthalmoscopy** *n.*

檢眼鏡，眼底鏡 檢查眼內部的儀器（見圖）。眼底鏡有兩類。直接檢眼鏡能把細小的光束照射到眼內，同時讓檢查者觀察光束在眼中的落點。檢查者和受檢者距離很近。在間接檢眼鏡中，眼內圖像在檢查者和受檢者之間形成；檢查者觀察的正是這個圖像。檢查者和受檢者幾乎只有一臂之遙。最近有人嘗試製造一種激光掃描檢眼鏡，它使用掃描照像機而不是人觀察眼內部。

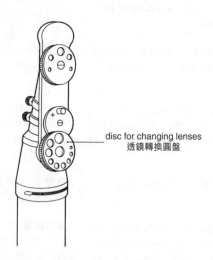

disc for changing lenses
透鏡轉換圓盤

An ophthalmoscope
檢眼鏡

ophthalmotomy *n.* the operation of making an incision in the eyeball.

眼球切開術 在眼球上造口的手術。

ophthalmotonometer (tonometer) *n*. a small instrument for measuring the pressure inside the eye. There are several types. The *applanation tonometer* measures the force required to flatten a known area of the cornea after a drop of local anaesthetic has made the cornea numb. A greater force is required when the pressure inside the eye is increased, and vice versa.

眼壓計　用於測量眼內壓力的小型儀器。眼壓計分許多種類。平壓式眼壓計測量局部麻醉使角膜麻木後壓平角膜的一個部分所需要的力量。眼內壓增加時，需要的力量要大，反之亦然。

-opia *suffix denoting* a defect of the eye or of vision. Example: *asthenopia* (eyestrain).

〔後綴〕視力不足　眼或視力的缺陷。如視力疲勞（眼疲勞）。

opiate *n*. one of a group of drugs derived from opium, which include *apomorphine, *codeine, *morphine, and *papaverine. Opiates depress the central nervous system: they relieve pain, suppress coughing, and stimulate vomiting. The most important opiate morphine and its synthetic derivative diamorphine (*see* heroin) are *narcotics, producing feelings of euphoria before inducing stupor. They are only used for severe pain since they cause *dependence.

阿片製劑　從阿片中提取的一組藥物，包括阿樸嗎啡、可待因、嗎啡及罌粟鹼。阿片製劑抑制中樞神經系統：鎮痛、止咳和刺激嘔吐。最重要的阿片製劑——嗎啡——及其合成衍生物二醋嗎啡（參閱 heroin）是麻醉藥，引起昏睡之前產生欣快感。能引起藥物依賴，僅在劇痛時使用。

opisth- (opistho-) *prefix denoting* **1.** dorsal; posterior. **2.** backwards.

〔前綴〕(1) 背的，後面的 (2) 向後的

opisthorchiasis *n*. a condition caused by the presence of the parasitic fluke *Opisthorchis* in the bile ducts. The infection is acquired through eating raw or undercooked fish that contains the larval stage of the parasite. Heavy infections can lead to considerable damage of the tissues of the bile duct and liver, progressing in advanced cases to *cirrhosis. Symptoms may include loss of weight, abdominal pain, indigestion, and sometimes diarrhoea. The disease, occurring in E Europe and the Far East, is treated with *chloroquine.

後睾吸蟲病　膽管中出現寄生性後睾吸蟲屬吸蟲引起的疾病。通過吃含此類寄生蟲幼蟲的生魚或半生魚引起感染。重度感染會導致膽管和肝組織的嚴重損害，以後發展為肝硬化。症狀可包括體重下降、腹痛、消化不良，有時產生腹瀉，此病在東歐和遠東發生，用氯奎治療。

Opisthorchis *n.* a genus of parasitic flukes occurring in E Europe and parts of SE Asia. *O. felineus* is normally a parasite of fish-eating mammals but accidental infections of man have occurred. The adult flukes, which live in the bile ducts, can cause *opisthorchiasis.

後睪吸蟲屬　產生於東歐和東南亞部分地區的寄生吸蟲屬。貓後睪吸蟲屬在正常情況下是食魚性哺乳動物的寄生蟲，但是偶爾傳染給人。成蟲生活在膽管中，能引起後睪吸蟲病。

opisthotonos *n.* the positon of the body in which the head, neck, and spine are arched backwards. It is assumed involuntarily by patients with tetanus and strychnine poisoning.

角弓反張　頭、頸和脊柱向後彎成弓形。它為破傷風和士的寧中毒患者的強迫體位。

opium *n.* an extract from the poppy *Papaver somniferum*, which has analgesic and narcotic action due to its content of *morphine. It has the same uses and side-effects as morphine and prolonged use may lead to *dependence. *See also* opiate.

阿片　罌粟屬植物罌粟中的提取物。由於它含有嗎啡，所以具有鎮痛和麻醉作用。和嗎啡的用途和副作用相同。長期使用會產生藥物依賴。參閱 opiate。

opponens *n.* one of a group of muscles in the hand that bring the digits opposite to other digits. For example, the *opponens pollicis* is the principal muscle causing opposition of the thumb.

對掌肌　手掌中的一組肌肉，它們使手指與其他手指對向運動。例如：拇指對掌肌是使拇指與其他手指對向的主要肌肉。

opportunistic *adj.* denoting a disease that occurs when the patient's immune system is impaired by, for example, an infection, another disease, or drugs. The infecting organism rarely causes the disease in healthy persons. Opportunistic infections, such as *Pneumocystis carinii* pneumonia, are common in patients with AIDS.

條件致病的　病人免疫系統受另一疾病，例如感染、或藥物損害時而生病。感染的生物體很少引起健康人生病。條件致病性感染，例如卡氏肺囊蟲肺炎常見於艾滋病患者。

opposition *n.* (in anatomy) the position of the thumb in relation to the other fingers when it is moved towards the palm of the hand.

對向　（解剖學）拇指向掌心運動時其位置與其他手指的關係。

-opsia *suffix denoting* a condition of vision. Example: *erythropsia* (red vision).

〔前綴〕視　例如：紅視。

opsonic index a numerical measurement of the power of a person's serum to attack invading bacteria and prepare them for destruction by *phagocytes. It is measured by dividing the average number of bacteria in the blood per phagocyte in the presence of immune serum by the corresponding number in the presence of normal serum. A vaccine increases the opsonic index.

調理指數 測量一個人的血清攻擊入侵細菌及吞噬細胞對入侵細菌吞噬能力的數據。免疫血清中每個吞噬細胞吞噬的血液中的細菌的平均數除以正常血清中的相應數目即為調理指數。疫苗接種能使調理指數增加。

opsonin n. a serum component that attaches itself to invading bacteria and apparently makes them more attractive to *phagocytes and thus more likely to be engulfed and destroyed.

調理素 一種血清成分，它依附到入侵細菌上，使細菌對吞噬細胞更具吸引力，從而更容易被吞噬和破壞。

opsonization n. the process by which opsonins render bacteria more attractive to *phagocytes by attaching themselves to their outer surfaces and changing their physical and chemical composition.

調理素作用 調理素依附於細菌外表面，使細菌對吞噬細胞更具有吸引力，並改變細菌的物理和化學成分的過程。

opt- (opto-) prefix denoting vision or the eye.

〔前綴〕視力，眼

optic adj. concerned with the eye or vision.

視力的，眼的 與眼或視力相關的。

optical activity the property possessed by some substances of rotating the plane of polarization of polarized light. A compound that rotates the plane to the left is described as laevorotatory (or l-); one that rotates the plane to the right is described as dextrorotatory (or d-).

旋光性 某些物質具有的能使偏振光的偏振面產生旋轉的特性。使偏振面向左旋轉的化合物叫左旋體；使偏振面向右旋轉的化合物叫右旋體。

optic atrophy degeneration of the optic nerve. It may be secondary to disease within the eye or it may follow damage to the nerve itself resulting from injury or inflammation. It is visible as pallor of the optic nerve as viewed inside the eye with an ophthalmoscope.

視神經萎縮 視神經的變性。可以是眼內的繼發性疾病，或者外傷或炎症引起的神經本身損害後發生。用檢眼鏡觀察眼底可見到視神經灰白。

optic chiasma (optic commissure) the X-shaped structure formed by the two optic nerves, which pass backwards from the eyeballs to meet in the midline beneath the brain, near the pituitary gland (see illustration). Nerve fibres from the nasal side of the retina of each eye cross over to join fibres from the lateral side of the retina of the opposite eye. The optic tracts resulting from the junction pass backwards to the occipital lobes.

視交叉　兩個視神經構成的X形結構，由眼球向後運行，在腦中綫下方，垂體附近會合（見圖）。每隻眼視網膜鼻側的神經纖維與對側眼視網膜外側的神經纖維相結合。由結合點產生的視束向後傳遞到達枕葉。

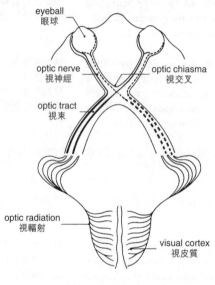

eyeball
眼球

optic nerve
視神經

optic chiasma
視交叉

optic tract
視束

optic radiation
視輻射

visual cortex
視皮質

The optic chiasma
視交叉

optic cup either of the paired cup-shaped outgrowths of the embryonic brain that form the retina and iris of the eyes.

視杯　構成眼視網膜和虹膜的胚胎期腦的一對杯狀突起。

optic disc (optic papilla) the start of the optic nerve, where nerve fibres from the rods and cones leave the eyeball. *See* blind spot.

視盤（視神經乳頭）　視神經的起點，神經纖維在此從視桿細胞和視錐細胞離開眼球。參閱 blind spot。

optic foramen the groove in the top of the *orbit that contains the optic nerve and the ophthalmic artery.

視神經管　含視神經和眼動脈的、位於眼窩頂部的槽。

optician *n.* a person who either makes and fits glasses (*dispensing optician*) or who can both test people for glasses and dispense glasses (*ophthalmic optician* or *optometrist*).

眼鏡師　製作和配眼鏡的人（配鏡師），或既驗光又配鏡的人。

optic nerve the second *cranial nerve (II), which is responsible for vision. Each nerve contains about one million fibres that receive information from the rod and cone cells of the retina. It passes into the skull behind the eyeball to reach the *optic chiasma, after which the visual pathway continues to the cortex of the occipital lobe of the brain on each side.

視神經　第二對腦神經，負責視力。每個視神經含大約一百萬根神經纖維，負責接收來自視網膜的視桿細胞和視錐細胞的信息。在眼球後進入顱內到達視交叉，然後視覺傳導路延伸到大腦兩側的枕葉皮質。

optic neuritis *see* retrobulbar neuritis.

視神經炎　參閱 retrobulbar neuritis。

optometer (refractometer) *n.* an instrument for measuring the *refraction of the eye. An *autorefractor* calculates the required spectacle lens correction automatically. Because the design and use of optometers is very complex, errors of refraction are usually determined using a *retinoscope.

視力計　測量眼屈光度的儀器。自動折射器自動計算所需要的眼鏡鏡片校正數。因為視力計的設計和用途非常複雜，屈光度的誤差通常用視網膜鏡確定。

optometrist *n. see* optician.

驗光師　參閱 optician。

oral *adj.* **1.** relating to the mouth. **2.** taken by mouth: applied to medicines, etc.

(1) 口腔的，口的　與口相關的。(2) 口服的　例如：口服用藥等。

oral cavity the mouth.

口腔　參閱 mouth。

oral contraceptive the Pill: a preparation, consisting of one or more synthetic female sex hormones, taken by women to prevent conception. Most oral contraceptive are combined pills, consisting of

口服避孕藥　婦女口服避孕用的、由一種或多種合成雌激素構成的一種藥丸。大多數口服避孕藥屬複合丸劑，由抑制正常排卵過程的雌激素和作用於

an *oestrogen, which blocks the normal process of ovulation, and a *progestogen, which acts on the pituitary gland to block the normal control of the menstrual cycle. Progestogens also alter the lining of the uterus and the viscosity of mucus in its outlet, the cervix, so that conception is less likely should ovulation occur. These pills are taken every day for three weeks and then stopped for a week, during which time menstruation occurs. Side-effects may include headache, weight gain, nausea, skin changes, and depression. There is also a small risk that blood clots may form in the veins, especially those of the legs (which may lead to *pulmonary embolism), or that prolonged use of hormonal contraceptives may reduce fertility. The unwanted pregnancy rate is less than 1 per 100 woman-years. With progestogen-only pills (sometimes known as *minipills*) the unwanted pregnancy rate is slightly higher (1–2 per 100 woman-years) but there are fewer side-effects (due to the absence of oestrogen).

Other hormonal contraceptives include injections and implants (*see* contraception). *See also* postcoital contraception.

oral hypoglycaemic drug one of the group of drugs that reduce that level of glucose in the blood and are taken by mouth for the treatment of noninsulin-dependent (Type II) *diabetes mellitus. They include the *sulphonylurea group (e.g. *chlorpropamide, *glibenclamide, and *tolbutamide) and *metformin (a biguanide).

oral rehabilitation the procedure of rebuilding a dentition that has been mutilated as a result of disease, wear, or trauma.

垂體腺抑制月經周期調節的孕激素構成。孕激素也改變子宮內膜及子宮口和子宮黏液稠度，這樣即使出現排卵也不大可能受孕。每日服用這些藥，連續三周，然後停藥一周，在此期間產生月經。副作用包括頭痛、體重增加、惡心、皮膚變化及抑鬱。也有靜脈，特別是腿部靜脈形成血栓（會導致肺血栓）的小危險，長期服用激素類避孕藥會降低生育能力。意外妊娠率每年不足 1/100 婦女。服用單純孕激素藥（有時稱小型丸劑）意外妊娠率略高（每年 1~2/100 婦女），但副作用較小（因為沒有雌激素）。

其他激素避孕藥包括注射劑和包埋劑（參閱 contraception）。參閱 postcoital contraception。

口服降血糖藥 降低血液中葡萄糖水平的一組藥物。口服，治療非胰島素依賴性糖尿病（II 型）。這些藥包括磺胺酰脲組（例如氯磺丙脲、格列本脲和甲苯磺丁脲）和甲福明（一種縮二胍）。

口腔康復 牙齒因為疾病、磨損或外傷造成損壞後的重新修復過程。

oral rehydration therapy (ORT) the administration of an isotonic solution of various sodium salts, potassium chloride, glucose, and water to treat acute diarrhoea, particularly in children. In developing countries it is the mainstay of treatment for cholera. Once the diarrhoea has settled, normal feeding is gradually resumed. Preparations in clinical use include *Dioralyte* and *Rehidrat*.

口服補液療法　使用各種鈉鹽、氯化鉀、葡萄糖和水的等滲溶液治療急性腹瀉，特別是兒童急性腹瀉。在發展中國家，它是治療霍亂的主要方法。腹瀉停止後，即可逐步恢復正常飲食。臨床使用的藥劑包括雙口服電解質液和復汗液。

Orbenin *n. see* cloxacillin sodium.

鄰氯青黴素鈉　參閱 cloxacillin sodium。

orbicularis *n.* either of two circular muscles of the face. The *orbicularis oris*, around the mouth, closes and compresses the lips. The *orbicularis oculi*, around each orbit, is responsible for closing the eye.

輪匝肌　面部的兩塊環形肌肉。口輪匝肌圍繞口，關閉並壓縮嘴唇。眼輪匝肌圍繞眼窩，負責閉合眼睛。

orbit *n.* the cavity in the skull that contains the eye. It is formed from parts of the frontal, sphenoid, zygomatic, lacrimal, ethmoid, palatine, and maxillary bones. **–orbital** *adj.*

眼窩　顱骨中容納眼球的腔。由部分額骨、蝶骨、顴骨、淚骨、篩骨、腭骨和上頜骨組成。

orchi- (orchido-, orchio-) *prefix denoting* the testis or testicle. Example: *orchioplasty* (plastic surgery of).

〔前綴〕睾丸　例如：睾丸成形術。

orchidalgia *n.* pain in the testicle. The pain may not be due to a primary condition of the testicle itself: it may be caused by a hernia in the groin, the presence of a stone in the lower ureter, or the presence of a *varicocele.

睾丸痛　睾丸疼痛。疼痛可能不是由睾丸本身的主要疾病引起：可能由腹股溝疝、輸尿管下部結石或精索靜脈曲張引起。

orchidectomy *n.* surgical removal of a testis, usually to treat such diseases as *seminoma (a malignant tumour of the testis). Removal of both testes (*castration) causes sterility.

睾丸切除術　一側睾丸的外科切除，常用於治療精原細胞瘤（睾丸惡性腫瘤）。雙側睾丸切除（閹割）引起不育。

orchidopexy *n.* the operation of mobilizing an undescended testis in the

睾丸固定術　使在腹股溝中不下降的睾丸固定在陰囊中的手

groin and fixing it in the scrotum. The operation should be performed well before puberty to allow the testis every chance of normal development (*see* cryptorchidism).

術。手術應在青春期前進行，使睾丸有正常發育的所有可能性（參閱 cryptorchidism）。

orchidotomy *n.* an incision into the testis, usually done to obtain *biopsy material for histological examination, particularly in men with few or no sperm in their semen (*see* azoospermia, oligospermia).

睾丸切開術 睾丸切開，常用於獲得供活組織檢查的材料，特別是精液中精子少或完全沒有的男性（參閱 azoospermia，oligospermia）。

orchitis *n.* inflammation of the testis. This causes pain, redness, and swelling of the scrotum, and may be associated with inflammation of the epididymis (*epididymo-orchitis*). The condition may affect one or both testes; it is usually caused by infection spreading down the vas deferens but can develop in mumps. Mumps orchitis affecting both testes may result in sterility. Treatment of epididymo-orchitis is by local support and by administration of analgesics and antibiotics; mumps orchitis often responds to *corticosteroids.

睾丸炎 睾丸的炎症。會引起陰囊疼痛、發紅及腫脹，並可與附睾的炎症（睾丸附睾炎）有關。此病可累及一側或雙側睾丸。通常由沿輸精管下行的炎症引起，但流行性腮腺炎中可出現。影響雙側睾丸的腮腺炎性睾丸炎會導致不育。睾丸附睾炎的治療有局部支持和使用鎮痛藥和抗生素；腮腺炎性睾丸炎對皮質類固醇治療有反應。

orciprenaline *n.* a drug used to relieve bronchitis and asthma. It has the same actions and side-effects as *isoprenaline. Trade name: **Alupent**.

奧西那林 用於解除支氣管炎和哮喘的藥物。作用和副作用與異丙腎上腺素相同。商品名：Alupent。

orf *n.* an infectious desease of sheep and goats caused by a *poxvirus. Those handling infected sheep may develop a painful nodule, 2–3 cm across, on the fingers or hands; it resolves spontaneously.

羊痘瘡 痘病毒引起的綿羊和山羊的傳染病。接觸被感染的綿羊的人手指或手上會產生直徑為 2~3 cm 的疼痛性節；可自行消失。

organ *n.* a part of the body, composed of more than one tissue, that forms a structural unit responsible for a particular function (or functions). Examples are the heart, lungs, and liver.

器官 身體的一部分，由幾種組織形成，有某一專門功能（或諸多功能）的結構性單位。例如：心臟、肺和肝臟。

organelle *n.* a structure within a cell that is specialized for a particular function. Examples of organelles are the nucleus, endoplasmic reticulum, Golgi apparatus, lysosomes, and mitochondria.

細胞器 細胞中專門負責一個特殊功能的一種結構。例如細胞核、內質網、高爾基體、溶酶體和綫粒體。

organic *adj.* **1.** relating to any or all of the organs of the body. **2.** describing chemical compounds containing carbon, found in all living systems.

(1) 器官的 與身體任何或所有器官相關的。(2) 有機的 在所有生物系統中含有碳的化合物。

organic disorder a disorder associated with changes in the structure of an organ or tissue. *Compare* functional disorder.

器質性疾病 與器官或組織的結構變化相關的疾病。與 functional disorder 對比。

organism *n.* any living thing, which may consist of a single cell (*see* microorganism) or a group of differentiated but interdependent cells.

生物體 任何有生命的東西。可由單細胞（參閱 microorganism）或一組不同但相互依靠的細胞組成。

organo- *prefix denoting* organ or organic. Examples: *organogenesis* (formation of); organopathy (disease of).

〔前級〕器官，器官的 例如：器官發生；器官病。

organ of Corti (spiral organ) the sense organ of the *cochlea of the inner ear, which converts sound signals into nerve impulses that are transmitted to the brain via the cochlear nerve.

科蒂器（螺旋器） 內耳耳蝸的感覺器官，它把聲音信號轉化成神經衝動，通過耳蝸神經傳入大腦。

organ of Jacobson (vomeronasal organ) a small blind sac in the wall of the nasal cavity. In man it never develops properly and has no function, but in lower animals (e.g. snakes) it is one of the major organs of olfaction.

雅各布森器（犁鼻器） 鼻腔內壁的一個小盲囊。在人類，它不全面發育且無功能，但在低等動物（如蛇），它是主要的嗅覺器官之一。

organotrophic *adj. see* heterotrophic.

器官營養的 參閱 heterotrophic。

orgasm *n.* the climax of sexual excitement, which in men occurs simultaneously with *ejaculation. In women its occurrence is much more variable, being dependent upon a number of physiological and psychological factors.

性慾高潮 性興奮的高峯，在男性，與射精同時產生。在女性，其變化有較大差異，取決於諸多生理和心理因素。

oriental sore (Baghdad boil, Delhi boil, Aleppo boil) a skin disease, occurring in tropical and subtropical Africa and Asia, caused by the parasitic protozoan *Leishmania tropica* (*see* leishmaniasis). The disease commonly affects children and takes the form of a slow-healing open sore or ulcer, which sometimes becomes secondarily infected with bacteria. Antibiotics are administered to combat the infection.

東方瘡（巴格達瘡、德里瘡、阿勒頗瘡） 發生於熱帶和亞熱帶非洲和亞洲，由寄生性原生蟲即熱帶利什曼原蟲引起的一種皮膚病（參閱 leishmaniasis）。此病通常影響兒童且表現為愈合緩慢的開放性瘡及潰瘍，常發生繼發性細菌感染。使用抗生素抗感染。

orientation *n.* (in psychology) awareness of oneself in time, space, and place. Orientation may be disturbed in such conditions as organic brain disease, toxic drug states, and concussion.

定向 （心理學）時間、空間及地點中的自我意識。器質性大腦疾病、藥物中毒狀態及腦震盪時定向會受影響。

origin *n.* (in anatomy) **1.** the point of attachment of a muscle that remains relatively fixed during contraction of the muscle. *Compare* insertion. **2.** the point at which a nerve or blood vessel branches from a main nerve or blood vessel.

起端 （解剖學）**(1)** 肌肉收縮過程中保持相對固定的肌肉附着點。與 insertion 對比。**(2)** 神經或血管從主要的神經或血管分支的點。

ornithine *n.* an *amino acid produced in the liver as a by-product during the conversion of ammonia to *urea.

鳥氨酸 氨轉化為尿素過程中作為副產品由肝臟產生的一種氨基酸。

Ornithodoros (Ornithodorus) *n.* a genus of soft *ticks, a number of species of which are important in various parts of the world in the transmission of *relapsing fever.

鈍緣蜱屬 軟蜱的一屬，其中許多種類在世界許多不同地區傳播回歸熱。

ornithosis *n. see* psittacosis.

鳥疫 參閱 psittacosis。

oro- *prefix denoting* the mouth.

〔前綴〕口

oroantral fistula a connection between the mouth and the maxillary sinus (antrum) as a sequel to tooth extraction. It may resolve or require surgical closure.

口腔上頜竇瘻 牙齒撥除後口腔和上頜竇之間的聯接（瘻道）。可愈合或需要手術縫合。

oropharynx *n.* the part of the *pharynx that lies between the soft palate and the hyoid bone (which is situated near the upper portion of the epiglottis).

口咽　位於軟齶和舌骨之間的咽部分（位於會厭上部附近）。

Oroya fever *see* bartonellosis.

奧羅亞熱　參閱 bartonellosis。

orphenadrine *n.* a drug that relieves spasm in muscle, used to treat all types of parkinsonism. It is administered by mouth or injection; side-effects may include dry mouth, sight disturbances, and difficulty in urination. Trade names: **Disipal**, **Norflex**.

奧芬那君　解除肌肉痙攣藥，用於治療各類帕金森症。口服或注射給藥；副作用可包括口乾、視力受干擾及排尿困難。商品名：Disipal，Norflex。

ORT *see* oral rehydration therapy.

口服補液療法　參閱 oral rehydration therapy。

ortho- *prefix denoting* **1.** straight. Example: *orthograde* (having straight posture). **2.** normal. Example: *orthocrasia* (normal reaction to drugs).

〔前綴〕**(1)** 直的　例如：直體步行的。**(2)** 正常的　例如：正常反應性（對藥物的正常反應）。

orthochromatic *adj.* describing or relating to a tissue specimen that stains normally.

正染的　形容正常着色的組織標本或與之相關的。

orthodiagraph *n.* an X-ray photograph designed to give an undistorted picture of part of the body so that accurate measurements may be made from it.

正影描記器　拍攝身體某一部分準確圖以便進行準確測量的 X 綫片。

orthodontic appliance an appliance used to move teeth as part of orthodontic treatment. A *fixed appliance* is fitted to the teeth by stainless steel bands or brackets and used to perform complex tooth movements; it is used by dentists with specialist training (*orthodontists*). A *removable appliance* is a dental plate with appropriate retainers and springs to perform simple tooth movements; it is removed from the mouth for cleaning by the patient.

正牙器　正牙治療時用於移動部分牙齒的裝置。固定正牙器用不銹鋼帶或圈固定在牙齒上，用於進行複雜的牙齒運動；由訓練有素的牙醫使用。活動正牙器是一個帶有適當的護圈和彈簧的托牙板，可進行簡單的牙齒運動。病人自己可從口中取出清洗。

orthodontics *n.* the branch of dentistry concerned with the growth and development of the dentition and the treatment of irregularities. *See* orthodontic appliance. **–orthodontic** *adj.*

正牙學　牙齒的生長及發育，治療牙齒不齊的牙科學分支。參閱 orthodontic appliance。

orthopaedics *n.* the science or practice of correcting deformities caused by disease of or damage to the bones and joints of the skeleton. This specialized branch of surgery may involve operation, manipulation, traction, *orthoses, or *prostheses. **–orthopaedic** *adj.*

矯形學　涉及矯正由疾病或損傷造成的骨及骨骼關節畸形的科學或操作。外科的這一專門分支可涉及手術、推拿、牽引、整直法或修復術。

orthophoria *n.* the condition of complete balance between the alignment of the two eyes, such that perfect alignment is maintained even when one eye is covered. This theoretically normal state is in fact rarely seen, since in most people there is a minimal tendency for the eyes to deviate (*see* heterophoria).

正視　雙目定位之間完全平衡的狀態，甚至一隻眼被遮住時，仍保持這種完美的定位。這種理論上的正常狀態實際中很罕見，因為在大多數人中，眼有輕度斜視趨向（參閱 heterophoria）。

orthopnoea *n.* breathlessness that prevents the patient from lying down, so that he has to sleep propped up in bed or sitting in a chair. **–orthopnoeic** *adj.*

端坐呼吸　病人臥位氣喘，以致不得不支撐在床上或坐在椅子上睡覺。

orthoptics *n.* the practice of using nonsurgical methods, particularly eye exercises, to treat abnormalities of vision and of coordination of eye movements (most commonly strabismus (squint) and amblyopia). Orthoptics also includes the detection and measurement of the degree of such abnormalities. **–orthoptist** *n.*

視軸矯正法　用非手術方法，特別是眼操治療視力異常和眼球運動協調異常（最常見的是斜視和弱視）的方法。視軸矯正法也包括對這類異常的檢查和測量。

orthoptoscope *n. see* amblyoscope.

視軸矯正器　參閱 amblyoscope。

orthosis *n.* an individually made surgical appliance that provides support for an unstable joint or joints. An example is a spinal brace.

整直法，矯正器　向不穩定關節提供支持的單個製造的外科裝置。例如：脊柱支架。

orthostatic *adj.* relating to the upright position of the body: used when describing this posture or a condition caused by it. *Orthostatic hypotension*, for example, is low blood pressure found in some patients when they stand upright.

直立的　與身體的直立位置相關的；用於描述這一體態或由此引起的病態。例如：直立性低血壓見於某些病人站立時產生的低血壓。

orthotics *n.* the science and practice of fitting surgical appliances to assist weakened joints.

矯形器修配學　安裝外科裝置輔助弱關節的科學及實踐。

os[1] *n.* (*pl.* **ossa**) a bone.

骨

os[2] *n.* (*pl.* **ora**) the mouth or a mouthlike part.

口腔，口狀物

osche- (oscheo-) *prefix denoting* the scrotum. Example: *occheocele* (a scrotal hernia).

〔前綴〕陰囊　例如：陰囊疝。

oscilloscope *n.* a cathode-ray tube designed to display electronically a wave form corresponding to the electrical data fed into it. Oscilloscopes are used to provide a continuous record of many different measurements, such as the activity of the heart and brain. *See* electrocardiography, electroencephalography.

示波器　用電子方法顯示輸入電子數據時形成波的陰極射綫管。示波器用於提供許多種類不同的檢測的連續記錄。例如：心臟和大腦的活動。參閱 electrocardiography，electroencephalography。

osculum *n.* (in anatomy) a small aperture.

小口　（解剖學）小孔。

Osgood-Schlatter disease inflammation and swelling of the tubercle at the top of the *tibia, i.e. the site of insertion of the patellar tendon (*see* osteochondritis). It is caused by repeated minor trauma resulting from physical activity and is most common in teenage boys. Most cases resolve with rest.

奧-施氏病　脛骨頂部結節，例如髕骨腱附着處的炎症及腫脹（參閱 osteochondritis）。由軀體活動產生的反覆性小外傷引起，最常見於男性少年。大多數病人通過休息可治愈。

-osis *suffix denoting* **1.** a diseased condition. Examples: *nephrosis* (of the kidney); *leptospirosis* (caused by *Leptospira* species). **2.** any condition.

〔前綴〕(1) 病態　例如：腎病（腎臟的疾病）；鈎端螺旋體病（由鈎端螺旋體屬引起）。(2) 狀態　例如：麻木狀態

Example: *narcosis* (of stupor). **3.** an increase or excess. Example: *leucocytosis* (of leucocytes).

（木僵狀態）。**(3)** 增加 例如：白細胞增多。

osm- (osmo-) *prefix denoting* **1.** smell or odour. **2.** osmosis or osmotic pressure.

〔前綴〕**(1)** 嗅，嗅覺 **(2)** 滲透，滲透壓

osmic acid *see* osmium tetroxide.

鋨酸 參閱 osmium tetroxide。

osmiophilic *adj.* describing a tissue that stains readily with osmium tetroxide.

嗜鋨的 形容易染四氧化鋨的組織的。

osmium tetroxide (osmic acid) a colourless or faintly yellowish compound used to stain fats or as a *fixative in the preparation of tissues for microscopical study. Osmium tetroxide evaporates readily, the vapour having a toxic action on the eyes, skin, and respiratory tract.

四氧化鋨（鋨酸） 一種無色或淡黃色化合物，用於脂肪染色或在顯微鏡檢查組織時作為固定液。四氧化鋨易蒸發，其蒸氣對眼、皮膚和呼吸道有毒害作用。

osmole *n.* a unit of osmotic pressure equal to the molecular weight of a solute in grams divided by the number of ions or other particles into which it dissociates in solution.

滲克分子 滲透壓單位，等於溶質的克分子量除以溶液離解的離子或其他粒子的數量。

osmoreceptor *n.* a group of cells in the *hypothalamus that monitor blood concentration. Should this increase abnormally, as in dehydration, the osmoreceptors send nerve impulses to the hypothalamus, which then increases the rate of release of *vasopressin from the posterior pituitary gland. Loss of water from the body in the urine is thus restricted until the blood concentration returns to normal.

滲透壓感受器 控制血液濃度的下丘腦中的細胞羣。如果血液濃度異常增加，例如在脫水時，滲透壓感受器向下丘腦發出神經衝動，下丘腦接着加速垂體後葉加壓素的釋放。從而制止體內水分在尿中的喪失，直到血液濃度恢復正常。

osmosis *n.* the passage of a solvent from a less concentrated to a more concentrated solution through a *semipermeable membrane. This tends to equalize the concentrations of the two solutions. In living organisms the solvent is water

滲透（作用） 溶液通過半透膜從較低濃度溶液流向較高濃度的溶液。滲透作用趨向於使兩種溶液間達到平衡。在生物體中，溶劑是水，細胞膜起半透膜作用。滲透（作用）過程在

and cell membranes function as semipermeable membranes, and the process of osmosis plays an important role in controlling the distribution of water. The *osmotic pressure* of a solution is the pressure by which water is drawn into it through the semipermeable membrane; the more concentrated the solution (i.e. the more solute molecules it contains), the greater its osmotic pressure. **–osmotic** *adj.*

控制水的分布中起重要作用。溶液的滲透壓是水被吸引通過半透膜進入溶液。溶液濃度越高（即含溶質分子越多），滲透壓越大。

osseous *adj.* bony: applied to the bony parts of the inner ear (cochlea, semicircular canals, labyrinth).

骨的 骨性的：指內耳的骨部分（耳蝸、半規管、迷路）。

ossicle *n.* a small bone. The *auditory ossicles* are three small bones (the incus, malleus, and stapes) in the middle *ear. They transmit sound from the outer ear to the labyrinth (inner ear).

小骨 小的骨頭。聽小骨是中耳內的三塊小骨（鐙骨、錘骨和砧骨）。它們把聲音從外耳傳向迷路（內耳）。

ossification (osteogenesis) *n.* the formation of *bone, which takes place in three stages by the action of special cells (osteoblasts). A meshwork of collagen fibres is deposited in connective tissue, followed by the production of a cementing polysaccharide. Finally the cement is impregnated with minute crystals of calcium salts. The osteoblasts become enclosed within the matrix as *osteocytes* (*bone cells*). In *intracartilaginous* (or *endochondral*) *ossification* the bone replaces cartilage. This process starts to occur soon after the end of the second month of embryonic life. *Intramembranous ossification* is the formation of a *membrane bone (e.g. a bone of the skull). This starts in the early embryo and is not complete at birth (*see* fontanelle).

骨化 骨的形成，在特殊細胞（成骨細胞）的作用下，分三個階段發生。膠原纖維網絡在纖維組織中沉積，接着是起黏固作用的黏多糖的產生；最後黏多糖中充滿了鈣鹽的結晶。成骨細胞作為骨細胞被包圍在基質中。在軟骨骨化中，骨代替了軟骨。此過程開始於胚胎期的第二個月末。膜內骨化是膜骨的形成過程（例如顱骨）。它開始於胚胎早期，出生時尚未完成（參閱fontanelle）。

ost- (oste-, osteo-) *prefix denoting* bone. Examples: *ostalgia* (pain in); *osteocarcinoma* (carcinoma of); *osteonecrosis*

〔前綴〕**骨** 如：骨痛；骨癌；骨壞死；骨成形術。

(death of); *osteoplasty* (plastic surgery of).

ostectomy *n.* the surgical removal of a bone or a piece of bone. *See also* osteotomy.

骨切除術 骨或骨的一部分手術切除術。參閱 osteotomy。

osteitis *n.* inflammation of bone, due to infection, damage, or metabolic disorder. *Osteitis fibrosa cystica* refers to the characteristic cystic changes that occur in bones during long-standing *hyperparathyroidism. *See also* Paget's disease (of bone) (osteitis deformans).

骨炎 感染、損傷或代謝疾病引起的骨的炎症。囊性纖維性骨炎指長期患甲狀旁腺功能亢進時骨中產生的特有的囊性變化。參閱 Paget's disease。

osteo- *prefix. see* ost-.

〔前綴〕骨 參閱 ost-。

osteoarthritis (osteoarthrosis) *n.* a disease of joint cartilage, associated with secondary changes in the underlying bone, which may ultimately cause pain and impair the function of the affected joint (most often the hip, knee, and thumb joints). The condition may result from trauma and is most common in those past middle life; it may also complicate many of the other disease involving joints, such as *rheumatoid arthritis (*secondary osteoarthritis*). Osteoarthritis is recognized on X-ray by narrowing of the joint space (due to loss of cartilage) and the presence of *osteophytes and irregularity at the bone margins. Treatment consists of aspirin and other analgesics, reduction of pressure across the joint (by weight loss and the use of a walking stick in osteoarthritis of the hip), and corrective and prosthetic surgery.

骨性關節炎 關節軟骨的疾病，與所屬骨的繼發性變化相關，最終會引起疼痛並損害受累關節的功能（經常是髖關節、膝關節和拇指關節）。此病常由外傷引起，最常見於年齡已過中年的人羣；它可併發於涉及關節的其他許多疾病，例如類風濕性關節炎（繼發性骨關節炎）。根據 X 綫片上的關節空間狹窄（由軟骨缺損引起）、骨贅的出現及骨緣不整齊可以診斷骨關節炎。治療包括使用阿司匹林及其他鎮痛藥、降低關節壓力（通過降低體重及讓髖關節的骨關節炎病人使用拐杖）、矯正和修復手術。

osteoarthropathy *n.* any disease of the bone and cartilage adjoining a joint. *Hypertrophic osteoarthropathy* is characterized by the formation of new bony tissue and occurs as a complication of chronic diseases of the chest, including

骨關節病 骨及軟骨關節頭的任何疾病。肥大性骨關節病特徵是形成新骨組織，也是肺膿腫、間皮瘤和肺癌等慢性胸部疾病的併發症。

pulmonary abscess, mesothelioma, and lung cancer.

osteoarthrosis *n. see* osteoarthritis.

骨關節病　　參閱　osteo-arthritis。

osteoarthrotomy *n.* surgical excision of the bone adjoining a joint.

骨關節頭切除術　骨關節頭的外科切除。

osteoblast *n.* a cell, originating in the mesoderm of the embryo, that is responsible for the formation of *bone. *See also* ossification.

成骨細胞　來源於胚胎的中胚層的細胞，負責骨的形成。參閱 ossification。

osteochondritis *n.* inflammation of a bone associated with pain: the deposition of abnormal bony tissue seen on X-ray (*see* osteosclerosis). The cause is not known and the condition is frequently self-limiting, but permanent deformity of the affected bone may result. Treatment is with analgesics. *See also* Köhler's disease, Legg-Calvé-Perthes disease, Osgood-Schlatter disease.

This condition was formerly known as *osteochondrosis*.

骨軟骨炎　併發疼痛的骨的炎症：X 綫片上可見異常骨組織的沉積（參閱 osteosclerosis）。病因不明，病程常為自限性的，但可產生受累骨的永久性畸形。用鎮痛藥治療。參閱 Köhler's disease，Legg-Calvé-Perthes disease，Osgood-Schlatter disease。

此病舊稱骨軟骨病。

osteochondritis dissecans release of a small fragment (or fragments) of bone and cartilage into a joint, most frequently the knee, with resulting pain, swelling, and limitation of movement. If the condition persists, or relapses frequently, *arthrotomy, followed by extraction of the bone fragments, may be required.

分離性骨軟骨炎　骨及軟骨碎片釋放進入關節，特別是進入膝關節，伴有疼痛、腫脹及活動受限制。如果此病長期存在或反覆發作，則需要作關節切開術，然後取出骨碎片。

osteochondroma *n.* (*pl.* **osteochondromata**) a bone tumour composed of cartilage-forming cells. It appears as a painless mass, usually at the end of a long bone, and is most common between the ages of 10 and 25. As a small proportion of these tumours become malignant if untreated, they are excised.

骨軟骨瘤　軟骨形成細胞構成的一種骨腫瘤。作為無痛團塊出現，通常出現在長骨端，10~25 歲人羣中最常見。如果不治療，有些可惡變，所以需要切除。

osteochondrosis *n. see* osteochondritis.

骨軟骨病　參閱　osteochondritis。

osteoclasia (osteoclasis) *n.* **1.** the deliberate breaking of a malformed or malunited bone, carried out by a surgeon to correct deformity. Also called: **osteoclasty**. **2.** dissolution of bone through disease (*see* osteolysis).

(1) 折骨術　為了糾正畸形，由外科醫生進行的有意折斷畸形的或連接不正的骨。也稱 osteoclasty。**(2) 骨質溶解**　疾病引起的骨的溶解（參閱 osteolysis）。

osteoclasis *n.* **1.** remodelling of bone by *osteoclasts, during growth or the healing of a fracture. **2.** *see* osteoclasia.

(1) 骨重建　發育或骨折愈合中通過破骨細胞產生的骨的重新成形。**(2) 折骨術**　參閱 osteoclasia。

osteoclast *n.* **1.** a large multinucleate cell that resorbs calcified bone. Osteoclasts are only found when bone is being resorbed and may be seen in small depressions on the bone surface. **2.** a device for fracturing bone for therapeutic purposes.

(1) 破骨細胞　再吸收已鈣化骨的大的多核細胞。破骨細胞僅見於骨被再吸收過程中，在骨表面可以看到小的凹陷。**(2) 折骨器**　為了治療目的所用的折斷骨的器械。

osteoclastoma *n.* a rare tumour of bone, caused by proliferation of *osteoclast cells.

成骨細胞瘤　破骨細胞增生引起的骨的一種罕見腫瘤。

osteocyte *n.* a bone cell: an *osteoblast that has ceased activity and has become embedded in the bone matrix.

骨細胞　一種骨細胞：活動停止並在骨基質中包埋的成骨細胞。

osteodystrophy *n.* any generalized bone disease resulting from a metabolic disorder. *Renal osteodystrophy* is the characteristic change in bones occurring in chronic kidney failure.

骨營養不良　代謝疾病引起的任何全身性骨病。腎病性骨營養不良是慢性腎臟衰竭時骨中出現的特徵性變化。

osteogenesis *n. see* ossification.

骨發生　參閱 ossification。

osteogenesis imperfecta (fragilias ossium) a congenital disorder in which the bones are unusually brittle and fragile. No treatment is available, but the tendency to fracture sometimes diminishes at adolescence.

成骨不全　骨質異常脆弱的一種先天性疾病。無法治療。但易骨折的趨向有時在青春期減小。

osteology *n.* the study of the structure and function of bones and related structures.

骨骼學　研究骨及其相關組織的結構和功能的科學。

osteolysis (osteoclasia) *n.* dissolution of bone through disease, commonly by infection or by loss of the blood supply (ischaemia) to the bone. In *acroosteolysis* the terminal bones of the fingers or toes are affected: a common feature of some disorders involving blood vessels (including *Raynaud's disease), *scleroderma, and systemic *lupus erythematosus.

骨質溶解　疾病引起的骨的溶解，常由感染或骨缺血（局部缺血）引起。肢端骨溶解患者指（趾）的末端骨受累，是某些涉及血管（包括雷諾病）、硬皮病和系統性紅斑狼瘡等病的共同特徵。

osteoma *n.* a benign bone tumour. A *cancellous osteoma* (*exostosis*) is an outgrowth from the end of a long bone, usually rising to point. A *compact osteoma* (*ivory tumour*) is usually harmless but it may rarely compress surrounding structures, as within the skull. An *osteoid osteoma* is an overgrowth of bone-forming cells, usually causing pain in the middle of a long bone. Compact and osteoid osteomas are treated by surgical excision.

骨瘤　良性骨腫瘤。鬆質骨瘤（外生骨疣）是長骨端的贅疣，常生長成一個尖。密質骨瘤（象牙樣瘤）通常是無害的，但偶爾可壓迫周圍組織，例如顱骨中的骨瘤。骨樣骨瘤是骨形成細胞的過度生長，常引起長骨中部的疼痛。密質骨瘤和骨樣骨瘤用外科切除治療。

osteomalacia *n.* softening of the bones caused by a deficiency of *vitamin D, either from a poor diet or lack of sunshine or both. It is the adult counterpart of *rickets. Vitamin D is necessary for the uptake of calcium from food; the deficiency therefore leads to progressive decalcification of bony tissues, often causing bone pain. The condition may become irreversible if treatment with vitamin D is not given.

骨軟化症　維生素 D 缺乏引起的骨的變化。可由食物中缺乏維生素 D 或日照不足引起，也可由兩種因素綜合引起，是佝僂病在成人中的對應名稱。維生素 D 對於從食物中吸收鈣是必不可少的。因此其缺乏會導致骨組織進行性脫鈣，常引起骨痛。如果不用維生素 D 治療，病情會變得不可逆轉。

osteomyelitis *n.* inflammation of the bone marrow due to infection. This is a hazard following compound fractures and must be rigorously guarded against whenever the marrow is exposed during

骨髓炎　感染造成的骨髓炎症。複合式骨折後出現有危害性。骨或關節手術時，如果骨髓暴露，必須嚴防骨髓炎發生。本病亦可由血源性微生物

bone or joint surgery. It may also be caused by blood-borne microorganisms. In *acute osteomyelitis*, most common in children, there is severe pain, swelling, and redness at the site, often in the shaft of a long bone, accompanied by general illness and high fever. *Chronic osteomyelitis* may follow the acute form or develop insidiously; tuberculosis and syphilis are occasional causes. Both forms are treated by antibiotics in high dosage, and in some cases drainage by surgery may be necessary. Delay in eradicating the infection may lead to bone shortening and deformity.

引起。急性骨髓炎常見於兒童，炎症部位，通常是長骨幹骺部，出現嚴重疼痛、腫脹及發紅，伴有全身性疾病和高燒。慢性骨髓炎可在急性骨髓炎後發生或潛隱性發生。結核病和梅毒偶爾會成為病因。兩種類型的骨髓炎都用大劑量抗生素治療。有些病例需要外科引流。如不及時消除感染可導致骨縮短和畸形。

osteopathy *n.* a system of diagnosis and treatment based on the theory that many diseases are associated with disorders of the musculoskeletal system. Diagnosis and treatment of these disorders involve palpation, manipulation, and massage. Osteopathy provides relief for many disorders of bones and joints, especially those producing back pain. **–osteopath** *n.* **–osteopathic** *adj.*

整骨療法 一種診斷和治療體系，其理論基礎是許多疾病都和肌骨骼系統疾病相關。這些疾病的診斷和治療包括觸診、推拿及按摩。整骨法解除了許多骨病和關節疾病，特別是那些造成背痛的疾病。

osteopetrosis (Albers-Schönberg disease, marble-bone disease) *n.* a congenital abnormality in which bones become abnormally dense and brittle and tend to fracture. Affected bones appear unusually opaque to X-rays. *See also* osteosclerosis.

骨硬化症（阿爾貝斯-舍恩貝格病，骨石化病） 一種先天性畸形，骨變得異常致密、易碎並有骨折趨向。受累骨在 X 綫片上變得異常模糊。參閱 osteosclerosis。

osteophyte *n.* a projection of bone, usually shaped like a rose thorn, that occurs at sites of cartilage degeneration or destruction near joints and intervertebral discs. Osteophyte formation is an X-ray sign of *osteoarthritis but is not a cause of symptoms in itself.

骨贅 骨的突起，形狀常類似於玫瑰刺，發生於軟骨變性部位或關節及椎間盤附近的破壞區域。骨贅是骨關節炎的 X 綫徵，但本身不是症狀的原因。

osteoporosis *n.* loss of bony tissue, resulting in bones that are brittle and

骨質疏鬆症 骨組織的缺乏，導致骨易碎及易發生骨折。感

liable to fracture. Infection, injury, and *synovitis can cause localized osteoporosis of adjacent bone. Generalized osteoporosis is common in the elderly, and in women often follows the menopause (see hormone replacement therapy). It is also a feature of *Cushing's disease and prolonged steroid therapy. Osteoporosis can be detected by *quantitative digital radiography.

osteosarcoma n. a malignant bone tumour. It is usually seen in children and adolescents but can occur in adults of all ages, occasionally in association with *Paget's disease of bone. In children the usual site for the tumour is the leg, particularly the femur. Secondary growths (metastases) are common, most frequently in the lungs (though other sites, such as the liver, may also be involved). The symptoms are usually pain and swelling at the site of the tumour and there is often a history of preceding trauma, although it is doubtful whether this contributes to the cause. Treatment of disease localized to the primary site was traditionally by amputation of the limb; limb-sparing surgery is now possible with replacement of the diseased bone by a metal prosthesis. Many centres also give *adjuvant chemotherapy in an attempt to kill any microscopic tumour that might have already spread. The drugs used include doxorubicin. cisplatin, vincristine, cyclophosphamide, and methotrexate.

osteosclerosis n. an abnormal increase in the density of bone, as a result of poor blood supply, chronic infection, or tumour. The affected bone is more opaque to X-rays than normal bone. See also osteopetrosis.

染、外傷和滑膜炎可引起鄰近骨的局部性骨質疏鬆。全身性骨質疏鬆常見於老人及更年期後婦女（參閱 hormone replacement therapy）。本病也是庫欣病及長期應用類固醇療法的一個特徵。用定量數字放射檢查可發現骨質疏鬆。

骨肉瘤 惡性骨腫瘤。常見於兒童及青少年，但可發生於各年齡段的成人，偶爾合併骨的佩吉特病。在兒童，骨肉瘤的常發部位是下肢，特別是股骨。繼發性生長（轉移）較常見，最頻繁的是在肺中（儘管其他部位，例如肝，也會受累）。症狀通常包括腫瘤部位的疼痛和腫脹。常有病前外傷史，但外傷是否為病因尚不清楚。局限於原發部位的骨肉瘤治療傳統上使用截肢，隨着用金屬假肢代替患病骨的出現，現在有可能進行肢體保留手術。許多中心也採用輔助化療試圖殺死有可能已經擴散的顯微腫瘤。使用的藥物包括阿黴素、順鉑、長春新鹼、環磷酰胺和甲氨蝶呤。

骨硬化 供血不足、慢性感染或腫瘤引起的骨質密度的異常增加。受累骨和正常骨相比更不透 X 綫。參閱 osteopetrosis。

osteotome *n.* a surgical chisel designed to cut bone (see illustration).

骨鑿　用於切骨的外科鑿子（見圖）。

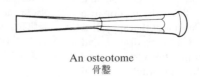

An osteotome
骨鑿

osteotomy *n.* a surgical operation to cut a bone into two parts, followed by realignment of the ends to allow healing. The operation is performed to reduce pain and disability in an arthritic joint, for cases in which conservative treatment has failed. Osteotomy of the jaws is performed to improve severe discrepancies in jaw relation.

骨切開術　把骨切成兩部分，然後再將切斷的兩端重新結合使其癒合的外科手術。保守療法失敗時，做這種手術可以減輕關節炎患者的疼痛和殘疾程度。頜骨切開術用於改進頜關節關係的嚴重分歧。

ostium *n.* (*pl.* **ostia**) (in anatomy) an opening. The *ostium abdominale* is the opening of the Fallopian tube into the abdominal cavity.

口　（解剖學）開口。腹腔口是輸卵管進入腹腔的開口。

-ostomy *suffix. see* -stomy.

〔後綴〕造口術，造瘻術，吻合術　參閱 -stomy。

ot- (oto-) *prefix denoting* the ear. Examples: *ototomy* (surgical incision of).

〔前綴〕耳　例如：耳切開術。

otalgia *n.* pain in the ear. Apart from local causes it may be due to diseases of the jaw joints, neck, throat, or teeth.

耳痛　耳的疼痛。除局部原因外，可因頜關節、頸部、咽喉或牙齒疾病引起。

OTC drug *see* over-the-counter drug.

非處方藥物　參閱 over-the-counter drug。

otic *adj.* relating to the ear.

耳的　與耳相關的。

otic capsule the cup-shaped cartilage in the head of an embryo that later develops into the bony *labyrinth of the ear.

耳囊　胚胎頭部中的杯狀軟骨，以後發育成耳的骨迷路。

otitis *n.* inflammation of the ear. *Otitis externa* is inflammation of the canal between the eardrum and the external opening of the ear (the external auditory meatus). *Acute otitis media* is inflammation, usually due to viral or bacterial infection, of the middle ear (the chamber lying behind the eardrum and containing the three bony ossicles that conduct sound to the inner ear). Symptoms include pain and a high fever. Treatment is with antibiotics and sometimes also by surgical drainage (*myringotomy). *Secretory otitis media* is a chronic accumulation of fluid in the middle ear, causing hearing loss (*see* glue ear). *Chronic suppurative otitis media* is chronic inflammation of the middle ear associated with perforations of the eardrum and in some instances with *cholesteatoma. The treatment involves surgical repair of perforations (*myringoplasty) or removal of the air cells in the mastoid bone (*mastoidectomy). *Labyrinthitis* (*otitis interna*) is inflammation of the inner ear causing vertigo, vomiting, loss of balance, and deafness.

otoconium *n. see* otolith.

otocyst *n.* a small cavity in the mesoderm of the head of an embryo that later develops into the membranous *labyrinth of the ear.

otolaryngology *n.* the study of diseases of the ears and larynx.

otolith (otoconium) *n.* one of the small particles of calcium carbonate associated with a macula in the *saccule or *utricle of the inner ear.

otology *n.* the study of diseases of the ear.

耳炎 耳的炎症。外耳炎是鼓膜及耳的外開口之間通道（外耳道）的炎症。急性中耳炎是常由病毒或細菌感染引起的中耳（位於鼓膜之後，含有三個向內耳傳導聲音的聽小骨的腔室）的炎症。症狀包括疼痛及高燒。治療用抗生素，有時也用外科引流（鼓膜切開術）。分泌性中耳炎是中耳內液體慢性聚積，可導致聽覺喪失（參閱 glue ear）。慢性化膿性中耳炎伴有鼓膜穿孔，有時伴有膽脂瘤。治療涉及外科修復穿孔（鼓膜成形術）或切除乳突骨中的空氣細胞（乳突切除術）。迷路炎（內耳炎）是內耳的炎症，引起眩暈、嘔吐、失衡及耳聾。

耳石 參閱 otolith。

聽囊 胚胎頭部中胚層內的小腔，以後發育成耳的膜迷路。

耳喉科學 研究耳和咽喉疾病的科學。

耳石 與內耳的球囊或橢圓囊斑相關的碳酸鈣微粒。

耳科學 研究耳病的科學。

-otomy *suffix. see* -tomy.

〔後綴〕**切開術** 參閱 -tomy。

otomycosis *n.* a fungus infection of the ear, causing irritation and inflammation of the canal between the eardrum and the external opening of the ear (external auditory meatus). It is one of the causes of *otitis externa.

耳真菌病 耳的真菌感染，造成鼓膜與耳的外口間的通道（外耳道）疼痛及炎症。是外耳炎的病因之一。

otoplasty (pinnaplasty) *n.* surgical repair or reconstruction of the ears after injury or in the correction of a congenital defect (such as 'bat ears').

耳成形術 受傷後或糾正先天性耳缺陷（例如蝙蝠耳）時耳的手術修復或重建。

otorhinolaryngology *n.* the study of ear, nose, and throat diseases (i.e. ENT disorders).

耳鼻喉科學 研究耳、鼻、喉科疾病（即 ENT 疾病）的科學。

otorrhagia *n.* bleeding from the ear.

耳出血 血液從耳流出。

otorrhoea *n.* any discharge from the ear, commonly a purulent discharge in chronic middle ear infection (*otitis media).

耳液溢 耳的任何排出物，通常是慢性中耳感染（中耳炎）時膿性排出物。

otosclerosis (otospongiosis) *n.* a hereditary disorder causing deafness in adult life. An overgrowth of the bone of the inner ear leads to the third ear ossicle (the stapes) becoming fixed to the fenestra ovalis, which separates the middle and inner ears, so that sounds cannot be conducted to the inner ear. *Deafness is progressive and may become very severe, but treatment by surgery is highly effective (*see* fenestration, stapedectomy).

耳硬化症 引起成年人耳聾的遺傳性疾病。內耳骨的過度增長導致第三聽骨（鐙骨）固定在前庭窗上，隔開了中耳和內耳，這樣聲音就不能傳進內耳。耳聾是進行性的，而且會變得很嚴重，但手術治療效果極佳（參閱 fenestration，stapedectomy）。

otoscope *n. see* auriscope.

耳鏡 參閱 auriscope。

otospongiosis *n. see* otosclerosis.

耳硬化症 參閱 otosclerosis。

ouabain *n.* a drug that stimulates the heart and is used to treat heart failure

毒毛花苷 G 刺激心臟，用於治療心力衰竭和其他心臟病的

and other heart conditions. It is administered by mouth or injection and has the same actions and side-effects as *digitalis.

藥物。口服或注射。作用及副作用同洋地黃。

outbreeding *n.* the production of offspring by parents who are not closely related. *Compare* inbreeding.

遠系繁殖 沒有親密血緣關係的父母生育的後代。與 inbreeding 對比。

outer ear the pinna and the external auditory meatus of the *ear.

外耳 耳的耳廓及外耳道。

out-of-the-body experience a form of *derealization in which there is a sensation of leaving one's body and visions of travelling through tunnels into light or of journeys on another plane of existence. It typically occurs after anaesthesia or severe illness and is often attributed to *anoxia of the brain.

飄飄欲仙之感 現實感喪失的一種形式，人有離開軀殼、看到自己通過光隧道漫游或在另一個有生命的星球上游歷之感。特別是麻醉或嚴重疾病後會出現。常由腦缺氧症引起。

out-patient *n.* a patient who receives treatment at a hospital, either at a single attendance or at a series of attendances, but is not admitted to a bed in a hospital ward. Large hospitals have *clinics at which out-patients with various complaints can be given specialist treatment. *Compare* in-patient.

門診病人 在醫院接受治療的病人，可以是一次護理或一系列護理，但不住院治療。大醫院有門診部，患各種病的門診病人可以在此接受專科治療。與 in-patient 對比。

oval window *see* fenestra (ovalis).

卵圓窗 參閱 fenestra (ovalis)。

ovari- (ovario-) *prefix denoting* the ovary.

〔前綴〕**卵巢**

ovarian cancer a malignant tumour of the ovary, usually a carcinoma. Because of its wide-ranging pathology and an imperfect understanding of its causes, ovarian cancer is not readily detected in the early stages of development, when the tumour is small and produces few suspicious symptoms. The incidence of the disease reaches a peak in post-

卵巢癌 卵巢的惡性腫瘤，常為癌症。因為病理學範圍大，對病因的了解不完全，所以腫瘤較小、產生少數可疑症狀時的早期卵巢癌不易被發現。此病發生率在更年期後婦女中達到最高峯。治療涉及手術，大多數病例還要配合化療及/或放療（參閱 taxol）。為了更好

menopausal women; treatment involves surgery and most cases also require combined chemotherapy and/or radiotherapy (*see also* taxol). In an attempt to facilitate a better understanding of the disease, and hence an earlier diagnosis and treatment, the World Health Organization (WHO) published in 1992 a revised Histological Classification of Ovarian Neoplasms and Tumour-like Lesions. An ultrasound screening test for ovarian cancer is being developed.

ovarian cyst a fluid-filled sac, one or more of which may develop in the ovary. Although most ovarian cysts are not malignant, they may reach a very large size, causing gross swelling of the abdomen and pressure on surrounding organs. The cyst may rotate on its stalk, thus cutting off its blood supply and causing severe abdominal pain and vomiting. In this case the cyst requires urgent surgical removal. Ovarian cysts that do become malignant may not be recognized until the tumour has advanced to a stage where treatment may be unsuccessful in eradicating the cancer. Screening programmes, based on ultrasound techniques, have been introduced in some areas to assist with the early detection of ovarian cysts and tumours.

ovariectomy *n. see* oophorectomy.

ovariotomy *n.* literally, incision of an ovary. However, the term commonly refers to surgical removal of an ovary (*oophorectomy).

ovaritis *n. see* oophoritis.

ovary *n.* the main female reproductive organ, which produces ova (egg cells) and steroid hormones in a regular cycle

地了解此病，從而達到早診斷和早治療，1992 年世界衛生組織修訂出版了《卵巢腫瘤和腫瘤樣損害的組織學分類》。用超聲波掃描檢查發現卵巢癌正在發展中。

卵巢囊腫 卵巢中發育的一個或多個充滿液體的囊。儘管大多數卵巢囊腫不是惡性的，但可長得很大，使腹部隆起，並壓迫周圍器官。囊腫會沿蒂部旋轉，因此切斷其血液供應，引起劇烈腹痛和嘔吐。這種病例需緊急手術切除囊腫。在腫瘤發展到用治療不能成功排除癌的程度之前，確實惡變的卵巢囊腫是辨認不出來的。以超聲波技術為基礎的篩查計劃已在某些地區使用，旨在幫助早期發現卵巢囊腫和腫瘤。

卵巢切除術 參閱 oophorectomy。

卵巢切開術，卵巢切除術 從字面意義上看指卵巢切開，但此術語常指卵巢切除（卵巢切除術）。

卵巢炎 參閱 oophoritis。

卵巢 主要的女性生殖器官，在前垂體產生的激素（促性腺激素）的作用下周期性（參

(*see* menstrual cycle) in response to hormones (*gonadotrophins) from the anterior pituitary gland. There are two ovaries, situated in the lower abdomen, one on each side of the uterus (*see* reproductive system). Each ovary contains numerous *follicles*, within which the ova develop (see illustration), but only a small proportion of them reach maturity (*see* Graafian follicle, oogenesis). The follicles secrete *oestrogen and small amounts of androgen. After ovulation a *corpus luteum forms at the site of the ruptured follicle and secretes progesterone. Oestrogen and progesterone regulate the changes in the uterus throughout the menstrual cycle and pregnancy. **–ovarian** *adj.*

閱 menstrual cycle）地產生卵子（卵細胞）和甾類激素。卵巢有兩個，位於下腹部，子宮兩側（參閱 reproductive system）。每個卵巢含無數卵泡，卵子在其中發育（見圖），但僅有很小比例的卵子能成熟（參閱 Graafian follicle，oogenesis）。卵泡分泌雌激素和少量雄激素。排卵後在破裂的卵泡部位黃體形成，並分泌孕酮。雌激素和孕酮在整個月經周期和妊娠期調節子宮的變化。

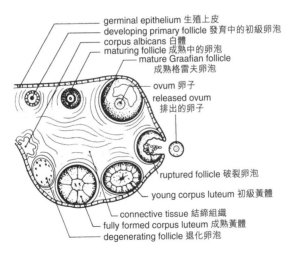

Section of the ovary showing ova in various stages of maturation
各種成熟階段卵子的卵巢斷面圖

overbite *n.* the vertical overlap of the upper incisor teeth over the lower ones.

overcompensation *n.* (in psychology) the situation in which a person tries to

覆殆　上切牙和下切牙的垂直重合。

過度補償　（心理學）一個人通過作出比實際需要更大的努力

overcome a disability by making greater efforts than are required. This may result in the person becoming extremely efficient in what he (or she) is trying to achieve; alternatively, excessive over-compensation may be harmful to the person.

盡力克服能力缺陷的情景。過度補償會使此人在他（或她）所做的事中極有效率，但過分的過度補償對此人可能有危害。

overjet *n.* the horizontal overlap of the upper incisor teeth in front of the lower ones.

覆蓋 上切牙與下切牙的水平重疊。

overt *adj.* plainly to be seen or detected: applied to diseases with observable signs and symptoms, as opposed to those whose presence may not be suspected for years despite the fact that they cause insidious damage. An infectious disease becomes overt only at the end of an incubation period.

明顯的 容易看到或檢查出來的：指有能觀察得到的體徵及症狀的疾病，而不是那些雖然引起隱性損害，但多年不被懷疑會出現的疾病。傳染病僅在潛伏期結束才變得明顯。

over-the-counter (OTC) drug a drug that may be purchased directly from a pharmacist without a doctor's pre-scription. Current government policy is to extend the range of OTC drugs: a number have already been derestricted (e.g. ibuprofen) and this trend is expected to increase, which will place an additional advisory responsibility on pharmacists.

非處方藥物 不用醫生的處方就可以直接從藥劑師處購買到的藥品。政府目前的政策是要擴大非處方藥物的範圍：有一部分藥已取消了限制（例如：布洛芬），這種趨勢有望增加。這會給藥劑師增加額外的咨詢義務。

ovi- (ovo-) *prefix denoting* an egg; ovum.

〔前綴〕蛋，卵

oviduct *n. see* Fallopian tube.

輸卵管 參閱 Fallopian tube。

ovulation *n.* the process by which an ovum is released from a mature *Graafian follicle. The fluid-filled follicle distends the surface of the ovary until a thin spot breaks down and the ovum floats out surrounded by a cluster of follicle cells (the cumulus oophoricus) and starts to travel down the Fallopian tube to the uterus. Ovulation is stimulated by

排卵 卵子從成熟的格雷夫卵泡中釋放的過程。充滿液體的卵泡使卵巢表面膨脹，在其薄弱點破裂，卵子被一團卵泡細胞（卵丘）包圍着流出，並開始由輸卵管下行至子宮。排卵在垂體前葉分泌的黃體生成素的刺激下發生。

the secretion of *luteinizing hormone by the anterior pituitary gland.

ovum (egg cell) *n.* the mature female sex cell (*see* gamete). The term is often applied to the secondary *oocyte although this is technically incorrect. The final stage of meiosis occurs only when the oocyte has been activated by fertilization.

卵子（卵細胞）　成熟的雌性性細胞（參閱 gamete）。此術語經常指次級卵母細胞，但從技術角度講，這是錯誤的。只有在受精激活初級卵母細胞時，才產生減數分裂的最後階段。

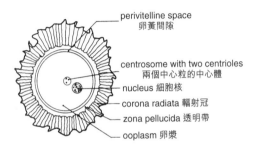

perivitelline space
卵黃間隙

centrosome with two centrioles
兩個中心粒的中心體

nucleus 細胞核

corona radiata 輻射冠

zona pellucida 透明帶

ooplasm 卵漿

A mature ovum (magnification about × 600)
成熟卵子（放大約 600 倍）

oxalic acid an extremely poisonous acid, $C_2H_2O_4$. It is a component of some bleaching powders and is found in many plants, including sorrel and the leaves of rhubarb. Oxalic acid is a powerful local irritant; when swallowed it produces burning sensations in the mouth and throat, vomiting of blood, breathing difficulties, and circulatory collapse. Treatment is with calcium lactate or other calcium salts, lime water, or milk.

草酸　劇毒性酸，$C_2H_2O_4$。是某些漂白粉的成分，存在於包括酸模和大黃葉在內的許多植物中。草酸是一種強力局部刺激藥。吞服時會產生口腔和咽喉的灼燒感、吐血、呼吸困難及循環性虛脫。治療應用乳酸鈣或其他鈣鹽、石灰水或奶汁。

oxalosis *n.* an inborn defect of metabolism causing deposition of oxalate in the kidneys and elsewhere and eventually leading to renal failure.

草酸血症　先天性代謝缺陷，引起草酸鹽在腎臟及其他部位沉積，最終導致腎衰。

oxaluria *n.* the presence in the urine of oxalic acid or oxalates, especially calcium oxalate. Excessive amounts of oxalates are excreted in *oxalosis.

草酸尿 尿中出現草酸或草酸鹽，特別是草酸鈣。草酸血症時，排出過量的草酸鹽。

oxatomide *n.* an *antihistamine drug used to treat hay fever. It is administered by mouth; possible side-effects include drowsiness and slowed reactions. Trade name: **Tinset**.

奧沙米特 用於治療枯草熱的一種抗組胺藥。口服。可能出現的副作用包括困倦和反應遲鈍。商品名：Tinset。

oxazepam *n.* a *benzodiazepine drug used to relieve anxiety and tension and for the treatment of alcoholism. It is administered by mouth and commonly causes drowsiness. *See also* tranquillizer.

奧沙西泮 用於解降焦慮和緊張、治療酒精中毒的一種苯二氮草類藥物。口服。常引起困倦。參閱 tranquillizer。

oxethazaine *n.* a local anaesthetic of skin and mucous membranes, used in indigestion mixtures (e.g. *Mucaine*) to relieve heartburn and pain due to inflammation of the digestive system. Mild side-effects, including dry mouth and nausea, may occur.

奧昔卡因 皮膚和黏膜的局部麻醉藥，以不易消化的混合物（例如黏卡因）形式使用，以解除消化系統炎症引起的胃灼熱和疼痛。可產生輕微副作用，包括口乾和惡心。

oxidase *n. see* oxidoreductase.

氧化酶 參閱 oxidoreductase。

oxidoreductase *n.* one of a group of enzymes that catalyse oxidation-reduction reactions. This class includes the enzymes formerly known either as *dehydrogenases* or as *oxidases*.

氧化還原酶 催化氧化-還原反應的一組酶。這類酶包括以前稱為脫氫酶或氧化酶的酶類。

oximeter *n.* an instrument for measuring the proportion of oxygenated haemoglobin (oxyhaemoglobin) in the blood.

血氧計 測量血液中充氧的血紅蛋白（氧合血紅蛋白）的比例的一種儀器。

oxprenolol *n.* a drug that controls the activity of the heart (*see* beta blocker), used to treat angina, high blood pressure, and abnormal heart rhythm. It is administered by mouth or injection; side-effects may include dizziness, drowsiness, headache, and digestive upsets. Trade name: **Trasicor**.

氧烯洛爾 控制心臟活動的藥物（參閱 beta blocker），用於治療心絞痛、高血壓及心律異常。口服或注射。副作用可包括頭暈、困倦、頭痛和消化不良。商品名：Trasicor。

oxybutinin *n.* a drug administered orally to reduce frequency and urgency of passing urine associated with an unstable bladder or instability of the *detrusor muscle of the bladder wall. It acts by relaxing the bladder muscle.

奧昔布寧　一種口服藥，用於降低與不穩定膀胱或由膀胱壁逼尿肌的不穩定相關的尿頻和尿急。通過鬆弛膀胱肌起作用。

oxycephaly (turricephaly) *n.* a deformity of the bones of the skull giving the head a pointed appearance. *See* craniosynosotosis. **–oxycephalic** *adj.*

尖頭（畸形）　頭呈尖形的顱骨畸形。參閱 craniosynostosis。

oxygen *n.* an odourless colourless gas that makes up one-fifth of the atmosphere. Oxygen is essential to most forms of life in that it combines chemically with glucose (or some other fuel) to provide energy for metabolic processes. In man oxygen is absorbed into the blood from air breathed into the lungs. Oxygen is administered therapeutically in various conditions in which the tissues are unable to obtain an adequate supply through the lungs (*see* oxygenator, (oxygen) tent). Symbol: O.

氧　占大氣的五分之一、無味、無色氣體。因為氧和葡萄糖（或其他能量）化合，為代謝過程提供能量，所以它對於大多數生命是必不可少的。在人類，氧從吸入肺的空氣中被吸收到血液中。組織通過肺得不到足夠氧氣供應時，可通過吸氧來治療（參閱 oxygenator，(oxygen) tent）。符號：O。

oxygenator *n.* a machine that oxygenates blood outside the body. It is used together with pumps to maintain the patient's circulation while he is undergoing open heart surgery (*see* heart lung machine) or to improve the circulation of a patient with heart or lung disorders that lower the amount of blood oxygen.

氧合器　體外血液充氧器械。患者接受心臟外科手術時，氧合器和泵一起使用，以維持其血液循環（參閱 heart lung machine），或病人患使血氧降低的心臟病或肺病時，用以增進血液循環。

oxygen deficit a physiological condition that exists in cells during periods of temporary oxygen shortage. During periods of violent exertion the body requires extra energy, which is obtained by the breakdown of glucose in the absence of oxygen, after the available oxygen has been used up. The breakdown products are acidic and cause muscle pain. The

缺氧　暫時缺氧時細胞中存在的生理狀態。身體劇烈運動時需要額外能量，這些能量在可獲得的氧氣耗盡後，在缺氧條件下通過分解葡萄糖獲取。分解物呈酸性，且引起肌肉疼痛，身體停止活動後，必須有供消除分解產物的氧（叫氧債）。

oxygen required to get rid of the break-down products (called the oxygen deficit) must be made available after the exertion stops.

oxygen tent *see* tent.

氧幕　參閱 tent。

oxyhaemoglobin *n.* the bright-red substance formed when the pigment *haemoglobin in red blood cells combines reversibly with oxygen. Oxyhaemoglobin is the form in which oxygen is transported from the lungs to the tissues, where the oxygen is released. *Compare* methaemoglobin.

氧合血紅蛋白　紅細胞中的色素即血紅蛋白與氧可逆性地結合時形成的鮮紅色物質。氧合血紅蛋白是氧從肺輸送到各組織並被釋放的形式。與 methaemoglobin 對比。

oxymetazoline *n.* a *sympathomimetic drug administered as a nasal spray to treat nasal congestion. Possible side-effects include irritation of the nose, headache, fast pulse, and insomnia. Trade name: **Afrazine**.

羥甲唑啉　一種擬交感神經藥，作為鼻噴劑給藥，用於治療鼻阻塞。可能的副作用包括鼻刺激、頭痛、脈搏加快及失眠。商品名：Afrazine。

oxymetholone *n.* a synthetic male sex hormone with *anabolic effects. Trade name: **Anapolon 50**.

羥甲烯龍　具有組成代謝作用的合成雄性性激素。商品名：Anapolon 50。

oxyntic cells (parietal cells) cells of the *gastric glands that secrete hydrochloric acid in the fundic region of the stomach.

泌酸細胞（壁細胞）　位於胃基底部，分泌鹽酸的胃腺細胞。

oxytetracycline *n.* an *antibiotic used to treat infections caused by a wide variety of bacteria. It is administered by mouth or injection or applied to the skin in a cream; side-effects are those of the other *tetracyclines. Trade names: **Imperacin**, **Terramycin**.

土黴素　治療細菌感染的廣譜抗生素。口服或注射或作為膏劑塗抹於皮膚。副作用同其他四環素類藥。商品名：Imperacin，Terramycin。

oxytocic *n.* any agent that induces or accelerates labour by stimulating the muscles of the uterus to contract. *See also* oxytocin.

催產藥　刺激子宮肌收縮誘使或加速分娩的藥物。參閱 oxytocin。

oxytocin *n.* *a* hormone, released by the pituitary gland, that causes contraction of the uterus during labour and stimulates milk flow from the breasts by causing contraction of muscle fibres in the milk ducts. Pituitary extract (*Syntocinon*) is used to induce uterine contractions and to control or prevent postpartum haemorrhage.

縮宮素　垂體釋放的一種激素，可引起分娩期間子宮收縮，並通過使乳腺管內肌纖維收縮刺激乳汁分泌。垂體提取物（催產素）用於誘導子宮收縮及控制或預防產後出血。

oxyuriasis *n.* *see* enterobiasis.

蟯蟲病　參閱 enterobiasis。

Oxyuris *n.* *see* pinworm.

尖尾綫蟲屬　參閱 pinworm。

ozaena *n.* a disorder of the nose in which the mucous membranes inside the nose become atrophied, with the production of an offensive discharge and crusts.

臭鼻症　鼻黏膜萎縮，產生刺激性分泌物並結痂的疾病。

ozone *n.* a poisonous gas containing three oxygen atoms per molecule. Ozone is a very powerful oxidizing agent and is formed when oxygen or air is subjected to electric discharge. Ozone is found in the atmosphere at very high altitudes (the *ozone layer*) and is responsible for destroying a large proportion of the sun's ultraviolet radiation. Without this absorption by ozone the earth would be subjected to a lethal amount of ultraviolet radiation.

臭氧　每個分子中含三個氧原子的一種毒氣。臭氧是一種強氧化劑，氧或空氣受放電現象影響時形成。臭氧可見於大氣層的高層（臭氧層），臭氧層能破壞大量的太陽紫外綫輻射，如果沒有臭氧的這種吸收能力，地球會受到致命量的紫外綫輻射。

P

Pacchionian body *see* arachnoid villus.

蛛網膜粒　參閱 arachnoid villus。

pacemaker *n.* **1.** a device used to produce and maintain a normal heart rate in patients who have *heart block. The unit consists of a battery that

(1) 起搏器　心臟傳導阻滯患者用於產生並維持正常心率的裝置。起搏器由一個電池構成，電池通過一根絕緣電極綫

stimulates the heart through an insulated electrode wire attached to the surface of the ventricle (*epicardial pacemaker*) or lying in contact with the lining of the heart (*endocardial pacemaker*). A pacemaker may be used as a temporary measure with an external battery or it may be permanent, when the whole apparatus is surgically implanted under the skin. Some pacemakers stimulate the heart at a fixed rate; others sense when the natural heart rate falls below a predetermined value and then stimulate the heart (*demand pacemaker*). **2.** the part of the heart that regulates the rate at which it beats: the *sinoatrial node.

與心室的表面相連（心外膜起搏器）或與心內膜相接（心內膜起搏器）以刺激心臟。起搏器可以作為帶有外接電池的臨時措施，也可以是永久性的，此時整個裝置被手術包埋於皮下。有些起搏器勻速刺激心臟，而另外一些在自然心率低於預定值時產生感應，然後刺激心臟（按需要起搏器）。**(2)** **起搏點** 調節心率的心臟部分：竇房節。

pachy- *prefix denoting* **1.** thickening of a part or parts. **2.** the dura mater.

〔前綴〕**(1)** 部分增厚　**(2)** 硬腦（脊）膜

pachydactyly *n.* abnormal enlargement of the fingers and toes, cocurring either as a congenital abnormality or as part of an acquired disease (such as *acromegaly).

指（趾）肥大 指（趾）的異常增大，可以是先天畸形，也可以是後天疾病的一部分（例如肢端肥大症）。

pachyglossia *n.* abnormal thickness of the tongue.

舌肥厚 舌的異常增厚。

pachymeningitis *n.* inflammation of the dura mater, one of the membranes (meninges) covering the brain and spinal cord (*see* meningitis).

硬腦（脊）膜炎 覆蓋大腦和脊髓的膜，即硬腦脊膜的炎症（參閱 meningitis）。

pachymeninx *n.* the *dura mater, outermost of the three meninges.

硬腦（脊）膜 三層腦膜中的最外層。

pachyonychia congenita a rare inherited condition characterized by thickening of the nails.

先天性甲肥厚 以指（趾）甲增厚為特點的一種罕見的遺傳疾病。

pachysomia *n.* thickening of parts of the body, which occurs in certain diseases.

軀體肥厚 某些疾病中出現的身體某些部分增厚。

pachytene *n.* the third stage of the first prophase of *meiosis, in which *crossing over begins.

粗綫期 減數分裂前期第一期的第三階段。在此期間染色體開始交換。

Pacinian corpuscles sensory receptors for touch in the skin, consisting of sensory nerve endings surrounded by capsules of membrane in 'onion-skin' layers. They are especially sensitive to changes in pressure and so detect vibration particularly well.

帕西尼小體，環層小體 皮膚中的觸覺感受器，由「洋葱皮」層中的膜囊包繞着的感覺神經末梢構成。它們對壓力變化很敏感，可很好地探知震動。

pack *n.* a pad of folded moistened material, such as cotton-wool, applied to the body or inserted into a cavity.

敷料 一種摺疊並弄濕的材料塊，如脱脂棉。用於包敷體表或填塞腔洞。

packed cell volume (haematocrit) the volume of the red cells (erythrocytes) in blood, expressed as a fraction of the total volume of the blood. The packed cell volume is determined by centrifuging blood in a tube and measuring the height of the red-cell column as a fraction of the total.

血細胞比容 血液中紅細胞的容積。用紅細胞占整個血液容積的分數表示。測定方法是把試管中的血液離心並作為總血量的百分比測量細胞柱高度。

pad *n.* cotton-wool, foam rubber, or other material used to protect a part of the body from friction, bruising, or other unwanted contact.

墊 用於保護身體的一部分避免受磨擦、挫傷或其他不必要接觸的脱脂棉、泡沫或其他材料。

paed- (paedo-) *prefix denoting* children.

〔前綴〕**兒童**

paederasty *n.* *sodomy with a boy or a young man.

雞姦兒童 雞姦男性兒童或男性青少年。

paediatrics *n.* the general medicine of childhood. Handling the sick child requires a special approach at every age from birth (or premature birth) to adolescence and also a proper understanding of parents. It also requires detailed knowledge of genetics, obstetrics, psychological development, management of handicaps at home and in school, and effects of social conditions on child

兒科學 兒科醫學的總稱。處理從出生（或早產）到青春期各階段的患兒都需要有特殊方法，並需要得到家長的正確理解。也需具備遺傳學、產科學、心理發育、家庭和學校對殘疾兒童的護理及社會環境對兒童健康的影響等方面的詳盡知識。與兒科學所有這些方面相關的預防措施是公共衞生醫

health. The preventive measures associated with all these aspects of paediatrics are the concern of *public health physicians and *community paediatricians. *See also* child health clinic. **–paediatrician** *n*.

師和社區兒科醫師所關注的事。參閱 child health clinic。

paedodontics *n*. the branch of dentistry concerned with the care and treatment of children's teeth.

兒童牙科學 涉及兒童牙齒護理及治療的牙科分支。

paedophilia *n*. sexual attraction to children (of either sex). Sexual activity with any children under the age of 16 is illegal in the UK. The condition is usually caused by psychological and social factors, which affect the development of sexuality. Paedophiles may seek treatment because of society's disapproval: *behaviour therapy can be used, or the sexual drive can be reduced by drug treatment. **–paedophile** *n*. **–paedophilic** *adj*.

戀童癖 對兒童產生的性吸引（可以是男性或女性兒童）。在英國，和 16 歲以下的兒童發生性關係是違法的。此病常由影響性慾發育的心理和社會因素引起。患者可能因社會反對就醫。可用行為療法治療或用藥療降低性衝動。

Paget's disease 1. a chronic disease of bones, occurring in the elderly and most frequently affecting the skull, backbone, pelvis, and long bones. Affected bones become thickened and their structure disorganized: X-rays reveal patchy *sclerosis. There are often no symptoms, but pain, deformity, and fracture can occur. Medical name: **osteitis deformans**. **2.** a malignant condition of the nipple, resembling eczema in appearance, associated with underlying infiltrating cancer of the breast. *See also* breast cancer. **3.** an uncommon condition of the vulva characterized by an epithelial lesion that histologically resembles the lesion of Paget's disease of the nipple. It may be associated with locally invasive *adenocarcinomas of the surrounding skin, as well as tumours at other sites.

佩吉特病 **(1) 變形性骨炎** 慢性骨病，發生於老年人，常影響顱骨、脊柱、骨盆和長骨。受累骨變厚，結構受破壞。X 綫下可見斑狀硬化。常無症狀，但可出現疼痛、畸形和骨折。醫學名：致密性骨炎，硬化性骨炎。**(2) 乳頭乳暈炎性癌變** 乳頭的惡性病變，外觀類似於濕疹，併發於潛伏的乳房浸潤癌。參閱 breast cancer。**(3) 外陰炎性癌變** 外陰的罕見疾病，特點為組織學上類似於乳頭乳暈性癌變的上皮損害。可併發周圍皮膚局部侵入性腺癌以及其他部位的腫瘤。

pain clinic a clinic that specializes in techniques of long-term pain relief. Pain clinics are usually directed by anaesthetists.

疼痛門診 專門從事除解長期疼痛技術的門診。疼痛門診常由麻醉師指導。

paint *n.* (in pharmacy) a liquid preparation that is applied to the skin or mucous membranes. Paints usually contain antiseptics, astringents, caustics, or analgesics.

塗劑 （藥劑學）塗於皮膚或黏膜的一種液體藥劑。常含有消毒劑、收斂劑、腐蝕劑或鎮痛藥。

palaeo- *prefix denoting* **1.** ancient. **2.** primitive.

〔前綴〕**(1)** 古，老，舊 **(2)** 原始的，初級的

palaeocerebellum *n.* the anterior lobe of the cerebellum. In evolutionary terms it is one of the earliest parts of the hindbrain to develop in mammals.

舊小腦 小腦的前葉。在進化意義上，它是哺乳動物後腦發育最早的部分。

palaeopathology *n.* the study of the diseases of man and other animals in prehistoric times, from examination of their bones or other remains. By examining the bones of specimens of Neanderthal man it has been discovered that spinal arthritis was a disease that existed at least 50,000 years ago.

古生物病理學 借助於檢查史前人類或其他動物的骨或其他遺骸研究其疾病的科學。通過檢查尼安德特人的骨標本，人們發現脊柱關節炎是一種至少五萬年前就已存在的疾病。

palaeostriatum *n. see* pallidum.

舊紋狀體 參閱 pallidum。

palaeothalamus *n.* the anterior and central part of the *thalamus, older in evolutionary terms than the lateral part, the neothalamus, which is well developed in apes and man.

舊丘腦 丘腦的前部及中部，在進化意義上比側部，即新丘腦，要陳舊些，新丘腦在人類與猿類發育良好。

palate *n.* the roof of the mouth, which separates the mouth from the nasal cavity and consists of two portions. The *hard palate*, at the front of the mouth, is formed by processes of the maxillae and palatine bones and is covered by mucous membrane. The *soft palate*, further back, is a movable fold of mucous membrane that tapers at the back of the mouth to

腭 口腔頂部，它將口腔與鼻腔分開，由兩部分組成。硬腭位於口腔的前方，由上頜骨突和腭骨構成，並被黏膜覆蓋。軟腭位於遠後部，是可移動的黏膜皺襞，皺襞在口腔後部變窄，形成一個組織的肉質懸垂瓣——懸雍垂。

form a fleshy hanging flap of tissue – the *uvula*.

palatine bone either of a pair of approximately L-shaped bones of the face that contribute to the hard *palate, the nasal cavity, and the orbits. *See* skull.

腭骨　面部的一對近似於 L 形的骨，參與構成硬腭、鼻腔和眼窩。參閱 skull。

palato- *prefix denoting* **1.** the palate. **2.** the palatine bone.

〔前綴〕**(1)** 腭　**(2)** 腭骨

palatoplasty *n.* plastic surgery of the roof of the mouth, usually to correct cleft palate or other defects present at birth.

腭成形術　口腔頂部的整形手術，常用於矯正出生時存在的腭裂或其他缺陷。

palatorrhaphy *n. see* staphylorrhaphy.

腭裂縫合術　參閱 staphylorrhaphy。

pali- (palin-) *prefix denoting* repetition or recurrence.

〔前綴〕重複，復發

palilalia *n.* a disorder of speech in which a word spoken by the individual is rapidly and involuntarily repeated. It is seen, with other tics, in the *Gilles de la Tourette syndrome. It is also encountered when encephalitis or other processes damage the *extrapyramidal system of the brain.

言語重複　一種語言障礙，患者把一個詞講得很快，且不自主地重複。和其他抽搐一起見於圖雷特綜合徵。腦炎或其他疾病引起腦椎體外系統受損時也可出現言語重複。

palindromic *adj.* relapsing: describing diseases or symptoms that recur or get worse.

復發的，再發的，回歸的　描述反覆發作或惡化的疾病。

palingraphia *n.* a disorder of writing in which words and letters are repeated. It is a feature of acquired brain disease, such as stroke.

書寫重複　重複單詞和字母的一種書寫障礙。是後天腦疾病，例如中風的一個特徵。

paliphrasia *n.* repetition of phrases while speaking: a form of *stammering or a kind of *tic.

言語重複　講話時反覆用某些短語：一種口吃或抽搐。

palliative *n.* a medicine that gives temporary relief from the symptoms of a

姑息劑　可以暫時解除疾病症狀但不能治癒疾病的一種藥。

disease but does not actually cure the disease. Palliatives are often used in the treatment of such diseases as cancer.

姑息劑常用於治療如癌症這樣的疾病。

pallidectomy *n.* a neurosurgical operation to destroy or modify the effects of the globus pallidus (*see* basal ganglia). This operation was used for the relief of *parkinsonism and other conditions in which involuntary movements are prominent.

蒼白球切開術 破壞或調節蒼白球（參閱 basal ganglia）作用的神經外科手術。此手術用於解除帕金森綜合徵和其他持久性不自主運動疾病。

pallidum (palaeostriatum) *n.* one of the dense collections of grey matter, deep in each cerebral hemisphere, that go to make up the *basal ganglia.

蒼白球 大腦灰質密集匯合之一，位於每側腦半球深部，構成基底神經節。

pallium *n.* the outer wall of the cerebral hemisphere as it appears in the early stages of evolution of the mammalian brain. In the modern brain it corresponds to the *cerebral cortex.

大腦蒼白質 哺乳動物大腦進化早期產生的腦半球外壁。在現代大腦中，它相當於大腦皮質。

pallor *n.* abnormal paleness of the skin, due to reduced blood flow or lack of normal pigments. Pallor may be associated with an indoor mode of life; it may also indicate shock, anaemia, cancer, or other diseases.

蒼白 血液流動減小或缺少正常色素引起的皮膚異常發白。蒼白可能與室內生活模式相關。也可以是休克、貧血、癌症或其他疾病的表現。

palmitic acid *see* fatty acid.

軟脂酸 參閱 fatty acid。

palpation *n.* the process of examining part of the body by careful feeling with the hands and fingertips. Using palpation it is possible, in many cases, to distinguish between swellings that are solid and those that are cystic (*see* fluctuation). Palpation is also used to discover the presence of a fetus in the uterus (*see* ballottement).

觸診 用手或指尖仔細觸摸檢查身體部位的過程。在許多病例中，用觸診能區別實性腫物與囊體腫物（參閱 fluctuation）。觸診也用於檢查子宮內存在的胎兒（參閱 ballottement）。

palpebral *adj.* relating to the eyelid (palpebra).

瞼的 與眼瞼相關的。

palpitation *n.* an awareness of the heart-beat. This is normal with fear, emotion, or exertion. It may also be a symptom of neurosis, arrhythmias, heart disease, and overactivity of the circulation (as in thyrotoxicosis).

心悸 覺察到心跳。恐懼、激動或用力過度時出現這種現象屬於正常。也可以是神經質、心律不齊、心臟病和血流過速（如在甲狀腺毒症中）的症狀。

palsy *n.* paralysis. This archaic word is retained in compound terms, such as *Bell's palsy, *cerebral palsy, and *Todd's palsy.

麻痺 這個過時的詞在複合術語中得以保留，例如貝爾麻痺、大腦性麻痺和托德麻痺。

paludism *n. see* malaria.

瘧疾 參閱 malaria。

pan- (pant(o)-) *prefix denoting* all; every: hence (in medicine) affecting all parts of an organ or the body; generalized.

〔前綴〕全部，廣泛 所有，每個，因此（醫學）影響器官或身體的所有部分；普遍性的。

panacea *n.* a medicine said to be a cure for all diseases and disorders, no matter what their nature. Unfortunately panaceas do not exist, despite the claims of many patent medicine manufacturers.

萬應藥 據說無論疾病性質如何，均可治愈的一種藥物。儘管許多專利藥品製造商宣稱已製造出此藥，但此藥並不存在。

Panadol *n. see* paracetamol.

醋氨酚 參閱 paracetamol。

pancarditis *n. see* endomyocarditis.

全心炎 參閱 endomyocarditis。

Pancoast syndrome pain and paralysis involving the lower branches of the brachial plexus due to infiltration by a malignant tumour of the apical region of the lung. *Horner's syndrome is also present.

潘科斯特綜合徵 臂叢下分支疼痛及癱瘓，病因是肺頂端區域惡性腫瘤的浸潤。也伴有霍納綜合徵。

pancreas *n.* a compound gland, about 15 cm long, that lies behind the stomach. One end lies in the curve of the duodenum; the other end touches the spleen. It is composed of clusters (*acini*) of cells that secrete *pancreatic juice. This contains a number of enzymes concerned in digestion. The juice drains into small

胰腺 長約15 cm，位於胃後的復合腺。一端位於十二指腸的彎曲部，另一端與脾相接。胰腺由分泌胰液的細胞團（腺泡）構成。胰液含有許多消化酶。胰液排入通向胰管的小導管。小導管與總導管相連，分泌液流入十二指腸。胰泡中分

ducts that open into the *pancreatic duct*. This unites with the common *bile duct and the secretions pass into the duodenum. Interspersed among the acini are the *islets of Langerhans – isolated groups of cells that secrete the hormones *insulin and *glucagon into the bloodstream.

布有胰島——向血液中分泌胰島素和高血糖素等激素的孤立細胞團。

pancreas divisum a congenital abnormality in which the pancreas develops in two parts draining separately into the duodenum, the small ventral pancreas through the main ampulla and the larger dorsal pancreas through an accessory papilla. In rare instances this is associated with recurrent abdominal pain, probably due to inadequate drainage of the dorsal pancreas. Diagnosis is made by *ERCP.

胰腺分離　一種先天性畸形，胰腺分兩部分發育，分別排入十二指腸，小的腹胰通過主胰管，大的背胰通過副胰管排入十二指腸。偶爾會併發反覆性腹痛，可能由背胰排泄不足所致。用內窺鏡逆行性胰管道造影術可以診斷。

pancreatectomy *n.* surgical removal of the pancreas. *Total pancreatectomy (Whipple's operation)* involves the entire gland and part of the duodenum. In *subtotal pancreatectomy* most of the gland is removed, usually leaving a small part close to the duodenum. In *partial pancreatectomy* only a portion of the gland is removed. The operations are performed for tumours in the gland or because of chronic or relapsing *pancreatitis. After total or subtotal pancreatectomy it is necessary to administer pancreatic enzymes with food to aid its digestion and insulin injections to replace that normally secreted by the gland.

胰腺切除術　手術切除胰腺。胰腺全切術（惠普爾手術）涉及整個胰腺和部分十二指腸。胰腺次全切除術切除大部分胰腺，通常保留靠近十二指腸的一小部分。胰腺部分切除術僅切除部分胰腺。胰腺腫瘤或慢性或反覆性胰腺炎時作胰腺切除術。胰腺全切術或次全切術之後，有必要在進食時服用胰酶以幫助消化並注射胰島素以代替胰腺的正常分泌。

pancreatic juice the digestive juice secreted by the *pancreas. Its production is stimulated by hormones secreted by the duodenum, which in turn is stimulated by contact with food from the stomach. If the duodenum produces the

胰液　胰腺分泌的消化液。其產生受十二指腸分泌的激素的刺激。該激素又受到與胃中食物接觸的刺激。如果十二指腸產生腸促胰液素，胰液就會含有大量的中和胃酸性物質的碳

hormone *secretin the pancreatic juice contains a large amount of sodium bicarbonate, which neutralizes the acidity of the stomach contents. Another hormone (see cholecystokinin) stimulates the production of a juice rich in digestive enzymes, including trypsinogen and chymotrypsinogen (which are converted to *trypsin and *chymotrypsin in the duodenum), *amylase, *lipase, and *maltase.

酸氫鈉。另外一種激素（參閱 cholecystokinin）刺激產生富含消化酶的液體，其中包括胰蛋白酶原和胰凝乳蛋白酶原（它們在十二指腸內被轉化為胰蛋白酶和胰凝乳蛋白酶）、澱粉酶、脂酶和麥牙糖酶。

pancreatin n. an extract obtained from the *pancreas, containing the pancreatic enzymes. Pancreatin is administered to treat conditions in which pancreatic secretion is deficient; for example, in pancreatitis.

胰酶 從胰腺中獲得的含有胰腺酶的提取物。用於治療胰分泌不足疾病，例如胰腺炎。

pancreatitis n. inflammation of the pancreas. *Acute pancreatitis* is a sudden illness in which the patient experiences severe pain in the upper abdomen and back, with shock; its cause is not always discovered, but it may be associated with gallstones or alcoholism. It may be mistaken for a perforated peptic ulcer but differs from this condition in that the level of the enzyme *amylase in the blood is raised. The main complication is the formation of a *pseudocyst. Treatment consists of intravenous feeding (no food or drink should be given by mouth), and *anticholinergic drugs. *Relapsing pancreatitis*, in which the above symptoms are recurrent and less severe, may be associated with gallstones or alcoholism; prevention is by removal of gallstones and avoidance of alcohol and fat. Operations may be done to improve drainage of the pancreatic duct. *Chronic pancreatitis* may produce symptoms similar to relapsing pancreatitis or may be painless; it leads to pancreatic failure causing *malabsorption and *diabetes mellitus. The pancreas often becomes calcified, producing

胰腺炎 胰腺的炎症。急性胰腺炎是一種突發病，患者會感到上腹及背部劇痛，伴有休克，病因不明確，可能與膽結石和酗酒有關。此病可以被誤診為十二指腸穿孔，但與十二指腸穿孔不同，因為血液中澱粉酶水平會增高。主要的併發症是形成假性囊腫。治療包括靜脈進食（不能經口腔進食或飲水）和使用抗膽鹼能藥。反覆性胰腺炎時上述症狀反覆發作，但不太嚴重。可能與膽石或酗酒有關。預防採取膽石切除和避免飲酒及食用脂肪。可手術增進胰管排液能力。慢性胰腺炎症狀與反覆性胰腺炎類似或可無痛；會導致胰腺衰竭，造成營養吸收不良和糖尿病。胰腺常會鈣化，X 綫片上可見陰影。營養吸收不良用低脂食物附加胰酶治療。糖尿病用胰島素治療。

visible shadowing on X-rays. The malabsorption is treated by a low-fat diet with pancreatic enzyme supplements, and the diabetes with insulin.

pancreatogram *n.* a radiographic image of the pancreatic ducts obtained by injecting a contrast medium into them by direct puncture under *ultrasound guidance, at the time of laparotomy or by *ERCP.

胰腺圖 剖腹術或內窺鏡逆行性胰膽管造影術時，在超聲波的指導下，直接穿刺胰腺注射造影劑所獲得的放射圖像。

pancreatotomy *n.* surgical opening of the duct of the pancreas in order to inspect the duct, to join the duct to the intestine, or to inject contrast material in order to obtain X-ray pictures of the duct system.

胰切開術 為了檢查胰管，把胰管和腸連接起來或注射造影劑以獲得胰系統的 X 綫片而切開胰管。

pancreozymin *n.* the name originally given to the fraction of the hormone *cholecystokinin that acts on the pancreas.

促胰酶素 作用於胰腺的縮膽囊素的舊名。

pancytopenia *n.* a simultaneous decrease in the numbers of red cells (*anaemia), white cells (*neutropenia), and platelets (*thrombocytopenia) in the blood. It occurs in a variety of disorders, including aplastic *anaemias, *hypersplenism, and tumours of the bone marrow.

全血細胞減少 血液中紅細胞（貧血）、白細胞（中性白細胞減少症）和血小板（血小板減少症）數量同時下降，出現於再生障礙性貧血、脾功能亢進和骨髓瘤等疾病中。

pandemic *n.* an *epidemic so widely spread that vast numbers of people in different countries are affected. The Black Death, the epidemic plague that ravaged Europe in the fourteenth century and killed over one third of the population, was a classical pandemic. AIDS is currently considered to be pandemic. **–pandemic** *adj.*

大流行病 不同國家中大量人受感染的流行病。黑死病是14世紀在歐洲猖獗的流行性瘟疫，造成1/3人口死亡，是典型的大流行病。艾滋病目前被認為是大流行病。

panic disorder a condition featuring recurrent brief episodes of acute distress,

驚慌病 特點為反覆發作的短期急性焦慮、思維紊亂和擔心

mental confusion, and fear of impending death. The heart beats rapidly, breathing is deep and fast, and sweating occurs. Overbreathing (hyperventilation) often makes the attack worse. These panic attacks usually occur about twice a week but may be more frequent and they are especially common in people with *agoraphobia. The condition tends to run in families and appears to be an organic disorder with a strong psychological component. Treatment is with *antidepressant drugs, especially the tricyclic group, and *MAO inhibitors. *Behaviour therapy can also be helpful.

死亡臨頭的一種疾病。患者心跳加速、呼吸急促和大汗淋漓。呼吸過快（換氣過度）常加劇發作。通常一周發生兩次，但可更多，且常見於曠野恐怖患者。此病趨向於在家中發作。表現為帶有強烈心理成分的器質性病變。治療使用抗抑鬱類藥，特別是三環類藥物及MAO抑制劑，行為療法亦有幫助。

panmixis *n.* random mating within a population, i.e. when there is no selection of partners on religious, racial, social, or other grounds.

隨機交配 人口的隨意配偶，即在不受宗教、種族、社會或其他因素影響的條件下選擇配偶。

panniculitis *n.* inflammation of the layer of fat beneath the skin, leading to multiple tender nodules in the legs and trunk.

脂膜炎 皮下脂肪層的炎症，可導致下肢及軀幹中出現多發性觸痛結節。

panniculus *n.* a membranous sheet of tissue. For example, the *panniculus adiposus* is the fatty layer of tissue underlying the skin.

膜 組織的膜狀表層。例如：脂膜是皮下脂肪層組織。

pannus *n.* invasion of the outer layers of the cornea of the eye by tissue containing many blood vessels, which grows in from the conjunctiva. It is seen as a result of inflammation of the cornea or conjunctiva, particularly in *trachoma.

血管翳，角膜翳 角膜外層受到從結膜中生長出來的、含許多血管的組織的侵襲。它被看作是角膜或結膜炎症，特別是沙眼的結果。

panophthalmitis *n.* inflammation involving the whole of the interior of the eye.

全眼球炎 涉及整個眼內部的炎症。

Panstrongylus *n.* a genus of large blood-sucking bugs (*see* reduviid). *P. megistus* is important in transmitting *Chagas' disease to man in Brazil.

錐蝽屬 大吸血臭蟲屬（參閱 reduviid）。在巴西，大錐蝽屬是傳播恰加斯病的重要途徑。

pant- (panto-) *prefix. see* pan-.

〔前綴〕總，全，泛　參閱 pan-。

pantothenic acid a B vitamin that is a constituent of *coenzyme A. It plays an important role in the transfer of acetyl groups in the body. Pantothenic acid is widely distributed in food and a deficiency is therefore unlikely to occur.

泛酸　一種 B 族維生素，輔酶 A的一種成分。在體內乙醯基的轉移中起重要作用。泛酸廣泛分布於食品，因此不大可能產生泛酸缺乏。

pantropic *adj.* describing a virus that can invade and affect many different tissues of the body, for example the nerves, skin, or liver, without showing a special affinity for any one of them.

泛向的　描述能夠侵入和影響身體許多組織的病毒，例如它可以侵犯並影響神經、皮膚或肝臟，不對任何一個組織表現出特殊的親和力。

papain *n.* a preparation that contains one or more protein-digesting enzymes. It is obtained from the pawpaw fruit and is used as a digestant.

番木瓜酶　含一種或多種蛋白質消化酶的藥劑。番木瓜酶從番木瓜汁中提取，用作消化劑。

Papanicolaou test (Pap test) *see* cervical smear.

帕帕尼克拉烏試驗　參閱 cervical smear。

papaverine *n.* an alkaloid, derived from opium, that relaxes smooth muscle. It is administered by injection as a preanaesthetic medication, usually in conjunction with *morphine. It may cause abnormal heart rate.

罌粟鹼　從阿片中提取的一種生物鹼，能鬆弛平滑肌。常和嗎啡一起作為前驅麻醉藥注射。可引起心律異常。

papilla *n.* (*pl.* **papillae**) any small nipple-shaped protuberance. Several different kinds of papillae occur on the *tongue, in association with the taste buds. The *optic papilla* is an alternative name for the *optic disc.

乳頭　乳頭狀小隆起。舌上生長有與味蕾相關的各種形式的乳頭。視神經乳頭是視神經盤的別稱。

papillitis *n.* inflammation of the first part of the optic nerve (the optic disc or optic papilla), i.e. where the nerve leaves the eyeball.

視神經乳頭炎　視神經第一部分（視神經盤或視神經乳頭），即神經自眼球的發出點的炎症。

papilloedema *n.* swelling of the first part of the optic nerve (the optic disc or optic papilla).

視神經乳頭水腫　視神經第一部分（視神經盤或視神經乳頭）的腫脹。

papilloma *n.* a benign nipple-like growth on the surface of skin or mucous membrane. Examples include *basal-cell papillomas* (*see* (seborrhoeic) keratosis) and *bladder papillomas*. **–papillomatous** *adj.*

乳頭狀瘤 皮膚或黏膜表面的良性乳頭狀生長物。例如基部細胞乳頭狀瘤（參閱 (seborrhoeic) keratosis）和膀胱乳頭狀瘤。

papillomatosis *n.* a condition in which many *papillomas grow on an area of skin or mucous membrane.

乳頭狀瘤病 皮膚或黏膜表面生長許多乳頭狀瘤的疾病。

papillotomy *n.* the operation of cutting the *ampulla of Vater to widen its outlet in order to improve bile drainage and allow the passage of stones from the common bile duct. It is usually performed using a diathermy wire through a *duodenoscope following *ERCP.

十二指腸乳頭切開術 手術切開十二指腸法特壺腹以擴大其出口，便於增加膽汁引流，使膽石能從普通膽管中通過。十二指腸乳頭切開術常為內窺鏡逆行性胰膽管造影術後通過十二指腸鏡用一根導管金屬綫進行。

papovavirus *n.* one of a group of small DNA-containing viruses producing tumours in animals (subgroup *polyomaviruses*) and in animals and man (subgroup *papillomaviruses*). *See also* human papillomavirus.

乳多泡病毒 在動物（多瘤病毒亞族）和動物及人類（乳頭病毒亞族）中造成腫瘤的含DNA的一組小病毒。參閱 human papillomavirus。

Pappataci fever *see* sandfly fever.

白蛉熱 參閱 sandfly fever。

papule *n.* a small raised spot on the skin, less than 5 mm in diameter.

丘疹 皮膚表面生長的直徑不足 5 mm 的小隆起。

papulo- *prefix denoting* a papule or pimple.

〔前綴〕 丘疹，膿疱

papulosquamous *adj.* describing a rash that is both papular and scaly.

丘疹鱗屑性的 描述既是丘疹又是鱗屑的皮疹。

para- *prefix denoting* **1.** beside or close to. Example: *paranasal* (near the nasal cavity). **2.** resembling. Example: *paradysentery* (a mild form of dysentery). **3.** abnormal. Example: *paralalia* (abnormal speech).

〔前綴〕 **(1)** 旁，附近 例如鼻旁的（靠近鼻腔）。**(2)** 類，副，似 例如：副痢疾（痢疾的輕微形式）。**(3)** 異常，倒錯，錯亂 例如：構音倒錯（語言異常）。

para-aminobenzoic acid a naturally occurring drug used in lotions and creams to prevent sunburn.

對氨苯甲酸 在洗劑和乳膏中使用的一種天然藥物。

para-aminosalicylic acid (PAS) a drug, chemically related to aspirin, used – in conjunction with isoniazid or streptomycin – to treat various types of tuberculosis. It is administered by mouth and commonly causes nausea, vomiting, diarrhoea, and rashes.

對氨水楊酸 化學上與阿司匹林相關的一種藥物，和異煙肼或鏈黴素共同使用治療各種結核病。口服，常引起惡心、嘔吐、腹瀉和皮疹。

paracentesis n. tapping: the process of drawing off excess fluid from a part of the body through a hollow needle or *cannula.

穿刺術 穿刺放液；用空心針或插管從身體某一部分引出積液的過程。

paracetamol (acetaminophen) n. an *analgesic drug that also reduces fever. It is used to treat mild or moderate pain, such as headache, toothache, and rheumatism. It is administered by mouth and may cause digestive upsets; overdosage causes liver damage. Trade names: **Calpol**, **Panadol**, **Panaleve**.

對乙酰氨基酚 同時具有退熱作用的鎮痛藥。用於治療輕度或中度疼痛，例如頭痛、牙痛和風濕病。口服，可引起消化不良；過量用藥會引起肝損害。商品名： Calpol，Panadol，Panaleve。

paracholia n. Archaic. disordered bile secretion.

泌膽障礙 （舊稱）膽汁分泌障礙。

Paracoccidioides n. a genus of yeast-like fungi causing infection of the skin and mucous membranes. The species *P. brasiliensis* causes a chronic skin disease, South American *blastomycosis.

芽生菌屬 引起皮膚和黏膜感染的酵母樣真菌屬。巴西芽生菌屬引起一種慢性皮膚病，即南美芽生菌病。

paracrine adj. describing a hormone that is secreted by an endocrine gland and affects the function of nearby cells, rather than being transported distally by the blood or lymph.

鄰泌激素 一種由內分泌腺分泌，影響鄰近細胞功能，而不是被血液或淋巴輸送到末梢的激素。

paracusis n. any abnormality of hearing.

聽覺倒錯 聽覺的任何異常。

paradidymis n. the vestigial remains of part of the embryonic *mesonephros

旁睾 見於成人睾丸附近的胚胎期中腎部分的退化器官的殘

that are found near the testis of the adult. Some of the mesonephric collecting tubules persist as the functional *vasa efferentia but the rest degenerate almost completely. A similar vestigial structure (the *paroophoron*) is found in females.

餘。中腎中某些集合管作為功能性輸出管繼續存在，而其餘的則幾乎完全退化。在女性可以發現類似結構（卵巢旁體）。

paradox *n.* (in *family therapy) a surprising interpretation or suggestion made in the course of therapy in order to demonstrate the relationship between a psychological symptom and a system of family relationships. For example, a child might be told to go on stealing from his parents because their concern about the symptom is all that is keeping their marriage intact.

佯謬奇異說法 （家庭療法）為了表明心理症狀和家庭體系之間的關係，在治療過程中所作的奇異解釋或暗示。例如可能會告知孩子要不斷地從其父母處偷竊，因為他們對此症狀的關注是唯一保持他們的婚姻關係的東西。

paradoxical breathing breathing movements in which the chest wall moves in on inspiration and out on expiration, in reverse of the normal movements. It may be seen in children with respiratory distress of any cause, which leads to indrawing of the intercostal spaces during inspiration. Patients with chronic airways obstruction also show indrawing of the lower ribs during inspiration, due to the distorted action of a depressed and flattened diaphragm. Crush injuries of the chest, with fractured ribs and sternum, can lead to a severe degree of paradoxical breathing.

反常呼吸 胸壁吸氣時向內運動，呼氣時向外運動，正好與正常運動相反的呼吸運動。見於任何原因所致的呼吸困難患兒，呼吸困難導致吸氣時肋間隙向內運動。慢性氣道阻塞患者因為膈膜受抑制和變平的扭曲作用，吸氣時也會表現出下肋骨向外運動。伴有肋骨和胸骨骨折的胸部壓碎性外傷可導致重症反常呼吸。

paraesthesiae *pl. n.* spontaneously occurring abnormal tingling sensations sometimes described as *pins and needles*. They may be symptoms of partial damage to a peripheral nerve, such as that caused by external pressure on the affected part, but can also result from damage to sensory fibres in the spinal cord. *Compare* dysaesthesiae.

感覺異常 自發產生的異常刺痛感，有時叫針刺感。可能是周圍神經部分損傷的症狀，例如：受損部位受外界壓力影響引起，但也可由脊髓感覺神經受損引起。與 dysaesthesiae 對比。

paraffin *n.* one of a series of hydrocarbons derived from petroleum. *Paraffin*

石蠟 石油中衍化出的一系列碳氫化合物之一。固體石蠟是

wax (*hard paraffin*), a whitish mixture of solid hydrocarbons melting at 45–60 °C, is used in medicine mainly as a base for ointments; it is also used for *embedding specimens for microscopical study. *Liquid paraffin* is a mineral oil, which has been used as a laxative.

固體碳氫化合物的一種白色混合物。熔點在45~60°C，在醫學中主要用作藥膏的基質，也可用於包埋標本供顯微鏡檢查。液體石蠟是一種礦物油，用作輕瀉劑。

paraganglion *n.* one of the small oval masses of cells found in the walls of the ganglia of the sympathetic nervous system, near the spinal cord. They are *chromaffin cells, like those of the adrenal gland, and may secrete adrenaline.

副神經節 見於脊髓附近交感神經系統節內壁中的小卵形細胞團。和腎上腺細胞一樣，它們是嗜鉻組織細胞，可分泌腎上腺素。

parageusia (parageusis) *n.* abnormality of the sense of taste.

味覺異常

paragonimiasis (endemic haemoptysis) *n.* a tropical disease that occurrs principally in the Far East, caused by the presence of the fluke *Paragonimus westermani* in the lungs. The infection is acquired by eating inadequately cooked shellfish, such as crayfish and crabs. Symptoms resemble those of chronic *bronchitis, including the coughing up of blood and difficulty in breathing (dyspnoea). Paragonimiasis is treated with the drugs bithionol and chloroquine.

並殖吸蟲病（寄生蟲性咯血） 主要發生在遠東地區的熱帶疾病，病因是肺中存在衛斯特曼並殖吸蟲。通過吃沒有烹熟的水生貝殼類動物，例如蝲蛄和蟹，引起感染。症狀類似於慢性支氣管炎，包括咳血和呼吸困難。用硫雙二氯酚和氯奎治療。

Paragonimus *n.* a genus of large tropical parasitic *flukes that are particularly prevalent in the Far East. The adults of *P. westermani* live in the lungs of man, where they cause destruction and bleeding of the tissues (*see* paragonimiasis). However, they may also be found in other organs of the body. Eggs are passed out in the sputum and the larvae undergo their development in two other hosts, a snail and a crab.

並殖吸蟲屬 主要在遠東地區流行的大的熱帶寄生蟲屬。衛斯特曼並殖吸蟲成蟲寄生於人類肺中，可引起這些組織的破壞和出血（參閱 paragonimiasis）。但牠們也見於人的其他器官。蟲卵隨痰排出。幼蟲在其他兩個宿主即蝸牛和蟹中發育。

paragranuloma *n.* an old term for one of the types of *Hodgkin's disease. It is

類肉芽腫 霍奇金病的一種類型的舊稱，現稱淋巴細胞主導

now known as *lymphocyte-predominant Hodgkin's disease* and has the best prognosis of all the types.

paragraphia *n.* a disorder of writing, involving the omission or transposition of letters or of whole words. The appearance of this in adult life is usually due to damage to the brain. In childhood it usually reflects a developmental delay in learning to write correctly.

parainfluenza viruses a group of large RNA-containing viruses that cause infections of the respiratory tract producing mild influenza-like symptoms. They are included in the paramyxovirus group (*see* myxovirus).

paraldehyde *n.* a *hypnotic and *anticonvulsant drug used to induce sleep in mental patients and to control convulsions in tetanus. It is administered by mouth, injection, or in suppositories; side-effects may include digestive upsets and, in large doses, prolonged unconsciousness. Both *tolerance and *dependence may result from prolonged use of the drug.

paralysis *n.* muscle weakness that varies in its extent, its severity, and the degree of *spasticity or flaccidity according to the nature of the underlying disease and its distribution in the brain, spinal cord, peripheral nerves, or muscles. *See also* diplegia, hemiplegia, paraplegia, poliomyelitis. **–paralytic** *adj.*

paramedian *adj.* situated close to or beside the *median plane.

paramedical *adj.* describing or relating to the professions closely linked to the medical profession and working in

型霍奇金病，在所有類型中預後最好。

書寫倒錯　一種書寫錯亂，字母或整個單詞被忽略或位置被顛倒。成年人中出現這種現象常由大腦受損引起。在兒童，常為學習書寫能力發育遲緩的表現。

副流感病毒　引起呼吸道感染產生輕度流感樣症狀的一組大型含 RNA 病毒。屬於副黏液病毒組（參閱 myxovirus）。

三聚乙醛　一種安眠和抗驚厥藥，用於誘使精神病人睡眠和控制破傷風病人抽搐。口服、注射或作為栓劑給藥。副作用可包括消化不良，大劑量使用時可產生長時間昏迷。長期使用可產生耐受性和藥物依賴。

麻痺、癱瘓　肌肉無力，因潛伏疾病的性質及其在大腦、脊髓、周圍神經或肌肉中的分布、肌無力範圍、嚴重程度、痙攣或鬆弛程度各不相同。參閱 diplegia，hemiplegia，paraplegia，poliomyelitis。

正中旁的　位於正中矢狀平面附近或旁邊的。

關係醫學的　描述與醫學專業密切相關並與之協同工作的專業。這些專業要求在某些領域

conjunction with them. Such professions require expert knowledge and experience in certain fields, but no medical degree. Paramedical personnel in a hospital include the radiographers, physiotherapists, and dietitians.

中具有專業知識和經驗，但沒有醫學學位。醫院內關係醫學工作者包括放射攝影師、理療師和營養師。

paramesonephric duct (Müllerian duct) either of the paired ducts that form adjacent to the mesonephric ducts in the embryo. In the female these ducts develop into the Fallopian tubes, uterus, and part of the vagina. However, in the male they degenerate almost completely.

副中腎管（米勒管） 胚胎期中腎管附近形成的一對導管之一。在女性，這些導管發育成輸卵管、子宮和陰道的一部分，而在男性，他們幾乎完全退化。

parameter *n*. (in medicine) a measurement of some factor, such as blood pressure, pulse rate, or haemoglobin level, that may have a bearing on the condition being investigated.

參數　（醫學）某種因素，例如血壓、脈搏或血紅蛋白水平的量度。它對正在觀察中的疾病有重要意義。

parametric test *see* significance.

參數試驗　參閱 significance。

parametritis (pelvic cellulitis) *n*. inflammation of the loose connective tissue and smooth muscle around the uterus (the parametrium). The condition may be associated with *puerperal infection.

子宮旁組織炎（盆腔蜂窩織炎） 子宮周圍的疏鬆結締組織和平滑肌炎（子宮旁組織）症。此病可能與產褥熱有關。

parametrium *n*. the layer of connective tissue surrounding the uterus.

子宮旁組織　圍繞子宮的結締組織層。

paramnesia *n*. a distorted memory, such as *confabulation or *déjà vu.

記憶錯誤　一種記憶障礙，例如虛談症或似曾相識症。

paramyoclonus multiplex a benign disorder of the nervous system that is characterized by brief and irregular twitchlike contractions of the muscles of the limbs and trunk.

多發性肌陣攣　神經系統的良性疾病，特點為四肢和軀幹肌肉的短暫、不規則抽搐狀收縮。

paramyotonia congenita a rare constitutional disorder in which prolonged contraction of muscle fibres (*see*

先天性肌強直病　一種罕見的器質性疾病，病人受冷時形成肌纖維長時間收縮（參閱

myotonia) develops when the patient is exposed to cold. This may be due to a disorder of potassium metabolism.

paramyxovirus *n. see* myxovirus.

paranasal sinuses the air-filled spaces, lined with mucous membrane, within some of the bones of the skull. They open into the nasal cavity, via the meatuses, and are named according to the bone in which they are situated. They comprise the *frontal sinuses* and the *maxillary sinuses* (one pair of each), the *ethmoid sinuses* (consisting of many spaces inside the ethmoid bone), and the two *sphenoid sinuses*. (See illustration.)

myotonia）。可能由鉀代謝病引起。

副黏液病毒 參閱 myxovirus。

鼻旁竇 位於顱骨某些骨中、襯有黏膜的充氣空隙。開口於鼻腔，穿過鼻道並根據其所處的骨命名。鼻旁竇包括額竇、上頜竇（每側各一對）、篩竇（由篩骨內許多空隙組成）和兩個蝶竇（見圖）。

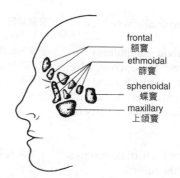

frontal
額竇
ethmoidal
篩竇
sphenoidal
蝶竇
maxillary
上頜竇

Paranasal sinuses projected to the surface
鼻旁竇表面投影

paraneoplastic syndrome signs or symptoms that may occur in a patient with cancer but are not due directly to local effects of the cancer cells. Removal of the cancer usually leads to resolution of the problem. An example is *myasthenia gravis secondary to a tumour of the thymus.

副腫瘤綜合徵 患者出現癌症體徵或症狀，但不是由癌細胞作用直接引起。切除腫瘤常會使問題得以解決。例如：重症肌無力的併發症胸腺瘤。

paranoia *n*. a mental disorder charcterized by *delusions organized into a system, without hallucinations or other marked symptoms of mental illness. It is a rare chronic condition; most people with such delusions will in time develop signs of other mental illness.

The same term is sometimes used more loosely for a state of mind in which the individual has a strong belief that he is persecuted by others. His behaviour is therefore suspicious and isolated. This can be a result of *personality disorder as well as mental illnesses causing *paranoid states.

偏執狂 一種精神性疾病，特點為系統性的妄想，不併發幻覺或其他明顯的精神病症狀。屬於一種罕見的慢性病；大多數有此類妄想的人會很快形成其他精神病體徵。

此術語有時泛指患者堅信他受到了他人迫害的精神狀態。其行為因此會多疑和孤癖。可能是人格障礙的結果。同時也是引起類偏狂狀態精神病的後果。

paranoid *adj*. **1.** describing a mental state characterized by fixed and logically elaborated *delusions. There are many causes, including paranoid *schizophrenia, *manic-depressive psychosis, organic psychoses such as *alcoholism, *paraphrenia, and severe emotional stress. **2.** describing a personality distinguished by such traits as excessive sensitivity to rejection by others, suspiciousness, hostility, and self-importance.

類偏狂 **(1)** 描寫一種精神狀態，其特徵為固定的和有邏輯的妄想。病因很多，包括類偏狂精神分裂症、躁狂抑鬱性精神病、酒精中毒、妄想癡呆和嚴重感情壓抑等器質性精神病。**(2)** 指一種性格，其突出特徵為對他人的拒絕態度過分敏感、多疑、對人存有敵意及狂妄自大。

paraparesis *n*. weakness of both legs, resulting from disease of the nervous system.

下肢輕癱 神經系統疾病導致的雙側下肢無力。

paraphasia *n*. a disorder of language in which unintended syllables, words, or phrases are interpolated in the patient's speech. A severe degree of paraphasia results in speech that is a meaningless jumble of words and sounds, called *jargon aphasia*.

言語錯亂 患者説話時加入多餘的音節、單詞或短語的一種語言障礙。重症言語錯亂會導致單詞和語音毫無意義、雜亂無章，稱作雜亂性失語。

paraphimosis *n*. retraction and constriction of the foreskin behind the glans penis. This occurs in some patients with *phimosis on erection of the penis: the tight foreskin cannot be drawn back

嵌頓包莖 包皮回縮至陰莖頭後部並形成狹窄。有些包莖患者陰莖勃起時產生包莖。緊繃的包皮不能回縮到陰莖頭，引起疼痛和腫脹。局部麻醉或全

over the glans and becomes painful and swollen. Manual replacement of the foreskin can usually be achieved under local or general anaesthesia, but *circumcision is required to prevent a recurrence.

麻時可施行包皮復位手法，但為了防止復發，需要進行包皮環切術。

paraphrenia *n.* a mental disorder characterized by systematic *delusions and prominent *hallucinations but without and other marked symptoms of mental illness. The only loss of contact with reality is in areas affected by the delusions and hallucinations. It is typically seen in the elderly and deaf. Some sufferers, if followed up over a period of years, eventually show other symptoms of *schizophrenia. It is therefore debatable whether paraphrenia constitutes a separate entity.

妄想癡呆　一種精神性疾病，其特點為系統性的妄想及明顯的幻覺，但無其他明顯的精神病症狀。與現實接觸的喪失僅限於受妄想和幻覺影響的部分。典型症狀見於老者和聾人。如果發生數年，有些患者會最終表現出精神分裂症和其他症狀。因此，妄想癡呆是否構成一個單獨的病類，尚有爭議。

paraplegia *n.* *paralysis of both legs, usually due to disease or injury of the spinal cord. It is often accompanied by loss of sensation below the level of the injury and disturbed bladder function. **–paraplegic** *adj.*, *n.*

截癱　雙側下肢癱瘓，常由脊髓疾病或受傷引起。常伴有受傷部位以下感覺喪失及膀胱功能受損。

paraprotein *n.* an abnormal protein of the *immunoglobulin series. Paraproteins appear in malignant disease of the spleen, bone marrow, liver, etc. Examples of paraproteins are *myeloma globulins, *Bence-Jones protein, and *macroglobulin.

病變蛋白，異型蛋白　免疫球蛋白系列的一種異常蛋白質。出現在脾、骨髓和肝等的惡性病中。例如骨髓瘤球蛋白、本斯-瓊斯蛋白和巨球蛋白等。

parapsoriasis *n.* a former name for the earliest phase of *mycosis fungoides.

類銀屑病　蕈樣真菌病最早期的舊稱。

parapsychology *n.* the study of *extrasensory perception, *psychokinesis, and other mental abilities that appear to defy natural law.

通靈學　研究超感知覺、精神驅動力及其他違反自然法則的精神能力的學科。

Paraquat *n. Trademark.* the chemical compound dimethyl dipyridilium, widely

百草枯　商標名。廣泛用作除草劑的二甲基二吡啶化合物。

used as a weed-killer. When swallowed it exerts its most serious effects upon the lungs, the tissues of which it destroys after a few days. Paraquat poisoning is almost invariably fatal.

parasite *n.* any living thing that lives in (*see* endoparasite) or on (*see* ectoparasite) another living organism (*see* host). The parasite, which may spend all or only part of its existence with the host, obtains food and/or shelter from the host and contributes nothing to its welfare. Some parasites cause irritation and interfere with bodily functions; others destroy host tissues and release toxins into the body, thus injuring health and causing disease. Human parasites include fungi, bacteria, viruses, protozoa, and worms. *See also* commensal, symbiosis. **–parasitic** *adj.*

parasiticide *n.* an agent that destroys parasites (excluding bacteria and fungi). *See also* acaricide, anthelmintic, trypanocide.

parasitology *n.* the study and science of parasites.

parasternal *adj.* situated close to the sternum. The *parasternal line* is an imaginary vertical line parallel to and midway between the lateral margin of the sternum and the vertical line through the nipple.

parasuicide *n.* a self-injuring act (such as an overdose of sleeping tablets) that is not motivated by a genuine wish to die. It differs from attempted *suicide in being common in young people who are distressed but not seriously mentally ill. However, many people who have acted in this way go on to attempt, or even to achieve, suicide. Help in sorting out their

吞服後會對肺造成最嚴重的影響，肺組織幾天後會被破壞。百草枯中毒幾乎都是致命的。

寄生蟲　任何生存在其他活的生物（參閱 host）體內（參閱 endoparasite）或體表（參閱 ectoparasite）的生物。寄生蟲可部分或終生與宿主在一起，從宿主處得到食物和／或處所，但對宿主沒有任何好處。有些寄生蟲引起刺激並干擾宿主的身體功能。其他的寄生蟲破壞宿主組織並向宿主體內釋放毒素，因此傷害宿主健康，引起疾病。人類寄生蟲包括真菌、細菌、病毒、原蟲和蠕蟲等。參閱 commensal，symbiosis。

殺寄生蟲藥　殺死寄生蟲（不包括細菌和真菌）的製劑。參閱 acaricide，anthelmintic，trypanocide。

寄生蟲學　研究寄生蟲的科學。

胸骨旁的　位於胸骨附近的。胸骨旁綫是一條假想的垂直綫，與胸骨外側緣和通過乳頭的垂直綫平行，並位於兩者中間。

假自殺　目的不在於求死的自傷行為（例如服用過量安眠片）。假自殺與企圖自殺不同，它常見於受壓抑，但沒有嚴重精神疾病的年輕人。但是許多有此行為者會反覆企圖自殺或甚至達到自殺目的。應幫助他們脫離困境。參閱 Samaritans。

difficulties should therefore be given. *See also* Samaritans.

parasympathetic nervous system one of the two divisions of the *autonomic nervous system, having fibres that leave the central nervous system from the brain and the lower portion of the spinal cord and are distributed to blood vessels, glands, and the majority of internal organs. The system works in balance with the *sympathetic nervous system, the actions of which it frequently opposes.

parasympatholytic *n.* a drug opposing the effects of the *parasympathetic nervous system. The actions of parasympatholytic drugs are *anticholinergic* (i.e. preventing acetylcholine from acting as a neurotransmitter); they include relaxation of smooth muscle, decreased secretion of saliva, sweat, and digestive juices, and dilation of the pupil of the eye. *Atropine and similar drugs have these effects; they are used in the treatment of peptic ulcers (e.g. *propantheline) and of parkinsonism (e.g. *benzhexol, *benztropine), to relieve spasm of smooth muscle (*see* spasmolytic), and as *mydriatics. Characteristic side-effects include dry mouth, thirst, blurred vision, dry skin, increased heart rate, and difficulty in urination.

parasympathomimetic *n.* a drug that has the effect of stimulating the *parasympathetic nervous system. The actions of parasympathomimetic drugs are *cholinergic* (resembling those of *acetylcholine) and include stimulation of skeletal muscle, *vasodilatation, depression of heart rate, increasing the tension of smooth muscle, increasing secretions (such as saliva), and constricting the pupil of the eye. They are used in

副交感神經系統 自主神經系統兩個分支中的一個。具有從大腦和脊髓下部分的中樞神經系統發出的神經纖維，分布於血管、腺體及大部分的內臟。此系統的功能和交感神經系統相互平衡，但作用常相反。

抗副交感神經藥 對抗副交感神經系統作用的藥物。作用是抗膽鹼能的（即防止乙醯膽鹼發揮神經遞質的作用）；包括鬆弛平滑肌、減少唾液、汗液和消化液的分泌及擴張瞳孔等。阿托品及類似藥物有這些作用；用於治療消化性潰瘍（如丙胺太林）和帕金森綜合徵（例如苯海索、苄扎托品）、解除平滑肌痙攣（參閱 spasmolytic）並作為擴瞳藥。典型副作用包括口乾、口渴、視力模糊、皮膚乾燥、心率加速及排尿困難。

擬副交感神經藥 刺激副交感神經系統作用藥物。具有膽鹼能的作用（類似於乙醯膽鹼的作用），包括刺激骨骼肌、擴張血管、降低心率、增加平滑肌張力、增加分泌（如唾液）及縮小瞳孔等。這些藥物用於治療重症肌無力（參閱 anticholinesterase）、青光眼（參閱 miotic）、某些心臟和血液循環疾病（例如卡巴膽鹼）和

the treatment of *myasthenia gravis (*see* anticholinesterase), glaucoma (*see* miotic), and some heart and circulatory conditions (e.g. *carbachol) and to restore intestinal and bladder function after surgery (e.g. *bethanechol).

手術後恢復腸及膀胱功能（例如烏拉膽鹼）。

paratenon *n.* the tissue of a tendon sheath that fills up spaces round the tendon.

腱旁組織　填充腱周圍空隙的腱鞘組織。

parathion *n.* an organic phosphorus compound, used as a pesticide, that causes poisoning when inhaled, ingested, or absorbed through the skin. Like several other organic phosphorus compounds it attacks, the enzyme *cholinesterase and causes excessive stimulation of the parasympathetic nervous system. The symptoms are headache, sweating, salivation, lacrimation, vomiting, diarrhoea, and muscular spasms. Treatment is by administration of *atropine.

對硫磷　用作殺蟲劑的一種有機磷化合物，吸入、攝入或經皮膚吸收後可引起中毒。像其他許多有機磷化合物一樣，它破壞膽鹼脂酶，引起副交感神經系統過度興奮。症狀包括頭痛、出汗、流涎、流淚、嘔吐、腹瀉和肌肉痙攣。用阿托品治療。

parathormone *n.* *see* parathyroid hormone.

甲狀旁腺素　參閱 parathyroid hormone。

parathyroidectomy *n.* surgical removal of the parathyroid glands usually as part of the treatment of *hyperparathyroidism.

甲狀旁腺切除術　手術切除甲狀旁腺，常作為治療甲狀旁腺機能亢進的一種方法。

parathyroid glands two pairs of yellowish-brown *endocrine glands that are situated behind, or sometimes embedded within, the *thyroid gland. They are stimulated to produce *parathyroid hormone by a decrease in the amount of calcium in the blood.

甲狀旁腺　位於甲狀腺之後，有時包埋於其中的兩對黃褐內分泌腺。甲狀旁腺在血液中鈣質降低的刺激下產生甲狀旁腺激素。

parathyroid hormone (parathormone) a hormone, synthesized and released by the parathyroid glands, that controls the distribution of calcium and phosphate in

甲狀旁腺激素　甲狀旁腺合成並釋放的一種激素，它控制血液中鈣和磷的分布。激素水平升高會導致鈣從骨向血液中轉

the body. A high level of the hormone causes transfer of calcium from the bones to the blood; a deficiency lowers blood calcium levels, causing *tetany. This condition may be treated by injections of the hormone. *Compare* thyrocalcitonin.

移。激素缺乏會降低血鈣水平，引起抽搐。此病可用注射甲狀旁腺激素治療。與 thyrocalcitonin 對比。

paratyphoid fever an infectious disease caused by the bacterium *Salmonella paratyphi A, B,* or *C.* Bacteria are spread in the faeces of patients or carriers, and outbreaks occur as a result of poor sanitation or unhygienic food-handling. After an incubation period of 1–10 days, symptoms, including diarrhoea, mild fever, and a pink rash on the chest, appear and last for about a week. Treatment with chloramphenicol is effective. Vaccination with *TAB provides temporary immunity against paratyphoid A and B.

副傷寒 甲、乙、丙型沙門傷寒菌引起的傳染病。細菌通過病人或帶菌者的糞便傳播。衛生條件差或食用不衛生的食物會導致疾病爆發。在 1~10 日潛伏期之後，腹瀉、低燒和胸部淡紅色丘疹等症狀會出現並持續大約一周。用氯黴素治療效果明顯。接種傷寒副傷寒菌苗可對甲、乙型傷寒產生暫時免疫。

pareidolia *n.* misperception of random stimuli as real things or people, as when faces are vividly seen in the flames of a fire.

幻想性錯覺 把隨意的刺激錯誤地感覺為真事或真人，例如在火焰中看到栩栩如生的面孔。

parenchyma *n.* the functional part of an organ, as opposed to the supporting tissue (*stroma*).

實質 器官的功能部分，與支持組織（基質）相對而言。

parental order *see* section 30 order.

親本法 參閱 section 30 order。

parenteral *adj.* administered by any way other than through the mouth: applied, for example, to the introduction of drugs or other agents into the body by injection.

腸胃外的 通過其他任何途徑而不是口腔給藥的，例如，通過注射向體內輸入藥物或其他製劑。

paresis *n.* muscular weakness caused by disease of the nervous system. It implies a lesser degree of weakness than *paralysis*, although the two words are often used interchangeably.

輕癱 神經系統疾病引起的肌無力。指比癱瘓程度較輕的肌無力，但這兩個詞常被交替使用。

paries *n*. (*pl.* **parietes**) **1.** the enveloping or surrounding part of an organ or other structure. **2.** the wall of a cavity.

parietal *adj*. **1.** of or relating to the inner walls of a body cavity, as opposed to the contents: applied particularly to the membranes lining a cavity (*see* peritoneum, pleura). **2.** of or relating to the parietal bone.

parietal cells either of a pair of bones forming the top and sides of the cranium. *See* skull.

parietal cells *see* oxyntic cells.

parietal lobe one of the major divisions of each cerebral hemisphere (*see* cerebrum), lying behind the frontal lobe, above the temporal lobe, and in front of the occipital lobe. It is thus beneath the crown of the skull. It contains the *sensory cortex and *association areas.

parity *n*. a term used to indicate the number of pregnancies a woman has had that have each resulted in the birth of an infant capable of survival. *See also* grand multiparity.

parkinsonism *n*. a clinical picture characterized by tremor, rigidity, and a poverty of spontaneous movements. The commonest symptom is tremor, which often affects one hand, spreading first to the leg on the same side and then to the other limbs. It is most pronounced in resting limbs, interfering with such actions as holding a cup. The patient has an expressionless face, an unmodulated voice, an increasing tendency to stoop, and a shuffling walk. Parkinsonism is a disease process affecting the basal ganglia of the brain and associated with

壁　**(1)** 器官或其他結構的包封部分或外圍部分。**(2)** 腔壁。

(1) 壁的　體腔內壁的或與之相關的,和其內容相對;特指腔室中的襯膜(參閱 peritoneum,pleura)。**(2) 頂骨的** 頂骨的或與之相關的。

頂骨　構成顱頂部及兩側的一對骨。參閱 skull。

壁細胞　參閱 oxyntic cells。

頂葉　每側腦半球(參閱 cerebrum)主要部分,位於額葉後部、顳葉上部和枕葉前部。因此在顱骨冠部之下。頂葉包含感覺皮層和聯想區。

經產狀況　用於指婦女懷孕次數並每次都產下活嬰的術語。參閱 grand multiparity。

帕金森綜合徵　以震顫、強直和自發運動缺乏為特點的臨床表現。最常見的症狀是震顫,常影響一隻手,首先擴散到同側下肢,然後擴散到其他肢體。休息時,症狀最明顯,妨礙像端杯子這樣的動作。病人面無表情,發音單調,有不斷加重的駝背傾向,拖步行走。帕金森綜合徵是影響大腦基底神經節並伴有神經遞質多巴胺缺乏的一種疾病過程。有時帕金森病(即一種和老齡相關的退化性疾病)和其他原因引起

a deficiency of the neurotransmitter *dopamine. Sometimes a distinction is made between *Parkinson's disease*, a degenerative disorder associated with ageing, and parkinsonism due to other causes. For example, it may be induced by the long-term use of *antipsychotic drugs and uncommonly it can be attributed to the late effects of *encephalitis or coal-gas poisoning or to *Wilson's disease. Relief of the symptoms may be obtained with anticholinergic drugs (*see* parasympatholytic), dopamine-receptor agonists (*see* dopamine), and *levodopa.

的帕金森綜合徵不同。例如它可能由長期使用抗精神病藥物誘發，偶爾可由腦炎、煤氣中毒或威爾遜病的後期作用引起。使用抗膽鹼藥（參閱 parasympatholytic）、多巴胺受體拮抗劑（參閱 dopamine）及左旋多巴來減輕症狀。

paromomycin *n*. an antibiotic, active against intestinal bacteria and amoebae, used mainly to treat dysentery. It is administered by mouth; side-effects include stomach pains, itching and heartburn.

巴龍黴素　對腸道細菌和阿米巴具有對抗作用的抗生素，主要用於治療痢疾。口服。副作用包括胃痛、瘙癢和胃灼熱等。

paronychia (whitlow) *n*. an inflamed swelling of the *nail folds. *Acute paronychia* is usually caused by infection with *Staphylococcus aureus*. *Chronic paronychia* occurs mainly in those who habitually engage in wet work; it is associated with secondary infection with *Candida albicans*. It is vital to keep the hands dry in order to control chronic paronychia.

甲溝炎　甲褶的炎性腫脹。急性甲溝炎常由金黃色葡萄球菌感染引起。慢性甲溝炎主要發生於日常從事潮濕作業的人，伴有繼發性念珠菌感染。為了控制慢性甲溝炎，保持雙手乾爽至關重要。

paroophoron *n*. the vestigial remains of part of the mesonephric duct in the female, situated next to each ovary. It is associated with a similar structure, the *epoophoron*. Both are without known function.

卵巢旁體　位於女性每側卵巢附近的中腎管的部分殘遺組織。它與一類似結構卵巢冠相關。兩者的功能尚不明晰。

parosmia *n*. any disorder of the sense of smell.

嗅覺倒錯　嗅覺的任何疾病。

parotid gland one of a pair of *salivary glands situated in front of each ear. The

腮腺　位於每只耳前部的一對唾液腺。腮腺管（斯滕森管）

openings of the parotid ducts (*Stensen's ducts*) are on the inner sides of the cheeks, opposite the second upper molar teeth.

開口於頰內側，與第二上磨牙相對。

parotitis *n.* inflammation of the parotid salivary glands. *See* mumps (infectious parotitis).

腮腺炎 腮涎腺的炎症。參閱 mumps (infectious parotitis)。

parous *adj.* having given birth to one or more children.

經產的 生過一個或更多孩子的。

paroxysm *n.* **1.** a sudden violent attack especially a spasm or convulsion. **2.** the abrupt worsening of symptoms or recurrence of disease. **–paroxysmal** *adj.*

(1) 發作 突然且猛烈地發作，特別是痙攣或抽搐。**(2) 陣發** 症狀突然加重或反覆發病。

parrot disease *see* psittacosis.

鸚鵡病 參閱 psittacosis。

pars *n.* a specific part of an organ or other structure, such as any of parts of the pituitary gland.

部分 器官或其他結構的一個特定部分，例如垂體的任何部分。

Part III accommodation accommodation provided by local authorities, under the terms of Part III of the National Assistance Act 1945, for those in need of care and attention whose income is below a certain minimum. Such accommodation replaced the workhouse, but the associated stigma – and dislike of the means test – deter many who are eligible from applying for help to which they are entitled.

第三部分收容所 （英國）依照國家救援法 (1945) 第三部分條文之規定，地方當局給那些收入低於某一最低標準的、需要治療和護理的人提供的收容所。這種收容所取代了濟貧院，但與之相關的壞名聲，以及厭惡調查其經濟狀況，使許多有權利申請得到救助的人對此敬而遠之。

parthenogenesis *n.* reproduction in which an organism develops from an unfertilized ovum. It is common in plants and occurs in some lower animals (e.g. aphids).

單性生殖 從一個未受精卵發育成生物體的繁殖。常見於植物並出現在某些低等動物（例如蚜蟲）中。

partially sighted register (in Britain) a list of persons who have poor sight but are not technically blind. In general their sight is adequate to permit the

弱視登記表 （英國）視力差但從技術角度講並非全盲人員的名單。一般來說，這些人的視力足以使他們從事需要一定視

performance of tasks for which some vision is essential. *Compare* blind register.

力的工作。與 blind register 對比。

partogram *n.* a graphic record of the course of labour.

產程圖 分娩過程的圖表記錄。

parturition *n.* childbirth. *See* labour.

分娩 參閱 labour。

parvi- *prefix denoting* small size.

〔前綴〕小

PAS *see* para-aminosalicylic acid.

對氨水楊酸 參閱 para-aminosalicylic acid。

pascal *n.* the *SI unit of pressure, equal to 1 newton per square metre. Symbol: Pa.

帕斯卡 壓力的國際單位，1 帕斯卡等於每平方米 1 牛頓。符號：Pa。

Paschen bodies particles that occur in the cells of skin rashes in patients with *cowpox or *smallpox; they are thought to be the virus particles.

帕申小體 牛痘和天花患者皮疹細胞中產生的微粒，它們被認為是病毒微粒。

passive movement movement not brought about by a patient's own efforts. Passive movements are induced by manipulation of the joints by a physiotherapist. They are useful in maintaining function when a patient has nerve or muscle disorders that prevent voluntary movement.

被動運動 非病人自己努力而產生的運動。被動運動是理療醫師推拿關節誘導產生的。病人患妨礙隨意運動的神經或肌肉疾病時，被動運動對維持功能很有用。

paste *n.* (in pharmacy) a medicinal preparation of a soft sticky consistency, which is applied externally.

糊劑 （藥劑學）外用的、軟而黏稠的藥劑。

Pasteurella a genus of small rodlike Gram-negative bacteria that are parasites of animals and man. The species *P. multocida* usually infects animals but may be transmitted to man through bites or scratches.

巴斯德菌屬 一種小桿狀革蘭氏陰性菌屬，寄生於動物和人。出血敗血性巴斯德菌屬常感染動物，但可通過咬傷或抓傷傳播給人。

pasteurization *n.* the treatment of milk by heating it to 65°C for 30 minutes, or to 72°C for 15 minutes, followed by rapid

巴斯德消毒法 把牛奶加熱至 65°C 維持 30 分鐘或至 72°C 維持 15 分鐘，然後快速冷

cooling, to kill such bacteria as those of tuberculosis and typhoid.

卻，以殺死諸如結核病及傷寒桿菌等細菌的處理方法。

pastille *n.* a medicinal preparation containing gelatine and glycerine, usually coated with sugar, that is dissolved in the mouth so that the medication is applied to the mouth or throat.

錠劑 一種含明膠和甘油的藥劑，常包於糖衣內，含服以便藥物作用於口腔或咽喉。

Patau syndrome a chromosome disorder in which there are three no. 13 chromosomes (instead of the usual two), causing mental retardation and defects in the heart, kidney, and scalp. Affected individuals rarely survive.

帕陶綜合徵 有三條第十三號染色體（而不是正常的兩條）的染色體疾病，引起智力低下和心臟、腎及頭皮缺陷。很少患者能存活。

patch test a test to discover which allergen is responsible for contact *dermatitis in a patient. Very low concentrations of common allergens (and any substances suspected of causing the dermatitis in the individual patient) are applied under a patch on the back. The patches are removed after 48 hours and the underlying skin is examined then and again after a further 48 hours. A positive test will show an eczematous reaction. The commonest allergens are nickel in women and chromium in men.

斑貼試驗 發現哪種過敏原引起接觸性皮炎的試驗。將濃度極低的普通過敏原（以及引起病人皮炎的任何可疑物質）塗於膠布貼在背上。48 小時後取掉膠布檢查此處皮膚，然後 48 小時後再重複一次。陽性試驗會呈現濕疹反應。最常見的過敏原在男性中是鎳，在女性中為鉻。

patella *n.* the lens-shaped bone that forms the kneecap. It is situated in front of the knee in the tendon of the quadriceps muscle of the thigh. *See also* sesamoid bone.

髕骨 構成膝蓋的透鏡形骨。髕骨位於膝蓋前方，與股四頭肌腱相連。參閱 sesamoid bone。

patellar reflex the knee jerk, in which stretching the muscle at the front of the thigh by tapping its tendon below the knee cap causes a *reflex contraction of the muscle, so that the leg kicks. This is a test of the connection between the sensory nerves attached to stretch receptors in the muscle, the spinal cord, and the motor neurones running from the

膝反射 叩擊膝蓋下部肌腱，使大腿前肌肉緊張，引起肌肉反射性收縮，腿向前踢。這是一種檢查肌肉牽張感受器、脊髓和從脊髓走向大腿肌肉的運動神經元之間聯繫的試驗，所有這些都涉及膝反射。疾病或損傷會導致膝反射缺失。

cord to the thigh muscle, all of which are involved in the reflex. Disease or damage may result in absence of the reflex.

patent ductus arteriosus *see* ductus arteriosus.

動脈導管　參閱 ductus arteriosus。

path- (patho-) *prefix denoting* disease. Example: *pathophobia* (morbid fear of).

〔前綴〕**病**　例如：疾病恐怖。

pathogen *n.* a microorganism, such as a bacterium, that parasitizes an animal (or plant) or man and produces a disease.

病原體　寄生於動物（或植物）或人、引起疾病的微生物。例如：細菌。

pathogenic *adj.* capable of causing disease. The term is applied to a parasitic microorganism (especially a bacterium) in relation to its host. **–pathogenicity** *n.*

致病性　能夠引起疾病的。此術語指寄生性微生物（特別是細菌）和其宿主的關係。

pathognomonic *adj.* describing a symptom or sign that is characteristic of or unique to a particular disease, the presence of such a sign or symptom allows positive diagnosis of the disease.

特殊病症的　描述某一疾病特徵性或獨有的症狀或體徵。這種體徵或症狀的出現可幫助確診。

pathological *adj.* relating to or arising from disease. For example, a pathological *fracture is one associated with disease of the bone.

病理性的　與疾病相關的或由疾病產生的。例如：病理性骨折與骨病有關。

pathology *n.* the study of disease processes with the aim of understanding their nature and causes. This is achieved by observing samples of blood, urine, faeces, and diseased tissue obtained from the living patient or at autopsy, by the use of X-rays, and by many other techniques. (*See* biopsy.) *Clinical pathology* is the application of the knowledge gained to the treatment of patients. **–pathologist** *n.*

病理學　研究疾病過程的科學，旨在理解疾病的性質和原因。通過觀察血、尿、糞便等標本及從患者活體或屍體解剖等獲得病變組織，使用 X 綫以及其他許多技術達到目的（參閱 biopsy）。臨床病理學指應用已獲得的知識治療病人。

-pathy *suffix denoting* **1.** disease. Example: *nephropathy* (of the kidney). **2.** therapy. Example: *osteopathy* (by manipulation).

〔前綴〕**(1)** **疾病**　例如：腎病。**(2)** **療法**　例如：骨療法（推拿術）。

pauciarthritis *n. see* arthritis.

少關節炎　參閱 arthritis。

pavementation (pavementing) *n.* the sticking of white blood cells to the linings of the finest blood vessels (capillaries) when inflammation occurs.

鋪壁　炎症發生時，白細胞黏附於最細小的血管（毛細血管）壁。

PCP *pneumocystis carinii* pneumonia. *See* Pneumocystis.

卡氏肺囊蟲肺炎　參閱 Pneumocystis。

PCR *see* polymerase chain reaction.

聚合酶鏈反應　參閱 polymerase chain reaction。

PDGF *see* growth factor.

血小板衍生生長因子　參閱 growth factor。

peau d'orange a dimpled appearance of the skin over a breast tumour, resembling the surface of an orange. The skin is thickened and the openings of hair follicles and sweat glands are enlarged.

橘皮現象　乳房腫瘤時皮膚的陷窩外觀，類似於橘子的表皮。皮膚變硬，毛孔及汗腺擴大。

pecten *n.* **1.** the middle section of the anal canal, below the anal valves (*see* anus). **2.** a sharp ridge on the upper branch of the pubis (part of the hip bone). **–pectineal** *adj.*

(1) 肛門梳　肛瓣下部肛管的中間部分（參閱 anus）。**(2) 恥骨梳**　恥骨上分支上的尖嵴（髖骨的一部分）。

pectoral *adj.* relating to the chest.

胸的　與胸相關的。

pectoral girdle *see* shoulder girdle.

肩岬帶　參閱 shoulder girdle。

pectoral muscles the chest muscles (see illustration). The *pectoralis major* is a large fan-shaped muscle that works over the shoulder joint, drawing the arm forward across the chest and rotating it medially. Beneath it, the *pectoralis minor* depresses the shoulder and draws the scapula down towards the chest.

胸肌　胸部肌肉（見圖）。胸大肌是一塊大的扇形肌肉，它在肩關節上起作用，牽拉手臂前移越過胸部，並向內旋轉。胸小肌位於胸大肌之下，它使肩關節下降，牽拉肩關節向下朝胸部運動。

pectoriloquy *n.* abnormal transmission of the patient's voice sounds through the chest wall so that they can be clearly

胸語言　病人的聲音通過胸壁異常傳播，以致用聽診器可以清楚地聽見聲音。耳語聲音

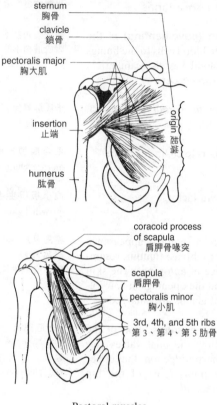

sternum 胸骨
clavicle 鎖骨
pectoralis major 胸大肌
insertion 止端
origin 起源
humerus 肱骨

coracoid process of scapula 肩胛骨喙突
scapula 肩胛骨
pectoralis minor 胸小肌
3rd, 4th, and 5th ribs 第3、第4、第5肋骨

Pectoral muscles
胸肌

heard through a stethoscope. Whispered sounds (*whispering pectoriloquy*) can be heard over the lung of a patient with pneumonia.

（低音胸語言）在肺炎患者的肺部可聽到。

pectus *n.* the chest or breast.

胸，乳

pectus carinatum *see* pigeon chest.

雞胸 參閱 pigeon chest。

pectus excavatum *see* funnel chest.

漏斗胸 參閱 funnel chest。

pedicle *n.* **1.** the narrow neck of tissue connecting some tumours to the normal tissue from which they have developed.

蒂 **(1)** 連接某些腫瘤與其賴以生長的正常組織的一種組織狹窄頸。**(2)**（整形外科）狹窄

2. (in plastic surgery) a narrow folded tube of skin by means of which a piece of skin used for grafting remains attached to its original site. A pedicle graft is used when the recipient site is unsuited to take an independent skin graft (for example, because of poor blood supply). *See also* flap, skin graft. **3.** (in anatomy) any slender stemlike process.

的皮膚摺疊管，用於移植的皮膚借助於它仍然依附於其原來的部位。接受植皮部位不適宜於獨立的皮膚移植時（例如：因為供血不足時），可使用蒂狀移植。參閱 flap，skin graft。**(3)**（解剖學）任何纖細的莖狀突起。

pediculicide *n.* an agent that kills lice; examples include *benzyl benzoate, *carbaryl, *lindane, *malathion, and *permethrin.

滅虱藥 殺滅虱子的藥物，例如苯甲酸苄酯、卡巴立、林旦、馬拉硫磷和苄氯菊酯。

Pediculoides (Pyemotes) *n.* a genus of widely distributed tiny predaceous mites. *P. ventricosus* occasionally attacks man and causes an allergic dermatitic called *grain itch*. This complaint most usually affects those people coming into contact with stored cereal products, such as hay and grain.

蒲蟎屬 分布廣泛的小捕食蟎屬。袋形虱蟎偶然侵襲人類，引起一種過敏性皮炎，即穀癢病。此病最常影響那些接觸倉貯穀物產品（例如乾草和穀物）的人。

pediculosis *n.* an infestation with lice, which causes intense itching; continued scratching by the patient may result in secondary bacterial infection of the skin. *Head lice* (*pediculosis humanis* var. *capitis*) are quite common in schoolchildren and do not indicate poor hygiene; they may be treated with *malathion or *carbaryl lotions. By contrast, *body lice* (*pediculosis corporis*) affect vagabonds and refugees; help is required from social services. *Pubic lice* (*Phthirus pubis*, the crab louse) are commonly sexually transmitted and respond to the same treatment as head lice.

虱病 感染虱子。可引起劇烈的瘙癢。病人不斷抓撓可導致皮膚繼發性細菌感染。頭虱常見於學齡兒童，並不能說明衛生條件差，可用馬拉硫磷或卡巴立洗液治療。相比之下，體虱侵襲流浪漢和難民；這些人需要社會服務的資助。陰虱（陰虱屬）常為性傳播疾病，治療方法和治療頭虱相同。

Pediculus *n.* a widely distributed genus of lice. There are two varieties of the species affecting man: *P. humanus capitis*, the head louse; and *P. humanus*

虱屬 分布廣泛的虱的一屬。侵襲人類的有兩個種類：頭虱和體虱。這些寄生蟲的出現會刺激皮膚（參閱 pediculo-

corporis, the body louse. The presence of these parasites can irritate the skin (*See* pediculosis), and in some parts of the world body lice are involved in transmitting *relapsing fever and *typhus.

sis），在世界有些地區，體虱傳播回歸熱和斑疹傷寒。

pedometer *n*. a small portable device that records the number of paces walked, and thus the approximate distance covered. A pedometer is usually attached to the leg or hung at the belt.

計步器，步數計 記錄走過的步數，因此可推算出行走的大約距離的小型便攜式裝備。計步器常繫在腿上或掛在皮帶上。

peduncle *n*. a narrow process or stalk-like structure, serving as a support or a connection. For example, the *middle cerebellar peduncle* connects the pons and cerebellum.

腳，蒂，莖 一狹窄突起或柄狀結構，起支持或連接作用。例如：小腦腳連接腦橋和小腦。

pellagra *n*. a nutritional disease due to a deficiency of *nicotinic acid (a B vitamin). Pellagra results from the consumption of a diet that is poor in either nicotinic acid or the amino acid tryptophan, from which nicotinic acid can be synthesized in the body. It is common in maize-eating communities. The symptoms of pellagra are scaly dermatitis on exposed surfaces, diarrhoea, and depression.

糙皮病 缺乏煙酸（一種維生素 B）造成的一種營養性疾病。糙皮病是因為攝取的食物中缺乏煙酸或色氨酸引起的，人體用色氨酸合成煙酸。糙皮病常發生於食用玉米的社區。症狀為暴露部位的脫屑性皮炎、腹瀉及抑鬱症。

pellicle *n*. a thin layer of skin, membrane, or any other substance.

表膜，表皮 一薄層的皮膚、膜或其他任何物質。

pelvic girdle (hip girdle) the bony structure to which the bones of the lower limbs are attached. It consists of the right and left *hip bones.

骨盆帶 下肢骨附着的骨結構。由左右髖骨組成。

pelvic inflammatory disease (PID) an acute or chronic condition in which the uterus, Fallopian tubes, and ovaries are infected. The inflammation is the result of infection spreading from an adjacent infected organ (such as the appendix) or ascending from the vagina; it may also

盆腔炎性疾病 子宮、輸卵管和卵巢受感染的一種急性或慢性疾病。炎症是鄰近受感染器官（例如：闌尾）炎症擴散的結果，或感染沿陰道上行造成。也可由血源性感染（例如結核病）引起。主要特徵是下

result from a blood-borne infection, such as tuberculosis. The main feature is lower abdominal pain that may, at times, be severe. An acute infection may respond to treatment with antibiotics, but in the chronic state, when pelvic *adhesions have developed, surgical removal of the diseased tissue may be necessary. Blocking of the Fallopian tubes is a common result of pelvic inflammatory disease.

pelvimetry *n.* the measurement of the four internal diameters of the pelvis (transverse, anteroposterior, left oblique, and right oblique). Pelvimetry helps in determining whether it will be possible for a fetus to be delivered in the normal way. Sufficient reduction of any one or more diameters may be an indication for Caesarean section.

pelvis *n.* (*pl.* **pelves**) **1.** the bony structure formed by the *hip bones, *sacrum, and *coccyx: the bony pelvis (see illustration). The hip bones are fused at the back to the sacrum to form a rigid

腹痛，有時會劇痛。急性炎症用抗生素治療效果明顯，慢性炎症中如果形成了骨盆黏連，需要手術切除病變組織。輸卵管阻塞是盆腔炎性疾病常見結果。

骨盆測量法 測量骨盆的四個內部直徑（橫徑、前後徑、左斜徑和右斜徑）。骨盆測量法有助於確定胎兒能否正常分娩。任何一個或多個直徑過分減小都預示着需要剖宮產手術。

(1) 骨盆 髖骨、骶骨和尾骨構成的骨結構（見圖）。髖骨在後方與骶骨融合形成堅硬的結構，保護下腹器官並為下肢骨和肌肉提供連接。**(2) 下腹**

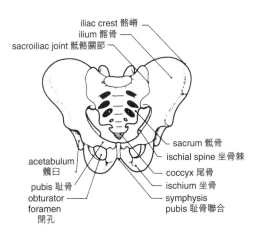

iliac crest 髂嵴
ilium 髂骨
sacroiliac joint 骶髂關節

sacrum 骶骨
ischial spine 坐骨棘
coccyx 尾骨
ischium 坐骨
symphysis pubis 耻骨聯合

acetabulum 髖臼
pubis 耻骨
obturator foramen 閉孔

The male pelvis (ventral view)
男性骨盆（前面觀）

structure that protects the organs of the lower abdomen and provides attachment for the bones and muscles of the lower limbs. **2.** the lower part of the abdomen. **3.** the cavity within the bony pelvis. **4.** any structure shaped like a basin, e.g. the expanded part of the ureter in the kidney (*renal pelvis.*) **–pelvic** *adj.*

部 **(3)** 骨盆內腔，盆腔 **(4)** 盆狀結構　任何盆狀結構，例如：輸尿管在腎臟中的增大部分（腎盂）。

pemoline *n.* a weak stimulant of the nervous system used to treat the *hyperkinetic syndrome in children. It is administered by mouth. Possible side-effects include headache, irritability, dizziness, sweating, palpitations, loss of appetite, weight loss, and dry mouth. Trade name: **volital**.

匹莫林　中樞神經系統弱興奮藥，用於治療兒童多動綜合徵。口服。副作用有頭痛、興奮、困倦、心悸、食慾不振、體重下降和口乾。商品名：Volital。

pemphigoid (bullous pemphigoid) *n.* a chronic itchy blistering disorder of the elderly. The blisters most commonly occur on the limbs and persist for several days, unlike those of *pemphigus. Pemphigoid is an *autoimmune disease and responds to treatment with corticosteroids or immunosuppressive drugs.

類天疱瘡（大疱性類天疱瘡）發生於老年人的慢性瘙癢疱瘡。與天疱瘡不同的是，類天疱瘡最常出現於四肢且可持續數日。類天疱瘡是一種自體免疫性疾病，用皮質類固醇或免疫抑制藥物治療，效果明顯。

pemphigus (pemphigus vulgaris) *n.* a rare but serious *autoimmune skin disease marked by successive outbreaks of blisters. The blisters are superficial and do not remain intact for long; the mouth and other mucous membranes, as well as the skin, are usually affected. A number of milder variants of the disease exist.

天疱瘡（尋常性天疱瘡）　一種罕見但嚴重的自體免疫性皮膚病，其特點為連續出現疱。疱為表面性的，會很快破裂。口腔及其他黏膜及皮膚常被感染。本病有許多症狀較輕的變型。

penetrance *n.* the frequency with which the characteristic controlled by a gene is seen in the individuals possessing it. Complete penetrance occurs when the characteristic is seen in all individuals known to possess the gene. If a percentage of individuals with the gene

外顯率　受某一個基因控制的特性在含該基因的個體中的出現頻率。當擁有該基因的所有個體中都有此特徵時，出現完全外顯率。如果帶有該基因的個體的百分比不能顯示其特點，外顯率則不完全。這樣，

do not show its effects, penetrance is incomplete. In this way a characteristic in a family may appear to 'skip' a generation.

家族的特點就會「跳過」一代人。

-penia *suffix denoting* lack or deficiency. Example: *neutropenia* (of neutrophils).

〔後綴〕**缺乏，減少** 例如中性白細胞減少症。

penicillamine *n*. a drug that binds metals and therefore aids their excretion (*see* chelating agent). It is used to treat *Wilson's disease, poisoning by metals such as lead, copper, and mercury, and severe rheumatoid arthritis. It is administered by mouth and commonly causes digestive upsets and allergic reactions. Trade names: **Distamine**, **Pendramine**.

青黴胺 與金屬結合，因此能幫助金屬排泄的藥物（參閱 chelating agent）。用於治療威爾遜病，鉛、銅、汞等金屬中毒及重症類風濕關節炎。口服。常引起消化不良及過敏反應。商品名：Distamine，Pendramine。

penicillin *n*. an *antibiotic that was derived from the mould *Penicillium rubrum* and first became available for treating bacterial infections in 1941. Since then, a number of naturally occurring penicillins have been developed to treat a wide variety of infections, notably *penicillin G* (*benzylpenicillin*), usually administered by injection but taken orally to treat dental abscesses, and *penicillin V* (*phenoxymethylpenicillin*), which is administered orally. There are few serious side-effects, but some patients are allergic to penicillin and develop such reactions as skin rashes, swelling of the throat, and fever. Similar drugs prepared from *Penicillium* moulds include *benethamine penicillin and *benzathine penicillin. All these penicillins are *beta-lactam antibiotics and are sensitive to penicillinase.

There are many antibiotics that are derived from the penicillins, including *amoxycillin, *ampicillin, *cloxacillin sodium, and *flucloxacillin; these are known as *semisynthetic penicillins*.

青黴素 從黴菌產黃青黴中提取的一種抗生素，1941 年首次用於治療細菌感染。從此以後，人類培養了許多自然產生的青黴素來治療各種感染，典型的有苄青黴素（青黴素 G），常注射給藥但可口服，用於治療牙膿腫，和口服苯氧甲基青黴素（青黴素 V）。嚴重副作用少見，但有些病人對青黴素過敏，會產生皮疹，咽喉腫脹及發熱。用青黴屬製成的類似藥劑有苄胺青黴素和苄星青黴素。所有這些青黴素都是β-內酰胺抗生素，對青黴素酶很敏感。

許多抗生素從青黴素衍生而來，其中包括阿莫西林、氨苄西林、鄰氯青黴素鈉和氟氯西林等，都是半合成青黴素。

penicillinase *n.* an enzyme, produced by some bacteria, that is capable of antagonizing the antibacterial action of penicillin and other *beta-lactam antibiotics. Purified penicillinase may be used to treat reactions to penicillin. It is also used in diagnostic tests to isolate microorganisms from the blood of patients receiving penicillin.

青黴素酶 某些細菌產生的一種酶，這種酶能夠對抗青黴素和其他 β-內醯胺抗生素藥物的抗菌作用。提純的青黴素酶可用於治療青黴素反應。也用於從使用青黴素患者的血液中分離微生物的診斷試驗。

Penicillium *n.* a genus of mouldlike fungi that commonly grow on decaying fruit, bread, or cheese. The species *P. rubrum* is the major natural source of the antibiotic *penicillin. Some species of *penicillium* are pathogenic to man, causing diseases of the skin and respiratory tract.

青黴屬 生長在腐爛水果、麵包或奶酪上的黴菌樣真菌屬。產黃青黴是生產抗生素青黴素的主要天然資源。有些青黴屬種類對人類有致病性，引起皮膚及呼吸道疾病。

penile prosthesis *see* prosthesis.

陰莖修復術 參閱 prosthesis。

penis *n.* the male organ that carries the *urethra, through which urine and semen are discharged (see illustration). Urination can occur in the normal hanging position. Most of the organ is composed of erectile tissue (*see* corpus

陰莖 帶有尿道的男性器官，尿液和精液通過它排出（見圖）。正常懸垂位置時可產生排尿。此器官的大部分由勃起組織（參閱 corpus cavernosum，corpus spongiosum）

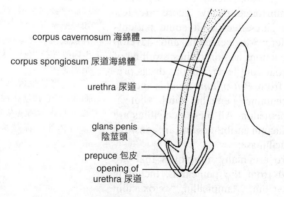

corpus cavernosum 海綿體
corpus spongiosum 尿道海綿體
urethra 尿道
glans penis 陰莖頭
prepuce 包皮
opening of urethra 尿道

The penis (median section)
陰莖（正中切面）

cavernosum, corpus spongiosum), which becomes filled with blood under conditions of sexual excitement so that the penis is erected. In this position it can act as a sexual organ, capable of entering the vagina and ejaculating semen. *See also* glans, prepuce.

組成，性興奮時，勃起組織充血，陰莖勃起。這時陰莖可以作為性器官，能夠進入陰道並射精。參閱 glans，prepuce。

pent- (penta-) *prefix denoting* five.

〔前綴〕五

pentaerythritol *n.* a drug that dilates blood vessels and is used in the treatment of angina and other heart conditions. It is administered by mouth and may cause headache and indigestion. Trade name: **Mycardol**.

季戊四醇　一種血管擴張藥，用於治療心絞痛及其他心臟病。口服，可引起頭痛和消化不良。商品名：Mycardol。

pentagastrin *n.* a synthetic hormone that has the same effects as *gastrin in stimulating the secretion of gastric juice from the stomach. It is injected to test for gastric secretion in the diagnosis of digestive disorders. Trade name: **Peptavlon**.

五肽胃泌素　一種合成激素，在刺激胃分泌消化液時，作用與胃泌素相同。診斷消化疾病時，注射用於檢查消化液。商品名：Peptavlon。

pentamidine *n.* a drug effective against protozoans and used in the treatment of *Pneumocystis carinii* pneumonia in AIDS patients, *trypanosomiasis, and *kala-azar. It is administered by injection or from an inhaler. Possible side-effects include low blood pressure, heart irregularity, low blood sugar (hypoglycaemia), low white blood cell count, and kidney damage. Trade names: **Pentam 300**, **Nebupent**.

噴他脒　一種能夠有效對抗原生動物的藥物，用於治療艾滋病人卡氏肺囊蟲肺炎、錐蟲病和黑熱病。注射或吸入給藥。副作用包括低血壓、心律不齊、低血糖、白細胞減少和腎損害。商品名：Pentam 300，Nebupent。

pentazocine *n.* a potent *analgesic drug used to relieve moderate or severe pain. It is administered by mouth, injection, or in suppositories; side-effects include dizziness and digestive upsets. Trade name: **Fortral**.

噴他佐　用於緩解中度或重度疼痛的一種強力鎮痛藥。口服，注射或栓劑給藥。副作用包括頭暈及消化不良。商品名：Fortral。

pentose *n.* a simple sugar with five carbon atoms: for example, ribose and xylose.

戊糖　帶有五個碳原子的單糖：例如核糖和木糖。

pentosuria *n.* an inborn defect of sugar metabolism causing abnormal excretion of pentose in the urine. There are no serious ill-effects.

Pentothal *n. see* thiopentone.

pepsin *n.* an enzyme in the stomach that begins the digestion of proteins by splitting them into peptones (*see* peptidase). It is produced by the action of hydrochloric acid on *pepsinogen*, which is secreted by the gastric glands. Once made, pepsin itself can act on pepsinogen to produce more pepsin.

pepsinogen *n. see* pepsin.

peptic *adj.* **1.** relating to pepsin. **2.** relating to digestion.

peptic ulcer a breach in the lining (mucosa) of the digestive tract produced by digestion of the mucosa by pepsin and acid. This may occur when pepsin and acid are present in abnormally high concentrations or when some other mechanism reduces the normal protective mechanisms of the mucosa; bile salts may play a part, especially in stomach ulcers. A peptic ulcer may be found in the oesophagus (*oesophageal ulcer*, which is associated with reflux *oesophagitis); the stomach (*see* gastric ulcer); duodenum (*see* duodenal ulcer); jejunum (*jejunal ulcer*, usually in the *Zollinger-Ellison syndrome); in a Meckel's *diverticulum; and close to a *gastroenterostomy (*stomal ulcer*, *anastomatic ulcer*, *marginal ulcer*).

peptidase *n.* one of a group of digestive enzymes that split proteins in the

戊糖尿　一種先天性糖代謝缺陷，引起尿中戊糖排泄異常。無嚴重的疾病後果。

硫噴妥鈉　參閱 thiopentone。

胃蛋白酶　一種胃酶，通過把蛋白質分解成蛋白腖開始消化蛋白質（參閱 peptidase）。胃蛋白酶是通過鹽酸對胃腺分泌的胃蛋白酶原的作用而產生的。胃蛋白酶一旦生成，本身就可以作用於胃蛋白酶原，生成更多的胃蛋白酶。

胃蛋白酶原　參閱 pepsin。

(1) 胃蛋白酶的　與胃蛋白酶相關的。**(2) 消化的**　與消化相關的。

消化性潰瘍　胃蛋白酶和胃酸對黏膜的消化作用而造成的消化道內壁（黏膜）的破壞。胃蛋白酶和胃酸濃度高於正常或其他機制降低了黏膜的正常保護作用時，會產生消化性潰瘍。膽汁酸鹽會起一定作用，特別是在胃潰瘍的形成中起作用。消化性潰瘍可見於食管（與食物返流性食管炎相關的食管潰瘍）、胃（參閱 gastric ulcer）、十二指腸（參閱 duodenal ulcer）、空腸（通常出現於佐-埃氏綜合徵中的空腸潰瘍）、梅克爾憩室及靠近施行過胃腸吻合術的地方（吻合口潰瘍、吻合處潰瘍和邊緣性潰瘍）。

肽酶　將胃和腸中的蛋白質分解成其構成成分氨基酸的一組

stomach and intestine into their constituent amino acids. The group is divided into the *endopeptidases and *exopeptidases.

peptide *n.* a molecule consisting of two or more *amino acids linked by bonds between the amino group (–NH) and the carboxyl group (–CO). This bond is known as a *peptide bond*. *See also* polypeptide.

peptone *n.* a large protein fragment produced by the action of enzymes on proteins in the first stages of protein digestion.

peptonuria *n.* the presence in the urine of *peptones, intermediate compounds formed during the digestion of proteins.

perception *n.* (in psychology) the process by which information about the world, as received by the senses, is analysed and made meaningful. Abnormalities of perception include *hallucinations, *illusions, and *agnosia.

percussion *n.* the technique of examining part of the body by tapping it with the fingers or an instrument (*plessor*) and sensing the resultant vibrations. With experience it is possible to detect the presence of abnormal solidification or enlargement in different organs and the presence of fluid, for example in the lungs.

percutaneous *adj.* through the skin: often applied to the route of administration of drugs in ointments, etc., which are absorbed through the skin.

percutaneous nephrolithotomy a technique of removing stones from the

消化酶之一。分為肽鏈內切酶和肽鏈外切酶。

肽 氨基團 (–NH) 以及羥基團 (–CO) 之間以鍵連接的由兩個或更多氨基酸組成的分子，這個鍵叫肽鍵。參閱 polypeptide。

蛋白腖 蛋白質消化第一階段中酶對蛋白質作用而產生的大的蛋白質碎片。

腖尿 尿中出現蛋白腖，蛋白腖是蛋白質消化過程中形成的中間化合物。

知覺 (心理學) 感覺器官接收到有關世界的信息、分析並賦予意義的過程。知覺異常包括幻覺、錯覺和失認症。

叩診 用手指或儀器 (叩診槌) 叩擊身體的一部分並感覺其產生的震動的檢查技術。如果檢查者有經驗，可探知不同器官中出現的異常實變或增大及出現積液，例如肺中出現積液。

經皮膚的 經過皮膚：常指以藥膏給藥為途徑等，藥物經皮膚被吸收。

經皮腎結石切除術 用一根導管提前在皮膚表面建立一個通

kidney via a *nephroscope passed into the kidney through a track from the skin surface previously established by the presence of a catheter.

往腎臟的通道，插入腎鏡，借助它從腎臟中取出腎石的技術。

percutaneous transhepatic cholangiopancreatography (PTC) a method for outlining the bile ducts and pancreatic ducts with radiopaque dyes, which are introduced by a catheter inserted into the ducts from the surface of the skin. *See* cholangiography.

經皮肝穿膽管胰造影術 把不透 X 綫染劑襯於膽管和胰腺管的方法，不透 X 綫染劑從插入皮膚表面下的導管引入體內。參閱 cholangiography。

perforation n. the creation of a hole in an organ, tissue, or tube. This may occur in the course of a disease (e.g. a *duodenal ulcer, colonic *diverticulitis, or stomach cancer), allowing the contents of the intestine to enter the peritoneal cavity, which causes acute inflammation (*peritonitis) with sudden severe abdominal pain and shock. Treatment is usually by surgical repair of the perforation, but conservative treatment with antibiotics may result in spontaneous healing. Perforation may also be caused accidentally be instruments – for example a gastroscope may perforate the stomach, a curette may perforate the uterus or by injury, for example to the eardrum.

穿孔 器官、組織或管道內孔的形成。可發生於疾病過程（例如十二指腸潰瘍，結腸憩室炎或胃癌等），使腸中物質進入腹腔，引起帶有突發性劇烈腹痛及休克的急性炎症（腹膜炎）。治療常採用穿孔手術修復，但用抗生素的保守療法可使穿孔自行愈合。穿孔偶然也可由使用儀器引起，例如：胃鏡可造成胃穿孔，刮匙可造成子宮穿孔，穿孔亦可由外傷引起，例如耳鼓室外傷引起穿孔。

perfusion n. **1.** the passage of fluid through a tissue, especially the passage of blood through the lung tissue to pick up oxygen from the air in the alveoli, which is brought there by *ventilation, and release carbon dioxide. If ventilation is impaired deoxygenated venous blood is returned to the general circulation. If perfusion is impaired insufficient gas exchange takes place. **2.** the deliberate introduction of fluid into a tissue, usually by injection into the blood vessels supplying the tissue.

灌注（法） **(1)** 液體流經組織，特別是血液流經肺組織，以便從肺泡中的空氣中獲得氧氣並釋放二氧化碳，空氣則是通過換氣被帶入肺泡的。如果換氣受損，脫氧的靜脈血就會返回血液循環。如果灌注受損會發生換氣不足。**(2)** 故意將液體引入組織，通常向給組織提供血液的血管中注射液體。

pergolide *n.* a drug that stimulates *dopamine receptors in the brain and is used in the treatment of *parkinsonism. It is administered by mouth. Possible side-effects include confusion, hallucinations, sleepiness, heart irregularity, nausea, breathing difficulties, and double vision. Trade name: **Celance**.

培高利特（硫丙麥角林） 一種刺激大腦中多巴胺受體的藥物，用於治療帕金森綜合徵。口服。副作用包括精神混亂、幻覺、嗜睡、心律不齊、惡心、呼吸困難及重視。商品名：Celance。

peri- *prefix denoting* near, around, or enclosing. Examples: *perianal* (around the anus); *pericardial* (around the heart); *peritonsillar* (around a tonsil).

〔前綴〕**附近，周圍** 例如：肛周的（肛門周圍），心包的（心臟周圍），扁桃體周的（扁桃體周圍）。

periadenitis *n.* inflammation of tissues surrounding a gland.

腺周炎 圍繞腺體的組織的炎症。

perianal haematoma (external haemorrhoid) a small painful swelling beside the anus, occurring after a bout of straining to pass faeces or coughing. Perianal haematomas are caused by the rupture of a small vein in the anus. They often heal spontaneously but occasionally rupture. Rarely this is followed by abscess formation. If severe pain continues, surgical removal can be undertaken. *See also* haemorrhoids.

肛門周圍血腫（外痔） 用力排大便或咳嗽之後，肛門附近產生的小的疼痛性腫脹。肛門周圍血腫由肛門中的小靜脈破裂引起。常可自愈，但偶然可破裂。很少出現膿腫。如果劇烈疼痛持久存在，應手術切除。參閱 haemorrhoids。

periapical *adj.* around an apex, particularly the apex of a tooth. The term is applied to bone surrounding the apex and to X-ray views of this area.

尖周的 尖（端）周圍的，特別是牙齒的尖端。此術語指尖（端）周圍的骨及 X 綫對此區域的圖像。

periarteritis nodosa *see* polyarteritis nodosa.

結節性動脈外膜炎 參閱 polyarteritis nodosa。

periarthritis *n.* inflammation of tissues around a joint capsule, including tendons and *bursae. *Chronic periarthritis*, which may be spontaneous or follow injury, is a common cause of pain and stiffness of the shoulder; it usually responds to local steroid injections or physiotherapy.

關節周炎 關節囊周圍組織，包括肌腱和黏液囊在內的炎症。慢性關節周炎可以是自發的或外傷之後產生。是肩關節疼痛和強直的常見原因。採用局部類固醇注射或理療常有效果。

pericard- (pericardio-) *prefix denoting* the pericardium.

〔前綴〕心包

pericardiectomy (pericardectomy) *n.* surgical removal of the membranous sac surrounding the heart (pericardium). It is used in the treatment of chronic constrictive pericarditis and chronic pericardial effusion (*see* pericarditis.)

心包切除術　手術切除包圍心臟的膜囊（心包）。用於治療慢性縮窄性心包炎和慢性心包積液（參閱 pericarditis）。

pericardiocentesis *n.* removal of excess fluid from within the sac (pericardium) surrounding the heart by means of needle *aspiration. *See* pericarditis, hydropericardium.

心包穿刺放液術　用針刺吸引術從包圍心臟的囊（心包）中排出多餘的積液。參閱 pericarditis，hydropericardium。

pericardiolysis *n.* the surgical separation of *adhesions between the heart and surrounding structures within the ribcage (*adherent pericardium*). The operation has now fallen into disuse.

心包鬆解術　手術分離胸腔內心臟與周圍組織的黏連物（黏連的心包）。此手術現已廢棄不用。

pericardiorrhaphy *n.* the repair of wounds in the membrane surrounding the heart (pericardium), such as those due to injury or surgery.

心包縫合術　修復包圍心臟的膜（心包）的創傷，例如：修復由外傷或手術造成的傷口。

pericardiostomy *n.* an operation in which the membranous sac around the heart is opened and the fluid within drained via a tube. It is sometimes used in the treatment of septic pericarditis.

心包造口術　打開包圍心臟的膜囊，用一根導管引流囊內液體的手術。有時用此術治療膿毒性心包炎。

pericardiotomy (pericardotomy) *n.* surgical opening or puncture of the membranous sac (pericardium) around the heart. It is required to gain access to the heart in heart surgery and to remove excess fluid from within the pericardium.

心包切開術　手術打開或穿刺包繞心臟的膜囊（心包）。心臟手術中要接近心臟或排出心包內過度積液時需要作心包切開術。

pericarditis *n.* acute or chronic inflammation of the membranous sac (pericardium) surrounding the heart. Pericarditis may be seen alone or as part of pancarditis (*see* endomyocarditis). It has numerous causes, including virus

心包炎　包繞心臟的膜囊（心包）的急性或慢性炎症。心包炎可單獨出現或作為全心炎的一部分出現（參閱 endomyocarditis）。病因眾多，包括病毒感染、尿毒症和癌症等。急

infections, uraemia, and cancer. *Acute pericarditis* is characterized by fever, chest pain, and a pericardial friction rub. Fluid may accumulate within the pericardial sac (*pericardial effusion*). Rarely, chronic thickening of the pericardium (*chronic constrictive pericarditis*) develops. This interferes with activity of the heart and has many features in common with *heart failure, including oedema, pleural effusions, ascites, and engorgement of the veins. Constrictive pericarditis most often results from tubercular infection.

The treatment of pericarditis is directed to the cause. Pericardial effusions may be aspirated by a needle inserted through the chest wall. Chronic constrictive pericarditis is treated by surgical removal of the pericardium (*pericardiectomy*).

pericardium *n.* the membrane surrounding the heart, consisting of two portions. The outer *fibrous pericardium* completely encloses the heart and is attached to the large blood vessels emerging from the heart. The internal *serous pericardium* is a closed sac of *serous membrane: the inner visceral portion (*epicardium*) is closely attached to the muscular heart wall and the outer parietal portion lines the fibrous pericardium. Within the sac is a very small amount of fluid, which prevents friction as the two surfaces slide over one another as the heart beats. **–pericardial** *adj.*

pericardotomy *n. see* pericardiotomy.

perichondritis *n.* inflammation of cartilage and surrounding soft tissues, usually due to chronic infection. A common site is the external ear.

性心包炎的特點是發熱、胸痛和心包摩擦。心包中會產生積液（心包滲出液）。在偶然情況下會產生慢性心包增厚（慢性狹窄性心包炎）。這會影響心臟的活動，和心衰有許多共同特徵，包括水腫、胸膜滲出液、腹水和靜脈充血等。狹窄性心包炎大多數由結核感染所致。

心包炎的治療在於治本。可經胸壁穿刺吸出心包滲出液。慢性狹窄性心包炎用手術切除心包（心包切除術）治療。

心包 由兩部分組成的、包繞心臟的膜。外層的心包纖維層包圍心臟並依附於心臟發出的大血管。內層的漿液性心包是一個封閉的漿膜囊：內部內臟部分（心外膜）與心肌壁緊密相連，外壁部分襯於心包纖維層。囊內有少量液體，心臟跳動時可防止兩層相互摩擦。

心包切開術 參閱 pericardiotomy。

軟骨膜炎 通常由慢性感染引起的軟骨及其周圍軟組織的炎症。常發部位是外耳。

perichondrium *n.* the dense layer of fibrous connective tissue that covers the surface of *cartilage.

軟骨膜 覆蓋軟骨表面的纖維結締組織的致密層。

pericoronitis *n.* inflammation around the crown of a tooth, particularly a partially erupted third molar.

牙冠周炎 牙冠周圍，特別是未完全萌出的第三磨牙周圍的炎症。

pericranium *n.* the *periosteum of the skull.

顱骨膜 顱骨的骨膜。

pericystitis *n.* inflammation in the tissues around the bladder, causing pain in the pelvis, fever, and symptoms of *cystitis. It usually results from infection in the Fallopian tubes or uterus, but can occasionally arise from severe infection in a *diverticulum of the bladder itself. Treatment of pericystitis is directed to the underlying cause and usually involves antibiotic therapy. Pericystitis associated with a pelvic abscess clears when the abscess is surgically drained.

膀胱周炎 膀胱周圍組織的炎症，可引起骨盆疼痛、發熱和膀胱炎的諸多症狀。常由輸卵管或子宮感染引起。但偶爾可由膀胱憩室本身的嚴重感染引起。膀胱周炎的治療針對其根本原因，常使用抗生素治療。伴有骨盆膿腫的膀胱周炎在膿腫手術引流後病情會消除。

periderm *n.* see epitrichium.

皮上層 參閱 epitrichium。

perihepatitis *n.* inflammation of the membrane covering the liver. It is usually associated with abnormalities of the liver (including liver abscess, cirrhosis, tuberculosis) or in chronic peritonitis.

肝周炎 覆蓋肝臟的膜的炎症。肝周炎常伴有肝異常（包括肝膿腫、肝硬化和肝結核）或慢性腹膜炎。

perikaryon *n.* see cell body.

核周體 參閱 cell body。

perilymph *n.* the fluid between the bony and membranous *labyrinths of the ear.

外淋巴 位於耳骨迷路和耳膜迷路之間的液體。

perimeter *n.* an instrument for mapping the extent of the *visual field (see illustration). The patient fixes his gaze on a target in the centre of the inner surface of the hemisphere. Objects are presented on this surface and the patient says if he sees them. The area of the visual field can be defined and any gaps in the field can

視野計 測量視野範圍的儀器（見圖）。病人把目光固定在半球內表面的中心上。半球內表面上出現物體，病人要說出他是否看見了這些物體，這樣可確定視野範圍，從而發現視野內任何缺陷。視野計多種多樣。固定視野計中，置於黑色

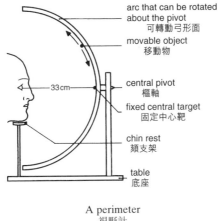

arc that can be rotated
about the pivot
可轉動弓形面

movable object
移動物

central pivot
樞軸

fixed central target
固定中心靶

33cm

chin rest
頦支架

table
底座

A perimeter
視野計

be detected. There are several types of perimeter. In the *static perimeter* the movable object is replaced by a system of tiny lights, set in a black background, that can be flashed briefly. If the patient has a field defect he will fail to see the lights that flash in the area of the defect. Modern visual field testing uses computerized machines that can detect very subtle field defects (*computerized perimetry*). **–perimetry** *n*.

perimetritis *n*. inflammation of the membrane on the outer surface of the uterus. The condition may be associated with *parametritis.

perimetrium *n*. the *peritoneum of the uterus.

perimysium *n*. the fibrous sheath that surrounds each bundle of *muscle fibres.

perinatal *adj*. relating to the period starting a few weeks before birth and including the birth and a few weeks after birth.

背景之中且可以短暫閃光的一系列小燈取代了可運動的物體。如果病人有視野缺陷，他就看不見此區域中閃光的燈泡。現代視野測量使用電腦化器械，它們可以測出非常細微的視野缺陷（電腦化視野計）。

子宮外膜炎 子宮外膜的炎症。此病可能與子宮旁組織炎相關。

子宮外膜 子宮的腹膜。

肌束膜 圍繞每束肌纖維的纖維鞘。

圍產期的 與分娩前幾周，包括分娩中及分娩後幾周這段時間有關的。

perinatal mortality rate *see* infant mortality rate.

圍產期死亡率 參閱 infant mortality rate。

perineal pouch *see* ileal pouch.

會陰囊 參閱 ileal pouch。

perineoplasty *n.* an operation designed to enlarge the vaginal opening by incising the hymen and part of the perineum (*Fenton's operation*).

會陰成形術 切開處女膜及部分會陰以增大陰道開口的手術（芬頓手術）。

perineorrhaphy *n.* the surgical repair of a damaged perineum. The damage is usually the result of a tear in the perineum sustained during childbirth.

會陰縫合術 受損會陰的手術修復。損傷通常為分娩期間會陰遭受撕裂的結果。

perinephric abscess a collection of pus around the kidney, usually secondary to *pyonephrosis.

腎周膿腫 腎臟周圍聚集膿液，通常為腎盂積膿的繼發症。

perinephritis *n.* inflammation of the tissues around the kidney. This is usually due to spread of infection from the kidney itself (*see* pyelonephritis, pyonephrosis). The patient has pain in the loins, fever, and fits of shivering. Prompt treatment of the underlying renal infection is required to prevent progression to an abscess.

腎周炎 腎臟周圍組織的炎症。腎周炎通常由腎臟本身感染擴散引起（參閱 pyelonephritis，pyonephrosis）。患者有腰痛、發熱和寒顫等症狀。為了防止膿腫擴展，需要迅速徹底治療感染。

perineum *n.* the region of the body between the anus and the urethral opening, including both skin and underlying muscle. In females it is perforated by the vaginal opening. **–perineal** *adj.*

會陰 肛門和尿道口之間的區域，包括皮膚及下層的肌肉。女性會陰有陰道開口。

perineurium *n.* the sheath of connective tissue that surrounds individual bundles (fascicles) of nerve fibres within a large *nerve.

神經束膜 大的神經中包裹單個神經纖維束（束）的結締組織鞘。

periodic acid–Schiff (PAS) reaction a test for the presence of glycoproteins, polysaccharides, certain mucopolysaccharides, glycolipids, and certain fatty

高碘酸-席夫反應 檢查組織切片中出現糖蛋白、多糖、某些黏多糖、糖脂和某些脂肪酸的試驗。組織先用高碘酸處理，

acids in tissue sections. The tissue is treated with periodic acid, followed by *Schiff's reagent. A positive reaction is the development of a red or magenta coloration.

然後用席夫試劑處理。陽性反應形成紅色或品紅色。

periodic fever *see* malaria.

周期熱 參閱 malaria。

periodontal *adj.* denoting or relating to the tissues surrounding the teeth.

牙周的 指圍繞牙的組織的，或與之相關的。

periodontal abscess an abscess that arises in the periodontal tissues and is invariably an acute manifestation of periodontal disease.

牙周膿腫 牙周組織中出現的膿腫，且幾乎全部是牙周疾病的急性表現。

periodontal disease disease of the tissues that support and attach the teeth – the gums, periodontal membrane, and alveolar bone. It is caused by the metabolism of bacterial *plaque on the surfaces of the teeth adjacent to these tissues. Periodontal disease includes *gingivitis and the more advanced stage of *periodontitis*, which results in the formation of spaces between the gums and the teeth (*periodontal pockets*), the loss of some fibres that attach the tooth to the jaw, and the loss of bone. The disease is widespread and is the most common cause of tooth loss in older people. Poor oral hygiene is a major contributory factor, but the resistance of the patient also has some influence; for example, the reduced resistance of AIDS patients may predispose to periodontal disease.

牙周病 支持和緊貼牙齒的組織——牙齦、牙周膜和牙槽骨等——的疾病。牙周病是由靠近這些組織的牙齒表面的菌斑的代謝引起的。牙周病包括牙齦炎和牙周炎的後期，導致牙齦和牙齒之間形成空隙（牙周袋）、連接牙齒與頜骨的某些纖維和骨的喪失。牙周病分布廣泛，是老人掉牙的最常見原因。口腔不衛生是一個主要的輔助因素，但病人的抵抗力亦有影響；例如艾滋病患者抵抗力下降，很容易感染牙周病。

periodontal membrane (periodontal ligament) the ligament around a *tooth, by which it is attached to the bone.

牙周膜（牙周韌帶） 牙齒周圍的韌帶，牙齒依靠它與骨相連。

periodontal pocket a space between the gingival tissues and tooth occurring in periodontitis. *See* periodontal disease.

牙周袋 牙周炎中產生的牙齦組織與牙齒之間的空隙。參閱 periodontal disease。

periodontics *n.* the branch of dentistry concerned with the tissues that support and attach the teeth and the prevention and treatment of *periodontal disease.

牙周病學　研究支持和緊貼牙齒的組織，預防和治療牙周病的牙科分支。

periodontium *n.* the tissues that support and attach the teeth: the gums (*see* gingiva), *periodontal membrane, alveolar bone, and *cementum.

牙周組織　支持和緊貼牙齒的組織：牙齦（參閱 gingiva）、牙周膜、牙槽骨和牙骨質。

periosteum *n.* a layer of dense connective tissue that covers the surface of a bone except at the articular surfaces. The outer layer of the periosteum is extremely dense and contains a large number of blood vessels. The inner layer is more cellular in appearance and contains osteoblasts and fewer blood vessels. The periosteum provides attachment for muscles, tendons, and ligaments.

骨膜　覆蓋不包括關節表面在內的骨表面的結締組織的致密層。骨膜的外層極致密並含有大量的血管。內層外觀呈蜂窩狀，含有成骨細胞和少數血管。骨膜為肌肉、肌腱和韌帶提供了連接。

periostitis *n.* inflammation of the membrane surrounding a bone (*see* periosteum). *Acute periostitis* results from direct injury to the bone and is associated with a *haematoma, which may later become infected. The uncomplicated condition subsides quickly with rest and anti-inflammatory analgesics. *Chronic periostitis* sometimes follows but is more often due to an inflammatory disease, such as tuberculosis or syphilis, or to a chronic ulcer overlying the bone involved. Chronic periostitis causes thickening of the underlying bone, which is evident on X-ray.

骨膜炎　包繞骨的膜（參閱 periosteum）的炎症。急性骨膜炎由骨的直接外傷引起，伴有血腫，以後可能形成感染。無併發症的骨膜炎通過休息及消炎鎮痛藥治療可以很快消除病情。慢性骨膜炎有時會隨後發生，但是更多的是由某種炎症疾病引起，例如由結核病或梅毒或由受累骨上方的慢性潰瘍引起。慢性骨膜炎下方骨增厚，這在 X 綫片上很明顯。

peripheral nervous system all parts of the nervous system lying outside the central nervous system (brain and spinal cord). It includes the *cranial nerves and *spinal nerves and their branches, which link the receptors and effector organs with the brain and spinal cord. *See also* autonomic nervous system.

周圍神經系統　位於中樞神經系統（大腦和脊髓）外的神經系統的所有部分。周圍神經系統包括腦神經、脊神經及其分支。這些分支將感受器和效應器與大腦和脊髓連接起來。參閱 autonomic nervous system。

periphlebitis *n.* inflammation of the tissues around a vein: seen as an extension of *phlebitis.

靜脈周炎　靜脈周圍組織的炎症，被看作是靜脈炎的擴散。

perisalpingitis *n.* inflammation of the peritoneal membrane on the outer surface of a Fallopian tube.

輸卵管腹膜炎　輸卵管外表面腹膜的炎症。

perisplenitis *n.* inflammation of the external coverings of the spleen.

脾周炎　脾臟外覆蓋層炎症。

peristalsis *n.* a wavelike movement that progresses along some of the hollow tubes of the body. It occurs involuntarily and is characteristic of tubes that possess circular and longitudinal muscles, such as the *intestines. It is induced by distension of the walls of the tube. Immediately behind the distension the circular muscle contracts. In front of the distension the circular muscle relaxes and the longitudinal muscle contracts, which pushes the contents of the tube forward. **–peristaltic** *adj.*

蠕動　沿身體某些空心管前進的波浪形運動。蠕動產生無隨意性，是具有環形和縱向肌的管（例如腸）的一個特徵。蠕動由管壁的擴張誘發。擴張後環形肌肉緊接着收縮。擴張前部環形肌舒張，縱向肌收縮，推動管內容物向前運動。

peritendineum *n.* the fibrous covering of a tendon.

腱鞘　腱的纖維覆蓋物。

peritendinitis *n. see* tenosynovitis.

腱鞘炎　參閱 tenosynovitis。

peritomy *n.* an eye operation in which an incision of the conjunctiva is made in a complete circle around the cornea.

球結膜環狀切開術　圍繞角膜作的完全性環形結膜切開的眼外科手術。

peritoneoscope *n. see* laparoscope.

腹腔鏡　參閱 laparoscope。

peritoneum *n.* the *serous membrane of the abdominal cavity (see illustration). The *parietal peritoneum* lines the walls of the abdomen, and the *visceral peritoneum* covers the abdominal organs. *See also* mesentery, omentum. **–peritoneal** *adj.*

腹膜　腹腔的漿膜（見圖）。腹膜壁層襯於腹壁，腹膜臟層覆蓋腹腔器官。參閱 mesentery，omentum。

peritonitis *n.* inflammation of the *peritoneum. *Primary peritonitis* is caused

腹膜炎　腹膜的炎症。原發性腹膜炎由經過血流傳播的細菌

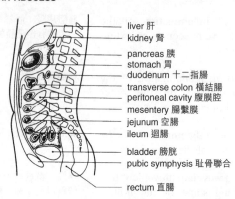

liver 肝
kidney 腎
pancreas 胰
stomach 胃
duodenum 十二指腸
transverse colon 橫結腸
peritoneal cavity 腹膜腔
mesentery 腸繫膜
jejunum 空腸
ileum 迴腸
bladder 膀胱
pubic symphysis 恥骨聯合
rectum 直腸

Sagittal section of the abdomen to show arrangement of the peritoneum
表示腹膜分布的腹腔縱切面圖

by bacteria spread via the bloodstream: examples are *pneumococcal peritonitis* and *tuberculous peritonitis*. Symptoms are diffuse abdominal pain and swelling, with fever and weight loss. Fluid may accumulate in the peritoneal cavity (*see* ascites) or the infection may complicate existing ascites. *Secondary peritonitis* is due to perforation or rupture of an abdominal organ (for example, a duodenal ulcer or the vermiform appendix), allowing access of bacteria and irritant digestive juices to the peritoneum. This produces sudden severe abdominal pain, first at the site of rupture but becoming generalized. Shock develops, and the abdominal wall becomes rigid; X-ray examination may reveal gas within the peritoneal cavity. Treatment is usually by surgical repair of the perforation, but in some cases conservative treatment using antibiotics and intravenous fluid may be used, *subphrenic abscess is a possible complication.

感染引起：例如肺炎球菌性腹膜炎和結核性腹膜炎。症狀有彌散性腹痛和腫脹，伴有發熱和體重下降。腹腔內會有積液（參閱 ascites）或感染可合併腹水。繼發性腹膜炎由腹腔器官穿孔或破裂（例如：十二指腸潰瘍或闌尾炎），使細菌及刺激性消化液進入腹膜引起。會產生突發性劇烈腹痛，首先開始於破裂部位但疼痛會擴散。可形成休克、腹壁變硬。X綫檢查可顯示腹腔內有氣體。常採用手術修復穿孔治療，但在有些病例中可使用抗生素及靜脈輸液等保守方法。可能出現的併發症是膈下膿腫。

peritonsillar abscess *see* quinsy.

扁桃體周膿腫   參閱 quinsy。

peritrichous *adj.* describing bacteria in which the flagella cover the entire cell surface.

周毛的　描述鞭毛覆蓋整個細胞表面的細菌。

perityphlitis *n. Archaic.* inflammation of the tissues around the caecum. *See* typhlitis.

盲腸周炎　（舊稱）盲腸周圍組織的炎症。參閱 typhlitis。

periureteritis *n.* inflammation of the tissues around a ureter. This is usually associated with inflammation of the ureter itself (*ureteritis) often behind an obstruction caused by a stone or stricture. Treatment is directed to relieving any obstruction of the ureter and controlling the infection with antibiotics.

輸尿管周炎　輸尿管周圍組織的炎症。此病常與輸尿管本身的炎症（輸尿管炎）相關，且常發生於由結石或狹窄引起的輸尿管阻塞部位之後。治療針對解除輸尿管的任何堵塞及使用抗生素控制感染。

perle *n.* a soft capsule containing medicine.

珠劑　含藥物的軟膠囊。

perleche *n.* dryness and cracking of the corners of the mouth, sometimes with infection. Perleche may be caused by persistent lip licking or by a vitamin deficient diet.

傳染性口角炎　口角變乾及破裂，有時伴有感染。傳染性口角炎可能由持久的舔唇或食物中缺乏維生素引起。

permethrin *n.* a synthetic derivative of the naturally occurring insecticide pyrethrin that is applied externally to treat head lice and scabies. Trade name: **Lyclear**.

苄氯菊酯　天然產生的殺蟲劑除蟲菊酯的一種合成衍生物，外用，治療頭虱和疥瘡。商品名：Lyclear。

pernicious *adj.* describing diseases that are highly dangerous or likely to result in death if untreated. *See also* pernicious anaemia.

惡性的　描述如不治療則非常危險或可能導致死亡的疾病。參閱 pernicious anaemia。

pernicious anaemia a form of *anaemia resulting from deficiency of *vitamin B_{12}. This in turn results either from failure to produce the substance (*intrinsic factor) that facilitates absorption of B_{12} from the bowel or from dietary deficiency of the vitamin. Pernicious anaemia is characterized by

惡性貧血　維生素 B_{12} 缺乏導致的一種貧血。維生素 B_{12} 的缺乏又由不能產生促進從腸中吸收維生素 B_{12} 的物質（內因子）或食物中缺乏該維生素引起。惡性貧血的特點是紅細胞生成缺陷及骨髓中出現巨幼紅細胞。重症惡性貧血中，神經

defective production of red blood cells and the presence of *megaloblasts in the bone marrow. In severe forms the nervous system is affected (*see* subacute combined degeneration of the cord). The condition is treated by injections of vitamin B_{12}.

系統會受到影響（參閱 subacute combined degeneration of the cord）。此病用注射維生素 B_{12} 治療。

pernio *n.* the medical name for a chilblain (*see* chilblains).

凍瘡　chilblain一詞的醫學名（參閱 chilblains）。

perniosis *n. see* chilblains.

凍瘡病　參閱 chilblains。

pero- *prefix denoting* deformity; defect. Example: *peromelia* (of the limbs).

〔前綴〕**畸形殘缺**　例如：四肢不全（畸形）。

peroneal *adj.* relating to or supplying the outer (fibular) side of the leg.

腓骨的，腓側的　與腿外側相關的或分布於腿的外側的。

peroneus *n.* one of the muscles of the leg that arises from the fibula. The *peroneus longus* and *peroneus brevis* are situated at the side of the leg and inserted into the metatarsal bones of the foot. They help to turn the foot outwards.

腓骨肌　發自腓骨的下肢肌肉。腓長肌和腓短肌位於腿的一側，附著於腳的跖骨。它們使腳向外旋轉。

peroxidase *n.* an enzyme, found mainly in plants but also present in leucocytes and milk, that catalyses the dehydrogenation (oxidation) of various substances in the presence of hydrogen peroxide (which acts as a hydrogen acceptor, being converted to water in the process).

過氧化物酶　一種酶，主要存在於植物之中，但也出現於白細胞和牛奶中，在有過氧化氫時，這種酶可催化各種物質的脫氫作用（過氧化氫作為氫的受體，在反應過程中被轉化成水）。

peroxisome *n.* a small structure within a cell that is similar to a *lysosome but contains different enzymes, some of which may take part in reactions involving hydrogen peroxide.

過氧化物酶體　細胞內類似於溶酶體，但含有不同酶的一種小結構，其中有些酶可參與過氧化氫的反應。

perphenazine *n.* a phenothiazine *antipsychotic drug used to relieve anxiety, tension, and agitation and to prevent nausea and vomiting. It is administered by mouth or injection;

奮乃靜　一種吩噻嗪類抗精神病藥，用於解除焦慮、緊張和激動、預防惡心和嘔吐。口服或注射，副作用與氯丙嗪類似。商品名：Fentazin。

side-effects are similar to those of *chlor-promazine. Trade name: **Fentazin**.

perseveration *n*. **1.** excessive persistence at a task that prevents the individual from turning his attention to new situations. It is a symptom of organic disease of the brain and sometimes of obsessional neurosis. **2.** the phenomenon in which an image continues to be perceived briefly in the absence of the object. This is a potentially serious neurological disorder.

persisitent vegetative state (PVS) the condition of living like a vegetable, without consciousness or the ability to initiate voluntary action, as a result of brain damage. People in the vegetative state may sometimes give the appearance of being awake and conscious, with open eyes. They may make random movements of the limbs or head and may pick or rub with the fingers, but there is no response to any form of communication and no reason to suppose that there is any awareness of the environment.

The vegetative state must be distinguished from apparently similar conditions, such as the psychiatric state of *catatonia, in which consciousness is retained and from which full recovery is possible, and the *locked-in syndrome* resulting from damage to brainstem, in which the patient is conscious but unable to speak or make any movement of any part of the body, except for blinking and upward eye movements, which permit signalling.

personality *n*. (in psychology) an enduring disposition to act and feel in particular ways that differentiate one individual from another. These patterns of behaviour are sometimes conceptualized

持續症 **(1)** 過度專注某一任務，從而妨礙了個人把注意力轉移到新的環境之中。這是大腦的器質性病變症狀，有時是強迫性神經官能症的症狀。**(2)** 物體消失後其影像繼續被發覺的現象。這可能是一種嚴重神經病。

持續植物樣狀態　由於大腦受損而導致的像植物樣的生活狀態，患者無意識或無能力進行自發運動。處於植物狀態的人睜開眼睛時有時呈現出清醒狀，他們會隨意運動四肢或搖頭，並用手指撿東西或摩擦手指，但對任何形式的交際均無反應，沒有理由可推斷病人能認知周圍環境。

　　植物樣狀態必須和與其表面上相似的狀態分開。例如：緊張症的精神病狀態，在這種狀態中患者保留着意識，可以完全康復，又如封閉綜合徵由腦幹損傷產生，患者有意識，但除了眨眼及眼向上運動傳遞信號外，不會講話，身體的任何一部分都不能運動。

人格　(心理學) 把一個人和另外一個人區分開來的，以特定方式運動或表達感情的持久性的氣質。這些行為的模式有時按不同組別（參閱 personality

as different categories (*see* personality disorder) and sometimes as different dimensions (*see* extroversion, neuroticism).

personality disorder a deeply ingrained and maladaptive pattern of behaviour, persisting through many years. It is usually manifest by the time the individual is adolescent. The abnormality of behaviour must be sufficiently severe that it causes suffering, either to the patient or to other people (or to both). Some individuals with such personalities mature into happier people. Most forms of psychotherapy claim to be of therapeutic value, but the worth of any treatment remains debatable. *See* anankastic, avoidant, borderline, dyssocial, hysterical, paranoid, schizoid.

perspiration *n.* *sweat or the process of sweating. *Insensible perspiration* is sweat that evaporates immediately from the skin and is therefore not visible; *sensible perspiration* is visible on the skin in the form of drops.

Perthes' disease *see* Legg-Calvé-Perthes disease.

pertussis *n. see* whooping cough.

pes *n.* (in anatomy) the foot or a part resembling a foot.

pes cavus *see* claw-foot.

pes planus *see* flat-foot.

pessary *n.* **1.** a plastic device, often ring-shaped, that fits into the vagina and keeps the uterus in position: used to treat *prolapse. The usual type is a *ring*

disorder），有時按不同範圍（參閱 extroversion，neuroticism）分類。

人格障礙 持續多年的一種根深蒂固的、適應不良的行為模式。常在患者處於青春期時表現出來。行為異常只有到了非常嚴重的程度才會對患者本人或他人（或者兩者）造成傷害。有些具有人格障礙的人隨着年齡增加可遇上較為幸福的生活。大多數心理療法稱其有療效，但治療價值尚有爭議。參閱 anankastic，avoidant，borderline，dyssocial，hysterical，paranoid，schizoid。

出汗 汗或出汗過程。不顯汗指汗從皮膚表面立即蒸發，因此看不見；顯汗指皮膚表面可觀察到的水珠。

佩特茲病，股骨頭骨骺骨軟骨病 參閱 Legg-Calvé-Perthes disease。

百日咳 參閱 whooping cough。

足，腳 （解剖學）足或與足相似的部分。

弓形足 參閱 claw-foot。

扁平足 參閱 flat-foot。

(1) 子宮托 常為環形的一種塑料裝置，安裝於陰道中保持子宮處於正常位置，用於治療子宮脫垂。常用類型為環形子

pessary but occasionally a *Hodge pessary* is used. **2.** a plug or cylinder of cocoa butter or some other soft material containing a drug that is fitted into the vagina for the treatment of gynaecological disorders (e.g. vaginitis) or for the induction of labour (a *Prostin pessary* containing prostaglandin). Also called: **vaginal suppository**.

宮托，偶爾可用霍奇子宮托。
(2) 陰道栓劑 含有藥物的可可脂或其他軟材料製成的栓劑，置於陰道中治療婦科疾病（例如陰道炎）或促進分娩（一種含前列腺素的普羅斯丁栓劑）。亦稱陰道栓劑。

pesticide *n.* a chemical agent used to kill insects or other organisms harmful to crops and other cultivated plants. Some pesticides, such as *parathion and *dieldrin, have caused poisoning in human beings and livestock after accidental exposure.

殺蟲劑 一種化學藥劑，用於殺滅對莊稼或其他農作物有害的昆蟲或其他生物。有些殺蟲劑，例如對硫磷和狄氏劑，在意外接觸後曾造成人畜中毒。

petechiae *pl. n.* small round flat dark-red spots caused by bleeding into the skin or beneath the mucous membrane. Petechiae occur, for example, in the *purpuras.

瘀斑 皮內或黏膜下出血引起的深紅色圓形扁平小點。例如紫癜病中產生的瘀斑。

pethidine (meperidine) *n.* a potent *analgesic drug with mild sedative action, used to relieve moderate or severe pain. It is administered by mouth or injection; side-effects may include nausea, dizziness, and dry mouth, and *dependence may occur with prolonged use.

哌替啶，度冷丁 帶有輕微鎮靜作用的強力鎮痛藥，用以緩解中度或重度疼痛。口服或注射，副作用可包括惡心、頭暈、口乾，長期使用可產生依賴。

petit mal *see* epilepsy.

癲癇小發作 參閱 epilepsy。

Petri dish a flat shallow circular glass or plastic dish with a pillbox-like lid, used to hold solid agar or gelatin media for culturing bacteria.

佩特里培養皿 帶有藥丸盒樣蓋的扁平圓形淺玻璃碟或塑料碟，用於盛放供培養細菌用的瓊脂或明膠。

petrissage *n.* kneading: a form of *massage in which the skin is lifted up, pressed down and squeezed, and pinched and rolled. Alternate squeezing and relaxation of the tissues stimulates the

揉捏法 一種按摩，作法是提、按、擠、捏和揉搓皮膚。組織的交替擠壓和鬆弛可刺激局部血液循環，在肌肉病症中具有緩解疼痛的作用。

local circulation and may have a pain-relieving effect in muscular disorders.

petrositis *n.* inflammation of the petrous part of the *temporal bone (which encloses the inner ear), usually due to an extension of *mastoiditis.

petrous bone *see* temporal bone.

Peutz-Jeghers syndrome a hereditary disorder in which the presence of multiple *polyps in the lining of the small intestine (intestinal *polyposis) is associated with pigmented areas (e.g. freckles) around the lips, on the inside of the mouth, and on the palms and soles. The polyps may bleed, resulting in anaemia, or may cause obstruction of the bowel.

-pexy *suffix denoting* surgical fixation. Example: *omentopexy* (of the omentum).

Peyer's patches oval masses of *lymphoid tissue on the mucous membrane lining the small intestine.

Peyronie's disease a dense fibrous plaque in the penis, which can be felt in the erectile tissue as an irregular hard lump. The penis curves or angulates at this point on erection and pain often results. The cause is unknown. The penis can be straightened surgically by means of *Nesbit's operation.*

pH a measure of the concentration of hydrogen ions in a solution, and therefore of its acidity or alkalinity. A pH of 7 indicates a neutral solution, a pH below 7 indicates acidity, and a pH in excess of 7 indicates alkalinity.

PHA *n. see* phytohaemagglutinin.

顳骨岩部炎 顳骨（顳骨包圍着內耳）岩部分的炎症，常由乳突炎擴散引起。

顳骨岩部 參閱 temporal bone。

普-杰氏綜合徵 一種遺傳性疾病，小腸內膜中多發性息肉（腸息肉病）與唇周圍，口腔內壁，手掌和跖上的色素沉積區（例如雀斑）有關。息肉可能出血，導致貧血或引起腸阻塞。

〔後綴〕固定術 手術固定。例如網膜固定術。

派伊爾結 小腸內黏膜淋巴組織的卵圓形塊。

佩羅尼病 陰莖內致密的纖維斑塊，在勃起組織中可以被觸知為一種不規則硬塊。陰莖勃起時在此部位彎曲或呈棱角形，常可導致疼痛。病因不明。借助於內斯比特手術可以手術整直陰莖。

pH值，氫離子指數 測量溶液中氫離子濃度，借此測量溶液的酸度或鹼度。pH 值為 7 時說明溶液呈中性，小於 7 時為酸性，大於 7 時為鹼性。

植物血細胞凝集素 參閱 phytohaemagglutinin。

phaco- (phako-) *prefix denoting* the lens of the eye.

〔前綴〕晶狀體

phacoemulsification (phakoemulsification) *n.* the process of breaking up the lens of the eye before removing it. A metal probe is inserted into the lens and the emulsification is performed by high-frequency vibration. This is now a popular method of performing cataract surgery.

晶狀體乳化　摘除晶狀體前使其破裂的過程。將一根金屬探針插入到晶狀體內，用高頻震波將晶狀體乳化。現在這是一種流行的白內障手術方法。

phaeochromocytoma *n.* a small vascular tumour of the inner region (medulla) of the adrenal gland. By its uncontrolled and irregular secretion of the hormones *adrenaline and *noradrenaline, the tumour causes attacks of raised blood pressure, increased heart rate, palpitations, and headache.

嗜鉻細胞瘤　腎上腺內部（髓質）的小血管瘤。嗜鉻細胞瘤通過其不加控制且不規則地分泌腎上腺素和去甲腎上腺等激素引起血壓升高、心率加快、心悸和頭痛等發作。

phag- (phago-) *prefix denoting* **1.** eating. **2.** phagocytes.

〔前綴〕**(1)** 吞噬　**(2)** 吞噬細胞

phage *n. see* bacteriophage.

噬菌體　參閱 bacteriophage。

-phagia *suffix denoting* a condition involving eating.

〔後綴〕噬　涉及吞食的狀態。

phagocyte *n.* a cell that is able to engulf and digest bacteria, protozoa, cells and cell debris, and other small particles, Phagocytes include many white blood cells (*see* leucocyte) and *macrophages, which play a major role in the body's defence mechanism. **–phagocytic** *adj.*

吞噬細胞　一種能吞噬並消化細菌、支原體、細胞碎片及其他小微粒的細胞。吞噬細胞包括許多白細胞（參閱 leucocyte）和巨噬細胞。它們在人體防禦機制中起重要作用。

phagocytosis *n.* the engulfment and digestion of bacteria and other foreign particles by a cell (*see* phagocyte). *Compare* pinocytosis.

吞噬作用　細胞吞食並消化細菌及其他異物（參閱 phagocyte）。與 pinocytosis 對比。

phako- *prefix. see* phaco-.

〔前綴〕晶狀體　參閱 phaco-。

phalangeal cells rows of supporting cells between the sensory hair cells of the organ of Corti (*see* cochlea).

指細胞 柯蒂替器（參閱 cochlea）感覺毛細胞間成排的支持細胞。

phalangectomy *n.* surgical removal of one or more of the small bones (phalanges) in the fingers or toes.

指（趾）骨切除術 手術切除指或趾一塊或多塊小骨（指（趾）骨）。

phalanges *n.* (*sing.* **phalanx**) the bones of the fingers and toes (digits). The first digit (thumb/big toe) has two phalanges. Each of the remaining digits has three phalanges. **–phalangeal** *adj.*

指（趾）骨 手指及腳趾的骨。第一手指（拇指）和腳趾（拇趾）有兩塊骨。其餘各指（趾）各有三塊指（趾）骨。

phalangitis *n.* inflammation of a finger or toe, causing swelling and pain. The condition may be caused by infection of the soft tissues, tendon sheaths, bone, or joints or by some rheumatic diseases, such as *psoriatic arthritis. *See also* dactylitis.

指（趾）骨炎 指或趾的炎症，可引起腫脹及疼痛。此病可由軟組織、腱鞘、骨或關節等的感染引起，或由某些風濕病，例如銀屑病性關節炎引起。參閱 dactylitis。

phalanx *n. see* phalanges.

指（趾）骨 參閱 phalanges。

phalloplasty *n.* surgical reconstruction or repair of the penis. It is required for congenital deformity of the penis, as in *hypospadias or *epispadias, and sometimes also following injury to the penis with loss of skin.

陰莖成形術 手術重建或修復陰莖。陰莖先天性畸形，例如尿道上裂和尿道下裂時，需要作此手術，有時陰莖外傷造成皮膚缺損時也需要作此手術。

phallus *n.* the embryonic penis, before the urethral duct has reached its final state of development.

初陰 尿道沒有發育到最後階段的胚胎期陰莖。

phanero- *prefix denoting* visible; apparent.

〔前綴〕可見的，明顯的

phaneromania *n.* an excessively strong impulse to touch or rub parts of one's own body.

自體觸摸癖 觸摸或摩擦自己身體某些部位的過度強烈衝動。

phantom limb the sensation that an arm or leg, or part of an arm or leg, is still

幻肢 臂或腿，或者是其一部分被截肢後，患者認為這部分

attached to the body after it has been amputated. Pain may seem to come from the amputated part. This may arise because of stimulation of the amputation stump, which contains severed nerves that formerly carried messages from the removed portion.

依舊連接在身體上的感覺。被截肢部位似乎有痛感。產生的原因可能是對殘肢刺激，殘肢含有從前被截去部分傳導信息的受損神經。

phantom pregnancy *see* pseudocyesis.

幻想妊娠 參閱 pseudocyesis。

phantom tumour a swelling, in the abdomen or elsewhere, caused by local muscular contraction or the accumulation of gases, that mimics a swelling caused by a tumour or other structural change. The condition is usually associated with emotional disorder, and the 'tumour' may disappear under anaesthesia.

幻想瘤 局部肌肉收縮或氣體積聚引起的腹部或其他部位的腫脹，它類似於腫瘤或其他結構變化引起的腫脹。此病常與情緒障礙相關，在麻醉狀態下，「腫瘤」可消失。

pharmaceutical *adj.* relating to pharmacy.

藥劑學的 與藥劑學相關的。

pharmacist *n.* a person who is qualified by examination and registered and authorized to dispense medicines or to keep open a shop for the sale and dispening of medicines.

藥劑師 經考核取得資格並註冊及被授權配藥或開店售藥及配藥的人。

pharmaco- *prefix denoting* drugs. Example: *pharmacophobia* (morbid fear of).

〔前綴〕藥 例如：藥物恐怖。

pharmacodynamics *n.* the interaction of drugs with cells. It includes such factors as the binding of drugs to cells, their uptake, and intracellular metabolism.

藥效學 藥物與細胞的相互作用，包括藥物與細胞的結合，藥物的吸收和細胞代謝等因素。

pharmacognosy *n.* the knowledge or study of pharmacologically active principles derived from plants.

生藥學 研究從植物中提取藥理學上有效成分的科學或知識。

pharmacokinetics *n.* the handling of a drug within the body, which includes its absorption, distribution in the body, metabolism, and excretion.

藥物動力學 體內藥物的處理，它包括藥物的吸收、在體內的分布、代謝及排泄。

pharmacology *n.* the science of the properties of drugs and their effects on the body. **–pharmacological** *adj.*

藥理學 研究藥物性質及其對人體作用的科學。

pharmacomania *n.* an abnormal desire for taking medicines.

藥物癖 想服藥的異常慾望。

pharmacopoeia *n.* a book containing a list of the drugs used in medicine, with details of their formulae, methods of preparation, dosages, standards of purity, etc.

藥典 包含醫用藥物名單、帶有藥物分子式、配製方法、劑量和純度標準等詳細資料的書籍。

pharmacy *n.* **1.** the preparation and dispensing of drugs. **2.** premises registered to dispense medicines and sell poisons.

(1) 藥劑學 藥物的配製及調劑。**(2)** 藥房 註冊配製及出售藥物和毒藥的商店。

pharyng- (pharyngo-) *prefix denoting* the pharynx. Example: *pharyngopathy* (disease of).

〔前綴〕咽 例如：咽病。

pharyngeal arch (**branchial** or **visceral arch**) any of the paired segmented ridges of tissue in each side of the throat of the early embryo that correspond to the gill arches of fish. Each arch contains a cartilage, a cranial nerve, and a blood vessel. Between each arch there is a *pharyngeal pouch.

咽弓，鰓弓 胚胎早期咽喉部兩側的成對分布弓狀組織，類似魚的鰓弓。每個弓含一軟骨、一根腦神經和一條血管。每個咽弓之間有咽囊。

pharyngeal cleft (**branchial** or **visceral cleft**) any of the paired segmented clefts in each side of the throat of the early embryo that correspond to the gills of fish. Soon after they have formed they close to form the *pharyngeal pouches, except for the first cleft, which persists as the external auditory meatus.

鰓裂 胚胎早期咽喉部兩側的成對分節裂縫之一，類似魚的鰓。它們形成後不久，除了第一鰓裂繼續作為外耳道外，其餘閉合形成咽囊。

pharyngeal pouch (**branchial** or **visceral pouch**) any of the paired

咽囊 胚胎早期咽喉側中成對的分節囊之一。發育成中耳鼓

segmented pouches in the side of the throat of the early embryo. They give rise to the tympanic cavity, the parathyroid glands, the thymus, and probably the thyroid gland.

室、甲狀旁腺、胸腺並且可能發育成甲狀腺。

pharyngectomy *n.* surgical removal of part of the pharynx.

咽（部分）切除術　咽的部分手術切除。

pharyngitis *n.* inflammation of the part of the throat behind the soft palate (pharynx). It produces *sore throat and may be associated with *tonsillitis.

咽炎　軟腭（咽）後部咽喉的部分炎症。它可引起咽喉痛並可伴有扁桃體炎。

pharyngocele *n.* a pouch or cyst opening off the pharynx (*see* branchial cyst).

咽突出　開口於咽的囊（參閱 branchial cyst）。

pharyngoplegia *n.* muscular paralysis of the pharynx.

咽肌麻痺　咽肌肉癱瘓。

pharyngoscope *n.* an *endoscope for the examination of the pharynx.

咽鏡　檢查咽的內窺鏡。

pharynx *n.* a muscular tube, lined with mucous membrane, that extends from the beginning of the oesophagus (gullet) up to the base of the skull. It is divided into the *nasopharynx, *oropharynx, and *laryngopharynx (see illustration) and it communicates with the posterior *nares, *Eustachian tube, the mouth, larynx, and oesophagus. The pharynx acts as a passageway for food from the mouth to the oesophagus, and as an air passage from the nasal cavity and mouth to the larynx. It also acts as a resonating chamber for the sounds produced in the larynx. **–pharyngeal** *adj.*

咽　從食管開始延伸到顱底的一種內襯黏膜的肌肉管道。咽分為鼻咽、口咽和喉咽（見圖）並與後鼻孔、咽鼓管、口腔、喉和食管相通。咽起着食物從口腔到食管的通道，空氣從鼻腔和口腔通向喉的通道的作用。也是喉中產生聲音的共鳴箱。

phenazocine *n.* an *analgesic drug used for rapid relief of moderate or severe pain. It is administered by mouth or injection; side-effects may include digestive upsets and dizziness, and prolonged

非那佐辛　用於快速解除中度和重度疼痛的一種鎮痛藥。口服或注射。副作用包括消化不良和頭暈，長期使用可導致依賴。商品名：Narphen。

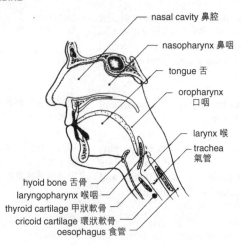

Longitudinal section of the pharynx
咽的縱切面圖

nasal cavity 鼻腔
nasopharynx 鼻咽
tongue 舌
oropharynx 口咽
larynx 喉
trachea 氣管
hyoid bone 舌骨
laryngopharynx 喉咽
thyroid cartilage 甲狀軟骨
cricoid cartilage 環狀軟骨
oesophagus 食管

use may lead to *dependence. Trade name: **Narphen**.

phenazopyridine *n.* an *analgesic drug used to relieve pain in inflammatory conditions of the bladder and urinary tract, such as cystitis and urethritis. It is administered by mouth and occasionally causes digestive upsets; in patients with *glucose-6-phosphate dehydrogenase deficiency it may damage the red blood cells. Trade name: **Pyridium**.

非那吡啶 一種鎮痛藥。用於解除膀胱及尿道炎症，如膀胱炎和尿道炎引起的疼痛。口服，偶爾可引起消化不良，葡萄糖-6-磷酸脫氫酶缺乏症患者用此藥可造成紅細胞破壞。商品名：Pyridium。

phenelzine *n.* a drug used to relieve depression and anxiety (*see* MAO inhibitor). It is administered by mouth; side-effects include dizziness, drowsiness, tiredness, and digestive upsets. Trade name: **Nardil**.

苯乙肼 用於解除抑鬱和焦慮的藥物（參閱 MAO inhibitor）。口服，副作用包括頭暈、嗜睡、困倦和消化不良。商品名：Nardil

phenindione *n.* an *anticoagulant drug used to treat thrombosis in the blood vessels of the heart and limbs. It is administered by mouth or injection; side-effects may include skin rashes,

苯茚二酮 治療心臟和四肢血管栓塞的抗凝血藥。口服或注射，副作用包括皮疹、發熱和腹瀉。商品名：Dindevan。

fever, and diarrhoea. Trade name: **Dindevan**.

pheniramine *n.* an *antihistamine used to treat allergic reactions such as hay fever and urticaria. It is administered by mouth or is applied to the skin in an ointment; side-effects may include drowsiness, digestive upsets, and skin reactions. Trade name: **Daneral**.

非尼拉敏　治療如枯草熱和蕁麻疹等過敏反應的抗組胺藥物。口服或作為油膏塗抹於皮膚上；副作用包括嗜睡、消化不良和皮膚反應。商品名：Daneral。

phenobarbitone *n.* a *barbiturate drug used to treat insomnia and anxiety and as an anticonvulsant in the treatment of epilepsy. It is administered by mouth or injection; side-effects may include drowsiness and skin sensitivity reactions, and dependence may result from continued use.

苯巴比妥，魯米那　用於治療失眠和焦慮，並作為抗驚厥藥治療癲癇的巴比妥酸鹽類藥。口服或注射，副作用可能包括嗜睡和皮膚過敏反應。長期使用可產生賴藥性。

phenol (carbolic acid) *n.* a strong *disinfectant used for cleansing wounds, treating inflammations of the mouth, throat, and ear, and as preservative in injections. It is administered as solution, ointments, and lotions and is highly toxic if taken by mouth.

苯酚　一種強力消毒劑，用於清洗傷口、治療口腔、咽喉和耳部炎症，並用作注射液中的防腐劑。作為溶液、油膏或洗劑給藥，口服具有劇毒。

phenolphthalein *n.* an irritant *laxative administered by mouth, usually given at night to act the following morning. Side-effects may include stomach cramps.

酚酞　口服刺激性輕瀉藥。常夜間給藥，次日早晨起作用。副作用可包括胃痛性痙攣。

phenolsulphonphthalein *n.* a red dye administered by injection in a test for kidney function.

酚磺酞，酚紅　腎功能試驗時注射的一種紅色染料。

phenothiazines *pl. n.* a group of chemically related compounds with various pharmacological actions. Some (e.g. *chlorpromazine and *trifluoperazine) are *antipsychotic drugs; others (e.g. *piperazine) are anthelmintics.

吩噻嗪　一種藥理作用各不相同的化學上的相關化合物。有些藥物（例如氯丙嗪和三氟拉嗪）屬於抗精神病藥；有些（例如哌嗪）屬於驅蟲藥。

phenotype *n.* **1.** the observable characteristics of an individual, which result

表型　(1) 個人擁有的基因（基因型）和環境之間互相作

from interaction between the genes he possesses (*genotype) and the environment. **2.** the expression in a person or on a cell of characteristics determined by genes that are not fully defined.

由沒有完全確定的基因決
定的個人或細胞的特徵表現。

phenoxybenzamine *n.* a drug that dilates blood vessels (*see* alpha blocker). It is used to reduce blood pressure and to treat conditions involving poor circulation, such as Raynaud's disease and chilblains. It is administered by mouth or injection and may cause dizziness and fast heartbeat. Trade name: **Dibenyline**.

酚苄明 一種血管舒張藥（參
閱 alpha blocker）。用於降低
血壓和治療涉及血液循環不良
的疾病，如雷諾病和凍瘡。口
服或注射，可引起頭暈和心跳
加快。商品名：Dibenyline。

phenoxymethylpenicillin (**penicillin V**) *n. see* penicillin.

苯氧甲基青黴素（青黴素 V）
參閱 penicillin。

phensuximide *n.* an *anticonvulsant drug used to prevent or reduce absence seizures in epilepsy. It is administered by mouth; side-effects may include dizziness, drowsiness, nausea, and loss of appetite.

苯琥胺 一種抗驚厥藥，用於
預防或降低癲癇失神發作。口
服，副作用包括頭暈、嗜睡、
惡心和食慾不振。

phentermine *n.* a *sympathomimetic drug that suppresses the appetite and is used in the treatment of obesity. It is administered by mouth; side-effects include dry mouth, nausea, and restlessness, and continued use produces *tolerance. Trade names: **Duromine**, **Ionamin**.

芬特明 抑制食慾的擬交感神
經藥，用於治療肥胖症。口
服，副作用包括口乾、惡心
和煩躁，連續使用可產生耐
受性。商品名：Duromine，
Ionamin。

phentolamine *n.* a drug that dilates blood vessels (*see* alpha blocker) and is used to reduce blood pressure in *phaeochromocytoma and to treat conditions of poor circulation such as Raynaud's disease and chilblains. It is administered by mouth or injection; side-effects include fast heartbeat and digestive upsets. Trade name: **Rogitine**.

酚妥拉明 一種血管舒張藥
（參閱 alpha blocker），在嗜鉻
細胞瘤中用於降低血壓及治療
如雷諾病和凍瘡等血液循環不
良疾病。口服或注射；副作用
包括心跳加快和消化不良。商
品名：Rogitine。

phenylalanine *n.* an *essential amino acid that is readily converted to tyrosine.

苯丙氨酸 一種很容易被轉化
為酪氨酸的必需氨基酸。這一

Blockade of this metabolic pathway gives rise to *phenylketonuria, which is associated with abnormally large amounts of phenylalanine and phenyl-pyruvic acid in the blood and retarded mental development.

代謝通道受阻會產生苯丙酮酸尿症，這一疾病伴有血液中含異常大量的苯丙氨酸和苯丙酮酸和智力發育遲緩。

phenylbutazone *n.* an *analgesic drug that reduces fever and inflammation and is used to relieve pain in rheumatic and related diseases. It is administered by mouth or injection; because of its adverse effect on the blood-forming tissues, its use has been restricted since 1984. Trade name: **Butazolidin**.

保泰松 一種具有退熱和消化作用的鎮痛藥，用於緩解風濕及相關疾病引起的疼痛。口服或注射。因為它對造血組織有不良反應，從 1984 年以來，此藥一直被限制使用。商品名：Butazolidin。

phenylephrine *n.* a drug that constricts blood vessels (*see* sympathomimetic). It is given by injection to increase blood pressure, in a nasal spray to relieve nasal congestion, and in eye drops to dilate the pupils. Irritation may occur when applied. Trade name: **Minims phenylephrine**.

苯福林 一種血管收縮藥（參閱 sympathomimetic）。注射以增加血壓，鼻腔噴霧以緩解充血，滴眼時可擴張瞳孔。用藥時可產生刺激作用。商品名：Minims phenylephrine。

phenylketonuria *n.* an inherited defect of protein metabolism causing an excess of the amino acid phenylalanine in the blood, which damages the nervous system and leads to severe mental retardation. Screening of newborn infants by testing a blood sample for phenylalanine (*see* Guthrie test) enables the condition to be detected soon enough for dietary treatment to prevent any brain damage: the baby's diet contains proteins from which phenylalanine has been removed. The gene responsible for phenylketonuria is recessive, so that a child is affected only if both parents are carriers of the defective gene.

苯丙酮酸尿 一種先天性蛋白質代謝缺陷，造成血液中含過量的苯丙氨酸，損壞神經系統，導致嚴重的智力低下。通過檢查新生兒血樣中的苯丙氨酸對新生兒進行篩查（參閱 Guthrie test）能夠及時發現此病，以便採取飲食療法預防大腦受損：嬰兒的食物中含有去掉苯丙氨酸的蛋白質。導致苯丙氨酸尿的基因是隱性的，只有雙親都是基因缺陷攜帶者時嬰兒才發病。

phenylpropanolamine *n.* a drug with actions similar to those of *ephedrine. It is used to relieve allergic conditions, such

苯丙醇胺 作用與麻黃鹼類似的一種藥。用於緩解過敏疾病，例如哮喘、枯草熱和鼻充

as asthma and hay fever, and nasal congestion, and is administered by mouth, injection, or by inhalation. Side-effects may include dizziness, headache, digestive disorders, sweating, and thirst.

血。口服、注射或吸入。副作用可能包括頭暈、頭痛、消化不良、出汗和口渴。

phenylthiocarbamide (PTC) *n.* a substance that tastes bitter to some individuals but is tasteless to others. Response to PTC appears to be controlled by a single pair of genes (*alleles): ability to taste PTC is *dominant to the inability to taste it.

苯硫脲 有些人感到有苦味，但還有人感到無味的一種物質。對於苯硫脲的反應好像受一對基因（等位基因）的控制：能嘗到苯硫脲苦味的人遠比嘗不出的人呈顯性。

phenytoin *n.* an *anticonvulsant drug used to control major and focal epileptic seizures. It is administered by mouth or injection; the side-effects include gum hypertrophy, hirsutism, and skin rashes. Overdosage causes unsteadiness. Trade name: **Epanutin**.

苯妥英 用於控制癲癇大發作和局部發作的一種抗驚厥藥。口服或注射，副作用包括牙齦肥大、多毛症和皮疹。用藥過量會使病情不穩定。商品名：Epanutin。

phial *n.* a small glass bottle for storing medicines or poisons.

瓶（形）管 用於存放藥物或毒物的小玻璃瓶。

-philia *suffix denoting* morbid craving or attraction. Example: *nyctophilia* (for darkness).

〔後綴〕**癖，嗜** 例如：嗜夜癖。

phimosis *n.* narrowing of the opening of the foreskin, which cannot therefore be drawn back over the underlying glans penis. This predisposes to inflammation (*see* balanitis, balanoposthitis), which results in further narrowing. Treatment is by surgical removal of the foreskin (*circumcision).

包莖 包皮開口狹窄，因此包皮不能回縮到下面的陰莖頭上。包莖可誘發炎症（參閱 balanitis，balanoposthitis），炎症又會造成進一步狹窄。治療為手術切除包皮（包皮環切術）。

phleb- (phlebo-) *prefix denoting* a vein or veins. Example: *phlebectopia* (abnormal position of).

〔前綴〕**靜脈** 例如：靜脈異位。

phlebectomy *n.* the surgical removal of a vein (or part of a vein), sometimes performed for the treatment of varicose veins in the legs (*varicectomy*).

靜脈切除術 手術切除靜脈（或靜脈的一部分），下肢靜脈曲張治療（曲張靜脈切除術）時有時作此手術。

phlebitis *n.* inflammation of the wall of a vein, which is most commonly seen in the legs as a complication of *varicose veins. A segment of vein becomes painful and tender and the surrounding skin feels hot and appears red. Thrombosis commonly develops (*see* thrombophlebitis). Treatment consists of elastic support together with drugs, such as phenylbutazone, to relieve the inflammation and pain. Anticoagulants are not used (*compare* phlebothrombosis). Phlebitis may also complicate sepsis (*see* pylephlebitis) or cancer, especially of the stomach, bronchus, or pancreas. In pancreatic cancer the phlebitis may affect a variety of veins (*thrombophlebitis migrans*).

靜脈炎　靜脈壁的炎症，作為靜脈曲張的併發症，最常見於下肢。一段靜脈發痛且有觸痛，周圍皮膚發熱並呈紅色。常發生栓塞（參閱 thrombophlebitis）。治療包括用彈性繃帶包紮結合用藥，例如保泰松類藥，以消炎止痛。不使用抗凝血藥（與 phlebothrombosis 對比）。靜脈炎也可合併膿毒血症（參閱 pylephlebitis）或癌症，特別是胃癌、支氣管癌或胰腺癌。在胰腺癌中，靜脈炎可累及多種靜脈（游走性血栓性靜脈炎）。

phlebography *n. see* venography.

靜脈造影術　參閱 venography。

phlebolith *n.* a stone-like structure, usually found incidentally on abdominal X-ray, that results from deposition of calcium in a venous blood clot. It appears as a small round white opacity in the pelvic region. It does not produce symptoms and requires no treatment.

靜脈石　通常在腹部 X 綫檢查時偶然發現的結石樣結構，它由靜脈血管凝塊中鈣的沉積產生。在骨盆區域，該結構呈白色圓形小的不透光物，不產生症狀，無需治療。

phlebosclerosis (venosclerosis) *n.* a rare degenerative condition, of unknown cause, that affects the leg veins of young men. The vein walls become thickened and feel like cords under the skin. It is not related to arteriosclerosis and needs no treatment.

靜脈硬化　一種病因不明，影響青年人下肢靜脈的罕見變性疾病。靜脈壁變厚，觸摸時皮下呈繩索狀。與動脈硬化無關，無需治療。

phlebothrombosis *n.* obstruction of a vein by a blood clot, without preceding inflammation of its wall. It is most common within the deep veins of the calf of the leg (in contrast to thrombophlebitis, which affects superficial leg veins (*see* phlebitis)). Prolonged bed

靜脈血栓形成　血液凝塊引起的靜脈阻塞，沒有靜脈壁的前期炎症。最常見於小腿的深層靜脈中（與血栓性靜脈炎不同，血栓性靜脈炎影響下肢淺表靜脈。參閱 phlebitis）。長期臥床休息、心衰、妊娠、外

rest, heart failure, pregnancy, injury, and surgery predispose to thrombosis by encouraging sluggish blood flow. Many of these conditions are associated with changes in the clotting factors in the blood that increase the tendency to thrombosis; these changes also occur in some women taking oral contraceptives.

The affected leg may become swollen and tender. The main danger is that the clot may become detached and give rise to *pulmonary embolism. Regular leg exercises help to prevent phlebothrombosis, and anticoagulant drugs (such as warfarin and heparin) are used in prevention and treatment. Large clots may be removed surgically in the operation of *thrombectomy* to relieve leg swelling.

傷和手術使血流緩慢導致栓塞。這些病例中的多數與血液中凝血因素的改變有關，這種改變增加了栓塞的可能性，也發生於口服避孕藥的某些婦女中。

受累的下肢可出現腫脹和觸痛。主要的危險在於凝血塊可脫落，引起肺栓塞。有規律的鍛煉下肢有助於預防靜脈血栓形成。預防和治療可使用抗凝血藥（如：華法林和肝素）。大的凝血塊可用血栓切除術去除以解除下肢腫脹。

Phlebotomus *n. see* sandfly.

白蛉屬　參閱 sandfly。

phlebotomy (venesection) *n.* the surgical opening or puncture of a vein in order to remove blood (in the treatment of *polycythaemia) or to infuse fluids, blood, or drugs in the treatment of many conditions. It may also be required for cardiac *catheterization and *angiocardiography.

靜脈切開術，放血術　手術切開或刺穿靜脈，用於放血（治療紅細胞增多症）或治療諸多疾病時用於輸液、輸血或給藥。作心臟導管插入術和心血管造影術時也需要作此手術。

phlegm *n.* a nonmedical term for *sputum.

黏痰　痰的非醫學術語。

phlegmasia alba dolens *see* thrombophlebitis.

栓塞性靜脈炎　參閱 thrombophlebitis。

phlegmon *n. Archaic.* inflammation of connective tissue, leading to ulceration.

蜂窩織炎　（舊稱）導致潰瘍的結締組織炎症。

phlycten *n.* a small pinkish-yellow nodule surrounded by a zone of dilated blood vessels that occurs in the conjunctiva or in the cornea. It develops into a small ulcer that heals without trace in the

水疱　發生於結膜或角膜的，被血管舒張區域所包圍的一種橘紅色小結節。水疱可發育成小潰瘍，愈合時角膜中無痕跡，但結膜中可產生殘留瘢

conjunctiva but produces some residual scarring in the cornea. Phlyctens, which are prone to recur, are thought to be due to a type of allergy to certain bacteria.

痕。水疱易復發，被看作是對某種細菌的一種過敏。

phobia *n.* a pathologically strong *fear of a particular event or thing. Avoiding the feared situation may severely restrict one's life and cause much suffering. The main kinds of phobia are *specific phobias* (isolated fears of particular things, such as sharp knives); *agoraphobia; *social phobias* of encountering people; and *animal phobias*, as of spiders, rats, or dogs (*see also* preparedness). Treatment is with behaviour therapy, especially *desensitization and *flooding. *Psychotherapy and drug therapy are also useful.

恐怖症 對某種特殊事件或物體的一種病理性強烈恐懼感。躲避所恐懼的情景會嚴重影響患者的生活並引起極度痛苦。主要的恐怖類型有：特殊物體恐怖（僅害怕特殊物體，例如利刃）、曠野恐怖、社交恐怖和動物恐怖，例如懼怕蜘蛛、老鼠或狗（參閱 preparedness）。用行為療法，特別是脫敏療法和以恐治恐法治療。心理療法和藥物療法也有效。

-phobia *suffix denoting* morbid fear or dread.

〔後綴〕**恐怖** 病態的害怕或恐懼。

phocomelia *n.* congenital absence of the upper arm and/or upper leg, the hands or feet or both being attached to the trunk by a short stump. The condition is extremely rare except as a side-effect of the drug *thalidomide taken during early pregnancy.

短肢畸形 上臂和／或大腿的先天性缺失，手或腳或者手腳都依靠一根短小的殘肢與軀體連接。除了妊娠早期服用沙利度胺藥所引起外，此病極為罕見。

pholcodine *n.* a drug that suppresses coughs and reduces irritation in the respiratory system (*see* antitussive). It is administered by mouth in cough mixtrues and sometimes causes nausea and drowsiness. Trade names: **Galenphol**, **Pholcomed**.

福爾可定 止咳和減輕呼吸系統刺激的一種藥（參閱 antitussive）。作為止咳合劑口服。有時可引起惡心和嗜睡。商品名：Galenphol，Pholcomed。

phon *n.* a unit of loudness of sound. The intensity of a sound to be measured is compared by the human ear to a reference tone of 2×10^{-5} pascal sound pressure and 1000 hertz frequency. The intensity of the reference tone is increased until it appears to be equal in loudness to the sound being measured;

昉 聲音的強度單位。所測音響的強度是用人耳對 2×10^{-5} 帕斯卡的參考音響與 1000 赫茲頻率的音響作以比較。參考聲音的強度被加大到聽起來等於要測量的聲音的強度；用昉表示的這一聲音的強度等於參考音升高的分貝數。

the loudness of this sound in phons is then equal to the number of decibels by which the reference tone has had to be increased.

phon- (phono-) *prefix denoting* sound or voice.

〔前綴〕**聲音**

phonasthenia *n.* weakness of the voice, especially when due to fatigue.

發音無力 聲音無力，特別是疲勞引起的發音無力。

phonation *n.* the production of vocal sounds, particularly speech.

發音 發出聲音，特別是語言。

phonocardiogram *n. see* electrocardio-phonography. **–phonocardiography** *n.*

心音圖 參閱 electrocardio-phonography。

-phoria *suffix denoting* (in ophthalmology) an abnormal deviation of the eyes or turning of the visual axis. Example: *heterophoria* (tendency to squint).

〔後綴〕**隱斜眼** （眼科學）眼的異常偏斜或視軸轉向偏差。例如：隱斜視。

Phormia *n.* a genus of non-bloodsucking flies, commonly known as blowflies. The maggot of *P. regina* normally breeds in decaying meat but it has occasionally been found in suppurating wounds, giving rise to a type of *myiasis.

黑花蠅屬 一種非吸血蠅屬，常稱為麗蠅。黑花蠅的蛆常在腐肉中繁殖，偶爾見於化膿性傷口，導致一種蠅蛆病。

phosgene *n.* a poisonous gas developed during World War I. It is a choking agent, acting on the lungs to produce *oedema, with consequent respiratory and cardiac failure.

光氣 第一次世界大戰期間生產的一種毒氣。這是一種窒息性毒氣，作用於肺引起水腫，從而導致呼吸困難和心力衰竭。

phosphagen *n.* creatine phosphate (*see* creatine).

磷酸肌酸 參閱 creatine。

phosphataemia *n.* the presence of phosphates in the blood. Sodium, calcium, potassium, and magnesium phosphates are normal constituents.

磷酸鹽血 血液中出現磷酸鹽。鈉、鈣、鉀、鎂的磷酸鹽是正常成分。

phosphatase *n.* one of a group of enzymes capable of catalysing the

磷酸酶 一組能夠催化磷酸酯水解的酶，例如葡萄糖-6-磷酸

hydrolysis of phosphoric acid esters. An example is glucose-6-phosphatase, which catalyses the hydrolysis of glucose-6-phosphate to glucose and phosphate. Phosphatases are important in the absorption and metabolism of carbohydrates, nucleotides, and phospholipids and are essential in the calcification of bone. *Acid phosphatase* is present in kidney, semen, serum, and the prostate gland. *Alkaline phosphatase* occurs in teeth, developing bone, plasma, kidney, and intestine.

酶催化葡萄糖-6-磷酸水解成葡萄糖和磷酸鹽。磷酸酶在碳水化合物、核苷酸和磷脂的吸收和代謝中起重要作用，對於骨的鈣化十分必要。酸性磷酸酶出現於腎臟、精液、血清和前列腺中。鹼性磷酸酶出現於牙齒、發育中的骨骼、血漿、腎臟和腸中。

phosphatidylcholine *n. see* lecithin.

磷脂酰膽鹼，卵磷脂 參閱 lecithin。

phosphatidylserine *n.* a cephalin-like phospholipid containing the amino acid serine. It is found in brain tissue. *See also* cephalin.

磷脂酰絲氨酸 含有絲氨酸這一氨基酸的腦磷脂樣磷脂。此物質存在於大腦組織中。參閱 cephalin。

phosphaturia (phosphuria) *n.* the presence of an abnormally high concentration of phosphates in the urine, making it cloudy. The condition may be associated with the formation of stones (calculi) in the kidneys or bladder.

磷酸鹽尿 尿中出現異常高濃度的磷酸鹽，使尿變渾濁。此病可能和腎或膀胱結石有關。

phosphocreatine *n.* creatine phosphate (*see* creatine).

磷酸肌酸 參閱 creatine。

phosphofructokinase *n.* an enzyme that catalyses the conversion of fructose-6-phosphate to fructose-1,6-diphosphate. This is an important reaction occurring during the process of *glycolysis.

磷酸果糖激酶 一種催化果糖-6-磷酸轉化成果糖-1,6-二磷酸的酶。這是糖酵解過程中發生的一個重要反應。

phospholipid *n.* a *lipid containing a phosphate group as part of the molecule. Phospholipids are constituents of all tissues and organs, especially the brain. They are synthesized in the liver and small intestine and are involved in many

磷脂 分子的一部分中含磷酸鹽團的一種脂類。磷脂是所有組織和器官，特別是大腦的成分。它們在肝和小腸中合成並參與身體的許多代謝過程。例如：腦磷脂、卵磷脂、縮醛磷

of the body's metabolic processes. Examples of phospholipids are *cephalins, *lecithins, plasmalogens, and phosphatidylserine.

脂和磷脂酰絲氨酸等都是磷脂。

phosphonecrosis *n*. the destruction of tissues caused by excessive amounts of phosphorus in the system. The tissues likely to suffer in phosphorus poisoning are the liver, kidneys, muscles, bones, and the cardiovascular system.

磷毒性壞死 組織系統中磷過量造成的組織損壞。可能遭受磷中毒的組織有肝、腎、肌肉、骨骼和血管系統。

phosphorus *n*. a nonmetallic element. Phosphorus compounds are major constituents in the tissues of both plants and animals. In man, phosphorus is mostly concentrated in *bone. However, certain phosphorus-containing compounds – for example adenosine triphosphate (*ATP) and *creatine phosphate – play an important part in energy conversions and storage in the body. In a pure state, phosphorus is toxic. Symbol: P.

磷 一種非金屬元素。磷化合物是動植物組織中的主要成分。磷在人體主要集中在骨骼,但某些含磷化合物——例如三磷酸腺苷(ATP)和磷酸肌酸——在人體能量轉化和貯存中起重要作用。磷在純淨狀態時有毒。符號:P。

phosphorylase *n*. any enzyme that catalyses the combination of an organic molecule (usually glucose) with a phosphate group (phosphorylation). Phosphorylase is found in the liver and kidney, where it is involved in the breakdown of glycogen to glucose-1-phosphate.

磷酸化酶 催化有機分子(通常為葡萄糖)和磷酸基團化合(磷酸化)的任何酶。磷酸化酶存在於肝和腎,在此將糖原分解為葡萄糖-1-磷酸。

phot- (photo-) *prefix denoting* light.

〔前綴〕光

photalgia *n*. pain in the eye caused by very bright light.

光痛 非常亮的光引起的眼痛。

photochemotherapy *n. see* PUVA.

光化學療法 參閱 PUVA。

photocoagulation *n*. the destruction of tissue by heat released from the absorption of light shone on it. In eye disorders the technique is used to destroy diseased retinal tissue, occurring, for example, as

光照性凝固法 用照射到組織上的光被吸收時釋放的熱量破壞組織。在眼科疾病中,此技術被用作破壞病變的視網膜組織,例如在糖尿病併發症(糖

a complication of diabetes (diabetic retinopathy); and to produce scarring between the retina and choroid, thus binding them together, in cases of *detached retina. Photocoagulation of the retina is usually done with an *argon or *diode laser.

尿病視網膜病）時使用。在視網膜脫離的病例中用於在視網膜和脈絡膜之間製造瘢痕，使之結合在一起。視網膜光照凝固法時常採用氫激光或二極管激光器。

photodermatosis *n.* any of various skin diseases caused by exposure to light of varying wavelength (*see* photosensitivity). The facial prominences and the 'V' of the neck are most commonly affected, the shadow areas behind the ears and below the chin being protected. A common photodermatosis is *polymorphic light eruption*, which affects 10% of the population. It appears with the first sunshine of spring and abates by late summer. The photodermatoses include certain *porphyrias, notably porphyria cutanea tarda. Photosensitivity reactions may also occur in those taking such drugs as tetracylines, phenothiazines, frusemide, and NSAIDs.

光照性皮膚病 暴露於不同波長的光引起的任何皮膚病（參閱 photosensitivity）。臉上的凸出部和頸的 V 字形部位最常受影響，耳後和頦下被遮蓋區域受到保護。常見的光照性皮膚病是多形性光疹，此病侵襲 10% 的人口。此病在春天的第一次光照時產生，夏天的後期消退。光照性皮膚病包括某些卟啉症，特別是遲緩性皮膚卟啉症。服用四環素、吩噻嗪、呋噻米和非甾類抗炎藥等藥物者也可產生光照過敏反應。

photomicrograph *n.* an enlarged photographic record of an object taken through an optical or electron mircoscope. *Compare* microphotograph.

顯微照片 通過光學或電子顯微鏡拍攝的一個物體的放大照片。與 microphotograph 對比。

photophobia *n.* an abnormal intolerance of light, in which exposure to light produces intense discomfort of the eyes with tight contraction of the eyelids and other reactions aimed at avoiding the light. In most cases the light simply aggravates already existing discomfort from eye disease. Photophobia may be associated with dilation of the pupils as a result of eye drops or with migraine, measles, German measles, or meningitis.

畏光 異常不耐光，患者暴露於光會產生眼極度不適，伴有眼瞼緊閉和其他旨在避光的反應。在大多數病例中，光只是加重已存在的眼病引起的不適。畏光可能與使用滴眼藥引起的瞳孔擴大，或與偏頭痛、麻疹、風疹或腦膜炎有關。

photophthalmia *n.* inflammation of the eye due to exposure to light. It is usually caused by the damaging effect of

強光眼炎 接觸光引起的眼的炎症。常由紫外綫對角膜的破壞作用引起，例如雪盲。

ultraviolet light on the cornea, for example in snow blindness.

photopic *adj.* relating to or describing conditions of bright illumination. For example, *photopic vision* is vision in bright light, in which the *cones of the retina are responsible for visual sensation. **–photopia** *n.*

明視的　描述亮光照明的狀態或與之相關的狀態。例如，明視覺指在亮光下的視覺，此時視錐細胞負責視覺。

photopsia *n.* the sensation of flashes of light caused by mechanical stimulation of the retina of the eye, usually due to traction by the attached vitreous humour when the eye is moved.

閃光幻覺　對視網膜的機械刺激作用引起的閃光感，通常由眼運動時依附的透明體液所致。

photoradiation *n.* a recently developed technique for the location and destruction of certain tumours that relies on the reaction to light of a substance that is derived from *haematoporphyrin (*haematoporphyrin derivative*; *HPD*). Injected into the body, HPD concentrates in tumour cells and glows when subjected to ultraviolet irradiation, thus allowing the tumour to be located. The tumour is then irradiated with red light, which breaks down HPD to release highly active oxygen that destroys the tumour cells without damaging surrounding normal tissue.

光輻射　新研製的確定某些腫瘤位置並破壞腫瘤的一種技術，其根據是從血卟啉中衍化出的物質（血卟啉衍化物；HPD）對光的反應。將 HPD 注射入體內，它會在腫瘤細胞內聚集，用紫外綫照射時，HPD 會發光，從而使人們能確定腫瘤位置。然後用紅光照射腫瘤，分解 HPD 使之釋放出活力極強的破壞腫瘤細胞的氧，而不會損壞周圍的正常組織。

photoretinitis *n.* damage to the retina of the eye caused by looking at the sun without adequate protection for the eyes. The retina may be burnt by the intense light focused on it; this affects the central part of the visual field, which may be permanently lost (*sun blindness*).

光照性視網膜炎　眼睛沒有充分保護時看太陽對視網膜造成的損害。視網膜可能被聚焦到視網膜上的強光灼傷；這會影響視野的中心部位，視力可能永久喪失（日光盲）。

photosensitivity *n.* abnormal reaction of the skin to sunlight. **–photosensitive** *adj.*

光敏感性　皮膚對陽光的異常反應。

photosynthesis *n.* the process whereby green plants and some bacteria

光合作用　植物和某些細菌利用葉綠素從太陽光吸收能，將

manufacture carbohydrates from carbon dioxide and water, using energy absorbed from sunlight by the green pigment chlorophyll. In green plants this complex process may be summarized thus: $6CO_2 + 6H_2O \rightarrow C_6H_{12}O_6 + 6O_2$

二氧化碳和水變成碳水化合物的過程。植物的光合作用可以總結為：$6CO_2 + 6H_2O \rightarrow C_6H_{12}O_6 + 6O_2$

phototaxis *n.* movement of a cell or organism in response to a stimulus of light.

趨光性 細胞或生物在光的刺激下運動。

photuria *n.* the excretion of phosphorescent urine, which glows in the dark, due to the presence of certain phosphorus-containing compounds derived from phosphates.

發光尿 一種磷光尿，夜間發光，原因是尿中有從磷酸鹽中衍化出的含磷化合物。

phren- (phreno-) *prefix denoting* **1.** the mind or brain. **2.** the diaphragm. **3.** the phrenic nerve.

〔前綴〕 **(1)** 精神，大腦 **(2)** 膈 **(3)** 膈神經

-phrenia *suffix denoting* a condition of the mind. Example: *hebephrenia* (schizophrenia affecting young adults).

〔後綴〕 **精神狀態** 例如：青春型精神分裂症。

phrenic avulsion the surgical removal of a section of the *phrenic nerve, which paralyses the diaphragm. The procedure was used as a means of resting a lung infected with tuberculosis.

膈神經抽出術 手術切除膈神經的一部分，使膈麻痺，此手術曾被用來使感染結核的肺休息。

phrenic crush surgical crushing of a portion of the *phrenic nerve. This paralyses the diaphragm on the side operated upon, which is then pushed upwards by the abdominal contents, thus pressing on the lung and partially collapsing it. This operation was formerly often combined with *pneumoperitoneum in the treatment of pulmonary tuberculosis.

膈神經壓榨術 手術壓榨部分膈神經。這使手術側的膈麻痺，被麻痺的膈部分被腹內容物上推。並擠壓在肺部，使肺部分萎縮。此手術在治療肺結核時曾和氣腹結合使用。

phrenic nerve the nerve that supplies the muscles of the diaphragm. On each side it arises in the neck from the third, fourth, and fifth cervical spinal roots and

膈神經 支配膈肌的神經。膈神經在每側都起自頸內第三、第四、第五頸脊神經根，從肺與心臟之間下行至膈。來自腦

passes downwards between the lungs and the heart to reach the diaphragm. Impulses through the nerves from the brain bring about the regular contractions of the diaphragm during breathing.

神經的衝動使膈在呼吸期間有節律的收縮。

phrenology *n.* the study of the bumps on the outside of the skull in order to determine a person's character. It is based on the mistaken theory that the skull becomes modified over the different functional areas of the cortex of the brain.

顱相學 研究頭蓋骨上的隆起部分以確定一個人的性格。顱相學建立在一個錯誤的理論基礎之上，即認為顱骨隨着大腦皮質的不同功能區域而產生變化。

Phthirus *n.* a widely distributed genus of lice. The crab (or pubic) louse, *P. pubis*, is a common parasite of man that lives permanently attached to the body hair, particularly that of the pubic or perianal regions but also on the eyelashes and the hairs in the armpits. Crab lice are not known to transmit disease but their bites can irritate the skin (*see* pediculosis). An infestation may be acquired during sexual intercourse or from hairs left on clothing, towels, and lavatory seats.

陰虱屬 一種分布廣泛的虱屬。陰虱是一種常見寄生蟲，它永久性地寄生於體毛，但也寄生於睫毛和腋毛。沒有發現陰虱會傳播疾病，但牠們的叮咬能刺激皮膚（參閱 pediculosis）。性交或留在衣服、毛巾及馬桶上的體毛能引起陰虱感染。

phthisis *n.* a former name for: **1.** any disease resulting in wasting of tissues; **2.** pulmonary *tuberculosis.

（舊稱）**(1) 消耗性疾病** 導致組織消耗的任何疾病。**(2) 肺結核**

phycomycosis *n.* a disease caused by parasitic fungi of the genera *Rhizopus*, *Absidia*, and *Mucor*. The disease affects the sinuses, the central nervous system, the lungs, and the skin tissues. The fungi are able to grow within the blood vessels of the lungs and nervous tissue, thus causing blood clots which cut off the blood supply (*see* infarction). Treatment with the antibiotic *amphotericin B has proved effective.

藻菌病 寄生性真菌根黴菌屬、犁頭黴菌屬和毛黴菌屬引起的疾病。此病影響鼻竇、中樞神經系統、肺和皮膚組織，真菌能夠在肺血管和神經組織中生長，引起凝血從而切斷血液供應（參閱 infarction）。用抗生素兩性黴素治療有效。

phylogenesis *n.* the evolutionary history of a species or individual.

系統發育，種系發生 物種或個體的進化史。

physi- (physio-) *prefix denoting* **1.** physiology. **2.** physical.

〔前綴〕**(1)** 生理學 **(2)** 物理的，軀體的

physical *adj.* (in medicine) relating to the body rather than to the mind. For example, a *physical sign* is one that a doctor can detect when examining a patient, such as abnormal dilation of the pupils or the absence of a knee-jerk reflex (*see also* functional disorder, organic disorder).

軀體的 （醫學）與身體而不是精神相關的。例如：體徵是醫生檢查病人時能發現的徵兆，如瞳孔異常擴大或膝反射缺失（參閱 functional disorder，organic disorder）。

physical medicine a medical specialty established by the Royal Society of Medicine in 1931. Initially the members pioneered clinics devoted to the diagnosis and management of rheumatic diseases, but later extended their interests to the *rehabilitation of patients with physical disabilities ranging from asthma and hand injuries to back trouble and poliomyelitis. The term has caused confusion in recent years, with many doctors preferring the description *rheumatology and rehabilitation* for this specialist activity. Since 1972, however, when the Royal College of Physicians approved it, physical medicine has become the generally accepted term. *See also* rheumatology.

物理醫學 皇家醫學會 1931 年建立的醫學專業。起初其成員率先開設了診斷和治療風濕性疾病的診所，後來診治範圍擴大到哮喘、手外傷、背痛到脊髓灰質炎等軀體殘疾患者的康復。近年來隨著許多醫生喜歡用風濕病學和康復醫學來描述這一醫學專業，此術語已引起了混亂。然而從 1972 年皇家內科醫學院認可此術語以來，它已被廣泛接受。參閱 rheumatology。

physician *n.* a registered medical practitioner who specializes in the diagnosis and treatment of disease by other than surgical means. In the USA the term is applied to any authorized medical practitioner. *See also* Doctor.

內科醫師 註冊行醫者，專門從事疾病的診斷和治療，但不能使用手術手段。在美國，此術語指任何被授權的行醫者。參閱 Doctor。

physiological solution one of a group of solutions used to maintain tissues in a viable state. These solutions contain specific concentrations of substances that are vital for normal tissue function (e.g. sodium, potassium, calcium, chloride,

生理溶液 一組用於維持組織處於存活狀態的溶液之一。這些溶液含有特定濃度的、對正常組織功能至關重要的物質（如鈉、鉀、鈣、氯、鎂、碳酸氫鹽、磷酸鹽離子、葡萄糖

magnesium, bicarbonate, and phosphate ions, glucose, and oxygen). An example of such a solution is *Ringer's solution.

和氧）。例如：林格溶液就是這種溶液。

physiology *n.* the science of the functioning of living organisms and of their component parts. **–physiological** *adj.* **–physiologist** *n.*

生理學　研究活生物和其組成部分功能的科學。

physiotherapy *n.* the branch of treatment that employs physical methods to promote healing, including the use of light, infrared and ultraviolet rays, heat, electric current, massage, manipulation, and remedial exercise.

物理治療，理療　採用物理方法促進康復的治療學分支，其中包括使用光、紅外綫、紫外綫、熱、電流、按摩、推拿和康復運動等。

physo- *prefix denoting* air or gas.

〔前綴〕空氣，氣

physostigmine (eserine) *n.* a *parasympathomimetic drug used mainly to constrict the pupil of the eye and to reduce pressure inside the eye in glaucoma. It is administered by injection, in eye drops, or in an ointment; side-effects include digestive upsets and salivation.

毒扁豆鹼　主要用於縮小瞳孔和降低青光眼病人眼壓的一種擬副交感神經藥。注射，作為滴眼藥或油膏給藥，副作用有消化不良和流涎。

phyt- (phyto-) *prefix denoting* plants; of plant origin.

〔前綴〕植物，植物源的

phytohaemagglutinin (PHA) *n.* a plant-derived alkaloid that stimulates T-lymphocytes to divide in the test tube.

植物血細胞凝集素　能夠刺激試管中 T 細胞分裂的植物鹼。

phytomenadione *n.* a form of *vitamin K occurring naturally in green plants but usually synthesized for use as an antidote to overdosage with anticoagulant drugs. It promotes the production of prothrombin, essential for the normal coagulation of blood. Trade name: **Konakion**.

維生素 K₁　綠色植物中自然存在的一種維生素 K，但常人工合成，作為抗血凝劑使用過量時的拮抗劑。維生素 K₁ 能產生正常凝血所必需的凝血酶。商品名：Konakion。

phytophotodermatitis *n.* an eruption of large blisters occurring after exposure to light in people who have been in

植物（性與）光照性皮炎　對於某些植物過敏，如對野生歐洲防風和歐芹過敏的人接觸了

contact with certain plants, such as wild parsnip or cow parsley, to which they are sensitive.

這些植物後又受光照而產生的大水疱疹。

phytotoxin *n.* any poisonous substance (toxin) produced by a plant, such as any of the toxins produced by fungi of the genus *Amanita*.

植物毒素 植物產生的任何有毒物質（毒素），例如：捕蠅蕈屬類真菌產生的任何毒素。

pia (pia mater) *n.* the innermost of the three *meninges surrounding the brain and spinal cord. The membrane is closely attached to the surface of the brain and spinal cord, faithfully following each fissure and sulcus. It contains numerous finely branching blood vessels that supply the nerve tissue within. The subarachnoid space separates it from the arachnoid.

軟腦膜 包圍大腦和脊髓的三層腦脊膜中最裏的一層。軟腦膜緊貼大腦和脊髓，深入到每個裂和溝。它含有無數供應腦內神經組織的細小血管分支。蛛網膜下腔把蛛網膜與軟腦膜隔開。

pian *n.* *see* yaws.

雅司病 參閱 yaws。

pica *n.* the indiscriminate eating of non-nutritious or harmful substances, such as grass, stones, or clothing. It is common in early childhood but may also be found in mentally handicapped and psychotic patients. Although previously thought to be completely non-adaptive, some evidence suggests that some patients showing pica may have particular mineral dificiencies (such as iron deficiency).

異食癖 不加區別地吃無營養或有害物質，例如草、石頭或衣服。常見於幼兒期，但也可見於心理缺陷患者和精神病患者。儘管以前人們認為異食癖是完全不適應環境，有證據表明有些異食癖患者可能缺乏某些特殊礦物質（例如缺鐵）。

Pick's disease a rare cause of dementia in middle-aged people. The damage is mainly in the frontal and temporal lobes of the brain, in contrast with the diffuse degeneration of *Alzheimer's disease.

皮克病 中年人痴呆病的一種罕見病因。主要是大腦額葉和顳葉受損，這與阿爾茨海默病的彌漫性變性相對。

pico- *prefix denoting* one million-millionth (10^{-12}).

〔前綴〕 沙，毫纖，微微（10^{-12}）。

picornavirus *n.* one of a group of small RNA-containing viruses (pico

細小核糖核酸病毒，微小RNA 病毒 一組含 RNA 的

= small; hence pico-RNA-virus). The group includes *Coxsackie viruses, *polioviruses, and *rhinoviruses.

小病毒之一（pico 表示小，因此 pico-RNA-virus 表示微小 RNA 病毒）。這組病毒有柯薩奇病毒，脊髓灰質炎病毒和鼻病毒。

picric acid (trinitrophenol) a yellow crystalline solid used as a dye and as a tissue *fixative.

三硝基（苯）酚，苦味酸 種用作染劑和組織固定劑的黃色結晶固體。

PID *see* pelvic inflammatory disease.

盆腔炎性疾病　參閱 pelvic inflammatory disease。

piedra *n.* a fungal disease of the hair in which the hair shafts carry hard masses of black or white fungus. The black fungus, *Piedraia hortai*, is found mainly in the tropics and the white variety, *Trichosporon cutaneum*, in temperate regions.

毛孢子菌病　一種毛髮的真菌性疾病，發病時毛幹攜帶黑色或白色真菌硬塊。黑色真菌為霍塔毛孢子菌，主要存在於熱帶地區，白色變種為皮膚毛孢子菌，發生於溫帶地區。

Pierre-Robin syndrome a congenital disease in which affected infants have a very small lower jawbone (mandible) and a cleft palate. They are susceptible to feeding and respiratory problems.

皮埃爾-羅賓綜合徵　一種先天性疾病，受累嬰兒下頜骨很小且腭裂。患兒進食困難，易患呼吸疾病。

pigeon chest forward protrusion of the breastbone resulting in deformity of the chest. The condition is painless and harmless. Medical name: **pectus carinatum**.

雞胸　胸骨向前突出，導致胸部畸形。這種病無痛、無害。醫學用語：鷄胸。

pigeon toes an abnormal posture in which the toes are turned inwards. It is often associated with *knock-knee.

鴿趾，內收足　腳趾向內的異常姿勢。鴿趾常和膝外翻有關。

pigment *n.* a substance giving colour. Physiologically important pigments include the blood pigments (especially *haemoglobin), *bile pigments, and retinal pigment (*see* rhodopsin). The pigment *melanin occurs in the skin and in the iris of the eye. Important plant pigments include *chlorophyll and the *carotenoids.

色素　着色物質。生理學意義上重要的色素有血色素（特別是血紅蛋白）、膽色素和視網膜色素（參閱 rhodopsin）。黑色素存在於皮膚和虹膜。重要的植物色素包括葉綠素和類胡蘿蔔素。

pigmentation *n*. coloration produced in the body by the deposition of one pigment, especially in excessive amounts. Pigmentation may be produced by natural pigments, such as bile pigments (as in jaundice) or melanin, or by foreign material, such as lead or arsenic in chronic poisoning.

pig-tail stents *see* stent.

piles *n. see*. haemorrhoids.

pili (fimbriae) *pl. n.* (*sing.* **pilus, fimbria**) hairlike processes present on the surface of certain bacteria. They are thought to be involved in adhesion of bacteria to other cells and in transfer of DNA during *conjugation.

pill *n*. **1**. a small ball of variable size, shape, and colour, sometimes coated with sugar, that contains one or more medicinal substances in solid form. It is taken by mouth. **2. the Pill** *see* oral contraceptive.

pillar *n*. (in anatomy) an elongated apparently supportive structure. For example, the *pillars of the fauces* are folds of mucous membrane on either side of the opening from the mouth to the pharynx.

pilo- *prefix denoting* hair. Example: *pilosis* (excessive development of).

pilocarpine *n*. a drug with actions and uses similar to those of *physostigmine. It is administered as eye drops and may cause digestive upsets and salivation if absorbed into the system. Trade name: **Minims pilocarpine**.

pilomotor nerves sympathetic nerves that supply muscle fibres in the skin,

色素沉着　體內色素沉積，特別是過量沉積引起的着色。色素沉着可能由自然色素產生，例如膽色素（如在黃疸中）、黑色素或異物引起，例如由慢性鉛或砷中毒引起。

雙 J 形引流條　參閱 stent。

痔　參閱 haemorrhoids。

菌毛　某些細菌表面出現的毛狀突起。據認為他們參與使細菌和其他細胞黏接在一起，以及在接合生殖期使 DNA 轉移。

(1) 藥丸　含一種或多種藥物，有時覆蓋有糖衣的大小、形狀和顏色各異的小球。口服。**(2)** 口服避孕藥　參閱 oral contraceptive。

弓，柱，腳　（解剖學）一種延長的明顯支持結構。例如：舌腭弓是口腔通往咽的開口兩側的黏膜皺襞。

〔前綴〕毛，髮　如：多毛。

毛果蕓香鹼　與毒扁豆鹼的作用和用途相似的一種藥物。作為滴眼藥給藥。被消化系統吸收可引起消化不良和流涎。商品名：Minims pilocarpine。

毛髮運動神經　支配皮膚中毛根周圍肌纖維的交感神經。交

around the roots of hairs. Activity of the sympathetic nervous system causes the muscles to contract, raising the hairs and giving the 'gooseflesh' effect of fear or cold.

感神經系統的活動使肌肉收縮，使頭髮豎起並產生恐懼或寒冷的「雞皮疙瘩」。

pilonidal sinus a short tract leading from an opening in the skin in or near the cleft at the top of the buttocks and containing hairs. The sinus may be recurrently infected, leading to pain and the discharge of pus. Treatment is by surgical opening and cleaning of the sinus.

藏毛竇，骶尾竇　由皮膚開口通向或接近臀部頂部裂的含毛短通道。骶尾竇可被反覆感染，導致疼痛及排膿。治療採取手術切開和清潔竇道。

pilosebaceous *adj.* relating to the hair follicles and their associated sebaceous glands.

毛囊（腺）皮質腺的　與毛囊及其皮脂腺相關的。

pilus *n.* a hair. *See also* pili.

毛，髮　參閱 pili。

pimel- (pimelo-) *prefix denoting* fat; fatty.

〔前綴〕脂肪，脂肪的

pimozide *n.* an *antipsychotic drug used to relieve hallucinations and delusions occurring in schizophrenia. It is administered by mouth; side-effects may include skin rashes, tremors, and abnormal movements. Trade name: **Orap**.

匹莫齊特　一種抗精神病藥，用於緩解精神分裂症中出現的幻覺和妄想。口服。副作用可包括皮疹、震顫和異常運動。商品名：Orap。

pimple *n.* a small inflamed swelling on the skin that contains pus. It may be the result of bacterial infection of a skin pore that has become obstructed with fatty secretions from the sebaceous glands. Pimples occurring in large numbers on the chest, back, and face are usually described as *acne, a common condition of adolescence.

小膿疱　皮膚上含膿的小炎症腫脹。它可能是皮脂腺的脂性分泌物阻塞了皮膚毛孔引起的細菌感染所致。胸、背和面部出現的大量小膿疱通常叫痤瘡，是青春期常見病。

pincement *n.* one of the techniques used in massage, in which pinches of the patient's flesh are taken between finger and thumb and twisted or rolled before release. This is said to improve the tone

撙按法　一種按摩技術，用手指和拇指捏起患者肌肉，撙或揉後再鬆開。據說這可以增加皮膚張力，改善血液循環並減輕按摩部位下方疼痛。

of the skin, improve circulation, and alleviate underlying pain.

pineal gland (pineal body) a pea-sized mass of nerve tissue attached by a stalk to the posterior wall of the third ventricle of the brain, deep between the cerebral hemispheres at the back of the skull. It functions as a gland, secreting the hormone *melatonin, the gland becomes calcified as age progresses, providing a useful landmark in X-rays of the skull. Anatomical name: **epiphysis**.

松果體　通過一根莖連接到大腦第三腦室後壁的一個豌豆大小的神經組織團，它位於顱後部大腦兩半球之間深處。作為一個腺體發揮作用，能分泌出褪黑激素。此腺體隨着人年齡增加會鈣化，在顱骨 X 綫檢查中提供了一個有用的界標。解剖學名：松果體。

pinguecula *n.* a degenerative change in the conjunctiva of the eye, seen most commonly in the elderly and in those who live in hot dry climates. Thickened yellow triangles develop on the conjunctiva at the inner and outer margins of the cornea.

結膜黃斑　眼結膜的退化性變化，最常見於老年人和生活在乾熱氣候中的人。角膜內外邊緣的結膜上形成變厚的黃色三角形。

pink disease a severe illness of children of the teething age, marked by pink cold clammy hands and feet, heavy sweating, raised blood pressure, rapid pulse, photophobia, loss of appetite, and insomnia. Affected infants are very prone to secondary infection, which may be fatal. It was been suggested that the condition is an allergic reaction to mercury, since it used to occur when teething powders, lotions, and ointments containing mercury were used. Although there is no definite proof of this, the disease has virtually disappeared since all mercury-containing paediatric preparations have been banned. Medical names: **acrodynia**, **erythroedema**, **erythromelalgia**.

紅皮病，肢痛症　出牙期兒童的一種嚴重疾病，特點為手腳發紅、冰冷、黏濕、多汗、血壓升高、脈搏急促、畏光、食慾不振和失眠等。患兒易發生繼發性感染，可引起死亡。因為此病常在使用含汞的牙粉、洗劑及膏劑後發生。所以人們認為此病是對汞的過敏反應。儘管尚無確鑿證據，但自從所有含汞的兒童用品被禁止後，此病已幾乎絕迹。醫學用語：肢痛症，紅皮水腫病，紅斑性肢痛病。

pink eye *see* conjunctivitis.

紅眼，急性結膜炎　參閱 conjunctivitis。

pinna (auricle) *n.* the flap of skin and cartilage that projects from the head at

耳廓　從頭部外耳道外開口處突出的皮和軟骨構成的瓣（見

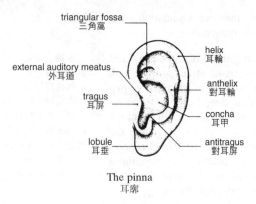

triangular fossa
三角窩

helix
耳輪

external auditory meatus
外耳道

anthelix
對耳輪

tragus
耳屏

concha
耳甲

lobule
耳垂

antitragus
對耳屏

The pinna
耳廓

the exterior opening of the external auditory meatus of the *ear (see illustration). In man the pinna is largely vestigial but it may be partly concerned with detecting the direction of sound sources.

pinnaplasty *n. see* otoplasty.

pinocytosis *n.* the intake of small droplets of fluid by a cell by cytoplasmic engulfment. It occurs in many white blood cells and in certain kidney and liver cells. *Compare* phagocytosis.

pinta *n.* a skin disease, prevalent in tropical America, that seems to affect only the dark-skinned races. It is caused by the *spirochaete *Treponema carateum*, a microorganism similar to those causing *yaws and *syphilis. The disease is thought to be transmitted either by direct contact between individuals or by flies that carry the infective spirochaetes on their bodies. Symptoms include thickening and eventual loss of pigment of the skin, particularly on the hands, wrists, feet, and ankles. Pinta is rarely disabling or fatal and is treated successfully with *penicillin.

圖）。耳廓在人類大部分已退化，但可能部分參與辨別聲源的方向。

耳廓整形術 參閱 otoplasty。

細胞吞飲作用 細胞通過胞漿的吞食作用攝食液體小滴。吞飲作用發生於許多白細胞、某些腎和肝細胞內。與 phagocytosis 對比。

品他病 流行於美洲熱帶地區，好像僅侵襲黑色人種的一種皮膚病。由品他病螺旋體引起，此螺旋體類似於引起雅司病和梅毒的微生物。人們認為此病的傳染途徑是人與人之間直接接觸或攜帶感染性螺旋體的蒼蠅。症狀有皮膚變厚及最後色素消失，特別是手、腕、足和踝部皮膚色素消失。偶爾可致殘或致命，用青黴素可有效治療。

pinworm (threadworm) *n.* a parasitic nematode worm of the genus *Enterobius* (*Oxyuris*), which lives in the upper part of the large intestine of man. The threadlike female worm, some 12 mm long, is larger than the male; it emerges from the anus in the evening to deposit its eggs, and later dies. If the eggs are swallowed by man and reach the intestine they develop directly into adult worms. Pinworms cause *enterobiasis, a disease common in children throughout the world.

蟯蟲（綫蟲） 生活在大腸上部的寄生性蟯蟲綫蟲。綫狀雌蟲長 12mm，比雄蟲大，夜間從肛門爬出產卵，然後死亡。如果蟲卵被人吞食且到達了腸，牠們會直接發育為成蟲，引起蟯蟲病，這是一種全球兒童常見病。

piperazine *n.* a drug used to treat infestations by roundworms and threadworms. It is administered by mouth; side-effects do not usually occur, but continued treatment at high doses may cause nausea, vomiting, headache, tingling sensations, and rashes. Trade name: **Pripsen**.

哌嗪 用於治療蛔蟲和蟯蟲感染的一種藥物。口服；常無副作用，但大劑量持續治療可引起惡心、嘔吐、頭痛、麻刺感及皮疹。商品名：Pripsen。

piriform fossae two pear-shaped depressions that lie on either side of the opening to the larynx.

梨狀隱窩 位於咽開口兩側的兩個梨狀凹陷。

piroxicam *n.* a nonsteroidal antiinflammatory drug (*see* NSAID) used to relieve pain and stiffness in osteoarthritis, rheumatoid arthritis, gout, and ankylosing spondylitis. It is administered by mouth; side-effects include dizziness, skin rash, and gastrointestinal symptoms. Trade name: **Feldene**.

吡羅昔康 一種非類固醇抗炎藥（參閱 NSAID），用於解除骨關節炎、風濕性關節炎、痛風、關節強硬性脊椎炎等病中疼痛和強直。口服；副作用有頭暈、皮疹和腸胃症狀。商品名：Feldene。

pisiform bone the smallest bone of the wrist (*carpus): a pea-shaped bone that articulates with the triquetral bone and, indirectly by cartilage, with the ulna.

豌豆骨 腕骨中最小的骨，呈豌豆形，它與三角骨相關節，並通過軟骨與尺骨間接構成關節。

pit *n.* (in anatomy) a hollow or depression, such as any of the depressions on the surface of an embryo marking the site of future organs.

窩，凹 （解剖學）凹或窩，如胚胎表面標誌着將來生長出器官的任何窩。

pithiatism *n.* the treatment of certain disorders by persuading the patient that all is well. Symptoms that disappear in these circumstances are regarded as manifestations of some psychological disturbance and are classified as hysterical symptoms.

説服療法　通過勸説病人使其相信其一切正常來治療某些疾病。在這些環境中消失的症狀被看作是心理障礙並被劃分為癔病性症狀。

pithing *n.* the laboratory procedure in which a part or the whole of the central nervous system of an experimental animal (such as a frog) is destroyed, usually by inserting a probe through the foramen magnum, in preparation for physiological or pharmacological experiments.

腦脊髓刺毀法　通常用一根探針刺透實驗動物（例如青蛙）的枕骨大孔，破壞其整個或部分中樞神經系統的實驗室操作，其目的在於進行病理學及藥理學實驗。

pitting *n.* the formation of depressed scars, as occurs on the skin following smallpox or acne. *Pitting oedema* is swelling of the tissues due to excess fluid in which fingertip pressure leaves temporary indentations in the skin.

凹陷，凹痕　下陷的瘢痕的形成，如天花或痤瘡後皮膚表面出現的凹陷。凹陷性水腫是因為組織過度積液引起的腫脹，手指尖按壓水腫部位會在皮膚上留下暫時性凹陷。

pituicyte *n.* a type of cell found in the posterior lobe of the pituitary gland. Similar in appearance to an *astrocyte, with numerous fine branches that end in contact with the lining membrane of the blood channels in the gland.

垂體（後葉）細胞　存在於垂體後葉的一類細胞，外觀上類似於星形（膠質）細胞，帶有無數細小分支，這些小分支的末梢與腺體血管襯膜相接觸。

pituitary gland (hypophysis) the master endocrine gland: a pea-sized body attached beneath the *hypothalamus in a bony cavity at the base of the skull. It has an anterior lobe (*adenohypophysis*), which secretes *thyroid-stimulating hormone, *ACTH (adrenocorticotrophic hormone), the *gonadotrophins, *growth hormone, *prolactin, *lipotrophin, and *melanocyte-stimulating hormone. The secretion of all these hormones is regulated by specific *releasing hormones*, which are produced in the hypothalamus (*see also* gonadotrophin-releasing

垂體　最重要的內分泌腺：垂體是顱基底部骨腔內附着於下丘腦下方的一個豌豆大小的腺體。它有一前葉（腺性垂體），能分泌促甲狀腺激素、促腎上腺皮質激素、促性腺激素、生長激素、催乳素、促脂解激素和促黑素細胞激素等。所有這些激素的分泌均受下丘腦產生的專門釋放激素的調節（參閱 gonadotrophin-releasing hormone）。後葉（神經性垂體）分泌加壓素和縮宮素，這些物質在下丘腦合成，輸送到垂體貯存，然後釋放。

hormone). The posterior lobe (*neuro-hypophysis*) secretes *vasopressin and *oxytocin, which are synthesized in the hypothalamus and transported to the pituitary, where they are stored before release.

pityriasis *n.* (originally) any of a group of skin diseases typified by the development of fine branlike scales. The term is now used only with a modifying adjective. *Pityriasis alba* is a common condition in children in which pale scaly patches occur on the face; it may be related to atopic *eczema. *Pityriasis rosea* is a common skin rash, believed to be viral in origin, that starts with a single patch of spots (a *herald patch*) on the trunk and is followed by an eruption of oval pink scaly *macules. The spots are often aligned along the ribs. The rash clears completely in about eight weeks. *Pityriasis versicolor* is a common chronic infection of the skin caused by the fungus *Pityrosporum orbiculare*, which is a normal inhabitant of the scalp. In susceptible people it changes to a pathogenic form called *Malassezia furfur* and produces a persistent depigmented scaly rash on the trunk. Treatment with *selenium sulphide (Selsun) shampoo readily kills the organism but the skin may take months to regain its normal colour. *See also* dandruff (pityriasis capitis).

Pityrosporum *n.* a genus of yeasts producing superficial infections of the skin. The species *P. orbiculare* is a normal inhabitant of the scalp but it can become pathogenic in susceptible individuals (*see* pityriasis).

pivampicillin *n.* a broad-spectrum *penicillin-type antibiotic administered by mouth to treat bronchitis, pneumonia,

糠疹 （原指）以形成細糠樣皮屑為特徵的一組皮膚病。此術語現在僅和一修飾性形容詞連用，白糠疹是一種兒童常見病，患兒面部產生鱗狀白斑，此病可能與特異反應性濕疹相關。玫瑰糠疹是一種常見皮疹，據說是病毒引起的，開始時軀幹上出現一小塊斑（前驅斑），然後爆發卵圓形鱗狀紅斑。斑塊常沿肋骨排列。大約八周後皮疹完全消退。花斑糠疹是由正圓瓶形酵母引起的常見慢性皮膚感染。這種真菌是頭皮的正常寄生物。在易感人羣中，它可能變成叫糠秕馬拉色黴菌的致病形式，並在人軀體上產生持續性色素脫離鱗狀皮疹。用硫化硒（二硫化硒）洗髮劑很容易殺死這種生物，但皮膚需數日後才能恢復正常顏色。參閱 dandruff (pityriasis capitis)。

瓶形酵母屬 產生皮膚表面感染的酵母菌屬，正圓瓶形酵母是頭皮上的正常寄生物，但在易感人羣中可變成致病因素（參閱 pityriasis）。

匹氨西林 口服廣譜青黴素類抗生素，用於治療支氣管炎、肺炎、皮膚感染、尿路感染和

skin infections, urinary infections, and gonorrhoea. Possible side-effects include allergic reactions, nausea, and vomiting. Trade name: **Pondocillin**.

淋病。副作用有過敏反應，惡心和嘔吐。商品名：Pondocillin。

pivmecillinam *n*. a *penicillin-type antibiotic used to treat urinary-tract and other infections. It is administered by mouth: possible side-effects include allergic reactions, nausea, and vomiting. Trade name: **Selexid**.

匹美西林　用於治療尿路及其他感染的青黴素類抗生素。口服，可能產生的副作用有過敏反應、惡心及嘔吐。商品名：Selexid。

pivot joint *see* trochoid joint.

車輪關節，旋轉關節　參閱 trochoid joint。

pizotifen *n*. an antihistamine drug used to prevent severe migraine attacks. Administered by mouth, it acts by inhibiting the effects of *serotonin. Possible side-effects include dizziness, drowsiness, and weight gain. Trade name: **Sanomigran**.

苯噻啶　用於預防嚴重偏頭痛的一種抗組胺藥。口服，通過抑制 5-羥色胺的作用起作用。可能出現的副作用有頭暈、嗜睡和體重增加。商品名：Sanomigran。

placebo *n*. a medicine that is ineffective but may help to relieve a condition because the patient has faith in its powers. New drugs are tested against placebos in clinical trials: the drug's effect is compared with the *placebo response*, which occurs even in the absence of any pharmacologically active substance in the placebo.

安慰劑　一種實際上無效，但因為病人相信其效力，因而可以幫助解除病情的一種藥物。在臨床試驗中，將新藥與安慰劑進行對照測試；新藥的作用與安慰劑的反應進行比較。即使安慰劑中沒有任何藥理學有效成分，安慰劑的反應也會發生。

placenta *n*. an organ within the uterus by means of which the embryo is attached to the wall of the uterus. Its primary function is to provide the embryo with nourishment, eliminate its wastes, and exchange respiratory gases. This is accomplished by the close proximity of the maternal and fetal blood systems within the placenta. It also functions as a gland, secreting *human chorionic gonadotrophin, *progesterone, and oestrogens, which regulate the

胎盤　子宮內器官，胚胎借之附着於子宮壁。其主要功能是給胚胎提供營養，排除廢料及交換呼吸氣體。這是通過胎盤內母體和胎兒血系統的緊密相連而獲得的。它也具有腺體的作用，分泌人絨（毛）膜促性腺激素、孕酮和雌激素，這些物質調節維持妊娠。參閱 afterbirth。

maintenance of pregnancy. *See also* afterbirth. **–placental** *adj.*

placenta praevia a placenta situated wholly or partially in the lower and non-contractile part of the uterus. when this becomes elongated and stretched during the last few weeks of pregnancy, and the cervix becomes stretched either before or during labour, placental separation and haemorrhage will occur. The cause is not known. In the more severe degrees of placenta praevia, where the placenta is situated entirely before the presenting part of the fetus, delivery must be by Caesarean section. In lesser degrees of placenta praevia, vaginal delivery may be undertaken with safety.

前置胎盤　全部或部分位於子宮下部以及無收縮力部分的胎盤。前置胎盤在妊娠最後幾周變長及牽張，宮頸在分娩前或分娩後過程中牽張時，胎盤會破裂並出血。原因尚不清楚。在較重程度的前置胎盤中，胚胎完全位於胎兒先露部分之前，這時需要作剖宮產手術。輕度前置胎盤時進行陰道分娩是安全的。

placentography *n.* *radiography of the pregnant uterus in order to determine the position of the placenta. This method is now superseded by the use of ultrasound (*see* ultrasonography).

胎盤造影術　妊娠子宮的放射照像術，目的在於確定胎盤的位置。這一方法現在已被超聲波（參閱 ultrasonography）代替。

placode *n.* any of the thickened areas of ectoderm in the embryo that will develop into nerve ganglia or the special sensory structures of the eye, ear, or nose.

基板　胚胎外胚層的任何增厚區域，發育成神經節或眼、耳或鼻的專門感覺結構。

plagiocephaly *n.* any distortion or lack of symmetry in the shape of the head, usually due to irregularity in the closure of the sutures between the bones of the skull.

斜頭（畸形）　頭顱形狀的任何變形或不對稱，常由顱骨間骨縫接合不規則所致。

plague *n.* **1.** any epidemic disease with a high death rate. **2.** an acute epidemic disease of rats and other wild rodents caused by the bacterium *Yersinia pestis*, which is transmitted to man by rat fleas. *Bubonic plague*, the most common form of the disease, has an incubation period of 2–6 days. Headache, fever, weakness, aching limbs, and delirium develop and

(1) 瘟疫　死亡率極高的任何流行病。**(2) 鼠疫**　由鼠疫耶爾森菌引起的老鼠及其他嚙齒動物的急性傳染病，由鼠蚤傳播給人。腺鼠疫是本病最常見的形式，潛伏期為 2~6 天。患者會出現頭痛、發熱、無力、四肢疼痛和譫妄；繼而出現淋巴結急性腫痛（參閱 bubo），

are followed by acute painful swellings of the lymph nodes (*see* bubo). In favourable cases the buboes burst after about a week, releasing pus, and then heal. In other cases bleeding under the skin, producing black patches, can lead to ulcers, which may prove fatal (hence the former name *Black Death*). In the most serious cases bacteria enter the bloodstream (*septicaemic plague*) or lungs (*pneumonic plague*); if untreated, these are nearly always fatal. Treatment with tetracycline, streptomycin, and chloramphenicol is effective; vaccination against the disease provides only partial protection.

在良好病例中，腹股溝淋巴結炎大約一周後破裂，釋放出膿，然後愈合。在其他病例中，皮下出血可產生黑斑，可導致潰瘍。這種病可導致死亡（因此舊名為黑死病）。在最嚴重的病例中，細菌進入血流（敗血性鼠疫）或肺（肺鼠疫）；如果不治療，病人幾乎全部會死亡。用四環素、鏈黴素和合黴素治療有效；接種僅產生部分保護。

plane *n.* a level or smooth surface, especially any of the hypothetical flat surfaces – orientated in various directions – used to divide the body; for example, the *coronal and *sagittal planes.

平面 水平或光滑的表面，特別是朝向不同方向，用於劃分身體的任何假想平面；例如冠狀面和矢狀面。

planoconcave *adj.* describing a structure, such as a lens, that is flat on one side and concave on the other.

平凹的 描述一種一面平而另一面凹陷的結構，如透鏡。

planoconvex *adj.* describing a structure, such as a lens, that is flat on one side and convex on the other.

平凸的 描述一種一面平而另一面凸起的結構，如透鏡。

plantar *adj.* relating to the sole of the foot (*planta*). *See also* flexion.

足底的，跖的 與腳底相關的。參閱 flexion。

plantar arch the arch in the sole of the foot formed by anastomosing branches of the plantar arteries.

足底弓 在足底內，由足底動脈的吻合支形成的動脈弓。

plantar reflex a reflex obtained by drawing a bluntly pointed object along the outer border of the sole of the foot from the heel to the little toe. The normal *flexor response* is a bunching and downward movement of the toes. An upward movement of the great toe is called an

跖反射，足底反射 用一個鈍頭的物體從足根沿足底外緣向小趾劃綫所引起的一種反射。正常的屈肌反射是腳趾屈曲向下運動。大拇趾向上的運動稱作伸肌反射（或稱巴賓斯基反射）。對於所有年滿 18 個月的

extensor response (or *Babinski reflex*). In all persons over the age of 18 months this is a sensitive indication of disease in the brain or spinal cord.

plantar wart a wart occurring in the skin on the sole of the foot. *See* wart.

plantigrade *adj.* walking on the entire sole of the foot: a habit of man and some animals.

plaque *n.* **1.** a layer that forms on the surface of a tooth, principally at its neck, composed of bacteria in an organic matrix. Under certain conditions the plaque may cause *gingivitis, *periodontal disease, or *dental caries. The purpose of oral hygiene is to remove plaque. **2.** raised patch on the skin, formed by *papules enlarging or coalescing to form an area 2 cm or more across. **3.** any flat and often raised patch, for example on mucous membrane, resulting from local damage.

-plasia *suffix denoting* formation; development. Example: *hyperplasia* (excessive tissue formation).

plasm- (plasmo-) *prefix denoting* **1.** blood plasma. **2.** protoplasm or cytoplasm.

plasma (blood plasma) *n.* the straw-coloured fluid in which the blood cells are suspended. It consists of a solution of various inorganic salts of sodium, potassium, calcium, etc., with a high concentration of protein (approximately 70 g/l) and a variety of trace substances.

plasmacytoma *n.* a malignant tumour of plasma cells, very closely allied to

人，這一反射都是檢查腦和脊髓病變的敏感指標。

足跖疣，跖疣 發生在足底皮膚中的一種疣。通常位於足趾的根部。參閱 wart。

跖行的 用整個足底走路。是人類和某些動物的習性。

(1) 牙斑，菌斑 主要是在牙頸表面由有機基質中的細菌形成的一層斑。在一定條件下，這種斑塊可能引起牙齦炎、牙周病或齲牙。口腔衛生的目的就在於清除這種菌斑。**(2)** 皮膚斑 由丘疹增大和融合而形成大於 2 cm 的皮膚突出區。**(3)** 斑 通常由於感染、局部損傷而引起的黏膜上的一種隆起的扁平斑塊。

〔後綴〕形成 發育。例如：增生（組織生長過度）。

〔前綴〕**(1)** 血漿 **(2)** 原生質或細胞質

血漿 懸浮有血細胞的淡黃色液體。它由鈉、鉀、鈣等各種無機鹽溶液、高濃度的蛋白質（約 70 g/l）和各種微量元素組成。

漿細胞瘤 漿細胞的一種惡性腫瘤。與骨髓瘤密切相關。通

*myeloma. It usually occurs as a solitary tumour of bone, but may be multiple. Less frequently it affects soft tissues, usually the upper air passages. All of these tumours may produce the abnormal gamma globulins that are characteristic of myeloma, and they may progress to widespread myeloma. The soft-tissue tumours often respond to radiotherapy and to such drugs as melphalan and cyclophosphamide; the bone tumours are less responsive. Tumours originating in soft tissue may spread to bone, producing an appearance on X-ray identical to myeloma deposits; these secondary growths often resolve completely after radiological treatment.

常以單一骨瘤的形式發生，但也可能有多發性的。有時侵犯上呼吸道的軟組織。這些腫瘤都可產生骨髓瘤所特有的異常丙種球蛋白，並可發展為擴散性骨髓炎。放射療法和苯丙氨酸氮芥及環磷酰胺類藥物對軟組織腫瘤通常有效，但對骨腫瘤療效較差。起源於軟組織的腫瘤可擴散到骨，在 X 綫檢查時顯示出與骨髓瘤相同的沉積物。這些繼發性生長物經放射治療後常全部消失。

plasmalogen n. a phospholipid, found in brain and muscle, similar in structure to *lecithin and *cephalin.

縮醛磷脂 存在於腦和肌肉中的一種磷脂。結構與卵磷脂和腦磷脂相似。

plasmapheresis n. a method of removing a quantity of plasma from the blood. Blood is withdrawn from the patient and allowed to settle in a container. The plasma is drawn off the top of the blood, and the blood cells are then transfused back into the patient.

血漿提取法 一種從血液中提取一定量血漿的方法。取患者血液置於容器內使之沉降。位於上層的血漿被提取，血細胞仍被回輸給患者。

plasmin (fibrinolysin) n. an enzyme that digests the protein fibrin. Its function is the dissolution of blood clots (*see* fibrinolysis). Plasmin is not normally present in the blood but exists as an inactive precursor, *plasminogen*.

纖維蛋白溶酶 一種消化蛋白纖維的酶。其功能是溶解血凝塊（參閱 fibrinolysis）。正常情況下纖維蛋白溶酶不存在於血液中，而是以無活性的前體纖維蛋白溶酶原的形式存在。

plasminogen n. a substance normally present in the blood plasma that may be activated to form *plasmin. *See* fibrinolysis, tissue plasminogen activator.

纖維蛋白溶酶原 正常情況下存在於血漿中，可被激活變成纖維蛋白溶酶的一種物質。參閱 fibrinolysis tissue plasminogen activator。

plasmoditrophoblast (syncytiotrophoblast) n. that part of the

合胞體滋養層 滋養層失去它的細胞結構而成為合胞體的那

*trophoblast that loses its cellular structure and becomes a *syncytium. This is the invasive part of the trophoblast, which erodes the maternal tissues and forms the villi of the placenta.

部分。這部分侵入母體組織而形成胎盤絨毛。

Plasmodium *n.* a genus of protozoans (*see* Sporozoa) that live as parasites within the red blood cells and liver cells of man. The parasite undergoes its asexual development (*see* schizogony) in man and completes the sexual phase of its development (*see* sporogony) in the stomach and digestive glands of a blood-sucking *Anopheles mosquito.* Four species cause *malaria in man: *P. vivax, P. ovale, P. falciparum, and P. malariae.*

瘧原蟲屬 寄生於人體紅細胞和肝細胞中的原蟲屬寄生蟲（參閱 Sporozoa）。該寄生蟲在人體內進行無性生殖（參閱 schizogony），而在吸血按蚊的胃和消化腺中完成其有性生殖期（參閱 sporogony）。引起瘧疾的四種原蟲為：間日瘧原蟲、卵形瘧原蟲、惡性瘧原蟲和三日瘧原蟲。

plasmolysis *n.* a process occurring in bacteria and plants in which the protoplasm shrinks away from the rigid cell wall when the cell is placed in a *hypertonic solution. Plasmolysis is due to withdrawal of water from the cell by *osmosis.

胞質皺縮 當將細菌和植物細胞放置於高滲溶液中時，原生質從堅硬的細胞壁脫離並收縮（退縮）的過程。胞質皺縮是由於水通過滲透作用從細胞內逸出所致。

plaster n. adhesive tape used in shaped pieces or as a bandage to keep a dressing in place.

膠布 可以以不同形狀黏貼用的橡皮膏，也可用作繃帶固定敷料。

plaster model (in dentistry) an accurate cast of the teeth and jaws made from modified plaster of Paris. A pair of models are used to study the dentition, particularly before treatment. Models are also used to construct dentures, orthodontic appliances, or such restorations as crowns.

石膏模型 （牙科學）用煅石膏加工製成的一種牙齒和下頜骨的精製模型。成對的模型常用於牙列研究，特別在治療前。模型也用於鑄造托牙、正牙器或牙冠修復。

plaster of Paris a preparation of gypsum (calcium sulphate) that sets hard when water is added. It is used in various modified forms in dentistry to make *plaster models. It is also used in orthopaedics for preparing plaster *casts.

煅石膏 加水時可變硬的一種石膏（硫酸鈣）製劑。牙科學中用以鑄造各種不同形狀的石膏模型，在矯形外科學中也用來製造石膏模型。

plastic lymph a transparent yellowish liquid produced in a wound or other site of inflammation, in which connective tissue cells and blood vessels develop during healing.

成形性淋巴 在創傷或其他炎症部位所產生的一種透明的淡黃色液體。當創傷愈合時,結締組織、細胞和血管在該液體中生長。

plastic surgery a branch of surgery dealing with the reconstruction of deformed or damaged parts of the body. It also includes the replacement of parts of the body that have been lost. If performed simply to improve appearances plastic surgery is called *cosmetic surgery*, but most plastic surgery involves the treatment and repair of burns or accidents and the correction of congenital defects, such as harelip and cleft palate.

整形外科 專門用於矯正人體畸形部位或修復人體損傷部位的外科分支學科。它也包括重建已喪失的人體部位。單純為改善容貌施行的整形外科稱作整容外科,但大部分整形外科是治療和修復燒傷或意外傷害,以及矯正先天性畸形,如兔唇和腭裂。

plastron *n.* the breastbone (*sternum) together with the costal cartilages attached to it.

胸板 胸骨與肋軟骨結合在一起的合稱。

-plasty *suffix denoting* plastic surgery. Example: *labioplasty* (of the lips).

〔後綴〕成形術,整形術 指整形外科手術,例如:唇成形術。

platelet (thrombocyte) *n.* a disc-shaped cell structure, 1–2 μm in diameter, that is present in the blood. With *Romanowsky stains platelets appear as fragments of pale-blue cytoplasm with a few red granules. They have several functions, all relating to the arrest of bleeding (*see* blood coagulation). There are normally $150–400 \times 10^9$ platelets per litre of blood. *See also* thrombopoiesis.

血小板 存在於血液中,1~2 μm 直徑的盤狀結構。用羅曼諾夫斯基染色劑染色的血小板,表現為帶有一些紅色顆粒的淺藍色胞漿碎片。它們具有數種功能,所有這些功能都與止血有關(參閱 blood coagulation)。正常人的每升血液中含有血小板為 $150~400 \times 10^9$。參閱 thrombopoiesis。

platelet-derived growth factor (PDGF) *see* growth factor.

血小板衍生生長因子 參閱 growth factor。

platy- *prefix denoting* broad or flat.

〔前綴〕寬或扁平

platyhelminth *n. see* flatworm.

扁蟲,扁形動物 參閱 flatworm。

platysma *n.* a broad thin sheet of muscle that extends from below the collar bone to the angle of the jaw. It depresses the jaw.

頸闊肌 是一塊從鎖骨下方延伸到（下）頜骨角的寬闊而薄的肌肉。它可以向下牽拉口角。

pledget *n.* a small wad of dressing material, such as lint, used either to cover a wound or sore or as a plug.

拭子（藥棉） 像絨布之類的一種小的敷料塊，用來敷蓋傷口、潰瘍或作為一種填塞物。

-plegia *suffix denoting* paralysis. Example: *hemiplegia* (of one side of the body).

〔後綴〕麻痺，癱瘓 例如（身體一側的）偏癱。

pleio- (pleo-) *prefix denoting* **1.** multiple. **2.** excessive.

〔前綴〕**(1)** 多的 **(2)** 過度的

pleiotropy *n.* a situation in which a single gene is responsible for more than one effect in the *phenotype. The mutation of such a gene will therefore have multiple effects. **–pleiotropic** *adj.*

（基因）多效性 在基因表型中，一個單一的基因具有多種影響作用的狀態。因而一種基因的突變也將有多種作用。

pleocytosis *n.* the presence of an abnormally large number of lymphocytes in the cerebrospinal fluid, which bathes the brain and spinal cord.

腦脊液淋巴細胞增多（症） 在浸泡腦和脊髓的腦脊液中異常地出現大量淋巴細胞。

pleomastia (polymastia) *n.* multiple breasts or nipples. These are usually symmetrically arranged along a line between the mid point of the collar bone and the pelvis (the nipple line).

多乳房 多個乳房或乳頭。這些乳房（或乳頭）通常沿着鎖骨中點和骨盆之間的連綫（乳頭綫）對稱地排列。

pleomorphism *n.* the condition in which an individual assumes a number of different forms during its life cycle. The malarial parasite (*Plasmodium*) displays pleomorphism.

多形性（多態性） 一個獨立的生物體在它的生命周期中以多種不同形態出現的現象。瘧原蟲就表現出多形性。

pleoptics *n.* special techniques practised by orthoptists (*see* orthoptics) for developing normal function of the macula (the most sensitive part of the retina), in people whose macular function has

弱視眼操練（治療）法 為了使那些由於弱視而使黃斑功能過早地受到影響的患者恢復黃斑（視網膜感光最敏銳的部位）的正常功能而由視軸矯正師

previously been disturbed because of strabismus (squint).

pleroceroid *n.* a larval stage of certain tapeworms, such as *Diphyllobothrium latum*. It differs from the *cysticercus (another larval form) in being solid and in lacking a cyst or bladder.

plessimetter (pleximeter) *n.* a small plate of bone, ivory, or other material pressed against the surface of the body and struck with a *plessor in the technique of *percussion.

plessor (plexor) *n.* a small hammer used to investigate nervous reflexes and in the technique of *percussion.

plethora *n.* any excess of any bodily fluid, especially blood (*see* hyperaemia). —**plethoric** *adj.*

plethysmography *n.* the process of recording the changes in the volume of a limb caused by alterations in blood pressure. The limb is inserted into a fluid-filled watertight casing (*oncometer*) and the pressure variations in the fluid are recorded.

pleur- (pleuro-) *prefix denoting* **1.** the pleura. **2.** the side of the body.

pleura *n.* the covering of the lungs (*visceral pleura*) and of the inner surface of the chest wall (*parietal pleura*). (See illustration.) The covering consists of a closed sac of *serous membrane, which has a smooth shiny moist surface due to the secretion of small amounts of fluid. This fluid lubricates the opposing visceral and parietal surfaces so that they can slide painlessly over each other during breathing. —**pleural** *adj.*

（參閱 orthoptics）指導的一種特殊操練技術。

全尾蚴，裂頭蚴 某些縧蟲（如闊節裂頭縧蟲）的幼蟲期。它與囊尾蚴（另一種幼蟲形式）的不同點在於實而無囊。

叩診板 用骨、象牙或其他材料製成的一種小板。叩診時，將其壓在身體的表面並用叩診槌敲擊它。

叩診槌 用來檢查神經反射和在叩診時用的一種小槌。

多血（質） 體液過多，尤其是指血液過多（參閱 hyperaemia）。

體積描記法 記錄由於血壓改變而引起的肢體體積變化的一種技術。將肢體插入一個充滿液體的密封筒（器官體積測量器）中，並記錄液體內壓力的變化。

〔前綴〕(1) 胸膜 **(2)** 身體側面

胸膜 覆蓋於肺（臟胸膜、肺胸膜）和胸壁內表面（壁胸膜）的膜（見圖）。由一個密封的漿膜囊構成。由於分泌少量的液體，胸膜的表面是平滑、光亮和濕潤的。這種液體對臟胸膜和壁胸膜表面起潤滑作用，以使在呼吸時，它們之間相互滑動而不產生疼痛。

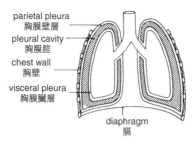

parietal pleura
胸膜壁層
pleural cavity
胸膜腔
chest wall
胸壁
visceral pleura
胸膜臟層
diaphragm
膈

The pleura
胸膜

pleural cavity the space between the visceral and parietal *pleura, which is normally very small as the pleural membranes are in close contact. The introduction of fluid (*pleural effusion*) or gas separates the pleural surfaces and increases the volume of the pleural space.

pleurectomy n. surgical removal of part of the *pleura, which is sometimes done to prevent further recurrences of spontaneous *pneumothorax or to remove diseased areas of pleura.

pleurisy n. inflammation of the *pleura, often due to pneumonia in the underlying lung. The normally shiny and slippery pleural surfaces lose their sheen and become slightly sticky, so that there is pain on deep breathing and a characteristic 'rub' can be heard through a stethoscope. Pleurisy is always associated with some other disease in the lung, chest wall, diaphragm, or abdomen.

pleurocele n. herniation of the pleura. *See* hernia.

pleurocentesis (thoracentesis, thoracocentesis) n. the insertion of a hollow

胸膜腔 臟胸膜和壁胸膜之間的空隙。正常情況下，由於兩層胸膜緊密相貼，所以胸膜腔非常狹小。如液體（胸膜腔積液）或氣體進入，將兩層胸膜表面分開，將會增加胸膜腔的容積。

胸膜（部分）切除術 有時為了防止自發性氣胸進一步復發或為了切除胸膜的病變區域而做的部分胸膜切除手術。

胸膜炎 通常由於胸膜深面的肺組織發炎而引起的胸膜炎症。正常情況下光滑的胸膜表面失去其光澤而變得有些粗糙不平，以致在深呼吸時引起疼痛，用聽診器可聽到一種特有的摩擦音。胸膜炎常與肺部、胸壁、膈或腹部的某些其他疾病有關。

胸膜疝 胸膜的突出。參閱 hernia。

胸腔穿刺術 為了抽出胸膜腔液體、血液、膿液或者氣體，

needle into the *pleural cavity through the chest wall in order to withdraw fluid, blood, pus, or air.

將一空心針經胸壁刺入胸膜腔的手術。

pleurodesis n. the artificial production of pleurisy by chemical or mechanical means to obliterate the *pleural cavity, in order to prevent recurrent, usually malignant, pleural effusions.

胸膜固定術 為了防止胸膜滲出（通常為惡性的）的反覆發作，用化學或機械方法造成人為的胸膜炎。

pleurodynia n. severe paroxysmal pain arising from the muscles between the ribs. It is often thought to be of rheumatic origin.

胸肌痛，胸膜痛 肋間肌肉產生的劇烈的陣發性痛，通常認為它是由風濕引起的。

pleurolysis (pneumolysis) n. surgical stripping of the parietal *pleura from the chest wall to allow the lung to collapse. The procedure was used in the days before effective antituberculous drugs to help tuberculosis to heal.

胸膜鬆解術 從胸壁剝離胸膜壁層以便使肺臟萎陷的手術。在沒有出現抗結核特效藥物之前，這種手術是一種常用的方法。

pleuropneumonia n. inflammation involving both the lung and pleura. *See* pleurisy, pneumonia.

胸膜肺炎 同時發生在肺和胸膜的炎症。參閱 pleurisy，pneumonia。

pleuropneumonia-like organisms (PPLO) n. see mycoplasma.

類胸膜肺炎菌 參閱 mycoplasma。

pleurotyphoid n. *typhoid fever involving the lungs.

胸膜型傷寒 合併肺部感染的傷寒。

pleximeter n. see plessimeter.

叩診板 參閱 plessimeter。

plexor n. see plessor.

叩診槌 參閱 plessor。

plexus n. a network of nerves or blood vessels. *See* brachial plexus.

叢 神經網或血管網。參閱 brachial plexus。

plica n. a fold of tissue; for example, the *plica sublingualis*, the mucous fold in the floor of the mouth. **–plicate** adj.

皺襞，褶 一種組織的皺褶。例如：舌下襞，即口底的黏膜皺襞。

plicamycin n. see mithramycin.

普卡黴素，光輝黴素 參閱 mithramycin。

plication *n.* a surgical technique in which the size of a hollow organ is reduced by taking tucks or folds in the walls.

摺疊術　在空腔性器官壁上打褶或摺疊，使其體積縮小的一種外科手術。

plombage *n.* **1.** a technique used in surgery for the correction of a *detached retina. A small piece of silicone plastic is sewn on the outside of the eyeball to produce an indentation over the retinal hole or tear to allow the retina to reattach. **2.** the insertion of plastic balls into the pleural cavity to cause collapse of the lung. This was done in the days before effective antituberculous drugs to help tuberculosis to heal.

充填術　**(1)** 矯正視網膜剝離的一種外科手術。將一小片硅塑料板縫到眼球的外表，以對視網膜孔所在部位產生一個壓力。**(2)** 將一些塑料球填入胸膜腔內以引起肺萎陷。在沒有抗結核特效藥物之前，該方法是用於治療結核病的一種輔助手段。

plumbism *n.* lead poisoning. *See* lead[1].

鉛中毒　參閱 lead[1]。

pluri- *prefix denoting* more than one; several.

〔前綴〕多數，多

pneo- *prefix denoting* breathing; respiration.

〔前綴〕呼吸

pneumat- (pneumato-) *prefix denoting* **1.** the presence of air or gas. **2.** respiration.

〔前綴〕**(1) 氣體**　含有空氣或氣體。**(2) 呼吸**

pneumatization *n.* the presence of air-filled cavities in bone, such as the sinuses of the skull.

氣腔　骨內形成的充滿氣體的腔。如顱骨中的竇。

pneumatocele *n.* herniation of lung tissue. *See* hernia.

肺膨出　肺組織突出。參閱 hernia。

pneumaturia *n.* the presence in the urine of bubbles of air or other gas, due to the formation of gas by bacteria infecting the urinary tract or to an abnormal connection (fistula) between the urinary tract and bowel.

氣尿　由於尿道的細菌感染或尿道與腸道的不正常溝通（瘻管）而在尿中出現含有空氣或其他氣體的氣泡。

pneumo- *prefix. See* pneum-.

〔前綴〕**(1) 氣，氣體　(2) 肺 (3) 呼吸**　參閱 pneum-。

pneumocephalus (pneumocele) *n*. the presence of air within the skull, usually resulting from a fracture passing through one of the air sinuses. There may be a leak of cerebrospinal fluid at the site of the fracture, manifested as a watery discharge from the nose. Pneumocephalus can be detected by plain X-rays of the skull, which show air and a fluid level inside a cavity, or by CT and MRI scanning.

顱腔積氣　通常由於顱骨骨折穿過氣竇而在顱內出現氣體。骨折處通常有腦脊液漏出。表現為從鼻子流出水樣液體。顱腔積氣可以通過顱骨 X 綫平片或計算機斷層掃描 (CT) 和磁共振 (MRI) 掃描而發現，在顱腔內出現氣體和液平面。

pneumococcus *n*. (*pl.* **pneumococci**) the bacterium **Streptococcus pneumoniae*, which is associated with pneumonia. **–pneumococcal** *adj*.

肺炎球菌　與肺炎有關的細菌：肺炎鏈球菌。

pneumoconiosis *n*. a group of lung diseases caused by inhaling dust. The dust particles must be less than 0.5 μm in diameter to reach the depths of the lung and there is usually a long period after initial exposure before shadows appear on the chest X-ray and breathlessness develops. In practice industrial exposure to coal dust (*see* coalworker's pneumoconiosis), silica (*see* silicosis), and asbestos (*see* asbestosis) produces most of the cases of pneumoconiosis. In Britain such cases are examined by the Medical Boarding Centres (Respiratory Diseases), on whose advice statutory compensation for industrial injury may be awarded.

塵肺，肺塵埃沉着病　由吸入性塵埃引起的一組肺部疾患。塵埃微粒直徑必須小於 0.5μm 才能進入肺的深部。從初次接觸塵埃到 X 綫檢查出現肺部陰影及哮喘之前，通常需經過一段較長時間。實際上，大多數肺塵埃沉着病都是由於接觸煤塵（參閱 coalworker's pneumoconiosis）、硅（參閱 silicosis）和石棉（參閱 asbestosis）等工業粉塵所致。在英國，這類疾病由呼吸性疾病醫療保健中心進行檢查，並按照他們的意見可能給予法定的工傷事故賠償。

Pneumocystis *n*. a genus of protozoans. The species *P. carinii* causes pneumonia in immunosuppressed patients, usually following intensive chemotherapy (*see also* AIDS). This *Pneumocystis carinii* pneumonia (PCP) is fatal in 10–30% of cases if untreated, but it can be overcome with high doses of *co-trimoxazole or *pentamidine.

肺囊蟲屬　原生動物的一個屬。通常在大劑量化學藥物治療後，卡氏肺囊蟲種可以引起免疫功能抑制患者的肺部炎症（參閱 AIDS）。卡氏肺囊蟲肺炎 (PCP) 如不治療，則可導致 10%~30% 患者的死亡，但大劑量的增效磺胺甲基異噁唑或噴他脒可以治愈該病。

pneumocyte *n*. a type of cell that lines the walls separating the air sacs (*see*

肺細胞　位於肺泡壁上的一類細胞（參閱 alveolus）。I 型肺

alveolus) in the lungs. Type I pneumocytes are flat and inconspicuous. Type II pneumocytes are cuboidal and secrete *surfactant.

pneumoencephalography *n.* a technique used in the X-ray diagnosis of disease within the skull. Air is introduced into the cavities (ventricles) of the brain to displace the cerebrospinal fluid, thus acting as a *contrast medium. X-ray photographs show the size and disposition of the ventricles and the subarachnoid spaces. The technique has largely been superseded by CT and MRI scanning.

pneumograph *n.* an instrument used to record the movements made during respiration.

pneumolysis *n. see* pleurolysis.

pneum- (pneumo-) *prefix denoting* **1.** the presence of air or gas. Example: *pneumocolon* (within the colon). **2.** the lung(s). Example: *pneumogastric* (relating to the lungs and stomach). 3. respiration.

pneumon- (pneumono-) *prefix denoting* the lung(s). Example: *pneumonopexy* (surgical fixation to the chest wall).

pneumonectomy *n.* surgical removal of a lung, usually for cancer.

pneumonia *n.* inflammation of the lung caused by bacteria, in which the air sacs (*alveoli) become filled with inflammatory cells and the lung becomes solid (*see* consolidation), the symptoms include those of any infection (fever, malaise, headaches, etc.), together with cough and chest pain. Pneumonias may be classified in different ways:

細胞呈扁平形，不明顯；II 型肺細胞呈立方形，能分泌表面活性物質。

氣腦造影術　是顱內疾患 X 綫診斷中應用的一種技術。將空氣注入到腦室以取代腦脊液，以此作為造影劑。X 綫照像可顯示腦室和蛛網膜下腔的大小和位置。這種技術現已基本被計算機斷層掃描和磁共振掃描技術所取代。

呼吸描記器　用來記錄呼吸運動的一種儀器。

（胸膜外）肺鬆解術　參閱 pleurolysis。

〔前綴〕**(1) 氣**　含有空氣或氣體。如結腸積氣。**(2) 肺**　如肺胃的（與肺和胃有關的）。**(3) 呼吸**

〔前綴〕**肺**　例如：肺固定術（將肺固定到胸壁上的手術）。

肺切除術　通常用來治療癌症所採用的切除肺的外科手術。

肺炎　由細菌引起的肺部發炎。此時炎症部位的肺泡被炎性細胞所填充，肺發生實變（參閱 consolidation）。其症狀同其他感染的症狀，包括發熱，不適及頭痛等，同時伴有咳嗽和胸痛。此病可按不同的方法進行分類：

　　(1) 根據 X 綫檢查表現分

(1) according to the X-ray appearance. *Lobar pneumonia* affects whole lobes and is usually caused by *Streptococcus pneumoniae*, while *lobular pneumonia* refers to multiple patchy shadows in a localized or segmental area. When these multiple shadows are widespread, the term *bronchopneumonia* is used. In bronchopneumonia, the infection starts in a number of small bronchi and spreads in a patchy manner into the alveoli.

(2) according to the infecting organism. The most common organism is *Streptococcus pneumoniae*, but *Haemophilus influenzae*, *Staphylococcus aureus*, *Legionella pneumophila*, and *Mycoplasma pneumoniae* (among others) may all be responsible for the infection. *See also* atypical pneumonia, viral pneumonia.

(3) according to the clinical and environmental circumstances under which the pneumonia is acquired. These infections are divided into *community-acquired pneumonia*, *hospital-acquired (nosocomial) pneumonia*, and pneumonias occurring in immunocompromised subjects (including those with AIDS). The organisms responsible for community-acquired pneumonia are totally different from those in the other groups.

Appropriate antibiotic therapy, based on the clinical situation and on microbiological studies, will result in complete recovery in the majority of patients.

pneumonitis *n*. inflammation of the lung that is confined to the walls of the air sacs (alveoli) and often caused by viruses or unknown agents. It may be acute and transient or chronic, leading to increasing respiratory disability. It does not respond to antibiotics but corticosteroids may be helpful. *Compare* pneumonia.

類。大葉性肺炎影響整個肺葉，通常它是由肺炎鏈球菌等引起的，而小葉性肺炎則表現為許多局部的小範圍的片狀陰影，當這許多小片狀陰影分布較廣泛時，則稱為支氣管肺炎。支氣管肺炎的感染開始於大量的小支氣管，繼而以斑片狀的方式擴散到肺泡。

(2) 根據感染的細菌劃分。最常見的是肺炎鏈球菌，但流感嗜血桿菌、金黃色葡萄球菌、嗜肺軍團桿菌和肺炎支原體都可能引起感染。參閱 atypical pneumonia，viral pneumonia。

(3) 根據臨床和肺炎發生的環境。其感染可分為社區獲得性肺炎（集體獲得性肺炎）、醫院獲得性肺炎及發生在免疫功能缺損者（包括艾滋病患者）的肺炎。引起社區獲得性肺炎的細菌完全不同於導致其他各類肺炎的細菌。

根據臨床情況及微生物學知識，適宜的抗生素治療可以使大多數患者完全康復。

局竈性肺炎 常由病毒引起或不明原因的，局限於肺泡壁上的肺部炎症。它可能是急性的和短暫的或是慢性的，可導致逐漸加重的呼吸困難。局竈性肺炎對抗生素不敏感，但皮質類固醇治療可能有效。與 pneumonia 對比。

pneumopericardium *n.* the presence of air within the membranous sac surrounding the heart. *See* hydropneumopericardium.

心包積氣　在心包腔內出現氣體。參閱 hydropneumopericardium。

pneumoperitoneum *n.* air or gas in the peritoneal or abdominal cavity, usually due to a perforation of the stomach or bowel. Pneumoperitoneum may be induced for diagnostic purposes (e.g. *laparoscopy). A former treatment of tuberculosis was the deliberate injection of air into the peritoneal cavity to allow the tuberculous lung to be rested (*artificial pneumoperitoneum*); this was frequently combined with *phrenic crush.

氣腹　通常由胃腸穿孔引起的腹膜腔積氣。氣腹可以用來作為診斷的手段（如腹腔鏡檢查）。早先治療肺結核時曾有意識地將氣體注入腹膜腔內以便使患結核的肺臟得到休息（人工氣腹）。這種方法常常和「膈神經壓榨術」聯合使用。

pneumoradiography *n.* X-ray examination of part of the body using a gas, such as air or carbon dioxide, as a *contrast medium. For example, introduction of air into the ventricles of the brain enables them to be distinguished by X-rays; in their normal (fluid-filled) state they are not sufficiently contrasted with the brain tissue itself.

充氣造影術　使用一種氣體（如空氣或二氧化碳）作為造影劑，對身體某部分進行 X 綫檢查的方法。例如，將空氣注入腦室以使其能被X綫檢查顯影。在正常狀態下腦室充滿液體，與腦組織本身難以區別。

pneumothorax *n.* air in the *pleural cavity. Any breach of the lung surface or chest wall allows air to enter the pleural cavity, causing the lung to collapse. The leak can occur without apparent cause, in otherwise healthy people (*spontaneous pneumothorax*), or result from injuries to the chest (*traumatic pneumothorax*). In *tension pneumothorax* a breach in the lung surface acts as a valve, admitting air into the pleural cavity when the patient breathes in but preventing its escape when he breathes out. This air must be let out by surgical incision.

A former treatment for pulmonary tuberculosis – *artificial pneumothorax* – was the deliberate injection of air into the pleural cavity to collapse the lung and allow the tuberculous areas to heal.

氣胸　胸膜腔積氣。肺表面或胸壁的任何裂口都可使空氣進入胸膜腔，引起肺萎陷。這種氣胸可不明原因地發生在各方面都健康的人身上（自發性氣胸）。或者由於胸部受傷而發生（外傷性氣胸）。在張力性氣胸中，肺表面的裂縫起着瓣膜的作用，當病人吸氣時，空氣得以進入胸膜腔，當病人呼氣時，則可阻止空氣逸出。這種積氣必須通過外科手術切開才能排出。

　　早先治療肺結核的方法——人工氣胸——即有意識地將空氣注入胸膜腔，使肺萎陷以便使患肺結核的部位得以痊愈。

-pnoea *suffix denoting* a condition of breathing. Example: *dyspnoea* (breathlessness).

〔後綴〕**呼吸狀態（症狀）** 例如：呼吸困難。

pock *n.* a small pus-filled eruption on the skin characteristic of *chickenpox and *smallpox rashes. *See also* pustule.

痘疱 水痘和天花所特有的，皮膚上一種充滿膿液的小疱疹。參閱 pustule。

pocket *n.* (in dentistry) *see* periodontal pocket.

袋（牙科學）參閱 periodontal pocket。

pod- *prefix denoting* the foot.

〔前綴〕**足，腳**

podagra *n.* gout of the foot, especially the big toe.

（足）痛風 足的痛風病，尤指大拇趾的痛風。

podalic version altering the position of a fetus in the uterus so that its feet will emerge first at birth. *See also* version.

胎足倒轉術 改變胎兒在子宮內的位置以便在分娩時，胎兒的雙腳先露的手術。參閱 version。

podopompholyx *n. see* pompholyx.

跖汗疱，足底汗疱 參閱 pompholyx。

-poiesis *suffix denoting* formation; production. Example: *haemopoiesis* (of blood cells).

〔後綴〕**形成，產生，生，造** 例如：血細胞生成。

poikilo- *prefix denoting* variation; irregularity.

〔前綴〕**異常，變異，不規則**

poikilocyte *n.* an abnormally shaped red blood cell (*erythrocyte). Poikilocytes may be classified into a variety of types on the basis of their shape; for example elliptocytes (ellipsoid) and schistocytes (semilunar). *See also* poikilocytosis.

異形紅細胞 一種異常形態的紅細胞。異形紅細胞根據其形狀可以分成各種類型。例如，橢圓形紅細胞（橢圓體）和裂紅細胞（半月形）。參閱 poikilocytosis。

poikilocytosis *n.* the presence of abnormally shaped red cells (*poikilocytes) in the blood. Poikilocytosis is particularly marked in *myelofibrosis but can occur to some extent in almost any blood disease.

異形紅細胞症 血液中出現異常形狀的紅細胞（異形紅細胞）。異形紅細胞症在骨髓纖維變性中特別明顯，但在幾乎所有的血液疾病中都能出現某種程度的異形紅細胞症。

poikiloderma *n.* a condition in which the skin atrophies and becomes pigmented, giving it a mottled appearance.

皮膚異色病　由於皮膚萎縮和色素沉着，而使其呈現一種花斑樣外觀的症狀叫皮膚異色病。

poikilothermic *adj.* cold-blooded: being unable to regulate the body temperature, which fluctuates according to that of the surroundings. Reptiles and amphibians are cold-blooded. *Compare* homoiothermic. **–poikilothermy** *n.*

冷血動物的，變溫動物的　冷血的、不能夠調節體溫的。體溫隨環境溫度變化而變化的。爬行類和兩棲類皆為冷血動物。與 homoiothermic 對比。

pointillage *n.* a procedure in massage in which the operator's fingers are pressed, fingertip first, deep into the patient's skin. This is done to manipulate underlying structures and break up adhesions that may have formed following injury.

指尖按摩法　操作者用拇指指尖深深地壓入病人皮膚的一種按摩手法。這種方法是為了按摩深部的結構及分離受傷後可能出現的黏連。

poison *n.* any substance that irritates, damages, or impairs the activity of the body's tissues. In large enough doses almost any substance acts as a poison, but the term is usually reserved for substances, such as arsenic, cyanide, and strychnine, that are harmful in relatively small amounts.

毒物　任何對人體組織的功能有刺激、破壞和損傷作用的物質。幾乎任何物質在足夠大的劑量時都會成為毒物。但該詞通常專指像砷、氰化物和士的寧這些僅用相當小的量即有損害作用的物質。

Poisson distribution *see* frequency distribution.

泊松分布　參閱 frequency distribution。

polar body one of the small cells produced during the formation of an ovum from an *oocyte that does not develop into a functional egg cell.

極體　在卵子形成期，從未發育為功能性卵細胞的卵母細胞中生長出的一種小細胞。

poldine *n.* a drug, similar to *atropine, that inhibits gastric secretion and is used to treat such disorders as gastric and duodenal ulcers. It is administered by mouth; side-effects may include dry mouth, blurred vision, difficulty in urination, and fast heartbeat. Trade name: **Nacton**.

泊爾定　一種類似於阿托品的藥物。可抑制胃的分泌功能。通常用於治療胃及十二指腸潰瘍之類的疾病。可通過口服給藥。副作用可能有口乾、視力模糊、排尿困難和心跳加快。商品名：Nacton。

pole *n.* (in anatomy) the extremity of the axis of the body, an organ, or a cell.

極　（解剖學），指身體、一個器官或一個細胞軸的末端。

poli- (polio-) *prefix denoting* the grey matter of the nervous system.

polioencephalitis *n.* a virus infection of the brain causing particular damage to the *grey matter of the cerebral hemispheres and the brainstem. The term is now usually restricted to infections of the brain by the poliomyelitis virus.

polioencephalomyelitis *n.* any virus infection of the central nervous system affecting the grey matter of the brain and spinal cord. *Rabies is the outstanding example.

poliomyelitis (infantile paralysis, polio) *n.* an infectious virus disease affecting the central nervous system. The virus is excreted in the faeces of an infected person and the disease is therefore most common where sanitation is poor. However, epidemics may occur in more hygienic conditions, where individuals have not acquired immunity to the disease during infancy. Symptoms commence 7–12 days after infection. In most cases paralysis does not occur: in *abortive poliomyelitis* only the throat and intestines are infected and the symptoms are those of a stomach upset or influenza; in *nonparalytic poliomyelitis* these symptoms are accompanied by muscle stiffness, particularly in the neck and back. *Paralytic poliomyelitis* is much less common. The symptoms of the milder forms of the disease are followed by weakness and eventual paralysis of the muscles: in *bulbar poliomyelitis* the muscles of the respiratory system are involved and breathing is affected.

There is no specific treatment, apart from measures to relieve the symptoms: cases of bulbar polio may require the use of a *respirator (ventilator).

〔前綴〕**灰質** 指神經系統的灰質。

腦灰質炎 一種對大腦半球和腦幹的灰質造成特殊損傷的腦部病毒感染。現在該詞通常僅指脊髓灰質炎病毒引起的腦部感染。

腦脊髓灰質炎 任何一種侵犯到腦和脊髓灰質的中樞神經系統的病毒感染。狂犬病是最顯著的例子。

脊髓灰質炎（小兒麻痺，脊髓灰質炎） 一種侵害中樞神經系統的病毒感染性疾病。這種病毒隨受感染病人的糞便排出，所以在環境衛生差的地區這種病最為常見。但是在衛生狀況較好的條件下，那些在嬰兒期，對該病未獲得免疫力的人，仍可能發生流行感染。感染後 7～12 天開始出現症狀。大多數病人不出現麻痺症狀；在頓挫性脊髓灰質炎，僅有喉及腸道感染，其症狀與胃腸功能紊亂或流行性感冒相似；非麻痺性脊髓灰質炎除上述症狀外，常伴有肌肉強直，特別是頸部和背部肌肉。麻痺性脊髓灰質炎較少見。該病較輕型的症狀是先有肌無力，最後是肌肉的麻痺；在延髓性脊髓灰質炎中，呼吸系統的肌肉受累而影響呼吸。

除了緩解症狀的措施外，尚無特殊的治療方法。延髓型脊髓灰質炎患者可能還需要使用呼吸機。免疫療法，口服薩賓疫苗或注射索爾克疫苗有顯著的效果。

Immunization, using the *Sabin vaccine (taken orally) or the *Salk vaccine (injected), is highly effective.

poliovirus *n.* one of a small group of RNA-containing viruses causing *poliomyelitis. They are included within the *picornavirus group.

脊髓灰質炎病毒　能引起脊髓灰質炎的一小組核糖核酸病毒中的一種。它們屬於細小核糖核酸病毒屬。

pollex *n.* (*pl.* **pollices**) the thumb.

拇指，拇

pollinosis *n.* a more precise term than *hay fever for an allergy due to the pollen of grasses, trees, or shrubs.

花粉病　比枯草熱更為確切的一個名詞，指由草、樹或灌木叢的花粉引起的一種變態反應性疾病。

poly- *prefix denoting* **1.** many; multiple. **2.** excessive. **3.** generalized; affecting many parts.

〔前綴〕**(1)** 多，多數 **(2)** 過分，過多，過度 **(3)** 廣泛的，全身的，多發的

polyarteritis nodosa (periarteritis nodosa) a disease of unknown cause in which there is patchy inflammation of the walls of the arteries. It is one of the *connective-tissue diseases. Common manifestations are arthritis, neuritis, asthma, skin rashes, hypertension, kidney failure, and fever. The inflammation is suppressed by corticosteroid drugs (such as prednisolone).

結節性多動脈炎　在多數動脈壁上出現炎症斑塊的一種不明原因的疾病。該病是一種結締組織性疾病。常見的表現有關節炎、神經炎、哮喘、皮疹、高血壓、腎衰和發燒。皮質類固醇藥，如強的松龍可控制炎症。

polyarthritis *n.* rheumatic disease involving several to many joints, either together or in sequence, causing pain, stiffness, swelling, tenderness, and loss of function. *Rheumatoid arthritis is the most common cause.

多關節炎　同時或進行性侵犯幾處乃至多處關節的風濕性疾病。此病能引起關節疼痛、強直、腫脹、觸疼及功能喪失。類風濕性關節炎是最常見的病因。

polychromasia (polychromatophilia) *n.* the presence of certain blue red blood cells (*erythrocytes) seen in blood films stained with *Romanowsky stains, as well as the normal pink cells. The cells that appear blue are juvenile erythrocytes (*see* reticulocyte).

多染（性）細胞增多　在用羅曼諾夫斯基染色劑染過的血片上，可看到某些帶藍色的紅細胞及正常的粉紅色血細胞。那些藍色的紅細胞是一些幼年紅細胞（未成熟紅細胞），參閱 reticulocyte。

polycoria *n.* a rare congenital abnormality of the eye in which there are one or more holes in the iris in addition to the pupil.

多瞳（畸形），多瞳症　一種罕見的先天性眼睛畸形。這種病人的眼睛除有瞳孔外，在虹膜內還有一個或多個孔。

polycystic disease of the kidneys an inherited disorder, transmitted as an autosomal *dominant, in which the substance of both kidneys is largely replaced by numerous cysts. Symptoms – including *haematuria, urinary tract infection, and hypertension – appear between the ages of 20 and 40 and are associated with chronic kidney failure.

多囊腎（腎的多囊病）　由常染色體顯性（等位基因）傳遞的一種遺傳性疾病。該病患者的兩腎實質大部分被許多囊腫所取代。患者常在 20~40 歲之間出現血尿、尿路感染和高血壓等症狀，並可併發慢性腎功能衰竭。

polycystic ovary syndrome (POS) a hormonal disorder characterized by incomplete development of *Graafian follicles in the ovary due to inadequate secretion of *luteinizing hormone; the follicles fail to ovulate and remain as multiple cysts distending the ovary. Further hormone imbalance results in obesity, hirsutism, and acne and the woman is infertile due to the lack of ovulation; this syndrome is known as the *Stein-Leventhal syndrome*. The treatment is administration of appropriate hormones.

多囊卵巢綜合徵　由於黃體生成素異常分泌，引起卵巢內格雷夫卵泡（囊性卵泡）發育不全的一種內分泌疾病。這種發育不全的卵泡不能排卵，並形成許多囊泡而使卵巢腫脹。進而，激素的失調導致肥胖，多毛和出現痤瘡。由於排卵不足，這些患者不能生育。這種症狀稱之為斯-利氏綜合徵，其治療是給予適當的激素。

polycythaemia *n.* an increase in the haemoglobin concentration of the blood. This may be due either to a decrease in the total volume of the plasma (*relative polycythaemia*) or to an increase in the total volume of the red cells (*absolute polycythaemia*). The latter may occur as a primary disease (*see* polycythaemia vera) or as a secondary condition in association with various respiratory or circulatory disorders that cause deficiency of oxygen in the tissues and with certain tumours, such as carcinoma of the kidney.

紅細胞增多　血液中血紅蛋白濃度增高。這可能是由於血漿總量的減少（相對紅細胞增多）或者由於紅細胞總量增加而引起（絕對紅細胞增多）。其後者（紅細胞總量增加）既可能是原發性疾病（參閱 polycythaemia vera），也可能併發於引起組織缺氧的各種呼吸或循環系疾病，或併發於某些腫瘤，如腎癌。

polycythaemia vera (polycythaemia rubra vera, erythraemia, Vaquez-Osler disease) a disease in which the number of red cells in the blood is greatly increased (*see also* polycythaemia). There is often also an increase in the numbers of white blood cells and platelets. Symptoms include headache, thromboses, *cyanosis, *plethora, and itching. Polycythaemia vera may be treated by blood-letting, but more severe cases are best treated by radiotherapy or cytotoxic drugs. The cause of the disease is not known.

原發性紅細胞增多症（紅細胞增多症，瓦-奧氏病） 血液中紅細胞大量增加的一種疾病（參閱 polycythaemia）。同時，常伴有白細胞和血小板數量的增高。症狀包括頭痛、血栓形成、紫紺、多血質外貌和皮膚瘙癢。原發性紅細胞增多可通過放血來治療，但是較嚴重病人最好使用放射療法或給予細胞毒素藥物。此病病因不明。

polydactylism *n. see* hyperdactylism.

多指（趾）畸形 參閱 hyperdactylism。

polydipsia *n.* abnormally intense thirst, leading to the drinking of large quantities of fluid. This is a symptom typical of diabetes mellitus and diabetes insipidus.

煩渴 能導致大量飲水的異常強烈的口渴現象。這是糖尿病和尿崩症的一種典型症狀。

polygene *n.* one of a number of genes that together control a single characteristic in an individual. Each polygene has only a slight effect and the expression of a set of polygenes is the result of their combined interaction. Characteristics controlled by polygenes are usually of a quantitative nature, e.g. height. *See also* multifactorial. **–polygenic** *adj.*

多基因 個體中共同調控一個單一性狀的數個基因中的一個，每個多基因僅發揮微小的作用，而一套多基因的表現則是它們聯合起來相互作用的結果。多基因所調控的性狀通常都是一種數量上的特徵，如高度。參閱 multifactorial。

polymastia *n. see* pleomastia.

多乳房 參閱 pleomastia。

polymer *n.* a substance formed by the linkage of a large number of smaller molecules known as *monomers*. An example of a monomer is glucose, whose molecules link together to form glycogen, a polymer. Polymers may have molecular weights from a few thousands to many millions. Polymers made up of a single type of monomer are known as

聚合物，聚合體，多聚體 由許多稱為單體的小分子物質結合起來形成的一種物質。一種單體的例子就是葡萄糖，它的分子連接在一起就形成糖原，一種多聚體（聚物）。聚合物的分子量可以從數千到數百萬。由單一種類的單體組成的聚合物稱同聚物，兩種或

homopolymers; those of two or more monomers as *heteropolymers*.

兩種以上單體組成的則叫雜聚物。

polymerase chain reaction (PCR) a sensitive technique of molecular genetics in which the DNA of a single cell, treated with polymerase enzymes, is induced to replicate many times. This enables the DNA to be amplified in sufficient quantities to enable genetic analysis. The technique may be utilized in the course of preimplantation diagnosis of genetic disorders (*see* prenatal diagnosis) and also in the identification of viruses in tissue samples, e.g. *human papillomavirus in cervical smears.

聚合酶鏈反應 **(PCR)** 一種敏感的分子遺傳學技術。用此技術，單細胞內的 DNA 在聚合酶的作用下可以複製許多次，這樣能使 DNA 擴增到足夠的量以便進行遺傳分析。此種技術可用於進行遺傳病的胚胎植入前診斷（參閱 prenatal diagnosis），也可用在組織標本中的病毒鑒別。如宮頸塗片中的人乳頭瘤病毒。

polymorph (polymorphonuclear leucocyte) *n. see* neutrophil.

多形核白細胞 參閱 neutrophil。

polymorphic light eruption *see* photodermatosis.

多形性光照性皮疹 參閱 photodermatosis。

polymorphism *n.* (in genetics) a condition in which a chromosome or a genetic character occurs in more that one form, resulting in the coexistence of more than one morphological type in the same population.

多態性，多形（態），多性變態 （遺傳學）一個染色體或一種遺傳特徵以多種形式出現，以致在同一羣體中出現多種形態特徵的共存。

polymyalgia rheumatica a rheumatic disease causing aching and progressive stiffness of the muscles of the shoulders and hips. The condition is most common in the elderly, rarely occurring before the age of 50. The symptoms respond rapidly and effectively to corticosteroid treatment, which must usually be continued for several years. It is sometimes associated with temporal *arteritis.

風濕性多肌痛 一種能引起肩部和髖部肌肉疼痛和逐漸強直的風濕性疾病。此病最常見於老年人，50 歲以前者少見。皮質類固醇治療，可使症狀迅速緩解，但通常必須持續用藥數年。該病有時併發顳動脈炎。

polymyositis *n.* a generalized disease of the muscles that may be acute or chronic. It particularly affects the muscles of the shoulder and hip girdles, which are weak

多肌炎 一種急性或慢性侵襲多處肌肉的常見疾病。該病尤易侵害肩部和髖部肌肉。觸診時該肌柔軟無力。在顯微鏡下

and tender to the touch. Microscopic examination of the affected muscles shows diffuse inflammatory changes, and relief of the symptoms is obtained with *corticosteroid drugs. The skin may be red and atrophic. *See also* dermatomyositis.

檢查，患肌呈彌漫性炎性改變。皮質類固醇類藥物可以緩解症狀。皮膚可發紅和萎縮。參閱 dermatomyositis。

polymyxin B an *antibiotic used to treat severe infections caused by Gram-negative bacteria. It is administered as a solution or ointment for ear and eye infections, often formulated with other drugs.

多黏菌素 B 治療由革蘭氏陰性菌引起的重症感染的一種抗生素。它常和其他藥物一起配製成溶液或軟膏治療耳或眼的感染。

polyneuritis *n.* any disorder involving all the peripheral nerves. The term is often used interchangeably with *poly-neuropathy although its specific use implies inflammation of the nerves.

多神經炎 累及整個周圍神經疾病。雖然該詞的含意專指神經炎症，但它往往與多發性神經病 (polyneuropathy) 一詞代替使用。

polyneuropathy *n.* any disease involving all the peripheral nerves. The symptoms first affect the tips of the fingers and toes (i.e. the extremities of the nerve fibres) and subsequently spread towards the trunk. The symptoms are usually roughly symmetrical. *See also* Guillain-Barré syndrome (postinfective polyneuropathy), neuropathy.

多神經病 累及整個周圍神經的疾病。症狀首先出現在指尖和趾尖（即神經纖維的末梢），進而向軀幹擴散。這些症狀往往是大致對稱分布的。參閱 Guillain-Barré syndrome（postinfective polyneuropathy），neuropathy。

polynucleotide *n.* a long chain of linked *nucleotides, of which molecules of DNA and RNA are made.

多核苷酸 由多個核苷酸連接而成的一條長鏈。脫氧核糖核酸及核糖核酸分子即由此長鏈構成。

polyopia *n.* the sensation of multiple images of one object. It is sometimes experienced by people with early cataract. *See also* diplopia.

視物顯多症 一物多像感。患早期白內障病人有時可有此症狀。參閱 diplopia。

polyorchidism *n.* a congenital abnormality resulting in more than two testes.

多睪（畸形） 長有兩個以上睪丸的先天畸形。

polyp (polypus) *n.* a growth, usually benign, protruding from a mucous

息肉 由黏膜上突出的一種生長物（瘤），通常為良性。息

membrane. Polyps are commonly found in the nose and sinuses, giving rise to obstruction, chronic infection, and discharge. They are often present in patients with allergic rhinitis, in whom they may develop in response to long-term antigenic stimulation. Other sites of occurrence include the ear, the stomach, and the colon, where they may eventually become malignant. *Juvenile polyps* occur in the intestine (usually colon or rectum) of infants or young people; sometimes they are multiple (*juvenile polyposis*). In the latter form there is a risk of malignant change (25% of cases) but most juvenile polyps are benign (*see also* Peutz-Jeghers syndrome). Polyps are usually removed surgically (*see* polypectomy).

肉通常見於鼻腔和鼻竇，引起梗阻、慢性炎症和溢液。息肉常見於變態反應性鼻炎（過敏性鼻炎）患者，它們可由長時期的抗原刺激而產生。息肉的其他好發部位包括耳、胃、結腸，這些部位的息肉最終都可能發生惡變。小的息肉常發生於嬰兒或青年人的腸道（通常為結腸或直腸），有時它們是多發的（幼年息肉病）。後者常有惡變的危險（25% 病例）。但大多數小息肉都是良性的（參閱 Peutz-Jeghers syndrome）。息肉通常採用外科手術切除（參閱 polypectomy）。

polypectomy n. the surgical removal of a *polyp. The technique used depends upon the site and size of the polyp, but it is often done by cutting across the base using a wire loop (snare) through which is passed a coagulating *diathermy current.

息肉切除術 切除息肉的外科手術。所採用的手術方法取決於息肉所在的部位及其大小。但通常用一個金屬環（勒除器）在息肉根部進行勒除。該金屬環可通電加熱以進行（傷口）凝固。

polypeptide n. a molecule consisting of three or more amino acids linked together by *peptide bonds. *Protein molecules are polypeptides.

多肽 三個或更多的氨基酸通過肽鏈連接在一起組成的一個分子。各種蛋白質分子都屬於多肽。

polyphagia n. gluttonous excessive eating.

貪食（症） 一種不知飽的暴食症。

polypharmacy n. treatment of a patient with more than one type of medicine.

複方藥劑，多味藥劑 讓病人服用多種藥物的治療方法。

polyphyletic adj. describing a number of individuals, species, etc., that have evolved from more than one ancestral group. *Compare* monophyletic.

多元的，多系的，多源的 描述從一個以上的祖系演化而來的許多個體或物種。與 monophyletic 對比。

polyploid adj. describing cells, tissues, or individuals in which there are three or

多倍體 指具有三套或更多套完整染色體的細胞、組織或個

more complete sets of chromosomes. *Compare* diploid, haploid. **–polyploidy** *n*.

體。與 diploid，haploid 對比。

polypoid *adj*. having the appearance of a *polyp.

息肉狀的　具有息肉樣外觀的。

polyposis *n*. a condition in which numerous *polyps form in an organ or tissue. *Familial polyposis* is a hereditary disease in which multiple polyps develop in the colon at puberty. As these polyps often become malignant, patients are usually advised to undergo total removal of the colon. *See also* Peutz-Jeghers syndrome. *Compare* pseudopolyposis.

息肉病　在一個器官或組織中形成許多息肉的情況。家族性結腸息肉病是一種遺傳性疾病。青春期，結腸內有多個息肉生長。因為這些息肉常常發生惡變，所以通常建議病人將結腸全部切除。參閱 Peutz-Jeghers syndrome，與 pseudopolyposis 對比。

polypus *n. see* polyp.

息肉　參閱 polyp。

polyradiculitis (polyradiculopathy) *n*. any disorder of the peripheral nerves (*see* neuropathy) in which the brunt of the disease falls on the nerve roots where they emerge from the spinal cord. An abnormal allergic response in the nerve fibres is thought to be the cause of this condition. The *Guillain-Barré syndrome is an example.

多發性神經根炎　一種主要侵害脊神經根部位的周圍神經性疾病（參閱 neuropathy）。人們認為該病的病因可能是神經纖維的一種異常變態反應（過敏反應）。吉-巴氏綜合徵（急性感染性多發性神經炎）就是一個例子。

polyribosome *n. see* polysome.

多聚核糖體，多聚核糖核蛋白體　參閱 polysome。

polysaccharide *n*. a *carbohydrate formed from many monosaccharides joined together in long linear or branched chains. Polysaccharides have two important functions: (1) as storage forms of energy; for example *glycogen in animals and man and *starch in plants, and (2) as structural elements; for example *mucopolysaccharides in animals and man and *cellulose in plants.

多糖　由多個單糖連接在一起形成長綫狀或支鏈形的一種碳水化合物。多糖有兩個重要功能：(1) 作為能量的貯存形式，如動物和人體內的糖原及植物內的澱粉。(2) 作為組織結構的組成成分，例如動物和人體內的黏多糖，植物中的纖維素。

polyserositis *n*. inflammation of the membranes that line the chest, abdomen,

多漿膜炎　胸腔、腹腔和關節處漿膜的炎症，並伴有腔內積

and joints, with accumulation of fluid in the cavities. Commonly the condition is inherited and intermittent and is termed *familial Mediterranean fever*. If complicated by infiltration of major organs by a glycoprotein (*see* amyloidosis) the disease usually proves fatal. Regular administration of colchicine will prevent the attacks in 95% of patients.

液。通常該病是遺傳性和間歇性的，並稱為家族性地中海熱。如果伴有主要器官的糖蛋白浸潤（參閱 amyloidosis），該病往往是致命的。常規給予秋水仙鹼可使 95% 的病人免於感染。

polysome (polyribosome) *n.* a structure that occurs in the cytoplasm of cells and consists of a group of *ribosomes linked together by *messenger RNA molecules: formed during protein synthesis.

多核糖體（多聚核糖體） 存在於細胞的胞漿中，由信使核糖核酸分子連接在一起形成的一組核糖體組成的結構，是在蛋白質合成過程中形成的。

polysomnograph *n.* a record of measurements of various bodily parameters during sleep. It is used in the diagnosis of sleep disorders, such as *obstructive sleep apnoea.

多功能睡眠測量儀 一種測量記錄睡眠中身體各種參數的儀器。它用於各種睡眠障礙的診斷。如阻塞性睡眠呼吸窒息。

polyspermia *n.* **1.** excessive formation of semen. **2.** *see* polyspermy.

(1) 精液過多 **(2)** 多精受精 參閱 polyspermy。

polyspermy (polyspermia) *n.* fertilization of a single ovum by more than one spermatozoon: the development is abnormal and the embryo dies.

多精受精 單個卵子與多精子相結合的受精過程。這種受精卵的發育是不正常的，胚胎不能存活。

polythelia *n.* a congenital excess of nipples (*see* pleomastia)

多乳頭畸形 一種先天性的乳頭過多畸形。參閱 pleomastia。

polyuria *n.* the production of large volumes of urine, which is dilute and of a pale colour. The phenomenon may be due simply to excessive liquid intake or to disease, particularly diabetes mellitus, diabetes insipidus, and kidney disorders.

多尿（症） 排出大量稀釋而又顏色淺淡的尿液。這種現象可能是由於單純的飲水過多，也可能由於某些疾病，特別是糖尿病、尿崩症和某些腎臟疾病引起。

pompholyx *n.* *eczema of the hands (*see also* cheiropompholyx) and feet (*podopompholyx*). Because the horny

汗疱 手部濕疹（參閱 cheiropompholyx）及足部濕疹（跖汗疱）。由於這些部位

layer of the skin in these parts is so thick the vesicles typical of eczema cannot rupture; they therefore persist in the skin, looking like sago grains. There is intense itching until the skin eventually peels. There may be secondary infection due to scratching. Pompholyx is most common in early adulthood and attacks occur suddenly, lasting up to six weeks. The disease may be recurrent or persist as a chronic condition.

皮膚的角質層太厚，水泡型的濕疹不能破裂，所以它們就存留在皮膚內，看上去像許多小米粒。（汗疱）有劇烈的奇癢，直到皮膚最後破損脫落。由於搔抓可能會引起繼發感染。汗疱在青壯年時期最為常見。並突然發病持續達六周。該病可能會反覆發作或者像慢性病一樣持續存在。

pons *n.* **1.** *see* pons Varolii. **2.** any portion of tissue that joins two parts of an organ.

(1) 腦橋　參閱 pons Varolii。
(2) 橋　連接一個器官兩個部位之間的組織部位。

pons Varolii (pons) the part of the *brainstem that links the medulla oblongata and the thalamus, bulging forwards in front of the cerebellum, from which it is separated by the fourth ventricle. It contains numerous nerve tracts between the cerebral cortex and the spinal cord and several nuclei of grey matter. From its front surface the *trigeminal nerves emerge.

腦橋　腦幹上連接延髓和中腦的部分。它在小腦前方向前膨出，並且和小腦間以第四腦室相隔。腦橋含有許多連接大腦皮質和脊髓的神經傳導束和一些灰質核團。三叉神經從腦橋的前表面發出。

pontic *n.* (in dentistry) *see* bridge.

橋體　（牙科學）參閱 bridge。

popliteus *n.* a flat triangular muscle at the back of the knee joint, between the femur and tibia, that helps to flex the knee. **–popliteal** *adj.*

膕肌　位於膝關節後面，股骨和脛骨之間的一塊扁平的三角形肌肉。它可幫助屈膝關節。

porcelain *n.* (in dentistry) a ceramic material that is used to construct tooth coloured crowns, inlays, or veneers.

瓷、瓷料　（牙科學）用於製作牙齒本色牙冠、嵌體或覆蓋物的一種陶瓷材料。

pore *n.* a small opening; for example, *sweat pores* are the openings of the sweat glands on the surface of the skin.

孔，門　一種小的開口。例如：汗孔就是皮膚表面汗腺的開口。

porencephaly *n.* an abnormal communication between the lateral *ventricle and the surface of the brain. This is

腦穿通（畸形）　側腦室與腦表面之間形成的一個異常通道。該畸形往往由腦外傷或腦血管

usually a consequence of brain injury or cerebrovascular disease; uncommonly it may be a developmental defect, when it would most likely affect both lateral ventricles.

疾病所致。雙側側腦室穿通畸形極可能是一種發育缺陷，但這並不多見。

porocephaliasis *n.* a rare infestation of the nasal cavities, windpipe, lungs, liver, or spleen by the nymphs of the parasitic arthropod *porocephalus*. Man becomes infected on consumption of water or uncooked vegetables contaminated with the parasite's eggs. There may be some abdominal pain while the parasite is in the gut but in many cases there are no symptoms. Porocephaliasis has been occasionally reported in negroes of central Africa.

蛇舌狀蟲病 是由寄生性節肢動物蛇舌狀蟲屬（洞頭蟲屬）的小成蟲（若蟲）引起的鼻腔、氣管、肺、肝或脾臟的一種罕見的感染。人可能由於飲用或進食被寄生蟲卵污染過的生水或生菜而引起感染。當寄生蟲進入腸道時病人可能有些腹痛，但大多數病人可無症狀。蛇舌狀蟲病在中非的黑人中曾偶爾有過報導。

Porocephalus *n.* a genus of wormlike arthropods occurring mainly in tropical Africa and India. The legless adults are parasites in the lungs of snakes. The eggs, which are ejected with the snake's bronchial secretions, may be accidentally swallowed by man. The larva bores through the gut wall and usually migrates to the liver, where it develops into a nymph (*see* porocephaliasis).

蛇舌狀蟲屬 一種主要存在於熱帶非洲和印度的蠕蟲樣節肢動物（屬）。這種無腿成蟲寄生於蛇的肺內。隨着蛇支氣管分泌物一起排出的蟲卵可能偶然被人吞服。其幼蟲穿過腸壁，通常遷移至肝臟，在肝臟發育成一個小成蟲（參閱 porocephaliasis）。

porphin *n.* a complex nitrogen-containing ring structure and parent compound of the *porphyrins.

卟吩 一種含有氮環結構的複合物，是卟啉的母體。

porphobilinogen *n.* a pigment that appears in the urine of individuals with acute *porphyria, causing it to darken if left standing.

卟吩膽色素原 急性卟啉症患者尿中出現的一種色素。如尿液靜置，則顏色可由淺變深。

porphyria *n.* one of a group of rare inherited disorders due to disturbance of the metabolism of the breakdown products (*porphyrins) of the red blood pigment haemoglobin. The defect may be primarily in the liver (*hepatic*

卟啉症，紫質症 由於血色素血紅蛋白分解產物（卟啉）代謝失調引起的一種罕見的遺傳性疾病。該遺傳性缺陷最初可能發生在肝臟（肝卟啉症）或骨髓（紅細胞生成性卟啉症）

porphyria) or in the bone marrow (*erythropoietic porphyria*) or both. The prominent features include the excretion of porphyrins and their derivatives in the urine, which may change colour on standing (*see* porphobilinogen); sensitivity of the skin to sunlight causing chronic inflammation or blistering; inflammation of the nerves (neuritis); mental disturbances; and attacks of abdominal pain. The commonest porphyria is *porphyria cutanea tarda*, which affects up to 1 in 5000 people in some countries. It is a hepatic porphyria in which light-exposed areas of the skin become blistered and fragile.

porphyrin *n.* one of a number of pigments derived from *porphin, which are widely distributed in living things. All porphyrins form chelates with iron, magnesium, zinc, nickel, copper, and cobalt. These chelates are constituents of *haemoglobin, *myohaemoglobin, the *cytochromes, and chlorophyll, and are thus important in many oxidation/reduction reactions in all living organisms. *See also* protoporphyrin IX.

porphyrinuria *n.* the presence in the urine of breakdown products of the red blood pigment haemoglobin (porphyrins), sometimes causing discoloration. *See* porphyria, porphobilinogen.

porta *n.* the aperture in an organ through which its associated vessels pass. Such an opening occurs in the liver (*porta hepatis*).

portacaval anastomosis (portacaval shunt) 1. a surgical technique in which the hepatic portal vein is joined to the inferior vena cava. Blood draining from the abdominal viscera is thus diverted

或兩者皆有。其主要特點是尿中有卟啉及其衍生物排出，如尿靜置，則可能改變顏色（參閱 porphobilinogen）；皮膚對日光過敏，引起慢性皮膚炎症或起疱；神經發炎（神經炎）；精神失常和腹痛。最常見的卟啉症是「遲發性皮膚卟啉症」，在某些國家，每五千人中就有一人患此病症。此病是一種肝卟啉症，皮膚被日光照射的部位產生水疱並變得脆弱。

卟啉 從卟吩衍生出來的多種色素中的一種。卟啉廣泛分布於生物體中。所有卟啉都和鐵、鎂、鋅、鎳、銅和鈷結合成螯合物。這些螯合物是血紅蛋白、肌紅蛋白、細胞色素和葉綠素的組成成分。因此它們在所有生物體的許多氧化還原反應中起重要作用。參閱 protoporphyrin IX。

卟啉尿 尿中出現血色素血紅蛋白的分解產物（卟啉）。有時可造成尿變色，參閱 porphyria，porphobilinogen。

門 一個器官中有關管道通過的孔。如肝上的一個開口（肝門）。

(1) 門腔靜脈吻合（門腔靜脈分流） 一種將肝臟門靜脈和下腔靜脈相連的外科手術。由腹腔器官回流的血液便可以繞過肝臟而回流。此手術用來治

past the liver. It is used in the treatment of *portal hypertension, since – by lowering the pressure within the veins of the stomach and oesophagus – it prevents serious bleeding into the gastrointestinal tract. **2.** any of the natural communications between the branches of the hepatic portal vein in the liver and the inferior vena cava.

療門靜脈高壓，因為通過它降低胃和食管靜脈壓力，所以可防止胃腸道的嚴重出血。**(2)** 指肝內門靜脈的分支與下腔靜脈之間的任何自然交通。

portal *adj.* **1.** relating to the portal vein or system. **2.** relating to a porta.

門的 **(1)** 與門靜脈或門靜脈系有關的。**(2)** 與門有關的（尤指肝門）。

portal hypertension a state in which the pressure within the hepatic *portal vein is increased, causing enlargement of the spleen, enlargement of veins in the oesophagus (gullet) (which may rupture to cause severe bleeding), and accumulation of fluid in the peritoneal cavity (ascites). The commonest cause is *cirrhosis, but other diseases of the liver or thrombosis of the portal vein will also produce it. Treatment is by *diuretic drugs, by surgery to join the portal vein to the inferior vena cava (bypassing the liver; *see* portacaval anastomosis), or by implanting a *stent within the liver to join portal tract veins to a hepatic vein tributary (*TIPSS – transcutaneous intrahepatic porto-systemic shunt*).

門靜脈高壓 肝臟門靜脈壓力增高，導致脾臟腫大，食管靜脈擴張（可發生破裂引起嚴重出血）和腹膜腔積液（腹水）。其最常見的原因是肝硬化，但肝臟的其他病變或門靜脈血栓形成也會引起門脈高壓。治療是使用利尿藥物、門靜脈與下腔靜脈吻合手術（繞過肝臟，參閱 portacaval anastomosis），或在肝內植入一個引流條以便將門靜脈的分支吻合到一個肝靜脈的屬支上（經皮肝內門腔靜脈分流術）。

portal system a vein or group of veins that terminates at both ends in a capillary bed. The best known is the *hepatic portal system*, which consists of the *portal vein and its tributaries (see illustration). Blood is drained from the spleen, stomach, pancreas, and small and large intestines into veins that merge to form the portal vein leading to the liver. Here the portal vein branches, ending in many small capillaries called *sinusoids. These permit the passage into the liver

門靜脈系統 兩端都終止於毛細血管床的一種靜脈或一組靜脈。最熟悉的就是肝門靜脈系，它由門靜脈及其分支組成（見圖）。由脾、胃、胰和大、小腸回流的血液進入各自的靜脈，然後匯合形成通向肝臟的門靜脈。在肝內，門靜脈的分支，終止於許多稱之為竇狀隙的小毛細血管。血液中從腸道吸收來的營養物質通過竇狀隙進入肝細胞。

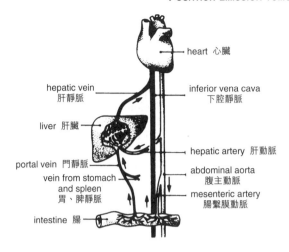

The hepatic portal system
肝門靜脈系統

cells of nutrients absorbed by blood from the intestines.

portal vein a short vein, about 8 cm long, forming part of the hepatic *portal system. It receives many tributaries, including the splenic vein from the spleen and pancreas, the gastric vein from the stomach, the mesenteric vein from the small and large intestines, and the rectal vein from the rectum and anus.

port-wine stain *see* naevus.

POS *see* polycystic ovary syndrome.

positron emission tomography (PET) a technique used to evaluate activity of brain tissues by measuring the emission of radioactive particles from molecules of radiation-labelled 2-deoxyglucose. This substance is accepted by brain cells in much the same way as glucose, but it

門靜脈 一條長約 8 cm 的短靜脈，為肝門靜脈系的組成部分。它接受許多分支，包括來自於脾、胰的脾靜脈，來自胃的胃靜脈，來自小腸和大腸的腸繫膜靜脈以及來自於直腸和肛門的直腸靜脈。

葡萄酒樣色素斑 參閱 naevus。

多囊卵巢綜合徵 參閱 polycystic ovary syndrome。

正電子發射 X 綫斷層攝影術 (PET) 通過測定放射性標記的 2-脫氧葡萄糖分子中放射性粒子的放射性來判定腦組織功能的一種技術。2-脫氧葡萄糖以和葡萄糖非常相似的方式被腦細胞所吸收，但被功能性神

is metabolized very slowly after uptake by functioning neurones. Metabolic activity is reduced in damaged brain tissues and radioactive emissions from these areas is absent or reduced considerably if scanned by tomography equipment designed to detect radiation. The 2-deoxyglucose, usually tagged with radioactive oxygen, is injected into the patient to be examined. PET examinations are employed in the diagnosis and treatment of patients suffering from cerebral palsy and similar types of brain damage. Other compounds may be labelled to study other aspects of brain metabolism and drug action. *See also* tomography. *Compare* computerized tomography (CT).

經元吸收後，代謝非常緩慢。受傷的腦組織中，新陳代謝活動減弱，這時如果使用專門為探測放射綫而設計的 X 綫斷層攝影儀進行掃描，可看到這些損傷部位的放射性消失或明顯減弱。2-脫氧葡萄糖通常用放射性氧作標記，注射入病人體內以備檢查。PET 檢查被用來診斷和治療患腦癱或其他類似腦損傷的病人。其他物質也可被標記以用來研究腦的其他方面的新陳代謝和藥物的作用。參閱 tomography，與 computerized tomography (CT) 對比。

posology *n*. the science of the dosage of medicines.

劑量學 研究藥物劑量的科學。

posset *n*. a small amount of milk that is regurgitated, usually with some wind, by many babies after feeding.

溢乳 許多嬰兒在吃奶後，在少量的奶汁吐出，並常帶有一些胃裏的氣。

Possum *n*. a device that enables severely paralysed patients to use typewriters, adding machines, telephones, and a wide variety of other machines. Modern Possums are operated by microswitches that require only the slightest movement in any limb. The original device worked by blowing and sucking a mouthpiece. The name derives from *Patient-Operated Selector Mechanism* (*POSM*).

自助裝備 一種能幫助嚴重癱瘓病人使用打字機、加數器、電話機及其他多種機器的裝置。這種現代化的裝備裝有微型按鈕，它只需要任何一個肢體的輕微動作就能操作。最初這種裝置是通過對咬嘴的吹吸來操作的。本詞是由 Patient-Operated Selector Mechanism 的字頭 (POSM) 衍生而來。

post- *prefix denoting* **1.** following; after. Example: *postepileptic* (after an epileptic attack). **2.** (in anatomy) behind. Example: *postoral* (behind the mouth).

〔前綴〕**(1)** 後的，在……之後 例如：一次癲癇發作以後。**(2)** （解剖學）後方的 例如：口後的。

postcentral *adj*. **1.** situated behind any centre. **2.** situated behind the central fissure of the brain.

中央後的 (1) 位於任何中央後的。**(2)** 位於大腦中央溝後的。

postcibal *adj.* occurring after eating.

食後的　發生在進食後的。

postcoital contraception prevention of pregnancy after intercourse has taken place. This can be achieved by three methods, which aim to prevent implantation of the fertilized ovum in the uterus: (1) the *Yuzpe method*, which consists of spaced oral doses of oestrogen and progestogen taken within 72 hours of unprotected intercourse; (2) a single oral dose of the anti-progesterone drug *mifepristone, taken within 72 hours of unprotected intercourse; and (3) insertion of an *IUCD within five days of unprotected intercourse.

事後避孕　性交後防止受孕。可以採取三種方法來防止受精卵在子宮內植入（着床）：(1) Yuzpe 方案：未加保護措施的性生活後，72 小時之內間隔服用口服劑量的雌激素和孕激素。(2) 未加保護措施的性生活後 72 小時內一次性服用口服劑量的抗孕酮（抗黃體酮）藥米非酮。(3) 在未加保護措施的性生活後五天之內放置一個宮內避孕器。

postcoital test a test used in the investigation of infertility. A specimen of cervical mucus, taken 6–24 hours after coitus, is examined under a microscope. The appearance of 10 or more progressively motile spermatozoa per high-power field in the specimen indicates that there is no abnormal reaction between spermatozoa and mucus. The test should be undertaken in the post-ovulatory phase of the menstrual cycle.

性交後試驗　在不育症調查中用的一種試驗。性交後 6~24 小時內採集的一份宮頸黏液樣品在顯微鏡下進行檢查。在該樣品中每個高倍視野下有十個或更多的活動良好的精子出現，說明在精子和宮頸黏液之間沒有異常反應。此檢查應在月經周期的排卵後期進行。

posterior *adj.* situated at or near the back of the body or an organ.

後的，後面的　位於或靠近身體或某一器官背側的。

postero- *prefix denoting* posterior. Example: *posterolateral* (behind and at the side of).

〔前綴〕後部，在後　指後面的。例如：後外側的（指在……的後外側方）。

posteroanterior *adj.* from the back to the front. In radiology it denotes a view in the *coronal plane.

後前位的　從後到前，在放射學中指冠狀平面的視象。

postganglionic *adj.* describing a neurone in a nerve pathway that starts at a ganglion and ends at the muscle or gland that it supplies. In the sympathetic nervous system, postganglionic fibres are

（神經）節後的　描述一個神經通路中起於一個神經節而止於它所支配的肌肉或腺體的一個神經元。在交感神經系，節後纖維是腎上腺素能的，在副

*adrenergic unlike those in the parasympathetic system, which are *cholinergic. *Compare* preganglionic.

交感神經系，並非如此，而是膽鹼能的。與 preganglionic 對比。

posthetomy *n.* an obsolete term for *circumcision.

包皮環切術 已廢用的 circumcision（包皮環切術）的名詞。

posthitis *n.* inflammation of the foreskin. This usually occurs in association with inflammation of the glans penis (*balanitis*; *see* balanoposthitis). Pain, redness, and swelling of the foreskin occurs due to bacterial infection. Treatment is by antibiotic administration, and subsequent *circumcision prevents further attacks.

包皮炎 包皮發炎。通常和陰莖頭炎同時發生（參閱 balanoposthitis），由於細菌感染，包皮發生疼痛，顏色暗紅並腫脹。其治療是應用抗生素類藥物，並接着作包皮環切手術以防止進一步感染。

posthumous birth 1. delivery of a child by *Caesarean section after the mother's death. **2.** birth of a child after the father's death.

遺腹分娩（遺腹出生）**(1)** 母親死後採用剖宮產手術使嬰兒分娩。**(2)** 父親死後嬰兒的分娩。

postmature *adj.* describing a baby born after 42 weeks of gestation (calculated from the first day of the last menstrual period). Such a birth can be associated with maternal diabetes or with *anencephaly in the fetus. **–postmaturity** *n.*

過度成熟的（嬰兒）指妊娠42 周以後（從末次月經的第一天算起）出生的嬰兒。這種分娩與母親患糖尿病有關或與胚胎期無腦畸型有關。

post mortem Latin: after death. *See* autopsy.

屍體解剖（拉丁語：死後）參閱 autopsy。

postnatal depression *see* baby blues, puerperal depression.

產後抑鬱 參閱 baby blues，puerperal depression。

postoperative *adj.* following operation: referring to the condition of a patient or to the treatment given at this time.

手術後的 做了手術以後的。指病人的手術後情況或術後這段時間所接受的治療。

postpartum *adj.* relating to the period of a few days immediately after birth.

產後的 有關產後數日內的。

post-traumatic stress disorder (PTSD) an anxiety disorder caused by

創傷後反應失調 人們在受到嚴重個人壓力或傷害後的表現

the major personal stress of a serious or frightening event, such as an injury, assault, rape, or exposure to warfare or a disaster involving many casualties. The reaction may be immediate or delayed for months. The sufferer experiences the persistent recurrence of images or memories of the event, together with nightmares, insomnia, a sense of isolation, guilt, irritability, and loss of concentration. Emotions may be deadened or depression may develop. The condition usually settles with time, but support and skilled counselling may be needed.

出的一種失衡狀態，如受傷、暴力、強姦、戰爭或意外事故等。這種反應可在數月後出現或立即出現，常再現於睡夢中，伴惡夢、失眠、孤獨、易惱怒、懷有內疚感、注意力減退等。這種反應隨時間推移可逐漸減退，也可進一步發展，所以進行必要的幫助和咨詢尤為重要。

postural muscles (antigravity muscles) muscles (principally extensors) that serve to maintain the upright posture of the body against the force of gravity.

體位肌（抗引力肌） 對抗地心引力，以維持身體直立姿勢的肌肉。

postviral fatigue syndrome *see* myalgic encephalomyelitis.

病毒後疲勞綜合徵 參閱 myalgic encephalomyelitis。

potassium *n.* a mineral element and an important constituent of the human body. It is the main base ion of intracellular fluid. Together with *sodium, it helps to maintain the electrical potential of the nervous system and is thus essential for the functioning of nerve and muscle. Normal blood levels are between 3.5 and 5 mmols/litre. High concentrations occur particularly in kidney failure and may lead to *arrhythmia and finally to cardiac arrest. Low values result from fluid loss e.g. due to vomiting or diarrhoea, and this may lead to general muscle paralysis. Symbol: K.

鉀 人體內一種重要的元素。是細胞內液的主要成分，與鈉一起維持神經系統的電位。也是肌肉、神經運動的基礎。正常血鉀水平維持在 3.5~5 mmol/l。高鉀會導致心律失常及心臟驟停，這常見於腎衰病人；而嘔吐或腹瀉會丟失大量的鉀從而使肌肉麻痺。符號：K。

potassium chloride a salt of potassium used to prevent and treat potassium deficiency, especially during treatment with certain diuretics. It is administered by mouth or injection; some irritation in the digestive system may occur after oral

氯化鉀 預防和治療鉀缺乏的一種鉀鹽，主要用於某些利尿劑治療時。口服或注射。口服後可能對消化系統有些刺激作用。商品名：Nu-K，Slow-K。

administration. Trade names: **Nu-K**, **Slow-K**.

potassium hydroxyquinoline a salt of potassium that has antifungal, antibacterial, and deodorant activities. It is applied to the skin in creams or lotions (e.g. in combination with *benzoyl peroxide as *Quinoderm* or *Quinoped*) to treat skin infections and occasionally causes skin irritation.

羥喹啉鉀　一種能夠抗真菌、細菌和具有除臭作用的鉀鹽。用法：將乳劑或洗液與過氧苯甲醯結合搽於皮膚上，以治療皮膚的感染。偶爾對皮膚有刺激作用。

potassium permanganate a salt of potassium used for disinfecting and cleansing wounds and as a general skin *antiseptic. It irritates mucous membranes and is poisonous if taken into the body.

高錳酸鉀　一種用作一般皮膚抗菌劑的鉀鹽，用於消毒和皮膚傷口的清洗。該藥有刺激黏膜的作用，如進入體內可引起中毒。

Potter syndrome a congenital condition characterized by absence of kidneys, resulting in decreased amniotic fluid (*see* oligohydramnios) and compression of the fetus. Babies have poorly developed lungs, a characteristic wrinkled and flattened facial appearance, and leg deformities and do not usually survive.

波特綜合徵　先天性的腎臟缺失。由於羊水減少及胎兒受壓（參閱 oligohydramnios），嬰兒發育不完善，特別是肺臟，以面部皺褶和扁平為特徵，下肢也有畸形，通常難以存活。

Pott's disease *tuberculosis of the backbone, usually transmitted by infected cows' milk. Untreated, it can lead to a hunchback deformity.

波特病　通過受感染乳牛的奶而感染的一種脊柱結核。如不治療，能引起駝背。

pouch *n.* **1.** (in anatomy) a small sac-like structure, especially occurring as an outgrowth of a larger structure. The *pouch of Douglas* is a pouch of peritoneum occupying the space between the rectum and uterus. **2.** (in surgery) a sac created from a loop of intestine and used to replace a section of rectum that has been surgically removed, for example for ulcerative colitis (*see* ileal pouch), or to replace the bladder after *cystectomy.

囊腔，腔　(1)　（解剖學）指一種小的袋狀結構，特別是在較大的結構上生長的囊，道格拉斯腔是位於子宮和直腸之間的囊。(2)　外科上用一段小腸袢來代替因外科手術而切除的直腸，如潰瘍性結腸炎（參閱 ileal pouch），或代替膀胱切除術後的膀胱。

poultice (fomentation) n. a preparation of hot moist material applied to any part of the body to increase local circulation, alleviate pain, or soften the skin to allow matter to be expressed from a boil. Poultices containing kaolin retain heat for a considerable period during use.

泥罨劑，泥敷劑　一種由熱的濕潤的材料配製的敷劑。該敷劑可塗抹於身體任何部位，以促進局部血液循環，減輕疼痛或軟化皮膚以使膿腫中的膿液易於擠出。為了使熱敷有效期延長，泥罨劑含有保溫的高嶺土。

Poupart's ligament *see* inguinal ligament.

普帕爾韌帶　參閱 inguinal ligament。

powder n. (in pharmacy) a medicinal preparation consisting of a mixture of two or more drugs in the form of fine particles.

散劑，粉劑　（藥劑學）一種由兩種或數種藥物混合配成的細小顆粒狀藥物製劑。

pox n. **1.** an infectious disease causing a skin rash. **2.** a rash of pimples that become pus-filled, as in *chickenpox and *smallpox.

痘　(1) 引起皮疹的傳染病。(2) 一種充滿膿液的小膿疱疹，例如水痘和天花。

poxvirus n. one of a group of large DNA-containing viruses including those that cause *smallpox (variola) and *cowpox (vaccinia) in man, and pox and tumours in animals.

痘病毒　一種大型脫氧核糖核酸病毒，包括引起人體天花和牛痘的病毒和引起動物痘疱和腫瘤的病毒。

PPLO *see* mycoplasma.

類胸膜肺炎菌，鳥型支原體　參閱 mycoplasma。

practice nurse a trained nurse caring for the patients of one or more general practitioners in the consulting room and on domiciliary consultations, rarely combining this with the duties of a receptionist. In Britain, practice nurses may be employed by District Health Authorities as *community nurses or directly by GPs, who can claim the standard contribution from the *Family Health Services Authority.

實習護士　一種經過培訓的護士，可在咨詢室內承擔一個或更多全科醫師的病人咨詢和家庭咨詢工作，很少承擔接待任務。在英國，實習護士可做為社區保健護士受僱於地段衛生局，或直接受僱於全科醫師，可從家庭健康服務管理局得到資助。

Prader-Willi syndrome a congenital condition in which obesity is associated

普-威氏綜合徵　一種先天性疾病，伴有肥胖表現及腦發育遲

with mental retardation and small genitalia; diabetes mellitus frequently develops in affected individuals.

緩與外生殖器細小。患者中，糖尿病多見。

pravastatin *n.* a drug used to reduce abnormally high levels of cholesterol in the blood. Its actions and side-effects are similar to those of *lovastatin. Trade name: **Lipostat**.

普伐他汀 一種能減少血中異常濃度膽固醇的藥物，它的作用效果和副作用與洛伐他汀相類似。商品名：Lipostat。

praziquantel *n.* an *anthelmintic drug used to eliminate tapeworms, schistosomes, liver flukes, and lung flukes. It is administered by mouth. Possible side-effects include nausea, abdominal discomfort, fever, sweating, and drowsiness. Trade name: **Biltricide**.

吡喹酮 一種能殺死絛蟲、血吸血、肝吸蟲及肺吸蟲的驅腸中藥物。口服給藥。可能的副作用有惡心、胃腸不適、發熱、出汗、困倦等表現。商品名：Biltricide。

prazosin *n.* a drug used in the treatment of high blood pressure (hypertension) by reducing peripheral vascular resistance (*see* alpha blocker). It is administered by mouth; common side-effects include dizziness, headache, palpitations, and nausea. Trade name: **Hypovase**.

哌唑嗪 一種通過減少外周血管阻力來治療高血壓的藥物。（參閱 alpha blocker）。口服給藥。常見的副作用有頭暈、頭痛、心悸、惡心。商品名：Hypovase。

pre- *prefix denoting* **1.** before; preceding. Example: *premenstrual* (before menstruation); *prenatal* (before birth). **2.** (in anatomy) in front of; anterior to. Example: *precardiac* (in front of the heart); *prepatellar* (in front of the patella).

〔前綴〕 **(1) 前** 例如月經前，產前。**(2) 前方的** （解剖學）如心前區或髕前的。

pre-agonal *adj.* relating to the phenomena that precede the moment of death. *See also* agonal.

瀕死的 有關死前瞬間的現象（症狀和體徵）。參閱 agonal。

precancerous *adj.* describing a non-malignant condition that is known to become malignant if left untreated. *Leukoplakia of the vulva is known to be a precancerous condition. *See also* metaplasia.

癌前期的 指一種雖然不是惡性的，但是如不治療，可以變為惡性的疾病。已知外陰白斑病就是一種癌前期的疾病。參閱 metaplasia。

precipitin *n.* any antibody that combines with its antigen to form a complex that comes out of solution and is seen as a precipitate. The antibody-antigen reaction is specific; the precipitin reaction is thus a useful means of confirming the identity of an unknown antigen or establishing that a serum contains antibodies to a known disease. This test may be performed in watery solution or in a semisolid medium such as agar gel. *See also* agglutination.

沉澱素　由任何抗體與其抗原結合而構成的一種複合物。這種物質在溶液中呈沉澱物析出。抗體-抗原反應是特異性的，因此沉澱反應對鑒定某種未知抗原或證實某種血清是否含有某種已知疾病抗體方面是一種有效的方法。該實驗可以在水溶液中或在半固體培養基（如瓊脂凝膠）中進行。參閱 agglutination。

precipitinogen *n.* any antigen that is precipitated from solution by a *precipitin.

沉澱原，沉澱素原　使用沉澱素從溶液中沉澱出來的任何抗原。

precision attachment (in dentistry) a special machined joint that holds certain types of partial *dentures in place. The attachment is in two parts, one fixed to the denture and the other fixed to a crown on one of the teeth abutting the denture.

精確附着，槽溝附着（牙科學）把某種類型的部分托牙固定在適當的位置上的一種經過特殊加工的接合體。該接合體一部分固定在托牙上，另一部分固定在橋基牙的牙冠上。

precocity *n.* an acceleration of normal development. The intellectually precocious child has a high IQ and may become isolated from his contemporaries or frustrated at school. Mental illness is less common than in those who develop normally. **–precocious** *adj.*

早熟　一種超常發育。智力早熟的兒童智商高，可能和他（她）的同齡人不合羣或在學校裏受到冷遇。早熟兒童患精神病者比發育正常兒童少。

precordium *n.* the region of the thorax immediately over the heart. **–precordial** *adj.*

心前區　胸部體表與心臟相應的部位。

precuneus *n.* an area of the inner surface of the cerebral hemisphere on each side, above and in front of the *corpus callosum. *See* cerebrum.

楔前葉　位於每側大腦半球內側面，胼胝體上方和前部的區域。參閱 cerebrum。

predisposition *n.* a tendency to be affected by a particular disease or kind of disease. Such a tendency may be

素質　具有易患某種特殊疾病或某類疾病的傾向。該傾向可以遺傳或者由於缺乏某種維生

hereditary or may arise because of such factors as lack of vitamins, food, or sleep. *See also* diathesis.

prednisolone *n.* a synthetic *corticosteroid used to treat rheumatic diseases and inflammatory and allergic conditions. It is administered by mouth, injected into joints, or applied in creams, lotions, and ointments (to treat skin conditions). Side-effects are those of *cortisone. Trade names: **Deltacortril, Deltastab, Precortisyl, Prednesol**.

prednisone *n.* a synthetic *corticosteroid used to treat rheumatic diseases, severe allergic conditions, inflammatory conditions, and leukaemia. It is administered by mouth and the side-effects are those of *cortisone. Trade name: **Decortisyl**.

pre-eclampsia (pregnancy-induced hypertension) *n.* high blood pressure (greater than 140/90 mmHg) developing during pregnancy in a woman whose blood pressure was previously normal. It is often accompanied by excessive fluid retention and less often by the presence of protein in the urine. *See also* eclampsia.

prefrontal lobe the region of the brain at the very front of each cerebral hemisphere (*see* frontal lobe). The functions of the lobe are concerned with emotions, memory, learning, and social behaviour. Nerve tracts in the lobe are cut during the operation of prefrontal *leucotomy.

preganglionic *adj.* describing fibres in a nerve pathway that end in a ganglion, where they form synapses with *postganglionic fibres that continue the pathway to the effector organ, muscle, or gland.

素、食物或睡眠等因素而產生。參閱 diathesis。

潑尼松龍 一種治療風濕性疾病、炎症和變態反應性疾病的合成皮質類固醇。口服，關節內注射或製成乳劑、洗劑和軟膏劑外用（適用於皮膚病）。副作用同可的松。商品名：Deltacortril，Deltastab，Precortisyl，Prednesol。

強的松 用於治療風濕性疾病、嚴重的變態反應疾病、炎症和白血病的一種合成皮質類固醇。口服。副作用同可的松。商品名：Decortisyl。

子癇前期（妊娠高血壓） 原來血壓正常的婦女妊娠晚期出現的一種高血壓（大於 140/90 mmHg）。常伴有組織間液增多與不常伴有蛋白尿。參閱 eclampsia。

額前葉 每側大腦半球最前部位（參閱 frontal lobe），該葉的功能與情感記憶、學習能力和社交行為有關。在做腦白質切除術時，額前葉神經束便被切斷。

神經節前 指在神經通路中終止於神經節的纖維。它們在該神經節中與繼續通向效應器、肌肉或腺體的節後纖維構成突觸。

pre-gangrene *n.* the penultimate stage of vascular insufficiency before *gangrene sets in; the term is usually applied to *ischaemia of the lower limb.

pregnancy *n.* the period during which a woman carries a developing fetus, normally in the uterus (*compare* ectopic pregnancy). Pregnancy lasts for approximately 266 days, from *conception until the baby is born, or 280 days from the first day of the last menstrual period (*see* Naegele rule). During pregnancy menstruation is absent, there may be a great increase in appetite, and the breasts increase in size; the woman may also experience *morning sickness. These and other changes are brought about by a hormone (*progesterone) produced at first by the ovary and later by the *placenta. Definite evidence of pregnancy is provided by various *pregnancy tests, by the detection of the heartbeat of the fetus, and by ultrasound. Medical name: **cyesis**. *See also* pseudocyesis (phantom pregnancy). **–pregnant** *adj.*

pregnancy-induced   hypertension (PIH) *see* pre-eclampsia.

pregnancy test any of several methods used to demonstrate whether or not a woman is pregnant. Most pregnancy tests are based on the detection of a hormone, *human chorionic gonadotrophin (HCG), in the urine. The sample of urine is mixed with serum containing antibodies to HCG and marker particles (sheep red cells or latex particles) coated with HCG. In the absence of pregnancy, the antibodies will cause *agglutination of the marker particles. If the urine is from a pregnant woman, the antibodies will be absorbed and no agglutination will occur. These tests may be positive for

壞疽前　壞疽發生前，血供不足的階段。該術語通常用來指下肢局部缺血。

妊娠　婦女在正常情況下，子宮內懷有正在發育的胎兒的時期，（與 ectopic pregnancy 對比）。從受孕直到嬰兒出生，妊娠期持續大約 266 天，或者從末次月經（參閱 Naegele rule）第一天開始 280 天。妊娠期月經停止，食慾大增，乳房增大。孕婦可有晨間惡心嘔吐。這些變化和其他一些變化均由最初從卵巢和後期從胎盤分泌的激素（孕酮）所引起。通過做各種妊娠試驗和聽到胎兒心音或超聲檢查可確診妊娠。醫學用語：妊娠。參閱 pseudocyesis。

妊娠高血壓　參閱 pre-eclampsia。

妊娠試驗　證實一位婦女是否懷孕的幾種方法中的任何一種。多數妊娠試驗以在尿中發現人絨毛膜促性腺激素為根據。尿液標本中加入含有人絨毛膜促性腺激素抗體的血清和人絨毛膜促性腺激素指示劑（羊紅細胞或膠乳劑）。在未妊娠婦女中，抗體會與標記物凝集。若尿液來自妊娠婦女，抗體將被吸收且無凝集出現，這種試驗在妊娠後 30 天內便有陽性表現，準確率為 98%。現在更新的試驗方法是用單克隆抗體（beta 人絨毛膜促性腺激

pregnancy as early as 30 days after the date of the last normal period and are 98% accurate. Newer tests using *monoclonal antibodies (*beta HCG*) are more easily interpreted. When carried out on serum rather than urine, these tests give even earlier positive results.

素），結果較容易分析。不用尿液而用血清進行這種試驗，可較早確診。

pregnanediol *n.* a steroid that is formed during the metabolism of the female sex hormone *progesterone. It occurs in the urine during pregnancy and certain phases of the menstrual cycle.

孕烷二醇　一種在女性激素孕酮的代謝過程中形成的固醇類化合物。見於妊娠期和月經周期某些階段的尿中。

pregnenolone *n.* a steroid synthesized in the adrenal glands, ovaries, and testes. Pregnenolone is an important intermediate product in steroid hormone synthesis and can – depending on the pathways followed – be converted to corticosteroids (glucocorticoids or mineralocorticoids), androgens, or oestrogens.

孕烯醇酮　一種在腎上腺、卵巢和睪丸中合成的固醇類化合物。孕烯醇酮在固醇類化合物激素的合成過程中是一種重要的中間產物。按照不同的途徑，孕烯醇酮能轉化為皮質激素類（糖皮質激素或鹽皮質激素），雄激素或雌激素。

preimplantation diagnosis *see* prenatal diagnosis.

胚胎植入前診斷　參閱 prenatal diagnosis。

premature beat *see* ectopic beat.

早產搏動　參閱 ectopic beat。

premature birth birth of a baby weighing less than 2.5 kg ($5^1/_2$ lb). Usually this is indicative of *preterm birth but it can also be caused by *intrauterine growth retardation (IUGR). Birth weights of less than 500 g are almost invariably incompatible with life.

早產　出生時的嬰兒體重小於 2.5 kg。通常這是早產的指徵，但也可能由於胎兒在子宮內發育障礙引起。出生體重小於 500 g 的嬰兒不易存活。

premature ejaculation emission of semen (and consequent loss of erection) during the initial stages of preparation for sexual intercourse, before insertion into the vagina or immediately afterwards.

射精過早，早洩　在準備性交的開始階段，陰莖還未插入陰道或剛插入陰道就發生射精（隨之發生陽痿）。

premedication *n.* drugs administered to a patient before an operation (usually

前驅給藥法，術前用藥法　在手術前給病人用藥（通常指麻

one in which an anaesthetic is used). Premedication usually comprises injection of a sedative, to calm the patient down, together with a drug, such as *atropine, to dry up the secretions of the lungs (which might otherwise be inhaled during anaesthesia).

醉劑），術前用藥法通常包括：為使病人安靜下來的鎮靜注射劑和使病人肺分泌物減少的藥物如阿托品，後者是為了避免在麻醉時將分泌物吸入。

premenstrual tension a condition of nervousness, irritability, emotional disturbance, headache, and/or depression affecting some women for up to about ten days before menstruation. The condition is associated with the accumulation of salt and water in the tissues. It usually disappears soon after menstruation begins. The hormone progesterone is believed to be a causative element and a deficiency of essential fatty acids has also been observed.

經前期緊張　有些婦女在月經前10天左右就開始出現神經過敏、易怒、情緒障礙、頭痛和/或抑鬱等症狀。該病與組織中鹽和水的瀦留有關。一旦月經來潮，以上症狀常立即消失。激素黃體酮被認為是病因之一，且發現缺少多種必需脂肪酸。

premenstruum *n.* the stage of the *menstrual cycle immediately preceding menstruation.

經前期　在月經周期中緊接來月經前的一段時間。

premolar *n.* either of the two teeth on each side of each jaw behind the canines and in front of the molars in the adult *dentition.

前磨牙，雙尖牙　在成人牙列中位於尖牙後和磨牙前的雙側頜骨上的兩顆牙齒。

premyelocyte *n. see* promyelocyte.

早幼粒細胞，前髓細胞　參閱promyelocyte。

prenatal diagnosis (antenatal diagnosis) diagnostic procedures carried out on pregnant women in order to discover genetic or other abnormalities in the developing fetus. Ultrasound scanning (*see* ultrasonography) remains the cornerstone of prenatal diagnosis. Other procedures include estimation of the level of *alpha-fetoprotein in the mother's serum and the amniotic fluid; chromosome and enzyme analysis of fetal cells obtained by *amniocentesis or,

產前診斷　對孕婦所進行的診斷過程，以發現正在生長發育中的胎兒在遺傳及其他方面的異常情況。超聲波掃描（參閱ultrasonography）仍是基本的方法。其他程序包括母體血清甲胎蛋白水平及羊水測定、分析通過羊膜穿刺或在妊娠早期通過絨膜絨毛取樣得到的胎兒細胞染色體和酶及檢查通過胎兒鏡或臍帶穿刺獲得的胎兒血液。若檢查結果顯示胎兒出生

at an earlier stage of pregnancy, by *chorionic villus sampling (CVS); and examination of fetal blood obtained by *fetoscopy or *cordocentesis. If the results indicate that the child is likely or certain to be born with severe malformation or abnormality, the possibility of abortion is discussed by the doctors involved with the parents.

Until recently, prenatal genetic diagnosis was dependent on CVS and amniocentesis, but it may now be extended to the earliest stages of embryonic development, before implantation occurs (*preimplantation diagnosis*). Access to these early embryos requires the removal and *in vitro fertilization of egg cells: three days after fertilization one or two cells are aspirated from the six- to eight-cell embryo; alternatively, tissue is removed from an embryo at five or six days, when it has reached the *blastocyst stage. Isolated cells can then be genetically analysed, using the *polymerase chain reaction amplification technique to produce enough DNA for genetic diagnosis. Even before pregnancy, this technique can be used to enable a prospective mother to be identified as the carrier of a gene defect, by means of the *mouthwash test. When a defect is detected, *genetic counselling is offered.

時很可能或肯定有嚴重畸形或異常，有關醫生和嬰兒父母可討論是否墮胎。

直到最近，胎兒基因診斷依賴於絨膜絨毛取樣檢查和羊膜穿刺術，但現在可持續到植入前的胚胎發育最早期（着床前診斷）。要獲得早期胚胎，需將卵細胞移出體外並在試管內受精。受精三天後，6~8 個細胞的胚胎變成 1 或 2 個細胞。5~6 天，當它到達胚泡階段時，從胚胎內取出組織。獨立的細胞已可以作基因分析，使用的是聚合酶鏈反應技術，以為基因診斷提供足夠的DNA。在妊娠前，這種技術甚至也可以只需通過嗽口液檢查來為未來的母親鑒別基因是否缺陷。若查出基因缺陷，應進行基因咨詢。

preoperative *adj.* before operation: referring to the condition of a patient or to treatment, such as sedation, given at this time.

手術前的 做手術以前的。術前這一段時間的病人情況或對病人的處理情況（如讓病人處於鎮靜狀態）。

preparedness *n.* (in psychology) a quality of some stimuli that makes them much more likely to give rise to a pathological fear. For example, animals or high places are much more likely to become the subject of a *phobia than are plants or clothes. One theory is that individuals

恐怖素質 在心理學中指某些刺激所具有的更容易引起病理性恐怖的性質。例如：動物和高處就比植物和衣服更易成為病理性恐怖的對象。有一種理論認為：從遺傳學的觀點來看，人對那些在人類進化過程

are genetically predisposed to *conditioning of fear to objects that have been a biological threat during the evolution of mankind.

中曾經成為威脅生命的物體，容易產生恐怖。

prepatellar bursitis *see* housemaid's knee.

髕前黏液囊炎 參閱 housemaid's knee。

prepubertal *adj.* relating to or occuring in the period before puberty.

青春期前的 有關或發生於青春期前時期的。

prepuce (foreskin) *n.* the fold of skin that grows over the end (glans) of the penis. On its inner surface modified sebaceous glands (*preputial glands*) secrete a lubricating fluid over the glans. The accumulation of this secretion is known as *smegma. The foreskin is often surgically removed in infancy (*see* circumcision). The fold of skin that surrounds the clitoris is also called the prepuce. **–preputial** *adj.*

包皮 生長並覆蓋於陰莖末端（龜頭）上面的皮膚皺褶。在包皮的內表面上有皮脂腺（包皮腺），該皮脂腺（包皮腺）能夠分泌一種潤滑液在龜頭上起潤滑作用。聚集的分泌物稱為包皮垢，包皮在嬰兒期常採用外科手術切除。陰蒂周圍的皮膚皺褶也稱為包皮。

preputial glands modified sebaceous glands on the inner surface of the *prepuce.

包皮腺 位於包皮內表面的起潤滑作用的皮脂腺。

prepyramidal *adj.* **1.** situated in the middle lobe of the cerebellum, in front of the *pyramid. **2.** describing nerve fibres in tracts that descend from the cerebral cortex to the before the crossing over that occurs at the pyramid of the medulla oblongata.

錐體前的 **(1)** 位於錐體前的小腦中葉內的。**(2)** 指從大腦皮質到脊髓的下行傳導束在延髓錐體交叉之前的神經纖維。

presby- (presbyo-) *prefix denoting* old age.

〔前綴〕**老年**

presbyacusis *n.* the progressive sensorineural *deafness that occurs with age.

老年性耳聾 見於老年人的進行性耳聾。

presbyopia *n.* difficulty in reading at the usual distance (about one foot from the eyes) and in performing other close

老視 老年人在看近距離物體時調節眼睛焦距的能力減弱，因此在通常的距離（離眼睛約一

work, due to the decline with age in the ability of the eye to alter its focus to see close objects clearly. This is caused by gradual loss of elasticity of the lens of the eye which thus becomes progressively less able to increase its curvature in order to focus on near objects.

英尺左右）閱讀和從事其他近距離工作有困難，這是由於眼球晶狀體的彈性逐漸消失所致。因此，為了聚焦於近距離物體時，要增加晶狀體的曲度，就變得越來越困難了。

prescribed disease one of a number of illnesses (currently 48) arising as a result of employment requiring close contact with a hazardous substance or circumstance. Examples include poisoning by such chemicals as mercury or benzene, decompression sickness in divers, and infections such as *anthrax in those handling wool. Some diseases that occur widely in the population may be prescribed in relation to a specific occupation (e.g. deafness in those working with pneumatic drills or tuberculosis in mortuary attendants). *See also* COSHH.

法定性職業病 由於在所從事的職業中不得不與有害物質或環境密切接觸而引起的一類疾病（現有 48 種），例如汞、苯等化學物質的中毒，潛水員的減壓病，羊毛操作工接觸感染的炭疽病等。有些在人羣中廣泛發生的疾病已被認定與某些特殊的職業有關（例如使用氣鑽的工人所患的耳聾病或停屍室的工作人員的結核病等，參閱 COSHH）。

prescription *n.* written direction from a registered medical practitioner to a pharmacist for preparing and dispensing a drug.

處方、藥方 醫生給藥劑師開的關於配製藥物與發藥的書面指示。

presenility *n.* premature ageing of the mind and body, so that a person shows the reduction in mental and physical abilities normally found only in old age. *See also* dementia, progeria. **–presenile** *adj.*

早老 身心早衰。一個人出現通常只有在老年人中才能見到的心理和生理功能減退。參閱 dementia，progeria。

presentation *n.* the part of the fetus that is closest to the birth canal and can be felt on inserting a finger into the vagina. Normally the head presents (*cephalic presentation*). However, the buttocks may present (*see* breech presentation) or, if the fetus lies transversely across the uterus, the shoulder or arm may present. In *placenta praevia the placenta may lie in front of the presenting fetal part.

先露 在分娩時用手指插入陰道檢查，在宮頸口接觸到的早先露出的嬰兒身體部分，正常應該是胎頭的出現（頭先露），然而，嬰兒的臀部（參閱 breech presentation）、肩和臂（橫位），都可能是先露出的部分。在前置胎盤時，胎盤可位於胎先露部的前方。在分娩時，這些不正常的先露均可

These abnormal presentations may cause complications during childbirth, and attempts may be made to correct them.

以導致難產，可採取措施加以糾正。

pressor *n.* an agent that raises blood pressure. *See* vasoconstrictor.

升壓藥　升高血壓的藥物。參閱 vasoconstrictor。

pressure index (PI) the ratio of the pressure in the posterior tibial artery to that in the brachial artery, which reflects the degree of arterial obstruction in the artery of the lower limb.

壓力指數　脛後動脈與肱動脈壓力之比值，反映了下肢動脈的動脈阻力。

pressure point a point at which an artery lies over a bone on which it may be compressed by finger pressure, to arrest haemorrhage beyond. For example, the femoral artery may be compressed against the pelvic bone in the groin.

壓迫點　動脈跨越骨上的某一點，在該處用手指壓迫動脈，可以阻止遠側的出血，例如：可在腹股溝處將股動脈壓向骨盆。

pressure sore *see* bedsore.

褥瘡　參閱 bedsore。

presymptomatic *adj.* describing or relating to a symptom that occurs before the typical symptoms of a disease. *See also* prodromal.

症狀發生前的　指發生在疾病典型症狀之前的症狀。參閱 prodromal。

presystole *n.* the period in the cardiac cycle just preceding systole.

收縮前期　心動周期中在剛開始收縮之前的時期。

preterm birth birth of a baby before 37 weeks (259 days) of gestation (calculated from the first day of the mother's last menstrual period); a birth at less than 23 weeks is at present incompatible with life. Such factors as *preeclampsia, multiple pregnancies (e.g. twins), maternal infection, and *cervical incompetence may all result in preterm births, but in the majority of cases the cause is unknown. Conditions affecting preterm babies may include *respiratory distress syndrome, feeding difficulties, inability to maintain normal body temperature, *apnoea, infection, *necrotizing enterocolitis, and

早產　懷孕 37 周（259 天）前生產嬰兒（從母親末次月經算起）。少於 23 周的不易存活。一些因素如子癇前期、多胎懷孕（如雙胞胎）、母體受感染，宮頸閉鎖不全都可造成早產，但主要病因仍不清楚。早產兒易出現呼吸窘迫綜合徵，哺乳困難，不能維持正常體溫、呼吸暫停、感染、壞死性小腸結腸炎及腦出血等，因此需對新生兒進行特別的護理；許多嬰兒被救活而並不留下後遺症，但孕期越短，問題越不易解決。

brain haemorrhages. Supportive treatment is provided in an incubator in a neonatal unit; many infants survive with no residual handicap but the shorter the gestation period, the more serious are the problems to be overcome.

prevalence rate a measure of morbidity based on current sickness in a population, estimated either at a particular time (*point prevalence*) or over a stated period (*period prevalence*). It can be expressed either in terms of sick people (persons) or episodes of sickness per 1000 individuals at risk. *Compare* incidence rate.

现患率 测定某特定时刻（时点患病率）或某段时刻（时间患病率）内人群中现有疾病的患病率。现患率可以每 1000 受威胁者中的病人数或发病次数表示。与 incidence rate 对比。

preventive dentistry the branch of dentistry concerned with the prevention of dental disease. It includes dietary counselling, advice on oral hygiene, and the application of *fluoride and *fissure sealants to the teeth.

预防牙医学 牙医学中关于牙病预防的分支学科。包括饮食咨询、口腔卫生指导，氟化物和牙裂隙充填剂的应用。

preventive medicine the branch of medicine whose main aim is the prevention of disease. This is a wide field, in which workers tackle problems ranging from the immunization of persons against infectious diseases, such as diphtheria or whooping cough, to finding methods of eliminating *vectors, such as malaria-carrying mosquitoes. *See also* World Health Organization.

预防医学 以预防疾病为基本目的的医学分支学科。这是一个广泛的领域，从抗白喉、百日咳之类传染病的人体免疫接种到寻找消灭病媒（如携带疟原虫的蚊子）的方法。参阅 World Health Organization。

preventive resin restoration a hybrid between a *fissure sealant and a conventional *filling that is used to treat early dental caries involving dentine on the occlusal surfaces of posterior teeth.

预防性的树脂修复 一种牙裂隙充填剂和常规填剂的混合充填物，治疗早期牙龋包括后牙𬌗面的牙质。

Priadel *n. see* lithium.

锂 参阅 lithium。

priapism *n.* persistent painful erection of the penis that requires decompression. A prolonged erection (i.e. of greater

阴茎异常勃起 阴茎持续性勃起，伴有疼痛感，并需要有减压来缓解。长期勃起（如超过

than six hours duration), resulting from administration of *papaverine or a similar drug, can be successfully treated by draining blood from the corpora cavernosa of the penis with a 19 SWG butterfly needle and instilling a *vasoconstrictor (e.g. aramine). Priapism may also occur in patients with sickle-cell trait and those undergoing *haemodialysis. An unrelieved priapism results in eventual fibrosis of the spongy tissue of the corpora and no further erections are possible.

prickle cells cells with cytoplasmic processes that form intercellular bridges. The germinative layer of the *epidermis is sometimes called the prickle cell layer.

prickly heat an itchy rash of small raised red spots. It occurs usually on the face, neck, back, chest, and thighs. Infants and obese people are susceptible to prickly heat, which is most common in hot moist weather. It is caused by blockage of the sweat ducts and the only treatment is removal of the patient to a cool (air-conditioned) place. Medical name: **miliaria**.

prilocaine *n.* a local *anaesthetic used particularly in ear, nose, and throat surgery and in dentistry. It is applied in a solution to mucous membranes or injected; high doses of the drug may cause methaemogolbinaemia and cyanosis. Prilocaine is also a constituent of *EMLA cream. Trade name: **Citanest**.

primaquine *n.* a drug used in the treatment of malaria. It is administered by mouth, usually in combination with other antimalarial drugs, such as *chloroquine. High doses may cause blood disorders (such as methaemoglobinaemia

六小時）是由於服用了罌粟鹼或類似藥物，可以通過抽取陰莖海綿體的血液及使用 19 SWG 蝶形針並注射血管收縮管藥物來治療（如阿拉明）。陰莖異常勃起也可發生於鐮狀細胞性遺傳病和其他曾作過血液透析的病人。長期不能緩解的陰莖異常勃起最終使海綿體纖維化而造成不能勃起。

棘細胞 以胞漿突起形成細胞間橋的細胞。表皮生發層有時稱為棘細胞層。

汗疹，痱子 一種伴瘙癢的小丘疹。常發生於顏面、頸項、背、胸和大腿皮膚。嬰兒和肥胖者易出汗疹，汗疹最多見於濕熱氣候，由於汗孔被堵塞所致，病人只需到涼爽（有空調）的地方即可。醫學用語：汗疹。

丙胺卡因 一種局部麻醉藥。主要用於耳鼻喉科手術和牙科。其溶液用於黏膜或注射，大劑量可引起高鐵血紅蛋白血症和紫紺，它也是 EMLA 霜的一種成分。商品名：Citanest。

伯氨喹 一種抗瘧藥物。口服，通常與其他抗瘧藥物（如氯喹）合用。大劑量可引起血液病變（如高鐵血紅蛋白血症或溶血性貧血）和胃腸紊亂。

or haemolytic anaemia) and digestive upsets.

primary health care health care provided by a *general practitioner or other health professional who has first contact with a patient seeking medical treatment, Primary health care services provided by the NHS include the general dental, ophthalmic, and pharmaceutical services, as well as the family doctor service, together with those community services outside the hospital service. *See also* community health, domiciliary services, general dental services, health centre. *Compare* secondary health care, tertiary health care.

初級衛生保健　由全科醫生或其他衛生專業人員為初次接觸就醫患者所提供的衛生保健。初級衛生保健服務由國民保健服務制包括牙科、眼科及藥物咨詢等，也包括家庭醫生服務和醫院服務以外的社區服務。參閱　community health，domiciliary services，general dental services，health centre。與 secondary health care，tertiary health care 對比。

prime *vb.* (in chemotherapy) to administer small doses of *cyclophosphamide prior to high-dose chemotherapy and/or radiotherapy. This causes proliferation of the primitive bone marrow cells and aids subsequent regeneration of the bone marrow.

基礎用藥　（化學治療）在大劑量化學治療和／或放射治療前給予小劑量環磷酰胺，以引起原始骨髓細胞增殖和促進隨後的骨髓再生。

prime mover *see* agonist.

主動肌　參閱 agonist。

primidone *n.* an *anticonvulsant drug used to treat major epilepsy. It is administered by mouth; common side-effects, which are usually transient, include drowsiness, muscle incoordination, digestive upsets, vertigo, and sight disturbances. Trade name: **Mysoline**.

撲米酮　一種治療癲癇大發作的抗驚厥藥。口服。常見副作用多為短暫的困倦、共濟失調、胃腸紊亂、眩暈和輕度視覺障礙等。商品名：Mysoline。

primigravida *n.* a woman experiencing her first pregnancy.

初孕婦　初次妊娠的婦女。

primipara *n.* a woman who has given birth to one infant capable of survival.

初產婦　分娩過一個活嬰的婦女。

primitive streak the region of the embryo that proliferates rapidly, producing mesoderm cells that spread outwards

原條　胚的一部分。該部迅速增殖，產生中胚層細胞，在內胚層和外胚層之間向外擴展。

between the layers of ectoderm and endoderm.

primordial *adj.* (in embryology) describing cells or tissues that are formed in the early stages of embryonic development.

原始的 （胚胎學）指胚胎發育早期形成的細胞和組織。

P–R interval the interval on an *electrocardiogram between the onset of atrial activity and ventricular activity. It represents the time required for the impulse from the *sinoatrial node to reach the ventricles.

P﹘R 間期 心房和心室興奮時表現在心電圖上的一個間期，代表衝動從竇房結到達心室的時間。

prion *n.* an agent that is apparently capable of replication and of causing infection but is of simpler constitution than any virus. Prions resist sterilization by normal methods and have been spread on surgical instruments and in donated human growth hormone. Prions are abnormal forms of a normal cell protein (PrP); they are produced by mutations in the gene that codes for PrP and are now widely accepted as being the causal agents of a range of serious diseases including Creutzfeldt-Jakob disease, Gerstmann-Straussler syndrome, and kuru, all of which are *spongiform encephalopathies. Different mutations in the PrP gene are believed to be responsible for the different forms of these so-called *prion diseases*.

朊病毒 一種有複製能力的因子。可引起感染但結構較病毒簡單。它可被正常的消毒方法滅活，可通過外科器械和合成的人類生長激素傳播。它是正常細胞蛋白的異型，是由細胞蛋白遺傳基因密碼突變而形成的，可造成一系列嚴重疾病，如克-雅氏綜合徵、格斯特曼綜合徵及庫魯病，這些都是海綿狀腦病。據認為細胞蛋白基因的不同突變形式引發了這些不同類型的所謂朊病毒疾病。

pro- *prefix denoting* **1.** before; preceding. **2.** a precursor. **3.** in front of.

〔前綴〕(1) 前 (2) 前體 (3) 在前面

probability *n. see* significance.

概率，機率 參閱 significance。

proband *n. see* propositus.

先證者 參閱 propositus。

probang *n.* a long flexible rod with a small sponge, ball, or tuft at the end, used to remove obstructions from the larynx

食管－氣管內除鯁器 為一可彎曲的長桿，末端裝有海綿或馬鬃，用於解除喉或食管阻

or oesophagus (gullet). A probang is also used to apply medication to these structures.

塞。還可用以對上述部位進行藥物治療。

probe *n.* **1.** a thin rod of pliable metal, such as silver, with a blunt swollen end. The instrument is used for exploring cavities, wounds, *fistulae, and sinus channels. **2. (gene probe)** a radioactively labelled cloned section of DNA that is used to detect identical sections of nucleic acid by means of pairing between complementary bases. *See* Northern blot analysis, Southern blot analysis.

探針 (1) 一種用柔韌金屬（如銀）製成的末端鈍圓的細桿。用於探測腔孔、創口、瘻管和竇道。**(2)**（基因探針）一種放射性標記的 DNA 克隆片斷，用來檢測核酸，通常用互補鹼基的配對方法。參閱 Northern blot analysis，Southern blot analysis。

probenecid *n.* a drug that reduces the level of uric acid in the blood (*see* uricosuric drug) and is used chiefly in the treatment of gout. It is administered by mouth; mild side-effects, such as digestive upsets, dizziness, and skin rashes, may occur. Trade name: **Benemid**.

丙磺舒 降低血中尿酸的一種藥物（參閱 uricosuric drug），主要用於治療痛風。口服用藥，可有輕度副作用，如胃腸紊亂、頭暈、皮疹。商品名：Benemid。

probucol *n.* a drug used to lower *cholesterol levels in the blood in patients with primary hypercholesterolaemia who have not responded to diet, weight reduction, and exercise. It acts by increasing the breakdown of low-density *lipoproteins and inhibits cholesterol synthesis. It is administered by mouth; side-effects include headache, skin rash, diarrhoea, and abdominal pain. Trade name: **Lurselle**.

普羅布考 一種用來降低血中膽固醇水平的藥物。用於原發性高膽固醇血症，經飲食治療、減肥、鍛煉等無效者，通過加速低密度脂蛋白的分解及抑制膽固醇的合成起作用。口服用藥。副作用有頭痛、皮疹、腹瀉和腹痛等。商品名：Lurselle。

procainamide *n.* a drug that slows down the activity of the heart and is used to control abnormal heart rhythm. It is administered by mouth or injection; side-effects may include digestive upsets, dizziness, and allergic reactions. Trade name: **Pronestyl**.

普魯卡因胺 抑制心臟活動的藥物。用於控制心律失常。口服或注射，副作用有胃腸紊亂、頭暈、變應性反應等。商品名：Pronestyl。

procaine (procaine hydrochloride) *n.* a local *anaesthetic administered by

普魯卡因（鹽酸普魯卡因） 局部麻醉藥。注射給藥。用於脊

---

injection for *spinal anaesthesia. It was formerly used in dentistry. Side-effects are uncommon, but allergic reactions may occur.

procaine penicillin G an *antibiotic, consisting of penicillin and procaine, used to treat infections caused by organisms sensitive to penicillin. It is injected into muscle so that the penicillin is released slowly and remains effective for some time. Trade names: **Bicillin**, **Triplopen**.

procarbazine *n.* a drug that inhibits growth of cancer cells by preventing cell division and is used to treat such cancers as Hodgkin's disease. It is administered by mouth; common side-effects include loss of appetite, nausea, vomiting, diarrhoea, and mouth sores. Trade name: **Natulan**.

process *n.* (in anatomy) a thin prominence or protuberance; for example, any of the processes of a vertebra.

prochlorperazine *n.* a phenothiazine *antipsychotic drug used to treat schizophrenia and other mental disorders, migraine, vertigo, nausea, and vomiting. It is administered by mouth, injection, or in suppositories; possible side-effects include drowsiness and dry mouth, and high doses may cause tremors and abnormal muscle movements. Trade name: **Stemetil**.

procidentia *n.* the complete downward displacement (*prolapse) of an organ, especially the uterus (*uterine procidentia*), which protrudes from the vaginal opening. Uterine procidentia may result from injury to the floor of the pelvic cavity, invariably the result of childbirth.

神經麻醉。過去一度用於牙科。副作用少見，可有變應性反應。

普魯卡因青黴素 由青黴素和普魯卡因組成的抗生素。用於治療對青黴素敏感的細菌感染。肌肉注射，因青黴素釋放緩慢，可使藥效維持一段時間。商品名：Bicillin，Triplopen。

丙卡巴肼 一種借阻止細胞分裂而抑制癌細胞生長的藥物，多用於治療霍奇金病之類的癌瘤。口服，常見副作用為食慾不振、惡心、嘔吐、腹瀉和口腔潰瘍。商品名：Natulan。

突 （解剖學）細小的突起或隆突。例如：所有脊椎骨上的突。

甲哌氯丙嗪 一種吩喹嗪類抗精神病藥。用於治療精神分裂症和其他精神障礙、偏頭痛、眩暈、惡心、嘔吐。口服、注射或製成栓劑。副作用有困倦、口乾，大劑量可引起震顫和異常肌活動。商品名：Stemetil。

脫垂 一個器官的完全下垂移位狀態（脫垂）。尤其是子宮脫垂時子宮可從陰道口突出。膀胱脫垂可因盆腔底部損傷或分娩而引起。

proct- (procto-) *prefix denoting* the anus and/or rectum.

〔前綴〕肛，直腸

proctalgia (proctodynia) *n.* pain in the rectum or anus. In *proctalgia fugax* severe pain suddenly affects the rectum and may last for minutes or hours; attacks may be days or months apart. There is no structural disease and the pain is probably due to muscle spasm (*see* irritable bowel syndrome). Relief is sometimes obtained from a bowel action, inserting a finger into the rectum, or from a hot bath, but it may be prevented by measures used in treating the irritable bowel syndrome.

肛痛　直腸或肛門部疼痛。患痙攣性肛痛時直腸突發劇烈疼痛，持續幾分鐘至幾小時，兩次發作可間隔幾天至幾個月。不能查出器質性病變，疼痛可能出自肌痙攣（參閱irritable bowel syndrome）。排便、用指插入肛門、或者行熱水坐浴、有時可解除疼痛。治療應激性大腸綜合徵的方法對此病有效。

proctatresia *n. see* imperforate anus.

肛門閉鎖　參閱 imperforate anus。

proctectasia *n.* enlargement or widening of the rectum, usually due to long-standing constipation (*see* dyschezia).

直腸擴張　直腸擴大或增粗，多為長時間便秘所致。參閱 dyschezia。

proctectomy *n.* surgical removal of the rectum. It is usually performed for cancer of the rectum and may require the construction of a permanent opening in the colon (*see* colostomy). If the anus is left, an *ileal pouch can be constructed to replace the rectum.

直腸切除術　外科手術切除直腸。通常用於直腸癌時施行，同時須於結腸建立一永久性開口（參閱 colostomy）。若保留肛門，可用迴腸囊來代替直腸。

proctitis *n.* inflammation of the rectum. Symptoms are ineffectual straining to empty the bowels (*tenesmus), diarrhoea, and often bleeding. Proctitis is invariably present in ulcerative *colitis and sometimes in *Crohn's disease, but may occur independently (*idiopathic proctitis*). Rarer causes include damage by irradiation (for example in radiation therapy for cervical cancer) or by *lymphogranuloma venereum.

直腸炎　直腸的炎症。症狀為竭力想排空大腸而總是徒勞（裏急後重），腹瀉、常有便血。直腸炎總與潰瘍性結腸炎伴存，有時伴有克羅恩病，但也可獨立存在（特發性直腸炎）。少見的原因是照射（如子宮頸癌的放射綫治療）或性病性淋巴肉芽腫造成的損害。

proctocele (rectocele) *n.* bulging or pouching of the rectum, usually a

直腸膨出　直腸膨脹或鼓凸，通常是向前突入陰道後壁，與

forward protrusion of the rectum into the posterior wall of the vagina in association with prolapse of the uterus. It is repaired by posterior *colporrhaphy.

子宮脫垂並存。可通過陰道縫合術加以修補。

proctoclysis *n.* an infusion of fluid into the rectum: formerly used to replace fluid but rarely employed now.

直腸滴注法　向直腸內注入液體。過去用於置換體液，現罕用。

proctocolectomy *n.* a surgical operation in which the rectum and colon are removed. In *panproctocolectomy* the whole rectum and colon are removed, necessitating either a permanent opening of the ileum (*see* ileostomy) or the construction of an *ileal pouch. This is usually performed for ulcerative *colitis.

直腸結腸切除術　切除直腸和結腸的外科手術。全直腸結腸切除術是將直腸和結腸全部切除，同時須將迴腸永久開口（參閱 ileostomy）或者建一個迴腸囊袋。此術常用於潰瘍性結腸炎。

proctocolitis *n.* inflammation of the rectum and colon, usually due to ulcerative *colitis. *See also* proctitis.

直腸結腸炎　通常由潰瘍性結腸炎所致的直腸和結腸炎症。參閱 proctitis。

proctodeum *n.* the site of the embryonic anus, marked by a depression lined with ectoderm. The membrane separating it from the hindgut breaks down in the third month of gestation. *compare* stomodeum.

肛道　胚胎時期肛門的部位，為覆蓋外胚層的凹窩。將肛道與後腸隔開的膜於妊娠第三個月消失。與 stomodeum 對比。

proctodynia *n. see* proctalgia.

肛部痛　參閱 proctalgia。

proctology *n.* the study of disorders of the rectum and anus.

肛腸病學　研究直腸和肛門疾病的學科。

proctorrhaphy *n.* a surgical operation to stitch tears of the rectum or anus.

直腸縫合術　直腸和肛門撕裂的外科縫合術。

proctoscope *n.* an illuminated instrument through which the lower part of the rectum and the anus may be inspected and minor procedures (such as injection therapy for haemorrhoids) carried out. **–proctoscopy** *n.*

直腸鏡　一種用於檢查直腸下部和肛門並可進行小手術（如注射藥物治療痔瘡）的照明裝置。

proctosigmoiditis *n.* inflammation of the rectum and the sigmoid (lower) colon. *See also* proctocolitis.

直腸乙狀結腸炎　直腸和乙狀結腸（下段結腸）的炎症。參閱 proctocolitis。

proctotomy *n.* incision into the rectum or anus to relieve *stricture (narrowing) of these canals or to open an imperforate (closed) anus.

直腸切開術　切開直腸或肛門以解除狹窄或為閉鎖肛門的開口的手術。

procyclidine *n.* a drug, similar in its effects to *atropine, used to reduce muscle tremor and rigidity in parkinsonism. It is administered by mouth or injection; common side-effects include dry mouth, blurred vision, and giddiness. Trade names: **Arpicolin**, **Kemadrin**.

丙環啶　一種作用類似阿托品的藥物。用以減輕震顫性麻痺的肌震顫和肌強直。口服或注射給藥。常見副作用為口乾、視物模糊、眩暈。商品名：Arpicolin，Kemadrin。

prodromal *adj.* relating to the period of time between the appearance of the first symptoms of an infectious disease and the development of a rash or fever. A *prodromal rash* is one preceding the full rash of an infectious disease.

前驅期的　指急性傳染病時從初始症狀出現到出現皮疹或發熱之間的那段時間。前驅疹是指傳染病在出現典型皮疹之前出現的疹子。

prodrome *n.* a symptom indicating the onset of a disease.

前驅症狀　疾病初起時的症狀。

proenzyme (zymogen) *n.* the inactive form in which certain enzymes (e.g. digestive enzymes) are originally produced and secreted. The existence of this inactive form prevents the enzyme from breaking down the cells in which it was made. Once the proenzyme has been secreted it is converted to the active from.

前酶（酶原）　某些酶（如消化酶）在剛產生和分泌時的無活性型。這種類型的存在不致使酶將製造它的細胞分解破壞。前酶一旦分泌，便轉變為活性型。

proerythroblast *n.* the earliest recognizable precursor of the red blood cell (erythrocyte). It is found in the bone marrow and has a large nucleus and a cytoplasm that stains deep blue with *Romanowsky stains. *See also* erythroblast, erythropoiesis.

原成紅細胞　紅細胞的最早可辨的前體細胞。可在骨髓內見到，有一巨大的核，胞漿用羅曼諾夫斯基染色法染成深藍色。參閱 erythroblast，erythropoiesis。

profunda *adj*. describing blood vessels that are deeply embedded in the tissues they supply.

profundaplasty *n*. surgical enlargement of the junction of the femoral artery and its deep branch, a common operation to relieve narrowing by atherosclerosis at this point.

progeria *n*. a very rare condition in which all the signs of old age appear and progress in a child, so that 'senility' is reached before puberty.

progesterone *n*. a steroid hormone secreted by the *corpus luteum of the ovary, the placenta, and also (in small amounts) by the adrenal cortex and testes. It is responsible for preparing the inner lining (endometrium) of the uterus for pregnancy. If fertilization occurs it maintains the uterus throughout pregnancy and prevents the further release of eggs from the ovary. *See also* menstrual cycle, progestogen.

progestogen *n*. one of a group of naturally occurring or synthetic steroid hormones, including *progesterone, that maintain the normal course of pregnancy. Progestogens are used to treat premenstrual tension, *amenorrhoea, and abnormal bleeding from the uterus. Because they prevent ovulation, progestogens are a major constituent of *oral contraceptives and other forms of hormonal *contraception. Synthetic progestogens may be taken by mouth but the naturally occurring hormone must be given by intramuscular injection or subcutaneous implant, as it is rapidly broken down in the liver.

proglottis *n*. (*pl*. **proglottids** or **proglottides**) one of the segments of a

深部的　用以描述深埋在由其供給營養的組織深面的血管。

深部成形術　股動脈及其深支吻合的擴張手術，是緩解因動脈粥樣硬化引起的動脈狹窄常用的手術。

早老，早衰　一種罕見的狀況，早在兒童期即出現全部老年期徵象，並逐漸發展以致未屆青春期即已衰老。

孕酮　由卵巢的黃體、胎盤以及（少量）由腎上腺皮質和睪丸分泌的一種固醇類激素。可使子宮內膜增生以適應妊娠需要。一旦受精，孕酮在整個妊娠期將使子宮維持在妊娠狀態並防止卵巢再次排卵。參閱　menstrual　cycle，progestogen。

孕激素　一類天然生成或人工合成的固醇類激素，其中包括維持正常妊娠進程的孕酮。多用於治療先兆流產、習慣性流產、月經前緊張症狀、閉經及子宮異常出血。因有抑制排卵作用，所以成為口服避孕藥和其他形式的激素類避孕藥的主要成分。合成的孕激素可口服，天然生成者，只能肌肉注射或皮下注射，因它可迅速被肝臟分解。

節片　縧蟲的一個體節。成熟的節片位於縧蟲的後端，每個

*tapeworm, Mature segments, situated at the posterior end of the worm, each consist mainly of a branched uterus packed with eggs.

節片主要由含卵的分支狀子宮組成。

prognathism *n.* the state of one jaw being markedly larger than the other and therefore in front of it. **–prognathic** *adj.*

凸頜 一頜明顯大於另一頜而呈向前凸出的狀態。

prognosis *n.* an assessment of the future course and outcome of a patient's disease, based on knowledge of the course of the disease in other patients together with the general health, age, and sex of the patient.

預後 對病人所患疾病的未來發展過程和結局的估計，預後是依據該病在別的病人身上發展過程的知識結合現病人的一般狀況、年齡、性別等而做出的。

proguanil *n.* a drug that kills malaria parasites and is used in the prevention and treatment of malaria. It is administered by mouth and rarely causes side-effects. Trade name: **Paludrine**.

氯胍 殺瘧原蟲藥。用於預防和治療瘧疾。口服。副作用罕見。商品名：Paludrine。

proinsulin *n.* a substance produced in the pancreas from which the hormone *insulin is derived.

前胰島素 在胰腺內生成的胰島素前體物質。

projection *n.* (in psychology) the attribution of one's own qualities to other people. This is one of the *defence mechanisms; people who cannot tolerate their own feelings (e.g. anger) may cope by imagining that other people have those feelings (e.g. are persecuting).

投射 （心理學）將自己的品質歸屬於他人。這是一種心理防禦機制；有的人對於自己的情感（如憤怒）不能容忍，卻老想像別人具有這種情感（如正在迫害他）。

projective test a way of measuring aspects of personality, in which the subject is asked to talk freely about ambiguous objects. His responses are then analysed. Examples are the *Rorschach test and the Thematic Apperception Test (in which the subject invents stories about a set of pictures).

投射試驗 一種測試性格諸方面的方法。要求受試者對相互矛盾的事物自由發表意見，然後對他的表現進行分析。屬於這類試驗的有羅爾沙赫試驗（墨迹試驗）和主題幻覺試驗（受試者對一組圖畫虛構故事）。

prolactin (lactogenic hormone, luteotrophic hormone, luteotrophin)

催乳素，生乳素，促黃體激素 一種在垂體前葉內合成和貯存

n. a hormone, synthesized and stored in the anterior pituitary gland, that stimulates milk production after childbirth and also stimulates production of *progesterone by the *corpus luteum in the ovary. In both sexes excessive secretion of prolactin gives rise to abnormal production of milk (galactorrhoea).

的激素。在分娩後刺激泌乳，並能刺激卵巢黃體產生孕酮。催乳素分泌過多可使女性和男性發生乳汁的異常分泌（乳溢）。

prolapse *n.* downward displacement of an organ or tissue form its normal position, usually the result of weakening of the supporting tissues. Prolapse of the uterus and/or vagina is, in most cases, caused by stretching and/or tearing of the supporting tissues during childbirth. The cervix may be visible at the vaginal opening or the uterus and vagina may be completely outside the opening (procidentia). Treatment is by surgical shortening of the supporting ligaments and narrowing of the vagina and vaginal orifice (*see* colporrhaphy, colpoperineorrhaphy). In prolapse of the rectum, the rectum descends to lie outside the anus.

脫垂，下垂 通常，由於支持組織的薄弱而使一個器官或組織由其正常位置向下脫垂。子宮和／或陰道脫垂，多數情況下皆因支持組織在分娩時過分緊張和／或拉傷引起。子宮頸可下降至陰道口水平或子宮和陰道完全脫出（脫垂），可通過外科手術拉緊支持組織和縮窄陰道及陰道口進行治療（參閱 colporrhaphy，colpoperineorrhaphy）。直腸脫垂指直腸下降至肛門以外。

prolapsed intervertebral disc (PID) a 'slipped disc': protrusion of the pulpy inner material of an *intervertebral disc through the fibrous outer coat, causing pressure on adjoining nerve roots, ligaments, etc. The condition often results from sudden twisting or bending of the backbone. Pressure on a nerve root causes *sciatica, and if severe may damage the nerve's function, leading to abnormalities or loss of sensation, muscle weakness, or loss of tendon reflexes. Treatment is by complete bed rest on a firm surface, manipulation, *traction, and analgesics; if these fail, the protruding portion of the disc is surgically removed (*see* laminectomy, microdiscectomy).

椎間盤脫出 椎間盤滑出。椎間盤內部的髓核穿過纖維環突出，使鄰近的神經根、韌帶受壓。通常由於脊柱突然扭曲或彎曲而產生。壓迫神經根引起坐骨神經痛，如壓迫嚴重，可使神經受損，導致感覺異常或喪失，肌無力或健反射消失。治療是睡硬床，徹底休息，手法推拿、牽引和服鎮靜藥。若上述治療無效，需外科手術切除椎間盤的突出部分。參閱 laminectomy，microdiscectomy。

proline *n.* an *amino acid found in many proteins.

脯氨酸　一種見於多種蛋白質中的氨基酸。

promazine *n.* a phenothiazine *antipsychotic drug used to relieve agitation, confusion, severe pain, anxiety, nausea, and vomiting and in the treatment of alcoholism and drug withdrawal symptoms. It is administered by mouth or injection; common side-effects are drowsiness and dizziness. Trade name: **Sparine**.

丙嗪　一種吩喹嗪類抗精神病藥。用以消除激動、精神混亂、嚴重疼痛、焦慮、惡心和嘔吐，並可治療酒精中毒和麻醉品戒斷綜合徵。口服或注射。常見副作用有困倦和眩暈。商品名：Sparine。

promegakaryocyte *n.* an immature cell, found in the bone marrow, that develops into a *megakaryocyte.

前巨核細胞　在骨髓中見到的一種不成熟細胞，以後分化為巨核細胞。

promethazine *n.* a powerful *antihistamine drug used to treat allergic conditions and – because of its sedative action – insomnia. It is also used as an *antitussive in cough mixtures. Promethazine is administered by mouth or injection; side-effects include drowsiness, dizziness, and confusion. Trade names: **Avomine**, **Phenergan**.

異丙嗪　一種強有力的抗阻胺藥。用於治療變應性疾病。因有鎮靜作用可治失眠，還可做為止咳合劑中的鎮咳藥。副作用有困倦、眩暈和精神混亂。商品名：Avomine，Phenergan。

prominence *n.* (in anatomy) a projection, such as a projection on a bone.

隆凸　（解剖學）凸起。如骨的凸起。

promontory *n.* (in anatomy) a projecting part of an organ or other structure.

岬　（解剖學）器官或其他結構的隆凸部分。

prompting *n.* a technique used in *behaviour modification to elicit a response not previously present. The subject is made to engage passively in the required behaviour by instructions or by being physically put through the movements. The behaviour can then be rewarded (*see* reinforcement). This is followed by *fading*, in which the prompting is gradually withdrawn and the reinforcement maintained.

激勵　在行為矯正中使用的一種技巧。旨在引出一個原本不存在的反應。通過指導或幫助患者完成某種運動，而使其被動地做出所要求的動作，此時可予以獎勵（參閱 reinforcement），接着進行淡化，即漸漸停止激勵，而獎勵繼續進行。

promyelocyte (premyelocyte) *n.* one of the series of cells that gives rise to the

早幼粒細胞　發育為粒細胞（血液血細胞的一個類型）的

*granulocytes (a type of white blood cell). It has abundant cytoplasm that, with *Romanowsky stains, appears blue with reddish granules (*compare* myeloblast, myelocyte). Promyelocytes are normally found in the blood-forming tissue of the bone marrow but may appear in the blood in a variety of diseases. *See also* granulopoiesis.

細胞系列中的一種細胞。胞漿豐富，羅曼諾夫斯基染色為藍色。含有紅色顆粒（與 myeloblast，myelocyte 對比）。正常見於骨髓造血組織，但許多疾病中可在血中出現。參閱 granulopoiesis。

pronation *n.* the act of turning the hand so that the palm faces downwards. In this position the bones of the forearm (radius and ulna) are crossed. *Compare* supination.

旋前　使手掌面朝後的旋轉動作，前臂在旋前時其前臂骨（尺骨和橈骨）的位置相互交叉。與 supination 對比。

pronator *n.* any muscle that causes pronation of the forearm and hand; for example, the *pronator teres*, a two-headed muscle arising from the humerus and ulna, close to the elbow, and inserted into the radius.

旋前肌　使前臂和手旋前的肌肉，例如，旋前圓肌以兩個頭起於肱骨和尺骨，緊貼肘，止於橈骨。

prone *adj.* **1.** lying with the face downwards. **2.** (of the forearm) in the position in which the palm of the hand faces downwards (*see* pronation). *Compare* supine.

(1) 俯臥　面朝下的。**(2) 旋前**在旋前狀態下，手掌面朝後（參閱 pronation）。與 supine 對比。

pronephros *n.* the first kidney tissue that develops in the embryo. It is not functional and soon disappears. *Compare* mesonephros, metanephros.

前腎　胚胎期最初發生的腎組織。無功能，且很快退化。與 mesonephros，metanephros 對比。

pronucleus *n.* (*pl.* **pronuclei**) the nucleus of either the ovum or spermatozoon after fertilization but before the fusion of nuclear material. The pronuclei are larger than the normal nucleus and have a diffuse appearance.

原核　受精後核物質融合前卵子或精子的核。原核較通常的核大，呈擴散外觀。

propantheline *n.* a drug that decreases activity of smooth muscle (*see* parasymptholytic) and is used to treat certain disorders of the digestive system,

丙胺太林　降低平滑肌活動的藥物（參閱 parasympatholytic），用於治療消化系統某些疾病，包括胃十二指腸潰

including stomach and duodenal ulcers, and enuresis (bed wetting). It is administered by mouth or injection; side-effects include dry mouth and blurred vision. Trade name: **Pro-Banthine**.

瘍和遺尿症（尿床）。口服或注射。副作用有口乾和視物模糊。商品名：Pro-Banthine。

properdin *n.* a group of substances in blood plasma that, in combination with *complement and magnesium ions, is capable of destroying certain bacteria and viruses. The properdin complex occurs naturally, rather than as the result of previous exposure to microorganisms, and its activity is not directed against any particular species. *Compare* antibody.

備解素 血漿內與補體和鎂離子結合後具有破壞某些細菌和病毒能力的一組物質。備解素複合物是天然存在的，並非經微生物預先作用產生，其作用不是直接針對任何特定的微生物。與 antibody 對比。

proper officer *see* public health physician.

專員 參閱 public health physician。

prophase *n.* the first stage of *mitosis and of each division of *meiosis, in which the chromosomes become visible under the microscope. The first prophase of meiosis occurs in five stages (*see* leptotene, zygotene, pachytene, diplotene, diakinesis).

前期 有絲分裂或每次減數分裂的第一階段，此時染色體在顯微鏡下可見。減數分裂的前期分 5 個階段（參閱 leptotene，zygotene，pachytene，diplotene，diakinesis）。

prophylactic *n.* an agent that prevents the development of a condition or disease. An example is *glyceryl trinitrate, which is used to prevent attacks of angina.

預防藥 防止疾病或症狀發生的藥物。例如：硝酸甘油用於預防心絞痛發作。

prophylaxis *n.* any means taken to prevent disease, such as immunization against diphtheria or whooping cough, or *fluoridation to prevent dental decay in children. **–prophylactic** *adj.*

預防 預防疾病的一切手段，如預防白喉和百日咳的免疫接種，預防兒童齲齒的氟化法等。

propositus (proband) *n.* the first individual studied in an investigation of several related patients with an inherited or familial disorder.

先證者 在對一些患某種遺傳病或家族性疾病的病人進行調查時第一個被研究的病人。

propranolol *n.* a drug (*see* beta blocker) used to treat abnormal heart rhythm,

普萘洛爾 一種治療心律失常、心絞痛、高血壓和解除焦

angina, and high blood pressure and also taken to relieve anxiety. It is administered by mouth or injection; common side-effects include digestive upsets, insomnia, and lassitude. Trade name: **Inderal**.

慮的藥物（參閱 beta blockers）。口服或注射，常見的副作用為胃腸紊亂、失眠和倦怠。商品名：Inderal。

proprietary name (in pharmacy) the trade name of a drug: the name assigned to it by the firm that manufactured it. For example, Zantac is the proprietary name for ranitidine.

藥品專利名 （藥劑學）藥物的商品名，由製造廠家命名，例如：Zantac 是雷尼替丁的藥品專利名稱。

proprioceptor *n.* a specialized sensory nerve ending (*see* receptor) that monitors internal changes in the body brought about by movement and muscular activity. Proprioceptors located in muscles and tendons transmit information that is used to coordinate muscular activity (*see* stretch receptor, tendon organ). *See also* mechanoreceptor.

本體感受器 一種特化的感覺神經末梢（參閱 receptor），監測由運動和肌活動引起的體內改變。位於肌肉或肌腱內的本體感受器傳遞信息以調整肌活動（參閱 stretch receptor，tendon organ）。參閱 mechanoreceptor。

proptometer *n. see* exophthalmometer.

突眼計 參閱 exophthalmometer。

proptosis *n.* forward displacement of an organ, especially the eye (*see* exophthalmos).

突出 器官（主要是眼球）前突移位（參閱 exophthalmos）。

propylthiouracil *n.* a drug that reduces thyroid activity and is used to treat *thyrotoxicosis and to prepare patients for surgical removal of the thyroid gland. It is administered by mouth; side-effects may include rashes and digestive upsets.

丙硫氧嘧啶 降低甲狀腺活性的藥物。用於治療甲狀腺毒症以及行甲狀腺切除術病人的術前準備。口服。副作用有皮疹和胃腸功能紊亂。

prorennin *n. see* rennin.

前凝乳酶 參閱 rennin。

Proscar *n. see* finasteride.

普洛斯卡 參閱 finasteride。

prosencephalon *n.* the forebrain.

前腦

prosop- (prosopo-) *prefix denoting* the face. Example: *prosopodynia* (pain in).

〔前綴〕面 例如：面痛。

prospective study 1. a forward-looking review of a group of individuals in relation to morbidity. **2.** *see* cohort study.

前瞻性研究 **(1)** 對一組患某種疾病的個體預見性調查。**(2)** 參閱 cohort study。

prostaglandin *n.* one of a group of hormone-like substances present in a wide variety of tissues and body fluids (including the uterus, brain, lungs, kidney, and semen). Prostaglandins have many actions; for example, they cause contraction of smooth muscle (including that of the uterus) and are mediators in the process of inflammation (aspirin and other *NSAIDs act by blocking their production). They are also involved in the production of mucus in the stomach, which provides protection against acid gastric juice; use of NSAIDs reduces this effect and predisposes to peptic ulceration, the principal side-effect of these drugs. Synthetic prostaglandins are used to induce labour or produce abortion (*see* dinoprost, gemeprost), to treat peptic ulcers (*see* misoprostol), and in the treatment of newborn babies with congenital heart disease (*see* alprostadil).

前列腺素 一種廣泛存在於組織和體液（包括子宮、腦、肺、腎、精液）中的一組激素樣物質。具有多種作用。例如，引起平滑肌收縮（包括子宮平滑肌）和做為炎症過程的介質（阿司匹林和其他非甾類抗炎藥物可抑制其產生）。前列腺素與胃黏液的產生有關。此種黏液可保護胃黏膜不受胃酸的侵害。用非甾類抗炎藥物可降低此種保護效應和促進消化性潰瘍的形成，這是這些藥的最主要的副作用。合成的前列腺素被用於引產或流產（參閱 dinoprost，gemeprost），治療消化性潰瘍（參閱 misoprostol）和用於治療新生兒先天性心臟病（參閱 alprostadil）。

prostate cancer a malignant tumour (*carcinoma) of the prostate gland, a common form of cancer in elderly men. It may progress slowly over many years and give symptoms similar to those of benign enlargement of the prostate (*see* prostate gland). Usually it has invaded locally, spread to regional lymph nodes, and metastasized to bone before clinical presentation. The tumour is associated with increased production of an enzyme, *prostatic specific antigen. Drug treatment aimed at suppressing the production or effects of androgen, on which the tumour is dependent, includes oestrogen therapy and the administration of *anti-androgens and *LHRH analogues.

前列腺癌 一種惡性前列腺腫瘤（癌），老年男性中常見的腫瘤。它可持續許多年，生長緩慢，其症狀類似一般前列腺增生（參閱 prostate gland）。它常發生局部侵犯，向局部淋巴結轉移。在出現臨床症狀之前可有骨轉移。該腫瘤與一種酶（前列腺特異性抗原）的增加有關。藥物治療主要是抑制腫瘤依賴的雄激素的產生或降低其效應。包括雌激素治療和給予抗雄激素和黃體生成素釋放激素類藥物，外科治療包括前列腺和睪丸切除術。

Surgical treatment includes radical
*prostatectomy and *orchidectomy.

prostatectomy *n.* surgical removal of
the prostate gland. The operation is necessary to relieve retention of urine due to
enlargement of the prostate or to cure
the symptoms of frequency and poor
urinary flow due to the same cause. The
operation can be performed through the
bladder (*transvesical prostatectomy*) or
through the surrounding capsule of the
prostate (*retropubic prostatectomy*). In
the operation of *transurethral prostatectomy* (or *transurethral resection*) some or
all the obstructing prostate can be
removed through the urethra using a
resectoscope (*see* resection). *Radical* (or
total) *prostatectomy* is undertaken for the
treatment of prostate cancer that is confined to the gland. It entails removal of
the prostate together with its capsule and
the seminal vesicles. Continuity of the
urinary tract is achieved by anastomosing the bladder to the divided urethra.

prostate gland a male accessory sex
gland that opens into the urethra just
below the bladder and vas deferens

前列腺切除術　外科切除前列
腺。為解除前列腺增大所致尿
瀦留、尿頻、尿流不暢等症
狀，須做前列腺切除術。手術
可經膀胱（經膀胱前列腺切除
術）或經前列腺包囊（恥骨後
前列腺切除術）進行。在經尿
道前列腺切除術（或經尿道切
除術）中，引起阻塞的前列腺
可部分或全部經尿道用前列腺
切除鏡切除（參閱 resec-
tion）。前列腺根治（全部）切
除術適用於前列腺瘤組織已侵
及腺體，所以須將前列腺及其
膜和精囊一起摘除，吻合尿道
與輸尿管，以保持尿道的通
暢。

前列腺　男性附屬性腺體，在
膀胱和輸精管下方開口於尿道
（見圖）。射精時前列腺分泌鹼

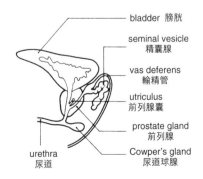

The prostate gland and associated structures (median view)
前列腺及其有關結構（正中斷面觀）

(see illustration). During ejaculation it secretes an alkaline fluid that forms part of the *semen. The prostate may become enlarged in elderly men (*benign prostatic hypertrophy*; *BPH*). This obstructs the neck of the bladder, impairing urination. The bladder dilates and the increased pressure is transmitted through the ureters to the kidney nephrons, leading to damage and impaired function of the kidneys. Treatment is by *prostatectomy or by means of drugs (*see* finasteride).

性液體，參與精液的形成。老年人可發生前列腺肥大（良性前列腺肥大），阻塞膀胱頸部而影響排尿。膀胱擴張及增高的內壓通過輸尿管傳到腎臟的腎單位，使腎受到損害導致腎功障礙。治療：前列腺切除術或藥物（參閱 finasteride）。

prostatic specific antigen (PSA) an enzyme produced by the glandular epithelium of the prostate. Increased quantities are secreted when the gland enlarges and levels of PSA in the blood are significantly elevated in cancer of the prostate, although there is no clear 'cut-off' level for normality. PSA levels tend to be much higher in advanced prostate cancer and the rate of fall on treatment is a good prognostic indicator of response.

前列腺特異性抗原 前列腺上皮分泌的一種酶類。雖然無明確的正常標準，但當腺體增大時，前列腺特異性抗原分泌增加，前列腺癌時，血中前列腺特異性抗原水平顯著上升。在即將發生前列腺癌時，前列腺特異性抗原的水平趨向於明顯升高，且對判定治療效果亦是一個很好的預測指標。

prostatitis *n.* inflammation of the prostate gland. This may be due to bacterial infection and can be either acute or chronic. In acute prostatitis the patient has all the symptoms of a urinary infection, including pain in the perineal area, temperature, and shivering. Treatment is by antibiotic administration. In chronic prostatitis the urinary symptoms are variable; if urinary obstruction develops, transurethral *prostatectomy is indicated.

前列腺炎 前列腺炎症。可由細菌感染引起，有急性與慢性之分。急性前列腺炎病人具有尿路感染的全部症狀，包括會陰疼痛、發熱和寒戰。用抗生素治療。慢性前列腺炎有不同的尿路症狀，如發生阻塞，則可行經尿道前列腺切除術。

prostatorrhoea *n.* an abnormal discharge of fluid from the prostate gland. This occurs in some patients with acute *prostatitis, who complain of a profuse discharge from the urethra. The discharge is usually thin and watery and is

前列腺液溢 前列腺排液異常。某些急性前列腺炎病人訴說尿道淋滴，排出的液體常呈稀薄水樣，細菌培養常陰性。當其原發前列腺炎得到控制後，排液隨着消失。

often sterile on culture. The discharge usually subsides when the underlying prostatitis is controlled.

prosthesis (*pl.* **prostheses**) *n.* any artificial device that is attached to the body as an aid. Prostheses include bridges, dentures, artificial parts of the face, artificial limbs, hearing aids and cochlear implants, implanted pacemakers, and many other substitutes for parts of the body that are missing or nonfunctional. *Penile prostheses* are malleable, semi-rigid, or inflatable rods inserted into the corpora cavernosa of the penis to produce rigidity sufficient for vaginal penetration in men with impotence. **–prosthetic** *adj.*

prosthetic dentistry the branch of dentistry that is concerned with the provision of *dentures, *bridges, and implant-retained prostheses.

protamine *n.* one of a group of simple proteins that can be conjugated with nucleic acids to form nucleoproteins. Protamine can also be combined with *insulin and zinc to form *protamine zinc insulin*, which – when injected – is absorbed much more slowly than ordinary insulin and thus reduces the frequency of injections.

protanopia *n.* a defect in colour vision in which affected individuals are insensitive to red light and confuse reds, yellows, and greens. *Compare* deuteranopia, tritanopia.

protease *n. see* proteolytic enzyme.

protein *n.* one of a group of organic compounds of carbon, hydrogen, oxygen,

假體　裝在身體上起輔助作用的人工裝置。假體包括齒橋托牙、人工面部、假肢、助聽器、耳蝸植入物、植入式起搏器以及其他許多身體上缺失或功能喪失部分的代用品。陰莖假體是可延伸的，半硬的，可充氣的柱狀物，植入陰莖海綿體內以產生足夠的硬度，來治療陽痿。

牙修復學　從事托牙製備，牙橋製備以及假牙的植入、維護的牙科學分支。

魚精蛋白，精蛋白　一種單純蛋白質，可與核酸結合成核蛋白。精蛋白還可與胰島素和鋅結合形成精蛋白鋅胰島素，本品注射後的吸收較普通胰島素慢得多，因而減少了注射次數。

紅色盲　對紅色光不敏感，不能區別紅、黃、綠色的色覺缺陷。與 deuteranopia，tritanopia 對比。

蛋白酶　參閱 preteolytic enzyme。

蛋白質　一類由碳、氫、氧、氮（還可有硫、磷）組成的有

and nitrogen (sulphur and phosphorus may also be present). The protein molecule is a complex structure made up of one or more chains of *amino acids, which are linked by peptide bonds. Proteins are essential constituents of the body; they form the structural material of muscles, tissues, organs, etc., and are equally important as regulators of function, as enzymes and hormones. Proteins are synthesized in the body from their constituent amino acids, which are obtained from the digestion of protein in the diet. Excess protein, not required by the body, can be converted into glucose and used as an energy source.

機化合物。蛋白質分子是由一條或多條由肽鏈連接的氨基酸鏈構成的複雜結構。蛋白質是機體的必需成分，它們形成肌肉、組織、器官等的結構物質，其重要性與功能的調節物——酶和激素等同。蛋白質在體內由其組成成分氨基酸合成。氨基酸則通過消化食物中的蛋白質獲得。機體不需要的過剩蛋白質則轉化為葡萄糖作為能源使用。

proteinuria *n.* the presence of protein in the urine. This may indicate the presence of damage to, or disease of, the kidneys. *See also* albuminuria.

蛋白尿 尿中出現蛋白質。表示腎臟受損或腎臟疾病。參閱 albuminuria。

proteolysis *n.* the process whereby complex protein molecules, obtained from the diet, are broken down by digestive enzymes in the stomach and small intestine into their constituent amino acids, which are then absorbed into the bloodstream. *See* endopeptidase, exopeptidase. **–proteolytic** *adj.*

蛋白分解 食物中的複雜蛋白質分子在胃和小腸內被消化酶分解為其組成成分氨基酸的過程。然後氨基酸被吸收進入血液。參閱 endopeptidase，exopeptidase。

proteolytic enzyme (protease) a digestive enzyme that causes the breakdown of protein. *See* endopeptidase, exopeptidase.

蛋白分解酶（蛋白酶） 分解蛋白質的消化酶，參閱 endopeptidase，exopetidase。

proteose *n.* a product of the hydrolytic decomposition of protein.

胨 蛋白質的水解產物。

Proteus *n.* a genus of rodlike Gram-negative flagellate highly motile bacteria common in the intestines and in decaying organic material. All species can decompose urea. Some species may cause disease in man: *P. vulgaris* can cause urinary tract infections.

變形桿菌屬 革蘭氏陰性、有鞭毛、活動性強的桿狀菌屬。通常存在於小腸與腐敗的有機物質中。所有的種均能分解尿素。某些變形桿菌可使人類致病：如普通變形桿菌能引起尿路感染。

prothrombin *n.* a substance, present in blood plasma, that is the inactive precursor from which the enzyme *thrombin is derived during the process of *blood coagulation. *See also* coagulation factors.

凝血酶原 凝血酶的無活性體。存在於血漿內，在凝血過程中轉化為凝血酶。參閱 coagulation factors。

prothrombin time (PT) the time taken for blood clotting to occur in a sample of blood to which calcium and thromboplastin have been added. A prolonged PT (compared with a control sample) indicates a deficiency of *coagulation factors, which – with calcium and thromboplastin – are required for the conversion of prothrombin to thrombin to occur in the final stages of blood coagulation. Measurement of PT is used to control anticoagulant therapy (e.g. with warfarin).

凝血酶原時間 是指加入鈣和凝血激酶的血液樣品中，血液凝結所用時間。凝結時間的延長（同對照樣品比較）表明，在血液凝固的最後階段中，凝血酶原變成凝血酶所需的帶鈣和凝血激酶的凝血因子缺乏。凝血時間的測定用來控制抗凝血治療（例如加入華法林）。

proto- *prefix denoting* **1.** first. **2.** primitive; early. **3.** a precursor.

〔前綴〕**(1)** 前，首先　**(2)** 原始，早　**(3)** 前體

protodiastole *n.* the short period in the cardiac cycle between the end of systole and the closure of the *aortic valve marking the start of diastole.

舒張前期 心動周期中在收縮結束和主動脈瓣關閉（表示舒張開始）之間的短暫瞬間。

proton pump the enzyme in the *oxyntic (parietal) cells of the stomach that causes acid secretion by prducing hydrogen ions in exchange for potassium ions.

質子泵 胃泌酸（壁）細胞中的一種酶，通過鉀離子的交換產生氫離子而分泌酸性物質。

proton-pump inhibitor a drug that reduces gastric acid secretion by blocking the *proton-pump within the *oxyntic (parietal) cells. Proton-pump inhibitors include *omeprazole; they are used for treating gastric and duodenal ulcers and reflux oesophagitis.

質子泵抑制劑 一種通過抑制胃泌酸細胞中的質子泵來減少胃酸分泌的藥物。質子泵抑制劑包括奧美拉唑。可用來治療胃及十二指腸潰瘍和返流性食管炎。

proto-oncogene *n.* a gene in a normal cell that is of identical structure to certain viral genes. Some are important

原癌基因 正常細胞內一種和病毒基因結構相同的基因。對細胞分裂起重要的調節作用。

regulators of cell division and damage may change them into *oncogenes.

任何損傷都會促使它們變成致癌基因。

protopathic *adj.* describing the ability to perceive only strong stimuli of pain, heat, etc. *Compare* epicritic.

粗覺的 指僅能感受強的疼痛和熱刺激的能力。與 epicritic 對比。

protoplasm *n.* the material of which living cells are made, which includes the cytoplasm and nucleus. **–protoplasmic** *adj.*

原生質、原漿 活細胞的構成物質，包括胞漿和胞核。

protoplast *n.* a bacterial or plant cell without its cell wall.

原生質體 失去細胞壁的細菌或植物細胞。

protoporphyrin IX the most common type of *porphyrin found in nature. It is a constituent of haemoglobin, myohaemoglobin, most of the cytochromes, and the commoner chlorophylls.

原卟啉 IX 自然界中最常見的卟啉類型。為血紅蛋白、肌紅蛋白、多數細胞色素以及普通葉綠素的組成成分。

Protozoa *n.* a group of microscopic single-celled animals. Most Protozoa are free-living but some are important disease-causing parasites of man; for example, *Plasmodium*, *Leishmania*, and *Trypanosoma* cause *malaria, *kalaazar, and *sleeping sickness respectively, *See also* amoeba.

原生動物門 一類僅能在顯微鏡下觀察到的單細胞動物。多數獨立生活，但有些為人類致病的寄生物。例如：瘧原蟲屬、利什曼原蟲屬、錐蟲屬。可分別引起瘧疾、黑熱病和昏睡病。參閱 amoeba。

protozoan *n.* a single-celled animal. *See* Protozoa.

原生動物 單細胞動物。參閱 protozoa。

protozoology *n.* the study of single-celled animals (*Protozoa).

原生動物學 研究單細胞動物（原生動物門）的科學。

protriptyline *n.* a tricyclic *antidepressant drug used to treat moderate or severe depression, especially in apathetic and withdrawn patients. It is administered by mouth; side-effects include dry mouth, blurred vision, fast heartbeat, digestive disturbances, and skin rashes. Trade name: **Concordin**.

普羅替林 一種三環結構的抗抑鬱藥。用於治療中度或重症抑鬱症，特別是表現淡漠或孤僻的病人。口服。副作用有口乾、視物模糊、心動過速、胃腸紊亂、皮疹。商品名：Concordin。

protrusion *n.* (in dentistry) **1.** forward movement of the lower jaw. **2.** a *malocclusion in which some of the teeth are further forward than usual. *Compare* retrusion.

前伸 （牙科學）**(1)** 下頜向前的運動。 **(2)** 部分牙過分前突的錯殆。與 retrusion 比。

protuberance *n.* (in anatomy) a rounded projecting part, e.g. the projecting part of the chin (*mental protuberance*).

隆凸 （解剖學）圓形隆起部。如下巴的隆凸部（頦隆凸）。

provitamin *n.* a substance that is not itself a vitamin but can be converted to a vitamin in the body. An example is β-carotene, which can be converted into vitamin A.

前維生素 本身不是維生素，然而能在體內轉化為維生素的物質。例如：β-胡蘿蔔素可轉化為維生素 A。

proximal *adj.* (in anatomy) situated close to the origin or point of attachment or close to the median line of the body. *Compare* distal.

近側的 （解剖學）緊臨起點或附着點的，或者靠近身體正中綫的。與 distal 對比。

prune belly syndrome a hereditary condition, occurring exclusively in males, characterized by a deficiency of abdominal muscles, complex malformation of the urinary tract, and bilateral undescended testes. The lungs may be underdeveloped. The name derives from the typically wrinkled appearance of the skin over the abdomen.

乾癟腹部綜合徵 一個僅發生於男性的遺傳性疾病。由於腹肌缺陷引起，並伴有複雜的泌尿道畸形，兩側肺部可能發育不健全。該名詞得名於腹部皮膚典型的皺褶表現。

prurigo *n.* a chronic intensely itchy skin disease of unknown cause. It usually starts in childhood with small pale pimples arising deep in the skin. Prurigo may occur in association with hay fever or asthma or start in warm weather. Treatment is unsatisfactory and relapses are frequent.

癢疹 一種原因不明的慢性皮膚瘙癢症。通常始發於兒童期，表現為由皮膚深層突起的蒼白丘疹。可與枯草熱或哮喘病同時存在，多在温暖季節發作。缺乏有效治療。常復發。

pruritus *n.* itching. Mediated by histamine and vasoactive chemicals, it is the predominant symptom of atopic *eczema, *lichen planus, and many other

瘙癢 由組胺和血管活性物質引起的癢感，是濕疹、扁平苔癬和其他許多皮膚病的主要症狀。它也發生於老年，可能是

skin diseases. It also occurs in the elderly and may be a manifestation of psychological illness. Perineal itching is common: itching of the vulva in women (*pruritus vulvae*) may be accompanied by itching of the anal region (*pruritus ani*), although the latter is more common in men. Causes of perineal itching include poor hygiene, *candidosis, *pinworms, and itchy skin diseases (such as eczema). Pruritus also occurs as a symptom of certain systemic disorders, such as chronic renal failure, *cholestasis, and iron deficiency. Treatment of pruritus is determined by the causes.

心理疾病的表現症狀。會陰部瘙癢普遍發生，婦女外陰瘙癢可能伴有肛門部瘙癢，儘管後者在男性更為普遍。會陰部瘙癢的原因是衛生不良、念珠菌病、蟯蟲和瘙癢性皮膚病（例如濕疹）。瘙癢也是某些生理系統紊亂的表現症狀，例如慢性腎衰竭、膽汁阻塞和缺鐵。治療措施視瘙癢原因而定。

prussic acid *see* hydrocyanic acid.

氫氰酸 參閱 hydrocyanic acid。

PSA *see* prostatic specific antigen.

前列腺特異性抗原 參閱 prostatic specific antigen。

psammoma *n.* a tumour containing gritty sandlike particles (*psammoma bodies*). It is typical of cancer of the ovary but may also be found in the meninges (the membranes surrounding the brain).

沙粒瘤 一種含沙樣顆粒（沙粒瘤小體）的腫瘤。是典型的卵巢部癌症，但也可見於腦膜處。

psellism *n.* a deficiency of articulation of speech, such as *stammering.

口吃 一種言語發音缺陷，如說話口吃。

pseud- (pseudo-) *prefix denoting* superficial resemblance to; false.

〔前綴〕表面相似，假的

pseudarthrosis (nearthrosis) *n.* a 'false' joint, formed around a displaced bone end after dislocation. Congenital hip dislocation may result in a pseudarthrosis.

假關節 脫位後在移位骨端周圍形成的假性連結。先天性髖關節脫位可導致假關節形成。

pseudoagglutination *n.* the misleading appearance of clumping that occurs during an antiserum-antigen test as a result of incorrect temperature or acidity of the solutions used.

假凝集 由於溫度或所用溶液酸度不合適，在抗血清-抗原試驗中出現的使人誤解的凝塊現象。

pseudocholinesterase *n.* an enzyme found in the blood and other tissues that – like *cholinesterase – breaks down acetylcholine, but much more slowly. Not being localized at nerve endings, it plays little part in the normal breakdown of acetylcholine in synapses and at neuromuscular junctions.

假膽鹼酯酶　血液和其他組織中存在的一種與膽鹼酯酶相似，能分解乙酰膽鹼但速度大為緩慢的酶。此酶因不存在於神經末梢，故在突觸內或神經肌肉接頭中的乙酰膽鹼正常分解中只起很小的作用。

pseudocoxalgia *n. see* Legg-Calvé-Perthes disease.

假性髖關節痛　參閱 Legg-Calvé-Perthes disease。

pseudocrisis *n.* a false crisis: a sudden but temporary fall of temperature in a patient with fever. The pseudocrisis is followed by a return to the fever.

假驟退　假的熱驟退：發熱病人體溫突然短時間下降，其後又升高。

pseudocryptorchidism *n.* apparent absence of the testes. This is quite common in young boys, who retract their testes into the groin due to involuntary or reflex contraction of the cremasteric muscle of the suspensory cord. The condition is only important in that it needs to be distinguished from true failure of descent of the testes into the scrotum, which requires early surgical treatment (*see* cryptorchidism).

假隱睾　外表缺乏睾丸的形態。較多見於青少年，係由於精索提睾肌不隨意性或反射性收縮使睾丸回縮在腹股溝部。這種狀態僅在需要與真性睾丸不能降入陰囊鑒別時才有意義。後者需早期外科手術。（參閱 cryptorchidism）。

pseudocyesis (phantom pregnancy, false pregnancy) *n.* a condition in which a nonpregnant woman exhibits symptoms of pregnancy, e.g. enlarged abdomen, increased weight, morning sickness, and absence of menstruation. The condition usually has an emotional basis.

假孕　未孕婦女顯示妊娠徵象（腹部膨隆，體重增加，晨起惡心，無月經）的狀況。通常為情緒性。

pseudocyst *n.* a fluid-filled space without a proper wall or lining, within an organ. A *pancreatic pseudocyst* may develop in cases of chronic pancreatitis or as a complication of acute pancreatitis. As the pseudocyst, which is filled with enzyme-rich pancreatic juice, slowly

假囊腫　器官內充滿液體而無固有包壁或內膜的腔。胰腺假囊腫可發生於慢性胰腺炎，或者是急性胰腺炎的合併症。當充盈富含酶的胰液的假囊腫慢慢增大時，可引起偶然的腹痛並伴有血中酶濃度增高。腹部

expands it may cause episodes of abdominal pain accompanied by a rise in the level of enzymes in the blood. It may be felt by abdominal examination or seen by radiology or ultrasound examination. Treatment is by surgical drainage, usually by the technique of joining the pseudocyst to the stomach (*marsupialization).

pseudogout *n.* joint pain and swelling, resembling gout, caused by crystals of calcium pyrophosphate in the synovial membrane and fluid. *See also* chondrocalcinosis.

pseudohermaphroditism *n.* a congenital abnormality in which the external genitalia of a male or a female resemble those of the opposite sex; for example, a woman would have enlarged labia and clitoris, resembling a scrotum and penis respectively.

pseudohypertrophy *n.* increase in the size of an organ or structure caused by excessive growth of cells that have a packing or supporting role but do not contribute directly to its functioning. The result is usually a decline in the efficiency of the organ although it becomes larger. **–pseudohypertrophic** *adj.*

pseudohypoparathyroidism *n.* a syndrome of mental retardation, restricted growth, and bony abnormalities due to a genetic defect that causes lack of response to the hormone secreted by the *parathyroid glands. Treatment with calcium and vitamin D can reverse most of the features.

pseudologia fantastica the telling of elaborate and fictitious stories as if they were true. Often some facts are woven into the tissue of lies. While not

檢查可觸知假囊腫，或可通過 X 綫或超聲波檢查而發現。治療一般為應用溝通假囊腫和胃的技術進行外科引流（造袋術，袋形縫術）。

假痛風 由焦磷酸鈣結晶沉着於滑膜和滑囊液內所致的類似痛風的關節腫痛。參閱 chondrocalcinosis。

假兩性畸形 一種先天性異常。表現為男性或女性外生殖器與異性相似。例如，女性的陰唇和陰蒂增大，相應地類似陰囊和陰莖。

假性肥大 僅起充填或支持作用的細胞過度生長所致的器官或結構的體積增大。器官或結構的功能並不能增強，結果往往器官增大而功能反而降低。

假甲狀旁腺功能減退 一種表現為智力低下、生長受阻和骨骼異常的綜合徵。係因基因缺陷而對甲狀旁腺分泌的激素缺乏反應所致。用鈣和維生素 D 治療可使多數症狀好轉。

幻想性謊言癖 繪聲繪色地將編造的故事說得如同真有其事。經常是將某些事實編織在謊言之中。這雖非一定是疾病

necessarily a symptom of illness, it is sometimes a feature of chronic mental illness and of personality disorders, particularly psychopathy.

pseudomembrane *n.* a false membrane, consisting of a layer of exudate on the surface of the skin or a mucous membrane. In diphtheria a pseudomembrane forms in the throat.

Pseudomonas *n.* a genus of rodlike motile pigmented Gram-negative bacteria. Most live in soil and decomposing organic matter; they are involved in recycling nitrogen, converting nitrates to ammonia or free nitrogen. The species *P. aeruginosa* is pathogenic to man, occurring in pus from wounds; it is associated with urinary tract infections. *P. pseudomallei* is the causative agent of *melioidosis.

pseudomutuality *n.* a disorder of communication within a family in which a superficial pretence of closeness and reciprocal understanding belies a lack of real feeling. It has been alleged, but not proved, to be a factor in the backgrounds of schizophrenics.

pseudomyxoma *n.* a mucoid tumour of the peritoneum, often seen in association with *myxomas of the ovary. In *pseudomyxoma peritonei* material from a myxoma, usually in the ovary, is spilled into the peritoneal cavity and continues to be produced within the abdomen, often to massive proportions.

pseudoneuritis *n.* a condition that resembles *retrobulbar neuritis but is not due to inflammation. The most usual cause is blockage of blood vessels in the optic nerve (*ischaemic optic neuropathy*).

症狀，但有時可為慢性精神疾病和人格障礙（尤其是精神變態）的表現。

假膜 皮膚或黏膜表面由一層滲出物構成的偽膜。白喉時喉內可形成假膜。

假單胞菌屬 革蘭氏陰性，有活動能力，含色素的桿狀菌屬。多數生存於土壤內，能分解有機物，參與氮的再循環，將硝酸鹽轉變為氨或游離氮。綠膿假單胞菌為人類致病菌，存在於創傷的膿內，與尿路感染有關。類鼻疽假單胞菌是類鼻疽病的病原菌。

假親密 家庭內部交往的障礙。表面上造作的親熱和相互理解掩飾着實際上的無感情。人們認為這是精神分裂症的背景因素之一，但此點未能證實。

假黏液瘤 腹膜的黏液樣瘤，常與卵巢黏液瘤並存。來自卵巢黏液瘤內的腹膜假黏液瘤物質溢出進入腹膜腔，並在腹膜腔內不斷生成，以致常可達到巨大程度。

假視神經炎 一種與球後視神經炎相似的非炎性疾病。最常見的原因是視神經內血管阻塞（缺血性視神經病）。

pseudo-obstruction *n.* obstruction of the alimentary canal without mechanical narrowing of the bowel. It is usually associated with abnormality of the nerve supply to the muscles of the bowel. *See also* ileus, Hirschsprung's disease.

假阻塞 腸管非機械性狹窄引起的營養運輸通路的堵塞。通常和腸道肌肉的神經支配異常有關。參閱 ileus，Hirschsprung's disease。

pseudophakos *n.* the state of the eye after the natural lens has been replaced by a plastic lens implanted inside the eye, approximately in the position previously occupied by the natural lens. This is the current form of surgery for cataract.

假晶狀體 眼內天然晶狀體被植入的塑料晶狀體取代（後者大致占據天然晶狀體原先的位置）。現在外科治療白內障使用此手術。

pseudoplegia *n.* paralysis of the limbs not associated with organic abnormalities. *See also* conversion disorder.

假癱 沒有器質性病變的肢體癱瘓。參閱 conversion disorder。

pseudopodium *n.* (*pl.* **pseudopodia**) a temporary and constantly changing extension of the body of an amoeba or an amoeboid cell (*see* phagocyte). Pseudopodia engulf bacteria and other particles as food and are responsible for the movements of the cell.

假足，偽足 阿米巴或阿米巴樣細胞體（參閱 phagocyte）的短暫或持續的延伸。假足能吞食細菌或其他顆粒，並使細胞運動。

pseudopolyposis *n.* a condition in which the bowel lining (mucosa) is covered by elevated or protuberant plaques (*pseudopolyps*) that are not true *polyps but abnormal growths of inflamed mucosa. It is usually found in patients with chronic ulcerative *colitis. The pseudopolyps may be seen with the *sigmoidoscope or the *colonoscope (through which they may be sampled for microscopic examination) or by barium enema examination.

假息肉症 腸黏膜表面覆蓋着突起或隆起斑塊的狀況（假息肉）。這些斑塊不是真正的息肉而是發炎黏膜的異常生長物。通常見於慢性潰瘍性結腸炎患者。可在乙狀結腸鏡或結腸鏡下（可取樣做顯微鏡檢查）或作鋇劑灌腸檢查發現。

pseudopseudohypoparathyroidism *n.* a condition in which all the symptoms of *pseudohypoparathyroidism are present but the patient's response to parathyroid hormone is normal. It is often found in families affected with pseudohypoparathyroidism.

假性假甲狀旁腺功能減退 具有假甲狀旁腺功能減退的全部症狀，但患者對甲狀旁腺激素的反應正常。常見於患有假甲狀旁腺功能減退病的家族成員中。

pseudotumour cerebri *see* benign intracranial hypertension.

假腦瘤　參閱 benign intracranial hypertension。

psilosis *n.* see sprue.

口炎性腹瀉　參閱 sprue。

psittacosis (parrot disease, ornithosis) *n.* an endemic infection of birds, especially parrots, budgerigars, canaries, finches, pigeons, and poultry, caused by a small intracellular bacterium, *Chlamydia psittaci*. The birds are often asymptomatic carriers. The infection is transmitted to humans by inhalation from handling the birds or by contact with feathers, faeces, or cage dust, but person-to-person transmission also occurs. The symptoms include fever, dry cough, severe muscle pain, and headache; occasionally a severe generalized systemic illness results. The condition responds to tetracycline or erythromycin.

鸚鵡熱　一種地方性鳥類傳染病，特別是鸚鵡、虎皮鸚鵡、金絲雀、雀科鳴禽、鴿子和家禽類，由一種小的細胞內細菌引起（鸚鵡熱衣原體）。鳥類常是無症狀攜帶者。人類通過觸摸鳥類或接觸鳥類羽毛、糞便或巢穴而吸入病菌被感染，但人類之間相互傳染同樣存在。症狀包括發熱、乾咳、肌肉劇痛和頭痛。偶爾也是一種嚴重的全身性疾病的結果。四環素或紅黴素治療有效。

psoas (psoas major) *n.* a muscle in the groin that acts jointly with the iliacus muscle to flex the hip joint (see illustration). A smaller muscle, *psoas minor* has the same action but is often absent.

腰大肌　腹股溝區的一塊肌肉，與髂肌聯合可以使髖關節屈曲（見圖）。另一塊小的肌肉叫腰小肌，具有相同功能，但常闕如。

psoralen *n.* see PUVA.

補骨脂素　參閱 PUVA。

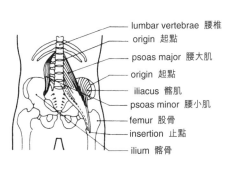

Psoas and iliacus muscles
腰肌與髂肌

psoriasis *n.* a chronic skin disease in which itchy scaly pink patches form on the elbows, knees, scalp, and other parts of the body. Psoriasis is one of the commonest skin diseases in Britain, affecting about 2% of the population, but its cause is not known. The disorder often runs in families, the commonest time of onset being in adolescence. It sometimes occurs in association with arthritis (*see* psoriatic arthritis). Occasionally the disease may be very severe, affecting much of the skin and causing considerable disability in the patient. While psychological stress may cause an exacerbation of psoriasis, the only significant event that precipitates the disease is a preceding streptococcal infection. Drugs, such as lithium or beta blockers, may occasionally be responsible.

Although there is as yet no cure, treatment of psoriasis has improved greatly in recent years. Tar and *dithranol are still used and topical corticosteroids remain popular. The vitamin D analogue *calcipotriol is a highly effective topical treatment, while *PUVA is an effective treatment for moderately severe disease. Systemic therapy, such as *methotrexate, *retinoids, or *cyclosporin, is reserved for the worst cases.

psoriatic arthritis arthritis associated with *psoriasis. It occurs in only a small minority of patients with psoriasis but may be painful and disabling. It often affects small joints, such as the terminal joints of the fingers and toes, or the spine (*spondylitis) and the sacroiliac joints (*sacroiliitis).

psych- (psycho-) *prefix denoting* **1.** the mind; psyche. **2.** psychology.

銀屑病　發生於肘部、膝部、頭部和身體其他部位的慢性皮膚病。表現為發癢的，鱗屑狀粉紅色斑塊。在英國是一種最常見的皮膚病，發病率大約為2％，但原因不明。此病常在家族中流行，最常見於青少年開始發病。有時與關節炎同時發生（參閱 psoriatric arthritis）。偶爾此病非常嚴重，會影響大部分皮膚，導致病人功能障礙。精神壓力可致銀屑病惡化。鏈球菌感染是此病唯一的明顯起因，藥物中如鋰和 β-受體阻滯劑或許引起此病。

　　雖然到目前為止還不能治愈，但治療手段近年來有了很大的改進。煤焦油與地蒽酚治療仍舊使用。局部皮質類固醇也很常用。局部應用維生素 D 類似物，鈣泊三醇非常有效。而光化學療法對於中等嚴重程度的銀屑病有效。系統治療如甲氨蝶呤、視黃酸或環孢菌素 A 用於最嚴重的病例。

銀屑病性關節炎　與銀屑病有關的關節炎。僅發生於未成年的銀屑病患者，可引起疼痛和殘疾。它常影響許多小關節如手指和腳趾關節，或脊柱（脊柱炎）及骶髂關節（骶髂關節炎）。

〔前綴〕**精神的**　(1) 意識的，精神　(2) 精神病學

psyche *n.* the mind or the soul; the mental (as opposed to the physical) functioning of the individual.

精神　意識或精神。指個體的精神功能（與軀體功能相對應）。

psychedelic *adj.* describing drugs that induce changes in the level of consciousness of the mind. Psychedelic drugs, which include *lysergic acid diethylamide (LSD) and *cannabis, are *hallucinogens and are used legally only for experimental purposes.

引起幻覺的　一種能夠引起腦內意識水平改變的藥物，引起幻覺的藥物，包括麥角二乙胺和大麻都是致幻劑，致幻劑只有用於科學實驗才是合法的。

psychiatrist *n.* a medically qualified physician who specializes in the study and treatment of mental disorders.

精神病學家　獲得專門資格的，治療和研究精神異常病人的內科醫生。

psychiatry *n.* the study of mental disorders and their diagnosis, management and prevention. –**psychiatric** *adj.*

精神病學　研究精神疾病及其診斷、處理和預防的科學。

psychic *adj.* **1.** of or relating to the *psyche. **2.** relating to parapsychological phenomena. **3.** describing a person who is endowed with extrasensory or psychokinetic powers.

(1) 精神的　(2) 心靈學的　(3) 超感覺的　（描述人）具有超感覺或精神驅動力的。

psychoanalysis *n.* a school of psychology and a method of treating mental disorders based upon the teaching of Sigmund Freud (1856–1939). Psychoanalysis employs the technique of *free association in the course of intensive *psychotherapy in order to bring repressed fears and conflicts to the conscious mind, where they can be dealt with (*see* repression). It stresses the dynamic interplay of unconscious forces and the importance of sexual development in childhood for the development of personality. –**psychoanalyst** *n.* –**psychoanalytic** *adj.*

精神分析　心理學學派之一，是一種以弗洛伊德 (1856~1939) 學說為基礎的精神障礙治療方法。精神分析在深入細緻的心理治療過程中應用自由聯想技術，使被壓抑的恐懼和衝突進入意識狀態以便進行治療（參閱 repression）。精神分析強調潛意識力量的相互作用以及兒童性發育在其人格發育中的重要性。

psychodrama *n.* a form of group psychotherapy in which individuals acquire

心理劇　一種羣體心理治療形式。在這種治療過程中，個體

insight into themselves by acting out situations from their past with other group members. *See* group therapy.

通過與羣體內其他成員表演他們以往體驗過的情景,從而獲得對於自我的認識。參閱 group therapy。

psychogenic *adj.* having an origin in the mind rather than in the body. The term is applied particularly to symptoms and illnesses.

精神性的,心理性的 起源於精神而非軀體的。該詞尤其用於對症狀和疾病進行描述。

psychogeriatrics *n.* the branch of psychiatry that deals with the mental disorders of old people. **–psychogeriatric** *adj.*

老年精神病學 精神病學的分支,主要研究老年人的精神紊亂。

psychokinesis *n.* a supposed ability of some individuals to alter the state or position of an object by the power of the mind alone, without any physical intervention. *See also* parapsychology.

精神驅動力 在某些人具有的設想依靠精神力量本身,而沒有任何軀體介入就能改變物體狀態和位置的能力。參閱 parapsychology。

psycholinguistics *n.* *see* cognitive psychology.

認識心理學,心理語言學 參閱 cognitive psychology。

psychologist *n.* a persons who is engaged in the scientific study of the mind. A psychologist may work in a university, in industry, in schools, or in a hospital. A *clinical psychologist* has been trained in aspects of the assessment and treatment of the ill and handicapped. He or she usually works in a hospital, often as one of a multidisciplinary team. An *educational psychologist* has been trained in aspects of the cognitive and emotional development of children. He or she usually works in close association with schools and advises on the management of children.

心理學家 從事心理科學研究工作的人。心理學家可以在大學、工廠、學校或醫院內工作。臨床心理學家接受過評定和治療疾病和殘疾的訓練,通常在醫院工作,並常作為多科性醫療隊的一員。教育心理學家則經過有關兒童認知和情緒發育方面的訓練,其工作通常與學校密切相關,並對兒童管理提出建議。

psychology *n.* the scientific study of behaviour and its related mental processes. Psychology is concerned with such matters as memory, rational and irrational thought, intelligence, learning, personality, perceptions, and emotions

心理學 研究行為以及與之相關的心理過程的科學。它涉及諸如記憶、理性和非理性思維、智力、學習、個性、知覺和情緒以及它們與行為的關係等方面。不同心理學派,其理

and their relationship to behaviour. Schools of psychology differ in their philosophy and methods. They include the introspectionist Freudian, Jungian, and Adlerian schools and the gestaltist, behaviourist, and cognitive schools; contemporary psychology tends strongly towards the latter (*see* cognitive psychology). Many practical psychologists profess not to belong to any school; some take an eclectic position. The branches of psychology, on the other hand, are functional or professional subspecialities based on practical considerations. They include abnormal, analytic, applied, clinical, comparative, developmental, educational, experimental, geriatric, industrial, infant, physiological, and social psychology. **–psychological** *adj.*

論和研究方法不同。他們包括內省主義者如弗洛伊德學派、榮格學派和阿德勒學派以及完形心理學派、行為主義者學派和認知學派；現代心理學強烈傾向於後者（參閱 cognitive psychology）。許多臨床心理學家聲稱他們不屬於任何學派；有些人採取兼收並蓄的態度。另一方面，心理學分支都是基於實用考慮的功能的或職業的下屬專業。它們包括異常的、分析的、應用的、臨床的、比較的、發育的、教育的、實驗的、老年的、工業的、嬰兒的、哲學的和社會的心理學。

psychometrics *n.* the measurement of individual differences in psychological functions (such as intelligence and personality) by means of standardized tests. **–psychometric** *adj.*

心理測驗 應用標準化的測試方法測定心理功能（如智力和個性）的個體差異。

psychomotor *adj.* relating to muscular and mental activity. The term is applied to disorders in which muscular activities are affected by cerebral disturbance.

精神運動的 與肌肉和精神活動有關的。該詞用於肌肉活動受大腦功能障礙影響的疾病。

psychomotor epilepsy *see* epilepsy.

精神運動性癲癇 參閱 epilepsy。

psychoneurosis *n.* a *neurosis that is manifest in psychological rather than organic symptoms.

精神性神經病 精神症狀比器質性症狀明顯的一種神經官能症。

psychopath *n.* a person who behaves in an antisocial way and shows little or no guilt for antisocial acts and little capacity for forming emotional relationships with others. Psychopaths tend to respond poorly to treatment but many mature as they age. *See also* dyssocial. **–psychopathic** *adj.* **–psychopathy** *n.*

精神變態者 以反社會方式行動，對其反社會行為無罪惡感，並且不能與他人建立感情關係的人。精神變態者對治療反應不佳，但許多患者到年老時會有好轉。參閱 dyssocial。

psychopathology *n.* **1.** the study of mental disorders, with the aim of explaining and describing aberrant behaviour. *Compare* psychiatry. **2.** the symptoms, collectively, of a mental disorder. **–psychopathological** *adj.*

精神病理學　**(1)** 研究精神紊亂，以解釋和描述異常行為的科學。與 psychiatry 對比。**(2)** 精神疾病的綜合症狀。

psychopharmacology *n.* the study of the effects of drugs on mental processes and behaviour, particularly *psychotropic drugs.

精神藥理學　研究藥物，尤其是精神治療藥物，對精神病變和行為的作用的科學。

psychophysiology *n.* the branch of psychology that records physiological measurements, such as the electrical resistance of the skin, the heart rate, the size of the pupil, and the electroencephalogram, and relates them to psychological events. **–psychophysiological** *adj.*

心理生理學　生理學的一個分支，它記錄各種生理學測量結果，諸如皮膚的電阻、心率、瞳孔的大小、腦電圖等，並把它們與心理活動相聯繫。

psychosexual development the process by which an individual becomes more mature in his sexual feelings and behaviour. Gender identity, sex-role behaviour, and choice of sexual partner are the three major areas of development. The phrase is sometimes used specifically for a sequence of stages, supposed by psychoanalytic psychologists to be universal, in which oral, anal, phallic, latency, and genital stages successively occur. These stages reflect the parts of the body on which sexual interest is concentrated during childhood development.

性心理發育　個體的性情感和行為變得更成熟的過程。性別確認、性行為和選擇性伴侶是發育的三個主要的方面。該術語有時特別用於性發育各期的出現次序，如口、肛、外生殖器、潛伏期和生殖期依次出現，精神分析派心理學家認為這種次序是普遍存在的。這些階段反映了兒童發育過程性興趣所集中的身體的部位。

psychosis *n.* one of a group of mental disorders that feature loss of contact with reality. The psychoses include *schizophrenia, major disorders of *affect (*see* manic-depressive psychosis), major *paranoid states, and organic mental disorders. Psychotic disorders manifest some of the following: *delusions,

精神病　以喪失與現實世界相接觸為特徵的精神紊亂性疾病之一。它包括精神分裂症、嚴重的情感紊亂（參閱 manic-depressive psychosis）、嚴重的狂躁狀態和器質性精神障礙。精神病表現出下列一些症狀：妄想、幻覺、嚴重思維障礙、

*hallucinations, severe thought disturbances, abnormal alteration of mood, poverty of thought, and grossly abnormal behaviour. Many cases of psychotic illness respond well to *antipsychotic drugs in that these drugs, while they are being taken, often induce a state of docility, acquiescence, apparent mental normality, and conformity with social norms. **–psychotic** *adj.*

情緒異常改變、思維貧乏和顯著的不正常行為。許多精神病患者在服用抗精神病藥物期間對藥物反應良好。該類藥物可使病人恢復溫和、默許等正常精神狀態和遵守社會規範。

psychosomatic *adj.* relating to or involving both the mind and body: usually applied to illnesses that are caused by the interaction of mental and physical factors. Certain physical illnesses, including asthma, eczema, and peptic ulcer, are thought to be in part a response to psychological and social stresses. Psychological treatments sometimes have a marked effect, but are usually much less effective than physical treatments for such illnesses.

身心的 與精神和軀體有關的或涉及兩者的。該詞常用於由精神和軀體因素相互作用引起的疾病。一些軀體性疾病，包括哮喘、濕疹和消化性潰瘍，被認為是在一定程度上對心理和社會壓力的應激。對於這些疾病，心理療法有時效果顯著，但通常遠不如軀體治療有效。

psychosurgery *n.* surgery on the brain to relieve psychological symptoms. The procedure is irreversible and is therefore reserved for the most severe and intractable of symptoms, particularly severe chronic anxiety, depression, and untreatable pain. Side-effects can be severe but are less common with modern selective operations. **–psychosurgical** *adj.*

精神外科學 以解除精神症狀為目的的腦外科手術。該手術是不可逆轉的，故專用於治療非常嚴重的和頑固的症狀，尤其是嚴重的慢性焦慮症、抑鬱症和頑固性疼痛。副作用可能很嚴重，但現代選擇性手術的副作用已不多見。

psychotherapy *n.* psychological (as opposed to physical) methods for the treatment of mental disorders and psychological problems. There are many different approaches to psychotherapy, including *psychoanalysis, *client-centred therapy, *group therapy, and *family therapy. These approaches share the views that the relationship between therapist and client is of prime

心理療法 治療精神障礙和心理問題的心理學（與軀體相對應）方法。心理療法有多種不同的手段，如精神分析、患者中心療法和集體治療和家庭治療等。這些療法都是基於如下觀點：醫生與患者間的關係是最重要的，治療的目標是幫助個體正常發育和全面認識自我而不只是消除症狀，醫生不指

importance, that the goal is to help personal development and self-understanding generally rather than only to remove symptoms, and that the therapist does not direct the client's decisions. They have all been very widely applied to differing clinical conditions but are of little or no value as treatments of mental illness. *See also* behaviour therapy, cognitive therapy, counselling. **–psychotherapeutic** *adj.* **–psychotherapist** *n.*

導患者對問題作出決定。上述療法已被廣泛用於治療各種臨床疾病，但用以治療精神疾患其效果尚不肯定。參閱 behaviour therapy，cognitive therapy，counselling。

psychoticism *n.* a dimension of personality derived from psychometric tests, which appears to indicate a degree of emotional coldness and some cognitive impairment.

心理評析法 一種源於心理測試的人格測量法，可顯示情緒的冷漠程度和一些認知損壞程度。

psychotropic *adj.* describing drugs that affect mood. *Antidepressants, *sedatives, *stimulants, and *tranquillizers are psychotropic.

治療精神病的 指對情緒有影響的藥物。如抗抑鬱藥、鎮靜藥、興奮劑和安定藥均是治療精神病的藥物。

psychro- *prefix denoting* cold.

〔前綴〕冷的

psychrophilic *adj.* describing organisms, especially bacteria, that grow best at temperatures of 0–25°C. *Compare* mesophilic, thermophilic.

嗜冷的 指能在 0~25°C 生長得很好的有機物，尤其是細菌。與 mesophilic，thermophilic 對比。

PTC 1. *see* percutaneous transhepatic cholangiopancreatography. **2.** *see* phenylthiocarbamide.

經皮肝穿膽管胰造影術 (1) 參閱 percutaneous transhepatic cholangiopancreatography。**(2)** 參閱 phenylthiocarbamide。

pterion *n.* the point on the side of the skull at which the sutures between the *parietal, *temporal, and *sphenoid bones meet.

翼點 顱骨側面上頂骨、顳骨和蝶骨間骨縫的匯合點。

pteroylglutamic acid *see* folic acid.

蝶酰穀氨酸 參閱 folic acid。

pterygium *n.* a triangular overgrowth of the cornea, usually the inner side, by

翼狀胬肉 角膜（通常為內側）上的三角形贅生物，由結膜增

thickened and degenerative conjunctiva. It is most commonly seen in people from dry hot dusty climates, and only rarely interferes with vision.

厚、變性所致；最常見於乾熱多塵氣候區的人們，有少數患者可影響視力。

pterygo- *prefix denoting* the pterygoid process of the sphenoid bone. Example: *pterygomaxillary* (of the pterygoid process and the maxilla).

〔前綴〕**翼**　蝶骨大翼。如翼上頜的（翼突和上頜的）。

pterygoid process either of two large processes of the *sphenoid bone.

翼突　蝶骨的兩個大突起。

ptomaine *n.* any of various substances produced in decaying foodstuffs and responsible for the unpleasant taste and smell of such foods. These compounds – which include putrescine, cadaverine, and neurine – were formerly thought to be responsible for food poisoning, but although they are often associated with toxic bacteria they themselves are harmless.

屍鹼　食物腐敗時產生的能使該食物具有惡臭口味和氣味的各種物質。這類物質包括腐胺、屍胺、神經鹼等，過去曾被認為是食物中毒的原因，儘管它們常常與毒性細菌相關，但它們本身是無害的。

ptosis *n.* drooping of the upper eyelid, for which there are several causes. It may be due to a disorder of the third cranial nerve (*oculomotor nerve), in which case it is likely to be accompanied by paralysis of eye movements causing double vision and an enlarged pupil. When part of *Horner's syndrome, ptosis is accompanied by a small pupil and an absence of sweating on that side of the face. It may be due to *myasthenia gravis, in which the ptosis increases with fatigue and is part of a more widespread fatiguable weakness. Ptosis may also occur as an isolated congenital feature or as part of a disease of the eye muscles, when it is associated with weak or absent eye movements.

上瞼下垂　各種原因引起的上眼瞼下垂。可由第三對腦神經（動眼神經）障礙引起，常伴有眼球運動麻痺，並引起複視和瞳孔增大。當作為霍納綜合徵的一部分時，上瞼下垂常伴有患側瞳孔縮小和面部汗閉。重症肌無力患者可有上瞼下垂，下垂的程度隨疲勞而增加，它是全身肌肉疲乏無力的一部分。上瞼下垂見於單獨的先天性病症或眼肌疾病的一部分，後者瞼下垂與眼球運動減弱或消失同時存在。

-ptosis *suffix denoting* a lowered position of an organ or part; prolapse. Example: *colpoptosis* (of the vagina).

〔後綴〕**下垂**　一個器官或器官的一部分的位置下降且超出正常範圍；脫垂。如陰道下垂。

PTSD *see* post-traumatic stress disorder.

ptyal- (ptyalo-) *prefix denoting* saliva. Example: *ptyalorrhoea* (excessive flow of).

〔前綴〕**唾液，涎**　如涎溢症（流涎過多）。

ptyalin *n*. an enzyme (an *amylase) found in saliva.

唾液澱粉酶　唾液中的一種酶（澱粉酶）。

ptyalism (sialorrhoea) *n*. the excessive production of saliva: a symptom of certain nervous disorders, poisoning (by mercury, mushrooms, or organophosphates), or infection (rabies). *Compare* dry mouth.

流涎　唾液分泌過多，為某些神經功能紊亂、中毒（汞、毒蕈、有機磷等）或感染（狂犬病）的一種症狀。與 dry mouth 對比。

ptyalith *n*. a stone (*calculus) in a salivary gland or duct.

涎石　唾液腺或導管中的石頭（結石）。

ptyalography *n*. *see* sialography.

涎管 X 綫造影術　參閱 sialography。

puberty *n*. the time at which the onset of sexual maturity occurs and the reproductive organs become functional. This is manifested in both sexes by the appearance of *secondary sexual characteristics (e.g. deepening of the voice in boys; growth of breasts in girls) and in girls by the start of *menstruation. These changes are brought about by an increase in sex hormone activity due to stimulation of the ovaries and testes by pituitary hormones. *See also* androgen, oestrogen. **–pubertal** *adj*.

青春期　性開始成熟，生殖器官開始發揮其功能的時期。這一時期兩性的第二性徵顯示出來（如男孩子嗓音低沉，女孩子乳房發育等），女性開始出現月經。這些變化是由於垂體激素刺激卵巢和睪丸，使其分泌的性激素作用增強而引起。參閱 androgen，oestrogen。

pubes *n*. **1.** the body surface that overlies the pubis, at the front of the pelvis. It is covered with *pubic hair*. **2.** *see* pubis. **–pubic** *adj*.

陰阜　**(1)** 骨盆前覆蓋恥骨的體表部分，長有陰毛。　**(2)** 參閱 pubis。

pubiotomy *n*. an operation to divide the pubic bone near the symphysis, the front midline where the left and right pubic

恥骨切開術　一種在恥骨聯合即左右恥骨連接的前正中綫附近分離恥骨的手術。該手術在

bones meet. Pubiotomy is performed during childbirth if it is found necessary to increase the size of an abnormally small pelvis to allow passage of the child and a Caesarean section is contraindicated. It is also done to facilitate access to the base of the bladder and the urethra during complex urological procedures (e.g. *urethroplasty).

分娩過程中骨盆過小又不可行剖宮產術,需擴大產道以利胎兒娩出時施行。該術也用於複雜的泌尿外科手術過程,以便容易進入到膀胱底和尿道(如尿道成形術)。

pubis *n.* (*pl.* **pubes**) a bone forming the lower and anterior part of each side of the *hip bone (*see also* pelvis). The two pubes meet at the front of the pelvis at the *pubic symphysis. See also* pubes.

耻骨 構成每側髖骨前下部的骨(參閱 pelvis)。兩塊耻骨在骨盆前部耻骨聯合處匯合。參閱 pubes。

Public Health Inspector (in Britain) the former title of the Environmental Health Officer.

公共衛生督察 (英國)環境衛生官員的舊稱。

Public Health Laboratory (in Britain) a regional service, with headquarters at Colindale, to assist with the investigation and control of infections. Such laboratories are a separate organization from hospital laboratories, which are under the control of District Health Authorities, but they can be located within a hospital and can contribute to the day-to-day diagnosis of hospital in-patients and out-patients.

公共衛生實驗室 (英國)總部設在科林代爾的地區性機構,幫助該地區對傳染病進行調查和控制。這類實驗室是從地段衛生局領導的醫院實驗室分離出來的獨立機構,但是可以設立在醫院內,並協助醫院對住院和門診患者進行日常診斷工作。

public health medicine the branch of medicine concerned with assessing needs and trends in health and disease of populations as distinct from individuals. Formerly known as *community medicine* or *social medicine*, it includes *epidemiology, *health promotion, *health service planning and evaluation, communicable disease control, and environmental hazards. *See also* public health physician.

公共衛生醫學 與評估非個體的公眾健康和疾病的需要和趨勢有關的醫學分支。舊稱社區醫學或社會醫學,它包括流行病學、健康促進、衛生事業規劃及評價,傳染性疾病控制和環境危害。參閱 public health physician。

public health nurse *see* health visitor.

公共衛生護士 參閱 health visitor。

public health physician (in Britain) a doctor of consultant status with special postgraduate training in public health medicine. Formerly known as *community physicians*, they undertake public health functions at each tier of the *National Health Service, either as *Regional (or District) Directors of Public Health* (formerly the Regional (or District) Medical Officers) or as other consultants in public health with responsibilities for such aspects of *health service planning as manpower, hospital building, or *health promotion as determined by the General Manager. In some districts the Director of Public Health may act as *proper officer* to the appropriate local authority, giving epidemiological and other medical advice to the *Environmental Health Officer. There are also specific posts as *consultants for communicable disease control* (*CCDC*), who are replacing the Medical Officers for Environmental Health (MOEH).

公共衛生醫師 （英國）在公共衛生醫學方面接受過特殊的研究生訓練的顧問醫生。舊稱社區醫師，無論是作為地區（或地段）公共衛生主任，（以前的地區或地段醫官），還是作為公共衛生方面的其他高級醫師，承擔衛生事業規劃方面諸如人力、醫院建設，或由總幹事決定的健康促進等方面的職責，它們都在國民保健服務制的各個層次上執行着公共衛生的職能。在有些地區，公共衛生主任可作為該地方當局的專員向環境衛生官員提出流行病學和其他醫學方面的建議。還有專職的傳染病控制高級醫師，正在取代環境衛生醫官。

pudendum *n.* (*pl.* **pudenda**) the external genital organs, especially those of the female (*see* vulva). **–pudendal** *adj.*

陰部 外生殖器，尤其是女性外生殖器。參閱 vulva。

puerperal *adj.* relating to childbirth or the period that immediately follows it.

產褥的 指分娩或緊接分娩後的一段時間。

puerperal depression a state of pathological sadness that sometimes affects a woman soon after the birth of her baby. The condition usually starts suddenly and without warning on the second or third day after delivery and usually resolves in about two months. In most cases the depression is not severe, but in about one case in 1000 it becomes serious enough to require admission to hospital. In these cases careful supervision and treatment are essential as there is a risk

產褥抑鬱症 有時在產婦剛剛分娩以後即影響產婦的一種病理悲傷狀態。這種情況常常於分娩的二三天後突然發作，並沒有先兆，又常常在約二個月後恢復。多數患者這種抑鬱不嚴重，但約千分之一患者會變得很嚴重，需入院治療。對於這些患者，仔細的引導和治療是必不可少的，因為她們有自殺或殺死嬰兒的危險。

that the woman may kill herself or her baby.

puerperal infection infection of the female genital tract arising as a complication of childbirth.

產褥感染 指分娩時合並發生的女性生殖道感染。

puerperal pyrexia a temperature of 38°C occurring on any two days within 14 days of childbirth or miscarriage.

產褥熱 在分娩或流產後 14 天的任何兩天內出現的 38°C 體温。

puerperium *n.* the period of up to about six weeks after childbirth, during which the uterus returns to its normal size (i.e. involution takes place).

產褥期 分娩後約六周的這段時間，子宮在此段時間恢復正常大小（復舊的發生）。

Pulex *n.* a genus of widely distributed *fleas. *P. irritans*, the human flea, is a common parasite of man and its bite may give rise to intense irritation and bacterial infection. It is an intermediate host for larvae of the tapeworms *Hymenolepis* and *Dipylidium*, which it can transmit to man, and it may also be involved in the transmission of plague.

蚤屬 一種廣泛分布的蚤。人蚤為常見的人體寄生蟲，咬人後可引起劇癢和細菌感染。牠是膜殼縧蟲和複孔縧蟲幼蟲的中間宿主，可將牠們傳播給人；還可參與鼠疫的傳播。

pulmo- (pulmon(o)-) *prefix denoting* the lung(s).

〔前綴〕肺

pulmonary *adj.* relating to, associated with, or affecting the lungs.

肺的 指與肺有關的、與肺有聯繫的或影響肺的。

pulmonary artery the artery that conveys blood from the heart to the lungs for oxygenation: the only artery in the body containing deoxygenated blood. It leaves the right ventricle and passes upwards for 5 cm before dividing into two, one branch going to each lung. Within the lungs each pulmonary artery divides into many fine branches, which end in capillaries in the alveolar walls. *See also* pulmonary circulation.

肺動脈 將來自心臟的血液運送至肺以獲取氧的動脈，是體內唯一含有脱氧血液的動脈。該動脈離開右心室上行 5cm 即分為 2 支，分別進入兩肺，在肺內又分成許多細支，止於肺泡壁的毛細血管。參閲 pulmonary circulation。

pulmonary capillary wedge pressure (PCWP) pressure of blood in the left

肺毛細血管楔壓 左心房內血液壓力，可反映肺循環的阻

atrium of the heart, which indicates the adequacy of the pulmonary circulation. It is measured using a catheter wedged in the most distal segment of the pulmonary artery. *See also* Swan-Ganz catheter.

力。該壓力的測量是用一導管插入到肺動脈最遠端進行的。參閱 Swan-Ganz catheter。

pulmonary circulation a system of blood vessels effecting transport of blood between the heart and lungs. Deoxygenated blood leaves the right ventricle by the pulmonary artery and is carried to the alveolar capillaries of the lungs. Gaseous exchange occurs, with carbon dioxide leaving the circulation and oxygen entering. The oxygenated blood then passes into small veins leading to the pulmonary veins, which leave the lungs and return blood to the left atrium of the heart. The oxygenated blood can then be pumped around the body via the *systemic circulation.

肺循環 在心臟與肺之間運輸血液的血管系統。由肺動脈攜帶脫氧血液離開右心室至肺泡毛細血管,進行氣體交換,二氧化碳離開循環,氧進入循環。氧合血液經小靜脈進入肺靜脈而返回左心房。接着氧合血液通過體循環流向全身。

pulmonary embolism obstruction of the *pulmonary artery or one of its branches by an *embolus, usually a blood clot derived from *phlebothrombosis of the leg veins. Large pulmonary emboli result in acute heart failure or sudden death. Smaller emboli cause death of sections of lung tissue, pleurisy, and haemoptysis (coughing of blood). Minor pulmonary emboli respond to the *anticoagulant drugs heparin and warfarin. Major pulmonary embolism is treated by *embolectomy or by dissolution of the blood colt with an infusion of *streptokinase. Recurrent pulmonary embolism may result in *pulmonary hypertension.

肺栓塞 肺動脈或其分支被栓子(通常為來自腿部靜脈血栓性靜脈炎的血凝塊)所阻塞。大的肺栓子可導致急性心力衰竭或猝死。較小的栓子可導致肺組織段(肺段)壞死、胸膜炎和咯血。抗凝血藥肝素和華法林對小的肺栓子有作用,而大的肺栓塞則需栓子切除術或注入鏈激酶以溶解血凝塊進行治療。反覆發作的肺栓塞可引起肺動脈高壓。

pulmonary hypertension a condition in which there is raised blood pressure within the blood vessels supplying the lungs (the pulmonary artery blood pressure is normally much lower than

肺動脈高壓 供應肺的血管內血壓升高(肺動脈血壓正常時遠低於主動脈及其分支的血壓)。肺動脈高壓可併發於肺栓塞、心間隔缺損、心力衰

the pressure within the aorta and its branches). Pulmonary hypertension may complicate pulmonary embolism, *septal defects, heart failure, diseases of the mitral valve, and chronic lung diseases. It may also develop without any known cause (*primary pulmonary hypertension*). The right ventricle enlarges and heart failure, fainting, and chest pain occur. The treatment is that of the cause; drugs used to control *hypertension are ineffective.

pulmonary stenosis congenital narrowing of the outlet of the right ventricle of the heart to the pulmonary artery. The defect may be in the pulmonary valve (*valvular stenosis*) or in the outflow tract of the right ventricle below the valve (*infundibular stenosis*). It may be isolated or combined with other heart defects (e.g. *tetralogy of Fallot). Severe pulmonary stenosis may produce angina pectoris, faintness, and heart failure. The defect is corrected by surgery.

pulmonary tuberculosis *see* tuberculosis.

pulmonary vein a vein carrying oxygenated blood from the lung to the left atrium. *See* pulmonary circulation.

pulp *n.* **1.** a soft mass of tissue (for example, of the spleen). **2.** the mass of connective tissue in the *pulp cavity*, at the centre of a *tooth. It is surrounded by dentine except where it communicates with the rest of the body at the apex. **3.** the fleshy cushion on the flexor surface of the fingertip.

pulp capping the procedure of covering an exposed tooth pulp following trauma with a medicament (usually

竭、二尖瓣病和慢性肺疾病。還可以不明原因地發現（原發性肺動脈高壓）。患者有右心室擴大、心力衰竭、昏厥和胸痛。治療針對病因進行，控制高血壓的藥物無效。

肺動脈狹窄 右心室出口至肺動脈的先天性狹窄。該缺陷可位於肺動脈瓣（瓣膜狹窄）或瓣膜下方右心室流出道（動脈圓錐狹窄）。它可以獨立發病也可合併其他心臟缺陷（如法樂四聯症）。嚴重的肺動脈狹窄可引起心絞痛、昏厥和心力衰竭。該缺陷須經手術進行糾正。

肺結核 參閱 tuberculosis。

肺靜脈 將氧合血從肺輸送至左心房的靜脈。參閱 pulmonary circulation。

髓 **(1)** 鬆軟的組織塊（如脾臟）。 **(2)** 在牙中央髓腔內的結締組織。牙髓四周為牙本質包圍，僅通過根尖孔與身體其他部分相通。 **(3)** 指端屈側面的肉質組織。

蓋髓術 一種用藥物覆蓋損傷後外露牙髓的方法，常常把藥物覆於氫氧化鈣上，然後再於

based on calcium hydroxide), which is then covered with a temporary or permanent *filling.

藥物上蓋以暫時或永久性填補物。

pulpitis *n*. inflammation of the pulp of a tooth: a frequent cause of toothache.

牙髓炎 牙髓的炎症,是牙痛的常見原因。

pulse *n*. a series of pressure waves within an artery caused by contractions of the left ventricle and corresponding with the heart rate (the number of times the heart beats per minute). It is easily detected on such superficial arteries as the radial artery near the wrist and the carotid artery in the neck. The average adult pulse rate at rest is 60–80 per minute, but exercise, injury, illness, and emotion may produce much faster rates.

脈搏 一系列由左心室收縮產生的與心率(每分鐘心跳的次數)一致的動脈內壓力波。在淺表的動脈,如腕部附近的橈動脈和頸部的頸動脈上,容易觸得。成年人安靜時的脈搏為每分鐘 60~80 次,但鍛煉、受傷、患病和情緒激動可使脈搏顯著加快。

pulseless disease *see* Takayasu's disease.

無脈病 參閱 Takayasu's disease。

pulsus paradoxus a large fall in systolic blood pressure and pulse volume when the patient breathes in. It is seen in constrictive *pericarditis, pericardial effusion, and asthma.

奇脈 病人吸氣時,心收縮期血壓和脈搏數顯著下降的現象。該體徵可見於縮窄性心包炎、心包積液和哮喘。

pulvinar *n*. the expanded posterior end of the *thalamus.

枕 丘腦膨大的後端。

punch-drunk syndrome a group of symptoms consisting of progressive *dementia, tremor of the hands, and epilepsy. It is a consequence of repeated blows to the head that have been severe enough to cause *concussion.

擊暈綜合徵 由進行性癡呆、手震顫和癲癇組成的一組症狀。是頭部遭受反覆的足以引起腦震盪的嚴重打擊的結果。

punctum *n*. (*pl*. **puncta**) (in anatomy) a point or small area, especially the *puncta lacrimalia* – the two openings of the tear ducts in the inner corners of the upper and lower eyelids (*see* lacrimal apparatus).

點 解剖學中的點和小區,主要指淚點,即上下眼瞼內眥部的淚小管的開口(參閱 lacrimal apparatus)。

puncture 1. *n.* a wound made accidentally or deliberately by a sharp object or instrument. Puncture wounds need careful treatment as a small entry hole in the skin can disguise serious injury in an underlying organ or tissue. Punctures are also performed for diagnostic purposes, in order to withdraw tissue or fluid for examination. *See also* lumbar puncture. **2.** *vb.* to pierce a tissue with a sharp instrument.

刺傷，穿刺　**(1)** 由尖銳的物體或工具意外或故意造成的外傷。由於小的皮膚入口可掩蓋深處器官組織的嚴重損傷，故刺傷須細心治療。穿刺可用於診斷目的，抽出組織或液體以供檢查。參閱 lumbar puncture。**(2)** 用尖銳的工具刺穿組織。

pupil *n.* the circular opening in the centre of the *iris, through which light passes into the lens of the eye. **–pupillary** *adj.*

瞳孔　虹膜中央的圓形孔，通過該孔光綫可穿透眼晶狀體。

pupillary reflex (light reflex) the reflex change in the size of the pupil according to the amount of light entering the eye. Bright light reaching the retina stimulates nerves of the *parasympathetic nervous system, which cause the pupil to contract. In dim light the pupil opens, due to stimulation of the *sympathetic nervous system. *See also* iris.

瞳孔反射（光反射）　瞳孔隨進入眼內光綫量而改變大小的反射。強光到達視網膜，刺激副交感神經系的神經，引起瞳孔縮小。在弱光下，由於交感神經系統的興奮，瞳孔開大。參閱 iris。

purgation *n.* the use of drugs to stimulate intestinal activity and clear the bowels. *See* laxative.

催瀉　用藥物刺激腸管活動，以清潔腸管。參閱 laxative。

purgative *n. see* laxative.

催瀉藥　參閱 laxative。

purine *n.* a nitrogen-containing compound with a two-ring molecular structure. Examples of purines are adenine and guanine, which form the *nucleotides of nucleic acids, and uric acid, which is the end-product of purine metabolism.

嘌呤　含雙環分子結構的含氮化合物。嘌呤的代表是腺嘌呤和鳥嘌呤，它們構成核酸的核苷酸，尿酸是嘌呤代謝的終產物。

Purkinje cells nerve cells found in great numbers in the cortex of the cerebellum. The cell body is flask-shaped, with numerous dendrites branching from the neck and extending fanwise among other

浦肯耶細胞　大量存在於小腦皮質內的神經細胞。胞體呈細頸燒瓶狀，有眾多樹突從頸部發出，並在其他細胞間呈扇狀伸向皮質表面，一條長的軸突

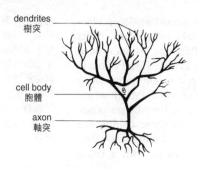

dendrites
樹突

cell body
胞體

axon
軸突

A Purkinje cell
浦肯耶細胞

cells towards the surface and a long axon that runs from the base deep into the cerebellum (see illustration).

Purkinje fibres *see* atrioventricular bundle.

purpura *n.* a skin rash resulting from bleeding into the skin from small blood vessels (capillaries); the individual purple spots of the rash are called *petechiae*. Purpura may be due either to defects in the capillaries (*nonthrombocytopenic purpura*) or to a deficiency of blood platelets (*thrombocytopenic purpura*). Acute idiopathic thrombocytopenic purpura is a disease of children in which antibodies are produce that destroy the patient's platelets. The child usually recovers without treatment. *See* thrombocytopenia, Henoch-Schönlein purpura.

purulent *adj.* forming, consisting of, or containing pus.

pus *n.* a thick yellowish or greenish liquid formed at the site of an established infection. Pus contains dead white blood

從基部伸向小腦深部 （見圖）。

浦肯耶纖維　參圖 atrioventricular bundle。

紫癜　由小血管（毛細血管）出血到皮膚內所造成的皮疹。皮疹上的單個紫色點稱為瘀點。紫癜可能由毛細血管缺陷（非血小板減少性紫癜）或血小板缺陷（血小板減少性紫癜）引起。急性特發性血小板性紫癜是一種兒童疾病，患兒產生破壞自身血小板的抗體。患兒一般可自愈。參閱 thrombocytopenia，Henoch-Schönlein purpura。

膿性的　生膿的，由膿構成的，含膿的。

膿　一種在感染部位形成的黏稠的、黃色或綠色的液體。膿含有死亡的白細胞、活的和死

cells, both living and dead bacteria, and fragments of dead tissue. *See also* mucopus, seropus.

的細菌以及壞死組織碎片。參閱 mucopus，seropus。

push-bang technique a technique for removing a stone from the ureter. It consists of 'pushing' the stone back into the renal pelvis, where it can be destroyed by *lithotripsy ('bang').

推-擊術 一種去除輸尿管結石的技術。該技術先把結石推回到腎盂，在腎盂內可將結石用碎石術粉碎（撞擊）。

pustule *n.* a small pus-containing blister on the skin.

膿疱 皮膚上的含膿小疱。

putamen *n.* a part of the lenticular nucleus (*see* basal ganglia).

殼 豆狀核的一部分（參閱 basal ganglia）。

putrefaction *n.* the process whereby proteins are decomposed by bacteria. This is accompanied by the formation of amines (such as *putrescine* and *cadaverine*) having a strong and very unpleasant smell.

腐敗 細菌分解蛋白質的過程。該過程同時有胺類（如腐胺和屍胺）產生，後者具有強烈惡臭氣味。

putrescine *n.* an amine formed during *putrefaction.

腐胺 腐敗過程中產生的一種胺。

PUVA (photochemotherapy) psoralen + ultraviolet A: the combination of *psoralen*, a light-sensitive drug, and exposure to long-wave (315–400 nm) ultraviolet light (UVA). It was used in the East in ancient times, using natural sunlight as the light source, for the treatment of *vitiligo. PUVA was introduced into Western medicine in 1973, principally for treating *psoriasis; a number of other conditions also respond. The psoralen is usually taken as tablets but may be administered in a bath. The UVA is administered by means of specially designed light cabinets containing large numbers of fluorescent tubes.

光化學療法 補骨脂素＋紫外綫 A：是一種應用名為補骨脂素的光敏感藥物和接受長波 (315~400 nm) 紫外光的綜合療法。該法用在古代東方，曾用自然陽光作光源進行治療白斑。光化學療法於 1973 年被引入西醫，主要用於治療銀屑病，對其他許多病也有效。補骨脂素通常以片劑使用，但也可以浴療。紫外綫是通過特殊設計的含有大量熒光管的光箱產生的。

PVS *see* persistent vegetative state.

永久植物狀態 參閱 persistent vegetative state。

py- (pyo-) *prefix denoting* pus; a purulent condition. Example: *pyoureter* (pus in a ureter).

〔前綴〕膿，化膿狀態 例如：輸尿管積膿。

pyaemia *n.* blood poisoning by pus-forming bacteria released from an abscess. The widespread formation of abscesses may occur, with fatal results. *Compare* sapraemia, septicaemia, toxaemia.

膿毒血症 化膿菌從膿腫釋放出來所致的血液中毒症。可發生廣泛性膿腫，造成致命的結果。與 sapraemia，septicaemia，toxaemia 對比。

pyarthrosis *n.* an infected joint filled with pus. Drainage, combined with antibiotic treatment, is necessary, though the joint may already be severely damaged if diagnosis is late.

關節積膿 關節感染且充滿膿液。如果診斷延誤，即使關節可能已嚴重受損，仍須切開引流，並聯合應用抗生素治療。

pyel- (pyelo-) *prefix denoting* the pelvis of the kidney. Example: *pyelectasis* (dilation of).

〔前綴〕腎盂 如腎盂擴張。

pyelitis *n.* inflammation of the pelvis of the kidney (the part of the kidney from which urine drains into the ureter). This is usually caused by a bacterial infection, which may develop in any condition causing obstruction to the flow of urine. The patient experiences pain in the loins, shivering, and a high temperature. Treatment is by the administration of a suitable antibiotic, together with analgesics and a high fluid intake. Any underlying abnormality of the urinary system must be relieved to prevent further attacks.

腎盂炎 腎盂（腎的一部分，尿經此排入輸尿管）的炎症。常由細菌感染引起，而後者可由任何尿路阻塞的疾病引起。病人有腰痛、寒戰、高熱。治療為給予適宜的抗生素，並用鎮痛劑以及大量飲水。泌尿系統的任何異常均須解除以預防進一步發作。

pyelocystitis *n.* inflammation of the renal pelvis and urinary bladder (*see* pyelitis, cystitis).

腎盂膀胱炎 腎盂和膀胱的炎症（參閱 pyelitis，cystitis）。

pyelogram *n. see* intravenous pyelogram, pyelography.

腎盂 X 綫片 參閱 intravenous pyelogram, pyelography。

pyelography (urography) *n.* X-ray examination of the kidneys using

腎盂 X 綫造影術 應用不透 X 綫的造影劑對腎臟進行 X 綫檢

*radiopaque contrast material. In *intravenous pyelography* (*excretion urography*) the contrast medium is injected into a vein and is concentrated and excreted by the kidneys (*see* intravenous pyelogram). In *retrograde pyelography*, fine catheters are passed up the ureter to the kidneys at *cystoscopy and contrast material is injected directly into the renal pelvis to allow X-ray examination. The X-ray pictures obtained from these procedures are called *pyelograms*.

查。在經靜脈腎盂造影術（排泄性腎 X 綫造影術）中造影劑被注入靜脈並被腎濃縮和排出（參閱 intravenous pyelogram）。在逆行性腎盂 X 綫造影術中，細導管在膀胱鏡檢查下向上經輸尿管被送至腎臟，並直接把造影劑注入腎盂以便進行 X 綫檢查。由此過程所獲得的 X 綫照片稱為腎盂 X 綫片。

pyelolithotomy *n.* surgical removal of a stone from the kidney through an incision made in the pelvis of the kidney. The incision is usually made into the posterior surface of the pelvis (*posterior pyelotomy*) to gain access to the stone, which can then be lifted clear.

腎盂結石切除術 經腎盂處做切口去除腎內結石的手術。切口常做在腎盂的後面（後側腎盂切開術），以接近和徹底清除結石。

pyelonephritis *n.* bacterial infection of the kidney substance. In *acute pyelonephritis*, the patient has pain in the loins, a high temperature, and shivering fits. Treatment is by the administration of an appropriate antibiotic, and a full urological investigation is conducted to determine any underlying abnormality and prevent recurrence. In *chronic pyelonephritis*, the kidneys become small and scarred and kidney failure ensues. *Vesicoureteric reflux in childhood is one of the causes.

腎盂腎炎 細菌所引起的腎實質感染。急性腎盂腎炎病人有腰痛、高熱和寒戰發作。治療用相應的抗生素，並進行泌尿系統全面檢查以發現任何潛在異常從而預防復發。在慢性腎盂腎炎、腎臟縮小、結疤，最終發生腎衰。兒童膀胱輸尿管返流是腎盂腎炎發病的原因之一。

pyeloplasty *n.* an operation to relieve obstruction at the junction of the pelvis of the kidney and the ureter. *See* hydronephrosis, Dietl's crisis.

腎盂成形術 為解除腎盂和輸尿管移行處的阻塞而進行的手術。參閱 hydronephrosis，Dietl's crisis。

pyelotomy *n.* surgical incision into the pelvis of the kidney. This operation is usually undertaken to remove a stone (*see* pyelolithotomy) but is also necessary when surgical drainage of the kidney is required by a catheter or tube.

腎盂切開術 切開腎盂的手術。該手術常用以去除結石（參閱 pyelolithotomy），當用導管進行腎臟外科引流時也是必須做的。

Pyemotes *n. see* Pediculoides.

虱形蟎　參閱 Pediculoides。

pyg- (pygo-) *prefix denoting* the buttocks.

〔前綴〕臀

pykno- *prefix denoting* thickness or density.

〔前綴〕濃厚，致密

pyknolepsy *n. Obsolete.* a very high frequency of absence seizures (*see* epilepsy).

癲癇小發作　廢用詞。頻度極高的失神發作（參閱 epilepsy）。

pyknosis *n.* the process in which the cell nucleus is thickened into a dense mass, which occurs when cells die. **–pyknotic** *adj.*

核固縮　細胞核濃縮為高密度團塊的過程，發生於細胞死亡時。

pyl- (pyle-) *prefix denoting* the portal vein.

〔前綴〕門靜脈

pylephlebitis (portal pyaemia) *n.* septic inflammation and thrombosis of the hepatic portal vein. This is a rare result of the spread of infection within the abdomen (as from appendicitis). The condition causes severe illness, with fever, liver abscesses, and *ascites. Treatment is by antibiotic drugs and surgical drainage of abscesses.

門靜脈炎（門靜脈膿血症）　肝門靜脈的敗血症和血栓形成。這是腹腔內感染（如源於闌尾炎）蔓延的罕見結果。該病可引起嚴重後果，有發熱、肝膿腫和腹水。治療為應用抗生素和膿腫外科引流。

pylethrombosis *n.* obstruction of the portal vein by a blood clot (*see* thrombosis). It can result from infection of the umbilicus in infants, pylephlebitis, cirrhosis of the liver, and liver tumours. *Portal hypertension is a frequent result.

門靜脈血栓形成　門靜脈被血凝塊阻塞（參閱 thrombosis）。該疾病可由嬰兒臍部感染、門靜脈炎、肝硬化和肝腫瘤引起。其常見結果為門靜脈高壓。

pylor- (pyloro-) *prefix denoting* the pylorus. Example: *pyloroduodenal* (of the pylorus and duodenum).

〔前綴〕幽門　如幽門和十二指腸的。

pylorectomy *n.* a surgical operation in which the muscular outlet of the stomach (*pylorus) is removed. *See* antrectomy, pyloroplasty.

幽門切除術　切除胃肌性出口（幽門）的外科手術。參閱 antrectomy，pyloroplasty。

pyloric stenosis narrowing of the muscular outlet of the stomach (*pylorus). This causes delay in passage of the stomach contents to the duodenum, which leads to repeated vomiting (sometimes of food eaten more than 24 hours earlier), and sometimes visible distension and movement of the stomach. If the condition persists the patient loses weight, becomes dehydrated, and develops *alkalosis. *Congenital hypertrophic pyloric stenosis* occurs in babies about 3–5 weeks old (particularly boys) in which the thickened pyloric muscle can be felt as a nodule. Treatment is by the surgical operation of *pyloromyotomy (Ramstedt's operation). Recovery is usually complete and the condition does not recur. Pyloric stenosis in adults is caused either by a *peptic ulcer close to the pylorus or by a cancerous growth invading the pylorus. Stenosis from peptic ulceration may be treated by healing the ulcer with an *antisecretory drug and dilating the pylorus with a *balloon, or by surgical removal or bypass (*see* gastroenterostomy). Surgery is required for cancerous obstruction.

幽門狹窄 胃肌性出口（幽門）狹窄。它可引起胃內容物進入十二指腸延遲，從而導致反覆的嘔吐（有時可嘔出 24 小時前所進食物），有時可見胃膨脹和胃蠕動。若該種情況持續存在，病人體重下降、脫水，進一步出現鹼中毒。先天性肥大性幽門狹窄出現在 3~5 周大的嬰兒（男孩居多），增厚的幽門肌肉觸診像一個結節。治療方法為進行幽門肌切開術（拉姆施蒂特手術），常常可完全恢復且不再復發。成人幽門狹窄可由靠近幽門的消化性潰瘍或癌生長侵襲幽門而引起。由消化性潰瘍引起的狹窄可通過服用抑制分泌藥和用氣囊擴張幽門的方法進行治療，也可外科切除或建立旁路（參閱 gastroenterostomy）。由癌腫引起的狹窄則須手術治療。

pyloromyotomy (Ramstedt's operation) *n.* a surgical operation in which the muscle around the outlet of the stomach (pylorus) is divided down to the lining (mucosa) in order to relieve congenital *pyloric stenosis.

幽門肌切開術（拉姆施蒂特手術） 將環繞胃出口（幽門）的肌肉分離至黏膜以解除先天性幽門狹窄的外科手術。

pyloroplasty *n.* a surgical operation in which the outlet of the stomach (pylorus) is widened by a form of reconstruction. It is done to allow the contents of the stomach to pass more easily into the duodenum, particularly after *vagotomy to treat peptic ulcers (which would otherwise cause delay in gastric emptying).

幽門成形術 胃出口（幽門）以重建方式被擴大的外科手術。此術目的在於使胃內容物更易進入十二指腸，尤其是在為治療消化性潰瘍而行迷走神經切斷術後（該手術可引起胃排空延遲）。

pylorospasm *n.* closure of the outlet of the stomach (pylorus) due to muscle spasm, leading to delay in the passage of stomach contents to the duodenum and vomiting. It is usually associated with duodenal or pyloric ulcers.

幽門痙攣 由肌肉痙攣引起的胃出口（幽門）關閉，可導致胃內容物進入十二指腸延遲和嘔吐。常與十二指腸或幽門潰瘍有關。

pylorus *n.* the lower end of the *stomach, which leads to the duodenum. It terminates at a ring of muscle – the *pyloric sphincter* – which contracts to close the opening by which the stomach communicates. with the duodenum. **–pyloric** *adj.*

幽門 胃的下端，與十二指腸相接。在其末端有一肌性環（幽門括約肌），該肌的收縮可關閉胃與十二指腸的交通口。

pyo- *prefix. see* py-.

〔前綴〕**膿** 參閱 py-。

pyocele *n.* a swelling caused by an accumulation of pus in a part of the body.

膿性囊腫 身體局部積膿所引起的腫脹。

pyocolpos *n.* the presence of pus in the vagina.

陰道積膿 陰道內有膿出現。

pyocyanin *n.* an antibiotic substance produced by the bacterium *Pseudomonas aeruginosa* and active principally against Gram-positive bacteria.

綠膿菌素 由綠膿假單胞菌產生的一種抗生素物質，主要用以治療革蘭氏陽性菌。

pyoderma gangrenosum an acute destructive ulcerating process of the skin, especially the legs and face. It may be associated with ulcerative *colitis of *Crohn's disease or with *rheumatoid arthritis or other forms of arthritis affecting many joints. Treatment is with high doses of corticosteroids.

皮膚化膿性壞疽病 一種皮膚急性破壞性潰瘍的過程，特別是下肢和面部，有時常和潰瘍性結腸炎、克羅恩病、類風濕性關節炎或其他形式的同時影響許多關節的關節炎並存。用大劑量的皮質激素治療。

pyogenic *adj.* causing the formation of pus. Pyogenic bacteria include *Staphylococcus aureus*, *Streptococcus hemolyticus*, and *Neisseria gonorrhoeae*.

生膿的 引起膿液生成。化膿性細菌包括有金黃色葡萄球菌、溶血性鏈球菌和奈瑟淋球菌。

pyogenic granuloma a common rapidly growing nodule on the surface of the skin. It is composed of small blood

化膿性肉芽腫 在皮膚表面常見的生長迅速的結節，它是由許多小的血管組成的，而且，

vessels and therefore bleeds readily after the slightest injury. It never becomes malignant and is treated by *curettage and cautery.

輕微損傷後容易出血；它永遠不癌變，通過刮除術和烙術治療。

pyometra *n.* the presence of pus in the uterus.

子宮積膿 在子宮內有膿。

pyometritis *n.* inflammation of the uterus, with the formation of pus.

化膿性子宮炎 伴有膿液形成的子宮炎。

pyomyositis *n.* bacterial or fungal infection of a muscle resulting in painful inflammation.

膿性肌炎 肌肉的細菌或真菌感染，導致痛性炎症。

pyonephrosis *n.* obstruction and infection of the kidney resulting in pus formation. A kidney stone is the usual cause of the obstruction, and the kidney becomes distended by pus and destroyed by the inflammation, which extends into the kidney substance itself and sometimes into the surrounding tissues (*see* perinephritis). Treatment is urgent *nephrectomy under antibiotic cover.

腎盂積膿 腎的阻塞和感染導致膿的生成。腎結石是常見的阻塞原因，腎臟由於膿及炎症的破壞而膨脹，膿有時進入腎實質，有時進入腎周圍組織（參閱 perinephritis）。治療是在抗生素控制下緊急施行腎切除術。

pyopneumothorax *n.* pus and gas or air in the *pleural cavity. The condition can arise if gas is produced by gas-forming bacteria as part of an *empyema or if air is introduced during attempts to drain the pus from an empyema. Alternatively a *hydropneumothorax may become infected.

膿氣胸 膿和氣體或空氣在胸膜腔內。當膿胸中的細菌為產氣菌，或者從膿胸引流時導入了空氣，即可發生膿氣胸。此外，液氣胸也可因感染而變成膿氣胸。

pyorrhoea *n.* a former name for *periodontal disease.

膿溢 牙周病的舊名。

pyosalpingitis *n.* inflammation of a Fallopian tube, with the formation of pus.

膿性輸卵管炎 伴有膿液形成的輸卵管炎。

pyosalpingo-oophoritis *n.* inflammation of an ovary and Fallopian tube, with the formation of pus.

膿性輸卵管卵巢炎 伴有膿液形成的卵巢、輸卵管炎。

pyosalpinx *n.* the accumulation of pus in a Fallopian tube.

輸卵管積膿　輸卵管內有膿蓄積。

pyosis *n.* the formation and discharge of pus.

化膿　膿生成和排膿。

pyothorax *n. see* empyema.

膿胸　參閱 empyema。

pyr- (pyro-) *prefix denoting* **1.** fire. **2.** a burning sensation. **3.** fever.

〔前綴〕**(1)** 火　**(2)** 燒灼感 **(3)** 發熱

pyramid *n.* **1.** one of the conical masses that make up the medulla of the *kidney, extending inwards from a base inside the cortex towards the pelvis of the kidney. **2.** one of the elongated bulging areas on the anterior surface of the *medulla oblongata in the brain, extending downwards to the spinal cord. **3.** one of the divisions of the vermis of the *cerebellum in the middle lobe. **4.** a protrusion of the medial wall of the vestibule of the middle ear.

錐體，圓錐　**(1)** 構成腎髓質的圓錐形團塊，基底在腎皮質下面，尖朝向腎盂。**(2)** 延髓腹側面一個狹長的隆起的區域，向下一直延續到脊髓。**(3)** 小腦中央葉蚓部的一部分。**(4)** 中耳鼓室內側壁上的錐狀隆起。

pyramidal cell a type of neurone found in the *cerebral cortex, with a pyramid-shaped cell body, a branched dendrite extending from the apex towards the brain surface, several dendrites extending horizontally from the base, and an axon running in the white matter of the hemisphere (see illustration).

錐體細胞　存在於大腦皮質中的一類神經元，胞體呈錐體狀，一條樹突由尖端發出，走向大腦表面，另有幾條樹突從基底水平向外伸展，一條軸突則在半球的髓質內走行（見圖）。

pyramidal system a collection of nerve tracts within the *pyramid of the medulla oblongata, en route from the cerebral cortex to the spinal cord. Within the pyramid fibres cross from one side of the brain to the opposite of the spinal cord; this is called the *decussation of the pyramids.*

錐體系　從大腦皮質到脊髓途經延髓錐體的所有神經纖維束。兩側的神經纖維在錐體內相互交叉，走向脊髓對側，稱為錐體交叉。

pyrantel *n.* an *anthelmintic drug used to treat infestations with intestinal worms, especially roundworms and

噻嘧啶　是一種驅腸蟲藥。用來治療腸蟲感染，特別是圓蟲和蟯蟲感染。口服。副作用

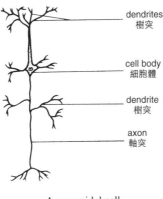

dendrites
樹突

cell body
細胞體

dendrite
樹突

axon
軸突

A pyramidal cell
錐體細胞

pinworms. It is administered by mouth. Side-effects occur only with large doses and include headache, dizziness, skin rash, and fever. Trade names: **Antiminth, Combantrin**.

只在大劑量用藥時產生,包括有頭痛、頭暈、皮疹、發熱。商品名:Antiminth,Combantrin。

pyrazinamide *n.* a drug administered by mouth, usually in combination with other drugs, to treat tuberculosis. Side-effects may include digestive upsets, joint pains, gout, fever, and rashes, and high doses may cause liver damage. Trade name: **Zinamide**.

吡嗪酰胺 一種口服藥,通常和其他藥物聯合用於治療結核病。副作用包括胃腸紊亂、關節痛、痛風、發熱、皮疹,大劑量可引起肝損害。商品名:Zinamide。

pyret- (pyreto-) *prefix denoting* fever.

〔前綴〕發熱

pyrexia *n. see* fever.

發熱 參閱 fever。

pyridostigmine *n.* an *anticholinesterase drug used in the treatment of *myasthenia gravis. It is administered by mouth or injection; side-effects may include nausea, vomiting, abdominal pain, diarrhoea, sweating, and increased salivation. Trade name: **Mestinon**.

吡斯的明 一種治療重症肌無力的抗膽鹼酯酶類藥。可口服,肌注。副作用有噁心、嘔吐、腹痛、腹瀉、出汗和唾液增加。商品名:Mestinon。

pyridoxal phosphate a derivative of vitamin B_6 that is an important *coenzyme in certain reactions of aminoacid metabolism. *See* transamination.

磷酸吡哆醛　維生素 B_6 的衍生物，為氨基酸代謝中某些反應的重要輔酶。參閱 transamination。

pyridoxine *n. see* vitamin B_6.

吡多辛　參閱 vitamin B_6。

pyrimethamine *n.* a drug administered by mouth for the prevention and treatment of *malaria, either alone or in combination with dapsone (in *Maloprim*); it is also used in the treatment of *toxoplasmosis. Possible side-effects include loss of appetite and vomiting, and prolonged use may interfere with red blood cell production. Trade name: **Daraprim**.

乙胺嘧啶，息瘧定　一種可口服用於預防和治療瘧疾的藥，可單獨用，也可和氨苯碸合用。也可以用來治療弓形蟲病。可能的副作用有食慾差和嘔吐，長時間使用可能影響紅細胞產生。商品名：Daraprim。

pyrimidine *n.* a nitrogen-containing compound with a ring molecular structure. The commonest pyrimidines are cytosine, thymine and uracil, which form the *nucleotides of nucleic acids.

嘧啶　一種帶單環分子結構的含氮化合物。最普通的嘧啶有胞嘧啶、胸腺嘧啶和尿嘧啶，三者參與生成核酸的核苷酸。

pyrogen *n.* any substance or agent producing fever. **–pyrogenic** *adj*.

致熱原　所有引起發熱的物質和因子。

pyromania *n.* an excessively strong impulse to set things on fire. **–pyromaniac** *adj. n.*

縱火癖　十分強烈的想放火燒東西的衝動。

pyrosis *n.* another term (chiefly US) for *heartburn.

胃灼熱　heartburn 的另一術語（主要在美國使用）。

pyruvic acid (pyruvate) a compound, derived from carbohydrates, that may be oxidized via a complex series of reactions in the *Krebs cycle to yield carbon dioxide and energy in the form of ATP.

丙酮酸　由碳水化合物衍化而來的一種化合物，可通過三羧酸循環中一系列反應，氧化生成二氧化碳和 ATP 形式的能量。

pyuria *n.* the presence of pus in the urine, making it cloudy. This is a sign of bacterial infection in the urinary tract.

膿尿　含有膿的混濁尿，為尿路細菌感染的症狀之一。

Q

qat *n. see* khat.

Q fever an acute infectious disease of cattle, sheep, and goats that is caused by a *rickettsia, *Coxiella burnetii*, and can be transmitted to man primarily through contaminated unpasteurized milk. The disease lasts about two weeks and causes fever, severe headache, and respiratory problems. Treatment with tetracyclines or chloramphenicol is effective. *See also* typhus.

qinghaosu *n.* a Chinese herbal drug used for 2000 years to treat *malaria. The active ingredient is sesquiterpene lactone that greatly reduces the number of malarial parasites in the blood. Trials of the drug have recently started in the West.

QRS complex the element of an *electrocardiogram that precedes the *S-T segment and indicates ventricular contraction.

Q-T interval the interval on an *electrocardiogram that contains the deflections that are produced by ventricular contraction.

quadrantanopia *n.* absence or loss of one quarter of the *visual field (i.e. upper nasal (inner), upper temporal (outer), lower nasal (inner), or lower temporal (outer)).

quadrate lobe one of the lobes of the *liver.

卡塔葉 參閱 khat。

Q 熱 一種由伯特納立克次體引起的牛、羊和山羊的急性傳染病。可主要通過污染的未經消毒的奶傳染給人。此病持續約兩周，可引起發熱，劇烈頭痛和呼吸道症狀。用四環素或氯黴素治療有效。參閱 typhus。

青蒿素 用於治療瘧疾已2000餘年的一種中草藥。它的活性成份倍半萜烯能減少血液中瘧原蟲的數量，藥物試驗在西方已開始。

QRS 複合波 在心電圖的S-T段之間的波，表示心室的收縮。

Q-T間期 心電圖上的一個間期，包括有心肌收縮產生的偏轉。

象限盲 四分之一視野（上鼻側、上顳側、下鼻側或下顳側）缺損或喪失。

肝方葉 肝臟的一葉。

quadratus *n.* any of various four-sided muscles. The *quadratus femoris* is a flat muscle at the head of the femur, responsible for lateral rotation of the thigh.

quadri- *prefix denoting* four. Example: *quadrilateral* (having four sides).

quadriceps *n.* one of the great extensor muscles of the legs. It is situated in the thigh and is subdivided into four distinct portions: the *rectus femoris* (which also flexes the thigh), *vastus lateralis*, *vastus medialis*, and *vastus intermedius* (see illustration).

方肌　四邊形的肌肉，股方肌是股骨頭上的一塊扁平的肌肉，可使大腿外旋。

〔前綴〕四　指四個。例如：四邊形的（有四條邊的）。

四頭肌　腿部最大的伸肌之一。位於大腿，被分為四個獨立的部分：股直肌（屈大腿），股外側肌，股內側肌及股中間肌（見圖）。

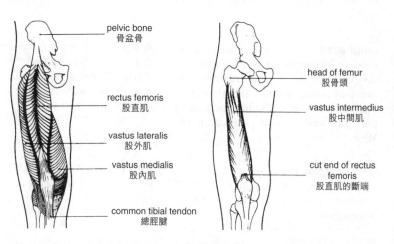

pelvic bone 骨盆骨	head of femur 股骨頭
rectus femoris 股直肌	vastus intermedius 股中間肌
vastus lateralis 股外肌	cut end of rectus femoris 股直肌的斷端
vastus medialis 股內肌	
common tibial tendon 總脛腱	

Components of the quadriceps femoris
四頭肌的組成

quadriplegia (tetraplegia) *n.* paralysis affecting all four limbs. **–quadriplegic** *adj.*, *n.*

quantitative digital radiography a method of detecting *osteoporosis. A narrow X-ray beam is directed at the area of interest (usually the spine and hip), which enables a measurement to be made of its calcium content (density).

四肢麻痺，四肢癱瘓　四個肢體的癱瘓。

定量數字放射攝影術　一種探知骨質疏鬆的方法，一束窄的X 綫光束直射研究區域（通常為脊柱和髖部），這可測出其鈣的含量（密度）。用這種方法可評價骨折發生的可能性和

In this way the likelihood of fracture can be assessed and preventive measures considered, e.g. *hormone replacement therapy.

考慮預防的措施，如激素替代療法。

quarantine *n.* the period for which a person (or animal) is kept in isolation in order to prevent the spread of a contagious disease. The original quarantine was a period of 40 days, but different diseases now have different quarantine periods.

檢疫期 為防止傳染病的播散而將人（或動物）隔離的期限。原來檢疫期為 40 天，但現在不同的疾病有不同的檢疫期限。

quartan fever *see* malaria.

三日瘧 參閱 malaria。

Queckenstedt test a part of the routine *lumbar puncture procedure. It is used to determine whether or not the flow of cerebrospinal fluid is blocked in the spinal canal.

克韋肯斯蒂特試驗 腰椎穿刺常規操作的一部分。用於測定椎管內腦脊液流動是否有阻塞。

quellung reaction a reaction in which antibodies against the bacterium *Streptococcus pneumoniae* combine with the bacterial capsule, which becomes swollen and visible to light microscopy.

莢膜腫脹反應 抗肺炎鏈球菌抗體與細菌莢膜結合的一種反應。此時莢膜腫脹，可在光學顯微鏡下檢查到。

quickening *n.* the first movement of a fetus in the uterus felt by the mother. Quickening is usually experienced after about 16 weeks of pregnancy, although it may occur earlier.

胎動初感 母親第一次感到子宮內胎兒的活動。通常約在妊娠 16 周後感受到胎動初感，雖然它可能發生較早。

quiescent *adj.* describing a disease that is in an inactive or undetectable phase.

靜止的 形容疾病在不活動或檢查不出的時期。

quinestradol *n.* a synthetic female sex hormone (*see* oestrogen) administered by mouth to treat inflammation of the vagina, particularly after the menopause. Side-effects do not usually occur. Trade name: **Pentovis**.

奎雌醇（雌三醇環戊醚） 一種人工合成的女性激素（參閱 oestrogen）。用於口服治療陰道炎症，尤其在絕經後。通常不發生副作用。商品名：Pentovis。

quinestrol *n.* a synthetic female sex hormone (*see* oestrogen) used to inhibit

炔雌醚 一種人工合成的女性性激素（參閱 oestrogen）。用

lactation in mothers not breast feeding. It is administered by mouth and side-effects are uncommon, though nausea and vomiting sometimes occur. Trade name: **Estrovis**.

於抑制斷奶後母親的泌乳。口服，副作用罕見，有時發生惡心、嘔吐。商品名： Estrovis。

quinidine *n.* a drug that slows down the activity of the heart and is administered by mouth to control abnormal and increased heart rhythm. Digestive upsets and symptoms of *cinchonism may occur as side-effects. Trade names: **Kinitard**, **Kinidin Durules**.

奎尼丁 減慢心臟活動的藥物。口服，用以控制心臟節律異常和增快。可能發生的副作用有消化道不適和金雞鈉中毒症狀。商品名： Kinitard, Kinidin Durules。

quinine *n.* a drug formerly used to prevent and treat *malaria, now largely replaced by more effective less toxic drugs. It is administered by mouth or injection; large doses can cause severe poisoning, symptoms of which include headache, fever, vomiting, confusion, and damage to the eyes and ears (*see* cinchonism).

奎寧 過去用於治療和預防瘧疾的藥物。現基本上已被毒性小且更有效的藥物替代。口服或注射，大劑量可引起嚴重中毒，其症狀有頭痛、發熱、嘔吐、精神錯亂以及眼和耳的損害（參閱 cinchonism）。

quinism *n.* the symptoms of overdosage or too prolonged treatment with quinine. *See* cinchonism.

奎寧中毒 由於奎寧治療用藥過量或時間過長引起的症狀。參閱 cinchonism。

quinolone *n.* one of a group of chemically related synthetic antibiotics that includes *nalidixic acid, *ofloxacin, and *enoxacin*. These drugs act by inactivating an enzyme, DNA gyrase, that is necessary for replication of the microorganisms and are often useful for treating infections with organisms that have become resistant to other antibiotics. They are administered by mouth. Possible side-effects include nausea, vomiting, diarrhoea, abdominal pain, headache, restlessness, and tiredness. Psychiatric disturbances occasionally occur.

喹諾酮 一組化學合成類抗生素之一，包括有萘啶酸、氧氟沙星和依諾沙星。這類藥通過抑制微生物複製所需的DNA旋轉酶而起作用，它常被用來治療對其他抗生素耐藥的細菌感染。可口服。可能的副作用包括惡心、嘔吐、腹瀉、腹痛、頭痛、不安和疲乏，有時發生精神紊亂。

quinsy *n.* pus in the space between the tonsil and the wall of the pharynx. The

扁桃體周膿腫 在扁桃體和咽壁之間的膿腫。病人可有嚴重

patient has severe pain with difficulty opening the mouth (*trismus) and swallowing. Treatment is with antibiotics. Surgical incision of the abscess may be necessary to release the collection of pus. Medical name: **peritonsillar abscess**.

quotidian fever *see* malaria.

Q wave the downward deflection on an *electrocardiogram that indicates the beginning of ventricular contraction.

的疼痛，並伴有張口困難（牙關緊閉）和吞咽困難。採用抗生素治療。為了排膿，手術切開膿腫可能是必要的。醫學用語：扁桃體周圍膿腫。

每日熱 參閱 malaria。

Q 波 在心電圖上向下移動的波，表示心室收縮開始。

R

rabbit fever *see* tularaemia.

rabies (hydrophobia) *n*. an acute virus disease of the central nervous system that affects all warm-blooded animals and is usually transmitted to man by a bite from an infected dog. Symptoms appear after an incubation period ranging from 10 days to over a year and include malaise, fever, difficulty in breathing, salivation, periods of intense excitement, and painful muscle spasms of the throat induced by swallowing. In the later stages of the disease the mere sight of water induces convulsions and paralysis; death occurs within 4–5 days.

Daily injections of rabies vaccine, together with an injection of rabies antiserum, may prevent the disease from developing in a person bitten by an infected animal. **–rabid** *adj*.

racemose *adj*. resembling a bunch of grapes. The term is applied particularly to a compound gland the secretory part of which consists of a number of small sacs.

兔熱病 參閱 tularaemia。

狂犬病（恐水病） 中樞神經系統的一種急性病毒性疾病，所有溫血動物都能受累。通常通過被感染的狗咬傷而傳染給人。在潛伏期（10天至1年以上）後出現症狀，有全身不適、發熱、呼吸困難、流涎，有一段時間高度興奮，以及因吞咽引起咽部痛性肌肉痙攣。疾病後期，一旦看見水就會引起驚厥和麻痺，4~5天內死亡。

每日注射狂犬疫苗，同時注射抗狂犬病血清可以防止被感染動物咬傷者的發病。

葡萄狀的 似一串葡萄。此詞特別用於形容那些其分泌部由許多小囊組成的複腺。

rachi- (rachio-) *prefix denoting* the spine.

〔前綴〕脊柱

rachis *n. see* backbone.

脊柱，脊椎 參閱 back-
bone。

rachischisis *n. see* spina bifida.

脊柱裂 參閱 spina bifida。

richitic *adj.* afflicted with rickets.

佝僂病的 患有佝僂病的。

rad *n.* a former unit of absorbed dose of ionizing radiation. It has been replaced by the *gray.

拉德 一種早期的離子放射吸
收劑量單位，現以戈瑞代替。

radial *adj.* relating to or associated with the radius (a bone in the forearm).

橈骨的 指與橈骨（前臂的一
根骨）有關的。

radial artery a branch of the brachial artery, beginning at the elbow and passing superficially down the forearm to the styloid process of the radius at the wrist. It then winds around the wrist and enters the palm of the hand, sending out branches to the fingers.

橈動脈 肱動脈的分支。起始
於肘部，通過前臂的淺部下降
達腕部橈骨莖突，繞過腕部並
進入手掌，發出分支到手指。

radial keratotomy an operation for shortsightedness (myopia). Deep cuts into the tissue of the cornea are placed radially around the outer two-third of the cornea; this flattens the curvature of the central part of the cornea and reduces the myopia. This procedure, used only for slight degrees of myopia, is being superseded by *excimer laser treatment.

放射狀角膜切開術 治療近
視眼手術。手術切口深達角
膜組織並放射狀環繞角膜外
緣 2/3。這可使角膜中心部分
的曲度變平，從而減少近視
度。這種療法僅適用於輕度近
視眼，正在被激態原子激光治
療所代替。

radial nerve an important mixed sensory and motor nerve of the arm, forming the largest branch of the *brachial plexus. It extends downwards behind the humerus, supplying muscles of the upper arm, to the elbow, which it supplies with branches, and then runs parallel with the radius. It supplies sensory branches to the base of the thumb and a small area of the back of the hand.

橈神經 臂部重要的感覺和運
動性混合神經，為臂叢的粗大
分支。在肱骨後方下行，支配
上臂肌肉，達肘部後發出分
支，然後與橈骨平行走行，並
發感覺支分布於拇指根部和手
背側一小部分區域。

radial reflex flexion of the forearm (and sometimes also of the fingers) that occurs when the lower end of the radius is tapped. It is due to contraction of the brachioradialis muscle, which is stimulated by tapping its point of insertion in the radius.

橈反射　輕叩橈骨下端時引起的前臂屈曲（有時手指亦屈曲）。這是由於敲打肱橈肌在橈骨上的附着點，使肱橈肌收縮所致。

radiation *n.* energy in the form of waves or particles, especially *electromagnetic radiation*, which includes (in order of increasing wavelength), *gamma rays, *X-rays, *ultraviolet rays, visible light, and infrared rays (radiant heat), and the particles.

輻射　以波或粒子形式發出的能量。尤指電磁輻射，它包括（按波長遞增的順序）γ射綫、X綫、紫外綫、可見光、紅外綫（輻射熱）以及粒子等。

radiation sickness any acute illness caused by exposure to rays emitted by radioactive substances, e.g. X-rays or gamma rays. Very high doses cause death within hours from destructive lesions of the central nervous system. Lower doses, which may still prove fatal, cause immediate symptoms of nausea, vomiting, and diarrhoea followed after a week or more by bleeding and other symptoms of damage to the bone marrow, loss of hair, and bloody diarrhoea.

放射性疾病　由於放射性物質的射綫（如X綫或γ射綫）照射引起的急性病。極大劑量時可由於中樞神經系統毀壞性病變，在幾小時內引起死亡。小劑量可立即引起惡心、嘔吐和腹瀉，在一周後出現血和骨髓受損的其他症狀，毛髮脱落和便血，最後可以致死。

radical treatment vigorous treatment that aims at the complete cure of a disease rather than the mere relief of symptoms. *Compare* conservative treatment.

根治　能幫助疾病痊愈的強有力的治療，而不只是緩解症狀。與 conservative treatment 對比。

radicle *n.* (in anatomy) **1.** a small *root. **2.** the initial fibre of a nerve or the origin of a vein. **–radicular** *adj.*

根（解剖學）　**(1)** 細小的根 **(2)** 神經起始部的纖維或靜脈的起端。

radiculitis *n.* inflammation of the root of a nerve. *See* polyradiculitis.

脊神經根炎　神經根發炎。參閲 polyradiculitis。

radio- *prefix denoting* **1.** radiation. **2.** radioactive substances.

〔前綴〕**(1)** 放射　**(2)** 放射性物質

radioactivity *n.* disintegration of the nuclei of certain elements, with the emission of energy in the form of alpha, beta, or gamma rays. As particles are emitted the elements 'decay' into other elements. Naturally occurring radioactive elements include radium and uranium. There are many artificially produced isotopes, including iodine-131 and cobalt-60, which are used in radiotherapy. *See* radioisotope. **–radioactive** *adj.*

radioautography *n. see* autoradiography.

radiobiology *n.* the study of the effects of radiation on living cells and organisms. Studies of the behaviour of cancer cells exposed to radiation have important applications in *radiotherapy, revealing why some tumours fail to respond to the treatment; this had led to the development of new radiotherapeutic techniques that make tumours more susceptible to attack by radiation.

radiodermatitis *n.* inflammation of the skin after its exposure to ionizing radiation. This may occur after a short dose of heavy radiation (radiotherapy or atomic explosions) or to prolonged exposure to small doses, as may happen accidentally to X-ray workers. The skin becomes dry, hairless, and atrophied, losing its colouring.

radiograph *n.* an image produced on a film by X-rays: an X-ray picture. *See* radiography.

radiographer *n.* **1. (diagnostic radiographer)** a person who is trained in the technique of taking X-ray pictures of parts of the body. **2. (therapeutic radiographer)** a person who is trained in the technique of treatment by *radiotherapy.

放射性　某些元素的核蛻變時發射α、β或γ射綫並釋放能量。元素在發射出粒子時衰變為另一種元素。天然的放射性元素有鐳和鈾。現在有許多人工生產的同位素，如[131]碘和[60]鈷，可被應用於放射治療。參閱 radioisotope。

放射自顯影術　參閱 autoradiography。

放射生物學　研究放射綫對活細胞和器官作用的科學。對接觸放射綫的癌細胞的活動的研究在放射治療上有重要的應用價值。已經弄清某些腫瘤對治療不反應的原因，這導致新的放射治療技術的發展，這種新技術使腫瘤對放射綫的攻擊更敏感。

放射性皮炎　放射性粒子照射後的皮膚炎症。可以發生於短時間重複照射（放射治療或原子爆炸）或長時間的小劑量照射後，例如偶可發生於 X 綫工作者。皮膚變乾燥，無毛或萎縮，脫色。

放射綫照片　X 綫在膠片上構成的影像，X 綫像片。參閱 radiography。

放射照像技術員　(1)（診斷放射照像技術員）經過訓練的拍照人體各部位 X 綫像片的技術人員。(2)（治療放射照像技術員）經過放射治療技術訓練的技術人員。

radiography *n.* diagnostic radiology: the technique of examining the body by directing *X-rays through it to produce images (*radiographs*) on photographic plates or fluorescent screens. Radiography is used in the diagnosis of such disorders as broken bones, gastric ulcers, and stones in the gall bladder or kidney, when inspection from outside the body is insufficient for diagnosis. It is also widely used in dentistry for detecting dental caries, periodontal disease, periapical disease, the presence and position of unerupted teeth, and disease of the jaws.

放射造影術　放射診斷學：用 X 綫透視人體，在照像底板或熒光屏上形成影像的檢查技術。放射照像檢查技術用於當體外檢查不足以診斷時，例如用於診斷骨折、胃潰瘍、膽囊結石或腎結石等疾病時。也廣泛應用於口腔檢查齲齒、牙周病、根尖周圍病變，有無未長出的牙齒和其位置以及頜骨病變。

radioimmunoassay *n.* the technique of using radioactive *tracers to determine the levels of particular antibodies in the blood. For example, radioactive iodine may be used to 'label' the hormone insulin. In some diabetic patients insulin provokes the formation of antiinsulin antibodies, which combine with the insulin. After the injection of the tracer insulin, samples of the patient's blood are analysed by *electrophoresis or *chromatography, and the antibody components of the blood are tested for the presence of radioactivity.

放射免疫測定法　應用放射性示踪劑測定血中特殊抗體的技術。例如放射性碘可以用來「標記」胰島素。有些糖尿病患者可產生與胰島素結合的抗胰島素抗體。注射胰島素示踪劑後，用電泳法或色譜法分析患者血標本，由於有放射性存在，就可測定血中抗體成分。

radioisotope *n.* an *isotope of an element that emits alpha, beta, or gamma radiation during its decay into another element. Artificial radioisotopes, produced by bombarding elements with beams of neutrons, are widely used in medicine as *tracers and as sources of radiation for the different techniques of *radiotherapy.

放射性同位素　一種元素的同位素。在其衰變為另一種元素時可放射出 α、β 或 γ 射綫。人工的放射性同位素是以中子流轟擊元素而產生的，在醫學上廣泛用作為「示踪劑」和不同放射治療技術的放射源。

radiologist *n.* a doctor specialized in the interpretation of X-rays and other scanning techniques for the diagnosis of disorders.

放射學家　專門從事分析 X 綫片來診斷病變的醫師。

radiology *n.* the branch of medicine that is concerned with the use of radiation, including X-rays, and radio active substances in the diagnosis and treatment of disease. *See also* interventional radiology, radiography (diagnostic radiology), radiotherapy (therapeutic radiology).

放射學　有關應用放射綫，包括X綫和放射性物質診斷和治療疾病的醫學分科。參閱 interventional radiology，radiography (diagnostic radiology)，radiotherapy (therapeutic radiology)。

radionecrosis *n.* necrosis (death) of tissue, commonly bone or skin, whose ability to heal has been markedly reduced by radiotherapy for a tumour. It can be induced by injury or surgery (such as tooth extraction) after irradiation.

放射性壞死　由於腫瘤的放射治療而引起的組織壞死，最常見於骨和皮膚，治愈的可能性很小。容易於放射治療後因損傷或手術（如拔牙）引起。

radionuclide *n.* a radioactive atomic nucleus used to label *tracers for diagnosis in nuclear medicine.

放射性核素　一種放射性原子核。被用於標記核醫學診斷中用的示踪劑。

radiopaque *adj.* having the property of absorbing, and therefore being opaque to, X-rays. Radiopaque materials, many of them containing iodine, are used as *contrast media in radiography (*see* diodone, iopanoic acid). Barium salts (e.g. *barium sulphate) are also radiopaque and used in barium 'meals' and enemas for the investigation of the digestive tract by X-rays.

不透 X 綫的　具有吸收 X 綫的特性，所以 X 綫不能透過。許多含有碘的不透 X 綫的物質作為造影劑用於放射造影術（參閱 diodone，iopanoic acid）。鋇鹽（例如硫酸鋇）也是不透 X 綫的，可在 X 綫檢查消化道時用作鋇餐或鋇灌腸。

radio pill a capsule containing a miniature radio transmitter that can be swallowed by a patient. During its passage through the digestive tract it transmits information about internal conditions (acidity, etc.) that can be monitored by means of a radio receiver near the patient.

放射性丸　能被病人吞咽的含有小型放射性傳遞質的膠囊。當通過消化道時能傳遞關於內在情況（酸度等等）的信息，可被放在病人身邊的放射性接收器所監測。

radioscopy *n.* examination of an X-ray image on a fluorescent screen (*see also* fluoroscope).

X 綫透視檢查　在熒光屏上的 X 綫影像檢查（參閱 fluoroscope）。

radiosensitive *adj.* describing certain forms of cancer cell that are

放射敏感的　描述某些類型癌細胞對放射綫具有特殊敏

particularly susceptible to radiation and are likely to be dealt with successfully by radiotherapy.

radiosensitizer *n*. a substance that increases the sensitivity of cells to radiation. The presence of oxygen and other compounds with a high affinity for electrons will increase radiosensitivity.

radiotherapist *n*. a doctor who specializes in treatment with radiotherapy.

radiotherapy *n*. therapeutic radiology: the treatment of disease with penetrating radiation, such as X-rays, beta rays, or gamma rays, which may be produced by machines or given off by radioactive isotopes. Beams of radiation may be directed at a diseased part from a distance (*see* telecurietherapy), or radioactive material, in the form of needles, wires, or pellets, may be implanted in the body. Many forms of cancer are destroyed by radiotherapy.

radium *n*. a radioactive metallic element that emits alpha and gamma rays during its decay into other elements. The gamma radiation is employed in *radiotherapy for the treatment of cancer. Because *radon, a radioactive gas, is released from radium, the metal must be enclosed in gas-tight containers during use. Radium is stored in lead-lined containers, which give protection from the radiation. Symbol: Ra. *See also* thorium-X.

radius *n*. the outer and shorter bone of the forearm (*compare* ulna). It partially revolves about the ulna, permitting *pronation and *supination of the hand. The head of the radius articulates with the *humerus. The lower end articulates

感性和用放射療法時易治療成功的。

放射致敏物 使細胞對放射綫敏感性增加的物質。對電子有高度親和力的氧和其他化合物，可增加放射敏感性。

放射治療學家 精通放療的醫生。

放射治療 放射治療學：用機器或放射性同位素放出穿透性射綫（X綫、β射綫或γ射綫）治療疾病。放射綫束可經一段距離直接達病變部位（參閱 telecurietherapy），或者把放射性物質以針、導絲或小球形式埋植在體內。放射治療可破壞多種癌瘤。

鐳 一種放射性金屬元素。在其衰變為其他元素時放射α和γ射綫。γ射綫用於癌的放射療法中。由於鐳可釋放放射性氣體氡，故在應用期間必須包裝於密封氣體的容器中。鐳貯存於襯有鉛的容器內以防止放射綫外射。符號：Ra。參閱 thorium-X。

橈骨 前臂外側的較短的骨（與 ulna 比較），它部分性地圍繞尺骨，可以使手旋前和旋後。橈骨頭與肱骨連成關節，下端與腕部舟狀骨和月狀骨連成關節，並與尺骨連成關

both with the scaphoid and lunate bones of the *carpus (wrist) and with the ulna (via the *ulnar notch* on the side of the bone). **–radial** *adj.*

節（依靠橈骨下端內側面的尺切迹）。

radix *n. see* root.

根　參閱 root。

radon *n.* a radioactive gaseous element that is produced during the decay of *radium. Sealed in small capsules called *radon seeds*, it is used in *radiotherapy for the treatment of cancer. It emits alpha and gamma radiation. Symbol: Rn.

氡　鐳衰變過程中產生的放射性氣體元素。封存於小膠囊中的氡叫「氡顆粒」，用於癌症的放射治療。它放射 α 與 γ 射綫。符號：Rn。

rale *n. see* crepitation.

囉音　參閱 crepitation。

Ramsay Hunt syndrome a form of *herpes zoster affecting the facial nerve, associated with facial paralysis and loss of taste. It also produces pain in the ear and other parts supplied by the nerve.

拉姆賽-亨特綜合徵（帶狀疱疹，膝狀神經節綜合徵）　一種侵犯面神經的帶狀疱疹，伴有面神經麻痺和味覺喪失。亦可引起耳痛和由該神經支配的其他部位疼痛。

Ramstedt's operation *see* pyloromyotomy.

拉姆施蒂特手術　先天性幽門狹窄環狀肌切斷術。參閱 pyloromyotomy。

ramus *n.* (*pl.* **rami**) **1.** a branch, especially of a nerve fibre or blood vessel. **2.** a thin process projecting from a bone, e.g. the rami of the *mandible.

分支　(1) 指神經纖維或血管的分支。(2) 支，指從骨上突出的細小突起，例如下頜支。

randomized controlled trial *see* intervention study.

隨機對照試驗　參閱 intervention study。

random sample a subgroup of a large population (the so-called *universe*) selected by a random process ensuring that each member of the universe has an equal chance of being included in the sample. It is sometimes *stratified* so that separate samples are drawn from each of several layers of the universe, usually on the basis of age, sex, and *social class.

隨機樣本　用隨機方法選擇的大組樣體（所謂總體）中的一個分組，以確保總體的每個成員有同等的機會入選樣本。有時採取分層抽樣。通常是根據年齡、性別和社會階層將單個樣本從總體的各層中抽出。有時通過預先確定個體羣（如鄉鎮或街道）可使選擇變得容

Selection is sometimes facilitated by identifying in advance groups of individuals (e.g. townships or neighbourhoods) whom it is deemed will together represent the whole (a so-called *sampling frame*).

易，這些個體羣被認為在一起代表整體（一個樣本框架）。

ranitidine *n.* an *antihistamine drug that inhibits gastric secretion and is used in the treatment of gastric and duodenal ulcers, oesophagitis, and the *Zollinger-Ellison syndrome. It is administered by mouth, intravenously, and intramuscularly; side-effects include headache, rash and drowsiness. Trade name: **Zantac**.

雷尼替丁　一種抑製胃酸分泌的抗組胺藥，用來治療胃和十二指腸潰瘍、食管炎及佐-埃氏綜合徵。口服、靜脈滴注或肌注用藥。副作用包括有頭痛、皮疹和倦睡。商品名：Zantac。

ranula *n.* a cyst found under the tongue, formed when the duct leading from a salivary or mucous gland is obstructed and distended.

舌下囊腫　唾液腺或黏液腺的導管阻塞和擴張形成的舌下囊腫。

raphe *n.* a line, ridge, seam, or crease in a tissue or organ, especially the line that marks the junction of two embryologically distinct parts that have fused to form a single structure in the adult. For example, the *raphe of the tongue* is the furrow that passes down the centre of the dorsal surface of the tongue.

縫　組織或器官上的綫，崤，縫或皺褶。是指在胚胎學上兩個不同部分聯接的標誌綫，而它在成人已融合成單一的結構。例如舌縫是指通過舌背側正中綫的溝。

rarefaction *n.* thinning of bony tissue sufficient to cause decreased density of bone to X-rays, as in osteoarthritis.

疏鬆　骨組織變稀疏以致在 X 綫上骨的密度減低，如在骨關節炎時。

rash *n.* a temporary eruption on the skin, usually typified by reddening – either discrete red spots or generalized reddening – which may be accompanied by itching. A rash may be a local skin reaction or the outward sign of a disorder affecting the body. Rashes commonly occur with infectious diseases, such as chickenpox and measles.

皮疹　皮膚暫時性皮疹。通常的特徵是發紅（可為散在的紅斑點，也可為全身性發紅），並伴有刺癢。皮疹可是局部皮膚的反應，或是體內病變的外表徵象。皮疹常發生於傳染病，如水痘和麻疹。

raspatory *n.* a filelike surgical instrument used for scraping the surface of bone (see illustration).

骨銼　銼刀樣的外科器械，用於刮骨頭表面（見圖）。

A rib raspatory
肋骨骨銼

rat-bite fever (sodokosis) a disease, contracted from the bite of a rat, due to infection by either the bacterium *Spirillum minus*, which causes ulceration of the skin and recurrent fever, or by the fungus *Streptobacillus moniliformis*, which causes inflammation of the skin, muscular pains, and vomiting. Both infections respond well to penicillin.

鼠咬熱　由鼠咬引起的疾病。因鼠咬熱螺旋體感染所致，可引起皮膚潰瘍，反覆發熱。或是因念珠狀鏈桿菌的真菌感染所致，可引起皮膚炎症，肌肉疼痛和嘔吐。青黴素治療對兩種感染均有效。

rationalization *n.* (in psychiatry) the explanation of events or behaviour in terms that avoid giving the true reasons. For example, a patient may explain not going to a party in terms of being too tired whereas he did not go because he was afraid of meeting new people.

文飾　（精神病學）解釋某事情或行為時避開講真實原因的表現。例如：一病人解釋他不去參加晚會是由於太疲乏，其實他不去的原因是怕遇見生人。

rauwolfia *n.* the dried root of the shrub *Rauwolfia serpentina*, which contains several alkaloids, including *reserpine. Rauwolfia and its alkaloids lower blood pressure and depress activity of the central nervous system. They were formerly used as tranquillizers in the treatment of mental illness but have been replaced by more effective and reliable drugs.

蘿芙木　印度蘿芙木的乾根。含有數種生物鹼，如利血平。蘿芙木與其生物鹼可降低血壓和抑製中樞神經系統活動。以往曾作為安定藥物治療精神病。現已由更有效和可靠的藥物替代。

Raynaud's disease a condition of unknown cause in which the arteries of the fingers are unduly reactive and enter

雷諾病　一種原因不明的病狀，當手遇冷時，手指動脈過度反應和發生痙攣（血管痙

spasm (*angiospasm* or *vasospasm*) when the hands are cold. This produces attacks of pallor, numbness, and discomfort in the fingers. A similar condition (*Raynaud's phenomenon*) may result from atherosclerosis, connective-tissue diseases, ingestion of ergot derivatives, or the frequent use of vibrating tools. Gangrene or ulceration of the fingertips may result from lack of blood to the affected part. Warm gloves and antispasmodic drugs (such as phenoxybenzamine) may relieve the condition. In unresponsive cases *sympathectomy is of value.

攣），可引起手指陣發性蒼白、麻木和不適。動脈粥樣硬化、膠原病、攝入麥角衍生物，以及經常使用振動的工具也可引起類似病狀（雷諾現象）。因指尖缺血可引起壞疽或潰瘍。溫暖的手套和抗痙攣藥（如酚苄明）可緩解此徵象。對無效病例作交感神經切除術是有價值的。

reaction formation (in psychoanalysis) a *defence mechanism by which unacceptable unconscious ideas are replaced by the opposite conscious attitude. For instance, a man might make an ostentatious show of affection to a person for whom he has an unconscious hatred.

反應形成 （精神分析）一種心理防禦機制，即潛意識的不能接受的想法被相反的有意識的態度所替代，例如：一個對他在潛意識中憎恨的人可能做出誇大的愛慕的表示。

reactive *adj.* describing mental illnesses that are precipitated by events in the psychological environment.

反應性的 描述心理環境中的重大事件所促發的精神病。

reagin *n.* a type of *antibody, formed against an allergen, that has special affinity for cell membranes and remains fixed in various tissues. Subsequent contact with the allergen causes damage to the tissues when the antigen-antibody reaction occurs. The damaged cells, particularly *mast cells, release histamine and serotonin, which are responsible for the local inflammation of an allergy or the very severe effects of anaphylactic shock (*see* anaphylaxis). Reagins belong to the IgE class of *immunoglobulins.

反應素 指針對某種變應原而形成的一種抗體，對細胞膜有特殊親和力，固定地留存在不同組織中。當以後再與變應原接觸時，就發生抗原抗體反應引起組織損傷。損傷的細胞，特別是肥大細胞，釋放組胺和5-羥色胺，引起局部的變態反應性炎症或過敏性休克等非常嚴重的後果（參閱 anaphylaxis）。反應素是屬於 IgE 類的免疫球蛋白。

reamer *n.* an instrument used in *endodontics to prepare the walls of a root canal for *root canal treatment.

擴孔鑽 牙髓病進行根管治療時用來製備牙根管壁的工具。

receptaculum *n.* the dilated portion of a tubular anatomical part. The *receptaculum* (or *cisterna*) *chyli* is the dilated end of the *thoracic duct, into which lymph vessels from the lower limbs and intestines drain.

接受池　解剖學上管狀結構的擴張部分。乳糜池是指胸導管起始端的擴張部，下肢與腸道的淋巴管匯入其中。

receptor *n.* a cell or group of cells specialized to detect changes in the environment and trigger impulses in the sensory nervous system. All sensory nerve endings act as receptors, whether they simply detect touch, as in the skin, or chemical substances, as in the nose and tongue, or sound or light, as in the ear and eye. *See* exteroceptor, interoceptor, mechanoreceptor, proprioceptor.

感受器　能探測到環境中的變化和觸發感覺神經衝動的一個或一羣特異細胞。所有感覺神經末梢都具有感受器的作用。例如，在皮膚中它們能感受觸覺，鼻與舌中能感受化學物質，而耳和眼中能感受到聲音和光綫。參閱　exteroceptor，interoceptor，mechanoreceptor，propriocepor。

recess *n.* (in anatomy) a hollow chamber or a depression in an organ or other part.

隱窩　（解剖學）器官或其他部分的凹窩或腔洞。

recessive *adj.* describing a gene (or its corresponding characteristic) whose effect is shown in the individual only when its *allele is the same, i.e. when two such alleles are present (the *double recessive* condition). Many hereditary diseases (including cystic fibrosis) are due to the presence of a defective gene as a double recessive. *Compare* dominant. **–recessive** *n.*

隱性的　形容一種基因（或它的相應特徵），這種基因的作用只有在等位基因相同情況下才會在個體上顯現出來。與dominant 對比。

recipient *n.* a person who receives something from a *donor, such as a blood transfusion or a kidney transplant.

受者　從供者接受某種物質者，例如輸血或腎移植。

recombinant DNA DNA that contains genes from different sources that have been combined by the techniques of *genetic engineering rather than by breeding experiments. Genetic engineering is therefore also known as *recombinant DNA technology.*

重組DNA　含有經過基因工程技術而不是繁殖實驗而組合起來的不同源基因的DNA，因此基因工程也叫重組DNA技術。

record linkage the means by which information about health events from several different sources (e.g. hospital attendance, vaccination, and consultation with general practitioners) are all related to a specific individual in a common file or more usually a computerized record. This contrasts with data in which events only are recorded (*see* Hospital In-Patient Enquiry) and two separate individuals treated for the same disease cannot be distinguished from one individual treated on two separate occasions.

連鎖記錄　一種記錄方法，能將某人健康情況的幾個不同來源的信息（例如：醫院的治療護理，預防注射情況，全科醫生的診治）歸併於一個共同的檔案內，或通常輸入電腦內。這與僅記錄事件的資料（參閱Hospital In-patient Enquiry）不同。在那種資料中，不能將兩個人因為同一疾病接受治療的記錄與一個人分別兩次接受治療的記錄加以區別。

recrudescence *n.* a fresh outbreak of a disorder in a patient after a period during which its signs and symptoms had died down and recovery seemed to be taking place.

復發　病人在症狀體徵消失和已康復後，經過一段時期，疾病又重新發作。

recruitment *n.* **1.** (in physiology) the phenomenon whereby an increase in the strength of a stimulus or repetition of the stimulus will stimulate increasing numbers of nerve cells to respond. **2.** the *loudness recruitment test*: a test of hearing used to distinguish deafness due to disease of the *cochlea (in the inner ear) from other causes of deafness. In cochlear deafness, while quiet sounds are heard with difficulty in the deaf ear compared with the normal one, louder sounds are heard equally well in both ears.

(1) 反射增進　（生理學）是指刺激強度的增加或重複刺激使更多的神經細胞受刺激而發生反應。**(2)** 複聽　指高聲複聽試驗，一種常用於區別耳蝸（內耳）病變所引起的耳聾和其他原因的耳聾的聽力試驗。在耳蝸性耳聾時，聾側耳朵聽較輕的聲音比正常耳朵困難，較響的聲音兩耳聽得同樣清楚。

rect- (recto-) *prefix denoting* the rectum. Examples: *rectouterine* (relating to the rectum and uterus); *rectovesical* (relating to the rectum and bladder).

〔前綴〕直腸　例如：直腸子宮的，直腸膀胱的。

rectocele *n. see* proctocele.

直腸突出　參閱 proctocele。

rectosigmoid *n.* the region of the large intestine around the junction of the sigmoid colon and the rectum.

直腸乙狀結腸　直腸與乙狀結腸相連處的大腸部分。

rectum *n.* the terminal part of the large *intestine, about 12 cm long, which runs from the sigmoid colon to the anal canal. Faeces are stored in the rectum before defecation. **–rectal** *adj.*

rectus *n.* any of several straight muscles. The *rectus muscles of the orbit* are some of the extrinsic *eye muscles. *Rectus abdominis* is a long flat muscle that extends bilaterally along the entire length of the front of the abdomen. The rectus muscles acting together serve to bend the trunk forwards; acting separately they bend the body sideways. The *rectus femoris* forms part of the *quadriceps.

recurrent *adj.* (in anatomy) describing a structure, such as a nerve or blood vessel, that turns back on its course, forming a loop.

red blood cell *see* erythrocyte.

redia *n.* (*pl.* **rediae**) the third-stage larva of a parasitic *fluke. Rediae develop within the body of a freshwater snail and undergo a process of asexual reproduction, giving rise to many fourth-stage larvae called *cercariae. *See also* miracidium, sporocyst.

reduction *n.* (in surgery) the restoration of a displaced part of the body to its normal position by manipulation or operation. The fragments of a broken bone are reduced before a splint is applied; a dislocated joint is reduced to its normal seating; or a hernia is reduced when the displaced organ or tissue is returned to its usual anatomical site.

reduction division the first division of *meiosis, in which the chromosome

直腸　大腸的終端部分，約12 cm 長，它始於乙狀結腸，下達肛門。在排便前糞便存於直腸。

直肌　有以下幾種：眼眶的直肌是幾條眼外肌。腹直肌是沿整個腹前部兩側延伸的長而扁平的肌肉，兩條直肌共同起作用時可使軀體前彎，一條直肌起作用時可使身體側彎。股直肌是股四頭肌的一部分。

返回的　（解剖學）形容一種結構如神經或血管在走行過程中折返回來形成一種祥。

紅細胞　參閱 erythrocyte。

雷蚴　吸蟲類寄生蟲的第三期幼蟲。雷蚴在淡水螺體內發育，並進行無性生殖，產生許多第四期幼蟲，稱為尾蚴。參閱 miracidium，sporocyst。

復位術　（外科學）通過手法或手術操作將身體的錯位部分回復到正常位置。治療骨折時在用夾板前先行斷骨復位；使脫位的關節恢復其正常位置；疝復位時，錯位的器官和組織被恢復至其正常的解剖部位。

減數分裂　成熟細胞分裂的第一次分裂，此時染色體數目減

number is halved. The term is sometimes used as a synonym for the whole of meiosis.

半。此術語有時用作為整個成熟細胞分裂的同義語。

reduplication *n.* doubling of the heart sounds, which may be heard in healthly individuals and shows variation with respiration due to the slightly asynchronous closure of the heart valves.

重疊音 可於健康人聽到的雙重心音，隨呼吸而變化，是由於心臟瓣膜輕度的關閉不同步所致。

reduviid *n.* any one of a group of winged insects (Reduviidae) whose mouthparts – adapted for piercing and sucking – take the form of a long proboscis that is tucked beneath the head when not in use. Some South American genera, notably *Panstrongylus*, *Rhodnius*, and *Triatoma* – the kissing bugs, are nocturnal blood-sucking insects that transmit the parasite causing *Chagas' disease in man.

獵蝽 一組有翅的昆蟲類（獵蝽科）。它的口部呈一個長喙狀，適於刺穿和吮吸，當不用時就卷藏在頭的下部。有些南美種類，如錐蝽屬，紅獵蝽屬和獵蝽屬，是天然的吸血昆蟲，並將寄生蟲傳播給人引起恰加斯病（南美洲錐蟲病）。

Reduvius *n.* a genus of predatory blood-sucking reduviid bugs. *R. personatus*, widely distributed in Europe, normally preys upon insects but occasionally attacks man. Its bite causes various allergic symptoms, including rash, nausea, and palpitations.

獵蝽屬 一屬食蟲的吸血昆蟲。廣泛分布於歐洲的偽裝獵蝽，通常捕食昆蟲，但有時也侵襲人類。被咬後可引起各種過敏症狀，如皮疹、惡心和心悸。

Reed-Sternberg cell *see* Sternberg-Reed cell.

里-斯氏細胞 參閱 Sternberg-Reed cell。

referred pain (synalgia) pain felt in a part of the body other than where it might be expected. An abscess beneath the diaphragm, for example, may cause a referred pain in the shoulder area, while heart disorders may cause pain in the left arm and fingers. The confusion arises because sensory nerves from different parts of the body share common pathways when they reach the spinal cord.

牽涉痛 不是在預期的身體部位發生的疼痛感覺。例如：膈下膿腫可引起肩部牽涉性疼痛，心臟病可引起左臂和手指疼痛，引起這種感覺錯位的原因是由於身體不同部位的感覺神經經過共同的通路到達脊髓。

reflex *n.* an automatic or involuntary activity brought about by relatively simple nervous circuits, without consciousness being necessarily involved. Thus a painful stimulus such as a pinprick will bring about the reflex of withdrawing the finger before the brain has had time to send a message to the muscles involved. *See* conditioned reflex, patellar reflex, plantar reflex.

反射　由比較簡單的神經回路引起而不需要意識參與的一種不隨意的自主性活動。例如，針刺這樣的疼痛刺激，在大腦輸送信息到有關的肌肉之前就引起手指回縮反射。參閱 conditioned reflex，patellar reflex，plantar reflex。

reflex arc the nervous circuit involved in a *reflex, being at its simplest a sensory nerve with a receptor, linked at a synapse in the brain or spinal cord with a motor nerve, which supplies a muscle or gland (see illustration). In a simple reflex (such as the *patellar reflex) only two neurones may be involved, but in other reflexes there may be several *interneurones in the arc.

反射弧　參與一個反射的神經回路，其最簡單的是一個連接感受器的感覺神經，與支配肌肉或腺體的運動神經在大腦或脊髓內形成突觸連接（見圖）。在一簡單反射中（例如膝反射）可能有兩個神經元參加，但另一些反射的反射弧中可有幾個中間神經元。

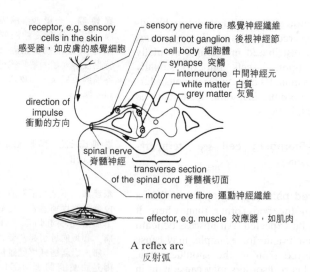

receptor, e.g. sensory cells in the skin 感受器，如皮膚的感覺細胞
sensory nerve fibre 感覺神經纖維
dorsal root ganglion 後根神經節
cell body 細胞體
synapse 突觸
interneurone 中間神經元
white matter 白質
grey matter 灰質
direction of impulse 衝動的方向
spinal nerve 脊髓神經
transverse section of the spinal cord 脊髓橫切面
motor nerve fibre 運動神經纖維
effector, e.g. muscle 效應器，如肌肉

A reflex arc
反射弧

reflux *n.* a backflow of liquid, against its normal direction of movement. *See also* (reflux) oesophagitis, vesicoureteric reflux.

返流　與其液體正常運動方向相反的逆流。參閱 (reflux) oesophagitis，vesicoureteric reflux。

refraction *n.* **1.** the change in direction of light rays when they pass obliquely from one transparent medium to another, of a different density. Refraction occurs as light enters the eye, when it passes from air to the media of the eye, i.e. cornea, aqueous humour, lens, and vitreous humour, to come to a focus on the retina. Errors of refraction, in which light rays do not come to a focus on the retina due to defects in the refracting media or shape of the eyeball, include astigmatism and long- and shortsightedness. **2.** determination of the power of refraction of the eye. This gives the degree to which the eye differs from normal, which will determine whether or not the patient needs glasses and, if so, how strong they should be.

(1) 折射 當光綫通過一個透明介質斜向射入另一個不同密度的介質時發生光綫方向改變。光綫進入眼睛時發生折射，當它從空氣到眼睛的介質，即角膜、房水、晶狀體和玻璃體，在視網膜形成一個聚光點。屈光不正時，由於折射介質或眼球外形有缺損，光綫不能在視網膜上形成聚光點，如散光、遠視和近視。**(2) 驗光** 眼睛折射力的測定。可以得知眼睛和正常相差的程度，由此決定患者是否需配眼鏡，以及眼鏡的度數。

refractometer *n.* *see* optometer.

屈光計　參閱 optometer。

refractory *adj.* unresponsive: applied to a condition that fails to respond satisfactorily to a given treatment.

難治性的　治療無效的，指治療未獲得滿意療效的狀況。

refractory period (in neurology) the time of recovery needed for a nerve cell that has just transmitted a nerve impulse or for a muscle fibre that has just contracted. During the refractory period a normal stimulus will not bring about excitation of the cell, which is undergoing *repolarization.

不應期　（神經病學）神經細胞剛傳遞過神經衝動或肌肉纖維剛收縮後需要的恢復時間。在不應期內，正常刺激將不會引起正處在復極化的細胞興奮。

refrigeration *n.* lowering the temperature of a part of the body to reduce the metabolic activity of its tissues or to provide a local anaesthetic effect.

降溫　為減少組織的代謝活動，或提供一個局部麻醉效應而降低身體某部分的溫度。

regimen *n.* (in therapeutics) a prescribed systematic form of treatment, such as a diet, course of drugs, or special exercises, for curing disease or improving health.

治療方案　（治療學）為治療疾病或改善健康而規定的系統治療方案，如膳食，藥物療程或特殊的鍛煉。

Regional Health Authority *see* National Health Service.

地區衛生局　參閱　National Health Service。

regional ileitis *see* Crohn's disease.

局限性結腸炎　參閱　Crohn's disease。

Regional Manpower Committee *see* manpower committee.

地區人力委員會　參閱　manpower committee。

Regional Medical Committee *see* medical committee.

地區醫學委員會　參閱　medical committee。

Regional Medical Officer *see* public health physician.

地區醫學官員　參閱　public health physician。

regional specialty *see* catchment area.

局限性專業　參閱　catchment area。

registrar *n.* (in a hospital) a relatively experienced trainee physician or surgeon responsible for the care of a number of patients with the assistance of junior doctors, whom he instructs. *Senior registrars* undergo highly specialist training after which they are normally promoted to a *consultant post; a senior registrar may work with one or more senior surgeons, physicians, or consultants.

主管醫師　(醫院內) 相對有經驗的內科醫師或外科醫師。他指導低年資醫師作為其助手，負責治療一定數量的病人。高年資主管醫師經過高水平專業培訓後，通常晉升為高級醫師。一位高年資主管醫師可與一個或多個高年資外科醫師、內科醫師或高級醫師共同工作。

regression *n.* **1.** (in psychiatry) reversion to a more immature level of functioning. The term may be applied to the state of a patient in hospital who becomes incontinent and demanding. It may also be applied to a single psychological function; for example, psychoanalysts speak of the *libido regressing to an early stage of development. **2.** the stage of a disease during which the signs and symptoms disappear and the patient recovers.

(1) 退化　(精神病學) 倒退至較不成熟的功能水平。此術語可用於住院病人處於失控或要求過分的狀態，也可應用於單一的心理學功能方面，例如，精神分析學家所提到的性慾退化至早期發育的階段。**(2) 消退**　病人的症狀和體徵消失或恢復時期。

regurgitation *n.* **1.** the bringing up of undigested material from the stomach to the mouth (*see* vomiting). **2.** the flowing

(1) 反胃　不消化的食物從胃返到口腔 (參閱 vomiting)。
(2) 回流　液體的流動方向和

back of a liquid in a direction opposite to the normal one, as when blood surges back through a defective valve in the heart after the heart has contracted.

正常相反，如心臟收縮後血液通過缺損的瓣膜向回流。

rehabilitation 1. (in *physical medicine) the treatment of an ill, injured, or disabled patient with the aim of restoring normal health and function or to prevent the disability from getting worse. **2.** any means for restoring the independence of a patient after diseases or injury, including employment retraining.

康復 **(1)**（理療學）用以治療疾病、外傷或殘疾，使病人恢復到正常的健康和功能，預防病情惡化的方法。**(2)** 任何使病後或受損傷後的病人恢復獨立能力的方法，包括就業再訓練。

reimplantation *n. see* replantation.

再植 參閱 replantation。

reinforcement *n.* (in psychology) the strengthening of a conditioned reflex (*see* conditioning). In classical conditioning this takes place when a conditioned stimulus is presented at the same time as – or just before – the unconditioned stimulus. In operant conditioning it takes place when a pleasurable event (or *reinforcer*), such as a reward, follows immediately after some behaviour. The *reinforcement schedule* governs how often and when such behaviour is rewarded. Different schedules produce different effects on behaviour.

強化 （心理學）指條件反射的強化（參閱 conditioning）。在經典的條件反射中，當條件刺激與非條件刺激同時出現，或稍早一些出現。在操作或條件反射時，強化作用發生在緊跟某行動之後立即給以愉快的事物（或強化劑），例如，在某些行動之後立即給予獎賞。強化的方案規定對這些行為的獎賞次數和時間。不同的方案產生不同的效應。

Reissner's membrane the membrane that separates the scala vestibuli and the scala media of the *cochlea of the ear.

前庭膜 將耳蝸前庭階和鼓階分隔的膜。

Reiter's syndrome a condition characterized by inflammation of the urethra (*see* urethritis), conjunctivitis, and arthritis. Horny areas may develop on the skin. No causative agent has been positively identified, although a virus may be implicated.

賴特爾綜合徵 以尿道炎（參閱 urethritis）、結膜炎和關節炎為特徵的狀態。皮膚上可發生角化區。病因未能確定，但可能與病毒有關。

rejection *n.* (in transplantation) the destruction by immune mechanisms

排異反應 （在移植中）從另一個人移植來的組織被免疫機制

of a tissue grafted from another individual. Antibodies, complement, clotting factors, and platelets are involved in the failure of the graft to survive. *Homograft rejection is a vigorous response that can be modified by drugs, such as cyclosporin A; *heterograft rejection is a violent acute response that is at present beyond therapeutic control.

所破壞。抗體、補體、凝血因子、血小板使移植物無法存活。同種移植排異是可用藥物限制的強烈反應，例如環孢菌素A；異種移植排異是目前超出治療控制以外的劇烈的急性反應。

relapse n. a return of disease symptoms after recovery had apparently been achieved or the worsening of an apparently recovering patient's condition during the course of an illness.

復發　指疾病明顯痊愈後，症狀又重新發生，或者在疾病過程中病人情況明顯恢復時又惡化。

relapsing fever an infectious disease caused by bacteria of the genus *Borrelia*, which is transmitted by ticks or lice and results in recurrent fever. The first episode of fever occurs about a week after infection: it is accompanied by severe headache and aching muscles and joints and lasts 2–8 days. Subsequent attacks are milder and occur at intervals of 3–10 days; untreated, the attacks may continue for up to 12 weeks. Treatment with antibiotics, such as tetracycline or erythromycin, is effective.

回歸熱　包柔螺旋體屬細菌引起的傳染病，由壁虱或體虱傳播，並引起反覆的發熱。第一次發熱大約發生於感染後一周，伴有頭痛，肌肉痛和關節痛，並持續 2~8 天。隨後的發作稍輕，間隔 3~10 天；若不治療，發作可持續 12 周。用抗生素治療有效，如四環素或紅黴素。

relative analgesia a sedation technique, used particularly in dentistry, in which a mixture of *nitrous oxide and oxygen is given. The patient remains conscious throughout; the technique is used to supplement local anaesthesia in nervous patients.

相對止痛法　一種鎮痛方法，特別應用於牙科，即給予氧化亞氮和氧的混合劑，病人始終保持意識清醒。此方法用於神經質病人，作局部麻醉的輔助手段。

relative density see specific gravity.

比重　參閱 specific gravity。

relaxant n. an agent that reduces tension and strain, particularly in muscles (see muscle relaxant).

鬆弛劑　主要減輕肌肉緊張和勞損的一種藥物（參閱 muscle relaxant）。

relaxation *n*. (in physiology) the diminution of tension in a muscle, which occurs when it ceases to contract: the state of a resting muscle.

鬆弛 （生理學）肌張力減弱，發生於肌肉停止收縮即肌肉靜息狀態時。

relaxation therapy treatment by teaching a patient to decrease his anxiety by reducing the tone in his muscles. This can be used by itself to help people cope with stressful situations or as a part of *desensitization to specific fears.

鬆弛療法 教病人通過降低肌肉張力來減輕病人的憂慮。人們可以用此方法幫助自己對付緊張狀態，或減少對特殊事物懼怕的敏感性。

relaxin *n*. a hormone, secreted by the placenta in the terminal stages of pregnancy, that causes the cervix (neck) of the uterus to dilate and prepares the uterus for the action of *oxytocin during labour.

弛緩素 妊娠末期胎盤所分泌的一種激素，也可引起子宮頸擴張，並使子宮對分娩時縮宮素的作用有所準備。

reline *n*. the procedure by which the fitting surface of a denture is rebased to make it fit a jaw that has undergone resorption since the denture was originally made. The procedure is often necessary for dentures that were fitted immediately after extraction of the teeth.

托牙墊底術 一種牙科技術，將假的吻合面重新墊底，以便與原先假牙配成後又發生骨質吸收的頜骨相符合。對拔牙後立即安裝的假牙常需要這種技術。

rem *n*. roentgen equivalent man: a former unit dose of ionizing radiation equal to the dose that gives the same biological effect as that due to one roentgen of X-rays. The rem has been replaced by the *sievert.

雷姆 人體倫琴當量，是過去用的電離輻射單位，相等於一個倫琴 X 綫所產生的同樣生物效應的劑量。雷姆現已被希（沃特）所代替。

REM rapid eye movement: describing a stage of *sleep during which the muscles of the eyeballs are in constant motion behind the eyelids. People woken up during this stage of sleep generally report that they were dreaming at the time.

快動眼睡眠 眼球快速運動：描述睡眠的一個時相，此時眼球在眼瞼後不斷地運動。在該睡眠時相醒來的人往往訴說他們此時正在做夢。

remedial profession any profession (including occupational therapy, physiotherapy, and speech therapy) in which

治療性職業 （包括職業治療、理療和語言治療）治療學家用他們的專業技術幫助殘疾人

the therapists use their skills to assist those with *handicap to achieve living and working standards as near normal as possible.

remission *n.* **1.** a lessening in the severity of symptoms or their temporary disappearance during the course of an illness. **2.** a reduction in the size of a cancer and the symptoms it is causing.

remittent fever *see* fever.

Remploy *n.* (in Britain) a nationally financed system of sheltered employment for those with severe *handicap in specially designed workshops managed and financed by the Department of Employment. Limited numbers of able-bodied craftsmen are included on the payroll to assist with administration and supervision and also to carry out tasks that would be potentially dangerous for those with handicap. Goods produced (especially furniture and luggage) are sold on the open market.

renal *adj.* relating to or affecting the kidneys.

renal artery either of two large arteries arising from the abdominal aorta and supplying the kidneys. Each renal artery divides into an anterior and a posterior branch before entering the kidney.

renal cell carcinoma *see* hypernephroma.

renal function tests tests for assessing the function of the kidneys. These include measurements of the specific gravity of urine, creatinine *clearance time, and blood urea levels; intravenous *pyelography; and renal angiography.

獲得盡可能正常的生活和工作水平。

(1) 緩解 在疾病的過程中症狀嚴重程度減輕或暫時消失。 **(2) 縮小，減輕** 由癌症所引起的症狀減輕或癌腫體積縮小。

弛張熱 參閱 fever。

殘疾人就業保障 （在英國）由國家撥款保護嚴重殘疾病人就業的制度。他們在專門設計的工廠中就業，這種工廠由就業部門管理和提供資金。為了幫助管理，監督和開展一些對殘疾人可能有危險的工作，在就業人員中包括有少數體格健全的手藝人。生產的產品（尤其是家具和皮箱）在公開市場上出售。

腎的 與腎臟相關或影響腎臟的。

腎動脈 來源於腹主動脈的供應腎臟的兩根大動脈，每一側腎動脈在人腎前分為前支與後支。

腎細胞癌 參閱 hypernephroma。

腎功能試驗 為評價腎的功能而做的試驗。包括尿比重、肌酐清除率和血的尿素水平等測量，靜脈腎盂造影和腎動脈造影。

renal transplantation *see* transplantation.

腎移植　參閱 transplantation。

renal tubule (uriniferous tubule) the fine tubular part of a *nephron, through which water and certain dissolved substances are reabsorbed back into the blood.

腎小管　腎單位的細管狀部分，水分與一些溶解的物質通過時被重新吸收入血液。

reni- (reno-) *prefix denoting* the kidney.

〔前綴〕腎（臟）

renin *n.* an enzyme released into the blood by the kidney in response to stress. It reacts with a substrate from the liver to produce *angiotensin, which causes constriction of blood vessels and thus an increase in blood pressure. Excessive production of renin results in the syndrome of renal *hypertension.

腎素　腎臟對應激狀態起反應而釋放至血液的酶。它與肝臟產生的一種物質起反應而生成血管緊張素，後者引起血管收縮而增高血壓。腎素形成過多會引起腎性高血壓綜合徵。

rennin *n.* an enzyme produced in the stomach that coagulates milk. It is secreted by the gastric glands in an inactive form, *prorennin*, which is activated by hydrochloric acid. Rennin converts caseinogen (milk protein) into insoluble casein in the presence of calcium ions. This ensures that the milk remains in the stomach, exposed to protein-digesting enzymes, for as long as possible. The largest amounts of rennin are present in the stomachs of young mammals.

凝乳酶　一種在胃內產生的凝固牛乳的酶。胃腺分泌的是無活性的前凝乳酶，後者被鹽酸激活。在鈣離子參與下可使酪蛋白原（牛乳蛋白）轉換成不溶解的酪蛋白。這可保證牛乳在胃內停留受蛋白消化酶作用的時間盡可能延長。在年幼的哺乳動物的胃內有大量的凝乳酶。

renography *n.* the radiological study of the kidneys by a *gamma camera following the intravenous injection of a radioactive substance, which is concentrated and excreted by the kidneys. The radioactive isotope (usually *technetium-99) emits gamma rays, which are recorded by the camera positioned over the kidneys. The resultant graph of each kidney gives information regarding function and rate of drainage.

腎造影術　將某種在腎臟濃集和由腎排泄的放射性物質由靜脈注射後，用 γ 照相機對腎臟進行放射學研究。放射性同位素（通常是 ⁹⁹ 鍀）放射出 γ 射綫，由位於腎臟上面的照相機記錄下來。對每個腎臟描繪的結果提供關於腎臟功能和排泄率的資料。

reovirus *n.* one of a group of small RNA-containing viruses that infect both respiratory and intestinal tracts without producing specific or serious diseases (and were therefore termed *r*espiratory *e*nteric *o*rphan viruses). *Compare* echovirus.

呼吸道腸道病毒 一組感染呼吸道和腸道的含核糖核酸的小病毒，不引起特異性的或嚴重的疾病（所以命名為呼吸道和腸道孤兒病毒）。與 echovirus 對比。

repetitive strain injury (RSI) pain with associated loss of function in a limb resulting from its repeated movement or sustained static loading. *Tenosynovitis and *tendovaginitis of the wrist associated with typing or operating a word processor is the injury most frequently encountered. When an industrial cause is identified and negligence of the employer proven, financial compensation is indicated.

重複緊張性損傷 因重複動作或持久不變的動作所引起與肢體功能喪失相聯繫的疼痛，與打字及操作文字處理機有關的腕部腱鞘炎，是最常見的損傷。當某一工業性原因被確定，而且證明被僱主忽視時，經濟賠償是必要的。

replacement bone a bone that is formed by replacing cartilage with bony material.

軟骨成骨 由骨質取代軟骨而形成的骨。

replantation *n.* **1.** a developing specialty for the reattachment of severed limbs (or parts of limbs) and other body parts (e.g. the nose). It employs techniques of *microsurgery to rejoin nerves and vessels. **2.** (also **reimplantation**) (in dentistry) the reinsertion of a tooth into its socket after its accidental or deliberate removal. **–replant** *vb.*

再植 **(1)** 是一門正在發展中的專業，它可使嚴重損傷的肢體（或肢體的部分）和身體其他部位（例如鼻）重新恢復形態和功能。該專業應用顯微外科技術使神經以及血管再接。**(2)**（牙科學中又稱再種植），指因意外或有意去掉牙後，重新將牙插入牙槽。

replication *n.* the process by which *DNA makes copies of itself when the cell divides. The two strands of the DNA molecule unwind and each strand directs the synthesis of a new strand complementary to itself (see illustration).

複製 細胞分裂時脱氧核糖核酸自身複製的過程。脱氧核糖核酸分子的雙鏈解鏈，每個鏈指導其新的互補鏈的合成（見圖）。

repolarization *n.* the process in which the membrane of a nerve cell returns to its normal electrically charged state after a nerve impulse has passed. During the

復極化 神經衝動經過後，神經細胞膜恢復其正常的帶電狀態。神經衝動經過時，膜分子結構的短暫改變使得大量離

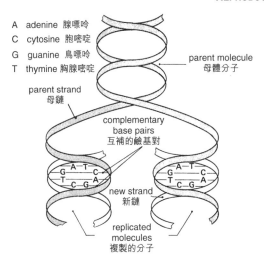

A adenine 腺嘌呤
C cytosine 胞嘧啶
G guanine 鳥嘌呤
T thymine 胸腺嘧啶

parent molecule
母體分子

parent strand
母鏈

complementary
base pairs
互補的鹼基對

new strand
新鏈

replicated
molecules
複製的分子

Replication of a DNA molecule
脫氧核糖核酸分子的複製

passage of a nerve impulse a temporary change in the molecular structure of the membrane allows a surge of ions across the membrane (*see* action potential). During repolarization ions diffuse back to restore the charge and the nerve becomes ready to transmit further impulses. *See* refractory period.

子通過細胞膜（參閱 action potential）。復極化時離子擴散回細胞，恢復電荷，神經也準備着傳遞下一個衝動。參閱 refractory period。

repositor *n.* an instrument used to return a displaced part of the body – for instance, a prolapsed uterus – to its normal position.

復位器　用於身體脫位部分回復原來位置的器械。例如將脫垂子宮回復到正常位置。

repression *n.* (in *psychoanalysis) the process of excluding an unacceptable wish or an idea from conscious mental life. The repressed material may give rise to symptoms. One goal of psychoanalysis is to return repressed material to conscious awareness so that it may be dealt with rationally.

壓抑　（精神分析）從有意識的精神生活中排除一種不能接受的願望和思想的過程。被壓抑的東西可能引起一些症狀。精神分析的目的之一是使被壓抑的東西回到意識中以便合理地進行治療。

reproduction rate *see* fertility rate.

生育率　參閱 fertility rate。

reproductive system the combination of organs and tissues associated with the process of reproduction. In males it includes the testes, vasa deferentia, prostate gland, seminal vesicles, urethra, and penis; in females it includes the ovaries, Fallopian tubes, uterus, vagina, and vulva. (See illustration.)

生殖系統 與生殖過程有關的器官和組織有機的聯繫在一起構成該系統。男性生殖系統包括睪丸、輸精管、前列腺、精囊腺，尿道和陰莖；女性生殖系統包括卵巢，輸卵管、子宮、陰道和外陰（見圖）。

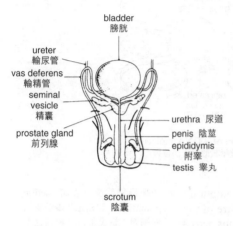

Male reproductive system
男性生殖系統

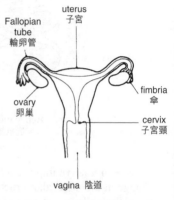

Female reproductive system
女性生殖系統

resection n. surgical removal of a portion of any part of the body. For example, a section of diseased intestine may be removed and the healthy ends sewn together. A *submucous resection* is removal of part of the cartilage septum (central division) of the nose that has become deviated, usually by injury. *Transurethral resection of the prostate* (*TUR* or *TURP*) – an operation performed when the prostate gland becomes enlarged – involves removal of portions of the gland through the urethra using an instrument called a *resectoscope*.

切除術 將身體任何一部分切除的外科手術。例如：將一段病變腸管切除，將健康的兩端互相縫合。黏膜下切除術就是將因外傷引起的鼻中隔軟骨彎曲部分切除的手術。經尿道前列腺切除術，就是當前列腺肥大時，用一種稱為切除器的器械，通過尿道將前列腺部分切除的手術。

resectoscope n. a type of surgical instrument (an **endoscope) used in resection of the prostate or in the removal of bladder tumours.

切除鏡 一種用於前列腺切除術或切除膀胱腫瘤手術的外科器械（內窺鏡之一）。

reserpine *n.* a drug extracted from *rauwolfia. Administered by mouth or injection, it has been used to lower high blood pressure. Side-effects often include mental depression, nasal congestion, and digestive upsets.

利血平　從蘿芙木中提取的一種藥物。用於口服或注射以降低高血壓。副作用常包括精神抑鬱、鼻充血和消化不良。

reserve volume the extra volume of air that an individual could inhale or exhale if he is not breathing to the limit of his capacity.

貯量　當呼吸不能達到肺活量限度時，人能吸入和呼出的額外空氣量。

residual volume the volume of air that remains in the lungs after the individual has breathed out as much as he can. This volume is increased in *emphysema.

殘氣量　個體在盡可能呼氣後，肺內殘留的氣量。當肺氣腫時殘氣量增加。

resistance *n.* **1.** the degree of *immunity that the body possesses: a measure of its ability to withstand disease. **2.** the degree to which a disease or disease-causing organism remains unaffected by antibiotics or other drugs.

(1) 抵抗力　機體具有的免疫程度，是其承受疾病能力的度量。(2) 耐藥性　疾病或致病細菌不受抗生素或其他藥物影響的程度。

resolution *n.* **1.** the stage during which inflammation gradually disappears. **2.** the degree to which individual details can be distinguished by the eye, as through a *microscope.

(1) 消散　炎症逐漸消失的階段。(2) 清晰度　用肉眼和通過顯微鏡可辨細微結構的程度。

resorcinol *n.* a drug that causes the skin to peel. It has been used in skin ointments to treat such conditions as acne, but with prolonged use the drug is absorbed into the body, causing under-activity of the thyroid gland (myxoedema) and convulsions.

雷瑣辛　可使皮膚脫皮的藥物，以軟膏外用於皮膚以治療諸如痤瘡等皮膚病。但延長使用該藥，會被機體吸收引起甲狀腺功能低下（黏液性水腫）和驚厥。

resorption *n.* loss of substance through physiological or pathological means.

吸收　物質以生理或病理方式消失。

respiration *n.* the process of gaseous exchange between an organism and its environment. This includes both *external respiration*, which involves *breathing, in

呼吸　機體與環境之間氣體交換的過程。包括外呼吸和內呼吸。外呼吸指肺泡毛細血管攝取氧，並將二氧化碳自血中釋

which oxygen is taken up by the capillaries of the lung *alveoli and carbon dioxide is released from the blood, and *internal respiration*, during which oxygen is released to the tissues and carbon dioxide absorbed by the blood. Blood provides the transport medium for the gases between the lungs and tissue cells. In addition, it contains a pigment, *haemoglobin, with special affinity for oxygen. Once inside the cell oxygen is utilized in metabolic processes resulting in the production of energy (*see* ATP), water, and waste materials (including carbon dioxide). *See also* lung. **–respiratory** *adj.*

放出機體。內呼吸時，氧被釋放入組織，而二氧化碳則被血液吸收。血液提供了肺與組織細胞間氣體運輸的媒介。此外，血液中含有色素，即血紅蛋白，與氧有特殊的親和力。在細胞內氧一旦被用於代謝過程，則引起能量的產生（參閱ATP），同時產生水和廢物（包括二氧化碳）。參閱 lung。

respirator *n.* **1.** a device used to maintain the breathing movements of paralysed patients. In the *positive-pressure respirator* air is blown into the patient's lungs via a tube passed either through the mouth into the trachea or through a *tracheostomy. Air is released from the lungs when the pressure from the respirator is relaxed. The *iron lung* is a type of respirator in which the patient is enclosed, except for the head, in an airtight container in which the air pressure is decreased and increased mechanically. This draws air into and out of the lungs, through the normal air passages. The *cuirass respirator* works on a similar principle, but leaves the limbs free. **2.** a face mask for administering oxygen or other gas or for filtering harmful fumes, dust, etc. *See also* artificial respiration.

(1) 呼吸機　用以維持麻痺病人呼吸運動的裝置。正壓呼吸機是經連接管通過口或氣管切開方式，將空氣吹入氣管。當呼吸機壓力解除時，空氣即從肺內排出。鐵肺是呼吸機的一種，它將病人除頭外全部包在一個密閉的容器內，容器內壓力機械性的降低和增加，如此將空氣經正常的呼吸道吸入肺內或自肺內呼出。胸甲式呼吸機工作原理與它相似，但肢體可以活動。**(2) 呼吸罩**　用於吸入氧氣或其他氣體，或過濾有害氣體和灰塵等的面罩。參閱 artificial respiration。

respiratory distress syndrome (hyaline membrane disease) the condition of a newborn infant in which the lungs are imperfectly expanded. Initial inflation and normal expansion of the lungs requires the presence of a substance (*surfactant) that reduces the surface

呼吸窘迫綜合徵（透明膜病）新生兒肺不能完全擴張的狀況。肺最初的充氣和正常擴張需要能夠降低肺泡表面張力和阻止細支氣管塌陷的物質（表面活性物質）存在。沒有表面活性物質則細支氣管塌陷，導

tension of the air sacs (alveoli) and prevents collapse of the small airways. Without surfactant the airways collapse, leading to inefficient and 'stiff' lungs. The condition is most common and serious among preterm infants, in whom surfactant is liable to be deficient. Breathing is rapid, laboured, and shallow, and microscopic examinations of lung tissue in fatal cases has revealed the presence of *hyaline material in the collapsed air sacs. The condition is treated by careful nursing, intravenous fluids, and oxygen, with or without positive pressure by a *respirator. Recently, surfactant administered at birth has produced encouraging results.

致肺功能降低和肺硬化。該綜合徵最常見於早產兒，其病情也最嚴重，因為早產兒容易缺乏表面活性物質。患兒呼吸快，且很費力。顯微鏡檢死亡病例肺組織，可見塌陷肺泡中有透明物質。治療需精心護理，經靜脈輸液，吸氧，也可用或不用正壓呼吸機。近來，在分娩時給予表面活性物質產生了令人鼓舞的效果。

respiratory quotient (RQ) the ratio of the volume of carbon dioxide transferred from the blood into the alveoli to the volume of oxygen absorbed into the alveoli. The RQ is usually about 0.8 because more oxygen is taken up than carbon dioxide excreted.

呼吸商 二氧化碳自血中轉運至肺泡的容積與肺泡吸入的氧氣的容積之比。呼吸商通常約為 0.8，因為氧的攝入量多於二氧化碳的排出量。

respiratory syncytial virus (RSV) a paramyxovirus (see myxovirus) that causes infections of the nose and throat. It is a major cause of bronchiolitis and pneumonia in young children. In tissue cultures infected with the virus, cells merge together to form a conglomerate (syncytium). RSV is thought to have a role in *cot deaths. Vulnerable children can be treated with *ribavirin.

呼吸合胞病毒 一種能夠引起鼻和喉感染的副黏病毒（參閱 myxovirus）。它是引起幼兒細支氣管炎與肺炎的主要病因。把病毒感染的組織進行培養，可見細胞融合在一起而形成一個球形團塊（合胞體）。呼吸合胞病毒被認為與嬰兒猝死有關。易感兒童可用利巴韋林治療。

respiratory system the combination of organs and tissues associated with *breathing. It includes the nasal cavity, pharynx, larynx, trachea, bronchi, bronchioles, and lungs and also the diaphragm and other muscles associated with breathing movements.

呼吸系統 與呼吸有關的器官和組織有機地結合在一起構成呼吸系統。包括鼻腔、咽、喉、氣管、支氣管、細支氣管和肺，以及與呼吸運動有關的膈肌和其他肌肉。

response *n.* the way in which the body or part of the body reacts to a *stimulus. For example, a nerve impulse may produce the response of a contraction in a muscle that the nerve supplies.

應答（反應） 機體或機體的某個部分對刺激所作出的反應。例如，某一神經衝動可使該神經支配的肌肉產生一種收縮反應。

response prevention a form of *behaviour therapy given for severe *obsessions. Patients are encouraged to abstain from rituals and repetitive acts while they are in situations that arouse anxiety. For example, a hand-washing ritual might be treated by stopping washing while being progressively exposed to dirt. The anxiety then declines, and with it the obsessions.

應答預防 對患有嚴重的強迫觀念的病人所進行的一種行為治療方法。當病人處於喚起焦慮的狀態時，鼓勵他們避免強迫和重複的行為（動作）。例如，當洗手強迫障礙的患者的手被進一步弄髒時，鼓勵他們不要洗手。這種焦慮就會伴隨着強迫觀念一起減輕。

restiform body a thick bundle of nerve fibres that conveys impulses from tracts in the spinal cord to the cortex of the anterior and posterior lobes of the cerebellum.

繩狀體 一個粗的神經纖維束，可將來自脊髓的神經衝動傳至小腦的前、後葉皮質。

resting cell a cell that is not undergoing division. *See* interphase.

靜止細胞 不進行分裂的細胞。參閱 interphase。

restoration *n.* (in dentistry) any type of dental *filling or *crown, which is aimed at restoring a tooth to its normal form, function, and appearance.

修復 （牙科學）各種牙齒充填或造冠，目的在於使牙恢復其正常的結構、功能和外觀。

rest pain pain, usually experienced in the feet, that indicates an extreme degree of *ischaemia.

靜息痛 常見於足的一種疼痛，表示缺血到了極高程度。

restriction enzyme (restriction endonuclease) an enzyme, obtained from bacteria, that cuts DNA into specific short segments. Restriction enzymes are widely used in *genetic engineering.

限制性內切酶 一種從細菌中獲得的酶，能夠將脫氧核糖核酸切成短的特異性片段。限制性內切酶廣泛用於基因工程。

resuscitation *n.* the restoration of a person who appears to be dead. It depends upon the revival of cardiac and

復蘇 指瀕臨死亡病人的復活。它依賴於心肺功能的復活。參閱 artificial respira-

respiratory function. *See also* artificial respiration, mouth-to-mouth respiration.

retainer *n.* (in dentistry) **1.** a component of a partial *denture that keeps it in place. **2.** an *orthodontic appliance that holds the teeth in position. **3.** a component of a *bridge that is fixed to a natural tooth.

retardation *n.* the slowing up of a process. *Psychomotor retardation* is a marked slowing down of activity and speech, which can reach a degree where a patient can no longer care for himself. It is a symptom of severe *depression. The term *mental retardation implies a delay in intellectual development rather than a qualitative defect.

retching *n.* repeated unavailing attempts to vomit.

rete *n.* a network of blood vessels, nerve fibres, or other strands of interlacing tissue in the structure of an organ. The *rete testis* is a network of tubules conducting sperm from the seminiferous tubules of the *testis to the vasa efferentia.

retention *n.* inability to pass urine, which is retained in the bladder. The condition may be acute and painful or chronic and painless. The commonest cause is enlargement of the prostate gland in men, although many other conditions may result in obstruction of bladder outflow. Retention is relieved by catheter drainage of the bladder, after which the underlying problem is dealt with. *See also* intermittent self catheterization.

retention defect (in psychology) a memory defect in which items that

tion，mouth-to-mouth respiration。

(1) 固位體 （牙科學）局部托牙的一個組成部分，可使假牙保持適當位置。**(2) 矯正器**一種正牙器，可使牙保持正常位置。**(3)** 固定在天然牙齒上的橋基的組成部分。

遲緩　指某一過程的減慢。精神運動遲緩是指活動和語言明顯的緩慢，可達到病人不再關心自己的程度。這是嚴重的抑鬱症的症狀之一。智力低下一詞表示智力發育延緩而不是器質性缺陷。

乾嘔　反覆無效的嘔吐。

網　器官結構中的血管、神經纖維的網絡，或其他交錯組織條索。如睪丸網是將精子從睪丸的精曲小管輸送至輸出小管的小管性網絡。

瀦留　存留在膀胱內的尿液不能排出去。這種情況可以是急性、疼痛的，也可以是慢性、無痛性的。最常見的原因是男性前列腺肥大，儘管許多其他情況也可以引起膀胱排尿阻塞。膀胱導尿可以解除尿瀦留，此後再治療原發疾病。參閱 intermittent self catheterization。

記憶缺損　（精神病學）一種記憶力缺失，已存貯於記憶中的

have been registered in the memory are lost from storage. It is a feature of *dementia.

項目被丟失。這是癡呆的一個特徵。

reticular activating system the system of nerve pathways in the brain concerned with the level of consciousness – from the states of sleep, drowsiness, and relaxation to full alertness and attention. The system integrates information from all of the senses and from the cerebrum and cerebellum and determines the overall activity of the brain and the autonomic nervous system and patterns of behaviour during waking and sleeping.

網狀激活系統 大腦內與覺醒水平相關的神經傳導系統,使人從睡眠、瞌睡和鬆弛狀態至完全覺醒和注意狀態。該系統把來自所有感官和來自大腦及小腦的信息整合,並決定腦和自主神經系的總體活動以及在清醒和睡眠時行為的方式。

reticular fibres microscopic, almost nonelastic, branching fibres of *connective tissue that join together to form a delicate supportive meshwork around blood vessels, muscle fibres, glands, nerves, etc. They are composed of a collagen-like protein (*reticulin*) and are particularly common in lymph nodes, the spleen, liver, kidneys, and muscles.

網狀纖維 顯微鏡下幾乎沒彈性的,呈分支狀的結締組織纖維,它們相互連結,在血管、肌纖維、腺體和神經等周圍形成一個纖細的支持性網絡。它們是由類膠原蛋白(網硬蛋白)組成的,尤常見於淋巴結、脾、肝、腎和肌肉。

reticular formation a network of nerve pathways and nuclei throughout the *brainstem, connecting motor and sensory nerves to and from the spinal cord, the cerebellum and the cerebrum, and the cranial nerves. It is estimated that a single neurone in this network may have synapses with as many as 25,000 other neurones.

網狀結構 神經傳導通路與神經核在腦幹內形成的網。連接通向和來自脊髓、小腦、大腦的運動和感覺神經以及顱神經。據估計,網狀結構內的單個神經元可與多達 25 000 個其他神經元形成突觸。

reticulin *n.* a protein that is the major constituent of *reticular fibres.

網硬蛋白 構成網狀纖維的一種主要蛋白。

reticulocyte *n.* an immature red blood cell (erythrocyte). Reticulocytes may be detected and counted by staining living red cells with certain basic dyes that result in the formation of a blue precipitate (*reticulum*) within the reticulocytes.

網織紅細胞 一種未成熟的紅細胞,可用某種鹼性染色劑使活的紅細胞染色的方法來測定和計數網織紅細胞。此種染色可在網織紅細胞內形成藍色沉澱(網狀組織)。為正常紅細

They normally comprise about 1% of the total red cells and are increased (*reticulocytosis*) whenever the rate of red cell production increases.

reticulocytosis *n.* an increase in the proportion of immature red blood cells (reticulocytes) in the bloodstream. It is a sign of increased output of new red cells from the bone marrow.

reticuloendothelial system (RES) a community of cells – *phagocytes – spread throughout the body. It includes *macrophages and *monocytes. The RES is concerned with defence against microbial infection and with the removal of worn-out blood cells from the bloodstream. *See also* spleen.

reticuloendotheliosis (histiocytosis X) *n.* overgrowth of cells of the *reticuloendothelial system, causing either isolated swelling of the bone marrow (*eosinophilic granuloma*) or destruction of the bones of the skull (*Hand-Schüller-Christian disease*). The most acute form, starting in infancy and usually rapidly fatal, is associated with tumours containing histiocytes in the internal organs (*Letterer-Siwe disease*).

reticulosis *n.* abnormal overgrowth, usually malignant, of any of the cells of the lymphatic glands or the immune system. *See* lymphoma, Hodgkin's disease, Burkitt's lymphoma.

reticulum *n.* a network of tubules or blood vessels. *See* endoplasmic reticulum, sarcoplasmic reticulum.

retin- (retino-) *prefix denoting* the retina. Example: *retinopexy* (fixation of a detached retina).

胞總數的 1%，每當紅細胞生成加速時，它就增加（網織紅細胞增多）。

網織紅細胞增多 血液中未成熟的紅細胞（網織紅細胞）比例增多。這是骨髓生成新的紅細胞增多的徵象。

網狀內皮系統 由分布於全身的吞噬細胞所組成的體系。包括巨噬細胞和單核細胞。網狀內皮系統被認為與抵抗細菌感染和清除血液中衰老血細胞有關。參閱 spleen。

網狀內皮組織增生（組織細胞增生症） 網狀內皮系統細胞的過度增生，引起骨髓孤立的腫脹（嗜酸性肉芽腫）或顱骨的破壞（漢-許-克氏病）。最多見急性型發生於嬰兒並常常迅速導致死亡，它與內臟組織細胞腫瘤有關（萊-賽氏病）。

網狀細胞增多症 淋巴腺或免疫系統任何細胞的異常過度增多，往往是惡性的。參閱 lymphoma，Hodgkin's disease，Burkitt's lymphoma。

網 小管或血管的網絡。參閱 endoplasmic reticulum，sarcoplasmic reticulum。

〔前綴〕**視網膜** 如：視網膜固定術（使剝離的視網膜固定）。

retina *n.* the light-sensitive layer that lines the interior of the eye. The outer part of the retina (*retinal pigment epithelium*; *RPE*), next to the *choroid, is pigmented to prevent the passage of light. The inner part, next to the cavity of the eyeball, contains *rods and *cones (light-sensitive cells) and their associated nerve fibres (see illustration). A large number of cones is concentrated in a depression in the retina at the back of the eyeball called the *fovea. **–retinal** *adj.*

視網膜　貼於眼球壁內的感光層。鄰接脈絡膜的視網膜外側部（視網膜色素上皮）具有色素沉着，可以阻止光綫通過。鄰接眼窩的內側部，含有視桿細胞和視錐細胞（感光細胞）以及與它們相連接的神經纖維（見圖）。大量視錐細胞聚集於位於眼球後部的被稱作「凹」的視網膜的凹陷處。

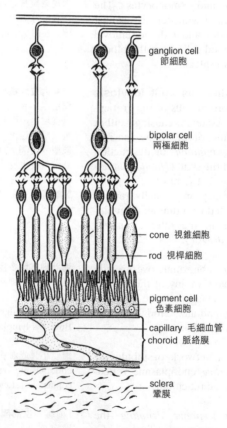

The structure of the retina
視網膜結構

retinaculum *n.* (*pl.* **retinacula**) a thickened band of tissue that serves to hold various tissues in place. For example, *flexor retinacula* are found over the flexor tendons in the wrist and ankle.

支持帶 使各種組織保持正常位置的粗的組織帶。例如，屈肌支持帶覆蓋於腕和踝部屈肌腱的上面。

retinal (retinene) *n.* the aldehyde of retinol (*vitamin A). *See also* rhodopsin.

視黃醛（維生素 A 醛） 視黃醇（維生素 A）的醛。參閱 rhodopsin。

retinene *n. see* retinal.

維生素 A 醛 參閱 retinal。

retinitis *n.* inflammation of the retina. In practice, the term is often used for conditions now known not to be inflammatory; for example for *retinitis pigmentosa*, a hereditary condition characterized by progressive degeneration of the retina. For such conditions the term *retinopathy is becoming more widely used.

視網膜炎 視網膜的炎症。實際上該術語常用於現在看來並非炎症的情況。例如，色素性視網膜炎是一種以視網膜進行性退變為特徵的遺傳性疾病。現在對這種情況更廣泛應用視網膜病這一醫學術語。

retinoblastoma *n.* a rare malignant tumour of the retina, occurring in infants.

視網膜胚細胞瘤 一種少見的發生於嬰兒的視網膜惡性腫瘤。

retinoid *n.* one of a group of drugs related to vitamin A that act on the skin to cause drying and peeling and a reduction in oil (sebum) production. These effects can be useful in the treatment of severe *acne, *psoriasis, *ichthyosis, and other skin disorders. Retinoids include *isotretinoin and *tretinoin; they are administered by mouth or applied as a cream. Possible side-effects, which may be serious, include severe fetal abnormalities (if taken by pregnant women), toxic effects on babies (if taken by breastfeeding mothers), liver and kidney damage, excessive drying, redness and itching of the skin, and muscle pain and stiffness.

視黃酸 與維生素 A 相關的藥物之一，作用於皮膚，可引起乾燥和脫皮以及油性分泌物減少。這些作用對治療嚴重的痤瘡、牛皮癬、魚鱗癬和其他皮膚病很有用。它包括異維生素 A 酸、維生素 A 酸，可口服吸收或製成單劑使用。可能產生的副作用有時可能很嚴重。孕婦服用可致嚴重胎兒畸形，哺乳期婦女服用可對嬰兒產生毒性作用，還會造成肝、腎損害，皮膚異常乾燥、發紅及瘙癢，肌肉疼痛和強直。

retinol *n. see* vitamin A.

視黃醇 參閱 vitamin A。

retinopathy *n.* any of various disorders of the retina resulting in impairment or loss of vision. It is usually due to damage to the blood vessels of the retina, occurring (for example) as a complication of diabetes (*diabetic retinopathy*), high blood pressure, or AIDS (*AIDS retinopathy*).

視網膜病　引起視力減弱或喪失的任何一種視網膜病變。常常由視網膜血管病變引起，如作為糖尿病、高血壓或艾滋病的併發症而發生。

retinoscope *n.* an instrument used to determine the power of spectacle lens required to correct errors of *refraction of the eye. It is held in the hand and casts a beam of light into the subject's eye. The examiner looks along the beam and sees the reflection in the subject's pupil. By interpreting the way the reflection moves when he moves the instrument, and by altering this by lenses held in his other hand near the subject's eye, he is able to detect long- or short-sightedness or astigmatism and to determine its degree. **–retinoscopy** *n.*

視網膜鏡　用於測量晶狀體糾正眼屈光不正能力的器械。用手持鏡，並用光照射至被檢者的眼內，然後檢查者沿光束查看，可看到被檢查者瞳孔內的映像。檢查者移動鏡子時映像亦移動，通過這一方法，檢查者調整靠近病人眼睛的另一種的鏡子，可以測出遠視、近視還是散光，並可測出其度數。

retraction *n.* **1.** (in obstetrics) the quality of uterine muscle fibres of remaining shortened after contracting during labour. This results in a gradual progression of the fetus downwards through the pelvis. The basal portion of the uterus becomes thicker and pulls up the dilating cervix over the presenting part. **2.** (in dentistry) the drawing back of one or more teeth into a better position by an *orthodontic appliance.

縮回　**(1)**（產科學）分娩時子宮肌纖維在收縮後保持縮短狀態的能力。該作用可使胎兒經過盆腔緩慢下行。子宮底部變厚並將蓋於先露部上的擴大的子宮頸向上拉。**(2)**（牙科學）用正牙器將一個或幾個牙齒收回到較好的位置。

retraction ring a depression in the uterine wall marking the junction between the actively contracting muscle fibres of the upper segment of the uterus and the muscle fibres of the lower segment. This depression is not always visible and is normal. In obstructed labour (e.g. contracted pelvis or malposition of the fetus resulting in shoulder

子宮收縮環　子宮壁上的凹陷，是子宮上部正在收縮肌纖維與下部肌纖維連接的標誌，該凹陷是正常的，也並不總能看見。在難產時（如因骨盆狹窄或胎位不正所致的肩先露），子宮上部的肌纖維縮短變厚；另一方面，下部肌纖維伸長變薄。當這兩部肌肉連接

presentation), the muscle fibres of the upper segment become shorter and thicker; the muscle fibres of the lower segment, on the other hand, become elongated and thinner. The junction between the two becomes more distinct as it rises into the abdomen from the pelvis. This abnormal ring is known as *Bandl's ring* and is a sign of impending rupture of the lower segment of the uterus, which becomes progressively thinner as Bandl's ring rises upwards. Immediate action to relieve the obstruction is then necessary, usually in the form of Caesarean section.

處由盆部向腹部上移時，該連接部位就更顯著了。這種異常的環被稱為班德爾環，它是子宮下部瀕臨破裂的一個徵兆，當班德爾環上移時，子宮下部肌肉進行性變薄。這時，需要立即採取措施，以解除難產，剖宮產術是常用的手段。

retractor *n.* a surgical instrument used to expose the operation site by drawing aside the cut edges of skin, muscle, or other tissues. There are several types of retractors for different operations (see illustration).

牽開器 為暴露手術視野將皮膚、肌肉或其他組織切緣牽向旁邊的外科器械。因手術不同，牽開器也有幾種不同類型（見圖）。

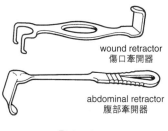

wound retractor
傷口牽開器

abdominal retractor
腹部牽開器

Retractors
牽開器

retro- *prefix denoting* at the back or behind. Examples: *retrobulbar* (at the back of the eyeball); *retroperitoneal* (behind the peritoneum).

〔前綴〕**後** 如：球後（眼球的背後）；腹膜後（腹膜的後方）。

retrobulbar neuritis (optic neuritis) inflammation of the optic nerve behind the eye, causing increasingly blurred vision. When the inflammation involves

球後視神經炎（視神經炎） 眼球後部視神經的炎症，引起進行性的視力模糊。當炎症侵犯神經的第一部分並能在視神經

the first part of the nerve and can be seen at the optic disc, it is called *optic papillitis*. Retrobulbar neuritis is one of the symptoms of multiple sclerosis but it can also occur as an isolated lesion, in the absence of any other involvement of the nervous system, with the patient recovering vision completely.

盤看到時，即稱為視乳頭炎。球後視神經炎是多發性硬化症的症狀之一，但也可作為獨立的損傷發生，而無任何其他神經系統疾病，此種病人的視力可完全恢復。

retroflexion *n.* the bending backward of an organ or part of an organ, especially the abnormal bending backward of the upper part of the uterus (i.e. the part furthest from the cervix).

後屈 指器官或器官的一部分向後彎曲，尤指子宮上部（例如遠離子宮頸的部分）異常向後彎曲。

retrograde *adj.* going backwards, or moving in the opposite direction to the normal. (*See* (retrograde) pyelography.) *Retrograde amnesia* is a failure to remember events immediately preceding an illness or injury.

逆行性 向後或與正常相反的方向移動。（參閱 (retrograde) pyelography）。逆行性遺忘是對患病或受傷前剛發生的事件失去記憶。

retrography *n.* writing in which letters are reversed so that they appear as mirror images. Adoption of this as a consistent style is usually a matter of voluntary choice or is *hysterical; very occasionally it follows brain damage. Mirror-image reversals of single letters are common in children learning to write and in older children whose language abilities are impaired.

反寫 看起來似鏡像而把字母反寫的字跡。把這種寫法作為一種一貫的方式常是一種主動選擇，或是癔病；也極偶然地出現在腦損傷後。單個字母的鏡像倒置發生在兒童學習寫字和較大兒童語言能力受損時是常見的。

retrolental fibroplasia *see* fibroplasia.

晶狀體後纖維組織增生 參閱 fibroplasia。

retroperitoneal fibrosis (RPF) a condition in which a dense plaque of fibrous tissue develops behind the peritoneum adjacent to the abdominal aorta. The ureters become encased and hence obstructed, causing acute *anuria and renal failure. The obstruction can be relieved by *nephrostomy or the insertion

腹膜後纖維變性 在接近腹主動脈的腹膜後部，纖維組織形成致密斑塊。這種情況下輸尿管被包裹，並可導致阻塞，引起急性無尿和腎衰竭。這種阻塞可通過腎造口術或插入雙 J 形引流條膜解除。在急性期給予類固醇對病情有所幫

of double J *stents. In the acute phase steroid administration may help, but in established RPF *ureterolysis is required.

助，但對已經形成的腹膜後纖維變性需行輸尿管鬆解術。

retroperitoneal space the region between the posterior pariental *peritoneum and the front of the *lumbar vertebrae. It contains important structures, including the kidneys, adrenal glands, pancreas, lumbar spinal nerve roots, sympathetic ganglia and nerves, and the abdominal *aorta and its major branches.

腹膜後間隙 位於腹膜後壁和腰椎前面之間的區域。該間隙內有重要的結構，包括腎、腎上腺、胰腺、腰部脊神經根、交感神經節和交感神經，以及腹主動脈和其主要分支。

retropulsion *n*. a compulsive tendency to walk backwards. It is a symptom of *parkinsonism.

後退步態 一種強迫性的向後走的傾向。它是帕金森綜合徵的症狀之一。

retrospective study a backward-looking review of the characteristics of a group of individuals in relation to morbidity, embracing some aspects of *cross-sectional and/or *case control studies. The term is sometimes loosely used as a synonym for such studies.

回顧性研究 對一組人羣有關發病率特點的回顧性總結，包括一些橫面的或病例對照的研究。該詞有時廣義地作為上述研究的同義詞。

retroversion *n*. an abnormal position of the uterus in which it is tilted backwards, with the base lying in the *pouch of Douglas, against the rectum, instead of on the bladder. It occurs in about 20% of women.

後傾 子宮向後傾斜的異常位置，同時子宮底位於道格拉斯腔內，靠着直腸而非膀胱，約有 20% 女性子宮後傾。

retrovirus *n*. an RNA-containing virus that can convert its genetic material into DNA by means of the enzyme *reverse transcriptase, which enables it to become integrated into the DNA of its host's cells. Retroviruses have been implicated in the development of some cancers and are associated with conditions characterized by an impaired immune system (*HIV is a retrovirus). They are also used as *vectors in gene therapy.

逆轉錄病毒 一種含核糖核酸的病毒，可通過逆轉錄酶將其遺傳物質轉移給脫氧核糖核酸。它能把病毒的遺傳物質整合到宿主細胞的脫氧核糖核酸中。逆轉錄病毒被認為與某些癌症的發生有關並與以免疫系統功能缺損為特徵的疾病相聯繫（如人類免疫缺陷病毒是一種逆轉錄病毒）。在基因治療中，逆轉錄病毒被用作媒介物。

retrusion *n.* (in dentistry) **1.** backward movement of the lower jaw. **2.** a malocclusion in which some of the teeth are further back than usual. *Compare* protrusion.

後移 （牙科學） **(1)** 下頜向後移動。**(2)** 錯𦧌，即有些牙齒比通常更向後。與 protrusion 對比。

Rett's syndrome a disorder affecting young girls, in which *stereotyped movements and social withdrawal appear during early childhood. Intellectual development is often impaired and special educational help is needed.

瑞特綜合徵 一種主要發生在年輕女性的疾病，這些女性在童年時期常有刻板動作和在公眾場合退縮不前的表現。她們的智力發育較差，需要接受特殊教育。

reverse transcriptase an enzyme, found mainly in *retroviruses, that catalyses the synthesis of DNA from RNA. It enables the viral RNA to be integrated into the host DNA.

逆轉錄酶 一種主要見於逆轉錄病毒的酶，它能催化促進從核糖核酸合成脫氧核糖核酸的反應，能使病毒的核糖核酸整合入宿主的脫氧核糖核酸中。

Reye's syndrome a rare disorder occurring in childhood. It is characterized by the symptoms of *encephalitis combined with evidence of liver failure. Often, the symptoms develop in the apparent recovery phase of a viral infection. Treatment is aimed at controlling cerebral *oedema and correcting metabolic abnormalities in order to allow spontaneous recovery, but there is still a significant mortality and there may be residual brain damage. The cause is not known, but *aspirin has been implicated and this drug should not be used in children below the age of 12 unless specifically indicated.

雷耶綜合徵 一種發生於兒童的罕見的疾病，它常以腦炎合併肝功能衰竭等症狀為特徵。通常症狀在病毒感染後顯著恢復期出現。治療主要針對控製腦水腫和糾正代謝紊亂以便自行恢復，但死亡率仍較高，並可殘留腦損害。原因不明，但已證實阿司匹林與之有關。因而對 12 歲以下兒童除非特殊需求不應使用該藥。

rhabdomyoma *n.* a rare benign tumour of skeletal muscle or heart muscle.

橫紋肌瘤 骨骼肌或心肌的一種罕見的良性腫瘤。

rhabdomyosarcoma *n.* a malignant tumour originating in, or showing the characteristics of, striated muscle. *Pleomorphic rhabdomyosarcoma* occurs in late middle age, in the muscles of the limbs. *Embryonal rhabdomyosarcomas*,

橫紋肌肉瘤 一種起源於橫紋肌或具有橫紋肌特徵的惡性腫瘤。多形性橫紋肌肉瘤發生於中晚年齡人的四肢肌肉。胚胎型橫紋肌肉瘤侵犯嬰兒、兒童及青年，它可分為葡萄簇狀的

affecting infants, children, and young adults, are classified as *botryoid* (in the vagina, bladder, ear, etc.), *embryonal* (most common in the head and neck, particularly the orbit); and *alveolar* (at the base of the thumb). The pleomorphic and alveolar types respond poorly to treatment; botryoid tumours are treated with a combination of radiotherapy, surgery, and drugs. The embryonal type, if treated at an early stage, can often be cured with a combination of radiotherapy and drugs (including vincristine, actinomycin D, and cyclophosphamide).

rhagades *pl. n.* cracks or long thin scars in the skin, particularly around the mouth or other areas of the body subjected to constant movement. The fissures around the mouth and nose of babies with congenital syphilis eventually heal to form rhagades.

rheo- *prefix denoting* **1.** a flow of liquid. **2.** an electric current.

rhesus factor (Rh factor) a group of *antigens that may or may not be present on the surface of the red blood cells; it forms the basis of the rhesus blood group system. Most people have the rhesus factor, i.e. they are *Rh-positive*. People who lack the factor are termed *Rh-negative*. Incompatibility between Rh-positive and Rh-negative blood is an important cause of blood transfusion reactions and *haemolytic disease of the newborn. *See also* blood group.

rheumatic fever (acute rheumatism) a disease affecting mainly children and young adults that arises as a delayed complication of infection of the upper respiratory tract with haemolytic streptococci (*see* Streptococcus). The main

（在陰道、膀胱、耳等），胚胎型的（最常見於頭、頸部，尤其是眼眶部），以及小泡狀的（在拇指的根部）。多形性的與小泡狀的這兩型的治療效果差。葡萄簇狀的腫瘤可用放射治療、外科手術和藥物聯合治療。若能在早期採用放射治療和藥物（如長春新鹼、放綫菌素 D 和環磷酰胺）的聯合療法，則胚胎型的往往能治愈。

皸裂 皮膚的裂口或細長瘢痕。尤其發生在經常活動的口周和身體其他部位，先天性梅毒的嬰兒口鼻周圍的裂隙最後愈合而形成皸裂。

〔前綴〕（1）流動的液體 （2）電流

Rh 因子 可存在或不存在於紅細胞表面的一組抗原，它形成 Rh 血型系統的基礎，大多數人有 Rh 因子，即他們是 Rh 陽性者。無 Rh 因子者稱為 Rh 陰性者。Rh 陽性與 Rh 陰性血液的配合禁忌是輸血反應和新生兒溶血性疾病的一個重要原因。參閱 blood group。

風濕熱（急性風濕病） 一種主要侵犯兒童和青年人的疾病，是上呼吸道溶血性鏈球菌（參閱 Streptococcs）感染的遲發併發症。主要特徵為發熱，進行性游走性關節炎，皮膚環形

features are fever, arthritis progressing from joint to joint, reddish circular patches on the skin, small painless nodules formed on bony prominences such as the elbow, abnormal involuntary movements of the limbs and head (Sydenham's *chorea), and inflammation of the heart muscle, its valves, and the membrane surrounding the heart. The condition may progress to *chronic rheumatic heart disease*, with scarring and chronic inflammation of the heart and its valves leading to heart failure, murmurs, and damage to the valves. The initial infection is treated with antibiotics (e.g. penicillin) and bed rest, with aspirin to relieve the joint pain. Following an acute attack, long-term prophylaxis with penicillin is often recommended to prevent a relapse. Rheumatic fever is becoming much less common in developed countrices, probably as a result of antibiotic use.

rheumatism *n.* any disorder in which aches and pains affect the muscles and joints. *See* rheumatoid arthritis, rheumatic fever, osteoarthritis, gout.

rheumatoid arthritis a form of *arthritis that is the second most common rheumatic disease (after *osteoarthritis). It typically involves the joints of the fingers, wrists, feet, and ankles and sometimes later the hips, knees, and shoulders: the joints are affected symmetrically and there is a considerable range of severity. Diagnosis is supported by a blood test, which in may patients shows the presence of *rheumatoid factor* in the serum (*see also* autoimmune disease), and by X-rays revealing typical changes (*rheumatoid erosions*) around the affected joints. A wide variety of treatments, usually based on anti-inflammatory analgesics, provide relief of symptoms, and some

紅斑，在骨的突出部位如肘部形成小的無痛性結節，肢體和頭部有異常的不自主活動（西登哈姆舞蹈病），和心肌、心瓣膜以及心包的炎症。這種病可以進一步發展為慢性風濕性心臟病，伴有心臟及其瓣膜的瘢痕形成和慢性炎症，導致心衰、心臟雜音和瓣膜損害。初期感染可用抗生素治療（如青黴素），臥床休息，用阿司匹林緩解關節疼痛，在急性發作後，長期預防性地使用青黴素常可以防止復發。風濕熱在發達國家愈來愈少見，可能是使用抗生素的結果。

風濕病　肌肉和關節疼痛的任何病。參閱 rheumatoid arthritis，rheumatic fever，osteoarthritis，gout。

類風濕性關節炎　關節炎的一種類型，這是第二位常見的風濕性疾病（在骨關節炎之後），典型的是侵犯指、腕、足和踝等關節，有時發生於髖、足和肩關節侵犯之後。關節的侵犯呈對稱性，且其嚴重程度很不相同。可通過查血診斷此病。在許多患者血漿中可查出類風濕因子（參閱 autoimmune disease），X綫可顯示於受侵犯關節周圍有典型的改變（類風濕性浸潤）。治療方法很多，通常以抗炎止痛藥物為基礎，能夠減輕症狀。對有些患病關節可通過修復外科手段進行替換（參閱 hip

diseased joints can be replaced by prosthetic surgery (*see* hip replacement). The condition may resolve spontaneously, but is usually relapsing and remitting or eventually progressive.

rheumatology *n.* the medical specialty concerned with the diagnosis and management of disease involving joints, tendons, muscles, ligaments, and associated structures. *See also* physical medicine. **–rheumatologist** *n.*

rhexis *n.* the breaking apart of a blood vessel, organ, or tissue.

Rh factor *see* rhesus factor.

rhin- (rhino-) *prefix denoting* the nose.

rhinencephalon *n.* the parts of the brain, collectively, that in early stages of evolution were concerned mainly with the sense of smell. The rhinencephalon includes the olfactory nerve, olfactory tract, and the regions now usually classified as belonging to the *limbic system.

rhinitis *n.* inflammation of the mucous membrane of the nose. It may be caused by virus infection (*acute rhinitis*; *see* (common) cold) or an allergic reaction (*allergic rhinitis*; *see* hay fever). In *atrophic rhinitis* the mucous membrane becomes thinned and fragile. In *perennial* (or *vasomotor*) *rhinitis* there is overgrowth of, and increased secretion by, the membrane.

rhinolith *n.* a stone (calculus) in the nose.

rhinology *n.* the branch of medicine concerned with disorders of the nose and nasal passages.

replacement）。該病亦可自行緩解，但通常復發和減輕或緩慢進展。

風濕病學 關於診斷和治療關節、肌腱、肌肉、韌帶和有關結構疾病的醫學專業。參閱 physical medicine。

破裂 血管、器官或組織的破碎分離。

Rh 因子 參閱 rhesus factor。

〔前綴〕**鼻**

嗅腦 大腦的一部分，在發育早期主要與嗅覺有關。嗅腦包括嗅神經、嗅束和嗅區，後者現在分類歸於邊緣系統。

鼻炎 鼻黏膜的炎症，可由病毒感染引起（急性鼻炎；參閱 cold）或因變態反應所致（過敏性鼻炎；參閱 hay fever）。患萎縮性鼻炎時，鼻黏膜變得薄而脆。患常年性（或血管舒縮性）鼻炎時，鼻黏膜過度增生，引起分泌增加。

鼻石 鼻內的結石。

鼻科學 關於鼻和鼻道疾病的醫學分支。

rhinomycosis *n.* fungal infection of the lining of the nose.

鼻真菌病　鼻腔內的真菌感染。

rhinophyma *n.* a bulbous craggy swelling of the nose, usually in men. It is a manifestation of *rosacea and in no way related to alcohol intake. Paring by plastic surgery may be necessary for cosmetic purposes.

肥大性酒渣鼻　鼻子持久性發紅和腫脹，常見於男性。它是酒渣鼻的一種表現，與飲酒無任何關聯，通過整形外科切除可達到整容的目的。

rhinoplasty *n.* surgery to alter the shape of the nose, sometimes using tissue (skin, cartilage, or bone) from elsewhere in the body or artificial implants.

鼻成形術　改變鼻外觀的外科手術，有時用身體其他部位（如皮膚、軟骨或骨）的組織或人工移植物。

rhinorrhoea *n.* a persistent watery mucous discharge from the nose, as in the common cold.

鼻溢　鼻腔持續地流出稀薄黏液，如發生在感冒時。

rhinoscleroma *n.* the formation of nodules in the interior of the nose and *nasopharynx, which become thickened. It is caused by bacterial infection (with *Klebsiella rhinoscleromatis*).

鼻硬結　鼻與鼻咽腔內側形成結節並增厚，此病由細菌感染引起（鼻硬結克雷白桿菌）。

rhinoscopy *n.* examination of the interior of the nose.

鼻鏡檢查　鼻內部的檢查。

rhinosporidiosis *n.* an infection of the mucous membranes of the nose, larynx, eyes, and genitals that is caused by the fungus *Rhinosporidium seeberi* and is characterized by the formation of tiny *polyps. It occurs most commonly in Asia.

鼻孢子蟲病　由西伯鼻孢子蟲引起的鼻黏膜、喉、眼睛和生殖器的感染，其特徵為形成小息肉。該病在亞洲最常見。

rhinovirus *n.* any one of a group of RNA-containing viruses that cause respiratory infections in man resembling the common cold. They are included in the *picornavirus group.

鼻病毒　一種含有核糖核酸的病毒，可引起類似感冒的呼吸道感染，屬細小核糖核酸病毒組。

Rhipicephalus *n.* a genus of hard *ticks widely distrbuted in the tropics. The dog tick (*R. sanguineus*) can suck the blood

扁頭蜱屬　廣泛分布於熱帶的硬蜱屬，犬蜱（血紅扁頭蜱）可吸吮人的血液，並傳播立克

of man and is commonly involved in the transmission of diseases caused by rickettsiae (*see* typhus).

次體引起的疾病（參閱 typhus）。

rhiz- (rhizo-) *prefix denoting* a root. Example: *rhizonychia* (the root of a nail).

〔前綴〕根　如甲根（指甲的根）。

rhizotomy *n.* a surgical procedure in which selected nerve roots are cut at the point where they emerge from the spinal cord. In *posterior rhizotomy* the posterior (sensory) nerve roots are cut for the relief of intractable pain in the organs served by these nerves. An *anterior rhizotomy* – the cutting of the anterior (motor) nerve roots – is sometimes done for the relief of severe muscle spasm.

脊神經根切斷術　選擇性地切斷從脊髓出來的神經根的外科手術。脊神經後根切斷術是切斷感覺神經根，以減輕它所支配的臟器的頑固性疼痛。脊神經前根切斷術是切斷運動神經根，有時是為減輕嚴重的肌痙攣。

Rhodnius *n.* a genus of large blood-sucking bugs (*see* reduviid). *R. prolixus* is important in the transmission of *Chagas' disease in Central America and the northern part of South America.

紅獵蝽屬　一種大型的吸血昆蟲屬（參閱 reduviid）。長紅獵蝽屬在中美洲和南美北部，是引起恰加斯病傳播的主要昆蟲。

rhodopsin (visual purple) *n.* a pigment in the retina of the eye, within the *rods, consisting of *retinal* – an aldehyde of retinol (*vitamin A) – and a protein. The presence of rhodopsin is essential for vision in dim light. It is bleached in the presence of light and this stimulates nervous activity in the rods.

視紫質　眼睛視網膜的一種色素，在視網膜視桿細胞內，由視黃醛（維生素 A）和一種蛋白質組成。視紫質的存在對光淺暗淡時的視覺是必需的，當有亮光時，它即脫色，此時就刺激了視桿細胞中的神經活性。

rhombencephalon *n. see* hindbrain.

菱腦　參閱 hindbrain。

rhomboid *n.* either of two muscles *rhomboid major* and *rhomboid minor*) situated in the upper part of the back, between the backbone and shoulder blade. They help to move the shoulder blade backwards and upwards.

菱形肌　位於背部上方在脊柱與肩胛骨之間的兩塊肌肉（大菱形肌和小菱形肌）。它們幫助肩胛骨向後和向上活動。

rhonchus *n.* (*pl.* **rhonchi**) an abnormal musical noise produced by air passing

乾囉音　空氣通過狹窄的支氣管產生的一種異常的音樂性噪

through narrowed bronchi. It is heard through a stethoscope, usually when the patient breathes out.

音，通常當病人呼氣時通過聽診器可聽到。

rhythm method a contraceptive method in which sexual intercourse is restricted to the *safe period* at the beginning and end of the *menstrual cycle. The safe period is calculated either on the basis of the length of the menstrual cycle or by reliance on the change of body temperature that occurs at ovulation. A third possible indicator (*see* Billings method) is the change that occurs with ovulation in the stickiness of the mucus at the neck (cervix) of the uterus. The method depends for its reliability on the woman having uniform regular periods and its failure rate is higher than with mechanical methods, approaching 25 pregnancies per 100 woman-years.

安全期避孕法 一種將性交限制在月經周期開始和末尾的「安全期」避孕方法。安全期的計算可據月經周期的時間長短，或依據排卵時體溫的變化。第三種可能的指標是排卵同時子宮頸黏液黏性的改變（參閱 Billings method）。此方法的可靠性是依賴於婦女有規律的月經周期，但失敗率高於用工具的避孕方法。每 100 個婦女一年有 25 個妊娠。

rib *n.* a curved, slightly twisted, strip of bone forming part of the skeleton of the thorax, which protects the heart and lungs. There are 12 pairs of ribs. The head of each rib articulates with one of the 12 thoracic vertebrae of the backbone; the other end is attached to a section of cartilage (*see* costal cartilage). The first seven pairs – the *true ribs* – are connected directly to the sternum by their costal cartilages. The next three pairs – the *false ribs* – are attached indirectly: each is connected by its cartilage to the rib above it. The last two pairs of ribs – the *floating ribs* – end freely in the muscles of the body wall. Anatomical name: **costa**.

肋骨 彎曲且呈輕度弓形的細長骨，形成胸廓骨骼的一部分，保護心臟和兩肺。肋骨有 12 對，每根肋骨頭與脊柱的 12 個胸椎之一相連接。另一端連着一段軟骨（參閱 costal cartilage）。第 1~7 對肋骨稱為真肋，直接以其肋軟骨和胸骨相連接。以後 3 對稱為假肋，不直接與胸骨相連，而是借其軟骨與上位肋骨的軟骨相連。最後 2 對肋骨稱浮肋，其前端游離於胸壁的肌肉中。

ribavirin *n.* an antiviral drug effective against a range of DNA and RNA viruses, including the herpes group, *respiratory syncytial virus, and those causing *hepatitis, several strains of influenza, and *Lassa fever. It is

利巴韋林（三氮唑核苷） 一種抗病毒藥，能有效地對抗一定範圍內的脫氧核糖核酸和核糖核酸病毒，包括疱疹病毒，呼吸合胞病毒，可引起肝炎、幾種流感和拉沙熱病毒。該藥可

administered by a small-particle aerosol inhaler and sometimes by intravenous injection. Possible side-effects include breathing difficulty, bacterial pneumonia, and *pneumothorax. Unfortunately, it antagonizes the action of *zidovudine against HIV. Trade name: **Virazole**.

以小顆粒噴霧劑吸入使用，有時也可以靜脈內注射。可能的副作用包括呼吸困難、細菌性肺炎和氣胸。遺憾的是，可抵銷齊多夫定對抗人類免疫缺陷病毒的作用。商品名：Virazole。

riboflavin *n. see* vitamin B₂.

核黃素　參閱 vitamin B₂。

ribonuclease *n.* an enzyme, located in the *lysosomes of cells, that splits RNA at specific places in the molecule.

核糖核酸酶　含於細胞溶酶體中的酶，它使核糖核酸在分子的特殊位置上分裂。

ribonucleic acid *see* RNA.

核糖核酸　參閱 RNA。

ribose *n.* a pentose sugar (i.e. one with free carbon atoms) that is a component of *RNA and several coenzymes. Ribose is also involved in intracellular metabolism.

核糖　一種戊糖（即有自由碳原子的糖），它是核糖核酸和幾種輔酶的成分。核糖也參與細胞內的代謝。

ribosome *n.* a particle, consisting of RNA and protein, that occurs in cells and is the site of protein synthesis in the cell (*see* translation). Ribosomes are either attached to the *endoplasmic reticulum or free in the cytoplasm as *polysomes. **–ribosomal** *adj.*

核糖體　細胞內由核糖核酸和蛋白質組成的一種顆粒，並是細胞內蛋白質合成的場所（參閱 translation）。核糖體可附着在內質網上，或以多聚核糖體的形式游離在細胞漿內。

ribozyme *n.* an RNA molecule that can act as an enzyme, catalysing changes to its own molecular structure (before the discovery of ribozymes it was assumed that all enzymes were proteins). Since replication of DNA and RNA cannot occur without enzymes, and since protein enzymes can only be produced by DNA coding, the question arose as to how nucleic acid molecules were able to replicate in the early stages of evolution. The discovery of ribozymes appears to resolve the enigma. Research is currently being undertaken to exploit the ability of genetically engineered ribozymes to

核酶　一種能像酶一樣催化自身分子結構發生變化的核糖核酸分子（在核酶發現以前，認為所有的酶均是蛋白質）。沒有酶，脫氧核糖核酸和核糖核酸就不能複製，蛋白性酶只能由脫氧核糖核酸編碼產生，所以就提出了核酸分子在進化早期如何進行複製的問題。發現核酶就像解謎一樣。為了利用基因工程核酶來破壞人類免疫缺陷病毒（艾滋病病毒）的核糖核酸，研究工作現正在進行。

destroy the RNA of HIV (the AIDS virus).

ricin *n.* a highly toxic albumin obtained from castor-oil seeds (*Ricinus communis*) that inhibits protein synthesis and becomes attached to the surface of cells, resulting in gastroenteritis, hepatic congestion and jaundice, and cardiovascular collapse. It is lethal to most species, even in minute amounts (1 µg/kg body weight); it is most toxic if injected intravenously or inhaled as fine particles. Ricin is being investigated as a treatment for certain lymphomas, which depends on its delivery to the exact site of the tumour in order to avoid destruction of healthy cells (*see* immunotoxin).

rickets *n.* a disease of childhood in which the bones do not harden due to a deficiency of *vitamin D. Without vitamin D, not enough calcium salts are deposited in the bones to make them rigid: consequently they become soft and malformed. This is particularly noticeable in the long bones, which become bowed, and in the front of the ribcage, where a characteristic rickety 'rosary' may become apparent. The deficiency of vitamin D may be dietary or due to lack of exposure to sunlight, which is important in the conversion of vitamin D to its active form. In the UK rickets is more common in Asian immigrant families.

Renal rickets is due to impaired kidney function causing bone-forming minerals to be excreted in the urine, which results in softening of the bones.

rickettsiae *pl. n.* (*sing.* **rickettsia**) a group of very small nonmotile spherical or rodlike parasitic organisms. They resemble bacteria in their cellular structure and method of asexual reproduction, but

蓖麻毒蛋白 從蓖麻籽中提取的高毒性白蛋白，它抑制蛋白合成，並結合於細胞表面引起胃腸炎、肝淤血和黃疸，以及心血管性虛脫。多數品種動物，即使小劑量(1µg/kg 體重)使用可引起死亡。靜脈注射或以小顆粒吸入時毒性最大。蓖麻毒蛋白被用以觀察治療某些淋巴瘤，依靠藥物釋放至腫瘤的確切位置以避免破壞健康細胞（參閱 immunotoxin）。

佝僂病 由於缺乏維生素 D 使骨變軟和變形的兒童疾病。缺了維生素 D，無足夠使骨變硬的鈣鹽沉積在骨內，因此骨骼變軟，變形。這在長骨尤其顯著。它們變得彎曲，且在胸廓前面可出現特徵性的佝僂病「串珠」。維生素 D 的缺乏可因食入不足或因為接受日照不足。日照對於維生素 D 轉變為活性維生素 D 具有重要的作用。在英國，佝僂病常見於亞洲移民家庭。

腎性佝僂病是由於腎功能損害導致構成骨的礦物質從尿中排出，從而引起骨骼的軟化。

立克次體 一組很小的不運動的球形或棒狀的寄生性微生物。在細胞結構和無性生殖方面與細菌相似，但它們又像病毒一樣不能在宿主的體外繁

– like viruses – they cannot reproduce outside the bodies of their hosts. Rickettsiae infect arthropods (ticks, mites, etc.), through whom they can be transmitted to mammals (including man), in which they can cause severe illness. The species *Rickettsia akari* causes *rickettsial pox, *R. conorii*, *R. prowazekii*, *R. tsutsugamushi*, and *R. typhi* cause different forms of *typhus, *R. rickettsii* causes *Rocky Mountain spotted fever, and *Coxiella burnetii* causes *Q fever. **–rickettsial** *adj.*

rickettsial pox a disease of mice caused by the microorganism *Rickettsia akari* and transmitted to man by mites: it produces chills, fever, muscular pain, and a rash similar to that of *chickenpox. The disease is mild and runs its course in 2–3 weeks. *See also* typhus.

ridge *n.* **1.** (in anatomy) a crest or a long narrow protuberance, e.g. on a bone. **2.** (in dental anatomy) *see* alveolus.

rifampicin *n.* an *antibiotic used to treat various infections, particularly tuberculosis. It is administered by mouth; digestive upsets and sensitivity reactions sometimes occur. Trade names: **Rifadin**, **Rimactane**.

Rift Valley fever a virus disease of East Africa transmitted from animals to man by mosquitoes and causing symptoms resembling those of *influenza.

rigidity *n.* (in neurology) resistance to the passive movement of a limb that persists throughout its range. It is a symptom of *parkinsonism. A smooth resistance is called *plastic* or *lead-pipe rigidity* while intermittent resistance is called *cogwheel rigidity*. *Compare* spasticity.

殖。立克次體感染節肢動物（蟎、蜱等），通過它們得以傳播到哺乳動物（包括人，並可引起哺乳動物嚴重疾病）。小蛛立克次體可引起立克次體痘，康諾爾立克次體、普氏立克次體、五日熱立克次體以及恙蟲熱立克次體引起不同類型的斑疹傷寒，立氏立克次體引起落基山斑疹熱，而伯納特立克次體引起 Q 熱。

立克次體痘　一種由微生物小蛛立克次體引起的鼠病，並由蟎傳播給人，引起寒戰、發熱、肌痛以及與水痘相似的皮疹。該病經過輕，病程為 2~3 周。參閱 typhus。

嵴　**(1)**（解剖學）骨頭上一條長而窄的隆起。**(2)**（牙科解剖）參閱 alveolus。

利福平　用於治療各種感染，特別是結核病的抗生素。為口服藥。有時可發生消化道不適和過敏反應。商品名：Rifadin，Rimactane。

裂谷熱　東非洲的一種病毒性疾病。通過蚊子從動物傳播給人，其症狀酷似流感。

強直　（神經病學）整個肢體對被動運動的持續性抵抗。這是帕金森病的一種症狀。呈均勻抵抗的強直稱為可塑性的或鉛管樣強直，而呈間斷性抵抗的強直稱為齒輪狀強直。與 spasticity 對比。

rigor *n.* **1.** an abrupt attack of shivering and a sensation of coldness, accompanied by a rapid rise in body temperature. This often marks the onset of a fever and may be followed by a feeling of heat, with copious sweating. **2.** *see* rigor mortis.

rigor mortis the stiffening of a body that occurs within some eight hours of death, due to chemical changes in muscle tissue. It starts to disappear after about 24 hours.

rima *n.* (in anatomy) a cleft. The *rima glottidis* (or glottis) is the space between the vocal cords.

rimiterol *n.* a drug, similar to *iso-prenaline, that is used as a *bronchodila-tor to relieve asthma and chronic bronchitis. It is administered by inhalation; side-effects, following large doses, may include dizziness, fainting, tremor, anxiety, and fast heart rate. Trade name: **Pulmadil**.

ring *n.* (in anatomy) *see* annulus.

Ringer's solution (Ringer's mixture) a clear colourless *physiological solution of sodium chloride (common salt), potassium chloride, and calcium chloride prepared with recently boiled pure water. The osmotic pressure of the solution is the same as that of blood serum. Ringer's solution is used for maintaining organs or tissues alive outside the animal or human body for limited periods. Sterile Ringer's solution may be injected intravenously to treat dehydration.

ringworm (tinea) *n.* a fungus infection of the skin, the scalp, or the nails. Ringworm is caused by the dermatophyte fungi – species of *Microsporum*,

(1) 寒戰 突然的戰栗發作和寒冷感，伴有體溫急劇升高。常為發熱開始的標誌，隨後可能有熱的感覺，並大量出汗。
(2) 屍僵 參閱 rigor mortis。

屍僵 死亡約 8 小時內出現的屍體僵硬，是由於肌組織內的化學變化所致。在約 24 小時後開始消失。

裂 （解剖學）一個裂隙。聲門裂（或聲門）是聲帶之間的縫隙。

利米特羅 與異丙腎上腺素相似的藥物，作為支氣管擴張藥用於減輕哮喘和慢性支氣管炎。用於吸入。大劑量的副作用可有頭暈、暈厥、震顫、焦慮和快心率。商品名：Pulmadil。

環 （解剖學）參閱 annulus。

林格溶液 一種透明無色的生理性溶液，為氯化鈉、氯化鉀和氯化鈣溶於新鮮煮沸的純淨水製成。其滲透壓與血漿相同，可用以維持器官或組織使其在動物或人體外存活一段時間。靜脈注射無菌的林格溶液可治療脫水。

癬，癬菌病 皮膚表面的真菌感染。好發於頭皮和足部，有時在指甲，由皮癬真菌引起，有小孢子菌屬、發癬菌和表皮

Trichophyton, and *Epidermophyton* – and also affects animals, a source of infection for man. It can be spread by direct contact or via infected materials. The lesions of ringworm may be ringlike (as its name suggests) and may cause intense itching. The commonest form of ringworm is *athlete's foot* (*tinea pedis*), which affects the skin between the toes. Another common type is ringworm of the scalp (*tinea capitis*), of which there is a severe form – *favus. Ringworm also affects the groin and thighs (*tinea cruris*: *see* dhobie itch) and the skin under a beard (*tinea barbae*). The disease is treated with antifungal agents taken by mouth (such as griseofulvin or terbinafine) or applied locally (there is now a wide choice of topical agents).

癬菌屬。它也可侵犯動物,而成為人類感染的來源。它可經直接接觸或通過被感染物傳播。癬的皮損可以是環形(正如其名字所顯示的),也可進一步引起瘙癢。最常見的癬是足癬,它侵犯足趾間的皮膚,另一種常見的癬類是頭癬,其嚴重型為黃癬。癬也可侵犯腹股溝區和股部(股癬:參閱 dhobie itch)以及鬍鬚下的皮膚(鬚癬)。此病的治療是口服或局部應用抗真菌劑(如灰黃黴素或特比萘芬,而局部劑也有許多可供選擇)。

Rinne's test a test to determine whether *deafness is conductive or sensorineural. A vibrating tuning fork is held first in the air, close to the ear, and then with its base placed on the bone (mastoid process) behind the ear. If the sound conducted by air is heard louder than the sound conducted by bone the test is positive and the deafness sensorineural; a negative result, when the sound conducted by bone is heard louder, indicates conductive deafness.

林內試驗 測定耳聾是傳導性或感音性的一種試驗。先將一振動的音叉持近耳邊,然後將音叉底部放在耳後的骨上(乳突),若由空氣傳導的聲音聽到時間長於骨傳導的聲音,則試驗為陽性,為感音性耳聾。若骨傳導的聲音持續時間長,則結果為陰性,提示為傳導性耳聾。

risk factor an attribute, such as a habit (e.g. cigarette smoking) or exposure to some environmental hazard, that leads the individual concerned to have a greater likelihood of developing an illness. The relationship is one of probability and as such can be distinguished from a *causal agent.

危險因素 導致某些人很可能患病的一種因素,諸如一種習慣(如吸煙)或接觸某些環境的危害極易引起個體患病。這種關係是一種可能性,與致病因素有所區別。

risk register a list of infants who have experienced some event in their obstetric and/or perinatal history known

危險登記 為一種嬰兒登記表。登記嬰兒在產科或在圍產期病史中的某些重要情況,這

to be correlated with a higher than average likelihood of serious abnormality; a similar listing is kept of children (and other vulnerable groups) whose social circumstances render them liable to abuse. Such children are subjected to extra surveillance from health and/or social services. Problems associated with risk registers include limiting the designation of predisposing conditions so as to contain the number on the register within reasonable proportions and ensuring that children not on the register receive adequate surveillance.

些情況發生嚴重畸形的可能性比正常高；或是一種類似的表格以登記那些社會環境致使他們易於形成惡習的孩子（和其他易受傷害的羣體）。這類兒童需接受特殊健康或社會服務監護。危險登記的問題包括為使登記表上的數字控制在合理比例內，對危險情況不能充分顯示，以及不能保證沒有登記的兒童接受適當的監護。

risus sardonicus an abnormal grinning expression resulting from involuntary prolonged contraction of facial muscles, as seen in *tetanus.

痙笑　不正常的咧嘴而笑的表情，由面部肌肉持續不隨意收縮引起，如見於破傷風。

Ritter's disease *see* staphylococcal scalded skin syndrome.

里特爾病，幼兒剝脫性皮炎　參閱 staphylococcal scalded skin syndrome。

river blindness *see* onchocerciasis.

河盲病　參閱 onchocerciasis。

RNA (ribonucleic acid) a *nucleic acid, occurring in the nucleus and cytoplasm of cells, that is concerned with synthesis of proteins (*see* messenger RNA, ribosome, transfer RNA, translation). In some viruses RNA is the genetic material. The RNA molecule is a single strand made up of units called *nucleotides.

核糖核酸　存在於細胞核和細胞漿內的一種核酸，與蛋白質合成有關（參閱 messenger RNA，ribosome，transfer RNA，translation）。有些病毒的核糖核酸是遺傳物質。核糖核酸分子是由核苷酸單位組成的單鏈。

Rocky Mountain spotted fever (spotted fever, tick fever) a disease of rodents and other small mammals in the USA caused by the microorganism *Rickettsia rickettsii* and transmitted to man by ticks. Symptoms include fever, muscle pains, and a profuse reddish rash like that of measles. If untreated the disease may be fatal, but treatment with

落基山斑疹熱（斑疹熱、蜱熱）美國囓齒動物和一些小哺乳動物的疾病，由立氏立克次體引起，並通過蜱傳播給人。症狀有發熱、肌痛，並有類似麻疹的彌散性紅色皮疹。該病若不治療，可以致死，但用四環素或氯黴素治療有效。參閱 typhus。

tetracycline or chloramphenicol is effective. *See also* typhus.

rod *n.* one of the two types of light-sensitive cells in the *retina of the eye (*compare* cone). The human eye contains about 125 million rods, which are necessary for seeing in dim light. They contain a pigment, *rhodopsin (or visual purple), which is broken down (bleached) in the light and regenerated in the dark. Breakdown of visual purple gives rise to nerve impulses; when all the pigment is bleached (i.e. in bright light) the rods no longer function. *See also* dark adaptation, light adaptation.

視桿細胞 眼視網膜內兩種感光細胞之一（與 cone 對比）。人眼約有 1.25 億個視桿細胞，該細胞在暗光下看東西時需要，它們包含有一種稱為視紫質的色素，它在亮光中破壞（脫色），在黑暗中再生。視紫質破壞時引起神經衝動；當所有色素都脫色（如在亮光裏）則視桿細胞不再起作用。參閱 dark adaptation，light adaptation。

rodent ulcer *see* basal cell carcinoma.

侵蝕性潰瘍 參閱 basal cell carcinoma。

roentgen *n.* a unit of exposure dose of X- or gamma-radiation equal to the dose that will produce 2.58×10^{-4} coulomb on all the ions of one sign, when all the electrons released in a volume of air of mass 1 kilogram are completely stopped.

倫琴 X 射綫或 γ 射綫輻射劑量單位：在質量為 1000 克的空氣中，當所有的電子停止釋放時輻射所產生的同符號離子的全部電荷量為 2.58×10^{-4} 庫倫。

role playing acting out another person's expected behaviour, usually in a contrived situation, in order to understand that person better. It is used in family psychotherapy, in teaching social skills to patients, and also in the training of psychiatric (and other) staff.

扮演角色 通常在預先計劃好的情況下，做出別人所預期的行為，以便使人更好地了解他們。此法用於家庭精神療法，教給病人社交能力，也可用以訓練精神病學（或其他的）工作人員。

Romaña's sign an early clinical sign of *Chagas' disease, appearing some three weeks after infection. There is considerable swelling of the eyelids of one or both eyes. This may be due to the presence of the parasites causing the disease but it may also be an allergic reaction to the repeated bites of their insect carriers.

羅曼尼亞徵（偏側性瞼結膜炎） 恰加斯病（南美洲錐蟲病）的早期臨床徵徵，在感染後約三周出現。一側或雙側眼瞼有明顯腫脹。可能是由致病寄生蟲引起，但也可能是病媒昆蟲反覆叮咬後的過敏反應。

Romanowsky stains a group of stains used for microscopical examination of blood cells, consisting of variable mixtures of thiazine dyes, such as azure B, with eosin. Romanowsky stains give characteristic staining patterns, on the basis of which blood cells are classified. The group includes the stains of Leishmann, Wright, May-Grünwald, Giemsa, etc.

Romberg's sign a finding on examination suggesting either a sensory disorder affecting those nerves that transmit information to the brain about the position of the limbs and joints and the tension in the muscles or a failure of the brain (cerebellum) to process this information. The patient is asked to stand upright. Romberg's sign is positive if he maintains his posture when his eyes are open but sways and falls when his eyes are closed.

rongeur *n.* powerful biting forceps for cutting tissue, particularly bone.

root *n.* **1.** (in neurology) a bundle of nerve fibres at its emergence from the spinal cord. The 31 pairs of *spinal nerves have two roots on each side, an anterior root containing motor nerve fibres and a posterior root containing sensory fibres. The roots merge outside the cord to form mixed nerves. **2.** (in dentistry) the part of a *tooth that is not covered by enamel and is normally attached to the alveolar *bone by periodontal fibres. **3.** the origin of any structure, i.e. the point at which it diverges from another structure. Anatomical name: **radix**.

root canal treatment (in *endodontics) the procedure of removing the remnants of the pulp of a tooth, cleaning and

羅曼諾夫斯基染劑　用於顯微鏡檢血細胞的一組染色劑。由噻嗪染劑（如天藍 B）與伊紅組成的各種不同混合劑。羅曼諾夫斯基染劑可以染出特徵性的染片，在此基礎上，可對血細胞進行分類。這類染色劑包括有利什曼、賴特、梅-格氏、吉姆薩染色劑等。

龍貝格徵　在檢查診斷是影響了傳遞有關肢體和關節位置以及肌張力等信息到大腦的神經引起的感覺性疾病或是腦（大腦）接受這些信息失敗時所得到的體徵。要求病人直立，若睜眼時能維持姿勢，而閉眼時則搖晃和摔倒，則為龍貝格徵陽性。

咬骨鉗　能切斷組織和骨頭的有力的咬鉗。

根　(1)（神經學）由脊髓發出的一束神經纖維。31 對脊神經每一對有左右兩個根。前根有運動神經纖維，後根有感覺神經纖維。兩神經根在脊髓外合併形成混合神經。(2)（牙科學）牙齒無釉質遮蓋的部分，正常時借助牙周纖維與牙槽骨連接。(3) 某種結構的起始部，即從其他結構的分出點。解剖學用語：根。

根管治療　（牙髓病學）去除殘留牙髓，使牙內根管清潔和成形，並作根管充填（參閱 root

shaping the canal inside the tooth, and filling the root canal (see root filling). The entire treatment usually extends over several visits. It is used to treat toothache and apical abscesses.

root filling 1. the final stage of *root canal treatment, in which the prepared canal inside a tooth root is filled with a suitable material. **2.** the material used to fill the canal in the root, usually a core of *gutta-percha with a thin coating of sealing cement.

root induction (in *endodontics) a procedure to allow continued root formation in an immature tooth with a damaged pulp.

Rorschach test a test to measure aspects of personality, consisting of ten inkblots, half of which are in various colours and the other half in black and white. The responses to the different inkblots are used to derive hypotheses about the subject. The use of the test for the diagnosis of brain damage or schizophrenia is no longer generally supported. See also projective test.

rosacea *n.* a chronic inflammatory disease of the face in which the skin becomes abnormally flushed. At times it becomes pustular and there may be an associated *keratitis. The disease occurs in both sexes and at all ages but is most common in women in their sixties; the cause is unknown. Treatment with oral tetracycline or topical metronidazole is very effective.

roseola (roseola infantum) *n.* a condition of young children in which a fever lasting for three or four days is followed by a rose-coloured maculopapular rash

filling）。全部的治療通常需要幾次，此法用於治療牙痛和根尖膿腫。

(1) 牙根充填 根管治療的最後階段，用適當物質充填在製備好的牙根根管內。**(2) 填料** 用於充填牙根管的物質，通常其中心是馬來乳膠，外面包有一層薄的水門汀封閉劑。

根誘導 （牙髓病學）使牙髓損壞的未成熟牙能繼續形成牙根的方法。

羅爾沙赫試驗 測定個性的一種試驗。由 10 種墨迹組成，其中半數是不同顏色的，另一半是黑白的。用對不同墨迹的反應來判斷病人的思想。用這種試驗來診斷大腦損害或精神分裂症已經不再得到廣泛支持。參閱 projective test。

酒渣鼻 一種面部的慢性炎症性疾病，其面部皮膚變得不正常的潮紅。有時它可變為膿疱性並合併角膜炎。該病可發生於任何年齡的男性和女性，但在女性 60 歲後最常見；原因不明。口服四環素或局部應用甲硝唑治療非常有效。

玫瑰疹 一種兒童疾病，病發時發熱持續 3 或 4 天，其後有玫瑰色的斑丘皮疹，2 天後皮疹退去。這種最常見的兒童發

that fades after two days. The commonest exanthematous fever in young children, it is caused by a recently discovered virus, human herpesvirus 6.

疹熱，由近年發現的人疱疹病毒 6 引起。

rostellum *n.* (*pl.* **rostella**) a mobile and retractable knob bearing hooks, present on the head (scolex) of certain *tapeworms, e.g. *Taenia* and *Echinococcus*.

頂突 某些絛蟲頭節上可動的和能回縮的帶鈎的突起。如絛蟲和棘球屬。

rostrum *n.* (*pl.* **rostra**) (in anatomy) a beaklike projection, such as that on the sphenoid bone. **–rostral** *adj.*

喙 （解剖學）一個鳥嘴狀的突起物，例如蝶骨上的喙。

rotator *n.* a muscle that brings about rotation of a part. The *rotatores* are small muscles situated deep in the back between adjacent vertebrae. They help to extend and rotate the vertebrae.

回旋肌 使某部位旋轉的肌肉。回旋肌是位於背深部兩個相鄰椎骨之間的小肌肉，可幫助伸展和旋轉椎骨。

Rothera's test a method of testing urine for the presence of acetone or acetoacetic acid: a sign of *diabetes mellitus. Strong ammonia is added to a sample of urine saturated with ammonium sulphate crystals and containing a small quantity of sodium nitroprusside. A purple colour confirms the presence of acetone or acetoacetic acid.

羅瑟拉試驗 測定尿內存在丙酮或乙酰乙酸的方法。尿內有丙酮或乙酰乙酸是糖尿病的一種徵象。將濃氨水加入飽含硫酸銨結晶和含有小量硝普鈉的尿標本中，出現紫色就可肯定有丙酮或乙酰乙酸。

Roth spot a pale area surrounded by haemorrhage sometimes seen in the retina, with the aid of an *ophthalmoscope, in those who have bacterial endocarditis, septicaemia, or leukaemia.

羅思斑 用檢眼鏡在患有細菌性心內膜炎、敗血症或白血病患者視網膜上看到的周圍有出血的白色區域。

roughage *n. see* dietary fibre.

粗糙食物 參閱 dietary fibre。

rouleau *n.* (*pl.* **rouleaux**) a cylindrical structure in the blood formed from several red blood cells piled one upon the other and adhering by their rims.

紅細胞錢串 血液內由若干紅細胞互相重疊，其邊緣黏連而形成的圓柱狀結構。

round window *see* fenestra (rotunda).

圓窗 參閱 fenestra (rotunda)。

roundworm *n. see* nematode.

蛔蟲　參閱 nematode。

-rrhagia (-rrhage) *suffix denoting* excessive or abnormal flow or discharge from an organ or part. Examples: *haemorrhage* (excessive bleeding); *menorrhagia* (excessive menstrual flow).

〔後綴〕**流出**　指有某種液體從某器官或身體某部過多或異常的流出或排出。例如：出血（過多的流出血液），月經過多（過多地流出經血）。

-rrhaphy *suffix denoting* surgical sewing; suturing. Example: *herniorrhaphy* (of a hernia).

〔後綴〕**縫合術**　指外科的縫合、縫術，如疝修補術。

-rrhexis *suffix denoting* splitting or rupture of a part.

〔後綴〕**裂**　指身體某部位的分裂或破裂。

-rrhoea *suffix denoting* a flow or discharge from an organ or part. Example: *rhinorrhoea* (from the nose).

〔後綴〕**溢**　指從某器官或部位流出或排出液體，例如鼻溢（從鼻流出）。

RSI *see* repetitive strain injury.

重複緊張性損傷　參閱 repetitive strain injury。

RSV *see* respiratory syncytial virus.

呼吸合胞病毒　參閱 respiratory syncytial virus。

rubber dam (in dentistry) a sheet of rubber used to isolate one or more teeth during treatment.

橡皮障　（牙科學）用於在治療時隔開一個或更多牙齒的一片橡皮。

rubefacient *n.* an agent that causes reddening and warming of the skin. Rubefacients are often used as *counterirritants for the relief of muscular pain.

發紅藥　一種使皮膚發紅和發熱的藥物，發紅藥常被用作抗刺激劑，以減輕肌肉疼痛。

rubella *n. see* German measles.

風疹　參閱 German measles。

rubeola *n. see* measles.

麻疹　參閱 measles。

rubidium-81 *n.* an artificial radioactive isotope that has a half-life of about four hours and decays into the radioactive gas *krypton-81m, emitting radiations as it does so. Symbol: ^{81}Rb.

^{81}銣　一種人工放射性同位素，其半衰期約4小時，衰變為放射性氣體^{81m}氪，同時放出射綫。符號：^{81}Rb。

rubor *n.* redness: one of the classical signs of inflammation in a tissue, the other three being *calor (heat), *dolor (pain) and *tumor (swelling). The redness of inflamed tissue is due to the increase in size of the small blood vessels in the area, which therefore contain more blood.

發紅　組織炎症的典型症狀之一，其他三個症狀是灼熱、疼痛和腫脹。炎症組織發紅的原因是局部小血管擴張，所以含血多。

rubrospinal tract a tract of *motor neurones that extends from the midbrain down to different levels in the spinal cord, carrying impulses that have travelled from the cerebral and cerebellar cortex via the nucleus ruber (red nucleus). The tract plays an important part in the control of skilled and dextrous movements.

紅核脊髓束　運動神經元的傳導束，從中腦下降到達脊髓的不同水平。傳遞來自大腦和小腦皮質經紅核的衝動。該傳導對於控制熟練和靈巧的運動極為重要。

ruga *n.* (*pl.* **rugae**) a fold or crease, especially one of the folds of mucous membrane that line the stomach.

皺褶　一種皺襞，特別指胃內黏膜皺襞。

rumination *n.* (in psychiatry) an obsessional type of thinking in which the same thoughts or themes are experienced repetitively, to the exclusion of other forms of mental activity. The patient commonly feels depressed and guilty after rumination. Rumination may be distinguished from morbid preoccupation in that the thoughts are irrational and resisted by the patient; they often involve abhorrent or aggressive feelings about events in the remote past and are accompanied by a lack of confidence in memory.

沉思　（精神病學）指一種不能擺脫的思想，即總是在重複體驗同樣的思想或問題而排斥了其他類型的精神活動。病人在沉思後往往覺得憂鬱和自咎。沉思與病態偏見，或出神的區別，在於其思想的不合理性，並為病人所反抗。他們常常對很久以前發生的事情有厭惡，憤怒和仇恨的感情，並對記憶缺乏信心。

rupture 1. *n. see* hernia. **2.** *n.* the bursting apart or open of an organ or tissue; for example, the splitting of the membranes enclosing an infant during childbirth. **3.** *vb.* (of tissues, etc.) to burst apart or open.

破裂　(1) 參閱 hernia。(2) 器官或組織的突然的破裂或裂開，例如，分娩時包住嬰兒的羊膜破裂。(3)（組織等）破裂或裂開。

Russell-Silver syndrome a congenital condition characterized by short stature, a triangular face with a small mandible (lower jaw), and asymmetry of the body.

拉西氏綜合徵　一種先天性疾病，其特徵為身材矮小，三角形臉，下頜小，身體不對稱。

Russian spring-summer encephalitis an influenza-like viral disease that affects the brain and nervous system and occurs in Russia and central Europe. It is transmitted to man either through the bite of forest-dwelling ticks of the species *Ixodes persulcatus* or by drinking the milk of infected goats. Infection of the meninges results in paralysis of the limbs and of the muscles of the neck and back. The disease, which is often fatal, can be prevented by vaccination.

俄羅斯春夏型腦炎　侵犯大腦和神經系統的一種流感樣病毒性疾病。發生在俄羅斯和中歐。通過棲息於森林的金鉤硬蜱叮咬或飲用感染的山羊奶而傳染給人。腦膜感染可引起肢體癱瘓，以及頸部和背部肌肉麻痺。該病常致死，但可通過接種進行預防。

Ryle's tube a thin flexible tube of rubber or plastic, inserted through the mouth or nose of a patient and used for withdrawing fluid from the stomach or giving a test meal.

賴耳管　一種橡膠或塑料的可曲性細管，通過病人口腔或鼻腔插入胃內，用於抽吸胃內液體或注入試餐。

S

Sabin vaccine an oral vaccine against poliomyelitis, prepared by culture of the virus under special conditions so that it loses its virulence (i.e. it becomes attenuated) but retains its ability to stimulate antibody production.

薩賓疫苗　口服脊髓灰質炎疫苗。在特殊條件下，通過培養病毒製成，使其失去致病力（減毒），但仍保留其刺激抗體產生的能力。

sac *n.* a pouch or baglike structure. Sacs can enclose natural cavities in the body, e.g. in the lungs (*see* alveolus) or in the *lacrimal apparatus of the eye, or they can be pathlological, as in a hernia.

囊　小袋或口袋樣結構。在體內圍成自然的腔，如肺（參閱 alveolus）或眼的淚器，或是病理性的，如疝。

sacchar- (saccharo-) *prefix denoting* sugar.

〔前綴〕糖

saccharide *n.* a carbohydrate. *See also* disaccharide, monosaccharide, polysaccharide.

糖類 碳水化合物。參閱 dis-accharide，monosaccharide，polysaccharide。

saccharine *n.* a sweetening agent. Saccharine is 400 times as sweet as sugar and has no energy content. It is very useful as a sweetener in diabetic and low-calorie foods. Saccharine is destroyed by heat and is not therefore used in cooking.

糖精 甜味劑。比糖甜 400 倍，但不含能量。常用作糖尿病或低卡食物的甜味劑。糖精受熱破壞，故不用於烹調。

Saccharomyces *n. see* yeast.

酵母屬 參閱 yeast。

saccule (sacculus) *n.* the smaller of the two membranous sacs within the vestibule of the ear: it forms part of the membranous *labyrinth. It is filled with fluid (endolymph) and contains a *macula. This responds to gravity and relays information to the brain about the position of the head.

球囊 耳的前庭內兩個膜囊中的較小者。構成部分膜迷路。球囊內充滿液體（內淋巴），並含有斑，可對重力作出反應，將頭部位置信息傳遞給腦。

saccus *n.* a sac or pouch. The *saccus endolymphaticus* is the small sac connected to the saccule and utricle of the inner ear by the *endolymphatic duct.

囊 小袋。內淋巴囊是由內淋巴管連接到內耳的球囊和橢圓囊的一個小囊。

sacralization *n.* abnormal fusion of the fifth lumbar vertebra with the sacrum.

腰椎骶化 第五腰椎與骶骨的異常融合。

sacral nerves the five pairs of *spinal nerves that emerge from the spinal column in the sacrum. The nerves carry sensory and motor fibres from the upper and lower leg and from the anal and genital regions.

骶神經 從脊柱骶部穿出的五對脊神經。含有支配大、小腿及肛門和生殖器部位的感覺和運動神經纖維。

sacral vertebrae the five vertebrae that are fused together to form the *sacrum.

骶椎 融合在一起組成骶骨的五塊椎骨。

sacro- *prefix denoting* the sacrum. Examples: *sacrococcygeal* (relating to the sacrum and coccyx); *sacrodynia* (pain in); *sacroiliac* (relating to the sacrum and ilium).

〔前綴〕骶（骨） 如骶尾的（與骶骨和尾骨相關的），骶（部）痛，骶髂的（與骶骨和髂骨相關的）。

sacroiliitis *n.* inflammation of the sacroiliac joint. Involvement of both joints is a common feature of ankylosing *spondylitis and associated rheumatic diseases, including *Reiter's syndrome and *psoriatic arthritis. The resultant low back pain and stiffness may be alleviated by rest and anti-inflammatory analgesics.

骶髂關節炎 骶髂關節的炎症。累及兩側骶髂關節，是關節強硬性脊椎炎和兼有風濕性疾病的共同特徵。包括賴特爾綜合徵和銀屑病性關節炎。本病引起的低位背痛和強直，可通過休息和使用抗炎止痛藥緩解。

sacrum *n.* (*pl.* **sacra**) a curved triangular element of the *backbone consisting of five fused vertebrae (*sacral vertebrae*). It articulates with the last lumbar vertebra above, the coccyx below, and the hip bones laterally. *See also* vertebra. **–sacral** *adj.*

骶骨 由五塊融合的椎骨（骶椎）組成的一個彎曲的三角形的脊柱部分。上部與最下一塊腰椎，下部與尾骨，側部與髖骨形成關節。參閱 vertebra。

saddle joint a form of *diarthrosis (freely movable joint) in which the articulating surfaces of the bones are reciprocally saddle-shaped. It occurs at the carpometacarpal joint of the thumb.

鞍狀關節 一種可動關節（可自由活動的關節）。兩骨的關節面呈交互鞍狀。見於拇指的腕掌關節。

sadism *n.* sexual excitement in response to inflicting or thinking about inflicting pain upon other people. *See also* masochism, sexual deviation. **–sadist** *n.* **–sadistic** *adj.*

施虐狂 使他人痛苦，或想到使人痛苦就能獲得的性興奮。參閱 masochism，sexual deviation。

SADS (seasonal affective disorder syndrome) a disorder in which the mood of the affected person is said to change according to the season of the year. Typically, with the onset of winter, there is depression, general slowing of mind and body, excessive sleeping, and overeating. These symptoms resolve with the coming of spring. The phenomenon may partly account for the known seasonal variation in suicide rates. SADS is not yet generally accepted as a clinical entity and the prevalence is unknown. There is evidence that mood is related to light, which suppresses the release of the hormone *melatonin from the pineal

季節性情感紊亂綜合徵 隨着一年中季節的改變，易感人羣情緒的紊亂。典型病例發生在冬季，抑鬱、腦力和體力活動通常變遲鈍、嗜睡並過量飲食。這些症狀隨着春季的來臨而消除。這種現象可以部分說明已知的自殺率的季節性改變。季節性情感紊亂綜合徵作為一種臨床病種尚未得到普遍接受，故其患病率不明。有證據證明情緒和光綫有關，此病抑制了松果體釋放褪黑激素。據說在白天暴露地在充足的光照下有時可緩解症狀。

gland. Exposure to additional light during the day is said sometimes to relieve symptoms.

safe period the days in each *menstrual cycle when conception is least likely. Ovulation generally occurs at the mid-point of each cycle, and in women with regular periods it is possible to calculate the days at the beginning and end of the cycle when coitus is unlikely to result in pregnancy. *See* rhythm method.

安全期　在每次月經周期內受孕可能性最小的日期。排卵通常發生在每個周期的中期。對經期有規律的婦女，可算出周期開始和終止時的日期，此時性交不會導致懷孕。參閱 rhythm method。

safranin (safranine) *n.* a group of water- and alcohol-soluble basic dyes used to stain cell nuclei and as counterstains for Gram-negative bacteria.

藏紅　一種溶於水和酒精的鹼性染料。用於染細胞核，並用作革蘭氏陰性細菌的複染劑。

sagittal *adj.* describing the dorsoventral plane that extends down the long axis of the body, dividing it into right and left halves (see illustration).

矢狀的　用以描述由背向腹的平面，此平面沿身體的長軸將身體分成左右兩半（見圖）。

sagittal suture *see* suture (def. 1).

矢狀縫　參閱 suture（釋義 1）。

salaam attacks *see* infantile spasms.

點頭狀發作　參閱 infantile spasms。

salbutamol *n.* a drug that stimulates beta-adrenergic receptors (*see* sympathomimetic); it is used as a *bronchodilator to relieve asthma, chronic bronchitis, and emphysema. It is administered by mouth, injection, or inhalation; side-effects may include dizziness, tremor, and fast heart rate, particularly after large doses. Trade name: **Ventolin**.

沙丁胺醇　一種刺激 β-腎上腺素能受體的藥物（參閱 sympathomimetic）。用作支氣管擴張藥，治療哮喘、慢性支氣管炎和肺氣腫。口服、注射或噴霧吸入。副作用可有眩暈、肌肉震顫、心率加快，大劑量使用後尤為多見。商品名：Ventolin。

salicylic acid a drug that causes the skin to peel and destroys bacteria and fungi. It is applied to the skin to treat ulcers, dandruff, eczema, psoriasis, warts, and corns. Skin sensitivity reactions may occur after continued use.

水楊酸　一種可引起表皮脫落、殺滅細菌和真菌的藥物。塗搽於皮膚治療潰瘍、頭皮屑、濕疹、銀屑病、疣和雞眼。連續使用可有皮膚過敏反應。

Sagittal plane of section through the body
身體矢狀平面

salicylism *n.* poisoning due to an overdose of aspirin or other salicylate-containing compounds. The main symptoms are headache, dizziness, ringing in the ears (tinnitus), disturbances of vision, vomiting, and – in severe cases – delirium and collapse. There is often severe *acidosis.

水楊酸中毒 過量阿司匹林或其他含有水楊酸鹽的藥物引起的中毒。主要症狀有頭痛、眩暈、耳鳴、視力減退、嘔吐，嚴重者可有譫妄和虛脫，並常有嚴重酸中毒。

saline (normal saline) *n.* a solution containing 0.9% sodium chloride. Saline may be used clinically as a diluent for drugs administered by injection and as a plasma substitute.

鹽水（生理鹽水） 含有 0.9% 氯化鈉的水溶液。臨床上用作注射劑的稀釋液和血漿代用品。

saliva *n.* the alkaline liquid secreted by the *salivary glands and the mucous membrane of the mouth. Its principal

唾液 由唾液腺和口腔黏膜分泌的鹼性液體。主要成分有水、黏液、緩衝物質和酶（如

constituents are water, mucus, buffers, and enzymes (e.g. amylase). The functions of saliva are to keep the mouth moist, to aid swallowing of food, to minimize changes of acidity in the mouth, and to digest starch. **–salivary** *adj.*

澱粉酶）。其作用是使口腔保持濕潤，幫助吞咽食物，使口腔酸度變化減到最小，以及消化澱粉。

salivary gland a gland that produces *saliva. There are three pairs of salivary glands: the *parotid glands, *sublingual glands, and *submandibular glands (see illustration). They are stimulated by reflex action, which can be initiated by the taste, smell, sight, or thought of food.

唾液腺　產生唾液的腺體。有三對唾液腺：腮腺、舌下腺和下頜下腺（見圖）。其分泌由味覺、嗅覺、視覺或想到食物的反射作用所引起。

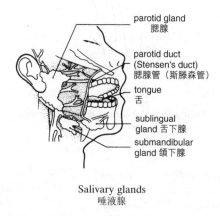

parotid gland
腮腺

parotid duct
(Stensen's duct)
腮腺管（斯滕森管）

tongue
舌

sublingual
gland 舌下腺

submandibular
gland 頜下腺

Salivary glands
唾液腺

salivation *n.* the secretion of saliva by the salivary glands of the mouth, increased in response to the chewing action of the jaws or to the thought, taste, smell, or sight of food. A small but regular flow of saliva is maintained to promote cleanliness in the mouth even when food is not being eaten. *See also* ptyalism.

流涎　由口腔唾液腺產生的唾液分泌。當咀嚼或者想到、嘗到、聞到或看到食物時，分泌即增加。甚或沒有進食，仍有少量唾液有規律地分泌，以保持口腔清潔。參閱 ptyalism。

Salk vaccine a vaccine against poliomyelitis, formed by treating the virus with formalin, which prevents it

索爾克疫苗　一種抗脊髓灰質炎的疫苗。用福爾馬林處理病毒製成。疫苗病毒不會致病，

from causing disease but does not impair its ability to stimulate antibody production. It is administered by injection.

但不影響其刺激抗體產生的能力。注射用。

salmeterol *n.* a *sympathomimetic bronchodilator drug used to treat severe asthma. It is administered by metered-dose areosol inhaler. Possible side-effects include a paradoxical worsening of the condition and a lowering of the blood potassium level. Trade name: **Serevent**.

沙美特羅 一種擬交感神經的支氣管擴張藥，用於治療嚴重的哮喘，計量氣霧吸入。可能的副作用有病情惡化以及血鉀水平降低。商品名：Serevent。

Salmonella *n.* a genus of motile rodlike Gram-negative bacteria that inhabit the intestines of animals and man and cause disease. They ferment glucose, usually with the formation of gas. The species *S. paratyphi* causes *paratyphoid fever, and *S. typhi* causes *typhoid fever. *Food poisoning, gastroenteritis, and septicaemia are caused by other species of *Salmonella*.

沙門菌屬 一種能運動的，桿狀的革蘭氏陰性菌屬。棲居於動物和人的腸道而致病。能發酵葡萄糖，常伴隨氣體的產生。副傷寒沙門菌引起副傷寒，傷寒沙門菌引起傷寒，其他沙門菌引起食物中毒、胃腸炎和敗血症。

salmonellosis *n.* an infestation of the digestive system by bacteria of the genus *Salmonella. See also* food poisoning.

沙門菌病 由沙門菌屬細菌引起的消化系統感染。參閱 food poisoning。

salping- (salpingo-) *prefix denoting* **1.** the Fallopian tube. **2.** the auditory tube (meatus).

〔前綴〕**(1)** 輸卵管 **(2)** 咽鼓管（耳道）

salpingectomy *n.* the surgical removal of a Fallopian tube. The operation involving both tubes is a permanent and completely effective method of contraception (*see* sterilization) since it prevents the egg cells passing from the ovaries to the uterus.

輸卵管切除術 外科切除輸卵管。手術切除兩側輸卵管是永久性的和完全有效的避孕方法（參閱 sterilization），因為阻止了卵子從卵巢進入子宮。

salpingitis *n.* inflammation of a tube, most commonly applied to inflammation of one or both of the Fallopian tubes caused by bacterial infection spreading from the vagina or uterus or carried in

輸卵管炎 輸卵管炎症。最常見於一側或兩側。經陰道或子宮或血液傳播的細菌感染引起。急性輸卵管炎時下腹部有劇烈疼痛，常可誤診為闌尾

the blood. In *acute salpingitis* there is a sharp pain in the lower abdomen, which may be mistaken for appendicitis, and the infection may spread to the membrane lining the abdominal cavity (*see* peritonitis). In severe cases the tubes may become blocked with scar tissue and the patient will be unable to conceive. The condition is treated with antibiotics and later, if necessary, by the surgical removal of the diseased tube(s).

炎。感染可傳播至腹膜（參閱 peritonitis）。嚴重病例，輸卵管可被瘢痕組織阻塞，患者不能受孕。治療可用抗生素，晚期必要時可手術切除病側輸卵管。

salpingography *n*. *radiography of one or both Fallopian tubes after a *radiopaque substance has been introduced into them via an injection into the uterus.

輸卵管造影術 經由子宮注射不透 X 綫物質，對一側或兩側輸卵管進行放射造影的技術。

salpingolysis *n*. a surgical operation carried out to restore patency to blocked Fallopian tubes; it involves the *division and removal of adhesions around the ovarian ends of the tubes.

輸卵管黏連分離術 一種使阻塞的輸卵管恢復開放的外科手術。治療採取分離和切除輸卵管的卵巢端周圍的黏連。

salpingo-oophoritis *n*. inflammation of a Fallopian tube and an ovary.

輸卵管卵巢炎 輸卵管和卵巢的炎症。

salpingostomy *n*. the operation performed to restore free passage through a blocked Fallopian tube. The blocked portion of the tube is removed surgically and the continuity is then restored. It is performed in women who have been sterilized previously by tubal occlusion (*see* sterilization) and in others whose Fallopian tubes have become blocked as a result of pelvic infection.

輸卵管復通術 使阻塞的輸卵管完全恢復復暢通的手術。輸卵管的阻塞部分被外科切除，然後恢復其連接。適用於以前通過結紮輸卵管的絕育手術（參閱 sterilization）以及由於盆腔感染造成輸卵管阻塞的女性。

salt depletion excessive loss of sodium chloride (common salt) from the body. This may result from sweating, persistent vomiting or diarrhoea, or loss of fluid in wounds. The main symptoms are muscular weakness and cramps. Miners and workers in hot climates are particularly

缺鹽 身體過度喪失氯化物（食鹽）。可由出汗、頑固性嘔吐或腹瀉，或創傷丟失液體所致。主要症狀為肌肉無力或痙攣。礦工和勞工們在炎熱氣候下尤為危險。常以服用鹽片作為預防措施。

at risk, and salt tablets are often taken as a preventive measure.

Salter and Harris classification *see* epiphysis.

Samaritans *n*. a British voluntary organization providing a telephone service for the suicidal and despairing. Started in 1953 by the Rev. Chad Varah in the cellars of a London church (St Stephen, Walbrook) with one telephone, it now has 187 branches throughout the country manned by some 22,000 volunteers. It offers a nonprofessional, confidential, and (if required) anonymous service at all hours. Samaritans will listen for as long as they are needed (sometimes called the listening therapy) and the service is free. They offer little advice, believing that their clients will be helped to make their own decisions by talking to someone who cares. They also offer a befriending service to support exceptionally distressed clients through a serious crisis.

sampling frame *see* random sample.

sanatorium *n*. **1.** a hospital or institution for the rehabilitation and convalescence of patients of any kind. **2.** an institution for patients who have suffered from pulmonary tuberculosis.

sandfly *n*. a small hairy fly of the widely distributed genus *Phlebotomus*. Adult sandflies rarely exceed 3 mm in length and have long slender legs. The blood-sucking females of certain species transmit various diseases, including *leishmaniasis, *sandfly fever, and *bartonellosis.

索特-哈利斯分類法 參閱 epiphysis。

撒瑪利亞社 英國的一個為可能自殺的人和絕望的人提供電話服務的志願組織。1953年由查德‧瓦拉牧師在倫敦一座教堂的地下室創辦,當時他只有一部電話。至今全國已有187個分支,22 000名志願者。該組織不分晝夜提供非職業性的、保密的和(如需要)匿名的服務。當有人求助於他們時,他們會耐心傾聽(有時稱作傾聽療法),而其服務是不收費的。他們很少給求助者出主意,相信求助者同關懷他的人交談後會得到幫助,做出自己的決定。他們也給遭遇嚴重危機而格外痛苦的求助人提供友好的援助服務。

抽樣設計 參閱 random sample。

療養院 **(1)** 使各類病人康復的醫院或機構。**(2)** 為肺結核病人設置的機構。

白蛉 一種多毛的白蛉屬微小雙翅昆蟲。分布很廣。成蟲的長度很少超過3 mm,腿細長。某幾種吸血的雌白蛉傳播多種疾病,包括利什曼病、白蛉熱和巴爾通體病。

sandfly fever (Pappataci fever) a viral disease transmitted to man by the bite of the sandfly *Phlebotomus papatasii*. Sandfly fever occurs principally in countries surrounding the Persian Gulf and the tropical Mediterranean; it occurs during the warmer months, does not last long, and is never fatal. Symptoms resemble those of influenza. There is no specific treatment apart from aspirin and codeine to relieve the symptoms.

白蛉熱 一種病毒性疾病。由巴浦白蛉叮咬人而傳播。主要發生於波斯灣和熱帶地中海周圍的國家。在較暖的月份內出現，為時不長，不致命。症狀類似流感。除用阿司匹林和可待因減輕症狀外，無特殊治療。

sandwich treatments combinations of treatment that 'sandwich' one type of treatment (e.g. a surgical operation) between exposures to another treatment (e.g. pre- and postoperative radiotherapy).

三明治療法 一種「三明治」式的複合治療（如外科手術），介於另外一種療法的兩次治療之間（如手術前後放射治療）。

sangui- (sanguino-) *prefix denoting* blood.

〔前綴〕血

sanguineous *adj.* **1.** stained, containing, or covered with blood. **2.** (of tissues) containing more than the normal quantity of blood.

血的 (1) 含血的，染血的或被血覆蓋的。(2)（組織）含有超過正常量的血液。

sanies *n.* a foul-smelling watery discharge from a wound or ulcer, containing serum, blood, and pus.

腐膿液 由傷口或潰瘍流出的有惡臭味的水樣物。含有血清、血和膿。

sanitarian *n. see* medical assistant.

公共衛生學家 參閱 medical assistant。

saphena *n. see* saphenous vein.

隱靜脈 參閱 saphenous vein。

saphena varix an abnormal dilatation of the terminal section of the long *saphenous vein in the groin.

隱靜脈曲張 長的隱靜脈的終末段在腹股溝的異常擴張。

saphenous nerve a large branch of the *femoral nerve that arises in the upper thigh, travels down on the inside of the leg, and supplies the skin from

隱神經 股神經的一個大分支。起於大腿上部，沿小腿內側下行。其感覺纖維分布於膝至踝以下的皮膚。

the knee to below the ankle with sensory nerves.

saphenous vein (saphena) either of two superficial veins of the leg, draining blood from the foot. The *long saphenous vein* – the longest vein in the body – runs from the foot, up the medial side of the leg, to the groin, where it joins the femoral vein. The *short saphenous vein* runs up the back of the calf to join the popliteal vein at the back of the knee.

隱靜脈 下肢的兩條淺靜脈。均收集足的血液。大隱靜脈是體內最長的靜脈，從足沿小腿內側上行至腹股溝，注入股靜脈。小隱靜脈沿腓腸肌背面上行，在膝的後方注入膕靜脈。

sapr- (sapro-) *prefix denoting* **1.** putrefaction. **2.** decaying matter.

〔前綴〕**腐** **(1)** 腐爛。 **(2)** 腐朽物。

sapraemia *n.* blood poisoning by toxins of saprophytic bacteria (bacteria living on dead or decaying matter). *Compare* pyaemia, septicaemia, toxaemia.

腐血症 血中毒。由腐物寄生菌（靠屍體或腐爛物質生活的細菌）的毒素引起。與 pyaemia，septicaemia，toxaemia 對比。

saprophyte *n.* any free-living organism that lives and feeds on the dead and putrefying tissues of animals or plants. *Compare* parasite. **–saprophytic** *adj.*

腐生物 任何靠動物、人的屍體和腐爛組織營養而生活的微生物。與 parasite 對比。

sarc- (sarco-) *prefix denoting* **1.** flesh or fleshy tissue. **2.** muscle.

〔前綴〕**(1)** 肉，肉樣組織 **(2)** 肌

sarcocele *n.* an obsolete term for a fleshy tumour (sarcoma) of the testis.

睾丸肉樣腫 睾丸肉樣瘤（肉瘤）的舊稱。

Sarcocystis *n.* a genus of parasitic protozoans (*see* Sporozoa) that infect birds, reptiles, and herbivorous mammals. *S. lindemanni*, which occasionally infects man, forms cylindrical cysts (*sarcocysts*) in the muscle fibres. In heavy infections these cysts can cause tissue degeneration and therefore provoke muscular pain and weakness. Sarcocysts have, in the few positively diagnosed cases, been

肉孢子蟲屬 寄生原蟲的一屬（參閱 Sporozoa）。感染鳥類、爬蟲類和食草的哺乳動物。林德曼肉孢子蟲偶可感染人，在肌組織內形成圓筒狀包囊（肉孢子蟲囊）。嚴重感染時包囊可導致組織變性，引起肌肉疼痛無力。少數確診病例見有肉孢子蟲囊位於心肌、上肢肌和喉。

located in the heart muscles, arm muscles, and larynx.

sarcoid 1. *adj.* fleshy. **2.** *n.* a fleshy tumour.

(1) 肉樣的　(2) 肉樣瘤，類肉瘤

sarcoidosis *n.* a chronic disorder of unknown cause in which the lymph nodes in many parts of the body are enlarged and small fleshy nodules (*see* granuloma) develop in the lungs, liver, and spleen. The skin, nervous system, eyes, and salivary glands are also commonly affected (*see* uveoparotitis), and the condition has features similar to *tuberculosis. Recovery is complete with minimal after-effects in two-thirds of all cases.

病肉樣瘤　一種病因未明的慢性疾患。體內許多部位的淋巴結腫大，並在肺、肝和脾內生長小的肉樣結節（參閱 granuloma）。皮膚、神經系統、眼和唾液腺亦常受累（參閱 uveoparotitis）。其症狀與結核有相似的特徵。可痊愈，僅三分之二的病例有極輕微的後遺症。

sarcolemma *n.* the cell membrane that encloses a muscle cell (muscle fibre).

肌膜　包着肌細胞（肌纖維）的細胞膜。

sarcoma *n.* any *cancer of connective tissue. These tumours may occur in any part of the body, as they arise in the tissues that make up an organ rather than being restricted to a particular organ. They can arise in fibrous tissue, muscle, fat, bone, cartilage, synovium, blood and lymphatic vessels, and various other tissues. *See also* chondrosarcoma, fibrosarcoma, leiomyosarcoma, liposarcoma, lymphangiosarcoma, osteosarcoma, rhabdomyosarcoma. **–sarcomatous** *adj.*

肉瘤　任何結締組織癌。肉瘤可發生於身體的任何部位，發生於構成器官的組織中而並非局限於某一器官。可發生於纖維組織、肌肉、脂肪、骨、軟骨、滑膜、血液、淋巴管以及其他各種組織。參閱 chondrosarcoma，fibrosarcoma，leiomyosarcoma，liposarcoma，lymphangiosarcoma，osteosarcoma，rhabdomyosarcoma。

sarcoma botryoides *see* carcinosarcoma.

葡萄樣肉瘤　參閱 carcinosarcoma。

sarcomatosis *n.* *sarcoma that has spread widely throughout the body, most commonly through the bloodstream. It is treated with drugs, typically one or a combination of the following: cyclophosphamide, ifosfamide, vincristine, actinomycin D, methotrexate, or doxorubicin. The prognosis is very poor.

肉瘤病　肉瘤已遍及全身的疾患。最常見通過血流播散。通常單獨或聯合使用下列藥物進行治療：環磷酰胺、異環磷酰胺、長春新鹼、放綫菌素 D、甲氨蝶呤或阿黴素。預後很差。

sarcomere *n.* one of the basic contractile units of which *striated muscle fibres are composed.

肌原纖維節　組成橫紋肌纖維的一個基本收縮單位。

Sarcophaga *n.* a genus of widely distributed non-bloodsucking flies, the flesh flies. Maggots are normally found in carrion or excrement but occasionally females will deposit their eggs in wounds or ulcers giving off a foul-smelling discharge; the presence of the maggots causes a serious *myiasis. Rarely, maggots may be ingested with food and give rise to an intestinal myiasis.

麻蠅屬　一種不吸血的蠅屬，或稱肉蠅。分布甚廣。通常在腐肉或糞便中找到蛆。偶見雌蠅排卵於傷口或潰瘍內，產生惡臭的排出物。蛆的存在可致嚴重的蠅蛆病。罕見蛆被攝食而引起腸道蛆病。

sarcoplasm (myoplasm) *n.* the cytoplasm of muscle cells.

肌質　肌細胞的胞漿。

sarcoplasmic reticulum an arrangement of membranous vesicles and tubules found in the cytoplasm of striated muscle fibres. The sarcoplasmic reticulum plays an important role in the transmission of nervous excitation to the contractile parts of the fibres.

肌質網　由膜小泡和膜小管排列組成。見於橫紋肌纖維的胞漿內。對傳遞神經興奮信息至肌的收縮纖維起重要作用。

Sarcoptes *n.* a genus of small oval mites. The female of *S. scabiei*, the scabies mite, tunnels into the skin, where it lays its eggs. The presence of the mites causes severe irritation, which eventually leads to *scabies.

疥蟎屬　一種小的橢圓形蟎屬。雌性疥蟎，即人疥蟎，穿入皮膚形成隧道，在該處產卵。疥蟎引起嚴重的皮膚刺激，最終導致疥瘡。

sarcostyle *n.* a bundle of muscle fibrils.

肌柱　一束肌纖維。

sartorius *n.* a narrow ribbon-like muscle at the front of the thigh, arising from the anterior superior spine of the ilium and extending to the tibia, just below the knee. The longest muscle in the body, the sartorius flexes the leg on the thigh and the thigh on the abdomen.

縫匠肌　一塊窄的帶狀肌肉，位於大腿前面，起自髂前上棘，延伸至脛骨，緊靠膝下方。是體內最長的肌肉，使小腿曲向大腿，大腿曲向腹部。

satyriasis *n.* an extreme degree of promiscuous heterosexual activity in men. *Compare* nymphomania.

男子色情狂　男子的一種極度亂交異性的活動。與 nymphomania 對比。

saucerization *n.* **1.** an operation in which tissue is cut away from a wound to form a saucer-like depression. It is carried out to facilitate healing and is commonly used to treat injuries or disorders in which bone is infected. **2.** the concave appearance of the upper surface of a vertebra that has been fractured by compression.

(1) 碟形手術 一種從傷口切除組織形成碟狀凹陷的手術。這種手術有利於傷口的愈合，通常用以治療損傷或骨受感染的疾患。**(2) 碟形凹陷** 椎骨受壓骨折，椎體上面呈凹形。

Sayre's jacket a plaster of Paris cast shaped to fit around and support the backbone. It is used in cases where the vertebrae have been severely damaged by disease, such as tuberculosis.

塞爾背心 一種圓柱形石膏夾。用以支持脊柱。當椎骨由於疾病，如結核，而嚴重損傷時使用之。

scab *n.* a hard crust of dried blood, serum, or pus that develops during the body's wound-healing process over a sore, cut, or scratch.

痂 由乾涸的血、血清或膿結成的硬殼。是潰瘍、切割傷或抓傷的傷口愈合過程中產生的。

scabicide *n.* a drug that kills the mites causing *scabies.

殺疥蟎藥 一種殺滅引起疥瘡的蟎的藥物。

scabies *n.* a skin infection caused by the mite *Sarcoptes scabiei*. Scabies is typified by severe itching (particularly at night), red papules, and often secondary infection. The female mite tunnels in the skin to lay her eggs and the newly hatched mites pass easily from person to person by contact. The intense itching represents a true allergic reaction to the mite, its eggs, and its faeces. Commonly infected areas are the penis, nipples, and the skin between the fingers. Treatment is by application of a scabicide, usually *permethrin, *lindane, or *malathion, to all areas of the body from the neck down; benzyl benzoate may also be used but causes irritation. All members of a family need treatment, but clothing and bedding need not be disinfested.

疥瘡 一種由疥蟎引起的皮膚感染。其徵象為奇癢（尤在夜間），有紅色丘疹，常繼發感染。雌蟎穿入皮膚形成隧道，在該處產卵。新孵化的蟎極易經人與人的接觸而傳播。強烈的瘙癢是由對蟎、它的卵以及糞便的真正變應性反應所引起。通常感染的部位有腹股溝、陰莖、乳頭和手指間的皮膚。治療通常應用苄氯菊酯、林旦和馬拉硫磷，頸部以下的所有部位都應用藥。苯甲酰基苯甲酸鹽亦可應用，但有刺激。家庭所有成員都需治療。衣物和床鋪不必消毒。

scala *n.* one of the spiral canals of the *cochlea. The *scala media* (*cochlear duct*) is the central membranous canal, containing the sensory apparatus of the cochlea; the *scala vestibuli* and *scala tympani* are the two bony canals of the cochlea.

階　為耳蝸螺旋管的一種。中階（蝸管）是中央膜管，含有耳蝸的感受器，前庭階和鼓階是耳蝸的兩個骨蝸管。

scald *n.* a *burn produced by a hot liquid or vapour, such as boiling water or steam.

燙傷　由熱的液體或蒸氣所致的燒傷。如沸水或水蒸氣。

scale 1. *n.* any of the flakes of dead epidermal cells shed from the skin. **2.** *vb.* to scrape deposits of calculus (tartar) from the teeth (*see* scaler).

(1) 鱗屑　由皮膚脱落的死亡的表皮細胞絮片。**(2) 刮治**　從牙齒刮除牙石（參閱 scaler）。

scalenus *n.* one of four paired muscles of the neck (*scalenus anterior*, *medius*, *minimus*, and *posterior*), extending from the cervical (neck) vertebrae to the first and second ribs. They are responsible for raising the first and second ribs in inspiration and for bending the neck forward and to either side.

斜角肌　頸部的四對肌肉（前、中、小和後斜角肌）。起自頸椎，止於第一和第二肋。可上提第一和第二肋，助吸氣。可使頸前屈和側屈。

scalenus syndrome (thoracic outlet syndrome) the group of symptoms caused by the scalenus anterior muscle compressing the subclavian artery and the lower roots of the brachial plexus against the fibrous and bony structures of the outlet of the upper thoracic vertebrae. Loss of sensation, wasting, and vascular symptoms may be found in the affected arm, which may also be painful.

前斜角肌綜合徵　鎖骨下動脈及臂叢下部神經根在前斜角肌與胸廓上口的骨和纖維組織之間受到壓迫所引起的一組症狀。患側臂可有感覺喪失、瘦弱和血管症狀，也可有痛覺。

scaler *n.* an instrument for removing calculus from the teeth. It may be a hand instrument or one energized by rapid ultrasonic vibrations.

刮器　一種可從牙上刮除牙石的器械。可以是手動或通過快速超聲振動來操作。

scalpel *n.* a small pointed surgical knife used by surgeons for cutting tissues. It

手術刀　一種小的帶尖頭的外科刀。外科醫生用以切割組

has a straight handle and usually detachable disposable blades of different shapes.

scan 1. *n.* examination of the body or a part of the body using *ultrasonography, *computerized tomography (CT), *magnetic resonance imaging (MRI), or scintigraphy (*see* scintigram). **2.** *n.* the image obtained from such an examination. **3.** *vb.* to examine the body using any of these techniques.

scanning laser ophthalmoscope *see* ophthalmoscope.

scanning speech a disorder of articulation in which the syllables are inappropriately separated and equally stressed. It is caused by disease of the cerebellum or its connecting fibres in the brainstem.

scaphocephaly *n.* an abnormally long and narrow skull due to premature closure of the suture between the two parital bones, along the top of the skull. **–scaphocephalic** *adj.*

scaphoid bone a boat-shaped bone of the wrist (*see* carpus). It articulates with the trapezium and trapezoid bones in front, with the radius behind, and with the capitate and lunate medially. It is commonly injured by falls on the wrist.

scapul- (scapulo-) *prefix denoting* the scapula.

scapula *n.* (*pl.* **scapulas** or **scapulae**) the shoulder blade: a triangular bone, a pair of which form the back part of the shoulder girdle (see illustration). The *spine* on its dorsal (back) surface ends at the *acromion process* at the top of the shoulder. This process turns forward and

纖。有一直刀柄，並裝有可拆卸的用後可丟棄的各式刀片。

(1) 掃描檢查　用超聲描記術、電子計算機斷層照相術、磁共振成像術或閃爍法（參閱 scintigram）進行查體或檢查身體的某一部分。**(2) 掃描圖** 從掃描檢查得到的圖像。**(3) 掃描**　用掃描檢查的任何技術進行查體。

激光掃描檢眼鏡　參閱 ophthalmoscope。

斷續言語　一種言語障礙。音節被不適當的隔開，並同等的重讀。由小腦的疾病或小腦與腦幹的連接纖維發生障礙所致。

舟狀頭　一種異常長而狹的頭顱。由於顱頂兩塊頂骨間的骨縫過早閉合所致。

舟骨　腕部的一塊船形小骨（參閱 carpus）。前面與大多角骨和小多角骨，後面與橈骨，內側與頭狀骨和月骨形成關節。通常腕部跌落易受傷。

〔前綴〕**肩胛**

肩胛骨　肩部的一塊三角形扁骨。一對肩胛骨形成肩胛帶的背側部分（見圖）。背側面的骨崤末端肩峯為肩部最高點。肩峯轉向前面與鎖骨形成肩鎖關節。肩鎖關節位於肩關節盂的上方。肱骨頭嵌入形成肩關

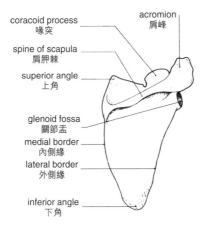

coracoid process
喙突

acromion
肩峰

spine of scapula
肩胛棘

superior angle
上角

glenoid fossa
關節盂

medial border
內側緣

lateral border
外側緣

inferior angle
下角

Right scapula (dorsal surface)
右肩胛骨（背面）

articulates with the collar bone (*clavicle) at the *acromioclavicular joint*; it overhangs the *glenoid fossa*, into which the humerus fits to form the socket of the shoulder joint. The *coracoid process* curves upwards and forwards from the neck of the scapula and provides attachment for ligaments and muscles. **–scapular** *adj.*

scar *n. see* cicatrix.

scarification *n.* the process of making a series of shallow cuts or scratches in the skin to allow a substance to penetrate the body. This was commonly performed during vaccination against smallpox; the vaccine was administered as a droplet left in contact with the scarified area.

scarlatina *n. see* scarlet fever.

scarlet fever a highly contagious disease, mainly of childhood, caused by bacteria of the genus *Streptococcus. It is transmitted either from a patient or

節球窩的盂內。喙突從肩胛頸的上前方彎曲突出，其上有肌肉和韌帶附着。

瘢痕　參閱 cicatrix。

劃痕　通過在皮膚上劃幾條淺的切口或痕道使某一物質得以透入體內的方法。常用於接種牛痘以預防天花，痘苗滴於劃痕部位。

猩紅熱　參閱 scarlet fever。

猩紅熱　一種具有高度傳染性的疾病。主要感染兒童，係鏈球菌屬的細菌所致。此病由病人或帶菌者（經咳嗽），或由

carrier (by coughing) or through contaminated milk. Symptoms commence 2–4 days after exposure and include fever, sickness, sore throat, and a widespread scarlet rash that spreads from the armpits and groin to the neck, chest, back, and limbs and also affects the tongue. Treatment with antibiotics shortens the disease and prevents such complications as ear and kidney infections and swollen neck glands. An infection usually confers immunity for life. Medical name: **scarlatina**. *Compare* German measles.

污染的牛奶傳播。感染後 2~4 日出現症狀,有發熱,惡心,咽喉炎,以及從腋部和腹股溝遍及頸、胸、背和四肢的猩紅色皮疹,舌上也可出現。用抗生素治療可縮短病程,並預防合併症的發生,如耳和腎的感染及頸淋巴結腫大。一次感染通常獲得終生免疫。醫學用語:猩紅熱。與 German measles 對比。

Scarpa's triangle *see* femoral triangle.

斯卡帕三角　參閱 femoral triangle。

scat- (scato-) *prefix denoting* faeces.

〔前綴〕糞

scatter diagram (in statistics) *see* correlation.

點圖　(統計學) 參閱 correlation。

SCC *see* squamous cell carcinoma.

鱗狀細胞癌　參閱 squamous cell carcinoma。

Scheuermann's disease *osteochondritis involving one or more of the vertebrae. The condition often arises in adolescence and causes spinal pain. It usually resolves spontaneously without deformity, causing sclerotic change in the affected bone.

脊柱骨軟骨病　骨軟骨炎累及一塊或更多椎骨。常在青春期發病並引起脊柱痛。一般自發性消除而無畸形,受累骨引起硬化改變。

Schick test a test to determine whether a person is susceptible to diphtheria. A small quantity of diphtheria toxin is injected under the skin; a patch of reddening and swelling shows that the person has no immunity and – if at particular risk – should be immunized.

希克試驗　檢查對白喉是否易感的試驗。用小量白喉毒素注於皮下,出現紅腫斑表示無免疫力,對處於有感染危險的人必須進行免疫接種。

Schiff's reagent aqueous *fuchsin solution decolourized with sulphur dioxide. A blue coloration develops in the presence of aldehydes.

席夫試劑　品紅水溶液,用二氧化硫作脫色劑。有醛類存在時即出現藍色。

Schilling test a test used to assess a patient's capacity to absorb vitamin B_{12} from the bowel. Radioactive vitamin B_{12} is given by mouth and urine collected for 24 hours. A normal individual will excrete at least 10% of the original dose over this period; a patient with *pernicious anaemia will excrete less than 5%.

席林試驗　檢查腸道對維生素 B_{12} 的吸收能力的試驗。口服放射性維生 B_{12}，並收集 24 小時尿。正常人在此期間至少排出原劑量的 10%，患惡性貧血的病人排出不足 5%。

schindylesis *n.* a form of *synarthrosis (immovable joint) in which a crest of one bone fits into a groove of another.

嵌合連接　不動關節的一種連接形式。在這種關節內，一骨之銳緣插入另一骨之深溝內。

-schisis *suffix denoting* a cleft or split.

〔後綴〕裂口，裂縫

schism *n.* a disorder of relationships within a family, in which parents quarrel and children are made to take sides. It was proposed as a cause of later schizophrenia in the children, but is more likely to be a nonspecific cause of psychological vulnerability.

分裂　家庭內的一種混亂關係。父母爭吵，子女被迫參與袒護一方。人們曾認為這是兒童日後患精神分裂症的一個病因，但這更可能是精神創傷的一個非特異性病因。

schisto- *prefix denoting* a fissure; split.

〔前綴〕分裂，裂縫

schistoglossia *n.* fissuring of the tongue. Congenital fissures are transverse, whereas those due to disease (such as syphilis) are usually longitudinal.

舌裂　舌的裂隙。先天性舌裂是橫向的，而因病（如梅毒）所致的舌裂常是縱向的。

Schistosoma (Bilharzia) *n.* a genus of blood *flukes, three species of which are important parasites of man causing one of the most serious of tropical diseases (*see* schistosomiasis). *S. japonicum* is common in the Far East; *S. mansoni* is widespread in Africa, the West Indies, and South and Central America; and *S. haematobium* occurs in Africa and the Middle East.

血吸蟲屬（裂體吸蟲屬）　一種血吸蟲屬。此屬中有三種是人的重要寄生蟲，可引起一種極為嚴重的熱帶病（參閱 schistosomiasis）。日本血吸蟲常見於遠東，曼森血吸蟲廣泛傳播於非洲、西印度羣島及中美與南美，埃及血吸蟲見於非洲和中東。

schistosomiasis (bilharziasis) *n.* a tropical disease caused by blood flukes of the genus *Schistosoma. Eggs present in the stools or urine of infected people

血吸蟲病（裂體吸蟲病）　由血吸蟲屬的血吸蟲引起的一種熱帶病。蟲卵存在於受感染者的糞和尿內，隨人的排洩物流入

undergo part of their larval development within freshwater snails living in water contaminated with human sewage. The disease is contracted when *cercaria larvae, released from the snails, penetrate the skin of anyone bathing in infected water. Adult flukes eventually settle in the blood vessels of the intestine (*S. mansoni* and *S. japonicum*) or the bladder (*S. haematobium*); the release of their spiked eggs causes anaemia, inflammation, and the formation of scar tissue. Additional intestinal symptoms are diarrhoea, dysentery, enlargement of the spleen and liver, and cirrhosis of the liver. If the bladder is affected, blood is passed in the urine and cystitis and cancer of the bladder may develop. The disease is treated with various drugs, including stibophen and other antimony-containing preparations, praziquantel, and niridazole.

水中。幼蟲的發育有一部分在淡水釘螺中進行。尾蚴離開釘螺，穿入在污染水中沐浴人的皮膚內，使感染致病。成蟲最終棲居於腸內血管中（日本血吸蟲和曼森血吸蟲）或膀胱中（埃及血吸蟲）。成蟲產卵呈窩狀堆積在一起，可導致貧血，炎症，以及形成瘢痕組織。此外腸道症狀有腹瀉、痢疾、脾和肝腫大，以及肝硬化。如膀胱受累，可見血尿，並可能發生膀胱炎和膀胱癌。此病可用多種藥物治療，包括胼波芬和其他含銻的製劑、吡喹酮以及尼立達唑。

schiz- (schizo-) *prefix denoting* a split or division.

〔前綴〕**裂，分裂**

schizogony *n.* a phase of asexual reproduction in the life cycle of a sporozoan (protozoan parasite) that occurs in the liver or red blood cells. The parasite grows and divides many times to form a *schizont*, which contains many *merozoites. The eventual release of merozoites of *Plasmodium*, the malaria parasite, from the blood cells produces fever in the patient.

裂殖生殖　孢子蟲（寄生原蟲）生活史中的無性生殖期。發生於肝或紅細胞內。原蟲生長，並多次分裂，形成裂殖體，含有許多裂殖子。瘧原蟲裂殖子從紅細胞內釋放出來，導致病人發熱。

schizoid personality a personality characterized by solitariness, emotional coldness to others, inability to experience pleasure, lack of response to praise and criticism, withdrawal into a fantasy world, excessive introspection, and eccentricity of behaviour. Some schizophrenics have this personality before

精神分裂樣人格　一種以孤獨、對他人冷漠、無力體驗喜悅、對表揚和批評缺乏反應、陷入迷幻世界、極度內省傾向、行為乖僻為特徵的人格。有些精神分裂症患者在其得病前即有這樣的人格，但大多有精神分裂樣人格者並沒有成為

their illness, but most schizoid personalities do not become schizophrenic. *See* personality disorder.

schizont *n*. one of the stages that occurs during the asexual phase of the life cycle of a sporozoan. *See* schizogony.

schizonticide *n*. any agent used for killing *schizonts.

schizophrenia *n*. a severe mental disorder (or group of disorders) characterized by a disintegration of the process of thinking, of contact with reality, and of emotional responsiveness. *Delusions and *hallucinations (especially of voices) are usual features, and the patient usually feels that his thoughts, sensations, and actions are controlled by, or shared with, others. He becomes socially withdrawn and loses energy and initiative. The main types of schizophrenia are *simple*, in which increasing social withdrawal and personal ineffectiveness are the major changes; *hebephrenic*, which starts in adolescence or young adulthood (*see* hebephrenia); *paranoid*, characterized by prominent delusions; and *catatonic*, with marked motor disturbances. The latter form is now rare.

Schizophrenia commonly – but not inevitably – runs a progressive course. The prognosis has improved with *antipsychotic drugs and with vigorous psychological and social management and rehabilitation. There are strong genetic factors in the causation, and environmental stress can precipitate illness. **–schizophrenic** *adj*.

schizotypal *adj*. describing a condition characterized by cold aloof feelings, eccentricities of behaviour, odd ways of thinking and talking, and

精神分裂症患者。參閱 personality disorder。

裂殖體 孢子蟲生活史中無性生殖階段的一期。參閱 schizogony。

殺裂殖體劑 任何殺滅裂殖體的藥物。

精神分裂症 一種嚴重的精神疾病（或一組精神障礙）。其特徵為：在思維過程、接觸現實和情感反應上有分裂現象。妄想和幻覺（尤其聽幻覺）也是常見的徵象。患者經常感到其思維、感覺和行動受他人控制或與他人分擔。患者回避與外界交往，喪失活力和進取精神。精神分裂症的主要類型有：單純型，主要症狀為與外界交往減少，活動能力減低；青春期痴呆型，始發於青春期或青年時期（參閱 hebephrenia）；妄想狂型，有突出的妄想特徵；緊張型，有明顯的運動障礙。後面的類型現在少見。

精神分裂症通常（但並非必定）表現為進行性病程。通過使用抗精神活動藥物，強有力的心理和環境治療，以及康復治療，使預後已有改進。精神分裂症的病因有明顯的遺傳因素，而環境壓力能助長其發病。

類精神分裂的 一種以表情冷漠，行為怪僻，說話和思維方式怪異，偶爾有短暫而嚴重的錯覺、幻覺或妄想樣思維為特

occasional short periods of intense illusions, hallucinations, or delusion-like ideas. The condition, known as *borderline schizophrenia*, is similar to some aspects of *schizophrenia and is more common in people who are genetically related to schizophrenics.

徵的精神狀態。該狀態稱之為擬精神分裂症,與精神分裂症的某些方面相似,並在與精神分裂症患者有遺傳關係的人羣中更為常見。

Schlemm's canal a channel in the eye, at the junction of the cornea and the sclera, through which the aqueous humour drains.

施勒姆管 眼內的一個管道。位於角膜和鞏膜接合處。房水經此管向靜脈回流。

Schönlein-Henoch purpura *see* Henoch-Schönlein purpura.

舍-亨氏紫癜 參閱 Henoch-Schönlein purpura。

school health service (in Britain) a service concerned with the early detection of physical, intellectual, and emotional abnormalities in schoolchildren and their subsequent treatment and surveillance. The service was formerly based on an ideal of three examinations at 5, 11, and 15 years by doctors and nurses specially employed by the Local Education Authority (LEA). It has now been changed to a system of selective examinations based on recommendations by teachers, *school nurses, or parental requests. The service is now the responsibility of the District Health Authority, but ascertainment and responsibility for allocation to *special schools remain the responsibility of the LEA.

學校衛生服務 (英國) 對學齡兒童的一種服務項目。目的是早日查出學童身體的、智力的和感情的異常,繼而給以治療和監測。這種服務早先基於由地方教育當局專門僱傭醫師和護士對 5、11 和 15 歲的學童做三次檢查。根據教師和學校護士的建議以及家長的請求現已改為對學童進行選擇性檢查的制度。這種服務現由地段衛生局負責,但對特種學校的確定和撥款,仍由地方教育當局負責。

school nurse a member of the *school health service who conducts routine examinations and/or treats minor ailments. *Health visitors may sometimes work in this capacity but State Registered and State Enrolled Nurses may also perform these tasks.

學校護士 學校保健服務系統的一個成員。擔任常規檢查及／或治療小傷小病的工作。保健員有時也擔任此項工作,而在政府註冊或擔任公職的護士也可執行這些任務。

Schwann cells the cells that lay down the *myelin sheath around the axon

施萬細胞 該細胞鋪於帶髓鞘神經纖維的軸突周圍形成髓

of a medullated nerve fibre. Each cell is responsible for one length of axon, around which it twists as it grows, so that concentric layers of membrane envelop the axon. The gap between adjacent Schwann cells forms a *node of Ranvier.

Schwannoma *n. see* neurofibroma.

sciatica *n.* pain felt down the back and outer side of the thigh, leg, and foot. It is usually caused by degeneration of an intervertebral disc, which protrudes laterally to compress a lower lumbar or an upper sacral spinal nerve root. The onset may be sudden, brought on by an awkward lifting or twisting movement. The back is stiff and painful. There may be numbness and weakness in the leg. Bed rest will often relieve the pain but surgical treatment is occasionally necessary.

sciatic nerve the major nerve of the leg and the nerve with the largest diameter. It runs down behind the thigh from the lower end of the spine; above the knee joint it divides into two main branches, the *tibial* and *common peroneal nerves*, which are distributed to the muscles and skin of the lower leg.

SCID severe combined immune deficiency: *see* adenosine deaminase deficiency.

scintigram *n.* a diagram showing the distribution of radioactive *tracer in a part of the body, produced by recording the flashes of light given off by a *scintillator as it is struck by radiation of different intensities. This technique is called *scintigraphy*. By scanning the body, section by section, a 'map' of the

鞘。每個細胞包繞一段軸突，並沿軸突周圍纏繞生長，使鞘膜的同心層得以包裹軸突。鄰近的兩個施萬細胞間的裂縫形成一個朗維埃結。

神經鞘瘤　參閱 neurofibroma。

坐骨神經痛　沿背部、大腿外側、小腿直至足部的一種疼痛。常因某一椎間盤的退行性變所致。椎間盤向側面突出，壓迫下部腰椎或上部骶椎的脊神經根。坐骨神經痛的發作可以是突然的，由一次笨拙的抬舉或扭轉運動引起。背部強直且疼痛，腿部麻木無力。臥床休息常可減輕疼痛，但外科治療有時也是必需的。

坐骨神經　腿部的主要神經，也是體內直徑最大的神經。起自脊柱下部末端，沿大腿後面下行至膝關節上方，分成二個主要分支，即脛神經和腓總神經，支配下肢的肌肉和皮膚。

嚴重聯合免疫缺陷　參閱 adenosine deaminase deficiency。

閃爍圖　一種顯示身體某一部位放射性示踪物分布情況的圖形。閃爍體受不同強度的放射綫碰撞，可產生閃爍光，錄製下來即成閃爍圖。這種技術稱為閃爍照相。對身體分段掃描，製成各部位的放射性"分布圖"，有助於診斷惡性腫瘤

radioactivity in various regions is built up, aiding the diagnosis of cancer or other disorders. Such a record is known as a *scintiscan*.

或其他疾患。這樣一種檢查稱為閃爍掃描。

scintillascope *n.* the instrument used to produce a *scintigram. It incorporates a *scintillator, a device to magnify the fluorescence produced in it by radiations, and a means of recording the results, often aided by a computer. *See also* gamma camera.

閃爍鏡 用以產生閃爍圖的儀器。它由下列部件合併組成：一個閃爍器，一個把由射綫產生的熒光放大的裝置，一個記錄器，常附有電腦。參閱 gamma camera。

scintillation counter (scintimeter) a device to measure and record the fluorescent flashes in a *scintillator exposed to high-energy radiation, as in a *scintillascope.

閃爍計數器 一種測量和記錄熒光閃爍的裝置。此裝置安裝在暴露於高能量射綫的閃爍體內，同樣可安裝在閃爍鏡內。

scintillator *n.* a substance that produces a fluorescent flash when struck by high-energy radiation, such as beta or gamma rays. In medicine the most commonly used scintillator is a crystal of thallium-activated sodium iodide. The fluorescence, magnified by a phototube multiplier, may be recorded photographically or electronically during the production of a *scintigram or scintiscan.

閃爍體 一種被高能射綫如 β 或 γ 射綫撞擊後可產生熒光閃爍的物質。在醫學上最常用的閃爍體是鉈激活的碘化鈉的結晶體。熒光被光電管倍增器放大，採用照相或電子技術製成閃爍圖或進行閃爍掃描。

scintiscan *n. see* scintigram.

閃爍掃描 參閱 scintigram。

scirrhous *adj.* describing carcinomas that are stony hard to the touch. Such a carcinoma (for example of the breast) is known as a *scirrhus*.

硬癌的 摸着如同石頭一樣堅硬的癌。這樣的癌（如乳癌）被稱為硬癌。

scissor leg a disability in which one leg becomes permanently crossed over the other as a result of spasticity of its *adductor muscles. The condition occurs in children with brain damage and in adults after strokes. A *tenotomy sometimes reduces the degree of disability.

剪形腿 一種殘疾。由於腿部內收肌處於強直狀態，致使這條腿永遠交叉於另一腿上方。這種情況發生於腦損傷的兒童和中風後的成人。施行腱切斷術有時可減輕殘疾程度。

scissura (scissure) *n.* a cleft or splitting, such as the splitting of the tip of a hair or the splitting open of tissues when a hernia forms.

分裂　裂開或裂口。如毛髮的尖端裂開，或疝形成時的組織裂口。

scler- (sclero-) *prefix denoting* **1.** hardening or thickening. **2.** the sclera. **3.** sclerosis.

〔前綴〕**(1)** 變硬，變厚　**(2)** 鞏膜　**(3)** 硬化

sclera (sclerotic coat) *n.* the white fibrous outer layer of the eyeball. At the front of the eye it becomes the cornea. *See* eye. **–scleral** *adj.*

鞏膜　眼球的白色纖維外層。在眼的前部成為角膜。參閱 eye。

sclerectomy *n.* an operation in which a portion of the sclera (the thick white layer of the eyeball) is removed.

鞏膜切除術　一種部分切除鞏膜（眼球的白色外層）的手術。

scleritis *n.* inflammation of the sclera (the white of the eye).

鞏膜炎　鞏膜（眼球的白色部分）的炎症。

scleroderma *n.* persistent hardening and contraction (sclerosis) of the body's connective tissue. It can affect any organ including the skin (which is thickened and waxy, mauve at first but ivory-coloured later), heart, kidney, lung, or oesophagus (gullet). Scleroderma may be localized (*see* morphoea) or it can spread slowly throughout the body, sometimes causing death. Although there is at present no cure for scleroderma, a number of drugs are available to treat most of its manifestations.

硬皮病　身體結締組織持久的硬化和收縮。可侵犯身體的任何器官，包括皮膚（厚並且蠟樣的，開始呈紫紅色，最後呈乳白色）、心、腎、肺或食管。硬皮病可以是局限性的（參閱 morphoea），或可緩慢地遍及全身，有時引起死亡。儘管目前對硬皮病無有效的治療，但許多藥物能夠治療該病的症狀。

scleromalacia *n.* thinning of the sclera (white of the eye) as a result of inflammation. Sometimes the sclera fades away completely in an area, and the underlying dark-bluish tissue (usually the ciliary body) bulges beneath the conjunctiva. This state is known as *scleromalacia perforans*.

鞏膜軟化　由於炎症引起鞏膜（眼的白色部分）變薄。有時鞏膜有一部分完全消失，其下層的黑藍色組織（通常是睫狀體）膨出於結膜下。這種狀況稱為穿通性鞏膜軟化。

sclerosis *n*. hardening of tissue, usually due to scarring (fibrosis) after inflammation or to ageing. It can affect the lateral columns of the spinal cord and the medulla of the brain (*amyotrophic lateral sclerosis*), causing progressive muscular paralysis (*see* motor neurone disease). It can also occur in scattered patches throughout the brain and spinal cord (*see* multiple sclerosis) or in the walls of the arteries (*see* arteriosclerosis, atherosclerosis). *See also* tuberous sclerosis.

硬化 組織變硬。常由於炎症後瘢痕形成（纖維化）或衰老所致。硬化可累及脊髓側索和延髓（肌萎縮性脊髓側索硬化），引起進行性肌麻痺（參閱 motor neurone disease）。硬化也可在腦和脊髓中到處發生（參閱 multiple sclerosis），有散發性斑塊形成，或可發生於動脈壁（參閱 arteriosclerosis，atherosclerosis）。參閱 tuberous sclerosis。

sclerotherapy *n*. treatment of varicose veins by the injection of an irritant solution. This causes thrombophlebitis, which encourages obliteration of the varicose vein by thrombosis and subsequent scarring. Sclerotherapy is also used for treating haemorrhoids and oesophageal varices.

硬化療法 通過注射一種刺激性溶液治療靜脈曲張的方法。此療法能引起血栓性靜脈炎，導致血栓形成，繼而結成瘢痕，而使曲張的靜脈得以閉塞。硬化療法也用來治療痔瘡和食管靜脈曲張。

sclerotic 1. (*or* **sclerotic coat**) *n. see* sclera **2.** *adj.* affected with *sclerosis.

(1) 鞏膜 參閱 sclera。(2) 硬化的

sclerotome *n*. **1.** a surgical knife used in the operation of *sclerotomy. **2.** (in embryology) the part of the segmented mesoderm (*see* somite) in the early embryo that gives rise to all the skeletal tissue of the body. The vertebrae and ribs retain the segmented structure, which is lost in the skull and limbs.

(1) 鞏膜刀 一種用於鞏膜切開術的外科刀。(2) 生骨節（胚胎學）胚胎早期中胚層的體節部分（參閱 somite）。身體所有的骨骼組織來源於此體節。椎骨和肋仍保留分節的結構，而在頭顱和四肢已消失。

sclerotomy *n*. an operation in which an incision is made in the sclera (white of the eye).

鞏膜切開術 在鞏膜（眼的白色部分）上作一切口的手術。

scolex *n*. (*pl.* **scolices**) the head of a *tapeworm. The presence of suckers and/or hooks on the scolex enables the worm to attach itself to the wall of its host's gut.

頭節 絛蟲的頭。頭節上有吸盤和／或鈎，使絛蟲得以附著在宿主的腸壁上。

scoliosis *n.* lateral (sideways) deviation of the backbone, caused by congenital or acquired abnormalities of the vertebrae, muscles, and nerves. Treatment may require spinal braces and, in cases of severe deformity, surgical correction by fusion or *osteotomy. *See also* kyphosis, kyphoscoliosis.

脊柱側凸　脊柱向側面偏斜。由先天的或後天的脊椎、肌肉、神經異常所致。治療需要脊柱支架，如畸形嚴重，可作骨融合或骨切開術矯正。參閱 kyphosis，kyphoscoliosis。

-scope *suffix denoting* an instrument for observing or examining. Example: *gastroscope* (instrument for examining the stomach).

〔後綴〕**鏡**　一種用來觀察或檢查的儀器。如胃鏡（檢查胃的儀器）。

scopolamine *n. see* hyoscine.

東莨菪鹼　參閱 hyoscine。

scorbutic *adj.* affected with scurvy.

壞血病的　受壞血病侵襲的。

scoto- *prefix denoting* darkness.

〔前綴〕**盲，暗**

scotoma *n.* (*pl.* **scotomata**) a small area of abnormally less sensitive or absent vision in the visual field, surrounded by normal sight. All people have a *blind spot in the visual field of each eye due to the small area inside the eye occupied by the optic disc, which is not sensitive to light. Similar islands of total visual loss in other parts of the field are referred to as *absolute scotomata*. A *relative scotoma* is a spot where the vision is decreased but still pressnt.

盲點　視野內光感異常弱或缺損的一個小區域，其周圍區域的光感正常。任何人每隻眼的視野內都有一個盲點。這是由於無感光作用的視盤占有而形成。在視網膜其他部分出現相似小島樣的光感完全缺損，稱為絕對盲點；而光感只是減弱但仍然存在的，則稱為相對盲點。

scotometer *n.* an instrument used for mapping defects in the visual field. *See also* campimetry, perimeter.

暗點計　一種用於給出視野缺損圖的儀器。參閱 campimetry，perimeter。

scotopic *adj.* relating to or describing conditions of poor illumination. For example, *scotopic vision* is vision in dim light in which the *rods of the retina are involved (*see* dark adaptation).

暗視的　描述微弱照明條件下的視力。例如：暗視力是弱光綫下的視力，視網膜的視桿細胞在弱光綫下起作用。參閱 dark adaptation。

screening test a simple test carried out on a large number of apparently healthy

篩查　在大數量外表健康的人羣中，對某種疾病進行普查的

people to separate those who probably have a specified disease from those who do not. Examples are the *Guthrie test and *cervical smears. Limitations depend on the severity and *frequency distribution of the disease and the efficiency and availability of treatment. Other factors to be taken into account are the safety, convenience, cost, and *sensitivity of the test. *See also* genetic screening.

一種簡單的方法。如加斯里試驗和宮頸塗片法。本法的適用範圍取決於該病的嚴重程度，疾病的頻數分布以及治療的效果和可靠程度。還要考慮其他因素，如安全、方便、價廉和檢查方法的敏感性。參閱 genetic screening。

scrofula *n.* *tuberculosis of lymph nodes, usually those in the neck, causing the formation of abscesses. Untreated, these burst through the skin and form running sores, which leave scars when they heal. Treatment with antituberculous drugs is effective. The disease, which is now rare, most commonly affects young children. **–scrofulous** *adj.*

瘰癧　淋巴結結核。通常見於頸部淋巴結，引起膿腫形成。如不治療，膿腫穿過皮膚破裂，形成一匐行性潰瘍，愈合後留下瘢痕。用抗結核藥治療有效。此病最常感染兒童，現已少見。

scrofuloderma *n.* tuberculosis of the skin in which the skin breaks down over suppurating tuberculous glands, with the formation of irregular-shaped ulcers with blue-tinged edges. Treatment is with antituberculous drugs, to which scrofuloderma responds better than *lupus vulgaris, another type of skin tuberculosis.

皮膚瘰癧　皮膚結核。患處皮膚潰爛，覆有化膿的結核性腺體，形成帶有藍色邊緣，形狀不規則的潰瘍。用抗結核藥治療，其對皮膚瘰癧的療效高於尋常狼瘡（另一類型的皮膚結核）的療效。

scrototomy *n.* an operation in which the scrotum is surgically explored, usually undertaken to investigate patients with probable obstructive *azoospermia.

陰囊切開術　一種對陰囊進行探查的手術。通常用來進行查明病人是否患有梗阻性精子缺乏。

scrotum *n.* the paired sac that holds the testes and epididymides outside the abdominal cavity. Its function is to allow the production and storage of spermatozoa to occur at a lower temperature than that of the abdomen. Further temperature control is achieved by contraction or relaxation of muscles in the scrotum. **–scrotal** *adj.*

陰囊　一對在腹腔外容納睾丸和附睾的囊。其作用是使得精子在溫度較腹腔內為低的條件下產生和貯存。更進一步的溫度控制由陰囊肌肉的收縮和鬆弛來完成。

scrub typhus (tsutsugamushi disease) a disease, widely distributed in SE Asia, caused by the parasitic micro-organism *Rickettsia tsutsugamushi* and transmitted to man through the bite of mites. Only larval mites of the genus *Tormbicula* are involved as vectors. Symptoms include headache, chills, high temperature (104°F), a red rash over most of the body, a cough, and delirium. A small ulcer forms at the site of the bite. Scrub typhus is treated with tetracycline and other broad-spectrum antibiotics. *See also* rickettsiae, typhus.

恙蟲病 一種廣泛分布於東南亞的疾病。由寄生微生物恙蟲熱立克次體引起。通過蟎的叮咬傳播給人。只有恙蟎屬的幼蟎起媒介作用。症狀包括頭痛、寒戰、高燒 (104°F)、身體的大部分起紅疹、咳嗽以及譫妄。在蟎叮咬處有小的潰瘍形成。本病用四環素類抗生素以及其他廣譜抗生素治療。參閱 rickettsiae，typhus。

scruple *n.* a unit of weight used in pharmacy. 1 scruple = 1.295 g (20 grains). 3 scruples = 1 drachm.

英分，吩 藥衡單位。1 英分 = 1.295 克 (20 英厘)。3 英分 = 1 英錢。

sculpting *n.* a technique of family psychotherapy, in which all the family members are seen together and one member is asked to arrange the others' physical positions to express their relationships and feelings. *See also* group therapy.

塑雕療法 一種家庭心理治療技術。全部家庭成員聚集在一起，要求其中一個成員來擺布其他成員的姿勢，以表達他們的相互關係和感情。參閱 group therapy。

scurvy *n.* a disease that is caused by a deficiency of *vitamin C (ascorbic acid). It results from the consumption of a diet devoid of fresh fruit and vegetables. The first sign of scurvy is swollen bleeding gums, and a rash of tiny bleeding spots around the hair follicles is characteristic. This may be followed by subcutaneous bleeding and the opening of previously healed wounds. Treatment with vitamin C soon reverses the effects.

壞血病 維生素 C (抗壞血酸) 缺乏引起的一種疾病。由於飲食內缺乏新鮮水果和蔬菜所引起。壞血病的第一體徵是牙齦腫脹，出血，毛囊周圍出現小出血點樣疹子是其特徵。繼而出現皮下出血或先前已愈合的傷口重新裂開。如用維生素 C 治療則可逆轉其病理過程。

scybalum *n.* a lump or mass of hard faeces.

硬糞塊 成團或成塊的硬糞。

seasickness *n. see* travel sickness.

暈船 參閱 travel sickness。

seasonal affective disorder syndrome *see* SADS.

季節性情感紊亂綜合徵　參閱 SADS。

sebaceous cyst 1. (wen) a pale or flesh-coloured dome-shaped cyst that commonly occurs in adults, especially on the face, neck, or trunk. It is firm, with a central dot, and contains keratin, not sebum; such cysts are therefore more correctly referred to as *epidermoid cysts*. They are usually removed surgically. **2.** a cyst of the sebaceous glands occurring in multiple form in a rare inherited condition, *steatocystoma multiplex*.

（女性）皮脂囊腫　**(1)**　一種蒼白色或肉色圓頂狀囊腫，一般發生於成年。尤其在面部、頸部或軀幹。它是堅硬的，有一個中心點，含有角蛋白而不是皮脂。這種囊腫更準確地應該稱為表皮樣囊腫。一般通過外科手術處理。**(2)**　在一種罕見的繼發狀態中，以多種形式發生的一種皮脂腺囊腫——皮脂囊腫病。

sebaceous gland any of the simple or branched glands in the *skin that secrete an oily substance, *sebum. They open into hair follicles and their secretion is produced by the disintegration of their cells. Some parts of the skin have many sebaceous glands, others few. Activity varies with age: the glands are most active at puberty.

皮脂腺　皮膚中分泌油性物質（皮脂）的，分支或不分支的腺體。皮脂腺開口於毛囊中，其細胞分解後即成為其分泌物。某些部位的皮膚具有許多皮脂腺，有些部位則幾乎沒有。皮脂腺的活動隨年齡而異，在青春期其活動最為旺盛。

seborrhoea *n.* excessive secretion of sebum by the *sebaceous glands. The glands are enlarged, especially beside the nose and other parts of the face. The condition predisposes to acne and is common at puberty, usually lasting for a few years. Seborrhoea may be associated with a kind of *eczema (seborrhoeic eczema). **–seborrhoeic** *adj.*

脂溢　皮脂腺分泌過多的皮脂。腺體常腫大，尤其鼻子附近和面部其他部位。常發生於青春期，易引起痤瘡，可持續幾年。脂溢可能和一種濕疹有關（脂溢性濕疹）。

sebum *n.* the oily substance secreted by the *sebaceous glands and reaching the skin surface through small ducts that lead into the hair follicles. Sebum provides a thin film of fat over the skin, which slows the evaporation of water; it also has an antibacterial effect.

皮脂　皮脂腺所分泌的一種油性物質。它可通過引向毛囊的小導管抵達皮膚表面。皮脂在皮膚表面形成一層薄膜，使水分蒸發減慢，它尚具有一種抗菌作用。

second *n.* the *SI unit of time, equal to the duration of 9,192,631,770 periods of

秒　時間的國際單位。等於基態下原子[133]銫兩個精度之間放

the radiation corresponding to the transition between two hyperfine levels of the ground state of the caesium-133 atom. This unit is now the basis of all time measurements. Symbol: s.

射周期的 9 192 631 770 倍。秒現在是時間度量的最基本單位。符號：s。

secondary health care health care provided by medical specialists or hospital staff members for a patient whose primary care was provided by the *general practitioner who first diagnosed or treated the patient. For example, a general practitioner who accepts a patient with an unusual skin condition provides primary care but if he refers the patient to a dermatologist, the skin specialist becomes the source of secondary care. *Compare* tertiary health care.

二級衛生保健 全科醫師為病人提供最初的診斷和治療，稱為該病人的初級衛生保健，然後由醫學專家或醫院的專職人員為該患者提供的保健，稱為二級衛生保健。例如，全科醫師接診了一個患有不同尋常皮膚病的患者，並為他提供初級保健，但如果他把該患者轉診給皮膚病專家，那麼皮膚病專家就成為二級衛生保健提供者。與 tertiary health care 對比。

secondary prevention the avoidance or alleviation of the serious consequences of disease by early detection. Best known methods include routine examinations, as in *child health clinics and the *school health service, or *screening tests applied to populations that are regarded as having a high risk of contracting specific diseases.

二級預防 通過早期探測，避免或減輕疾病的嚴重後果。公認的最佳方法包括諸如在兒童保健站和學校衛生服務進行的常規檢查，或對被認為可能罹患某些特殊疾病的高危人羣進行篩查。

secondary sexual characteristics the physical characteristics that develop after puberty as a result of sexual maturation. In boys they include the growth of facial and pubic hair and the breaking of the voice. In girls they include the growth of pubic hair and the development of the breasts.

第二性徵 青春期後身體發育的性別特徵。它是性成熟的結果。男孩的第二性徵包括有鬍鬚和陰毛的生長，發聲的變調。女孩的第二性徵包括有陰毛生長和乳房發育。

second messenger an organic molecule that acts within a cell to initiate the response to a signal carried by a chemical messenger (e.g. a hormone) that does not itself enter the cell. Examples of

第二信使 一種在細胞內活動的有機分子。該分子對化學信使（如激素）所攜帶的信號產生最初的應答，但化學信使自身不進入細胞。第二信

second messengers are *inositol triphosphate and cyclic *AMP.

使有肌醇三磷酸鹽和環磷酸腺苷。

secretin *n.* a hormone secreted from the small intestine (duodenum) when acidified food leaves the stomach. It stimulates the secretion of relatively enzyme-free alkaline juice by the pancreas (*see* pancreatic juice) and of bile by the liver.

分泌素，腸促胰液素 酸化食物離開胃時，小腸（十二指腸）分泌的一種激素。分泌素刺激胰腺（參閱 pancreatic juice），分泌含酶較少的鹼性液體，並刺激肝臟分泌膽汁。

secretion *n.* **1.** the process by which a gland isolates constituents of the blood or tissue fluid and chemically alters them to produce a substance that it discharges for use by the body or excretes. The principal methods of secretion – *apocrine, *holocrine, and *merocrine – are illustrated in the diagram. **2.** the substance that is produced by a gland.

(1) 分泌 某一腺體將血液或組織液中某些成分離析出來的過程。同時使這些成分發生化學變化，使之產生一種物質為機體所利用或排出體外。分泌的主要方式有：頂分泌、全分泌和部分分泌三種（見圖）。
(2) 分泌物 腺體所分泌的物質。

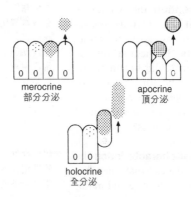

merocrine
部分分泌

apocrine
頂分泌

holocrine
全分泌

Methods of secretion
分泌方式

secretor *n.* a person in whose saliva and other body fluids are found traces of the water-soluble A, B, or O agglutinogens that determine *blood group.

血型物質分泌者 在唾液和其他體液中有決定 ABO 血型微量水溶性凝集原的人。

section 1. *n.* (in surgery) the act of cutting (the cut or division made is also

(1) 切開（術），切（斷）面 （外科學）切割動作（切口也

called a section). For example, an *abdominal section* is performed for surgical exploration of the abdomen (*see* laparotomy). A *transverse section* is a cut made at right angles to a structure's long axis. *See also* Caesarean section. **2.** *n.* (in microscopy) a thin slice of the specimen to be examined under a microscope. **3.** *vb.* to issue an order for *compulsory admission to a psychiatric hospital under the appropriate section of the *Mental Health Act.

用此詞）。如外科剖腹探查就是一個腹部切開術（參閱 laparotomy）。對一個組織結構的長軸作一垂直切割叫作橫切。參閱 Caesarean section。
(2) 切片　（顯微鏡檢查）顯微鏡下檢查的一種薄標本切片。
(3)（動詞）根據精神保健法令相應條文發布強制性收入精神病醫院的指令。

section 30 order (parental order) a court order made under the Human Fertilization and Embryology Act 1990 that enables a married couple to be regarded as the legal parents of a child born to a *surrogate mother commissioned by that couple. Application must be made within six months of the child's birth and the child's home must be with the husband and wife at the time of the application.

第三十款法令（親本法）　（英國）根據人類受精和胚胎學法案 1990 制定的法庭法令。該法令可使一對已婚夫婦作為一個由替身母親生的孩子的法律父母親，替身母親是由這對已婚夫婦選定的。這種申請必需在孩子出生後六個月之內提出，而且在申請時，孩子必需與父母居住。

security object a particular item that brings comfort and a sense of security to a young child, often for a number of years. Security objects are usually associated in some way with bed and are often made of soft material. A scrap of an old blanket or of a former night garment, a teddy bear, even an old nappy may be chosen as a comforter and these are often pressed to the face as the child settles down to sleep. There is no reason to suppose that security objects are in any way undesirable, at any age.

安全物　為小孩帶來舒適和安全感的特殊物品。常持續使用數年。在某種程度上，安全物常和床有關並用軟物製成。一條舊毛毯的碎片，或一件從前的睡袍，或一個玩具熊，甚至一片舊尿布都可能被選擇作為一個安全物，小孩常把它挨在臉上睡覺。沒有理由認為任何年齡以任何方式使用安全物是不理想的。

sedation *n.* the production of a restful state of mind, particularly by the use of drugs (*see* sedative).

鎮靜作用　產生心情平靜狀態的作用。特別在服用某些藥物以後（參閱 sedative）。

sedative *n.* a drug that has a calming effect, relieving anxiety and tension. Sedatives are *hypnotic drugs administered

鎮靜劑　一種具有鎮定並減緩焦慮和緊張作用的藥物。催眠藥用作鎮靜劑時，用量應小於

at lower doses than those needed for sleep (drowsiness is a common side effect). *See also* tranquillizer.

催眠劑量（常見副作用為倦睡）。參閱 tranquillizer。

sedimentation rate the rate at which solid particles sink in a liquid under the influence of gravity. *See also* ESR (erythrocyte sedimentation rate).

沉降率　在重力的影響下，固體微粒在一個液體內沉降的速率。參閱 ESR (erythrocyte sedimentation rate)。

segment *n.* (in anatomy) a portion of a tissue or organ, usually distinguishable from other portions by lines of demarcation. *See also* somite.

節段　（解剖學）某一組織或器官的一部分。常可根據分界綫和其他部分相區別。參閱 somite。

selegiline *n.* a selective *MAO inhibitor used in the treatment of parkinsonism. Administered by mouth, selegiline is thought to retard the breakdown of *dopamine. Possible side-effects include faintness on standing up, nausea, involuntary movements, and confusion. Trade name: **Eldepryl**.

司來吉蘭　一種用於治療帕金森綜合徵的選擇性單胺氧化酶抑制劑。通過口服該藥，認為可延遲多巴胺的分解。可能的副作用包括站立不穩、惡心、不自主運動以及意識模糊。商品名：Eldepryl。

selenium *n.* a *trace element recently found to be an essential component of the enzyme deiodinase, which catalyses the production of triiodothyronine (T_3) from thyroxine (T_4) in the thyroid gland. Selenium deficiency prevents the formation of T_3. Symbol: Se.

硒　一種微量元素。近期發現它是脫碘酶的基本成分。在甲狀腺內，可催化四碘甲狀腺原氨酸 (T_4) 變成三碘甲狀腺原氨酸 (T_3)。硒缺乏可阻止 T_3 的形成。符號：Se。

selenium sulphide a selenium compound with antifungal properties, used to treat *dandruff and scalp infections. It is administered in a shampoo. Trade names: **Lenium**, **Selsun**.

硫化硒　一種硒的化合物。具有抗真菌特性，用於治療頭皮屑和頭皮感染。常含於洗髮香液中。商品名：Lenium，Selsun。

sella turcica a depression in the body of the sphenoid bone that encloses the pituitary gland.

蝶鞍　容納垂體的蝶骨體的凹陷部分。

semeiology *n.* see symptomatology.

症狀學　參閱 symptomatology。

semen (seminal fluid) *n.* the fluid ejaculated from the penis at sexual climax. Each ejaculate may contain 300–500 million spermatozoa suspended in a fluid secreted by the *prostate gland and *seminal vesicles with a small contribution from *Cowper's glands. It contains fructose, which provides the spermatozoa with energy, and *prostaglandins, which affect the muscles of the uterus and may therefore assist transport of the spermatozoa. **–seminal** *adj.*

精液　性慾高潮時陰莖射出的液體。一次射精可含有 3 億~5 億個精子，混懸在前列腺、精囊腺和一小部分考珀腺分泌液內。精液內含有的果糖可向精子提供能量；含有的前列腺素能影響子宮肌肉從而協助精子的移動。

semi- *prefix denoting* half.

〔前綴〕半

semicircular canals three tubes that form part of the membranous *labyrinth of the ear. They are concerned with balance and each canal registers movement in a different plane. At the base of each canal is a small swelling (an *ampulla*), which contains a *crista. When the head moves the fluid (endolymph) in the canals presses on the cristae, which register the movement and send nerve impulses to the brain.

半規管　形成內耳膜迷路部分的三個小管。它們涉及身體平衡。每個半規管感受不同平面的運動。每個半規管基部有一個小的膨大（壺腹），內含有一個壺腹嵴。當頭部動作移動半規管內液體（內淋巴）壓迫這些嵴時，嵴感知這一運動，並把神經衝動傳入大腦。

semilunar cartilage one of a pair of crescent-shaped cartilages in the knee joint situated between the femur and tibia.

關節半月板　位於股骨和脛骨之間膝關節內的一對半月形軟骨。

semilunar valve either of the two valves in the heart situated at the origin of the aorta (*aortic valve*) and the pulmonary artery (*pulmonary valve*). Each consists of three flaps (cusps), which maintain the flow of blood in one direction.

半月瓣　位於心臟主動脈根部（主動脈瓣）和肺動脈根部（肺動脈瓣）的瓣膜。每個瓣膜由三片（瓣）組成。使血流保持向一個方向流動。

seminal analysis analysis of a specimen of semen, which should be obtained after five days of abstinence from coitus, in order to assess male fertility. Normal values are as follows: volume of ejaculate: 2–6.5 ml; liquefaction complete in

精液分析　精液標本的分析。節制性交五天後收集精液標本，用於評價男性生育。正常值如下：射精量：2~6.5 ml；30 分鐘完全液化；精子濃度：0.2 億~2 億 / ml（精子計數參

30 minutes; sperm concentration: 20–200 million spermatozoa per ml (*sperm count* refers to the total number of spermatozoa in the ejaculate); motility: 60% moving progressively at 30 minutes to 3 hours; abnormal forms: less than 20%. Analysis of three separate specimens is necessary before confirming the presence of an abnormal result.

考射出精子的總數）；活動性：30 分鐘到 3 小時，60% 精子向前移動；不正常形態：少於 20%。得出異常結果前，三次精液分離標本的分析是必需的。

seminal vesicle either of a pair of male accessory sex glands that open into the vas deferens before it joins the urethra. The seminal vesicles secrete most of the liquid component of *semen.

精囊腺 一對男性附屬性腺。它和輸精管匯合，共同開口於尿道。大部分精液成分由精囊腺分泌。

seminiferous tubule any of the long convoluted tubules that make up the bulk of the *testis.

曲細精管 構成睾丸大部分的卷曲細長小管。

seminoma *n.* a malignant tumour of the testis, appearing as a swelling, often painless, in the scrotum. It tends to occur in an older age group than the *teratomas. The best treatment for localized disease is surgery involving removal of the testis (*see* orchidectomy). Secondary tumours in the lungs can be treated with chemotherapy and radiotherapy to the draining lymph nodes. A similar tumour occurs in the ovary (*see* dysgerminoma).

精原細胞瘤 一種睾丸的惡性腫瘤。它表現為陰囊腫大，無痛。常出現於較畸胎瘤更大的年齡組。睾丸切除術是局限性病變的最佳療法（參閱 orchidectomy）。繼發的肺轉移瘤可用化療和放療方法處理淋巴結。卵巢可有類似腫瘤（參閱 dysgerminoma）。

semipermeable membrane a membrane that allows the passage of some molecules but not others. *Cell membranes are semipermeable. Semipermeable membranes are used clinically in *haemodialysis for patients with kidney failure.

半透膜 允許某些分子通過而不允許其他分子通過的膜。細胞膜是半透膜。臨床利用半透膜作腎功能衰竭患者的血液透析之用。

semiprone *adj.* describing the position of a patient lying face downwards, but with one or both knees flexed to one side so that the body is not lying completely flat. *Compare* prone, supine.

半俯臥位 一種俯臥病人的體位。其一個或兩個膝關節向一側屈曲。因此其軀體並非完全平臥。與 prone，supine 對比。

senescence *n.* the condition of ageing, which is often marked by a decrease in physical and mental abilities. **–senescent** *adj.*

衰老　機體的老化狀態。常以體力和精力減退為標誌。

senile dementia loss of the intellectual faculties often associated with behavioural deterioration, beginning for the first time in old age. *See also* dementia.

老年性痴呆　老年人才出現的智力喪失，常伴隨行為退化。參閱 dementia。

senior house officer *see* consultant.

主治醫師　參閱 consultant。

senna *n.* the dried fruits of certain shrubs of the genus *Cassia*, used as an irritant *laxative to relieve constipation and to empty the bowels before X-ray examination. It is administered by mouth; side-effects do not usually occur, but severe diarrhoea may follow large doses. Trade name: **Senokot**.

番瀉葉　某些番瀉屬灌木的乾葉。係一種刺激性輕瀉劑，用以減輕便秘或 X 綫檢查前排空大腸。口服。一般無副作用，但大劑量可引起嚴重腹瀉。商品名：Senokot。

sensation *n.* a feeling: the result of messages from the body's sensory receptors registering in the brain as information about the environment. Messages from *exteroceptors are interpreted as specific sensations – smell, taste, temperature, pain, etc. – in the conscious mind. Messages from *interoceptors, however, rarely reach the consciousness to produce sensation.

感覺　來自感覺器的信號作為環境的信息被大腦感知的結果。來自外感受器的信號在人的意識中產生特異性感覺——嗅覺、味覺、溫覺、痛覺等。來自內感受器的信號，很少變為意識性感覺的。

sense *n.* one of the faculties by which the qualities of the external environment are appreciated – sight, hearing, smell taste, or touch.

（感）覺　一種鑒別外界環境的質的能力——視覺，聽覺，嗅覺或觸覺。

sense organ a collection of specialized cells (*receptors), connected to the nervous system, that is capable of responding to a particular stimulus from either outside or inside the body. Sense organs can detect light (the eyes), heat, pain, and touch (the skin), smell (the nose), and taste (the taste buds).

感覺器官　一種特異性細胞的集合體（感覺器）。它與神經系統相連接，應答來自體內外某一特定的刺激。感覺器官可察覺光（眼）、熱、痛和觸（皮膚）、氣味（鼻）和味道（味蕾）。

sensibility n. the ability to be affected by, and respond to, changes in the surroundings (*see* stimulus). Sensibility is a characteristic of cells of the nervous system.

感受性　對周圍環境變化的感受和反應能力（參閱 stimulus）。感受性是神經系統細胞的一個特徵。

sensitive adj. possessing the ability to respond to a *stimulus. The cells of the retina, for example, are sensitive to the stimulus of light and respond by sending nerve impulses to the brain. Other *receptors are sensitive to different specific stimuli, such as pressure or the presence of chemical substances.

能感受的，敏感的　具有對一個刺激產生反應的能力。如視網膜細胞對光刺激是能感受的，且能產生反應——將神經衝動傳到大腦。其他不同的感受器感受各種不同的特異性刺激，諸如壓力或各種化學性刺激。

sensitivity n. (in preventive medicine) a measure of the reliability of a *screening test based on the proportion of people with a specific disease who react positively to the test (the higher the sensitivity the fewer false negatives). This contrasts with *specificity*, which is the proportion of people free from disease who react negatively to the test (i.e. the higher the specificity the fewer the false positives). Though these are theoretically independent variables, most screening tests are so designed that if the sensitivity is increased the specificity is reduced and the number of false positives may rise to wasteful proportions.

敏感性　（預防醫學）衡量篩查可靠性的一種方法。根據某一特異疾病患者中該試驗呈陽性反應的百分數而定（敏感性越高、假陰性越少）。相反，特異性則只在無病的人羣中該試驗呈陰性的百分數（即特異性越高，假陽性越少）。雖然，在理論上，這些都是獨立的度量，但實際上大多數篩查的設計均相同，如果敏感性增加，特異性即降低，因而假陽性率增加，造成浪費。

sensitization n. **1.** alteration of the responsiveness of the body to the presence of foreign substances. In the development of an *allergy, an individual becomes sensitized to a particular allergen and reaches a state of *hypersensitivity. The phenomena of sensitization are due to the production of antibodies. **2.** (in behaviour therapy) a form of *aversion therapy in which anxiety-producing stimuli are associated with the unwanted behaviour. In *covert sensitization* the behaviour and an unpleasant

(1) 致敏（感作用）　機體對外源性物質反應的改變。在形成過敏過程中，機體被某一特殊過敏原致敏，而進入過敏狀態。抗體形成是致敏現象的原因。**(2) 致過敏，敏感化**　（行為療法）厭惡療法的一種形式。是把產生焦慮的刺激與不良的行為聯繫起來。隱性致過敏是通過語言暗示，在一種不良行為的同時喚起一種不愉快感覺（如厭惡）。

feeling (such as disgust) are evoked simultaneously by verbal cues.

sensory *adj.* relating to the input division of the nervous system, which carries information from *receptors throughout the body towards the brain and spinal cord.

感覺的　和神經系統的傳入部分有關。它把遍及全身感受器得到的信息帶給大腦和脊髓。

sensory cortex the region of the *cerebral cortex responsible for receiving incoming information relayed by sensory nerve pathways from all parts of the body. Different areas of cortex correspond to different parts of the body and to the various senses. *Compare* motor cortex.

感覺皮質　大腦皮質中，負責接受感覺神經通路從全身各部分傳入的信息的區域。不同的大腦皮質區和機體不同部位以及各種不同感覺相對應。與 motor cortex 對比。

sensory deprivation the state in which there is a major reduction in incoming sensory information. Prolonged sensory deprivation is damaging as the body depends for health and normal function on constant stimulation. The main input sensory channels are the eyes, ears, skin, and nose. If input from all of these is blocked, there is loss of the sense of reality, distortion of time and imagined space, hallucinations, bizarre thought patterns, and other indications of neurological dysfunction. Even minimal sensory deprivation in early childhood can have a serious effect on the future personality. An eye covered for a few months in infancy remains effectively blind for life. Early deprivation of normal hearing can produce severe intellectual and educational damage. Deprivation of the normal contact and stimulation provided for the baby by the mother can cause personality disturbance in later life.

感覺喪失　傳入感覺信息嚴重減少的一種狀態。延遲性感覺喪失指的是身體賴以健康和正常功能的連續性刺激受到損害。主要傳入感覺通道有眼、耳、皮膚和鼻。如果所有這些傳入被阻斷，就會出現真性感覺喪失、時空感覺失真、幻覺、奇異的思維模式以及其他神經性功能紊亂的徵象。在兒童早期甚至極小的感覺喪失在未來的人格中也會出現嚴重影響。在嬰兒期，眼被蓋住幾個月後，生活中殘留有效的盲區。正常聽力的早期喪失，可產生嚴重的智力及教育上的損害。嬰兒通過和母親的正常接觸和刺激的喪失可引起嬰兒在以後生活中人格紊亂。

sensory nerve a nerve that carries information inwards, from an outlying

感覺神經　把信息從機體外圍部位傳向中樞神經系統的神

part of the body towards the central nervous system. Different sensory nerves convey information about temperature, pain, touch, taste, etc., to the brain. *Compare* motor nerve.

經。不同的感覺神經分別向大腦傳遞溫、痛、觸、味等感覺。與 motor nerve 對比。

separation anxiety a state of distress and fear at the prospect of leaving secure surroundings, such as is experienced by some children when they must leave parents to go to school. It is often caused by insecure *attachment.

分離焦慮 對於將要離開安全可靠的環境感到苦悶和恐懼的狀態。如某些兒童必須離開家長去上學時的感受。常由不可靠的依戀所引起。

sepsis *n.* the putrefactive destruction of tissues by disease-causing bacteria or their toxins.

膿毒症 致病菌或其毒素引起的組織的腐敗性破壞。

sept- (septi-) *predfix denoting* **1.** seven. **2.** (or **septo-**) a septum, especially the nasal septum. **3.** sepsis.

〔前綴〕**(1)** 七 **(2)** 中隔 尤指鼻中隔。**(3)** 膿毒症

septal defect a hole in the partition (septum) between the left and right halves of the heart. This abnormal communication is congenital due to an abnormality of heart development in the fetus. It may be found between the two atria (*atrial septal defect*; *ASD*) or between the ventricles (*ventricular septal defect*; *VSD*). A septal defect permits abnormal circulation of blood from the left side of the heart, where pressures are higher, to the right. This abnormal circulation is called a *shunt* and results in excessive blood flow through the lungs. *Pulmonary hypertension develops and *heart failure may occur with large shunts. A heart *murmur is normally present. Large defects are closed surgically but small defects do not require treatment. Recent intrauterine surgical techniques enable a fetus in which an ASD has been detected to proceed to full term by using the placental circulation as a substitute for the *extracorporeal

間隔缺損 心臟左右半側之間的間隔上的一個洞口。這一異常交通口來源於胎兒期心臟的先天性發育畸形。可位於兩個心房間（房間隔缺損，ASD）或兩個心室間（室間隔缺損，VSD）。間隔缺損的存在引起血液從壓力較高的左側流向右側，產生異常血循環。這種異常血循環叫做分流。它導致大量血流通過肺。大量分流情況下可產生肺動脈高壓和心力衰竭。通常有心臟雜音存在。大的缺損應作外科修補，但小缺損不需治療。近期，宮內外科技術能夠探測到胎兒房間隔缺損，能在懷孕全程中用胎盤循環替代體外循環。

circulation that would otherwise be required.

septic *adj.* relating to or affected with *sepsis.

膿毒性的　與膿毒症有關的，或罹患膿毒症的。

septicaemia *n.* widespread destruction of tissues due to absorption of disease-causing bacteria or their toxins from the bloodstream. The term is also used loosely for any form of *blood poisoning. *Compare* pyaemia, sapraemia, toxaemia.

敗血症　血流內致病菌或致病毒素的吸收引起組織的廣泛破壞。在不嚴格的情況下，該術語也用於任何敗血症的形成。與 pyaemia，sapraemia，toxaemia 對比。

Septrin *n. see* co-trimoxazole.

複方新諾明　參閱 co-trimoxazole。

septum *n.* (*pl.* **septa**) a partition or dividing wall within an anatomical structure. For example, the *atrioventricular septum* divides the atria of the heart from the ventricles. **–septal** *adj.* **–septate** *adj.*

間隔　某解剖結構中的分隔部分。如心房和心室的房室隔。

sequela *n.* (*pl.* **sequelae**) any disorder or pathological condition that results from a preceding disease or accident.

後遺症，併發症　任何由先天的疾病或意外事故所造成的功能障礙或病理狀態。

sequestration *n.* the formation of a fragment of dead bone (*see* sequestrum) and its separation from the surrounding tissue.

死骨形成　形成死骨片（參閱 sequestrum）並和周圍組織分離。

sequestrectomy *n.* surgical removal of a *sequestrum.

死骨切除術　切除死骨片的手術。

sequestrum *n.* (*pl.* **sequestra**) a portion of dead bone formed in an infected bone in chronic *osteomyelitis. It is surrounded by an envelope (*involucrum*) of sclerotic bone and fibrous tissue and can be seen as a dense area within the bone on X-ray. It can cause irritation and the formation of pus, which may discharge through a *sinus, and is usually surgically removed (*sequestrectomy*).

死骨（片）　慢性骨髓炎患者骨感染時形成的死骨的一部分。它的周圍常被硬化性骨質和纖維組織所包裹（死骨包殼），X 綫照片上骨體內有致密區。它可引起刺激性疼痛和膿液形成。膿可由竇道流出，常需手術切除（死骨切除術）。

ser- (sero-) *prefix denoting* **1.** serum. **2.** serous membrane.

〔前綴〕**(1)** 血清 **(2)** 漿膜

serine *n. see* amino acid.

絲氨酸 參閱 amino acid。

seroconvert *vb.* to produce specific antibodies in response to the presence of an antigen (e.g. a vaccine or a virus). **—seroconversion** *n.*

血清轉化 （對疫苗產生抗體）通過對抗原存在（如一種疫苗或一種病毒）的應答產生特異性抗體。

serofibrinous *adj.* describing an exudate of serum that contains a high proportion of the protein fibrin.

漿液纖維蛋白性的 含有大量纖維蛋白的漿液性滲出物。

serology *n.* the study of blood serum and its constituents, particularly their contribution to the protection of the body against disease. *See* agglutination, complement fixation, precipitin. **—serological** *adj.*

血清學 研究血清及其成分的科學。尤其研究其保護機體抵抗疾病的作用。參閱 agglutination，complement fixation，precipitin。

sero-negative arthritis *see* (ankylosing) spondylitis.

血清陰性關節炎 參閱 (ankylosing) spondylitis。

seropus *n.* a mixture of serum and pus, which forms, for example, in infected blisters.

漿液性膿 漿液和膿的混合物。例如感染性水泡內形成的混合物。

serosa *n. see* serous membrane.

漿膜 參閱 serous membrane。

serositis *n.* inflammation of a *serous membrane, such as the lining of the thoracic cavity (pleura). *See* polyserositis.

漿膜炎 漿膜的炎症。如覆蓋於胸膜內面的膜（胸膜）的炎症。參閱 polyserositis。

serotherapy *n.* the use of serum containing known antibodies (*see* antiserum) to treat a patient with an infection or to confer temporary passive *immunity upon a person at special risk. The use of antisera prepared in animals carries its own risks (for example, a patient may become hypersensitive to horse protein); the risk is reduced if the serum is taken from an immune human being.

血清療法 應用含有已知抗體的血清（參閱 antiserum），治療某種感染的患者。或給予某一高危患者的暫時性被動免疫。應用動物製備的抗血清可帶來它本身的危險性（如某些患者可對馬的血清蛋白過敏）。使用取自免疫的人的血清可減少危險。

serotonin (5-hydroxytryptamine) *n.* a compound widely distributed in the tissues, particularly in the blood platelets, intestinal wall, and central nervous system. Serotonin is thought to play a role in inflammation similar to that of *histamine and it also acts as a *neurotransmitter, especially concerned with the process of sleep.

5-羟色胺 廣泛分布於組織中的一種化合物。在血小板、小腸壁和中樞神經系統內的含量較多。在炎症中它被認為和組胺起相似的作用。它也可能起神經遞質的作用，尤其是參與睡眠過程中的神經介質。

serotype *n.* a category into which material is placed based on its serological activity, particularly in terms of the antigens it contains or the antibodies that may be produced against it. Thus bacteria of the same species may be subdivided into serotypes that produce slightly different antigens. The serotype of an infective organism is important when treatment or prophylaxis with a vaccine is being considered.

血清型 根據血清學活性，尤其根據所含抗原或抗體物質所作的血清學分類。因此，同種細菌可分為抗原稍有不同的若干種血清型。當考慮應用一種疫苗作為治療或預防時，選擇感染性病原體的血清型是重要的。

serous *adj.* **1.** relating to or containing serum. **2.** resembling serum or producing a fluid resembling serum.

血清的，漿液的 **(1)** 與血清有關的，或含有血清的。**(2)** 與血清相似的，或產生類似血清液體的。

serous membrane (serosa) a smooth transparent membrane, consisting of *mesothelium and underlying elastic fibrous connective tissue, lining certain large cavities of the body. The *peritoneum of the abdomen, *pleura of the chest, and *pericardium of the heart are all serous membranes. Each consists of two portions: the *parietal* portion lines the walls of the cavity, and the *visceral* portion covers the organs concerned. The two are continuous, forming a closed sac with the organs essentially outside the sac. The inner surface of the sac is moistened by a thin fluid derived from blood serum, which allows frictionless movement of organs within their cavities. *Compare* mucous membrane.

漿膜 光滑而透明的膜。它由間皮及其下的彈性結締組織組成，覆蓋於某些巨大體腔的內表面。腹膜、胸膜和心包膜均係漿膜。每一漿膜由兩個部分組成：壁層位於腔壁，臟層覆蓋臟器。壁層與臟層互相連續，構成一個密閉的囊袋。臟器位於囊袋之外，囊袋的內面常由來自血清的一薄層液體所濕潤，以便腔內臟器活動時不產生摩擦。與 mucous membrane 對比。

serpiginous *adj.* describing a creeping or extending skin lesion, especially one with a wavy edge.

匐行的　描述一種爬行或蔓延性皮膚病變，尤其具有波狀的邊緣。

serratus *n.* any of several muscles arising from or inserted by a series of processes that resemble the teeth of a saw. An example is the *serratus anterior*, a muscle situated between the ribs and shoulder blade in the upper and lateral parts of the thorax. It is the chief muscle responsible for pushing and punching movements.

鋸肌　起始部或附着部呈一連串鋸齒狀的肌肉。如前鋸肌位於胸廓上部肋骨與肩胛骨間，是管理推擊動作的主要肌肉。

Sertoli cells cells found in the walls of the seminiferous tubules of the *testis. Compared with the germ cells they appear large and pale. They anchor and probably nourish the developing germ cells, especially the *spermatids, which become partly embedded within them. A *Sertoli-cell tumour* is a rare testicular tumour causing *feminization.

塞爾托利細胞，足細胞　睪丸輸出小管（細精管）的壁細胞。與生殖細胞相比較，形態大且蒼白。它們支持並可能營養正在發育中的生殖細胞，尤其是精細胞。部分精細胞包埋於其中。足細胞腫瘤是一種罕見的、可導致男子女性化的睪丸腫瘤。

serum (blood serum) *n.* the fluid that separates from clotted blood or blood plasma that is allowed to stand. Serum is essentially similar in composition to *plasma but lacks fibrinogen and other substances that are used in the coagulation process.

血清　從凝血塊或血漿中分離出來的液體。血清和血漿的成分基本相似，只是血清中缺少纖維蛋白原和其他在凝血過程中被消耗的物質。

serum hepatitis *see* hepatitis.

血清性肝炎　參閱 hepatitis。

serum sickness a reaction that sometimes occurs 7–12 days after injection of a quantity of foreign serum, such as horse serum used in the preparation of antitetanus injections. The usual symptoms are rashes, fever, joint pains, and enlargement of the lymph nodes. The reaction is due to the presence of antigenic material still in the circulation by the time that the body has started producing antibodies against it; it is

血清病　發生於注射一定量的異體蛋白後 7~12 天出現的一種反應。如抗破傷風製劑中的馬血清。常見症狀為：皮疹、發熱、關節痛和周圍淋巴結腫大。反應的機制為機體開始產生抗體的時候，血循環仍有抗原性物質。因此，它是一種遲發性過敏反應。此病罕見有嚴重者。

therefore a form of delayed *hypersensitivity reaction. The condition is rarely serious.

sesamoid bone an oval nodule of bone that lies within a tendon and slides over another bony surface. The patella (kneecap) and certain bones in the hand and foot are sesamoid bones.

籽骨　位於肌腱之中，而在另一骨面滑動的卵圓形骨結節。臏骨（膝蓋骨）以及某些手足骨均係籽骨。

sessile *adj.* (of a tumour) having no stalk.

無柄的，無蒂的，固着的，無蒂的（腫瘤）

seton *n.* an outmoded form of treatment in which a thread was passed through a pinch of skin and tied in a loop. This acted as a counterirritant to pain elsewhere and produced a running sore thought to be useful for the drainage of harmful materials from the body.

掛綫，串綫　一種過時療法。將一根綫穿過一塊皮膚，並打成結。它可起到減少別處疼痛的作用，同時產生一個潰瘍。據認為這可以把有害的物質引流到體外。

sexarche *n.* the age when a person first engages in sexual intercourse.

初交　初次性交的年齡。

sex chromatin *chromatin found only in female cells and believed to represent a single X chromosome in a nondividing cell. It can be used to discover the sex of a baby before birth by examination of cells obtained by *amniocentesis or *chorionic villus sampling. There are two main kinds: (1) the *Barr body*, a small object that stains with basic dyes, found on the edge of the nucleus just inside the nuclear membrane; (2) a drumstick-like appendage to the nucleus in neutrophils (a type of white blood cell).

性染色質　只存在於雌性細胞內的染色質。它在一個未分裂細胞內代表單一Ｘ染色體。檢查羊膜穿刺術或絨膜絨毛取樣術獲得的細胞中有無性染色體，可在嬰兒出生前鑒定其性別。它有兩個主要類別：(1)巴爾體，呈鹼性染色的小體，緊貼於細胞核膜的內側；(2)中性白細胞核的鼓槌狀物附近。

sex chromosome a chromosome that is involved in the determination of the sex of the individual. Women have two *X chromosomes; men have one X chromosome and one *Y chromosome. *Compare* autosome.

性染色體　決定性別的染色體。女性有兩個Ｘ染色體，男性有一個Ｘ染色體和一個Ｙ染色體。與 autosome 對比。

sex hormone any steroid hormone, produced mainly by the ovaries or testes, that is responsible for controlling sexual development and reproductive function. *Oestrogens and *progesterone are the female sex hormones; *androgens are the male sex hormones.

性激素　主要由卵巢和睪丸分泌的固醇類激素。它負責性發育和生殖功能的控制，雌激素和黃體酮係雌性激素；雄激素是雄性性激素。

sex-limited *adj.* describing characteristics that are expressed differently in the two sexes but are controlled by genes not on the sex chromosomes, e.g. baldness in men.

限性的　在兩性中表現出不同特徵，但只受性染色體以外的基因控制，如男性禿頭。

sex-linked *adj.* describing genes (or the *characteristics controlled by them) that are carried on the sex chromosomes, usually the *X chromosome. The genes for certain disorders such as *haemophilia, are carried on the X chromosome. Since these sex-linked genes are *recessive, men are more likely to have the diseases since they have only one X chromosome; women can carry the genes but their harmful effects are usually masked by the dominant (normal) alleles on their second X chromosome.

性連鎖（伴性的）　描述由性染色體（通常由 X 染色體）攜帶的某些基因（或由這些基因控制的）特徵。某些疾病，如血友病，其基因由 X 染色體攜帶。由於這些性連鎖基因是隱性的，而男性只有一個染色體，所以患這些疾病的可能性較大。女性雖也能攜帶這些基因，但其有害作用常被其第二個 X 染色體上的顯性（正常）等位基因掩蓋。

sexology *n.* the study of sexual matters, including anatomy, physiology, behaviour, and techniques.

性學　研究性的科學。包括性解剖學、生理學、行為學和性技術。

sex ratio the proportion of males to females in a population, usually expressed as the number of males per 100 females. The *primary sex ratio*, at the time of fertilization, is in theory 50% male. The *secondary sex ratio*, found at birth, usually indicates slightly fewer girls than boys.

兩性比率，性（別）比率　人羣中的男女比例。通常用相對於每 100 個女性的男性數來表示。在理論上，受精期的最初性比率是 50% 為男性。出生時的實際比率常表現女嬰稍少於男嬰。

sexual abuse *see* child abuse, paedophilia.

性濫用　參閱 child abuse，paedophilia。

sexual deviation any sexual behaviour regarded as abnormal by society. The deviation may relate to the sexual object (as in *fetishism) or the activity engaged in (for example, *sadism and *exhibitionism). The activity is sexually pleasurable.

The definition of what is normal varies with different cultures, and treatment is appropriate only when the deviation causes suffering. Some people may find that *counselling helps them to adjust to their deviation. Others may wish for treatment to change the deviation: *aversion therapy is used, also *conditioning normal sexual fantasies to pleasurable behaviour. The only helpful effect of drugs is to reduce sexual drive generally.

sexually transmitted disease (STD) any disease transmitted by sexual intercourse, formerly known as *venereal disease*. STDs include *AIDS, *syphilis, *gonorrhoea, genital *herpes, and *soft sore. The medical specialty concerned with STDs is *genitourinary medicine*.

SFD small for dates: *see* intrauterine growth retardation.

SGOT serum glutamic oxaloacetic transaminase. *See* glutamic oxaloacetic transaminase.

SGPT *n.* serum glutamic pyruvic transaminase. *See* glutamic pyruvic transaminase.

shaking palsy an archaic name for *parkinsonism.

shaping *n.* a technique of *behaviour modification used in the teaching of complex skills or in encouraging rare

性偏離 被社會認為不正常的性行為。這種性偏離可以與性對象（如戀物癖）或強迫行為（如施虐狂和露陰癖）有關。這種行為可獲得性滿足。

性偏離的概念隨文化不同而不同，並且只有當這種行為引起痛苦時治療才是適當的。某些人可通過咨詢幫助他們糾正性偏離。另外一些人要求治療：使用厭惡療法，也可用對正常性幻想的條件反射來獲得性滿足。藥物唯一有效的幫助是減少一般的性衝動。

性傳播疾病 因性交而傳播的疾病，即從前人們熟知的性病。性傳播疾病包括艾滋病、梅毒、淋病、生殖器疱疹和軟下疳。治療性傳播疾病的藥物是生殖泌尿系藥物。

足月小樣兒 參閱 intrauterine growth retardation。

血清穀草轉氨酶 血清穀氨酸草酰乙酸轉氨酶。參閱 glutamic oxaloacetic transaminase。

血清穀丙轉氨酶 血清穀氨酸丙酮酸轉氨酶。參閱 glutamic pyruvic transaminase。

震顫麻痹 帕金森綜合徵的舊稱。

塑造療法 一種改變行為的技術，用以教授某些複雜機能或鼓勵某些罕見的行為方式。首

forms of behaviour. At first the therapist rewards actions that are similar to the desired behaviour; thereafter the therapist rewards successively closer approximations, until eventually only the desired behaviour is rewarded and thereby learned.

先，醫師對於患者所做的與預期行為相似的動作給予獎勵，爾後對一次比一次更加近似的動作給予報償，直到最後做出完全與預期目標符合的行為，終於學會它。

sheath *n.* **1.** (in anatomy) the layer of connective tissue that envelops structures such as nerves, arteries, tendons, and muscles. **2.** a *condom.

鞘　**(1)**（解剖學）包被神經、動脈、肌腱和肌肉的結締組織層。**(2)** 避孕套。

Sheehan's syndrome a condition in which *amenorrhoea and infertility follow a major haemorrhage in pregnancy. It is caused by necrosis (death) of the anterior lobe of the pituitary gland as a direct result of the haemorrhage reducing the blood supply to the gland. *Compare* Asherman syndrome.

希恩綜合徵　在妊娠期，繼大出血後的閉經或不育狀態。直接的原因是由於大出血減少了垂體的血供，引起垂體前葉壞死。與 Asherman syndrome 對比。

sheltered housing specially converted (or adapted) accommodation, often in the form of a flatlet, designed to meet the special needs of the elderly who are capable of a degree of self-care. A warden is generally in attendance. The extent to which meals and other services are provided on a continuous basis varies; so too in Britain does the *per capita* payment from the appropriate social service department.

老人公寓　一種經過改建（或適應某種目的）的特殊住所。通常為生活能自理的老人們的特殊需要設計成小套間的形式。一般配備一名管理員。連續不斷供應膳食和其他服務項目因地而異。在英國，為每一位來此居住的老人從相應的社會服務部門支出的經費因人而異。

Shigella *n.* a genus of nonmotile rod-like Gram-negative bacteria normally present in the intestinal tract of warm-blooded animals and man. They ferment carbohydrates without the formation of gas. Some *Shigella* species are pathogenic. *S. dysenteriae* is associated with bacillary *dysentery.

志賀（桿）菌屬　熱血動物和人類腸道內正常存在的、無運動的、革蘭氏陰性桿菌。它們使碳水化合物發酵，不產氣。若干種有致病性。痢疾志賀菌能引起細菌性痢疾。

shigellosis *n.* an infestation of the digestive system by bacteria of the genus *Shigella*, causing bacillary *dysentery.

志賀菌病，志賀菌痢疾　志賀菌屬細菌所引起的消化道感染，即細菌性痢疾。

shingles *n.* herpes zoster (*see* herpes).

带状疱疹 参阅 herpes。

shock *n.* the condition associated with circulatory collapse, when the arterial blood pressure is too low to maintain an adequate supply of blood to the tissues. The patient has a cold sweaty pallid skin, a weak rapid pulse, irregular breathing, dry mouth, dilated pupils, and a reduced flow of urine.

Shock may be due to a decrease in the volume of blood, as occurs after internal or external *haemorrhage, burns, dehydration, or severe vomiting or diarrhoea. It may be caused by reduced activity of the heart, as in coronary thrombosis, myocardial infarction, or pulmonary embolism. It may also be due to widespread dilation of the veins so that there is insufficient blood to fill them. This may be caused by the presence of bacteria in the bloodstream (*bacteraemic* or *toxic shock*), a severe allergic reaction (*anaphylactic shock: see* anaphylaxis), overdosage with such drugs as narcotics or barbiturates, or the emotional shock due to a personal tragedy or disaster (*neurogenic shock*). Sometimes shock may result from a combination of any of these causes, as in *peritonitis. The treatment of shock is determined by the cause.

休克 动脉压太低，难以维持足够的血液供应机体组织时所出现的循环衰竭状态。患者皮肤苍白、出冷汗、脉搏快而弱、呼吸不规则、口乾，瞳孔扩大以及尿量减少。

休克可由血容量减少引起，如内出血、外出血、脱水、烧伤、严重呕吐或腹泻。它也可由心肌活动力减低引起，如冠状动脉血栓形成，心肌梗死或肺栓塞。它也可由静脉普遍扩张，静脉血液充盈不足引起。其原因有：血流内细菌存在（菌血症性休克）；严重过敏性反应（过敏性休克：参阅 anaphylaxis）；药物过量，如麻醉药或巴比妥类；或由某一悲剧事件或灾难所引起的情绪性休克（神经性休克）。有时，休克可由上述几种原因的组合所引起，如腹膜炎。休克的治疗取决于其病因。

short-sightedness *n. see* myopia.

近视 参阅 myopia。

shoulder *n.* the ball-and-socket joint (*see* enarthrosis) between the glenoid cavity of the *scapula and the upper end (head) of the humerus. It is a common site of dislocation. The joint is surrounded by a capsule closely associated with many tendons: it is the site of many strains and inflammations ('cuff injuries').

肩，肩关节 球窝关节。由肩胛骨的肩胛盂和肱骨上端（头）构成（参阅 enarthrosis）。易于脱位。肩关节关节囊周围被一些肌腱紧密包裹。扭伤和炎症（肩袖损伤）多见。

shoulder girdle (pectoral girdle) the bony structure to which the bones of the upper limbs are attached. It consists of the right and left *scapulas (*shoulder blades*) and clavicles (collar bones).

肩帶骨　上肢骨附着的骨骼結構。它由左右肩胛骨和鎖骨構成。

shunt *n.* a passage connecting two anatomical channels and diverting blood or other fluid (e.g. cerebrospinal fluid) from one to the other. It may occur as a congenital abnormality (as in *septal defects of the heart) or be surgically created. *See also* anastomosis.

分流　連接兩個解剖管腔的通道，使血液或其他體液（如腦脊液）改道從一個管腔流向另一個管腔。它可以是先天畸形（如心臟間隔缺損）或由手術形成，參閱 anastomosis。

sial- (sialo-) *prefix denoting* **1.** saliva. **2.** a salivary gland.

〔前綴〕**(1)** 涎，唾液　**(2)** 涎腺，唾液腺

sialadenitis *n.* inflammation of a salivary gland.

涎腺炎　涎（唾液）腺的炎症。

sialagogue *n.* a drug that promotes the secretion of saliva. *Parasympathomimetic drugs have this action.

催涎藥　促進涎腺分泌的藥物。擬副交感神經藥物有此功能。

sialic acid an amino sugar. Sialic acid is a component of some *glycoproteins, *gangliosides, and bacterial cell walls.

涎（唾液）酸　一種氨基酸，涎酸是某些糖蛋白、神經節苷脂和細菌細胞壁的成分。

sialography (ptyalography) *n.* X-ray examination of the salivary glands, after introducing a quantity of radiopaque material into the ducts of the salivary glands in the mouth. It enables the presence of calculi or obstruction to be detected.

涎管造影術　把不透 X 綫的物質注入口內涎腺導管所做的涎腺 X 綫檢查。它能檢查涎腺管內存在的阻塞。

sialolith *n.* a stone (calculus) in a salivary gland or duct, most often the duct of the submandibular gland. The flow of saliva is obstructed, causing swelling and intense pain.

涎石　存在於涎腺或導管內，尤其常見於下頜下腺內的石頭（結石）。唾液腺的分泌液受阻，引起涎腺腫脹和劇痛。

sialorrhoea *n.* see ptyalism.

流涎，涎漏　參閱 ptyalism。

Siamese twins (conjoined twins) identical twins that are physically joined together at birth. The condition ranges from twins joined only by the umbilical blood vessels (*allantoido-angiopagous twins*) to those in whom conjoined heads or trunk are inseparable.

塞米斯雙胎　生下時呈連體的單卵性雙胎。包括臍血管相連（即尿囊血管雙胎）、頭部或軀幹相連等各種情況。

sib *n. see* sibling.

血親，同胞　參閱 sibling。

sibilant *adj.* whistling or hissing. The term is applied to certain high-pitched abnormal sounds heard through a stethoscope.

嘶音的　笛聲或嘶嘶聲。描述聽診器聽到的某些高音調的異常音所用的術語。

sibling (sib) *n.* one of a number of children of the same parents, i.e. a brother or sister.

同胞　同一父母的子女中的一個。即兄弟或姊妹。

sickle-cell disease (drepanocytosis) *n.* a hereditary blood disease that mainly affects people of African ancestry but also occurs in the Mediterranean region and reaches high frequencies in parts of Saudi Arabia and India. It occurs when the sickle-cell gene has been inherited from both parents and is characterized by the production of an abnormal type of *haemoglobin – sickle-cell haemoglobin (Hbs)* – which precipitates in the red cells when the blood is deprived of oxygen, forming crystals that distort the cells into the characteristic sickle shape: this process is known as *sickling*. Sickle cells are rapidly removed from the circulation, leading to anaemia and jaundice. There is no satisfactory treatment; the highest mortality is in childhood but some patients may live to an age of 60–70 years. The carrier condition (*sickle-cell trait*) occurs when the defective gene is inherited from only one parent. It generally causes no symptoms but confers some protection from malaria, which accounts for the high frequency of the

鐮狀細胞病　非洲裔人罹患的一種遺傳性血液病。同樣也發生於地中海地區，沙特阿拉伯和印度也是高發區。當從父母雙方接受鐮狀細胞基因遺傳後即發此病。其特徵為紅細胞內產生一種異常血紅蛋白，即鐮狀細胞血紅蛋白。當血液失氧以後此種血紅蛋白在紅細胞內沉澱，變為不溶性結晶，使紅細胞變為特殊的鐮刀形，這一過程被稱為鐮狀化。鐮狀細胞很快地從血液中除去，導致貧血和黃疸。現在尚無滿意的治療方法，在兒童期死亡率很高，但一些病人可以活到60~70歲。攜帶狀況（鐮狀細胞性狀）僅發生於從父母一方遺傳來的缺陷基因。常無症狀但可從瘧疾中得到一些保護，因此在瘧疾區，這種基因較常見。如果給這種狀態的患者全身麻醉，麻醉師應警惕。

gene in malarious areas. If a general anaesthetic is to be given to a patient with this condition, the anaesthetist should be alerted.

sickness benefit (in the UK) a non-meanstested benefit paid, under the Social Security Act 1975, to those who do not qualify for statutory sick pay but are incapable of work because of some specific disease or bodily or mental disablement. Entitlement depends on an adequate record of national insurance contributions (except in the case of people whose incapacity is due to an accident at work or a *prescribed disease). Claims can be made by self-certification for the first seven days of incapacity and production of a *medical certificate thereafter. Increased payments are made for certain adult dependants. Entitlement continues for the first 28 weeks of incapacity (including any period during which statutory sick pay has been paid). After this, *invalidity benefit* becomes payable if incapacity continues. People who do not qualify for sickness benefit, or for whom income from sickness benefit is insufficient, may be eligible for *income support.

From April 1995 sickness and invalidity benefit has been replaced by an *incapacity benefit*, which requires stricter medical proof of entitlement.

side-effect *n.* an unwanted effect produced by a drug in addition to its desired therapeutic effects. Side-effects are often undesirable and may be harmful.

sidero- *refix denoting* iron.

sideroblast *n.* a red blood cell precursor (*see* erythroblast) in which of iron-containing granules can be demonstrated

疾病津貼 （英國）一種不測定收入的津貼支付。按照 1975 年社會保險法規定，該津貼給予無資格領取法定疾病津貼但又因為某些特殊疾病或體力、腦力殘疾而喪失工作能力的人。此權利依賴國民保險捐助的適當記錄（除外由於工傷或遵照醫囑治療疾病的無工作能力的人）。喪失工作能力後七天內可出示自我證明書，並在領取醫療證明後提出申請。某些成年受贍養者可增加支付。喪失工作能力28周內可繼續享受該權利（包括在此期間已被付給的法定疾病津貼）。此後如果繼續無能力工作可享受喪失工作能力津貼。無資格領取疾病津貼的人或疾病津貼不足的人可以申請收入資助。

1995 年 4 月起，疾病津貼以及喪失工作能力津貼被無能力津貼所替代，享受該津貼權利要求嚴格的醫療證明。

副作用 某一藥物除了預期的治療作用以外，尚產生一些無用的作用。副作用常是令人討厭的，且可能是有害的。

〔前綴〕鐵

鐵粒幼紅細胞 紅細胞的前體（參閱 erythroblast）。適當的染色技術可顯示該細胞內有含

by suitable staining techniques. Sideroblasts may be seen in normal individuals and are absent in iron deficiency. A certain type of anaemia (*sideroblastic anaemia*) is characterized by the presence of abnormal *ringed sideroblasts*. **–sideroblastic** *adj.*

鐵顆粒。鐵粒幼紅細胞存在於正常人，不存在於鐵缺乏者。出現異型環狀鐵粒幼紅細胞是某些類型貧血的特徵。

siderocyte *n.* a red blood cell in which granules of iron-containing protein (*Pappenheimer bodies*) can be demonstrated by suitable staining techniques. These granules are normally removed by the spleen and siderocytes are characteristically seen when the spleen is absent.

高鐵紅細胞 用適當染色技術可顯示含鐵蛋白顆粒（帕彭海默小體）的一種紅細胞。正常情況下，這些顆粒由脾清除。如脾闕如則可看到特徵性高鐵紅細胞。

sideropenia *n.* iron deficiency. This may result from dietary inadequacy; increased requirement of iron by the body, as in pregnancy or childhood; or increased loss of iron from the body, usually due to chronic bleeding. The most important manifestation of iron deficiency is *anaemia, which is readily corrected by iron therapy.

鐵（質）缺乏（症） 可因飲食內缺少鐵元素，或因機體對鐵的需要增加所致。如妊娠期或兒童期；或因機體失鐵過多，但一般多因慢性失血所致。貧血是鐵缺乏的最重要表現。此種貧血可迅速被鐵劑治療所糾正。

siderosis *n.* the deposition of iron oxide dust in the lungs, occurring in silver finishers, arc welders, and haematite miners. Iron oxide itself is inert, but pulmonary *fibrosis may develop if fibrogenic dusts such as silica are also inhaled.

肺鐵末沉着病，鐵塵肺 氧化鐵塵末在肺內沉着。見於銀器精製工、電焊工和赤鐵礦工。氧化鐵本身無活性，但是，如果與致纖維化粉塵（如與硅塵）同時吸入，則可發展為肺纖維化。

SIDS sudden infant death syndrome: *see* cot death.

嬰兒猝死綜合徵 參閱 cot death。

siemens *n.* the *SI unit of electrical conductance, equal to the conductance between two points on a conductor when a potential difference of 1 volt between these points causes a current of 1 ampere to flow between them. Symbol: S.

西（門子） 電導的國際單位。當一導體的兩點之間 1 伏特的電位差引起 1 安培的電流時，電導等於 1 西（門子）。符號：S。

sievert *n.* the *SI unit of dose equivalent, being the dose equivalent when the absorbed dose of ionizing radiation multiplied by the stipulated dimensionless factors is 1 J kg^{-1}. As different types of radiation cause different effects in biological tissue a weighted absorbed dose, called the dose equivalent, is used in which the absorbed dose is modified by multiplying it by dimensionless factors stipulated by the International Commission on Radiological Protection. The sievert has replaced the *rem. Symbol: Sv.

希（沃特） 劑量當量的國際單位。當電離輻射的吸收劑量乘規定的無量綱因子是 1 焦爾／千克時，劑量當量就是 1 希（沃特）。因為不同類型的輻射在生物體組織中引起不同的效應，故使用加權的吸收劑量，即所謂劑量當量，劑量當量是吸收劑量乘以國際放射防護委員會規定的無量綱因子的乘積。舊單位雷姆已為希（沃特）所替代。符號：Sv。

sigmoid- *prefix denoting* the sigmoid colon. Example: *sigmoidotomy* (incision into).

〔前級〕乙狀結腸 例如：乙狀結腸切開術。

sigmoid colon (sigmoid flexure) the S-shaped terminal part of the descending *colon, which leads to the rectum.

乙狀結腸 降結腸的 S 形終末部分，和直腸相接。

sigmoidectomy *n.* removal of the sigmoid colon by surgery. It is performed for tumours, severe *diverticular disease, or for an abnormally long sigmoid colon that has become twisted (*see* volvulus).

乙狀結腸切除術 手術切除乙狀結腸。切除的原因有腫瘤、嚴重憩室性疾病，或因乙狀結腸過長所引起的腸扭轉。參閱 volvulus。

sigmoidoscope *n.* an instrument in serted through the anus in order to inspect the interior of the rectum and sigmoid colon. In its commonest form it consists of a steel or chrome tube, 25 cm long and 3 cm in diameter, with some form of illumination and a bellows to inflate the bowel, but flexible fibre-optic instruments, 60 cm long, are increasingly being used.

乙狀結腸鏡 一種通過肛門插入直腸和乙狀結腸內的器械。最常用的由鋼管或鉻鋼管組成，長 25cm，內徑 3cm。附有不同類型照明裝置和一個手用吹氣器，給結腸充氣。而柔軟的纖維內窺鏡（長 60cm），應用越來越廣泛。

sigmoidoscopy *n.* examination of the rectum and sigmoid colon with a *sigmoidoscope. It is used in the investigation of diarrhoea or rectal bleeding, particularly to detect colitis or cancer

乙狀結腸鏡檢查 使用乙狀結腸鏡作直腸和乙狀結腸檢查。用以檢查腹瀉或直腸出血。特別是用以查出結腸炎或直腸癌。有時應給予全身麻醉，尤

of the rectum. A general anaesthetic is sometimes given, especially if the procedure is expected to be painful or uncomfortable, but flexible fibreoptic instruments make this unnecessary.

其如果事先預料到這一檢查給患者帶來痛苦或不適時。但使用柔軟的纖維內窺鏡時則不需要。

sign *n.* an indication of a particular disorder that is observed by a physician but is not apparent to the patient. *Compare* symptom.

體徵　由醫師觀查到的一個特殊病徵，但患者自己並不覺察。與 symptom 對比。

significance *n.* (in statistics) a relationship between two groups of observations indicating that the difference between them (e.g. between the percentages of smokers and nonsmokers respectively who die from lung cancer) is unlikely to have occurred by chance alone. An assumption is made that there is no difference between the two populations from which the two groups come (*null hypothesis*). This is tested, and a calculation indicating that there is a *probability* of less than 5% (P < 0.05) that the observed difference or a larger one could have arisen by chance is regarded as being *statistically significant* and the null hypothesis is rejected. Some tests are *parametric*, based on the assumption that the range of observations are distributed by chance in a *normal* or *Gaussian distribution*, where 95% lie within two *standard deviations of the *mean (*Student's t test* to compare means). Nonparametric tests (*Mann-Whitney U tests*) make no assumptions about distribution patterns. *See also* frequency distribution, standard error.

顯著性　（統計學）兩個觀察值之間相互關係，表明其差別偶然發生的可能性不大（如死於肺癌的患者中，吸煙者和非吸煙者的兩個組百分數之間的關係）。假設這兩組觀察值所屬的兩個羣體之間沒有差別（零假設或無效假設）。經過檢驗計算表明，這一被觀察到的差別（或更大的差別）是偶然發生的可能性小於 5%（P < 0.05），則差別被認為有統計學顯著性，於是零假設就被否定。有些檢驗是參數性的，基於如下假設：觀察值的頻數範圍呈隨機的正態分布（或高斯分布），分布於平均值的兩個標準差之間的觀察值占 95%（t 檢驗，常用於兩平均數的比較）。非參數性檢驗對於分布態不作假設。參閱 frequency distribution，standard error。

silicosis *n.* a lung disease – a form of *pneumoconiosis – produced by inhaling silica dust particles. It affects workers in hard-rock mining and tunnelling, quarrying, stone dressing, sand blasting, and boiler scaling. Silica stimulates *fibrosis

矽肺，硅肺，石末沉着病　肺塵埃沉着病（塵肺）的一種類型。由吸入二氧化硅粒引起。採礦工人、採石工人、鍋爐清理工易患此病。二氧化硅刺激肺組織纖維化，引起氣喘逐漸

of lung tissue, which produces progressive breathlessness and considerably increased susceptibility to tuberculosis.

silver nitrate a salt of silver with *astringent, *caustic, and *disinfectant properties. It is applied in solutions or creams to destroy warts and to treat skin injuries, including burns. Application discolours the skin bluish-black (*see* argyria).

simethicone *n.* a silicone-based material with antifoaming properties, used in the treatment of flatulence and often incorporated into antacid remedies. Simethicone is also used as in barrier creams for the management of napkin rash and other skin disorders.

Simmond's disease loss of sexual function, loss of weight and other features of failure of the pituitary gland (*hypopituitarism) caused by trauma or tumours or occurring in women after childbirth complicated by bleeding (postpartum haemorrhage).

Simulium *n. see* black fly.

simvastatin *n.* a drug used to reduce abnormally high levels of cholesterol in the blood. Its actions and side-effects are similar to those of *lovastatin. Trade name: **Zocor**.

sinew *n.* a tendon.

singer's nodule a pearly white nodule that may develop on the vocal cords of professional singers.

single photon emission computed tomography (SPECT) a radiological technique for the early diagnosis of brain damage. Brain cells impaired by loss of

硝酸銀 銀的一種鹽類，具有收斂、腐蝕、消毒等性能，其溶液或乳霜可用以消除疣，治療包括燒傷在內的皮膚創傷。可使黑色皮膚脫色（參閱 argyria）。

二甲硅油 一種硅鹼基物質。帶有抗泡沫性質。用於胃腸脹氣的治療。常混合於抗酸藥物，也可做成保護膏被用於尿布疹及其他皮膚病的治療。

西蒙茲病 性機能喪失，體重減輕和有其他垂體機能衰竭徵象（垂體機能減退症）的疾病，見於損傷、腫瘤或發生在產後出血時。

蚋屬 參閱 black fly。

普伐司丁 一種能減低血中膽固醇異常高水平的藥物，其作用和副作用與洛伐它汀相似。商品名：Zocor。

腱

結節性聲帶炎 一種白色環狀結節，常發生在職業歌手的聲帶上。

單光子發射計算機照相術 一種用於診斷早期腦損傷的放射學技術。腦的細胞損傷是由於缺血造成的，由於損傷或突然

blood supply due to injury or stroke release glutamate, which triggers a series of biochemical reactions that may cause irreversible brain damage. In this new technique the patient is injected with a chemical tracer that binds to glutamate and can be scanned by special *computerized tomography equipment to locate the site of the initial injury and determine the amount of glutamate released. The glutamate can then be neutralized by appropriate drugs before its harmful effects cause permanent brain damage.

釋放穀氨酸，觸發一系列生化反應使腦細胞發生不可逆的損傷。用這種新技術，給病人注射一種化學示踪劑與穀氨酸結合，可用特殊的電腦斷層照相裝置掃描到最初損傷部位及測定穀氨酸的釋放量，在它引起永久性腦損傷的有害作用前就可用一種適當的藥物來中和它。

singultus *n. see* hiccup.

呃逆　參閱 hiccup。

sinistr- (sinistro-) *prefix denoting* left or the left side.

〔前綴〕左或左側的

sino- (sinu-) *prefix denoting* **1.** a sinus. **2.** the sinus venosus.

〔前綴〕**(1)** 竇　**(2)** 靜脈竇

sinoatrial node (SA node) the pacemaker of the heart: a microscopic area of specialized cardiac muscle located in the upper wall of the right atrium near the entry of the vena cava. Fibres of the SA node are self-excitatory, contracting rhythmically at around 70 times per minute. Following each contraction, the impulse spreads throughout the atrial muscle and into fibres connecting the SA node with the *atrioventicular node. The SA node is supplied by fibres of the autonomic nervous system; impulses arriving at the node accelerate or decrease the heart rate.

竇房結　心臟起搏點。位於上腔靜脈入口附近，右房壁上部的特殊心肌的顯微結構。竇房結纖維具有自主應激性，每分鐘呈 70 次左右規律性收縮。隨着每次收縮，衝動經心房肌向竇房結和房室結間纖維傳遞。竇房結的神經分布來自自主神經系統。衝動抵達竇房結，使心率加速或減慢。

sinus *n.* **1.** an air cavity within a bone, especially any of the cavities within the bones of the face or skull (*see* paranasal sinus). **2.** any wide channel containing blood, usually venous blood. *Venous sinuses* occur, for example, in the dura mater and drain blood from the brain.

竇　**(1)** 骨內含氣腔。特別是面頰骨或頭顱骨內的含氣腔（參閱 paranasal sinus）。**(2)** 含有血液，通常是靜脈血管的變大管腔，如硬腦膜靜脈竇，可從大腦引流出血液。**(3)** 在一個管狀器官，尤其是在血管內

3. a pocket or bulge in a tubular organ, especially a blood vessel; for example, the *carotid sinus. **4. (sinus tract)** an infected tract leading from a focus of infection to the surface of the skin or a hollow organ. *See* pilonidal sinus.

sinus arrhythmia a normal variation in the heart rate, which accelerates slightly on inspiration and slows on expiration. It is common in healthy individuals.

sinusitis *n.* inflammation of one or more of the mucous-membrane-lined air spaces in the facial bones that communicate with the nose (the paranasal sinuses). It is often caused by infection spreading from the nose. Symptoms include headache and tenderness over the affected sinus, which may become filled with a purulent material that is discharged through the nose. In persistent cases treatment may require the affected sinus to be washed out or drained by a surgical operation.

sinusoid *n.* a small blood vessel found in certain organs, such as the adrenal gland and liver. Large numbers of sinusoids occur in the liver. They receive oxygen-rich blood from the hepatic artery and nutrients from the intestines via the portal vein. Oxygen and nutrients diffuse through the capillary walls into the liver cells. The sinusoids are drained by the hepatic veins. *See also* portal system.

sinus venosus a chamber of the embryonic heart that receives blood from several veins. In the adult heart it becomes part of the right atrium.

siphonage *n.* the transfer of liquid from one container to another by means of a bent tube. The procedure is used

出現的一個小袋或膨出，如頸動脈竇。**(4)** 竇道感染性病竈通向體表或一個中空臟器的感染性通道。參閱 pilonidal sinus。

竇性心率不齊 心率的正常變異。吸氣時輕度增快，呼氣時變慢。一般見於健康者。

竇炎 與鼻腔相通的面頰骨內的一個或一個以上的含氣黏膜腔（副鼻竇）的炎症。通常由鼻腔的感染蔓延引起。症狀有頭痛，鼻竇部壓痛，可被膿性物質充填。膿性物質可從鼻腔流出。頑固性病例需作病竇沖洗治療或手術引流治療。

竇狀隙 腎上腺和肝臟等若干臟器內的小血管。肝臟內可有大量竇狀隙。它們從肝動脈內接受含氧血液，通過門靜脈從腸內接受營養素。氧和營養素經毛細血管壁彌散滲入肝細胞。竇狀隙內的血液由肝靜脈引流。參閱 portal system。

靜脈竇 胚胎期心臟的一個腔室，它同時接受幾條靜脈的血液。在成年期的心臟中它變成為右房的一部分。

虹吸法 用一根曲管把液體從一容器移到另一容器，本法可用作胃灌洗術。通過一個漏斗

in gastric *lavage, when the stomach is filled with water through a funnel and rubber tube, and the tube is then bent downwards to act as a siphon and empty the stomach of its contents.

和橡皮管把水灌入胃內，爾後把橡皮管向下彎曲，起到虹吸作用，把胃內容物排空。

Siphunculina *n.* a genus of flies. *S. funicola,* the eye fly of India, feeds on the secretions of the tear glands and in landing on or near the eyes contributes to the spread of *conjuctivits.

眼蠅 蠅的一個屬。印度眼蠅以淚腺的分泌物為食物，寄生於眼內或眼的附近，傳播結膜炎。

sirenomelia *n. see* sympodia.

（無足）並腿畸形 參閱 sympodia。

sito- *prefix denoting* food.

〔前綴〕**食物**

sitz bath a fairly shallow hip bath in which the person is seated. Sitz baths of cold and hot water, rapidly alternated, were formerly used for the treatment of a variety of sexual disorders.

坐浴 一種淺水臀部坐浴。從前曾用冷水和熱水快速交替以治療各種性慾障礙。

SI units (Système International d'Unités) the internationally agreed system of units now in use for all scientific purposes. SI units are based on the metre-kilogram-second system and have seven base units and two supplementary units. Measurements of all other physical quantities are expressed in derived units, consisting of two or more base units. Tables 1 and 2 (Appendix) list the base units and the derived units having special names; all these units are defined in the dictionary.

Decimal multiples of SI units are expressed using specified prefixes; where possible a prefix representing 10 raised to a power that is a multiple of three should be used. Prefixes are listed in Table 3 (Appendix).

國際單位 目前在科學上所使用的都是國際單位制。根據米-公斤-秒制國際單位，共有 7 個基本單位和兩個增補單位。所有其他的物理量的測定都是上述的導出單位，它由兩個或兩個以上的基本單位組成。各種基本單位和具有專門名稱的導出單位均列於表 1 和表 2 （附錄）。所有這些單位的含義均可在本詞典中查到。

國際單位的 10 的倍數用特殊的前綴表示。應盡可能使用 3 的倍數來作 10 的冪。各種前綴列於表 3 （附錄）。

Sjögren's syndrome a condition in which the patient complains of a *dry

斯耶格倫綜合徵，乾燥綜合徵 患者主訴因唾液腺耗竭而口

mouth, caused by wasting of the salivary glands. It is associated with rheumatoid arthritis and dryness of the eyes.

乾，並伴類風濕性關節炎和兩眼乾燥的一種疾病。

skatole (methyl indole) *n.* a derivative of the amino acid tryptophan, excreted in the urine and faeces.

糞臭素（甲基吲哚）　在尿和糞內排出的一種氨基酸色氨酸衍化物。

skeletal muscle *see* striated muscle.

骨骼肌　參閱　striated muscle。

skeleton *n.* the rigid framework of connected *bones that gives form to the body, protects and supports its soft organs and tissues, and provides attachments for muscles and a system of levers essential for locomotion. The 206 named bones of the body are organized into the *axial skeleton* (of the head and trunk) and the *appendicular skeleton* (of the limbs). (See illustration.) **–skeletal** *adj.*

骨骼　許多骨連接在一起的堅硬框架。它構成身體的外形，保護並支撐着體內柔軟的臟器和組織，它提供肌肉的附着和一個為運動所必要的槓桿系統。機體共 206 塊有名稱的骨組成中軸骨骼（頭顱和軀幹）以及附屬骨骼（四肢）（見圖）。

skew *n.* a disorder of relationships within a family, in which one parent is overpowering and the other is submissive and there is a general avoidance of anxiety-provoking situations. It was proposed as a specific cause of schizophrenia in the children, but this has not been confirmed.

反常家庭　家庭內部關係的反常。父母的一方專制，一方順從。一般總存在避免引起焦慮的情況。曾認為這是兒童精神分裂症的一種特異性病因，但尚未確定。

skew deviation a neurological condition of the eyes in which one eye turns down while the other turns up. It is seen in disorders of the *cerebellum or *brainstem.

偏斜視　眼睛的一種神經病學症狀。眼球向下向內轉動時，另一眼球卻向上或向外側轉動。本病見於小腦或腦幹病變。

skia- *prefix denoting* shadow.

〔前綴〕影

skiagram *n.* a 'shadow-photography', such as an X-ray photograph produced in radiography. **–skiagraphy** *n.*

影像（照）片　一張影像照片。如 X 綫照相術的一張 X 綫照片。

skin *n.* the outer covering of the body, consisting of an outer layer, the

皮膚　身體外面的覆蓋物。它由外層的表皮和內層的真皮組

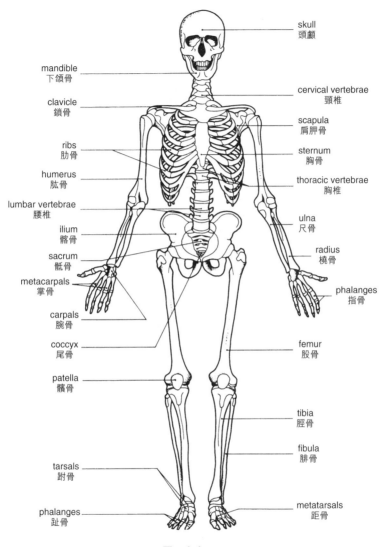

The skeleton
骨骼

skull 頭顱	
mandible 下頜骨	
clavicle 鎖骨	cervical vertebrae 頸椎
ribs 肋骨	scapula 肩胛骨
humerus 肱骨	sternum 胸骨
lumbar vertebrae 腰椎	thoracic vertebrae 胸椎
ilium 髂骨	ulna 尺骨
sacrum 骶骨	radius 橈骨
metacarpals 掌骨	phalanges 指骨
carpals 腕骨	femur 股骨
coccyx 尾骨	tibia 脛骨
patella 髕骨	fibula 腓骨
tarsals 跗骨	metatarsals 距骨
phalanges 趾骨	

*epidermis, and an inner layer, the *dermis (see illustration). Beneath the dermis is a layer of fatty tissue. The skin has several functions. The epidermis protects the body from injury and also from

成（見圖）。真皮下有一層脂肪組織。皮膚有多種功能。表皮保護機體免受創傷和寄生蟲的侵襲，同時也協助機體預防脫水。皮膚內能豎立的汗毛、

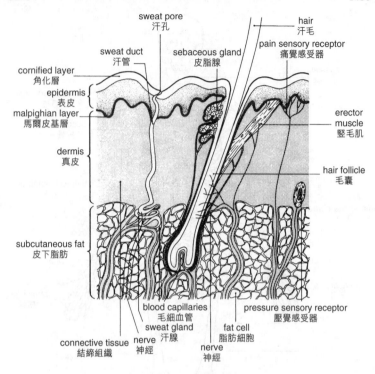

Section through the skin
皮膚切面示意圖

invasion by parasites. It also helps to prevent the body from becoming dehydrated. The combination of erectile hairs, *sweat glands, and blood capillaries in the skin form part of the temperature-regulating mechanism of the body. When the body is too hot, loss of heat is increased by sweating and by the dilation of the capillaries. When the body is too cold the sweat glands are inactive, the capillaries contract, and a layer of air is trapped over the epidermis by the erected hairs. The skin also acts as an organ of excretion (by the secretion of *sweat) and as a sense organ (it contains receptors that are sensitive to heat, cold, touch, and pain). The layer of fat underneath

汗腺和毛細血管構成體溫調節機制的一個部分。當機體太熱時，加強出汗，擴張毛細血管以增加散熱；當機體太冷時，汗腺停止工作，毛細血管收縮，汗毛豎起把一層空氣吸附在表皮上。皮膚也是一個分泌器官（分泌汗）和感覺器官（它含有對冷熱和觸痛覺的感受器）。真皮下的脂肪層具有貯存營養和水分的功能。解剖學用語：皮膚。

the dermis can act as a reservoir of food and water. Anatomical name: **cutis**.

skin graft a portion of healthy skin cut from one area of the body and used to cover a part that has lost its skin, usually as a result of injury, burns, or operation. A skin graft is normally taken from another part of the body of the same patient (an *autograft), but occasionally skin may be grafted from one person to another as a temporary healing measure (a *homograft). The full thickness of skin may be taken for a graft (*see* flap) or the surgeon may use three-quarters thickness, thin sheets of skin (*see* Thiersch's graft), or a pinch skin graft. The type used depends on the condition and size of the damaged area to be treated.

skull *n.* the skeleton of the head and face, which is made up of 22 bones. It can be divided into the cranium, which encloses the brain, and the face (including the lower jaw (mandible)). (See illustration.) The *cranium* consists of eight bones. The frontal, parietals (two), occipital, and temporals (two) form the vault of the skull (*calvaria*) and are made up of two thin layers of compact bone separated by a layer of spongy bone (*diploë*). The remaining bones of the cranium – the sphenoid and ethmoid – form part of its base. The 14 bones that make up the face are the nasals, lacrimals, inferior nasal conchae, maxillae, zygomatics, and palatines (two of each), the vomer, and the mandible. All the bones of the skull except the mandible are connected to each other by immovable joints (*see* suture). The skull contains cavities for the eyes (*see* orbit) and nose (*see* nasal cavity) and a large opening at its base (*foramen magnum*) through which the spinal cord passes.

皮移植片　從身體某部切下一塊健康皮膚用以覆蓋缺損皮膚部分。此種缺損通常由皮膚創傷、燒傷或手術造成。正常情況下，皮移植皮片取自自身的另一部位皮膚（自體移植）。偶爾作為暫時性治療措施，移植皮片取自另一人的皮膚（同種移植）。移植皮片應取足夠厚度（參閱 flap）。外科醫師也可用 3/4 厚度的皮膚或紙片樣薄皮片（參閱 Thiersch's graft）或點狀皮片。植皮類型取決於損傷皮膚的情況和面積。

顱骨　頭和面的骨骼，由 22 塊骨組成。它可分為腦顱骨（包圍腦）和面顱骨（包括下頜骨）（見圖）。腦顱骨由 8 塊骨組成：額骨、頂骨（兩塊），枕骨和顳骨（兩塊），共同形成頭顱的穹窿（顱蓋）。所有顱骨均由兩層細密骨質組成，兩層之間被一層海綿狀骨質所分開（板障）。其餘的腦顱骨（蝶骨和篩骨）組成顱骨的基底部。其他組成面部的 14 塊骨頭包括鼻骨、淚骨、上鼻甲、上頜骨、顴骨、腭骨（以上各有兩塊），梨骨和下頜骨。除了下頜骨以外，其餘所有骨均直接連接在一起（參閱 suture）。顱骨前面有眼眶（參閱 orbit）和鼻（參閱 nasal cavity），顱底有一大孔（枕骨大孔），脊髓由此通過。

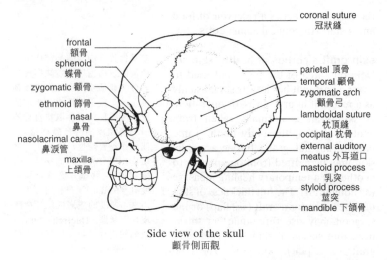

Side view of the skull
顱骨側面觀

coronal suture
冠狀縫

frontal
額骨
sphenoid
蝶骨
zygomatic 顴骨
ethmoid 篩骨
nasal
鼻骨
nasolacrimal canal
鼻淚管
maxilla
上頜骨

parietal 頂骨
temporal 顳骨
zygomatic arch
顴骨弓
lambdoidal suture
枕頂縫
occipital 枕骨
external auditory
meatus 外耳道口
mastoid process
乳突
styloid process
莖突
mandible 下頜骨

SLE systemic lupus erythematosus. *See* lupus erythematosus.

sleep *n.* a state of natural unconsciousness, during which the brain's activity is not apparent (apart from the continued maintenance of basic bodily functions, such as breathing) but can be detected by means of an electroencephalogram (EEG). Different stages of sleep are recognized by different EEG wave patterns. Drowsiness is marked by short irregular waves; as sleep deepens the waves become slower, larger, and more irregular. This slow-wave sleep is periodically interrupted by episodes of paradoxical, or *REM (rapid-eye-movement), sleep, when the EEG pattern is similar to that of an awake and alert person. Dreaming occurs during REM sleep. The two states of sleep alternate in cycles of from 30 to 90 minutes, REM sleep constituting about a quarter of the total sleeping time.

sleep apnoea *n.* cessation of breathing during sleep, which may be *obstructive*,

系統性紅斑狼瘡 參閱 lupus erythematosus。

睡眠 一種正常的無意識狀態。此時大腦活動不外顯（除了機體的基本機能，如呼吸機能繼續維持以外），但仍可記錄到腦電圖 (EEG)。根據腦電圖的不同波型可把睡眠分為不同的期。瞌睡時是不規則低波；睡眠加深時腦電波變為更不規則的慢高波。這一慢波睡眠週期性地被反常的時相睡眠，即快動眼睡眠（眼球快速運動）所中斷。此時腦電波型和覺醒狀態相似。夢出現於快動眼睡眠時。上述兩種睡眠狀態每隔 30~90 分鐘呈週期性交替。快動眼睡眠大約占整體睡眠時間的 1/4。

睡眠呼吸暫停 由於上呼吸道阻塞，造成呼吸無效。在睡眠

due to frustrated efforts to breathe against blocked upper airways (*see* obstructive sleep apnoea), or *central*, in which there is no evidence of any voluntary effort.

時出現呼吸停止或由於中樞無任何迹象的自發的結果。

sleeping sickness (African trypanosomiasis) a disease of tropical Africa caused by the presence in the blood of the parasitic protozoans *Trypanosoma gambiense* or *T. rhodesiense*. The parasites are transmitted to man through the bite of *tsetse flies. Initial symptoms include fever, headache, and chills, followed later by enlargement of the lymph nodes, anaemia, and pains in the limbs and joints. After a period of several months or even years, the parasites invade the minute blood vessels supplying the central nervous system. This causes drowsiness and lethargy, and ultimately – if untreated – the patient dies. Rhodesian sleeping sickness is the more virulent form of the disease. The drugs *suramin, *pentamidine, and *eflornithine are used to treat the early curable stages of sleeping sickness; drugs containing arsenic (*see* tryparsamide) are administered after the brain is affected. Eradication of tsetse flies helps prevent spread of the infection.

昏睡病 熱帶非洲的一種疾病。由於血液內存在的寄生性原蟲，岡比亞錐蟲或羅德西亞錐蟲所引起。寄生原蟲通過采采蠅的叮咬而傳入人體內。早期症狀有發熱、頭痛和寒戰，隨後繼以淋巴結腫大、貧血及肢體和關節疼痛。數月或數年以後，寄生原蟲侵及供應中樞神經的微血管，從而引起瞌睡和昏睡。然後（如未予治療），患者死亡。羅德西亞昏睡病是本病中較嚴重的一型。藥物蘇拉明，或噴他脒和依氟鳥氨酸可用以治療早期可治型昏睡病。如大腦被侵害以後，則使用含砷製劑（參閱 tryparsamide）。徹底撲滅采采蠅有助於預防這一傳染性疾病的傳播。

sleep-walking *n. see* somnambulism.

夢游 參閱 somnambulism。

sling *n.* a bandage arranged to support and rest an injured limb so that healing is not hindered by activity. The most common sling is a *triangular bandage tied behind the neck to support the weight of a broken arm. The arm is bent at the elbow and held across the body.

懸帶 懸吊的绷帶。用以支撐和固定一個受傷的肢體，以免活動影響痊愈。三角绷帶最為常用。它懸吊在頸上，以支撐傷臂的重量，肘部屈曲，手托在身體的一邊。

slipped disc a colloquial term for a *prolapsed intervertebral disc.

滑出盤 椎間盤脫出的俗稱。

slit lamp a device for providing a narrow beam of light, used in conjunction with a special microscope. It can be used to examine minutely the structures within the eye, one layer at a time.

裂隙燈　一種可產生一個窄光束並和一架專門顯微鏡相連接的裝置。用以檢查眼內細微結構，每次檢查一個層次。

slough *n*. dead tissue, such as skin, that separates from healthy tissue after inflammation or infection.

腐肉　壞死的組織。如一塊皮膚在一次炎症或感染以後，和正常組織呈分離狀態。

slow virus one of a group of infective disease agents that resemble *viruses in some of their biological properties but whose physical properties (e.g. sensitivity to radiation) suggest that they may not contain nucleic acid. They are now more commonly known as *prions.

慢病毒　一組傳染性疾病的病原體，在生物特性上與病毒相似，但生理特性不同（如對射綫的敏感度），提示它們可能不含核酸。它們現在較常稱為朊病毒。

SMA *see* spinal muscular atrophy.

脊髓性肌肉萎縮　參閱 spinal muscular atrophy。

small for dates (SFD) *see* intrauterine growth retardation.

足月小樣兒　參閱 intrauterine growth retardation。

smallpox *n*. an acute infectious virus disease causing high fever and a rash that scars the skin. It is transmitted chiefly by direct contact with a patient. Symptoms commence 8–18 days after exposure and include headache, backache, high fever, and vomiting. On the third day, as the fever subsides, red spots appear on the face and spread to the trunk and extremities. Over the next 8–9 day all the spots (macules) change to pimples (papules), then to pea-sized blisters that are at first watery (vesicles) but soon become pus-filled (pustules). The fever returns, often causing delirium. On the 11th or 12th day the rash and fever abate. Scabs formed by drying out of pustules fall off 7–20 days later, leaving permanent scars. The patient remains infectious until all scabs have been shed. Most patients recover but serious complications, such

天花　一種急性病毒性感染，可引起高熱和使皮膚形成癥痕的皮疹。主要由於與患者直接接觸而被感染。接觸後的第8~18 天開始出現症狀。包括頭痛、背痛、高熱和嘔吐。發病第三天在高熱減退時，臉部出現紅斑，且向軀幹和四肢蔓延。再經 8~9 天，全部斑點變為膿疱丘疹，爾後變為豆大的疱疹，起初為水泡，不久即變為膿疱。體溫重新上升，常伴譫妄。第 11~12 天，皮疹和體溫消退。膿疱乾燥結痂。7~20天以後脫落，造成永久性癥痕。患者的感染狀態持續到全部痂脫落為止。大部分患者可恢復健康但可發生某些嚴重併發症，諸如腎炎和肺炎。氨硫脲治療有效。一次感染可終身免疫。目前，抗天花免疫接種

as nephritis or pneumonia, may develop. Treatment with thiosemicarbazone is effective. An attack usually confers immunity; immunization against smallpox has now totally eradicated the disease. Medical name: **variola**. *see also* alastrim, cowpox.

已徹底消滅了此病。醫學用語：天花。參閱 alastrim，cowpox。

smear *n.* a specimen of tissue or other material taken from part of the body and smeared on a microscope slide for examination. *See* cervical smear.

塗片 從身體某一部分取下的組織和其他材料的標本，塗成顯微鏡薄片，以供檢查。參閱 cervical smear。

smegma *n.* the secretion of the glands of the foreskin (*prepuce), which accumulates under the foreskin and has a white cheesy appearance. It becomes readily infested by a harmless bacterium that resembles the tubercle bacillus.

陰垢 包皮腺的分泌物。在包皮內積累。呈白色奶酪樣外觀，它很易沾染上一種類似於結核桿菌的無害細菌。

Smith's fracture a fracture just above the wrist, across the lower end of the radius, resulting in forward displacement of the hand and wrist below the fracture. It is the reverse of *Colles' fracture.

史密斯骨折 腕關節上方骨折。骨折綫位於橈骨下端。由於手部向前着地而受力引起。腕關節在骨折處下方。與其相對的是科利斯骨折。

smooth muscle (involuntary muscle) muscle that produces slow long-term contractions of which the individual is unaware. Smooth muscle occurs in

平滑肌 一種肌肉，能產生緩慢的長時間收縮，本人卻不察覺。平滑肌存在於各種空腔臟器。如：胃、腸、血管、膀

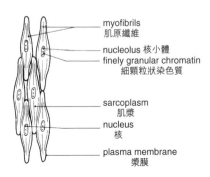

myofibrils
肌原纖維
nucleolus 核小體
finely granular chromatin
細顆粒狀染色質
sarcoplasm
肌漿
nucleus
核
plasma membrane
漿膜

Arrangement of smooth muscle cells
平滑肌細胞排列

hollow organs, such as the stomach, intestine, blood vessels, and bladder. It consists of spindle-shaped cells within a network of connective tissue (see illustration) and is under the control of the autonomic nervous system. *Compare* striated muscle.

snare *n.* an instrument consisting of a wire loop designed to remove polyps, tumours, and other projections of tissue, particularly those occurring in body cavities (see illustration). The loop is used to encircle the base of the tumour and is then pulled tight. *See also* diathermy.

胱，它由結締組織網內的許多梭狀細胞（見圖）組成。由自主神經系統控制。與 striated muscle 對比。

勒除器 由鋼絲套圈組成的器械。用以除去存在於體內的息肉、腫瘤和其他隆起組織（見圖）。用套圈套住腫瘤的基部，後把套圈收緊。參閱 diathermy。

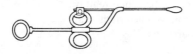

A nasal snare
鼻勒除器

sneeze 1. *n.* an involuntary violent reflex expulsion of air through the nose and mouth provoked by irritation of the mucous membrane lining the nasal cavity. **2.** *vb.* to produce a sneeze.

噴嚏 (1) 鼻腔內黏膜受刺激而引起一種非隨意性強烈反射。將空氣從鼻腔和口腔噴出。**(2)** 打噴嚏。

Snellen chart the commonest chart used for testing sharpness of distant vision (*see* visual acuity). It consists of rows of capital letters, called *test types*, the letters of each row becoming smaller down the chart. The large letter at the top is of such a size that it can be read by a person with normal sight from a distance of 60 metres. A normally sighted person can read successive lines of letters from 36, 24, 18, 12, 9, 6, and 5 metres respectively. There is sometimes a line for 4 metres. The subject sits 6 metres from the chart and one eye is tested at a time. If he can only read down as far as the 12-metre line the visual acuity is expressed as 6/12.

斯內倫視力表 用以測量遠（距）視力敏銳度的最常用表（參閱 visual acuity）。它由數排大寫字母組成。表的下方每排字母小於上排的字母。最上方的大寫字母可由一個正常視力的人從 60 米以外讀認。一個正常視力的人分別可以從 36、24、18、12、9、6、5 米外讀出第一排以下相應各排的字母。有時有一排可在 4 米外讀出。被檢查者在離表 6 米處用一隻眼睛測視，如果只能讀出 12 米這一排字母，那麼其視敏度可用 6/12 表示，正常人被檢時應能讀出 6 米這一排字

Normally sighted people can read the 6-metre line, i.e. normal acuity is 6/6, and many people read the 5-metre line with ease. A smaller chart on the same principle is available for testing near vision. In North America the test is done at a distance of 20 feet: 20/20 vision is the same as 6/6.

母，即正常視敏度為 6/6。很多人可以很容易地讀出 5 米這一排字母。一種與以上原理相同的類似小表可供近距視力測視。在北美洲這種測視的距離為 20 英尺：20/20 視敏度與此種測試 6/6 相當。

snore 1. *vb.* to breathe in such a way as to cause vibration of the soft palate of the roof of the mouth, resulting in a hoarse noise. Snoring usually occurs during sleep. **2.** *n.* the sound made by breathing in this way.

(1) 打鼾　引起口腔頂部軟齶振動的一種呼吸方式。它產生一種噪音，通常發生於睡眠時。**(2) 鼾聲**　以這種方式呼吸所發出的聲音。

snow blindness a painful disorder of the cornea of the eye due to excessive exposure to ultraviolet light reflected from the snow. Recovery usually follows within 24 hours of covering the eyes.

雪盲　過度暴露於雪反射的紫外綫而致眼角膜疼痛性疾患。眼睛覆蓋後，通常於 24 小時內恢復。

snuffles *n.* **1.** partial obstruction of breathing in infants, caused by the common cold. **2.** (formerly) discharge through the nostrils associated with necrosis of the nasal bones: seen in infants with congenital syphilis.

嬰兒鼻塞　(1) 由普通感冒引起嬰兒呼吸道部分阻塞。**(2)**（舊稱）鼻孔流出物內伴壞死性鼻骨：見於嬰兒先天性梅毒。

social class any one of the subdivisions of the population made by the Office of Population Censuses and Surveys based on occupation, as indicated in the ten-yearly census. Such groupings are intended to stratify the population according to standard of living and income (all married women and children up to school-leaving age are classified in accordance with the occupation of husband/father). Five classes are recognized: I professional/self-employed; II administrative; III (nonmanual) clerical and (manual) skilled manual workers; IV semi-skilled; V unskilled. An alternative subdivision into *socio-economic groups*

社會階層　在（英國）人口調查局每 10 年進行的一次調查中，根據職業劃分人口詳細分類之一。按照生活水平和收入（已婚婦女或在學兒童，依據其丈夫或父親分類），把人口分成 5 個階層：(1) 專業人員或自由職業者；(2) 行政管理人員；(3)（非體力）職員及熟練體力工人；(4) 半熟練工人；(5) 非熟練工人。另一種分類是將人羣分成若干社會經濟羣。許多社會學家認為此種分類方法更正確反應職業等級。但此法較複雜，一般不採納。

is believed by many sociologists to reflect employment grades more accurately, but it is more complicated and tends to be less generally applied.

social medicine *see* public health medicine.

social services advice and practical help with problems due to social circumstances. Every local authority is responsible for establishing and staffing a social service department, although block exchequer grants monitored by the *Department of Social Security meet some of the costs. An increasing proportion of the *social workers* in these departments are professionally trained. The present policy is to train generic social workers, but there are special social workers with medical and psychiatric training who are seconded for work in hospitals (*see* medical social worker). Social workers assess the eligibility of clients for such social services as home helps and meals on wheels or refer them to the appropriate statutory or voluntary services; difficulties may sometimes arise when the hospital *catchment area* is not coterminous with the local authority. In relation to mental health, social workers may obtain court orders for *compulsory admission where necessary and provide surveillance and support for those being treated at home or in designated hostel accommodation, including those discharged from hospital. (*See also* aftercare.) *Case work* involves identifying the cause of the client's problem and, where appropriate, advising how best to correct it and/or adept to the circumstances.

social worker *see* social services.

社會醫學　參閱 public health medicine。

社會福利　對由社會環境引起的問題提供建議或實際幫助。每一地方政府負責組建一個社會福利部，儘管由社會福利部支配的經費補貼可滿足某些開支。這些部門的社會福利工作者之中，接受過專門訓練的人日益增多。目前的方針是培訓一般社會福利工作者，但還有一些接受過醫學和心理學訓練的專門社會福利工作者，被調派到醫院工作（參閱 medical social worker）。社會福利工作者審定當事人是否有資格獲取某類社會服務，例如：家務服務，流動送餐，或介紹當事人到適當的法定或民辦服務機構。有時當醫院的保健地段與地方當局的管轄區不同時，會出現困難。關於精神保健方面，社會福利工作者在必要時可獲得法院強行住院的命令和給在家庭或指定場所接受治療的病人，包括出院病人，提供監護和支持（參閱 after-care）。病案調查工作包括辨明當事人發生困難的原因，並適當地給予如何解決這些問題及適應環境的建議。

社會福利工作者　參閱 social services。

socio-economic group *see* social class.

socket *n.* (in anatomy) a hollow or depression into which another part fits, such as the cavity in the alveolar bone of the jaws into which the root of a tooth fits. *See also* dry socket.

sodium *n.* a mineral element and an important constituent of the human body (average sodium content of the adult body is 4000 mmol). Sodium controls the volume of extracellular fluid in the body and maintains the acid-base balance. It also helps maintain electrical potentials in the nervous system and is thus necessary for the functioning of nerves and muscles. Sodium is contained in most foods and is well absorbed, the average daily intake in the UK being 200 mmol. The amount of sodium in the body is controlled by the kidneys. An excess of sodium leads to the condition of *hypernatraemia*, which often results in *oedema. This may develop in infants fed on bottled milk, which has a much higher sodium content than human milk. Since babies are less able to remove sodium from the body than adults the feeding of a high-sodium diet to babies is dangerous and may lead to dehydration. Sodium is also implicated in hypertension: a high-sodium diet is thought to increase the risk of hypertension in later life. Symbol: Na.

sodium bicarbonate a salt of sodium that neutralizes acid and is used to treat stomach and digestive disorders, *acidosis, and sodium deficiency. It is administered by mouth or injection; high doses may cause digestive upsets. *See also* antacid.

社會經濟群　參閱　social class。

槽，臼，窩　(解剖學) 一個中空或凹陷的結構，其中有其他組織充填，例如上下牙槽骨的孔穴由牙根充填。參閱　dry socket。

鈉　一種無機元素。也是人體的一個重要成分（成人體內平均含鈉 4000 mmol）。鈉控制機體細胞外液容量，維持酸鹼平衡。它並參與神經系統電位差的維持，因而它為神經、肌肉功能所必需。大部分食物內均含鈉，且吸收良好。英國人每日鈉攝取量為 200 mmol，體內總鈉量由腎臟控制，鈉過多導致高鈉血症，常引起水腫。牛奶含鈉量遠高於人奶，高鈉血症可發生於牛奶餵養的嬰兒。嬰兒從體內排鈉的能力低於成人，因此嬰兒高鈉飲食餵養可以引起脫水。鈉也參與高血壓的發病：高鈉膳食被認為能增加後半生的高血壓危險。符號：Na。

碳酸氫鈉　一種能中和酸的鈉鹽。用以治療胃腸道疾病、酸中毒、鈉缺乏症。可供口服或注射，大劑量引起消化道不適。參閱　antacid。

sodium chloride common salt: a salt of sodium that is present in all tissues and is important in maintaining the *electrolyte balance of the body. Sodium chloride infusions are the basis of fluid replacement therapy after operations and for conditions associated with salt depletion, including shock and dehydration. Sodium chloride is also a basic constituent of *oral rehydration therapy.

氯化鈉，普通鹽 一種鈉鹽，存在於各種組織中，在維持電解質平衡中起重要作用。生理鹽水是手術後治療低鈉血症，糾正休克和脫水補液的基本液體。它也是口服補液治療的基本成分。

sodium fluoride a salt of sodium used to prevent tooth decay. It is administered by mouth or applied to the teeth as paste or solution. Taken by mouth, it may cause digestive upsets and large doses may cause fluorine poisoning. *See also* fluoridation. Trade name: **Fluor-a-day**.

氟化鈉 一種預防齲齒的鈉鹽。口服或者以膏劑或溶液直接塗敷牙齒。口服可引起消化道不適感，大劑量口服則可引起氟中毒。參閱 fluoridation。商品名：Fluor-a-day。

sodium fusidate an *antibiotic used mainly to treat infections caused by *Staphylococcus*. It is administered by mouth or injection or applied in an ointment for skin infections; common side-effects are mild digestive upsets. Trade name: **Fucidin**.

夫西地酸鈉 一種主要用於治療葡萄球菌感染的抗生素。可供口服或注射。皮膚感染時則用油膏製劑。常見的副作用為消化道不適感。商品名：Fucidin。

sodium hydroxide (caustic soda) a powerful alkali in widespread use as a cleaning agent. It attacks the skin, causing severe chemical burns that are best treated by washing the area with large quantities of water. When swallowed it causes burning of the mouth and throat, which should be treated by giving water, milk, or other fluid to dilute the stomach contents, and by gastric lavage.

氫氧化鈉 一種廣泛用於清潔劑的強鹼，它強烈刺激皮膚，可引起皮膚化學性灼燒傷。此時最好用大量的水沖洗創面，如果是吞下後引起的口腔和喉部灼傷，應給飲水、牛奶或其它飲料治療，旨在使胃內容物稀釋，並進行胃灌洗治療。

sodium nitrite a sodium salt used, with sodium thiosulphate, to treat cyanide poisoning. It is administered by injection and may cause digestive upsets, dizziness, headache, fainting, and cyanosis. It also has effects similar to *glyceryl trinitrate and has been used to treat angina.

亞硝酸鈉 一種鈉鹽，和硫代硫酸鈉合用治療氰化物中毒，供注射用。可引起消化道不適、頭暈、頭痛、暈厥和紫紺。它尚具有和硝酸甘油相似的作用，可用於治療心絞痛。

sodium salicylate a drug with actions and side-effects similar to those of *aspirin. It is used mainly to treat rheumatic fever.

水楊酸鈉 一種和阿司匹林作用及副作用相似的藥物，主要用於治療風濕熱。

sodium thiosulphate a salt of sodium used, with *sodium nitrite, to treat cyanide poisoning. It is administered by intravenous injection.

硫代硫酸鈉 一種鈉鹽，與亞硝酸鈉合用治療氰化物中毒，供靜脈注射用。

sodium valproate an *anticonvulsant drug used to treat all types of epilepsy. It is administered by mouth; side-effects may include digestive upsets, drowsiness, and muscle incoordination. Trade name: **Epilim**.

丙戊酸鈉 用於治療各種癲癇的抗驚厥藥，供口服，副作用為消化道不適、倦睡和共濟失調。商品名：Epilim。

sodokosis *n. see* rat-bite fever.

鼠咬熱 參閱 rat-bite fever。

sodomy *n.* sexual intercourse using the anus. This may be homosexual, heterosexual, or between man and beast. *See also* sexual deviation.

雞姦，獸姦 通過肛門性交。可在同性、異性或人獸間進行。參閱 sexual deviation。

soft sore (chancroid) a sexually transmitted disease caused by the bacterium *Haemophilus ducreyi*, resulting in enlargement and ulceration of lymph nodes in the groin. Treatment with sulphonamides is effective.

軟下疳 一種由杜克雷嗜血桿菌引起的性病，它導致腹股溝淋巴結腫大和潰瘍，磺胺類藥物治療有效。

solarium *n.* a room in which patients are exposed to either sunlight or artificial sunlight (a blend of visible light and infrared and ultraviolet radiation directed from special lamps).

日光浴室 患者接受太陽光或人工陽光照射的房間。人工太陽光是由專門的燈發出的可見光、紅外綫、紫外綫輻射的混合光組成。

solar plexus (coeliac plexus) a network of sympathetic nerves and ganglia high in the back of the abdomen.

腹腔（神經）叢 一種交感神經和神經節組成的網狀結構，位於腹腔後上部。

soleus *n.* a broad flat muscle in the calf of the leg, beneath the *gastrocnemius muscle. The soleus flexes the foot, so that the toes point downwards.

比目魚肌 小腿後部的一個寬而扁平的肌肉，位於腓腸肌的深層。可使足跖屈，趾尖向下。

soma *n.* **1.** the entire body excluding the germ cells. **2.** the body as distinct from the mind.

體，軀體 **(1)** 指生殖細胞以外的整個身體。**(2)** 指和精神有區別的軀體。

somat- *prefix denoting* **1.** the body. **2.** somatic.

〔前綴〕**(1)** 身體 **(2)** 軀體的

somatic *adj.* **1.** relating to the non-reproductive parts of the body. A somatic mutation cannot be inherited. **2.** relating to the body wall (i.e. excluding the viscera), e.g. somatic *mesoderm. *Compare* splanchnic. 3. relating to the body rather than the mind.

身體的，軀體的，體壁的 **(1)** 與身體非生殖部分有關的，軀體的突變不能被遺傳。**(2)** 體壁有關的（即內臟除外），如體壁中胚層。與 splanchnic 對比。**(3)** 與軀體有關而與精神無關。

somatization disorder (Briquet's syndrome) a psychiatric disorder characterized by multiple recurrent changing physical symptoms in the absence of physical disorders that could explain them. The disorder is chronic and is often accompanied by depression and anxiety. It can disrupt personal and family relationships and lead to unnecessary medical and surgical treatment. It is sometimes treated with *cognitive therapy, *psychotherapy, and/or *antidepressants.

軀體化的（精神錯亂）紊亂（布里奎特綜合徵） 一種精神錯亂，以多重聯想為特點的生理綜合徵，但不能以生理功能紊亂來解釋。此種精神紊亂是一種慢性的常伴精神上的壓力和焦慮，它可以使人格瓦解和家庭關係破裂。無需藥物和外科治療，有時可以通過認知療法、心理治療和／或抗抑鬱藥進行治療。

somatomedin *n.* a protein hormone, produced by the liver in response to stimulation by growth hormone, that stimulates protein synthesis and promotes growth. It is biochemically similar to *insulin and has some actions similar to insulin; it is therefore sometimes said to have *insulin-like activity* (*ILA*) or is referred to as *insulin-like growth factor* (*IGF*).

促生長因子 一種蛋白質激素，在生長激素刺激下由肝細胞產生，能刺激蛋白質合成和促進生長。它的生物化學性質與胰島素相似，同時具有一些與胰島素相似的功能，因而它有時被認為有胰島素樣作用 (ILA) 或指胰島素樣生長因子 (IGF)。

somatopleure *n.* the body wall of the early embryo, which consists of a simple layer of ectoderm lined with mesoderm. The amnion is a continuation of this

胚體壁（外胚層和體壁中胚層） 早期胚胎的體壁，它是由外胚層和中胚層組成的一個單一層，羊膜是這一結構在胚外的

structure outside the embryo. *Compare* splanchnopleure.

延續。與 splanchnopleure 對比。

somatostatin (growth-hormone-release inhibiting factor) a hormone, produced by the hypothalamus and some extraneural tissues, including the gastrointestinal tract and pancreas (*see* islets of Langerhans), that inhibits *growth hormone (somatotrophin) release by the pituitary gland. Both growth-hormone releasing hormone and somatostatin are controlled by complex neural mechanisms related to sleep rhythms, stress, neurotransmitters, blood glucose, and exercise. Its inhibitory effect on gastrointestinal secretions is used to reduce flow from *fistulae from the pancreas or bowel to the body surface. Its effect on reducing abdominal blood flow is used to reduce bleeding from *oesophageal varices.

生長激素釋放抑制因子 一種由下丘腦和一些神經系統以外組織、胃腸道、胰臟產生的激素（參閱 islets of Langerhans）。它抑制垂體釋放生長激素。生長激素釋放激素和生長激素都由複雜的神經機制控制，與睡眠節律、應激反應、神經遞質、血糖和體質有關，它對胃腸道激素的抑制作用用於減少胰液、腸內容物從瘻流出到體外。它降低胃腸道血流速度的作用用於降低食管靜脈曲張的血流速度。

somatotrophin *n. see* growth hormone.

促生長素 參閱 growth hormone。

somatotype *n. see* body type.

體型 參閱 body type。

somite *n.* any of the paired segmented divisions of *mesoderm that develop along the length of the early embryo. The somites differentiate into voluntary muscle, bones, connective tissue, and the deeper layers of the skin (*see* dermatome, myotome, sclerotome).

體節 沿着早期胚胎的長軸發育的中胚層的任一成對節段。體節可區分為隨意肌、骨、結締組織和皮膚較深層組織。參閱 dermatome，myotome，sclerotome。

somnambulism (noctambulation) *n.* sleep-walking: walking about and performing other actions in a semiautomatic way during sleep without later memory of doing so. It is common during childhood and may persist into adult life. It can also arise spontaneously or as the result of stress or hypnosis. **–somnambulistic** *adj.*

夢游症 睡眠中起來行走或做出其他一些半自主動作，爾後不能記憶做過的事情，一般常見於兒童期，可持續到成年期，亦可在應激或催眠狀態中自發產生。

somniloquence *n.* talking in one's sleep. *See also* somnambulism.

夢囈，夢語 夢中講話。參閱 somnambulism。

somnolism *n.* a hypnotic trance. *See* hypnosis.

催眠狀態 一種催眠性迷睡狀態。參閱 hypnosis。

sonoplacentography *n.* the technique of using *ultrasound waves to determine the position of the placenta during pregnancy. This has an advantage over using X-rays in that the fetus is not subjected to possibly harmful radiation.

超聲胎盤造影術 妊娠期間，應用超聲波確定胎盤位置的一種技術。因為胎兒不能耐受可能有害的放射線，所以，此技術比 X 綫造影術優越。

sonotopography *n.* the use of *ultrasound waves to determine the position of structures within the body, such as the position of a fetus within the uterus or the midline of the brain within the skull.

超聲斷層檢查術 應用超聲波檢查體內各種結構的位置，如胎兒在子宮內的位置或顱內大腦中綫的位置。

soporific *n. see* hypnotic.

催眠藥 參閱 hypnotic。

sorbitol *n.* a carbohydrate with a sweet taste, used by diabetics as a substitute for cane sugar. It is also used in disorders of carbohydrate metabolism and in drip feeding. It is administered by mouth or injection; large doses taken by mouth may cause digestive upsets.

山梨（糖）醇 一種帶有甜味的碳水化合物。糖尿病患者用作蔗糖的代替物，它亦用於碳水化合物代謝障礙和滴注餵養患者。供口服或注射，大劑量口服可引起消化道不適感。

sordes *pl. n.* the brownish encrustations that form around the mouth and teeth of patients suffering from fevers.

口垢 發熱患者口腔和牙齒附近形成的帶褐色痂皮。

sore *n.* a lay term for any ulcer or other open wound of the skin or mucous membranes, which may be caused by injury or infection. *See also* bedsore, soft sore.

瘡，潰瘍 皮膚或黏膜的各種潰瘍或開放性傷口的一個俗稱。它們可由外傷或感染引起。參閱 bedsore，soft sore。

sore throat pain at the back of the mouth, commonly due to bacterial or viral infection of the tonsils (*tonsillitis) or the pharynx (*pharyngitis). If infection persists the lymph nodes in the neck may become tender and enlarged (cervical adenitis).

咽喉痛 口腔後壁痛，一般常由扁桃體（扁桃體炎）或咽（咽炎）的細菌性或病毒性感染引起。如感染持續存在，則頸部淋巴結可腫大和觸痛（頸部淋巴結炎）。

sotalol *n.* a drug (*see* beta blocker) used to treat abnormal heart rhythm, angina, and high blood pressure and to relieve symptoms in *thyrotoxicosis. It is administered by mouth or injection; side-effects may include digestive upsets, tiredness, and dizziness. Trade names: **Beta-Cardone**, **Sotacor**.

索他洛爾 一種用於治療心率失常、心絞痛和高血壓的藥物（參閱 beta blocker）。並可減輕甲狀腺毒症的症狀。可口服或注射，副作用有消化道不適感、乏力、頭暈。商品名：Beta-Cardone，Sotacor。

souffle *n.* a soft blowing sound heard through the stethoscope, usually produced by blood flowing in vessels.

雜音，吹氣音 用聽診器聽到的一種柔和吹風樣音。通常由於血管內血液流動所產生。

sound (in surgery) **1.** *n.* a long rodlike instrument, often with a curved end, used to explore body cavities (such as the bladder) or to dilate *strictures in the urethra or other canals. **2.** *vb.* to explore a cavity using a sound.

探子（外科學） **(1)** 一種長柱樣器械，末端常有一個彎曲，常用以探查體腔（如膽囊與膀胱）或用以擴張狹窄的尿道或其他管腔。**(2)** 用探子探查某一個腔孔。

Southern blot analysis a technique for identifying a specific form of DNA in cells. The DNA is extracted from the cells and restriction enzymes used to cut it into small fragments. The fragments are separated and a gene *probe known to match the DNA fragment being sought is used. *Compare* Northern blot analysis, Western blot analysis.

DNA 印迹分析 一個鑒別細胞內特異型 DNA 的技術，DNA 從細胞內提取，用限制性內切酶把它切成小段，小段彼此分開，用已知基因探針來測量被尋找的 DNA 片斷。與 Northern blot analysis，Western blot analysis 對比。

Southey's tubes fine-calibre tubes for insertion into subcutaneous tissue to drain excess fluid. They are rarely used in practice today.

索西管 一種極細的管子，用來插入皮下組織去排除過多的體液，目前極少應用。

space maintainer an orthodontic appliance that maintains an existing space in the dentition.

牙間隙保持器 牙正畸器械，它保持牙列間隙的存在。

Spanish fly the blister beetle, *Lytta vesicatoria*: source of the irritant and toxic chemical compound *cantharidin.

西班牙蠅，斑蝥，西班牙綠芫菁 具有刺激性和毒性，是複方斑蝥素製劑的來源。

sparganosis *n.* a disease caused by the migration of certain tapeworm larvae

裂頭蚴病 某種縧蟲的幼蟲移行所引起的疾病（參閱 spar-

(see sparganum) in the tissues beneath the skin, between the muscles, and occasionally in the viscera and brain. The larvae, which normally develop in frogs and reptiles, are accidentally transferred to man by eating the uncooked flesh of these animals or by drinking water contaminated with minute crustaceans infected with the tapeworm larvae. The larvae cause inflammation, swelling, and fibrosis of the tissues. Treatment of the condition, common in the Far East, involves intravenous injections of neosalvarsan and surgical removal of the larvae.

ganum），幼蟲存在於皮下組織、肌肉間，偶見於內臟和大腦內。正常情況下，這些幼蟲在蛙和爬行動物體內發育。偶然傳播給人的途徑是吃了這些未煮熟的宿主動物的肉，或飲用了含有被絛蟲幼蟲污染的甲殼綱動物的水，幼蟲可引起機體組織的炎症、腫脹和纖維化。遠東地區常用的治療是靜脈注射新胂凡納明以及手術取出幼蟲。

sparganum *n*. the larvae of certain tapeworms, including species of *Diphyllobothrium and Spirometra, which may accidentally infect man (see sparganosis). They are actually *plerocercoids, but the generic name Sparganum is sometimes given to them since they fail to develop into adults and definite classification of the species is not possible from the larvae alone.

裂頭蚴屬 某些絛蟲的幼蟲，包括裂頭絛蟲和疊宮絛蟲，牠們可以偶然地感染人（參閱 sparganosis）。實際上，牠們是全尾裂頭蚴，但通俗稱牠們為裂頭蚴屬，因為牠們不能發育成成蟲。而又無法單獨根據幼蟲作出明確分類。

spasm *n*. a sustained involuntary muscular contraction, which may occur either as part of a generalized disorder, such as a *spastic paralysis, or as a local response to an otherwise unconnected painful condition. *Carpopedal spasm* affects the muscles of the hands and feet and is caused by a deficiency of available calcium in the body.

痙攣 肌肉呈持久不隨意收縮。可為全身性疾病的一個部分，如痙攣性麻痺；也可以是對另一個不相關疼痛狀態的局部反應。手足痙攣可侵及手足肌肉，它由體內缺鈣引起。

spasmo- *prefix denoting* spasm.

〔前綴〕痙攣

spasmodic *adj*. occurring in spasms or resembling a spasm.

痙攣的 出現了痙攣或與痙攣類似的。

spasmolytic *n*. a drug that relieves spasm of smooth muscle; examples are *aminophylline and *papaverine.

解痙劑，鎮痙劑 一種緩解平滑肌痙攣的藥物，如氨茶鹼和罌粟鹼。解痙劑可用作解除氣

Spasmolytics may be used as *bronchodilators to relieve spasm in bronchial muscle, to stimulate the heart in the treatment of angina, or to relieve colic due to spasm of the digestive system.

管肌痙攣的支氣管擴張藥；在心絞痛治療中，它興奮心臟，或用於緩解消化系統痙攣引起的腸絞痛。

spasmus nutans a combination of symptoms including a slow nodding movement of the head, *nystagmus (involuntary movements of the eyes), and spasm of the neck muscles. It affects infants and it normally disappears within a year or two.

點頭狀痙攣 一組混合症狀，包括緩慢點頭動作、眼球震顫（眼球的非隨意運動）和頸部肌肉痙攣。它侵及嬰兒，正常情況下 1~2 年內症狀消失。

spastic colon *see* irritable bowel syndrome.

痙攣性結腸 參閱 irritable bowel syndrome。

spasticity *n.* resistance to the passive movement of a limb that is maximal at the beginning of the movement and gives way as more pressure is applied. It is a symptom of damage to the corticospinal tracts in the brain or spinal cord. It is usually accompanied by weakness in the affected limb (*see* spastic paralysis). *Compare* rigidity.

痙攣狀態，強直（狀態） 對肢體被動性動作的抵抗。動作開始時抵抗最強，需要用較強的力量才能使之動作。它是大腦或脊髓內皮質脊髓束受損的一個症狀。常伴有病側肢體無力（參閱 spastic paralysis）。與 rigidity 對比。

spastic paralysis weakness of a limb or limbs associated with increased reflex activity. This results in resistance to passive movement of the limb (*see* spasticity). It is caused by disease affecting the nerve fibres of the corticospinal tract, which in health not only initiate movement but also inhibit the stretch reflexes to allow the movements to take place. *See* cerebral palsy.

痙攣性麻痺 一個或兩個肢體運動減弱伴反射增強。病肢對運動有抵抗（參閱 spasticity）。係由皮質脊髓束神經纖維的疾病所引起。正常人的皮質脊髓束不僅可使肢體運動，而且可抑制牽張反射，從而保證動作的完成。參閱 cerebral palsy。

spatula *n.* an instrument with a blunt blade used to spread ointments or plasters and, particularly in dentistry, to mix materials.

藥刀，藥鏟 一種醫療器械。有一個鈍的刀刃，用以使油膏或硬膏鋪開。尤多在牙科用以調合材料。

special hospitals hospitals for the care of mentally ill patients who are also

專科醫院 治療精神病患者的醫院。這些患者有危險性，因

dangerous and must therefore be kept securely. There are four in the UK: Broadmoor, Rampton, Ashworth, and Carstairs. Most (but not all) patients are there compulsorily under a hospital order made by a court according to the *Mental Health Act.

special school (in Britain) an education establishment for handicapped children. The discovery and assessment (*ascertainment*) of those needing to attend a special school may occur long before school age (2 years or younger); the responsibility for deciding who attends a special school lies with the local education authority. Special schools exist for each of the following 11 groups of handicapped children: blind, partially sighted, deaf, partially deaf, delicate (those with such medical handicaps as congenital heart disease or cystic fibrosis), educationally subnormal, mentally handicapped (in which learning potential is limited and independent living may prove impossible), maladjusted (those with behavioral difficulties), physically handicapped (by such conditions as poliomyelitis, muscular dystrophy, or limb absence from thalidomide), epileptic, and those with speech defects. Some special schools cater for combinations of two or more of these handicaps. Special education for the blind and for those with other severe handicaps may start as early as 2 years, deaf children requiring special education from the date of discovery.

species *n*. the smallest unit used in the classification of living organisms. Members of the same species are able to interbreed and produce fertile offspring. Similar species are grouped together within one *genus.

此必須保持安全。在英國有四所此類醫院：布羅德穆、蘭普頓、阿什沃爾斯和卡斯素爾斯。根據精神保健法，大部分（但不是全部）患者應接受醫院強制管理。

特種學校 （英國）為殘疾兒童辦的教育機構。應發現並確定（查明）需要在學齡前（2 歲或 2 歲前）進入特種學校的殘疾兒童，決定殘疾兒童進入特種學校是地方教育當局的責任。如以下 11 個組的殘疾兒童可進此特種學校：全盲、半盲、全聾、半聾、殘疾者（如先天性心臟病、囊性纖維性變）、弱智、精神殘疾（學習困難、不能獨立生活）、適應不良（行動困難）、軀體殘疾（如脊髓灰質炎、肌營養不良，或因服用沙利度胺而致缺肢畸形），癲癇以及語言缺陷者。若干特種學校接收以上兩種或兩種以上殘疾兒童。盲童及其他殘疾兒童的教育開始於 2 歲，聾兒則一經發現，應立即開始特種教育。

物種 生物分類中使用的最小單位。同種成員可雜交並產生能生育的後代。相近的種則聚合成屬。

specific 1. *n.* a medicine that has properties especially useful for the treatment of a particular disease. **2.** *adj.* (of a disease) caused by a particular microorganism that causes no other disease. **3.** *adj.* of or relating to a species.

(1) 特效藥 對某種特定疾病的治療特別有效的藥。**(2) 特異性的** (指疾病) 由某種專門微生物引起,該微生物不引發其他疾病。**(3) 物種的** 屬於某物種的或與某一物種有關的。

specific gravity the ratio, more correctly known as *relative density*, of the density of a substance at 20°C to the density of water at its temperature of maximum density (4°C). Measurement of the specific gravity of urine is one of the tests of renal function.

比重 一種物質在 20°C 時的密度與水在最大密度溫度 (4°C) 時的密度之比例,更準確地稱為相對密度。測定尿比重是腎功能的檢查之一。

specificity *n.* (in screening tests) *see* sensitivity.

特異性 (在篩查中) 參閱 sensitivity。

SPECT *see* single photon emission computed tomography.

單光子發射計算機照相術 參閱 single photon emission computed tomography。

spectinomycin *n.* an *antibiotic used to treat various infections, particularly gonorrhoea. It is administered by injection; side-effects may include nausea, dizziness, fever, and rash. Trade name: **Trobicin**.

壯觀黴素 一種用於治療各類感染,尤其是淋病的抗生素,注射用藥。副作用包括惡心、頭昏、發燒及皮疹。商品名: Trobicin。

spectrograph *n.* an instrument (a *spectrometer or *spectroscope) that produces a photographic record (*spectrogram*) of the intensity and wavelength of electromagnetic radiations.

光譜儀 一種顯示電磁輻射強度及波長的影像記錄 (光譜圖) 儀器 (分光計或分光鏡)。

spectrometer *n.* any instrument for measuring the intensity and wavelengths of visible or invisible electromagnetic radiations. *See also* spectroscope.

分光計 任何測量可視及非可視電磁射綫強度及波長的儀器。參閱 spectroscope。

spectrophotometer *n.* an instrument (a spectrometer) for measuring the intensity of the wavelengths of the components of light (visible or ultraviolet).

分光光度計 一種測定光 (可見光或紫外綫) 的波長強度的儀器 (分光計)。

spectroscope *n*. an instrument used to split up light or other radiation into components of different wavelengths, the simplest spectroscope uses a prism, which splits white light into the rainbow colours of the visible spectrum.

分光鏡　用來將光或射綫分解為不同波長的組成部分的儀器。最簡單的分光鏡使用一個鏡，將白色光綫分成可見的彩虹光譜。

specular reflection (in *ultrasonics) the reflection of sound waves from the surface of an internal structure, which can be used to produce a picture of the surface as an echogram (*see* echography). A specular reflection contrasts with vaguer diffuse echoes produced by minor differences in tissue density.

鏡面反射　(超聲波學) 來自體內結構表面的聲波的反射，該反射能產生該表面的圖像，像回聲圖 (參閱 echography)。鏡面反射與因組織密度的微小差別而產生的模糊而彌散的回聲形成了鮮明的對照。

speculum *n*. (*pl.* **specula**) a metal instrument for inserting into and holding open a cavity of the body, such as the vagina, rectum, or nasal orifice, in order that the interior may be examined (see illustration).

窺器　一種金屬儀器，用來插入或撐開身體的某個孔腔，如陰道、直腸或鼻腔，以便檢查其內部情況 (見圖)。

speech therapy the rehabilitation of patients who are unable to speak coherently because of congenital causes, accidents, or illness (e.g. stroke). Speech therapists have special training in this field but are not medically registered.

語言療法　對因先天性原因，意外事故或疾病 (如中風) 引起的不能連貫講話的病人的康復治療。語言治療師在這一領域受過特別訓練，但無行醫註冊執照。

sperm *n*. *see* spermatozoon.

精子，精液　參閱 spermatozoon。

sperm- (spermi(o)- spermo-) *prefix denoting* sperm or semen.

〔前綴〕精，精液

spermat- (spermato-) *prefix denoting* **1.** sperm. **2.** organs or ducts associated with sperm.

〔前綴〕(1) 精子，精液 (2) 精子器官　與精子、精液有關的器官或導管。

spermatic artery either of two arteries that originate from the abdominal aorta and travel downwards to supply the testes.

精索動脈　自腹主動脈下行給睪丸供血的兩條精索動脈之一。

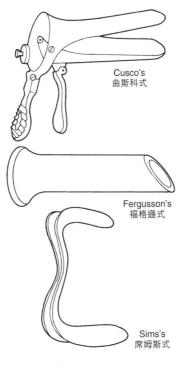

Cusco's
曲斯科式

Fergusson's
福格遜式

Sims's
席姆斯式

Vaginal specula
陰道窺器示意圖

spermatic cord the cord, consisting of the *vas deferens, nerves, and blood vessels, that runs from the abdominal cavity to the testicle in the scrotum. The *inguinal canal, through which the spermatic cord passes, becomes closed after the testes have descended.

精索 由輸精管、神經及血管構成，起自腹腔終止於陰囊中的睪丸。精索所經過的腹股溝管在睪丸下降後呈閉鎖狀態。

spermatid *n.* a small cell produced as an intermediate stage in the formation of spermatozoa. Spermatids become embedded in *Sertoli cells in the testis. They are transformed into spermatozoa by the process of spermiogenesis (*see* spermatogenesis).

精細胞，精子細胞 精子生成過程中作為中間階段產生的小細胞。它們包嵌在睪丸內的塞爾托利細胞中，在精子形成的過程中轉變成精子。（參閱 spermatogenesis）

spermatocele *n.* a cystic swelling in the scrotum containing sperm. The cyst

精子囊腫 含精子的陰囊的囊性腫脹。囊腫產生於附睪（從

arises from the epididymis (the duct conveying sperm from the testis) and can be felt as a lump above the testis. Needle *aspiration of the cyst reveals a milky opalescent fluid that contains sperm. Treatment is by surgical removal.

睾丸運輸精子的導管），觸摸如一腫塊在睾丸上。從囊腫處用針抽吸可見牛奶狀乳白色中液體內含精子。治療通過手術切除。

spermatocyte *n*. a cell produced as an intermediate stage in the formation of spernatozoa (*see* spermatogenesis). Spermatocytes develop from spermatogonia in the walls of the seminiferous tubules of the testis; they are known as either *primary* or *secondary spermatocytes* according to whether they are undergoing the first or second division of meiosis.

精母細胞 精子形成過程所產生的中期細胞。（參閱 spermatogenesis）。精母細胞發育自睾丸生精細管壁上的精原細胞。根據其是否進行第一次或第二次減數分裂，分別稱為初級或二級精母細胞。

spermatogenesis *n*. the process by which mature spermatozoa are produced in the testis (see illustration). *Spermatogonia, in the outermost layer of the seminiferous tubules, multiply throughout reproductive life. Some of them divide by meiosis into *spermatocytes, which produce haploid *spermatids. These are transformed into mature spermatozoa by the process of *spermiogenesis*, the whole process takes 70–80 days.

精子發生 成熟精子在睾丸產生的過程（見圖）。輸精管外層的精原細胞在生殖期內都可繁殖。其中一些通過減數分裂成產生單倍精子的精母細胞。通過精子發生過程轉變為成熟精子。整個過程為 70~80 天。

spermatogonium *n*. (*pl.* **spermatogonia**) a cell produced at an early stage in the formation of spermatozoa (*see* spermatogenesis). Spermatogonia first appear in the testis of the fetus but do not multiply significantly until after puberty. They act as stem cells in the walls of the seminiferous tubules, dividing continuously by mitosis and giving rise to *spermatocytes.

精原細胞 精子形成早期階段產生的細胞（參閱 spermatogenesis）。該細胞最早出現於胎兒睾丸內，但顯著增殖是在青春期後。在輸精管壁上該細胞起著幹細胞作用，並以有絲分裂繼續分裂產生精母細胞。

spermatorrhoea *n*. the involuntary discharge of semen without orgasm. Semen is usually produced by ejaculation at

遺精，精溢 無性慾高潮下的不隨意排精。通常在性慾高潮時射精，且正常時其他時間不

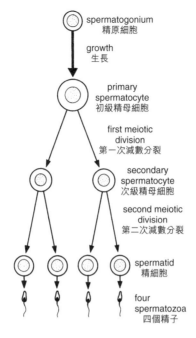

Spermatogenesis
精子發生示意圖

orgasm and does not normally discharge at other times. If, however, the mechanism of ejaculation is lost, spermatorrhoea may occur.

spermatozoon (sperm) *n.* (*pl.* **spermatozoa**) a mature male sex cell (*see* gamete). The tail of a sperm enables it to swim, which is important as a means for reaching and fertilizing the ovum (although muscular movements of the uterus may assist its journey from the vagina). *See also* acrosome, fertilization.

spermaturia *n.* the presence of spermatozoa in the urine. Spermatozoa are occasionally seen on microscopic examination of the urine and their presence is not abnormal. If present in large

排精。但如果射精機制喪失，遺精則會發生。

精子 一種成熟的雄性性細胞（見圖，參閱 gamete）。精子的尾巴使其能夠游動，這是精子接近卵子並使其受精的重要途徑（儘管子宮肌肉的運動也可協助精子自陰道游入）。參閱 acrosome，fertilization。

精液尿 尿中精子的存在。在尿顯微鏡檢查中偶見精子，而其存在並非異常。如有大量精子，通常在排尿結束時尿液變混濁。性高潮時非正常的向膀

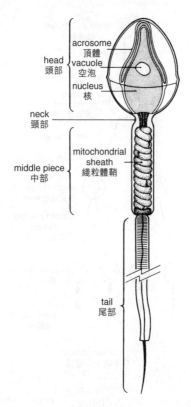

head 頭部
acrosome 頂體
vacuole 空泡
nucleus 核

neck 頸部

middle piece 中部
mitochondrial sheath 綫粒體鞘

tail 尾部

A spermatozoon
精子

numbers, the urine becomes cloudy, usually towards the end of micturition. Abnormal ejaculation into the bladder on orgasm (retrograde ejaculation) may occur after *prostatectomy or other surgical procedures or in neurological conditions that destroy the ability of the bladder neck to close on ejaculation.

sperm count *see* seminal analysis.

spermicide *n.* an agent that kills spermatozoa. Creams and jellies containing

胱射精（逆向射精）可發生在前列腺切除術後或其他外科手術後或因神經系統疾病使射精時膀胱莖的關閉功能受損傷。

精子計數 參閱 seminal analysis。

殺精子劑 一種殺死精子的物質，含有化學殺精劑的油劑或

chemical spermicides are used – in conjunction with a *diaphragm – as contraceptives. **–spermicidal** *adj.*

膠凍，常常與子宮帽一起使用，或用作為避孕藥。

spermiogenesis *n.* the process by which spermatids become mature spermatozoa within the seminiferous tubules of the testis. *See* spermatogenesis.

精子發生 精細胞在睾丸輸精管內變為成熟精子的過程。參閱 spermatogenesis。

spheno- *prefix denoting* the sphenoid bone. Examples: *sphenomaxillary* (relating to the sphenoid and maxillary bones); *sphenopalatine* (relating to the sphenoid bone and palate).

〔前綴〕**蝶骨** 例如蝶上頜的（與蝶骨及上頜骨相關）；蝶腭的（與蝶骨及腭骨相關）。

sphenoid bone a bone forming the base of the cranium behind the eyes. It consists of a *body*, containing air spaces continuous with the nasal cavity (*see* paranasal sinuses); two *wings* that form part of the orbits; and two *pterygoid processes* projecting down from the point where the two wings join the body. *See* skull.

蝶骨 一構成兩眼後顱骨基底的一塊骨頭。它由一個體兩個翼構成。體是與鼻腔相連的氣腔（參閱 paranasal sinuses），雙翼構成眼眶的部分。兩翼突自兩翼與體的結合點向下突出。參閱 skull。

spherocyte *n.* an abnormal form of red blood cell (*erythrocyte) that is spherical rather than disc-shaped. In blood films spherocytes appear smaller and stain more densely than normal red cells. They are characteristically seen in some forms of haemolytic anaemia. Spherocytes tend to be removed from the blood as they pass through the spleen. *See also* spherocytosis.

球形紅細胞 一種球形而非盤形的非正常血紅細胞。該細胞在血膜中較正常紅細胞小且染色濃度大。在某種溶血性貧血中作為特有的現象可見該細胞存在。該細胞在通過脾臟時傾向於從血液中除掉。參閱 spherocytosis。

spherocytosis *n.* the presence in the blood of abnormally shaped red cells (*spherocytes). Spherocytosis may occur as a hereditary disorder (*hereditary spherocytosis*) or in certain haemolytic *anaemias.

球形紅細胞症 血液中異形紅細胞（球形紅細胞）的存在。該病可作為一遺傳性疾病發生，也可出現在某種溶血性貧血中。

sphincter *n.* a specialized ring of muscle that surrounds an orifice. Contractions of

括約肌 圍繞體腔口的特殊肌環。收縮該肌可完全或部分地

the sphincter partly or completely close the orifice. Sphincters are found, for example, around the anus (*anal sphincter*) and at the opening between the stomach and duodenum (*pyloric sphincter*).

閉合腔口。例如在肛門周圍可見該肌（肛門括約肌），在胃及十二指腸間開口處亦可見括約肌（幽門括約肌）。

sphincter- *prefix denoting* a sphincter.

〔前綴〕**括約肌**

sphincterectomy *n.* the surgical removal of any sphincter muscle.

括約肌切除術　任何切除括約肌的手術。

sphincterotomy *n.* **1.** surgical division of any sphincter muscle. *See also* anal fissure. **2.** surgical removal of part of the iris in the eye at the border of the pupil.

括約肌切開術　**(1)** 任何切開括約肌的手術。參閱 anal fissure。**(2)** 切除眼瞳孔邊緣的部分虹膜手術。

sphingomyelin *n.* a *phospholipid that contains sphingosine, a fatty acid, phosphoric acid, and choline. Sphingomyelins are found in large amounts in brain and nerve tissue.

鞘髓磷脂　一種含神經鞘氨醇、脂肪酸、磷酸及膽鹼的磷脂，該磷脂常大量見於大腦及神經組織內。

sphingosine *n.* a lipid alcohol that is a constituent of sphingomyelin and cerebrosides.

鞘氨醇　一種由鞘髓磷脂和腦苷組成的脂醇。

sphygmo- *prefix denoting* the pulse.

〔前綴〕**脈，脈搏**

sphygmocardiograph *n.* an apparatus for producing a continuous record of both the heartbeat and the subsequent pulse in one of the blood vessels. The recording can be shown on a moving tape or on an electronic screen.

心動脈搏描記器　一種連續記錄心搏和隨後某一血管脈搏的儀器。該記錄顯示在移動帶或電子屏幕上。

sphygmograph *n.* an apparatus for producing a continuous record of the pulse in one of the blood vessels, showing the strength and rate of the beats.

脈搏描記儀、脈搏計　一種用於連續記錄一根血管脈搏、顯示搏動力量和速率的儀器。

sphygmomanometer *n.* an instrument for measuring *blood pressure in the arteries. It consists of an inflatable cuff connected via a rubber tube to a column

血壓計　一種測量動脈血壓的儀器。由一個可充氣的袖套通過橡皮管與有刻度的水銀柱連接構成。將袖套纏在一肢體上

of mercury with a graduated scale. The cuff is applied to a limb (usually the arm) and inflated to exert pressure on a large artery until the blood flow stops. The pressure is then slowly released and, with the aid of a stethoscope to listen to the pulse, it is possible to determine both the systolic and diastolic pressures (which can be read on the scale).

（通常是臂上），對其充氣向一根大動脈施加壓力，直至血流被阻斷。而後，緩緩地減壓，借助聽診器聽脈搏可確定收縮壓和舒張壓（在刻度表上可讀這些數字）。

sphygmophone *n*. a device to record the heartbeat or pulse in the form of amplified sound waves played through a loudspeaker or earphones.

脈音聽診器 一種記錄心跳或脈搏的裝置，聲波放大後通過喇叭或耳機傳出。

sphygmoscope *n*. a device for showing the heartbeat or pulse as a visible signal, especially a continuous wave signal on a cathode-ray tube.

脈搏檢視器 一種以可視信號方式顯示心搏和脈搏的裝置，特別是在陰極射線管上顯示的連續波信號。

spica *n*. a bandage wound spirally around an injured limb. At each turn it is given a twist so that the slack material is taken up at the overlap.

人字形繃帶 螺旋狀纏在受傷的肢體上的繃帶。每繞一圈，繃帶反摺一次，使其鬆弛部分在重疊時收緊。

spicule *n*. a small splinter of bone.

骨刺 骨的小碎片。

spina bifida (rachischisis) a developmental defect in which the newborn baby has part of the spinal cord and its coverings exposed through a gap in the backbone. The symptoms may include paralysis of the legs, incontinence, and mental retardation from the commonly associated brain defect, *hydrocephalus. Spina bifida is associated with an abnormally high level of *alpha-fetoprotein in the amniotic fluid surrounding the embryo. The condition can be diagnosed at about the 16th week of pregnancy by a maternal blood test and confirmed by amniocentesis and ultrasound, so making termination of the pregnancy possible. Recent evidence suggests that the risk of spina bifida is reduced if extra *folic acid

脊柱裂 新生兒的部分脊髓和脊膜由脊柱的裂口處暴露在外的一種先天發育性疾病。症狀有下肢麻痺、大小便失禁及常常合併有腦部缺陷——腦積水而導致智力發育遲緩。脊柱裂伴隨有胚胎周圍羊水甲胎蛋白高於正常水平。此病可在妊期約 16 周時通過檢查母親的血液診斷出來和通過羊膜穿刺和超聲技術來證實。因此中止妊娠是可能的。新近的研究表明如果孕婦的飲食中加入葉酸，脊柱裂的危險會減少。參閱 neural tube defects。

is included in the diet of pregnant women. *See also* neural tube defects.

spina bifida occulta a defect in the bony arch of the spine that (unlike spina bifida) has a normal skin covering; there may be an overlying hairy patch. The condition is usually an incidental finding on X-ray and it is not associated with neurological involvement.

spinal accessory nerve *see* accessory nerve.

spinal anaesthesia 1. suppression of sensation, usually in the lower part of the body, by the injection of a local anaesthetic into the spaces surrounding the spinal cord. There are two types used for surgery: *subarachnoid* and *epidural*. In the latter the anaesthetic is injected between the dura and the surrounding bony vertebral foramen, using a special blunt needle with a side-hole to reduce the chance of penetrating the dura. In the former a very fine needle is used to reduce the amount of cerebrospinal fluid that escapes as the needle penetrates the dura. Both techniques have complications, especially the subarachnoid route (headache, sepsis, paraplegia). The injection site for subarachnoid spinal anaesthetics is most often in the lumbar region of the vertebral column, the needle being inserted between the vertebrae (anywhere between the second and fifth). For epidural anaesthetics, the sacral and caudal regions are often used. The extent of the area anaesthetized depends upon the amount and strength of local anaesthetic injected. Dilute local anaesthetic solutions are used when the sensory nerves are targeted rather than the motor nerves. In many instances a fine catheter is passed through the needle to

隱性脊柱裂　脊柱骨弓缺陷。該病（不同於脊柱裂）外表皮膚正常，有時見有毛斑覆蓋。常在 X 綫檢測時偶然發現。此病不伴有神經系統疾病。

脊髓副神經　參閱 accessory nerve。

(1) 脊神經麻醉　通過向脊髓周圍的腔注射局部麻醉劑，從而阻滯身體下半部分感覺。用於外科手術的麻醉有兩類：蛛網膜下和硬膜外麻醉。後者為減少穿透硬脊膜的機率使用特製的鈍頭針，針眼在側翼，麻醉劑注入硬脊膜與其周圍的椎管之間。前者為防止腦脊液在穿過硬脊膜注射時流出則使用極細的針頭。此兩種方式，尤其是蛛網膜下的途徑都會引發併發症（頭痛、膿毒病、截癱）。蛛網膜下的脊神經麻醉區多在腰椎之間（腰 II 及腰 IV 間的任一椎間）。硬膜外麻醉則常在骶骨及尾骨部分進行。麻醉程度取決於局部麻醉藥注射的量與濃度。當麻醉目標僅為感覺神經而不涉及運動神經時使用稀釋過的麻醉劑。在很多情況下針頭上穿有極細的導管以便能反覆或連續地注入麻醉劑，有些病人如患胸部感染，或處於生產過程中的，因身體情況要求減少全身麻醉而不能進行全身麻醉；或者在某些情況下不能馬上找到進行全身麻醉的熟練的麻醉師時脊髓麻醉都是十分有用的。此技術在斯堪地納維亞及美國使用

enable repeated or continuous injections of anaesthetic solution. Spinal anaesthesia is useful in patients whose condition makes them unsuitable for a general anaesthetic, perhaps because of chest infection; for certain obstetric procedures; to reduce the requirements for general anaesthetic drugs; or in circumstances where a skilled anaesthetist is not readily available to administer a general anaesthetic. The technique is more commonly used in Scandinavia and the USA than in Britain. **2.** loss of sensation in part of the body as a result of injury or disease to the spinal cord. The area of the body affected depends upon the site of the lesion: the lower it is in the cord the less the sensory disability.

得較為普遍，英國則較少。**(2)** **脊髓性感覺缺失** 因外傷或脊髓疾病導致身體某部位感覺缺失。受影響的範圍取決於受損部位：部位越靠脊髓的下方，感覺缺失的範圍越小。

spinal column *see* backbone.

脊柱 參閱 backbone。

spinal cord the portion of the central nervous system enclosed in the vertebral column, consisting of nerve cells and bundles of nerves connecting all parts of the body with the brain. It

脊髓 脊柱中含中樞神經系統的部分，由將身體各部分與大腦相連的神經細胞及神經束構成。內含有一白色物質所包圍的灰色物質核心（見圖）。外

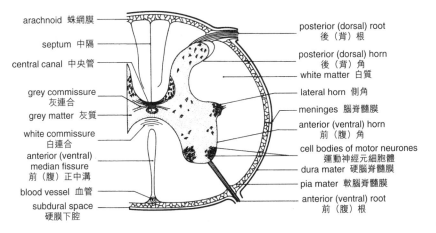

arachnoid 蛛網膜
septum 中隔
central canal 中央管
grey commissure 灰連合
grey matter 灰質
white commissure 白連合
anterior (ventral) median fissure 前（腹）正中溝
blood vessel 血管
subdural space 硬膜下腔

posterior (dorsal) root 後（背）根
posterior (dorsal) horn 後（背）角
white matter 白質
lateral horn 側角
meninges 腦脊髓膜
anterior (ventral) horn 前（腹）角
cell bodies of motor neurones 運動神經元細胞體
dura mater 硬腦脊髓膜
pia mater 軟腦脊髓膜
anterior (ventral) root 前（腹）根

Transverse section through the spinal cord
脊髓橫斷面示意圖

contains a core of grey matter surrounded by white matter (see illustration). It is enveloped in three layers of membrane, the *meninges, and extends from the medulla oblongata in the skull to the level of the second lumbar vertebra. From it arise 31 pairs of *spinal nerves.

spinal muscular atrophy (SMA) a hereditary condition in which cells of the spinal cord die and the muscles in the arms and legs become progressively weaker. The gene responsible has been located: in affected children it is inherited as a double *recessive. SMA usually develops between the ages of 2 and 12. Eventually the respiratory muscles are affected and death usually results from respiratory infection. Most affected individuals are wheelchair-bound by the age of 20 and few survive beyond the age of 30. *Infantile spinal muscular atrophy* is an acute aggressive form of the condition (see Werdnig-Hoffmann disease).

spinal nerves the 31 pairs of nerves that leave the spinal cord and are distributed to the body, passing out from the vertebral canal through the spaces between the arches of the vertebrae (see illustration). Each nerve has two *roots, an anterior, carrying motor nerve fibres, and a posterior, carrying sensory fibres. Immediately after the roots leave the spinal cord they merge to form a mixed spinal nerve on each side.

spindle *n.* a collection of fibres seen in a cell when it is dividing. The fibres radiate from the two ends (*poles*) and meet at the centre (the *equator*) giving a structure shaped like two cones placed base to base. It plays an important part in

裏三層膜，即腦脊膜，從頭顱中的延髓質延展至腰椎第二節的位置。其中產生 31 對脊神經。

脊髓性肌肉萎縮症 由於脊髓中細胞死亡而使上、下肢肌肉患有進行性無力的遺傳性疾病。致病基因已經找出：在病孩中以雙隱性基因遺傳下來。此病通常在 2~12 歲間發病。最終呼吸肌受影響，並常因呼吸系統感染導致死亡。多數患者 20 歲時行動依靠輪椅，少數人能活過 30 歲。嬰兒脊髓性肌肉萎縮症是此病的一種急性侵襲型（參閱 Werdnig-Hoffmann disease）。

脊神經 由椎管經過椎弓間隙從脊髓發出遍布全身的 31 對神經（見圖）。每一神經都有兩個根，前根含運動神經纖維，後根含感覺神經纖維。二者一經離開脊髓便在兩側形成混合的脊髓神經。

梭，紡錘體 細胞分裂時細胞中見到的細絲的集團。細絲在細胞兩端（極）呈輻射狀向中央（中緯綫）集合，結構尤如兩個底靠底圓錐。在有絲分裂及減數分裂的染色體運動中起

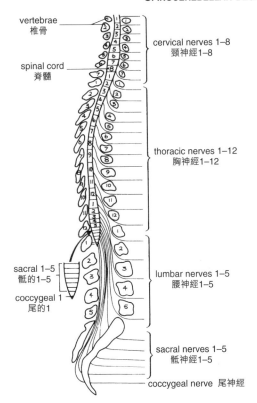

Origins of the spinal nerves (one side only)
脊髓神經起源（限於側面）

chromosome movement in *mitosis and *meiosis and is also involved in division of the cytoplasm.

着重要作用，也涉及胞漿的分裂。

spine *n*. **1.** a sharp process of a bone. **2.** the vertebral column (*see* backbone). **–spinal** *adj*.

(1) 棘 骨的尖銳突起。**(2) 脊柱** 參閱 backbone。

spino- *prefix denoting* **1.** the spine. **2.** the spinal cord.

〔前級〕**(1) 棘，脊柱 (2) 脊髓**

spinocerebellar degeneration any of a group of inherited disorders of the

脊髓小腦變性 腦內小腦及皮層脊髓束的遺傳性疾病羣。以

cerebellum and corticospinal tracts in the brain. They are characterized by *spasticity of the limbs and cerebellar *ataxia.

四肢痙攣及小腦運動失調為特徵。

spiral bandage a bandage wound round a part of the body, overlapping the previous section at each turn.

螺旋形繃帶 身體某部分纏繞的繃帶，每繞一圈繃帶疊加覆蓋在前一圈上。

spiral organ *see* organ of Corti.

螺旋器 參閱 organ of Corti。

Spirillum *n.* a genus of highly motile rigid spiral-shaped bacteria usually found in fresh and salt water containing organic matter. They bear tufts of flagella at one or both ends of the cell. Most species are saprophytes, but *S. minus* causes *ratbite fever.

螺菌屬 一種活動力強，堅硬的螺旋形菌屬。常在含有有機物的淡水和鹽水中發現。細胞的一端或兩端長有鞭毛。多數菌種係腐物寄生菌，但小螺菌引發鼠咬熱。

spiro- *prefix denoting* **1.** spiral. **2.** respiration.

〔前綴〕**(1)** 螺旋 **(2)** 呼吸

spirochaete *n.* any one of a group of spiral-shaped bacteria that lack a rigid cell wall and move by means of muscular flexions of the cell. The group includes the genera *Borrelia*, *Leptospira*, and *Treponema*.

螺旋體 螺旋形細胞羣中的任意一種。缺乏堅硬的細胞壁，靠細胞肌性屈曲而移動。該細胞羣包括包柔螺旋體屬，鈎端螺旋體屬和密螺旋體屬。

spirograph *n.* an instrument for recording breathing movements. The record (a tracing) obtained is called a *spirogram*. **–spirography** *n.*

呼吸描記器 記錄呼吸運動的儀器。所得記錄（一種描記）稱為呼吸描記圖。

spirometer *n.* an instrument for measuring the volume of air inhaled and exhaled. It is used in tests of *ventilation. **–spirometry** *n.*

肺量計 計量吸入及呼出空氣體積的儀器。用於肺換氣測驗。

spironolactone *n.* a synthetic *corticosteroid that inhibits the activity of the hormone *aldosterone and is used to treat heart failure, high blood pressure, and fluid retention (oedema). It is administered by mouth; side-effects may

螺內酯 一種抑制醛固酮激素活性的人工合成的皮質類固醇，用於治療心力衰竭、高血壓和液體瀦留（水腫）。口服。副作用可有頭痛、胃不適及嗜睡。因動物實驗發現該物

include headache, stomach upsets, and drowsiness and since 1988 its use has been restricted as it was found to cause carcinomas in animals. Trade name: **Aldactone**.

Spitz-Holter valve a one-way valve used to drain cerebrospinal fluid in order to control *hydrocephalus. The device is inserted into the ventricles of the brain and passes via a subcutaneous tunnel to drain into either the right atrium or the peritoneum.

splanch- (splanchno-) *prefix denoting* the viscera.

splanchnic *adj.* relating to the viscera, e.g. splanchnic *mesoderm. *Compare* somatic (def. 2).

splanchnic nerves the series of nerves in the sympathetic system that are distributed to the blood vessels and viscera, passing forwards and downwards from the chain of sympathetic ganglia near the spinal cord to enter the abdomen and branch profusely.

splanchnocranium *n.* the part of the skull that is derived from the *pharyngeal arches, i.e. the mandible (lower jaw).

splanchnopleure *n.* the wall of the embryonic gut, which consists of a layer of endoderm with a layer of mesoderm outside it. The yolk sac is a continuation of this structure. *Compare* somatopleure.

spleen *n.* a large dark-red ovoid organ situated on the left side of the body below and behind the stomach. It is enclosed within a fibrous capsule that extends into the spongy interior – the *splenic pulp* – to form a supportive

質可引起癌症，從 1988 年起其使用受到限制。商品名：Aldactone。

施-霍氏瓣 為控制腦積水而採用的一種單向瓣膜，用以排出腦脊髓液。該裝置可插入腦室內，經過皮下渠道將腦脊髓液引流至右心房或腹膜。

〔前綴〕**內臟**

內臟的 與內臟有關的，例如：臟壁中的胚層。與 somatic 釋義 2 對比。

內臟神經 分布於血管及內臟的一組交感神經，始於靠近脊髓的交感神經節，向前及向下延伸，進入腹腔，發出許多分支。

臟顱 由咽弓，即下頜骨發生的顱骨部分。

胚臟壁，臟層 胚胎內臟的壁，該壁內含內胚層，外裹中胚層。卵黃囊是該結構的延續。與 somatopleure 對比。

脾 大的暗紅色的卵形器官，位於身體的左下側，胃的後方。它的外面包裹着纖維性囊以形成支持性框架，纖維囊再向裏為海綿狀的內部脾髓。脾髓是由淋巴組織的聚合體（白

framework. The pulp consists of aggregates of *lymphoid tissue (*white pulp*) within a meshwork of *reticular fibres packed with red blood cells (*red pulp*). The spleen is a major component of the *reticuloendothelial system, producing lymphocytes in the newborn and containing *phagocytes, which remove worn-out red blood cells and other foreign bodies from the blood-stream. It also acts as a reservoir for blood and, in the fetus, as a source of red blood cells. Anatomical name: **lien. –splenic** *adj.*

髓）組成的，淋巴組織周圍是網狀纖維結構，網眼內擠滿了紅細胞（紅髓）。脾是網狀內皮系統的主要組成部分，能在新生兒體內產生淋巴細胞並內含有能清除衰老的紅細胞和其他異物的吞噬細胞。該器官還充當着血液貯存庫，在胚胎期內又是紅細胞的供應源泉。解剖學用語：脾。

splen- (spleno-) *prefix denoting* the spleen. Example: *splenorenal* (relating to the spleen and kidney).

〔前綴〕**脾** 例如：脾腎的（與脾和腎有關的）。

splenectomy *n.* surgical removal of the spleen. This is sometimes necessary in the emergency treatment of bleeding from a ruptured spleen and in the treatment of some blood diseases. Splenectomy in children may diminish the immune response to infections.

脾切除術 脾外科手術切除。在緊急處理因脾破裂引起的大出血及在治療某些血液病時，該手術有必要施行。兒童進行該手術可能會降低對傳染病的免疫反應。

splenitis *n.* inflammation of the spleen. *See also* perisplenitis.

脾炎 脾的炎症。參閱 perisplenitis。

splenium *n.* the thickest part of the *corpus callosum, rounded and protruding backwards over the thalami, the pineal gland, and the midbrain.

壓部 胼胝體最厚的部分，圓形，向丘腦、松果體及中腦後凸起。

splenomegaly *n.* enlargement of the spleen. It most commonly occurs in *malaria, *schistosomiasis, and other disorders caused by parasites; in infections; in blood disorders, including some forms of anaemia and lack of platelets (*thrombocytopenia); in *leukaemia; and in *Hodgkin's disease. *See also* hypersplenism.

巨脾 脾增大。多發於瘧疾、血吸蟲病及其他寄生蟲病；傳染病及一些包括某些類型的貧血、血小板減少症、白血病及霍奇金病在內的血液病。參閱 hypersplenism。

splenorenal anastomosis a method of treating *portal hypertension by joining the splenic vein to the left renal vein. *Compare* portacaval anastomosis.

脾腎靜脈吻合術 通過將脾靜脈與左腎靜脈相吻合來治療門脈高壓症的方法。與 portacaval anastomosis 對比。

splint *n.* a rigid support to hold broken bones in position until healing has occurred.

夾板 骨折時為固定斷骨位置直至其痊愈而使用的硬性支托物。

splinter haemorrhage a linear haemorrhage below the nails, usually the result of trauma but also occurring in such conditions as subacute bacterial *endocarditis or severe rheumatoid arthritis.

裂片形出血 指甲下的綫狀出血，通常由外傷造成，但也可在亞急性細菌性心內膜炎及嚴重的類風濕關節炎時發生。

splitting *n.* a *defence mechanism by which people deal with an emotional conflict by viewing some people as all good and others as all bad: they fail to integrate themselves or other people into complex but coherent images.

分裂 一種心理防禦機制，通過該機制人們在處理情感矛盾時將一些人視為好人，而將其他人視為壞人；他們無法形成一完整的關於他們自己或其他人的複雜但同時又是連貫的意像。

spondyl- (spondylo-) *prefix denoting* a vertebra or the spine.

〔前綴〕**脊椎、脊柱**

spondylitis *n.* inflammation of the synovial joints of the backbone. *Ankylosing spondylitis* is a *sero-negative arthritis*, one of a group of arthritides that do not exhibit rheumatoid factors in the serum. 90% of cases carry the tissue-type antigen HLA B27 (*see* HLA system). Ankylosing spondylitis predominantly affects young males and the inflammation affects the joint capsules and their attached ligaments and tendons, principally the intervertebral joints and sacroiliac joints (*see* sacroiliitis). The resultant pain and stiffness are treated by analgesics and regular daily exercises. The disorder can lead to severe deformities of the spine (*see* kyphosis, ankylosis).

脊椎炎 脊柱滑膜關節的炎症。關節強硬性脊椎炎是一種血清陰性的關節炎，一種在血清中無類風濕性因子存在的關節炎病症羣之一。90% 的病例都帶有組織類型抗原 HLA B27（參閱 HLA system）。此病多發於青年男性，且炎症將影響到關節囊及附着的韌帶、肌腱，其中主要是椎骨間關節及骶髂關節（參閱 sacroiliitis）。病發導致的疼痛和強直，可通過鎮痛劑及每日規律的鍛煉得到治療。該病可能會導致嚴重的脊椎變形（參閱 kyphosis，ankylosis）。

spondylolisthesis *n.* a forward shift of one vertebra upon another, due to a defect of the joints that normally bind them together. This may be congenital or develop after injury. The majority of cases in which pain is present are treated with rest and a surgical belt or corset; in a small minority, showing severe disability or pressure on nerve roots, surgical fusion may be required.

脊椎前移 脊椎逐個向前移位，由正常時連接脊椎的關節缺陷所致。此病可能是先天造成的，也可能是因外傷發展的。大多數有痛感的病例，採用休息療法或穿着外科束帶或背心治療，少數有嚴重行動不便或壓迫神經根的病例需外科融合術。

spondylosis. *n.* a spinal condition resulting from degeneration of the intervertebral discs in the cervical, thoracic, or lumbar regions. Symptoms include pain and restriction of movement. Spondylosis produces a characteristic appearance on X-ray, including narrowing of the space occupied by the disc and the presence of *osteophytes; these feature of the disease (*radiological spondylosis*) may not be accompanied by any signs and symptoms. Pain is relieved by wearing a collar (when the neck region is affected) or a surgical belt (for the lower spine), which prevents movement. Very severe cases sometimes require surgical fusion.

脊椎關節強直 椎間盤在頸椎、胸椎或腰椎發生變性而導致脊柱病。症狀有疼痛及活動受限（不便）。此病在 X 綫檢查時呈特異性表現，其中包括椎間盤變窄及骨贅的出現。該病的這些特徵（放射學所見的脊椎關節強直）也可能不伴有體徵或病症。通過戴領圈（頸椎受累時）、繫外科束帶（脊椎下位受累時）來避免脊椎間活動從而緩解病痛。有時病情十分嚴重者需作外科融合手術。

spondylosyndesis *n.* surgical fusion of the intervertebral joints of the backbone.

脊柱制動術 脊柱椎間關節之外科融合手術。

spongiform encephalopathy any one of a group of rapidly progressive degenerative neurological diseases that include scrapie in sheep, bovine spongiform encephalopathy (BSE) in cattle, and *kuru and *Creutzfeldt-Jakob disease* in humans. In humans the spongiform encephalopathies are characterized by rapidly progressive dementia associated with myoclonic jerks (*see* myoclonus); on pathological examination the brains of affected individuals show a characteristic cystic degeneration. The diseases are

海綿狀腦病 一種或一組發展迅速的退行性神經性疾病，其中包括羊的瘙癢病，牛的牛海綿狀腦病 (BSE) 及人的庫魯病和克-雅氏綜合徵。對於人類該病以迅速進行性癡呆伴有震顫為特徵（參閱 myoclonus），患者的腦病理檢查顯示出典型囊性變性。該病被認為是由非常規的傳染性病原體（參閱 prion）所引起的。

thought to be caused by unconventional transmissible agents (*see* prion).

spongioblast *n.* a type of cell that forms in the early stages of development of the nervous system, giving rise to *astrocytes and *oligodendrocytes.

成膠質細胞　神經系統發展過程中早期形成的一類細胞，該細胞使星形膠質細胞和少突膠質細胞產生。

spongioblastoma *n. see* glioblastoma.

成膠質細胞瘤　參閱 glioblastoma。

spontaneous *adj.* arising without apparent cause or outside aid. The term is applied in medicine to certain conditions, such as pathological fractures, that arise in the absence of outside injury; also to recovery from a disease without the aid of specific treatment.

自發的，特發的　無明顯原因或外因相助而發生的。該術語在醫學中適用於下列情況：無外傷而發生的病理性骨折；不經特殊治療而痊愈的疾病。

sporadic *adj.* describing a disease that occurs only occasionally or in a few isolated places. *Compare* endemic, epidemic.

散發性的　用來描述某疾病僅偶然發生或僅在某幾個孤立地區發生。與 endemic，epidemic 對比。

spore *n.* a small reproductive body produced by plants and microorganisms. Some kinds of spores function as dormant stages of the life cycle, enabling the organism to survive adverse conditions. Other spores are the means by which the organism can spread vegetatively. *See also* endospore.

孢子，芽胞　植物或微生物產生的一種有繁殖能力的微體。有些類型的孢子在生命周期中處於一種休眠狀態，使有機體在逆境中生存下去。其他類型的孢子是有機體無性繁殖的手段。參閱 endospore。

sporicide *n.* an agent that kills spores (e.g. bacterial spores). Some disinfectants that liberate chlorine are sporicides, but most other germicides are ineffective since spores are very resistant to chemical action. **–sporicidal** *adj.*

殺孢子劑　能殺死孢子（如細菌牙胞）的藥劑。一些能釋放氯的消毒劑是殺孢子劑，但大多數的殺蟲劑沒有殺死孢子的效用，因為孢子對化學作用的抵抗力強。

sporocyst *n.* the second-stage larva of a parasitic *fluke, found within the tissues of a freshwater snail. A sporocyst develops from a first stage larva (*see* miracidium) and gives rise either

包蚴　寄生性吸蟲第二階段的幼蟲。在淡水螺的組織內寄生。包蚴由第一階段的幼蟲（參閱 miracidium）發育而來，並再發育成下一階段的幼

to the next larval stage (*see* redia) or daughter sporocysts. The latter develop directly into the final larval stage (*see* cercaria) without the intermediate redia stage.

蟲（參閱 redia）或子包蚴。子包蚴可不經過中間的雷蚴期而直接發育成最後階段的幼蟲（參閱 cercaria）。

sporogony *n*. the formation of *sporozoites during the life cycle of a sporozoan. The contents of the zygote, formed by the fusion of sex cells, divide repeatedly and eventually release a number of sporozoites. *Compare* schizogony.

孢子生殖　孢子蟲生命周期裏形成的子孢子。由性細胞融合形成的合子成分反覆分裂並最終釋放出大量的子孢子。與 schizogony 對比。

sporotrichosis *n*. a chronic infection of the skin and superficial lymph nodes that is caused by the fungus *Sporothrix schenckii* and results in the formation of abscesses and ulcers.

孢子絲菌病　皮膚及淺表淋巴結的慢性炎症，該病是由申克孢子絲菌屬真菌引起的，並將導致膿腫及潰瘍的形成。

Sporozoa *n*. a group of parasitic Protozoa that includes *Plasmodium, the malaria parasite. Most sporozoans do not have cilia or flagella. Sporozoan life cycles are complex and usually involve both sexual and asexual stages. Some sporozoans are parasites of invertebrates, and the parasites are passed to new hosts by means of spores. Sporozoans that parasitize vertebrates are transmitted from host to host by invertebrates, which act as intermediate hosts. For example, the mosquito *Anopheles* is the intermediate host of *Plasmodium*.

孢子蟲綱　寄生性原生動物羣，其中包括瘧原蟲，瘧疾寄生蟲。大多數孢子蟲綱無纖毛或鞭毛。其生活周期十分複雜，通常既包括有性繁殖期也包括無性繁殖期。有些孢子蟲寄生於無脊椎動物內，並通過孢子將寄生蟲傳給其新宿生。寄生於脊椎動物體內的孢子蟲，通過無脊椎動物這個中間宿主從一個宿主傳播到另一個宿主。例如，蚊子就是瘧原蟲的中間宿主。

sporozoite *n*. one of the many cells formed as a result of *sporogony during the life cycle of a sporozoan. In *Plasmodium sporozoites are formed by repeated divisions of the contents of the *oocyst inside the body of the mosquito. The released sporozoites ultimately pass into the insect's salivary glands and await transmission to a human host at the next blood meal.

子孢子　孢子蟲生命周期內因孢子生殖而產生的眾多細胞之一。對於瘧原蟲其子孢子是通過在蚊子體內的卵囊成分不斷分裂而來的。釋放出的子孢子最終進入蚊子的唾液腺，並等待着在下一次吸血時轉入人類宿主。

sports injury any injury related to the practice of a sport, often resulting from the overuse and stretching of muscles, tendons, and ligaments. Sports medicine is a developing specialty concerned with the treatment of sports injuries and measures designed to prevent or minimize them (e.g. in the design of sports equipment).

運動損傷 與體育鍛煉有關的損傷，常因肌肉、肌腱及韌帶的過勞及拉傷所致。運動醫學是一門新興的學科，涉及運動損傷的治療及設計預防或減少損傷的途徑（如在體育器械的設計方面）。

spotted fever *see* meningitis, Rocky Mountain spotted fever, typhus.

斑疹熱 參閱 meningitis，Rocky Mountain spotted fever，typhus。

sprain *n.* injury to a ligament, caused by sudden overstretching. As the ligament is not severed it gradually heals, but this may take several months. Sprains should be treated by cold compresses (ice-packs) at the time of injury, and later by restriction of activity.

扭傷 韌帶損傷，由突然過度伸展所致。如韌帶沒有嚴重扭傷，會在數月後漸愈。受傷當時用冷敷（冰袋）治療，過後限制活動。

Sprengel's deformity a congenital abnormality of the scapula (shoulder blade), which is small and positioned high in the shoulder. It is caused by failure of the normal development of this bone.

施普倫格爾畸形 肩胛骨的先天性畸形，患者的肩胛骨小而且位置向上。此病由肩胛骨的不正常發育引起。

sprue (psilosis) *n.* deficient absorption of food due to disease of the small intestine. *Tropical sprue* is seen in people from temperate regions who stay in tropical climates for weeks or months. It is characterized by diarrhoea (usually *steatorrhoea), an inflamed tongue (glossitis), anaemia, and weight loss; the lining of the small intestine is inflamed and atrophied, probably because of infection. Treatment with antibiotics and *folic acid is usually effective, but the condition often improves spontaneously on return to a temperate climate. *See also* coeliac disease (nontropical sprue), malabsorption.

口炎性腹瀉 因小腸疾病導致的食物吸收不良。熱帶口炎性腹瀉常見於由溫帶到熱帶停留幾周或數月的人。其特徵為腹瀉（通常為脂肪痢）、口炎、貧血、體重下降、小腸黏膜可能因感染而發炎並萎縮。一般情況用抗生素及葉酸治療即可見效。而且病症常會在返回溫帶地區後自然緩解。參閱 coeliac disease (nontropical sprue)，malabsorption。

spud *n.* a blunt needle used for removing foreign bodies embedded in the cornea of the eye.

眼科刮針　用以清除眼角膜內異物的鈍頭針。

spur *n.* a sharp projection, especially one of bone.

刺　尖銳突出物，尤指骨的尖銳突出物。

sputum *n.* material coughed up from the respiratory tract. Its characteristics, including colour, consistency, volume, smell, and the appearance of any solid material within it, often provide important information affecting the diagnosis and management of respiratory disease. Pathological examination of sputum for microorganisms and for abnormal cells may add further information.

痰　由呼吸道咳出的物質。其包括顏色、稠度、多少、氣味及痰中硬物質在內的各種特徵，可提供呼吸疾病的診斷及治療重要信息。對痰的微生物及非正常細胞的病理檢驗能進一步提供有關信息。

squalene *n.* an unsaturated hydrocarbon (a terpene), synthesized in the body, from which *cholesterol is derived.

角鯊烯　一種在體內合成的不飽和烴（萜烯），該物質衍生出膽固醇。

squama *n.* (*pl.* **squamae**) **1.** a thin plate of bone. **2.** a scale, such as any of the scales from the cornified layer of the *epidermis.

(1) 鱗　骨的薄片。(2) 鱗屑　如出自表皮角質層的任何一種鱗屑。

squamo- *prefix denoting* **1.** the squamous portion of the temporal bone. **2.** squamous epithelium.

〔前綴〕(1) 顳骨鱗部　(2) 鱗狀上皮

squamous bone *see* temporal bone.

顳骨鱗部　參閱 temporal bone。

squamous cell carcinoma (SCC) the second commonest form of skin cancer (after *basal cell carcinoma), occurring usually in late-middle and old age. Sunlight is the commonest cause but other environmental carcinogens may be responsible. SCC is mainly found on areas exposed to light and is three times more common in men than in women. SCC grows faster than basal cell carcinoma; it spreads locally at first but later

鱗狀（上皮）細胞癌　第二種最常見的皮膚癌類型（僅次於基底細胞癌），發病年齡多見於中老年。陽光是最常見的病因，但其他來自環境的致癌物也可能有關。此病主要發生在日光曝曬的部分且男性發病較女性多 3 倍。該病的發展較基底細胞癌要快，起初擴散到局部地區，但以後也可能擴散到遠離病源的地區（參閱 metas-

may spread to sites distant from its origin (*see* metastasis). Treatment is usually by surgical excision or radiotherapy.

tasis）。治療主要為外科切除手術和放射療法。

squamous epithelium *see* epithelium.

鱗狀上皮 參閱 epithelium。

squint *n. see* strabismus.

斜視 參閱 strabismus。

SSPE *see* subacute sclerosing panencephalitis.

惡急性硬化性全腦炎 參閱 subacute sclerosing panencephalitis。

stadium *n.* (*pl.* **stadia**) a stage in the course of a disease; for example, the *stadium invasionis* is the period between exposure to infection and the onset of symptoms.

期 病程中的一個階段，如侵入期是指從接觸感染到症狀出現的一段時間。

stage *vb.* (in oncology) to determine the presence and site of metastases from a primary tumour in order to plan treatment. In addition to clinical examination, a variety of imaging and surgical techniques may be employed to provide a more accurate assessment.

分期 （腫瘤學）確定原發性腫瘤是否轉移及轉移部位，從而制訂治療計劃。為了作出更精確的估計，除臨床檢查外還要動用各種各樣的影象及外科技術手段。

staghorn calculus a branched stone forming a cast of the collecting system of the kidney and therefore filling the calyces and pelvis. The stone is usually associated with infected urine, the commonest organism being *Proteus vulgaris*. The combination of obstruction and infection can cause *pyonephrosis and, if neglected, a *perinephric abscess.

鹿角結石 側支結石形成管型的腎收集系統，因此填塞腎盞及腎盂。常伴有尿道感染，其最常見的生物體為普通變形桿菌。阻塞與感染相結合將導致腎盂積膿，而且如果忽視會導致腎周膿腫。

stagnant loop syndrome *see* blind loop syndrome.

腸袢鬱滯綜合徵 參閱 blind loop syndrome。

stain 1. *n.* a dye used to colour tissues and other specimens for microscopical examination. In an *acid stain* the colour is carried by an acid radical and the stain is taken up by parts of the specimen having a basic (alkaline) reaction. In a

(1) 染劑 顯微檢驗時使組織及其他標本着色的染料。酸性染劑中酸基攜帶顏色，標本中發生鹼反應的部分將吸收染劑。鹼性染劑中鹼基帶有顏色，發生酸反應的部分標本將

basic stain the colour, carried by a basic radical, is attracted to parts of the specimen having an acidic reaction. *Neutral stains* have neither acidic nor basic affinities. A *contrast stain* is used to give colour to parts of a tissue not affected by a previously applied stain. A *differential stain* allows different elements in a tissue to be distinguished by staining them in different colours. **2.** *vb.* to treat a specimen for microscopical study with a stain.

吸收染劑。中性染劑不具有酸、鹼親和性。對比染劑使組織中對先前使用的染劑無反應的部分着色。鑑別性染劑用來區別標本的成分，它使各種成分染上不同的色。**(2) 染色** 用染劑來處理做顯微檢查的標本。

Stamey procedure an operation devised to cure stress incontinence of urine in women in which specially designed needles are employed to sling or hitch up the neck of the bladder to the anterior abdominal wall with unabsorbable suture material. *See also* colposuspension.

斯塔梅手術 一種用以治療婦女腹部壓迫性小便失禁的手術，該手術用專門設計的針和不吸收性縫綫將膀胱頭紮起懸吊到前腹腔壁。參閱 colposuspension。

stammering (stuttering) *n.* halting articulation with interruptions to the normal flow of speech and repetition of the initial consonants of words or syllables (*compare* cluttering). It usually first appears in childhood and the symptoms are most severe when the stammerer is under any psychological stress. It is not a symptom of organic disease and it will usually respond to the re-education of speech by a trained therapist. Medical name: **dysphemia**. **–stammerer** *n.*

口吃 發音停滯，中斷正常語流，詞語的第一個輔音或音節出現重複（與 cluttering 對比）。口吃多首次出現在兒童期，患者受到心理壓力便有極嚴重表現。口吃不是器質性疾病的症狀，由受過訓練的治療師進行語言再教育，往往會有收效。醫學用語：訥吃。

standard deviation (in statistics) a measure of the scatter of observations about their arithmetic *mean, which is calculated from the square root of the *variance* of the readings in the series. The arithmetic sum of the amounts by which each observation varies from the mean must be zero, but if these variations are squared before being summated, a positive value is obtained: the mean of this

標準差 （統計學）用以衡量一組觀察資料的計算平均值的離散度的度量，該數值由這組讀數方差的平方根求得。每個觀察值與平均值之差的算術和一定為零，但如先將這些差平方再求和，則結果一定為正值，這個正數值的平均數即方差。事實上，差平方和除以總觀察數減一後求得的平均值是一更

value is the variance. In practice a more reliable estimate of variance is obtained by dividing the sum of the squared deviations by one *less* than the total number of observations. *See also* significance.

為可靠的方差估計方法。參閱 significance。

standard error (of a *mean) the extent to which the means of several different samples would vary if they were taken repeatedly from the same population. Differences between means are said to have statistical *significance when they are greater than twice the standard error of those means, since the probability of this difference or a larger one occurring by chance is less than 5%.

標準誤差 （指一個平均數）從同一羣體反覆取樣時，幾個不同的樣本的平均值變化的程度。當平均值之差高於其標準誤差的兩倍以上時，這些平均值的差別被認為具有統計意義，因為這一差別的概率或者說更大數值出現的機率小於5%。

stanozolol *n.* an *anabolic steroid used to treat the effects of deep vein thrombosis and systemic sclerosis. Trade name: **Stromba.**

司坦唑，同化類固醇 一種合成代謝的甾類化合物，用於治療深靜脈血栓形成及全身性硬皮病。商品名：Stromba。

St Anthony's fire an old colloquial name for the inflammation of the skin associated with ergot poisoning. *See* ergotism.

聖安東尼熱 由麥角中毒引發的皮炎的舊稱。參閱ergotism。

stapedectomy *n.* surgical removal of the third ear ossicle (stapes), enabling it to be replaced with a prosthetic bone in the treatment of *otosclerosis.

鐙骨切除術 切除第三塊聽小骨（鐙骨）的手術，該手術在治療耳硬化症時使鐙骨的作用能夠由假骨取代。

stapes *n.* a stirrup-shaped bone in the middle *ear that articulates with the incus and is attached to the membrane of the fenestra ovalis. *See* ossicle.

鐙骨 馬鐙形骨，位於中耳，與砧骨構成關節，並貼附在前庭卵圓窗的膜上。參閱ossicle。

staphylectomy *n.* surgical removal of the uvula (the back of the soft palate).

懸雍垂切除術 切除懸雍垂（軟腭後部）的手術。

staphylococcal scalded skin syndrome (Lyell's disease, Ritter's disease) a disease of young infants that is caused by bacteria of the genus *Staphylococcus* affecting the skin, which

葡萄球菌性鱗片皮膚綜合徵（萊爾病，里特爾病） 新生兒皮膚因感染葡萄球菌屬的細菌而導致的疾病，病兒皮膚發紅並片狀剝落。該病可突然發

becomes reddened and flakes off. It can occur as outbreaks and affected children need careful handing and appropriate antibiotic treatment. Medical name: **toxic epidermal necrolysis**.

作，患兒需細心護理並用合適的抗生素治療。醫學用語：毒性表皮溶解壞死症。

Staphylococcus *n.* a genus of Gram-positive nonmotile spherical bacteria occurring in grapelike clusters. Some species are saprophytes; others parasites. Many species produce *exotoxins. The species *S. aureus* is commonly present on skin and mucous membranes; it causes boils and internal abscesses. More serious infections caused by staphylococci include pneumonia, bacter-aemia, osteomyelitis, and enterocolitis. –**staphylococcal** *adj.*

葡萄球菌屬　一屬革蘭氏陽性非運動性球菌，呈現葡萄串狀。其中某些種為腐物寄生菌，其餘為一般寄生菌。許多種產生外毒素。金黃色葡萄球菌普遍存在於皮膚及黏膜表面，可引起癤腫和深部膿腫。由葡萄球菌引起的更為嚴重的感染包括肺炎、菌血症、骨髓炎、小腸結腸炎。

staphyloma *n.* abnormal bulging of the cornea or sclera (white) of the eye. *Anterior staphyloma* is a bulging scar in the cornea to which a part of the iris is attached. It is usually the site of a healed corneal ulcer that has penetrated right through the cornea; the iris blocks the hole and prevents the further leakage of fluid from the front chamber of the eye. In *ciliary staphyloma* the sclera bulges over the ciliary body as a result of high pressure inside the eyeball. A bulging of the sclera at the back of the eye (*posterior staphyloma*) occurs in some severe cases of short-sightedness.

葡萄腫　眼角膜或鞏膜的異常凸出。前葡萄腫是角膜上有瘢痕凸出，其下有部分虹膜黏着。該部位常為角膜潰瘍的愈合處，該處潰瘍曾穿透角膜，穿透孔被虹膜堵塞以防止眼睛前房液的溢出。睫狀體葡萄腫為鞏膜在睫狀體部位向外凸出，是眼球內眼壓過高的結果。在眼後的鞏膜凸出（後葡萄腫）發生於某些高度近視患者。

staphylorrhaphy (**palatorrhaphy, uraniscorrhaphy**) *n.* surgical suture of a cleft palate.

軟腭縫合術（**腭裂縫合術，腭修補術**）　縫合腭裂的手術。

starch *n.* the form in which *carbohydrates are stored in many plants and a major constituent of the diet. Starch consists of linked glucose units and occurs in two forms, α-*amylose* and *amylopectin*. In α-*amylose* the units are in the form of

澱粉　碳水化合物在眾多植物中的貯存形式，是食物的主要成分。澱粉由葡萄糖單位連接而成，有兩種存在形態：α-直鏈澱粉及支鏈澱粉。在 α-直鏈澱粉中葡萄糖單位以不分支的

a long unbranched chain; in amylopectin they form a branched chain. The presence of starch can be detected using iodine: α-amylose gives a blue colour with iodine; amylopectin a red colour. Starch is digested by means of the enzyme *amylase. *See also* dextrin.

長鏈形式存在，而支鏈澱粉的葡萄糖單位則形成分支的鏈。澱粉的存在可用碘來測定：α-直鏈澱粉遇碘成藍色；支鏈澱粉遇碘成紅色。澱粉通過澱粉酶被消化。參閱 dextrin。

Starling's law a law stating that a muscle, including the heart muscle, responds to increased stretching at rest by an increased force of contraction when stimulated.

斯塔林定律 這一定律闡述：包括心肌在內的肌肉靜息時拉得越長，刺激時收縮力越大。

starvation *n. see* malnutrition.

飢餓 參閱 malnutrition。

stasis *n.* stagnation or cessation of flow; for example, of blood or lymph whose flow is obstructed or of the intestinal contents when onward movement (peristalsis) is hindered.

停滯，鬱積 流動液體的停滯或靜止狀態，例如血流或淋巴液的流動受阻，腸內容物的前移運動（蠕動）受阻。

-stasis *suffix denoting* stoppage of a flow of liquid; stagnation. Example: *haemostasis* (of blood).

〔後綴〕**停滯** 液體流動的停止；停滯。例如：血流停滯。

static reflex the reflex maintenance of muscular tone for posture.

靜位反射 為保持某種姿勢而肌肉持續緊張的反射。

status asthmaticus a severe attach of asthma, which often follows a period of poorly controlled asthma. Patients are distressed and very breathless and may die from respiratory failure if not vigorously treated with inhaled oxygen, nebulized or intravenous bronchodilators, and corticosteroid therapy; sedatives are absolutely contraindicated. These patients need hospital care in an intensive care unit.

哮喘持續狀態 哮喘病的嚴重發作，常持續一段時間控制不住的哮喘。病人十分痛苦，呼吸極其困難，並且如不採取強有力的治療措施，可能會因呼吸衰竭而死亡。此時治療方式有吸氧，使用霧化支氣管擴張藥，或靜脈內注射支氣管擴張藥，或使用皮質類固醇，絕對禁止使用鎮靜藥。病人需在監護室內住院看護。

status epilepticus the occurrence of repeated epileptic seizures without any recovery of consciousness between them. Its control is a medical emergency, since

癲癇持續狀態 癲癇反覆發作，其間無意識狀態恢復。需緊急醫治控制病情，因延長的癲癇持續狀態可能導致死亡。

prolonged status epilepticus may lead to the patient's death.

status lymphaticus enlargement of the thymus gland and other parts of the lymphatic system, formerly believed to be a predisposing cause to sudden death in infancy and childhood associated with hypersensitivity to drugs or vaccines.

淋巴體質　胸腺及淋巴系統其他部分的增大，過去認為是嬰幼兒對藥物和疫苗過敏而突然死亡的素質性原因。

STD *see* sexually transmitted disease.

性傳播疾病　參閱 sexually trasnsmitted disease。

steapsin *n. see* lipase.

胰脂酶　參閱 lipase。

stearic acid *see* fatty acid.

脂肪酸　參閱 fatty acid。

steat- (steato-) *prefix denoting* fat; fatty tissue.

〔前綴〕脂肪，脂肪組織

steatoma *n.* any cyst or tumour of a sebaceous gland.

脂瘤　皮脂腺的任何囊腫或腫瘤。

steatopygia *n.* the accumulation of large quantities of fat in the buttocks. In the Hottentots of Africa this is a normal condition, thought to be an adaptation that allows fat storage without impeding heat loss from the rest of the body.

臀脂過多　大量脂肪堆積在臀部。對於非洲霍屯督人，此為正常現象，據認為這是一適應性的表現，脂肪蓄積於臀部但並不影響身體其他部分的熱量散發。

steatorrhoea *n.* the passage of abnormally increased amounts of fat in the faeces (more than 5 g/day) due to reduced absorption of fat by the intestine (*see* malabsorption). The faeces are pale, smell offensive, may look greasy, and are difficult to flush away.

脂肪痢　因腸內脂肪吸收減少（參閱 malabsorption），故而有異常增多的脂肪隨糞便（每日超過 5g）排出的症狀。大便色蒼白、味惡，外觀油膩，難以沖洗。

steatosis *n.* infiltration of *hepatocytes with fat. This may occur in pregnancy, alcoholism, malnutrition, or with some drugs.

脂肪變性　肝細胞有脂肪浸入。可能在懷孕、嗜酒、營養不良或服用某些藥物時發生。

stellate fracture a star-shaped fracture of the kneecap caused by a direct blow.

星形骨折　由直接撞擊所致的髕骨骨折，該骨折呈星形。髕

The bone may be either split or severely shattered; if the fragments are displaced, the bone may need to be surgically removed (*patellectomy*).

骨可能會有裂隙，嚴重時碎成幾片。如果碎片移位，需作髕骨切除手術（髕骨切除術）。

stellate ganglion a star-shaped collection of sympathetic nerve cell bodies in the root of the neck, from which sympathetic nerve fibres are distributed to the face and neck and to the blood vessels and organs of the thorax.

星形神經節　頸根部交感神經細胞體的交匯之處，狀如星形，由此處交感神經纖維發出分支到面部、頸部及胸腔的血管和器官。

Stellwag's sign apparent widening of the distance between the upper and lower eyelids (the palpebral fissure) due to retraction of the upper lid and protrusion of the eyeball. It is a sign of exophthalmic *goitre.

施特爾瓦格徵　上、下瞼之間距離明顯增大（瞼裂），係上瞼收縮及眼球突出所致。為突眼性甲狀腺腫的體徵。

stem cell an immortal cell that is able to produce all the cells within an organ. The term is most usually applied to the *haemopoietic stem cells of the bone marrow.

幹細胞　器官內可產生所有細胞的永生細胞。這一術語通常用以指骨髓造血幹細胞。

steno- *prefix denoting* **1.** narrow. Example: *stenocephaly* (narrowness of the head). **2.** constricted.

〔前綴〕**(1) 狹窄**　例如：頭狹窄（頭部的狹窄）。**(2) 收縮的**

stenopaeic *adj.* (in ophthalmology) describing an optical device consisting of an opaque disc punctured with a fine slit or hole (or holes), which is placed in front of the eye in the same position as glasses and enables sharper vision in cases of gross long- or short-sightedness or astigmatism. It sharpens the image formed on the retina because it confines the light reaching the eye to one or more fine beams. The same principle is used in the pin-hole camera.

裂隙鏡　（眼科學）一種光學裝置，該裝置為一不透明的圓片上面有一處極細的裂隙或一小孔（或幾個小孔），此裝置可像眼鏡一樣戴在眼前，對於高度遠視、近視或散光的情況可提高視力。因為它能將進入眼睛的光聚成一條或幾條光束從而提高視網膜成像的能力。針孔攝影機亦應用了這一原理。

stenosis *n.* the abnormal narrowing of a passage or opening, such as a blood vessel or heart valve. *See* aortic,

狹窄　通過或開口處的異常狹窄，如血管及心臟瓣膜。參閱　aortic，carotid-artery，

carotid artery, mitral, pulmonary, and pyloric stenosis.

mitral，pulmonary及pyloric stenosis。

stenostomia (stenostomy) *n.* the abnormal narrowing of an opening, such as the opening of the bile duct.

口狹窄 開口處的異常狹窄，如膽管口。

Stensen's duct the long secretory duct of the *parotid salivary gland.

斯滕森管 長的腮腺分泌導管。

stent *n.* a splint placed inside a duct or canal, such as the ureter or bile duct. It may be used at operation to aid healing of an anastomosis, or placed across an obstruction to maintain an open lumen, e.g. in a bile duct obstructed by a tumour or stricture. *Double J* (or *pigtail*) *stents* are slender catheters with side holes that are passed over a guide wire either through an endoscope or at open operation to drain urine from the kidney pelvis to the bladder via the ureter. On removal of the guide wire both the upper and lower extremities of the stent assume a J-shape, hence preventing both upward and downward migration. They are commonly used to splint a damaged ureter and to relieve obstruction.

引流條 置於導管或腔內的條形體。用於手術時幫助吻合處愈合或穿透阻塞處放置以保持腔的敞開，如膽管因腫瘤或狹窄而阻塞時。雙 J（辮形）形引流條為很薄的導管，兩端有孔，孔上有導絲通過，在內窺鏡或開腔手術時通過輸尿管將尿液自腎盂引流入膀胱。在去掉導管上下兩端的導絲後，導管將恢復 J 形，從而防止上、下移動。常用來輸導以解除輸尿管受損而造成的阻塞。

sterco- *prefix denoting* faeces.

〔前綴〕**糞**

stercobilin *n.* a brownish-red pigment formed during the metabolism of the *bile pigments biliverdin and bilirubin, which are derived from haemoglobin. Stercobilin is subsequently excreted in the urine or faeces.

糞膽素 源自血紅蛋白的膽綠素及膽紅素在代謝過程中形成的棕紅色素。該物質隨後由尿或糞排出。

stercolith *n.* a stone formed of dried compressed faeces.

糞石 糞因乾燥而成的結石。

stercoraceous *adj.* composed of or containing faeces.

糞的 由糞便組成的或含有糞便的。

stereognosis *n.* the ability to recognize the three-dimensional shape of an object

實體覺 僅靠觸覺就可認識到物體三維形狀的能力。該能力

by touch alone. This is a function of the *association areas of the parietal lobe of the brain. *See also* agnosia.

係大腦頂葉聯合區的一種功能。參閱 agnosia。

stereoisomers *pl. n.* compounds having the same molecular formula but different three-dimensional arrangements of their atoms. The atomic structures of stereoisomers are mirror images of each other.

立體異構體 具備同樣的分子式但原子的三維排列不同的化合物。其原子結構互為鏡像對應。

stereoscopic vision perception of the shape, depth, and distance of an object as a result of having *binocular vision. The brain receives two distinct images from the eyes, which it interprets as a single three-dimensional image.

立體視覺 雙眼視覺所產生的對物體形狀、深度及距離的認識。大腦從雙眼得到兩個不同的映像並將這兩者轉化為單一的三維像。

stereotaxy *n.* a surgical procedure in which a deep-seated area in the brain is operated upon after its position has been established very accurately by three-dimensional measurements. The operation may be performed using an electrical current or by heat, cold, or mechanical techniques. *See also* leucotomy.

立體定位法 一種運用三維計量來準確定位方可進行大腦深層區的手術的外科操作。手術可用電擊、高熱、冷凍及機械方法進行。參閱 leucotomy。

stereotypy *n.* the constant repetition of a complex action, which is carried out in the same way each time. It is seen in *catatonia and infantile *autism; sometimes it is an isolated symptom in mental retardation. It is more common in patients who live in institutions where they are bored and unstimulated. It can prevent a patient from carrying on normal life, and sometimes causes physical injury to the patient. Drugs, such as *phenothiazines, and behaviour therapy are sometimes used in treating the condition.

刻板症 對一複雜動作的不斷重複，每一次均以同樣的方式進行。此病見於緊張症和幼兒孤獨癖患者，有時也作為智力低下的孤立症狀出現。更常見於一些生活環境單調枯燥的患者。此病可能會妨礙病人過正常生活，有時會給病人帶來身體傷害。其治療可用藥物如吩噻嗪，亦可用行為療法。

sterile *adj.* **1.** (of a living organism) barren; unable to reproduce its kind

(1) 不育的 （指一個生命有機體）不會生育的，沒有繁殖後

(see sterility). **2.** (of inanimate objects) completely free from bacteria, fungi, viruses, or other microorganisms that could cause infection.

sterility *n.* inability to have children, either due to *infertility or (in someone who has been fertile) deliberately induced by surgical procedures as a means of contraception (see sterilization). Sterility may also be an incidental result of an operation or drug treatment undertaken for other reasons, such as removal of the uterus (*hysterectomy) because of cancer.

sterilization *n.* **1.** a surgical operation or any other process that induces *sterility in men or women. In women, hysterectomy and bilateral oophorectomy (surgical removal of both ovaries) are 100% effective and permanent. Alternatively, the Fallopian tubes may be removed (see salpingectomy) or divided and/or ligated. These operations can be performed through the abdomen or the vagina. The modern technique (*tubal occlusion*) is to occlude (close) permanently the inner (lower) half of the Fallopian tube through a *laparoscope. The occluding device is usually a clip (the *Hulka-Clemens* or *Filshie clips*) or a small plastic ring (*Falope ring*); *diathermy coagulation carries greater dangers (e.g. bowel burns) and is now little used. A more recent method is the use of a rapid-setting plastic introduced into the tubes through a *hysteroscope. Men are usually sterilized by *vasectomy. *See also* castration. **2.** the process by which all types of microorganisms (including spores) are destroyed. This is achieved by the use of heat, radiation, chemicals, or filtration. *See also* autoclave.

代能力的（參閱 sterility）。**(2) 完全無菌的**（指無生命物體）完全不受細菌、真菌、病毒或其他微生物感染的。

不育 無生育能力。因不育症或（對於某些已生育的）作為節育措施，人為地採用外科手段而導致的這一狀態（參閱 sterilization）。不育也可能是因其他原因而進行的手術或服用藥物所產生的伴隨性結果，如因癌切除子宮的手術（子宮切除術）。

(1) 絕育 導致男性或女性無生育能力的外科手術或任何其他過程。女性子宮切除術及雙側卵巢摘除術（外科摘除雙側卵巢）的有效率為 100% 且有永久性絕育效果。或者可將輸卵管摘除（參閱 salpingectomy），切斷或結紮亦可達到絕育目的。手術可通過腹部或陰道施行。現代技術手段（輸卵管閉合）是通過腹腔鏡來永久地閉合（關閉）輸卵管的內半部（下半部）。此閉合裝置常為一小夾（Hulka-Clemens 或 Filshie 夾）或為一小塑料環（輸卵管環）；透熱凝結法常帶有較大危險（如腸燒傷）因而現在很少使用。通過子宮鏡向輸卵管內引入快速定型的塑料是一種比較新的絕育手段，男性通常是作輸精管切除術來絕育。參閱 castration。**(2) 消毒** 殺滅各種類型微生物（包括孢子）的方法。這一效果是通過使用熱、射綫、化學物質或濾過作用來達到的。參閱 autoclave。

stern- (sterno-) *prefix denoting* the sternum. Example: *sternocostal* (relating to the sternum and ribs).

〔前綴〕**胸骨**　例如：胸肋的（與胸骨及肋骨相關的）。

Sternberg-Reed cell (Reed-Sternberg cell) a large binucleate cell that is characteristic of *Hodgkin's disease.

斯-里氏細胞　雙核巨細胞，霍奇金病的典型細胞。

sternebra *n.* (*pl.* **sternebrae**) one of the four parts that fuse during development to form the body of the sternum.

胸骨節　共四塊，在胸骨發育成一體時將四小部分合在一起之處。

sternocleidomastoid muscle *see* sternomastoid muscle.

胸鎖乳突肌　參閱 sternomastoid muscle。

sternohyoid *n.* a muscle in the neck, arising from the sternum and inserted into the hyoid bone. It depresses the hyoid bone.

胸骨舌骨肌　頸肌，起自胸骨，又插入舌骨，可使舌骨下降。

sternomastoid muscle (sternocleido-mastoid muscle) a long muscle in the neck, extending from the mastoid process to the sternum and clavicle. It serves to rotate the neck and flex the head.

胸鎖乳突肌　頸部一條長肌，自乳突延展至胸骨及鎖骨。功能：轉頸，屈頭。

sternomastoid tumour a small painless nonmalignant swelling in the lower half of the *sternomastoid muscle, appearing a few days after birth. It occurs when the neck of the fetus is in an abnormal position in the uterus, which interferes with the blood supply to the affected muscle, and it is most common after breech births. The tumour may cause a slight tilt of the head towards the tumour and turning of the face to the other side. This can be corrected by physiotherapy aimed at increasing all movements of the body, but without stretching the neck.

胸鎖乳突肌腫瘤　胸鎖乳突肌下半部的無痛、良性小腫物，出生後數日出現。該病見於胎兒頸在子宮內位置不正，影響到這些相關肌肉的正常供血，最常見於臀位分娩後。可引起頭部向該側微傾，面部轉向另一側。可用物理療法治療，其目的在於不牽拉頸部的情況下增強全身運動。

sternotomy *n.* surgical division of the breastbone (sternum), performed to allow access to the heart and its major vessels.

胸骨切開術　切開胸骨的外科手術，以通向心臟及其大血管。

sternum *n.* (*pl.* **sterna**) the breastbone: a flat bone, 15–20 cm long, extending from the base of the neck to just below the diaphragm and forming the front part of the skeleton of the thorax. The sternum articulates with the collar bones (*see* clavicle) and the costal cartilages of the first seven pairs of ribs. It consists of three sections: the middle and longest section – the *body* or *gladiolus* – is attached to the *manubrium at the top and the *xiphoid (or ensiform) process at the bottom. The manubrium slopes back from the body so that the junction between the two parts forms an angle (*angle of Louis* or *sternal angle*). **–sternal.** *adj.*

胸骨　胸骨：一塊扁骨，長15~20 cm，自頸根部延至膈下，構成胸前的骨架。胸骨與鎖骨（參閱 clavicle）及第 1~7 對肋骨的軟骨關節相連。它由三部分組成：中部也是最長的部分——胸骨體——上承胸骨柄，下接劍突。胸骨柄從胸骨體向後傾斜以使這兩部分匯合之處能形成一個角度（路易斯角或胸骨角）。

steroid *n.* one of a group of compounds having a common structure based on the *steroid nucleus*, which consists of three six-membered carbon rings and one five-membered carbon ring. The naturally occurring steroids include the male and female sex hormones (*androgens and *oestrogens), the hormones of the adrenal cortex (*see* corticosteroid), *progesterone, *bile salts, and *sterols. Synthetic steroids have been produced for therapeutic purposes.

類固醇，甾類　一族以甾核為基礎，結構相同的化合物。甾核由三個六碳環和一個五碳環組成。天然的類固醇包括雄性激素和雌性激素（雄激素和雌激素）、腎上腺皮質激素（參閱 corticosteroid）、孕酮、膽鹽和固醇。人工類固醇已經生產出來，用於治療。

sterol *n.* one of a group of *steroid alcohols. The most important sterols are *cholesterol and *ergosterol.

固醇，甾醇　類固醇中的一類，其中最重要的固醇為膽固醇及麥角固醇。

stertor *n.* a snoring type of noisy breathing heard in deeply unconscious patients.

鼾息　在深度昏迷的病人中呼吸時發出鼾聲樣的噪音。

steth- (stetho-) *prefix denoting* the chest.

〔前綴〕胸

stethoscope *n.* an instrument used for listening to sounds within the body, such as those in the heart and lungs (*see* auscultation). A simple stethoscope usually

聽診器　用以聽取體內聲音的儀器，如心音及肺呼吸音（參閱 auscultation）。簡單的聽診器通常由一隔膜或一敞開的鐘

consists of a diaphragm or an open bell-shaped structure (which is applied to the body) connected by rubber or plastic tubes to shaped earpieces for the examiner. More complicated devices may contain electronic amplification systems to aid diagnosis.

形結構（用以接觸身體）靠塑料或橡皮管與診斷者的耳廓相連，較複雜的裝置可能有電子擴音系統以輔助診斷。

sthenia *n.* a state of normal or greater than normal strength. *Compare* asthenia. **–sthenic** *adj.*

強壯 體力狀態正常或超過正常。與 asthenia 對比。

stibophen *n.* a sodium-containing salt of antimony used to treat *schistosomiasis. It is administered by injection; side-effects may include digestive upsets, slow heart rate, and anaemia.

睇波芬 一含鈉銻鹽，用以治療血吸蟲病。注射給藥，副作用：消化道不適，心率減慢及貧血。

stigma *n.* (*pl.* **stigmata**) **1.** a mark that characterizes a particular disease, such as the *café au lait spots characteristic of neurofibromatosis. **2.** any spot or lesion on the skin.

(1) 病斑 某疾病特有的斑記，如神經纖維病特有的咖啡牛乳色斑。**(2) 皮膚斑** 皮膚上的斑點或病損。

stilboestrol *n.* a synthetic female sex hormone (*see* oestrogen) used to relieve menstrual disorders and symptoms of the menopause, to treat prostate and breast cancer, and to suppress lactation. It is administered by mouth or injection; side-effects are those of other synthetic oestrogens.

己烯雌酚 人工合成的雌性激素（參閱 oestrogen），用以緩解月經不調和經絕期症狀，治療前列腺癌、乳腺癌、抑制乳汁分泌。口服或注射；副作用同其他合成雌激素。

stilet (stylet, stylus) *n.* **1.** a slender probe. **2.** a wire placed in the lumen of a catheter to give it rigidity while the instrument is passed along a body canal (such as the urethra).

(1) 細探子 一根細的探針。**(2) 導管絲** 導管腔內放置的金屬絲，該絲在導管通過體內管道（例如尿道）時，賦予導管一定的硬度。

stillbirth *n.* birth of a fetus that shows no evidence of life (heartbeat, respiration, or independent movement) at any time later than 24 weeks after conception. Under the Stillbirth (Definition) Act 1992, there is a legal obligation to notify

死產 妊娠 24 周後任意時間產下的無生命特徵（心跳、呼吸或自主活動）的胎兒。根據（英國）1992 年的死產（定義）法，生下死產後必須通知適當的政府當局。每 1000 次分娩

all stillbirths to the appropriate author-ity. The number of such births expressed per 1000 births (live and still) is known as the *stillbirth rate*. In legal terms, via-bility is deemed to start at the 24th week of pregnancy and a fetus born dead before this time is known as an *abortion or miscarriage. However, some fetuses born alive before the 24th week may now survive as a result of improved perinatal care.

（活嬰或死嬰）中的死產數稱為死產率。法律上講自妊娠 24 周起產下胎兒被認為是能存活的，而在這之前產下胎兒，胎兒出生時死夭被認為是流產。然而一些在 24 周前產下的胎兒現在仍能存活，係早產嬰兒護理技術進步之原因。

Still's disease chronic arthritis devel-oping in children before the age of 16. There are several different forms of arthritis affecting children, and some authorities confine the diagnosis of Still's disease to the following: a disease of childhood marked by arthritis (often involving several joints) with a swinging fever and a transitory red rash. There is sometimes severe illness affecting the entire body and the condition may be complicated by enlargement of the spleen and lymph nodes and inflamma-tion of the pericardium and iris.

斯蒂爾病 16 歲前兒童患上的慢性關節炎。侵害兒童的關節炎有幾種不同的形式，一些專家將該病的診斷限制在以下幾點：兒童期得病，特徵為關節炎（常涉及幾個關節），高燒和一過性紅色皮疹。嚴重時影響全身，並可合併脾和淋巴結腫大、心包炎及虹膜炎。

stimulant *n.* an agent that promotes the activity of a body system or func-tion. Amphetamine and *caffeine are stimulants of the central nervous system.

興奮劑 提高身體系統活動或功能的藥劑。苯丙胺和咖啡因是中樞神經系統的興奮劑。

stimulator *n.* any apparatus designed to stimulate nerves and muscles for a variety of purposes. It can be used to stimulate particular areas of the brain or to block pain (as in *transcutaneous electrical nerve stimulation).

刺激儀 因不同目的用於刺激神經和肌肉的任何器械。可用於刺激大腦的特定區域或阻滯疼痛（例如經皮電神經刺激）。

stimulus *n.* (*pl.* **stimuli**) any agent that provokes a response, or particular form of activity, in a cell, tissue, or other struc-ture, which is said to be *sensitive* to that stimulus.

刺激物 任何能在對該物有敏感性的細胞、組織或其他結構中激發起反應或某種活動形式的物質。

stippling *n.* a spotted or speckled appearance, such as is seen in the retina in certain eye diseases or in abnormal red blood cells stained with basic dyes.

點彩　斑狀或點狀表現，如見於某些眼疾病的視網膜上或用鹼性染色的異常紅細胞內。

stirrup *n.* (in anatomy) *see* stapes.

鐙骨　（解剖學）參閱 stapes。

stitch *n.* **1.** a sharp localized pain, commonly in the abdomen, associated with strenuous physical activity (such as running), especially shortly after eating. It is a form of cramp. **2.** *see* suture.

(1) 刺痛　局部銳痛，常見於腹部，與緊張的體力活動（如跑步）有關，尤其是飯後立即進行的活動。為痛性痙攣的一種類型。**(2) 縫綫**　參閱 suture。

stock culture *see* culture.

存貯培養　參閱 culture。

Stokes-Adams syndrome (Adams-Stokes syndrome) attacks of temporary loss of consciousness that occur when blood flow ceases due to ventricular *fibrillation or to *asystole. This syndrome may complicate *heart block. It is treated by means of a battery-operated *pacemaker.

阿-斯綜合徵　突發的暫時性意識喪失，發生於因心室纖維性顫動或心搏停止引起的血流停滯。此綜合徵可併發心傳導阻滯。用電起搏器治療。

stoma *n.* (*pl.* **stomata**) **1.** (in anatomy) the mouth or any mouthlike part. **2.** (in surgery) the artificial opening of a tube (e.g. the colon or ileum) that has been brought to the abdominal surface (*see* colostomy, ileostomy). *Stoma therapists* are nurses specially trained in the care of these artificial openings and the appliances used with them. **–stomal** *adj.*

(1) 口　（解剖學）口或任何開口型部分。**(2) 造口**　（外科學）植於腹壁表面的管道（如結腸或迴腸）的人工開口（參閱 colostomy，ileostomy）。造口術治療員係指對這類造口護理及其用具操作方面受過專門訓練的護士。

stomach *n.* a distensible saclike organ that forms part of the alimentary canal between the oesophagus (gullet) and the duodenum (see illustration). It communicates with the former by means of the *cardiac orifice* and with the latter by the *pyloric sphincter*. The stomach lies just below the diaphragm, to the right of the spleen and partly under the liver. Its

胃　可擴張的囊袋狀器官，構成消化道中食管和十二指腸之間的部分（見圖）。胃由賁門與食管相通，由幽門括約肌與十二指腸相通。其位置恰在膈下，脾右，部分在肝下。其功能為繼續口腔開始的消化過程，黏膜內的胃腺分泌胃液，胃液中含有助於化學性消化的

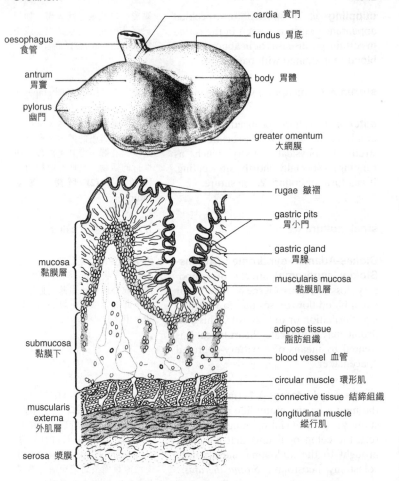

Regions of the stomach seen from the front (above); layers of the
stomach wall (below)
胃的分區前面觀（上圖）；胃壁各層（下圖）

function is to continue the process of
digestion that begins in the mouth.
*Gastric juice, secreted by gastric glands
in the mucosa, contains hydrochloric acid
and the enzyme *pepsin, which contribute to chemical digestion. This –
together with the churning action of the
muscular layers of the stomach – reduces

鹽酸和胃蛋白酶。化學性消化
再加上胃肌層的攪拌作用，將
食物變成已部分消化的半流體
狀物質，然後進入十二指腸。

the food to a semiliquid partly digested mass that passes on to the duodenum.

stomat- (stomato-) *prefix denoting* the mouth.

〔前綴〕口腔

stomatitis *n.* inflammation of the mucous lining of the mouth.

口炎 口腔黏膜層的炎症。

stomatology *n.* the branch of medicine concerned with diseases of the mouth.

口腔學 關於口腔疾病的醫學分支。

stomodeum *n.* the site of the embryonic mouth, marked by a depression lined with ectoderm from which the teeth develop. The membrane separating it from the foregut breaks down by the end of the first month of pregnancy. *Compare* proctodeum.

口凹 胚胎口腔的位置，表現為外胚層所蓋的凹陷，以後由該處長出牙齒。分隔口凹和原腸的膜在妊娠 1 個月末時破裂。與 proctodeum 對比。

-stomy (-ostomy) *suffix denoting* a surgical opening into an organ or part. Example: *colostomy* (into the colon).

〔後綴〕造口術 指在器官或身體某部位進行外科造口。例如結腸造口術（在結腸上）。

stone *n. see* calculus.

結石 參閱 calculus。

stool *n.* *faeces discharged from the anus.

糞 由肛門排出的糞便。

stop needle a surgical needle with a shank that has a protruding collar to stop it when the needle has been pushed a prescribed distance into the tissue. A stop needle has the eye at the tip.

有擋針 外科用針，帶有針柄，柄上有突起的圓擋。當針刺入組織達到預定距離阻止進針。其針尖部有針眼。

strabismus (heterotropia) *n.* squint: any abnormal alignment of the two eyes. The strabismus is most commonly horizontal – *convergent strabismus* (or *esotropia*) or *divergent strabismus* (*exotropia*) – but it may be vertical (*hypertropia*, in which the eye looks upwards, or *hypotropia*, in which it looks downwards). In rare cases both eyes look towards the same point but one is twisted

斜視 兩眼視綫不正常的成綫。其中最常見的為水平向斜視——會聚性斜視（內斜視）或散開性斜視（外斜視）——但其中也有垂直向斜視（上斜視，其一眼向上視，或下斜視，其一眼向下視）。罕見有兩眼看前方同一點時，一眼與另一眼相關，發生順時針或逆時針轉動（旋轉斜視）。複視

clockwise or anticlockwise in relation to the other (*cyclotropia*). Double vision is possible, but the image from the deviating eye usually becomes ignored. In cyclotropia the image is not separated from the normal one but rotated across it. Most strabismus is *concomitant*, i.e. the abnormal alignment of the two eyes remains fairly constant, in whatever direction the person is looking. This is usual with childhood squints. Strabismus acquired by injury or disease is usually *incomitant*, i.e. the degree of misalignment varies in different directions of gaze. *See also* cover test, heterophoria.

有可能，但來自背離雙眼的影像常被忽視。旋轉斜視中，斜視眼的影像並不與正常眼的影像分離，而是與之斜交叉。絕大多數斜視眼是共同性斜視，即不論向何方注視，兩眼不正常成綫始終保持恆定。這種情況常見於兒童期斜視，由外傷或疾病造成的斜視則通常為非共同性斜視，即隨着注視方向不同，兩眼不正常成綫的程度發生變化。參閱 cover test，heterophoria。

strain 1. *n.* excessive stretching or working of a muscle, resulting in pain and swelling of the muscle. *Compare* sprain. **2.** *n.* a group of organisms, such as bacteria, obtained from a particular source or having special properties distinguishing them from other members of the same species. **3.** *vb.* to damage a muscle by overstretching.

(1) 勞損 肌肉過度牽伸或作用，引起肌肉疼腫，與 sprain 對比。**(2) 株** 一羣有機體，如細菌，通過特定來源方可得到或具有使其與同種中的其他成員相區別的不同的特徵。**(3) 拉傷** 因過度拉伸而損傷肌肉。

strain gauge a sensitive instrument for measuring tension and alterations in pressure. It is extensively used in medical instruments.

壓力表 計量壓力及壓力變化的敏感儀器。廣泛使用於醫療器械。

strangulated *adj.* describing a part of the body whose blood supply has been interrupted by compression of a blood vessel, as may occur in a loop of intestine trapped in a *hernia.

絞窄的 描述身體某部位血管受壓而供血中斷的狀況，如可發生於小腸袢嵌入疝內時。

strangulation *n.* the closure of a passage, such as the main airway to the lungs (resulting in the cessation of breathing), a blood vessel, or the gastrointestinal tract.

絞窄 通路的封閉，如通向肺的主要氣道的絞窄（致使呼吸中斷），血管或胃腸道的絞窄。

strangury *n.* severe pain in the urethra referred from the base of the bladder and

痛性尿淋瀝 由膀胱底傳出的尿道劇痛，同時伴有強烈尿

associated with an intense desire to pass urine. It occurs when the base of the bladder is irritated by a stone or an indwelling catheter. It is also noted in patients with an invasive cancer of the base of the bladder or severe *cystitis or *prostatitis, when the strong desire to urinate is accompanied by the painful passage of a few drops of urine.

意。發生於膀胱底受結石或留置導尿管刺激時。在膀胱底侵襲性癌或嚴重的膀胱炎或前列腺炎病人中也有發生，其表現為尿意強烈，排尿時痛苦而且僅能排出幾滴尿液。

Strassman procedure an operation to correct a double uterus (*see* uterus didelphys). It has now largely been replaced by techniques involving the use of a *hysteroscope.

斯特拉斯曼手術　手術矯正雙子宮（參閱　uterus didelphys）。現大量地已由使用子宮鏡的有關技術所取代。

stratum *n.* a layer of tissue or cells, such as any of the layers of the *epidermis of the skin (the *stratum corneum* is the outermost layer).

層　一組織層或細胞層，如皮膚表皮各層（角質層為其最外層）。

strawberry mark (strawberry naevus) *see* naevus.

草莓斑（草莓狀痣）　參閱 naevus。

streak *n.* (in anatomy) a line, furrow, or narrow band. *See also* primitive streak.

條，紋　（解剖學）一綫條，溝紋或窄條。參閱　primitive streak。

Streptobacillus *n.* a genus of Gram-negative aerobic nonmotile rodlike bacteria that tend to form filaments. The single species, *S. moniliformis*, is a normal inhabitant of the respiratory tract of rats but causes *rat-bite fever in man.

鏈桿菌屬　一屬革蘭氏陰性、需氧、無活動力、桿狀細菌，有形成菌絲傾向，其中一念珠狀鏈桿菌為大鼠呼吸道正常寄生菌，但能使人患鼠咬熱。

streptococcal toxic shock syndrome a bacterial disease of children characterized by fever, shock, and multiple organ failure. It is similar to the *toxic shock syndrome caused by staphylococci, but in these cases the infecting organisms are of the genus *Streptococcus*.

鏈球菌中毒性休克綜合徵　兒童所患的細菌病，特徵為發燒、休克、多器官功能喪失。與葡萄球菌中毒引起的休克綜合徵相似，但本徵中的感染性有機體為鏈球菌。

Streptococcus *n.* a genus of Gram-positive nonmotile spherical bacteria

鏈球菌屬　一屬革蘭氏陽性、無活動能力，呈鏈狀排列的球

occurring in chains. Most species are saprophytes; some are pathogenic. Many pathogenic species are *haemolytic*, i.e. they have the ability to destroy red blood cells in blood agar. This provides a useful basis for classifying the many different strains. Strains of *S. pyogenes* (the β-haemolytic streptococci) are associated with many infections, including *scarlet fever, and produce many *exotoxins. Strains of the α-haemolytic streptococci are associated with bacterial *endocarditis. The species *S. pneumoniae* (formerly *Diplococcus pneumoniae*) – the *pneumococcus* – is associated with pneumonia. It occurs in pairs, surrounded by a capsule (*see* quellung reaction). *S. mutans* has been shown to cause dental caries. *See also* Lancefield classification, streptokinase. **–streptococcal** *adj.*

streptodornase *n.* an enzyme produced by some haemolytic bacteria of the genus *Streptococcus* that is capable of liquefying pus. *See also* streptokinase.

streptokinase *n.* an enzyme produced by some haemolytic bacteria of the genus *Streptococcus* that is capable of liquefying blood clots (*see also* fibrinolytic). It is injected to treat blockage of blood vessels, including infarction and pulmonary embolism. It is also used in combination with streptodornase, applied topically or taken by mouth or injection, to liquefy pus and relieve inflammation. Side-effects may include digestive upsets, fever, and haemorrhage. Trade names: **Kabikinase, Streptase**.

streptolysin *n.* an *exotoxin that is produced by strains of *Streptococcus* bacteria and destroys red blood cells.

菌。其中多數種為腐物寄生菌，有些可致病。致病種中多數為溶血性，即具在血瓊脂培養基中破壞紅細胞之能力。這一特點提供了對多種菌株進行分類的有用依據。化膿鏈球菌株（β 溶血性鏈球菌）與包括猩紅熱在內的許多傳染病有關，且能產生多種外毒素。綠色鏈球菌株（α 溶血性鏈球菌）則與細菌性心內膜炎有關。肺炎鏈球菌種（過去稱為肺炎雙球菌）——肺炎球菌——與肺炎有關。此菌成對存在，外包莢膜（參閱 quellung reaction）。突變鏈球菌亦被證明可引起齲齒。參閱 Lancefield classification，streptokinase。

鏈脫酶 鏈球菌屬中某些溶血性球菌產生的能使膿液化的酶。參閱 streptokinase。

鏈激酶 鏈球菌屬中某些溶血性鏈球菌產生的可使血塊液化的酶（參閱 fibrinolytic）。注射可治療血管阻塞，包括梗塞和肺栓塞。亦可與鏈脫酶聯合使用，採取局部外用、口服或注射，使膿液化，減輕炎症，副作用有消化道不適、發熱和出血。商品名：Kabikinase，Streptase。

鏈球菌溶血素 鏈球菌屬產生的一種可破壞紅細胞的外毒素。

Streptomyces *n.* a genus of aerobic mouldlike bacteria. Most species live in the soil, but some are parasites of animals, humans, and plants; in humans they cause *Madura foot. They are important medically as a source of such antibiotics as *streptomycin, *actinomycin. *chloramphenicol, and *neomycin.

鏈黴菌屬　需氧黴菌屬。屬中多數種生活於土壤中，有些寄生於動物、人和植物中；在人身上可引起足分支黴病。在醫學上是鏈黴素、放綫菌素、氯黴素和新黴素等抗生素的來源而占有重要地位。

streptomycin *n.* an *antibiotic, derived from the bacterium *Streptomyces griseus*, that is effective against a wide range of bacterial infections; it is administered by intramuscular injection. In tuberculosis therapy streptomycin is given in conjunction with other drugs (e.g. *isoniazid) because bacteria soon become resistant to it. Side-effects causing ear and kidney damage may develop in some patients.

鏈黴素　從灰色鏈黴菌中提取的抗生素，具廣譜抗細菌感染作用。肌注施藥。治療結核病時，將該藥與其他藥物合用（如異烟肼），係細菌對該藥很快會產生抵抗力之故。有些患者可能會有耳和腎損害的副作用。

stress *n.* any factor that threatens the health of the body or has an adverse effect on its functioning, such as injury, disease, or worry. The existence of one form of stress tends to diminish resistance to other forms. Constant stress brings about changes in the balance of hormones in the body.

應激　危及身體健康或有害於身體功能的任何因素，如受傷、患病或憂慮。一種應激形式的存在可能會導致對其他應激形式抵抗能力的降低。持續的應激狀態會引起體內激素平衡失調。

stretch receptor a cell or group of cells found between muscle fibres that responds to stretching of the muscle by transmitting impulses to the central nervous system through the sensory nerves. Stretch receptors are part of the *proprioceptor system necessary for the performance of coordinated muscular activity.

牽張感受器　存在於肌纖維間的單個細胞或一組細胞對肌肉的牽張作出反應，其衝動通過感覺神經傳到中樞神經系統。是本體感受器系統的一部分，為肌肉協調活動所必需。

stretch reflex (myotatic reflex) the reflex contraction of a muscle in response to its being stretched.

牽張反向（肌伸長反射）　對牽拉肌肉作出的肌肉收縮的反應。

stria *n.* (*pl.* **striae**) (in anatomy) a streak, line, or thin band. The *striae gravidarum* (stretch marks) are the lines that appear on the skin of the abdomen of pregnant women, due to excessive stretching of the elastic fibres. Red or purple during pregnancy, they become white after delivery. The *stria terminalis* is a white band that separates the thalamus from the ventricular surface of the caudate nucleus in the brain.

紋 （解剖學）條紋、綫條或細帶。妊娠紋（伸張紋記）為孕婦腹部皮膚出現的條紋，係彈性纖維過度拉長之故。妊娠期間紅或紫色，分娩後白色。終紋是腦內隔開丘腦及尾狀核腦室面的白色條帶。

striated muscle a tissue comprising the bulk of the body's musculature. It is also known as *skeletal muscle*, because it is attached to the skeleton and is responsible for the movement of bones, and *voluntary muscle*, because it is under voluntary control. Striated muscle is composed of parallel bundles of multinucleate fibres (each containing many *myofibrils*), which reveal cross-banding

橫紋肌 構成身體肌肉系統主體的組織。又名骨骼肌，因其附着在骨骼上並負責骨的運動之故，亦名隨意肌，因其受意志支配之故。由大量的多核肌纖維（其下含大量肌原纖維束平行構成，顯微鏡下觀察呈帶狀交錯）。這是因每條肌原纖維內的肌動蛋白絲和肌凝蛋白絲交錯排列的結果（見圖）。

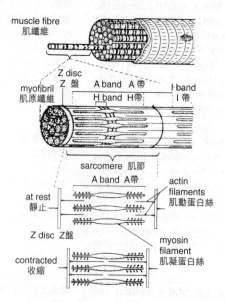

Structure of striated muscle
橫紋肌的構造

when viewed under the microscope. This effect is caused by the alternation of *actin* and *myosin* protein filaments within each myofibril (see illustration). When muscle contraction takes place, the two sets of filaments slide past each other, so reducing the length of each unit (*sarcomere*) of the myofibril. The sliding is caused by a series of cyclic reactions resulting in a change in orientation of projections on the myosin filaments; each projection is first attached to an actin filament but contracts and releases it to become reattached at a different site.

肌肉收縮時，這兩組肌絲在相互之間滑動，故而縮短了肌原纖維每一單位的長度（肌長）。肌絲的滑動是由一系列周期性反應所引起的，反應結果是使肌凝蛋白絲上的突起發生方向變化，每個突起先是觸及一條肌動蛋白，然後收縮，繼而脫離後者並在另一位置接觸肌動蛋白絲。

stricture *n*. a narrowing of any tubular structure in the body, such as the oesophagus (gullet), bowel, ureter, or urethra. A stricture may result from inflammation, muscular spasm, growth of a tumour within the affected part, or from pressure on it by neighbouring organs. For example, a *urethral stricture* is a fibrous narrowing of the urethra, usually resulting from injury or inflammation. The patient has increasing difficulty in passing urine and may develop *retention. The site and length of the stricture is assessed by *urethrography and urethroscopy, and treatment is by periodic dilatation of the urethra using *sounds *urethrotomy, or *urethroplasty. Strictures in the alimentary canal are dilated by *balloon or *stricturoplasty.

狹窄 體內管狀結構如食管、腸、輸尿管、尿道的狹窄。狹窄由受累部分的炎症、肌肉痙攣、腫瘤生長所致，也可由毗鄰器官的壓迫產生。例如：尿道狹窄常常是因外傷或炎症所致的纖維性狹窄。患者的排尿困難逐漸加重，並可發展成尿瀦留。狹窄的部位和長度可用尿道 X 綫造影術或尿道鏡檢查來加以確定。其治療為定期用探子擴張尿道、尿道切開術或尿道成形術。消化道狹窄可用氣囊擴張或狹窄成形術。

stricturoplasty *n*. an operation in which a stricture (usually in the small intestine) is widened by cutting it.

狹窄整復術 手術切開以拓寬狹窄（常為小腸處）。

stridor *n*. the noise heard on breathing in when the trachea or larynx is obstructed. It tends to be louder and harsher than *wheeze.

喘鳴 氣管或咽喉堵塞時呼吸發出的噪聲。此聲比哮鳴大而且粗。

strobila *n.* (*pl.* **strobilae**) the entire chain of segments that make up the body of an adult *tapeworm.

鏈體 構成縧蟲成蟲身體的整條節片鏈。

stroke (apoplexy) *n.* a sudden attack of weakness affecting one side of the body. It is the consequence of an interruption to the flow of blood to the brain. The primary disease is in the heart or blood vessels and the effect on the brain is secondary. The flow of blood may be prevented by clotting (*thrombosis*), a detached clot that lodges in an artery (*embolus*), or, rupture of an artery wall (*haemorrhage*). Prolonged reduction of blood pressure may result in similar brain damage. A stroke can vary in severity from a passing weakness or tingling in a limb (*see* transient ischaemic attack) to a profound paralysis, coma, and death. *See also* cerebral haemorrhage.

中風（卒中）突發性的身體一側無力。係大腦血液供應中斷之故。原發病在心臟或血管，繼發於大腦。血流受阻的原因可能是血凝塊（血栓形成），血凝塊脫落而堵塞動脈（栓塞）或動脈壁破裂（出血）。中風的嚴重程度不同，輕則僅有一過性虛弱無力或肢體刺痛（參閱 transient ischaemic attack），重則可致深度癱瘓、昏迷以至死亡（參閱 cerebral haemorrhage）。

stroma *n.* the connective tissue basis of an organ, as opposed to the functional tissue (*parenchyma*). For example, the stroma of the erythrocytes is the spongy framework of protein strands within a red blood cell in which the blood pigment haemoglobin is packed; the stroma of the cornea is the transparent fibrous tissue making up the main body of the cornea.

基質 器官的結締組織基礎，是與器官的功能組織（實質）相對而言的。例如，紅細胞基質是由紅細胞內蛋白質纖維構築的海綿狀結構，血紅蛋白包裹於其中；角膜基質為透明纖維組織，構成了角膜主體。

Strongyloides *n.* a genus of small slender nematode worms that live as parasites inside the small intestines of mammals. *S. stercoralis* infects the human small intestine (*see* strongyloidiasis); its larvae, which are passed out in the stools, develop quickly into infective forms.

類圓綫蟲屬 一屬寄生在哺乳動物小腸內的細小綫蟲。糞類圓綫蟲感染人的小腸（參閱 strongyloidiasis）；其幼蟲隨糞便排出並迅速發育成感染型綫蟲。

strongyloidiasis (strongyloidosis) *n.* an infestation of the small intestine with

糞圓綫蟲病 小腸內因糞圓綫蟲寄生所致的感染，常見於潮

the parasitic nematode worm *Strongyloides stercoralis*, common in humid tropical regions. Larvae, present in soil contaminated with human faeces, penetrate the skin of a human host and may produce an itching rash. They migrate to the lungs, where they cause tissue destruction and bleeding, and then via the windpipe and gullet to the intestine. Adult worms burrow into the intestinal wall and may cause ulceration, diarrhoea, abdominal pain, nausea, anaemia, and weakness. Treatment involves use of the drug *thiabendazole.

濕的熱帶地區。存在於為人糞所污的土壤中的幼蟲。穿透人類宿主的皮膚並造成發癢的皮疹。又遷移到肺部，引起肺組織損害及出血，再通過氣管及食管進入腸內。成蟲鑽入腸道壁可引起潰瘍、腹瀉、腹痛、惡心、貧血及體虛。用噻苯達唑治療。

strontium *n.* a yellow metallic element, absorption of which causes bone damage when its atoms displace calcium in bone. The radioactive isotope *strontium*-90, which emits beta rays, is used in radiotherapy for the *contact therapy of skin and eye tumours. Symbol: Sr.

鍶 黃色金屬元素，吸收該元素後它將取代骨鈣而引起骨損害。放射性同位素 ^{90}鍶釋放 β 射綫，可在放射治療中用於皮膚和眼腫瘤的接觸放射綫療法。符號：Sr。

struma *n.* (*pl.* **strumae**) a swelling of the thyroid gland (*see* goitre). *Riedel's struma* is a rare chronic inflammation of the thyroid (*see* thyroiditis), which becomes firm and enlarged and is eventually destroyed.

甲狀腺腫 甲狀腺腫大（參閱 goitre）。里德爾甲狀腺腫是一種罕見的甲狀腺慢性炎症（參閱 thyroiditis），其甲狀腺變硬，增大，最終破壞。

strychnine *n.* a poisonous alkaloid produced in the seeds of the East Indian tree *Strychnos nux-vomica*. In small doses it was formerly widely used in 'tonics'. Poisoning causes painful muscular spasms similar to those of tetanus; the back becomes arched (the posture known as *opisthotonos*) and death is likely to occur from spasm in the respiratory muscles.

士的寧 毒性生物鹼，產生於東印度馬錢樹種子中。過去小劑量地廣泛使用於「強壯劑」中。中毒時引起類似破傷風的疼痛的肌肉痙攣，背部彎成弓形（此姿勢稱為角弓反張），並且因呼吸肌痙攣可致命。

S-T segment the segment on an *electrocardiogram that represents the interval preceding the last phase of the *cardiac cycle, when the heart recovers from contraction. The S-T segment is

S-T 段 心電圖段，表示在心動周期中一階段前的間隔，為心臟收縮後的恢復期。常由急性心肌缺血而延長；通常在康復後可回到正常。

usually raised by acute *ischaemia of the heart muscle: it usually returns to normal with recovery.

Student's t test *see* significance.

stupe *n*. any piece of material, such as a wad of cottonwool, soaked in hot water (with or without medication) and used to apply a poultice.

stupor *n*. a condition of near unconsciousness, with apparent mental inactivity and reduced ability to respond to stimulation.

Sturge-Weber syndrome *see* angioma.

stuttering *n. see* stammering.

St Vitus' dance an archaic name Sydenham's *chorea.

Stycar tests Standard Tests for Young Children and Retardates: tests developed by the paediatrician Mary Sheridan to assess visual development.

stye *n*. acute inflammation of a gland at the base of an eyelash, caused by bacterial infection. The gland becomes hard and tender and a pus-filled cyst develops at its centre. Styes are treated by bathing in warm water or removal of the eyelash involved. Medical name: **hordeolum**.

stylet *n. see* stilet.

stylo- *prefix denoting* the styloid process of the temporal bone. Example: *stylomastoid* (relating to the styloid and mastoid processes).

---

t 檢驗 參閱 significance。

熱敷布 一塊布料，如棉毛軟墊，浸入熱水中（加或不加藥物），用以包敷泥罨劑。

木僵 近乎於意識喪失的狀態，伴有明顯的智力遲鈍，對刺激反應力降低。

斯 - 韋 氏 綜 合 徵 參 閱 angioma。

口吃 參閱 stammering。

聖維圖斯舞蹈 西德納姆舞蹈病的舊稱。

斯蒂卡測試 少年兒童與弱智者的標準測驗。由兒科醫生瑪麗莎瑞旦制定，用來評估其視力發育。

瞼腺炎，麥粒腫 由細菌所致的睫毛基部腺體的急性炎症。腺體變硬有觸痛感，在其中心周圍形成一充滿膿的囊。治療用熱敷或將受累睫毛拔除。醫學用語：瞼緣炎。

導 管 絲 ， 細 探 子 參 閱 stilet。

〔前綴〕**莖突** 顳骨的莖狀突起。例如莖突乳突（與莖突及乳突有關的）。

styloglossus *n.* a muscle that extends from the tongue to the styloid process of the temporal bone. It serves to draw the tongue upwards and backwards.

茎突舌肌　起自舌部止於顳骨茎突的一塊肌肉。用於牽動舌向後、向上活動。

stylohyoid *n.* a muscle that extends from the styloid process of the temporal bone to the hyoid bone. It serves to draw the hyoid bone backwards and upwards.

茎突舌骨肌　由顳骨茎突延伸到舌骨的一塊肌肉，其作用為牽拉舌骨向後、向上活動。

styloid process 1. a long slender downward-pointing spine projecting from the lower surface of the *temporal bone of the skull. It provides attachment for muscles and ligaments of the tongue and hyoid bone. **2.** any of various other spiny projections; occurring, for example, at the lower ends of the ulna and radius.

(1) 茎突　由顳顳骨的下表面伸出，指向下方的一塊細長棘狀突起，為舌、舌骨的肌肉及韌帶提供附着處。**(2) 棘狀突起**　各種其他的棘狀突起；例如見於尺骨和橈骨下端。

stylus *n.* **1.** a pencil-shaped instrument, commonly used for applying external medication; for example, to apply silver nitrate to warts. **2.** *see* stilet.

(1) 棒　筆狀工具，常用於施用外用藥，例如，用硝酸銀棒治療疣。**(2) 導管絲，細探子**　參閱 stilet。

styptic *n. see* haemostatic.

止血劑　參閱 haemostatic。

sub- *prefix denoting* **1.** below; underlying. Examples: *subcostal* (below the ribs); *sublingual* (below the tongue); *submandibular* (below the mandible). **2.** partial or slight.

〔前綴〕**(1) 下，下面的**　例如：骨下的（肋骨下的）；舌下的（舌頭下面的）；下頜下的（下頜下面的）。**(2) 亞**　部分地或輕度地。

subacute *adj.* describing a disease that progresses more rapidly than a *chronic condition but does not become *acute.

亞急性的　描述某疾病的過程快於慢性但又非急性病。

subacute combined degeneration of the cord the neurological disorder complicating a deficiency of *vitamin B$_{12}$ and pernicious anaemia. There is selective damage to the motor and sensory nerve fibres in the spinal cord, resulting in *spasticity of the limbs and a sensory *ataxia. It may also be accompanied by damage to the peripheral nerves and the

亞急性脊髓混合變性　一種神經系統疾病，合併有維生素 B$_{12}$ 缺乏與惡性貧血。脊髓運動和感覺神經纖維選擇性受損，導致肢體痙攣與感覺性共濟失調。亦可伴有周圍神經和視神經損害及癡呆症。注射維生素 B$_{12}$ 治療。

optic nerve and by dementia. It is treated by giving vitamin B$_{12}$ injections.

subacute sclerosing panencephalitis (SSPE) a rare and late complication of *measles characterized by a slow progressive neurological deterioration that is usually fatal. It can occur four to ten years after the initial infection.

亞急性硬化性全腦炎 少見的麻疹晚期併發症，以常常是致命的緩慢進行性神經系統衰退為特徵。首次感染後 4~6 年內可以發病。

subarachnoid haemorrhage bleeding into the subarachnoid space surrounding the brain, which causes severe headache with stiffness of the neck. The usual source of such a haemorrhage is a cerebral *aneurysm that has burst. The diagnosis is confirmed by CT scan or by finding blood-stained cerebrospinal fluid at *lumbar puncture. Identification of the site of the aneurysm, upon which decisions about treatment will be based, is achieved by cerebral *angiography.

蛛網膜下（腔）出血 圍繞腦的蛛網膜下腔內出血，引發劇烈頭痛和頸部強直。這種出血通常源自腦動脈瘤破裂。可通過 CT 掃描或腰椎穿刺發現血染的腦脊液來確診。動脈瘤的定位，將為治療方案決策提供依據，可做腦血管造影來獲得。

subarachnoid space the space between the arachnoid and pia *meninges of the brain and spinal cord, containing circulating cerebrospinal fluid and large blood vessels. Several large spaces within it are known as *cisternae*.

蛛網膜下腔 腦與脊髓的蛛網膜和軟膜間的空腔，腔內含腦脊髓液和大血管。腔內的幾個大的腔隙被稱為池。

subclavian artery either of two arteries supplying blood to the neck and arms. The right subclavian artery branches from the innominate artery; the left subclavian arises directly from the aortic arch.

鎖骨下動脈 向頸和臂供血的兩條動脈之一。右鎖骨下的動脈由無名動脈分枝而來，左鎖骨下動脈則直接發自主動脈弓。

subclavian steal syndrome diversion of blood from the vertebral artery to the subclavian artery when the latter is blocked proximally. It causes attacks of diminished consciousness (*syncope).

鎖骨下動脈分流綜合徵 鎖骨下動脈臨近堵塞時血從脊椎動脈轉向流入鎖骨下動脈。引發意識減弱（暈厥）。

subclinical *adj.* describing a disease that is suspected but is not sufficiently

亞臨床的 描述某一疾病受到懷疑，但在病人身上尚未發展

developed to produce definite signs and symptoms in the patient.

到足以產生體徵或症狀的程度。

subconscious *adj.* **1.** describing mental processes of which a person is not aware. **2.** (in psychoanalysis) denoting the part of the mind that includes memories, motives, and intentions that are momentarily not present in consciousness but can more or less readily be recalled to awareness. *Compare* unconscious.

(1) 下意識的　描述人無意識時的精神過程。**(2) 潛意識的**（精神分析）指思維部分包括記憶，動機和意向在片刻間不存在於意識之內，但又多少能很容易地恢復到意識狀態。與 unconscious 對比。

subcutaneous *adj.* beneath the skin. A *subcutaneous injection* is given beneath the skin. *Subcutaneous tissue* is loose connective tissue, often fatty, situated under the dermis.

皮下的　皮膚下面的。皮下注射就是注射到皮膚下面，皮下組織是疏鬆的結締組織，常為脂肪，位於真皮之下。

subdural *adj.* below the dura mater (the outermost of the meninges); relating to the space between the dura mater and arachnoid. *See also* haematoma.

硬膜下　硬膜（腦膜的最外層）之下的，與硬膜和蛛網膜之間的腔隙相關的。參閱 haematoma。

subglottis *n.* that part of the *larynx that lies below the vocal cords.

聲門下部　聲門下的喉部。

subinvolution *n.* failure of the uterus to revert to its normal size during the six weeks following childbirth.

子宮復舊不全　分娩後 6 周子宮未能恢復到正常大小。

sublimation *n.* the replacement of socially undesirable means of gratifying motives or desires by means that are socially acceptable. *See also* defence mechanism, repression.

昇華　以社會所接受的方式來取代社會所不滿意的方式從而滿足心願與願望。參閱 defence mechanism，repression。

subliminal *adj.* subconscious: beneath the threshold of conscious perception.

閾下的，下意識的　在意識知覺的閾值之下的。

sublingual gland one of a pair of *salivary glands situated in the lower part of the mouth, one on either side of the tongue. The sublingual glands are the smallest salivary glands; each gland has about 20 ducts, most of which

舌下腺　位於口腔底部，舌兩側的一對唾液腺之一。它是最小的唾液腺，每一腺體有近 20 個導管，其中多數開口在腺體上，直接朝口腔。

open into the mouth directly above the gland.

subluxation *n*. partial *dislocation of a joint, so that the bone ends are misaligned but still in contact.

不全脫位　關節部分脫位，故而關節頭錯位但仍有接觸。

submandibular gland (submaxillary gland) one of a pair of *salivary glands situated below the parotid glands. Their ducts (*Wharton's ducts*) open in two papillae under the tongue, on either side of the frenulum.

下頜下腺　位於腮腺下的一對唾液腺之一。其導管（下頜下腺管）在舌下，繫帶兩側上的兩個乳突處開口。

submaxillary gland *see* submandibular gland.

下頜下腺　參閱 submandibular gland。

submentovertical (SMV) *adj*. (in radiology) denoting a horizontal view of the base of the skull.

頦下水平位的　（放射學）顱底水平位觀察所見的。

submucosa *n*. the layer of loose connective (*areolar) tissue underlying a mucous membrane; for example, in the wall of the intestine. **–submucosal** *adj*.

黏膜下層　位於黏膜之下的疏鬆的（蜂窩狀）結締組織層；例如：腸壁內黏膜下。

subphrenic abscess a collection of pus in the space below the diaphragm, usually on the right side, between the liver and diaphragm. Causes include postoperative infection (particularly after the stomach or bowel have been opened) and perforation of an organ (e.g. perforated peptic ulcer). Prompt treatment by antibiotics may be effective, but more frequently the abscess requires surgical drainage.

膈下膿腫　膈肌下腔內積膿，常在右側，肝與膈肌之間。病因包括術後感染（尤其是胃腸手術切開後）和器官穿孔（如消化性潰瘍穿孔）。用抗生素立即治療也許有效，但更常見膿腫須作外科手術引流。

substitution *n*. **1.** (in psychoanalysis) the replacement of one idea by another: a form of *defence mechanism. **2.** *symptom substitution* is the supposed process whereby removing one psychological symptom leads to another symptom appearing if the basic

(1) 替代　（精神分析）一個觀念被另一個所取代：心理防禦機制的一種形式。**(2) 症狀更替**　據說只要基本的精神病因未除，一個精神症狀的消失會導致另一症狀的產生。是否如此，尚無定論。

psychological cause has not been removed. It is controversial whether this happens.

substitution therapy treatment by providing a less harmful alternative to a drug or remedy that a patient has been receiving. It is used when the patient has become addicted to a drug or is placing too much reliance upon a particular remedy. The patient is weaned off the 'hard' drug to which he has become addicted by the gradual substitution of a nonaddictive drug with a similar or a sedative effect.

替代療法 用一種副作用較小的藥物或治療來代替病人一直在使用的藥物或治療。該療法用於病人對某治療成癖或過分依賴某治療時。通過給予病人作用相似的或鎮靜性非成癮藥物，逐步取代病人對之成癮的藥物，從而使病人戒除麻醉品。

substrate *n.* the specific substance or substances on which a given *enzyme acts. For example, starch is the substrate for salivary amylase; RNA is the substrate for ribonuclease.

底物 特定的酶對之起作用的一種或幾種特殊物質。例如：澱粉是唾液澱粉酶的底物，核糖核酸是核糖核酸酶的底物。

subsultus *n.* abnormal twitching or tremor of muscles, such as may occur in feverish conditions.

顫跳 肌肉的異常抽搐，可能發生於發燒狀態下。

subtertian fever a form of *malaria resulting from repeated infection by *Plasmodium falciparum* and characterized by continuous fever.

惡性瘧 因惡性瘧原蟲重複感染產生的一種瘧疾類型，其特徵為持續發熱。

subthalamic nucleus a collection of grey matter, shaped like a biconvex lens, lying beneath the *thalamus and close to the *corpus striatum, to which it is connected by nerve tracts. It has connections with the cerebral certex and several other nuclei nearby.

下丘腦核團 灰質的集合體，形似雙凸鏡，位於丘腦下方，緊靠紋狀體，並通過神經束與之相連。核團與大腦皮質及附近其他幾個神經核均有聯繫。

subzonal insemination (Suzi) a method of assisting conception in cases of infertility caused by inability of the spermatozoa to penetrate the barriers surrounding the ovum. Using *in vitro fertilization techniques, a small number

帶下授精 在精子不能穿透卵子障壁而引起不育的情況下一種幫助受孕的方法。運用試管內授精技術，一小組精子（不超過 6 個）通過透明帶注射到卵黃周區（卵膜外圍）。若隨

of spermatozoa (no more than six) are injected through the *zona pellucida into the perivitelline space (which surrounds the egg membrane). If fertilization subsequently occurs, the blastocyst is implanted in the mother's uterus.

後發生受精，再將胚泡植入母體子宮內。

succus *n.* any juice or secretion of animal or plant origin.

汁，液 源自植物或動物的任何汁液或分泌物。

succus entericus (intestinal juice) the clear alkaline fluid secreted by the glands of the small intestine. It contains mucus and digestive enzymes, including *enteropeptidase, *erepsin, *lactase, and *sucrase.

腸液 由小腸內腺體分泌出的清亮鹼性液體。腸液內含腸肽酶、乳糖酶、蔗糖酶等消化酶。

succussion *n.* a splashing noise heard when a patient who has a large quantity of fluid in a body cavity, such as the pleural cavity, moves suddenly or is deliberately shaken.

振盪音 體腔，如胸腔內有大量液體的病人在突然活動或故意振動時發出的水濺般的聲響。

sucralfate *n.* an aluminium-containing drug that forms a protective coating over the stomach or duodenal lining. Administered by mouth, sucralfate is used in the treatment of peptic ulcer. A fairly common side-effect is constipation. Trade name: **Antepsin**.

硫糖鋁 含鋁藥物，可在胃及十二指腸壁內形成一保護層。口服，用於治療消化性潰瘍。常見的副作用為便秘。商品名：Antepsin。

sucrase *n.* an enzyme, secreted by glands in the small intestine, that catalyses the hydrolysis of sucrose into its components (glucose and fructose).

蔗糖酶 一種小腸腺分泌的酶，可催化蔗糖水解為其各成分（葡萄糖及果糖）。

sucrose *n.* a carbohydrate consisting of glucose and fructose. Sucrose is the principal constituent of cane sugar and sugar beet; it is the sweetest of the natural dietary carbohydrates. The increasing consumption of sucrose in the last 50 years has coincided with an increase in the incidence of dental caries, diabetes, coronary heart disease, and obesity.

蔗糖 由葡萄糖及果糖組成的碳水化合物。為甘蔗糖和甜菜糖的主要成分；天然碳水化合物性食物中最甜的一類。隨著近 50 年來人們對其消費的增加，齲病、糖尿病、冠狀動脈性心臟病及肥胖症的發病率也隨之增加。

suction *n.* the use of reduced pressure to remove unwanted fluids or other material through a tube for disposal. Suction is often used to clear secretions from the airways of newly born infants to aid breathing. During surgery, suction tubes are used to remove blood from the area of operation and to decompress the stomach (*nasogastric suction*) and the pleural space of air and blood (*chest suction*).

抽吸 用減壓的原理通過導管將不要的液體或其他物質吸出來廢棄掉。常用來清除嬰兒呼吸道中的分泌物以助其呼吸。手術中,吸管用來清除手術區的血液,使胃部 (鼻胃抽吸) 及胸腔 (胸部抽吸) 的空氣及血液減壓。

Sudan stains a group of azo compounds used for staining fats. The group includes *Sudan I*, *Sudan II*, *Sudan III*, *Sudan IV*, and *Sudan black*.

蘇丹染液 一組偶氮化合物,用作脂肪染色,其中包括蘇丹 I、蘇丹 II、蘇丹 III、蘇丹 IV 及蘇丹黑。

sudden infant death syndrome (SIDS) *see* cot death.

嬰兒猝死綜合徵 參閱 cot death。

Sudek's atrophy rapid development of *osteoporosis in a hand or foot, sometimes resulting from injury, infection, or malignancy.

祖德克萎縮 骨質疏鬆症在手或足部的急性發展,有時由外傷、感染或惡性腫瘤所致。

sudor *n. see* sweat.

汗 參閱 sweat。

sudorific *n. see* diaphoretic.

發汗藥 參閱 diaphoretic。

suffocation *n.* cessation of breathing as a result of drowning, smothering, etc., leading to unconsciousness or death (*see* asphyxia).

窒息 因溺水或濃烟燻嗆等引起的,導致失去知覺或死亡的呼吸停止 (參閱 asphyxia)。

suffusion *n.* the spreading of a flush across the skin surface, caused by changes in the local blood supply.

漲紅 皮膚表面的泛紅,因局部供血變化所致。

sugar any *carbohydrate that dissolves in water, is usually crystalline, and has a sweet taste. Sugars are classified chemically as *monosaccharides or *disaccharides. Table sugar is virtually 100% pure *sucrose and contains no other nutrient; brown sugar is less highly refined sucrose. Sugar is used as both a sweetening

糖 任何可水解的碳水化合物,常為結晶態,具甜味。化學上將其分為單糖或二糖。食糖實際上為 100% 的純蔗糖,不含其他營養成分;紅糖的加工精要度稍差些。糖用作甜味劑和保存劑。參閱 fructose,glucose,lactose。

and preserving agent. *See also* fructose, glucose, lactose.

suggestion *n.* (in psychology) the process of changing people's beliefs, attitudes, or emotions by telling them that they will change. It is sometimes used as a synonym for *hypnosis. See also* autosuggestion.

暗示 （心理學）通過告訴人其信仰、態度或情感將會有所變化而使其在這些方面改變的過程。有時作為「催眠」的同義詞使用。參閱 autosuggestion。

suicide *n.* self-destruction as a deliberate act. Distinction is usually made between *attempted suicide*, when death is averted although the person concerned intended to kill himself (or herself), and *parasuicide*, when the attempt is made for reasons other than actually killing oneself. In the UK 4547 people killed themselves in 1991 (3494 of whom were men). Some 22% of these suicides were caused by overdoses and 29% by toxic gases.

自殺 蓄意進行的自我毀滅行為。常常要與企圖自殺區別開，企圖自殺是當事人有自殺企圖但自殺未遂；還要與假自殺相區別：假自殺目的並非真正要殺死自己。1991 年英國有 4547 起自殺（其中 3494 起為男性自殺）。其中 22% 是服用過劑量藥物，29% 是使用毒氣。

sulcus *n.* (*pl.* **sulci**) **1.** one of the many clefts or infoldings of the surface of the brain. The raised outfolding on each side of a sulcus is termed a *gyrus*. **2.** any of the infoldings of soft tissue in the mouth, for example between the cheek and the alveolus.

(1) 溝 大腦表面的眾多縫隙與皺褶。其兩邊凸出的褶被稱為回。**(2)** 溝 口內軟組織皺褶，例如頰與牙槽間的溝。

sulfametopyrazine *n. see* sulphonamide.

磺胺林 參閱 sulphonamide。

sulphacetamide *n.* a drug of the *sulphonamide group that is used in eye drops to treat such infections as conjunctivitis. Transient irritation may occur with higher doses. Trade names: **Albucid, Ocusol**.

乙醯磺胺 磺胺類藥物之一，製成滴眼劑治療諸如結膜炎之類的感染。大劑量可引起短暫的刺激。商品名：Albucid，Ocusol。

sulphadiazine *n. see* sulphonamide.

磺胺嘧啶 參閱 sulphonamide。

sulphadimidine *n. see* sulphonamide.

磺胺二甲嘧啶 參閱 sulphonamide。

sulpha drug *see* sulphonamide.

sulphamethoxazole *n.* a drug of the *sulphonamide group. It is taken by mouth and is effective in the treatment of infections of the respiratory tract (including bronchitis), the urinary and gastrointestinal tracts, and the skin. The drug is frequently administered in a combined preparation with trimethoprim (*see* co-trimoxazole (Bactrim, Septrin)).

sulphasalazine *n.* a drug of the *sulphonamide group, used in the treatment of ulcerative colitis. It is given by mouth or in the form of suppositories. The most common side-effects are nausea, loss of appetite, and raised temperature. Trade name: **Salazopyrin**.

sulphinpyrazone *n.* a *uricosuric drug given by mouth for the treatment of chronic gout. The main side-effects are nausea and abdominal pain; the drug may also activate a latent duodenal ulcer and it should not be taken by patients with impaired kidney function. Trade name: **Anturan**.

sulphonamide (sulpha drug) *n.* one of a group of drugs, derived from sulphanilamide (a red dye), that prevent the growth of bacteria (i.e. they are bacteriostatic). Sulphonamides are usually given by mouth and are effective against a variety of infections. Because many sulphonamides are rapidly excreted and very soluble in the urine, they are used to treat infections of the urinary tract, especially in combination with other drugs (such as *trimethoprim).

A variety of side-effects may occur with sulphonamide teatment, including nausea, vomiting, headache, and loss of

磺胺藥　參閱 sulphonamide。

磺胺甲基異噁唑　磺胺類藥物之一。口服，對於治療呼吸道感染（包括支氣管炎在內），尿道、胃腸道及皮膚感染有效。常與磺胺甲氧苄啶製成合劑片服用（參閱 co-trimoxazole (Bactrim，Septrin)）。

柳氮磺胺吡啶　磺胺類藥物之一，用以治療潰瘍性結腸炎。口服或製成栓劑。最常見的副作用是惡心、無食慾及體溫升高。商品名：Salazopyrin。

苯磺唑酮　一種促尿酸尿藥物，口服，治療慢性痛風。主要副作用是惡心及腹痛，亦可激活潛在的十二指腸潰瘍。腎功能不全者禁用。商品名：Anturan。

磺胺（磺胺藥）　源自氨苯磺胺（一種紅色顏料）的一類藥物，具有抑止細菌生長的（抑菌）作用。口服，治療多種感染有效。許多磺胺能迅速排泄並且易於在尿中溶解，所以用來治療尿道感染，特別是採取與其他藥物聯合用藥的方式（如甲氧苄啶）。

　　磺胺類治療可產生多種副作用，如惡心、嘔吐、頭痛、無食慾；更為嚴重的副作用還有紫紺、血液疾病、皮疹和發熱。因細菌對磺胺類藥物的抵抗力在增加，並且隨着更有效

appetite; more severe effects include *cyanosis, blood disorders, skin rashes, and fever. Because of increasing bacterial resistance to sulphonamides, and with the development of more effective less toxic antibiotics, the clinical use of these drugs has declined. Those still used include *sulphacetamide, *sulphamethoxazole, *sulphasalazine, *sulphadimidine*, *sulphadiazine*, and *sulfametopyrazine*.

且毒性更小的抗生素的發展，這類藥物的臨床應用已經減少。仍在使用的包括：乙醯磺胺、磺胺甲基異噁唑、柳氮磺胺吡啶、磺胺二甲嘧啶、磺胺嘧啶及磺胺林。

sulphone *n.* one of a group of drugs closely related to the *sulphonamides in structure and therapeutic actions. Sulphones possess powerful activity against the bacteria that cause leprosy and tuberculosis. The best known sulphone is *dapsone.

碸 在結構與治療作用上與磺胺非常相近的一組藥物。具有強大的抗麻風病和結核病菌的作用。其中最著名的是氨苯碸。

sulphonylurea *n.* one of a group of *oral hypoglycaemic drugs, derived from a *sulphonamide, that are used in the treatment of noninsulin-dependent diabetes mellitus; they act by stimulating the islet cells in the pancreas to produce more insulin. The group includes *chlorpropamide, *tolazamide, *glibenclamide, and *tolbutamide.

磺胺醯脲 一組口服降血糖藥，由磺胺衍生而來，用於治療非胰島素依賴性糖尿病。通過刺激胰島細胞產生更多的胰島素來起作用。該組藥中有氯磺丙脲，妥拉磺脲，格列本脲和甲苯磺丁脲。

sulphur *n.* a nonmetallic element that is active against fungi and parasites. It is a constituent of ointments and other preparations used in the treatment of skin disorders and infections (such as psoriasis and dermatitis).

硫 一種非金屬元素，抗真菌及寄生蟲作用活躍。含硫軟膏和其他製劑的組成部分，用於治療皮膚病和感染（如銀屑病及皮炎）。

sulphuric acid a powerful corrosive acid, H_2SO_4, widely used in industry. Swallowing the acid causes severe burning of the mouth and throat and difficulty in breathing, speaking, and swallowing. The patient should drink large quantities of milk or water or white of egg; gastric lavage should not be delayed.

硫酸 強腐蝕性酸，分子式為 H_2SO_4，廣泛應用於工業。吞咽該酸引起口腔、咽部嚴重燒傷及呼吸、講話和吞咽困難，病人需飲入大量乳、水或蛋清，立即洗胃，不得拖延。皮膚或眼接觸者用水沖洗傷處。

Skin or eye contact should be treated by flooding the area with water.

sumatriptan *n.* a drug that blocks the effects of *serotonin and is effective in the treatment of acute *migraine by selectively constricting blood vessels to the brain. It is administered by mouth or by subcutaneous injection. Possible side-effects include dizziness, drowsiness, fatigue, chest pain, and a rise in blood pressure. Trade name: **Imigran**.

sunburn *n.* damage to the skin by prolonged or unaccustomed exposure to the sun's rays. Sunburn may vary from reddening of the skin to the development of large painful fluid-filled blisters, which may cause shock if they cover a large area (*see* burn). Fair-skinned red-haired people are more susceptible to sunburn than others.

sunstroke *n. see* heatstroke.

super- *prefix denoting* **1.** above; overlying. **2.** extreme or excessive.

superciliary *adj.* of or relating to the eye-brows (supercilia).

superego *n.* (in psychoanalysis) the part of the mind that functions as a moral conscience or judge. It is also responsible for the formation of ideals for the *ego. The superego is the result of the incorporation of parental injunctions into the child's mind.

superfecundation *n.* the fertilization of two or more ova of the same age by spermatozoa from different males. *See* superfetation.

superfetation *n.* the fertilization of a second ovum some time after the start of

舒馬坦 抑制 5-羥色胺作用的一種藥物，治療急性偏頭痛有效，作用途徑是有選擇地收縮通向大腦的血管。口服或皮下注射給藥。可能出現的副作用包括有頭暈、嗜睡、四肢無力，胸部疼痛、血壓升高。商品名：Imigran。

曬傷 長時間日光曝曬或皮膚不適應日光曝曬而造成的損害。其程度變化不等，從皮膚發紅到疼痛的大水泡出現，後者如面積大可致休克（參閱 burn）。膚色白皙、髮色紅棕者比其他人更易受到曬傷。

日射病 參閱 heatstroke。

〔前綴〕(1) 在上　上面的。**(2)** 極，超

眉的 眼眉的或與眼眉有關的。

超我 （精神分析）作為道德良心或道德裁判起作用的那部分意識。亦負責構築自我理想。超我是父母作用與兒童心理結合為一體的結果。

同期複孕 同期的二個或多個卵子由來自不同的精子同時受精的現象。參閱 superfetation。

異期受孕 在妊娠開始後的一段時間內有第二個卵子受精，

pregnancy, resulting in two fetuses of different maturity in the same uterus.

造成同一子宮內存在兩個不同成熟程度的胎兒的現象。

superficial *adj.* (in anatomy) situated at or close to a surface. Superficial blood vessels are those close to the surface of the skin.

淺表的 （解剖學）位於或靠近表面的。淺血管是指那些靠近皮膚表層的血管。

superinfection *n.* an infection arising during the course of another infection and caused by a different microorganism, which is usually resistant to the drugs used to treat the primary infection. The infective agent may be a normally harmless inhabitant of the body that becomes pathogenic when other harmless types are removed by the drugs or it may be a resistant variety of the primary infective agent.

重複感染 在某一感染過程中出現的另一種由不同微生物引發的感染。這種微生物常對原發感染的治療藥物有抗藥性。這種微生物正常時是身體的無害棲居者，而在當其他類無害菌被藥物清除後它則變為致病性的，或者它也可以是原發感染病菌中的一種耐藥菌株。

superior *adj.* (in anatomy) situated uppermost in the body in relation to another structure or surface.

在上的 （解剖學）與其他結構或表面相比較居於身體的最上面的。

supernumerary *n.* (in dentistry) an additional tooth.

額外牙 （牙科學）一顆多餘的牙。

superovulation 1. controlled hyperstimulation of the ovary to produce more follicles with oocytes. Usually induced by drugs (e.g. *clomiphene), it is performed in *in vitro fertilization and other procedures of assisted conception in order to improve the pregnancy rates. **2.** uncontrolled hyperstimulation of the ovary (*ovarian hyperstimulation syndrome*), an abnormal response of the ovaries leading to multiple follicle production. It may be associated with abdominal pain, ascites, oliguria, or even renal failure. Thromboembolism is the most dangerous complication.

排卵過多 **(1)** 有控制下的卵巢過度興奮以從卵母細胞產生更多卵泡。常由藥物（如氯米芬）引發，用於試管內授精和其他人工授精中，以提高受孕比率。**(2)** 無控制下的卵巢過度興奮（卵巢過度興奮綜合徵），卵巢的非正常反應將導致卵泡生產的倍增。可能會伴有腹痛、腹水、少尿或甚至腎衰竭。最危險的併發症為血栓栓塞。

supination *n.* the act of turning the hand so that the palm is uppermost. *Compare* pronation.

旋後 轉動手從而使手掌朝上的動作。與 pronation 對比。

supinator *n.* a muscle of the forearm that extends from the elbow to the shaft of the radius. It supinates the forearm and hand.

旋後肌　自肘部延展到橈骨幹的前臂肌肉。使前臂與手旋後。

supine *adj.* **1.** lying on the back or with the face upwards. **2.** (of the forearm) in the position in which the palm of the hand faces upwards. *Compare* prone.

(1) 仰臥的　靠背躺下，面朝上的。**(2) 旋後的**　（前臂的）手掌面朝上的位置的。與 prone 對比。

supplementary benefit a cash payment formerly made from exchequer funds to those over 16 whose income was below a certain minimum. From April 1988 it was replaced by *income support.

補充救濟金　（英國）過去，從國庫基金中支給 16 歲以上、收入低於某一最低綫之人的現金。從 1988 年 4 月起已由收入津貼所取代。

suppository *n.* a medicinal preparation in solid form suitable for insertion into the rectum or vagina. *Rectal suppositories* may contain simple lubricants (e.g. glycerin); drugs that act locally in the rectum or anus (e.g. corticosteroids, local anaesthetics); or drugs that are absorbed and act at other sites (e.g. *bronchodilators). *Vaginal suppositories* are used in the treatment of some gynaecological disorders (*see* pessary).

栓劑　固體醫學製劑，適用於塞入直腸或陰道內。直腸栓劑可含有單一的潤滑劑（如甘油）；局部作用於直腸或肛門的藥物（如皮質類固醇，局部麻醉劑）；或吸收後在其他部位發揮作用的藥物（如支氣管擴張藥）。陰道栓劑用於治療某些婦科病（參閱 pessary）。

suppression *n.* **1.** the cessation or complete inhibition of any physiological activity. **2.** treatment that removes the outward signs of an illness or prevents its progress. **3.** (in psychology) a *defence mechanism by which a person consciously and deliberately ignores an idea that is unpleasant to him.

(1) 抑制　生理活動的靜息或完全被抑制住的狀態。**(2) 控制**　消除疾病的外在體徵或阻止其進展的治療。**(3) 壓抑**（心理學）一種心理防禦機制，通過壓抑使人有意識地、蓄意地忽視某些使他不愉快的思想。

suppuration *n.* the formation of pus.

化膿　膿液的形成。

supra- *prefix denoting* above; over. Examples: *supraclavicular* (above the clavicle); *suprahyoid* (above the hyoid bone); *suprarenal* (above the kidney).

〔前綴〕在上，上方的　例如：鎖骨上的（在鎖骨上的），舌骨上的（在舌骨上的），腎上的（在腎上的）。

supraglottis *n.* that part of the *larynx that lies above the vocal cords and includes the *epiglottis.

supraorbital *adj.* of or relating to the area above the eye orbit.

supraorbital reflex the closing of the eyelids when the supraorbital nerve is struck, due to contraction of the muscle surrounding the orbit (orbicularis oculi muscle).

supraregional specialty *see* catchment area.

suprarenal glands *see* adrenal glands.

supravital staining the application of a *stain to living tissue, particularly blood cells, removed from the body.

suramin *n.* a nonmetallic drug used in the treatment of *trypanosomiasis. It is usually given by slow intravenous injection. Side-effects, which vary in intensity and frequency and are related to the nutritional state of the patient, include nausea, vomiting, shock, and loss of consciousness.

surfactant *n.* a wetting agent. *Pulmonary surfactant*, secreted by type I *pneumocytes, is a complex mixture of compounds (including lipids, protein, and carbohydrates) that prevents the air sacs (alveoli) of the lungs from collapsing by reducing surface tension. In its absence, as in the immature lungs of premature babies, *atelectasis and *respiratory distress syndrome will develop.

surgeon *n.* a qualified medical practitioner who specializes in surgery. *See* Doctor.

聲門上的　聲帶上方的喉部，包括會厭在內。

眶上的　眼眶上方區域的或與該區域有關的。

眶上反射　眶上神經受到碰擊時，由於眶周圍肌（眼輪匝肌）收縮，使眼瞼閉合。

跨地區專科　參閱 catchment area。

腎上腺　參閱 adrenal glands。

體外活體染色　對活組織、特別是離體血細胞加以染色。

蘇拉明　非金屬藥物，用於治療錐蟲病。常以緩慢的靜脈注射給藥。副作用因用藥強度與頻率的不同而不同，與病人的營養狀況有關，其中有惡心、嘔吐、休克及意識喪失。

表面活性物質　濕潤劑。由 I 型肺細胞分泌的肺表面活性物質，是一種多種化合物（包括脂類、蛋白質和碳水化合物）組成的複合物，可防止因表面張力降低引起的肺泡塌陷。在早產兒尚未成熟的肺中，因缺乏這種物質，可發生肺塌陷及呼吸窘迫綜合徵。

外科醫師　獲得行醫資格，專修外科的醫師。參閱 Doctor。

surgery *n.* the branch of medicine that treats injuries, deformities, or disease by operation or manipulation. *See also* cryosurgery, microsurgery. **–surgical** *adj.*

外科學 用手術或手法操作治療外傷、畸形及疾病的醫學分支。參閱 cryosurgery，microsurgery。

surgical neck the constriction of the shaft of the *humerus, below the head. It is frequently the point at which fracture of the humerus occurs.

外科頸 肱骨頭下，骨幹的狹窄部分，在此位置好發肱骨骨折。

surgical spirit methylated spirit, usually with small amounts of castor oil and oil of wintergreen: used to sterilize the skin before surgery, injections, etc.

外科酒精 含甲醇之酒精，常含少量蓖麻油及冬青油：用於手術、注射等前的皮膚消毒。

surrogate *n.* **1.** (in psychology) a person or object in someone's life that functions as a substitute for another person. In the treatment of sexual problems, when the patient does not have a partner to cooperate in treatment, a surrogate provided by the therapist acts as a sexual partner who gives service to the patient up to and including intercourse. According to psychoanalysts, people and objects in dreams can be surrogates for important individuals in a person's life. **2.** (in reproduction) *see* surrogate mother.

(1) 替身 （心理學）一個人或物在某人的生活中起着作為另外一人的替代品的作用。在性生活障礙之治療中，如病人沒有治療合作伙伴，由治療師提供的替身就要充當病人的性伴侶，該人要給病人提供服務並包括與病人性交。據精神分析學家認為：夢中的人或物可能是個人生活中重要人物的替身。**(2) 替身母親** （繁殖）參閱 surrogate mother。

surrogate mother a woman who becomes pregnant (by artificial insemination or embryo insertion) following an arrangement made with another party (usually a couple unable themselves to have children) in which she agrees to hand over the child she carries to that party when it is born. Such an arrangement is made on the understanding that no payment is involved between either parties. Certain activities in connection with surrogacy are regulated by the Surrogacy Arrangements Act 1985: it is unlawful for any form of advertisement to be employed, and for

替身母親 一婦女按照與另一對夫婦（常為自己不能懷孩子的夫婦）所訂的協議受孕（通過人工受精或胚胎植入的方式）。協議中她同意在她所懷的孩子出世時把孩子交給那對夫婦。協議是基於理解雙方之間不涉及任何付款問題而制定的。（在英國）與此相關的某些活動由 1985 年替身受孕安排法來加以規範：使用任何形式的廣告為非法行為，任何從事替身母親委托業務商業性代辦處亦為非法。

commercial agencies to commission surrogate mothers.

susceptibility *n.* lack of resistance to disease. It is partly a reflection of general health but is also influenced by vaccination or other methods of increasing resistance to specific diseases.

易感性　缺乏抗病能力。易感性部分地反映了全身的健康體狀況，但亦可通過接種疫苗或其他方法來提高對特定疾病的抵抗力。

suspensory bandage a bandage arranged to support a hanging part of the body. Examples include a sling used to hold an injured lower jaw in position and a bandage used to support the scrotum in various conditions of the male genital organs.

懸吊帶　一種為支托身體懸吊部分所用的繃帶。例如用以使受傷下頜保持合適位置的吊帶及患不同男性生殖器疾病時用以支托陰囊的繃帶。

suspensory ligament a ligament that serves to support or suspend an organ in position. For example, the suspensory ligament of the lens is a fibrous structure attached to the ciliary processes (*see* ciliary body) by means of which the lens of the eye is held in position.

懸韌帶　用來將器官支住或懸吊於適當位置的韌帶。例如，晶狀體懸韌帶是纖維性結構，附着於睫狀突（參閱 ciliary body），它將眼晶狀體保持在適當的位置上。

sustentaculum *n.* any anatomical structure that supports another structure. **–sustentacular** *adj.*

支持物　任何支持其他結構的解剖結構。

suture 1. *n.* (in anatomy) a type of immovable joint, found particularly in the skull, that is characterized by a minimal amount of connective tissue between the two bones. The cranial sutures include the *coronal suture*, between the frontal and parietal bones; the *lambdoidal suture*, between the parietal and occipital bones; and the *sagittal suture*, between the two parietal bones (see illustration). **2.** *n.* (in surgery) the closure of a wound or incision with material such as silk or catgut, to facilitate the healing process. There is a wide variety of suturing techniques developed to meet the differing circumstances of injuries to and incisions in the body

(1) 縫　（解剖學）一種不能活動的關節類型，多見於顱骨，以兩骨間極少量的結締組織為特徵。顱縫包括：冠狀縫，位於額骨及頂骨之間；人字縫，位於頂骨及枕骨之間；矢狀縫，位於兩頂骨之間（見圖）。(2) 縫合術　（外科學）用絲線或腸線等材料使傷口或創口縫合住從而促進愈合過程。針對身體組織不同的損傷及創口情況有多種多樣的縫合技術（見圖）。(3) 縫線　用來縫合創口的材料例如絲線、腸線、尼龍線或金屬絲。(4) 縫合　用縫線來合住傷口。

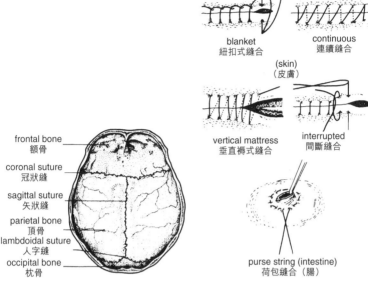

blanket
紐扣式縫合

continuous
連續縫合

(skin)
（皮膚）

vertical mattress
垂直褥式縫合

interrupted
間斷縫合

purse string (intestine)
荷包縫合（腸）

Types of surgical suture
各種外科縫合術式

frontal bone
額骨

coronal suture
冠狀縫

sagittal suture
矢狀縫

parietal bone
頂骨

lambdoidal suture
人字縫

occipital bone
枕骨

Sutures of the skull (internal surface of
the vault)
顱骨諸縫（顱骨穹窿的內表面）

tissues (see illustration). **3.** *n.* the material – silk, catgut, nylon, or wire – used to sew up a wound. **4.** *vb.* to close a wound by suture.

suxamethonium *n.* a drug that relaxes voluntary muscle (*see* muscle relaxant). It is administered by intravenous injection and is used mainly to produce muscle relaxation during surgery carried out under general anaesthesia and to reduce muscular movements occurring during *electroconvulsive therapy. Trade names: **Anectine**, **Scoline**.

琥珀膽鹼　鬆弛隨意肌的藥物（參閱 muscle relaxant）。靜脈注射，主要用於在全身麻醉情況下進行外科手術時產生肌肉鬆弛以及在電驚厥治療中減少肌肉活動。商品名：Anectine，Scoline。

Suzi *see* subzonal insemination.

帶下授精　參閱 subzonal insemination。

swab *n.* a pad of absorbent material (such as cotton), sometimes attached to

拭子，藥簽　一小塊吸水性材料（如棉花），有時貼附於細

a stick or wire, used for cleaning out or applying medication to wounds, operation sites, or body cavities. In operations, gauze swabs are used to clean blood from the site; such swabs are always carefully counted and contain a *radiopaque 'tag' to facilitate identification should it by mischance remain in the body after operation.

棍或金屬絲上，用以對創口、手術部位或體腔進行清潔或給藥。手術時，拭子用以清除手術部位血液；這些拭子需經常仔細清點數目並帶有不透 X 綫標記以便於萬一由於手術後疏忽遺留在體內時方便查出。

swallowing (deglutition) *n.* the process by which food is transferred from the mouth to the oesophagus (gullet). Voluntary raising of the tongue forces food backwards towards the pharynx. This stimulates reflex actions in which the larynx is closed by the epiglottis and the nasal passages are closed by the soft palate, so that food does not enter the trachea (windpipe). Lastly, food moves down the oesophagus by *peristalsis and gravity.

吞咽 食物由口進入食管的過程。舌隨意的抬起迫使食物向後朝咽部運動。這一刺激引起反射活動：喉部被會厭閉合，鼻通道為軟腭關閉，因此食物不會進入氣管。最後借食管蠕動及重力作用，食物沿食管下行。

Swan-Ganz catheter a catheter with an inflatable balloon at its tip, which can be inserted into the pulmonary artery via the right chambers of the heart. Inflation of the balloon enables measurement of pressure in the left atrium and hence pulmonary artery pressure.

斯-甘氏導管 一頭帶有一可充氣的小氣球的管子，由左心室可將該管植入肺動脈。將小球充氣，能夠測出左心房的壓力進而可測出肺動脈壓。

sweat *n.* the watery fluid secreted by the *sweat glands. Its principal constituents in solution are sodium chloride and urea. The secretion of sweat is a means of excreting nitrogenous waste; at the same time it has a role in controlling the temperature of the body – the evaporation of sweat from the surface of the skin has a cooling effect. Therefore an increase in body temperature causes an increase in sweating. Other factors that increase the secretion of sweat include pain, nausea, nervousness, and drugs (*diaphoretics). Sweating is reduced by colds, diarrhoea,

汗 由汗腺分泌的水樣液體。其溶液中的主要組成成分為氯化鈉和尿素。分泌汗液是一種排除氮廢物途徑，同時在控制體溫方面亦起到一定作用：汗從表皮蒸發走具有降溫效應。其他增加汗分泌的因素有疼痛、惡心、緊張及藥物（發汗藥）。寒冷、腹瀉及某些藥物則減少泌汗。解剖學用語：汗。

and certain drugs. Anatomical name: **sudor**.

sweat gland a simple coiled tubular *exocrine gland that lies in the dermis of the *skin. A long duct carries its secretion (*sweat) to the surface of the skin. Sweat glands occur over most of the surface of the body; they are particularly abundant in the armpits, on the soles of the feet and palms of the hands, and on the forehead.

汗腺　皮膚真皮層內一圈一圈纏繞起來的單管外分泌腺。有一長導管將分泌物（汗）引向皮膚表面。汗腺在大部分體表均有分布，尤其以腋窩、腳底、手掌以及額部最為豐富。

sycosis *n.* inflammation of the hair follicles caused by infection with *Staphylococcus aureus*; it commonly affects the beard area (*sycosis barbae*) of men in their thirties or forties. The infection usually spreads unless treated by applying antibiotic ointments or giving antibiotics by mouth.

鬚瘡　金黃色葡萄球菌感染所致的毛囊發炎；三四十歲男性的鬍鬚部位常受感染（葡萄球菌性鬚瘡）。除非使用抗生素軟膏或口服抗生素治療，否則感染會擴大。

symbiosis *n.* an intimate and obligatory association between two different species of organism (*symbionts*) in which there is mutual aid and benefit. *Compare* commensal, mutualism, parasite.

共生　兩個不同種的有機體（共生物）之間親密及相互依存的聯繫，而這種聯繫是互助互利性質的。與 commensal，mutualism，parasite 對比。

symblepharon *n.* a condition in which the eyelid adheres to the eyeball. It is usually the result of chemical (especially alkali) burns to the conjunctiva lining the eyelid and eyeball.

瞼球黏連　眼瞼與眼球黏在一起。通常為眼瞼和眼球的結膜被化學物質（尤其是鹼）灼傷所致。

symbolism *n.* (in psychology) the process of representing an object or an idea by something else. Typically an abstract idea is represented by a simpler and more tangible image. Psychoanalytic theorists hold that conscious ideas frequently act as symbols for unconscious thoughts and that this is particularly evident in dreaming, in *free association, and in the formation of psychological

象徵主義　（心理學）以其他某物代表某客體或觀念的過程。以較簡單或較實在的表象來代表一抽象概念是一種典型。精神分析學家認為意識觀念常充當非意識觀念的象徵，這一點在夢中、在自由聯想中、在精神病症狀的形成中尤為明顯。根據這一理論，一個症狀（如吞咽困難）可能是一種無意識

symptoms. According to this theory, a symptom (such as difficulty in swallowing) might be a symbolic representation of an unconscious idea (such as a fantasy of oral intercourse). **–symbolic** *adj.*

觀念（如經口性交幻想）的象徵性符號。

symmelia *n.* a developmental abnormality in which the legs appear to be fused.

並腿畸形 一種出現兩腿融合的非正常發育。

symmetry *n.* (in anatomy) the state of opposite parts of an organ or parts at opposite sides of the body corresponding to each other.

對稱 （解剖學）器官的兩個相對部分或身體的兩側相互一致的狀況。

sympathectomy *n.* the surgical *division of sympathetic nerve fibres. It is done to minimize the effects of normal or excessive sympathetic activity. Most often it is used to improve the circulation to part of the body; less commonly to inhibit excess sweating or to relieve the *photophobia induced by an abnormally dilated pupil of the eye.

交感神經切除術 外科分離交感神經纖維。這樣做是為了將正常或過高的交感神經活動減到最小。最常用來改善身體某部分的循環；其次為抑制泌汗過多，或解除眼瞳孔異常擴大所致的畏光。

sympathetic nervous system one of the two divisions of the *autonomic nervous system, having fibres that leave the central nervous system, via a chain of ganglia close to the spinal cord, in the thoracic and lumbar regions. Its nerves are distributed to the blood vessels, heart, lungs, intestines and other abdominal organs, sweat glands, salivary glands, and the genitals, whose functions it governs by reflex action, in balance with the *parasympathetic nervous system.

交感神經系統 自主神經系統的兩部分之一，其纖維發自中樞神經系統，通過緊鄰脊柱的胸腰部神經節鏈繼續行走。其神經分布於血管、心臟、肺部、腸及其他腹部器官、汗腺、唾液腺及生殖器，其神經通過反射活動調控這些器官的功能，與副交感神經系統相協調。

sympathin *n.* the name given by early physiologists to the substances released from sympathetic nerve endings, now known to be a mixture of *adrenaline and *noradrenaline.

交感素 早期生理學家為交感神經末梢釋放物質所起名稱，現已知為腎上腺素和去甲腎上腺素的混合物。

sympathoblast *n.* one of the small cells formed in the early development of nerve tissue that eventually become the neurones of the sympathetic nervous system.

成交感神經細胞　神經組織早期發育時生成的一種小細胞，最終將成為交感神經系統的神經元。

sympatholytic *n.* a drug that opposes the effects of the sympathetic nervous system. Drugs such as *guanethidine and *methyldopa block the transmission of impulses along adrenergic nerves; they are used to treat high blood pressure. *Alpha blockers, such as *phentolamine, block alpha-adrenergic receptors, causing – in particular – dilatation of peripheral blood vessels; they are used for disorders of the circulation or to lower the blood pressure. *Beta blockers, such as *propranolol, selectively block the beta-adrenergic receptors and principally affect the heart.

抗交感神經藥，交感神經阻滯藥　對抗交感神經系統效應的藥物。像胍乙啶和甲基多巴之類的藥物具阻斷沿腎上腺素能神經傳導衝動之作用，可用以治療高血壓。α-受體阻滯劑，諸如酚妥拉明，阻斷 α-腎上腺素能受體，引起（主要為）外周血管擴張，用於治療循環障礙與降低血壓。β-受體阻滯劑，諸如普萘洛爾，選擇性阻斷 β-腎上腺素能受體，並且主要影響心臟。

sympathomimetic *n.* a drug that has the effect of stimulating the *sympathetic nervous system. The actions of sympathomimetic drugs are *adrenergic* (resembling those of *noradrenaline). *Alpha-adrenergic* stimulants, such as *phenylephrine, constrict blood vessels in the skin and intestine and are used in nasal decongestants; *beta-adrenergic* drugs, such as *salbutamol, *salmeterol, and *terbutaline, relax bronchial smooth muscle and are used as *bronchodilators. Some beta-adrenergic drugs, e.g. *ephedrine and *isoprenaline, are less selective and also stimulate beta receptors in the heart, producing an increased heart rate; if used as bronchodilators, these drugs may have unwanted side-effects on the heart.

擬交感神經藥　具有刺激交感神經系統興奮作用的藥。其作用為腎上腺素能性（類似去甲腎上腺素）。α-腎上腺素能藥物，如苯福林，收縮皮膚和腸道的血管，且可用於消除鼻充血；β-腎上腺素能藥，諸如沙丁胺醇、沙美特羅、及特布他林，鬆弛支氣管平滑肌，故可用作支氣管擴張藥。某些 β-腎上腺素能藥，如麻黃素和異丙腎上腺素，其作用的選擇性較少且刺激心臟內的 β-受體，產生心跳加快；故而如用作支氣管擴張藥，這些藥會對心臟產生意外的副作用。

sympathy *n.* (in physiology) a reciprocal influence exercised by different parts of the body on one another.

交感作用　（生理學）身體不同部位相互間受到對方的影響。

symphysiotomy *n.* the operation of cutting through the front of the pelvis at the pubic *symphysis in order to enlarge the diameter of the pelvis and aid delivery of a fetus whose head is too large to pass through the pelvic opening. This procedure is now rarely employed.

恥骨聯合切開術 由骨盆前面手術切開到恥骨聯合處，以擴大骨盆直徑，幫助頭部過大的嬰兒通過骨盆開口處分娩。此技術現已很少使用。

symphysis *n.* **1.** a joint in which the bones are separated by fibrocartilage, which minimizes movement and makes the bony structure rigid. Examples are the *pubic symphysis* (the joint between the pubic bones of the pelvis) and the joints of the backbone, which are separated by intervertebral discs (see illustration). **2.** the line that marks the fusion of two bones that were separate at an early stage of development, such as the symphysis of the *mandible.

聯合 **(1)** 以纖維軟骨隔開兩骨的關節，這種關節將骨活動降至最低限度並使骨結構硬直。例如恥骨聯合（骨盆兩恥骨間的關節）以及脊柱關節，該關節由椎間盤隔開（見圖）。**(2)** 標記出發育早期兩骨曾分離後又融合的綫。如下頜聯合。

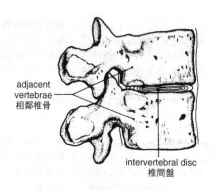

adjacent vertebrae
相鄰椎骨

intervertebral disc
椎間盤

Symphysis between two vertebrae
兩椎骨間的聯合

sympodia (sirenomelia) *n.* a developmental abnormality in which there is fusion of the legs with absence of the feet.

無足並腿畸形 兩腿融合且無雙足的非正常發育。

symptom *n.* an indication of a disease or disorder noticed by the patient himself.

症狀 由病人自己覺察到的疾病或障礙的表現。出現的當前

A *presenting symptom* is one that leads a patient to consult a doctor. *Compare* sign.

症狀是促使病人就醫的原因。與 sign 對比。

symptomatology (semeiology) *n*. **1.** the branch of medicine concerned with the study of symptoms of disease. **2.** the symptoms of a disease, collectively.

病症學 **(1)** 關於症狀研究的醫學分支。**(2)** 某疾病所有症狀之總稱。

syn- (sym-) *prefix denoting* union or fusion.

〔前綴〕聯合，融合

synalgia *n*. see referred pain.

連帶痛 參閱 referred pain。

synapse *n*. the minute gap across which *nerve impulses pass from one neurone to the next, at the end of a nerve fibre. Reaching a synapse, an impulse causes the release of a *neurotransmitter, which diffuses across the gap and triggers an electrical impulse in the next neurone. Some brain cells have more than 15,000 synapses. *See also* neuromuscular junction.

突觸 神經衝動在神經纖維末梢由一個神經元傳到下一個神經元所要跨越的微小間隙。衝動抵達突觸時引起神經遞質的釋放，遞質擴散此間隙，觸發下一個神經元產生電衝動。某些大腦細胞具有15 000個以上突觸。參閱 neuromuscular junction。

synarthrosis *n*. an immovable joint in which the bones are united by fibrous tissue. Examples are the cranial *sutures. *See also* gomphosis, schindylesis.

不動關節 由纖維組織將兩骨聯在一起的不活動關節。例如顱骨縫。參閱 gomphosis，schindylesis。

synchilia (syncheilia) *n*. congenital fusion of the lips.

並唇畸形 先天性雙唇融合。

synchondrosis *n*. a slightly movable joint (*see* amphiarthrosis) in which the surfaces of the bones are separated by hyaline cartilage, as occurs between the ribs and sternum. This cartilage may become ossified in later development, as between the *epiphyses and shaft of a long bone.

軟骨結合 有輕微活動性的關節（參閱 amphiarthrosis）。兩骨面由透明軟骨隔開，如肋骨與胸骨之間的關節。發育晚期時透明軟骨骨化，例如長骨骺和幹之間的軟骨。

syncope (fainting) *n*. loss of consciousness induced by a temporarily insufficient flow of blood to the brain. It

暈厥 失去意識，因腦部短暫血流不足所致。常見於其他方面健康的人，由於情緒打擊、

commonly occurs in otherwise healthy people and may be caused by an emotional shock, by standing for prolonged periods, or by injury and profuse bleeding. An attack comes on gradually, with lightheadedness, sweating, and blurred vision. Recovery is normally prompt and without any persisting ill-effects.

長時站立、外傷、大出血引起。發作逐漸開始,頭暈眼花、出汗及視力模糊漸次出現。一般能迅速恢復,並且不留任何持續性不良後果。

syncytiotrophoblast *n. see* plasmoditrophoblast.

合胞體滋養層 參閱 plasmoditrophoblast。

syncytium *n.* (*pl.* **syncytia**) a mass of *protoplasm containing several nuclei. Muscle fibres are syncytia. **–syncytial** *adj.*

合胞體 多核的原漿質體。肌纖維即為合胞體。

syndactyly *n.* congenital fusion of the fingers or toes. It varies in severity from no more than marked webbing of two or more fingers to virtually complete union of all the digits.

並指(趾)畸形 手指或腳趾的先天性融合。其嚴重程度不等,輕則兩或多指(趾)間有不明顯的指(趾)蹼,重則所有指(趾)節完全融合。

syndesm- (syndesmo-) *prefix denoting* connective tissue, particularly ligaments.

〔前綴〕**結締組織** 尤指韌帶。

syndesmology *n.* the branch of anatomy dealing with joints and their components.

韌帶學 研究關節及其組成部分的解剖學分支。

syndesmophyte *n.* a vertical outgrowth of bone from a vertebra, seen in ankylosing *spondylitis, *Reiter's syndrome, and *psoriatic arthritis. Fusion of syndesmophytes across the joints between vertebrae contributes to rigidity of the spine, seen in advanced cases of these diseases.

韌帶骨贅 脊柱骨上長出的與之垂直的突出物,見於強直性脊椎炎、賴特爾綜合徵及銀屑病性關節炎中。韌帶骨贅在脊椎間發生跨關節的融合可致脊椎強直,見於上述疾病的嚴重情況下。

syndesmosis *n.* an immovable joint in which the bones are separated by connective tissue. An example is the articulation between the bases of the tibia and fibula (see illustration).

韌帶聯合 由結締組織隔開的不活動關節。脛骨與腓骨底之間關節便是一個例子(見圖)。

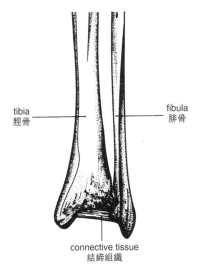

tibia
脛骨

fibula
腓骨

connective tissue
結締組織

A syndesmosis
韌帶聯合

syndrome *n.* a combination of signs and/or symptoms that forms a distinct clinical picture indicative of a particular disorder.

綜合徵 構成某種特殊病患有暗示作用的獨特的臨床徵像之體徵和／或症狀的集合。

synechia *n.* an adhesion between the iris and another part of the eye. An *anterior synechia* is between the iris and the cornea or the part of the sclera that normally hides the extreme outer edge of the iris from view. A *posterior synechia* is between the iris and the lens.

虹膜黏連 虹膜與眼其他部分的黏連。虹膜前黏連是虹膜與正常時將其最外緣遮蓋住的角膜或鞏膜之一部分黏連。虹膜與晶狀體黏連是虹膜後黏連。

syneresis *n.* contraction of a blood clot. When first formed, a blood clot is a loose meshwork of fibres containing various blood cells. Over a period of time this contracts, producing a firm mass that seals the damaged blood vessels.

血塊凝縮 血凝塊的收縮。血凝塊生成之初為含多種血細胞的疏鬆網狀物。一段時間之後，凝塊收縮，產生堅實的團塊封住受損的血管。

synergist *n.* **1.** a drug that interacts with another to produce increased activity, which is greater than the sum of the

(1) 協同劑 與其他藥物協同作用以產生更大活性的藥物，其效力大於兩藥分別使用時的

effects of the two drugs given separately. Some synergists may have dangerous effects, as when MAO inhibitors enhance the effects of antihistamine and anticholinergic drugs. **2.** a muscle that acts with an *agonist in making a particular movement. **–synergism** *n*.

效力之和。某些協同劑也可以產生危險的效果，如單氨氧化酶抑制劑可增加抗組胺藥與抗膽鹼能藥的作用。**(2)** 協同肌與主動肌共同作用產生某特定動作之肌肉。

syngeneic *adj*. describing grafted tissue that is genetically identical to the recipient's tissue, as when the donor and recipient are identical twins.

同基因的，同源的　描述被移植的組織在基因上與受體的組織是一致的，如當器官捐獻者與接受者是相等的雙胞胎時。

synoptophore *n*. see amblyoscope.

同視鏡　參閱 amblyoscope。

synostosis *n*. the joining by ossification of two adjacent bones. It occurs, for example, at the *sutures between the bones of the skull.

骨性聯接　相鄰兩骨因骨化而聯接起來。如發生於顱骨縫。

synovectomy *n*. surgical removal of the synovium of a joint. This is performed in cases of chronic synovitis, when other measures have been ineffective, in order to reduce pain in the joint and prevent further destruction.

滑膜切除術　手術切除關節滑膜。用於慢性滑膜炎且在其他治療措施不能奏效的情況下為減輕關節疼痛，防止進一步的破壞而採用的手術。

synovia (synovial fluid) the thick colourless lubricating fluid that surrounds a joint or a bursa and fills a tendon sheath. It is secreted by the synovial membrane.

滑液　無色黏稠潤滑性液體，包裹著關節和滑囊內面，充盈於腱鞘。由滑膜分泌。

synovial joint *see* diarthrosis.

滑膜關節　參閱 diarthrosis。

synovial membrane (synovium) the membrane, composed of mesothelium and connective tissue, that forms the sac enclosing a freely movable joint (*see* diarthrosis). It secretes the lubricating synovial fluid.

滑膜　由間皮和結締組織構成的膜，該膜形成了封閉的能自由活動的關節囊（參閱 diarthrosis）。由該膜分泌潤滑性的滑液。

synovioma *n*. a benign or malignant tumour of the synovial membrane. Benign synoviomas occur on tendon

滑膜瘤　滑膜的良性或惡性腫瘤。良性滑膜瘤發生於腱鞘，惡性滑膜瘤（滑膜肉瘤）可能

sheaths; malignant synoviomas (*synovial sarcomas*) may occur where synovial tissue is not normally found, e.g. in the oesophagus.

發生於正常無滑膜組織的部位，如食管內。

synovitis *n.* inflammation of the membrane (synovium) that lines a joint capsule, resulting in pain and swelling (arthritis). It is caused by injury, infection, or rheumatic disease. Treatment depends on the underlying cause; to determine this, samples of the synovial fluid or membrane are taken for examination.

滑膜炎 包裹着關節囊內面的膜（滑膜）所發炎症，導致疼痛和腫脹（關節炎）。由外傷、感染或風濕病引起。治療要針對病因進行；取滑液或滑膜標本作檢查以確定病因。

synovium *n. see* synovial membrane.

滑膜 參閱 synovial membrane。

syphilide (syphilid) *n.* the skin rash that appears in the second stage of *syphilis, usually two months to two years after primary infection. Syphilides occur in crops that may last from a few days to several months. They denote a highly infectious stage of the disease.

梅毒疹 出現在梅毒二期的皮疹，常在原發感染後的兩個月到兩年的時間內出現。梅毒疹出現時成片，可持續數天到數月。其出現提示梅毒高度感染期到來。

syphilis *n.* a chronic sexually transmitted disease caused by the bacterium *Treponema pallidum*, resulting in the formation of lesions throughout the body. Bacteria usually enter the body during sexual intercourse, through the mucous membranes of the vagina or urethra, but they may rarely be transmitted through wounds in the skin or scratches. Bacteria may also pass from an infected pregnant woman across the placenta to the developing fetus, resulting in the disease being present at birth (*congenital syphilis*).

The primary symptom – a hard ulcer (*chancre) at the site of infection – forms 2–4 weeks after exposure. Neighbouring lymph nodes enlarge about two weeks later. Secondary stage symptoms appear about two months after infection and

梅毒 一種慢性性病，由蒼白密螺旋體菌引起，導致全身性的損害。該菌通常在性交過程中進入體內，通過陰道或尿道黏膜侵入人體，但極少數的情況下也可通過皮膚創口或擦傷處侵入。該菌還可由受感染的婦女通過胎盤傳給發育中的胎兒，以致出生時即已患病（先天性梅毒）。

初期症狀——感染部位的硬性潰瘍（下疳），形成於接觸後的 2~4 周。鄰近的淋巴結 2 周後腫大。二期症狀感染 2 個月後出現，其中包括發熱、不適、全身性淋巴結腫大及胸部出現持續 1~2 周的淡紅色皮疹。數月甚至數年後該菌進入第三期，此時全身廣泛出現腫瘤樣團塊（梅毒瘤）。三期梅

include fever, malaise, general enlarge-ment of lymph nodes, and a faint red rash on the chest that persists for 1–2 weeks. After months, or even years, the disease enters its tertiary stage with widespread formation of tumour-like masses (*gummas). Tertiary syphilis may cause serious damage to the heart and blood vessels (*cardiovascular syphilis*) or to the brain and spinal cord (*neurosyphilis*), resulting in *tabes dorsalis, blindness, and *general paralysis of the insane.

Treatment with penicillin is fully effec-tive if administered in the early weeks of the infection. Syphilis can be diagnosed by several tests. *Compare* bejel. **–syphilitic** *adj.*

毒可對心臟及血管造成嚴重損害（心血管梅毒），對腦及脊髓嚴重損害（神經梅毒），導致脊髓癆，失明及麻痺性癡呆。

如在感染最初幾周使用青黴素治療可獲充分療效。可由幾種化驗來確診。與 bejel 對比。

syring- (syringo-) *prefix denoting* a tube or long cavity, especially the central canal of the spinal cord.

〔前綴〕**管，腔** 一根管或一個長腔，尤指脊髓中央管。

syringe *n.* an instrument consisting of a piston in a tight-fitting tube that is at-tached to a hollow needle or thin tube. A syringe is used to give injections, remove material from a part of the body, or to wash out a cavity, such as the outer ear.

注射器 一種由針栓和一與之緊密相配的針管所組成的器械。針管上配有一空芯針頭或細管，用於注射，從身體某部位吸出物質，或沖洗腔室，如洗外耳室。

syringobulbia *n. see* syringomyelia.

延髓空洞症 參閱 syringomyelia。

syringoma *n.* a multiple benign tumour of the sweat glands, which shows as small hard swellings usually in the face, neck, or chest.

汗腺腺瘤 汗腺的多發性良性腫瘤，常在面部頸部、胸部呈小硬腫塊狀。

syringomyelia *n.* a disease of the spinal cord in which longitudinal cavities form within the cord in the cervical (neck) region. The centrally situated cavity (*syrinx*) is especially likely to damage the motor nerve cells and the nerve fibres that transmit the sensations of pain and temperature. Characteristically there is

脊髓空洞症 在脊髓頸段內形成長條形腔洞的一種脊髓疾病，位於中央的腔洞（瘻）特別易於損害運動神經細胞及痛覺和溫度覺的傳導神經纖維。典型表現為手部肌肉無力，消瘦，伴有痛覺及溫度覺缺失。空洞向上擴展到腦幹下部時稱

weakness and wasting of the muscles in the hands with a loss of awareness of pain and temperature. An extension of the cavitation into the lower brainstem is called *syringobulbia*. Cerebellar *ataxia, a partial loss of pain sensation in the face, and weakness of the tongue and palate may occur.

為延髓空洞症，其時可產生小腦性共濟失調、面部部分喪失痛覺、舌和腭無力。

system *n.* (in anatomy) a group of organs and tissues associated with a particular physiological function, such as the *nervous system or *respiratory system.

系統 （解剖學）由特定生理功能聯繫起來的一組器官及組織，例如神經系統和呼吸系統。

systemic *adj.* relating to or affecting the body as a whole, rather than individual parts and organs.

系統的，全身的 影響或與全身有關而非個別部分或器官的。

systemic circulation the system of blood vessels that supplies all parts of the body except the lungs. It consists of the aorta and all its branches, carrying oxygenated blood to the tissues, and all the veins draining deoxygenated blood into the vena cava. *Compare* pulmonary circulation.

體循環 除肺部外供給全身各部分的血管系統。由將氧合血輸送到組織的主動脈及其所有分支再加將脫氧的血引入腔靜脈的所有靜脈血管組成。與 pulmonary circulation 對比。

systole *n.* the period of the cardiac cycle during which the heart contracts. The term usually refers to *ventricular systole*, which lasts about 0.3 seconds. *Atrial systole* lasts about 0.1 seconds. **–systolic** *adj.*

收縮期 心動周期中的心收縮階段。該術語通常指心室收縮期，持續約 0.3 秒。心房收縮期持續約為 0.1 秒。

systolic pressure *see* blood pressure.

收縮壓 參閱 blood pressure。

T

tabes dorsalis (locomotor ataxia) a form of neurosyphilis occurring 5–20 years after the original sexually transmitted infection. The infecting organisms

脊髓癆（運動性共濟失調） 一種神經梅毒的形式，首次感染性病後 5~20 年內發生。感染菌進行性地破壞感覺神經。常見

progressively destroy the sensory nerves. Severe stabbing pains in the legs and trunk, an unsteady gait, and loss of bladder control are common. Some patients have blurred vision caused by damage to the optic nerves. Penicillin is used to arrest the progression of this illness. *See also* syphilis, general paralysis of the insane.

有腿部和軀幹嚴重的刺痛感、步態不穩、膀胱失控。有些病人因視神經損害引起視力模糊。青黴素可用來阻止病情的發展。參閱 syphilis，general paralysis of the insane。

tablet *n.* (in pharmacy) a small disc containing one or more drugs, made by compressing a powdered form of the drug(s). It is usually taken by mouth but may be inserted into a body cavity (*see* suppository).

片劑 （藥劑學）一小圓片，含一種或多種藥，將粉狀藥物壓製而成。常為口服，也可植入體腔（參閱 suppository）。

tabo-paresis *n.* a late effect of syphilitic infection of the nervous system is which the patient shows features of *tabes dorsalis and *general paralysis of the insane.

脊髓癆性麻痺性痴呆 梅毒神經系統感染的遲發反應。其患者常顯示出有脊髓癆及麻痺性痴呆的特徵。

TAB vaccine a combined vaccine used to produce immunity against the diseases typhoid, paratyphoid A, and paratyphoid B.

傷寒副傷寒菌苗 用於產生免疫以抵抗傷寒、副傷寒 A 及副傷寒 B 的聯合疫苗。

tachy- *prefix denoting* fast; rapid.

〔前綴〕快，迅速

tachycardia *n.* an increase in the heart rate above normal. *Sinus tachycardia* may occur normally with exercise or excitement or it may be due to illness, such as fever. *Arrhythmias may also produce tachycardia (*ectopic tachycardia*).

心動過速 心率增加超過正常，如竇性心動過速。正常時可發生於體育鍛煉或情緒激動時，也可因疾病如發熱引起。心率失常時也可產生心動過速（異位性心動過速）。

tachyphylaxis *n.* a falling-off in the effects produced by a drug during continuous use or constantly repeated administration, common in drugs that act on the nervous system.

快速減敏 持續用藥或經常性的重複用藥致使藥物效果減退，常見於作用於神經系統的藥物上。

tachypnoea *n.* rapid breathing.

呼吸急促 呼吸快。

tactile *adj.* relating to or affecting the sense of touch.

觸覺的　與觸覺相關或影響觸覺的。

taenia *n.* (*pl.* **taeniae**) a flat ribbon-like anatomical structure. The *taeniae coli* are the longitudinal ribbon-like muscles of the colon.

帶　扁平帶狀解剖結構。結腸帶為結腸的長條形帶狀肌。

Taenia *n.* a genus of large tapeworms, some of which are parasites of the human intestine. The 4–10 m long beef tapeworm, *T. saginata*, is the commonest tapeworm parasite of man. Its larval stage (*see* cysticercus) develops within the muscles of cattle and other ruminants, and man becomes infected on eating raw or undercooked beef. *T. solium*, the pork tapeworm, is 2–7 m long. Its larval stage may develop not only in pigs but also in man, in whom it may cause serious disease (*see* cysticercosis). *See also* taeniasis.

絛蟲屬　一屬大絛蟲，其中有些為人腸道寄生蟲。4~10米長的無鉤絛蟲是最常見的寄生於人體的絛蟲。幼蟲期（參閱 cysticercus）是在牛和其他反芻動物的肌肉中發育。而人是在吃下生的未熟的牛肉後被感染的。有鉤絛蟲為2~7米長。其幼蟲期可不僅在豬而且可在人身上發育，並導致嚴重疾病（參閱 cysticercosis）。參閱 taeniasis。

taeniacide (taenicide) *n.* an agent that kills tapeworms.

殺絛蟲劑　殺死絛蟲的藥劑。

taeniafuge *n.* an agent, such as *niclosamide, that eliminates tapeworms from the body of their host.

驅絛蟲劑　可以將絛蟲從宿主體內清除掉的一種藥劑，如氯硝柳胺。

taeniasis *n.* an infestation with tapeworms of the genus *Taenia*. Man becomes infected with the adult worms following ingestion of raw or undercooked meat containing the larval stage of the parasite. The presence of a worm in the intestine may occasionally give rise to increased appetite, hunger pains, weakness, and weight loss. Worms are expelled from the intestine using various anthelmintics, including *niclosamide. *See also* cysticercosis.

絛蟲病　因絛蟲屬的絛蟲所引發的感染。人在食入生的或未煮熟的帶有絛蟲幼蟲的肉後遭受感染。該蟲在腸內的存在偶爾會引起食慾增加、飢餓性疼痛、體虛無力及體重下降。可用各種腸蟲驅蟲劑，其中包括氯硝柳胺，加以驅除。參閱 cysticercosis。

Tagamet *n. see* cimetidine.

甲氰咪胍　參閱 cimetidine。

Takayasu's disease (pulseless disease) progressive occlusion of the arteries arising from the arch of the aorta (including those to the arms and neck), resulting in the absence of pulses in the arms and neck. Symptoms include attacks of unconsciousness (syncope), paralysis of facial muscles, and transient blindness, due to an inadequate supply of blood to the head.

高安病（無脈病） 動脈的進行性閉合，從主動脈弓（包括臂及頸部）產生，導致手臂及頸部的脈搏缺失，腦供血不足產生的症狀包括失去意識（暈厥）、面部肌肉麻痺及短暫失明。

tal- (talo-) *prefix denoting* the ankle bone (talus).

〔前綴〕踝骨（距骨）

talampicillin *n.* a penicillin-type antibiotic chemically related to *ampicillin, effective against Gram-positive and many Gram-negative organisms (*see* Gram's stain). It is administered by mouth; a possible side-effect is a severe penicillin hypersensitivity reaction. Trade name: **Talpen**.

酞氨西林 一種青黴素類抗生素，化學上屬氨苄西林，能有效地抗革蘭氏陽性菌及多種革蘭氏陰性菌（參閱 Gram's stain）。口服，可能引起的副作用有嚴重的青黴素過敏反應。商品名：Talpen。

talc *n.* a soft white powder, consisting of magnesium silicate, used in dusting powders ad skin applications. Talc used to dust surgical rubber gloves causes irritation of serous membranes, resulting in adhesions, if not washed off prior to an operation.

滑石粉 一種柔軟的白色粉末，含鎂硅酸鹽，用於撒粉及皮膚用藥。撲撒在外科用橡皮手套上的滑石粉，若不在術前沖洗掉，會引起漿膜發癢，導致黏連。

talipes *n. see* club-foot.

畸形足 參閱 club-foot。

talus (astragalus) *n.* the ankle bone. It forms part of the *tarsus, articulating with the tibia above, with the fibula to the lateral (outer) side, and with the calcaneus below.

距骨 踝骨。組成部分跗骨，上連脛骨，側（朝外的）連腓骨，下接跟骨。

tambour *n.* a recording drum consisting of an elastic membrane stretched over one end of a cylinder. It is used in various instruments for recording changes in air pressure.

氣鼓 一種記錄用鼓。由繃在圓筒一端的彈性膜構成。用於記錄氣壓變化的各種儀器上。

tamoxifen *n.* a drug used in the treatment of *breast cancer: it combines with hormone receptors in the tumour to inhibit the effect of oestrogens (*see* antioestrogen). Side-effects are uncommon but include facial flushing, tumour pain, and hypercalcaemia. Tamoxifen is being investigated for its effects in preventing breast cancer in those women considered to be at risk of developing the disease. Trade name: **Nolvadex**.

他莫昔芬　用於治療乳腺癌的藥物；它與癌腫中的激素感受器相結合以抑製雌激素的作用（參閱 anti-oestrogen）。副作用不常見，但其中有面紅、癌腫疼痛和高鈣血症。該藥對於被認為處於乳腺癌發病危險期內的婦女所起的預防作用正在調查中。商品名：Nolvadex。

tampon *n.* a pack of gauze, cotton wool, or other absorbent material used to plug a cavity or canal in order to absorb blood or secretions. A vaginal tampon is commonly used by women to absorb the menstrual flow.

塞子　一塊紗布、藥棉、或其他吸水材料，用來填塞腔管以吸收血液或分泌物。陰道塞子通常為婦女所使用以吸收月經血。

tamponade *n.* **1.** the insertion of a tampon. **2.** abnormal pressure on a part of the body; for example, as caused by the presence of excessive fluid between the pericardium (sac surrounding the heart) and the heart.

(1) 填塞　插入塞子的動作。**(2) 壓迫，壓塞**　對身體某部位的不正常壓迫；例如，由於心包膜（包裹住心臟的囊）和心臟之間液體過多所致。

tantalum *n.* a rare heavy metal used in surgery as it is easily moulded and does not corrode. For example, tantalum sutures and plates are used for repair of defects in the bones of the skull. Symbol: Ta.

鉭　一稀有重金屬，用於外科，係它有易於鑄造以及不被腐蝕的特點之故。例如，鉭縫綫和鉭板用以修補顱骨缺損。符號：Ta。

tapetum *n.* **1.** a layer of specialized reflecting cells in the *choroid behind the retina of the eye. **2.** a band of nerve fibres that form the roof and wall of the lower posterior part of the *corpus callosum.

毯　**(1)** 視網膜後的脈絡膜裏的一層特殊的反射細胞。**(2)** 一束神經纖維構成了胼胝體下後部之頂部和壁部。

tapeworm *n.* any of a group of flatworms that have a long thin ribbon-like body and live as parasites in the intestines of man and other vertebrates. The body of a tapeworm consists of a head (*scolex*), a short neck, and a *strobila* made up of a

絛蟲　一組扁形蟲類，身體呈細長帶狀，寄居於人類及其他脊椎動物的腸道。由頭部、短頸和多節段（節片）的鏈狀體部構成。成熟的節片充滿了蟲卵，蟲卵將從成蟲的游離端釋

chain of separate segments (*proglottides*). Mature proglottides, full of eggs, are released from the free end of the worm and pass out in the host's stools. Eggs are then ingested by an intermediate host, in whose tissues the larval stages develop (*see* plerocercoid, cysticercus, hydatid). Man is the primary host for some tapeworms (*see* Taenia, Hymenolepis). However, other genera are also medically important (*see* Diphyllobothrium, Dipylidium, Echinococcus).

放出來,並隨宿主的大便排出體外。之後蟲卵被中間宿主攝入,在其組織中縧蟲的蟲卵發育成幼蟲(參閱 plerocercoid,cysticercus,hydatid)。人是有些縧蟲(參閱 Taenia,Hymenolepis)的終宿主,但其他種類的縧蟲也有醫學意義(參閱 Diphyllobothrium,Dipylidium,Echinococcus)。

tapotement *n.* a technique used in *massage in which a part of the body is struck rapidly and repeatedly with the hands. Tapotement of the chest wall in bronchitic patients often helps to loosen mucus within the air passages so that it can be coughed up.

叩撫法 一種用手迅速叩擊反覆敲打身體某部位的按摩法。給支氣管病人的胸壁施行叩撫法常有助於氣管內黏液的鬆解,使之能被咳出。

tapping *n. see* paracentesis.

穿刺放液法 參閱 paracentesis。

target cell (in haematology) an abnormal form of red blood cell (*erythrocyte) in which the cell assumes the ringed appearance of a 'target' in stained blood films. Target cells are a feature of several types of anaemia, including those due to iron deficiency, liver disease, and abnormalities in haemoglobin structure.

靶細胞 (血液病學)一種形狀不正常的紅細胞,在染色的血片中該細胞呈現為靶環狀。為幾種貧血類型的特徵,例如由缺鐵和血紅蛋白結構異常所致的貧血。

target organ the specific organ or tissue upon which a hormone, drug, or other substance acts.

靶器官 激素、藥物或其他物質所要作用的特定器官或組織。

tars- (tarso-) *prefix denoting* **1.** the ankle; tarsal bones. **2.** the edge of the eyelid.

〔前綴〕**(1)** **跗骨** 踝,踝部七塊骨。**(2)** **眼瞼緣**

tarsal 1. *adj.* relating to the bones of the ankle and foot (*tarsus). **2.** *adj.* relating to the eyelid, esp. to its supporting tissue

(1) **跗骨的** 與踝骨及足骨有關的。**(2)** **眼瞼的** 與眼瞼相關的,尤指其支持組織(瞼板)

(tarsus). **3.** *n.* any of the bones forming the tarsus.

tarsalgia *n.* aching pain arising from the tarsus in the foot.

tarsal glands *see* meibomian glands.

tarsectomy *n.* **1.** surgical excision of the tarsal bones of the foot. **2.** surgical removal of a section of the tarsus of the eyelid.

tarsitis *n.* inflammation of the eyelid.

tarsoplasty *n. see* blepharoplasty.

tarsorrhaphy *n.* an operation in which the upper and lower eyelids are joined together, either completely or along part of their length. It is performed to protect the cornea or to allow a corneal injury to heal.

tarsus *n.* (*pl.* **tarsi**) **1.** the seven bones of the ankle and proximal part of the foot (see illustration). The tarsus articulates with the metatarsals distally and with the tibia and fibula proximally. **2.** the firm fibrous connective tissue that forms the basis of each eyelid.

tartar *n.* an obsolete term for *calculus, the hard deposit that forms on the teeth.

taste *n.* the sense for the appreciation of the flavour of substances in the mouth. The sense organs responsible are the *taste buds on the surface of the *tongue, which are stimulated when food dissolves in the saliva in the mouth. It is generally held that there are four basic taste sensations – sweet, bitter, sour, and salt –

的。**(3)** **跗骨** 構成跗節的任何骨。

跗骨痛 發自足部跗骨的疼痛。

瞼板腺 參閱 meibomian glands。

(1) **跗骨切除術** 切除足跗骨的手術。**(2)** **瞼板切除術** 眼瞼板的切除手術。

瞼板炎 眼瞼炎症。

瞼成形術 參閱 blepharoplasty。

瞼縫合術 將上、下眼瞼縫合在一起的手術。或完全縫合或部分縫合。其目的是為了保護角膜或使角膜處傷口愈合。

(1) **跗骨** 踝的七塊骨頭和足的近端部分（見圖）。跗骨遠端與跖骨相聯接，近端與脛骨、腓骨相接。**(2)** **瞼板** 構成眼瞼基部的堅韌纖維結締組織。

牙石 牙垢的過時術語，指在牙齒上形成的硬沉積物。

味覺 識別口腔內物質味道的感覺。負責味覺的感覺器官為舌表面的味蕾，當口腔裏的唾液將食物溶解時，味覺就會受到刺激。通常認為味覺主要有四種——甜、苦、酸和鹹——但另外兩種味——鹹味和金屬味——有時也算在內。

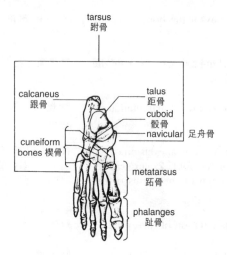

Bones of the right ankle and foot
右踝和足骨

but two others – alkaline and metallic –
are sometimes added to this list.

taste buds the sensory receptors
concerned with the sense of taste (see
illustration). They are located in the
epithelium that covers the surface of the
*tongue, lying in the grooves around
the papillae, particularly the circumvallate papillae. Taste buds are also present
in the soft palate, the epiglottis, and parts
of the pharynx. When a taste cell is
stimulated by the presence of a dissolved
substance impulses are sent via nerve
fibres to the brain. From the anterior
two-thirds of the tongue impulses pass
via the facial nerve. The taste buds in the
posterior third of the tongue send impulses via the glossopharyngeal nerve.

taurine *n.* an amino acid that is a constituent of the *bile salt taurocholate and
also functions as a *neurotransmitter in
the central nervous system.

味蕾 與味覺有關的感覺感受
器（見圖）。味蕾在覆蓋於舌
表面的上皮層內，存在於舌乳
頭（尤指輪廓乳頭）周圍的溝
紋裏。味蕾也出現在軟腭、會
厭及部分咽部。當味覺細胞由
溶解物質刺激時，衝動就通過
神經纖維傳送至大腦，舌前三
分之二產生的衝動由面神經傳
遞，味蕾通過舌咽神經傳送舌
後三分之一產生的衝動。

牛磺酸 一種氨基酸，係牛磺
膽酸鹽之組成部分，亦在中樞
神經系統中起神經遞質之作
用。

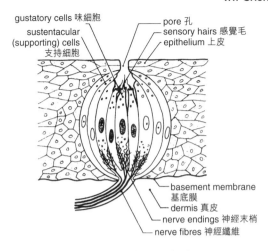

gustatory cells 味細胞
sustentacular
(supporting) cells
支持細胞
pore 孔
sensory hairs 感覺毛
epithelium 上皮
basement membrane
基底膜
dermis 真皮
nerve endings 神經末梢
nerve fibres 神經纖維

Structure of a taste bud
味蕾的結構

taurocholic acid *see* bile acids.

taxis *n.* (in surgery) the returning to a normal position of displaced bones, organs, or other parts by manipulation only, unaided by mechanical devices.

taxol *n.* an anticancer drug formerly obtainable only from the bark of the Pacific yew tree but now synthesized; it has also been produced by biotechnological methods. Taxol interacts with tubulin, a protein involved in cell division, and has been found to exercise control on the growth of ovarian, breast, and lung cancers. Results of clinical trials of taxol in the treatment of ovarian cancer are encouraging.

Tay-Sachs disease (amaurotic familial idiocy) an inherited disorder of lipid metabolism (*see* lipidosis) in which abnormal accumulation of lipid in the brain leads to blindness, mental retardation, and death in infancy. The gene

牛磺膽酸 參閱 bile acids。

整復法 （外科學）用手法而不借助醫療器械使錯位的骨、器官或其他部分恢復正常位置。

紫杉酚 一種抗癌藥物，原先僅可從太平洋紫杉樹皮中提取，現可人工合成，已經可以用生物技術生產。紫杉酚作用於微管蛋白，即細胞分裂中涉及的蛋白，且已發現能控製卵巢癌、乳腺癌及肺癌的生長。在治療卵巢癌方面的臨床試驗結果令人鼓舞。

泰-薩氏病（家族性黑蒙性白痴） 遺傳性脂肪代謝障礙疾病（參閱 lipidosis），此病中脂肪在腦內不正常的蓄積導致失明，智力發育遲緩，及嬰兒期死亡。其致病基因為隱性，並且由於

responsible for the disorder is *recessive, and the disease can now be largely prevented by genetic counselling in communities known to be affected.

在已知的患病社區中開展遺傳咨詢，目前此病已基本上得到預防。

TCP *Trade name*. a solution of trichlorphenol: an effective *antiseptic for minor skin injuries and irritations. It may also be used as a gargle for colds and sore throats.

三氯苯酚 三氯苯酚溶液之商品名：用於輕微的皮膚外傷及瘙癢的有效抗菌劑。也可用作含漱劑治療感冒及喉痛。

TCR T-cell receptor: an important component of the surface of T-*lymphocytes, by which antigen is recognized.

T 細胞受體 T 淋巴細胞表面的重要組成部分，據此辨認抗原。

TCRE *see* transcervical resection of the endometrium.

經宮頸子宮內膜切除術 參閱 transcervical resection of the endometrium。

tear gas any of the several kinds of gas used in warfare and by the police to produce temporary incapacitation. Most tear gases produce stinging pain in the eyes and streaming from the eyes and nose. *See also* CS gas.

催淚毒氣 戰爭中或警察使用的幾種毒氣以使人暫時失去能力。多數催淚氣可引起眼睛刺痛並引起從眼和鼻流淚和流涕。參閱 CS gas。

tears *pl. n.* the fluid secreted by the lacrimal glands (*see* lacrimal apparatus) to keep the front of the eyeballs moist and clean. Tears contain *lysozyme, an enzyme that destroys bacteria. Irritation of the eye, and sometimes emotion, cause excessive production of tears. *See also* blinking.

眼淚 用來使眼球前方保持濕潤和清潔，由淚腺（參閱 lacrimal apparatus）分泌的液體。淚中含一種殺滅細菌的溶菌酶。眼睛受刺激或感情激動時引起過多的眼淚產生。參閱 blinking。

technetium-99 *n.* an isotope of the artificial radioactive element technetium. It emits gamma radiation and is used as a *tracer for the examination of the brain, thyroid gland, and other organs in the technique of scintigraphy (*see* scintigram).

^{99}鍀 人工放射性鍀元素之同位素。釋放 γ 射綫，並在閃爍照相中作為示踪劑檢查腦和甲狀腺（參閱 scintigram）。

tectospinal tract a tract that conveys nerve impulses from the midbrain, across

頂蓋脊髓束 傳遞神經衝動的傳導束，從中腦經中綫下行至

the midline as it descends, to the spinal cord in the cervical (neck) region. It contains important *motor neurones.

tectum *n.* the roof of the *midbrain, behind and above the *cerebral aqueduct. From the nerve tissue protrude two pairs of rounded swellings called the *superior* and *inferior colliculi*, which contain cells concerned with reflexes involving vision and hearing, respectively.

teeth *pl. n. see* tooth.

tegmen *n.* (*pl.* **tegmina**) a structure that covers an organ or part of an organ. For example the *tegmen tympani* is the bony roof of the middle ear.

tegmentum *n.* the region of the *midbrain below and in front of the *cerebral aqueduct. It contains the nuclei of several cranial nerves, the *reticular formation, and other ascending and descending nerve pathways linking the forebrain and the spinal cord.

teichopsia *n.* shimmering coloured lights, accompanied by blank spots in the visual field (*transient scotomata*), often seen by sufferers at the beginning of an attack of migraine.

tel- (tele-, telo-) *prefix denoting* **1.** end or ending. **2.** distance.

tela *n.* any thin weblike tissue, particularly the *tela choroidea*, a folded double layer of *pia mater containing numerous small blood vessels that extends into several of the *ventricles of the brain.

telangiectasis (*pl.* **telangiectases**) a localized collection of distended blood

頸髓區，其中含有重要的運動神經元。

頂蓋　中腦頂部，大腦導水管後上方。從神經組織突出兩對圓形隆起稱為上、下丘，上、下丘中含有分別與視覺和聽覺反射有關的細胞。

牙　參閱 tooth。

蓋　覆蓋一器官或覆蓋部分器官之結構。例如鼓室蓋是中耳的骨質頂部。

大腦腳蓋　大腦導水管前下方的中腦部位。內含多種腦神經核、網狀結構及其他聯繫前腦與脊髓之上行或下行的神經通路。

閃光暗點　視野中有色光綫在閃爍，同時伴有空白點（短暫暗點）。常見於偏頭痛患者發作開始之時。

〔前綴〕**(1)** 末端　**(2)** 距離

網狀組織　任何薄的蛛網狀組織，尤指脈絡組織，該組織為摺疊的雙層軟腦膜，內含眾多小血管，該膜一直延伸至大腦若干個腦室。

毛細血管擴張　擴張的毛細血管之局部聚集。形狀如紅斑

capillary vessels. It is recognized as a red spot, sometimes spidery in appearance, that blanches on pressure. Telangiectases may be found in the skin or the lining of the mouth, gastrointestinal, respiratory, and urinary passages. The condition in which multiple telangiectases occur is termed *telangiectasia*. It may be seen as an inherited condition associated with a bleeding tendency (*haemorrhagic telangiectasia*). Accessible bleeding telangiectases (e.g. in the nose) may be obliterated by cauterization.

塊，有時狀若蜘蛛，壓迫後褪色，可因此識別。毛細血管擴張見於皮膚、口腔內層、胃腸道、呼吸道和尿道。有多發性毛細血管擴張時稱之為毛細血管擴張症。可以看作是一種遺傳性疾病伴有出血傾向（出血性毛細血管擴張症）。易於出血的毛細血管擴張（如鼻腔內）可用燒灼法使血管閉塞。

telangiitis *n.* inflammation of the smallest blood vessels (*see* angiitis).

毛細血管炎 最小血管之炎症（參閱 angiitis）。

teleceptor *n.* a sensory *receptor that is capable of responding to distant stimuli. An example is the eye, which is capable of detecting changes and events at a great distance, unlike touch receptors, which depend on close contact.

距離感受器 可以對有一定距離的刺激作出反應的一種感覺感受器，眼睛是一個例子，眼睛可以探察到遠處發生的變化及事件，這不同於需要密切接觸的觸覺感受器。

telecurietherapy *n.* a form of *radiotherapy in which penetrating radiation is directed at a patient from a distance. Originally radium was used as the radiation source; today artificial radioactive isotopes, such as cobalt-60, are used.

遠距離治療 一種類型的放射性治療，其穿透性射綫在一段距離外射向病人。起初鐳曾被用作放射源，今天使用的是人工放射性同位素，如 ^{60}鈷。

telegony *n.* the unsubstantiated theory that mating with one male has an effect on the offspring of later matings with other males.

前父遺傳 一種未證實的理論，指與一個男人結過婚會影響後來與其他男人結婚所生的後代。

telencephalon *n. see* cerebrum.

端腦 參閱 cerebrum。

teleradiography *n.* a form of *radiography in which the X-ray source is situated about 2 metres from the patient, which produces X-ray pictures with less distortion.

遠距離放射造影術 一種形式的放射造影術，X 綫放射源在距患者約 2 米之處，故所得到的 X 綫圖像很少失真。

telocentric *n.* a chromosome in which the centromere is situated at either of its ends. **–telocentric** *adj.*

端着絲粒　一種染色體，其着絲粒位於兩個末端。

telodendron *n.* one of the branches into which the *axon of a neurone divides at its destination. Each telodendron finishes as a terminal *bouton*, which takes part in a *synapse or a *neuromuscular junction.

終樹突　神經元的軸索在其終點的分支。每個終樹突末端如一個終鈕，它參與形成突觸或神經肌肉連接。

telogen *n. see* anagen.

調聚體　參閱 anagen。

telophase *n.* the final stage of *mitosis and of each of the divisions of *meiosis, in which the chromosomes at each end of the cell become long and thin and the nuclear membrane reforms around them. The cytoplasm begins to divide.

末期　有絲分裂的最後期和每次減數分裂的最末期。此時在細胞兩側的染色體變得長而細，並在其周圍重新形成核膜，細胞漿開始分裂。

temazepam *n.* a *benzodiazepine used for the treatment of insomnia associated with diffculty falling asleep, frequent nocturnal awakenings, or early morning awakening. It is given by mouth; common side-effects include drowsiness, dizziness, and loss of appetite. Trade name: **Normison**.

替馬西泮　苯並二氮草類藥物，用以治療伴有難以入睡、夜醒頻繁、晨醒過早的失眠。口服，常見副作用有嗜睡、頭暈及無食慾。商品名：Normison。

temple *n.* the region of the head in front of and above each ear.

顳部　耳前上方的頭部區。

temporal *adj.* of or relating to the temple.

顳的　顳部的或與顳部有關的。

temporal arteritis *see* arteritis.

顳動脈炎　參閱 arteritis。

temporal artery a branch of the external carotid artery that supplies blood mainly to the temple and scalp.

顳動脈　頸外動脈的分支，主要向顳部及頭皮供血。

temporal bone either of a pair of bones of the cranium. The *squamous* portion forms part of the side of the cranium. The *petrous* part contributes to the base of the

顳骨　頭顱兩側的一對骨。其鱗狀部構成顳骨的側面部分。岩部用於形成頭顱的基底部分，並包括中耳和內耳。其下方為

skull and contains the middle and inner ears. Below it are the *mastoid process, *styloid process, and zygomatic process (*see* zygomatic arch). *See also* skull.

乳突、莖突和顴突（參閱 zygomatic arch）。參閱 skull。

temporalis *n.* a fan-shaped muscle situated at the side of the head, extending from the temporal fossa to the mandible. This muscle lifts the lower jaw, thus closing the mouth.

顳肌 頭部側面之扇狀肌肉，起於顳窩下至頜骨。該肌抬起下頜，從而使嘴閉合。

temporal lobe one of the main divisions of the *cerebral cortex in each hemisphere of the brain, lying at the side within the temple of the skull and separated from the frontal lobe by a cleft, the *lateral sulcus*. Areas of the cortex in this lobe are concerned with the appreciation of sound and spoken language.

顳葉 大腦兩半球腦皮質的主要部分之一，位於頭顳兩側的顳部內，其與額葉由一裂隙，即側溝，相分隔。該葉的皮質區與聲音及語言的感受相關。

temporal lobe epilepsy *see* epilepsy.

顳葉癲癇 參閱 epilepsy。

temporo- *prefix denoting* **1.** the temple. **2.** the temporal lobe of the brain.

〔前綴〕**(1)** 顳部 **(2)** 大腦顳葉

temporomandibular joint the articulation between the *mandible and the *temporal bone: a hinge joint (*see* ginglymus).

顳下頜關節 下頜骨與顳骨間之關節：係屈戌關節（參閱 ginglymus）。

temporomandibular joint syndrome a condition in which the patient has painful temporomandibular joints, tenderness in the muscles that move the jaw, clicking of the joints, and limitation of jaw movement. Stress, resulting in clenching the jaws and grinding the teeth, is thought to be a causal factor.

顳下頜關節綜合徵 此病徵中病人顳下頜關節疼痛，運動下頜的肌肉有觸痛，關節有咔嗒聲，且下頜活動受限。由緊張所致的緊咬牙關和磨牙被認為是其病因之一。

tenaculum *n.* **1.** a sharp wire hook with a handle. The instrument is used in surgical operations to pick up pieces of tissue or the cut end of an artery. **2.** a band of fibrous tissue that holds a part of the body in place.

(1) 把持鈎 帶柄的銳利的金屬絲鈎。用於外科手術以提起一塊組織或切割動脈的一端。
(2) 支持體 將身體某部分保持於恰當位置的纖維組織帶。

tendinitis *n.* inflammation of a tendon. It occurs most commonly after excessive overuse but is sometimes due to bacterial infection (e.g. *gonorrhoea), or a generalized rheumatic disease (e.g. *rheumatoid arthritis or ankylosing spondylitis). Treatment is by rest, achieved sometimes by splinting the adjacent joint, and corticosteroid injection into the tender area around the tendon. Tendinitis at the insertion of the supraspinatus muscle is a frequent cause of pain and restricted movement in the shoulder. *See also* tennis elbow. *Compare* tenosynovitis.

tendon *n.* a tough whitish cord, consisting of numerous parallel bundles of collagen fibres, that serves to attach a muscle to a bone. Tendons are inelastic but flexible; they assist in concentrating the pull of the muscle on a small area of bone. Some tendons are surrounded by *tendon sheaths* – these are tubular double-layered sacs lined with synovial membrane and containing synovial fluid. Tendon sheaths enclose the flexor tendons at the wrist and ankle, where they minimize friction and facilitate movement. *See also* aponeurosis. **–tendinous** *adj.*

tendon organ (Golgi tendon organ) a sensory *receptor found within a tendon that responds to the tension or stretching of the tendon and relays impulses to the central nervous system. Like stretch receptors in muscle, tendon organs are part of the *proprioceptor system.

tendovaginitis (tenovaginitis) *n.* inflammatory thickening of the fibrous sheath containing one or more tendons, usually caused by repeated minor injury. It usually occurs at the back of the thumb

肌腱炎　肌腱的炎症。最常見於過度運動之後，但也有因細菌感染所致（如淋病），或由全身性風濕性關節炎（如類風濕性關節炎或强直性脊椎炎）引起。治療靠休息：用夾板固定鄰近關節和在肌腱周圍壓痛區注射皮質類固醇。岡上肌肌肉附着處肌腱炎是肩痛及肩活動受限的常見病因。與 tenosynovitis 對比。

肌腱　堅韌的白色索帶，由眾多平行的膠原纖維束構成。其作用為使肌肉附着於骨上。肌腱無彈性但可彎曲，它們協助將肌肉的牽拉力集中於骨上的一小區域內。有的肌腱由腱鞘所包圍。腱鞘是內襯滑膜和含有滑液的管形雙層囊。腱鞘包裹腕和踝的屈肌肌腱，可將摩擦降至最低程度並使活動方便。參閱 aponeurosis。

腱感受器（高爾基腱器）　感覺感受器，存在於肌腱內，對肌腱的張力牽拉作出反應，並向中樞神經系統傳遞衝動。與肌肉的牽拉感受器相似，腱感受器是本體感受器系統的一部分。

腱鞘炎　含有一個或幾個肌腱的纖維鞘因發炎而增厚，常因反覆的輕微損傷所致。常發生於拇指背面（奎爾萬腱鞘炎），並致使手腕活動時疼

(*de Quervain's tendovaginitis*) and results in pain on using the wrists. Treatment is by rest, injection of cortisone into the tendon sheath, and, if these fail, surgical incision of the sheath.

痛。治療為休息，及腱鞘內注射可的松，如這些均未奏效，採用手術切開腱鞘。

tenesmus *n.* a sensation of the desire to defecate, which is continuous or recurs frequently, without the production of significant amounts of faeces (often small amounts of mucus or blood alone are passed). This uncomfortable symptom may be due to *proctitis, prolapse of the rectum, rectal tumour, or *irritable bowel syndrome.

裏急後重 持續或反覆的想要排便的感覺，而無足夠量的大便排出（常僅為小量黏液和血）。這種不適症狀可能因直腸炎、直腸脫垂、直腸腫瘤或應激性腸綜合徵引起。

tennis elbow a painful inflammation of the tendon at the outer border of the elbow, caused by overuse of the forearm muscles. Treatment is by rest, massage, and local corticosteroid injection. *See also* tendinitis.

網球肘 肘外緣肌腱的疼痛性炎症，由前臂肌肉勞損引起。治療為休息、按摩及局部注射皮質類固醇。參閱 tendinitis。

teno- *prefix denoting* a tendon.

〔前綴〕**腱**

Tenon's capsule the fibrous tissue that lines the orbit and surrounds the eyeball.

特農囊 內襯於眼眶和外裹眼球的纖維組織。

tenoplasty *n.* surgical repair of a ruptured or severed tendon.

腱成形術 外科修復破裂的或斷開的肌腱。

tenoposide *n.* a drug used in the treatment of certain cancers, particularly in childhood. It is very similar to *etoposide.

替尼泊甙 用於治療某些癌症的藥物，尤其用於兒童。與依托泊甙十分相似。

tenorrhaphy *n.* the surgical operation of uniting the ends of divided tendons by suture.

腱縫合術 外科手術縫合肌腱斷開的各端。

tenosynovitis (peritendinitis) *n.* inflammation of a tendon sheath, producing pain, swelling, and an audible creaking on movement. It may result from a bacterial infection or occur as

腱鞘炎 產生疼痛、腫脹及活動時發出可聽到的吱嘎聲之腱鞘炎症。可因細菌感染引起或者是引發滑膜炎的風濕性疾病的一部分。

part of a rheumatic disease causing *synovitis.

tenotomy *n.* surgical *division of a tendon. This may be necessary to correct a joint deformity caused by tendon shortening or to reduce the imbalance of forces caused by an overactive muscle in a spastic limb. *See also* scissor leg.

tenovaginitis *n. see* tendovaginitis.

TENS *see* transcutaneous electrical nerve stimulation.

tensor *n.* any muscle that causes stretching or tensing of a part of the body.

tent *n.* **1.** an enclosure of material (usually transparent plastic) around a patient in bed, into which a gas or vapour can be passed as part of treatment. An *oxygen tent* is relatively inefficient as a means of administering oxygen; a face mask or intranasal oxygen are used where possible. **2.** a piece of dried vegetable material, usually a seaweed stem, shaped to fit into an orifice, such as the cervical canal. As it absorbs moisture it expands, providing a slow but forceful means of dilating the orifice.

tentorium *n.* a curved infolded sheet of *dura mater that dips inwards from the skull and separates the cerebellum below from the occipital lobes of the cerebral hemispheres above.

terat- (terato-) *prefix denoting* a monster or congenital abnormality.

teratogen *n.* any substance, agent, or process that induces the formation of developmental abnormalities in a fetus.

腱切斷術　肌腱分離術。在矯正因肌腱變短而引起的關節畸形時或減少因痙攣肢體肌肉過度活躍引起肌肉不平衡之力量時，均有做這種手術之必要。參閱 scissor leg。

腱鞘炎　參閱 tendovaginitis。

經皮下電神經刺激　參閱 transcutaneous electrical nerve stimulation。

張肌　使身體某部分伸長或緊張之肌肉。

(1) 帷幕　臥床病人床周圍的帷帳（通常為透明塑料），其內可充入氣體或蒸氣，作為治療的一部分。氧氣帷幕是一種效率較低的給氧方式，如有可能則用面罩或鼻管吸氧。**(2)** 塞條　一條乾的植物材料，常為海藻莖，製成適合進入管口的形狀，例如子宮頸管。因其吸水後膨脹，提供了一種緩慢但有效的方式來擴張管口。

幕　彎曲摺疊的硬腦膜。向顱骨內插入，將下面的小腦與上面的大腦半球枕葉隔開。

〔前級〕**畸胎，先天性異常**

致畸形物　任何導致胎兒發育畸形的物質、藥劑及過程。已知的致畸形物包括以下藥物：

Known teratogens include such drugs as *thalidomide and alcohol; such infections as German measles and cytomegalovirus; and also irradiation with X-rays and other ionizing radiation. *Compare* mutagen. **–teratogenic** *adj.*

沙利度胺和乙醇；以下感染：風疹和巨細胞病毒；及 X 綫和其他電離輻射的刺激。與 mutagen 對比。

teratogenesis *n.* the process leading to developmental abnormalities in the fetus.

畸形生成 導致胎兒發育性畸形的過程。

teratology *n.* the study of developmental abnormalities and their causes.

畸形學 研究發育異常及其原因的學科。

teratoma *n.* a tumour composed of a number of tissues not usually found at that site. Teratomas most frequently occur in the testis and ovary, possibly derived from remnants of embryological cells that have the ability to differentiate into many types of tissue. *Malignant teratoma of the testis* is found in young men: it is most common in the undescended testis. Like *seminoma, it frequently occurs as a painless swelling of one testis (pain is not a good indication that the swelling is benign). Treatment is by *orchidectomy avoiding an incision into the scrotum. The tumour can spread to lymph nodes, lungs, and bone, treatment of which may involve the use of radiotherapy and drugs such as vinblastine, bleomycin, cisplatin, and etoposide. Teratomas often produce *alphafetoprotein, beta human chorionic gonadotrophin, or both; the presence of these substances (*tumour markers) in the blood is a useful indication of the amount of tumour and the effect of treatment.

畸胎瘤 由許多在該部位不常見的組織構成的腫瘤。畸胎瘤最常見於睪丸及卵巢，可能來源於能分化成多種類型組織的胚胎細胞。睪丸惡性畸胎瘤見於年輕人：在未下降的睪丸中最常見。類似於精原細胞瘤，常見於一側睪丸並且無痛性腫脹（疼痛不是良性腫瘤的可靠指標）。治療採用睪丸切除術，避免切開陰囊。該腫瘤可擴散到淋巴結、肺和骨。擴散後可採用放射治療和藥物治療，如長春鹼、博來黴素、順鉑及依托泊甙。該腫瘤常產生甲胎蛋白、β-人絨毛膜促性腺激素，或兩者都有；這些物質（腫瘤標記）在血液中的出現對於腫瘤大小及治療效果都是十分有用的指標。

teratospermia *n.* see oligospermia.

畸形精子（症） 參閱 oligospermia。

terbinafine *n.* an antifungal drug used to treat severe ringworm. It is administered

特必萘芬 治療嚴重癬病的抗真菌藥物。口服，可能產生副

by mouth; possible side-effects include nausea, abdominal pain, and allergic skin rashes. Trade name: **Lamisil**.

terbutaline *n.* a *bronchodilator drug (*see* sympathomimetic) used in the treatment of asthma, bronchitis, and other respiratory disorders. It may be given by mouth, injection, or inhalation; common side-effects include nervousness and dizziness. Trade name: **Bricanyl**.

teres *n.* either of two muscles of the shoulder, extending from the scapula to the humerus. The *teres major* draws the arm towards the body and rotates it inwards; the *teres minor* rotates the arm outwards.

terfenadine *n.* an antihistamine used for the treatment of the symptoms of hay fever, such as sneezing, itching, and watering of the eyes. It is administered by mouth; commonest side-effects are drowsiness, headache, and gastrointestinal upsets. Trade name: **Triludan**.

terlipressin *n.* a drug that releases *vasopressin over a period of hours. It is used to help to control bleeding from *oesophageal varices by constricting the small arteries in the intestinal tract.

terpene *n.* any of a group of unsaturated hydrocarbons many of which are found in plant oils and resins and are responsible for the scent of these plants (e.g. mint). Larger terpenes include vitamin A, squalene, and the carotenoids.

Terramycin *n. see* oxytetracycline.

tertian fever *see* malaria.

作用有惡心、腹痛及過敏性皮疹。商品名：Lamisil。

特布他林（叔丁喘寧素） 支氣管擴張藥（參閱 sympathomimetic），用於治療哮喘、支氣管炎及其他呼吸系統疾病。口服、注射或吸入均可，常見副作用有緊張或頭暈。商品名：Bricanyl。

圓肌 肩部的兩塊肌肉，從肩胛骨延伸到肱骨。大圓肌使上臂向身體內收並內旋，小圓肌使上臂外旋。

特非那定 抗組胺藥，治療花粉病的各種症狀，如打噴嚏、發癢及眼睛流淚。口服，最常見的副作用有嗜睡、頭痛、胃腸不適。商品名：Triludan。

特利加壓素 一種藥物，每隔數小時之後釋放出加壓素，用以控制因腸道小動脈收縮而引起的食管靜脈曲張出血。

萜 一組未飽和的碳氫化合物，多見於植物油和樹脂中，並富有這些植物的香味（如薄荷）。較大的萜類包括維生素A、角鯊烯以及類胡蘿蔔素。

土黴素 參閱 oxytetracycline。

間日瘧 參閱 malaria。

tertiary health care the services provided by specialized hospitals equipped with diagnostic and treatment facilities not available at general hospitals or by doctors who are uniquely qualified to treat unusual disorders that do not respond to therapy that is available at secondary care centres. *Compare* primary health care, secondary health care.

三級衛生保健 由專科醫院提供的服務，該醫院裝備有在綜合醫院所沒有的診斷及治療設施，或者該醫院的醫生獨具資格，能對二級醫療中心治療無效的罕見病進行治療。與 primary health care，secondary health care 對比。

tesla *n.* the *SI unit of magnetic flux density, equal to a density of 1 weber per square metre. Symbol: T.

特（斯拉） 磁通量密度之國際單位，1 特斯拉等於每平方米 1 韋（伯）的密度。符號：T。

testicle *n.* either of the pair of male sex organs within the scrotum. It consists of the *testis and its system of ducts (the vasa efferentia and epididymis).

睾丸 陰囊內的一對男性性器官。其中包括睾丸與輸精管道系統（輸精管與附睾）。

testis *n.* (*pl.* **testes**) either of the pair of male sex organs that produce spermatozoa and secrete the male sex hormone *androgen under the control of *gonadotrophins from the pituitary gland. The testes of the fetus form within the abdomen but descend into the *scrotum in order to maintain a lower temperature that favours the production and storage of spermatozoa. The bulk of the testis is made up of long convoluted *seminiferous tubules* (see illustration), in which the spermatozoa develop (*see* spermatogenesis). The tubules also contain *Sertoli cells, which may nourish developing sperm cells. Spermatozoa pass from the testis to the *epididymis to complete their development. The *interstitial* (*Leydig*) *cells*, between the tubules, are the major producers of androgen.

睾丸 一對男性性器官之一，產生精子並在垂體促性腺激素控制之下分泌男性激素雄激素。胎兒的睾丸在腹腔內形成，但以後下降到陰囊，以保持一個利於精子產生及貯存的較低溫度。睾丸的主要部分由長的曲細精管構成（見圖），精子在曲細精管內發育生長（參閱 spermatogenesis）。曲細精管中還有塞爾托利細胞，這些細胞滋養正在發育中的精子細胞。由睾丸到附睾精子完成了其發育過程。曲細精管之間的間質細胞（萊迪希細胞）是主要的雄激素產生者。

test meal a standard meal given to stimulate secretion of digestive juices, which can then be withdrawn by tube and measured as a test of digestive

試餐 一種標準餐，用以刺激消化液分泌。之後消化液可由管子抽吸，並加以測定，以此作為對消化功能的一種試驗。

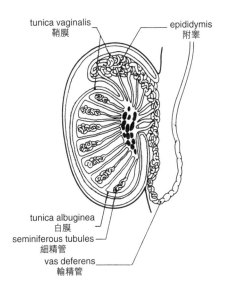

tunica vaginalis 鞘膜　　　epididymis 附睪

tunica albuginea 白膜
seminiferous tubules 細精管
vas deferens 輸精管

Longitudinal section through a testis
睪丸的縱切面

function. A *fractional test meal* was a gruel preparation to stimulate gastric secretion, whose acid content was measured. This has been replaced by tests using histamine or pentagastrin as secretory stimulants. The *Lundh test meal* is a meal of oil and protein to stimulate pancreatic secretion, which is withdrawn from the duodenum and its trypsin content measured as a test of pancreatic function.

分段試餐為糊劑，刺激胃分泌，測定酸含量。此種試餐已被作為分泌刺激劑的組胺或五肽胃泌素取代。倫德試餐，是一種油和蛋白的膳食，用以刺激胰腺的分泌，從十二指腸處抽吸胰液，並測定其中胰蛋白酶的含量，以此作為對胰腺功能的一種試驗。

testosterone *n*. the principal male sex hormone (*see* androgen).

睪酮　主要的男性激素（參閱 androgen）。

test-tube baby a baby born to a woman as a result of fertilization of one of her ova by her partner's sperm outside her body. *See* in vitro fertilization.

試管嬰兒　一位婦女的一個卵子與其伴侶的精子於體外受精後產下的嬰兒。參閱 in vitro fertilization。

tetan- (tetano-) *prefix denoting* **1.** tetanus. **2.** tetany.

〔前綴〕**(1)** 破傷風 **(2)** 手足搐搦

tetanolysin *n*. a toxin produced by tetanus bacilli in an infected wound, causing the local destruction of tissues.

破傷風菌溶血素　由破傷風桿菌在其感染的傷口產生的一種毒素，引起局部組織的破壞。

tetanospasmin *n*. a toxin produced by tetanus bacilli in an infected wound. The toxin diffuses along nerves, causing paralysis, and may reach the spinal cord and brain, when it causes violent muscular spasms and the condition of lockjaw.

破傷風痙攣毒素　由破傷風桿菌在其感染的傷口處產生的一種毒素。該毒素沿神經彌散，引起癱瘓，並可能到達脊髓和大腦，其時引起劇烈的肌肉痙攣及牙關緊閉。

tetanus (lockjaw) *n*. an acute infectious disease, affecting the nervous system, caused by the bacterium *Clostridium tetani*. Infection occurs by contamination of wounds by bacterial spores. Bacteria multiply at the site of infection and produce a toxin that irritates nerves so that they cause spasmodic contraction of muscles. Symptoms appear 4–25 days after infection and consist of muscle stiffness, spasm, and subsequent rigidity, first in the jaw and neck then in the back, chest, abdomen, and limbs; in severe cases the spasm may affect the whole body, which is arched backwards (*see* opisthotonos). High fever, convulsions, and extreme pain are common. If respiratory muscles are affected, a *tracheostomy or intubation and ventilation is essential to avoid death from asphyxia. Mortality is high in untreated cases but prompt treatment with penicillin and antitoxin is effective. An attack does not confer immunity. Immunization against tetanus is effective but temporary. **–tetanic** *adj*.

破傷風　一種急性傳染性疾病，損害神經系統。該病是由破傷風梭狀芽胞桿菌引發。細菌芽胞污染傷口而引起感染。在感染部位細菌增殖，並產生刺激神經進而引起肌肉痙攣性收縮之毒素。症狀在感染後4~25天內出現，其症狀有肌肉僵硬、痙攣及繼而發生的強直。強直先在下頜及頸部，以後波及背部、胸部、腹部及四肢；病情嚴重時發生全身性痙攣，背部向後彎曲成弓形（參閱 opisthotonos）。高熱、驚厥及劇痛常見。如影響到呼吸肌，為避免因窒息而死亡，做氣管切開、喉管插入和換氣是非常必要的。不治療的患者中死亡率很高，但迅速果斷地應用青黴素和抗毒素治療是有效的。一次患病後並不產生免疫。抗破傷風的免疫法是有效的，但效果是暫時的。

tetany *n*. spasm and twitching of the muscles, particularly those of the face, hands, and feet. Tetany is caused by a reduction in the blood calcium level, which may be due to underactive parathyroid glands, rickets, or *alkalosis.

手足搐搦　肌肉痙攣或抽搐，尤見於面部肌肉，手足肌肉。該症是因血鈣水平降低而引起的，而低血鈣可能起因於甲狀旁腺功能低下、佝僂病或鹼中毒。

tetra- *prefix denoting* four.

〔前級〕四

tetracycline *n.* **1.** one of a group of *antibiotic compounds derived from cultures of *Streptomyces* bacteria. These drugs, which include *chlortetracycline, *doxycycline, *oxytetracycline, and tetracycline, are effective against a wide range of bacterial infections. They are usually given by mouth to treat various conditions, including respiratory-tract infections, syphilis, and acne. Side-effects such as nausea, vomiting, and diarrhoea are fairly common. In addition, suppression of normal intestinal bacteria may make the patient susceptible to infection with tetracycline-resistant organisms. Tetracyclines should not be administered after the fourth month of pregnancy and their use should be avoided in young children to prevent unsightly staining of the permanent teeth. **2.** a particular antibiotic of the tetracycline group. Trade nemes: **Achromycin, Tetrabid**.

(1) 四環素族 一組抗菌化合物，衍生於鏈球菌屬培養物。這類藥物包括有金黴素、多西環素、土黴素及四環素，具有廣譜抗菌作用。常口服以治療各種疾病，如呼吸道感染、梅毒和痤瘡。副作用，如惡心、嘔吐及腹瀉，較為常見。此外，正常腸道細菌受四環素族抑制後，會使病人易受對四環素族耐藥細菌感染。妊娠四個月後的婦女不應服用四環素族藥，幼兒也要避免服用此類藥，以防止恆牙被染成難看的顏色。**(2) 四環素** 四環素族中某一特定的抗生素。商品名：Achromycin，Tetrabid。

tetrad *n.* (in genetics) **1.** the four cells resulting from meiosis after the second telophase. **2.** the four chromatids of a pair of homologous chromosomes (*see* bivalent) in the first stage of meiosis.

(1) 四裂體 （遺傳學）第二次減數分裂末期之後形成的四個細胞。**(2) 四分體** 在第一期減數分裂時一對同源染色體（參閱 bivalent）的四個染色單體。

tetradactyly *n.* a congenital abnormality in which there are only four digits on hand or foot.

四指（趾） 一先天性異常，其手或腳僅有四指（趾）。

tetrahydrocannabinol *n.* a derivative of marijuana that has antiemetic activity and also produces euphoria. These two properties are utilized in the prevention of chemotherapy-induced sickness.

四氫大麻酚 大麻的衍生物，有止吐作用，並能產生欣快感，這兩種特性被用於預防化療引起的嘔吐。

tetrahydrozoline *n.* a drug that constricts blood vessels and is used as a nasal decongestant. *See* vasoconstrictor.

四氫唑啉 收縮血管之藥物，作為鼻腔減少充血劑使用。參閱 vasoconstrictor。

tetralogy of Fallot a form of congenital heart disease in which there is *pulmonary stenosis, enlargement of the right ventricle, a ventricular *septal defect, and in which the origin of the aorta lies over the septal defect. The affected child is blue (cyanosed) and frequently squats. The defect is corrected surgically.

法樂四聯症 先天性心臟病的一種形式，包括有肺動脈狹窄、右心室肥大、室間隔缺損以及主動脈源於缺損間隔上方。患病兒童紫紺並常常蹲坐。此種缺陷可用手術矯正。

tetraplegia *n. see* quadriplegia.

四肢癱瘓 參閱 quadriplegia。

tetrodotoxin *n.* puffer-fish toxin, one of the most powerful known nerve toxins with a mortality of about 50%. There is no known antidote.

河豚毒素 河豚科魚類毒素，為一種現知的最劇烈的神經毒素，其致死率約50%。現尚無解藥。

T-group *n.* a group of people who meet in order to increase their sensitivity and their skills in human relationships by discussing themselves and their relationships. Such groups are sometimes formed in the training of psychiatric staff (the *T* stands for *training*).

T人群 聚在一起的一組人，他們通過討論自己以及討論他們與其他人之間的關係來增強其在人際關係方面的敏感性和技能。在培訓精神病學工作人員時有時組織這樣的小組（T代表訓練）。

thalam- (thalamo-) *prefix denoting* the thalamus. Example: *thalamolenticular* (relating to the thalamus and lenticular nucleus of the brain).

〔前綴〕**丘腦** 例如：丘腦豆狀核的（與丘腦和大腦豆狀核相關的）。

thalamencephalon *n.* the structures, collectively, at the anterior end of the brainstem, comprising the *epithalamus, *thalamus, *hypothalamus, and subthalamus, all of which are concerned with the reception and processing of information that enters from sensory nerve pathways.

丘腦 集中於腦幹前端的一組結構，由丘腦上部、丘腦、丘腦下部及丘腦底部構成，各部分均與接收和處理來自感覺神經通路的信息有關。

thalamic syndrome a raised threshold to pain stimuli combined with a highly unpleasant burning quality to any pain that is experienced once the threshold is exceeded. It is caused by disease affecting the *thalamus.

丘腦綜合徵 疼痛刺激的閾值增高，並伴有對任何疼痛極不適的燒灼感。一旦超過此閾值就會感受這種疼痛。由丘腦患病所致。

thalamotomy *n.* an operation on the brain in which a lesion is made in a precise part of the *thalamus. It has been used to control psychiatric symptoms of severe anxiety and distress, in which cases the lesion is made in the dorsomedial nucleus of the thalamus, which connects with the frontal lobe. *See also* psychosurgery.

丘腦切開術　一種腦部手術，對丘腦中的一精確部位造成一種損傷。此法用以控制有嚴重焦慮和痛苦的精神症狀。在這種情況時要對與額葉相連的丘腦核造成損傷。參閱 psychosurgery。

thalamus *n.* (*pl.* **thalami**) one of two egg-shaped masses of grey matter that lie deep in the cerebral hemispheres in each side of the forebrain. The thalami are relay stations for all the sensory messages that enter the brain, before they are transmitted to the cortex. All sensory pathways, except that for the sense of smell, are linked to nuclei within the thalamus, and it is here that the conscious awareness of messages as sensations – temperature, pain, touch, etc. – probably begins.

丘腦　兩個卵形灰質團之任一，位於前腦兩側的大腦半球深處。丘腦是所有進入大腦的感覺信息在傳入大腦皮質前的中繼站。所有的感覺通路，除嗅覺外，都與丘腦內的核相連，並且就在此處可能開始了對感覺信息——温度、疼痛、觸覺等等——的有意識辨認。

thalassaemia (Cooley's anaemia) *n.* a hereditary blood disease, widespread in the Mediterranean countries, Asia, and Africa, in which there is an abnormality in the protein part of the *haemoglobin molecule. The affected red cells cannot function normally, leading to anaemia. Other symptoms include enlargement of the spleen and abnormalities of the bone marrow. Individuals inheriting the disease from both parents are severely affected (*thalassaemia major*), but those inheriting it from only one parent are usually symptom-free. Patients with the major disease are treated with repeated blood transfusions. The disease can be detected by prenatal diagnosis.

地中海貧血（庫利貧血）　一種遺傳性疾病，廣泛分布於地中海地區國家、亞洲和非洲，其血紅蛋白分子中的蛋白部分發生異常。受侵犯的紅細胞不能正常工作，致使貧血發生。其他症狀包括脾腫大和骨髓異常。受父母雙方遺傳患病的個體病變嚴重（重型地中海貧血），但從父母中一方遺傳患病者常無症狀。重型地中海貧血者要進行反覆輸血治療。可通過產前診斷發現該病。

thalassotherapy *n.* treatment by means of remedial bathing in sea water.

海水療法　在海水中進行治療性洗浴的療法。

thalidomide *n.* a drug that was formerly used as a sedative. If taken during the first three months of pregnancy, it was found to cause fetal abnormalities involving limb malformation and has now been withdrawn.

沙利度胺 以往用作鎮靜劑的藥物。如在妊娠頭三個月內服用此藥，據發現可引起包括肢體畸形在內的胎兒發育異常，故該藥現已停止使用。

thallium *n.* a leadlike element that has several dangerously poisonous compounds. The poison is cumulative and causes liver and nerve damage and bone destruction. The victim's hair is likely to fall out and does not grow again. Treatment is by administration of *chelating agents. Symbol: Tl.

鉈 一種類似鉛的元素，有幾種危險性的毒性化合物。毒物蓄積，造成肝及神經損傷，並引起骨破壞。受害者的頭髮可能脫落並不再重長。採用螯合劑治療。符號：Tl。

thallium scan a method of studying blood flow through the heart muscle (myocardium) and diagnosing myocardial *ischaemia using an injection of the radioisotope thallium-201. Defects of perfusion, such as a recent infarct, emit little or no radioactivity and are seen as 'cold spots' when an image is formed using a *gamma camera and computer. Exercise may be used to provoke 'cold spots' in the diagnosis of ischaemic heart disease.

鉈掃描 一種通過研究心臟肌肉（心肌層）之血流來對心肌缺血加以確診的方法，其時要注射放射性同位素 201鉈。心臟灌注的缺陷，如最新梗塞處，將有很少或沒有放射性釋放，並且在 γ 照相機及計算機所形成的圖像上可看見「冷點」。在對缺血性心臟疾病診斷時用運動鍛煉法可激發「冷點」的出現。

theca *n.* a sheathlike surrounding tissue. For example, the *theca folliculi* is the outer wall of a *Graafian follicle.

膜 組織周圍所包裹的鞘狀物。例如，卵泡膜是格雷夫卵泡的外壁。

theine *n.* the active volatile principle found in tea (*see* caffeine).

茶鹼，咖啡因 茶中發現的揮發性活素（參閱 caffeine）。

thenar *n.* **1.** the palm of the hand. **2.** the fleshy prominent part of the hand at the base of the thumb. *Compare* hypothenar. **–thenar** *adj.*

(1) 手掌 (2) 魚際 手拇指根部肉厚的隆起部分。與 hypothenar 對比。

theobromine *n.* an alkaloid, occurring in cocoa, coffee, and tea, that has a weak diuretic action and dilates coronary and

可可鹼 一種生物鹼，見於可可、咖啡和茶葉內，有微弱的利尿作用並能擴張冠狀動脈和

other arteries. It was formerly used to treat angina.

其他動脈。以往曾廣泛用於治療心絞痛。

theophylline *n.* an alkaloid, occurring in the leaves of the tea plant, that has a diuretic effect and relaxes smooth muscles, especially of the bronchi. Theophylline preparations, particularly *aminophylline, are used mainly to control bronchial asthma. Trade names: **Lasma, Pro-Vent**.

茶鹼 一種生物鹼，見於茶樹的葉內，具有利尿作用，還可鬆弛平滑肌，特別是支氣管平滑肌。茶鹼製劑，尤其是氨茶鹼，主要用於控制支氣管哮喘。商品名：Lasma，Pro-Vent。

therapeutic index the ratio of a dose of a therapeutic agent that produces damage to normal cells to the dose that is necessary to have a defined level of anti-cancer activity. It indicates the relative efficacy of a treatment against tumours.

治療指數 治療劑對正常細胞產生危害的劑量與其達到明顯抗癌效果所必需的劑量之比率。它顯示出抗癌治療的相對效力。

therapeutics *n.* the branch of medicine that deals with different methods of treatment and healing (*therapy*), particularly the use of drugs in the cure of disease.

治療學 研究不同治療及治愈方法的醫學分支，尤指治病中的藥物使用。

therm *n.* a unit of heat equal to 100,000 British thermal units. 1 therm = 1.055 × 10^8 joules.

克卡 熱量單位，相當於 10 萬英國熱單位。1 克卡 = 1.055 × 10^8 焦耳。

therm- (thermo-) *prefix denoting* **1.** heat. **2.** temperature.

〔前綴〕**(1)** 熱 **(2)** 溫度

thermoalgesia (thermalgesia) *n.* an abnormal sense of pain that is felt when part of the body is warmed. It is a type of *dysaesthesia and is a symptom of partial damage to a peripheral nerve or to the fibre tracts conducting temperature sensation to the brain.

熱性痛覺 身體某部分在暖熱時所感到的一種異常疼痛的感覺。係感覺障礙之一種類型。也是周圍神經或向大腦傳導溫度覺的纖維束部分受損時的症狀。

thermoanaesthesia *n.* absence of the ability to recognize the sensations of heat and coldness. When occurring as an isolated sensory symptom it indicates damage to the spinothalamic tract in the

溫覺缺失 對冷熱感覺辨認能力的缺失。當其作為一孤立的感覺症狀出現時，提示脊髓中的脊髓丘腦束受損，而該部分將溫度衝動向丘腦傳送。

spinal cord, which conveys the impulses of temperature to the thalamus.

thermocautery *n.* the destruction of unwanted tissues by heat (*see* cauterize).

thermocoagulation *n.* the coagulation and destruction of tissues by cautery.

thermography *n.* a technique for measuring and recording the heat produced by different parts of the body: by using photographic film sensitive to infrared radiation. The picture produced is called a *thermogram*. The heat radiated from the body varies in different parts according to the flow of blood through the vessels; thus areas of poor circulation produce less heat. On the other hand a tumour with an abnormally increased blood supply may be revealed on the thermogram as a 'hot spot'. The technique is used in the diagnosis of tumours of the breast (*mammothermography*).

thermolysis *n.* (in physiology) the dissipation of body heat by such processes as the evaporation of sweat from the skin surface.

thermometer *n.* a device for registering temperature. A *clinical thermometer* consists of a sealed narrow-bore glass tube with a bulb at one end. It contains mercury, which expands when heated and rises up the tube. The tube is calibrated in degrees, and is designed to register temperatures between 35°C (95°F) and 43.5°C (110°F). An *oral thermometer* is placed in the mouth; a *rectal thermometer* is inserted into the rectum.

thermophilic *adj.* describing organisms, especially bacteria, that grow best at

熱烙術 用熱破壞不要的組織（參閱 cauterize）。

熱凝固術 用燒灼術將組織凝固或破壞掉。

溫度記錄法 一用以計量和記錄身體各部分所產生熱量的技術；使用對紅外綫輻射敏感的照相底片。所得照片稱為溫度記錄圖。身體各部分的熱輻射隨其血管中的血流情況而不同；這樣循環不好的部位所產熱量較少。相反，血液供應異常增加的腫瘤則會在溫度記錄圖上以「熱點」顯示出來。此技術用於診斷乳房腫瘤（乳房溫度記錄法）。

熱放散 （生理學）通過皮膚表面蒸發汗液這樣的過程使身體熱量散發。

溫度計 記錄溫度的裝置。臨床用體溫計由一端帶有小球的一個密封的細玻璃管構成。其小球內含有水銀，受熱時膨脹並上升到玻璃管內。玻璃管上標有刻度，可記錄 35°C（95°F）到 43.5°C（110°F）之間的溫度。口溫度計置於口中，而肛門溫度計則插入直腸。

嗜熱的 描述微生物，特別是細菌，在 48~85°C 時處於最佳

temperatures of 48–85°C. *Compare* mesophilic, psychrophilic.

狀態。與 mesophilic，psychrophilic 比較。

thermophore *n.* any substance that retains heat for a long time, such as kaolin, which is often used in hot poultices.

保熱劑　任何在長時間內保熱的物質，如高嶺土，常被用於熱泥敷療中。

thermoreceptor *n.* a sensory nerve ending that responds to heat or to cold. Such *receptors are scattered widely in the skin and in the mucous membrane of the mouth and throat.

溫度感受器　對冷、熱作出反應的感覺神經末梢。此類感受器廣泛分布於皮膚及口腔和咽部的黏膜。

thermotaxis *n.* the physiological process of regulating or adjusting body temperature.

體溫調節　調節和調整身體溫度的生理過程。

thermotherapy *n.* the use of heat to alleviate pain and stiffness in joints and muscles and to promote an increase in circulation. *Diathermy provides a means of generating heat within the tissues themselves.

溫熱療法　用熱來減輕關節和肌肉的疼痛及僵直，並用以增加血液循環。透熱療法是使組織自身產熱的方法。

thiabendazole *n.* an *anthelmintic used to treat infestations of threadworms and other intestinal worms. It is administered orally and may cause vomiting, vertigo, and gastric discomfort. Trade name: **Mintezol**.

噻苯達唑　用以治療蟯蟲及其他腸寄生蟲傳染的驅蟲藥。口服，可能會引起嘔吐、眩暈及胃部不適。商品名：Mintezol。

thiacetazone (thioparamizone) *n.* a drug that can be used in the treatment of tuberculosis (in combination with *isoniazid). It is administered by mouth. Toxic effects, though infrequent, are severe and include anorexia, hepatitis, and exfoliative dermatitis.

氨硫脲　一種治療結核（與異煙肼合併使用）的藥物。口服，毒性反應雖然少見，但卻嚴重，包括食慾喪失、肝炎和剝脫性皮炎。

thiamin *n. see* vitamin B_1.

硫胺（素）　參閱 vitamin B_1。

thiazide diuretic *see* diuretic.

噻嗪類利尿藥　參閱 diuretic。

Thiersch's graft (split-skin graft) a type of skin graft in which thin partial thicknesses of skin are cut in narrow strips or sheets and placed onto the wound area to be healed.

蒂爾施移植片（分層皮移植片）一種皮膚移植類型，其皮膚的薄分層被切成窄條或片，置於傷口區上面，以使其愈合。

thioguanine *n.* a drug that prevents the growth of cancer cells and is used in the treatment of leukaemia. It is given by mouth and commonly reduces the numbers of white blood cells and platelets. Other side-effects include nausea, vomiting, loss of appetite, and jaundice. Trade name: **Lanvis**.

硫鳥嘌呤 防止癌細胞生長的藥物，用以治療白血病。口服，常常會減少白細胞及血小板。其他副作用還有惡心、嘔吐、無食慾和黃疸。商品名：Lanvis。

thioparamizone *n. see* thiacetazone.

氨硫脲 參閱 thiacetazone。

thiopentone *n.* a short-acting *barbiturate. It is given by intravenous injection to produce general *anaesthesia or as a premedication prior to surgery. Possible complications of thiopentone anaesthesia can include respiratory depression, laryngeal spasm, and thrombophlebitis. The drug is not used when respiratory obstruction is present. Trade names: **Intraval, Pentothal**.

硫噴妥鈉 短效巴比妥酸鹽。通過靜脈注射以產生全身麻醉或作為外科術前用藥。硫噴妥鈉麻醉可能引發的併發症有呼吸抑制、喉痙攣、血栓性靜脈炎。當有呼吸道阻塞時，禁用此藥。商品名：Intraval，Pentothal。

thiophilic *adj.* growing best in the presence of sulphur or sulphur compounds. The term is usually applied to bacteria.

嗜硫的 在有硫或硫化物存在時生長處於最佳狀態的。該術語常用來指細菌。

thioridazine *n.* a phenothiazine *antipsychotic drug used in the treatment of a wide range of mental and emotional disturbances, including schizophrenia and senile dementia. The drug is given by mouth; side-effects include faintness, dizziness, dry mouth, and impairment of sexual function. Trade name: **Melleril**.

硫利達嗪 一種吩噻嗪類抗精神病藥，廣泛用於治療精神及情緒紊亂，如精神分裂症及老年性癡呆。口服，副作用包括暈厥、頭暈、口乾、及性功能減退。商品名：Melleril。

thioxanthene *n. see* antipsychotic.

噻噸 參閱 antipsychotic。

thorac- (thoraco-) *prefix denoting* the thorax or chest.

〔前綴〕胸，胸廓

thoracentesis *n. see* pleurocentesis.

胸腔穿刺術　參閱 pleurocentesis。

thoracic cavity the chest cavity. *See* thorax.

胸腔　胸部的腔。參閱 thorax。

thoracic duct one of the two main trunks of the *lymphatic system. It receives lymph from both legs, the lower abdomen, left thorax, left side of the head, and left arm and drains into the left innominate vein.

胸導管　淋巴系統的兩個主幹之一。它接受來自雙側下肢、下腹、左胸、頭部左側及左臂的淋巴液，並將淋巴液導入左側無名靜脈。

thoracic vertebrae the 12 bones of the *backbone to which the ribs are attached. They lie between the cervical (neck) and lumbar (lower back) vertebrae and are characterized by the presence of facets for articulation with the ribs. *See also* vertebra.

胸椎　脊柱與肋骨相連的 12 個脊椎骨。它們位於頸椎與腰椎之間，其特徵為肋骨相接處有一小關節面。參閱 vertebra。

thoracocentesis *n. see* pleurocentesis.

胸腔穿刺術　參閱 pleurocentesis。

thoracoplasty *n.* a former treatment for pulmonary tuberculosis involving surgical removal of parts of the ribs, thus allowing the chest wall to fall in and collapse the affected lung.

胸廓成形術　以往治療肺結核的方法，包括手術切除部分肋骨，使胸腔壁下陷致使結核侵襲的肺部萎陷。

thoracoscope *n.* an instrument used to inspect the *pleural cavity. **–thoracoscopy** *n.*

胸腔鏡　用以探查胸腔的器械。

thoracotomy *n.* surgical opening of the chest cavity to inspect or operate on the heart, lungs, or other structures within.

胸廓切開術　手術切開胸腔，以檢查心、肺或其他內在結構或對這些部分進行手術。

thorax *n.* the chest: the part of the body cavity between the neck and the diaphragm. The skeleton of the thorax is formed by the sternum, costal cartilages, ribs, and thoracic vertebrae of the backbone. It encloses the lungs, heart,

胸廓　胸部：頸與膈之間的體腔部分。胸廓的骨架是由胸骨、肋軟骨、肋骨和脊柱的胸椎構成的。它將肺、心臟、食管及相關結構圍在其中。與 abdomen 對比。

oesophagus, and associated structures. *Compare* abdomen. **–thoracic** *adj.*

thorium-X *n.* the radioactive isotope radium-224, which emits alpha radiation and was formerly used in *radiotherapy. *See also* radium.

釷-X　放射性同位素 ^{224}鐳，可放出 α 射綫，以往用於放射治療中。參閱 radium。

thought-stopping *n.* a technique of *behaviour therapy used in the treatment of obsessional thoughts. Attention is voluntarily withdrawn from these thoughts and focused on some other vivid image or engrossing activity.

思維停止　行為療法的一項技術，用以治療強迫意念。注意力被有意地從這些觀念中撤回，並集中在其他一些生動的想象或吸引人的活動上。

threadworm *n. see* pinworm.

綫蟲　參閱 pinworm。

threonine *n.* an *essential amino acid. *See also* amino acid.

蘇氨酸　一種必需的氨基酸。參閱 amino acid。

threshold *n.* (in neurology) the point at which a stimulus begins to evoke a response, and therefore a measure of the sensitivity of a system under particular conditions. A *thermoreceptor that responds to an increase in temperature of only two degrees is said to have a much lower threshold than one that will only respond to a change in temperature of ten degrees or more. In this example the threshold can be measured directly in terms of degrees.

閾值　（神經病學）刺激開始激起反應的起始點，因此也是對特定情況下的系統敏感的一種測量。溫度僅增加 2 度時便可作出反應的溫度感受器比溫度變化 10 度或更多時才作出反應的溫度感受器閾值要低得多。此例中的閾值可直接拿度數來衡量。

thrill *n.* a vibration felt on placing the hand on the body. A heart murmur that is felt by placing the hand on the chest wall is said to be accompanied by a thrill.

震顫　將手放到身體上所感受到的震動。據稱，把手放在胸壁能感覺到的心臟雜音伴有震顫。

-thrix *suffix denoting* a hair or hairlike structure.

〔後綴〕毛　毛髮或類似毛髮的結構。

thromb- (thrombo-) *prefix denoting* **1.** a blood clot (thrombus). **2.** thrombosis. **3.** blood platelets.

〔前綴〕**(1)** 血凝塊（血栓）**(2)** 血栓形成 **(3)** 血小板

thrombasthenia n. a hereditary blood disease in which the function of the *platelets is defective although they are present in normal numbers. The manifestations are identical to those of thrombocytopenic *purpura.

血小板機能不全 遺傳性血液病，其血小板有功能缺陷，儘管其數值正常。臨床表現與血小板減少性紫癜相似。

thrombectomy n. a surgical procedure in which a blood clot (thrombus) is removed from an artery or vein (*see* endarterectomy, phlebothrombosis).

血栓切除術 一種將血凝塊（血栓）從動脈或靜脈中切除（參閱 endarterectomy，phlebothrombosis）的外科手術。

thrombin n. a substance (*coagulation factor) that acts as an enzyme, converting the soluble protein fibrinogen to the insoluble protein fibrin in the final stage of *blood coagulation. Thrombin is not normally present in blood plasma, being derived from an inactive precursor, *prothrombin*.

凝血酶 一種起着酶作用的物質（凝血因子），在凝血過程中的最後階段該物質由可溶性纖維蛋白原轉變為不溶性纖維蛋白。正常情況下血漿內不存在該物質，它是從非活性前體——凝血酶原——衍生而來的。

thromboangiitis obliterans *see* Buerger's disease.

血栓閉塞性脈管炎 參閱 Buerger's disease。

thrombocyte n. see platelet.

血小板 參閱 platelet。

thrombocythaemia n. a disease in which there is an abnormal proliferation of the cells that produce blood *platelets (*megakaryocytes), leading to an increased number of platelets in the blood. This may result in an increased tendency to form clots within blood vessels (thrombosis); alternatively the function of the platelets may be abnormal, leading to an increased tendency to bleed. Treatment is by radiotherapy or by *cytotoxic drugs.

血小板增多症 產生血小板的細胞（巨核細胞）異常增多，致使血液中血小板數量增多的疾病。這可能會引起血管內血凝塊（血栓）形成的傾向增加。另一方面血小板的功能可能不正常，致使出血的傾向增加。用放射治療或細胞毒素藥物加以治療。

thrombocytopenia n. a reduction in the number of *platelets in the blood. This results in bleeding into the skin (*see* purpura), spontaneous bruising, and prolonged bleeding after injury. Thrombocytopenia may result from failure of

血小板減少症 血液中血小板數減少。這將引起皮膚出血（參閱 purpura）、自發性皮膚青腫、以及損傷後出血不止。該病可由血小板生成障礙或過度受損引起。

platelet production or excessive destruction of platelets. **–thrombocytopenic**
adj.

thrombocytosis *n.* an increase in the
number of *platelets in the blood. It may
occur in a variety of diseases, including
chronic infections, cancers, and certain
blood diseases and is likely to cause an
incresed tendency to form blood clots
within vessels (thrombosis).

血小板增多　血液中血小板數
增多。可出現在多種疾病中，
包括慢性感染、癌症和某些血
液病，並很可能引起血管內血
凝塊形成（血栓形成）的傾向
增加。

thromboembolism *n.* the condition
in which a blood clot (thrombus), formed
at one point in the circulation, becomes
detached and lodges at another point.
It is most commonly applied to the
association of phlebothrombosis and
*pulmonary embolism (*pulmonary
thromboembolic disease*).

血栓栓塞　在血液循環內某點
形成的血凝塊（血栓）脫落並
停留在其他點上。這最常指的
是由靜脈血栓形成所併發的肺
栓塞（肺血栓栓塞性疾病）。

thromboendarterectomy *n.* *see*
endarterectomy.

血栓動脈內膜切除術　參閱
endarterectomy。

thromboendarteritis *n.* thrombosis
complicating *endarteritis, seen in temporal *arteritis, *polyarteritis nodosa,
and syphilis. It may cause death of part
of the organ supplied by the affected
artery.

血栓性動脈內膜炎　血栓形成
並合併有動脈內膜炎，見於顳
動脈炎、結節性多動脈炎及梅
素。可引起由受損動脈供血的
器官部分壞死。

thrombokinase *n. see* thromboplastin.

凝血激酶　參閱 thromboplas-
tin。

thrombolysis *n.* the dissolution of a
blood clot (thrombus) by the infusion
of an enzyme, such as *streptokinase,
into the blood (*see also* tissue plasminogen activator). It may be used in
the treatment of *phlebothrombosis,
*pulmonary embolism, and coronary
thrombosis.

血栓溶解　因血內注入一種
酶，如鏈激酶（參閱 tissue
plasminogen activator），而使
血凝塊（血栓）溶解。可用於
治療靜脈血栓形成、肺栓塞和
冠狀動脈血栓形成。

thrombolytic *adj.* describing an agent
that breaks up blood clots (thrombi).

溶解血栓的　能使血凝塊（血
栓）分解的藥物。參閱

See fibrinolytic, tissue plasminogen activator.

thrombophlebitis *n.* inflammation of the wall of a vein (*see* phlebitis) with secondary thrombosis occurring within the affected segment of vein. Pregnant women are more prone to thrombophlebitis because of physiological changes in the blood and the effects of pressure within the abdomen. It may involve superficial or deep veins of the legs (the latter being less common in pregnancy than the former). Thrombophlebitis of the femoral vein may produce *phlegmasia alba dolens* (painful white leg), which was a common accompaniment to puerperal fever (now fortunately rare). Deep-vein thrombosis may precede *pulmonary embolism.

thromboplastin (thrombokinase) *n.* a substance formed during the earlier stages of *blood coagulation. It acts as an enzyme, converting the inactive substance prothrombin to the enzyme *thrombin.

thrombopoiesis *n.* the process of blood *platelet production. Platelets are formed as fragments of cytoplasm shed from giant cells (*megakaryocytes) in the bone marrow by a budding process.

thrombosis *n.* a condition in which the blood changes from a liquid to a solid state and produces a blood clot (*thrombus*). Thrombosis may occur within a blood vessel in diseased states. Thrombosis in an artery obstructs the blood flow to the tissue it supplies: obstruction of an artery to the brain is one of the causes of a *stroke and thrombosis in an artery supplying the heart – *coronary thrombosis – results in a heart attack (*see*

fibrinolytic，tissue plasminogen activator。

血栓性靜脈炎 靜脈壁發炎（參閱 phlebitis），同時靜脈在患病部分有繼發性血栓形成。孕婦更易患上此病，因其血液中發生生理變化及腹壓的影響。可能會侵犯到雙腿的表層或深層靜脈（對於孕婦後者較前者少見）。股靜脈發生的血栓性靜脈炎可能會引發股白腫（痛苦的腿部泛白），該病常合併有產褥熱（慶幸的是現已少見）。深層靜脈的血栓形成可能會導致栓塞。

凝血激酶 形成於凝血早期的一種物質。起酶之作用，將無活性凝血酶原轉變成凝血酶。

血小板形成 血小板生成之過程。由巨細胞（巨核細胞）在骨髓內發育過程中脫落胞漿的碎片形成。

血栓形成 血液由液態變為固態並生成血凝塊（血栓）的情況。這種情況可發生於病變的血管內。動脈血栓形成將阻塞血液流向其所供應的組織：腦動脈阻塞是中風的原因之一，而供應心臟之動脈血栓形成──冠狀動脈血栓形成──將引起心臟病的發作（參閱 myocardial infarction）。靜脈亦可能有血栓形成，且可併發

myocardial infarction). Thrombosis can also occur in a vein, and it may be associated with inflammation (*see* phlebitis, phlebothrombosis). The thrombus may become detached from its site of formation and carried in the blood to lodge in another part (*see* embolism).

有炎症（參閱 phlebitis，phlebothrombosis）。血栓可從其形成的部位脫落並被血液帶到其他部位停留（參閱 embolism）。

thrombus *n.* a blood clot (*see* thrombosis).

血栓 血凝塊（參閱 thrombosis）。

thrush *n. see* candidosis.

鵝口瘡 參閱 candidosis。

thym- (thymo-) *prefix denoting* the thymus.

〔前綴〕**胸腺**

thymectomy *n.* surgical removal of the thymus gland.

胸腺切除術 切除胸腺的外科手術。

-thymia *suffix denoting* a condition of the mind. Example: *cyclothymia* (alternations of mood).

〔後綴〕**心境** 心理狀態。例如：循環情感性氣質（精神狀態明顯的交替變換）。

thymic aplasia failure of development of the *thymus gland. This was formerly thought to predispose to *hypersensitivity reactions and to infection and so to death in childhood (*see* status lymphaticus), a concept no longer held.

胸腺發育不全 胸腺發育不良。過去認為這種情況易患過敏反應及感染，並且因此致使兒童夭折（參閱 status lymphaticus），但人們現已不再持此觀點。

thymidine *n.* a compound containing thymine and the sugar ribose. *See also* nucleoside.

胸腺嘧啶核苷 含有胸腺嘧啶與核糖之化合物。參閱 nucleoside。

thymine *n.* one of the nitrogen-containing bases (*see* pyrimidine) occurring in the nucleic acids DNA and RNA.

胸腺嘧啶 存在於DNA及RNA核酸中的一種含氮鹼基（參閱 pyrimidine）。

thymitis *n* inflammation of the thymus gland (the mass of lymphatic tissue behind the breastbone).

胸腺炎 胸腺（胸骨後的淋巴組織）的炎症。

thymocyte *n.* a lymphocyte within the *thymus.

胸腺細胞 胸腺內的淋巴細胞。

thymoma *n.* a benign or malignant tumour of the *thymus gland. It is sometimes associated with *myasthenia gravis, a chronic disease in which muscles tire easily. Surgical removal of the tumour may result in improvement of the muscle condition, but the response is often slow.

胸腺瘤　胸腺的良性或惡性腫瘤。有些情況下伴有重症肌無力，是一種肌肉易疲勞的慢性病。外科手術切除胸腺瘤可能會導致肌肉情況的改善，但這種反應往往是緩慢的。

thymoxamine *n.* an *alpha blocker drug that causes peripheral blood vessels to dilate (*see* vasodilator). It is administered by mouth in the treatment of Raynaud's disease and similar conditions. Side-effects include mild nausea, diarrhoea, headache, and flushing. The drug should be used with caution in patients with diabetes mellitus or heart disease. Trade name: **Opilon**.

莫西賽利　一種使末梢血管擴張的 α-受體阻滯藥（參閱 vasodilator）。口服，用以治療雷諾病及類似疾病。副作用包括輕微惡心、腹瀉、頭痛及面紅。對糖尿病和心臟病患者慎用。商品名：Opilon。

thymus *n.* a bilobed organ in the root of the neck, above and in front of the heart. The thymus is enclosed in a capsule and divided internally by cross walls into many lobules, each full of T-lymphocytes (white blood cells associated with antibody production). In relation to body size the thymus is largest at birth. It doubles in size by puberty, after which it gradually shrinks, its functional tissue being replaced by fatty tissue. In infancy the thymus controls the development of *lymphoid tissue and the immune response to microbes and foreign proteins (accounting for allergic response, autoimmunity, and the rejection of organ transplants). T-lymphocytes migrate from the bone marrow to the thymus, where they mature and differentiate until activated by antigen. **–thymic** *adj.*

胸腺　頸根部、心臟前上方的一雙葉器官。胸腺包裹在被膜中，其內部被縱橫交叉的壁隔成許多小葉，每個小葉內充滿了 T-淋巴細胞（與抗體產生相關的白細胞）。與身體大小相比，胸腺在出生時最大。青春期時達到其出生時的兩倍，隨後逐漸萎縮，其功能性組織被脂肪組織所取代。嬰兒期胸腺控制着淋巴組織的發育及對微生物及異體蛋白的免疫反應（為變態反應、自體免疫及排斥移植器官的原因）。T-淋巴細胞從骨髓轉移到胸腺，在胸腺內該細胞成熟並在被抗體激活時分化。

thyro- *prefix denoting* the thyroid gland. Example: *thyroglossal* (relating to the thyroid gland and tongue).

〔前綴〕**甲狀腺**　例如：甲狀舌的（與甲狀腺及舌相關的）。

thyrocalcitonin (calcitonin) *n.* a hormone, produced by certain cells in the thyroid gland, that lowers the levels of calcium and phosphate in the blood. Thyrocalcitonin is given by infection to treat hypercalcaemia and Paget's disease of the bone. *Compare* parathyroid hormone.

降鈣素 一種激素，由甲狀腺的某種細胞所產生，能降低血液中鈣和磷的濃度。注射以治療高鈣血症和骨的佩吉特病。與 parathyroid hormone 對比。

thyrocele *n.* a swelling of the thyroid gland. *See* goitre.

甲狀腺腫 甲狀腺腫大。參閱 goitre。

thyroglobulin *n.* a protein in the thyroid gland from which the *thyroid hormones (thyroxine and triiodotyrosine) are synthesized.

甲狀腺球蛋白 在甲狀腺內合成甲狀腺激素（甲狀腺素與三碘酪氨酸）的一種蛋白。

thyrohyoid *adj.* relating to the thyroid cartilage and hyoid bone. The *thyrohyoid ligaments* form part of the *larynx; contraction of the *thyrohyoid muscle* raises the larynx.

甲狀腺舌骨的 與甲狀軟骨及舌骨相關的。甲狀腺舌骨韌帶組成喉的一部分。甲狀腺舌骨肌收縮時將喉部向上抬動。

thyroid cartilage the main cartilage of the *larynx, consisting of two broad plates that join at the front to form a V-shaped structure. The thyroid cartilage forms the *Adam's apple* in front of the larynx.

甲狀軟骨 喉部的主要軟骨，由兩個在前緣結合形成一 V 字結構的寬片組成。該軟骨構成喉前部的喉結。

thyroidectomy *n.* surgical removal of the thyroid gland. In *partial thyroidectomy*, only the diseased part of the gland is removed; in *subtotal thyroidectomy*, a method of treating *thyrotoxicosis, the surgeon removes 90% of the gland.

甲狀腺切除術 外科切除甲狀腺。部分甲狀腺切除術中僅有部分甲狀腺被切除，而在甲狀腺次全切除手術中外科醫生將 90% 的腺體切除，該方法用以治療甲狀腺毒症。

thyroid gland a large *endocrine gland situated in the base of the neck (see illustration). It consists of two lobes, one on either side of the trachea, that are joined by an *isthmus* (sometimes a third lobe extends upwards from the isthmus). The thyroid gland consists of a large number of closed follicles inside which is a jelly-like colloid, which contains the principal

甲狀腺 位於頸根部的大的內分泌腺（見圖）。由兩葉構成，氣管的一側各有一葉，兩葉以峽部相接（有時從峽部向上伸出第三葉）。甲狀腺由大量的封閉濾泡組成，其中為凝膠狀的膠體，它含有甲狀腺分泌的主要活性物質。通過分泌甲狀腺激素，甲狀腺參與調節

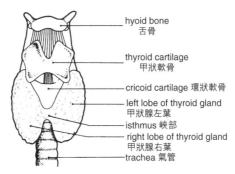

hyoid bone
舌骨

thyroid cartilage
甲狀軟骨

cricoid cartilage 環狀軟骨
left lobe of thyroid gland
甲狀腺左葉
isthmus 峽部
right lobe of thyroid gland
甲狀腺右葉
trachea 氣管

Position of the thyroid gland
甲狀腺的位置

active substances that are secreted by the gland. The thyroid gland is concerned with regulation of the metabolic rate by the secretion of *thyroid hormone, which is stimulated by *thyroid-stimulating hormone from the pituitary gland and requires trace amounts of iodine. Thyroid extract is used in the treatment of thyroid deficiency diseases.

代謝率,而其分泌則受垂體中促甲狀腺激素的刺激,並需要微量的碘。甲狀腺浸出物可用來治療甲狀腺功能低下症。

thyroid hormone an iodine-containing substance, synthesized and secreted by the thyroid gland, that is essential for normal metabolic processes and mental and physical development. There are two thyroid hormones, *triiodothyronine* and *thyroxine*. Lack of these hormones gives rise to *cretinism in infants and *myxoedema in adults. Excessive production of thyroid hormones gives rise to *thyrotoxicosis.

甲狀腺激素 含碘物質,由甲狀腺合成並分泌,該物質是正常的新陳代謝過程、智力與身體發育所必需的。有兩種甲狀腺激素,即三碘甲狀腺氨酸與甲狀腺素。缺少這種激素會使嬰兒患克汀病,成人患黏液性水腫。甲狀腺激素的過多分泌會導致甲狀腺毒症。

thyroiditis *n.* inflammation of the thyroid gland. *Acute thyroiditis is* due to bacterial infection; *chronic thyroiditis* is commonly caused by an abnormal immune response (*see* autoimmunity) in which lymphocytes invade the tissues of the gland. *See* Hashimoto's disease, struma.

甲狀腺炎 甲狀腺之炎症。急性甲狀腺炎由細菌感染引起;慢性甲狀腺炎則常由異常免疫反應(參閱 autoimmunity)引起,在該反應中淋巴細胞侵入甲狀腺組織內。參閱 Hashimoto's disease,struma。

thyroid-stimulating hormone (TSH, thyrotrophin) a hormone, synthesized and secreted by the anterior pituitary gland under the control of *thyrotrophin-releasing hormone, that stimulates activity of the thyroid gland. Defects in TSH production lead to over- or under-secretion of *thyroid hormones. TSH may be given by injection to test thyroid gland function.

促甲狀腺激素　由垂體前葉分泌、合成的一種激素，該激素在促甲狀腺激素釋放激素的支配下，可刺激甲狀腺的活力。該激素的生成障礙將導致甲狀腺激素分泌的過多或過少。注射該激素可用以測定甲狀腺功能。

thyrotomy *n.* surgical incision of either the thyroid cartilage in the neck or of the thyroid gland itself.

甲狀腺切開術　外科切除頸部之甲狀腺軟骨或者切除甲狀腺本身。

thyrotoxicosis *n.* the syndrome due to excessive amounts of thyroid hormones in the bloodstream, causing a rapid heartbeat, sweating, tremor, anxiety increased appetite, loss of weight, and intolerance of heat. Causes include simple overactivity of the gland, a hormone-secreting benign tumour or carcinoma of the thyroid, and *Grave's disease* (*exophthalmic goitre*), in which there are additional symptoms including swelling of the neck (*goitre*) due to enlargement of the gland and protrusion of the eyes (*exophthalmos*). Treatment may be by surgical removal of the thyroid gland, administration of radioactive iodine to destroy part of the gland, or by the use of drugs (such as *carbimazole or *propylthiouracil) that interfere with the production of thyroid hormones. **–thyrotoxic** *adj.*

甲狀腺毒症　因血流中存在有過量的甲狀腺激素而引起的綜合徵。導致心跳加快、出汗、震顫、焦慮、食慾增加、體重下降及怕熱。病因包括單純的甲狀腺功能亢進，分泌激素的良性腫瘤或甲狀腺瘤及格雷夫病（突眼性甲狀腺腫），後者還有因甲狀腺腫大而頸部腫脹（甲狀腺腫）及突眼（眼球突出）等額外的症狀。治療時可切除甲狀腺，使用放射性碘破壞部分腺體，或服用阻礙甲狀腺激素產生的藥物（如卡比馬唑或丙硫氧嘧啶）。

thyrotrophin *n. see* thyroid-stimulating hormone.

促甲狀腺激素　參閱 thyroid-stimulating hormone。

thyrotrophin-releasing hormone (TRH) a hormone from the hypothalamus (in the brain) that acts on the anterior pituitary gland to stimulate the release of *thyroid-stimulating hormone.

促甲狀腺激素釋放激素　來自下丘腦（大腦內）的激素，該激素作用於垂體前葉並刺激它釋放甲狀腺刺激激素。通過靜脈注射該激素可測定甲狀腺功

TRH is given by intravenous injection to test thyroid gland function and to estimate reserves of thyroid-stimulating hormone in the pituitary.

能並估量出垂體內甲狀腺刺激激素的貯備。

thyroxine *n.* one of the hormones synthesized and secreted by the thyroid gland (*see* thyroid hormone). Thyroxine can be administered by mouth to treat underactivity of the thyroid gland (*see* cretinism, myxoedema).

甲狀腺素　由甲狀腺合成並分泌的激素之一（參閱 thyroid hormone）。口服該激素可治療甲狀腺功能低下（參閱 cretinism，myxoedema）。

TIA *see* transient ischaemic attack.

一過性腦缺血　參閱 transient ischaemic attack。

tibia *n.* the shin bone: the inner and larger bone of the lower leg (see illustration). It articulates with the *femur above, with the *talus below, and with the *fibula to the side (at both ends); at the lower end is a projection, the medial *malleolus, forming part of the articulation with the talus.

脛骨　小腿內側的大骨（見圖），該骨在上方與股骨相關節，在下與距骨相關節，在兩側（兩端）與腓骨相關節；其下端有一隆突，即內踝，是其與距骨形成關節的部分。

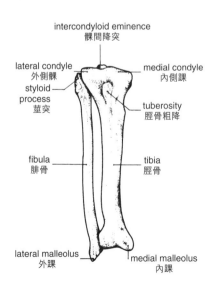

Right tibia and fibula
右側脛骨與腓骨

tibialis *n.* either of two muscles in the leg, extending from the tibia to the metatarsal bones of the foot. The *tibialis anterior* turns the foot inwards and flexes the toes backwards. Situated behind it, the *tibialis posterior* extends the toes and inverts the foot.

脛骨肌 腿部的兩塊肌肉之一，該肌從脛骨延展至足部跖骨。脛骨前肌使足內翻，並使腳趾向腳背彎曲。脛骨後肌，位於前肌後方，使腳趾伸展和足反轉。

tibio- *prefix denoting* the tibia. Example: *tibiofibular* (relating to the tibia and fibula).

〔前綴〕**脛骨，脛** 例如脛腓的（與脛骨及腓骨相關的）。

tic *n.* a repeated and largely involuntary movement varying in complexity from the twitch of a muscle to elaborate well-coordinated actions. Simple tics occur in about a quarter of all children and usually disappear within a year. Tics most often become prominent when the individual is exposed to emotional stress. *See also* Gilles de la Tourette syndrome.

抽搐 反覆發生的，大都為不隨意的運動，其複雜程度從肌肉顫動到精細協調的動作各有不同。簡單的抽搐在四分之一的兒童身上均可見到，但通常在一年內消失。當患者處於心理情緒壓力之中時，症狀多變得顯著。參圖 Gilles de la Tourette syndrome。

ticaricillin *n.* a *penicillin-type antibiotic useful for its action against the bacterium *Pseudomonas aeruginosa*.

替卡西林 青黴素類抗生素，其作用可抵抗綠膿假單胞菌。

tic douloureux *see* neuralgia.

三叉神經痛 參閱 neuralgia。

tick *n.* a bloodsucking parasite belonging to the order of arthropods (the Acarina) that also includes the *mites. Tick bites can cause serious skin lesions and occasionally paralysis (*see* Ixodes, Amblyomma), and certain tick species transmit *typhus, *Lyme disease, and *relapsing fever. Dimethyl phthalate is used as a tick repellent. There are two families: Argasidae (soft ticks), including *Ornithodoros*, with mouthparts invisible from above and no hard shield (*scutum*) on the dorsal surface; and Ixodidae (hard ticks), which includes *Dermacentor*, *Haemaphysalis*, and *Rhipicephalus*, with clearly visible mouthparts and a definite scutum.

蜱（壁虱） 屬於節肢動物類（蟎目）的一種吸血性寄生蟲，其中也包括蟎在內。叮咬會引起嚴重的皮膚損害，且偶爾會引起癱瘓（參閱 Ixodes，Amblyomma），有的蜱類傳播斑疹傷寒、萊姆病及回歸熱。酞酸二甲酯被用作蜱的驅除劑。蜱有兩種：隱喙蜱科（軟蜱），及硬蜱科（硬蜱）；前者包括鈍喙蜱屬，該屬的口部從上面可以見到，但其背部表面無硬的盾殼（盾片）；後者中包括革蜱屬、立蜱屬，有明顯可見的口部及明確的盾片。

tick fever any infectious disease transmitted by ticks, especially *Rocky Mountain spotted fever.

蜱熱　由蜱傳播的任何傳染性疾病，尤指落基山斑疹熱。

Tietze's syndrome (costochondritis) a painful swelling of a rib in the region of the chest, over the junction of bone and cartilage. The cause is unknown and the condition usually resolves without treatment, but in some cases local injections of corticosteroids are required.

蒂策綜合徵（肋骨軟骨炎）　胸腔部肋骨的疼痛性腫脹，發生在肋骨與軟骨的連接處。病因不明，病情常無須治療就自愈，但有時需局部注射皮質類固醇。

time sampling (in psychology) a way of recording behaviour in which the presence or absence of particular kinds of behaviour is noted during each of several fixed prearranged periods of time. *See also* event sampling.

時間抽樣　（心理學）一種記錄行為的方式，在幾段預先安排的固定時間內，對每一段時間中某特殊行為的發生或沒有發生予以記錄。參閱 event sampling。

timolol *n.* a *beta blocker used in the treatment of high blood pressure (hypertension), long-term prophylaxis after an acute myocardial infarction, and *glaucoma. It is administered by mouth or in solution as eye drops; side-effects include decreased heart rate, hypotension, and dizziness. Trade names: **Betim, Blocadren, Timoptol**.

哇嗎洛爾　一種 β-受體阻滯劑，用於治療血壓高，可長效預防急性心肌梗死及青光眼。口服或作眼藥水滴注；副作用有心率減慢、低血壓，及頭暈。商品名：Betim，Blocadren，Timoptol。

tincture *n.* an alcoholic extract of a drug derived from a plant.

酊劑　從一種植物中提取的酒精浸出物藥。

tinea *n. see* ringworm.

癬　參閱 ringworm。

Tinel's sign a method for checking the regeneration of a nerve: direct tapping over the sheath of the nerve elicits a distal tingling sensation (*see* paraesthesiae), which indicates the beginning of regeneration.

蒂內爾徵　檢查神經是否再生的一種方法：直接叩診神經鞘引出遠端的麻刺感（參閱 paraesthesiae），提示再生開始。

tinnitus *n.* any noise (buzzing, ringing, etc.) in the ear. The many causes include wax (*cerumen) in the ear; damage to the eardrum; diseases of the inner ear, such

耳鳴　耳內有某種噪聲（嗡嗡聲、叮吟聲等等）。病因有多種，如耳內耵聹（耳垢）；鼓膜損傷；內耳疾病，如耳硬化

as *otosclerosis and *Ménière's disease; drugs such as aspirin and quinine, and abnormalities of the auditory nerve and its connections within the brain.

症和梅尼埃爾病；藥物影響，例如阿司匹林和奎寧；以及聽神經及其在大腦內的傳導發生異常。

tintometer *n.* an instrument for measuring the depth of colour in a liquid. The colour can then be compared with those on standard charts so that the concentration of a particular compound in solution can be estimated.

液體比色器 衡量液體顏色深度之儀器。將待測液體的顏色與標準比色表相比較，就可估計溶液內某特殊化合物的濃度。

TIPSS (transcutaneous intrahepatic porto-systemic shunt) *see* portal hypertension.

經皮肝門靜脈系統分流 參閱 portal hypertension。

tissue *n.* a collection of cells specialized to perform a particular function. The cells may be of the same type (e.g. in nervous tissue) or of different types (e.g. in connective tissue). Aggregations of tissues constitute organs.

組織 專門執行某種功能的細胞的集合體。可屬於同類胞（如神經組織中），也可屬於不同類型的細胞（如結締組織中）。組織的聚集構成器官。

tissue culture the culture of living tissues, removed from the body, in a suitable medium supplied with nutrients and oxygen.

組織培養 對人體取出的活組織的培養，將其置於適宜的培養基中，並供以營養及氧氣。

tissue plasminogen activator (tPA, TPA) a natural protein, found in the body and now able to be manufactured by genetic engineering (*see* alteplase), that can break up a thrombus (*see* thrombolysis). It requires the presence of *fibrin as a cofactor and is able to activate *plasminogen on the fibrin surface, which distinguishes it from the other plasminogen activators, *streptokinase and *urokinase.

組織纖維蛋白溶酶原激活酶 一種自然蛋白，見於體內，現在可由基因工程（參閱 alteplase）生產，該蛋白可溶解血栓（參閱 thrombolysis）。需用纖維蛋白作為輔助因子，這樣才可能激活纖維蛋白表面的纖維蛋白溶酶原，這使其不同於其他纖維蛋白溶酶原激活酶、鏈激酶及尿激酶。

tissue typing determination of the *HLA profiles of tissues to assess their compatibility. It is the most important predictor of success or failure of a transplant operation.

組織配型 確定組織的 HLA 特性以評估其相容性。對於移植手術的成功與失敗這將是一個最重要的預示。

titre *n.* (in immunology) the extent to which a sample of blood serum containing antibody can be diluted before losing its ability to cause agglutination of the relevant antigen. It is used as a measure of the amount of antibody in the serum.

滴度 （免疫學）指一種程度，在這一程度時含有抗體的血清標本被稀釋至將失去與相關抗原起凝集作用的能力。該指標用以衡量血清中抗體的含量。

titubation *n.* a rhythmical nodding movement of the head, sometimes involving the trunk. Occasionally the use of this term is extended to include a stumbling gait.

顛搖 有節奏的點頭運動，有時包括軀幹。有時此術語的使用擴大到涵蓋蹣跚的步態。

T-lymphocyte *n. see* lymphocyte.

T－淋巴細胞 參閱 lymphocyte。

TNM classification a classification defined by the American Joint Committee on Cancer for the extent of spread of a cancer. T refers to the size of the tumour, N the presence and extent of lymph node involvement, and M the presence of distant spread.

TNM 分級 由美國癌症聯合委員會所確定的一種分級制度。T 指腫瘤大小，N 指淋巴結受累及其程度，M 指擴散存在。

tobacco *n.* the dried leaves of the plant *Nicotiana tabacum* or related species, used in smoking and as snuff. Tobacco contains the stimulant but poisonous alkaloid *nicotine, which enters the bloodstream during smoking. The volatile tarry material also released during smoking contains carcinogenic chemicals (*see* carcinogen).

煙草 煙草植物或其近緣品種的乾葉，用於吸煙或用作鼻煙。煙草中含興奮劑，但吸煙時有毒的生物鹼尼古丁（煙鹼）進入血流。吸煙時釋放出的揮發性柏油狀物質還含有致癌的化學物質（參閱 carcinogen）。

tobramycin *n.* an antibiotic used to treat septicaemia, external eye infections, and lower respiratory, urinary, skin, abdominal, and central nervous system infections. It is administered by intravenous or intramuscular injections or applied by ointment or solution to the eye. Kidney damage or hearing impairment may occur with high doses or prolonged use. Trade names: **Nebcin**, **Tobralex**.

妥布黴素 一種抗生素，用於治療敗血症、外眼感染，及下呼吸道、尿道、皮膚、腹腔及中樞神經系統感染。給藥方法：靜脈注射、肌注、外塗油膏或滴眼藥水。大劑量、長時間用藥可能會損害腎及損傷聽力。商品名：Nebcin，Tobralex。

tocainide *n.* an *anti-arrhythmic drug used to treat life-threatening cardiac arrest due to ventricular *fibrillation. It is administered by mouth. Possible side-effects include nausea, vomiting, dizziness, tremor, and reduced white blood cell production. Trade name: **Tonocard**.

妥卡尼 一種抗心律失常藥，用於治療因心室纖維性顫動引起的心動停止。口服。可引起的副作用有惡心、嘔吐、頭暈、震顫及白細胞減少。商品名：Tonocard。

toco- *prefix denoting* childbirth or labour.

〔前綴〕分娩，生育

tocopherol *n. see* vitamin E.

生育酚 參閱 vitamin E。

toddler's diarrhoea a disorder of young children characterized by the passage of frequent loose, offensive, and bulky stools in which partially digested or undigested food may be visible (the 'peas and carrot' stool). There is no other definable abnormality and the children gain weight normally. Management consists of excluding other causes of diarrhoea and reassurance that the disorder is benign and self-limiting (it resolves by school age).

小兒腹瀉 一種幼兒疾病，其特徵為排出的糞便量大、鬆散且有惡臭，其中半消化的或未消化的食物仍可見（「豆及胡蘿蔔」便）。患兒無其他明顯異常之處，且體重正常增長。此病的處理要排除其他腹瀉病因，並要保證使患兒放心此症為良性的，且病程為自限性的（到入學年齡時消失）。

Todd's paralysis (Todd's palsy) transient paralysis of a part of the body that has previously been involved in a focal epileptic seizure (*see* epilepsy).

托德麻痺 身體某一部分發生的暫時性麻痺，該症出現前有局竈性癲癇發作（參閱 epilepsy）。

Tofranil *n. see* imipramine.

丙咪嗪 參閱 imipramine。

tolazamide *n.* a drug administered by mouth in the treatment of noninsulin-dependent diabetes. Side-effects include nausea, loss of appetite, diarrhoea, weakness, and lethargy. Trade name: **Tolanase**. *See also* sulphonylurea.

妥拉磺脲 口服藥，用以治療非胰島素依賴型糖尿病。副作用包括惡心、無食慾、腹瀉、體虛及嗜睡。參閱 sulphonylurea。商品名：Tolanase。

tolbutamide *n.* a drug taken by mouth in the treatment of noninsulin-dependent diabetes mellitus. It acts directly on the pancreas to stimulate

甲苯磺丁脲 口服藥，用於治療非胰島素依賴型糖尿病。該藥直接作用於胰腺，刺激其產生胰島素，尤其對老年病人的

insulin production and is particularly effective in elderly patients with mild diabetes (*see* sulphonylurea). Side-effects are similar to those of the *sulphonamides and include skin reactions and transient jaundice. Trade names: **Pramidex, Rastinon**.

tolerance *n.* the reduction or loss of the normal response to a drug or other substance that usually provokes a reaction in the body. *Drug tolerance* may develop after taking a particular drug over a long period of time. In such cases increased doses are necessary to produce the desired effect. Some drugs that cause tolerance also cause *dependence. *See also* glucose tolerance test, immunological tolerance, tachyphylaxis.

tolnaftate *n.* an antiseptic applied topically as a cream, powder, or solution in the treatment of various fungal infections of the skin, including ringworm. It is not effective in candidosis. Trade names: **Tinactin, Tinaderm**.

toluidine blue a dye used in microscopy for staining *basophilic substances in tissue specimens.

-tome *suffix denoting* a cutting instrument. Example: *microtome* (instrument for cutting microscopical sections).

tomo- *prefix denoting* **1.** section or sections. **2.** surgical operation.

tomography *n.* the technique of using X-rays or ultrasound waves to produce an image of structures at a particular depth within the body, bringing them into sharp focus while deliberately blurring structures at other depths. The visual record of this technique is called a

輕型糖尿病（參閱 sulphonylurea）有效。副作用類似於磺胺類藥物，包括皮膚反應和一過性黃疸。商品名：Pramidex，Rastinon。

耐受性 對藥物或其他常能在體內激起反應的物質的正常反應力減低或喪失。藥物耐受性可在較長一段時間服用某藥物後產生。此時增大劑量是達到理想藥效所必需的。某些引起耐受性的藥物亦可引起藥物依賴。參閱 glucose tolerance test，immunological tolerance，tachyphylaxis。

托萘酯 一種抗菌劑，作為乳膏、粉劑或溶液應用於表皮以治療包括癬在內的各種皮膚真菌感染。該藥對念珠菌病無效。商品名：Tinactin，Tinaderm。

甲苯胺藍 顯微鏡下給組織標本中嗜鹼物質染色時使用的一種染劑。

〔後綴〕**刀具** 例如：切片機（製備顯微鏡切片的器具）。

〔前綴〕**(1) 切面，節 (2) 外科手術**

體層照相術 應用 X 綫或超聲波來產生身體內某一深層結構之圖像的技術，將這一深層的結構置於清晰的焦點之下而有意使其他深層的結構模糊不清。該技術的視覺記錄被稱為體層照相（參閱 dental pan-

tomogram (*see also* dental pantomogram). *See* computerized tomography, positron emission tomography, ultrasonotomography.

tomogram）。參閱 computerized tomography，positron emission tomography，ultrasonotomography。

-tomy (-otomy) *suffix denoting* a surgical incision into an organ or part. Example: *gastrotomy* (into the stomach).

〔後綴〕**切開術** 手術切開某一器官或部分。例如：胃切開術（將胃切開的）。

tone *n. see* tonus.

緊張性 參閱 tonus。

tongue *n.* a muscular organ attached to the floor of the mouth. It consists of a *body* and a *root*, which is attached by muscles to the hyoid bone below, the styloid process behind, and the palate above. It is covered by mucous membrane, which is continuous with that of the mouth and pharynx. On the undersurface of the tongue a fold of mucous membrane, the *frenulum linguae*, connects the midline of the tongue to the floor of the mouth. The surface of the tongue is covered with minute projections (*papillae*), which give it a furred appearance (see illustration). *Taste

舌 與口腔底部相連的肌肉器官。由體和根組成，由肌肉使其根在下方與舌骨相附，在後方與莖突相連，在上方與腭相連。其表面由黏膜覆蓋，此黏膜又與口腔和咽部黏膜相續接。在舌的下表面有一黏膜皺襞，即舌繫帶，該皺襞將舌中部與口底部連接起來。舌表面布滿小的突起（乳頭），這些小突起使舌表面呈絨毛狀（見圖）。味蕾分布於乳頭周圍的溝內，特別是蕈狀乳頭和輪廓乳頭的周圍。舌有三大主要功能。在咀嚼和吞咽食物時協助

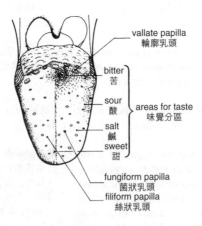

The upper surface of the tongue
舌的上表面

buds are arranged in grooves around the papillae, particularly the fungiform and cirumvallate papillae. The tongue has three main functions. It helps in manipulating food during mastication and swallowing; it is the main organ of taste; and it plays an important role in the production of articulate speech. Anatomical name: **glossa**.

攪拌食物，是味覺的主要器官；並在產生清晰發音的過程中起重要作用。解剖學用語：舌。

tongue-tie *n.* a disorder of young children in which the tongue is anchored in the floor of the mouth more firmly than usual. No treatment is required unless the condition is extreme and associated with forking of the tongue.

結舌 少兒疾病，患兒的舌頭比通常更緊固在口底部。除非情況極其嚴重並伴有舌分叉者無需治療。

tonic 1. *adj.* **a.** relating to normal muscle tone. **b.** marked by continuous tension (contraction), e.g. a tonic muscle *spasm. **2.** *n.* a medicinal substance purporting to increase vigour and liveliness and produce a feeling of well-being: beneficial effects of tonics are probably due to their placebo action.

(1) 緊張的 a. 與正常的肌肉緊張相關的。b. 由持續性緊張（收縮）表現出來的。例如，緊張性肌肉痙攣。**(2) 強壯劑** 一種增加精力和活力並產生健康感覺的藥劑。強壯劑的有益影響可能來自其安慰作用。

tonicity *n.* **1.** the normal state of slight contraction, or readiness to contract, of healthy muscle fibres. **2.** the effective osmotic pressure of a solution. *See* hypertonic, hypotonic, osmosis.

(1) 緊張性 健康肌纖維略微收縮或準備收縮的正常狀態。**(2) 張力** 溶液的有效滲透壓力。參閱 hypertonic，hypotonic，osmosis。

tono- *prefix denoting* **1.** tone or tension. **2.** pressure.

〔前綴〕**(1) 緊張，張力 (2) 壓力**

tonofibril *n.* a tiny fibre occurring in bundles in the cytoplasm of cells that lie in contact, as in epithelial tissue. Tonofibrils are concerned with maintaining contact between adjacent cells. *See* desmosome.

張力原纖維 在細胞胞漿中成束出現、互相接觸的細纖維，例如在上皮組織內。該纖維與維持相鄰細胞之間的接觸有關。參閱 desmosome。

tonography *n.* measurement of the pressure within the eyeball in such a way as to allow a record to be made on a chart

張力描記術 眼球內壓力之測量法。該方法可將每次若干分鐘內的壓力變化描記在圖上。

of variations in pressure occurring over a period of several minutes.

tonometer *n.* an instrument for measuring pressure in a part of the body, e.g. the eye (*see* ophthalmotonometer).

壓力計　身體某部分，如眼睛（參閱　ophthalmotonometer）壓力之測量器。

tonsil *n.* a mass of *lymphoid tissue on either side of the back of the mouth. It is concerned with protection against infection. The term usually refers to either of the *palatine tonsils*, but below the tongue is another pair, the *lingual tonsils*. *See also* adenoids (nasopharyngeal tonsil).

扁桃體　口腔後部兩側的淋巴組織團。它與預防感染有關。該術語通常指兩腭扁桃體之任一，但舌下有另一對扁桃體，即舌扁桃體。參閱　adenoids (nasopharyngeal tonsil)。

tonsillectomy *n.* surgical removal of the tonsils.

扁桃體切除術　外科摘除扁桃體。

tonsillitis *n.* inflammation of the tonsils due to bacterial or viral infection, causing a sore throat, fever, and difficulty in swallowing. If tonsillitis due to streptococcal infection is not treated (by antibiotics) it may lead to *rheumatic fever or *nephritis.

扁桃體炎　因細菌或病毒引起的扁桃體炎症，造成咽喉痛、發燒及吞咽困難。如果鏈球菌感染所致的扁桃體炎不加治療（用抗生素），它將導致風濕熱或腎炎。

tonus (tone) *n.* the normal state of partial contraction of a resting muscle, maintained by reflex activity.

緊張　靜止肌肉的正常部分收縮狀態，由反射活動來維持。

tooth *n.* (*pl.* **teeth**) one of the hard structures in the mouth used for cutting and chewing food. Each tooth is embedded in a socket in part of the jawbone (mandible or maxilla) known as the *alveolar bone* (or *alveolus*), to which it is attached by the *periodontal membrane. The exposed part of the tooth (*crown*) is covered with *enamel and the part within the bone (*root*) is coated with *cementum; the bulk of the tooth consists of *dentine enclosing the *pulp (see illustration). The group of embryological cells that gives rise to a tooth is known as the *tooth germ*.

牙　口腔內用來切、嚼食物的堅硬結構之一。每顆牙都嵌入牙槽骨（上頜骨或下頜骨）的窩臼內，以牙周膜相連接。牙齒暴露部分（牙冠）被牙釉質覆蓋，埋在骨中的部分（牙根）則由牙骨質覆蓋；牙之主體由牙本質構成，牙髓包裹於其內部（見圖）。使牙生長的一組胚胎期細胞稱為牙胚。

　　牙共有四種不同類型（參閱 canine，incisor，premolar，molar）。參閱 dentition。

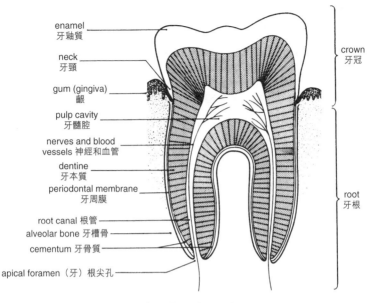

enamel
牙釉質

neck
牙頸

gum (gingiva)
齦

pulp cavity
牙髓腔

nerves and blood
vessels 神經和血管

dentine
牙本質

periodontal membrane
牙周膜

root canal 根管

alveolar bone 牙槽骨

cementum 牙骨質

apical foramen（牙）根尖孔

crown
牙冠

root
牙根

Section of a molar tooth
磨牙的切面

There are four different types of tooth (*see* canine, incisor, premolar, molar). *See also* dentition.

tooth extraction *see* extraction.

拔牙　參閱 extraction。

topagnosis *n.* inability to identify a part of the body that has been touched. It is a symptom of disease in the parietal lobes of the brain. The normal ability to localize touch is called *topognosis*.

位置感覺缺乏　不能確定身體被觸及之部位的狀況。係大腦頂葉病變之症狀。確定被觸及部位的正常能力被稱為位置感覺。

tophus *n.* (*pl.* **tophi**) a hard deposit of crystalline uric acid and its salts in the skin, cartilage (especially of the ears), or joints; a feature of *gout.

痛風石　尿酸結晶及其鹽的堅硬沉積物，見於皮膚、軟骨（特別是耳）及關節處，為痛風的特徵。

topical *adj.* local: used for the route of administration of a drug that is applied directly to the part being treated (e.g. to the skin or eye).

局部的　用指給藥途徑，將藥直接施用於治療部位（如用於皮膚或眼）。

topo- *prefix denoting* place; position; location.

〔前綴〕地方，位置，局部

topography *n.* the study of the different regions of the body, including the description of its parts in relation to the surrounding structures. **–topographical** *adj.*

局部解剖　對身體不同部位的研究，包括描述該部位與周圍結構之關係。

tormina *n. see* colic.

絞痛　參閱 colic。

torpor *n.* a state of sluggishness and diminished responsiveness: a characteristic of certain mental disorders and a symptom of certain forms of poisoning or metabolic disorder.

遲鈍　呆滯及反應力減退之狀態：是某些精神病的特徵和某種形式的中毒及代謝紊亂的症狀。

torsion *n.* twisting. Abnormal twisting of a testis within the scrotum or of a loop of bowel in the abdomen may impair blood and nerve supplies to these parts and cause severe damage.

扭轉　捩轉。陰囊內的睪丸或腹腔的腸袢之不正常的扭轉。可損傷這些部位的血液供應及神經支配並造成嚴重損害。

torticollis (wryneck) *n.* an irresistible turning movement of the head that becomes more persistent, so that eventually the head is held continually to one side. The spasm of the muscles is often painful and the patient is sensitive about his appearance. It may be caused by a birth injury to the sternomastoid muscle (*see* sternomastoid tumour). Relief may be obtained by cutting the motor nerve roots of the spinal nerves in the neck region or by injection of the affected muscles with *botulinum toxin.

斜頸　不可控制的轉頭運動，該動作變得愈發頑固並最終使頭持續地向一側歪斜。這種肌肉痙攣常常是痛苦的，而且病人對其外表十分敏感。可能是由於分娩時損傷胸鎖乳突肌造成的（參閱 sternomastoid tumour）。切斷頸部脊神經的運動神經根或向病變肌肉注射肉毒桿菌毒素可緩解症狀。

toruloma *n.* a tumour-like lesion in the lungs resulting from *cryptococcosis.

隱球菌結節　由隱球菌病所致的肺部腫瘤樣病變。

torulosis *n. see* cryptococcosis.

隱球菌病　參閱 cryptococcosis。

Tourette's syndrome (TS) *see* Gilles de la Tourette syndrome.

圖雷特綜合徵　參閱 Gilles de la Tourette syndrome。

tourniquet *n.* a device to press upon an artery and prevent flow of blood through it, usually a cord, rubber tube, or tight bandage bound around a limb. Tourniquets are no longer recommended as a first-aid measure to stop bleeding from a wound because of the danger of reducing the supply of oxygen to other tissues (direct pressure on the wound itself is considered less harmful). However, a temporary tourniquet to increase the distension of veins when a sample of blood is being taken does no harm.

止血帶　壓迫動脈以阻止血液從動脈流出的用具，通常是圍繞肢體縛緊的一根帶子、橡皮管或繃帶。止血帶已不再被推薦為傷口止血的急救措施，因為它有減少向其他組織供氧的危險（直接壓迫傷口本身現認為傷害性小些）。然而，在抽取血樣時為增加靜脈擴張而短時間的使用止血帶是無害的。

tow *n.* the teased-out short fibres of flax, hemp or jute, used in swabs for cleaning, in *packs or *stupes for the application of poultices, and for a variety of other purposes.

麻短纖維　從亞麻、大麻或黃麻梳下來的短纖維，用作擦洗用的拭子、泥敷劑的敷料或熱敷巾，及其他諸多目的。

Towne's projection a *posteroanterior X-ray film to show the entire skull and mandible.

湯氏（額枕位）投照　前後位 X 綫片用以顯示整個頭顱及下頜骨。

tox- (toxi-, toxo-, toxic(o)-) *prefix denoting* **1.** poisonous; toxic. **2.** toxins or poisoning.

〔前綴〕**(1)** 有毒的，中毒的 **(2)** 毒素，中毒

toxaemia *n.* blood poisoning that is caused by toxins formed by bacteria growing in a local site of infection. It produces generalized symptoms, including fever, diarrhoea, and vomiting. *Compare* pyaemia, sapraemia, septicaemia.

毒血症　血液中毒症，因細菌在局部感染處繁殖產生毒素所致。引起全身症狀，包括發燒、腹瀉及嘔吐。與 pyaemia，sapraemia，septicaemia 對比。

toxic *adj.* having a poisonous effect; potentially lethal.

有毒的　具有毒性作用的，潛在致死性的。

toxicity *n.* the degree to which a substance is poisonous. *See also* LD_{50}.

毒性　某物質有毒的程度。參閱 LD_{50}。

toxicology *n.* the study of poisonous materials and their effects upon living organisms. **–toxicologist** *n.*

毒理學　研究毒物及其對生物的作用。

toxicosis *n.* the deleterious effects of a toxin; poisoning: includes any disease caused by the toxic effects of any substances.

中毒　毒素的有害作用，包括由任何物質的毒性作用所致的各種疾病。

toxic shock syndrome a state of acute *shock due to *septicaemia. The commonest cause is a retained foreign body (e.g. a tampon or IUCD) combined with the presence of staphylococci (*see also* streptococcal toxic shock syndrome). The condition can be life-threatening if not treated aggressively with appropriate antibiotics and supportive care (including fluid and electrolyte replacement).

中毒性休克綜合徵　因敗血症引起的急性休克狀態。最常見的病因為異物滯留（如棉塞或宮內避孕器）合併有葡萄球菌的存在（參閱　streptococcal toxic shock syndrome）。該病如不積極予以適當的抗生素治療並給以支持性護理（包括補充液體及電解質），病人的生命將受到威脅。

toxin *n.* a poison produced by a living organism, especially by a bacterium (*see* endotoxin, exotoxin). In the body toxins act as *antigens, and special *antibodies (*antitoxins*) are formed to neutralize their effects.

毒素　由活的有機體，尤其是細菌所產生的毒質（參閱 endotoxin，exotoxin）。在體內毒素起抗原作用，並形成特異性抗體（抗毒素）以中和其作用。

Toxocara *n.* a genus of large nematode worms that are intestinal parasites of vertebrates. *T. canis* and *T. cati*, the common roundworms of dogs and cats respectively, have life cycles similar to that of the human roundworm, *Ascaris lumbricoides*. See toxocariasis.

弓蛔蟲屬　一屬大型綫蟲，係脊椎動物的腸道寄生蟲。犬弓蛔蟲和貓弓蛔蟲，分別為犬和貓的最為常見的綫蟲，其生活周期類似於人蛔蟲。參閱 toxocariasis。

toxocariasis (visceral larva migrans) *n.* an infestation with the larvae of the dog and cat roundworms, *Toxocara canis* and *T. cati*. Man, who is not the normal host, becomes infected on swallowing eggs of *Toxocara* present on hands or in food and drink contaminated with the faeces of infected domestic pets. The larvae, which migrate around the body, cause destruction of various tissues; the liver becomes enlarged and the lungs inflamed (*see* pneumonitis). Symptoms may include fever, joint and muscle pains, vomiting, an irritating rash, and

弓蛔蟲病　對犬弓蛔蟲及貓弓蛔蟲之幼蟲的感染。正常情況下，人並不是這兩類寄生蟲的宿主，但在吞下手上沾染的蟲卵或受感染寵物的糞便污染的飲食中的蟲卵時，人也會被感染。在全身游走的幼蟲會引起對各種組織的破壞；肝臟腫大，肺部發炎（參閱 pneumonitis）。症狀包括發燒、關節及肌肉疼痛、嘔吐、刺激性皮疹和驚厥。幼蟲亦有可能停留在眼視網膜內，並引起炎症和肉芽腫。該病廣泛分布於世

convulsions. Larvae can also lodge in the retina of the eye where they cause inflammation and *granuloma. The disease, widely distributed throughout the world, primarily affects children. Severe cases are treated with thiabendazole.

界各地，主要侵犯兒童。病情嚴重時用噻苯達唑治療。

toxoid *n.* a preparation of the poisonous material (toxin) that is produced by dangerous infective organisms, such as those of tetanus and diphtheria, and has been rendered harmless by chemical treatment while retaining its antigenic activity. Toxoids are used in *vaccines.

類毒素 某些危險的致病微生物，如破傷風和白喉桿菌，所產生的有毒物質（毒素）的製劑，可通過化學處理使它變成無毒性，而又同時保留它的抗原作用。類毒素用於預防接種。

Toxoplasma *n.* a genus of crescent-shaped sporozoans that live as parasites within the cells of various tissues and organs of vertebrate animals, especially birds and mammals, and complete their life cycle in a single host, the cat. *T. gondii* infects sheep, cattle, dogs and man, sometimes provoking an acute illness (*see* toxoplasmosis).

弓形體屬 一屬半月形的孢子蟲，寄生於脊椎動物，特別是鳥類和哺乳動物體內的各器官和組織的細胞內，該屬寄生蟲只在一個宿主上完成其生活周期。鼠弓形體會侵犯羊、牛、狗及人，有時引發急性病（參閱 toxoplasmosis）。

toxoplasmosis *n.* a disease of mammals and birds due to the protozoan *Toxoplasma gondii*, which is transmitted to man via undercooked meat, contaminated soil, or by direct contact (especially with infected cats). Generally symptoms are mild (swollen lymph nodes and an influenza-like illness), but severe infection of lymph nodes can occur in patients whose immune systems are compromised. *Congenital toxoplasmosis*, in which a woman infected during pregnancy transmits the organism to her fetus, can produce blindness or mental retardation in the newborn. Severe cases have been treated with sulphonamides and pyrimethamine.

弓形蟲病 由鼠弓形體原蟲引起的疾病，可通過未煮熟的肉、被污染的土或直接接觸（特別是已被感染的貓）傳播給人。一般症狀較輕（淋巴結腫大及流感狀疾病），但淋巴結的嚴重感染會發生在那些免疫系統遭到損害的患者身上。先天性弓形蟲病是由妊娠期感染的孕婦將此類微生物傳給胎兒的，會引起新生兒失明或智力低下。嚴重時用磺胺類藥加乙胺嘧啶治療。

tPA (TPA) *see* tissue plasminogen activator.

組織纖維蛋白溶酶原激活酶 參閱 tissue plasminogen activator。

Tpot an acronym for *the pot*ential doubling time, the time taken for a tumour to double its cells in the absence of cell loss (i.e. by radiation). It is related to the rate constant for cell production (kP), where kP = log2/Tpot, and enables direct measurement of the rate of cell proliferation by tumours.

腫瘤潛在倍增時間　一首字母縮略詞，指在沒有細胞丟失的情況下（如通過放射療法）腫瘤細胞增加一倍所需的時間。它與細胞繁殖的恆定速率 (kP) 有關，即 kP = log2/Tpot，因此就可以直接計量出腫瘤繁殖的速率。

trabecula *n.* (*pl.* **trabeculae**) **1.** any of the bands of tissue that pass from the outer part of an organ to its interior, dividing it into separate chambers. For example, trabeculae occur in the penis. **2.** any of the thin bars of bony tissue in spongy *bone. **–trabecular** *adj.*

小梁　(1) 從器官外到器官裏的組織帶，它將組織隔成小室。例如，陰莖小梁。(2) 鬆質骨的骨組織內的纖細梁柱。

trabeculectomy *n.* an operation for glaucoma, one part of which is the removal of a small segment of tissue from part of the wall of *Schlemm's canal. This area is known as the *trabecular meshwork*. Trabeculectomy allows aqueous fluid to filter out of the eye under the conjunctiva, thus reducing the pressure inside the eye.

小梁切除術　治療青光眼的一種手術，手術中的一部分是將施勒姆管壁的一小部分切除。該區域稱作小梁網。該手術將使眼房水在結膜下滲出眼睛，因此減輕了眼內壓力。

trace element an element that is required in minute concentrations for normal growth and development. Trace elements include fluorine (*see* fluoride), manganese, zinc, copper, *iodine, cobalt, *selenium, molybdenum, chromium, and silicon. They may serve as *cofactors or as constituents of complex molecules (e.g. cobalt in vitamin B_{12}).

痕量元素　正常生長發育所必需的有微小含量的元素。其中包括氟（參閱 fluoride）、錳、鋅、銅、碘、鈷、硒、鉬、鉻及硅。這些元素起輔助因子或複雜分子的組成成分之作用（例如維生素 B_{12} 中的鈷）。

tracer *n.* a substance that is introduced into the body and whose progress can subsequently be followed so that information is gained about metabolic processes. Radioactive tracers, giving off radiation that can be detected on a *scintigram or with a *gamma camera, are used for a variety of purposes, such

示蹤劑　引入體內後其動向被跟蹤觀察從而得到關於代謝過程信息的一種物質。放射性示蹤劑在放出射綫時可在閃爍圖上或用 γ 照相機探知，它可用於多種目的，例如檢查甲狀腺疾病或疑有腦腫瘤時使用。

as the investigation of thyroid disease or possible brain tumours.

trache- (tracheo-) *prefix denoting* the trachea.

〔前綴〕**氣管**

trachea *n.* the windpipe: the part of the air passage between the *larynx and the main *bronchi, i.e. from just below the Adam's apple, passing behind the notch of the *sternum (breastbone) to behind the angle of the sternum. The upper part of the trachea lies just below the skin, except where the thyroid gland is wrapped around it. **–tracheal** *adj.*

氣管 喉與主支氣管間的空氣通道的一部分，即喉結以下的部分，從胸骨切迹的後面到胸骨角的後面。除了被甲狀腺裹住的部分，上部氣管位於皮下。

tracheal tugging a sign that is indicative of an *aneurysm of the aortic arch: a downward tug is felt on the windpipe when the finger is placed in the midline at the root of the neck.

氣管牽引感 主動脈弓動脈瘤的提示性體徵，當把手指置於頸根部中綫處時，可感覺到氣管上有向下的牽拉感。

tracheitis *n.* inflammation of the *trachea, usually secondary to bacterial or viral infection in the nose or throat. Tracheitis causes soreness in the chest and a painful cough and is often associated with bronchitis. In babies it can cause asphyxia, particularly in *diphtheria. Treatment includes appropriate antibacterial drugs, humidification of the inhaled air or oxygen, and mild sedation to relieve exhaustion due to persistent coughing.

氣管炎 氣管的炎症，通常繼發於鼻或咽喉部的細菌或病毒感染。該病引起胸痛及咳嗽時的疼痛，並經常併發支氣管炎。嬰兒氣管炎，特別是白喉有可能引起窒息。治療包括：使用合適的抗菌藥，吸入濕化過的空氣或氧氣，以及使用較輕的鎮靜劑來減輕持續性咳嗽引起的疲憊。

tracheostomy (tracheotomy) *n.* a surgical operation in which a hole is made into the *trachea through the neck to relieve obstruction to breathing, as in diphtheria. A curved metal, plastic, or rubber tube is usually inserted through the hole and held in position by tapes tied round the neck. It may be possible for the patient to speak by occluding the opening with his fingers. The tube must

氣管造口術（氣管切開術） 一外科手術，在頸部氣管造「口」以減輕呼吸阻塞，例如在白喉時。通常將一彎曲的金屬、塑料或橡皮管子通過此「口」插入氣管，並用膠帶圍繞頸部將其固定。以手指堵住該「口」時病人可講話。管子必須保持清潔暢通。該術也可與人工呼吸聯合使用，此時它不僅能確

be kept clean and unblocked. Tracheostomy is also used in conjuction with artificial respiration, when it serves not only to secure the airway but also provides a route for sucking out secretions and protects the airway against the inhalation of pharyngeal contents. *See also* minitracheostomy.

保氣道暢通，也可為吸出分泌物提供路徑，並保證氣道不吸入咽內物質。參閱 minitracheostomy。

tracheotomy *n. see* tracheostomy.

氣管切開術（氣管造口術） 參閱 tracheostomy。

trachoma *n.* a chronic contagious eye disease – a severe form of *conjunctivitis – caused by the virus-like bacterium *Chlamydia trachomatis*; it is common in some hot countries. The conjunctiva of the eyelids becomes inflamed, leading to discharge of pus. If untreated, the conjunctiva becomes scarred and shrinks, causing the eyelids to turn inwards so that the eyelashes scratch the cornea (*trichiasis); blindness can be a late complication. Treatment with tetracyclines is effective in the early stages of the disease.

沙眼 慢性接觸性傳染眼病——結膜炎的一種嚴重型——由類病毒的細菌沙眼衣原體引起，常見於炎熱地區。眼瞼結膜發炎，會引起膿物分泌。如不予治療，結膜出現瘢痕並收縮，致使眼瞼內翻，這樣又造成睫毛摩擦角膜（倒睫）；失明係其晚期的併發症。用四環素治療常在該病早期時見效。

tract *n.* **1.** a group of nerve fibres passing from one part of the brain or spinal cord to another, forming a distinct pathway, e.g. the spinothalamic tract, pyramidal tract, and corticospinal tract. **2.** an organ or collection of organs providing for the passage of something, e.g. the digestive tract.

(1) 束 一組神經纖維，這些神經纖維從大腦或脊髓的某一部位向其另一部位形成一獨特通路，如脊髓丘腦束、錐體丘腦束以及皮層丘脊髓束。**(2) 管道** 器官或器官的集合，能夠給某些物質提供通路，例如消化道。

traction *n.* the application of a pulling force, especially as a means of counteracting the natural tension in the tissues surrounding a broken bone. This tension makes correct alignment of the fragments difficult. Considerable force, exerted with weights, ropes, and pulleys, may be necessary to ensure that a broken femur is kept correctly positioned during the early stages of healing.

牽引 應用牽引力以抵抗骨折周圍組織的自然張力的方法。這種張力使斷骨的復位困難。為保證骨折的股骨在治療早期保持正確的位置，需要用重錘、繩索和滑輪來產生相當大的拉力。

tractotomy *n.* a neurosurgical operation for the relief of intractable pain. The nerve fibres that carry painful sensation to consciousness travel from the spinal cord through the brainstem in the spinothalamic tracts. This procedure is designed to sever the tracts within the medulla oblongata. *See also* cordotomy.

神經束切斷術　神經外科手術，用以減輕難以治愈的疼痛。向知覺傳遞疼痛感覺的神經循脊髓丘腦束經脊髓到達腦幹。神經束切斷術旨在切斷延髓內的神經束。參閱 cordotomy。

tragus *n.* the projection of cartilage in the *pinna of the outer ear that extends back over the opening of the external auditory meatus.

耳屏　外耳耳廓上的軟骨隆起，該隆起向後延展到外耳道開口的上方。

Training Opportunities Scheme (TOPS) formerly, a scheme that included training those with severe disabilities to help them obtain employment. *See* Employment Service.

就業培訓大綱　（英國）過去推行的計劃，其中包括培訓嚴重殘疾人使其就業的計劃。參閱 Employment Service。

trance *n.* a state in which reaction to the environment is diminished although awareness is not impaired. It can be caused by hypnosis, meditation, catatonia, conversion disorder, drugs (such as hallucinogens), and religious ecstasy.

恍惚　對周圍環境的反應減退而意識尚未受損的一種狀態。可由催眠、沉思、緊張症、癌症、藥物（例如致幻劑）及宗教狂引起。

tranexamic acid a drug that prevents the breakdown of blood clots in the circulation (*fibrinolysis) by blocking the activation of plasminogen to form *plasmin, i.e. it is an *antifibrinolytic* drug. It is administered by mouth as an antidote to overdosage by *fibrinolytic drugs and to control severe bleeding, for example in haemophiliacs. Possible side-effects include nausea and vomiting. Trade name: Cyklokapron.

氨甲環酸　一種防止血液循環中的血凝塊溶解（纖維蛋白溶解）的藥物，該藥物阻斷纖維蛋白溶酶原被激活形成纖維蛋白溶酶，即一種抗溶解纖維蛋白藥物。口服，用作過劑量服用纖維蛋白溶解性藥物的解藥，及控制嚴重的出血，例如在血友病中。可能的副作用有惡心及嘔吐。商品名：Cyklokapron。

tranquillizer *n.* a drug that produces a calming effect, relieving anxiety and tension. *Antipsychotic drugs (formerly known as *major tranquillizers*) have this effect and are used to treat severe mental disorders (psychoses), including

安定藥　產生鎮定作用的藥，可減輕焦慮及緊張。精神抑制藥（昔稱強安定藥）具有此類作用並用來治療嚴重的神經錯亂（精神病），包括精神分裂症及躁狂。弱安定藥，如苯二

schizophrenia and mania. The *minor tranquillizers*, such as benzodiazepines (e.g. *chlordiazepoxide and *diazepam) and *meprobamate, are, used to treat neuroses and to relieve anxiety and tension due to various causes. Common side-effects of these drugs are drowsiness and dizziness, and prolonged use may result in *dependence.

氮䓬類（如氯氮䓬和地西泮）及甲丙氨酯，用於治療神經官能症和減輕不同原因引起的焦慮和緊張，這類藥物的常見副作用是嗜睡和頭暈，長期使用有時可產生藥物依賴。

trans- *prefix denoting* through or across. Example: *transurethral* (through the urethra).

〔前綴〕**經，透過**　例如：經尿道的（通過尿道的）。

transaminase *n.* an enzyme that catalyses the transfer of an amino group from an amino acid to an α-keto acid in the process of *transamination. Examples include *glutamic oxaloacetic transaminase (GOT), which catalyses the transamination of glutamate and oxaloacetate to α-ketoglutarate and aspartate, and *glutamic pyruvic transaminase (GPT), converting glutamate and pyruvate to α-ketoglutarate and alanine.

轉氨酶　在一種氨基酸向 α-酮酸轉移的過程中催化氨基轉移的一種酶。例如穀氨酸草酰乙酸轉氨酶（GOT）催化穀氨酸及草酰乙酸轉移為 α-酮戊二酸和天門冬氨酸，而穀氨酸丙酮酸轉氨酶（GPT）則將穀氨酸和丙酮酸轉化為 α-酮戊二酸和丙氨酸。

transamination *n.* a process involved in the metabolism of amino acids in which amino groups (–NH$_2$) are transferred from amino acids to certain α-keto acids, with the production of a second keto acid and amino acid. The reaction is catalysed by enzymes (*see* transaminase), which require pyridoxal phoshate as a coenzyme.

氨基轉移（作用）　氨基酸的新陳代謝作用過程，其中氨基（–NH$_2$）從氨基酸轉移到某種 α-酮酸，同時形成另一個酮酸和氨基酸。該反應由酶催化（參閱 transaminase），需要磷酸吡哆醛作為輔酶。

transcervical resection of the endometrium (TCRE) an operation, which is performed under local anaesthetic, in which the membrane lining the uterus (*see* endometrium) is cut away by a form of *electrosurgery using a *resectoscope, which is introduced through the cervix. Like *endometrial ablation,

經宮頸子宮內膜切除術　在局部麻醉下經子宮頸引入內膜切除鏡以電外科的形式將子宮內襯膜（參閱 endometrium）切除的手術。與子宮內膜摘除術相似，該手術作為子宮切除術的替代辦法用以治療經期異常大出血。

TCRE is used as an alternative to hysterectomy to treat abnormally heavy menstrual bleeding.

transcription *n.* the process in which the information contained in the *genetic code is transferred from DNA to RNA: the first step in the manufacture of proteins in cells. *See* messenger RNA, translation.

轉錄作用 將基因密碼內所含信息從脫氧糖核酸轉移至核糖核酸的過程：係細胞內蛋白製造之第一步。參閱 messenger RNA，translation。

transcutaneous electrical nerve stimulation (TENS) the introduction of pulses of low-voltage electricity into tissue for the relief of pain. It is effected by means of a small portable battery-operated unit with leads connected to electrodes attached to the skin; the strength and frequency of the pulses, which prevent the passage of pain impulses to the brain, can be adjusted by the patient. TENS is used mainly for the relief of rheumatic pain; as a method of producing pain relief in labour, it is less frequently used than epidural anaesthesia (*see* spinal anaesthesia), which has a much wider application for pain relief in obstetrics.

經皮電神經刺激 向組織內導入低伏特的電脈衝以緩解疼痛。它由一個小的便攜式電池操縱器，用導綫與附在皮膚上的電極相連而起作用，它將阻隔痛覺衝動向大腦的傳遞，該操縱器可由患者自行調節。該方法主要用於減輕風濕性疾病的痛苦；作為緩解分娩時產生疼痛的方法，不如硬膜外麻醉（參閱 spinal anaesthesia）常用，硬膜外麻醉如今在產科對於緩解疼痛有着更為廣泛的應用。

transduction *n.* the transfer of DNA from one bacterium to another by means of a *bacteriophage (phage). Some bacterial DNA is incorporated into the phage. When the host bacterium is destroyed the phage infects another bacterium and introduces the DNA from its previous host, which may become incorporated into the new host's DNA.

轉導作用 通過噬菌體脫氧核糖核酸從一種細菌轉移至另一種細菌的過程。一些細菌的脫氧核糖核酸併入噬菌體。當受體細菌被破壞時，噬菌體就感染另外的細菌，並將來自以前受體的脫氧核糖核酸釋放出來，與新受體的脫氧核糖核酸相結合。

transection *n.* **1.** a cross section of a piece of tissue. **2.** cutting across the tissue of an organ (*see also* section).

橫切 **(1)** 一塊組織的橫切面。**(2)** 將一器官的組織橫切（參閱 section）。

transfection *n.* the direct transfer of DNA molecules into a cell.

轉變感染 脫氧核糖核酸分子直接轉送進細胞。

transferase *n.* an enzyme that catalyses the transfer of a group (other than hydrogen) between a pair of substrates.

轉移酶 在一對物質之間的基團（不是氫）轉移中起催化作用的酶。

transference *n.* (in psychoanalysis) the process by which a patient comes to feel and act towards the therapist as though he or she were somebody from the patient's past life, especially a powerful parent. The patient's transference feelings may be of love or of hatred, but they are inappropriate to the actual person of the therapist. *Countertransference* is the reaction of the therapist to the patient, which is similarly based on past relationships.

移情 （精神分析）病人逐漸把感情和行動轉向治療者，把他當作病人過去生活中的某個人，特別是其有權威的父母，這一過程叫移情。這種移情既可出於愛也可出於恨，但都與現實中的這位治療者不相干。反移情作用是反映治療者對病人的反應，也同樣是基於其過去的人際關係而形成的。

transferrin (siderophilin) *n.* a *glycoprotein, found in the blood plasma, that is capable of binding iron and thus acts as a carrier for iron in the bloodstream.

轉鐵蛋白 一種血漿糖蛋白，可在血流中與鐵結合併作為鐵的攜帶者。

transfer RNA a type of RNA whose function is to attach the correct amino acid to the protein chain being synthesized at a *ribosome. *See also* translation.

轉移核糖核酸 一類核糖核酸，其功能是將相應的氨基酸結合到核糖體中正在合成的多肽鏈上。參閱 translation。

transformation zone the area of the *cervix of the uterus where the squamous epithelium, which covers the vaginal portion of the cervix, joins with the columnar epithelium, which forms the lining (endocervix) of the cervical canal.

上皮移形區 子宮頸的部分區域，該區中覆蓋子宮頸陰道部分的鱗狀上皮與形成宮頸道內層（子宮頸內膜）的柱狀上皮相匯合。

transfusion *n.* **1.** the injection of a volume of blood obtained from a healthy person (the *donor*) into the circulation of a patient (the *recipient*) whose blood is deficient in quantity or quality, through accident or disease. Direct transfusion from one person to another is rarely performed; usually bottles of carefully stored blood of different *blood groups are kept in *blood banks for use as

(1) 輸血 把從健康人（供血者）身上採來的一定量的血注入患者的血液循環中，該患者因意外或疾病而導致血液量或質的不足。直接把血從一個人輸向另一人的例子很少，通常是把不同血型的血液裝在瓶中，再小心保存在血庫以供需要時使用。輸血時血液通過插入靜脈的針頭在重力作用下滴

necessary. During transfusion the blood is allowed to drip, under gravity, through a needle inserted into one of the recipient's veins. Blood transfusion is routine during major surgical operations in which much blood is likely to be lost. **2.** the administration of any fluid, such as plasma or saline solution, into a patient's vein by means of a *drip.

入。在可能出現較多失血的大手術中輸血是常規。**(2) 輸液** 用靜脈輸注器將各種液體，如血漿或鹽溶液輸入病人靜脈。

transient ischaemic attack (TIA) the result of temporary disruption of the circulation to part of the brain due to *embolism, *thrombosis to brain arteries, or spasm of the vessel walls. The symptoms may be similar to those of a *stroke but patients recover within 24 hours.

一過性腦缺血 因栓塞、腦動脈血栓形成、血管壁痙攣致使大腦局部血液循環受到暫時性的中斷所造成的結果。症狀與中風相似，但患者在 24 小時內得以恢復。

transillumination *n.* the technique of shining a bright light through part of the body to examine its structure. Transillumination of the sinuses of the skull is a means of detecting abnormalities.

透照法 用亮光通過身體某部以檢查其結構的方法。對顱骨竇的透照是檢查其異常的方法。

translation *n.* (in cell biology) the manufacture of proteins in a cell, which takes place at the ribosomes. The information for determining the correct sequence of amino acids in the protein is carried to the ribosomes by *messenger RNA, and the amino acids are brought to their correct position in the protein by *transfer RNA.

轉譯 （細胞生物學）細胞內核糖體對蛋白質的製造。信使核糖核酸攜帶確定蛋白質中氨基酸正確序列的信息，該信息被傳給核糖體，而轉移核糖核酸則將氨基酸帶至其在蛋白質中的正確位置。

translocation *n.* (in genetics) a type of chromosome mutation in which a part of a chromosome is transferred to another part of the same chromosome or to a different chromosome. This changes the order of the genes on the chromosomes and can lead to serious genetic disorders, e.g. chronic myeloid leukaemia.

易位 （遺傳學）染色體突變的一種類型，其中染色體的一部分轉移至同一染色體的另一部分或不同的染色體中去。這改變了基因在染色體上的排列，並可能引起嚴重的遺傳性病變，例如慢性粒細胞性白血病。

transmethylation *n.* the process whereby an amino acid donates its

甲基轉移 氨基酸為其他化合物甲基化的過程提供甲基末端

terminal methyl (–CH₃) group for the methylation of other compounds. Methionine is the principal methyl donor in the body and the donated methyl group may subsequently be involved in the synthesis of such compounds as choline or creatinine or in detoxification processes.

（–CH₃）。蛋氨酸是體內主要的甲基供體，它提供的甲基可隨後參與一些化合物的合成，如膽鹼或肌酐，或參與解毒過程。

transmigration *n.* the act of passing through or across, e.g. the passage of blood cells through the intact walls of capillaries and venules (*see* diapedesis).

移行（血細胞滲出） 通過或透過某物的動作。例如血細胞通過完整的毛細血管壁或小靜脈壁（參閱 diapedesis）。

transplantation *n.* the implantation of an organ or tissue (*see* graft) from one part of the body to another or from one person (the donor) to another (the recipient). Success for transplantation depends on the degree of compatibility between donor and graft: it is greatest for *autografts (self-grafts), less for *homografts (between individuals of the same species), and least for *heterografts (between different species). Skin and bone grafting are examples of transplantation techniques in the same individual. A kidney transplant involves the grafting of a healthy kidney from a donor to replace the diseased kidney of the recipient: renal transplantation is the second commonest example of human transplant surgery using homografts (after corneal grafts – *see* keratoplasty). Heart transplants have also been carried out with success and liver transplants have also been attempted. Transplanting organs or tissues between individuals is a difficult procedure because of the natural rejection processes in the recipient of the graft. Special treatment (e.g. with *immunosuppressive drugs) is needed to prevent graft rejection.

移植術 將器官或組織從身體的某一部位移植（參閱 graft）到另一部位或從某個人（供者）移植到另一個人（受者）。移植的成功取決於供者與移植物的相容性：自體移植最易成功，同種移植（同種的不同個體之間）次之，異種移植（不同種之間）最次。皮膚及骨移植為同體移植的例子。腎移植是用供者的健康腎臟來取代受者有病的腎臟的移植：腎移植是應用同體移植的人體移植外科中第二常見的例子（僅次於角膜移植。參閱 keratoplasty）。心臟移植現也能成功地施行，肝移植也有嘗試。在不同個體間進行器官或組織移植是個困難的過程，因為受體對移植物有自然的排斥作用。需要用特殊治療（例如免疫抑制藥）以防止移植物的排異反應。

transposition *n*. the abnormal positioning of a part of the body such that it is on the opposite side to its normal site in the body. For example, it may involve the heart (*see* dextrocardia).

錯位（反位） 身體某部分所處的異常位置，該位置恰與正常位置相反。例如，累及心臟的錯位：右位心（參閱 dextrocardia）

transposition of the great vessels a congenital abnormality of the heart in which the aorta arises from the right ventricle and the pulmonary artery from the left ventricle. Life is impossible unless there is an additional abnormality, such as a septal defect, that permits the mixing of blood between the pulmonary and systemic (aortic) circulations. Few of those untreated survive infancy and childhood, but the defect may be improved or corrected surgically.

大血管錯位 一種先天性心臟畸形，其中主動脈起始於右心室而肺動脈起始於左心室，除非另有畸形，如中隔缺損，致使肺循環和體循環主動脈的血液相匯合，否則就不能存活。不治療的患者很少能活過嬰、幼兒期，此缺陷可通過手術來改善或矯正。

transsexualism *n*. the condition of one who firmly believes that he (or she) belongs to the sex opposite to his (or her) biological gender. The roots of such a belief usually go back to childhood. Children with such beliefs are treated with encouragement to engage in the activities appropriate to their biological sex and to work through their difficulties in psychotherapy. Adults with such beliefs can seldom be persuaded to change them; surgical sex reassignment is sometimes justifiable, to make the externals of the body conform to the individual's view of himself (or herself). **–transsexual** *adj.*, *n*.

異性轉化心理變態 堅定地認為自己的性別與其生理性別相反的一種病態。這種想法的根源常可追溯到兒童時期。有這樣想法的兒童可用鼓勵其參加適合其生理性別活動的辦法加以心理治療。而有此想法的成人很少能被說服改變自己的觀念。有時需做性徵再造手術使他們的身體外表符合其觀點。

transudation *n*. the passage of a liquid through a membrane, especially of blood through the wall of a capillary vessel. The liquid is called the *transudate*.

漏出 液體通過膜，特別是血液通過毛細血管壁透出。此液體稱作漏出液。

transuretero-ureterostomy *n*. the operation of connecting one ureter to the other in the abdomen. The damaged/obstructed ureter is cut above the

經輸尿管-輸尿管吻合術 在腹部將輸尿管相接的手術。受損壞或受阻的輸尿管在其病變或受阻節段上方被切斷，並將其

diseased or damaged segment and joined end-to-side to the other ureter.

尾端連接到其他輸尿管的側面。

transurethral resection of the prostate (TUR, TURP) *see* resection.

經尿道前列腺切除術 參閱 resection。

transvaginal ultrasonography *ultrasonography using a vaginal probe instead of an abdominal transducer. It allows the use of a higher frequency, thus providing superior resolution and therefore an earlier and more accurate identification of fetal structures.

陰道超聲波檢查 使用陰道探子而非腹部轉導器的超聲波檢查。這樣的檢查允許使用較高的頻率,因而能產生較佳的分辨力,和進而提供胎兒結構的更為早期和更精確的識別。

transverse *adj.* (in anatomy) situated at right angles to the long axis of the body or an organ.

橫的 (解剖學)與身體或器官之長軸成直角的。

transverse process the long projection from the base of the neural arch of a *vertebra.

橫突 脊椎神經弓基底部發出的長突。

transvestism (cross-dressing) *n.* dressing in clothes normally associated with the opposite sex, which may occur in both heterosexual and homosexual people. Cross-dressing may be practised by transsexuals (*see* transsexualism), in whom it is not sexually arousing. Other transvestites are fetishistic; in these cross-dressing is sexually arousing and may lead to masturbatory or other sexual behaviour. Treatment may be by behavioural techniques, such as *aversion therapy, but is not always needed. *See also* sexual deviation. **–transvestite** *n.*

易裝癖 穿着的服裝常與異性有關,在異性戀者和同性戀者中均有發生。易裝行為可由異性轉化心理變態者作出(參閱 transsexualism),但此舉並不引起性感覺。其他易裝癖者可能為戀物癖者;對於這些人易裝可喚起性覺並可導致手淫和其他性行為。可通過行為療法,如厭惡療法予以治療,但不一定需要治療。參閱 sexual deviation。

tranylcypromine *n.* an antidepressant drug – one of the *MAO inhibitors given by mouth for the treatment of severe mental depressive states. Common side-effects include restlessness, insomnia, giddiness, and a fall in blood pressure. Trade name: **Parnate**.

反苯環丙胺 一種抗抑鬱藥,是一種單胺氧化酶抑製劑,口服以治療嚴重的精神抑鬱狀態。常見的副作用有焦慮、失眠、眩暈及血壓低。商品名: Parnate。

trapezium *n.* a bone of the wrist (*see* carpus). It articulates with the scaphoid bone behind, with the first metacarpal in front, and with the trapezoid and second metatarsal on either side.

大多角骨 腕部的一塊骨（參閱 carpus）。在後面與舟骨，在前面與第一掌骨，在兩側與小多角骨及第二掌骨相關節。

trapezius *n.* a flat triangular muscle covering the back of the neck and shoulder. It is important for movements of the scapula and it also draws the head backwards to either side.

斜方肌 扁平三角肌，覆蓋頸背及肩部。對肩胛骨的運動起重要作用，並使頭部向後仰以轉向兩側中的任何一側。

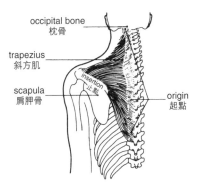

occipital bone
枕骨

trapezius
斜方肌

scapula
肩胛骨

insertion 止點

origin
起點

Left trapezius muscle
左斜方肌

trapezoid bone a bone of the wrist (*see* carpus). It articulates with the second metatarsal bone in front, with the scaphoid bone behind, and with the trapezium and capitate bones on either side.

小多角骨 腕部的一塊骨（參閱 carpus）。在前與第二掌骨，在後與舟骨，在兩側與大多角骨及頭狀骨連成關節。

trauma *n.* **1.** a physical wound or injury, such as a fracture or blow. *Trauma scores* are numerical systems for assessing the severity and prognosis of serious injuries. **2.** (in psychology) an emotionally painful and harmful event. Theorists have speculated that some events (such as birth) are always traumatic. Symptoms of neurosis may follow an overwhelmingly

(1) 外傷 身體創傷或損傷，如骨折或跌打。外傷比數是評估損傷的嚴重程度和預後的數字體系。**(2) 創傷** （心理學）感情上受痛苦或受傷害的事件。理論家推測有些事情（如分娩）總是創傷性的。神經症狀可能在極為緊張的事件，如戰鬥或嚴重外傷之後出現。

stressful event, such as battle or serious injuty. **–traumatic** *adj.*

traumatic fever a fever resulting from a serious injury.

創傷性發熱 由嚴重外傷所致的發燒。

traumatology *n.* accident surgery: the branch of surgery that deals with wounds and disabilities arising from injuries.

創傷學 事故外科學：外科學分支，研究創傷及外傷所致的殘疾。

travel sickness (motion sickness) nausea, vomiting, and headache caused by motion during travel by sea, road, or air. The symptoms are due to overstimulation of the balance organs in the *inner ear by repeated small changes in the position of the body and are aggravated by movements of the horizon. Sedative antihistamine drugs (*see* antiemetic) are effective in preventing motion sickness.

旅行病（暈動病） 由乘船、乘車或乘飛機旅行時的運動引起的惡心、嘔吐、頭痛。該症狀是由於體位反覆的小變化使內耳的平衡器官過度興奮，並被水平移動加重。用鎮靜的抗組胺藥物（參閱 antiemetic）預防暈動病有效。

trazodone *n.* a drug used in the treatment of depression with and without anxiety. It is administered by mouth; side-effects include dry mouth, nausea, excitement, and skin rash. Trade name: **Molipaxin**.

曲唑酮 一種藥物，用於治療由焦慮或非焦慮引起的抑鬱。口服，副作用有口乾、惡心、興奮及皮疹。商品名：Molipaxin。

Treacher Collins syndrome (Treacher Collins deformity) a hereditary disorder of facial development. The precursors of the ear fail to develop, which results in a variety of ear and facial malformations.

特-科氏綜合徵（特-科氏畸形） 先天性面部發育疾病。耳前體未能發育，造成耳部、面部的各種畸形。

trematode *n. see* fluke.

吸蟲 參閱 fluke。

tremor *n.* a rhythmical and alternating movement that may affect any part of the body. The *physiological tremor* is a feature of the normal mechanism for maintaining posture. It may be more apparent in states of fatigue or anxiety. *Essential tremor* is slower and particularly affects the hands. It can be

震顫 累及身體任何部位的有節律的交替運動。生理性震顫是維持姿勢的正常機制特徵。疲勞或焦慮時較為明顯。特發性震顫較慢，特別好發於手。它可能會令人尷尬或不方便，但並不伴有其他症狀。在同一家庭的幾個成員身上或在老年

embarrassing and inconvenient but it is not accompanied by any other symptoms. A similar tremor may also occur in several members of one family and also in elderly people. Resting tremor is a prominent symptom of *parkinsonism. An *intention tremor* occurs when a patient with disease of the cerebellum tries to touch an object. The closer the object is approached the wilder become the movements.

人身上都可產生類似的震顫。靜止性震顫是帕金森病的突出症狀。意向性震顫發生於有小腦疾病的患者試圖去拿物體時。手愈近物體，震顫愈烈。

trench foot (immersion foot) blackening of the toes and the skin of the foot due to death of the superficial tissues and caused by prolonged immersion in cold water or exposure to damp and cold.

浸泡足　因淺表組織壞死或長時間浸泡在冷水中和暴露於潮濕陰冷之中引起的腳趾或足部皮膚發黑。

Trendelenburg position a special operating-table posture for patients undergoing surgery of the pelvis or for patients suffering from shock. The patient is laid on his back with the pelvis higher than the head, inclined at an angle of about 45°.

特倫德倫貝格臥位　骨盆手術病人或休克病人在手術臺上的一種特殊體位。病人平躺骨盆高於頭部，成 45° 傾斜。

trephine *n.* a surgical instrument used to remove a circular area of tissue, usually from the cornea of the eye or from bone (the latter for microscopical examination). It consists of a hollow tube with a serrated cutting edge. It is used during the preliminary stages of craniotomy.

環鑽，環鋸　外科用具，用於切除組織的環狀區域，通常為角膜或骨的環狀區域（後者為顯微鏡檢查用）。由一個帶鋸齒切割邊緣的中空管構成。用於穿顱術的初期。

Treponema *n.* a genus of anaerobic spirochaete bacteria. All species are parasitic and some cause disease in animals and man: *T. carateum* causes *pinta, *T. pallidum* *syphilis, and *T. pertenue* *yaws.

密螺旋體　一屬厭氧螺旋體，其中各種均為寄生性的，有些可使動物及人致病。品他病密螺旋體引起品他病，蒼白密螺旋體引起梅毒，細弱密螺旋體引起雅司病。

treponematosis *n.* any infection caused by spirochaete bacteria of the genus *Treponema*. See pinta, syphilis, yaws.

密螺旋體病　由密螺旋體屬細菌引起的感染。參閱 pinta，syphilis，yaws。

tretinoin *n.* a *retinoid drug used in the treatment of acne. It is administered topically as a cream, gel, or liquid; side-effects include blistering, altered pigmentation, increased sensitivity to sunlight, and fetal abnormalities. Trade name: **Retin-A**.

維生素 A 酸，維甲酸　視黃酸類藥物，用於治療痤瘡、粉刺。以油膏、凝膠體或液體形式局部施用，副作用包括發水疱，改變色素沉着，增加對陽光的敏感度，及胎兒畸形。商品名：Retin-A。

triad *n.* (in medicine) a group of three united or closely associated structures or three symptoms or effects that occur together. A *portal triad* in a portal canal of the liver consists of a branch of the portal vein, a branch of the hepatic artery, and an interlobular bile tubule.

三聯（徵）　（醫學）三個聯合或密切相關的一組結構，或三個同時發生的症狀或作用。肝門三聯即由門靜脈分支、肝動脈分支及葉間膽小管組成。

triage *n.* a system whereby a group of casualties or other patients is sorted according to the seriousness of their injuries or illnesses so that treatment priorities can be allocated between them. In emergency situations it is designed to maximize the number of survivors.

傷員鑒別分類　將一羣傷亡人員或其他病人按其嚴重程度分類的系統，這樣可在他們中分配治療的主次。在急診情況下，該作法旨在使生存的人數達到最大。

triamcinolone *n.* a synthetic corticosteroid hormone with uses similar to *cortisone; it reduces inflammation but does not cause salt and water retention. It is administered by mouth and common side-effects include headache, dizziness, somnolence, muscle weakness, and a fall in blood pressure, particularly on the sudden withdrawal of treatment. Trade names: **Adcortyl, Ledercort**.

曲安西龍　合成的皮質類固醇激素，作用與可的松相似；可減輕炎症，但不引起鹽和水瀦留。口服，副作用包括頭痛、頭暈、嗜睡、肌無力及血壓下降，尤其是在突然中止治療時。商品名：Adcortyl，Ledercort。

triamterene *n.* a *diuretic that is given by mouth and produces an effect within two hours. It causes the loss of sodium and chloride from the kidneys and is used in the treatment of various forms of fluid retention (oedema). Common side-effects include nausea, vomiting, weakness, reduced blood pressure, and digestive disorders. Trade name: **Dytac**.

氨苯蝶啶　口服利尿劑，兩小時之內起效。可使腎臟喪失鈉和氯，用於治療各種液體瀦留（水腫）。常見副作用為惡心、嘔吐、無力、血壓下降及消化不良。商品名：Dytac。

triangle *n.* (in anatomy) a three-sided structure or area; for example, the *femoral triangle.

三角 （解剖學）三邊結構或三邊區，例如股三角。

triangular bandage a piece of material cut or folded into a triangular shape and used for making an arm sling or holding dressings in position.

三角帶 剪成或摺疊成的一塊材料，用作為手臂懸帶或將敷料固定在位。

Triatoma *n.* a genus of bloodsucking bugs (*see* reduviid). *T. infestans* is important in transmitting *Chagas' disease in Argentina, Uruguay, and Chile.

錐蝽屬 一屬吸血昆蟲（參閱 reduviid）。騷擾錐蝽是在阿根廷、烏拉圭和智利傳播恰加斯病的重要昆蟲。

triceps *n.* a muscle with three heads of origin, particularly the *triceps brachii*, which is situated on the back of the upper arm and contracts to extend the forearm. It is the *antagonist of the *brachialis.

三頭肌 起點有三頭的肌肉，特別指肱三頭肌，位於上臂後側，收縮時可伸展前臂。它是肱肌的拮抗肌。

trich- (tricho-) *prefix denoting* hair or hairlike structures.

〔前綴〕毛髮，毛髮狀結構

trichiasis *n.* a condition in which the eyelashes rub against the eyeball, producing discomfort and sometimes ulceration of the cornea. It may result from inflammation of the eyelids, which makes the lashes grow out in abnormal directions, or when scarring of the conjunctiva (lining membrane) turns the eyelid inwards. It accompanies all forms of *entropion.

倒睫 睫毛摩擦眼球，引起不適並時有角膜潰瘍發生的情況。可由眼瞼炎症造成，使睫毛向不正常方向生長；亦可由結膜（內襯膜）出現瘢痕造成，使眼瞼內翻，倒睫伴隨各種眼瞼內翻。

Trichinella *n.* a genus of minute parasitic nematode worms. The adults of *T. spiralis* live in the small intestine of man, where the females release large numbers of larvae. These bore through the intestinal wall and can cause disease (*see* trichinosis). The parasite can also develop in pigs and rats.

毛綫蟲屬 一屬微小的寄生性綫蟲。旋毛綫蟲的成蟲寄居於人的小腸，雌蟲在此產下大量的幼蟲。這些幼蟲穿過腸壁可引起疾病（參閱 trichinosis）。這些寄生蟲亦可在豬和大鼠中生長。

trichiniasis *n. see* trichinosis.

旋毛蟲病 參閱 trichinosis。

trichinosis (trichiniasis) *n.* a disease of cold and temperate regions caused by the larvae of the nematode worm *Trichinella spiralis*. Humans contract trichinosis after eating imperfectly cooked meat infected with the parasite's larval cysts. Larvae, released by females in the intestine, penetrate the intestinal wall and cause diarrhoea and nausea. They migrate around the body and may cause fever, vertigo, delirium, and pains in the limbs. The larvae eventually settle within cysts in the muscles, and this may result in pain and stiffness. Trichinosis, rarely a serious disease, is treated with thiabendazole.

旋毛蟲病　在寒帶和溫帶地區由旋毛綫蟲引起的疾病。人在食入被其幼蟲包囊感染的未徹底煮熟的肉時患上旋毛蟲病。在腸內由雌蟲釋放的幼蟲穿透腸壁引起腹瀉及惡心。牠們游走全身，又可引起發燒、眩暈、譫妄及肢體疼。幼蟲最終留在肌肉中的包囊內，可造成疼痛及僵硬。該病不是重病，可用噻苯達唑治療。

trichloracetic acid an *astringent used in solution for a variety of skin conditions. It is also applied topically to produce sloughing, especially for the removal of warts.

三氯乙酸　一種用於治療各種皮膚病的溶液收斂劑。也可外用以產生腐肉脫落，特別是用於去除疣贅。

trichobezoar *n.* hairball: a mass of swallowed hair in the stomach. It may be the patient's own hair or animal hairs. *See* bezoar.

毛團　毛髮團：吞入胃內的一團毛髮。可以是病人自己的毛髮也可以是動物的毛髮。參閱 bezoar。

Trichocephalus *n. see* whipworm.

鞭毛蟲　參閱 whipworm。

trichoglossia *n.* hairiness of the tongue, due to the growth of fungal organisms infecting its surface.

毛舌　因感染舌表面的真菌生長而引起的毛樣舌。

trichology *n.* the study of hair.

毛髮學　研究毛髮之學科。

Trichomonas *n.* a genus of parasitic flagellate protozoans that move by means of a wavy membrane, bearing a single flagellum, projecting from the body surface. *T. vaginalis* often infects the vagina, where it may cause severe irritation and a foul-smelling discharge (*see* vaginitis), and sometimes also the male *urethra; it

毛滴蟲屬　一屬有鞭毛的寄生性原蟲，靠波狀膜移動，長有一單根鞭毛，從其體表伸出。陰道毛滴蟲常感染陰道，可在陰道內引起嚴重刺激及惡臭分泌物（參閱 vaginitis），有時亦感染男性尿道；可通過性交傳播。人毛滴蟲和口腔毛滴蟲分

can be transmitted during sexual intercourse. *T. hominis* and *T. tenax* live in the large intestine and mouth respectively. *See also* trichomoniasis.

trichomoniasis *n.* **1.** an infection of the digestive system by the protozoa *Trichomonas hominis*, causing dysentery. **2.** an infection of the vagina due to the protozoan *Trichomonas vaginalis*, causing inflammation of genital tissues with vaginal discharge (*see* vaginitis). It can be transmitted to males in whom it causes urethral discharge. Treatment is with *metronidazole.

trichomycosis *n.* any hair disease that is caused by infection with a fungus.

Trichophyton *n.* a genus of fungi, parasitic to man, that frequently infect the skin, nails, and hair and cause *ringworm. *See also* dermatophyte.

trichorrhexis nodosa a condition in which the hairs break easily. It may be due to a hereditary condition or it may occur as a consequence of repeated physical or chemical injury. The latter condition may follow the use of heat or bleach on the hair or be caused by persistent rubbing.

Trichosporon *n.* a genus of fungi, parasitic to man, that infect the scalp and beard (*see* piedra).

trichotillomania *n.* loss of hair caused by a person persistently rubbing or pulling it.

trichromatic *adj.* describing or relating to the normal state of colour vision, in

別生活在大腸及口腔。參閱 trichomoniasis。

毛滴蟲病 (1) 由致痢疾的人毛滴蟲原蟲引起的消化系統感染。(2) 由陰道毛滴蟲原蟲引起的陰道感染，可引起生殖器官感染及陰道分泌物增多（參閱 vaginitis）。該蟲可傳染給男性，引起其尿道分泌物。用甲硝唑治療。

毛髮菌病 由真菌感染引起的毛髮疾病。

髮癬菌屬 一屬真菌，寄生於人體，頻繁侵犯人的皮膚、指甲及毛髮，可引起癬病。參閱 dermatophyte。

結節性脆髮病 一種頭髮易斷的病。可由遺傳因素或由反覆的物理、化學損傷所致。後者可在頭髮熱燙或漂白之後出現，也可由持久性摩擦引起。

毛孢子菌屬 一屬真菌，寄生於人，侵犯頭皮及鬍鬚（參閱 piedra）。

拔毛髮狂 一種由人持續地摩擦及扯拉頭髮引起的頭髮脫失。

三色視的 形容或與正常的色覺狀態有關的，在該狀態下該

which a person is sensitive to all three of the primary colours (red, green, and blue) and can match any given colour by a mixture of these three. *Compare* dichromatic, monochromat.

人對三原色（紅、綠、藍）都敏感，並且能夠將此三色混合配出任何指定的顏色。與 dichromatic，monochromat 對比。

trichuriasis *n*. an infestation of the large intestine by the *whipworm, *Trichuris trichiura*; it occurs principally in humid tropical regions. Man acquires the infection by eating food contaminated with the worms' eggs. Symptoms, including bloody diarrhoea, anaemia, weakness, and abdominal pain, are evident only in heavy infestations. Trichuriasis can be treated with various anthelmintics, including thiabendazole and piperazine salts.

鞭蟲病　毛首鞭蟲在人大腸寄生所引起的疾病。發病主要見於潮濕的熱帶地區。因食入被鞭蟲卵污染的食物而感染此病，症狀包括血性腹瀉、貧血、無力及腹痛，只在感染嚴重時症狀才明顯，用包括噻苯達唑和哌嗪鹽類在內的各種驅蟲藥治療均可。

Trichuris *n. see* whipworm.

鞭蟲屬　參閱 whipworm。

tricuspid valve the valve in the heart between the right atrium and right ventricle. It consists of three cusps that channel the flow of blood from the atrium to the ventricle and prevent any backflow.

三尖瓣　心臟內右心房和右心室間的瓣膜。由三個尖瓣組成，它使血液由心房流到心室，但又阻止血液返流。

tricyclic antidepressant *see* antidepressant.

三環抗抑鬱藥　參閱 antidepressant。

tridactyly *n*. a congenital abnormality in which there are only three digits on a hand or foot.

三指（趾）　先天性畸形，手、足只長有三個指（趾）。

trifluoperazine *n*. an *antipsychotic drug (a phenothiazine) with uses and effects similar to those of *chlorpromazine. Common side-effects include drowsiness, dryness of mouth, dizziness, and muscular spasm and tremor. Trade name: **Stelazine**.

三氟拉嗪　一種抗精神病的藥物（吩噻嗪），應用和效果與氯丙嗪相似。常見副作用有嗜睡、口乾、頭暈、肌肉痙攣及震顫。商品名：Stelazine。

trifluridine *n. see* antiviral drug.

曲氟尿苷　參閱 antiviral drug。

trifocal lenses lenses in which there are three segments. The upper provides a clear image of distant objects; the lower is used for reading and close work; and the middle one for the intermediate distance. Musicians sometimes find the middle segment useful for reading the score during performance.

三焦距鏡片　分成三段的眼鏡鏡片。上段呈現遠距離物體的清晰物像，下段用於閱讀及做精細工作，而中段用於中距離視物。音樂家有時在演出時用中段閱讀樂譜。

trigeminal nerve the fifth and largest *cranial nerve (V), which is split into three divisions: the ophthalmic, maxillary, and mandibular nerves (see illustration). The motor fibres are responsible for controlling the muscles involved in chewing, while the sensory fibres relay information about temperature, pain, and touch from the whole front half of the head (including the mouth) and also from the meninges.

三叉神經　第五對，亦是最大的腦神經，分為三支：眼神經、上頜神經和下頜神經（見圖）。運動神經纖維負責支配咀嚼肌，而感覺神經纖維傳遞來自整個頭的前半部（包括口）及腦膜的溫度、疼痛及觸覺信息。

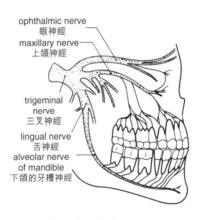

ophthalmic nerve
眼神經
maxillary nerve
上頜神經
trigeminal nerve
三叉神經
lingual nerve
舌神經
alveolar nerve of mandible
下頜的牙槽神經

The trigeminal nerve
三叉神經

trigeminal neuralgia (tic douloureux) *see* neuralgia.

三叉神經痛　參閱 neuralgia。

trigeminy *n.* a condition in which the heartbeats can be subdivided into groups

三聯搏症　心臟搏動可被分為每三搏一組的病症。第一搏正

of three. The first beat is normal, but the second and third are premature beats (*see* ectopic beat).

常，但第二、第三搏為期前搏動（參閱 ectopic beat）。

trigger finger an impairment in the ability to extend a finger, resulting either from a nodular thickening in the flexor tendon sheath. On unclenching the fist, the affected finger (usually the third or fourth) at first remains bent and then, on overcoming the resistance, suddenly straightens ('triggers'). Treatment is by incision of the tendon sheath.

扳機狀指 手指伸展能力的損傷，因屈肌肌腱結節狀增厚或因其腱鞘狹窄所致。在鬆開拳頭時，患指（常為第三指或第四指）先是保持彎曲狀，隨後，在克服阻力之後，突然伸直（「扳機」）。切開腱鞘予以治療。

triglyceride *n.* a lipid or neutral *fat consisting of glycerol combined with three fatty-acid molecules. Triglycerides are synthesized from the products of digestion of dietary fat: they are the form in which fat is stored in the body.

甘油三酯 脂類或中性脂肪，由甘油與三個脂肪酸分子組成。它合成於飲食脂肪的消化產物：是體內貯存脂肪的形式。

trigone *n.* a triangular region or tissue, such as the triangular region of the wall of the bladder that lies between the openings of the two ureters and the urethra.

三角區 三角形區域或組織，如位於兩輸尿管開口及尿道口之間的膀胱壁的三角區。

trigonitis *n.* inflammation of the trigone (base) of the urinary bladder. This can occur as part of a generalized *cystitis or it can be associated with inflammation in the urethra, prostate, or cervix (neck) of the uterus. The patient experiences an intense desire to pass urine frequently; treatment includes the clearing of any underlying infection by antibiotic administration.

膀胱三角炎 膀胱三角區發炎。它可能是整個膀胱炎的一部分，也可能是尿道炎、前列腺炎或子宮頸炎的併發症。患者有頻繁排尿的強烈慾望；治療包括用抗生素清除感染。

trigonocephaly *n.* a deformity of the skull in which the vault of the skull is sharply angled just in front of the ears, giving the skull a triangular shape. **–trigonocephalic** *adj.*

三角頭 頭顱畸形，其中顱骨穹窿於兩耳前方呈陡角，使顱骨成三角形。

triiodothyronine *n.* one of the hormones synthesized and secreted by the thyroid gland. *See* thyroid hormone.

三碘甲狀腺氨酸　由甲狀腺合成並分泌的一種激素。參閱 thyroid hormone。

trimeprazine *n.* an *antihistamine drug (a *phenothiazine derivative) that also possesses sedative properties. Given by mouth, it is mainly used in the treatment of pruritus (itching) and urticaria (nettle rash). Common side-effects include drowsiness, dizziness, dryness of mouth, muscular tremor and incoordination and confusion. Trade name: **Vallergan**.

阿利馬嗪　一種抗組胺藥（吩噻嗪衍生物），也具有鎮靜特性。口服，主要用於治療瘙癢及蕁麻疹。常見副作用有嗜睡、頭暈、口乾、肌肉震顫、肌肉不協調和精神混亂。商品名：Vallergan。

trimester *n.* (in obstetrics) any one of the three successive three-month periods (the *first*, *second*, and *third trimesters*) into which a pregnancy may be divided.

三月期　（產科學）連續三個月為一期來劃分的妊娠分期（第一、第二和第三個三月期）。

trimethoprim *n.* an antiseptic that is active against a range of microorganisms. It is used mainly in the treatment of chronic urinary-tract infections and malaria and is often administered, by mouth, in a combined preparation with sulphamethoxazole (*see* co-trimoxazole (Bactrim, Septrin)). Long-term treatment may cause depression of the bone marrow function. Trade names: **Ipral, Trimopan**.

甲氧苄啶　一抗菌藥，對治療一系列微生物均有效。主要用於治療慢性尿道感染和瘧疾，常口服給藥，與磺胺甲基異噁唑合用（參閱 co-trimoxazole）。長期使用可致骨髓功能受抑。商品名：Ipral，Trimopan。

trimipramine *n.* a tricyclic *antidepressant drug that also possesses sedative properties. It is given by mouth or by injection for the treatment of acute or chronic mental depression. Common side-effects include drowsiness, dizziness, dry mouth, and a fall in blood pressure. Trade name: **Surmontil**.

曲米帕明　一種三環結構的抗抑鬱藥，兼具鎮靜性。口服或注射以治療急、慢性精神抑鬱症。常見副作用包括嗜睡、頭暈、口乾及血壓下降。商品名：Surmontil。

trinitrophenol *n. see* picric acid.

三硝基酚　參閱 picric acid。

triose *n.* a carbohydrate with three carbon units: for example, glyceraldehyde.

丙糖　含有三個碳單位的碳水化合物：例如，甘油醛。

triple marker test a blood test used in the prenatal diagnosis of *Down's syndrome, which can be performed at about the 16th week of pregnancy. Levels of *alpha-fetoprotein (afp), unconjugated *oestriol (uE₃), and *human chorionic gonadotrophin in the serum are computed with maternal age to determine the statistical likelihood of the fetus being affected. If the risk is high, the diagnosis can be confirmed by chromosome analysis.

三重（組）標記測驗　約在妊娠 16 周時進行的血液測驗以在出生前診斷唐氏綜合徵。血清中甲胎蛋白、未配對的雌（甾）三醇，及人絨毛膜促性腺激素的水平與母親的年齡一起計算用以得出嬰兒受感染的統計概率。如果概率大，可用染色體分析加以證實。

triploid *adj.* describing cells, tissues, or individuals in which there are three complete chromosome sets. *Compare* haploid, diploid. **–triploid** *n.*

三倍體　描述有三個完整染色體組的細胞、組織或個體。與 haploid，diploid 對比。

triprolidine *n.* an *antihistamine drug used to treat allergy and, in combination with other drugs (e.g. dextromethorphan in *Actifed*), to relieve the symptoms of the common cold. Trade name: **Actidil**.

曲普利啶　抗組胺藥，用以治療過敏，與其他藥物（如右美沙芬）聯用，緩解普通感冒的症狀。商品名：Actidil。

triquetrum (triquetral bone) *n.* a bone of the wrist (*see* carpus). It articulates with the ulna behind and with the pisiform, hamate, and lunate bones in the carpus.

三角骨　腕關節的一塊骨（參閱 carpus）。在後與尺骨連成關節，並與腕骨的豌豆骨、鈎骨及月骨連成關節。

trismus *n.* spasm of the jaw muscles, keeping the jaws tightly closed. This is the characteristic symptom of *tetanus but it also occurs less dramatically as a sensitivity reaction to certain drugs and in diorders of the *basal ganglia.

牙關緊閉　咬肌痙攣，使上下頜緊閉。是破傷風的典型症狀，但也在某些藥物的過敏反應中或基底神經節疾病中出現的不甚顯著的症狀。

trisomy *n.* a condition in which there is one extra chromosome present in each cell in addition to the normal (diploid) chromosome set. A number of chromosome disorders are due to trisomy, including *Down's syndrome and *Klinefelter's syndrome. **–trisomic** *adj.*

三倍體病　在每一個細胞內除正常染色體組（二倍體）之外，又存在一個額外的染色體的疾病。許多染色體病都是由三位體引起的，其中包括唐氏綜合徵及克蘭費爾特綜合徵。

tritanopia *n.* a rare defect of colour vision in which affected persons are insensitive to blue light and confuse blues and greens. *Compare* deuteranopia, protanopia.

藍色盲　一種罕見的視色缺陷，患者對藍色光不敏感，並且將藍色和綠色混淆。與 deuteranopia，protanopia 對比。

tritium *n.* an isotope of hydrogen that emits beta particles (electrons) during its decay. It has been used as a *tracer in the investigation of diseases of the heart and the lungs. Symbol: T or ^{3}H.

氚　氫的同位素，衰變時釋放出 β 粒子（電子）。用作為示踪劑檢查心、肺疾病。符號：T 或 ^{3}H。

trocar *n.* an instrument used combined with a *cannula to draw off fluids from a body cavity (such as the peritoneal cavity). It comprises a metal tube containing a removable shaft with a sharp three-cornered point; the shaft is withdrawn after the trocar has been inserted into the cavity.

套針　和套管共同使用從體腔（如腹腔）抽取液體的一種器械。它有一個金屬套管，管內有一可抽出的針芯，針芯有一銳利的三角針尖；將套針插入腔中後即將針芯拔出。

trochanter *n.* either of the two protuberances that occur below the neck of the *femur.

轉子　股骨頸下存在的二個隆突之一。

troche *n.* a medicinal lozenge, taken by mouth, used to treat conditions of the mouth or throat and also of the alimentary canal.

錠劑　藥用糖錠，含化以治療口腔、咽喉及消化道疾病。

trochlea *n.* an anatomical part having the structure or function of a pulley; for example the groove at the lower end of the *humerus or the fibrocartilaginous ring in the frontal bone (where it forms part of the orbit), through which the tendon of the superior oblique eye muscle passes. **–trochlear** *adj.*

滑車　一解剖部分，具有滑輪樣的結構或功能；例如，肱骨下端的溝，或額骨（組成眼眶的一部分）的纖維軟骨環，眼上斜肌腱即通過該環。

trochlear nerve the fourth *cranial nerve (IV), which supplies the superior oblique muscle, one of the muscles responsible for movement of the eyeball in its socket. The action of the trochlear nerve is coordinated with that of

滑車神經　第四對腦神經，支配上斜肌，而上斜肌為負責眼球在眼眶內運動的肌肉之一。滑車神經的作用是協調動眼神經和展神經。

the *oculomotor and the *abducens nerves.

trochoid joint (pivot joint) a form of *diarthrosis (freely movable joint) in which a bone moves round a central axis, allowing rotational movement. An example is the joint between the atlas and axis vertebrae.

車軸關節，旋轉關節　一種類型的動關節（自由移動的關節），骨頭在其中繞中軸作旋轉移動。在寰椎和樞椎間的關節便是其中的一例。

Troisier's sign enlarged lymph nodes at the base of the neck on the left side associated with a carcinoma of the stomach.

特魯瓦西埃徵　左側頸基部淋巴結腫大，與胃癌有關。

Trombicula *n*. a genus of widely distributed mites – the harvest mites. The six-legged parasitic larvae (chiggers) are common in fields during the autumn and frequently attack man, remaining attached to the skin for several days while feeding on the lymph and digested skin tissues. Their bite causes intense irritation and a severe dermatitis. Various repellents, e.g. benzyl benzoate, can be applied to clothing. *Trombicula* larvae transmit scrub typhus in southeast Asia.

恙蟎屬　一屬分布廣泛的蟎——沙蟎。秋天田地中常見六腿寄生幼蟲（沙蟎），該蟲頻繁侵襲人類，附着在人的皮膚上達數天，以淋巴液及分解了的皮膚組織為食。其叮咬引起劇烈的刺激及嚴重的皮炎。可將各種驅蟲劑，如苯甲酸苄酯噴灑在衣服上。恙蟎幼蟲在東南亞地區傳播恙蟲病。

troph- (tropho-) *prefix denoting* nourishment or nutrition.

〔前綴〕**營養**

trophoblast *n*. the tissue that forms the wall of the *blastocyst. At implantation it forms two layers, an inner cellular layer (*cytotrophoblast*) and an outer syncytial layer (*plasmoditrophoblast*), which forms the outermost layer of the placenta and attains direct contact with the maternal bloodstream.

　　Trophoblast sampling was the name originally given to the technique now known as *chorionic villus sampling.

滋養層　形成胚泡壁的組織。在植入時它形成兩層，即內部細胞層（細胞滋養層）和外部細胞層（合體滋養層），後者形成胚胎最外層，直接與母血接觸。

　　滋養層取樣檢驗技術是現名為絨膜絨毛取樣檢驗的舊名。

trophozoite *n*. a stage in the life cycle of the malarial parasite (*Plasmodium*) that develops from a merozoite in the red

滋養體原蟲　瘧原蟲生活周期中的一期，在紅細胞中由裂殖子發育而來。滋養體具有一環

blood cells. The trophozoite, which has a ring-shaped body and a single nucleus, grows steadily at the expense of the blood cell; eventually its nucleus and cytoplasm undergo division to form a *schizont containing many merozoites.

狀體及一單核，靠消耗血細胞穩步生長，最終核和胞漿分裂，形成含有許多裂殖子的裂殖體。

-trophy *suffix denoting* nourishment, development, or growth Example: *dystrophy* (defective development).

〔後綴〕**營養，發育，生長**例如：營養障礙（發育不全）。

-tropic *suffix denoting* **1.** turning towards. **2.** having an affinity for; influencing. Example: *inotropic* (muscle).

〔後綴〕**(1) 趨向……的 (2)有親和力的，影響……的** 例如：影響收縮力的（指肌肉）。

tropical medicine the study of diseases more commonly found in tropical regions than elsewhere, such as *malaria, *leprosy, *trypanosomiasis, *schistosomiasis, and *leishmaniasis.

熱帶醫學 研究常發生於熱帶地區而非其他地區之疾病的科學，例如瘧疾、麻風病、錐蟲病、血吸蟲病及利什曼病。

tropical ulcer (Naga sore) a skin disease prevalent in wet tropical regions. A large open sloughing sore usually develops at the site of a wound or abrasion. The ulcer, commonly located on the feet and legs, is often infected with spirochaetes and bacteria and may extend deeply and cause destruction of muscles and bones. Treatment involves the application of mild antiseptic dressings and intramuscular doses of *penicillin. Skin grafts may be necessary in more serious cases. The exact cause of the disease has not yet been determined.

熱帶潰瘍（那加潰瘍） 一種流行於潮濕熱帶地區的皮膚病。在傷口或擦傷處通常有大塊的開放性爛瘡長出。這種潰瘍常位於腳和腿部，常受螺旋體和細菌感染，並可向深度擴展引起肌肉及骨骼的損傷。治療可用緩和的抗菌敷料包紮及肌注青黴素。在病情較嚴重時有必要作植皮。其確切病因尚未確定。

tropicamide *n.* a drug used in the form of eye drops to dilate the pupil so that the inside of the eye can more easily be examined or operated upon. Trade name: **Mydriacyl.**

托吡卡胺 一種藥物，作為滴眼劑使用，用以擴張瞳孔以便更易檢查眼的內部或在眼內做手術。商品名：Mydriacyl。

tropocollagen *n.* the molecular unit of *collagen. It consists of a helix of three

膠原單位 膠原蛋白的分子單位。它是由三個膠原蛋白分子

collagen molecules: this arrangement confers on the fibres structural stability and resistance to stretching.

組成的一個螺旋結構：該種排列能穩定纖維結構並抗牽拉。

truncus *n.* a *trunk: a main vessel or other tubular organ from which subsidiary branches arise.

幹 一條主管道或其他管狀器官，由此分出從屬分支。

truncus arteriosus the main arterial trunk arising from the fetal heart. It develops into the aorta and pulmonary artery.

動脈幹 從胎兒心臟發出的主動脈幹。它發育成主動脈及肺動脈。

trunk *n.* **1.** the main part of a blood vessel, lymph vessel, or nerve, from which branches arise. **2.** the body excluding the head and limbs.

(1) 主幹 血管、淋巴管和神經的主要部分，其分支由此分出。**(2) 軀幹** 不包括頭和四肢在內的身體。

truss *n.* a device for applying pressure to a hernia to prevent it from protruding. It usually consists of a pad attached to a belt with straps or spring strips and it is worn under the clothing.

疝帶 一種向疝施以壓力以防止其突出的器械。通常由一個連接到搭扣帶上的腰帶或彈性布條做成，穿着於衣服裏面。

trust *n.* (in the NHS) *see* hospital.

托管 （在國家衛生局）參閱 hospital。

trypanocide *n.* an agent that kills trypanosomes and is therefore used to treat infestations caused by these parasites (*see* trypanosomiasis). The main trypanocides are arsenic-containing compounds.

殺錐蟲劑 一種可殺死錐蟲的藥劑，故用於治療由錐蟲類寄生蟲引起的感染（參閱 trypanosomiasis）。主要的殺錐蟲劑為含砷化合物。

Trypanosoma *n.* a genus of parasitic protozoans that move by means of a long trailing flagellum and a thin wavy membrane, which project from the body surface. Trypanosomes undergo part of their development in the blood of a vertebrate host. The remaining stages occur in invertebrate hosts, which then transmit the parasites back to the vertebrates. *T. rhodesiense* and *T. gambiense*, which are transmitted through the bite of

錐蟲屬 寄生性原蟲一屬，靠拖着的長鞭毛及突出於體表的薄波動膜運動。在脊椎動物宿主的血中完成其部分生長發育。其餘生長期將在無脊椎運動宿主身上進行，然後再傳播給脊椎動物。由采采蠅叮咬傳播的羅德西亞錐蟲和岡比亞錐蟲，在非洲引起昏睡病。克氏錐蟲由豬椿攜帶，在南美引起恰加斯病。

*tsetse flies, cause *sleeping sickness in Africa. *T. cruzi*, carried by *reduviid bugs, causes Chagas' disease in South America.

trypanosomiasis *n.* any disease caused by the presence of parasitic protozoans of the genus *Trypanosoma*. The two most important diseases are *Chagas' disease (South American trypanosomiasis) and *sleeping sickness (African trypanosomiasis).

tryparsamide *n.* a drug used in the treatment of trypanosomiasis (sleeping sickness). Usually given by injection, it penetrates the cerebrospinal fluid and is highly active against the infective organism (*Trypanosoma gambiense*). Trade name: **Tryparsam.**

trypsin *n.* an enzyme that continues the digestion of proteins by breaking down peptones into smaller peptide chains (*see* peptidase). It is secreted by the pancreas in an inactive form, trypsinogen, which is converted in the duodenum to trypsin by the action of the enzyme enteropeptidase.

trypsinogen *n. see* trypsin.

tryptophan *n.* an *essential amino acid. *See also* amino acid.

tsetse *n.* a large bloodsucking fly of tropical Africa belonging to the genus *Glossina*. Tsetse flies, which have slender forwardly projecting biting mouthparts, feed during the day on man and other mammals. They transmit the blood parasites that cause *sleeping sickness. *G. palpalis* and *G. tachinoides*, which are found along river banks, transmit *Trypanosoma gambiense*; *G. morsitans*, *G.*

錐蟲病　由錐蟲屬寄生性原蟲引發的疾病。其中最主要的兩種病為恰加斯病（南美錐蟲病）及昏睡病（非洲錐蟲病）。

錐蟲腫胺　用於治療錐蟲病（昏睡病）的藥物。常注射給藥，可通過腦脊液，對抗傳染性有機體（岡比亞錐蟲）十分有效。商品名：Tryparsam。

胰蛋白酶　一種酶，它通過將蛋白腖分解成小肽鏈（參閱 peptidase）來繼續消化蛋白。它由胰腺分泌成一種非活性的形式，即胰蛋白酶原，該物質在十二指腸內經腸肽酶的作用轉化為胰蛋白酶。

胰蛋白酶原　參閱 trypsin。

色氨酸　一種必需氨基酸。參閱 amino acid。

采采蠅　熱帶非洲的一種大型吸血蠅，屬於舌蠅屬。采采蠅具有一細長向前突出的叮咬嘴部，白天取食於人和其他哺乳動物。牠們傳播引起昏睡病的血液寄生蟲。見於河流沿岸的鬚舌蠅傳播岡比亞錐蟲；見於熱帶草原國家的刺舌蠅、淡足舌蠅等傳播羅德西亞錐蟲。

swynnertoni, and *G. pallidipes*, which are found in savannah country, transmit *T. rhodesiense*.

TSH *see* thyroid-stimulating hormone.

促甲狀腺激素　參閱　thyroid-stimulating hormone。

tsutsugamushi disease *see* scrub typhus.

恙蟲病　參閱 scrub typhus。

tubal occlusion blocking of the Fallopian tubes. This is achieved by surgery as a means of *sterilization; it is also a result of *pelvic inflammatory disease.

輸卵管閉塞　輸卵管的阻斷。作為絕育措施可用手術方法獲得；也可由盆腔炎症所致。

tubal pregnancy *see* ectopic pregnancy.

輸卵管妊娠　參閱 ectopic pregnancy。

tube *n.* (in anatomy) a long hollow cylindrical structure, e.g. a *Fallopian tube.

管　（解剖學）一長而中空的圓柱狀結構，如輸卵管。

tuber *n.* (in anatomy) a thickened or swollen part. The *tuber cinereum* is a part of the brain situated at the base of the hypothalamus, connected to the stalk of the pituitary gland.

結節　（解剖學）變厚或腫脹的部位。灰結節是大腦的一部分，位於下丘腦基底，與垂體莖相連接。

tubercle *n.* **1.** (in anatomy) a small rounded protuberance on a bone. For example, there are two tubercles at the upper end of the humerus. **2.** the specific nodular lesion of *tuberculosis.

(1) 小結節　（解剖學）骨骼上的圓形小突起。例如肱骨上端的兩個小結節。**(2) 結核結節**　特異性結節狀結核病病變。

tubercular *adj.* having small rounded swellings or nodules, not necessarily caused by tuberculosis.

結節性的　具有圓形的小腫脹或結節，並非一定由結核病引起。

tuberculide *n.* an eruption of the skin that arises in response to an internal focus of tuberculosis.

結核疹　皮膚發疹，產生於內部結核病病竈。

tuberculin *n.* a protein extract from cultures of tubercle bacilli, used to test whether a person has suffered from or been in contact with tuberculosis. In the

結核菌素　從結核菌培養基中提取的一種蛋白，用於檢查一個人是否患有結核病或與該病有過接觸。芒圖試驗是將一定

Mantoux test a quantity of tuberculin is injected beneath the skin and a patch of inflammation appearing in the next 48–72 hours is regarded as a positive reaction, meaning that a degree of immunity is present.

tuberculoma *n.* a mass of cheeselike material resembling a tumour, seen in some cases of *tuberculosis. Tuberculomas are found in a variety of sites, including the lung or brain, and a single mass may be the only clinical evidence of disease. Treatment is by surgical excision, together with antituberculous drugs.

tuberculosis *n.* an infectious disease caused by the bacillus *Mycobacterium tuberculosis* (first identified by Koch in 1882) and characterized by the formation of nodular lesions (*tubercles*) in the tissues.

In *pulmonary tuberculosis* – formerly known as *consumption* and *phthisis* (wasting) – the bacillus is inhaled into the lungs where it sets up a primary tubercle and spreads to the nearest lymph nodes (the *primary complex*). Natural immune defences may heal it at this stage; alternatively the disease may smoulder for months or years and fluctuate with the patient's resistance. Many people become infected but show no symptoms. Others develop a chronic infection and can transmit the bacillus by coughing and sneezing. Symptoms of the active disease include fever, night sweats, weight loss, and the spitting of blood. In some cases the bacilli spread from the lungs to the bloodstream, setting up millions of tiny tubercles throughout the body (*miliary tuberculosis*), or migrate to the meninges to cause tuberculous *meningitis. Bacilli entering by the mouth, usually in infected cows' milk, set up a primary

量的結核菌素注射於皮下，48~72 小時內有炎症斑塊出現被認為是陽性，意味着存在一定程度的免疫。

結核瘤 一團乾酪狀物質，酷似腫瘤，見於某些結核病例中。結核瘤見於諸多部位，包括肺或腦，且單獨的一個腫塊可能是該病僅有的臨床證據。施行外科切除及合併使用抗結核藥為治療方法。

結核病 一種傳染性疾病，由結核分支桿菌（1882 年首次被科赫確認）引起，其特徵為在組織內形成小結節狀病變（結核結節）。

肺結核——以前稱謂為癆病或肺病——是結核菌被吸入肺，在肺部形成原發性結節，並擴散到附近的淋巴結（原發綜合徵）。在此階段，自然免疫防禦可治愈該徵；或者該病可遷延數月或數年，並隨病人的抵抗力而波動。許多被感染的人並無症狀顯示。其他人則發展為慢性感染並能通過咳嗽、打噴嚏傳播桿菌。活動性結核病的症狀有發燒、夜汗、體重下降及咯血。在有些情況下，結核分支桿菌由肺部擴散到血液中，在全身引起數萬個結節（粟粒型結核），或游走到腦膜引起結核性腦膜炎。經口進入人體的結核桿菌常存在於受感染的奶牛牛奶中，引發腹部淋巴結的原發綜合徵，導致腹膜炎，有時可播散到其他器官、關節及骨骼（參閱 Pott's disease）。

該病通過合併使用抗生素

complex in abdominal lymph nodes, leading to *peritonitis, and sometimes spread to other organs, joints, and bones (see Pott's disease).

Tuberculosis is curable by various combinations of the antibiotics *streptomycin, *ethambutol, *isoniazid (INH), *rifampicin, and *pyrazinamide. Preventive measures in the UK include the detection of cases by X-ray screening of vulnerable populations and inoculation with *BCG vaccine of those with no immunity to the disease (the *tuberculin test identifies which people require vaccination).

鏈黴素、乙胺丁醇，異烟胼（INH），利福平及吡嗪酰胺可以治愈。在英國預防措施包括對易感人羣進行 X 綫篩查以確定攜帶者及對無免疫力的人接種卡介苗（用結核菌素試驗確定需要接種者）。

tuberose see tuberous.

結節狀的　參閱 tuberous。

tuberosity n. a large rounded protuberance on a bone. For example, there is a tuberosity at the upper end of the tibia.

粗隆　骨骼上的圓形大突起。例如，脛骨上端的一粗隆。

tuberous (tuberose) adj. knobbed; having nodules or rounded swellings.

結節狀的　結節的；有結節的或有圓形腫脹的。

tuberous sclerosis (epiloia) a hereditary disorder in which the brain, skin, and other organs are studded with small plaques or tumours. Symptoms include epilepsy and mental retardation.

結節性硬化（結節性腦硬化）一種先天性病變，腦、皮膚及其他器官遍布小斑塊或小腫物。其症狀有癲癇及智力低下。

tubo- prefix denoting a tube, especially a Fallopian tube or auditory tube (meatus).

〔前綴〕管　尤指輸卵管或咽鼓管。

tuboabdominal adj. relating to or occurring in a Fallopian tube and the abdomen.

輸卵管腹腔的　有關於或發生於輸卵管及腹腔的。

tubocurarine n. a drug given by intravenous injection to produce relaxation of voluntary muscles before surgery and in such conditions as tetanus, encephalitis, and poliomyelitis (see muscle relaxant). Toxic side-effects are usually only seen

筒箭毒鹼　術前鬆弛隨意肌以及破傷風、腦炎和脊髓灰質炎等病中使用的靜脈注射藥（參閱 muscle relaxant）。毒性副作用常僅見於過量時，此時因呼吸肌麻痺可能發生呼

with overdosage, when respiratory failure due to paralysis of respiratory muscles may occur. Trade names: **Jexin**, **Tubarine**.

tubo-ovarian *adj.* relating to or occurring in a Fallopian tube and an ovary.

tubotympanal *adj.* relating to the tympanic cavity and the *Eustachian tube.

tubule *n.* (in anatomy) a small cylindrical hollow structure. *See also* renal tubule, seminiferous tubule.

tularaemia (rabbit fever) *n.* a disease of rodents and rabbits, caused by the bacterium *Francisella tularensis*, that is transmitted to man by deer flies (*see* Chrysops), by direct contact with infected animals, by contamination of wounds, or by drinking contaminated water. Symptoms include an ulcer at the site of infection, enlarged lymph nodes, headache, aching pains, loss of weight, and a fever lasting several weeks. Treatment with chloramphenicol, streptomycin, or tetracycline is effective.

tulle gras a soft dressing consisting of open-woven silk (or other material) impregnated with a waterproof soft paraffin wax.

tumbu fly a large non-bloodsucking fly, *Cordylobia anthropophaga*, widely distributed in tropical Africa. The female fly lays her eggs on ground contaminated with urine or excreta or on clothing tainted with sweat or urine. The maggots are normally parasites of rats, but if they come into contact with man they penetrate the skin, producing boil-like swellings (*see also* myiasis). The maggots

吸衰竭。商品名：Jexin，Tubarine。

輸卵管-卵巢的 有關於或發生於輸卵管和卵巢的。

咽鼓管鼓室的 與鼓室及咽鼓管相關的。

小管 （解剖學）小而中空的柱狀結構。參閱 renal tubule，seminiferous tubule。

兔熱病 嚙齒動物和兔類的一種疾病，由土拉桿菌引起，通過鹿虻（參閱 Chrysops）、與被感染動物的直接接觸、傷口感染或飲用被污染的水，將此病傳播給人。症狀有感染部位發生潰瘍、淋巴結腫大、頭痛、全身酸痛、體重下降和持續數周的發燒。用氯黴素、鏈黴素或四環素治療有效。

潤膚薄紗 一種用質地稀疏的絲織品（或其他材料）在浸透防水軟石蠟後製成的柔軟敷料。

嗜人瘤蠅 一種大的非吸血蠅，即嗜人瘤蠅屬，廣泛分布於熱帶非洲。雌蠅或產卵於被尿液污染的土地上，或產卵於被汗水及尿液沾污的衣服上。其蛆常寄生於大鼠類，但若接觸到人，即會穿過皮膚，引起癤樣腫物（參閱 myiasis）。在腫處塗抹油膏可逐漸將蛆排出。

can be gently eased out by applying oil to the swellings.

tumefaction *n.* the process in which a tissue becomes swollen and tense by accumulation within it of fluid under pressure.

腫脹　在壓力下，組織內液體積聚使組織腫脹而緊張的過程。

tumescence *n.* a swelling, or the process of becoming swollen, usually because of an accumulation of blood or other fluid within the tissues.

腫　腫脹或腫脹的過程，常係組織內血液或其他液體聚積之故。

tumid *adj.* swollen.

腫脹的　參閱 swollen。

tumor *n.* swelling: one of the classical signs of *inflammation in a tissue, the other three being *calor (heat), *rubor (redness), and *dolor (pain). The swelling of an inflamed area is due to the leakage from small blood vessels of clear protein-containing fluid, which accumulates between the cells.

腫脹　組織內炎症的典型體徵之一，其他三個體徵為熱、紅及痛。發炎區的腫脹是由清亮的含蛋白液體從小血管中滲出，聚積於細胞間所致。

tumour *n.* any abnormal swelling in or on a part of the body. The term is usually applied to an abnormal growth of tissue, which may be *benign or *malignant. *Compare* cyst.

腫瘤　身體某部位內或該部位上發生的任何異常腫ъ。該術語常用來指組織的異常生長，這種生長可為良性的或惡性的。與 cyst 對比。

tumour-associated antigen a protein produced by cancer cells. Its presence in the blood can be revealed by means of a simple blood test, which could provide a basis for the diagnosis of malignant melanoma and other cancers at their earliest – and most treatable – stages of development.

腫瘤相關抗原　癌細胞產生的蛋白。血液中該蛋白的存在可通過簡單的驗血來揭示，這為在最早發展階段，即最可治療的階段，診斷惡性腫瘤及其他癌症奠定基礎。

tumour-infiltrating lymphocyte (TIL) a lymphoid cell that can infiltrate solid tumours. Such cells can be cultured in vitro, in the presence of *interleukin 2, and have been used as vehicles for *tumour-necrosis factor in gene therapy trials for cancer.

腫瘤浸潤的淋巴細胞　能浸入堅固腫瘤的淋巴細胞。該細胞可在白細胞介素-2 存在的情況下，在試管中培養出來。在基因治療癌症的試驗中該細胞被用作腫瘤壞死因素的載體。

tumour marker a substance produced by a tumour that can be used to monitor the size of the tumour and the effects of treatment. An example is *alpha-fetoprotein, which is used to monitor treatment of testicular *teratomas.

tumour necrosis factor (TNF) a specific protein that causes destruction of tumours. The gene encoding TNF has been used in gene therapy trials for cancer.

Tunga *n.* a genus of sand fleas found in tropical America and Africa. The fertilized female of *T. penetrans*, the chigoe or jigger, burrows beneath the skin of the foot, where it becomes enclosed in a swelling of the surrounding tissues and causes intense itching and inflammation. Surgical removal of the fleas is recommended.

tunica *n.* a covering or layer of an organ or part; for example, a layer of the wall of a blood vessel (*see* adventitia, intima, media). The *tunica albuginea* is a fibrous membrane comprising one of the covering tissues of the ovary, penis, and testis.

tunnel *n.* (in anatomy) a canal or hollow groove. *See also* carpal tunnel.

TUR (TURP) transurethral resection (of the prostate). *See* resection.

turbinate bone *see* nasal concha.

turbinectomy *n.* the surgical removal of one of the bones forming the nasal cavity (nasal conchae, or turbinate bones).

turgescence *n.* a swelling, or the process by which a swelling arises in

腫瘤標記　由腫瘤產生的一種物質，該物質可用於檢驗腫瘤大小及治療效果。例如甲胎蛋白被用於監測睪丸畸胎瘤的治療。

腫瘤壞死因素　摧毀腫瘤的特定蛋白。含該物質編碼的基因被用於癌症的基因治療試驗。

潛蚤屬　一屬發現於熱帶美洲及非洲的沙蚤。受精的雌性穿皮潛蚤、沙蚤鑽藏到腳皮膚下，封閉於腫脹的周圍組織中，引起劇烈刺癢及炎症。建議手術去除沙蚤。

膜　器官或器官部分的覆蓋層或被膜，例如血管壁的一層（參閱 adventitia，intima，media）。白膜是一纖維膜，構成卵巢、陰莖和睪丸的覆蓋組織之一。

隧道　（解剖學）管道或凹溝。參閱 carpal tunnel。

經尿道（前列腺）切除術　經尿道切除（前列腺）。參閱 resection。

鼻甲　參閱 nasal concha。

鼻甲切除術　手術切除構成鼻腔的骨（鼻甲骨）之一。

腫脹　一腫物或腫脹在組織內產生的過程，通常係血液

tissues, usually by the accumulation of blood or other fluid under pressure.

或其他液體聚積壓迫組織之故。

turgor *n*. a state of being swollen or distended.

脹滿 腫脹或鼓脹的狀態。

Turner's syndrome a genetic defect in women in which there is only one X chromosome instead of the usual two. Affected women are infertile: they have female external genitalia but no ovaries and therefore no menstrual periods (*see* amenorrhoea). Characteristically they are short and have variable developmental defects, which may include webbing of the neck.

特納綜合徵 婦女的一種遺傳缺陷，患者只有一個染色體，而不是一般的兩個染色體。患病婦女不育：她們有女性的外生殖器但無卵巢，因此無月經期（參閱 amenorrhoea）。最典型性的是她們身材矮小，有各種發育缺陷，包括有蹼頸。

turricephaly *n*. *see* oxycephaly.

尖頭 參閱 oxycephaly。

tussis *n*. the medical name for *coughing.

咳 咳嗽之醫學名詞。

twilight state a condition of disturbed consciousness in which the individual can still carry out some normal activities but is impaired in his awareness and has no memory of what he has done. It is encountered after epileptic attacks, in alcoholism, and in organic states of confusion. It may be associated with other symptoms, such as physical and mental slowing, episodes of rage, and hallucinations. Twilight states last only for a short time, commonly a few hours.

朦朧狀態 一種意識混亂的狀態，病人仍可繼續進行某些正常活動，但其知覺受損，並對其所做之事無記憶。此病發生於癲癇發作之後、酒精中毒或器質性精神錯亂時。該狀態下病人常伴有其他症狀，如體力和腦力活動減慢、暴怒發作及幻覺。該狀態僅持續短時間，通常為數小時。

twins *n*. two individuals who are born at the same time and of the same parents. *Fraternal* (or *dizygotic*) *twins* are the result of the simultaneous fertilization of two egg cells; they may be of different sexes and are no more alike than ordinary siblings. *Identical* (or *monozygotic*) *twins* result from the fertilization of a single egg cell that subsequently divides to give two separate fetuses. They are of

雙胎兒（孿生） 同時由同父母所生的兩個個體。雙卵性（或雙合子的）雙胎係兩個卵細胞同時受精之結果，他們可能性別不同，而且並不比一般的兄弟姐妹長得更相像。單卵性（單合子的）雙胎則為一個受精卵細胞隨後分裂為兩個胎兒的結果。他們性別相同，且其他方面的遺傳性也相同；其外

the same sex and otherwise genetically identical; any differences in their appearance are due to environmental influences. *See also* Siamese twins.

表方面的任何不同都出於環境影響。參閱 Siamese twins。

tylosis *n.* diffuse *keratosis occurring especially on the palms and soles.

胼胝形成 彌漫性角化形成，尤其在手掌及腳跟處。

tympan- (tympano-) *prefix denoting* **1.** the eardrum. Example: *tympanectomy* (surgical excision of). **2.** the middle ear.

〔前綴〕**(1) 鼓膜** 例如：鼓膜切除術（外科手術切除鼓膜）。**(2) 中耳**

tympanic cavity *see* middle ear.

鼓室 參閱 middle ear。

tympanic membrane (eardrum) the membrane at the inner end of the external auditory meatus, separating the outer and middle ears. It is formed from the outer wall of the lining of the tympanic cavity and the skin that lines the external auditory meatus. When sound waves reach the ear the tympanum vibrates, transmitting these vibrations to the malleus – one of the auditory *ossicles in the middle ear – to which it is attached.

鼓膜 外耳道內端的膜，分隔外耳和中耳。由鼓室外壁的上皮及外耳道的上皮形成。當聲波到達耳部，振動鼓膜，鼓膜又將這些振動傳遞到錘骨，即中耳的一塊聽小骨，該骨是與鼓膜相連的。

tympanites (meteorism) *n.* distension of the abdomen with air or gas: the abdomen is resonant (drumlike) on *percussion. Causes include intestinal obstruction, the *irritable bowel syndrome, and *aerophagy.

鼓脹（腸脹氣） 腹部因空氣或氣體而脹鼓：叩診時腹部有共鳴。病因有腸梗阻、應激性腸道綜合徵及吞氣症。

tympanoplasty *n.* surgical repair of defects of the eardrum and middle ear ossicles. *See* myringoplasty.

鼓膜成形術 手術修復鼓膜及中耳聽小骨的缺陷。參閱 myringoplasty。

tympanotomy *n.* a surgical operation to expose the middle ear and allow access to the ossicles. It is usually performed by incising around the eardrum and turning it forwards.

鼓膜切開術 外科手術以露出中耳和接近聽小骨。常圍繞鼓膜邊切開並將鼓膜向前提。

tympanum *n*. the *middle ear (tympanic cavity) and/or the eardrum (*tympanic membrane).

鼓室　中耳（鼓室腔）和／或鼓膜。

typhlitis *n*. *Obsolete* inflammation of the caecum: formerly a common diagnosis of the condition now recognized as appendicitis.

盲腸炎　（廢用詞）盲腸發炎：過去常診斷為盲腸炎，現認為是闌尾炎。

typhlosis *n*. an obsolete term for *blindness.

視覺缺失　失明的舊稱。

typho- *prefix denoting* **1.** typhoid fever. **2.** typhus.

〔前綴〕　**(1)** 傷寒　**(2)** 斑疹傷寒

typhoid fever an infection of the digestive system by the bacterium *Salmonella typhi*, causing general weakness, high fever, a rash of red spots on the chest and abdomen, chills, sweating, and in serious cases inflammation of the spleen and bones, delirium, and erosion of the intestinal wall leading to haemorrhage. It is transmitted through food or drinking water contaminated by the faeces or urine of patients or carriers. In most cases recovery occurs naturally but treatment with such antibiotics as ampicillin, amoxicillin, ciprofloxacin, or chloramphenicol reduces the severity of symptoms. Vaccination with *TAB provides temporary immunity. *Compare* paratyphoid fever.

傷寒　傷寒沙門菌引起的消化系統感染，造成全身無力、高熱、胸腹部紅色斑疹、寒戰、出汗，嚴重的病例有脾和骨骼發炎、譫妄以及導致出血的腸壁糜爛。通過被病人或帶菌者的糞便、尿液所污染的食物及飲水傳播。多數情況該病可自愈，但用氨苄青黴素、阿莫西林、環丙沙星或氯黴素之類的抗生素治療可減輕症狀的嚴重性。接種傷寒菌苗可獲得暫時性免疫。與 paratyphoid fever 對比。

typhus (spotted fever) *n*. any one of a group of infections caused by *rickettsiae and characterized by severe headache, a widespread rash, prolonged high fever, and delirium. They all respond to treatment with chloramphenicol or tetracyclines. *Epidemic typhus* (also known as *classical* or *louseborne typhus*) is caused by infection with *Rickettsia prowazekii* transmitted by lice.

斑疹傷寒　（斑疹熱）立克次體引起的一組傳染病，其特徵是嚴重的頭痛，廣泛分布的皮疹，長時間高燒和譫妄。用氯黴素及四環素治療均有效。流行性斑疹傷寒（亦稱典型性或虱傳斑疹傷寒）是由虱傳播的普氏立克次體引起的。過去曾在擁擠及不衛生的情況下（如戰爭及飢荒時期）廣泛流行，

It was formerly very prevalent in over-crowded insanitary conditions (as during wars and famines), with a mortality rate approaching 100%. *Endemic typhus* (*murine* or *flea-borne typhus*) is a disease of rats due to *Rickettsia mooseri*; it can be transmitted to man by rat fleas, causing a mild typhus fever. There are in addition several kinds of *tick typhus* (in which the rickettsiae are transmitted by ticks), including *Rocky Mountain spotted fever, and typhus transmitted by mites (*see* rickettsial pox, scrub typhus).

病死率近 100%。地方性斑疹傷寒（鼠型斑疹傷寒或蚤傳斑疹傷寒）是由莫氏立克次體引起的鼠病；可由鼠蚤傳播於人，引起輕型斑疹傷寒。另外，還有幾種蜱傳斑疹熱（由蜱傳播立克次體），其中包括落基山斑疹熱，以及由蟎傳播的斑疹傷寒（參閱 rickettsial pox，scrub typhus）。

tyramine *n.* an amine naturally occurring in cheese. It has a similar effect in the body to that of *adrenaline. This effect can be dangerous in patients taking *MAO inhibitors (antidepressants), in whom blood pressure may become very high. Cheese is therefore not advised when such drugs are prescribed.

酪胺　奶酪中天然存在的一種胺。在體內與腎上腺素作用相似。此作用可能對服用單胺氧化酶抑制劑的患者有危險性，其血壓可能會十分高。建議病人用這類藥時不要吃奶酪。

Tyroglyphus *n. see* Acarus.

粉蟎屬　參閱 Acarus。

tyrosine *n. see* amino acid.

酪氨酸　參閱 amino acid。

tyrosinosis *n.* an inborn defect of metabolism of the amino acid tyrosine that causes excessive excretion of parahydroxyphenylpyruvic acid in the urine, giving it abnormal reducing power.

酪氨酸代謝紊亂症　先天性酪氨酸代謝障礙，造成尿液中過多地排出羥苯丙酮酸，使尿具有異常的還原能力。

tyrothricin *n.* an *antibiotic derived from the bacterium *Bacillus brevis*. It is used, alone or in combination with some other drugs (e.g. benzocaine in *Tyrozets*), in the form of skin applications and lozenges in the treatment of infections of the mouth, throat, and skin, and of wounds and burns.

短桿菌素　取自短桿菌的抗生素。可單獨或與其他藥物（如苯佐卡因）聯合用作皮膚用藥或錠劑以治療口腔、咽喉、皮膚、創口或燒傷處的感染。

U

ubiquinone *n.* a *coenzyme that acts as an electron transfer agent in the mitochondria of cells (*see* electron transport chain).

輔酶 Q 一種輔酶，在細胞綫粒體內起電子轉移作用（參閱 electron transport chain）。

UICC *see* Union international contre le cancer.

國際抗癌聯合會 參閱 Union international contre le cancer。

ulcer *n.* a break in the skin extending to all its layers, or a break in the mucous membrane lining the alimentary tract, that fails to heal and is often accompanied by inflammation. Of the many types of skin ulcer, the most common is the venous (or hypostatic) leg ulcer, known incorrectly as a *varicose ulcer*, which is caused by increased venous pressure and usually occurs in older women. *See also* bedsore.

For ulcers of the alimentary tract, *see* aphtha, duodenal ulcer, gastric ulcer, peptic ulcer.

潰瘍 擴展到皮膚各層的破潰或消化道黏膜的破潰，這種破潰難以愈合且常伴有炎症。在眾多皮膚潰瘍中，最常見的為腿部靜脈（或附積性的）潰瘍，被誤稱為靜脈曲張性潰瘍，係靜脈壓力增加之故，常見於老年婦女。參閱 bedsore。

關於消化道潰瘍，參閱 aphtha，duodenal ulcer，gastric ulcer，peptic ulcer。

ulcerative colitis inflammation and ulceration of the colon and rectum. *See* colitis.

潰瘍性結腸炎 結腸與直腸的炎症及潰瘍。參閱 colitis。

ulcerative gingivitis acute painful gingivitis with ulceration, in which the tissues of the gums are rapidly destroyed. Occurring mainly in debilitated patients, it is associated with anaerobic microorganisms (*see* Fusobacterium, Bacteroides) and is accompanied by an unpleasant odour. Treatment is with *metronidazole and a careful and thorough regime of oral hygiene supplemented with oxidizing mouthwashes. In the past ulcerative gingivitis has been

潰瘍性齦炎 其時有潰瘍形成的急性疼痛性齒齦炎，齒齦組織被快速毀壞。主要見於衰弱患者，併發有厭氧菌感染（參閱 Fusobacterium，Bacteroides），伴有難聞氣味發出。治療：應用滅滴靈，嚴格口腔衛生制度，輔之以有氧化作用的含漱劑。舊稱樊尚咽峽炎，並將其嚴重型稱為走馬疳。

called *Vincent's angina*; in its severe form it is known as *noma.

ule- (ulo-) *prefix denoting* **1.** scars; scar tissue. **2.** the gums.

ulna *n.* the inner and longer bone of the forearm (see illustration). It articulates with the humerus and radius above and with the radius and indirectly with the wrist bones below. At its upper end is the *olecranon process and *coronoid process; at the lower end is a cone-shaped *styloid process.* **–ulnar** *adj.*

〔前綴〕**(1)** 瘢痕，瘢痕組織 **(2)** 牙齦

尺骨　前臂內側之長骨（見圖）。在上與肱骨、橈骨，在下與橈骨，並間接地與腕骨相關節。在其上端有鷹嘴突和喙狀突，在其下端有錐形莖突。

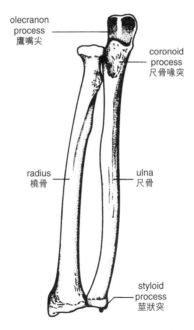

olecranon
process
鷹嘴尖

coronoid
process
尺骨喙突

radius
橈骨

ulna
尺骨

styloid
process
莖狀突

Right ulna and radius (front view)
右尺骨与橈骨（前面）

ulnar artery a branch of the brachial artery arising at the elbow and running deep within the muscles of the medial

尺動脈　肱動脈的一分支，起於肘部，走行於前臂中間肌深處。該動脈穿入手掌與橈動脈

side of the forearm. It passes into the palm of the hand, where it unites with the arch of the radial artery and gives off branches to the hand and fingers.

弓匯合，並向手及手指分出動脈分支。

ulnar nerve one of the major nerves of the arm. It originates in the neck, from spinal roots of the last cervical and first thoracic divisions, and runs down the inner side of the upper arm to behind the elbow. In the forearm it supplies the muscles with motor nerves; lower down it divides into several branches that supply the skin of the palm and fourth and fifth fingers.

尺神經 主要的臂神經之一。源自頸部，從最後一個頸神經根及第一胸神經根出發，沿上臂內側下行至肘背。在前臂它以運動神經支配肌肉，再向下尺神經又分成若干分支以支配手掌皮膚及第四、第五指。

ultra- *prefix denoting* **1.** beyond. **2.** an extreme degree (e.g. of large or small size.)

〔前綴〕**(1)** 超，超出 **(2)** 極度 如最大的極端或最小的極端。

ultracentrifuge *n.* a *centrifuge that works at extremely high speeds of rotation: used for separating large molecules, such as proteins.

超速離心機 轉速極高的離心機：用來分離大分子，如蛋白。

ultrafiltration *n.* filtration under pressure. In the kidney, blood is subjected to ultrafiltration to remove the unwanted water, urea, and other waste material that goes to make up urine.

超濾法 加壓過濾。在腎臟，血液受到超濾，以排出多餘的水分、尿素和組成尿液的其他廢物。

ultramicroscope *n.* a microscope for examining particles suspended in a gas or liquid under intense illumination from one side. Light is scattered or reflected from the particles, which can be seen through the eyepiece as bright objects against a dark background.

超顯微鏡 在一側強光照明之下用以檢查氣體、液體中懸浮粒子的顯微鏡。光綫遇粒子時被散射或反射，通過目鏡觀察到黑暗背景上的發亮物體。

ultramicrotome *n.* an instrument for cutting extremely thin sections of tissue (not more than 0.1 μm thick) for electron microscopy. *See also* microtome.

超微切片機 切割供電子顯微鏡檢查使用的極薄組織切片（厚度不超過 0.1 μm）的器械。參閱 microtome。

ultrasonics *n.* the study of the uses and properties of sound waves of very high frequency (*see* ultrasound). **–ultrasonic** *adj.*

超聲學　對超高頻聲波之特徵及用途進行研究的學科（參閱 ultrasound）。

ultrasonography *n.* the use of *ultrasound above 30,000 Hz to produce pictures of structures within the body. A controlled beam is directed into the body via an abdominal transducer (*compare* transvaginal ultrasonography) and the echoes of reflected sound are used to form an electronic image of various structures of the body. Based on the principles of underwater detection of ships, it allows ultrasonic visualization of the fetus in the uterus. Its uses include the diagnosis of pregnancy; assessment of gestational age; diagnosis of a multiple pregnancy, *malpresentations, and *hydatidiform moles; location of the placental site; and detection of fetal abnormalities.

超聲描記術　應用 30 000 Hz 以上的超聲產生關於人體內部結構的照片。一束受控光柱由腹部換能器導入體內（與 transvaginal ultrasonography 對比），並將反射的回聲用來形成體內各種結構的圖像。根據水下探測船的原理，這項技術將提供子宮中胎兒的超聲圖像。其用途包括懷孕確診、孕齡估算、確診多胎妊娠、先露異常及水泡狀胎塊、胎定位和胎兒異常探查。

ultrasonotomography (echotomography) *n.* the use of *ultrasound to examine the internal structure of the body by producing images of the reflections from different depths. A picture of the structures within a 'slice' of the body can be built up, much in the same way as X-rays can be employed to produce a tomogram (*see* tomography).

超聲體層攝影術（回聲體層攝影術）　用超聲波檢驗身體內部結構以產生其不同深層的反射圖像。與 X 綫用來產生體層攝影圖（參閱 tomography）的方法相同，超聲波可用來產生身體某一層的結構圖像。

ultrasound (ultrasonic waves) *n.* sound waves of extremely high frequency (above 20,000 Hz), inaudible to the human ear. Ultrasound can be used to examine the structure of the inside of the body, in the same way that X-rays can be used to build up pictures but with the advantages that the patient is not submitted to potentially harmful radiation and that structures not opaque to X-rays can be seen (*see* ultrasonography). The

超聲（超聲波）　超高頻率（20 000 Hz 以上）的聲波，係人耳聽不到的聲波。超聲波可用於檢查人體內的結構，其方法與 X 綫產生圖像之方法相同，但其優點是病人不受射綫的潛在危害，並且不透 X 綫的結構亦能由超聲波顯現（參閱 ultrasonography）。超聲波的振動作用還可用於治療各種組織深層疾病，甚至用於腎及

vibratory effect of these sound waves can also be used in the treatment of various disorders of deep tissues, and even to break up stones in the kidney or elsewhere. Ultrasonic instruments are used in dentistry to remove *calculus from the surfaces of teeth and to remove debris from the root canals of teeth in *root canal treatment. *See also* echography.

其他部位的碎石。超聲波儀在牙科中用以清除牙表面的結石及在牙根管治療中清除管中碎片。參閱 echography。

ultrasound marker the appearance, on *ultrasound examination of a pregnant woman, of a particular physical abnormality in the fetus at a specific stage in fetal development. Such markers suggest the presence of specific chromosomal or developmental abnormalities. For example, the *nuchal marker* – a dark area in the neck region of the fetus – is one of the markers for Down's syndrome.

超聲標記 胎兒在其某一發育期中呈現出某種身體異常的表象,這些表現出現於孕婦的超聲波檢查上。這些表象提示有某種染色體及發育異常存在。例如頸部標記——胎兒頸部的黑色區——即為唐氏綜合徵之標記。

ultraviolet rays invisible shortwavelength radiation beyond the violet end of the visible spectrum. Sunlight contains ultraviolet rays, which are responsible for the production of both suntan and – on overexposure – sunburn. The dust and gases of the earth's atmosphere absorb most of the ultraviolet rays in sunlight (*see* ozone). If this did not happen, the intense ultraviolet radiation from the sun would be lethal to living organisms.

紫外綫 可見光譜中紫綫端以外的看不見的短波射綫。陽光中含紫外綫,故而能曬黑皮膚,並在過度照射時曬傷皮膚。地球大氣層中的灰塵及氣體吸收了陽光中大部分的紫外綫(參閱 ozone)。若非如此,陽光中強烈的紫外綫會殺死生物。

umbilical cord the strand of tissue connecting the fetus to the placenta. It contains two arteries that carry blood to the placenta and one vein that returns it to the fetus. It also contains remnants of the *allantois and *yolk sac and becomes ensheathed by the *amnion.

臍帶 連接胎兒與胎盤的組織紐帶。它有兩條向胎盤輸送血液的動脈,有一條使血液回流到胎兒的靜脈。臍帶也含有尿囊及卵黃囊的殘餘,並且不被羊膜覆蓋。

umbilicus (omphalus) *n.* the navel: a circular depression in the centre of the abdomen marking the site of attachment

臍 肚臍:腹部中心的圓形凹窩,為胎兒臍帶接點的記號。

of the *umbilical cord in the fetus. **–umbilical** *adj.*

umbo *n.* a projecting centre of a round surface, especially the projection of the inner surface of the eardrum to which the malleus is attached.

突 圓形表面的中央突起，尤指與錘骨相連的鼓膜內表面突起。

unciform bone *see* hamate bone.

鈎骨 參閱 hamate bone。

uncinate fits a form of temporal lobe *epilepsy in which hallucinations of taste and smell and inappropriate chewing movements are prominent features.

鈎回發作 顳葉癲癇的一種形式，味覺和嗅覺的幻覺以及不合適的咀嚼運動為其突出特徵。

unconscious *adj.* **1.** in a state of unconsciousness. **2.** describing those mental processes of which a person is not aware. **3.** (in psychoanalysis) denoting the part of the mind that includes memories, motives, and intentions that are not accessible to awareness and cannot be made conscious without overcoming resistances. *Compare* subconscious.

(1) 神志不清的 處於不省人事之狀態。**(2) 無意識的** 描述一個人並無意識自覺的心理過程。**(3) 潛意識的** （精神分析）表示包括記憶、動機及意圖等在內的部分心智，它們沒有達到意識水平，並且若不克服阻力就不能達到意識狀態。與 subconscious 對比。

unconsciousness *n.* a condition of being unaware of one's surroundings, as in sleep, or of being unresponsive to stimulation. An unnatural state of unconsciousness may be caused by factors that produce reduced brain activity, such as lack of oxygen, *head injuries, poisoning, blood loss, and many diseases, or it may be brought about deliberately during general *anaesthesia. *See also* coma.

意識喪失 對周圍事物失去知覺的狀態，像在睡眠中一樣，或者為對刺激物無反應的狀態。非自然的意識喪失狀態可能由導致及腦活動減低的因素所致，如缺氧，頭部損傷、中毒、失血及多種疾病，或在全身麻醉過程中故意造成此狀態。參閱 coma。

uncus *n.* any hook-shaped structure, especially a projection of the lower surface of the cerebral hemisphere that is composed of cortex belonging to the temporal lobe.

鈎 任何鈎狀結構，尤指大腦半球下表面、構成顳葉皮層的隆起。

undecenoic acid an antifungal agent, applied to the skin in the form of powder,

十一烯酸 抗真菌藥劑，以粉劑、軟膏、洗劑或氣霧劑的形

ointment, lotion, or aerosol spray for the treatment of such infections as athlete's foot. Trade name: **Mycota**.

式外用於皮膚，以治療感染，如腳癬。商品名：Mycota。

undine *n.* a small rounded container, usually made of glass, for solutions used to wash out the eye. It has a small neck for filling and a long tapering spout with a narrow outlet to deliver a fine stream of fluid to the eye.

洗眼壺　小的圓形容器，常由玻璃製成，盛有洗眼用的溶液。有一短頸以填充液體，和一細長的流出管以向眼睛傾注細流。

undulant fever *see* brucellosis.

波狀熱　參閱 brucellosis。

ungual *adj.* relating to the fingernails or toenails (ungues).

指（趾）甲的　有關指（趾）甲的。

unguentum (in pharmacy) *n.* an ointment.

軟膏　（藥劑學）油膏。

unguis *n.* a fingernail or toenail. *See* nail.

指（趾）甲　手指甲或腳趾甲。參閱 nail。

uni- *prefix denoting* one.

〔前綴〕單一

unicellular *adj.* describing organisms or tissues that consist of a single cell. Unicellular organisms include the Protozoa, most bacteria, and some fungi.

單細胞的　描述器官或組織由一個單一細胞組成的。單細胞有機體包括原蟲、大多數細菌以及某些真菌。

unilateral *adj.* (in anatomy) relating to or affecting one side of the body or one side of an organ or other part.

單側的　（解剖學）有關或影響一側身體、一側器官或一側其他部位的。

union *n.* (in a fractured bone) the successful result of healing of a fracture, in which the previously separated bone ends have become firmly united by newly formed bone. Failure of union (*non-union*) may result if the bone ends are not immobilized or from infection or bone diseases. *Compare* malunion.

愈合　（折斷的骨骼中）骨折處的成功愈合，原先分開的骨端因新骨形成而牢固地結合在一起。如果骨端沒有固定，或發生感染或骨病，可造成愈合失敗（不愈合）。與 malunion 對比。

Union international contre le cancer (UICC) an international body promoting cancer prevention and treatment.

國際抗癌聯合會　促進癌症預防與治療的國際機構。

unipolar *adj.* (in neurology) describing a neurone that has one main process extending from the cell body. *Compare* bipolar.

單極的 （神經病學）描述神經元只有一個從細胞體伸出的主突。與 bipolar 對比。

UPPP *n. see* uvulopalatopharyngoplasty.

懸雍垂軟腭咽成形術 　參閱 uvulopalatopharyngoplasty。

urachus *n.* the remains of the cavity of the *allantois, which usually disappears during embryonic development. In the adult it normally exists in the form of a solid fibrous cord connecting the bladder with the umbilicus, but it may persist abnormally as a patent duct. **–urachal** *adj.*

臍尿管 　殘餘的尿管囊腔，通常該腔在胚胎發育期間消失。在成人中，以連接膀胱與臍的堅韌纖維帶的形式正常地存在，但也可以未閉管道的形式異常地存在。

uracil *n.* one of the nitrogen-containing bases (*see* pyrimidine) occurring in the nucleic acid RNA.

尿嘧啶 　一種含氮鹼基（參閱 pyrimidine），見於核糖核酸內。

uraemia *n.* the presence of excessive amounts of urea and other nitrogenous waste compounds in the blood. These waste products are normally excreted by the kidneys in urine; their accumulation in the blood occurs in kidney failure and results in nausea, vomiting, lethargy, drowsiness, and eventually (if untreated) death. Treatment may require *haemodialysis on a kidney machine. **–uraemic** *adj.*

尿毒症 　血液內過多地存在尿素和其他含氮廢物。這些廢物正常時經腎由尿排出，在腎衰時他們積於血液中導致惡心、嘔吐、昏睡和嗜睡，並最終（如不予治療）導致死亡。需用人工腎機器進行血液透析治療。

uramustine *n.* a *cytotoxic drug used in the treatment of various forms of cancer, particularly chronic lymphatic leukaemia. Uramustine is administered by intravenous injection and it is highly toxic; common side-effects are nausea, vomiting and diarrhoea, and depression of bone marrow function.

烏拉莫司汀 　細胞毒素藥物，用於治療各種癌症，尤其是慢性淋巴細胞性白血病。靜脈注射，毒性大，常見副作用有惡心、嘔吐、腹瀉和骨髓功能受抑。

uran- (urano-) *prefix denoting* the palate.

〔前綴〕腭

urataemia *n.* the presence in the blood of sodium urate and other urates, formed by the reaction of uric acid with bases. In *gout, urataemia leads to deposition of urates in various parts of the body.

尿酸鹽血症 血液中尿酸鹽及其他尿酸鹽的存在，由尿酸與鹼作用形成。痛風時，該症導致身體各部分沉積有尿酸鹽。

uraturia *n.* the presence in the urine of urates (salts of uric acid). Abnormally high concentrations of urates in urine occur in *gout.

尿酸鹽尿 尿酸鹽在尿液中的存在。尿內尿酸鹽濃度之異常升高見於痛風。

urea *n.* the main breakdown product of protein metabolism. It is the chemical form in which unrequired nitrogen is excreted by the body in the urine. Urea is formed in the liver from ammonia and carbon dioxide in a series of enzyme-mediated reactions (the *urea cycle*). Accumulation of urea in the bloodstream together with other nitrogenous compounds is due to kidney failure and gives rise to *uraemia.

尿素 蛋白代謝的主要分解產物。身體將不需要的氮以這種化學物質的形式由尿排出。尿素是在一系列酶的介入反應（尿素循環）下在肝內由氨與二氧化碳形成的。血流中尿素及其他含氮化合物的蓄積係腎功不全之故，並會引發尿毒症。

urease *n.* an enzyme that catalyses the hydrolysis of urea to ammonia and carbon dioxide.

尿素酶 一種酶，催化尿素水解成氨和二氧化碳。

urecchysis *n.* the escape of uric acid from the blood into spaces in the connective tissue.

尿浸潤 尿酸從血液向結締組織空隙中滲漏。

ureter *n.* either of a pair of tubes, 25–30 cm long, that conduct urine from the pelvis of kidneys to the bladder. The walls of the ureters contain thick layers of smooth muscle, which contract to force urine into the bladder, between an outer fibrous coat and an inner mucous layer. **–ureteral**, **ureteric** *adj.*

輸尿管 一對長 25~30 cm 的管道，將尿液從腎盂導入膀胱。其管壁為厚厚的平滑肌層，故而可在其收縮時將尿液擠壓入膀胱，該肌層外有纖維膜，內有黏膜層。

ureter- (uretero-) *prefix denoting* the ureter(s). Example: *ureterovaginal* (relating to the ureters and vagina).

〔前綴〕輸尿管 例如：輸尿管陰道的（有關輸尿管和陰道的）。

ureterectomy *n.* surgical removal of a ureter. This usually includes removal

輸尿管切除術 手術切除輸尿管。常將有關的腎臟同時切除

of the associated kidney as well (*see* nephroureterectomy). If previous nephrectomy has been performed to remove a kidney that has been destroyed by *vesicoureteric reflux or because of a tumour of the renal pelvis, subsequent ureterectomy may be necessary to cure reflux into the stump of the ureter or tumour in the ureter, respectively.

（參閱 nephroureterectomy）。如果以前因膀胱輸尿管返流或因腎盂腫瘤而做了腎切除術，則隨後可能需做輸尿管切除術以治療輸尿管殘端中的尿液返流或治療輸尿管腫瘤。

ureteritis *n.* inflammation of the ureter. This usually occurs in association with inflammation of the bladder (*see* cystitis), particularly if caused by *vesicoureteric reflux. Tuberculosis of the urinary tract can also cause ureteritis, which progresses to *stricture formation.

輸尿管炎 輸尿管發炎。通常與膀胱炎有關（參閱 cystitis），尤其是當膀胱炎是由膀胱輸尿管返流引起時。尿路結核也可引起輸尿管炎，進而形成狹窄。

ureterocele *n.* a cystic swelling of the wall of the ureter at the point where it passes into the bladder. It is associated with stenosis of the opening of the ureter and it may cause impaired drainage of the kidney with dilatation of the ureter and *hydronephrosis. If urinary obstruction is present, the ureterocele should be dealt with surgically.

輸尿管疝 輸尿管壁在通入膀胱處發生的囊性腫脹。與輸尿管開口狹窄有關，可引起因輸尿管擴張和腎盂積水導致的腎臟排尿障礙。如出現尿路阻塞，則需做手術處理。

ureteroenterostomy *n.* an artificial communication, surgically created, between the ureter and the bowel. In this form of urinary diversion, which bypasses the bladder, the ureters are attached to the sigmoid colon (*see* ureterosigmoidostomy).

輸尿管吻合術 在輸尿管與腸腔之間人為地用手術建立起的通道。這種尿路改道是繞過膀胱將輸尿管連接到乙狀結腸上（參閱 ureterosigmoidostomy）。

ureterolithotomy *n.* the surgical removal of a stone from the ureter (*see* calculus). The operative approach depends upon the position of the stone within the ureter. If the stone occupies the lower portion of the ureter, it may be extracted by *cystoscopy, thus avoiding open surgery.

輸尿管石切除術 手術去除輸尿管結石（參閱 calculus）。手術方法取決於輸尿管中結石的位置。如結石位於輸尿管的下部，可通過膀胱鏡取出，而避免做切開手術。

ureterolysis *n.* an operation to free one or both ureters from surrounding fibrous tissue causing an obstruction.

輸尿管鬆解術　將一個或兩個輸尿管從引起阻塞的纖維組織中鬆開的手術。

ureteroneocystostomy *n.* the surgical reimplantation of a ureter into the bladder. This is most commonly performed to cure *vesicoureteric reflux. The ureter is reimplanted obliquely through the bladder wall to act as a valve and prevent subsequent reflux. The operation is usually referred to as an *antireflux procedure* or simply *reimplantation of ureter*.

輸尿管膀胱吻合術　將輸尿管再植入膀胱的手術。最常用於治療膀胱輸尿管返流。將輸尿管傾斜地再植入膀胱壁中，以起活瓣的作用防止以後的返流。該手術常稱為抗返流術或簡單稱為輸尿管再植術。

ureteronephrectomy *n. see* nephroureterectomy.

輸尿管腎切除術　參閱 nephroureterectomy。

ureteroplasty *n.* surgical reconstruction of the ureter using a segment of bowel or a tube of bladder (*see* Boari flap). This is necessary if a segment of ureter is damaged by disease or injury.

輸尿管成形術　用腸或膀胱管之一段重建輸尿管的手術（參閱 Boari flap）。在由於疾病或外傷使輸尿管的一段受損時，有必要做該手術。

ureteropyelonephritis *n.* inflammation involving both the ureter and the renal pelvis (*see* ureteritis, pyelitis).

輸尿管腎盂腎炎　涉及輸尿管及腎盂的炎症（參閱 ureteritis，pyelitis）。

ureteroscope *n.* a rigid or flexible instrument that can be passed into the ureter and up into the pelvis of the kidney. Usually, the ureter needs to be dilated before the instrument is passed. It is most commonly used to visualize a stone in the ureter and remove it safely under direct vision with a stone basket or forceps. Larger stones can be fragmented with an ultrasound or electrohydraulic *lithotripsy probe, passed through the instrument.

輸尿管鏡　一種固定或可活動的器具，可通過輸尿管插入並上行至腎盂。通常在其插入之前需擴張輸尿管。此工具常用來觀察輸尿管處的結石，並在直視下用取石籃或取石鉗安全地取走結石。大塊結石可由穿入此工具的超聲波或電液壓電震碎石探針擊碎。

ureteroscopy *n.* the inspection of the lumen of the ureter with a *ureteroscope.

輸尿管鏡檢查　用輸尿管鏡對輸尿管腔進行的檢查。

ureterosigmoidostomy *n.* the operation of implanting the ureters into the

輸尿管乙狀結腸吻合術　將輸尿管植入乙狀結腸的手術（參

sigmoid colon (*see* ureterenterostomy). This method of permanent urinary diversion may be used after *cystectomy or to bypass a diseased or damaged bladder. The urine is passed together with the faeces, and continence depends upon a normal anal sphincter. The main advantage of this form of diversion is the avoidance of an external opening and appliance to collect the urine; the disadvantages include possible kidney infection and acidosis.

閱 ureterenterostomy）。這個永久性尿路改道的方法可用於膀胱切除術後，或用於繞過患病或受損的膀胱。尿與糞便同時排出，並由正常的肛門括約肌控制。這種改道的主要優點是避免了外開口和應用收集尿液的器械；其缺點是可能發生腎臟感染和酸中毒。

ureterostomy *n.* the surgical creation of an external opening into the ureter. This usually involves bringing the ureter to the skin surface so that the urine can drain into a suitable appliance (*cutaneous ureterostomy*). The divided dilated ureter can be brought through the skin to form a spout, but ureters of a normal size need to be implanted into a segment of bowel used for this purpose (*see* ileal conduit) to avoid narrowing and obstruction.

輸尿管造口術　輸尿管上造一外開口的手術。這常包括將尿液引到皮膚表面，以使尿液排入一合適的器具內（皮膚輸尿管造口術）。分離後擴張了的輸尿管可以直接拉出皮膚形成一出口，但正常大小的輸尿管則需植入一節腸管內（參閱 ileal conduit）來達到防止狹窄和阻塞的目的。

ureterotomy *n.* surgical incision into the ureter. The commonest reason for performing this is to allow removal of a stone (*see* ureterolithotomy).

輸尿管切開術　切開輸尿管的手術。最常見的原因是為摘除結石（參閱 ureterolithotomy）。

urethr- (urethro-) *prefix denoting* the urethra.

〔前級〕尿道

urethra *n.* the tube that conducts urine from the bladder to the exterior. The female urethra is quite short (about 3.5 cm) and opens just within the *vulva, between the clitoris and vagina. The male urethra is longer (about 20 cm) and runs through the penis. As well as urine, it receives the secretions of the male accessory sex glands (prostate and Cowper's glands and seminal vesicles) and spermatozoa from the *vas deferens;

尿道　將尿從膀胱排向體外之管道。女性尿道很短（約3.5 cm），並在陰蒂與陰道之間的外陰處開口。男性尿道較長（約20 cm），通過陰莖。除尿液外，亦接受男性附屬性腺（前列腺、考珀腺及精囊）分泌物以及輸精管來的精子，故而也起到射精管的作用。

thus it also serves as the ejaculatory duct.

urethritis *n.* inflammation of the urethra. This may be due to gonorrhoea (*specific urethritis*), another sexually transmitted infection, often infection with *Chlamydia trachomatis* (*nongonococcal urethritis*, *NGU*; or *nonspecific urethritis*, *NSU*), or to the presence of a catheter in the urethra. The symptoms are those of urethral discharge with painful or difficult urination (*dysuria). Treatment of urethritis due to infection is by administration of appropriate antibiotics after the causative organisms have been isolated from the discharge. Untreated or severe urethritis results in a urethral *stricture.

尿道炎 尿道發炎。可由淋病（特異性尿道炎）、其他性傳播感染，常為沙眼衣原體感染（非淋病尿道炎）；或非特異性尿道炎），或尿道中放置導管引起。症狀為排尿疼痛及排尿困難。因感染引起尿道炎的治療是在尿液中分離出致病菌後使用相應的抗生素。未治療或嚴重的尿道炎會造成尿道狹窄。

urethrocele *n.* prolapse of the urethra into the vaginal wall causing a bulbous swelling to appear in the vagina, particularly on straining. The condition is associated with previous childbirth. Treatment usually involves surgical repair of the lax tissues to give better support to the urethra and the vaginal wall.

尿道突出 尿道向陰道壁脱垂，在陰道上呈現泡狀隆起特別發生於用力時。該症與前次分娩有關。治療：手術修復鬆弛組織使其更好地支持尿道及陰道壁。

urethrography *n.* X-ray examination of the urethra, after the introduction of a *radiopaque fluid, so that its outline and any narrowing or other abnormalities may be observed in X-ray photographs (*urethrograms*). In *ascending urethrography* a radiopaque jelly is injected up the urethra using a special syringe and penile clamp. In *descending urethrography* (or *micturating cystourethrography*, *MCUG*), X-rays of the urethra can be taken during the passing of water-soluble contrast material previously inserted into the bladder.

尿道 X 綫造影術 在導入不透X 綫的液體後進行的尿道 X 綫檢查，這樣可在 X 綫照片上（尿道像片）觀察到尿道外形、尿道狹窄或其他異常。在上行尿道 X 綫造影時，用特殊的注射器及陰莖夾把造影劑注入尿道。在下行尿道造影（排洩性膀胱尿道造影術）時，可在預先注入膀胱的水溶性造影劑通過尿道時，進行 X 綫照像。

urethroplasty *n.* surgical repair of the urethra, especially a urethral *stricture. The operation entails the insertion of a flap or patch of skin from the scrotum or perineum into the urethra at the site of the stricture, which is laid widely open. The operation can be performed in one stage, although two stages are usual in the reconstruction of a posterior urethral stricture (*see* urethrostomy). *Transpubic urethroplasty* is performed to repair a ruptured posterior urethra following a fractured pelvis. Access to the damaged urethra is achieved by partial removal of the pubic bone.

尿道成形術　外科手術修復尿道，尤指修復尿道狹窄。手術的任務是將取自陰囊或會陰的皮瓣或皮片植入尿道狹窄處，以增大其開口。雖然手術可一步完成，但後尿道狹窄的重建通常分兩步完成（參閱 urethrostomy）。經恥骨的尿道成形術用於修復骨盆骨折後破裂的後尿道。進入損傷尿道的途徑是將恥骨部分切除。

urethrorrhaphy *n.* surgical restoration of the continuity of the urethra. This may be required following laceration of the urethra.

尿道縫合術　手術恢復尿道的貫通。尿道撕裂後有必要做此手術。

urethrorrhoea *n.* a discharge from the urethra. This is a symptom of *urethritis.

尿道液溢　從尿道不斷流出滲液。為尿道炎症狀之一。

urethroscope *n.* an *endoscope, consisting of a fine tube fitted with a light and lenses, for examination of the interior of the male urethra, including the prostate region. **–urethroscopy** *n.*

尿道鏡　一種內窺鏡，由配有光源和透鏡的細管組成，用於檢查男性尿道內部，包括前列腺區。

urethrostenosis *n.* a *stricture of the urethra.

尿道狹窄　狹窄之尿道。

urethrostomy *n.* the operation of creating an opening of the urethra in the perineum in men. This can be permanent, to bypass a severe *stricture of the urethra in the penis, or it can form the first stage of an operation to cure a stricture of the posterior section of the urethra (*urethroplasty).

尿道造口術　在男性會陰部建立一尿道開口的手術。可為永久性的，以繞過陰莖內嚴重狹窄的尿道，或作為治療後尿道狹窄手術（尿道成形術）的第一步。

urethrotomy *n.* the operation of cutting a *stricture in the urethra. It is usually performed with a *urethrotome*. This

尿道切開術　切開尿道狹窄處之手術。常用尿道刀來施行。這種器械是一種內窺鏡，由一

instrument, a type of *endoscope, consists of a sheath down which is passed a fine knife, which is operated by the surgeon viewing the stricture down an illuminated telescope.

帶鞘小刀構成，外科醫生通過照明鏡觀察狹窄來操作小刀。

-uria *suffix denoting* **1.** a condition of urine or urination. Example: *polyuria* (passage of excess urine). **2.** the presence of a specified substance in the urine. Example: *haematuria* (blood in).

〔後綴〕尿　**(1)** 尿或排尿之情況。例如：多尿（排尿過多）。**(2)** 尿中存在特殊物質。如血尿（血在尿中）。

uric acid a nitrogen-containing organic acid that is the end-product of nucleic acid metabolism and is a component of the urine. Crystals of uric acid are deposited in the joints of people suffering from *gout.

尿酸　含氮有機酸，係核酸代謝之終產物，亦為尿液的一組成部分。尿酸結晶在痛風患者的關節內沉積。

uricosuric drug a drug, such as *probenecid or *sulphinpyrazone, that increases the amount of *uric acid excreted in the urine. Uricosuric drugs are used to treat gout and other conditions in which the levels of uric acid in the blood are increased, as during treatment with some *diuretics. Uricosuric drugs are sometimes administered with certain antibiotics (such as penicillin) to maintain high blood levels since they inhibit their excretion.

促尿酸尿藥物　一種藥物，如丙磺舒及苯磺唑酮，可增加尿液中排出的尿酸量。該類藥物用於治療痛風及其他血中尿酸量增加的病症，例如在用某些利尿劑治療期間。有時可與某種抗生素（如青黴素）合用，以維持高血藥水平，因為促尿酸尿藥物抑制排出抗生素。

uridine *n.* a compound containing uracil and the sugar ribose. *See also* nucleoside.

尿苷　一種化合物，含有尿嘧啶及核糖。參閱 nucleoside。

uridrosis *n.* the presence of excessive amounts of urea in the sweat; when the sweat dries, a white flaky deposit of urea may remain on the skin. The phenomenon occurs in *uraemia.

尿汗症　汗中有過多尿素存在；汗乾時皮膚上殘留白色絮片狀尿素沉積物。此現象見於尿毒症。

urin- (urino-, uro-) *prefix denoting* urine or the urinary system.

〔前綴〕尿，泌尿系統

urinalysis *n.* the analysis of *urine, using physical, chemical, and microscopical

尿分析　用物理、化學及顯微鏡檢查來分析尿液，從而判斷

tests to determine the proportions of its normal constituents and to detect alcohol, drugs, sugar, or other abnormal constituents.

其正常成分的比例，及檢測酒精、藥物、糖或其他異常成分。

urinary bladder *see* bladder.

膀胱 參閱 bladder。

urinary diversion any of various techniques for the collection and diversion of urine away from its usual excretory channels, after the bladder has been removed (*see* cystectomy) or bypassed. These techniques include *ureterosigmoidostomy and the construction of an *ileal conduit. *Continent diversion*, usually after cystectomy, may be achieved by constructing a reservoir or pouch from a section of small or large intestine or a combination of both. This can be emptied by catheterization via a small *stoma and has the advantage over an ileal conduit in that a urinary drainage bag is not required.

泌尿改道 膀胱切除後（參閱 cystectomy）或繞開膀胱後從通常排泄渠道排出的尿液被收集或改道的各種技術。這些技術包括輸尿管乙狀結腸吻合術及構建迴腸導水管。節制性改道，常在膀胱切除術後，通過用小腸或大腸（或二者）的一部分構建一個貯器或貯囊來實現。通過一小孔插入的導管來排空貯器，與迴腸導管相比其優越在於無需泌尿引流袋。

urinary tract the entire system of ducts and channels that conduct urine from the kidneys to the exterior. It includes the ureters, the bladder, and the urethra.

尿路 將尿由腎排出體外的整個管道系統。它包括輸尿管、膀胱及尿道。

urination (micturition) *n*. the periodic discharge of urine from the bladder through the urethra. It is initiated by voluntary relaxation of the sphincter muscle below the bladder and maintained by reflex contraction of the muscles of the bladder wall.

排尿 由膀胱經尿道的周期性排尿。排尿開始於膀胱下括約肌的隨意鬆弛，然後由膀胱壁肌肉收縮反射維持尿液排出。

urine *n*. the fluid excreted by the kidneys, which contains many of the body's waste products It is the major route by which the end-products of nitrogen metabolism – *urea, *uric acid, and *creatinine – are excreted. The other major constituent is sodium chloride. Over 100 other substances are usually

尿 由腎臟排出的液體，含多種身體廢棄產物。是氮和陳代謝終產物——尿素、尿酸及肌酸酐排出體外的主要途徑。另外的主要成分是氯化鈉。還有百餘種其他物質存在於尿中，但其含量極微。診斷疾病時常用尿液的生物化學分析

present, but only in trace amounts. Biochemical analysis of urine is commonly used in the diagnosis of diseases (for example, there are high levels of urinary glucose in diabetes and of ketone bodies in ketonuria); immunological analysis of urine is the basis of most *pregnancy tests.

（例如，糖尿病中尿糖水平高，酮尿症中酮體水平高），尿液的免疫學分析是大多數妊娠試驗的基礎。

uriniferous tubule *see* renal tubule.

腎小管 參閱 renal tubule。

urinogenital (urogenital) *adj*. of or relating to the organs and tissues concerned with both excretion and reproduction, which are anatomically closely associated.

泌尿生殖的 泌尿和生殖器官及組織的或與之有關的，這兩部分在解剖學上密切相關。

urinogenital sinus the duct in the embryo that receives the ureter and mesonephric and paramesonephric ducts and opens to the exterior. The innermost portion forms most of the bladder and the remainder forms the urethra with its associated glands. Part of it may also contribute towards the vagina.

泌尿生殖竇 胚胎中接受輸尿管、中腎管、副中腎管並開口於體外的管道。其最內部分形成膀胱的大部分，其餘部分形成尿道及與尿道相關的腺體。該竇的一部分也可形成陰道。

urinometer *n*. a hydrometer for measuring the specific gravity of urine.

尿比重計 一比重計，用於測量尿液比重。

urobilinogen *n*. a colourless product of the reduction of the *bile pigment bilirubin. Urobilinogen is formed from bilirubin in the intestine by bacterial action. Part of it is reabsorbed and returned to the liver; part of it is excreted in the faeces (a trace may also appear in the urine). When exposed to air, urobilinogen is oxidized to a brown pigment, *urobilin*.

尿膽素原 一種膽汁色素的無色還原產物。該物質在腸內通過細菌作用由膽紅素形成。它的一部分被再度吸收並還原到肝；部分隨糞便排出（尿中有痕量顯示）。暴露於空氣中時，該物質被氧化成褐色色素，即尿膽素。

urocele *n*. cystic swelling in the scrotum, containing urine that has escaped from the urethra. This may arise following urethra injury. Immediate treatment is to

陰囊積液 陰囊的囊性腫脹，內含由尿道溢出的尿液。尿道損傷後可發生。及時治療是作恥骨弓上的膀胱切開術以排

divert the urine by suprapubic *cystotomy, local drainage of the swelling, and antibiotic administration.

尿，或作腫脹處局部引流以及應用抗生素。

urochesia *n.* the passage of urine through the rectum. This may follow a penetrating injury involving both the lower urinary tract and the bowel.

肛門排尿　經直腸的排尿。可發生於下部尿路及腸道穿透性損傷後。

urodynamics *n.* the recording of pressures within the bladder by the use of special equipment that can also record urethral sphincter pressures. It is an essential investigation in the study of urinary incontinence.

泌尿動力學　用某種特殊器械記錄膀胱內壓力，並同時記錄尿道括約肌壓力。是研究排尿無節制的根本性調查。

urogenital *adj. see* urinogenital.

泌尿生殖的　參閱 urinogenital。

urography *n. see* pyelography.

尿道造影術　參閱 pyelography。

urokinase *n.* an enzyme produced in the kidney that is capable of breaking up blood clots (*see* fibrinolytic). It activates *plasminogen directly to plasmin, which dissolves blood clots. When injected, it has a short half-life, which makes it more useful in certain cases. It is used in the treatment of pulmonary embolism, deep-vein thrombosis, acute myocardial infarction, and other causes of thrombosis. Trade name: **Ukidan**.

尿激酶　腎產生的一種酶，可分解血凝塊（參閱 fibrinolytic）。它將纖維蛋白溶酶原直接激活為溶解血液凝塊的纖維蛋白溶酶。注入人體後，其排出期很短，這使它在某些情況下更為有用。它用於治療肺栓塞、深靜脈血栓形成、急性心肌缺血及其他血栓形成性疾病。商品名：Ukidan。

urolith *n.* a stone in the urinary tract. *See* calculus.

尿石　尿路結石。參閱 calculus。

urology *n.* the branch of medicine concerned with the study and treatment of diseases of the urinary tract. **–urological** *adj.* **–urologist** *n.*

泌尿科學　一醫學分支，與研究及治療尿路疾病有關。

uroporphyrin *n.* a porphyrin that plays an intermediate role in the synthesis

尿卟啉　一種卟啉，在合成原卟啉 IX 中起中介作用。大量

of *protoporphyrin IX It is excreted in significant amounts in the urine in porphyria.

的尿卟啉，在卟啉症時隨尿排出。

ursodeoxycholic acid a drug used to dissolve cholesterol gallstones; it is administered by mouth. Side-effects are infrequent but include diarrhoea and indigestion. Trade names: **Destolit**, **Ursofalk**.

熊去氧膽酸 用於化解膽固醇膽石的一種藥物；口服。副作用少見，但包括腹瀉及消化不良。商品名：Destolit，Ursofalk。

urticaria (nettle rash, hives) *n*. an itchy rash resulting from the release of *histamine by *mast cells. Individual swellings (weals) appear rapidly and resolve spontaneously within hours. *Acute urticaria* is common and represents an immediate response to such allergens as seafood or strawberries. *Chronic urticaria* is not an allergic condition and may persist for years. *Angio-oedema* occurs when the weals involve the lips, eyes, or tongue, which may swell alarmingly and constitute a medical emergency. Urticaria can be prevented by taking antihistamines regularly.

蕁麻疹 因肥大細胞釋放組胺引起的發癢皮疹。一個又一個腫團很快出現但數小時內又會自然化解掉。急性蕁麻疹常見並出現於對如海鮮、草莓等過敏性物質立即反應時。慢性蕁麻疹不是過敏性病症，可持續數年。血管水腫見於蕁麻疹累及唇、眼或舌時，會出現令人驚恐的腫脹，並構成急症。定期服用抗組胺藥物可預防該病。

uter- (utero-) *prefix denoting* the uterus. Examples: *uterocervical* (relating to the cervix (neck) of the uterus); *uterovaginal* (relating to the uterus and vagina); *uterovesical* (relating to the uterus and bladder).

〔前綴〕**子宮** 例如：子宮頸的（有關子宮頸的）；子宮陰道的（有關子宮及陰道的）；子宮膀胱的（有關子宮及膀胱的）。

uterine *adj*. of or relating to the uterus.

子宮的 子宮的或有關子宮的。

uterography *n*. *radiography of the uterus.

子宮造影術 對子宮進行的放射綫照像術。

uterosalpingography (hysterosalpingography) *n*. *radiography of the interior of the uterus and the Fallopian tubes following injection of a *radiopaque fluid.

子宮輸卵管造影術 注入不透X綫液體後對子宮及輸卵管內部進行的放射綫照像術。

uterus (womb) *n.* the part of the female reproductive tract that is specialized to allow the embryo to become implanted in its inner wall and to nourish the growing fetus from the maternal blood. The nonpregnant uterus is a pearshaped organ, about 7.5 cm long. It is suspended in the pelvic cavity by means of peritoneal folds (ligaments) and fibrous bands. The upper part is connected to the two *Fallopian tubes and the lower part joins the vagina at the cervix. The uterus has an inner mucous lining (*endometrium) and a thick wall of smooth muscle (*myometrium). During childbirth the myometrium undergoes strong contractions to expel the fetus through the cervix and vagina. In the absence of pregnancy the endometrium undergoes periodic development and degeneration (*see* menstrual cycle). **–uterine** *adj.*

子宮　女性生殖道之一部分，專門供胚胎在其內壁植入以及從母血中給生長的胎兒提供營養。未妊娠子宮呈梨形，長約 7.5 cm。由腹膜韌帶及纖維束懸於盆腔內。上部連接兩個輸卵管，下部與陰道相連。子宮有內黏膜層（子宮內膜）及厚厚的平滑肌壁（子宮肌層）。分娩時平滑肌層進行強有力的收縮，將胎兒通過子宮頸及陰道娩出。未妊娠的子宮內膜進行周期性增生及退化（參閱 menstrual cycle）。

uterus didelphys (double uterus) a congenital condition resulting from the incomplete midline fusion of the two *paramesonephric (Müllerian) ducts during early embryonic development. The usual result is a double uterus with one or two cervices and a single vagina. Complete failure of fusion results in a double uterus with double cervices and two separate vaginae.

雙子宮　在早期胚胎發育中，兩個副中腎管中綫融合不完全引起的一種先天性疾病。通常雙子宮有一個或兩個子宮頸及一個陰道。完全不融合的情況會造成帶有雙子宮頸及雙陰道的雙子宮。

utricle (utriculus) *n.* **1.** the larger of the two membranous sacs within the vestibule of the ear: it forms part of the membranous *labyrinth. It is filled with fluid (endolymph) and contains a *macula. This responds to gravity and relays information to the brain about the position of the head. **2.** a small sac (the *prostatic utricle*) extending out of the urethra of the male into the substance of the prostate gland.

(1) 橢圓囊　內耳前庭部分兩個膜性囊中較大的一個：它形成膜迷路的一部分。它充滿液體（內淋巴）並含有聽斑。它對重力有反應，並將有關頭部位置的信息傳給大腦。**(2) 小囊**（前列腺囊）從男性尿道伸到前列腺實質中的小囊。

uvea (uveal tract) *n.* the vascular pigmented layer of the eye, which lies beneath the outer layer (sclera). It consists of the *choroid, *ciliary body, and *iris. **–uveal** *adj.*

眼色素層　眼內的血管色素層，位於眼球外層（鞏膜）之下。由脈絡膜、睫狀體和虹膜組成。

uveal tract *see* uvea.

眼色素層　參閱 uvea。

uveitis *n.* inflammation of any part of the uveal tract of the eye, either the iris (*iritis*), ciliary body (*cyclitis*), or choroid (*choroiditis*). Inflammation confined to the iris and ciliary body, which are commonly inflamed together, is called *anterior uveitis* that confined to the choroid is termed *posterior uveitis*. In general, the causes of anterior and posterior uveitis are different; anterior uveitis (unlike choroiditis) is usually painful. All types may lead to visual impairment, and uveitis is an important cause of blindness. In most cases the disease appears to originate in the uveal tract itself, but it may occur secondarily to disease of other parts of the eye, particularly of the cornea and sclera.

Treatment consists of the use of drugs that suppress the inflammation, combined with measures to relieve the discomfort and more specific drug treatment if a specific cause of the uveitis is found. The drugs may be given as drops, injections, or tablets, often in combination.

眼色素層炎　眼色素層任一組成部分所發生的炎症，可以是虹膜（虹膜炎）、睫狀體（睫狀體炎）或脈絡膜（脈絡膜炎）。局限於虹膜及睫狀體的炎症，稱作前眼色素層炎，常同時發炎。通常前眼色素炎與後眼色素炎的病因不同；前眼色素層炎（不同於脈絡膜炎）常十分疼痛。無論哪種類型的眼色素層炎都會導致視力損傷，而且此炎症是引起失明的一個重要原因。多數情況下該炎症源自眼色素層本身，但也可繼發於眼睛其他部分疾病之後，尤其是角膜及鞏膜病之後。

治療使用抑制炎症的藥物，同時採取緩解不適的措施，且在找出眼色素層炎特殊病因時用特異性藥物治療。這些藥物可用滴劑、注射或片劑，常聯合使用。

uveoparotitis (uveoparotid fever) *n.* inflammation of the iris, ciliary body, and choroid regions of the eye (the uvea) and swelling of the parotid salivary gland: one of the manifestations of the chronic disease *sarcoidosis.

眼色素層腮腺炎　眼內虹膜、睫狀體、脈絡膜的炎症與腮腺腫同時發生：為慢性結節病的表現之一。

uvula *n.* a small soft extension of the soft palate that hangs from the roof of the

懸雍垂　軟腭的一小塊柔軟延伸物，懸自舌根上方的口腔根

mouth above the root of the tongue. It is composed of muscle, connective tissue, and mucous membrane.

uvulectomy *n.* surgical removal of the uvula.

uvulitis *n.* inflammation of the uvula.

uvulopalatopharyngoplasty (UPPP) *n.* a surgical operation to remove the uvula, part of the soft palate, and the tonsils in the treatment of snoring.

部。由肌肉、結締組織及黏膜組成。

懸雍垂切除術　切除懸雍垂之手術。

懸雍垂炎　懸雍垂之炎症。

懸雍垂軟腭扁桃體切除術　手術切除懸雍垂、部分軟腭及扁桃體，用於治療打鼾。

V

vaccination *n.* a means of producing immunity to a disease by using a *vaccine, or a special preparation of antigenic material, to stimulate the formation of appropriate antibodies. The name was applied originally only to treatment with vaccinia (cowpox) virus, which gives protection not only against cowpox itself but also against the related smallpox. However, it is now used synonymously with *inoculation* as a method of *immunization against any disease. Vaccination is often carried out in two or three stages, as separate doses are less likely to cause unpleasant side-effects. A vaccine is usually given by injection but may be introduced into the skin through light scratches; for some diseases, oral vaccines are available.

接種　一種對疾病產生免疫力的方法，該方法通過用疫苗或抗原材料的特殊製劑來刺激形成與疾病相應的抗體。這一名詞原僅用在使用牛痘病毒疫苗上，該疫苗不僅可預防牛痘且可抵抗天花。然而現在該名詞被用作對任何疾病進行免疫接種的同義詞。接種常分二步或三步來進行，因為分劑量較不易引起不適的副作用。接種常採用注射的方法，但也可用輕劃痕而將疫苗導入皮膚的方法，對有些疾病，也有口服疫苗。

vaccine *n.* a special preparation of antigenic material that can be used to stimulate the development of antibodies and thus confer active *immunity against a specific disease or number of diseases.

疫苗　一種特異性抗原材料製劑，可用於刺激抗體產生，故而對某一特殊疾病或數種疾病產生自動免疫，許多疫苗的製造方法是通過培養細菌及病

Many vaccines are produced by culturing bacteria or viruses under conditions that lead to a loss of their virulence but not of their antigenic nature. Other vaccines consist of specially treated toxins (*toxoids) or of dead bacteria that are still antigenic. Examples of live but attenuated (weakened) organisms in vaccines are those against tuberculosis, rabies, and smallpox. Dead organisms are used against cholera and typhoid; precipitated toxoids are used against diphtheria and tetanus. *See* immunization.

毒，使之喪失毒力，但保持其抗原性。其他疫苗則由特殊處理過的仍有抗原性的毒素（類毒素）或死菌構成。例如毒力減弱的活菌（病毒）用於抗結核病、狂犬病及天花等疫苗。死菌疫苗用於抗霍亂和傷寒；沉澱類毒素用於抗白喉及破傷風疫苗。參閱 immunization。

vaccinia *n. see* cowpox.

牛痘　參閱 cowpox。

vaccinoid *adj.* resembling a local infection with vaccinia (cowpox) virus. A vaccinoid reaction is one of the possible results of vaccination against smallpox in indivduals who already have partial immunity. The swelling, reddening, and blistering are considerably less than the so-called primary reaction that occurs after the inoculation of a person with no immunity against smallpox.

假牛痘的　類似於因牛痘病毒引起的局部感染。假牛痘反應是對天花已產生部分免疫的人進行接種可能引起的結果之一。腫脹、發紅和水疱比無天花免疫者在種痘後發生的所謂初發反應明顯地輕。

vacuole *n.* a space within the cytoplasm of a cell, formed by infolding of the cell membrane, that contains material taken in by the cell. White blood cells form vacuoles when they surround and digest bacteria and other foreign material.

空泡　細胞胞漿內的空間，由細胞膜內褶形成，其中含有被細胞攝入的物質。當白細胞包圍並消化細菌及其他異物時該細胞形成空泡。

vacuum extractor (ventouse) a device to assist delivery consisting of a suction cup that is attached to the head of the fetus: traction is then applied slowly. Introduced in 1954, it has been widely used but has not been accepted as a substitute for obstetric forceps.

真空吸取器　一種助娩器械，其中有一吸杯可連接到胎兒頭部然後慢慢施以吸力。於 1954 年投入使用，現已廣泛使用但仍沒有作為產鉗的替代品被接受。

vagin- (vagino-) *prefix denoting* the vagina.

〔前綴〕陰道

vagina *n*. the lower part of the female reproductive tract: a muscular tube, lined with mucous membrane, connecting the cervix of the uterus to the exterior. It receives the erect penis during coitus: semen is ejaculated into the upper part of the vagina and from there the sperms must pass through the cervix and uterus in order to fertilize an ovum in the Fallopian tube. The wall of the vagina is sufficiently elastic to allow the passage of the newborn child. **–vaginal** *adj*.

陰道　女性生殖道的下部：是一個肌肉管道，管道內覆有黏膜，該管道連接子宮頸和外部。性交時接受勃起的陰莖，精液射入陰道上部，然後精子必須通過子宮頸和子宮腔才能在輸卵管內使卵受精。陰道壁彈性充足可使新生兒通過。

vaginismus *n*. sudden and painful contraction of the muscles surrounding the vagina, usually in response to the *vulva or vagina being touched. Sexual intercourse may be impeded, and the condition may be associated with fear of or aversion to coitus. Other causative factors include vaginal injury or ulceration, dryness or shrinkage of the lining membrane of the vagina, and inflammation of the vagina or bladder. *See also* dyspareunia.

陰道痙攣　陰道周圍肌肉之突然的疼痛性收縮，通常為外陰或陰道被觸碰時的反應。這種情況可能會妨礙性交，並可能與性交恐懼及反感有關。陰道損傷或潰瘍、陰道黏膜乾燥或皺縮以及陰道或膀胱的炎症是致病的其他原因。參閱 dyspareunia。

vaginitis *n*. inflammation of the vagina, which may be caused by infection (most commonly with *Trichomonas vaginalis*), dietary deficiency, or poor hygiene. There is often itching (*see* pruritus), increased vaginal discharge, and pain on passing urine. Vaginitis may indicate the presence of sexually transmitted disease. *Postmenopausal* (or *atrophic*) *vaginitis* is caused by a deficiency of female sex hormones.

陰道炎　陰道炎症，可由感染（常為陰道滴蟲）、營養不足及衛生不佳引起。常有癢感（參閱 pruritus）、陰道分泌物增加及排尿時疼痛。該病可能提示性傳播疾病的存在。月經後陰道炎係女性激素不足之故。

vaginoplasty (colpoplasty) *n*. a tissue-grafting operation on the vagina.

陰道成形術　陰道處的組織移植手術。

vaginoscope *n. see* colposcope.

陰道鏡　參閱 colposcope。

vago- *prefix denoting* the vagus nerve.

〔前綴〕迷走神經

vagotomy *n.* the surgical cutting of any of the branches of the vagus nerve. This is usually performed to reduce secretion of acid and pepsin by the stomach in order to cure a peptic ulcer. *Truncal vagotomy* is the cutting of the main trunks of the vagus nerve; in *selective vagotomy* the branches of the nerve to the gall bladder and pancreas are left intact. *Highly selective (or proximal) vagotomy* is the cutting of the branches of the vagus nerve to the body of the stomach, leaving the branches to the outlet (pylorus) intact: this makes additional surgery to permit emptying of the stomach contents unnecessary.

迷走神經切斷術　手術切斷迷走神經分支。常用於為治療消化性潰瘍而減少胃酸及胃蛋白酶的分泌。迷走神經幹切斷術是將迷走神經的主幹切斷；選擇性迷走神經切斷術保留支配膽囊及胰腺的神經分支的完整。高度選擇性（或近端）迷走神經切斷術是切斷支配胃體部的迷走神經，而保留支配幽門分支的完整；故無需做使胃內容物排空的附加手術。

vagus nerve the tenth *cranial nerve (X), which supplies motor nerve fibres to the muscles of swallowing and parasympathetic fibres to the heart and organs of the chest cavity and abdomen. Sensory branches of the vagus carry impulses from the viscera and the sensation of taste from the mouth.

迷走神經　第十對腦神經，該神經以運動神經纖維支配吞咽肌，以副交感神經纖維支配心臟、胸及腹腔的臟器。該神經的感覺分支接受來自內臟的衝動及來自口腔的味覺。

valgus *adj.* describing any deformity that displaces the hand or foot away from the midline. *See* club-foot (talipes valgus), hallux valgus, knock knee (genu valgum).

外翻的　形容手或足離開中綫的錯位畸形。參閱 club-foot（talipes valgus）、hallux valgus，knock knee（genu valgum）。

validity *n.* an indication of the extent to which a clinical sign or test is a true indicator of disease. Reduced validity can arise if the tests produce different results when conducted several times on the same person under identical conditions (i.e. *reduced reproducibility*, *reliability*, or *repeatability*). This may be because the same observer gets different results on successive occasions (*intraobserver error*) or because a series of different observers fail to obtain the same result (*interobserver error*). Such errors

準確性　指一個臨床徵像或試驗作為疾病指標的準確程度。對同一個病人在相同條件下進行幾次試驗所得結果不同時，可能發生準確性降低（即再現性、可靠性和重複性減少）。這種情況可能是由於同一觀察者對逐次的情況得出了不同的結果（觀察者誤差），也可能由於不同的觀察者們不能得出同樣的結果（觀察者之間誤差）。此類誤差之產生可能是由於在觀察方面或解釋方面存

may arise because of a true difference in observation and/or interpretation or because of a preconceived notion (often unconscious) by the observer, which influences either his judgment or the tone and manner with which he questions the patient. *Compare* intervention study.

在有真正的差異，也可能是由於觀察者有先入之見（常常是無意識的），這樣就會影響到觀察者的判斷，也會影響到他向病人詢問時的語調及態度。與 intervention study 對比。

valine *n.* an *essential amino acid. *See also* amino acid.

纈氨酸 一種必需氨基酸。參閱 amino acid。

Valium *n. see* diazepam.

安定 參閱 diazepam。

vallecula *n.* a furrow or depression in an organ or other part. On the undersurface of the cerebellum a vallecula separates the two hemispheres.

谷 器官或其他部位上的溝或凹陷。位於小腦下部表面的溝將其分為兩個半球。

valve *n.* a structure found in some tubular organs or parts that restricts the flow of fluid within them to one direction only. Valves are important structures in the heart, veins, and lymphatic vessels. Such a valve consists of two or three *cusps fastened like pockets to the walls of the vessel. Blood flowing in the right direction flattens the cusps to the walls, but when flow is reversed the cusps become filled with blood or lymph and dilate to block the opening (see illustration). *See also* mitral valve, tricuspid valve, semilunar valve.

瓣膜 一種存在於管道器官或其他部分內部的結構，用以限制該器官或該部分內的液體只沿一個方向流動。瓣膜是心臟、靜脈、淋巴管的重要結構。此類瓣膜有兩三個瓣尖，瓣尖如口袋附於管壁上。正方向的血流使瓣尖倒向管壁，但當逆流時，瓣尖則被血液或淋巴液所充滿而膨脹，故而堵塞管口（見圖）。參閱 mitral valve，tricuspid valve，semilunar valve。

valvotomy (valvulotomy) *n.* surgical cutting through a valve. The term is usually used to describe the operation to relieve obstruction caused by stenosed valves in the heart.

瓣膜切開術 手術切開瓣膜。此術語常指手術減輕因心臟瓣膜狹窄引起的阻塞。

valvula *n.* (*pl.* **valvulae**) a small valve. The *valvulae conniventes* are circular folds of mucous membrane in the small intestine.

瓣（襞） 小的瓣膜。環狀襞是小腸黏膜的環形皺襞。

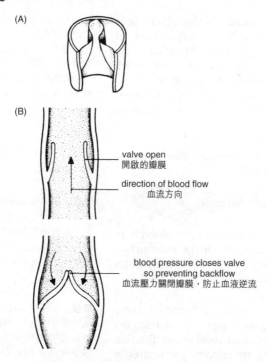

(A) cut vein showing the two cusps of a valve;
切斷的靜脈顯示一個瓣膜的兩個瓣尖
(B) action of a venous valve
靜脈瓣的功用

valvulitis *n*. inflammation of one or more valves, particularly the heart valves. This may be acute or chronic and is most often due to rheumatic fever (*see* endocarditis).

瓣膜炎 一個或多個瓣膜發炎，特別是心臟瓣膜。可為急性或慢性，最常見的原因是風濕熱（參閱 endocarditis）。

vancomycin *n*. an *antibiotic, derived from the bacterium *Streptomyces orientalis*, that is effective against most Gram-positive organisms (e.g. streptococci and staphylococci). It is given by intravenous infusion for infections due to strains that are resistant to other antibiotics. It usually has a low toxicity but may

萬古黴素 一種抗生素，取自東方鏈球菌屬，對抗多數的革蘭氏陽性菌（例如：葡萄球菌及鏈球菌）均有效。靜脈輸注用於治療對其他抗生素耐藥菌株引起的感染。該藥毒性低，但也可引起耳聾或血栓性靜脈炎。商品名：Vancocin。

cause deafness or thrombophlebitis. Trade name: **Vancocin**.

van den Bergh's test a test to determine whether jaundice in a patient is due to *haemolysis or to disease of the liver or bile duct. A sample of serum is mixed with sulphanilic acid, hydrochloric acid, and sodium nitrite. The immediate appearance of a violet colour is called a *direct reaction* and indicates that the jaundice is due to liver damage or obstruction of the bile duct. If the colour appears only when alcohol is added, this is an *indirect reaction* and points to haemolytic jaundice.

範登伯格試驗　一種試驗，用以決定病人的黃疸是溶血引起還是肝、膽道疾病引起。將血清標本與對氨基苯磺酸、鹽酸及亞硝酸鈉相混合。其後立即出現紫色的叫直接反應，表示黃疸是由肝損傷或膽道堵塞所致。如只有在加入酒精後才有此顏色顯示，則為間接反應，提示為溶血性黃疸。

vaporizer *n.* a piece of equipment for producing an extremely fine mist of liquid droplets by forcing a jet of liquid through a narrow nozzle with a jet of air. Vaporizers are used to produce aerosols of various medications for use in inhalation therapy.

霧化器　一種器具，用以產出有極細小液滴的薄霧，該器具借助空氣射流使液體通過狹窄的嘴管噴射出來。噴霧器通過使各種藥物產生氣溶膠（氣霧劑）而用於吸入療法。

Vaquez-Osler disease *see* polycythaemia vera.

瓦-奧氏病　參閱　polycythaemia vera。

variable *n.* (in biostatistics) a characteristic (e.g. morbidity, life style, or habit) relating to a single individual or group. *Qualitative variables* are descriptive characteristics, such as sex, race, or occupation, *quantitative variables* relate to a numerical scale and are subdivided into *discrete variables*, found only at fixed points (e.g. number of children), and *continuous variables*, found at any point on a scale (e.g. weight).

變量　（生物統計學）有關個人或一組人羣的特徵（如發病率、生活方式或習慣）。質的變量是描述諸如性別、種族或職業等特徵；量的變量則與數的大小相關，並進一步分為只存在於幾個固定點（如兒童的數量）的離散型變量以及存在於坐標上任何點的連續型變量（如重量）。

variance *n. see* standard deviation.

方差　參閱　standard deviation。

varicectomy *n. see* phlebectomy.

曲張靜脈切除術　參閱　phlebectomy。

varicella *n. see* chickenpox.

水痘　參閱 chickenpox。

varices *pl. n. see* varicose veins.

靜脈曲張　參閱 varicose veins。

varicocele *n.* a collection of dilated veins in the spermatic cord, more commonly affecting the left side of the scrotum than the right. It usually produces no symptoms apart from occasional aching discomfort. In some cases varicocele is associated with a poor sperm count (*see* oligospermia) sufficient to cause infertility. Surgical correction of the varicocele in such patients (*varicocelectomy*) usually results in a considerable improvement in the quality and motility of the sperm.

精索靜脈曲張　擴張的靜脈集聚於精索，左側陰囊受累往往多於右側。除偶有疼痛不適之外常無症狀。在有些病例中該症伴有精子計數不足致孕（參閱 oligospermia）。這類患者在手術治療精索靜脈曲張（曲張精索靜脈切除術）後，精子的數量及運動能力都可大大改善。

varicose veins veins that are distended, lengthened, and tortuous. The superficial veins (saphenous veins) of the legs are most commonly affected; other sites include the oesophagus (*see* oesophageal varices) and tests (*varicocele). There is an inherited tendency to varicose veins but obstruction to blood flow is responsible in some cases. Complications including thrombosis, *phlebitis, and haemorrhage may occur. Treatment includes elastic support and *sclerotherapy, but *avulsion (stripping) or excision (*phlebectomy) is required in some cases. Medical name: **varices**.

靜脈曲張　擴張、拉長或彎曲的靜脈。最常侵犯腿部表淺靜脈（隱靜脈）；其他受累部位有食管（參閱 oesophageal varices）及睾丸（精索靜脈曲張）。該病有一定的遺傳傾向，但有些發病是由於血流阻塞所致。併發症可包括血栓形成、靜脈炎及出血。治療可有彈性支持法和硬化療法，但有些病例需做撕脫術（剝脫）或切除術（靜脈切除術）。醫學用語：靜脈曲張。

varicotomy *n.* incision into a varicose vein (*see* phlebectomy).

曲張靜脈切開術　切開曲張的靜脈（參閱 phlebectomy）。

variola *n. see* smallpox.

天花　參閱 smallpox。

varioloid 1. *n.* a mild form of smallpox in people who have previously had smallpox or have been vaccinated against it. **2.** *adj.* resembling smallpox.

(1) 輕天花　以前患有天花或已接種天花者所得的一種輕型天花。**(2) 天花樣的**　與天花相像的。

varix *n.* (*pl.* **varices**) a single *varicose vein.

静脈曲張　一支曲張的靜脈。

varus *adj.* describing any deformity that displaces the hand or foot towards the midline. *See* bowleg (genu varum), club-foot (talipes varus), hallux varus.

內翻的　形容手或腳朝中綫錯位的畸形。參閱 bowleg (genu varum)，　club-foot (talipes varus)，hallux varus。

vas *n.* (*pl.* **vasa**) a vessel or duct.

脈管或管道

vas- (vaso-) *prefix denoting* **1.** vessels, especially blood vessels. **2.** the vas deferens.

〔前綴〕**(1)** 脈管　尤指血管。**(2)** 輸精管

vasa efferentia (*sing.* **vas efferens**) the many small tubes that conduct spermatozoa from the testis to the epididymis. They are derived from some of the excretory tubules of the *mesonephros.

輸出管　將精子從睾丸導入附睾的許多小管。衍生於胚胎中腎管的一些排泄管道。

vasa vasorum *pl. n.* the tiny arteries and veins that supply the walls of blood vessels.

血管滋養管　供養血管壁的非常細小的動脈和靜脈。

vascular *adj.* relating to or supplied with blood vessels.

血管的　有關血管或由血管供養的。

vascularization *n.* the development of blood vessels (usually capillaries) within a tissue.

血管化　組織內血管的形成（常為毛細血管）。

vascular system *see* cardiovascular system.

血管系統　參閱 cardiovascular system。

vasculitis *n. see* angiitis.

血管炎　參閱 angiitis。

vas deferens (*pl.* **vasa deferentia**) either of a pair of ducts that conduct spermatozoa from the *epididymis to the *urethra on ejaculation. It has a thick muscular wall the contraction of which assists in ejaculation.

輸精管　射精時將精子從附睾傳送到尿道的一對管之一。具有厚的肌層，肌層收縮可助射精。

vasectomy *n.* the surgical operation of severing the duct (vas deferens)

輸精管切除術　切除將睾丸與精囊及尿道相連的輸精管之外

connecting the testis to the seminal vesicle and urethra. Vasectomy of both ducts causes sterility and is an increasingly popular means of birth control. Vasectomy does not affect sexual desire or potency.

科手術。兩側輸精管切除術導致不育，現已成為日益普及的絕育方法。該手術並不影響性慾或性交能力。

vaso- *prefix. see* vas-.

〔前綴〕**血管** 參閱 vas-。

vasoactive *adj.* affecting the diameter of blood vessels, especially arteries. Examples of vasoactive agents are emotion, pressure, carbon dioxide, and temperature. Some exert their effect directly, others via the *vasomotor centre in the brain.

血管活性的 影響血管，尤其是動脈管徑的。情緒、血壓、二氧化碳及體溫均為血管活性因素的例子。其中一些因素可直接發揮作用，另一些則要通過大腦中的血管運動中樞。

vasoconstriction *n.* a decrease in the diameter of blood vessels, especially arteries. This results from activation of the *vasomotor centre in the brain, which brings about contraction of the muscular walls of the arteries and hence an increase in blood pressure.

血管收縮 血管，尤指動脈管徑的縮小。係腦部血管運動中樞活動引起動脈肌層收縮，從而導致血壓升高之故。

vasoconstrictor *n.* an agent that causes narrowing of the blood vessels and therefore a decrease in blood flow. Examples are *metaraminol and *phenylephrine. Vasoconstrictors are used to raise the blood pressure in disorders of the cirulation, shock, or severe bleeding and to maintain blood pressure during surgery. Some vasoconstrictors (e.g. *xylometazoline) have a rapid effect when applied to mucous membranes and may be used to relieve nasal congestion. If the blood pressure rises too quickly headache and vomiting may occur. A vasoconstrictor is often added to local anaesthetic solutions used in dentistry to prolong their effectiveness.

血管收縮藥 引起血管變窄，因而使血流減少的藥劑。間羥胺及苯福林就是其中的例子。該類藥物用於循環障礙、休克、嚴重出血時血壓升高及在手術時維持血壓。其中某些藥物（如賽洛唑啉）用於黏膜時有速效，可用以減輕鼻充血。如血壓升高過快，可發生頭痛及嘔吐。該藥常加入局麻溶液，在牙科中使用以延長局部麻醉之作用。

vasodilatation *n.* an increase in the diameter of blood vessels, especially

血管舒張 血管，尤指動脈管徑之增大。係腦部運動中樞活

arteries. This results from activation of the *vasomotor centre in the brain, which brings about relaxation of the arterial walls and a consequent lowering of blood pressure.

動引起動脈壁鬆弛，因而導致血壓下降之故。

vasodilator *n.* a drug that causes widening of the blood vessels and therefore an increase in blood flow. Vasodilators are used to lower blood pressure in cases of hypertension. *Coronary vasodilators*, such as *glyceryl trinitrate and *pentaerythritol, increase the blood flow through the heart and are used to relieve and prevent angina. Large doses of coronary vasodilators cause such side-effects as flushing of the face, severe headache, and fainting. *Peripheral vasodilators*, such as *alpha blockers and *nicotinyl, affect the blood vessels of the limbs and are used to treat conditions of poor circulation, such as acrocyanosis, chilblains, and Raynaud's disease.

血管舒張藥　引起血管擴張，從而使血壓下降之藥物。用於高血壓症中以降低血壓。冠狀血管擴張劑，如硝酸甘油和季戊四醇，增加通過心臟的血流，以減輕和防止心絞痛。大劑量使用冠狀血管擴張劑會引起面部潮紅、嚴重頭痛及暈厥等副作用。外周血管舒張藥，如 α-受體阻滯劑及煙醇，作用於四肢血管以治療血液循環不佳的病變，如手足發紺，凍瘡及雷諾病。

vaso-epididymostomy *n.* the operation of joining the vas deferens to the epididymis in a side-to-side manner in order to bypass an obstruction to the passage of sperm from the testis. The obstruction, which may be congenital or acquired, is usually present in the mid-portion or tail of the epididymis. Vaso-epididymostomy is therefore usually performed by anastomosing the head of the epididymis to a longitudinal incision in the lumen of the adjacent vas.

輸精管附睾吻合術　使輸精管與附睾以側與側方相吻合之手術，用以繞過精子從睾丸排出的阻塞。該阻塞可以是先天的，亦可是後天的，常存在於附睾的中部或尾部。因此該手術使附睾頭部與鄰近輸精管切口相吻合。

vasoligation *n.* the surgical tying of the vas deferens (the duct conveying sperm from the testis). This is performed to prevent infection spreading from the urinary tract and causing recurrent *epididymitis. It is sometimes performed at the same time as *prostatectomy to

輸精管結紮術　結紮輸精管（精子自睾丸輸出之管道）之手術。用以防止感染自尿道擴散引起復發性附睾炎。有時也用於前列腺切除術時防止術後併發附睾炎。

prevent the complication of epididymitis in the postoperative period.

vasomotion *n.* an increase or decrease in the diameter of blood vessels, particularly the arteries. *See* vasoconstriction, vasodilatation.

血管舒縮　血管管徑，尤指動脈，之增加或縮小。參閱 vasoconstriction，vasodilatation。

vasomotor *adj.* controlling the muscular walls of blood vessels, especially arteries, and therefore their diameter.

血管舒縮的　支配血管肌層的，特別是動脈，從而控制血管管徑的。

vasomotor centre a collection of nerve cells in the medulla oblongata that receives information from sensory receptors in the circulatory system (*see* baroreceptor) and brings about reflex changes in the rate of the heartbeat and in the diameter of blood vessels, so that the blood pressure can be adjusted. The vasomotor centre also receives impulses from elsewhere in the brain, so that emotion (such as fear) may also influence the heart rate and blood pressure. The centre works through *vasomotor nerves of the sympathetic and parasympathetic systems.

血管運動中樞　延髓內的一個神經細胞集合體，它從循環系統的感受器（參閱 baroreceptor）接受信息，並引起心率及血管管徑的反射變化，從而調節血壓。該中樞亦從大腦其他地方接收衝動，故而情緒（特別是恐懼）亦可影響到心率及血壓。該中樞通過血管運動神經的交感和副交感系統來起作用。

vasomotor nerve any nerve, usually belonging to the autonomic nervous system, that controls the circulation of blood through blood vessels by its action on the muscle fibres within their walls or its action on the heartbeat. The *vagus nerve slows the heart and reduces its output, but sympathetic nerves increase the rate and output of the heart and increase blood pressure by causing the constriction of small blood vessels at the same time.

血管運動神經　常係自主神經系統的神經，通過作用於血管壁的肌纖維或作用於心臟跳動來控制血液循環。迷走神經減慢心臟活動，並減少其輸出量，而交感神經則加快心率並增加心輸出量，同時引起小血管收縮而升高血壓。

vasopressin (antidiuretic hormone, ADH) *n.* a hormone, released by the pituitary gland, that increases the reabsorption of water by the kidney, thus

加壓素（抗利尿激素）　一種激素，由垂體釋放，可增加腎對水的重吸收，從而防止身體失水過多。該激素亦可收縮血

preventing excessive loss of water from the body. Vasopressin also causes constriction of blood vessels. It is administered either nasally or by injection to treat *diabetes insipidus. Intravenous injections of vasopressin are used to control bleeding from *oesophageal varices by restricting arterial blood flow to the liver.

管。鼻吸入法或注射以治療尿崩症。靜脈注射該藥以限制流入肝臟的動脈血流，從而控制因食管靜脈曲張引起的大出血。

vasopressor *adj.* stimulating the contraction of blood vessels and therefore bringing about an increase in blood pressure.

血管加壓的 刺激血管收縮以使血壓升高的。

vasospasm *n. see* Raynaud's disease.

血管痙攣 參閱 Raynaud's disease。

vasotomy *n.* a surgical incision into the vas deferens (the duct conveying sperm from the testis). This is usually undertaken to allow catheterization of the vas and the injection of radiopaque contrast material for X-ray examination (*vasography*), to test for patency of the duct in patients with *azoospermia.

輸精管造口術 切開輸精管（精子從睾丸輸出的管道）之手術。此手術常用於作導管插入術及不透 X 綫對比劑注入以檢查精子缺乏症患者輸精管是否蔽塞。

vasovagal *adj.* relating to the action of impulses in the *vagus nerve on the circulation. The vagus reduces the rate at which the heart beats, and so lowers its output.

血管迷走神經的 與迷走神經衝動對血液循環之作用相關的。該神經減慢心率從而減少心輸出量。

vasovagal attack excessive activity of the vagus nerve, causing slowing of the heart and a fall in blood pressure, which leads to fainting. *See* syncope.

血管迷走神經性發作 迷走神經過度興奮致使心跳減慢及血壓下降，故而引起暈厥。參閱 syncope。

vasovasostomy *n.* the surgical operation of reanastomosing the vas deferens after previous vasectomy: the reversal of vasectomy, undertaken to restore fertility.

輸精管吻合術 在前輸精管切除術後重新將輸精管吻合的外科手術：逆轉輸精管切除術用以恢復生育力。

vasovesiculitis *n.* inflammation of the *seminal vesicles and *vas deferens.

輸精管精囊炎 精囊和輸精管發炎。常併發前列腺炎，引起

This usually occurs in association with *prostatitis and causes pain in the perineum, groin, and scrotum and a high temperature. On examination the vasa and seminal vesicles are thickened and tender. Treatment includes administration of antibiotics.

會陰、腹股溝、陰囊的疼痛及高燒。檢查時，輸精管和精囊增厚並有觸痛。抗生素治療。

vastus *n.* any of three muscles (*vastus intermedius*, *vastus lateralis*, and *vastus medialis*) that form part of the *quadriceps muscle of the thigh.

股肌 構成大腿股四頭肌的三塊肌肉（股中間肌、股外肌和股內肌）之一。

vector *n.* **1.** an animal, usually an insect or a tick, that transmits parasitic microorganisms – and therefore the diseases they cause – from person to person or from infected animals to human beings. Mosquitoes, for example, are vectors of malaria, filariasis, and yellow fever. **2.** an agent used to insert a foreign gene or DNA fragment into a bacterial or other cell in *genetic engineering and *gene therapy. Viruses, especially retroviruses, are often used as vectors: once inside the host cell, the virus can replicate and thus produce copies (*clones) of the gene.

(1) 媒介物 一動物，常為昆蟲或蜱，傳播寄生性微生物，並因此引起疾病——使之從人傳給人或從已感染的動物傳播給人。例如：蚊子是瘧疾、絲蟲病及黃熱病的媒介物。**(2) 媒介因子** 基因工程或基因療法中植入細菌或其他細胞中的異質基因或異質脫氧核糖核酸片斷。病毒，尤其是逆轉錄病毒，常用作媒介因子：一旦植入宿主細胞，該病毒可複製產生基因複本（克隆）。

vectorcardiography *n. see* electrocardiography.

心向量描記術 參閱 electrocardiography。

vegetation *n.* (in pathology) an abnormal outgrowth from a membrane, fancied to resemble a vegetable growth. In ulcerative endocarditis, such outgrowths, consisting of *fibrin with enmeshed blood cells, are found on the membrane lining the heart valves.

贅生物 （病理學）膜上長出的異常贅疣，假想與植物的生長相似。在潰瘍性心內膜炎中，這樣的贅疣由纖維蛋白及其網絡中的血細胞組成，可見覆於心瓣膜上。

vegetative *adj.* **1.** relating to growth and nutrition rather than to reproduction. **2.** functioning unconsciously; autonomic.

(1) 生長的 有關生長及營養的，而無關生殖的。**(2) 植物性的** 無意識地發生作用的；自主的。

vehicle *n.* (in pharmacy) any substance that acts as the medium in which a drug is administered. Examples are sterile water, isotonic sodium chloride, and dextrose solutions.

載劑 （藥劑學）投藥時的載藥物質。例如：蒸餾水、等滲氯化鈉和葡萄糖溶液。

vein *n.* a blood vessel conveying blood towards the heart. All veins except the *pulmonary vein carry deoxygenated blood from the tissues, via the capillaries, to the vena cava. The walls of veins consist of three tissue layers, but these are much thinner and less elastic than those of arteries (see illustration). Veins contain *valves that assist the flow of blood back to the heart. Anatomical name: **vena. –venous** *adj.*

靜脈 向心臟運輸血液的血管。各靜脈，不含肺靜脈，借毛細血管從各組織攜帶脫氧的血液進入腔靜脈。靜脈壁由三層組織構成，但這些組織層比動脈組織層要薄得多並且彈性小（見圖）。靜脈具有幫助血液流回心臟的瓣膜。解剖學用語：靜脈。

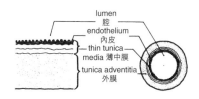

Transverse section through a vein
靜脈橫切面

velamen (velamentum) *n.* a covering membrane.

膜 覆蓋膜。

vellus *n.* the fine hair that occurs on the body before puberty is reached.

毫毛 青春期到來之前身體所長的細毛。

velum *n.* (in anatomy) a veil-like covering The *medullary velum* is either of two thin layers of tissue that form part of the roof of the fourth ventricle of the brain.

帆 （解剖學）帆狀覆蓋物。髓帆是兩片薄層組織，構成第四腦室頂部。

vena *n.* (*pl.* **venae**) *see* vein.

靜脈 參閱 vein。

vena cava either of the two main veins, conveying blood from the other veins to the right atrium of the heart. The *inferior*

腔靜脈 兩條主靜脈之一，將血液從其他靜脈送回到右心房。下腔靜脈由左、右髂總靜

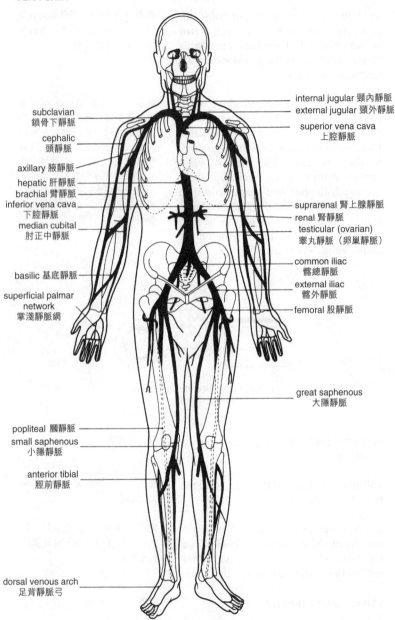

internal jugular 頸內靜脈
external jugular 頸外靜脈
superior vena cava 上腔靜脈
subclavian 鎖骨下靜脈
cephalic 頭靜脈
axillary 腋靜脈
hepatic 肝靜脈
brachial 臂靜脈
inferior vena cava 下腔靜脈
median cubital 肘正中靜脈
suprarenal 腎上腺靜脈
renal 腎靜脈
testicular (ovarian) 睪丸靜脈（卵巢靜脈）
common iliac 髂總靜脈
external iliac 髂外靜脈
femoral 股靜脈
basilic 基底靜脈
superficial palmar network 掌淺靜脈網
great saphenous 大隱靜脈
popliteal 膕靜脈
small saphenous 小隱靜脈
anterior tibial 脛前靜脈
dorsal venous arch 足背靜脈弓

The principal veins of the body
人體主要靜脈

vena cava, formed by the union of the right and left common iliac veins, receives blood from parts of the body below the diaphragm. The *superior vena cava*, originating at the junction of the two innominate veins, drains blood from the head, neck, thorax, and arms.

脈連接而成，接受來自膈以下部位的血液。上腔靜脈起自兩無名靜脈連接處，收集來自頭、頸、胸和上肢的血液。

vene- (veno-) *prefix denoting* veins.

〔前綴〕**靜脈**

veneer *n*. a facing of *composite resin or *porcelain applied to the surface of a tooth to give improved shape and/or colour. The tooth requires minimal preparation and the facing is retained by enamel that has been treated by the *acid-etch technique. Veneers are a more conservative way of treating discoloured teeth than by *crowns.

覆蓋，鑲蓋　合成樹脂或瓷料牙面，塗於牙齒表面以改進牙齒形狀和/或顏色。牙齒需要最小的製劑，使牙面通過酸蝕法處理的釉質得以保留。和造冠術相比，覆蓋是一種較為保守的治療牙齒褪色的方法。

venene *n*. a mixture of two or more *venoms; used to produce antiserum against venoms (*antivenene*).

蛇毒　兩種或多種毒液的混合物，用於製成抗毒血清（抗蛇毒素）。

venepuncture (venipuncture) *n*. the puncture of a vein for any therapeutic purpose; for example, to extract blood for laboratory tests. *See also* phlebotomy.

靜脈穿刺　為治療目的而穿刺靜脈；例如，為實驗室檢查而採血。參閱 phlebotomy。

venereal disease (VD) *see* sexually transmitted disease.

性病　參閱 sexually transmitted disease。

venesection *n. see* phlebotomy.

靜脈切開術　參閱 phlebotomy。

veno- *prefix. see* vene-.

〔前綴〕**靜脈**　參閱 vene-。

venoclysis *n*. the continuous infusion into a vein of saline or other solution.

靜脈輸注　向靜脈內連續輸入鹽水或其他溶液。

venography (phlebography) *n*. X-ray examination to show up the course of veins in a particular region of the body. A *radiopaque contrast medium is injected slowly into a vein and X-ray photographs (*venograms*) taken as the

靜脈造影術　X 綫檢查以顯示身體某一部分靜脈流程。緩緩將不透 X 綫造影劑注入靜脈，當該化合物流向心臟時進行 X 綫照像（靜脈照像）。在該造影劑未將靜脈完全充滿或出

compound is carried towards the heart. Damage, obstruction, or abnormal communication with other vessels will be seen where the medium does not fill the vein properly or apparently leaks from it. *See also* angiography.

現明顯滲漏時，可觀察到靜脈損傷、阻塞或與其他脈管交通不正常的情況。參閱 angiography。

venom *n.* the poisonous material produced by snakes, scorpions, spiders, and other animals for injecting into their prey or enemies. Some venoms produce no more than local pain and swelling; others produce more general effects and can prove lethal.

毒液 蛇、蝎、蜘蛛或其他動物產生的用以注入其獵物或敵人體內的有毒物質。有些毒液產生局部疼痛腫脹，有些則引起全身反應並可致命。

venosclerosis *n. see* phlebosclerosis.

靜脈硬化 參閱 phlebosclerosis。

ventilation *n.* the passage of air into and out of the respiratory tract. The air that reaches only as far as the conducting airways cannot take part in gas exchange and is known as *dead space ventilation* – this may be reduced by performing a *tracheostomy. In the air sacs of the lungs (alveoli) gas exchange is most efficient when matched by adequate blood flow (*perfusion). Ventilation/perfusion imbalance (ventilation of underperfused alveoli or perfusion of underventilated alveoli) is an important cause of *anoxia and *cyanosis.

通氣 空氣出入呼吸道的流通。空氣只能到達導氣管而不能參加空氣交換，並被稱為死腔樣通氣，這可通過做氣管造口術使之減少。肺泡的氣體交換（彌散）在有充足的血流相配時最為有效。通氣／血流比例失調（肺泡低彌散性通氣或肺泡低通氣性彌散）是缺氧和紫紺的主要原因。

ventilator *n.* **1.** a device to ensure a supply of fresh air. **2.** equipment that is manually or mechanically operated to maintain a flow of air into and out of the lungs of a patient who is unable to breathe normally. *See also* respirator.

(1) 通風機 保證新鮮空氣供應的一種機械。**(2) 呼吸機** 手動或機械操作的裝置，用以維持無法正常呼吸的患者氣流進出肺部。參閱 respirator。

ventouse *n. see* vacuum extractor.

吸（療）杯 參閱 vacuum extractor。

ventral *adj.* relating to or situated at or close to the front of the body or to the anterior part of an organ.

腹的，前側的 有關、位於、接近身體或器官前部的。

ventricle *n*. **1.** either of the two lower chambers of the *heart, which have thick muscular walls. The left ventricle, which is thicker than the right, receives blood from the pulmonary vein via the left atrium and pumps it into the aorta. The right ventricle pumps blood received from the venae cavae (via the right atrium) into the pulmonary artery. **2.** one of the four fluid-filled cavities within the brain (see illustration). The paired first and second ventricles (*lateral ventricles*), one in each cerebral hemisphere, communicate with the third ventricle in the midline between them. This in turn leads through a narrow channel, the *cerebral aqueduct*, to the fourth ventricle in the hindbrain, which is continuous with the spinal canal in the centre of the spinal cord. *Cerebrospinal fluid circulates through all the cavities. **–ventricular** *adj*.

室 **(1)** 心臟的兩個下腔，有厚厚的肌肉壁。左室厚於右室，接受通過左心房來自肺靜脈的血液並將血液泵入主動脈。右室將來自腔靜脈的血（通過右心房）泵入肺動脈。**(2)** 腦內四個由腦脊液充滿的腔（見圖）之一。第一及第二腦室（側腦室）成對，各在一大腦半球，與中綫上的第三腦室相通，接着經過狹窄的大腦導水管通到後腦的第四室，第四室與脊髓中央管相連續。腦脊髓液通過所有這些腦室循環。

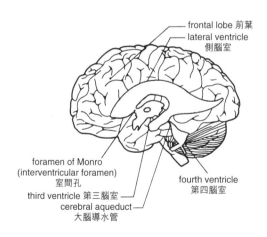

frontal lobe 前葉
lateral ventricle 側腦室
foramen of Monro (interventricular foramen) 室間孔
third ventricle 第三腦室
cerebral aqueduct 大腦導水管
fourth ventricle 第四腦室

Ventricles of the brain (side view)
腦室（側面）

ventricul- (ventriculo-) *prefix denoting* a ventricle (of the brain or heart).

〔前綴〕室　腦室或心室。

ventricular folds *see* vocal cords.

室襞　參閱 vocal cords。

ventricular septal defect (VSD) *see* septal defect.

室中隔缺損　參閱 septal defect。

ventriculitis *n*. inflammation in the ventricles of the brain, usually caused by infection. It may result from the rupture of a cerebral abscess into the cavity of the ventricle or from the spread of a severe form of *meningitis from the subarachnoid space.

腦室炎　腦室發炎，常由感染引起，起因於腦膿腫破潰進入腦室腔，或源於重型腦膜炎自蛛網膜下腔的擴散。

ventriculoatriostomy *n*. an operation for the relief of raised pressure due to the build-up of cerebrospinal fluid that occurs in *hydrocephalus. Using a system of catheters, the fluid is drained into the jugular vein in the neck.

腦室心房造口（引流）術　減輕腦積水中因腦脊液聚集導致的壓力升高的一種手術。使用導管系統，將腦脊液導入頸靜脈。

ventriculography *n*. X-ray examination of the ventricles of the brain after the introduction of a contrast medium, such as air or radiopaque material. This procedure has been largely made redundant by CT and MRI scanning.

腦室造影術　導入對比劑，如空氣或不透X綫物質，之後對腦室進行的X綫檢查。因使用CT及MRI掃描，該方法已顯得多餘。

ventriculoscopy *n*. observation of the ventricles of the brain through a fibre-optic instrument. *See* endoscope, fibre optics.

腦室鏡　借助光學纖維儀器以觀察腦室。參閱 endoscope，fibre optics。

ventriculostomy *n*. an operation to introduce a hollow needle (cannula) into one of the lateral ventricles (cavities) of the brain. This may be done to relieve raised intracranial pressure, to obtain cerebrospinal fluid from the ventricle for examination, or to introduce antibiotics or contrast material for X-ray examination.

腦室造口引流術　將中空針管（套管）引入大腦側腦室的手術。用於減輕顱內壓的升高，從腦室取腦脊液作檢查，注入抗生素，或注入作X綫檢查用的造影劑。

ventro- *prefix denoting* **1.** ventral. **2.** the abdomen.

〔前綴〕**(1)** 前側的　**(2)** 腹

ventrofixation *n. see* ventrosuspension.

子宮懸吊術　參閱 ventrosus-
pension。

ventrosuspension (ventrofixation) *n.*
surgical fixation of a displaced uterus to
the anterior abdominal wall. This may
be achieved by shortening the round
ligaments at their attachment either to
the uterus or to the abdominal wall.

子宮懸吊術　將異位的子宮手
術固定在前腹壁上。可以通過
縮短圓韌帶與子宮或腹壁的連
接達到此目的。

venule *n.* a minute vessel that drains
blood from the capillaries. Many venules
unite to form a vein.

小靜脈　從毛細血管排出血液
的細小血管。眾多小靜脈匯成
一個靜脈。

verapamil *n.* a *calcium antagonist used
in the treatment of essential hypertension, angina, and arrhythmia. It is administered by mouth; side-effects include
constipation, nausea, and hypotension.
Trade names: **Cordilox**, **Securon**,
Univer.

維拉帕米　一種鈣拮抗藥，用
於原發性高血壓、咽峽炎及
心律失常。口服，副作用包
括便秘、惡心以及低血壓。
商品名：Cordilox，Securon，
Univer。

verbigeration *n.* repetitive utterances of
the same words over and over again. This
is a kind of *stereotypy affecting speech
and is most common in institutionalized
schizophrenics.

言語重複　反複講同樣的詞
語。係累及言語的刻板症，常
見於住院的精神分裂症患者。

vermicide *n.* a chemical agent used to
destroy parasitic worms living in the
intestine. *Compare* vermifuge.

殺蟲劑　一種化學製劑，用於
驅除生活在腸內的寄生蟲。與
vermifuge 對比。

vermiform appendix *see* appendix.

闌尾　參閱 appendix。

vermifuge *n.* any drug or chemical agent
used to expel worms from the intestine.
See also anthelmintic.

驅蟲劑　用於驅除腸內寄生蟲
的任何藥物或化學製劑。參閱
anthelmintic。

vermis *n.* the central portion of the
*cerebellum, lying between its two
lateral hemispheres and immediately
behind the pons and the medulla
oblongata of the hindbrain.

蚓部　小腦的中間部分，位於
兩側小腦中間半球中，緊接後
腦的橋腦和延髓。

vermix *n.* the vermiform *appendix.

闌尾　蠕蟲樣的闌尾。

vernal conjunctivitis conjunctivitis of allergic origin, often associated with hay fever or other forms of *atopy.

vernier *n.* a device for obtaining accurate measurements of length, to 1/10th, 1/100th or smaller fractions of a unit. It consists of a fixed graduated main scale against which a shorter vernier scale slides. The vernier scale is graduated into divisions equal to nine-tenths of the smallest unit marked on the main scale. The vernier scale is often adjusted by means of a screw thread. A reading is taken by observing which of the markings on the scales coincide.

vernix caseosa the layer of greasy material which covers the skin of a fetus or newborn baby. It is produced by the oil-secreting glands of the skin and contains skin scales and fine hairs.

verruca (plantar wart) *n.* (*pl.* **verrucae**) *see* wart.

verrucous carcinoma an *indolent preinvasive wartlike carcinoma of the oral cavity, which is associated with chewing tobacco.

version *n.* a manoeuvre to alter the position of a fetus in the uterus to facilitate delivery. For example, the fetus may be turned from a transverse to a longitudinal position or from a buttocks-first to a head-first presentation (*see* cephalic version).

vertebra *n.* (*pl.* **vertebrae**) one of the 33 bones of which the *backbone is composed. Each vertebra typically consists of a *body*, or *centrum*, from the back of which arises an arch of bone (the *neural arch*) enclosing a cavity (the *vertebral*

春季結膜炎 過敏源性結膜炎，常伴發花粉病或其他形式的特異反應。

游標尺 一種精確的長度測量儀器，精確到 1/10、1/100 或更小分數。由一個固定在有刻度的主標尺上滑動的小游標尺構成。其刻度等於主標尺上的最小單位的十分之九。常用螺紋調整游標刻度。通過觀察標尺刻度的重合之處獲得讀數。

胎兒皮脂 一層覆蓋胎兒或新生兒周身的油脂層。由皮脂腺產生，包括皮鱗屑及細毛。

疣 參閱 wart。

疣狀癌 一種難愈合的局限性口腔疣狀癌，它與嚼煙草有關。

胎位倒轉術 為便於分娩而改變胎兒在子宮內位置的手法。例如，胎兒可由橫向位置轉為縱向位置或從臀先露改為頭先露（參閱 cephalic version）。

椎骨 組成脊柱的三十三塊骨之一。每一個椎骨的構成特徵是有一個椎體，背面形成一骨弓（神經弓），弓圍成一個腔，脊髓自腔內通過。神經弓具有一個棘突和供肌肉附着的

canal, or foramen) through which the spinal cord passes. The neural arch bears one *spinous process* and two *transverse processes*, providing anchorage for muscles, and four *articular processes*, with which adjacent vertebrae articulate (see illustration). Individual vertebrae are bound together by ligaments and *intervertebral discs. **–vertebral** *adj.*

兩個橫突，以及四個與臨近椎骨連成關節的關節突（見圖）。單個的椎骨被韌帶及椎間盤連接在一起。

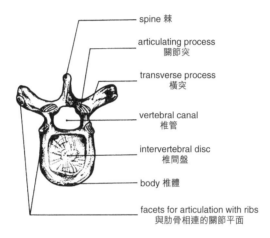

spine 棘

articulating process
關節突

transverse process
橫突

vertebral canal
椎管

intervertebral disc
椎間盤

body 椎體

facets for articulation with ribs
與肋骨相連的關節平面

A typical thoracic vertebra (from above)
典型胸椎（上面觀）

vertebral column *see* backbone.

脊柱　參閱 backbone。

vertigo *n.* a disabling sensation in which the affected individual feels that either he himself or his surroundings are in a state of constant movement. It is most often a spinning sensation but there may be a feeling that the ground is tilting. It is a symptom of disease either in the *labyrinth of the inner ear or in the *vestibular nerve or its nuclei in the brainstem, which are involved in the sense of balance.

眩暈　一種失去能力的感覺，患者感到他本人或其周圍環境處於持續運動狀態。常有旋轉感但也有地面傾斜的感覺。係與平衡感覺有關的內耳迷路、腦幹前庭神經或其核之病變症狀。

vesical *adj.* relating to or affecting a bladder, especially the urinary bladder.

vesicant *n.* an agent that causes blistering of the skin.

vesicle *n.* **1.** a very small blister in the skin, often no bigger than a pinpoint, that contains a clear fluid (serum). Vesicles occur in a variety of skin disorders, including eczema and herpes. **2.** (in anatomy) any small bladder, especially one filled with fluid. **–vesicular** *adj.*

vesico- *prefix denoting* the urinary bladder. Example: *vesicovaginal* (relating to the bladder and vagina).

vesicofixation *n. see* cystopexy.

vesicostomy *n.* the surgical creation of an artificial channel between the bladder and the skin surface for the passage of urine. It is sometimes combined with closure of the urethra.

vesicoureteric reflux the backflow of urine from the bladder into the ureters. This is due to defective valves (which normally prevent reflux). Infection is conveyed to the kidneys, causing recurrent attacks of acute *pyelonephritis and scarring of the kidneys in childhood. Children with urinary infection must be investigated for reflux by *cystoscopy; if the condition does not settle with antibiotic therapy corrective surgery must be performed.

vesicovaginal fistula an abnormal communication between the bladder and the vagina causing urinary incontinence. This may result from surgical damage to the bladder during a gynaecological

囊泡的　有關或影響囊泡的，特別是膀胱的。

起疱劑　使皮膚起疱的藥劑。

(1) 小泡　皮膚上很小的疱，通常不超過針尖大小，內含清亮的液體（血清）。見於各種皮膚病，包括濕疹及疱疹。(2) 小囊　（解剖學）任何小囊，特別是有液體充滿的小囊。

〔前綴〕膀胱　例如：膀胱陰道的（有關膀胱及陰道的）。

膀胱固定術　參閱 cystopexy。

膀胱造口術　用手術在皮膚表面與膀胱間建立人工通道以使尿液流過。該手術有時與尿道閉合術同時進行。

膀胱輸尿管返流　尿液從膀胱向輸尿管返流。這是因瓣膜缺損（正常時瓣膜阻止返流）所致。當感染傳到腎臟時，引起急性腎盂腎炎的反覆發作和童年期腎瘢痕形成。泌尿系統感染的兒童必須用膀胱鏡檢查有無返流；在抗生素治療無效時需做矯正手術。

膀胱陰道瘺　膀胱、陰道間存在的不正常的連通，致使小便失禁。係婦科手術（如子宮切除術）造成膀胱損害或繼放射治療骨盆惡性腫瘤後造成放射

operation (e.g. hysterectomy) or radiation damage following radiotherapy for pelvic malignancy. In Third World countries it is often caused by necrosis associated with prolonged obstructed labour.

性傷害之故。第三世界國家中此病常由於長時間梗阻性分娩引起壞死造成。

vesicular breathing *see* breath sounds.

肺泡性呼吸　參閱　breath sounds。

vesiculectomy *n.* surgical removal of a *seminal vesicle. This operation, which is rarely undertaken, may be performed for a tumour of the seminal vesicles.

精囊切除術　切除精囊之手術。此手術罕用，可治療精囊腫瘤。

vesiculitis *n.* inflammation of the seminal vesicles. *See* vasovesiculitis.

精囊炎　精囊發炎。參閱 vasovesiculitis。

vesiculography *n.* X-ray examination of the seminal vesicles. This is usually performed by injecting radiopaque contrast material into the exposed vasa deferentia. It can also be undertaken by inserting a catheter into the ejaculatory duct (which discharges semen from the vesicle into the vas deferens) via an *endoscope. This examination is rarely undertaken for the specific purpose of outlining the seminal vesicles; it is more commonly performed to test for the patency of the vas deferens in patients with *azoospermia.

精囊造影術　X 綫檢查精囊。常通過向暴露的輸精管注射不透 X 綫造影劑進行。也可通過內窺鏡向射精管（此管將精子從精囊排入輸精管）內插一導管來施行。本檢查偶用於觀察精囊輪廓這樣的具體目的，較常用於檢查精子缺乏症患者輸精管的開放情況。

vessel *n.* a tube conveying a body fluid, especially a blood vessel or a lymphatic vessel.

脈管　運輸體液，尤指血液或淋巴液的管道。

vestibular glands the two pairs of glands that open at the junction of the vagina and vulva. The more posterior of the two are the *greater vestibular glands* (*Bartholin's glands*); the other pair are the *lesser vestibular glands*. Their function is to lubricate the entrance to the vagina during coitus.

前庭腺　兩對腺體，開口於陰道及外陰道連接處。其中較靠後的一對為前庭大腺（巴托林腺），另一對為前庭小腺。功能：性交時潤滑陰道入口處。

vestibular nerve the division of the *vestibulocochlear nerve that carries impulses from the semicircular canals, utricle, and saccule of the inner ear to the brain, conveying information about the body's posture and movements in space and allowing coordination and balance.

前庭神經　前庭耳蝸神經之一部分，從內耳的半規管、橢圓囊及球囊向大腦傳導衝動，傳遞體位和空間運動信息，主管協調和平衡。

vestibule *n.* (in anatomy) a cavity situated at the entrance to a hollow part. The vestibule of the ear is the cavity of the bony *labyrinth that contains the *saccule and *utricle – the organs of equilibrium.

前庭　（解剖學）位於一凹陷入口處的腔。耳前庭是骨迷路腔，它包括平衡器——球囊及橢圓囊。

vestibulocochlear nerve (acoustic nerve, auditory nerve) the eighth cranial nerve (VIII), responsible for carrying sensory impulses from the inner ear to the brain. It has two branches, the *vestibular nerve* and the *cochlear nerve*. The cochlear nerve carries impulses from the spiral *cochlea and is therefore the nerve of hearing, while the vestibular nerve serves equilibrium, carrying impulses from the semicircular canals, utricles, and saccules with information about posture, movement, and balance.

前庭耳蝸神經（聽神經）　負責向大腦傳遞內耳的感覺衝動的第八對腦神經。有兩支，即前庭神經和耳蝸神經。耳蝸神經從螺旋管將衝動傳出，故而為聽神經，而前庭神經則起平衡器作用，從半規管、球囊及橢圓囊傳出有關位置、運動及平衡信息的衝動。

vestigial *adj.* existing only in a rudimentary form. The term is applied to organs whose structure and function have diminished during the course of evolution until only a rudimentary structure exists.

退化的　僅以痕迹形式存在的。用於指進化過程中器官的結構及功能減退至存留殘餘結構的情況。

viable *adj.* capable of living a separate existence. The legal age of viability of a fetus is 24 weeks, but some fetuses now survive birth at an even earlier age.

能存活的　能夠以獨立存在的方式活下來的。胎兒的法定可存活年齡為 24 周，但現在有些胎兒可以在比這個更小的年齡時出生並存活下來。

Vibramycin *n. see* doxycycline.

強力黴素　參閱 doxycycline。

vibrator *n.* a machine used to generate vibrations of different frequencies, which

振動器　用以產生不同頻率的振動的機器，將不同頻率作用

have a stimulating effect when applied to different parts of the body. A vibrator may also be used to loosen thick mucus in the sinuses or air passages.

於身體不同部位時，可產生刺激作用。該機亦可用於排出鼻竇或氣道內的濃稠黏液。

Vibrio *n.* a genus of Gram-negative motile comma-shaped bacteria widely distributed in soil and water. Most species are saprophytic but some are parasites, including *V. cholerae*, which causes *cholera.

弧菌　一屬革蘭氏陰性並能運動的弧形菌，廣泛分布於泥土或水中。多數係腐生細菌類，但也有一些是寄生性的，其中包括致霍亂的霍亂弧菌。

vibrissa *n.* (*pl.* **vibrissae**) a stiff coarse hair, especially one of the stiff hairs that lie just inside the nostrils.

鼻毛　硬且粗的毛，尤指鼻孔內的硬毛。

vicarious *adj.* describing an action or function performed by an organ not normally involved in the function. For example, *vicarious menstruation* is a rare disorder in which monthly bleeding occurs from places other than the vagina, such as the sweat glands, breasts, nose, or eyes.

異位的　指一個器官產生在其正常情況下所沒有的作用或功能。例如，異位月經為一少見病變，表現為從非陰道部位如汗腺、乳房、鼻或眼按月出血。

vidarabine *n.* an antiviral drug that inhibits DNA synthesis and is used to treat herpes simplex, herpes zoster (shingles), and *cytomegalovirus infections. It is administered by intravenous infusion. Possible side-effects include weakness and skin rashes. Trade name: **Vira-A**.

阿糖腺苷　一種抗病毒藥，抑制脫氧核糖核酸合成，並用於治療單純性疱疹、帶狀疱疹及巨細胞病毒感染。靜脈輸注給藥。副作用可有體虛和皮疹。商品名：Vira-A。

villus *n.* (*pl.* **villi**) one of many short finger-like processes that project from some membranous surfaces. Numerous *intestinal villi* line the small *intestine. Each contains a network of blood capillaries and a *lacteal. Their function is to absorb the products of digestion and they greatly increase the surface area over which this can take place. *Chorionic villi* are folds of the *chorion (the outer membrane surrounding a fetus) from

絨毛　從一些膜狀表面伸出的許多短指狀突起。大量小腸絨毛位於小腸表面，每個絨毛含有毛細血管網和乳糜管。其作用是吸收消化產物，並大大增加了吸收表面。絨毛膜（胎兒周圍的外膜）的絨毛是絨毛膜的皺褶，由此形成胎兒胎盤。他們為母親和胎兒血液之間氧、二氧化碳、食物以及廢物等的交換提供了廣大的區域。

which the fetal part of the *placenta is formed. They provide an extensive area for the exchange of oxygen, carbon dioxide, nutrients, and waste products between maternal and fetal blood. *See also* arachnoid villus, chorionic villus sampling.

參閱 arachnoid villus，chorionic villus sampling。

vinblastine *n.* a *cytotoxic drug that is given by intravascular injection mainly in the treatment of cancers of the lymphatic system, such as Hodgkin's disease. It is highly toxic, since it also acts on normal tissues; common side-effects include nausea, vomiting, diarrhoea, and depression of bone marrow function. Trade name: **Velbe**.

長春鹼 細胞毒藥物，靜脈注射，主要用於治療淋巴系統腫瘤，如霍奇金病。具有高毒性，因其對正常組織亦有作用，常見副作用有惡心、嘔吐、腹瀉和骨髓功能受抑。商品名：Velbe。

vinca alkaloid one of a group of antimitotic drugs (*see* cytotoxic drug) derived from the periwinkle (*Vinca rosea*). Vinca alkaloids, which are used especially to treat leukaemias and lymphomas, include *vinblastine, *vincristine, and *vindesine.

長春生物鹼 一組生物鹼藥物之一（參閱 cytotoxic drug），衍生於小蔓長春花。該藥主要用於治療白血病及淋巴腫瘤，此藥中包括長春鹼、長春新鹼及長春地辛。

Vincent's angina an obsolete term for *ulcerative gingivitis.

樊尚咽峽炎 潰瘍性牙齦炎的舊稱。

vincristine *n.* a cytotoxic drug with uses and side-effects similar to those of vinblastine. Trade name: **Oncovin**.

長春新鹼 細胞毒類藥物，其用途及不良反應類似於長春鹼。商品名：Oncovin。

vinculum *n.* (*pl.* **vincula**) a connecting band of tissue. The *vincula tendinum* are threadlike bands of synovial membrane that connect the flexor tendons of the fingers and toes to their point of insertion on the phalanges.

紐 組織的連接帶。腱紐是滑膜的綫狀帶，將指（趾）的屈肌肌腱連接到指（趾）骨的附着點。

vindesine *n.* a cytotoxic drug with similarities to *vinblastine and vincristine. Additional side-effects include alopecia and peripheral neuropathy. Trade name: **Eldisine**.

長春地辛 細胞毒素藥物，類似於長春花鹼及長春新鹼。另外的副作用還有脫髮及周圍神經病變。商品名：Eldisine。

VIP (vasoactive intestinal peptide) a protein produced by cells of the pancreas. Large amounts of this protein cause severe diarrhoea.

血管活性腸肽 胰腺細胞產生的一種蛋白。大量的此類蛋白引起嚴重腹瀉。

vipoma *n.* a tumour of islet cells of the pancreas that secrete *VIP.

舒血管腸肽瘤 分泌血管活性腸肽的胰腺胰島細胞腫瘤。

viraemia *n.* the presence in the blood of virus particles.

病毒血症 血液中存有病毒顆粒。

viral pneumonia an acute infection of the lung caused by any one of a number of viruses, such as *respiratory syncytial virus, adenovirus, influenza and parainfluenza viruses, and enteroviruses. It is characterized by headache, fever, muscle pain, and a cough that produces a thick sputum. The pneumonia can often occur with or subsequent to a systemic viral infection. Treatment is by supportive care, but antibiotics are administered if a bacterial infection is superimposed.

病毒性肺炎 由多種病毒，如呼吸合胞病毒、腺病毒、流感及副流感病毒以及腸病毒等引起的肺部急性感染。特徵為頭痛、發燒、肌肉疼痛及產生膿痰的咳嗽。肺炎常在全身性病毒感染當時或之後發生。治療採用支持療法。但如伴有細菌感染，需用抗生素治療。

virilism *n.* the development in a female of a combination of increased body hair, muscle bulk, and deepening of the voice (*masculinization) and male psychological characteristics.

男性化 女性發育中出現體毛增多、肌肉發達及嗓音低沉（男性化）和男性心理特徵的綜合徵。

virilization *n.* the most extreme result of excessive androgen production (*hyperandrogenism) in women. It is characterized by temporal balding, a male body form, muscle bulk, deepening of the voice, enlargement of the clitoris, and *hirsutism. Virilization in prepubertal boys may be caused by some tumours (*see* Leydig tumour).

男性化 女性中因雄性激素分泌過多（雄激素過多症）而引起的最嚴重後果。特徵為暫時性禿頂、男性體格、肌肉發達、嗓音低沉、陰蒂增大及多毛症。青春期前的男孩出現男性化可能是因某種腫瘤所致（參閱 Leydig tumour）。

virology *n.* the science of viruses. *See also* microbiololgy.

病毒學 關於病毒的科學。參閱 microbiology。

virulence *n.* the disease-producing (pathogenic) ability of a microorganism. *See also* attenuation.

毒力 微生物之致病力。參閱 attenuation。

virus *n.* a minute particle that is capable of replication but only within living cells. Viruses are too small to be visible with a light microscope and too small to be trapped by filters. They infect animals, plants, and microorganisms (*see* bacteriophage). Each consists of a core of nucleic acid (DNA or RNA) surrounded by a protein shell. Some bear an outer lipid capsule. Viruses cause many diseases, including the common cold, influenza, measles, mumps, chickenpox, herpes, AIDS, polio, and rabies. *Antiviral drugs are effective against some of them, and many viral diseases are controlled by means of vaccines. **–viral** *adj.*

病毒　僅在活細胞內有複製能力的微小顆粒。病毒太小以致在光學顯微鏡下無法觀察到，並且也無法用過濾器阻留。它們侵襲動物、植物及微生物（參閱 bacteriophage）。每個病毒由蛋白殼包裹的核酸核心（DNA 或 RNA）組成。有些病毒具有脂質外囊。病毒能引起多種疾病，如普通感冒、流感、麻疹、流行性腮腺炎、水痘、疱疹、艾滋病、脊髓灰質炎及狂犬病。抗病毒藥物對有些病毒有效，但許多病毒性疾病要通過疫苗來控制。

viscera *pl. n.* (*sing.* **viscus**) the organs within the body cavities, especially the organs of the abdominal cavities (stomach, intestines, etc.). **–visceral** *adj.*

內臟　體腔內各器官，尤指腹腔內器官（胃，腸等）。

visceral arch *see* pharyngeal arch.

鰓弓　參閱 pharyngeal arch。

visceral cleft *see* pharyngeal cleft.

鰓裂　參閱 pharyngeal cleft。

visceral pouch *see* pharyngeal pouch.

咽囊　參閱 pharyngeal pouch。

viscero- *prefix denoting* the viscera.

〔前綴〕內臟的

viscus *n. see* viscera.

內臟　參閱 viscera。

visual acuity sharpness of vision. How well one sees things depends on how well they are illuminated and upon such factors as practice and motivation, but the essential requirements are a healthy retina and the ability of the eye to focus incoming light to form a sharp image on the retina. The commonest way of assessing visual acuity is the *Snellen chart, which measures the *resolving power* of the eye.

視敏度　視覺的敏銳性。一個人視物的清晰度取決於物體被照明的強度，以及實踐和動機等因素，但基本的要求是要有健全的視網膜及眼睛集中光綫於視網膜上形成清晰影像的能力。評定視敏度最常見的方法是斯內倫視力表，該表衡量眼睛的分辨能力。

visual field the area in front of the eye in any part of which an object can be seen without moving the eye. With both eyes open and looking, straight forward it is possible to see well-illuminated objects placed anywhere in front of the eyes, although the eyebrows and eyelids reduce the extent of the field somewhat. This is the *binocular visual field*. With only one eye open the field is *uniocular* and is restricted inwards by the nose. If the object is small or poorly illuminated it will not be seen until it is moved closer to the point at which the eye is actually looking, i.e. nearer to the centre of the visual field. Similarly, coloured objects are not seen so far away from the centre as are white objects of the same size and brightness. This is because the retina is not uniformly sensitive to light of different colours or intensities (*see* rod, cone): retinal sensitivity increases towards its centre (the *macula). Thus, while there is an absolute visual field beyond which things cannot be seen, no matter how large or bright they are, a relative field exists for objects of different brightness, size, and colour. The most common visual field loss is due to *glaucoma. *See also* campimetry, perimeter.

visual purple *see* rhodopsin.

vital capacity the maximum volume of air that a person can exhale afer maximum inhalation. It is usually measured on an instrument called a *spirometer*.

vital centre any of the collections of nerve cells in the brain that act as governing centres for different vital body functions – such as breathing, heart, rate, blood pressure, temperature control etc. – making reflex adjustments according

視野　不動眼睛可看見眼前區域中任一部位上的物體，這一區域稱為視野。儘管眼眉及眼瞼會在某種程度上縮小視野的範圍，但在雙眼睜開，並直視前方時可以看見眼前任何地方照明好的物體。這便是雙眼視野。若僅有一隻眼睜開，則是單眼視野，該視野內側受鼻限制。如果物體小或照明差，只有將它移近眼睛直視之處，即接近視中央才能看見。同樣，有色物體在遠離中央處亦無法看見，而同樣大小及亮度的白色物體卻是可見的。這是因視網膜對不同顏色及明暗程度的敏感性不同（參閱 rod，cone）：靠近中央處（黃斑）視網膜的敏感度增加。故而有一個絕對視野，還有一個相對視野。前者，無論物體多麼大和多麼亮，超出它就不能看見；後者則因物體顏色、大小、亮度的不同而不同。最常見的視野喪失係青光眼之故。參閱 campimetry，perimeter。

視紫質　參閱 rhodopsin。

肺活量　一個人在最大吸氣後呼出的最大氣體容積，常以被稱為肺量計的儀器進行測量。

生命中樞　腦內神經細胞的集體，為身體不同生命活動的控制中樞——如呼吸、心率、血壓和體溫調節等——按照身體需要作出反射調節。大多數位於下丘腦和腦幹。

to the body's needs. Most lie in the hypothalamus and brainstem.

Vitallium *n. Trademark.* an alloy of chromiun and cobalt that is used in instruments, prostheses, surgical appliances, and dentures.

鈷合金 （商品名）鉻與鈷的合金，用於儀器、修復體、外科器械以及假牙。

vital staining (intravital staining) the process of staining a living tissue by injecting a stain into the organism. *Compare* supravital staining.

活體染色法 將染劑注入有機體內以使活體組織染色的過程。與 supravital staining 對比。

vital statistics *see* biostatistics.

生命統計學 參閱 biostatistics。

vitamin *n.* any of a group of substances that are required, in very small amounts, for healthy growth and development: they cannot be synthesized by the body and are therefore essential constituents of the diet. Vitamins are divided into two groups, according to whether they are soluble in water or fat. The water-soluble group includes the vitamin B complex and vitamin C; the fat-soluble vitamins are vitamins A, D, E, and K. Lack of sufficient quantities of any of the vitamins in the diet results in specific vitamin deficiency diseases.

維生素 一組健康生長和發育所必需的含量極小的物質：它們不能在身體內合成，故而成為膳食中的重要組成部分。按其是否溶於水或脂肪可劃分為兩類。水溶性類包括維生素 B 複合物及維生素 C，脂溶性類有維生素 A、D、E 及 K。膳食中任何一種維生素的含量不足導致特異性維生素缺乏病。

vitamin A (retinol) a fat-soluble vitamin that occurs preformed in foods of animal origin (especially milk products, egg yolk, and liver) and is formed in the body from the pigment β-*carotene, present in some vegetable foods (for example cabbage, lettuce, and carrots). Retinol is essential for growth, vision in dim light, and the maintenance of soft mucous tissue. A deficiency causes stunted growth, night blindness, *xerophthalmia, *keratomalacia, and eventual blindness. The recommended daily intake is 750 µg retinol equivalents for an adult (1 µg

維生素 A（維生素 A 醇）一種脂溶性維生素。自然存在於動物源性食物（特別是奶製品、蛋黃及肝）中，在體內可從 β-胡蘿蔔素這種色素中形成，該色素存在於一些蔬菜中（例如卷心菜、萵苣和胡蘿蔔）。維生素 A 醇為生長、暗視覺及維持柔軟的黏膜組織所必需，缺乏該物質可引起生長障礙、夜盲、乾眼病、角膜軟化、甚至最終失明。建議成人每日攝取 750µg 維生素 A 醇當量（1µg 維生素A醇當量 =

retinol equivalent = 1 µg retinol or 6 µg β-carotene).

vitamin B any one of a group of water-soluble vitamins that, although not chemically related, are often found together in the same kinds of food (milk, liver, cereals, etc.) and all function as *coenzymes. *See* vitamins B$_1$, B$_2$, B$_6$, B$_{12}$, biotin, folic acid, nicotinic acid, pantothenic acid.

vitamin B$_1$ (thiamin, aneurine) a vitamin of the B complex that is active in the form of *thiamin pyrophosphate*, a coenzyme in decarboxylation reactions in carbohydrate metabolism. A deficiency of vitamin B$_1$ leads to *beriberi. Good sources of the vitamin are cereals, beans, meat, potatoes, and nuts. The recommended daily intake is 1 mg for an adult.

vitamin B$_2$ (riboflavin) a vitamin of the B complex that is a constituent of the coenzymes *FAD (flavine adenine dinucleotide) and *FMN (flavine mononucleotide). Riboflavin is therefore important in tissue respiration. A deficiency of riboflavin causes a condition known as *ariboflavinosis, which is not usually serious. Good sources of riboflavin are liver, milk, and eggs. The recommended daily intake for an adult is 1.7 mg.

vitamin B$_6$ (pyridoxine) a vitamin of the B complex from which the coenzyme *pyridoxal phosphate, involved in the transamination of amino acids, is formed. The vitamin is found in most foods and a deficiency is therefore rare.

vitamin B$_{12}$ (cyanocobalamin) a vitamin of the B complex. The form of

1µg 維生素 A 醇或 6µg β-胡蘿蔔素）。

維生素 B 一組水溶性維生素，這些維生素雖無化學聯繫，但卻常發現共同存在於同類食物中（奶、肝、穀類等），並都起輔酶作用。參閱 vitamin B$_1$，B$_2$，B$_6$，B$_{12}$，biotin，folic acid，nicotinic acid，pantothenic acid。

維生素 B$_1$（硫胺） 一維生素 B 複合物。硫胺焦磷酸鹽型具有活性，為糖代謝中脫羧反應的輔酶。維生素 B$_1$ 缺乏可致腳氣病。此維生素之重要來源係穀類、豆類、肉、土豆及堅果。成人每日建議攝入量為 1 mg。

維生素 B$_2$（核黃素） 一維生素 B 複合物，為輔酶 FAD（黃素腺嘌呤二核苷酸）和 FMN（黃素單核苷酸）中的一組成部分。因此核黃素對組織呼吸是重要的。維生素 B$_2$ 缺乏將引起核黃素缺乏症，此症一般不嚴重。肝、奶、蛋為其重要來源，成人每日建議攝入量為 1.7 mg。

維生素 B$_6$（吡多辛） 維生素 B 複合物中的一種，它形成磷酸吡哆醛，後者參與氨基酸的轉氨基反應。該物質見於大多數食物中故而罕見有維生素 B$_6$ 缺乏症。

維生素 B$_{12}$ B 族維生素中的一類。維生素 B$_{12}$ 具有輔酶活

vitamin B_{12} with coenzyme activity is 5-*deoxyadenosyl cobalamin*, which is necessary for the synthesis of nucleic acids, the maintenance of *myelin in the nervous system, and the proper functioning of *folic acid, another B vitamin. The vitamin can be absorbed only in the presence of *intrinsic factor*, a protein secreted in the stomach. A deficiency of vitamin B_{12} affects nearly all the body tissues, particularly those containing rapidly dividing cells. The most serious effects of a deficiency are *pernicious anaemia and degeneration of the nervous system. Vitamin B_{12} is manufactured only by certain microorganisms and is contained only in foods of animal origin. Good sources are liver, fish, and eggs The daily recommended adult intake is 3–4 µg.

vitamin C (ascorbic acid) a water-soluble vitamin with *antioxidant properties that is essential in maintaining healthy connective tissues and the integrity of cell walls. It is necessary for the synthesis of collagen. A deficiency of vitamin C leads to *scurvy. The recommended daily intake is 30 mg for an adult; rich sources are citrus fruits and vegetables.

vitamin D a fat-soluble vitamin that enhances the absorption of calcium and phosphorus from the intestine and promotes their deposition in the bone. It occurs in two forms: *ergocalciferol* (*vitamin D_2, calciferol*), which is manufactured by plants when the sterol ergosterol is exposed to ultraviolet light, and *cholecalciferol* (*vitamin D_3*), which is produced by the action of sunlight on 7-dehydrocholesterol, a sterol widely distributed in the skin. A deficiency of vitamin D, either from a poor diet or lack

性，係 5-脱氧腺苷鈷胺，後者是合成核酸及維持神經系統中的髓鞘質必需的，也是使質葉酸及其他維生素 B 發揮正常作用必需的。維生素 B_{12} 只在胃分泌的一種蛋白，即內因子存在的情況下才可被吸收。維生素 B_{12} 缺乏幾乎影響到全身組織，尤其是那些含快速分裂細胞的組織。維生素 B_{12} 缺乏症最嚴重的後果為惡性貧血與神經系統變性。維生素 B_{12} 只由某些微生物產生，並且只存在於動物性食物中，其重要來源為肝、魚以及蛋。成人每日建議攝入量為 3~4µg。

維生素 C（抗壞血酸）一水溶性維生素，具有抗氧化特性，在維持結締組織的健全及細胞壁的完整方面十分重要。也是膠原合成所必需。維生素 C 缺乏症導致壞血病。成人每日建議攝入量 30 mg；柑橘類水果及蔬菜中含量豐富。

維生素 D 一脂溶性維生素，可增強鈣和磷在腸道吸收和促進鈣磷在骨中沉積。以兩種形式出現：麥角鈣化醇（維生素 D_2）及膽鈣化醇（維生素 D_3），前者由植物中麥角固醇暴露於紫外綫而生成，後者由廣泛分布於皮膚中的膽固醇類，即 7-脱氫膽固醇在陽光作用下生成。無論是因膳食不良或因缺乏日曬造成的維生素 D 缺乏，都可導致骨骼脱鈣發展為佝僂病與軟骨病。肝

of sunlight, leads to decalcified bones and the development of *rickets and *osteomalacia. Good sources of vitamin D are liver and fish oils. The recommended daily intake is 10 μg for a child up to five years and 2.5 μg thereafter. Vitamin D is toxic and large doses must therefore be avoided.

和魚肝油是維生素 D 的豐富來源。五歲前兒童每日建議攝入量為 10 μg，五歲後每日 2.5 μg。維生素 D 有毒性，因此要避免大劑量應用。

vitamin E any of a group of chemically related compounds (*tocopherols* and *tocotrienols*) that have *antioxidant properties and are thought to stabilize cell membranes by preventing oxidation of their unsaturated fatty acid components. The most potent of these is *α-tocopherol*. Good sources of the vitamin are vegetable oils, eggs, butter, and wholemeal cereals. It is fairly widely distributed in the diet and a deficiency is therefore unlikely.

維生素 E 一組化學上相關的化合物（生育酚和生育三烯酚類）中的任何一種，具抗氧化劑特性，據認為它能防止不飽和脂肪酸氧化而使細胞膜穩定。最常見的成分為 α-生育酚。其重要來源為植物油、蛋、黃油、粗麵粉和穀類。膳食中廣泛存在，故罕見其缺乏症。

vitamin K a fat-soluble vitamin occurring in two main forms: *phytomenadione* (of plant origin) and *menaquinone* (of animal origin). It is necessary for the formation of *prothrombin in the liver, which is essential for blood clotting, and it also regulates the synthesis of other clotting factors. A dietary deficiency does not often occur as the vitamin is synthesized by bacteria in the large intestine and is widely distributed in green leafy vegetables and meat.

維生素 K 脂溶性維生素，見於兩種主要形式：維生素 K_1（植物源性）及維生素 K_2（動物源性）。維生素 K 是肝臟形成凝血酶原所必需，而凝血酶原是凝血中必不可少的。因維生素 K 可由大腸內細菌合成並廣泛存在於綠葉蔬菜和肉類中，故而其食源性缺乏症罕見發生。

vitellus *n.* the yolk of an ovum.

卵黃 卵子的黃。

vitiligo *n.* a common disorder in which symmetrical white or pale *macules appear on the skin. It affects all races, but is more conspicuous in dark-skinned races. Vitiligo is an *autoimmune disease and may occur with other such diseases (e.g. thyroid disease or pernicious anaemia). It is usually progressive,

白斑（白斑病） 一種皮膚出現對稱性白斑或發白斑塊的常見病。感染所有人種。但在膚色深的人種中更為明顯。該病為自體免疫性疾病，並可與其他疾病（如甲狀腺病或惡性貧血病）同時發生。儘管色素沉着可再度發生，它常為進行性

although spontaneous repigmentation may occur. Treatment with *PUVA may be effective in darker-skinned people; pale-skinned sufferers can best be helped by using potent sunscreens or by cosmetic camouflage.

vitrectomy *n.* the removal of the whole or part of the vitreous humour of the eye, including vitreous haemorrhage. It is often necessary in surgery to repair a *detached retina.

vitreous humour (vitreous body) the transparent jelly-like material that fills the chamber behind the lens of the eye.

viviparous *adj.* describing animal groups (including most mammals) in which the embryos develop within the body of the mother so that the young are born alive rather than hatch from an egg. –**viviparity** *n.*

vivisection *n.* a surgical operation on a living animal for experimental purposes.

vocal cords (vocal folds) the two folds of tissue which protrude from the sides of the *larynx to form a narrow slit (glottis) across the air passage (see

的。膚色較深者用光化學療法可能有效，膚色較淺者用強力防曬霜或化妝品遮蓋可有所幫助。

玻璃體摘除術　全部或部分摘除眼內玻璃體，包括玻璃體出血。修復脫落視網膜時常有必要做此手術。

玻璃體　充滿晶狀體後腔的透明膠樣物質。

胎生的　形容一類動物（包括大多數哺乳動物），其胚胎在母體內生長發育，故而出生時為活的幼小動物而非從卵孵化的動物。

活體解剖　為實驗目的而對活動物進行的手術。

聲帶　兩條組織皺襞，從咽部兩側伸出，在呼吸道上形成一條狹縫（聲門）（見圖）。它們對呼吸的氣流進行控制調節，

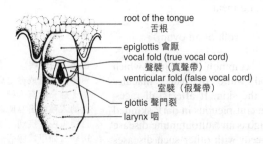

root of the tongue
舌根

epiglottis 會厭
vocal fold (true vocal cord)
聲襞（真聲帶）
ventricular fold (false vocal cord)
室襞（假聲帶）

glottis 聲門裂
larynx 咽

The vocal cords
聲帶

illustration). Their controlled interference with the expiratory air flow produces audible vibrations that make up speech, song, and all other vocal noises. Alterations in the vocal cords themselves or in their nerve supply by disease interferes with phonation.

產生可聽見的振動，這便是説話、唱歌及其他的嗓音。疾病引起的聲帶自身或其神經支配發生的變化可影響發音。

vocal fremitus *see* fremitus.

語言震顫 參閱 fremitus。

vocal resonance the sounds heard through the stethoscope when the patient speaks ("ninety nine"). These are normally just audible but become much louder (*bronchophony*) if the lung under the stethoscope is consolidated, when they resemble the sounds heard over the trachea and main bronchi. Vocal resonance is lost over pleural fluid except at its upper surface, when it has a bleating quality and is called *aegophony*. *See also* pectoriloquy.

語響 當患者説話（例如説 ninety nine）時，借助聽診器聽到的聲音。這些聲音在正常情況下剛可聽到，若聽診器下的肺發生實變時，聲音會顯着變大（支氣管語言），與氣管及支氣管上聽到的聲音相似。胸腔積液部位語響消失，但在積液以上的表面則不同，此時聽到的音像羊叫，稱為「羊音」。參閱 pectoriloquy。

volar *adj.* relating to the palm of the hand or the sole of the foot (the *vola*).

掌的（蹠的） 有關手掌或腳底（蹠）的。

Volkmann's contracture fibrosis and shortening of muscles due to inadequate blood supply. It is a complication that arises after fractures have been encased by constricting bandages and plaster casts. *See also* compartment syndrome.

福爾克曼攣縮 因供血不足引起的纖維變性及肌肉縮短。骨折後因用緊繃的繃帶或石膏模固定而產生的併發症。參閱 compartment syndrome。

volsellum (vulsellum) *n.* surgical forceps with clawlike hooks at the ends of both blades.

雙爪鉗 外科用鉗，兩個葉片末端都有爪樣鉤。

volt *n.* the *SI unit of electric potential, equal to the potential difference between two points on a conducting wire through which a constant current of 1 ampere flows when the power dissipated between these points is 1 watt. Symbol: V.

伏特 電位差的國際單位，等於 1 安培恆定電流通過一導綫上所耗電功率為 1 瓦特時兩點間的電位差。符號：V。

voluntary admission entry of a patient into a psychiatric hospital with his (or her) agreement. *Compare* compulsory admission.

自願入院　經病人同意住入精神病院。與 compulsory admission 對比。

voluntary muscle *see* striated muscle.

隨意肌　參閱 striated muscle。

volvulus *n.* twisting of part of the digestive tract, usually leading to partial or complete obstruction and sometimes reducing the blood supply, causing gangrene. A volvulus may untwist spontaneously or by manipulation, but surgical exploration is usually performed. *Gastric volvulus* is a twist of the stomach, usually in a hiatus *hernia. *Small-intestinal volvulus* is twisting of part of the bowel around an *adhesion. *Sigmoid volvulus* is a twist of the sigmoid colon, usually when this loop is particularly long.

腸扭轉　消化道部分扭轉，常引起部分或全部阻塞，有時引起血液供應減少，導致壞死。腸扭轉可自然緩解或通過手法操作緩解，但常需施行手術探查。胃扭轉常發生於食管孔疝。小腸扭轉為黏連周圍的部分腸扭轉。乙狀結腸扭轉則常因該段腸袢特別長而發生。

vomer *n.* a thin plate of bone that forms part of the nasal septum (*see* nasal cavity). *See also* skull.

梨骨　薄板狀骨，它構成鼻中隔部分。參閱 skull。

vomica *n.* **1.** an abnormal cavity in an organ, usually a lung, sometimes containing pus. **2.** *n.* the abrupt expulsion from the mouth of a large quantity of pus or decaying matter originating in the throat or lungs.

(1) 空洞　器官內的異常空腔，常在肺部，有時含膿液。(2) 咳膿痰　口腔中突然排出來自喉部或肺部之大量膿液或腐爛物。

vomit 1. *vb.* to eject the contents of the stomach through the mouth (*see* vomiting). **2.** *n.* the contents of the stomach ejected during vomiting. Medical name: **vomitus**.

(1) 嘔吐　胃內容物從口腔中排出（參閱 vomiting）。(2) 嘔吐物　嘔吐時排出的胃內容物。醫學用語：嘔吐。

vomiting *n.* the reflex action of ejecting the contents of the stomach through the mouth. Vomiting is controlled by a special centre in the brain that may be stimulated by drugs (e.g. *apomorphine) acting directly on it; or by impulses transmitted through nervous pathways either

嘔吐　經口排出胃內容物的反射活動。該活動由大腦特殊中樞控制，該中樞可受藥物直接作用而興奮（例如：阿樸嗎啡），也可由神經通路傳遞來的衝動引起興奮，包括胃的衝動（例如：在食入刺激性食物

from the stomach (e.g. after ingesting irritating substances, in gastritis and other stomach diseases), the intestine (e.g. in intestinal obstruction), or from the inner ear (in travel sickness). The stimulated vomiting centre sets off a chain of nerve impulses producing coordinated contractions of the diaphragm and abdominal muscles, relaxation of the muscle at the entrance to the stomach, etc., causing the stomach contents to be expelled. Medical name: **emesis**.

von Hippel-Lindau disease an inherited syndrome in which *haemangioblastomas, particularly in the cerebellum, are associated with renal and pancreatic cysts, *angiomas in the retina (causing blindness), cancer of the kidney cells, and red birthmarks.

von Recklinghausen's disease 1. a syndrome due to excessive secretion of *parathyroid hormone (hyperparathyroidism), characterized by loss of mineral from bones, which become weakened and fracture easily, and formation of kidney stones. Medical name: **osteitis fibrosa. 2.** *see* neurofibromatosis.

Von Rosen's sign *see* congenital dislocation of the hip.

von Willebrand's disease an inherited disorder of the blood that is characterized by episodes of spontaneous bleeding similar to *haemophilia. It may or may not be associated with deficiency of *Factor VIII and is inherited as an autosomal *dominant.

voyeurism *n.* the condition of obtaining sexual pleasure by watching other people undressing or enjoying sexual relations. *See also* sexual deviation. **–voyeur** *n.*

後，胃炎及其他胃病時），腸的衝動（例如：腸梗阻）或內耳衝動（旅行病）等。嘔吐中樞興奮時引起一連串神經衝動，產生膈肌與腹肌協調收縮，胃入口處肌肉鬆弛等，使胃內容物排出。醫學用語：嘔吐。

希-林氏病 一種綜合徵，在此病中成血管細胞瘤特別是小腦中的成血管細胞瘤伴有腎和胰腺囊腫、視網膜血管瘤、腎細胞癌及紅色胎痣。

馮雷克林豪森病 (1) 因甲狀旁腺激素分泌過多（甲狀旁腺機能亢進）引起的綜合徵，特徵為骨中喪失礦物質而變得脆弱易折，以及形成腎結石。醫學用語：纖維性骨炎。**(2)** 神經纖維瘤病。參閱 neurofibromatosis。

馮羅森徵 參閱 congenital dislocation of the hip。

馮維勒布蘭德病，遺傳性假血友病 遺傳性血液疾病，特徵為自發性與血友病相似的流血發作。它可能與第八因子缺乏有關，也可能與之無關，並且以正常基因顯性遺傳。

窺淫癖 通過觀其他人裸體或性交而獲得性快樂的一種病態。參閱 sexual deviation。

vulsellum *n. see* volsellum.

雙爪鉗 參閱 volsellum。

vulv- (vulvo-) *prefix denoting* the vulva.

〔前綴〕外陰

vulva *n.* the female external genitalia. Two pairs of fleshy folds – the *labia majora* and *labia minora* – surround the openings of the vagina and urethra and extend forward to the clitoris (see illustration). *See also* vestibular glands.

外陰 女性外生殖器。兩對多肉皺襞——大陰唇及小陰唇——圍繞於陰道及尿道開口，向前展至陰蒂（見圖）。參閱 vestibular glands。

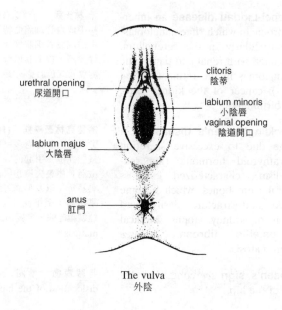

urethral opening
尿道開口

clitoris
陰蒂

labium minoris
小陰唇

vaginal opening
陰道開口

labium majus
大陰唇

anus
肛門

The vulva
外陰

vulvectomy *n.* surgical removal of the external genitals (*see* vulva) of a woman. *Simple vulvectomy* involves excision of the labia majora, labia minora, and clitoris and is carried out for a nonmalignant growth. *Radical vulvectomy* is a much more extensive operation carried out for a malignant growth, e.g. cancer of the vulva. It involves wide excision of

外陰切除術 切除女性外生殖器（參閱 vulva）的手術。簡單外陰切除術包括切除大陰唇、小陰唇及陰蒂，在非惡性新生物時使用。根據性外陰切除術是範圍更廣的手術，用於惡性新生物時，如外陰癌。除在外陰兩側徹底摘除淋巴結外，該手術還廣泛涉及切除大

the labia majora and minora and the clitoris in addition to complete removal of all regional lymph nodes on both sides. The skin covering these areas is also removed, leaving an extensive raw area that is allowed to heal by *granulation.

陰唇、小陰唇和陰蒂，覆蓋這些部位的皮膚也要切除，留下大片創傷區域，通過肉芽生長來愈合。

vulvitis *n.* inflammation of the vulva, which is often accompanied by intense itching (see pruritus).

外陰炎 外陰發炎，常伴有劇烈瘙癢（參閱 pruritus）。

vulvovaginitis *n.* inflammation of the vulva and vagina (*see* pruritus, vaginitis).

外陰陰道炎 外陰及陰道發炎（參閱 pruritus，vaginitis）。

W

wafer *n.* a thin sheet made from moistened flour, formerly used to enclose a powdered medicine that is taken by mouth.

糯米紙 糯米粉加水製成的薄紙，過去常用於包裹口服藥粉。

waiting list a list of the names of patients who are awaiting admission to hospital after having been assessed either as an outpatient or on a domiciliary consultation involving a specialist. In general the patients are offered places in the order in which their names were placed on the list, but in certain circumstances (e.g. if the condition is potentially dangerous or painful) the consultant may recommend urgent or even immediate admission. One of the facts recorded in relation to hospital admissions is the length of time between the name being placed on the list and the patient being admitted (*waiting time*). General practitioners may also request *direct admission* (immediate) for urgent cases who have not been seen by the consultant; such admission may be arranged by phone

入院候診單 等候入院的病人名單，他們或者是門診上確定要入院的病人，或是地段上通過專家會診確定的入院病人。通常，病人入院以名單為序，但在某些情況下（例如病情有危險或疼痛），經治醫師可建議緊急或甚至立即接收入院。入院登記的目的之一就是確定從名單上登記的時間到得到入院的時間長短（等候時間）。全科醫師推薦一些未經治醫師診斷的緊急病人直接入院，可通過電話與經治醫師或他的代理人聯繫，或者是通過醫院急診室安排病人入院。

with the consultant or his or her deputy or channelled through the accident and emergency department of the hospital.

Waldeyer's ring the ring of lymphoid tissue formed by the tonsils.

瓦爾戴爾扁桃體環　扁桃體構成的淋巴組織環。

Wallerian degeneration fatty degeneration of a ruptured nerve fibre that occurs within the nerve sheath distal to the point of severance.

沃勒變性　破裂神經纖維的脂肪變性，產生於遠離裂點的神經鞘內。

warfarin *n.* an *anticoagulant used mainly in the treatment of coronary or venous thrombosis to reduce the risk of embolism. It is given by mouth or injection. The principal toxic effect is local bleeding, usually from the gums and other mucous membranes. Warfarin has also been used as a rat poison. Trade name: **Marevan**.

華法林（苄丙酮香豆素）　一種抗凝藥物，主要用於治療冠狀動脈或靜脈血栓形成，從而減少栓塞危險性。口服或注射。主要毒性反應為局部出血，通常見於牙齦部及其他黏膜。該藥也可用作滅鼠藥。商品名：Marevan。

wart *n.* benign growth on the skin caused by infection with *human papillomavirus. *Common warts* are firm horny papules. 1–10 mm in diameter, found mainly on the backs of the hands. Most will clear spontaneously within two years. *Plantar warts* (or *verrucae*) occur on the soles and are often tender. Plane warts are flat and skin coloured – and therefore difficult to see; they are usually found on the face and may be present in very large numbers. *Genital warts* are frequently associated with other genital infections and affected women have an increased risk of developing cervical cancer. Treatment of warts is with OTC (over-the-counter) remedies, such as lactic and salicylic acids, but *cryotherapy with liquid nitrogen is probably more effective. Occasionally curettage and cautery are used: surgical excision is never indicated.

疣　皮膚上長出的良性新生物，因感染人乳頭狀瘤病毒引起。普通疣為尖硬的角狀丘疹，直徑 1~10mm，主要見於手背。兩年內大多數會自然消除。足底疣見於足跟，常較柔軟。扁平疣平扁，且與皮膚同色，故而難以發現，常見於面部，並大量存在。生殖器疣常常與其他生殖器感染有關，且患病婦女有患宮頸癌的更大危險。治療使用非處方藥物，如乳酸及水楊酸，但冷凍療法可能更為有效。偶爾用刮除術及烙術：外科手術除疣從不使用。

Warthin's tumour (adenolymphoma) a tumour of the parotid salivary glands, containing epithelial and lymphoid tissues with cystic spaces.

沃爾信瘤（腺淋巴瘤） 一種腮腺唾液腺腫瘤，它含有帶囊腔的上皮和淋巴組織。

Wassermann reaction formerly, the most commonly used test for the diagnosis of *syphilis. A sample of the patient's blood is examined, using a *complement-fixation reaction, for the presence of antibodies to the organism *Treponema pallidum*. A positive reaction (WR+) indicates the presence of antibodies and therefore infection with syphilis.

瓦塞爾曼反應 以前為最常用的診斷梅毒的檢驗。用補體結合反應來檢查病人的血標本中梅毒螺旋體的抗體。陽性反應（WR+）表明抗體存在，因此有梅毒感染。

water bed a bed with a flexible water-containing mattress. The surface of the bed adapts itself to the patient's posture, which leads to greater comfort and fewer bedsores.

充水床墊 一種柔軟可變形的充水床墊。床表面因病人姿勢而變，使病人感覺更加舒適及少患褥瘡。

waterbrash *n.* a sudden filling of the mouth with dilute saliva. This often accompanies dyspepsia, particularly if there is nausea.

泛酸 口腔內突然充滿稀薄唾液。常伴有消化不良，特別是惡心。

Waterhouse-Friderichsen syndrome acute haemorrhage in the adrenal glands with haemorrhage into the skin associated with the sudden onset of acute bacteraemic *shock. It is usually caused by meningococcal septicaemia (*see* meningitis).

沃-弗氏森綜合徵 急性腎上腺出血，伴有皮膚內出血，合併有突發性急性菌血症休克。常係腦膜炎雙球菌敗血症（參閱 meningitis）之故。

Water's projection a *posteroanterior X-ray film to show the maxillae, maxillary sinuses, and zygomatic bones.

沃特投影 顯示上頜骨、上頜竇及顴骨的前後位 X 綫片。

watt *n.* the *SI unit of power, equal to 1 joule per second. In electrical terms it is the energy expended per second when a current of 1 ampere flows between two points on a conductor between which there is a potential difference of 1 volt. 1 watt = 10^7 ergs per second. Symbol: W.

瓦特 功率的國際單位。相當於 1 焦耳／秒。電學術語中指 1 安培／秒的電流通過導體中電位差為 1 伏的兩點所耗的電能。1 瓦特 = 10^7 爾格／秒。符號：W。

weal *n.* a transient swelling, confined to a small area of the skin, that is characteristic of *urticaria and occurs following *dermographism.

風塊 限於皮膚上一小區域內的暫時性隆起，為蕁麻疹之特徵，常繼皮膚畫痕現象之後出現。

weber *n.* the *SI unit of magnetic flux, equal to the flux linking a circuit of one turn that produces an e.m.f. of 1 volt when reduced uniformly to zero in 1 second. Symbol: Wb.

韋伯 磁通量的國際單位，等於電路中 1 個綫圈中 1 伏電動勢均勻減到零時產生的電磁通量。符號：Wb。

Weber-Christian disease *see* panniculitis.

韋-克氏病 參閱 panniculitis。

Weber's test a hearing test in which a vibrating tuning fork is placed at the midpoint of the forehead. A normal individual hears it equally in both ears, but if one ear is affected by conductive *deafness the sound appears louder in the affected ear.

韋貝爾試驗 聽力試驗，將振動的音叉放到額部中點，正常人兩耳聽到的聲響相同，但如其中一耳患傳導性耳聾，該耳聽到的聲響較大。

web space the soft tissue between the bases of the fingers and toes.

蛛網腔 指（趾）基底間的軟組織。

Wechsler scales standardized scales for the measurement of *intelligence quotient (IQ) in adults and children. They are administered by a chartered psychologist. *See* intelligence test.

韋克斯勒等級 標準化等級，用於衡量兒童與成人之智商。經特許的心理專家進行評估。參閱 intelligence test。

Wegener's granulomatosis an autoimmune disease predominantly affecting the nasal passages, lungs, and kidneys, characterized by *granuloma formation in addition to arteritis. Untreated the disease is usually fatal, but it can be controlled (sometimes for years) with steroids, cyclophosphamide, and azathioprine.

韋格納肉芽腫 一種自體免疫性疾病，主要侵犯鼻、肺及腎。特徵為動脈炎之外有肉芽腫形成。不予治療，此病常會致命，但此病可通過甾類化合物、環磷酰胺和硫唑嘌呤控制（有時長達數年）。

Weil-Felix reaction a diagnostic test for typhus. A sample of the patient's serum is tested for the presence of antibodies against the organism *Proteus vulgaris*.

韋-費氏反應 斑疹傷寒之診斷試驗。檢測這種病人血清中有無普通變形桿菌的抗體。雖然這種相對無害的桿菌不是引起

Although this relatively harmless organism is not the cause of typhus, it possesses certain antigens in common with the causative agent of the disease and can therefore be used instead of it in laboratory tests. Typhus is suspected if antibodies are found to be present.

斑疹傷寒的病原體，但它與致病菌有某種相同的抗原成分，故而在實驗室試驗中可用之代替。如發現抗體則可懷疑為斑疹傷寒。

Weil's disease *see* leptospirosis.

韋爾病　參閱 leptospirosis。

Welch's bacillus *see* Clostridium.

韋爾什桿菌　參閱 Clostridium。

wen *n. see* sebaceous cyst.

皮脂囊腫　參閱 sebaceous cyst。

Werdnig-Hoffmann disease a hereditary disorder – a severe form of *spinal muscular atrophy – in which the cells of the spinal cord begin to die between birth and the age of six months, causing a symmetrical muscle weakness in affected infants that starts proximally. Respiratory and facial muscles become affected. Children usually die by the age of 20 months from respiratory failure and there is no treatment. *Genetic counselling is required for parents of an affected child as each of their subsequent children has a one in four chance of being affected.

韋-霍氏病　一種遺傳性疾病，是脊髓性肌萎縮之嚴重型。其脊髓細胞在出生之後到六個月期間開始死亡，引起患兒對稱性肌肉無力。呼吸肌及面部肌肉亦會受侵犯。患兒常在 20 個月齡時死亡。此病無法治療。患兒父母需進行遺傳咨詢，因為他們以後所生的孩子有 1/4 的患病機率。

Wernicke's encephalopathy mental confusion or delirium occurring in combination with paralysis of the eye muscles, *nystagmus, and an unsteady gait. It is caused by a deficiency of vitamin B_1 (thiamin) and is most commonly seen in alcoholics and in patients with persistent vomiting. Treatment with thiamin relieves the symptoms.

韋尼克腦病　伴有眼肌麻痺、眼球震顫及步態不穩的精神錯亂或譫妄。係維生素 B_1（硫胺）缺乏之故，常見於酒精中毒者及持久性嘔吐病人。硫胺治療可緩解症狀。

Wertheim's hysterectomy a radical operation performed for cervical cancer, in which the uterus, Fallopian tubes,

韋特海姆子宮切除術　為治療子宮頸癌而作的根除性手術，手術時要切除子宮、輸卵管、

ovaries, upper vagina, broad ligaments, and regional lymph nodes are removed.

卵巢、上陰道、闊韌帶及局部淋巴結。

Western blot analysis a technique for the detection of specific proteins. After separation by *electrophoresis, the proteins are bound to radioactively labelled antibodies and identified by X-ray. *Compare* Northern blot analysis, Southern blot analysis.

蛋白質印跡分析 探查特異性蛋白的一項技術。電泳分離後，這些蛋白與放射性標誌的抗體結合並由 X 綫鑒定。與 Northern blot analysis, Southern blot analysis 對比。

wet-and-dry bulb hygrometer *see* hygrometer.

乾濕球濕度計 參閱 hygrometer。

Wharton's duct the secretory duct of the submandibular *salivary gland.

沃頓管，下頜下腺管 下頜下唾液腺之分泌管。

Wharton's jelly the mesoderm tissue of the umbilical cord, which becomes converted to a loose jelly-like *mesenchyme surrounding the umbilical blood vessels.

沃頓膠 臍帶中胚層組織，它轉變為圍繞臍血管的疏鬆、膠樣間質。

wheeze *n.* an abnormal high-pitched (sibilant) or low-pitched sound heard-either by the unaided human ear or through the stethoscope – mainly during expiration. Wheezes occur as a result of narrowing of the airways, such as results from *bronchospasm or increased secretion and retention of sputum; they are commonly heard in patients with asthma or chronic bronchitis.

哮鳴 異常的高音（嘶音的）或低音，可由未加助聽器的人耳或通過聽診器聽到——主要在呼氣時。哮鳴係氣道狹窄之故，如因支氣管痙攣，或因痰分泌及滯留增多所致；常見於哮喘或慢性支氣管炎病人。

whiplash injury damage to the ligaments, vertebrae, spinal cord, or nerve roots in the neck region, caused by sudden jerking back of the head and neck. In its most severe form (a *cervical fracture*), death or permanent paralysis (*quadriplegia or *paraplegia) may result. Sudden deceleration in a motor accident is the commonest cause. Immobilization using a special collar is the principal treatment.

頭部衝擊傷 韌帶、脊柱、脊髓及頸部神經根損傷，由於頭和頸部被猛烈後推引起。其中最嚴重者（頸骨折）可致死或永久性癱瘓（四肢癱瘓或截癱）。汽車事故中突然減速是其最常見的原因。用特殊硬領固定是其主要治療方法。

Whipple's disease a rare disease, occurring only in males, in which absorption of digested food in the intestine is reduced. As well as symptoms and signs of *malabsorption there is usually skin pigmentation and arthritis. Diagnosis is made by *jejunal biopsy; microorganisms have been found in the mucosa, and the disease usually responds to prolonged antibiotic treatment.

惠普爾病　一種罕見病，僅見於男性，腸道內消化食物的吸收減退。除營養不良的症狀和體徵外，通常還有皮膚色素沉着及關節炎。借助空腸活組織檢查來診斷，檢查時可發現黏膜中存在微生物，長期抗生素治療對該病有效。

Whipple's operation *see* pancreatectomy.

惠普爾手術　參閱 pancreatectomy。

Whipple's triad a combination of three clinical features that indicate the presence of an *insulinoma; (1) attacks of fainting, dizziness, and sweating on fasting; (2) severe hypoglycaemia present during the attacks; (3) relief from the attacks achieved by administering glucose.

惠普爾三聯徵　提示患有胰島瘤的三個同時存在的臨床特徵：(1) 空腹時暈厥、頭昏、出汗；(2) 在發病的過程中存在嚴重低血糖；(3) 施用葡萄糖可緩解發作。

whipworm *n.* a small parasitic whiplike nematode worm, *Trichuris trichiura* (*Trichocephalus dispar*), that lives in the large intestine. Eggs are passed out of the body with the faeces and human infection (*see* trichuriasis) results from the consumption of water of food contaminated with faecal material. The eggs hatch in the small intestine but mature worms migrate to the large intestine.

鞭蟲　小的寄生性鞭毛樣綫蟲，即毛首鞭蟲，生活在大腸內。蟲卵通過糞便排出體外，人通過食入被糞便污染的水及食物而感染（參閱 trichuriasis）。蟲卵在小腸孵化，但成蟲移行至大腸。

white blood cell *see* leucocyte.

白細胞　參閱 leucocyte。

white leg *see* thrombophlebitis.

股白腫　參閱 thrombophlebitis。

white matter nerve tissue of the central nervous system that is paler in colour than the associated *grey matter because it contains more nerve fibres and thus larger amounts of the insulating material

白質　中樞神經系統的神經組織，其顏色較相鄰灰質白些，因它含有較多的神經纖維及較大量的隔離物質髓鞘。在大腦中，白質位於大腦皮層灰質層

*myelin. In the brain the white matter lies within the grey layer of cerebral cortex; in the spinal cord it is between the arms of the X-shaped central core of grey matter.

內;在脊髓裏,它則位於 X 形中央灰質柱之間。

whitlow *n. see* paronychia.

瘭疽 參閱 paronychia。

WHO *see* World Health Organization.

世界衛生組織 參閱 World Health Organization。

whoop *n.* a noisy convulsive drawing in of the breath following the spasmodic coughing attack characteristic of *whooping cough.

哮吼 百日咳典型的痙攣性咳嗽發作後的聲音很大的痙攣性吸氣。

whooping cough an acute infectious disease, primarily affecting children, due to infection of the mucous membranes lining the air passages by the bacterium *Bordetella pertussis*. After an incubation period of 1–2 weeks catarrh, mild fever, coughing, and loss of appetite gradually develop and persist for 1–2 weeks. The cough becomes paroxysmal: series of short coughs are followed by involuntary drawing in of the breath, which produces the whooping sound. Bleeding from the nose and mouth and vomiting often occur after a paroxysm. This stage lasts about two weeks and the child is infectious throughout. Over the following 2–3 weeks symptoms slowly decline but the cough may persist for many weeks. Whooping cough is seldom serious but it may occasionally be followed by pneumonia. Immunization reduces the incidence and severity of the disease: the vaccine is usually given in a combined form (*see* DPT vaccine). An attack usually also confers immunity. Medical name: **pertussis**.

百日咳 急性傳染病,主要侵犯兒童,係呼吸道內黏膜受百日咳嗜血桿菌感染之故。 1~2 周潛伏期後逐漸發生卡他、低熱、咳嗽、食慾喪失,並持續 1~2 周。繼而咳嗽變為發作性:一陣短促咳嗽後,發生伴有哮吼聲的不自主吸氣。陣咳發作後常發生鼻腔出血及嘔吐,該期持續 2~3 周,此期內患兒一直有傳染性。 2~3 周後症狀漸輕,但咳嗽可持續多周。百日咳一般不嚴重,但偶爾可伴發肺炎。免疫接種可降低疾病的發病率及嚴重性。常用聯合疫苗接種(參閱 DPT vaccine)。一次患病往往可獲得免疫。醫學用語:百日咳。

Widal reaction an *agglutination test for the presence of antibodies against the

魏達反應 一種檢驗抗傷寒沙門菌抗體的凝集試驗。是診斷

Salmonella organisms that cause typhoid fever. It is thus a method of diagnosing the presence of the disease in a patient and also a means of identifying the organisms in infected material.

傷寒病及鑒定感染物質中細菌種類的方法。

Wilms' tumour *see* nephroblastoma.

維爾姆斯瘤　參閱 nephroblastoma。

Wilson's disease an inborn defect of copper metabolism in which there is a deficiency of *caeruloplasmin (which normally forms a nontoxic complex with copper). The free copper may be deposited in the liver, causing jaundice and cirrhosis, or in the brain, causing mental retardation and symptoms resembling *parkinsonism. There is a characteristic brown ring in the cornea (the *Kayser-Fleischer ring*). If the excess copper is removed from the body by regular treatment with *penicillamine both mental and physical development may be normal. Medical name: **hepato-lenticular degeneration**.

威爾遜病　先天性銅代謝障礙，本病中銅藍蛋白（正常時與銅形成無毒性絡合物）缺乏。游離的銅可以在肝臟沉積，引起黃疸及肝硬化；或沉積在腦，引起智力低下和酷似帕金森病的症狀。在角膜有一特徵性的褐色環（凱 - 弗氏環）。若用青黴胺定期治療能使過多的銅排出體外，智力和體力的發育都可正常。醫學用語：肝豆狀核變性。

windigo *n.* a delusion of having been transformed into a *windigo*, a mythical monster that eats human flesh. It is often quoted as an example of a syndrome confined to one culture (that of some North American Indian tribes, such as the Cree).

溫第高妄想　一種變成溫第高的妄想，溫第高為神話中吃人肉的怪物。常用於描述僅有在某種文化中（北美印第安部落文化，如克里族）出現的綜合徵。

windpipe *n. see* trachea.

氣管　參閱 trachea。

wisdom tooth the third *molar tooth on each side of either jaw, which erupts normally around the age of 20.

智齒　上下頜兩側的第三個磨牙，正常在 20 歲左右萌出。

witch hazel (hamamelis) a preparation made from the leaves and bark of the tree *Hamamelis virginiana*, used as an *astringent, especially for the treatment of sprains and bruises.

北美金縷梅　一種製劑，用北美金縷梅的葉和樹皮製成，用作收斂劑，特別是用作治療扭傷和青腫。

withdrawal *n.* **1.** (in psychology) the removal of one's interest from one's surroundings. *Thought withdrawal* is the experience of one's thoughts being removed from one's head, which is characteristic of *schizophrenia. **2.** *see* coitus interruptus.

(1) 退縮 （心理學）某人對周圍環境失去興趣。思想退縮（被奪）是指某人感到思想從其頭腦中被去掉的體驗，是精神分裂症的一個特徵。**(2) 中斷性交** 參閱 coitus interruptus。

withdrawal symptoms *see* dependence.

戒斷綜合徵 參閱 dependence。

Wohlfahrtia *n.* a genus of non-bloodsucking flies. Females of the species *W. magnifica* and *W. vigil* deposit their parasitic maggots in wounds and the openings of the body. This causes *myiasis, particularly in children.

肉蠅屬 一屬非吸血性蠅。雌性壯麗肉蠅及獨居肉蠅把牠們產生的蛆堆積於傷口及人體孔口處，引起蠅蛆病，尤見於兒童。

Wolffian body *see* mesonephros.

沃爾夫小體 參閱 mesonephros。

Wolffian duct the mesonephric duct (*see* mesonephros).

沃爾夫管 中腎管（參閱 mesonephros）。

Wolff-Parkinson-White syndrome a congenital abnormality of heart rhythm caused by the presence of an accessory conduction pathway between the atria and ventricles (*see* atrioventricular bundle). It results in premature excitation of one ventricle and is characterized by an abnormal wave (*delta wave*) at the start of the *QRS complex on the electrocardiogram.

沃-帕-懷氏綜合徵 先天性心臟節律異常，因房室間存在附屬傳導通路（參閱 atrioventricular bundle）引起。它起因於心預激，在心電圖上顯示 QRS 複合波開始時存在非正常波的特徵。

womb *n.* *see* uterus.

子宮 參閱 uterus。

woolsorter's disease *see* anthrax.

羊毛分揀工病 參閱 anthrax。

word blindness *see* alexia.

失讀症 參閱 alexia。

World Health Organization (WHO) an international organization, membership of which is open to every country, with

世界衛生組織 一國際組織，各國都可成為其會員，根據財力收取會費，該組織討論健康

subscription according to means; health issues are discussed and policies evolved mainly through working groups, including acknowledged authorities, and published reports. Staff are seconded by invitation to advise on self-help to solve problems (especially infectious disease control). WHO handles information on the internationally *notifiable diseases, publishes the *International Classification of Diseases, and awards fellowships to enable health staff from poorer countries to obtain further training.

問題，通過工作小組，即公認的權威機構，和發布的報告來制訂政策。其工作人員應邀請提供自立解決問題的咨詢（尤其是傳染性疾病控制方面）。該組織處理國際法定傳染病信息，出版《國際疾病分類》並向較貧窮國家的衛生工作人員提供深造的獎學金。

worm *n.* any member of several groups of soft-bodied legless animals, including flatworms, nematode worms, earthworms, and leeches, that were formerly thought to be closely related and classified as a single group – Vermes.

蠕蟲 幾種無腿軟體動物，包括扁蟲、綫蟲、蚯蚓及水蛭。以前這些動物被認為是密切相關的，並被分類為一個單獨的組——蠕蟲類。

wormian bone one of a number of small bones that occur in the cranial sutures.

縫間骨 顱骨骨縫處的眾多小骨之一。

wound *n.* a break in the structure of an organ or tissue caused by an external agent. Bruises, grazes, tears, cuts, punctures, and burns are all examples of wounds.

創傷 外界因素造成的某一器官或組織結構的破壞。挫傷、擦傷、撕裂傷、刀割傷、刺傷及燒傷都為創傷的例子。

wrist *n.* **1.** the joint between the forearm and hand. It consists of the proximal bones of the *carpus, which articulate with the radius and ulna. **2.** the whole region of the wrist joint, including the carpus and lower parts of the radius and ulna.

(1) 腕關節 前臂與手之間的關節。由與近端腕骨構成關節的橈骨和尺骨組成。**(2) 腕部** 腕關節的全部區域，包括腕部以及橈骨和尺骨的下部。

wrist drop paralysis of the muscles that raise the wrist, which is caused by damage to the *radial nerve. This may result from compression of the nerve against the humerus in the upper arm or from selective damage to the nerve, which is a feature of *lead poisoning.

腕下垂 由橈神經受損造成的抬腕肌麻痹。可繫上臂肱骨處神經受壓迫或選擇性損害神經之故。後者為鉛中毒的特徵。

wryneck *n. see* torticollis.

斜頸　參閱 torticollis。

Wuchereria *n.* a genus of white thread-like parasitic worms (*see* filaria) that live in the lymphatic vessels. *W. bancrofti* is a tropical and subtropical species that causes *elephantiasis, lymphangitis, and chyluria. The immature forms concentrate in the lungs during the day. At night they become more numerous in the blood vessels of the skin, from which they are taken up by blood-sucking mosquitoes, acting as carriers of the diseases they cause.

吳策綫蟲屬　一屬生活在淋巴管內的白色綫樣寄生蟲（參閱 filaria）。班氏吳策綫蟲為一熱帶或亞熱帶種，引發象皮病、淋巴管炎與乳糜尿。白天未成熟幼蟲集中於肺部，夜間出現於皮膚血管中，如這時被吸血蚊子吸走，則成為傳播本病的媒介。

X

xamoterol *n.* a drug that stimulates beta receptors in the heart (*see* sympathomimetic) and used in the treatment of long-term mild heart failure. It is administered by mouth. Possible side-effects include headache, dizziness, muscle cramps, palpitations, and skin rashes. Trade name: **Corwin**.

扎莫特羅　一種刺激心臟 β 受體藥物（參閱 sympathomimetic），用於治療長期輕型心力衰竭。口服。副作用包括頭痛、頭昏、肌肉痙攣、心悸及皮疹。商品名：Corwin。

xanthaemia (carotenaemia) *n.* the presence in the blood of the yellow pigment *carotene, from excessive intake of carrots, tomatoes, or other vegetables containing the pigment.

胡蘿蔔素血症　因過多攝入胡蘿蔔、西紅柿及其他含胡蘿蔔素的蔬菜致使血液中存在黃色色素——胡蘿蔔素。

xanthelasma *n.* yellow *plaques occurring symmetrically around the eyelids. In elderly people it is quite common and of no more than cosmetic importance, but in some cases it may be a manifestation of disorders of fat metabolism (hyperlipidaemia).

黃斑瘤　眼周皮膚出現對稱性黃斑。常見於老年人，僅為容貌問題，但在有些病人中，為脂肪代謝障礙的表現（高脂血症）。

xanthine *n.* a nitrogenous breakdown product of the purines adenosine and guanine. Xanthine is an intermediate

黃嘌呤　腺嘌呤及鳥嘌呤的氮分解物。係核酸分解為尿酸的中間產物。

product of the breakdown of nucleic acids to uric acid.

xanthinuria *n.* excess of the purine derivative *xanthine in the urine, usually the result of an inborn defect of metabolism. It is both rare and symptomless.

xantho- *prefix denoting* yellow colour.

xanthochromia *n.* yellow discoloration, such as may affect the skin (for example, in jaundice) or the cerebrospinal fluid (when it contains the breakdown products of haemoglobin from red blood cells that have entered it).

xanthoma *n.* (*pl.* **xanthomata**) a yellowish skin lesion associated with any of various disorders of lipid metabolism. There are several types of xanthomata. *Tuberous xanthomata* are found on the knees and elbows; *tendon xanthomata* involve the extensor tendons of the hands and feet and the Achilles tendon. Crops of small yellow papules at any site are known as *eruptive xanthomata*, while larger flat lesions are called *plane xanthomata*.

xanthomatosis *n.* the presence of multiple xanthomata in the skin. *See* xanthoma.

xanthophyll *n.* a yellow pigment found in green leaves. An example of a xanthophyll is *lutein*.

xanthopsia *n.* yellow vision: the condition in which all objects appear to have a yellowish tinge. It is sometimes experienced in digitalis poisoning.

X chromosome the sex chromosome present in both sexes. Women have two

黃嘌呤尿 尿內有過多由嘌呤衍生的黃嘌呤，常為先天性代謝障礙的結果。該病罕見發生且無症狀出現。

〔前綴〕**黃色**

黃變 變成黃色，例如使皮膚（例如黃疸時）或腦脊液變黃（當腦脊液中有紅細胞的血紅蛋白分解產物時）。

黃瘤 發黃的皮膚損傷，與各種脂類代謝障礙有關。該症有多種類型。結節狀黃瘤見於膝肘；腱黃瘤涉及手足的伸肌腱及艾基利斯跟腱。跟腱任何部位出現的小黃丘疹均被稱為出疹性黃瘤，而大的扁平損害則叫作扁平黃瘤。

黃瘤病 皮膚中存在多發性黃瘤。參閱 xanthoma。

胡蘿蔔醇 綠葉中存在的黃色色素。例如葉黃素。

黃視症 黃色視覺。視任何物體都呈黃顏色色調的病態。在洋地黃中毒時，有時可體驗到。

X 染色體 兩性中都存在的性染色體。女性有兩個 X 染色

X chromosomes and men one. Genes for some important genetic disorders, including *haemophilia, are carried on the X chromosomes; these genes are described as *sex-linked. *Compare* Y chromosome.

體，男性只有一個。某些重要的遺傳病變基因，如血友病，位於其上。這些基因稱為性連鎖基因。與 Y chromosome 對比。

xeno- *prefix denoting* different; foreign; alien.

〔前綴〕不同的，外來的，相異的

xenodiagnosis *n.* a procedure for diagnosing infections transmitted by insect carriers. Uninfected insects of the species known to carry the disease in question are allowed to suck the blood of a patient suspected of having the disease. A positive diagnosis is made if the disease parasites appear in the insects. This method has proved invaluable for diagnosing Chagas' disease, using reduviid bugs (the carriers), since the parasites are not always easily detected in blood smears.

動物接種診斷　診斷由昆蟲載體傳播的傳染病之方法。用已知能傳播該病但未感染的昆蟲去刺吸懷疑有此病的患者血液。若該病寄生蟲出現在昆蟲體內，則為陽性診斷。診斷恰加斯病時用獵蝽（病媒），此方法已被證明十分有用，因為其寄生蟲很難使用血塗片找到。

xenogeneic *adj,* describing grafted tissue derived from a donor of a different species.

異種基因的　描述取自不同種供體的移植組織。

xenograft *n. see* heterograft.

異種移植物　參閱 heterograft。

xenophobia *n.* excessive fear of strangers and foreigners. *See* phobia.

生客恐怖　過分害怕生人或外國人。參閱 phobia。

Xenopsylla *n.* a genus of tropical and subtropical fleas, with some 40 species. The rat flea, *X. cheopis*, occasionally attacks man and can transmit plague from an infected rat population; it also transmits murine typhus and two tapeworms, *Hymenolepis nana* and *H. diminuta*.

客蚤屬　一屬熱帶、亞熱帶蚤，有 40 餘種。鼠蚤，即印鼠客蚤，偶爾侵襲人類，並可將鼠疫從感染的鼠羣中傳染給人；它也可以傳播鼠型斑疹傷寒和兩種縧蟲：短膜殼縧蟲及縮小膜殼縧蟲。

xero- *prefix denoting* a dry condition.

〔前綴〕乾燥

xeroderma *n.* a mild form of the hereditary disorder *ichthyosis, in which the skin develops slight dryness and forms branlike scales. It is common in the elderly.

乾皮病 輕型遺傳性鱗癬病變，患者皮膚輕度乾燥並有糠皮樣鱗屑形成。

xerophthalmia *n.* a progressive nutritional disease of the eye due to deficiency of vitamin A. The cornea and conjunctiva become dry, thickened, and wrinkled. This may progress to *keratomalacia and eventual blindness.

乾眼病 維生素 A 缺乏所致的進行性營養眼病。角膜及結膜變得乾燥、增厚及起皺，可發展成角膜軟化及最後失明。

xeroradiography *n.* X-ray imaging produced on photoconductive paper. It is usually used for screening the breast for cancer (*xeromammography*).

乾板 X 綫照相術 X 綫成像於光照傳導性紙上。常用於檢查乳腺癌（乳房乾板 X 綫照相術）。

xerosis *n.* abnormal dryness of the conjunctiva, the skin, or the mucous membranes. Xerosis affecting the conjunctiva is due not to decreased production of tears but to changes in the membrane itself, which becomes thickened and grey in the area exposed when the eyelids are open.

乾燥病 眼結膜、皮膚或黏膜異常乾燥。累及眼結膜的乾燥病不是因為眼淚分泌減少，而是結膜本身改變，在眼瞼睜開時的暴露區結膜變厚和變灰。

xerostomia *n. see* dry mouth. *Compare* ptyalism.

口腔乾燥 參閱 dry mouth。與 ptyalism 對比。

xiphi- (xipho-) *prefix denoting* the xiphoid process of the sternum. Example: *xiphocostal* (relating to the xiphoid process and ribs).

〔前綴〕劍 胸骨劍突，如劍突肋骨的（有關劍突及肋骨的）。

xiphisternum *see* xiphoid process.

劍突 參閱 xiphoid process。

xiphoid process (xiphoid cartilage) the lowermost section of the breastbone (*see* sternum): a flat pointed cartilage that gradually ossifies until it is completely replaced by bone, a process not completed until after middle age. It does not articulate with any ribs. Also called: **ensiform process** *or* **cartilage**, **xiphisternum**.

劍突（劍突軟骨） 胸骨最下端處的一塊扁平尖形骨（參閱 sternum）：此軟骨逐漸骨化直至完全被骨代替。這一過程在中年後完成。劍突不與任何肋骨形成關節。亦稱劍形軟骨或軟骨劍突。

X-rays *n.* electromagnetic radiation of extremely short wavelength (beyond the ultraviolet), with great penetrating powers in matter opaque to light. X-rays are produced when high-energy beams of electrons strike matter. They are used in diagnosis in the techniques of *radiography and also in *radiotherapy. Great care is needed to avoid unnecessary exposure, because the radiation is harmful to all living things. *See* radiation sickness.

X 綫 波長特別短（短於紫外綫）的電磁波射綫，有穿過不透光綫物體的強穿透力。高能電子束撞擊物質時發出 X 綫，用於放射診斷與某種類型的放射治療。由於大劑量照射對所有生物均有害，故需注意避免不必要的照射。參閱 radiation sickness。

xylene (dimethylbenzene) *n.* a liquid used for increasing the transparency of tissues prepared for microscopic examination after dehydration. *See* clearing.

二甲苯 在脱水後製備顯微檢查組織標本時，用以增加透明度的液體。參閱 clearing。

xylometazoline *n.* a drug that constricts blood vessels (*see* vasoconstrictor). It is rapidly acting and long lasting and is applied topically as a nasal decongestant in the relief of the common cold and sinusitis. Toxic effects are rare. Trade name: **Otrivine**.

賽洛唑啉 血管收縮藥（參閱 vasoconstrictor）。作用快且持續時間長，作為鼻的減充血劑，用於局部以減輕感冒及鼻竇炎症狀。毒性反應少見。商品名：Otrivine。

xylose *n.* a pentose sugar (i.e. one with five carbon atoms) that is involved in carbohydrate interconversions within cells. It is used as a diagnostic aid for intestinal function.

木糖 戊糖（含五個碳原子）。參與細胞內碳水化合物互變。用於腸功能的輔助診斷。

Y

YAG laser yttrium–aluminium–garnet laser: a type of *laser used for cutting tissue, for example in lens *capsulotomy or *iridotomy.

釔-鋁-石榴石激光 用於切割組織的一種激光，例如：晶狀體囊切除術及虹膜切開術中。

yawning *n.* a reflex action in which the mouth is opened wide and air is drawn

呵欠 張大嘴使空氣吸入肺，然後再慢慢呼出的一種反射活

into the lungs then slowly released. It is a result of drowsiness, fatigue, or boredom.

yaws (pian, framboesia) *n.* a tropical infectious disease caused by the presence of the spirochaete *Treponema pertenue* in the skin and its underlying tissues. Yaws occurs chiefly in conditions of poor hygiene. It is transmitted by direct contact with infected persons and their clothing and possibly also by flies of the genus *Hippelates*. The spirochaetes enter through abrasions on the skin. Initial symptoms include fever, pains, and itching, followed by the appearance of small tumours, each covered by a yellow crust of dried serum, on the hands, face, legs, and feet. These tumours may deteriorate into deep ulcers. The final stage of yaws, which may appear after an interval of several years, involves destructive and deforming lesions of the skin, bones, and periosteum (*see also* gangosa, goundou). Yaws, which commonly affects children, is prevalent in hot humid lowlands of equatorial Africa, tropical America, the Far East, and the West Indies. It responds well to treatment with *penicillin and other antibiotics.

Y chromosome a sex chromosome that is present in men but not in women; it is believed to carry the genes for maleness. *Compare* X chromosome.

yeast *n.* any of a group of fungi in which the body (mycelium) consists of individual cells, which may occur singly, in groups of two or three, or in chains. Yeasts reproduce by budding and by the formation of sexual spores (in the case of the perfect yeasts) or asexual spores (in the case of the imperfect yeasts). The

動。是瞌睡、疲勞、厭煩的結果。

雅司病 一種熱帶傳染病,由皮膚及皮下組織存在細弱密螺旋體所致。其發生主要因為衛生條件差,可通過接觸患者或其衣服而感染,也可通過潛蠅屬的蒼蠅傳播,螺旋體通過皮膚破損處進入人體。開始症狀為發燒、疼痛及瘙癢,繼而在手、臉、腿及腳出現小腫塊,每個腫塊都覆蓋有乾血清黃痂。腫塊可惡化變成深的潰瘍。其最後階段可間隔數年後才出現,有皮膚、骨、骨膜的破壞及變形病變(參閱gangosa,goundou)。該病常侵襲兒童,流行於赤道非洲國家、美洲熱帶地區、遠東及印度羣島潮濕炎熱的低地。用青黴素及其他抗生素治療效果良好。

Y 染色體 只存在於男性而不存在於女性的性染色體,據認為該染色體攜有男性基因。與X chromosome 對比。

酵母 一組真菌中的任何一種,其體(菌絲體)為單個細胞,單獨、兩、三成羣或成鏈狀出現。酵母菌以無性芽生和有性孢子形成的方式進行繁殖。其中包括麵包師酵母(酵母屬),它參與碳水化合物發酵,產生酒精和二氧化碳,在

group includes baker's yeast (*Saccharomyces*), which ferments carbohydrates to produce alcohol and carbon dioxide and is important in brewing and breadmaking. Some yeasts are a commercial source of proteins and of vitamins of the B complex. Yeasts that cause disease in man include *Candida, *Cryptococcus, and *Pityrosporum.

釀造飲料和製作麵包中很重要。某些酵母還是蛋白質和 B 族維生素的商品原料。在人體內致病的酵母有念珠菌屬、隱球菌屬及瓶形酵母屬。

yellow fever an infectious disease, caused by an *arbovirus, occurring in tropical Africa and the northern regions of South America. It is transmitted by mosquitoes, principally *Aëdes aegypti*. The virus causes degeneration of the tissues of the liver and kidneys. Symptoms, depending on severity of infection, include chill, headache, pains in the back and limbs, fever, vomiting, constipation, a reduced flow of urine (which contains high levels of albumin), and *jaundice. The more serious cases may prove fatal, but recovery from a first attack confers subsequent immunity. The disease is treated by fluid replacement and can be prevented by vaccination.

黃熱病　由蟲媒病毒引起的傳染病，發生於熱帶非洲及南美洲北部。由蚊子傳播，尤其是埃及伊蚊。其病毒引起肝、腎組織變性，症狀取決於感染嚴重程度，有寒戰、頭痛、背部和肢體痛、發燒、嘔吐、便秘、尿量減少（含較多白蛋白）及黃疸。病情嚴重者可致命，但第一次得病後恢復可獲得免疫。此病可通過液體置換治療並用接種預防。

yellow spot *see* macula (lutea).

黃斑　參閱 macula (lutea)。

Yersinia *n.* a genus of aerobic or facultatively anaerobic Gram-negative bacteria that are parasites of animals and man. The species *Y. pestis* causes bubonic *plague, and *Y. enterocolitica* causes intestinal infections.

耶爾森菌屬　一種寄生於人和動物中的需氧或厭氧革蘭氏陽性菌。鼠疫耶爾森菌可引起腺鼠疫，而小腸結腸炎耶爾森菌可引起腸炎。

yohimbine *n.* an alkaloid with *sympatholytic effects: it lowers blood pressure and controls arousal and anxiety and has been used to treat both physical and psychogenic impotence.

育亨賓寧鹼　一種具有抗交感神經作用的鹼：降低血壓、控制喚醒及焦慮狀態，現用於治療身體及精神性陽痿。

yolk (deutoplasm) *n.* a substance, rich in protein and fat, that is laid down

卵黃（滋養質）　富有蛋白及脂肪的物質。作為胚胎營養物

within the egg cell as nourishment for the embryo. It is absent (or nearly so) from the eggs of mammals (including man) whose embryos absorb nutrients from their mother.

質而存在於卵細胞中。哺乳動物（包括人）的卵中沒有（或幾乎沒有）卵黃，這些動物胚胎從母體中吸收營養物質。

yolk sac (vitelline sac) the membranous sac, composed of mesoderm lined with endoderm, that lies ventral to the embryo. Its initially wide communication with the future gut is later reduced to a narrow duct passing through the *umbilicus. It probably assists in transporting nutrients to the early embryo and is one of the first sites where blood cells are formed.

卵黃囊　一膜狀囊，由中胚層組成，內襯內胚層，位於胚盤腹側。早期與原腸廣泛相通，以後變成一狹窄的通過臍的管道。該物質可能有助於向早期胚胎運輸營養，也是最早生成血細胞的部位。

yttrium-90 *n.* an artificial radioactive isotope of the element yttrium, used in *radiotherapy. Yttrium-90, which emits beta rays, can be used in the form of 1 mm spheres scattered around a tumour or injected directly into a tumour in the form of a solution.

[90]釔　釔元素的人工放射性同位素，用於放療。[90]釔發射出 β 射綫，可採用直徑 1 mm 的球圍繞腫瘤散射形式，或以溶液形式直接注入腫瘤。

Z

zalcitabine *n.* a drug, similar to *didanosine, that is used in attempts to prolong the lives of AIDS patients. It is administered by mouth. Possible side-effects include reversible nerve damage, ulceration of the gullet, skin rashes, severe pancreatitis, nausea, vomiting, and headache.

扎西他賓　一種藥物，與地丹諾辛相似，用於試圖延長艾滋病患者的生命。口服，副作用可包括可逆神經損害、咽潰瘍、皮疹、嚴重胰腺炎、惡心、嘔吐及頭痛。

Zantac *n. see* ranitidine.

甲胺呋硫　參閱 ranitidine。

zein *n.* a protein found in maize.

玉米蛋白　玉米中發現的蛋白。

zidovudine *n.* an antiviral drug used in the treatment of AIDS and of AIDS-related complex. It is not approved for HIV-positive patients who are asymptomatic. The drug slows the growth of HIV infection in the body, but is not curative. It is administered by mouth and intravenously; the most common side-effects are nausea, headache, and insomnia, and it may damage the blood-forming tissues of the bone marrow. Trade name: **Retrovir.**

齊多夫定 抗病毒藥，用於治療艾滋病及其併發症。該藥尚未批准對 HIV 陽性，而無症狀出現的患者使用。該藥減緩 HIV 在體內的感染，但並不能治愈。口服或靜脈注射，最常見副作用有惡心、頭痛和失眠，並可損傷骨髓造血組織。商品名：Retrovir。

zinc oxide a mild *astringent used in various skin conditions, usually mixed with other substances. It is applied as a cream, ointment, dusting powder, or as a paste, sometimes in the form of an impregnated bandage.

氧化鋅 溫和收斂劑，用於各種皮膚病，常與其他物質合用。製成乳膏、粉劑或糊劑使用，有時也用於加固繃帶。

zinc sulphate a preparation used in the treatment of proven zinc deficiency. It is administered by mouth. Trade names: **Solvazinc, Z Span Spansule.**

硫酸鋅 用於治療已證實的鋅缺乏症。口服。商品名：Solvazinc，Z Span Spansule。

zinc undecenoate (zinc undecylenate) an antifungal agent with uses similar to those of *undecenoic acid.

十一烯酸鋅 抗真菌藥劑，其作用與十一烯酸相似。

Zollinger-Ellison syndrome a rare disorder in which there is excessive secretion of gastric juice due to high levels of circulating *gastrin, which is produced by a pancreatic tumour (*see* gastrinoma) or an enlarged pancreas. The high levels of stomach acid cause diarrhoea and peptic ulcers, which may be multiple, in unusual sites (e.g. jejunum), or which may quickly recur after *vagotomy or partial *gastrectomy. Treatment with a histamine-blocking drug, by removal of the tumour (if benign), or by total gastrectomy is usually effective.

佐-埃氏綜合徵 一種罕見疾病，由於胰腺腫瘤（參閱 gastrinoma）或胰腺增生使血循環中胃泌素的含量很高而造成胃液分泌過多。高胃酸可引起腹瀉和消化性潰瘍，呈多發性，並可發生在罕發部位（如空腸），或在迷走神經切斷及部分胃切除術後很快復發。使用組胺阻滯劑，切除腫瘤（如為良性）或全胃切除治療往往有效。

zona pellucida the thick membrane that develops around the mammalian oocyte within the ovarian follicle. It is penetrated by at least one spermatozoon at fertilization and persists around the *blastocyst until it reaches the uterus. *See* ovum.

zonula *n. see* zonule.

zonule (zonula) *n.* (in anatomy) a small band or zone; for example the *zonule of Zinn* (*zonula ciliaris*) is the suspensory ligament of the eye. **–zonular** *adj.*

zonulolysis *n.* dissolution of the suspensory ligament of the lens of the eye (the *zonule of Zinn*) by means of an enzyme solution injected behind the iris, which facilitates removal of the lens in cases of cataract. This technique is not used for modern cataract surgery.

zoo- *prefix denoting* animals.

zoonosis *n.* an infectious disease of animals that can be transmitted to man. *See* anthrax, brucellosis, cat-scratch fever, cowpox, glanders, Q fever, Rift Valley fever, rabies, rat-bite fever, toxoplasmosis, tularaemia, typhus.

zoophilism *n.* sexual attraction to animals, which may be manifest in stroking and fondling animals or in sexual intercourse (*bestiality*). **–zoophilic** *adj.*

zoophobia *n.* excessively strong fear of animals. *See* phobia.

zoopsia *n.* visual hallucinations of animals. These can occur in any condition causing hallucinations but are most typical of *delirium tremens.

透明帶　哺乳動物卵泡中圍繞卵細胞生長的一層厚膜。受精時至少可被一個精子穿透，在受精卵抵達子宮前一直存在於胚泡周圍。參閱 ovum。

小帶　參閱 zonule。

小帶　（解剖學）小帶狀物或條形物，例如睫狀小帶是眼球中的懸韌帶。

睫狀小帶鬆解法　在虹膜後注入一種酶溶液，鬆解眼晶狀體的懸韌帶（睫狀小帶）以便在治療白內障時切除晶狀體。現代外科治療白內障不使用此法。

〔前綴〕動物

動物源性疾病　可傳播給人的動物傳染病。參閱 anthrax，brucellosis，cat-scratch fever，cowpox，glanders，Q fever，Rift Valley fever，rabies，rat-bite fever，toxoplasmosis，tularaemia，typhus。

嗜獸癖　對動物發生的性戀，可表現為愛撫動物或與之性交（獸姦）。

動物恐怖　對動物過分強烈的恐懼。參閱 phobia。

動物幻視　幻視中出現動物。可發生在任何幻覺時，但主要見於震顫性譫妄。

zwitterion *n.* an ion that bears a positive and a negative charge. Amino acids can yield zwitterions.

兩性離子　一個既有正電荷又有負電荷的離子。氨基酸便可產生這種離子。

zygoma *n. see* zygomatic arch, zygomatic bone.

顴骨　參閱 zygomatic arch，zygomatic bone。

zygomatic arch (zygoma) the horizontal arch of bone on either side of the face, just below the eyes, formed by connected processes of the zygomatic and temporal bones. *See* skull.

顴弓　位於兩面頰、眼正下方的水平位骨弓，由顴骨及顬骨的突起連接而成。參閱 skull。

zygomatic bone (zygoma, malar bone) either of a pair of bones that form the prominent part of the cheeks and contribute to the orbits. *See* skull.

顴骨　構成面頰突出部分的一對骨之一，也是眼眶的一部分。參閱 skull。

zygote *n.* the fertilized ovum before *cleavage begins. It contains both male and female pronuclei.

合子　卵裂開始前的受精卵。含有男性及女性的原核。

zygotene *n.* the second stage of the first prophase of *meiosis, in which the homologous chromosomes form pairs (bivalents).

偶綫　減數分裂第一期的第二階段，在此期同源染色體形成配對（二價體）。

zym- (zymo-) *prefix denoting* **1.** an enzyme. **2.** fermentation.

〔前綴〕 **(1)** 酶　**(2)** 發酵

zymogen *n. see* proenzyme.

酶原　參閱 proenzyme。

zymology *n.* the science of the study of yeasts and fermentation.

酶學　對酵母及發酵進行研究的科學。

zymolysis *n.* the process of *fermentation or digestion by an enzyme.

酶解作用　酶促發酵或消化過程。

zymosis *n.* **1.** the process of *fermentation, brought about by yeast organisms. **2.** the changes in the body that occur in certain infectious diseases, once thought to be the result of a process similar to fermentation. **–zymotic** *adj.*

(1) 發酵　由酵母菌引起的發酵過程。　**(2)** 發酵病　過去認為在患傳染病時體內出現的一種類似發酵過程的變化。

zymotic disease an old name for a contagious disease, which was formerly thought to develop within the body following infection in a process similar to the fermentation and growth of yeast.

發酵病 傳染病的舊名，以前認為在感染後，傳染病在體內的發展與發酵及酵母生長過程相類似。

Appendix 附錄

Table 1. Base and Supplementary SI Units
表 1. 基本的和增補的國際單位

physical quantity 物理量	*name of unit* 單位名稱	*symbol for unit* 單位符號
length 長度	metre 米	m
mass 質量	kilogram 千克	kg
time 時間	second 秒	s
electric current 電流	ampere 安培	A
thermodynamic temperature 熱學力溫度	kelvin 開爾文	K
luminous intensity 光強度	candela 堪德拉	cd
amount of substance 物理量	mole 摩爾	mol
*plane angle 平面角	radian 弧度	rad
*solid angle 立體角	steradian 球面度	sr

*supplementary units 增補單位

Table 2. Derived SI Units with Special Names
表 2. 派生的國際單位及其名稱

physical quantity	name of unit	symbol for unit
物理量	單位名稱	單位符號
frequency	hertz	Hz
頻率	赫茲	
energy	joule	J
能量	焦耳	
force	newton	N
力	牛頓	
power	watt	W
功率	瓦特	
pressure	pascal	Pa
壓力	帕斯卡	
electric charge	coulomb	C
電荷	庫侖	
electric potential difference	volt	V
電位差（電壓）	伏特	
electric resistance	ohm	Ω
電阻	歐姆	
electric conductance	siemens	S
電導	西門子	
electric capacitance	farad	F
電容	法拉第	
magnetic flux	weber	Wb
磁通量	韋伯	
inductance	henry	H
電感	亨利	
magnetic flux density (magnetic induction)	tesla	T
磁通量密度（磁感）	特斯拉	
luminous flux	lumen	lm
光通量	流明	
luminance (illumination)	lux	lx
照明	勒	
absorbed dose	gray	Gy
吸收劑量	格雷	
activity	becquerel	Bq
活性	貝可（勒爾）	
dose equivalent	sievert	Sv
劑量當量	西沃特	

Table 3. Decimal Multiples and Submultiples to be used with SI Units

表 3. 國際單位使用的 10 的倍數和因數

submultiple	prefix	symbol	multiple	prefix	symbol
因數	前綴	符號	倍數	前綴	符號
10^{-1}	deci-	d	10^{1}	deca-	da
10^{-2}	centi-	c	10^{2}	hecto-	h
10^{-3}	milli-	m	10^{3}	kilo-	k
10^{-6}	micro-	μ	10^{6}	mega-	M
10^{-9}	nano-	n	10^{9}	giga-	G
10^{-12}	pico-	p	10^{12}	tera-	T
10^{-15}	femto-	f	10^{15}	peta-	P
10^{-18}	atto-	a	10^{18}	exa-	E
10^{-21}	zepto-	z	10^{21}	zetta-	Z
10^{-24}	yocto-	y	10^{24}	yotta-	Y